2001
WRITER'S MARKET

8,000 EDITORS WHO BUY WHAT YOU WRITE

EDITOR

KIRSTEN C. HOLM

WRITER'S DIGEST BOOKS
CINCINNATI, OHIO

Praise for *Writer's Market*

"No writer should be without the *Writer's Market* . . . This is the biggest and best book in the industry for American markets." **—American Markets Newsletter**

"The *Writer's Market* is by far and away the premier source for [finding a publication or publisher] for writers in all stages in ther career(s)." **—John Austin, Book of the Month**

"The *Writer's Market* is another must-have book for writers seeking to profit from their writing endeavors." **—Writer's Write, The Internet Writing Journal**

"An invaluable resource that lays out the nuts and bolts of getting published." **—Library Journal**

"The writer's bible and best friend. If you're serious about selling what you write and submit material regularly, you need a new copy every year." **—Freelance Writer's Report**

"This volume is a freelancer's working tool, as important as the basic computer or typewriter." **—The Bloomsbury Review**

If your company or contest would like to be considered for a listing in the next edition of *Writer's Market* or www.WritersMarket.com, send a message specifying which section of the book you wish to be in by e-mail to writersmarket.com or by mail to Writer's Market—Questionnaire, 1507 Dana Ave., Cincinnati OH 45207.

All listings in *Writer's Market* must be paying markets.

Managing Editor, Annuals Department: Doug Hubbuch
Editorial Director, Annuals Department: Barbara Kuroff
Production Editors: Anne Bowling, Terri See, Robert Lee Brewer

Writer's Market Website: www.WritersMarket.com

Writer's Digest Website: www.writersdigest.com

Library of Congress Catalog Number 31-20772
International Standard Serial Number 0084-2729
International Standard Book Number 0-89879-977-5
International Standard Book Number 0-89879-982-1 (Internet Edition)

Attention Booksellers: This is an annual directory of F&W Publications. Return deadline for this edition is December 31, 2001.

contents at a glance

Using Your *Writer's Market* to Sell Your Writing   **2**
How to use this book

Getting Published   **5**
Articles and information for previously unpublished writers

Personal Views   **40**
Interviews with successful bestselling authors

The Business of Writing   **55**
Information for the more experienced writer

The Listings:

   Literary Agents   **93**

   Book Publishers   **125**

   Canadian & International Book Publishers   **345**

   Small Press   **366**

   Book Producers   **379**

   Consumer Magazines   **383**

   Trade Magazines   **811**

   Scriptwriting   **938**

   Syndicates   **976**

   Greeting Cards & Gift Ideas   **982**

   Contests & Awards   **988**

   Resources   **1049**

Book Publishers Subject Index   **1061**

General Index   **1085**

Contents

1 From the Editor

2 Using Your Writer's Market to Sell Your Writing

4 Important Listing Information

GETTING PUBLISHED

5 Before Your First Sale

The basics of writing for publication. Freelance magazine writer **Helen Zelon** shares her approach to queries, contracts and writing in general on **page 7**.

5 Develop your ideas, then target the markets	**11** Professionalism and courtesy	**14** Photographs and slides
	11 Writing tools	**14** Photocopies
6 Query and cover letters	**13** Manuscript format	**15** Mailing submissions
9 Book proposals	**13** Estimating word count	**16** Recording submissions
9 A word about agents		

17 Writing Queries That Work, by Don McKinney

A long-time editor and writing instructor examines the seven elements every query letter must have. After all, you only get one chance to make a first impression!

21 Query Letter Clinic, by Don Prues

Eight new, real-life examples of queries that succeeded and queries that failed, with plenty of comments to help you understand why. Two checklists—what not do in your query and a quick review before you mail it—help you fine tune that letter.

32 Sell What You Write, by Greg Dougherty

You have the sample copies, now what do you do? A successful freelancer shows you how to study a magazine for clues that will help you find the right markets for your ideas.

36 First Bylines, by Lynn Wasnak

The path to publication is different for everyone. Three writers share their individual journeys to that first magazine sale.

PERSONAL VIEWS

40 Edward Ball: Bestselling Author Reveals Secrets for Writing the Compelling Memoir, by Anne Bowling

Research was critical to writing his National Book Award-winning *Slaves in the Family*. Here Edward Ball shares some of his experiences in researching and writing the 300-year history of his family.

44 Alan Cheuse: Writing Across the Spectrum, by Paula Deimling

Novelist, journalist, essayist, reviewer and professor, Alan Cheuse has advice for writers working in multiple fields. Whether you are writing fiction or nonfiction, he says, the story is what makes your work shine.

48 Elizabeth Graver: Quiet Style Brings Power, by Anne Bowling

Writing is a continual learning process for Elizabeth Graver, winner of the Drue Heinz Award and author of two highly-acclaimed novels and a short story collection. Working within a community of writers makes writing less solitary, she says, and keeps the emphasis on writing, not publishing.

52 Jerry Jenkins: Christian Fiction Enters the Mainstream,

by Chantelle Bentley

Six volumes and counting, the Left Behind series, an international blockbuster success, details the events of the Book of Revelations. Jerry Jenkins discusses the challenges of writing for the Christian market in a secular world and the phenomenal crossover success of the series.

THE BUSINESS OF WRITING

55 Minding the Details

Information for the more experienced writer on negotiating and securing fair agreements, managing your rights and handling your earnings legally.

55 Contracts and agreements	**56** Types of rights	**58** Copyright
56 Rights and the writer	**57** Selling subsidiary rights	**59** Finances and taxes

61 How Much Should I Charge?, by Lynn Wasnak

Take advantage of the expertise of hundreds of working freelancers surveyed for our newly revised annual guide to pay ranges for typical freelance jobs. With tips and trends in the current market, this article will give you a leg up in accurately figuring how much you, and your time, is worth.

74 Book Contract Clinic: Quick Fixes for Bad Clauses,

by Stephen Gillen, Esq.

Contracts may be the most confusing aspect of getting published. Examine the small print with an intellectual property lawyer and find out what to do when good clauses go bad.

85 First Books, by Lynn Wasnak

Publishing your first book can be exhilirating, exhausting and surprising. Three authors share insights and experiences of their individual journies to publication.

89 Publishers and Their Imprints

Faster than a speeding takeover, large-scale shifts in the publishing universe affect the ownership of many imprints. Here's a snapshot of how the major publishers fall out . . . for the moment.

LITERARY AGENTS

Looking for a literary agent? Here's where to start your search, with 55 reputable literary agents that are open to new and previously published writers and 18 WGA Signatory script agents.

94 Literary Agents: The Listings

LITERARY AGENTS SUBJECT INDEX

| 119 Fiction | 120 Nonfiction | 123 Scripts |

THE MARKETS

125 Book Publishers
From A&B Publishers to Zondervan, hundreds of places to sell your book ideas. The introduction to this section helps you refine your approach to publishers.

345 Canadian & International Book Publishers
The introduction to this section covers how to submit your work to international markets.

366 Small Presses
Companies publishing three or fewer books a year are listed here. Small presses often have narrowly tailored subjects—be sure to read each listing closely.

379 Book Producers
Book producers, or packagers as they are sometimes called, assemble the elements of books, (writers, editors, designers and illustrators) for publishers.

383 Consumer Magazines
This section offers plentiful opportunities for writers with hundreds of listings for magazines on nearly every subject under the sun. Six freelancers in very different subject areas discuss the value of establishing a "beat" on pages **431, 470, 494, 594, 604,** and **779,** and **Emily Hancock,** editor of Moxie magazine talks about creating an alternative magazine for real women on **page 805.**

386 Animal	444 Consumer Services &	504 History
394 Art & Architecture	Business Opportunity	507 Hobby & Craft
399 Associations	447 Contemporary Culture	529 Home & Garden
402 Astrology, Metaphysical &	451 Detective & Crime	540 Humor
New Age	451 Disabilities	540 Inflight
405 Automotive & Motorcycle	455 Entertainment	544 Juvenile
409 Aviation	460 Ethnic/Minority	558 Literary & "Little
413 Business and Finance	469 Food & Drink	581 Men's
422 Career, College, & Alumni	474 Games & Puzzles	584 Military
430 Child Care & Parental	474 Gay & Lesbian Interest	588 Music
Guidance	479 General Interest	591 Mystery
444 Comic Books	492 Health & Fitness	593 Nature, Conservation & Ecology

603	Personal Computers	700	Rural		Backpacking, Hockey, Horse
607	Photography	703	Science		Racing, Hunting & Fishing,
609	Politics & World Affairs	706	Science Fiction, Fantasy &		Martial Arts, Miscellaneous,
613	Psychology & Self-		Horror		Motor Sports, Running,
	Improvement	712	Sex		Skiing & Snow Sports,
614	Regional	717	Sports		Soccer, Tennis, Water,
664	Relationships		Archery & Bowhunting,		Sports, Wrestling
666	Religious		Baseball, Bicycling, Boating,	770	Teen & Young Adult
696	Retirement		Gambling, General Interest,	778	Travel, Camping & Trailer
699	Romance & Confession		Golf, Guns, Hiking &	796	Women's

811 Trade, Technical & Professional Journals

Magazines listed in this section serve a wide variety of trades and professions. The introduction tells how to break in and establish yourself in the trades.

812	Advertising, Marketing & PR	860	Farm	905	Lumber
813	Art, Design & Collectibles		Agricultural Equipment,	905	Machinery & Metal
816	Auto & Truck		Crops & Soil Management,	906	Maintenance & Safety
821	Aviation & Space		Dairy Farming, Livestock,	908	Management & Supervision
822	Beauty & Salon		Management, Miscellaneous,	909	Marine & Maritime Industries
824	Beverages & Bottling		Regional	910	Medical
826	Book & Bookstore	866	Finance	914	Mining & Minerals
827	Brick, Glass & Ceramics	870	Fishing	914	Music
828	Building Interiors	870	Florists, Nurseries &	916	Office & Environment &
828	Business Management		Landscapers		Equipment
835	Church Administration &	877	Groceries & Food Products	917	Paper
	Ministry	880	Hardware	918	Pets
842	Clothing	880	Home Furnishings &	918	Plumbing, Heating, Air
842	Confectionary and Snack		Household Goods		Conditioning & Refrigeration
	Foods	880	Hospitals, Nursing & Nursing	919	Printing
842	Construction & Contracting		Homes	920	Professional Photography
846	Drugs, Healthcare & Medical	883	Hotels, Motels, Clubs,	921	Real Estate
	Products		Resorts & Restaurants	924	Resources & Waste
848	Education & Counseling	885	Industrial Operations		Distribution
852	Electronics &	887	Information Systems	925	Selling & Merchandising
	Communication	892	Insurance	930	Sport Trade
853	Energy & Utilities	893	Jewelry	933	Stone, Quarry & Mining
855	Engineering & Technology	894	Journalism & Writing	934	Transportation
857	Entertainment & the Arts	902	Law	935	Travel
		904	Leather Goods	937	Veterinary

938 Scriptwriting

Markets for film and television scripts and stageplays are listed here.

940 Business & Educational Writing
942 Playwriting
966 Screenwriting

976 Syndicates

Newspaper syndicates distribute writers' works around the nation and the world. The introduction offers advice for breaking into this market.

982 Greeting Cards & Gift Ideas

Greeting card and gift markets provide outlets for a wide variety of writing styles. The introduction to this section tells you how to approach these companies professionally.

988 Contests & Awards

Contests and awards offer many opportunities for writers, and can launch a successful writing career. Playwright.

989 General	1019 Playwriting & Scriptwriting	1036 Translation
990 Nonfiction	1030 Journalism	1037 Multiple Writing Areas
999 Fiction	1033 Writing for Children &	1044 Arts & Councils Foundations
1008 Poetry	Young Adults	

RESOURCES

1049 Publications

1051 Websites

1055 Organizations

1057 Glossary

1061 BOOK PUBLISHERS SUBJECT INDEX

1061 Fiction	1065 Nonfiction

1085 General Index

COMPLAINT PROCEDURE

If you feel you have not been treated fairly by a listing in **Writer's Market**, we advise you to take the following steps:

- First try to contact the listing. Sometimes one phone call or a letter can quickly clear up the matter.
- Document all your correspondence with the listing. When you write to us with a complaint, provide the details of your submission, the date of your first contact with the listing and the nature of your subsequent correspondence.
- We will enter your letter into our files and attempt to contact the listing.
- The number and severity of complaints will be considered in our decision whether or not to delete the listing from the next edition.

From the Editor

My mother was lamenting the loss of my daughter's company on Thursdays, now that she's attending school fulltime. "Don't worry," my daughter said to comfort her. "Everything changes, Grandmommy, everything changes."

I've posted those words over my computer this past year. While every year is challenging, this year was particularly so, as we were not only producing this, the usual 100% updated print book but also working on an exciting new direction for this long-standing resource. For the past year we've been constructing **www.WritersMarket.com**, which begins as an online database of all the publishing opportunities contained in *Writer's Market* and then takes off for points not entirely known even to us yet.

The print book remains our primary concern. Filling it, even stuffing it, with useful information and markets for writers just beginning to sell their work as well as for more seasoned professionals turning straight to the markets, is never easy. Balancing articles and markets is a delicate task, even with 1100+ pages to play with. This year I'm particularly pleased to offer some nuts-and-bolts book contract information for those readers looking for some guidance in this thorny area. The interviews with six successful freelancers on how to establish a niche contain really useful advice on how to make a career out of writing. First Bylines and First Books talks with writers about achieving their all-important first steps into publication. And as always, we present a broad range of markets in as many respects as possible—pay rates, subject areas, size, openness to new writers, new markets, older markets, book publishers, magazines.

Writer's Market is still packed with helpful information about how and where to get your work published. Our new database, however, combines the customized search capabilities the previous CD-ROM offered (you can focus on markets specific to your writing interests) with the immediacy of the web (we can provide you with current changes in those markets). Reporting changes of address or policies without having to wait until the next paper edition comes out is an exciting prospect. Also exciting is the opportunity to include markets we painstakingly collected only to find we didn't have room to include them all in the print edition. Now this "bonus" information is available to you on WritersMarket.com. We're also lining up a steady flow of interesting and informative articles and interviews, offering information we'd like to include in print but just don't have as much space for as we'd like.

I'm always amazed at how *Writer's Market* readers personalize this book as their own. (99.9% of the time in a positive way!) I frequently get friendly e-mails from readers alerting me to a change of address or policy for one of our listed markets. I welcome this information, and think of those kind writers who take a moment out of the freelance wars as kind of foot soldiers sending posts from the front line. With this new venture I'd welcome all the help that the *Writer's Market* family can give. At the risk of receiving 3,000 e-mails that one magazine editor has changed, please send any changes *you* come across to **WMOnline@fwpubs.com**.

So, as my daughter wisely observed, "Everything changes." A lot will change in the coming year about *how* we do what we do here at *Writer's Market* and WritersMarket.com. But *what* we do won't ever change. Helping writers make sense of the writing world, in whatever ways they need us to do so, will always come first and foremost.

Wishing you the best of luck and a successful year full of changes of your own.

Kirsten Campbell Holm

Kirsten Campbell Holm, Editor, *Writer's Market*
writersmarket@fwpubs.com

Using Your *Writer's Market* to Sell Your Writing

Writer's Market is here to help you decide where and how to submit your writing to appropriate markets. Each listing contains information about the editorial focus of the market, how it prefers material to be submitted, payment information and other helpful tips.

WHAT'S NEW?

Writer's Market has always given you the important information you need to know in order to approach a market knowledgeably. We've continued to search out improvements to help you access that information more efficiently.

Symbols. Scanning through the listings to find the right publisher for your book manuscript just got easier. The key symbol (⚷) quickly sums up a publisher's interests, along with information on what subjects are currently being emphasized or phased out. In Consumer Magazines the ⚷ zeroes in on what areas of that market are particularly open to freelancers to help you break in. Other symbols let you know, at a glance, whether a listing is new, a book publisher accepts only agented writers, comparative pay rates for a magazine, and more. A key to the symbols appears on the front and back inside covers.

Literary agents. Recognizing the increasing importance of literary agents in the book publishing field, we've researched and included 75 literary and script agents at the beginning of the listings on page 93. All of these agents have indicated a willingness to work with new, previously unpublished writers as well as more established authors. Most are members of the Association of Authors' Representatives (AAR), or the Writers Guild of America (WGA).

More names, royalty rates and advances highlighted. In the Book Publishers section we identify acquisition editors with the word **Acquisitions** to help you get your manuscript to the right person. Royalty rates and advances are highlighted in boldface, as well as important information on the percentage of first-time writers, unagented writers, the number of books published and manuscripts received.

Names, pay rates and percentage freelance-written highlighted. Can you send an editor a query by e-mail? We asked editors if they accept e-queries as well as by mail, fax or phone. In Consumer Magazines, who to send your article to at each magazine is identified by the boldface word **Contact**. In addition, the percentage of a magazine that is freelance written, the number of articles and pay rates for features, columns and departments, and fillers are also highlighted, quickly identifying the information you need to know when considering whether or not to submit your work.

New articles. Be sure to check out the new articles geared to more experienced writers in Minding the Details. In Book Contract Clinic, a consultation with intellectual property attorney Stephen Gillen shows you how to improve typical book contract clauses to favor you, the author. In First Books, Lynn Wasnak details the journey of three authors breaking into the book market. M.J. Rose discusses the power of marketing on her success in the e-publishing world. Become an expert in an area and command higher fees is the advice of six freelancers we interviewed for the Consumer Magazines section this year. Don't miss these Insider Reports on making a niche your home on pages 431, 470, 494, 594, 604 and 779.

Interviews with bestselling authors. Personal Views offers interviews with bestselling authors on writing and success. Edward Ball, Elizabeth Graver, Alan Cheuse and Jerry Jenkins offer insights into their writing life and advice for yours.

As always, all of the listings have been checked and verified, with more e-mail addresses and websites added.

IF *WRITER'S MARKET* IS NEW TO YOU . . .

A quick look at the Table of Contents will familiarize you with the arrangement of *Writer's Market*. The three largest sections of the book are the market listings of Book Publishers; Consumer Magazines; and Trade, Technical & Professional Journals. You will also find other sections of market listings for Scriptwriting, Syndicates, Greeting Cards and Contests & Awards. The section introductions contain specific information about trends, submission methods and other helpful resources for the material included in that section.

The articles in the first section, Getting Published, are included with newer, unpublished writers in mind. In Writing Queries That Work, Don McKinney spells out what your letter needs to cover and why. Query Letter Clinic shows you eight real-life examples of letters that hit the mark and those that missed it. Sell What You Write, by Greg Daugherty, shows you how to analyze a magazine like a writer, a writer looking to make a sale. Putting it all together, Lynn Wasnak's First Bylines talks to three writers about how they made their first sale.

Narrowing your search

After you've identified the market categories you're interested in, you can begin researching specific markets within each section.

Book Publishers are categorized, in the Book Publishers Subject Index, according to types of books they are interested in. If, for example, you plan to write a book on a religious topic, simply turn to the Book Publishers Subject Index and look under the Religion subhead in Nonfiction for the names and page numbers of companies that publish such books.

Consumer Magazines and Trade, Technical & Professional Journals are categorized by subject to make it easier for you to identify markets for your work. If you want to publish an article dealing with some aspect of retirement, you could look under the Retirement category of Consumer Magazines to find an appropriate market. You would want to keep in mind, however, that magazines in other categories might also be interested in your article (for example, women's magazines publish such material as well). Keep your antennae up while studying the markets: less obvious markets often offer the best opportunities.

Interpreting the markets

Once you've identified companies or publications that cover the subjects you're interested in, you can begin evaluating specific listings to pinpoint the markets most receptive to your work and most beneficial to you.

In evaluating an individual listing, first check the location of the company, the types of material it is interested in seeing, submission requirements, and rights and payment policies. Depending upon your personal concerns, any of these items could be a deciding factor as you determine which markets you plan to approach. Many listings also include a reporting time, which lets you know how long it will typically take for the publisher to respond to your initial query or submission. (We suggest that you allow an additional month for a response, just in case your submission is under further review or the publisher is backlogged.)

Check the Glossary at the back of the book for unfamiliar words. Specific symbols and abbreviations are explained in the key appearing on the front and back inside covers. The most important abbreviation is SASE—self-addressed, stamped envelope. Always enclose one when you send unsolicited queries, proposals or manuscripts. This requirement is not included in most of the individual market listings because it is a "given" that you must follow if you expect to receive a reply.

A careful reading of the listings will reveal that many editors are very specific about their needs. Your chances of success increase if you follow directions to the letter. Often companies do not accept unsolicited manuscripts and return them unread. Read each listing closely, heed the tips given, and follow the instructions. Work presented professionally will normally be given more serious consideration.

Whenever possible, obtain writer's guidelines before submitting material. You can usually obtain them by sending a SASE to the address in the listing. Magazines often post their guidelines on their website as well. You should also familiarize yourself with the company's publications. Many of the listings contain instructions on how to obtain sample copies, catalogs or market lists. The more research you do upfront, the better your chances of acceptance, publication and payment.

Additional help

The book contains many articles on a variety of helpful topics. Insider Reports—interviews with writers, editors and publishers—offer advice and an inside look at publishing. Some listings contain editorial comments, indicated by a bullet (●), that provide additional information discovered during our compilation of this year's *Writer's Market*. E-mail addresses and websites have been included for many markets. Publications in the Resources section includes some, but by no means all, trade magazines, directories and sources of information on writing-related topics. The Websites section points you to writing-related material on the Web.

Newer or unpublished writers should be sure to read Before Your First Sale. Minding the Details offers valuable information about rights, taxes and other practical matters. There is also a helpful section titled How Much Should I Charge? that offers guidance for setting your freelance fees.

Important Listing Information

- Listings are based on editorial questionnaires and interviews. They are not advertisements; publishers do not pay for their listings. The markets are not endorsed by *Writer's Market* editors. F&W Publications, Inc., Writer's Digest Books and its employees go to great effort to ascertain the validity of information in this book. However, transactions between users of the information and individuals and/or companies are strictly between those parties.
- All listings have been verified before publication of this book. If a listing has not changed from last year, then the editor told us the market's needs have not changed and the previous listing continues to accurately reflect its policies.
- *Writer's Market* reserves the right to exclude any listing.
- When looking for a specific market, check the index. A market may not be listed for one of these reasons:
    1. It doesn't solicit freelance material.
    2. It doesn't pay for material.
    3. It has gone out of business.
    4. It has failed to verify or update its listing for this edition.
    5. It was in the middle of being sold at press time, and rather than disclose premature details, we chose not to list it.
    6. It hasn't answered *Writer's Market* inquiries satisfactorily. (To the best of our ability, and with our readers' help, we try to screen out fraudulent listings.)
    7. It buys few manuscripts, constituting a very small market for freelancers.
- Individual markets that appeared in last year's edition but are not listed in this edition are included in the General Index, with a notation giving the basis for their exclusion.

Getting Published

Before Your First Sale

Many writers new to the craft feel that achieving publication—and getting paid for their work—is an accomplishment so shrouded in mystery and magic that there can be little hope it will ever happen to *them*. Of course, that's nonsense. All writers were newcomers once. Getting paid for your writing is not a matter of insider information or being handed the one "key" to success. There's not even a secret handshake.

Making money from your writing will require three things of you:

- Good writing
- Knowledge of writing markets (magazines and book publishers) and how to approach them professionally
- Persistence

Good writing without marketing know-how and persistence might be art, but who's going to know if it never sells? A knowledge of markets without writing ability or persistence is pointless. And persistence without talent and at least a hint of professionalism is simply irksome. But a writer who can combine the above-mentioned virtues stands a good chance of not only selling a piece occasionally, but enjoying a long and successful writing career.

You may think a previously unpublished writer has a difficult time breaking into the field. As with any profession, experience is valued, but that doesn't mean publishers are closed to new writers. While it is true some editors prefer working with established writers, most are open to professional submissions and good ideas from any writer, and quite a few magazine editors like to feature different styles and voices.

In nonfiction book publishing, experience in writing or in a particular subject area is valued by editors as an indicator of the author's ability and expertise in the subject. As with magazines, the idea is paramount, and new authors break in every year with good, timely ideas.

As you work in the writing field, you may read articles or talk to writers and editors who give conflicting advice. There are some norms in the business, but they are few. You'll probably hear as many different routes to publication as writers you talk to.

The following information on submissions has worked for many writers, but it's not the *only* method you can follow. It's easy to get wrapped up in the specifics of submitting (should my name go at the top left or right of the manuscript?) and fail to consider weightier matters (is this idea appropriate for this market?). Let common sense and courtesy be your guides as you work with editors, and eventually you'll develop your own most effective submission methods.

DEVELOP YOUR IDEAS, THEN TARGET THE MARKETS

Writers often think of an interesting story, complete the manuscript and then begin the search for a suitable publisher or magazine. While this approach is common for fiction, poetry and screenwriting, it reduces your chances of success in many other writing areas. Instead, try choosing categories that interest you and study those sections in *Writer's Market*. Select several listings that you consider good prospects for your type of writing. Sometimes the individual listings will even help you generate ideas.

Next, make a list of the potential markets for each idea. Make the initial contact with markets using the method stated in the market listings. If you exhaust your list of possibilities, don't give up. Reevaluate the idea or try another angle. Continue developing ideas and approaching markets with them. Identify and rank potential markets for an idea and continue the process.

As you submit to the various periodicals listed in *Writer's Market*, it's important to remember that every magazine is published with a particular slant and audience in mind. Probably the number one complaint we hear from editors is that writers often send material and ideas that are completely wrong for their magazines. The first mark of professionalism is to know your market well. That knowledge starts here in *Writer's Market*, but you should also search out back issues of the magazines you wish to write for and learn what specific subjects they have published in past issues and how those subjects have been handled. Websites can be an invaluable source. Not only do many magazines post their writer's guidelines on their site, many publish some or all of the current issue, as well as an archive of past articles. This will give you clues as to what they're interested in and what they've already published.

Prepare for rejection and the sometimes lengthy wait. When a submission is returned, check your file folder of potential markets for that idea. Cross off the market that rejected the idea and immediately mail an appropriate submission to the next market on your list. If the editor has given you suggestions or reasons as to why the manuscript was not accepted, you might want to incorporate these when revising your manuscript.

About rejection. Rejection is a way of life in the publishing world. It's inevitable in a business that deals with such an overwhelming number of applicants for such a limited number of positions. Anyone who has published has lived through many rejections, and writers with thin skin are at a distinct disadvantage. The key to surviving rejection is to remember that it is not a personal attack—it's merely a judgment about the appropriateness of your work for that particular market at that particular time. Writers who let rejection dissuade them from pursuing their dream or who react to each editor's "No" with indignation or fury do themselves a disservice. Writers who let rejection stop them do not publish. Resign yourself to facing rejection now. You will live through it, and you will eventually overcome it.

QUERY AND COVER LETTERS

A query letter is a brief but detailed letter written to interest an editor in your manuscript. It is a tool for selling both nonfiction magazine articles and nonfiction books. With a magazine query you are attempting to interest an editor in buying your article for her periodical. A book query's job is to get an editor interested enough to ask you for either a full proposal or the entire manuscript. (Note: Some book editors accept proposals on first contact. Refer to individual listings for contact guidelines.) Some beginners are hesitant to query, thinking an editor can more fairly judge an idea by seeing the entire manuscript. Actually, most nonfiction editors prefer to be queried.

There is no query formula that guarantees success, but there are some points to consider when you begin. Queries should:

- Be limited to one page, single-spaced, and address the editor by name (Mr. or Ms. and the surname).
- Grab the editor's interest with a strong opening. Some magazine queries begin with a paragraph meant to approximate the lead of the intended article.
- Indicate how you intend to develop the article or book. Give the editor some idea of the work's structure and content.
- Let the editor know if you have photos available to accompany your magazine article (never send original photos—send photocopies or duplicates).
- Mention any expertise or training that qualifies you to write the article or book. If you've published before, mention it; if not, don't.
- End with a direct request to write the article (or, if you're pitching a book, ask for the go-ahead to send in a full proposal or the entire manuscript). Give the editor an idea of the expected length and delivery date of your manuscript.

Tricks of the magazine trade

Helen Zelon's goals as a magazine freelancer are basic: "To keep writing, to get better at the craft, to tell more stories to more readers, and to remain curious and open to new ideas and experiences in my work." Basic, she says, "but not always easy."

Zelon, who has made a career of freelancing, got started "in editorial work, as a proofreader and a copy editor, and later, as a medical editor and ghostwriter." For the past four years, she has been writing freelance pieces for magazines and already has several impressive credits on her resume, including *Family Circle Magazine, Cosmopolitan, Family Life, Moment,* and contributions to a nonfiction book, *Totally Brooklyn* (Workman Publishing Co.).

Through her experiences, Zelon has developed several insider's tips that help achieve her freelance goals more easily. For starters, she has learned the importance of liking her stories' subjects. "I definitely consider my interests when taking on a story," she says. "If I don't feel enthusiasm for the content, it will be a dull read (and a dull writing job, too). I think the writer's feelings show all over the page, even when a story is not a first-person piece. The stronger the writer's affinity for a subject, the better the story." Her interests even gave Zelon and her daughter an opportunity to attend NASA's Space Camp for a piece she covered for *Scientific American: Explorations.*

While Zelon often works on assignment, she says, "Proposing ideas is a big part of the fun of the work, coming up with an idea that you can't shake, one that's intriguing to write. And ideas are everywhere. The problem is not getting the idea but taking the time to do a thorough job researching the idea to craft a credible pitch."

Preliminary research is the key to a strong query, says Zelon. "I do a lot of background work before I pitch a story, including some interviews. It can feel as if you're doing all the research you'd have to do to write the piece even before the idea is sold, but I believe in the strength of a good pitch and spend a lot of time on them." And editors are naturally more impressed by writers who approach them well prepared.

After gathering material for a story, Zelon looks for a place to sell it before she starts writing. "I've not had a lot of experience with submitting finished pieces blind," she explains, "because I tend to write with a specific audience in mind." Once an editor accepts her proposal, she is then able to tailor the story to the magazine's audience. Zelon takes a practical approach to writing for different types of readers, claiming "it is like talking to different people—we do it every day without thinking."

When it comes to contacting editors, Zelon targets perspective markets. "The idea dictates where I pitch the story, for example, an education piece for *Family Life.* Finding new markets is driven by the story idea you want to sell. Where would you read a similar story? That's where you pitch it."

Having a contact at the magazine is also extremely beneficial. Zelon was fortunate enough to meet an editor for *Family Circle Magazine* in a writing workshop. She later contacted that editor and made her first sale.

Through her experience, Zelon has found that "the best editors I've worked with have been readily accessible and open to ideas, whether they are ideas that turn into stories or ideas that emerge to change the focus of the piece in the course of working on a story. Good editors want good ideas from writers and are not afraid to let stories evolve."

Of course, Zelon has also encountered some editors she wished she had never met. "I had a bad experience some time ago when an idea I pitched verbally was later produced by the publisher, exactly as I had proposed but with another writer. I will never pitch again to her, and I learned to submit every pitch on paper, but there are no guarantees. There's an old maxim, 'Once burned, twice shy,' that applies to freelancing stories. If you've had a bad experience with a magazine, don't go back to them. If an editor has been unpleasant or cold, don't pursue her. If your story has been mishandled, offer the next one elsewhere, and chalk it up to experience. It can be frustrating, but there's little to be gained from hollering at an editor after the story's in print. Let it go, and take your stories to another market."

Telling the good markets from the bad ones can be difficult for a freelancer. As Zelon points out, "Good people work at big magazines and at little magazines, and less-scrupulous people can be found in both locations as well." Nevertheless, the publisher's contract can be a clue to how it works. Therefore, it is important to understand completely each aspect of the contract before you sign. "Read your contract or letter of agreement *carefully* so you understand when you'll be paid and, of equal importance, what rights you grant the magazine by selling them the story. Some magazines request Internet and other publication rights, others only want first North American rights. No matter how excited you are to receive the contract, make sure you know what you're signing before you send it back."

Through all her experiences as a freelancer, perhaps the most important lesson Zelon has learned is to work hard and not get discouraged during times when work is hard to find. "You have to be able to work on deadline, to hustle—at least a little bit—and you have to be able to sustain the intervals between jobs both psychologically and economically. Freelancers can get their work read if they present ideas—magazines need content; they are always looking for writers and stories."

—Donya Dickerson

Some writers state politely in their query letters that after a specified date (slightly beyond the listed reporting time), they will assume the editor is not currently interested in their topic and will submit the query elsewhere. It's a good idea to do this only if your topic is a timely one that will suffer if not considered quickly.

A brief single-spaced cover letter enclosed with your manuscript is helpful in personalizing a submission. If you have previously queried the editor on the article or book, the cover letter should be a brief reminder, not a sales pitch. "Here is the piece on goat herding, which we discussed previously. I look forward to hearing from you at your earliest convenience."

If you are submitting to a market that considers unsolicited complete manuscripts, your cover letter should tell the editor something about your manuscript and about you—your publishing history and any particular qualifications you have for writing the enclosed manuscript.

Once your manuscript has been accepted, you may offer to get involved in the editing process, but policy on this will vary from magazine to magazine. Most magazine editors don't send galleys to authors before publication, but if they do, you should review the galleys and return them as soon as possible. Book publishers will normally involve you in rewrites whether you like it or not.

The Query Letter Clinic on page 21 presents several specific real-life query letters, some that worked (and some that didn't), along with editors' comments on why the letter was successful or where the letter failed to garner an assignment.

For more information about writing query letters, read *How to Write Irresistible Query Letters*, by Lisa Collier Cool, or *How To Write Attention-Grabbing Query & Cover Letters*, by John Wood (both Writer's Digest Books).

Querying for fiction

Fiction is sometimes queried, but most fiction editors don't like to make a final decision until they see the complete manuscript. Most editors will want to see a synopsis and sample chapters for a book, or a complete short story manuscript. Consult individual listings for specific fiction guidelines. If a fiction editor does request a query, briefly describe the main theme and story line, including the conflict and resolution. For more information on what goes into a novel synopsis, *The Marshall Plan for Novel Writing*, or *Your Novel Proposal: From Creation to Contract*, by Blythe Camenson and Marshall J. Cook (both by Writer's Digest Books).

BOOK PROPOSALS

Most nonfiction books are sold by book proposal, a package of materials that details what your book is about, who its intended audience is, and how you intend to write it. Most fiction is sold either by complete manuscript, especially for first-time authors, or by two or three sample chapters. Take a look at individual listings to see what submission method editors prefer.

The nonfiction book proposal includes some combination of a cover or query letter, an overview, an outline, author's information sheet and sample chapters. Editors also want to see information about the audience for your book and about titles that compete with your proposed book.

If a listing does not specify, send as much of the following information as you can.

- The cover or query letter should be a short introduction to the material you include in the proposal.
- An overview is a brief summary of your book. For nonfiction, it should detail your book's subject and give an idea of how that subject will be developed. If you're sending a synopsis of a novel, cover the basic plot.
- An outline covers your book chapter by chapter. The outline should include all major points covered in each chapter. Some outlines are done in traditional outline form, but most are written in paragraph form.
- An author's information sheet should—as succinctly and clearly as possible—acquaint the editor with your writing background and convince her of your qualifications to write about the subject.
- Many editors like to see sample chapters, especially for a first book. In fiction it's essential. In nonfiction, sample chapters show the editor how well you write and develop the ideas from your outline.
- Marketing information—i.e., facts about how and to whom your book can be successfully marketed—is now expected to accompany every book proposal. If you can provide information about the audience for your book and suggest ways the book publisher can reach those people, you will increase your chances of acceptance.
- Competitive title analysis is an integral part of the marketing information. Check the *Subject Guide* to *Books in Print* for other titles on your topic. Write a one- or two-sentence synopsis of each. Point out how your book differs and improves upon existing titles.

For more detailed information on what your book proposal should contain, see *How to Write a Book Proposal*, by Michael Larsen (Writer's Digest Books).

A WORD ABOUT AGENTS

Recognizing the importance of literary agents in publishing today, we've included a section of 75 agents, 50 handling books and 25 handling scripts, beginning on page 92. We've selected agents who describe themselves as open to both previously published and newer writers and who do not charge a fee to look at work. The literary agents belong to the Association of Authors'

COVER LETTER

COVER PAGE

OVERVIEW

MARKETING INFORMATION

COMPETITION

AUTHOR INFORMATION

CHAPTER OUTLINE

SAMPLE CHAPTERS

ATTACHMENTS

A nonfiction book proposal will usually consist of the elements illustrated above. Their order is less important than the fact that you have addressed each component.

Representatives (AAR), a voluntary professional organization. We've also included a few who are not members of AAR but have come to agenting after a notable career in editing and publishing. The script agents are all signatory agencies of The Writers Guild of America.

An agent represents a writer's work to buyers, negotiates contracts, follows up to see that contracts are fulfilled and generally handles a writer's business affairs, leaving the writer free to write. Effective agents are valued for their contacts in the publishing industry, their savvy about which publishers and editors to approach with which ideas, their ability to guide an author's career, and their business sense.

While most book publishers listed in *Writer's Market* publish books by unagented writers, some of the larger ones are reluctant to consider submissions that have not reached them through a literary agent. Companies with such a policy are noted by a symbol ($) at the beginning of the listing, as well as in the submission information within the listing.

For more information about finding and working with a literary agent, as well as 550 listings of literary and script agents, see *Guide to Literary Agents* (Writer's Digest Books). The *Guide* offers listings similar to those presented here, as well as a wealth of informational articles on the author-agent relationship and publishing processes.

PROFESSIONALISM AND COURTESY

Publishers are as crunched for time as any other business professional. Between struggling to meet deadlines without exceeding budgets and dealing with incoming submissions, most editors find that time is their most precious commodity. This state of affairs means an editor's communications with new writers, while necessarily a part of his job, have to be handled efficiently and with a certain amount of bluntness.

But writers work hard, too. Shouldn't editors treat them nicely? Shouldn't an editor take the time to point out the *good* things about the manuscript he is rejecting? Is that too much to ask? Well, in a way, yes. It *is* too much to ask. Editors are not writing coaches; much less are they counselors or therapists. Editors are in the business of buying workable writing from people who produce it. This, of course, does not excuse editors from observing the conventions of common business courtesy. Good editors know how to be polite (or they hire an assistant who can be polite for them).

The best way for busy writers to get along with (and flourish among) busy editors is to develop professional business habits. Correspondence and phone calls should be kept short and to the point. Don't hound editors with unwanted calls or letters. Honor all agreements, and give every assignment your best effort. Pleasantness, good humor, honesty and reliability will serve you as well in publishing as they will in any other area of life.

You will occasionally run up against editors and publishers who don't share your standard of business etiquette. It is easy enough to withdraw your submissions from such people and avoid them in the future.

WRITING TOOLS

Typewriters and computers. For many years, *the* tool of the writer's trade was the typewriter. While many writers continue to produce perfectly acceptable material on their manual or electric typewriters, more and more writers have discovered the benefits of writing on a computer. Editors, too, have benefited from the change; documents produced on a computer are less likely to present to the editor such distractions as typos, eraser marks or globs of white correction fluid. That's because writing composed on a computer can be corrected before it is printed out.

If you think computers are not for you, you should reconsider. A desktop computer, running a good word processing program, can be the greatest boon to your writing career since the dictionary. For ease of manipulating text, formatting pages and correcting spelling errors, the computer handily outperforms the typewriter. Many word processing programs will count words for you, offer synonyms from a thesaurus, construct an index and give you a choice of typefaces to print out your material. Some will even correct your grammar (if you want them to). When you consider that the personal computer is also a great way of tracking your submissions and staying on top of all the other business details of a writing career—and a handy way to do research if you have a modem—it's hard to imagine how we ever got along without them.

Many people considering working with a computer for the first time are under the mistaken impression that they face an insurmountable learning curve. That's no longer true. While learning computer skills once may have been a daunting undertaking, today's personal computers are much more user-friendly than they once were. And as prices continue to fall, good systems can be had for under $1,000.

Whether you're writing on a computer or typewriter, your goal should be to produce pages of clean, error-free copy. Stick to standard typefaces, avoiding such unusual styles as script or italic. Your work should reflect a professional approach and consideration for your reader. If you are printing from a computer, avoid sending material printed from a low-quality dot-matrix printer, with hard-to-read, poorly shaped characters. Many editors are unwilling to read these manuscripts. New laser and ink jet printers, however, produce high-quality pages that *are* acceptable to editors. Readability is the key.

Electronic submissions. Many publishers are accepting or even requesting that final manuscript submissions be made on computer disk. This saves the magazine or book publisher the expense of having your manuscript typeset, and can be helpful in the editing stage. The publisher will simply download your finished manuscript into the computer system they use to produce their product. Be sure to mention if you are able to submit the final manuscript on disk. The editors will let you know what computer format they use and how they would like to receive your material.

Some publishers who accept submissions on disk also will accept electronic submissions by modem. Modems are computer components that can use your phone line to send computerized files to other computers with modems. It is an extremely fast way to get your manuscript to the publisher. However, you must work out submission information with the editor *before* you send something via modem. Causing the editor's system to crash, or unwittingly infecting his system with a virus, does not make for a happy business relationship.

Fax machines and e-mail. Fax machines transmit copy across phone lines. E-mail addresses are for receiving and sending electronic mail over a computer network, most commonly the Internet. Those publishers who wanted to list their fax machine numbers and e-mail addresses have done so.

Between businesses, the fax has come into standard daily use for materials that have to be sent quickly. Fax machines are in airports, hotels, libraries and even grocery stores. Many libraries, schools, copy shops and even "cyber cafés" offer computer time for free or for a low hourly rate. However, do not fax or e-mail queries, proposals or entire manscripts to editors unless they indicate they are willing to receive them. A proposal on shiny fax paper curling into itself on the editor's desk makes an impression—but not the one you want. If your proposal is being considered, it will probably be routed to a number of people for their reactions. Fax paper won't stand up well to that amount of handling. Writers should continue to use traditional means for sending manuscripts and queries and use the fax number or e-mail address we list only when an editor asks to receive correspondence by this method.

Letters and manuscripts sent to an editor for consideration should be neat, clean and legible. That means typed (or computer-printed), double spaced, on $8\frac{1}{2} \times 11$ inch paper. Handwritten materials will most often not be considered at all. The typing paper should be at least 16 lb. bond (20 lb. is preferred).

The first impression an editor has of your work is its appearance on the page. Why take the chance of blowing that impression with a manuscript or letter that's not as appealing as it could be?

You don't need fancy letterhead for your correspondence with editors. Plain bond paper is fine. Just type your name, address, phone number and the date at the top of the page—centered or in the right-hand corner. If you want letterhead, make it as simple and businesslike as possible. Keep the cute clip art for the family newsletter. Many quick print shops have standard typefaces and can supply letterhead stationery at a relatively low cost. Never use letterhead for typing your manuscripts. Only the first page of queries, cover letters and other correspondence should be typed on letterhead.

MANUSCRIPT FORMAT

When submitting a manuscript for possible publication, you can increase its chances of making a favorable impression by adhering to some fairly standard matters of physical format. Many professional writers use the format described here. Of course, there are no "rules" about what a manuscript must look like. These are just guidelines—some based on common sense, others more a matter of convention—that are meant to help writers display their work to best advantage. Strive for easy readability in whatever method you choose and adapt your style to your own personal tastes and those of the editors to whom you submit.

Most manuscripts do not use a cover sheet or title page. Use a paper clip to hold pages together, not staples. This allows editors to separate the pages easily for editing. Scripts should be submitted with plain cardstock covers front and back, held together by Chicago or Revere screws.

The upper corners of the first page of an article manuscript contain important information about you and your manuscript. This information should be single-spaced. In the upper *left* corner list your name, address and phone number. If you are using a pseudonym for your byline, your legal name still should appear in this space. In the upper *right* corner, indicate the approximate word count of the manuscript, the rights you are offering for sale and your copyright notice (© 1999 Ralph Anderson). A handwritten copyright symbol is acceptable. (For more information about rights and copyright, see Minding the Details on page 55.) For a book manuscript include the same information with the exception of rights. Do not number the first page of your manuscript.

Center the title in capital letters one-third of the way down the page. Set the spacing to double-space. Type "by" and your name or pseudonym centered one double-space beneath that.

After the title and byline, drop down two double-spaces, paragraph indent, and begin the body of your manuscript. Always double-space your manuscript and use standard paragraph indentations of five spaces. Margins should be about 1¼ inches on all sides of each full page of the manuscript.

On every page after the first, type your last name, a dash and the page number in either the upper left or right corner. The title of your manuscript may, but need not, be typed on this line or beneath it. Page number two would read: Anderson—2. Follow this format throughout your manuscript.

If you are submitting novel chapters, leave the top one-third of the first page of each chapter blank before typing the chapter title. Subsequent pages should include the author's last name, the page number, and a shortened form of the book's title: Anderson—2—Skating. (In a variation on this, some authors place the title before the name on the left side and put the page number on the right-hand margin.)

When submitting poetry, the poems should be typed single-spaced (double-space between stanzas), one poem per page. For a long poem requiring more than one page, paper clip the pages together. You may want to write "continued" at the bottom of the page, so if the pages are separated, editors, typesetters and proofreaders won't assume your poem ends at the bottom of the first page.

For more information on manuscript formats, see *Formatting & Submitting Your Manuscript*, by Jack and Glenda Neff and Don Prues (Writer's Digest Books).

ESTIMATING WORD COUNT

Many computers will provide you with a word count of your manuscript. Your editor will count again after editing the manuscript. Although your computer is counting characters, an editor or production editor is more concerned with the amount of space the text will occupy on a page. Several small headlines, or subheads, for instance, will be counted the same by your computer as any other word of text. An editor may count them differently to be sure enough space has been estimated for larger type.

For short manuscripts, it's often quickest to count each word on a representative page and multiply by the number of pages. You can get a very rough count by multiplying the number of pages in your manuscript by 250 (the average number of words on a double-spaced typewritten page). Do not count words for a poetry manuscript or put the word count at the top of the manuscript.

To get a more precise count, add the number of characters and spaces in an average line and divide by six for the average words per line. Then count the number of lines of type on a representative page. Multiply the words per line by the lines per page to find the average number of words per page. Then count the number of manuscript pages (fractions should be counted as fractions, except in book manuscript chapter headings, which are counted as a full page). Multiply the number of pages by the number of words per page you already determined. This will give you the approximate number of words in the manuscript.

PHOTOGRAPHS AND SLIDES

The availability of good quality photos can be a deciding factor when an editor is considering a manuscript. Many publications also offer additional pay for photos accepted with a manuscript. Check the magazine's listing when submitting black & white prints for the size an editor prefers to review. The universally accepted format for transparencies is 35mm; few buyers will look at color prints. Don't send any transparencies or prints with a query; wait until an editor indicates interest in seeing your photos.

On all your photos and slides, you should stamp or print your copyright notice and "Return to:" followed by your name, address and phone number. Rubber stamps are preferred for labeling photos since they are less likely to cause damage. You can order them from many stationery or office supply stores. If you use a pen to write this information on the back of your photos, be careful not to damage the print by pressing too hard or by allowing ink to bleed through the paper. A felt tip pen is best, but you should take care not to put photos or copy together before the ink dries.

Captions can be typed on adhesive labels and affixed to the back of the prints. Some writers, when submitting several transparencies or photos, number the photos and type captions (numbered accordingly) on a separate 8½ × 11 sheet of paper.

Submit prints rather than negatives or consider having duplicates made of your slides or transparencies. Don't risk having your original negative or slide lost or damaged when you submit it.

PHOTOCOPIES

Make copies of your manuscripts and correspondence before putting them in the mail. Don't learn the hard way, as many writers have, that manuscripts get lost in the mail and that publishers sometimes go out of business without returning submissions. You might want to make several good quality copies of your manuscript while it is still clean and submit them while keeping the original manuscript as a file copy.

Some writers include a self-addressed postcard with a photocopied submission and suggest in the cover letter that if the editor is not interested in the manuscript, it may be tossed out and a reply returned on the postcard. This practice is recommended when dealing with international markets. If you find that your personal computer generates copies more cheaply than you can pay to have them returned, you might choose to send disposable manuscripts. Submitting a disposable manuscript costs the writer some photocopy or computer printer expense, but it can save on large postage bills.

MAILING SUBMISSIONS

No matter what size manuscript you're mailing, always include a self-addressed, stamped envelope (SASE) with sufficient return postage that is large enough to contain your manuscript if it is returned. The website for the U.S. Postal Service, http://www.usps.gov, and the website for the Canadian Postal Service, http://www.canadapost.ca, both have handy postage calculators if you are unsure of how much you'll need.

A manuscript of fewer than six pages may be folded in thirds and mailed as if it were a letter using a #10 (business-size) envelope. The enclosed SASE can be a #10 folded in thirds or a #9 envelope which will slip into the mailing envelope without being folded. Some editors also appreciate the convenience of having a manuscript folded into halves in a 6×9 envelope. For manuscripts of six pages or longer, use 9×12 envelopes for both mailing and return. The return SASE may be folded in half.

A book manuscript should be mailed in a sturdy, well-wrapped box. Enclose a self-addressed mailing label and paper clip your return postage to the label. Unfortunately, new mailing restrictions make it more difficult to mail packages of 12 ounces and over, causing some publishers to discontinue returning submissions of this size.

Always mail photos and slides First Class. The rougher handling received by standard mail could damage them. If you are concerned about losing prints or slides, send them certified or registered mail. For any photo submission that is mailed separately from a manuscript, enclose a short cover letter of explanation, separate self-addressed label, adequate return postage and an envelope. Never submit photos or slides mounted in glass.

To mail up to 20 prints, you can buy photo mailers that are stamped "Photos—Do Not Bend" and contain two cardboard inserts to sandwich your prints. Or use a 9×12 manila envelope, write "Photos—Do Not Bend" and make your own cardboard inserts. Some photography supply shops also carry heavy cardboard envelopes that are reusable.

When mailing a number of prints, say 25-50 for a book with illustrations, pack them in a sturdy cardboard box. A box for typing paper or photo paper is an adequate mailer. If, after packing both manuscript and photos, there's empty space in the box, slip in enough cardboard inserts to fill the box. Wrap the box securely.

To mail transparencies, first slip them into protective vinyl sleeves, then mail as you would prints. If you're mailing a number of sheets, use a cardboard box as for photos.

Types of mail service

- **First Class** is an expensive way to mail a manuscript, but many writers prefer it. First Class mail generally receives better handling and is delivered more quickly. Mail sent First Class is also forwarded for one year if the addressee has moved, and is returned automatically if it is undeliverable.
- **Priority mail** reaches its destination within two to three days. To mail a package of up to 2 pounds costs $3.20, less than either United Parcel Service or Federal Express. First Class mail over 11 ounces is classified Priority. Confirmation of delivery is an additional 35¢.
- **Standard mail** rates are available for packages, but be sure to pack your materials carefully because they will be handled roughly. To make sure your package will be returned to you if it is undeliverable, print "Return Postage Guaranteed" under your address.
- **Certified Mail** must be signed for when it reaches its destination. If requested, a signed receipt is returned to the sender. There is a $1.40 charge for this service, in addition to the required postage, and a $1.25 charge for a return receipt.
- **Registered Mail** is a high-security method of mailing where the contents are insured. The package is signed in and out of every office it passes through, and a receipt is returned to the sender when the package reaches its destination. The cost depends on the weight, destination and whether you obtain insurance.
- If you're in a hurry to get your material to your editor, you have a lot of choices. In

addition to fax and computer technologies mentioned earlier, overnight and two-day mail services are provided by both the U.S. Postal Service and several private firms. More information on next day service is available from the U.S. Post Office or check your Yellow Pages under "Delivery Services."

Other correspondence details

Use money orders if you are ordering sample copies or supplies and do not have checking services. You'll have a receipt, and money orders are traceable. Money orders for up to $700 can be purchased from the U.S. Postal Service for an 80 cents service charge. Banks, savings and loans, and some commercial businesses also carry money orders; their fees vary. *Never* send cash through the mail for sample copies.

Insurance is available for items handled by the U.S. Postal Service but is payable only on typing fees or the tangible value of the item in the package—such as typing paper—so your best insurance when mailing manuscripts is to keep a copy of what you send. Insurance is 85 cents for $50 or less and goes up to a $45.70 plus postage maximum charge for $5,000.

When corresponding with publishers in other countries, International Reply Coupons (IRCs) must be used for return postage. Surface rates in other countries differ from those in the U.S., and U.S. postage stamps are of use only within the U.S.

U.S. stamps can be purchased online with a credit card at http://www.usps.gov or by calling 1-800-STAMP24. Non-U.S. residents can call (816)545-1000 or (816)545-1011 to order stamps. Canadian postage can be purchased online at http://www.canadapost.ca.

Because some post offices don't carry IRCs (or because of the added expense), many writers dealing with international mail send photocopies and tell the publisher to dispose of them if the manuscript is not appropriate. When you use this method, it's best to set a deadline for withdrawing your manuscript from consideration, so you can market it elsewhere.

International money orders are also available from the post office for a charge of $3 or $7.50, depending on the destination.

RECORDING SUBMISSIONS

Once you begin submitting manuscripts, you'll need to manage your writing business by keeping copies of all manuscripts and correspondence, and by recording the dates of submissions.

One way to keep track of your manuscripts is to use a record of submissions that includes the date sent, title, market, editor and enclosures (such as photos). You should also note the date of the editor's response, any rewrites that were done, and, if the manuscript was accepted, the deadline, publication date and payment information. You might want to keep a similar record just for queries.

Also remember to keep a separate file for each manuscript or idea along with its list of potential markets. You may want to keep track of expected reporting times on a calendar, too. Then you'll know if a market has been slow to respond and you can follow up on your query or submission. It will also provide you with a detailed picture of your sales over time.

Writing Queries That Work

BY DON McKINNEY

The most important element in any magazine article sale is not the idea, or even the skill with which the article is written, but the query letter you send to the editor. It seems obvious, but I'll say it anyway: If you don't impress that first person to read your letter, you'll never get a chance to impress anyone else.

So who do you send this query to? And how do you know that anyone will even read it, let alone offer you any encouragement? To answer the second question first, magazines are hungry for good ideas, and they will encourage a strong and suitable query letter no matter what the background of the writer proposing it.

What is a good query letter? Very simply, it is one that catches an editor's attention, suggests an article that fits the magazine's format and gives enough information about both subject and writer to persuade the editor you can produce a publishable piece.

But let's get back to my first question. To begin with, you don't send it to "The Editor" or even to the editor by name. Manuscripts sent to nobody in particular end up reaching nobody in particular. They pile up in somebody's office, or maybe even an empty space next to the water cooler, where they are known as part of the "slush pile." Slush isn't something you want on your sidewalk and, for the most part, editors don't want it in their magazines, either.

Some magazines don't read unsolicited manuscripts at all and simply return them with a brief form letter to that effect. In most cases they pile up until somebody is embarrassed enough by the stack of dog-eared material to sit down and go through it, usually with little or no expectation that anything publishable will be found. Expecting nothing, they find nothing; the main goal is to get rid of the stuff before somebody complains. Sometimes "slush" pieces do sell; I've bought some myself. But the odds are not far from those of winning $5 million from Ed McMahon.

AVOIDING THE SLUSH PILE

So how do you avoid the dreaded slush pile? Simply pick a name off the masthead and write directly to them. Not the editor, who is too busy, or the managing editor or executive editor, and probably not even the articles editor, although that person would seem logical. Instead, I'd pick somebody lower down on the masthead, somebody whose job is to find new talent and who will win recognition by discovering a new writer. This person will probably be listed as an associate editor or perhaps assistant articles editor, and he or she will be ambitious, not pressed by daily deadlines, and would love to be on your side if you have something to offer. He or she will be your contact if the decision is made to encourage you to go further. You will have a live editor, a friend in court, and you will have avoided the slush pile forever.

WHAT IS A GOOD QUERY?

Let me start by saying that a query has two aims in life: (1) to convince an editor that you have a good idea and (2) to convince that editor you can turn it into a publishable manuscript.

DON McKINNEY *was a magazine editor for thirty-one years with magazines such as* True, The Saturday Evening Post *and* McCall's. *He took over the magazine sequence at the University of South Carolina at Columbia, and continued teaching magazine writing after his retirement. He has written dozens of magazine articles and short stories. This article is excerpted from his book* Magazine Writing That Sells *(Writer's Digest Books).*

To achieve these purposes, you have to provide a number of things, all of which should add up to no more than two double-spaced typewritten pages, less if possible.

I think of the elements that make up a good query as the seven W's and an L. They are:

- Lead
- What about
- Why now
- Who from
- What treatment
- What length
- Why you
- When deliver

Lead

Some writers on writing suggest that the lead should be the same as the lead you plan for the finished article, and while that will sometimes work, it can present problems. The lead you plan for the article may be far too long for a two-page query. A query lead should be kept to one paragraph; two at most. Also, you may not know what your lead is going to be until you've finished your research, and maybe not even then.

Just keep in mind that your lead has to catch somebody's attention. It might be a brief anecdote that helps explain your idea. It might be a provocative quote ("I know there are American prisoners of war being held in China because I've been in regular touch with them," says W. Eugene South, a prominent . . .). It could begin with some startling statistics, or a straight statement. An Atlanta writer named Maxine Rock once began a query to *Nova* magazine: "It has been man's dream to talk to the animals. Here in Atlanta, that dream is reality."

If you were an editor, could you stop reading?

What about

Your lead may explain some of this, but probably not as fully as will be necessary to ensure that the editors know exactly what you have in mind. Try to summarize the point of your article as simply as you can, ideally in one sentence, no more than one paragraph.

Why now

It's not enough to propose a good topic; you also need to explain why this is the right time to publish an article on it. Perhaps there's an anniversary coming up; you might, for instance, be proposing an article on the proven effectiveness of the air bag on the whatever-it-is anniversary of its first use. There might be a new study that sheds light on something like aspirin, or sodium use or the value of aerobics. Perhaps a newspeg is coming up; you're proposing a major takeout on some city because it will be celebrating its bicentennial in five months, or on the current state of the abortion controversy because of an upcoming Supreme Court decision.

Perhaps this is simply a subject that is frequently in the news, like genetic engineering, and you are proposing a major story to tell readers what they need to know to understand the breaking news. Maybe you're suggesting a profile of a person—a teacher, say, who has had great success in an inner city school and whose experience might point to some solutions for a national problem.

You don't have to say "This is a good time to do this story because . . . ," but you do have to give the editors a reason to decide that the timing is, indeed, right.

Who from

Very simply, where are you getting your information? Who are your sources and have they agreed to talk to you? If there have been surveys, studies or reports you plan to draw on, list them. If you plan to back up your article with quotes from other written sources, you might indicate you know of their existence. Editors want the assurance of knowing you know where to get the information you need.

What treatment

Very simply, how do you plan to handle this story? Lots of anecdotes? Straight exposition? With plenty of interviews and, if so, with whom? With humor? And what is your point of view? I don't mean you have to take sides on a subject like, say, school busing to achieve integration, or a national health plan, but you do need to make clear what your approach will be. Will you be advocating one side or another, or will you simply be presenting both sides and allowing readers to reach their own decision?

This isn't necessarily something you need to address directly, but the general tone of the query should clearly indicate your point of view.

What length

Just tell the editor what you have in mind ("I see this as an article of about fifteen hundred words . . . "), but don't sound rigid, as the editor may be looking for short pieces or extra-long ones and will be the ultimate judge of what length would be most suitable.

Why you

In short, what can you say that might encourage an editor to entrust this idea to you? If you have had numerous sales to major magazines, you probably don't need to say much more. But if you haven't, think about why you might be a good person to take on this assignment. Is there something in your background that makes you uniquely qualified to write this piece? If it's about education, are you a teacher? If you want to write about children, are you a parent? If it deals with health, do you have firsthand knowledge of the field? Does your job or hobby or education give you some special insight?

Perhaps you've written on this subject for a local or regional publication. Think about what led you to suggest an article on this subject in the first place, and see if that doesn't suggest some reason why you'd be a good person to write it.

When deliver

This doesn't have to be an ironclad promise, but it will give the editor an idea of when it might be available for scheduling purposes. It's also a good opportunity to remind the editor that this idea hasn't just popped into your head: "I've been looking into this for several weeks and have interviewed a number of the people I'd need to talk to. I've also checked out the material already published on the subject. For these reasons, I think I could have a finished manuscript within four weeks of your go-ahead. . . ."

Some writers wind up their queries by saying they're "looking forward to your response," but I don't see a world of point in this. As an editor, I know they are hoping for my approval or they wouldn't have written me in the first place. I'd recommend simply winding up on a businesslike note—perhaps a statement saying when a piece could be delivered—and then send it off and start work on another query. You can't have too many queries out to editors.

Then what?

The sad fact is that, even though your proposal is only a page or two, it may take six weeks or longer to get an answer. That eager junior editor has to hustle it to a less junior editor, who will pass it on to the articles editor, and, if it is still alive, to the managing editor and probably the editor. All this is going to take time, and an attempt to hurry the process could result in somebody just sending it back to get rid of you.

So be patient and get something else—a lot of something elses—in the works. Successful writers usually have a half dozen or more ideas circulating all the time. If that first query hasn't gotten a response in six weeks, I see no harm in a postcard asking if they've received it. Offer to send another copy in case the first one has gone astray.

Don't sound too impatient; don't threaten to take your idea to another magazine. Threats will get you nowhere. That second inquiry ought to get results. If it doesn't, and you haven't heard anything in a few more weeks, feel free to submit your idea somewhere else.

MULTIPLE SUBMISSIONS

So why not just do that in the first place? The answer is: Most editors don't like it. It may not be fair, and it may mean that it takes far too long to get an okay on your idea, but if the word gets around that you go in for multiple submissions, this may work against you.

Remember, the world of magazine editors is a fairly small one. They know each other, and they meet and talk over their work, and word on writers—good or bad—gets around. Also, think of how you'd handle it if you got an okay from one magazine and then another one called up and asked for the piece. Even if you lie successfully, Editor No. 2 is going to see your piece in Magazine No. 1 and know what you did.

On the other hand, there may be times when your subject is so hot, so timely, that you need to make a quick sale before somebody else beats you to it. Maybe that POW who was being held in China has come back and you have a chance to interview him. Then, I think, you can send off a query to a number of magazines, providing you tell each one in your query what you're doing. Just simply say that, because of the timeliness of the story and your fear that another writer will get to it first, you're sending similar proposals to magazines X, Y and Z. You will be delighted to do the story for the magazine that contacts you first.

Query Letter Clinic

BY DON PRUES

The most indispensable companion to an unsold piece of writing is its query letter. Whether you're trying to sell a 100-word sidebar, a 4,000-word feature article, a 60,000-word nonfiction book or a 100,000-word novel, you need a darn good query letter to go with it. Period.

The *Writer's Encyclopedia* defines a query letter as "a sales letter to an editor that is designed to interest him in an article or book idea." With so many submissions to evaluate, editors tend to make fast judgments. So you must pitch a tight and concise query that explains the gist of your piece, why readers will want to read it, and why you're the perfect person to write it.

PRE-QUERY PROVISIONS

Identifying what to omit and what to include in your query can mean the difference between earning a sale or receiving a rejection, so take precautions before submitting.

Trust the editor and suppress your paranoia. Some writers exclude important information from a query fearing the editor will "steal" their idea. Bad move. Editors aren't thieves, and leaving important information out of your query will only increase your chances of keeping yourself out of print. As will mentioning fees in your query; it will send your query straight to the can. If you're an unpublished writer, don't mention that either. Finally, never include a separate cover letter with your query letter. The query is your cover letter, your letter of inquiry, and your letter of intent—all packed into one tightly-wrapped, single-spaced page.

While some rules are meant to be broken, the rule of keeping a query to one page remains intact. If you can't explain your idea in less than a page, you're probably not too clear about the idea itself.

Just because a query is simply one page don't assume it is simple to compose. A saleable query demands you include all the right information in a small space. Addressing your query to the appropriate editor is most important. Ensure this by calling the editorial office and asking who handles the type of material you're submitting. If you want to write a travel piece for a magazine, call and ask for the name and title of the travel editor. That's it. Don't ask to speak with the travel editor; merely get the correct spelling of his name. Always type or word process your query and put it on simple letterhead—editors want good ideas, not fancy fonts and cute clip art. Make your salutation formal; no "Dear Jim" or "Hello" (just today I saw two queries with these exact salutations!). And always offer an estimated word count and delivery date.

COMPOSING THE QUERY

You're ready to write your letter. Introduce your idea in a sentence or two that will make the editor curious, such as an interesting fact, an intriguing question, or maybe something humorous. Then state your idea in one crisp sentence to grab the editor's attention. But don't stop there. Reel in the editor with one or two paragraphs expounding upon your idea. Walk through the

---

DON PRUES *is the co-author of* Formatting & Submitting Your Manuscript *(Writer's Digest Books).*

Query Letter Checklist

Before sending queries, ask yourself:
- Have I addressed the query to the right person at the magazine, and have I double-checked spellings, particularly of all proper nouns?
- Is my query neatly typed and free of errors?
- Is my idea to the point?
- Have I outlined the story or given at least a good idea of the direction the story will take?
- Have I included sources I have interviewed or plan to interview?
- Do I know which department or section my piece best fits and have I told the editor?
- Have I included clips that show my talent?
- Have I noted why I'm the right writer for this story?
- Have I included a self-addressed, stamped envelope (SASE) for reply?
- Does my letter note my address, telephone and fax numbers and e-mail address?
- Have I recorded the query's topic, the date and the target publication in a log?
  (If I don't hear back in six to twelve weeks, I can follow up with a letter reminding the editor about my query or a postcard withdrawing the idea.)

from *The Writer's Market Companion*, by Joe Feiertag and Mary Cupito (Writer's Digest Books)

steps of your project and explain why you're the perfect person to write what you're proposing. List your sources, particularly if you have interviews lined up with specialists on your topic, as this will help establish the credibility of your work.

The tone of your writing is also important. Create a catchy query laden with confidence but devoid of cockiness. Include personal information only if it will help sell your piece, such as previous writing experience with the topic and relevant sample clips. And never forget a SASE.

Most questions about queries revolve around whether to send simultaneous submissions. Sending simultaneous queries to multiple editors is typically okay if you inform all editors you're doing so. But some editors refuse to read simultaneous queries (*Writer's Market* listings indicate if an editor is not receptive to them) because they want an exclusive option to accept or reject your submission. This can be a problem if editors do not respond quickly; it keeps you from submitting to other markets. The two clear advantages to sending simultaneous queries are that you have many lines in the water at once and it prompts a rapid reply—an editor excited by your query will be more apt to get back to you knowing the competition could get to you first.

WHAT THE CLINIC SHOWS YOU

Unpublished writers wonder how published writers break into print. It's not just a matter of luck; published writers construct compelling queries. What follows are ten actual queries submitted to editors (names and addresses have been altered). Five queries are strong; five are not. Detailed comments from the editors show what the writer did and did not do to secure a sale. As you'll see, there's no such thing as a boilerplate "good" query; every winning query works its own magic.

FOR MORE EXAMPLES of queries that hit the mark and queries that missed it, check the expanded Query Letter Clinic on the web at www.WritersMarket.com

Fourteen Things Not to Do In Your Query Letter

1. Don't try any cute attention-getting devices, like marking the envelope "Personal." This also includes fancy stationery that lists every publication you've ever sold to, or "clever" slogans. As Jack Webb used to say on Dragnet, "Just the facts, ma'am."

2. Don't talk about fees. If the fee you mention is too high, it will turn the editor off. If it's too low, he'll think you don't value your work.

3. Keep your opinions to yourself. If you're proposing an article on some public figure, for instance, your personal views are not relevant. Bear in mind that you're offering your services as a reporter, not the author of an editorial or personal opinion column.

4. Don't tell the editors what others you've shown the idea to think of it. ("Several of my friends have read this and think it's marvelous . . .") is a certain sign of the amateur writer. The same goes for comments from other editors. Sometimes you'll hear from an editor who wanted to buy your idea, but was over-ruled, and that editor might say nice things about it and might even offer the suggestion that "It might be just right for Magazine X." Don't pass that praise along. Let Magazine X decide for itself.

5. Don't name drop. Editors will not be impressed that you once babysat for the state governor or had dinner with Bill and Hillary. However, if you do know somebody who works for that magazine, or writes for it, or if you know an editor on another magazine who has bought your work and likes it, say so. Contacts are valuable; dropping names to show what a big deal you are isn't.

6. Don't try to soft soap the editor by telling him or her how great the magazine is, but definitely make it clear that you read it. You could say that you particularly enjoyed a certain article, to show that you're paying attention, but too much praise sounds phony.

7. Don't send in any unnecessary enclosures, such as a picture of yourself (or your prize-winning Labrador Retriever). Just send in material that will sell the idea, which is usually nothing more than the query itself.

8. Don't offer irrelevant information about yourself. Simply tell the editor what there might be in your background that qualifies you to write this story.

9. Don't offer such comments as "I never read your magazine, but this seems to be a natural . . ." or "I know you don't usually publish articles about mountain-climbing, but . . ." Know the magazine, and send only those ideas that fit the format.

10. Don't ask for a meeting to discuss your idea further. If the editor feels this is necessary, he or she will suggest it.

11. Don't ask for advice, such as "If you don't think you can use this, could you suggest another magazine that could?" Or, "If you don't think this works as it is, do you have any suggestions for ways in which I could change it?" Editors are paid to evaluate ideas and to offer suggestions for revision; they'll do this without your prompting. What they won't do is offer extensive advice on pieces they don't want.

12. Don't offer to rewrite, as this implies you know it's not good enough as you have submitted it. Again, editors will ask for rewrites if necessary, and they usually are.

13. Don't make threats such as, "If I don't hear from you within four weeks I'll submit it elsewhere." If the editor is dubious about the idea anyway, that takes away any reason to make a decision.

14. Don't include a multiple-choice reply card, letting the editor check a box to indicate whether he likes it or not. I never got one of those that accompanied an idea I wanted to encourage.

*From *Magazine Writing That Sells*, by Don McKinney (Writer's Digest Books)

Robert Ware
One Winning Query Avenue
Publish City, SC 29288

Ms. Judy Carl-Hendrick
Managing Director, Intercultural Press, Inc.
P.O. Box 700
Yarmouth, ME 04096

RE: New Book Proposal

Dear Ms. Carl-Hendrick:

My name is Robert Ware. I write you today with a book proposal for *e-Commerce: The International Perspective.*

e-Commerce: The International Perspective addresses the single most important hurdle facing America's e-business firms: the challenge of multicultural interfacing. Multicultural interfacing can be broadly defined as how culture affects the distribution, use, perceptions, and expectations of the Internet. At its core, it assumes that all Internet users are not alike and that cultural differences will manifest themselves in how the Internet is distributed, used and perceived.

There is a void in the fast growing market of e-commerce business education. First, there are very few management texts in this area. Second, texts that address the international growth of the e-commerce industry are virtually nonexistent. Third, no text to date addresses the influence of culture on Internet-based services. To fill this void, I propose a 50,000-word book aimed at the college, graduate, and professional markets that will discuss how cultural differences affect the use and acceptance of the Internet, e-services, and e-commerce. I envision a web site that would act as a companion to the text.

I am uniquely qualified to author this text. First, my doctoral research focuses on how the Internet affects the internationalization of firms. I am building a timely and current understanding of the challenges commerce firms face as they expand internationally. Second, I have fifteen years of international business experience in the information services and consumer industries. I am sensitive to how culture affects business operations. I have degrees from Harvard, the MIT Sloan School of Management, and am working on my Ph. D. in international business at the University of South Carolina.

Current e-commerce courses are technical and domestic in focus. In the near future, however, this focus will shift to the international dimension of e-commerce. The reason for this is the 161.5 million Internet users outside the U.S. who represent over 58% of total Internet users, and are the fastest growing geography segment on the Internet.

The primary market for this book are the over four million students in over 1,000 MBA programs around the world. The secondary market are the managers of the 15.7 million e-business web sites on the Internet. *Enterprise e-Commerce* by Peter Fingen et al, an e-commerce book currently in print, is rated 418 on Amazon.com's bestseller list. Lastly, at 50,000 words, *e-Commerce: The International Perspective* is short enough not to be cost prohibitive to most publishing houses.

It is my sincerest hope that you will favorably receive and review this query. I hope that we may converse in some detail about this project in the near future.

Regards,

Robert Ware

Handwritten annotations:

Good

Author has done his homework; the letter is addressed to the correct person (me).

Gives his name and the proposed book's title right up front.

Introduces the problem and defines his terms. This is all concise and clearly worded.

Tells me there's a void and offers three clear ways to fill it.
Elaborates on how the proposed book will fill the void (gives specifics about length and the market he's going to target).

His qualifications are excellent for authoring a book of this sort, and he's not overly boastful when telling me about them.

Further reasons for publishing this book.

Good, compelling use of statistics, including the books potential audience, and helpful marketing research.

The layout of the letter is clean, clear and professional.

This letter is one of the best I have received in recent memory. On one page the author has related all critical information in a concise, professional, articulate manner. No annoying typos or spelling errors. He writes coherently which is so important in a query. Moreover, he has researched our company enough to know his proposed book is appropriate for our publishing house.

Comments provided by Judy Carl-Hendrick, managing editor of Intercultural Press

Bad

Wrong Market Man
333 Try Again Blvd.
Unpublished, CA 90210

September 15, 1999
Ms. Judy Carl-Hendrick   — *The author has researched at least enough to know to address the letter to me.*
Intercultural Press, Inc.
P.O. Box 700
Yarmouth, ME 04096

— *Incorrect punctuation.*

Dear Ms. Carl-Hendrick;   *Immediate turnoff.*

    Are you ready for this? Everyone from movie stars to Internet wizards are start-
ing to do it. Doing what you ask? They are all taking courses to learn to make
money teaching conversational English. That's right, now schools around the world
are starting to look into this new way to make large financial gains. Yes, even the
government is demanding that kids take English conversation beginning in elementary school.   *What government? I assume Japan's?*

Simply not true (it's a gradual process).

This should have been introduced earlier.

    I have been teaching English conversation in Japan for over ten years. I've
decided to take what I know to the typewriter, which is why I'm proposing that
you consider publishing my manuscript, *Teaching English in Japan: The Goldmine
of the 21st Century.*

A real turnoff for a serious publisher.

    And since I've been teaching ESL, numerous potential teachers have contacted
me because they've heard how much money can be made teaching English as a
second language. And when I talk to them they are always shocked when I tell
them they don't need anything more than a BA in any subject from any American
university to teach English in Japan. And anybody with any degree can teach. And
what's great is that you teach just English conversation and so they don't have to
worry about any grammar or punctuation or writing skills. You can make up to
$100 per hour teaching and it's all tax free. And you only have to work for about
six months, so the rest of the year is vacation time. So how come nobody has heard
about this? Because there hasn't been the necessary BOOK to tell them about it.
Now there is.

Doubtful.

Seems like a direct contra- diction to first sentence of this para- graph.

    Teaching English in Japan: The Goldmine of the 21st Century contains and
outlines everything someone needs to know to teach English in Japan, from finding
an employer to teaching techniques, to obtaining work permits to how to survive
the move. And I have names for over 1,000 potential employers. And I also provide
a chart of over 200 suggestions as to what to do and what not to do once you get
to Japan. So this is both a user-friendly guidebook and a directory of important
facts and information. The material found in this book cannot be found in any other
book.   *What does this mean?*

No reason for italics or caps.

Mixes up directory and teaching points—not wise.

For your information, I would like to let you know that this is a simultaneous
submission and any information you can provide pertaining to this matter would
be greatly appreciated.   *Aside from being uncompelling, this letter contains a number of grammar and punctuation errors, especially*
Thank you for your time.   *for an ESL teacher (notice all the sentences that*
Sincerely,   *begin with "And"). Finally, the major mistake here is that this letter shouldn't have even been sent to us.*

Wrong Market Man   *The author failed to research what we publish; we never publish ESL books, just cross-cultural books.*

Comments provided by Judy Carl-Hendrick, managing editor of Intercultural Press

Tells in one brief sentence why she's writing me and what she has to offer.

Provides a clear description of the project with a hook in the first paragraph after intro (A "How to" book with an attitude). Always good to get this information in toward the beginning of the letter.

Shows her strong qualifications for being the right person to author this book.

Clearly shows why there's need for this book (lists changes occurring in the work force and address questions workers are asking themselves).

Highlights compelling facts about the booming market (and attributes these facts to reliable sources).

Offers a brief but effective overview of the competition for this book and how the book will fit into its particular publishing niche.

Good

Doris S. Michaels
Doris Michaels Literary Agency
1841 Broadway, Suite 903
New York, NY 10023

— Addresses letter to correct agent (me).

Dear Ms. Michaels,

I am looking for an agent to represent my book and am delighted to submit the proposal for your consideration. *The Age of Advantage: Issues, Options and Strategies for Mid-Life Career Transition* is a "How-to" book with an attitude:

- It provokes thoughtful consideration about mid-life career transition;
- It motivates readers to challenge their own expectations and stretch their limits;
- It teaches specific strategies and techniques for getting a job when the competition is stiff and you're no longer 35.

Author Jean Erickson Walker, Ed.D has over 20 years' experience as a career counselor, management consultant, educator, and public speaker. She has worked with over 3,000 people in career transition, the majority of whom are mid-age.

Downsizing, right-sizing, layoffs, terminations, acquisitions and mergers have taken their toll on corporate America and people at mid-age have been by far the hardest hit. Their job searches are much more difficult and over twice as long as those of younger people.

The Age of Advantage answers the questions:
1. What specific strategies can mid-agers take to position themselves effectively in the marketplace?
2. What are the personal blocks that keep them from understanding they have options, and taking the risks involved to change careers?
3. What keeps them in jobs, and even life styles, they no longer enjoy or want?
4. What are the issues that make mid-life career transition so difficult?
5. How is job loss affecting this group's self-confidence?

The market for this book is extensive:
- 33 million people over the age of 50 in the United States:
- 11 million still in the workforce;
- 18 million have stated they want to work or get a better job.
- 76% of retirees would like to be working (AARP statistics).
- A Baby Boomer will reach age 50 every 7½ seconds for the next 10 years (*Wall Street Journal*, 1/20/96).
- 785 professionals in 226 Corporate Outplacement Firms are expected to counsel 50,000 executives who have lost their jobs this year, the majority of whom will be mid-age (*Peterson's Guide to Outplacement Firms*).

"How to" books on job search and career transition fill the shelves. Most deal with the general category of job search, while others target specific audiences such as recent college graduates, women, and people in highly technical fields. Several focus on résumé writing, interviewing, finding job openings, preparing cover letters, and even negotiating. Only one specifically deals with older Americans, and its target audience is post-retirement. An increasing number of books are beginning to deal with traumas of mid-life transitions, mid-life crises, etc. However, there is no other resource that specifically pulls together all aspects of mid-life career transitions.

Thank you for your consideration.

Sincerely,   *Politely closes the letter (shows she's not demanding or desperate).*

Jean Erickson Walker

The entire query letter is so well organized. The author doesn't try to convince me she's a great writer or that this is a worthwhile project. She gets to her points quickly, and outlines those points with lists.

Bad

Not addressed to the agent personally (never write a To Whom It May Concern letter in publishing—you're certain not to be taken seriously).

Terry Terrible Query
1234 Not Even Close Road
Slushpile, NY 10025
terryt@badwriters.com

Wordy and awkward (especially the "which means of course I need an agent"—almost sounds a little mean).

To Whom it May Concern:

Fails to tell me much about the novel. She just gives the plot a label (episodic/adventure/etc.) and drops in a few vague bits about the story.

I have just completed my first novel (it's called *Melanie's Miracles*), and I would like to sell it to a publisher, which means of course I need an agent. That's why I am writing this letter to you.

Melanie's Miracles is sixty thousand words or two hundred and five pages long. It is geared toward adult readers. The novel is written in first person, singular and revolves around Melanie, a recent retiree who tells the story of her life after leaving the workforce. The plot could best be described as episodic/adventure/etc. Melanie fills us in on what she has learned as she has travelled through life. She give detailed information about stages of life and its key events. But the story is more about the people Melanie meets than it is about Melanie, which means that she is really just a window through which one (the reader) looks to see the crazy, strange, characters who pass through our lives.

The diction and word choice are terrible. Why put (the reader) in parentheses like that?

Since this is my first novel it was challenging, but I had a lot of fun writing it also. In the past I've written short stories that dealt with romance, drama, villains and other typical story elements, but this time I wrote a more personalized work about real people. These are people you know and I know and readers will know once they read about Melanie's miracles. The miracles, of course, are the people she has encountered throughout her life.

It doesn't matter whether she found the process of writing the novel challenging and fun; what matters is that the novel is worthy of being published, which it isn't.

I'd like to close by saying that I think with the right editor's input and expertise this novel has the potential to become very popular and could benefit all involved.

Thanks.

How could it benefit "all involved?" Who are we talking about? Very unclear.

If she is looking for "the right editor's input and expertise," then why is she soliciting an agent and not the help of an editor?

The author doesn't mention any writing credentials, just topics and character types she's written about in the past.

Terry Terrible Query

The basic gist and plot of the novel is not condensed into a compelling, comprehensive paragraph. There's no clear organization here either.

This is obviously a poor query. I know little about the novel or the writer, but I do know enough to pass on this query. The writing meanders and seems as if it's written by a child—I can only imagine how painful it would be to read the novel in its entirety!

Comments provided by Doris Michaels of the Doris S. Michaels Literary Agency

Salvo Press was new, so it was nice to see that published authors were looking at us. I could see that he was a professional writer.

A starred review in Publishers Weekly was impressive. He also sent me copies of these reviews.

I already know that many books were optioned, but few ever made it to the big screen. Still, someone in the movie industry had found quality in his writing.

He got my interest with the description of the book. I had a feeling this would be more that a genre mystery, and I was right. The synopsis that accompanied the query letter further detailed the quality I would find in the manuscript.

He was looking for a small press to highlight his talent. Many mid-list authors at major New York publishing houses had been cut recently; he was looking for a niche publisher.

Gerald Duff
111 To The Printer Way
Publishersville, NY 12343

Salvo Press
P.O. Box 9095
Bend, OR 97708

Dear Mr. Schmidt,

I write to ask if you would consider my new novel for publication by Salvo Press. I have published three novels to date: *Indian Giver* in 1983 with Indiana University Press, *Graveyard Working* in 1994 at Baskerville and *That's All Right, Mama: The Unauthorized Life of Elvis's Twin* in the following year, also at Baskerville.

That's All Right, Mama received a starred review in *Publishers Weekly* and was subsequently reviewed favorably in *The Washington Post, Boston Globe, Entertainment Weekly, New Orleans Times-Picayune, Dallas Morning News, Orlando Sentinel, Tulsa World, International Herald-Tribune, Baltimore Sun* and in over one hundred other newspapers and magazines, including originals and the syndications of the *Post, Sentinel* and *Globe* reviews. It went into a second printing and attracted attention from numerous reprint houses, motion picture production companies and foreign publishers. It has been optioned by Janet Burrows at Warner Brothers. My previous novel, *Graveyard Working*, had good reviews as well, in newspapers and in the *Atlantic Monthly*. I've enclosed copies of some of these reviews of both novels for your perusal.

Unfortunately, Baskerville has not enjoyed financial success with many of its other books and has suspended its publication of fiction for the time being. Thus my search for a new publisher. This novel is entitled *Memphis Ribs*, and it's a genre-bending, hard-boiled mystery about a Memphis homicide detective named J.W. Ragsdale. It's set in Memphis and in the Mississippi Delta in May, the time of the International Barbecue Contest and the Cotton Carnival, two events spanning Memphis society and culture. Like all my novels, it's an amalgam of humor and what the *Atlantic Monthly* called in its review of an earlier book, "Mr. Duff's grotesquely amusing and bloody version of the southern Gothic genre." I have enclosed a summary of it, for your information, and I'd be glad, of course, to send part or all of the manuscript (97,000 words) if and when appropriate.

I'm at a point in my writing career where my work is receiving wider attention of a gratifyingly favorable kind, and I believe that, given some of the mysteries you've published at Salvo Press, *Memphis Ribs* may be of interest to you. I certainly hope so.

Thanks for your attention. I look forward to hearing from you.

Sincerely,

Gerald Duff

Although this letter does not contain every element I like, it got my attention and I asked to see more. Memphis Ribs by Gerald Duff went on to great reviews and sales. Duff's next book, Snake Song, was released in the Fall 2000.

P.S. I enclosed a brief list of publishing credits and a self-addressed, stamped envelope for return of materials, should you be unable to consider my request.

Comments provided by Scott Schmidt, publisher of Salvo Press

There were so many problems with this letter, it was difficult to choose which errors to highlight. I couldn't even imagine how the manuscript would look.

Bad

Loser Letterman
9999 Need Help Rd.
Unpublished, OH 45234

Salvo Press
P.O. Box 9095
Bend, OR 97708

Dear Mr. Schmidt,

Hatred: prejudiced hostility or animosity.

Who in this world has gone through life feeling hatred for someone else? And who hasn't been tempted to act on that sense of hatred by hurting or killing the hated person? Inside each of us lives a rainy-day self that wants to act on these feelings. Although most of the time we take a minute to think before we act, sometimes that mean and convincing philosophical being inside our soul makes us give in to our impulses. Why do we do this knowing that two wrongs do not make a right? Because in our spirit's mind, carrying out the hatred we feel is all we can do to keep sane.

My novel's goal is not to figure out everything about hatred, but to take the reader on a journey through that mind's reality of what it's like to feel hatred. It shows why sometimes we feel we must take the highway to hell and not the road to heaven, even though we know which path we should take.

Stan is the main character who's filled with hate because his twin brother was killed and he feels his life won't be complete unless he murders the murderer. He thinks committing that vengeful act will end the hatred that's been consuming his life. He wants to revel to the world how he feels about the killer. He also wants the killer to feel the pain his brother must of suffered at the killer's hands. Stan ends up feeling bad about wanting to kill and so he starts to wonder if he's justified or is he just being stupid. He begins to ask himself lots of introspective questions and we get to know him better with each one he asks.

Hate has a length of about seventy thousand words and touches on such areas of human emotion as hatred, loss, love, anger, suicide, and remorse. If you would like to publish this novel, I will be glad to send you the entire manuscript or a few sample chapters. I am also submitting this query letter to other publishers and agents.

Thanks and I look forward to hearing from you soon.

Sincerely,

Loser Letterman

Handwritten margin notes:

If I don't even know the definition of hatred, I shouldn't be in the publishing business.

"Rainy-Day Self"? So, you only have these feelings when it's raining? I forced myself to keep reading.

Philosophical being? This makes no sense at all to me.

This is one of the many clichés in the letter. I can only guess how many would be contained in a 70,000 word novel.

Now we have a "spirit's mind"—what's that?

Another cliché.

I think he means must "have," not must "of." Little errors like this are real turn-offs.

I think he means reveal, not "revel."

Thank God.

Hate. Now that's an original title.

Comments provided by Scott Schmidt, publisher of Salvo Press

Sally Writes
111 High Hopes Lane
Nice Pitch, TN 45222
Phone (653)333-444
Fax (653)333-5555
swrites@xyz.com

Good

September 28, 2001

Frederick Raborg
Editor
Amelia Magazine
329 "E" Street
Bakersfield, CA 93304-2031

The author has used a textbook approach, which, in this case, seems to work.

Dear Mr. Raborg,

Enclosed is my short story, "Second Sister" (2,500 words). It's about Susan Demp-sey, an abortion-rights activist who spends every weekend staging protests against pro-life organizations. But Susan's routine changes when Kristin Comb comes into town and reveals to Susan that they're sisters, born two years apart. Susan had heard about a second sister but always thought her mother aborted that child. The child, of course, wasn't aborted and is now a thriving, loving, well-adjusted adult. The two sisters become great friends, leading Susan to abandon her weekly protests and become a luke-warm pro-choice advocate (at best). The question is: Has Susan lost part of herself by gaining a sister?

A tightly conceived query for short fiction is extremely difficult to compose, but I like the direct, concise approach used in this query. It covers briefly all of the major editorial concerns—length, situation, conflict and conclusion. It also reassures the editor that the story actually has been written and that the query isn't one of speculation only.

Suggests well-rounded characters, though there is little hint of local color or ambiance, which would have been helpful.

I have published three previous stories. You are the first editor I'm soliciting with this story. I will wait six weeks for your response befire I approach another maga-zine.

Thank you for considering "Second Sister."

Sincerely,

Repeating the story's title locks it in the editor's mind.

Implies experience through prior publication and grants exclusivity while affording patience for a decision.

Sally Writes

Encl: Short story, "Second Sister"
SASE

Good to let me know what is enclosed in the submission package.

Comments provided by Frederick Raborg, Jr., editor of *Amelia Magazine*

Bad

Alice Noscribe
2222 Poor Query Lane
Try Again, ID 83298
(656) 848-4848

Frederick A. Raborg
Amerlia Magazine
329 E Street
Bakersfield, CA 93304-2301

Dear Mr. Raborg,

— Correctly addresses the letter.

Wrong word—poor professionalism (which is evident throughout the letter).

*"Alice, come here for a minute, sweetheart. There's something I need to tell you,"
Wendy nervously called.
"I don't have time for talking Wendy. I'm really in a hurry right now. Tony is on
his way here and I need to jump into the shower and be ready by 11:00." Whenever
Tony picked me up I was always running late, every single time. This was a Saturday
and that meant it was the day I had to take my kids to there fathers, had to do
laundry, had to work the evening shift, and had to do all the chores around the
restaurant to get everything ready for the beginning of the new week on Sunday.
Then I had to shower and get ready for Tony."*

Opening a query with a quote out of context is dangerous. Read like clutter and delays the effect of the query.

Well, "there's something I need to tell you;" are about the worst words one person
can tell another. You know your only going to get bad news. I didn't want to hear
any bad news. After all my life was staring to take shape, I recently turned twenty-
five, just started college, finally got divorced from the jerk who fathered my two
kids, and at last was in a health relationship. My life was only going forward and
I didn't want any bad news to get in it's way.

Lots of careless typos, misspellings and improper punctuation throughout.

*"Sugar I'm sorry to tell you, but Tony's mother called me today and told me he
killed himself. She said to tell you about it because I'm your best friend and she
wanted somebody close to you to break the news."*

*Those few minutes talking with Wendy had really changed my life forever. I'd never
known anyone who died much less anyone who had killed themselves, and now here
I was all of the sudden having to deal with my beloved boyfriend's suicide. Death
was staring me in the eyes and life didn't seem so promising anymore. You never
know when your number is up.*   Why is it geared toward our audience?

Poor syntax and trite phrasing.

How can it help them?

My story is geared toward your magazine's audience. It will help them confront
death and be prepared for it when someone close to them dies. I am purposing a
2,5000 word story, which would start at the beginning, go all the way up to Tony's
death, and then end showing how it crumbled my world and how I've learned to
deal with it.   Where else? Again, another terrible slip of professionalism.

Should be "proposing."

I will be glad to send you the portion of the story I've written so far. I could have
the entire manuscript finished and ready for you in three weeks if you're interested.

I don't want a portion of the story. The story should have been finished before sending the query.

Cordially,

Finally, this query tells me much too little on which to make a decision, and the lengthy quotes are only dead weight.

It's dangerous to be so concrete until an editorial deadline has been decided.

Alice Noscribe

Comments provided by Frederick Raborg, Jr., editor of *Amelia Magazine*

Sell What You Write

BY GREG DAUGHERTY

"Study the magazine."

That may be the most clichéd advice ever offered to people who want to write for magazines. It may also be the best.

If you wanted to work for, say, a steel mill, you'd do what you could to learn about the kind of steel it made, try to get its annual report and so forth. But with a magazine, everything is there in black and white and a lot of other colors.

For most of your life you've probably read magazines. But unless you've been writing professionally, you've read them like a reader. Here we look at how to read a magazine like a writer—a writer who wants to sell it something. The process, as you'll see, can be very different.

THE COVER

What a magazine puts on its cover can tell you a lot about who it thinks its readers are and what it believes they're interested in. Does it favor articles about health, money, travel, sex, relationships? Does it seem to be addressing men, women or both? Young readers or older ones? Does it treat its material seriously or with a sense of humor?

Consider these two cover lines on the subject of cordless screwdrivers from the magazines *Consumer Reports* and *Verge*. "Screwdrivers"—*Consumer Reports*. "Screw anywhere"—*Verge*. Which magazine do you think fancies itself a title for hip young men?

THE TABLE OF CONTENTS

Somewhere, usually in the first dozen pages of the magazine, will be a list of its entire fare for that issue. Reading it will give you a more rounded picture of what the magazine wants than its cover alone will. Here, for example, you'll see whether the magazine runs personal essays—a genre unlikely to make it to the magazine's cover but possibly a regular part of its mix nonetheless.

Here, too, you'll usually see bylines. They can tell you whether the magazine leans heavily on big-name writers or is open to newcomers. A quick comparison of the bylines on the table of contents and the names of staffers listed on the masthead can tell you whether the magazine is largely staff written or freelance written. A contributor's column, if the magazine has one, can give you further insight into what kind of writers that magazine generally uses.

THE MASTHEAD

Not every magazine has a masthead. *The New Yorker*, for example, is famous for not having one. When a magazine does not list its staff, you can scan it for a likely name to address your query to. Here are some of the job titles you're likely to see, starting at the top:

Editor-in-Chief (sometimes just Editor)—the person in charge of the editorial part of the

---

GREG DAUGHERTY *has been a successful freelance writer and magazine editor for over twenty years. His writing has appeared in many magazines, from trade journals to general interest publications, and he has held senior editorial positions for* Reader's Digest, Money, Consumer Reports *and* Success *magazines. Currently he is editor-in-chief of* New Choices *and a correspondent for* Writer's Digest. *This article is excerpted from his book,* You Can Write for Magazines *(Writer's Digest Books).*

magazine. Except on magazines with very small staffs, the editor in chief may not work directly with many writers, especially new ones. Sometimes, though, he or she is the best person to address a query to, since it's likely to be passed on to the appropriate editor.

Executive Editor—another editor who may not work directly with many writers but may instead manage other editors.

Managing Editor—often an editor in charge of getting the magazine out on schedule. Some managing editors work with freelance writers, but most, in my experience, don't.

Articles Editor—pretty much what it sounds like. The articles editor, if the magazine has one, is often the best person to address your query to.

Senior editor, associate editor, assistant editor, etc.—editors with varying degrees of authority who may or may not work with freelance writers. Sometimes an editor who is relatively low on the masthead will be a good bet because he or she may take more interest in you than more experienced editors who are already working with as many writers as they can handle. Other times, junior editors will simply be too preoccupied with advancing their own careers to show much interest in yours. So you take your chances.

THE DEPARTMENTS

The biggest difference between departments and articles is the length. Departments run shorter pieces—often much shorter ones. While a full-length article may run 2,000 words or longer, a department may only be 750 to 1,000 words. So if you're interested in writing short pieces, study the departments, which you'll usually find in the front and back of the magazine. Here are a few questions to ask as you do:

- What are the regular departments in the magazine, and what subject area does each one cover?
- Do they appear to be written by a regular columnist or open to a variety of writers?
- Are the writers on staff (check the masthead) or freelance?

ARTICLES

Articles often appear in what's referred to as a "well," more or less in the middle of the magazine. Some magazines open their wells with that issue's cover story. Others simply start with any article that seems appropriate. Either way, when the little departments in the front of the magazine end (and before the little ones in the back begin), you'll typically find the magazine's longest features, often page after glossy page of them, uninterrupted by ads. What can you learn from the articles you find there? Here are a few things:

- How does the magazine usually begin its articles? With an anecdote? With the latest news on the subject? Or with some other type of lead?
- Does it run any essays or pieces written in the first person?
- Does it like humor?
- Does it often use sidebars?
- Does it run seasonal articles?
- How long are its articles, in general? (To get a quick estimate, count the words in an average paragraph and multiply by the number of paragraphs.)

Ideally, you should go through this process with at least two or three recent issues of your target magazine. But if all you can scrounge up is a single copy, you can still get a clue to what past issues have covered by reading the letters to the editor, if the magazine prints any. Many magazines also run a box with short blurbs about the future articles, which can give you a hint of what's coming up.

THE ADVERTISING

Yes, you can even learn something from a magazine's advertising. Thomas Clark, former editor of *Writer's Digest*, notes that the products in ads offer a lot of clues to the kinds of people

Editorial Etiquette in Five Easy No-Nos

The writer/editor relationship, alas, is rarely an equal one. Editors can often get away with being rude to writers, but writers don't get anywhere unless they're perfectly polite in return. The rules change once you're famous, of course. But in the meantime, here are five rules any writer would do well to heed:

No-No 1: Don't phone unless you're invited to. You could be interrupting crucial work or just ruining a lusty daydream. Either way, the editor is likely to be less open-minded about whatever you called to discuss than if you had put it on paper. Editors are better at dealing with paper anyway.

No-No 2: Don't fax, either. The magazine could be waiting for a last-minute article or an urgent take-out menu.

No-No 3: Don't miss any deadlines you agree to. By the same token, don't agree to any deadlines you couldn't possibly make.

No-No 4: Don't complain about the difficulty of the assignment, the lousy pay or whatever. Editors won't hesitate to annoy you, but that doesn't mean you're allowed to annoy them.

No-No 5: Don't try to build up your work by making fun of something the magazine published. Sure, that last article on your favorite topic may have gotten all the facts wrong. But if you point that out, the editor may take it personally. Believe it or not, underneath their tough hides, editors can be very sensitive creatures.

who are reading the magazine. For example, says Clark, "Are we talking about a 30-something urbanite who is single or a 40-year-old midwestern housewife with two kids?"

So even if you normally whiz past the ads, give them a look. A magazine stuffed with pitches for expensive watches, luxury automobiles and pricey perfumes probably goes to a wealthier audience than one whose advertisers are promoting economy cars and canned soup. A magazine with ads for baby diapers presumably reaches younger readers than one with ads for the adult kind.

WRITER'S GUIDELINES

You can also glean some of the above information by sending for the writer's guidelines many magazines offer in return for a self-addressed, stamped envelope. The problem with guidelines is that they're often out of date; magazines change quickly these days, and revising their editorial guidelines is seldom a high priority.

Can you learn anything of use from guidelines? Sometimes. A magazine's guidelines may, for example, tell you how far ahead it works. That can be helpful if you're hoping to propose an article that should run at a specific time of year. The guidelines may also tell you whether the magazine wants you to supply photos and, if so, what format it prefers.

Perhaps most useful of all, guidelines often tell you what the magazine is not interested in. For example, the guidelines for *Smithsonian Magazine* note that, "We do not consider fiction, poetry, travel features, political and news events, or previously published articles." *Popular Mechanics* magazine's guidelines tell would-be automotive writers that, "We do all our own road testing and conduct our own owner surveys. Please don't query us about submitting driving reports on specific models or articles about what it's like to own a specific car."

THE MAGAZINES MOST OPEN TO NEW WRITERS

Some magazines are more receptive to new writers than others. Here are five types of publications that are almost always looking for fresh talent:

1. New magazines. Some eight hundred to nine hundred new magazines are launched each year, according to Samir A. Husni, a University of Mississippi journalism professor who compiles an annual guide to new magazines. Half will fail within a year, Husni says, and only three of every ten will still be in business after four years. But while they are around, they'll need writers—and lots of them.

New magazines are especially receptive to new writers for a couple of reasons. One, obviously, is that they don't have a vast network of writers in place yet. Another is that new magazines usually don't have the editorial budgets of larger ones, so they're often willing to take a chance on less-experienced (in other words, cheaper) writers.

How do you find out about new magazines before they're old magazines? The easiest way is to keep checking both your local newsstand and the supermarket magazine racks for titles you've never seen before.

Another good source of information on new magazines and ones still on the drawing board are the trade magazines that people in the publishing business read. Among the most useful are *Advertising Age, Adweek* and *Folio: The Magazine for Magazine Management. Writer's Digest* can also tip you off to new magazines. So, on occasion, will *The Wall Street Journal* and the business sections of *The New York Times* and other major newspapers.

And never underestimate the value of your own mailbox. What may be mere junk mail to your neighbors could be valuable information to you. Years ago I received a mailing from *Yankee* magazine, announcing a new spin-off called *Collectibles Illustrated*. I wrote to the editor of the new magazine, enclosed some clippings of articles I've done and offered my services in case he ever needed a correspondent where I lived. Within weeks I had an assignment, and over the next three years, until the magazine's ultimate demise, I wrote more than a dozen pieces.

2. Old magazines with new owners. When a magazine gets a new owner, things tend to change. A new owner almost inevitably means a new team of editors and, sometimes, a new approach to whatever the magazine covers. Any change of that sort means an opportunity for writers.

The best way to keep track of ownership changes is to read the trade magazines mentioned previously. Another is to take note when a magazine alters its logo or overall design. A new design may mean a new art director, another near inevitability after an ownership change.

3. Magazines that are changing frequency. A magazine expanding from six issues a year to twelve may need twice as much editorial material to fill its pages. Even a magazine going from ten issues a year to twelve may need twenty percent more. Any frequency boost is likely to mean the magazine is more open to new writers. Again, it pays to check those trade publications now and then and to watch the newsstand like a pro.

4. Magazines that are changing focus. Sometimes magazines take a new direction even without changing owners. That, too, may spell opportunity, since not all of the magazine's current writers will be right for the new and improved model.

5. Small magazines. Whether they're under new management or have been run by the same family since the War of 1812, small-circulation magazines tend to be more open to new writers than their giant competitors. Small magazines also tend to have smaller budgets, which means they often have to take talent where they find it. You may never make a living by writing for small magazines, but they can be a terrific place to gain some experience and accumulate a few good clips. What's more, the editors who work for small magazines often move on to bigger magazines as their own careers progress, taking their best writers along with them.

First Bylines

BY LYNN WASNAK

How sweet it is to break into print for the first time! Here, three nonfiction writers—a newspaper journalist, a freelancer for national magazines, and a writer with an intensely personal essay to sell—share their success stories. Through hard work and dogged persistence, they found the right freelance outlets for their writing and from that beginning have gone on to the pleasure and security of steady work.

DAVID STRINGER
First Publication: *Ann Arbor Observer*

Sometimes the best place to start a writing career is in your own backyard. When David Stringer faced retirement after thirty-two years teaching English to high school students, he knew what he wanted to do, and that was to write. He'd published nonfiction in academic journals before, and had a few poems published, but had never written for pay.

So before his official retirement two years ago, Stringer tested the writing waters in two directions, simultaneously. He began working for his brother, a management consultant, preparing case studies for executive training. And he started doing freelance writing for the *Ann Arbor Observer*.

Stringer chose the *Ann Arbor Observer* because it was close at hand. He'd enjoyed reading it for years, so he had a good sense of its style and what its editors might be able to use. Also, he had an "in" with the staff. A former student had written some features for the *Observer*, and told him the editor, John Hilton, was helpful and accessible. He suggested that Stringer contact Hilton.

Stringer's first article for the *Observer* was a profile of a fellow teacher, focused on cultural identity issues. "It was not very good, but it was good enough. They edited it heavily, and published it, so I was in."

How did he feel about that "heavy editing," after thirty years of teaching kids to write? "Well, I was chagrined . . . until I saw that it came out better. I simply had to learn how to do that kind of writing. I'd been teaching kids how to write an analysis of *Hamlet*, the "getting-ready-for-college" kind of writing. You don't have to grab people in your lead in a piece your English teacher is paid to read. It's not the piece I'm proudest of," Stringer admits, "But it is my first. Kind of like the first time you're having sex. It's not the best, but damn I'm glad I did it."

Since that first article appeared, Stringer worked avidly at building his writing career. He's written more (and better) features for the *Observer*. One, about high-school kids' spring break trips to Cancun, was "full of juicy horror stories," he says. "I got thank-you phone calls from parents and there were classroom discussions about it; the kids were having to negotiate permis-

LYNN WASNAK *has been a fulltime freelance writer for more than twenty years, and thanks the newly published writers here for sharing their insights and experience.*

sion from their parents to go on spring break trips. People ran off copies and sent them to friends. All that was very gratifying." Stringer is also being published in *Parenting* Magazine.

Business writing works, too. "I'm finding that people pay a lot for writing. Not for poetry or fiction, unless you're Stephen King," says Stringer. But when a corporate newsletter job opened to freelance, he was asked his fee. "I said, 'I charge $100 an hour.' The guy didn't even blink."

Recently, Stringer and his brother were waiting for confirmation of a contract for a business book. "In December, the publisher—a large, reputable company—said, 'We've got a contract,' but here it is March, and I still haven't seen it. I can't reach the editor or publisher on the phone or voice mail. I got one e-mail that said, 'It's a go-ahead, can I call you tomorrow?' I replied, 'Sure, call me tomorrow, 9 a.m.,' and that was three weeks ago!"

This sort of frustration comes with the freelance territory, Stringer believes. "When you get a gig, suddenly there's this bunch of money. Then you might have, as I did, three months with nothing and a lot of postage on query letters."

He admits he has a special advantage to help deal with uncertainty that other writers might not enjoy. "I have a pension that pays half to two-thirds of the money I need each month. That's the way to be a writer. My food and rent are taken care of."

Even better, he's creating a new identity for himself as a writer. "It's a form of reincarnation. I've got a lot more energy. It's been kind of a rebirth for me."

What's the moral of Stringer's story? There's lots of writing to be done and money to be made at it. "Do your first article well, so there's a second one. There's plenty of work for English majors," he says, "but you've got to find it."

JULIE JOELLE
First Publication: *Mademoiselle*

In 1998, Julie JoElle came back from a Key West vacation of sun, sand, and all-night writing binges, determined to write for women's magazines. "I sat in the Columbus, Ohio, library and sank into a stack of books on how to write and sell," she says. "I learned that most of the advice suggested I start small with local papers or little magazines. I found this so-called 'encouragement' really depressing!"

"It made me feel small," she adds, "and if I followed that advice I wouldn't be where I am today," with articles in large-circulation national and international magazines, a movie contract, a book under way and more.

How did JoElle, then a twenty-something high-school-dropout, pull off this amazing feat? She read the how-to publish books and listened to her gut. And she had a very strong story to tell. That combination led her to parlay an intensely personal story into a freelance story idea.

To get started, JoElle researched the magazines she wanted to write for, reading at least six months' of back issues. One publication she studied was *Redbook*, where she found an article about Munchausen by proxy (MBP). In this rare psychiatric disorder, an adult (usually a mother) deliberately causes "symptoms" in a child, who then suffers needless and painful medical treatments. "The writer of that article didn't understand why the mother did what she did. I was a MBP victim, too—but I'd been an older child, and I *did* understand why my mom did it. The story in *Redbook* created a burning desire for me to tell people what happened."

JoElle followed the usual new writer's advice and sent queries to five small magazines. Then, just for kicks, she followed her instincts and wrote individual, tailored queries for *Mademoiselle*, *Cosmo*, and *Ladies Home Journal*.

The small magazines quickly rejected her idea. "Soon the only ones I hadn't heard from were the biggies, and I figured they would get around to it." Instead, she got a letter from *Cosmopolitan*, asking for the article on spec. Then the next morning, *Mademoiselle* phoned, asking to purchase the story outright for $1.75 a word. Three hours later, *Ladies Home Journal* called, as well. Presto—three big opportunities and her first major sale!

The experience taught her a whole new perspective on marketing her work. "Most books say 'Keep it small. Don't expect a lot.' I say, 'Expect exactly what you want.' "

With her check from *Mademoiselle*, JoElle moved to Los Angeles, and soon sold the story to *Marie Claire* in Australia and other international publications. Then she got an offer from a company interested in movie rights. "That really excited me, but also made me realize I couldn't do this alone. I needed to have an agent to represent the work for the most monetary value, and also to make sure I didn't sign my rights away."

Once again, as JoElle researched "how to do it," the discouraging messages were everywhere. Once again, she ignored them, went straight to the Writer's Guild website, got a list of credited agents and started cold-calling. "You have to go through the watch dog system, so I blurted out a forty-second soundbite: 'A TV show is calling me, and someone offered to buy my movie rights, and I need representation.' "

After a few tries, she landed Norman Kurland of Broder, Kurland, Webb and Uffner, one of the top literary agencies for TV writers. This firm now represents her movie of the week idea, and sent her to well-known agent Joel Gotler at AMG/Renaissance, who will market her book when it's finished.

"When you want to go into a new career, or have a dream, there are so many people around to say 'You'll never make it,' or 'Don't give up your day job.' Those little messages can be very daunting."

Instead JoElle advises new writers to "Search your heart and take a real assessment of what you feel you can do. Start at that level. Don't start at rock bottom, because you might not be rock bottom. Start where you feel capable of starting, then work backwards, if you must."

When a rejection happens, JoElle takes it with a shrug and a view that "working for that magazine is not right for me," instead of thinking "Oh God, I got shot down again!" "If you're not right for them, they're not right for you. You just need to find the people who are right for you," she says.

HELEN HARRIS
First Publication: *Modern Maturity*

Speaking to Helen Harris, one is immediately struck by her vibrant life force, a quickly discernable passion. Harris dug deep into that life force to generate the writing that resulted in her first sale.

Her article, titled "Touch and Go: my silent craving for body contact," describes in wrenching detail the sensual anguish of a new widow. She says out loud what many think, but would not dare to say.

Harris credits her teachers, especially Bill Kittredge of the MFA program at University of Montana, for steering her in the right direction after twenty-five years of rejection slips: "When I went there, after my husband died, I was fifty-four—the oldest student, older than the teachers. But it was such fun," she says. "The heart of the program is a seminar once a week. We had an opportunity to write a lot and have a very attentive audience. That's how the piece got started, with all these marked-up drafts.

© Anne Hamersky

"Bill Kittredge would say 'Dig deeper. You must write about the things that keep you awake at night. You must write about the things you do not dare write about. It's hard to do that, but that's why people read.' That made perfect sense to me, because that's what I read," she says.

Harris relied on books long before she spent twenty-four years as an English teacher at the junior high and high-school level. "When I was a girl," she says, "I didn't have any real access to information about sex, and so I would go to the dictionary. I just appreciated that so. There it would be, written down, and it wouldn't tell on me. That's what really thrills me. The way people are in a library or a bookstore—the way they are engaged with the page and the secret things going on there." While the lessons she learned in the MFA program were important, the contacts she made proved more so. "Bill Kittredge was instrumental in connecting me with John Wood, the editor at *Modern Maturity*," she says.

The first piece she submitted to Wood was turned down. "But he turned it down with such a generous amount of praise, and he said, 'Think of us whenever you write.' So I sent him other pieces." But nothing happened for over three years and she didn't recontact him. "I'm so shy of editors; I'm terrified of them," she admits. "I'd forgotten he even had 'Touch and Go,' when he wrote me back and asked, 'Have you sold this elsewhere? Can we use it?' I said, 'My God, are you out of your mind? Of course you can use it!' "

To add to the tension of first publication, there was a slight complication. After years of handling in an editorial office, Wood's copy of her manuscript was missing a page. "I spent days looking through my place," says Harris. "I had six different drafts, none of which was the one he had. Finally, because I didn't have it on the computer, I had to hold my breath and patch together some plausible wording between pages four and six, and hope he wouldn't notice!"

Apparently the patch job worked, because her piece appeared in *Modern Maturity*'s August 1999 issue. Since then, she placed the article that *Modern Maturity* initially rejected. And with Kittredge's help, she found an agent for the novel she worked on while completing her MFA program. Kittredge asked his own agent to look at it. After she rejected it, Kittredge told Harris, "Do not let this sit around!" and said to send it to fifty agents.

"The copying and postage was several hundred dollars, because I submitted a bulky package, with several chapters. Of the fifty, I was rejected by forty-eight, and it took me a full year to get up my courage to send the rest of it to the one agent who said she'd look at it," Harris says. That agent is currently shopping her novel around, while Harris edits a group of pieces done about the same time as the one that appeared in *Modern Maturity*. This collection will be titled *Widow Making: a Memoir of Death and Sex*. "I always really loved to write, and there were a couple of times when I really did think I had something fresh to say."

It seems that now there is no stopping her.

Bestselling Author Reveals Secrets for Writing the Compelling Memoir

BY ANNE BOWLING

Edward Ball's is the kind of man-bites-dog story that makes pretty big news in publishing. Ball, an art critic for the *Village Voice*, decides to tackle his first book project—a 300-year family history. And with his memoir he hits a literary grand slam: the manuscript is taken on by one of publishing's preeminent editors, and *Slaves in the Family* (Farrar, Straus & Giroux, 1998) goes on to win the National Book Award for nonfiction. The memoir, called "a brilliant blend of archival research and oral history" by *The New Yorker*, draws the kind of attention its bestselling predecessor *Angela's Ashes* attracted for Frank McCourt. Following that comes the author tour, with book signings, readings, lectures.

Edward Ball

© Sigrid Estrada

But all that must have been the easy part for Ball, whose bestselling scholarly memoir traces the history of South Carolina's Ball family, the rice and cotton plantations they ran and the people they enslaved. The real work was the research and writing, which for Ball was a fulltime job for three years. During that time he reviewed 10,000 pages of family records, letters and papers spanning some 300 years; interviewed hundreds of people, both Ball family members and descendents of Ball family slaves to record oral histories; and spent months "roaming the halls of libraries and reading other works to learn the rules of research and history." Public reception, Ball says, was icing on the cake.

"When you're writing a book, you only think about whether you can finish it. I didn't have the luxury of saying 'this will all be worth it in the end,' " he says. "I was trying to do something that took every fiber of my intelligence, and an enormous exertion of strength, and I was just thinking 'can I actually do this?' This is the first book I've written, and like a lot of writers, I wasn't exactly sure what it would be like after publication."

While the recognition Ball's book has received makes his story a bit of an anomaly, more writers than ever are taking a crack at memoir. The form is alluring now, both because it has exploded in popularity, and because everyone has a story to tell. But before writers sit down to craft that life story, whether it's a 300-year family history or an intimate personal account, a little instruction can go a long way: Where do you find the archives and documents that create the roadmap for your story? Can you rely on memory alone, or do you need to corroborate that with records? What can you do to prevent causing rifts in the family you're writing about? What should you know when you sit down to do the actual writing?

Here Ball discusses the path he followed to write *Slaves in the Family*, and shares advice from the trail for writers considering tackling their own life stories.

ANNE BOWLING *is editor of* Novel & Short Story Writer's Market.

To cover such a detailed and extensive period of history, what research methods did you use, and which were most helpful?

Apart from the Ball family papers, which were extensive, I relied on interviews, military records, wills, plats, tax records, marriage records, census records, all kinds of government documents, and that's the order in which they were important. The interviews were probably the most important, because many families have oral tradition passed down from generation to generation. So family members would give their accounts of events from the distant past, and I would take those accounts to whatever records pertained to them, and try to corroborate their accounts in documentation.

When you began your research, did you know what you were doing, or did you learn as you went along?

I had to teach myself how to do historical research, and handle different forms of evidence. I had no degree in history—I was an art critic writing for the *Village Voice*—so it took me many months of roaming the halls of libraries and reading other works to learn the rules of history and research. I was self-taught, I guess, but there's no special science in writing memoir based on historical background. It can be done by practically anyone, if you're passionate enough about it.

Did you discover pitfalls during your research you could warn others about?

The main pitfall I try to warn people away from is the desire to cover up the hard realities of the past. There's a natural tendency to soften one's family's poverty or involvement in nefarious acts, one's family's adultery or illegitimate children. If you go into a memoir project with the goal of burnishing some kind of family tradition, you might as well not attempt anything at all. It wouldn't be interesting to anyone, and it would provide no psychological journey worth attempting.

How aware were you when you began the project that there would be obstacles in your way by way of living family members, social reaction?

I was pretty aware that what I wanted to do could be unpopular in my own family. Once in a while I became gun-shy and stopped working, because I didn't want to hurt anybody. I was also aware it could be painful for black people I didn't even know, and that also sometimes gave me pause, and made me slow down.

But I had a couple of things working in my favor. One was an enormous horde of family papers, and those 10,000 pages of records I studied to write the book were not in the attic of an aunt of mine. They were in libraries and could be looked at by anybody, so I didn't have to rely on the goodwill of cousins to tell me what actually happened on the Ball plantations. I was also fortunate that the black families I met were courageous enough to try to come to terms with the painful things we shared.

I knew this was incendiary material, but I had to decide whether the peace of mind of my own family—let's say 100 people—was more important than the peace of mind of tens of thousands of Americans whose ancestors lived in slavery on our family's plantations. And although this was a terrible equation to have to solve, I decided it was important to go ahead.

To what extent is the published *Slaves in the Family* different from your first draft?

I worked on the book for three years full time, and during that time wrote drafts and sketches, many of which I threw away. When I finally turned in a draft I was happy with, my editor made almost no changes whatsoever, just a line edit here or there.

My editor, Jonathan Galassi at Farrar, Straus & Giroux, made one important suggestion that I incorporated. I had thought I would write a chronological narrative that started 300 years ago on the first Ball plantation, and ended in the 20th century with where everybody went, in a linear narrative. But my editor suggested I use a flashback/flashforward structure, one chapter in the past, one chapter in the present. It worked because I don't think anyone would sit still for 200 years of plantation history before we got to living people.

What's attractive about this story, for many people, is the connection of the living to the dead, and the idea that we can connect living people to moments in American history. But if you have to go through 200 pages of history to get to the living, the book might have sold to an academic market, but not to a popular market.

To what do you attribute the current mass popularity of memoir?

One explanation is that we have realized that living people contain multitudes of stories that connect to deeper streams in American society. We are fascinated by the living, and so many examples of recent memoir writing are from people who are telling exemplary stories about the past—experience in war, experience as a black person, as an immigrant from a Jewish family. It's the way we Americans get interested in history, the testimony of a living person on something of importance to all of us as a nation.

I think that's the ingredient in my book that links it to memoir. It's really a hybrid book, part memoir and part history. But what's appealing to people is the testimony of the living, about things important to all of us having to do with our nation's history.

The memoirist is a sort of stand-in for something else. I think for better and worse, I represent access to the plantation past. My book is a kind of window on the past, and I think that can be said for a lot of memoir writers.

I thought it was unusual that you turned over such large spaces in your book to straight quotes, in some cases letting your interview subjects speak uninterrupted for pages. Why does this technique work?

I did it because people had stories to tell that I couldn't tell by research, or by working as a ventriloquist. I didn't want to interrogate people, and make their stories bend to my perception. Their stories were powerful enough without me intruding on them. With the black families, my presence in their lives was already shocking to them because of who I am, and I could not—and didn't want to—conduct myself like an interrogator. So I asked leading questions and let people talk. It works in a lot of cases, in some it doesn't. That was also the case with the white folks I talked to, my own family members who have strong views about our family legacy. In the interviews I did with Ball cousins, also, it was important to let people talk and state their opinions.

Did you develop any interview methods you could share? In particular those that helped you break the ice with reluctant subjects?

A lot of it's in the way you approach people. If you show that you have respect for people's secrets, and their stories, then they'll talk to you. People are very frightened that you will mishandle their secrets and make them into tabloid exposé, but if you approach people in a way that shows you respect their experience, usually they'll talk to you.

In my case, I would go talk to people usually with a file folder of information about their family, or about our family, that they did not have. And it would be like a kind of gift, so you don't approach people merely as someone who's going to take from them—take their stories and their testimony—but you bring something of equal value to share.

In research areas where the facts were sketchy or nonexistent, how much latitude did you allow yourself to fill in the blanks with conjecture or composite information? And how did you let the reader know when you hit those areas?

I thought I had to make my best effort to tell what actually went on between people—black people and white people, in this case. Because I knew that if I made something up, somebody was going to call me on it. With my own family, for example, if I had invented a story of interracial sex between my family members and African-American women that our family enslaved, somebody was going to call me on that. On the other hand, if I had painted a sentimental picture of relationships between good Ball masters and subservient Ball slaves, then black people were going to call me on that. So I felt my only choice was to tell what I found had happened.

To write history is to write a narrative and to interpret evidence. It is an act of imagination, but if you're aware of that, you make your best attempt to play by the rules. Here's an example: a great grandfather of mine fought in the Civil War and kept a diary throughout the war. It was a very terse diary, with short entries like "We had a fire fight with Sherman's advance guard today," or "It rained all day." I knew this was an unusual thing, the personal diary of a Civil War soldier, but it wasn't enough to tell a story. So I went to other places to find out what was going on around this person, to the army reports and to the company histories that were written after the war, so that I could give a feeling to what his experience might have been. But I tried my best to stick as closely as I could to the facts. I think memoirists serve their readers to the extent that they try to stick to the facts. The way people tend to mythologize the past and their own experiences puts off a lot of readers.

What was one of the most gratifying moments to you in writing this memoir?

For the second to last chapter, called "A Reckoning," I interviewed an elderly woman named Emily Frayer. She was black and 94 at the time of the interview. She told me about the day her grandmother and grandfather became free on a Ball plantation. It's a story she used to hear when she was a child about the arrival of the Yankees to liberate Limerick Plantation. And she used the most vivid descriptions of what happened, as though she had actually been there. After hearing her story, which was almost photographic in its recall, I was skeptical that this was the way things had actually happened. But I found a diary written by a Ball woman who was living on this plantation at the time describing the events of that day. They were identical, minute by minute, to the events that this black woman had described to me. So the written record of the Ball family and the oral tradition of a black family that I had never met, and our family had not spoken to for 100 years, were identical. It was the thing I was hoping for.

Alan Cheuse: Writing Across the Spectrum

BY PAULA DEIMLING

You probably know the speaking voice of Alan Cheuse. On the airwaves of National Public Radio, he's the calm, thoughtful commentator on books, but behind this voice is a writer who brings to the job firsthand knowledge of what an author goes through to write a book. His own work as novelist, journalist, essayist and professor has taught him much—so much more than he ever imagined as a child when he'd see his father typing in the alcove of the family's small apartment, and "got the notion I could do that."

Alan Cheuse

Until five years ago, Cheuse wrote at the typewriter too, but since has switched to a personal computer. He works every morning at fiction unless he's at the end of a long book, when the writing spills over into the afternoons. Most afternoons are set aside for essays, reviews and journalism. The temptation of his younger days just to dabble, instead of buckling down to the real work of writing, is long gone.

"I started writing late, and I didn't get very far. I hadn't read enough," Cheuse says. "You hope that the fallow time was somehow preparatory, but in my case it wasn't. I just wasn't ready. I wasted time."

Despite his "late" start, Cheuse has a hefty body of work to show for his discipline. He is the author of three novels, *The Bohemians* (Apple-wood Books, Inc.), *The Light Possessed* (Peregrine Smith Books) and *The Grandmothers' Club* (Peregrine); several collections of short stories, including his most recent collection, *Lost and Old Rivers* (Southern Methodist University Press); and a memoir titled *Fall Out of Heaven*. His articles and essays have appeared in *The New York Times*, *The Chicago Tribune*, *The Dallas Morning News* and *Redbook*, among other places. He has also co-edited two short story anthologies, *The Sound of Writing* and *Listening to Ourselves* (both Anchor Books).

TURNING POINTS

Some of Cheuse's best lessons have come from a career change he hadn't planned on. In the 1970s, Cheuse was writing fiction in his spare time, while teaching at Bennington College and working toward tenure. Bennington offered him a one-year contract, but for a devoted teacher and academic, the college's decision was tantamount to being fired. He left Bennington and moved to Knoxville, Tennessee, where he began writing fulltime. He wrote articles, essays and fiction. He'd vowed to break through as a fiction writer by age forty, but until that happened, it was the nonfiction that helped pay the bills. Then, in 1979, one month before his fortieth birthday, a check from *The New Yorker* for a short story Cheuse had written proved he had what it took to go the distance from writing nonfiction to creating fiction.

PAULA DEIMLING *is a full-time writer and former editor of* Writer's Market. *She is one of the authors of* The Writer's Essential Desk Reference *(Writer's Digest Books). Past interviews have included Isaac Asimov, Russell Banks and Jane Smiley.*

"Choose subjects you care about and want to know more about," Cheuse says of writing salable nonfiction. "If someone gives you an assignment that seems dull, look for the people in it. Let them reveal themselves and the dullness will dissipate. As much as you can, people your piece with characters as you would a story, except that they are real folks, and you make them shine in your story by employing the facts of their presences, and lives.

"Story is the operative word here," Cheuse says. "Organize your facts, but tell the story, with beginning, middle and end—just as if you were writing a mystery. In the beginning, you'll have an important deed or difficulty, then comes learning how to solve it, then comes the solution."

Today, as a teacher in George Mason University's Graduate Creative Writing Program, Cheuse will sometimes hear students say, "I don't want to include too many details." But, he points out, writers have to cross over the line and realize that the story—whether it's nonfiction or a short story—is made up of details: "Articles fall flat when the writer does not dig deeply enough, or gaze sharply enough, to discern those details that make the subject the distinct thing it is. As in, say, the particular way Chicago police book a criminal, a routine that is generally the same in every city in America. But in Chicago, or New York, or Miami, or Boise, it's done in a particular fashion. Get the details. God, as the man said, is in the details. Make me see, and make me feel, the motives of the subjects in your stories."

But, if details are the substance of fiction and nonfiction, Cheuse insists writers must master the art of the sentence in order to transform details into fine writing. The major turning point in his writing, Cheuse says, was "when I was capable of making serious sentences in a sure, steady way. Writing is about making one sentence after another." And then building on the sentences, page after page. One important component of creating sentences that sing to the reader—in fiction, nonfiction or essay—is the rhythm of those sentences, Cheuse says. "You read to catch the rhythm of the greats, and you model your sentences on theirs until you find your own particular rhythms emerging out of the material. One sentence at a time—like rungs on a ladder leading up to the hayloft, sentences must be functional and one must necessarily lead to the other." Look at the opening paragraphs of *The Great Gatsby*, *A Farewell to Arms* or *To the Lighthouse*, he points out.

Cheuse likens the process of creating deft sentences to walking on the rocks to get across a raging stream: "First you have to find the first rock, and then the next and the next and the next, one at a time, until you can do it so deftly that instead of stepping and standing, you're eventually stepping and walking, stepping and hopping along across the water."

Practice is the way to achieve this deftness in writing, Cheuse believes. And reading—voracious reading. Cheuse's studies in comparative literature—earning a doctorate from Rutgers University in 1974—set in motion for him a lifetime pattern of reading. "Looking back, the work I had to do prepared me for writing, because I had to read most of the greats of Western literature. Not that reading automatically translates into good writing, but it's a rare successful writer who doesn't become a professional reader," he says. "Imagine a painter who didn't know the great art of the world, or a would-be composer who didn't know the history of music. Unless you're a genius, you have to study your art form."

THE POWER OF LANGUAGE

What's so fascinating about writing is that we use language every day, Cheuse says, and yet look at what language can accomplish when used in aesthetic and symbolic ways. Cheuse points out that Gertrude Stein made the distinction between ordinary language (literal) and literary language (symbolic), and emphasized the plastic nature of literary language—that it may be shaped and formed in the same way stone is shaped by a sculptor. "So the young writer has to allow himself the frightening freedom to break free of a subject and freely invent, the way a composer makes variations on a theme. And by inventing, recognize the closed system of meaning within all symbolic art, including the art we happen to be trying to make," he says. "Or, to try to bring this down to ground level, work like a shoemaker making shoes for a figure in his own imagination.''

In 1986, Cheuse traveled to what was then the Soviet Union, on a personal journey prompted by a visit to his father's gravesite. There, Cheuse says, he heard the voice of his father, urging him to travel to Khiva, in Uzbekistan, where the elder Cheuse had spent part of his youth. The result of Cheuse's journey was the publication of *Fall Out of Heaven*, a memoir which details his coming to terms with the man he'd observed typing sketches years before. ''The battle between us was one of an old father, a new son, a man of Old World ways, and a boy trying to make an American life.'' Woven into *Fall Out of Heaven* is a memoir written by his father, who had been a pilot in the Red Army air force. Narration is the common ground between fiction and nonfiction, Cheuse says. And while the forms are very different, in either case you want a story that turns a recollected experience into something alive and vital and moving. Because of that, Cheuse says, ''writing fiction prepares you for writing nonfiction. It's usually not the other way around, as most novels by serious journalists will show. Some nonfiction writers will never become novelists. And those who do may never become good novelists. Research is useful for a certain sort of novel—I know because I have done a lot of it—but all the research in the world can't make the novel catch fire if the spark isn't there.''

When writing nonfiction, Cheuse looks for a central scene or event upon which to build the story. For instance, in researching a 16,000-word piece for the *San Diego Weekly Reader*, he spent a week on the late shift at the San Ysidro border station. The first things he noticed were the drug-sniffing dogs. ''I knew from the beginning that the piece would begin with the dogs, and then I'd burrow deeper and deeper into the subject.''

With fiction, the inspiration comes to Cheuse in one of many ways. ''I never consciously choose to cast a story or a novel in first person or third, and stories come to me in pieces, sometimes the middle, sometimes the end, sometimes the beginning, usually with an image or a voice.''

Cheuse was researching a magazine article on the Jews of Tijuana when, in the national archives of Mexico, he learned about Hernando Alonso, the first Jew to travel to Mexico with the explorer Cortés in 1521. One passage in particular caught his attention—just three lines— and after completing the article, he wrote the short story ''Hernando Alonso'' (included in *Lost and Old Rivers*). ''Out of three lines I tried to make a world, a life, and a death,'' says Cheuse.

Cheuse acknowledges that both frustrations and joys await the nonfiction writer who decides to write short stories or a novel. The truth is, not everyone can successfully write both. ''Certainly writing nonfiction doesn't as a rule disqualify you from writing good fiction. But a sprinter isn't necessarily a good cross-country athlete. The novel is the decathlon of art,'' he says. ''You need to have skills and talents, some of which can come from writing nonfiction, but not necessarily.''

OTHER AUTHORS' BOOKS

As the book commentator for NPR's ''All Things Considered'' since 1983, Cheuse sees the gamut of books published each year. Receiving 1,000 to 2,000 books in the mail annually, he reads across the spectrum, not only literary work but also science fiction and thrillers. ''Nights are for reading,'' he says.

Cheuse reviews fifty to fifty-five books a year, making sure to review books by known and unknown authors. There's no set criteria for which books are reviewed, but a book must have significant distribution across the country in view of the nearly nine million listeners. ''As for what I look for, I want a book that sings to me, stirs me deeply, and does it with deftness, daring and high skill,'' Cheuse says. He can usually sense in a couple of pages if a book is on the mark. ''A story must begin in the right place,'' he says. ''You have to feel its innate beginning-ness.''

Sometimes, a story doesn't seem right; the character in the opening says or knows too much, or too little. Had the editor noticed this, such a problem could have been remedied with revision. Or sometimes a book isn't ready; ''the writer hasn't grasped the essence of his own material,''

Cheuse observes. "The writer needs to develop that sense of certainty about the work. . . . The writer needs to find that opening that establishes the sure direction of the story."

As Cheuse reads beyond the opening of a book, he wants to be thrilled and surprised, and have the book's innate inevitability be fulfilled. And then there are those extraordinary books where the author's words seem to "leap on ice," according to Cheuse. "How is it possible to leap on ice?" Cheuse asks. "Discover how to write the right sentences about the right material," he says.

We live in a Silver Age of fiction, Cheuse says, pointing to the work of Saul Bellow, Norman Mailer, Flannery O'Connor and Eudora Welty. There are large numbers of first-rate writers among us now whose work may or may not last, he says. "Whether any of us is great is not for us to figure." The Golden Age, by contrast, starts with Herman Melville and onward, William Faulkner, F. Scott Fitzgerald and Ernest Hemingway. "We're in a Golden Age of nonfiction," he says, a time of many fine writers including Joan Didion, Frank Conroy, Barry Lopez and Peter Matthiessen.

Cheuse recently received a piano as a birthday gift from his wife. "At twenty minutes a day, in a hundred years I may become a piano player. It's the same for new writers. You have to work at it at least as much as a professional musician. You have got to behave professionally, not in an amateurish way." That means practice, he says. Practice. 'Til the phrases flow deftly.

Quiet Style Brings Power to the Fiction of Elizabeth Graver

By ANNE BOWLING

Elizabeth Graver

As Oprah peddles what critics are calling the new women's fiction, off in the distance and out of the fray Elizabeth Graver rises like a quiet star on the literary horizon. Not for her the sometimes hyperbolic sentimentality of the Oprah picks—Graver's fiction is characterized by a more modulated, understated grace which critics have called "exquisitely poignant" and "genuinely haunting."

"If you'd asked me when I was six what I wanted to be, I would have said a writer. I would have said that at every point along the way," says Graver, author of the 1997 title *Unravelling* (Hyperion), and more recently *The Honey Thief* (Hyperion, 1999). "I'm not sure why I've been so single-minded. I always knew I would write no matter what, but whether or not I could get published or earn a living at it was a much harder question."

In pursuit of her answer, Graver prepared herself for the long haul. Ten years, she told herself, would be enough time to master her craft, find her way into publication, and discover whether fiction writing was a place she could call a professional home. So when in 1991 her short story collection *Have You Seen Me* was picked by Richard Ford for the Drue Heinz Literature Prize, and published by the University of Pittsburgh Press, Graver was, well, surprised. "I remember this kind of startled feeling," she says, "and then thinking there had been a door way ahead of me, and it was going to take a long time to get through it, but now I was through."

It was another six years before Graver's first novel, *Unravelling*, was published, and there were not enough superlatives to go around. "This finely crafted exploration of a young woman clinging to tenderness even as she acquires a somber and unsettling wisdom makes *Unravelling*, no matter its 19th Century setting, an absolutely affecting portrait of adolescence," wrote a critic for *The Chicago Tribune*. Others compared its evocation of historical setting to Charles Frazier's National Book Award winning *Cold Mountain*. The novel was named a *New York Times* Notable Book for 1997, and was a finalist for the PEN/New England L.L. Winship Award.

The story of Aimee Slater, born in 1829 on a small New Hampshire farm, *Unravelling* traces her path from the farm to work in the textile mills in nearby Lowell, and finally to a cabin on the rim of her parents' property, where she lives in relative isolation. The novel's quiet, interior focus links it stylistically with Graver's second novel *The Honey Thief*, a contemporary novel set in upstate New York. Told alternately through the eyes of eleven-year-old Eva Baruch and her mother, that novel also traces the inner journey of the women whose lives it explores.

A self-confessed writer "who needs readers," Graver carved a place for herself in the writing community throughout her apprenticeship, and availed herself of the collegiality, direction and financial support of a network of writers. Her fellowship to Washington University kept her among a writing community as she earned her MFA, and retreats to the Bread Loaf Writer's

---

ANNE BOWLING *is editor of* Novel & Short Story Writer's Market.

Conference and McDowell Colony gave her extended periods among other writers to work at her craft. She also received fellowships from the National Endowment for the Arts and the Guggenheim Foundation, and even after publication of her second novel she participates in a writer's group. Graver might say her apprenticeship continues.

"I have a contract for my next novel, but I'm still struggling with all sorts of things about how to write it," Graver says. "I think I almost naively thought there was one door you get through in publishing, and then you're through. In terms of continuing to hone your craft, and pushing the boundaries of your work, and in terms of the capriciousness of the publishing world, it's not actually like there's one door. You never quite know."

Here Graver talks about how she found financial and emotional support for her journey, the benefits of belonging to a writing community, and how she creates her memorable stories.

Are there writers who have influenced your distinctive style, and if so, how do they show up in your work?

It's hard to tell whether I'm drawn to certain writers because they echo the sensibility I had in the first place, or whether the work I'm now producing reflects their sensibilities. I think it's probably a combination, and a movement back and forth for me. I'm drawn to language that's beautiful, and also strong in a certain way. I'm also very drawn to writers who manage to map the contours of interior life in intricate and subtle ways.

A writer like Alice Munro, for example, I go back to again and again for how she takes the form of the short story and within it, manages to make you feel like you're reading a sliver of someone's life, but that they have an entire life. There's just an incredible density, and feeling of wholeness and complexity to her characters that I'm sort of stunned by. That, and what she does with time, the way she can jump forward forty years in a page.

When do you see the most concentrated period of development as you were learning to write fiction?

I think probably in graduate school at Washington University in St. Louis, and then maybe after that and since then was the time I really dove deep into the whole thing, instead of sort of playing around on the edges. Those two years, when I was on a fellowship and didn't have to worry about earning a living and was surrounded by other people who were writing, were very fruitful and incredibly exciting.

I had written one horrible little thesis of short stories before I got to graduate school. I remember writing my first short stories and thinking they felt incredibly awkward. I didn't know how to move characters around, or how to handle time, and I particularly recall having this sort of grim feeling that I had to make more happen. And resisting that. In graduate school I started to figure out, in my own very idiosyncratic way, how to create a kind of arc, or movement, in a story on my own terms, so it could be an internal movement, or a small shift. And at that time somehow my sense of the story, and the possibilities of the form, became more fluid.

Did you find the environment of the MFA program particularly helpful?

I did. I've always created through an institution or created some kind of writing community, and I've always been in a writer's group. So I'm someone who needs readers. I'm not sure it's necessary to get that through the particular structure of an MFA program, although for me one of the main benefits of it was a grant. Before that, I'd been a secretary and a teacher, and just worked like crazy to pay the rent. Being in that kind of space, where writing should be your first priority, was very valuable.

As a writer who values working within a community of colleagues, what have you found valuable about writers' groups?

The one I was in the longest now has splintered into several factions. A friend and I started it when I was twenty-two. At the time we were four young women—Pagan Kennedy and Lauren

Slater, and a writer I met at the Bread Loaf Writer's Conference named Audrey Schulman. We were all unpublished, and very passionate and serious. But also had a lot of fun together—we'd cook dinner, and Audrey had a washing machine, so we would do our laundry at her house.

But then we'd sit and talk, and read our work out loud. It was incredibly sustaining, particularly at that stage when we were all unpublished and were getting no external support from anybody. At this point everybody in that group has now published at least two books. I think a lot of it was talent, but probably even more it was willpower, sweat, supporting each other and having this be an incredibly regular part of our lives. It's always helped me to produce, knowing I'm going to be meeting with people and they're producing. And you're expected to bring something to the group. I think that can make it less solitary, and give you steps along the way, so that the whole publishing thing in some ways is given less importance.

Tell me a little bit about shopping *Unravelling* around. You said it was difficult to find a publisher?

It was a long process, and I remember thinking "What if this never gets published?" and having two reactions to that: partly thinking that it would be years of work, and that would be really sad and frustrating, and then also partly thinking I learned an incredible amount writing this book, and I liked it. Somehow, on some level, I never lost faith in it as something that had meaning in my life.

Your voice is so distinctive, quiet and almost elegiac. How many years had you written before you found that voice?

It's interesting that you ask. It's hard for me to see my voice from the outside, although I'm sure it has developed in some ways. I would say the more I write, the more defined my voice gets, but on the other hand the more I write, the more I'm conscious of wanting to expand my voice. I know I have a very strong sense of rhythm and cadence, and that never seems to go away—my sense of the way the words should fall is really strong.

You're a very atmospheric writer and, like Alice McDermott, you're able to finely sketch scenes with a minimum of detail. Is that something writers can be taught, or is it more individual than that?

I think so. I often quote to my students Henry James, who said, "Try to be someone on whom nothing is lost." With my students, I talk a lot about looking closely at the world through their own lens, and trying to find language of their own to express it, and being wary of language that's too familiar or overused.

Also, different writers have different senses that tend to be primary. I'm quite visual, and I don't know whether that can be taught. I think what you tend to notice in the world comes very early. I remember Grace Paley once said she never described what her characters looked like because it didn't interest her at all. Meanwhile, her characters had these incredible voices and a sense of living in these dense, rich communities, so it didn't matter what they looked like. That's not what they're about. But I tend to notice color and texture, and I love antiques and old things and weathered things, and I've always been interested in the way the physical seems to carry history or human association with it. So for me the tactile world of the story is very seductive, and also important in terms of being a way to get into a more interior world.

You alternate point of view in *The Honey Thief*, from Eva to her mother and back again. How did you arrive at the decision to approach the novel this way, and did you see it as risky?

For me, *The Honey Thief* was originally about Eva. But as I started to get farther into it, it became very much about the whole process of memory and withholding, and the gaps between people. And in that way having the multiple points of view enacted what the novel was about;

if it was just through her point of view you would never see what it was she didn't know, and you would never see the spaces between her and her mother in quite the same way. So having those multiple points of view allowed me to play with the multiplicity of perspectives. That way, one person knows something someone else doesn't know; one person experiences a moment in time that another person can't remember. It actually makes the narrative itself enact those gaps.

How did you handle switching point of view?

I tried to imagine each of the characters as fully as possible so each of their stories would be compelling enough, and also to make it clear enough in terms of how time was working so it wasn't just completely muddled.

Also, I think the fact that I told it in third person gave it a kind of continuity. If it had been in first person and I kept switching voices, it might have been more awkward. I often have this reaction to multiple-points-of-view novels told in first person: either the voices sound strained, as if you really hear the author each time and it doesn't really sound like three different people; or, the voices sound like the writer's been trying too hard to make them distinct. And for some reason, that particular approach doesn't usually work for me. So with the third person, there was the sense of a narrator who was in control of the story.

In your teaching at Boston College, are there common stumbling blocks you find among your writing students?

I find it often takes students awhile to get to the heart of their story. They'll often start chronologically—say, at the beginning of a day—and it takes them awhile to get to the knot of tension or the moment of real interest in the story. That's fine, they're finding their way toward it, but what I often encourage them to do is use that early draft as very rough and elastic and subject to change, and have them think about starting at the end or in the middle. I think there's often a circling around the heart of things with beginning writers, and even with non-beginning writers. They're finding out what they want to say through the saying of it. But making it really work often involves recasting and moving things around and lopping off the beginning.

I encourage my students to be very playful and loose and unselfconscious at first, and to try to not be self-critical in the early drafts, and allow themselves to roam. But then I encourage them to be very disciplined about revising. For me, writing is a real mixture of playfulness and looseness, and then shaping. And it's hard to balance those two things, because if your critical voice is too loud at the beginning, you'll never get anything out, but if you believe that everything that pours out is fine, you'll never get anything that has a shape.

There is a great deal of talk these days about the shrinking commercial market for literary short fiction. What's your outlook?

I think in terms of story collections being published by commercial presses, it's very hard to do. But then there are all these things like the contests, the Drue Heinz that I was published through, and the Flannery O'Connor prize, and the Associated Writing Programs prize. They all do a fantastic job of publishing collections, which get out there and get reviewed. Mine went into paperback. So I think there are avenues that have been formed partly to help alleviate that deficit. In terms of the whole question of magazines, I think it's also true there are far fewer mainstream periodicals that publish short fiction, but there are so many good literary magazines, and new ones keep popping up, so that there are a lot of ways in which publishing has become more democratic. So it doesn't seem entirely grim to me.

Also, reading the literary magazines is really important, and I always subscribe to at least one, partly in the desire to support them and partly because I think it is where you find writing that is not necessarily making it into the more commercial presses. And one way to find a good place to send your stories is to find a magazine filled with writers whose work you love.

Jerry Jenkins: Christian Fiction Enters the Mainstream

BY CHANTELLE BENTLEY

With nearly 20 million in sales and inclusion on the *New York Times* Bestseller List, Jerry B. Jenkins, co-author with Dr. Tim La-Haye of the *Left Behind* series, has taken the prophetic story contained within the Book of Revelations to millions of readers around the world and even brought some of those readers to a new faith. "Dr. LaHaye and I have heard from more than 2,000 people in person, via e-mail, snail mail, or phone who say they have become believers in Christ through reading these books," says Jenkins.

Jerry Jenkins

Besides authoring the *Left Behind* series, Jenkins has had a successful writing career with more than 100 books to his credit—including biographies of Hank Aaron, Orel Hershiser, Nolan Ryan and Brett Butler. Jenkins also assisted Billy Graham with his bestselling memoir *Just As I Am*. In addition, Jenkins writes on the topics of marriage and family life, and has written numerous fiction titles for both children and adults.

Jenkins also has years of editing experience. He has worked as the sports editor of a daily newspaper, the managing editor of a periodical, executive editor of a magazine, and, finally, as editor of *Moody Magazine* where he currently serves as writer-in-residence.

While preparing to begin writing the next book in the *Left Behind* series, Jenkins took a few moments to discuss his writing life and his recent success.

While reviewing your list of published titles I was amazed by the volume of books you've written over the past twenty years. How do you maintain such a hectic pace while also writing on such a wide variety of subjects?

I don't sing or dance or preach. This is all I do. I don't find it hectic, if I maintain my family priorities. I have never written while my kids were at home and awake, which allowed me to write—when I did have the time—without guilt. Until 1990, I wrote only from nine in the evening to midnight. Now I write during the day when my high schooler is at school.

How has your editing experience affected your writing ability and how you promote your work?

When I arrived at the Moody Institute in October of 1974, I had already published eight or nine books. But because of all my editing experience, I've become a better rewriter and editor of my own work, doing that kind of thing to other people's writing all day.

As far as the ability to sell my work, I suppose my visibility didn't hurt and I may have gotten the benefit of the doubt. But I had already been fairly fortunate in that regard, having learned to sell on the basis of queries and proposals. I have always been able to sell my stuff. I

CHANTELLE BENTLEY *is the former editor of* Poet's Market.

have been turned down on ideas, but not on written work, having learned to write only after getting a green light.

Which genre is most challenging to write and why?

Most challenging is writing for kids, because naturally you must use a limited vocabulary. As-told-to autobiographies are tricky, but I've learned to catch the subject's voice and write as he would if he were a writer, rather than as I would if I were him.

What kind of research do you do for the books in the *Left Behind* series?

The idea for fictionalizing an account of the Rapture and the Tribulation was Dr. LaHaye's, and he has been studying prophecy and theology since before I was born. I have become, in essence, his protégé and now own everything he has written or read on these subjects. He provides a chronology of biblical events and I get the fun part of making up the stories and writing the novels.

After connecting with Dr. LaHaye through literary agent Rick Christian and deciding to write *Left Behind*, how did you find a publisher for the series?

I wrote and Rick shopped an early version of chapter one (which did not even include Buck, the second protagonist) among several publishers. We got solid offers from five, top offers from two, and eventually selected Tyndale.

Was the entire series proposed to potential publishers or was the first book sold and then interest in a series developed from there?

After contracting with Tyndale, I wrote half of the first (and only, at that time) title, realizing that I had covered only one week of the seven-year period. Tyndale agreed to a trilogy. In the middle of book two, I told them it would likely take six books, and they agreed. Then we decided on seven.

When book four took us only to the two-and-one-half year mark, the publisher asked if I really thought I could finish the series in just three more books. I said I could but that it would become plot driven rather than character driven. He said, how many if you stay at the same pace? I said twelve. That's where we stand now. Book six took us to the half-way point. Six more should finish it. The story is told at the same pace, but I'm writing two a year now, rather than one.

Does Tyndale House have much input over what goes into each book?

They have that right, but Dr. LaHaye is considered the leading evangelical scholar on these matters, and the fiction seems to have worked, so they're thrilled and trust us. Of course we count on them for their part of the editing process too.

How does publishing the *Left Behind* series compare with finding a publisher for some of your own work?

It's the same. We pitch ideas, get a contract, and I write.

With the publicity and attention brought to you through the success of the *Left Behind* series, do you have a more difficult time finding that space within yourself that is required to write?

Yes. I always thought writing full-time would give me unlimited blocks of time to write. But the business of writing (media, etc.) has become my new full-time job and I still must carve out the time to write.

Do you feel the quality of the writing in the later books in the series has been affected by the speed at which you have to write them?

I never rush the writing. I write at the same speed as always, but of course I have less down time between finishing each book. The people closest to the project (Tyndale, an agent, my first readers, etc.) feel each book is better than the last. I want each to be better and work hard at that.

Do you have any advice for other Christian writers who struggle to sell their work in the secular publishing market?

A Christian publisher, two Christian authors, and a story as overtly evangelical as it can be combine to produce the biggest Christian crossover success ever. The lesson is apparently to not hold back or try to soft-sell the message. Readers tell us they have fallen in love with the characters and loved to keep turning the pages, so clearly the fundamentals of fiction still apply.

Do you believe that Christian writers are at a greater disadvantage when it comes to publishing and selling their work?

The general market seems thrilled with anything that entertains and sells, so where there might have seemed to be a prejudice against Christian themes, that has been dispelled by several bestsellers (not just our own).

The Business of Writing
Minding the Details

Writers who have had some success in placing their work know that the effort to publish requires an entirely different set of skills than does the act of writing. A shift in perspective is required when you move from creating your work to selling it. Like it or not, successful writers—*career writers*—have to keep the business side of the writing business in mind as they work.

Each of the following sections discusses a writing business topic that affects anyone selling his writing. We'll take a look at contracts and agreements—the documents that license a publisher to use your work. We'll consider your rights as a writer and sort out some potentially confusing terminology. We'll cover the basics of copyright protection—a topic of perennial concern for writers. And for those of you who are already making money with your writing, we'll offer some tips for keeping track of financial matters and staying on top of your tax liabilities.

Our treatment of the business topics that follow is necessarily limited. Look for complete information on each subject at your local bookstore or library—both in books (some of which we mention) and periodicals aimed at writers. Information is also available from the federal government, as indicated later in this article.

CONTRACTS AND AGREEMENTS

If you've been freelancing even a short time, you know that contracts and agreements vary considerably from one publisher to another. Some magazine editors work only by verbal agreement; others have elaborate documents you must sign in triplicate and return before you begin the assignment. As you evaluate any contract or agreement, consider carefully what you stand to gain and lose by signing. Did you have another sale in mind that selling all rights the first time will negate? Does the agreement provide the publisher with a number of add-ons (electronic rights, advertising rights, reprint rights, etc.) for which they won't have to pay you again?

In contract negotiations, the writer is usually interested in licensing the work for a particular use but limiting the publisher's ability to make other uses of the work in the future. It's in the publisher's best interest, however, to secure rights to use the work in as many ways as possible, both now and later on. Those are the basic positions of each party. The negotiation is a process of compromise and capitulation on questions relating to those basic points—and the amount of compensation to be given the writer for his work.

A contract is rarely a take-it-or-leave-it proposition. If an editor tells you that his company will allow *no* changes on the contract, you will then have to decide how important the assignment is to you. But most editors are open to negotiation, and you should learn to compromise on points that don't matter to you while maintaining your stand on things that do.

When it's not specified, most writers assume that a magazine publisher is buying first rights. Some writers' groups can supply you with a sample magazine contract to use when the publisher doesn't supply one, so you can document your agreement in writing. Members of The Authors

Guild are given a sample book contract and information about negotiating when they join. For more information about contracts and agreements, see *Business and Legal Forms for Authors & Self-Publishers*, by Tad Crawford (Allworth Press, 1990); *From Printout to Published*, by Michael Seidman (Carroll & Graf, 1992) or *The Writer's Guide to Contract Negotiations*, by Richard Balkin (Writer's Digest Books, 1985), which is out of print but should be available in libraries.

RIGHTS AND THE WRITER

A creative work can be used in many different ways. As the originator of written works, you enjoy full control over how those works are used; you are in charge of the rights that your creative works are "born" with. When you agree to have your work published, you are giving the publisher the right to use your work in one or more ways. Whether that right is simply to publish the work for the first time in a periodical or to publish it as many times as he likes and in whatever form he likes is up to you—it all depends on the terms of the contract or agreement the two of you arrive at. As a general rule, the more rights you license away, the less control you have over your work and the more money you should be paid for the license. We find that writers and editors sometimes define rights in different ways. For a classification of terms, read Types of Rights, below.

Sometimes editors don't take the time to specify the rights they are buying. If you sense that an editor is interested in getting stories but doesn't seem to know what his and the writer's responsibilities are regarding rights, be wary. In such a case, you'll want to explain what rights you're offering (preferably one-time or first serial rights only) and that you expect additional payment for subsequent use of your work.

You should strive to keep as many rights to your work as you can from the outset, otherwise, your attempts to resell your writing may be seriously hampered.

The Copyright Law that went into effect January 1, 1978, said writers were primarily selling one-time rights to their work unless they—and the publisher—agreed otherwise in writing. Book rights are covered fully by the contract between the writer and the book publisher.

TYPES OF RIGHTS

- **First Serial Rights**—First serial rights means the writer offers a newspaper or magazine the right to publish the article, story or poem for the first time in any periodical. All other rights to the material remain with the writer. The qualifier "North American" is often added to this phrase to specify a geographical limit to the license.

    When material is excerpted from a book scheduled to be published and it appears in a magazine or newspaper prior to book publication, this is also called first serial rights.
- **One-Time Rights**—A periodical that licenses one-time rights to a work (also known as simultaneous rights) buys the *nonexclusive* right to publish the work once. That is, there is nothing to stop the author from selling the work to other publications at the same time. Simultaneous sales would typically be to periodicals without overlapping audiences.
- **Second Serial (Reprint) Rights**—This gives a newspaper or magazine the opportunity to print an article, poem or story after it has already appeared in another newspaper or magazine. Second serial rights are nonexclusive—that is, they can be licensed to more than one market.
- **All Rights**—This is just what it sounds like. If you license away all rights to your work, you forfeit the right to ever use it again. If you think you'll want to use the material later, you must avoid submitting to such markets or refuse payment and withdraw your material. Ask the editor whether he is willing to buy first rights instead of all rights before you agree to an assignment or sale. Some editors will reassign rights to a writer after a given period, such as one year. It's worth an inquiry in writing.
- **Electronic Rights**—These rights cover usage in a broad range of electronic media, from

online magazines and databases to CD-ROM magazine anthologies and interactive games. The magazine contract should specify if—and which—electronic rights are included. The presumption is that unspecified rights are kept by the writer.

- **Subsidiary Rights**—These are the rights, other than book publication rights, that should be covered in a book contract. These may include various serial rights; movie, television, audiotape and other electronic rights; translation rights, etc. The book contract should specify who controls these rights (author or publisher) and what percentage of sales from the licensing of these sub rights goes to the author.

- **Dramatic, Television and Motion Picture Rights**—This means the writer is selling his material for use on the stage, in television or in the movies. Often a one-year option to buy such rights is offered (generally for 10 percent of the total price). The interested party then tries to sell the idea to other people—actors, directors, studios or television networks, etc. Some properties are optioned over and over again, but most fail to become dramatic productions. In such cases, the writer can sell his rights again and again—as long as there is interest in the material. Though dramatic, TV and motion picture rights are more important to the fiction writer than the nonfiction writer, producers today are increasingly interested in nonfiction material; many biographies, topical books and true stories are being dramatized.

SELLING SUBSIDIARY RIGHTS

The primary right in the world of book publishing is the right to publish the book itself. All other rights (such as movie rights, audio rights, book club rights, electronic rights and foreign

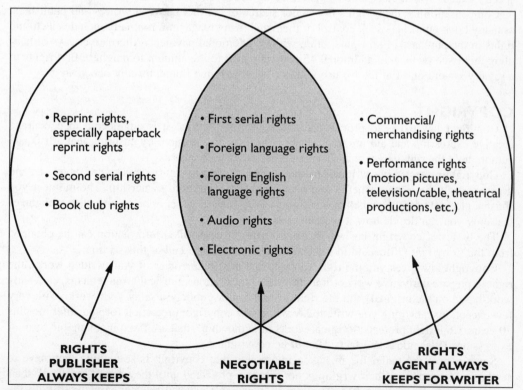

- Reprint rights, especially paperback reprint rights
- Second serial rights
- Book club rights

- First serial rights
- Foreign language rights
- Foreign English language rights
- Audio rights
- Electronic rights

- Commercial/ merchandising rights
- Performance rights (motion pictures, television/cable, theatrical productions, etc.)

RIGHTS PUBLISHER ALWAYS KEEPS

NEGOTIABLE RIGHTS

RIGHTS AGENT ALWAYS KEEPS FOR WRITER

Some subsidiary rights are always granted to the publisher. Some should always be retained by the author. The remainder are negotiable, and require knowledgeable advice from a literary agent or attorney in deciding whether it is more advantageous to grant them to the publisher or reserve them.

rights) are considered secondary, or subsidiary, to the right to print publication. In contract negotiations, authors and their agents traditionally try to avoid granting the publisher subsidiary rights that they feel capable of marketing themselves. Publishers, on the other hand, typically hope to obtain control over as many of the sub rights as they can. Philosophically speaking, subsidiary rights will be best served by being left in the hands of the person or organization most capable of—and interested in—exploiting them profitably. Sometimes that will be the author and her agent, and sometimes that will be the publisher.

Larger agencies have experience selling foreign rights, movie rights and the like, and many authors represented by such agents prefer to retain those rights and let their agents do the selling. Book publishers, on the other hand, have subsidiary rights departments, which are responsible for exploiting all sub rights the publisher was able to retain during the contract negotiation.

That job might begin with a push to sell foreign rights, which normally bring in advance money which is divided among author, agent and publisher. Further efforts then might be made to sell the right to publish the book as a paperback (although many book contracts now call for hard/soft deals, in which the original hardcover publisher buys the right to also publish the paperback version).

Any other rights which the publisher controls will be pursued, such as book clubs and magazines. Publishers usually don't control movie rights to a work, as those are most often retained by author and agent.

The marketing of electronic rights to a work, in this era of rapidly expanding capabilities and markets for electronic material, can be tricky. With the proliferation of electronic and multimedia formats, publishers, agents and authors are going to great pains these days to make sure contracts specify exactly *which* electronic rights are being conveyed (or retained).

Compensation for these rights is a major source of conflict between writers and publishers, as many book publishers seek control of them and many magazines routinely include electronic rights in the purchase of all rights, often with no additional payment. Alternative ways of handling this issue include an additional 15 percent added to the amount to purchase first rights to a royalty system or a flat fee for use within a specified time frame, usually one year.

COPYRIGHT

Copyright law exists to protect creators of original works. It is engineered to encourage creative expression and aid in the progress of the arts and sciences by ensuring that artists and authors hold the rights by which they can profit from their labors.

Copyright protects your writing, unequivocally recognizes you (its creator) as its owner, and grants you all the rights, benefits and privileges that come with ownership. The moment you finish a piece of writing—whether it is a short story, article, novel or poem—the law recognizes that only you can decide how it is to be used.

The basics of copyright law are discussed here. More detailed information can be obtained from the Copyright Office and in the books mentioned at the end of this section.

Copyright law gives you the right to make and distribute copies of your written works, the right to prepare derivative works (dramatizations, translations, musical arrangements, etc.—any work based on the original) and the right to perform or publicly display your work. With very few exceptions, anything you write today will enjoy copyright protection for your lifetime plus 70 years. Copyright protects "original works of authorship" that are fixed in a tangible form of expression. Titles, ideas and facts can *not* be copyrighted.

Some people are under the mistaken impression that copyright is something they have to send away for, and that their writing is not properly protected until they have "received" their copyright from the government. The fact is, you don't have to register your work with the Copyright Office in order for your work to be copyrighted; any piece of writing is copyrighted the moment it is put to paper. Registration of your work does, however, offer some additional protection (specifically, the possibility of recovering punitive damages in an infringement suit) as well as legal proof of the date of copyright.

Registration is a matter of filling out an application form (for writers, that's generally Form TX) and sending the completed form, a nonreturnable copy of the work in question and a check for $30 to the Library of Congress, Copyright Office, Register of Copyrights, 101 Independence Ave. SE, Washington DC 20559-6000. If the thought of paying $30 each to register every piece you write does not appeal to you, you can cut costs by registering a group of your works with one form, under one title for one $30 fee.

Most magazines are registered with the Copyright Office as single collective entities themselves; that is, the individual works that make up the magazine are *not* copyrighted individually in the names of the authors. You'll need to register your article yourself if you wish to have the additional protection of copyright registration. It's always a good idea to ask that your notice of copyright (your name, the year of first publication, and the copyright symbol ©) be appended to any published version of your work. You may use the copyright notice regardless of whether or not your work has been registered.

One thing writers need to be wary of is "work for hire" arrangements. If you sign an agreement stipulating that your writing will be done as work for hire, you will not control the copyright of the completed work—the person or organization who hired you will be the copyright owner. Work for hire arrangements and transfers of exclusive rights must be in writing to be legal, but it's a good idea to get every publishing agreement in writing before the sale.

You can obtain more information about copyright from the Copyright Office, Library of Congress, Washington DC 20559. To get answers to specific questions about copyright, call the Copyright Public Information Office at (202)707-3000 weekdays between 8:30 a.m. and 5 p.m. eastern standard time. To order copyright forms by phone, call (202)707-9100. Forms can also be downloaded from the Library of Congress website at http://lcweb.loc.gov/copyright. The website also includes information on filling out the forms, general copyright information and links to other websites related to copyright issues. A thorough (and thoroughly enjoyable) discussion of the subject of copyright law as it applies to writers can be found in Stephen Fishman's *The Copyright Handbook: How to Protect and Use Written Works* (Nolo Press, 1994). A shorter but no less enlightening treatment is Ellen Kozak's *Every Writer's Guide to Copyright & Publishing Law* (Henry Holt, 1990).

FINANCES AND TAXES

As your writing business grows, so will your obligation to keep track of your writing-related finances and taxes. Keeping a close eye on these details will help you pay as little tax as possible and keep you apprised of the state of your freelance business. A writing business with no systematic way of tracking expenses and income will soon be no writing business at all. If you dislike handling finance-related tasks, you can always hire someone else to handle them for a fee. If you do employ a professional, you must still keep the original records with an eye to providing the professional with the appropriate information.

If you decide to handle these tasks yourself—or if you just want to know what to expect of the person you employ—consider these tips:

Accurate records are essential, and the easiest way to keep them is to separate your writing income and expenses from your personal ones. Most professionals find that separate checking accounts and credit cards help them provide the best and easiest records.

Get in the habit of recording every transaction (both expenses and earnings) related to your writing. You can start at any time; you don't need to begin on January 1. Because you're likely to have expenses before you have income, start keeping your records whenever you make your first purchase related to writing—such as this copy of *Writer's Market*.

Any system of tracking expenses and income will suffice, but the more detailed it is, the better. Be sure to describe each transaction clearly—including the date; the source of the income (or the vendor of your purchase); a description of what was sold or bought; whether the payment was by cash, check or credit card; and the amount of the transaction.

The other necessary component of your financial record-keeping system is an orderly way to store receipts related to your writing. Check stubs, receipts for cash purchases, credit card receipts and similar paperwork should all be kept as well as recorded in your ledger. Any good book about accounting for small business will offer specific suggestions for ways to track your finances.

Freelance writers, artists and photographers have a variety of concerns about taxes that employees don't have, including deductions, self-employment tax and home office credits. Many freelance expenses can be deducted in the year in which they are incurred (rather than having to be capitalized, or depreciated, over a period of years). For details, consult the IRS publications mentioned later.

There also is a home office deduction that can be claimed if an area in your home is used *exclusively* and *regularly* for business and you have no other fixed location where you conduct substantial activities for your business. Contact the IRS for information on requirements and limitations for this deduction. If your freelance income exceeds your expenses, regardless of the amount, you must declare that profit. If you make $400 or more after deductions, you must pay Social Security tax and file Schedule SE, a self-employment form, along with your Form 1040 and Schedule C tax forms.

While we cannot offer you tax advice or interpretations, we can suggest several sources for the most current information.

- Check the IRS website, http://www.irs.ustreas.gov/. Full of helpful tips and information, the site also provides instant access to important IRS forms and publications.
- Call your local IRS office. Look in the white pages of the telephone directory under U.S. Government—Internal Revenue Service. Someone will be able to respond to your request for IRS publications and tax forms or other information. Ask about the IRS Tele-tax service, a series of recorded messages you can hear by dialing on a touch-tone phone. If you need answers to complicated questions, ask to speak with a Taxpayer Service Specialist.
- Obtain the basic IRS publications. You can order them by phone or mail from any IRS office; most are available at libraries and some post offices. Start with *Your Federal Income Tax* (Publication 17) and *Tax Guide for Small Business* (Publication 334). These are both comprehensive, detailed guides—you'll need to find the regulations that apply to you and ignore the rest. There are many IRS publications relating to self-employment and taxes; Publication 334 lists many of these publications—such as *Business Use of Your Home* (Publication 587) and *Self-Employment Tax* (Publication 533).
- Consider other information sources. Many public libraries have detailed tax instructions available on tape. Some colleges and universities offer free assistance in preparing tax returns. And if you decide to consult a professional tax preparer, the fee is a deductible business expense on your tax return.

How Much Should I Charge?

BY LYNN WASNAK

If you are reading this article with serious intent, chances are you agree with Dr. Samuel Johnson when he said, "No man but a blockhead ever wrote except for money." He knew in the 1700s what we have to remind ourselves en route to the millennium—while it is not at all easy to get rich being a writer, it is definitely possible to earn a living freelancing. You may not be able to afford that vacation home you dreamed of or the 30-foot yacht. But every year, real people not much different from you put food on the table, a roof overhead and even pay for the kids' dental bills with their freelance writing income.

This is said despite the well-established reality that writers in general are underpaid and, according to surveys conducted by the Author's Guild and others, writer's wages on the whole are stagnant or declining. Most recent information from the National Writers Union says only 15 percent of working writers make more than $30,000 annually. There is no doubt this is a problem, and writers need to band together through organizations such as the NWU, American Society of Journalists and Authors and others to rattle corporate cages everywhere and give professional writers more respect and more cash.

But we take the glass-is-half-full side of the argument here, because there is data from *Writer's Market*'s newest survey of freelance income that shows a substantial number of writers earn $30,000 to $40,000 and more (sometimes well into 6 figures) by freelance writing activities.

So how are some writers able to "make it" while others are stewing in credit card juice? The money-making writers have certain traits in common. Most are solid, experienced writers who spent some time learning their craft, either independently or as employees in PR departments, ad agencies, magazines, newspapers or book publishers. They have talent, they are reliable professionals who respect deadlines, and most of the better earners specialize in subjects or types of writing in which they have developed "insider" knowledge and expertise. There appears to be more money for more writers in business and technology markets (including advertising and PR) than there is in magazine or book publishing/editing, though some writers prefer the variety and/or prestige offered in traditional publishing arenas. For most freelancers, newspapers are not the way to go if income is a priority. However, they may be useful as a source of initial clips to promote work in better-paying markets, and they may be helpful to specialists or self-publishers who benefit from the publicity.

But the real difference between the haves and the have-nots among freelancers is sheer, unglamorous business savvy. In short, the money-earning freelancer puts effort into developing and refining all small business skills, especially the key element: marketing. There is reason to argue that writers' pay in general is low partly because so few writers care much about the business aspects of this occupation. In this, freelance writing is similar to other creative fields. Hobby artists, photographers, potters and musicians love what they're doing and get paid "hobby" rates, if at all. Professionals in those fields, if they also have good business sense, earn a living with what they do.

So let's assume you are an aspiring freelancer with fairly well-developed writing skills, or

LYNN WASNAK *has been a full-time freelancer for more than 20 years. She is intimately acquainted with the peaks, valleys and sinkholes of this fascinating business, and looks forward to making more mistakes (and learning from them) as time goes on.*

an active freelancer who wants to earn more or break into new areas. We'll also assume you would like to be (sooner rather than later) in that giddy realm of the NWU's top 15 percent who earn more than $30,000. The meat of this article is in the rates that follow (gleaned, as previously mentioned, from our survey participants and other writing income analysis). But before you get to the meat, let's tackle the bread-making ingredients of the freelance business.

WHERE THE JOBS ARE

Where do freelancers find their jobs? According to our survey participants, the top job-getter is a toss-up between networking with fellow writers and prior contact with the editor/writing buyer. Both score high. Other strong job leads come from e-mail and/or hard-copy queries, networking with businesses (through Chambers of Commerce and specialized industry meetings), and of course, *Writer's Market*, *Writer's Digest* and topic-specific publications such as *The Travelwriter Marketletter*. Some writers send samples and résumés out cold to potential clients, or do cold-calling on the phone to set up interviews or present samples. (Cold-calling is more acceptable among general business and technology firms than in magazine and book publishing.) Some writers have used direct mail self-promotions successfully, though others said they found it a waste of money.

Obviously, you'll want to stay abreast of developments in the particular industries that you focus on (or would like to enter). Book writers/editors find *Publishers Weekly* a must-read, and business writers of most every stripe will find possible stories or clients in *The Wall Street Journal*. (Both publications and many others have classified want ads that sometimes seek writing or creative talent.) If you have access to press events or conferences where editors and writers mingle, by all means take full advantage. Don't forget to carry a few samples along with your nicely printed brochure and business cards (you *do* have them, don't you?)

But whether or not you have access to the editorial party scene, don't miss the newest wave of writers' marketing opportunities on the Internet. If your freelance activities don't yet include a computer (you need this ASAP, plus fax machine, organized file cabinets etc.), visit your local library, log on and take a peek at websites such as http://www.inkspot.com. This site and several others provide information on both contract (freelance) and staff jobs for writers.

But by far, the most credible referrals for future jobs come about when a past client tells someone you're a top-notch writer. So as you do each assignment, even the most tedious, give your absolute best effort. That person you're writing for might become the best job recruiter you've ever had!

HOW TO CHOOSE YOUR OWN SALARY

Can you really choose your own salary? As an independent business person, unlike an employee, you not only can, you *must* set your own goals. That includes income. You may also set a time frame in which you either expect to meet or exceed these goals—or rethink your business plan. (And yes, it's a very good idea to set down a written plan for your freelancing activity. It doesn't have to be as formal as the business plan for a bank or a retail store, but if you want to earn money, you have to figure out what writing skills you have to sell, who might want them and how you will persuade them that you are the best writer for the job.)

To determine your income requirements, start off with your required annual income and add 30 percent for current expenses and the additional expenses you may have to incur as a new freelancer. Don't forget to figure in approximately another 30 percent for health insurance, social security, retirement and other benefits that may be paid in whole or in part by your present employer. (If you need to get health insurance, check out some of the writers' organizations which offer insurance as a membership option.) This number is your basic income requirement.

Next, figure a standard hourly rate, or rate range. Some business plans suggest arriving at an hourly rate by dividing the basic income requirement above by 2,080 (the number of hours in a 40-hour work week, 52 weeks a year). But this calculation is not too helpful for freelance

Figuring an Hourly Rate

$$\frac{\text{required annual income} + 30\% \text{ (expenses)} + 30\% \text{ (benefits)}}{\text{billable hours worked per year}}$$

For example,

$$\frac{\$30,000 + \$9,000 + \$9,000}{1,500 \text{ hours}} = \$32/\text{hour}$$

writers, most of whom are set up as sole proprietorships, unless you plan to work more hours. That's because, as a sole proprietor, you are not likely to bill clients for 40 hours each week, unless you put in a lot of overtime. Full-time freelancers may bill as few as 800 hours annually, because running a writing business means doing it *all*. Researching markets, preparing samples, interviewing prospective clients, putting together proposals, creating your webpage, networking—all these vital tasks eat up time. (Occasionally the office needs a good vacuuming, too. Without a helpful partner, the crumbs will stay unless *you* sweep them up.) Few writers have secretaries to do their filing, or accountants to handle the routine jobs of invoicing and check writing. (Many writers do employ outside accountants to handle their taxes, including the somewhat cumbersome Business Schedule C. These suppliers may also serve as on-the-fly financial consultants and an accountant might be a useful critic for your business plan.) Most of us who freelance also want a few days of vacation here or there. So subtract these nonbillable hours to get a more realistic number. Divide the realistic billable number into your income goal to come up with a basic hourly rate that will allow you to hit your income target.

When you look at that rate, it may seem extremely high. Maybe it is, maybe it isn't. Your next step is to study the rate guidelines that follow this introduction to see if your hourly fee is in the ballpark. Then do more job-specific research on your own. Ask other writers in your locale (or those who work for the same kind of organization, if it is elsewhere) what they charge. You'll need to factor the competitive rate into your personal equation.

If you follow the job hunting and income guidelines, with a little luck you will be asked to bid on a job. Nearly every one of the freelancers who were earning adequate income stressed the requirement: "Don't sell yourself short!" Most professional freelancers suggest starting your estimate somewhere in the middle range, and being willing to negotiate. They say it is far easier to negotiate your fee downward than the reverse.

HOW LONG DOES IT TAKE?

Hourly rates are a good place to start your process of estimates and billing, but sometimes it's hard to get a handle on how long a project will take. In our survey, we asked participants to estimate the time it takes them to complete various writing assignments. The results pointed out, once again, what wide variables there are among writers, both in the type of work they commonly produce and in the speed of their writing.

This is not a scientific sample by any means, but it may give you some clues to the amount of work time to expect. Of course the best way to figure your own hours once you're active is to keep a detailed work log per project—and don't omit any part of it. (If you have to have

Project Time Guidelines

(Writing time estimates, assuming research at hand)

4-page brochure:
Extremes: 2 hours, low/15 days, high; Typical: 1-2 days

700-word technical article:
Extremes: 45 minutes, low/6 weeks, high; Typical: 2-4 hours

Feature article (2,000 words):
Extremes: 2 hours, low/12 weeks, high; Typical: 10 hours to 1 week

2-page PR release:
Extremes: 20 minutes, low/1 week, high; Typical: 2-4 hours

Speech for corporate executive:
Extremes: 2 hours, low/3 weeks, high; Typical: 3-5 days

8-page newsletter:
Extremes: 4 hours, low/5 weeks, high; Typical: 2-4 days

"thinking time," put that on the log, even if you don't bill the client the full amount.) By keeping good time records of specific project types, before too long you will be able to discern a pattern. Some writers use this pattern to determine their "per project" fees, multiplying their usual hours times their hourly rate (often adding a cushion to cover extraordinary circumstances). Writers who prefer "project fees" may gain speed with experience, and thereby earn higher hourly rates without the client feeling any pain.

Again, the following work times are given as a very rough guideline, not gospel. You've got to take the time it takes you to do the job properly, while keeping the market rates in mind.

ADVERTISING, COPYWRITING & PR

Advertising copywriting: $400 low, $1,000 mid-range, $2,000 high/full page ad depending on the size and kind of client; $50 low, $75 mid-range, $100 high/hour; $250 and up/day; $500 and up/week; $1,000-2,000 as a monthly retainer. In Canada, rates range from $40-80/hour.

Advertorials: $25-35/hour; up to $1/word or by flat fee ($300/700 words is typical). In Canada, 40-80¢/word; $35-75/hour.

Book jacket copywriting: $100-600/front cover jacket plus flaps and back jacket copy summarizing content and tone of the book.

Campaign development or product launch: $3,500 low, $7,000 mid-range, $12,000 high/project.

Catalog copywriting: $25-$45/hour or $85 and up/project.

Copyediting for advertising: $25-35/hour.

Direct mail copywriting: $25-45/hour; $75 and up/item or $400-800/page.

Direct mail packages: This includes copywriting direct mail letter, response card and advertising materials. $50 low, $75 mid-range, $115 high/hour; $2,500-10,000/project, depending on complexity. Additional charges for production such as desktop publishing, addressing, etc.

Direct mail response card for a product: $250-500/project.

Direct mail production (DTP): $50-60/hour.

Event promotions/publicity: $40 low, $60 mid-range, $70 high/hour; $500-750/day.

Fundraising campaign brochure: $50-75 for research (20 hours) and copywriting (30 hours); up to $5,000 for major campaign brochure, including research, writing and production (about 50 hours of work).

High-tech marketing materials: $85 low, $125 mid-range, $250 high/hour.

New product release: $20-35/hour or $300-500/release.

News release: *See Press/news release.*

Political campaigns, public relations: Small town or state campaigns, $10-50/hour; congressional, gubernatorial or other national campaigns, $25-100/hour or up to 10% of campaign budget.

Promotion for events: $20-30/hour. For conventions and longer events, payment may be per diem or a flat fee of $500-2,500. *See also Press/news release.*

Press kits: $50 low, $70 mid-range, $125 high/hour; $1,000-5,000/project.

Press/news release: $40 low, $70 mid-range, $150 high/hour; $150 low, $350 mid-range, $500 high/project.

Print advertisement: $200-500/project. In Canada, $100-200/concept. *See also Advertising copywriting.*

Product information: $30-60/hour; $400-500/day or $100-300/page. *See also Sales and services brochures and fliers.*

Promotion for tourism, museums, art shows, etc.: $20-$50 and up/hour for writing or editing promotion copy. Additional charges for production, mailings, etc.

Public relations for businesses: $250-600/day plus expenses average—more for large corporations.

Public relations for government: $25-50/hour or a monthly retainer based on number of hours per period. Lower fees for local government agencies, higher for state-level and above.

Public relations for organizations or nonprofits: $15-35/hour. If working on a monthly retainer, $100-500/month.

Public relations for schools or libraries: $15-20/hour for small districts or libraries; up to $35/hour for larger districts.

Public relations monthly retainers: $500 low, $800 mid-range, $1,000 high (fee includes press releases, modest events etc.).

Radio advertisement: $50 low, $75 mid-range, $125 high/hour; $400 low, $750 mid-range, $2,000 high/spot; $200-400/week for part-time positions writing radio ads, depending on the size of the city (and market).

Sales and services brochures and fliers: $30 low, $65 mid-range, $100 high/hour; $500 low, $1,000 mid-range, $2,500 high/4-page project depending on size and type of business (small nonprofit organization to a large corporation), the number of pages (usually from 1-16) and complexity of the job.

Sales letters: $2/word; $40 low, $70 mid-range, $125 high/hour; $400 low, $750 mid-range, $2,000 high/project.

Speech editing or evaluation: $50 low, $90 mid-range, $125/high, $200 very high/finished minute. In Canada, $75-125/hour or $70-100/minute of speech.

Speechwriting (general): $50 low, $90 mid-range, $125 high, $200 very high/finished minute. In Canada, $75-125/hour or $70-100/minute of speech.

Speechwriting for business owners or executives: Up to $80/hour or a flat fee of about $100 for a short (6- or 7-minute speech); $500-3,000 for up to 30 minutes. Rates also depend on size of the company and the event.

Speechwriting for government officials: $4,000/20 minutes plus up to $1,000 for travel and expenses.

Speechwriting for political candidates: $250 and up for local candidates (about 15 minutes); $375-800 for statewide candidates and $1,000 or more for national congressional candidates.

TV commercial: 30 second spot: $950-1,500. In Canada, $60-130/minute of script (CBC pays Writers Guild rates, CTV pays close to that and others pay less. For example, TV Ontario pays $70-100/script minute).

AUDIOVISUALS & ELECTRONIC COMMUNICATIONS

(See Technical for computer-related services)

Audiocassette scripts: $10-50/scripted minute, assuming written from existing client materials, with no additional research or meetings; otherwise $85-100/minute, $750 minimum.

Audiovisuals: For writing, $250-350/requested scripted minute; includes rough draft, editing conference with client, and final shooting script. For consulting, research, producing, directing, soundtrack oversight, etc. $400-600/day plus travel and expenses. Writing fee is sometimes 10% of gross production price as billed to client. Some charge flat fee of $1,500-2,100/package.

Book summaries for film producers: $50-100/book. *Note: You must live in the area where the business is located to get this kind of work.*

Business film scripts (training and information): $50 low, $85 mid-range, $200 high/hour; $75 low, $100 mid-range, $175 high/finished minute.

Copyediting audiovisuals: $20-25/hour.

Educational/training film scripts: $50 low, $85 mid-range, $200 high/hour; $100/finished minute.

Industrial product film: $125-150/minute; $500 minimum flat fee.

Novel synopsis for film producer: $150-300/5-10 pages typed, single spaced.

Options (feature films): $1,500 low, $15,000 mid-range, $50,000 high, $400,000 very high/project.

Radio continuity writing: $5/page to $150/week, part-time. In Canada, $40-80/minute of script; $640/show for a multi-part series.

Radio copywriting: *See Advertising, Copywriting & PR.*

Radio documentaries: $258/60 minutes, local station.

Radio editorials: $10-30/90-second to 2-minute spots.

Radio interviews: For National Public Radio, up to 45 seconds, $25; 2 minutes and longer, $62/minute. Small radio stations would pay approximately 50% of the NPR rate; large stations, double the NPR rate.

Script synopsis for business: $40/hour.

Script synopsis for agent or film producer: $75/2-3 typed pages, single-spaced.

Scripts for nontheatrical films for education, business, industry: Prices vary among producers, clients, and sponsors and there is no standardization of rates in the field. Fees include $75-120/minute for one reel (10 minutes) and corresponding increases with each successive reel; approximately 10% of the production cost of films that cost the producer more than $1,500/release minute.

Screenwriting: $6,000 and up/project.

Slide presentation: Including visual formats plus audio, $150-600/10-15 minutes.

Slide/single image photos: $75 flat fee.

Slide/tape script: $50 low, $75 mid-range, $100 high/hour; $100 low, $300 high/finished minute; $1,500-3,000/finished project.

TV commercial: *See Advertising, Copywriting & PR.*

TV documentary: 30-minute 5-6 page proposal outline, $1,839 and up; 15-17 page treatment, $1,839 and up; less in smaller cities. In Canada research for a documentary runs about $6,500.

TV editorials: $35 and up/1-minute, 45 seconds (250-300 words).

TV filmed news and features: From $10-20/clip for 30-second spot; $15-25/60-second clip; more for special events.

TV information scripts: Short 5- to 10-minute scripts for local cable TV stations, $10-15/hour.

TV, national and local public stations: For programs, $35-100/minute down to a flat fee of $5,000 and up/30- to 60-minute script.

TV news film still photo: $3-6 flat fee.

TV news story/feature: $60 low, $95 mid-range, $140 high.

TV scripts: (non-theatrical): $50 low, $75 mid-range, $85 high/hour; $300 per finished minute; $3,000/project.

TV scripts: (Teleplays/mow): $15,000/30-minute sitcom.

BOOK PUBLISHING

Abstracting and abridging: $40 low, $60 mid-range, $85 high/hour; $30-35/hour for reference and professional journals; $600/5,000 word book summary.

Anthology editing: Variable advance plus 3-15 percent of royalties. Advance should cover reprint fees or fees are handled by the publisher. Flat-fee-per-manuscript rates range from $500-5,000 and up.

Book jacket copywriting: *See Advertising, Copywriting & PR.*

Book proposal consultation: $20-75/hour or a flat rate of $100-250.

Book proposal writing: 50¢/word; $45 low, $65 mid-range, $85 high/hour: $2,000-3,500/project, depending on length and whether the client provides full information or the writer must do research, and whether a sample chapter is required.

Book query critique: $50 for critique of letter to the publisher and outline.

Book summaries for book clubs: $50-100/book.

Book writing (own): $20 low, $40 mid-range, $50 high/hour; (advances) $15 low, $35 mid-range, $45 high/hour.

Content editing (scholarly): $14 low, $22 mid-range, $32 high, $100 very high/hour.

Content editing (textbook): $14 low, $35 mid-range, $65 high, $100 very high/hour.

Content editing (trade): $30 low, $60 mid-range, $100 high/hour; $800 low, $1,200 mid-range, $6,000 high/project.

Copyediting: $17 low, $30 mid-range, $50 high, $75 very high/hour; $3-5/page. Lower-end rates charged for light copyedit (3-10 pages/hour) of general, trade material. Higher-end rates charged for substantive copyediting or for textbooks and technical material (2-5 pages/hour).

Ghostwriting, as told to: This is writing for a celebrity or expert either for a self-published book or for a publisher. Author gets full advance plus 50 percent of royalties, typically $15,000 low, $25,000 high/project plus a percentage of ownership and 'with' credit line. Hourly rates for subjects who are self-publishing are $25 low, $55 mid-range, $85 high/hour; $125 low, $175 high/book page. In Canada, author also gets full advance and 50 percent of royalties or $10,000-20,000 flat fee per project. Research time is charged extra.

Ghostwriting, no credit: Projects may include writing for an individual planning to self publish or for a book packager, book producer, publisher, agent or corporation. Rates range from $5,000 very low, $15,000 low, $25,000 mid-range, $50,000 high/project (plus expenses); packagers pay flat fee or combination of advance plus royalties. For self-published clients, ask for one-fourth down payment, one-fourth when book is half-finished, one-fourth at the three-quarters mark and one-fourth upon completion.

Indexing: $15 low, $25 mid-range, $40 high, $95 very high/hour; charge higher hourly rate if using a computer index program that takes fewer hours. Also can charge $2-6/indexable page; 40-70¢/line of index or a flat fee of $250-500 depending on length.

Manuscript evaluation and critique: $150-200/outline and first 20,000 words: $300-500/up to 100,000 words. Also $15-35/hour for trade books, slightly less for nonprofits. Page rates run from $1.50-2.50/page.

Movie novelization: $3,500-15,000 depending on writer's reputation, amount of work to be done and amount of time writer is given.

Novel synopsis for a literary agent: $150/5-10 pages typed, single-spaced.

Page layout (desktop publishing/camera-ready copy): $25 low, $40 mid-range, $50 high/hour. Higher per-page rates may be charged if material involves complex technical material and graphics.

Production editing/project management: $15 low, $30 mid-range, $75 high, $150 very high/ hour. This is overseeing the production of a project, coordinating editing and production stages, etc.

Proofreading: $15 low, $30 mid-range, $55 high/hour; $4-6/page. High-end rates are charged for technical, scientific and reference material.

Research for writers or book publishers: $20-40/hour and up; $150 and up/day plus expenses. A flat rate of $300-500 may be charged, depending on complexity of the job.

Rewriting: $18-50/hour; $5-7/page. Some writers receive royalties on book projects.

Summaries for book clubs/catalogues: $20 low, $40 mid-range, $75 high/hour.

Textbooks: $20 low, $40 mid-range, $60 high/hour.

Translation (literary): 10¢/word, $30-35/hour; also $95-125/1,000 English words.

Typesetting: $20-45/hour or $5-10/page.

BUSINESS

Annual reports: A brief report with some economic information and an explanation of figures, $35 low, $70 mid-range, $100 high, $150 very high/hour; $300 low, $600 high/page; $500/ day; $3,000 low, $6,000 mid-range, $12,000 high/project if extensive research and/or writing is involved in a large project. A report that must meet Securities and Exchange Commission (SEC) standards and reports requiring legal language could bill $75-150/hour. Bill separately if desktop publication (typesetting, page layout, etc.) is involved (some smaller firms and nonprofits may ask for writing/production packages).

Associations and organizations (writing for): $15-25/hour for small organizations; up to $50/ hour for larger associations or a flat fee depending on the length and complexity of the project. For example, $500-1,000 for an association magazine article (2,000 words) or $1,000-1,800 for a 10-page informational booklet.

Audiovisuals/audiocassette scripts: *See Audiovisuals & Electronic Communications.*

Book summaries for businesses: $25-50/page or $20-35/hour.

Brochures, fliers, booklets for business: $25-40/hour for writing or from $500-$4,000 and up/ project (12-16 pages and more). Additional charges for desktop publishing, usually $20-40/ hour; $20-30/page or a flat fee per project. *See also Copyediting for business or Manuscript editing/evaluation for trade journals.*

Business editing (general): $25 low, $40 mid-range, $85 high/hour.

Business letters: $25 low, $65 mid-range, $100 high/hour, depending on the size of the business and the length/complexity of the material, or $2/word.

Business plan: $1/word; $200/manuscript page or up to $1,500/project. High-end rates are charged if extensive research is involved. Sometimes research is charged separately per hour or per day.

Business writing (general): $30-80/hour. In Canada, $1-2/word or $50-100/hour. *See other entries in this section and in Advertising, Copywriting & PR for specific projects such as brochures, copywriting, speechwriting, brochures or business letters. For business film script-writing see Audiovisuals & Electronic Communications.*

Business writing seminars: $500 for a half-day seminar, plus travel expenses or $1,000-5,000/ day. Rates depend on number of participants as well as duration. Average per-person rate is $50/person for a half-day seminar. *See also Educational and Literary Services.*

Catalogs for business: $25-40/hour or $25-600/printed page; more if tables or charts must be reworked for readability or consistency. Additional charges for desktop publishing ($20-40/ hour is average).

Collateral materials for business: *See individual pieces (brochures, catalogs, etc.) in this section and in Advertising, Copywriting & PR.*

Commercial reports for business, insurance companies, credit agencies: $6-15/page.

Consultation on communications: $25 low, $50 mid-range, $85 high/hour; $600 low, $2,000 high/day (includes travel). Lower-end fees charged to nonprofits and small businesses.

Consumer complaint letters (answering): $25-30/letter.

Copyediting for business: $20-40/hour or $20-50/manuscript page, up to $40/hour for business proposals. Charge lower-end fees ($15-25/hour) to nonprofits and very small businesses.

Corporate histories: $30 low, $70 mid-range, $100 high/hour; $500/day; $7,500/project.

Corporate periodicals, editing: $20 very low, $40 low, $60 mid-range, $85 high/hour.

Corporate periodicals, writing: $25 very low, $40 low, $70 mid-range, $120 high/hour, depending on size and nature of the corporation. Also $1-3/word. In Canada, $1-2/word or $40-90/hour.

Corporate profile: $1,250-2,500 flat fee for up to 3,000 words or charge on a per word basis, up to $1/word.

Financial presentation: $1,500-4,500 for a 20-30 minute presentation.

Fundraising campaign brochure: *See Advertising, Copywriting & PR.*

Ghostwriting for business (usually trade magazine articles or business columns): $25-100/hour; $200 or more/day plus expenses (depending on amount of research involved, length of project).

Government research: $35-50/hour.

Government writing: $30-50/hour. In Canada, $50-80/hour.

Grant proposal writing for nonprofits: $30-100/hour or flat fee.

Indexing for professional journals: $20-40/hour.

Industrial/service business training manual: $25-40/hour; $50-100/manuscript page or a flat fee, $1,000-4,000, depending on number of pages and complexity of the job.

Industry training film scripts: *See Business film scripts in Audiovisuals & Electronic Communications.*

Industrial product film script: *See Audiovisuals & Electronic Communications.*

Job application letters: $20-40/letter.

Manuals/documentation: $25-60/hour. *See also Computers, Scientific & Technical.*

Manuscript editing/evaluation for trade journals: $20-40/hour.

Market research survey reports: $25-50/hour or $500-1,500/day; also flat rates of $500-2,000/project.

Newsletters, abstracting: $30/hour.

Newsletters, desktop publishing/production: $25 low, $40 mid-range, $85 high/hour. Higher-end rates for scanning photographs, advertising layout, illustration or design. Editing charged extra.

Newsletters, editing: $25 low, $45 mid-range, $85 high/hour; $200-500/issue; $2/word. Higher-end fees charged if writing or production is included. Editors who produce a regular newsletter on a monthly or quarterly basis tend to charge per month or per issue—and find them easier to do after initial set up.

Newsletters, writing: $35 low, $50 mid-range, $100 high/hour; $500 low, $1,350 mid-range, $2,500 high/project; $200 and up/page. In Canada, $45-70/hour.

Nonprofit editing: $15 low, $30 mid-range, $55 high/hour.

Nonprofit writing: $15 very low, $25 low, $50 mid-range, $70 high/hour.

Programmed instruction consultation fees: *See Educational & Literary Services.*

Programmed instruction materials for business: *See Educational & Literary Services.*

Proofreading for business: $15-50/hour; low-end fees for nonprofits.

Public relations: *See Advertising, Copywriting and PR.*

Résumé writing: $30 low, $55 mid-range, $100 high.

Retail newsletters for customers: Charge regular newsletter rates or $175-300/4-page project. Additional charges for desktop publishing.

Sales brochures, fliers, letters, other advertising materials: *See Advertising, Copywriting & PR.*

Scripts for business/training films: *See Audiovisuals & Electronic Communications.*

Translation, commercial: $30-45/hour; $115-125/1,000 words. Higher-end fees for non-European languages into English.

Translation for government agencies: $30-45; up to $125/1,000 words. Higher-end fees for non-European languages into English.

Translation through translation agencies: Agencies pay 33⅓% average less than end-user clients and mark up translator's prices by as much as 100% or more.

Translation, technical: $30-45/hour; $125 and up/1,000 words, depending on complexity of the material.

COMPUTER, SCIENTIFIC & TECHNICAL

Abstracting, CD-ROM: $50/hour.

Abstracting, online: $40/hour.

Computer documentation, general (print): $35 low, $60 mid-range, $100 high/hour; $100-150/page. *See also Software manual writing.*

Computer documentation (online): $20 low, $50 mid-range, $85 high/hour.

Demonstration software: $70 and up/hour.

Legal/government editing: $15 very low, $25 low, $50 mid-range, $65 high/hour.

Legal/government writing: $15 very low, $30 low, $50 mid-range, $65 high/hour.

Medical and science editing: $20 low, $60 mid-range, $85 high/hour, depending on the complexity of the material and the expertise of the editor.

Medical and science proofreading: $15-30/hour.

Medical and science writing: $35 low, $70 mid-range, $150 high/hour; $1-3/word, depending on the complexity of the project and the writer's expertise.

Online editing: $25 low, $40 mid-range, $68 high/hour.

Software manual writing: $15 low, $50 mid-range, $100 high/hour for research and writing.

Technical editing: $20-60/hour or $150-1,000/day.

Technical typesetting: $4-7/page; $25-35/hour; more for inputting of complex material.

Technical writing: $30-75/hour; $20-30/page. *See also Computer documentation and Software manual writing.*

Technical translation: *See item in Business.*

Webpage design: $50 low, $85 mid-range, $125 high/hour..

Webpage writing/editing: $50 low, $85 mid-range, $125 high/hour; $170 mid-range, $500 high/page.

EDITORIAL/DESIGN PACKAGES

Business catalogs: *See Business.*

Desktop publishing: For 1,000 dots-per-inch type, $5-15/camera-ready page of straight type; $30/camera-ready page with illustrations, maps, tables, charts, photos; $100-150/camera-ready page for oversize pages with art. Also $25-50/hour depending on graphics, number of photos, and amount of copy to be typeset. Packages often include writing, layout/design, and typesetting services.

Greeting cards ideas (with art included): Anywhere from $30-300, depending on size of company.

Newsletters: *See Desktop publishing (this section) and Newsletters (Business).*

Picture editing: $20-40.

Photo brochures: $700-15,000 flat fee for photos and writing.

Photo research: $15-30/hour.

Photography: $10-150/b&w photo; $25-300/color photo; also $800/day.

EDUCATIONAL & LITERARY SERVICES

Business writing seminars: *See Business.*

Consultation for individuals (in business): $250-1,000/day.

Consultation on communications: *See Business.*

Developing and designing courses for business or adult education: $250-$1,500/day or flat fee.

Editing for individual clients: $10-50/hour or $2-7/page.

Educational consulting and educational grant and proposal writing: $250-750/day or $30-75/hour.

Lectures at national conventions by well-known authors: $2,500-20,000 and up, plus expenses; less for panel discussions.

Lectures at regional writers' conferences: $300 and up, plus expenses.

Lectures to local groups, librarians or teachers: $50-150.

Lectures to school classes: $25-75; $150/day; $250/day if farther than 100 miles.

Manuscript evaluation for theses/dissertations: $15-30/hour.

Poetry manuscript critique: $25/16-line poem.

Programmed instruction consultant fees: $300-1,000/day, $50-75/hour.

Programmed instruction materials for business: $50/hour for inhouse writing and editing; $500-1,000/day plus expenses for outside research and writing. Alternate method: $2,000-5,000/hour of programmed training provided depending on technicality of subject.

Public relations for schools: *See Advertising, Copywriting & PR.*

Readings by poets, fiction writers: $25-600 depending on author.

Scripts for nontheatrical films for education: *See Audiovisuals & Electronic Communications.*

Short story manuscript critique: 3,000 words, $40-60.

Teaching adult education course: $15 low, $45 mid-range, $125 high/hour; $1,750-2,500/ continuing education course; fee usually set by school, not negotiated by teachers.

Teaching adult seminar: $20 low, $40 mid-range, $60 high/hour; $750-1,000/3-day course. In Canada, $35-50/hour.

Teaching business writing to company employees: *See Consultation on communications in Business.*

Teaching college course or seminar: $15-70/class hour.

Teaching creative writing in school: $15-70/hour of instruction, or $1,500-2,000/12-15 week semester; less in recessionary times.

Teaching elementary and middle school teachers how to teach writing to students: $75-150/1- to 1½ hour session.

Teaching home-bound students: $5-15/hour.

Tutoring: $25/1- to 1½ hour private session.

TV instruction taping: $150/30-minute tape; $25 residual each time tape is sold.

Workshop instructing: $25 low, $50 mid-range, $75 high/hour; $2,500-3,500/13-week course.

Writer-in-schools: Arts council program, $130/day; $650/week. Personal charges plus expenses vary from $25/day to $100/hour depending on school's ability to pay.

Writer's workshop: Lecturing and seminar conducting, $50-150/hour to $750/day plus expenses; local classes, $35-50/student for 10 sessions.

Writing for individual clients: $25-100/hour, depending on the situation. *See also Business writing in Business.*

Writing for scholarly journals: $75/hour.

MAGAZINES & TRADE JOURNALS

Abstracting: $20-30/hour for trade and professional journals; $20 low, $30 mid-range, $60 high/hour for scholarly journals.

Advertorial: $650 low, $1,000 high/printed page.

Article manuscript critique: $40/3,000 words.

Arts reviewing: $35-100 flat fee or 20-30¢/word, plus admission to events or copy of CD (for music).

Book reviews: $22 low, $50 mid-range, $175 high, $750 very high/piece; 25¢-$1/word.

Consultation on magazine editorial: $1,000-1,500/day plus expenses.

Copyediting magazines: $16-30/hour.

Editing: General, $25-500/day or $250-2,000/issue; religious publications, $200-500/month or $15-30/hour.

Fact checking: $26 low, $50 mid-range, $75 high/hour.

Feature articles: Anywhere from 20¢-$4/word; or $150-2,750/1,500 word article, depending on size (circulation) and reputation of magazine.

Ghostwriting articles (general): Up to $2/word; or $300-3,000/project.

Indexing: $15-40/hour.

Magazine, city, calendar of events column: $50-150/column.

Magazine column: 25¢ low, $1.50 mid-range, $4 high/word; $25 low, $200 mid-range, $2,500 high/piece. Larger circulation publications pay fees related to their regular word rate.

Magazine copyediting: $15 low, $25 mid-range, $50 high, $100 very high/hour.

Magazine editing: $15 low, $30 mid-range, $60 high/hour.

Magazine research: $20 low, $40 mid-range, $75 high/hour.

Manuscript consultation: $25-50/hour.

Manuscript criticism: $40-60/article or short story of up to 3,000 words. Also $20-25/hour.

Picture editing: *See Editorial/Design Packages.*

Permission fees to publishers to reprint article or story: $75-500; 10-15¢/word; less for charitable organizations.

Production editing: $15-30/hour.

Proofreading: $12-25/hour.

Research: $20-25/hour.

Rewriting: Up to $80/manuscript page; also $100/published page.

Science writing for magazines: $2,000-5,000/article. *See also Computer, Scientific & Technical.*

Special news article: For a business's submission to trade publication, $250-500/1,000 words. In Canada, 25-45¢/word.

Stringing: 20¢-$1/word based on circulation. Daily rate: $150-250 plus expenses; weekly rate: $900 plus expenses. Also $10-35/hour plus expenses; $1/column inch.

Trade journal ad copywriting: *See Advertising, Copywriting & PR.*

Trade journal feature article: For business client, $400-1,000. Also $1-2/word.

NEWSPAPERS

Ads for small business: $25/small, one-column ad, or $10/hour and up. *See also Advertising, Copywriting & PR.*

Arts reviewing: For weekly newspapers, $15-50 flat fee; for dailies, $50 and up; for Sunday supplements, $100-400. Also admission to event or copy of CD (for music).

Book reviews: For small newspapers, byline and the book only; for larger publications, $35-200 and a copy of the book.

Column, local: $40 low, $125 mid-range, $300 high/hour, depending on circulation.

Copyediting: $10-30/hour; up to $40/hour for large daily paper.

Copywriting: *See Advertising, Copywriting & PR.*

Dance criticism: $25-400/article.

Drama criticism: Local, newspaper rates; non-local, $50 and up/review.

Editing/manuscript evaluation: $25/hour.

Fact checking: *See Magazines & Trade Journals.*

Feature: $25 low, $200 mid-range, $500 high/piece, depending on circulation. In Canada, $15-40/word, but rates vary widely.

Obituary copy: Where local newspapers permit lengthier than normal notices paid for by the funeral home (and charged to the family), $15-25. Writers are engaged by funeral homes.

Picture editing: *See Editorial/Design Packages.*

Proofreading: $16-20/hour.

Reporting: $25 low, $45 mid-range, $100 high/piece (small circulation); $60 low, $175 high/per piece (large circulation).

Science writing for newspapers: *See Computer, Scientific & Technical.*

Stringing: $10 low, $25 mid-range, $40 high/piece; $1/column inch, sometimes with additional mileage payment.

Syndicted column, self-promoted: $5-10 each for weeklies; $10-25/week for dailies, based on circulation.

MISCELLANEOUS

Comedy writing for nightclub entertainers: Gags only, $5-25 each. Routines, $100-1,000/minute. Some new comics may try to get a 5-minute routine for $150; others will pay $2,500 for a 5-minute bit from a top writer.

Comics writing: $35-50/page and up for established comics writers.

Contest judging: Short manuscripts, $10/entry; with one-page critique, $15-25. Overall contest judging: $100-500.

Corporate comedy skits: $300-800/half-hour skit (used at meetings, conventions).

Craft ideas with instructions: $50-200/project.

Encyclopedia articles: Entries in some reference books, such as biographical encyclopedias, 500-2,000 words; pay ranges from $60-80/1,000 words. Specialists' fees vary.

Family histories: Fees depend on whether the writer edits already prepared notes or does extensive research and writing; and the length of the work, $500-15,000.

Institutional (church, school) history: $200-1,000/15-50 pages, or $20-35/hour.

Manuscript typing: Depending on manuscript length and delivery schedule, $1.25-2/page with one copy; $15/hour.

Party toasts, limericks, place card verses: $1.50/line.

Research for individuals: $5-30/hour, depending on experience, geographic area and nature of work.

Special occasion booklet: Family keepsake of a wedding, anniversary, Bar Mitzvah, etc., $120 and up.

Book Contract Clinic: Quick Fixes for Bad Clauses

BY STEPHEN E. GILLEN ESQ.

If you've been published, then you've seen it before—a WHEREAS and a THEREFORE followed by eight or more pages of pre-printed, pedantic prose offered up by the editor as his/her "standard publishing contract." Other than a few tiny spaces for your name, the title of your work, and the manuscript delivery date, the bulk of it looks as though it were long ago locked down in Century Schoolbook type.

But the truth is that there is more to review than the spelling of your name, choice of title, and projected completion date, and more to negotiate than you might realize. Here, then, are three critical points to get you in the right frame of mind, followed by an explanation of six typical clauses to help you understand what is (or ought to be) worthy of negotiation.

POINT #1—YOU HAVE MORE LEVERAGE THAN YOU THINK

Editors are under ever increasing pressure to sign new titles, meet publication dates, and deliver sales results. For many of them, these factors have a direct bearing on their year end compensation (a circumstance that can work to your significant bargaining advantage as year end approaches). While there are many aspiring first-time authors out there, only a relative handful will be published. If you have attracted interest or a contract offer, then you have already made the cut. A reasonable list of tactfully stated concerns and requested amendments will only reinforce the impression that you are a competent and thorough professional. Moreover, the editor will have invested a significant amount of time in reviewing your proposal, perhaps getting outside reviews, preparing a pro forma profit and loss analysis, and drafting a publication plan and recommendation for his/her superiors—if you are not signed, all of this effort will have been for naught and the editor will be back to square one.

POINT #2—YOU HAVE TO DO YOUR HOMEWORK

Negotiations are ultimately influenced by which side knows the most about the other side's positions. The editor starts this contest with an advantage gained from experience in the market, experience doing other similar deals (undoubtedly many more than you have done), and the benefits of your perspective as reflected in your proposal. The way you get on an even footing with your editor/publisher is to learn more about your publisher's plans for, and expectations of, your work—information that will help you evaluate your leverage and your editor's weaknesses. Ask about these issues in the context of negotiating a book contract and the editor will evade them, hedge, or refuse to answer. Ask about them after the editor has indicated an interest in your work but before you engage in active, contract-focused negotiations—in the context of learning more about your editor/publisher, more about their list and their business, more about the market and your potential competition—and you may catch the editor still in his or her

STEPHEN E. GILLEN *is a partner with the firm of Frost & Jacobs LLP in Cincinnati, Ohio. His practice is concentrated in publishing, licensing, copyrights, trademarks, and related matters. The firm maintains a web site at http://www.frojac.com where additional articles and links to other sites of interest to writers can be found.*

selling mode. Ask them yourself and in person or over the phone. Negotiations may be formal and may be best handled by your attorney or agent in order to preserve your relationship with your editor. But information gathering will be most effective if you do it in person. A question perceived as innocuous when asked by you will be viewed with suspicion if posed by your agent or attorney. It may take some prodding, probing, wheedling, and cajoling, but the information you gather will prove valuable so take copious notes.

POINT #3—DECIDE WHAT'S IMPORTANT TO YOU

There is no one-size-fits-all solution. If you make your living as a professional writer, then money issues will likely be at the top of your list—advances, grants, royalties, re-use rights should be the focus of your attention. If, on the other hand, you're an academic living by the "publish or perish" mantra and in search of the inner peace that tenure will bring, then the money issues may well take a back seat to ensuring that your work is actually published—on schedule and intact. If you are a professional of another sort (doctor, lawyer, accountant) and you view your book not so much as a revenue generator, but more as a promotional piece and as your professional bona fides, then your principal focus may well be on the non-compete provision and ensuring that it does not preclude you from engaging in the kind of professional writing, speaking, and consulting that does pay the bills. Keep your goals firmly in mind as you review the clauses and the better/best alternatives that follow.

Odds are, you will not prevail on all of these issues. But odds are equally as good that you will not lose on all of them either. In any event, you will not get that for which you do not ask. So ask away . . . at the end of the day you will have a better deal and a more informed relationship with your publisher.

AUTHOR WARRANTIES, REPRESENTATIONS, AND INDEMNITIES. *The Author hereby warrants and represents that: (i) the Author has the right to enter into this Agreement and to grant the rights herein granted and the Author has not and will not assign, pledge, or encumber such rights; (ii) the Author is the sole Author of the Work and, except for material of others permission for use of which has been obtained by the Author pursuant to Paragraph _____, the Work is original and previously unpublished; (iii) the Work is not in the public domain; (iv) neither the Work nor its title will contain any material that would violate or infringe any personal, proprietary, or other right of any person or entity or that would violate any contract of the Author, express or implied, or that would disclose any information given to the Author in confidence or on the understanding it would not be disclosed or published; (v) no material in the Work is inaccurate; (vi) the use of any instruction, material, or formula contained in the Work will not result in injury; and (vii) appropriate warnings will be contained in the Work concerning any particular hazards that may be involved in carrying out experiments described in the Work or involved in the use of instructions, materials, or formulas in the Work, and descriptions of relevant safety precautions. The Author hereby indemnifies and agrees to hold the Publisher, its licensees, and any seller of the Work harmless from any liability, damage, cost, and expense, including reasonable attorney's fees and costs of settlement, for or in connection with any claim, action, or proceeding inconsistent with the Author's warranties or representations herein, or based upon or arising out of any contribution of the Author to the Work. The Publisher will notify the Author of any claim, action, or proceeding, and the Publisher may use counsel of its own selection to defend the same. The Author may participate in the defense, at the Author's own expense, with counsel of the Author's own choosing. The Publisher will have the right to withhold payment of sums otherwise payable to the Author under this or any other agreement with the Author, and to apply the sums withheld to such liability. The warranties, representations, and indemnity of the Author herein will survive termination of this Agreement for any reason and will extend to any licensees, distributors, and assigns of the Publisher.*

Publishers usually require their authors to make certain representations and warranties about the work submitted—that it isn't libelous, that it doesn't infringe third party copyrights, and so on. This is generally a reasonable request because, in many respects, only the Author is in a position to know whether or not the Author's work is original and non-infringing. Be careful, however, that these representations apply only to work as supplied by you and not to the work of other contributors or editors. Also, we all know that every editor likes to put his mark on a work by changing the title. Be sure that you do not warrant that the title does not infringe trademark or other rights (unless, of course, it is indeed your title and you have taken appropriate steps to clear its use).

Most contracts will also require you to indemnify the publisher for any damage or cost incurred as a result of your breach of the foregoing warranties. It is reasonable for you to ask that such indemnification be limited to defects as determined by a court of competent jurisdiction and also to ask that your obligation to indemnify the publisher be capped at the total royalties and other payments you actually receive from the publisher's exploitation of your work, or that you be added as a named insured on the publisher's media perils policy. While the latter may sound like a happy compromise, understand that the deductibles (for which you would still be liable) are generally very large.

Better:

AUTHOR WARRANTIES, REPRESENTATIONS, AND INDEMNITIES. *The Author hereby warrants and represents, with respect only to the Author's contributions to the Work, that: (i) the Author has the right to enter into this Agreement and to grant the rights herein granted and the Author has not and will not assign, pledge, or encumber such rights; (ii) the Author is the sole Author of the Work and, except for material of others permission for use of which has been obtained by the Author pursuant to Paragraph _____, the Work is original and previously unpublished; (iii) the Work is not in the public domain; (iv) the Work contains no material that would violate or infringe any personal, proprietary, or other right of any person or entity or that would violate any contract of the Author, express or implied, or that would disclose any information given to the Author in confidence or on the understanding it would not be disclosed or published; (v) to the best of the Author's knowledge no* *material in the Work is inaccurate; and (vi) the use of any instruction, material, or formula contained in the Work will not result in injury; and appropriate warnings will be contained in the Work concerning any particular hazards that may be involved in carrying out experiments described in the Work or involved in the use of instructions, materials, or formulas in the Work, and descriptions of relevant safety precautions. The Author hereby indemnifies and agrees to hold the Publisher, its licensees, and any seller of the Work harmless from any liability, damage, cost, and expense, including reasonable attorney's fees and costs of settlement, for or in connection with any claim, action, or proceeding based upon a breach (as determined by the final and non-appealable verdict of a court of competent jurisdiction) of the Author's warranties or representations herein. The Publisher will notify the Author of any claim, action, or proceeding, and the Publisher may use counsel of its own selection to defend the same. The Author may participate in the defense, at the Author's own expense, with counsel of the Author's own choosing. The Author shall not be responsible for any settlement of a claim, action, or proceeding with respect to which the Author has reasonably withheld the Author's approval. The Publisher will have the right to withhold its reasonable estimate of the total liability of the Author (including reasonable attorney's fees) from sums otherwise payable to the Author under this or any other agreement with the Author, and to apply the sums withheld to such liability.*

Best:

AUTHOR WARRANTIES, REPRESENTATIONS, AND INDEMNITIES. *The Author hereby warrants and represents, with respect only to the Work as submitted by the Author, that, to the best of the Author's actual knowledge: (i) the Author has the right to enter into this Agreement and to grant the rights herein granted and the Author has not and will not assign, pledge, or encumber such rights; (ii) the Author is the sole Author of the Work and, except for material of others permission for use of which has been obtained by the Author pursuant to Paragraph __, the Work is original and previously unpublished; (iii) the Work is not in the public domain; (iv) and the Work contains no material that would violate or infringe any personal, proprietary, or other right of any person or entity or that would violate any contract of the Author, express or implied, or that would disclose any information given to the Author in confidence or on the understanding it would not be disclosed or published. The Author hereby indemnifies and agrees to hold the Publisher, its licensees, and any seller of the Work harmless from any liability, damage, cost, and expense, including reasonable attorney's fees and costs of settlement, for or in connection with any claim based upon a breach of the Author's warranties or representations herein as determined by the final and non-appealable judgment of a court of competent jurisdiction; provided that the Publisher promptly notifies the Author of any such claim and cooperates with the Author in its defense. The Author shall not be responsible for any settlement of a claim, action, or proceeding with respect to which the Author has reasonably withheld the Author's approval. The Publisher shall add the Author as a named insured on the Publisher's media perils policy of insurance.*

Strategy:

The publisher may have a limited ability to alter the language in these clauses as a result of the requirements of its policy of insurance. In any event, your exposure under these clauses is largely within your control. If there is something about the nature of your work that makes it susceptible to attack (e.g., it's an expose of a private figure), it is in your best interest to be sure that the publisher is fully aware of the issues and that you work closely with the publisher and its media perils insurer to minimize the likelihood of a successful challenge.

ROYALTIES. *Except as otherwise provided below, the Publisher will pay to the Author a royalty of _____% based upon the Publisher's net receipts from sales by it of copies of the Work, revisions thereof, or reprints of all or portions thereof. A royalty at one half the aforementioned rate will be applied to the Publisher's net receipts:*

(a) from sales by it in foreign markets of special editions, adaptations, or regular editions of the Work, or from sales by it in the domestic or foreign markets of foreign language editions or adaptations of the Work;

(b) from sales by it of visual or sound reproductions or adaptations, motion pictures, educational and commercial television versions, braille and large-type editions, microfilm or microfiche editions, and microcomputer adaptations of the Work;

(c) from the sales by its subsidiaries or business affiliates through trade channels, mail order or coupon advertising campaigns, and solicitation by radio and television.

(d) from the Publisher's use or adaptation of the Work (or any portion thereof) in conjunction with any other work as a part of a database or custom published work through any means of storage, transmission, or copying now known or hereafter devised. With respect to this subsection (d), the Author's royalty shall be applied to a pro rata portion of the net receipts, said portion to be determined through use of a reasonable and objective method of relative valuation to be selected by the Publisher in its sole discretion.

The Publisher will pay to the Author 50% of the Publisher's net proceeds:

(e) from agreements to transfer, sell, or license to others the right to reprint all or portions of the Work, to include the Work in an electronic database, or to make visual or sound reproductions or adaptations, motion pictures, educational and commercial television versions, Braille and large-type editions, microfilm, or microfiche editions, microcomputer adaptations, electronic versions, translations, or foreign editions or adaptations either in English or in foreign languages.

No royalty shall be paid on copies sold at a discount of more than 50% or below the cost of manufacture. Publisher may set up a reserve sufficient in its opinion to allow for returns.

The royalty clause generally provides for a base rate on the cash actually received by the publisher from sales though its traditional distribution channels, with much lower rates on sales through a number of secondary channels. Recently, it has become common for publishers to provide for some discretionary mechanism for allocating the sales proceeds from special bundling deals and from exploitation of electronic rights (d above). On rights sales (e above) as opposed to product sales, the publisher typically splits the proceeds 50/50 with the author. Sometimes the publisher takes a larger share, only with some significant effort will you get the publisher to take less. Understanding these provisions means understanding the publisher's distribution and accounting models, which can be labyrinthine. Include an audit clause, and leave this to the sharp pencils.

Better:

ROYALTIES. *Except as otherwise provided below, the Publisher will pay to the Author a royalty of:*
_____% on the first _____ copies in any single edition
_____% on the next _____ copies in any single edition
_____% on all copies thereafter in any single edition
based upon the Publisher's net receipts from sales by it of copies of the Work, revisions thereof, or reprints of all or portions thereof ("net receipts" means cash received by the Publisher less returns, exchanges, and any amounts separately itemized on the customer's invoice for shipping, handling, or taxes). Author shall have the right, upon reasonable notice and during usual business hours but not more than once each year, to have the books and records of Publisher examined at the place where the same are regularly maintained insofar as they relate to the Work, by an independent public accountant. Such examination shall be at the cost of Author unless the net of all errors aggregate to more than three percent (3%) of the total sum accrued to Author are found to Author's disadvantage, in which case the cost of such examination shall be borne by Publisher. Any amounts disclosed by the examination to be due to the Author shall be promptly paid together with interest at the highest allowable statutory rate calculated from the date the payment should have been made.

Best:

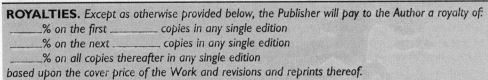

ROYALTIES. *Except as otherwise provided below, the Publisher will pay to the Author a royalty of:*
_____% on the first _____ copies in any single edition
_____% on the next _____ copies in any single edition
_____% on all copies thereafter in any single edition
based upon the cover price of the Work and revisions and reprints thereof.
The Publisher will pay to the Author 50% of the Publisher's net proceeds from agreements to transfer, sell, or license to others the right to exercise any of the Subsidiary Rights granted herein. Author shall have the right, upon reasonable notice and during usual business hours but not more than once each year, to have the books and records of Publisher examined at the place where the same are regularly maintained insofar as they relate to the Work, by an independent public accountant. Such examination shall be at the cost of Author unless the net of all errors aggregate to more than three percent (3%) of the total sum accrued to Author are found to Author's disadvantage, in which case the cost of such examination shall be borne by Publisher. Any amounts disclosed by the examination to be due to the Author shall be promptly paid together with interest at the highest allowable statutory rate calculated from the date the payment should have been made.

Strategy:

Royalties are the proverbial two birds in the bush. Far better to negotiate for non-refundable advances—these represent a bird in the hand and, if they are significant, increase the publisher's stake in promoting your work to ensure its commercial success. In any event, know whether your royalties will be based on cover price, invoice price, or net receipts. And if they are based on the latter, ask the publisher to define the "net" in net receipts so you know what will be deducted. Also ask for a copy of the publisher's discount schedule and for some historical averages (i.e., how much of the publisher's sales are typically done at each discount rate) so that you can compare apples to apples in the event you are the happy holder of two or more contract offers. What is a good royalty rate and how much should you ask for? Unfortunately, there is no pat answer to this question. If you do your homework, however, you will at least be able to ask for a tiered royalty structure—a base rate up to the publisher's break even volume, a higher rate on sales over break even, and a higher rate still on sales over the volume at which the publisher achieves its target margin. Watch out for an unlimited ability to reserve for returns—any such right should be subject to a cap based upon the publisher's historical experience. If you are successful in obtaining substantial advances, be sure that they are paid upon submission of manuscript (and not on the publisher's acceptance, which might be delayed) and that they are not cross-collateralized (i.e., recoverable from royalties earned by other titles that you might have written or might yet write for the same publisher).

SUBMISSION OF MANUSCRIPT. *The Author will deliver to the Publisher, on or before date, a complete and legible typewritten manuscript (and word processed text-file) of the Work satisfactory to the Publisher in form and content. If the manuscript for the complete Work is not delivered on or before the date specified above, or if the manuscript is not satisfactory to the Publisher in form or content, the Publisher may, at its option: (a) allow the Author to finish, correct or improve the manuscript by a date specified by the Publisher, (b) have the manuscript properly prepared by such other Author(s) as it may select and the Publisher may deduct the cost of obtaining such Author's services, whether compensated by fee or royalties, from the Author's royalties or (c) terminate this agreement by written notice to the Author, in which case any manuscript shall be returned and all rights therein shall revert to the Author, and any amounts which may have been advanced to the Author will be promptly refunded to the Publisher. In the event circumstances since the date of this Agreement have, in the sole judgment of the Publisher, caused the market for the Work to change or evaporate, the Publisher may reject the Work. In such event, the Publisher shall so notify the Author. the Author shall be entitled to retain one half the advance specified in Paragraph _____ as a kill fee, all rights in the Work shall revert to the Author, and neither the Author nor the Publisher shall have any further obligations hereunder.*

It's one thing to be signed to a publishing contract, but unfortunately (and perhaps unfairly) quite another actually to be published. Editors come and go and markets change. An open-ended manuscript acceptability standard (like the one above) can leave you holding an unpublished manuscript. Most form contracts will require that you deliver a completed manuscript that is acceptable to the publisher in form and content. This arguably allows the publisher to reject your completed work for any reason (provided it is not acting in bad faith). You should strive for an acceptability clause that requires only that the finished manuscript conform in coverage and quality to the sample chapters provided with your prospectus or, alternatively, a clause that requires the manuscript to be professionally competent and fit for publication. You should also ask for language that obliges the publisher to provide you with detailed editorial comments and at least one opportunity to revise. And you should not permit the publisher to complete or otherwise use your work and charge any third party costs against your account without your consent.

Better:

SUBMISSION OF MANUSCRIPT. *The Author will deliver the completed Work on or before date. The Publisher acknowledges and agrees that the manuscript will be deemed acceptable so long as it professionally competent and fit for publication in the good faith exercise of the Publisher's reasonable judgment.*

Best:

SUBMISSION OF MANUSCRIPT. *The Author will deliver the completed Work on or before date. The Publisher acknowledges and agrees that the manuscript will be deemed acceptable so long as it conforms in content, coverage, style, and rigor to the outline and prospectus previously provided (a copy of which is attached hereto as Exhibit 1). In the event the publisher deems any submission not acceptable, it will so advise the Author in writing within 30 days of the date of submission and will describe with particularity the deficiencies therein and the changes required to make the submission acceptable, in which event that Author shall have 30 days to make the required improvements. The Publisher's failure to so advise the Author in the time and manner specified shall be deemed the Publisher's acceptance as to the tendered submission.*

Strategy:

Don't assume that just because you were offered a contract based upon your tender of a completed first draft manuscript, that the publisher will necessarily publish your work. If the acquiring editor moves on, you will be back to square one with a new editor who may not have the same level of interest in or commitment to your work. When seeing your work in print is an important objective, make sure you close and lock the publisher's back door.

> **CONFLICTING WORKS.** *During the life of this Agreement, the Author will not without the prior written consent of the Publisher participate in the preparation or publication of any work on a similar subject, which might tend to interfere with or injure the sale of the Work, and will not authorize the use of the Author's name in connection with any such work.*
>
> *OPTION. Author grants the Publisher the option to publish the Author's next book-length work. The Author shall submit the completed manuscript for such work to the Publisher and the Publisher shall have 90 days within which to notify the Author of whether it will exercise its option and to tender to the Author a publishing agreement for same on substantially the same terms as are provided herein. During the option term, the Author shall not offer such work to any other publisher and thereafter shall not offer such work to any other publisher except on terms more favorable than those offered by the Publisher.*

Almost every publishing contract will include a "non-compete" provision calculated to ensure that the publisher has a monopoly on your work on a particular subject and that you do not publish or assist in publishing any other work that might compete. These restrictions are usually very broadly drafted and open-ended in scope. As such, they may be unenforceable as an unreasonable restraint of trade. Better, however, to try to narrow them before you sign. Also common, though slightly less so, is an options clause that gives the publisher dibs on your next manuscript. Strike the option clause and tell the publisher that if they do a great job with the current one, you will certainly be back with the next.

Better:

> **COMPETING WORKS.** *During the life of this Agreement, the Author will not without the prior written consent of the Publisher participate in the preparation or publication of any directly competing work. For purposes of this Section, a "directly competing work" shall be defined as any book-length work on the subject of be as specific as possible.*

Best:

> **COMPETING WORKS.** *During the life of this Agreement, the Author will not without the prior written consent of the Publisher participate in the preparation or publication of any directly competing work. For purposes of this Section, a "directly competing work" shall be defined as any book-length work on the subject of be as specific as possible and intended primarily for distribution and sale to be as specific as possible through specify channels. The Publisher acknowledges that the Author has in process the following works, provisionally entitled:*
>
> *specify*
>
> *and agrees that these works do not constitute directly competing works. The Publisher further agrees that the Author's activities as a specify, and any work that she/he might write or present in connection with the performance of those activities (and not constituting a book-length work for trade distribution) shall not be deemed a breach of the provisions of this Section. Nor shall the use of her/his name or likeness in connection with such activities be deemed a breach thereof.*

Strategy:

The narrower the non-compete, the better. The more precisely you can define what it is you will not do and what it is you are free to do, the less opportunity there will be for misunderstandings. If the publisher expresses a reluctance to more precisely define the boundaries, ask for a quid pro quo—i.e., a parallel commitment from the publisher to refrain from publishing the works of other authors on the same subject. It is highly unlikely that the publisher would entertain such a prospect, but the mere thought may make them more reasonable about the scope of your non-compete.

> **GRANT OF RIGHTS.** *The Author acknowledges that the Work was specially commissioned by the Publisher and intended as an instructional text and agrees that the Work shall be considered a work-made-for-hire, with the Publisher deemed the author and sole owner thereof for copyright purposes. In addition, and against the possibility that the Work might ultimately be deemed incapable of characterization as a work-made-for-hire as a matter of law, the author hereby irrevocably grants to the Publisher all right, title and interest (including, without limitation, all copyrights throughout the world and all other legal and equitable rights in all media, whether now known or hereafter invented) to the Work. The Author acknowledges that she/he shall not acquire any rights of any kind in the Work as a result of his/her services under this Agreement.*

The grant of rights clause spells out the breadth of rights being acquired by the publisher—and there is a broad range of possibilities here. Least favorable to the author are "work-for-hire" provisions (like the one above), which transfer the broadest possible rights to the publisher and deprive the author of certain statutory protections. While relatively uncommon in trade book deals, they are often used in educational publishing (especially at lower curricular levels). More common (and slightly more favorable to the author) are grants of "all right, title, and interest," (also included above, as the publisher's fall back position in the event the work at issue does not qualify for work-for-hire treatment). While appearing to be all encompassing, the "all rights" grant at least leaves the author with her/his statutory protections intact. But in the final analysis, there is little reason for the publish to get rights that it does not intend to exploit. If your publisher intends only to publish a hard cover edition for distribution in North America, then the grant of rights should convey North American hard cover rights only. Alternate editions can be addressed by amendment to your book contract if and when the publisher expresses an interest in publishing them. The following provisions represent possible compromises that allocate rights in the work more equitably.

Better:

> **CONDITIONAL GRANT OF ALL RIGHTS.** *The Author hereby grants to the Publisher the sole and exclusive right and license to publish, promote, distribute and sell (or permit others to do so) the Work in all languages, in all media, and throughout the world; provided, however, that the right to publish the Work in any form other than book form (the "Subsidiary Rights") shall become non-exclusive as to those Subsidiary Rights which have not been commercially exploited by the Publisher within two years after first publication of the Work in book form and the Author expressly reserves the non-exclusive right also to exploit said unexercised Subsidiary Rights, free of any obligation to pay royalties to the Publisher, but agrees to cooperate with the Publisher to ensure that any such exploitation shall not interfere with the Publisher's exclusive right to produce and publish the Work in book form.*

Best:

> **GRANT OF EXCLUSIVE BOOK PUBLISHING RIGHTS.** *The Author hereby grants to the Publisher the sole and exclusive right and license to publish, promote, distribute and sell (or permit others to do so) the Work in the English language only, in book form only, and only for distribution in North America. All other rights in the Work are expressly reserved exclusively to the Author.*

Strategy:

In this day and age, most publishers are in fact positioned to exploit (through subsidiaries, affiliates, and standing relationships) more than book publishing rights and it is in your best interests to let them have everything they will effectively commercialize. The extent to which you bargain to retain some of these rights will depend upon the nature of your work and whether it lends itself to these alternative uses, the publisher's ability and interest in exploiting them for you, and your ability to do this independently. But you should resist the temptation to get sloppy here and you should endeavor to force the publisher to specify which, if any, of the following rights they truly need and are presently positioned to exploit:

- hardcover
- trade paperback
- mass market paperback
- digest
- abridgement
- condensation
- selection
- anthology
- collection

- book club
- reprint edition
- first serial
- second serial
- syndication
- merchandising
- motion picture (theatrical)
- television
- dramatic adaptation (live theatrical)

- radio
- audio (books on tape)
- multimedia (interactive digital and games)
- electronic (text only database and information retrieval—on disk or on-line)

The list goes on and on. To the extent these rights are licensed by the publisher to some other, they are referred to as "subsidiary rights" (i.e., rights subsidiary to the publisher's principal line of business).

WHAT SHOULD YOU ASK YOUR EDITOR?

Your first task is to loosen up the editor with some questions about his/her background. Get the editor talking freely about himself/herself and you are well on your way:

How long have you been with Publisher X? Editors move from house to house and it will be helpful to know how long your editor has been in his/her current position.

Where were you before? The experience he/she gained at other houses will tell you something about his/her knowledge of the market and the business.

Did you come up through the sales side or through editorial? The editor with a sales background will have a significantly different negotiating focus from the editor with an editorial background.

Tell me about your current list.
- How many titles are there?
- What disciplines (if an educational work)?
- What curricular level (if an educational work)?
- What is (are) your lead title(s)?
- What sort of market share do they have?
- Are any of them market leaders?

The answers to these questions will tell you something about your editor's place in the pecking order and about how much attention your project is likely to get.

Next, find out how important your project is to his/her bonus (no editor will knowingly tell you, but the answers to these questions may provide a few clues):

How many new books do you sign in a typical year? The answer to this question will tell you something about the editors annual signing goals.

How many have you signed so far this year? The answer to this question will give you some idea of where the editor is in relation to his/her goals. If the editor is close to his/her annual average, it could well be that signing you will make the difference between earning or not earning a bonus. You will probably never know for certain how important your project is, but you may at least get a clue.

Find out where your book fits in:

How would you envision positioning my book in relation to the competition? This will tell you what your editor sees as your work's competitive advantages-information that will prove useful should you decide to approach other publishers with your project.

Who are your principal competitors in this market? If you have not already submitted tothese competitors, you should seriously consider doing so immediately. The best leverage you can have in negotiating a book contract is to know that there is another interested publisher in the wings.

Do you have any titles (published or signed) similar to mine? For obvious reasons, you want to know if the editor will have divided loyalties. Moreover, when it comes time to talk about the scope of your non-compete clause, it is very helpful to be able to point out specifically that the publisher is not similarly constrained.

If the proposal or partial manuscript has been reviewed, check the reviews to see who is identified as a competitor. Again, you want to know about the other publishers who might also be interested in your work.

Get the numbers (the answers to these questions will help you back into a reasonable advance against royalties) :

How big a market are we talking about? This will give you a sense of how the publisher views your book and whether you both see it the same way

What sort of market penetration does Publisher X generally expect with a new book? In combination with the answer to question #11, this will give you a way of corroborating the editor's sales projections.

How many units would an average book do in the market for which my book is targeted?
• First year?
• Lifetime?
• How many do you think the market leader does?

The answers to these questions, once you know the cover price, will let you estimate revenues and royalties so that you can make a credible, objectively supportable request for advances.

How many units does a book like mine have to do to break even? The answer to this question will tell you at what volume the publisher covers its costs.

How many would it have to do before you would consider it a roaring success? The answer to this question will tell you at what point the publisher has made its customary margin. The break-even volume and the volume necessary to a target margin are natural break points for a sliding royalty scale. Consider accepting the rate first offered up to break even, but ask for a higher rate up to the target margin, and ask for the moon beyond that.

How would you see it priced? As noted, this information helps you project revenues and royalties, but it also will tell you something about the titles your editor views as competitive-because they will necessarily fall in the same price range.

Do you think it would travel well? If the editor says no, then it will be very hard for him/her to push for exclusive, perpetual foreign and translation rights.

Tell me about Publisher X's foreign sales ability? sub rights licensing (translations and adaptations)? new media capability? Again, rights that the editor is not positioned to aggressively exploit should not be part of the package.

Get the promotion plan:

What would you envision doing to promote a book like mine?
• Promotional brochure (how many pages? full color? how big a mailing?)
• How many review copies/comps?
• Presentation at sales conference? author appearance?
• Newspaper/Journal ads?
• Anything else?

Most publishing contracts say very little indeed about what the publisher will do to market and promote your work. If you get a sales pitch from the editor, make an effort to reduce it to writing and reference it in the publishing contract.

Check the back door:

Roughly what percent of the titles you sign actually make it into print? The answer to this question will tell you how important it is to introduce an objective acceptability standard into the manuscript delivery clause.

Is there anything else I should know about you or about how you see my book fitting into your list? If you editor is still talking, you should still be taking notes.

You will not get answers to all of these questions. And you will not get answers to any of them without a fair amount of prodding. But the time and effort you spend will tell you volumes about your editor and will pay many dividends when the time comes to negotiate that contract.

Knock 'em dead!

—*Stephen E. Gillen*

First Books

BY LYNN WASNAK

Is publishing a first book all it's cracked up to be? Beyond the initial struggle of writing the book in the first place, what else should writers be prepared for? Here are the stories of three very different "First Books": the stories of getting a novel, giftbook/journal, and self-published how-to title from manuscripts to the bookstore shelves. So whether you're writing novels or memoir, how-to or inspirational, you may find in these authors' stories some useful tools for the trail.

BINO A. REALUYO
The Umbrella Country, (Random House, 1999)

To Bino Realuyo, selling his first novel brought a mixture of pleasure and pain. "I wrote this novel while holding down a full-time job and a part-time job," the Philippine-born writer says. "I always write with a sense of urgency, as if no time can possibly go wasted." The pleasure was in the act of writing, he says: "I love the whole process of discovery."

Realuyo didn't think about agents as he refined his coming-of-age story, set in Manila. An agent had contacted him after his first fiction reading in Boston and stayed in touch over the years. So when *The Umbrella Country* was finished, Realuyo sent it to her with confidence. But she turned it down. "She said she didn't love it enough," he says. "This was a great setback. I didn't know anything about finding agents."

Recovering from the shock of his manuscript's rejection, Realuyo queried other agents who responded quickly, but negatively—all very discouraging. Finally a writer friend introduced him to her agent, who signed him up. Realuyo's relief was followed by a second stream of rejections. Editors liked his writing and sent long, encouraging letters, invariably ending the same way: "We can't sell this book."

As a published poet and founder of the Asian American Writers Workshop in New York, Realuyo knew what was happening. The market for serious fiction is small, especially for unknowns. The Filipino theme limited sales prospects. "As far as publishers were concerned, I was a good writer, but a great commercial risk. That's when I started thinking seriously about sales," he says. "I thought the agent-writer relationship should be interactive. I wanted to know the backgrounds of editors who were reading my book." So when a Random House editor rejected his work (after another writer-friend steered it her way) Realuyo hesitated only briefly. "I told my agent to give the editor a call. I wanted to meet her." Face to face, he liked this editor's insight and vision. "I offered to revise my novel. She said okay." Two weeks' intense revision (skipping Thanksgiving dinner) yielded a manuscript the editor praised. But her colleagues at Random House said "No—not enough sales potential." She was also an associate editor at

LYNN WASNAK *has been a fulltime freelance writer for more than twenty years, and thanks the newly published writers here for sharing their insights and experience.*

Ballantine. They said "No" too, but this time Realuyo promptly faxed the publishers a two-page sales pitch. "Five minutes later, the book was sold for a five-figure advance," he says.

Initial publishing plans sounded great. His novel would debut in Ballantine's new literary imprint. Then, abruptly, the vagaries of the publishing field interceded again. The imprint never materialized. Everything went on hold until Ballantine Reader's Circle (BRC) planned to publish the title as an original paperback. BRC incorporates a reader's guide targeted to reading groups, which Realuyo calls "an excellent way to introduce a new author. Reading groups buy a bagload at once."

Though hardcover books typically garner more prestige and reviews, Realuyo was reasonably satisfied. "At least I didn't have to worry whether my book would come out in paperback," he says.

To compensate for a limited promotional budget, Realuyo had to be a strong promoter himself. He set up a personal website at www.geocities.com/realuyo to help Internet visitors learn about his work. Without a paid tour, "I sent myself to the West Coast, L.A. and San Francisco, because some reading venues invited me and the Filipino community is there."

For years, Realuyo had paid attention to Barnes & Noble's "Discover Great New Writers" series. So he convinced Ballantine to submit *The Umbrella Country* for competition. It was selected in Spring 1999, received prominent display in stores, and was a finalist for B&N's Discover award. It also made *Booklist*'s "Top Ten Novels for 1999." And in a little over a year, *The Umbrella Country* has gone into a third printing.

"Writers need to know that the publishing struggle does not end with a book being printed," says Realuyo. "One must work really hard to promote; simply take off the writer's hat, put on the publicist's hat, and move on. It is not an easy life, but I am blessed for being given the opportunity to publish. And I am so glad there are places like Barnes & Noble, which promote our kinds of books in their special way."

LISA AND GENE C. FANT
Expectant Moments: Devotions for Expectant Couples, (Zondervan, 1999)

Thanks to thorough research, solid marketing strategy and possible divine intervention, Lisa and Gene Fant birthed two babies and a book in the same year. *Expectant Moments* sold, in proposal form, to the first publisher who saw it.

This remarkable feat had a long gestation. The Fants, of Clinton, Mississippi, are both English teachers and devout Christians. When they planned to start their family, Gene scoured bookstores for devotions about pregnancy as a gift to Lisa, but found none on the shelves.

Next he checked out Amazon.com and Barnesandnoble.com, again with no results. Thinking ahead to the costs of parenting, this seemed like a ripe opportunity to improve income and serve others simultaneously. Neither Gene nor his wife had written a book, but they'd written for academia and placed a few articles. So Gene got out *Writer's Market* and started whittling down possible publishers. "We're both voracious readers, so we already knew where to start," he says.

Gene chose about three publishers, looked up the websites, and read their catalogs, looking for devotional and parenting books. Zondervan stood out right away. It presented clear writer's guidelines, covered the right subjects, and its track record of using both first-time writers and unagented writers was excellent. Knowing that Zondervan had been purchased by the much-larger HarperCollins was the clincher. "I knew it would have access to any market we could possibly wish for," he says.

Gene didn't use an agent, partly because he felt pressed for time with babies on the way. Besides, he'd done his homework. "My professors at Old Dominion University in Virginia said you can't just let inspiration strike you. You've got to have a clear idea about what you want to do, decide what your market is, and know who's in that market," he explains.

He had no editor's name, but the proposal he prepared (ten samples and an outline, plus bios) got past the interns who read unsolicited manuscripts. "When the editor called me, she said 'None of us could believe there was no such book,' which told me they were going to buy it," says Gene. The Fants received the actual signed contract when their twins were about two months old.

Without telling Lisa, Gene had volunteered her services as co-writer. "We'd painted rooms together, but we'd never written together. At first I thought, 'No way,' " says Lisa, of her part in their writing team. "But it turned out to be a wonderful experience."

The Fants say the writing process was a total collaboration, done mostly after the twins were put to bed each night. "Sometimes we worked with a baby on each lap," says Gene.

Both praise Zondervan's editorial staff for encouragement and advice. Their final revision was about 70 percent longer, following editorial suggestions. "The editors pulled a lot of things out of us, trying to get more meat," says Gene.

The promotion budget was limited, but Zondervan sent books to its media contacts. One big success was a full-page writeup in the state's biggest newspaper.

Now Gene has taken on the job of promotion manager, soliciting TV and radio interviews and book signings. "I used to be a songwriter. Didn't have much success, but I learned about networking. I like to talk to people. When I meet people in my travels, I keep a file." One friend who'd been a station manager at a small local TV station arranged an interview. Gene then used that experience as leverage to get other stations interested.

Their first print run sold out in about three weeks, largely to the gift market, and more printings followed. The Fants hope their book will have a long lifespan. "People are always having babies," says Lisa, "and we tried to eliminate time references. We feel there was some kind of supernatural guidance going on that we can't quite understand," she adds. "Hopefully, God wants to use what we can give."

More books may come, but not immediately. Two babies can exhaust the most dedicated writers. Says Gene, "We have two two-year-olds. It's 'NO' in stereo. In the evening, we used to sit down at 7:30 and write on the book for a couple hours. Now at 7:30 we fall into bed. But people like us who read get ideas, and we'll continue having lots of ideas until our heads explode."

FRANCES ANNE HERNAN
The ABCs of Hiring a Nanny, (Nationwide Printing, 1999)

Frances Hernan was in her late fifties when she wrote her first book *The ABCs of Hiring a Nanny.* Even more challenging, she chose to self-publish it.

"Every bit of writing I did was training for the writing I was going to do," says Hernan. She began as a teenager, writing radio continuity at an Ohio radio station, followed by years of helping military wives, politicians, businesspeople and non-profit group members through her writing and public presentations.

An empty-nester, Hernan craved change. She moved to New York to be a nanny for a year. To her surprise, she enjoyed it. One year stretched into ten.

Still a writer at heart, she kept her eyes and ears open. Soon she realized that parents needed information to make smart choices about

© Steven R. Attig

nannies. Hernan decided to prepare a step-by-step guide to this vital service and present it at workshops. She embarked on an extensive research effort lasting about a year. "You cannot imagine the number of letters I had to write and phone calls I had to make to get my material," she says.

On investigation, workshops seemed a too costly way to reach an audience. So she devised an alternative format, combining a book, companion computer disk, and website.

The book was an essential element, but Hernan barely explored traditional publishing. "I didn't feel my credits were strong enough to attract a major publisher. Besides, I wanted complete control!" she says. She envisioned a long shelf-life for her book and many unconventional ways to market it: as handouts for pediatricians and obstetricians, corporate recruitment packets, and as an organizational fundraiser. "I couldn't target the way I wanted to if I relied solely on booksellers," she says.

Hernan checked out subsidy publishing, but decided it was a scam. "Fees are too high and non-negotiable; you get very little service, and subsidy lacks credibility in the marketplace," she says.

So she turned to self-publishing, taking responsibility for printing cost and marketing. "I asked several printers for pricing. The quotes were too high. So I retooled the idea." She planned to prepare a few samples to show potential investors. One printer, Nationwide, got really excited about the project. The owner offered to print quantities as needed, and work out payment when the book took off. They've joined forces on the project ever since.

Promotion is Hernan's area of expertise, a necessity for self-publishing success. "I knew I could make this work if I approached it like the political campaigns I managed. Essentially, I hired myself."

She studied markets in ten key cities. "I know what kind of bookstores are in those cities even if I haven't been there. I call it my 'yellow brick road' campaign. Brick by brick we're establishing a market," she says.

The Internet helped in getting the word out (http://abcnanny.bizland.com), as well as Amazon-.com and Borders.com, Hernan says. She is also giving seminars on the topic in selected book-stores and libraries.

"It's been a slow process establishing my credibility with organizations," she admits. "It's interesting how an address, fax number, charge machine, business cards, and letterhead add credibility, with each little step you take," she says.

Hernan never stops selling. "I went out to buy a blouse the other day, and sold books to the store recruiter and the general manager," she says. She writes letters, sends flyers, makes phone calls, and pursues TV time on local cable stations. "I've talked to Welcome Wagons. Selling this as a fundraiser may be just as good an idea for me as going through the conventional market, though that might not work with very many books," she says.

"I want to emphasize how much help writing courses, groups, and conferences were in the production and promotion of the book," she adds. "When you're doing something and don't know exactly what you're doing, you have to draw from every resource that's available to you.

"My father used to tell me, 'Frances, you don't get the tomato until you plant the seed. You don't see the tomato for a long time.' I think about that analogy a lot, because a lot of these things I've done I keep doing, over and over, like I'm watering a garden," she says. "Eventually the seed is going to sprout."

Publishers and Their Imprints

Keeping up with the heavy wave of buying, selling, merging, consolidating and dissolving among publishers and their imprints over the last few years can leave even the most devout *Publishers Weekly* reader dizzy. To help curious writers sort it out, we offer this breakdown of major publishers, who owns whom, and which imprints are under which umbrella. Remember, this list is just a snapshot of how things are shaped at our press time—due to the dynamic nature of the publishing world, it's subject to change at any moment.

SIMON & SCHUSTER (Viacom, Inc.)

Pocket Books
Archway Paperbacks
Minstrel Books
MTV Books
Pocket Books Hardcover
Pocket Books Trade Paperbacks
Pocket Pulse
Sonnet
Washington Square Press

Simon & Schuster Children's Publishing
Aladdin Paperbacks
Atheneum Books for Young Readers
Little Simon
Margaret K. McElderry Books
Simon & Schuster Books for Young Readers
Simon Spotlight
Simon & Schuster Interactive

Simon & Schuster Audio

Simon & Schuster Trade
Fireside
The Free Press
Scribner
    Lisa Drew Books
    Rawson Associates
Simon & Schuster
Simon & Schuster Editions
Simon & Schuster Libros en Espanol
Touchstone

HARPERCOLLINS (U.K.)

Harper General Books Group
Access Press
Avon Books
Cliff Street Books
The Ecco Press
Eos
HarperAudio
HarperBusiness
HarperCollins
HarperEntertainment
HarperResource
HarperSan Francisco
Perennial
Quill
Regan Books
William Morrow

Harper Children's Books Group
Avon
Joanna Cotler Books
Laura Geringer Books
Greenwillow Books
HarperCollins Children's Books
HarperFestival
HarperTrophy
Tempest

Harper Around the World
HarperAustralia
HarperCanada
HarperCollins UK
Zondervan

RANDOM HOUSE, INC. (Bertelsmann Book Group)

The Ballantine Publishing Group
Ballantine Books
Del Rey
Fawcett
Ivy
Library of Contemporary Thought
One World
Wellspring

Bantam Dell Publishing Group
Bantam
Delacorte Press
Dell Books
Delta Books
Dial Press
DTP
Island Books

Doubleday Broadway Publishing Group
Broadway Books
Currency
Doubleday
Doubleday Religious Publishing
Doubleday/Image
Nan A. Talese
WaterBrook Press

Knopf Publishing Group
Everyman's Library
Alfred A. Knopf Inc.
Pantheon Books
Schocken Books
Vintage Anchor Publishing
    Anchor
    Vintage Books

The Crown Publishing Group
Bell Tower
Clarkson Potter
Crown Business
Crown Publishers Inc.
Discovery Books
Harmony Books
House of Collectibles
Sierra Club Books
Three Rivers Press
Times Books

Random House Audio Publishing Group
Bantam Doubleday Dell Audio Publishing
Listening Library
Random House AudioBooks

Random House Children's Media Group
Bantam Books for Young Readers
Crown Books for Young Readers
CTW Publishing
Delacorte Press Books for Young Readers
Doubleday Books for Young Readers
Dragonfly Books
Knopf Books for Young Readers
Laurel Leaf
Random House Books for Young Readers
Random House Home Video
Yearling Books

Random House Diversified Publishing Group
Random House Large Print Publishing
Random House Value Publishing

Random House International

Random House New Media

Random House Trade Group
The Modern Library
Random House Trade Books
Villard Books

Random House Information Group
Fodor's Travel Publications
Living Language
Princeton Review
Random House Puzzles and Games
Random House Reference & Information
    Publishing

PENGUIN PUTNAM INC. (Pearson—U.K.)

The Penguin Group
Allen Lane
Arkana
DAW Books
Dutton
Mentor
Meridian
Onyx
Pelham
Penguin
Penguin Classics
Penguin Press
Penguin Studio
Plume
ROC
Signet
Signet Classics
Topaz
Viking

The Putnam Berkley Group
Ace
Ace/Putnam
Berkley Books
Boulevard
Grosset/Putnam
HP Books
Jove
Perigee
Price Stern Sloan, Inc.
Prime Crime
G.P. Putnam's Sons
Riverhead
Jeremy P. Tarcher

Penguin Putnam Books for Young Readers
Dial Books for Young Readers
Dutton Children's Books
Grosset & Dunlap
Philomel Books
Price Stern Sloan, Inc.
Puffin
    PaperStar
G.P. Putnam's Sons
Viking Children's Books
Frederick Warne
Wee Sing

TIME WARNER (U.S.)

Warner Books
Mysterious Press
Warner Aspect
Warner Romance
Warner Vision

Time Life Inc.

Time Warner Audiobooks

Little, Brown and Company
Back Bay Books
Bullfinch Press
Little, Brown Books for Children and
    Young Adults
Megan Tingley Books

HOLTZBRINCK (Germany)

Farrar Straus & Giroux
Faber & Faber Inc.
Farrar Straus & Giroux Books for Young
  Readers
    Aerial Fiction
    Francis Foster Books
    Mirasol/Libros
    R and S Books
    Sunburst Paperbacks
Hill and Wang
Noonday Press
North Point Press
Sunburst Books

Henry Holt & Co.
Henry Holt & Co. Books for Young Readers
John Macrae Books
Metropolitan Books
Owl Books

St. Martin's
Bedford Books
Buzz Books
Dead Letter
Tom Doherty Associates
    TOR
    Forge
Thomas Dunne Books
Griffin
Let's Go
Picador
St. Martin's Paperbacks
St. Martin's Press
St. Martin's Scholarly & Reference
Stonewall Inn
Truman Talley Books

Literary Agents

The publishing world is never static. There's the quiet ebb and flow of imprints expanding and editors moving, and then there's the cataclysmic explosion when publishing giants collide. Through it all, the literary agent has become an increasingly important mediator, connecting writers, ideas and publishers to form books.

With an increasing emphasis on profit margins, many of the larger publishers have eliminated the entry level editorial assistants primarily responsible for reading manuscripts sent in by writers—"over the transom" to the "slush pile," in the jargon. As a result, agents have taken over some of this task, separating the literary wheat from the chaff and forwarding the promising manuscripts on to possible publishers. Most publishers remain open to receiving at least query letters directly from authors, but some of the largest publishers accept agented submissions only.

As you look through the Book Publishers section of *Writer's Market*, you will see the symbol Ⓐ at the beginning of some listings. This symbol denotes publishers that accept submissions only from agents. If you find a book publisher that is a perfect market for your work but only reads agented manuscripts, contacting an agent is your next logical step.

Finding an agent is *not* easier than finding a publisher. It may even be harder, since there are far fewer agents than publishing companies. However, if you do secure representation, your "reach" into the publishing world has extended to include everyone that agent knows.

CHOOSING AND USING AN AGENT

Literary agents, like authors, come in all shapes and sizes, with different areas of interest and expertise. It's to your advantage to take the time and choose an agent who is most closely aligned to your interests and your manuscript's subject.

The agents listed in this section have all indicated that they are open to working with new, previously unpublished writers as well as published writers. None of the agents listed here charge a reading fee, which is money paid to an agent to cover the time and effort in reading a manuscript or a few sample chapters. While there is nothing wrong with charging a reading fee (after all, agents have to make a living too), we encourage writers to first try agents that do not.

Most of the agents listed here are members of AAR, the Association of Authors' Representatives. The AAR is a voluntary professional organization, whose members agree to abide by a strict code of ethics that prohibits charging fees for reading a manuscript or editorial services or receiving "consideration fees" for successful referrals to third parties.

We also present a small section of script agents, all members of the Writers' Guild of America (WGA). WGA signatory agencies are prohibited from charging fees from WGA members; most do not charge fees of nonmembers, as well.

The listings that follow contain the information you need to determine if an agent is suitable for your work. Read each listing carefully to see if an agency specializes in your subject areas. Or go straight to the Literary Agent Subject Index found after the listings to compile a list of agencies specifically interested in the subjects you write. We've broken the Subject Index into three main categories: Nonfiction, Fiction and Scripts.

Literary & Script Agents:
The Listings

This section consists of 75 individual agency listings, followed by a Subject Index of nonfiction and fiction book and script categories which list the names of agencies that have expressed an interest in manuscripts on that subject. We've included listings for both literary and script agents. Literary agents are interested in nonfiction and fiction book manuscripts while script agents read only television and movie scripts.

You can approach the information listed here in two ways. You can skim through the listings and see if an agent stands out as particularly right for your manuscript and proceed from there. Or you can check the Subject Indexes that follow these listings to focus your search more narrowly. Cross-referencing categories and concentrating on those agents interested in two or more aspects of your manuscript might increase your chances of success.

Either way, it is important to carefully read the information contained in the listing. Each agency has different interests, submission requirements and response times. They'll tell you what they want, what they don't want, and how they want to receive it. Try to follow their directions as closely as possible. For these agents in particular, time is extremely important, and wasting theirs won't help your case.

There are several sections to each listing. The first paragraph lists the agency's name, address and contact information. It also includes when the agency was established, how many clients it represents and what percentage of those clients are new/previously unpublished writers. It offers the agency's self-described areas of specialization and a breakdown of the different types of manuscripts it handles (nonfiction, fiction, movie scripts, etc.).

The first subsection is **Members Agents**, which lists the individuals who work at the agency. The next is **Handles**, which outlines the different nonfiction and fiction categories an agency will look at. **How to Contact** specifies how agents want to receive material and how long you should wait for their response. **Needs** identifies subjects they are particularly interested in seeing, as well as what they definitely do not handle and will not look at. **Recent Sales** is pretty self-explanatory. **Terms** offers information on the commission an agent takes (domestic and foreign), if a written contract is offered, and whether and what miscellaneous expenses are charged to an author's account. **Writers' Conferences** identifies conferences that agent attends. And **Tips** presents words of advice an agent might want to give prospective authors.

FOR MORE ON THE SUBJECT . . .

The *Guide to Literary Agents* (Writer's Digest Books) offers 550 agent listings and a wealth of informational articles on the author/agent relationship and other related topics.

LITERARY AGENTS

N: LINDA ALLEN LITERARY AGENCY, 1949 Green St., Suite 5, San Francisco CA 94123-4829. (415)921-6437. **Contact:** Linda Allen or Amy Kossow. Estab. 1982. Member of AAR. Represents 35-40 clients. Specializes in "good books and nice people."
Represents: Nonfiction, novels (adult). **Considers these nonfiction areas:** anthropology/archaeology; art/architecture/design; biography; business; child guidance/parenting; computers/electronics; ethnic/cultural interests; gay/lesbian issues; government/politics/law; history; music/dance/theater/film; nature/environment; popular culture; psychology; soci-

ology; women's issues/women's studies. **Considers these fiction areas:** action/adventure; contemporary issues; detective/police/crime; ethnic; feminist; gay; glitz; horror; lesbian; literary; mainstream; mystery/suspense; psychic/supernatural; regional; thriller/espionage.

How to Contact: Query with SASE. Considers simultaneous queries. Responds in 3 weeks to queries. Returns materials only with SASE.

Needs: Obtains new clients "by referral mostly."

Recent Sales: Prefers not to share information on specific sales.

Terms: Agent receives 15% commission. Charges for photocopying.

BETSY AMSTER LITERARY ENTERPRISES, P.O. Box 27788, Los Angeles CA 90027-0788. **Contact:** Betsy Amster. Estab. 1992. Member of AAR. Represents over 50 clients. 40% of clients are new/unpublished writers. Currently handles: 65% nonfiction books; 35% novels.

• Prior to opening her agency, Ms. Amster was an editor at Pantheon and Vintage for 10 years and served as editorial director for the Globe Pequot Press for 2 years. "This experience gives me a wider perspective on the business and the ability to give focused editorial feedback to my clients."

Represents: Nonfiction books, novels. **Considers these nonfiction areas:** biography/autobiography; business; child guidance/parenting; cyberculture; ethnic/cultural interests; gardening; health/medicine; history; how-to; money/finance/economics; popular culture; psychology; self-help/personal improvement; sociology; women's issues/women's studies. **Considers these fiction areas:** ethnic; literary.

How to Contact: For fiction, send query and first page. For nonfiction, send query only. For both, "include SASE or no response." Responds in 1 month to queries; 2 months to mss.

Needs: Actively seeking "outstanding literary fiction (the next Jane Smiley or Wally Lamb) and high profile self-help/psychology." Does not want to receive poetry, children's books, romances, westerns, science fiction. Obtains new clients through recommendations from others, solicitation, conferences.

Recent Sales: *Esperanza's Box of Saints*, by Maria Amparo Escandón; *The Tribes of Palos Verdes*, by Joy Nicholson (St. Martin's); *How to be a Chicana Role Model*, by Michele M. Serros (Riverhead); *The Blessing of a Skinned Knee: Using Jewish Spiritual Wisdom to Solve Everyday Parenting Problems*, by Wendy Mogel (Scribner); *What They Don't Teach You at Film School*, by Camille Landau & Tiare White (Hyperion); *Sports Her Way: Motivating Girls to Start & Stay with Sports*, by Susan M. Wilson (Simon & Schuster); *The Medicine Wheel Garden*, by E. Barrie Kavasch (Bantam).

Terms: Agent receives 15% commission on domestic sales. Offers written contract, binding for 1-2 years. 60 days notice must be given to terminate contract. Charges for photocopying, postage, long distance phone calls, messengers and galleys and books used in submissions to foreign and film agents and to magazines for first serial rights.

Writers' Conferences: Squaw Valley, Maui Writers Conference; Pacific Northwest Conference; San Diego Writers Conference; UCLA Writers Conference.

LORETTA BARRETT BOOKS INC., 101 Fifth Ave., New York NY 10003. (212)242-3420. Fax: (212)691-9418. E-mail: lbarbooks@aol.com. President: Loretta A. Barrett. **Contact:** Kirsten Lundell or Loretta A. Barrett. Estab. 1990. Member of AAR. Represents 70 clients. Specializes in general interest books. Currently handles: 25% fiction; 75% nonfiction.

• Prior to opening her agency, Ms. Barrett was vice president and executive editor at Doubleday for 25 years.

Represents: Considers all areas of nonfiction. Considers these fiction areas: action/adventure; confessional; contemporary issues; detective/police/crime; ethnic; experimental; family saga; feminist; gay; glitz; historical; humor/satire; lesbian; literary; mainstream; mystery/suspense; psychic/supernatural; religious/inspirational; romance; sports; thriller/espionage. "No children's or juvenile."

How to Contact: Query first with SASE. Considers simultaneous queries and submissions. Responds in 6 weeks to queries. Returns materials only with SASE.

Recent Sales: *Inviting God to Your Wedding*, by Martha Williamson (Harmony); *Line of Sight*, by Jack Kelly (Hyperion).

Terms: Agent receives 15% commission on domestic sales; 20% on foreign sales. Offers written contract. Charges for shipping and photocopying.

Writers' Conferences: San Diego State University Writer's Conference; Maui Writer's Conference.

[N] JENNY BENT, LITERARY AGENT, GRAYBILL & ENGLISH, L.L.C., 1920 N St. NW, #620, Washington DC 20036. Fax: (202)457-0662. E-mail: jenlbent@aol.com. **Contact:** Jenny Bent. Estab. 1997. Member of AAR. Represents 40 clients. 50% of clients are new/unpublished writers. Currently handles: 75% nonfiction books; 25% novels.

• Prior to joining her agency, Ms. Bent worked as an editor in book publishing and magazines.

Represents: Nonfiction books, novels. **Considers these nonfiction areas:** animals; biography/autobiography; child guidance/parenting; ethnic/cultural interests; gay/lesbian issues; health/medicine; history; language/literature/criticism; New Age/metaphysics; popular culture; psychology; religious/inspirational; science/technology; self-help/personal improvement; women's issues/women's studies. **Considers these fiction areas:** contemporary issues; detective/crime/police (hard-boiled detective); ethnic; family saga; gay/lesbian; literary; romance; suspense.

How to Contact: Query. Send outline/proposal and SASE. "Please always include a bio or résumé with submissions or queries." *No calls please.* Accepts queries by e-mail. Considers simultaneous submissions. Responds in 2 weeks to queries; 1 month to mss. Returns material only with SASE.

Needs: Actively seeking quality fiction from well-credentialed authors. Does not want to receive science fiction, New Age fiction, thrillers, children's, self-help from non-credentialed writers. Obtains new clients through recommendations, solicitations, conferences.

Recent Sales: Sold 15 titles in the last year. *If Men Were Angels*, by Reed Karaim (W.W. Norton); *Angelhead: A Crime Memoir*, by Greg Bottoms (Crown).

Terms: Agent receives 15% commission on domestic sales; 25% on foreign sales. Offers written contract. 30 days notice must be given to terminate contract. Charges for office expenses, postage, photocopying, long distance.

Writer's Conferences: Hurston-Wright (Richmond, VA, summer); Washington Independent Writers Spring Writers Conference (Washington DC, May); Washington Romance Writers Spring Retreat; Virginia Romance Writers Conference (Williamsburg, VA, March).

Reading List: Reads *New Age Journal* and *Psychology Today* to find new clients. Looks for "writers with strong credentials."

Tips: "Since Graybill & English is both a literary agency and a law firm, we can offer our clients essential legal services."

PAM BERNSTEIN & ASSOCIATES, INC., 790 Madison Ave., Suite 310, New York NY 10021. (212)288-1700. Fax: (212)288-3054. **Contact:** Pam Bernstein or Donna Downing. Estab. 1992. Member of AAR. Represents 50 clients. 20% of clients are new/previously unpublished writers. Specializes in commercial adult fiction and nonfiction. Currently handles: 60% nonfiction books; 40% fiction.

● Prior to becoming agents, Ms. Bernstein served as vice president with the William Morris Agency; Ms. Downing was in public relations.

Represents: Considers these nonfiction areas: child guidance/parenting; cooking/food/nutrition; current affairs; health/medicine; how-to; popular culture; psychology; religious/inspirational; self-help/personal improvement; sociology; true crime/investigative; women's issues/women's studies. **Considers these fiction areas:** contemporary issues; ethnic; historical; mainstream; mystery/suspense; romance (contemporary); thriller.

How to Contact: Query. Responds in 2 weeks to queries; 1 month to mss. Include postage for return of ms.

Recent Sales: Sold 25 titles in the last year. *The Bipolar Child*, by Janice and Demitri Papolos (Broadway); *The Wholeness of a Broken Heart* (Riverhead); *The Barefoot Contessa Cookbook* (Clarkson Potter).

Terms: Agent receives 15% commission on domestic sales; 20% on foreign sales. Offers written contract, binding for 3 years, with 30 day cancellation clause. 100% of business is derived from commissions on sales. Charges for postage and photocopying.

[N] BLEECKER STREET ASSOCIATES, INC., 532 LaGuardia Place, New York NY 10012. (212)677-4492. Fax: (212)388-0001. **Contact:** Agnes Birnbaum. Estab. 1984. Member of AAR, RWA, MWA. Represents 60 clients. 20% of clients are new/previously unpublished writers. "We're very hands-on and accessible. We try to be truly creative in our submission approaches. We've had especially good luck with first-time authors." Currently handles: 65% nonfiction books; 25% novels; 10% syndicated material.

● Prior to becoming an agent, Ms. Birnbaum was an editor at Simon & Schuster, Dutton/Signet and other publishing houses.

Represents: Nonfiction books, novels, short story collections. **Considers these nonfiction areas:** animals; anthropology/archaeology; biography/autobiography; business; child guidance/parenting; computers/electronics; cooking/food/nutrition; current affairs; ethnic/cultural interests; gay/lesbian issues; government/politics/law; health/medicine; history; how-to; humor; juvenile nonfiction; memoirs; military/war; money/finance/economics; nature/environment; New Age/metaphysics; popular culture; psychology; religious/inspirational; science/technology; self-help/personal improvement; sociology; sports; true crime/investigative; women's issues/women's studies. **Considers these fiction areas:** detective/police/crime; erotica; ethnic; family saga; feminist; gay/lesbian; historical; literary; mystery; psychic/supernatural; romance; thriller/espionage.

How to Contact: Query with SASE. Does not accept queries by fax or e-mail. Considers simultaneous queries. Responds in 1 week to queries "if interested"; 1 month on mss. Returns materials only with SASE.

Needs: Does not want to receive science fiction, westerns, poetry, children's books, academic/scholarly/professional books, plays, scripts. Obtains new clients through recommendations from others, queries, conferences. "Plus, I will approach someone with a letter if his/her work impresses me."

Recent Sales: Sold 35 titles in the last year. *Star Spangled Banner*, by Irvin Molotsky (Dutton); *Salt In Your Sock*, by Lillian Beard, M.D. (Times Books); *Sabrina*, by Pat Barnes-Svarney (Archway); *Healing Companion*, by Jeff Kane, M.D. (Harper SF).

Terms: Agent receives 15% commission on domestic sales; 25% on foreign sales if co-agent is used, if not, 15% on foreign sales. Offers written contract, exclusive on all work. 30-day notice must be given to terminate contract. Charges for postage, long distance, fax, messengers, photocopies, not to exceed $150.

Writer's Conferences: PennWriters (Pittsburgh PA, May).

Tips: "Keep query letters short and to the point; include only information pertaining to book or background as writer. Try to avoid superlatives in description. Work needs to stand on its own, so how much editing it may have received has no place in a query letter."

CURTIS BROWN LTD., 10 Astor Place, New York NY 10003-6935. (212)473-5400. Member of AAR; signatory of WGA. **Contact:** Perry Knowlton, chairman; Timothy Knowlton, CEO; Peter L. Ginsberg, president.

Member Agents: Laura Blake Peterson; Ellen Geiger; Emilie Jacobson, vice president; Maureen Walters, vice president; Virginia Knowlton; Timothy Knowlton (film, screenplays, plays); Marilyn Marlow, executive vice president; Ed Wintle (film, screenplays, plays); Andrew Pope; Clyde Taylor; Mitchell Waters; Elizabeth Harding, Douglas Stewart, Dave Barbor (translation rights).
Represents: Nonfiction books, juvenile books, novels, novellas, short story collections, poetry books. **Considers all categories of nonfiction and fiction.**
Also Handles: Movie scripts, feature film, TV scripts, TV MOW, stage plays. **Considers these script subject areas:** action/adventure; comedy; detective/police/crime; ethnic; feminist; gay; historical; horror; lesbian; mainstream; mystery/suspense; psychic/supernatural; romantic comedy and drama; thriller; westerns/frontier.
How to Contact: No unsolicited mss. Query first with SASE. Responds in 3 weeks tn queries; 5 weeks to mss (only if requested).
Needs: Obtains new clients through recommendations from others, solicitation, at conferences and query letters.
Recent Sales: Prefers not to share information on specific sales.
Terms: Offers written contract. Charges for photocopying, some postage.

SHEREE BYKOFSKY ASSOCIATES, INC., 16 W. 36th St., 13th Floor, New York NY 10018. Website: www.sheree bee.com. **Contact:** Sheree Bykofsky. Estab. 1984. Incorporated 1991. Member of AAR, ASJA, WNBA. Represents "a limited number" of clients. Specializes in popular reference nonfiction. Currently handles: 80% nonfiction; 20% fiction.
• Prior to opening her agency, Ms. Bykofsky served as executive editor of The Stonesong Press and managing editor of Chiron Press. She is also the author or co-author of more than 10 books.
Represents: Nonfiction, commercial and literary fiction. **Considers all nonfiction areas,** especially biography/autobiography; business; child guidance/parenting; cooking/foods/nutrition; current affairs; ethnic/cultural interests; gay/lesbian issues; health/medicine; history; how-to; humor; music/dance/theater/film; popular culture; psychology; inspirational; self-help/personal improvement; true crime/investigative; women's issues/women's studies. "I have wide-ranging interests, but it really depends on quality of writing, originality, and how a particular project appeals to me (or not). I take on very little fiction unless I completely love it—it doesn't matter what area or genre."
How to Contact: Query with SASE. No unsolicited mss or phone calls. Considers simultaneous queries. Responds in 1 week to short queries; 1 month to solicited mss. Returns materials only with SASE.
Needs: Does not want to receive poetry, material for children, screenplays. Obtains new clients through recommendations from others.
Recent Sales: Sold 50 titles in the last year. *Falling Flesh Just Ahead*, by Lee Potts (Longstreet); *Tripping*, by Charles Hayes (Viking).
Terms: Agent receives 15% commission on domestic sales; 15% on foreign sales. Offers written contract, binding for 1 year "usually." Charges for postage, photocopying and fax.
Writers' Conferences: ASJA (NYC); Asilomar (Pacific Grove CA); Kent State; Southwestern Writers; Willamette (Portland); Dorothy Canfield Fisher (San Diego); Writers Union (Maui); Pacific NW; IWWG; and many others.
Tips: "Read the agent listing carefully, and comply with guidelines."

RUTH COHEN, INC. LITERARY AGENCY, P.O. Box 7626, Menlo Park CA 94025. (650)854-2054. **Contact:** Ruth Cohen. Estab. 1982. Member of AAR, Authors Guild, Sisters in Crime, RWA, SCBWI. Represents 45 clients. 15% of clients are new/previously unpublished writers. Specializes in "quality writing in contemporary fiction, women's fiction, mysteries, thrillers and juvenile fiction." Currently handles: 60% fiction, 35% juvenile, 5% nonfiction.
• Prior to opening her agency, Ms. Cohen served as directing editor at Scott Foresman & Company (now HarperCollins).
Represents: Adult novels, juvenile books. **Considers these nonfiction areas:** ethnic/cultural interests; juvenile nonfiction; women's issues/women's studies. **Considers these fiction areas:** detective/police; ethnic; historical; juvenile; contemporary; thriller; literary; mainstream; mystery/suspense; picture books; romance (historical, long contemporary); young adult.
How to Contact: *No unsolicited mss.* Send outline plus 2 sample chapters. "Please indicate your phone number or e-mail address." *Must include SASE.* Responds in 3 weeks to queries.
Needs: Does not want to receive poetry, westerns, film scripts or how-to books. Obtains new clients through recommendations from others and through submissions.
Recent Sales: Prefers not to share information on specific sales.
Terms: Agent receives 15% commission on domestic sales; 20% on foreign sales, "if a foreign agent is involved." Offers written contract, binding for 1 year "continuing to next." Charges for foreign postage, phone calls, photocopying submissions and overnight delivery of mss when appropriate.
Tips: "As the publishing world merges and changes, there seem to be fewer opportunities for new writers to succeed in the work that they love. We urge you to develop the patience, persistence and perseverance that have made this agency so successful. Prepare a well-written and well-crafted manuscript, and our combined best efforts can help advance both our careers."

ROBERT CORNFIELD LITERARY AGENCY, 145 W. 79th St., New York NY 10024-6468. (212)874-2465. Fax: (212)874-2641. E-mail: rbcbc@aol.com. **Contact:** Robert Cornfield. Estab. 1979. Member of AAR. Represents 60 clients. 20% of clients are new/previously unpublished writers. Specializes in film, art, literary, music criticism, food, fiction. Currently handles: 60% nonfiction books; 20% scholarly books; 20% novels.

● Prior to opening his agency, Mr. Cornfield was an editor at Holt and Dial Press.

Represents: Nonfiction books, novels. **Considers these nonfiction areas:** animals; anthropology/archaeology; art/architecture/design; biography/autobiography; cooking/food/nutrition; history; language/literature/criticism; music/dance/theater/film. **Considers literary fiction.**

How to Contact: Query with SASE. Responds in 3 weeks to queries.

Needs: Obtains new clients through recommendations.

Recent Sales: Sold 15-20 titles in the last year. *Mixed Signals*, by Richard Barrios (Routledge); *Multiple Personalties*, by Joan Acorella (Jossey-Bass).

Terms: Agent receives 10% commission on domestic sales; 20% on foreign sales. No written contract. Charges for postage, excessive photocopying.

RICHARD CURTIS ASSOCIATES, INC., 171 E. 74th St., Suite 2, New York NY 10021. (212)772-7363. Fax: (212)772-7393. E-mail: Jhacrworth@curtisagency.com. Website: www.curtisagency.com. **Contact:** Pam Valvera. Estab. 1969. Member of AAR, RWA, MWA, WWA, SFWA, signatory of WGA. Represents 100 clients. 5% of clients are new/previously unpublished writers. Specializes in general and literary fiction and nonfiction, as well as genre fiction such as science fiction, romance, horror, fantasy, action-adventure. Currently handles: 50% nonfiction books; 50% novels.

● Prior to opening his agency, Mr. Curtis was an agent with the Scott Meredith Literary Agency for 7 years and has authored over 50 published books.

Member Agents: Amy Victoria Meo, Jennifer Hackrworth, Richard Curtis.

Represents: Nonfiction books, scholarly books, novels. **Considers all nonfiction and fiction areas.**

How to Contact: "We do not accept fax or e-mail queries, conventional queries (outline and 3 sample chapters) must be accompanied by SASE." Responds in 1 month to queries; 1 month to mss.

Needs: Obtains new clients through recommendations from others, solicitations and conferences.

Recent Sales: Sold 100 titles in the last year. *Courtney Love: The Real Story*, by Poppy Z. Brite (Simon & Schuster); *Darwin's Radio*, by Greg Bear (Del Rey/Random House); *Expendable*, by James Gardner (Avon). Other clients include Dan Simmons, Jennifer Blake, Leonard Maltin, Earl Mindell and Barbara Parker.

Terms: Agent receives 15% commission on domestic sales; 20% on foreign sales. Offers written contract, binding on a "book by book basis." Charges for photocopying, express, fax, international postage, book orders.

Writers' Conferences: Romance Writers of America; Nebula Science Fiction Conference.

DARHANSOFF & VERRILL LITERARY AGENTS, 179 Franklin St., 4th Floor, New York NY 10013. (212)334-5980. Fax: (212)334-5470. Estab. 1975. Member of AAR. Represents 100 clients. 10% of clients are new/previously unpublished writers. Specializes in literary fiction. Currently handles: 25% nonfiction books; 60% novels; 15% short story collections.

Member Agents: Liz Darhansoff, Charles Verrill, Leigh Feldman, Tal Gregory.

Represents: Nonfiction books, novels, short story collections. **Considers these nonfiction areas:** anthropology/archaeology; biography/autobiography; current affairs; health/medicine; history; language/literature/criticism; nature/environment; science/technology. **Considers literary and thriller fiction.**

How to Contact: Query letter only. Responds in 2 weeks to queries.

Needs: Obtains new clients through recommendations from others.

Recent Sales: *Cold Mountain*, by Charles Frazier (Atlantic Monthly Press); *At Home in Mitford*, by Jan Karon (Viking).

JOAN DAVES AGENCY, 21 W. 26th St., New York NY 10010. (212)685-2663. Fax: (212)685-1781. **Contact:** Jennifer Lyons, director; Heather Currier, assistant. Estab. 1960. Member of AAR. Represents 100 clients. 10% of clients are new/previously unpublished writers. Specializes in literary fiction and nonfiction, also commercial fiction.

Represents: Nonfiction books, novels. **Considers these nonfiction areas:** biography/autobiography; gay/lesbian issues; popular culture; translations; women's issues/women's studies. **Considers these fiction areas:** ethnic, family saga; gay; literary; mainstream.

How to Contact: Query. Considers simultaneous submissions. Responds in 3 weeks to queries; 6 weeks to mss. Returns materials only with SASE.

Needs: Obtains new clients through editors' and author clients' recommendations. "A few queries translate into representation."

Recent Sales: Sold 70 titles in the last year. *Strange Fire*, by Melvin Jules Bukiet (W.W. Norton); *JLVT! Growing Up Female with a Bad Reputation*, by Leora Tannenbaum; and *Candor and Perversion*, by Roger Shattuck (W.W. Norton).

Terms: Agent receives 15% commission on domestic sales; 20% on foreign sales. Offers written contract, on a per book basis. Charges for office expenses. 100% of business is derived from commissions on sales.

Reading List: Reads *The Paris Review, Missouri Review*, and *Voice Literary Supplement* to find new clients.

DH LITERARY, INC., P.O. Box 990, Nyack NY 10960-0990. (212)753-7942. E-mail: dhendin@aol.com. **Contact:** David Hendin. Estab. 1993. Member of AAR. Represents 50 clients. 20% of clients are new/previously unpublished writers. Specializes in trade fiction, nonfiction and newspaper syndication of columns or comic strips. Currently handles: 60% nonfiction books; 10% scholarly books; 20% fiction; 10% syndicated material.

● Prior to opening his agency, Mr. Hendin served as president and publisher for Pharos Books/World Almanac as well as senior vp and COO at sister company United Feature Syndicate.

Represents: Nonfiction books, novels, syndicated material. **Considers these nonfiction areas:** animals; anthropology/archaeology; biography/autobiography; child guidance/parenting; current affairs; ethnic/cultural interests; government/politics/law; health/medicine; history; how-to; language/literature/criticism; money/finance/economics; nature/environment; popular culture; psychology; science/technology; self-help/personal improvement; true crime/investigative; women's issues/women's studies. **Considers these fiction areas:** literary; mainstream; mystery; thriller/espionage.
How to Contact: Responds in 6 weeks to queries. Accepts queries by e-mail, "but no downloads." Considers simultaneous queries. Returns materials only with SASE.
Needs: Obtains new clients through referrals from others (clients, writers, publishers).
Recent Sales: Sold 18-20 titles in the last year. *Pink Flamingo Murders*, by Elaine Viets (Dell); *Age of Anxious Anxiety*, by Tom Tiede (Grove Atlantic); *History of American Etiquette*, by Judith Martin (Norton).
Terms: Agent receives 15% commission on domestic sales; 20% on foreign sales. Offers written contract, binding for 1 year. Charges for out of pocket expenses for postage, photocopying manuscript, and overseas phone calls specifically related to a book.
Tips: "Have your project in mind and on paper before you submit. Too many writers/cartoonists say 'I'm good . . . get me a project.' Publishers want writers with their own great ideas and their own unique voice. No faxed submissions."

N⃞ DHS LITERARY, INC., 6060 N. Central Expwy., Suite 624, Dallas TX 75206-5209. (214)363-4422. Fax: (214)363-4423. **Contact:** David Hale Smith, president. Estab. 1994. Represents 40 clients. 50% of clients are new/previously unpublished writers. Specializes in commercial fiction and nonfiction for adult trade market. Currently handles: 50% nonfiction books; 50% novels.
• Prior to opening his agency, Mr. Smith was an editor at a newswire service.
Represents: Nonfiction books, novels. **Considers these nonfiction areas:** biography/autobiography; business; child guidance/parenting; computers/electronics; cooking/food/nutrition; current affairs; ethnic/cultural interests; gay/lesbian issues; popular culture; sports; true crime/investigative. **Considers these fiction areas:** detective/police/crime; erotica; ethnic; feminist; gay; historical; horror; literary; mainstream; mystery/suspense; sports; thriller/espionage; westerns/frontier.
How to Contact: Query for fiction; send outline/proposal and sample chapters for nonfiction. Considers simultaneous queries and submissions. Responds in 1 month to queries; 4 months to mss. Returns materials only with SASE, otherwise discards.
Needs: Actively seeking thrillers, mysteries, suspense, etc., and narrative nonfiction. Does not want to receive poetry, short fiction, children's books. Obtains new clients through referrals from other clients, editors and agents, presentations at writers conferences and via unsolicited submissions.
Recent Sales: Sold 29 titles in the last year. *Shooting At Midnight*, by Greg Rucka (Bantam); *Food & Mood*, by Elizabeth Somer (Holt).
Terms: Agent receives 15% commission on domestic sales; 25% on foreign sales. Offers written contract, with 10-day cancellation clause or upon mutual consent. Charges for client expenses, i.e., postage, photocopying. 100% of business is derived from commissions on sales.
Reading List: Reads *Outside Magazine*, STORY, *Texas Monthly*, *Kenyon Review*, *Missouri Review* and *Mississippi Mud* to find new clients. "I like to see good writing in many formats. So I'll often call a writer who has written a good short story, for example, to see if she has a novel."
Tips: "Remember to be courteous and professional, and to treat marketing your work and approaching an agent as you would any formal business matter. When in doubt, always query first—in writing—with SASE."

SANDRA DIJKSTRA LITERARY AGENCY, PMB 515, 1155 Camino del Mar, Del Mar CA 92014-2605. (619)755-3115. **Contact:** Sandra Zane. Estab. 1981. Member of AAR, Authors Guild, PEN West, Poets and Editors, MWA. Represents 100 clients. 30% of clients are new/previously unpublished writers. "We specialize in a number of fields." Currently handles: 60% nonfiction books; 5% juvenile books; 35% novels.
Member Agents: Sandra Dijkstra.
Represents: Nonfiction books, novels. **Considers these nonfiction areas:** anthropology; biography/autobiography; business; child guidance/parenting; nutrition; current affairs; ethnic/cultural interests; government/politics; health/medicine; history; literary studies (trade only); military/war (trade only); money/finance/economics; nature/environment; psychology; science/technology; self-help/personal improvement; sociology; sports; true crime/investigative; women's issues/women's studies. **Considers these fiction areas:** contemporary issues; detective/police/crime; ethnic; family saga; feminist; literary; mainstream; mystery/suspense; thriller/espionage.
How to Contact: Send "outline/proposal with sample chapters for nonfiction, synopsis and first 50 pages for fiction and SASE." Responds in 6 weeks.
Needs: Obtains new clients primarily through referrals/recommendations, but also through queries and conferences and often by solicitation.
Recent Sales: *The Mistress of Spices*, by Chitra Divakaruni (Anchor Books); *The Flower Net*, by Lisa See (HarperCollins); *Outsmarting the Menopausal Fat Cell*, by Debra Waterhouse (Hyperion).
Terms: Agent receives 15% commission on domestic sales; 20% on foreign sales. Offers written contract, binding for 1 year. Charges for expenses "from years we are *active* on author's behalf to cover domestic costs so that we can spend time selling books instead of accounting expenses. We also charge for the photocopying of the full manuscript or nonfiction proposal and for foreign postage."

Writers' Conferences: "Have attended Squaw Valley, Santa Barbara, Asilomar, Southern California Writers Conference, Rocky Mountain Fiction Writers, to name a few. We also speak regularly for writers groups such as PEN West and the Independent Writers Association."

Tips: "Be professional and learn the standard procedures for submitting your work. Give full biographical information on yourself, especially for a nonfiction project. Always include SASE with correct return postage for your own protection of your work. Query with a 1 or 2 page letter first and always include postage. Nine page letters telling us your life story, or your book's, are unprofessional and usually not read. Tell us about your book and write your query well. It's our first introduction to who you are and what you can do! Call if you don't hear within a reasonable period of time. Be a regular patron of bookstores and study what kind of books are being published. READ. Check out your local library and bookstores—you'll find lots of books on writing and the publishing industry that will help you! At conferences, ask published writers about their agents. Don't believe the myth that an agent has to be in New York to be successful— we've already disproved it!"

DONADIO AND OLSON, INC., 121 W. 27th St., Suite 704, New York NY 10001. (212)691-8077. Fax: (212)633-2837. **Contact:** Neil Olson. Estab. 1970. Member of AAR. Represents approximately 100 clients. Specializes in literary fiction and nonfiction. Currently handles: 40% nonfiction; 50% novels; 10% short story collections.
Member Agents: Edward Hibbert (literary fiction); Neil Olson; Ira Silverberg; Peter Steinberg.
Represents: Nonfiction books, novels, short story collections.
How to Contact: Query with 50 pages and SASE. Considers simultaneous queries and submissions. Returns materials only with SASE.
Recent Sales: Sold over 15 titles in the last year. Prefers not to share information on specific sales.
Terms: Agent receives 15% commission on domestic sales; 20% on foreign sales.

JANE DYSTEL LITERARY MANAGEMENT, One Union Square West, Suite 904, New York NY 10003. (212)627-9100. Fax: (212)627-9313. Website: www.dystel.com. **Contact:** Miriam Goderich, Todd Keithley. Estab. 1994. Member of AAR. Presently represents 200 clients. 50% of clients are new/previously unpublished writers. Specializes in commercial and literary fiction and nonfiction plus cookbooks. Currently handles: 65% nonfiction books; 25% novels; 10% cookbooks.
Member Agents: Stacey Glick; Jessica Jones; Todd Keithley; Charlotte Ho (foreign rights); Jane Dystel; Miriam Goderich; Jo Fagan; Kyong Cho.
Represents: Nonfiction books, novels, cookbooks. **Considers these nonfiction areas:** animals; anthropology/archaeology; biography/autobiography; business; child guidance/parenting; cooking/food/nutrition; current affairs; education; ethnic/cultural interests; gay/lesbian issues; government/politics/law; health/medicine; history; humor; military/war; money/finance/economics; New Age/metaphysics; popular cultures; psychology; religious/inspirational; science/technology; true crime/investigative; women's issues/women's studies. **Considers these fiction areas:** action/adventure; contemporary issues; detective/police/crime; ethnic; family saga; gay; lesbian; literary; mainstream; thriller/espionage.
How to Contact: Query with SASE. Reports in 3 weeks on queries; 6 weeks on mss.
Needs: Obtains new clients through recommendations from others, solicitation, at conferences.
Recent Sales: *The Sparrow* and *Children of God*, by Mary Russell; *Water Carry Me*, by Thomas Moran; *Syrup*, by Maxx Barry.
Terms: Agent receives 15% commission on domestic sales; 19% of foreign sales. Offers written contract on a book to book basis. Charges for photocopying. Galley charges and book charges from the publisher are passed on to the author.
Writers' Conferences: West Coast Writers Conference (Whidbey Island WA, Columbus Day weekend); University of Iowa Writer's Conference; Pacific Northwest Writer's Conference; Pike's Peak Writer's Conference; Santa Barbara Writer's Conference.

JEANNE FREDERICKS LITERARY AGENCY, INC., 221 Benedict Hill Rd., New Canaan CT 06840. Phone/fax: (203)972-3011. E-mail: jflainc@ix.netcom.com. **Contact:** Jeanne Fredericks. Estab. 1997. Member of AAR. Represents 80 clients. 10% of clients are new/unpublished writers. Specializes in quality adult nonfiction by authorities in their fields. Currently handles: 98% nonfiction books; 2% novels.
● Prior to opening her agency, Ms. Fredericks was an agent and acting director with the Susan P. Urstadt Inc. Agency.
Represents: Nonfiction books. **Considers these nonfiction areas:** animals; anthropology/archeaology; art/architecture; biography/autobiography; business; child guidance/parenting; cooking/food/nutrition; crafts/hobbies; current affairs; health/medicine/alternative health; history; horticulture; how-to; interior design/decorating; money/finance/economics; nature/environment; photography; psychology; science; self-help/personal improvement; sports; women's issues. **Considers these fiction areas:** family saga; historical; literary.
How to Contact: Query first with SASE, then send outline/proposal or outline and 1-2 sample chapters with SASE. No fax queries. Accepts queries by e-mail. "If short—no attachments." Considers simultaneous queries and submissions. Responds in 3 weeks to queries; 6 weeks to mss. Returns material only with SASE.
Needs: Obtains new clients through referrals, submissions to agency, conferences.
Recent Sales: Sold 22 titles in the last year. *Gaining Ground: Creating Big Gardens in Small Spaces*, by Maureen Gilmer (NTC/Contemporary); *The Book of Five Rungs for Executives*, by Donald Krause (Nicholas Brealey—US & Britain; Meberneuter-Germany; Lyon—Portugal; Makron—Brazil; etc.).

Terms: Agent receives 15% commission on domestic sales; 20% on foreign sales; 25% with foreign co-agent. Offers written contract, binding for 9 months. 2 months notice must be given to terminate contract. Charges for photocopying of whole proposals and mss, overseas postage, priority mail and Federal Express.

Writers' Conferences: PEN Women Conference (Williamsburg VA, February); Connecticut Press Club Biennial Writers' Conference (Stamford CT, April); ASJA Annual Writers' Conference East (New York NY, May); BEA (Chicago, June).

Tips: "Be sure to research the competition for your work and be able to justify why there's a need for it. I enjoy building an author's career, particularly if s(he) is professional, hardworking, and courteous. Aside from eight years of agenting experience, I've had ten years of editorial experience in adult trade book publishing that enables me to help an author polish a proposal so that it's more appealing to prospective editors. My MBA in marketing also distinguishes me from other agents."

SANFORD J. GREENBURGER ASSOCIATES, INC., 55 Fifth Ave., New York NY 10003. (212)206-5600. Fax: (212)463-8718. **Contact:** Heide Lange. Estab. 1945. Member of AAR. Represents 500 clients.

Member Agents: Heide Lange, Faith Hamlin, Beth Vesel, Theresa Park, Elyse Cheney, Dan Mandel, Francis Greenburger.

Represents: Nonfiction books, novels. **Considers all nonfiction areas. Considers these fiction areas:** action/adventure; contemporary issues, detective/police/crime; ethnic; family saga; feminist; gay; glitz; historical; humor/satire; lesbian; literary; mainstream; mystery/suspense; psychic/supernatural; regional; sports; thriller/espionage.

How to Contact: Query first. Responds in 3 weeks to queries; 2 months to mss.

Needs: Does not want to receive romances or westerns.

Recent Sales: Sold 200 titles in the last year. Prefers not to share information on specific sales. Clients include Andrew Ross, Margaret Cuthbert, Nicholas Sparks, Mary Kurcinka, Linda Nichols, Edy Clarke and Peggy Claude Pierre.

Terms: Agent receives 15% commission on domestic sales; 20% on foreign sales. Charges for photocopying, books for foreign and subsidiary rights submissions.

REECE HALSEY NORTH, 98 Main St., PMB 704, Tiburon CA 94920. (415)789-9191. Fax: (415)789-9177. E-mail: bookgirl@worldnet.att.net. **Contact:** Kimberley Cameron. Estab. 1957. Member of AAR. Represents 40 clients. 30% of clients are new/previously unpublished writers. Specializes in mystery, literary and mainstream fiction, excellent writing. Currently handles: 30% nonfiction books; 70% fiction.

● The Reece Halsey Agency has an illustrious client list largely of established writers, including the estate of Aldous Huxley and has represented Upton Sinclair, William Faulkner and Henry Miller. Ms. Cameron has recently opened a Northern California office and all queries should be addressed to her at the Tiburon office.

Member Agents: Dorris Halsey (by referral only, LA office); Kimberley Cameron (Reese Halsey North).

Represents: Fiction and nonfiction. **Considers these nonfiction areas:** biography/autobiography; current affairs; history; language/literature/criticism; memoirs; popular culture; spiritualism; true crime/investigative; women's issues/women's studies. **Considers these fiction areas:** action/adventure; contemporary issues; detective/police/crime; ethnic; family saga; historical; literary; mainstream; mystery/suspense; science fiction; thriller/espionage; women's fiction.

How to Contact: Query with SASE. Responds in 3 weeks to queries; 3 months to mss.

Recent Sales: Prefers not to share information on specific sales.

Terms: Agent receives 15% commission on domestic sales of books. Offers written contract, binding for 1 year. Requests 6 copies of ms if representing an author.

Writers' Conferences: BEA and various writer conferences, Maui Writers Conference.

Reading List: Reads *Glimmer Train*, *The Sun* and *The New Yorker* to find new clients. Looks for "writing that touches the heart."

Tips: Obtains new clients through recommendations from others and solicitation. "Please send a polite, well-written query and include a SASE with it!"

[N] RICHARD HENSHAW GROUP, 132 W. 22nd St., 4th Floor, New York NY 10011. (212)414-1172. Fax: (212)721-4208. E-mail: rhgagents@aol.com. Website: www.rich.henshaw.com. **Contact:** Rich Henshaw. Estab. 1995. Member of AAR, SinC, MWA, HWA, SFWA. Represents 35 clients. 20% of clients are new/previously unpublished writers. Specializes in thrillers, mysteries, science fiction, fantasy and horror. Currently handles: 20% nonfiction books; 10% juvenile books; 70% novels.

● Prior to opening his agency, Mr. Henshaw served as an agent with Richard Curtis Associates, Inc.

Represents: Nonfiction books, juvenile books, novels. **Considers these nonfiction areas:** animals; biography/autobiography; business; child guidance/parenting; computers/electronics; cooking/food/nutrition; current affairs; gay/lesbian issues; government/politics/law; health/medicine; how-to; humor; juvenile nonfiction; military/war; money/finance/economics; music/dance/theater/film; nature/environment; New Age/metaphysics; popular culture; psychology; science/technology; self-help/personal improvement; sociology; sports; true crime/investigative; women's issues/women's studies. **Considers these fiction areas:** action/adventure; detective/police/crime; ethnic; family saga; fantasy; glitz; historical; horror; humor/satire; juvenile; literary; mainstream; psychic/supernatural; science fiction; sports; thriller/espionage; young adult.

How to Contact: Query with SASE. Responds in 3 weeks to queries; 6 weeks to mss.

Needs: Obtains new clients through recommendations from others, solicitation, at conferences and query letters.

Recent Sales: Sold 17 titles in the last year. *Out For Blood*, by Dana Stabenow (Dutton/Signet); *Deadstick*, by Megan Mallory Rust (Berkley); *And Then There Were None*, by Stephen Solomita (Bantam); *The Well Trained Mind*, by Susan Wise Bauer and Jessie Wise (W.W. Norton).

Terms: Agent receives 15% commission on domestic sales; 20% on foreign sales. No written contract. Charges for photocopying manuscripts and book orders. 100% of business is derived from commission on sales.

Tips: "Always include SASE with correct return postage."

INTERNATIONAL CREATIVE MANAGEMENT, 40 W. 57th St., New York NY 10019. (212)556-5600. Fax: (212)556-5665. West Coast office: 8942 Wilshire Blvd., Beverly Hills CA 90211. (310)550-4000. Fax: (310)550-4100. **Contact:** Literary Department. Member of AAR, signatory of WGA.

Member Agents: Esther Newberg and Amanda Urban, department heads; Lisa Bankoff; Kristine Dahl; Mitch Douglas; Suzanne Gluck; Sloan Harris; Heather Schroder; Denise Shannon; Richard Abate, Sam Cohn.

Terms: Agent receives 10% commission on domestic sales; 15% on UK sales; 20% on translations.

JAMES PETER ASSOCIATES, INC., P.O. Box 772, Tenafly NJ 07670-0751. (201)568-0760. Fax: (201)568-2959. E-mail: bertholtje@compuserve.com. **Contact:** Bert Holtje. Estab. 1971. Member of AAR. Represents 54 individual authors and 5 corporate clients (book producers). 15% of clients are new/previously unpublished writers. Specializes in nonfiction, all categories. "We are especially interested in general, trade and reference." Currently handles: 100% nonfiction books.

  ● Prior to opening his agency, Mr. Holtje was a book packager, and before that, president of an advertising agency with book publishing clients.

Represents: Nonfiction books. **Considers these nonfiction areas:** anthropology/archaeology; art/architecture/design; biography/autobiography; business; child guidance/parenting; current affairs; ethnic/cultural interests; gay/lesbian issues; government/politics/law; health/medicine; history; language/literature/criticism; memoirs (political or business); military/war; money/finance/economics; music/dance/theater/film; popular culture; psychology; self-help/personal improvement; travel; women's issues/women's studies.

How to Contact: Send outline/proposal and SASE. Prefers to be only reader. Responds in 1 month to queries. Returns materials only with SASE.

Needs: Actively seeking "good ideas in all areas of adult nonfiction." Does not want to receive "children's and young adult books, poetry, fiction." Obtains new clients through recommendations from other clients and editors, contact with people who are doing interesting things, and over-the-transom queries.

Recent Sales: Sold 34 titles in the last year. *Patton on Management*, by Dr. Alan Axelrod (Prentice-Hall); *Out of the Ordinary: A Biographical Dictionary of Women Explorers*, by Sarah Purcell and Edward Purcell (Routledge); *Ace Your Mid Terms and Finals—A 5-book series*, by The Ian Samuel Group (McGraw-Hill).

Terms: Agent receives 15% commission on domestic sales; 20% on foreign sales. Offers written contract on a per book basis.

JCA LITERARY AGENCY, 27 W. 20th St., Suite 1103, New York NY 10011. (212)807-0888. Fax: (212)807-0461. **Contact:** Jeff Gerecke, Tony Outhwaite. Estab. 1978. Member of AAR. Represents 100 clients. 20% of clients are new/unpublished writers. Currently handles: 20% nonfiction books; 5% scholarly books; 75% novels.

Member Agents: Jeff Gerecke; Tony Outhwaite, Jane Cushman.

Represents: Nonfiction books, scholarly books, novels. **Considers these nonfiction areas:** anthropology/archaeology; biography/autobiography; business; current affairs; government/politics/law; health/medicine; history; language/literature/criticism; memoirs; military/war; money/finance/economics; music/dance/theater/film; nature/environment; popular culture; science/technology; sociology; sports; translations; true crime/investigative; women's issues/women's studies. **Considers these fiction areas:** action/adventure; contemporary issues; detective/police/crime; family saga; historical; literary; mainstream; mystery; sports; thriller/espionage.

How to Contact: Query with SASE. Does not accept queries by fax or e-mail. Considers simultaneous queries and submissions. "We occasionally may ask for an exclusive look." Responds in 2 weeks to queries; 6 weeks to mss. Returns materials only with SASE.

Needs: Does not want to receive screenplays, poetry, children's books, science fiction/fantasy, genre romance. Obtains new clients through recommendations, solicitations, conferences.

Recent Sales: *The Lost Glass Plates of Wilfred Eng*, by Thomas Orton (Counterpoint); *Sharp Shooter*, by David Healey (The Berkley Publishing Group/Jove); *A Healthy Place to Die*, by Peter King (St. Martin's Press). Other clients include Ernest J. Gaines, W.E.B. Griffin, Polly Whitney, David J. Garrow.

Terms: Agent receives 15% commission on domestic sales; 20% on foreign sales. No written contract. "We work with our clients on a handshake basis." Charges for postage on overseas submissions, photocopying, mss for submission, books purchased for subrights submission, and bank charges, where applicable. "We deduct the cost from payments received from publishers."

Tips: "We do not ourselves provide legal, accounting, or public relations services for our clients, although some of the advice we give falls somewhat into these realms. In cases where it seems necessary we will recommend obtaining outside advice or assistance in these areas from professionals who are not in any way connected to the agency."

N **HARVEY KLINGER, INC.**, 301 W. 53rd St., New York NY 10019. (212)581-7068. Fax: (212)315-3823. Contact: Harvey Klinger. Estab. 1977. Member of AAR. Represents 100 clients. 25% of clients are new/previously unpublished writers. Specializes in "big, mainstream contemporary fiction and nonfiction." Currently handles: 50% nonfiction books; 50% novels.

Member Agents: David Dunton (popular culture, parenting, home improvement, thrillers/crime); Laurie Liss (literary fiction, human interest, politics, women's issues).

Represents: Nonfiction books, novels. **Considers these nonfiction areas:** biography/autobiography; cooking/food/nutrition; health/medicine; psychology; science/technology; self-help/personal improvement; spirituality; sports; true crime/investigative; women's issues/women's studies. **Considers these fiction areas:** action/adventure; detective/police/crime; family saga; glitz; literary; mainstream; thriller/espionage.

How to Contact: Query with SASE. "We do not accept queries by fax or e-mail." Responds in 1 month to queries; 2 months to mss.

Needs: Obtains new clients through recommendations from others.

Recent Sales: Sold 20 titles in the last year. *Secrets About Life Every Woman Should Know*, by Barbara De Angelis (Hyperion); *Torn Jeans: Levi Strauss and the Denim Dynasty*, by Ellen Hawkes (Lisa Drew Books/Scribner); *The Looking Glass*, by Richard Paul Evans (Simon & Schuster); *The Women of Troy Hill*, by Clare Ansberry (Harcourt Brace); *Exit Music: The Radiohead Story*, by Mac Randall (Dell).

Terms: Agent receives 15% commission on domestic sales; 25% on foreign sales. Offers written contract. Charges for photocopying manuscripts, overseas postage for mss.

N **THE KNIGHT AGENCY**, P.O. Box 550648, Atlanta GA 30355. Or: 2407 Matthews St., Atlanta GA 30319. (404)816-9620. E-mail: deidremk@aol.com. Website: www.knightagency.net. **Contact:** Deidre Knight. Estab. 1996. Member of AAR, RWA, Authors Guild. Represents 30 clients. 40% of clients are new/previously unpublished writers. Currently handles: 50% nonfiction books; 50% novels.

Represents: Nonfiction books, novels. **Considers these nonfiction areas:** biography/autobiography; business; child guidance/parenting; computers/electronics; cooking/food/nutrition; current affairs; ethnic/cultural interests; health/medicine; history; how-to; money/finance/economics; music/dance/theater/film; popular culture; psychology; religious/inspirational; self-help/personal improvement; sports; true crime/investigative; women's issues/women's studies. **Considers these fiction areas:** ethnic; literary; mainstream; mystery/suspense; regional; religious/inspirational; romance (contemporary, historical, inspirational); women's fiction; commercial fiction.

How to Contact: Query with SASE. Considers simultaneous queries and submissions. Responds in 2 weeks to queries; 6 weeks to mss.

Needs: "We are looking for a wide variety of fiction and nonfiction. In the nonfiction area, we're particularly eager to find personal finance, business investment, pop culture, self-help/motivational and popular reference books. In fiction, we're always looking for romance, women's fiction, ethnic and commercial fiction."

Recent Sales: Sold 20 titles in the last year. *Panic-Proof Parenting*, by Debra Holtzman (NTC/Contemporary); *Simple Strategies for Electronic Daytrades*, by Tori Turner (Adams Media); and *Abbey Road to Zapple Records: A Beatles Encyclopedia*, by Judson Knight (Taylor Publishing).

Terms: Agent receives 15% commission on domestic sales; 25% on foreign sales. Offers written contract, binding for 1 year. 60 days notice must be given to terminate contract. Charges clients for photocopying, postage, overnight courier expenses.

BARBARA S. KOUTS, LITERARY AGENT, P.O. Box 560, Bellport NY 11713. (631)286-1278. **Contact:** Barbara Kouts. Estab. 1980. Member of AAR. Represent 50 clients. 10% of clients are new/previously unpublished writers. Specializes in adult fiction and nonfiction and children's books. Currently handles: 20% nonfiction books; 60% juvenile books; 20% novels.

Represents: Nonfiction books, juvenile books, novels. **Considers these nonfiction areas:** biography/autobiography; child guidance/parenting; current affairs; ethnic/cultural interests; health/medicine; history; juvenile nonfiction; music/dance/theater/film; nature/environment; psychology; self-help/personal improvement; women's issues/women's studies. **Considers these fiction areas:** contemporary issues; family saga; feminist; historical; juvenile; literary; mainstream; mystery/suspense; picture book; young adult.

How to Contact: Query with SASE. Responds in 2-3 days to queries; 4-6 weeks to mss.

Needs: Obtains new clients through recommendations from others, solicitation, at conferences, etc.

Recent Sales: *Dancing on the Edge*, by Han Nolan (Harcourt Brace); *Cendrillon*, by Robert San Souci (Simon & Schuster).

Terms: Agent receives 10% commission on domestic sales; 20% on foreign sales. Charges for photocopying.

Tips: "Write, do not call. Be professional in your writing."

MICHAEL LARSEN/ELIZABETH POMADA LITERARY AGENTS, 1029 Jones St., San Francisco CA 94109-5023. (415)673-0939. E-mail: larsenpoma@aol.com. Website: www.Larsen-Pomada.com. **Contact:** Mike Larsen or Elizabeth Pomada. Estab. 1972. Members of AAR, Authors Guild, ASJA, NWA, PEN, WNBA, California Writers Club. Represents 100 clients. 40-45% of clients are new/unpublished writers. Eager to work with new/unpublished writers. Currently handles: 70% nonfiction books; 30% novels.

● Prior to opening their agency, both Mr. Larsen and Ms. Pomada were promotion executives for major publishing houses. Mr. Larsen worked for Morrow, Bantam and Pyramid (now part of Berkley), Ms. Pomada worked at Holt, David McKay, and The Dial Press.

Member Agents: Michael Larsen (nonfiction), Elizabeth Pomada (fiction, books of interest to women).

Represents: Adult nonfiction books, novels. **Considers these nonfiction areas:** anthropology/archaeology; art/architecture/design; biography/autobiography; business; cooking/food/nutrition; current affairs; ethnic/cultural interests; futurism; gay/lesbian issues; government/politics/law; health/medicine; history; how-to; humor; interior design/decorating; language/literature/criticism; memoirs; money/finance/economics; music/dance/theater/film; nature/environment; New Age/metaphysics; parenting; photography; popular culture; psychology; religious/inspirational; science/technology; self-help/personal improvement; sociology; sports; travel; true crime/investigative; women's issues/women's studies. **Considers these fiction areas:** action/adventure; contemporary issues; detective/police/crime; ethnic; experimental; family saga; fantasy; feminist; gay; glitz; historical; humor/satire; lesbian; literary; mainstream; mystery/suspense; psychic/supernatural; religious/inspirational; romance (contemporary, gothic, historical).

How to Contact: Query with synopsis and first 10 pages of completed novel. Responds in 2 months to queries. For nonfiction, "please read Michael's book *How to Write a Book Proposal* (Writer's Digest Books) and then mail or e-mail the title of your book and a promotion plan." Always include SASE. Send SASE for brochure and title list.

Needs: Actively seeking commercial and literary fiction. "Fresh voices with new ideas of interest to major publishers. Does not want to receive children's books, plays, short stories, screenplays, pornography.

Recent Sales: *Black Raven* (10th book in the Deverry Series), by Katharine Kerr (Bantam/Spectra); *If Life Is a Game, These Are The Rules*, by Cherie Carter-Scott (Broadway Books); *The Center at the Edge, Seeking the Inner Meaning of Outer Space*, by Wyn Wachhorst (Basic Books).

Terms: Agent receives 15% commission on domestic sales; 15% on dramatic sales; 20-30% on foreign sales. May charge for printing, postage for multiple submissions, foreign mail, foreign phone calls, galleys, books, and legal fees.

Writers' Conferences: Book Expo America; Santa Barbara Writers Conference (Santa Barbara); Maui Writers Conference (Maui); ASJA.

Tips: "We have very diverse tastes. We look for fresh voices and new ideas. We handle literary, commercial and genre fiction, and the full range of nonfiction books."

LEVANT & WALES, LITERARY AGENCY, INC., 108 Hayes St., Seattle WA 98109-2808. (206)284-7114. Fax: (206)284-0190. E-mail: waleslit@aol.com. **Contact:** Elizabeth Wales or Adrienne Reed. Estab. 1988. Member of AAR, Pacific Northwest Writers' Conference, Book Publishers' Northwest. Represents 65 clients. Specializes in mainstream nonfiction and fiction, as well as narrative nonfiction and literary fiction. Currently handles: 60% nonfiction books; 40% novels.

● Prior to becoming an agent, Ms. Wales worked at Oxford University Press and Viking Penguin.

Represents: Nonfiction books, novels. **Considers these nonfiction areas:** animals; biography/autobiography; business; current affairs; education; ethnic/cultural interests; gay/lesbian issues; health; language/literature/criticism; lifestyle; memoirs; nature; New Age; popular culture; psychology; science; self-help/personal improvement; women's issues/women's studies—open to creative or serious treatments of almost any nonfiction subject. **Considers these fiction areas:** cartoon/comic/women's; ethnic; experimental; feminist; gay; lesbian; literary; mainstream (no genre fiction).

How to Contact: Query first with SASE. "To Query: Please send cover letter, writing sample (no more than 30 pp.) and SASE." Accepts queries by e-mail. "Only short queries, no attachments." Considers simultaneous queries and submissions. Responds in 3 weeks to queries; 6 weeks to mss. Returns materials only with SASE.

Recent Sales: Sold 14 titles in the last year. *The Amazon.com Way*, by Robert Spector (HarperCollins); *The Kid*, by Dan Savage (Dutton); *Memoir of My Life with Animals*, by Brenda Peterson (Norton); *Harvest Son*, by David Mascmoto (Norton).

Terms: Agent receives 15% commission on domestic sales. "We make all our income from commissions. We offer editorial help for some of our clients and help some clients with the development of a proposal, but we do not charge for these services. We do charge, after a sale, for express mail, manuscript photocopying costs, foreign postage and outside USA telephone costs."

Writers' Conferences: Pacific NW Writers Conference (Seattle, July).

Tips: "We are interested in published and not-yet-published writers. Especially encourages writers living in the Pacific Northwest, West Coast, Alaska and Pacific Rim countries."

ELLEN LEVINE LITERARY AGENCY, INC., 15 E. 26th St., Suite 1801, New York NY 10010. (212)889-0620. Fax: (212)725-4501. **Contact:** Ellen Levine. Estab. 1980. Member of AAR. Represents over 100 clients. 20% of clients are new/previously unpublished writers. Currently handles: 55% nonfiction books; 5% juvenile books; 40% fiction.

Member Agents: Elizabeth Kaplan, Diana Finch, Louise Quayle, James E. Rogers, Ellen Levine.

Represents: Nonfiction books, juvenile books, novels, short story collections. **Considers these nonfiction areas:** anthropology; biography; current affairs; health; history; memoirs; popular culture; psychology; science; women's issues/women's studies; books by journalists. **Considers these fiction areas:** literary; mystery; women's fiction; thrillers.

How to Contact: Query with SASE. Reports in 3 weeks to queries, if SASE provided; 6 weeks to mss, if submission requested.

Needs: Obtains new clients through recommendations from others.

Recent Sales: *The Day Diana Died*, by Christopher Andersen (William Morrow); *Maxing Out: Why Women Sabotage Their Financial Security*, by Colette Dowling (Little, Brown).

Terms: Agent receives 15% commission on domestic sales; 20% on foreign sales. Charges for overseas postage, photocopying, messenger fees, overseas telephone and fax, books ordered for use in rights submissions.
Tips: "My three younger colleagues at the agency (Louise Quayle, Diana Finch and Elizabeth Kaplan) are seeking both new and established writers. I prefer to work with established writers, mostly through referrals."

LOWENSTEIN ASSOCIATES, INC., 121 W. 27th St., Suite 601, New York NY 10001. (212)206-1630. Fax: (212)727-0280. President: Barbara Lowenstein. Estab. 1976. Member of AAR. Represents 150 clients. 20% of clients are new/unpublished writers. Specializes in multicultural books (fiction and nonfiction), medical experts, commercial fiction, especially suspense, crime and women's issues. "We are a full-service agency, handling domestic and foreign rights, film rights, and audio rights to all of our books." Currently handles: 60% nonfiction books; 40% novels.
Member Agents: Barbara Lowenstein (president); Nancy Yost (agent); Eileen Cope (agent); Melena Fancher (agent); Norman Kurz (business affairs).
Represents: Nonfiction books, novels. **Considers these nonfiction areas:** animals; anthropology/archaeology; biography/autobiography; business; child guidance/parenting; craft/hobbies; current affairs; education; ethnic/cultural interests; gay/lesbian issues; government/politics/law; health/medicine; history; how-to; humor; language/literature/criticism/; memoirs; money/finance/economics; music/dance/theater/film; nature/environment; New Age/metaphysics, popular culture; psychology; religious/inspirational; science/technology; self-help/personal improvement; sociology; sports; travel; true crime/investigative; women's issues/women's studies. **Considers these fiction areas:** contemporary issues; detective/police/crime; erotica; ethnic; feminist; gay; historical; lesbian; literary mainstream; mystery/suspense; romance (contemporary, historical, regency); medical thrillers.
How to Contact: Send query with SASE, "otherwise will not respond." For fiction, send outline and 1st chapter. No unsolicited mss. "Please do not send manuscripts." Prefers to be only reader. Reports in 6 weeks to queries. Returns materials only with SASE.
Needs: Obtains new clients through "referrals, journals and magazines, media, solicitations and a few conferences."
Recent Sales: Sold approximately 75 titles in the last year. *Getting Everything You Can out of All You've Got*, by Jay Abraham (St. Martin's); *Work As a Spiritual Practice*, by Lewis Richmond (Broadway); *Acts of Malice*, by Perri O'Shaughnessy (Delacorte). Other clients include Gina Barkhordar Nahai, Ishmael Reed, Michael Waldholz, Myrlie Evers Williams, Barry Yourgrau, Deborah Crombie, Jan Burke and Leslie Glass.
Terms: Agent receives 15% commission on domestic sales; 20% on foreign sales; 20% on dramatic sales. Offers written contract on a book-by-book basis. Charges for large photocopy batches and international postage.
Writer's Conference: Malice Domestic; Bouchercon.
Tips: "Know the genre you are working in and READ!"

CAROL MANN AGENCY, 55 Fifth Ave., New York NY 10003. (212)206-5635. Fax: (212)675-4809. E-mail: cmlass @aol.com. **Contact:** Carol Mann. Estab. 1977. Member of AAR. Represents over 100 clients. 25% of clients are new/ previously unpublished writers. Specializes in current affairs; self-help; psychology; parenting; history. Currently handles: 70% nonfiction books; 30% novels.
Member Agents: Ms. Gareth Esersky (contemporary nonfiction); Jim Fitzgerald (literary, cinematic, Internet projects).
Represents: Nonfiction books. **Considers these nonfiction areas:** anthropology/archaeology; art/architecture/design; biography/autobiography; business; child guidance/parenting; current affairs; ethnic/cultural interests; government/politics/law; health/medicine; history; money/finance/economics; psychology; self-help/personal improvement; sociology; women's issues/women's studies. **Considers literary fiction.**
How to Contact: Query with outline/proposal and SASE. Responds in 3 weeks to queries.
Needs: Actively seeking "nonfiction: pop culture, business and health; fiction: literary fiction." Does not want to receive "genre fiction (romance, mystery, etc.)."
Recent Sales: *Radical Healing*, by Rudolph Ballentine, M.D. (Harmony); *Timbuktu*, by Paul Auster (Holt); *Stopping Cancer Before It Starts*, by American Institute for Cancer Research (Golden). Other clients include Dr. William Julius Wilson, Barry Sears (*Mastering The Zone*), Dr. Judith Wallerstein, Lorraine Johnson-Coleman (*Just Plain Folks*), Pulitzer Prize Winner Fox Butterfield and James Tobin, NBCC Award Winner for *Ernie Pyle* (Free Press).
Terms: Agent receives 15% commission on domestic sales; 20% on foreign sales. Offers written contract.
Tips: "No phone queries. Must include SASE for reply."

MANUS & ASSOCIATES LITERARY AGENCY, INC., 375 Forest Ave., Palo Alto CA 94301. (650)470-5151. Fax: (650)470-5159. E-mail: manuslit@manuslit.com. Website: www.manuslit.com. **Contact:** Jillian Manus. Also: 417 E. 57th St., Suite 5D, New York NY 10022. (212)644-8020. Fax: (212)644-3374. **Contact:** Janet Manus. Estab. 1985. Member of AAR. Represents 75 clients. 30% of clients are new/previously unpublished writers. Specializes in commercial literary fiction, narrative nonfiction, thrillers, health, pop psychology, women's empowerment. "Our agency is unique in the way that we not only sell the material, but we edit, develop concepts and participate in the marketing effort. We specialize in large, conceptual fiction and nonfiction, and always value a project that can be sold in the TV/ feature film market." Currently handles: 55% nonfiction books; 5% juvenile books; 40% novels.
● Prior to becoming agents, Jillian Manus was associate publisher of two national magazines and director of development at Warner Bros. and Universal Studios; Janet Manus has been a literary agent for 20 years.

Member Agents: Jandy Nelson (self-help, health, memoirs, narrative nonfiction, literary fiction, multicultural fiction, thrillers); Jill Maverick (self-help, health, memoirs, dramatic nonfiction, women's fiction, commercial literary fiction, Southern writing, thrillers); Stephanie Lee (self-help, memoirs, dramatic nonfiction, commercial literary fiction, multicultural fiction, quirky/edgy fiction).

Represents: Nonfiction books, novels. **Considers these nonfiction areas**: biography/autobiography; business; child guidance/parenting; computers/electronics; current affairs; ethnic/cultural interests; health/medicine; how-to; memoirs; money/finance/economics; nature/environment; popular culture; psychology; science/technology; self-help/personal improvement; women's issues/women's studies; dramatic/narrative nonfiction; Gen X and Gen Y issues. **Considers these fiction areas**: literary; thriller/espionage; women's fiction; commercial literary fiction; multicultural fiction; Southern fiction; quirky/edgy fiction.

How to Contact: Query with SASE. Accepts queries by fax and e-mail. If requested, send outline and 2-3 sample chapters. Considers simultaneous queries and submissions. Responds in 2 months to queries; 6 weeks to mss. Returns materials only with SASE.

Needs: Actively seeking high-concept thrillers, commercial literary fiction, women's fiction, celebrity biographies, memoirs, multicultural fiction, popular health, women's empowerment. Does not want to receive horror, science fiction/fantasy, romance, westerns, young adult, children's, poetry, cookbooks, magazine articles. Usually obtains new clients through recommendations from editors, clients and others; conferences; and unsolicited materials.

Recent Sales: *Catfish & Mandala*, by Andrew X. Pham (Farrar, Straus & Giroux); *Jake & Mimi*, by Frank Baldwin (Little, Brown); *Wishing Well*, by Paul Pearsall, Ph.D. (Hyperion); *Balancing the Equation*, by Dr. Lorraine Zappart (Pocket Books/Simon & Schuster). Other clients include Marcus Allen, Carlton Stowers, Alan Jacobson, Ann Brandt, Dr. Richard Marrs, Mary Loverde, Lisa Huang Fleishman, Judy Carter, Daryl Ott Underhill, Glen Klein.

Terms: Agent receives 15% commission on domestic sales; 20-25% on foreign sales. Offers written contract, binding for 2 years. 60 days notice must be given to terminate contract. Charges for copying and postage.

Writer's Conferences: Maui Writers Conference (Maui HI, Labor Day); San Diego Writer's Conference (San Diego CA, January); Willamette Writers Conference (Willamette OR, July).

Tips: "Research agents using a variety of sources, including *LMP*, guides, *Publishers Weekly*, conferences and even acknowledgements in books similar in tone to yours."

ELAINE MARKSON LITERARY AGENCY, 44 Greenwich Ave., New York NY 10011. (212)243-8480. Fax: (212)691-9014. Estab. 1972. Member of AAR and WGA. Represents 200 clients. 10% of clients are new/unpublished writers. Specializes in literary fiction, commercial fiction, trade nonfiction. Currently handles: 35% nonfiction books; 55% novels; 10% juvenile books.

Member Agents: Geri Thoma, Sally Wofford-Girand, Elizabeth Sheinkman, Elaine Markson.

Represents: Quality fiction and nonfiction.

How to Contact: Obtains new clients by recommendation only.

Recent Sales: *The First Horseman*, by John Case (Ballantine); *Life, the Movie*, by Neal Gabler (Knopf); *The Hidden Jesus*, by Donald Spoto (St. Martins).

Terms: Agent receives 15% commission on domestic sales; 20% on foreign sales. Charges for postage, photocopying, foreign mailing, faxing, and other special expenses.

MARGRET McBRIDE LITERARY AGENCY, 7744 Fay Ave., Suite 201, La Jolla CA 92037. (858)454-1550. Fax: (858)454-2156. Estab. 1980. Member of AAR, Authors Guild. Represents 50 clients. 15% of clients are new/unpublished writers. Specializes in mainstream fiction and nonfiction.

 ● Prior to opening her agency, Ms. McBride served in the marketing departments of Random House and Ballantine Books and the publicity departments of Warner Books and Pinnacle Books.

Represents: Nonfiction books, novels, audio, video film rights. **Considers these nonfiction areas:** biography/autobiography; business; child guidance/parenting; cooking/food/nutrition; current affairs; ethnic/cultural interests; gay/lesbian issues; government/politics/law; health/medicine; history; how-to; money/finance/economics; music/dance/theater/film; popular culture; psychology; religious/inspirational; science/technology; self-help/personal improvement; sociology; sports; true crime/investigative; women's issues/women's studies. **Considers these fiction areas:** action/adventure; detective/police/crime; ethnic; historical; humor; literary; mainstream; mystery/suspense; thriller/espionage; westerns/frontier.

How to Contact: Query with synopsis or outline. Considers simultaneous queries. *No unsolicited mss.* Responds in 6 weeks to queries. Returns materials only with SASE.

Needs: Does not want to receive screenplays.

Recent Sales: Sold 20 titles in the last year. *Special Circumstances*, by Sheldon Siegel (Bantam); *Instant Emotional Healing*, by George Pratt Ph.D. and Peter Lambrou Ph.D. (Broadway); *Leadership by the Book*, by Ken Blanchard (Morrow).

Terms: Agent receives 15% commission on domestic sales; 10% on dramatic sales; 25% on foreign sales charges for overnight delivery and photocopying.

⟦N⟧ WILLIAM MORRIS AGENCY, INC., 1325 Ave. of the Americas, New York NY 10019. (212)586-5100. West Coast Office: 151 El Camino Dr., Beverly Hills CA 90212. **Contact:** Mel Berger, vice president. Member of AAR.

Member Agents: Owen Laster; Robert Gottlieb; Mel Berger; Matt Bialer; Claudia Cross; Joni Evans; Tracy Fisher; Marcy Posner; Dan Strone; George Lane; Bill Conrad; Peter Franklin; Samuel Liff; Gilbert Parker.

Represents: Nonfiction books, novels.

How to Contact: Query with SASE. Does not accept queries by fax or e-mail.

Recent Sales: Prefers not to share information on specific sales.

Terms: Agent receives 10% commission on domestic sales; 20% on foreign sales.

[N] HENRY MORRISON, INC., 105 S. Bedford Rd., Suite 306A, Mt. Kisco NY 10549. (914)666-3500. Fax: (914)241-7846. **Contact:** Henry Morrison. Estab. 1965. Signatory of WGA. Represents 48 clients. 5% of clients are new/previously unpublished writers. Currently handles: 5% nonfiction books; 5% juvenile books; 85% novels; 5% movie scripts.

Represents: Nonfiction books, novels. **Considers these nonfiction areas:** anthropology/archaeology; biography; government/politics/law; history; juvenile nonfiction. **Considers these fiction areas:** action/adventure; detective/police/crime; family saga.

How to Contact: Query. Responds in 2 weeks to queries; 3 months to mss.

Needs: Obtains new clients through recommendations from others.

Recent Sales: Sold 10 titles in the last year. *Untitled*, by Robert Ludlum (St. Martin's); *The Pearl*, by Eric Lustbader (TOR); *Burnt Sienna*, by David Morrell (Warner Books); *Rock & Scissors*, by Steve Samuel (Simon & Schuster). Other clients include Joe Gores, Samuel R. Delany, Beverly Byrnne, Patricia Keneally-Morrison and Molly Katz.

Terms: Agent receives 15% commission on domestic sales; 25% on foreign sales. Charges for ms copies, bound galleys and finished books for submission to publishers, movie producers, foreign publishers.

[N] JEAN V. NAGGAR LITERARY AGENCY, 216 E. 75th St., Suite 1E, New York NY 10021. (212)794-1082. **Contact:** Jean Naggar. Estab. 1978. Member of AAR, Women's Media Group and Women's Forum. Represents 100 clients. 20% of clients are new/previously unpublished writers. Specializes in mainstream fiction and nonfiction, literary fiction with commercial potential. Currently handles: 35% general nonfiction books; 5% scholarly books; 15% juvenile books; 45% novels.

Member Agents: Frances Kuffel (literary fiction and nonfiction, New Age); Alice Tasman (spiritual/New Age, medical thrillers, commercial/literary fiction); Anne Engel (academic-based nonfiction for general readership).

Represents: Nonfiction books, novels. **Considers these nonfiction areas among others:** biography/autobiography; child guidance/parenting; current affairs; government/politics/law; health/medicine; history; juvenile nonfiction; memoirs; New Age/metaphysics; psychology; religious/inspirational; self-help/personal improvement; sociology; travel; women's issues/women's studies. "We would, of course, consider a query regarding an exceptional mainstream manuscript touching on any area." **Considers these fiction areas:** action/adventure; contemporary issues; detective/police/crime; ethnic; family saga; feminist; historical; literary; mainstream; mystery/suspense; psychic/supernatural; thriller/espionage.

How to Contact: Query with SASE. Prefers to be only reader. Responds in 24 hours to queries; approximately 2 months to mss. Returns materials only with SASE.

Needs: Obtains new clients through recommendations from publishers, editors, clients and others, and from writers' conferences.

Recent Sales: *The Young Irelanders*, by Ann Moore (N.A.L.); *Empires of Sand*, by David Ball (Bantam); *Hotel Alleluja*, by Lucinda Roy (HarperCollins); *The Missing Moment*, by Robert Pollack (Houghton Mifflin); *Fiona Range*, by Mary McGarry Morris (Viking-Penguin); *La Cucina*, by Lily Prior (HarperCollins).

Terms: Agent receives 15% commission on domestic sales; 20% on foreign sales. Offers written contract. Charges for overseas mailing; messenger services; book purchases; long-distance telephone; photocopying. "These are deductible from royalties received."

Writers' Conferences: Willamette Writers Conference; Pacific Northwest Writers Conference; Breadloaf Writers Conference; Virginia Women's Press Conference (Richmond VA), Marymount Manhattan Writers Conference.

Tips: "Use a professional presentation. Because of the avalanche of unsolicited queries that flood the agency every week, we have had to modify our policy. We will now only guarantee to read and respond to queries from writers who come recommended by someone we know. Our areas are general fiction and nonfiction, no children's books by unpublished writers, no multimedia, no screenplays, no formula fiction, no mysteries by unpublished writers."

[N] NATIONAL WRITERS LITERARY AGENCY, a division of NWA, 3140 S. Peoria #295, Aurora CO 80014. (303)751-7844. Fax: (303)751-8593. E-mail: aajwiii@aol.com. **Contact:** Andrew J. Whelchel III. Estab. 1987. Represents 52 clients. 20% of clients are new/previously unpublished writers. Currently handles: 60% nonfiction books; 20% juvenile books; 12% novels; 1% novellas; 1% poetry; 6% scripts.

Member Agents: Andrew J. Whelchel III (screenplays, nonfiction); Jason S. Cangialosi (nonfiction); Shayne Sharpe (novels, screenplays, fantasy).

Represents: Nonfiction books, juvenile books, textbooks. **Considers these nonfiction areas:** animals; biography/autobiography; child guidance/parenting; education; government/politics/law; how-to; juvenile nonfiction; popular culture; science/technology; sports; travel. **Considers these fiction areas:** action/adventure; juvenile; mainstream; picture book; science fiction; sports; young adult.

How to Contact: Query with outline. Accepts queries by e-mail. Considers simultaneous queries. Responds in 2 weeks to queries; 2 months to mss. Returns materials only with SASE.

Needs: Actively seeking "music, business, cutting edge novels, pop culture, compelling true stories, science and technology." Does not want to receive "concept books, westerns, over published self-help topics." Obtains new clients at conferences or over the transom.

Recent Sales: Sold 12 titles in the last year. *Escapade*, by Natalie Cosby (Orly Adelson Productions); *Love One Another* (3 book series), by Gloria Chisholm (Waterbrook Press/Random House).

Terms: Agent receives 15% commission on domestic sales; 20% on foreign sales; 10% on film. Offers written contract, binding for 1 year with 30-day termination notice.

Writers' Conferences: National Writers Association (Denver, CO, 2nd weekend in June); Sandpiper (Miami, FL, 1st weekend in October).

Reading List: Reads *Popular Mechanics*, *The Futurist*, *Industry Standard*, *Money*, *Rolling Stone*, *Maxim*, *Details*, *Spin* and *Buzz* to find new clients.

Tips: "Query letters should include a great hook just as if you only had a few seconds to impress us. A professional package gets professional attention. Always include return postage!"

NEW ENGLAND PUBLISHING ASSOCIATES, INC., P.O. Box 5, Chester CT 06412-0645. (203)345-READ and (203)345-4976. Fax: (203)345-3660. E-mail: nepa@nepa.com. Website: www.pcnet.nepa.com/~nepa. **Contact:** Elizabeth Frost-Knappman, Edward W. Knappman, Kristine Sciavi, Ron Formica, or Victoria Harlow. Estab. 1983. Member of AAR, ASJA, Authors Guild, Connecticut Press Club. Represents over 100 clients. 15% of clients are new/previously unpublished writers. Specializes in adult nonfiction books of serious purpose.

Represents: Nonfiction books. **Considers these nonfiction areas:** biography/autobiography; business; child guidance/parenting; government/politics/law; health/medicine; history; language/literature/criticism; military/war; money/finance/economics; nature/environment; psychology; science/technology; personal improvement; sociology; true crime/investigative; women's issues/women's studies. **"Occasionally considers crime fiction."**

How to Contact: Send outline/proposal with SASE. Considers simultaneous queries. Responds in 3 weeks to queries; 5 weeks to mss. Returns materials only with SASE.

Recent Sales: Sold 50 titles in the last year. *The Woman's Migraine Survival Handbook*, by Christina Peterson and Christine Adamec (HarperCollins); *Dreams in the Key of Blue, A Novel*, by John Philpin (Bantam); *Ice Blink: The Mysterious Fate of Sir John Franklin's Lost Polar Expedition*, by Scott Cookman (Wiley); *Susan Sontag*, by Carl Rollyson and Lisa Paddock (Norton).

Terms: Agent receives 15% commission on domestic sales; 20% foreign sales (split with overseas agent). Offers written contract, binding for 6 months.

Writers' Conferences: BEA (Chicago, June); ALA (San Antonio, January); ALA (New York, July).

Tips: "Send us a well-written proposal that clearly identifies your audience—who will buy this book and why."

PINDER LANE & GARON-BROOKE ASSOCIATES, LTD., 159 W. 53rd St., Suite 14E, New York NY 10019-6005. (212)489-0880. **Contact:** Robert Thixton, vice president. Member of AAR, signatory of WGA. Represents 80 clients. 20% of clients are new/previously unpublished writers. Specializes in mainstream fiction and nonfiction. Currently handles: 25% nonfiction books; 75% novels.

Member Agents: Nancy Coffey, Dick Duane, Robert Thixton.

Represents: Nonfiction books, novels. **Considers these nonfiction areas:** biography/autobiography; child guidance/parenting; gay/lesbian issues; health/medicine; history; memoirs; military/war; music/dance/theater/film; psychology; self-help/personal improvement; true crime/investigative. **Considers these fiction areas:** contemporary issues; detective/police/crime; family saga; fantasy; gay; literary; mainstream; mystery/suspense; romance; science fiction.

How to Contact: Query with SASE. Responds in 3 weeks to queries; 2 months to mss.

Needs: Does not want to receive screenplays, TV series teleplays or dramatic plays. Obtains new clients through referrals and from queries.

Recent Sales: Sold 15 titles in the last year. *Nobody's Safe*, by Richard Steinberg (Doubleday); *The Kill Box*, by Chris Stewart (M. Evans); *Return to Christmas*, by Chris Heimerdinger (Ballantine).

Terms: Agent receives 15% on domestic sales; 30% on foreign sales. Offers written contract, binding for 3-5 years.

Tips: "With our literary and media experience, our agency is uniquely positioned for the current and future direction publishing is taking. Send query letter first giving the essence of the manuscript and a personal or career bio with SASE."

AARON M. PRIEST LITERARY AGENCY, 708 Third Ave., 23rd Floor, New York NY 10017. (212)818-0344. Fax: (212)573-9417. **Contact:** Aaron Priest or Molly Friedrich. Estab. 1974. Member of AAR. Currently handles: 25% nonfiction books; 75% fiction.

Member Agents: Lisa Erbach Vance, Paul Cirone.

Represents: Nonfiction books, fiction.

How to Contact: Query only (must be accompanied by SASE). Unsolicited mss will be returned unread.

Recent Sales: *Absolute Power*, by David Baldacci (Warner); *Three To Get Deadly*, by Janet Evanovich (Scribner); *How Stella Got Her Groove Back*, by Terry McMillan (Viking); *Day After Tomorrow*, by Allan Folsom (Little, Brown); *Angela's Ashes*, by Frank McCourt (Scribner); *M as in Malice*, by Sue Grafton (Henry Holt).

Terms: Agent receives 15% commission on domestic sales. Charges for photocopying, foreign postage expenses.

HELEN REES LITERARY AGENCY, 123 N. Washington St., 2nd Floor, Boston MA 02114. (617)723-5232, ext. 233 or 222. **Contact:** Joan Mazmanian. Estab. 1981. Member of AAR. Represents 50 clients. 50% of clients are new/ previously unpublished writers. Specializes in general nonfiction, health, business, world politics, autobiographies, psychology, women's issues. Currently handles: 60% nonfiction books; 40% novels.
Represents: Nonfiction books, novels. **Considers these nonfiction areas:** biography/autobiography; business; current affairs; government/politics/law; health/medicine; history; money/finance/economics; women's issues/women's studies. **Considers these fiction areas:** contemporary issues; historical; literary; mainstream; mystery/suspense; thriller/espionage.
How to Contact: Query with outline plus 2 sample chapters and SASE. Responds in 2 weeks to queries; 3 weeks to mss.
Needs: Obtains new clients through recommendations from others, solicitation, at conferences, etc.
Recent Sales: *The Mentor*, by Sebastian Stuart (Bantam); *Managing the Human Animal*, by Nigel Nicholson (Times Books); *Just Revenge*, by Alan Dershowitz (Warner).
Terms: Agent receives 15% commission on domestic sales; 20% on foreign sales.

[N] ANGELA RINALDI LITERARY AGENCY, P.O. Box 7877, Beverly Hills CA 90212-7877. (310)842-7665. Fax: (310)837-8143. E-mail: e2arinaldi@aol.com. **Contact:** Angela Rinaldi. Estab. 1994. Member of AAR. Represents 50 clients. Currently handles: 50% nonfiction books; 50% novels.
● Prior to opening her agency, Ms. Rinaldi was an editor at New American Library, Pocket Books and Bantam, and the manager of book development of *The Los Angeles Times*.
Represents: Nonfiction books, novels, TV and motion picture rights. **Considers these nonfiction areas:** biography/ autobiography; business; child guidance/parenting; food/nutrition; current affairs; health/medicine; money/finance/economics; popular culture; psychology; self-help/personal improvement; sociology; true crime/investigative; women's issues/women's studies. **Considers literary and commercial fiction.**
How to Contact: For fiction, send the first 100 pages and brief synopsis. For nonfiction, query first or send outline/ proposal, include SASE for both. Responds in 6 weeks. Accepts queries by e-mail. Considers simultaneous queries and submissions. "Please advise if this is a multiple submission to another agent." Returns materials only with SASE.
Needs: Actively seeking commercial and literary fiction. Does not want to receive scripts, category romances, children's books, westerns, science fiction/fantasy and cookbooks.
Recent Sales: *The Starlite Drive-In*, by Marjorie Reynolds (William Morrow & Co.); *Twins: Pregnancy, Birth and The First Year of Life*, by Agnew, Klein and Ganon (HarperCollins); *The Thyroid Solution*, by Dr. Ridha Arem; *Quiet Time*, by Stephanie Kane (Bantam).
Terms: Agent receives 15% commission on domestic sales; 20% on foreign sales. Offers written contract. Charges for photocopying ("if client doesn't supply copies for submissions"). 100% of business is derived from commissions on sales. Foreign, TV and motion picture rights for clients only.

[N] THE GAIL ROSS LITERARY AGENCY, 1666 Connecticut Ave. NW, #500, Washington DC 20009. (202)328-3282. Fax: (202)328-9162. **Contact:** Jennifer Manguera. Estab. 1988. Member of AAR. Represents 200 clients. 75% of clients are new/previously unpublished writers. Specializes in adult trade nonfiction. Currently handles: 90% nonfiction books; 10% novels.
Member Agent(s): Gail Ross (nonfiction).
Represents: Nonfiction books, novels. **Considers these nonfiction areas:** anthropology/archaeology; biography/autobiography; business; cooking/food/nutrition; education; ethnic/cultural interests; gay/lesbian issues; government/politics/ law; health/fitness; humor; money/finance/economics; nature/environment; psychology; religious/inspirational; science/ technology; self-help/personal improvement; sociology; sports; true crime/investigative. **Considers these fiction areas:** ethnic; feminist; gay; literary.
How to Contact: Query with SASE. Responds in 1 month.
Needs: Obtains new clients through referrals.
Recent Sales: Prefers not to share information on specific sales.
Terms: Agent receives 15% commission on domestic sales; 25% on foreign sales. Charges for office expenses (i.e., postage, copying).

THE DAMARIS ROWLAND AGENCY, 510 E. 23rd St., #8-G, New York NY 10010-5020. (212)475-8942. Fax: (212)358-9411. **Contact:** Damaris Rowland or Steve Axelrod. Estab. 1994. Member of AAR. Represents 50 clients. 10% of clients are new/previously unpublished writers. Specializes in women's fiction. Currently handles: 75% novels, 25% nonfiction.
Represents: Nonfiction books, novels. **Considers these nonfiction areas:** animals; cooking/food/nutrition; health/ medicine; nature/environment; New Age/metaphysics; religious/inspirational; women's issues/women's studies. **Considers these fiction areas:** detective/police/crime; historical; literary; mainstream; psychic/supernatural; romance (contemporary, gothic, historical, regency).
How to Contact: Send outline/proposal with SASE. Responds in 6 weeks.
Needs: Obtains new clients through recommendations from others, at conferences.
Recent Sales: *The Perfect Husband*, by Lisa Gardner (Bantam); *Soul Dating To Soul Mating, On The Path To Spiritual Partnership*, by Basha Kaplan and Gail Prince (Putnam Books); *My Dearest Enemy*, by Connie Brockway (Dell).

Terms: Agent receives 15% commission on domestic sales; 20% on foreign sales. Offers written contract, with 30 day cancellation clause. Charges only if extraordinary expenses have been incurred, e.g., photocopying and mailing 15 ms to Europe for a foreign sale. 100% of business is derived from commissions on sales.

Writers' Conferences: Novelists Inc. (Denver, October); RWA National (Texas, July), Pacific Northwest Writers Conference.

VICTORIA SANDERS & ASSOCIATES, 241 Avenue of the Americas, New York NY 10014-4822. (212)633-8811. Fax: (212)633-0525. **Contact:** Victoria Sanders and/or Diane Dickensheid. Estab. 1993. Member of AAR, signatory of WGA. Represents 75 clients. 25% of clients are new/previously unpublished writers. Currently handles: 50% nonfiction books; 50% novels.

Represents: Nonfiction, novels. **Considers these nonfiction areas:** biography/autobiography; current affairs; ethnic/cultural interests; gay/lesbian issues; govenment/politics/law; history; humor; language/literature/criticism; music/dance/theater/film; popular culture; psychology; translations; women's issues/women's studies. **Considers these fiction areas:** action/adventure; contemporary issues; ethnic; family saga; feminist; gay; lesbian; literary; thriller/espionage.

How to Contact: Query with SASE. Considers simultaneous queries. Responds in 1 week to queries; 1 month to mss. Returns materials only with SASE.

Needs: Obtains new clients through recommendations, "or I find them through my reading and pursue."

Recent Sales: Sold 15 titles in the last year. *Blindsighted*, by Karin Slaughter (Morrow); *Redemption Song*, by Dr. Bertice Berry (Doubleday).

Terms: Agent receives 15% commission on domestic sales; 20% on foreign sales. Offers written contract binding at will. Charges for photocopying, ms, messenger, express mail and extraordinary fees. If in excess of $100, client approval is required.

Tips: "Limit query to letter, no calls, and give it your best shot. A good query is going to get a good response."

WENDY SHERMAN ASSOCIATES, INC., 450 Seventh Ave., Suite 3004, New York NY 10123. (212)279-9027. Fax: (212)279-8863. E-mail: wendy@wsherman.com. **Contact:** Wendy Sherman. Estab. 1999. Represents 20 clients. 30% of clients are new/unpublished writers. "We specialize in developing new writers as well as working with more established writers. My experience as a publisher is a great asset to my clients." Currently handles: 50% nonfiction books; 50% novels.

● Prior to becoming an agent, Ms. Sherman worked for Aaron Priest agency and was vice president, executive director of Henry Holt, associate publisher, subsidiary rights director, sales and marketing director.

Member Agents: Jessica Litchenstein (mystery and romance); Wendy Sherman.

Represents: Nonfiction books, novels. **Considers these nonfiction areas:** biography/autobiography; child guidance/parenting; ethnic/cultural interests; memoirs; psychology; self-help/personal improvement; true crime/investigative. **Considers these fiction areas:** contemporary issues; mainstream; mystery/suspense; romance; thriller/espionage.

How to Contact: Query with SASE or send outline/proposal and 1 sample chapter. Accepts queries by e-mail. Responds in 1 month to queries; 6 weeks to mss. Returns unwanted material only with SASE.

Needs: Obtains most new clients through referrals from clients, writers, editors.

Recent Sales: Sold 8 titles in the last year. *The Judgement*, by D.W. Buffa (Warner Books); *Rescuing Jeffrey*, by Richard Galli (Algonquin); *These Granite Islands*, by Sarah Stouich (Little Brown); *Mad Dog in the Jungle*, by Alan Eisenstock (Pocket Books). Other clients include Howard Bahr, George Quesnelle, Lundy Bancroft, Lise Friedman, Tom Schweich.

Terms: Agent receives 15% commission on domestic sales; 20% on foreign sales. Offers written contract. Charges for photocopying of ms, messengers, FedEx, etc. (reasonable, standard expenses).

IRENE SKOLNICK LITERARY AGENCY, 22 W. 23rd St., 5th Floor, New York NY 10010. (212)727-3648. Fax: (212)727-1024. E-mail: sirene35@aol.com. **Contact:** Irene Skolnick. Estab. 1993. Member of AAR. Represents 45 clients. 75% of clients are new/previously unpublished writers.

Represents: Adult nonfiction books, adult fiction. **Considers these nonfiction areas:** biography/autobiography; current affairs. **Considers these fiction areas:** contemporary issues; historical; literary.

How to Contact: Query with SASE, outline and sample chapter. No unsolicited mss. Accepts queries by fax. Considers simultaneous queries and submissions. Responds in 1 month to queries. Returns materials only with SASE.

Recent Sales: Sold 15 titles in the last year. *An Equal Music*, by Vikram Seth; *Kaaterskill Falls*, by Allegra Goodman; *Taking Lives*, by Michael Pye.

Terms: Agent receives 15% commission on domestic sales; 20% on foreign sales. Sometimes offers criticism service. Charges for international postage, photocopying over 40 pages.

ROBIN STRAUS AGENCY, INC., 229 E. 79th St., New York NY 10021. (212)472-3282. Fax: (212)472-3833. E-mail: springbird@aol.com. **Contact:** Robin Straus. Estab. 1983. Member of AAR. Specializes in high-quality fiction and nonfiction for adults. Currently handles: 65% nonfiction books; 35% novels.

● Prior to becoming an agent, Robin Straus served as a subsidiary rights manager at Random House and Doubleday and worked in editorial at Little, Brown.

Represents: Nonfiction, novels. **Considers these nonfiction areas:** animals; anthropology/archaeology; art/architecture/design; biography/autobiography; child guidance/parenting; cooking/food/nutrition; current affairs; ethnic/cultural

Agent guides writers through publishing process

For the last several months, you've labored painstakingly on your novel—crafting characters who captivate and prose that dazzles. Or, maybe you've poured all your efforts into your nonfiction book, and now you're confident that it far surpasses any other like it on the market. Writing your masterpiece has taken an *unbelievable* amount of time. And if you have to wait another second before it's on the shelves, you just might burst.

But everything in publishing seems to move at a snail's pace. Everyone is telling you to be realistic, but you don't know what qualifies as reasonable and what doesn't. That's where having an agent comes in handy. Not only do agents have personal connections with editors to help sell your book faster, but they are also advantageous to any writer trying to navigate the rocky waters of publishing. "The more I can share with my clients," says literary agent Wendy Sherman, "the better equipped they are to understand the publishing process and have realistic expectations. That includes how the process works from the moment you send in a book to when it's actually published and thereafter. A lot of authors get frustrated because they feel left in the dark. I feel it's my job to be with them through the entire process."

Although Sherman is new to agenting, her twenty years of publishing experience—including time as publisher at Henry Holt & Company—puts her in an excellent position to help her clients understand this process. "I always knew I wanted to be an agent," says Sherman, "because it allows me to use my publishing knowledge directly for the benefit of the writer."

When the opportunity to join the Aaron M. Priest Literary Agency arose, Sherman says, "I could not imagine a better place to work. I learned everything I possibly could—the basics of who to deal with and how things are done, how to run an agency and what editors are acquiring what kinds of books. It was good to work with people who are so professional and so good at what they do."

Nevertheless, after nine months at Aaron Priest, Sherman decided to open her own agency. "It became increasingly clear to me that I wanted to work for myself and fully devote my time to my own clients." And that client list grew quickly. "Becoming an agent has been a smooth transition for me. I worked with several authors at Holt who didn't have agents and who were happy to come with me." Those include legal suspense writer D.W. Buffa, whose next novel, *The Judgment*, Sherman sold to Warner Books; and Howard Bahr, author of *The Black Flower* and *The Year of Jubilo*, both published by Henry Holt & Company, Inc.

Working with an agent whose background is in publishing helps speed up the process once an editor accepts a book. Sherman explains, "I've sat in hundreds of editorial board meetings and dozens of sales conferences and marketing meetings. I know what issues come up. I can anticipate them and present my material in a way that makes it easier for my books to be acquired. An editor falling in love with a project is only the first step; they still have to convince other people. It's my job to give editors the tools and the information to allow that next step to happen."

Nevertheless, part of knowing how a publishing company works is having a realistic understanding of its limits. "Authors need to learn what publishers can and can't do for them," says Sherman. "Publishers are incredibly overworked, and today, in many cases, authors have to do their own legwork to get their name out there. It's a collaborative effort."

There are even times when it's better to push the deadline for a book *back*—which can be difficult for an eager writer. Sherman encountered this situation when she sold *Rescuing Jeffery*, by Richard Galli, to Algonquin Books of Chapel Hill. "It's an incredible story about a father whose seventeen-year-old son is injured in a swimming pool accident. The book focuses on the ten days in the hospital after the accident when the father and family decide if they should allow the boy to live. The book was originally supposed to be published in March, but there was great interest from television and magazines who wanted to make the story a big event for Father's Day, so Algonquin pushed the publication back to June."

Sherman is also realistic when deciding who to take on as a client. "Obviously, I want to love the material and see that it has great potential to be sold. I look for writers who are substantive enough to have more than one book in them and who have a great story to tell— whether it's fiction or nonfiction."

An example of Sherman's dream client is novelist Sarah Stonich. "Everything attracted me to her book, *These Granite Islands*," she explains. "I fell in love with the manuscript instantly and was completely dazzled by her writing. While reading her manuscript, I found that I was pinching myself thinking I can't believe something this good has come my way so soon. We spent a lot of time on it—she is very hardworking. I was delighted with the response we got from publishers. Even the ones that didn't ultimately acquire the book loved it. It's been a dream from beginning to end. And now the book is one of Little, Brown's lead fall titles, and it's been sold to publishers around the world."

Sherman will read both nonfiction and fiction, but she says her tastes are varied. "My fiction tastes tend to be everywhere from upmarket quality fiction to somewhat literary to commercial. On the nonfiction side, I represent narrative nonfiction, memoir, and some broad self-help titles. I look for books that help you live your life better. I'm not looking for anything spiritual, and I'm not strong in the science fiction or horror genres."

Above all, Sherman looks for books she feels passionate enough about to back them every step of the way. And she looks for clients who understand the importance of this passion. "I was talking to a new client last week who said, 'I'm so glad I'm working with you because you really get my book.' When you write a book, you have a vision of what it is. What you want is an agent who reads it and says, 'Yes, I completely agree.' You want someone who has the same commitment and belief that you have."

—*Donya Dickerson*

interests; government/politics/law; health/medicine; history; language/literature/criticism; music/dance/theater/film; nature/environment; popular culture; psychology; science/technology; sociology; women's issues/women's studies. **Considers these fiction areas:** contemporary issues; family saga; historical; literary; mainstream; thriller/espionage.
How to Contact: Query with sample pages. "Will not download e-mail inquiries." SASE ("stamps, not metered postage") required for response and return of material submitted. Responds in 1 month to queries and mss.
Needs: Takes on very few new clients. Most new clients obtained through recommendations from others.
Recent Sales: Prefers not to share information on specific sales.
Terms: Agent receives 15% commission on domestic sales; 20% on foreign sales. Offers written contract when requested. Charges for "photocopying, UPS, messenger and foreign postage, etc. as incurred."

N: UNITED TRIBES, 240 W. 35th St., #500, New York NY 10001. (212)534-7646. E-mail: janguerth@aol.com. Website: www.unitedtribes.com. **Contact:** Jan-Erik Guerth. Estab. 1998. Represents 40 clients. 10% of clients are new/

unpublished writers. Specializes in the "Spirituality of Everyday Life" and ethnic, social, gender and cultural issues; comparative religions; self-help and wellness; science and arts; history and politics; nature and travel; and any fascinating future trends. Currently handles: 99% nonfiction books, 1% novels.

● Prior to becoming an agent, Mr. Guerth was a comedian, journalist, radio producer and film distributor.

Represents: Nonfiction books, novels. **Considers these nonfiction areas:** anthropology/archaeology; art/architecture/design; biography/autobiography; business; child guidance/parenting; cooking/food/nutrition; current affairs; education; ethnic/cultural interests; gay/lesbian issues; government/politics/law; health/medicine; history; how-to; language/literature/criticism; memoirs; money/finance/economics; music/dance/theater/film; nature/enviornment; popular culture; psychology; religious/inspirational; science/technology (popular); self-help/personal improvement; sociology; translations; women's issues/women's studies. **Considers these fiction areas:** ethnic; historical; religious/inspirational.

How to Contact: Send outline and 3 sample chapters with SASE, include résumé. Accepts queries by e-mail. Prefers to be only reader. Responds in 2 weeks to queries; 1 month to mss. Returns materials only with SASE.

Needs: Obtains new clients through recommendations from others, solicitations and conferences.

Recent Sales: Prefers not to share information on specific sales.

Terms: Agent receives 15% commission on domestic sales; 20% on foreign sales.

[N] SCOTT WAXMAN AGENCY, INC., 1650 Broadway, Suite 1011, New York NY 10019. (212)262-2388. Fax: (212)262-0119. E-mail: gracem@swagency.net. Website: www.swagency.net. **Contact:** Grace Madamba. Estab. 1997. Member of AAR. Represents 60 clients. 50% of clients are new/unpublished writers. Specializes in "both commercial fiction and nonfiction. We are particularly strong in the areas of crime fiction, sports and religion. Will look at literary fiction." Currently handles: 60% nonfiction books; 40% novels.

● Prior to opening his agency, Mr. Waxman was editor for five years at HarperCollins.

Member Agents: Scott Waxman (all categories of nonfiction, commercial fiction); Giles Anderson (literary fiction, commercial fiction).

Represents: Nonfiction books, novels. **Considers these nonfiction areas:** biography/autobiography; business; ethnic/cultural interests; health/medicine; history; money/finance/economics; popular crime; religious/inspirational; self-help/personal improvement; sports. **Considers these fiction areas:** action/adventure; ethnic; historical; literary; hard-boiled detective; religious/inspirational; romance (contemporary, historical); sports; suspense.

How to Contact: Query with SASE. Accepts queries by e-mail. Considers simultaneous queries. Responds in 2 weeks to queries; 6 weeks to mss. Discards unwanted or unsolicited mss. Returns materials only with SASE.

Needs: Actively seeking strong, high-concept commercial fiction, narrative nonfiction. Obtains new clients through recommendations, writers conferences, Internet, magazines.

Recent Sales: Sold 40 titles in the last year. *Mid-Life Irish*, by Frank Gannon (Wagner); *All Good Things*, by John Reed (Delacorte); *She Got Game*, by Cynthia Cooper (Warner Books); *Cinderella Story*, by Bill Murray (Doubleday).

Terms: Agent receives 15% commission on domestic sales; 20% on foreign sales. Offers written contract. 60 days notice must be given to terminate contract. Charges for photocopying, express mail, fax, international postage, book orders. Refers to editing services for clients only. 0% of business is derived from editing service.

Writers' Conferences: Celebration of Writing in the Low Country (Beaufort SC, August 6-9, 1999); Golden Triangle Writers Guild Conference (Beaumont TX, October 1999); FIU/Seaside Writers Conference (FL, October).

Reading List: Reads *Witness*, *Boulevard*, *Literal Latté*, *Mississippi Review*, *Zoetrope*, and many others to find new clients.

[N] WRITERS HOUSE, 21 W. 26th St., New York NY 10010. (212)685-2400. Fax: (212)685-1781. Estab. 1974. Member of AAR. Represents 280 clients. 50% of clients were new/unpublished writers. Specializes in all types of popular fiction and nonfiction. No scholarly, professional, poetry or screenplays. Currently handles: 25% nonfiction books; 35% juvenile books; 40% novels.

Member Agents: Albert Zuckerman (major novels, thrillers, women's fiction, important nonfiction); Amy Berkower (major juvenile authors, women's fiction, art and decorating, psychology); Merrilee Heifetz (quality children's fiction, science fiction and fantasy, popular culture, literary fiction); Susan Cohen (juvenile and young adult fiction and nonfiction, Judaism, women's issues); Susan Ginsburg (serious and popular fiction, true crime, narrative nonfiction, personality books, cookbooks); Fran Lebowitz (juvenile and young adult, popular culture); Michele Rubin (serious nonfiction); Karen Solem (contemporary and historical romance, women's fiction, narrative nonfiction, horse and animal books); Robin Rue (commercial fiction and nonfiction, YA fiction); Jennifer Lyons (literary, commercial fiction, international fiction, nonfiction and illustrated).

Represents: Nonfiction books, juvenile books, novels. **Considers these nonfiction areas:** animals; art/architecture/design; biography/autobiography; business; child guidance/parenting; cooking/food/nutrition; health/medicine; history; interior design/decorating; juvenile nonfiction; military/war; money/finance/economics; music/dance/theater/film; nature/environment; psychology; science/technology; self-help/personal improvement; true crime/investigative; women's issues/women's studies. **Considers any fiction area.** "Quality is everything."

FOR LISTINGS OF OVER 500 literary and script agents, consult the *Guide to Literary Agents*.

How to Contact: Query. Responds in 1 month to queries.
Needs: Obtains new clients through recommendations from others.
Recent Sales: *The New New Thing*, by Michael Lewis (Norton); *The First Victim*, by Ridley Pearson (Hyperion); *Into the Garden*, by V.C. Andrews (Pocket); *Fearless*, by Francine Pascal (Pocket).
Terms: Agent receives 15% commission on domestic sales; 20% on foreign sales. Offers written contract, binding for 1 year.
Tips: "Do not send manuscripts. Write a compelling letter. If you do, we'll ask to see your work."

SUSAN ZECKENDORF ASSOC. INC., 171 W. 57th St., New York NY 10019. (212)245-2928. **Contact:** Susan Zeckendorf. Estab. 1979. Member of AAR. Represents 15 clients. 25% of clients are new/previously unpublished writers. Currently handles: 50% nonfiction books; 50% fiction.
   • Prior to opening her agency, Ms. Zeckendorf was a counseling psychologist.
Represents: Nonfiction books, novels. **Considers these nonfiction areas:** art/architecture/design; biography/autobiography; child guidance/parenting; health/medicine; history; music/dance; psychology; science; sociology; women's issues/women's studies. **Considers these fiction areas:** contemporary issues; detective/police/crime; ethnic; family saga; glitz; historical; literary; mainstream; mystery/suspense; thriller/espionage.
How to Contact: Query with SASE. Considers simultaneous queries and submissions. Responds in 10 days to queries; 3 weeks to mss. Obtains new clients through recommendations, listings in writer's manuals. Returns materials only with SASE.
Needs: Actively seeking mysteries, literary fiction, mainstream fiction, thrillers, social history, parenting, classical music, biography. Does not want to receive science fiction, romance. "No children's books."
Recent Sales: Sold 6 titles in the last year. *The Four Hundred: New York in the Gilded Age*, by Jerry E. Patterson (Rizzoli); *The Power of Myth in Storytelling*, by James N. Frey (St. Martin's).
Terms: Agent receives 15% commission on domestic sales; 20% on foreign sales. Charges for photocopying, messenger services.
Writers' Conferences: Central Valley Writers Conference; the Tucson Publishers Association Conference; Writer's Connection; Frontiers in Writing Conference (Amarillo, TX); Golden Triangle Writers Conference (Beaumont TX); Oklahoma Festival of Books (Claremont OK); Mary Mount Writers Conference.
Tips: "We are a small agency giving lots of individual attention. We respond quickly to submissions."

SCRIPT AGENTS

N **BERMAN BOALS AND FLYNN INC.**, 208 W. 30th St., #401, New York NY 10001. (212)868-1068. **Contact:** Judy Boals or Jim Flynn. Estab. 1972. Member of AAR, Signatory of WGA. Represents about 35 clients. Specializes in dramatic writing for stage, film, TV.
Represents: Feature film, TV scripts, stage plays.
How to Contact: Query with SASE.
Needs: Obtains new clients through recommendations from others.
Recent Sales: Prefers not to share information on specific sales.
Terms: Agent receives 10% commission.

THE MARSHALL CAMERON AGENCY, 19667 NE 20th Lane, Lawtey FL 32058. Phone/fax: (904)964-7013. E-mail: marshall_cameron@hotmail.com. **Contact:** Margo Prescott. Estab. 1986. Signatory of WGA. Specializes in feature films. Currently handles: 100% movie scripts.
Member Agents: Margo Prescott; Ashton Prescott; John Pizzo (New York co-agent).
Represents: Feature film. **Considers these script subject areas:** action/adventure; comedy; detective/police/crime; drama (contemporary); mainstream; thriller/espionage.
How to Contact: Query by letter with SASE or by e-mail. No phone queries. Accepts queries by e-mail. Considers simultaneous queries. Responds in 1 week to queries; 2 months to mss. Returns materials only with SASE.
Recent Sales: Prefers not to share information on specific sales.
Terms: Agent receives 10% commission on domestic sales; 20% on foreign sales. Offers written contract, binding for 1 year.
Tips: "Often professionals in film will recommend us to clients. We also actively solicit material. Always enclose SASE with your query."

N **CIRCLE OF CONFUSION LTD.**, 666 Fifth Ave., Suite 303, New York NY 10103. (212)969-0653. Fax: (718)997-0521. E-mail: circleltd@aol.com. **Contact:** Rajeev K. Agarwal, Lawrence Mattis. Estab. 1990. Signatory of WGA. Represents 25 clients. 60% of clients are new/previously unpublished writers. Specializes in screenplays for film and TV. Currently handles: 5% novels; 5% novellas; 90% movie scripts.
Member Agents: Rajeev Agarwal; Lawrence Mattis; Annmarie Negretti; John Sherman.
Represents: Feature film. **Considers all script subject areas.**
Also Handles: Nonfiction books, novels, novellas, short story collections. **Considers all nonfiction and fiction areas.**
How to Contact: Query with SASE. Responds in 1 month to queries; 2 months to mss.
Needs: Obtains new clients through queries, recommendations and writing contests.

Recent Sales: *Movie/TV MOW scripts optioned/sold: The Matrix*, by Wachowski Brothers (Warner Brothers); *Ghosts of October*, by Chabot/Peterka (Dreamworks); *Blood of the Gods*, by Jaswinski (Warner Brothers); *Droid*, by Massa (Warner Brothers).
Terms: Agent receives 10% commission on domestic sales; 10% on foreign sales. Offers written contract, binding for 1 year.
Tips: "We look for screenplays and other material for film and television."

DOUROUX & CO., 445 S. Beverly Dr., Suite 310, Beverly Hills CA 90212-4401. (310)552-0900. Fax: (310)552-0920. E-mail: douroux@relaypoint.net. Website: www.relaypoint.net/~douroux. **Contact:** Michael E. Douroux. Estab. 1985. Signatory of WGA, member of DGA. 20% of clients are new/previously unpublished writers. Currently handles: 50% movie scripts; 50% TV scripts.
Member Agents: Michael E. Douroux (chairman/CEO).
Represents: Movie scripts, feature film, TV scripts, TV MOW, episodic drama, sitcom, animation. **Considers these script subject areas:** action/adventure; comedy; detective/police/crime; family saga; fantasy; historical; mainstream; mystery/suspense; romantic comedy and drama; science fiction; thriller/espionage; westerns/frontier.
How to Contact: Query with SASE.
Recent Sales: Prefers not to share information on specific sales.
Terms: Agent receives 10% commission. Offers written contract, binding for 2 years. Charges for photocopying only.

THE BARRY FREED CO., 2040 Ave. of the Stars, #400, Los Angeles CA 90067. (310)277-1260. Fax: (310)277-3865. E-mail: blfreed@aol.com. **Contact:** Barry Freed. Signatory of WGA. Represents 15 clients. 95% of clients are new/unpublished writers. Currently represents: 100% movie scripts.
• Prior to opening his agency, Mr. Freed worked for ICM.
Represents: Feature film, TV MOW. **Considers these script subject areas:** action/adventure; comedy; contemporary issues; detective/police/crime; ethnic; family saga; horror; mainstream; mystery/suspense; science fiction; sports; teen; thriller/espionage.
How to Contact: Query with SASE. Responds immediately to queries; in 3 moths tn mss.
Needs: Actively seeking adult drama, comedy, romantic comedy, science fiction. Does not want to receive period, westerns. Obtains new clients through recommendations from others.
Recent Sales: Prefers not to share information on specific sales.
Terms: Offers written contract binding for 2 years.
Tips: "Our clients are a highly qualified small roster of writers who write comedy, action adventure/thrillers, adult drama, romantic comedy."

SAMUEL FRENCH, INC., 45 W. 25th St., New York NY 10010-2751. (212)206-8990. Fax: (212)206-1429. **Contact:** Lawrence Harbison, editors. Estab. 1830. Member of AAR. Represents plays which it publishes for production rights.
Member Agents: Brad Lohrenz; Alleen Hussung; Linda Kirkland; Charles R. Van Nostrand.
Represents: Theatrical stage play, musicals, variety show. **Considers these script subject areas:** comedy; contemporary issues; detective/police/crime; ethnic; experimental; fantasy; horror; mystery/suspense; religious/inspirational; thriller.
How to Contact: Query or send entire ms. Replies "immediately" on queries; decision in 2-8 months regarding publication. "Enclose SASE."
Recent Sales: Prefers not to share information on specific sales.
Terms: Agent usually receives 10% professional production royalties; variable amateur production royalties.

:N: CAROLYN HODGES AGENCY, 1980 Glenwood Dr., Boulder CO 80304-2329. (303)443-4636. Fax: (303)443-4636. E-mail: hodgesc@earthlink.net. **Contact:** Carolyn Hodges. Estab. 1989. Signatory of WGA. Represents 15 clients. 90% of clients are new/previously unpublished writers. Represents only screenwriters for film and TV MOW. Currently handles: 15% movie scripts; 45% TV scripts.
• Prior to opening her agency, Ms. Hodges was a freelance writer and founded the Writers in the Rockies Screenwriting Conference.
Represents: Movie scripts, feature film, TV scripts, TV MOW. **Considers these script subject areas:** action/adventure; comedy; contemporary issues; erotica; experimental; horror; mainstream; mystery/suspense; psychic/supernatural; romance (comedy, drama).
How to Contact: Query with 1-page synopsis and SASE. Accepts queries by fax or e-mail. Considers simultaneous queries and submissions. Responds in 1 week to queries; 10 weeks to mss. "Please, no queries by phone." Returns materials only with SASE.
Needs: Obtains new clients by referral only.
Recent Sales: Sold 3 projects in the last year. *Fantasy Land*, by Robert Lilly (Gallus Enterprises); *Ribit*, by Janie Norris (K. Peterson); *Two Hour Layover*, by Steven Blake (River Road Enterprises).
Terms: Agent receives 10% on domestic sales; foreign sales "depend on each individual negotiation." Offers written contract, standard WGA. No charge for criticism. "I always try to offer concrete feedback, even when rejecting a piece of material." Charges for postage. "Sometimes we request reimbursement for long-distance phone and fax charges."
Writers' Conferences: Director and founder of Writers in the Rockies Film Screenwriting Conference (Boulder CO, August).

Tips: "Become proficient at your craft. Attend all workshops accessible to you. READ all the books applicable to your area of interest. READ as many 'produced' screenplays as possible. Live a full, vital and rewarding life so your writing will have something to say. Get involved in a writer's support group. Network with other writers. Receive 'critiques' from your peers and consider merit of suggestions. Don't be afraid to re-examine your perspective."

N: HUDSON AGENCY, 3 Travis Lane, Montrose NY 10548. (914)737-1475. Fax: (914)736-3064. E-mail: hudagency@juno.com. **Contact:** Susan or Pat Giordano. Estab. 1994. Signatory of WGA. Represents 30 clients. 50% of clients are new/previously unpublished writers. Specializes in feature film and TV. Also specializes in animation writers. Currently handles: 50% movie scripts; 50% TV scripts and TV animation.
Member Agents: Sue Giordano (TV animation); Michele Perri (books); Cheri Santone (features and animation); Sunny Bik (Canada contact).
Represents: Feature film, documentary, animation, TV MOW, miniseries, sitcom; PG or PG-13 only. **Considers these script subject areas:** action/adventure; cartoon/animation; comedy; contemporary issues; detective/police/crime; family saga; fantasy; juvenile; mystery/suspense; romantic comedy and drama; teen; westerns/frontier.
How to Contact: Send outline and sample pages with SASE. Accepts queries by fax or e-mail. Responds in 1 week to queries; 3 weeks to mss. Returns material only with SASE.
Needs: Actively seeking "writers with television and screenwriting education or workshops under their belts." Does not want to receive "R-rated material, no occult, no one that hasn't taken at least one screenwriting workshop." Obtains new clients through recommendations from others and listing on WGA agency list.
Recent Sales: Prefers not to share information on specific sales.
Terms: Agent receives 10% commission on domestic sales; 10% on foreign sales.
Tips: "Yes, we may be small, but we work very hard for our clients. Any script we are representing gets excellent exposure to producers. Our network has over 1,000 contacts in the business and growing rapidly. We are GOOD salespeople. Ultimately it all depends on the quality of the writing and the market for the subject matter. Do not query unless you have taken at least one screenwriting course and read all of Syd Field's books."

N: LARCHMONT LITERARY AGENCY, 444 N. Larchmont Blvd., Suite 200, Los Angeles CA 90004. (323)856-3070. Fax: (323)856-3071. E-mail: agent@larchmontlit.com. **Contact:** Joel Millner. Estab. 1998. Signatory of WGA, member of DGA. Specializes in feature writers and feature writer/directors. "We maintain a small, highly selective client list and offer a long-term career management style of agenting that larger agencies can't provide." Currently handles: 5% novels, 90% movie scripts, 5% cable or TV films.
 • Prior to becomning an agent, Mr. Millner attended NYU Film School and participated in The William Morris agent training program.
Represents: Movie scripts, feature film, novels. **Considers these script subject areas:** action/adventure; biography/autobiography; animation; comedy; contemporary issues; detective/police/crime; fantasy; historical; horror; mainstream; mystery/suspense; psychic/supernatural; romantic comedy; romantic drama; science fiction; sports; thriller/espionage.
Also Handles: Considers these fiction areas: action/adventure; contemporary issues; detective/police crime; family saga; fantasy; historical; horror; humor/satire; juvenile; literary; mainstream; mystery; psychic/supernatural; romance; science fiction; sports; thriller/espionage.
How to Contact: Query with SASE. Accepts queries by e-mail. Prefers to be the only reader. Responds in 2 weeks. *No unsolicited scripts.* Discards unwanted queries and mss.
Needs: Actively seeking spec feature scripts or established feature writers. Obtains new clients through recommendations from current clients, producers, studio execs, and university writing programs, national writing contests.
Recent Sales: Prefers not to share information on specific sales.
Terms: Agent receives 10% commission on domestic sales. No written contract.
Writers' Conferences: NYU Film School (Los Angeles, June 1999).
Tips: "Please do not send a script until it is in its best possible draft."

MONTEIRO ROSE AGENCY, 17514 Ventura Blvd., #205, Encino CA 91316. (818)501-1177. Fax: (818)501-1194. E-mail: monrose@ix.netcom.com. Website: www.monteiro-rose.com. **Contact:** Milissa Brockish. Estab. 1987. Signatory of WGA. Represents over 50 clients. Specializes in scripts for animation, TV and film. Currently handles: 40% movie scripts; 20% TV scripts; 40% animation.
Member Agents: Candace Monteiro (literary); Fredda Rose (literary); Milissa Brockish (literary); Jason Dravis (literary).
Represents: Feature film, animation, TV MOW, episodic drama. **Considers these script subjects:** action/adventure; cartoon/animation; comedy; contemporary issues; detective/police/crime; ethnic; family saga; historical; juvenile; mainstream; mystery/suspense; psychic/supernatural; romantic comedy and drama; science fiction; teen; thriller.
How to Contact: Query with SASE. Accepts queries by fax, "but cannot guarantee reply without SASE." Responds in 1 week to queries; 2 months to mss. Returns materials only with SASE.
Needs: Obtains new clients through recommendations from others in the entertainment business and query letters.
Recent Sales: Prefers not to share information on specific sales.
Terms: Agent receives 10% commission on domestic sales. Offers standard WGA 2 year contract, with 90-day cancellation clause. Charges for photocopying.

Tips: "It does no good to call and try to speak to an agent before they have read your material, unless referred by someone we know. The best and only way, if you're a new writer, is to send a query letter with a SASE. If agents are interested, they will request to read it. Also enclose a SASE with the script if you want it back."

PANDA TALENT, 3721 Hoen Ave., Santa Rosa CA 95405. (707)576-0711. Fax: (707)544-2765. **Contact:** Audrey Grace. Estab. 1977. Signatory of WGA, SAG, AFTRA, Equity. Represents 10 clients. 80% of clients are new/previously unpublished writers. Currently handles: 5% novels; 40% TV scripts; 50% movie scripts; 5% stage plays.
Story Readers: Steven Grace (science fiction/war/action); Vicki Lima (mysteries/romance); Cleo West (western/true stories).
Represents: Feature film, TV MOW, episodic drama, sitcom. **Considers these script subject areas:** action/adventure; animals; comedy; detective/police/crime; ethnic; family saga; military/war; mystery/suspense; romantic comedy and drama; science fiction; true crime/investigative; westerns/frontier.
How to Contact: Query with treatment. Responds in 3 weeks to queries; 2 months to mss. Must include SASE.
Recent Sales: Prefers not to share information on specific sales.
Terms: Agent receives 10% commission on domestic sales; 10% on foreign sales.

N: PREFERRED ARTISTS TALENT AGENCY, 16633 Ventura Blvd., Suite 1421, Encino CA 91436. (818)990-0305. Fax: (818)990-2736. **Contact:** Kimber Wheeler. Estab. 1985. Signatory of WGA. 90% of clients are new/previously unpublished writers. Currently handles: 90% movie scripts, 10% novels.
Represents: Movie scripts, novels. **Considers these script areas:** action/adventure; biography/autobiography; cartoon/comic; comedy; contemporary issues; detective/police/crime; ethnic; family saga; fantasy; feminist; gay; horror; lesbian; mystery/suspense; psychic/supernatural; romance; science fiction; sports; thriller/espionage.
How to Contact: Query with outline/proposal and SASE.
Recent Sales: Prefers not to share information on specific sales.
Terms: Agent receives 10% commission on domestic sales. Offers written contract, binding for 1 year. WGA rules on termination apply.
Tips: "A good query letter is important. Use any relationship you have in the business to get your material read."

STANTON & ASSOCIATES LITERARY AGENCY, 4413 Clemson Dr., Garland TX 75042-5246. (972)276-5427. Fax: (972)276-5426. E-mail: preston8@onramp.net. Website: rampages.onramp.net/~preston8. **Contact:** Henry Stanton, Harry Preston. Estab. 1990. Signatory of WGA. Represents 36 clients. 90% of clients are new screenwriters. Specializes in screenplays. Currently handles: 50% movie scripts; 40% TV scripts; 10% books.
● Prior to joining the agency, Mr. Preston was with the MGM script department and an author and screenwriter for 40 years.
Represents: Feature film, TV MOW. **Considers these script subject areas:** action/adventure; comedy; romantic comedy; romantic drama; thriller.
How to Contact: Query with SASE. Accepts queries by fax or e-mail. Considers simultaneous queries and submissions. Responds in 1 week to queries; 1 month to screenplays (review). Returns materials only with SASE.
Needs: Does not want to see science fiction, fantasy or horror. Obtains new clients through WGA listing, *Hollywood Scriptwriter*, word of mouth (in Dallas).
Recent Sales: *A Tale Worth Telling* (*The Life of Saint Patrick*), (Angelic Entertainment); *Chipita* (uprize Productions); *Today I Will Nourish My Inner Martyr* (Prima Press); *Barbara Jordan, The Biography* (Golden Touch Press).
Terms: Agent receives 15% commission on domestic sales. Offers written contract, binding for 2 years on individual screenplays. Returns scripts with reader's comments.
Tips: "We have writers available to edit or ghostwrite screenplays and books. Fees vary dependent on the writer. All writers should always please enclose a SASE with any queries."

N: SYDRA TECHNIQUES CORP., 481 Eighth Ave. E 24, New York NY 10001. (212)631-0009. Fax: (212)631-0715. E-mail: sbuck@virtualnews.com. **Contact:** Sid Buck. Estab. 1988. Signatory of WGA. Represents 30 clients. 80% of clients are new/unpublished writers. Currently handles: 30% movie scripts; 10% novels; 30% TV scripts; 10% nonfiction books; 10% stage plays; 10% multimedia.
● Prior to opening his agency, Mr. Buck was an artist's agent.
Represents: Feature film, TV MOW, sitcom, animation. **Considers these script subject areas:** action/adventure; cartoon/animation; comedy; contemporary issues; detective/police/crime; family saga; biography/autobiography; mainstream; mystery/suspense; science fiction; sports.
How to Contact: Send outline/proposal with SASE. Responds in 1 month.
Needs: "We are open." Obtains new clients through recommendations.
Recent Sales: Prefers not to share information on specific sales.
Terms: Agent receives 10% commission on domestic sales; 15% on foreign sales. Offers written contract, binding for 2 years. 120 day notice must be given to terminate contract.

N: TALENT SOURCE, 107 E. Hall St., P.O. Box 14120, Savannah GA 31416-1120. (912)232-9390. Fax: (912)232-8213. E-mail: mshortt@ix.netcom.com. Website: www.talentsource.com. **Contact:** Michael L. Shortt. Estab. 1991. Signatory of WGA. 35% of clients are new/previously unpublished writers. Currently handles: 75% movie scripts; 25% TV scripts.

• Prior to becoming an agent, Mr. Shortt was a television program producer.

Represents: Feature film, episodic drama, TV MOW, sitcom. **Considers these script areas:** comedy; contemporary issues; detective/police/crime; erotica; family saga; horror; juvenile; mainstream; mystery/ suspense; romance (comedy, drama); teen. Also handles CD-Roms, direct videos.

How to Contact: Send outline with character breakdown. Include SASE. Responds in 10 weeks to queries.

Needs: Actively seeking "character-driven stories (e.g., *Sling Blade, Sex Lies & Videotape*)." Does not want to receive "big budget special effects science fiction." Obtains new clients through word of mouth.

Recent Sales: Prefers not to share information on specific sales.

Terms: Agent receives 10% commission on domestic sales; 15% on foreign sales. Offers written contract.

PEREGRINE WHITTLESEY AGENCY, 345 E. 80 St., New York NY 10021. (212)737-0153. Fax: (212)734-5176. **Contact:** Peregrine Whittlesey. Estab. 1986. Signatory of WGA. Represents 30 clients. 50% of clients are new/previously unpublished writers. Specializes in playwrights who also write for screen and TV. Currently handles: 20% movie scripts, 80% stage plays.

Represents: Feature film, stage plays.

How to Contact: Query with SASE. Responds in 1 week to queries; 1 month to mss.

Needs: Obtains new clients through recommendations from others.

Recent Sales: *The Stick Wife* and *0 Pioneers!*, by Darrah Cloud (Dramatic Publishing); *Alabama Rain*, by Heather McCutchen (Dramatic Publishing).

Terms: Agent receives 10% commission on domestic sales; 15% on foreign sales. Offers written contract, binding for 2 years.

THE WRIGHT CONCEPT, 1612 W. Olive Ave., Suite 205, Burbank CA 91506. (818)954-8943. Fax: (818)954-9370. E-mail: mrwright@www.wrightconcept.com. Website: www.wrightconcept.com. **Contact:** Marcie Wright. Estab. 1985. Signatory of WGA, DGA. Specializes in TV comedy writers and feature comedy writers. Currently handles: 50% movie scripts; 50% TV scripts.

Member Agents: Marcie Wright (TV/movie).

Represents: Feature film, TV MOW, episodic drama, sitcom, variety show, animation, syndicated material. **Considers these script subject areas:** action/adventure, teen; thriller. Also handles CD-Rom games.

How to Contact: Query with SASE. Responds in 2 weeks.

Needs: Obtains new clients through recommendations and queries.

Recent Sales: *Movie/TV MOW script(s) optioned/sold:* Mickey Blue Eyes (Castlerock); *The Pentagon Wars* (HBO); *Shot Through the Heart* (HBO).

Terms: Agent receives 10% commission on sales. Offers written contract, binding for 1 year, with 90 day cancellation clause. 100% of business is derived from commissions on sales.

Writers' Conferences: Speaks at UCLA 3-4 times a year; Southwest Writers Workshop (Albuquerque, August); *Fade-In Magazine* Oscar Conference (Los Angeles, May); *Fade-In Magazine* Top 100 People in Hollywood (Los Angeles, August); University of Georgia's Harriett Austin Writers Conference; Houston Film Festival.

N: WRITERS & ARTISTS AGENCY, 19 W. 44th St., Suite 1000, New York NY 10036. (212)391-1112. Fax: (212)575-6397. **Contact:** William Craver, Nicole Graham, Jeff Berger. Estab. 1970. Member of AAR, signatory of WGA. Represents 100 clients. West Coast location: 8383 Wilshire Blvd., Suite 550, Los Angeles CA 90211. (323)866-0900. Fax: (323)659-1985.

Represents: Movie scripts, feature film, TV scripts, TV MOW, miniseries, episodic drama, stage plays. **Considers all script subject areas.**

How to Contact: Query with brief description of project, bio and SASE. Responds in 1 month to queries only when accompanied by SASE. No unsolicited mss accepted.

Recent Sales: Prefers not to share specific information on specific sales.

Subject Index

LITERARY AGENTS/FICTION

Action/Adventure: Allen, Linda; Barrett Books, Loretta; Dystel, Jane; Greenburger Assoc., Sanford J.; Halsey North, Reece; Henshaw Group, Richard; JCA; Klinger, Harvey; Larsen/Elizabeth Pomada, Michael; McBride, Margret; Morrison, Henry; Naggar, Jean V.; National Writers; Sanders, Victoria; Waxman, Scott; Zeckendorf Assoc., Susan

Cartoon/comic: Levant & Wales

Confessional: Barrett Books, Loretta
JCA

Contemporary issues: Allen, Linda; Barrett Books, Loretta; Bent, Literary Agent, Jenny, Graybill & English, L.L.C.; Bernstein & Assoc., Pam; Dijkstra, Sandra; Dystel, Jane; Greenburger Assoc., Sanford J.; Halsey North, Reece; JCA; Kouts, Barbara S.; Larsen/Elizabeth Pomada, Michael; Lowenstein Assoc.; Naggar, Jean V.; Pinder Lane & Garon-Brooke Assoc.; Rees, Helen; Sanders, Victoria; Sherman Assoc., Wendy; Skolnick, Irene; Straus, Robin; Zeckendorf Assoc., Susan

Detective/police/crime: Allen, Linda; Barrett Books, Loretta; Bent, Literary Agent, Jenny, Graybill & English, L.L.C.; Bleecker St. Assoc.; Cohen, Ruth; DHS Literary; Dijkstra, Sandra; Dystel, Jane; Greenburger Assoc., Sanford J.; Halsey North, Reece; Henshaw Group, Richard; JCA; Klinger, Harvey; Larsen/Elizabeth Pomada, Michael; Lowenstein Assoc.; McBride, Margret; Morrison, Henry; Naggar, Jean V.; Pinder Lane & Garon-Brooke Assoc.; Rowland, Damaris; Zeckendorf Assoc., Susan

Erotica: Bleecker St. Assoc.; DHS Literary; Lowenstein Assoc.

Ethnic: Allen, Linda; Amster, Betsy; Barrett Books, Loretta; Bent, Literary Agent, Jenny, Graybill & English, L.L.C.; Bernstein & Assoc., Pam; Bleecker St. Assoc.; Cohen, Ruth; Daves, Joan; DHS Literary; Dijkstra, Sandra; Dystel, Jane; Greenburger Assoc., Sanford J.; Halsey North, Reece; Henshaw Group, Richard; JCA; Knight Agency; Larsen/Elizabeth Pomada, Michael; Levant & Wales; Lowenstein Assoc.; McBride, Margret; Naggar, Jean V.; Ross, The Gail; Sanders, Victoria; United Tribes; Waxman, Scott; Zeckendorf Assoc., Susan

Experimental: Barrett Books, Loretta; JCA; Larsen/Elizabeth Pomada, Michael; Levant & Wales; Manus & Assoc.

Family saga: Barrett Books, Loretta; Bent, Literary Agent, Jenny, Graybill & English, L.L.C.; Bleecker St. Assoc.; Daves, Joan; Dijkstra, Sandra; Dystel, Jane; Fredericks, Jeanne; Greenburger Assoc., Sanford J.; Halsey North, Reece; Henshaw Group, Richard; JCA; Klinger, Harvey; Kouts, Barbara S.; Larsen/Elizabeth Pomada, Michael; Morrison, Henry; Naggar, Jean V.; Pinder Lane & Garon-Brooke Assoc.; Sanders, Victoria; Straus, Robin; Zeckendorf Assoc., Susan

Fantasy: Henshaw Group, Richard; Larsen/Elizabeth Pomada, Michael; Pinder Lane & Garon-Brooke Assoc.

Feminist: Allen, Linda; Barrett Books, Loretta; Bleecker St. Assoc.; DHS Literary; Dijkstra, Sandra; Greenburger Assoc., Sanford J.; JCA; Kouts, Barbara S.; Larsen/Elizabeth Pomada, Michael; Levant & Wales; Lowenstein Assoc.; Naggar, Jean V.; Ross, The Gail; Sanders, Victoria

Gay: Allen, Linda; Barrett Books, Loretta; Bent, Literary Agent, Jenny, Graybill & English, L.L.C.; Bleecker St. Assoc.; Daves, Joan; DHS Literary; Dystel, Jane; Greenburger Assoc., Sanford J.; JCA; Larsen/Elizabeth Pomada, Michael; Levant & Wales; Lowenstein Assoc.; Pinder Lane & Garon-Brooke Assoc.; Ross, The Gail; Sanders, Victoria

Glitz: Allen, Linda; Barrett Books, Loretta; Greenburger Assoc., Sanford J.; Henshaw Group, Richard; JCA; Klinger, Harvey; Larsen/Elizabeth Pomada, Michael; Zeckendorf Assoc., Susan

Historical: Barrett Books, Loretta; Bernstein & Assoc., Pam; Bleecker St. Assoc.; Cohen, Ruth; DHS Literary; Fredericks, Jeanne; Greenburger Assoc., Sanford J.; Halsey North, Reese; Henshaw Group, Richard; JCA; Kouts, Barbara S.; Larsen/Elizabeth Pomada, Michael; Lowenstein Assoc.; McBride, Margret; Naggar, Jean V.; Rees, Helen; Rowland, Damaris; Skolnick, Irene; Straus, Robin; United Tribes; Waxman, Scott; Zeckendorf Assoc., Susan

Horror: Allen, Linda; Cohen, Ruth; DHS Literary; Henshaw Group, Richard; JCA; Kouts, Barbara S.; National Writers; Barrett Books, Loretta

Humor/satire: Greenburger Assoc., Sanford J.; Henshaw Group, Richard; JCA; Larsen/Elizabeth Pomada, Michael; McBride, Margret

Juvenile: Cohen, Ruth; Henshaw Group, Richard; Kouts, Barbara S.; National Writers

Open to all fiction categories: Barrett Books, Loretta; Bernstein & Assoc., Pam; Bleecker St. Assoc.; Brown, Curtis; Cohen, Ruth; Curtis Assoc., Richard; Knight Agency; Larsen/Elizabeth Pomada, Michael; Lowenstein Assoc.; Pinder Lane & Garon-Brooke Assoc.; Rowland, Damaris; Sherman Assoc., Wendy; Waxman, Scott; Writers House

Religious/inspiration: Allen, Linda; Barrett Books, Loretta; Dystel, Jane; Greenburger Assoc., Sanford J.; Larsen/ Elizabeth Pomada, Michael; Levant & Wales; Lowenstein Assoc.; Sanders, Victoria

Romance: Allen, Linda; Amster, Betsy; Barrett Books, Loretta; Bent, Literary Agent, Jenny, Graybill & English, L.L.C.; Bleecker St. Assoc.; Cohen, Ruth; Cornfield, Robert; Darhansoff & Verrill; Daves, Joan; DH Literary; DHS Literary; Dijkstra, Sandra; Dystel, Jane; Fredericks, Jeanne; Greenburger Assoc., Sanford J.; Halsey North, Reece; Henshaw Group, Richard; JCA; Klinger, Harvey; Knight Agency; Kouts, Barbara S.; Larsen/Elizabeth Pomada, Michael; Levant & Wales; Levine, Ellen; Lowenstein Assoc.; Mann, Carol; Manus & Assoc.; Markson, Elaine; McBride, Margret; Naggar, Jean V.; Pinder Lane & Garon-Brooke Assoc.; Rees, Helen; Ross, The Gail; Rowland, Damaris; Sanders, Victoria; Skolnick, Irene; Straus, Robin; Waxman, Scott; Zeckendorf Assoc., Susan

Science fiction: Allen, Linda; Barrett Books, Loretta; Bernstein & Assoc., Pam; Cohen, Ruth; Daves, Joan; DH Literary; DHS Literary; Dijkstra, Sandra; Dystel, Jane; Greenburger Assoc., Sanford J.; Halsey North, Reece; Henshaw Group, Richard; JCA; Klinger, Harvey; Knight Agency; Kouts, Barbara S.; Larsen/Elizabeth Pomada, Michael; Levant & Wales; Lowenstein Assoc.; Markson, Elaine; McBride, Margret; Naggar, Jean V.; National Writers; Pinder Lane & Garon-Brooke Assoc.; Rees, Helen; Rowland, Damaris; Sherman Assoc., Wendy; Straus, Robin; Zeckendorf Assoc., Susan

Sports: Allen, Linda; Barrett Books, Loretta; Bernstein & Assoc., Pam; Bleecker St. Assoc.; Cohen, Ruth; DH Literary; DHS Literary; Dijkstra, Sandra; Greenburger Assoc., Sanford J.; Halsey North, Reece; JCA; Knight Agency; Kouts, Barbara S.; Larsen/Elizabeth Pomada, Michael; Levine, Ellen; Lowenstein Assoc.; McBride, Margret; Naggar, Jean V.; Pinder Lane & Garon-Brooke Assoc.; Rees, Helen; Sherman Assoc., Wendy; Waxman, Scott; Zeckendorf Assoc., Susan

Thriller/espionage: Cohen, Ruth; Kouts, Barbara S.; National Writers

Westerns/frontier: Allen, Linda; Barrett Books, Loretta; Bleecker St. Assoc.; Greenburger Assoc., Sanford J.; Henshaw Group, Richard; Larsen/Elizabeth Pomada, Michael; Naggar, Jean V.; Rowland, Damaris

Young adult: Allen, Linda; Greenburger Assoc., Sanford J.; Knight Agency; Manus & Assoc.

LITERARY AGENTS/NONFICTION

Agriculture/horticulture: Amster, Betsy; Fredericks, Jeanne

Animals: Bent, Literary Agent, Jenny, Graybill & English, L.L.C.; Bleecker St. Assoc.; Cornfield, Robert; DH Literary; Dystel, Jane; Fredericks, Jeanne; Henshaw Group, Richard; JCA; Levant & Wales; Lowenstein Assoc.; National Writers; Rowland, Damaris; Straus, Robin; Writers House

Anthropology: Allen, Linda; Bent, Literary Agent, Jenny, Graybill & English, L.L.C.; Bleecker St. Assoc.; Cornfield, Robert; Darhansoff & Verrill; DH Literary; Dijkstra, Sandra; Dystel, Jane; Fredericks, Jeanne; James Peter Assoc.; JCA; Larsen/Elizabeth Pomada, Michael; Levine, Ellen; Lowenstein Assoc.; Mann, Carol; Morrison, Henry; Ross, The Gail; Straus, Robin; United Tribes

Art/architecture/design: Allen, Linda; Bent, Literary Agent, Jenny, Graybill & English, L.L.C.; Cornfield, Robert; Fredericks, Jeanne; James Peter Assoc.; JCA; Larsen/Elizabeth Pomada, Michael; Mann, Carol; Straus, Robin; United Tribes; Writers House; Zeckendorf Assoc., Susan

Biography/autobiography: Allen, Linda; Amster, Betsy; Bent, Literary Agent, Jenny, Graybill & English, L.L.C.; Bleecker St. Assoc.; Bykofsky Assoc., Sheree; Cornfield, Robert; Darhansoff & Verrill; Daves, Joan; DH Literary; DHS Literary; Dijkstra, Sandra; Dystel, Jane; Fredericks, Jeanne; Halsey North, Reece; Henshaw Group, Richard; James Peter Assoc.; JCA; Klinger, Harvey; Knight Agency; Kouts, Barbara S.; Larsen/Elizabeth Pomada, Michael; Levant & Wales; Levine, Ellen; Lowenstein Assoc.; Mann, Carol; Manus & Assoc.; McBride, Margret; Morrison, Henry; Naggar, Jean V.; National Writers; New England Pub. Assoc.; Pinder Lane & Garon-Brooke Assoc.; Rees, Helen; Rinaldi, Angela; Ross, The Gail; Sanders, Victoria; Sherman Assoc., Wendy; Skolnick, Irene; Straus, Robin; United Tribes; Waxman, Scott; Writers House; Zeckendorf Assoc., Susan

Business: Allen, Linda; Amster, Betsy; Bleecker St. Assoc.; Bykofsky Assoc., Sheree; DHS Literary; Dijkstra, Sandra; Dystel, Jane; Fredericks, Jeanne; Henshaw Group, Richard; James Peter Assoc.; JCA; Knight Agency; Larsen/Elizabeth Pomada, Michael; Levant & Wales; Lowenstein Assoc.; Mann, Carol; Manus & Assoc.; McBride, Margret; New England Pub. Assoc.; Rees, Helen; Rinaldi, Angela; Ross, The Gail; United Tribes; Waxman, Scott; Writers House

Child guidance/parenting: Allen, Linda; Amster, Betsy; Bent, Literary Agent, Jenny, Graybill & English, L.L.C.; Bernstein & Assoc., Pam; Bleecker St. Assoc.; Bykofsky Assoc., Sheree; DH Literary; DHS Literary; Dijkstra, Sandra; Dystel, Jane; Fredericks, Jeanne; Henshaw Group, Richard; James Peter Assoc.; JCA; Knight Agency; Kouts, Barbara S.; Larsen/ Elizabeth Pomada, Michael; Lowenstein Assoc.; Mann, Carol; Manus & Assoc.; McBride, Margret; Naggar, Jean V.; National Writers; New England Pub. Assoc.; Pinder Lane & Garon-Brooke Assoc.; Rinaldi, Angela; Sherman Assoc., Wendy; Straus, Robin; United Tribes; Writers House; Zeckendorf Assoc., Susan

Computers/electronics: Allen, Linda; Bleecker St. Assoc.; DHS Literary; Henshaw Group, Richard; JCA; Knight Agency; Manus & Assoc.

Cooking/food/nutrition: Bernstein & Assoc., Pam; Bleecker St. Assoc.; Bykofsky Assoc., Sheree; Cornfield, Robert; DHS Literary; Dijkstra, Sandra; Dystel, Jane; Fredericks, Jeanne; Henshaw Group, Richard; Klinger, Harvey; Knight Agency; Larsen/Elizabeth Pomada, Michael; McBride, Margret; Rinaldi, Angela; Ross, The Gail; Rowland, Damaris; Straus, Robin; United Tribes; Writers House

Crafts/hobbies: Fredericks, Jeanne; Lowenstein Assoc.

Current affairs: Bernstein & Assoc., Pam; Bleecker St. Assoc.; Bykofsky Assoc., Sheree; Darhansoff & Verrill; DH Literary; DHS Literary; Dijkstra, Sandra; Dystel, Jane; Fredericks, Jeanne; Halsey North, Reece; Henshaw Group, Richard; James Peter Assoc.; JCA; Knight Agency; Kouts, Barbara S.; Larsen/Elizabeth Pomada, Michael; Levant & Wales; Levine, Ellen; Lowenstein Assoc.; Mann, Carol; Manus & Assoc.; McBride, Margret; Naggar, Jean V.; Rees, Helen; Rinaldi, Angela; Sanders, Victoria; Skolnick, Irene; Straus, Robin; United Tribes

Education: Dystel, Jane; Halsey North, Reece; Henshaw Group, Richard; Levant & Wales; Lowenstein Assoc.; National Writers; Pinder Lane & Garon-Brooke Assoc.; Ross, The Gail; United Tribes

Ethnic/cultural interests: Allen, Linda; Amster, Betsy; Bent, Literary Agent, Jenny, Graybill & English, L.L.C.; Bleecker St. Assoc.; Bykofsky Assoc., Sheree; Cohen, Ruth; DH Literary; DHS Literary; Dijkstra, Sandra; Dystel, Jane; James Peter Assoc.; JCA; Knight Agency; Kouts, Barbara S.; Larsen/Elizabeth Pomada, Michael; Levant & Wales; Lowenstein Assoc.; Mann, Carol; Manus & Assoc.; McBride, Margret; Ross, The Gail; Sanders, Victoria; Sherman Assoc., Wendy; Straus, Robin; United Tribes; Waxman, Scott

Gay/lesbian issues: Allen, Linda; Bent, Literary Agent, Jenny, Graybill & English, L.L.C.; Bleecker St. Assoc.; Bykofsky Assoc., Sheree; Daves, Joan; DHS Literary; Dystel, Jane; Henshaw Group, Richard; James Peter Assoc.; JCA; Larsen/Elizabeth Pomada, Michael; Levant & Wales; Lowenstein Assoc.; McBride, Margret; Pinder Lane & Garon-Brooke Assoc.; Ross, The Gail; Sanders, Victoria; United Tribes

Government/politics/law: Allen, Linda; Bleecker St. Assoc.; DH Literary; Dijkstra, Sandra; Dystel, Jane; Henshaw Group, Richard; James Peter Assoc.; JCA; Larsen/Elizabeth Pomada, Michael; Lowenstein Assoc.; Mann, Carol; McBride, Margret; Morrison, Henry; Naggar, Jean V.; National Writers; New England Pub. Assoc.; Rees, Helen; Ross, The Gail; Sanders, Victoria; Straus, Robin; United Tribes

Health/medicine: Amster, Betsy; Bent, Literary Agent, Jenny, Graybill & English, L.L.C.; Bernstein & Assoc., Pam; Bleecker St. Assoc.; Bykofsky Assoc., Sheree; Darhansoff & Verrill; DH Literary; Dijkstra, Sandra; Dystel, Jane; Fredericks, Jeanne; Henshaw Group, Richard; James Peter Assoc.; JCA; Klinger, Harvey; Knight Agency; Kouts, Barbara S.; Larsen/Elizabeth Pomada, Michael; Levant & Wales; Levine, Ellen; Lowenstein Assoc.; Mann, Carol; Manus & Assoc.; McBride, Margret; Naggar, Jean V.; New England Pub. Assoc.; Pinder Lane & Garon-Brooke Assoc.; Rees, Helen; Rinaldi, Angela; Ross, The Gail; Rowland, Damaris; Straus, Robin; United Tribes; Waxman, Scott; Writers House; Zeckendorf Assoc., Susan

History: Allen, Linda; Amster, Betsy; Bent, Literary Agent, Jenny, Graybill & English, L.L.C.; Bleecker St. Assoc.; Bykofsky Assoc., Sheree; Cornfield, Robert; Darhansoff & Verrill; DH Literary; Dijkstra, Sandra; Dystel, Jane; Fredericks, Jeanne; Halsey North, Reece; James Peter Assoc.; JCA; Knight Agency; Kouts, Barbara S.; Larsen/Elizabeth Pomada, Michael; Levine, Ellen; Lowenstein Assoc.; Mann, Carol; McBride, Margret; Morrison, Henry; Naggar, Jean V.; New England Pub. Assoc.; Pinder Lane & Garon-Brooke Assoc.; Rees, Helen; Sanders, Victoria; Straus, Robin; United Tribes; Waxman, Scott; Writers House; Zeckendorf Assoc., Susan

How-to: Amster, Betsy; Barrett Books, Loretta; Bernstein & Assoc., Pam; Bleecker St. Assoc.; Bykofsky Assoc., Sheree; DH Literary; DHS Literary; Fredericks, Jeanne; Greenburger Assoc., Sanford J.; Henshaw Group, Richard; JCA; Knight Agency; Larsen/Elizabeth Pomada, Michael; Lowenstein Assoc.; Manus & Assoc.; McBride, Margret; National Writers; United Tribes; Waxman, Scott

Humor: Allen, Linda; Barrett Books, Loretta; Bernstein & Assoc., Pam; Bleecker St. Assoc.; Bykofsky Assoc., Sheree; Darhansoff & Verrill; DH Literary; DHS Literary; Dijkstra, Sandra; Dystel, Jane; Greenburger Assoc., Sanford J.; Halsey North, Reece; Henshaw Group, Richard; JCA; Klinger, Harvey; Larsen/Elizabeth Pomada, Michael; Levine, Ellen; Lowenstein Assoc.; Manus & Assoc.; McBride, Margret; Naggar, Jean V.; Rees, Helen; Ross, The Gail; Sanders, Victoria; Sherman Assoc., Wendy; Straus, Robin; Zeckendorf Assoc., Susan

Interior design/decorating: Fredericks, Jeanne; Larsen/Elizabeth Pomada, Michael; Writers House

Juvenile nonfiction: Bleecker St. Assoc.; Cohen, Ruth; Henshaw Group, Richard; Kouts, Barbara S.; Morrison, Henry; Naggar, Jean V.; National Writers; Writers House

Language/literature/criticism: Bent, Literary Agent, Jenny, Graybill & English, L.L.C.; Cornfield, Robert; Darhansoff & Verrill; DH Literary; Dijkstra, Sandra; Halsey North, Reece; James Peter Assoc.; JCA; Larsen/Elizabeth Pomada, Michael; Levant & Wales; Lowenstein Assoc.; New England Pub. Assoc.; Sanders, Victoria; Straus, Robin; United Tribes

Memoirs: Bleecker St. Assoc.; Halsey North, Reece; James Peter Assoc.; JCA; Larsen/Elizabeth Pomada, Michael; Levant & Wales; Levine, Ellen; Lowenstein Assoc.; Manus & Assoc.; Naggar, Jean V.; Pinder Lane & Garon-Brooke Assoc.; Sherman Assoc., Wendy; United Tribes; Zeckendorf Assoc., Susan

Military/war: Bleecker St. Assoc.; Dijkstra, Sandra; Dystel, Jane; Henshaw Group, Richard; James Peter Assoc.; JCA; New England Pub. Assoc.; Pinder Lane & Garon-Brooke Assoc.; Writers House

Money/finance/economics: Amster, Betsy; Bleecker St. Assoc.; DH Literary; Dijkstra, Sandra; Dystel, Jane; Fredericks, Jeanne; Henshaw Group, Richard; James Peter Assoc.; JCA; Knight Agency; Larsen/Elizabeth Pomada, Michael; Lowenstein Assoc.; Mann, Carol; Manus & Assoc.; McBride, Margret; New England Pub. Assoc.; Rees, Helen; Rinaldi, Angela; Ross, The Gail; United Tribes; Waxman, Scott; Writers House

Music/dance/theater/film: Allen, Linda; Bykofsky Assoc., Sheree; Cornfield, Robert; Henshaw Group, Richard; James Peter Assoc.; JCA; Knight Agency; Kouts, Barbara S.; Larsen/Elizabeth Pomada, Michael; Lowenstein Assoc.; McBride, Margret; Pinder Lane & Garon-Brooke Assoc.; Sanders, Victoria; Straus, Robin; United Tribes; Writers House; Zeckendorf Assoc., Susan

Nature/environment: Allen, Linda; Bleecker St. Assoc.; Darhansoff & Verrill; DH Literary; Dijkstra, Sandra; Fredericks, Jeanne; Henshaw Group, Richard; JCA; Kouts, Barbara S.; Larsen/Elizabeth Pomada, Michael; Levant & Wales; Lowenstein Assoc.; Manus & Assoc.; New England Pub. Assoc.; Ross, The Gail; Rowland, Damaris; Straus, Robin; United Tribes; Writers House

New Age/metaphysics: Bent, Literary Agent, Jenny, Graybill & English, L.L.C.; Bleecker St. Assoc.; Dystel, Jane; Henshaw Group, Richard; JCA; Larsen/Elizabeth Pomada, Michael; Levant & Wales; Lowenstein Assoc.; Naggar, Jean V.; Rowland, Damaris

Open to all nonfiction categories: Barrett Books, Loretta; Brown, Curtis; Curtis Assoc., Richard; Greenburger Assoc., Sanford J.; Levant & Wales; Barrett Books, Loretta; Knight Agency; Larsen/Elizabeth Pomada, Michael; United Tribes; Waxman, Scott

Photography: Fredericks, Jeanne; JCA; Larsen/Elizabeth Pomada, Michael

Popular culture: Allen, Linda; Amster, Betsy; Bent, Literary Agent, Jenny, Graybill & English, L.L.C.; Bernstein & Assoc., Pam; Bleecker St. Assoc.; Bykofsky Assoc., Sheree; Daves, Joan; DH Literary; DHS Literary; Dystel, Jane; Halsey North, Reece; Henshaw Group, Richard; James Peter Assoc.; JCA; Knight Agency; Larsen/Elizabeth Pomada, Michael; Levant & Wales; Levine, Ellen; Lowenstein Assoc.; Manus & Assoc.; McBride, Margret; National Writers; Rinaldi, Angela; Sanders, Victoria; Straus, Robin; United Tribes; Waxman, Scott

Psychology: Allen, Linda; Amster, Betsy; Bent, Literary Agent, Jenny, Graybill & English, L.L.C.; Bernstein & Assoc., Pam; Bleecker St. Assoc.; Bykofsky Assoc., Sheree; DH Literary; Dijkstra, Sandra; Dystel, Jane; Fredericks, Jeanne; Henshaw Group, Richard; James Peter Assoc.; JCA; Klinger, Harvey; Knight Agency; Kouts, Barbara S.; Larsen/Elizabeth Pomada, Michael; Levant & Wales; Levine, Ellen; Lowenstein Assoc.; Mann, Carol; Manus & Assoc.; McBride, Margret; Naggar, Jean V.; New England Pub. Assoc.; Pinder Lane & Garon-Brooke Assoc.; Rinaldi, Angela; Ross, The Gail; Sanders, Victoria; Sherman Assoc., Wendy; Straus, Robin; United Tribes; Writers House; Zeckendorf Assoc., Susan

Religious/inspirational: Bent, Literary Agent, Jenny, Graybill & English, L.L.C.; Bernstein & Assoc., Pam; Bleecker St. Assoc.; Bykofsky Assoc., Sheree; Dystel, Jane; Knight Agency; Larsen/Elizabeth Pomada, Michael; Lowenstein Assoc.; McBride, Margret; Naggar, Jean V.; Ross, The Gail; Rowland, Damaris; Waxman, Scott

Science/technology: Bent, Literary Agent, Jenny, Graybill & English, L.L.C.; Bent, Literary Agent, Jenny, Graybill & English, L.L.C.; Bleecker St. Assoc.; Darhansoff & Verrill; DH Literary; Dijkstra, Sandra; Dystel, Jane; Fredericks, Jeanne; Henshaw Group, Richard; JCA; Klinger, Harvey; Larsen/Elizabeth Pomada, Michael; Levant & Wales; Levine, Ellen; Lowenstein Assoc.; Manus & Assoc.; McBride, Margret; National Writers; New England Pub. Assoc.; Ross, The Gail; Straus, Robin; United Tribes; Writers House; Zeckendorf Assoc., Susan

Self-help/personal: Amster, Betsy; Bent, Literary Agent, Jenny, Graybill & English, L.L.C.; Bernstein & Assoc., Pam; Bleecker St. Assoc.; Bykofsky Assoc., Sheree; DH Literary; Dijkstra, Sandra; Fredericks, Jeanne; Henshaw Group, Richard; James Peter Assoc.; Klinger, Harvey; Knight Agency; Kouts, Barbara S.; Larsen/Elizabeth Pomada, Michael; Levant & Wales; Lowenstein Assoc.; Mann, Carol; Manus & Assoc.; McBride, Margret; Naggar, Jean V.; New England Pub. Assoc.; Pinder Lane & Garon-Brooke Assoc.; Rinaldi, Angela; Ross, The Gail; Sherman Assoc., Wendy; United Tribes; Waxman, Scott; Writers House

Sociology: Allen, Linda; Amster, Betsy; Bernstein & Assoc., Pam; Bleecker St. Assoc.; Dijkstra, Sandra; Henshaw Group, Richard; JCA; Larsen/Elizabeth Pomada, Michael; Lowenstein Assoc.; Mann, Carol; McBride, Margret; Naggar, Jean V.; New England Pub. Assoc.; Rinaldi, Angela; Ross, The Gail; Straus, Robin; United Tribes; Zeckendorf Assoc., Susan

Sports: Bleecker St. Assoc.; DHS Literary; Dijkstra, Sandra; Fredericks, Jeanne; Henshaw Group, Richard; JCA; Klinger, Harvey; Knight Agency; Larsen/Elizabeth Pomada, Michael; Lowenstein Assoc.; McBride, Margret; National Writers; Ross, The Gail; Waxman, Scott

Translations: Daves, Joan; JCA; Sanders, Victoria; United Tribes

True crime/investigative: Bernstein & Assoc., Pam; Bleecker St. Assoc.; Bykofsky Assoc., Sheree; DH Literary; DHS Literary; Dijkstra, Sandra; Dystel, Jane; Halsey North, Reece; Henshaw Group, Richard; JCA; Klinger, Harvey; Knight Agency; Larsen/Elizabeth Pomada, Michael; Lowenstein Assoc.; McBride, Margret; New England Pub. Assoc.; Pinder Lane & Garon-Brooke Assoc.; Rinaldi, Angela; Ross, The Gail; Sherman Assoc., Wendy; Writers House; Zeckendorf Assoc., Susan

Women's issues/women's studies: Allen, Linda; Amster, Betsy; Bent, Literary Agent, Jenny, Graybill & English, L.L.C.; Bernstein & Assoc., Pam; Bleecker St. Assoc.; Bykofsky Assoc., Sheree; Cohen, Ruth; Daves, Joan; DH Literary; Dijkstra, Sandra; Dystel, Jane; Fredericks, Jeanne; Halsey North, Reece; Henshaw Group, Richard; James Peter Assoc.; JCA; Klinger, Harvey; Knight Agency; Kouts, Barbara S.; Larsen/Elizabeth Pomada, Michael; Levant & Wales; Levine, Ellen; Lowenstein Assoc.; Mann, Carol; Manus & Assoc.; McBride, Margret; Naggar, Jean V.; New England Pub. Assoc.; Rees, Helen; Rinaldi, Angela; Rowland, Damaris; Sanders, Victoria; Straus, Robin; United Tribes; Writers House; Zeckendorf Assoc., Susan

SCRIPT AGENTS SUBJECT INDEX

Action/adventure: Douroux & Co.; Freed Company; Hodges, Carolyn; Hudson Agency; Larchmont; Monteiro Rose; Panda Talent; Preferred Artists; Stanton & Assoc.; Sydra Technique Corp.; Wright Concept

Animation: Douroux & Co.; Hudson Agency; Monteiro Rose; Panda Talent; Sydra Technique Corp.; Wright Concept

Biography/autobiography: Larchmont; Preferred Artists; Sydra Technique Corp.

Cartoon/animation: Hudson Agency; Larchmont; Monteiro Rose; Preferred Artists; Sydra Technique Corp.

Comedy: Cameron, Marshall; Douroux & Co.; Freed Company; French, Samuel; Hodges, Carolyn; Hudson Agency; Larchmont; Monteiro Rose; Panda Talent; Preferred Artists; Stanton & Assoc.; Sydra Technique Corp.; Talent Source

Contemporary issues: Freed Company; French, Samuel; Hodges, Carolyn; Hudson Agency; Larchmont; Momentum Marketing; Monteiro Rose; Preferred Artists; Sydra Technique Corp.; Talent Source

Detective/police/crime: Cameron, Marshall; Douroux & Co.; Freed Company ; French, Samuel; Hudson Agency; Larchmont; Monteiro Rose; Panda Talent; Preferred Artists; Sydra Technique Corp.; Talent Source

Documentary: Hudson Agency

Episodic drama: Douroux & Co.; Monteiro Rose; Panda Talent; Talent Source; Wright Concept; Writers & Artists

Erotica: Hodges, Carolyn; Talent Source

Ethnic: Freed Company; French, Samuel; Monteiro Rose; Panda Talent; Preferred Artists

Experimental: French, Samuel; Hodges, Carolyn

Family saga: Douroux & Co.; Freed Company; Hudson Agency; Larchmont; Monteiro Rose; Panda Talent; Preferred Artists; Sydra Technique Corp.; Talent Source

Fantasy: Douroux & Co.; French, Samuel; Hudson Agency; Larchmont; Preferred Artists

Feature film: Berman Boals & Flynn; Cameron, Marshall; Circle of Confusion; Douroux & Co.; Freed Company; Hodges, Carolyn; Hudson Agency; Larchmont; Monteiro Rose; Panda Talent; Stanton & Assoc.; Sydra Technique Corp.; Talent Source; Whittlesey, Peregrine; Wright Concept; Writers & Artists

Feminist: Preferred Artists

Gay: Preferred Artists

Historical: Douroux & Co.; Larchmont; Monteiro Rose

Horror: Freed Company; French, Samuel; Hodges, Carolyn; Larchmont; Preferred Artists; Talent Source

Juvenile: Hudson Agency; Monteiro Rose; Talent Source

Lesbian: Preferred Artists

Mainstream: Cameron, Marshall; Douroux & Co.; Freed Company; Hodges, Carolyn; Larchmont; Momentum Marketing; Monteiro Rose; Sydra Technique Corp.; Talent Source

Multimedia: Talent Source

Mystery/suspense: Douroux & Co.; Freed Company; French, Samuel; Hodges, Carolyn; Hudson Agency; Larchmont; Monteiro Rose; Panda Talent; Preferred Artists; Sydra Technique Corp.; Talent Source; Writers & Artists

Open to all categories: Circle of Confusion; Writers & Artists

Psychic/supernatural: Hodges, Carolyn; Larchmont; Monteiro Rose; Preferred Artists

Religious/inspirational: French, Samuel

Romance: Panda Talent; Preferred Artists

Romantic comedy: Douroux & Co.; Hodges, Carolyn; Hudson Agency; Larchmont; Monteiro Rose; Panda Talent; Stanton & Assoc.; Talent Source; Douroux & Co.; Hodges, Carolyn; Hudson Agency; Larchmont; Monteiro Rose; Panda Talent; Stanton & Assoc.; Talent Source

Science fiction: Douroux & Co.; Freed Company; Larchmont; Momentum Marketing; Monteiro Rose; Panda Talent; Preferred Artists; Sydra Technique Corp.

Sitcom: Douroux & Co.; Hudson Agency; Panda Talent; Sydra Technique Corp.; Talent Source; Wright Concept

Sports: Freed Company; Larchmont; Preferred Artists; Sydra Technique Corp.

TV movie of the week: Douroux & Co.; Freed Company; Hodges, Carolyn; Hudson Agency; Monteiro Rose; Panda Talent; Stanton & Assoc.; Sydra Technique Corp.; Talent Source; Wright Concept; Writers & Artists

Teen: Freed Company; Hudson Agency; Monteiro Rose; Talent Source; Wright Concept

Theatrical stage play: Berman Boals; French, Samuel; Whittlesey, Peregrine; Writers & Artists

Thriller/espionage: Cameron, Marshall; Douroux & Co.; Freed Company; French, Samuel; Larchmont; Monteiro Rose; Preferred Artists; Stanton & Assoc.; Wright Concept

Travel: James Peter Assoc.; Larsen/Elizabeth Pomada, Michael; Lowenstein Assoc.; Naggar, Jean V.; National Writers

Variety show: French, Samuel; Wright Concept

Westerns/frontier: Douroux & Co.; Hudson Agency; Larchmont; Panda Talent;

MARKET CONDITIONS are constantly changing! If this is 2002 or later, buy the newest edition of *Writer's Market* at your favorite bookstore or order directly from Writer's Digest Books at (800)289-0963.

The Markets

Book Publishers

The book business, for the most part, runs on hunches. Whether the idea for a book comes from a writer, an agent or the imagination of an acquiring editor, it is generally expressed in these terms: "This is a book that I *think* people will like. People will *probably* want to buy it." The decision to publish is mainly a matter of the right person, or persons, agreeing that those hunches are sound.

THE PATH TO PUBLICATION

Ideas reach editors in a variety of ways. They arrive unsolicited every day through the mail. They come by phone, sometimes from writers but most often from agents. They arise in the editor's mind because of his daily traffic with the culture in which he lives. The acquisitions editor, so named because he is responsible for securing manuscripts for his company to publish, sifts through the deluge of possibilities, waiting for a book idea to strike him as extraordinary, inevitable, profitable.

In some companies, acquisitions editors possess the authority required to say, "Yes, we will publish this book." In most publishing houses, though, the acquisitions editor must prepare and present the idea to a proposal committee made up of marketing and administrative personnel. Proposal committees are usually less interested in questions of extraordinariness and inevitability than they are in profitability. The editor has to convince them that it makes good business sense to publish this book.

Once a contract is signed, several different wheels are set in motion. The author, of course, writes the book if he hasn't done so already. While the editor is helping to assure that the author is making the book the best it can be, promotion and publicity people are planning mailings of review copies to influential newspapers and review periodicals, writing catalog copy that will help sales representatives push the book to bookstores, and plotting a multitude of other promotional efforts (including interview tours and bookstore signings by the author) designed to dangle the book attractively before the reading public's eye.

When the book is published, it usually receives a concerted promotional push for a month or two. After that, the fate of the book—whether it will "grow legs" and set sales records or sit untouched on bookstore shelves—rests in the hands of the public. Publishers have to compete with all of the other entertainment industries vying for the consumer's money and limited leisure time. Successful books are reprinted to meet the demand. Unsuccessful books are returned from bookstores to publishers and are sold off cheaply as "remainders" or are otherwise disposed of.

THE STATE OF THE BUSINESS

The book publishing industry is beginning to recover from the difficulties experienced in the last few years. Publishers sell their products to bookstores on a returnable basis, which means the stores usually have 120 days to either pay the bill or return the order. With independent bookstores continuing to close and superstores experiencing setbacks as well, many publishers were hit with staggering returns. This has slowed somewhat, but continues to be a concern. While there are many more outlets to *buy* books, including online bookstores such as Amazon.com,

Borders.com and Barnesandnoble.com, this doesn't necessarily translate into more books being *bought*. Some feel the superstore phenomenon has proved a mixed blessing. The greater shelf area means there are more materials available, but also drives a need for books as "wallpaper" that is continually refreshed by returning older books and restocking with newer ones.

But that's not to say publishers are rushing to bring esoteric or highly experimental material to the marketplace. The blockbuster mentality—publishing's penchant for sticking with "name brand" novelists—still drives most large publishers. It's simply a less risky venture to continue publishing authors whom they know readers like. On the other hand, the prospects for nonfiction authors are perhaps better than they have been for years. The boom in available shelf space has provided entree to the marketplace for books on niche topics that heretofore would not have seen the light of day in most bookstores. The superstores position themselves as one-stop shopping centers for readers of every stripe. As such, they must carry books on a wide range of subjects.

The publishing community as a whole is stepping back from the multimedia hype and approaching the market more cautiously, if not abandoning it entirely. While the possibilities offered by CD-ROM technology still exist, publishers realize that marrying format and content are crucial for a successful, profitable product. Online publishing seems to offer promise, if only publishers can figure out how to make money from this new and different format.

HOW TO PUBLISH YOUR BOOK

The markets in this year's Book Publishers section offer opportunities in nearly every area of publishing. Large, commercial houses are here as are their smaller counterparts; large and small "literary" houses are represented as well. In addition, you'll find university presses, industry-related publishers, textbook houses and more.

The Book Publishers Subject Index is the place to start. You'll find it in the back of the book, before the General Index. Subject areas for both fiction and nonfiction are broken out for the over 1,200 total book publisher listings. Not all of them buy the kind of book you've written, but this Index will tell you which ones do.

When you have compiled a list of publishers interested in books in your subject area, read the detailed listings. Pare down your list by cross-referencing two or three subject areas and eliminating the listings only marginally suited to your book. When you have a good list, send for those publishers' catalogs and any manuscript guidelines available or check publishers' websites, which often contain catalog listings, manuscript preparation guidelines, current contact names and other information helpful to prospective authors. You want to make sure your book idea is in line with a publisher's list but is not a duplicate of something already published. Visit bookstores and libraries to see if their books are well represented. When you find a couple of books they have published that are similar to yours, write or call the company to find out who edited these books. This last, extra bit of research could be the key to getting your proposal to precisely the right editor.

Publishers prefer different kinds of submissions on first contact. Most like to see a one-page query with SASE, especially for nonfiction. Others will accept a brief proposal package that might include an outline and/or a sample chapter. Some publishers will accept submissions from agents only. Virtually no publisher wants to see a complete manuscript on initial contact, and sending one when they prefer another method will signal to the publisher "this is an amateur's submission." Editors do not have the time to read an entire manuscript, even editors at small presses who receive fewer submissions. Perhaps the only exceptions to this rule are children's picture book manuscripts and poetry manuscripts, which take only as much time to read as an outline and sample chapter anyway.

In your one-page query, give an overview of your book, mention the intended audience, the competition (check *Books in Print* and local bookstore shelves), and what sets your book apart. Detail any previous publishing experience or special training relevant to the subject of your book. All of this information will help your cause; it is the professional approach.

Only one in a thousand writers will sell a book to the first publisher they query, especially if the book is the writer's first effort. Make a list of a dozen or so publishers that might be interested in your book. Try to learn as much about the books they publish and their editors as you can. Research, knowing the specifics of your subject area, and a professional approach are often the difference between acceptance and rejection. You are likely to receive at least a few rejections, however, and when that happens, don't give up. Rejection is as much a part of publishing, if not more, than signing royalty checks. Send your query to the next publisher on your list. Multiple queries can speed up the process at this early stage.

Personalize your queries by addressing them individually and mentioning what you know about a company from its catalog or books you've seen. Never send a form letter as a query. Envelopes addressed to "Editor" or "Editorial Department" end up in the dreaded slush pile.

If a publisher offers you a contract, you may want to seek advice before signing and returning it. An author's agent will very likely take 15% if you employ one, but you could be making 85% of a larger amount. Some literary agents are available on an hourly basis for contract negotiations only. For more information on literary agents, contact the Association of Authors' Representatives, 10 Astor Place, 3rd Floor, New York NY 10003, (212)353-3709. Also check the current edition of *Guide to Literary Agents* (Writer's Digest Books). Attorneys will only be able to tell you if everything is legal, not if you are getting a good deal, unless they have prior experience with literary contracts. If you have a legal problem, you might consider contacting Volunteer Lawyers for the Arts, 1 E. 53rd St., 6th Floor, New York NY 10022, (212)319-2787.

AUTHOR-SUBSIDY PUBLISHER'S LISTINGS NOT INCLUDED

Writer's Market is a reference tool to help you sell your writing, and we encourage you to work with publishers that pay a royalty. Subsidy publishing involves paying money to a publishing house to publish a book. The source of the money could be a government, foundation or university grant, or it could be the author of the book. Publishers offering nonauthor-subsidized arrangements have been included in the appropriate section. If one of the publishers listed here offers you an author-subsidy arrangement (sometimes called "cooperative publishing," "co-publishing" or "joint venture"), asks you to pay for all or part of the cost of any aspect of publishing (printing, advertising, etc.) or to guarantee the purchase of any number of the books yourself, we would like you to let us know about that company immediately.

Sometimes newer publishers will offer author-subsidy contracts to get a leg up in the business and plan to become royalty-only publishers once they've reached a firm financial footing. Some publishers feel they must offer subsidy contracts to expand their lists beyond the capabilities of their limited resources. This may be true, and you may be willing to agree to it, but we choose to list only those publishers paying a royalty without requiring a financial investment from the author. In recent years, several large subsidy publishers have suddenly gone out of business, leaving authors without their money, their books, and in some cases, without the copyright to their own manuscripts.

WHAT'S NEW

We've added several features to make *Writer's Market* even more helpful in your search for the right publisher for your work, features you won't find in any other writer's guide.

The "key" to successful submissions

You may have written the most wonderful historical romance to ever grace the page. But if you submit it to a publisher of history textbooks, you're not likely to get too far. To help you quickly skim the listings for the right publisher, we've added a key symbol (⚷) with a brief summary of what that publisher does produce, as well as areas of interest they are currently emphasizing and areas they are de-emphasizing.

Information at a glance

Most immediately noticeable, we've added a number of symbols at the beginning of each listing to quickly convey certain information at a glance. In the Book Publisher sections, these symbols identify new listings (🅽), "opportunity" markets that buy at least 50 percent from unagented or first-time writers (🖾), and publishers that accept agented submissions only (💲). Different sections of *Writer's Market* include other symbols; check the front and back inside covers for an explanation of all the symbols used throughout the book.

How much money? What are my odds?

We've also highlighted important information in boldface, the "quick facts" you won't find in any other market guide but should know before you submit your work. This includes: how many manuscripts a publisher buys per year; how many from first-time authors; how many from unagented writers; the royalty rate a publisher pays; and how large an advance is offered.

Publishers, their imprints and how they are related

In this era of big publishing—and big mergers—the world of publishing has grown even more intertwined. A "family tree" on page 89 lists the imprints and often confusing relationships of the largest conglomerate publishers.

In the listings, "umbrella" listings for these larger houses list the imprints under the company name. Imprint names in boldface indicate a separate, individual listing, easily located alphabetically, which provides much more detailed information about that imprint's specific focus, needs and contacts.

Each listing includes a summary of the editorial mission of the house, an overarching principle that ties together what they publish. Under the heading **Acquisitions:** we list many more editors, often with their specific areas of expertise. We have also increased the number of recent titles to help give you an idea of the publishers' scope. We have included the royalty rates for those publishers willing to disclose them, but contract details are closely guarded and a number of larger publishers are reluctant to publicly state these terms. Standard royalty rates for paperbacks generally range from 7½ to 12½ percent, for hardcovers from 10 to 15 percent. Royalty rates for children's books are often lower, generally ranging from 5 to 10 percent.

Finally, we have listed a number of publishers who only accept agented submissions. This benefits the agents who use *Writer's Market*, those writers with agents who use the book themselves, and those as yet unagented writers who want to know more about a particular company.

For a list of publishers according to their subjects of interest, see the nonfiction and fiction sections of the Book Publishers Subject Index. Information on book publishers and producers listed in the previous edition of *Writer's Market* but not included in this edition can be found in the General Index.

A&B PUBLISHERS GROUP, 1000 Atlantic Ave., Brooklyn NY 11238. (718)783-7808. Fax: (718)783-7267. E-mail: maxtay@webspan.net. **Acquisitions:** Maxwell Taylor, production manager (children's, adult nonfiction); Wendy Gift, editor (fiction). Estab. 1992. Publishes hardcover originals and trade paperback originals and reprints. **Publishes 12 titles/year. Receives 120 queries and 150 mss/year. 30% of books from first-time authors; 30% from unagented writers. Pays 5-12% royalty on net price. Offers $500-2,500 advance.** Publishes book 12-18 months after acceptance of ms. Accepts simultaneous submissions. Responds in 2 months to queries and proposals, 5 months to mss. Book catalog free.

⚷ The audience for A&B Publishers Group is African-Americans. Currently emphasizing children's books. **Nonfiction:** Children's/juvenile, coffee table book, cookbook, illustrated book. Subjects include cooking/foods/nutrition, history. Query. Reviews artwork/photos as part of ms package. Send photocopies.

Fiction: Query.
Recent Title(s): *Nutricide*, by Llaila O. Afrika (nonfiction).
Tips: "Read, read, read. The best writers are developed from good reading. There is not enough attention to quality."

A ABBEVILLE PUBLISHING GROUP, 22 Cortland St., New York NY 10007. (212)577-5555. Fax: (212)577-5579. Website: www.abbeville.com. Estab. 1977. Publishes illustrated hardcover and trade paperback originals. **Pays royalty.** Publishes book 18 months after acceptance of ms. *Agented submissions only.*
   ● Abbeville publishes high-quality illustrated trade nonfiction.
Imprint(s): Abbeville Press, Abbeville Kids, Artabras (promotional books), Cross River Press, Modern Masters.

N ABDO PUBLISHING COMPANY, 4940 Viking Dr., Edina MN 55435. (612)831-1317. Fax: (612)831-1632. E-mail: info@abdopub.com. Website: www.abdopub.com. **Acquisitions:** Paul Abdo, editor-in-chief (nonfiction, sports, history); Bob Italia, senior editor (science, history). Publishes hardcover originals. **Publishes 120 titles/year. Each imprint publishes 40 titles/year. Receives 300 queries and 100 mss/year. 10% of books from first-time authors; 90% from unagented writers. Makes outright purchase $500-1,200. No advance.** Publishes book 6 months after acceptance of ms. Accepts simultaneous submissions. Responds in 2 months to queries, 4 months to proposals, 6 months to mss. Book catalog and ms guidelines free on request.
   ○➤ ABDO publishes nonfiction children's books (pre-kindergarten to 6th grade) for school and public libraries—mainly history, sports and biography.
Imprints: ABDO & Daughters, Checkerboard Library, SandCastle.
Nonfiction: Biography, children's/juvenile, how-to. Subjects include animals, history, sports. Query with SASE.
Recent Title(s): *Civil War*, by Ann Guines (children's nonfiction); *Ricky Martin*, by Paul Joseph (children's biography).

N ABI PROFESSIONAL PUBLICATIONS, P.O. Box 5243, Arlington VA 22205. (703)538-5750. Fax: (703)536-9644. E-mail: vandamere@netzero.net. Website: www.abipropub.com. **Acquisitions:** Art Brown, publisher/editor-in-chief (prosthetics, rehabilitation, dental/medical research). Publishes hardcover and trade paperback originals. **Publishes 10 titles/year. Receives 20-30 queries and 5-10 mss/year. 25% of books from first-time authors; 100% from unagented writers. Pays royalty on revenues generated. Offers small advance.** Publishes book 1 year after acceptance of ms. Accepts simultaneous submissions. Responds in 3 months. Book catalog and manuscript guidelines on website.
Nonfiction: Reference, technical, textbook. Health/medicine subjects. Submit proposal package, including outline, representative chapter and author bio or submit complete ms. Reviews artwork/photos as part of ms package. Send photocopies.
Recent Title(s): *Cleft Palate Dentistry*, by Robert McKinstry (dental text); *Managing Stroke*, by Paul R. Rao and John E. Toerge (rehabilitation).
Tips: Audience is Allied health professionals, dentists, researchers, patients undergoing physical rehabilitation.

ABINGDON PRESS, The United Methodist Publishing House, 201 Eighth Ave. S., Nashville TN 37203. (615)749-6000. Fax: (615)749-6512. Website: www.abingdon.org. President/Publisher: Neil M. Alexander. Senior Vice President/Publishing: Harriett Jane Olson. **Acquisitions:** Robert Ratcliff, senior editor (professional clergy); Peg Augustine, editor (children's); Joseph A. Crowe, editor (general interest). Estab. 1789. Publishes hardcover and paperback originals; church supplies. **Publishes 120 titles/year. Receives 3,000 queries and 250 mss/year. Few books from first-time authors; 85% of books from unagented writers. Generally pays 7½% royalty on retail price.** Publishes book 2 years after acceptance. Book catalog free. Manuscript guidelines for SASE. Responds in 2 months.
   ○➤ Abingdon Press, America's oldest theological publisher, provides an ecumenical publishing program dedicated to serving the Christian community—clergy, scholars, church leaders, musicians and general readers—with quality resources in the areas of Bible study, the practice of ministry, theology, devotion, spirituality, inspiration, prayer, music and worship, reference, Christian education and church supplies.
Imprint(s): Abingdon Press, Cokesbury, Dimensions for Living.
Nonfiction: Religious-lay and professional, gift book, reference, children's religious books, academic texts. Query with outline and samples only.
Recent Title(s): *Celtic Praise*, by Van de Weyer (gift).

N ABIQUE, 1700 Amelia Court, #423, Plano TX 75075. E-mail: abique@lycosmail.com. Website: http://members.xoom.com/abique. **Acquisitions:** Tom Kyle, editorial director. Publishes hardcover and trade paperback originals. **Publishes 20 titles/year. Pays 10% royalty on wholesale price.** Publishes book 6 months after acceptance of ms. Accepts simultaneous submissions. Responds in 1 month to queries.
   ○➤ "We are somewhat like a university press in that we seek books with too narrow an audience for other publishers to consider." Currently emphasizing history, law, local interest. De-emphasizing fiction, textbooks, illustrated and photo books.
Nonfiction: Reference, technical, academic disciplines. Subjects include anthropology/archaeology, government/politics, health/medicine, history, nature/environment, philosophy, science, sociology. Query first with SASE. Reviews artwork/photos as part of the ms package. Send photocopies.
Recent Title(s): *America's Worst Train Disaster*, by Don Moody (nonfiction); *Answering the Call*, by Michael Long (nonfiction).

Tips: "We specialize in books aimed directly at a small specialized audience. Our authors are experts who write for a limited audience. We rely on them to direct us to that audience and to know what that audience wants to read. We want authors who will work to promote their book."

HARRY N. ABRAMS, INC., La Martinière Groupe, 100 Fifth Ave., New York NY 10011. (212)206-7715. Fax: (212)645-8437. Website: www.abramsbooks.com. Publisher/Editor-in-Chief: Paul Gottlieb. **Acquisitions:** Eric Himmel, executive editor. Estab. 1949. Publishes hardcover and "a few" paperback originals. **Publishes 150 titles/year. Pays royalty. Offers variable advance.** Publishes book 2 years after acceptance of ms. Responds in 3 months. Book catalog for $5.

  O→ "We publish *only* high-quality illustrated art books, i.e., art, art history, museum exhibition catalogs, written by specialists and scholars in the field."

Nonfiction: Art, architecture, nature and science, outdoor recreation. Requires illustrated material for art and art history, museums. Submit outline, sample chapters and illustrations. Reviews artwork/photos as part of ms package.

Tips: "We are one of the few publishers who publish almost exclusively illustrated books. We consider ourselves the leading publishers of art books and high-quality artwork in the U.S. Once the author has signed a contract to write a book for our firm the author must finish the manuscript to agreed-upon high standards within the schedule agreed upon in the contract."

ABSEY & CO., 23011 Northcrest Dr., Spring TX 77389. (281)257-2340. E-mail: abseyandco@aol.com. Website: www.absey.com. **Acquisitions:** Trey Hall, editor-in-chief. Publishes hardcover, trade paperback and mass market paperback originals. **Publishes 6-10 titles/year. 50% of books from first-time authors; 50% from unagented writers. Royalty and advance vary.** Publishes book 1 year after acceptance of ms. No e-mail submissions. Responds in 3 months to queries, 9 months to mss. Manuscript guidelines for #10 SASE or on website.

  O→ "Our goal is to publish original, creative works of literary merit." Currently emphasizing educational, young adult literature. De-emphasizing self-help.

Nonfiction: Educational subjects and language arts, as well as general nonfiction. Query with SASE.

Fiction: "Since we are a small, new press, we are looking for book-length manuscripts with a firm intended audience." Query with SASE.

Poetry: Publishes the "Writers and Young Writers Series." Interested in thematic poetry collections of literary meit. Query with SASE.

Recent Title(s): *The Legacy of Roxaboxen*, by Alice MeLerran (nonfiction); *Dragonfly*, by Alice McLerran (fiction); *Where I'm From*, by George Ella Lyon (poetry).

  ● *Where I'm From* was named "2000" New York Public Library's Best Book for the Teen Age.

Tips: "We work closely and attentively with authors and their work."

ACADEMY CHICAGO PUBLISHERS, 363 W. Erie St., Chicago IL 60610-3125. (312)751-7300. Fax: (312)751-7306. E-mail: academy363@aol.com. Website: www.academychicago.com. **Acquisitions:** Anita Miller, editorial director/senior editor. Estab. 1975. Publishes hardcover originals and trade paperback reprints. **Publishes 15 titles/year. Receives approximately 2,000 submissions/year. Publishes first-time and unagented authors. Pays 7-10% royalty on wholesale price. Modest advances.** Publishes book 18 months after acceptance. Book catalog for 9 × 12 SAE with 6 first-class stamps. Manuscript guidelines for #10 SASE. Responds in 2 months. "No electronic submissions."

  O→ "We publish quality fiction and nonfiction. Our audience is literate and discriminating. No novelized biography or history."

Nonfiction: Biography. Subjects include history, travel. Submit proposal package, including outline, first 3 chapters and author information.

Recent Title(s): *Hitler: The Man & The Military Leader*, by Percy Ernst Schramm; *Too Late for the Festival*, by Rhiannon Paine.

Fiction: Historical, mainstream/contemporary, military/war, mystery. "We look for quality work, but we do not publish experimental, avant garde novels." Submit proposal package, including synopsis, first 3 chapters.

Recent Title(s): *The Other Rebecca*, by Maureen Freely (novel); *Glass Hearts*, by Terri Paul (novel); *Man Who Once Played Catch with Nellie Fox*, by John Mandarino (humorous sports novel).

Tips: "At the moment, we are looking for good nonfiction; we certainly want excellent original fiction, but we are swamped. No fax queries, no disks. We are always interested in reprinting good out-of-print books."

ACE SCIENCE FICTION AND FANTASY, The Berkley Publishing Group, Penguin Putnam Inc., 375 Hudson St., New York NY 10014. (212)366-2000. Website: www.penguinputnam.com. **Acquisitions:** Anne Sowards, editor. Estab. 1953. Publishes hardcover, paperback originals and reprints. **Publishes 75 titles/year.** Responds in 6 months. Manuscript guidelines for #10 SASE.

  O→ Ace publishes exclusively science fiction and fantasy.

Fiction: Science fiction, fantasy. *Agented submissions only.* Query first with SASE.

Recent Title(s): *Obsidian Butterfly*, by Laurell K. Hamilton; *All Tomorrow's Parties*, by William Gibson.

ACROPOLIS BOOKS, INC., 8601 Dunwoody Pl., Suite 303, Atlanta GA 30350. (770)643-1118. Fax: (770)643-1170. E-mail: acropolisbooks@mindspring.com. Website: www.acropolisbooks.com. **Acquisitions:** W. Allen Marsh, managing editor (spiritual unfoldment, spiritual experience). Estab. 1958. Publishes hardcover and trade paperback originals and reprints. **Publishes 20 titles/year; imprint publishes 5-10 titles/year. Receives 150 queries and 80 mss/year. 30% of books from first-time authors; 90% from unagented writers. Royalties or outright purchases negotiable. Advances negotiable.** Publishes book an average of 1 year after acceptance of ms. Responds in 1 month to queries and proposals, 2 months to mss. Book catalog and ms guidelines for #10 SASE.

> ⛗ "It is the mission of Acropolis Books to publish books at the highest level of consciousness, commonly referred to as mysticism. This was the consciousness demonstrated by revelators of every religion in the world. Our commitment is the publication of mystical literature—the spiritual principles of Omnipresence, Omnipotence and Omniscience and its expression."

Imprint(s): I-Level, Awakening.

Nonfiction: Inspirational. Subjects include philosophy, religion and mysticism. "We publish books of higher consciousness and books that are a bridge to higher consciousness. Writers must understand our focus." Submit 4 sample chapters with SASE. Reviews artwork/photos as part of ms package. Send photocopies.

Fiction: Mysticism/inspirational. "Our books encompass the spiritual principles of Omniprescence, Omnipotence and Omniscience; and further bring home the mystical realization that everyone in this world is an individual instrument of God in expression." Submit 4 sample chapters with SASE.

Poetry: Submit complete ms.

Recent Title(s): *The Contemplative Life*, by Joel S. Goldsmith (nonfiction); *The Osford Book of English Mystical Verse* (poetry).

Tips: "Clearly understand our focus by reading or understanding books that we have published. We accept very few manuscripts."

⊠ **ACTA PUBLICATIONS**, 4848 N. Clark St., Chicago IL 60640-4711. Fax: (773)271-7399. E-mail: gfapierce@aol .com. **Acquisitions:** Gregory F. Augustine Pierce. Estab. 1958. Publishes trade paperback originals. **Publishes 10 titles/year. Receives 50 queries and 15 mss/year. 50% of books from first-time authors; 90% from unagented writers. Pays 10-12% royalty on wholesale price.** Publishes book 1 year after acceptance of ms. Responds in 2 months to proposals. Book catalog and author guidelines for SASE.

> ⛗ ACTA publishes non-academic, practical books aimed at the mainline religious market.

Nonfiction: Religion. Submit outline and 1 sample chapter. Reviews artwork/photos. Send photocopies.

Recent Title(s): *Protect Us from All Anxiety: Meditations for the Depressed*, by William Burke (self-help).

Tips: "Don't send a submission unless you have read our catalog or one of our books."

ADAMS MEDIA CORPORATION, 260 Center St., Holbrook MA 02343. (781)767-8100. Fax: (781)767-0994. E-mail: editors@adamsmedia.com. Website: www.adamsmedia.com. **Acquisitions:** Edward Walters, editor-in-chief (humor, personal finance, popular reference and parenting); Pamela Liflander, senior editor (health, New Age, religion, spirituality, history and biography); Jere Calmes, senior business editor (history, investing, marketing, management, small business and entrepreneurship); Paula Munier Lee, senior editor (self-help, psychology, lifestyle, alternative medicine and women's issues); Cheryl Kimball, acquisitions editor (health, self-help, cooking, gardening and general lifestyle); William McNeill, associate editor (careers, job hunting, nature, sports, recreation and personal finance). senior business editor; Cheryl Kimball. Estab. 1980. Publishes hardcover originals, trade paperback originals and reprints. **Publishes 200 titles/year. Receives 5,000 queries and 1,500 mss/year. 25% of books from first-time authors; 25% from unagented writers. Pays standard royalty or makes outright purchase. Offers variable advance.** Publishes book 1 year after acceptance of ms. Accepts simultaneous submissions. Responds in 3 months.

> ⛗ Adams Media publishes commercial nonfiction, including career titles, innovative business and self-help books.

Nonfiction: Biography, cookbook, gift book, how-to, humor, illustrated book, reference, self-help. Subjects include Americana, animals, business/economics, child guidance/parenting, cooking/foods/nutrition, gardening, government/politics, health/medicine, history, hobbies, language/literature, military/war, money/finance, nature/environment, psychology, regional, science, sports, women's issues/studies. Submit outline. Does not return unsolicited materials.

Recent Title(s): *Dream Big*, by Cynthia Stewart-Copier; *Heart Warmers*, by Azriela Jaffe.

⊠ **ADAMS-BLAKE PUBLISHING**, 8041 Sierra St., Fair Oaks CA 95628. (916)962-9296. Website: www.adams-blake.com. Vice President: Paul Raymond. **Acquisitions:** Monica Blane, senior editor. Estab. 1992. Publishes trade paperback originals and reprints. **Publishes 10-15 titles/year. Receives 150 queries and 90 mss/year. 90% of books from first-time authors; 90% from unagented writers. Pays 15% royalty on wholesale price.** Publishes book 6 months after acceptance of ms. Accepts simultaneous submissions. Responds in 3 months to mss.

> ⛗ Adams-Blake Publishing is looking for business, technology and finance titles as well as data that can be bound/packaged and sold to specific industry groups at high margins. "We publish technical and training material we can sell to the corporate market. We are especially looking for 'high ticket' items that sell to the corporate market for prices between $100-300." Currently emphasizing technical, computers, technology. De-emphasizing business, management.

Nonfiction: How-to, technical. Subjects include business/economics, computers/electronics, health/medicine, money/finance, software. Query with sample chapters or complete ms. Reviews artwork/photos as part of ms package. Send photocopies.

Recent Title(s): *Success From Home*, by Alan Canton.

Tips: "We will take a chance on material the big houses reject. Since we sell the majority of our material directly, we can publish material for a very select market. This year we seek niche market material that we can Docutech™ and sell direct to the corporate sector. Author should include a marketing plan. Sell us on the project!"

ADDAX PUBLISHING GROUP, INC., 8643 Hauser Dr., Suite 235, Lenexa KS 66215. (913)438-5333. Fax: (913)438-2079. E-mail: addax1@addaxpublishing.com. **Acquisitions:** Submissions Editor. Estab. 1992. Publishes hardcover and trade paperback originals. **Publishes 20 titles/year. 50% of books from first-time authors; 75% from unagented writers. Pays royalty. No advance.** Publishes book 1 year after acceptance of ms. Accepts simultaneous submissions.

    ○━ Addax Publishing Group publishes sports books on and with athletes and teams in both professional and college sports. "In addition, we publish children's books for holidays, goal-oriented children's books with sports themes, select inspiration, motivation, how-to, and humor books. Our titles have both regional and national emphasis."

Nonfiction: Biography, children's/juvenile, coffee table book. Subjects include sports and entertainment. Submit completed ms.

Recent Titles: *George Brett from Here to Cooperstown*; *Favre Family Cookbook*; *The Tigers and Their Den*.

Tips: "We have a fairly tightly defined niche in sports-related areas."

ADDICUS BOOKS, INC., P.O. Box 45327, Omaha NE 68145. (402)330-7493. **Acquisitions:** Rod Colvin, president. Website: www.AddicusBooks.com. Estab. 1994. Publishes trade paperback originals. **Publishes 8-10 titles/year. 70% of books from first-time authors; 60% from unagented writers. Pays royalty on retail price.** Publishes book 9 months after acceptance of ms. Accepts simultaneous submissions. Responds in 1 month to proposals. Guidelines for #10 SASE. "No electronic submissions, please."

    ○━ Addicus Books, Inc. seeks mss with strong national or regional appeal.

Nonfiction: How-to, self-help. Subjects include Americana, business/economics, health/medicine, psychology, regional, true-crime. Query with outline and 3-4 sample chapters.

Recent Title(s): *Lung Cancer—A Guide to Diagnosis & Treatment*, by Walter Scott, M.D. (health); *The Marital Compatibility Test*, by Susan Adams (relationships).

Tips: "We are looking for quick-reference books on health topics. Do some market research to make sure the market is not already flooded with similar books. We're also looking for good true-crime manuscripts, with an interesting story, with twists and turns, behind the crime."

ADIRONDACK MOUNTAIN CLUB, INC., 814 Goggins Rd., Lake George NY 12845-4117. (518)668-4447. Fax: (518)668-3746. E-mail: pubs@adk.org. Website: adk.org. **Acquisitions:** Andrea Masters, publications director (all titles); Neal Burdick, editor (*Adirondac* magazine, published bimonthly). Publishes hardcover and trade paperback originals and reprints. **Publishes 34 titles/year. Receives 36 queries and 12 mss/year. 95% of books from first-time authors; 95% from unagented writers. Pays 6-10% royalty on retail price. Offers $250-500 advance.** Publishes book 8 months after acceptance of ms. Responds in 3 months to queries, 4 months to proposals and mss. Book catalog free on request and on website. Manuscript guidelines free on request.

    ○━ "Our main focus is recreational guides to Adirondack and Catskill parks; however, our titles continue to include natural, cultural and literary histories of these regions. Our main interest is in protecting the resource with environmental publications. This is the focus of our magazine, *Adirondac*, as well."

Nonfiction: Reference. Subjects include nature/environment, recreation, regional, sports, travel, trail maps. Query with SASE or submit proposal package, including outline, 1-2 sample chapters and proposed illustrations and visuals. Reviews artwork/photos as part of the ms package. Send photocopies.

Recent Title(s): *Trailside Notes: A Naturalist's Companion to Adirondack Plants*, by Ruth Schottman; *Kids on the Trail! Hiking with Children in the Adirondacks*, by Rose Rivezzi.

Tips: "Our audience consists of outdoors people interested in muscle-powered recreation, natural history, and 'armchair traveling' in the Adirondacks and Catskills. Bear in mind the educational mandate implicit in our organization's mission. Note range of current ADK titles."

AHA PRESS, American Hospital Association, One N. Franklin, Chicago IL 60606. (312)893-6800. Fax: (312)422-4500. E-mail: hill@healthforum.com. Website: www.healthforum.com. **Acquisitions:** Editorial Director. Estab. 1979. Publishes hardcover and trade paperback originals. **Publishes 15-20 titles/year. Receives 75-100 submissions/year. 20% of books from first-time authors; 100% from unagented writers. Pays 10-12% royalty on net sale. Offers $1,000 average advance.** Publishes book 1 year after acceptance. Responds in 6 months. Book catalog and ms guidelines for 9×12 SAE with 7 first-class stamps.

    ○━ AHA Press publishes books on health care administration primarily for senior and middle management of health care institutions, as well as for trustees and other community leaders. Currently emphasizing comprehensive reference works and handbooks. De-emphasizing monographs.

Nonfiction: Reference, technical, textbook. Subjects include business/economics (specific to health care institutions); health/medicine (never consumer oriented). Need field-based, reality-tested responses to changes in the health care field directed to hospital CEO's, planners, boards of directors, or other senior management. No personal histories, untested health care programs or clinical texts. Query with SASE.

Recent Title(s): *Error Reduction in Health Care*; *Technology and the Future of Health Care*.

Tips: "The successful proposal demonstrates a clear understanding of the needs of the market and the writer's ability to succinctly present practical knowledge of demonstrable benefit that comes from genuine experience that readers will recognize, trust and accept."

ALASKA NORTHWEST BOOKS, Graphic Arts Center Publishing. Editorial offices: P.O. Box 10306, Portland OR 97296-0306. (503)226-2402. Fax: (503)223-1410. **Acquisitions:** Tricia Brown. Estab. 1999. Publishes hardcover and trade paperback originals and reprints. Publishes 12 titles/year. Receives hundreds of submissions/year. 10% of books from first-time authors; 90% from unagented writers. Pays 10-15% royalty on wholesale price. Buys mss outright (rarely). Offers advance. Publishes book an average of 1 year after acceptance. Accepts simultaneous submissions. Responds in 6 months to queries. Book catalog and ms guidelines for 9×12 SAE with 6 first-class stamps.

   O→ "Our book needs are as follows: one-half Alaskan focus, one-quarter Northwest, one-eighth Pacific coast, one-eighth national (looking for logical extensions of current subjects)."

Nonfiction: "All written for a general readership, not for experts in the subject." Subjects include nature and environment, travel, cookbooks, Native American culture, adventure, outdoor recreation and sports, the arts, children's books. Submit outline/synopsis and sample chapters.

Recent Title(s): *Through Yup'ik Eyes*, by Colin Chisholm (memoir).

Tips: "Book proposals that are professionally written and polished, with a clear market receive our most careful consideration. We are looking for originality. We publish a wide range of books for a wide audience. Some of our books are clearly for travelers, others for those interested in outdoor recreation or various regional subjects. If I were a writer trying to market a book today, I would research the competition (existing books) for what I have in mind, and clearly (and concisely) express why my idea is different and better. I would describe the bookbuyers (and readers)—where they are, how many of them are there, how they can be reached (organizations, publications), why they would want or need my book."

ALBA HOUSE, 2187 Victory Blvd., Staten Island NY 10314-6603. (718)761-0047. Fax: (718)761-0057. E-mail: albabooks@aol.com. Website: www.albahouse.org. **Acquisitions:** Edmund C. Lane, S.S.P., editor. Estab. 1961. Publishes hardcover, trade paperback and mass market paperback originals. **Publishes 24 titles/year. Receives 300 queries and 150 mss/year. 20% of books from first-time authors; 100% from unagented writers. Pays 7-10% royalty. No advance.** Publishes book 9 months after acceptance of ms. Responds in 1 month to queries and proposals, 2 months to mss. Book catalog and ms guidelines free.

   O→ Alba House is the North American publishing division of the Society of St. Paul, an International Roman Catholic Missionary Religious Congregation dedicated to spreading the Gospel message.

Nonfiction: Reference, textbook. Religious subjects. Manuscripts which contribute, from a Roman Catholic perspective, to the personal, intellectual and spiritual growth of individuals in the following areas: Scripture, theology and the Church, saints (their lives and teachings), spirituality and prayer, religious life, marriage and family life, liturgy and homily preparation, pastoral concerns, religious education, bereavement, moral and ethical concerns, philosophy, psychology. Reviews artwork/photos as part of ms package. Send photocopies.

Recent Title(s): *Christian Spirituality*, by Charles J. Healey, S.J.

THE ALBAN INSTITUTE, 7315 Wisconsin Ave., Suite 1250 W., Bethesda MD 20814-3211. (301)718-4407. Fax: (301)718-1958. Website: www.alban.com. **Acquisitions:** David Lott, managing editor (multicultural/diversity; faith & health); Beth Gaede, acquisitions editor (women's issues; congregational size issues; faith, money & lifestyle). For submissions to the journal *Congregations*, send to Lisa Kinney. Estab. 1974. Publishes trade paperback originals. **Publishes 12 titles/year. Receives 100 submissions/year. 100% of books from unagented writers. Pays 7-10% royalty on books;** makes outright purchase of $50-100 on publication for 450-2,000 word articles relevant to congregational life—practical—ecumenical. Publishes book 1 year after acceptance. Responds in 4 months. Book catalog and ms guidelines for 9×12 SAE with 3 first-class stamps.

   O→ "Our publications have a focus on practical, how-to materials, usually based on extensive research, that reaches an ecumenical and sometimes interfaith audience without a particular theological slant." Emphasizing multiculturalism; faith & health; mission & purpose; technology. De-emphasizing sexuality issues; pastoral searches; geriatrics.

Nonfiction: Religious—focus on local congregation—ecumenical. Must be accessible to general reader. Research preferred. Needs mss on the task of the ordained leader in the congregation, the career path of the ordained leader in the congregation, problems and opportunities in congregational life, and ministry of the laity in the world and in the church. No sermons, biblical studies, devotional, children's titles, novels, inspirational or prayers. Query for guidelines. Proposals only, no unsolicited mss.

Recent Title(s): *Letters to Lee: Mentoring the New Minister*, by Paul C. Clayton (nonfiction).

Tips: "Our audience is comprised of intelligent, probably liberal mainline Protestant and Catholic clergy and lay leaders, executives and seminary administration/faculty—people who are concerned with the local church at a practical level and new approaches to its ministry. We are looking for titles on congregations, the clergy role, calling and career; visions, challenges, how-to's; and the ministry of the laity in the church and in the world."

ALBURY PUBLISHING, P.O. Box 470406, Tulsa OK 74147. **Acquisitions:** Elizabeth Sherman, editorial development manager. Publishes hardcover and trade paperback originals and reprints. **Publishes 20 titles/year. Receives 200 queries**

and 360 mss/year. **1% of books from first-time authors; 50% from unagented writers. Pays royalty or makes outright purchase.** Publishes book 2 years after acceptance of ms. Responds in 6 months to proposals. Book catalog for 9×12 SAE and 5 first-class stamps. Manuscript guidelines for #10 SASE.

○━ "We are a Christian publisher with an upbeat presentation."

Nonfiction: Bible teaching, humor, self-help, compilations of historic Christian leaders and devotionals. "Most of our authors are established ministers and friends of the house. In order to break into our market, writers must exhibit a clearly defined, professionally presented proposal that shows they know and understand our market." Submit outline, complete ms, marketing plan, itinerary and author bio with SASE.

Recent Title(s): *Jesus Freaks,* by dc Talk; *Voice of the Martyrs.*

ALEF DESIGN GROUP, 4423 Fruitland Ave., Los Angeles CA 90058. (213)585-7312. Website: www.alefdesign.com. **Acquisitions:** Jane Golub. Estab. 1990. Publishes hardcover and trade paperback originals. **Publishes 25 titles/year; imprint publishes 10 titles/year. Receives 30 queries and 30 mss/year. 80% of books from first-time authors; 100% from unagented writers. Pays 10% royalty.** Publishes book 3 years after acceptance of ms. Accepts simultaneous submissions. Responds in 6 months to mss. Book catalog for 9×12 SAE and 10 first-class stamps.

○━ The Alef Design Group publishes books of Judaic interest only. Currently de-emphasizing picture books.

Nonfiction: Children's/juvenile, textbook. Subjects include language/literature (Hebrew), religion (Jewish). Query with SASE. Reviews artwork/photos as part of ms package. Send photocopies.

Fiction: Juvenile, religious, young adult. "We publish books of Judaic interest only." Query with SASE.

Recent Title(s): *Scripture Windows,* by Peter Pitzele (nonfiction); *The Road to Exile,* by Didier Nebot (fiction).

N ALEXANDER BOOKS, Creativity, Inc., 65 Macedonia Rd., Alexander NC 28701. (828)252-9515. Fax: (828)255-8719. E-mail: sales@abooks.com. Website: www.abooks.com. **Acquisitions:** Pat Roberts, acquisitions editor. Publishes hardcover originals and trade paperback and mass market paperback originals and reprints. **Publishes 15-20 titles/year. Receives 200 queries and 100 mss/year. 10% of books from first-time authors; 75% from unagented writers. Pays 12-15% royalty on wholesale price. Advances seldom given (minimum $100).** Publishes book 18 months after acceptance of ms. Book catalog and ms guidelines for 9×12 SASE with $1.01 postage.

○━ Alexander Books publishes mostly nonfiction national titles, both new and reprints.

Imprint(s): Farthest Star (classic science fiction, very few new titles), Mountain Church (mainline Protestant material).

Nonfiction: Biography, how-to, reference, self-help. Subjects include computers/electronics, government/politics, collectibles, history, regional, religion, travel. "We are interested in large niche markets." Query or submit 3 sample chapters and proposal package, including marketing plans with SASE. Reviews artwork/photos as part of ms package. Send photocopies.

Fiction: Historical, mainstream/contemporary, mystery, science fiction, western. "We prefer local or well-known authors or local interest settings". Query or submit synopsis and 3 sample chapters with SASE.

Recent Title(s): *Sanders Price Guide to Autographs,* 5th ed., by Sanders and Roberts; *Birthright,* by Mike Resnick.

Tips: "Send well-proofed manuscripts in final form. We will not read first rough drafts. Know your market."

ALGONQUIN BOOKS OF CHAPEL HILL, Workman Publishing, P.O. Box 2225, Chapel Hill NC 27515-2225. (919)967-0108. Website: www.algonquin.com. Editorial Director: Shannon Ravenel. **Acquisitions:** Editorial Department. Estab. 1982. "We're a very small company that tries to give voice to new writers." Publishes hardcover originals, trade paperback originals and reprints of own titles. **Publishes 24 titles/year.** Query by mail before submitting work. No phone, e-mail, or fax queries or submissions. Visit our website for full submission policy.

○━ Algonquin Books publishes quality literary fiction and nonfiction.

N ALLEGRO PRESS, 102 46th St., Holmes Beach FL 34217-1814. (941)778-1953. Fax: (941)778-7146. E-mail: publisher@allegro-press.com. Website: www.allegro-press.com. **Acquisitions:** Acquisitions Editor. Publishes trade paperback originals. **Publishes 6 titles/year. 80% of books from first-time authors; 100% from unagented writers. Pays 90% royalty on net sales after direct expenses met. Publishes book 6 months after acceptance of ms. Responds in 1 month to mss.** Book catalog on website.

○━ Allegro Press works almost exclusively with solicited authors.

Nonfiction: Children's/juvenile, technical. Subjects include government/politics, military/war, philosophy, religion, science. Submit completed ms. Reviews artwork/photos as part of ms package. Send photocopies.

Fiction: History or allegory only (allegory may take form of mystery, romance, science fiction, spiritual, suspense). Submit completed ms.

Recent Title(s): *Shall We Clone a Man?,* by Alonso (religion/philosophy); *Melisande* (allegory).

Tips: "A non-majority viewpoint will be treated with serious consideration."

N ALLIGATOR PRESS, INC., P.O. Box 49158, Austin TX 78765. (512)454-0496. Fax: (512)380-0098. E-mail: kkimball@alligatorpress.com. Website: www.alligatorpress.com. **Acquisitions:** Kirk Markin, editor (literature, fiction, romance, humor); Rachelle Cruz, editor (women's subjects, mystery); Wendy Broadwater, editor (gay/lesbian). Publishes hardcover, trade paperback and mass market paperback originals. **Publishes 8 titles/year. Pays 5-10% royalty on retail price. Offers $500-5,000 advance.** Publishes book 8 months after acceptance of ms. Accepts simultaneous submissions. Responds in 1 month to queries, 2 months to proposals, 3 months to mss. Manuscript guidelines on website.

Nonfiction: Self-help. Subjects include gay/lesbian, language/literature. Query with SASE or submit proposal package, including outline and 5 sample chapters or submit completed ms. Reviews artwork/photos as part of ms package. Send transparencies.

Fiction: Adventure, erotica, ethnic, feminist, gay/lesbian, horror, literary, mainstream/contemporary, military/war, multicultural, mystery, poetry, romance, science fiction, suspense. Query with SASE or submit proposal package, including synopsis and 5 sample chapters or submit completed ms.

Poetry: Query, submit 5 sample poems or submit complete ms.

Recent Title(s): *Cuando cantan los lagartos*, by Miguel Santana (historial romance); *Cloven*, by Chae Waters (mystery/suspense).

ALLISONE PRESS, Star Rising Publishers, P.O. Box 494, Mt. Shasta CA 96067-0494. Phone/fax: (877)249-6894. E-mail: publisher@allisonepress.com. Website: www.allisonepress.com. **Acquisitions:** Robin May, publisher (New Age, metaphysical); Kristen B. May, editor (poetry, fiction); Leondra, editor (Earth-based religions, occult, paranormal). Publishes trade paperback originals. **Publishes 5-6 titles/year; imprints publish 2-3 titles/year. Receives 100 queries and 75 mss/year. 90% of books from first-time authors; 90% from unagented writers. Pays 10-20% royalty on retail price or makes outright purchase of $500-5000. No advance.** Publishes book 18 months after acceptance of ms. Accepts simultaneous submissions. Responds in 1 month to queries and proposals, 4 months to mss. Book catalog and ms guidelines for #10 SASE or on website.

   O—π "We like books that help someone to understand how to do something. We cater to a wide audience, from the layperson to the expert." Currently emphasizing New Age, Wiccan, pagan. De-emphasizing science fiction, children's titles.

Imprint(s): Allisone (contact Robin May), Star Rising (contact Kristen May).

Nonfiction: How-to, self-help. Subjects include creative nonfiction, philosophy, religion, spirituality, astrology, occult, witchcraft, Earth religions, New Age, channeling, metaphysical. Submit complete ms. *Writer's Market* recommends query with SASE first.

Fiction: Fantasy, occult, poetry, religious, short story collections, spiritual. Submit complete ms. *Writer's Market* recommends query with SASE first. "We are looking for 'new writers' with that creative flow and uninhibited expression."

Poetry: Submit complete ms. *Writer's Market* recommends query with SASE first.

Recent Title(s): *Walk Like an Egyptian*, by Ramona Louise Wheeler (religion); *From the Beats to the B Sides*, by John Hulse (poetry).

Tips: "Be creative and don't judge your work too harshly. Free up the creativity that we all possess."

ALLWORTH PRESS, 10 E. 23rd St., Suite 510, New York NY 10010-4402. Fax: (212)777-8261. E-mail: pub@allworth.com. Website: www.allworth.com. **Acquisitions:** Tad Crawford, publisher; Nicole Potter, editor. Estab. 1989. Publishes hardcover and trade paperback originals. **Publishes 25-30 titles/year.** Responds in 3 months to queries and proposals. Book catalog and ms guidelines free on request.

   O—π Allworth Press publishes business and self-help information for artists, designers, photographers, authors and film and performing artists, as well as books about business, money and the law for the general public. The press also publishes the best of classic and contemporary writing in art and graphic design. Currently emphasizing photography, film, video and theater.

Nonfiction: How-to, reference. Subjects include the business aspects of art, design, photography, performing arts, writing, as well as business and legal guides for the public. Query.

Recent Title(s): *Sculpture in the Age of Doubt*, by Thomas McEvilley; *The Swastika*, by Steven Heller.

Tips: "We are trying to give ordinary people advice to better themselves in practical ways—as well as helping creative people in the fine and commercial arts."

ALLYN & BACON, Pearson Education Group, 160 Gould St., Needham Heights MA 02494. (781)455-1200. Website: www.abacon.com. **Acquisitions:** Nancy Forsyth, editorial director. *Education:* Arnis Burvikovs, editor (educational technology, reading/emergent literacy, language arts, children's literature, ESL/bilingual methods, education administration, vocational-ed methods); Traci Mueller, editor (C&I, social studies, curriculum, multicultural ed, math & science, early childhood); Paul Smith, editor (ed psych); Virginia Lanigan, editor (special ed, counseling); Steve Dragin, editor (special-path, aud, deaf study/ed, higher ed, foundations of education). *English:* Joe Opiela, editor (English comp plus developmental, authors with last name A-K and all developmental authors); Eben Ludlow, editor (English comp, authors with last name L-Z). *Communication:* Karen Bowers, editor (mass communication, speech communication, journalism, drama). *Psychology:* Becky Pascal, editor (psych, clinical, abnormal, statistics, human sexuality); Jeff Lasser, editor (psych, developmental); Carolyn Merrill, editor (intro, physio, social, cognitive); Joe Burns, editor (health, phys ed, dance, human sexuality). *Sociology:* Karen Hanson, editor (sociology/intro, crime, criminal justice); Judy Fifer, editor (social work, family therapy); Sarah Kelbaugh, editor (advanced sociology, anthropology). Publishes hardcover and trade paperback originals. **Publishes 300 titles/year. 5-10% of books from first-time authors; 95% from unagented writers. Pays 10-15% royalty on net price. Advance varies.** Publishes book 1-3 years after acceptance of ms. Accepts simultaneous submissions. Responds in 2 months to queries. Book catalog and ms guidelines free or on website.

   O—π Allyn & Bacon publishes college texts, freshman through graduate level, and professional reference books, in the areas of education, the humanities and the social sciences.

Nonfiction: Reference, technical, textbook; primarily college texts; some titles for professionals. Subjects include education, health, psychology, sociology, criminal justice, social work, speech, mass communication. Query with outline, 2-3 sample chapters, table of contents, author's vita and SASE. Reviews artwork/photos as part of ms package. Send photocopies.

Recent Title(s): *Social Psychology: Unraveling the Mystery,* by Kenrick Douglas, Steven Neubug and Robert Cialdini.

Tips: "We focus on a few areas and cover them thoroughly; publishing vertically, from freshman level through graduate level. We also publish a number of titles within each discipline, same area but different approach. So, just because we have titles in an area already, it doesn't mean we aren't interested in more."

ALYSON PUBLICATIONS, INC., 6922 Hollywood Blvd., Suite 1000, Los Angeles CA 90028. (323)860-6065. Fax: (323)467-0152. E-mail: mail@alyson.com. Website: www.alyson.com. **Acquisitions:** Attn. Editorial Dept.; Scott Brassart, associate publisher (fiction, science); Angela Brown, associate editor (women's fiction, arts). Estab. 1979. Publishes trade paperback originals and reprints. **Publishes 40 titles/year. Receives 1,500 submissions/year. 40% of books from first-time authors; 70% from unagented writers. Pays 8-15% royalty on net price. Offers $1,500-15,000 advance.** Publishes book 18 months after acceptance. Responds in 2 months. Book catalog and ms guidelines for 6×9 SAE with 3 first-class stamps.

Oₐ Alyson Publications publishes books for and about gay men and lesbians from all economic and social segments of society, and explores the political, legal, financial, medical, spiritual, social and sexual aspects of gay and lesbian life, and contributions to society. They also consider bisexual and transgender material. Emphasizing medical, legal and financial nonfiction titles.

Imprint(s): Alyson Wonderland, Alyson Classics Library.

Nonfiction: Gay/lesbian subjects. "We are especially interested in nonfiction providing a positive approach to gay/lesbian/bisexual issues." Accepts nonfiction translations. Submit 2-page outline with SASE. No dissertations. Reviews artwork/photos as part of ms package.

Fiction: Gay novels. Accepts fiction translations. No short stories, poetry. Submit 1-2 page synopsis with SASE.

Recent Title(s): *The New York Years,* by Felice Picano (fiction); *No Mercy,* by Pat Califia (nonfiction).

Tips: "We publish many books by new authors. The writer has the best chance of selling to our firm well-researched, popularly written nonfiction on a subject (e.g., some aspect of gay history) that has not yet been written about much. With fiction, create a strong storyline that makes the reader want to find out what happens. With nonfiction, write in a popular style for a nonacademic audience. We also look at manuscripts aimed at kids of lesbian and gay parents."

AMACOM BOOKS, American Management Association, 1601 Broadway, New York NY 10019-7406. (212)903-8417. Fax: (212)903-8083. Website: www.amanet.org. CEO: Weldon P. Rackley. President and Publisher: Hank Kennedy. **Acquisitions:** Adrienne Hickey, executive editor (management, human resources development, organizational effectiveness, strategic planning); Ellen Kadin, senior acquisitions editor (marketing, sales, customer service, personal development); Ray O'Connell, senior acquisitions editor (manufacturing, finance, project management); Jacquie Flynn, acquisitions editor (information technology, training). Estab. 1923. Publishes hardcover and trade paperback originals, professional books in various formats. **Publishes 90-100 titles/year. Receives 800 submissions/year. 50% of books from first-time authors; 70% from unagented writers. Pays 10-15% royalty on net receipts by the publisher. Publishes book 9 months after acceptance. Responds in 2 months. Book catalog and proposal guidelines free.**

Oₐ Amacom is the publishing arm of the American Management Association, the world's largest training organization for managers and executives. Amacom publishes books on business issues, strategies and tasks to enhance organizational and individual effectiveness. Currently emphasizing e-commerce. De-emphasizing small-business management, job-finding.

Nonfiction: Publishes business books of all types, including management, marketing, training, technology applications, finance, career, professional skills for retail, direct mail, college and corporate markets. Query or submit outline/synopsis, sample chapters, résumé.

Recent Title(s): *eBay the Smart Way,* by Joseph T. Sinclair; *Generations at Work,* by Ron Zemke, Claire Raines and Bob Filipczak.

AMBASSADOR BOOKS, INC., 71 Elm St., Worcester MA 01609. (508)756-2893. Fax: (508)757-7055. Website: www.ambassadorbooks.com. **Acquisitions:** Kathryn Conlan, acquisitions editor. Publishes hardcover and trade paperback originals. **Publishes 7 titles/year. Receives 50 queries and 25 mss/year. 50% of books from first-time authors; 90% from unagented writers. Pays 8-12% royalty on retail price.** Publishes book 10 months after acceptance. Accepts simultaneous submissions. Responds in 3 months. Book catalog free on request or on website.

Oₐ "We look for books of intellectual and/or spiritual excellence."

Nonfiction: Biography, children's/juvenile, coffee table book, illustrted book, self-help. Subjects include creative nonfiction, history, military/war, regional, religion, spirituality, sports. Query with SASE or submit completed ms. Reviews artwork/photos as part of the ms package. Send photocopies.

Fiction: Juvenile, literary, picture books, religious, spiritual, sports, young adult. Query with SASE or submit completed ms.

Recent Title(s): *Men of Spirit, Men of Sports,* by Wally Carew (sports and spirituality); *The Anonymous Disciple,* by Gerard Goggins (literary and spiritual).

AMBER BOOKS PUBLISHING, 1334 E. Chandler Blvd., Suite 5-D67, Phoenix AZ 85048. (602)460-1660. Fax: (602)283-0991. E-mail: amberbk@aol.com. Website: www.amberbooks.com. **Acquisitions:** Tony Rose, publisher (self help/African-American entertainment bios); Tenny Iuony, editor (African-American fashion, style). Estab. 1997. Publishes trade paperback and mass market paperback originals. **Publishes 5-10 titles/year. Receives 30 queries and 15 mss/year. 100% of books from first-time authors; 100% from unagented writers. Pays 10-15% royalty on wholesale price. No advance.** Publishes book 2 months after acceptance of ms. Accepts simultaneous submissions. Responds in 1 month. Book catalog free on request or on website.

   O─¬ Amber Books publishes entertainment bios on the latest African-American rappers and singers, self-help, finance, credit and how-to books.

Nonfiction: Biography, children's/juvenile, how-to, self-help. Subjects include multicultural, sports. Submit completed ms. Reviews artwork/photos as part of ms package. Send photocopies.

Fiction: Comic books, erotica, humor, romance (Black), sports. Submit completed ms.

Recent Titles: *Get That Cutie in Commercials, Television Films and Videos*, by Kanbias Conba; *The African-American Woman's Guide to Successful Make-Up and Skin Care*, by Alfred Fornay.

Tips: The goal of Amber Books is to build a strong catalog comprised of "self-help" books, celebrity bio books, and children's books, in print and on software, along with computer games which pertain to, about, and for the African-American population.

AMERICA WEST PUBLISHERS, P.O. Box 2208, Carson City NV 89702-2208. (775)585-0700. Fax: (877)726-2632. E-mail: global@nidlink.com. Website: www.hohoax.com. **Acquisitions:** George Green, president. Estab. 1985. Publishes hardcover and trade paperback originals and reprints. **Publishes 20 titles/year. Receives 150 submissions/year. 90% of books from first-time authors; 90% from unagented writers. Pays 10% on wholesale price. Offers $300 average advance.** Publishes book 6 months after acceptance. Accepts simultaneous submissions. Responds in 1 month. Book catalog and ms guidelines free.

   O─¬ America West seeks the "other side of the picture," political cover-ups and new health alternatives.

Imprint(s): Bridger House Publishers, Inc.

Nonfiction: Subjects include economic, health/medicine (holistic self-help), political (including cover-up), UFO—metaphysical. Submit outline/synopsis and sample chapters. Reviews artwork/photos as part of ms package.

Recent Title(s): *Psychokinesiology*, by Dr. Alec Halub.

Tips: "We currently have materials in all bookstores that have areas of UFOs; also political and economic nonfiction."

AMERICAN ATHEIST PRESS, P.O. Box 5733, Parsippany NJ 07054-6733. (908)259-0700. Fax: (908)259-0748. E-mail: editor@atheists.org. Website: www.atheists.org. **Acquisitions:** Frank Zindler, editor. Estab. 1959. Publishes trade paperback originals and reprints. **Publishes 12 titles/year. Receives 200 submissions/year. 40-50% of books from first-time authors; 100% from unagented writers. Pays 5-10% royalty on retail price.** Publishes book within 2 years after acceptance. Accepts simultaneous submissions. Responds in 4 months to queries. Book catalog for 6½×9½ SAE. Publishes quarterly journal, *American Atheist*, for which are needed articles of interest to atheists. Writer's guidelines for 9×12 SAE.

   O─¬ "We are interested in books that will help Atheists gain a deeper understanding of Atheism, improve their ability to critique religious propaganda, and assist them in fighting to maintain the 'wall of separation between state and church.'" Currently emphasizing the politics of religion, science and religion. De-emphasizing biblical criticism (but still doing some).

Imprint(s): Gustav Broukal Press.

Nonfiction: Biography, reference, general. Subjects include history (of religion and atheism, of the effects of religion historically); philosophy and religion (from an atheist perspective, particularly criticism of religion); politics (separation of state and church, religion and politics); atheism (particularly the lifestyle of atheism; the history of atheism; applications of atheism). "We would like to see more submissions dealing with the histories of specific religious sects, such as the L.D.S., the Worldwide Church of God, etc." Submit outline and sample chapters. Reviews artwork/photos.

Fiction: Humor (satire of religion or of current religious leaders); anything of particular interest to atheists. "We rarely publish any fiction. But we have occasionally released a humorous book. No mainstream. For our press to consider fiction, it would have to tie in with the general focus of our press, which is the promotion of atheism and free thought." Submit outline/synopsis and sample chapters.

Recent Title(s): *Living in the Light: Freeing Your Child from the Dark Ages*, by Anne Stone (rearing atheist children).

Tips: "We will need more how-to types of material—how to argue with creationists, how to fight for state/church separation, etc. We have an urgent need for literature for young atheists."

AMERICAN BAR ASSOCIATION BOOK PUBLISHING, 750 N. Lake Shore Dr., Book Publishing 8.1, Chicago IL 60611. (312)988-5000. Fax: (312)988-6030. E-mail: rockwelm@staff.abanet.org. Website: www.ababooks.org. **Acquisitions:** Mary Kay Rockwell, director. Estab. 1878. Publishes hardcover and trade paperback originals. **Publishes 100 titles/year. Receives 50 queries/year. 20% of books from first-time authors; 95% from unagented writers. Pays 5-15% royalty on wholesale or retail price.** Publishes book 18 months after acceptance of ms. Accepts simultaneous submissions. Responds in 1 months to queries and proposals, 3 months to mss. Book catalog for $7.95. Manscript guidelines free.

   O─¬ "We are interested in books that will help lawyers practice law more effectively whether it's help in handling clients, structuring a real estate deal or taking an antitrust case to court."

Nonfiction: How-to (in the legal market), reference, technical. Subjects include business/economics, computers/electronics, money/finance, software, legal practice. "Our market is not, generally, the public. Books need to be targeted to lawyers who are seeking solutions to their practice problems. We rarely publish scholarly treatises." Query with SASE.

Recent Title(s): *Freedom of Speech in the Public Workplace* (municipal law).

Tips: "ABA books are written for busy, practicing lawyers. The most successful books have a practical, reader-friendly voice. If you can build in features like checklists, exhibits, sample contracts, flow charts, and tables of cases, please do so." The Association also publishes over 50 major national periodicals in a variety of legal areas. Contact Susan Yessne, executive editor, at the above address for guidelines.

AMERICAN CHEMICAL SOCIETY, 1155 16th St. NW, Washington DC 20036. (202)872-4564. Fax: (202)452-8913. E-mail: a_wilson@acs.org. **Acquisitions:** Anne Wilson, senior product manager. Estab. 1876. Publishes hardcover originals. **Publishes 35 titles/year. Pays royalty.** Accepts simultaneous submissions. Does not return submissions. Responds in 2 months to proposals. Book catalog free on request.

O→ American Chemical Society publishes symposium-based books for chemistry.

Nonfiction: Technical, semi-technical. Subjects include science. "Emphasis is on meeting-based books."

Recent Nonfiction Title(s): *Infrared Analysis of Peptides and Proteins*, edited by Singh.

AMERICAN COLLEGE OF PHYSICIAN EXECUTIVES, (ACPE PUBLICATIONS), 4890 W. Kennedy Blvd., Suite 200, Tampa FL 33609. (813)287-2000. E-mail: wcurry@acpe.org. Website: www.acpe.org. **Acquisitions:** Wesley Curry, managing editor. Estab. 1975. Publishes hardcover and trade paperback originals. **Publishes 12-15 titles/year. Receives 6 queries and 3 mss/year. 80% of books from first-time authors; 100% from unagented writers. Pays 10-15% royalty on wholesale price or makes outright purchase of $1,000-4,000.** Publishes book 8 months after acceptance of ms. Responds in 1 month to queries and ms, 2 months to proposals. Book catalog and ms guidelines free.

O→ "Our books are aimed at physicians in their roles as managers within the health care delivering and financing system."

Nonfiction: Technical, textbook. Subjects include business/economics, health/medicine. Query and submit outline. Reviews artwork/photos as part of ms package. Send photocopies.

Recent Title(s): *Digital Doctors*, by Marshall Ruffin; *Top Docs*, by George Longshore.

AMERICAN CORRECTIONAL ASSOCIATION, 4380 Forbes Blvd., Lanham MD 20706. (301)918-1800. Fax: (301)918-1896. E-mail: afins@aca.org. Website: www.corrections.com/aca. **Acquisitions:** Alice Fins, managing editor. Estab. 1870. Publishes hardcover and trade paperback originals. **Publishes 18 titles/year. Receives 40 submissions/year. 90% of books from first-time authors; 100% from unagented writers. Pays 10% royalty on net sales.** Publishes book 1 year after acceptance. Responds in 4 months. Book catalog and ms guidelines free.

O→ American Correctional Association provides practical information on jails, prisons, boot camps, probation, parole, community corrections, juvenile facilities and rehabilitation programs, substance abuse programs and other areas of corrections.

Nonfiction: How-to, reference, technical, textbook, correspondence courses. "We are looking for practical, how-to texts or training materials written for the corrections profession. No autobiographies or true-life accounts by current or former inmates or correctional officers, theses, or dissertations." No fiction. No poetry. Query with SASE. Reviews artwork/photos as part of ms package.

Recent Title(s): *No Time to Play: Youthful Offenders in Adult Correctional Systems*, by Barry Glick, Ph.D., William Sturgeon with Charles Venator-Santiago.

Tips: Authors are professionals in the field of corrections. "Our audience is made up of corrections professionals and criminal justice students. No books by inmates or former inmates." This publisher advises out-of-town freelance editors, indexers and proofreaders to refrain from requesting work from them.

AMERICAN COUNSELING ASSOCIATION, 5999 Stevenson Ave., Alexandria VA 22304-3300. (703)823-9800. **Acquisitions:** Carolyn C. Baker, director of publications. Estab. 1952. Scholarly paperback originals. **Publishes 10-15 titles/year. Receives 200 queries and 125 mss/year. 5% of books from first-time authors; 90% from unagented writers. Pays 10-15% royalty on net sales.** Publishes book within 7 months after acceptance of final draft. Accepts simultaneous submissions. Responds in 2 months to queries and proposals, 4 months to mss. Manuscript guidelines free.

O→ The American Counseling Association is dedicated to promoting public confidence and trust in the counseling profession. "We publish scholarly books for graduate level students and mental health professionals. We do not publish books for the general public."

Nonfiction: Reference, textbooks for professional counselors. Subjects include education, gay/lesbian, health/medicine, psychology, religion, sociology, women's issues/studies. ACA does not publish self-help books or autobiographies. Query with proposal package, including outline, 2 sample chapters and vitae and SASE.

Recent Title(s): *Critical Incidents in School Counseling*, by Paul Pedersen and Lawrence Tyson.

Tips: "Target your market. Your books will not be appropriate for everyone across all disciplines."

AMERICAN FEDERATION OF ASTROLOGERS, P.O. Box 22040, Tempe AZ 85285. (480)838-1751. Fax: (480)838-8293. E-mail: afa@msn.com. Website: www.astrologers.com. **Acquisitions:** Kris Brandt Riske, publications manager. Estab. 1938. Publishes trade paperback originals and reprints. **Publishes 10-15 titles/year. Receives 10 queries**

and 20 mss/year. **50% of books from first-time authors; 100% from unagented writers. Pays 10% royalty.** Publishes book 10 months after acceptance of ms. Accepts simultaneous submissions. Responds in 6 months to mss. Book catalog for $2. Manuscript guidelines free.

O-π American Federation of Astrologers publishes astrology books, calendars, charts and related aids.

Nonfiction: Astrology. Submit complete ms.

Recent Title(s): *Road Map to Your Future*, by Bernie Ashman.

AMERICAN NURSES PUBLISHING, American Nurses Foundation, an affiliate of the American Nurses Association, 600 Maryland Ave. SW, #100 West, Washington DC 20024-2571. (202)651-7213. Fax: (202)651-7003. **Acquisitions:** Luanne Crayton, editor/project manager; Rosanne O'Connor, publisher. Publishes professional and trade paperback originals and reprints. **Publishes 15-20 titles/year. Receives 40 queries and 10 mss/year. 75% of books from first-time authors; 100% from unagented writers. Pays 10% royalty on retail price.** Publishes book 4 months after acceptance of ms. Responds in 4 months to proposals and mss. Catalog and ms guidelines free.

O-π American Nurses publishes books designed to help professional nurses in their work and careers. Through the publishing program, the Foundation fulfills one of its core missions—to provide nurses in all practice settings with publications that address cutting-edge issues and form a basis for debate and exploration of this century's most critical health care trends.

Nonfiction: Reference, technical and textbook. Subjects include advanced practice, computers, continuing education, ethics, human rights, health care policy, managed care, nursing administration, psychiatric and mental health, quality, research, workplace issues, key clinical topics. Submit outline and 1 sample chapter. Reviews artwork/photos as part of ms package. Send photocopies.

Recent Title(s): *Competencies for Telehealth Technologies in Nursing*, ANA; *Scope and Standards of Public Health Nursing Practice*, Quad Council of Public Health Nursing Organizations.

AMERICAN PRESS, 28 State St., Suite 1100, Boston MA 02109. Phone/fax: (617)247-0022. **Acquisitions:** Jana Kirk, editor. Estab. 1911. Publishes college textbooks. **Publishes 25 titles/year. Receives 350 queries and 100 mss/year. 50% of books from first-time authors; 90% from unagented writers. Pays 5-15% royalty on wholesale price.** Publishes book 9 months after acceptance of ms. Responds in 3 months. Book catalog free.

Nonfiction: Technical, textbook. Subjects include agriculture/horticulture, anthropology/archaeology, art/architecture, business/economics, education, government/politics, health/medicine, history, music/dance, psychology, science, sociology, sports. "We prefer that our authors actually teach courses for which the manuscripts are designed." Query or submit outline with tentative table of contents. No complete mss.

Recent Title(s): *Basic Communications Course Annual 1999*, edited by Lawrence W. Hugenberg.

[N] [★] AMERICAN QUILTER'S SOCIETY, Schroeder Publishing, P.O. Box 3290, Paducah KY 42002-3290. (270)898-7903. Fax: (270)898-8890. E-mail: meredith@aqsquilt.com or editor@aqsquilt.com. Website: www.AQSquilt.com. **Acquisitions:** Barbara Smith, executive book editor (primarily how-to and patterns, but other quilting books sometimes published). Estab. 1984. Publishes hardcover and trade paperback originals. **Publishes 18 titles/year. Receives 300 queries and 60 proposals/year. 60% of books from first-time authors; 100% from unagented writers. Pays 5% royalty on retail price.** No advance. Publishes book 11 months after receipt of ms. Accepts simultaneous submissions. Responds in same day to queries, 2 months to proposals. Book catalog and manuscript guidelines free.

O-π American Quilter's Society publishes how-to and pattern books for quilters (beginners through intermediate skill level).

Nonfiction: Coffee table book, how-to, reference, technical, about quilting. Subjects include creative nonfiction, hobbies, about quilting. Query with SASE or submit proposal package, including outline, 2 sample chapters, photos and patterns (if available). Reviews artwork/photos as part of ms package. Send photocopies, slides and drawings are also acceptable for a proposal.

Recent Title(s): *Favorite Redwork Designs*, by Betty Alderman (embroidery and applique patterns).

AMERICAN SOCIETY OF CIVIL ENGINEERS PRESS, 1801 Alexander Bell Dr., Reston VA 20191-4400. (703)295-6275. Fax: (703)295-6278. E-mail: ascepress@asce.org. Website: www.pubs.asce.org. **Acquisitions:** Joy E. Chau, acquisitions editor: . Estab. 1988. **Publishes 15-20 titles/year. 50% of books from first-time authors; 100% from unagented writers. Pays 10% royalty. No advance.** Accepts simultaneous submissions. Request ASCE book proposal submission guidelines.

O-π ASCE Press publishes technical volumes that are useful to both practicing civil engineers and undergraduate and graduate level civil engineering students. "We publish books by individual authors and editors to advance the civil engineering profession." Currently emphasizing geotechnical, hydrology, structural engineering and bridge engineering. De-emphasizing highly specialized areas with narrow scope.

Nonfiction: Civil engineering. "We are looking for topics that are useful and instructive to the engineering practitioner." Query with outline, sample chapters and cv.

Recent Title(s): *Design of Shallow Foundations*, by Samuel French.

Tips: "ASCE Press is a book publishing imprint of ASCE and produces authored and edited applications-oriented books for practicing civil engineers and graduate level civil engineering students. All proposals and manuscripts undergo a vigorous review process."

AMERICAN WATER WORKS ASSOCIATION 6666 W. Quincy Ave., Denver CO 80235. (303)794-7711. Fax: (303)794-7310. E-mail: cmurcray@awwa.org. Website: www.awwa.org. **Acquisitions:** Colin Murcray, senior acquisitions editor; Mindy Burke, senior technical editor. Estab. 1881. Publishes hardcover and trade paperback originals. **Publishes 100 titles/year. Receives 200 queries and 35 mss/year. 30% of books from first-time authors; 100% from unagented writers. Pays 15% royalty on wholesale or retail price. No advance.** Publishes book 1 year after acceptance of ms. Responds in 3 months. Accepts e-mail submissions. Book catalog and manuscript guidelines free.

    O—π AWWA strives to advance and promote the safety and knowledge of drinking water and related issues to all audiences—from kindergarten through post-doctorate.

Nonfiction: Subjects include nature/environment, science, software, drinking water-related topics. Query or submit outline, 3 sample chapters and author biography. Reviews artwork/photos as part of ms package. Send photocopies.

Recent Title(s): *The Drinking Water Dictionary*, by Jim Symons, et al.

AMHERST MEDIA, INC., 155 Rano St., Suite 300, Buffalo NY 14207. (716)874-4450. Fax: (716)874-4508. E-mail: amherstmed@aol.com. Website: www.AmherstMediaInc.com. **Acquisitions:** Craig Alesse, publisher. Estab. 1974. Publishes trade paperback originals and reprints. **Publishes 30 titles/year. Receives 50 submissions/year. 80% of books from first-time authors; 100% from unagented writers. Pays 6-8% royalty on retail price.** Publishes book 1 year after acceptance. Accepts simultaneous submissions. Responds in 2 months. Book catalog and ms guidelines free.

    O—π Amherst Media publishes how-to photography books.

Nonfiction: Photography how-to. "Looking for well-written and illustrated photo books." Query with outline, 2 sample chapters and SASE. Reviews artwork/photos as part of ms package.

Recent Title(s): *The Art of Portrait Photography*, by Michael Grecco (nonfiction).

Tips: "Our audience is made up of beginning to advanced photographers. If I were a writer trying to market a book today, I would fill the need of a specific audience and self-edit in a tight manner."

ANCESTRY INCORPORATED, 266 W. Center St., Orem UT 84057. (801)426-3500. Fax: (801)426-3501. E-mail: mwright@myfamilyinc.com. Book Editor: Matthew Wright. *Ancestry* magazine Editor: Jennifer Utley. **Acquisitions:** Loretto Szucs, executive editor. Estab. 1983. Publishes hardcover, trade and paperback originals and *Ancestry* magazine. **Publishes 12-20 titles/year. Receives over 100 submissions/year. 70% of books from first-time authors; 100% from unagented writers. Pays 8-12% royalty or makes outright purchase. No advance.** Accepts simultaneous submissions. Responds in 2 months. Book catalog for 9×12 SAE with 2 first-class stamps.

    O—π "Our publications are aimed exclusively at the genealogist. We consider everything from short monographs to book length works on topics such as immigration, migration, record collections and heraldic topics, among others."

Nonfiction: How-to, reference, genealogy. Subjects include Americana, historical methodology and genealogical research techniques. No mss that are not genealogical or historical. Query, or submit outline/synopsis and sample chapters with SASE. Reviews artwork/photos.

Recent Title(s): *Printed Sources*, by Kory L. Meyerink.

Tips: "Genealogical and historical reference, how-to, and descriptions of source collections have the best chance of selling to our firm. Be precise in your description. Please, no family histories or genealogies."

[A] ANCHOR PUBLISHING MARYLAND, Box 2630, Landover Hills MD 20784. (301)459-0738. Fax: (301)552-0225. E-mail: tomantion@aol.com. Website: www.antion.com. **Acquisitions:** Tom Antion, president. Estab. 1988. Publishes trade paperback originals. **Publishes 5-10 titles/year. Receives 10 queries and 1 ms/year. 0% of books from first-time authors; 0% from unagented writers. Makes outright purchase of $500-1,000. No advance.** Publishes book 1 year after acceptance of ms. Responds in 3 months to mss.

Nonfiction: How-to, humor. Subjects include business/economics. *Agented submissions only.*

Recent Title(s): *Wake Em Up Business Presentation.*

[logo] ANCHORAGE PRESS, INC., P.O. Box 8067, New Orleans LA 70182-8067. (504)283-8868. Fax: (504)899-9217. **Acquisitions:** Orlin Corey, editor. Publishes hardcover originals. Estab. 1935. **Publishes 10 titles/year. Receives 450-900 submissions/year. 50% of books from first-time authors; 80% from unagented writers. Pays 10-15% royalty on retail price. Playwrights also receive 50-75% royalties.** Publishes book 1-2 years after acceptance. Responds in 1 month to queries, 4 months to mss. Book catalog and ms guidelines free.

    O—π "We are an international agency for plays for young people. First in the field since 1935."

Nonfiction: Textbook, plays. Subjects include education, language/literature, plays. "We are looking for play anthologies; and texts for teachers of drama/theater (middle school and high school.)" Query. Reviews artwork/photos.

Plays: Plays of juvenile/young people's interest. Query.

Recent Title(s): *The Taste of Sunrise*, by Suzan L. Zeder; *Lincoln's Log*, by Barry Kornhauser.

[N] [logo] AND BOOKS, 702 S. Michigan, South Bend IN 46601. (219)232-3134. Fax: (312)803-0887. E-mail: andbooks@ripco.com. Editor: Janos Szebedinsky. Estab. 1980. Publishes trade paperback originals. **Publishes 10 titles/year. Receives 1,000 submissions/year. 50% of books from first-time authors; 90% from unagented writers. Pays 6-10% royalty on retail price.** Accepts simultaneous submissions. Publishes books 1 year after acceptance. Responds in up to 3 months. Book catalog for #10 SASE.

Nonfiction: Subjects include computers (consumer-level), current affairs, social justice, psychology, religion, music: blues, classical. Especially needs books on computers and electronic publishing. No biography, humor or diet books. *Writer's Market* recommends sending a query with SASE first.

Tips: "Attempt to get an intro or foreword by a respected authority on your subject. Include comments by others who have reviewed your material. Research the potential market and include the results with your proposal. In other words, make every effort to communicate your knowledge of the publishing process. A little preliminary legwork and market investigation can go a long way to influence a potential publisher. No longer interested in books on sports or law."

WILLIAM ANDREW/NOYES PUBLISHING, (formerly William Andrew, Inc.), 169 Kinderkamack Rd., Park Ridge IL 07656. (201)505-4955. Fax: (201)505-4955. E-mail: editorial@williamandrew.com. Website: www.williamand rew.com. **Acquisitions:** Dudley Kay, publisher (industrial hygiene and safety, chemical and general welding); George Narita, senior editor (semiconductor manufacturing, advanced materials); William Woishnis, editorial director (plastics and special chemicals). Estab. 1989. **Publishes hardcover originals. Publishes 30 titles/year. Receives 100 queries and 20 mss/year. 40% of books from first-time authors; 100% from unagented writers. Pays 12% royalty on net proceeds. Offers $1,000-5,000 advance, depending on author's reputation and nature of book.** Publishes book 6 months after acceptance of ms. Accepts simultaneous submissions. Responds in 1 month to queries, 2 months to proposals and mss. Book catalog and ms guidelines free.

> O→ William Andrew, Inc. specializes in technical information, both for printed and electronic publishing, primarily of interest to academic and research scientists and engineers. Currently emphasizing semiconductor manufacturing and industrial hygiene. De-emphasizing environmental protection.

Nonfiction: Reference, technical, textbook. Subjects include industrial processing, science, engineering, materials science, economic books pertaining to chemistry, chemical engineering food, textiles, energy electronics, pollution control, semiconductor material and process technology. Submit outline and SASE. Length: 50,000-250,000 words. Reviews artwork/photos as part of ms package. Send photocopies.

Recent Title(s): *Handbook of Ceramic Grinding and Polishing*, by Marinescu et al.

A **ANDREWS McMEEL UNIVERSAL**, 4520 Main St., Kansas City MO 64111-7701. (816)932-6700. Website: www.uexpress.com. **Acquisitions:** Christine Schillig, vice president/editorial director. Estab. 1973. **Publishes hardcover and paperback originals. Publishes 300 titles/year. Pays royalty on retail price. Offers advance.**

> O→ Andrews McMeel publishes general trade books, humor books, miniature gift books, calendars, greeting cards, and stationery products.

Nonfiction: General trade, humor, how-to, pop culture. Also produces gift books, posters and kits. Query only. *Agented submissions only.*

Recent Title(s): *The Millionaire Mind*, by Thomas J. Stanley, PhD.

ANGELINES™ PUBLISHING, (formerly AngeLines™ Productions), P.O. Box 2094, Westport CT 06880. **Acquisitions:** J. Weber, editor-in-chief. **Publishes trade paperback originals. Publishes 6 titles/year. Receives 2,000 queries and 200 mss/year. 10% of books from first-time authors; 75% from unagented writers. Royalty on retail price varies. No advance.** Publishes book 1 year after publication of ms. Accepts simultaneous submissions, if so noted. Responds in 2 months to proposals. Manuscript guidelines for #10 SASE.

> O→ AngeLines publishes books for metaphysically and spiritually aware adults. "We aim to be the premier publisher of channeled and psychic material from the most reputable channels and psychics." Currently emphasizing unique comprehensive material for advanced metaphysicians. De-emphasizing beginner, intro, "me-too" books.

Nonfiction: Self-help, self-actualization. Subjects include money/finance, psychology, metaphysics, spirituality. "We currently are producing a 16-volume series of articles, *ACP Oracles™*, by psychic/channel Amie Angeli. Most of our books published/contracted are channeled material." Submit proposal, chapter outline and 1-3 sample chapters with SASE. Reviews artwork/photos as part of the ms package. Send photocopies.

Recent Title(s): *The Colors in Our Lives*, by Amie Angeli (ACP Oracles series); *Father to Daughter: Thoughts from Another World*, by Shirley Buck Welton (channeled material).

Tips: "Our ideal author is an advanced metaphysician with journalist experience, previously published; international experience is a real plus—our books are sold internationally."

APPALACHIAN MOUNTAIN CLUB BOOKS, 5 Joy St., Boston MA 02108. Fax: (617)523-0722. Website: www.o utdoors.org. **Acquisitions:** Beth Krusi, publisher/editor. Estab. 1897. **Publishes trade paperback originals. Publishes 6-10 titles/year. Receives 200 queries and 20 mss/year. 30% of books from first-time authors; 90% from unagented writers. Pays 6-10% royalty on retail price. Offers modest advance.** Publishes book 10 months after acceptance of ms. Accepts simultaneous submissions. Responds in 3 months to proposals. Book catalog for 8½×11 SAE with 4 first-class stamps. Manuscript guidelines for #10 SASE.

> O→ Appalachian Mountain Club publishes hiking guides, water-recreation guides (non-motorized), nature, conservation and mountain-subject guides for America's Northeast. "We connect recreation to conservation."

Nonfiction: How-to, guidebooks. Subjects include history (mountains, Northeast), nature/environment, recreation, regional (Northeast outdoor recreation). Writers should avoid submitting: proposals on Appalachia (rural southern mountains); not enough market research; too much personal experience—autobiography." Query. Reviews artwork/photos as part of ms package. Send photocopies and transparencies "at your own risk."

Recent Title(s): *Not Without Peril; Journey North.*

Tips: "Our audience is outdoor recreationalists, conservation-minded hikers and canoeists, family outdoor lovers, armchair enthusiasts. Our guidebooks have a strong conservation message. Visit our website before querying."

A-R EDITIONS, INC., 801 Deming Way, Madison WI 53717. (608)836-9000. Fax: (608)831-8200. Website: www.are ditions.com. **Acquisitions:** Paul Ranzini, managing editor, Recent Researches music editions; James L. Zychowicz, managing editor, Computer Music and Digital Audio Series. Estab. 1962. **Publishes 25 titles/year. Receives 40 queries and 24 mss/year. 50% of books from first-time authors; 100% from unagented writers. Pays royalty or honoraria.** Responds in 1 month to queries, 3 months to proposals and 6 months to mss. Book catalog and newsletter free. Manuscript guidelines free (check website).

> ○━ A-R Editions publishes modern critical editions of music based on current musicological research. Each edition is devoted to works by a single composer or to a single genre of composition. The contents are chosen for their potential interest to scholars and performers, then prepared for publication according to the standards that govern the making of all reliable, historical editions.

Nonfiction: Historical music editions, computers and electronics, software; also titles related to computer music and digital audio. Query or submit outline with SASE.
Recent Title(s): *Fundamentals of Digital Audio*, by Alan Kefauver.

■▲ ARABESQUE, BET Books, 850 Third Ave., 16th Floor, New York NY 10022. (212)407-1500. Website: www.arab esque.com. **Acquisitions:** Karen Thomas, senior editor. Publishes mass market paperback originals. **Publishes 60 titles/ year. 30-50% of books from first-time authors; 50% from unagented writers. Pays royalty on retail price, varies by author. Advance varies by author.** Publishes book 18 months after acceptance of ms. Accepts simultaneous submissions. Responds in 3 months to mss. Book catalog for #10 SASE.

> ○━ Arabesque publishes contemporary romances about African-American couples.

Fiction: Multicultural romance. Query with synopsis and SASE. *No unsolicited mss.*
Recent Title(s): *More Than Gold*, by Shirley Hailstock.

▲ ARCADE PUBLISHING, 141 Fifth Ave., New York NY 10010. (212)475-2633. **Acquisitions:** Webb Younce, senior editor; Coates Bateman, editor; Richard Seaver, publisher/editor-in-chief; Jeannette Seaver, publisher/executive editor. Estab. 1988. Publishes hardcover originals, trade paperback originals and reprints. **Publishes 45 titles/year. 5% of books from first-time authors. Pays royalty on retail price. Offers $3,000-50,000 advance.** Publishes book within 18 months after acceptance of ms. Responds in 3 months to queries.

> ○━ Arcade prides itself on publishing top-notch commercial nonfiction and literary fiction, with a significant proportion of foreign writers.

Nonfiction: Biography, cookbook, general nonfiction. Subjects include cooking/foods/nutrition, government/politics, history, nature/environment and travel. *Agented submissions only.* Reviews artwork/photos. Send photocopies.
Fiction: Ethnic, historical, humor, literary, mainstream/contemporary, mystery, short story collections, suspense. *Agented submissions only.*
Recent Title(s): *The Banyan Tree*, by Christopher Nolan.

■▲ ARCADIA PUBLISHING, Tempus Publishing, 2-A Cumberland St., Charleston SC 29401. (843)853-2070. Fax: (843)853-0044. E-mail: sales@arcadiapublishing.com. Website: www.arcadiaimages.com. **Acquisitions:** Patrick Catel, publisher (Midwest); Amy Sutton, publisher (North); Mark Berry, publisher (South); Allison Carpenter, publisher (Southwest). Query with SASE. Publishes mass market paperback originals. **Publishes 800 titles/year; imprint publishes 350 titles/year. Receives 100 queries and 20 mss/year. 80% of books from first-time authors; 95% from unagented writers. Pays 10% royalty.** Accepts simultaneous submissions. Responds in 1 month to queries. Book catalog on website. Manuscript guidelines for #10 SASE.

> ○━ "Arcadia publishes photographic regional histories. We have more than 1,000 in print in our 'Images of America' series. We have expanded our program to include Midwest and West Coast locations." Currently emphasizing local history, oral history, Civil War history, college histories, African-American history.

Nonfiction: Coffee table book. Subjects include pictorial history, local history, African-American history, postcard history, sports history, college history, oral history, Civil War history. Local, national and regional publications. Query with SASE. Reviews artwork/photos as part of ms package. Send photocopies.
Recent Title(s): *My Texas Family: An Uncommon Journey to Prosperity*, by Rick and Ronda Hyman; *General Motors: A Photographic History*, by Michael Davis.
Tips: "Writers should know that we only publish history titles. The majority of our books are on a city or region, and are pictorial in nature. We are beginning new series, including oral histories, sports histories, black histories and college histories."

▲ ARCHWAY PAPERBACKS, Pocket Books for Young Readers, Simon & Schuster, 1230 Avenue of the Americas, New York NY 10020. (212)698-7669. Website: www.simonsayskids.com. Publishes mass market paperback originals and reprints. **Publishes approximately 100 titles/year. Receives over 1,000 submissions/year. Pays 6-8% royalty on retail price.** Publishes book 2 years after acceptance. Responds in 3 months.

> ○━ Archway Paperbacks publishes fiction and current nonfiction for young adult readers ages 12-18.

Nonfiction: Young adult, ages 12-18. Subjects include current popular subjects or people, sports. *Agented submissions only.*

Fiction: Young adult horror, mystery, suspense thrillers, contemporary fiction, romances for YA, ages 12-18. *Agented submissions only.*
Recent Title(s): *Buffy the Vampire Slayer* and *Dawson's Creek* (TV-tie-in titles).

ARDEN PRESS INC., P.O. Box 418, Denver CO 80201-0418. (303)697-6766. Fax: (303)697-3443. Fax: (303)697-3443. **Acquisitions:** Susan Conley, publisher. Estab. 1980. Publishes hardcover and trade paperback originals and reprints. 95% of books are originals; 5% are reprints. **Publishes 4-6 titles/year. Receives 600 submissions/year. 20% of books from first-time authors; 80% from unagented writers. Pays 8-15% royalty on wholesale price. Offers $2,000 average advance.** Publishes book 6 months after acceptance. Accepts simultaneous submissions. Responds in 2 months to queries. Manuscript guidelines free.
  O─┐ Arden Press publishes nonfiction on women's history and women's issues. "We sell to general and women's bookstores as well as public and academic libraries. Many of our titles are adopted as texts for use in college courses."
Nonfiction: Women's issues/studies subjects. No personal memoirs or autobiographies. Query with outline/synopsis and sample chapters.
Recent Title(s): *Whatever Happend to the Year of the Woman?*, by Amy Handlin.
Tips: "Writers have the best chance selling us nonfiction on women's subjects. If I were a writer trying to market a book today, I would learn as much as I could about publishers' profiles *then* contact those who publish similar works."

ARKANSAS RESEARCH, P.O. Box 303, Conway AR 72033. (501)470-1120. Fax: (501)470-1120. E-mail: desmond @ipa.net. **Acquisitions:** Desmond Walls Allen, owner. Estab. 1985. Publishes hardcover originals and trade paperback originals and reprints. **Publishes 20 titles/year. 90% of books from first-time authors; 100% from unagented writers. Pays 5-10% royalty on retail price. Offers no advance.** Publishes book 6 months after acceptance of ms. Responds in 1 month. Book catalog for $1. Manuscript guidelines free.
  O─┐ "Our company opens a world of information to researchers interested in the history of Arkansas."
Imprint(s): Research Associates.
Nonfiction: How-to (genealogy), reference, self-help. Subjects include Americana, ethnic, history, hobbies (genealogy), military/war, regional, all Arkansas-related. "We don't print autobiographies or genealogies about one family." Query with SASE. Reviews artwork/photos as part of ms package. Send photocopies.
Recent Title(s): *Life & Times from The Clay County Courier Newspaper Published at Corning, Arkansas, 1893-1900.*

JASON ARONSON, INC., 230 Livingston St., Northvale NJ 07647-1726. (201)767-4093. Fax: (201)767-4330. Website: www.aronson.com. Editor-in-chief: Arthur Kurzweil. **Acquisitions:** Arthur Kurzweil, (Judaica), vice president/editor-in-chief; Ann Marie Dooley, editor (psychotherapy). Estab. 1967. Publishes hardcover and trade paperback originals and reprints. **Publishes 250 titles/year. 50% of books from first-time authors; 95% from unagented writers. Pays 10-15% royalty on retail price.** Publishes book an average of 1 year after acceptance. Responds in 1 month. *Writer's Market* recommends allowing 2 months for reply. Catalog and ms guidelines free.
  O─┐ "We are looking for high quality, serious, scholarly books in two fields: psychotherapy and Judaica."
Nonfiction: Subjects include history, philosophy, psychology, religion translation. Query or submit outline and sample chapters. Reviews artwork/photos as part of ms packages. Send photocopies.
Recent Title(s): *The Candle of God*, by Adin Steinsaltz (Judaica).

▓ ARTE PUBLICO PRESS, University of Houston, Houston TX 77204-2174. (713)743-2841. Fax (713)743-2847. Website: www.arte.uh.edu. **Acquisitions:** Nicolas Kanellos, editor. Estab. 1979. Publishes hardcover originals, trade paperback originals and reprints. **Publishes 36 titles/year. Receives 1,000 queries and 500 mss/year. 50% of books from first-time authors; 80% from unagented writers. Pays 10% royalty on wholesale price. Offers $1,000-3,000 advance.** Publishes book 2 years after acceptance of ms. Accepts simultaneous submissions. Responds in 1 month to queries and proposals; 4 months to mss. Book catalog free. Manuscript guidelines for #10 SASE.
  O─┐ "We are a showcase for Hispanic literary creativity, arts and culture. Our endeavor is to provide a national forum for Hispanic literature."
Imprint(s): Pinata Books.
Nonfiction: Children's/juvenile, reference. Subjects include ethnic, language/literature, regional, translation, women's issues/studies. "Nonfiction is definitely not our major publishing area." Query with outline/synopsis, 2 sample chapters and SASE. "Include cover letter explaining why your manuscript is unique and important, why we should publish it, who will buy it, etc."
Fiction: Ethnic, literary, mainstream/contemporary. Query with synopsis, 2 sample chapters and SASE.
Poetry: Submit 10 sample poems.
Recent Title(s): *Chicano! The History of the Mexican American Civil Rights Movement*, by F. Arturo Rosales (history/nonfiction); *Project Death*, by Richard Bertematti (novel/mystery); *I Used to Be a Superwoman*, by Gloria Velasquez (poetry collection/inspirational).

ASA, AVIATION SUPPLIES & ACADEMICS, 7005 132nd Place SE, Newcastle WA 98059. (425)235-1500. Fax: (425)235-0128. Website: www.asa2fly.com. Director of Operations: Mike Lorden. Editor: Jennifer Trerise. **Acquisitions:**

Fred Boyns, controller; Jacqueline Spanitz, curriculum director and technical advisor (pilot and aviation educator). **Publishes 25-40 titles/year. 100% of books from unagented writers.** Publishes book 9 months or more after acceptance. Book catalog free.

O→ ASA is an industry leader in the development and sales of aviation supplies, publications, and software for pilots, flight instructors, flight engineers and aviation technicians. All ASA products are developed by a team of researchers, authors and editors.

Nonfiction: How-to, technical, education. All subjects must be related to aviation education and training. "We are primarily an aviation publisher. Educational books in this area are our specialty; other aviation books will be considered." Query with outline. Send photocopies.

Recent Title(s): *The Savvy Flight Instructor: Secrets of the Successful CFI*, by Greg Brown (nonfiction).

Tips: "Two of our specialty series include ASA's *Focus Series*, and ASA *Aviator's Library*. Books in our *Focus Series* concentrate on single-subject areas of aviation knowledge, curriculum and practice. The *Aviator's Library* is comprised of titles of known and/or classic aviation authors or established instructor/authors in the industry, and other aviation specialty titles."

N: ASCP PRESS, American Society of Clinical Pathologists, 2100 W. Harrison St., Chicago IL 60612. (312)738-4864. Fax: (312)738-1619. Website: www.ascp.org. **Acquisitions:** Joshua R. Weikersheimer, publisher. Estab. 1959. Publishes hardcover originals. **Publishes 10 titles/year. Receives 700 queries and 90 mss/year. 1% of books from first-time authors; 100% from unagented writers. Sometimes pays by grants, 15% maximum royalty on retail price.** Publishes book 5 months (non-illustrated) or 7 months (color-illustrated) after acceptance of ms. Responds immediately to queries. *Writer's Market* recommends allowing 2 months for reply. Book catalog and ms guidelines free. Website offers complete catalog, ms guidelines and editorial contact information.

O→ "ASCP Press publishes the art of medicine."

Nonfiction: Illustrated book, reference, textbook. Subjects include health/medicine, science. Submit outline, 1 sample chapter, cv, precis with SASE.

Tips: Audience is researchers, physicians, non-allied health.

N: ASM INTERNATIONAL, 9639 Kinsman Rd., Materials Park OH 44073-0002. (440)338-5151. Fax: (440)338-4634. E-mail: cust-srv@po.asm-intl.org. Website: www.asm-intl.org. **Acquisitions:** Veronica Flint, manager of book acquisitions (metallurgy/materials processing). Publishes hardcover originals. **Publishes 15-20 titles/year. Receives 50 queries and 10 mss/year. 50% of books from first-time authors; 100% from unagented writers. Pays 5-15% royalty on wholesale price or makes outright purchase. Offers $500-1,000 advance.** Publishes book 9 months after acceptance of ms. Responds in 1 month to queries, 2 months to proposals and mss. Book catalog free on request or on website. Manuscript guidelines free on request.

O→ ASM focuses on practical information related to materials selection and processing.

Nonfiction: Reference, technical, textbook. Subjects include engineering reference. Submit proposal package, including outline, 1 sample chapter and author credentials. Reviews artwork/photos as part of the ms package. Send photocopies.

Recent Title(s): *Corrosion: Understanding the Basics*, by J.R. Davis; *Metallurgy for the Non-Metallurgist*, by H. Chandler.

Tips: "Our audience consists of technically trained people seeking practical information on metals and materials to help them solve problems on the job."

ASSOCIATION FOR SUPERVISION AND CURRICULUM DEVELOPMENT, 1703 N. Beauregard St., Alexandria VA 22311. (703)578-9600. Fax: (703)575-5400. Website: www.ascd.com. **Acquisitions:** John O'Neil, acquisitions director. Estab. 1943. Publishes trade paperback originals. **Publishes 24-30 titles/year. Receives 100 queries and 100 mss/year. 50% of books from first-time authors; 100% from unagented writers. Pays negotiable royalty on actual monies received or makes outright purchase. Offers advance.** Publishes book 1 year after acceptance of ms. Accepts simultaneous submissions. Responds in 6 months to proposals. Book catalog and ms guidelines free or on website.

O→ ASCD publishes professional books for educators.

Nonfiction: How-to, professional books for education field. Education subjects. Submit outline and 2 sample chapters. Reviews artwork/photos as part of the ms package. Send photocopies.

Recent Titles: *Teaching with the Brain in Mind*, by Eric Jensen.

ATHENEUM BOOKS FOR YOUNG READERS, Simon & Schuster, 1230 Avenue of the Americas, New York NY 10020. (212)698-2715. Website: www.simonsayskids.com. Associate Publisher/Vice President/Editorial Director: Jonathan J. Lanman. **Acquisitions:** Marcia Marshall, executive editor (nonfiction, fantasy); Anne Schwartz, editorial director, Anne Schwartz Books; Caitlyn Dlouhy, senior editor. Estab. 1960. Publishes hardcover originals. **Publishes 70 titles/year. Receives 15,000 submissions/year. 8-12% of books from first-time authors; 50% from unagented writers. Pays 10% royalty on retail price. Offers $2,000-3,000 average advance.** Publishes book 18 months after acceptance. Responds in 3 months. Manuscript guidelines for #10 SASE.

O→ Atheneum Books for Young Readers publishes books aimed at children from pre-school age, up through high school.

Nonfiction: Biography, history, science, humor, self-help, all for juveniles. Subjects include: Americana, animals, art, business/economics, health, music, nature, photography, politics, psychology, recreation, religion, sociology, sports and travel. "Do remember, most publishers plan their lists as much as two years in advance. So if a topic is 'hot' right now, it may be 'old hat' by the time we could bring it out. It's better to steer clear of fads. Some writers assume juvenile books are for 'practice' until you get good enough to write adult books. Not so. Books for young readers demand just as much professionalism in writing as adult books. So save those 'practice' manuscripts for class, or polish them before sending them. *Query letter only for all submissions. We do not accept unsolicited mss."*

Fiction: Adventure, ethnic, experimental, fantasy, gothic, historical, horror, humor, mainstream, mystery, science fiction, suspense, western, all in juvenile versions. "We have few specific needs except for books that are fresh, interesting and well written. Again, fad topics are dangerous, as are works you haven't polished to the best of your ability. (The competition is fierce.) Other things we don't need at this time are safety pamphlets, ABC books, coloring books and board books. In writing picture book texts, avoid the coy and 'cutesy,' such as stories about characters with alliterative names. *Query letter only for all submissions. We do not accept unsolicited mss."* Send art samples under separate cover to Ann Bobco at the above address.

Poetry: "At this time there is a growing market for children's poetry. However, we don't anticipate needing any for the next year or two."

Recent Title(s): *The Century that Was*, by Giblin (nonfiction); *Horace and Morris But Mostly Dolores*, by Howe (fiction); *Doodle Dandies*, by Lewis (poetry).

ATL PRESS, INC., P.O. Box 4563, Shrewsbury MA 01545. (508)898-2290. Website: www.atlpress.com. **Acquisitions**: Paul Lucio, acquisitions manager. Estab. 1992. Publishes hardcover and trade paperback originals. **Publishes 8-12 titles/ year. Receives 100 queries/year. 25% of books from first-time authors. Pays royalty on retail price.** Publishes book 3 months after acceptance of ms. Responds in 2 months to queries. Book catalog and ms guidelines for #10 SASE.

O➡ ATL specializes in science and technology publications for both the professional and the popular audience.

Nonfiction: Children's/juvenile, multimedia (CD-ROM), reference, technical, textbook. Subjects include business and economics, education, health/medicine, money/finance, nature/environment, science. "We look for well-written manuscripts in subjects with either broad, general interest topics of leading-edge professional topics. Avoid too narrow a focus." Submit outline and 3-4 sample chapters with SASE.

Recent Title(s): *New Technologies for Healthy Foods*, by M. Yalpani.

Tips: "Audience is educated, open-minded adults, juveniles, parents, educators, professionals. Realistically evaluate your manuscript against competition. We publish only titles for which there is an actual demand. We are committed to produce authoritative and thought-provoking titles that are distinguished both in their content and appearance."

AUBURN HOUSE, Greenwood Publishing Group, 88 Post Rd. W., Westport CT 06881. (203)226-3571. Fax: (203)222-1502. Website: www.greenwood.com. **Acquisitions:** Editorial Offices. Publishes hardcover and trade paperback originals. **Publishes 16 titles/year. Pays variable royalty on net price. Rarely offers advance.** Publishes book 1 year after acceptance of ms. Accepts simultaneous submissions. Responds in 6 months to queries and proposals. Book catalog and ms guidelines online.

O➡ "Auburn publishes books and advanced texts in health studies, education and social policy."

Nonfiction: Subjects include business/economics, government/politics, health/medicine. Query with proposal package, including: scope, whether a complete ms is available or when it will be, CV or résumé and SASE. *No unsolicited mss.*

Recent Title(s): *Adoption Policy and Special Needs Children*, edited by Rosemary Avery (sociology).

Tips: Greenwood Publishing maintains an excellent website offering catalog, ms guidelines and editorial contacts.

AUSTIN & WINFIELD PUBLISHERS, The University Press of America, 4720 Boston Way, Lanham MD 20706. (301)731-9527. Fax: (301)306-5357. E-mail: rwest@univpress.com. Website: www.univpress.com. **Acquisitions:** Dr. Robert West, publisher, editorial director. Estab. 1992. Publishes hardcover originals and reprints. **Publishes 120 titles/ year; imprint publishes 41 titles/year. Receives 300 queries and 180 mss/year. 60% of books from first-time authors; 100% from unagented writers. Pays 8% royalty on wholesale price. No advance.** Publishes book 5 months after acceptance of ms. Accepts simultaneous submissions. Responds in 1 month. Book catalog free for #10 SASE or on website. Manuscript guidelines free for #10 SASE.

O➡ Austin & Winfield is an international scholarly publisher specializing in law, criminal justice and legal policy. "We publish monographs and revised dissertations—this is what we are seeking."

Nonfiction: Reference, technical, textbook. Subjects include government/politics, philosophy, sociology. Submit proposal package, including outline, 2 sample chapters and résumé.

Recent Title(s): *Constitutional Law in the United States*, 3rd ed., by Randall Bland and Joseph Brogan.

Tips: "Scholarly/library market is our main focus—we are like a university press in standards and expectations."

AUTONOMEDIA, P.O. Box 568, Williamsburgh Station, Brooklyn NY 11211. (718)963-2603. Fax: (718)963-2603. E-mail: info@autonomedia.org. Website: www.autonomedia.org. **Acquisitions:** Kevin Coogan, acquisitions editor. Estab. 1984. Publishes trade paperback originals and reprints. **Publishes 25 titles/year. Receives 350 queries/year. 30% of books from first-time authors; 90% from unagented writers. Pays variable royalty. Offers $100 advance.** Publishes book 6 months after acceptance of ms. Accepts simultaneous submissions. Responds in 2 months. Book catalog for $1. Submission guidelines on website.

O➡ Autonomedia publishes radical and marginal books on culture, media and politics.

Nonfiction: Subjects include anthropology/archaeology, art/architecture, business/economics, gay/lesbian, government/ politics, history, nature/environment, philosophy, religion, translation, women's issues/studies. Submit outline with SASE. Reviews artwork/photos as part of ms package. Send photocopies.

Fiction: Erotica, experimental, feminist, gay/lesbian, literary, mainstream/contemporary, occult, science fiction, short story collections. Submit synopsis with SASE.
Poetry: Submit sample poems.
Recent Title(s): *The Anarchists*, by John Henry MacKay.

AVALON BOOKS, Thomas Bouregy & Co., Inc., 160 Madison Ave., New York NY 10016. (212)598-0222. Fax: (212)223-5251. E-mail: avalon-books@att.net. Website: www.avalonbooks.com. **Acquisitions:** Erin Cartwright, senior editor; Veronica Mixon, editor; Mira Son, assistant editor. Estab. 1950. **Publishes 60 titles/year. 80% of books from unagented writers. Pays royalty.** Publishes book 6 months after acceptance. Responds in 4 months. Manuscript guidelines for #10 SASE.
   O➥ "We publish wholesome fiction. We're the 'Family Channel' of publishing. We try to make what we publish suitable for anybody in the family." Currently de-emphasizing romantic suspense.
Fiction: "We publish wholesome romances, mysteries, westerns. Our books are read by adults as well as teenagers, and the characters are all adults. All the romances and mysteries are contemporary; all the westerns are historical." Length: 40,000-50,000 words. Submit first 3 chapters, synopsis and SASE. "Manuscripts that are too long will not be considered."
Recent Title(s): *Cyber Bride*, by Annette Couch-Jareb (romance); *Ten and Me*, by Johnny D. Boggs (western); *Endangered*, by Eric C. Evans (mystery).
Tips: "We are looking for love stories, heroines who have interesting professions, and we are actively seeking new authors. We do accept unagented manuscripts, and we do publish first novels. Right now we are concentrating on finding talented new mystery and romance writers with solid storytelling skills."

AVANYU PUBLISHING INC., P.O. Box 27134, Albuquerque NM 87125. (505)341-1280. Fax: (505)341-1281. E-mail: brentric@aol.com. **Acquisitions:** J. Brent Ricks, president. Estab. 1984. Publishes hardcover and trade paperback originals and reprints. **Publishes 4 titles/year. Receives 40 submissions/year. 30% of books from first-time authors; 90% from unagented writers. Pays 8% maximum royalty on wholesale price.** Publishes book 1 year after acceptance. Responds in 2 months. Book catalog for #10 SASE.
   O➥ Avanyu publishes highly-illustrated, history-oriented books and contemporary Indian/Western art.
Nonfiction: Biography, illustrated book, reference, Southwest Americana. Subjects include Americana, anthropology/ archaeology, art/architecture, ethnic, history, photography, regional, sociology. Query with SASE. Reviews artwork/ photos as part of ms package.
Recent Titles: *Kachinas Spirit Beings of the Hopi*; *Mesa Verde Ancient Architecture*, by Pendleton Woolen Mills.
Tips: "Our audience consists of libraries, art collectors and history students. We publish subjects dealing with modern and historic American Indian matters of all kinds."

◼ **AVERY**, Penguin Putnam, 375 Hudson St., New York NY 10014. (212)366-2000. Fax: (212)366-2365. Website: www.penguinputnam.com. **Acquisitions:** John Duff, publisher; Norman Goldfind, vice president, marketing and product development (health, alternative medicine). Estab. 1976. Publishes trade paperback originals. **Publishes 25 titles/year. Receives 3,000 queries and 1,000 mss/year. 70% of books from first-time authors; 90% from unagented writers. Pays royalty. Conservative advances offered.** Publishes book 1 year after acceptance of ms. Accepts simultaneous submissions. Responds in 2 weeks to queries, 3 weeks to proposals and manuscripts. *Writer's Market* recommends allowing 2 months for reply. Book catalog and ms guidelines free.
   O➥ Avery specializes in health, nutrition, alternative medicine, and fitness.
Nonfiction: "We generally do not publish personal accounts of health topics unless they outline a specific plan that covers all areas of the topic." Submit outline with proposal package, including cover letter, author biography, table of contents, preface with SASE.
Recent Title(s): *Dr. Art Ulene's Complete Guide to Vitamins, Minerals, and Herbs*.
Tips: "Our mission is to enable people to improve their health through clear and up-to-date information."

AVIATION PUBLISHERS, Markowski International Publishers, 1 Oakglade Circle, Hummelstown PA 17036-9525. (717)566-0468. Fax: (717)566-6423. E-mail: avipub@excite.com. **Acquisitions:** Michael A. Markowski, editor-in-chief. Guidelines for #10 SASE with 2 first-class stamps.
   O➥ Aviation Publishers publishes books to help people learn more about aviation and model aviation through the written word.
Nonfiction: How-to and historical. Subjects include radio control, free flight, indoor models, electric flight, rubber powered flying models, micro radio control, aviation history, homebuilt aircraft, ultralights and hang gliders.
Recent Title(s): *Birdflight as the Basis of Aviation*, by Otto Lilienthal.
Tips: "Our focus is on books of short to medium length that will serve the emerging needs of the hobby. We want to help youth get started and enhance everyone's enjoyment of the hobby."

AVISSON PRESS, INC., 3007 Taliaferro Rd., Greensboro NC 27408. Fax: (336)288-6989. **Acquisitions:** M.L. Hester, editor. Estab. 1994. Publishes hardcover originals and trade paperback originals and reprints. **Publishes 9-10 titles/year. Receives 600 queries and 400 mss/year. 5% of books from first-time authors; 90% from unagented writers. Pays**

8-10% royalty on wholesale price. Offers occasional small advance. Publishes book 15 months after acceptance of ms. Accepts simultaneous submissions, if so noted. Responds in 1 week to queries and proposals, 3 months to mss. Book catalog for #10 SASE.

    O⌐ Avisson Press publishes helpful nonfiction for senior citizens, minority topics and young adult biographies (African-American, women). Currently emphasizing young-adult biography only.

Nonfiction: Biography, reference, self-help (senior citizens and teenagers), regional or North Carolina, textbook (creative writing text). Subjects include history (Southeast or North Carolina), language/literature, psychology, regional, sports, women's issues/studies. Query or submit outline and 1-3 sample chapters.

    ● Avission Press no longer accepts fiction or poetry.

Recent Title(s): *Blackball Superstars*, by Ace Collins and John Hillman (nonfiction); *Eight Who Made a Difference: Pioneer Women in the Arts*, by Erica Stux (nonfiction).

Tips: Audience is primarily public and school libraries.

AVON BOOKS, 1350 Avenue of the Americas, New York NY 10019. Website: www.avonbooks.com. **Acquisitions:** Editorial Submissions. Estab. 1941. Publishes mass market paperback originals and reprints. **Publishes 400 titles/year. Royalty and advance negotiable.** Publishes ms 2 years after acceptance of ms. Accepts simultaneous submissions. Responds in 3 months. Guidelines for SASE.

Imprint(s): Avon Eos.

Nonfiction: How-to, popular psychology, self-help, health, history, war, sports, business/economics, biography, politics. No textbooks. Query only with SASE.

Fiction: Romance (contemporary, historical), science fiction, fantasy, men's adventure, suspense/thriller, mystery, western. Query only with SASE.

Recent Title(s): *Joining*, by Johanna Lindsey.

AVON EOS, Avon Books, 1350 Avenue of the Americas, New York NY 10019. (212)261-6800. Website: www.avonbooks.com/eos. **Acquisitions:** Jennifer Brehl, executive editor; Caitlin Blasdell, senior editor; Diana Gill, editor. Publishes hardcover originals, trade and mass market paperback originals and reprints. **Publishes 55-60 titles/year. Receives 2,500 queries and 800 mss/year. 25% of books from first-time authors; 5% from unagented writers. Pays royalty on retail price, range varies.** Publishes book 18-24 months after acceptance of ms. Accepts simultaneous submissions, if so noted. Responds in 6 months. Manuscript guidelines for #10 SASE.

    O⌐ "We put out quality science fiction/fantasy with broad appeal."

Fiction: Fantasy, science fiction. No horror or juvenile topics. "We look for original work that will break traditional boundaries of this genre." Query with full synopsis of book, 3 sample chapters and SASE.

Recent Title(s): *Expendable*, by James Alan Gardener.

Tips: "We strongly advise submitting via a literary agent. If you make an unsolicited, unagented submission, follow our guidelines (i.e., do not send an entire manuscript; send query, synopsis and sample chapters only)."

AZTEX CORP., P.O. 50046, Tucson AZ 85703-1046. (520)882-4656. Website: www.aztexcorp.com. **Acquisitions:** Elaine Jordan, editor. Estab. 1976. Publishes hardcover and paperback originals. **Publishes 10 titles/year. Receives 250 submissions/year. 100% of books from unagented writers. Pays 10% royalty.** Publishes book 18 months after acceptance. Responds in 3 months.

Nonfiction: "We specialize in transportation subjects (how-to and history)." Accepts nonfiction translations. Submit outline and 2 sample chapters. "Queries without return envelopes or postage are not responded to." Reviews artwork/photos as part of ms package.

Tips: "We look for accuracy, thoroughness and interesting presentation."

BACKCOUNTRY GUIDES, (formerly Backcountry Publications), The Countryman Press, P. O. Box 748, Woodstock VT 05091-0748. (802)457-4826. Fax: (802)457-1678. E-mail: countrymanpress@wwnorton.com. Website: www.countrymanpress.com. **Acquisitions:** Ann Kraybill, managing editor. Publishes trade paperback originals. **Publishes 15 titles/year. Receives 1,000 queries and a few mss/year. 25% of books from first-time authors; 75% from unagented writers. Pays 7-10% royalty on retail price. Offers $1,500-2,500 advance.** Publishes book 18 months after acceptance of ms. Accepts simultaneous submissions. Returns submissions only with SASE. Responds in 2 months to proposals. Book catalog free. Ms guidelines for #10 SASE.

    O⌐ Backcountry Guides publishes guidebooks that encourage physical fitness and appreciation for and understanding of the natural world, self-sufficiency and adventure. "We publish several series of regional destination guidebooks to outdoor recreation. They include: the 50 Hikes series; 25 Bicycle Tours series; Trout Streams series; and a paddling (canoeing and kayaking) series." Currently emphasizing kayaking; bicycling the national parks.

Nonfiction: Subjects include nature/environment, outdoor recreation: bicycling, hiking, canoeing, kayaking, fly fishing, walking, guidebooks and series. Query with outline, 50 sample pages and proposal package including market analysis and SASE.

Recent Title(s): *Bicycling America's National Parks: California*, by David Story; *Kayaking the Maine Coast*, by Dorcas Miller.

Tips: "Look at our existing series of guidebooks to see how your proposal fits in."

BAEN PUBLISHING ENTERPRISES, P.O. Box 1403, Riverdale NY 10471-0671. (718)548-3100. Website: baen.c om. **Acquisitions:** Jim Baen, editor-in-chief; Toni Weisskopf, executive editor. Estab. 1983. Publishes hardcover, trade paperback and mass market paperback originals and reprints. **Publishes 120 titles/year. Receives 5,000 submissions/ year. 5% of books from first-time authors; 50% from unagented writers. Pays royalty on retail price.** Responds in 8 months to queries and proposals, 1 year to complete mss. Book catalog free. Manuscript guidelines for #10 SASE.
   O— "We publish books at the heart of science fiction and fantasy."
Fiction: Fantasy, science fiction. Submit outline/synopsis and sample chapters or complete ms.
Recent Title(s): *Ashes of Victory*, by David Weber.
Tips: "See our books before submitting. Send for our writers' guidelines."

BAKER BOOK HOUSE COMPANY, P.O. Box 6287, Grand Rapids MI 49516-6287. (616)676-9185. Fax: (616)676-2315. Website: www.bakerbooks.com.
Imprint(s): Baker Academic, **Baker Books**, Baker Bytes, Brazos Press, **Chosen**, **Fleming H. Revell**, Spire, Wynwood.

BAKER BOOKS, Baker Book House Company, P.O. Box 6287, Grand Rapids MI 49516-6287. (616)676-9185. Fax: (616)676-9573. Website: www.bakerbooks.com. Director of Publications: Don Stephenson. **Acquisitions:** Rebecca Cooper, assistant editor. Estab. 1939. Publishes hardcover and trade paperback originals and trade paperback reprints. **Publishes 80 titles/year. 10% of books from first-time authors; 85% from unagented writers. Pays 14% royalty on net receipts.** Publishes book within 1 year after acceptance. Accepts simultaneous submissions, if so noted. Responds in 2 months to proposals. Book catalog for 8½ × 11 SAE with 6 first-class stamps or on website. Manuscript guidelines for #10 SASE or on website.
   O— "Baker Books publishes popular religious nonfiction and fiction, children's books, academic and reference books, and professional books for church leaders. Most of our authors and readers are evangelical Christians, and our books are purchased from Christian bookstores, mail-order retailers, and school bookstores."
Imprint(s): Hamewith, Hourglass, Labyrinth, Raven's Ridge, Spire Books.
Nonfiction: Anthropology, archaeology, biography, CD-ROM, children's/juvenile, contemporary issues, giftbook, illustrated book, parenting, psychology, reference, self-help, seniors' concerns, singleness, textbook, women's concerns, children's books, Christian doctrine, reference books, books for pastors and church leaders, textbooks for Christian colleges and seminaries. Query with proposal, including chapter summaries or outlines, sample chapters, résumé and SASE. Reviews artwork as part of ms package. Send 1-2 photocopies.
Fiction: Literary novels focusing on women's concerns, mainstream/contemporary, religious, mysteries, juvenile, picture books, young adult. Query with synopsis/outline, sample chapters, résumé and SASE.
Recent Title(s): *The Last Days According to Jesus*, by R.C. Sproul (theology); *Resting in the Bosom of the Lamb*, by Augusta Trobaugh (southern fiction).

BALCONY PRESS, 512 E. Wilson, Suite 306, Glendale CA 91206. (818)956-5313. E-mail: ann@balconypress.com. **Acquisitions:** Ann Gray, publisher. Publishes hardcover and trade paperback originals. **Publishes 6-8 titles/year. Pays 10% royalty on wholesale price. No advance.** Responds in 1 month to queries and proposals; 3 months to mss. Book catalog free.
Nonfiction: Coffee table books and illustrated books. Subjects include art/architecture, ethnic, gardening, history (relative to design, art and architecture) and regional. "We are interested in the human side of design as opposed to technical or how-to. We like to think our books will be interesting to the general public who might not otherwise select an architecture or design book." Query by telephone or letter. Submit outline and 2 sample chapters with introduction if applicable.
Recent Title(s): *Photographing Architecture & Interiors*, by Julius Shulman.
Tips: Audience consists of architects, designers and the general public who enjoy those fields. "Our books typically cover California subjects but that is not a restriction. It's always nice when an author has strong ideas about how the book can be effectively marketed. We are not afraid of small niches if a good sales plan can be devised." We also now publish *LA Architect* magazine focusing on contemporary architecture and design in Southern California. Editor: Danette Riddle.

BALE BOOKS, Bale Publications, 5121 St. Charles Ave., Suite #13, New Orleans LA 70115. **Acquisitions:** Don Bale, Jr, editor-in-chief. Estab. 1963. Publishes hardcover and paperback originals and reprints. **Publishes 10 titles/ year. Receives 25 submissions/year. 50% of books from first-time authors; 90% from unagented writers. Offers standard 10-12½-15% royalty contract on wholesale or retail price; sometimes makes outright purchases of $500. No advance.** Publishes book 3 years after acceptance. Responds in 3 months. Book catalog for #10 SAE with 2 first-class stamps.
   O— "Our mission is to educate numismatists about coins, coin collecting and investing opportunities."
Nonfiction: Numismatics. "Our specialties are coin and stock market investment books; especially coin investment books and coin price guides." Submit outline and 3 sample chapters.
Recent Title(s): *How to Find Valuable Old & Scarce Coins*, by Jules Penn.
Tips: "Most of our books are sold through publicity and ads in the coin newspapers. We are open to any new ideas in the area of numismatics. Write for a teenage through adult level. Lead the reader by the hand like a teacher, building chapter by chapter. Our books sometimes have a light, humorous treatment, but not necessarily. We look for good English, construction and content, and sales potential."

N: BALL PUBLISHING, 335 N. River St., Batavia IL 60510. (630)208-9080. Fax: (630)208-9350. E-mail: info@ball publishing.com. Website: www.ballpublishing.com. **Acquisitions:** Rick Blanchette, book editor (floriculture, horticulture, agriculture). Publishes hardcover and trade paperback originals. **Publishes 6-10 titles/year. Receives 15 queries and 3 mss/year. 20% of books from first-time authors; 100% from unagented writers. Pays 10-15% royalty on wholesale price, makes outright purchase of $500. Offers up to $3,000 advance.** Publishes book 8 months after acceptance of ms. Accepts simultaneous submissions. Responds in 2 months. Book catalog for 8½×11 SASE with 3 first-class stmps.

O—¬ "Our books have been primarily published for professionals in the floriculture and horticulture fields. We are open to books on gardening for the consumer, but that is not our primary focus."

Nonfiction: How-to, reference, technical, textbook. Subjects include floriculture, agriculture/horticulture, gardening. Query with SASE or submit proposal package, including outline and 2 sample chapters. Reviews artwork/photos as part of the ms package. Send photocopies.

Recent Title(s): *Pests and Diseases of Herbaceous Perennials*, by Stanton Gill, David L. Clement, Ethel Dutky (technical); *Ball Culture Guide, (3rd edition), by Jim Nau (technical).*

Tips: "Professional growers and retailers in floriculture and horticulture make up the majority of our audience. Serious gardeners are a secondary audience. Make sure you know your subject well and present the material in a way that will be of interest to professionals. We do not publish for the inexperienced gardener. Include photos if they are critical to your proposal."

A: BALLANTINE BOOKS, Random House, Inc., 1540 Broadway, New York NY 10036. (212)782-9000. Website: www.randomhouse.com/BB. Publishes hardcover and trade paperback originals. President: Gina Centrello. **Acquisitions**: Maureen O'Neal, editorial director (literary and commercial fiction, nonfiction); Leona Nevler, editor (all kinds of fiction and nonfiction); Peter Borland, editorial director (commercial fiction, pop culture); Joe Blades, associate publisher (mystery); Elizabeth Zack, editor (motivational, inspirational, women's sports, career, seasonal tie-ins); Joanne Wyckoff, senior editor (religion, history, biography, spirituality, nature/pets, psychology); Shauna Summers, senior editor (historical and contemporary romance, commercial women's fiction, general fiction, thrillers/suspense); Dan Smetanka, senior editor (literary fiction, narrative nonfiction). Estab. 1952. Publishes hardcover, trade paperback, mass market paperback originals.

O—¬ Ballantine Books publishes a wide variety of nonfiction and fiction.

Nonfiction: How-to, humor, self-help. Subjects include animals, child guidance/parenting, cooking/foods/nutrition, health/medicine. *No unsolicited mss. Agented submissions only.*

Fiction: Historical fiction, women's mainstream, multicultural and general fiction.

Recent Title(s): *The Orchid Thief*, by Susan Orlean (nonfiction); *L.A. Requiem*, by Robert Crais (fiction).

BANCROFT PRESS, P.O. Box 65360, Baltimore MD 21209-9945. (410)358-0658. Fax: (410)764-1967. E-mail: bruceb@bancroftpress.com. Website: www.bancroftpress.com. **Acquisitions:** Bruce Bortz, publisher (health, investments, politics, history, humor); Fiction Editor (literary novels, poetry, mystery/thrillers). Publishes hardcover and trade paperback originals. **Publishes 4 titles/year. Pays various royalties on retail price.** Also packages books for other publishers (no fee to authors). Publishes book up to 3 years after acceptance of ms. Responds in 4 months to proposals. Book catalog for #10 SASE.

O—¬ Bancroft Press is a general trade publisher specializing in books by journalists. Currently emphasizing health and adult books for young adults. De-emphasizing celebrity fiction.

Nonfiction: Biography, how-to, humor, self-help. Subjects include business/economics, government/politics, health/medicine, money/finance, regional, sports, women's issues/studies, popular culture, essays. We advise writers to visit website www.bancroftpress.com." Submit proposal package, including outline, 2 sample chapters and competition/market survey.

Fiction: Literary, mystery, poetry, thrillers. Query with outline and 2 sample chapters.

Recent Nonfiction Title(s): *A Cry Unheard: New Insights into the Medical Consequences of Loneliness*, by James J. Lynch, Ph.D. (nonfiction); *The Reappearance of Sam Webber*, by Jonathon Scott Fuqua (fiction).

BANTAM DELL PUBLISHING GROUP, Random House, Inc., Dept. WM, 1540 Broadway, New York NY 10036. (212)354-6500. Website: www.bantamdell.com. Senior Vice President/Deputy Publisher: Nita Taublib. **Acquisitions:** Toni Burbank (nonfiction: self-help, health/medicine, nature, spirituality, philosophy, mythology); Jackie Cantor (fiction: literary, women's fiction, historical romance); Kara Cesare (fiction: romance, women's fiction); Beth DeGuzman (fiction: romance, women's fiction, suspense); Tracy Devine (fiction: literary, women's fiction, general commercial fiction, suspense, romance); Anne Groell (fiction: fantasy, science fiction); Jackie Farber (fiction: women's fiction, general commercial fiction); Katie Hall (fiction and nonfiction: military, historical, sociological); Susan Kamil (The Dial Press, fiction and nonfiction: literary, memoir, sociological, historical); Kathleen Jayes (fiction and nonfiction: literary, self-help, sociological, philosophy, mythology); Robin Michaelson (nonfiction: self-help, child care/parenting, psychology); Kate Miciak (fiction: mystery, suspense, historical fiction); Wendy McCurdy (fiction: romance, women's fiction); Daniel Perez (nonfiction: Americana, self-help, health/medicine); Beth Rashbaum (nonfiction: health, psychology, self-help, women's issues, Judaica, history, memoir); Tom Spain (fiction and nonfiction: Americana, memoir, sociology, historical); Mike Shohl (fiction: fantasy, science fiction). Estab. 1945. Publishes hardcover, trade paperback and mass market paperback originals; mass market paperback reprints. **Publishes 500 titles/year.** Publishes book an average of 1 year after ms is accepted. Accepts simultaneous submissions from agents.

O→ Bantam Dell is a division of Random House, publishing both fiction and nonfiction.

Imprint(s): Bantam, Delacorte Press, Dell, Delta, The Dial Press, DTP, Island.

Nonfiction: Biography, how-to, humor, self-help. Subjects include Americana, business/economics, child care/parenting, diet/fitness, cooking/foods/nutrition, government/politics, health/medicine, history, language/literature, military/war, mysticism/astrology, nature, philosophy/mythology, psychology, religion/inspiration, science, sociology, spirituality, sports, true crime, women's studies. Agent submissions or single-page query letter briefly describing the work (including category and subject matter) and author biography. *SASE a must.*

Fiction: Adventure, fantasy, feminist, historical, literary, mainstream/contemporary, mystery, romance, science fiction, suspense. Agent submissions or single-page query letter briefly describing the work (including category and subject matter) and author biography. *SASE a must.*

Recent Title(s): *Irresistible Forces*, by Danielle Steel (Delacorte, fiction); *The Testament*, by John Grisham (Dell, fiction); *The Plutonium Files*, by Eileen Welsom (The Dial Press, nonfiction).

Tips: No unsolicited mss; send one-page queries only.

BANTAM DOUBLEDAY DELL BOOKS FOR YOUNG READERS, Random House Children's Publishing, Random House, Inc., 1540 Broadway, New York NY 10036. (212)782-9000. Fax: (212)782-9452. Website: www.randomhouse.com/kids. Vice President/Associate Publisher/Editor-in-Chief: Beverly Horowitz. Editorial Director: Michelle Poploff.

Acquisitions: Wendy Lamb, executive editor; Francoise Bui, executive editor; Karen Wojtyla, editor; Wendy Loggia, editor; Diana Capriotti, associate editor. Publishes hardcover, trade paperback and mass market paperback series originals, trade paperback reprints. **Publishes 300 titles/year. Receives thousands of queries/year. 10% of books from first-time authors; few from unagented writers. Pays royalty. Advance varies.** Publishes book 2 years after acceptance of ms. Responds in 2 months. Book catalog for 9×12 SASE.

O→ "Bantam Doubleday Dell Books for Young Readers publishes award-winning books by distinguished authors and the most promising new writers."

Imprint(s): Delacorte Press Books for Young Readers, Doubleday Books for Young Readers, Laurel Leaf (ya), Picture Yearling, Skylark, Starfire, Yearling (middle grade).

• The best way to break in to this market is through its two contests, the **Marguerite de Angeli Contest** and the **Delacorte Press Contest for a First Young Adult Novel**, listed in the Contests & Awards section of this book.

Nonfiction: "Bantam Doubleday Dell Books for Young Readers publishes a very limited number of nonfiction titles."

Fiction: Adventure, fantasy, humor, juvenile, mainstream/contemporary, mystery, picture books, suspense, young adult. Query with SASE. *No unsolicited material.*

Recent Title(s): *Bud, Not Buddy*, by Christopher Paul Curtis (Newbery Award winner); *My Friend John*, by Charlotte Zolotow (picture book); *Ties That Bind, Ties That Break*, by Lensey Namiska (fiction).

▲ **BARBOUR PUBLISHING, INC.**, P.O. Box 719, Uhrichsville OH 44683. (740)922-6045. **Acquisitions:** Susan Schlabach, senior editor (all areas); Rebecca Germany, managing editor (fiction). Estab. 1981. Publishes hardcover, trade paperback and mass market paperback originals and reprints. **Publishes 100 titles/year. Receives 520 queries and 625 mss/year. 40% of books from first-time authors; 95% from unagented writers. Pays 0-12% royalty on net price or makes outright purchase of $500-5,000. Offers $500-2,500 advance.** Publishes book 2 years after acceptance of ms. Accepts simultaneous submissions. Responds in 1 month to queries, 3 months to proposals and mss. Book catalog for 9×12 SAE and 2 first-class stamps. Manuscript guidelines for #10 SASE.

O→ Barbour Books publishes mostly devotional material that is non-denominational and evangelical in nature; Heartsong Presents publishes Christian romance. "We're a Christian evangelical publisher."

Imprint(s): Heartsong Presents (contact Rebecca Germany, managing editor), Promise Press (contact Susan Schlabach, senior editor).

Nonfiction: Biography, children's/juvenile, cookbook, gift book, humor, illustrated book, reference. Subjects include child guidance/parenting, cooking/foods/nutrition, money/finance, religion (evangelical Christian), women's issues/studies. "We are always looking for biographical material for adults and children on heroes of the faith. Always looking for humor! Some writers do not explain their purpose for writing the book and don't specify who their audience is. Many proposals are sketchy, non-specific and difficult to understand. If I can't decipher the proposal, I certainly won't accept a manuscript." Submit outline and 3 sample chapters with SASE. Reviews artwork/photos as part of the ms package. Send photocopies. "Send sufficient postage if you want your materials returned."

Fiction: Historical, humor, mainstream/contemporary, religious, romance, short story collections, Western. "All of our fiction is 'sweet' romance. No sex, no bad language, etc. Audience is evangelical/Christian, and we're looking for wholesome material for young as well as old. Common writer's mistakes are a sketchy proposal, an unbelievable story and a story that doesn't fit our guidelines for inspirational romances." Submit synopsis and 3 sample chapters with SASE.

Recent Title(s): *God Is In the Small Stuff*, by Bruce Bickel and Stan Jantz (nonfiction); *Short Stories for Long Rainy Days*, by Katherine Douglas (fiction).

Tips: "Audience is evangelical/Christian conservative, non-denominational, young and old. We're looking for *great concepts*, not necessarily a big name author or agent. We want to publish books that will sell millions, not just 'flash in the pan' releases. Send us your ideas!"

BARNEGAT LIGHT PRESS, Pine Barrens Press, P.O. Box 607, 3959 Rt. 563, Chatsworth NJ 08019-0607. (609)894-4415. Fax: (609)894-2350. **Acquisitions:** R. Marilyn Schmidt, publisher. Publishes trade paperback originals. **Publishes**

4 titles/year. Receives 50 queries and 30 mss/year. 0% of books from first-time authors; 100% from unagented writers. Makes outright purchase. Publishes book 6 months after acceptance of ms. Responds in 1 month. *Writer's Market* recommends allowing 2 months for reply. Book catalog free on request or on website.

> O→ "We are a regional publisher emphasizing the mid-Atlantic region. Areas concerned are gardening and cooking."

Imprint(s): Pine Barrens Press.

Nonfiction: Cookbook, how-to, illustrated book. Subjects include agriculture/horticulture, cooking/foods/nutrition, gardening, regional, travel. Query with SASE. Reviews artwork/photos as part of the ms package. Send photocopies.

Recent Title(s): *Exploring the Pine Barrens: A Guide*, by R.M. Schmidt (travel); *Cranberry Cookery Complete*, by R.M. Schmidt.

BARRICADE BOOKS INC., 150 Fifth Ave., Suite 700, New York NY 10011-4311. (212)627-7000. Fax: (212)627-7028. **Acquisitions:** Carole Stuart, publisher. Estab. 1991. Publishes hardcover and trade paperback originals and trade paperback reprints. **Publishes 30 titles/year. Receives 200 queries and 100 mss/year. 80% of books from first-time authors; 50% from unagented writers. Pays 10-12% royalty on retail price for hardcover. Advance varies.** Publishes book 18 months after acceptance of ms. Responds in 1 month to queries. Book catalog for $3.

> O→ "We look for nonfiction, mostly of the controversial type, and books we can promote with authors who can talk about their topics on radio and television and to the press."

Nonfiction: Biography, how-to, reference, self-help. Subjects include business/economics, ethnic, gay/lesbian, government/politics, health/medicine, history, nature/environment, psychology, sociology, women's issues/studies. Query with outline and 1-2 sample chapters with SASE or material will not be returned. Reviews artwork/photos as part of ms package. Send photocopies.

Recent Title(s): *The Animal in Hollywood*, by John L. Smith (crime/mafia).

Tips: "Do your homework. Visit bookshops to find publishers who are doing the kinds of books you want to write. Always submit to a *person*—not just 'editor.' Always enclose SASE or you may not get a response."

BARRON'S EDUCATIONAL SERIES, INC., 250 Wireless Blvd., Hauppauge NY 11788. (631)434-3311. Fax: (631)434-3217. Website: barronseduc.com. **Acquisitions:** Wayne Barr, managing editor/director of acquisitions. Estab. 1941. Publishes hardcover, paperback and mass market originals and software. **Publishes 400 titles/year. Reviews 2,000 queries and 1,000 mss/year. 40% of books from first-time authors; 75% from unagented writers. Pays 14-16% royalty on both wholesale and retail price or makes outright purchase of $2,500-5,000. Offers $2,500-5,000 advance.** Publishes book 2 years after acceptance of ms. Accepts simultaneous submissions. Responds in 1 month to queries, 8 months to ms. Book catalog free.

> O→ Barron's tends to publish series of books, both for adults and children. "We are always on the lookout for creative nonfiction ideas for children and adults."

Nonfiction: Adult education, art, business, cookbooks, crafts, foreign language, review books, guidance, pet books, travel, literary guides, parenting, health, juvenile, young adult sports, test preparation materials and textbooks. Reviews artwork/photos as part of ms package. Query or submit outline/synopsis and 2-3 sample chapters. Accepts nonfiction translations.

Fiction: Juvenile, young adult. Submit complete ms.

Recent Title(s): *A Book of Magical Herbs*, by Margaret Picton; *Family Gardener*, by Lucy Peel.

Tips: "Audience is mostly educated self-learners and hobbyists. The writer has the best chance of selling us a book that will fit into one of our series. SASE must be included for the return of all materials. Please be patient for replies."

BATTELLE PRESS, Battelle Memorial Institute, 505 King Ave., Columbus OH 43201. (614)424-6393. Fax: (614)424-3819. E-mail: press@battelle.org. Website: www.battelle.org/bookstore. **Acquisitions:** Joe Sheldrick. Estab. 1980. Publishes hardcover and paperback originals and markets primarily by direct mail. **Publishes 15 titles/year. Pays 10% royalty on wholesale price. No advance.** Publishes book 6 months after acceptance of ms. Accepts simultaneous submissions. Responds in 1 month. Book catalog free.

> O→ Battelle Press strives to be a primary source of books and software on science and technology management.

Nonfiction: "We are looking for management, leadership, project management and communication books specifically targeted to engineers and scientists." Query. Reviews artwork/photos as part of ms package. Send photocopies. Returns submissions with SASE only by writer's request.

Recent Title(s): *Managing the Industry/University Cooperative Research Center*; *Project Manager's Survival Guide*.

Tips: Audience consists of engineers, researchers, scientists and corporate researchers and developers.

BAY BOOKS, (formerly KQED Books), 555 DeHaro St., #220, San Francisco CA 94107. (415)252-4350. **Acquisitions**: James Connolly, editorial director. Publishes hardcover originals, trade paperback originals and reprints. **Publishes 10 titles/year. Receives 20 queries/year. 70% of books from first-time authors. Royalties vary substantially. Offers $0-25,000 advance.** Publishes book 6 months after acceptance of ms. Accepts simultaneous submissions. Responds in 1 month. *Writer's Market* recommends allowing 2 months for reply. Book catalog for 9×12 SASE and 3 first-class stamps.

Nonfiction: Coffee table book, cookbook, gift book, how-to, humor, illustrated book. Subjects include Americana, child guidance/parenting, cooking, food & nutrition, education, health/medicine, history, hobbies, nature/environment, religion, travel (Armchair Travel), cable/PBS series companions. "We only publish titles related to public and cable television series." Query.

Recent Title(s): *Savor the Southwest*, by Barbara Fenzl (cooking).

Tips: "Audience is people interested in Public Broadcasting subjects: history, cooking, how-to, armchair travel, etc."

N: BAYLOR UNIVERSITY PRESS, P.O. Box 97363, Waco TX 76798. (254)710-3164. Fax: (254)710-3440. E-mail: David_Holcomb@baylor.edu. Website: www.baylor.edu/~BUPress. **Acquisitions:** J. David Holcomb, editor. Publishes hardcover and trade paperback originals. **Publishes 5 titles/year. Pays 10% royalty on wholesale price.** Publishes book 6 months after acceptance of ms. Responds in 2 months to proposals.

Imprint(s): Markham Press Fund.

Nonfiction: Scholarly. Subjects include anthropology/archaeology, history, regional, religion, women's issues/studies. Submit outline and 1-3 sample chapters.

Recent Title(s): *A Year at the Catholic Worker: A Spiritual Journey Among the Poor*, by Marc H. Ellis (Literature and the Religious Spirit Series).

Tips: "We publish contemporary and historical scholarly works on religion, ethics, church-state studies, and oral history, particularly as these relate to Texas and the Southwest." Currently emphasizing religious studies, history. De-emphasizing art, archaeology.

BAYWOOD PUBLISHING CO., INC., 26 Austin Ave., Amityville NY 11701. (631)691-1270. Fax: (631)691-1770. E-mail: baywood@baywood.com. Website: www.baywood.com. **Acquisitions:** Stuart Cohen, managing editor. Estab. 1964. **Publishes 25 titles/year. Pays 7-15% royalty on retail price.** Publishes book within 1 year after acceptance of ms. Catalog and ms guidelines free.

○→ Baywood Publishing publishes original and innovative books in the humanities and social sciences, including areas such as health sciences, gerontology, death and bereavement, psychology, technical communications and archaeology.

Nonfiction: Technical, scholarly. Subjects include anthropology/archaeology, computers/electronics, gerontology, imagery, labor relations, education, death/dying, drugs, nature/environment, psychology, public health/medicine, sociology, technical communications, women's issues/studies. Submit outline/synopsis and sample chapters.

Recent Title(s): *Eighteenth-Century British Aesthetics*, by Dabney Townsend.

BEACHWAY PRESS, 300 W. Main St., Suite A, Charlottesville VA 22903. (804)245-6800. Fax: (804)297-0569. E-mail: writers@beachway.com. Website: www.outside-america.com. **Acquisitions:** Scott Adams, publisher. **Publishes 10-15 titles/year. Pays 7½% royalty on wholesale price. Offers $2,500 advance.** Publishes book 1 year after acceptance of ms. Responds in 2 months to queries and proposals. Manuscript guidelines for #10 SASE or on website.

○→ Beachway Press publishes books designed to open up new worlds of experiences for those anxious to explore, and to provide the detailed information necessary to get them started.

Nonfiction: Innovative outdoor adventure and travel guidebooks. "We welcome ideas that explore the world of adventure and wonder; from day hikes to mountain bikes, from surf to skis." Query with outline, 2 sample chapters, methods of research and SASE. Reviews artwork/photos as part of ms package. Send proof prints.

Recent Title(s): *Mountain Bike America*™ (guidebook series).

Tips: "Someone interested in writing for us should be both an avid outdoors person and an expert in their area of interest. This person should have a clear understanding of maps and terrain and should enjoy sharing their adventurous spirit and enthusiasm with others. E-mail queries get fastest response."

BEACON PRESS, 25 Beacon St., Boston MA 02108-2892. (617)742-2110. Fax: (617)723-3097. E-mail: kdaneman@beacon.org. Website: www.beacon.org/Beacon. Director: Helene Atwan. **Acquisitions:** Deborah Chasman, editorial director (African-American, Asian-American, Latino, Native American, Jewish and gay and lesbian studies, anthropology); Deanne Urmy, executive editor (child and family issues, environmental concerns); Tisha Hooks, associate editor (cultural studies, Asian and Caribbean studies, women and spirituality); Amy Caldwell, assistant editor (poetry, gender studies, gay/lesbian studies and Cuban studies). Estab. 1854. Publishes hardcover originals and paperback reprints. **Publishes 60 titles/year. Receives 4,000 submissions/year. 10% of books from first-time authors. Pays royalty. Advance varies.** Accepts simultaneous submissions. Responds in 3 months.

○→ Beacon Press publishes general interest books that promote the following values: the inherent worth and dignity of every person; justice, equity, and compassion in human relations; acceptance of one another; a free and responsible search for truth and meaning; the goal of world community with peace, liberty and justice for all; respect for the interdependent web of all existence. Currently emphasizing innovative nonfiction writing by people of all colors. De-emphasizing poetry, children's stories, art books, self-help.

Imprint(s): Bluestreak Series (contact Deb Chasman, editor, innovative literary writing by women of color).

Nonfiction: General nonfiction including works of original scholarship, religion, women's studies, philosophy, current affairs, anthropology, environmental concerns, African-American, Asian-American, Native American, Latino and Jewish studies, gay and lesbian studies, education, legal studies, child and family issues, Irish studies. Query with outline/synopsis, cv or résumé and sample chapters with SASE. *Strongly prefers agented submissions.*

Recent Title(s): *Five Thousand Days Like This One*, by Jane Brox (nonfiction); *The Healing*, by Gayl Jones (fiction).

Tips: "We probably accept only one or two manuscripts from an unpublished pool of 4,000 submissions per year. No fiction, children's book, or poetry submissions invited. Authors should have academic affiliation."

[N] BEEMAN JORBENSEN, INC., 7510 Allisonville Rd., Indianapolis IN 46250. (317)841-7677. Fax: (317)849-2001. **Acquisitions:** Brett Johnson, president (automotive/auto racing). Publishes hardcover and trade paperback originals and hardcover reprints. **Publishes 4 titles/year. Receives 10 queries/year. 50% of books from first-time authors; 100% from unagented writers. Pays 15-30% royalty on wholesale price. Offers advance up to $1,000.** Publishes book 8 months after acceptance of ms. Responds in 1 month to queries, 2 months to proposals. Book catalog free.
Nonfiction: Coffee table book, illustrated book, reference. Subjects include automotive, auto racing. Query with SASE or submit proposal package, including outline and 1 sample chapter.
Recent Title(s): *Porsche Speedster*, by Michel Thiriar (coffee table); *Road America*, by Tom Schultz (illustrated book); *Volkswagon KdF, 1934-1945*, by Terry Shuler (illustrated book).
Tips: Audience is automotive enthusiasts, specific marque owners/enthusiasts, auto racing fans and participants.

[N] BEHRMAN HOUSE INC., 11 Edison Place, Springfield NJ 07081. (973)379-7200. Fax: (973)379-7280. E-mail: webmaster@behrmanhouse.com. Website: www.behrmanhouse.com. **Acquisitions:** David Behrman. Estab. 1921. **Publishes 20 titles/year. Receives 200 submissions/year. 20% of books from first-time authors; 95% from unagented writers. Pays 2-10% on wholesale price or retail price or makes outright purchase of $500-10,000. Offers $1,000 average advance.** Publishes book 18 months after acceptance. Accepts simultaneous submissions. Responds in 2 months. Book catalog free.
　○► "Behrman House publishes quality books of Jewish content—history, Bible, philosophy, holidays, ethics, Israel, Hebrew—for children and adults."
Nonfiction: Juvenile (ages 1-18), reference, textbook. Religious subjects. "We want Jewish textbooks for the el-hi market." Query with outline and sample chapters.
Recent Title(s): *Living As Partners with God*, by Gila Gevirtz (theology).

FREDERIC C. BEIL, PUBLISHER, INC., 609 Whitaker St., Savannah GA 31401. (912)233-2446. Fax: (912)234-3978. E-mail: beilbook@beil.com. Website: www.beil.com. **Acquisitions:** Mary Ann Bowman, editor. Estab. 1982. Publishes hardcover originals and reprints. **Publishes 13 titles/year. Receives 1,800 queries and 13 mss/year. 80% of books from first-time authors; 100% from unagented writers. Pays 7½% royalty on retail price.** Publishes book 20 months after acceptance. Accepts simultaneous submissions. Responds in 1 month to queries. Book catalog free.
　○► Frederic C. Beil publishes in the fields of history, literature, biography, books about books, and the book arts.
Imprint(s): The Sandstone Press, Hypermedia, Inc.
Nonfiction: Biography, general trade, illustrated book, juvenile, reference. Subjects include art/architecture, history, language/literature, book arts. Query. Reviews artwork/photos as part of ms package. Send photocopies.
Fiction: Historical and literary. Query.
Recent Title(s): *Joseph Jefferson: Dean of the American Theatre*, by Arthur Bloom; *Goya, Are You With Me Now?*, by H.E. Francis.
Tips: "Our objectives are (1) to offer to the reading public carefully selected texts of lasting value; (2) to adhere to high standards in the choice of materials and in bookmaking craftsmanship; (3) to produce books that exemplify good taste in format and design; and (4) to maintain the lowest cost consistent with quality."

BELLWETHER-CROSS PUBLISHING, 18319 Highway 20 W., East Dubuque IL 61025. (815)747-6255 or (888)516-5096. Fax: (815)747-3770. E-mail: jcrow@shepherd.clrs.com. **Acquisitions:** Janet White, senior developmental editor. Publishes college textbooks. **Publishes 18 titles/year. Receives 100 mss/year. 80% of books from first-time authors; 100% from unagented writers. Pays 10% royalty on wholesale price. No advance.** Publishes book 6 months after acceptance of ms. No simultaneous submissions. Responds in 1 month. Manuscript guidelines available.
　○► Bellwether-Cross concentrates on college environmental books and nontraditional textbooks with mainstream possibilities.
Nonfiction: Textbook. Submit complete ms., including cover letter. Reviews artwork as part of ms package. Send photocopies and SASE.
Recent Title(s): *Experiences in Environmental Science*, by Barbara Krumhardt and Danielle Wirth (college textbook); *Plant Biology in the Laboratory*, by Steven Herbert, Anne Sylvester and Clifford Weil.

THE BENEFACTORY, INC., 925 N. Milwaukee, Suite 1010, Wheeling IL 60090. (847)919-1777. Fax: (847)919-2777. E-mail: benefactory@aol.com. Website: www.readplay.com. **Acquisitions:** Cynthia A. Germain, senior manager, product development. Estab. 1990. Publishes hardcover and trade paperback originals and reprints. **Publishes 9 titles/year. 50% of books from first-time authors; 50% from unagented writers. Pays 3-5% royalty on wholesale price. Offers $3,000-5,000 advance.** Publishes book 1 year after acceptance of ms. Accepts simultaneous submissions. Responds in 6 months to queries and proposals, 8 months to mss. Book catalog and ms guidelines free.
　○► The Benefactory's mission is to foster animal protection, motivate reading, teach core values and encourage children to become creative, responsible individuals.
Nonfiction: Children's/juvenile. Subjects include animals, nature/environment. "Each story must be a true story about a real animal and contain educational details. Both prose and verse are accepted." Submit outline and SASE. Reviews artwork/photos as part of ms package. Send photocopies.

Recent Title(s): *Caesar, On Deaf Ears,* by Loren Spiotta DiMare (nonfiction).

BENTLEY PUBLISHERS, Automotive Publishers, 1734 Massachusetts Ave., Cambridge MA 02138-1804. (617)547-4170. **Acquisitions:** Janet Barnes, senior editor. Estab. 1949. Publishes hardcover and trade paperback originals and reprints. **Publishes 15-20 titles/year. 20% of books are from first-time authors; 95% from unagented writers. Pays 10-15% royalty on net price or makes outright purchase. Advance negotiable.** Publishes book 1 year after acceptance. Responds in 6 weeks. Book catalog and ms guidelines for 9×12 SAE with 4 first-class stamps.

   O→ Bentley Publishers publishes books for automotive enthusiasts.
Nonfiction: How-to, technical, theory of operation, coffee table. Automotive subjects only; this includes motor sports. Query or submit outline and sample chapters. Reviews artwork/photos as part of ms package.
Recent Title(s): *A French Kiss with Death,* by Michael Keyser.
Tips: "Our audience is composed of serious, intelligent automobile, sports car, and racing enthusiasts, automotive technicians and high-performance tuners."

N. BERGIN & GARVEY, Greenwood Publishing Group, 88 Post Rd. W., Westport CT 06881. (203)226-3571. Fax: (203)222-1502. Website: www.greenwood.com. **Acquisitions:** Editorial Offices. Publishes hardcover and trade paperback original nonfiction in the areas of education, anthropology, alternative medicine and parenting for libraries, educational groups and university scholars. **Publishes 25 titles/year. Receives 1000s of queries/year. 50% of books from first-time authors. Pays variable royalty on net price. Rarely offers advance.** Publishes book 1 year after acceptance of ms. Accepts simultaneous submissions. Responds in 6 months to queries and proposals. Book catalog and ms guidelines online.
Nonfiction: Subjects include anthropology/archaeology, child guidance/parenting, education. Query with proposal package, including scope, organization, length of project, whether a complete ms is available or when it will be, CV or résumé and SASE. *No unsolicited mss.*

THE BERKLEY PUBLISHING GROUP, Penguin Putnam, Inc., 375 Hudson St., New York NY 10014. (212)366-2000. Website: www.penguinputnam.com. **Acquisitions:** Denise Silvestro, senior editor (general nonfiction, business); Judith Stern Palais, senior editor (women's general, literary and romance fiction); Tom Colgan, senior editor (history, business, inspiration, biography, suspense/thriller, mystery, adventure); Gail Fortune, senior editor (women's fiction, romance, mystery); Martha Bushko, assistant editor (mystery, literary fiction, suspense/thriller); Kimberly Waltemyer, editor (adult western, romance, mystery); Brent Wittmer, editor (history, nonfiction, literary fiction). Estab. 1954. Publishes paperback and mass market originals and reprints. **Publishes approximately 800 titles/year. Few books from first-time authors; 1% from unagented writers. Pays 4-15% royalty on retail price. Offers advance.** Publishes book 2 years after acceptance of ms. Responds in 6 weeks to queries.

   O→ The Berkley Publishing Group publishes a variety of general nonfiction and fiction including the traditional categories of romance, mystery and science fiction.
Imprint(s): Ace Science Fiction, Berkley, **Boulevard**, Jove, Prime Crime.
Nonfiction: Biography, reference, self-help, how-to. Subjects include business management, job-seeking communication, positive thinking, gay/lesbian, health/fitness, psychology/self-help, women's issues/studies, general commercial publishing. No memoirs or personal stories. Query with SASE. Prefers agented submissions.
Fiction: Mystery, romance, western, young adult. No adventure or occult fiction. Prefers agented material. Query with SASE.
Recent Title(s): *Tom Clancy's Rainbow Six,* by Tom Clancy (novel); *Meditations from Conversations with God,* by Neale Donald Walsch (inspiration).

BERKSHIRE HOUSE PUBLISHERS, INC., 480 Pleasant St., Suite #5, Lee MA 01238. (413)243-0303. Fax: (413)243-4737. E-mail: info@berkshirehouse.com. Website: www.berkshirehouse.com. President: Jean J. Rousseau. **Acquisitions:** Philip Rich, editorial director. Estab. 1966. **Publishes 10-15 titles/year. Receives 100 queries and 6 mss/year. 50% of books from first-time authors; 80% from unagented writers. Pays 5-10% royalty on retail price. Offers $500-5,000 advance.** Publishes book 18 months after acceptance. Accepts simultaneous submissions. Responds in 1 month to proposals. Book catalog free.

   O→ "We publish a series of travel guides, the Great Destinations™ Series, about specific U.S. destinations, guides to appeal to discerning travelers. We also specialize in books about our own region (the Berkshires and New England), especially recreational activities such as outdoor exploration and gardening. We occasionally publish cookbooks related to New England or country living/country inns in general. We offer books of historical interest in our American Classics™ Series." Currently emphasizing Great Destinations™ series, outdoor recreation. De-emphasizing cookbooks except those related to New England or country living and country inns. Please refer to website for more information.
Nonfiction: Subjects include US travel, American culture, history, nature/environment, recreation (outdoors), wood crafts, regional cookbooks. "To a great extent, we choose our topics then commission the authors, but we don't discourage speculative submissions. We just don't accept many. Don't overdo it; a well-written outline/proposal is more useful than a full manuscript. Also, include a cv with writing credits."
Recent Title(s): *The Napa & Sonoma Book: A Complete Guide,* by Tim Fish and Peg Melnik.
Tips: "Our readers are literate, active, interested in travel, especially in selected 'Great Destinations' areas and outdoor activities and cooking."

N **BETHANY HOUSE PUBLISHERS**, 11400 Hampshire Ave. S., Minneapolis MN 55438. (952)829-2500. Fax: (952)829-2768. Website: www.bethanyhouse.com. Publisher: Gary Johnson. **Acquisitions:** Sharon Madison, ms review editor; Steve Laube, senior editor (nonfiction); David Horton, senior editor (adult fiction); Barbara Lilland, senior editor (adult fiction); Rochelle Gloege, senior editor (children and youth). Estab. 1956. "The purpose of Bethany House Publishers' publishing program is to relate biblical truth to all areas of life—whether in the framework of a well-told story, of a challenging book for spiritual growth, or of a Bible reference work." Publishes hardcover and trade paperback originals, mass market paperback reprints. **Publishes 120-150 titles/year. 93% of books are from unagented writers; 2% of books from first-time authors. Pays negotiable royalty on net price. Offers negotiable advance.** Publishes ms 1 year after acceptance of ms. Accepts simultaneous submissions. Responds in 3 months. Book catalog for 9×12 SAE with 5 first-class stamps. Manuscript guidelines free or on website.

  • Bethany House Publishers specializes in books that communicate biblical truth and assist people in both spiritual and practical areas of life. New interest in contemporary fiction.

Nonfiction: Biography, gift book, how-to, references, self-help. Subjects include personal growth, devotional, contemporary issues, marriage and family, reference, applied theology and inspirational. "Prospective authors must have credentials, credibility and well-honed writing." Submit proposal package including outline, 3 sample chapters, author information, and qualifications for writing with SASE. Reviews artwork/photos as part of ms package. Send photocopies. No phone, fax or e-mail queries.

Recent Nonfiction Title(s): *Becoming a Vessel God Can Use*, by Donna Partow (self-help); *The Compact Guide to World Religions*, by Dean C. Halverson (reference); *When God Says No*, by Leith Anderson (meditation and prayer).

Fiction: Adult historical fiction, teen/young adult, children's fiction series (age 8-12) and Bethany Backyard (age 6-12). Send SASE for guidelines.

Recent Title(s): *Taking Up Your Cross*, by Tricia McCary Rhodes (nonfiction); *The Crossroad*, by Beverly Lewis (fiction).

Tips: "We are seeking high quality fiction and nonfiction that will inspire and challenge our audience."

BETTERWAY BOOKS, F&W Publications, 1507 Dana Ave., Cincinnati OH 45207. (513)531-2690. **Acquisitions:** Jack Heffron (genealogy, theater and the performing arts; lifestyle, including home organization). Estab. 1982. Publishes hardcover and trade paperback originals, trade paperback reprints. **Publishes 30 titles/year. Pays 10-20% royalty on net receipts. Offers $3,000-5,000 advance.** Accepts simultaneous submissions, if so noted. Publishes book an average of 18 months after acceptance. Responds in 1 month. Book catalog for 9×12 SAE with 6 first-class stamps.

  • Betterway books are instructional books that are to be *used*. "We like specific step-by-step advice, charts, illustrations, and clear explanations of the activities and projects the books describe."

Nonfiction: How-to, illustrated book, reference and self-help. "Genealogy and family traditions are topics that we're particularly interested in. We are interested mostly in original material, but we will consider republishing self-published nonfiction books and good instructional or reference books that have gone out of print before their time. Send a sample copy, sales information, and reviews, if available. If you have a good idea for a reference book that can be updated annually, try us. We're willing to consider freelance compilers of such works." No cookbooks, diet/exercise, psychology self-help, health or parenting books. Query with outline and sample chapters. Reviews artwork/photos as part of ms package.

Recent Title(s): *Organizing Your Family History Search*, by Sharon DeBartolo Carmack (genealogy).

Tips: "Keep the imprint name well in mind when submitting ideas to us. What is the 'better way' you're proposing? How will readers benefit *immediately* from the instruction and information you're giving them?"

BICK PUBLISHING HOUSE, 307 Neck Rd., Madison CT 06443. (203)245-0073. Fax: (203)245-5990. E-mail: bickpubhse@aol.com. Website: www.bickpubhouse.com. **Acquisitions:** Dale Carlson, president (psychology); Hannah Carlson (special needs, disabilities); Irene Ruth (wildlife). Estab. 1994. Publishes trade paperback originals. **Publishes 4 titles/year. Receives 4-6 queries and mss/week. 55% of books from first-time authors; 55% from unagented writers. Pays 10% royalty on net price. Offers $500-1,000 advance.** Publishes book 1 year after acceptance of ms. Responds in 1 month to queries, 2 months to proposals, 3 months to mss. Book catalog free. Manuscript guidelines for #10 SASE.

  • Bick Publishing House publishes step-by-step, easy-to-read professional information for the general adult public about physical, psychological and emotional disabilities or special needs. Teenage psychology series. Wildlife rehabilitation series. Currently emphasizing teen psychology for teens.

Nonfiction: Subjects include animals (wildlife rehabilitation), health/medicine (disability/special needs), teen psychology. Submit proposal package, including outline, 3 sample chapters, résumé with SASE. Reviews artwork/photos as part of ms package. Send photocopies.

Recent Title(s): *Stop the Pain: Teen Meditations*; *Stop the Pain: Adult Meditation*, both by Dale Carlson.

BIRCH BROOK PRESS, P.O. Box 81, Delhi NY 13753. (212)353-3326. Fax: (607)746-7453. E-mail: birchbrkpr@prodigy.net. Website: www.birchbrookpress.com. **Acquisitions:** Tom Tolnay, editor. Estab. 1982. Publishes hardcover and trade paperback originals. **Publishes 4-6 titles/year. Receives hundreds of queries and mss/year. 95% of books from unagented writers. Royalty varies. Offers modest advance.** Publishes book 1 year after acceptance of ms. Accepts simultaneous submission, if informed. Responds in 1 month to queries, 2 months to mss. Book catalog and manuscript guidelines free for #10 SASE.

O‑w Birch Brook Press is a popular culture and literary publisher of handcrafted books and art, featuring letterpress editions produced at its own printing, typesetting and binding facility. Currently emphasizing short stories of flyfishing, hiking and Adirondack outdoors.

Imprint(s): Birch Book Press, Birch Brook Impressions, Persephone Press.

Nonfiction: Literary. Subjects include literature, books on books, baseball, fly fishing, opera. "We have a very limited nonfiction publishing program, mostly generated inhouse in anthologies." Query with SASE and ms sample. Reviews artwork as part of ms package. Send art photocopies to Frank C. Eckmair, art director.

Fiction: Literary, popular culture. "Mostly we do anthologies around a particular theme generated inhouse." Query with synopsis with sample chapter and SASE.

Poetry: Submit complete ms.

● This publisher recently took over the poetry publishing company Persephone Press.

Recent Titles: *A Brief Illustrated History of the Bookshelf*, art and text by Marshall Brooks (nonfiction); *Kilimanjaro Burning*, by John B. Robinson (fiction); *Risking the Wind* by Warren Carrier (poetry).

Tips: "Audience is college educated, readers and collectors. Our books are mostly letterpress editions printed from metal type and therefore tend to be short with content suitable to antique printing methods."

BK MK PRESS, University of Missouri-Kansas City, 5101 Rockhill Rd., Kansas City MO 64110-2499. (816)235-2558. Fax: (816)235-2611. E-mail: bkmk@umkc.edu. **Acquisitions:** Jim McKinley, executive editor (fiction/nonfiction); Michelle Boisseau, associate editor (poetry); Ben Furnish, managing editor. Estab. 1971. Publishes hardcover and trade paperback originals. **Publishes 5-6 titles/year. Receives 200-250 queries and 350 mss/year. 40% of books from first-time authors; 70% from unagented writers. Pays 10% royalty on wholesale price. No advance.** Publishes book 1 year after acceptance of ms. Accepts simultaneous submissions. Responds in 4 months to queries, 8 months to mss. Manuscript guidelines for #10 SASE.

O‑w Bk Mk Press publishes fine literataure.

Nonfiction: Subjects include creative nonfiction. Query with SASE.

Fiction: Literary, poetry in translation, short story collections. Submit proposal package, including 50 pages, cover letter and SASE.

Poetry: Submit 10 sample poems.

Recent Titles: *The Man in the Buick*, by Kathleen George (fiction); *Wolf Howl*, by Francis Blessfington (poetry).

Tips: "We skew toward readers of literature, particularly contemporary writing. Because of our limited number of titles published per year, we discourage apprentice writers or 'scattershot' submissions."

BLACK DOG & LEVENTHAL PUBLISHERS INC., 151 W. 19th St., 12th Floor, New York NY 10011. (212)647-9336. Fax: (212)647-9332. Publishes hardcover originals and reprints. **Publishes 30-40 titles/year. Receives 12 queries and 12 mss/year. Pays royalty on retail price or on net receipts or makes outright purchase. Offers $1,500-20,000 advance.** Publishes book 6 months after acceptance of ms. Accepts simultaneous submissions. Responds in 6 months. Book catalog free.

O‑w "We look for very commercial books that will appeal to a broad-based audience."

Nonfiction: Biography, children's/juvenile, coffee table book, cookbook, gift book, how-to, humor, illustrated book, multimedia (CD format), reference, self-help, technical. Subjects include americana, animals, art/architecture, child guidance/parenting, cooking/foods/nutrition, gardening, health/medicine, history, hobbies, language/literature, memoirs, military/war, multicultural, music/dance, nature/environment, photography, recreation, regional, sex, sociology, sports, travel. Submit proposal package, including outline, 3 sample chapters and SASE. Reviews artwork/photos as part of ms package. Send transparencies.

Fiction: Mystery, suspense. "We very rarely publish fiction." Query with SASE.

Recent Title(s): *Moments: The Pulitzer Prize Photographs*, by Hal Buell (photo journalism); *Skyscrapers*, by Judith Dupre (architecture).

Tips: "We look for books that are very commercial and that can be sold in an array of outlets such as bookstores, catalogs, warehouse clubs, K-mart, Costco, book clubs, etc."

BLACKBIRCH PRESS, INC., P.O. Box 3573, Woodbridge CT 06525. (203)387-7525. E-mail: staff@blackbirch. com. Website: www.blackbirch.com. **Acquisitions:** Beverly Larson, editorial director. Estab. 1990. Publishes hardcover and trade paperback originals. **Publishes 70-90 titles/year. Receives 400 queries and 75 mss/year. 100% of books from unagented writers. Pays 4-8% royalty on net price or makes outright purchase. Offers $1,000-5,000 advance.** Publishes book 1 year after acceptance of ms. Accepts simultaneous submissions. Replies only if interested. Manuscript guidelines free. "We cannot return submissions or send guidelines/replies without an enclosed SASE."

O‑w Blackbirch Press publishes juvenile and young adult nonfiction and fiction titles.

Nonfiction: Children's/juvenile: biography, illustrated books, reference. Subjects include animals, anthropology/archeology, art/architecture, education, health/medicine, history, nature/environment, science, sports, travel, women's issues/studies. "No proposals for adult readers, please." Publishes in series—6-8 books at a time. Query with SASE. *No unsolicited mss or proposals. No phone calls.* Cover letters and résumés are useful for identifying new authors. Reviews artwork/photos as part of ms package. Send photocopies.

Recent Title(s): *A Whale on Her Own: The True Story of Wilma the Whale*, by Brian Skerry; *Flies*, by Elaine Pascoe.

JOHN F. BLAIR, PUBLISHER, 1406 Plaza Dr., Winston-Salem NC 27103-1470. (336)768-1374. Fax: (336)768-9194. **Acquisitions:** Carolyn Sakowski, editor. Estab. 1954. Publishes hardcover originals and trade paperbacks. **Publishes 20 titles/year. Receives 2,000 submissions/year. 20-30% of books from first-time authors; 90% from unagented writers. Royalty negotiable.** Publishes book 18 months after acceptance. Responds in 3 months. Book catalog and ms guidelines for 9×12 SAE with 5 first-class stamps.

    O→ John F. Blair publishes in the areas of travel, history, folklore and the outdoors for a general trade audience, most of whom live or travel in the southeastern U.S.

Nonfiction: Especially interested in travel guides dealing with the Southeastern US. Also interested in Civil War, outdoors, travel and Americana; query on other nonfiction topics. Looks for utility and significance. Submit outline and first 3 chapters. Reviews artwork/photos as part of ms package.

Fiction: "We publish one work of fiction per season relating to the Southeastern U.S." No category fiction, juvenile fiction, picture books, short story collections or poetry. *Writer's Market* recommends sending a query with SASE first.

BLOOMBERG PRESS, Bloomberg L.P., 100 Business Park Dr., P.O. Box 888, Princeton NJ 08542-0888. Website: www.bloomberg.com/books. **Acquisitions:** Jared Kieling, editorial director; Kathleen Peterson, senior acquisitions editor. Estab. 1995. Publishes hardcover and trade paperback originals. **Publishes 18-22 titles/year. Receives 90 queries and 17 mss/year. 45% of books from unagented writers. Pays negotiable, competitive royalty. Offers negotiable advance.** Publishes book 9 months after acceptance of ms. Accepts simultaneous submissions. Responds in 1 month to queries. Book catalog for 10×13 SAE with 5 first-class stamps.

    O→ Bloomberg Press publishes professional books for practitioners in the financial markets and finance and investing books for informed personal investors, entrepreneurs and consumers. "We publish commercially successful, very high-quality books that stand out clearly from the competition by their brevity, ease of use, sophistication, and abundance of practical tips and strategies; books readers need, will use and appreciate."

Imprint(s): Bloomberg Personal Bookshelf, Bloomberg Professional Library, Bloomberg Small Business.

Nonfiction: How-to, reference, technical. Subjects include small business, current affairs, money/finance, new economy, personal finance and investing for consumers, professional books on finance, investment and financial services. "We are looking for authorities and experienced service journalists. We are looking for original solutions to widespread problems and books offering fresh investment opportunities. Do not send us management books—we don't publish them—or unfocused books containing general information already covered by one or more well-established backlist books in the marketplace." Submit outline, sample chapters and SAE with sufficient postage.

Recent Title(s): *Zero Gravity*, by Steve Harmon.

Tips: "*Bloomberg Professional Library*: Audience is upscale financial professionals—traders, dealers, brokers, planners and advisors, financial managers, money managers, company executives, sophisticated investors. *Bloomberg Personal Bookshelf:* audience is upscale consumers and individual investors. *Bloomberg Personal Finance:* Authors are experienced business and financial journalists and/or financial professionals nationally prominent in their specialty for some time who have proven an ability to write a successful book. Research Bloomberg and look at our specially formatted books in a library or bookstore, read *Bloomberg Personal Finance* and *Bloomberg* magazines and peruse our website."

BLUE HERON PUBLISHING, 1234 SW Stark St., Portland OR 97205. (503)221-6841. Fax: (503)221-6843. E-mail: bhp@teleport.com. Website: www.teleport.com/~bhp. **Acquisitions:** Dennis Stovall, publisher; Daniel Urban, associate editor. Estab. 1985. Publishes trade paperback originals and reprints. **Publishes 12 titles/year.** Responds in 6 weeks. Book catalog for #10 SASE.

    O→ Blue Heron Publishing publishes books on writing and the teaching of writing, young adult and adult literature, western outdoor photography, and left-wing novels of mystery and suspense. Now considering ethnic cookbooks. Currently emphasizing books on writing and the teaching of writing, mysteries. De-emphasizing young adult.

Nonfiction: Looking for books that sell in educational markets as well as the trade. Query with SASE.

Recent title(s): *Travel Writing in Fiction & Fact*, by Jane Edwards (nonfiction); *The Adventures of Elizabeth Fortune*, by K. Follis Cheatham (fiction); *Millenniel Spring*, edited by Michael Malan and Peter Sears (poetry).

Tips: "We publish in several overlapping markets from an editorial perspective of fostering cultural diversity, encouraging new literary voices, and promulgating progressive positions on social and political issues through fine fiction and nonfiction."

BLUE MOON BOOKS, INC., Avalon Publishing Group, 841 Broadway, New York NY 10003. (212)614-7880. Fax: (212)614-7887. E-mail: tmpress@aol.com. Website: www.bluemoonbooks.com. **Acquisitions:** Gayle Watkins, editor. Estab. 1987. Publishes trade paperback and mass market paperback originals. **Publishes 30-40 titles/year. Receives 1,000 queries and 500 mss/year. Pays 7½-10% royalty on retail price. Offers $500 and up advance.** Publishes book 1 year after acceptance of ms. Responds in 2 months. Book catalog free.

    O→ "Blue Moon Books is strictly an erotic press; largely fetish-oriented material, B&D, S&M, etc."

Nonfiction: Trade erotic and sexual nonfiction. *No unsolicited mss.*

Fiction: Erotica. *No unsolicited mss.*

Recent Title(s): *Patong Sisters: An American Woman's View of the Bangkok Sex World*, by Cleo Odzer; *J and Seventeen*, by Kenzaburo Oe.

BLUE POPPY PRESS, 3450 Penrose Place, Suite 110, Boulder CO 80301. (303)447-8372. Fax: (303)245-8362. E-mail: bluepp@compuserve.com. Website: www.bluepoppy.com. **Acquisitions:** Bob Flaws, editor-in-chief. Estab. 1981. Publishes hardcover and trade paperback originals. **Publishes 9-12 titles/year. Receives 50-100 queries and 20 mss/year. 40-50% of books from first-time authors; 100% from unagented writers. Pays 10-15% royalty "of sales price at all discount levels."** Publishes book 1 year after acceptance of ms. Responds in 1 month. Book catalog and ms guidelines free.

O→ Blue Poppy Press is dedicated to expanding and improving the English language literature on acupuncture and Asian medicine for both professional practitioners and lay readers.

Nonfiction: Self-help, technical, textbook related to acupuncture and Oriental medicine. "We only publish books on acupuncture and Oriental medicine by authors who can read Chinese and have a minimum of five years clinical experience. We also require all our authors to use Wiseman's *Glossary of Chinese Medical Terminology* as their standard for technical terms." Query or submit outline, 1 sample chapter and SASE.

Recent Title(s): *Managing Menopause Naturally*, by Honora Wolfe.

Tips: Audience is "practicing acupuncturists, interested in alternatives in healthcare, preventive medicine, Chinese philosophy and medicine."

THE BLUE SKY PRESS, Scholastic Inc., 555 Broadway, New York NY 10012. (212)343-6100. Website: www.scholastic.com. Editorial Director: Bonnie Verburg. **Acquisitions:** The Editors. Estab. 1982. Publishes hardcover originals. **Publishes 15-20 titles/year. Receives 2,500 queries/year. 1% of books from first-time authors; 75% from unagented writers. Pays 10% royalty on wholesale price, between authors and illustrators.** Publishes book 2 1/2 years after acceptance of ms. Responds in 6 months to queries.

O→ Blue Sky Press publishes primarily juvenile picture books—cutting edge, exciting books for children. Currently de-emphasizing historical fiction.

Fiction: Juvenile: adventure, fantasy, historical, humor, mainstream/contemporary, picture books, multicultural, folktales. Accepting queries (with SASE) from previously published authors only.

● Because of a large backlog of books, The Blue Sky Press is not accepting unsolicited submissions.

Recent Title(s): *No, David!*, by David Shannon (fiction).

N: BLUE/GRAY BOOKS, Creativity, Inc., 65 Macedonia Rd., Alexander NC 28701. (828)252-9515. Fax: (828)255-8719. Website: www.blue-gray.com. **Acquisitions:** Pat Roberts, acquisitions editor. Publishes trade paperback originals and reprints. **Publishes 4 titles/year. Pays negotiable royalty on wholesale price. Seldom offers advance.** Publishes book 18 months after acceptance of ms. Book catalog and ms guidelines for 9×12 SASE with $1.01 postage.

O→ Blue/Gray Books specializes in Civil War history.

Nonfiction: Civil War subjects include Americana, government/politics, biography, history, military/war. Query or submit proposal package, including original book if wanting reprint with SASE. Reviews artwork/photos as part of ms package. Send photocopies. Query or submit synopsis and 3 sample chapters with SASE.

Recent Title(s): *Rebel Boast*, by Manly Wade Wellman.

N: BLUEWOOD BOOKS, The Siyeh Group, Inc., P.O. Box 689, San Mateo CA 94401. (650)548-0754. Fax: (650)548-0654. E-mail: bluewoodb@aol.com. **Acquisitions:** Richard Michaels, director. Publishes trade paperback originals. **Publishes 8 titles/year. 20% of books from first-time authors; 100% from unagented writers. Makes work for hire assignments—fee depends upon book and writer's expertise. Offers advance of ⅓ fee.**

O→ "We are looking for qualified writers for nonfiction series—history and biography oriented."

Nonfiction: Biography, illustrated book. Subjects include Americana, anthropology/archaeology, art/architecture, business/economics, government/politics, health/medicine, history, military/war, multicultural, science, sports, women's issues/studies. Query with SASE.

Recent Title(s): *American Politics in the 20th Century*, by J. Bonasia (political history); *100 Families Who Shaped World History*, by Samuel Crompton (world history).

Tips: "Our audience consists of adults and young adults. Our books are written on a newspaper level—clear, concise, well organized and easy to understand. We encourage potential writers to send us a résumé, providing background, qualifications and references."

BNA BOOKS, The Bureau of National Affairs, Inc., 1231 25th St. NW, Washington DC 20037-1165. (202)452-4343. Fax: (202)452-4997. E-mail: books@bna.com. Website: www.bna.com/bnabooks. **Acquisitions:** Tim Darby, new product director (labor and employment law, employee benefits); Jim Fattibene, acquisitions manager (legal practice, intellectual property, health law). Estab. 1929. Publishes hardcover and softcover originals. **Publishes 35 titles/year. Receives 200 submissions/year. 20% of books from first-time authors; 95% from unagented writers. Pays 5-15% royalty on net cash receipts. Offers $500 average advance.** Publishes book 1 year after acceptance of ms. Accepts simultaneous submissions. Responds in 3 months to queries. Book catalog and ms guidelines free.

O→ BNA Books publishes professional reference books written by lawyers, for lawyers. Currently emphasizing health law.

Nonfiction: Legal reference, professional/scholarly. Subjects include labor and employment law, health law, legal practice, labor relations and intellectual property law. No fiction, biographies, bibliographies, cookbooks, religion books, humor or trade books. Submit detailed table of contents or outline.

Recent Title(s): *Fair Labor Standards Act; Intellectual Property Law in Cyberspace*.

Tips: "Our audience is made up of practicing lawyers and business executives; managers, federal, state, and local government administrators; unions; and law libraries. We look for authoritative and comprehensive works that can be supplemented or revised every year or two on subjects of interest to those audiences."

BOA EDITIONS, LTD., 260 East Ave., Rochester NY 14604. (716)546-3410. Fax: (716)546-3913. E-mail: boaedit@fr ontiernet.net. Website: www.boaeditions.org. **Acquisitions:** Steven Huff, publisher/managing editor; Thom Ward, editor. Estab. 1976. Publishes hardcover and trade paperback originals. **Publishes 10 titles/year. Receives 1,000 queries and 700 mss/year. 15% of books from first-time authors; 90% from unagented writers. Pays 7½-10% royalty on retail price. Advance varies, usually $500.** Publishes book 18 months after acceptance of ms. Accepts simultaneous submissions. Responds in 1 week to queries, 4 months to mss. Book catalog and ms guidelines free.
> ○━ BOA Editions publishes distinguished collections of poetry and poetry in translation. "Our goal is to publish the finest American contemporary poetry and poetry in translation."

Poetry: Accepting mss for publication in 2001 and beyond. Query with full ms and SASE.
Recent Title(s): *Dusty Angel*, by Michael Blumenthal; *Blessing the Boats*, by Lucille Clifton.
Tips: "Readers who, like Whitman, expect of the poet to 'indicate more than the beauty and dignity which always attach to dumb real objects . . . they expect him to indicate the path between reality and their souls,' are the audience of BOA's books."

BONUS BOOKS, INC., Precept Press, 160 E. Illinois St., Chicago IL 60611. (312)467-0580. Fax: (312)467-9271. E-mail: db@bonus-books.com. Website: www.bonus-books.com. Managing Editor: Michael Olsen. Estab. 1985. Publishes hardcover and trade paperback originals and reprints. **Publishes 30 titles/year. Receives 400-500 submissions/year. 40% of books from first-time authors; 60% from unagented writers. Royalties vary. Rarely offers advance.** Publishes book 8 months after acceptance. Accepts simultaneous submissions, if so noted. Responds in 2 months to queries. Book catalog for 9×11 SASE. Manuscript guidelines for #10 SASE.
> ○━ Bonus Books is a publishing and audio/video company featuring subjects ranging from human interest to sports to gambling.

Nonfiction: Subjects include automotive/self-help, biography/current affairs, broadcasting, business/self-help, Chicago people and places, collectibles, cookbooks, education/self-help, fund raising, handicapping winners, home and health, humor, entertainment, regional, sports and women's issues/studies. Query with outline, sample chapters and SASE. Reviews artwork/photos as part of ms package. All submissions and queries must include SASE.
Recent Title(s): *Method Marketing*, by D. Hatch.

▨ BOOKHOME PUBLISHING, P.O. Box 5900, Navarre FL 32566. (850)936-4050. Fax: (850)939-4953. E-mail: editor@bookidea.com. Website: www.bookhome.com. **Acquisitions:** Scott Gregory, publisher (small business, relationships, lifestyles, self-help). Publishes hardcover and trade paperback originals. **Publishes 5 titles/year. Receives 100 queries and 100 mss/year. 50% of books from first-time authors; 50% from unagented writers. Pays 7-12% royalty on wholesale price. Offers $0-1,000 advance.** Publishes book 1 year after acceptance of ms. Accepts simultaneous submissions. Responds in 2 months to proposals. Book catalog for #10 SAE with 2 first-class stamps. Manuscript guidelines for #10 SASE.
> ○━ "Our readers want to live better lives and build better businesses." Currently emphasizing writing/publishing, Florida travel. De-emphasizing self-help.

Nonfiction: How-to, self-help. Subjects include business, creative nonfiction, lifestyles, career. Submit proposal package, including outline, marketing plan, 2 sample chapters and SASE.
Recent Title(s): *Get Published Get Paid*, by Janet Groene.
Tips: "Ask for our guidelines (include SASE) or review our guidelines at our website. Do your homework, then make your proposal irresistible! Make sure a publicity plan is part of your proposal. We work hard to tell the world about our wonderful books, and we expect our authors to do the same."

▨ BOOKS IN MOTION, 9922 E. Montgomery, Suite 31, Spokane WA 99206. (509)922-1646. **Acquisitions:** Gary Challender, president. Publishes unabridged audiobook originals. **Publishes 100-120 titles/year. 25% of books from first-time authors; 90% from unagented writers. Pays 10% royalty on wholesale or retail price.** Accepts simultaneous submissions. Reporting time varies. Book catalog and ms guidelines on request.
Fiction: Adventure, fantasy, historical, mainstream/contemporary, mystery, religious, science fiction, suspense, western. "Minimal profanity and no gratuitous sex. We like series using the same charismatic character." Query with synopsis and first chapter.
Recent Title(s): *Kiss of the Bees*, by J.A. Jance.
Tips: "Our audience is 20% women, 80% men. Many of our audience are truck drivers, who want something interesting to listen to."

BOOKWORLD, INC./BLUE STAR PRODUCTIONS, 9666 E. Riggs Rd., #194, Sun Lakes AZ 85248. (602)895-7995. Fax: (602)895-6991. E-mail: bookworldinc@earthlink.net. Website: www.bkworld.com. **Acquisitions:** Barbara DeBolt, editor. Publishes trade and mass market paperback originals. **Publishes 10-12 titles/year. Receives thousands of queries and mss/year. 75% of books from first-time authors; 90% from unagented writers. Pays royalty on wholesale or retail price. No advance for new authors.** Responds in 8 months to queries, 16 months to mss. Book catalog on website. Manuscript guidelines for #10 SASE or on website.

○━ Book World, Inc. publishes mainstream and specialty books. Blue Star Productions focuses on UFOs, the paranormal, metaphysical, angels, psychic phenomena, visionary fiction, spiritual—both fiction and nonfiction.

Nonfiction/Fiction: UFO-related subjects, anything pertaining to the paranormal. "To save time and reduce the amount of paper submissions, we are encouraging e-mail queries and submissions (no downloads or attachments), or disk submissions formatted for Windows 95, using Word Perfect or Microsoft Word. Our response will be via e-mail so no SASE will be needed in these instances, unless the disk needs to be returned. For those without computer access, a SASE is a must and we prefer seeing the actual manuscript, a query letter. *No phone queries.*"

Recent Title(s): *Time Travelers from Our Future*, by Dr. Bruce Goldberg; *The Raven's Way*, by Michael Patton.

Tips: "Know our guidelines. We are now accepting manuscripts on disk using WordPerfect 6.0 and higher."

N: BOTTOM DOG PRESS, %Firelands College of BGSU, Huron OH 44839. (419)433-5560. **Acquisitions:** Dr. Larry Smith, director. "We are Midwest-focused and somewhat literary." Publishes hardcover, trade paperback and mass market paperback originals, hardcover and trade paperback reprints. **Publishes 4 titles/year. Receives 300 queries and 250 mss/year. 30% of books from first-time authors, 90% from unagented writers. Pays 7-15% royalty on wholesale price. Offers $100-300 advance.** Publishes book 1 year after acceptance of ms. Accepts simultaneous submissions (if notified). Responds in 1 months to queries and proposals, 4 months to mss. Books catalog and ms guidelines free.

Nonfiction: Biography. Subjects include writing, nature/environment, photography, regional (Midwest), women's issues/studies, working class issues. Query then submit outline and 2 sample chapters with SASE. Reviews artwork/photos as part of ms package. Send photocopies.

Fiction: Ethnic, literary, mainstream/contemporary, working class. "We do one fiction book/year, Midwest-based with author on locale." Query then submit synopsis, 2 sample chapters and SASE.

Poetry: Midwest, working class focus. "Read our books before submitting." Query first then submit 10 sample poems.

Recent Title(s): *Writing Work: Writers on Working-Class Writing* (collection); *No Pets: Stories*, by Jim Ray Daniels; *Blind Horse: Poems*, by Jeanne Beyner.

Tips: "We publish for broad yet literate public. Do not get an agent—try the small presses first." Currently emphasizing working-class writing.

A BOULEVARD, Penguin Putnam Inc., 375 Hudson St., New York NY 10014. (212)366-2000. Website: www.penguinputnam.com. **Acquisitions:** Acquisitions Editor. Estab. 1995. Publishes trade paperback and mass market paperback originals and reprints. **Publishes 85 titles/year.** *Agented submissions only.*

BOWLING GREEN STATE UNIVERSITY POPULAR PRESS, Bowling Green State University, Bowling Green OH 43403-1000. (419)372-7866. Fax: (419)372-8095. E-mail: abrowne@bgnet.bgsu.edu. Website: www.bgsu.edu/college/library/press/press.html. **Acquisitions:** (Ms.) Pat Browne, director (popular culture); Alma MacDougall, editor (popular culture and literature). Estab. 1967. Publishes hardcover originals and trade paperback originals. **Publishes 20 titles/year. Receives 350 queries and 75 mss/year. 50% of books from first-time authors; 100% from unagented writers. Pays 5-12% royalty on wholesale price or makes outright purchase.** Publishes book 9 months after acceptance of ms. Responds in 3 months. Book catalog and ms guidelines free.

○━ Publishes books on literature and popular culture for an academic audience.

Nonfiction: Biography, reference, textbook. Subjects include Americana, art/architecture, ethnic, history, language/literature, regional, sports, women's issues/studies. Submit outline and 3 sample chapters.

Recent Title(s): *Stephen King's America*, by Jonathan Davis.

Tips: "Our audience includes university professors, students, and libraries."

BOYDS MILLS PRESS, *Highlights for Children*, 815 Church St., Honesdale PA 18431-1895. (570)253-1164. Website: www.boydsmillspress.com. Publisher: Kent L. Brown. **Acquisitions:** Beth Troop, manuscript coordinator; Larry Rosler, editorial director. Estab. 1990. Publishes hardcover originals and trade paperback originals and reprints. **Publishes 50 titles/year; imprint publishes 2-6 titles/year. Receives 10,000 queries and mss/year. 20% of books are from first-time authors; 20% from unagented writers. Pays 8-15% royalty on retail price. Advance varies.** Accepts simultaneous submissions. Responds in 1 month. Book catalog and ms guidelines for $2 postage and SAE.

○━ Boyds Mill Press, the book publishing arm of *Highlights for Children*, publishes a wide range of children's books of literary merit, from preschool to young adult. Currently emphasizing novels (but no fantasy, romance or horror).

Imprint(s): Wordsong (poetry).

Nonfiction: Juvenile subjects include agriculture/horticulture, animals, ethnic, history, hobbies, nature/environment, regional, religion, sports, travel. "Nonfiction should be accurate, tailored to young audience. Accompanying art is preferred, as is simple, narrative style, but in compelling, evocative language. Too many overwrite for the young audience and get bogged down in minutia. Boyds Mills Press is not interested in manuscripts depicting violence, explicit sexuality, racism of any kind or which promote hatred. We also are not the right market for self-help books or romances." Query with proposal package, including outline, 1 sample chapter, some art samples (photos, drawings), with SASE.

Fiction: Adventure, ethnic, historical, humor, juvenile, mystery, picture books, suspense, western, young adult. "Don't let a personal agenda dominate to the detriment of plot. In short, tell a good story. Too many writers miss the essence of a good story: beginning, middle, end; conflict and resolution because they're more interested in making a sociological statement." Submit outline/synopsis and 3 sample chapters for novel or complete ms for picture book.

Poetry: "Poetry should be appropriate for young audiences, clever, fun language, with easily understood meaning. Too much poetry is either too simple and static in meaning or too obscure." Submit 6 sample poems. Collections should have a unifying theme.

Recent Title(s): *Sybil's Night Ride*, by Karen B. Winnick (nonfiction); *Waiting for Dolphins*, by Carole Crowe (fiction); *Fly with Poetry*, by Avis Harley (poetry).

Tips: "Our audience is pre-school to young adult. Concentrate first on your writing. Polish it. Then—and only then— select a market. We need primarily picture books with fresh ideas and characters—avoid worn themes of 'coming-of-age,' 'new sibling,' and self-help ideas. We are always interested in multicultural settings. Please—no anthropomorphic characters."

BRANDEN PUBLISHING CO., INC., 17 Station St., Box 843, Brookline Village MA 02447. Fax: (617)734-2046. Website: www.branden.com. **Acquisitions:** Adolph Caso, editor. Estab. 1965. Publishes hardcover and trade paperback originals, reprints and software. **Publishes 15 titles/year. Receives 1,000 submissions/year. 80% of books from first-time authors; 90% from unagented writers. Pays 5-10% royalty on net. Offers $1,000 maximum advance.** Publishes book 10 months after acceptance. Responds in 1 month. *Writer's Market* recommends allowing 2 months for reply.

　　○✦ Branden publishes books by or about women, children, military, Italian-American or African-American themes.

Imprint(s): International Pocket Library and Popular Technology, Four Seas and Brashear.

Nonfiction: Biography, illustrated book, juvenile, reference, technical, textbook. Subjects include Americana, art, computers, health, history, music, photography, politics, sociology, software, classics. Especially looking for "about 10 manuscripts on national and international subjects, including biographies of well-known individuals." No religion or philosophy. Paragraph query only with author's vita and SASE. *No unsolicited mss.* No telephone inquiries, e-mail or fax inquiries. Reviews artwork/photos as part of ms package.

Fiction: Ethnic (histories, integration); religious (historical-reconstructive). No science, mystery or pornography. Paragraph query only with author's vita and SASE. *No unsolicited mss.* No telephone, fax or e-mail inquiries.

Recent Title(s): *Straddling the Border*, by Martha Cummings (summer stay in Italy), *Snowball in Hell*, by Roland Hopkins (Nazi mystery).

BRASSEY'S, INC., (formerly Batsford Brassey, Inc.), 22841 Quicksilver Dr., Dulles VA 20166. (703)661-1548. Fax: (703)661-1547. E-mail: djacobs@booksintl.com. **Acquisitions:** Don McKeon, publisher (military history, national and international affairs, defense, sports). Estab. 1984. Publishes hardcover and trade paperback originals and reprints. **Publishes 80 titles/year. Receives 900 queries/year. 30% of books from first-time authors; 80% from unagented writers. Pays 6-12% royalty on wholesale price. Offers $20,000 maximum advance.** Publishes book 1 year after acceptance of ms. Accepts simultaneous submissions. Responds in 2 months to proposals. Book catalog and ms guidelines for 9×12 SASE.

　　○✦ Brassey's specializes in national and international affairs, military history, biography, intelligence, foreign policy, defense, transportation and sports. "We are seeking to build our biography, military history and national affairs lists and have also created a new imprint, Brassey's Sports."

Imprint(s): Brassey's Sports.

Nonfiction: Biography, coffee-table book, reference, textbook. Subjects include government/politics, national and international affairs, history, military/war, intelligence studies and sports. When submitting nonfiction, be sure to include sufficient biographical information (e.g., track records of previous publications), and "make clear in proposal how your work might differ from other such works already published and with which yours might compete." Submit proposal package, including outline, 1 sample chapter, bio, analysis of book's competition, return postage and SASE. Reviews artwork/photos as part of ms package. Send photocopies.

Recent Title(s): *The Outpost War: U.S. Marines in Korea, 1952*, vol. 1, by Lee Ballenger; *Hitler: The Pathology of Evil*, by George Victor.

Tips: "Our audience consists of military personnel, government policymakers, and general readers with an interest in military history, biography, national/international affairs, defense issues, intelligence studies and sports." No fiction.

BRASSEY'S SPORTS, Brassey's, Inc. 22841 Quicksilver Dr., Dulles VA 20166. (703)661-1548. Fax: (703)661-1547. E-mail: djacobs@booksintl.com. **Acquisitions:** Don McKeon, publisher. Publishes hardcover and trade paperback originals and reprints. **Publishes 80 titles/year. Receives 900 queries/year. 30% of books from first-time authors; 80% from unagented writers. Pays 6-12% royalty on wholesale price. Offers maximum $20,000 advance.** Publishes book 1 year after acceptance of ms. Accepts simultaneous submissions. Responds in 2 months. Book catalog free. Manuscript guidelines for 9×12 SAE and 4 first-class stamps.

Nonfiction: Biography, coffee table book, reference. Subjects include americana, history, sports. Query with SASE. Reviews artwork/photos as part of ms package. Send photocopies.

Recent Title(s): *Baseball Prospectus 2000 Edition*, by Chris Kahrl et. al. (annual reference).

BREVET PRESS, INC., P.O. Box 1404, Sioux Falls SD 57101. **Acquisitions:** Donald P. Mackintosh, publisher (business); Peter E. Reid, managing editor (technical); A. Melton, editor (Americana); B. Mackintosh, editor (history). Estab. 1972. Publishes hardcover and paperback originals and reprints. **Publishes 15 titles/year. Receives 40 submis-**

sions/year. **50% of books from first-time authors; 100% from unagented writers. Pays 5% royalty. Offers $1,000 average advance.** Publishes book 1 year after acceptance. Accepts simultaneous submissions. Responds in 2 months. Book catalog free.

O→ Brevet Books seeks nonfiction with "market potential and literary excellence."

Nonfiction: Specializes in business management, history, place names, and historical marker series. Subjects include Americana, business, history, technical books. Query with SASE. "After query, detailed instructions will follow if we are interested." Reviews artwork/photos as part of ms package. Send photocopies.

Tips: "Keep sexism out of the manuscripts."

BREWERS PUBLICATIONS, Association of Brewers, 736 Pearl St., Boulder CO 80302. (303)447-0816. Fax: (303)447-2825. E-mail: bp@aob.org. Website: beertown.org. **Acquisitions:** Toni Knapp, publisher. Estab. 1986. Publishes hardcover and trade paperback originals. **Publishes 8 titles/year. 50% of books from first-time authors; 50% from unagented writers. Pays royalty on net receipts. Advance negotiated.** Publishes book within 18 months of acceptance of ms. Accepts simultaneous submissions. Responds in 3 months. Book catalog free.

O→ Brewers Publications is the largest publisher of books on beer-related subjects.

Nonfiction: "We publish books on history, art, culture, literature, brewing and science of beer. In a broad sense, this also includes biographies, humor, cooking and suspense/mystery fiction." Query first with brief proposal and SASE.

Fiction: Suspense/mystery with a beer theme. Query.

Recent Title(s): *Independence Days: Essays of Ordinary Moments*, by Justin Matolt.

Tips: "We're moving into suspense fiction: Beer must be at the central theme and must 'educate'—as in other niche/genre mystery fiction such as culinary, etc."

BRIDGE WORKS PUBLISHING CO., Box 1798, Bridge Lane, Bridgehampton NY 11932. (516)537-3418. Fax: (516)537-5092. E-mail: bap@hamptons.com. **Acquisitions:** Barbara Phillips, editor/publisher. Estab. 1992. Publishes hardcover originals and reprints. **Publishes 4-6 titles/year. Receives 1,000 queries and mss/year. 50% of books from first-time authors; 80% from unagented writers. Pays 10% royalty on retail price. Offers $1,000 advance.** Publishes book 1 year after acceptance of ms. Responds in 1 month to queries and proposals, 2 months to mss. Book catalog and ms guidelines for #10 SASE.

O→ "Bridge Works is a small press dedicated to mainstream quality fiction and nonfiction. We have no niche other than the propagation of information, education and entertainment."

Nonfiction: Biography, history, language/literature, public policy. "We *do not* accept multiple submissions. We prefer a query first." Query or submit outline and proposal package with SASE.

Fiction: Literary, mystery, short story collections. "Query with SASE before submitting ms. First-time authors should have manuscripts vetted by freelance editors before submitting. We do not accept or read multiple submissions." Query or submit synopsis and 2 sample chapters with SASE.

Poetry: "We publish only *one* collection every 5 years." Query and submit sample poems.

Recent Title(s): *Duty*, by Jim R. Lane; *A Window Facing West*, by John L. Tarlton.

Tips: "Query letters should be one page, giving general subject or plot of the book and stating who the writer feels is the audience for the work. In the case of novels or poetry, a portion of the work could be enclosed."

BRIGHTON PUBLICATIONS, INC., P.O. Box 120706, St. Paul MN 55112-0706. (612)636-2220. Fax: (612)636-2220. **Acquisitions:** Sharon E. Dlugosch, editor. Estab. 1977. Publishes trade paperback originals. **Publishes 4 titles/year. Receives 100 queries and 100 mss/year. 50% of books from first-time authors; 100% from unagented writers. Pays 10% royalty on wholesale price.** Accepts simultaneous submissions. Responds in 3 months. Book catalog and ms guidelines for #10 SASE.

O→ Brighton Publications publishes books on celebration or seasonal how-to parties and anything that will help to give a better party such as activities, games, favors, and themes. Currently emphasizing games for meetings, annual parties, picnics, etc., celebration themes, and party/special event planning.

Nonfiction: How-to, games, tabletop, party themes. "We're interested in topics telling how to live any part of life well. Query. Submit outline and 2 sample chapters.

Recent Title(s): *Installation Ceremonies for Every Group: 26 Memorable Ways to Install New Officers*, by Pat Hines; *Meeting Room Games: Getting Things Done in Committees*, by Nan Booth.

BRISTOL FASHION PUBLICATIONS, P.O. Box 20, Enola PA 17025. Website: www.BFPBOOKS.com **Acquisitions:** John Kaufman, publisher. Publishes hardcover and trade paperback originals. **Publishes 25 titles/year. Receives 150 queries and 100 mss/year. 50% of books from first-time authors; 100% from unagented writers. Pays 7-11% royalty on retail price. No advance.** Publishes books 3 months after acceptance of ms. Responds in 1 month. Book catalog for 6½×9 SAE and 99¢ postage. Ms guidelines for #10 SASE.

O→ Bristol Fashion publishes books on boats and boating.

Nonfiction: How-to, reference and general interest relating to boats and boating. "We are interested in any title which relates to these fields. Query with a list of ideas. Include phone number. This is a fast changing market. Our title plans rarely extend past 6 months, although we know the type and quantity of books we will publish over the next 2 years. We prefer good knowledge with simple to understand writing style containing a well-rounded vocabulary." Query first, including brief outline, writing samples, tearsheets or sample chapters with SASE. Reviews artwork/photos as part of the ms package. Send photocopies or JPEG files on CD.

Recent Title(s): *Building a Fiberglass Boat.*

Tips: "All of our staff and editors are boaters. As such, we publish what we would want to read relating to boats. Our audience is generally boat owners or expected owners who are interested in learning about boats and boating. Keep it easy and simple to follow. Use nautical terms where appropriate. Do not use complicated technical jargon, terms or formulas without a detailed explanation of same. Use experienced craftsmen as a resource for knowledge."

BRISTOL PUBLISHING ENTERPRISES, 14692 Wicks Blvd., San Leandro CA 94577. (800)346-4889. Fax: (510)895-4459. **Acquisitions:** Pat Hall, managing editor. Estab. 1988. Publishes trade paperback originals. **Firm publishes 10-15 titles/year. Receives 50-75 queries/year. 25% of books from first-time authors; 100% from unagented writers. Pays 6% royalty on wholesale price or makes varying outright purchase.** Publishes book 1 year after acceptance of ms. Accepts simultaneous submissions. Responds in 4 months. Book catalog free. Manuscript guidelines for #10 SASE.

Imprint(s): Nitty Gritty cookbooks, The Best 50 Recipe Series.

Nonfiction: Cookbook, how-to. Subjects include cooking/foods/nutrition, entertaining. "Send a proposal or query first; editor will contact if interested in seeing manuscript. Most cookbooks are related to housewares products and/or hot culinary trends. Readers are novice cooks who want to know more about what is going on. Research our company before submitting." Query with outline and 1-2 samples chapters

Recent Title(s): *The Weekend Chef*, by Robin O'Neill.

Tips: "We encourage new authors. Sending a completed manuscript is useful but not necessary. A comprehensive outline, 6-10 sample recipes and writing sample is satisfactory. Our books educate without intimidating. We require our authors to have some form of food industry background."

BROADCAST INTERVIEW SOURCE, INC., Free Library, 2233 Wisconsin Ave., NW #301, Washington DC 20007. (202)333-4904. Fax: (202)342-5411. E-mail: davis@yearbooknews.com. Website: www.freelibrary.com. **Acquisitions:** Mitchell P. Davis, nonfiction editor; Randal Templeton, travel editor; Simon Goldfarb, fiction editor/information-oriented titles. Estab. 1984. Publishes trade paperback originals and reprints. **Publishes 14 titles/year. Receives 750 queries and 110 mss/year. 20% of books from first-time authors; 40% from unagented writers. Pays 5-15% royalty on wholesale price or makes outright purchase of $2,000-10,000. Offers $2,000 advance, but rarely.** Publishes book 1 month after acceptance. Accepts simultaneous submissions. Responds in 1 month. Book catalog and ms guidelines free on request or on website.

> ○┑ Broadcast Interview Source develops and publishes resources for publicists and journalists. Currently emphasizing nonfiction. De-emphasizing fiction.

Nonfiction: Biography, cookbook, gift book, how-to, humor, multimedia, reference, self-help, technical, textbook, catalogs, almanacs. Subjects include agriculture/horiticulture, Americana, business/economics, computers/electronics, education, history, hobbies, military/war, money/finance, psychology, recreation, religion, translation. Submit proposal package including outline and 3 sample chapters.

Fiction: Adventure, erotica, experimental, historical, humor, literary, mainstream/contemporary, military/war, plays, religious, translation, western. Submit proposal package, including synopsis and 2 sample chapters.

Recent Titles: *Talk Show Yearbook* (Licamele).

Tips: "We expect authors to be available for radio interviews at www.radiotour.com."

Ⓐ BROADWAY BOOKS, Doubleday Broadway Publishing Group, Random House, Inc., 1540 Broadway, New York NY 10036. (800)223-6834. Fax: (212)782-9411. E-mail: (first initial + last name)@randomhouse.com. Website: www.broadwaybooks.com. **Acquisitions:** Lauren Marino, editor (pop culture, entertainment, spirituality); Suzanne Oaks, senior editor (business); Charles Conrad, vice president and executive editor (general nonfiction); Gerald Howard, vice president/executive editor; Jennifer Josephy (cookbooks); Luke Dempsey, senior editor (sports, media, fiction); Ann Campbell, editor (psychology/self-help, parenting, health). Estab. 1995. Publishes hardcover and trade paperback originals and reprints.

> ○┑ Broadway publishes general interest nonfiction and fiction for adults.

Nonfiction: General interest adult books. Subjects include biography/memoirs, business, child care/parenting, cookbooks, current affairs, diet/nutrition, health, history, New Age/spirituality, money/finance, travel narrative, motivational/inspirational, sports, politics, popular culture, psychology, women's studies, sex/erotica, consumer reference, golf. *Agented submissions only.*

Fiction: Publishes a limited list of commercial literary fiction.

Recent Title(s): *A Walk in the Woods*, by Bill Bryson; *Under the Tuscan Sun*, by Frances Mayes.

Ⓝ BROOKS BOOKS, 4634 Hale Dr., Decatur IL 62526. (217)877-2966. E-mail: brooksbooks@q-com.com. Website: www.family-net.net/~brooksbooks. **Acquisitions:** Randy Brooks, editor (haiku poetry, tanka poetry). Publishes hardcover and trade paperback originals. **Publishes 3-5 titles/year. Receives 100 queries and 25 mss/year. 10% of books from first-time authors; 100% from unagented writers. Pays 10-15% royalty on retail price or makes outright purchase of $100-500.** Publishes book 16 months after acceptance of ms. Responds in 1 month to queries, 3 months to proposals, 6 months to mss. Book catalog for #10 SASE or on website. Manuscript guidelines for #10 SASE.

> ○┑ Brooks Books, formerly High/Coo Press, publishes English-language haiku books, chapbooks, magazines and bibliographies.

Imprints: High/Coo Press, Brooks Books.

Poetry: Submit 10 sample poems.

Recent Title(s): *Amost Unseen: Selected Haiku of George Swede*, by George Swede; *Fresh Scent*, by Lee Gurga (both haiku).

Tips: "Our readers enjoy contemporary haiku based on the literary tradition of Japanese aesthetics (not 5-7-5 Internet jokes)."

BRYANT & DILLON PUBLISHERS, INC., 100 N. Wyoming Ave, S, Orange NJ 07079. (973)763-1470. Fax: (973)763-2533. **Acquisitions:** James Bryant, editor (women's issues, film, photography). Estab. 1993. Publishes hardcover and trade paperback originals. **Publishes 8-10 titles/year. Receives 500 queries and 700 mss/year. 100% of books from first-time authors; 90% from unagented writers. Pays 6-10% royalty on retail price.** Publishes book 1 year after acceptance of ms. Accepts simultaneous submissions. Responds in 3 months to proposals.

    O━ Bryant & Dillon publishes books that speak to an African-American audience and others interested in the African-American experience.

Nonfiction: Biography, how-to, self-help. Subjects include Black studies, business/economics, education, ethnic, film, government/politics, history, language/literature, money/finance, women's issues/studies. "Must be on subjects of interest to African-Americans." Submit cover letter, author's information sheet, marketing information, outline and 3 sample chapters with SASE (envelope large enough for contents sent). "No faxes or phone calls!" No poetry or children's books.

BUCKNELL UNIVERSITY PRESS, Lewisburg PA 17837. (570)577-3674. Fax: (570)577-3797. E-mail: clingham@bucknell.edu. Website: www.departments.bucknell.edu/univ_press. **Acquisitions:** Greg Clingham, director. Estab. 1969. Publishes hardcover originals. **Publishes 40-45 titles/year. Receives 400 inquiries and submissions/year. 20% of books from first-time authors; 99% from unagented writers. Pays royalty.** Publishes accepted works within 18 months of delivery of finished ms. Responds in 1 month to queries. Book catalog free.

    O━ "In all fields, our criteria are scholarly excellence, critical originality, and interdisciplinary and theoretical expertise and sensitivity."

Nonfiction: English and American literary criticism, literary theory and cultural studies, historiography (including the history of law, medicine and science), art history, modern languages, classics, philosophy, anthropology, ethnology, psychology, sociology, religion, political science, cultural and political geography, and interdisciplinary combinations of the aforementioned. Series: Bucknell Studies in Eighteenth-Century Literature and Culture, Bucknell Studies in Latin American Literature and Theory, Bucknell Studies in Historiography. Biannual Journal: *The Bucknell Review: A Scholarly Journal of Letters, Arts, and Sciences*. Query with SASE.

Recent Title(s): *Aesthetics and Gender in American Literature: Portraits of the Woman as Artist*, by Deborah Barker.

Tips: "An original work of high-quality scholarship has the best chance. We publish for the scholarly community."

BULFINCH PRESS, Little, Brown & Co., 3 Center Plaza, Boston MA 02108. (617)263-2797. Fax: (617)263-2857. Website: www.bulfinchpress.com. Publisher: Carol Judy Leslie. **Acquisitions:** Sarah Gurney, department assistant. Publishes hardcover and trade paperback originals. **Publishes 60-70 titles/year. Receives 500 queries/year. Pays variable royalty on wholesale price. Advance varies.** Publishes book 18 months after acceptance of ms. Accepts simultaneous submissions. Responds in 2 months to proposals.

    O━ Bulfinch Press publishes large format art books.

Nonfiction: Style books, gift books, illustrated books. Subjects include art/architecture, gardening, photography. Query with outline, sample artwork and SASE. Send color photocopies or laser prints.

Recent Title(s): *Life: Our Century in Pictures; 100 Flowers*, by Harold Feinstein.

THE BUREAU FOR AT-RISK YOUTH, P.O. Box 760, Plainview NY 11803-0760. (516)349-5520. Fax: (516)349-5521. E-mail: info@at-risk.com. Website: www.at-risk.com. **Acquisitions:** Sally Germain, editor-in-chief. Estab. 1988. **Publishes 25-50 titles/year. Receives hundreds of submissions/year. Most books from first-time authors; 100% from unagented writers. Pays royalty of 10% maximum on selling price. Advance varies.** Publication 1 year after acceptance of ms. Accepts simultaneous submissions. Responds in 1-8 months. Book catalog free if appropriate after communication with author.

    O━ Publishes how-to prevention curriculum or short booklets, pamphlet series, curriculum and other educational materials on guidance topics for educators, parents, mental health and juvenile justice professionals.

Nonfiction: Educational materials for parents, educators and other professionals who work with youth. Subjects include child guidance/parenting, education. "The materials we publish are curriculum, book series, workbook/activity books or how-to-oriented pieces tailored to our audience. They are generally not single book titles and are rarely book length." Query.

Recent Title(s): *101 Ready-to-Use Drug Prevention Activities*.

Tips: "Publications are sold exclusively through direct mail catalog. We do not publish book-length pieces. Writers whose expertise is appropriate to our customers should send query or proposal since we tailor everything very specifically to meet our audience's needs."

BURFORD BOOKS, P.O. Box 388, Short Hills NJ 07078. (973)258-0960. Fax: (973)258-0113. **Acquisitions:** Peter Burford, publisher. Estab. 1997. Publishes hardcover originals, trade paperback originals and reprints. **Publishes 25**

titles/year. Receives 300 queries and 200 mss/year. 30% of books from first-time authors; 60% from unagented writers. Pays royalty on wholesale price. Accepts simultaneous submissions. Publishes book 18 months after acceptance of ms. Responds in 1 month to queries and proposals, 2 months to mss. Book catalog and ms guidelines free.

O─π Burford Books publishes books on all aspects of the outdoors, from gardening to sports, practical and literary.

Nonfiction: How-to, illustrated book. Subjects include horticulture, animals, cooking/foods/nutrition, gardening, hobbies, military/war, nature/environment, recreation, sports, travel. Query with outline with SASE. Reviews artwork/photos as part of the ms package. Send photocopies.

Recent Title(s): *Three-Shot Golf for Women*, by Janet Coles.

BURNHAM PUBLISHERS, (formerly Nelson-Hall Publishers), 111 N. Canal St., Chicago IL 60606. (312)930-9446. Senior Editor: Richard O. Meade. **Acquistions:** Editorial Director. Estab. 1999. Publishes hardcover and paperback originals. **Publishes 30 titles/year. Receives 200 queries and 20 mss/year. 90% of books submitted by unagented writers. Pays 5-15% royalty on wholesale price.** Publishes book 1 year after acceptance. Accepts simultaneous submissions. Responds in 1 month to queries.

O─π Burnham publishes college textbooks and, more rarely, general scholarly books in the social sciences.

Nonfiction: Subjects include anthropology/archaeology, government/politics, criminology, psychology, sociology. Query with outline, 2 sample chapters, cv.

Recent Title(s): *Cities in the Third Wave*, by Leonard Ruchelman.

BUSINESS McGRAW-HILL, The McGraw Hill Companies, 2 Penn Plaza, 11th Floor, New York NY 10121. (212)904-2000. Fax: (212)904-6096. Website: www.books.mcgraw-hill.com/business/contact.html. Publisher: Philip Ruppel. **Acquisitions:** Jeffrey Krames, editorial director; Mary Glenn, senior editor; Michelle Reed, editor; Amy Murphy. **Publishes 100 titles/year. Receives 1,200 queries and 1,200 mss/year. 30% of books from first-time authors; 60% from unagented writers. Pays 10-15% royalty on net price. Offers $5,000 advance and up.** Publishes book 6 months after acceptance of ms. Accepts simultaneous submissions. Responds in 3 months. Book catalog and ms guidelines free on request with SASE.

O─π "McGraw Hill's business division and trade reference is the world's largest business publisher, offering nonfiction trade and paperback originals in more than ten areas, including management, sales and marketing, careers, trade reference, self-help, training, finance and science."

Nonfiction: How-to, reference, self-help. Subjects include business, money/finance. "Current, up-to-date, original ideas are needed. Good self-promotion is key." Submit proposal package, including outline, toc, concept.

Recent Nonfiction Title(s): *The 12 Simple Secrets of Microsoft Management*, by David Thielen; *Rethinking the Sales Force*, by Neil Rackham.

BUTTERWORTH-HEINEMANN, Reed-Elsevier (USA) Inc., 225 Wildwood Ave., Woburn MA 01801-2041. (800)470-1199. Fax: (781)904-2640. Website: www.bh.com. **Acquisitions:** Jim DeWolf, vice president of technical publishing (engineering, electronics, computing, media and visual); Marie Lee, publisher (Focal Press); Phil Sutherland, publisher (Digital Press); Susan Pioli, publishing director (Medical); Candy Hall, senior editor (Newnes). Estab. 1975. Publishes hardcover and trade paperback originals. **Publishes 150 titles/year. Each imprint publishes 25-30 titles/year. 25% of books from first-time authors; 95% from unagented writers. Pays 10-12% royalty on wholesale price. Offers modest advance.** Publishes book 9 months after acceptance of ms. Responds in 1 month to proposals. Book catalog and ms guidelines free.

O─π Butterworth-Heinemann publishes technical professional and academic books in technology, medicine and business; no fiction.

Imprint(s): Butterworth-Heinemann (engineering, medical, security and criminal justice, business), Medical, Digital Press (computing), **Focal Press** (media and visual technology), Newnes (electronics), Security & Criminal Justice.

Nonfiction: How-to (in our selected areas), reference, technical, textbook. Subjects include business, computers/electronics, health/medicine, photography, security/criminal justice, audio-video broadcast, communication technology. Submit outline, 1-2 sample chapters, competing books and how yours is different/better, with SASE. Reviews artwork/photos as part of ms package. Send photocopies.

Tips: Butterworth-Heinemann has been serving professionals and students for over five decades. "We remain committed to publishing materials that forge ahead of rapidly changing technology and reinforce the highest professional standards. Our goal is to give you the competitive advantage in this rapidly changing digital age."

CADENCE JAZZ BOOKS, Cadence Building, Redwood NY 13679. (315)287-2852. Fax: (315)287-2860. **Acquisitions:** Bob Rusch, Carl Ericson. Estab. 1992. Publishes trade paperback and mass market paperback originals. **Publishes 15 titles/year. Receives 10 queries and 10 mss/year. 90% of books from first-time authors; 100% from unagented writers. Pays royalty or makes outright purchase.** Publishes book 6 months after acceptance of ms. Responds in 1 month.

O─π Cadence publishes jazz histories and discographies.

Nonfiction: Jazz music biographies, discographies and reference works. Submit outline and sample chapters and SASE. Reviews artwork/photos as part of ms package. Send photocopies.

Recent Title(s): *The Earthly Recordings of Sun Ra*, by Robert L. Campbell (discography).

CAMBRIDGE EDUCATIONAL, P.O. Box 2153, Charleston WV 25328-2153. (888)744-0100. Fax: (304)744-9351. Website: www.cambridgeeducational.com. Subsidiaries include: Cambridge Parenting and Cambridge Job Search. President: Stephen Jones. **Acquisitions:** Amy Pauley, managing editor. Estab. 1981. Publishes supplemental educational products. **Publishes 30-40 titles/year. Receives 200 submissions/year. 20% of books from first-time authors; 90% from unagented writers. Makes outright purchase of $1,500-4,000. Occasional royalty arrangement.** Publishes book 8 months after acceptance. Accepts simultaneous submissions.

   O→ "We are known in the education industry for guidance-related and career search programs." Currently emphasizing social studies and science.

Nonfiction: Subjects include child guidance/parenting, cooking/foods/nutrition, education, health/medicine, money/finance, career guidance, social studies and science. "We are looking for scriptwriters in the same subject areas and age group. We only publish books written for young adults and primarily sold to libraries, schools, etc. We do not seek books targeted to adults or written at high readability levels." Query or submit outline/synopsis and sample chapters. Does not respond unless interested. Reviews artwork/photos as part of ms package.

Recent Title(s): *6 Steps to Getting a Job for People with Disabilities*, by Wayne Forster.

Tips: "We encourage the submission of high-quality books on timely topics written for young adult audiences at moderate to low readibility levels. Call and request a copy of all our current catalogs, talk to the management about what is timely in the areas you wish to write on, thoroughly research the topic, and write a manuscript that will be read by young adults without being overly technical. Low to moderate readibility yet entertaining, informative and accurate."

CAMINO BOOKS, INC., P.O. Box 59026, Philadelphia PA 19102. (215)732-2491. Fax: (215)732-8288. Website: www.caminobooks.com. **Acquisitions:** E. Jutkowitz, publisher. Estab. 1987. Publishes hardcover and trade paperback originals. **Publishes 8 titles/year. Receives 500 submissions/year. 20% of books from first-time authors. Pays 6-12% royalty on net price. Offers $1,000 average advance.** Publishes book 1 year after acceptance. Responds in 2 weeks to queries. *Writer's Market* recommends allowing 2 months for reply.

   O→ Camino publishes nonfiction of regional interest to the Mid-Atlantic states.

Nonfiction: Biography, cookbook, how-to, juvenile. Subjects include agriculture/horticulture, Americana, art/architecture, child guidance/parenting, cooking/foods/nutrition, ethnic, gardening, government/politics, history, regional, travel. Query with outline/synopsis and sample chapters with SASE.

Tips: "The books must be of interest to readers in the Middle Atlantic states, or they should have a clearly defined niche, such as cookbooks."

CANDLEWICK PRESS, Walker Books Ltd. (London), 2067 Massachusetts Ave., Cambridge MA 02140. (617)661-3330. Fax: (617)661-0565. **Acquisitions:** Liz Bicknell, editor-in-chief (poetry, picture books, fiction); Mary Lee Donovan, executive editor (nonfiction/fiction); Gale Pryor, editor (nonfiction/fiction); Amy Ehrlich, editor-at-large (picture books); Kara LaReau, associate editor; Cynthia Platt, associate editor; Danielle Sadler, editorial assistant. Estab. 1991. Publishes hardcover originals, trade paperback originals and reprints. **Publishes 200 titles/year. Receives 1,000 queries and 1,000 mss/year. 5% of books from first-time authors; 40% from unagented writers. Pays 10% royalty on retail price. Advance varies.** Publishes book 3 years after acceptance of ms for illustrated books, 1 year for others. Accepts simultaneous submissions, if so noted. Responds in 10 weeks to mss.

   O→ Candlewick Press publishes high-quality, illustrated children's books for ages infant through young adult. "We are a truly child-centered publisher."

Nonfiction: Children's/juvenile. "Good writing is essential; specific topics are less important than strong, clear writing."

Fiction: Juvenile.

Recent Title(s): *It's So Amazing*, by Robie Harris, illustrated by Michael Emberley (nonfiction); *Burger Wuss*, by M.T. Anderson (fiction); *Weslandia*, by Paul Fleischman, illustrated by Kevin Hawkes (picture book).

C&T PUBLISHING, 1651 Challenge Dr., Concord CA 94520. Fax: (925)677-0374. E-mail: ctinfo@ctpub.com. Website: www.ctpub.com. **Acquisitions:** Liz Aneloski, editor. Estab. 1983. Publishes hardcover and trade paperback originals. **Publishes 18-26 titles/year. Receives 80 submissions/year. 10% of books from first-time authors; 100% from unagented writers. Pays 5-10% royalty on retail price. Offers $1,000 average advance.** Accepts simultaneous submissions. Responds in 2 months. Free book catalog and proposal guidelines. No SASE required.

   O→ "C&T publishes well-written, beautifully designed books on quilting, dollmaking, fiber arts and ribbonwork."

Nonfiction: Quilting books, primarily how-to, occasional quilt picture books, quilt-related crafts, wearable art, needlework, fiber and surface embellishments, other books relating to fabric crafting. "Please call or write for proposal guidelines." Extensive proposal guidelines are also available on their website.

Recent Title(s): *Start Quilting with Alex Anderson*; *The Photo Transfer Handbook*, by Jean Ray Laury.

Tips: "In our industry, we find that how-to books have the longest selling life. Quiltmakers, sewing enthusiasts, needle artists and fiber artists are our audience. We like to see new concepts or techniques. Include some great examples and you'll get our attention quickly. Dynamic design is hard to resist, and if that's your forté, show us what you've done."

N: CANDYCANE PRESS, Ideals Publications, 535 Metroplex Dr., Suite 250, Nashville TN 37211. (615)333-0478. Publisher: Patricia Pingry. **Acquisitions:** Copy Editor. **Publishes 5-10 titles/year. Advance varies.** Responds in 2 months.

☞ CandyCane uses Christian stories for children ages 3-8; holiday-oriented manuscripts and picture books for the Christian market.

Fiction: Juvenile, religious. Submit completed ms.

Recent Title(s): *Barefoot Days* (children's poetry); *The Story of David* (board book); *Jolly Old Santa Claus*.

⃞Ⓝ CAPSTONE PRESS, P.O. Box 669, Mankato MN 56002. (507)388-6650. Fax: (507)625-4662. Website: www.cap stone-press.com. **Acquisitions:** Helen Moore, product planning editor (nonfiction for students grades K-12). Publishes hardcover originals. **Publishes 250-300 titles/year. Receives 100 queries/year. No unsolicited mss. 5% of books from first-time authors. Makes outright purchase; payment varies by imprint.** Responds in 3 months to queries. Book catalog on website.

☞ Capstone publishes nonfiction children's books for schools and libraries.

Imprints: Capstone Books, Blue Earth Books, Bridgestone Books, Pebble Books, LifeMatters.

Nonfiction: Children's/juvenile. Subjects include Americana, animals, child guidance/parenting, cooking/foods/nutrition, health/medicine, history, military/war, multicultural, nature/environment, recreation, science, sports. Query with SASE. "We do not accept proposals or manuscripts. Authors interested in writing for Capstone Press can request an author's brochure."

Recent Title(s): *Downhill In-Line Skating*, by Nick Cook; *The Nez Perce Tribe*, by Allison Lassieur.

Tips: Audience is made up of elementary, middle school, and high school students who are just learning how to read, who are experiencing reading difficulties, or who are learning English. Capstone Press does not publish unsolicited mss submitted by authors, and it rarely entertains proposals. Instead, Capstone hires freelance authors to write on nonfiction topics selected by the company. Authors may send an SASE to request a brochure.

THE CAREER PRESS, INC., Box 687, 3 Tice Rd., Franklin Lakes NJ 07417. (201)848-0310. Fax: (201)848-1727. Website: www.careerpress.com. President: Ronald Fry. **Acquisitions:** Michael Lewis, acquisitions editor. Estab. 1985. **Publishes 65 titles/year. Receives 300 queries and 1,000 mss/year. 10% of books from first-time authors; 10% from unagented writers. Pays royalty on net receipts.** Publishes book up to 6 months after acceptance of ms. Accepts simlultaneous submissions. Responds in 1 month. Book catalog and ms guidelines free.

☞ Career Press publishes primarily paperback and some hardcover nonfiction originals in the areas of job hunting and career improvement, including reference and education; as well as management philosophy titles for a small business and management audience. Career Press also offers a line of personal finance titles for a general readership. New Page Books, established in 2000, publishes paperback and some hardcover originals in the areas of New Age, Judaica, health, parenting, and weddings/entertaining.

Imprint(s): New Page Books.

Nonfiction: How-to, reference, self-help. Subjects include business/economics, money/finance, financial planning/ careers. "Look through our catalog; become familiar with our publications. We like to select authors who are specialists on their topic." Query with outline, 1-2 sample chapters and SASE.

Recent Title(s): *101 Great Answers to Tough Interview Questions*, by Ron Fry (career); *Urban Legends*, by Richard Roeper (reference).

CAROLRHODA BOOKS, INC., Lerner Publishing Group., 241 First Ave. N., Minneapolis MN 55401. (612)332-3344. Fax: (612)332-7615. Website: www.lernerbooks.com. **Acquisitions:** Rebecca Poole, submissions editor. Estab. 1969. Publishes hardcover originals. **Publishes 50-60 titles/year. Receives 2,000 submissions/year. 10% of books from first-time authors; 90% from unagented writers. Pays royalty on wholesale price, makes outright purchase or negotiates payments of advance against royalty. Advance varies.** Publishes book 18 months after acceptance. Accepts submissions from March 1-31 and October 1-31 *only*. Submissions received at other times of the year will be returned to sender. No phone calls. Responds in 6 months. Book catalog for 9×12 SAE with $3 for postage. Manuscript guidelines for #10 SASE.

☞ Carolrhoda Books is a children's publisher focused on producing high-quality, socially conscious nonfiction and fiction books with unique and well-developed ideas and angles for young readers that help them learn about and explore the world around them. Currently de-emphasizing picture books, biographies on more obscure figures.

Nonfiction: Children's/juvenile (pre-kindergarten to 6th grade). Subjects include biography, ethnic, nature/environment, science, sports. Carolrhoda Books seeks creative children's nonfiction "We are always interested in adding to our biography series. Books on the natural and hard sciences are also of interest." Query with SASE for return of ms. Reviews artwork/photos as part of ms package. Send photocopies.

Fiction: Juvenile, historical, picture books. "We only publish about one picture book per year. Not looking for folktales or anthropomorphic animal stories." Query with SASE, send complete ms for picture books.

Recent Title(s): *Revolutionary Poet: A Story about Phillis Wheatley* (Creative Minds Biography series), by Maryann N. Weidt; *Allen Jay and the Underground Railroad* (On My Own History series), by Marlene Targ Brill (fiction).

Tips: The Lerner Publishing Group does not publish alphabet books, puzzle books, song books, text books, work books, religious subject matter or plays.

Ⓐ CARROLL & GRAF PUBLISHERS INC., Avalon Publishing Group, 19 W. 21st St., Suite 601, New York NY 10010. (212)627-8590. Fax: (212)627-8490. **Acquisitions:** Kent Carroll, publisher; Phillip Turner, executive editor.

Estab. 1983. Publishes hardcover and trade paperback originals. **Publishes 120 titles/year. 10% of books from first-time authors. Pays 10-15% royalty on retail price for hardcover, 7½% for paperback. Offers $5,000-100,000 advance.** Publishes book 9 months after acceptance of ms. Responds in 1 month to queries. Book catalog free.

O→ Carroll and Graf Publishers offers quality fiction and nonfiction for a general readership. Carroll and Graf is owned by Publishers Group West.

Nonfiction: Biography, reference, self-help. Subjects include business/economics, history, contemporary culture, true crime. Publish general trade listings; are interested in developing long term relations with authors. Query. *Agented submissions only.*

Fiction: Literary, mystery, science fiction, suspense, thriller. Query. *Agented submissions only.*

Recent Title(s): *Faust's Metropolis: A History of Berlin*, by Alexandra Richie (history); *Master Georgie*, by Beryl Bainbridge (fiction).

CARTWHEEL BOOKS, Scholastic, Inc., 555 Broadway, New York NY 10012. (212)343-6100. Fax: (212)343-4444. Website: www.scholastic.com. Vice President/Editorial Director: Bernette Ford. **Acquisitions:** Grace Maccarone, executive editor; Sonia Black, editor; Jane Gerver, executive editor; Liza Baker, acquisitions editor. Estab. 1991. Publishes hardcover originals. **Publishes 85-100 titles/year. Receives 250 queries/year; 1,200 mss/year. 1% of books from first-time authors; 50% from unagented writers. Pays royalty on retail price. Offers advance.** Publishes book 2 years after acceptance of ms. Accepts simultaneous submissions. Responds in 4 months to queries; 3 months to proposals; 6 months to mss. Book catalog for 9×12 SAE. Manuscript guidelines free.

O→ Cartwheel Books publishes innovative books for children, up to age 8. "We are looking for 'novelties' that are books first, play objects second. Even without its gimmick, a Cartwheel Book should stand alone as a valid piece of children's literature."

Nonfiction: Children's/juvenile. Subjects include animals, history, music/dance, nature/environment, recreation, science, sports. "Cartwheel Books publishes for the very young, therefore nonfiction should be written in a manner that is accessible to preschoolers through 2nd grade. Often writers choose topics that are too narrow or 'special' and do not appeal to the mass market. Also, the text and vocabulary are frequently too difficult for our young audience." *Agented submissions or previously published authors only.* Reviews artwork/photos as part of ms package.

Fiction: Humor, juvenile, mystery, picture books. "Again, the subject should have mass market appeal for very young children. Humor can be helpful, but not necessary. Mistakes writers make are a reading level that is too difficult, a topic of no interest or too narrow, or manuscripts that are too long." *Agented submissions or previously published authors only.*

Recent Title(s): *I Spy*, by Jean Marzollo and Walter Wick (picture book).

Tips: Audience is young children, ages 3-9. "Know what types of books the publisher does. Some manuscripts that don't work for one house may be perfect for another. Check out bookstores or catalogs to see where your writing would 'fit' best."

CATBIRD PRESS, 16 Windsor Rd., North Haven CT 06473-3015. (203)230-2391. Website: www.catbirdpress.com. **Acquisitions:** Robert Wechsler, publisher. Estab. 1987. Publishes hardcover and trade paperback originals and trade paperback reprints. **Publishes 4-5 titles/year. Receives 1,000 submissions/year. 5% of books from first-time authors; 80% from unagented writers. Pays 10% royalty on retail price. Offers $2,000 average advance.** Publishes book 1 year after acceptance. Accepts simultaneous submissions, if so noted. Responds in 1 month to queries if SASE is included. *Writer's Market* recommends allowing 2 months for reply. Manuscript guidelines for #10 SASE or on website.

O→ Catbird publishes sophisticated, humorous, literary fiction and nonfiction with fresh styles and approaches.

Imprint(s): Garrigue Books (Czech works in translation).

Nonfiction: Humor, law, general. "We are looking for up-market prose humorists. No joke or other small gift books. We are also interested in very well-written general nonfiction that takes fresh, sophisticated approaches." Submit outline, sample chapters and SASE.

Fiction: Literary, humor, translations. "We are looking for writers of well-written literature who have a comic vision, take a fresh approach, and have a fresh, sophisticated style. No genre, wacky, or derivative mainstream fiction." Submit outline/synopsis, sample chapter and SASE.

Recent Title(s): *A Double Life*, by Frederic Raphael (fiction); *Performing Without a Stage: The Art of Literary Translation*, by Robert Wechsler (nonfiction); *The Poetry of Jarslav Seifert*, translated by Ewald Osers (poetry).

Tips: "First of all, we want writers, not books. Second, we are only interested in writing that is not like what is out there already. The writing should be highly sophisticated, but not obscure; the approach or, better, approaches should be fresh and surprising. Writers more interested in content than in style should look elsewhere."

CATHOLIC UNIVERSITY OF AMERICA PRESS, 620 Michigan Ave. NE, Washington DC 20064. (202)319-5052. Fax: (202)319-4985. E-mail: cua-press@cua.edu. Website: http://cuapress.cua.edu. **Acquisitions:** Dr. David J. McGonagle, director. Estab. 1939. **Publishes 20 titles/year. Receives 100 submissions/year. 50% of books from first-time authors; 100% from unagented writers. Pays variable royalty on net receipts.** Publishes book 2 years after acceptance. Responds in 6 months. Book catalog for SASE.

O→ The Catholic University of America Press publishes in the fields of history (ecclesiastical and secular), literature and languages, philosophy, political theory, social studies, and theology. "We have interdisciplinary emphasis on patristics, medieval studies and Irish studies. Our principal interest is in works of original scholarship intended for scholars and other professionals and for academic libraries, but we will also consider manuscripts whose chief contribution is to offer a synthesis of knowledge of the subject which may be of interest to a wider audience or suitable for use as supplementary reading material in courses."

Nonfiction: History, languages and literature, philosophy, religion, church-state relations, political theory. No unrevised doctoral dissertations. Length: 80,000-200,000 words. Query with outline, sample chapter, cv and list of previous publications.

Recent Title(s): *Hesburgh: A Biography*, by Michael O'Brien.

Tips: "Scholarly monographs and works suitable for adoption as supplementary reading material in courses have the best chance."

CATO INSTITUTE, 1000 Massachusetts Ave. NW, Washington DC 20001. (202)842-0200. Website: www.cato.org. **Acquisitions:** David Boaz, executive vice president. Estab. 1977. Publishes hardcover originals, trade paperback originals and reprints. **Publishes 12 titles/year. Receives 50 submissions/year. 25% of books from first-time authors; 90% from unagented writers. Makes outright purchase of $1,000-10,000.** Publishes book 9 months after acceptance. Accepts simultaneous submissions. Responds in 3 months. Book catalog free.

➺ Cato Institute publishes books on public policy issues from a free-market or libertarian perspective.

Nonfiction: Public policy *only*. Subjects include foreign policy, economics, education, government/politics, health/medicine, monetary policy, sociology. Query.

Recent Title(s): *A New Deal for Social Security*, by Peter Ferrara and Michael Tanner.

CAXTON PRESS, (formerly The Caxton Printers, Ltd.), 312 Main St., Caldwell ID 83605-3299. (208)459-7421. Fax: (208)459-7450. Website: caxtonprinters.com. President: Gordon Gipson. **Acquisitions:** Wayne Cornell, managing acquisitions editor (Western Americana, regional nonfiction). Estab. 1907. Publishes hardcover and trade paperback originals. **Publishes 6-10 titles/year. Receives 250 submissions/year. 50% of books from first-time authors; 60% from unagented writers. Pays royalty. Offers advance.** Publishes book 18 months after acceptance. Accepts simultaneous submissions. Responds in 3 months. Book catalog for 9×12 SASE.

➺ "Western Americana nonfiction remains our focus. We define Western Americana as almost any topic that deals with the people or culture of the west, past and present." Currently emphasizing regional issues—primarily Pacific Northwest. De-emphasizing "coffee table" or photographic intensive books.

Nonfiction: Americana, Western Americana. "We need good Western Americana, especially the Northwest, emphasis on serious, narrative nonfiction." Query. Reviews artwork/photos as part of ms package.

Recent Title(s): *Dreamers: On the Trail of the Nez Perce*, by Martin Stadius.

Tips: "Books to us never can or will be primarily articles of merchandise to be produced as cheaply as possible and to be sold like slabs of bacon or packages of cereal over the counter. If there is anything that is really worthwhile in this mad jumble we call the twentieth century, it should be books."

CCC PUBLICATIONS, 9725 Lurline Ave., Chatsworth CA 91311. (818)718-0507. **Acquisitions:** Cliff Carle, editorial director. Estab. 1983. Publishes trade paperback and mass market paperback originals. **Publishes 40-50 titles/year. Receives 1,000 mss/year. 50% of books from first-time authors; 50% of books from unagented writers. Pays 8-12% royalty on wholesale price.** Publishes book 6 months after acceptance. Accepts simultaneous submissions. Responds in 3 months. Catalog for 10×13 SAE with 2 first-class stamps.

➺ CCC publishes humor that is "today" and will appeal to a wide demographic. Currently emphasizing "short, punchy pieces with *lots* of cartoon illustrations, or very well-written text if long form."

Nonfiction: Humorous how-to/self-help. "We are looking for *original*, *clever* and *current* humor that is not too limited in audience appeal or that will have a limited shelf life. All of our titles are as marketable five years from now as they are today. No rip-offs of previously published books, or too special interest manuscripts." Query or send complete ms with SASE. Reviews artwork/photos as part of ms package.

Recent Title(s): *The Difference Between Men & Women*, by Fred Sahner (nonfiction).

Tips: "Humor—we specialize in the subject and have a good reputation with retailers and wholesalers for publishing super-impulse titles. SASE is a must!"

CEDAR FORT, INC., 925 N. Main, Springville UT 84663. (801)489-4084. Fax: (801)489-9432. E-mail: skybook@earthlink.net. Website: www.cedarfort.com. **Acquisitions:** Lee Nelson, editor (fiction); Lyle Mortimer, editor (inspirational); Cindy Bunce, editor (how-to). Publishes hardcover and trade paperback originals. **Publishes 50 titles/year; imprint publishes 10-17 titles/year. Receives 200 queries and 500 mss/year. 50% of books from first-time authors; 98% from unagented writers. Pays 6-12% royalty on wholesale price.** Publishes book 6 months after acceptance of ms. Accepts simultaneous submissions. Responds in 1 month to queries and proposals, 2 months to mss. Book catalog and ms guidelines free. Send photocopies.

➺ Cedar Fort is looking for books of "broad national appeal."

Imprints: CFI (Lyle Mortimer), Council Press (Cindy Bunce) and Bonneville Books (Lee Nelson).

Nonfiction: Biography, how-to, self-help. Subjects include child guidance/parenting, religion, sociology, spirituality. Submit proposal package, including outline, 1 sample chapter, author bio and vita. Reviews artwork/photos as part of ms package.

Fiction: Adventure, historical, humor, juvenile, literary, mainstream/contemporary, regional, religious, romance, spiritual, sports, suspense, western, young adult. Submit proposal package, including synopsis, 3 sample chapters and author info.

Recent Title(s): *Gold of Carre Shinot*, by Kerry Boren (treasure hunter); *Doug's Dilemma*, by Chad Daybell (regional fiction).

CENTERSTREAM PUBLICATIONS, P.O. Box 17878, Anaheim Hills CA 92807. (714)779-9390. Fax: (714)779-9390. E-mail: centerstrm@aol.com. **Acquisitions:** Ron Middlebrook, Cindy Middlebrook, owners. Estab. 1980. Publishes hardcover and mass market paperback originals, trade paperback and mass market paperback reprints. **Publishes 12 titles/year. Receives 15 queries and 15 mss/year. 80% of books from first-time authors; 100% from unagented writers. Pays 10-15% royalty on wholesale price. Offers $300-3,000 advance.** Publishes book 8 months after acceptance of ms. Accepts simultaneous submissions. Responds in 3 months to queries. Book catalog and ms guidelines for #10 SASE.

　○━ Centerstream publishes music history and instructional books.

Nonfiction: Music history and music instructional book. Query with SASE.

Recent Title(s): *Hawaiian Ukulele, the Early Methods* (music); *Aloha* (collection of Hawaiian songs).

CHALICE PRESS, Christian Board of Publication, P.O. Box 179, St. Louis MO 63166. (314)231-8500. Fax: (314)231-8524. E-mail: chalice@cbp21.com. Website: www.chalicepress.com. **Acquisitions:** Dr. David P. Polk, editor-in-chief (religion: general); Dr. Jon L. Berquist, academic editor (religion: academic). Publishes hardcover and trade paperback originals. **Publishes 50 titles/year. Receives 500 queries and 400 mss/year. 15% of books from first-time authors; 100% from unagented writers. Pays 14-18% royalty on wholesale price. Offers $500 advance.** Publishes book 1 year after acceptance of ms. Accepts simultaneous submissions. Responds in 1 month to queries, 2 months to proposals, 3 months to mss. Book catalog free for #10 SASE or on website. Manuscript guidelines free or on website.

Nonfiction: Textbook, general religious. Subjects include religion, spirituality. Submit proposal package, including outline and 1-2 sample chapters.

Recent Title(s): *Touchstones*, by Scott Colglazier (nonfiction, spirituality).

Tips: "We publish for both professional and lay Christian readers."

CHANDLER HOUSE PRESS, Rainbow New England Corp., 335 Chandler St., Worcester MA 01602. (508)756-7644. Fax: (508)756-9425. E-mail: clairecs@tatnuck.com. Website: www.tatnuck.com. President: Lawrence J. Abramoff. **Acquisitions:** Claire Cousineau, publisher. Estab. 1993. Publishes hardcover and trade paperback originals and reprints. **Publishes 12 titles/year. Receives 200 queries and 50 mss/year. 50% of books from first-time authors; 70% from unagented writers. Pays royalty on net sales.** Publishes book 6-12 months after acceptance of ms. Accepts simultaneous submissions. Responds in 1 month. *Writer's Market* recommends allowing 2 months for reply. Book catalog and manuscript guidelines free. "We focus mainly on regional interest titles, custom publishing, and various nonfiction titles with a highly defined niche audience."

　○━ Chandler House Press is a general interest nonfiction publisher.

Nonfiction: Biography, gift book, how-to, illustrated book, reference, self-help. Subjects include regional Americana, business, regional history, parenting, personal finance, pets, recreation, relationships, sports, women's issues. Submit outline, 1-3 sample chapters and SASE. Reviews artwork/photos as part of ms package. Send photocopies.

Recent Title(s): *SPAG: An American Business Legend* (biography/regional).

CHARIOT/VICTOR PUBLISHING, Cook Communications Ministries, 4050 Lee Vance View, Colorado Springs CO 80918. (719)536-3271. Fax: (719)536-3269. **Acquisitions:** Patty Ralston, administrative assistant. Estab. 1875. Publishes hardcover and trade paperback originals, both children's and adult, fiction and nonfiction. **Publishes 150 titles/year. 10% of books from first-time authors; 50% from unagented writers. Pays variable royalty on net price. Advance varies.** Publishes book 1-2 years after acceptance of ms. Accepts simultaneous submissions, if so noted. Responds in 2 months to queries. Manuscript guidelines for #10 SASE.

　○━ Chariot/Victor publishes children's and family spiritual growth books. Books "must have strong underlying Christian themes or clearly stated Biblical value."

Imprint(s): Chariot Books (children), **Lion Publishing**, Rainfall (toys, media, games), Victor Adult Books.

Nonfiction: Biography, children's/juvenile. Child guidance/parenting, history, religion. Query with SASE.

　● No longer publishing fiction.

Recent Title(s): *The Reflective Life*, by Ken Gire (nonfiction); *Loving a Prodigal*, by Norm Wright (family issues); *Dr. Laura: A Mother In America* (contemporary issues).

Tips: "All books must in some way be Bible-related by authors who themselves are evangelical Christians with a platform. Chariot Victor, therefore, is not a publisher for everybody. Only a small fraction of the manuscripts received can be seriously considered for publication. Most books result from contacts that acquisitions editors make with qualified authors, though from time to time an unsolicited proposal triggers enough excitement to result in a contract. A writer has the best chance of selling Chariot Victor a well-conceived and imaginative manuscript that helps the reader apply Christianity to her life in practical ways. Christians active in the local church and their children are our audience."

CHARLES RIVER MEDIA, P.O. Box 417, 403 VFW Dr., Rockland MA 02370. (781)871-4184. Fax: (781)871-4376. E-mail: chrivmedia@aol.com. Website: www.charlesriver.com. **Acquisitions:** David Pallai, president (networking,

Internet related); Jennifer Niles, publisher (computer graphics, animation game programming). Publishes trade paperback originals. **Publishes 24 titles/year. Receives 1,000 queries and 250 mss/year. 30% of books from first-time authors; 90% from unagented writers. Pays 5-30% royalty on wholesale price. Offers $3,000-20,000 advance.** Publishes book 1 month after acceptance of ms. Accepts simultaneous submissions. Responds in 1 month. Book catalog for #10 SASE. Manuscript guidelines on website.

　　O┱ "Consult our website for proposal outlines. Manuscripts must be completed within 6 months of contract signing."

Nonfiction: Multimedia (Win/Mac format), reference, technical. Subjects include computers/electronics. Query with SASE or submit proposal package, including outline, 2 sample chapters and résumé. Reviews artwork/photos as part of ms package. Send photocopies or GIF, TIFF or PDF files.

Recent Title(s): *Web Site Usability*, by Mark Pearrow; *3D Lighting Techniques*, by Arnold Gallardo.

Tips: "We are very receptive to detailed proposals by first-time or non-agented authors."

CHARLESBRIDGE PUBLISHING, School Division, 85 Main St., Watertown MA 02472. (617)926-0329. Fax: (617)926-5720. E-mail: books@charlesbridge.com. Website: www.charlesbridge.com. Estab. 1980. Publishes hardcover and trade paperback nonfiction children's picture books (80%) and fiction picture books for school programs and supplementary materials. **Acquisitions:** Elena Dworkin Wright, vice president school division. **Publishes 2-4 titles plus school materials and curriculum. Receives 2,500 submissions/year. 10-20% from first-time authors; 80% from unagented writers.** Publishes books 2-4 years after acceptance of ms.

　　O┱ "We're looking for fiction to use as literature in the math curriculum and kids activity books (not coloring)."

Nonfiction: School or craft books that involve problem solving, building, projects or crafts, books written with humor and expertise in the field. Submit complete ms with cv and SASE.

Fiction: Math concepts in non-rhyming story.

Recent Title(s): *The Ugly Vegetables*, written and illustrated by Grace Lin.

CHARLESBRIDGE PUBLISHING, Trade Division, 85 Main St., Watertown MA 02472. (617)926-0329. Fax: (617)926-5270. E-mail: books@charlesbridge.com. Website: www.charlesbridge.com. Estab. 1980. Publishes hardcover and trade paperback nonfiction children's picture picture books (80%) and fiction picture books for the trade and library markets, as well as school programs and supplementary materials. **Acquisitions:** Harold Underdown, editorial director; Yolanda LeRoy, editor. **Publishes 30 titles/year. Receives 2,500 submissions/year. 10-20% from first-time authors; 80% from unagented writers.** Publishes books 2-4 years after acceptance of ms.

　　O┱ "We're always interested in innovative approaches to a difficult genre, the nonfiction picture book. No novels or books for older children." Currently emphasizing nature, science, multiculturalism. De-emphasizing folk tales, poems.

Imprints: Talewinds (2 fiction titles/season).

Nonfiction: Strong interest in nature, environment, social studies and other topics for trade and library markets. Exclusive submissions only.

Fiction: "Strong, realistic stories with enduring themes." Exclusive submissions only.

Recent Title(s): *Say It Again*, by Brian Capie, illustrated by David Mooney.

CHELSEA GREEN PUBLISHING COMPANY, P.O. Box 428, #205 Gates-Briggs Bldg., White River Junction VT 05001-0428. (802)295-6300. Fax: (802)295-6444. Website: www.chelseagreen.com. **Acquisitions:** Jim Schley, editor-in-chief (environmentalism, ecology, nature, renewable energy, alternative building); Ben Watson, senior editor (organic gardening and farming). Estab. 1984. Publishes hardcover and trade paperback originals and reprints. **Publishes 16-20 titles/year; imprint publishes 3-4 titles/year. Receives 300-400 queries and 200-300 mss/year. 30% of books from first-time authors; 80% from unagented writers. Pays royalty on publisher's net. Offers $2,500-10,000 advance.** Publishes book 18 months after acceptance of ms. Responds in 1 month to queries, 2 months to proposals and mss. Book catalog and ms guidelines free or on website.

　　O┱ Chelsea Green publishes and distributes books relating to issues of sustainability with a special concentration on books about nature, the environment, independent living, organic gardening, renewable energy and alternative or natural building techniques. The books reflect positive options in a world of environmental turmoil.

Imprint(s): Real Goods Solar Living Book series.

Nonfiction: Biography, cookbook, how-to, reference, self-help, technical. Subjects include agriculture/horticulture, art/architecture, cooking/foods/nutrition, gardening, memoirs, money/finance, nature/environment, regional, forestry. Query with SASE or submit proposal package, including outline and 1-2 sample chapters. Reviews artwork/photos as part of ms package. Send "whatever is most representatiave and appropriate."

Recent Titles: *New Organic Grower*, by Eliot Coleman (gardening/farming).

Tips: "Our readers are passionately enthusiastic about ecological solutions for contemporary challenges in construction, energy harvesting, agriculture and forestry. Our books are also carefully and handsomely produced to give pleasure to bibliophiles of a practical bent. It would be very helpful for prospective authors to have a look at several of our current books, as well as our catalog and website. For certain types of book, we are the perfect publisher, but we are exceedingly focused on particular areas."

CHESS ENTERPRISES, 107 Crosstree Rd., Caraopolis PA 15108-2607. Fax: (412)262-2138. E-mail: bgdudley@com puserve.com. **Acquisitions:** Bob Dudley, owner. Estab. 1981. Publishes trade paperback originals. **Publishes 10 titles/**

year. Receives 20 queries and 12 mss/year. 10% of books from first-time authors; 100% from unagented writers. Makes outright purchase of $500-3,000. No advance. Publishes book 4 months after acceptance of ms. Accepts simultaneous submissions. Responds in 1 month.

O— Chess Enterprises publishes books on how to play the game of chess.

Nonfiction: Game of chess only. Query.

Recent Title(s): *Checkmate!*, by Koltanowsky and Finklestein.

Tips: "Books are targeted to chess tournament players, book collectors."

CHICAGO REVIEW PRESS, 814 N. Franklin, Chicago IL 60610-3109. (312)337-0747. Fax: (312)337-5985. E-mail: csherry@ipgbook.com or yuval@ipgbook.com. Website: www.ipgbook.com. **Acquisitions:** Cynthia Sherry, executive editor (general nonfiction, children's); Yuval Taylor, editor (African, African-American and performing arts). Estab. 1973. Publishes hardcover and trade paperback originals and trade paperback reprints. **Publishes 30-35 titles/year. Receives 200 queries and 600 manuscripts/year. 50% of books from first-time authors; 50% from unagented writers. Pays 7-12½% royalty. Offers $1,500-5,000 average advance.** Publishes book 18 months after acceptance. Accepts simultaneous submissions. Responds in 3 months. Book catalog for $3.50. Manuscript guidelines for #10 SASE or on website.

O— Chicago Review Press publishes intelligent nonfiction on timely subjects for educated readers with special interests.

Imprint(s): Lawrence Hill Books, A Capella Books (contact Yuval Taylor).

Nonfiction: Creative nonfiction, children's/juvenile (activity books only), cookbooks (specialty only), how-to. Subjects include art/architecture, child guidance/parenting/pregnancy, creative nonfiction, education, ethnic, gardening (regional), health/medicine, history, hobbies, memoirs, multicultural, music/dance, nature/environment, recreation, regional. Query with outline, toc and 1-2 sample chapters. Reviews artwork/photos.

Recent Title(s): *The Civil War for Kids*, by Janis Herbert.

Tips: "Along with a table of contents and 1-2 sample chapters, also send a cover letter and a list of credentials with your proposal. Also, provide the following information in your cover letter: audience, market and competition—who is the book written for and what sets it apart from what's already out there."

CHILD WELFARE LEAGUE OF AMERICA, 440 First St. NW, Third Floor, Washington DC 20001. (202)638-2952. Fax: (202)638-4004. E-mail: books@cwla.org. Website: www.cwla.org. **Acquisitions:** Acquisitions Editor. Publishes hardcover and trade paperback originals. **Publishes 30-50 titles/year. Receives 300 submissions/year. 95% of books from unagented writers. 50% of books are nonauthor-subsidy published. Pays 0-10% royalty on net domestic sales.** Publishes book 1 year after acceptance of ms. Responds to queries in 3 months. Book catalog and ms guidelines free.

O— CWLA is a privately supported, nonprofit, membership-based organization committed to preserving, protecting and promoting the well-being of all children and their families.

Imprint(s): CWLA Press (child welfare professional publications), Child & Family Press (children's books and parenting books for the general public).

Nonfiction: Subjects include children's books, child guidance/parenting, sociology. Submit complete ms.

Recent Title(s): *An American Face* (children's book); *Seven Sensible Strategies for Drug Free Kids*.

Tips: "We are looking for positive, kid friendly books for ages 3-9. We are looking for books that have a positive message . . . a feel-good book."

CHILDREN'S PRESS, Grolier Publishing, 90 Sherman Turnpike, Danbury CT 06816. (203)797-6802. Fax: (203)797-6986. Website: www.grolier.com. Publisher: John Selfridge. **Acquisitions:** Melissa Stewart, executive editor; Halley Gatenby, senior editor (geography). Estab. 1946. Publishes nonfiction hardcover originals. **Publishes 200 titles/year. Makes outright purchase for $500-1,000. No advance.** Publishes book 20 months after acceptance. Book catalog and submission guidelines available for SASE.

O— Children's Press publishes nonfiction for the school and library market. "Our books support textbooks and closely relate to the elementary and middle-school curriculum."

Nonfiction: Children's/juvenile. Subjects include animals, anthropology/archaeology, art/architecture, ethnic, health/medicine, history, hobbies, music/dance, nature/environment, science and sports. Query with SASE. "We publish nonfiction books that supplement the elementary school curriculum." No fiction, poetry, folktales, cookbooks or novelty books.

● Grolier was recently purchased by Scholastic, Inc.

Recent Title(s): *Columbia*, by Marion Morison; *Mount Rushmore*, by Andrew Sandella; *Extraordinary Women of the West*, by Judy Alter.

Tips: Most of this publisher's books are developed inhouse; less than 5% come from unsolicited submissions. However, they publish several series for which they always need new books. Study catalogs to discover possible needs.

CHINA BOOKS & PERIODICALS, INC., 2929 24th St., San Francisco CA 94110-4126. (415)282-2994. Fax: (415)282-0994. Website: www.chinabooks.com. **Acquisitions:** Greg Jones, editor (language study, health, history); Baolin Ma, senior editor (music, language study); Chris Robyn, editor (language study, poetry, history). Estab. 1960. Publishes hardcover and trade paperback originals. **Averages 5 titles/year. Receives 300 submissions/year. 10% of**

books from first-time authors; **95% from unagented writers. Pays 6-8% royalty on net receipts. Advance negotiable.** Publishes book 1 year after acceptance. Accepts simultaneous submissions. Responds in 3 months to queries. Book catalog free. Manuscript guidelines for #10 SASE or on website.

○━ China Books is the main importer and distributor of books and magazines from China, providing an ever-changing variety of useful tools for travelers, scholars and others interested in China and Chinese culture. "We are looking for original book ideas, especially in the areas of language study, children's books, history and culture, all relating to China." Currently emphasizing language study. De-emphasizing art, fiction.

Nonfiction: "*Important*: *All* books *must* be on topics related to China or East Asia, or Chinese-Americans. Books on China's history, politics, environment, women, art/architecture; language textbooks, acupuncture and folklore." Query with outline and sample chapters. Reviews artwork/photos as part of ms package.

Recent Titles: *Flowing the Tai Chi Way*, by Peter Uhlmann (nonfiction); *Drinking with the Moon*, by Jeannette Faurot (poetry).

Tips: "We are looking for original ideas, especially in language study, children's education, adoption of Chinese babies, or health issues relating to traditional Chinese medicine."

CHOSEN BOOKS PUBLISHING CO., LTD., Baker Book House Company, 3985 Bradwater St., Fairfax VA 22031-3702. (703)764-8250. Fax: (703)764-3995. E-mail: jecampbell@aol.com. Website: www.bakerbooks.com. **Acquisitions:** Jane Campbell, editor. Estab. 1971. Publishes hardcover and trade paperback originals. **Publishes 8 titles/year. Receives 500 submissions/year. 15% of books from first-time authors; 99% from unagented writers. Pays royalty on net receipts.** Publishes book 18 months after acceptance. Accepts simultaneous submissions. Responds in 3 months. Manuscript guidelines for #10 SASE. Catalog not available.

○━ "We publish well-crafted books that recognize the gifts and ministry of the Holy Spirit, and help the reader live a more empowered and effective life for Jesus Christ."

Nonfiction: Expositional books on narrowly focused themes. "We publish books reflecting the current acts of the Holy Spirit in the world, books with a charismatic Christian orientation." No New Age, poetry, fiction, autobiographies, biographies, compilations, Bible studies, booklets, academic or children's books. Submit synopsis, chapter outline, résumé, 2 sample chapters and SASE. No response without SASE. No e-mail submissions; brief query only by e-mail. *No complete mss.*

Recent Title(s): *Healing the Nations: A Call to Global Intercession*, by John Sandford.

Tips: "We look for solid, practical advice for the growing and maturing Christian from authors with professional or personal experience platforms. No conversion accounts or chronicling of life events, please. State the topic or theme of your book clearly in your cover letter."

CHRISTIAN ED. PUBLISHERS, P.O. Box 26639, San Diego CA 92196. (858)578-4700. Fax: (858)578-2431. E-mail: BibleClubs@cepub.com. Website: www.christianedwarehouse.com. **Acquisitions:** Dr. Lon Ackelson, senior editor. **Publishes 64 titles/year. Makes outright purchase of 3¢/word.** Responds in 3 months on assigned material. No queries or proposals. Book catalog for 9×12 SASE and 4 first-class stamps. Manuscript guidelines for #10 SASE.

○━ Christian Ed. Publishers is an independent, non-denominational, evangelical company founded nearly 50 years ago to produce Christ-centered curriculum materials based on the Word of God for thousands of churches of different denominations throughout the world. "Our mission is to introduce children, teens, and adults to a personal faith in Jesus Christ and to help them grow in their faith and service to the Lord. We publish materials that teach moral and spiritual values while training individuals for a lifetime of Christian service." Currently emphasizing Bible curriculum for preschool through preteen ages.

Nonfiction: Bible Club curriculum. "All subjects are on assignment." Query with SASE.

Fiction: "All writing is done on assignment." Query with SASE.

Recent Title(s): *All-Stars for Jesus: Bible Curriculum for Juniors*.

Tips: "Read our guidelines carefully before sending us a manuscript. All writing is done on assignment only and must be age appropriate (preschool-6th grade)."

CHRISTIAN PUBLICATIONS, INC./HORIZON BOOKS, 3825 Hartzdale Dr., Camp Hill PA 17011. (717)761-7044. Fax: (717)761-7273. E-mail: editors@cpi-horizon.com. Website: www.cpi-horizon.com or www.christianpublications.com. Managing Editor: David E. Fessenden. **Acquisitions:** George McPeek, editorial director. Estab. 1883. Publishes hardcover originals; mass market and trade paperback originals and reprints. **Publishes 35 titles/year (about 50% are reprints of classic authors). Receives 200 queries and 400 mss/year. 25% of books from first-time authors; 90% from unagented writers. Pays 5-10% royalty on retail price or makes outright purchase. Advance varies.** Publishes book 18 months after acceptance of ms. Accepts simultaneous submissions; "We do *not* reprint other publishers' material." Responds in 1 month to queries, 3 months to proposals and mss. Book catalog for 9×12 SAE with 7 first-class stamps. Manuscript guidelines for #10 SASE or on website.

○━ "Our purpose is to propagate the gospel of Jesus Christ through evangelistic, deeper life and other publishing, serving our denomination and the wider Christian community. All topics must be from an evangelical Christian viewpoint."

Imprint(s): Horizon Books.

Nonfiction: Biography, gift book, how-to, humor, reference (reprints *only*), self-help, textbook, teen/young adult. Subjects include Americana, religion (Evangelical Christian perspective), child guidance, parenting, spirituality. Query with SASE or submit proposal package, including chapter synopsis, 2 sample chapters (including chapter 1), audience and market ideas, author bio. Reviews artwork/photos as part of ms package. Send photocopies.

Fiction: Historical, humor, mainstream/contemporary, mystery, religious, spiritual, young adult. "We are not considering unsolicited fiction at this time. No poetry." *All unsolicited ms returned unopened.*

Recent Title(s): *All Mothers Are Working Mothers*, by Laura Sabin Riley (devotional); *Song of the Second Fiddle*, by Todd Hahn (Christian living).

Tips: "We are owned by The Christian and Missionary Alliance denomination; while we welcome and publish authors from various denominations, their theological perspective must be compatible with The Christian and Missionary Alliance. We are especially interested in fresh, practical approaches to deeper life—sanctification with running shoes on. Readers are evangelical, regular church-goers, mostly female, usually leaders in their church. Your book should grow out of a thorough and faithful study of Scripture. You need not be a 'Bible scholar,' but you should be a devoted student of the Bible."

CHRONICLE BOOKS, Chronicle Publishing Co., 85 Second St., 6th Floor, San Francisco CA 94105. (415)537-3730. Fax: (415)537-4440. E-mail: frontdesk@chronbooks.com. Website: www.chronbooks.com. President: Jack Jensen. **Acquisitions:** Bill LeBlond, editor (cookbooks); Amy Novesky, managing editor (children's); (Mr.) Nion McEvoy, editor (general); Leslie Jonath, editor (lifestyle); Alan Rapp, (art and design); Sarah Malarky (popular culture). Estab. 1966. Publishes hardcover and trade paperback originals. **Publishes 250 titles/year. Receives 22,500 submissions/year. 20% of books from first-time authors. 15% from unagented writers.** Publishes book 18 months after acceptance. Accepts simultaneous submissions. Responds in 3 months to queries. Book catalog for 11 × 14 SAE with 5 first-class stamps. Guidelines available on website.

> O→ "Chronicle Books specializes in high-quality, reasonably priced illustrated books for adults and children." Titles include best-selling cookbooks; fine art, design, photography, and architecture titles; and full-color nature books.

Imprint(s): Chronicle Books for Children, GiftWorks (ancillary products, such as stationery, gift books).

Nonfiction: Coffee table book, cookbook, architecture, art, design, gardening, gift, health, nature, nostalgia, photography, recreation. Query or submit outline/synopsis with artwork and sample chapters.

Recent Title(s): *Batman: The Complete History*, by Les Daniels (popular culture); *Weber's Art of the Grill*, by Jamie Purviance (cookbook).

CHRONICLE BOOKS FOR CHILDREN, Chronicle Books, 85 Second St., 6th Floor, San Francisco CA 94105. (415)537-3730. Fax: (415)537-4420. E-mail: frontdesk@chroniclebooks.com. Website: www.chroniclebooks.com/Kids. **Acquisitions:** Victoria Rock, director of Children's Books (nonfiction/fiction); Amy Novesky, managing editor (nonfiction/fiction plus middle grade and young adult); Jennifer Vetter, editor; Summer Laurie, editorial assistant. Publishes hardcover and trade paperback originals. **Publishes 40-50 titles/year. Receives 20,000 submissions/year. 5% of books from first-time authors; 25% from unagented writers. Pays 8% royalty. Advance varies.** Publishes book 18 months after acceptance of ms. Accepts simultaneous submissions if so noted. Responds in 2-18 weeks to queries; 5 months to mss. Book catalog for 9 × 12 SAE and 3 first-class stamps. Manuscript guidelines for #10 SASE.

> O→ Chronicle Books for Children publishes an eclectic mixture of traditional and innovative children's books. "Our aim is to publish books that inspire young readers to learn and grow creatively while helping them discover the joy of reading. We're looking for quirky, bold artwork and subject matter." Currently emphasizing picture books, holiday titles. De-emphasizing young adult.

Nonfiction: Biography, children's/juvenile, illustrated book, nonfiction books for ages 8-12 years, and nonfiction picture books for ages up to 8 years. Subjects include animals, multicultural and bilingual, nature/environment, art, science. Query with outline and SASE. Reviews artwork/photos as part of the ms package.

Fiction: Fiction picture books, middle grade fiction, young adult projects. Mainstream/contemporary, multicultural, picture books, young adult, chapter books. Query with synopsis and SASE. Send complete ms for picture books.

Recent Title(s): *The Truth About Great White Sharks* (nonfiction); *Sylvia Long's Mother Goose (fiction)*.

Tips: "We are interested in projects that have a unique bent to them—be it in subject matter, writing style, or illustrative technique. As a small list, we are looking for books that will lend our list a distinctive flavor. Primarily we are interested in fiction and nonfiction picture books for children ages up to eight years, and nonfiction books for children ages up to twelve years. We publish board, pop-up, and other novelty formats as well as picture books. We are also interested in early chapter books, middle grade fiction, and young adult projects."

N: CHURCH GROWTH INSTITUTE, P.O. Box 7000, Forest VA 24551. (804)525-0022. Fax: (804)525-0608. E-mail: cgimail@churchgrowth.org. Website: www.churchgrowth.org. **Acquisitions:** Cindy Spear, director of resource development. Estab. 1984. Publishes trade paperback originals. **Publishes 4 titles/year. Pays 5% royalty on retail price.** Publishes book 1 year after acceptance of ms. Accepts simultaneous submissions. Responds in 3 months to queries. Resource catalog for 9 × 12 SAE with 4 first-class stamps. Manuscript guidelines given after query and outline is received.

> O→ "Our mission is to provide cutting-edge seminars and publish practical resources to help pastors, churches and

individuals reach their potential for Christ; to promote spiritual and numerical growth in churches, thereby leading Christians to maturity and lost people to Christ; and to equip pastors so they can equip their church members to do the work of the ministry."

Nonfiction: How-to manuals. Subjects include religious education (church-growth related). "Material should originate from a conservative Christian view and cover topics that will help churches grow, through leadership training, new attendance or stewardship programs, and new or unique ministries, or enhancing existing ministries. Accepted manuscripts will be adapted to our resource packet format. All material must be practical and easy for the *average* Christian to understand." Query or submit outline and brief explanation of what the packet will accomplish in the local church and whether it is leadership or lay-oriented. Reviews artwork/photos as part of ms package. Send photocopies or transparencies. Recent title: *Stop Child Abuse Before It Happens*, by Bill Harper.

● The Church Growth Institute is not accepting freelance submissions for 2000 but may reconsider for 2001.

Tips: "We are not publishing many *textbooks*. Concentrate on how-to manuals, video curriculum for small group studies and complete resource packets (planning a campaign, program or ministry, step-by-step agenda, resource list, etc., plus audio- or video-cassettes)."

CIRCLET PRESS INC., 1770 Massachusetts Ave., #278, Cambridge MA 02140. (617)864-0492. Fax: (617)864-0663. E-mail: circlet-info@circlet.com. Website: www.circlet.com. **Acquisitions:** Cecilia Tan, publisher/editor. Estab. 1992. Publishes hardcover and trade paperback originals. **Publishes 6-10 titles/year. Receives 50-100 queries and 500 mss/ year. 50% of stories from first-time authors; 90% from unagented writers. Pays 4-12% royalty on retail price or makes outright purchase (depending on rights); also pays in books if author prefers.** Publishes stories 18 months after acceptance of ms. Accepts simultaneous submissions. Responds in 1 month to queries, 6-18 months to mss. Book catalog and ms guidelines for #10 SASE.

O─┐ "Circlet Press publishes science fiction/fantasy short stories which are too erotic for the mainstream and to promote literature with a positive view of sex and sexuality, which celebrates pleasure and diversity. We also publish other books celebrating sexuality and imagination with our imprints—The Ultra Violet Library and Circumflex."

Imprint(s): The Ultra Violet Library (gay and lesbian science fiction and fantasy. "These books will not be as erotic as our others."); Circumflex (erotic and sexual nonfiction titles, how-to and essays).

Fiction: Erotic science fiction and fantasy short stories only. Gay/lesbian stories needed but all persuasions welcome. "Fiction must combine both the erotic and the fantastic. The erotic content needs to be an integral part of a science fiction story, and vice versa. Writers should not assume that any sex is the same as erotica." Submit full short stories up to 10,000 words between April 15 and August 31. Manuscripts received outside this reading period are discarded. Queries only via e-mail.

Recent Title(s): *Nymph*, by Francesca Lia Block; *Through A Brazen Mirror*, by Delia Sherman.

Tips: "Our audience is adults who enjoy science fiction and fantasy, especially the works of Anne Rice, Storm Constantine, Samuel Delany, who enjoy vivid storytelling and erotic content. Seize your most vivid fantasy, your deepest dream and set it free onto paper. That is at the heart of all good speculative fiction. Then if it has an erotic theme as well as a science fiction one, send it to me. No horror, rape, death or mutilation! I want to see stories that *celebrate* sex and sexuality in a positive manner. Please write for our guidelines as each year we have a specific list of topics we seek."

■ **CITY & COMPANY**, 22 W. 23rd St., New York NY 10010. (212)366-1988. Fax: (212)242-0412. E-mail: cityco@ bway.net. Website: cityandcompany.com. **Acquisitions:** Helene Silver, publisher. Estab. 1994. Publishes hardcover and trade paperback originals. **Publishes 10 titles/year. Receives 75 queries and 10 mss/year. 50% of books from first-time authors; 75% from unagented writers. Pays 5-10% royalty on wholesale price. Offers advance.** Publishes book 6 months after acceptance of ms. Accepts simultaneous submissions. Responds in 3 months to queries. Book catalog free.

O─┐ City & Company specializes in single subject New York city guide books.

Nonfiction: Must have New York focus. Giftbook, illustrated book, reference, travel guidebooks. Subjects include child guidance/parenting, gardening, music/dance, nature/environment, recreation, regional, sports, travel, single subject city guide. Submit proposal package, including outline, 3 sample chapters and author bio. Reviews artwork/photos as part of ms package.

CLEAR LIGHT PUBLISHERS, 823 Don Diego, Santa Fe NM 87501-4224. (505)989-9590. E-mail: clpublish@aol.c om. **Acquisitions:** Harmon Houghton, publisher. Estab. 1981. Publishes hardcover and trade paperback originals. **Publishes 20-24 titles/year. Receives 100 queries/year. 10% of books from first-time authors; 50% from unagented writers. Pays 10% royalty on wholesale price. Offers advance, a percent of gross potential.** Publishes book 1 year after acceptance of ms. Accepts simultaneous submissions. Responds in 3 months to queries. Book catalog free.

O─┐ Clear Light publishes books that "accurately depict the positive side of human experience and inspire the spirit."

Nonfiction: Biography, coffee table book, cookbook. Subjects include Americana, anthropology/archaelogy, art/architecture, cooking/foods/nutrition, ethnic, history, nature/environment, philosophy, photography, regional (Southwest). Query with SASE. Reviews artwork/photos as part of ms package. Send photocopies (no originals).

Recent Title(s): *Utopian Legacies*, by John Mohawk; *Native Science*, by Gregory Cajete.

CLEIS PRESS, P.O. Box 14684, San Francisco CA 94114-0684. (415)575-4700. Fax: (415)575-4705. Website: www.cleispress.com. **Acquisitions:** Frederique Delacoste. Estab. 1980. Publishes trade paperback originals and reprints. **Publishes 20 titles/year. 10% of books are from first-time authors; 90% from unagented writers. Pays variable royalty on retail price.** Publishes book 2 years after acceptance of ms. Accepts simultaneous submissions "only if accompanied by an original letter stating where and when ms was sent." Responds in 1 month. Book catalog for #10 SAE with 2 first-class stamps.

O→ Cleis Press specializes in gay/lesbian fiction and nonfiction.

Nonfiction: Subjects include feminist, gay/lesbian and human rights. "We are interested in books by and about women in Latin America; on lesbian and gay rights; on sexuality; topics which have not already been widely documented. We do not want religious/spiritual tracts; we are not interested in books on topics which have been documented over and over, unless the author is approaching the topic from a new viewpoint." Query or submit outline and sample chapters.

Fiction: Feminist, gay/lesbian, literary. "We are looking for high quality fiction by women and men. No romances." Submit complete ms. *Writer's Market* recommends sending a query with SASE first.

Recent Title(s): *Gore Vidal: Sexually Speaking* (nonfiction); *The Woman Who Rode to the Moon*, by Bett Reece Johnson (fiction).

Tips: "Be familiar with publishers' catalogs; be absolutely aware of your audience; research potential markets; present fresh new ways of looking at your topic; avoid 'PR' language and include publishing history in query letter."

CLEVELAND STATE UNIVERSITY POETRY CENTER, R.T. 1813, Cleveland State University, Cleveland OH 44115-2440. (216)687-3986. Fax: (216)687-6943. E-mail: poetrycenter@csuohio.edu. **Acquisitions:** David Evett, Bonnie Jacobson, Ted Lardner and Ruth Schwartz, editors. Poetry Center Coordinator: Rita M. Grabowski. Estab. 1962. Publishes trade paperback and hardcover originals. **Publishes 4 titles/year. Receives 500 queries and 1,000 mss/year. 60% of books from first-time authors; 100% from unagented writers. 30% of titles subsidized by CSU, 20% by government subsidy. CSU Poetry Series pays one-time, lump-sum royalty of $200-400, plus 50 copies; Cleveland Poets Series (Ohio poets only) pays 100 copies. $1,000 prize for best full-length ms each year. No advance.** Accepts simultaneous submissions. Responds in 1 month to queries, 8 months to mss. Book catalog for $2. Manuscript guidelines for SASE. Manuscripts are not returned.

Poetry: No light verse, inspirational, or greeting card verse. ("This does not mean that we do not consider poetry with humor or philosophical/religious import.") Query; ask for guidelines. Submit only November-January. Charges $20 reading fee. Reviews artwork/photos only if applicable (e.g., concrete poetry).

Recent title(s): *Buried Treasure*, by Dan Bellm.

Tips: "Our books are for serious readers of poetry, i.e. poets, critics, academics, students, people who read *Poetry*, *Field*, *American Poetry Review*, etc. Trends include movement away from 'confessional' poetry; greater attention to form and craftsmanship. Project an interesting, coherent personality; link poems so as to make coherent unity, not just a miscellaneous collection. Especially need poems with *mystery*, i.e., poems that suggest much, but do not tell all."

CLOUD PEAK, 730 W. 51st St., Casper WY 82601. (307)265-6196. Fax: (305)265-6922. E-mail: pharwitz@isis-intl.com. **Acquisitions:** Paul Harwitz. Publishes hardcover originals and reprints, trade paperback originals and reprints, mass market paperback originals and reprints. **Publishes 36 titles/year. Receives 200 queries and 80 mss/year. 10% of books are from first-time authors; 50% from unagented writers. Pays 10% royalty for nonfiction, percentage for fiction varies. No advance.** Publishes book 1-2 years after acceptance of ms. Accepts simultaneous submissions. Responds in 2 months to queries, 3 months to proposals, 2 months to mss. Book catalog and ms guidelines for #10 SASE or on website.

O→ Cloud Peak is currently emphasizing nonfiction books about Indians, African-Americans, Asians, Hispanics and other "minorities" in the West.

Nonfiction: Biography, children's juvenile, how-to, humor. Subjects include Americana (Western), education, history, military/war, multicultural, sports, women's issues/women's studies. "Submissions to our 'Women of the West' line of nonfiction will receive special consideration." Query with SASE. *All unsolicited submissions returned unopened.* Reviews artwork/photos as part of ms package. Send photocopies, transparencies or computer files on 3½″ floppy disk.

Fiction: Adventure, fantasy, historical, horror, humor, juvenile, military/war, multicultural, multimedia, mystery, poetry, science fiction, suspense, western, Native American. "Do everything you can to make the book a real 'page-turner,' Plots and sub-plots must be plausible and suited to the locale(s). Main and secondary characters must speak dialog which matches their respective personality traits. Blacks, Spanish-speaking people and other 'minorities' must *not* be portrayed stereotypically. Historical accuracy is important." Query with SASE. *All unsolicited mss returned unopened.*

Poetry: "We publish Western/cowboy/Indian poetry in single-author collections and multi-author anthologies." Query with 3 sample poems or send complete ms.

Recent Title(s): *Soldiers Falling Into Camp: The Battles at the Rosebud and Little Bighorn*, by Robert Kammen, Frederick Lefthand and Joe Marshall (military history); *The Watcher*, by Robert Kammen (Western/supernatural/ecological); *Riders of the Leafy Spurge*, by Bill Lowman (cowboy poetry).

Tips: "Buy, read and study the *Writer's Market* each year. Writing must flow. Imagine you are a reader visiting a bookstore. Write the first page of the book in such a way that the reader feels *compelled* to buy it. It helps a writer to work from an outline. When we solicit a manuscript for consideration, we like to receive both a hard copy and a floppy disk."

COACHES CHOICE, P.O. Box 1828, Monterey CA 93942. (888)229-5745. Fax: (831)393-1102. E-mail: info@h ealthylearning.com. Website: www.coacheschoiceweb.com. **Acquisitions:** Sue Peterson, general manager (sports); Jim Peterson, director of acquisitions (sports); Shannon Romano, director of operations. Publishes trade paperback originals and reprints. **Publishes 40 titles/year. Receives 100 queries and 60 mss/year. 50% of books from first-time authors; 95% from unagented writers. Pays 10-15% royalty. As a rule, does not offer advances.** Publishes book 1 year after receipt of ms. Accepts simultaneous submissions. Responds in 2 months. Book catalog and ms guidelines free.

    O─╖ "We publish books for anyone who coaches a sport or has an interest in coaching a sport—all levels of competition."

Nonfiction: How-to, reference. Subjects include sports, sports specific training, general physical conditioning. Submit proposal package, including outline, 2 sample chapters and résumé. Reviews artwork/photos as part of ms package. Send photocopies and diagrams.

Recent Title(s): *101 Winning Drills from the AVCA*, edited by Kinda Lenberg (volleyball expert).

COFFEE HOUSE PRESS, 27 N. Fourth St., Suite 400, Minneapolis MN 55401. Fax: (612)338-4004. Publisher/ Editor: Allan Kornblum. **Acquisitions:** Chris Fischbach, managing editor. Estab. 1984. Publishes hardcover and trade paperback originals. **Publishes 14 titles/year. Receives 5,000 queries and mss/year. 75% of books are from unagented writers. Pays 8% royalty on retail price.** Publishes book 18-24 months after acceptance. Responds in 1 month to queries or samples, 6 months to mss. Book catalog and ms guidelines for #10 SAE with 2 first-class stamps.

Fiction: Literary novels, short story collections. No genre. Query first with samples and SASE.

Poetry: Full-length collections.

Recent Title(s): *The Cockfighter*, by Frank Manley (fiction); *Avalanche*, by Quincy Troupe (poetry).

Tips: "Look for our books at stores and libraries to get a feel for what we like to publish. No phone calls, e-mails, or faxes."

COLLECTORS PRESS, INC., P.O. Box 230986, Portland OR 97281-0986. (503)684-3030. Fax: (503)684-3777. Website: www.collectorspress.com. **Acquisitions:** Richard Perry, publisher. Estab. 1992. Publishes hardcover and trade paperback originals. **Publishes 20 titles/year. Receives 500 queries and 200 mss/year. 75% of books from first-time authors; 75% from unagented writers. Pays royalty.** Publishes book 1 year after acceptance of ms. Responds in 1 month. Book catalog and ms guidelines free.

    O─╖ Collectors Press Inc. publishes award-winning popular-culture coffee table and gift books on 20th century and modern collections and interests.

Nonfiction: Art, illustration, science-fiction art, fantasy art, graphic design, photography, comic art, magazine art, historical art, poster art, architecture, and genre-specific art. Submit proposal package, including market research, outline, 2 sample chapters and SASE. Reviews artwork/photos as part of ms package. Send transparencies or *very* clear photos.

Recent Title(s): *Science Fiction of the 20th Century: An Illustrated History.*

Tips: "Your professional package must be typed. No computer disks accepted."

COLLEGE PRESS PUBLISHING COMPANY, P.O. Box 1132, Joplin MO 64802. (417)623-6280. Website: www.co llegepress.com. **Acquisitions:** John Hunter, acquisitions editor. Estab. 1959. Publishes hardcover and trade paperback originals and reprints. **Publishes 25-30 titles/year. Receives 400 queries and 300 mss/year. 25% of books from first-time authors; 90% from unagented writers. Pays 5-15% royalty on wholesale price.** Publishes book 6 months after acceptance of ms. Accepts simultaneous submissions. Responds in 3 months to proposals. Book catalog for 9 × 12 SAE and 5 first-class stamps. Manuscript guidelines for #10 SASE.

    O─╖ "College Press is an organization dedicated to support the mission and work of the church. Its mission is the production and distribution of materials which will facilitate the discipling of the nations as commanded by our Lord Jesus Christ." Denomination affiliation with Christian churches/Churches of Christ.

Nonfiction: Textbook, Christian textbooks and small group studies. Subjects include religion, Christian Apologetics. "We seek textbooks used in Christian colleges and universities—leaning toward an Arminian and an amillennial mindset." Query with proposal package, including synopsis, author bio, 3 sample chapters with SASE.

Recent Title(s): *Newcomer's Guide to the Bible*, by Mike Armour.

Tips: "Our core market is Christian Churches/Churches of Christ and conservative evangelical Christians. Have your material critically reviewed prior to sending it. Make sure that it is non-Calvinistic and that it leans more amillennial (if it is apocalyptic writing)."

COMBINED PUBLISHING, INC., 476 W. Elm St., P.O. Box 307, Conshohocken PA 19428. (610)828-2595. Fax: (610)828-2603. E-mail: combined@combinedpublishing.com. Website: www.combinedpublishing.com. **Acquisitions:** Kenneth S. Gallagher, senior editor. Estab. 1985. Publishes hardcover originals and trade paperback reprints. **Publishes 12-14 titles/year. 30% of books from first-time authors; 100% from unagented writers. Pays 8-10% royalty on wholesale price. Offers $1,000-1,500 advance.** Publishes book 1 year after acceptance of ms. Responds in 4 months. Book catalog free.

    O─╖ "Our focus is military nonfiction, usually books of about 75,000 words. Civil War and World War II are the periods most heavily covered. We publish a series called Great Campaigns. Authors should be aware of the editorial formula of this series."

Nonfiction: Military history. Submit outline, 1 sample chapter and SASE. Reviews artwork/photos as part of ms package. Send photocopies only.

Recent Title(s): *Joshua Chamberlain*, by Edward G. Longacre.

N ⚏ COMMON COURAGE PRESS, One Red Barn Rd., Box 702, Monroe ME 04951. (207)525-0900 or (800)497-3207. Fax: (207)525-3068. E-mail: orders-info@commoncouragepress.com. Website: www.commoncouragep ress.com. **Acquisitions:** Ms. Flic Shooter, publisher (leftist political literature). Publishes hardcover and trade paperback originals and trade paperback reprints. **Publishes 12 titles/year. Receives 50 queries and 200 mss/year. 50% of books from first-time authors; 100% from unagented writers. Pays 10% royalty on wholesale price. Offers advance.** Publishes book 9 months after acceptance of ms. Accepts simultaneous submissions. Responds in 1 month. Book catalog free or on website. Manuscript guidelines on website.

○─┐ "Nonfiction leftist, activist, political, history, feminist, media issues are our niche."

Imprints: Odonian Press (Greg Bates, publisher).

Nonfiction: Biography, humor, illustrated book, reference, textbook. Subjects include anthropology/archaeology, creative nonfiction, ethnic, gay/lesbian, government/politics, health/medicine, history, military/war, multicultural, nature/environment, science, spirituality. Query with SASE or submit proposal package, including outline or submit completed ms. Reviews artwork/photos as part of ms package.

Poetry: Activist only. Submit 10 sample poems or submit complete ms.

Recent Title(s): *New Military Humanism*, by Noam Chomsky (leftist political); *Habits of Highly Deceptive Media*, by Norman Solomon (media bias).

Tips: Audience consists of left-wing activists, college audiences.

COMPANION PRESS, P.O. Box 2575, Laguna Hills CA 92654. Fax: (949)362-4489. E-mail: sstewart@companionpr ess.com. Website: www.companionpress.com. **Acquisitions:** Steve Stewart, publisher. Publishes trade paperback originals. **Publishes 6 titles/year. Receives 50 queries and 25 mss/year. 50% of books from first-time authors; 100% from unagented writers. Pays 6-8% royalty on retail price or makes outright purchase.** Publishes book 9 months after acceptance of ms. Responds in 1 month. *Writer's Market* recommends allowing 2 months for reply. Book catalog and ms guidelines online.

○─┐ "We only publish gay adult books for men." Currently emphasizing biographies.

Fiction and Nonfiction: Biographies, anthologies, novels, video guidebooks. Subjects niche: gay/sexuality. Query. Reviews artwork/photos as part of ms package. Send photocopies.

Recent Title(s): *The Gay Adult Video Star Directory* (nonfiction); *Rent Boys, Hustlers & Escorts* (erotic anthology).

COMPASS AMERICAN GUIDES INC., Fodor's, Random House. 5332 College Ave., Suite 201, Oakland CA 94618. **Acquisitions:** Kit Duane, managing editor; Christopher Burt, creative director. Publishes trade paperback originals. **Publishes 10 titles/year. Receives 50 queries and 5 mss/year. 5% of books from first-time authors; 90% from unagented writers. Makes outright purchase of $5,000-10,000. Offers $1,500-3,000 advance.** Publishes book an average of 8 months after acceptance of ms. Accepts simultaneous submissions. Responds in 6 months. Book catalog for $1.

○─┐ Compass American Guides publishes guides to U.S. and Canadian states, provinces or cities.

Nonfiction: Travel guides. "We cannot guarantee the return of any submissions." Query this publisher about its specific format. Reviews artwork/photos as part of ms package. Photographers should send duplicate slides.

CONARI PRESS, 2550 Ninth St., Suite 101, Berkeley CA 94710. (510)649-7175. Fax: (510)649-7190. E-mail: conari @conari.com. Website: www.conari.com. **Acquisitions:** Heather McArthur, managing editor. Estab. 1987. Publishes hardcover and trade paperback originals. **Publishes 36 titles/year. Receives 1,000 submissions/year. 50% of books from first-time authors; 50% from unagented writers. Pays 12-16% royalty on net price. Offers $5,000 average advance.** Publishes book 1-3 years after acceptance. Accepts simultaneous submissions. Responds in 3 months. Manuscript guidelines for 6×9 SASE.

○─┐ Conari Press seeks to be a catalyst for profound change by providing enlightening books on topics ranging from relationships, personal growth, and parenting to women's history and issues, social issues and spirituality. "We value integrity, process, compassion and receptivity, both in the books we publish and in our internal workings."

Nonfiction: Psychology, spirituality, women's issues, parenting. No poetry or fiction! Submit proposal and complete ms, attn: Heather McArthur. Reviews artwork/photos as part of ms package.

Recent Title(s): *The Courage for Peace*, by Louise Diamond; *The Courage to Give*, by Jackie Waldman.

Tips: "Writers should send us well-targeted, specific and focused manuscripts. No recovery issues. We have a commitment to publish quality books that contribute positively to society—books that reveal, explore, and incite us to grow spiritually and emotionally."

CONCORDIA PUBLISHING HOUSE, 3558 S. Jefferson Ave., St. Louis MO 63118-3968. (314)268-1187. Fax: (314)268-1329. E-mail: boverton@cphnet.org. Website: www.cph.org. **Acquisitions:** Dawn Weinstock, managing editor (adult nonfiction, devotionals, youth fiction); Jane Wilke, acquisitions editor (children's product, teaching resources); Ken Wagener, senior editor (adult nonfiction on Christian spirituality and culture, academic works of interest in Lutheran markets). Estab. 1869. Publishes hardcover and trade paperback originals. **Publishes 150 titles/year. Receives 2,500**

submissions/year. **10% of books from first-time authors; 95% from unagented writers. Pays royalty or makes outright purchase.** Publishes book 15 months after acceptance of ms. Simultaneous submissions discouraged. Responds in 3 months to queries. Manuscript guidelines for #10 SASE.

◕ Concordia publishes Protestant, inspirational, theological, family and juvenile material. All manuscripts must conform to the doctrinal tenets of The Lutheran Church—Missouri Synod. Currently emphasizing practical parenting books.

Nonfiction: Juvenile, adult. Subjects include child guidance/parenting (in Christian context), inspirational, how-to, religion. Query with SASE first.

Fiction: Juvenile. "We will consider preteen and children's fiction and picture books. All books must contain Christian content. No adult Christian fiction." Query with SASE first.

Recent Title(s): *Standing Up Against the Odds*, by Debra and Robert Bruce and Ellen Oldacro (nonfiction); *Horsefeathers* series, by Dandi Daley Mackall (fiction).

Tips: "Our needs have broadened to include writers of books for lay adult Christians."

CONFLUENCE PRESS, INC., Lewis-Clark State College, 500 Eighth Ave., Lewiston ID 83501-1698. (208)799-2336. Fax: (208)799-2324. **Acquisitions:** James R. Hepworth, publisher. Estab. 1975. Publishes hardcover originals and trade paperback originals and reprints. **Publishes 4-5 titles/year. Receives 500 queries and 150 mss/year. 50% of books from first-time authors; 50% from unagented writers. Pays 10-15% royalty on net sales price. Offers $100-2,000 advance.** Publishes book 18 months after acceptance of ms. Accepts simultaneous submissions. Responds in 2 months to queries, 1 month to proposals, 3 months to mss. Book catalog and ms guidelines free.

◕ "We are increasingly moving toward strictly regional books by regional authors and rarely publish writers from outside the western United States." Currently emphasizing essay collections, biography, autobiography. De-emphasizing novels, short stories.

Nonfiction: Subjects include Americana, ethnic, history, language/literature, nature/environment, regional, translation. Query.

Fiction: Ethnic, literary, mainstream/contemporary, short story collections. Query.

Poetry: Submit 6 sample poems.

Recent Title(s): *A Little Bit of Wisdom: Conversations with a Nez Perce Elder* (nonfiction); *The Names of Time*, by Mary Ann Waters (poetry).

CONSORTIUM PUBLISHING, 640 Weaver Hill Rd., West Greenwich RI 02817-2261. (401)397-9838. Fax: (401)392-1926. **Acquisitions:** John M. Carlevale, chief of publications. Estab. 1990. Publishes trade paperback originals and trade paperback reprints. **Publishes 12 titles/year. Receives 150 queries and 50 mss/year. 50% of books from first-time authors; 95% from unagented writers. Pays 10-15% royalty.** Publishes book 3 months after acceptance of ms. Responds in 2 months. Book catalog and ms guidelines for #10 SASE.

◕ Consortium publishes books for all levels of the education market.

Nonfiction: How-to, humor, illustrated book, reference, self-help, technical, textbook. Subjects include business/economics, child guidance/parenting, education, government/politics, health/medicine, history, music/dance, nature/environment, psychology, science, sociology, women's issues/studies. Query or submit proposal package, including table of contents, outline, 1 sample chapter and SASE. Reviews artwork/photos as part of ms package. Send photocopies.

Recent Title(s): *Teaching the Child Under Six, 4th edition*, by James L. Hymes, Jr. (education).

Tips: Audience is college and high school students and instructors, elementary school teachers and other trainers.

CONSUMER PRESS, 13326 SW 28 St., Suite 102, Ft. Lauderdale FL 33330. (954)370-9153. Fax: (954)472-1008. **Acquisitions:** Joseph Pappas, editorial director. Estab. 1989. Publishes trade paperback originals. **Publishes 2-5 titles/year. Receives 2,000 queries and 1,000 mss/year. 50% of books from first-time authors; 70% from unagented writers. Pays royalty on wholesale price or on retail price, as per agreement.** Publishes book 6 months after acceptance of ms. Accepts simultaneous submissions. Book catalog free.

Imprint(s): Women's Publications.

Nonfiction: How-to, self-help. Subjects include homeowner guides, building/remodeling, child guidance/parenting, health/medicine, money/finance, women's issues/studies. Query by mail with SASE.

Recent Title(s): *The Ritalin Free Child*, by Diana Hunter.

COPPER CANYON PRESS, P.O. Box 271, Port Townsend WA 98368. (360)385-4925. E-mail: coppercanyonpress@olympus.net. **Acquisitions:** Sam Hamill, editor. Estab. 1972. Publishes trade paperback originals and occasional clothbound editions. **Publishes 12 titles/year. Receives 1,500 queries/year and 500 mss/year. 10% of books from first-time authors; 95% from unagented writers. Pays 7-10% royalty on retail price.** Publishes book 2 years after acceptance of ms. Responds in 2 months. Book catalog free.

◕ Copper Canyon Press is dedicated to publishing poetry in a wide range of styles and from a full range of the world's many cultures.

Poetry: No unsolicited mss. "First and second book manuscripts are considered only for our Hayden Carruth Awards, presented annually." Send SASE for entry form in September of each year.

Recent Title(s): *East Window: The Asian Translations*, by W.S. Merwin; *The Shape of the Journey: Collected Poems*, by Jim Harrison; *Configurations: New & Selected Poems*, by Clarence Major; *Rave: Selected Poems*, by Olga Broumas.

CORNELL MARITIME PRESS, INC., P.O. Box 456, Centreville MD 21617-0456. (410)758-1075. Fax: (410)758-6849. E-mail: cornell@crosslink.net. **Acquisitions:** Charlotte Kurst, managing editor. Estab. 1938. Publishes hardcover originals and quality paperbacks for professional mariners and yachtsmen. **Publishes 7-9 titles/year. Receives 150 submissions/year. 80% of books from first-time authors; 99% from unagented writers. "Payment is negotiable but royalties do not exceed 10% for first 5,000 copies, 12½% for second 5,000 copies, 15% on all additional.** Royalties for original paperbacks are invariably lower. Revised editions revert to original royalty schedule." Publishes book 1 year after acceptance. Responds in 2 months. Book catalog for 10×13 SAE with 5 first-class stamps.

○━ Cornell Maritime Press publishes books for the merchant marine and a few recreational boating books.

Imprint: Tidewater (regional history, folklore and wildlife of the Chesapeake Bay and the Delmarva Peninsula).

Nonfiction: Marine subjects (highly technical), manuals, how-to books on maritime subjects. Query first, with writing samples and outlines of book ideas.

Recent Title(s): *Modern Marine Engineer's Manual* (Volume I, 3rd edition), by Everett Hunt, editor.

CORNELL UNIVERSITY PRESS, Sage House, 512 E. State St., Ithaca NY 14850. (607)277-2338. Fax: (607)277-2374. Website: www.cornellpress.cornell.edu. **Acquisitions:** Frances Benson, editor-in-chief. Estab. 1869. Publishes hardcover and paperback originals. **Pays royalty. Offers $0-5,000 advance.** Publishes book 1 year after acceptance of ms. Sometimes accepts simultaneous submissions. Catalog and ms guidelines available via website or upon request.

○━ Cornell Press is an academic publisher of nonfiction with particular strengths in anthropology, Asian studies, biological sciences, classics, history, labor and business, literary criticism, politics and international relations, psychology, women's studies, Slavic studies. Currently emphasizing sound scholarships that appeals beyond the academic community.

Imprint(s): Comstock (contact Peter J. Prescott, science editor), **ILR Press**.

Nonfiction: Biography, reference, textbook. Subjects include agriculture/horticulture, anthropology/archaeology, art/architecture, business and economics, education, ethnic, gay/lesbian, government/politics, history, language/literature, military/war, music/dance, philosophy, psychology, regional, religion, science, sociology, translation, women's issues/studies. Submit cover letter, résumé and prospectus.

Recent Title(s): *The Measuring of Life: Virginia Woolf's Last Years*, by Herbert Marder; *You Don't Always Get What You Pay For*, by Elliot Sclar.

Tips: "Cornell University Press is the oldest university press in the country. From our beginnings in 1869, we have grown to be a major scholarly publisher, offering 150 new titles a year in many disciplines."

CORWIN PRESS, INC., 2455 Teller Rd., Thousand Oaks CA 91320. (805)499-9734. Fax: (805)499-5323. E-mail: jay.whitney@corwinpress.com. **Acquisitions:** Jay Whitney, director of acquisitions (early childhood); Robb Clouse, editor (special education); Rachel Livsey, editor (curriculum and instruction). Estab. 1990. Publishes hardcover and paperback originals. **Publishes 70 titles/year. Pays 10% royalty on net sales.** Publishes book 7 months after acceptance of ms. Responds in 1 month to queries. Manuscript guidelines for #10 SASE.

○━ Corwin Press, Inc. publishes leading-edge, user-friendly publications for education professionals.

Nonfiction: Curriculum activities and professional-level publications for administrators, teachers, school specialists, policymakers, researchers and others involved with early childhood-12 education. Seeking fresh insights, conclusions and recommendations for action. Prefers theory or research based books that provide real-world examples and practical, hands-on strategies to help busy educators be successful. No textbooks that simply summarize existing knowledge or mass-market books. Query.

Recent Title(s): *25 Biggest Mistakes Teachers Make and How to Avoid Them*, by Carolyn Orange; *The Biological Brain in a Cultural Classroom*, by Robert Slywester.

Ⓝ COUNTRY MUSIC FOUNDATION PRESS, 4 Music Square E., Nashville TN 37203. (615)256-1639. Fax: (615)255-2245. Website: www.countrymusichalloffame.com and www.vanderbilt.edu/vupress. **Acquisitions:** Paul Kingsbury, deputy director (country music history, biography); Chris Dickinson, associate editor (current country performers, criticism). Publishes hardcover originals and trade paperback originals and reprints. **Publishes 2-4 titles/year. Receives 12 queries/year. Pays 10% royalty on wholesale price. Offers $1,000-5,000 advance.** Publishes book 1 year after acceptance of ms. Accepts simultaneous submissions. Responds in 2 months to queries, 3 months to proposals, 4 months to mss. Book catalog on website. Manuscript guidelines free.

○━ "We publish biographies and histories for the most part. All our books have some connection to country music."

Nonfiction: Biography, illustrated book, reference. Subjects include americana, history, music/dance, regional. Query with SASE or submit proposal package, including outline, 1 sample chapter and introduction. Reviews artwork/photos as part of ms package. Send photocopies.

Recent Title(s): *A Good-Natured Riot: The Birth of the Grand Ole Opry*, by Charles Wolfe (history); *True Adventures with the King of Bluegrass*, by Tom Piazza (memoir).

Tips: "Our audience is a balance between educated country music fans and scholars. Submit queries or proposals only if you are very knowledgeable about your subject. Our books are in-depth studies written by experts or by music insiders. We aren't especially receptive to inexperienced beginners."

THE COUNTRYMAN PRESS, P.O. Box 748, Woodstock VT 05091-0748. (802)457-4826. Fax: (802)457-1678. E-mail: countrymanpress@wwnorton.com. Website: www.countrymanpress.com. Editor-in-Chief: Helen Whybrow. **Ac-**

quisitions: Ann Kraybill, managing editor. Estab. 1973. Publishes hardcover originals, trade paperback originals and reprints. **Publishes 25 titles/year. Receives 1,000 queries/year. 30% of books from first-time authors; 70% from unagented writers. Pays 5-15% royalty on retail price. Offers $1,000-5,000 advance.** Publishes book 18 months after acceptance of ms. Accepts simultaneous submissions. Responds in 2 months to proposals. Book catalog free. Manuscript guidelines for #10 SASE.

　　O—¬ Countryman Press publishes books that encourage physical fitness and appreciation for and understanding of the natural world, self-sufficiency and adventure.

Imprint(s): Backcountry Guides.

Nonfiction: How-to, guidebooks, general nonfiction. Subjects include gardening, nature/environment, recreation, New England, travel, country living. "We publish several series of regional recreation guidebooks—hiking, bicycling, walking, fly-fishing, canoeing, kayaking—and are looking to expand them. We're also looking for books of national interest on travel, gardening, rural living, nature and fly-fishing." Submit proposal package including outline, 3 sample chapters, market information, author bio with SASE. Reviews artwork/photos as part of ms package. Send photocopies.

Recent Title(s): *King Philip's War*, by Eric Schultz and Michael Tougias (history); *Cider, Hard and Sweet*, by Ben Watson (how-to).

COUNTRYSPORT PRESS, Building 116, Craig Industrial Park, Selma AL 36701. (334)872-6400. Fax: (334)872-6443. E-mail: countrysport@tomnet.com. Website: www.countrysport.com. **Acquisitions:** Bob Hunter, publisher. Estab. 1988. Publishes hardcover originals and reprints. **Publishes 12 titles/year. 20% of books from first-time authors; 90% from unagented writers. Pays royalty on wholesale price. Advance varies by title.** Publishes book 1 year after acceptance of ms. Accepts simultaneous submissions. Responds in 1 month to queries; 3 months to proposals and mss. Book catalog free via website or with SASE.

　　O—¬ "Our audience is upscale sportsmen with interests in wingshooting, fly fishing, fine guns and other outdoor activities."

Nonfiction: Coffee table book, how-to, illustrated book, other. Subjects include wingshooting, fly fishing, fine guns, outdoor-related subjects. "We are looking for high-quality writing that is often reflective, anecdotal, and that offers a complete picture of an outdoor experience." Query with outline and 3 sample chapters.

Recent Title(s): *The Best Guns*, by Michael McIntosh.

CQ PRESS, Congressional Quarterly, Inc., 1414 22nd St. NW, Washington DC 20037. (202)887-8500. Fax: (202)822-6583. E-mail: dtarr@cq.com. Website: www.books.cq.com. **Acquisitions:** David Tarr; Patricia Gallagher (library/reference); Brenda Carter, Clarisse Kiino (college/political science); Debra Mayberry (directory), acquisitions editors. Estab. 1945. **Publishes 50-70 hardcover and paperback titles/year. 95% of books from unagented writers. Pays college or reference royalties or fees. Sometimes offers advance.** Publishes book an average of 1 year after acceptance. Accepts simultaneous submissions. Responds in 3 months. Book catalog free.

　　O—¬ CQ seeks "to educate the public by publishing authoritative works on American and international government and politics."

Imprint(s): CQ Press; College/Political Science, Library/Reference, Directory.

Nonfiction: All levels of college political science texts. "We are interested in American government, public administration, comparative government, and international relations." Academic reference books, information directories on federal and state governments, national elections, international/state politics and governmental issues. Submit proposal, outline and bio.

Recent Title(s): *Guide to Congress*.

Tips: "Our books present important information on American government and politics, and related issues, with careful attention to accuracy, thoroughness and readability."

CRAFTSMAN BOOK COMPANY, 6058 Corte Del Cedro, Carlsbad CA 92009-9974. (760)438-7828 or (800)829-8123. Fax: (760)438-0398. E-mail: jacobs@costbook.com. Website: www.craftsman-book.com. **Acquisitions:** Laurence D. Jacobs, editorial manager. Estab. 1957. Publishes paperback originals. **Publishes 12 titles/year. Receives 50 submissions/year. 85% of books from first-time authors; 98% from unagented writers. Pays 7½-12½% royalty on wholesale price or retail price.** Publishes book 2 years after acceptance. Accepts simultaneous submissions. Responds in 2 months. Book catalog and ms guidelines free.

　　O—¬ Craftsman books are loaded with step-by-step instructions, illustrations, charts, reference data, checklists, forms, samples, cost estimates, rules of thumb and examples that solve actual problems in the builder's office and in the field. Every book covers a limited subject fully, becomes the owner's primary reference on that subject, has a high utility-to-cost ratio, and will help the owner make a better living in his profession." Currently emphasizing data via the Internet.

Nonfiction: How-to, technical. All titles are related to construction for professional builders. Query with SASE. Reviews artwork/photos as part of ms package.

Recent Title(s): *Commercial Metal Stud Framing*, by Ray Clark.

Tips: "The book should be loaded with step-by-step instructions, illustrations, charts, reference data, forms, samples, cost estimates, rules of thumb, and examples that solve actual problems in the builder's office and in the field. The book must cover the subject completely, become the owner's primary reference on the subject, have a high utility-to-cost ratio, and help the owner make a better living in his chosen field."

CREATION HOUSE, Strang Communications, 600 Rinehart Rd., Lake Mary FL 32746. (407)333-3132. **Acquisitions:** Allen Quain, acquisitions editor; Rick Nash, director of product development; Jerry Lenz, curriculum manager (children's curriculum). Publishes hardcover and trade paperback originals. **Publishes 40-50 titles/year. Receives 100 queries and 600 mss/year. 2% of books from first-time authors; 95% from unagented writers. Pays 4-18% royalty on retail price. Offers $1,500-5,000 advance.** Publishes book 9 months after acceptance of ms. Accepts simultaneous submissions. Responds in 2 months to proposals, 3 months to mss. Manuscript guidelines for #10 SASE.

   O→ Creation House publishes books for the Pentecostal/charismatic Christian market.

Nonfiction: Christian, spirit-filled interest, charismatic, cookbook, giftbook, health and fitness. Subjects include religion, spirituality (charismatic). Query with outline, 3 sample chapters, author bio and SASE.

Recent Title(s): *The Bible Cure*, by Dr. Reginald Cherry (health and spirit); *Thus Saith the Lord?*, by John Revere (charismatic interest).

CREATIVE HOMEOWNER, 24 Park Way, Upper Saddle River NJ 07458. (201)934-7100. Fax: (201)934-7541. E-mail: laurad@chp-publisher.com. Website: www.creativehomeowner.com. **Acquisitions:** Tim Bakke, editorial director; Miranda Smith, editor; Nancy Engel, editor; Kathie Robits, editor (home decorating/design). Estab. 1978. Publishes trade paperback originals. **Publishes 12-16 titles/year. Receives dozens of queries and mss/year. 50% of books from first-time authors; 98% from unagented writers. Makes outright purchase of $8,000-35,000.** Publishes book 16 months after acceptance of ms. Responds in 6 months to queries. Book catalog free.

   O→ Creative Homeowner Press is the one source for the largest selection of quality how-to books, booklets and project plans.

Nonfiction: How-to, illustrated book. Subjects include gardening, hobbies, home remodeling/building, home repairs, home decorating/design. Query or submit proposal package, including competitive books (short analysis) and outline and SASE. Reviews artwork/photos as part of ms package.

Recent Title(s): *Adding Value to Your Home*, by Sid Davies; *Complete Guide to Water Gardens*, by Kathleen Fisher.

N CREATIVE PUBLISHING CO., The Early West, Box 9292, College Station TX 77842-0292. (409)693-0808. Fax: (409)764-7758. E-mail: earlywest@aol.com. Website: www.Earlywest.com. **Acquisitions:** Theresa Earle. Estab. 1978. Publishes hardcover originals. **Receives 20-40 submissions/year. 50% of books from first-time authors; 100% from unagented writers. Royalty varies on wholesale price.** Publishes book 8 months after acceptance. *Writer's Market* recommends allowing 2 months for reply. Free book catalog.

   O→ Publisher of nonfiction books on the Old West. Most involve a famous gunfighter, lawman, or outlaw personality. De-emphasizing the frontier.

Nonfiction: Biography. Subjects include Americana (western), history. No mss other than 19th century Western America. Query. Reviews artwork/photos as part of ms package.

Recent Title(s): *Harvey Logan in Knoxville*, by Sylvia Lynch.

CRICKET BOOKS, Carus Publishing, 332 S. Michigan Ave., #1100, Chicago IL 60604. (312)939-1500. E-mail: cricketbooks@caruspub.com. Website: www.cricketmag.com. **Acquisitions:** Laura Tillotson, senior editor. Estab. 1999. Publishes hardcover originals. **Publishes 12 titles/year. Receives 300 queries and 600 mss/year. 50% of books from first-time authors; 50% from unagented writers. Pays up to 10% royalty on retail price. Offers advance of $2,000 and up.** Publishes book 18 months after acceptance. Accepts simultaneous submissions. Responds in 1 month to queries and proposals, 2 months to mss. Manuscript guidelines for #10 SASE.

   O→ Cricket Books publishes picture books, chapter books and middle-grade novels for children ages 7-12.

Fiction: Juvenile. Submit complete ms. *Writer's Market* recommends sending query first.

Recent Title(s): *The Boy Trap*, by Nancy Matson, illustrated by Michael Chesworth.

Tips: Audience is children ages 7-12. "Take a look at the fiction magazines we publish, *Spider* and *Cricket*, to see what sort of material we're interested in."

CROSS CULTURAL PUBLICATIONS, INC., P.O. Box 506, Notre Dame IN 46556. (219)273-6526. Fax: (219)273-5973. E-mail: crosscult@aol.com. Website: www.crossculturalpub.com. **Acquisitions:** Cyriac Pullapilly, general editor. Estab. 1980. Publishes hardcover and softcover originals and hardcover and trade paperback reprints. **Publishes 5-20 titles/year. Receives 5,000 queries and 2,000 mss/year. 40% of books from first-time authors; 90% from unagented writers. Pays 10% royalty on wholesale price. No advance.** Publishes book 6 months after acceptance of ms. Accepts simultaneous submissions. Responds in 2 months to queries; 3 months to proposals, 4 months to mss. Book catalog and ms guidelines free on request or on website. *Writer's Market* recommends allowing 2 months for reply. Book catalog free.

   O→ "We publish to promote intercultural and interfaith understanding." Currently emphasizing religious and philosophical books.

Nonfiction: Biography, coffeetable book, cookbook, reference, textbook. Subjects include anthropology/archaeology, business/economics, ethnic, government/politics, history, memoirs multicultural, nature/environment/philosophy, psychology, religion, sociology, spirituality, translation, travel, women's issues/studies. Submit proposal package, including outline. "We publish scholarly books that deal with intercultural topics—regardless of discipline. Books pushing into new horizons are welcome, but they have to be intellectually sound and balanced in judgement."

Fiction: Historical, religious, romance, science fiction. "Should have a serious plot and message." Query with SASE or submit proposal package including synopsis.

Poetry: "Exceptionally good poetry with moving message." Query with sample poems or submit complete ms.
Recent Title(s): *Zero: What Number Is God?* by Sarah Voss, Ph.D.; *Connections and Disconnections: Between Linguistics, Morality, Religion and Democracy,* by Tim Cooney and Beth Preddy.

THE CROSSING PRESS, 97 Hangar Way, Watsonville CA 95019. (408)722-0711. Fax: (408)772-2749. Website: www.crossingpress.com. **Acquisitions:** Caryle Hirshberg, acquisitions editor; Elaine Goldman Gill, publisher. Estab. 1967. Publishes trade paperback originals. **Publishes 40-50 titles/year. Receives 2,000 submissions/year. 10% of books from first-time authors; 75% from unagented writers. Pays royalty.** Publishes book 18 months after acceptance of ms. Accepts simultaneous submissions. Responds in 2 months to queries. Book catalog free.
> ○━ The Crossing Press publishes titles on a theme of "tools for personal change" with an emphasis on health, spiritual growth, healing and empowerment.

Nonfiction: Natural and alternative health, spirituality, personal growth/transformation, empowerment, self-help, cookbooks. Submit detailed outline, sample chapter, market anaylsis, timetable and detailed vita.
Recent Title(s): *Single Mother's Survival Guide.*
Tips: "Simple intelligent query letters do best. No come-ons, no cutes. It helps if you have credentials. Authors should research our website first to see what sort of books we currently publish."

CROSSWAY BOOKS, Good News Publishers, 1300 Crescent St., Wheaton IL 60187-5800. Fax: (630)682-4785. Editorial Director: Marvin Padgett. **Acquisitions:** Jill Carter. Estab. 1938. Publishes hardcover and trade paperback originals. **Publishes 95 titles/year. Receives 2,500 submissions/year. 2% of books from first-time authors; 75% from unagented writers. Pays negotiable royalty. Offers negotiable advance.** Publishes book 18 months after acceptance. Responds in up to 2 months. Book catalog for 9×12 SAE with 7 first-class stamps. Manuscript guidelines for #10 SASE.
> ○━ " 'With making a difference in people's lives for Christ' as its maxim, Crossway Books lists titles written from an evangelical Christian worldview."

Nonfiction: "Books that provide fresh understanding and a distinctively Christian examination of questions confronting Christians and non-Christians in their personal lives, families, churches, communities and the wider culture. The main types include: (1) Issues books that typically address critical issues facing Christians today; (2) Books on the deeper Christian life that provide a deeper understanding of Christianity and its application to daily life; and, (3) Christian academic and professional books directed at an audience of religious professionals. Be sure the books are from an evangelical Christian worldview. Writers often give sketchy information on their book's content." Query with SASE. No phone queries.
Fiction: "We publish fiction that falls into these categories: (1) Christian realism, or novels set in modern, true-to-life settings as a means of telling stories about Christians today in an increasingly post-Christian era; (2) Supernatural fiction, or stories typically set in the 'real world' but that bring supernatural reality into it in a way that heightens our spiritual dimension; (3) Historical fiction, using historical characters, times and places of interest as a mirror for our own times; (4) Some genre-technique fiction (mystery, western); and (5) Children's fiction. "We are not interested in romance novels, horror novels, biblical novels (i.e., stories set in Bible times that fictionalize events in the lives of prominent biblical characters), issues novels (i.e., fictionalized treatments of contemporary issues), and end times/prophecy novels. We do not accept full manuscripts or electronic submissions." Submit synopsis with 2 sample chaptes and SASE.
Recent Title(s): *The Legacy of Sovereign Joy*, by John Piper (nonfiction); *All That Glitters*, by Gilbert Morris (fiction).
Tips: "All of our fiction must have 'Christian' content—combine the Truth of God's Word with a passion to live it out. Writers often submit without thinking about what a publisher actually publishes. They also send full manuscripts without a synopsis. Without a synopsis, the manuscript does not get read."

CROWN BUSINESS, (formerly Times Business), Random House, Inc., 299 Park Ave., New York NY 10171. (212)572-2275. Fax: (212)572-4949. Website: www.randomhouse.com. **Acquisitions:** John Mahaney, executive editor. Estab. 1995. Publishes hardcover and trade paperback originals. **Publishes 20-25 titles/year. 50% of books from first-time authors; 15% from unagented writers. Pays negotiable royalty on list price; hardcover on invoice price. Advance negotiable.** Publishes book 9 months after acceptance of ms. Accepts simultaneous submissions. Responds in 1 month on proposals. Book catalog free from Random House (same address). Manuscript guidelines for #10 SASE.
Nonfiction: Subjects include business/economic, money/finance, management, technology and business. Query with proposal package including outline, 1-2 sample chapters, market analysis and SASE.
Recent Title(s): *Profit Zone*, by Adrian Zlywotzky and David Morrison.

CUMBERLAND HOUSE PUBLISHING, 431 Harding Industrial Dr., Nashville TN 37211. (615)832-1171. Fax: (615)832-0633. E-mail: cumbhouse@aol.com. **Acquisitions:** Ron Pitkin, president; Julia M. Pitkin (cooking/lifestyle). Estab. 1996. Publishes hardcover, trade paperback and mass market originals, and hardcover, trade paperback and mass market reprints. **Publishes 60 titles/year; imprint publishes 5 titles/year. Receives 3,000 queries and 500 mss/year. 30% of books from first-time authors; 80% from unagented writers. Pays 10-20% royalty on wholesale price. Offers $1,000-10,000 advance.** Publishes book an average of 8 months after acceptance. Accepts simultaneous submissions. Responds in 6 months to queries and proposals, 4 months or more to mss. Book catalog for 8×10 SAE and 4 first-class stamps. Manuscript guidelines free.
Imprint(s): Cumberland House Hearthside (contact Julia M. Pitkin, editor-in-chief).

Nonfiction: Cookbook, gift book, how-to, humor, reference. Subjects include Americana, cooking/foods/nutrition, government/politics, history, military/war, recreation, regional, sports, travel. Query or submit outline. Reviews artwork/photos as part of ms package. Send photocopies.

Fiction: Mystery. Writers should know "the odds are really stacked against them." Query.

Recent Title(s): *Smokehouse Ham, Spoon Bread and Scuppernong Wine*, by Joe Dabney (winner of 1999 James Beard Cookbook of the Year Award); *Skeleton Crew*, by Beverly Connor (mystery).

Tips: Audience is "adventuresome people who like a fresh approach to things. Writers should tell what their idea is, why it's unique and why somebody would want to buy it—but don't pester us."

△ CURRENCY, Doubleday Broadway Publishing Group, Random House, Inc., 1540 Broadway, New York NY 10036. (212)782-9730. Fax: (212)782-8911. E-mail: rscholl@randomhouse.com. **Acquisitions:** Roger Scholl, executive editor. Estab. 1989. **Pays 7½-15% royalty on retail price. Offers advance.** Publishes ms 1 year after acceptance.

O— Currency publishes "business books for people who want to make a difference, not just a living."

Nonfiction: Business/economics subjects. *Agented submissions only.*

Recent Title(s): *Six Sigma*, by Mike Harry and Richard Schroeder; *Eight Steps to Seven Figures*, by Charles Carlson.

CURRENT CLINICAL STRATEGIES PUBLISHING, 27071 Cabot Rd., Suite 126, Laguna Hills CA 92653. (949)348-8404. Fax: (949)348-8405. E-mail: info@ccspublishing.com. Website: www.ccspublishing.com. **Acquisitions:** Camille deTonnancour, editor. Estab. 1988. Publishes trade paperback originals. **Publishes 20 titles/year. Receives 10 queries and 10 mss/year. 50% of books from first-time authors; 50% from unagented writers. Pays royalty.** Publishes book 6 months after acceptance of ms.

O— Current Clinical Strategies is a medical publisher for healthcare professionals.

Nonfiction: Technical. Health/medicine subjects. Submit 6 sample chapters. *Physician authors only.* Reviews artwork/photos as part of ms package. Send file by e-mail only.

Recent Title(s): *Family Medicine 2000*, by Paul D. Chan, M.D.; *Pediatrics Five Minute Reviews 2001*, by Karen Scruggs, M.D..

CYPRESS PUBLISHING GROUP, 11835 ROE #187, Leawood KS 66211. (913)681-9875. Fax: (913)341-5158. E-mail: cpa@kcnet.com. Vice President Marketing: Carl Heintz. **Acquisitions:** William S. Noblitt, JoAnn Heinz. Publishes hardcover and trade paperback originals. **Publishes 10 titles/year. 80% of books from first-time authors; 90% from unagented writers. Pays 10-15% royalty on wholesale price.** Publishes book 8 months after acceptance of ms. Responds in 2 weeks to queries, 1 month to proposals and mss. *Writer's Market* recommends allowing 2 months for reply. Book catalog free.

O— "We are an innovative niche publisher of business and finance books, including training materials." Currently emphasizing business, finance, investing.

Nonfiction: How-to, illustrated book, self-help, technical, textbook. Subjects include business/economics, computers/electronics (business related), hobbies (amateur radio, antique radio), money/finance, psychology (business related), software (business related). Query with proposal package, including outline, 1-3 sample chapters, overview of book. Send photocopies.

Recent Title(s): *Money Manager*, by Alex Grant.

Tips: "Our editorial plans change—we are always looking for outstanding submissions. Many writers fail to consider what other books on the topics are available. The writer must think about the fundamental book marketing question: Why will a customer *buy* the book?"

DANTE UNIVERSITY OF AMERICA PRESS, INC., P.O. Box 843, Brookline Village MA 02447. Fax: (617)734-2046. E-mail: danteu@usa1.com. Website: www.danteuniversity.org/dpress.html. **Acquisitions:** Adolph Caso, president. Estab. 1975. Publishes hardcover and trade paperback originals and reprints. **Publishes 5 titles/year. Receives 50 submissions/year. 50% of books from first-time authors; 50% from unagented writers. Pays royalty. Negotiable advance.** Publishes book 10 months after acceptance of ms. Responds in 2 months.

O— "The Dante University Press exists to bring quality, educational books pertaining to our Italian heritage as well as the historical and political studies of America. Profits from the sale of these publications benefit the Foundation, bringing Dante University closer to a reality."

Nonfiction: Biography, reference, reprints, translations from Italian and Latin. Subjects include general scholarly nonfiction, Renaissance thought and letter, Italian language and linguistics, Italian-American history and culture, bilingual education. Query first with SASE. Reviews artwork/photos as part of ms package.

Fiction: Translations from Italian and Latin. Query first with SASE.

Poetry: "There is a chance that we would use Renaissance poetry translations."

Recent Title(s): *Trapped in Tuscany*, by Tullio Bertini (World War II nonfiction); *Rogue Angel*, by Carol Damioli (mystery).

DARLINGTON PRODUCTIONS, INC., P.O. Box 5884, Darlington MD 21034. (410)457-5400. E-mail: dpi14@aol .com. Website: www.darlingtonproductions.com. **Acquisitions:** Jeffrey D. McKaughan, president. Publishes hardcover originals, trade paperback originals and reprints. **Publishes 9 titles/year. Receives 20 queries/year. 75% of books**

published are from first-time writers; **100% from unagented writers. Pays 10% royalty on retail price and small bulk fee at time of release. No advance.** Publishes book 6 months after acceptance. Accepts simultaneous submissions. Responds in 1 month to queries and proposals, 3 months to mss. Book catalog and ms guidelines free.

O→ Darlington publishes military history/war reference and illustrated titles.

Nonfiction: Illustrated book, reference, technical. Military history/war subjects. Query with outline. Reviews artwork/photos as part of ms package. Send photocopies.

Recent Nonfiction Title(s): *Russian/Soviet Armor and Artillery Design Practices 1945-Present*, by Zaloga, Hull and Markov.

JONATHAN DAVID PUBLISHERS, INC., 68-22 Eliot Ave., Middle Village NY 11379-1194. (718)456-8611. Fax: (718)894-2818. E-mail: info@jdbooks.com. Website: www.jdbooks.com. **Acquisitions:** Alfred J. Kolatch, editor-in-chief. Estab. 1948. Publishes hardcover and trade paperback originals and reprints. **Publishes 20-25 titles/year. 50% of books from first-time authors; 90% from unagented writers. Pays royalty or makes outright purchase.** Publishes book 18 months after acceptance of ms. Responds in 1 month to queries and proposals, 2 months to mss. Book catalog on website. Manuscript guidelines for #10 SASE or on website.

O→ Jonathan David publishes "popular Judaica." Currently emphasizing projects geared toward children.

Nonfiction: Biography, children's/juvenile, coffee table book, cookbook, gift book, how-to, humor, illustrated book, reference, self-help. Subjects include creative nonfiction, ethnic, memoirs, multicultural, religion, spirituality, sports, popular Judaica. Query with SASE or submit proposal package, including outline, 3 sample chapters and author biography. Reviews artwork/photos as part of ms package. Send photocopies.

Recent Title(s): *Drawing a Crowd*, by Bill Gallo (sports cartoons/memoir); *Hear My Story*, by Michael Garbutt (Jewish identity).

DAVIS PUBLICATIONS, INC., 50 Portland St., Worcester MA 01608. (508)754-7201. Fax: (508)753-3834. **Acquisitions:** Claire Mowbray Golding, editorial director (grades K-8); Helen Ronan, editorial director (grades 9-12). Estab. 1901. **Publishes 5-10 titles/year. Pays 10-12% royalty.** Publishes book 1 year after acceptance of ms. Book catalog for 9×12 SAE with 2 first-class stamps. Authors guidelines for SASE.

O→ Davis publishes art, design and craft books for the elementary and high school markets.

Nonfiction: Publishes technique-oriented art, design and craft books for the educational market, as well as books dealing with art and culture, and art history. "Keep in mind the intended audience. Our readers are visually oriented. All illustrations should be collated separately from the text, but keyed to the text. Photos should be good quality transparencies and black and white photographs. Well-selected illustrations should explain, amplify, and enhance the text. We average 2-4 photos/page. We like to see technique photos as well as illustrations of finished artwork, by a variety of artists, including students. Recent books have been on printmaking, clay sculpture, design, jewelry, drawing and watercolor painting." Submit outline, sample chapters and illustrations. Reviews artwork/photos as part of ms package.

Recent Title(s): *The Great Clay Adventure*, by Ellen Kong; *You Can Weave!*, by Kathy Monahan.

DAW BOOKS, INC., 375 Hudson St., 3rd Floor, New York NY 10014-3658. (212)366-2096. Fax: (212)366-2090. E-mail: daw@penguinputnam.com. Website: www.dawbooks.com. Publishers: Elizabeth Wollheim and Sheila Gilbert. **Acquisitions:** Peter Stampfel, submissions editor. Estab. 1971. Publishes hardcover and paperback originals and reprints. **Publishes 60-80 titles/year. Pays in royalties with an advance negotiable on a book-by-book basis.** Sends galleys to author. Simultaneous submissions "returned unread at once, unless prior arrangements are made by agent." Responds in 6 weeks "or longer, if a second reading is required." Book catalog free.

O→ DAW Books publishes science fiction and fantasy.

Fiction: "We are interested in science fiction and fantasy novels. We need science fiction more than fantasy right now, but we're still looking for both. We like character-driven books with attractive characters. We're not looking for horror novels, but we are looking for mainstream suspense thrillers. We accept both agented and unagented manuscripts. Long books are absolutely not a problem. We are not seeking collections of short stories or ideas for anthologies. We do not want any nonfiction manuscripts." Query with SASE first.

Recent Title(s): *Mountains of Black Glass*, by Tad Williams (science fiction).

DEARBORN, 155 N. Wacker Dr., Chicago IL 60606-1719. (312)836-4400. Fax: (312)836-1021. E-mail: zigmund@dearborn.com. Website: www.dearborntrade.com. **Acquisitions:** Cynthia Zigmund, associate publisher (finance); Jean Iversen, senior acquisitions editor (general business/management); Mary B. Good, acquisitions editor (entrepreneurship, consumer real estate, business biographies). Estab. 1959. Publishes hardcover and paperback originals. **Publishes 50 new titles/year. Receives 400 submissions/year. 50% of books from first-time authors; 50% from unagented writers. Pays 10-15% royalty on wholesale price.** Publishes book 6 months after acceptance. Accepts simultaneous submissions. Responds in 1 month. Book catalog and ms guidelines free.

O→ The trade division of Dearborn publishes practical, solutions-oriented books for individuals and corporations on the subjects of finance, consumer real estate, business and entrepreneurship. Currently emphasizing finance, general business/management, consumer real estate. De-emphasizing small business.

Nonfiction: How-to, reference, textbooks. Subjects include small business, real estate, insurance, banking, securities, money/finance. Query.

Recent Title(s): *The 100 Best Stocks to Own for Under $20*, by Gene Walden; *Digital Day Trading*, by Howard Abell.

IVAN R. DEE, INC., The Rowman & Littlefield Publishing Group, 1332 N. Halsted St., Chicago IL 60622-2637. (312)787-6262. Fax: (312)787-6269. E-mail: elephant@ivanrdee.com. Website: www.ivanrdee.com. **Acquisitions:** Ivan R. Dee, president. Estab. 1988. Publishes hardcover originals and trade paperback originals and reprints. **Publishes 50 titles/year. 10% of books from first-time authors; 75% from unagented writers. Pays royalty.** Publishes book 9 months after acceptance of ms. Responds in 1 month to queries. *Writer's Market* recommends allowing 2 months for reply. Book catalog free.

O→ Ivan R. Dee publishes serious nonfiction for general informed readers. Currently de-emphasizing literary criticism.

Imprint(s): Elephant Paperbacks, New Amsterdam Books.

Nonfiction: History, literature and letters, biography, politics, contemporary affairs, theater. Submit outline and sample chapters. Reviews artwork/photos as part of ms package.

Recent Title(s): *Dawning of the Raj*, by Jeremy Bernstein; *Matinee Idylls*, by Richard Schickel.

Tips: "We publish for an intelligent lay audience and college course adoptions."

A DEL REY BOOKS, Ballantine Publishing Group, Random House, Inc., 1540 Broadway, 11th Floor-J, New York NY 10036. (212)782-8393. E-mail: delrey@randomhouse.com. Website: www.randomhouse.com/delrey/. Associate Publisher: Kuo-Yu Liang. **Acquisitions:** Shelly Shapiro, editorial director (science fiction, fantasy); Steve Saffel, senior editor (fantasy, alternate history); Chris Schluep, assistant editor (science fiction). Estab. 1977. Publishes hardcover, trade paperback, and mass market originals and mass market paperback reprints. **Publishes 70 titles/year. Receives 1,900 submissions/year. 10% of books from first-time authors; 0% from unagented writers. Pays royalty on retail price. Offers competitive advance.** Publishes book 1 year after acceptance. Responds in 6 months, occasionally longer. Writer's guidelines for #10 SASE.

O→ Del Rey publishes top level fantasy, alternate history, and science fiction.

Fiction: Fantasy ("should have the practice of magic as an essential element of the plot"), alternate history ("novels that take major historical events, such as Civil War, and bend history in a new direction, sometimes through science fiction or fantasy devices"), science fiction ("well-plotted novels with good characterization, exotic locales, and detailed alien cultures"). *Agented submissions only.*

Recent Title(s): *Darwin's Radio*, by Greg Bear; *The Great War: Walk in Hell*, by Harry Turtledove.

Tips: "Del Rey is a reader's house. Pay particular attention to plotting, strong characters, and dramatic, satisfactory conclusions. It must be/feel believable. That's what the readers like. In terms of mass market, we basically created the field of fantasy bestsellers. Not that it didn't exist before, but we put the mass into mass market."

A DELACORTE PRESS, Bantam Dell Publishing Group, Random House, Inc., 1540 Broadway, New York NY 10036. (212)354-6500. Editor-in-Chief: Leslie Schnur. **Acquisitions:** (Ms.) Jackie Cantor (women's fiction); Tom Spain (commercial nonfiction and fiction). Publishes hardcover and trade paperback originals. **Publishes 36 titles/year.**

Nonfiction and Fiction: *Agented submissions only.*

Recent Title(s): *Why Not Me?*, by Al Franken (nonfiction); and *Be Cool*, by Elmore Leonard (fiction).

A DELTA, Bantam Dell Publishing Group, Random House, Inc., 1540 Broadway, New York NY 10036. (212)354-6500. **Acquisitions:** Tom Spain, editorial. **Publishes 36 titles/year.**

O→ Delta Trade Paperbacks publishes serious nonfiction and literary fiction.

Nonfiction: Biography, memoir. Subjects include ethnic, health/medicine, music. *Agented submissions only.*

Fiction: Literary, short story collections. *Agented submissions only.*

Recent Title(s): *Do They Hear You When You Cry*, by Fanziya Kassindja with Lagli Miller Zashir (nonfiction/women's studies); *Charming Billy*, by Alice McDermott (fiction).

◪ THE DESIGN IMAGE GROUP INC., 231 S. Frontage Rd., Suite 17, Burr Ridge IL 60521. (630)789-8991. Fax: (630)789-9013. E-mail: dig1956@aol.com. Website: www.designimagegroup.com. **Acquisitions:** Editorial Committee. Estab. 1984. Publishes trade paperback originals. **Publishes 6 titles/year. Receives 400 queries and 1,200 mss/year. 75% of books from first-time authors; 90% of books from unagented writers. Pays 10-15% royalty on wholesale price. Offers $3,000-3,600 advance.** Accepts simultaneous submissions. Responds in 1 month to queries; 2 months to mss. Book catalog for 6×9 SAE with 2 first-class stamps. Manuscript guidelines for #10 SASE.

O→ The Design Image Group publishes "traditional supernatural, human form, monster-based horror fiction."

Fiction: Horror. Query. Submit 3 sample chapters and SASE. "Please, no complete ms. Absolutely no phone queries! Absolutely no fax queries!"

Recent Titles: *Carmilla: The Return*, by Kyle Marffin; *A Face Without a Heart*, by Rick Reed.

Tips: "Best advice to understand what we seek: send for our guidelines! They spell out quite clearly what we're looking for . . . and what we don't want to see. Horror is a small genre—only a fraction of the size of sci-fi or romance. Don't expect to ever get rich in this genre. Write horror because you love to do so. Show us something that's been rejected by the major New York trade publishers, and we might surprise you! Nontheless, we demand the same quality writing, suspenseful plotting and engaging characters any mass market publisher would; don't confuse the small press with amateur or experimental publishing. We seek mass market appeal for our smaller audience."

DIAL BOOKS FOR YOUNG READERS, Penguin Putnam Inc., 345 Hudson St., 3rd Floor, New York NY 10014. (212)366-2800. President/Publisher: Nancy Paulsen. Assistant Editor: Jocelyn Wright. **Acquisitions:** Submissions Editor. Publishes hardcover originals. **Publishes 50 titles/year. Receives 5,000 queries and submissions/year. 10% of books from first-time authors. Pays variable royalty and advance.** Responds in 4 months.

> Dial Books for Young Readers publishes quality picture books for ages 18 months-8 years, lively, believable novels for middle readers and young adults, and well-researched manuscripts for young adults and middle readers.

Imprint(s): Phyllis Fogelman Books.

Nonfiction: Juvenile picture books, middle grade and young adult books. Especially looking for "quality picture books and well-researched young adult and middle-reader manuscripts that lend themselves to attractive illustration." Not interested in alphabet books, riddle and game books, and early concept books. Responds to query letters outlining book and giving writer's credentials. Include SASE. *No unsolicited mss.*

Fiction: Juvenile picture books, middle grade readers, young adult books. Subjects include adventure, fantasy, historical, humor, mystery. Especially looking for "lively and well-written novels for middle grade and young adult children involving a convincing plot and believable characters. The subject matter or theme should not already be overworked in previously published books. The approach must not be demeaning to any minority group, nor should the roles of female characters (or others) be stereotyped, though we don't think books should be didactic, or in any way message-y. No topics inappropriate for the juvenile, young adult, and middle grade audiences. No plays." *Agented mss only.* Responds to query letter with SASE outlining book and author's credentials only. *No unsolicited mss.*

Recent Title(s): *Parts*, by Ted Arnold; *Jazmin's Notebook*, by Nikki Grimes.

Tips: "Our readers are anywhere from preschool age to teenage. Picture books must have strong plots, lots of action, unusual premises, or universal themes treated with freshness and originality. Humor works well in these books. A very well thought out and intelligently presented book has the best chance of being taken on. Genre isn't as much of a factor as presentation."

A DIAL PRESS, Bantam Dell Publishing Group, Random House, Inc., 1540 Broadway, New York NY 10036. (212)354-6500. Fax: (212)782-8414. Website: www.bbd.com. **Acquisitions:** Susan Kamil, vice president, editorial director. Estab. 1924. **Publishes 6-12 titles/year. Receives 200 queries and 450 mss/year. 75% of books from first-time authors. Pays royalty on retail price. Offers advance.** Publishes book 18 months after acceptance of ms. Accepts simultaneous submissions.

> Dial Press publishes quality fiction and nonfiction. *Agented submissions only.*

Nonfiction: Biography, memoirs, serious nonfiction, cultural criticism. Subjects include Americana, art/architecture, government/politics, health/medicine, history, psychology, women's issues/studies. *Agented submissions only*; query by letter with SASE.

Fiction: General literary fiction.

Recent Title(s): *Letters of the Century* (nonfiction); *City of Light* (fiction).

DIMI PRESS, 3820 Oak Hollow Lane, SE, Salem OR 97302-4774. (503)364-7698. Fax: (503)364-9727. E-mail: dickbook@aol.com. Website: http://members.aol.com/dickbook/dimi_press.html. **Acquisitions:** Dick Lutz, president. Publishes trade paperback originals. **Publishes 5 titles/year. Receives 100-150 queries and 20-25 mss/year. 80% of books from first-time authors; 90% from unagented writers. Pays 10% royalty on net receipts. No advance.** Publishes book 9 months after acceptance of ms. Accepts simultaneous submissions. Responds in 2 weeks to queries and proposals, 1 month to mss. Book catalog and ms guidelines for #10 SASE.

> "We provide accurate information about unusual things in nature." Currently de-emphasizing self-help books.

Nonfiction: "Soliciting manuscripts on unusual things in nature, such as unusual animals or natural formations. Also natural disasters such as volcanic eruptions, earthquakes, or floods. Preferably of the world's 'worst.' Also related manuscripts on nature/travel/environment. No travel guides." Query with outline and 1 sample chapter and SASE, if answer is desired. Reviews artwork/photos as part of ms package. Send photocopies.

Recent Title(s): *Across African Sand*, by Deutschle.

Tips: "Audience is adults who wish to learn something and are interested in unusual travel excursions. Please send for guidelines before submitting."

N: DIOGENES PUBLISHING, SA14 #253-1615, 965 Alamo Dr., Unit 336, Vacaville CA 95687. (707)447-6482. Fax: (707)447-6482. E-mail: sales@diogenespublishing.com. Website: www.diogenespublishing.com. **Acquisitions:** Chris Primi, marketing director. Publishes trade paperback originals. **Publishes 6 titles/year. Receives 50 queries and 25 mss/year. 75% of books from first-time authors; 75% from unagented writers. Pays 10% royalty on wholesale price.** No advance. Publishes book 1 year after acceptance of ms. Responds in 2 months to queries and mss, 4 months to proposals. Book catalog on website.

> Diogenes is a nonfiction publisher seeking "quality writing, original thinking."

Nonfiction: Nonfiction cultural studies, satire, sociology. Subjects include creative nonfiction, philosophy, psychology, sociology, satire. Query with SASE. Reviews artwork/photos as part of ms package. Send photocopies.

Recent Title(s): *Happiness & Other Lies*, by Mary Massaro; *Self-Esteem for Children*, by John Prosper.

DISCOVERY ENTERPRISES, LTD., 31 Laurelwood Dr., Carlisle MA 01741. (978)287-5401. Fax: (978)287-5402. E-mail: deldeitch1@aol.com. **Acquisitions:** JoAnne W. Deitch, president (plays for Readers Theatre, on American history). Publishes trade paperback originals **Publishes 10 titles/year. Receives 50 queries and 20 mss/year. Publishes 5% from first-time authors; 90% from unagented writers. Pays 15-20% royalty on wholesale price or makes outright purchase of $500-1,000. No advance.** Publishes book 6 months after acceptance of ms. Accepts simultaneous submissions. Responds in 1 month. Book catalog for 6×9 SAE with 3 first-class stamps. No guidelines.

Nonfiction: Reference. Subjects include government/politics, history (American history, world history—primary source documents and analyses). Submit proposal package, including outline and cv.

Plays: "We're interested in 40-minute plays (reading time) for students in grades 4-10 on topics in U.S. history." Query about topics prior to sending completed play for review. Query with SASE, then submit complete ms.

Recent Title(s): *The Beat Generation*, by Juliet H. Mofford (nonfiction); *Sister Anna*, by Wim Coleman and Pat Perrin (fiction).

Tips: "Call or send query on topic prior to sending manuscript for plays or proposals for American history books."

DORAL PUBLISHING, INC., 10451 W. Palmeras Dr., Suite 225, Sun City AZ 85373-2072. (623)875-2057. Fax: (623)875-2059. E-mail: doralpub@mindspring.com. Website: www.doralpubl.com. **Acquisitions:** Alvin Grossman, publisher; Luana Luther, editor-in-chief (pure bred dogs); Mark Anderson, editor (general dog books). Estab. 1986. Publishes hardcover and trade paperback originals. **Publishes 7 titles/year. Receives 30 queries and 15 mss/year. 60% of mss from first-time authors, 85% from unagented writers. Pays 10% royalty on wholesale price.** Publishes book 6 months after acceptance of ms. *Writer's Market* recommends allowing 2 months for reply. Book catalog free. Manuscript guidelines for #10 SASE.

    ○┅ Doral Publishing publishes only books about dogs and dog-related topics, mostly geared for pure-bred dog owners and showing. Currently emphasizing breed books. De-emphasizing children's work.

Nonfiction: How-to, children's/juvenile, reference. Subjects must be dog-related (showing, training, agility, search and rescue, health, nutrition, etc.). "We are looking for new ideas. No flowery prose. Manuscripts should be literate, intelligent, but easy to read." Query first or submit outline and 2 sample chapters with SASE. Reviews artwork/photos as part of the ms package. Send photocopies.

Fiction: Children's/juvenile. Subjects must center around dogs. Either the main character should be a dog or a dog should play an integral role. Query with SASE.

Recent Title(s): *The Mastiff*; *The Welsh Terrier*.

Tips: "We are currently expanding and are looking for new topics and fresh ideas while staying true to our niche. While we will steadfastly maintain that market—we are always looking for excellent breed books—we also want to explore more 'mainstream' topics."

DORCHESTER PUBLISHING CO., INC., 276 Fifth Ave., Suite 1008, New York NY 10001-0112. (212)725-8811. Fax: (212)532-1054. E-mail: dorchedit@dorchesterpub.com.
Imprint(s): Love Spell (romance), **Leisure Books**.

A DOUBLEDAY, Doubleday Broadway Publishing Group, Random House, Inc., 1540 Broadway, New York NY 10036. (212)782-8911. Fax: (212)782-9700. Website: www.randomhouse.com. Vice President/Editor-in-Chief: William Thomas. Estab. 1897. Publishes hardcover and trade paperback originals and reprints. **Publishes 200 titles/year. Receives thousands of queries and mss/year. 30% of books from first-time authors. Pays royalty on retail price. Advance varies.** Publishes book 1 year after acceptance of ms. Responds in 6 months to queries.

    ○┅ Doubleday publishes high-quality fiction and nonfiction.

Imprint(s): Anchor Books; **Currency**; **Doubleday Religious Division**; **Image Books**; Nan A. Talese.

Nonfiction: Biography, cookbook, gift book, how-to, humor, illustrated book, self-help. Subjects include agriculture/horticulture, Americana, animals, anthropology, art/architecture, business/economics, child guidance/parenting, computers/electronics, cooking/foods/nutrition, education, ethnic, gardening, gay/lesbian, government/politics, health/medicine, history, hobbies, language/literature, military/war, money/finance, music/dance, nature/environment, philosophy, photography, psychology, recreation, regional, religion, science, sociology, software, sports, translation, travel, women's issues/studies. *Agented submissions only.*

Fiction: Adventure, confession, erotica, ethnic, experimental, feminist, gay/lesbian, historical, horror, humor, literary, mainstream/contemporary, mystery, picture books, religious, short story collections, suspense. *Agented submissions only.*

Recent Title(s): *The Street Lawyer*, by John Grisham (fiction).

A DOUBLEDAY RELIGIOUS PUBLISHING, Doubleday Broadway Publishing Group, Random House, Inc., 1540 Broadway, New York NY 10036. (212)354-6500. Fax: (212)782-8911. Website: www.randomhouse.com. **Acquisitions:** Eric Major, vice president, religious division; Trace Murphy, senior editor; Andrew Corben, editor. Estab. 1897. Publishes hardcover originals and reprints, trade paperback originals and reprints. **Publishes 45-50 titles/year; each imprint publishes 12 titles/year. Receives 1,000 queries/year; receives 500 mss/year. 30% of books are from first-time authors; 3% from unagented writers. Pays 7½-15% royalty. Advance varies.** Publishes book 1 year after acceptance of ms. Accepts simultaneous submissions. Responds in 3 months to proposals. Book catalog for SAE with 3 first-class stamps.

Imprint(s): Image Books, Anchor Bible Commentary, Anchor Bible Reference, Galilee, New Jerusalem Bible.

Nonfiction: Biography, cookbook, gift book, reference, self-help. Subjects include child guidance/parenting, cooking/foods/nutrition, history, language/literature, memoirs, money/finance, religion, spirituality. *Agented submissions only.*

Fiction: Religious. *Agented submissions only.*

Recent Title(s): *The Lamb's Supper*, by Scott Hahn.

DOUBLEDAY/IMAGE, Doubleday Broadway Publishing Group, Random House, Inc., 1540 Broadway, New York NY 10036. (212)354-6500. Fax: (212)782-9735. Website: www.randomhouse.com. **Acquisitions:** Trace Murphy, senior editor. Estab. 1956. Publishes hardcover originals and reprints, trade paperback originals and reprints, mass market paperback originals and reprints. **Publishes 12 titles/year. Receives 500 queries/year; receives 300 mss/year. 10% of books from first-time writers; no unagented writers. Pays royalty on retail price. Advance varies.** Publishes book 18 months after acceptance of ms. Accepts simultaneous submissions. Responds in 3 months on proposals.

   O—π Image Books has grown from a classic Catholic list to include a variety of current and future classics, maintaining a high standard of quality as the finest in religious paperbacks. Also publish Doubleday paperbacks/ hardcovers for general religion, spirituality, including works based in Buddhism, Islam, Judaism.

Nonfiction: Biography, cookbook, gift book, how-to, humor, illustrated book, reference, self-help. Subjects include philosophy, psychology, religious/inspirational, world wisdom traditions, women's issues/studies. Query. Prefers agented submissions. Reviews artwork as part of ms package. Send photocopies.

Recent Title(s): *No Future without Forgiveness*, by Desmond Tutu.

DOVER PUBLICATIONS, INC., 31 E. 2nd St., Mineola NY 11501. (516)294-7000. Fax: (516)873-1401. E-mail: dover@inch.com. **Acquisitions:** Paul Negri, editor-in-chief; John Grafton (math/science reprints). Estab. 1941. Publishes trade paperback originals and reprints. **Publishes 500 titles/year. Makes outright purchase.** Book catalog free.

Nonfiction: Biography, children's/juvenile, coffee table book, cookbook, how-to, humor, illustrated book, textbook. Subjects include agriculture/horticulture, Americana, animals, anthropology/archaeology, art/architecture, cooking/food/ nutrition, health/medicine, history, hobbies, language/literature, music/dance, nature/environment, philosophy, photography, religion, science, sports, translation, travel. Publishes mostly reprints. Accepts original paper doll collections, game books, coloring books (juvenile). Query. Reviews artwork/photos as part of ms package.

Recent Title(s): *The Waning of the Middle Ages*, by John Huizenga.

DOWN EAST BOOKS, Down East Enterprise, Inc., P.O. Box 679, Camden ME 04843-0679. Fax: (207)594-7215. E-mail: msteere@downeast.com. Senior Editor: Karin Womer. **Acquisitions:** Chris Cornell, editor (Silver Quill); Michael Steere, associate editor (general). Estab. 1967. Publishes hardcover and trade paperback originals, trade paperback reprints. **Publishes 20-24 titles/year. Receives 800 submissions/year. 50% of books from first-time authors; 90% from unagented writers. Pays 10-15% royalty on receipts. Offers $200 average advance.** Publishes book 1 year after acceptance. Accepts simultaneous submissions. Responds in 3 months. Manuscript guidelines for 9 × 12 SAE with 3 first-class stamps.

   O—π Down East Books publishes books, calendars and videos which capture and illuminate the astonishing beauty and unique character of New England's people, culture, and wild places: the very aspects that distinguish New England from the rest of the United States.

Imprint(s): Silver Quill (fly fishing and wing-shooting market; Chris Cornell, editor, e-mail: ccornell@downeast.com).

Nonfiction: Books about the New England region, Maine in particular. Subjects include Americana, history, nature, guide books, crafts, recreation, field guides. "All of our regional books must have a Maine or New England emphasis." Query. Reviews artwork/photos as part of ms package.

Fiction: "We publish 1-2 juvenile titles/year (fiction and nonfiction), and 1-2 adult fiction titles/year." *Writer's Market* recommends sending a query with SASE first.

Recent Title(s): *Profiles in Saltwater Angling* (nonfiction); *Summer of the Osprey* (fiction); *Acadia: Visions and Verse* (poetry).

DOWN THE SHORE PUBLISHING, Box 3100, Harvey Cedars NJ 08008. (609)978-1233. E-mail: shore@att.n et. Website: www.down-the-shore.com. **Acquisitions:** Leslee Ganss, associate editor. Publishes hardcover and trade paperback originals and reprints. **Publishes 3-5 titles/year. Receives 200 queries and 20 mss/year. 80% of books from first-time authors; 100% from unagented writers. Pays royalty on wholesale or retail price or makes outright purchase.** No advance. Publishes book 1-2 years after acceptance of ms. Accepts simultaneous submissions. Responds in 3 months. Book catalog for 8 × 10 SAE with 2 first-class stamps or on website. Manuscript guidelines for #10 SASE or on website.

   O—π "Bear in mind that our market is regional—New Jersey, the Jersey Shore, the mid-Atlantic, and seashore and coastal subjects."

Nonfiction: Children's/juvenile, coffee table book, gift book, illustrated book, regional history. Subjects include Americana, art/architecture, history, nature/environment, regional, spirituality. Query with SASE or submit proposal package, including outline and 1 sample chapter. Reviews artwork/photos as part of ms package. Send photocopies.

Fiction: Regional. Query with SASE or submit proposal package, including synopsis and 1 sample chapter.

Poetry: "We do not publish poetry, unless it is to be included as part of an anthology."

Recent Title(s): *Shore Chronicles: Diaries and Travelers' Tales from the Jersey Shore 1764-1955*, Margaret Thomas Buchholz, editor (nonfiction); *Shore Stories: An Anthology of the Jersey Shore*, Rich Youmans, editor (fiction).

Tips: "Carefully consider whether your proposal is a good fit for our established market."

LISA DREW BOOKS, Simon & Schuster, 1230 Avenue of the Americas, New York NY 10020. (212)698-7000. Website: www.simonsays.com. **Acquisitions:** Lisa Drew, publisher. Publishes hardcover originals. **Publishes 10-14**

titles/year. Receives 600 queries/year. 10% of books from first-time authors. Pays royalty on retail price, varies by author and project. Advance varies. Publishes book 1 year after acceptance of ms. Accepts simultaneous submissions, if so noted. Responds in 1 month to queries. Book catalog free through Scribner (same address).
O➝ "We publish *reading* books; nonfiction that tells a story, not '14 ways to improve your marriage.' "
Nonfiction: Subjects include government/politics, history, women's issues/studies, law, entertainment. *Agented submissions only.* No unsolicited material.

DRY BONES PRESS, P.O. Box 597, Roseville CA 95678. Phone/fax: (415)707-2129. Website: www.drybones.com. **Acquisitions:** J. Rankin, editor/publisher. Publishes hardcover and trade paperback originals and reprints and mass market paperback originals. "We now work with Ingram/LPI, Borders/Sprint, and PublishingOnline.com routinely." **Publishes 6-10 titles/year. Pays 6-10% royalty on retail price.** Publishes book 2 years after acceptance of ms. Accepts simultaneous submissions, if so noted. Responds in 2 months, if possible.
Nonfiction: California Gold Rush, reference, technical. Subjects include health/medicine, history, philosophy, regional, religion, translation, nursing patient writing. Submit outline, 1-2 sample chapters and proposal package, including marketing ideas with SASE. Recent title: *Old Catholic Missal & Ritual* (nonfiction); *Mind Play* (fiction); *Seeded Puffs* (poetry).
Fiction: Historical, humor/satire, mainstream/contemporary, mystery, plays, religious, science fiction. "Looking for unique items, with solid quality. No maudlin sentimentality or failure to develop insight or characters." Submit synopsis, 1-2 sample chapters with SASE. Recent title: *Aquarius*, by Richard Epstein (satire/social commentary).

[A] DTP, Bantam Dell Publishing Group, Random House, Inc. 1540 Broadway, New York NY 10036. (212)354-6500. **Acquisitions**: Tom Spain, editorial director. Publishes trade paperback originals. **Publishes 36 titles/year.**
O➝ Dell Trade Paperbacks publishes light, humorous material and books on pop culture.
Nonfiction: Humor, self-help, pop culture. *Agented submissions only.*
Recent Title(s): *What Einstein Didn't Know*, by Robert Wolke.

DUFOUR EDITIONS, P.O. Box 7, Chester Springs PA 19425. Phone/fax: (610)458-5005. E-mail: dufour8023@aol.com. Website: http://members.aol.com/Dufour8023/Index.html. **Acquisitions**: Thomas Lavoie, associate publisher. Estab. 1948. Publishes hardcover originals, trade paperback originals and reprints. **Publishes 5-6 titles/year. Receives 100 queries and 15 mss/year. 20-30% of books from first-time authors; 50% from unagented writers. Pays 6-10% royalty on net receipts. Offers $500-1,000 advance.** Publishes book 18 months after acceptance of ms. Accepts simultaneous submissions. Responds in 3 months to queries and proposals, 6 months to mss. Book catalog and ms guidelines free.
O➝ "We're a small literary house and distribute a number of quality fiction, poetry and nonfiction titles from the U.K. and Irish publishers as well. We have not been doing any poetry lately."
Nonfiction: Biography. Subjects include history, translation. Query with SASE. Reviews artwork/photos as part of ms package. Send photocopies.
Fiction: Ethnic, historical, literary, short story collections. Query with SASE.
Poetry: Query.
Recent Title(s): *The Case of the Pederast's Wife*, by Clare Elfman.
Tips: "Audience is sophisticated, literate readers especially interested in foreign literature and translations, and a strong Irish-Celtic focus. Check to see if the publisher is really a good match for your subject matter."

THOMAS DUNNE BOOKS, St. Martin's Press, 175 Fifth Ave., New York NY 10010. (212)674-5151. **Acquistions:** Tom Dunne, publisher; Peter J. Wolverton, associate publisher; Ruth Cavin, associate publisher (mysteries). Publishes hardcover originals, trade paperback originals and reprints. **Publishes 90 titles/year. Receives 1,000 queries/year. 20% of books from first-time authors; less than 5% from unagented writers. Pays 10-15% royalty on retail price for hardcover, 7½% for paperback. Advance varies with project.** Publishes book 1 year after acceptance of ms. Accepts simultaneous submissions. Responds in 2 months to queries. Ms guidelines for #10 SASE.
O➝ Thomas Dunne publishes a wide range of fiction and nonfiction.
Nonfiction: Biography. Subjects include government/politics, history, political commentary. "Author's attention to detail is important. We get a lot of manuscripts that are poorly proofread and just can't be considered." Query or submit outline and 100 sample pages with SASE. Reviews artwork/photos as part of ms package. Send photocopies.
Fiction: Mainstream/contemporary, thrillers, suspense, women's. Query or submit synopsis and 100 sample pages with SASE.
Recent Title(s): *An Ocean Apart*, by Robin Pilcher (commercial fiction).

DUQUESNE UNIVERSITY PRESS, 600 Forbes Ave., Pittsburgh PA 15282-0101. (412)396-6610. Fax: (412)396-5984. Website: www.duq.edu/dupress. **Acquisitions:** Susan Wadsworth-Booth, director. Estab. 1927. Publishes hardcover and trade paperback originals. **Publishes 8-12 titles/year. Receives 500 queries and 75 mss/year. 30% of books from first-time authors; 95% from unagented writers. Pays royalty on net price.** Publishes book 1 year after acceptance of ms. Responds in 1 month to proposals, 3 months to mss. Book catalog and ms guidelines free with SASE.
O➝ Duquesne publishes scholarly monographs in the fields of literary studies (medieval & Renaissance), philosophy, ethics, religious studies and psychology. "We also publish a series, *Emerging Writers in Creative Nonfiction*, for first-time authors of creative nonfiction for a general readership."

Nonfiction: Creative nonfiction, scholarly/academic. Subjects include language/literature, philosophy, religion. "We look for quality of scholarship." For scholarly books, query or submit outline, 1 sample chapter and SASE. For creative nonfiction, submit 2 copies of ms.

Recent Title(s): *The Last Settlers*, by Jennifer Brice and Charles Mason.

DUTTON CHILDREN'S BOOKS, Penguin Putnam Inc., 345 Hudson St., New York NY 10014. (212)414-3700. Fax: (212)414-3397. Website: www.penguinputnam.com. **Acquisitions:** Lucia Monfried, associate publisher/editor-in-chief (picture books, easy-to-read books); Stephanie Owens Lurie, president and publisher (picture books and middle grade fiction); Donna Brooks, editorial director (books for all ages with distinctive narrative style); Susan Von Metre, senior editor (character-oriented picture books and middle grade fiction); Sarah Ketchersid, editor (character-oriented picture books and middle grade fiction); Meredith Mundy Wasinger, editor (nonfiction). Estab. 1852. Publishes hardcover originals as well as novelty formats. **Publishes 100 titles/year. 15% from first-time authors. Pays royalty on retail price.**

    O— Dutton Children's Books publishes high-quality fiction and nonfiction for readers ranging from preschoolers to young adults on a variety of subjects. Currently emphasizing picture books and middle-grade fiction that offer a fresh perspective. De-emphasizing photographic nonfiction.

Nonfiction: For preschoolers to young adults; including animals/nature, U.S. history and science. Query with SASE.

Fiction: Dutton Children's Books has a diverse, general-interest list that includes picture books; easy-to-read books; and fiction for all ages, from "first-chapter" books to young adult readers. Query with SASE and letter only.

Recent Title(s): *The Little Red Hen (Makes a Pizza)*, by Philemon Sturge, illustrated by Amy Walrod (fiction); *Sitting Bull*, by Al Marrin (nonfiction).

A DUTTON PLUME, Penguin Putnam Inc., 375 Hudson St., New York NY 10014. (212)366-2000. President: Carol Baron. **Acquisitions:** Lori Lipsky, publisher (business, mainstream fiction); Brian Tart, editor-in-chief (commercial fiction, self-help/spirituality); Rosemary Ahern, senior editor (literary fiction, narrative nonfiction); Laurie Chittenden, senior editor (multicultural and women's fiction, narrative nonfiction); Jennifer Dickerson, associate editor (women's commercial fiction, literary fiction, spirituality, self-help); Mitch Hoffman, editor (commercial fiction); Kimberly Perdue, assistant editor (Gen-X fiction, humor, self-help). Estab. 1852. **Publishes 60 titles/year. Receives 20,000 queries and 10,000 mss/year. 30-40% of books from first-time authors; 2% from unagented writers. Advance negotiable.** Publishes book 18 months after acceptance. Responds in 6 months.

    O— Dutton publishes hardcover, original, mainstream, and contemporary fiction and nonfiction in the areas of biography, self-help, politics, psychology, and science for a general readership.

Nonfiction: Biography, gift book, how-to, humor, reference, self-help. Subjects include Americana, animals, anthropology/archaeology, art/architecture, business/economics, child guidance/parenting, cooking/foods/nutrition education, ethnic, gardening, gay/lesbian, government/politics, health/medicine, history, hobbies, language/literature, military/war, money/finance, music/dance, nature/environment, philosophy, photography, psychology, recreation, regional, religion, science, sociology, sports, translation, women's issues/studies. *Agented submissions only.*

Fiction: Adventure, erotica, ethnic, gay/lesbian, historical, literary, mainstream/contemporary, mystery, occult, short story collections, suspense. "We are looking for novelists who can write a book a year with consistent quality." *Agented submissions only.*

Recent Title(s): *Reaching to Heaven: A Spiritual Journey Through Life and Death*, by James Van Praagh (inspirational).

Tips: "Write the complete manuscript and submit it to an agent or agents. They will know exactly which editor will be interested in a project."

EAGLE'S VIEW PUBLISHING, 6756 N. Fork Rd., Liberty UT 84310. Fax: (801)745-0903. E-mail: eglcrafts@aol.com. **Acquisitions:** Denise Knight, editor-in-chief. Estab. 1982. Publishes trade paperback originals. **Publishes 4-6 titles/year. Receives 40 queries and 20 mss/year. 90% of books from first-time authors; 100% from unagented writers. Pays 8-10% royalty on net selling price.** Publishes book 1 year or more after acceptance of ms. Accepts simultaneous submissions. Responds in 1 year to proposals. Book catalog and ms guidelines for $3.

    O— Eagle's View publishes primarily how-to craft books with a subject related to historical or contemporary Native American/Mountain Man/frontier crafts. Currently emphasizing bead-related craft books. De-emphasizing earring books.

Nonfiction: How-to, Indian, mountain man and American frontier (history and craft). Subjects include anthropology/archaeology (Native American crafts), ethnic (Native American), history (American frontier historical patterns and books), hobbies (crafts, especially beadwork, earrings). "We are expanding from our Indian craft base to more general but related crafts." Submit outline and 1-2 sample chapters. Reviews artwork/photos as part of ms package. Send photocopies or sample illustrations. "We prefer to do photography in house."

Recent Title(s): *The Art of Simulating Eagle Feathers*, by Bob Gutierrez.

Tips: "We will not be publishing any new beaded earrings books for 1-2 years. We are interested in other craft projects using seed beads, especially books that feature a variety of items, not just different designs for one item."

★ EAKIN PRESS/SUNBELT MEDIA, INC., P.O. Box 90159, Austin TX 78709-0159. (512)288-1771. Fax: (512)288-1813. E-mail: eakinpub@sig.net. Website: www.Eakinpress.com. **Acquisitions:** Edwin M. Eakin, editorial director; Virginia Messer, associate publisher. Estab. 1978. Publishes hardcover and paperback originals and reprints.

Publishes 60 titles/year. Receives 1,500 submissions/year. 50% of books from first-time authors; 90% from un-agented writers. Pays 10-12-15% royalty on net sales. Publishes book 18 months after acceptance. Accepts simultaneous submissions. Responds in 3 months. Book catalog for $1.25. Manuscript guidelines for #10 SASE.

    O⌐ Eakin specializes in Texana and Western Americana for adults and juveniles. Currently emphasizing women's studies. De-emphasizing World War II.

Imprint(s): Eakin Press, Nortex Press.

Nonfiction: Adult nonfiction: Western Americana, African American studies, business, sports, biographies, Civil War, regional cookbooks, Texas history, World War II. Juvenile nonfiction: includes biographies of historic personalities, prefer with Texas or regional interest, or nature studies; and easy-read illustrated books for grades 1-3. Query with SASE.

Fiction: No adult fiction. Juvenile fiction for grades K-12, preferably relating to Texas and the Southwest or contemporary. Query or submit outline/synopsis and sample chapters.

Recent Title(s): *Inside Russia*, by Inez Jeffery; *Black, Buckskin and Blue*, by Art Burton.

EASTERN NATIONAL, 470 Maryland Dr., Fort Washington PA 19034. (215)283-6900. Fax: (215)283-6925. Website: www.nationalparkbooks.org. **Acquisitions:** Jason Scarpello, publishing manager. Estab. 1948. Publishes trade paperback originals and reprints. **Publishes 50-60 titles/year. Receives 20 queries and 10 mss/year. 5% of books from first-time authors; 50% from unagented writers. Pays 1-10% royalty on retail price or makes outright purchase of $6,000 maximum.** Publishes book 2 years after acceptance of ms. Responds in 1 month to queries. *Writer's Market* recommends allowing 2 months for reply. Book catalog on website or by request.

    O⌐ "Our mission is to continue to strengthen our relationship with the National Park Service and other partners."

Imprint(s): Eastern Acorn Press.

Nonfiction: Biography, children's/juvenile. Subjects include Americana, history, military/war, nature/environment. "Requests for editorial plans are only accepted from member agencies." Query. *All unsolicited mss returned unopened.*

Recent Title(s): *National Parks on the Great Lakes*, by Ron Thomson.

THE ECCO PRESS, HarperCollins, 10 E. 53rd St., New York NY 10022. (212)207-7000. Fax: (212)702-2460. Website: www.harpercollins.com. Editor-in-Chief: Daniel Halpern. **Acquisitions:** address queries to Submissions Editor. Estab. 1970. Publishes hardcover and trade paperback originals and reprints. **Publishes 60 titles/year. Receives 3,000 queries/year. Pays royalty. Offers advance.** Publishes book 1 year after acceptance of ms. Book catalog and ms guidelines free.

    O⌐ "The Ecco Press publishes finely crafted books of high literary merit, establishing a reputation as one of the most important literary publishers worldwide."

Nonfiction: Biography/autobiography, cookbook. Subjects include cooking/foods, literature, sports, translations. Query with SASE. All unsolicited mss and book proposals will be returned unread.

Fiction: Literary, short story collections. Query with SASE.

Recent Title(s): *Blonde*, by Joyce Carol Oates; *Swarm*, by Jorie Graham.

ECS LEARNING SYSTEMS, INC., P.O. Box 791437, San Antonio TX 78279-1437. (830)438-4262. Fax: (830)438-4263. E-mail: ecslearn@gvtc.com or educyberstor@gvtc.com. Website: www.educyberstore.com. **Acquisitions:** Lori Mammen, editor (educational material). Estab. 1982. **Publishes 15-25 titles/year. Receives 120 queries and 50 mss/year. 25% of books from first-time authors; 100% from unagented writers. Pays 10% royalty on wholesale price. No advance.** Publishes book 18 months after acceptance of ms. Responds in 2 months to queries, 4 months to proposals and mss. Book catalog and ms guidelines free.

    O⌐ ECS Learning Systems publishes practical educational material for teachers, parents and students including fun, motivating ideas to make children want to learn. Currently emphasizing reading and math learning activities. No fiction.

Nonfiction: Educational resource books for teachers, parents, students. Query with SASE. Reviews artwork/photos as part of ms package. Send photocopies.

Recent Title(s): *Wake-Up Brains* series, by Michelle Ball and Barbara Morris.

Tips: "Our audience breaks down into three groups—busy teachers looking for great, ready-to-use teaching ideas; supportive parents looking for ways to enhance their children's education; and discerning kids looking for learning activities/challenges outside the classroom. Submit practical, motivating material for learning. We are *not* interested in dry, theoretical material."

[N] [■] **EDICIONES NUEVO ESPACIO**, 28 Park Lane, Fair Haven NJ 07704. (732)933-0692. Fax: (732)933-1075. E-mail: ednuevoespacio@aol.com or editores@editorial-ene.com. Website: http://editorial-ene.com. **Acquisitions:** Gustavo Gac-Artigas, senior editor (fiction); Maria C. Cintron, editor (fiction and academia). Publishes trade paperback originals and reprints. **Publishes 100 titles/year. Receives 1,000 queries and 500 mss/year. 30% of books from first-time authors; 100% from unagented writers. Pays 10-15% royalty; on CD Books pays 10-18% royalty.** No advance. Accepts simultaneous submissions. Does not return submissions Responds in 2 weeks to queries, 1 month to proposals, 2 months to mss. Book catalog and ms guidelines on website.

    O⌐ "We publish book length (108-700 pages) critical studies on subjects related to Spanish, Spanish-American and USA Latino/a literature, and proceedings of conferences on Spanish and Spanish-American Literature."

Imprints: Gutenberg (traditional books), Platinum (CD books), Academia (scholarly studies).

Nonfiction: Reference, scholar and proceedings of literary conferences. Subjects include language/literature, memoirs, multicultural, translation, women's issues/studies. Query by e-mail to ednuevoespacio@aol.com or submit completed ms including the names of 3 experts in the field to editores@editorial-ene.com.

Fiction: Feminist, historical, literary, multicultural, mystery, plays, poetry, poetry in translation, romance, short story collections, suspense, translation, young adult. Submit an e-mail query, and later, the ms by e-mail in Word or rich-text format.

Poetry: "We publish poetry collections with a minimum of 108 pages in Spanish, English or bilingual edition. The quality determines publication. We reprint poetry books." E-mail query to ednuevoespacio@aol.com or submit attached complete ms to editores@editorial-ene.com.

Recent Title(s): *The Ricardo Sánchez Reader: Critical Essays and Anthology*, edited by Dr. Arnoldo Carlos Vento (Academia, CD book); *Prepucio Carmesi*, by Pedro Granados (Perú, novel); and *Ropero de un lacónico*, by Luis Tomás Martínez (Dominican Republic, poetry).

Tips: "Be sure that your manuscript is ready to be published, that the minimum length of the book is 108 pages, that you own the rights, and that you send it to the appropriate imprint."

THE EDUCATION CENTER, INC., 3511 W. Market St., Suite 200, Greensboro NC 27403. Fax: (336)547-1590. Estab. 1973. **Publishes 100 titles/year. Receives 300 queries and 100 mss/year. Under 5% of books from first-time authors; 100% from unagented writers. Purchases ms with one-time payment. "Payment amount negotiated when contract signed."** Publishes book 1-2 years after acceptance of ms. Responds in 6 months to proposals.

    ○━ The Education Center publishes supplementary resource books for elementary teachers: preschool/grade 6. Currently emphasizing preschool books in a series.

Nonfiction: Teacher resource/supplementary materials. Subjects include education P/K-6, language/literature. Submit outline and 1 sample chapter.

Recent Title(s): *Busy Kids™ for Preschool-Kindergarten*, an 8-book series; *The Mailbox® Math Series*, an 8-book series for grades 4 and 5.

Tips: "We place a strong emphasis on materials that teach the basic language arts and math skills. We are also seeking materials for teaching science and literature-based activities. Technical, complex or comprehensive manuscripts (such as textbooks and theory/practice articles) are not accepted."

EDUCATOR'S INTERNATIONAL PRESS, INC., 18 Colleen Rd., Troy NY 12180. (518)271-9886. **Acquisitions:** Sarah J. Biondello, publisher/acquisitions editor. Estab. 1996. Publishes hardcover and trade paperback originals and reprints. **Publishes 10-12 titles/year. Receives 50 queries and 50 mss/year. 50% of books from first-time authors; 98% from unagented writers. Pays 3-15% royalty on wholesale price.** Publishes book 1 year after acceptance of ms. Accepts simultaneous submissions. Responds in 2 months to queries and proposals, 3 months to mss. Book catalog and ms guidelines free.

    ○━ Educator's International publishes books in all aspects of education, broadly conceived, from pre-kindergarten to postgraduate. "We specialize in texts, professional books, videos and other materials for students, faculty, practitioners and researchers. We also publish a full list of books in the areas of women's studies, and social and behavioral sciences."

Nonfiction: Textbook, supplemental texts, conference proceedings. Subjects include education, gay/lesbian, language/literature, philosophy, psychology, software, women's issues/studies. Submit table of contents, outline, 2-3 chapters, résumé with SASE. Reviews artwork/photos as part of ms package.

Recent Title(s): *Our Sons Were Labeled Behavior Disordered*, by Joy-Ruth Mickelson.

Tips: Audience is professors, students, researchers, individuals, libraries.

EDUCATORS PUBLISHING SERVICE, INC., 31 Smith Place, Cambridge MA 02138-1089. (617)547-6706. Fax: (617)547-3805. Website: www.epsbooks.com. **Acquisitions:** Dorothy Miller, vice president and executive editor. Estab. 1952. **Publishes 26 titles/year. Receives 400 queries and 400 mss/year. 50% of books come from first-time authors; 100% from unagented writers. Pays 5-12% royalty on retail price.** Publishes book 8 months minimum after acceptance of ms. Accepts simultaneous submissions. Responds in 1 month to queries and 3 months to proposals and mss. Book catalog and ms guidelines free on request.

    ○━ EPS is looking for supplementary materials for the regular K-12 classroom. "We are particularly interested in workbook series, but will gladly consider any proposals for high-quality material that is useful to teachers and students." Currently emphasizing math workbooks K-6.

Nonfiction: Workbooks (language arts and math) and some professional books. Language/literature subjects. Query. Reviews artwork/photos as part of ms package. Send photocopies.

Recent Title(s): *Claims to Fame: 12 Short Biographies*, by Carol Einstein; *Handprints: An Early Reading Program*, by Ann Staman.

Tips: Teacher, students (K-adult) audiences.

EDUPRESS, 1140-A Calle Cordillera, San Clemente CA 92673. (949)366-9499. Fax: (949)366-9441. E-mail: edupress @pacbell.net. Website: www.edupressinc.com. **Acquisitions:** Kathy Rogers, production manager. Estab. 1979. Publishes trade paperback originals. **Publishes 40 titles/year. Receives 20 queries and 20 mss/year. 25% of books from first-time authors. Makes outright purchase.** Publishes book 1 year after acceptance of ms. Responds in 2 months to queries, 5 months to mss. Book catalog and ms guidelines free.

O—π Edupress publishes supplemental resources for classroom curriculum. Currently emphasizing more science, math, writing emphasis than in the past.

Nonfiction: Educational resources for pre-school through middle school. Submit proposal package, including ms copy, outline, 1 sample chapter and SASE. Reviews artwork/photos as part of ms package. Send photocopies. "We use inhouse artists but will consider submitted art."

Recent Title(s): *Renaissance Activity Book*, by Linda Milliken.

Tips: Audience is classroom teachers and homeschool parents.

EDUTAINMENT MEDIA, P.O. Box 15274, Portland ME 04112. (207)780-1653. E-mail: scribe68@yahoo.com. Website: www.edutainmentmedia.com. **Acquisitions:** Jason Raschack, publisher (biography, how-to, memoirs); Celeste McMann, acquisitions editor (photography, political books). Publishes hardcover originals and trade paperback originals and reprints. **Publishes 4 titles/year. 50% of books from first-time authors; 50% from unagented writers. Pays 6-8% royalty on retail price. Offers $1,000 advance.** Publishes book 1 year after acceptance of ms. Accepts simultaneous submissions. Responds in 1 month. Book catalog free. Manuscript guidelines for #10 SASE.

O—π Future plans call for submissions on the following specific subject areas: welfare reform, education reform and libertarian political philosophy.

Nonfiction: Biography, how-to, illustrated book, self-help. Subjects include business/economics, history, hobbies, memoirs, photography. Query with SASE. All unsolicited mss returned unopened. Reviews artwork/photos as part of ms package. Send photocopies.

Fiction: Comic books, erotica, gothic, historical, military/war. Submit completed ms.

Recent Title(s): *Comic Book Publishing, A How-to Manual*, by J. Raschack; *Women: A Success Guide for Men; Men: A Success Guide for Women*.

Tips: "Our audience consists of highly educated people that follow all publications on subjects they are interested in."

EERDMANS BOOKS FOR YOUNG READERS, William B. Eerdmans Publishing Co., 255 Jefferson Ave. SE, Grand Rapids MI 49503. (616)459-4591. Fax: (616)459-6540. **Acquisitions:** Judy Zylstra, editor. Publishes picture books and middle reader and young adult fiction and nonfiction. **Publishes 12-15 titles/year. Receives 3,000 submissions/year. Pays 5-7½% royalty on retail price.** Publishes middle reader and YA books 1 year after acceptance. Publishes picture books 2-3 years after acceptance. Accepts simultaneous submissions, if noted. Responds in 6 weeks to queries. Book catalog for large SASE.

O—π "We publish books for children and young adults that deal with spiritual themes—but never in a preachy or heavy-handed way. Some of our books are clearly religious, while others (especially our novels) look at spiritual issues in very subtle ways. We look for books that are honest, wise and hopeful." Currently emphasizing general picture books (also picture book biographies), novels (middle reader and YA). De-emphasizing YA biographies, retellings of Bible stories.

Nonfiction and Fiction: Children's books. Picture books, middle reader, young adult fiction and nonfiction. Submit complete mss for picture books and novels or biographies under 200 pages with SASE. For longer books, send query letter and 3 or 4 sample chapters with SASE. "Do not send illustrations unless you are a professional illustrator." Send color photocopies rather than original art.

Recent Title(s): *A Bird or Two: A Story about Henri Matisse*, written and illustrated by Bijou Le Tord; *At Break of Day*, written by Nikki Grimes, illustrated by Paul Morin.

WILLIAM B. EERDMANS PUBLISHING CO., 255 Jefferson Ave. SE, Grand Rapids MI 49503. (616)459-4591. Fax: (616)459-6540. E-mail: sales@eerdmans.com. **Acquisitions:** Jon Pott, editor-in-chief; Charles Van Hof, managing editor (history); Judy Zylstra, children's book editor. Estab. 1911. Publishes hardcover and paperback originals and reprints. **Publishes 120-130 titles/year. Receives 3,000-4,000 submissions/year. 10% of books from first-time authors; 95% from unagented writers. Pays royalty.** Publishes book 1 year after acceptance. Accepts simultaneous submissions if noted. Responds in 6 weeks to queries. Book catalog free.

O—π "Approximately 80% of our adult publications are religious and most of these are academic or semi-academic in character (as opposed to inspirational or celebrity books), though we also publish books on the Christian life. Our nonreligious titles, most of them in regional history or on social issues, aim, similarly, at an educated audience."

Imprint(s): Eerdmans Books for Young Readers (Judy Zylstra, editor).

Nonfiction: Religious, reference, textbooks, monographs, children's books. Subjects include biblical studies, theology, ethics, literature, religious history, philosophy of religion, psychology, sociology, regional history. "We prefer that writers take the time to notice if we have published anything at all in the same category as their manuscript before sending it to us." Accepts nonfiction translations. Query with outline, 2-3 sample chapters and SASE for return of ms. Reviews artwork/photos.

Recent Title(s): *The Story of Ruth*, by Joan D. Chittister and John August Swanson; *Abraham Lincoln: Redeemer President*, by Allen C. Guelzo.

ELDER BOOKS, P.O. Box 490, Forest Knolls CA 94933. (415)488-9002. E-mail: info@elderbooks.com. Website: www.elderbooks.com. **Acquisitions:** Carmel Sheridan, director. Estab. 1987. Publishes trade paperback originals. **Pub-**

lishes 6-10 titles/year. **Receives 200 queries and 50 mss/year. 50% of books from first-time authors; 50% from unagented writers. Pays 7% royalty on retail price. No advance.** Publishes book 9 months after acceptance of ms. Responds in 3 months to queries. Book catalog free.

    ○━ Elder Books is dedicated to publishing practical, hands-on guidebooks for family and professional caregivers of persons with Alzheimer's.

Nonfiction: Gift book, how-to, self-help. Subjects include parenting, education, health/medicine, money/finance, psychology, senior issues, Alzheimer's disease, women's issues/studies. Submit outline, 2 sample chapters. Reviews artwork/photos as part of ms package. Send photocopies.

Recent Title(s): *Coping With Caring: Daily Reflections for Alzheimer's Caregivers*, by Lyn Roche.

Tips: "Our books are written in a style that is user-friendly and nontechnical, presenting key information on caregiver concerns including: how to keep the person engaged through meaningful activities, prevent caregiver burnout, cope with wandering and organize a search in the event the person disappears, deal with difficult behaviors."

■ ELECTRIC WORKS PUBLISHING, 605 Ave. C.E., Bismarck ND 58501. (701)255-0356. E-mail: editors@electricpublishing.com. Website: www.electricpublishing.com. **Acquisitions:** James R. Bohe, editor-in-chief. Publishes digital books. **Publishes 50 titles/year. Receives 30 queries and 250 mss/year. 60% of books from first-time authors; 99% from unagented writers. Pays 36-40% royalty on wholesale price. No advance.** Publishes book 3 months after acceptance of ms. Accepts simultaneous submissions. Responds in 2 months. Book catalog and ms guidelines on website.

    ○━ Digital publisher offering a wide range of subjects.

Nonfiction: Biography, children's/juvenile, cookbook, how-to, humor, illustrated book, multimedia (CD-ROM, disk), reference, self-help, technical. Subjects include agriculture/horticulture, Americana, animals, anthropology/archaeology, art/architecture, business/economics, child guidance/parenting, computers/electronics, cooking/foods/nutrition, creative nonfiction, education, ethnic, gardening, government/politics, health/medicine, history, hobbies, language/literature, memoirs, military/war, money/finance, multicultural, music/dance, nature/environment, philosophy, photography, psychology, recreation, regional, religion, science, sociology, software, spirituality, sports, translation, travel, women's issues/women's studies. Submit entire ms in digital format. Reviews artwork/photos as part of ms package. Send files in JPEG or GIF format.

Fiction: Adventure, ethnic, experimental, fantasy, gothic, historical, horror, humor, juvenile, literary, mainstream/contemporary, military/war, multicultural, multimedia, mystery, occult, plays, poetry, poetry in translation, regional, religious, romance, science fiction, short story collections, spiritual, sports, suspense, translation, western, young adult. Submit complete ms electronically.

Poetry: Submit complete ms.

Recent Title(s): *The Captive Fiction Writer*, by Jean M. Goldstrom; *Formidable Enemy*, by Terry Bramlett.

Ⓝ ELEPHANT BOOKS, Creativity, Inc., 65 Macedonia Rd., Alexander NC 28701. (828)252-9515. Fax: (828)255-8719. E-mail: sales@abooks.com. Website: www.elephant.alexander.nc.us. **Acquisitions:** Pat Roberts, acquisitions editor. Publishes trade paperback originals and reprints. **Publishes 8 titles/year. Receives 100 queries and 50 mss/year. 90% of books from first-time authors; 80% from unagented writers. Pays 12-15% royalty on wholesale price. Seldom offers advance.** Publishes book 18 months after acceptance of ms. Book catalog and manuscript guidelines for 9×12 SASE with $1.01 postage.

Imprint(s): Blue/Gray Books (contact Ralph Roberts, Civil War history).

Nonfiction: Cookbooks, history subjects. Interested in Civil War and innovative cookbooks. Query or submit outline with 3 sample chapters and proposal package, including potential marketing plans with SASE. Reviews artwork/photos as part of ms package. Send photocopies.

Recent Title(s): *Women of the War*, by Frank Moore.

EMC/PARADIGM PUBLISHING INC., EMC Corporation, 875 Montreal Way, St. Paul MN 55102. (651)290-2800. Fax: (651)290-2828. E-mail: educate@emcp.com. Website: www.emcp.com. **Acquisitions:** George Provol, publisher; Wesley J. Lawton, executive editor (information technology/allied health). Estab. 1980. **Publishes 50 titles/year. Receives 60 queries and 35 mss/year. 20% of books from first-time authors; 100% from unagented writers. Pays 6-10% royalty on net.** Publishes book 1 year after acceptance of ms. Accepts simultaneous submissions. Responds in 2 months to proposals. Book catalog for 8×12 SAE with 4 first-class stamps. Manuscript guidelines free.

    ○━ EMC/Paradigm focuses on textbooks for business and office, computer information systems, and allied health education marketed to proprietary business schools and community colleges.

Nonfiction: Textbook, multimedia. Subjects include business and office, communications, computers, allied health, accounting, keyboarding, staff development. Submit outline and 2 sample chapters.

Recent Title(s): *Microsoft Word 2000 Signature Series*, by Nita Rutkosky.

Tips: "We are looking more seriously at materials for skills-based learning. Let us know what ideas you have."

EMIS, INC., P.O. Box 820062, Dallas TX 75382-0062. Website: www.emispub.com. President: Lynda Blake. Publishes trade paperback originals. **Publishes 4 titles/year. Pays 12% royalty on retail price.** Responds in 3 months. Book catalog and manuscript guidelines free.

    ○━ "Our books are published as a medical text designed for physicians to fit in the lab coat pocket as a quick means of locating information." Currently emphasizing infectious diseases. De-emphasizing medical program management.

Nonfiction: Reference. Subjects include women's health/medicine and psychology. Submit 3 sample chapters with SASE.
Recent title(s): *Managing Contraceptive Pill Patients.*
Tips: Audience is medical professionals and medical product manufacturers and distributors.

EMPIRE PUBLISHING SERVICE, P.O. Box 1344, Studio City CA 91614-0344. (818)789-4980. **Acquisitions:** Joseph Witt. Publishes hardcover reprints and trade paperback originals and reprints. **Publishes 40 titles/year; imprint publishes 15 titles/year. Receives 500 queries and 85 mss/year. 50% of books from first-time authors; 95% from unagented writers. Pays 6-10% royalty on retail price. Offers variable advance.** Publishes book up to 2 years after acceptance of ms. Responds in 1 month to queries, 2 months to proposals, up to 1 year to mss. Book catalog for SAE and 5 first-class stamps. Manuscript guidelines $1 with #10 SASE.
○→ "Submit only Sherlock Holmes, performing arts and health."
Imprints: Gaslight Publications, Gaslight Books, Empire Publications.
Nonfiction: How-to, humor, reference, technical, textbook. Subjects include health/medicine, music/dance, Sherlock Holmes. Query with SASE. Reviews artwork/photos as part of ms package. Send photocopies.
Fiction: Sherlock Holmes. Query with SASE.
Recent Title(s): *Sherlock Holmes and the Curse of the Mummy's Tomb*, by J. Harries (mystery, music and suspense); *Sherlock Holmes in the Deerstalker*, by T. Mustoo/D. Flack (musical, mystery).

ENCOUNTER BOOKS, 116 New Montgomery St., Suite 206, San Francisco CA 94105-3640. (415)538-1460. Fax: (415)538-1461. Website: www.encounterbooks.com. **Acquisitions:** Peter Collier, publisher. Hardcover originals and trade paperback reprints. **Publishes 12-20 titles/year. Receives 200 queries and 100 mss/year. 40% of books from first-time authors; 60% from unagented writers. Pays 7-10% royalty on retail price. Offers $2,000-25,000 advance.** Publishes book 22 months after acceptance of ms. Accepts simultaneous submissions. Responds in 2 months to queries, 4 months to proposals and mss. Book catalog and ms guidelines free or on website.
○→ Encounter Books publishes serious nonfiction—books that can alter our society, challenge our morality, stimulate our imaginations. Currently emphasizing history, culture, social criticism and politics.
Nonfiction: Biography, reference. Subjects include anthropology/archaeology, business/economics, child guidance/parenting, creative nonfiction, education, ethnic, government/politics, health/medicine, history, language/literature, memoirs, military/war, money/finance, multicultural, nature/environment, philosophy, psychology, religion, science, sex, sociology, spirituality, women's issues/studies, gender studies. Submit proposal package, including outline and 1 sample chapter.
Recent Titles: *Creating Equal: My Fight Against Race Preferences*, by Ward Connerly.

ENSLOW PUBLISHERS INC., 40 Industrial Rd., Box 398, Berkeley Heights NJ 07922. (973)771-9400. Website: www.enslow.com. **Acquisitions:** Brian D. Enslow, editor. Estab. 1977. Publishes hardcover originals. **Publishes 150 titles/year. 10% require freelance illustration. Pays royalty on net price. Offers advance.** Publishes book 1 year after acceptance of ms. Responds in 1 month. *Writer's Market* recommends allowing 2 months for reply. Writer's guidelines for SASE.
○→ Enslow publishes hardcover nonfiction books for young adults and school-age children, mostly as part of a series.
Nonfiction: Interested in new ideas for series of books for young people. Some areas of interest are social studies, science, health, biography, history, reference topics, and recreations such as sports. No fiction, fictionalized history or dialog.
Recent Title(s): *Advertising*, by Nancy Day; *Holocaust Rescuers*, by David Lyman.
Tips: "We love to receive résumés from experienced writers with good research skills who can think like young people."

EPICENTER PRESS, INC., P.O. Box 82368, Kenmore WA 98028. (425)485-6822. Fax: (425)481-8253. E-mail: epipress@aol.com. Website: www.epicenterpress.com. **Acquisitions:** Kent Sturgis, publisher. Estab. 1987. Publishes hardcover and trade paperback originals. **Publishes 10 titles/year. Receives 200 queries and 100 mss/year. 75% of books from first-time authors; 90% from unagented writers. Advance negotiable.** Publishes book 1-2 years after acceptance of ms. Responds in 2 months to queries. Book catalog and ms guidelines on website or by request.
○→ "We are a regional press founded in Alaska whose interests include but are not limited to the arts, history, environment, and diverse cultures and lifestyles of the North Pacific and high latitudes."
Nonfiction: Biography, coffee table book, gift books, humor. Subjects include animals, art/architecture, ethnic, history, nature/environment, photography, recreation, regional, travel, women's issues/studies. "Our focus is the Pacific Northwest and Alaska. We do not encourage nonfiction titles from outside Alaska and the Pacific Northwest, nor travel from beyond Alaska, Washington, Oregon and California." Submit outline and 3 sample chapters. Reviews artwork/photos as part of ms package. Send photocopies.
Recent Title(s): *Good Time Girls of the Alaska-Yukon Gold Rush*, by Lael Morgan.

PAUL S. ERIKSSON, PUBLISHER, P.O. Box 125, Forest Dale VT 05745-4210. (802)247-4210. Fax: (802)247-4256. **Acquisitions:** Paul S. Eriksson, publisher/editor; Peggy Eriksson, associate publisher/co-editor. Estab. 1960. Publishes hardcover and paperback trade originals, paperback trade reprints. **Publishes 5 titles/year. Receives 1,500**

submissions/year. **25% of books from first-time authors; 95% from unagented writers. Pays 10-15% royalty on retail price. Offers advance if necessary.** Publishes book 6 months after acceptance of ms. *Writer's Market* recommends allowing 1 month for reply. Catalog for #10 SASE.

O— "We look for intelligence, excitement and saleability."

Nonfiction: Americana, birds (ornithology), art, biography, business/economics, cooking/foods/nutrition, health, history, hobbies, how-to, humor, nature, politics, psychology, recreation, self-help, sociology, sports, travel. Query with SASE. No simultaneous submissions.

Fiction: Serious, literary. Query with SASE.

Recent Title(s): *The Headmaster's Wife*, by Richard A. Hawley (novel); *Writing Dramatic Nonfiction*, by William Noble.

ETC PUBLICATIONS, 700 E. Vereda Sur, Palm Springs CA 92262-4816. (760)325-5352. Fax: (760)325-8841. **Acquisitions:** Dr. Richard W. Hostrop, publisher (education and social sciences); Lee Ona S. Hostrop, editorial director (history and works suitable below the college level). Estab. 1972. Publishes hardcover and paperback originals. **Publishes 6-12 titles/year. Receives 100 submissions/year. 75% of books from first-time authors; 90% from unagented writers. Offers 5-15% royalty, based on wholesale and retail price.** Publishes book 9 months after acceptance. *Writer's Market* recommends allowing 2 months for reply.

O— ETC publishes works that "further learning as opposed to entertainment."

Nonfiction: Educational management, gifted education, futuristics, textbooks. Accepts nonfiction translations in above areas. Submit complete ms with SASE. *Writer's Market* recommends query first with SASE. Reviews artwork/photos as part of ms package.

Recent Title(s): *The Internet for Educators and Homeschoolers*, by Steve Jones, Ph.D.

Tips: "Special consideration is given to those authors who are capable and willing to submit their completed work in camera-ready, typeset form. We are particularly interested in works suitable for *both* the Christian school market and homeschoolers; e.g., state history texts below the high school level with a Christian-oriented slant."

EVAN-MOOR EDUCATIONAL PUBLISHERS, 18 Lower Ragsdale Dr., Monterey CA 93940-5746. (831)649-5901. Fax: (831)649-6256. E-mail: editorial@evan-moor.com. Website: www.evan-moor.com. **Acquisitions:** Marilyn Evans, senior editor. Estab. 1979. Publishes teaching materials. **Publishes 50-60 titles/year. Receives 50 queries and 100 mss/year. 1% of books from first-time authors; 100% from unagented writers. Makes outright purchase minimum of $1,000.** Publishes book 1 year after acceptance of ms. Accepts simultaneous submissions. Responds in 3 months. Book catalog and ms guidelines free or on website.

O— "Our books are teaching ideas, lesson plans, and blackline reproducibles for grades PreK-6 in all curriculum areas except music and bilingual." Currently emphasizing writing/language arts. De-emphasizing thematic materials.

Nonfiction: Teaching materials, grade PreK-6. Submit proposal package, including outline and 3 sample chapters.

Recent Titles: *Daily Math Practice*, one book each grades 1-6 (nonfiction); *More Read & Understand, Stories and Activities*, one book each grades 1-3 (fiction); *Writing Poetry with Children*, by Jo Ellen Moore (poetry).

Tips: "Writers should know how classroom/educational materials differ from trade publications. They should request catalogs and submissions guidelines before sending queries or manuscripts."

M. EVANS AND CO., INC., 216 E. 49th St., New York NY 10017-1502. Fax: (212)688-2810. E-mail: mevans@sprynet.com. **Acquisitions:** George C. deKay, editor-in-chief (general trade); P.J. Dempsey, senior editor (general nonfiction). Estab. 1960. Publishes hardcover and trade paperback originals. Pays negotiable royalty. **Publishes 30-40 titles/year. 5% of books from unagented writers. Publishes book 8 months after acceptance.** Responds in 2 months. Book catalog for 9×12 SAE with 3 first-class stamps.

O— Evans has a strong line of health and self-help books but is interested in publishing quality titles on a wide variety of subject matters. "We publish a general trade list of adult nonfiction, cookbooks and semi-reference works. The emphasis is on selectivity, publishing commercial works with quality." Currently emphasizing health, relationships, nutrition.

Nonfiction: "Our most successful nonfiction titles have been related to health and the behavioral sciences. No limitation on subject." Query. *No unsolicited mss.*

Fiction: "Our very small general fiction list represents an attempt to combine quality with commercial potential. We publish no more than one novel per season." Query. *No unsolicited mss.*

Recent Title(s): *Dr. Atkins' New Carbohydrate Gram Counter* (health); *New Encyclopedia of Vitamins and Minerals*.

Tips: "A writer should clearly indicate what his book is all about, frequently the task the writer performs least well. His credentials, although important, mean less than his ability to convince this company that he understands his subject and that he has the ability to communicate a message worth hearing. Writers should review our book catalog before making submissions."

EXECUTIVE EXCELLENCE PUBLISHING, 1344 E. 1120 S., Provo UT 84606. (800)304-9782. Fax: (801)377-5960. E-mail: calvinh@eep.com. Website: www.eep.com. **Acquisitions:** Calvin W. Harper, manager, book division (business, self-help, leadership). Estab. 1984. Publishes hardcover and trade paperback originals and trade paperback reprints. **Publishes 16-20 titles/year. Receives 300 queries and 150 mss/year. 35% of books from first-time authors;**

95% from unagented writers. Pays 15% on cash received and 50% of subsidiary rights proceeds. No advance. Publishes book 6-9 months after acceptance of ms. Accepts simultaneous submissions. Responds in 1 month to queries and proposals, 3 months to mss. Book catalog free on request or on website.

O➤ Executive Excellence publishes business and self-help titles. "We help you—the busy person, executive or entrepreneur—to find a wiser, better way to live your life and lead your organization." Currently emphasizing business innovations for general management and leadership (from the personal perspective). De-emphasizing technical or scholarly textbooks on operational processes and financial management or workbooks.

Nonfiction: Self-help. Subjects include business/leadership/management, entrepreneurship, career, small business, motivational. Submit proposal package, including outline, 1-2 sample chapters and author bio, company information.

Recent Title(s): *Attracting Customer Love*, by Chip Bell; *Pioneering Organizations*, by Larry Davis.

Tips: "Executive Excellence Publishing is an established publishing house with a strong niche in the marketplace. Our magazines, *Executive Excellence* and *Personal Excellence*, are distributed monthly in twelve countries across the world and give us and our authors massive market exposure. Our authors are on the cutting edge in their fields of leadership, self-help and business and organizational development. We usually publish only the biggest names in the field, but we are always looking for strong new talent with something to say, and a burning desire to say it."

FACTS ON FILE, INC., 11 Penn Plaza, 15th Floor, New York NY 10001. (212)967-8800. Fax: (212)967-9196. E-mail: llikoff@factsonfile.com. Website: www.factsonfile.com. **Acquisitions:** Laurie Likoff, editorial director (science, music, history); Frank Darmstadt (science, nature, multi-volume reference); Nicole Bowen, senior editor (American history, women's studies, young adult reference); James Chambers, trade editor (health, pop culture, sports); Gary Goldstein, trade. Estab. 1941. Publishes hardcover originals and reprints. **Publishes 135 titles/year. Receives approximately 2,000 submissions/year. 25% of books from unagented writers. Pays 10-15% royalty on retail price. Offers $10,000 average advance.** Accepts simultaneous submissions. Responds in 2 months to queries. Book catalog free.

O➤ Facts on File produces high-quality reference materials on a broad range of subjects for the school library market and the general nonfiction trade.

Imprint(s): Checkmark Books.

Nonfiction: Reference. Informational books on careers, education, health, history, entertainment, natural history, philosophy, psychology, recreation, religion, language, sports, multicultural studies, science, popular culture. "We publish serious, informational books for a targeted audience. All our books must have strong library interest, but we also distribute books effectively to the book trade. Our library books fit the junior and senior high school curriculum." No computer books, technical books, cookbooks, biographies (except YA), pop psychology, humor, fiction or poetry. Query or submit outline and sample chapter with SASE. No submissions returned without SASE.

Tips: "Our audience is school and public libraries for our more reference-oriented books and libraries, schools and bookstores for our less reference-oriented informational titles."

FAIRLEIGH DICKINSON UNIVERSITY PRESS, 285 Madison Ave., Madison NJ 07940. (973)443-8564. Fax: (973)443-8364. E-mail: fdupress@fdu.edu. **Acquisitions:** Harry Keyishian, director. Estab. 1967. Publishes hardcover originals. **Publishes 45 titles/year. Receives 300 submissions/year. 33% of books from first-time authors; 95% from unagented writers.** "Contract is arranged through Associated University Presses of Cranbury, New Jersey. We are a *selection* committee only." Nonauthor subsidy publishes 2% of books. Publishes book 1 year after acceptance of ms. Responds in 2 weeks to queries. *Writer's Market* recommends allowing 2 months for reply.

O➤ Fairleigh Dickinson publishes books for the academic market.

Nonfiction: Reference, scholarly books. Subjects include art, business/economics, Civil War, film, history, Jewish studies, literary criticism, music, philosophy, politics, psychology, sociology, women's studies. Looking for scholarly books in all fields; no nonscholarly books. Query with outline and sample chapters. Reviews artwork/photos as part of ms package.

Recent Title(s): *Between Old Worlds and New: Occasional Writings on Music*, by Wilfrid Mellers.

Tips: "Research must be up to date. Poor reviews result when authors' bibliographies and notes don't reflect current research. We follow *Chicago Manual of Style* (14th edition) style in scholarly citations. We will consider collections of unpublished conference papers or essay collections, if they relate to a strong central theme and have scholarly merit."

FAIRVIEW PRESS, 2450 Riverside Ave. S., Minneapolis MN 55454. (800)544-8207. Fax: (612)672-4980. Website: www.press.fairview.org. **Acquisitions:** Lane Stiles, director; Stephanie Billecke, editor. Estab. 1988. Publishes hardcover and trade paperback originals and reprints. **Publishes 8-12 titles/year. Receives 3,000 queries and 500 mss/year. 40% of books from first-time authors; 65% from unagented writers. Advance and royalties negotiable.** Publishes book 1 year after acceptance of ms. Accepts simultaneous submissions. Responds in 6 months to proposals. Book catalog and ms guidelines free.

O➤ Fairview Press currently publishes books and related materials emphasizing health, medicine, seniors/aging and grief.

Nonfiction: Reference, self-help. Subjects include health, medicine, aging, grief and bereavement, and patient education. "Manuscripts that are essentially one person's story are rarely saleable." Submit proposal package, including outline, 2 sample chapters, author information, marketing ideas and SASE. Send photocopies.

Recent Title(s): *Living Well with Heart Disease*, by Fairview Health Services.

Tips: Audience is general reader, especially families. "Tell us what void your book fills in the market; give us an angle. Tell us who will buy your book. We have moved away from recovery books and have focused on health and medical issues."

FALCON PUBLISHING, INC., Landmark Communications, Box 1718, Helena MT 59624. (406)442-6597. Fax: (406)442-0384. E-mail: falcon@falcon.com. Website: www.falcon.com. **Acquisitions:** Glenn Law, editorial director; Charlene Patterson, editorial assistant (Two Dot Books: regional and western history, western Americana). Estab. 1978. Publishes hardcover and trade paperback originals. **Publishes 80 titles/year. Receives 350 queries and 30 mss/year. 20% of books from first-time authors; 95% from unagented writers. Pays royalty on net sales.** Publishes book 1-2 years after acceptance of ms. Accepts simultaneous submissions. Responds in 2 months to queries. Book catalog for $2.50.

O━ Falcon Press is primarily interested in ideas for recreational guidebooks and books on regional outdoor subjects. "Falcon is committed to the concept of 'green publishing': promoting the responsible and safe use of the natural environment, as well as its preservation. We consider ideas for recreational guidebooks and books on regional outdoor subjects." Currently emphasizing outdoor recreation, regional themes, regional history.

Imprint(s): Chockstone, Falcon Guide, Insiders', Sky House, ThreeForks (cookbooks), **Two Dot**.
Nonfiction: Illustrated book, guide books. Subjects include nature/environment, recreation, travel. Query with SASE. "We can only respond to queries submitted on the topics listed above. No fiction, no poetry." Reviews artwork/photos as part of the ms package. Send transparencies.
Recent Title(s): *Allen and Mike's Really Cool Telemark Tips*, by Allen O'Bannon and Mike Clelland.
Tips: "Authors of guidebooks must hike the hikes and ride the trails."

FARRAR, STRAUS & GIROUX BOOKS FOR YOUNG READERS, Farrar Straus Giroux, Inc., 19 Union Square West, New York NY 10003. (212)741-6900. Fax: (212)633-2427. **Acquisitions:** Margaret Ferguson, editorial director. Estab. 1946. Publishes hardcover and trade paperback originals. **Publishes 50 titles/year. Receives 6,000 queries and mss/year. 10% of books from first-time authors; 50% from unagented writers. Pays 6% royalty on retail price for paperbacks, 10% for hardcovers. Offers $4,000-25,000 advance.** Publishes book 18 months after acceptance of ms. Accepts simultaneous submissions, if informed. Responds in 2 months to queries, 3 months to mss. Book catalog for 9×12 SAE with $1.87 postage. Manuscript guidelines for #10 SASE.

O━ "We publish original and well-written material for all ages."

Imprint(s): Aerial Fiction, Frances Foster Books, Mirasol/Libros Juveniles, R&S Books, Sunburst Paperbacks.
Fiction: Juvenile, picture books, young adult. Query with SASE; considers complete ms. "We still look at unsolicited manuscripts, but for novels we prefer synopsis and sample chapters. Always enclose SASE for any materials author wishes returned. Query status of submissions in writing—no calls, please."
Recent Title(s): *Holes*, by Louis Sachar (Newbery Medal Book, ages 10 and up); *Trolls*, by Polly Horvath; *Francie*, by Karen English; *Snow*, by Uri Shulevitz (Caldecott Honor Book).
Tips: Audience is full age range, preschool to young adult. Specializes in literary fiction.

FARRAR, STRAUS & GIROUX, INC., 19 Union Square West, New York NY 10003. Fax: (212)633-2427. Estab. 1946. Publishes hardcover originals. **Publishes 120 titles/year. Receives 5,000 submissions/year. Pays variable royalty. Offers advance.** Publishes book 18 months after acceptance.

O━ Farrar, Straus & Giroux is one of the most respected publishers of top-notch commercial-literary fiction and specialized nonfiction, as well as cutting-edge poetry.

Imprint(s): Faber & Faber Inc. (UK-originated books), **Farrar, Straus & Giroux Paperbacks, Farrar, Straus & Giroux Books for Young Readers, Hill & Wang, North Point Press**, Sunburst Books.
Nonfiction and Fiction: Query.
Recent Title(s): *Slaves in the Family*, by Edward Ball (nonfiction); *Gain*, by Richard Powers (fiction); *Birthday Letters*, by Ted Hughes (poetry).

FARRAR, STRAUS & GIROUX PAPERBACKS, (formerly Noonday Press), 19 Union Square W., New York NY 10003. (212)741-6900. Fax: (212)633-9385. **Acquisitions:** Elisabeth Dyssegaard, executive editor. Publishes trade paperback originals and reprints. **Publishes 70 titles/year. Receives 1,500-2,000 queries/mss per year. Pays 6% royalty on retail price. Advance varies.** Accepts simultaneous submissions. Responds in 2 months on queries and proposals. Book catalog and ms guidelines free.

O━ Noonday emphasizes literary nonfiction and fiction, as well as fiction and poetry reprints.

Nonfiction: Biography. Subjects include child guidance/parenting, education, language/literature. Query with outline, 2-3 sample chapters, cv, cover letter discribing project and SASE. *No unsolicited mss.*
Fiction: Literary. Mostly reprints of classic authors.
Recent Title(s): *Message from My Father*, by Calvin Trillin (memoir); *Enemies: A Love Story*, by Isaac Bashevis Singer (fiction).

N ☒ FREDERICK FELL PUBLISHERS, INC., 2131 Hollywood Blvd., Hollywood FL 33020. (954)925-5242. Fax: (954)925-5244. E-mail: fellpub@aol.com. Website: www.fellpub.com. **Acquisitions:** Virginia Wells, senior editor. Publishes hardcover and trade paperback originals. **Publishes 25 titles/year. Receives 1,500-2,000 queries and 1,000**

mss/year. **95% of books from first-time authors; 95% from unagented writers. Pays negotiable royalty on retail price. Offers up to $10,000 advance.** Publishes book 1 year after acceptance of ms. Accepts simultaneous submissions. Responds in 1 month to queries, 3 months to proposals and mss. Manuscript guidelines for #10 SASE.

○╼ Independent publisher with titles in 13 genres.

Nonfiction: How-to, reference, self-help. Subjects include business/economics, child guidance/parenting, education, ethnic, health/medicine, hobbies, money/finance, spirituality. Submit proposal package, including outline, 3 sample chapters, author bio, publicity ideas, market analysis. Reviews artwork/photos as part of ms package. Send photocopies.

Recent Title(s): *How to Prevent, Control & Cure Diabetes*, by Seymour Alterman, MD (health/medicine); *The Leader Within You*, by Robert Danzic (business/inspiration).

Tips: "We are most interested in well-written, timely nonfiction with strong sales potential. We will not consider topics that appeal to a small, select audience. Learn markets and be prepared to help with sales and promotion. Show us how your book is unique or better than the competition."

FERGUSON PUBLISHING COMPANY, 200 W. Jackson, 7th Floor, Chicago IL 60606. Website: www.fergpubco.com. **Acquisitions:** Andrew Morkes, managing editor, career publications. Estab. 1940. Publishes hardcover originals. **Publishes 30 titles/year. Responds in 6 months to queries. Pays by project.**

○╼ "We are primarily a career education publisher that publishes for schools and libraries."

Nonfiction: Reference. "We publish work specifically for the elementary/junior high/high school/college library reference market. Works are generally encyclopedic in nature. Our current focus is career encyclopedias. We consider manuscripts that cross over into the trade market. No mass market, poetry, scholarly, or juvenile books, please." Query or submit outline and 1 sample chapter.

Recent Title(s): *Encyclopedia of Careers and Vocational Guidance, 11th Edition*; *Great Careers in Two Years: The Associate Degree Option*.

Tips: "We like writers who know the market—former or current librarians or teachers or guidance counselors."

FILTER PRESS, P.O. Box 95, Palmer Lake CO 80133-0095. (719)481-2420. Fax: (719)481-2420. E-mail: filter.press@prodigy.net. **Acquisitions:** Doris Baker, president. Estab. 1956. Publishes trade paperback originals and reprints. **Publishes 4-6 titles/year. Pays 10-12% royalty on wholesale price.** Publishes ms an average of 8 months after acceptance.

○╼ Filter Press specializes in nonfiction of the West. De-emphasizing cooking, foods and nutrition.

Nonfiction: Subjects include Americana, anthropology/archaeology, cooking/foods/nutrition, crafts and crafts people of the Southwest, memoirs, women writers of the West. "We're interested in the history and natural history of the West." Query with outline and SASE. Reviews artwork/photos as part of ms package.

Recent Title(s): *Viva el Amor, A Latino Wedding Planner*, by Dr. Edna Bautista (nonfiction); *Fittle Fex's Secret*, by Mary Peace Finley (children's fiction).

FIRE ENGINEERING BOOKS & VIDEOS, PennWell Publishing Co., Park 80 W., Plaza 2, Saddle Brook NJ 07663. (201)845-0800. Fax: (201)845-6275. E-mail: 74677.1505@compuserve.com. **Acquisitions:** William Manning, editor; Diane Feldman, managing editor; James Bacon, book editor. Publishes hardcover and softcover originals. **Publishes 10 titles/year. Receives 24 queries/year. 75% of books from first-time authors; 100% from unagented writers. Pays 15% royalty on net sales.** Publishes book 1 year after acceptance of ms. No simultaneous submissions. Responds in 3 months to proposals. Book catalog free.

○╼ Fire Engineering publishes textbooks relevant to firefighting and training. Training firefighters and other emergency responders. Currently emphasizing reserve training, preparedness for terrorist threats, natural disasters, first response to fires and emergencies.

Nonfiction: Reference, technical, textbook. Subjects include firefighter training, public safety. Submit outline and 2 sample chapters, and biographical sketch.

Recent Title(s): *Truck Company Operations*, by John W. Mittendorf.

Tips: "No human interest stories, technical training only."

FIREBRAND BOOKS, LPC Group, 141 The Commons, Ithaca NY 14850. (607)272-0000. Website: www.firebrandbooks.com. **Acquisitions:** Nancy K. Bereano, publisher. Estab. 1985. Publishes hardcover and trade paperback originals. **Publishes 6-8 titles/year. Receives 400-500 submissions/year. 50% of books from first-time authors; 90% from unagented writers. Pays 7-9% royalty on retail price, or makes outright purchase.** Publishes book 18 months after acceptance. Accepts simultaneous submissions, if so noted. Responds in 1 month to queries. *Writer's Market* recommends allowing 2 months for reply. Book catalog free.

○╼ "Our diverse audience includes feminists, lesbians, ethnic audiences, and other progressive people."

Nonfiction: Personal narratives, essays. Subjects include feminism, lesbianism. Submit complete ms.

Fiction: Considers all types of feminist and lesbian fiction.

● Firebrand was recently acquired by LPC Group, which plans to continue publishing under the Firebrand imprint.

FISHER BOOKS, LLC, Perseus Book Group 5225 W. Massingale Rd., Tucson AZ 85743. (520)744-6110. Fax: (520)744-0944. Website: www.fisherbooks.com. **Acquisitions:** Sarah Trotta, managing editor. Estab. 1987. Publishes trade paperback originals and reprints. **Publishes 23 titles/year. 25% of books from first-time authors; 75% from unagented writers. Pays 10-15% royalty on wholesale price.** Accepts simultaneous submissions. Book catalog for 8½×11 SAE with 3 first-class stamps.

O→ Fisher Books publishes how-to and self-help titles focusing on pregnancy and childcare. Currently emphasizing pregnancy, childcare, parenting. De-emphasizing business.

Nonfiction: Subjects include automotive, business, cooking/foods/nutrition, pregnancy/childcare, regional gardening, family health, self-help. Submit outline and sample chapter with SASE.

Recent Title(s): *Your Pregnancy: Every Woman's Guide.*

• Fisher Books was recently acquired by Perseus Book Group.

FLORICANTO PRESS, Inter American Corp., 650 Castro St., Suite 120-331, Mountain View CA 94041. (415)552-1879. Fax: (415)793-2662. E-mail: acquisitions@floricantopress.com. Website: www.floricantopress.com. Publishes hardcover and trade paperback originals and reprints. **Publishes 6 titles/year. Receives 200 queries/year. 60% of books from first-time authors; 5% from unagented writers. Pays 5% royalty on wholesale price. Offers $500-1,500 advance.** Rejected mss destroyed. Responds in 3 months to queries, 7 months to mss. Book catalog for #10 SASE.

O→ Floricanto Press is "dedicated to promoting Latino thought and culture." Currently emphasizing biographies, women's studies, history. De-emphasizing poetry.

Nonfiction: Biography, cookbook, reference. Subjects include anthropology/archaeology, ethnic (Hispanic), health/medicine, history, language/literature, psychology, women's issues/studies. "We are looking primarily for nonfiction popular (but serious) titles that appeal the general public on Hispanic subjects." Submit outline and sample chapter(s).

Fiction: Adventure, erotica, ethnic (Hispanic), literary, occult, romance, short story collections. "On fiction we prefer contemporary works and themes." Submit synopsis and 1 sample chapter.

Recent Title(s): *Far from My Mother's Home* (short stories); *Love & Riot in Los Angeles* (nonfiction).

Tips: Audience is general public interested in Hispanic culture. "Submit material as described, on DOS disk, graphic art for cover. We need authors that are willing to promote their work heavily."

[N] FLORIDA ACADEMIC PRESS, P.O. Box 540, Gainesville FL 32602. (352)332-5104. Fax: (352)331-6003. E-mail: FAPress@worldnet.att.net. **Acquisitions:** Max Vargas, CEO (nonfiction/self-help); Sam Decalo, managing editor (academic); Florence Dusek, assistant editor (fiction). Publishes hardcover and trade paperback originals. **Publishes 4 titles/year. Receives 60 queries and 20 mss/year. 20% of books from first-time authors; 100% from unagented writers. Pays 5-8% royalty on retail price.** Publishes book 3 months after acceptance of ms. Responds in 3 months to mss. Book catalog and ms guidelines free.

O→ Florida Academic Press publishes self-help, nonfiction and fiction books.

Nonfiction: How-to, reference, self-help. Subjects include government/politics, history, scholarly Third World. Submit completed ms. Reviews artwork/photos as part of ms package. Send photocopies.

Fiction: Literary, regional. Submit completed ms.

Recent Title(s): *Complete Publishers Resource Manual*, by Linda Able (reference); *Civil-Military Relations in Africa*, by Samuel Decalo (history).

Tips: Considers complete mss only. "Manuscripts we decide to publish must be submitted in camera-ready form."

[N] FLYING BOOKS, Sky Media, LLC, P.O. Box 2245, Inver Grove Hts. MN 55076-8245. (651)453-1875. Fax: (651)453-1895. E-mail: histaviate@earthlink.net. Website: www.aviationhistory.com. **Acquisitions:** G.E. Herrick, publisher (aviation history). Publishes hardcover and trade paperback originals and hardcover and trade paperback reprints. **Publishes 12 titles/year; imprint publishes 2/year. Receives 30 queries and 15 mss/year. 30% of books from first-time authors; 90% from unagented writers. Pays 10% royalty on wholesale price. Responds in 1 month to queries and proposals, 2 months to mss. Book catalog free.**

O→ "Aviation and aviation history are our strong points. Illustrations, photographs and other documentation appeal to our customers. We like to see the story told: how did this aircraft 'fit,' what did it do, how did it impact peoples lives?"

Nonfiction: History. Subjects include military/war, aviation. Reviews artwork/photos as part of ms package. Send photocopies.

Recent Title(s): *Mystery Ship!*, by Edward Phillips (aviation history); *Wings of Stearman*, by Peter Bowers (aviation history).

Tips: "Our buyers are interested in aviation history and aircraft in general. Of particular interest are nonfiction works covering specific aircraft types, manufacturers or military aircraft. Research and accuracy are of paramount importance."

FOCAL PRESS, Butterworth Heinemann, Reed Elsevier (USA) Inc., 225 Wildwood Ave., Woburn MA 01801-2041. Fax: (781)904-2640. E-mail: marie.lee@bhusa.com. Website: www.focalpress.com. **Acquisitions:** Marie Lee, publisher; Terri Jadick, associate editor; Charles McEnerney, associate editor. Estab. US, 1981; UK, 1938. Publishes hardcover and paperback originals and reprints. **Publishes 40-45 UK-US titles/year; entire firm publishes 200 titles/year. Receives 500-700 submissions/year. 25% of books from first-time authors; 90% from unagented writers. Pays 10-12% royalty on net receipts. Offers modest advance.** Publishes book 9-12 months after acceptance. Accepts simultaneous submissions. Responds in 2 months. Book catalog and ms guidelines for SASE.

O→ Focal Press publishes reference material in all areas of the media, from audio, broadcasting, and cinematography, through to journalism, radio, television, video, and writing. Currently emphasizing graphics, animation and multimedia.

Nonfiction: How-to, reference, technical and textbooks in media arts: photography, film and cinematography, broadcasting, theater and performing arts and audio, sound and media technology. High-level scientific/technical monographs are also considered. "We do not publish collections of photographs or books composed primarily of photographs. Our books are text-oriented, with artwork serving to illustrate and expand on points in the text." Query preferred, or submit outline and sample chapters. Reviews artwork/photos as part of ms package.

Recent Title(s): *IFP West Independent Filmmaker's Manual*, by Nicole Shay LoLoggia and Eden Wurmfeld.

Tips: "Our advances and royalties are more carefully determined with an eye toward greater profitability for all our publications."

N FOCUS PUBLISHING, INC., P.O. Box 665, Bemidji MN 56619. (218)759-9817. Fax: (218)751-2183. E-mail: focus@paulbunyan.net. Website: www.paulbunyan.net/focus. **Acquisitions:** Jan Haley, vice president. Estab. 1994. Publishes hardcover and trade paperback originals and reprints. **Publishes 4-6 titles/year. Receives 250 queries and 100 mss/year. 90% of books from first-time authors; 100% from unagented writers. Pays 7-10% royalty on retail price.** Publishes book 1 year after acceptance of ms. Responds in 2 months. Book catalog free.

　　O→ "Focus Publishing is a small press primarily devoted to Christian books and appropriate to children and home-schooling families."

Nonfiction: Children's/juvenile. Subjects include religion, women's issues/studies. Submit proposal package, including marketing ideas with SASE. Reviews artwork/photos as part of the ms package. Send photocopies.

Fiction: Juvenile, picture books, religious, young adult. "We are looking for Christian books for men and young adults. Be sure to list your target audience." Query and submit synopsis.

Poetry: "We are not especially interested in poetry at this time." Query.

Recent Title(s): *Success in School*, by Vicki Caruana; *The Exemplary Husband*, by Dr. Stuart Scott.

Tips: "I prefer SASE inquiries, synopsis and target markets. Please don't send 5 lbs. of paper with no return postage. Our focus is on Christian living books for adults and children. Only Biblically-sound proposals considered."

FODOR'S TRAVEL PUBLICATIONS, INC., Random House, Inc. 201 E. 50th, New York NY 10022. **Acquisitions:** Karen Cure, editorial director. Estab. 1936. Publishes trade paperback originals. **Publishes 300 titles/year. Receives 100 queries and 4 mss/year. Most titles are collective works, with contributions as works for hire. Most contributions are updates of previously published volumes.** Publishes book 1 year after acceptance of ms. Accepts simultaneous submissions. Responds in 2 months to queries. Book catalog free.

　　O→ Fodor's publishes travel books on many regions and countries.

Nonfiction: Travel guides, some illustrated, and travel how-to books. "We're not interested in travel literature or in proposals for general travel guidebooks. We are interested in unique approaches to favorite destinations. Writers seldom review our catalog or our list and often query about books on topics that we're already covering. Beyond that, it's important to review competition and to say what the proposed book will add." Query or submit outline, sample chapter(s) and proposal package, including competition review and review of market with SASE. "Do not send originals without first querying as to our interest in the project."

Recent Title(s): *France '00*, by Fodor's (travel guide).

Tips: "In preparing your query or proposal, remember that it's the only argument Fodor's will hear about why your book will be a good one and why you think it will sell; and it's also best evidence of your ability to create the book you propose. Craft your proposal well and carefully so that it puts your best foot forward."

FOGHORN OUTDOORS, Avalon Travel Publishing, Avalon Publishing Group, 5855 Beaudry St., Emeryville CA 94608. (510)595-3664. Website: www.foghorn.com. **Acquisitions:** Pauli Galin, editorial director. Estab. 1985. Publishes trade paperback originals and reprints. **Publishes 30 titles/year. Receives 500 queries and 200 mss/year. 10% of books from first-time authors; 98% from unagented writers. Pays 12% royalty on wholesale price; occasional work-for-hire.** Publishes book 18 months after acceptance of ms. Accepts simultaneous submissions. Responds in 1 month to queries, 2 months to proposals and mss. Book catalog free.

　　O→ Foghorn publishes outdoor recreation guidebooks.

Nonfiction: Outdoor recreation guidebooks. Subjects include nature/environment, recreation (camping, hiking, fishing), sports, outdoors, leisure. Query first with SASE, Attn: acquisitions editor.

Tips: "We are expanding our list nationally in the formats we already publish (camping, hiking, fishing, dogs) as well as developing new formats to test California."

FORGE, Tom Doherty Associates, LLC., 175 Fifth Ave., 14th Floor, New York NY 10010. (212)388-0100. Fax: (212)388-0191. E-mail: inquiries@tor.com. Website: www.tor.com. **Acquisitions:** Patrick Nielsen Hayden, senior editor (science fiction and fantasy, techno-thriller, alternate history); Melissa Ann Singer, senior editor (historicals, thrillers with medical, ecological, or biotech elements, contemporary mysteries, women's fiction, nonfiction on women's or health issues, horror/occult); Natalia Aponte, senior editor (biotech and medical thrillers, women's fiction, historicals); Claire Eddy, editor (science fiction and fantasy, mystery, historical, suspense); Jenna Felice, editor (science fiction and fantasy, general fiction). Publishes hardcover, trade paperback and mass market paperback originals, trade and mass market paperback reprints. **Receives 5,000 mss/year. 2% of books from first-time authors; a few from unagented writers. Royalties: paperback, 6-8% first-time authors, 8-10% established authors; hardcover, 10% first 5,000, 12½% second 5,000, 15% thereafter. Offers advance.** Responds in 4 months to proposals. Book catalog for 9×12 SASE with 2 first-class stamps.

　　O→ "TDA publishes the best of past, present, and future—meaning that we cover all ground in fiction from historicals set in prehistory to the sharpest contemporary fiction to the acknowledged best in science fiction and fantasy. We are a little more interested in quality horror fiction than we were a year ago. We are less interested in apocalyptic or millennial thrillers, obviously. We're not much interested in serial killers either."

Nonfiction: Subjects include health/medicine, science, women's issues/studies. Query with outline and 3 sample chapters.

Fiction: Historical, horror, mainstream/contemporary, mystery, suspense, thriller; general fiction of all sorts. "We handle a wide range of books; if you're not sure if a project is right for us, phone us and ask." Query with synopsis and 3 sample chapters.

Recent Title(s): *Peace, War & Politics*, by Jack Anderson (nonfiction); *Vengeance*, by Stuart M. Kaminsky (fiction).

N FORT ROSS INC. RUSSIAN-AMERICAN PUBLISHING PROJECTS, 26 Arthur Place, Yonkers NY 10701. (914)375-6448. Fax: (914)375-6439. E-mail: ftross@ix.netcom.com. **Acquisitions:** Dr. Vladimir P. Kartsev, executive director (romance, mystery, science fiction, fantasy, nonfiction). Publishes paperback originals. **Publishes 12 titles/year. Receives 100 queries and 100 mss/year. Pays 4-7% royalty on wholesale price or makes outright purchase of $500-1,500. Offers $500 advance.** Publishes book 1 year after acceptance of ms. Accepts simultaneous submissions. Responds in 1 month to queries and proposals, 3 months to mss.

O→ "Generally, we publish Russia-related books in English or Russian. Sometimes we publish books in collaboration with the Russian and Polish publishers in translation into Russian and Polish. In this case we are looking for the books of 'all-in-one' character, 'how-to' books, books for teens, romance, mystery, science fiction and adventure."

Nonfiction: Biography, illustrated book, technical. Subjects include art/architecture, business/economics, memoirs. Query with SASE. Reviews artwork/photos as part of ms package. Send photocopies.

Fiction: Adventure, fantasy, horror, mainstream/contemporary, mystery, romance, science fiction, suspense. "We are looking for the manuscripts (books) of well-established authors to publish them in Russian and Polish languages in collaboration with the Russian and Polish publishers in the USA or abroad." Query with SASE.

Recent Title(s): *The Cosack Galopped Far Away*, by N. Feodorov (biography in English); *Diaries of Lo*, by Pia Pera (fiction).

FORUM, Prima Publishing, 3000 Lava Ridge Court, Roseville CA 95661. (916)787-7000. Fax: (916)787-7005. Website: primalifestyles.com. **Acquisitions:** Steven Martin, publisher. Publishes hardcover and trade paperback originals and reprints. **Publishes 10-15 titles/year. 25% of books from first-time authors; 5% from unagented writers. Pays variable advance and royalty.** Publishes book 1 year after acceptance of ms. Accepts simultaneous submissions. Responds in 1 month to queries and proposals, 2 months to mss.

O→ "Forum publishes books that contribute to the marketplace of ideas."

Nonfiction: Subjects include libertarian/conservative thought, trends in business, technology and society, government/politics, history, religion, current affairs, individual empowerment. Query with outline, 1 sample chapter and SASE.

Recent Title(s): *Let Us Talk of Many Things*, by William F. Buckley, Jr.; *The Rise and Fall of the Soviet Empire*, by Brian Crozier.

N FORUM PUBLISHING COMPANY, 383 E. Main St., Centerport NY 11721. (631)754-5000. Fax: (631)754-0630. Website: www.forum123.com. **Acquisitions:** Martin Stevens. Estab. 1981. Publishes trade paperback originals. Publishes 12 titles/year. Receives 200 queries and 25 mss/year. 75% of books from first-time authors; 75% from unagented writers. No advance. Makes outright purchase of $250-750. Publishes book 4 months after acceptance. Accepts simultaneous submissions. Responds in 1 month to mss. *Writer's Market* recommends allowing 2 months for reply. Book catalog free.

O→ Forum publishes only business titles.

Nonfiction: Subjects include business/economics, money/finance. Submit outline. Reviews artwork/photos as part of ms package. Send photocopies.

Recent Nonfiction Title(s): *Selling Information By Mail*, by Glen Gilcrest.

★ FORWARD MOVEMENT PUBLICATIONS, 412 Sycamore St., Cincinnati OH 45202. (513)721-6659. Fax: (513)721-0729. E-mail: egleason@forwardmovement.org. Website: www.forwardmovement.org. **Acquisitions:** Reverend Edward S. Gleason, editor and director. Estab. 1934. Publishes trade and mass market paperback originals, trade paperback reprints and tracts. **Publishes 6 titles/year. Receives 1,000 queries and 300 mss/year. 30% of books from first-time authors; 100% from unagented writers. Pays one-time honorarium. No advance.** Responds in 1 month to queries and proposals, 2 months to mss. Book catalog and ms guidelines free.

O→ "Forward Movement was established 'to help reinvigorate the life of the church.' Many titles focus on the life of prayer, where our relationship with God is centered, death, marriage, baptism, recovery, joy, the Episcopal Church and more." Currently emphasizing prayer/spirituality.

Nonfiction: Biography, children's/juvenile, reference and self-help publications about religion and prayer. "We publish a variety of types of books, but they all relate to the lives of Christians. We are an agency of the Episcopal Church." Query with SASE or submit completed ms.

Fiction: Episcopal for middle school (ages 8-12) readers. Query with SASE.

Recent Title(s): *God Is Not in the Thesaurus*, by Bo Don Cox (nonfiction); *Dare to Imagine*, by Sydney Von Lehn (fiction).

Tips: Audience is primarily Episcopalians and other Christians.

FOUR WALLS EIGHT WINDOWS, 39 W. 14th St., Room 503, New York NY 10011. Fax: (212)206-8799. E-mail: edit@fourwallseightwindows.com. Website: www.fourwallseightwindows.com. Estab. 1987. Publisher: John Oakes. **Acquisitions:** Acquisitions Editor. Estab. 1987. Publishes hardcover originals, trade paperback originals and reprints. **Publishes 28 titles/year. Receives 3,000 submissions/year. 15% of books from first-time authors; 50% from unagented writers. Pays royalty on retail price. Advance varies widely.** Publishes book 1-2 years after acceptance. Responds in 2 months to queries. Book catalog for 6×9 SAE with 3 first-class stamps.

    ○➤ Emphasizing fine literature and quality nonfiction, Four Walls Eight Windows has a reputation for carefully edited and distinctive books.

Imprint(s): No Exit.

Nonfiction: Political, investigative. Subjects include art/architecture, government/politics, history, language/literature, nature/environment, science. No New Age. Query with outline and SASE. All mss without SASE discarded.

Fiction: Feminist, literary, science fiction. "No romance, popular." Query first with outline/synopsis and SASE.

Recent Title(s): *Genesis: The Story of Apollo 8*, by Robert Zimmerman (science); *Arcade*, by Gordon Lish (fiction).

FOX CHAPEL PUBLISHING, 1970 Broad St., East Petersburg PA 17520. (717)560-4703. Fax: (717)560-4702. E-mail: editors@carvingworld.com. Website: www.carvingworld.com. **Acquisitions:** Alan Giagnocave. Publishes hardcover and trade paperback originals and trade paperback reprints. **Publishes 12-20 titles/year. 80% of books from first-time authors; 100% from unagented writers. Pays royalty or makes outright purchase. Advance varies.** Publishes book 6-18 months after acceptance of ms. Accepts simultaneous submissions. Responds in 2 months to queries.

    ○➤ Fox Chapel publishes woodworking and woodcarving titles for professionals and hobbyists.

Nonfiction: Woodworking, woodcarving and related titles. Query. Reviews artwork/photos as part of ms package. Send photocopies.

Recent Title(s): *Carving the Human Face*, by Jeff Pharen; *Capturing Character & Expression in Wood*.

Tips: "We're looking for knowledgeable artists, woodworkers first, writers second to write for us. Our market is for avid woodworking hobbyists and professionals."

THE FREE PRESS, Simon & Schuster, 1230 Avenue of the Americas, New York NY 10020. (212)698-7000. Fax: (212)632-4989. Website: www.simonsays.com. **Acquisitions:** Liz Maguire, editorial director; Chad Conway, associate editor (history/current events); Robert Wallace, senior editor (business); Bruce Nichols, senior editor (history); Paul Golob, senior editor (current events/politics); Philip Rapapport, editor (psychology/social work/self-help); Steven Morrow, editor (science, math, literature, art). Estab. 1947. **Publishes 120 titles/year. Receives 3,000 submissions/year. 15% of books from first-time authors; 50% of books from unagented writers. Pays variable royalty.** Publishes book 1 year after acceptance of ms. Responds in 2 months.

    ○➤ The Free Press publishes serious adult nonfiction.

Nonfiction: professional books and college texts in the social sciences, humanities and business. Reviews artwork/photos as part of ms package. "We look for an identifiable target audience, evidence of writing ability." Accepts nonfiction translations. Query with 1-3 sample chapters, outline before submitting mss.

Recent Title(s): *The Educated Child*, by William Bennett; *Eye of the Storm*, by Robert Sneden.

FREE SPIRIT PUBLISHING INC., 400 First Ave. N., Suite 616, Minneapolis MN 55401-1724. (612)338-2068. Fax: (612)337-5050. E-mail: help4kids@freespirit.com. Website: www.freespirit.com. Publisher: Judy Galbraith. **Acquisitions:** Acquisitions Editor. Estab. 1983. Publishes trade paperback originals and reprints. **Publishes 30 titles/year. 25% of books from first-time authors; 75% from unagented writers. Offers advance.** Book catalog and ms guidelines free.

    ○➤ "We believe passionately in empowering kids to learn to think for themselves and make their own good choices."

Imprint(s): Self-Help for Kids®, Free Spirited Classroom® Series, Self-Help for Teens®.

Nonfiction: Self-Help for Kids®. Subjects include child guidance/parenting, education (pre-K-12, but not textbooks or basic skills books like reading, counting, etc.), health (mental/emotional health—*not* physical health—for/about children), psychology (for/about children), sociology (for/about children). No fiction, poetry or autobiographies. Query with outline, 2 sample chapters and SASE. Send photocopies. "Many of our authors are teachers, counselors or others involved in helping kids."

Recent Title(s): *Can You Relate? Real-World Advice for Teens on Guys, Girls, Growing Up, and Getting Along*, by Annie Fox, M.Ed.

Tips: "Our audience is children, teens, teachers, parents and youth counselors. We are concerned with kids' mental/emotional well-being and are especially looking for books written directly to kids in a language they can understand. We are not looking for academic or religious materials, nor books that analyze problems with the nation's school systems. Instead we want books that offer practical, positive advice so kids can help themselves."

Ⓝ FROMM INTERNATIONAL PUBLISHING CORPORATION, 560 Lexington Ave., New York NY 10022. (212)308-4010. **Acquisitions:** Fred Jordan, executive director; Henry Lincoln. Estab. 1982. Publishes hardcover originals, trade paperback originals and reprints. **Publishes 20-25 titles/year. Receives 200 mss/year. 10% of books from**

first-time authors; 10% from unagented writers. **Pays 10-15% royalty. Offers $2,500 advance.** Publishes book 1 year after acceptance of ms. Accepts simultaneous submissions. Responds in 1 month to queries and proposals, 2 months to mss. Book catalog free.

Nonfiction: Biography, illustrated book, reference. Subjects include Americana, art/architecture, health/medicine, history, language/literature, psychology, popular culture. Submit 3 sample chapters and table of contents with SASE. Reviews artwork/photos as part of ms package. Send photocopies.

Recent Title(s): *Breakout*, by Martin Russ.

Tips: Audience is the general trade, both popular and "high brow."

[N] FRONT STREET, 20 Battery Park Ave. #403, Asheville NC 28801. (828)236-3097. Fax: (828)236-3098. E-mail: jrn@frontstreetbooks.com. Website: www.frontstreetbooks.com. **Acquisitions:** Stephen Roxburgh, president and publisher; Joy Neaves, assistant editor. Publishes hardcover originals. **Publishes 12-24 titles/year; imprint publishes 6-12 titles/year. 20% of books from first-time authors; 80% from unagented writers. Pays royalty on retail price. Offers $1,500-8,500 advance.** Publishes book 1 year after acceptance of ms. Accepts simultaneous submissions. Responds in 1 month to queries, 2 months to proposals, 3 months to mss. Book catalog for 6×9 SAE with 77¢ in stamps or on website. Manuscript guidelines for #10 SASE or on website.

O▬ "We publish only for children and young adults."

Imprints: Front Street/Cricket Books (Laura Tillotson, editor); Front Street/Lemniscant Books (Stephen Roxburgh).

Nonfiction: Children's/juvenile, gift book, illustrated book.

Fiction: Adventure, fantasy, feminist, historical, horror, humor, juvenile, literary, picture books, poetry, romance, science fiction, young adult. Query with SASE or submit proposal package, including synopsis and 3 sample chapters or submit completed ms.

GATF PRESS, Graphic Arts Technical Foundation, 200 Deer Run Rd., Sewickley PA 15143-2600. (412)741-6860. Fax: (412)741-2311. E-mail: poresick@gatf.com. Website: www.gatf.org. **Acquisitions:** Peter Oresick, director of publications; Tom Destree, editor in chief; Amy Woodall, managing editor (graphic arts, communication, book publishing, printing). Estab. 1924. Publishes trade paperback originals and hardcover reference texts. **Publishes 15 titles/year. Receives 25 submissions/year. 50% of books from first-time authors; 100% from unagented writers. Pays 5-15% royalty on retail price.** Publishes book 6 months after acceptance. Responds in 1 month to queries. *Writer's Market* recommends allowing 2 months for reply. Book catalog for 9×12 SAE with 2 first-class stamps. Manuscript guidelines for #10 SASE.

O▬ "GATF's mission is to serve the graphic communications community as the major resource for technical information and services through research and education." Currrently emphasizing career guides for graphic communications.

Nonfiction: How-to, reference, technical, textbook. Subjects include printing/graphic communications and electronic publishing. "We primarily want textbook/reference books about printing and related technologies. However, we are expanding our reach into electronic communications." Query with SASE or submit outline, sample chapters and SASE. Reviews artwork/photos as part of ms package.

Recent Title(s): *Practical Proofreading*, by Matthew Willen; *Understanding Graphic Communication*, by Harvey Levenson.

Tips: "We are publishing titles that are updated more frequently, such as *On-Demand Publishing*. Our scope now includes reference titles geared toward general audiences interested in computers, imaging, and Internet as well as print publishing."

GAY SUNSHINE PRESS and LEYLAND PUBLICATIONS, P.O. Box 410690, San Francisco CA 94141-0690. Website: www.gaysunshine.com. **Acquisitions:** Winston Leyland, editor. Estab. 1970. Publishes hardcover originals, trade paperback originals and reprints. **Publishes 6-8 titles/year. Pays royalty or makes outright purchase.** Responds in 6 weeks to queries. Book catalog for $1.

O▬ Gay history, sex, politics, and culture are the focus of the quality books published by Gay Sunshine Press. Leyland Publications publishes books on popular aspects of gay sexuality and culture. "We seek innovative literary nonfiction and fiction depicting gay themes and lifestyles."

Nonfiction: How-to and gay lifestyle topics. "We're interested in innovative literary nonfiction which deals with gay lifestyles." No long personal accounts, academic or overly formal titles. Query. "After we respond positively to your query, submit outline and sample chapters with SASE." *All unsolicited mss are returned unopened.*

Fiction: Erotica, ethnic, experimental, historical, mystery, science fiction, translation. "Interested in well-written novels on gay themes; also short story collections. We have a high literary standard for fiction." Query. "After we respond positively to your query, submit outline/synopsis and sample chapters with SASE." *All unsolicited mss returned unopened.*

Recent Title(s): *Partings at Dawn: An Anthology of Japanese Gay Literature.*

[N] [★] GENESIS PRESS, INC., 315 Third Ave. N, Columbus MS 39701. (662)329-9927. Fax: (662)329-9399. E-mail: books@genesis-press.com. Website: www.genesis-press.com. **Contact:** Gary Frazier, editor-in-chief. Publishes hardcover and trade paperback originals and reprints. **Publishes 36 titles/year. Receives 100-200 queries and 75-100**

mss/year. **50% of books from first-time authors; 90% from unagented writers. Pays 6-15% royalty on wholesale price. Offers $500-5,000 advance.** Publishes book 1 year after acceptance of ms. Responds in 2 months to queries, 6 months to mss. Book catalog for $1.50. Manuscript guidelines for #10 SASE.

O→ Genesis publishes a diverse line including African-American and mainstream romance, Southern fiction, children's books and mainstream nonfiction.

Nonfiction: Biography, children's/juvenile, humor. Subjects include history. Query with SASE, outline and first 3 chapters.

Fiction: Erotica, ethnic, literary, multicultural, mystery, regional, romance, young adult. Query with SASE, synopsis and first 3 chapters.

Recent Title(s): *Lasting Valor*, by Vernon Baker (biography); *Soul to Soul*, by Donna Hill (romance).

Tips: "Be professional. Always include a cover letter and SASE. Follow the submission guidelines posted on our website or send SASE for a copy."

LAURA GERINGER BOOKS, HarperCollins Children's Books, 1350 Avenue of the Americas, New York NY 10019. (212)207-7000. Website: www.harpercollins.com. **Acquisitions:** Laura Geringer, senior vice president/publisher. Publishes hardcover originals. **Publishes 15-20 titles/year. 5% of books from first-time authors; 25% from unagented writers. Pays 10-12½% on retail price. Advance varies.** Publishes ms 6-12 months after acceptance of ms for novels, 1-2 years after acceptance of ms for picture books. Responds in 3 months to queries and proposals, 4 months to mss. Book catalog for 8×10 SAE with 3 first-class stamps. Manuscript guidelines for #10 SASE.

O→ "We look for books that are out of the ordinary, authors who have their own definite take, and artists that add a sense of humor to the text."

Fiction: Children's, adventure, fantasy, humor, literary, picture books, young adult. "A mistake writers often make is failing to research the type of books an imprint publishes, therefore sending inappropriate material." Query with SASE for picture books; submit complete ms with SASE for novels.

Recent Title(s): *If You Give a Pig a Pancake*, by Laura Nurmeroff; illustrated by Felicia Bond.

GESSLER PUBLISHING CO., INC., 10 E. Church Ave., Roanoke VA 24011. (540)345-1429. Fax: (540)342-7172. E-mail: usa@ggroupplc.com. Website: www.ggroupusa.com. **Acquisitions:** John Stanley, director of US operations. Estab. 1932. Publishes trade paperback originals and reprints. **Publishes 75 titles/year. Receives 50 queries and 25 mss/year. 5% of books from first-time authors; 90% from unagented writers, "very few, if any, are agented." Pays 10-20% royalty on retail price. Offers $250-500 advance.** Publishes book 9 months after acceptance of ms. Accepts simultaneous submissions. Responds in 3 days to queries, 3 weeks to mss. *Writer's Market* recommends allowing 2 months for reply. Book catalog free.

O→ Gessler publishes high-quality language-learning materials for the education market.

Nonfiction: Textbook. Subjects include education, language/literature, multicultural. "We publish supplementary language learning materials. Our products assist teachers with foreign languages, ESL, and multicultural activities." Query first, then submit outline/synopsis with 2-3 sample chapters or complete ms with cover letter and SASE. Reviews artwork/photos as part of ms package. Send photocopies.

Recent Title(s): *Buenviaje*, by Maria Koonce (Spanish workbook).

Tips: Elementary/middle school/high school audience. "Writers need to be more open-minded when it comes to understanding not everyone learns the same way. They may have to be flexible when it comes to revising their work to accommodate broader teaching/learning methods."

GIFTED EDUCATION PRESS, 10201 Yuma Court, P.O. Box 1586, Manassas VA 20109. (703)369-5017. E-mail: mdfish@cais.com. Website: www.giftedpress.com. **Acquisitions:** Maurice Fisher, publisher. Estab. 1981. Publishes mass market paperback originals. **Publishes 10 titles/year. Receives 75 queries and 25 mss/year. 90% of books from first-time authors; 100% from unagented writers. Pays 10-12% royalty on retail price.** Publishes book 3 months after acceptance of ms. Accepts simultaneous submissions. Responds in 1 month. Book catalog free. Manuscript guidelines for #10 SASE.

O→ Gifted Education Press publishes books on multiple intelligences, humanities education for gifted children and how to parent gifted children. Currently emphasizing multiple intelligences and problems/issues of educating gifted children.

Nonfiction: Reference, textbook, teacher's guides. Subjects include child guidance/parenting, computers/electronics, education, language/literature, philosophy, psychology, science. "Writers must indicate their expertise in the subject and propose challenging topics for teachers and gifted students." Query or submit outline with SASE. *All unsolicited mss returned.* Reviews artwork/photos as part of ms package.

Recent Title(s): *Bright Child*, by Lynn Fox; *Multiple Intelligences in the World*, by Maurice Fisher.

Tips: Audience is parents and teachers of gifted students, university professors and graduate students. "We are looking for clear, straight forward and well-organized writing. Expertise in the topical areas is required."

GLENBRIDGE PUBLISHING LTD., 6010 W. Jewell Ave., Denver CO 80232-7106. Fax: (303)987-9037. **Acquisitions:** James A. Keene, editor. Estab. 1986. Publishes hardcover originals and reprints, trade paperback originals. **Publishes 6-8 titles/year. Pays 10% royalty.** Publishes book 1 year after acceptance of ms. Accepts simultaneous submissions. Responds in 2 months to queries. Book catalog for 6×9 SASE. Manuscript guidelines for #10 SASE.

O→ "Glenbridge has an eclectic approach to publishing. We look for titles that have long-term capabilities."

Nonfiction: Subjects include Americana, business/economics, history, music, philosophy, politics, psychology, sociology, cookbooks. Query with outline/synopsis, sample chapters and SASE.
Recent Title(s): *Train Your Dog in One Hour*, by Sandy Butler.

THE GLENLAKE PUBLISHING COMPANY, LTD., 1261 W. Glenlake, Chicago IL 60660. (773)262-9765. Fax: (773)262-9436. E-mail: glenlake@ix.netcom.com. Website: www.glenlake.com. **Acquisitions:** Barbara Craig, editor. Estab. 1995. Publishes hardcover originals. **Publishes 20 titles/year. Receives 50 queries and 5 mss/year. 25% of books from first-time authors; 100% from unagented writers. Pays 10-15% royalty on wholesale price. Offers $1,500 average advance.** Publishes book 2 months after acceptance of ms. Accepts simultaneous submissions. Responds in 1 month to queries. Book catalog available via website or with SASE.

   O–π "Glenlake is an independent book publisher whose primary objective is to promote the advancement of critical thinking in the areas of business, finance, economics, applied statistics, computer applications to business and statistics, and environmental science and engineering."

Nonfiction: Subjects include business/economics, computers/electronics, money/finance. Submit proposal package, including author's bio, outline, 1 sample chapter and SASE.
Recent Title(s): *International Handbook of Corporate Finance*, by Brian Terry.

THE GLOBE PEQUOT PRESS, INC., P.O. Box 480, Guilford CT 06437. (203)458-4500. Fax: (203)458-4604. Website: www.globe-pequot.com. President/Publisher: Linda Kennedy. **Acquisitions:** Shelley Wolf, submissions editor. Estab. 1947.Publishes paperback originals, hardcover originals and reprints. **Publishes 150 titles/year. Receives 1,500 submissions/year. 30% of books from first-time authors; 70% from unagented writers. Average print order for a first book is 4,000-7,500. Makes outright purchase or pays 10% royalty on net price. Offers advance.** Publishes book 1 year after acceptance of ms. Accepts simultaneous submissions. Responds in 3 months. Book catalog for 9×12 SASE.

   O–π Globe Pequot is among the top sources for travel books in the United States and offers the broadest selection of travel titles of any vendor in this market. Currently emphasizing outdoor recreation list.

Nonfiction: Regional travel guidebooks and outdoor recreation guides. No doctoral theses, fiction, genealogies, memoirs, poetry or textbooks. Submit brief synopsis of work, table of contents or outline, sample chapter, résumé/vita, definition of target audience, and an analysis of competing titles. Reviews artwork/photos.
Recent Title(s): *Great American Rail Journeys* (Curiosities Series); *Derek Hutchinson's Expedition Kayaking* (Winter Trails Series).

DAVID R. GODINE, PUBLISHER, INC., 9 Hamilton Place, Boston MA 02108. Website: www.godine.com. Estab. 1970. Publishes hardcover and trade paperback originals and reprints. **Publishes 25 titles/year. Pays royalty on retail price.** Publishes book 3 years after acceptance of ms. Book catalog for 5×8 SAE with 3 first-class stamps.

   O–π "Our particular strengths are books about the history and design of the written word, literary essays, and the best of world fiction in translation. We also have an unusually strong list of children's books, all of them printed in their entirety with no cuts, deletions, or side-stepping to keep the political watchdogs happy."

Nonfiction: Biography, coffee table book, cookbook, illustrated book, children's/juvenile. Subjects include Americana, art/architecture, gardening, nature/environment, photography, literary criticism, current affairs. *No unsolicited mss.*
Fiction: Literary, novel, short story collection, children's/juvenile. *No unsolicited manuscripts.*
Recent Title(s): *The Corner in the Marais: Memoir of a Paris Neighborhood*, by Alex Karmel (nonfiction); *The Disobedience of Water*, by Sena Jeter Naslund (fiction); *Beyond*, by Albert Goldbarth (poetry).

GOLDEN WEST PUBLISHERS, 4113 N. Longview, Phoenix AZ 85014. (602)265-4392. Fax: (602)279-6901. Website: www.goldenwestpublishers.com. **Acquisitions:** Hal Mitchell, editor. Estab. 1973. Publishes trade paperback originals. **Publishes 15-20 titles/year. Receives 200 submissions/year. 50% of books from first-time authors; 100% from unagented writers. Prefers mss on work-for-hire basis. No advance.** Publishes book an average of 6 months after acceptance. Accepts simultaneous submissions. Responds in 1 month to queries, 2 months to mss.

   O–π "We seek to provide quality, affordable cookbooks and books about the Southwest to the marketplace. We are currently featuring Cooking Across America Cook Book Series™ plus state and regional cookbooks." Currently emphasizing cooking across America. De-emphasizing southwest history.

Nonfiction: Cookbooks, books on the Southwest and West. Subjects include cooking/foods, Southwest history and outdoors, recreation, travel. Query. Reviews artwork/photos as part of ms package.
Recent Title(s): *Minnesota Cookbook*, by Wade; *Oklahoma Cookbook*, by Lilley.
Tips: "We are interested in Arizona and Southwest material, and regional and state cookbooks for the entire country, and welcome material in these areas."

GOLLEHON PRESS, INC., 6157 28th St., SE, Grand Rapids MI 49546. (616)949-3515. Fax: (616)949-8674. Website: www.gollehonbooks.com. **Acquisitions:** Lori Adams, editor. Publishes hardcover and trade paperback originals and mass market paperback originals. **Publishes 6-8 titles/year. Receives 100 queries and 30 mss/year. 85% of books from first-time authors; 90% from unagented writers. Pays 7% royalty on retail price. Offers $500-1,000 advance.** Publishes book 6 months after acceptance of ms. Accepts simultaneous submissions. Reponds in 1 month to queries and proposals if interested, 2 months to mss. Book catalog and ms guidelines on website.

   O–π Currently emphasizing trivia how-to titles and books for seniors. *No unsolicited mss*; brief proposals only.

Nonfiction: Children's/juvenile, how-to, humor, self-help. Subjects include animals, anthropology/archaeology, business/economics, gardening, health/medicine, hobbies, money/finance, psychology, games. Submit brief proposal package. No SASE (we do not return mss). Reviews artwork/photos as part of ms package, but send photocopies only if requested.

Tips: "Mail brief book proposal and few sample pages only. We will request full manuscript if interested. We cannot respond to all queries. Full manuscripts will be returned if we requested it and writer provides SASE. We do not return proposals. Simultaneous submissions are encouraged."

GOVERNMENT INSTITUTES/ABS., 4 Research Place, Suite 200, Rockville MD 20850-3226. (301)921-2355. Fax: (301)921-0373. E-mail: giinfo@govinst.com. Website: www.govinst.com. **Acquisitions:** Russ Bahorsky, acquisitions editor (occupational safety and health, quality, ISO 9000 risk and reliability); Charlene Ikonomou (environmental compliance and sciences, marine industry), editors. Estab. 1973. Publishes hardcover and softcover originals and CD-ROM/disk products. **Publishes 45 titles/year. Receives 100 submissions/year. 50% of books from first-time authors; 100% from unagented writers. Pays royalty or makes outright purchase.** Publishes book 5 months after acceptance. Accepts simultaneous submissions, if so noted. Responds in 2 months. Book catalog free.

    O─┒ "Our mission is to be the leading global company providing practical, accurate, timely and authoritative information desired by people concerned with environment, health and safety, telecommunications, and other regulatory and technical topics." Currently emphasizing practical information for the business community. De-emphasizing books on issues and theories.

Nonfiction: Reference, technical. Subjects include environmental law, occupational safety and health, environmental engineering, telecommunications, employment law, FDA matters, industrial hygiene and safety, real estate with an environmental slant, management systems, Quality, ISO 9000 risk and reliability. Needs professional-level titles in those areas. Also looking for international environmental topics. Submit outline and at least 1 sample chapter.

Recent Title(s): *Environmental Guide to the Internet*, by Murphy/Briggs-Erickson.

Tips: "We also conduct courses. Authors are frequently invited to serve as instructors."

THE GRADUATE GROUP, P.O. Box 370351, West Hartford CT 06137-0351. (860)233-2330. Fax: (860)233-2330. E-mail: graduategroup@hotmail.com. Website: www.GraduateGroup.com. **Acquisitions:** Mara Whitman, president; Robert Whitman, vice president. Estab. 1964. Publishes trade paperback originals. **Publishes 50 titles/year. Receives 100 queries and 70 mss/year. 60% of books from first-time authors; 85% from unagented writers. Pays 20% royalty on retail price.** Publishes book 3 months after acceptance of ms. Accepts simultaneous submissions. Responds in 1 month. Book catalog and ms guidelines free.

    O─┒ "The Graduate Group helps college and graduate students better prepare themselves for rewarding careers and helps people advance in the workplace." Currently emphasizing test preparation, career advancement and materials for prisoners.

Nonfiction: Reference. Subjects include test taking, directories, dictionaries, career/internships, law, medicine, law enforcement, corrections, how to succeed, self-motivation, education, professional development, building self-esteem, learning networking skills, working with the disabled and gifted, summer/year round opportunities for students, assisting the elderly, financial planning, business, international. Send complete ms and SASE with sufficient postage.

Recent Title(s): *Real Life 101: Winning Secrets You Won't Find in Class*, by Debra Yergen; *Getting In: Applicant's Guide to Graduate School Admissions*, by David Burrell.

Tips: Audience is career planning offices; college, graduate school and public libraries. "We are open to all submissions, especially those involving career planning, internships and other nonfiction titles. Looking for books on law enforcement, books for prisoners and reference books on subjects/fields students would be interested in. We want books on helping students and others to interview, pass tests, gain opportunity, understand the world of work, networking, building experience, preparing for advancement, preparing to enter business, improving personality and building relationships."

GRANITE PUBLISHING, LLC, (formerly Wild Flower Press), Blue Water Publishing, P.O. Box 1429, Columbus NC 28756. (828)894-8444. Fax: (828)894-8454. E-mail: bluewaterp@aol.com. Website: www.5thworld.com. President: Pam Meyer. **Acquisitions:** Brian Crissey. Publishes hardcover originals and trade paperback originals and reprints. **Publishes 6 titles/year. Receives 50 queries and 25 mss/month. 80% of books from first-time authors; 90% from unagented writers. Pays 7½-15% royalty.** Publishes book 16 months after acceptance of ms. Accepts simultaneous submissions. Responds in 2 months on mss. Book catalog and ms guidelines for SASE with 55¢ postage.

    O─┒ "Granite Publishing strives to preserve the Earth by publishing books that develop new wisdom about our emerging planetary citizenship, bringing information from the outerworlds to our world."

Nonfiction: Books about extraterrestrial research and experiences. Submit proposal. Reviews artwork/photos as part of ms package. Send photocopies.

Recent Title(s): *Zeta Talk*, by Nancy Lieder.

GRAYWOLF PRESS, 2402 University Ave., Suite 203, St. Paul MN 55114. (651)641-0077. Fax: (651)641-0036. Website: www.graywolfpress.org. Editor/publisher: Fiona McCrae. Executive Editor: Anne Czarniecki. **Acquisitions:** Jeffrey Shotts (poetry, nonfiction); Katie Dublinski, editorial assistant (fiction, nonfiction). Estab. 1974. Publishes trade cloth and paperback originals and reprints. **Publishes 16 titles/year. Receives 2,500 queries/year. 20% of books from**

first-time authors; 50% from unagented writers. **Pays royalty on retail price. Offers $1,000-6,000 advance on average.** Publishes book 18 months after acceptance of ms. Responds in 3 months to queries. Book catalog free. Manuscript guidelines for #10 SASE.

   O→ Graywolf Press is an independent, nonprofit publisher dedicated to the creation and promotion of thoughtful and imaginative contemporary literature essential to a vital and diverse culture.

Nonfiction: Language/literature/culture. Query with SASE.

Fiction: Literary. "Familiarize yourself with our list first." Query with SASE.

Poetry: "We are interested in linguistically challenging work." Query sample with SASE.

Recent Title(s): *A Hundred White Daffodils*, by Jane Kenyon (nonfiction); *How the Body Prays*, by Peter Weltner (fiction); *Things and Flesh*, by Linda Gregg (poetry).

GREAT QUOTATIONS PUBLISHING, 1967 Quincy Ct., Glendale Heights IL 60139. (630)582-2800. Fax: (630)582-2813. **Acquisitions:** Diane Voreis, acquisitions editor (humor, relationships, Christian); Jan Stob, acquisitions editor (children's). Estab. 1991. **Publishes 30 titles/year. Receives 1,500 queries and 1,200 mss/year. 50% of books from first-time authors; 80% from unagented writers. Pays 3-5% royalty on net sales.** Publishes book 6 months after acceptance of ms. "We publish new books twice a year, in July and in January." Accepts simultaneous submissions. Responds in 6 months with SASE. Book catalog for $2. Manuscript guidelines for #10 SASE.

   O→ Great Quotations seeks original material for the following general categories: children, humor, inspiration, motivation, success, romance, tributes to mom/dad/grandma/grandpa, etc. Currently emphasizing humor, Christian, relationships. De-emphasizing poetry, self-help.

Nonfiction: Humor, illustrated book, quotes. Subjects include business/economics, child guidance/parenting, nature/environment, religion, sports, women's issues/studies. "We look for subjects with identifiable markets, appealing to the general public. We publish children's books or others requiring multicolor illustration on the inside. We don't publish highly controversial subject matter." Submit outline and 2 sample chapters. Reviews artwork/photos as part of ms package. Send photocopies, transparencies.

Poetry: "We would be most interested in upbeat and juvenile poetry."

Recent Title(s): *Memories for My Grandchild*, by Millie Mackiney; *Chocolate Temptations*, by Christine Lacey.

Tips: "Our books are physically small and generally a very quick read. They are available at gift shops and book shops throughout the country. We are aware that most of our books are bought on impulse and given as gifts. We need strong, clever, descriptive titles; beautiful cover art and brief, positive, upbeat text. Be prepared to submit final manuscript on computer disk, according to our specifications. (It is not necessary to try to format the typesetting of your manuscript to look like a finished book.)"

GREENHAVEN PRESS, INC., P.O. Box 289009, San Diego CA 92198-9009. (858)485-7424. Fax: (858)485-9549. Website: www.greenhaven.com. **Acquisitions:** Stuart Miller, managing editor. Estab. 1970. **Publishes approximately 100 anthologies/year; all anthologies are works for hire. Makes outright purchase of $1,000-3,000.** Publishes ms 1 year after acceptance of ms. Book catalog for 9 × 12 SAE with 3 first-class stamps or on website.

   O→ Greenhaven Press publishes hard and softcover educational supplementary materials and (nontrade) nonfiction anthologies on contemporary issues, literary criticism and history for high school and college readers. These anthologies serve as supplementary educational material for high school and college libraries and classrooms. Currently emphasizing literary and historical topics, and social-issue anthologies.

Nonfiction: "We produce tightly formatted anthologies on contemporary issues, literary criticism, and history for high school- and college-level readers. We are looking for freelance book editors to research and compile these anthologies; we are not interested in submissions of single-author manuscripts. Each series has specific requirements. Potential book editors should familiarize themselves with our catalog and anthologies." Query. No unsolicited mss.

Recent Title(s): *Biomedical Ethics* (Opposing Viewpoints Series).

GREENWILLOW BOOKS, HarperCollins Publishers, 1350 Avenue of the Americas, New York NY 10019. (212)261-6500. Website: www.harpercollins.com. Senior Editor: Elizabeth Shub. **Acquisitions:** Editorial Department, Greenwillow Books. Estab. 1974. Publishes hardcover originals and reprints. **Publishes 60-70 titles/year. 1% of books from first-time authors; 30% from unagented writers. Pays 10% royalty on wholesale price for first-time authors. Advance varies.** Publishes ms 2 years after acceptance of ms. Accepts simultaneous submissions, if so noted. Responds in 3 months to mss. Book catalog for 9 × 12 SASE with $2.00 postage. Manuscript guidelines for #10 SASE.

   O→ Greenwillow Books publishes quality picture books and fiction for young readers of all ages, and nonfiction primarily for children under seven years of age.

Fiction: Juvenile, picture books: fantasy, historical, humor, literary, mystery. Send complete ms with SASE. Reviews artwork with submissions. Send photocopies.

Recent Title(s): *Earthdance*, by Lynne Reiser; *All Alone in the Universe*, by Lynne Rae Perkins.

GREENWOOD PRESS, Greenwood Publishing Group, 88 Post Rd. W., Westport CT 06881. (203)226-3571. Fax: (203)222-1502. Website: www.greenwood.com. **Acquisitions:** Peter Kracht, executive editor. Establ 1967. Publishes hardcover originals. **Publishes 200 titles/year. Receives 1,000 queries/year. 25% of books from first-time authors. Pays variable royalty on net price. Offers advance rarely.** Publishes book 1 year after acceptance of ms. Accepts simultaneous submissions. Responds in 6 months to queries. Book catalog and ms guidelines online.

○━ Greenwood Press publishes reference materials for the entire spectrum of libraries, as well as scholarly monographs in the humanities and the social and behavioral sciences.

Nonfiction: Reference. Query with proposal package, including scope, organization, length of project, whether a complete ms is available or when it will be, cv or résumé and SASE. *No unsolicited mss.*

Recent Title(s): *John Grisham: A Critical Companion*, by Mary Beth Pringle.

GREENWOOD PUBLISHING GROUP, Reed-Elsevier (USA) Inc.,, 88 Post Rd. W, Westport CT 06881. (203)226-3571. Fax: (203)222-1502. Website: www.greenwood.com. **Acquisitions:** Academic, reference and trade—George Butler (anthropology, education, literature, drama and sociology, ext. 461‹gbutler@greenwood.com›); Cynthia Harris (history and economics, ext. 460 ‹charris@greenwood.com›); Nita Romer (multicultural and women's studies, gerontology, media, political science and law, psychology, ext. 445 ‹nromer@greenwood.com›); Pam St. Clair (art and architecture, music and dance, philosophy and religion, popular culture); Interdisciplinary studies, such as African-American studies are handled by all editors; contact js@greenwood.com. Secondary School Reference—Emily Birch (sociology, psychology, arts, religion, sports and recreation, ext. 448 ‹ebirch@greenwood.com›); Jane Garry (library science, pregnancy, parenting, alternative medicine, education, and anthropology, ext. 480 ‹jgarry@greenwood.com›); Barbara Rader (literature, history, women's studies, school librarianship, ext. 442 ‹brader@greenwood.com›); Heather Staines (history and military studies, ext. 214 ‹hstaines@greenwood.com›). Professional Publishing: Eric Valentine (Quorum Books, ext. 471 ‹evalentine@greenwood.com›). Publishes hardcover and trade paperback originals. **Publishes 700 titles/year. Pays royalty on net price. Offers advance rarely.** Publishes book 1 year after acceptance of ms. Accepts simultaneous submissions. Book catalog and ms guidelines online.

○━ The Greenwood Publishing Group consists of five distinguished imprints with one unifying purpose: to provide the best possible reference, professional, text, and scholarly resources in the humanities and the social and behavioral sciences.

Imprint(s): Auburn House, Bergin & Garvey, **Greenwood Press**, **Praeger Publishers**, Quorum Books.

Nonfiction: Reference, textbook. Subjects include anthropology/archaeology, business/economics, child guidance/parenting, education, government/politics, history, language/literature, military/war, music/dance, philosophy, psychology, religion, sociology, sports, women's issues/studies. Query with proposal package, including scope, organization, length of project, whether a complete ms is available or when it will be, cv or résumé and SASE. *No unsolicited mss.*

Recent Title(s): *From the Unthinkable to the Unavoidable*, edited by Carol Rittner and John Roth (religion/Holocaust studies); *The Feminist Encyclopedia of German Literature*, edited by Friederike Eigler and Susanne Kord; *The Fighting Pattons*, by Brian Sobel (military).

Tips: "No interest in fiction, drama, poetry—looking for serious, scholarly, analytical studies of historical problems." Greenwood Publishing maintains an excellent website, providing complete catalog, ms guidelines and editorial contacts.

GROLIER PUBLISHING, Grolier Inc., 90 Sherman Turnpike, Danbury CT 06816. (203)797-3500. Fax: (203)797-3197. Estab. 1895. Publishes hardcover and trade paperback originals.

○━ "Grolier Publishing is a leading publisher of reference, educational and children's books. We provide parents, teachers and librarians with the tools they need to enlighten children to the pleasure of learning and prepare them for the road ahead."

Imprint(s): Children's Press, Grolier Educational, **Orchard Books**, **Franklin Watts**.

● Grolier was recently purchased by Scholastic, Inc.

Ⓐ GROSSET & DUNLAP PUBLISHERS, Penguin Putnam Inc., 345 Hudson St., New York NY 10014. Art Director: Creston Ely. **Acquisitions:** Jane O'Connor, president. Estab. 1898. Publishes hardcover (few) and paperback originals. **Publishes 175 titles/year.** Publishes book 18 months after acceptance. Responds in 2 months.

○━ Grosset & Dunlap publishes children's books that examine new ways of looking at the world of a child.

Imprint(s): Planet Dexter, **Price Stern Sloan**.

Nonfiction: Juveniles. Subjects include nature, science. *Agented submissions only.*

Fiction: Juveniles. *Agented submissions only.*

Recent Title(s): *Dragon Slayers' Academy* series, *Zack Files* series.

Tips: "Nonfiction that is particularly topical or of wide interest in the mass market; new concepts for novelty format for preschoolers; and very well-written easy readers on topics that appeal to primary graders have the best chance of selling to our firm."

GROUP PUBLISHING, INC., 1515 Cascade Ave., Loveland CO 80538. (970)669-3836. Fax: (970)669-1994. E-mail: kloesche@grouppublishing.com. Website: www.grouppublishing.com. **Acquisitions:** Kerri Loesche, editorial assistant. Estab. 1974. Publishes trade paperback originals. **Publishes 24 titles/year. Receives 200 queries and 50 mss/year. 40% of books from first-time authors; 95% from unagented writers. Pays up to 10% royalty on wholesale price or makes outright purchase or work for hire. Offers up to $1,000 advance.** Publishes book 18 months after acceptance of ms. Accepts simultaneous submissions. Responds in 1 month to queries, 6 months to proposals and mss. Book catalog for 9×12 SAE with 2 first-class stamps. Manuscript guidelines for #10 SASE.

○━ "Our mission is to encourage Christian growth in children, youth and adults."

Imprint(s): Group.

Nonfiction: How-to, adult, youth and children's ministry resources. Subjects include education, religion and any subjects pertinent to adult, youth or children's ministry in a church setting. "We're an interdenominational publisher of resource materials for people who work with adults, youth or children in a Christian church setting. We also publish materials for use directly by youth or children (such as devotional books, workbooks or Bibles stories). Everything we do is based on concepts of active and interactive learning as described in *Why Nobody Learns Much of Anything at Church: And How to Fix It*, by Thom and Joani Schultz. We need new, practical, hands-on, innovative, out-of-the-box ideas—things that no one's doing . . . yet." Query with SASE or submit proposal package, including outline, 3 sample chapters, cover letter and introduction to the book (written as if the reader will read it), and sample activities if appropriate.

Recent Title(s): *Aqua Church*, by Leonard Sweet (church leadership); *The Dirt on Learning*, by Thom and Joani Schultz (effective teaching and learning).

Tips: "Our audience consists of pastors, Christian education directors and Sunday school teachers. We're seeking proposals for CD-ROM projects. Submit same as proposal package above."

GROVE/ATLANTIC, INC., 841 Broadway, New York NY 10003. (212)614-7850. Fax: (212)614-7886. Publisher: Morgan Entrekin. **Acquisitions:** Joan Bingham, executive editor; Elizabeth Schmitz, senior editor/director of subsidiary rights; Andrew Miller, editor. Estab. 1952. Publishes hardcover originals, trade paperback originals and reprints. **Publishes 60-70 titles/year. Receives 1000s queries/year. 10-15% of books from first-time authors; "very few" from unagented writers. Pays 7½-15% royalty on retail price. Advance varies considerably.** Publishes book 1 year after acceptance of ms. Accepts simultaneous submissions. "Because of volume of queries, Grove/Atlantic can only respond when interested—though SASE might generate a response." Book catalog free.

○━ Grove/Atlantic publishes serious nonfiction and literary fiction.

Imprint(s): Grove Press (estab. 1952), Atlantic Monthly Press (estab. 1917).

Nonfiction: Biography. Subjects include government/politics, history, travel. Query with SASE. *No unsolicited mss.*

Fiction: Experimental, literary, translation. Query with SASE. *No unsolicited mss.*

Poetry: "We try to publish at least one volume of poetry every list." Query. *No unsolicited mss.*

Recent Title(s): *Black Hawk Dawn: A Story of Modern War*, by Mark Bowden.

ALDINE DE GRUYTER, Walter de Gruyter, Inc., 200 Saw Mill River Rd., Hawthorne NY 10532. (914)747-0110. Fax: (914)747-1326. E-mail: rkoffler@degruyterny.com. Website: www.degruyter.de. **Acquisitions**: Dr. Richard Koffler, executive editor. Publishes hardcover and academic paperback originals. **Publishes 15-25 titles/year. Receives several hundred queries and 100 mss/year. 15% of books from first-time authors; 99% from unagented writers. Pays 7½-10% royalty on net sales.** Publishes book 9 months after acceptance of ms. Accepts simultaneous submissions. Responds in 2 months to proposals. Book catalog free. Ms guidelines only after contract.

○━ Aldine de Gruyter is an academic nonfiction publisher.

Nonfiction: Textbook (rare), course-related monographs and edited volumes. Subjects include anthropology (biological); sociology, human services, evolutionary psychology. "Aldine's authors are academics with Ph.D's and strong publication records. No poetry or fiction." Submit 1-2 sample chapters, proposal package, including c.v., market, competing texts, etc., reviews of earlier work.

Recent Title(s): *The Politics of Medicine*, by Theodore R. Marmon.

Tips: Audience is professors and upper level and graduate students.

GRYPHON PUBLICATIONS, P.O. Box 209, Brooklyn NY 11228. **Acquisitions:** Gary Lovisi, owner/publisher. Publishes trade paperback originals and reprints. **Publishes 10 titles/year. Receives 500 queries and 1,000 mss/year. 60% of books from first-time authors; 90% from unagented writers. No advance.** Makes outright purchase by contract, price varies. Publishes book 2 years after acceptance of ms. Responds in 1 month to queries. *Writer's Market* recommends allowing 2 months for reply. Book catalog and ms guidelines for #10 SASE.

Imprint(s): Paperback Parade Magazine, Hardboiled Magazine, Other Worlds Magazine, Gryphon Books, Gryphon Doubles.

Nonfiction: Reference, bibliography. Subjects include hobbies, literature and book collecting. "We need well-written, well-researched articles, but query first on topic and length. Writers submit material that is not fully developed/researched." Query with SASE. Reviews artwork/photos as part of ms package. Send photocopies (slides, transparencies may be necessary later).

Fiction: Mystery, science fiction, suspense, urban horror, hardboiled fiction. "We want cutting-edge fiction, under 3,000 words with impact!" For short stories, query or submit complete ms. For novels, send 1-page query letter with SASE.

Tips: "We are very particular about novels and book-length work. A first-timer has a better chance with a short story or article. On anything over 6,000 words *do not* send manuscript, send *only* query letter with SASE."

GUILFORD PUBLICATIONS, INC., 72 Spring St., New York NY 10012. (212)431-9800. Fax: (212)966-6708. E-mail: info@guilford.com. Website: www.guilford.com. **Acquisitions:** Seymour Weingarten, editor-in-chief; Rochelle Serwator, editor (neuropsychology, speech and language); Kitty Moore, executive editor (psychology/psychiatry, child clinical, culture); Christopher Jennison, senior editor (education, school psychology); Jim Nageotte, senior editor (family, social work, culture, clinical psychology); Peter Wissoker, editor (geography, communication, social theory). Estab. 1978. Publishes hardcover and trade paperback originals and trade paperback reprints. **Publishes 75 titles/year. Receives 200 queries and 50 mss/year. 30% of books from first-time authors; 90% from unagented writers. Pays 0-15%**

royalty on wholesale price. Offers $500-5,000 advance. Publishes book 7 months after acceptance of ms. Accepts simultaneous submissions. Responds in 1 month to queries and proposals, 2 months to mss. Book catalog and ms guidelines free or on website.

O→ Guilford Publications publishes quality trade and professional titles in psychology, psychiatry and the behavioral sciences, including addictions, gender issues and child abuse; as well as cultural studies, philosophy, politics, geography, communication and education. Products include books, journals and videos.

Nonfiction: Self-help, technical, textbook. Subjects include child guidance/parenting, education, gay/lesbian, government/politics, health/medicine, philosophy, psychology, sociology, women's issues/studies. Query with SASE. Submit proposal package, including outline, 2 sample chapters and curriculum vitae.

Recent Titles: *Reconciliable Differences*, by Christensen and Jacobson.

Tips: "Projects must be solidly research-based."

GULF PUBLISHING COMPANY, P.O. Box 2608, Houston TX 77252-2608. (713)529-4301. Fax: (713)520-4438. E-mail: kilmerk@gulfpub.com or calkt@gulfpub.com. Website: www.gpcbooks.com or www.gulfpub.com. **Acquisitions:** Tim Calk, acquisitions editor (science/technical); Kim Kilmer, acquisitions editor (field guides, cookbooks, Texana business, children's, dog training). Estab. 1916. Publishes hardcover and trade paperback originals and reprints. **Publishes 60-65 titles/year. Receives 1,000 queries and 400 mss/year. 50% of books from first-time authors; 90% from unagented writers. Pays royalty.** Publishes book 18 months after acceptance of ms. Accepts simultaneous submissions. Responds in 1 month to queries, 3 months to proposals and mss. Book catalog and ms guidelines with SASE.

O→ Gulf publishes technical and Texana titles. "We are expanding to publish books for a more general nonfiction audience. The titles include, but are not necessarily limited to, outdoor field guides, general cookbooks, business books, dog training books, and books on human resources and training."

Imprint(s): Maverick (Hank the Cowdog Audiobooks); Lonestar (Texana); Cashman Dudley (business).; Barker Heeler (dog training); Enchanted Rock (children's).

Nonfiction: Cookbook, how-to, reference, dog training, technical, Texana. Subjects include business/economics, cooking/foods/nutrition, money/finance, nature/environment, regional. Submit proposal package, including cover letter, outline, résumé, sample chapters and SASE. Reviews artwork/photos as part of ms package. Send color copies, slides or actual photos.

Fiction: Juvenile, picture books. "Primarily, we are interested in picture books for young readers (ages 3-9)." Submit synopsis, sample chapter and SASE.

Recent Title(s): *The Common Sense Approach, Surviving Puppyhood*, by Kay Guetzloff; *Executive Leadership*, by Joseph Olmstead.

HALF HALT PRESS, INC., P.O. Box 67, Boonsboro MD 21713. (301)733-7119. Fax: (301)733-7408. E-mail: hhpress@aol.com. Website: www.halfhaltpress.com. **Acquisitions:** Elizabeth Carnes, publisher. Estab. 1986. Publishes 90% hardcover and trade paperback originals and 10% reprints. **Publishes 15 titles/year. Receives 150 submissions/year. 25% of books from first-time authors; 50% from unagented authors. Pays 10-12½% royalty on retail price. Offers advance by agreement.** Publishes book 1 year after acceptance of ms. Responds in 1 month to queries. *Writer's Market* recommends allowing 2 months for reply. Book catalog for 6×9 SAE with 2 first-class stamps.

O→ "We publish high-quality nonfiction on equestrian topics, books that help riders and trainers do something better."

Nonfiction: Instructional: horse and equestrian-related subjects only. "We need serious instructional works by authorities in the field on horse-related topics, broadly defined." Query with SASE. Reviews artwork/photos as part of ms package.

Recent Title(s): *Dressage in Harmony*, by Walter Zettl.

Tips: "Writers have the best chance selling us well-written, unique works that teach serious horse people how to do something better. If I were a writer trying to market a book today, I would offer a straightforward presentation, letting the work speak for itself, without hype or hard sell. Allow publisher to contact writer, without frequent calling to check status. They haven't forgotten the writer but may have many different proposals at hand; frequent calls to 'touch base,' multiplied by the number of submissions, become an annoyance. As the publisher/author relationship becomes close and is based on working well together, early impressions may be important, even to the point of being a consideration in acceptance for publication."

ALEXANDER HAMILTON INSTITUTE, 70 Hilltop Rd., Ramsey NJ 07446-1119. (201)825-3377. Fax: (201)825-8696. Website: www.ahipubs.com. **Acquisitions:** Brian L.P. Zevnik, editor-in-chief; Gloria Ju, editor; Amy Knierim, editor. Estab. 1909. Publishes 3-ring binder and paperback originals. **Publishes 5-10 titles/year. Receives 50 queries and 10 mss/year. 25% of books from first-time authors; 95% from unagented writers. Pays 5-8% royalty on retail price or makes outright purchase ($3,500-7,000). Offers $3,500-7,000 advance.** Publishes book 10 months after acceptance. Accepts simultaneous submissions. Responds in 1 month to queries, 2 months to mss.

O→ Alexander Hamilton Institute publishes "non-traditional" management books for upper-level managers and executives. Currently emphasizing legal issues for HR/personnel. De-emphasizing how-to business management.

Nonfiction: Executive/management books. The first audience is overseas, upper-level managers. "We need how-to and skills building books. *No* traditional management texts or academic treatises." The second audience is US personnel executives and high-level management. Subject is legal personnel matters. "These books combine court case research and practical application of defensible programs." Submit outline, 3 paragraphs on each chapter, examples of lists, graphics, cases.

Recent Title(s): *Employer's Guide to Record-Keeping Requirements*.

Tips: "We sell exclusively by direct mail to managers and executives around the world. A writer must know his/her field and be able to communicate practical systems and programs."

HAMPTON ROADS PUBLISHING COMPANY, INC., 1125 Stoney Ridge Rd., Charlottesville VA 22902. (804)296-2772. Fax: (804)296-5096. E-mail: hrpc@hrpub.com. Website: hrpub.com. **Acquisitions:** Frank DeMarco, chief editor (metaphysical/visionary fiction); Robert S. Friedman, president (metaphysical, spiritual, inspirational, self-help); Ken Eagle Feather, marketing director (spiritual paths/Toltec); Richard Leviton, senior editor (alternative medicine). Estab. 1989. Publishes hardcover and trade paperback originals. **Publishes 35-40 titles/year. Receives 1,000 queries and 1,500 mss/year. 50% of books from first-time authors; 70% from unagented writers. Pays royalty. Offers $1,000-100,000 advance.** Usually publishes book 1 year after acceptance of ms. Accepts simultaneous submissions. Responds in 2 months to queries and proposals, 6 months to mss. Book catalog free. Manuscript guidelines free.

O— "Our reason for being is to impact, uplift and contribute to positive change in the world. We publish books that will enrich and empower the evolving consciousness of mankind."

Imprint(s): Young Spirit (children's spiritual).

Nonfiction: How-to, illustrated book, self-help. Spirituality subjects. Query or submit synopsis with SASE. Reviews artwork/photos as part of the ms package. Send photocopies.

Fiction: Spiritual, visionary fiction. "Fiction should have one or more of the following themes: spiritual, inspirational, metaphysical, i.e., past life recall, out of body experiences, near death experience, paranormal." Query or submit synopsis with full ms and SASE.

Recent Title(s): *Jonah*, by Dana Redfield (fiction); *Emir's Education and the Proper Use of Magical Powers*, by Jane Roberts (Young Spirit imprint).

■ HANCOCK HOUSE PUBLISHERS, 1431 Harrison Ave., Blaine WA 98230-5005. (604)538-1114. Fax: (604)538-2262. E-mail: david@hancockwildlife.org. Website: www.hancockwildlife.org. **Acquisitions:** David Hancock, publisher. Estab. 1971. Publishes hardcover and trade paperback originals and reprints. **Publishes 14 titles/year. Receives 300 submissions/year. 50% of books from first-time authors; 90% from unagented writers. Pays 10% royalty.** Accepts simultaneous submissions. Publishes book up to 1 year after acceptance. Book catalog free. Manuscript guidelines for #10 SASE.

O— Hancock House Publishers, seeks agriculture, natural history, animal husbandry, conservation and popular science titles with a regional (Pacific Northwest), national or international focus.

Nonfiction: Biography, how-to, reference, technical. Pacific Northwest history and biography, nature guides, native culture, and international natural history. "Centered around Pacific Northwest, local history, nature guide books, international ornithology and Native Americans." Submit outline, 3 sample chapters and proposal package, including selling points with SASE. Reviews artwork/photos as part of ms package. Send photocopies.

Recent Title(s): *Bushplanes of the North*, by Robert Grant (aviation/history).

HANSER GARDNER PUBLICATIONS, 6915 Valley Ave., Cincinnati OH 45244. (513)527-8977. Fax: (513)527-8950. Website: www.hansergardner.com. **Acquisitions:** Woody Chapman. Estab. 1993. Publishes hardcover and paperback originals and reprints. **Publishes 5-10 titles/year. Receives 40-50 queries and 5-10 mss/year. 75% of books from first-time authors; 100% from unagented writers. Pays 10-15% royalty on net receipts. No advance.** Publishes book 10 months after acceptance of ms. Accepts simultaneous submissions. Responds in 2 weeks to queries, 1 month to proposals and mss. Book catalog and ms guidelines free.

O— Hanser Gardner publishes training and practical application titles for metalworking, machining and finishing shops/plants.

Nonfiction: How-to, technical, textbook. Subjects include metalworking and finishing processes, and related management topics. "Our books are primarily basic introductory-level training books and books that emphasize practical applications. Strictly deal with subjects shown above." Query with résumé, preface, outline, sample chapter, comparison to competing or similar titles. Reviews artwork/photos as part of ms package. Send photocopies.

Recent Title(s): *Industrial Painting*, by Norman R. Roobol (industrial reference).

Tips: "Our readers and authors occupy various positions within small and large metalworking, machining and finishing shops/plants. We prefer that interested individuals write, call, or fax us with their queries first, so we can send them our proposal guideline form."

HARBOR PRESS, 5713 Wollochet Dr. NW, Gig Harbor WA 98335. Fax: (253)851-5191. E-mail: info@harborpress.com. Website: www.harborpress.com. President/Publisher: Harry R. Lynn. **Acquisitions:** Deborah Young, senior editor (please direct submissions to Harbor Press, 5 Glen Dr., Plainview NY 11803). Estab. 1985. Publishes hardcover and trade paperback originals and reprints. **Publishes 8-10 titles/year. Negotiates competitive royalties on wholesale price or makes outright purchase.**

O— Harbor Press publishes consumer-oriented health and self-improvement titles for both trade and mail-order markets.

Nonfiction: Health, self-improvement. Subjects include health/medicine, nutrition. Query with proposal package, including outline, 3 sample chapters, synopsis and SASE. Reviews artwork as part of ms package. Send photocopies.
Recent Title(s): *Healing Back Pain Naturally: The Mind-Body Program Proven to Work*, by Art Brownstein, M.D.

HARCOURT INC., Children's Books Division, 525 B St., Suite 1900, San Diego CA 92101. (619)261-6616. Fax: (619)699-6777. Website: www.harcourtbooks.com/Childrens/childrn.html. Publisher: Louise Pelan. Estab. 1919. Publishes hardcover originals and trade paperback reprints.

    O━ Harcourt Inc. owns some of the world's most prestigious publishing imprints which produce quality products for the juvenile, educational, scientific, technical, medical, professional and trade markets worldwide.
Imprint(s): Harcourt Children's Books, Gulliver Books, Silver Whistle, Red Wagon Books, Harcourt Young Classics, Green Light Readers, Voyager Books/Libros Viajeros, Harcourt Paperbacks, Odyssey Classics, Magic Carpet Books.
Nonfiction and Fiction: No unsolicited mss or queries accepted. No phone calls.
    ● At press time Harcourt was exploring the sale of the company
Recent Title(s): *Home Run*, by Robert Burleigh; *My Name is Georgia*, by Jeanette Winter.

HARCOURT INC., Trade Division, 525 B St., Suite 1900, San Diego, CA 92101. (619)699-6560. Fax: (619)699-5555. Website: www.harcourtbooks.com. **Acquisitions**: David Hough, managing editor; Jane Isay, editor-in-chief (science, math, history, language); Drenka Willen, senior editor (poetry, fiction in translation, history); Walter Bode, editor (history, geography, American fiction). Publishes hardcover and trade paperback originals and trade paperback reprints. **Publishes 120 titles/year. 5% of books from first-time authors; 5% from unagented writers. Pays 6-15% royalty on retail price. Offers $2,000 minimum advance.** Accepts simultaneous mss.

    O━ Harcourt Inc. owns some of the world's most prestigious publishing imprints—imprints which distinguish quality products for the juvenile, educational, scientific, technical, medical, professional and trade markets worldwide. Currently emphasizing science and math.
Imprint(s): Harvest (contact Andre Bernard).
Nonfiction: Publishes all categories *except* business/finance (university texts), cookbooks, self-help, sex. Agented submissions or query letters only with SASE. *No unsolicited mss.*
    ● At press time Harcourt was exploring the sale of the company
Recent Title(s): *The Feeling of What Happens*, by Antonio Damasio (nonfiction); *Blindness*, by Jose Saramago (fiction); *Open Closed Open*, by Yehuda Amichai (poetry).

Ⓐ HARPERBUSINESS, HarperCollins Publishers, 10 E. 53rd St., New York NY 10022. (212)207-7000. Website: www.harpercollins.com. **Acquisitions**: Adrian Zackheim, senior vice president/publisher; David Conti, executive editor; Laureen Rowland, senior editor; Zachary Schisgal, senior editor. Estab. 1991. Publishes hardcover, trade paperback and mass market paperback originals, hardcover and trade paperback reprints. **Publishes 50-55 titles/year. Receives 500 queries and mss/year. 1% of books from first-time authors; 0% from unagented writers. Pays royalty on retail price; varies. Offers advance.** Accepts simultaneous submissions. Responds in 2 months to agented proposals and mss. Book catalog free.

    O━ HarperBusiness publishes "the inside story on ideas that will shape business practices and thinking well into the next millennium, with cutting-edge information and visionary concepts." Currently emphasizing finance, motivation, technology.
Nonfiction: Biography (economics); business/economics, marketing subjects. "We don't publish how-to, textbooks or things for academic market; no reference (tax or mortgage guides), our reference department does that. Proposals need to be top notch. We tend not to publish people who have no business standing. Must have business credentials." *Agented submissions only.*
Recent Title(s): *Now or Never*, by Mary Modahl; *Consulting Demons*, by Lewis Pinault.
Tips: Business audience: managers, CEOs, consultants, some academics.

HARPERCOLLINS CHILDREN'S BOOKS, HarperCollins Publishers, 1350 Avenue of the Americas, New York NY 10019. (212)261-6500. Website: www.harpercollins.com. Editor-in-Chief: Kate Morgan Jackson. **Acquisitions**: Alix Reid, editorial director; Robert Warren, editorial director; Phoebe Yeh, editorial director. Publishes hardcover originals. **Publishes 350 titles/year. Receives 200 queries and 5,000 mss/year. 5% of books from first-time authors; 25% from unagented writers. Pays 10-12½% royalty on retail price. Advance varies.** Publishes novel 1 year, picture books 2 years after acceptance of ms. Accepts simultaneous submissions. Responds in 1 month to queries and proposals, 4 months to mss. Book catalog for 8×10 SASE with 3 first-class stamps. Ms guidelines for #10 SASE.

    O━ "We have no rules for subject matter, length or vocabulary, but look instead for ideas that are fresh and imaginative, good writing that involves the reader is essential."
Imprint(s): Joanna Cotler Books (Joanna Cotler, editorial director); **Laura Geringer Books** (Laura Geringer, editorial director); Harper Festival (Suzanne Daghlian, editorial director); Avon; Harper Tempest (Elise Howard, vice president publisher); Harper Trophy (Ginee Seo, editorial director).
Fiction: Adventure, fantasy, historical, humor, juvenile, literary, picture books, young adult. Query *only* with SASE. no unsolicited mss.
Recent Title(s): *Today I Feel Silly*, by Jamie Lee Curtis (picture book); *Ella Enchanted*, by Gail Carson Levine (novel).

HARPERENTERTAINMENT, HarperCollins Publishers, 10 E. 53rd St., New York NY 10022. (212)207-7000. E-mail: lara.comstock@harpercollins.com. Editorial Director/Vice President: Hope Innelli. **Acquisitions:** Lara Comstock, editor. Estab. 1997. **20% of books from first-time authors. Writer-for-hire arrangements mostly. Fees vary.** Responds in 3-12 months to mss. Book catalog and mss guidelines not available.

    O⊸ "A newly formed imprint, HarperEntertainment is dedicated to publishing sports, movie and TV tie-ins, celebrity bios and books reflecting trends in popular culture."

Nonfiction: Children's/juvenile, biographies, movie and TV-tie ins. "The bulk of our work is done by experienced writers for hire, but we are open to original ideas." Query with outline and SASE.

Fiction: Humor, juvenile, movie and TV tie-ins. Query with synopsis and SASE.

Recent Title(s): *Mary-Kate & Ashley's New Adventures.*

A **HARPERPERENNIAL**, HarperCollins Publishers, 10 E. 53rd St., New York NY 10022. (212)207-7000. Website: www.harpercollins.com. **Acquisitions:** Acquisitions Editor. Estab. 1963. Publishes trade paperback originals and reprints. **Publishes 100 titles/year. Receives 500 queries/year. 5% of books from first-time authors.**

    O⊸ Harper Perennial publishes a broad range of adult literary fiction and nonfiction paperbacks.

Nonfiction: Biography, cookbook, how-to, humor, illustrated book, reference, self-help. Subjects include Americana, animals, business/economics, child guidance/parenting, education, ethnic, gay/lesbian,history, language/literature, mental health, military/war, money/finance, music/dance, nature/environment, philosophy, psychology/self-help psychotherapy, recreation, regional, religion/spirituality, science, sociology, sports, translation, travel, women's issues/studies. "Our focus is ever-changing, adjusting to the marketplace. Mistakes writers often make are not giving their background and credentials—why they are qualified to write the book. A proposal should explain why the author wants to write this book; why it will sell; and why it is better or different from others of its kind." *Agented submissions only.*

Fiction: Ethnic, feminist, literary. "Don't send us novels—go through hardcover." *Agented submissions only.*

Poetry: "Don't send poetry unless you have been published in several established literary magazines already." *Agented submissions only.* Query with 10 sample poems.

Tips: "See our website for a list of titles or write to us for a free catalog."

HARPERSANFRANCISCO, HarperCollins Publishers, 353 Sacramento St., Suite 500, San Francisco CA 94111-3653. (415)477-4400. Fax: (415)477-4444. E-mail: hcsanfrancisco@harpercollins.com. Vice President/Associate Publisher: Stephen Hanselman. **Acquisitions:** Liz Perle, editor-at-large (women's studies, psychology, personal growth, inspiration); Douglas Abrams, senior editor (Hebrew Bible, Judaism, religion, health, sexuality); John Loudon, executive editor (religious studies, biblical studies, psychology/personal growth, Eastern religions); David Hennessy, associate editor (New Age, gay and lesbian nonfiction, inspiration, general nonfiction); Gideon Weil, associate editor (general nonfiction, self-help, inspiration, Judaica.) Estab. 1977. Publishes hardcover originals, trade paperback originals and reprints. **Publishes 75 titles/year. Receives about 10,000 submissions/year. 5% of books from first-time authors. Pays royalty.** Publishes book within 18 months after acceptance.

    O⊸ HarperSanFrancisco publishes books that "nurture the mind, body and spirit; support readers in their ongoing self-discovery and personal growth; explore the essential religious and philosophical issues of our time; and present the rich and diverse array of the wisdom traditions of the world to a contemporary audience."

Nonfiction: Biography, how-to, reference, self-help. Subjects include psychology, religion, self-help, spirituality. Query. *No unsolicited mss.*

Recent Title(s): *The Legacy of Luna*, by Julia Butterfly Hill (nonfiction); *Weaving the Web*, by Tim Berners-Lee (nonfiction).

HARVARD BUSINESS SCHOOL PRESS, Harvard Business School Publishing Corp., 60 Harvard Way, Boston MA 02163. (617)783-7400. Fax: (617)783-7489. E-mail: bookpublisher@hbsp.harvard.edu. Website: www.hbsp.harvard.edu. Director: Carol Franco. **Acquisitions:** Marjorie Williams, executive editor; Kirsten Sandberg, senior editor; Melinda Adams Merino, senior editor; Hollis Heimbouch, senior editor; Nikki Sabin, acquisitions editor. Estab. 1984. Publishes hardcover originals. **Publishes 35-45 titles/year. Pays escalating royalty on retail price. Advances vary widely depending on author and market for the book.** Accepts simultaneous submissions. Responds in 1 month to proposals and mss. Book catalog and ms guidelines available on website.

    O⊸ The Harvard Business School Press publishes books for an audience of senior and general managers and business scholars. HBS Press is the source of the most influential ideas and conversations that shape business worldwide.

Nonfiction: Subjects include general management, marketing, finance, digital economy, technology and innovation, human resources. Submit proposal package, including outline with sample chapters.

Recent Title(s): *Digital Capital*, by Don Tapscott, David Ticoll and Alex Lowry.

Tips: "Take care to really look into the type of business books we publish. They are generally not handbooks, how-to manuals, policy-oriented, dissertations, edited collections, or personal business narratives."

THE HARVARD COMMON PRESS, 535 Albany St., Boston MA 02118-2500. (617)423-5803. Fax: (617)423-0679 or (617)695-9794. Website: www.harvardcommonpress.com. **Acquisitions:** Bruce P. Shaw, president/publisher. Associate Publisher: Dan Rosenberg. Estab. 1976. Publishes hardcover and trade paperback originals and reprints. **Publishes 12 titles/year. Receives 1,000 submissions/year. 20% of books from first-time authors; 40% of books**

from unagented writers. **Pays royalty. Offers average $4,000 advance.** Publishes book 1 year after acceptance of ms. Accepts simultaneous submissions. Responds in 2 months. Book catalog for 9×12 SAE with 3 first-class stamps. Manuscript guidelines for SASE.

    O→ "We want strong, practical books that help people gain control over a particular area of their lives." Currently emphasizing cooking, childcare/parenting, health. De-emphasizing general instructional books, travel.

Imprint(s): Gambit Books.

Nonfiction: Subjects include cooking, childcare/parenting, health, travel. "A large percentage of our list is made up of books about cooking, child care and parenting; in these areas we are looking for authors who are knowledgeable, if not experts, and who can offer a different approach to the subject. We are open to good nonfiction proposals that show evidence of strong organization and writing, and clearly demonstrate a need in the marketplace. First-time authors are welcome." Accepts nonfiction translations. Submit outline and 1-3 sample chapters. Reviews artwork/photos.

Recent Title(s): *The New England Cookbook*, by Brooke Dojny.

Tips: "We are demanding about the quality of proposals; in addition to strong writing skills and thorough knowledge of the subject matter, we require a detailed analysis of the competition."

HASTINGS HOUSE, Eagle Publishing Corp., 9 Mott Ave., Suite 203, Norwalk CT 06850. (203)838-4083. Fax: (203)838-4084. E-mail: Hhousebks@aol.com. Website: www.hastingshousebooks.com. Publisher: Peter Leers. **Acquisitions:** Rachel Borst, senior editor (nonfiction: history, biography, architecture); Earl Steinbicker, travel editor (edits our Daytrips series of guides). Publishes hardcover and trade paperback originals and reprints. **Publishes 20 titles/year. Receives 600 queries and 900 mss/year. 10% of books from first-time authors; 40% from unagented writers. Pays 8-10% royalty on retail price on trade paperbacks. Offers $1,000-10,000 advance.** Publishes book 6-10 months after acceptance of ms. Responds in 2 months.

    O→ "We are looking for books that address consumer needs. We are primarily focused on expanding our Daytrips Travel Series nationally and internationally along with related travel books and select nonfiction." Currently de-emphasizing foods, nutrition, cookbooks.

Nonfiction: Biography, cookbook, how-to, reference, self-help, consumer. Subjects include business/economics, cooking/foods/nutrition, health/medicine, psychology, travel, writing. Query or submit outline.

Recent Title(s): *Great American Mansions*, (revised edition) by Merril Folsom.

HATHERLEIGH PRESS, 5-22 46th Ave. #200, Long Island City NY 11101-5215. (212)832-1584. Fax: (212)832-1502. E-mail: info@hatherleigh.com. Website: www.hatherleigh.com. Editor-In-Chief: Frederic Flach, M.D. **Acquisitions:** Kevin J. Moran, associate publisher. Estab. 1995. Publishes hardcover originals, trade paperback originals and reprints. **Publishes 10-12 titles/year. Receives 20 queries and 20 mss/year. Pays 5-15% royalty on retail price or makes outright purchase. Offers $500-5,000 advance.** Publishes book 6 months after acceptance of ms. Responds in 2 months to queries. Book catalog free.

    O→ Hatherleigh Press publishes general self-help titles and reference books for mental health professionals. Currently emphasizing fitness, popular medicine. De-emphasizing self-help.

Imprint(s): Red Brick Books—new fiction imprint (Kevin J. Moran, acquisitions editor); Getfitnow.com Books.

Nonfiction: Reference, self-help, technical. Subjects include health/medicine, psychology. Submit outline and 1 sample chapter with SASE. Reviews artwork/photos as part of ms package. Send photocopies.

Recent Title(s): *I Can't Believe It's Yoga*, by Lisa Trivell.

Tips: Audience is mental health professionals. Submit a clear outline, including market and audience for your book.

[N] HAVEN PUBLICATIONS, GPO Box 8101, New York NY 10116-8101. **Acquisitions:** R. Hayes, vice president (philosophy). Publishes hardcover originals. **Publishes 8-12 titles/year. Receives 30 queries and 30 mss/year. 4% of books from first-time authors; 100% from unagented writers. Pays 6-10% royalty on retail price. No advance.** Publishes book 16 months after acceptance of ms. Responds in 1 month to queries and proposals, 6 months to mss. Book catalog free.

    O→ Publisher of philosophical and theoretical academic titles.

Nonfiction: Technical, textbook. Subjects include philosophy, psychology, religion, science, sociology. Submit completed ms.

Recent Title(s): *Developments in Semantics*, by Orenstein (logic); *The Emotions*, by Irani (theory).

[N] HAWK PUBLISHING GROUP, 6420 S. Richmond Ave., Tulsa OK 74136. Website: www.hawkpub.com. **Acquisitions:** William Bernhardt, publisher. Publishes hardcover and trade paperback originals, hardcover and trade paperback reprints and mass market paperback reprints. **Publishes 10-15 titles/year. 10% of books from first-time authors; 10% from unagented writers (but we accept unagented submissions). Pays royalty. Advance varies.** Publishes book 9 months after acceptance of ms. Accepts simultaneous submissions. Responds in 1 month to mss.

    O→ "The best way to learn what HAWK publishes is to examine previous HAWK books. Search at www.hawkpub. com to see what we've done in the past."

Nonfiction: Biography, how-to, self-help. Subjects include anthropology/archaeology, business and economics, child guidance/parenting, education, health/medicine, history, hobbies, language/literature, money/finance, nature/environment, philosophy, recreation. Submit proposal package, including outline, ms or 3 sample chapters with SASE. Queries by e-mail are welcome. Reviews artwork/photos as part of ms package. Send photocopies.

Fiction: Adventure, fantasy, historical, horror, humor, juvenile, literary, mainstream/contemporary, mystery, picture books, science fiction, suspense, young adult. Send query with ms or synopsis and 3 sample chapters and SASE. Queries by e-mail are welcome.

Poetry: Submit complete ms. Queries by e-mail are welcome.

Recent Title(s): *Remnants of Glory*, by Teresa Miller (novel); *Old Fears*, by John Wooley & Ron Wolfe (novel).

THE HAWORTH PRESS, INC., 10 Alice St., Binghamton NY 13904. (607)722-5857. Fax: (607)722-8465. Website: www.haworthpressinc.com. **Acquisitions:** Bill Palmer, managing editor. Estab. 1973. Publishes hardcover and trade paperback originals. **Publishes 100 titles/year. Receives 500 queries and 250 mss/year. 60% of books from first-time authors; 98% from unagented writers. Pays 7½-15% royalty on wholesale price. Offers $500-1,000 advance.** Publishes book 1 year after acceptance of ms. Responds in 2 months to proposals. Manuscript guidelines free.

   O⊸ The Haworth Press is primarily a scholarly press.

Imprint(s): The Harrington Park Press, Haworth Pastoral Press, Haworth Food Products Press.

Nonfiction: Reference, textbook. Subjects include agriculture/horticulture, business/economics, child guidance/parenting, cooking/foods/nutrition, gay/lesbian, health/medicine, money/finance, psychology, sociology, women's issues/studies. "No 'pop' books." Submit proposal package, including outline and 1-3 sample chapters and author bio. Reviews artwork/photos as part of ms package. Send photocopies.

Recent Title(s): *Reviving the Tribe*, by Eric Rofes (gay & lesbian).

HAY HOUSE, INC., P.O. Box 5100, Carlsbad CA 92018-5100. (760)431-7695. Fax: (760)431-6948. E-mail: jkramer @hayhouse.com. Website: www.hayhouse.com. **Acquisitions:** Jill Kramer, editorial director. Estab. 1985. Publishes hardcover and trade paperback originals. **Publishes 40 titles/year. Receives 1,200 submissions/year. 10% of books are from first-time authors; 25% from unagented writers. Pays standard royalty.** Publishes book 10-15 months after acceptance of ms. Accepts simultaneous submissions (through the mail only—no e-mail submissions). Responds in 3 weeks. *Writer's Market* recommends allowing 2 months for reply. Book catalog free. Does not respond or return mss without SASE.

   O⊸ "We publish books, audios and videos that help heal the planet."

Imprint(s): Astro Room, Hay House Lifestyles.

Nonfiction: Primarily self-help, Subjects include relationships, mind/body health, nutrition, education, astrology, environment, health/medicine, money/finance, nature, philosophy/New Age, psychology, spiritual, sociology, women's and men's issues/studies. "Hay House is interested in a variety of subjects as long as they have a positive self-help slant to them. No poetry, children's books or negative concepts that are not conducive to helping/healing ourselves or our planet." Query or submit outline, sample chapters and SASE.

Recent Title(s): *Sixth Sense*, by Stuart Wilde (nonfiction).

Tips: "Our audience is concerned with our planet, the healing properties of love, and general self-help principles. If I were a writer trying to market a book today, I would research the market thoroughly to make sure there weren't already too many books on the subject I was interested in writing about. Then I would make sure I had a unique slant on my idea. SASE a must!"

HAZELDEN PUBLISHING, P.O. Box 176, Center City MN 55012. Website: www.hazelden.org. **Acquisitions:** Rebecca Post, executive editor. Estab. 1954. Publishes hardcover and trade paperback originals and trade paperback reprints. **Publishes 100 titles/year. Receives 2,500 queries and 1,000 mss/year. 30% of books from first-time authors; 50% from unagented writers. Pays 8% royalty on retail price. Offers advance based on first year sales projections.** Publishes book 1 year after acceptance of ms. Accepts simultaneous submissions. Responds in 6 months. Book catalog or ms guidelines free.

   O⊸ Hazelden is a trade, educational and professional publisher specializing is psychology, self-help, and spiritual books that help enhance the quality of people's lives. Products include gift books, curriculum, workbooks, audio and video, computer-based products and wellness products. "We specialize in books on addiction/recovery, spirituality/personal growth, chronic illness and prevention topics related to chemical and mental health."

Nonfiction: Gift book, how-to, self-help. Subjects include child guidance/parenting, gay/lesbian, health/medicine, memoirs, psychology, spirituality. Query with SASE. Submit proposal package, including outline, 2 sample chapters, market analysis and author qualifications.

Recent Title(s): *Playing It By Heart*, by Melody Beattie (self-help); *I Closed My Eyes: Revelations of a Battered Woman*, by Michelle Weldon.

Tips: Audience includes "consumers and professionals interested in the range of topics related to chemical and emotional health, including spirituality, self-help and addiction recovery."

HEALTH COMMUNICATIONS, INC., 3201 SW 15th St., Deerfield Beach FL 33442. (954)360-0909. Fax: (954)360-0034. Website: www.hci-online.com. **Acquisitions:** Christine Belleris, editorial director; Susan Tobias, editor; Allison Janse, editor; Lisa Drucker, editor. Publishes hardcover and trade paperback originals. Estab. 1976. **Publishes 40 titles/year. 20% of books from first-time authors; 90% from unagented writers. Pays 15% royalty on net price.** Publishes book 9 months after acceptance of ms. Accepts simultaneous submissions. Responds in 1 month to queries, 3 months to proposals and mss. Book catalog for 8½×11 SASE. Manuscript guidelines for #10 SASE.

O━ "We are the Life Issues Publisher. Health Communications, Inc., strives to help people grow and improve their lives from physical and emotional health to finances and interpersonal relationships." Currently emphasizing books for a teenage audience with a new interest in books for active senior citizens.

Nonfiction: Self-help. Subjects include child guidance/parenting, inspiration, psychology, spirituality, women's issues/ studies, recovery. Submit proposal package, including outline, 2 sample chapters, vitae, marketing study and SASE. No phone calls. Reviews artwork/photos as part of ms package. Send photocopies.

Recent Title(s): *Chicken Soup for the Couple's Soul* by Canfield, Hansen, DeAngelis and Donnelly (nonfiction); *Wings of Destiny*, by Catherine Lanigan (fiction).

Tips: Audience is composed primarily of women, aged 25-60, interested in personal growth and self-improvement. "Please do your research in your subject area. We publish general self-help books and are expanding to include new subjects such as business self-help and possibly alternative healing. We need to know why there is a need for your book, how it might differ from other books on the market and what you have to offer to promote your work."

HEALTH INFORMATION PRESS (HIP), PMIC (Practice Management Information Corp.), 4727 Wilshire Blvd., Los Angeles CA 90010. (323)954-0224. Fax: (323)954-0253. Website: medicalbookstore.com. **Acquisitions:** Kathryn Swanson, managing editor. Publishes hardcover originals, trade paperback originals and reprints. **Publishes 8-10 titles/ year. Receives 1,000 queries and 50 mss/year. 10% of books from first-time authors; 90% from unagented writers. Pays 10-15% royalty on net receipts. Offers $3,000 average advance.** Publishes books 18 months after acceptance of ms. Responds in 6 months. Book catalog and ms guidelines for #10 SASE.

O━ Health Information Press publishes books for consumers who are interested in taking an active role in their health care.

Nonfiction: How-to, illustrated book, reference, self-help. Subjects include health/medicine, psychology, science. "We seek to simplify health and medicine for consumers." Submit proposal package, including outline, 3-5 sample chapters, curriculum vitae or résumé and letter detailing who would buy the book and the market/need for the book. Reviews artwork/photos as part of the ms package.

Recent Title(s): *Living Longer with Heart Disease*, by Howard Wayne, M.D.; *A Spy in the Nursing Home*, by Eileen Kraatz.

HEALTHWISE PUBLICATIONS, Piccadilly Books Ltd., P.O. Box 25203, Colorado Springs CO 80936-5203. (719)550-9887. Website: www.piccadillybooks.com. Publisher: Bruce Fife. **Acquisitions**: Submissions Department. Publishes hardcover and trade paperback originals and trade paperback reprints. **Pays 10% royalty on retail price.** Publishes book within 1 year after acceptance of ms. Accepts simultaneous submissions.

O━ Healthwise specializes in the publication of books on health and fitness written with a holistic or natural health viewpoint.

Nonfiction: Diet, nutrition, exercise, alternative medicine and related topics. Query with sample chapters. Responds only if interested, unless accompanied by a SASE.

Recent Title(s): *Saturated Fat May Save Your Life!*, by Bruce Fife, N.D. (health/nutrition).

WILLIAM S. HEIN & CO., INC., 1285 Main St., Buffalo NY 14209-1987. (716)882-2600. Fax: (716)883-8100. E-mail: mail@wshein.com. **Acquisitions:** Sheila Jarrett, publications manager. Estab. 1961. **Publishes 30 titles/year. Receives 80 queries and 40 mss/year. 20% of books from first-time authors; 100% from unagented writers. Pays 10-25% royalty on net price.** Publishes book 9 months after acceptance of ms. Accepts simultaneous submissions. Does not return submissions. Responds in 3 months. Book catalog free.

O━ William S. Hein & Co. publishes reference books for law librarians, legal researchers and those interested in legal writing. Currently emphasizing law, government.

Nonfiction: Reference. Subjects include law and librarianship. Submit proposal package, including outline, 3 sample chapters and intended audience.

Recent Title(s): *Acing Your First Year of Law School: The Ten Steps to Success You Won't Learn in Class*, by Shana Noyes and Henry Noyes; *Legal Education for the 21st Century*, by Donald King.

■▲ **HEINEMANN**, Reed Elsevier (USA) Inc., 361 Hanover St., Portsmouth NH 03801. (603)431-7894. Fax: (603)431-7840. Website: www.heinemann.com. **Acquisitions:** Leigh Peake, executive editor (education); Lisa Barnett, senior editor (performing arts); William Varner, acquisitions editor (literacy); Lisa Luedeke, acquisitions editor (Boynton/ Cook). Estab. 1977. Publishes hardcover and trade paperback originals. **Publishes 80-100 titles/year. 50% of books from first-time authors; 75% from unagented writers. Pays royalty on wholesale price. Advance varies widely.** Accepts simultaneous submissions. Responds in 3 months to proposals. Book catalog free. Manuscript guidelines for #10 SASE.

O━ Heinemann specializes in theater and education titles. "Our goal is to offer a wide selecton of books that satisfy the needs and interests of educators from kindergarten to college." Currently emphasizing literacy education, K-12 education through technology.

Imprint(s): Boynton/Cook Publishers.

Nonfiction: How-to, reference. Subjects include parenting as it relates to school education, education, gay/lesbian issues, language arts, women's issues/studies, drama. "Our goal is to provide books that represent leading ideas within our niche markets. We publish very strictly within our categories. We do not publish classroom textbooks." Query. Submit proposal package, including table of contents, outline, 1-2 sample chapters.

Recent Title(s): *Word Matters*, by Irene Fountas and Gay-sa Pirrell.
Tips: "Keep your queries (and manuscripts!) short, study the market, be realistic and prepared to promote your book!"

HELIX BOOKS, Perseus Publishing, 11 Cambridge Center, Cambridge MA 02142 (617)252-5250. Fax: (617)252-5285. Website: www.aw.com. **Acquisitions:** Jeffrey Robbins, executive editor (physics, astronomy, complexity); Amanda Cook, editor (biology, evolution, complexity). Estab. 1992. Publishes hardcover and trade paperback originals and reprints. **Publishes 30 titles/year. Receives 160 queries/year. 50% of books from first-time authors; 60% from unagented writers. Pays 7½-15% royalty on retail price "sliding scale based on number of copies sold." Offers $5,000 and up advance.** Publishes book 6 months after acceptance of ms. Accepts simultaneous submissions but prefers exclusive. Responds in 1 month to queries. Book catalog free.

    ○┅ "Helix Books presents the world's top scientists and science writers sharing with the general public the latest discoveries and their human implications, across the full range of scientific disciplines." Currently emphasizing physics/astronomy, biology, evolution, complexity. De-emphasizing earth sciences, philosophy of science, neuroscience.

Nonfiction: Science. Query or submit outline, 2 sample chapters and proposal package, including market analysis, competition analysis, audience description, chapter outlines/table of contents, why topic is hot, why author is the one to write this book, 25-word synopsis that explains why the proposed book will be the best ever written about this topic.

HELLGATE PRESS, PSI Research, 300 N. Valley Dr., Grants Pass OR 97526. (503)479-9464. Fax: (503)476-1479. Website: www.psi-research.com/hellgate.htm. **Acquisitions:** Emmett Ramey, president. Estab. 1996. **Publishes 20-25 titles/year. Pays royalty.** Publishes books 6 months after acceptance of ms. Accepts simultaneous submissions. Responds in 2 months to queries. Book catalog and ms guidelines for #10 SASE.

    ○┅ Hellgate Press specializes in military history, other military topics and travel.

Nonfiction: Subjects include history, military/war, travel. Query with outline, sample chapter and SASE. Reviews artwork/photos as part of the ms package. Send photocopies.
Recent Title(s): *Pilots, Man Your Planes!*, by Wilbur Morrison.

HENDRICK-LONG PUBLISHING CO., INC., P.O. Box 25123, Dallas TX 75225-1123. (214)358-4677. Fax: (214)352-4768. E-mail: hendrick-long@worldnet.att.net. **Acquisitions:** Joann Long. Estab. 1969. Publishes hardcover and trade paperback originals and hardcover reprints. **Publishes 8 titles/year. Receives 500 submissions/year. 90% of books from unagented writers. Pays royalty on selling price.** Publishes book 18 months after acceptance. Responds in 1 month to queries, 2 months if more than query sent. Book catalog for 8½×11 or 9×12 SAE with 4 first-class stamps. Manuscript guidelines for #10 SASE.

    ○┅ Hendrick-Long publishes historical fiction and nonfiction primarily about Texas and the Southwest for children and young adults.

Nonfiction: Biography, history. Texas and Southwest-focused material for *children and young adults*. Query or submit outline and 2 sample chapters. Reviews artwork/photos as part of ms package; send photocopies, no original art.
Fiction: Texas and the Southwest-focused material for *kindergarten through young adult*. Query or submit outline/synopsis and 2 sample chapters.
Recent Title(s): *Lone Star Justice: Supreme Court Justice Tom C. Clark*, by Evan Young (young adult); *Terror from the Gulf: A Hurricane in Galveston*, by Martha T. Jones.

HENDRICKSON PUBLISHERS, INC., 140 Summit St., P.O. Box 3473, Peabody MA 01961-3473. Fax: (978)531-8146. E-mail: DPenwell@hendrickson.com. **Acquisitions:** Dan Penwell, manager of trade products. Estab. 1983. Publishes hardcover and trade paperback originals and reprints. **Publishes 35 titles/year. Receives 200 submissions/year. 10% of books from first-time authors; 90% from unagented writers.** Publishes book an average of 1 year after acceptance of ms. Accepts simultaneous submissions (if so notified). Responds in 2 months. Book catalog and ms guidelines for SASE.

    ○┅ Hendrickson publishes "books that give insight into Bible understanding (academically) and encourage spiritual growth (popular trade)." Currently emphasizing Bible reference. De-emphasizing fiction.

Nonfiction: Religious subjects. "We will consider any quality manuscript specifically related to biblical studies and related fields. Also, nonfiction books in a more popular vein that give a hunger to studying, understanding and applying Scripture; books that encourage spiritual growth, such as personal devotionals." Submit outline and sample chapters.
Recent Title(s): *Day by Day with the Early Church Fathers*, edited by Hudsan, Sharrer and Vanker; *12 Steps to Becoming a More Organized Woman (Tips from Proverbs 31)*, by Lane Jordan.

HENSLEY PUBLISHING, (formerly Virgil Hensley), 6116 E. 32nd St., Tulsa OK 74135-5494. (918)664-8520. E-mail: terri@hensleypublishing.com. Website: www.hensleypublishing.com. **Acquisitions:** Terri Kalfas, editor. Estab. 1965. Publishes hardcover and paperback originals. **Publishes 5-10 titles/year. Receives 800 submissions/year. 50% of books from first-time authors; 50% from unagented writers.** Publishes ms 18 months after acceptance of ms. Responds in 2 months to queries. Manuscript guidelines for #10 SASE. No electronic submissions.

    ○┅ Hensley Publishing publishes Bible-centered books, devotionals and curriculum that offer the reader a wide range of topics. Currently emphasizing shorter studies.

Nonfiction: Bible study curriculum. Subjects include child guidance/parenting, money/finance, men's and women's Christian education, prayer, prophecy, Christian living, large and small group studies, discipleship, adult development, parenting, personal growth, pastoral aids, church growth, family. "We do not want to see anything non-Christian." No New Age, poetry, plays, sermon collections. Query with synopsis and sample chapters.

Recent Title(s): *Love's Got Everything to Do with It*, by Rosemarie Karlebach.

Tips: "Submit something that crosses denominational lines directed toward the large Christian market, not small specialized groups. We serve an interdenominational market—all Christian persuasions. Our goal is to get readers back into studying their Bible instead of studying about the Bible."

HERITAGE BOOKS, INC., 1540-E Pointer Ridge Place, Bowie MD 20716-1859. (301)390-7708. Fax: (301)390-7193. **Acquisitions:** Karen Ackerman, editorial supervisor. Estab. 1978. Publishes hardcover and paperback originals and reprints. **Publishes 100 titles/year. Receives 300 submissions/year. 25% of books from first-time authors; 100% from unagented writers. Pays 10% royalty on list price.** Accepts simultaneous submissions. Responds in 1 month. *Writer's Market* recommends allowing 2 months for reply. Book catalog for SAE.

   O–¬ "We particularly desire to publish nonfiction titles dealing with history and genealogy."

Nonfiction: History and genealogy including how-to and reference works, as well as conventional histories and genealogies. "Ancestries of contemporary people are not of interest. The titles should be either of general interest or restricted to Eastern U.S. and Midwest, United Kingdom, Germany. Material dealing with the present century is usually not of interest." Query or submit outline with SASE. Reviews artwork/photos.

Tips: "The quality of the book is of prime importance; next is its relevance to our fields of interest."

HEYDAY BOOKS, Box 9145, Berkeley CA 94709-9145. Fax: (510)549-1889. E-mail: heyday@heydaybooks.com. Website: www.heydaybooks.com. **Acquisitions:** Malcolm Margolin, publisher; Carolyn West, managing editor. Estab. 1974. Publishes hardcover originals, trade paperback originals and reprints. **Publishes 12-15 titles/year. Receives 200 submissions/year. 50% of books from first-time authors; 90% of books from unagented writers. Pays 8-10% royalty on net price.** Publishes book 8 months after acceptance of ms. Responds in 2 weeks to queries, 2 months to mss. *Writer's Market* recommends allowing 2 months for reply. Book catalog for 7×9 SAE with 3 first-class stamps.

   O–¬ Heyday Books publishes nonfiction books and literary anthologies with a strong California focus. "We publish books about native Americans, natural history, history, literature, and recreation, with a strong California focus."

Nonfiction: Books about California only. Subjects include Americana, history, nature, travel. Query with outline and synopsis. Reviews artwork/photos.

Recent Title(s): *A World Transformed: Firsthand Accounts of California Before the Gold Rush*, edited by Joshua Paddison (nonfiction); *California Shorts* (anthology), edited by Steven Gilbar (fiction); *The Geography of Home: California Poetry of Place* (anthology), edited by Christopher Buckley and Gary Young (poetry).

[N] HIDDENSPRING, Paulist Press. 997 Macarthur Blvd., Mahwah NY 07430. (201)825-7300. Fax: (201)825-8345. Website: www.hiddenspringsbooks.com. **Acquisitions:** Jan-Erik Guerth, senior editor (nonfiction/spirituality). Publishes hardcover and trade paperback originals and trade paperback reprints. **Publishes 10-12 titles/year. 5% of books from first-time authors; 20% from unagented writers. Royalty varies on wholesale or retail price. Advance varies.** Accepts simultaneous submissions. Responds in 1 month. Manuscript guidelines on website.

   O–¬ "Books should always have a spiritual angle—nonfiction with a spiritual twist."

Nonfiction: Biography, gift book, how-to, self-help. Subjects include americana, anthropology/archaeology, art/architecture, business/economics, child guidance/parenting, cooking/foods/nutrition, creative nonfiction, ethnic, gardening, gay/lesbian, government/politics, health/medicine, history, memoirs, money/finance, multicultural, music/dance, nature/environment, philosophy, psychology, regional, religion, science, sociology, spirituality, travel, women's issues/studies. Submit proposal package, including outline, 5 sample chapters and SASE.

Recent Title(s): *Conversation*, by Theodore Zeldin (self-help); *The God Experiment*, by Russell Stannard (science and religion).

HIGHSMITH PRESS, P.O. Box 800, Fort Atkinson WI 53538-0800. (920)563-9571. Fax: (920)563-4801. E-mail: hpress@highsmith.com. Website: www.hpress.highsmith.com. **Acquisitions:** Donald J. Sager, publisher. Estab. 1990. Publishes hardcover and paperback originals. **Publishes 20 titles/year. Receives 500-600 queries and 400-500 mss/year. 30% of books from first-time authors; 100% from unagented writers. Pays 10-12% royalty on net sales price. Offers $250-1,000 advance.** Publishes book 6 months after acceptance of ms. Accepts simultaneous submissions. Responds in 1 month to queries, 2 months to proposals, 3 months to mss. Book catalog and ms guidelines free.

   O–¬ Highsmith Press publishes educational, professional, and informational resources to meet the practical needs of librarians, educators, readers, library users, colleges, media specialists, schools and related institutions, and to help them fulfill their valuable functions.

Imprint(s): Alleyside Press, Upstart Books (creative supplemental reading, library and critical thinking skills materials designed to expand the learning environment).

Nonfiction: Professional resources for teachers (K-12) and libraries. "We are primarily interested in manuscripts that stimulate or strengthen reading, library and information-seeking skills and foster critical thinking." Query with outline and 1-2 sample chapters. Reviews artwork/photos as part of ms package. Send transparencies.

Fiction: No longer accepting children's picture book mss. "Our current emphasis is on storytelling collections for preschool-grade 6. We prefer stories that can be easily used by teachers and children's librarians, multicultural topics, and manuscripts that feature fold and cut, flannelboard, tangram, or similar simple patterns that can be reproduced."
Recent Title(s): *Library Celebrations*, by Cindy Dingwall; *Literature Online*, by Karen Moran.

HILL AND WANG, Farrar Straus & Giroux, Inc., 19 Union Square W., New York NY 10003. (212)741-6900. Fax: (212)633-9385. **Acquisitions:** Elisabeth Sifton, publisher; Lauren Osborne, senior editor. Estab. 1956. Publishes hardcover and trade paperbacks. **Publishes 12 titles/year. Receives 1,500 queries/year. 50% of books from first-time authors; 50% from unagented writers. Pays 7½% royalty on retail price. Advances "vary widely from a few hundred to several thousand dollars."** Publishes book 1 year after acceptance of ms. Accepts simultaneous submissions. Responds in 2 months. Book catalog free.
  ○▪ Hill and Wang publishes serious nonfiction books, primarily in history and the social sciences.
Nonfiction: Cross-over academic and trade books. Subjects include government/politics, history (primarily American, some European and African history), public policy, women's issues, some drama. Submit outline, sample chapters, letter explaining rationale for book and SASE.
Fiction: *Not* considering new fiction, drama or poetry.
Recent Title(s): *Ungentlemanly Acts: The Army's Notorious Incest Trial*, by Louise Barnett.

HIPPOCRENE BOOKS INC., 171 Madison Ave., New York NY 10016. (212)685-4371. Fax: (212)779-9338. E-mail: hippocre@ix.netcom.com. Website: www.hippocrenebooks.com. President/Publisher: George Blagowidow. **Acquisitions:** Carol Chitnis, managing editor (cooking, history, travel, nonfiction reference); Caroline Gates, associate editor (foreign language, dictionaries, language guides); Kara Migliorelli, associate editor (illustrated histories, weddings, proverbs). Estab. 1971. Publishes hardcover and trade paperback originals. **Publishes 250 titles/year. Receives 250 submissions/year. 10% of books from first-time authors; 95% from unagented writers. Pays 6-10% royalty on retail price. Offers $2,000 advance.** Publishes book 16 months after acceptance of ms. Accepts simultaneous submissions. Responds in 2 months. Book catalog for 9×12 SAE with 5 first-class stamps. Manuscript guidelines for #10 SASE.
  ○▪ Hippocrene publishes reference books of international interest, often bilingual, in the fields of cookery, travel, language and literature. It specializes in foreign language dictionaries and learning guides. We also publish ethnic cuisine cookbooks, travel and history titles. Currently emphasizing cookbooks, foreign language dictionaries. De-emphasizing military, travel.
Nonfiction: Reference. Subjects include foreign language, Judaic reference, ethnic and special interest travel, military history, bilingual love poetry, bilingual proverbs, international cookbooks, Polish interest, foreign language, dictionaries and instruction. Submit proposal including outline, 2 sample chapters, toc.
Recent Title(s): *Ladino-English/English-Ladino Concise Encyclopedia Dictionary*, by Dr. Elli Kohen (nonfiction reference); *Old Havana Cookbook: Cuban Recipes in Spanish and English* (cooking).
Tips: "Our recent successes in publishing general books considered midlist by larger publishers is making us more of a general trade publisher. We continue to do well with reference books like dictionaries, atlases and language studies. We ask for proposal, sample chapter, and table of contents. We then ask for material if we are interested."

HI-TIME PFLAUM, (formerly Hi-Time Publishing), N90 W16890 Roosevelt Dr., Menomonee Falls WI 53051-7933. (262)502-4222. Fax: (262)502-4224. E-mail: kcannizzo@hi-time.com. **Acquisitions:** Karen A. Cannizzo, publisher. **Publishes 20 titles/year. Payment method may be outright purchase, royalty or down payment plus royalty.** Book catalog and ms guidelines free.
  ○▪ "Hi-time*Pflaum, a division of Peter Li, Inc., serves the spacialized market of religious education, primarily Roman Catholic. We provide quality, theologically sound, practical, and affordable resources that assist religious educators of and ministers to children from preschool through senior high school."
Nonfiction: Textbook, religion. "We publish religious education material for Catholic junior high through adult programs. Most of our material is contracted in advance and written by persons with theology or religious education backgrounds." Query with SASE.
Recent Title(s): *Active Learning for Catholic Kids* (series); *Conversations with Teens: Catholic Perspectives* (series).

HOHM PRESS, P.O. Box 2501, Prescott AZ 86302. Fax: (520)717-1779. E-mail: pinedr@goodnet.com. **Acquisitions:** Regina Sara Ryan, managing editor. Estab. 1975. Publishes hardcover and trade paperback originals. **Publishes 6-8 titles/year. 50% of books from first-time authors. Pays 10-15% royalty on net sales. No advance.** Publishes book 18 months after acceptance of ms. Accepts simultaneous submissions. Responds in 3 months to queries.
  ○▪ Hohm Press publishes a range of titles in the areas of psychology and spirituality, herbistry, alternative health methods and nutrition. Currently emphasizing health alternatives.
Nonfiction: Self-help. Subjects include alternative health/medicine, philosophy, religious (Hindu, Buddhist, Sufi or translations of classic texts in major religious traditions). "We look for writers who have an established record in their field of expertise. The best buy of recent years came from two women who fully substantiated how they could market their book. We believed they could do it. We were right." Query with SASE.
Poetry: "We are not accepting poetry at this time except for translations of recognized religious/spiritual classics." Query.

Recent Title(s): *The Yoga Tradition,* by Georg Feuerstein (nonfiction); *For Love of the Dark One: Songs of Mirabai,* by Andrew Schelling (poems).

HOLIDAY HOUSE INC., 425 Madison Ave., New York NY 10017. (212)688-0085. Fax: (212)421-6134. Editor-in-Chief: Regina Griffin. **Acquisitions:** Suzanne Reinoehl, associate editor. Estab. 1935. Publishes hardcover originals. **Publishes 50 titles/year. Receives 3,000 submissions/year. 2-5% of books from first-time authors; 50% from unagented writers. Pays royalty on list price, range varies. Offers $2,000-10,000 advance.** Publishes book 1-2 years after acceptance of ms. Query. Manuscripts not returned without SASE. Manuscript guidelines for #10 SASE.

   O— Holiday House publishes children's and young adult books for the school and library markets. "We have a commitment to publishing first-time authors and illustrators. We specialize in quality hardcovers from picture books to young adult, both fiction and nonfiction, primarily for the school and library market." Currently emphasizing literary middle-grade novels.

Nonfiction: American history, biography, natural history, science. Submit query only with SASE. Reviews artwork/photos as part of ms package. Send photocopies only—no originals—to Claire Counihan, art director.

Fiction: Adventure, ethnic, historical, humor, juvenile, picture books, easy readers. Query first with SASE.

Recent Title(s): *In the Line of Fire: Presidents' Lives at Stake,* by Judith St. George (nonfiction); *A Child's Calendar,* by John Updike, illustrated by Trina Schart Hyman.

Tips: "We are not geared toward the mass market, but toward school and library markets. We need picturebook texts with strong stories and writing. We do not publish board books or novelties."

N: HOLMES & MEIER PUBLISHERS, INC., East Building, 160 Broadway, New York NY 10038. (212)374-0100. Fax: (212)374-1313. E-mail: hmpl60@aol.com. Website: www.holmesandmeier.com. **Acquisitions:** Maggie Kennedy, managing editor. Publisher: Miriam H. Holmes. Estab. 1969. Publishes hardcover and paperback originals. **Publishes 20 titles/year. Pays royalty.** Publishes book an average of 18 months after acceptance. Responds in up to 6 months. Query with SASE. Book catalog free.

   O— "We are noted as an academic publishing house and are pleased with our reputation for excellence in the field. However, we are also expanding our list to include books of more general interest."

Imprint(s): Africana Publishing Co.

Nonfiction: Africana, art, biography, business/economics, history, Judaica, Latin American studies, literary criticism, politics, reference and women's studies. Accepts translations. Query first with outline, sample chapters, cv and idea of intended market/audience.

HOLMES PUBLISHING GROUP, P.O. Box 623, Edmonds WA 98020. E-mail: HPubG@aol.com. CEO: J.D. Holmes. **Acquisitions:** L.Y. Fitzgerald. Estab. 1983. Publishes hardcover and trade paperback originals and reprints. **Publishes 40 titles/year. Receives 120 queries and 80 mss/year. 20% of books from first-time authors; 20% from unagented writers. Pays 10% royalty on net revenue.** Publishes book 4 months after acceptance of ms. Responds in 2 months.

   O— Holmes publishes informative spiritual titles on philosophy, metaphysical and religious subjects, and alternative medicine and health.

Imprint(s): Alchemical Press, Alexandrian Press, Contra/Thought, Sure Fire Press.

Nonfiction: Self-help. Subjects include health/medicine, occult, philosophy, religion, metaphysical. "We do not publish titles that are more inspirational than informative." Query only with SASE.

   • Holmes Publishing Group no longer publishes fiction.

Recent Title(s): *An Age for Lucifer: Predatory Spirituality and the Quest for Godhood,* by Robert Tucker; *The Historic Structure of the Original Golden Dawn Temples,* by Darcy Kuntz.

HENRY HOLT & COMPANY BOOKS FOR YOUNG READERS, Henry Holt & Co., Inc., 115 W. 18th St., New York NY 10011. (212)886-9200. Associate Publisher: Laura Godwin (picture books, chapter books and middle grade). Senior Editor: Marc Aronson (young adult). Senior Editor: Christy Ottaviano (picture books, chapter books and middle grade). Senior Editor: Nina Ignatowicz (picture books and chapter books). Editor: Reka Simonsen (picture books, chapter books and middle grade). **Acquisitions:** BYR Submissions. Estab. 1866 (Holt). Publishes hardcover originals. **Publishes 70-80 titles/year. 5% of books from first-time authors; 50% from unagented writers. Pays royalty on retail price. Offers $3,000 and up advance.** Publishes book 18 months after acceptance of ms. Responds in 5 months to queries and mss. Book catalog and ms guidelines free with SASE.

   O— "Henry Holt Books for Young Readers publishes highly original and cutting-edge fiction and nonfiction for all ages, from the very young to the young adult."

Imprint(s): Books by Michael Hague, Books by Bill Martin Jr. and John Archambault; Owlet Paperbacks; Redfeather Books (chapter books for ages 7-10).

Nonfiction: Children's/juvenile, illustrated book. Query with SASE.

Fiction: Juvenile: adventure, animal, contemporary, fantasy, history, humor, multicultural, sports, suspense/mystery. Picture books: animal, concept, history, humor, multicultural, sports. Young adult: contemporary, fantasy, history, multicultural, nature/environment, problem novels, sports. Query with SASE.

Recent Title(s): *When Zachary Beaver Came to Town,* by Kimberly Willis Holt (juvenile fiction); *Little Bunny on the Move,* by Peter McCarty (picture book).

HENRY HOLT & COMPANY, INC., 115 W. 18th St., New York NY 10011. (212)886-9200. President and Publisher: John Sterling. **Acquisitions**: Sara Bershtel, associate publisher of Metropolitan Books (literary fiction, politics, history); Elizabeth Stein, adult trade editor; David Sobel, senior editor (science, culture, history, health); Jennifer Barth, executive editor (adult literary fiction, narrative nonfiction); Deb Brady, senior editor (lifestyle, health, self help, parenting). Query before submitting.

O→ Holt is a general interest publisher of quality fiction and nonfiction. Currently emphasizing narrative nonfiction. De-emphasizing cooking, gardening.

Imprint(s): John Macrae Books, Metropolitan Books, **Henry Holt & Company Books for Young Readers** (Books by Michael Hague, Books by Bill Martin Jr. and John Archambault, Owlet Paperbacks, Redfeather Books, W5 Reference).
Recent Title(s): *M: The Man Who Became Caravaggio*; *Wild Minds*, by Marc Hanser.

HOLY CROSS ORTHODOX PRESS, Hellenic College, 50 Goddard Ave., Brookline MA 02445. Fax: (617)850-1460. **Acquisitions:** Anton C. Vrame, Ph.D., managing editor. Estab. 1974. Publishes trade paperback originals. **Holy Cross publishes 8 titles/year; Hellenic College imprint publishes 2 titles/year. Receives 10-15 queries and 10-15 mss/year. 85% of books from first-time authors; 100% from unagented writers. Pays 8-12% royalty on retail price.** Publishes book 18 months after acceptance of ms. Accepts simultaneous submissions. Responds in 6 months to mss. Book catalog free.

O→ Holy Cross publishes titles that are rooted in the tradition of the Eastern Orthodox Church.

Imprint(s): Holy Cross Orthodox Press, Hellenic College Press.
Nonfiction: Academic. Subjects include ethnic, religion (Greek Orthodox). "Holy Cross Orthodox Press publishes scholarly and popular literature in the areas of Orthodox Christian theology and Greek letters. Submissions are often far too technical usually with a very limited audiences." Submit outline and complete ms. Reviews artwork/photos as part of the manuscript package. Send photocopies.
Recent Title(s): *Christianity: Lineaments of a Sacred Tradition*, by Philip Sherrard.

HOME PLANNERS, LLC, 3275 West Ina Rd., #110, Tucson AZ 85741. (520)297-8200. Fax: (520)297-6219. E-mail: paulette@torchlake.com. Website: www.homeplanners.com. **Acquisitions:** Paulette Mulvin, special projects and acquisitions editor. Estab. 1946. Publishes hardcover and trade paperback originals. **Publishes 12-15 titles/year. Receives 8-10 queries and 2-3 mss/year. 80% of books from first-time authors; 100% from unagented writers. Pays outright purchase of $5,000-18,000. No advance.** Publishes book 6 months after acceptance of ms. Accepts simultaneous submissions. Responds in 2 months to queries, 4 months to proposals, 6 months to mss. Book catalog free.

O→ Home Planners publishes home plan, landscape, interior design books and magazines and construction plans. "We are primarily interested in how-to or reference titles. We may consider personal experience or technical stories but only if unusual and exceptionally well done."

Nonfiction: How-to, reference. Subjects include art/architecture, gardening, homebuilding/home improvement/remodeling. Query with SASE. Submit proposal package, including outline and 1 sample chapter. Reviews artwork/photos as part of ms package. Send photocopies.
Recent Titles: *The Home Building Process*, by Rick Binsacca (nonfiction).
Tips: "Have some experience in architecture, building or remodeling. Previous publishing or magazine writing in the field preferred."

HONOR BOOKS, P.O. Box 55388, Tulsa OK 74155. (918)496-9007. Fax: (918)496-3588. E-mail: info@honorbooks.com. Website: www.honorbooks.com. **Acquisitions:** Catherine Dodd, acquisitions coordinator. Publishes hardcover and trade paperback originals. **Publishes 60 titles/year. Receives 2,000 queries and 1,300 mss/year. 2% of books from first-time authors. 50% of books from unagented writers. Pays royalty on wholesale price, makes outright purchase or assigns work for hire. Advance negotiable.** Publishes book 14 months after acceptance of ms. Accepts simultaneous submissions. Responds in 1 month to queries, 4 months to proposals. Ms guidelines for #10 SASE.

O→ "We are a Christian publishing house with a mission to inspire and encourage people to draw near to God and to enjoy His love and grace." Currently emphasizing humor, personal and spiritual growth, children's books. De-emphasizing devotions, personal stories.

Nonfiction: Devotionals, motivation, seasonal/holiday gift books, "portable" inspiration. Subjects are geared toward the "felt needs" of people. No autobiographies or teaching books. Query with outline, writing sample and proposal package, including table of contents, synopsis and author bio, SASE. Reviews artwork/photos as part of the ms package. Send photocopies.
Recent Title(s): *Love Letters from God*; *Snickers from the Front Pew*.
Tips: "Our books are for busy, achievement-oriented people who are looking for a balance between reaching their goals and knowing that God loves them unconditionally. Our books encourage spiritual growth, joyful living and intimacy with God. Write about what you are for and not what you are against. We look for scripts that are biblically based and which inspire readers."

HOUGHTON MIFFLIN BOOKS FOR CHILDREN, Houghton Mifflin Company, 222 Berkeley St., Boston MA 02116. (617)351-5959. Fax: (617)351-1111. E-mail: Children's_Books@hmco.com. Website: www.hmco.com. **Acquisitions:** Hannah Rodgers, submissions coordinator. Publishes hardcover and trade paperback originals and reprints. **Firm publishes 100 titles/year. Receives 5,000 queries and 12,000 mss/year. 10% of books from first-time authors; 70%**

from unagented writers. **Pays 5-10% royalty on retail price. Advance dependent on many factors.** Publishes book 18 months after acceptance of ms. Accepts simultaneous submissions. Responds in 4 months. Book catalog for 9×12 SASE with 3 first-class stamps. Manuscript guidelines for #10 SASE.

O—¬ "Houghton Mifflin gives shape to ideas that educate, inform, and above all, delight."

Imprint(s): Sandpiper Paperback Books (Eden Edwards, editor).

Nonfiction: Biography, children's/juvenile, humor, illustrated book. Subjects include agriculture/horticulture, Americana, animals, anthropology, art/architecture, ethnic, gardening, history, language/literature, music/dance, nature/environment, recreation, regional, science, sports, travel. Interested in "innovative science books, especially about scientists 'in the field' and what they do." Submit outline and 2 sample chapters with SASE. Mss not returned without appropriate-sized SASE. Reviews artwork/photos as part of ms package. Send photocopies.

Fiction: Adventure, ethnic, historical, humor, juvenile (early readers), literary, mystery, picture books, suspense, young adult, board books. Submit full ms with appropriate-sized SASE.

Recent Title(s): *Top of the World*, by Steve Jenkins (nonfiction); *Signs and Wonders*, by Pat Lowery Collins (fiction); *Dutch Sneakers and Flea Keepers*, by Calet Brown (poetry).

Tips: "Faxed or e-mailed manuscripts and proposals are not considered."

HOUGHTON MIFFLIN COMPANY, 215 Park Ave. S., New York NY 10003. (212)420-5800. Fax: (212)420-5899. Website: www.hmco.com. Executive Vice President: Wendy J. Strothman. Editor-in-Chief, Adult Books: Janet Silver. Publisher, Children's Books: Anita Silvey. **Acquisitions:** Submissions Editor. Estab. 1832. Publishes hardcover and trade paperback originals and reprints. **Publishes 60 hardcovers, 30-40 paperbacks/year. 10% of books from first-time authors; 20% from unagented writers. Hardcover: pays 10-15% royalty on retail price, sliding scale or flat rate based on sales; paperback: 7½% flat fee, but negotiable. Advance varies.** Publishes book 1-2 years after acceptance of ms. Accepts simultaneous submissions. Responds in 3 months. Book catalog and ms guidelines free.

O—¬ "Houghton Mifflin gives shape to ideas that educate, inform and delight. In a new era of publishing, our legacy of quality thrives as we combine imagination with technology, bringing you new ways to know."

Imprint(s): Clarion Books, Walter Lorraine Books, **Houghton Mifflin Books for Children**, Mariner Paperbacks, Sandpiper Paperbacks, Frances Tenenbaum Books.

Nonfiction Biography, childrens/juvenile, language/literature, military/war, money/finance, music/dance, nature/environment, philosophy, photography, psychology, recreation, regional, religion, science, sociology, sports, travel, women's issues/studies. "We are not a mass market publisher. Our main focus is serious nonfiction. We do practical self-help but not pop psychology self-help." Query with outline, 1 sample chapter and SASE. Reviews artwork/photos as part of ms package. Send photocopies.

Fiction: Adventure, confession, ethnic, fantasy, feminist, gay/lesbian, historical, humor, literary, mainstream/contemporary, mystery, short story collections, suspense. "We are not a mass market publisher. Study the current list." Query with 3 sample chapters or complete mss and SASE.

Poetry: "At this point we have an established roster of poets we use. It is hard for first-time poets to get published by Houghton Mifflin."

Recent Title(s): *Interpreter of Maladies*, by Jhumpa Lahiri; *Woman*, by Natalie Angier; *The Human Stain*, by Philip Roth.

HOUSE OF COLLECTIBLES, Ballantine Publishing Group, Random House, Inc., 299 Park Ave., New York NY 10171. Website: www.randomhouse.com. **Acquisitions:** Linda Loewenthal, editor. Publishes trade and mass market paperback originals. **Publishes 25-28 titles/year. Receives 200 queries/year. 1% of books from first-time authors; 85% from unagented writers. Pays royalty on retail price, varies. Offers advance against royalties, varies.** Publishes book 6 months after acceptance of ms. Book catalog free from Ballantine. No unsolicited mss or query letters.

O—¬ "One of the premier publishing companies devoted to books on a wide range of antiques and collectibles, House of Collectibles publishes books for the seasoned expert and the beginning collector alike."

Imprint(s): Official Price Guide series.

Nonfiction: How-to (related to collecting antiques and coins), reference books. Subjects include hobbies, recreation.

Recent Title(s): *Official Price Guide to Records*, by Jerry Osborne.

Tips: "We have been publishing price guides and other books on antiques and collectibles for over 35 years and plan to meet the needs of collectors, dealers and appraisers well into the 21st century."

HOWELL PRESS, INC., 1713-2D Allied Lane, Charlottesville VA 22903. (804)977-4006. Fax: (804)971-7204. E-mail: howellpres@aol.com. Website: www.howellpress.com. **Acquisitions:** Ross A. Howell, president; Meghan Mitchell, editor. Estab. 1985. **Publishes 10-13 titles/year. Receives 500 submissions/year. 10% of books from first-time authors; 80% from unagented writers. Pays 5-7% royalty on net retail price.** "We generally offer an advance, but amount differs with each project and is generally negotiated with authors on a case-by-case basis." Publishes book 18 months after acceptance of ms. Responds in 2 months. Book catalog for 9×12 SAE with 4 first-class stamps. Manuscript guidelines for #10 SASE.

O—¬ Howell Press publishes and distributes books in the categories of history, transportation, gardening, cooking and regional (Mid-Atlantic and Southeastern U.S.) interest. Currently emphasizing military aviation, Civil War history, cooking. De-emphasizing memoirs (military).

Nonfiction: Illustrated books, historical texts. Subjects include aviation, military history, cooking, wine appreciation, maritime history, motor sports, gardening, transportation, quilting, travel and regional (Mid-Atlantic and Southeastern

U.S.). "Generally open to most ideas, as long as writing is accessible to average adult reader. Our line is targeted, so it would be advisable to look over our catalog before querying to better understand what Howell Press does." Query with outline and sample chapters with SASE. Reviews artwork/photos as part of ms package. Does not return mss without SASE.

Recent Title(s): *First and Second Maryland Cavalry, C.S.A.*, by Robert Driver (nonfiction).

Tips: "Focus of our program has been illustrated books, but we will also consider nonfiction manuscripts that would not be illustrated."

HUDSON HILLS PRESS, INC., 122 E. 25th St., 5th Floor, New York NY 10010-2936. (212)674-6005. Fax: (212)674-6045. **Acquisitions:** Paul Anbinder, president/publisher. Estab. 1978. Publishes hardcover and paperback originals. **Publishes 15 titles/year. Receives 50-100 submissions/year. 15% of books from first-time authors; 90% from unagented writers. Pays 4-6% royalty on retail price. Offers $3,500 average advance.** Publishes book 1 year after acceptance of ms. Accepts simultaneous submissions. Responds in 2 months. Book catalog for 6×9 SAE with 2 first-class stamps.

    O➤ Hudson Hills Press publishes books about art and photography, including monographs.

Nonfiction: Art, photography. Query first, then submit outline and sample chapters. Reviews artwork/photos as part of ms package.

Recent Title(s): *Hollis Sigler's Breast Cancer Journal*, by Hollis Sigler and Susan M. Love, M.D.

HUMAN KINETICS PUBLISHERS, INC., P.O. Box 5076, Champaign IL 61825-5076. (217)351-5076. Fax: (217)351-2674. E-mail: hk@hkusa.com. Website: www.HumanKinetics.com. **Acquisitions:** Ted Miller, vice president and director (trade); Rainer Martens, president and director STM; Martin Barnard, trade senior acquisitions editor (fitness, running, golf, tennis, cycling, fishing); Scott Wikgren, HPERD director (health, physical education, recreation, dance); Mike Bahrke, STM acquisitions editor (scientific, technical, medical); Loarn Robertson, STM acquisitions editor (biomechanics, anatomy, athletic training, cardiac rehab, test/measurement); Judy Wright, HPERD acquisitions editor (dance, motor, learning/behavior/performance/development, gymnastics, adapted physical education, older adults); Linda Bump, STM acquisitions editor (sport psychology, sport history, sport sociology, sport management, women and sport, recreation and leisure); John Klein, American fitness alliance director (youth fitness, fitness testing); Jeff Riley, trade acquisitions editor (team sports, soccer, basketball, football, bowling). Publisher: Rainer Martens. Estab. 1974. Publishes hardcover and paperback text and reference books, trade paperback originals, software and audiovisual. **Publishes 120 titles/year. Receives 300 submissions/year. 30% of books from first-time authors; 90% of books from unagented writers. Pays 10-15% royalty on net income.** Publishes book an average of 18 months after acceptance. Accepts simultaneous submissions. Responds in 2 months. Book catalog free.

    O➤ Human Kinetics publishes books which accurately interpret sport and fitness training and techniques, physical education, sports sciences and sports medicine for coaches, athletes and fitness enthusiasts and professionals in the physical action field.

Imprint(s): HK Trade, HK Academic.

Nonfiction: How-to, reference, self-help, technical and textbook. Subjects include health, recreation, sports, sport sciences and sports medicine, and physical education. Especially interested in books on fitness; books on all aspects of sports technique or how-to books and coaching books; books which interpret the sport sciences and sports medicine, including sport physiology, sport psychology, sport pedagogy and sport biomechanics. No sport biographies, sport record or statistics books or regional books. Submit outline and sample chapters. Reviews artwork/photos as part of ms package.

Recent Title(s): *The Baseball Coaching Bible*, by John Winkin and Jerry Kendall (trade); *Physiology of Sport and Exercise*, by Jack H. Wilmore and David S. Costill (STM nonfiction).

HUMANICS PUBLISHING GROUP, P.O. Box 7400, Atlanta GA 30357. (404)874-2176. Fax: (404)874-1976. E-mail: humanics@mindspring.com. Website: http://humanicspub.com. **Acquisitions:** W. Arthur Bligh, editor. Estab. 1976. Publishes trade paperback originals. **Publishes 20 titles/year; imprints: Humanics Trade Paperback, 10; Humanics Learning, 12. Receives 5,000 queries/year. 70% of books from first-time authors. Pays 10% royalty on wholesale price. Offers $500-3,000 advance.** Publishes book 1-12 months after acceptance of ms. Accepts simultaneous submissions, if so noted. Responds only if interested. Book catalog free. Manuscript guidelines for #10 SASE.

    O➤ "We publish books which will target the New Age market (i.e., self-help, eastern philosophy, metaphysics, psychology). We also publish teacher resource guides and activity books for early childhood development." Currently emphasizing Feng Shui, Taoism, learning (phonics, reading, parent involvement). De-emphasizing children's books.

Imprint(s): Humanics Trade Paperback, Humanics Learning.

Nonfiction: Children's/juvenile, illustrated book, self-help. Subjects include child guidance/parenting, psychology, philosophy, spirituality (e.g., taoism), New Age. Query with outline, 1 sample chapter and SASE.

Recent Title(s): *Lifestyles for the 21st Century*, by Marcus Wells; *Tao of an Unclutted Life*, by Karen Hicks.

Tips: "For our activity books, audience is parents and educators looking for books which will enrich their children's lives. For our trade books, audience is anyone interested in positive, healthy self-development. We are looking for quality and creativity. As a small publisher, we don't waste our time or an author's time on books that are not of lasting importance or value. Taoism and Zen high interest."

■ **HUNTER HOUSE**, P.O. Box 2914, Alameda CA 94501. (510)865-5282. Fax: (510)865-4295. E-mail: acquisition s@hunterhouse.com. Website: www.hunterhouse.com. Publisher: Kiran S. Rana. **Acquisitions:** Jeanne Brondino, acquisitions editor. Estab. 1978. Publishes hardcover and trade paperback originals and reprints. **Publishes 18 titles/year. Receives 200-300 queries and 100 mss/year. 50% of books from first-time authors; 80% from unagented writers. Pays 12-15% royalty on net receipts, defined as selling price. Offers $500-3,000 advance.** Publishes book 1-2 years after acceptance of final ms. Accepts simultaneous submissions. Responds in 2 months to queries, 3 months to proposals, 6 months to mss. Book catalog and ms guidelines for 8½ × 11 SAE with 3 first-class stamps.

   O→ Hunter House publishes health books (especially women's health), self-help health, sexuality and couple relationships, violence prevention and intervention. Currently emphasizing health, sexuality, violence prevention. De-emphasizing reference, self-help psychology.

Nonfiction: Reference, (only health reference); self-help, social issues. "Health books (especially women's health) should focus on emerging health issues or current issues that are inadequately covered and be written for the general population. Family books: Our current focus is sexuality and couple relationships, and alternative lifestyles to high stress. Community topics include violence prevention/violence intervention. We also publish specialized curricula for counselors and educators in the areas of violence prevention and trauma in children." Query with proposal package, including synopsis, table of contents and chapter outline, sample chapter, target audience information, competition and what distinguishes the book. Send photocopies, proposals generally not returned, requested mss returned with SASE. Reviews artwork/photos as part of ms package.

Recent Title(s): *The Feisty Woman's Breast Cancer Book*, by Elaine Radner; *Pocket Book of Foreplay*, by Richard Craze.

Tips: Audience is concerned people who are looking to educate themselves and their community about real-life issues that affect them. "Please send as much information as possible about *who* your audience is, *how* your book addresses their needs, and *how* you reach that audience in your ongoing work."

HUNTER PUBLISHING, INC., 130 Campus Dr., Edison NJ 08818. Fax: (561)546-8040. E-mail: hunterp@bellsouth. net. Website: www.hunterpublishing.com. **Acquisitions:** Kim André, editor; Lissa Dailey. President: Michael Hunter. Estab. 1985. **Publishes 100 titles/year. Receives 300 submissions/year. 10% of books from first-time authors; 75% from unagented writers. Pays royalty. Offers negotiable advance.** Publishes book 5 months after acceptance of ms. Accepts simultaneous submissions. Responds in 3 weeks to queries, 1 month on ms. *Writer's Market* recommends allowing 2 months for reply. Book catalog for #10 SAE with 4 first-class stamps.

   O→ Hunter Publishing publishes practical guides for travelers going to the Caribbean, U.S., Europe, South America, and the far reaches of the globe.

Imprint(s): Adventure Guides, Romantic Weekends Guides, Alive Guides.

Nonfiction: Reference, travel guides. "We need travel guides to areas covered by few competitors: Caribbean Islands, South and Central America, regional U.S. from an active 'adventure' perspective." No personal travel stories or books not directed to travelers. Query or submit outline/synopsis and sample chapters. Reviews artwork/photos as part of ms package.

Recent Title(s): *Adventure Guide to Canada's Atlantic Provinces*, by Barbara Radcliffe-Rogers.

Tips: "Guides should be destination-specific, rather than theme-based alone. Thus, 'travel with kids' is too broad; 'Florida with Kids' is OK. Make sure the guide doesn't duplicate what other guide publishers do. We need active adventure-oriented guides and more specialized guides for travelers in search of the unusual."

N **IBEX PUBLISHERS**, P.O. Box 30087, Bethesda MD 20824. (301)718-8188. Fax: (301)907-8707. E-mail: info@i bexpub.com. Website: www.ibexpub.com. Publishes hardcover and trade paperback originals, hardcover and trade paperback reprints. **Publishes 6-10 titles/year. Pay varies.** Accepts simultaneous submissions. Book catalog free.

   O→ IBEX publishes books about Iran and the Middle East.

Imprints: Iranbooks Press.

Nonfiction: Biography, cookbook, reference, textbook. Subjects include cooking/foods/nutrition, language/literature. Query with SASE or submit proposal package, including outline and 2 sample chapters.

Poetry: Translations of Persian poets will be considered.

■ **ICONOGRAFIX, INC.**, 1830A Hanley Rd., P.O. Box 446, Hudson WI 54016. (715)381-9755. Fax: (715)381-9756. E-mail: iconogfx@spacestv.net. **Acquisitions:** Dylan Frautschi, acquisitions manager (transportation). Estab. 1992. Publishes trade paperback originals. **Publishes 24 titles/year. Receives 100 queries and 20 mss/year. 50% of books from first-time authors; 100% from unagented writers. Pays 8-12½% royalty on wholesale price or makes outright purchase of $1,000-3,000. Offers $1,000-3,500 advance.** Publishes book 1 year after acceptance of ms. Accepts simultaneous submissions. Responds in 1 month to queries, 3 months to proposals and mss. Book catalog and ms guidelines free.

   O→ Iconografix publishes special historical interest photographic books for transportation equipment enthusiasts.

Nonfiction: Photo albums, coffee table book, illustrated book. Subjects include Americana, hobbies, transportation. Query with SASE or submit proposal package, including outline. Reviews artwork/photos as part of ms package. Send photocopies.

Recent Title(s): *Volunteer & Rural Fire Apparatus*, by Wood & Sorenson (photo collection); *Mario Andretti Photo Album*, by Peter Nygaard (race photos); *Trains of the Twin Ports*, by Marv Nielsen (train photos).

IDEALS CHILDREN'S BOOKS, Hambleton-Hill Publishing, Inc., 1501 County Hospital Rd., Nashville TN 37218. **Acquisitions:** Bethany Snyder, editor. Publishes children's hardcover and trade paperback originals. **Publishes 25 titles/ year. Receives 300 queries and 2,000-2,500 mss/year. 10% of books from first-time authors; 10% from unagented writers. Pay determined by individual contract.** Publishes book up to 2 years after acceptance of ms. Responds in 6 months to queries, proposals and mss. Manuscript guidelines for #10 SASE.

    O→ Ideals Children's Books publishes fiction and some nonfiction for toddlers to 8-year-olds. This publisher accepts only unsolicited manuscripts from agents, members of the Society of Children's Book Writers & Illustrators, and previously published book authors who may submit with a list of writing credits. Currently emphasizing realistic fiction for picture books. De-emphasizing anthropomorphism, concept books (ABC, colors, etc.).

Nonfiction: Children's. Subjects include Americana, nature/environment, science, sports. Submit proposal package.
Fiction: Submit complete ms with SASE. No middle grade or young adult novels.
Recent Title(s): *Discovery Readers* (science/nature series); *Twice Upon a Time Tale* series, by Alan Osmond (fiction).
Tips: "We are not interested in anthropomorphism or alphabet books. We are seeking original, child-centered fiction for the picture book format."

IDEALS PUBLICATIONS INC., 535 Metroplex Dr., Suite 250, Nashville TN 37211. (615)333-0478. Publisher: Patricia Pingry. **Acquisitions:** Copy Editor. Estab. 1944. Uses short prose and poetry. Also publishes *Ideals* magazine. **Publishes 8-10 hardbound books, 12-14 childrens titles. Advance varies. Most material from unagented submissions.** Accepts simultaneous submissions. Accepts previously published material. Send information about when and where the piece previously appeared. Publishes book 18 months after acceptance of ms. Responds in 2 months only with SASE. Manuscript guidelines free with SASE.

    O→ Ideals publishes highly illustrated seasonal, nostalgic, inspirational and patriotic coffee table books, including a travel book series, and children's picture and board books.

Imprint(s): Candy Cane Press (children's holiday-oriented).
Nonfiction: Biography, coffee table books. Subjects include travel, inspirational, nostalgic, patriotic, historical, how-to, self-help.
Recent Title(s): *Barefoot Days* (children's poetry).

N A IDG BOOKS WORLDWIDE, Business Group, 645 N. Michigan Ave., Suite 800, Chicago, IL 60611. (312)482-8460. Fax: (312)482-8561. E-mail: kwelton@idgbooks.com. Website: www.idgbooks.com. **Acquisitions:** Kathleen A. Welton, vice president/publisher; Mark Butler, senior acquisitions editor (personal finance, taxes, small business, e-commerce); Holly McGuire, senior acquisitions editor (technical/how-to, management and skills training, business self-help); Karen Hansen, acquisitions editor (careers); Stacy Collins (sports). Publishes trade paperback originals. **Pays 10-15% royalty. Offers $0-25,000 advance.** Publishes book 3 months after acceptance of ms. Responds in 2 months. Manuscript guidelines free.

    O→ "IDG Books dedicates itself to publishing innovative, high-quality titles on the most popular business, self-help and general reference topics."

Nonfiction: How-to, illustrated book, reference, self-help, technical. Subjects include business/economics (small business, e-commerce, careers), education (management and skills training), money/finance (personal finance, taxes), sports. *Agented submissions only.*
Recent Title(s): *Investing For Dummies*, by Eric Tyson.

N A IDG BOOKS WORLDWIDE, Education Group, 10475 Crosspoint Blvd., Indianapolis IN 46256. (317)572-3075. E-mail: dsteele@idgbooks.com. Website: www.idgbooks.com. **Acquisitions:** Diane Steele, vice president/publisher. Publishes trade paperback originals. **Pays 10-15% royalty. Offers $0-25,000 advance.** Publishes book 3 months after acceptance of ms. Responds in 2 months. Manuscript guidelines free.

    O→ "IDG Books dedicates itself to publishing innovative, high-quality titles on the most popular business, self-help and general topics."

Nonfiction: How-to, reference, self-help. Subjects include education. *Agented submissions only.*

N A IDG BOOKS WORLDWIDE, Lifestyle Group, 1633 Broadway, New York NY 10019. (212)654-8153. E-mail: knebenhaus@idgbooks.com. Website: www.idgbooks.com. **Acquisitions:** Kathleen Nebenhause, vice president/ publisher (manages editorial and sports, self-help, health/medicine); Mike Spring, vice president/publisher (travel); Jennifer Feldman, assistant vice president/publisher (cooking, gardening); Dominique DeVito, assistant vice president/ publisher (pets). Publishes trade paperback originals. **Pays 10-15% royalty. Offers $0-25,000 advance.** Publishes book 3 months after acceptance of ms. Responds in 2 months. Manuscript guidelines free.

    O→ "IDG Books dedicates itself to publishing innovative, high-quality titles on the most popular business, self-help and general reference topics."

Nonfiction: Cookbook, gift book, how-to, illustrated book, reference, self-help. Subjects include pets, child guidance/ parenting, cooking/foods/nutrition, health/medicine, gardening, recreation, sports, travel. *Agented submissions only.*
Recent Title(s): *How to Cook Everything*, by Mark Bittman.

ILR PRESS, Cornell University Press, Sage House, 512 E. State St., Ithaca NY 14850. (607)277-2338 ext. 232. Fax: (607)277-2374. **Acquisitions:** F. Benson, editor. Estab. 1945. Publishes hardcover and trade paperback originals and reprints. **Publishes 12-15 titles/year. Pays royalty.** Responds in 2 months to queries. Book catalog free.

○── "We are interested in manuscripts with innovative perspectives on current workplace issues that concern both academics and the general public."

Nonfiction: All titles relate to industrial relations and/or workplace issues including relevant work in the fields of history, sociology, political science, economics, human resources, and organizational behavior. Needs for the next year include mss on workplace problems, employment policy, immigration, current history, and dispute resolution for academics and practitioners. Query or submit outline and sample chapters.

Recent Title(s): *Manufacturing Advantage: Why High-Performance Systems Pay Off*, by Eileen Appelbaum, et al; *The Working Class Majority: America's Best Kept Secret*, by Michael Leveig.

Tips: "Manuscripts must be well documented to pass our editorial evaluation, which includes review by academics in related fields."

IMPACT PUBLICATIONS, 9104 Manassas Dr., Suite N, Manassas Park VA 20111-5211. (703)361-7300. Fax: (703)335-9486. E-mail: submit@impactpublications.com. Website: www.impactpublications.com. **Acquisitions:** Caryl Krannich, vice president. Publishes hardcover and trade paperback originals and reprints. **Publishes 15-20 titles/year. Receives 30 queries and 20 mss/year. 30% of books from first-time authors; 100% from unagented writers. Pays 10-15% royalty on wholesale price.** Publishes book 10 months after acceptance of ms. Accepts simultaneous submissions. Responds in 2 months. Book catalog on website. Manuscript guidelines for #10 SASE or on website.

○── Impact Publications publishes business, career and travel books.

Imprints: Impact Guides.

Nonfiction: Reference, self-help. Subjects include business/economics, travel, career. Submit proposal package, including outline, 1 sample chapter and marketing plan. Reviews artwork/photos as part of ms package. Send photocopies.

Recent Title(s): *Savvy Interviewing*, by Ron and Caryl Krannich (career/business); *Take This Job and Thrive*, by Anita Bruzzese (business/career).

INCENTIVE PUBLICATIONS, INC., 3835 Cleghorn Ave., Nashville TN 37215-2532. (615)385-2934. Fax: (615)385-2967. E-mail: comments@incentivepublications.com. Website: www.incentivepublications.com. **Acquisitions:** Angela Reiner, editor. Estab. 1970. Publishes paperback originals. **Publishes 25-30 titles/year. Receives 350 submissions/year. 25% of books from first-time authors; 100% from unagented writers. Pays royalty or makes outright purchase.** Publishes book an average of 1 year after acceptance. Responds in 1 month to queries.

○── Incentive publishes developmentally appropriate teacher/parent resource materials and educational workbooks for children in grades K-12. Currently emphasizing primary material. De-emphasizing science.

Nonfiction: Teacher resource books in pre-K through 12th grade. Query with synopsis and detailed outline.

Recent Title(s): *The BASIC/Not Boring Grade Book Series* (Grades 1-5), by Imogene Forte and Marjorie Frank; *Internet Quest*, by C. Cook and J. Pfeifer.

INFORMATION TODAY, INC., 143 Old Marlton Pike, Medford NJ 08055. (609)654-6266. Fax: (609)654-4309. E-mail: jbryans@infotoday.com. Website: www.infotoday.com. **Acquisitions:** John B. Bryans, editor-in-chief. Publishes hardcover and trade paperback originals. **Publishes 15-20 titles/year. Receives 100 queries and 30 mss/year. 30% of books from first-time authors; 90% from unagented writers. Pays 10-15% royalty on wholesale price. Offers $500-2,500 advance.** Publishes book 9 months after acceptance of ms. Accepts simultaneous submissions. Responds in 1 month to queries, 2 months to proposals, 3 months to mss. Book catalog free on request or on website. Manuscript guidelines free on request or via e-mail as attachment.

○── "We look for highly-focused coverage of cutting-edge technology topics, written by established experts and targeted to a tech-savvy readership. Virtually all our titles focus on how information is accessed, used, shared and transformed into knowledge that can benefit people, business and society."

Imprints: ITI (academic, scholarly, library science); CyberAge Books (high-end consumer and business technology books—emphasis on Internet/WWW topics including online research).

Nonfiction: Biography, how-to, reference, technical. Subjects include business/economics, computers/electronics, education, Internet and cyberculture; library and information science. Query with SASE. Reviews artwork/photos as part of ms package. Send photocopies.

Recent Title(s): *The Extreme Searcher's Guide to Web Search Engines*, by Ran Hock (how-to/reference); *Electronic Democracy: Using the Internet to Transform American Politics*, by G. Browning.

Tips: "Our readers include scholars, academics, indexers, librarians, information professionals (ITI imprint) as well as high-end consumer and business users of Internet/www/online technologies, and people interested in the marriage of technology with issues of social significance (i.e., cyberculture)."

INNER TRADITIONS INTERNATIONAL, P.O. Box 388, 1 Park St., Rochester VT 05767. (802)767-3174. Fax: (802)767-3726. E-mail: info@innertraditions.com. Website: www.innertraditions.com. Managing Editor: Rowan Jacobsen. **Acquisitions:** Jon Graham, editor. Estab. 1975. Publishes hardcover and trade paperback originals and reprints. **Publishes 60 titles/year. Receives 3,000 submissions/year. 10% of books from first-time authors; 20% from unagented writers. Pays 8-10% royalty on net receipts. Offers $1,000 average advance.** Publishes book 1 year after acceptance of ms. Responds in 3 months to queries, 6 months to mss. Book catalog and ms guidelines free.

○── Inner Traditions publishes works representing the spiritual, cultural and mythic traditions of the world and works on alternative medicine and holistic health that combine contemporary thought with the knowledge of the world's great healing traditions. Currently emphasizing alternative health.

Imprint(s): Destiny Audio Editions, Destiny Books, Destiny Recordings, Healing Arts Press, Inner Traditions, Inner Traditions En Español, Inner Traditions India, Park Street Press.

Nonfiction: Subjects include anthropology/archaeology, natural foods, cooking, nutrition, health/alternative medicine, history and mythology, indigenous cultures, music/dance, nature/environment, ethnobotany business, esoteric philosophy, psychology, world religions, women's issues/studies, New Age. "We are interested in the relationship of the spiritual and transformative aspects of world cultures." Query or submit outline and sample chapters with SASE. Does not return mss without SASE. Reviews artwork/photos as part of ms package.

Recent Title(s): *The Temple of Man*, by Schwaller de Lubicz.

Tips: "We are not interested in autobiographical stories of self-transformation. We do not accept any electronic submissions (via e-mail). We are not currently looking at fiction."

N INTERCONTINENTAL PUBLISHING, 6451 Steeple Chase Lane, Manassas VA 20111-2611. (703)369-4992. Fax: (703)670-7825. E-mail: icpub@worldnet.att.net. **Acquisitions:** H.G. Smittenaar, publisher. Publishes hardcover and trade paperback originals. **Publishes 6 titles/year. Pays 5% minimum royalty.** Accepts simultaneous submissions. Responds in 2 months to queries and mss.

○→ Intercontinental publishes mystery and suspense novels.

Fiction: Mystery, suspense. Submit proposal package, including 1-3 sample chapters, estimated word count and SASE.

Recent Title(s): *The Cop Was White as Snow*, by Spizer (mystery); *Dekok and Murder in Ecstasy*, by Baantjer (police procedural).

Tips: "Be original, write proper English, be entertaining."

INTERCULTURAL PRESS, INC., P.O. Box 700, Yarmouth ME 04096. (207)846-5168. Fax: (207)846-5181. E-mail: books@interculturalpress.com. Website: www.interculturalpress.com. **Acquisitions:** Judy Carl-Hendrick, managing editor. Estab. 1980. Publishes hardcover and paperback originals. **Publishes 8-12 titles/year. Receives 50-80 submissions/year. 50% of books from first-time authors; 95% of books from unagented writers. Pays royalty. Offers small advance occasionally.** Publishes book within 2 years after acceptance. Accepts simultaneous submissions. Responds in 2 months. Book catalog and ms guidelines free.

○→ Intercultural Press publishes materials related to intercultural relations, including the practical concerns of living and working in foreign countries, the impact of cultural differences on personal and professional relationships and the challenges of interacting with people from unfamiliar cultures, whether at home or abroad. Currently emphasizing international business.

Nonfiction: Reference, textbook and theory. "We want books with an international or domestic intercultural or multicultural focus, especially those on business operations (how to be effective in intercultural business activities), education (textbooks for teaching intercultural subjects, for instance) and training (for Americans abroad or foreign nationals coming to the United States). Our books are published for educators in the intercultural field, business people engaged in international business, managers concerned with cultural diversity in the workplace, and anyone who works in an occupation where cross-cultural communication and adaptation are important skills. No manuscripts that don't have an intercultural focus." Accepts nonfiction translations. Query with outline or proposal. *No unsolicited mss.*

Recent Title(s): *Reading Between the Sign*, by Anna Mindess; *The Third Culture Kid Experience*, by David C. Pillock and Ruth E. Van Reken.

INTERLINK PUBLISHING GROUP, INC., 46 Crosby St., Northampton MA 01060. (413)582-7054. Fax: (413)582-7057. E-mail: info@interlinkbooks.com. Website: www.interlinkbooks.com. **Acquisitions:** Michel Moushabeck, publisher. Estab. 1987. Publishes hardcover and trade paperback originals. **Publishes 50 titles/year. Receives 600 submissions/year. 30% of books from first-time authors; 50% from unagented writers. Pays 6-8% royalty on retail price.** Publishes book 18 months after acceptance. Accepts simultaneous submissions. Responds in 1 month to queries. *Writer's Market* recommends allowing 2 months for reply. Book catalog and ms guidelines free.

○→ Interlink publishes a general trade list of adult fiction and nonfiction with an emphasis on books that have a wide appeal while also meeting high intellectual and literary standards.

Imprint(s): Crocodile Books, USA; Interlink Books; Olive Branch Press.

Nonfiction: World travel, world history and politics, ethnic cooking, world music. Submit outline and sample chapters.

Fiction: Ethnic, international feminist. "Adult fiction—We are looking for translated works relating to the Middle East, Africa or Latin America. Juvenile/Picture Books—Our list is full for the next two years. No science fiction, romance, plays, erotica, fantasy, horror." Submit outline/synopsis and sample chapters.

Recent Title(s): *House of the Winds*, by Mia Yun.

Tips: "Any submissions that fit well in our publishing program will receive careful attention. A visit to our website, your local bookstore, or library to look at some of our books before you send in your submission is recommended."

N INTERNATIONAL CITY/COUNTY MANAGEMENT ASSOCIATION, 777 N. Capitol St., NE, Suite 500, Washington DC 20002. (202)962-3648. Website: www.icma.com. **Acquisitions:** Christine Ulrich, editorial director; Barbara Moore, director of publishing/data services. Estab. 1914. "Our mission is to enhance the quality of local government and to support and assist professional local administrators in the United States and other countries." Publishes hardcover and paperback originals. **Publishes 10-15 titles/year. Receives 50 queries and 20 mss/year. 20% of books from first-time authors; 100% from unagented writers. Makes negotiable outright purchase.** Publishes book 18 months after acceptance of ms. Responds in 3 months. Book catalog and ms guidelines free via website.

Nonfiction: Reference, textbook, training manuals. Subjects include local government. Query with outline and 1 sample chapter. Reviews artwork/photos as part of ms package. Send photocopies.

Recent Nonfiction Title(s): *Records Management,* by Julian L. Mims; *Telecommunications: Planning for the Future; Accountability for Performance,* edited by David N. Ammons (performance measurement).

INTERNATIONAL FOUNDATION OF EMPLOYEE BENEFIT PLANS, P.O. Box 69, Brookfield WI 53008-0069. (262)786-6700. Fax: (262)786-8780. E-mail: books@ifebp.org. Website: www.ifebp.org. **Acquisitions:** Dee Birschel, senior director of publications. Estab. 1954. Publishes hardcover and trade paperback originals. **Publishes 10 titles/year. Receives 20 submissions/year. 15% of books from first-time authors; 80% from unagented writers. Pays 5-15% royalty on wholesale and retail price.** Publishes book 1 year after acceptance. Responds in 3 months to queries. Book catalog free. Manuscript guidelines for SASE.

O━ IFEBP publishes general and technical monographs on all aspects of employee benefits—pension plans, health insurance, etc.

Nonfiction: Reference, technical, consumer information, textbook. Subjects limited to health care, pensions, retirement planning, and employee benefits. Query with outline.

Recent Title(s): *Integratio Disability Management: An Employers Guide,* by Janet R. Douglas.

Tips: "Be aware of interests of employers and the marketplace in benefits topics, for example, how AIDS affects employers, health care cost containment."

INTERNATIONAL MARINE, The McGraw-Hill Companies, P.O. Box 220, Camden ME 04843-0220. (207)236-4838. Fax: (207)236-6314. **Acquisitions:** Jonathan Eaton, editorial director (boating, marine nonfiction). Estab. 1969. Publishes hardcover and paperback originals. **Publishes 40 titles/year. receives 500-700 mss/year. 30% of books from first-time authors; 80% from unagented writers. Pays standard royalties based on net price. Offers advance.** Publishes book 1 year after acceptance. Responds in 2 months. Book catalog and ms guidelines for SASE.

O━ International Marine publishes "good books about boats."

Imprint(s): Ragged Mountain Press (sports and outdoor books that take you off the beaten path).

Nonfiction: "Marine and outdoor nonfiction. A wide range of subjects include: sea stories, seamanship, boat maintenance, etc." All books are illustrated. "Material in all stages welcome." Query first with outline and 2-3 sample chapters. Reviews artwork/photos as part of ms package.

Recent Nonfiction Title(s): *Fatal Storm,* by Rob Mundle (nonfiction); *The Elements of Boat Strength,* by Dave Gerr (how-to).

Tips: "Writers should be aware of the need for clarity, accuracy and interest. Many progress too far in the actual writing."

INTERNATIONAL MEDICAL PUBLISHING, P.O. Box 479, McLean VA 22101-0479. (703)356-2037. Fax: (703)734-8987. E-mail: masterso@patriot.net. Website: www.medicalpublishing.com. **Acquisitions:** Thomas Masterson, MD, editor. Estab. 1991. Publishes mass market paperback originals. **Publishes 30 titles/year. Receives 50 queries and 20 mss/year. 5% of books from first-time authors; 100% from unagented writers. Pays royalty on gross receipts.** Publishes book 8 months after acceptance of ms. Responds in 2 months to queries.

O━ IMP publishes books to make life easier for doctors in training. "We're branching out to also make life easier for people with chronic medical problems."

Nonfiction: Reference, textbook. Health/medicine subjects. "We distribute only through medical and scientific bookstores. Think about practical material for doctors-in-training. We are interested in handbooks. Online projects are of interest." Query with outline.

Recent Title(s): *Day-by-Day Diabetes Calendar,* by Resa Levetan.

INTERNATIONAL SCHOLARS PUBLICATIONS, INC., The University Press of America, 4720 Boston Way, Lanham MD 20706. (301)731-9527. Fax: (301)306-5357. E-mail: rwest@univpress.com. Website: www.univpress.com. **Acquisitions:** Dr. Robert West, publisher/editorial director. Estab. 1993. Publishes hardcover and trade paperback originals, hardcover reprints. **Publishes 32 titles/year. Receives 200 queries and 140 mss/year. 80% of books from first-time authors; 100% from unagented writers. Pays 5-8% royalty on wholesale price.** Publishes book 5 months after acceptance of ms. Accepts simultaneous submissions. Responds in 1 month. Book catalog and ms guidelines for #10 SASE or via website.

O━ International Scholars Publications is an independent publishing house founded by scholars from a variety of traditions united by the goal of affirming the richness and diversity of contemporary scholarship.

Imprint(s): Catholic Scholars Publications, Christian Universities Press, University Press for West Africa.

Nonfiction: Biography, reference, scholarly, textbook. Subjects include art/architecture, education, ethnic, government/politics, history, language/literature, military/war, money/finance, philosophy, psychology, religion, science, sociology, women's issues/studies, Africa. "Research monographs and revised dissertations welcome. Some submissions do not contain enough information or have work condition problems." Query with outline, 2 sample chapters, cv and SASE.

Recent Title(s): *Aspects of Personal Faith,* by Barnett Friel; *Paradoxical Feminism: The Novels of Rebecca West,* by Ann Norton.

Tips: "Audience are upscale readers who enjoy an intellectual challenge. Focus on concept, contents, size of work and why it should be released."

INTERNATIONAL WEALTH SUCCESS, P.O. Box 186, Merrick NY 11570-0186. (516)766-5850. Fax: (516)766-5919. **Acquisitions:** Tyler G. Hicks, editor. Estab. 1967. **Publishes 10 titles/year. Receives 100 submissions/year. 100% of books from first-time authors; 100% from unagented writers. Pays 10% royalty on wholesale or retail price. Buys all rights. Offers usual advance of $1,000, but this varies depending on author's reputation and nature of book.** Publishes book 4 months after acceptance. Responds in 1 month. Book catalog and ms guidelines for 9×12 SAE with 3 first-class stamps.

○━ "We publish nonfiction books and periodicals to help Beginning Wealth Builders choose, start, finance, and succeed in their own home-based or externally-quartered small business. Currently looking for books on business bootstrap financing, income real estate, e-commerce."

Nonfiction: Self-help, how-to. "Techniques, methods, sources for building wealth. Highly personal, how-to-do-it with plenty of case histories. Books are aimed at wealth builders and are highly sympathetic to their problems. These publications present a wide range of business opportunities while providing practical, hands-on, step-by-step instructions aimed at helping readers achieve their personal goals in as short a time as possible while adhering to ethical and professional business standards." Financing, business success, venture capital, etc. Length: 60,000-70,000 words. Query. Reviews artwork/photos.

Recent Title(s): *How to Make Fast Cash in Real Estate with No Money Down Deals*, by Rod L. Griffin.

Tips: "With the mass layoffs in large and medium-size companies there is an increasing interest in owning your own business. So we focus on more how-to hands-on material on owning—and becoming successful in—one's own business of any kind. Our market is the BWB—Beginning Wealth Builder. This person has so little money that financial planning is something they never think of. Instead, they want to know what kind of a business they can get into to make some money without a large investment. Write for this market and you have millions of potential readers. Remember—there are a lot more people *without* money than *with* money."

INTERSTATE PUBLISHERS, INC., 510 N. Vermilion St., P.O. Box 50, Danville IL 61834-0050. (217)446-0500. Fax: (217)446-9706. E-mail: info-ipp@ippinc.com. Website: www.ippinc.com. **Acquisitions:** Ronald L. McDaniel, vice president, editorial. Estab. 1914. Publishes hardcover originals. **Publishes 20 titles/year. Receives 100 queries and 25 mss/year. 50% of books from first-time authors; 100% from unagented writers. Pays 10% royalty on actual money received from sales.** Publishes book 6 months after acceptance of ms. Accepts simultaneous submissions, if so noted. Responds in 2 months to proposals. Book catalog (specify high school or college) for 9×12 SAE with 4 first-class stamps.

○━ Interstate Publishers publishes textbooks and related materials that infuse science concepts into agricultural education.

Nonfiction: Textbook, ancillary materials for each textbook. Subjects include agriculture/horticulture, education (middle school, high school, college). Submit proposal package, including prospectus, outline, 2 sample chapters and SASE. Reviews artwork/photos as part of ms package. Send photocopies.

Recent Title(s): *Floriculture: Greenhouse Production to Floral Design*, by Ronald J. Biondo and Dianne A. Noland; *Biotechnology*, by Jasper S. Lee, et al.

Tips: "Our audience is students who are interested in agriculture. They may simply want to become literate on the subject, or they may be preparing for a career in the new science-oriented agriculture. The career may well be off the farm and in areas such as landscaping, food technology, biotechnology, plant and soil science, etc. Educational texts must demonstrate fair and balanced treatment of the sexes, minorities, and persons with disabilities."

INTERVARSITY PRESS, P.O. Box 1400, Downers Grove IL 60515. (630)734-4000. Fax: (630)734-4200. E-mail: mail@ivpress.com. Website: www.ivpress.com. **Acquisitions:** David Zimmerman, assistant editor; Linda Doll, editor (general, Christian living); Andy Le Pean, editorial director (academic); Jim Hoover, assistant editorial director (academic, reference); Cindy Bunch-Hotaling, editor (Bible study, Christian living). Estab. 1947. Publishes hardcover originals, trade paperback and mass market paperback originals. **Publishes 70-80 titles/year. Receives 1,500 queries and 1,000 mss/year. 15% of books from first-time authors; 85% from unagented writers. Pays negotiable flat fee or royalty on retail price. Offers negotiable advance.** Publishes book 2 years after acceptance of ms. Accepts simultaneous submissions. Responds in 3 months to proposals. Book catalog for 9×12 SAE and 5 first-class stamps. Manuscript guidelines available via e-mail or with #10 SASE.

○━ InterVarsity Press publishes a full line of books from an evangelical Christian perspective targeted to an open-minded audience. "We serve those in the university, the church and the world, by publishing books from a Christian evangelical perspective."

Imprint(s): Academic (contact: Andy LePean); Bible Study; General; Popular; Reference (contact Dan Reid).

Nonfiction: Religious subjects. Writers need cv/résumé and detailed table of contents with query and SASE.

Recent Title(s): *Apologetic Preaching*, by Craig Loscalzo; *Science and Its Limits*, by Del Ratzsch.

INTERWEAVE PRESS, 201 E. Fourth St., Loveland CO 80537. (970)669-7672. Fax: (970)667-8317. **Acquisitions:** Marilyn Murphy, editorial director. Estab. 1975. Publishes hardcover and trade paperback originals. **Publishes 10-15 titles/year. Receives 50 submissions/year. 60% of books from first-time authors; 98% from unagented writers. Pays 10% royalty on net receipts.** Publishes book 1 year after acceptance of ms. Accepts simultaneous submissions, if so noted. Responds in 2 months. Book catalog and ms guidelines free.

○━ Interweave Press publishes instructive and inspirational titles relating to the fiber arts and herbal topics.

Nonfiction: How-to, technical. Subjects limited to fiber arts—basketry, spinning, knitting, dyeing and weaving—and herbal topics—gardening, cooking, medical herbs and lore. Submit outline/synopsis and sample chapters. Reviews artwork/photos as part of ms package.
Recent Title(s): *What the Labels Won't Tell You*, by Logan Chamberlain.
Tips: "We are looking for very clear, informally written, technically correct manuscripts, generally of a how-to nature, in our specific fiber and herb fields only. Our audience includes a variety of creative self-starters who appreciate inspiration and clear instruction. They are often well educated and skillful in many areas."

N IRON GATE PUBLISHING, P.O. Box 999, Niwot CO 80544-0999. (303)530-2551. Fax: (303)530-5273. E-mail: irongate@estreet.com. Website: www.irongate.com. **Acquisitions:** Dina C. Carson, publisher (how-to, genealogy); Risa J. Johnson, editor (reunions). Publishes hardcover and trade paperback originals. **Publishes 6-10 titles/year; imprint publishes 2-6 titles/year. Receives 100 queries and 20 mss/year. 30% of books from first-time authors; 10% from unagented writers. Pays royalty on a case-by-case basis.** Publishes book 1 year after acceptance of ms. Accepts simultaneous submissions. Responds in 2 months. Book catalog free or on website. Manuscript guidelines on website.
  O— "Our readers are people who are looking for solid, how-to advice on planning reunions or self-publishing a genealogy."
Imprints: Reunion Solutions Press, KinderMed Press.
Nonfiction: How-to, multimedia, reference. Subjects include child guidance/parenting, health/medicine, hobbies, reunions, genealogy. Query with SASE or submit proposal package, including outline, 2 sample chapters and marketing summary. Reviews artwork/photos as part of ms package. Send photocopies.
Recent Title(s): *The Genealogy and Local History Researcher's Self-Publishing Guide*; *Reunion Solutions: Everything You Need to Know to Plan a Family, Class, Military, Association or Corporate Reunion.*
Tips: "Please look at the other books we publish and tell us in your query letter why your book would fit into our line of books."

A ISLAND, Bantam Dell Publishing Group, Random House, Inc., 1540 Broadway, New York NY 10036. (212)354-6500. **Acquisitions:** Maggie Crawford, editorial director. Publishes mass market paperback originals and reprints. Publishes bestseller fiction and nonfiction. **Publishes 12 titles/year.**
Fiction: Mystery, romance, suspense. *Agented submissions only.*
Recent Title(s): *Runaway Jury*, by John Grisham (suspense).

N ★ ISLAND PRESS, Shearwater Books. 1718 Connecticut Ave. NW, Washington DC 20009. (202)232-7933. Fax: (202)234-1328. E-mail: info@islandpress.org. Website: www.islandpress.org. **Acquisitions:** Barbara Dean, executive editor (ecosystems management); Todd Baldwin, senior editor (business/economics); Heather Boyer, sponsoring editor (land use/community issues). Publishes hardcover and trade paperback originals and trade paperback reprints. **Publishes 50 titles/year; imprint publishes 10 titles/year. Receives 50-75 queries and 5-10 mss/year. 50% of books from first-time authors; 60% from unagented writers. Pays 10-15% royalty on wholesale price.** Publishes book 1 year after acceptance of ms. Accepts simultaneous submissions. Responds in 1 month to queries and proposals, 2 months to mss. Book catalog and ms guidelines free or on website.
  O— Island Press specializes in books about environmental problems.
Imprints: Shearwater Books (Jonathan Cobb, editor).
Nonfiction: Biography, reference, textbook, scholarly and professional. Subjects include anthropology/archaeology, business/economics, nature/environment, science, land use and planning. Query with SASE or submit proposal package, including outline and 2 sample chapters. Reviews artwork/photos as part of ms package. Send photocopies.
Recent Title(s): *Earth Rising: American Environmentalism in the 21st Century*, by Philip Shabecoff; *All the Wild and Lonely Places, Journeys in a Desert Landscape*, by Lawrence Hogue.
Tips: "We're looking for solutions-oriented information for professionals, students and concerned citizens working to solve environmental problems."

N LEE JACOBS PRODUCTIONS, Box 362, Pomeroy OH 45769-0362. (740)992-5208. Fax: (740)992-0616. E-mail: LJacobs@frognet.net. Website: LeeJacobsProductions.com. **Acquisitions:** Lee Jacobs, president. Publishes hardcover and trade paperback originals and reprints. **Publishes 5 titles/year. Receives 5 queries and 5 mss/year. 10% of books from first-time authors; 90% from unagented writers. Pays 5% royalty or makes outright purchase of $100-5,000.** Publishes book 6 months after acceptance of ms. Responds in 1 month to queries and proposals, 6 months to mss. Book catalog for $5 or on website.
  O— Lee Jacobs Productions publishes books about magic, comedy and entertainment.
Nonfiction: Biography, coffee table book, how-to, humor, illustrated book, reference, technical, textbook. Subjects include history, hobbies, memoirs, money/finance, photography, psychology, recreation. Query with SASE. Reviews artwork/photos as part of ms package.
Tips: Audience is magicians, comedians, pro entertainers, mentalists.

JAMESON BOOKS INC., 722 Columbus St., P.O. Box 738, Ottawa IL 61350. (815)434-7905. Fax: (815)434-7907. **Acquisitions:** Jameson G. Campaigne, publisher/editor. Estab. 1986. Publishes hardcover originals. **Publishes 12 titles/**

year. **Receives 500 queries/year; 300 mss/year. 33% of books from first-time authors; 33% from unagented writers. Pays 6-15% royalty on retail price. Offers $1,000-25,000 advance.** Publishes book 1 year after acceptance of ms. Accepts simultaneous submissions. Responds in 6 months to queries. Book catalog for 8×10 SASE.

➥ Jameson Books publishes conservative politics and economics; Chicago area history; and biographies.

Nonfiction: Biography. Subjects include business/economics, history, politics, regional (Chicago area). Query with sample chapter and SASE (essential). *Submissions not returned without SASE.*

Fiction: Interested in pre-cowboy frontier fiction. Query with 1 sample chapter and SASE.

Recent Title(s): *Politics as a Noble Calling*, by F. Clifton White (memoirs); *Yellowstone Kelly: Gentleman and Scout*, by Peter Bowen (fiction).

[N] [↗] JEWISH LIGHTS PUBLISHING, LongHill Partners, Inc., P.O. Box 237, Sunset Farms Offices, Rt. 4, Woodstock VT 05091. (802)457-4000. Editor: Stuart Matlins. **Acquisitions:** Acquisitions Editor. Estab. 1990. Publishes hardcover and trade paperback originals, trade paperback reprints. **Publishes 25 titles/year. Receives 500 queries and 250 mss/year. 50% of books from first-time authors; 99% from unagented writers. Pays royalty on net sales, 10% on first printing, then increases.** Publishes book 1 year after acceptance of ms. Accepts simultaneous submissions. Responds in 3 months. Book catalog and ms guidelines free.

➥ "We publish books which fall under the category of religion, theology, philosophy, history and spirituality which can be read by people of all faiths and all backgrounds."

Nonfiction: Children's/juvenile, illustrated book, reference, self-help, spirituality, inspiration. Subjects include business/economics (with spiritual slant, finding spiritual meaning in one's work), health/medicine, healing/recovery, wellness, aging, life cycle, history, nature/environment, philosophy, theology, religion, women's issues/studies. "We do *not* publish haggadot, biography, poetry, cookbooks or books aiming to be most successfully sold during any specific holiday season." Submit proposal package, including cover letter, table of contents, 2 sample chapters and SASE. (Postage must cover weight of ms.) Reviews artwork/photos as part of ms package. Send photocopies.

Recent Title(s): *A Heart of Many Rooms: Celebrating the Many Voices within Judaism*, by David Hartman; *Good Whispers: Stories of the Soul, Lessons of the Heart*, by Karyn D. Kedar.

Tips: "We publish books for all faiths and backgrounds. Many also reflect the Jewish wisdom tradition."

JIST WORKS, INC., 8902 Otis Ave., Indianapolis IN 46216-1033. (317)613-4200. Fax: (317)613-4309. E-mail: jistworks@aol.com. Website: www.jistworks.com. **Acquisitions:** Michael Cunningham, editor-in-chief. Estab. 1981. Publishes trade paperback originals and reprints. **Publishes 60 titles/year. Receives 150 submissions/year. 60% of books from first time authors; majority from unagented writers. Pays 5-12% royalty on wholesale price or makes outright purchase (negotiable).** Publishes book 1 year after acceptance. Accepts simultaneous submissions. Responds in 3 months to queries. Book catalog and ms guidelines for 9×12 SAE with 6 first-class stamps.

➥ "Our purpose is to provide quality career, job search, and other living skills information, products, and services that help people manage and improve their lives—and the lives of others."

Imprint(s): Park Avenue Publications (business and self-help that falls outside of the JIST topical parameters).

Nonfiction: How-to, career, reference, self-help, software, video, textbook. Specializes in job search, self-help and career related topics. "We want text/workbook formats that would be useful in a school or other institutional setting. We also publish trade titles, all reading levels. Will consider books for professional staff and educators, appropriate software and videos." Query with SASE. Reviews artwork/photos as part of ms package.

Recent Title(s): *The Quick Résumé & Cover Letter Book*, by J. Michael Farr.

Tips: "Institutions and staff who work with people of all reading and academic skill levels, making career and life decisions or people who are looking for jobs are our primary audience, but we're focusing more on business and trade topics for consumers."

[N] JOHNSON BOOKS, Johnson Publishing Co., 1880 S. 57th Court., Boulder CO 80301. (303)443-9766. Fax: (303)443-1106. **Acquisitions:** Stephen Topping, editorial director. Estab. 1979. Publishes hardcover and paperback originals and reprints. **Publishes 10-12 titles/year. Receives 500 submissions/year. 30% of books from first-time authors; 90% from unagented writers. Royalties vary.** Publishes book 1 year after acceptance. Responds in 3 months. Book catalog and ms guidelines for 9×12 SAE with 5 first-class stamps.

➥ Johnson Books specializes in books on the American West, primarily outdoor, "useful" titles that will have strong national appeal.

Imprint(s): Spring Creek Press.

Nonfiction: General nonfiction, books on the West, environmental subjects, natural history, paleontology, geology, archaeology, travel, guidebooks, outdoor recreation. Accepts nonfiction translations. "We are primarily interested in books for the informed popular market, though we will consider vividly written scholarly works." Submit outline/synopsis and 3 sample chapters. Looks for "good writing, thorough research, professional presentation and appropriate style. Marketing suggestions from writers are helpful."

Recent Title(s): *Women of Consequence*, by Jeanne Varnell (western biography).

JOURNEY BOOKS, Bob Jones University Press, 1700 Wade Hampton Blvd., Greenville SC 29614-0001. (864)370-1800. Fax: (864)298-0268. E-mail: jb@bjup.com. Website: www.bjup.com. **Acquisitions:** Gloria Repp, juvenile fiction editor (fiction suitable for ages two through teens); Suzette Jordan, nonficiton editor (nonfiction suitable for juvenile and adult readers). Estab. 1974. Publishes trade paperback originals and reprints. **Publishes 11 titles/year. Receives**

180 queries and 570 mss/year. 10% of books from first-time authors; 100% from unagented writers. Makes outright purchase of $500-1,250; royalties to established authors. Publishes book 18 months after acceptance of ms. Accepts simultaneous submissions. Responds in 2 months to mss. Book catalog and ms guidelines free.

O➝ Journey Books publishes nonfiction and fiction "reflecting a Christian perspective. Journey rarely publishes biblical fiction and doesn't publish romance, poetry or drama." Now accepting nonfiction manuscripts for adult market.

Nonfiction: Biography, children's/juvenile and adult. Subjects include animals, gardening, history, sports. "We're looking for concept books on almost any subject suitable for children. We also like biographies." Submit outline and 3 sample chapters.

Fiction: Juvenile, young adult. "We're looking for well-rounded characters and plots with plenty of action suitable for a Christian audience." Submit synopsis and 5 sample chapters or complete ms.

Recent Title(s): *Seven Wonders of the World*, by Ron Tagliapietra (nonfiction); *Songbird*, by Nancy Lohr (fiction).

Tips: "Our readers are children ages two and up, teens and young adults. We're looking for high-quality writing that reflects a Christian standard of thought and features well-developed characters capable of dynamic changes, in a convincing plot. Most open to: first chapter books, adventure, biography."

N: JUDAICA PRESS, 123 Ditmas Ave., Brooklyn NY 11218. (718)972-6200. Fax: (718)972-6204. E-mail: judaicapr @aol.com. Website: www.judaicapress.com. **Acquisitions:** Bonnie Goldman, senior editor. Estab. 1963. Publishes hardcover and trade paperback originals and reprints. **Publishes 8 titles/year. No advance.** Responds in 3 months to queries. Book catalog available via website.

O➝ "We cater to the traditional, Orthodox Jewish market."

Nonfiction: "Looking for very traditional Judaica, especially children's books." Query with outline, 1 sample chapter.

Recent Title(s): *Invisible Chains*, Eva Vogiel; *New Beginnings*, by C.B. Weinfeld.

JUDSON PRESS, P.O. Box 851, Valley Forge PA 19482-0851. (610)768-2128. Fax: (610)768-2441. E-mail: judsonpres s@juno.com. Website: www.judsonpress.com. Publisher: Kristy Arnesen Pullen. **Acquisitions:** Randy Frame. Estab. 1824. Publishes hardcover and paperback originals. **Publishes 20-30 titles/year. Receives 750 queries/year. Pays royalty or makes outright purchase.** Publishes book 10 months after acceptance of ms. Accepts simultaneous submissions. Responds in 3 months. Enclose return postage. Book catalog for 9×12 SAE with 4 first-class stamps. Manuscript guidelines for #10 SASE.

O➝ "Our audience is mostly church members and leaders who seek to have a more fulfilling personal spiritual life and want to serve Christ in their churches and other relationships. We have a large African American readership." Currently emphasizing worship resources/small group resources. De-emphasizing biography, poetry.

Nonfiction: Adult religious nonfiction of 30,000-80,000 words. Query with outline and sample chapter.

● Judson Press also publishes a quarterly journal, *The African American Pulpit*; call for submission guidelines.

Recent Title(s): *Journey Into Day: Meditations for New Cancer Patients*, by Rusty Freeman.

Tips: "Writers have the best chance selling us practical books assisting clergy or laypersons in their ministry and personal lives. Our audience consists of Protestant church leaders and members. Be sensitive to our workload and adapt to the market's needs. Books on multicultural issues are very welcome. Also seeking books that heighten awareness and sensitivity to issues related to the poor and to social justice."

KALMBACH PUBLISHING CO., 21027 Crossroads Circle, P.O. Box 1612, Waukesha WI 53187-1612. Fax: (414)798-6468. E-mail: tspohn@kalmbach.com. Website: books.kalmbach.com. Editor-in-Chief: Dick Christianson (model railroading, scale modeling, toy trains, railfanning). **Acquisitions:** Kent Johnson, acquisitions editor (model railroading, toy trains). Estab. 1934. Publishes hardcover and paperback originals, paperback reprints. **Publishes 15-20 titles/year. Receives 100 submissions/year. 85% of books from first-time authors; 100% from unagented writers. Pays 10% royalty on net. Offers $1,500 average advance.** Publishes book 18 months after acceptance. Responds in 2 months.

O➝ Kalmbach publishes reference materials and how-to publications for serious hobbyists in the railfan, model railroading, plastic modeling and toy train collecting/operating hobbies.

Nonfiction: Hobbies, how-to, amateur astronomy, railroading. "Our book publishing effort is in railroading and hobby how-to-do-it titles *only*." Query first. "I welcome telephone inquiries. They save me a lot of time, and they can save an author a lot of misconceptions and wasted work." In written query, wants detailed outline of 2-3 pages and a complete sample chapter with photos, drawings, and how-to text. Reviews artwork/photos as part of ms package.

Recent Title(s): *Basics of Ship Modeling*, by Mike Ashey.

Tips: "Our books are about half text and half illustrations. Any author who wants to publish with us must be able to furnish good photographs and rough drawings before we'll consider contracting for his book."

N: KAMEHAMEHA SCHOOLS PRESS, Kamehameha Schools, 1887 Makuakane St., Honolulu HI 96817-1887. (808)842-8880. Fax: (808)842-8876. E-mail: kspress@ksbe.edu. Website: www.ksbe.edu/pubs/KSPress/catalog/html. **Acquisitions:** Henry Bennett. Publishes hardcover and trade paperback originals and reprints. **Publishes 3-5 titles/year. 10-25% of books from first-time authors; 100% from unagented writers. Makes outright purchase.** Publishes book up to 2 years after acceptance of ms. Responds in 3 months. Book catalog for #10 SASE.

○┐ "Only writers with substantial and documented expertise in Hawaiian history, Hawaiian culture, Hawaiian language, and/or Hawaiian studies should consider submitting to Kamehameha Schools Press. We prefer to work with writers available to physically meet at our Honolulu offices."

Imprints: Kamehameha Schools, Kamehameha Schools Bishop Estate.

Nonfiction: Biography, children's/juvenile, reference, textbook. Subjects include education, history, regional, translation. Query with SASE. Reviews artwork/photos as part of ms package. Send photocopies.

KAR-BEN COPIES, INC., 6800 Tildenwood Ln., Rockville MD 20852. (800)452-7236. Fax: (301)881-9195. E-mail: karben@aol.com. Website: www.karben.com. **Acquisitions:** Madeline Wikler, editor (juvenile Judaica). Estab. 1976. Publishes hardcover and trade paperback originals. **Publishes 8-10 titles/year. Receives 50-100 queries and 300-400 mss/year. 5% of books from first-time authors; 100% from unagented writers. Pays 5-8% royalty of net sales. Offers $500-2,500 advance.** Publishes book 10 months after acceptance of ms. Accepts simultaneous submissions. Responds in 1 month. Book catalog free or on website. Manuscript guidelines for 9 × 12 SAE with 2 first-class stamps.

○┐ Kar-Ben Copies publishes Jewish books, calendars and cassettes, fiction and nonfiction, for preschool and primary children interested in Jewish holidays and traditions.

Nonfiction: Children's/juvenile (Judaica only). Religious subjects. "Jewish themes only!" Submit complete ms.

Fiction: Juvenile, religious. "Jewish themes and young kids only!"

Recent Title(s): *Too Many Cooks*, by Edie Stoltz Zolkower; *Baby's Bris*, by Susan Wilkowsky.

Tips: "Do a literature search to make sure similar title doesn't already exist."

A KENSINGTON PUBLISHING CORP., 850 Third Ave., 16th Floor, New York NY 10022. (212)407-1500. Fax: (212)935-0699. Website: www.kensingtonbooks.com. **Acquisitions:** Ann LaFarge, executive editor (romance, fiction); Tracy Bernstein, editorial director (pop culture, spiritual, New Age, parenting, health); Paul Dinas, editor-in-chief (nonfiction, true crime thrillers, epic westerns); Kate Duffy, editorial director (historical romance, regency, romance, Ballad, erotica); John Scognamiglio, editorial director (romance, regency, mystery, thrillers, pop culture); Clare Gerus, editor (alternative health, general nonfiction); Karen Haas, editor (romance, true crime, westerns); Amy Garvey, editor (romance, regency, Precious Gems historical romances); Tomasita Ortiz, editor (romance, Encanto Hispanic romances); Karen Thomas, senior editor (Arabesque romance, African American fiction and nonfiction); Diane Stockwell, editor (Encanto Hispanic romances); Hillary Sares, editor (Precious Gem romances). Estab. 1975. Publishes hardcover originals, trade paperback, and mass market paperback originals. **Kensington publishes 300 titles/year; Pinnacle 60; Zebra 140-170; Arabesque 48. Receives 6,000 queries/year. 3-5% of books from first-time authors. Pays royalty on retail price; advance and royalty vary by author and type of book.** Publishes book 18 months after acceptance of ms. Accepts simultaneous submissions. Responds in 1 month to queries; 3 months to mss. Book catalog for #10 SASE. Manuscript guidelines on website.

• Kensington recently purchased the Carol Publishing Group.

Imprint(s): Arabesque, Ballad, Bouquet, Encanto, **Kensington,** **Pinnacle,** Precious Gems, **Zebra.**

Nonfiction: Self-help. Subjects include alternative health/medicine, pop culture, true crime, biography, humor, current events. Query with synopsis and SASE. *No unsolicited mss.*

Fiction: Mystery, romance, suspense, women's, thriller, gay fiction, epic westerns. Query with synopsis and SASE. *No unsolicited mss. No unagented writers.*

Recent Title(s): *Landing It*, by Scott Hamilton (nonfiction); *Celebration*, by Fern Michaels (fiction).

Tips: Agented submissions only, except for submissions to Arabesque, Ballad, Bouquet, Encanto and Precious Gems.

KENT STATE UNIVERSITY PRESS, P.O. Box 5190, Kent OH 44242-0001. (330)672-7913. Fax: (330)672-3104. **Acquisitions:** John T. Hubbell, director (history, regional); Joanna H. Craig, editor-in-chief (literary criticism). Estab. 1965. Publishes hardcover and paperback originals and some reprints. **Publishes 30-35 titles/year. Nonauthor subsidy publishes 20% of books. Standard minimum book contract on net sales. Offers advance rarely.** Responds in 3 months. Book catalog free.

○┐ Kent State publishes primarily scholarly works and titles of regional interest. Currently emphasizing US history, literary criticism. De-emphasizing European history.

Nonfiction: Especially interested in "scholarly works in history and literary studies of high quality, any titles of regional interest for Ohio, scholarly biographies, archaeological research, the arts, and general nonfiction. Always write a letter of inquiry before submitting manuscripts. We can publish only a limited number of titles each year and can frequently tell in advance whether or not we would be interested in a particular manuscript. This practice saves both our time and that of the author, not to mention postage costs. If interested we will ask for complete manuscript. Decisions based on inhouse readings and two by outside scholars in the field of study." Enclose return postage.

Recent Title(s): *Taken at the Flood: Robert E. Lee & Confederate Strategy in the Maryland Campaign of 1862*, by Joseph L. Harsh.

Tips: "We are cautious about publishing heavily-illustrated manuscripts."

N. MICHAEL KESEND PUBLISHING, LTD., 1025 Fifth Ave., New York NY 10028. (212)249-5150. Publisher: Michael Kesend. **Acquisitions:** Judy Wilder, editor. Estab. 1979. Publishes hardcover and trade paperback originals and reprints. **Publishes 4-6 titles/year. Receives 300 submissions/year. 20% of books from first-time authors; 40% from unagented writers. Pays 6% royalty on wholesale price. Advance varies.** Publishes book 18 months after acceptance. Responds in 2 months to queries. Guidelines for #10 SASE.

O┰ Michael Kesend publishes guidebooks and other nonfiction titles for sale in bookstore chains and independents, in museum stores, parks or similar outlets. Currently emphasizing travel guidebooks. De-emphasizing health/animals/hobbies.

Nonfiction: Biography, how-to, self-help, sports, travel guides (regional and national). Subjects include animals, health, history, nature, sports, travel, the environment, guides to several subjects. Needs sports, and environmental awareness guides. No photography mss. Submit outline and sample chapters. Reviews artwork/photos as part of ms package.

Recent Title(s): *West Coast Garden Walks*, by Alice Joyce.

Tips: "Looking for national guides, outdoor travel guides, sports nonfiction, art or garden-related guides and/or others suitable for museum stores, natural history and national or state park outlets."

ALFRED A. KNOPF AND CROWN BOOKS FOR YOUNG READERS, Random House, Inc., 1540 Broadway, New York NY 10036. (212)782-5623. Website: www.randomhouse.com/kids. Vice President/Publishing Director: Simon Boughton. Associate Publishing Director: Andrea Cascardi. Editor: Nancy Siscoe. Senior Editor: Tracy Gates. **Acquisitions:** Send mss to Crown/Knopf Editorial Department. Publishes hardcover originals, trade paperback reprints. **Publishes 60 titles/year. 10% of books from first-time authors; 40% from unagented writers. Pays 4-10% royalty on retail price. Offers advance of $3,000 and up.** Publishes book 1-2 years after acceptance of ms. Accepts simultaneous submissions. Responds in 3 months to mss. Book catalog for 9×12 SASE. Manuscript guidelines free.

O┰ Knopf is known for high quality literary fiction, and is willing to take risks with writing styles. It publishes for children ages 4 and up. Crown is known for books young children immediately use and relate to. It focuses on children ages 2-6. Crown also publishes nonfiction for all ages.

Imprint(s): Alfred A. Knopf Books for Young Readers, Crown Books for Young Readers, Knopf Paperbacks, Dragonfly.

Nonfiction: Children's/juvenile, biography. Subjects include ethnic, history, nature/environment, science. Query with entire ms and SASE.

Fiction: Juvenile, literary, picture books, young adult. Query with entire ms and SASE.

Recent Title(s): *Sammy Keyes and the Hotel Thief*, by Wendelin van Draanen (fiction); *Emeline at the Circus*, by Marjorie Priceman (picture book).

ALFRED A. KNOPF, INC., Knopf Publishing Group, Random House, Inc., 299 Park Ave., New York NY 10171. (212)751-2600. Website: www.aaknopf.com. **Acquisitions:** Senior Editor. Estab. 1915. Publishes hardcover and paperback originals. **Publishes 200 titles/yearly. 15% of books from first-time authors; 30% from unagented writers. Royalty and advance vary.** Publishes book 1 year after acceptance of ms. Accepts simultaneous submissions, if so noted. Responds in 3 months. Book catalog for 7½×10½ SAE with 5 first-class stamps.

O┰ Knopf is a general publisher of quality nonfiction and fiction.

Nonfiction: Book-length nonfiction, including books of scholarly merit. Preferred length: 50,000-150,000 words. "A good nonfiction writer should be able to follow the latest scholarship in any field of human knowledge, and fill in the abstractions of scholarship for the benefit of the general reader by means of good, concrete, sensory reporting." Query. Reviews artwork/photos as part of ms package.

Fiction: Publishes book-length fiction of literary merit by known or unknown writers. Length: 40,000-150,000 words. Query with sample chapters.

Recent Title(s): *Time, Love, Memory*, by Jonathan Weiner (nonfiction); *Gertrude and Claudius*, by John Updike (fiction); *Handwriting*, by Michael Ondaatje (poetry).

KOGAN PAGE U.S., Kogan Page Ltd., 163 Central Ave., #2, Dover NH 03820. (603)749-9171. Fax: (603)749-6155. E-mail: bizbks@aol.com. Website: www.kogan-page.co.uk. **Acquisitions:** Spencer Smith (business). Publishes hardcover and trade paperback originals. **Publishes 100 titles/year. Pays royalty. Advances vary.** Publishes book 1 year after acceptance of ms. Accepts simultaneous submissions. Responds in 1 month to queries, 2 months to proposals. Book catalog on request or on website.

O┰ Kogan Page U.S. publishes books in business, management, finance, international business and education for business people and educators.

Nonfiction: How-to, reference, self-help, textbook. Subjects business/economics. Query with SASE. Submit outline, 2 sample chapters, competition and market analysis. Reviews artwork/photos as part of ms package. Send photocopies.

Recent Title(s): *Millennium Countdown*, by Kusmirak (business/computer).

N H.J. KRAMER, INC., P.O. Box 1082, Tiburon CA 94920. (415)435-5367. Fax: (415)435-5364. E-mail: hjkramer@jps.net. **Acquisitions:** Jan Phillips, managing editor. Estab. 1984. Publishes hardcover and trade paperback originals. **Publishes 5 titles/year. Receives 1,000 queries and 500 mss/year. 20% of books from first-time authors. Advance varies.** Publishes book 18 months after acceptance of ms. Book catalog free.

O┰ "The books we publish are our contribution to an emerging world based on cooperation rather than on competition, on affirmation rather than on self-doubt, and on the certainty that all humanity is connected. Our goal is to touch as many lives as possible with a message of hope for a better world."

Imprint(s): Starseed Press Children's Books.

Nonfiction: Children's/juvenile, illustrated book, spiritual themes. Adult subjects include health/medicine, spiritual, New Age, metaphysical.

Fiction: Juvenile. "Prospective authors please note: Kramer's list is selective and is normally fully slated several seasons in advance. Submissions closed.

Recent Title(s): *Blowing Zen*, by Ray Brooks (nonfiction); *My Spiritual Alphabet Book*, by Holly Bea, illustrated by Kim Howard (fiction).

Tips: "Our books are for people who are interested in personal growth and consciousness-raising. We are not interested in personal stories unless it has universal appeal."

KRAUSE PUBLICATIONS, 700 E. State, Iola WI 54990. (715)445-2214. Website: www.krause.com. **Acquisitions:** Acquisitions Editor. Publishes hardcover and trade paperback originals. **Publishes 150 titles/year. Receives 300 queries and 30 mss/year. 10% of books from first-time authors; 90% from unagented writers. Pays 6-12.5% royalty on wholesale price or makes outright purchase of $500-10,000. Offers advance up to $3,500.** Publishes book 3 months after acceptance of ms. Accepts simultaneous submission. Responds in 1 month to proposals and mss. Book catalog free or on website. Manuscript guidelines free.

○➤ "We are the world's largest hobby and collectibles publisher."

Nonfiction: Cookbook, how-to, illustrated book, reference, self-help, technical. Subjects include Americana, business/economics, cooking/foods/nutrition, hobbies, recreation, sports. Submit proposal package, including outline, 1-3 sample chapters and letter explaining your project's unique contributions. Reviews artwork/photos as part of ms package. Send sample photos.

Recent Title(s): *Golf Collectibles*, by C. Furjamie (reference/price guide); *Outdoor Survival*, by Fears (how-to).

Tips: Audience consists of serious hobbyists. "Your work should provide a unique contribution to the special interest."

KREGEL PUBLICATIONS, Kregel, Inc., P.O. Box 2607, Grand Rapids MI 49501. (616)451-4775. Fax: (616)451-9330. E-mail: kregelbooks@kregel.com. Website: www.kregel.com. **Acquisitions:** Dennis R. Hillman, publisher. Estab. 1949. Publishes hardcover and trade paperback originals and reprints. **Publishes 90 titles/year. Receives 400 queries and 100 mss/year. 10% of books from first-time authors; 90% from unagented writers. Pays 8-16% royalty on wholesale price. Offers $200-2,000 advance.** Publishes book 14 months after acceptance of ms. Accepts simultaneous submissions. Responds in 3 months. Book catalog free. Manuscript guidelines for #10 SASE or on website.

○➤ "Our mission as an evangelical Christian publisher is to provide—with integrity and excellence—trusted, biblically-based resources that challenge and encourage individuals in their Christian lives. Works in theology and biblical studies should reflect the historic, orthodox Protestant tradition."

Imprint(s): Editorial Portavoz (contact Luis Seaone).

Nonfiction: Biography (Christian), gift book, reference. Religious and spiritual subjects. "We serve evangelical Christian readers and those in career Christian service." Query with SASE.

Fiction: Religious. Fiction should be geared toward the evangelical Christian market. Query with SASE.

Recent Title(s): *Eusebius: The Church History*, by Paul L. Maier (church history); *Joy to the World*, by Ken Osbeck (inspirational); *Lethal Harvest*, by William Cutrer (mystery).

Tips: "Our audience consists of conservative, evangelical Christians, including pastors and ministry students. Think through very clearly the intended audience for the work."

KRIEGER PUBLISHING CO., P.O. Box 9542, Melbourne FL 32902-9542. (321)724-9542. Fax: (321)951-3671. E-mail: info@krieger-publishing.com. Website: www.krieger-publishing.com. **Acquisitions:** Elaine Harland, manager/editor (natural history/sciences and veterinary medicine); Michael W. Galbraith, series editor (adult education); Gordon Patterson, series editor (essays compiled to explore issues and concerns of scholars); Donald M. Waltz, series editor (space sciences). Estab. 1969. Publishes hardcover and paperback originals and reprints. **Publishes 30 titles/year. Receives 100 submissions/year. 30% of books from first-time authors; 100% from unagented writers. Pays royalty on net price.** Publishes book 1 year after acceptance of ms. Responds in 3 months. Book catalog free.

○➤ "We provide accurate and well-documented scientific and technical titles for text and reference use, college level and higher."

Imprint(s): Anvil Series, Orbit Series, Public History.

Nonfiction: College reference, technical, textbook. Subjects include history, space science, herpetology, chemistry, physics, engineering, adult education, veterinary medicine, natural history, math. Query. Reviews artwork/photos as part of ms package.

Recent Title(s): *The Turfgrass Disease Handbook*, by Houston B. Couch; *A Veterinary Guide to Parasites of Reptiles; Volume II: Anthropods*, by Susan M. Barnard.

KROSHKA BOOKS, 227 Main St., Suite 100, Huntington NY 11743. (631)424-6682. Fax: (631)424-4666. E-mail: novascience@earthlink.net. **Acquisitions:** Frank Columbus, editor-in-chief; Nadya Columbus, editor. Publishes hardcover and paperback originals. **Publishes 150 titles/year. Receives 1,000 queries/year. Pays royalty.** Publishes book 6-12 months year after acceptance. Accepts simultaneous submissions. Responds in 1 month.

○➤ "Virtually all areas of human endeavor fall within our scope of interest."

Imprint: Troitsa Books.

Nonfiction: Biography, technical. Subjects include anthropology, business/economics, computers/electronics, nutrition, education, government/politics, health/medicine, history, money/finance, nature/environment, philosophy, psychology, recreation, religion, science, sociology, software, sports, childhood development. Query. Reviews artwork/photos as part of ms package. Send photocopies.

Recent Title(s): *Firemania*, by Carl Chiarelli.

KUMARIAN PRESS, INC., 14 Oakwood Ave., West Hartford CT 06119-2127. (860)233-5895. Fax: (860)233-6072. E-mail: kpbooks@aol.com. Website: www.kpbooks.com. **Acquisitions:** Linda Beyus, acquisitions editor. Estab. 1977. Publishes hardcover and trade paperback originals. **Publishes 8-12 titles/year. Pays royalty of 7-10% of net.** Accepts simultaneous submissions, if so noted. Responds in 1 month to queries and proposals. Book catalog and ms guidelines free.

> O— Kumarian Press publishes books that will have a positive social and economic impact on the lives of people living in "Third World" conditions, no matter where they live. "We publish books for professionals, academics, students interested in global affairs which includes international development, peace and conflict resolution, environmental sustainability, globalization, NGOs, women and gender."

Nonfiction: Professional, academic. Subjects include economics, government/politics, environment, sociology, women and gender studies, microenterprise, globalization, international development, sustainability. "Kumarian Press looks for scholarly mss that address world issues and promote change." Submit proposal package including outline, 1-2 sample chapters, cv or résumé, intended readership, detailed table of contents and projected word count with SASE. No e-mail submissions.

Recent Title(s): *Inequity in the Global Village: Recycled Rhetoric and Disposable People*, by Jan Knippers Black.

LAKE CLAREMONT PRESS, 4650 N. Rockwell St., Chicago IL 60625. (773)583-7800. Fax: (773)583-7877. E-mail: lcp@lakeclaremont.com. Website: www.lakeclaremont.com. **Acquisitions:** Sharon Woodhouse, publisher. Publishes trade paperback originals. **Publishes 5-7 titles/year. Receives 20-40 queries and 3-10 mss/year. 55% of books from first-time authors; 100% from unagented writers. Pays 10-15% royalty on wholesale price. Offers $250-2,000 advance.** Publishes book 8 months after acceptance of ms. Accepts simultaneous submissions. Responds in 1 month to queries and mss, 2 months to proposals. Book catalog on website.

> O— "We currently specialize in books on the Chicago area and its history, and are beginning to expand into general nonfiction, especially regional titles for other areas. We also like nonfiction books on ghosts, graveyards and folklore."

Nonfiction: Subjects include Americana, ethnic, history, regional, travel. Query with SASE or submit proposal package, including outline and 2 sample chapters, or submit completed ms (e-mail queries and proposals preferred).

Recent Title(s): *Chicago Haunts: Ghostlore of the Windy City*, by Ursula Bielski; *Hollywood on Lake Michigan: 100 Years of Chicago and the Movies*, by Arnie Bernstein.

Tips: "Please include a market analysis in proposals (who would buy this book & where?) and an analysis of similar books available for different regions. Please know what else is out there."

LANGENSCHEIDT PUBLISHING GROUP, 46-35 54th Rd., Maspeth NY 11378. (800)432-MAPS. Fax: (718)784-0640. E-mail: spohja@langenscheidt.com. **Acquisitions:** Sue Pohja, acquisitions; Christine Cardone, editor. Estab. 1983. Publishes hardcover and trade paperback. **Publishes over 150 titles/year. Receives 50 queries and 15 mss/year. 100% of books from unagented writers. Pays royalty or makes outright purchase.** Publishes book 6 months after acceptance of ms. Accepts simultaneous submissions. Responds in 2 months to proposals. Book catalog free.

> O— Langenscheidt Publishing Group publishes maps, travel guides, foreign language dictionary products, world atlases and educational materials."

Imprint(s): ADC Map, American Map, Arrow Map, Creative Sales, Hagstrom Map, Hammond Map, Insight Guides, Hammond World Atlas Corp., Trakker Map.

Nonfiction: Reference. Foreign language subjects. "Any foreign language that fills a gap in our line is welcome." Submit outline and 2 sample chapters (complete ms preferred.)

Recent Title(s): *Pocket Vietnamese*; *Atlas of the 20th Century*.

Tips: "Any item related to our map, foreign language dictionary, atlas and travel lines could have potential for us. Particularly interested in titles that are viable and have little in the way of good competition."

LARK, a division of Sterling Publishing, 50 College St., Asheville NC 28801. E-mail: carol.taylor@larkbooks.com. Website: www.larkbooks.com. **Acquisitons:** Carol Taylor, publisher. Estab. 1976. Publishes hardcover and trade paperback originals and reprints. **Publishes over 50 titles/year. Receives 300 queries and 100 mss/year. 80% of books from first-time authors; 90% from unagented writers. Offers up to $3,000 advance.** Publishes book 1 year after acceptance of ms. Accepts simultaneous submissions. Responds in 2 months.

> O— Lark Books publishes high quality, highly illustrated books, primarily in the crafts/leisure markets celebrating the creative spirit. We work closely with bookclubs. Our books are either how-to, 'gallery' or combination books."

Nonfiction: Coffee table book, cookbook, how-to, do-it-yourself, home/style, illustrated book, children's/juvenile. Subjects include gardening, hobbies, nature/environment, crafts. Query first. If asked, submit outline and 1 sample chapter, sample projects, table of contents. Reviews artwork/photos as part of ms package. Send transparencies if possible.

Recent Title(s): *Complete Book of Floorcloths*, by Cathy Cooper.

Tips: "We publish both first-time and seasoned authors. In either case, we need to know that you have substantial expertise on the topic of the proposed book—that we can trust you to know what you're talking about. If you're great at your craft but not so great as a writer, you might want to work with us as a coauthor or as a creative consultant."

[N] LARSON PUBLICATIONS/PBPF, 4936 Rt. 414, Burdett NY 14818-9729. (607)546-9342. Fax: (607)546-9344. E-mail: larson@lightlink.com. Website: www.lightlink.com/larson. **Acquisitions:** Paul Cash, director. Estab. 1982. "We look for studies of comparative spiritual philosophy or personal fruits of independent (transsectarian viewpoint) spiritual research/practice." Publishes hardcover and trade paperback originals. **Publishes 4-5 titles/year. Receives 1,000 submissions/year. 5% of books from first-time authors. Pays 7½% royalty on retail price or 10% cash received. Rarely offers advance.** Publishes book 1 year after acceptance. Accepts simultaneous submissions. Responds in 4 months to queries. Unsolicited mss not accepted; queries only. Book catalog for 9×12 SAE with 3 first-class stamps.

Nonfiction: Spiritual philosophy. Subjects include philosophy, psychology and religion. Query or submit outline and sample chapters. Reviews artwork/photos as part of ms package.

Recent Title(s): *The Art of Napping at Work*, by William and Camille Anthony.

[N] LATIN AMERICAN LITERARY REVIEW PRESS, 121 Edgewood Ave., Pittsburgh PA 15218. (412)371-9023. Fax: (412)371-9025. E-mail: lalrp@aol.com. Website: www.lalrp.org. **Acquisitions:** Maria G. Trujillo, assistant editor (Latin American fiction). Estab. 1980. Publishes trade paperback originals. **Publishes 12 titles/year. Receives 40 queries and 50 mss/year. 25% of books from first-time authors; 75% from unagented writers. Pays 7-10% royalty on wholesale price or makes outright purchase.** Publishes book 14 months after acceptance of ms. Accepts simultaneous submissions. Responds in 6 months to mss. Book catalog and ms guidelines available via website or with SASE.

   O→ "We focus on English translations of works that were originally written in Spanish or Portuguese."

Nonfiction: Subjects include language/literature (Latin American), translation, women's issues/studies. Query with SASE. Reviews artwork/photos as part of ms package. Send photocopies.

Fiction: Literary, multicultural, short story collections, translation. Send complete ms with SASE.

Poetry: Poetry, poetry in translation. "Translated poetry should be by a recognized name." Submit complete ms.

Recent Title(s): *Clara*, by Luisa Valenzuela; *The Medicine Man*, by Francisco Rojas Gonzalez.

Tips: Publishes for the general adult and college level audiences.

MERLOYD LAWRENCE BOOKS, Perseus Book Group, 102 Chestnut St., Boston MA 02108. **Acquisitions:** Merloyd Lawrence, president. Estab. 1982. Publishes hardcover and trade paperback originals. **Publishes 7-8 titles/year. Receives 400 submissions/year. 25% of books from first-time authors; 20% from unagented writers. Pays royalty on retail price.** Publishes book 1 year after acceptance of ms. Accepts simultaneous submissions.

Nonfiction: Child development, health/medicine, nature/environment, psychology, social science. Query with SASE only. *All queries with SASE read and answered.* No unsolicited mss read.

Recent Title(s): *Mayhem: Violence as Public Entertainment*, by Sissela Bok; *Rattling the Cage: Towards Legal Rights for Animals*, by Steven Wise.

[N] LAWYERS & JUDGES PUBLISHING CO., P.O. Box 30040, Tucson AZ 85751-0040. (520)323-1500. Fax: (520)323-0055. E-mail: sales@lawyersandjudges.com. Website: www.lawyersandjudges.com. **Acquisitions:** Steve Weintraub, president. Estab. 1982. Publishes professional hardcover originals. **Publishes 15 titles/year. Receives 200 queries and 30 mss/year. 5% of books from first-time authors; 100% from unagented writers. Pays 7-10% royalty on retail price.** Publishes book 5 months after acceptance of ms. Accepts simultaneous submissions. Responds in 2 months. Book catalog free.

   O→ Lawyers & Judges is a highly specific publishing company, reaching the legal and insurance fields and accident reconstruction."

Nonfiction: Reference. Legal/insurance subjects. "Unless a writer is an expert in the legal/insurance areas, we are not interested." Submit proposal package, including full or *very* representative portion of ms.

Recent Title(s): *Forensic Aspects of Vision and Highway Safety*, by Allen, Abrams, Ginsburg and Weintraub.

[N] [✶] LE GESSE STEVENS PUBLISHING, 3333 Midway Dr., Unit 102, San Diego CA 92110. (619)221-8252. Fax: (619)758-9040. **Acquisitions:** Helen Chung, acquisitions editor (fiction, adventure); Sharon Carey, editor (children's books, poetry); Virginia Field, editor (cookbooks, nonfiction); Barry Lomax, editor (fiction). Publishes hardcover, trade paperback and mass market paperback originals. **Publishes 200 titles/year. Receives 1,800 queries and 760 mss/year. 70% of books from first-time authors; 95% from unagented writers. Pays 8-19% royalty on wholesale price.** Publishes book 6 months after acceptance of ms. Accepts simultaneous submissions. Responds in 1 month to queries, 2 months to proposals, 3 months to mss. Book catalog and manuscript guidelines free.

   O→ "Our goal is to reach a wide audience exposing new talented authors with subjects ranging from fiction, poetry, children's books, biographies and adventure stories."

Nonfiction: Biography, children's/juvenile, coffee table book, cookbook, gift book, how-to, humor, illustrated book, self-help, technical, textbook. Subjects include agriculture/horticulture, Americana, animals, anthropology/archaeology, art/architecture, business/economics, child guidance/parenting, computers/electronics, cooking/foods/nutrition, creative nonfiction, education, ethnic, gardening, gay/lesbian, government/politics, health/medicine, history, hobbies, language/literature, memoirs, military/war, money/finance, multicultural, music/dance, nature/environment, philosophy, photography, psychology, recreation, regional, religion, science, sex, sociology, software, spirituality, sports, translation, travel, women's issues/studies. Submit completed ms. Reviews artwork/photos as part of ms package. Send photocopies.

Fiction: Adventure, confession, ethnic, experimental, fantasy, feminist, gay/lesbian, gothic, hi-Lol, historical, horror, humor, juvenile, literary, mainstream/contemporary, military/war, multicultural, mystery, occult, picture books, plays, regional, religious, romance, science fiction, short story collections, spiritual, sports, suspense, translation, western, young adult. Submit completed ms.

Poetry: Submit complete ms.

Recent Title(s): *Women Can Find Shipwrecks Too*, by Margaret Brandeis (biography); *The Aqualene Chase*, by Harold R. Miller (detective fiction); *Fantasies in Rhyme*, by Donald Beynon (poetry).

LEARNING PUBLICATIONS, INC., 5351 Gulf Dr., Holmes Beach FL 34217. (941)778-6651. Fax: (941)778-6818. E-mail: info@learningpublications.com. Website: www.learningpublications.com. **Acquisitions**: Ruth Erickson, editor. Estab. 1975. Publishes trade paperback originals and reprints. **Publishes 10-15 titles/year. Receives 150 queries and 50 mss/year. 50% of books from first-time authors; 100% from unagented writers. Pays 5-10% royalty.** Publishes book 1 year after acceptance of ms. Accepts simultaneous submissions. Responds in 1 month to queries and proposals, 4 months to mss. Book catalog free. Manuscript guidelines for #10 SASE.

    O→ "We specifically market by direct mail to education and human service professionals materials to use with students and clients."

Nonfiction: Reference, textbook, curricula and manuals for education and human service professionals. Subjects include education, psychology, sociology, women's issues/studies. "Writers interested in submitting manuscripts should request our guidelines first." Query and submit outline and/or table of contents, 1 sample chapter, proposal package, including one-page synopsis and résumé with SASE. Reviews artwork/photos as part of ms package. Send photocopies.

Tips: "Learning Publications has a limited, specific market. Writers should be familiar with who buys our books."

LEBHAR-FRIEDMAN BOOKS, Lebhar-Friedman, Inc., 425 Park Ave., New York NY 10022-3556. (212)756-5204. Fax: (212)756-5128. E-mail: fscatoni@lf.com. Website: www.lfbooks.com. **Acquisitions:** Frank R. Scatoni, acquisitions editor; Geoff Golson, publisher. Publishes hardcover originals and reprints, trade paperback originals and reprints. **Publishes 25-30 titles/year. Receives over 500 queries and over 300 mss/year. 50% of books from first-time authors; 20% from unagented writers. Pays 7½-15% royalty on retail price. Offers competitive advances.** Publishes book 1 year after acceptance of ms. Accepts simultaneous submissions. Responds in 1 month to queries, 2 months to proposals, 3 months to mss. Book catalog and ms guidelines on website.

Nonfiction: Biography, coffee table book, cookbook, gift book, how-to, humor, illustrated book, multimedia, reference, self-help, technical, textbook. Subjects include agriculture/horticulture, Americana, animals, anthropology/archaeology, art/architecture, business/economics, child guidance/parenting, computers/electronics, cooking/foods/nutrition, creative nonfiction, education, ethnic, gardening, government/politics, health/medicine, history, hobbies, language/literature, memoirs, money/finance, nature/environment, philosophy, photography, psychology, recreation, regional, religion, science, sociology, software, spirituality, travel, women's issues/women's studies. Query with SASE or submit proposal package, including outline and 2 sample chapters. Reviews artwork as part of ms package. Reviews photocopies, not originals.

Recent Title(s): *The New York Times Book of Women's Health*, by Jane E. Brody (health); *Life Under a Leaky Roof*, by David Owen (essays).

LEE & LOW BOOKS, 95 Madison Ave., New York NY 10016. (212)779-4400. Fax: (212)683-1894. Website: www.lee andlow.com. **Acquisitions:** Louise May, senior editor. Estab. 1991. **Publishes 12 titles/year.** Send complete ms with SASE. Responds in 5 months. Encourages new writers. Manuscript guidelines on website.

    O→ "Our goals are to meet a growing need for books that address children of color, and to present literature that all children can identify with. We only consider multicultural children's picture books." Currently emphasizing material for 2-10 year olds.

Recent Title(s): *Crazy Horse's Vision*, by Joseph Bruchac, illustrated by S.D. Nelson.

Tips: "Of special interest are stories set in contemporary America. We are interested in fiction as well as nonfiction. We do not consider folktales, fairy tales or animal stories."

⟦N⟧ ⟦▲⟧ LEGACY PRESS, Rainbow Publishers, P.O. Box 261129, San Diego CA 92196. (858)271-7600. Fax: (858)578-4795. E-mail: rbbooks@earthlink.net. Website: www.rainbowpublishers.com. **Acquisitions:** Christy Allen, editor. Publishes hardcover and trade paperback originals. **Publishes 30 titles/year; imprint publishes 10 titles/year. Receives 250 queries and 250 mss/year. 50% of books from first-time authors; 100% from unagented writers. Pays 8-12% royalty on wholesale price. Advance starts at $500.** Publishes book 18 months after acceptance of ms. Accepts simultaneous submissions. Responds in 3 months. Book catalog for 9×12 SAE with 2 first-class stamps. Manuscript guidelines for #10 SASE.

    O→ "We are focusing on our Criss Cross Collection for pre-teen girls."

Nonfiction: Children's/juvenile. Subjects include cooking/foods/nutrition, creative nonfiction, gardening, hobbies, recreation, religion, spirituality. Submit proposal package, including outline, 3-5 sample chapters and market analysis.

Recent Title(s): *Gotta Have God* (3-book series of devotionals for boys); *My Bible Journey*, by Mary J. Davis (journal/devotional).

Tips: Audience consists of kids ages 4-12, particularly evangelical Christian. "Tell us why your manuscript is unique. For our girls books, think of Christian versions of general market nonfiction themes."

LEHIGH UNIVERSITY PRESS, Linderman Library, 30 Library Dr., Lehigh University, Bethlehem PA 18015-3067. (610)758-3933. Fax: (610)974-2823. E-mail: inlup@lehigh.edu. **Acquisitions:** Philip A. Metzger, director. Estab. 1985. Publishes hardcover originals. **Publishes 10 titles/year. Receives 90-100 queries and 50-60 mss/year. 70% of books from first-time authors; 100% from unagented writers. Pays royalty.** Publishes book 18 months after acceptance of ms. Accepts simultaneous submissions. Responds in 3 months. Book catalog and ms guidelines free.

O─m Lehigh University Press is an academic press publishing scholarly monographs. "We are especially interested in works on 18th century studies and the history of technology, but consider works of quality on a variety of subjects."

Nonfiction: Biography, reference, academic. Subjects include Americana, art/architecture, history, language/literature, science. Submit 1 sample chapter and proposal package.

Recent Title(s): *Exiles in Hollywood: Major European Film Directors in America*, by Gene D. Phillips; *Reforging Shakespeare: The Story of a Theatrical Scandal*, by Jeffrey Kahan.

LEISURE BOOKS, Dorchester Publishing Co., Inc., 276 Fifth Ave., Suite 1008, New York NY 10001-0112. (212)725-8811. Fax: (212)532-1054. E-mail: dorchedit@dorchesterpub.com. Website: www.dorchesterpub.com. **Acquisitions:** Joanna Rulf, editorial assistant; Kate Seaver, editorial assistant; Alicia Condon, editorial director; Don D'Auria, senior editor (Westerns, technothrillers, horror); Christopher Keeslar, editor. Estab. 1970. Publishes mass market paperback originals and reprints. **Publishes 160 titles/year. Receives thousands of mss/year. 20% of books from first-time authors; 20% from unagented writers. Pays royalty on retail price. Advance negotiable.** Publishes book 18 months after acceptance of ms. Responds in 6 months to queries. Book catalog free (800)481-9191. Manuscript guidelines for #10 SASE or on website.

O─m Leisure Books is seeking historical romances, westerns, horror and technothrillers.

Imprint(s): Love Spell (romance), **Leisure** (romance, western, techno, horror).

Fiction: Historical romance (90,000-100,000 words); time-travel romance (90,000 words); futuristic romance (90,000 words); westerns (75,000-115,000 words); horror (90,000 words); technothrillers (90,000 words). "We are strongly backing historical romance. All historical romance should be set pre-1900. Horrors and westerns are growing as well. No sweet romance, science fiction, erotica, contemporary women's fiction, mainstream or action/adventure." Query or submit outline/synopsis and first 3 sample chapters only. "No material returned without SASE."

Recent Title(s): *Mine to Take*, by Dara Joy (romance).

LERNER PUBLISHING GROUP, 241 First Ave. N., Minneapolis MN 55401. (612)332-3344. Fax: (612)332-7615. Website: www.lernerbooks.com. Editor-in-Chief: Mary Rodgers. **Acquisitions:** Jennifer Zimian, editor. Estab. 1959. Publishes hardcover originals, trade paperback originals and reprints. **Publishes 150-175 titles/year; First Avenue Edition, 30; Carolrhoda, 50-60; Runestone Press, 3. Receives 1,000 queries and 300 mss/year. 20% of books from first-time authors; 95% from unagented writers. Pays 3-8% royalty on net price (approximately 60% of books) or makes outright purchase of $1,000-3,000 (for series and work-for-hire). Offers $1,000-3,000 advance.** Publishes book 2 years after acceptance of ms. Submissions accepted in March and October only. Accepts simultaneous submissions. Responds in 4 months to proposals. Catalog for 9×12 SAE with 6 first-class stamps. Manuscript guidelines for #10 SASE. "Requests for catalogs and submissions guidelines must be clearly addressed as such on envelope."

O─m "Our goal is to publish books that educate, stimulate and stretch the imagination, foster global awareness, encourage critical thinking and inform, inspire and entertain." Currently emphasizing biographies. De-emphasizing fiction.

Imprint(s): Carolrhoda Books; First Avenue Editions (paperback reprints for hard/soft deals only); Lerner Publications; Runestone Press.

Nonfiction: Children's/juvenile (grades 3-10). Subjects include art/architecture, biography, ethnic, history, nature/environment, science, sports, aviation, geography. Query with outline, 1-2 sample chapters, SASE.

Fiction: Juvenile (middle grade). "We are not actively pursuing fiction titles." Query with synopsis, 1-2 sample chapters and SASE.

Recent Title(s): *Emily Dickinson: Singular Poet*, by Carol Dommermuth-Costa (biography).

N ARTHUR LEVINE BOOKS, Scholastic Inc., 555 Broadway, New York NY 10012. (212)343-4436. **Acquisitions:** Arthur Levine, publisher. "Arthur Levine Books is looking for distinctive literature, for whatever's extraordinary. **Publishes 8-12 titles/year. "We are willing to work with first-time authors, with or without agent." Pays variable royalty on retail price. Advance varies.** Book catalog for 9×12 SASE.

Fiction: Juvenile, picture books. Query only, include SASE.

Recent Title(s): *Beautiful Warrior*, by Emily Arnold McCully; *Ghost Cats*, by Susan Shreve.

N ★ LIBRARIES UNLIMITED, INC., P.O. Box 6633, Englewood CO 80155. (303)770-1220. Fax: (303)220-8843. E-mail: lu-editorial@lu.com. Website: www.lu.com. **Acquisitions:** Barbara Ittner, acquisitions editor (school library titles); Edward Kurdyla, general manager (academic/reference titles). Estab. 1964. Publishes hardcover originals. **Publishes 75 titles/year; Ukranian, 45; Teacher Ideas, 30. Receives 400 queries and 100 mss/year. 50% of books from first-time authors; 100% from unagented writers. Pays 8-15% royalty on wholesale price.** Publishes book 1 year after acceptance of ms. Accepts simultaneous submissions. Responds in 1 month to queries, 2 months to proposals and mss. Book catalog and manuscript guidelines available via website or with SASE.

O─m Libraries Unlimited publishes resources for libraries, librarians and educators.

Imprint(s): Teacher Ideas Press (Susan Zernial, acquisitions editor); Ukrainian Academic Press.

Nonfiction: Reference, textbook, teacher resource and activity books. Reference books on these topics for libraries: agriculture/horticulture, anthropology/archaeology, art/architecture, business/economics, education, ethnic, health/medicine, history, language/literature, military/war, music/dance, philosophy, psychology, religion, science, sociology, women's issues/studies. Interested in reference books of all types (annotated bibliographies, sourcebooks and handbooks; curriculum enrichment/support books for teachers K-12 and school librarians). Submit proposal package, including brief description of book, outline, 1 sample chapter, author credentials, comparison with competing titles, audience and market. Reviews artwork/photos as part of ms package. Send photocopies.

Recent Title(s): *Genreflecting: A Guide to Reading Interest in Genre Fiction*, by Diana Herald; *Multicultural Information Quests*, by Marie E. Rodger.

Tips: "We welcome any ideas that combine professional expertise, writing ability, and innovative thinking. Audience is librarians (school, public, academic and special) and teachers (K-12)."

LIFETIME BOOKS, INC., 2131 Hollywood Blvd., Suite 305, Hollywood FL 33073. (954)925-5242. Fax: (954)925-5244. E-mail: lifeline@aol.com. Website: www.lifetimebooks.com. **Acquisitions:** Virginia Wells, senior editor. Estab. 1943. Publishes hardcover and trade paperback originals. **Publishes 20-25 titles/year. Receives 1,500-2,00 queries and 1,000 mss/year. 95% of books from first-time authors; 95% from unagented writers. Pays negotiable royalty on retail price. Offers advance of $0-10,000.** Publishes book 4 months after acceptance. Accepts simultaneous submissions. Responds in 1 month to queries and proposals, 2 months to mss. Book catalog and ms guidelines for #10 SASE.

> O→ "Lifetime Books is committed to inspiring readers to improve all aspects of their lives by providing how-to and self-help information which can help them obtain such a goal."

Imprint(s): Compact Books (contact Donald Lessne); Fell Publishers; Lifetime Periodicals.

Nonfiction: Children's/juvenile, cookbooks, giftbooks, reference, how-to, self-help. Subjects include animals, business and sales, child guidance/parenting, cooking/food/nutrition, education, ethnic, health/medicine, hobbies, bio/exposé, money/finance, philosophy, psychology, religion, sports. "We are interested in material on business, health and fitness, self-improvement and reference. We will not consider topics that only appeal to a small, select audience." Submit outline, author bio, publicity ideas, proposals and 3 sample chapters. Reviews artwork as part of ms package. Send photocopies. No poetry, no fiction, no short stories, no children's.

Recent Title(s): *The Leader Within You*, by Robert Danzig (business); *The Tiniest Acorn*, by Marsha T. Danzig (fiction).

Tips: "We are most interested in well-written, timely nonfiction with strong sales potential. Our audience is very general. Learn markets and be prepared to help with sales and promotion. Show us how your book is unique, different or better than the competition."

LIGUORI PUBLICATIONS, One Liguori Dr., Liguori MO 63057. (636)464-2500. Fax: (636)464-8449. E-mail: jbauer@liguori.org. Website: www.liguori.org. Publisher: Harry Grile. **Acquisitions:** Judith A. Bauer, managing editor (Trade Group); Lauren Borstal, managing editor (Pastorlink, electronic publishing). Estab. 1943. The Trade Group publishes hardcover and trade paperback originals and reprints under the Liguori and Liguori/Triumph imprints; publishes 30 titles/year. The Catechetical and Pastoral Resources Group publishes paperback originals and reprints under the Liguori and Libros Liguori imprints: **Publishes 50 titles/year, including Spanish-language titles. The Electronic Publishing Division publishes 4 titles/year under the Faithware® imprint. Royalty varies or purchases outright. Advance varies.** Publishes 2 years after acceptance of ms. Prefers no simultaneous submissions. Responds in 2 months to queries and proposals, 3 months to mss. Author guidelines available via website.

> O→ Liguori Publications, faithful to the charism of Saint Alphonsus, is an apostolate within the mission of the Denver Province. Its mission, a collaborative effort of Redemptorists and laity, is to spread the gospel of Jesus Christ primarily through the print and electronic media. It shares in the Redemptorist priority of giving special attention to the poor and the most abandoned. Currently emphasizing practical spirituality, spiritual slant on secular topics.

Imprint(s): Faithware®, Libros Liguori, Liguori Books, Liguori/Triumph.

Nonfiction: Inspirational, devotional, prayer, Christian-living, self-help books. Religious subjects. Mostly adult audience; limited children/juvenile. Query with annotated outline, 1 sample chapter, SASE. Query for CD-ROM and Internet publishing. Publishes very few electronic products received unsolicited.

Recent Title(s): *In the Fullness of Time*, by Fulton J. Sheen (spirituality).

LIMELIGHT EDITIONS, Proscenium Publishers, Inc., 118 E. 30th St., New York NY 10016. Fax: (212)532-5526. E-mail: jjlmlt@idt.net. Website: www.limelighteditions.com. **Acquisitions:** Melvyn B. Zerman, president; Roxanna Font, associate publisher. Estab. 1983. Publishes hardcover and trade paperback originals, trade paperback reprints. **Publishes 14 titles/year. Receives 150 queries and 40 mss/year. 15% of books from first-time authors; 20% from unagented writers. Pays 7½ (paperback)-10% (hardcover) royalty on retail price. Offers $500-2,000 advance.** Publishes book 10 months after acceptance of ms. Responds in 1 month to queries and proposals, 3 months to mss. Book catalog and ms guidelines free.

> O→ Limelight Editions publishes books on film, theater, music and dance. "Our books make a strong contribution to their fields and deserve to remain in print for many years."

Nonfiction: Biography, historical, humor, instructional—most illustrated—on music/dance or theater/film. "All books are on the performing arts *exclusively*." Query with proposal package, including 2-3 sample chapters, outline with SASE. Reviews artwork/photos as part of ms package. Send photocopies.
Recent Title(s): *Detours and Lost Highways: A Map of Neo-Noir*, by Foster Hirsch (film); *Actors Talk: Profiles and Stories from the Acting Trade*, by Dennis Brown.

N LION BOOKS, Sayre Ross Co., 210 Nelson Rd., Scarsdale NY 10583. (914)725-2280. Fax: (914)725-3572. **Acquisitions:** Harriet Ross, editor. Estab. 1966. Publishes hardcover originals and reprints, trade paperback reprints. **Publishes 14 titles/year. Receives 60-150 queries and 100 mss/year. 60% of books from first-time authors. Pays 7-15% royalty on wholesale price or makes outright purchase of $500-5,000.** Publishes book 5 months after acceptance of ms. Responds in 1 week to queries, 1 month to mss.
Nonfiction: Biography, how-to. Subjects include Americana, ethnic, government/politics, history, recreation, sports. No fiction, please! Submit complete ms with SASE. *Writer's Market* recommends query with SASE first.

LIPPINCOTT WILLIAMS & WILKINS, 530 Walnut St., Philadelphia PA 19106. (215)521-8300. Fax: (215)521-8902. Website: www.LWW.com. **Acquisitions:** Doug Symington, vice president/editor-in-chief. Estab. 1792. Publishes hardcover and softcover originals. **Publishes 325 titles/year. Pay rates vary depending on type of book, whether the author is the principal or contributing author and amount of production necessary.** Accepts simultaneous submissions, if so noted. Responds in 3 months to proposals.
O—ᴋ Lippincott Williams & Wilkins publishes books on healthcare information, including basic science, for medical and nursing students and ongoing education for practicing nursing and clinicians.
Imprint(s): Lippincott; Lippincott Williams & Wilkins.
Nonfiction: Reference, textbook, manuals, atlases on health/medicine subjects. "We do not publish for the layperson." Query with proposal package including outline, table of contents, cv, proposed market and how your ms differs from already-published material, estimate number of trim size pages and number and type of illustrations (line drawing, halftone, 4-color).
Recent Title(s): *Radiology of the Foot and Ankle*; *Problems in Anesthesia*.
Tips: Audience includes physicians, medical scientists, medical and nursing students, practicing nurses and clinicians.

N LISTEN & LIVE AUDIO, INC., P.O. Box 817, Roseland NJ 07068. (201)798-3830. Fax: (201)798-3225. E-mail: alfred@listenandlive.com. Website: www.listenandlive.com. **Acquisitions:** Alisa Weberman, publisher (manuscripts for audio). **Publishes 10 titles/year. Receives 100 mss/year. Pays 10% royalty on wholesale price.** Publishes book 6 months after acceptance of ms. Accepts simultaneous submissions. Responds in 3 months to mss. Book catalog on website.
O—ᴋ Listen & Live publishes fiction and nonfiction books on audio cassette.
Imprints: South Bay Entertainment.
Nonfiction: Multimedia (audio format). Subjects include business/economics, self-help, relationship. Submit completed ms.
Fiction: Young adult. Submit completed ms.
Recent Title(s): *Rough Water: Stories of Survival from the Sea (audio)*, by various authors (outdoor adventure); *The World's Shortest Stories (audio)*, by various artists (short short stories).

A LITTLE, BROWN AND CO., CHILDREN'S BOOKS, 3 Center Plaza, Boston MA 02108. (617)227-0730. Website: www.littlebrown.com. Editorial Director/Associate Publisher: Maria Modugno. **Acquisitions:** Leila Little. Estab. 1837. Publishes hardcover originals, trade paperback originals and reprints. **Firm publishes 60-70 titles/year. Pays royalty on retail price. Offers advance to be negotiated individually.** Publishes book 2 years after acceptance of ms. Accepts simultaneous submissions, if so noted. Responds in 1 month to queries, 2 months to proposals and mss.
O—ᴋ Little, Brown and Co. publishes books on a wide variety of nonfiction topics which may be of interest to children and are looking for strong writing and presentation, but no predetermined topics.
Imprints: Megan Tingley Books.
Nonfiction: Children's/juvenile, middle grade and young adult. Subjects include animals, art/architecture, ethnic, gay/lesbian, history, hobbies, nature/environment, recreation, science, sports. Writers should avoid "looking for the 'issue' they think publishers want to see, choosing instead topics they know best and are most enthusiastic about/inspired by." *Agented submissions only.*
Fiction: All juvenile/young adult; picture books. Categories include adventure, ethnic, fantasy, feminist, gay/lesbian, historical, humor, mystery, science fiction and suspense. "We are looking for strong fiction for children of all ages in any area, including multicultural. We always prefer full manuscripts for fiction." *Agented submissions only.*
Recent Title(s): *The Tale I Told Sasha*, by Nancy Willard, illustrated by David Christiana.
Tips: "Our audience is children of all ages, from preschool through young adult. We are looking for quality material that will work in hardcover—send us your best."

LITTLE, BROWN AND CO., INC., Time Warner Inc., 1271 Avenue of the Americas, New York NY 10020. (212)522-8700. Website: www.twbookmark.com. Editor-in-Chief: Michael Pietsch. **Acquisitions:** Editorial Department,

Trade Division. Estab. 1837. Publishes hardcover originals and paperback originals and reprints. **Publishes 100 titles/ year. "Royalty and advance agreements vary from book to book and are discussed with the author at the time an offer is made."**

O— "The general editorial philosophy for all divisions continues to be broad and flexible, with high quality and the promise of commercial success as always the first considerations."

Imprint(s): Back Bay Books; **Bulfinch Press**; **Little, Brown and Co. Children's Books**.

Nonfiction: "Issue books, autobiography, biographies, culture, cookbooks, history, popular science, nature and sports." Query *only. No unsolicited mss or proposals.*

Fiction: Contemporary popular fiction as well as fiction of literary distinction. Query *only. No unsolicited mss.*

Recent Title(s): *All Too Human*, by George Stephanopoulos; *Void Moon*, by Michael Connelly (fiction).

LITTLE SIMON, Simon & Schuster Children's Publishing Division, Simon & Schuster, 1230 Avenue of the Americas, New York NY 10020. (212)698-7200. Fax: (212)698-2794. Website: www.simonsayskids.com. Vice President/Publisher: Robin Corey. **Acquisitions:** Cindy Alvarez, editorial director; Eva Molta, senior editor. Publishes novelty books only. **Publishes 75 titles/year. 5% of books from first-time authors; 5% from unagented writers. Pays 2-5% royalty on retail price for original, non-licensed mss.** Publishes book 6 months after acceptance of ms. Responds to queries in 8 months.

O— "Our goal is to provide fresh material in an innovative format for pre-school to age eight. Our books are often, if not exclusively, illustrator driven."

Nonfiction: Children's/juvenile novelty books. "Novelty books include many things that do not fit in the traditional hardcover or paperback format, such as pop-up, board book, scratch and sniff, glow in the dark, open the flap, etc." Query only with SASE. *All unsolicited mss returned unopened.*

Recent Title(s): *Look Who's in the Thanksgiving Play*, by Andrew Clements.

LIVINGSTON PRESS, Station 22, University of West Alabama, Livingston AL 35470. E-mail: jwt@univ.westal.edu. **Acquisitions:** Joe Taylor, director. Estab. 1984. Publishes hardcover and trade paperback originals. **Publishes 4-6 titles/ year; imprint publishes 1 title/year. 20% of books from first-time authors; 90% from unagented writers. Pays 12½% of book run.** Publishes book 18 months after acceptance of ms. Accepts simultaneous submissions. Responds in 1 month to queries; 1 year to mss.

O— Livingston Press publishes topics such as southern literature and quirky fiction. Currently emphasizing short stories. De-emphasizing poetry.

Imprint(s): Swallow's Tale Press.

Nonfiction: Local history, folklore only. Query. *All unsolicited mss returned.*

Fiction: Experimental, literary, short story collections. Query with SASE.

Poetry: "We publish very little poetry, mostly books we have asked to see." Query with SASE.

Recent Title(s): *Flight From Valhalla*, by Michael Bugeja (poetry); *Partita in Venice*, by Curt Leviant (fiction).

Tips: "Our readers are interested in literature, often quirky literature."

LLEWELLYN PUBLICATIONS, Llewellyn Worldwide, Ltd., P.O. Box 64383, St. Paul MN 55164-0383. (612)291-1970. Fax: (612)291-1908. E-mail: lwlpc@llewellyn.com. Website: www.llewellyn.com. **Acquisitions:** Nancy J. Mostad, acquisitions manager (New Age, metaphysical, occult, self-help, how-to books); Barbara Wright, acquisitions editor (kits and decks). Estab. 1901. Publishes trade and mass market paperback originals. **Publishes 100 titles/year. Receives 2,000 submissions/year. 30% of books from first-time authors; 90% from unagented writers. Pays 10% royalty on moneys received both wholesale and retail.** Accepts simultaneous submissions. Responds in 3 months. Book catalog for 9×12 SAE with 4 first-class stamps. Manuscript guidelines for SASE.

O— Llewellyn publishes New Age fiction and nonfiction exploring "new worlds of mind and spirit." Currently emphasizing astrology, wicca, alternative health and healing, tarot. De-emphasizing fiction, channeling.

Nonfiction: How-to, self-help. Subjects include nature/environment, health and nutrition, metaphysical/magic, astrology, tarot, women's issues/studies. Submit outline and sample chapters. Reviews artwork/photos as part of ms package.

Fiction: Metaphysical/occult, which is authentic and educational, yet entertaining.

Recent Title(s): *The Green Guide to Herb Gardening*, by Deborah Harding (nonfiction).

LOCUST HILL PRESS, P.O. Box 260, West Cornwall CT 06796-0260. (860)672-0060. Fax: (860)672-4968. E-mail: locusthill@snet.net. **Acquisitions:** Thomas C. Bechtle, publisher. Estab. 1985. Publishes hardcover originals. **Publishes 12 titles/year. Receives 150 queries and 20 mss/year. 100% of books from unagented writers. Pays 12-18% royalty on retail price.** Publishes book 6 months after acceptance of ms. Accepts simultaneous submissions. Responds in 1 month. *Writer's Market* recommends allowing 2 months for reply. Book catalog free.

O— Locust Hill Press specializes in scholarly reference and bibliography works for college and university libraries worldwide, as well as monographs and essay collections on literary subjects.

Nonfiction: Reference. Subjects include ethnic, language/literature, women's issues/studies. "Since our audience is exclusively college and university libraries (and the occasional specialist), we are less inclined to accept manuscripts in 'popular' (i.e., public library) fields. While bibliography has been and will continue to be a specialty, our Locust Hill Literary Studies is gaining popularity as a series of essay collections and monographs in a wide variety of literary topics." Query.

Recent Title(s): *Denise Levertov: New Perspectives*, by Anne C. Little and Susie Paul.

Tips: "Remember that this is a small, very specialized academic publisher with no distribution network other than mail contact with most academic libraries worldwide. Please shape your expectations accordingly. If your aim is to reach the world's scholarly community by way of its libraries, we are the correct firm to contact. But *please*: no fiction, poetry, popular religion, or personal memoirs."

LONE EAGLE PUBLISHING CO., 1024 N. Orange Ave., Hollywood CA 90038. (310)471-8066 or 1-800-FILM-BKS. Fax: (310)471-4969. E-mail: info@loneeagle.com. Website: www.loneeagle.com. **Acquisitions:** Jeff Black, editor. Estab. 1982. Publishes perfectbound and trade paperback originals. **Publishes 15 titles/year. Receives 100 submissions/ year. 50% of books from unagented writers. Pays 10% royalty minimum on net income wholesale. Offers $2,500-5,000 average advance.** Publishes book 1 year after acceptance of ms. Accepts simultaneous submissions. Responds quarterly to queries. Book catalog free.
   O— Lone Eagle Publishing Company publishes reference directories that contain comprehensive and accurate cred-
       its, personal data and contact information for every major entertainment industry craft. Lone Eagle also publishes
       many 'how-to' books for the film production business, including books on screenwriting, directing, budgeting
       and producing, acting, editing, etc. Lone Eagle is broadening its base to include general entertainment titles.
Nonfiction: Technical, how-to, reference. Film and television subjects. "We are looking for books in film and television, related topics or biographies." Submit outline toc and sample chapters. Reviews artwork/photos as part of ms package.
Recent Title(s): *Elements of Style for Screenwriters*, by Paul Argentina; *1001: A Video Odyssey*, by Steve Tathan.
Tips: "A well-written, well-thought-out book on some technical aspect of the motion picture (or video) industry has the best chance. Pick a subject that has not been done to death, make sure you know what you're talking about, get someone well-known in that area to endorse the book and prepare to spend a lot of time publicizing the book. Completed manuscripts have the best chance for acceptance."

LONELY PLANET PUBLICATIONS, 150 Linden St., Oakland CA 94607-2538. (510)893-8555. Fax: (510)893-8563. E-mail: info@lonelyplanet.com. Website: www.lonelyplanet.com. **Acquisitions:** Mariah Bear, publishing manager (travel guide books); Roslyn Bullas, publishing manager (Pisces). Estab. 1973. Publishes trade paperback originals. **Publishes 60 titles/year. Receives 500 queries and 100 mss/year. 5% of books from first-time authors; 100% from unagented writers. Makes outright purchase or negotiated fee—⅓ on contract, ⅓ on submission, ⅓ on approval.** Publishes book 2 years after acceptance of ms. Accepts simultaneous submissions. Responds in 3 months to queries. Manuscript guidelines for #10 SASE.
   O— Lonely Planet publishes travel guides, atlases, travel literature, diving and snorkeling guides.
Nonfiction: Travel guides, phrasebooks atlases and travel literature exclusively. "Request our catalog first to make sure we don't already have a similar book or call and see if a similar book is on our production schedule." Submit outline or proposal package. Reviews artwork/photos as part of ms package. Send photocopies.
Recent Title(s): *Great Lakes States*.

[A] LONGSTREET PRESS, INC., 2140 Newmarket Parkway, Suite 122, Marietta GA 30067. (770)980-1488. Fax: (770)859-9894. Website: www.longstreetpress.net. President/Editor: Scott Bard. **Acquisitions:** Tysie Whitman, senior editor (general nonfiction, regional interest); John Yow, senior editor (business, self-help, Southern memoir, Southern fiction). Estab. 1988. Publishes hardcover and trade paperback originals. **Publishes 45 titles/year. Receives 2,500 submissions/year. 10% of books from first-time authors; none from unagented writers. Pays royalty.** Publishes book 1 year after acceptance of ms. Accepts simultaneous submissions. Responds in 3 months. Book catalog for 9×12 SAE with 4 first-class stamps. Manuscript guidelines for #10 SASE.
   O— Although Longstreet Press publishes a number of genres, their strengths in the future will be general nonfiction
       such as business, self-help and Southern biography, guidebooks, and fiction. "As Southern publishers, we look
       for regional material." Currently emphasizing quality nonfiction for a wide audience (memoir, business, self-
       help). De-emphasizing humor, cookbooks, gift and illustrated books.
Nonfiction: Subjects include Americana, gardening, history, Southern biography, nature/environment, self-help, regional, sports. "No poetry, scientific or highly technical, textbooks of any kind, erotica." *Agented submissions only.*
Fiction: Literary, contemporary Southern fiction. *Agented fiction only.*
Recent Title(s): *No Higher Honor: The USS Yorktown and the Battle of Midway*, by Jeff Nesmith (nonfiction); *Home Across the Road*, by Nancy Peacock (fiction).

LOOMPANICS UNLIMITED, P.O. Box 1197, Port Townsend WA 98368-0997. Fax: (360)385-7785. E-mail: loompseditor@olympus.net. Website: www.loompanics.com. President: Michael Hoy. **Acquisitions:** Gia Cosindas, editor. Estab. 1975. Publishes trade paperback originals. **Publishes 15 titles/year. Receives 500 submissions/year. 40% of books from first-time authors; 100% from unagented writers. Pays 10-15% royalty on wholesale or retail price or makes outright purchase of $100-1,200. Offers $500 average advance.** Publishes book 1 year after acceptance of ms. Accepts simultaneous submissions. Responds in 2 months. Author guidelines free. Book catalog for $5, postpaid.
   O— The mission statement offered by Loompanics is "no more secrets—no more excuses—no more limits! We
       publish how-to books with an edge. We are always looking for beat-the-system books on crime, tax avoidance,
       survival, drug manufacture, revenge and self-sufficiency."
Nonfiction: How-to, reference, self-help. "In general, works about outrageous topics or obscure-but-useful technology written authoritatively in a matter-of-fact way." Subjects include the underground economy, crime, drugs, privacy, self-sufficiency, anarchism and "beat the system" books. "We are looking for how-to books in the fields of espionage,

investigation, the underground economy, police methods, how to beat the system, crime and criminal techniques. We are also looking for similarly-written articles for our catalog and its supplements. No cookbooks, inspirational, travel, management or cutesy-wutesy stuff." Query or submit outline/synopsis and sample chapters. Reviews artwork/photos.

Recent Title(s): *Drink as Much as You Want and Live Longer*, by Fred Beyerlein.

Tips: "Our audience is young males looking for hard-to-find information on alternatives to 'The System.' Your chances for success are greatly improved if you can show us how your proposal fits in with our catalog."

LOUISIANA STATE UNIVERSITY PRESS, P.O. Box 25053, Baton Rouge LA 70894-5053. (225)388-6294. Fax: (225)388-6461. **Acquisitions:** L.E. Phillabaum, director; Maureen G. Hewitt, assistant director and editor-in-chief; John Easterly, executive editor; Sylvia Frank, acquisitions editor. Estab. 1935. Publishes hardcover originals, hardcover and trade paperback reprints. **Publishes 70-80 titles/year. Receives 800 submissions/year. 33% of books from first-time authors. 95% from unagented writers. Pays royalty on list and net price.** Publishes book 1 years after acceptance of ms. Responds in 1 month to queries. *Writer's Market* recommends allowing 2 months for reply. Book catalog and ms guidelines free.

Nonfiction: Biography and literary poetry collections. Subjects include art/architecture, ethnic, government/politics, history, language/literature, military/war, music/dance, photography, regional, women's issues/studies. Query or submit outline and sample chapters.

Recent Title(s): *The Collected Poems of Robert Penn Warren* (poetry); *Lee and His Generals in War and Memory*, by Gary W. Gallagher (history).

Tips: "Our audience includes scholars, intelligent laymen, general audience."

THE LOVE AND LOGIC PRESS, INC., Cline/Fay Institute, Inc., 2207 Jackson St., Golden CO 80401. (800)LUV-LOGIC. Fax: (303)278-3894. Website: www.loveandlogic.com. **Acquisitions:** Jim Fay, president/publisher (multiculturalism, social change, community organizing, progressive social work practice); Carol Thomas, product development specialist (education, design). Publishes hardcover and trade paperback originals. **Publishes 5-12 titles/year. 10% of books from first-time authors; 100% from unagented writers. Pays 7½-12% royalty on wholesale price. Offers $500-5,000 advance.** Publishes book 18 months after acceptance of ms. Accepts simultaneous submissions. Responds in 1 month to queries and proposals; 3 months to mss. Book catalog free.

O— "We publish titles which help empower parents, teachers and others who help young people, and which help these individuals become more skilled and happier in their interactions with children. Our titles stress building personal responsibility in children and helping them become prepared to function well in the world." Currently emphasizing parenting, classroom management. De-emphasizing psychology, self-help.

Nonfiction: Self-help. Subjects include child guidance/parenting, education, health/medicine, psychology, sociology, current social issue trends. "We consider any queries/proposals falling into the above categories (with the exception of parenting) but especially psychology/sociology and current social issues and trends." No mss or proposals in New Age category, personal recovery stories, i.e., experiences with attempted suicide, drug/alcohol abuse, institutionalization or medical experiences. Query with SASE. Reviews artwork/photos as part of ms package. Send photocopies.

Recent Title(s): *Humor, Play and Laughter: Stress-proofing Life With Your Kids*, by Joseph Michelli, Ph.D.

LOVE SPELL, Dorchester Publishing Co., Inc., 276 Fifth Ave., Suite 1008, New York NY 10001-0112. (212)725-8811. Website: www.dorchesterpub.com. **Acquisitions:** Joanna Rulf, editorial assistant; Kate Seaver, editorial assistant; Christopher Keeslar, editor. Publishes mass market paperback originals. **Publishes 48 titles/year. Receives 1,500-2,000 queries and 150-500 mss/year. 30% of books from first-time authors; 25-30% from unagented writers. Pays 4% royalty on retail price for new authors. Offers $2,000 average advance for new authors.** Publishes book 1 year after acceptance of ms. Responds in 6 months to mss. Book catalog free (800)481-9191. Manuscript guidelines for #10 SASE or on website.

O— Love Spell publishes the quirky sub-genres of romance: time-travel, paranormal, futuristic. "Despite the exotic settings, we are still interested in character-driven plots." Love Spell has two humor lines including both contemporary and historical romances.

Fiction: Romance: historical, time-travel, paranormal, futuristic, gothic. Query or submit synopsis and first 3 sample chapters only. "No material will be returned without a SASE. "Books industry-wide are getting shorter; we're interested in 90,000 words."

Recent Title(s): *Love Me Tender*, by Sandra Hill.

LOWELL HOUSE, NTC/Contemporary, 2020 Avenue of the Stars, Suite 300, Los Angeles CA 90067. (310)552-7555. Fax: (310)552-7573. E-mail: lperigo@tribune.com. **Acquisitions:** Hudson Perigo, Lowell House senior editor (trade health, nonfiction, mental health, parenting); Peter Hoffman, Keats senior editor (natural and alternative trade titles); Rachel Livesy, Roxbury Park editor (adult nonfiction, juvenile fiction and nonfiction). Publishes hardcover originals, trade paperback originals and reprints. **Publishes 120 titles/year. 60% of books from first-time authors; 75% from unagented writers. Pays royalty on retail price.** Publishes book 20 months after acceptance of ms. Accepts simultaneous submissions. Responds in 3 months to proposals. Book catalog for 9 × 12 SAE with $3 postage.

O— Lowell House publishes reference titles in health, parenting and adult education. Keats emphasizes alternative, natural health.

Imprint(s): Keats, Roxbury Park.

Nonfiction: Reference. Subjects include child guidance/parenting, nutrition, education, health/medicine, money/finance, psychology, recreation, sports, women's issues/studies. Query or submit outline, 1 sample chapter and SASE.
Recent Title(s): *The Thyroid Sourcebook*, by M. Sara Rosenthal (Lowell House); *Prescription Alternatives*, by Earl Mindel (Keats); *101 Ways to Raise a Happy Baby*, by Lisa McCourt and Virginia Hopkin (Roxbury Park).
Tips: "Submit a well-constructed proposal that clearly delineates the work's audience, its advantages over previously published books in the area, a detailed outline, and synopsis and the writer's cv or background."

LOYOLA PRESS, 3441 N. Ashland Ave., Chicago IL 60657-1397. (773)281-1818 ext. 300. Fax: (773)281-0152. E-mail: editors@loyolapress.com. Website: www.loyolapress.org. **Acquisitions:** Jim Manney, acquisitions editor (religion, spirituality); Linda Schlafer, acquisitions editor (Ignatian spirituality, children's). Estab. 1912. Publishes hardcover and trade paperback originals. **Publishes 30 titles/year. Receives 500 queries/year. 5% of books from first-time authors; 50% from unagented writers. Pays 10% royalty on wholesale price or purchases outright. Offers advance up to $6,000.** Publishes book 13 months after acceptance of ms. Accepts simultaneous submissions. Responds in 1 month to queries, 3 months to proposals and mss. Book catalog and guidelines on website.
Imprint(s): Jesuit Way, Seeker's Guides, Wild Onion.
Nonfiction: Practical spirituality with Catholic Christian flavor. Subjects include child guidance/parenting with spiritual slant, prayer and meditation, personal relationships, spiritual wisdom for everyday life, scripture study for nonspecialists, the Catholic tradition. *Jesuit Way* books focus on Jesuit history, biography, and spirituality. *Seeker's Guides* are short introductions to various aspects of Christian living. *Wild Onion* books highlight religion in Chicago. Query before submitting ms.
Recent Title(s): *God in the Moment*, by Kathy Coffey; *The Seeker's Guide to Reading the Bible*, by Steve Mueller.
Tips: "Audience is general readers of religion books, with Catholic or sacramental interests. We do not publish academic books or books for religious professionals. We do publish in the area of Catholic faith formation. Study our guidelines. We get many inappropriate submissions because authors do not know we are a trade publisher of religion books for a non-professional market."

N ⌘ LRP PUBLICATIONS, INC., P.O. Box 980, Horsham PA 19044-0980. (215)784-0860. Fax: (215)784-9639. E-mail: custserve@lrp.com. Website: www.lrp.com. **Acquisitions:** Gary Bagin, director of publishing. Estab. 1978. Publishes hardcover and trade paperback originals. **Publishes 20 titles/year. Receives 15 queries and 12 mss/year. 95% of books from first-time authors; 100% from unagented writers. Royalties vary. Offers $0-1,000 advance.** Publishes book 9 months after acceptance of ms. Responds in 1 month to queries, 2 months to proposals, 3 months to mss. Book catalog and manuscript guidelines free.
    ○➔ LRP Publications, Inc., publishes reference books for human resource managers, attorneys, risk managers, school administrators, consulting experts in litigation.
Nonfiction: Reference. Subjects include education, law, workers compensation, bankruptcy, employment. Submit proposal package, including outline, cv, market analysis, competition.
Recent Title(s): *Preventing and Responding to Workplace Sexual Harassment*, by Christopher McNeill.

LUCENT BOOKS, P.O. Box 289011, San Diego CA 92198-9011. (619)485-7424. Fax: (619)485-8019. **Acquisitions:** Lori Shein, managing editor. Estab. 1988. Publishes hardcover educational supplementary materials and (nontrade) juvenile nonfiction. **Publishes 150 books/year. 10-15% of books from first-time authors; 95% from unagented writers. Makes outright purchase of $2,500-3,000.** Query for book catalog and ms guidelines; send 9×12 SAE with 3 first-class stamps.
    ○➔ Lucent publishes nonfiction for a middle school audience providing students with resource material for academic studies and for independent learning.
Nonfiction: Juvenile. "We produce tightly formatted books for middle grade readers. Each series has specific requirements. Potential writers should familiarize themselves with our material." Series deal with history, current events, social issues. All are works for hire, by assignment only. No unsolicited mss. "Once title is assigned, authors submit outline and first chapter."
Recent Title(s): *Teen Parenting*, by Gail B. Stewart; *Life Under the Jim Crow Laws*, by Charles George.
Tips: "We expect writers to do thorough research using books, magazines and newspapers. Biased writing—whether liberal or conservative—has no place in our books. We prefer to work with writers who have experience writing nonfiction for middle grade students. We are looking for experienced writers, especially those who have written nonfiction books at young adult level."

THE LYONS PRESS, 123 W. 18th St., New York NY 10011. (212)620-9580. Fax: (212)929-1836. Website: www.lyons press.com. **Acquisitions:** Becky Koh, editor (sports, health); Richard Rothschild, managing editor; Lilly Golden, editor-at-large; Enrica Gadler, editor; Jay Cassell, editor; J. McCullogh, associate editor; Brando Skyhorse, assistant editor. Estab. 1984 (Lyons & Burford), 1997 (The Lyons Press). Publishes hardcover and trade paperback originals and reprints. **Publishes 180 titles/year. 30% of books from first-time authors; 60% from unagented writers. Pays varied royalty on retail price.** Publishes book 1 year after acceptance of ms. Accepts simultaneous submissions. Responds in 3 weeks to queries. *Writer's Market* recommends allowing 2 months for reply. Book catalog free.
    ● The Lyons Press has teamed up to develop books with L.L. Bean, *Field & Stream*, The Nature Conservancy and *Golf Magazine*.

Nonfiction: Subjects include Americana, animals, cooking/foods/nutrition, gardening, health, hobbies, nature/environment, science, sports, travel. Query.

Recent Title(s): *On the Beaten Path: An Appalachian Pilgrimage*, by Robert Alden Rubin.

Tips: The Lyons Press publishes practical and literary books, chiefly centered on outdoor subjects—natural history, all sports, gardening, horses, fishing. Currently emphasizing adventure, sports. De-emphasizing hobbies, travel.

MACADAM/CAGE PUBLISHING INC., 155 Sansome St., Suite 520, San Francisco CA 94104. (415)986-7502. Fax: (415)986-7414. E-mail: ecom@earthlink.net. Website: www.macadamcage.com. **Acquisitions**: Patrick Walsh, editor; David Poindexter, publisher. Publishes hardcover and trade paperback originals. **Publishes 10-20 titles/year. Receives 300 queries and 300 mss/year. 75% of books from first-time authors; 25% from unagented writers. Pays negotiable royalty.** Publishes book up to 1 year after acceptance of ms. Accepts simultaneous submissions. "We like to keep in close contact with writers." Responds in 2 months. Manuscript guidelines for #10 SASE.

○━ Enthusiastic new publisher wants to publish quality retail hardcover fiction and nonfiction with a West Coast emphasis. Currently interested in contemporary literature.

Nonfiction: Coffee table book, gift book. Subjects include regional. Submit proposal package, including outline and 3 sample chapters and SASE.

Fiction: Historical, literary, mainstream/contemporary. Submit proposal package, including synopsis, 3 sample chapters and SASE.

Recent Titles: *Infidelity: A Memoir*, (nonfiction); *The Beggar's Throne* (fiction).

Tips: "We publish for readers of quality fiction and nonfiction. We accept submissions on disk (Microsoft format), if accompanied by written synopsis."

MACMILLAN COMPUTER PUBLISHING USA, 201 W. 103rd St., Indianapolis IN 46290. (317)581-3500. Website: www.mcp.com.

Imprint(s): Brady Games, Macmillan Online, **Que**, **Sams**.

MACMURRAY & BECK, 4101 E. Louisiana, Suite 100, Denver CO 80246. (303)753-7565. Fax: (303)753-6566. Website: www.macmurraybeck.com. **Acquisitions:** Frederick Ramey, executive editor; Leslie Koffler, associate editor; Greg Michelson, fiction. Estab. 1989. Publishes hardcover and trade paperback originals. **Publishes 5-8 titles/year. 80% of books from first-time authors; 20% from unagented writers. Pays 8-12% royalty on retail price. Offers $2,000-5,000 advance.** Publishes book 18 months after acceptance of ms. Accepts simultaneous submissions. Responds in 3 months to queries and proposals, 6 months to mss. Book catalog $2. Manuscript guidelines free.

○━ "We are interested in reflective personal narrative of high literary quality both fiction and nonfiction."

Nonfiction: "We are looking for personal narratives and extraordinary perspectives." Submit outline and 2 sample chapters with SASE. Reviews artwork/photos as part of ms package. Send photocopies.

Fiction: Literary. "We are most interested in debut novels that explore the way we live our lives, but we select for voice and literary merit far more than for subject or narrative." Writers often make the mistake of "submitting genre fiction when we are in search of strong literary fiction." Submit synopsis and 3 sample chapters with SASE.

Recent Title(s): *Girl in Hyacinth Blue*, by Susan Vreeland; *Hummingbird House*, by Patricia Henley.

MADISON BOOKS, Rowman and Littlefield Publishing Group, 4720 Boston Way, Lanham MD 20706. (301)459-3366. Fax: (301)459-2118. **Acquisitions:** Alyssa Theodore, acquisitions editor. Estab. 1984. Publishes hardcover originals, trade paperback originals and reprints. **Publishes 40 titles/year. Receives 1,200 submissions/year. 15% of books from first-time authors; 65% from unagented writers. Pays 10-15% royalty on net price.** Publishes ms 1 year after acceptance. Responds in 2 months. Book catalog and ms guidelines for 9×12 SAE with 4 first-class stamps.

Nonfiction: History, biography, contemporary affairs, trade reference. Query or submit outline and sample chapter. *No unsolicited mss.*

MAGE PUBLISHERS INC., 1032 29th St. NW, Washington DC 20007. (202)342-1642. Fax: (202)342-9269. E-mail: info@mage.com. Website: www.mage.com. **Acquisitions:** Amin Sepehri, assistant to publisher. Estab. 1985. Publishes hardcover originals and reprints, trade paperback originals. **Publishes 4 titles/year. Receives 40 queries and 20 mss/year. 10% of books from first-time authors; 95% from unagented writers. Pays variable royalty. Offers $250-1,500 advance.** Publishes book 8-16 months after acceptance of ms. Accepts simultaneous submissions. Responds in 1 month to queries and proposals, 3 months to mss. Book catalog free.

○━ Mage publishes books relating to Persian/Iranian culture.

Nonfiction: Biography, children's/juvenile, coffee table book, cookbook, gift book, illustrated book. Subjects include anthropology/archaeology, art/architecture, cooking/foods/nutrition, ethnic, history, language/literature, music/dance, sociology, translation. Query. Reviews artwork/photos as part of ms package. Send photocopies.

Fiction: Ethnic, feminist, historical, literary, mainstream/contemporary, short story collections. Must relate to Persian/Iranian culture. Query.

Poetry: Must relate to Persian/Iranian culture. Query.

Recent Title(s): *A Taste of Persia*, by N. Batmanglis (cooking); *The Lion and the Throne*, by Ferdowsi (mythology).

Tips: Audience is the Iranian-American community in America and Americans interested in Persian culture.

⌗ THE MAGNI GROUP, INC., 7106 Wellington Point Rd., McKinney TX 75070. (972)540-2050. Fax: (972)540-1057. E-mail: info@magnico.com. Website: www.magnico.com. **Acquisitions:** Evan Reynolds, president. Publishes hardcover and trade paperback originals and trade paperback reprints. **Publishes 5-10 titles/year. Receives 20 queries and 10-20 mss/year. 50% of books from first-time authors; 80% from unagented writers. Pays royalty on wholesale price or makes outright purchase.** Publishes book 6 months after acceptance of ms. Responds in 2 months. Book catalog and ms guidelines on website.
Imprints: Magni Publishing.
Nonfiction: Cookbook, how-to, self-help. Subjects include child guidance/parenting, cooking/foods/nutrition, health/medicine, money/finance, sex. Submit completed ms. Reviews artwork/photos as part of ms package. Send photocopies.
Recent Title(s): *Slim & Fit with Pu-Erh Tea*; *Healthy & Beautiful with Tea Tree Oil* (both health titles).

MANATEE PUBLISHING, P.O. Box 6467, Titusville FL 32782. (407)267-9800. Fax: (407)267-8076. **Acquisitions:** Frank Hudak, publisher. Publishes trade paperback originals and reprints. **Publishes 6 titles/year. Receives 200 queries and 100 mss/year. 90% of books from first-time authors; 100% from unagented writers. Pays 10-15% royalty on wholesale price.** Publishes book 1 year after acceptance of ms. Accepts simultaneous submissions. Responds in 1 month. Book catalog and ms guidelines for #10 SASE.
   ○╌ "We publish fiction (crisp, clear writing with a strong story line) and nonfiction (informative and useful to the reader)."
Nonfiction: Business, how-to, history, self-help.
Fiction: Young adult, adult contemporary/mainstream, mystery, historical.

★ MARCH STREET PRESS, 3413 Wilshire, Greensboro NC 27408. Phone/fax: (336)282-9754. E-mail: rbixby@aol.com. Website: users.aol.com/marchst. **Acquisitions:** Robert Bixby, editor/publisher. Publishes literary chapbooks. **Publishes 6-10 titles/year. Receives 12 queries and 30 mss/year. 50% of books from first-time authors; 100% from unagented writers. Pays 15% royalty. Offers advance of 10 copies.** Estab. 1988. Publishes book 6 months after acceptance of ms. Accepts simultaneous submissions. Responds in 3 months to mss. Book catalog and ms guidelines for #10 SASE.
   ○╌ March Street publishes poetry chapbooks.
Poetry: "My plans are based on the submissions I receive, not vice versa." Submit complete ms.
Recent Title(s): *Everything I Need*, by Keith Taylor.
Tips: "March Street Press is purely an act of hedonistic indulgence. The mission is to enjoy myself. Just as authors express themselves through writing, I find a creative release in designing, editing and publishing. Audience is extremely sophisticated, widely read graduates of M.A., M.F.A. and Ph.D. programs in English and fine arts. Also lovers of significant, vibrant and enriching verse regardless of field of study or endeavor. Most beginning poets, I have found, think it beneath them to read other poets. This is the most glaring flaw in their work. My advice is to read ceaselessly. Otherwise, you may be published, but you will never be accomplished."

⌗ MARKETSCOPE BOOKS, 119 Richard Court, Aptos CA 95003. (831)688-7535. **Acquisitions:** Ken Albert, editor-in-chief. Estab. 1985. Publishes hardcover and trade paperback originals. **Publishes 10 titles/year. 50% of books from first-time authors; 50% from unagented writers. Pays 10-15% royalty on wholesale price.** Publishes book 1 year after acceptance. Accepts simultaneous submissions. Responds in 1 week to queries. *Writer's Market* recommends allowing 2 months for reply.
Nonfiction: Biography, how-to, humor, self-help. Subjects include sexuality, health/medicine, hobbies, money/finance, nature/environment, recreation, regional. Query. Reviews artwork/photos as part of the ms package.

MARLOWE & COMPANY, Avalon Publishing Group, 841 Broadway, 4th Floor, New York NY 10003. (212)614-7880. Publisher: Neil Ortenberg. **Acquisitions:** Gayle Watkins, acquisitions editor. Estab. 1993. Publishes hardcover and trade paperback originals and reprints. **Publishes 60 titles/year. Receives 800 queries/year. 5% of books from first-time authors; 5% from unagented writers. Pays 10% royalty on retail price for hardcover, 6% for paperback. Offers advance of 50% of anticipated first printing.** Publishes book 1 year after acceptance of ms. Book catalog free.
   ○╌ Currently emphasizing spirituality, health, religion.
Nonfiction: Health/medicine, New Age, history. Query with SASE. *No unsolicited submissions.*
Fiction: Literary. "We are looking for literary, rather than genre fiction." *No unsolicited submissions.*
   ● Marlowe & Company is closed to submissions at this time.
Recent Title(s): *Dog Soldiers: Societies of the Plains*, by Thomas Mails (history); *Amistad*, by David Pesci (fiction).

⌗ MAXIMUM PRESS, 605 Silverthorn Rd., Gulf Breeze FL 32561. (850)934-0819. **Acquisitions:** Jim Hoskins, publisher. Publishes trade paperback originals. **Publishes 10-12 titles/year. Receives 10 queries and 10 mss/year. 40% of books from first-time authors; 90% from unagented writers. Pays 7½-15% royalty on wholesale price. Offers $1,000-5,000 advance.** Publishes book 3 months after acceptance of ms. Responds in 1 month. *Writer's Market* recommends allowing 2 months for reply. Book catalog free.
   ○╌ "Maximum Press is a premier publisher of books that help readers apply technology efficiently and profitably. Special emphasis is on books that help individuals and businesses increase revenue and reduce expenses through the use of computers and other low-cost information tools." Currently emphasizing e-business.

Nonfiction: How-to, technical. Subjects include business, computers and Internet. Query with proposal package, including credentials.

Recent Title(s): *Marketing on the Internet*, by Jan Zimmerman (computer/Internet); *101 Ways to Promote Your Web Site*, by Susan Sweeney (e-business).

MAYFIELD PUBLISHING COMPANY, 1280 Villa St., Mountain View CA 94041. Fax: (650)960-0826. Website: www.mayfieldpub.com. **Acquisitions:** Ken King, (philosophy, religion); Holly Allen, (communications); Frank Graham, (psychology, parenting); Jan Beatty, (anthropology, theater, art); Renee Deljon, (English); Michele Sordi, (health, physical eduction); Serina Beauparlant (sociology, women's studies). Estab. 1947. **Publishes 80-90 titles/year.** Accepts simultaneous submissions. Manuscript guidelines free.

O→ Mayfield publishes textbooks for college level courses in the humanities and social sciences.

Nonfiction: Textbook (*college only*). Subjects include anthropology/archaeology, art, child guidance/parenting, communications/theater, health/physical education, English composition, music/dance, philosophy, psychology, religion, sociology, women's studies. Submit proposal package including outline, table of contents, sample chapter, description of proposed market.

MBI PUBLISHING, 729 Prospect Ave., P.O. Box 1, Osceola WI 54020-0001. (715)294-3345. Fax: (715)294-4448. E-mail: mbibks@motorbooks.com. Website: www.motorbooks.com. Publishing Director: Zack Miller. **Acquisitions:** Lee Klancher, editor-in-chief (tractors, stock car racing, motorcycles); Mike Haenggi, acquisitions editor (aviation, military history); Keith Mathiowetz, acquisitions editor (American cars, Americana, railroading collectibles); Paul Johnson, acquisitions editor (automotive how-to, boating); John Adams-Graf, acquisitions editor (foreign cars, vintage racing); Steve Hendrickson, acquisitions editor (hot rods). Estab. 1973. Publishes hardcover and paperback originals. **Publishes 125 titles/year. Receives 200 queries and 50 mss/year. 95% of books from unagented writers. Pays 12% royalty on net receipts. Offers $5,000 average advance.** Publishes book 1 year after acceptance. Accepts simultaneous submissions. Responds in 3 months. Free book catalog. Manuscript guidelines for #10 SASE.

O→ MBI is a transportation-related publisher: cars, motorcycles, racing, trucks, tractors, boats, bicycles—also Americana, aviation and military history.

Imprint(s): Bay View, Bicycle Books, Crestline, Zenith Books.

Nonfiction: Coffeetable book, gift book, how-to, illustrated book. Subjects include Americana, history, hobbies, how-to, military war, photography (as they relate to cars, trucks, motorcycles, motor sports, aviation—domestic, foreign and military). Accepts nonfiction translations. Query with SASE. "State qualifications for doing book." Reviews artwork/photos as part of ms package. Send photocopies.

Recent Title(s): *America's Special Forces*, by David Bohrer (modern military).

N: McBOOKS PRESS, 120 W. State St., Ithaca NY 14850. (607)272-2114. E-mail: mcbooks@mcbooks.com. Website: www.mcbooks.com. Publisher: Alexander G. Skutt. **Acquisitions:** (Ms.) S.K. List, editorial director. Estab. 1979. Publishes trade paperback and hardcover originals and reprints. **Publishes 20 titles/year. Pays 5-10% royalty on retail price. Offers $1,000-5,000 advance.** Responds in 1 month to queries, 2 months to proposals.

O→ Currently emphasizing New York state regional nonfiction.

Nonfiction: Subjects include vegetarianism, regional (New York state) nonfiction, period nautical/military historical fiction. "Authors' ability to promote a plus." Query with SASE. No unsolicited mss.

Recent Title(s): *Waterfalls of the Adirondacks & Catskills*, by Derek Doeffinger and Keith Boas; *The New Vegetarian Baby*, by Sharon Yntema and Christine Beard.

McDONALD & WOODWARD PUBLISHING CO., 325 Dorrence Rd., Granville OH 43023. (740)321-1140. Fax: (740)321-1141. Website: www.mwpubco.com. **Acquisitions:** Jerry N. McDonald, managing partner/publisher. Estab. 1986. Publishes hardcover and trade paperback originals. **Publishes 8 titles/year. Receives 100 queries and 20 mss/year. 50% of books from first-time authors; 100% from unagented writers. Pays 10% royalty on net receipts.** Publishes book 1 year after acceptance of ms. Accepts simultaneous submissions. Responds in 2 weeks. Book catalog free.

O→ "McDonald & Woodward publishes books in natural and cultural history." Currently emphasizing travel, history, natural history. De-emphasizing self-help.

Nonfiction: Biography, coffee table book, how-to, illustrated book, self-help. Subjects include Americana, animals, anthropology, ethnic, history, nature/environment, science, travel. Query or submit outline and sample chapters. Reviews artwork/photos as part of ms package. Send photocopies.

Recent Title(s): *The Carousel Keepers: An Oral History of American Carousels*, by Carrie Papa; *The Mammals of Virginia*, by Donald W. Linzey.

Tips: "We are especially interested in additional titles in our 'Guides to the American Landscape' series. Should consult titles in print for guidance. We want well-organized, clearly written, substantive material."

MARGARET K. McELDERRY BOOKS, Simon & Schuster Children's Publishing Division, Simon & Schuster, 1230 Sixth Ave., New York NY 10020. (212)698-2761. Fax: (212)698-2796. Website: www.simonsayskids.com. Vice President/Publisher: Brenda Bowen. Editor-at-Large: Margaret K. McElderry. **Acquisitions:** Emma D. Dryden, executive editor (books for preschoolers to 16-year-olds); Krissy McCurry, assistant editor. Estab. 1971. Publishes quality material for preschoolers to 16-year-olds, but publishes only a few YAs. Publishes hardcover originals. **Publishes 25 titles/year.**

Receives 5,000 queries/year. 10% of books from first-time authors; 50% from unagented writers. **Average print order is 4,000-6,000 for a first teen book; 7,500-10,000 for a first picture book. Pays royalty on retail price: 10% fiction; picture book, 5% author, 5% illustrator. Offers $5,000-6,000 advance for new authors.** Publishes book up to 2 years after contract signing. Manuscript guidelines for #10 SASE.

O→ "We are more interested in superior writing and illustration than in a particular 'type' of book." Currently emphasizing young picture books. De-emphasizing picture books with a lot of text.

Nonfiction: Children's/juvenile, adventure, biography, history. "Read. The field is competitive. See what's been done and what's out there before submitting. Looks for originality of ideas, clarity and felicity of expression, well-organized plot and strong characterization (fiction) or clear exposition (nonfiction); quality. We will accept one-page query letters with SASE for picture books or novels." *No unsolicited mss.*

Fiction: Middle grade or YA. Adventure, fantasy, historical, mainstream/contemporary, mystery. Send one-page query letter with SASE. *No unsolicited mss.*

Poetry: Query with 3 sample poems.

Recent Title(s): *Star in the Storm*, by Joan Hiatt Harlow (middle grade fiction); *Mrs. Hen's Big Surprise*, by Christel Desmoinaux (picture book fiction).

Tips: "Freelance writers should be aware of the swing away from teen-age novels to books for younger readers and of the growing need for beginning chapter books for children just learning to read on their own."

McFARLAND & COMPANY, INC., PUBLISHERS, Box 611, Jefferson NC 28640. (336)246-4460. Fax: (336)246-5018. E-mail: info@mcfarlandpub.com. Website: www.mcfarlandpub.com. **Acquisitions:** Robert Franklin, president/editor-in-chief (chess, general); Steve Wilson, senior editor (automotive, general); Virginia Tobiassen, editor (general); Marty McGee, assistant editor. Estab. 1979. Publishes reference books and scholarly, technical and professional monographs. Publishes mostly hardcover and a few "quality" paperback originals; a non-"trade" publisher. **Publishes 175 titles/year. Receives 1,200 submissions/year. 70% of books from first-time authors; 95% from unagented writers. Pays 10-12½% royalty on net receipts. No advance.** Publishes book 10 months after acceptance. Responds in 1 month.

O→ McFarland publishes serious nonfiction in a variety of fields, including general reference, performing arts, sports (particularly baseball); women's studies, librarianship, literature, Civil War, history and international studies. Currently emphasizing medieval history, automotive history. De-emphasizing memoirs.

Nonfiction: Reference books and scholarly, technical and professional monographs. Subjects include African American studies (very strong), art, business, chess, Civil War, drama/theater, cinema/radio/TV (very strong), health, history, librarianship (very strong), music, pop culture, sociology, sports/recreation (very strong), women's studies (very strong), world affairs (very strong). Reference books are particularly wanted—fresh material (i.e., not in head-to-head competition with an established title). "We prefer manuscripts of 250 or more double-spaced pages." No fiction, New Age, exposés, poetry, children's books, devotional/inspirational works, Bible studies or personal essays. Query with outline and sample chapters. Reviews artwork/photos as part of ms package.

Recent Title(s): *Self, Taught, Outsider and Folk Art*, by Betty-Carol Sellen with Cynthia J. Johanson.

Tips: "We want well-organized knowledge of an area in which there is not information coverage at present, plus reliability so we don't feel we have to check absolutely everything. Our market is worldwide and libraries are an important part." McFarland also publishes the *Journal of Information Ethics*.

McGREGOR PUBLISHING, 4532 W. Kennedy Blvd., Suite 233, Tampa FL 33609. (813)805-2665 or (888)405-2665. Fax: (813)832-6777. E-mail: mcgregpub@aol.com. **Acquisitions:** Dave Rosenbaum, acquisitions editor; J.C. Fifer, subsidiary rights and sales. Publishes hardcover and trade paperback originals. **Publishes 6-10 titles/year. Receives 150 queries and 20 mss/year. 75% of books from first-time authors; 80% from unagented writers. Pays 10-12% on retail price; 13-16% on wholesale price. Advances vary.** Publishes book 1 year after acceptance of ms. Accepts simultaneous submissions. Responds in 2 months to queries and proposals, 3 months to mss. Book catalog and ms guidelines free.

O→ "We publish nonfiction books that tell the story behind the story."

Nonfiction: Biography, how-to, self-help. Subjects include business/economics, ethnic, history, money/finance, regional, sports. "We're always looking for regional nonfiction titles, and especially for sports, biographies, true crime, self-help and how-to books." Query or submit outline with 2 sample chapters.

● McGregor no longer publishes fiction.

Recent Title(s): *Messier: Hockey's Dragonslayer*, by Rick Carpiniello; *An Hour to Kill*, by Hudson/Hills.

Tips: "We pride ourselves on working closely with an author and producing a quality product with strong promotional campaigns."

MEADOWBROOK PRESS, 5451 Smetana Dr., Minnetonka MN 55343. (612)930-1100. Fax: (612)930-1940. Website: www.meadowbrookpress.com. **Acquisitions:** Joseph Gredler, poetry submissions editor (children's and adult poetry); Megan McGinnis, general submissions editor (general submissions, fiction). Estab. 1975. Publishes trade paperback originals and reprints. **Publishes 20 titles/year. Receives 1,500 queries/year. 15% of books from first-time authors. Pays 10% royalty.** Publishes book 1 year after acceptance. Accepts simultaneous submissions. Responds in 3 months to queries. Book catalog and ms guidelines for #10 SASE.

O─ Meadowbrook is a family-oriented press which specializes in parenting books, party books, humorous quote books, humorous children's poetry books, children's activity books and juvenile fiction. Currently emphasizing parenting and party books. De-emphasizing joke and quote books.

Nonfiction: How-to, humor, reference. Subjects include baby/childcare, cooking/foods/nutrition, senior citizens, children's activities, relationships. No academic or autobiography. Query with outline and sample chapters. "We prefer a query first; then we will request an outline and/or sample material." Send for guidelines.

Fiction: Children's fiction ages 7-12. Query with SASE.

Poetry: Children's humorous poetry and light verse for adults. Query with SASE.

Recent Title(s): *Preschool Play & Learn*, by Penny Warner (nonfiction); *Girls to the Rescue #7*, by Bruce Lansky (fiction); *If Pigs Could Fly and Other Deep Thoughts*, by Bruce Lansky (poetry).

Tips: "Always send for fiction and poetry guidelines before submitting material. We do not accept unsolicited picture book submissions." Meadowbrook has several series, including Girls to the Rescue, Newfangled Fairy Tales and Kids Pick the Funniest Poems.

MEDICAL PHYSICS PUBLISHING, 4513 Vernon Blvd., Madison WI 53705. (608)262-4021. Fax: (608)265-2121. E-mail: mpp@medicalphysics.org. Website: www.medicalphysics.org. **Acquisitions:** John Cameron, president; Betsey Phelps, managing editor. Estab. 1985. Publishes hardcover and trade paperback originals and reprints. **Publishes 10-12 titles/year; imprint publishes 3-5 titles/year. Receives 10-20 queries/year. 100% of books from unagented writers. Pays 10% royalty on wholesale price.** Publishes book 6 months after acceptance of ms. Accepts simultaneous submissions. Responds in 6 months to mss. Book catalog available via website or upon request.

O─ "We are a nonprofit, membership organization publishing affordable books in medical physics and related fields." Currently emphasizing biomedical engineering. De-emphasizing books for the general public.

Nonfiction: Reference books, textbooks, and symposium proceedings in the fields of medical physics and radiology. Also distribute Ph.D. theses in these fields. Submit entire ms. Reviews artwork/photos as part of ms package. Send disposable copies.

Recent Nonfiction Title(s): *The Modern Technology of Radiation Oncology*, edited by Jacob Van Dyk; *Physics of the Body*, by John R. Cameron, James G. Skofronick and Roderick M. Grant.

MERIWETHER PUBLISHING LTD., 885 Elkton Dr., Colorado Springs CO 80907-3557. (719)594-4422. Fax: (719)594-9916. E-mail: merpcds@aol.com. **Acquisitions:** Arthur Zapel, Theodore Zapel, Rhonda Wray, editors. Estab. 1969. Publishes paperback originals and reprints. **Publishes 10-12 books/year; 50-60 plays/year. Receives 1,200 submissions/year. 50% of books from first-time authors; 90% from unagented writers. Pays 10% royalty on retail price or makes outright purchase.** Publishes book 6 months after acceptance. Accepts simultaneous submissions. Responds in 2 months. Book catalog and ms guidelines for $2.

O─ Meriwether publishes theater books, games and videos; speech resources; plays, skits and musicals; and resources for gifted students. "We specialize in books on the theatre arts and religious plays for Christmas, Easter and youth activities. We also publish musicals for high school performers and churches." Currently emphasizing how-to books for theatrical arts and church youth activities.

Nonfiction: How-to, reference, educational, humor. Also textbooks. Subjects include art/theater/drama, music/dance, recreation, religion. "We publish unusual textbooks or trade books related to the communication or performing arts and how-to books on staging, costuming, lighting, etc. We are not interested in religious titles with fundamentalist themes or approaches—we prefer mainstream religion titles." Query or submit outline/synopsis and sample chapters.

Recent Title(s): *Audition Monologs for Student Actors*, by Roger Ellis; *Let's Put on a Show*, by Adrea Gibbs.

Fiction: Plays and musicals—humorous, mainstream, mystery, religious, suspense.

Tips: "Our educational books are sold to teachers and students at college, high school and middle school levels. Our religious books are sold to youth activity directors, pastors and choir directors. Our trade books are directed at the public with a sense of humor. Another group of buyers is the professional theatre, radio and TV category. We focus more on books of plays and short scenes and textbooks on directing, staging, make-up, lighting, etc."

▨ ✠ MERRIAM PRESS, 218 Beech St., Bennington VT 05201-2611. (802)447-0313. Fax: (305)847-5978. E-mail: ray@merriam-press.com. Website: www.merriam-press.com. Publishes hardcover originals and reprints and trade paperback originals and prints. **Publishes 12 titles/year. Receives 50 queries and 30 mss/year. 70-90% of books from first-time authors; 90% from unagented writers. Pays 10% royalty on retail price.** Publishes book 1 year after acceptance of ms. Accepts simultaneous submissions. Responds in 1 month. Book catalog for $3 or on website. Manuscript guidelines for #10 SASE or on website.

O─ Merriam Press specializes in military subjects, especially World War II.

Nonfiction: Biography, illustrated book, reference, technical. Subjects include military/war. Query with SASE or submit proposal package, including outline and 1 sample chapter or submit completed ms. Reviews artwork/photos as part of ms package. Send photocopies.

Recent Title(s): *Marine Chaplain 1943-1946*, by George W. Wickersham II; and *Mount Up! We're Moving Out!*, by Vernon H. Brown Jr.

Tips: "Our books are geared for WWII/military history historians, collectors, model kit builders, war gamers, veterans, general enthusiasts."

MESORAH PUBLICATIONS, LTD., 4401 Second Ave., Brooklyn NY 11232. (718)921-9000. Fax: (718)680-1875. E-mail: artscroll@mesorah.com. Website: www.artscroll.com. **Acquisitions:** (Mrs.) D. Schechter, literary editor. Estab. 1976. Publishes hardcover and trade paperback originals. **Publishes 50 titles/year. Receives 50 queries and 200 mss/ year. 30% of books from first-time authors; 100% from unagented writers. Pays 3-10% royalty on retail price. No advance.** Publishes book 1 year after acceptance of ms. Accepts simultaneous submissions. Responds in 2 months.

    O↔ Mesorah publishes Judaica, Bible study, Talmud, liturgical materials, history, books on the Holocaust for an Orthodox Jewish audience.

Imprints: Shaar Press, Tamar Books.

Nonfiction: Biography, children's/juvenile, coffee table book, cookbook, gift book, reference, self-help, textbook. Subjects include business/economics, child guidance/parenting, creative nonfiction, education, ethnic, history, memoirs, philosophy, religion, spirituality, translation. Query with SASE, or submit proposal package, including outline and 2 sample chapters or completed ms. Reviews artwork/photos as part of ms package. Send photocopies.

Fiction: Adventure, historical, juvenile, mainstream/contemporary, mystery, religious. Query with SASE, or submit proposal package, including synopsis and 2 sample chapters, or completed ms.

Recent Title(s): *Twerski on Spirituality*, by Dr. A.J. Twerski (spirituality); *The Runaway*, by Chaim Eliav (suspense).

METAL POWDER INDUSTRIES FEDERATION, 105 College Rd. E., Princeton NJ 08540. (609)452-7700. Fax: (609)987-8523. E-mail: info@mpif.org. Website: www.mpif.org. **Acquisitions:** Cindy Jablonowski, publications manager; Peggy Lebedz, assistant publications manager. Estab. 1946. Publishes hardcover originals. **Publishes 10 titles/ year. Pays 3-12½% royalty on wholesale or retail price. Offers $3,000-5,000 advance.** Responds in 1 month.

    O↔ Metal Powder Industries publishes monographs, textbooks, handbooks, design guides, conference proceedings, standards, and general titles in the field of powder metullary or particulate materials.

Nonfiction: Work must relate to powder metallurgy or particulate materials.

Recent Title(s): *Advances in Powder Metallurgy and Particulate Materials* (conference proceeding).

MICHIGAN STATE UNIVERSITY PRESS, 1405 S. Harrison Rd., Manly Miles Bldg., Suite 25, East Lansing MI 48823-5202. (517)355-9543. Fax: (800)678-2120; local/international (517)432-2611. E-mail: msupress@msu.edu. Website: www.msu.edu/unit/msupress. **Acquisitions:** Martha Bates, acquisitions editor. Estab. 1947. Publishes hardcover and softcover originals. **Publishes 35 titles/year. Receives 1,000 submissions/year. 75% of books from first-time authors; 100% from unagented writers. Royalties vary.** Publishes ms 18 months after acceptance of ms. Book catalog and ms guidelines for 9×12 SASE.

    O↔ Michigan State University publishes scholarly books that further scholarship in their particular field. In addition they publish nonfiction that addresses, in a more contemporary way, social concerns, such as diversity, civil rights, the environment.

Imprint(s): Lotus, Colleagues.

Nonfiction: Scholarly, trade. Subjects include Afro-American studies, American regional history, American literature and criticism, American studies, business, Canadian studies, contemporary African studies, contemporary civil rights history, creative nonfiction, Great Lakes regional, labor studies, legal studies, Native American studies, women's studies. Series: Canadian Series, Schoolcraft Series, Rhetoric and Public Affairs Series, Native American Series, Colleagues Books. Query with outline and sample chapters. Reviews artwork/photos.

Recent Title(s): *Peninsula*, edited by Michael Steinberg.

MIDDLE ATLANTIC PRESS, 10 Twosome Dr., Box 600, Moorestown NJ 08057. (856)235-4444. Fax: (856)727-6914. E-mail: ABD@koen.com. Website: www.koen.com/midatindex.html. **Acquisitions:** Terence Doherty, acquisitions editor; Robert Koen, publisher. Publishes trade paperback originals and mass market paperback originals and reprints. **Publishes 2-4 titles/year. Receives 50 queries and 12 mss/year. 5% of books from first-time authors; 50% from unagented writers. Offers $1,500-5,000 advance.** Publishes book 3 months after acceptance of ms. Accepts simultaneous submissions. Responds in 1 week to queries, 1 month to proposals.

    O↔ Middle Atlantic Press is a regional publisher of nonfiction focusing on New York, New Jersey, Pennsylvania, Delaware and Maryland. Currently emphasizing books of information (i.e., guides, travel). De-emphasizing juvenile titles.

Imprint(s): MAP.

Nonfiction: Cookbooks. Subjects include history, recreation, regional, sports. Submit proposal package, outline with 3 sample chapters and SASE. Sometimes reviews artwork/photos as part of ms package. Send photocopies.

Recent Title(s): *Phantom of the Pines* (history/folklore); *Crab Cookbook*; *535 Wonderful Things to Do This Week*, by Mitch Kaplan (regional travel).

N: THE MIDKNIGHT CLUB, P.O. Box 25, Brown Mills NJ 08015. (609)735-9043. Fax: E-mail: info@midknightclub.net. Website: www.midknightclub.net. **Acquisitions:** Faith Ann Hotchkin, editor-in-chief. Publishes hardcover and trade paperback originals and trade paperback reprints. **Publishes 4-6 titles/year. Receives 300 queries and 200 mss/ year. 65% of books from first-time authors; 100% from unagented writers. Pays 10-15% royalty on wholesale price.** Publishes book 8 months after acceptance of ms. Accepts simultaneous submissions. Responds in 1 month to queries, 2 months to proposals and mss. Book catalog on website. Manuscript guidelines for #10 SASE or on website.

    O↔ "We're interested in religions of the ages and occult matters that have existed for a long time. No New Age fads."

Nonfiction: How-to, self-help. Subjects include philosophy, religion, spirituality. Submit proposal package, including outline, 3 sample chapters, marketing plans and how it stacks up to the competition. Reviews artwork/photos as part of ms package. Send photocopies.
Fiction: Horror, occult, religious, science fiction. "Make it unique." Query with SASE.
Recent Title(s): *Out the In Door*, by Michael Szul (dreams); *Shangri-La*, by Michael Szul (horror).

MILKWEED EDITIONS, 1011 Washington Ave. S., Suite 300, Minneapolis MN 55415. (612)332-3192. Website: www.milkweed.org. **Acquisitions:** Emilie Buchwald, publisher; Elisabeth Fitz, manuscript coordinator (fiction, children's fiction, poetry); City as Home editor (literary writing about cities); World as Home editor (literary writing about the natural world). Estab. 1980. Publishes hardcover originals and paperback originals and reprints. **Publishes 20 titles/year. Receives 3,000 submissions/year. 30% of books from first-time authors; 70% from unagented writers. Pays 7½% royalty on list price. Advance varies.** Publishes work 1-2 years after acceptance. Accepts simultaneous submissions. Responds in 6 months. Book catalog for $1.50. Manuscript guidelines for SASE.
    ○┓ Milkweed Editions publishes literary fiction for adults and middle grade readers, nonfiction, memoir and poetry. "Our vision is focused on giving voice to writers whose work is of the highest literary quality and whose ideas engender personal reflection and cultural action." Currently emphasizing nonfiction about the natural world.
Nonfiction: Literary. Subjects include nature/environment and human community. Send ms with SASE for our response.
Fiction: Literary. Novels for adults and for readers aged 8-13. High literary quality. Send ms with SASE.
Recent Title(s): *Ecology of a Cracker Childhood*, by Janisse Ray (nonfiction); *Falling Dark*, by Tim Tharp (fiction); *Butterfly Effect*, by Harry Humes (poetry).
Tips: "We are looking for excellent writing in fiction, nonfiction, poetry, and children's novels, with the intent of making a humane impact on society. Send for guidelines. Acquaint yourself with our books in terms of style and quality before submitting. Many factors influence our selection process, so don't get discouraged. Nonfiction is focused on literary writing about the natural world, including living well in urban environments. We no longer publish children's biographies. We read poetry in January and June only."

MILKWEEDS FOR YOUNG READERS, Milkweed Editions, 1011 Washington Ave. S., Suite 300, Minneapolis MN 55415. (612)332-3192. Fax: (612)332-6248. Website: www.milkweed.org. Children's Reader: Elisabeth Fitz. Estab. 1984. Publishes hardcover and trade paperback originals. **Publishes 1-2 titles/year. 25% of books from first-time authors; 70% from unagented writers. Pays 7½% royalty on retail price. Advance varies.** Publishes book 1 year after acceptance of ms. Accepts simultaneous submissions. Responds in 2 months to queries, 6 months to mss. Book catalog for $1.50. Manuscript guidelines for #10 SASE.
    ○┓ "Milkweeds for Young Readers are works that embody humane values and contribute to cultural understanding." Currently emphasizing natural world, urban environments. De-emphasizing fantasy.
Fiction: For ages 8-12: adventure, animal, fantasy, historical, humor, environmental, mainstream/contemporary. Query with 2-3 sample chapters and SASE.
Recent Title(s): *The Ocean Within*, by V.M. Caldwell.

THE MILLBROOK PRESS INC., 2 Old New Milford Rd., Brookfield CT 06804. Fax: (203)775-5643. Website: www.millbrookpress.com. Senior Vice President/Publisher: Jean Reynolds. Amy Shields and Laura Walsh, senior editors. **Acquisitions:** Bridget Noujaim, manuscript coordinator. Estab. 1989. Publishes hardcover and paperback originals. **Publishes 185 titles/year. Pays varying royalty on wholesale price or makes outright purchase. Advance varies.** Publishes book 1 year after acceptance of ms. Responds in 1 month to queries and proposals. Book catalog for 9×12 SAE with 4 first-class stamps. Manuscript guidelines for #10 SASE.
    ○┓ Millbrook Press publishes quality children's books of curriculum-related nonfiction for the school/library market.
Imprint(s): Twenty-First Century Books (Pat Culleton, publisher); Dominic Barth, editor.
Nonfiction: Children's/juvenile. Subjects include animals, anthropology/archaeology, ethnic, government/politics, health/medicine, history, hobbies, nature/environment, science, sports. Specializes in general reference, social studies, science, arts and crafts, multicultural and picture books. "Mistakes writers most often make when submitting nonfiction are failure to research competing titles and failure to research school curriculum." Query or submit outline and 1 sample chapter.
Recent Title(s): *The Valiant Women of the Viet Nam War*, by Karen Zeinert.

MINNESOTA HISTORICAL SOCIETY PRESS, Minnesota Historical Society, 345 Kellogg Blvd. W., St. Paul MN 55102-1906. (651)296-2264. Fax: (651)297-1345. Website: www.mnhs.org. **Acquisitions:** Gregory M. Brith, director; Ann Regan, managing editor. Estab. 1849. Publishes hardcover and trade paperback originals, trade paperback reprints. **Publishes 10 titles/year; each imprint publishes 5 titles/year. Receives 100 queries and 25 mss/year. 50% of books from first-time authors; 100% from unagented writers. Royalties are negotiated.** Publishes book 14 months after acceptance. Responds in 1 month to queries. *Writer's Market* recommends allowing 2 months for reply. Book catalog free.
    ○┓ Minnesota Historical Society Press publishes both scholarly and general interest books that contribute to the understanding of Minnesota and Midwestern history.
Imprint(s): Borealis Books (reprints only); Midwest Reflections (memoir and personal history).

Nonfiction: Regional works only: biography, coffee table book, cookbook, illustrated book, reference. Subjects include anthropology/archaeology, art/architecture, history, memoir, photography, regional, women's issues/studies, Native American studies. Query with proposal package including letter, outline, vita, sample chapter. Reviews artwork/photos as part of ms package. Send photocopies.

Recent Title(s): *Frederick Manfred: A Daughter Remembers*, by Freya Manfred; *The Girls Are Coming*, by Peggie Carlson.

Tips: Minnesota Historical Society Press is getting many inappropriate submissions from their listing. A regional connection is required.

MINSTREL BOOKS, Pocket Books for Young Readers, Simon & Schuster, 1230 Avenue of the Americas, New York NY 10020. (212)698-7669. Website: www.simonsayskids.com. Editorial Director: Patricia MacDonald. **Acquisitions:** Attn: Manuscript proposals. Estab. 1986. Publishes hardcover originals and reprints, trade paperback originals. **Publishes 125 titles/year. Receives 1,200 queries/year. Less than 25% from first-time authors. Pays 6-8% royalty on retail price. Advance varies.** Publishes book 2 years after acceptance of ms. Accepts simultaneous submissions. Responds in 3 months to queries. Book catalog and ms guidelines free.

　　O→ "Minstrel publishes fun, kid-oriented books, the kinds kids pick for themselves, for middle grade readers, ages 8-12."

Nonfiction: Children's/juvenile—middle grades, ages 8-12. Subjects include celebrity biographies and books about TV shows.

　　● "This publisher accepts agented submissions only."

Fiction: Middle grade fiction for ages 8-12: animal stories, fantasy, humor, juvenile, mystery, science fiction, suspense. No picture books. "Thrillers are very popular, and 'humor at school' books."

Recent Title(s): *Snow Day*, by Mel Odom; *I Was a Sixth Grade Alien* series, by Bruce Coville.

Tips: "Hang out with kids to make sure your dialogue and subject matter are accurate."

MITCHELL LANE PUBLISHERS, INC., P.O. Box 200, Childs MD 21916-0200. (410)392-5036. Fax: (410)392-4781. **Acquisitions:** Barbara Mitchell, publisher. Estab. 1993. Publishes hardcover and trade paperback originals. **Publishes 22-27 titles/year. Receives 100 queries and 5 mss/year. 0% of books from first-time authors; 100% from unagented writers. Makes outright purchase on work-for-hire basis. No advance.** Publishes book 1 year after acceptance of ms. Responds only if interested. Book catalog free.

　　O→ Mitchell Lane publishes multicultural biographies for children and young adults."

Nonfiction: Multicultural, biography. Ethnic subjects. All unsolicited mss returned unopened.

Recent Title(s): *Britney Spears* (Real-Life Reader Biography), by Ann Gaines (juvenile); *Ricky Martin* (Real-Life Reader Biography), by Valerie Menard (juvenile).

Tips: "We hire writers on a 'work-for-hire' basis to complete book projects we assign. Send résumé and writing samples that do not need to be returned."

MODERN LANGUAGE ASSOCIATION OF AMERICA, Dept. WM, 10 Astor Pl., New York NY 10003. (212)475-9500. Fax: (212)477-9863. **Acquisitions:** Joseph Gibaldi, director of book acquisitions and development. Director of MLA Book Publications: Martha Evans. Estab. 1883. Publishes hardcover and paperback originals. **Publishes 15 titles/year. Receives 125 submissions/year. 100% of books from unagented writers. Pays 5-10% royalty on net proceeds.** Publishes book 1 year after acceptance. Responds in 2 months to mss. Book catalog free.

　　O→ The MLA publishes on current issues in literary and linguistic research and teaching of language and literature at postsecondary level.

Nonfiction: Scholarly, professional. Language and literature subjects. No critical monographs. Query with outline.

M MOMENTUM BOOKS, LTD., 1174 E. Big Beaver Rd., Troy MI 48083-1934. (248)689-0936. Fax: (248)689-0956. E-mail: momentumbooks@glis.net. **Acquisitions:** Franklin Foxx, editor. Estab. 1987. **Publishes 6 titles/year. Receives 100 queries and 30 mss/year. 95% of books from first-time authors; 100% from unagented writers. Pays 10-15% royalty. No advance.**

　　O→ Momentum Books publishes regional books and general interest nonfiction.

Nonfiction: Biography, cookbook, guides. Subjects include cooking/foods/nutrition, government/politics, history, memoirs, military/war, sports, travel. Submit proposal package, including outline, 3 sample chapters and marketing outline.

Recent Title(s): *Thus Spake David E.*, by David E. Davis, Sr. (automotive); *Rockin' Down the Dial*, by David Carson (regional history).

MONACELLI PRESS, 10 E. 92nd St., New York NY 10128. (212)831-0248. **Acquisitions:** Andrea Monfried, editor. Estab. 1994. Publishes hardcover and trade paperback originals. **Publishes 25-30 titles/year. Receives over 100 queries and mss/year. 10% of books from first-time authors; 90% from unagented writers. Pays royalty on retail price. Offers occasional advance, amount negotiable.** Publishes book 18 months after acceptance of ms. Accepts simultaneous submissions. Responds in 3 months to queries. Book catalog free.

　　O→ Monacelli Press produces high-quality illustrated books in architecture, fine arts, decorative arts, landscape and photography.

Nonfiction: Coffee table book. Subjects include art/architecture. Query with outline, 1 sample chapter and SASE. Reviews artwork/photos as part of ms package. Send transparencies, duplicate slides best. (Monacelli does not assume responsibility for unsolicited artwork; call if you are uncertain about what to send.)

Recent Title(s): *Jim Dine: The Alchemy of Images*, text by Marco Livingstone with commentary by Jim Dine.

MOODY PRESS, Moody Bible Institute, 820 N. LaSalle Blvd., Chicago IL 60610. (800)678-8001. Fax: (800)678-0003. Website: www.moodypress.org. Vice President/Executive Editor: Greg Thorton. **Acquisitions:** Acquisitions Coordinator. Estab. 1894. Publishes hardcover, trade and mass market paperback originals and hardcover and mass market paperback reprints. **Publishes 60 titles/year; imprint publishes 5-10 titles/year. Receives 1,500 queries and 2,000 mss/year. Less than 1% of books from first-time authors; 99% from unagented writers. Royalty varies. Offers $500-5,000 advance.** Publishes book 9-12 months after acceptance of ms. Accepts simultaneous submissions but prefers not to. Responds in 2 months. Book catalog for 9×12 SAE with 4 first-class stamps. Guidelines for #10 SASE.

○─ "The mission of Moody Press is to educate and edify the Christian and to evangelize the non-Christian by ethically publishing conservative, evangelical Christian literature and other media for all ages around the world; and to help provide resources for Moody Bible Institute in its training of future Christian leaders."

Imprint(s): Northfield Publishing, Moody Children & Youth.

Nonfiction: Children's/juvenile, gift book, general Christian living. Subjects include child guidance/parenting, money/finance, religion, women's issues/studies. "Look at our recent publications, and convince us of what sets your book apart from all the rest on bookstore shelves and why it's consistent with our publications. Many writers don't do enough research of the market or of our needs." Query with outline, 3 sample chapters, table of contents, author's own market study showing why book will be successful and SASE.

Recent Nonfiction Title(s): *Relational Parenting*, by Ross Campbell, M.D.

Fiction: Religious. "We are not currently accepting fiction submissions."

Tips: "Our audience consists of general, average Christian readers, not scholars. Know the market and publishers. Spend time in bookstores researching."

MOON PUBLICATIONS, INC., Avalon Travel Publishing, Avalon Publishing Group, 5855 Beaudry St., Emeryville CA 94608. (510)595-3664. Website: www.moon.com. Publisher: Bill Newlin. Editorial Director: Pauli Galin. Estab. 1973. Publishes trade paperback originals. **Publishes 15 titles/year. Receives 100-200 submissions/year. 50% from first-time authors; 95% from unagented writers. Pays royalty on net price. Offers advance of up to $10,000.** Publishes book an average of 9 months after acceptance. Accepts simultaneous submissions. Responds in 2 months. Book catalog and proposal guidelines for 7½×10½ SAE with 2 first-class stamps.

○─ "Moon Publications publishes comprehensive, articulate travel information to North and South America, Asia and the Pacific."

Imprint(s): John Muir Publications.

Nonfiction: "We specialize in travel guides to Asia and the Pacific Basin, the United States, Canada, the Caribbean, Latin America and South America, but are open to new ideas. Our guides include in-depth cultural and historical background, as well as recreational and practical travel information. We prefer comprehensive guides to entire countries, states, and regions over more narrowly defined areas such as cities, museums, etc. Writers should write first for a copy of our guidelines. Proposal required with outline, table of contents, and writing sample. Author should also be prepared to provide photos, artwork and base maps. No fictional or strictly narrative travel writing; no how-to guides." Reviews artwork/photos as part of ms package.

Recent Nonfiction Title(s): *New York Handbook*, by Christiane Bird (travel); *Tennessee Handbook*, by Jeff Bradley (travel); *Dominican Republic Handbook*, by Gaylord Dold (travel).

Tips: "Moon Travel Handbooks are designed by and for independent travelers seeking the most rewarding travel experience possible. Our Handbooks appeal to all travelers because they are the most comprehensive and honest guides available. Check our website."

⟦N⟧ THOMAS MORE PUBLISHING, Resources for Christian Living, 200 E. Bethany Dr., Allen TX 75002. (972)390-6923. Fax: (972)390-6620. E-mail: dhampton@rcl-enterprises.com. Website: www.rclweb.com. **Acquisitions:** Debra Hampton, marketing and sales director (religious publishing). Publishes hardcover, trade paperback, mass market paperback originals and hardcover, trade paperback and mass market paperback reprints. **Publishes 25 titles/year. Receives 250 queries and 150 mss/year. 25% of books from first-time authors; 50% from unagented writers. Pays 8-12% royalty on wholesale price. Offers $2-10,000 advance.** Publishes book 8 months after acceptance of ms. Accepts simultaneous submissions. Responds in 3 months to proposals and mss. Book catalog free.

○─ Thomas More specializes in self-help and religious titles.

Imprints: Christian Classics (contact: Debra Hampton).

Nonfiction: Self-help. Subjects include religion, spirituality, women's issues/studies. Submit proposal package, including outline and 3 sample chapters. Reviews artwork/photos as part of ms package. Send photocopies.

Recent Title(s): *Soul Moments: Times When Heaven Touches Earth*, by Isabel Anders (women's spirituality); *Grow Yourself a Life You'll Love*, by Barbara Garro (self-help).

MOREHOUSE PUBLISHING CO., 4475 Linglestown Rd., Harrisburg PA 17112. (717)541-8130. Fax: (717)541-8136. E-mail: morehouse@morehouse.com. Website: www.morehousegroup.com. **Acquisitions:** Mark Fretz, editorial director. Estab. 1884. Publishes hardcover and paperback originals. **Publishes 35 titles/year. 50% from first-time authors. Pays 10% net royalties. Offers small advance.** Publishes books within 18 months of acceptance. Accepts simultaneous submissions. Responds in 2 months. Guidelines available upon request.

O→ Morehouse Publishing has traditionally published for the Episcopal Church and the Anglican Communion.

Nonfiction: "In addition to its line of books for the Episcopal church, it also publishes books of practical value from within the Christian tradition for clergy, laity, academics, professionals, and seekers." Subjects include spirituality, biblical studies, liturgics, congregational resorces, women's issues, devotions and meditations, and issues around Christian life. Submit outline, 1-2 sample chapters, résumé or cv.

Fiction: Christian children's picture books for ages 3-8. Submit entire ms (no more than 1,500 words) and résumé/cv.

Recent Title(s): *Living with Contradiction: An Introduction to Benedictine Spirituality*, by Esther de Waal; *Jenny's Prayer*, by Annette Griessman, illustrated by Mary Ann Lard.

[N] MORNINGSIDE HOUSE, INC., Morningside Bookshop, 260 Oak St., Dayton OH 45410. (937)461-6736. Fax: (937)461-4260. E-mail: msbooks@erinet.com. Website: www.morningsidebooks.com. **Acquisitions:** Robert J. Younger, publisher. Publishes hardcover and trade paperback originals and reprints. **Publishes 10 titles/year; imprint publishes 5 titles/year. Receives 30 queries and 10 mss/year. 20% of books from first-time authors; 80% from unagented writers. Pays 10% royalty on retail price. Offers $1,000-2,000 advance.** Publishes ms 15 months after acceptance. Accepts simultaneous submissions. Book catalog for $4 or on website.

O→ Morningside publishes books for readers interested in the history of the American Civil War.

Imprints: Morningside Press, Press of Morningside Bookshop.

Nonfiction: Subjects include history, military/war. Query with SASE or submit completed ms. Reviews artwork/photos as part of ms package. Send photocopies.

Recent Title(s): *Arkansas Confederates in the Western Theater*, by James Willis (Civil War history).

[A] WILLIAM MORROW, HarperCollins, 10 E. 53rd St., New York NY 10022. (212)207-7000. Fax: (212)207-7145. Website: www.harpercollins.com. Editorial Director: Lisa Queen. Managing Editor: Kim Lewis. **Acquisitions:** Acquisitions Editor. Estab. 1926. **Publishes 200 titles/year. Receives 10,000 submissions/year. 30% of books from first-time authors. Pays standard royalty on retail price. Advance varies.** Publishes book 2 years after acceptance of ms. Responds in 3 months.

O→ William Morrow publishes a wide range of titles that receive much recognition and prestige. A most selective house.

Nonfiction and Fiction: Publishes adult fiction, nonfiction, history, biography, arts, religion, poetry, how-to books, cookbooks. Length: 50,000-100,000 words. *Agented submissions only. No unsolicited mss or proposals.*

Recent Title(s): *From this Day Forward*, by Cokie and Steve Roberts; *Stiffed*, by Susan Faludi.

[M] MOUNTAIN N'AIR BOOKS, P.O. Box 12540, La Crescenta CA 91224. (818)951-4150. Website: www.mountain-n-air.com. **Acquisitions:** Gilberto d'Urso, owner. Publishes trade paperback originals. **Publishes 6 titles/year. Receives 50 queries and 35 mss/year. 75% of books from first-time authors; 100% from unagented writers. Pays 5-10% royalty on retail price or makes outright purchase. No advance.** Publishes book 6 months after acceptance with ms. Responds in 2 weeks to queries and 2 months to mss. Manuscript guidelines available via website or upon request with #10 SASE.

O→ Mountain N'Air publishes books for those generally interested in the outdoors and travel.

Imprint(s): Bearly Cooking.

Nonfiction: Biography, cookbook, how-to. Subjects include cooking/foods/nutrition, nature/environment, recreation, travel/adventure. Submit outline with 2 sample chapters. Reviews artwork/photos as part of the ms package. Send photocopies.

Recent Title(s): *Thinking Out Loud Through the American West*, by Pete Sinclair; *The Adventures of a Naturalist in the Himalya*, by Laurence Swan.

[M] MOUNTAIN PRESS PUBLISHING COMPANY, P.O. Box 2399, Missoula MT 59806-2399. (406)728-1900. Fax: (406)728-1635. E-mail: mtnpress@montana.com. Website: www.mtnpress.com. **Acquisitions:** Kathleen Ort, editor-in-chief (natural history/science/outdoors); Gwen McKenna, editor (history); Jennifer Carey, assistant editor (Roadside Geology and Tumbleweed Series). Estab. 1948. Publishes hardcover and trade paperback originals. **Publishes 15 titles/year. Receives 250 submissions/year. 50% of books from first-time authors; 90% from unagented writers. Pays 7-12% on wholesale price.** Publishes book 2 years after acceptance. Responds in 3 months. Book catalog free.

O→ "We are expanding our Roadside Geology, Geology Underfoot and Roadside History series (done on a state by state basis). We are interested in well-written regional field guides—plants, flowers and birds—and readable history and natural history."

Nonfiction: Western history, nature/environment, regional, earth science, creative nonfiction. "No personal histories or journals." Query or submit outline and sample chapters. Reviews artwork/photos as part of ms package.

Recent Title(s): *From Earth to Herbalist: An Earth Conscious Guide to Medicinal Plants*, by Gregory Tilford; *William Henry Jackson: Framing the Frontier*, by Douglas Waitley.

Tips: "Find out what kind of books a publisher is interested in and tailor your writing to them; research markets and target your audience. Research other books on the same subjects. Make yours different. Don't present your manuscript to a publisher—*sell* it to him. Give him the information he needs to make a decision on a title. Please learn what we publish before sending your proposal. We are a 'niche' publisher."

THE MOUNTAINEERS BOOKS, 1001 SW Klickitat Way, Suite 201, Seattle WA 98134-1162. (206)223-6303. Fax: (206)223-6306. E-mail: mbooks@mountaineers.org. Website: www.mountaineersbooks.org. Executive Director: Art Freeman. Managing Editor: Kathleen Cubley. **Acquisitions:** Margaret Foster, editor-in-chief. Estab. 1961. Publishes 95% hardcover and trade paperback originals and 5% reprints. **Publishes 40 titles/year. Receives 150-250 submissions/ year. 25% of books from first-time authors; 98% from unagented writers. Pays royalty on net sales. Offers advance.** Publishes book 1 year after acceptance. Responds in 3 months. Book catalog and ms guidelines for 9 × 12 SAE with $1.33 postage.

> O→ Mountaineers Books specializes in expert, authoritative books dealing with mountaineering, hiking, backpacking, skiing, snowshoeing, canoeing, bicycling, etc. These can be either how-to-do-it or where-to-do-it (guidebooks). Currently emphasizing regional conservation and natural history.

Nonfiction: Guidebooks for national and international adventure travel, recreation, natural history, conservation/environment, non-competitive self-propelled sports, outdoor how-to. Does *not* want to see "anything dealing with hunting, fishing or motorized travel." Submit author bio, outline and minimum of 2 sample chapters. Accepts nonfiction translations. Looks for "expert knowledge, good organization." Also interested in nonfiction adventure narratives.

Recent Title(s): *Ghosts of Everest: The Search for Mallory and Irvine*, by Hemmleb, Johnson and Simonson; *Bradford Washburn: Mountain Photography*, edited by Anthony Decaneas.

> • See the Contests and Awards section for information on the Barbara Savage/"Miles From Nowhere" Memorial Award for outstanding adventure narratives offered by Mountain Books.

Tips: "The type of book the writer has the best chance of selling our firm is an authoritative guidebook (*in our field*) to a specific area not otherwise covered; or a how-to that is better than existing competition (again, *in our field*)."

MULTNOMAH PUBLISHERS, INC., P.O. Box 1720, Sisters OR 97759. (541)549-1144. Website: www.multnomahb ooks.com. **Acquisitions:** Rod Morris, editor (general fiction); Karen Ball, editor. Estab. 1987. Publishes hardcover and trade paperback originals. **Publishes 120 titles/year. Receives 2,400 queries and 1,200 mss/year. 2% of books from first-time authors; 50% from unagented writers. Pays royalty on wholesale price.** Publishes book 1-2 years after acceptance of ms. Accepts simultaneous submissions. Responds in 3 months to queries. Manuscript guidelines via website or upon request with #10 SASE.

> O→ Multnomah publishes books on Christian living and family enrichment, devotional and gift books and fiction.

Imprint(s): Alabaster, Multnomah Books, Palisades.

> • Gold'n'Honey children's books was sold to Zondervan for the Zonderkidz imprint.

Nonfiction: Children, coffee table book, gift book, humor, illustrated book. Subjects include child guidance/parenting, religion. Submit proposal package, including outline/synopsis, 3 sample chapters and market study with SASE. Reviews artwork/photos as part of ms package. Send photocopies.

Fiction: Adventure, historical, humor, mystery, religious, romance, suspense, western. Submit synopsis, 3 sample chapters with SASE.

Recent Title(s): *Refiners Fire*, by Sylvia Bambola (fiction); *I Kissed Dating Goodbye*, by Joshua Harris (nonfiction).

MUSTANG PUBLISHING CO., P.O. Box 770426, Memphis TN 38177-0426. Website: www.mustangpublishing.c om. **Acquisitions:** Rollin Riggs, editor. Estab. 1983. Publishes hardcover and trade paperback originals. **Publishes 10 titles/year. Receives 1,000 submissions/year. 50% of books from first-time authors; 90% of books from unagented writers. Pays 6-8% royalty on retail price.** Publishes book 1 year after acceptance. Accepts simultaneous submissions. Responds in 1 month. *Writer's Market* recommends allowing 2 months for reply. Book catalog for $2 and #10 SASE. No phone calls, please.

> O→ Mustang publishes general interest nonfiction for an adult audience.

Nonfiction: How-to, humor, self-help. Subjects include Americana, hobbies, recreation, sports. "Our needs are very general—humor, travel, how-to, etc.—for the 18-to 60-year-old market." Query or submit outline and sample chapters with SASE. Reviews artwork as part of ms package. Send photocopies.

Recent Title(s): *Medical School Admissions: The Insider's Guide*, by Zebala (career); *The Complete Book of Golf Games*, by Johnston (sports).

Tips: "From the proposals we receive, it seems that many writers never go to bookstores and have no idea what sells. Before you waste a lot of time on a nonfiction book idea, ask yourself, 'How often have my friends and I actually *bought* a book like this?' We are not interested in first-person travel accounts or memoirs."

Ⓐ THE MYSTERIOUS PRESS, Warner Books, 1271 Avenue of the Americas, New York NY 10020. (212)522-7200. Fax: (212)522-7990. Website: www.twbookmark. **Acquisitions:** William Malloy, executive editor; Sara Ann Freed, editor-in-chief. Estab. 1976. Publishes hardcover and mass market editions. **Publishes 36 titles/year. No unagented writers. Pays standard, but negotiable, royalty on retail price. Amount of advance varies widely.** Publishes book an average of 1 year after acceptance of ms. Responds in 2 months.

> O→ The Mysterious Press publishes well-written crime/mystery/suspense fiction.

Fiction: Mystery, suspense, crime/detective novels. No short stories. Query.

Recent Title(s): *The Hook*, by Donald Westlake; *Beneath the Skin*, by Nicci French.

THE NAIAD PRESS, INC., P.O. Box 10543, Tallahassee FL 32302. (850)539-5965. Fax: (850)539-9731. Website: www.naiadpress.com. **Acquisitions:** Barbara Grier, editorial director. Estab. 1973. Publishes paperback originals. **Publishes 32 titles/year. Receives over 1,500 submissions/year. 20% of books from first-time authors; 99% from unagented writers. Pays 15% royalty on wholesale or retail price. No advance.** Publishes book 2 years after acceptance. Responds in 4 months. Book catalog and ms guidelines for 6×9 SAE and $1.50 postage and handling.

○→ The Naiad Press publishes lesbian fiction, preferably lesbian/feminist fiction.

Fiction: "We are not impressed with the 'oh woe' school and prefer realistic (i.e., happy) novels. We emphasize fiction and are now heavily reading manuscripts in that area. We are working in a lot of genre fiction—mysteries, short stories, fantasy—all with lesbian themes, of course. We have instituted an inhouse anthology series, featuring short stories only by our own authors (authors who have published full length fiction with us or those signed to do so)." Query.

Recent Title(s): *Murder Undercover*, by Claire McNab (mystery).

● The Naiad Press downsized recently, and will continue to publish three of its authors while working with Bella Books which will publish the remaining books under contract.

Tips: "There is tremendous world-wide demand for lesbian mysteries from lesbian authors published by lesbian presses, and we are doing several such series. We are no longer seeking science fiction. Manuscripts under 50,000 words have twice as good a chance as over 50,000."

NARWHAL PRESS, INC., 1629 Meeting St., Charleston SC 29405-9408. (843)853-0510. Fax: (843)853-2528. E-mail: shipwrex@aol.com. Website: www.shipwrecks.com. **Acquisitions:** Dr. E. Lee Spence, chief editor (marine archaeology, shipwrecks); Dr. Robert Stockton, managing editor (novels, marine histories, military); Roni L. Smith, associate editor (novels, children's books). Estab. 1994. Publishes hardcover and quality trade paperback originals. **Publishes 10 titles/year. Receives 100 queries and 50 mss/year. 75% of books from first-time authors; 100% from unagented writers. Pays 10-15% royalty on wholesale price. Offers $1,000-2,000 advance.** Publishes book at least 3 months after acceptance of ms, depending on revisions and other considerations. Accepts simultaneous submissions. Responds in 2 weeks to queries, 1 month to mss.

○→ Narwhal Press specializes in books about shipwrecks and marine archaeology and military history.

Nonfiction: Biography, children's/juvenile, how-to, reference. Subjects include anthropology/archaeology, history, memoirs, military/war. "We are constantly searching for titles of interest to shipwreck divers, marine archaeologists, Civil War buffs, etc., but we are expanding our titles to include novels, children's books, modern naval history, World War II, Korea, Vietnam and personal memoirs." Query or submit outline and 3 sample chapters and SASE. Reviews artwork/photos as part of ms package. Send photocopies.

Fiction: Historical, juvenile, mainstream/contemporary, military/war, young adult, dive-related. "We prefer novels with a strong historical context. We invite writers to submit fiction about undersea adventures. Best to call or write first." Query, then submit synopsis and 3 sample chapters and SASE.

Recent Title(s): *Tempest, Fire and Foe*, by Lew Andrews (destroyer escorts of WWII); *Confrontation Zone*, by Rod Lenahan (US invasion of Panama).

Tips: "Become an expert in your subject area. Polish and proofread your writing."

N NASW PRESS, National Association of Social Workers, 750 First St. NE, Suite 700, Washington DC 20002-4241. (202)408-8600. Fax: (202)336-8312. E-mail: press@naswdc.org. Website: www.naswpress.org. Executive Editor: Paula Delo. Estab. 1956. **Publishes 10-15 titles/year. Receives 100 submissions/year. 20% of books from first-time authors; 100% from unagented writers. Pays 10-15% royalty on net prices.** Publishes book 1 year after acceptance of ms. Responds within 4 months on submissions. Book catalog and ms guidelines website or free with SASE.

○→ NASW Books "provides outstanding information tools for social workers and other human service professionals to advance the knowledge base in social work and social welfare." Currently emphasizing health, policy, substance abuse and aging books.

Nonfiction: Textbooks of interest to professional social workers. "We're looking for books on social work in health care, mental health, multicultural competence and substance abuse. Books must be directed to the professional social worker and build on the current literature." Submit outline and sample chapters with SASE. Rarely reviews artwork/photos as part of ms package.

Recent Title(s): *Close to Home: Human Services and the Small Community*, by Emilia E. Martinez-Brawley.

Tips: "Our audience includes social work practitioners, educators, students and policy makers. They are looking for practice-related books that are well grounded in theory. The books that do well have direct application to the work our audience does. New technology, AIDS, welfare reform and health policy will be of increasing interest to our readers. We are particularly interested in manuscripts for fact-based practice manuals that will be very user-friendly."

NATUREGRAPH PUBLISHERS, INC., P.O. Box 1047, Happy Camp CA 96039. (530)493-5353. Fax: (530)493-5240. E-mail: nature@sisgtel.net or naturgraph@aol.com. Website: members.aol.com/naturegraph/homepage.htm or www.naturegraph.com. **Acquisitions:** Barbara Brown, editor-in-chief; Keven Brown, editor. Estab. 1946. Publishes trade paperback originals. **Publishes 5 titles/year. Pays 8-10% royalty on wholesale price. No advance.** Responds in 1 month to queries, 2 months to proposals and mss.

○→ Naturegraph publishes "books for a better world. Within our niches of nature and Indian subjects, we hope the titles we choose to publish will benefit the world in some way."

Nonfiction: Primarily publishes nonfiction for the layman in natural history (biology, geology, ecology, astronomy); American Indian (historical and contemporary); outdoor living (backpacking, wild edibles, etc.); crafts and how-to. "Our primary niches are nature and Native American subjects with adult level, non-technical language and scientific accuracy. First, send for our free catalog. Study what kind of books we have already published." Submit outline and 2 sample chapters with SASE.

Recent Title(s): *Guide to California's Freshwater Fishes*, by Bob Madgic; *Greengrass Pipe Dancers, A Story of Crazy Horse's Pipebag*, by Lionel Pinn.

Tips: "Please—always send a stamped reply envelope. Publishers get hundreds of manuscripts yearly; not just yours."

THE NAUTICAL & AVIATION PUBLISHING CO., 1250 Fairmont Ave., Mt. Pleasant SC 29464. (843)856-0561. Fax: (843)856-3164. E-mail: nautical.aviation.publishing@worldnet.att.net. Website: www.sonic.net/~bstone/nautical. **Acquisitions:** Jan Snouck-Hurgronje, editor; Amanda M. McCall, acquisitions editor; Jamie T. Sgubin, copy editor; Pam Gilbert, editor. Estab. 1979. Publishes hardcover originals and reprints. **Publishes 10-12 titles/year. Receives 500 submissions/year. Pays 10-14% royalty on net selling price. Rarely offers advance.** Accepts simultaneous submissions. Book catalog free.

    O— The Nautical & Aviation Publishing Co. publishes military history—fiction and reference.

Nonfiction: Reference. Subjects include history, American wars. Query with synopsis and 3 sample chapters. Reviews artwork/photo as part of package.

Fiction: Historical. Submit outline/synopsis and sample chapters.

Recent Title(s): *Southern Campaigns of the American Revolution*, by Dan Morril (nonfiction); *Celia Garth*, by Gwen Bristow (fiction).

Tips: "We are primarily a nonfiction publisher, but will review historical fiction of military interest of literary merit."

◼ **NAVAL INSTITUTE PRESS**, US Naval Institute, 291 Wood Ave., Annapolis MD 21402-5035. (410)268-6110. Fax: (410)295-1084. E-mail: esecunda@usni.org. Website: www.usni.org. Press Director: Ronald Chambers. **Acquisitions:** Paul Wilderson, executive editor; Tom Cutler, senior acquisitions editor; Eric Mills, acquisitions editor. Estab. 1873. **Publishes 80-90 titles/year. Receives 700-800 submissions/year. 50% of books from first-time authors; 85% from unagented writers. Pays 5-10% royalty on net sales.** Publishes book 1 year after acceptance. Book catalog free with 9×12 SASE. Manuscript guidelines for #10 SASE.

    O— The U.S. Naval Institute Press publishes general and scholarly books of professional, scientific, historical and literary interest to the naval and maritime community.

Imprint(s): Bluejacket Books (paperback reprints).

Nonfiction: "We are interested in naval and maritime subjects and in broad military topics, including government policy and funding. Specific subjects include: tactics, strategy, navigation, history, biographies, aviation, technology and others." Query letter strongly recommended.

Fiction: Limited fiction on military and naval themes.

Recent Title(s): *Dog Company Six*, by Edwin Simmons (fiction).

◼ **NEAL-SCHUMAN PUBLISHERS, INC.**, 100 Varick St., New York NY 10013. (212)925-8650. Fax: (212)219-8916. E-mail: charles@neal-schuman.com. Website: www.neal-schuman.com. **Acquistions:** Charles Harmon, director of publishing. Estab. 1976. Publishes hardcover and trade paperback originals. **Publishes 30 titles/year. Receives 500 submissions/year. 75% of books from first-time authors; 90% from unagented writers. Pays 10% royalty on net sales. Offers advances infrequently.** Publishes book 4 months after acceptance. Responds in 1 month to proposals. *Writer's Market* recommends allowing 2 months for reply. Book catalog and ms guidelines free.

    O— "Neal-Schuman publishes books about libraries, information science and the use of information technology, especially in education and libraries."

Nonfiction: Reference, Internet guides, textbook, texts and professional books in library and information science. "We are looking for many books about the Internet." Submit proposal package, including vita, outline, preface and sample chapters.

Recent Title(s): *Internet Power Searching*, by Phil Bradley.

THOMAS NELSON PUBLISHERS, NelsonWord Publishing Group, Box 141000, Nashville TN 37214-1000. Corporate address does not accept unsolicited mss; no phone queries. **Acquisitions:** Acquisitions Editor. **Publishes 150-200 titles/year. Pays royalty on net sales with rates negotiated for each project.** Publishes books 1-2 years after acceptance. Responds in 3 months. Accepts simultaneous submissions, if so noted.

    O— Thomas Nelson publishes Christian lifestyle nonfiction and fiction.

Imprint(s): Janet Thoma Books, Oliver-Nelson Books.

Nonfiction: Adult inspirational, motivational, devotional, self-help, Christian living, prayer and evangelism, reference/Bible study. Query with SASE, then send brief, prosaic résumé, 1-page synopsis and 1 sample chapter with SASE.

Fiction: Seeking successfully published commercial fiction authors who write for adults from a Christian perspective. Send brief, prosaic résumé, 1-page synopsis and 1 sample chapter with SASE.

Recent Title(s): *Success God's Way*, by Charles Stanley; *The Death of Innocence*, by John and Patsy Ramsey.

TOMMY NELSON, Thomas Nelson, Inc., 404 BNA Dr., Bldg. 200, Suite 508, Nashville TN 37217. Fax: (615)902-2415. Website: www.tommynelson.com. Publishes hardcover and trade paperback originals. **Publishes 50-75 titles/**

year. **Receives 1,000 mss/year. 5% of books from first-time authors; 50% from unagented writers. Pays royalty on wholesale price or makes outright purchase. Pays $1,000 minimum advance.** Publishes book 18 months after acceptance of ms. No simultaneous submissions.

O─ Tommy Nelson publishes children's Christian nonfiction and fiction for boys and girls up to age 14. "We honor God and serve people through books, videos, software and Bibles for children that improve the lives of our customers."

Imprint(s): Word Kids.

Nonfiction: Children's/juvenile. Religious subjects (Christian evangelical). *No unsolicited submissions.*

Fiction: Adventure, juvenile, mystery, picture books, religious. "No stereotypical characters without depth." *No unsolicited submissions.*

Recent Title(s): *50 Money Making Ideas for Kids*, by Allen & Lauree Burkett (money making projects); *Butterfly Kisses*, by Bob Carlisle (father's reflections on daughter).

Tips: "Know the CBA market. Check out the Christian bookstores to see what sells and what is needed."

N **NESHUI PUBLISHING,** 1345 Bellevue, St. Louis MO 63117. (314)905-6942. E-mail: info@neshui.com. Website: www.neshui.com. **Acquisitions:** Bradley Hodge, editor. Publishes trade paperback originals. **Publishes 4 titles/ year. Receives 400 queries and 500 mss/year. 30% of books from first-time authors; 80% from unagented writers. Pays 6-12% royalty on retail price. Offers $500-1,000 advance.** Publishes book 9 months after acceptance of ms. Accepts simultaneous submissions. Responds in 1 month to queries, 2 months to proposals and mss. Book catalog on website. Manuscript guidelines free or on website.

O─ Neshui Publishing is currently emphasizing fiction, pulp, American pop culture.

Nonfiction: Biography, self-help, textbook. Subjects include Americana, creative nonfiction, ethnic, gay/lesbian, government/politics, history, language/literature, memoirs, military/war, philosophy, psychology, religion, science, sex, travel, women's issues/studies. Query with SASE.

Fiction: Adventure, comic books, confession, erotica, ethnic, experimental, fantasy, feminist, gay/lesbian, gothic, hi-Lol, historical, horror, humor, juvenile, literary, mainstream/contemporary, military/war, multicultural, multimedia, mystery, occult, plays, poetry, poetry in translation, regional, religious, romance, science fiction, short story collections, spiritual, suspense, western, young adult. "Please submit on disk." Query with SASE.

Poetry: Query.

Recent Title(s): *The First Step*, by William Jackson (fiction); *Now*, by Nick Luedde (poetry).

Tips: General audience. "Please be positive and we look forward to reading your novel."

A **NEW AMERICAN LIBRARY,** Penguin Putnam Inc., 375 Hudson St., New York NY 10014. (212)366-2000. Website: www.penguin.com. Executive Director: Carolyn Nichols. **Acquisitions:** Ellen Edwards, executive editor (commercial women's fiction—mainstream novels and contemporary romances; mysteries in a series and single title suspense; nonfiction of all types for a general audience); Laura Anne Gilman, executive editor (science fiction/fantasy/horror, mystery series, New Age); Audrey LaFehr, executive editor (contemporary and historical romance, women's suspense, multicultural fiction); Hilary Ross, associate executive editor (romances, Regencies); Doug Grad, senior editor (thrillers, suspense novels, international intrigue, technothrillers, military fiction and nonfiction, adventure nonfiction); Joe Pittman, senior editor (mysteries, suspense, thrillers, horror, commerical fiction); Dan Slater, senior editor (historical fiction, adult westerns, thrillers, military fiction and nonfiction, true crime, media tie-ins); Cecilia Oh, associate editor (romance, Regency, commercial women's fiction, inspirational nonfiction); Genny Ostertag, associate editor (suspense, multicultural commercial fiction, women's fiction). Publishes mass market paperback originals and reprints. **Publishes 500 titles/year. Receives 20,000 queries and 10,000 mss/year. 30-40% of books from first-time authors; 5% from unagented writers. Advance and royalty negotiable.** Publishes book 1-2 years after acceptance of ms. Responds in 6 months.

O─ NAL publishes commercial fiction and nonfiction for the popular audience.

Imprint(s): Mentor, Onyx, **ROC**, Signet, Signet Classic, Signet Reference, Topaz.

Nonfiction: Biography, how-to, reference, self-help. Subjects include animals, child guidance/parenting, cooking/ foods/nutrition, ethnic, health/medicine, language/literature, military/war, money/finance, psychology, sports. "Looking for reference and annual books." *Agented submission only.*

Fiction: Erotica, ethnic, fantasy, historical, horror, literary, mainstream/contemporary, mystery, occult, romance, science fiction, suspense, western. "Looking for writers who can deliver a book a year (or faster) of consistent quality." *Agented submissions only.*

Recent Title(s): *Suspicion of Betrayal*, by Barbara Parker; *The Medusa Stone*, by Jack DuBrul.

THE NEW ENGLAND PRESS, INC., P.O. Box 575, Shelburne VT 05482. (802)863-2520. Fax: (802)863-1510. E-mail: nep@together.net. Website: www.nepress.com. **Acquisitions:** Mark Wanner, managing editor. Publishes hardcover and trade paperback originals. **Publishes 6-8 titles/year. Receives 500 queries and 200 mss/year. 50% of books from first-time authors; 90% from unagented writers. Pays royalty on wholesale price. No advance.** Estab. 1978. Publishes book 15 months after acceptance of ms. Accepts simultaneous submissions. Responds in 3 months. Book catalog free.

O─ The New England Press publishes high-quality trade books of regional northern New England interest. Currently emphasizing young adult historical, Vermont history.

Nonfiction: Biography, young adult, illustrated book. Subjects include nature, history, regional, Vermontiana. "Nonfiction submissions must be based in Vermont and have northern New England topics. No memoirs or family histories. Identify potential markets and ways to reach them in cover letter." Submit outline and 2 sample chapters with SASE. Reviews artwork/photos as part of the ms package. Send photocopies.

Fiction: "We look for very specific subject matters based on Vermont history and heritage. We are also interested in historical novels for young adults based in New Hampshire and Maine. We do not publish contemporary adult fiction of any kind." Submit synopsis and 2 sample chapters with SASE.

Recent Title(s): *Green Mountain Boys of Summer: Vermonters in the Big Leagues, 1882-1993*, by Tom Simon, ed., (nonfiction); *Father by Blood*, by Louella Bryant (fiction).

Tips: "Our readers are interested in all aspects of Vermont and northern New England, including hobbyists (railroad books) and students (young adult fiction and biography). No agent is needed, but our market is extremely specific and our volume is low, so send a query or outline and writing samples first. Sending the whole manuscript is discouraged. We will not accept projects that are still under development or give advances."

NEW HARBINGER PUBLICATIONS, 5674 Shattuck Ave., Oakland CA 94609. (510)652-0215. Fax: (510)652-5472. E-mail: nhelp@newharbinger.com. Website: www.newharbinger.com. **Acquisitions:** Jenli Gastwirth, acquisitions editor (balanced living); Catharine Sutker, acquisitions editor (psychology); Angela Watrors, acquisitions editor (contemporary issues); Kristin Bede, acquisitions manager (human sexuality, parenting). Estab. 1979. **Publishes 40 titles/year. Receives 750 queries and 200 mss/year. 60% of books from first-time authors; 80% from unagented writers. Pays 12% royalty on wholesale price. Offers $0-3,000 advance.** Publishes book 1 year after acceptance of ms. Accepts simultaneous submissions. Responds in 1 month to queries and proposals, 2 months to mss. Book catalog and ms guidelines free.

   O—ⁿ "We look for psychology and health self-help books that teach the average reader how to master essential skills. Our books are also read by mental health professionals who want simple, clear explanations of important psychological techniques and health issues." Currently emphasizing workbooks, contemporary women's issues.

Nonfiction: Self-help (psychology/health), textbooks. Subjects include anger management, anxiety, coping, health/medicine, psychology. "Authors need to be a qualified psychotherapist or health practitioner to publish with us." Submit proposal package, including outline, 3 sample chapters, competing titles and why this one is special.

Recent Title(s): *Why Are We still Fighting?*, by Maureen Lassen; *Multiple Chemical Sensitivity: A Survival Guide*, by Pamela Gibson, Ph.D.

Tips: Audience includes psychotherapists and lay readers wanting step-by-step strategies to solve specific problems. "Our definition of a self-help psychology or health book is one that teaches essential life skills. The primary goal is to train the reader so that, after reading the book, he or she can deal more effectively with problems."

NEW HOPE PUBLISHERS, Division of Woman's Missionary Union, P.O. Box 12065, Birmingham AL 35202-2065. (205)991-8100. Fax: (205)991-4015. E-mail: new_hope@wmu.org. Website: www.newhopepubl.com. **Acquisitions:** Acquisitions Editor. **Publishes 18-24 titles/year. Receives 100 queries and 250 mss/year. 25% of books from first-time authors; 98% from unagented writers. Pays 7-10% royalty on retail price or makes outright purchase.** Publishes book 2 years after acceptance of ms. Responds in 6 months to mss. Book catalog for 9×12 SAE with 3 first-class stamps. Manuscript guidelines for #10 SASE.

   O—ⁿ "Our goal is to provide resources to motivate and equip women to share the hope of Christ."

Imprint(s): New Hope, Woman's Missionary Union.

Nonfiction: How-to, children's/juvenile (religion), personal spiritual growth. Subjects include child guidance/parenting (from Christian perspective), education (Christian church), religion (Christian faith—must relate to missions work, culture and multicultural issues, Christian concerns, Christian ethical issues, spiritual growth, etc.), women's issues/studies from Christian perspective. "We publish Christian education materials that focus on missions work or educational work in some way. Teaching helps, spiritual growth material, ideas for working with different audiences in a church, etc.—missions work overseas or church work in the U.S., women's spiritual issues, guiding children in Christian faith." Submit outline and 3 sample chapters for review. Submit complete ms for acceptance decision.

Recent Title(s): *A Seeking Heart: Rediscovering True Worship*, by Alicia Williamson and Sarah Groves; *Cassie, You're a Winner!*, by Renée Kent.

◪ NEW HORIZON PRESS, P.O. Box 669, Far Hills NJ 07931. (908)604-6311. Fax: (908)604-6330. E-mail: nhp@newhorizonpressbooks.com. Website: www.newhorizonpressbooks.com. **Acquisitions:** Dr. Joan S. Dunphy, publisher (nonfiction, social cause, true crime). Estab. 1983. Publishes hardcover and trade paperback originals. **Publishes 12 titles/year. 90% of books from first-time authors; 50% from unagented writers. Pays standard royalty on net price. Pays advance.** Publishes book 2 years after acceptance of ms. Accepts simultaneous submissions. Book catalog and ms guidelines free.

   O—ⁿ New Horizon publishes adult nonfiction featuring true stories of uncommon heroes, true crime, social issues and self help. Introducing a new line of children's self-help.

Imprints: Small Horizons.

Nonfiction: Biography, children's/juvenile, how-to, self-help. Subjects include child guidance/parenting, creative nonfiction, government/politics, health/medicine, nature/environment, psychology, women's issues/studies, true crime. Submit proposal package, including outline, 3 sample chapters, author bio with photo, résumé and marketing information.

Recent Title(s): *Tainted Roses*, by Margie Danielsen.

Tips: "We are a small publisher, thus it is important that the author/publisher have a good working relationship. The author must be willing to sell his book."

NEW RIVERS PRESS, 420 N. Fifth St., Suite 1180, Minneapolis MN 55401-1384. E-mail: eric@newriverspr ess.org. Website: www.newriverspress.org. **Acquisitions:** Eric Braun, editor. Estab. 1968. Publishes trade paperback originals and occasional jacketed cloth editions. **Publishes 8-10 titles/year. Receives 500 queries and 1,000 mss/year. 95% of books from first-time authors; 99.9% from unagented writers. Pays royalty; pays $500 honoraria for contest winners.** Publishes book 2 years after acceptance. Book catalog free. Send SASE for manuscript guidelines to the Minnesota Voices Project (Minnesota authors only), and the Headwaters Literary Competition (writers from North America). There is a $10 reading fee for Headwaters; no fee for Minnesota Voices.

O— "New Rivers publishes the best poetry, fiction and creative nonfiction from new and emerging writers in our region, nation and world." Currently emphasizing national authorship.

Nonfiction: Creative prose. "We publish memoirs, essay collections, and other forms of creative nonfiction." Query.
Fiction: Literary and short story collections. Query with synopsis and 2 sample chapters.
Poetry: Submit 10-15 sample poems.
Recent Title(s): *Music of the Inner Lakes*, by Roger Sheffer (fiction); *Vendettas, Charms, and Prayers*, by Pamela Gemin (poetry).

NEW VICTORIA PUBLISHERS, P.O. Box 27, Norwich VT 05055-0027. Phone/fax: (802)649-5297. E-mail: newvic@aol.com. Website: www.opendoor.com/NewVic/. **Acquisitions:** Claudia Lamperti, editor; ReBecca Béguin, editor. Estab. 1976. Publishes trade paperback originals. **Publishes 8-10 titles/year. Receives 100 submissions/ year. 50% of books from first-time authors; most books from unagented writers. Pays 10% royalty.** Publishes book 1 year after acceptance. Responds to queries in 1 month. Book catalog free.

O— "New Victoria is a nonprofit literary and cultural organization producing the finest in lesbian fiction and nonfiction." Emphasizing fantasy. De-emphasizing coming-of-age stories.

Nonfiction: History. "We are interested in feminist history or biography and interviews with or topics relating to lesbians. No poetry." Submit outline and sample chapters.
Fiction: Adventure, erotica, fantasy, historical, humor, mystery, romance, science fiction, western. "We will consider most anything if it is well written and appeals to lesbian/feminist audience." Submit outline/synopsis and sample chapters. "Hard copy only—no disks."
Recent Title(s): *Queer Japan*, by Barbara Summerhawk (nonfiction); *Talk Show*, by Melissa Hartman (fiction).
Tips: "Try to appeal to a specific audience and not write for the general market. We're still looking for well-written, hopefully humorous, lesbian fiction and well-researched biography or nonfiction."

NEW WORLD LIBRARY, 14 Pamaron Way, Novato CA 94949. (415)884-2100. Fax: (415)884-2199. E-mail: escort@ nwlib.com. Website: www.nwlib.com. Publisher: Marc Allen. **Acquisitions:** Georgia Hughes, editorial director; Jason Gardner, managing editor. Estab. 1979. Publishes hardcover and trade paperback originals and reprints. **Publishes 35 titles/year. 10% of books from first-time authors; 50% from unagented writers. Pays 12-16% royalty on wholesale price for paperback; 12-20% royalty on wholesale price for hardcover. Offers $0-200,000 advance.** Publishes book 18 months after acceptance of ms. Accepts simultaneous submissions. Responds in 2 months. Book catalog and ms guidelines free.

O— NWL is dedicated to publishing books that inspire and challenge us to improve the quality of our lives and our world. Currently emphasizing illustrated books, natural health, parenting.

Imprint(s): Nataraj.
Nonfiction: Gift book, self-help. Subjects include business/prosperity, cooking/foods/nutrition, ethnic (African-American, Native American), money/finance, nature/environment, personal growth, parenting, natural health, psychology, religion, women's issues/studies. Query or submit outline, 1 sample chapter and author bio with SASE. Reviews artwork/ photos as part of ms package. Send photocopies.
Recent Title(s): *The Power of Now*, by Eckhart Tolle; *The Mystic Heart*, by Wayne Teasdale.

NEW YORK UNIVERSITY PRESS, 838 Broadway, New York NY 10003. (212)998-2575. Fax: (212)995-3833. Website: www.nyupress.nyu.edu. **Acquisitions:** Eric Zinner (cultural studies, literature, media, anthropology); Jennifer Hammer (Jewish studies, psychology, religion, women's studies); Niko Pfund (business, history, law); Stephen Magro (social sciences). Estab. 1916. Publishes hardcover and trade paperback originals. **Publishes 150 titles/year. Receives 800-1,000 queries/year. 30% of books from first-time authors; 90% from unagented writers. Advance and royalty on net receipts varies by project.** Publishes book 8 months after acceptance of ms. Accepts simultaneous submissions. Responds in 1 month to proposals (peer reviewed).

O— New York University Press embraces ideological diversity. "We often publish books on the same issue from different poles to generate dialogue, engender and resist pat categorizations."

Nonfiction: Subjects include anthropology/archaeology, art/architecture, business/economics, computers/electronics, education, ethnic, gay/lesbian, government/politics, health/medicine, history, language/literature, military/war, money/ finance, music/dance, nature/environment, philosophy, photography, psychology, regional, religion, sociology, sports, travel, women's issues/studies. Submit proposal package, including outline, 1 sample chapter and with SASE. Reviews artwork/photos as part of the ms package. Send photocopies.
Fiction and Poetry: Publishes *only* contest winners for the NYU Press Prizes.

Recent Title(s): *Kosovo: A Short History*, by Noel Malcolm.

N: NICHOLS PUBLISHING, P.O. Box 6036, E. Brunswick NJ 08816. (732)297-2862. Fax: (732)940-0549. Vice President and Publisher: Fran Van Dalen. **Acquisitions:** Fran Lubrano, editorial director. Estab. 1979. Publishes hardcover and paperback originals. Publishes 50 titles/year. 15% of books from first-time authors; 98% from unagented writers. Pays 5-15% royalty on wholesale price. Offers $300-500 average advance. Publishes book 9 months after acceptance. Simultaneous submissions OK. Responds to queries in 1 month. *Writer's Market* recommends allowing 2 months for reply. Book catalog free.

O→ Nichols publishes training and management reference books.

Nonfiction: Reference, technical. Subjects include management, education, training. Submit outline and sample chapters. "We need more books on training."

Recent Title(s): *Assembling Course Materials*, by Nicolay and Barrett.

Tips: "No longer seeking books on architecture, computers/electronics, or engineering."

NO STARCH PRESS, 555 Dettaro St., Suite 250, San Francisco CA 94107. (415)863-9900. Fax: (415)863-9950. E-mail: info@nostarch.com. Website: www.nostarch.com. **Acquisitions:** William Pollock, publisher. Estab. 1994. **Publishes trade paperback originals. Publishes 10-12 titles/year. Receives 100 queries and 5 mss/year. 80% of books from first-time authors; 90% from unagented writers. Pays 10-15% royalty on wholesale price.** Publishes book 4 months after acceptance of ms. Accepts simultaneous submissions. Book catalog free.

O→ No Starch Press publishes informative, easy to read computer books for non-computer people to help them get the most from their hardware and software. Currently emphasizing Linux and trade nonfiction related to the technology business and/or cyberculture.

Imprint(s): Linux Journal Press.

Nonfiction: How-to, reference, technical. Subjects include computers/electronics, Linux, software. Submit outline, 1 sample chapter, bio, market rationale. Reviews artwork/photos as part of ms package. Send photocopies.

Recent Title(s): *The No B.S. Guide to Red Hut Linux 6*, by Bob Rankin; *Astronomer's Computer Companion*, by Jeff Foust and Ron Lafen.

Tips: "No fluff—content, content, content or just plain fun. Understand how your book fits into the market. Tell us why someone, anyone, will buy your book. Be enthusiastic."

N: NOLO.COM, (formerly Nolo Press), 950 Parker St., Berkeley CA 94710. (510)549-1976. Fax: (510)548-5902. E-mail: info@nolo.com. Website: www.nolo.com. **Acquisitions:** Barbara Kate Repa, senior editor. Estab. 1971. Publishes trade paperback originals. **Publishes 25 titles/year. 10% of books from first-time authors; 98% from unagented writers. Pays 10-12% royalty on net sales.** Accepts simultaneous submissions. Responds within 2 weeks to queries.

O→ "Our goal is to publish 'plain English' self-help law books, software and various electronic products for consumers."

Nonfiction: How-to, reference, self-help. Subjects include legal guides in various topics including employment, consumer, small business, intellectual property landlord/tenant and estate planning. "We do some business and finance titles, but always from a legal perspective, i.e., bankruptcy law." Query with outline, 1 sample chapter and SASE. Welcome queries but majority of titles are produced inhouse.

Recent Title(s): *Avoid Employee Lawsuits*, by Barbara Kate Repa; *Using Divorce Mediation*, by Katherine E. Stoner.

NORTH LIGHT BOOKS, F&W Publications, 1507 Dana Ave., Cincinnati OH 45207. Editorial Director: Greg Albert. **Acquisitions:** Acquisitions Coordinator. Publishes hardcover and trade paperback how-to books. **Publishes 40-45 titles/year. Pays 10% royalty on net receipts. Offers $4,000 advance.** Accepts simultaneous submissions. Responds in 1 month. Book catalog for 9×12 SAE with 6 first-class stamps.

O→ North Light Books publishes art, craft and design books, including watercolor, drawing, colored pencil and decorative painting titles that emphasize illustrated how-to art instruction. Currently emphasizing table-top crafts using materials found in craft stores like Michael's, Hobby Lobby.

Nonfiction: Watercolor, drawing, colored pencil, decorative painting, craft and graphic design instruction books. Interested in books on watercolor painting, basic drawing, pen and ink, colored pencil, decorative painting, table-top crafts, basic design, computer graphics, layout and typography. Do not submit coffee table art books without how-to art instruction. Query or submit outline and examples of artwork (transparencies and photographs).

Recent Title(s): *Crafting Your Own Heritage Album*, by Bev Kirschner Braun.

NORTH POINT PRESS, Farrar Straus & Giroux, Inc., 19 Union Square W., New York NY 10003. (212)741-6900. Fax: (212)633-9385. Editorial Director: Rebecca Saletan. Editor: Ethan Nosowsky. **Acquisitions:** Katrin Wilde. Estab. 1980. Hardcover and trade paperback originals. **Publishes 25 titles/year. Receives hundreds of queries and hundreds of mss/year. 20% of books from first-time authors. Pays standard royalty rates. Advance varies.** Publishes book 18 months after acceptance of ms. Accepts simultaneous submissions. Responds in 2 months to queries and proposals, 3 months to mss. Manuscript guidelines for #10 SAE.

O→ "We are a broad-based literary trade publisher—high quality writing only."

Nonfiction: Subjects include nature/environment, food/gardening, history, religion (no New Age), music, memoir/biography, sports, travel. "Be familiar with our list. No genres." Query with outline, 1-2 sample chapters and SASE.

Recent Title(s): *Tigers in the Snow*, by Peter Matthiessen; *My Kitchen Wars*, by Betty Fussell.

NORTHEASTERN UNIVERSITY PRESS, 360 Huntington Ave., 416CP, Boston MA 02115. (617)373-5480. Fax: (617)373-5483. Website: www.neu.edu/nupress. **Acquisitions**: William Frohlich, director (music, criminal justice); John Weingartner, senior editor (history, law and society); Elizabeth Swayze, editor (women's studies). Estab. 1977. Publishes hardcover originals and trade paperback originals and reprints. **Publishes 40 titles/year. Receives 500 queries and 100 mss/year. 50% of books from first-time authors; 90% from unagented writers. Pays 5-15% royalty on wholesale price. Offers $500-5,000 advance.** Publishes book 1 year after acceptance of ms. Accepts simultaneous submissions. Responds in 1 month. Book catalog and ms guidelines free.

    ○⊸ Northeastern University Press publishes scholarly and general interest titles in the areas of American history, criminal justice, law and society, women's studies, African-American literature, ethnic studies and music. Currently emphasizing American studies. De-emphasizing literary studies.

Nonfiction: Biography, adult trade scholarly monographs. Subjects include Americana, criminal justice, ethnic, law/society, history, memoirs, music/dance, regional, women's issues/studies. Query or submit proposal package, including outline, 1-2 sample chapters and SASE. Reviews artwork/photos as part of ms package. Send photocopies.

Fiction: Literary. Majority of fiction titles are reissues. Query.

Recent Title(s): *The Diary of Alice James*, by Alice James; *The Northeastern Dictionary of Women's Biography*, by Jennifer S. Uglow.

NORTHERN ILLINOIS UNIVERSITY PRESS, 310 N. Fifth St., DeKalb IL 60115-2854. (815)753-1826/753-1075. Fax: (815)753-1845. **Acquisitions**: Mary L. Lincoln, director/editor-in-chief; Martin Johnson, acquisitions editor (history, politics). Estab. 1965. **Publishes 18-20 titles/year. Pays 10-15% royalty on wholesale price.** Book catalog free.

    ○⊸ NIU Press publishes both specialized scholarly work and books of general interest to the informed public. "We publish mainly history, politics, anthropology, and other social sciences. We are interested also in studies on the Chicago area and midwest and on literature in translation." Currently emphasizing literature in translation. De-emphasizing literary criticism.

Nonfiction: "Publishes mainly history, political science, social sciences, philosophy, literary criticism and regional studies. No collections of previously published essays, no unsolicited poetry." Accepts nonfiction translations. Query with outline and 1-3 sample chapters.

Recent Title(s): *A Birder's Guide to the Chicago Region*, by Lynne Carpenter and Joel Greenberg.

NORTHFIELD PUBLISHING, Moody Press, 215 W. Locust St., Chicago IL 60610. (800)678-8001. Fax: (312)329-2019. **Acquisitions**: Acquisitions Coordinator. **Publishes 5-10 titles/year. Less than 1% of books from first-time authors; 95% from unagented writers. Pays royalty on net receipts. Offers $500-50,000 advance.** Publishes books 1 year after acceptance of ms. Accepts simultaneous submissions, but prefers not to. Responds in 2 months to queries. Book catalog for 9×12 SAE with 2 first-class stamps. Manuscript guidelines for #10 SASE.

    ○⊸ "Northfield publishes a line of books for non-Christians or those exploring the Christian faith. While staying true to Biblical principles, we eliminate some of the Christian wording and scriptual references to avoid confusion."

Nonfiction: Biographies (classic). Subjects include business/economics, child guidance/parenting, finance. Query with outline, 2-3 sample chapters, table of contents, author's market study of why this book will be successful and SASE.

Recent Title(s): *The Five Love Languages of Teens*, by Gary Chapman.

NORTHLAND PUBLISHING CO., INC., P.O. Box 1389, Flagstaff AZ 86002-1389. (520)774-5251. Fax: (520)774-0592. E-mail: editorial@northlandpub.com. Website: www.northlandpub.com. **Acquisitions:** Brad Melton, adult editor (Native American and Western history, popular culture, lifestyle and cookery); Aimee Jackson, kids editor (picture books, especially humor). Estab. 1958. Publishes hardcover and trade paperback originals. **Publishes 25 titles/year. Imprint publishes 10-12 titles/year. Receives 4,000 submissions/year. Adult list: 25% from first-time authors; 75% from unagented writers. Children's list: 20% from first-time authors; 20% from unagented writers. Pays royalty on net and list receipts. Offers advance.** Publishes book 2 years after acceptance. Accepts simultaneous submissions. Responds in 3 months. Call for book catalog and ms guidelines.

    ○⊸ "Northland has an excellent reputation for publishing quality nonfiction books that emphasize the American West. Our strengths include Native American and Western history, culture, art and cookbooks. Under our imprint, Rising Moon, we publish picture books for children, with universal themes and national appeal." Currently emphasizing popular culture, lifestyle, cookery, regional sports and women's history. De-emphasizing natural history.

Imprint(s): Rising Moon (books for young readers).

Nonfiction: Biography, children's/juvenile, coffee table book, cookbook, gift book. Subjects include anthropology/archaeology (Native America), art/architecture, cooking/foods/nutrition (cookbooks, Southwest), ethnic (Native Americans, Hispanic), popular culture (film, nostalgia), history (natural, military and Native American), hobbies (collecting/arts), nature/environment (picture books), regional (Southwestern and Western US). Submit outline and 2-3 sample chapters with SASE. No fax or e-mail submissions. Reviews artwork/photos as part of the ms package. "Artwork should be sent to the Art Director unless it is critical to understanding the proposal."

Fiction: Picture books. Send complete manuscript with SASE.

Recent Title(s): *Cinema Southwest: An Illustrated Guide to the Movies and their Locations*, by John Murray (adult); *Jane vs. the Tooth Fairy*, by Betsy Jay (children's).

Tips: "Our audience is composed of general interest readers."

N A NORTH-SOUTH BOOKS, Nord-Sud Verlag AG, 1123 Broadway, Suite 800, New York NY 10010. (212)463-9736. **Acquisitions:** Julie Amper. Website: www.northsouth.com. Estab. 1985. **Publishes 100 titles/year. Receives 5,000 queries/year. 5% of books from first-time authors. Pays royalty on retail price.** Publishes book an average of 2 years after acceptance of ms. Returns submissions accompanied by SASE "but is very low priority." Does not respond unless interested.

> O─ "The aim of North-South is to build bridges—bridges between authors and artists from different countries and between readers of all ages. We believe children should be exposed to as wide a range of artistic styles as possible with universal themes."

Fiction: Picture books, easy-to-read. "We are currently accepting only picture books; all other books are selected by our German office." *Agented submissions only. All unsolicited mss returned unopened.*

Recent Title(s): *The Rainbow Fish & the Big Blue Whale*, by Marcus Pfister (picture).

NORTHWORD PRESS, Creative Publishing International, Inc., 5900 Green Oak Dr., Minnetonka MN 55343. (612)936-4700. Fax: (612)933-1456. **Acquisitions:** Barbara K. Harold, editorial director. Estab. 1984. Publishes hardcover and trade paperback originals. **Publishes 15-20 titles/year. Receives 600 submissions/year. 50% of books are from first-time authors; 90% are from unagented writers. Pays 10-15% royalty on wholesale price. Offers $2,000-20,000 advance.** Publishes book 1 year after acceptance. Accepts simultaneous submissions. Responds in 3 months to queries. Book catalog for 9×12 SASE with 7 first-class stamps. Manuscript guidelines for SASE.

> O─ NorthWord Press publishes exclusively nature and wildlife titles for adults, teens, and children.

Nonfiction: Coffee table books, introductions to wildlife and natural history, guidebooks, children's illustrated books; nature and wildlife subjects exclusively. Query with outline, sample chapters and SASE.

Recent Title(s): *Daybreak 2000*, by Roger Tefft; *Greenland Expedition*, by Lonnie Dupre.

Tips: "No poetry, fiction or memoirs. We have expanded to include exotic and non-North American topics."

W.W. NORTON CO., INC., 500 Fifth Ave., New York NY 10110. Fax: (212)869-0856. Website: www.wwnorton.com. **Acquisitions:** Starling Lawrence, editor-in-chief; Robert Weil, executive editor; Edwin Barber; Jill Bialosky (literary fiction, biography, memoirs); Amy Cherry (history, biography, women's issues, African-American, health); Carol Houck-Smith (literary fiction, travel memoirs, behavioral sciences, nature); Angela von der Leppe (trade nonfiction, behavioral sciences, earth sciences, astronomy, neuro-science, education); Jim Mairs (history, biography, illustrated books); Alane Mason (serious nonfiction cultural and intellectual history, illustrated books, literary fiction and memoir); W. Drake McFeely, president (nonfiction, particularly science and social science). Estab. 1923. Publishes hardcover and paperback originals and reprints. **Publishes 300 titles/year. Pays royalty.** Responds in 2 months.

> O─ General trade publisher of fiction, poetry and nonfiction, educational and professional books. "W. W. Norton Co. strives to carry out the imperative of its founder to 'publish books not for a single season, but for the years' in the areas of fiction, nonfiction and poetry."

Imprint(s): Backcountry Publication, Countryman Press, W.W. Norton.

Nonfiction and Fiction: Subjects include antiques and collectibles, architecture, art/design, autobiography/memoir, biography, business, child care, cooking, current affairs, family, fiction, games, health, history, law, literature, music, mystery, nature, nautical topics, photography, poetry, politics/political science, reference, religion, sailing, science, self-help, transportation, travel. *College Department:* Subjects include biological sciences, economics, psychology, political science, and computer science. *Professional Books* specializes in psychotherapy. "We are not interested in considering books from the following categories: juvenile or young adult, religious, occult or paranormal, genre fiction (formula romances, sci-fi or westerns), and arts and crafts. Please give a brief description of your submission, your writing credentials, and any experience, professional or otherwise, which is relevant to your submission. Submit 2 or 3 sample chapters, one of which should be the first chapter, with SASE. No phone calls. Address envelope and letter to The Editors."

Recent Title(s): *Hitler*, by Ian Kershaw (nonfiction); *Voyage of the Narwhal*, by Andrea Barrett (fiction).

NTC/CONTEMPORARY PUBLISHING GROUP, 4255 W. Touhy Ave., Lincolnwood IL 60712. (847)679-5500. Fax: (847)679-2494. E-mail: ntcpub2@aol.com. Vice President and Publisher-Trade Division: John T. Nolan. **Acquisitions:** Danielle Egan-Miller, business editor; Rob Taylor, associate editor; Denise Betts, assistant editor; Betsy Lancefield, senior editor. Estab. 1947. Publishes hardcover originals and trade paperback originals and reprints. **Publishes 850 titles/year. Receives 9,000 submissions/year. 10% of books from first-time authors; 25% of books from unagented writers. Pays 6-15% royalty on retail price.** Publishes book 1 year after acceptance. Accepts simultaneous submissions. Responds in 2 months. Manuscript guidelines for SASE.

> O─ "We are a midsize, niche-oriented, backlist-oriented publisher. We publish exclusively nonfiction in general interest trade categories plus travel, reference and quilting books."

Imprint(s): Contemporary Books, Country Roads Press, Keats Publishing, **Lowell House, Masters Press,** NTC Business Books, **NTC Publishing Group, National Textbook Company,** Passport Books, Peter Bedrick Books, **The Quilt Digest Press, VGM Career Horizons.**

Nonfiction: Cookbooks, how-to, reference, self-help. Subjects include business, careers, child guidance/parenting, crafts (especially quilting), marketing and advertising, cooking, health/fitness, nutrition, pet care, popular culture, psychology, sports, travel. Submit outline, sample chapters and SASE. Reviews artwork/photos as part of ms package.

Recent Title(s): *The Fondue Cookbook*, by Gina Steer; *Tales from the Ballpark*, by Mike Shannon.

OAK KNOLL PRESS, 310 Delaware St., New Castle DE 19720. (302)328-7232. Fax: (302)328-7274. E-mail: oakknoll @oakknoll.com. Website: www.oakknoll.com. **Acquisitions:** Editor. Estab. 1976. Publishes hardcover and trade paperback originals and reprints. **Publishes 35 titles/year. Receives 100 queries and 100 mss/year. 50% of books from first-time authors; 100% from unagented writers. Pays 10% royalty on income.** Publishes book 18 months after acceptance of ms. Accepts simultaneous submissions. Responds in 1 month to queries. *Writer's Market* recommends allowing 2 months for reply. Book catalog free.

    O─┐ Oak Knoll specializes in books about books—preserving the art and lore of the printed word.

Nonfiction: Book arts. Subjects include printing, papermaking, bookbinding, book collecting, etc. Query. Reviews artwork/photos as part of ms package. Send photocopies.

Recent Title(s): *Historical Scripts*, by Stan Knight; *Printing on the Iron Handpress*, by Richard-Gabriel Rummonds.

OASIS PRESS, PSI Research, 300 N. Valley Dr. Grants Pass OR 97526, Grants Pass OR 97526. (503)479-9464. Fax: (503)476-1479. **Acquisitions:** Emmett Ramey, president. Estab. 1975. Publishes hardcover, trade paperback and binder originals. **Publishes 20-30 books/year. Receives 90 submissions/year. 60% of books from first-time authors; 90% from unagented writers. Pays 10% royalty on the net received, except wholesale sales. No advance.** Publishes book 6 months after acceptance. Accepts simultaneous submissions. Responds in 2 months (initial feedback) to queries. Book catalog and ms guidelines for SASE.

    O─┐ Oasis Press publishes books for small business or individuals who are entrepreneurs or owners or managers of small businesses (1-300 employees).

Imprint(s): Hellgate Press.

Nonfiction: How-to, reference, textbook. Subjects include business/economics, computers, education, money/finance, retirement, exporting, franchise, finance, marketing/public relations, relocations, environment, taxes, business start up and operation. Needs information-heavy, readable mss written by professionals in their subject fields. Interactive where appropriate. Authorship credentials less important than hands-on experience qualifications. Query for unwritten material or to check current interest in topic and orientation. Submit outline/synopsis and sample chapters. Reviews artwork/photos as part of ms package.

Recent Title(s): *Before You Go Into Business, Read This*, by Ira Nottonson.

Tips: "Best chance is with practical, step-by-step manuals for operating a business, with worksheets, checklists. The audience is made up of entrepreneurs of all types: small business owners and those who would like to be; attorneys, accountants and consultants who work with small businesses; college students; dreamers. Make sure your information is valid and timely for its audience, also that by virtue of either its content quality or viewpoint, it distinguishes itself from other books on the market."

OHIO STATE UNIVERSITY PRESS, 1070 Carmack Rd., Columbus OH 43210. (614)292-6930. Fax: (614)292-2065. E-mail: ohiostatepress@osu.edu. Website: www.ohiostatepress.org. **Acquisitions:** Malcolm Litchfield, director. Estab. 1957. **Publishes 30 titles/year. Pays royalty.** Responds in 3 months; ms held longer with author's permission.

    O─┐ Ohio State University Press publishes scholarly nonfiction, and offers short fiction and short poetry prizes. Currently emphasizing criminal justice and American history. De-emphasizing political science and European studies.

Nonfiction: Scholarly studies with special interests in business and economics, American history, criminology, literary criticism, political science, regional studies, women's studies, women's health. Query with outline and sample chapters and SASE.

Recent Title(s): *Seasoning: A Poet's Year*, by David Young (memoir); *Women Drinking Benedictine*, by Sharon Dilworth.

Tips: "Publishes some poetry and fiction in addition to the prizes. Query first."

OHIO UNIVERSITY PRESS, Scott Quadrangle, Athens OH 45701. (740)593-1155. Fax: (740)593-4536. Website: www.ohiou.edu/oupress/. **Acquisitions:** Gillian Berchowitz, senior editor (contemporary history, African studies, Appalachian studies); David Sanders, director (literature, literary criticism, midwest and frontier studies, Ohioana). Estab. 1964. Publishes hardcover and trade paperback originals and reprints. **Publishes 45-50 titles/year. Receives 500 queries and 50 mss/year. 20% of books from first-time authors; 95% from unagented writers. Pays 7-10% royalty on net sales. No advance.** Publishes book 1 year after acceptance of ms. Responds in 1 month to queries and proposals, 2 months to mss. Book catalog free. Manuscript guidelines for #10 SASE.

    O─┐ Ohio University Press publishes and disseminates the fruits of research and creative endeavor, specifically in the areas of literary studies, regional works, philosophy, contemporary history, African studies and frontier Americana. Its charge to produce books of value in service to the academic community and for the enrichment of the broader culture is in keeping with the university's mission of teaching, research and service to its constituents.

Imprint(s): Ohio University Monographs in International Studies (Gillian Berchowitz); Swallow Press (David Sanders, director).

Nonfiction: Biography, reference, scholarly. Subjects include African studies, agriculture/horticulture, Americana, animals, anthropology/archaeology, art/architecture, ethnic, gardening, government/politics, history, language/literature, military/war, nature/environment, philosophy, regional, sociology, travel, women's issues/studies. Query with proposal package, including outline, sample chapter and SASE. "We prefer queries or detailed proposals, rather than manuscripts, pertaining to scholarly projects that might have a general interest. Proposals should explain the thesis and details of the subject matter, not just sell a title." Reviews artwork/photos as part of ms package. Send photocopies.

Recent Title(s): *Amy Levy: Her Life and Letters*, by Linda Hurt Beckman; *Broken English*, by P.L. Gaos.

Tips: "Rather than trying to hook the editor on your work, let the material be compelling enough and well-presented enough to do it for you."

THE OLIVER PRESS, INC., 5707 W. 36th St., Minneapolis MN 55416-2510. (952)926-8981. Fax: (952)926-8965. E-mail: queries@oliverpress.com. Website: www.oliverpress.com. **Acquisitions:** Denise Sterling, editor. Estab. 1991. Publishes hardcover originals. **Publishes 10 titles/year. Receives 100 queries and 20 mss/year. 10% of books from first-time authors; 100% from unagented writers.** Publishes book up to 2 years after acceptance of ms. Accepts simultaneous submissions. Responds in 2 months to queries. Book catalog for 9×12 SAE with 4 first-class stamps. Manuscript guidelines for #10 SASE.

   O→ "We publish collective biographies for ages 10 and up. Although we cover a wide array of subjects, all are published in this format." Currently emphasizing subjects connected to school curriculum; history of technology.

Nonfiction: Children's/juvenile collective biographies only. Subjects include business/economics, ethnic, government/politics, health/medicine, military/war, nature/environment, science. Query with SASE.

Recent Title(s): *Explorers, Missionaries, and Trappers: Trailblazers of the West*, by Kieron Doherty.

Tips: "Audience is primarily junior and senior high school students writing reports."

ONE ON ONE COMPUTER TRAINING, Mosaic Media, 2055 Army Trail Rd., Suite 100, Addison IL 60101. (630)628-0500. Fax: (630)628-0550. E-mail: oneonone@pincom.com. Website: www.oootraining.com. **Acquisitions:** Natalie Young, manager product development. Estab. 1976. **Publishes 10-20 titles/year. 100% of material from unagented writers. Pays 5-10% royalty (rarely) or makes outright purchase of $3,500-10,000. Advance depends on purchase contract.** Publishes book 3 months after acceptance of ms. Responds in 1 month. Catalog free.

   O→ OneOnOne Computer Training publishes computer training in newsletter and CD-Rom formats. Currently emphasizing soft skills for IT professionals, as well as programming.

Imprint(s): OneOnOne Computer Training.

Nonfiction: How-to, self-help, technical. Subjects include computers, software, IT, Internet programming, software certification and computer security. Query. All unsolicited mss returned unopened.

Recent Title(s): *Working Smarter With the Internet*; *Best Practices in IT Management*.

ONJINJINKTA PUBLISHING, The Betty J. Eadie Press, 909 S.E. Everett Mall Way, Everett WA 98208. Fax: (425)290-7809. E-mail: peter@onjinjinkta.com. Website: www.onjinjinkta.com. **Acquisitions:** Peter Orullian, senior editor; Bret Sable, associate editor. Publishes hardcover, trade paperback and mass market paperback originals and reprints. **Publishes 8-12 titles/year; imprint publishes 4-6 titles/year. Receives 2,000 queries and 600 mss/year. 50% of books from first-time authors; 80% from unagented writers. Pays 5-15% royalty on retail price. Offers $1,000-10,000 advance.** Publishes book 18 months after acceptance of ms. Accepts simultaneous submissions. Responds in 2 months to queries and proposals, 3 months to mss. Manuscript guidelines for #10 SASE.

   O→ Onjinjinkta publishes the future work of Betty Eadie (*Embraced by the Light*) and inspirational works by other writers.

Imprint(s): Wanbli Publishing (contact Peter Orullian, editor)

Nonfiction: Children's/juvenile, humor, self-help. Subjects include Americana, creative nonfiction, military/war, music/dance, nature/environment, regional, religion, spirituality. Submit proposal package, including outline, 1 sample chapter, author bio and SASE.

Fiction: Adventure, fantasy, horror, humor, mainstream/contemporary, military/war, mystery, regional, religious, science fiction, spiritual, suspense. Submit proposal package including synopsis, 1 sample chapter and author bio.

Poetry: Query.

Recent Title(s): *The Ripple Effect*, by Betty J. Eadie; *Jack & Jill, Why They Kill: Saving Our Children, Saving Ourselves*, by James E. Shaw, Ph.D.

Tips: "Nonfiction audience is thoughtful, hopeful individuals who seek self-awareness. Fiction audience is readers who desire to be engaged in the high art of escapism. We can only publish a short list each year; your book must target its market forcefully, and its story must express and invoke fresh ideas on the ancient themes."

⟦N⟧ OPEN ROAD PUBLISHING, P.O. Box 284, Cold Spring Harbor NY 11724. (516)692-7172. Fax: (516)692-7193. E-mail: Jopenroad@aol.com. Website: openroadpub.com. **Acquisitions:** Jonathan Stein, publisher; Dillard Bentwright, acquisitions editor. Publishes trade paperback originals. **Publishes 22-27 titles/year. Receives 100 queries and 50 mss/year. 30% of books from first-time authors; 98% from unagented writers. Pays 5-6% royalty on retail price. Offers $1,000-5,000 advance.** Publishes book 3 months after acceptance of ms. Accepts simultaneous submissions. Responds in 1 month to queries, 2 months to proposals. Book catalog and ms guidelines free.

   O→ Open Road publishes travel guides.

Nonfiction: How-to. Subjects include travel. Query with SASE. No unsolicited mss.

Recent Title(s): *China Guide*, by Ruth Lor Malloy; *Arizona Guide*, by Larry Ludmer.

ORANGE FRAZER PRESS, INC., 37½ W. Main St., P.O. Box 214, Wilmington OH 45177. (937)382-3196. Fax: (937)383-3159. Website: www.orangefrazer.com. **Acquisitions:** John Baskin, editor (Ohio sports, Ohio history); Marcy Hawley, editor (Ohio reference, Ohio travel). Publishes hardcover and trade paperback originals and reprints. **Publishes 10 titles/year. Receives 50 queries and 40 mss/year. 50% of books from first-time authors; 99% from unagented writers. Pays 10-12% royalty on wholesale price.** Publishes book 18 months after acceptance of ms. Accepts simultaneous submissions. Responds in 2 months to queries, 1 month to proposals and mss. Book catalog free.
Nonfiction: Biography, coffee table book, cookbook, gift book, humor, illustrated book, reference, textbook. Subjects include art/architecture, cooking/foods/nutrition, education, history, memoirs, nature/environment, photography, recreation, regional (Ohio), sports, travel, women's issues/women's studies. Submit proposal package, including outline, 1 sample chapter and SASE. Reviews artwork/photos as part of ms package. Send photocopies or transparencies.
Recent Title(s): *The Notion of Family*, by Eleanor Mallet.

ORCHARD BOOKS, Grolier, 95 Madison Ave., New York NY 10016. (212)951-2600. Fax: (212)213-6435. E-mail: jwilson@Grolier.com. Website: www.grolier.com. President/Publisher: Judy V. Wilson. **Acquisitions:** Rebecca Davis, senior editor; Ana Cerro, editor; Lisa Hammond, assistant editor; Tamson Weston, assistant editor. Estab. 1987. Publishes hardcover and trade paperback originals. **Publishes 60-70 titles/year. Receives 3,000 queries/year. 25% of books from first-time authors; 50% from unagented writers. Pays 6-10% royalty on retail price. Advance varies.** Publishes book 1 year after acceptance of ms. Responds in 3 months to queries.
> O➤ Orchard specializes in children's picture books. Currently emphasizing picture books and middle grade novels (ages 8-12). De-emphasizing young adult.
Nonfiction: Children's/juvenile, illustrated book. Subjects include animals, history, nature/environment. Query with SASE. *"No unsolicited mss at this time. Queries only! Be as specific and enlightening as possible about your book."* Reviews artwork/photos as part of the ms package. Send photocopies.
● Grolier was recently purchased by Scholastic, Inc.
Fiction: Picture books, young adult, middle reader, board book, novelty. Query with SASE. *No unsolicited mss, please.*
Recent Title(s): *Wolf!*, by Bloom and Piet; *Mouse in Love*, by Aruego and Dewey.
Tips: "Go to a bookstore and read several Orchard Books to get an idea of what we publish. Write what you feel and query us if you think it's 'right.' It's worth finding the right publishing match."

OREGON STATE UNIVERSITY PRESS, 101 Waldo Hall, Corvallis OR 97331-6407. (541)737-3166. Fax: (541)737-3170. Website: http://osu.orst.edu/dept/press. **Acquisitions:** Mary Braun, acquiring editor. Estab. 1965. Publishes hardcover and paperback originals. **Publishes 15-20 titles/year. Receives 100 submissions/year. 75% of books from first-time authors; 100% of books from unagented writers. Pays royalty on net receipts. No advance.** Publishes book 1 year after acceptance. Responds in 3 months. Book catalog and ms guidelines available via website or upon request with 2 first-class stamps and 6×9 SAE.
> O➤ Oregon State University Press publishes several scholarly and specialized books and books of particular importance to the Pacific Northwest. "OSU Press plays an essential role by publishing books that may not have a large audience, but are important to scholars, students and librarians in the region."
Nonfiction: Publishes scholarly books in history, biography, geography, literature, natural resource management, with strong emphasis on Pacific or Northwestern topics. Submit outline and sample chapters.
Recent Title(s): *Tongrass: Pulp Politics and the Fight for the Alaska Rain Forest*, by Kathie Durbin.
Tips: Send for an authors' guidelines pamphlet.

ORYX PRESS, 4041 N. Central Ave., Suite 700, Phoenix AZ 85012. (602)265-2651. Fax: (602)265-6250. E-mail: info@oryxpress.com. Website: www.oryxpress.com. President: Phyllis B. Steckler. **Acquisitions:** Donna Sanzone, Eleanora Von Dehsen, Henry Rasof, acquisitions editors; Martha Wilke (submission). Estab. 1975. **Publishes 50 titles/year. Receives 500 submissions/year. 40% of books from first-time authors; 80% from unagented writers. Pays 10% royalty on net receipts. Offers moderate advances.** Publishes book 9 months after acceptance of manuscript. Proposals via Internet welcomed. Responds in 1 month. Book catalog and author guidelines available via website or upon request.
> O➤ Oryx Press publishes print and/or electronic reference resources for public, college and university, K-12 school, business and medical libraries, and professionals.
Nonfiction: Directories, dictionaries, encyclopedias, in print and electronic formats (online and CD-ROM), and other general reference works; special subjects: business, education, science, technology, consumer health care, government information, gerontology, social sciences. Query or submit outline/rationale and samples. Queries/mss may be routed to other editors in the publishing group.
Recent Title(s): *Science and Technology Almanac*, edited by William Allstetter; *Encyclopedia of Smoking and Tobacco*, by Arlene Hirschfelder.
Tips: "We are accepting and promoting more titles over the Internet. We are also looking for up-to-date, relevant ideas to add to our established line of print and electronic works."

OSBORNE MEDIA GROUP, The McGraw-Hill Companies, 2600 10th St., Berkeley CA 94710. (510)548-2805. Fax: (510)549-6603. Website: www.osborne.com. **Acquisitions:** Scott Rogers, associate editor; Wendy Rinaldi, editorial director; Gareth Hancock, editorial director; Roger Stewart, editorial director. Estab. 1979. Publishes computer trade paperback originals. **Publishes 250 titles/year. Receives 600 submissions/year. 30% of books from first-time authors. Pays 8-12% royalty on wholesale price. Offers $8,000-10,000 average advance.** Publishes book an average of 6 months after acceptance. Accepts simultaneous submissions. Responds in 2 months. Book catalog free.

    O→ Osborne publishes technical computer books and software.

Nonfiction: Software, technical. Computer and e-commerce subjects. Query with outline and sample chapters. Reviews artwork/photos as part of ms package.

Recent Title(s): *Java 2.0: The Complete Reference*, by Herbert Scholdt.

Tips: "A leader in self-paced training and skills development tools on information technology and computers."

OSPREY PUBLISHING LIMITED, SBM Inc., 443 Park Ave. S., #801, New York NY 10016. (212)685-5560. Fax: (212)685-5836. E-mail: ospreyusa@aol.com. Website: www.osprey-publishing.co.uk. **Acquisitions:** Lee Johnson, managing editor (military, uniforms, battles). Publishes hardcover and trade paperback originals. **Publishes 78 titles/year. Receives "hundreds" queries/year. 25% of books from first-time authors; 100% from unagented writers. Makes outright purchases of $1,000-5,000. Offers advance.** Publishes book 1 year after acceptance of ms. Responds in 2 months. Book catalog free or on website.

    O→ Osprey Publishing produces high-quality nonfiction series in the areas of military and aviation history and automotive titles. Lines include Air Combat, Aircraft of the Aces, Campaign, Elite, Men at Arms, New Vanguard, Warrior.

Nonfiction: Biography, illustrated book, military history, aviation, automotive. Subjects include history, hobbies, military/war. Query with SASE. Reviews artwork/photos as part of ms package. Send photocopies.

Recent Title(s): *Caesar's Legions: Roman Soldier 753 BC-117AD*, by Sekunda, et al.

Tips: "Osprey history books appeal to everyone with an interest in history: Teachers, students, history buffs, re-enactors, model makers, researchers, writers, movie production companies, etc. Known for meticulous research and attention to detail, our books are considered accurate and informative. Please do not send manuscript. We publish mainly in series in specific monographic format. Please provide academic credentials and subject matter of work. Artist references must be provided by author."

OUR SUNDAY VISITOR, INC., 200 Noll Plaza, Huntington IN 46750-4303. (219)356-8400. Fax: (219)359-9117. E-mail: booksed@osv.com. Website: osv.com. Editor-in-Chief: Greg Erlandson. **Acquistions:** Jacquelyn Lindsey and Michael Dabruiel, acquisitions editors. Estab. 1912. Publishes paperback and hardbound originals. **Publishes 20-30/year. Receives over 500 submissions/year. 10% of books from first-time authors; 90% from unagented writers. Pays variable royalty on net receipts. Offers $1,500 average advance.** Publishes book 1 year after acceptance. Responds in 3 months. Author's guide and catalog for SASE.

    O→ "We are a Catholic publishing company seeking to educate and deepen our readers in their faith." Currently emphasizing reference, apologetics and catechetics. De-emphasizing inspirational.

Nonfiction: Catholic viewpoints on current issues, reference and guidance, family, prayer and devotional books, and Catholic heritage books. Prefers to see well-developed proposals as first submission with annotated outline and definition of intended market. Reviews artwork/photos as part of ms package.

Recent Title(s): *Our Sunday Visitor's Treasury of Catholic Stories*, by Gerald Costello.

Tips: "Solid devotional books that are not first-person, well-researched Church histories or lives of the saints and catechetical books have the best chance of selling to our firm. Make it solidly Catholic, unique, without pious platitudes."

A THE OVERLOOK PRESS, Distributed by Penguin Putnam, 386 W. Broadway, New York NY 10012. (212)965-8400. Fax: (212)965-9839. Publisher: Peter Mayer. **Acquisitions:** (Ms.) Tracy Carns, editor. Estab. 1971. Publishes hardcover and trade paperback originals and hardcover reprints. **Publishes 40 titles/year. Receives 300 submissions/year. Pays 3-15% royalty on wholesale or retail price.** Responds in 5 months. Book catalog free.

    O→ Overlook Press publishes fiction, children's books and nonfiction.

Imprint(s): Elephant's Eye, Tusk Books.

Nonfiction: Art, architecture, biography, current events, design, film, health/fitness, history, how-to, lifestyle, martial arts, music, popular culture, New York State regional. No pornography. *Agented submissions only.*

Fiction: Literary fiction, fantasy, foreign literature in translation. *Agented submissions only.*

■ THE OVERMOUNTAIN PRESS, P.O. Box 1261, Johnson City TN 37605. (423)926-2691. Fax: (423)929-2464. E-mail: bethw@overmtn.com. Website: www.overmtn.com. **Acquisitions:** Elizabeth L. Wright, editor. Estab. 1970. Publishes hardcover and trade paperback originals and hardcover and trade paperback reprints. **Publishes 15-20 titles/year. Receives 500 queries and 100 mss/year. 50% of books from first-time authors; 100% from unagented writers. Pays 7½-15% royalty on wholesale price. No advance.** Publishes book 1 year after acceptance of ms. Accepts simultaneous submissions. Responds in 1 month to queries, 6 months to proposals and mss. Book catalog and ms guidelines free.

    O→ The Overmountain Press publishes primarily Appalachian history. Audience is people interested in history of Tennessee, Virginia, North Carolina, Kentucky, and all aspects of this region—Revolutionary War, Civil War, county histories, historical biographies, etc. Currently emphasizing history, nonfiction, Southern mysteries. De-emphasizing fiction, poetry, reminiscences, memoirs.

Imprint(s): Silver Dagger Mysteries.

Nonfiction: Biography, children's/juvenile, cookbook. Subjects include Americana, cooking/foods/nutrition, history, military/war, nature/environment, photography, regional, Native American. Submit proposal package, including outline, 3 sample chapters and marketing suggestions. Reviews artwork/photos as part of ms package. Send photocopies.
Fiction: Picture books.
Recent Title(s): *Between the States: Bristol TN/VA During the Civil War*, by V.N. "Bud" Phillips (nonfiction); *Appalachian ABCs*, by Francie Hall (children's ABC book).
Tips: "Please submit a proposal. Please no phone calls."

RICHARD C. OWEN PUBLISHERS INC., P.O. Box 585, Katonah NY 10536. Website: www.RCowen.com. **Acquisitions:** Janice Boland, director of children's books; Amy Finney, project editor (professional development, teacher-oriented books). Estab. 1982. Publishes hardcover and paperback originals. **Publishes 23 titles/year. Receives 150 queries and 1,000 mss/year. 99% of books from first-time authors; 100% from unagented writers. Pays 5% royalty on wholesale price.** Publishes book 3-5 years after acceptance of ms. Accepts simultaneous submissions, if so noted. Responds in 1 month to queries and proposals, 2 months to mss. Manuscript guidelines for SASE with 52¢ postage.
- "Our focus is literacy education in addition to stories for 5- to 6-year-olds by providing children with good, meaningful stories. We are also seeking manuscripts for our new collection of short, snappy stories for children in third grade. Subjects include humor, careers, mysteries, science fiction, folktales, women, fashion trends, sports, music, myths, journalism, history, inventions, planets, architecture, plays, adventure, technology, vehicles."
Nonfiction: Children's/juvenile humor, illustrated book. Subjects include animals, nature/environment, gardening, music/dance, recreation, science, sports. "Our books are for 5-7-year-olds. The stories are very brief—under 200 words—yet well structured and crafted with memorable characters, language and plots." Send for ms guidelines, then submit complete ms with SASE.
Fiction: Picture books. "Brief, strong story line, believable characters, natural language, exciting—child-appealing stories with a twist. No lists, alphabet or counting books." Send for ms guidelines, then submit full ms with SASE.
Poetry: Poems that excite children are fun, humorous, fresh and interesting. No jingles. Must rhyme without force or contrivance. Send for ms guidelines, then submit complete ms with SASE.
Recent Title(s): *Strange Plants*, by Nic Bishop (nonfiction); *Archie's Dollar*, by Nathan Zimclman (fiction); *Tiger Dave*, by Carter Boucher (limerick).
Tips: "We don't respond to queries. Please do not fax or e-mail us. Because our books are so brief it is better to send entire ms. We publish books with intrinsic value for young readers—books they can read with success. We believe students become enthusiastic, independent, life-long learners when supported and guided by skillful teachers. The professional development work we do and the books we publish support these beliefs."

OWL BOOKS, Henry Holt & Co., Inc., 115 W. 18th St., New York NY 10011. (212)886-9200. Website: www.hholt.com. **Acquisitions:** David Sobel, senior editor. Estab. 1996. Publishes trade paperback originals. **Firm publishes 135-140 titles/year; imprint publishes 50-60 titles/year. 30% of books from first-time authors. Pays 6-7½% royalty on retail price.** Advance varies. Publishes book 1 year after acceptance of ms. Accepts simultaneous submissions. Responds in 3 months to proposals.
- "We are looking for original, great ideas that have commercial appeal, but that you can respect."
Nonfiction: "Broad range." Subjects include art/architecture, biography, cooking/foods/nutrition, gardening, health/medicine, history, language/literature, nature/environment, regional, sociology, sports, travel. Query with outline, 1 sample chapter and SASE.
- "This publisher accepts agented submissions only."
Fiction: Literary fiction. Query with synopsis, 1 sample chapter and SASE.
Recent Title(s): *White Boy Shuffle*, by Paul Beatty; *The Debt to Pleasure*, by John Lanchester.

PACIFIC BOOKS, PUBLISHERS, P.O. Box 558, Palo Alto CA 94302-0558. (650)965-1980. **Acquisitions:** Henry Ponleithner, editor. Estab. 1945. **Publishes 6-12 titles/year. Pays 7½-15% royalty. No advance.** Estab. 1945. Responds in 1 month. *Writer's Market* recommends allowing 2 months for reply. Book catalog and guidelines for 9×12 SASE.
- Pacific Books publishes general interest and scholarly nonfiction including professional and technical books, and college textbooks.
Nonfiction: General interest, professional, technical and scholarly nonfiction trade books. Specialties include western Americana and Hawaiiana. Looks for "well-written, documented material of interest to a significant audience." Also considers text and reference books for high school and college. Accepts artwork/photos and translations. Query with outline and SASE.
Recent Title(s): *How to Choose a Nursery School: A Parents' Guide to Preschool Education*, by Ada Anbar, 2nd Edition.

PACIFIC PRESS PUBLISHING ASSOCIATION, Book Division, P.O. Box 5353, Nampa ID 83653-5353. (208)465-2511. Fax: (208)465-2531. E-mail: editor.book@pacificpress.com. Website: www.pacificpress.com. **Acquisitions:** Tim Lale (children's stories, devotional, biblical). Estab. 1874. Publishes hardcover and trade paperback originals and reprints. **Publishes 35 titles/year. Receives 600 submissions and proposals/year. Up to 35% of books from first-**

time authors; **100% from unagented writers. Pays 8-16% royalty on wholesale price. Offers $300-1,500 average advance depending on length.** Publishes book 10 months after acceptance. Responds in 3 months. Manuscript guidelines available at website or send #10 SASE.

> O— Pacific Press is an exclusively religious publisher of the Seventh-day Adventist denomination. "We are looking for practical, how-to oriented manuscripts on religion, health, and family life that speak to human needs, interests and problems from a Biblical perspective. We publish books that promote a stronger relationship with God, deeper Bible study, and a healthy, helping lifestyle."

Nonfiction: Biography, cookbook (vegetarian), how-to, juvenile, self-help. Subjects include cooking/foods (vegetarian only), health, nature, religion, family living. "We can't use anything totally secular or written from other than a Christian perspective." Query or request information on how to submit a proposal. Reviews artwork/photos.

Recent Title(s): *Walking with Angel*, by Lonnie Melashenko and Brian Jones; *Anticipation*, by Hyveth Williams.

Tips: "Our primary audience is members of the Seventh-day Adventist denomination. Almost all are written by Seventh-day Adventists. Books that are doing well for us are those that relate the Biblical message to practical human concerns and those that focus more on the experiential rather than theoretical aspects of Christianity. We are assigning more titles, using less unsolicited material—although we still publish manuscripts from freelance submissions and proposals."

PACIFIC VIEW PRESS, P.O. Box 2657, Berkeley CA 94702. **Acquisitions:** Pam Zumwalt, acquisitions editor. Estab. 1992. Publishes hardcover and trade paperback originals. **Publishes 4-6 titles/year. 50% of books from first-time authors; 100% from unagented writers. Pays 10% maximum royalty on net. Offers $1,000-5,000 advance.** Publishes book 1 year after acceptance. Accepts simultaneous submissions. Responds in 2 months to queries and proposals. Book catalog free. Writer's guidelines for #10 SASE.

> O— Pacific View Press publishes books for persons professionally/personally aware of the growing importance of the Pacific Rim and/or the modern culture of these countries, especially China.

Nonfiction: Children's/juvenile (Asia/multicultural only), reference, textbook (Chinese medicine only), contemporary Pacific Rim affairs. Subjects include business/economics (Asia and Pacific Rim only), health/medicine (Chinese medicine), history (Asia), regional (Pacific Rim), travel (related to Pacific Rim). Query with proposal package including outline, 1-2 chapters, target audience and SASE.

Recent Title(s): *Made in China: Ideas and Inventions from Ancient China*, by Suzanne Williams (illustrated Chinese history for kids).

Tips: "Audience is business people, academics, travelers, etc."

PALADIN PRESS, P.O. Box 1307, Boulder CO 80306-1307. (303)443-7250. Fax: (303)442-8741. E-mail: editoria l@paladin-press.com. Website: www.paladin-press.com. President/Publisher: Peder C. Lund. **Acquisitions:** Jon Ford, editorial director. Estab. 1970. Publishes hardcover and paperback originals and paperback reprints. **Publishes 50 titles/ year. 50% of books from first-time authors; 100% from unagented writers. Pays 10-12-15% royalty on net sales.** Publishes book 1 year after acceptance. Accepts simultaneous submissions. Responds in 2 months. Book catalog free.

> O— Paladin Press publishes the "action library" of nonfiction in military science, police science, weapons, combat, personal freedom, self-defense, survival, "revenge humor." Currently emphasizing personal freedom, financial freedom.

Imprint(s): Sycamore Island Books.

Nonfiction: "Paladin Press primarily publishes original manuscripts on military science, weaponry, self-defense, personal privacy, financial freedom, espionage, police science, action careers, guerrilla warfare, fieldcraft and 'creative revenge' humor. If applicable, send sample photographs and line drawings with complete outline and sample chapters." Query with outline and sample chapters.

Recent Title(s): *Street Smarts, Firearms, and Personal Security*, by Jim Grover.

Tips: "We need lucid, instructive material aimed at our market and accompanied by sharp, relevant illustrations and photos. As we are primarily a publisher of 'how-to' books, a manuscript that has step-by-step instructions, written in a clear and concise manner (but not strictly outline form) is desirable. No fiction, first-person accounts, children's, religious or joke books. We are also interested in serious, professional videos and video ideas (contact Michael Janich)."

PANTHEON BOOKS, Knopf Publishing Group, Random House, Inc., 201 E. 50th St., 25th Floor, New York NY 10022. (212)751-2600. Fax: (212)572-6030. Editorial Director: Dan Frank. Senior Editors: Shelley Wanger, Deborah Garrison. Executive Editor: Erroll McDonald. **Acquisitions:** Adult Editorial Department. Estab. 1942. **Pays royalty. Offers advance.**

> O— Pantheon Books publishes both Western and non-Western authors of literary fiction and important nonfiction.

Nonfiction: History, travel, science, memoir, biography, literary and international fiction.

Recent Title(s): *Mercies*, by Anne Lamott; *Waiting*, by Ha Jin.

PAPIER-MACHE PRESS

> • Papier-Mache Press was sold to LPC Group.

PARACLETE PRESS, P.O. Box 1568, Orleans MA 02653. (508)255-4685. Fax: (508)255-5705. **Acquisitions:** Lillian Miao, CEO. Estab. 1981. Publishes hardcover and trade paperback originals. **Publishes 14 titles/year. Receives 156**

queries and 60 mss/year. **80% of books from unagented writers. Pays 10-12% royalty. May offer advance.** Publishes book up to 2 years after acceptance of ms. Accepts simultaneous submissions. Responds in 2 months to queries, proposals and mss. Book catalog and ms guidelines for 8½×11 SASE and 4 first-class stamps.

O→ Publisher of Christian classics, personal testimonies, devotionals, new editions of classics, compact discs and videos.

Nonfiction: Prayer, spirituality. religious subjects. No poetry or children books. Submit outline with sample chapters.

Recent Title(s): *A Grief Unveiled*, by Gregory Floyd; *Religious Poetry and Prose of John Donne*, edited by Henry L. Carrigan Jr.

PARAGON HOUSE PUBLISHERS, 2700 University Ave. W., Suite 200, St. Paul MN 55114-1016. (651)644-3087. Fax: (651)644-0997. E-mail: paragon@paragonhouse.com. Website: www.paragonhouse.com. **Acquisitions:** Laureen Enright, acquisitions editor (general). Estab. 1982. Publishes hardcover and trade paperback originals and trade paperback reprints. **Publishes 12-15 titles/year; each imprint publishes 2-5 titles/year. Receives 400 queries and 75 mss/year. 7% of books from first-time authors; 90% from unagented writers. Pays 7-15% royalty on net sales. Offers $500-1,500 advance.** Publishes book 1 year after acceptance of ms. Accepts simultaneous submissions. Responds in 3 months. Book catalog on website. Manuscript guidelines for #10 SASE.

Imprints: PWPA Books (Dr. Gordon L. Anderson); Althena Books (Laureen Enright); New Era Books (Laureen Enright); ICUS Books (Laureen Enright).

O→ "We publish general interest titles and textbooks that provide the readers greater understanding of society and the world." Currently emphasizing religion, philosophy. De-emphasizing spirituality.

Nonfiction: Textbook. Subjects include government/politics, multicultural, nature/environment, philosophy, religion, sociology, spirituality, women's issues/studies. Submit proposal package, including outline, 2 sample chapters and summary, market breakdown and SASE for return of material.

Recent Titles: *Horyo: Memoirs of an American POW*, by Richard Gordon; *Ethics after the Holocaust: Perspectives, Critiques, and Responses*, ed. by John K. Roth.

⟦N⟧ PARLAY INTERNATIONAL, P.O. Box 8817, Emeryville CA 94662-0817. (510)601-1000. Fax: (510)601-1008. E-mail: info@parlay.com. Website: www.parlay.com. **Acquisitions:** Maria Sundeen, director of production development. Publishes hardcover, trade paperback, mass market paperback originals and trade paperback reprints. **Publishes 10 titles/year. Pays 10% royalty on wholesale price or makes outright purchase for negotiable flat fee.** Publishes book 10 months after acceptance of ms. Accepts simultaneous submissions. Responds in 1 month to queries and proposals, 3 months to mss. Book catalog and ms guidelines free or on website.

O→ Parlay International specializes in health, safety, and productivity subjects.

Nonfiction: Biography, multimedia (CD-ROM format), reference, self-help, technical, Kopy Kits® reproducible materials. Subjects include business/economics, child guidance/parenting, cooking/foods/nutrition, health/medicine, money/finance, translation, women's issues/studies, safety, communications. Query with SASE or submit proposal package, including outline, minimum 2 sample chapters and market summary.

Recent Title(s): *Safety & Health* and *Managing Work & Family*, both book/Kopy Kit®/CD-ROM packages.

Tips: "Parlay International publishes books for training, education and communication. Our three primary areas of information include health, safety and productivity topics. We have historically been providers of materials for educators, healthcare providers, business professionals, newsletters and training specialists. We are looking to expand our customer base to include not only business to business sales but mass market and consumer trade sales as well. Any suggested manuscript should be able to sell equally to our existing customer base as well as to the mass market, while retaining a thematic connection to our three specialty areas. Our customer base and specialty areas are very specific. Please review our website or catalogs before submitting a query."

⟦N⟧ PARNASSUS IMPRINTS, 105 Cammett Rd., Marstons Mills MA 02648. (508)790-1175. Fax: (508)790-1176. **Acquisitions:** Susan R. Klein, editor. Estab. 1981. Publishes hardcover originals, trade paperback originals and reprints. **Publishes 6-8 titles/year. Receives 50 queries and 15-20 mss/year. 25% of books from first-time authors; 50% from unagented writers. Pays 7-10% royalty on retail price. Offers variable advance.** Publishes book 1 year after acceptance of ms. Accepts simultaneous submissions. Responds in 1 month to queries, 2 months to proposals and mss. Book catalog for $1 postage.

O→ "The primary focus of the Parnassus Imprints list is nonfiction for readers interested in subjects relating to New England, particularly Cape Cod."

Nonfiction: Subjects include regional Americana, anthropology/archaeology, art/architecture, cooking/food/nutrition, gardening, history, hobbies, nature/environment, recreation, sports, travel. "One or more books per list will be of national interest." Query with outline, proposal, 3 sample chapters and SASE. Reviews artwork/photos as part of ms package. Send photocopies.

Recent Title(s): *A Most Remarkable Enterprise*, by Capt. William Sturgis; *Murder Hill*, by Theresa Barbo.

Tips: Audience is readers interested in Cape Cod/New England subjects.

PASSEGGIATA PRESS, P.O. Box 636, Pueblo CO 81002. (For Packages: 222 "B" St., Pueblo CO 81003.) (719)544-1038. **Acquisitions:** Donald E. Herdeck, publisher/editor-in-chief; Harold Ames, Jr., general editor. Estab. 1973. Publishes hardcover and paperback originals. **Publishes 10-20 titles/year. Receives 200 submissions/year. 15% of books**

from first-time authors; **99% from unagented writers. Nonauthor-subsidy publishes 5% of books. Pays 10% royalty. Offers advance "only on delivery of complete manuscript which is found acceptable; usually $300."** Accepts simultaneous submissions. Responds in 1 month.

> O→ "We search for books that will make clear the complexity and value of non-Western literature and culture. Mostly we do fiction in translation." Currently emphasizing criticism of non-Western writing (Caribbean, Latin American, etc.). De-emphasizing poetry.

Nonfiction: Specializes in African, Caribbean, Middle Eastern (Arabic and Persian) and Asian-Pacific literature, criticism and translation, Third World literature and history, fiction, poetry, criticism, history and translations of creative writing, including bilingual texts (Arabic language/English translations). Query with outline, table of contents. Reviews artwork/photos as part of ms package. State availability of photos/illustrations.

Fiction: Query with synopsis, plot summary (1-3 pages).

Poetry: Submit 5-10 sample poems.

Recent Title(s): *Not Yet African* (travel); *I Am a Martinican Woman (fiction); An Ocean of Dreams* (poetry).

Tips: "We are always interested in genuine contributions to understanding non-Western culture. We need a *polished* translation, or original prose or poetry by non-Western authors *only*. Critical and cross-cultural studies are accepted from any scholar from anywhere."

PATHFINDER PUBLISHING OF CALIFORNIA, 3600 Harbor Blvd., #82, Oxnard CA 93035. (805)984-7756. Fax: (805)985-3267. E-mail: bmosbrook@earthlink.net. Website: www.pathfinderpublishing.com. Publishes hardcover and trade paperback originals. **Publishes 4 titles/year. Receives 75 queries and 50 mss/year. 80% of books from first-time authors; 70% from unagented writers. Pays 9-15% royalty on wholesale price. Offers $200-1,000 advance.** Publishes book 4 months after acceptance of ms. Responds in 1 month. Book catalog free or on website.

> O→ Pathfinder Publishing of California was founded to seek new ways to help people cope with psychological and health problems resulting from illness, accidents, losses, or crime.

Nonfiction: Self-help. Subjects include creative nonfiction, health/medicine, hobbies, psychology, sociology. Submit completed ms. Reviews artwork/photos as part of ms package. Send photocopies.

Recent Title(s): *The Men's Club*, by Gottlieb (cancer); and *When Work Equals Life*, by S. Anthony Baron et. al (violence prevention).

PAULINE BOOKS & MEDIA, Daughters of St. Paul, 50 St. Paul's Ave., Jamaica Plain MA 02130-3491. (617)522-8911. Fax: (617)541-9805. Website: www.pauline.org. **Acquisitions:** Sister Mary Mark Wickenheiser, FSP, acquisitions (adult); Sister Patricia Edward Jablonski, acquisitions (children); Sister Madonna Ratliff, FSP, acquisitions editor (adult). Estab. 1948. Publishes trade paperback originals and reprints. **Publishes 25-35 titles/year. Receives approximately 1,300 proposals/year. Pays authors 8-12% royalty on net sales.** Publishes ms 2-3 years after acceptance. Responds in 3 months. Book catalog for 9×12 SAE with 4 first-class stamps.

> O→ "As a Catholic publishing house, we serve the Church by responding to the hopes and needs of all people with the Word of God, in the spirit of St. Paul. Pauline Books and Media publishes in the areas of faith and moral values, family formation, spiritual growth and development, children's faith formation, instruction in the Catholic faith for young adults and adults. Works consonant with Catholic theology are sought." Currently emphasizing saints/biographies, popular presentation of Catholic faith, biblical prayer. De-emphasizing pastoral ministry, teen fiction.

Nonfiction: Saints' biographies, juvenile, spiritual growth and faith development. Subjects include child guidance/parenting, religion teacher resources, Scripture. No strictly secular mss. Query with SASE. *No unsolicited mss.*

Fiction: Juvenile. Query only with SASE. *No unsolicited mss.*

Recent Title(s): *Images for Prayer: Matthew, Mark, Luke, John*, by Robert J. Knopp (nonfiction); *Poetry as Prayer: The Hound of Heaven* (poetry).

PAULIST PRESS, 997 MacArthur Blvd., Mahwah NJ 07430. (201)825-7300. Fax: (201)825-8345. E-mail: info@paulistpress.com. Website: www.paulistpress.com. **Acquisitions:** Lawrence E. Boadt, president/editorial director; Donna Crilly, editor (liturgy and catechetics); Joseph Scott, editor (adult theology, Catholic faith issues). Managing Editor: Maria Maggi. Estab. 1865. Publishes hardcover and paperback originals and paperback reprints. **Publishes 90-100 titles/year. Receives 500 submissions/year. 5-8% of books from first-time authors; 95% from unagented writers. Nonauthor subsidy publishes 1-2% of books. Usually pays royalty on net, but occasionally on retail price. Usually offers advance.** Publishes book 10 months after it enters production. Responds in 2 months.

> O→ Paulist Press publishes Christian and Catholic theology, spirituality and religion titles.

Nonfiction: Philosophy, religion, self-help, textbooks (religious). Accepts nonfiction translations from German, French and Spanish. "We would like to see theology (Catholic and ecumenical Christian), popular spirituality, liturgy, and religious education texts." Submit outline and 2 sample chapters. Reviews artwork/photos as part of ms package.

Recent Title(s): *Pius XII and the Second World War*, by Pierre Blet; *Celtic Spirituality*, by Oliver Davies (Classics of Western Spirituality).

PBC INTERNATIONAL INC., 1 School St., Glen Cove NY 11542. (516)676-2727. Fax: (516)676-2738. Publisher: Mark Serchuck. **Acquisitions:** Lisa Maruca, managing director. Estab. 1980. Publishes hardcover and paperback originals. **Publishes 20 titles/year. Receives 100-200 submissions/year. Most of books from first-time authors and unagented writers done on assignment. Pays royalty and/or flat fees.** Accepts simultaneous submissions. Responds in 2 months. Book catalog for 9×12 SASE.

> O→ PBC International is the publisher of full-color visual idea books for the design, marketing and graphic arts professional. "Edited for trend-making design professionals and style-conscious consumers, our books bring the reader a fresh contemporary point of view—one that presents spaces that are inviting and employ a mix of elements, a depth of composition and, above all, are current and modern."

Nonfiction: Subjects include design, graphic art, architecture/interior design, packaging design, marketing design, product design. No submissions not covered in the above listed topics. Query with outline and sample chapters with SASE. Reviews artwork/photos as part of ms package.

PEACHTREE CHILDREN'S BOOKS, Peachtree Publishers, Ltd. 494 Armour Circle NE, Atlanta GA 30324-4088. (404)876-8761. Fax: (404)875-2578. E-mail: peachtree@mindspring.com. Website: www.peachtree-online.com. President/Publisher: Margaret Quinlin. **Acquisitions:** Helen Harriss, submissions editor. Publishes hardcover and trade paperback originals. **Publishes 20 titles/year. 25% of books from first-time authors; 25% from unagented writers. Pays royalty on retail price. Advance varies.** Publishes book 18 months after acceptance of ms. Accepts simultaneous submissions. Responds in 3 months to queries, 4 months on manuscripts. Book catalog for $1.35 first-class postage. Manuscript guidelines for #10 SASE.

> O→ "We publish a broad range of subjects and perspectives, with emphasis on innovative plots and strong writing."

Imprint(s): Freestone, Peachtree Jr.

Nonfiction: Children's/juvenile/YA. Subjects include health, history, natural science. Submit complete ms with SASE. *Writer's Market* recommends a query with SASE first.

Fiction: Juvenile, picture books, young adult. Submit ms with SASE.

Recent Title(s): *About Mammals*, by Cathryn Sill (children's picture book); *Polar Star*, by Sally Grindley.

PEACHTREE PUBLISHERS, LTD., 494 Armour Circle NE, Atlanta GA 30324-4888. (404)876-8761. Fax: (404)875-2578. E-mail: peachtree@mindspring.com. Website: www.peachtree-online.com. **Acquisitions:** Helen Harriss, submissions editor (all unsolicited mss); Sarah Helyar Smith (children's, juvenile, young adult, adult), Amy Sproull (regional/outdoors). Estab. 1978. Publishes hardcover and trade paperback originals. **Publishes 20-25 titles/year.** Approximately 65% of Peachtree's list consists of children's books. **Receives up to 18,000 submissions/year. 25% of books from first-time authors; 75% from unagented writers. Prefers to work with previously published authors. Pays 7½-15% royalty.** Publishes book 2 years after acceptance. Responds in 6 months to queries. Book catalog for 9×12 SAE with 3 first-class stamps.

> O→ Peachtree Publishers specializes in children's books, juvenile chapter books, young adult, regional guidebooks, parenting and self-help. Currently emphasizing young adult, self help, children's, juvenile chapter books. De-emphasizing cooking, gardening, adult fiction.

Imprint(s): Peachtree Children's Books (Peachtree Jr., Free Stone).

Nonfiction: General. Subjects include children's titles and juvenile chapter books, history, health, humor, biography, general gift, recreation, self-help. No technical or reference. Submit outline and sample chapters. Reviews artwork/photos as part of ms package. Send photocopies.

Fiction: Literary, juvenile, young adult, mainstream. No fantasy, science fiction or romance. Submit sample chapters.

Recent Title(s): *Vaccinating Your Child*, by Humiston and Good; *Eleanor's Story: An American Girl in Hitler's Germany*, by Eleanor Garner.

PELICAN PUBLISHING COMPANY, 1000 Burmaster, P.O. Box 3110, Gretna LA 70053. (504)368-1175. Website: www.pelicanpub.com. President/Publisher: Milburn Calhoun. **Acquisitions:** Nina Kooij, editor-in-chief. Estab. 1926. Publishes hardcover, trade paperback and mass market paperback originals and reprints. **Publishes 70 titles/year. Receives 5,000 submissions/year. 15% of books from first-time authors; 90% from unagented writers. Pays royalty on actual receipts.** Publishes book 9-18 months after acceptance. Responds in 1 month to queries. Writer's guidelines for SASE on on website.

> O→ "We believe ideas have consequences. One of the consequences is that they lead to a bestselling book. We publish books to improve and uplift the reader." Currently emphasizing business titles.

Nonfiction: Biography, coffee table book (limited), popular history, sports, architecture, illustrated book, juvenile, motivational, inspirational, Scottish, Irish, editorial cartoon. Subjects include Americana (especially Southern regional, Ozarks, Texas, Florida and Southwest); business (popular motivational, if author is a speaker); music (American artforms: jazz, blues, Cajun, R&B); politics (special interest in conservative viewpoint); religion (for popular audience mostly, but will consider others). *Travel*: Regional and international. *Motivational*: with business slant. *Inspirational*: author must be someone with potential for large audience. *Cookbooks*: "We look for authors with strong connection to restaurant industry or cooking circles, i.e., someone who can promote successfully." Query with SASE. "We require that a query be made first. This greatly expedites the review process and can save the writer additional postage expenses." No multiple queries or submissions. Reviews artwork/photos as part of ms package. Send photocopies only.

Fiction: Historical, Southern, juvenile. "We publish maybe one novel a year, usually by an author we already have. Almost all proposals are returned. We are most interested in historical Southern novels." No young adult, romance, science fiction, fantasy, gothic, mystery, erotica, confession, horror, sex or violence. Submit outline/synopsis and 2 sample chapters with SASE.

Recent Title(s): *The Majesty of the French Quarter*, by Kerri McCaffety (architecture); *The Warlord's Puzzle*, by Virginia Walton Pilegard (juvenile).

Tips: "We do extremely well with cookbooks, travel, popular histories, and some business. We will continue to build in these areas. The writer must have a clear sense of the market and knowledge of the competition. A query letter should describe the project briefly, give the author's writing and professional credentials, and promotional ideas."

PENCIL POINT PRESS, INC., 277 Fairfield Rd., Fairfield NJ 07004. **Acquisitions:** Gene Garone, publisher (all areas). **Publishes 4-12 titles/year. Receives 4-12 queries and 12 mss/year. 100% of books from first-time authors. Pays 5-16% royalty or makes outright purchase of $25-50/page. No advance.** Publishes book 1 year after acceptance. Accepts simultaneous submissions. Responds in 2 months to proposals. Book catalog free.

    O─ Pencil Point publishes educational supplemental materials for teachers of all levels. Currently emphasizing mathematics and science. De-emphasizing language arts.

Nonfiction: Reference, technical, textbook. Education subjects, including professional reference, music, science, mathematics, language arts, ESL and special needs. Prefers supplemental resource materials for teachers grades K-12 and college (especially mathematics). Submit proposal package, including outline, 2 sample chapters and memo stating rationale and markets.

Recent Title(s): *Earthscope: Exploring Relationships Affecting Our Global Environment*, by Wright H. Gwyn.

Tips: Audience is K-8 teachers, 9-12 teachers and college-level supplements. No children's trade books or poetry.

PENGUIN PUTNAM INC., 375 Hudson St., New York NY 10014. Website: www.penguinputnam.com. President: Phyllis Grann. General interest publisher of both fiction and nonfiction.

Imprint(s): The Penguin Group: *Hardcover:* Allen Lane, **DAW,** Donald I. Fine, **Dutton,** Penguin Press, Penguin Studio, Viking. *Paperback:* Arkana, **DAW**, Donald I. Fine, Mentor, Meridian, Onyx, Penguin, Penguin Classics, Plume, **Roc, Signet,** Signet Classics, Topaz; *Children's:* **Dial Books for Young Readers, Dutton Children's Books, Puffin, Viking Children's Books,** Frederick Warne. **The Putnam Berkley Publishing Group:** *Hardcover:* Ace/Putnam, **Boulevard,** Grosset/Putnam, **Price Stern Sloan,** Putnam, **G.P. Putnam's Sons,** Riverhead, **Jeremy P. Tarcher**; *Paperback:* Ace, **Berkley Books, Boulevard,** HP Books, Jove, **Perigee, Price Stern Sloan,** Prime Crime, Riverhead Books; *Children's:* **Grosset & Dunlap,** PaperStar, **Philomel Books, Price Stern Sloan, G.P. Putnam's Sons,** Wee Sing.

PENNSYLVANIA HISTORICAL AND MUSEUM COMMISSION, Commonwealth of Pennsylvania, P.O. Box 1026, Harrisburg PA 17108-1026. (717)787-8099. Fax: (717)787-8312. Website: www.state.pa.us. **Acquisitions:** Diane B. Reed, chief, publications and sales division. Estab. 1913. Publishes hardcover and paperback originals and reprints. **Publishes 6-8 titles/year. Receives 25 submissions/year. Pays 5-10% royalty on retail price. Makes outright purchase or sometimes makes special assignments.** Publishes book 18 months after acceptance. Accepts simultaneous submissions. Responds in 4 months. Prepare mss according to the *Chicago Manual of Style*.

    O─ "We are a public history agency and have a tradition of publishing scholarly and reference works, as well as more popularly styled books that reach an even broader audience interested in some aspect of Pennsylvania."

Nonfiction: All books must be related to Pennsylvania, its history or culture: biography, illustrated books, reference, technical and historic travel. No fiction. "The Commission seeks manuscripts on Pennsylvania, specifically on archaeology, history, art (decorative and fine), politics and biography." Query or submit outline and sample chapters. Guidelines and proposal forms available.

Recent Title(s): *Pennsylvania Architecture*, by Richard Webster and Deborah Stephens Burns.

Tips: "Our audience is diverse—students, specialists and generalists—all of them interested in one or more aspects of Pennsylvania's history and culture. Manuscripts must be well researched and documented (footnotes not necessarily required depending on the nature of the manuscript) and interestingly written. Manuscripts must be factually accurate, but in being so, writers must not sacrifice style."

■ **PENNYWHISTLE PRESS,** P.O. Box 734, Tesuque NM 87574. (505)982-0000. Fax: (505)982-0066. E-mail: pennywhistlebook@aol.com. **Acquisitions:** Victor di Suvero, publisher. **Publishes 6 titles/year. Receives 400 queries and 500 mss/year. 30% of books from first-time authors; 100% from unagented writers. Pays $100, chapbook plus 30 copies of book to author.** Publishes book 1 year after acceptance. Accepts simultaneous submissions. Responds in 1 month to queries, 2 months to proposals, 3 months to mss. Book catalog for 4 × 12 SAE with 1 first-class stamp. Manuscript guidelines free.

    O─ Pennywhistle publishes poetry chapbooks, books and anthologies. This year Pennywhistle Press inaugurates its Ariadne imprint under which it will publish a series of books of interest primarily to women.

Imprint(s): Ariadne.

Poetry: Submit 30 sample poems.

Recent Title(s): *¡ Saludos! Poems of New Mexico*, the first bilingual collection of the poetry of New Mexico; *Naked Heart*, poems by Victor di Suvero.

PERFECTION LEARNING CORPORATION, 10520 New York Ave., Des Moines IA 50322-3775. (515)278-0133. Fax: (515)278-2980. Website: www.perfectionlearning.com. **Acquisitions:** Sue Thies, senior editor (books division); Terry Ofner, senior editor (curriculum division). Estab. 1926. Publishes hardcover and trade paperback originals. **Publishes 50-60 fiction and informational; 150 teacher's resources titles/year. Pays 5-8% royalty on retail price. Offers $300-500 advance.** Responds in 5 months to proposals.

○→ "Perfection Learning is dedicated to publishing books and literature-based materials that enhance teaching and learning in pre-K-12 classrooms and libraries." Emphasizing hi/lo fiction and nonfiction books. De-emphasizing literature-based teacher resources.

Imprint(s): Cover-to-Cover.

Nonfiction: Publishes nonfiction and curriculum books, including workbooks, literature anthologies, teacher guides, literature tests, and niche textbooks for grades 3-12. "We are publishing hi-lo informational books for students in grades 2-8, reading levels 1-4." Query or submit outline with SASE; for curriculum books, submit proposal and writing sample with SASE.

Fiction: "We are publishing hi-lo fiction in a variety of genres for students in grades 2-8, reading levels 1-4." Submit 2-3 sample chapters with SASE.

Recent Title(s): *The Secret Room*, by Cynthia Mercati (hi-lo historical fiction); *Ancient Egypt: Moments in History*, by Shirley Jordan (hi-lo informational book).

PERIGEE BOOKS, Penguin Putnam Inc., 375 Hudson St., New York NY 10014. (212)366-2000. **Acquisitions:** John Duff, editor. Publishes trade paperback originals and reprints. **Publishes 12-15 titles/year. Receives hundreds of queries/year; 30 proposals/year. 30% first-time authors; 10% unagented writers. Pays 7½-15% royalty. Offers $5,000-150,000 advance.** Publishes book 18 months after acceptance of ms. Responds in 2 months. Catalog free. Manuscript guidelines given on acceptance of ms.

Nonfiction: Prescriptive books. Subjects include health/fitness, child care, spirituality. Query with outline. Prefers agented mss, but accepts unsolicited queries.

THE PERMANENT PRESS/SECOND CHANCE PRESS, 4170 Noyac Rd., Sag Harbor NY 11963. (631)725-1101. (631)725-1101. Fax: (631)725-8215. E-mail: thepermanentpress.com. Website: www.thepermanentpress.com. **Acquisitions:** Judith Shepard, editor. Estab. 1978. Publishes hardcover originals. **Publishes 20 titles/year. Receives 7,000 submissions/year. 60% of books from first-time authors; 60% from unagented writers. Pays 10-15% royalty on wholesale price. Offers $1,000 advance for Permanent Press books; royalty only on Second Chance Press titles.** Publishes book 18 months after acceptance. Accepts simultaneous submissions. Responds in 6 months to queries. Book catalog for 8×10 SAE with 7 first-class stamps. Manuscript guidelines for #10 SASE.

○→ Permanent Press publishes literary fiction. Second Chance Press devotes itself exclusively to re-publishing fine books that are out of print and deserve continued recognition. "We endeavor to publish quality writing—primarily fiction—without regard to authors' reputations or track records." Currently emphasizing literary fiction. No poetry, short story collections.

Nonfiction: Biography, autobiography, historical. No scientific and technical material, academic studies. Query.

Fiction: Literary, mainstream, mystery. Especially looking for high line literary fiction, "artful, original and arresting." No genre fiction, poetry or short stories. Query with first 20 pages.

Recent Title(s): *Harry's Absence: Looking for My Father on the Mountain*, by Dr. Jonathan Scott (nonfiction); *Whompyjawed*, by Mitch Cullin (fiction).

Tips: "Audience is the silent minority—people with good taste. We are interested in the writing more than anything and long outlines are a turn-off. The SASE is vital to keep track of things, as we are receiving ever more submissions. No fax queries will be answered. We aren't looking for genre fiction but a compelling, well-written story." Permanent Press does not employ readers and the number of submissions it receives has grown. If the writer sends a query or manuscript that the press is not interested in, a reply may take six weeks. If there is interest, it may take 3 to 6 months.

■ **PETER PAUPER PRESS, INC.**, 202 Mamaroneck Ave., White Plains NY 10601-5376. **Acquisitions:** Lynn Rosen, editorial director. Estab. 1928. Publishes hardcover originals. **Publishes 40-50 titles/year. Receives 700 queries and 300 mss/year. 5% of books from first-time authors; 90% from unagented writers. Makes outright purchase only.** Publishes ms 1 year after acceptance. Responds in 1 month. *Writer's Market* recommends allowing 2 months for reply. Manuscript guidelines for #10 SASE.

○→ PPP publishes small format, illustrated gifts for occasions and in celebration of specific relationships such as Mom, sister, friend, teacher, grandmother, granddaughter.

Nonfiction: Subjects include specific relationships or special occasions (graduation, Mother's Day, Christmas, etc.). "We do not publish narrative works. We publish brief, original quotes, aphorisms, and wise sayings. *Please do not send us other people's quotes.*" Submit outline with SASE.

Recent Title(s): *A Friend for All Seasons*, compiled by Helen H. Moore.

Tips: "Our readers are primarily female, age 20 and over, who are likely to buy a 'gift' book in a stationery, gift, book or boutique store. Writers should become familiar with our previously published work. We publish only small-format illustrated hardcover gift books of between 750-4,000 words. We have no interest in work aimed at men."

◨ ■ **PETERSON'S**, P.O. Box 2123, Princeton NJ 08543-2123. (800)338-3282. Fax: (609)243-9150. Website: www.petersons.com. **Acquisitions:** Denise Rance, executive assistant, editorial. Estab. 1966. Publishes trade and reference books. **Publishes 75-100 titles/year. Receives 250-300 submissions/year. 60% of books from first-time authors; 90% from unagented writers. Pays 7½-12% royalty on net sales. Offers advance.** Publishes book 1 year after acceptance. Responds in 3 months. Book catalog free.

○→ "Peterson's publishes well-known references as its guides to graduate and professional programs, colleges and universities, financial aid, distance learning, private schools, standardized test-prep, summer programs, international study, executive education, job hunting and career opportunities, as well as a full line of software offering career guidance and information for adult learners and workplace solutions for education professionals."

Nonfiction: Careers, education, authored titles, as well as education and career directories. Submit complete ms or table of contents, introduction and 2 sample chapters with SASE. *Writer's Market* recommends query with SASE first. Looks for "appropriateness of contents to our markets, author's credentials, and writing style suitable for audience."

Recent Title(s): *The Ultimate High School Survival Guide*, by Julianne Dueber.

Tips: Many of Peterson's reference works are updated annually. Peterson's markets strongly to libraries and institutions, as well as to the corporate sector.

N: PHAIDON PRESS, 180 Varick St., 14th Floor, New York NY 10014. (212)652-5400. Fax: (212)652-5419. **Acquisitions:** Karen Stein, editorial director (art and architecture, design, photography). Publishes hardcover and trade paperback originals and reprints. **Publishes 100 titles/year. Receives 500 mss/year. 20% of books from first-time authors; 80% from unagented writers. Pays royalty on wholesale price.** Publishes book 1 year after acceptance of ms. Accepts simultaneous submissions. Responds in 3 months to proposals. Book catalog free.

Imprints: Phaidon.

Nonfiction: Subjects include art/architecture, photography. Submit proposal package, including outline or submit completed ms. Reviews artwork/photos as part of ms package. Send photocopies.

Recent Title(s): *Lost Revolutions: The South in the 1950s*, by Pete Daniel; *Our Own Backyard, The United States in Central America, 1977-1992*, by William M. Leogrande.

PHI DELTA KAPPA EDUCATIONAL FOUNDATION, P.O. Box 789, Bloomington IN 47402. (812)339-1156. Fax: (812)339-0018. E-mail: special.pubs@pdkintl.org. Website: www.pdkintl.org. **Acquisitions:** Donovan R. Walling, editor of special publications. Estab. 1906. Publishes hardcover and trade paperback originals. **Publishes 24-30 titles/ year. Receives 100 queries and 50-60 mss/year. 50% of books from first-time authors; 100% from unagented writers. Pays honorarium of $500-5,000.** Publishes book 9 months after acceptance of ms. Responds in 3 months to proposals. Book catalog and ms guidelines free.

O–ᴦ "We publish books for educators—K-12 and higher education. Our professional books are often used in college courses but are never specifically designed as textbooks."

Nonfiction: How-to, reference, essay collections. Subjects include child guidance/parenting, education, legal issues. Query with outline and 1 sample chapter. Reviews artwork/photos as part of ms package.

Recent Title(s): *The ABC's of Behavior Change*, by Frank J. Sparzo; *American Overseas Schools*, edited by Robert J. Simpson and Charles R. Duke.

PHILOMEL BOOKS, Penguin Putnam Inc., 345 Hudson St., New York NY 10014. (212)414-3610. **Acquisitions:** Patricia Lee Gauch, editorial director; Michael Green, senior editor. Estab. 1980. Publishes hardcover originals. **Publishes 20-25 titles/year. Receives 2,600 submissions/year. 15% of books from first-time authors; 30% from unagented writers. Pays standard (7½-15%) royalty. Advance negotiable.** Publishes book 1-2 years after acceptance. Responds in 3 months to queries. Book catalog for 9×12 SAE with 4 first-class stamps. Request book catalog from marketing department of Putnam Publishing Group.

O–ᴦ "We look for beautifully written, engaging manuscripts for children and young adults."

Fiction: Children's picture books (ages 3-8); middle-grade fiction and illustrated chapter books (ages 7-10); young adult novels (ages 10-15). Particularly interested in picture book mss with original stories and regional fiction with a distinct voice. Historical fiction OK. Unsolicited mss accepted for picture books only; query first for long fiction. Always include SASE. No series or activity books.

Recent Title(s): *Blue Willow*, by Pam Conrad, illustrated by S. Saelig Gallagher; *Elyimpics*, by X.J. Kennedy, illustrated by Graham Percy.

Tips: "We prefer a very brief synopsis that states the basic premise of the story. This will help us determine whether or not the manuscript is suited to our list. If applicable, we'd be interested in knowing the author's writing experience or background knowledge. We try to be less influenced by the swings of the market than in the power, value, essence of the manuscript itself."

PICADOR USA, St. Martin's Press, 175 Fifth Ave., New York NY 10010. **Acquisitions:** Publisher. Estab. 1994. Publishes hardcover originals and trade paperback originals and reprints. **Publishes 70-80 titles/year. 30% of books from first-time authors. Publishes "few" unagented writers. Pays 7½-12½% royalty on retail price. Advance varies.** Publishes book 18 months after acceptance of ms. Accepts simultaneous submissions. Responds in 2 months to queries. Book catalog for 9×12 SASE and $2.60 postage. Manuscript guidelines for #10 SASE.

O–ᴦ Picador publishes high-quality literary fiction and nonfiction. "We are open to a broad range of subjects, well written by authoritative authors."

Nonfiction: Subjects include language/literature, philosophy, biography/memoir, cultural history, narrative books with a point of view on a particular subject. "When submitting queries, be aware of things outside the book, including credentials, that may affect our decision." Query only with SASE. No phone queries.

Fiction: Literary. Query only with SASE.

Recent Title(s): *James Dickey*, by Henry Hart (biography); *Not Even My Name*, by Thea Halo (memoir history); *Grange House*, by Sarah Blake (fiction).

PICCADILLY BOOKS LTD., (formerly Piccadilly Books), P.O. Box 25203, Colorado Springs CO 80936-5203. (719)550-9887. Website: www.piccadillybooks.com. Publisher: Bruce Fife. **Acquisitions:** Submissions Department. Estab. 1985. Publishes hardcover and trade paperback originals and trade paperback reprints. **Publishes 5-8 titles/year. Receives 120 submissions/year. 70% of books from first-time authors; 95% from unagented writers. Pays 10% royalty on retail price.** Publishes book within 1 year of acceptance. Accepts simultaneous submissions. Responds only if interested, unless accompanied by a SASE.

O⚓ Picadilly publishes books on humor, entertainment, performing arts, skits and sketches, and writing.

Nonfiction: How-to books on entertainment, humor, performing arts, writing and small business. "We have a strong interest in subjects on clowning, magic, puppetry and related arts, including comedy skits and dialogs." Query with sample chapters.

Recent Title(s): *The World's Funniest Clown Skits*, by Barry DeChant.

Tips: "Experience has shown that those who order our books are either kooky or highly intelligent or both. If you like to laugh, have fun, enjoy games, or have a desire to act like a jolly buffoon, we've got the books for you."

PICTON PRESS, Picton Corp., P.O. Box 250, Rockport ME 04856-0250. (207)236-6565. Fax: (207)236-6713. E-mail: sales@pictonpress.com. Website: www.pictonpress.com. **Acquisitions:** Candy McMahan Perry, office manager. Publishes hardcover and mass market paperback originals and reprints. **Publishes 30 titles/year. Receives 30 queries and 15 mss/year. 50% of books from first-time authors; 100% from unagented writers. Pays 0-10% royalty on wholesale price or makes outright purchase.** Publishes book 6 months after acceptance of ms. Responds in 2 months to queries and proposals, 3 months to mss. Book catalog free.

O⚓ "Picton Press is one of America's oldest, largest and most respected publishers of genealogical and historical books specializing in research tools for the 17th, 18th and 19th centuries."

Imprint(s): Cricketfield Press, New England History Press, Penobscot Press, **Picton Press**.

Nonfiction: Reference, textbook. Subjects include Americana, genealogy, history, vital records. Query with outline.

Recent Title(s): *Nemesis At Potsdam*, by Alfred de Zayas.

THE PILGRIM PRESS, United Church of Christ, United Church Press, 700 Prospect Ave. E., Cleveland OH 44115-1100. (216)736-3715 or (216)736-3704. Fax: (216)736-3703. E-mail: stavet@ucc.org. Website: www.pilgrimpress.com. **Acquisitions:** Timothy G. Staveteig, publisher. Estab. 1621. Publishes hardcover and trade paperback originals. **Publishes 25 titles/year. 30% of books from first-time authors; 80% from unagented writers. Pays standard royalties and advances where appropriate.** Publishes book an average of 18 months after acceptance. Responds in 3 months to queries. Book catalog and ms guidelines free.

• See also United Church Press.

Nonfiction: Ethics, social issues with a strong commitment to justice—addressing such topics as public policy, sexuality and gender, economics, medicine, gay and lesbian concerns, human rights, minority liberation and the environment—primarily in a Christian context, but not exclusively.

Recent Title(s): *Still Groovin'*, by Ruth Beckford.

Tips: "We are concentrating more on academic and trade submissions. Writers should send books about contemporary social issues. Our audience is liberal, open-minded, socially aware, feminist, church members and clergy, teachers and seminary professors."

PIÑATA BOOKS, Arte Publico Press, University of Houston, Houston TX 77204-2174. (713)743-2841. Fax: (713)743-2847. Website: www.arte.uh.edu. **Acquisitions:** Nicolas Kanellos, president. Estab. 1994. Publishes hardcover and trade paperback originals. **Publishes 10-15 titles/year. 60% of books from first-time authors. Pays 10% royalty on wholesale price. Offers $1,000-3,000 advance.** Publishes book 2 years after acceptance of ms. Accepts simultaneous submissions. Responds in 1 month to queries, 6 months to mss. Book catalog and ms guidelines available via website or with #10 SASE.

O⚓ Piñata Books is dedicated to the publication of children's and young adult literature focusing on U.S. Hispanic culture.

Nonfiction: Children's/juvenile. Ethnic subjects. "Pinata Books specializes in publication of children's and young adult literature that authentically portrays themes, characters and customs unique to U.S. Hispanic culture." Query with outline/synopsis, 2 sample chapters and SASE.

Fiction: Adventure, juvenile, picture books, young adult. Query with synopsis, 2 sample chapters and SASE.

Poetry: Appropriate to Hispanic theme. Submit 10 sample poems.

Recent Title(s): *Silent Dancing: A Partial Remembrance of a Puerto Rican Childhood*, by Judith Ortiz-Cofer (memoir, ages 11-adult); *Tun-ta-ca-tun*, edited by Sylvia Pena (children's poetry, preschool to young adult).

Tips: "Include cover letter with submission explaining why your manuscript is unique and important, why we should publish it, who will buy it, etc."

PINEAPPLE PRESS, INC., P.O. Box 3899, Sarasota FL 34230. (941)359-0886. **Acquisitions:** June Cussen, editor. Estab. 1982. Publishes hardcover and trade paperback originals. **Publishes 20 titles/year. Receives 1,500 submissions/year. 20% of books from first-time authors; 80% from unagented writers. Pays 6½-15% royalty on net price. Seldom offers advance.** Publishes book 18 months after acceptance. Accepts simultaneous submissions. Responds in 3 months. Book catalog for 9×12 SAE with $1.24 postage.

O⚓ "We are seeking quality nonfiction on diverse topics for the library and book trade markets."

Nonfiction: Biography, how-to, reference, regional (Florida), nature. Subjects include animals, history, gardening, nature. "We will consider most nonfiction topics. Most, though not all, of our fiction and nonfiction deals with Florida." No pop psychology or autobiographies. Query or submit outline/brief synopsis, sample chapters and SASE.

Fiction: Literary, historical, mainstream, regional (Florida). No romance or science fiction. Submit outline/brief synopsis and sample chapters.

Recent Title(s): *Best Back Roads of Florida*, by Douglas Waitley; *The Return*, by Mark Mustian (novel).

Tips: "Learn everything you can about book publishing and publicity and agree to actively participate in promoting your book. A query on a novel without a brief sample seems useless."

PLATINUM PRESS INC., 311 Crossways Park Dr., Woodbury NY 11797. (516)364-1800. Fax: (516)364-1899. **Acquisitions:** Herbert Cohen (mysteries, detective). Estab. 1990. Publishes hardcover reprints. **Offers $500-750 advance.**

○➤ Platinum Press publishes reprints of previously published detective and mystery books.

Imprint(s): Detective Book Club, Platinum Press.

Fiction: Mystery, suspense. Query with SASE.

PLAYERS PRESS, INC., P.O. Box 1132, Studio City CA 91614-0132. (818)789-4980. **Acquisitions:** Robert W. Gordon, vice president, editorial. Estab. 1965. Publishes hardcover and trade paperback originals, and trade paperback reprints. **Publishes 35-70 titles/year. Receives 200-1,000 submissions/year. 15% of books from first-time authors; 80% from unagented writers. Pays royalty on wholesale price.** Publishes book within 2 years of acceptance. Reports to queries in 1 month, up to 1 year to mss. Book catalog and guidelines for 9×12 SAE with 5 first-class stamps.

○➤ Players Press publishes support books for the entertainment industries: theater, film, television, dance and technical. Currently emphasizing plays. De-emphasizing children's.

Nonfiction: Juvenile and theatrical drama/entertainment industry. Subjects include the performing arts, costume, theater and film crafts. Needs quality plays and musicals, adult or juvenile. Query. Reviews artwork/photos as part of package.

Plays: Subject matter includes adventure, confession, ethnic, experimental, fantasy, historical, horror, humor, mainstream, mystery, religious, romance, science fiction, suspense, western. Submit complete ms for theatrical plays only. Plays must be previously produced. "No novels or story books are accepted."

Recent Title(s): *50 Scenes To Go*, by Mila Johnson.

Tips: "Plays, entertainment industry texts, theater, film and TV books have the only chances of selling to our firm."

■▲ **PLEASANT COMPANY PUBLICATIONS**, 8400 Fairway Pl., Middleton WI 53562. Fax: (608)836-1999. Website: www.americangirl.com. **Acquisitions:** Erin Falligant, submissions editor. Estab. 1986. Publishes hardcover and trade paperback originals. **Publishes 50-60 title/year. Receives 500 queries and 800 mss/year. 90% of books from unagented writers. "Payment varies extremely depending on the nature of the work." Advance varies.** Accepts simultaneous submissions. Responds in 2 months. Book catalog for SASE.

○➤ Pleasant Company publishes fiction and nonfiction for girls 7-12.

Imprint(s): The American Girls Collection, American Girl Library, AG Fiction, History Mysteries.

Nonfiction: Children's/juvenile for girls, ages 7-12. Subjects include contemporary lifestyle, activities, how-to. Query.

Fiction: Juvenile for girls, ages 7-12. Subjects include contemporary and historical fiction, mysteries. "We are seeking strong, well-written fiction, historical and contemporary, told from the perspective of a middle-school-age girl. We are also seeking fresh picture-book concepts and proposals. No romance, fantasy, picture books, rhyme or stories about talking animals." Query or send ms.

Recent Title(s): *A Song for Jeffrey*, by Constance Foland; *The Smuggler's Treasure*, by Sarah M. Buckey.

PLEXUS PUBLISHING, INC., 143 Old Marlton Pike, Medford NJ 08055-8750. (609)654-6500. Fax: (609)654-4309. E-mail: jbryans@infotoday.com. **Acquisitions:** John B. Bryans, editor-in-chief (regional fiction and nonfiction [southern NJ], health/medicine, nature, ecology, field guides). Estab. 1977. Publishes hardcover and paperback originals. **Publishes 4-5 titles/year. Receives 30-60 submissions/year. 70% of books from first-time authors; 90% from unagented writers. Pays 17½% royalty on wholesale price; buys some booklets outright for $250-1,000. Offers $500-1,000 advance.** Accepts simultaneous submissions. Responds in 3 months. Book catalog and guidelines for 10×13 SAE with 4 first-class stamps.

○➤ Plexus publishes mainly regional-interest (southern NJ) fiction and nonfiction including mysteries, field guides, history. Also health/medicine, biology, ecology, botony, astronomy.

Nonfiction: Mostly regional (southern NJ) natural and historical references. Other subjects include botany, medicine, biology, ecology, astronomy. "We will consider any book on a nature/biology subject, particularly those of a reference (permanent) nature that would be of lasting value to high school and college audiences, and/or the general reading public (ages 14 and up). Authors should have authentic qualifications in their subject area, but qualifications may be by experience as well as academic training." No gardening, philosophy or psychology; generally not interested in travel but will consider travel that gives sound ecological information. Also interested in mss of about 20-40 pages in length for feature articles in *Biology Digest* (guidelines available with SASE). Query. Reviews artwork as part of ms package. Send photocopies.

Fiction: Mysteries and literary novels with a strong regional (southern NJ) angle. Query.

Recent Title(s): *Patriots, Pirates & Pineys: Sixty Who Shaped New Jersey*, by Robert Peterson; *Cape Mayhem*, by Jane Kelly (fiction).

N̄ POCKET BOOKS, Simon & Schuster, 1230 Avenue of the Americas, New York NY 10020. (212)698-7000. **Acquisitions:** Tracy Behar, vice president/editorial director. Publishes paperback originals and reprints, mass market and trade paperbacks and hardcovers. **Publishes 250 titles/year. Receives 2,500 submissions/year. 25% of books from first-time authors; less than 25% from agented writers. Pays 6-8% royalty on retail price.** Publishes book an average of 2 years after acceptance. Book catalog free. Manuscript guidelines for #10 SASE.

    O→ Pocket Books publishes general interest nonfiction and adult fiction.

Nonfiction: History, biography, reference and general nonfiction, humor, calendars. Query with SASE.

Fiction: Adult (mysteries, thriller, psychological suspense, Star Trek ® novels, romance, westerns). Query with SASE.

Recent Title(s): *All I Really Need to Know in Business I Learned at Microsoft*, by Julie Brick (nonfiction); *Star Trek Avenger*, by William Shatner (fiction).

N̄ PONTALBA PRESS, 4417 Dryades St., New Orleans LA 70115. (877)891-4474. Fax: (504)899-6573. E-mail: wayne@pontalbapress.com. Website: www.pontalbapress.com. **Acquisitions:** Christian Allman, director (fiction, nonfiction, art/photography, motivational, alternative culture, biography). Publishes hardcover, trade and mass market paperback originals. **Publishes 6-10 titles/year; imprint publishes 1-2/year. Receives 600-800 queries and 300-400 mss/year. 50% of books from first-time authors; 75% from unagented writers. Pays 3-8% royalty on retail price.** Publishes book 10 months after acceptance of ms. Accepts simultaneous submissions. Responds in 1 month to queries, 4 months to proposals, 6 months to mss. Book catalog and ms guidelines for #10 SASE or on website.

Imprints: Autumn, Spring, Winter, Summer, ICAN.

    O→ "Pontalba Press is dedicated to publishing unique, cutting-edge fiction, nonfiction, and art/photography books by both first-time and established authors."

Nonfiction: Biography, coffee table book, cookbook, gift book, humor, illustrated book, multimedia, self-help. Subjects include Americana, anthropology/archaeology, art/architecture, business/economics, cooking/food/nutrition, creative nonfiction, education, ethnic, gay/lesbian, government/politics, history, language/literature, memoirs, military/war, multicultural, music/dance, philosophy, photography, psychology, regional, religion, science, sex, spirituality, sports, travel, women's issues/studies. Submit proposal package, including 3 sample chapters, author bio and art sampler (if any) and market potential. Reviews artwork/photos as part of ms package.

Fiction: Adventure, confession, erotica, ethnic, experimental, fantasy, feminist, gay/lesbian, gothic, historical, horror, humor, literary, mainstream/contemporary, military/war, multimedia, mystery, occult, regional, romance, science fiction, spiritual, sports, suspense. Submit proposal package, including synopsis, 3 sample chapters or submit completed ms.

Recent Title(s): *Obituary Cocktail: The Great Saloons of New Orleans*, by Kerri McCaffet (nonfiction).

◪ POPULAR CULTURE INK, P.O. Box 1839, Ann Arbor MI 48106. (734)677-6351. **Acquisitions:** Tom Schultheiss, publisher. Estab. 1989. Publishes hardcover originals and reprints. **Publishes 4-6 titles/year. Receives 50 queries and 20 mss/year. 100% of books from first-time authors; 100% from unagented writers. Pays variable royalty on wholesale price. Offers variable advance.** Publishes book 2 years after acceptance. Accepts simultaneous submissions. Responds in 1 month. *Writer's Market* recommends allowing 2 months for reply. Book catalog and ms guidelines free.

    O→ Popular Culture Ink publishes directories and reference books for radio, TV, music and other entertainment subjects.

Nonfiction: Reference. Subjects include music, popular entertainment. Query with SASE.

Recent Title(s): *Surfin' Guitars*, by Robert Dalley (1960s surf music).

Tips: Audience is libraries, avid collectors. "Know your subject backwards. Make sure your book is unique."

POPULAR WOODWORKING BOOKS, F&W Publications, 1507 Dana Ave., Cincinnati OH 45207. (513)531-2690. **Acquisitions:** Mark Thompson, acquisitions editor. Publishes hardcover and trade paperback originals and reprints. **Publishes 10-12 titles/year. Receives 30 queries and 10 mss/year. 50% of books from first-time authors; 95% from unagented writers. Pays 10-20% royalty on net receipts. Offers $3,000-5,000 advance.** Publishes book 1 year after acceptance of ms. Accepts simultaneous submissions. Responds in 1 month. Book catalog and ms guidelines for 9 × 12 SAE with 6 first-class stamps.

Nonfiction: How-to, illustrated book, woodworking/wood crafts. "We publish heavily illustrated how-to woodworking books that show, rather than tell, our readers how to accomplish their woodworking goals." Query with proposal package, including outline, transparencies and SASE. Reviews artwork/photos as part of ms package. Send transparencies. "Always submit copies of transparencies. We will not be responsible for lost or stolen transparencies!"

Recent Title(s): *How to Build Classic Garden Furniture*, by Danny Proulx.

Tips: "Our books are for 'advanced beginner' woodworking enthusiasts."

◪ POSSIBILITY PRESS, One Oakglade Circle, Hummelstown PA 17036-9525. (717)566-0468. Fax: (717)566-6423. E-mail: posspress@excite.com. Website: www.possibilitypress.com. **Acquisitions:** Mike Markowski, publisher; Marjorie L. Markowski, editor-in-chief. Estab. 1981. Publishes trade paperback originals. **Publishes 10-20 titles/year. Receives 1,000 submissions/year. 90% of books from first-time authors; 100% from unagented writers. Royalties vary.** Publishes book approximately 1 year after acceptance. Responds in 2 months. Manuscript guidelines for #10 SAE and 2 first-class stamps.

    O→ "Our mission is to help the people of the world grow and become the best they can be, through the written and spoken word." No longer interested in health issues.

Imprint(s): Aviation Publishers, Possibility Press.

Nonfiction: How-to, self-help. Subjects include business, current significant events, pop-psychology, success/motivation, inspiration, entrepreneurship, sales marketing, network marketing and homebased business topics, and human interest success stories.
Recent Title(s): *The Electronic Dream*, by John Fuhrman.
Tips: "Our focus is on creating and publishing bestsellers written by authors who speak and consult. We're looking for authors who are serious about making a difference in the world."

N: CLARKSON POTTER, The Crown Publishing Group, Random House, Inc., 299 Park Ave., New York NY 10171. (212)751-2600. Website: www.randomhouse.com. Editor: Roy Finamore. Senior Editors: Annetta Hanna, Katie Workman. Executive Editor: Pam Krauss. **Acquisitions:** Lauren Shakely, editorial director. Estab. 1959. Publishes hardcover and trade paperback originals. **Publishes 55 titles/year. 15% of books from first-time authors.** Responds in 3 months to queries and proposals.
   O→ Clarkson Potter specializes in publishing cooking books, decorating and other around-the-house how-to subjects.
Nonfiction: Publishes art/architecture, biography, child guidance/parenting, crafts, cooking and foods, decorating, design gardening, how-to, humor, photography, and popular psychology. Query or submit outline and sample chapter with tearsheets from magazines and artwork copies (e.g.—color photocopies or duplicate transparencies).
   • "This publisher accepts agented submissions only."
Recent Title: *Martha Stewart's Hors d'oeuvres Handbook.*

PPI PUBLISHING, P.O. Box 292239, Kettering OH 45429. (937)294-5057. **Acquisitions:** Shary Price, managing editor. Publishes age-specific paperback originals. **Publishes 10-15 titles/year. Receives 200 queries and 50 mss/year. 90% of books from first-time authors; 100% from unagented writers. Pays 10% royalty on retail price.** Publishes book 10 months after acceptance of ms. Accepts simultaneous submissions. Responds in 2 months to queries, 3 months to proposals, 2 months to mss. Catalog and guidelines for 9 × 12 SASE and 2 first-class stamps. Manuscript guidelines for #10 SASE.
   O→ "PPI Publishing seeks to provide top-quality, well researched, up-to-the-minute information on the 'hot' issues for teens with distribution mostly to schools and public libraries."
Nonfiction: Children/young adult, how-to, self-help. Subjects include motivational; social issues such as AIDS, abortion, teenage drinking; environmental issues such as the Rainforest and the ozone layer; teen sexuality; "hot youth topics;" career guidance. Publishes books in the Fall. Query or submit outline with 3 sample chapters with SASE. Reviews artwork/photos as part of the ms package. Send photocopies.
Recent Title(s): *AIDS: Facts, Issues, Choices*, by Faith H. Brynie, Ph.D.
Tips: Readers are students in grades 7-12 and their teachers. "We're looking for quality material on 'hot' topics that will appeal to middle school/high school students. Submit fresh topics with logical thought and writing."

PRACTICE MANAGEMENT INFORMATION CORP. (PMIC), 4727 Wilshire Blvd., #300, Los Angeles CA 90010. (323)954-0224. Fax: (323)954-0253. E-mail: pmiceditor@aol.com. Website: www.medicalbookstore.com. **Acquisitions:** Kathryn Swanson, managing editor. Estab. 1986. Publishes hardcover originals. **Publishes 21 titles/year. Receives 100 queries and 50 mss/year. 10% of books from first-time authors; 90% from unagented writers. Pays 12½% royalty on net receipts. Offers $1,000-5,000 advance.** Publishes book 18 months after acceptance of ms. Responds in 6 months to queries. Book catalog and ms guidelines for #10 SASE.
   O→ PMIC helps healthcare workers understand the business of medicine by publishing books for doctors, medical office and hospital staff, medical managers, insurance coding/billing personnel.
Imprint(s): PMIC, Health Information Press.
Nonfiction: Reference, technical, textbook, medical practice management, clinical, nonfiction. Subjects include business/economics, health/medicine, science. Submit proposal package, including outline and letter stating who is the intended audience, the need/market for such a book, as well as outline, 3-5 sample chapters and curriculum vitae/résumé.
Recent Title(s): *ICD-9-CM Coding Made Easy*, by James Davis; *Medicare Rules & Regulations*, by Maxine Lewis; *Collections Made Easy*, by Michael Berry.

PRAEGER PUBLISHERS, The Greenwood Publishing Group, Inc., 88 Post Road W., Westport CT 06881. (203)226-3571. Fax: (203)226-6009. Publisher: Peter Kracht. **Acquisitions:** Heather Stainer (history, military); Nita Romer (psychology); Elizabeth Clinton (sociology); Cynthia Harris (economics); Pamela St. Clair (cultural studies, media); James Sabin (politics). Estab. 1949. Publishes paperback originals. **Publishes 250 titles/year. Receives 1,200 submissions/ year. 5% of books from first-time authors; 90% from unagented writers. Pays 6½-12% royalty on net sales. Rarely offers advance.** Publishes book an average of 1 year after acceptance. Accepts simultaneous submissions. Responds in 1 month. *Writer's Market* recommends allowing 2 months for reply. Book catalog and manuscript guidelines available on website.
   O→ Praeger publishes scholarly trade and advanced texts in the the social and behavioral sciences and communications, international relations and military studies.
Nonfiction: "We are looking for scholarly works in women's studies, sociology, psychology, contemporary history, military studies, political science, economics, international relations. No language and literature." Query with proposal package, including: scope, organization, length of project; whether a complete ms is available, or when it will be; cv or résumé with SASE. No unsolicited ms.

Recent Title(s): *An American Paradox: Censorship in a Nation of Free Speech*, by Patrick Garry; *Black and Right: The Bold New Voice of Black Conservatives in America*, edited by Stan Faryna, Brad Stetson and Joseph G. Conti.

PRAIRIE OAK PRESS, 821 Prospect Place, Madison WI 53703. (608)255-2288. Fax: (608)255-4204. E-mail: popjama @aol.com. **Acquisitions:** Jerry Minnich, president. Estab. 1991. Publishes hardcover originals, trade paperback originals and reprints. **Publishes 6-8 titles/year. Pays royalty or makes outright purchase. Offers $500-1,000 advance.** Responds in 3 months to proposals.

O→ Prairie Oak publishes exclusively Upper Great Lakes regional nonfiction. Currently emphasizing travel, sports, recreation.

Imprint(s): Prairie Classics, Acorn Guides.

Nonfiction: History, folklore, gardening, sports, travel, architecture, other general trade subjects. "Any work considered must have a strong tie to Wisconsin and/or the Upper Great Lakes region." Query or submit outline and 1 sample chapter with SASE.

Recent Title(s): *Wisconsin Lighthouses*, by Ken and Barb Wardius.

Tips: "When we say we publish regional works only, we mean Wisconsin, Minnesota, Michigan, Illinois. Please do not submit books of national interest. We cannot consider them."

PRECEPT PRESS, Bonus Books, 160 E. Illinois St., Chicago IL 60611. (312)467-0580. Fax: (312)467-9271. E-mail: bb@bonus-books.com. Website: www.bonus-books.com. **Acquisitions:** Michael Olsen, editor. Estab. 1970. Publishes hardcover and trade paperback originals. **Publishes 20 titles/year. Receives 300 queries and 100 mss/year. 25% of books from first-time authors; 90% from unagented writers. Pays royalty.** Publishes book 8 months after acceptance. Accepts simultaneous submissions if so noted. Responds in 3 months to proposals. Manuscript guidelines for #10 SASE.

O→ Precept Press features a wide variety of books for the technical community. Currently emphasizing cultural and film theory.

Nonfiction: Reference, technical, clinical, textbook. Subjects include business, CD-ROM, medical and oncology texts. Query with SASE.

Recent Title(s): *Handbook of Chemotherapy Regimens for Gynecologic Cancers*, by Maurie Markman.

PRESIDIO PRESS, 505B San Marin Dr., Suite 300, Novato CA 94945-1340. (415)898-1081, ext. 125. Fax: (415)898-0383. **Acquisitions:** E.J. McCarthy, executive editor. Estab. 1974. Publishes hardcover originals and reprints. **Publishes 24 titles/year. Receives 1,600 submissions/year. 35% of books from first-time authors; 65% from unagented writers. Pays 15-20% royalty on net receipts. Advance varies.** Publishes book 18 months after acceptance. Responds within 1 month to queries. Book catalog and ms guidelines for 7½ × 10½ SAE with 4 first-class stamps.

O→ "We publish the finest and most accurate military history and military affairs nonfiction, plus entertaining and provocative fiction related to military affairs."

Imprint(s): Lyford Books.

Nonfiction: Subjects include military history and military affairs. Query with SASE. Reviews artwork/photos as part of ms package. Send photocopies.

Fiction: Military. Query with SASE.

Recent Title(s): *The Biographical History of World War II*, by Mark M. Boatner III; *Proud Legions*, by John Antal (military fiction).

Tips: "Study the market. Find out what publishers are publishing, what they say they want and so forth. Then write what the market seems to be asking for, but with some unique angle that differentiates the work from others on the same subject. We feel that readers of hardcover fiction are looking for works of no less than 80,000 words."

▓N▓ THE PRESS AT THE MARYLAND HISTORICAL SOCIETY, 201 W. Monument St., Baltimore MD 21201. (410)685-3750. Fax: (410)385-2105. E-mail: rcottom@mdhs.org. Website: www.mdhs.org. **Acquisitions:** Robert I. Cottom, publisher (MD/regional history). Publishes hardcover and trade paperback originals and trade paperback reprints. **Publishes 4-6 titles/year. Receives 12-15 queries and 8-10 mss/year. 50% of books from first-time authors; 100% from unagented writers. Pays 6-10% royalty on retail price.** Publishes book 1 year after acceptance of ms. Accepts simultaneous submissions. Responds in 1 month to queries and proposals, 6 months to mss. Book catalog on website.

O→ The Press at the Maryland Historical Society specializes in Maryland state and regional subjects.

Nonfiction: Biography, children's/juvenile, illustrated book, textbook (general interest/scholarly history). Subjects include history. Query with SASE or submit proposal package, including outline and 1-2 sample chapters.

Recent Title(s): *History of the Maryland Penitentiary*, by Wallace Shugg (history); *The Life of Benjamin Banneker*, by Silvio A. Bedini (biography).

Tips: "Our audience consists of intelligent readers of Maryland/Chesapeake regional history and biography."

PRICE STERN SLOAN, INC., Penguin Putnam Inc., 345 Hudson, New York NY 10014. (212)414-3610. Fax: (212)414-3396. Publisher: Jon Anderson. **Acquisitions:** Submissions Editor (juvenile submissions); Calendars Editor (calendar submissions). Estab. 1963. **Publishes 80 titles/year (95% children's). Makes outright purchase. Offers advance.** Responds in 3 months. Catalog for 9 × 12 SAE with 5 first-class stamps. Manuscript guidelines for SASE. Address to "Catalog Request" or "Manuscript Guidelines."

O→ Price Stern Sloan publishes quirky mass market novelty series for children and adult page-a-day calendars.

Imprint(s): Doodle Art®, I Can Read Comics, Mad Libs®, Mad Mysteries®, Mr. Men & Little Miss™, Plugged In®, Serendipity®, Travel Games to Go, Troubador Press, Wee Sing®.

Nonfiction and Fiction: Mass market juvenile series and adult page-a-day calendars only. Do not send *original* artwork or ms. *No unsolicited mss.* "Most of our titles are unique in concept as well as execution."

Recent Title(s): The *Plugged In™ When Your Parents Split Up* . . Alys Swan Jackson (nonfiction); *Kermit's ABC*, illustrated by Stef de Renver (fiction).

Tips: "Price Stern Sloan has a unique, humorous, off-the-wall feel."

PRIDE & IMPRINTS, 7419 Ebbert Dr. SE, Port Orchard WA 98367. Website: www.windstormcreative.com. **Acquisitions:** (Ms.) Cris Newport, senior editor. Estab. 1989. Publishes trade paperback originals and reprints. **Publishes 50 titles/year. Receives 5,200 queries and 15,000 mss/year. Pays 10-15% royalty on wholesale price.** Publishes book 1-2 years after acceptance of ms. Responds in 6 months to mss.

 ⦿ Publisher of fiction and poetry. Will review work by previously published authors only.

Fiction: Science fiction, fantasy, gay/lesbian/bisexual adult fiction, young adult novels, historical novels, contemporary fiction. No children's books, horror, "bestseller" fiction, spy or espionage novels, "thrillers," any work which describes childhood sexual abuse or in which this theme figures prominently. Query with cover letter and a one page synopsis of the ms which details the major plot developments.

Recent Title(s): *Bones Become Flowers*, by Jess Mowry (contemporary fiction); *Annabel and I*, by Chris Anne Wolfe (lesbian fiction); *Journey of a Thousand Miles*, by Peter Kasting (gay fiction).

Tips: "Visit website for detailed submission instructions."

PROFESSIONAL PUBLICATIONS, INC., 1250 Fifth Ave., Belmont CA 94002-3863. (650)593-9119. Fax: (650)592-4519. E-mail: amagee@ppi2pass.com. **Acquisitions:** Aline Magee, acquisitions editor. Estab. 1975. Publishes hardcover and paperback originals, video and audio cassettes, CD-ROMs. **Publishes over 30 titles/year. Receives 100-200 submissions/year.** Publishes book 18 months after acceptance of ms. Accepts simultaneous submissions. Responds in 2 weeks to queries. *Writer's Market* recommends allowing 2 months for reply. Book catalog and ms guidelines free.

 ⦿ PPI publishes for engineering, architecture, land surveying, and interior design professionals preparing to take examinations for national licensing. Professional Publications wants only professionals practicing in the field to submit material. Currently emphasizing engineering exam review. De-emphasizing architecture exam review.

Nonfiction: Reference, technical, textbook. Subjects include engineering mathematics, engineering, land surveying, architecture, interior design. Especially needs "review books for all professional licensing examinations." Query or submit outline and sample chapters. Reviews artwork/photos as part of ms package.

Recent Title(s): *Civil Engineering Reference Manual for the PE Exam*, by Michael R. Lindeburg, PE.

Tips: "We specialize in books for working professionals: engineers, architects, land surveyors, interior designers, etc. The more technically complex the manuscript is the happier we are. We love equations, tables of data, complex illustrations, mathematics, etc. In technical/professional book publishing, it isn't always obvious to us if a market exists. We can judge the quality of a manuscript, but the author should make some effort to convince us that a market exists. Facts, figures, and estimates about the market—and marketing ideas from the author—will help sell us on the work."

PROMETHEUS BOOKS, 59 John Glenn Dr., Buffalo NY 14228. (716)691-0133. Fax: (716)564-2711. E-mail: SLMPBBOOKS@aol.com. Website: www.prometheusbooks.com. **Acquisitions:** Steven L. Mitchell, editor-in-chief; Eugene O'Connor, acquisitions editor (Humanity Books, scholarly and professional works in philosophy, social science); Linda Greenspan Regan, executive editor (Prometheus, popular science, health, psychology, criminology). Estab. 1969. Publishes hardcover originals, trade paperback originals and reprints. **Publishes 85-100 titles/year. Receives 2,500 queries and mss/year. 25% of books from first-time authors; 50% from unagented writers. Pays 10-15% royalty on wholesale price; other for paper. Offers $1,000-3,000 advance; advance rare, if ever, for children's books.** Publishes book 18 months after acceptance of ms. Accepts simultaneous submissions, if so noted. Responds in 1 month to queries and proposals, 4 months to mss. Book catalog free. Manuscript guidelines for #10 SASE.

 ⦿ "Prometheus Books is a leading independent publisher in philosophy, popular science and critical thinking. We publish authoritative and thoughtful books by distinguished authors in many categories. We are a niche, or specialized, publisher that features *critiques* of the paranormal and pseudoscience, religious extremism and right wing fundamentalism and creationism; Biblical and Koranic criticism: human sexuality, etc. Currently emphasizing popular science, health, psychology, social science.

Imprint(s): Humanity Books (scholarly and professionals monographs in philosophy, social science, sociology, archaeology, Marxist studies, etc.).

Nonfiction: Biography, children's/juvenile, reference. Subjects include contemporary issues, current events, education, government/politics, health/medicine, history, Islamic studies, language/literature, law, philosophy, psychology, popular science, reference, religion (not religious, but critiquing), critiques of the paranormal and UFO sightings, etc., self-help,

---

FOR INFORMATION on book publishers' areas of interest, see the nonfiction and fiction sections in the Book Publishers Subject Index.

sexuality. "Ask for a catalog, go to the library, look at our books and others like them to get an idea of what our focus is." Submit proposal package including outline, synopsis and a well-developed query letter with SASE. Reviews artwork/ photos as part of ms package. Send photocopies.

Recent Title(s): *Gardner's Whys and Wherefores*, by Martin Gardner (science and paranormal).

Tips: "Audience is highly literate with multiple degrees; an audience that is intellectually mature and knows what it wants. They are aware, and we try to provide them with new information on topics of interest to them in mainstream and related areas."

PROMPT PUBLICATIONS, Howard W. Sams & Co., 2647 Waterfront Parkway E. Dr., Indianapolis IN 46214-2041. (317)298-5400. Fax: (800)552-3910. E-mail: atripp@hwsams.com. Website: www.hwsams.com. **Acquisitions:** Alice J. Tripp, managing editor. Publishes trade paperback originals and reprints. **Publishes 18-30 titles/year. Receives 50-75 queries and 30 mss/year. 40% of books from first-time authors; 90% from unagented writers. Pays royalty on retail price based on author's experience. Advance varies.** Book catalog free.

   O-¬ "Our mission is to produce quality and reliable electronics technology publications in book form, to meet the needs of the engineer, technician, hobbyist and average consumer." Currently emphasizing cutting-edge electronics technology. De-emphasizing electronics project books.

Nonfiction: How-to, reference, technical. Subjects include audio/visual, computers/electronics, electronics repair, energy, science (electricity). "Books should be written for beginners *and* experts, hobbyists *and* professionals. We do not publish books about software. We like manuscripts about cutting-edge technology, consumer electronics, troubleshooting and repair, component cross-references." Established authors query; new authors send complete ms or proposal with SASE. Reviews artwork/photos as part of ms package.

Tips: Audience is consumers, electronics/technical hobbyists, professionals needing reference books. "Remember that it takes a while for a book to be published, so keep notes on updating your material when the book is ready to print. When submitting, above all, *be patient*. It can take up to a year for a publisher to decide to publish your book."

◤◢ PROSTAR PUBLICATIONS INC., 3 Church Circle, #109, Annapolis MD 21401. (310)577-1975. Fax: (310)577-9272. Website: www.nauticalbooks.com. **Acquisitions:** Peter Griffes, president (marine-related/how-to/business/technical); Susan Willson, editor (history/memoirs). Estab. 1965. Publishes trade paperback originals. **Publishes 35 titles/year; imprint publishes 10-15. Receives 60 queries and 25 mss/year. 50% of books from first-time authors; 100% from unagented writers. Pays 15% royalty on wholesale price. Rarely offers advance.** Publishes book 1 year after acceptance of ms. Accepts simultaneous submissions. Responds in 1 month to queries, 3 months to proposals. Book catalog on website.

   O-¬ "Originally, ProStar published only nautical books. At present, however, we are expanding. Any quality nonfiction book would be of interest."

Imprints: Lighthouse Press (Peter Griffes).

Nonfiction: Coffee table book, how-to, illustrated book, reference, technical. Subjects include art/architecture, business/economics, history, memoirs, nature/environment, nautical, travel. Query. Reviews artwork/photos as part of ms package. Send photocopies.

Recent Titles: *The Steeples of Old New England*, by Kirk Chivell; *Memories, Memories*, by Lily Margules.

Tips: "We prefer to work directly with the author; we seldom work with agents. Send in a well-written query letter, and we will give your book serious consideration."

PRUETT PUBLISHING, 7464 Arapahoe Rd., Suite A-9, Boulder CO 80303. (303)449-4919. Fax: (303)443-9019. E-mail: pruettbks@aol.com. **Acquisitions:** Jim Pruett, publisher. Estab. 1959. Publishes hardcover paperback and trade paperback originals and reprints. **Publishes 10-15 titles/year. 60% of books are from first-time authors; 100% from unagented writers. Pays 10-12% royalty on net income.** Publishes book 18 months after acceptance of ms. Accepts simultaneous submissions. Responds in 2 months to queries. Book catalog and ms guidelines free.

   O-¬ "Pruett Publishing strives to convey to our customers and readers a respect of the American West, in particular the spirit, traditions, and attitude of the region. We publish books in the following subject areas: outdoor recreation, regional history, environment and nature, travel and culture. We especially need books on outdoor recreation."

Nonfiction: Regional history, guidebooks, nature, biography. Subjects include Western Americana, archaeology (Native American), Western history, nature/environment, recreation (outdoor), regional/ethnic cooking/foods (Native American, Mexican, Spanish), regional travel, regional sports (cycling, hiking, fishing). "We are looking for nonfiction manuscripts and guides that focus on the Rocky Mountain West." Submit proposal package. Reviews artwork/photos and formal proposal as part of ms package.

Recent Title(s): *Flyfishing the Texas Coast: Back Country Flats to Bluewater*, by Chuck Scales and Phil Shook, photography by David J. Sams; *Trout Country: Reflections on Rivers, Flyfishing & Related Addictions*, by Bob Saile; *Rocky Mountain Christmas*, by John H. Monnett.

Tips: "There has been a movement away from large publisher's mass market books and towards small publisher's regional interest books, and in turn distributors and retail outlets are more interested in small publishers. Authors don't need to have a big name to have a good publisher. Look for similar books that you feel are well produced—consider design, editing, overall quality and contact those publishers. Get to know several publishers, and find the one that feels right—trust your instincts."

N ⋆ PRUFROCK PRESS, P.O. Box 8813, Waco TX 76714. (254)756-3337. Fax: (254)756-3339. E-mail: prufrock @prufrock.com or mcintosh@prufrock.com. Website: www.prufrock.com. **Acquisitions:** Joel McIntosh, publisher. Publishes trade paperback originals and reprints. **Publishes 15 titles/year. Receives 150 queries and 50 mss/year. 50% of books from first-time authors; 100% from unagented writers. Pays 10% royalty on sale price.** Publishes book 9 months after acceptance of ms. Responds in 2 months. Book catalog and ms guidelines free.

○━ "Prufrock Press provides exciting, innovative and current resources supporting the education of gifted and talented learners."

Nonfiction: Children's/juvenile, how-to, textbook. Subjects include child guidance/parenting, education. "We publish for the education market. Our readers are typically teachers or parents of gifted and talented children. Many authors send us classroom activity books. Our product line is built around professional development books for teachers. While some of our books may include activities, many are included to illustrate a teaching concept on strategies, or strategy in use at an application level." Request query package from publisher.

Recent Title(s): *Coping for Capable Kids*, by Dr. Leonora M. Cohen and Dr. Erica Frydenberg.

Tips: "We are one of the larger independent education publishers; however, we have worked hard to offer authors a friendly, informal atmosphere. Authors should feel comfortable calling up and bouncing an idea off of us or writing us to get our opinion of a new project idea."

PUFFIN BOOKS, Penguin Putnam Inc., 345 Hudson St., New York NY 10014-3657. (212)414-2000. Website: www.penguinputnam.com/childrens. President/Publisher: Tracy Tang. **Acquisitions:** Sharyn November, senior editor; Kristin Gilson, executive editor; Joy Peskin, associate editor. Publishes trade paperback originals and reprints. **Publishes 175-200 titles/year. Receives 300 queries and mss/year. 1% of books by first-time authors; 5% from unagented writers. Royalty and advance vary.** Publishes book 1 year after acceptance of ms. Responds in 3 months to mss. *No unsolicited mss.* Book catalog for 9×12 SASE with 7 first-class stamps; send request to Marketing Department.

○━ Puffin Books publishes high-end trade paperbacks and paperback reprints for preschool children, beginning and middle readers, and young adults.

Imprint(s): PaperStar.

Nonfiction: Biography, children's/juvenile, illustrated book, young children's concept books (counting, shapes, colors). Subjects include education (for teaching concepts and colors, not academic), women in history. " 'Women in history' books interest us." Query. *No unsolicited mss.*

Fiction: Picture books, young adult novels, middle grade and easy-to-read grades 1-3. "We publish mostly paperback reprints. We do very few original titles." Query. *No unsolicited mss.*

Tips: "Our audience ranges from little children 'first books' to young adult (ages 14-16). An original idea has the best luck."

PURDUE UNIVERSITY PRESS, 1207 South Campus Courts, Bldg. E, West Lafayette IN 47907-1207. (765)494-2038. Website: www.thepress.purdue.edu. **Acquisitions:** Thomas Bacher, director (technology, business, veterinary medicine, philosophy); Margaret Hunt, managing editor (Central European studies, regional, literature). Estab. 1960. Publishes hardcover and trade paperback originals and trade paperback reprints. **Publishes 14-20 titles/year. Receives 600 submissions/year. Pays 7½-15% royalty.** Publishes book 9 months after acceptance. Responds in 2 months. Book catalog and ms guidelines available via website or 9×12 SASE.

○━ "We look for books that look at the world as a whole and offer new thoughts and insights into the standard debate." Currently emphasizing technology, human-animal issues, business. De-emphasizing literary studies.

Nonfiction: "We publish work of quality scholarship and titles with regional (Midwest) flair. Especially interested in innovative contributions to the social sciences and humanities that break new barriers and provide unique views on current topics. Expanding into veterinary medicine, engineering and business topics. Always looking for new authors who show creativity and thoroughness of research." Print and electronic projects accepted. Query before submitting.

Recent Title(s): *Women Succeeding in the Sciences*, by Jody Bart.

G.P. PUTNAM'S SONS, (Adult Trade), Penguin Putnam, Inc., 375 Hudson, New York NY 10014. (212)366-2000. Fax: (212)366-2666. Website: www.putnam.com. **Acquisitions:** Acquisitions Editor. Publishes hardcover and trade paperback originals. **5% of books from first-time authors; none from unagented writers. Pays variable advance on retail price.** Accepts simultaneous submissions. Responds in 6 months to queries. Request book catalog through mail order department. Manuscript guidelines free.

Imprint(s): Perigee, Price Stern Sloan, Putnam (children's), **Jeremy P. Tarcher**.

Nonfiction: Biography, celebrity-related topics, contemporary affairs, cookbook, self-help. Subjects include animals, business/economics, child guidance/parenting, cooking/foods/nutrition, health/medicine, military/war, nature/environment, religion/inspirational, science, sports, travel, women's issues/studies. Query with SASE. *No unsolicited mss.*

Fiction: Adventure, literary, mainstream/contemporary, mystery, suspense, women's. Query with synopsis, *brief* writing sample (the shorter the better) and SASE. Prefers agented submissions.

Recent Title(s): *Lindbergh*, by A. Scott Berg (nonfiction); *Rainbow Six*, by Tom Clancy (adventure).

G.P. PUTNAM'S SONS BOOKS FOR YOUNG READERS, Penguin Putnam Books for Young Readers, Penguin Putnam Inc., 345 Hudson St., New York NY 10014. (212)414-3610. Website: www.penguinputnam.com. **Acquisitions:** Manuscript editor. Publishes hardcover originals. **Publishes 40 titles/year. Receives 2,500 submissions/year. 20% of**

books from first-time authors; 30% from unagented writers. Pays standard royalty. Advance negotiable. Publishes book 2 years after acceptance of ms. Responds in 2 months to queries and unsolicited mss. Book catalog and ms guidelines for SASE.

Fiction: Children's picture books (ages 3-8); middle-grade fiction and illustrated chapter books (ages 7-10); older middle-grade fiction (ages 10-14) some young adult (ages 14-18). Particularly interested in middle-grade fiction with strong voice, literary quality, high interest for audience, poignancy, humor, unusual settings or plots. Historical fiction OK. Query or submit proposal package, including outline, table of contents and 3 sample chapters with SASE. Always include SASE or no response. No science fiction, no series or activity books, no board books.

Recent Title(s): *Getting Near to Baby*, by Audrey Couloumbis; *26 Fairmount Avenue*, by Tomie dePaola; *Next Stop Grand Central*, by Maira Kalman.

QUE, Macmillan Computer Publishing USA, 201 W. 103rd St., Indianapolis IN 46290. (317)581-3500. Website: www.mcp.com/que/. Vice President/Publisher: Paul Boger. **Acquisitions:** Holly Allender, acquisitions editor (Linux networking, programming, ERP); Gretchen Ganser, acquisitions editor (Linux networking, programming, ERP); Stephanie McComb, acquisitions editor (Idiot's Guides, Easy Series, Quick Reference Series); Jill Byus, acquisitions editor (Windows 2000, hardware, certification); Tracy Williams, acquisitions editor (Windows 2000, hardware, certification); Angelina Ward, Heather Kane, Jenny Watson (desktop applications, graphics, hardware, certification); Michelle Newcomb, Loretta Yates, Todd Green, Katie Purdum (database, ERP, consumer programming, networking, Linux). Publishes hardcover, trade paperback and mass market paperback originals and reprints. **Publishes 200 titles/year. 85% of books from unagented writers. Pays variable royalty on wholesale price or makes work-for-hire arrangements. Advance varies.** Accepts simultaneous submissions. Responds in 1 month to proposals. Catalog and ms guidelines free.

Nonfiction: Computer books.

Recent Title(s): *XML Web Documents from Scratch*.

QUEST BOOKS, Theosophical Publishing House, P.O. Box 270, Wheaton IL 60189. (630)665-0130. Fax: (630)665-8791. E-mail: questbooks@aol.com. Website: htpp://www.theosophica.org. **Acquisitions:** Sharon Brown Dorr, publishing manager; Brenda Rosen, acquisitions editor. Publishes hardcover originals and trade paperback originals and reprints. **Publishes 12-15 titles/year. Receives 500 queries and 100 mss/year. 50% of books from first-time authors; 75% from unagented writers. Pays 10-13% on wholesale price. Offers $3,000-10,000 advance.** Publishes book 20 months after acceptance of ms. Accepts simultaneous submissions. Responds in 1 month to queries, 2 months to proposals, 3 months to mss. Book catalog and ms guidelines free.

    Oⁿ "TPH is dedicated to the promotion of the unity of humanity and the encouragement of the study of religion, philosophy and science, to the end that we may better understand ourselves and our place in the universe."

Nonfiction: Biography, illustrated book, self-help. Subjects include anthropology/archaeology, art/architecture, health/medicine, music/dance, nature/environment, travel, self-development, self-help, philosophy (holistic), psychology (transpersonal), Eastern and Western religions, theosophy, comparative religion, men's and women's spirituality, Native American spirituality, holistic implications in science, health and healing, yoga, meditation, astrology. "Our speciality is high-quality spiritual nonfiction with a self-help aspect. Great writing is a must. We seldom publish 'personal spiritual awakening' stories. No submissions accepted that do not fit the needs outlined above." Accepts nonfiction translations. Query or submit proposal package, including author bio, contents, sample chapter and SASE. Reviews artwork/photos as part of ms package. Send photocopies.

Recent Title(s): *The Illustrated Encyclopedia of Buddhist Wisdom*, by Gill Farrer-Halls; *God Is at Eye Level: Photography as a Healing Art*, by Jan Phillips.

Tips: "Our audience includes the 'New Age' community, seekers in all religions, general public, professors, and health professionals. Read a few recent Quest titles. Know our books and our company goals. Explain how your book or proposal relates to other Quest titles. Quest gives preference to writers with established reputations/successful publications."

QUILL DRIVER BOOKS/WORD DANCER PRESS, 8386 N. Madsen Ave., Clovis CA 93611. (559)322-5917. Fax: (559)322-5967. E-mail: sbm12@csufresno.edu. **Acquisitions:** Stephen Blake Mettee, publisher. Publishes hardcover and trade paperback originals and reprints. **Publishes 10-12 titles/year. (Quill Driver Books: 4/year, Word Dancer Press: 6-8/year). 50% of books from first-time authors; 95% from unagented writers. Pays 4-10% royalty on retail price. Offers $500-5,000 advance.** Publishes book 9 months after acceptance. Accepts simultaneous submissions. Responds in 1 month to queries and proposals, 3 months to mss. Book catalog and ms guidelines for #10 SASE.

    Oⁿ "We publish a modest number of books per year, each of which, we hope, makes a worthwhile contribution to the human community, and we have a little fun along the way." Currently emphasizing books to enhance the lifestyles of those over 50.

Nonfiction: Biography, how-to, reference, general nonfiction. Subjects include Californiana, regional, fund-raising, writing. Query with proposal package. Reviews artwork/photos as part of ms package. Send photocopies.

Recent Title(s): *Damn! Why Didn't I Write That?: How Ordinary People are Raking in $100,000.00 or More Writing Niche Books & How You Can Too!*, by Marc McClutcheon.

THE QUILT DIGEST PRESS, NTC/Contemporary Publishing Group, 4255 W. Touhy, Lincolnwood IL 60712-1975. (847)679-5500. Fax: (847)679-2494. **Acquisitions:** Anne Knudsen, executive editor. Publishes hardcover and trade paperback originals. **Publishes 10-12 titles/year. Receives 100 queries and 30 mss/year. 20% of books from first-time authors; 80% from unagented writers. Pays royalty on wholesale price.** Publishes book 1 year after acceptance of ms. Accepts simultaneous submissions. Responds in 2 months. Book catalog and ms guidelines free.

O━ Quilt Digest Press publishes quilting and sewing craft books.

Nonfiction: How-to. Subjects include hobbies, crafts/quilting. Submit outline, bio, sample, photos and SASE. Reviews artwork/photos as part of ms package. Send color photocopies.

Recent Title(s): *Circles of the East*, by Kumiko Sudo.

QUITE SPECIFIC MEDIA GROUP LTD., 260 Fifth Ave., Suite 703, New York NY 10001. (212)725-5377. Fax: (212)725-8506. E-mail: info@quitespecificmedia.com. Website: www.quitespecificmedia.com. **Acquisitions:** Ralph Pine, editor-in-chief. Estab. 1967. Publishes hardcover originals, trade paperback originals and reprints. **Publishes 12 titles/year. Receives 300 queries/year and 100 mss/year. 75% of books from first-time authors; 85% from unagented writers. Pays royalty on wholesale price. Advance varies.** Publishes book 18 months after acceptance. Accepts simultaneous submissions. Responds "as quickly as possible." Book catalog available via website or upon request and ms guidelines free.

O━ Quite Specific Media Group is an umbrella company of five imprints specializing in costume and fashion, theater and design.

Imprint(s): Costume & Fashion Press, Drama Publishers, By Design Press, Entertainment Pro, Jade Rabbit

Nonfiction: Texts, guides, manuals, directories, reference and multimedia—for and about performing arts theory and practice: acting, directing; voice, speech, movement; makeup, masks, wigs; costumes, sets, lighting, sound; design and execution; technical theater, stagecraft, equipment; stage management; producing; arts management, all varieties; business and legal aspects; film, radio, television, cable, video; theory, criticism, reference; playwriting; theater and performance history; costume and fashion. Accepts nonfiction and technical works in translations also. Query with 1-3 sample chapters and SASE; no complete mss. Reviews artwork/photos as part of ms package.

Recent Title(s): Recently co-published books with the Victoria and Albert Museum, London.

[N] **QUORUM BOOKS**, Greenwood Publishing Group, 88 Post Rd. W., Westport CT 06881. (203)226-3571. Fax: (203)222-1502. Website: www.greenwood.com. **Acquisitions:** Eric Valentine, publisher. **Publishes 75 titles/year. 50% of books from first-time authors. Pays 7½-15% royalty on net price. Rarely offers advances.** Publishes book an average of 1 year after acceptance on ms. Accepts simultaneous submissions. Responds in 2 months to queries and proposals. Website offers a catalog, ms guidelines and editorial contacts.

O━ Quorum Books publishes professional and academic books in all areas of business and business-related law.

Nonfiction: Subjects include business, economics, finance. Query with proposal package, including scope, organization, length of project, whether a complete ms is available or when it will be, cv or résumé and SASE. *No unsolicited mss.*

Recent Nonfiction Title(s): *The Practice of Multinational Banking: Macro-Policy Issues and Key International Concepts, 2nd edition*, by Dara Khambata.

Tips: "We are not a trade publisher. Our products are sold almost entirely by mail, in hardcover and at relatively high list prices."

RAGGED MOUNTAIN PRESS, International Marine/The McGraw-Hill Companies, P.O. Box 220, Camden ME 04843-0220. (207)236-4837. Fax: (207)236-6314. **Acquisitions:** Thomas McCarthy, acquisitions editor; Jonathan Eaton, editorial director. Estab. 1969. Publishes hardcover and trade paperback originals and reprints. **Publishes 40 titles/year; imprint publishes 15, remainder are International Marine. Receives 200 queries and 100 mss/year. 30% of books from first-time authors; 90% from unagented writers. Pays 10-15% royalty on net price. Offers advance.** Publishes book 1 year after acceptance of ms. Accepts simultaneous submissions. Responds in 1 month to queries. *Writer's Market* recommends allowing 2 months for reply. Book catalog for 9×12 SAE with 10 first-class stamps. Manuscript guidelines for #10 SASE.

O━ Ragged Mountain Press publishes books that take you off the beaten path.

Nonfiction: Outdoor-related how-to, guidebooks, essays, adventure, sports. Subjects include camping, fly fishing, snowshoeing, backpacking, canoeing, outdoor cookery, skiing, snowboarding, survival skills and wilderness know-how, birdwatching, natural history, climbing and kayaking. "Ragged Mountain publishes nonconsumptive outdoor and environmental issues books of literary merit or unique appeal. Be familiar with the existing literature. Find a subject that hasn't been done or has been done poorly, then explore it in detail and from all angles." Query with outline and 1 sample chapter. Reviews artwork/photos as part of ms package. Send photocopies.

Recent Title(s): *Advanced Backpacker*, by Chris Townsend; *The Baffled Parent's Guide to Coaching Youth Soccer*, by Bobby Clark.

[N] **RAINBOW BOOKS**, Rainbow Publishers, P.O. Box 261129, San Diego CA 92196. (858)271-7600. Fax: (858)578-4795. E-mail: rbbooks@earthlink.net. Website: www.rainbowpublishers.com. **Acquisitions:** Christy Allen, editor. Publishes trade paperback originals. **Publishes 30 titles/year; imprint publishes 20 titles/year. Receives 250 queries and 250 mss/year. 50% of books from first-time authors; 100% from unagented writers. Makes outright purchase of at least $500.** Publishes book 18 months after acceptance. Accepts simultaneous submissions. Responds in 3 months. Book catalog for 9×12 SAE with 2 first-class stmps. Manuscript guidelines for #10 SASE.

O→ "We are looking for activity books for kids' teachers in a Christian setting (church, Christian school, home school, etc.)."

Nonfiction: Subjects include animals, cooking/foods/nutrition, creative nonfiction, education, gardening, nature/environment, recreation, religion, spirituality. Query with SASE or submit proposal package, including outline, 3-5 sample chapters and market analysis.

Recent Title(s): *Favorite Bible Children* (4-book series); *Big Puzzles for Little Hands*, by Carla Williams (4-book series).

Tips: Audience consists of teachers of kids 2-12 who want to provide a fun Bible learning environment. "Send for our catalog first to see what we've published then tell us why your topic is unique."

RAINBOW BOOKS, INC., P.O. Box 430, Highland City FL 33846. (863)648-4420. Fax: (863)647-5951. E-mail: rbibooks@aol.com. **Acquisitons:** Betsy A. Lampe, editorial director. Estab. 1979. Publishes hardcover and trade paperback originals. **Publishes 12-15 titles/year. Receives 300 queries and 100 mss/year. 90% of books from first-time authors; 80% from unagented writers. Pays 6-12% royalty on retail price. Offers advance.** Publishes book 1 year after acceptance of ms. Accepts simultaneous submissions. Responds in 1 month to queries and proposals, 2 months to mss. Manuscript guidelines for #10 SASE.

O→ Rainbow Books publishes self-help/how-to books for the layman, and is also interested in seeing the same type of nonfiction books for ages 8 to 14 years. "We have begun a limited line of mystery fiction, up to approximately 80,000 words. We publish no other fiction."

Nonfiction: Biography, children's/juvenile, how-to, self-help. Subjects include animals, business/economics, child guidance/parenting, education, gardening, hobbies, money/finance, nature/environment, philosophy, psychology, recreation, science, sociology, sports, women's issues/studies. "We want books that provide authoritative answers to questions in layman language. We have also begun a list of 3rd-to-8th grade titles for young people along the same lines as our adult general nonfiction. Writers must include background credentials for having written the book they propose." Query with SASE. Reviews artwork/photos as part of ms package. Send photocopies.

Fiction: "Mainly, we're looking for well-written mystery books that deserve to be published." Submit synopsis and 1st chapter and SASE with sufficient postage.

Recent Title(s): *How to Stay Married Without Going Crazy*, by Rebecca Ward, MSW (nonfiction); *Biotechnology is Murder*, by Dirk Wyle (fiction).

Tips: "We are addressing an adult population interested in answers to questions, and also 8- to 14-year-olds of the same mindset. Be professional in presentation of queries and manuscripts, and always provide a return mailer with proper postage attached in the event the materials do not fit our list. In mystery fiction, we don't want to see books with violence for violence's sake."

RANDOM HOUSE BOOKS FOR YOUNG READERS, (formerly Random House Children's Publishing), Random House, Inc., 201 E. 50th St., New York NY 10022. (212)751-2600. Fax: (212)940-7685. Website: www.randomh ouse/com/kids. Vice President/Publishing Director: Kate Klimo. **Acquisitions:** Mallory Loehr, senior editor/licensing director (Stepping Stones); Heidi Kilgras, editor (Step into Reading); Naomi Kleinberg, senior editor (Picturebacks). Estab. 1935. Publishes hardcover, trade paperback, and mass market paperback originals and reprints. **Publishes 200 titles/year. Receives 1,000 queries/year. Pays 1-6% royalty or makes outright purchase. Advance varies.** Publishes book 1 year after acceptance of ms. Accepts simultaneous submissions. Responds in within 6 months. Book catalog free.

O→ "Random House Books aim to create books that nurture the hearts and minds of children, providing and promoting quality books and a rich variety of media that entertain and educate readers from 6 months to 12 years."

Imprint(s): Random House Books for Young Readers, **Alfred A. Knopf and Crown Children's Books**, Dragonfly Paperbacks.

Nonfiction: Children's/juvenile. Subjects include animal, history, nature/environment, popular culture, science, sports. *Agented submissions only. No unsolicited mss.*

Fiction: Humor, juvenile, mystery, picture books, young adult. "Familiarize yourself with our list. We look for original, unique stories. Do something that hasn't been done." *Agented submissions only. No unsolicited mss.*

Recent Title(s): *Gerald McBoing Boing*, by Dr. Seuss.

RANDOM HOUSE, INC., 201 E. 50th St., New York NY 10022. (212)751-2600. Website: www.randomhouse.com.
Imprint(s): *Ballantine Publishing Group:* **Ballantine Books, Del Rey**, Fawcett, Ivy, Library of Contemporary Thought, One World. Wellspring. *The Bantam Dell Publishing Group:* Bantam, **Delacorte Press**, Dell, **Delta, The Dial Press**, DTP (Dell Trade Paperbacks), **Island**. *The Crown Publishing Group:* Bell Tower, **Clarkson Potter, Crown Business**, Crown Publishers, Discovery Books, Harmony Books, **House of Collectibles, Sierra Club Books**, Three Rivers Press, Times Books. *The Doubleday Broadway Publishing Group:* **Broadway Books, Currency, Doubleday, Doubleday Religious Publishing**, Doubleday/Image, **Nan A. Talese**, Waterbrook Press. *The Knopf Publishing Group:* Alfred A. Knopf, Everyman's Library, **Pantheon Books, Schocken Books, Vintage Anchor Publishing**. *Random House Audio Publishing Group:* Bantam Doubleday Dell Audio Publishing, Listening Library, Random House AudioBooks. *Random House Children's Media Group:* **Alfred A. Knopf Books for Young Readers**, Bantam Books for Young Readers, **Crown Books for Young Readers**, CTW Books (Children's Television Workshop), Delacorte Press Books for Young Readers, Doubleday Books for Young Readers, Dragonfly Books, Laurel-Leaf Books, **Random House Books for Young**

Readers, Yearling Books, Random House Home Video. *Random House Diversified Publishing Group:* Random House Large Print Publishing, Random House Value Publishing. *Random House Information Group:* **Fodor's Travel Publications**, Living Language, Princeton Review, Random House Puzzles & Games, Random House Reference & Information Publishing. *The Random House Trade Publishing Group:* **Random House Trade Books, Villard Books**, The Modern Library.

RANDOM HOUSE TRADE PUBLISHING GROUP, Random House, Inc., 201 E. 50th St., 11th Floor, New York NY 10022. (212)751-2600. Website: www.randomhouse.com. Estab. 1925. **Publishes 120 titles/year. Receives 3,000 submissions/year. Pays royalty on retail price.** Accepts simultaneous submissions. Responds in 2 months. Book catalog free. Manuscript guidelines for #10 SASE.

    ○━ "Random House is the world's largest English-language general trade book publisher. It includes an array of prestigious imprints that publish some of the foremost writers of our time—in hardcover, trade paperback, mass market paperback, electronic, multimedia and other formats."

Imprint(s): Modern Library, Random House Trade Books, **Villard**.

Nonfiction: Biography, cookbook, humor, illustrated book, self-help. Subjects include Americana, art, business/economics, classics, cooking and foods, health, history, music, nature, politics, psychology, religion, sociology and sports. No juveniles or textbooks (separate division).

    ● "This publisher accepts agented submissions only."

Fiction: Adventure, confession, experimental, fantasy, historical, horror, humor, mainstream, mystery, and suspense. Submit outline/synopsis, 3 sample chapters and SASE.

Recent Title(s): *Sex On Campus*, by Elliott and Brantley; *The Gospel According to the Son*, by Norman Mailer.

RED HEN PRESS, Valentine Publishing Group, P.O. Box 902587, Palmdale CA 93590-2587. (818)831-0649. Fax: (818)831-6659. E-mail: redhen@vpg.net. Website: www.vpg.net. **Acquisitions:** Mark E. Cull, publisher/editor (fiction); Katherine Gale, poetry editor (poetry, literary fiction). Estab. 1993. Publishes trade paperback originals. **Publishes 10 titles/year. Receives 2,000 queries and 500 mss/year. 10% of books from first-time authors; 90% from unagented writers. Pays 10% royalty on retail price.** Publishes book 1 year after acceptance of ms. Accepts simultaneous submissions. Responds in 1 month to queries, 2 months to proposals, 3 months to mss. Book catalog and ms guidelines available vie website or free upon request.

    ○━ Red Hen Press specializes in literary fiction and poetry.

Nonfiction: Biography, children's/juvenile, cookbooks. Subjects include anthropology/archaeology, ethnic, gay/lesbian, language/literature, travel, women's issues/studies. Query with SASE. Reviews artwork/photos as part of ms package. Send photocopies.

Fiction: Ethnic, experimental, feminist, gay/lesbian, historical, literary, mainstream/contemporary, poetry, poetry in translation, short story collections. "We prefer high-quality literary fiction." Query with SASE.

Poetry: Query with 5 sample poems.

Recent Titles: *Unfree Association: Holocaust Memoir*, by Dr. Bloch; *Tisch*, by Stephan Dixon.

Tips: "Audience reads poetry, literary fiction, intelligent nonfiction. If you have an agent, we may be too small since we don't pay advances. Write well. Send queries first. Be willing to help promote your own book."

REFERENCE SERVICE PRESS, 5000 Windplay Dr., Suite 4, El Dorado Hills CA 95762. (916)939-9620. Fax: (916)939-9626. E-mail: findaid@aol.com. Website: www.rspfunding.com. **Acquisitions:** Stuart Hauser, acquisitions editor. Estab. 1977. Publishes hardcover originals. **Publishes 10-20 titles/year. 100% of books from unagented writers. Pays 10% royalty or higher.** Publishes book 6 months after acceptance. Accepts simultaneous submissions. Responds in 2 months. Book catalog for #10 SASE.

    ○━ Reference Service Press publishes only directories and monographs dealing with financial aid.

Nonfiction: Reference for financial aid seekers. Subjects include education, ethnic, military/war, women's issues/studies, disabled. Submit outline and sample chapters.

Recent Title(s): *College Student's Guide to Merit and Other No-Need Funding, 2000-2002.*

Tips: "Our audience consists of librarians, counselors, researchers, students, re-entry women, scholars and other fundseekers."

Ⓐ **REGAN BOOKS**, HarperCollins, 10 E. 53rd St., New York NY 10022. (212)207-7400. Fax: (212)207-6951. Website: www.harpercollins.com. **Acquisitions:** Judith Regan, president/publisher. Estab. 1994. Publishes hardcover and trade paperback originals. **Publishes 30 titles/year. Receives 7,500 queries and 5,000 mss/year. Pays royalty on retail price. Advance varies.** Publishes book 1 year after acceptance of ms. Accepts simultaneous submissions. Responds in 3 months to proposals.

    ○━ Regan Books publishes general fiction and nonfiction: biography, self-help, style and gardening books, and is known for contemporary topics and controversial authors and titles.

Nonfiction: Biography, coffee table book, cookbook, gift book, illustrated book, reference, self-help. All subjects. *Agented submissions only. No unsolicited mss.* Reviews artwork as part of ms package. Send photocopies.

Fiction: All categories. *Agented submissions only. No unsolicited mss.*

Recent Title(s): *I Know This Much Is True*, by Wally Lamb.

A̲ REGNERY PUBLISHING, INC., Eagle Publishing, One Massachusetts Ave., NW, Washington DC 20001. (202)216-0600. Website: www.regnery.com. Publisher: Alfred S. Regnery. **Acquisitions:** Harry Crocker, executive editor (bestsellers); Erica Rogers, editor (health, exercise, diet); Jed Donahue, editor (biography, American history). Estab. 1947. Publishes hardcover and paperback originals and reprints. **Publishes 30 titles/year. 0% of books from unagented writers. Pays 8-15% royalty on retail price. Offers $0-50,000 advance.** Publishes book 1 year after acceptance. No fax submissions. Responds in 3 months to queries, proposals, mss.

O— Regnery publishes conservative, well-written, well-produced, sometimes controversial books. Currently emphasizing health books.

Imprint(s): Gateway Editions Classics, LifeLine Health Books.

Nonfiction: Biography, business/economics, current affairs, health/medicine, history, money/finance, politics. *Agented submissions only. No unsolicited mss.*

Recent Title(s): *A Republic, Not an Empire*, by Patrick J. Buchanan (nonfiction).

Tips: "We seek high-impact, headline-making, bestseller treatments of pressing current issues by established experts in the field."

RENAISSANCE BOOKS, Renaissance Media, 5858 Wilshire Blvd., Suite 200, Los Angeles CA 90036. (323)939-1840. **Acquisitions:** Kimbria Hays, production coordinator; Arthur Morey, managing editor; James Robert Parish, editor (show business); Richard F.X. O'Connor, editor (general nonfiction); Joe McNeely, editor (New Age/psychology). Publishes hardcover and trade paperback originals. **Publishes 50-60 titles/year. Receives 400 queries/year. 5% of books from first-time authors; 10% from unagented writers. Pays royalty on retail price. Advance varies widely.** Publishes book 7 months after acceptance of ms. Accepts simultaneous submissions. Responds in 2 months to proposals. Book catalog free.

O— Renaissance publishes a wide range of nonfiction trade books.

Nonfiction: Biography, cookbook, how-to, reference, self-help. Subjects include Americana, animals, business and economics, child guidance/parenting, cooking/foods/nutrition, government/politics, health/medicine, history, hobbies, money/finance, psychology, recreation, sociology, sports, entertainment, show business. Submit outline and 2 sample chapter with SASE.

Recent Title(s): *The America We Deserve*, by Donald Trump; *Who Killed Hollywood*, by Peter Bart.

Tips: "Include as much marketing information as possible in your proposal. Why will your book sell in today's marketplace?"

REPUBLIC OF TEXAS PRESS, Wordware Publishing, Inc., 2320 Los Rios Blvd., Suite 200, Plano TX 75074. (972)423-0090. Fax: (972)881-9147. E-mail: gbivona@wordware.com. Website: www.wordware.com. **Acquisitions:** Ginnie Bivona. Publishes trade and mass market paperback originals. **Publishes 28-32 titles/year. Receives 400 queries and 300 mss/year. 95% of books from unagented writers. Pays 8-10% royalty on net price.** Publishes book within 6 months after acceptance of ms. Responds in 2 months. Book catalog and ms guidelines for SASE.

O— Republic of Texas Press specializes in Texas history and general Texana.

Nonfiction: Old West, cuisine, sports, nature, travel guides, Texas military and ethnic history, ghost and mystery stories, humor, trivia and biography. Submit table of contents, 2 sample chapters, target audience, author bio, and SASE.

Recent Title(s): *The Alamo Story: From Early History to Current Conflicts*, by J.R. Edmondson; *Exploring Ft. Worth with Children*, by Michael Bumagin, M.D.

Tips: "We are interested in anything relating to Texas. From the wacky to the most informative, any nonfiction concept will be considered. Our market is primarily adult, but we will consider material for children aged 10-14."

RESOURCE PUBLICATIONS, INC., 160 E. Virginia St., Suite #290, San Jose CA 95112-5876. (408)286-8505. Fax: (408)287-8748. E-mail: info@rpinet.com. Website: www.rpinet.com/ml/ml.html. **Acquisitions:** Nick Wagner, editorial director (religious books). Estab. 1973. Publishes trade paperback originals. **Produces 12-18 titles/year. 30% of books from first-time authors; 99% from unagented writers. Pays 8% royalty (for a first project). Offers $250-1,000 advance.** Responds in 10 weeks. Book catalog and ms guidelines on website.

O— Resource Publications publishes books to help liturgists and ministers make the imaginative connection between liturgy and life.

Nonfiction: How-to, reference, self-help. Subjects include child guidance/parenting, education, music/dance, religion, professional ministry resources for worship, education, clergy and other leaders, for use in Roman Catholic and mainline Protestant churches. Submit proposal, including résumé. Reviews artwork as part of freelance ms package.

Fiction: Fables, anecdotes, faith sharing stories, any stories useful in preaching or teaching. Query.

Recent Title(s): *Cultivating Character: Month-by-Month Resources for Parents and Teachers, Performing Parables.*

Tips: "We are publishers and secondarily we are book packagers. Pitch your project to us for publication first. If we can't take it on on that basis, we may be able to take it on as a packaging and production project."

FLEMING H. REVELL PUBLISHING, Baker Book House, P.O. Box 6287, Grand Rapids MI 49516. Fax: (616)676-2315. Website: www.bakerbooks.com. **Acquisitions:** Linda Holland, editorial director; Bill Petersen, senior acquisitions editor; Lonnie Hull DuPont, senior editor; Jane Campbell, senior editor (Chosen Books). Estab. 1870. Publishes hardcover, trade paperback and mass market paperback originals and reprints. **Publishes 50 titles/year; imprint publishes**

10 titles/year. Receives 750 queries and 1,000 mss/year. 1% of books from first-time authors; 75% from unagented writers. Pays 14-18% royalty on wholesale price. Publishes book 1 year after acceptance of ms. Accepts simultaneous submissions. Responds in 3 months. Manuscript guidelines for #10 SASE.

O➤ Revell publishes to the heart (rather than to the head). For 125 years, Revell has been publishing evangelical books for the personal enrichment and spiritual growth of general Christian readers.

Imprint(s): Chosen Books, Spire Books.

Nonfiction: Biography, coffee table book, how-to, self-help. Subjects include child guidance/parenting, Christian Living. Query with outline and 2 sample chapters.

Fiction: Religious. Submit synopsis and 2 sample chapters.

Recent Title(s): *Making Children Mind without Losing Yours*, by Dr. Kevin Leman (nonfiction); *Triumph of the Soul*, by Michael R. Joens (fiction).

■ REVIEW AND HERALD PUBLISHING ASSOCIATION, 55 W. Oak Ridge Dr., Hagerstown MD 21740. (301)393-3000. E-mail: jjohnson@rhpa.org. **Acquisitions:** Jeannette R. Johnson, acquisitions editor. Estab. 1861. Publishes hardcover, trade paperback and mass market paperback originals and reprints. **Publishes 40-50 titles/year. Receives 200 queries and 350 mss/year. 50% of books from first-time authors; 95% from unagented writers. Pays 7-16% royalty. Offers $500-1,000 advance.** Publishes book 18-24 months after acceptance of ms. Accepts simultaneous submissions. Responds in 1 month to queries and proposals, 2 months to mss. Book catalog for 10×13 SASE. Manuscript guidelines for #10 SASE.

O➤ "Through print and electronic media, the Review and Herald Publishing Association nurtures a growing relationship with God by providing products that teach and enrich people spiritually, mentally, physically and socially as we near Christ's soon second coming. We belong to the Seventh-day Adventist denomination."

Nonfiction: Biography, children's/juvenile, cookbook, gift book, humor, multimedia, reference, self-help, textbook, Christian lifestyle, inspirational. Subjects include animals, anthropology/archaeology, child guidance/parenting, cooking/foods/nutrition, education, health/medicine, history, nature/environment, philosophy, religion, women's issues/studies. Submit proposal package, including 3 sample chapters and cover letter with SASE.

Fiction: Adventure, historical, humor, juvenile, mainstream/contemporary, religious, all Christian-living related. Submit synopsis and or 3 sample chapters.

Recent Title(s): *The Great Kidsboro Takeover*, by Marshal Younger (children's); *Ten Christian Values Every Kid Should Know*, by Donna Habenicht (child guidance); *Highly Effective Marriage*, by Nancy Van Pelt (marriage).

■ MORGAN REYNOLDS PUBLISHING, 620 S. Elm St., Suite 383-384, Greensboro NC 27406. Fax: (336)275-1152. E-mail: info@morganreynolds.com. Website: www.morganreynolds.com. **Acquisitions:** Laura Shoemaker, editor. Publishes hardcover originals. **Publishes 10-12 titles/year. Receives 250-300 queries and 100-150 mss/year. 50% of books from first-time authors; 100% from unagented writers. Pays 8-12% royalty on wholesale price. Offers $500-1,000 advance.** Publishes book 8 months after acceptance of ms. Accepts simultaneous submissions. Responds in 3 months.

O➤ Morgan Reynolds publishes nonfiction books for juvenile and young adult readers. "We prefer lively, well-written biographies of interesting contemporary and historical figures for our biography series. Books for our Great Events series should be insightful and exciting looks at critical periods. We are interested in more well-known subjects rather than the esoteric."

Nonfiction: Subjects include young adult/juvenile oriented Americana, business/economics, government/politics, history, language/literature, military/war, money/finance, and women's issues/studies. No children's books, picture books or fiction. We publish titles in the following series: Notable Americans, World Writers, Great Events, Champions of Freedom, Great Athletes, Masters of Music, Great Scientists, American Business Tycoons, Makers of the Media, as well as high-quality non-series works. Submit outline and 3 sample chapters or complete ms. Include SASE.

Recent Title(s): *George Gershwin: American Composer*, by Catherine Reef; *The Pullman Strike of 1894: American Labor Comes of Age*, by Rosemary Laughlin.

Tips: "Research the markets before submitting. We spend too much time dealing with manuscripts that shouldn't have been submitted. Request our writer's guidelines and visit our website. We will be happy to send a catalog if provided with 65 cents postage."

■ RICHBORO PRESS, P.O. Box 947, Southampton PA 18966-0947. (215)355-6084. Fax: (215)364-2212. E-mail: betapersii@2000_@yahoo.com. Website: www.richboropress.com. **Acquisitions:** George Moore, editor. Estab. 1979. Publishes hardcover, trade paperback originals and software. **Publishes 4 titles/year. Receives 500 submissions/year. 90% of books from unagented writers. Pays 10% royalty on retail price.** Publishes book 1 year after acceptance. Electronic submissions preferred. Responds in 2 months to queries. Free book catalog. Manuscript guidelines for $1 and #10 SASE.

O➤ Richboro specializes in cooking titles.

Nonfiction: Cookbook, how-to, gardening. Subjects include cooking/foods. Query.

RISING TIDE PRESS, 3831 N. Oracle Rd., Tucson AZ 85705-3254. (520)888-1140. Fax: (520)888-1123. Website: www.risingtide.com. **Acquisitions:** Debra Tobin, partner (mystery, adventure, nonfiction); Brenda Kazen, partner (science fiction, young adult fiction). Estab. 1991. Publishes trade paperback originals. **Publishes 10-15 titles/year. Receives**

1,000 queries and 600 mss/year. 75% of books from first-time authors; 100% from unagented writers. Pays royalty on wholesale price. Publishes book 15 months after acceptance. *No* simultaneous submissions. Responds in 1 week to queries, 1 months to proposals, 3 months to mss. Book catalog for $1. Writer's guidelines for #10 SASE.

O→ "We are committed to publishing books about strong women and their lives. We seek to provide readers with images of women aspiring to be more than their prescribed roles dictate. Books that stir the imagination." Currently more interested in books for young adults.

Nonfiction: Lesbian nonfiction. Query with outline, entire ms and *large* SASE. *Writer's Market* recommends a query with SASE first. Reviews artwork/photos as part of ms package. Send photocopies.

Fiction: Woman's fiction only. Adventure, erotica, fantasy, historical, horror, humor, literary, mainstream/contemporary, mystery, occult, romance, science fiction, suspense, mixed genres. "Major characters must be women and stories must depict strong women characters." Query with synopsis or entire ms and SASE.

Recent Title(s): *Feathering Your Nest: An Interactive Workbook & Guide to a Loving Lesbian Relationship,* by Gwen Leonhard and Jennie Mast (nonfiction); *Agenda For Murder,* by Joan Alberella (fiction).

Tips: "We welcome unpublished authors. We do *not* consider agented authors. Any material submitted should be proofed. No multiple submissions."

ROC BOOKS, Penguin Putnam Inc., 375 Hudson St., New York NY 10014. (212)366-2000. Website: www.penguinput nam.com. **Acquisitions:** Laura Anne Gilman, executive editor; Jennifer Heddle, assistant editor. Publishes mass market, trade and hardcover originals. **Publishes 36 titles/year. Receives 500 queries/year. Pays royalty. Advance negotiable.** Accepts simultaneous submissions. Report in 2-3 months to queries.

O→ "Roc tries to strike a balance between fantasy and science fiction. We're looking for books that are a good read, that people will want to pick up time and time again."

Fiction: Fantasy, horror, science fiction. Query with synopsis and 1-2 sample chapters. *"We discourage unsolicited submissions."*

Recent Title(s): *Queen of the Darkness,* by Anne Bishop; *On the Oceans of Eternity,* by S.M. Stirling.

ROCKBRIDGE PUBLISHING CO., Howell Press, P.O. Box 351, Berryville VA 22611-0351. (540)955-3980. Fax: (540)955-4126. E-mail: cwpub@visuallink.com. Website: rockbpubl.com. **Acquisitions:** Katherine Tennery, publisher. Estab. 1989. Publishes hardcover original and reprints, trade paperback originals. **Publishes 4-6 titles/year. Pays royalty on wholesale price. No advance.** Responds in 3 months to proposals. Writer's guidelines available on website.

O→ Rockbridge publishes nonfiction books about the Civil War, Virginia tour guides, Virginia/Southern folklore and ghost stories.

Nonfiction: "We are developing a series of travel guides to the country roads in various Virginia counties. The self-guided tours include local history, identify geographic features, etc. We are also looking for material about the Civil War, especially biographies, and expanding interests from Virginia to other southern states, notably Georgia." Query with outline, 3 sample chapters, author credentials and SASE.

Recent Title(s): *The Burning: Sheridan in the Shenandoah Valley,* by John Heatwole.

N RONIN PUBLISHING, INC., P.O. Box 522, Berkeley CA 94701. (510)420-3669. Fax: (510)420-3672. E-mail: info@roninpub.com. Website: www.roninpub.com. **Acquisitions:** Beverly Potter, publisher; Dan Joy, editor. Estab. 1983. Publishes trade paperback originals and reprints. **Publishes 8 titles/year; imprint publishes 1-2 titles/year. Receives 10 queries and 10 mss/year. Pays royalty on net only. Offers $500-1,000 advance.** Publishes book 1 year after acceptance of ms. Responds in 3 months to queries, 6 months to proposals and mss. Book catalog free.

O→ "Ronin publishes book as tools for personal development, visionary alternatives and expanded consciousness."

Imprint(s): 20th Century Alchemist (Contact: Beverly Potter, editor-in-chief).

Nonfiction: Reference, self-help. Subjects include agriculture/horticulture, business/economics, cooking/foods/nutrition, gardening, health/medicine, psychology, spirituality, counterculture/psychedelia. "Our publishing purview is highly specific, as indicated in our catalog. We have rarely if ever published a book which initially arrived as an unsolicited manuscript. Please send queries only." Query with SASE. Agented submissions only. No unsolicited mss, please.

Recent Title(s): *Timothy Leary Turn on Tune in Drop Out.*

Tips: "Our audience is interested in hard information and often buys several books on the same subject. Please submit query only. If on the basis of the query, we are interested in seeing the proposal or manuscript, we will let you know. No response to the query indicates that we have no interest. Become familiar with our interests through our catalog."

N ROSE PUBLISHING, 4455 Torrance Blvd., #259, Torrance CA 90503. (310)370-8962. Fax: (310)370-7492. E-mail: rosepubl@aol.com. Website: www.rose-publishing.com. **Acquisitions:** Carol R. Witte, editor. **Publishes 5-10 titles/year. 5% of books from first-time authors; 100% from unagented writers. Pays royalty or makes outright purchase.** Publishes book 18 months after acceptance of ms. Accepts simultaneous submissions. Responds in 3 months to proposals, 2 months to mss. Book catalog free.

O→ "We publish only Bible-based materials in chart, poster or pamphlet form, easy-to-understand and appealing to children, teens or adults on Bible study, prayer, basic beliefs, scripture memory, salvation, sharing the gospel and worship."

Nonfiction: Reference, pamphlets, group study books. Subjects include archaeology, Bible studies, Christian history, counseling aids, cults/occult, curriculum, Christian discipleship, evangelism/witnessing, Christian living, marriage, prayer, prophecy, creation, singles issues, spirituality. Submit proposal package, including outline, 3 sample chapters and photocopies of chart contents or poster artwork. Reviews artwork/photos as part of the ms package. Send photocopies.
Recent Title(s): *Creation & Evolution* (chart and pamphlet); *Prophecies Fulfilled by Jesus* (chart).
Tips: Audience includes both church (Bible study leaders, Sunday school teachers (all ages), pastors, youth leaders) and home (parents, home schoolers, children, youth, high school and college).

THE ROSEN PUBLISHING GROUP, 29 E. 21st St., New York NY 10010. (212)777-3017. Fax: (212)253-6915. E-mail: rosened@mail.rosenpub.com. **Acquisitions:** Erin M. Hovanec, young adult editorial division leader. Estab. 1950. Publishes nonfiction hardcover originals. **Publishes 300 titles/year. Receives 150 queries and 75 mss/year. 50% of books from first-time authors; 95% from unagented writers. Pays 6-10% royalty on retail price or makes outright purchase of $175-1,200. May offer $500 advance.** Publishes books 9 months after acceptance of ms. Responds in 2 months to proposals. Book catalog and ms guidelines free.
    O── The Rosen Publishing Group publishes young adult titles for sale to school and public libraries. Each book is aimed at teenage readers and addresses them directly.
Imprint(s): PowerKids Press (nonfiction for grades K-4 that are supplementary to the curriculum. Topics include conflict resolution, character-building, health, safety, drug abuse prevention, history, self-help, religion, science and multicultural titles. **Contact:** Kristen Eck, PowerKids Press editorial division leader). Rosen Central (nonfiction for grades 5-8 on a wide range of topics, guidance topics or material related to the curriculum. Topics include social issues, health, sports, self-esteem, history and science. **Contact:** Erin M. Hovanec, young adult editorial division).
Nonfiction: Juvenile, self-help, young adult, reference. Submit outline and 1 sample chapter. Areas of particular interest include multicultural ethnographic studies; careers; coping with social, medical and personal problems; values and ethical behavior; drug abuse prevention; self-esteem; social activism; religion; science; and social studies.
Recent Title(s): *The Divorce Resource Series*; *Psyched for Science.*
Tips: "The writer has the best chance of selling our firm a book on vocational guidance or personal social adjustment, or high-interest, low reading-level material for teens."

N. ROUTLEDGE, INC., 29 W. 35th St., New York NY 10001-2299. (212)216-7800. Fax: (212)563-2269. Website: routledge-ny.com. **Acquisitions:** Kenneth Wright, vice president/publisher. Estab. 1836. **Publishes 175 titles/year in New York. 10% of books from first-time authors; 95% of books from unagented authors. Pays royalty.** Publishes book 1 year after acceptance. Accepts simultaneous submissions. Responds in 3 months to queries.
    O── The Routledge list includes humanities, social sciences, reference. Monographs, reference works, hardback and paperback upper-level texts, academic general interest.
Imprint(s): Theatre Arts Books.
Nonfiction: Academic subjects include philosophy, literary criticism, social sciences, history, women's studies, lesbian and gay studies, race and ethnicity, political science, anthropology, education, reference. Query with proposal package, including toc, intro, sample chapter, overall prospectus, cv and SASE.
Recent Title(s): *Teaching to Transgress,* by bell hooks.

ROWMAN & LITTLEFIELD PUBLISHING GROUP, 4720 Boston Way, Lanham MD 20706. (301)459-3366. Publishes hardcover and trade paperback originals and reprints. **Publishes 1,000 titles/year.**
Imprint(s): AltaMira Press, **Ivan R. Dee,** Derrydale Press, Lexington Books, New Amsterdam Books, **Rowman & Littlefield Publishers, Madison Books, Scarecrow Press,** University Press of America, Vestal Press.
Tips: "We have a scholarly audience."

ROXBURY PUBLISHING CO., P.O. Box 491044, Los Angeles CA 90049. (310)473-3312. **Acquisitions:** Claude Teweles, publisher. Estab. 1981. Publishes hardcover and paperback originals and reprints. **Publishes 25-30 titles/year. Pays royalty.** Accepts simultaneous submissions. Responds in 2 months.
    O── Roxbury publishes college textbooks in the humanities and social sciences only.
Nonfiction: College-level textbooks and supplements *only.* Subjects include speech, communication, political science, family studies, sociology, criminology, criminal justice. Query, submit outline/synopsis and sample chapters, or submit complete ms. *Writer's Market* recommends a query with SASE first.

RUMINATOR BOOKS, (formerly Hungry Mind Press), 1648 Grand Ave., St. Paul MN 55105. (651)699-7038. Fax: (651)699-7190. E-mail: books@ruminator.com. Website: www.ruminator.com. **Acquisitions:** Pearl Kilbride. Publishes hardcover originals, trade paperback originals and reprints. **Publishes 10-12 titles/year. Receives 300 queries and 500 mss/year. 40% of books from unagented writers. Royalties and advances vary.** Publishes book 1 year after acceptance of ms. Accepts simultaneous submissions. Responds in 2 months to proposals. Book catalog for 6×9 SAE and 2 first-class stamps. Manuscript guidelines for #10 SASE.
    O── Ruminator Books is an independent press dedicated to publishing literary works from diverse voices, books that bring a political, social, or cultural idea to a wide and varied readership. Currently emphasizing cultural, political, social commentary and nature subjects.
Nonfiction and Fiction: Literary, adult fiction and nonfiction. No how-to or self-help/instructional mss. Submit proposal package, including letter, outline and at least one sample chapter with SASE.

Recent Title(s): *Nellie Stone Johnson: The Life of an Activist*, with David Braver (nonfiction); *River Warren*, by Kent Megers.

RUNNING PRESS BOOK PUBLISHERS, 125 S. 22nd St., Philadelphia PA 19103. (215)567-5080. Fax: (215)568-2919. President/Publisher: Stuart Teacher. **Acquisitions:** Carlo DeVito, publisher; Jennifer Worick, editorial director; Justin Loeber, publicity director; Bill Jones, design director; John Whalen, sales director; Bill Luckey, production director. Estab. 1972. Publishes hardcover originals, trade paperback originals and reprints. **Publishes 150 titles/year. Receives 600 queries/year. 50% of books from first-time authors; 30% from unagented writers. Payment varies. Advances varies.** Publishes book 6-18 months after acceptance of ms. Accepts simultaneous submissions. Responds in 2 months to queries. Book catalog free. Manuscript guidelines for #10 SASE.

   O↦ "Running Press and Courage Books publish nonfiction trade and promotional titles, including pop culture books, cookbooks, quote books, children's learning kits, photo-essay books, journals, notebooks, literary classics, inspirational, crossword puzzles."

Imprint(s): Courage Books.

Nonfiction: Children's/juvenile, how-to, self-help. Subjects include art/architecture, cooking/foods/nutrition, recreation, science, craft, how-to. Query with outline, contents, synopsis and SASE. Reviews artwork/photos as part of the ms package. Send photocopies; "no originals."

Recent Title(s): *Strange Fruit*, by David Margolick; *It's Slinky!*, by Lou Harry.

RUTGERS UNIVERSITY PRESS, 100 Joyce Kilmer Ave., Piscataway NJ 08854-8099. (732)445-7762. Fax: (732)445-7039. E-mail: marlie@rci.rutgers.edu. Website: rutgerspress.rutgers.edu. **Acquisitions**: Leslie Mitchner, editor-in-chief/associate director (humanities); David Myers, acquiring editor (social sciences); Helen Hsu, senior editor (science, regional books). Estab. 1936. Publishes hardcover originals and trade paperback originals and reprints. **Publishes 80 titles/year. Receives up to 1,500 queries and up to 300 books/year. Up to 30% of books from first-time authors; 70% from unagented writers. Pays 7½-15% royalty on retail or net price. Offers $1,000-10,000 advance.** Publishes book 1 year after acceptance of ms. Accepts simultaneous submissions, if so noted. Responds in 1 month to proposals. Book catalog and ms guidelines available via website or with SASE.

   O↦ "Our press aims to reach audiences beyond the academic community with accessible scholarly and regional books."

Nonfiction: Books for use in undergraduate courses. Subjects include anthropology, African-American studies, Asian-American studies, education, gay/lesbian, government/politics, gender studies, health/medicine, history of science, literature, literary criticism, multicultural studies, nature/environment, regional, religion, human evolution, sociology, translation, women's studies, ecology, media studies. Submit outline and 2-3 sample chapters. Reviews artwork/photos as part of the ms package. Send photocopies.

Recent Title(s): *The Great American Road Trip: U.S. 1, Maine to Florida*, by Peter Genovese.

Tips: Both academic and general audiences. "Many of our books have potential for undergraduate course use. We are more trade-oriented than most university presses. We are looking for intelligent, well-written and accessible books. Avoid overly narrow topics."

RUTLEDGE HILL PRESS, Thomas Nelson, P.O. Box 141000, Nashville TN 37214-1000. (615)244-2700. Fax: (615)244-2978. Website: www.rutledgehillpress.com. **Acquisitions:** Lawrence Stone, publisher. Estab. 1982. Publishes hardcover and trade paperback originals and reprints. **Publishes 40-50 titles/year. Receives 1,000 submissions/year. 40% of books from first-time authors; 80% from unagented writers. Pays royalty. Offers advance.** Publishes book 10 months after acceptance. Responds in 8 months. Book catalog for 9×12 SAE with 4 first-class stamps. Manuscript guidelines for #10 SASE.

   O↦ "We are a publisher of market-specific books, focusing on particular genres or regions."

Nonfiction: Biography, cookbook, humor, regional travel, Civil War history, quilt books, sports. "The book should have a unique marketing hook other than the subject matter itself. Books built on new ideas and targeted to a specific U.S. region are welcome. Please, no fiction, children's, academic, poetry or religious works, and we won't even look at *Life's Little Instruction Book* spinoffs or copycats." Submit cover letter that includes brief marketing strategy and author bio, outline and sample chapters. Reviews artwork/photos as part of ms package.

Recent Title(s): *A Gentleman Entertains*, by John Bridges and Bryan Curtis; *101 Secrets a Good Dad Knows*, by Walter Browder and Sue Ellen Browder; *Pilgrims: Sinners, Saints and Prophets*, by Marty Stuart.

   ● Rutledge Hill was acquired last year by the large Christian publisher Thomas Nelson.

SAFARI PRESS INC., 15621 Chemical Lane, Building B, Huntington Beach CA 92649-1506. (714)894-9080. Fax: (714)894-4949. E-mail: info@safaripress.com. Website: www.safaripress.com. **Acquisitions:** Jacqueline Neufeld, editor. Estab. 1984. Publishes hardcover originals and reprints and trade paperback reprints. **Publishes 20-25 titles/year. 50% of books from first-time authors; 99% from unagented writers. Pays 8-15% royalty on wholesale price.** No simultaneous submissions. Book catalog for $1. "Request our 'Notice to Prospective Authors.' "

   O↦ Safari Press publishes books *only* on big-game hunting, firearms, and wingshooting; this includes African, North American, European, Asian, and South American hunting and wingshooting.

Nonfiction: Biographies of hunters, "how-to" hunting and wingshooting stories, hunting adventure stories. Subjects include hunting, firearms, wingshooting—"nothing else. We discourage autobiographies, unless the life of the hunter or firearms maker has been exceptional. We routinely reject manuscripts along the lines of 'Me and my buddies went hunting for . . . and a good time was had by all!' No fishing." Query with outline and SASE.
Recent Title(s): *Campfire Lies of a Canadian Guide*, by Fred Webb; *The Adventurous Life of a Vagabond Hunter*, by Sten Cedergrin.
- The editor notes that she receives many manuscripts outside the areas of big-game hunting, wingshooting and sporting firearms.

SAGAMORE PUBLISHING, 804 N. Neil St., Suite 100, Champaign IL 61820. (217)363-2072. Fax: (217)363-2073. E-mail: books@sagamorepub.com. Website: www.sagamorepub.com. **Acquisitions:** Joseph Bannon, CEO (parks, recreation, leisure); Tom Bast, director of acquistions (outdoor recreation). Estab. 1974. Publishes hardcover and trade paperback originals. **Publishes 10-12 titles/year. Receives 30-40 queries and 25-30 mss/year. 40% of books from first-time authors; 100% from unagented writers. Pays 7-15% royalty. No advance.** Publishes book 6 months after acceptance of ms. Accepts simultaneous submissions. Responds in 1 month. Book catalog and ms guidelines free or on website.
- "Sagamore Publishing has been a leader in the parks and recreation field for over 20 years. We are now expanding into the areas of tourism and recreation for special populations such as people with autism or ADD/ADHD, and outdoor adventure and wildlife."
Nonfiction: Reference, textbook. Subjects include education, health/medicine, nature/environment, recreation, outdoor adventure, tourism. Submit proposal package, including outline, 1 sample chapter and market projections. Reviews artwork/photos as part of ms package. Send photocopies.
Recent Titles: *Outdoor Recreation in American Life*, by Ken Cordell (textbook/reference).
Tips: "We strongly encourage potential authors to submit a marketing prospective with any manuscript they submit."

ST. ANTHONY MESSENGER PRESS, 1615 Republic St., Cincinnati OH 45210-1298. (513)241-5615. Fax: (513)241-0399. E-mail: stanthony@americancatholic.org. Website: www.americancatholic.org. Publisher: The Rev. Jeremy Harrington, O.F.M. **Acquisitions:** Lisa Biedenbach, managing editor. Estab. 1970. Publishes trade paperback originals. **Publishes 15-25 titles/year. Receives 200 queries and 50 mss/year. 5% of books from first-time authors; 99% from unagented writers. Pays 10-12% royalty on net receipts of sales. Offers $1,000 average advance.** Publishes book 18 months after acceptance. Responds in 1 month on queries, 2 months on proposals and mss. Book catalog for 9×12 SAE with 4 first-class stamps. Manuscript guidelines free.
- "St. Anthony Messenger Press/Franciscan Communications seeks to communicate the word that is Jesus Christ in the styles of Saints Francis and Anthony. Through print and electronic media marketed in North America and worldwide, we endeavor to evangelize, inspire and inform those who search for God and seek a richer Catholic, Christian, human life. Our efforts help support the life, ministry and charities of the Franciscan Friars of St. John the Baptist Province, who sponsor our work."
Nonfiction: History, religion, Catholic identity and teaching, prayer and spirituality resources, scripture study. Children's books with Catholic slant, family-based religious education programs. Query with outline and SASE. Reviews artwork/photos as part of ms package.
Recent Title(s): *Mary's Flowers: Gardens, Legends and Meditations*, by Vincenzina Krymon; *Bible Stories Revisited: Discover Your Story in the Old Testament*, by Maevina Scott, O.S.F.
Tips: "Our readers are ordinary 'folks in the pews' and those who minister to and educate these folks. Writers need to know the audience and the kind of books we publish. Manuscripts should reflect best and current Catholic theology and doctrine." St. Anthony Messenger Press especially seeks books which will sell in bulk quantities to parishes, teachers, pastoral ministers, etc. They expect to sell at least 5,000 to 7,000 copies of a book.

ST. AUGUSTINE'S PRESS, P.O. Box 2285, South Bend IN 46680-2285. (219)-291-3500. Fax: (219)291-3700. E-mail: bruce@staugustine.net. Website: wwwstaugustine.net. **Acquisitions:** Bruce Fingerhut, president (philosophy). Publishes hardcover originals and trade paperback originals and reprints. **Publishes 50 titles/year. Receives 200 queries and 100 mss/year. 5% of books from first-time authors; 95% from unagented writers. Pays 6-20% royalty. Offers $500-5,000 advance.** Publishes book 8 months after acceptance of ms. Accepts simultaneous submissions. Responds in 2 months on queries, 3 months on proposals, 4 months on mss. Book catalog free.
- "Our market is scholarly in the humanities. We publish in philosophy, religion, cultural history, and history of ideas only."
Imprints: Carthage Reprints.
Nonfiction: Biography, textbook. Subjects include history of ideas, cultural history, philosophy, religion. Query with SASE. Reviews artwork/photos as part of ms package. Send photocopies.
Recent Title(s): *Plato's Symposium*, by S. Rosen (philosophy); *Xanthippic Dialogues*, by R. Scruton (philosophy).

ST. BEDE'S PUBLICATIONS, St. Scholastica Priory, P.O. Box 545, Petersham MA 01366-0545. (978)724-3407. Fax: (978)724-3574. President: Mother Mary Clare Vincent. **Acquisitions:** Acquisitions Editor. Estab. 1977. Publishes hardcover originals, trade paperback originals and reprints. **Publishes 8-12 titles/year. Receives 100 submissions/year. 30-40% of books from first-time authors; 98% from unagented writers. Nonauthor subsidy publishes 10% of**

books. Pays 5-10% royalty on wholesale price or retail price. No advance. Publishes book 2 years after acceptance of ms. Accepts simultaneous submissions. Responds in 2 months. Book catalog and ms guidelines for 9 × 12 SAE and 2 first-class stamps.

O➤ St. Bede's Publications is owned and operated by the Roman Catholic nuns of St. Scholastica Priory. The publications are seen as as apostolic outreach. Their mission is to make available to everyone quality books on spiritual subjects such as prayer, scripture, theology and the lives of holy people.

Nonfiction: Textbook (theology), religion, prayer, spirituality, hagiography, theology, philosophy, church history, related lives of saints. No submissions unrelated to religion, theology, spirituality, etc., and no poetry, fiction or children's books. Query or submit outline and sample chapters with SASE. Does not return submissions without adequate postage.

Recent Title(s): *Truthful Living*, by Michael Casey; *The Invisible Father*, by Louis Bouyer (translated from French).

Tips: "There seems to be a growing interest in monasticism among lay people, and we will be publishing more books in this area. For our theology/philosophy titles our audience is scholars, colleges and universities, seminaries, etc. For our other titles (i.e. prayer, spirituality, lives of saints, etc.) the audience is above-average readers interested in furthering their knowledge in these areas."

ST. MARTIN'S PRESS, 175 Fifth Ave., New York NY 10010. Estab. 1952. Publishes hardcover, trade paperback and mass market originals. **Publishes 1,500 titles/year. Pays royalty. Offers advance.** General interest publisher of both fiction and nonfiction.

Imprint(s): Bedford Books, Buzz Books, **Dead Letter, Thomas Dunne Books, Forge, Picador USA**, St. Martin's Press Scholarly & Reference, **Stonewall Inn Editions, TOR Books**.

Nonfiction: General nonfiction, reference, scholarly, textbook. Biography, business/economics, contemporary culture, cookbooks, self-help, sports, true crime.

Fiction: General fiction. Fantasy, historical, horror, literary, mainstream, mystery, science fiction, suspense, thriller, Western (contemporary).

ST. MARTIN'S PRESS, SCHOLARLY & REFERENCE DIVISION, St. Martin's Press, 175 Fifth Ave., New York NY 10010. (212)982-3900. Fax: (212)777-6359. **Acquisitions:** Michael Flamini, editorial director (history, politics, education, religion); Karen Wolny, senior editor (politics); Krsiti Long, editor (literary criticism, cultural studies, anthropology); Anthony Wahl, editor (political economy, political theory, Asian studies). Publishes hardcover and trade paperback originals. **Firm publishes 700 titles/year. Receives 500 queries and 600 mss/year. 25% of books from first-time authors; 75% from unagented writers. Pays royalty: trade, 7-10% list; other, 7-10% net. Advance varies.** Publishes book 7 months after acceptance of ms. Accepts simultaneous submissions. Responds in 1 month on proposals. Book catalog and ms guidelines free.

O➤ "We remain true to our origin as a scholarly press . . . with the backing of St. Martin's Press we are able to make books more accessible."

Nonfiction: Reference, scholarly. Subjects include business/economics, government/politics, history, language/literature, philosophy, religion, sociology, women's issues/studies, humanities, social studies. No fiction or poetry. "We are looking for good solid scholarship." Query with proposal package including outline, 3-4 sample chapters, prospectus, cv and SASE. "We like to see as much completed material as possible." Reviews artwork/photos as part of ms package.

● St. Martin's Press, Scholarly and Reference Division merged with Macmillan UK and will be called Palgrave.

Recent Title(s): *Joan of Arc: Her Story*, by Régine Pernoud and Marie-Véronique Clin, revised and translated by Jeremy Duquesnay Adams.

■■ **SAINT MARY'S PRESS**, 702 Terrace Heights, Winona MN 55987-1320. (800)533-8095. Fax: (800)344-9225. Website: www.smp.org. **Acquisitions:** Steve Nagel, editor (young adult fiction). Estab. 1943. Publishes trade paperback originals. **Publishes 20 titles/year. Receives 300 queries and 150 mss/year. 70% of books from first-time authors; 95% from unagented writers. Pays 8-12% royalty on wholesale price. No advance.** Publishes book 14 months after acceptance of ms. Accepts simultaneous submissions. Book catalog free or on website. Ms guidelines free.

Nonfiction: Subjects include memoirs, regional, spirituality. Titles for Catholic youth and their parents, teachers and youth ministers. Query with SASE or proposal package, including outline, 1 sample chapter and brief author bio.

Fiction: Religious, young adult. "We are looking for character-driven young adult novels of 40,000 words that: portray the struggle toward adulthood, whatever the genre or historical circumstances. We want unforgetable characters."

Recent Titles: *Catholic Youth Bible*, edited by B. Singer-Towns; *Neighbors and Traitors*, by C. Duncan Buckman.

Tips: "Do research of Saint Mary's Press books lives before submitting your proposal."

SALINA BOOKSHELF, 624½ North Beaver Street, Flagstaff AZ 86001. (520)527-0070. Website salinabookshelf.com. Editor: Louise Lockard. Publishes trade paperback originals and reprints. **No books from first-time authors; 100% from unagented writers. Pays 20% minimum royalty.** Publishes book 6 months after acceptance. Accepts simultaneous submissions. Responds in 3 months.

Nonfiction: Children's/juvenile, textbook (Navajo language). Ethnic subjects. "We publish childrens' bilingual readers. Nonfiction should be appropriate to science and social studies curriculum grades 3-8." Query. Reviews artwork/photos as part of ms package. Send photocopies.

Fiction: Juvenile. "Submissions should be in English/a language taught in Southwest classrooms." Query.

Recent Title(s): *Dine Bizaad: Speak, Read, Write Navajo*, by Irvy W. Goossen.

Poetry: "We accept poetry in English/Southwest language for children." Submit 3 sample poems.

SALVO PRESS, P.O. Box 9095, Bend OR 97708. Phone/fax: (541)330-8746. E-mail: sschmidt@bendnet.com. Website: www.salvopress.com. **Acquisitions:** Scott Schmidt, publisher. Publishes trade paperback originals and e-books. **Publishes 6 titles/year. Receives 500 queries and 100 mss/year. 50% of books from first-time authors; 50% from unagented writers. Pays 8-15% royalty on retail price. No advance.** Publishes book 9 months after acceptance of ms. Responds in 1 month to queries, 2 months on mss. Book catalog and ms guidelines on website.
Fiction: Mystery, suspense, espionage, thriller. Query with SASE. "Our needs change. Check our website." Recent title: *Snake Song*, by Gerald Duff (mystery).
Tips: "Salvo Press also sponsors the annual Mystery Novel Award. Send SASE for guidelines or check the website."

SAMS, Macmillan Computer Publishing USA, 201 W. 103rd St., Indianapolis IN 46290. (317)581-3500. Website: www.mcp.com/sams/. Publisher: Dean Miller/non-window applications. **Acquisitions:** Angela Kozlowski, acquisitions editor; Steve Anglin, acquisitions editor (operating systems, certification, professional programming); Randi Roger, acquisitions editor (applications, web); Sharon Cox, acquisitions editor (programming); Neil Rowe, Geoff Mukhtar, Danielle Bird (Microsoft programming, operating systems/servers, networking); William Brown, Carol Ackerman (non-Microsoft programming, networking); Jeff Schultz, Betsy Brown, Shelley Johnston (consumer applications and operating systems, graphics, Web development). Estab. 1951. Publishes trade paperback originals. **Publishes 160 titles/year. 30% of books from first-time authors; 95% from unagented writers. Pays royalty on wholesale price, negotiable. Advance negotiable.** Publishes book 1 year after acceptance of ms. Accepts simultaneous submissions if noted; "however, once contract is signed, Sams Publishing retains first option rights on future works on same subject." Responds in 6 weeks on queries. Manuscript guidelines free.
 O— Sams has made a major commitment to publishing books that meet the needs of computer users, programmers, administrative and support personnel, and managers.
Nonfiction: Computer subjects. Query with SASE.
Recent Title(s): *Microsoft Windows 2000 Server Unleashed.*

[N] SANDLAPPER PUBLISHING CO., INC., P.O. Box 730, Orangeburg SC 29116-0730. (803)531-1658. Fax: (803)534-5223. E-mail: agallman@theisp.net. **Acquisitions:** Amanda Gallman, managing editor. Estab. 1982. Publishes hardcover and trade paperback originals and reprints. **Publishes 6 titles/year. Receives 200 submissions/year. 80% of books from first-time authors; 95% from unagented writers. Pays 15% maximum royalty on net receipts.** Publishes book 20 months after acceptance. Accepts simultaneous submissions, if so noted. Responds in 3 months. Book catalog and ms guidelines for 9 × 12 SAE with 4 first-class stamps.
 O— "We are an independent, regional book publisher specializing in nonfiction relating to South Carolina."
Nonfiction: History, biography, illustrated books, humor, cookbook, juvenile (ages 9-14), reference, textbook. Subjects are limited to history, culture and cuisine of the Southeast and especially South Carolina. "We are looking for manuscripts that reveal under-appreciated or undiscovered facets of the rich heritage of our region. If a manuscript doesn't deal with South Carolina or the Southeast, the work is probably not appropriate for us. We don't do self-help books, children's books about divorce, kidnapping, etc., and absolutely no religious manuscripts." Query or submit outline and sample chapters "if you're not sure it's what we're looking for, otherwise complete ms." *Writer's Market* recommends query with SASE first. Reviews artwork/photos as part of ms package.
Recent Nonfiction Title(s): *The Man Who Loved the Flag*; *South Carolina a Day at a Time.*
Fiction: "We do not need fiction submissions at present, and will not consider any horror, romance or religious fiction." Query or submit outline/synopsis and sample chapters. "Submit books dealing with regional nature, science and outdoor subjects on South Carolina."
Tips: "Our readers are South Carolinians, visitors to the region's tourist spots, and friends and family that live out-of-state. We are striving to be a leading regional publisher for South Carolina. We will be looking for more history, travel and biography."

SANTA MONICA PRESS LLC, P.O. Box 1076, Santa Monica CA 90406. Website: www.santamonicapress.com. **Acquisitions:** Acquistions Editor. Estab. 1991. Publishes trade paperback originals. **Publishes 6-10 titles/year. Receives 200-300 queries and mss/year. 75% of books from first-time authors; 75% from unagented writers. Pays 4-10% royalty on wholesale price. Offers $500-2,500 advance.** Publishes book 1 year after acceptance of ms. Accepts simultaneous submissions. Responds in 2 months on proposals. Book catalog and ms guidelines for SASE with 55 cents postage.
 O— Santa Monica Press Publishes two lines of books: general how-to books written in simple, easy-to-understand terms; and books which explore popular culture from an offbeat perspective.
Nonfiction: Gift book, how-to, illustrated book reference. Subjects include Americana, pop culture, health/medicine, music/dance, sports, theater, film, general how-to. Submit proposal package, including outline, 2-3 sample chapters, biography, marketing potential of book with SASE. All unsolicited mss returned unopened. Reviews artwork/photos as part of the ms package. Send photocopies.
Recent Title(s): *Quack! Tales of Medical Fraud from the Museum of Questionable Medical Devices*, by Bob McCoy (nonfiction); *The Seven Sacred Rites of Menopause*, by Kristi Boylan (nonfiction).
Tips: "Our how-to books provide readers with practical guidance in a wide variety of subjects, from letter writing to health care. These handy guides are written in simple, easy-to-understand terms. Our offbeat books explore popular culture from an offbeat perspective. These large format books feature hundreds of graphics and photos and are written for the naturally curious reader who possesses a healthy sense of humor."

SARABANDE BOOKS, INC., 2234 Dundee Rd., Suite 200, Louisville KY 40205. (502)458-4028. Fax: (502)458-4065. E-mail: sarabandeb@aol.com. Website: www.sarabandebooks.org. **Acquisitions**: Sarah Gorham, editor-in-chief. Publishes hardcover and trade paperback originals. **Publishes 8 titles/year. Receives 500 queries and 2,000 mss/year. 35% of books from first-time authors; 75% from unagented writers. Pays 10% royalty on actual income received. Offers $500-2,000 advance.** Publishes book 18 months after acceptance of ms. Accepts simultaneous submissions. Responds in 3 months on queries, 6 months on mss. Book catalog free. Manuscript guidelines for #10 SASE.
> O— "Sarabande Books was founded to publish poetry and short fiction, as well as the occasional literary essay collection. We look for works of lasting literary value. We are actively seeking novellas, as well as essays on the writing life."

Fiction: Literary, novellas, short story collections. "We do not publish novels." Query with 1 sample story, 1 page bio, listing of publishing credits and SASE. *Submissions in September only.*

Poetry: "Poetry of superior artistic quality. Otherwise no restraints or specifications." Query and submit 10 sample poems. *Submissions in September only.*

Recent Title(s): *How She Knows What She Knows About Yo-Yos*, by Mary Ann Taylor-Hall (fiction); *On Sleeping*, by Michael Burkard (poetry).

Tips: Sarabande publishes for a general literary audience. "Know your market. Read—and buy—books of literature." Sponsors contests.

N: SARPEDON PUBLISHERS, 49 Front St., Rockville Centre NY 11570. **Acquisitions**: Steven Smith. Estab. 1991. Publishes hardcover originals and trade paperback reprints. **Publishes 15 titles/year. Receives 100 queries/year. 14% of books from first-time authors; 20% from unagented writers. Pays royalty. Offers $250-1,250 advance.** Publishes book 6-9 months after acceptance of ms. Accepts simultaneous submissions. Responds in 1 months on queries, 2 months on proposals, 3 months on mss. Book catalog and ms guidelines for #10 SASE.

Nonfiction: Biography. Subjects include Americana, government, exploration, European history, military/war. Submit outline, 2 sample chapters and synopsis. Reviews artwork/photos as part of ms package. Send photocopies.

SAS INSTITUTE INC., SAS Campus Dr., Cary NC 27513-2414. (919)677-8000. Fax: (919)677-4444. E-mail: sasbbu @.sas.com. Website: www.sas.com. **Acquisitions**: Julie M. Platt, editor-in-chief. Estab. 1976. Publishes hardcover and trade paperback originals. **Publishes 40 titles/year. Receives 30 submissions/year. 50% of books from first-time authors; 100% from unagented writers. Payment negotiable. Offers negotiable advance.** Responds in 2 weeks on queries. Book catalog and ms guidelines are available via website or with SASE.
> O— SAS Institute publishes books for SAS software users, "both new and experienced."

Nonfiction: Software, technical, textbook, statistics. "SAS Institute's Publications Division publishes books developed and written inhouse. Through the Books by Users program, we also publish books by SAS users on a variety of topics relating to SAS software. We want to provide our users with additional titles to supplement our primary documentation and to enhance the users' ability to use the SAS System effectively. We're interested in publishing manuscripts that describe or illustrate using any of SAS Institute's software products. Books must be aimed at SAS software users, either new or experienced. Tutorials are particularly attractive, as are descriptions of user-written applications for solving real-life business, industry or academic problems. Books on programming techniques using the SAS language are also desirable. Manuscripts must reflect current or upcoming software releases, and the author's writing should indicate an understanding of the SAS System and the technical aspects covered in the manuscript." Query. Submit outline/synopsis and sample chapters. Reviews artwork/photos as part of ms package.

Recent Title(s): *The Little SAS Book: A Primer*, by Lora D. Delunch and Susan J. Slaughter.

Tips: "If I were a writer trying to market a book today, I would concentrate on developing a manuscript that teaches or illustrates a specific concept or application that SAS software users will find beneficial in their own environments or can adapt to their own needs."

SASQUATCH BOOKS, 615 Second Ave., Suite 260, Seattle WA 98104. (206)467-4300. Fax: (206)467-4301. E-mail: books@sasquatchbooks.com. Website: www.sasquatchbooks.com. President: Chad Haight. **Acquisitions**: Gary Luke, editorial director; Kate Rogers, editor (travel). Estab. 1986. Publishes regional hardcover and trade paperback originals. **Publishes 30 titles/year. 20% of books from first-time authors; 75% from unagented writers. Pays royalty on cover price. Offers wide range of advances.** Publishes ms 6 months after acceptance. Responds in 3 months. Book catalog for 9 × 12 SAE with 2 first-class stamps.
> O— Sasquatch Books publishes adult nonfiction from the Northwest, specializing in travel, cooking, gardening, history and nature.

Nonfiction: Subjects include regional art/architecture, cooking, foods, gardening, history, nature/environment, recreation, sports, travel and outdoors. "We are seeking quality nonfiction works about the Pacific Northwest and West Coast regions (including Alaska to California). In this sense we are a regional publisher, but we do distribute our books nationally." Query first, then submit outline and sample chapters with SASE.

Recent Title(s): *West Coast Seafood*, by Jay Harlow; *NW Herb Lover's Handbook*, by Mary Precis.

Tips: "We sell books through a range of channels in addition to the book trade. Our primary audience consists of active, literate residents of the West Coast."

SCARECROW PRESS, INC., Rowman & Littlefield Publishing Group, 4720 Boston Way, Lanham MD 20706. (301)459-3366. Fax: (301)459-2118. Website: www.scarecrowpress.com. **Acquisitions**: Sue Easun, acquisitions editor (library and information science, knowledge management); Bruce Phillips, acquisitions editor (music); Tom Koerner, editorial director (educational administration). Estab. 1950. Publishes hardcover originals. **Publishes 165 titles/year. Receives 600-700 submissions/year. 70% of books from first-time authors; 99% from unagented writers. Pays 8% royalty on net of first 1,000 copies; 10% of net price thereafter. No advance.** Publishes book 18 months after receipt of ms. Responds in 2 months. Book catalog for 9×12 SAE and 4 first-class stamps.

> Scarecrow Press publishes several series: The Historical Dictionary series, which includes countries, religious, international organizations; and Composers of North America. "We consider any scholarly title likely to appeal to libraries. Emphasis is on reference material." Currently emphasizing educational administration, music, information science, Internet, knowledge management.

Nonfiction: Reference books and meticulously prepared annotated bibliographies, indices and books on women's studies, ethnic studies, music, movies, stage. library and information science, parapsychology, fine arts and handicrafts, social sciences, religion, sports, literature and language. Query.

Recent Title(s): *Fantasy and Horror,* by Neil Barron.

SCHENKMAN BOOKS, INC., 118 Main Street, Rochester VT 05767. (802)767-3702. Fax: (802)767-9528. E-mail: schenkma@sover.net. Website: www.sover.net/~schenkma/. **Acquisitions:** Joe Schenkman, editor. Estab. 1961. Publishes hardcover and trade paperback originals and reprints. **Publishes 6 titles/year. Receives 100 queries and 25 mss/year. 80% of books from first-time authors; 95% from unagented writers. Pays 10% royalty on net receipts.** Accepts simultaneous submissions. Book catalog and ms guidelines free.

> "Schenkman Books specializes in publishing scholarly monographs for the academic community. For almost forty years we have brought revolutionary works to the public to fuel discourse on important issues. It is our hope that the material we make available contributes to the efforts toward peace and humanitarianism throughout the world."

Nonfiction: Biography, self-help, textbook, scholarly monographs. Subjects include anthropology, ethnic, government/politics, history, music, philosophy, psychology, sociology, women's issues/studies, African studies, African-American studies, Asian studies, Caribbean studies. Query with outline. Reviews art as part of the package. Send photocopies.

Recent Title(s): *Work Abuse,* by Judith Wyatt and Chauncey Hare (self-help/management relations).

SCHOCKEN BOOKS, Knopf Publishing Group, Random House, Inc., 201 E. 50th St., New York NY 10022. (212)572-2559. Fax: (212)572-6030. Website: www.randomhouse.com/schocken. **Acquisitions:** Susan Ralston, editorial director; Altie Karper, editor. Estab. 1931. Publishes hardcover originals and reprints, trade paperback originals and reprints. **Publishes 12-15 titles/year. A small percentage of books are from first-time writers; small percentage from unagented writers. Advance varies.** Accepts simultaneous submissions.

> "Schocken publishes a broad list of serious, solid fiction and nonfiction books with commercial appeal, as well as reprints of classics." Schocken has a commitment to publishing Judaica, and also specializes in the areas of religious, cultural and historical studies.

Nonfiction: Subjects include education, government/politics, history, Judaica, nature/environment, philosophy, cultural studies, religion, women's issues/studies. Submit proposal package, including detailed outline and sample chapter.

Recent Title(s): *The Monk and The Philosopher: A Father and Son Discuss Life's Eternal Questions.*

SCHOLASTIC INC., Book Group, 555 Broadway, New York NY 10012. (212)343-6100. Estab. 1920. Website: www.scholastic.com. Vice President/Publisher: Jean Feiwel. Publishes trade paperback originals for children ages 4-young adult. Publishes juvenile hardcover picture books, novels and nonfiction. **All divisions: Pays advance and royalty on retail price.** Responds in 6 months. Manuscript guidelines for #10 SASE.

> "We are proud of the many fine, innovative materials we have created—such as classroom magazines, book clubs, book fairs, and our new literacy and technology programs. But we are most proud of our reputation as 'The Most Trusted Name in Learning.' "

Imprint(s): Blue Sky Press (contact Bonnie Verburg), **Cartwheel Books** (contact Bernette Ford), Arthur Levine Books (contact Arthur Levine), Mariposa (contact Susanna Pasternac), **Scholastic Press** (contact Elizabeth Szabla), Scholastic Reference & Gallimard (contact Wendy Barish), Scholastic Trade Paperback (contact Craig Walker).

● Scholastic recently purchased Grolier, Inc.

Nonfiction: Publishes nonfiction for children ages 4 to teen. Query.

Fiction: Hardcover—open to all subjects suitable for children. Paperback—family stories, mysteries, school, friendships for ages 8-12, 35,000 words. YA fiction, romance, family and mystery for ages 12-15, 40,000-45,000 words for average to good readers. Queries welcome. No unsolicited mss.

Recent Title(s): *The Great Fire,* by Jim Murphy; *Out of the Dust,* by Karen Hesse.

Tips: New writers for children should study the children's book field before submitting.

SCHOLASTIC PRESS, Scholastic Inc., 555 Broadway, New York NY 10012. (212)343-6100. Website: www.scholastic.com. **Acquisitions:** Elizabeth Szabla, editorial director. Publishes hardcover originals. **Publishes 50 titles/year. Receives 2,500 queries/year. 5% of books from first-time authors. Pays royalty on retail price. Royalty and advance vary.** Publishes book 18-24 months after acceptance of ms. Responds in 6 months on queries.

> Scholastic Press publishes a range of picture books, middle grade and young adult novels.

Nonfiction: Children's/juvenile, general interest. *Agented submissions only.*

Fiction: Juvenile, picture books. *Agented submissions only.*

Recent Title(s): *Adaline Falling Star*, by Mary Pope Osborne (fiction).

SCHOLASTIC PROFESSIONAL PUBLISHING, Scholastic, Inc., 555 Broadway, New York NY 10012. Website: www.scholastic.com. Vice President/Editor-in-Chief: Terry Cooper. **Acquisitions:** Adriane Rozier, editorial production coordinator. Estab. 1989. **Publishes 80-100 books/year. Offers standard contract.** Responds in 3 months. Book catalog for 9×12 SASE.

Nonfiction: Elementary and middle-school level enrichment—all subject areas, including math and science and theme units, integrated materials, writing process, management techniques, teaching strategies based on personal/professional experience in the classroom and technology ideas. Production is limited to printed matter: resource and activity books, professional development materials, reference titles. Length: 6,000-12,000 words. Query with table of contents, outline and sample chapter.

Recent Titles(s): *Getting the Most out of Morning Message & Other Shared Writing Lessons*, by Carleen DaCruz Payne and Mary Browning Schulman; *150 Totally Terrific Writing Prompts*, by Justin Martin.

Tips: "Writer should have background working in the classroom with elementary or middle school children, teaching pre-service students, and/or solid background in developing supplementary educational materials for these markets."

A SCRIBNER, Simon & Schuster, 1230 Avenue of the Americas, New York NY 10020. (212)698-7000. Publishes hardcover originals. **Publishes 70-75 titles/year. Receives thousands of queries/year. 20% of books from first-time authors; none from unagented writers. Pays 7½-12½% royalty on wholesale price. Advance varies.** Publishes book 9 months after acceptance of ms. Accepts simultaneous submissions. Responds in 3 months on queries.

Imprint(s): Rawson Associates; **Lisa Drew Books**; Scribner Classics (reprints only); Scribner Poetry (by invitation only).

Nonfiction: Subjects include education, ethnic, gay/lesbian, health/medicine, history, language/literature, nature/environment, philosophy, psychology, religion, science, biography, criticism. *Agented submissions only.*

Fiction: Literary, mystery, suspense. *Agented submissions only.*

Poetry: Publishes few titles; by invitation only.

Recent Title(s): *Angela's Ashes*, by Frank McCourt (memoir, National Book Award and Pulitzer Prize winner); *Underworld*, by Don DeLillo.

N SCRIVENERY PRESS, P.O. Box 740969-180, Houston TX 77274-0969. (713)665-6760. Fax: (713)665-8838. E-mail: books@scrivenery.com. Website: www.scrivenery.com. **Acquisitions:** Kevin Miller, associate editor (nonfiction); Chris Coleman, associate editor (fiction/general); Leila B. Joiner, editor (fiction/literary). Publishes hardcover originals and trade paperback originals and reprints. **Publishes 20 titles/year. Receives 400 queries and 30 mss/year. 25% of books from first-time authors; 50% from unagented writers. Pays 8½-15% royalty on retail price. Electronic and other subsidiary rights at 50% publisher's net; motion picture rights remain with author. Seldom offer an advance; never more than $1,000.** Publishes book 7 months after acceptance of ms. Accepts simultaneous submissions. Responds in 2 months on queries and proposals, 3 months on mss. Book catalog for $2 or on website. Manuscript guidelines for #10 SASE or on website.

> O— "Our primary needs are in the humanities: English literatuare (history and/or analyses); literary theory (for a general, educated audience); science, technology, and culture, and natural history (e.g., Edward O. Wilson, Stephen Jay Gould); and history. Biography (no memoirs or autobiography) is also needed; we prefer figures from arts, letters and science rather than political/military figures."

Nonfiction: Biography, how-to, self-help, humanities. Subjects include Americana, creative nonfiction, history, hobbies, language/literature, nature/environment, philosophy, science, translation. Submit proposal package, including outline and 3 sample chapters. All unsolicited manuscripts returned unopened. Reviews artwork/photos as part of ms package. Send photocopies, line-art only; no photos.

Fiction: Adventure, experimental, historical, literary, mainstream/contemporary, mystery, regional, short story collections, suspense, translation. "Our greatest interest is in mainstream and literary fiction; we prefer literary crossover in all genres." Submit proposal package, including synopsis and 3 sample chapters. All unsolicited mss returned unopened.

Recent Title(s): *Young Men with Unlimited Capital: The Story of Woodstock*, by Rosenman, Roberts and Pilpel (history); *Good King Sauerkraut*, by Barbara Paul (mystery).

Tips: "In both fiction and nonfiction, we market to an adult, educated audience who seek the pleasure of expertly-wielded language in addition to well-crafted story. Scrivenery Press is open to unpublished talent, but not writers new to the craft. Polish your manuscript as best you can; expect to be judged against seasoned pros. In fiction, we prefer polished, literate work that could be construed as a crossover between genre and literary fiction; examples would be, in mystery, Umberto Eco's *The Name of the Rose*; in mainstream, David Guterson's *Snow Falling on Cedars* or Annie Proulx's *The Shipping News*; in the history genre, Charles Frazier's *Cold Mountain*, or our recent release by E.A. Blair, *A Journey to the Interior*. In nonfiction we seek thoughtful work, but material not specifically geared to an academic market."

SEAL PRESS, 3131 Western Ave., Suite 410, Seattle WA 98121. Fax: (206)285-9410. E-mail: sealpress@sealpress.com. Website: www.sealpress.com. **Acquisitions:** Faith Conlon, editor/publisher. Jennie Goode, managing editor. Publishes hardcover and trade paperback originals. **Publishes 6 titles/year. Receives 500 queries and 500 mss/year. 25%**

of books from first-time authors; **70% from unagented writers. Pays 7-10% royalty on retail price. Offers $500-2,000 advance.** Publishes book 18 months after acceptance of ms. Accepts simultaneous submissions. Responds in 2 months on queries. Book catalog and ms guidelines for SASE.

O→ "Seal Press is an independent feminist book publisher interested in original, lively, radical, empowering and culturally diverse nonfiction by women addressing contemporary issues from a feminist perspective or speak positively to the experience of being female." Currently emphasizing women outdoor adventurists, young feminists. De-emphasizing fiction unless lesbian.

Imprint(s): Adventura Books, Djuna Books, Live Girls.

Nonfiction: Self-help, literary nonfiction essays. Subjects include child guidance/parenting, ethnic, gay/lesbian, health/medicine, nature/outdoor writing, travel, women's issues/studies, popular culture, memoir. Query with SASE. Reviews artwork/photos as part of ms package. Send photocopies.

Fiction: Ethnic, feminist, gay/lesbian, literary. "We are interested in alternative voices." Query with synopsis and SASE. *No unsolicited mss.*

Recent Title(s): *Pilgrimage: One Woman's Return to a Changing India*, by Pramila Jayapal (nonfiction); *Bruised Hibiscus*, by Elizabeth Nunez (fiction).

● Seal Press is not publishing poetry or mysteries at this time.

Tips: "Our audience is generally composed of women interested in reading about contemporary issues addressed from a feminist perspective."

N ☆ SEEDLING PUBLICATIONS, INC., 4522 Indianola Ave., Columbus OH 43214-2246. (614)267-7333. Fax: (614)267-4205. E-mail: sales@seedlingpub.com. Website: www.seedlingpub.com. **Acquisitions:** Josie Stewart, vice president. Estab. 1992. Publishes in an 8-, 12-, or 16-page format for beginning readers. **Publishes 8-10 titles/year. Receives 50 queries and 450 mss/year. 50% of books from first-time authors; 100% from unagented writers. Pays royalty or makes outright purchase.** Publishes book 1 year after of acceptance of ms. Accepts simultaneous submissions. Responds in 6 months. Book catalog for #10 SAE and 3 first-class stamps. Manuscript guidelines for #10 SASE.

O→ Seedling publishes books for young children to "keep young readers growing."

Nonfiction: Children's/juvenile. Science, math or social studies concepts are considered. Submit outline with SASE. Reviews artwork/photos as part of ms package. Send photocopies.

Fiction: Juvenile. Submit outline with SASE. Reviews artwork/photos as part of ms package. Send photocopies.

Recent Title(s): *Look! Bugs . . .*, by Karen Hooker (nonfiction in a very simple format told in 32 words); *Not Too Small At All*, by Deborah Holt Williams (folktale element at a beginning reader level).

Tips: "Follow our guidelines. Do not submit full-length picture books or chapter books. Our books are for children, ages 5-7, who are just beginning to read independently. We do not accept stories that rhyme or poetry at this time. Try a manuscript with young readers. Listen for spots in the text that don't flow when the child reads the story. Rewrite until the text sounds natural to beginning readers."

☆ SELF-COUNSEL PRESS, 1704 N. State St., Bellingham WA 92225. (360)676-4530. Website: www.self-counsel.com. **Acquisitions:** Richard Day, managing editor. Estab. 1977. Publishes trade paperback originals and reprints. **Publishes 30 titles/year. Receives 1,000 queries/year. 30% of books from first-time authors; 90% from unagented writers. Pays 10% royalty on net price. Rarely pays advance.** Publishes book 8 months after acceptance of ms. Accepts simultaneous submissions. Responds in 2 months. Book catalog and ms guidelines available via website or upon request.

O→ Self-Counsel Press publishes a range of quality self-help publication books written in practical, non-technical style by recognized experts in the fields of business, financial, personal or legal guidance for people who want to help themselves. "We also publish a writing series."

Nonfiction: How-to, reference, self-help. Subjects include business/economics, computers/electronics, money/finance, legal issues for laypeople. Submit proposal package, including outline, 2 sample chapters and résumé.

Recent Title(s): *Tax This!*, by Scott Estill; *Writing Horror*, by Edo Van Belkom.

● This publisher also has offices in Canada.

☆ ▢ SERENDIPITY SYSTEMS, P.O. Box 140, San Simeon CA 93452. (805)927-5259. E-mail: bookware@thegrid.net. Website: www.s-e-r-e-n-d-i-p-i-t-y.com. or www.thegrid.net/bookware/bookware.htm. **Acquisitions:** John Galuszka, publisher. **Publishes 6-12 titles/year; each imprint publishes 0-6 titles/year. Receives 600 queries and 150 mss/year. 95% of books from unagented writers. Pays 33% royalty on wholesale price or on retail price, "depending on how the book goes out."** Publishes book 2 months after acceptance of ms. Accepts simultaneous submissions. Electronic submissions required. "We publish on disks, the Internet and CD-ROMs, plus Rocket Editions for Nuvo Media's Rocket eBook reader device." Responds in 1 month on mss. *Writer's Market* recommends allowing 2 months for reply. Book catalog available online. Manuscript guidelines for #10 SASE, or on the Internet.

O→ "Since 1986 Serendipity Systems has promoted and supported electronic publishing with electronic books for IBM-PC compatible computers."

Imprint(s): Books-on-Disks™, Bookware™.

Nonfiction: "We only publish reference books on literature, writing and electronic publishing." Query first with SASE. Submit entire ms on disk in ASCII or HTML files. Queries by e-mail; mss, summaries with sample chapters and long documents should be sent by postal mail.

Fiction: "We want to see *only* works which use (or have a high potential to use) hypertext, multimedia, interactivity or other computer-enhanced features. No romance, religious, occult, New Age, fantasy, or children's mss. Submit entire ms on disk in ASCII or HTML files. Query first.

Recent Title(s): *The Electronic Publishing Forum* (nonfiction); *Sideshow*, by Marian Allen.

Tips: "Check our guidelines on the Internet for the latest information."

SERGEANT KIRKLAND'S PRESS, 8 Yakama Trail, Spotsylvania VA 22553-2422. (540)582-6296. Fax: (540)582-8312. E-mail: seagraver@kirklands.org. Website www.Kirklands.org. **Acquisitions:** Pia S. Seagrave, Phd.D., editor-in-chief. Publishes hardcover and trade paperback originals, hardcover reprints. **Publishes 22-24 titles/year. Receives 300 queries and 120 mss/year. 70% of books from first-time authors; 90% from unagented writers. Pays 8-10% royalty on wholesale price. No advance.** Publishes book 6 months after acceptance of ms. Accepts simultaneous submissions. Responds in 2 months on queries and proposals; 4 months on mss. Book catalog free. Manuscript guidelines for #10 SASE.

　　O→ Currently emphasizing American history of academic and regional interest—colonial, Civil War, WWII and Vietnam periods.

Nonfiction: Biography, reference. Subjects include Americana, anthropology/archaeology, ethnic, government/politics, history, military/war, regional. Submit complete ms. *Writer's Market* recommends a query first. Reviews artwork/photos as part of ms package. Send photocopies.

Recent Titles: *Absolution*, by Charles Boyle (Vietnam).

Tips: "Have your work professionally edited and be sure it meets the general standards of The Chicago Manual of Style."

SEVEN STORIES PRESS, 140 Watts St., New York NY 10013. (212)226-8760. Fax: (212)226-1411. E-mail: info@sevenstories.com. Website: www.sevenstories.com. **Acquisitions:** Daniel Simon, Greg Ruggiero, Michael Manekin, Vidaine Husman. Estab. 1995. Publishes hardcover and trade paperback originals. **Publishes 20-25 titles/year. 15% of books from first-time authors; 15% from unagented writers. Pays 7-15% royalty on retail price.** Publishes book 1-3 years after acceptance. Accepts simultaneous submissions. Responds in 3 months. Book catalog and manuscript guidelines free.

　　O→ Seven Stories Press publishes literary/activist fiction and nonfiction "on the premise that both are works of the imagination and that there is no contradiction in publishing the two side by side." Currently emphasizing politics, social justice, biographies, foreign writings.

Nonfiction: Biography. Subjects include general nonfiction. Query only. No unsolicited ms. Responds only if interested.

Fiction: Contemporary. Query only. SASE required. *No unsolicited mss.*

Recent Title(s): *All Things Censored*, by Mumia Abu Jamal (nonfiction); *So Vast the Prison*, by Assia Djebar (fiction); *Poems for the Nation*, edited by Allen Ginsberg (poetry).

HAROLD SHAW PUBLISHERS, Waterbrook Press, 5446 Academy Blvd., #200, Colorado Springs CO 80918. (719)590-4999. Fax: (719)590-8977. **Acquisitions:** Erin Healy, editor. Estab. 1967. Publishes mostly trade paperback originals and reprints. **Publishes 30 titles/year. Receives 1,000 submissions/year. 10-20% of books from first-time authors; 90% from unagented writers. Offers 10-12% royalty on net receipts. Sometimes makes outright purchase of $375-2,500 for Bible studies and compilations.** Publishes book 18 months after acceptance of ms. Responds in 3-6 months. Guidelines for #10 SASE. Catalog for 9×12 SAE with 5 first-class stamps.

　　O→ "We publish a wide range (full circle) of books from a Christian perspective for use by a broad range of readers."

Nonfiction: Subjects include marriage, family and parenting, self-help, mental health, spiritual growth, Bible study and literary topics. "We are looking for adult general nonfiction with different twists—self-help manuscripts with fresh insight and colorful, vibrant writing style. No unsolicited mss.

Recent Title(s): *In All Thy Ways*, by Joan Walsh Anglund.

SHEED & WARD BOOK PUBLISHING, 7373 S. Lovers Lane Rd., Franklin WI 53132. (800)558-0580. Fax: (800)369-4448. E-mail: sheed@execpc.com. Website: www.bookmasters.com/sheed. **Acquisitions:** Jeremy W. Langford, editor-in-chief (Catholicism). Publishes hardcover and trade paperback originals. **Publishes 25-30 titles/year. Receives 600-1,000 queries and 600-1,000 mss/year. 25% of books from first-time authors; 90% from unagented writers. Pays 6-12% royalty on retail price. Offers $500-2,000 advance.** Publishes book 8 months after acceptance of ms. Responds in 1 month on queries, 2 months on proposals, 2 months on mss. Book catalog and ms guidelines free or on website.

　　O→ "We are looking for books that help our readers, most of whom are college educated, gain access to the riches of the Catholic/Christian tradition. We publish in the areas of history, biography, spirituality, prayer, ethics, ministry, justice, liturgy."

Nonfiction: Biography, gift book, reference. Subjects include religion, spirituality. Submit proposal package, including outline and 2 sample chapters and strong cover letter indicating why the project is unique and compelling. Reviews artwork/photos as part of ms package. Send photocopies.

Recent Title(s): *Why Do We Suffer? A Scriptural Approach to the Human Condition*, by Daniel Harrington; *Job: And Death No Dominion*, by Daniel Berrigan.

Tips: "We prefer that writers get our author guidelines either from our website or via mail before submitting proposals."

SIERRA CLUB BOOKS, 85 Second, San Francisco CA 94105. (415)977-5500. Fax: (415)977-5793. **Acquisitions:** James Cohee, senior editor. Estab. 1962. Publishes hardcover and paperback originals and reprints. **Publishes 30 titles/ year. Receives 1,000 submissions/year. 50% of books from unagented writers. Royalties vary by project. Offers $5,000-15,000 average advance.** Publishes book 18 months after acceptance. Responds in 2 months.

O─ The Sierra Club was founded to help people to explore, enjoy and preserve the nation's forests, waters, wildlife and wilderness. The books program publishes quality trade books about the outdoors and the protection of natural resources.

Nonfiction: A broad range of environmental subjects: outdoor adventure, descriptive and how-to, women in the outdoors; landscape and wildlife pictorials; literature, including travel and works on the spiritual aspects of the natural world; travel and trail; natural history and current environmental issues, including public health and uses of appropriate technology; gardening; general interest. "Specifically, we are interested in literary natural history, environmental issues such as nuclear power, self-sufficiency, politics and travel." Does *not* want "proposals for large color photographic books without substantial text; how-to books on building things outdoors; books on motorized travel; or any but the most professional studies of animals." Query first, then submit outline and sample chapters. Reviews artwork/photos as part of ms package. Send photocopies.

Recent Title(s): *Seven Wonders: Timeless Travels for a Healthier Planet.*

SILHOUETTE BOOKS, 300 E. 42nd St., New York NY 10017. (212)682-6080. Fax: (212)682-4539. Website: www.eHarlequin.com. Editorial Director, Silhouette Books, Harlequin Historicals: Tara Gavin. **Acquisitions:** Mary Theresa Hussey, senior editor (Silhouette Romance); Karen Taylor Richman, senior editor (Silhouette Special Editions); Joan Marlow Golan, senior editor (Silhouette Desires); Leslie Wainger, executive senior editor (Silhouette Intimate Moments); Tracy Farrell, senior editor/editorial coordinator (Harlequin Historicals). Estab. 1979. Publishes mass market paperback originals. **Publishes 350 titles/year. Receives 4,000 submissions/year. 10% of books from first-time authors; 50% from unagented writers. Pays royalty.** Publishes book 1-3 years after acceptance. Manuscript guidelines for #10 SASE.

O─ Silhouette publishes contemporary adult romances.

Imprint(s): *Silhouette Romance* (contemporary adult romances, 53,000-58,000 words); *Silhouette Desire* (contemporary adult romances, 55,000-60,000 words); *Silhouette Intimate Moments* (contemporary adult romances, 80,000 words); *Harlequin Historicals* (adult historical romances, 95,000-105,000 words); *Silhouette Special Edition* (contemporary adult romances, 75,000-80,000 words).

Fiction: Romance (contemporary and historical romance for adults). "We are interested in seeing submissions for all our lines. No manuscripts other than the types outlined. Manuscript should follow our general format, yet have an individuality and life of its own that will make it stand out in the readers' minds." Send query letter, 2 page synopsis and SASE to head of imprint. *No unsolicited mss.*

Recent Title(s): *Enchanted*, by Nora Roberts.

Tips: "The romance market is constantly changing, so when you read for research, read the latest books and those that have been recommended to you by people knowledgeable in the genre. We are actively seeking new authors for all our lines, contemporary and historical."

[N] ▣ SILVER DAGGER MYSTERIES, The Overmountain Press, P.O. Box 1261, Johnson City TN 37605. (423)926-2691. Fax: (423)929-2464. E-mail: alexfoster@silverdaggerstore.com. Website: www.silverdaggerstore.com. **Acquisitions:** Alex Foster, acquisitions editor (P.O. Box 35, New Johnsonville TN 37134-0035). Publishes hardcover and trade paperback originals and reprints. **Publishes 30 titles/year; imprint publishes 15 titles/year. Receives 100 queries and 50 mss/year. 50% of books from first-time authors; 50% from unagented writers. Pays 15% royalty on wholesale price.** No advance. Publishes book 1 year after acceptance of ms. Accepts simultaneous submissions. Responds in 1 month on queries, 3 months on proposals, 6 months on mss. Book catalog and ms guidelines on website.

O─ Silver Dagger publishes mysteries that take place in the American South.

Fiction: Mystery. "We look for average-length books of 60-80,000 words." Query with SASE or submit proposal package, including synopsis, 2 sample chapters and author biography. All unsolicited mss returned unopened.

Recent Title(s): *All the Hungry Mothers*, by Deborah Adams; *Midnight Hour*, by Mary Saums.

Tips: "We publish cozies, hard-boiled and police procedural mysteries. Check the website for specific guidelines and submission dates. Due to a large number of submissions, we only review at certain times of the year."

SIMON & SCHUSTER, 1230 Avenue of the Americas, New York NY 10020. Website: www.simonsays.com. *Adult Trade*: Simon & Schuster Trade (Fireside, **The Free Press**, Kaplan, **Scribner [Lisa Drew, Rawson Associates**, Scribner], Simon & Schuster, Touchstone, Scribner Paperback Fiction); *Simon & Schuster Children's Publishing* (Aladdin Paperbacks, **Atheneum Books for Young Readers, Margaret K. McElderry Books**), Nickelodeon, Simon Spotlight [**Little Simon**], **Simon & Schuster Books for Young Readers**, Simon & Schuster New Media; *Mass Market*: Pocket Books (Pocket Books for Young Adults [**Archway Paperbacks, Minstrel Books**, Pocket Books for Young Adults Pocket Pulse], MTV Books, Nickelodeon, *Star Trek*, Washington Square Press, Pocket Pulse).

SIMON & SCHUSTER BOOKS FOR YOUNG READERS, Simon & Schuster Children's Publishing Division, 1230 Avenue of the Americas, New York NY 10020. (212)698-2851. Fax: (212)698-2796. Website: www.simonandschuster.com. or www.simonsayskids.com. **Acquisitions:** Stephen Geck, editorial director, vice president/associate publisher (humorous picture books, fiction, nonfiction); Kevin Lewis, editor (African-American/multicultural picture books, humorous picture books, middle-grade); David Gale, senior editor (young adult/middle grade novels); Jessica Schulte, editor (picture books, young adult); Amy-Hampton Knight, editor (character-centered picture books and poetry). Publishes hardcover originals. **Publishes 80-90 titles/year. Receives 2,500 queries and 10,000 mss/year. 5-10% of books from first-time authors; 40% from unagented writers. Pays 4-12% royalty on retail price. Advance varies.** Publishes book 1-3 years after acceptance of ms. Accepts simultaneous submissions. Responds in 2 months on queries. Manuscript guidelines for #10 SASE.

> ☞ "The three adjectives we use to describe our imprint are fresh, family-oriented and accessible. We're looking for writing-edge fiction, family-oriented picture books that are character-oriented." Currently emphasizing middle grade humor/adventure stories. De-emphasizing nonfiction.

Nonfiction: Children's/juvenile. Subjects include animals, ethnic, history, nature/environment. "We're looking for innovative, appealing nonfiction especially for younger readers. Please don't submit education or textbooks." Query with SASE only. *All unsolicited mss returned unread.*

Fiction: Fantasy, historical, humor, juvenile, mystery, picture books, science fiction, young adult. "Fiction needs to be fresh, unusual and compelling to stand out from the competition. We're not looking for problem novels, stories with a moral, or rhymed picture book texts." Query with SASE only. *All unsolicited mss returned unread.*

Poetry: "Most of our poetry titles are anthologies; we publish very few stand-alone poets." No picture book ms in rhymed verse. Query.

Recent Title(s): *Ghosts of the White House*, by Charyl Harness (nonfiction); *Heaven*, by Angela Johnson (fiction); *Climb Into My Lap*, selected by Lee Bennett Hopkins (poetry).

Tips: "We're looking for fresh, original voices and unexplored topics. Don't do something because everyone else is doing it. Try to find what they're *not* doing. We publish mainly for the bookstore market, and are looking for books that will appeal directly to kids."

SKIDMORE-ROTH PUBLISHING, INC., 400 Inverness Dr., S. #260, Englewood CO 80112. (303)662-8793. Fax: (303)662-8079. E-mail: info@skidmore-roth.com. Website: www.skidmore-roth.com. **Acquisitions:** Lynn Kendall, editor. Estab. 1987. Publishes trade paperback originals. **Publishes 24 titles/year. Receives 10 queries and 24 mss/year. 50% of books from first-time authors; 100% from unagented writers. Pays 4-8% royalty on wholesale price or makes outright purchase of $2,500-10,000.** Publishes book 9 months after acceptance of ms. Accepts simultaneous submissions. Responds in 2 weeks on proposals.

> ☞ Skidmore-Roth publishes medical books and material for medical professionals worldwide.

Nonfiction: Reference, textbook. Health/medicine subjects . "We are looking for proposals in areas where there is currently a lack of publication."

Recent Title(s): *EMS Field Protocol Manual*, by Jon Apfelbaum.

Tips: "Audience is licensed nurses working in hospitals, long term care facilities, subacute centers, home health, HMO's and medical clinics, nurse assistants and nurse aides, nursing students and other allied health professions."

⟨N⟩ SKINNER HOUSE BOOKS, The Unitarian Universalist Association, 25 Beacon St., Boston MA 02108. (617)742-2100, ext 601. Fax: (617)742-7025. E-mail: skinner_house@uua.org. Website: www.uua.org/skinner. **Acquisitions:** Johanna Bates, marketing coordinator. Estab. 1975. Publishes trade paperback originals and reprints. **Publishes 8-10 titles/year. 50% of books from first-time authors; 100% from unagented writers. Pays 5-10% royalty on net sales. Offers $100 advance.** Publishes book 1 year after acceptance of ms. Responds in 3 months on queries. Book catalog for 6×9 SAE with 3 first-class stamps, "or e-mail bookstore@uua.org, or visit our website." Manuscript guidelines for #10 SASE.

> ☞ Skinner House publishes books for Unitarian Universalists, ministers, lay leaders, religious educators, parents, youth, feminists, GLBT and social activists.

Nonfiction: Biography, children's/juvenile, church leadership. Subjects include gay/lesbian/bisexual/transgender, history, religion, women's issues/studies, inspirational. "We publish titles in Unitarian Universalist faith, history, biography, worship, and issues of social justice. We also publish a selected number of inspirational titles of poetic prose and at least one volume of meditations per year. Writers should know that Unitarian Universalism is a liberal religious denomination committed to progressive ideals." Query. Reviews artwork/photos as part of ms package. Send photocopies.

Recent Nonfiction Title(s): *This Very Moment*, by James Ishmael Ford (Zen Buddhism for Unitarian Universalists); *Alabaster Village*, by Christine Morgan (autobiography, Transylvania); *Green Mountain Spring*, by Gary Kowalski (meditation and inspiration).

Fiction: Juvenile. "The only fiction we publish is for children, usually in the form of parables or very short stories (500 words) on liberal religious principles or personal development. Fiction for adults is not accepted." Query.

Tips: "From outside our denomination, we are interested in manuscripts that will be of help or interest to liberal churches, Sunday School classes, parents, ministers and volunteers. Inspirational/spiritual and children's titles must reflect liberal Unitarian Universalist values. Fiction for youth is being considered."

SLACK INC., 6900 Grove Rd., Thorofare NJ 08086. (856)848-1000. Fax: (856)853-5991. E-mail: adrummond@slackinc.com. Website: www.slackinc.com. **Acquisitions:** Amy E. Drummond, editorial director. Estab. 1960. Publishes hardcover and softcover originals. **Publishes 32 titles/year. Receives 80 queries and 23 mss/year. 75% of books from first-time authors; 100% from unagented writers. Pays 10% royalty.** Publishes book 8 months after acceptance. Accepts simultaneous submissions. Responds in 4 months on queries, 1 month on proposals, 3 months on mss. Book catalog and ms guidelines free.

O━ Slack publishes academic textbooks and professional reference books on various medical topics.

Nonfiction: Textbook (medical). Subjects include ophthalmology, athletic training, physical therapy, occupational therapy. Submit proposal package, including outline, 2 sample chapters, market profile and cv. Reviews artwork/photos as part of ms package. Send photocopies.

Recent Title(s): *Occupational Therapy: Enabling Function and Well Being*, by Christiansen and Baum.

SMITH AND KRAUS PUBLISHERS, INC., P.O. Box 127, Lyme NH 03768. (603)643-6431. Fax: (603) 643-1831. **Acquisitions:** Marisa Smith, president/publisher. Estab. 1990. Publishes hardcover and trade paperback originals. **Publishes 35-40 books/year. 10% of books from first-time authors; 10-20% from unagented writers. Pays 10% royalty of net on retail price. Offers $500-2,000 advance.** Publishes book 1 year after acceptance. Responds in 1 month on queries, 2 months on proposals, 4 months on mss. Book catalog free.

Nonfiction and Fiction: Drama, theater. Query with SASE. Does not return submissions.

Recent Title(s): *Horton Foote: Collected Plays Volume III*; *Plays of Fairy Tales (Grades K-3)*, by L.E. McCullough.

GIBBS SMITH, PUBLISHER, P.O. Box 667, Layton UT 84041. (801)544-9800. Fax: (801)544-5582. E-mail: info@gibbs-smith.com. Website: www.gibbs~smith.com. **Acquisitions:** Madge Baird, editorial director (humor, western); Gail Yngve, editor (gift books, architecture, interior decorating, poetry); Suzanne Taylor, editor (children's, rustic living, outdoor activities and picture); Linda Nimori, editor. Estab. 1969. Publishes hardcover and trade paperback originals. **Publishes 50 titles/year. Receives 1,500-2,000 submissions/year. 8-10% of books from first-time authors; 50% from unagented writers. Pays 6-15% royalty on gross receipts. Offers $2,000-3,000 advance.** Publishes book 1-2 years after acceptance of ms. Accepts simultaneous submissions, if so noted. Responds in 1 month on queries, 10 weeks on proposals and mss. Book catalog for 9 × 12 SAE and $2.13 in postage. Manuscript guidelines free.

O━ "We publish books that enrich and inspire humankind." Currently emphasizing interior decorating and design, home reference. De-emphasizing novels and short stories.

Imprint(s): Gibbs Smith Junior.

Nonfiction: Children's/juvenile, illustrated book, textbook. Subjects include architecture, humor, interior design, nature, regional. Query or submit outline, several completed sample chapters and author's cv. Reviews artwork/photos as part of the ms package. Send sample illustrations if applicable.

Fiction: No novels. No short stories. Only short works oriented to gift market. Submit synopsis with sample illustration if applicable.

Poetry: "Our annual poetry contest accepts entries only in April. Charges $15 fee. Prize: $500." Submit complete ms.

Recent Title(s): *Log Cabin Living*, by Daniel Mack (nonfiction); *The Lesson*, by Carol Lynn Pearson (fiction).

N **★** **SOFT SKULL PRESS INC.**, 98 Suffolk, #3A, New York NY 10002. (212)673-2502. Fax: (212)673-0787. E-mail: sander@softskull.com. Website: www.softskull.com. **Acquisitions:** Nick Mamatas, editor (political science); Sander Hicks, editor-in-chief (everything). Publishes hardcover and trade paperback originals. **Publishes 12-15 titles/year. Receives 100 queries and 100 mss/year. 80% of books from first-time authors; 50% from unagented writers. Pays 7-10% royalty. Offers $100-15,000 advance.** Publishes book 6 months after acceptance of ms. Responds in 2 months on queries and proposals, 3 months on mss. Book catalog free or on website. Manuscript guidelines on website.

O━ "We're really into political science from a left-of-center, under-35 perspective."

Nonfiction: Biography. Subjects include art/architecture, gay/lesbian, government/politics, military/war, music/dance, philosophy. Query with SASE or submit proposal package, including outline and 2 sample chapters. Agented submissions are encouraged.

Fiction: Confession, experimental, historical, literary, mainstream/contemporary, multicultural, short story collections. "We love Richard Ford, Hemmingway, Dennis Cooper and Denis Johnson." Query with SASE or submit proposal package, including synopsis and 1 sample chapter. Agented submissions encouraged.

Poetry: Query with no more than ten poems. "We're not doing as much as we used to. Must be exceptional."

Recent Title(s): *Fortunate Son*, by J.H. Hatfield (biography); *Outline of My Lover*, by Douglas A. Martin (literary/erotica); *Riot in the Charm Factory*, by Todd Colby (post-punk poetry).

Tips: "Our audience is passionate, radical, angry, dissatisfied with the current political and cultural status quo."

SOHO PRESS, INC., 853 Broadway, New York NY 10003. (212)260-1900. Website: www.sohopress.com. **Acquisitions:** Juris Jurjevics, publisher/editor-in-chief; Laura Hruska, associate publisher; Melanie Fleishman, editor/director of marketing. Estab. 1986. Publishes hardcover and trade paperback originals. **Publishes 40 titles/year. Receives 7,000 submissions/year. 75% of books from first-time authors; 40% from unagented writers. Pays 10-15% royalty on retail price. Offers advance.** Publishes book within 1 year after acceptance. Accepts simultaneous submissions. Responds in 2 months. Book catalog for 6 × 9 SAE with 2 first-class stamps.

O━ Soho Press publishes literary fiction, thrillers, mysteries set overseas and in the U.S., multicultural fiction and nonfiction."

Nonfiction: Literary nonfiction: travel, autobiography, biography, etc. No self-help. Submit outline and sample chapters.

Fiction: Adventure, ethnic, feminist, historical, literary, mainstream/contemporary, mystery, suspense. Submit complete ms with SASE. *Writer's Market* recommends query with SASE first.

Recent Title(s): *Hokkaido Highway Blues: Hitchhiking Japan*, by Will Ferguson (nonfiction); *The Farming of Bones*, by Edwidge Danticat (fiction).

Tips: "Soho Press publishes discerning authors for discriminating readers, finding the strongest possible writers and publishing them." Soho Press also publishes two book series: Hera (historical fiction reprints with accurate and strong female lead characters) and Soho Crime (mysteries set overseas, noir, procedurals).

N: SOMA BOOKS, (formerly KQED Books), 555 DeHaro St., #220, San Francisco CA 94107. (415)252-4350. **Acquisitions**: James Connolly, editorial director. Publishes hardcover originals, trade paperback originals and reprints. **Publishes 10 titles/year. Receives 20 queries/year. 70% of books from first-time authors. Royalties vary substantially. Offers $0-25,000 advance.** Publishes book 6 months after acceptance of ms. Accepts simultaneous submissions. Responds in 1 month. *Writer's Market* recommends allowing 2 months for reply. Book catalog for 9×12 SASE and 3 first-class stamps.
Nonfiction: Coffee table book, cookbook, gift book, how-to, humor, illustrated book. Subjects include Americana, child guidance/parenting, cooking, food & nutrition, education, health/medicine, history, hobbies, nature/environment, religion, travel (Armchair Travel), cable/PBS series companions. "We only publish titles related to public and cable television series." Query.
Recent Title(s): *Savor the Southwest*, by Barbara Fenzl (cooking).
Tips: "Audience is people interested in Public Broadcasting subjects: history, cooking, how-to, armchair travel, etc."

SOUNDPRINTS, The Trudy Corp., 353 Main Ave., Norwalk CT 06851. (203)846-2274. Fax: (203)846-1776. E-mail: sndprnts@ix.netcom.com. Website: www.soundprints.com. **Acquisitions**: Sandy Wells, editorial assistant. Estab. 1988. Publishes hardcover originals. **Publishes 12-14 titles/year. Receives 200 queries/year. 20% of books from first-time authors; 90% of books from unagented writers. Makes outright purchase. No advance.** Publishes book 2 years after acceptance of ms. Accepts simultaneous submissions. Responds to queries in 3 months. Book catalog and ms guidelines available via website or upon request.
    O⊸ Soundprints publishes picture books that portray a particular animal and its habitat. All books are reviewed for accuracy by curators from the Smithsonian Institution and other wildlife experts.
Nonfiction: Children's/juvenile, animals. "We focus on worldwide wildlife and habitats. Subject animals must be portrayed realistically and must not be anthropomorphic. Meticulous research is required." Query with SASE. Does not review photos. (All books are illustrated in full color.)
Fiction: Juvenile. "Most of our books are under license from the Smithsonian Institution and are closely curated fictional stories based on fact. We never do stories of anthropomorphic animals. When we publish juvenile fiction, it will be about wildlife or history and all information in the book *must* be accurate." Query.
Recent Title(s): *Bumblebee at Apple Tree Lane*, by Laura Gates Galvin; *Sockeye's Journey Home: The Story of a Pacific Salmon*, by Barbara Gaines Winkelman.
Tips: "Our books are written for children from ages four through eight. Our most successful authors can craft a wonderful story which is derived from authentic wildlife or historic facts. First inquiry to us should ask about our interest in publishing a book about a specific animal or habitat."

SOURCEBOOKS, INC., P.O. Box 4410, Naperville IL 60567. (630)961-3900. Fax: (630)961-2168. Website: www.sourcebooks.com. Publisher: Dominique Raccah. **Acquisitions:** Todd Stocke, managing editor (nonfiction trade); Deborah Werksman (Hysteria Publications). Estab. 1987. Publishes hardcover and trade paperback originals. **Publishes 100 titles/year. 50% of books from first-time authors; 75% from unagented writers. Pays 6-15% royalty on wholesale price.** Publishes book 1 year after acceptance. Accepts simultaneous submissions. Responds in 3 months on queries. Book catalog and ms guidelines for 9×12 SASE.
    O⊸ Sourcebooks publishes many forms of nonfiction titles, generally in the how-to and reference areas, including books on parenting, self-help/psychology, business and health. Focus is on practical, useful information and skills. It also continues to publish in the reference, New Age, history, current affairs and travel categories. Currently emphasizing humor, gift, women's interest, New Age.
Imprint(s): Casablanca Press (love/relationships), Sphinx Publishing (self-help legal), Hysteria Publications (women's humor/gift book).
Nonfiction: *Small Business Sourcebooks:* books for small business owners, entrepreneurs and students. "A key to submitting books to us is to explain how your book helps the reader, why it is different from the books already out there (please do your homework) and the author's credentials for writing this book." *Sourcebooks:* gift books, self-help, general business, and how to. "Books likely to succeed with us are self-help, art books, parenting and childcare, psychology, women's issues, how-to, house and home, humor, gift books or books with strong artwork." Query or submit outline and 2-3 sample chapters (not the first). *No complete mss.* Reviews artwork/photos as part of ms package.
Recent Title(s): *And the Crowd Goes Wild*, by Joe Garner (sports); *911 Beauty Secrets*, by Diane Irons (health/beauty).
    ● Planning a fiction line within the next 2 years. Will seek books with strong story lines which communicate to a wide audience.
Tips: "Our market is a decidedly trade-oriented bookstore audience. We also have very strong penetration into the gift store market. Books which cross over between these two very different markets do extremely well with us. Our list is a solid mix of unique and general audience titles and series-oriented projects. In other words, we are looking for products that break new ground either in their own areas or within the framework of our series of imprints. We love to develop books in new areas or develop strong titles in areas that are already well developed."

SOUTH END PRESS, 7 Brookline St., Cambridge MA 02139. (617)547-4002. Fax: (617)547-1333. E-mail: southend @igc.org. Website: www.lbbs.org/sep/sep.htm. **Acquisitions:** Acquisitions Department. Estab. 1977. Publishes library and trade paperback originals and reprints. **Publishes 10 titles/year. Receives 400 queries and 100 mss/year. 30% of books from first-time authors; 95% from unagented writers. Pays 11% royalty on wholesale price. Occasionally offers $500-2,500 advance.** Publishes book 9 months after acceptance. Accepts simultaneous submissions. Responds in up to 3 months on queries and proposals. Book catalog and ms guidelines free.

○━ South End Press publishes nonfiction political books with a new left/feminist/multicultural perspective.

Nonfiction: Subjects include economics, education, ethnic, gay/lesbian, government/politics, health/medicine, history, nature/environment, philosophy, science, sociology, women's issues/studies, political. Query or submit 2 sample chapters including intro or conclusion and annotated toc. Reviews artwork as part of ms package. Send photocopies.

Recent Title(s): *Marx in Soho*, by Howard Zinn; *Rogue States*, by Noam Chomsky.

SOUTHERN ILLINOIS UNIVERSITY PRESS, P.O. Box 3697, Carbondale IL 62902-3697. (618)453-2281. Fax: (618)453-1221. Website: www.siu.edu/-siupress. **Acquisitions:** Jim Simmons, editorial director (film, theater, aviation, American history); Karl Kageff, sponsoring editor (composition, rhetoric, criminology); Rick Stetter, director (military history, criminology, trade nonfiction). Estab. 1956. Publishes hardcover and trade paperback originals and reprints. **Publishes 50-60 titles/year; imprint publishes 4-6 titles/year. Receives 800 queries and 300 mss/year. 45% of books from first-time authors; 100% from unagented writers. Pays 5-10% royalty on wholesale price. Rarely offers advance.** Publishes book 1 year after receipt of a final ms. Responds in 3 months. Book catalog and ms guidelines free.

○━ "To serve the academy and serious readers of the Mississippi Valley." Currently emphasizing theater, film, rhetoric, American history. De-emphasizing literary criticism, philosophy.

Imprint(s): Shawnee Books (contact Lisa Bayer, director of marketing).

Nonfiction: Biography, reference, textbook. Subjects include Americana, history, regional, sports, women's issues/studies. Query with proposal package, including synopsis, table of contents, author's vita with SASE.

Recent Title(s): *American Goddess at the Rape of Nanking*, by Hua-ling Hu (nonfiction); *Off0Season*, by Eliot Asinof (fiction); *The Young American Poets: An Anthology*, by Kevin Prufer, editor (poetry).

SOUTHERN METHODIST UNIVERSITY PRESS, P.O. Box 750415, Dallas TX 75275-0415. Fax: (214)768-1432. Website: www.smu.edu/~press. **Acquisitions:** Kathryn Lang, senior editor. Estab. 1937. Publishes hardcover and trade paperback originals and reprints. **Publishes 10-15 titles/year. Receives 500 queries and 500 mss/year. 75% of books from first-time authors; 95% from unagented writers. Pays up to 10% royalty on wholesale price. Offers $500 advance.** Publishes book 1 year after acceptance. Responds in 1 month on queries and proposals, 1 year on mss.

○━ Southern Methodist University publishes in the fields of literary fiction, ethics and human values, film and theater, regional studies and theological studies. Currently emphasizing literary fiction. De-emphasizing scholarly, narrowly focused studies.

Nonfiction: Subjects include medical ethics/human values, film/theater, regional history, theology. Query with outline, 3 sample chapters, table of contents and author bio. Reviews artwork/photos as part of the ms package. Send photocopies.

Fiction: Literary novels and short story collections. Query.

Recent Title(s): *One Day's Perfect Weather*, by Daniel Stern (story collection); *You Can Sleep While I Drive*, by Liza Weiland (story collection).

THE SPEECH BIN, INC., 1965 25th Ave., Vero Beach FL 32960-3062. (561)770-0007. **Acquisitions:** Jan J. Binney, senior editor. Estab. 1984. Publishes trade paperback originals. **Publishes 10-20 titles/year. Receives 500 mss/year. 50% of books from first-time authors; 90% from unagented writers. Pays negotiable royalty on wholesale price.** Publishes ms 1 year after acceptance. Responds within 3 months if SASE included. Book catalog for 9×12 SASE and $1.48 postage.

○━ Publishes professional materials for specialists in rehabilitation, particularly speech-language pathologists and audiologists, special educators, occupational and physical therapists, and parents and caregivers of children and adults with developmental and post-trauma disabilities."

Nonfiction: How-to, illustrated book, juvenile (preschool-teen), reference, textbook, educational material and games for both children and adults. Subjects include health, communication disorders and education for handicapped persons. Query or submit outline and sample chapters with SASE. Reviews artwork as part of ms package. Send photocopies.

Fiction: "Booklets or books for children and adults about handicapped persons, especially with communication disorders." Query or submit outline/synopsis and sample chapters. "This is a potentially new market for The Speech Bin."

Recent Title(s): *Living Skills for the Head-Injured Child*, by Julie Buxton and Kelly Godfree (nonfiction); *Artic-Pic*, by Denise Grigas.

Tips: "Books and materials must be clearly presented, well written and competently illustrated. We have added books and materials for use by other allied health professionals. We are also looking for more materials for use in treating adults and very young children with communication disorders. Please do not fax manuscripts to us." The Speech Bin is increasing their number of books published per year and is especially interested in reviewing treatment materials for adults and adolescents.

SPENCE PUBLISHING COMPANY, 111 Cole St., Dallas TX 75207. (214)939-1700. Fax: (214)939-1800. E-mail: mitchmuncy@aol.com. Website: www.spencepublishing.com. **Acquisitions:** Mitchell Muncy, editor-in-chief. Estab. 1995. Publishes hardcover and trade paperback originals. **Publishes 8-10 titles/year. Pays 12% royalty on net receipts.**

No advance. Accepts simultaneous submissions. Responds in 1 month on queries, 2 months on proposals. Book catalog free or on website. Manuscript guidelines for #10 SASE. No proposal accepted without prior request for guidelines. Under no circumstances send manuscript before query.

O— Spence publishes nonfiction books of commentary on culture and society. Currently emphasizing feminism, religion and public life, marriage and family.

Nonfiction: Subjects include education, government/politics, philosophy, religion, sociology, women's issues/studies.
Recent Title(s): *Hating Whitey*, by David Horowitz (nonfiction); *The Church Impotent*, by Leon Podles.
Tips: "We publish books on culture and society from a generally (though not exclusively) conservative point of view. We seek books with a fresh approach to serious questions of public and private life that propose constructive alternatives to the status quo."

SPINSTERS INK, 32 E. First St., #330, Duluth, MN 55802. (218)727-3222. Fax: (218)727-3119. E-mail: spinster@spinsters-ink.com. Website: www.spinsters-ink.com. **Acquisitions:** Nancy Walker. Estab. 1978. Publishes trade paperback originals and reprints. **Publishes 6 titles/year. Receives 400 submissions/year. 50% of books from first-time authors; 95% from unagented writers. Pays 7-11% royalty on retail price.** Publishes book 18 months after acceptance. Responds in 4 months. Book catalog free. Manuscript guidelines for SASE.

O— "Spinsters Ink publishes novels and nonfiction works that deal with significant issues in women's lives from a feminist perspective: books that not only name these crucial issues, but—more important—encourage change and growth. We are committed to publishing works by women writing from the periphery, fat women, Jewish women, lesbians, old women, poor women, rural women, women examining classism, women of color, women with disabilities, women who are writing books that help make the best in our lives more possible."

Nonfiction: Feminist analysis for positive change. Subjects include women's issues. "We do not want to see work by men or anything that is not specific to women's lives (humor, children's books, etc.)." Query. Reviews artwork/photos as part of ms package.
Fiction: Ethnic, women's, lesbian. "We do not publish poetry or short fiction. We are interested in fiction that challenges, women's language that is feminist, stories that treat lifestyles with the diversity and complexity they deserve. We are also interested in genre fiction, especially mysteries." Submit outline/synopsis and sample chapters.
Recent Title(s): *Sugar Land*, by Joni Rodgers (fiction).

[N:] SPOTTED DOG PRESS, INC., P.O. Box 1721, 2399 N. Sierra Hwy., Bishop CA 93514. (760)872-1524. Fax: (760)872-1319. E-mail: spdogpress@qnet.com. Website: www.spotteddogpress.com. **Acquisitions**: Wynne Benti, publisher (cultural & natural history); Andrew Zdon, senior editor (outdoor). Publishes trade softcover originals and reprints. **Publishes 6-10 titles/year. Receives 10-25 queries and 5-10 mss/year. 50% of books from first-time authors; 100% from unagented writers. Pays negotiable royalty on wholesale price. Offers advance and/or a bonus based on sales.** Publishes book 1 year after acceptance of ms. Prefers no simultaneous submissions. Responds in 1 month. Book catalog and manuscript guidelines for #10 SASE or on website.

O— Spotted Dog Press specializes in outdoor travel and guide books.

Nonfiction: How-to, travel & guide books. Subjects include nature/environment, travel, climbing, hiking, mountaineering, world & outdoor adventure, historic travel guides. Query with SASE, table of contents, outline, 2 sample chapters and résumé of experience. Reviews artwork/photos as part of ms package. Send photocopies or good quality color inkjet or laserjet samples.
Recent Title(s): *Out From Las Vegas*, by Florine Lawlor (desert travel); *Climbing Mt. Whitney*, by Walt Wheelock/Wynne Benti (mountain guide book).
Tips: "Our guide books are written for the outdoor audience looking for adventure or challenge within their own reach. We'll consider travel or guide books with interesting or colorful cultural or historical qualities or author narrative in a specialized or 'niche' market not covered by other outdoor publishers. We won't consider gonzo 4-wheel drive, hunting, fishing or similar subjects. Authors should also be able to submit their own photos for their book."

STACKPOLE BOOKS, 5067 Ritter Rd., Mechanicsburg PA 17055. Fax: (717)796-0412. E-mail: jschnell@stackpolebooks.com. Website: www.stackpolebooks.com. **Acquisitions:** Judith Schnell, editorial director (fly fishing, sports); William C. Davis, editor (history); Mark Allison, editor (nature, photography); Ed Skender, editor (military guides); Kyle Weaver, editor (Pennsylvania). Estab. 1935. Publishes hardcover and paperback originals and reprints. **Publishes 75 titles/year. Pays industry standard royalty.** Publishes book 1 year after acceptance. Responds in 1 month. *Writer's Market* recommends allowing 2 months for reply.

O— "Stackpole maintains a growing and vital publishing program by featuring authors who are experts in their fields, from outdoor activities to Civil War history."

Nonfiction: Outdoor-related subject areas—nature, wildlife, outdoor skills, outdoor sports, fly fishing, paddling, climbing, crafts and hobbies, photography, history especially Civil War and military guides. Query. Does not return unsolicited mss. Reviews artwork/photos as part of ms package.
Recent Title(s): *Exploring the Appalachian Trail Guides* (5-book hiking series).
Tips: "Stackpole seeks well-written, authoritative manuscripts for specialized and general trade markets. Proposals should include chapter outline, sample chapter and illustrations and author's credentials."

STANDARD PUBLISHING, Standex International Corp., 8121 Hamilton Ave., Cincinnati OH 45231. (513)931-4050. Website: www.standardpub.com. Publisher/Vice President: Mark Taylor. **Acquisitions:** Lise Caldwell (children's books); Ruth Frederick (children's ministry resources); Dale Reeves (Empowered Youth Products); Jim Eichenberger (Solid Foundation Resources for ministry to adults). Estab. 1866. Publishes hardcover and paperback originals and reprints. **Pays royalty.** Publishes book 18 months after acceptance. Responds in 3 months. Manuscript guidelines for #10 SASE; send request to Jolene Goldschmidt.

O⤙ Standard specializes in religious books for children and religious education. De-emphasizing board books.
Nonfiction: Children's picture books, Christian education (teacher training, working with volunteers), quiz, puzzle, crafts (to be used in Christian education). Query with SASE.
Recent Title(s): *My Good Night Bible*, by Susan Lingo (nonfiction); *Can God See Me?*, by JoDee McConnaughhay (fiction); *Edible Object Talks*, by Susan Lingo (poetry).

STANFORD UNIVERSITY PRESS, Stanford CA 94305-2235. (650)723-9434. Fax: (605)725-3457. Website: www.s up.org. Editorial Director: Pamela Holway. Senior Editor: Muriel Bell. Humanities Editor: Helen Tartar. **Acquisitions:** Norris Pope, director. Estab. 1925. **Publishes 120 titles/year. Receives 1,500 submissions/year. 40% of books from first-time authors; 95% from unagented writers. Pays up to 15% royalty ("typically 10%, often none"). Sometimes offers advance.** Publishes book 14 months after receipt of final ms. Responds in 6 weeks.

O⤙ Stanford University Press publishes scholarly books in the humanities, social sciences and natural history, high-level textbooks and some books for a more general audience.
Nonfiction: History and culture of China, Japan and Latin America; literature, criticism, and literary theory; political science and sociology; European history; anthropology, linguistics and psychology; archaeology and geology; medieval and classical studies. Query with prospectus and an outline. Reviews artwork/photos as part of ms package.
Recent Title(s): *The Leisure Ethic*, by William A. Gleason and Charles W. Chesnutt.
Tips: "The writer's best chance is a work of original scholarship with an argument of some importance."

STARBURST PUBLISHERS, P.O. Box 4123, Lancaster PA 17604. (717)293-0939. Fax: (717)293-1945. E-mail: editorial@starburstpublishers.com. Website: www.starburstpublishers.com. **Acquisitions:** Editorial Department. Estab. 1982. Publishes hardcover and trade paperback originals. **Publishes 15-20 titles/year. Receives 1,000 queries and mss/ year. 50% of books from first-time authors, 75% from unagented writers. Pays 6-16% royalty on wholesale price. Advance varies.** Publishes book 1 year after acceptance of ms. Accepts simultaneous submissions. Responds in 1 month on queries. *Writer's Market* recommends allowing 2 months for reply. Book catalog for 9 × 12 SASE with 4 first-class stamps. Manuscript guidelines for #10 SASE.

O⤙ Starburst publishes quality self-help, health and inspirational titles for the trade and religious markets. Currently emphasizing inspirational gift, how-to and health books. De-emphasizing fiction.
Nonfiction: General nonfiction, cookbook, gift book, how-to, self-help, Christian. Subjects include business/economics, child guidance/parenting, cooking/foods/nutrition, counseling/career guidance, education, gardening, health/medicine, home, money/finance, nature/environment, psychology, real estate, recreation, religion. "We are looking for books that inspire, teach and help today's average American." Submit proposal package including outline, 3 sample chapters, author's biography and SASE. Reviews artwork/photos as part of ms package. Send photocopies.
Fiction: Inspirational. "We are only looking for good wholesome fiction that inspires or fiction that teaches self-help principles." Submit outline/synopsis, 3 sample chapters, author's biography and SASE.
Recent Title(s): *The Bible*, by Larry Richards (nonfiction); *The Weekly Feeder*, by Cort Kirkpatrick (nonfiction).
Tips: "Fifty percent of our line goes into the Christian marketplace, fifty percent into the general marketplace. We have direct sales representatives in both the Christian and general (bookstore, catalog, price club, mass merchandiser, library, health and gift) marketplace. Write on an issue that slots you on talk shows and thus establishes your name as an expert and writer."

STEEPLE HILL, Harlequin Enterprises, 300 E. 42nd St., New York NY 10017. Website: www.@harlequin.com. **Acquisitions**: Tara Gavin, editorial director; Tracy Farrell, senior editor. Acquisitions Editors: Ann Leslie Tuttle, Patience Smith, Karen Kosztolnyik and all Silhouette/Harlequin Historicals editors. Estab. 1997. Publishes mass market paperback originals. **Pays royalty.** Manuscript guidelines for #10 SASE.

O⤙ "This series of contemporary, inspirational love stories portrays Christian characters facing the many challenges of life, faith and love in today's world."
Imprint(s): Love Inspired.
Fiction: Christian romance (70,000 words). Query or submit synopsis and 3 sample chapters with SASE.
Recent Title(s): *A Mother at Heart*, by Carolyne Aarsen.
Tips: "Drama, humor and even a touch of mystery all have a place in this series. Subplots are welcome and should further the story's main focus or intertwine in a meaningful way. Secondary characters (children, family, friends, neighbors, fellow church members, etc.) may all contribute to a substantial and satisfying story. These wholesome tales of romance include strong family values and high moral standards. While there is no premarital sex between characters, a vivid, exciting romance that is presented with a mature perspective, is essential. Although the element of faith must clearly be present, it should be well integrated into the characterizations and plot. The conflict between the main characters should be an emotional one, arising naturally from the well-developed personalities you've created. Suitable stories should also impart an important lesson about the powers of trust and faith."

STENHOUSE PUBLISHERS, P.O. Box 360, York ME 03909. (207)363-9198. Fax: (207)363-9730. E-mail: philippa @stenhouse.com. Website: www.stenhouse.com. **Acquisitions:** Philippa Stratton, editorial director. Estab. 1993. Publishes paperback originals. **Publishes 15 titles/year. Receives 300 queries/year. 30% of books from first-time authors; 99% from unagented writers. Pays royalty on wholesale price. Offers "very modest" advance.** Publishes book 6 months after delivery of final ms. Responds in 1 month on queries, 2 months on proposals, 3 months on mss. Book catalog and ms guidelines free or on website.

O⊸ Stenhouse publishes books that support teachers' professional growth by connecting theory and practice, and specializes in literacy education.

Nonfiction: Exclusively education, specializing in literacy. "All our books are a combination of theory and practice." Query with outline. Reviews artwork/photos as part of ms package. Send photocopies.

Recent Title(s): *Methods that Matter: Six Structures for Best Practice Classrooms*, by Harvey Daniels and Marilyn Bizar; *Strategies That Work: Teaching Comprehension to Enhance Understanding*, by Stephanie Harvey and Anne Goudvis.

STERLING PUBLISHING, 387 Park Ave. S., New York NY 10016. (212)532-7160. Fax: (212)213-2495. Website: www.sterlingpub.com. **Acquisitions:** Sheila Anne Barry, acquisitions manager. Estab. 1949. Publishes hardcover and paperback originals and reprints. **Publishes 350 titles/year. Pays royalty. Offers advance.** Publishes book 1 year after acceptance. Responds in 4 months. Guidelines for SASE.

O⊸ Sterling publishes highly illustrated, accessible, hands-on, practical books for adults and children.

Imprint(s): Sterling/Chapelle; **Lark**; Sterling/Tamos; Sterling/Silver; Sterling/Godsfield; Sterling/SIR.

Nonfiction: Fiber arts, games and puzzles, health, how-to, hobbies, children's humor, children's science, nature and activities, pets, recreation, reference, sports, wine, gardening, art, home decorating, dolls and puppets, ghosts, UFOs, woodworking, crafts, medieval, Celtic subjects, alternative health and healing, new consciousness. Query or submit detailed outline and 2 sample chapters with photos if applicable.

Recent Title(s): *The Great Rubber Stamp Book*, by Dee Gruenig.

⟨N⟩ STILL WATERS POETRY PRESS, 459 Willow Ave., Galloway Township NJ 08201. Website: wwww.netcom.com/~salake/stillwaterspoetrypress. **Acquisitions:** Shirley A. Lake, editor. Estab. 1989. Publishes trade paperback originals and chapbooks. **Publishes 2 titles/year. Receives 50 queries and 500 mss/year. 80% of books from first-time authors; 100% from unagented writers. Pays in copies for first press run; 10% royalty for additional press runs. No advance.** Publishes book 4 months after acceptance of ms. Accepts simultaneous submissions. Responds in 1 month on queries and proposals, 3 months on mss. Book catalog and ms guidelines available via website or with #10 SASE.

O⊸ "Dedicated to significant poetry for, by or about women, we want contemporary themes and styles set on American soil. We don't want gay, patriarchal religion, lesbian, simple rhyme or erotic themes."

Poetry: "We publish chapbooks only, 20-30 pages, one author at a time. Do not expect publication of a single poem. Enclose SASE. Query then submit complete ms.

Recent Title(s): *Suzy and Her Husband*, By Edward Mast; *Moving Expenses*, by Lori Shpunt.

Tips: "Don't send manuscripts via certified mail. It wastes your money and my time."

STIPES PUBLISHING CO., P.O. Box 526, Champaign IL 61824-9933. (217)356-8391. Fax: (217)356-5753. E-mail: stipes@soltec.com. Website: www.stipes.com. **Acquisitions:** Benjamin H. Watts, (engineering, science, business); Robert Watts (agriculture, music and physical education). Estab. 1925. **Publishes hardcover and paperback originals. Publishes 15-30 titles/year. Receives 150 submissions/year. 50% of books from first-time authors; 95% from unagented writers. Pays 15% maximum royalty on retail price.** Publishes book 4 months after acceptance. Responds in 2 months.

O⊸ Stipes Publishing is "oriented towards the education market and educational books with some emphasis in the trade market."

Nonfiction: Technical (some areas), textbooks on business/economics, music, chemistry, CADD, agriculture/horticulture, environmental education, and recreation and physical education. "All of our books in the trade area are books that also have a college text market. No books unrelated to educational fields taught at the college level." Submit outline and 1 sample chapter.

Recent Title(s): *The Microstation J Workbook*, by Michael Ward.

STOEGER PUBLISHING COMPANY, 5 Mansard Court, Wayne NJ 07470. (973)872-9500. Fax: (973)872-2230. E-mail: stoegerindustries@msn.com. **Acquisitions:** David Perkins, vice president. Estab. 1925. Publishes trade paperback originals. **Publishes 12-15 titles/year. Royalty varies, depending on ms.** Accepts simultaneous submissions. Responds in 1 month. Book catalog for #10 SAE with 2 first-class stamps.

O⊸ Stoeger publishes books on hunting, shooting sports, fishing, cooking, nature and wildlife.

Nonfiction: Specializing in reference and how-to books that pertain to hunting, fishing and appeal to gun enthusiasts. Submit outline and sample chapters.

Recent Title(s): *Complete Book of Whitetail Hunting*, by Toby Bridges; *Complete Guide to Modern Rifles*, by Gene Gangarosa, Jr.

STONE BRIDGE PRESS, P.O. Box 8208, Berkeley CA 94707. (510)524-8732. Fax: (510)524-8711. E-mail: sbp@stonebridge.com. Website: www.stonebridge.com/. **Acquisitions:** Peter Goodman, publisher. Estab. 1989. Publishes hardcover and trade paperback originals. **Publishes 8 titles/year; imprint publishes 2 titles/year. Receives 100 queries**

and 75 mss/year. **15-20% of books from first-time authors; 90% from unagented writers. Pays royalty on wholesale price. Advance varies.** Publishes book 2 years after acceptance. Accepts simultaneous submissions. Responds in 1 month on queries and proposals, 4 months on mss. Book catalog free.

O— Stone Bridge Press strives "to publish and distribute high-quality informational tools about Japan."

Imprint(s): The Rock Spring Collection of Japanese Literature.

Nonfiction: How-to, reference. Subjects include art/architecture, business/economics, government/politics, language/literature, philosophy, translation, travel, women's issues/studies. "We publish Japan- (and some Asia-) related books only." Query with SASE. Reviews artwork/photos as part of ms package. Send photocopies.

Recent Title(s): *Huyao Miyuzaki: Master of Japanese Animation*; *Tokyo Q: Annual Guide to the City*; *The Japanese Way of the Flower.*

Tips: Audience is "intelligent, worldly readers with an interest in Japan based on personal need or experience. No children's books or commercial fiction. Realize that interest in Japan is a moving target. Please don't submit yesterday's trends or rely on a view of Japan that is outmoded. Stay current!"

STONEWALL INN, St. Martin's Press, 175 Fifth Ave., New York NY 10010. (212)674-5151. Website: www.stonewall inn.com. **Acquisitions:** Keith Kahla, general editor. Publishes trade paperback originals and reprints. **Publishes 20-23 titles/year. Receives 3,000 queries/year. 40% of books from first-time authors; 25% from unagented writers. Pays standard royalty on retail price. Advance varies.** Publishes book 1 year after acceptance of ms. Accepts simultaneous submissions. Responds in 6 months on queries. Book catalog free.

O— Stonewall Inn is an imprint for gay and lesbian themed fiction, nonfiction and mysteries. Currently emphasizing literary fiction. De-emphasizing mysteries.

Nonfiction: Subjects include nearly every aspect of gay/lesbian studies. "We are looking for well-researched sociological works; author's credentials count for a great deal." Query with SASE.

Fiction: Gay/lesbian, literary, mystery. "Anybody who has any question about what a gay novel is should go out and read half a dozen. For example, there are hundreds of 'coming out' novels in print." Query with SASE.

Recent Title(s): *The Pleasure Principle*, by Michael Bronski (nonfiction); *An Arrow's Flight*, by Mark Merlis (fiction).

STONEYDALE PRESS, 523 Main St., Stevensville MT 59870. (406)777-2729. Fax: (406)777-2521. E-mail: daleburk @montana.com. **Acquisitions:** Dale A. Burk, publisher. Estab. 1976. Publishes hardcover and trade paperback originals. **Publishes 4-6 titles/year. Receives 40-50 queries and 6-8 mss/year. 90% of books from unagented writers. Pays 12-15% royalty.** Publishes book 18 months after acceptance of ms. Responds in 2 months. Book catalog available.

O— "We seek to publish the best available source books on big game hunting, historical reminiscence and outdoor recreation in the Northern Rocky Mountain region."

Nonfiction: How-to hunting books, historical reminiscences. Query.

Recent Title(s): *Lewis & Clark on the Upper Missouri*, by Jeanne O'Neil; *Montana's Bitterroot Valley*, by Russ Lawrence.

STOREY PUBLISHING, Schoolhouse Rd., Pownal VT 05261. (802)823-5200. Fax: (802)823-5819. Website: www.st orey.com. **Acquisitions:** Margaret J. Lydic, editorial director; Deborah Balmuth (natural beauty and healing/health, crafts, herbs); Deborah Burns (animals, horses, birds, farming); Gwen Steege (gardening, crafts). Estab. 1983. Publishes hardcover and trade paperback originals and reprints. **Publishes 45 titles/year. Receives 600 queries and 150 mss/year. 25% of books from first-time authors; 80% from unagented writers. Pays royalty or makes outright purchase.** Publishes book within 2 years of acceptance. Accepts simultaneous submissions. Responds in 1 month to queries, 3 months on proposals and mss. Book catalog and ms guidelines available via website or free upon request.

O— "We publish practical information that encourages personal independence in harmony with the environment."

Nonfiction: Subjects include garden and home, herbs, natural health and beauty, birds and nature, animals, beer and wine, cooking and crafts, building, home-based business. Occasionally reviews artwork/photos as part of the ms package.

Recent Title(s): *The Vegetable Gardener's Bible*, by Edward C. Smith; *Everyday Antiques*, by JJ Despain.

STORY LINE PRESS, Three Oaks Farm, P.O. Box 1240, Ashland OR 97520-0055. (541)512-8792. Fax: (541)512-8793. E-mail: mail@storylinepress.com. Website: www.storylinepress.com. **Acquisitions:** Robert McDowell, publisher/editor. Estab. 1985. Publishes hardcover and trade paperback originals. **Publishes 12-16 titles/year. Receives 500 queries and 1,000 mss/year. 10% of books from first-time authors; most from unagented writers. Pays 10-15% royalty on retail price or makes outright purchase of $250-1,500. Offers $0-3,000 advance.** Publishes book 1-2 years after acceptance of ms. Accepts simultaneous submissions. Responds in 1 month on queries, 3 months on mss. Book catalog free. Manuscript guidelines for #10 SASE.

O— "Story Line Press exists to publish the best stories of our time in poetry, fiction and nonfiction. Seventy-five percent of our list includes a wide range of poetry and books about poetry. Our books are intended for the general and academic reader. We are working to expand the audience for serious literature."

Nonfiction: Literary. Subjects include authors/literature. Query with SASE.

Fiction: Literary, no popular genres. "We currently have a backlist through the year 2000. Please send query letter first." Query with SASE.

Poetry: Backlist for publication is through the year 2000.

Recent Title(s): *New Expansive Poetry*, by R.S. Gwynn, editor (nonfiction); *Quit Monks Or Die!*, by Maxine Kumin (fiction); *Questions for Ecclesiastes*, by Mark Jarman (poetry).

Tips: "We strongly recommend that first-time poetry authors submit their book-length manuscripts in the Nicholas Roerich Poetry Contest or the Three Oaks Fiction Contest." See the Contests & Awards section for details.

STYLUS PUBLISHING, LLC, 22883 Quicksilver Dr., Sterling VA 20166. **Acquisitions**: John von Knorring, publisher. Estab. 1996. Publishes hardcover and trade paperback originals. **Publishes 6-10 titles/year. Receives 50 queries and 6 mss/year. 50% of books from first-time authors; 100% from unagented writers. Pays 5-10% royalty on wholesale price.** Publishes book 6 months after acceptance of ms. Responds in 1 month. Book catalog and ms guidelines free.

    ○ "We publish books for administrators, faculty developers, educational technologists and leaders in higher education as well as books for corporate trainers and managers."

Nonfiction: Subjects include business and training, education. Query or submit outline, 1 sample chapter with SASE. Reviews artwork/photos as part of ms package. Send photocopies.

Recent Title(s): *Thinking about Teaching and Learning*; *Job Search in Academe*.

SUCCESS PUBLISHING, 3419 Dunham Rd., Warsaw NY 14569-9735. (716)786-5663. **Acquisitions:** Allan H. Smith, president (home-based business); Ginger Smith (business), Dana Herbison (home/craft), Robin Garretson (fiction). Estab. 1982. Publishes mass market paperback originals. **Publishes 6 titles/year. Receives 175 submissions/year, 10 mss/year. 90% of books from first-time authors; 100% from unagented writers. Pays 7-12% royalty.** Offers $500-1,000 advance. Publishes book 10 months after acceptance. Accepts simultaneous submissions. Responds in 2 months. Book catalog and ms guidelines for #10 SAE with 2 first-class stamps.

    ○ Success publishes guides that focus on the needs of the home entrepeneur to succeed as a viable business. Currently emphasizing starting a new business. De-emphasizing self-help/motivation books.

Nonfiction: Children's/juvenile, how-to, self-help. Subjects include child guidence/parenting, business/economics, hobbies, money/finance, craft/home-based business. "We are looking for books on how-to subjects such as home business and sewing." Query.

Recent Title(s): *How to Find a Date/Mate*, by Dana Herbison.

    ● Success Publishing notes that it is looking for ghostwriters.

Tips: "Our audience is made up of housewives, hobbyists and owners of home-based businesses."

SUDBURY PRESS, Profitable Technology, Inc., 40 Maclean Dr., Sudbury MA 01776. Fax: (978)443-0734. E-mail: press@intertain.com. Website: www.sudburypress.com. **Acquisitions:** Susan Gray, publisher. Publishes hardcover and mass market paperback originals. **Publishes 4 titles/year. Receives 100 queries and 100 mss/year. 100% of books from first-time authors; 100% from unagented writers. Pays 10% royalty on wholesale price. Offers $3,000 advance.** Publishes book 12 months after acceptance. Responds in 6 months. Book catalog on Internet.

    ○ Sudbury Press publishes autobiographies and biographies of women.

Nonfiction: "We want biographies and autobiographies of ordinary women in extraordinary circumstances."

Recent Title(s): *To Auschwitz and Back: My Personal Journey*, by Ruth Bindefeld Neray.

THE SUMMIT PUBLISHING GROUP, 2000 E. Lamar Blvd., Suite 600, Arlington TX 76006. (817)588-3013. Fax: (817)462-4014. E-mail: jbertolet@flashwave.com. Website: www.summitpeaks.com. **Acquisitions:** Jill Bertolet, publisher; Sarah Nahhas, acquisitions manager. Estab. 1990. Publishes hardcover originals, trade paperback originals and reprints. **Publishes 10 titles/year. 80% of books from first-time authors; 80% from unagented writers. Pays 15% royalty on wholesale price. Offers $2,000 and up advance**, depending on author's credibility. Publishes book 6 months after acceptance of ms. Accepts simultaneous submissions. Responds in 1 month on queries and proposals, 6 months on mss.

    ○ Summit Publishing Group publishes contemporary books with a nationwide appeal. "We target the adult market with biography, self-help, how-to, gift and coffee table books." Currently emphasizing self-help, biography, cookbooks. De-emphasizing children's/juvenile.

Imprints: Legacy Books (corporate private label organizational publications).

Nonfiction: Biography, coffee table book, cookbook, gift book, how-to, humor, self-help. Subjects include art/architecture, business/economics, cooking, ethnic, gardening, government/politics, health/medicine, history, hobbies, military/war, money/finance, nature/environment, recreation, regional, religion, science, sociology, sports, women's issues/studies. Submit proposal package including outline, 2 sample chapters, table of contents, proposal marketing letter and résumé with SASE. Reviews artwork/photos as part of ms package. Send photocopies.

Recent Title(s): *On the Brink*, by Norman Brinker.

Tips: "Books should have obvious national-distribution appeal, be of a contemporary nature and be marketing-driven: author's media experience and contacts a strong plus."

SUNSTONE PRESS, P.O. Box 2321, Santa Fe NM 87504-2321. (505)988-4418. Website: www.sunstonepress.com. **Acquisitions:** James C. Smith, Jr., president. Estab. 1971. Publishes paperback and hardcover originals. **Publishes 25 titles/year. Receives 400 submissions/year. 70% of books from first-time authors; 100% from unagented writers. Pays 7½-15% royalty on wholesale price.** Publishes book 18 months after acceptance. Responds in 1 month.

    ○ "After firmly establishing ourselves as a regional publisher of southwestern U.S. themes, Sunstone Press has been interested—and had success—in the launching of mainstream fiction by first-time novelists in the last five years. We continue our focus on regional subjects for our nonfiction titles, especially biographies."

Imprint(s): Sundial Publications.
Nonfiction: How-to series craft books. Books on the history, culture and architecture of the Southwest. "Looks for strong regional appeal (Southwestern)." Query with SASE. Reviews artwork/photos as part of ms package.
Fiction: Publishes material with various themes. Query with SASE.
Recent Title(s): *Breakdown: How the Secrets of the Atomic Bomb Were Stolen During World War II*, by Richard Melzer, Ph.D. (nonfiction); *Buckskin and Satin*, by Romain Wilhelmsen.
Tips: This publisher's focus is the Southwestern US but it receives many, many submissions outside this subject.

SWEDENBORG FOUNDATION PUBLISHERS, 320 North Church St., West Chester PA 19380. (610)430-3222. Fax: (610)430-7982. E-mail: acquisition@swedenborg.com. Website: www.swedenborg.com. Executive Director/Publisher: Deborah Forman. **Acquisitions:** Susan Poole, acquisitions editor. Estab. 1849. Publishes hardcover and trade paperback originals and reprints. **Publishes 10-15 titles/year; imprints publish 1 title/year. Pays 10% royalty on net receipts or makes outright purchase. Offers $1000 minimum advance.** Responds in 3 months on queries, 6 months on proposals, 9 months on mss. Book catalog and ms guidelines free.
　　O﹣ "The Swedenborg Foundation publishes books by and about Emanuel Swedenborg (1688-1772), his ideas, how his ideas have influenced others, and related topics. A Chrysalis book is an adventurous, spiritually focused book presented with a nonsectarian perspective that appeals to open-minded, well-educated seekers of all traditions. Appropriate topics include—but are not limited to—science, mysticism, spiritual growth and development, wisdom traditions, healing and spirituality, as well as subjects that explore Swedenborgian concepts, such as: near-death experience, angels, biblical interpretation, mysteries of good and evil, etc. These books will foster a searching approach to the spiritual basis of reality."
Imprint(s): Chrysalis Books, Swedenborg Foundation Press.
Nonfiction: Spiritual growth and development, science and spirituality. Subjects include philosophy, psychology, religion. Query with proposal package, including synopsis, outline, sample chapter and SASE. Reviews artwork/photos as part of ms package. Send photocopies.
Recent Nonfiction Title(s): *The Fashioning of Angels: Partnership as Spiritual Practice*, by Stephen and Robin Larsen.
　　● The Swedenborg Foundation also publishes *Chrysalis Reader*, listed in Consumer Magazines/Religious.
Tips: "Most readers of our books are thoughtful, well-read individuals seeking resources for their philosophical, spiritual or religious growth. Especially sought are nonfiction works that bridge contemporary issues to spiritual insights."

N SYBEX, INC., 1151 Marina Village Pkwy., Alameda CA 94501. (510)523-8233. Fax: (510)523-2373. E-mail: proposals@sybex.com. Website: www.sybex.com. Publisher: Jordan Gold. **Acquisitions:** Kristine O'Callaghan, contracts and licensing manager. Estab. 1976. Publishes paperback originals. **Publishes 180 titles/year. Pays standard royalties. Offers competitive advance.** Publishes book 3 months after acceptance. Accepts simultaneous submissions. Responds in up to 6 months. Free book catalog.
　　O﹣ Sybex publishes computer and software titles.
Nonfiction: Computers, computer software. "Manuscripts most publishable in the field of PC applications software, hardware, programming languages, operating systems, computer games, Internet/Web certification and networking." Submit outline and 2-3 sample chapters. Looks for "clear writing, logical presentation of material; and good selection of material such that the most important aspects of the subject matter are thoroughly covered; well-focused subject matter; clear understanding of target audience; and well-thought-out organization that helps the reader understand the material." Views artwork/photos, disk/CD as part of ms package.
Recent Nonfiction Title(s): *Mastering Windows 98,* second edition, by Robert Cowart; *The Complete PC Upgrade and Maintenance Guide,* 10th edition, by Mark Minasi; *CCNA™: Cisco® Certified Network Associate Study Guide*, by Todd Lammle.
Tips: Queries/mss may be routed to other editors in the publishing group. Also seeking freelance writers for revising existing works and as contributors in multi-author projects.

SYRACUSE UNIVERSITY PRESS, 621 Skytop Road, Suite 110, Syracuse NY 13244-5290. (315)443-5534. Fax: (315)443-5545. Website: http://sumweb.syr.edu/su_press/. **Acquisitions:** Robert A. Mandel, director. Estab. 1943. **Averages 80 titles/year. Receives 600-700 submissions/year. 25% of books from first-time authors; 75% from unagented writers. Nonauthor subsidy publishes 20% of books. Pays royalty on net sales.** Publishes book an average of 15 months after acceptance of ms. Simultaneous submissions discouraged. Book catalog for 9×12 SAE with 3 first-class stamps.
　　O﹣ Currently emphasizing television, Jewish studies, Middle East topics. De-emphasizing peace studies.
Nonfiction: "Special opportunity in our nonfiction program for freelance writers of books on New York state, sports history, Jewish studies, the Middle East, religious studies, television and popular culture. Provide precise descriptions of subjects, along with background description of project. The author must make a case for the importance of his or her subject." Query with outline and at least 2 sample chapters. Reviews artwork/photos as part of ms package.
Recent Title(s): *Exposing the Wilderness: Early Twentieth-Century Adirondack Postcard Photographers*, by Robert Bogdan (nonfiction); *The Reason for Wings*, by Joyce Reiser Kornblatt (fiction); *A Cup of Sin: Selected Poems*, by Simin Behbahani, translated by Farzaneh Milani (poetry).
Tips: "We're seeking well-written and well-researched books that will make a significant contribution to the subject areas listed above and will be well-received in the marketplace."

A **NAN A. TALESE**, Doubleday Broadway Publishing Group, Random House, Inc., 1540 Broadway, New York NY 10036. (212)782-8918. Fax: (212)782-9261. Website: www.nantalese.com. **Acquisitions:** Nan A. Talese, editorial director. Publishes hardcover originals. **Publishes 15 titles/year. Receives 400 queries and mss/year. Pays variable royalty on retail price. Advance varies.** Publishes book 1 year after acceptance of ms. Accepts simultaneous submissions. Responds in 1 week to queries, 2 weeks to proposals and mss.

　　Oⁿ Nan A. Talese publishes nonfiction with a powerful guiding narrative and relevance to larger cultural trends and interests, and literary fiction of the highest quality.

Nonfiction: Biography, history, sociology, popular sciences. Subjects include art/architecture, history, philosophy, current trends. *Agented submissions only.*

Fiction: Well written narratives with a compelling story line, good characterization and use of language. We like stories with an edge. *Agented submissions only.*

Recent Title(s): *The Blind Assassin*, by Margaret Atwood (fiction).

Tips: "Audience is highly literate people interested in story, information and insight. We want well-written material. See our website."

TAYLOR PUBLISHING COMPANY, 1550 W. Mockingbird Lane, Dallas TX 75235. (214)819-8334. Fax: (214)819-8580. Website: www.taylorpub.com. President: Craig Von Pelt. Publisher/Editorial Director: Lynn Brooks. **Acquisitions:** Michael Emmerich, senior editor (sports, history, pop culture, gardening, health); Camille N. Cline, senior editor (pop culture, history, health, gardening). Estab. 1981. Publishes hardcover and softcover originals. **Publishes 35 titles/year. Receives 1,500 submissions/year. 25% of books from first-time authors; 25% from unagented writers.** Publishes book 1-2 years after acceptance. Accepts simultaneous submissions. Responds in 3 months. Book catalog and ms guidelines for 10×13 SASE.

　　Oⁿ "We publish solid, practical books that should backlist well. We look for authors who are expert authors in their field and already have some recognition through magazine articles, radio appearances or their own TV or radio show. We also look for speakers or educators."

Nonfiction: Gardening, sports, popular culture, parenting, health, home improvement, how-to, popular history, biography, miscellaneous nonfiction. Submit outline, sample chapter, an overview of the market and competition and an author bio as it pertains to proposed subject matter. Reviews artwork as part of ms package.

Recent Title(s): *Where's Harry*, by Steve Stone; *ESPN: The Uncensored History*, by Michael Freeman.

TCU PRESS, P.O. Box 298300, TCU, Fort Worth TX 76129. (817)257-7822. Fax: (817)257-5075. **Acquisitions:** Judy Alter, director; James Ward Lee, acquisitions consultant. Estab. 1966. Publishes hardcover originals, some reprints. **Publishes 12 titles/year. Receives 100 submissions/year. 10% of books from first-time authors; 75% from unagented writers. Nonauthor-subsidy publishes 10% of books. Pays 10% royalty on net price.** Publishes book 16 months after acceptance. Responds in 3 months on queries.

　　Oⁿ TCU publishes "scholarly works and regional titles of significance focusing on the history and literature of the American West."

Nonfiction: American studies, literature and criticism. Query. Reviews artwork/photos as part of ms package.

Fiction: Regional fiction, by invitation only. *Please do not query.*

Recent Title(s): *Larry L. King: A Writer's Life in Letters*, ed. Richard Holland (nonfiction); *Alamo Heights*, by Scott Zesch (fiction).

Tips: "Regional and/or Texana nonfiction has best chance of breaking into our firm."

TEACHERS COLLEGE PRESS, 1234 Amsterdam Ave., New York NY 10027. (212)678-3929. Fax: (212)678-4149. Website: www.tc.columbia.edu/tcpress. Director: Carole P. Saltz. **Acquisitions:** Brian Ellerbeck, executive acquisitions editor. Estab. 1904. Publishes hardcover and paperback originals and reprints. **Publishes 60 titles/year. Pays industry standard royalty.** Publishes book 1 year after acceptance. Responds in 2 months. Catalog free.

　　Oⁿ Teachers College Press publishes a wide range of educational titles for all levels of students: early childhood to higher education. "Publishing books that respond to, examine and confront issues pertaining to education, teacher training and school reform."

Nonfiction: "This university press concentrates on books in the field of education in the broadest sense, from early childhood to higher education: good classroom practices, teacher training, special education, innovative trends and issues, administration and supervision, film, continuing and adult education, all areas of the curriculum, computers, guidance and counseling and the politics, economics, philosophy, sociology and history of education. We have recently added women's studies to our list. The Press also issues classroom materials for students at all levels, with a strong emphasis on reading and writing and social studies." Submit outline and sample chapters.

Recent Title(s): *How Schools Might Be Governed and Why*, by Seymour Sarason.

TEACHING & LEARNING COMPANY, 1204 Buchanan St., P.O. Box 10, Carthage IL 62321-0010. (217)357-2591. Fax: (217)357-6789. E-mail: tandlcom@adams.net. Website: www.teachinglearning.com. **Acquisitions:** Jill Eckhardt, managing editor. Estab. 1994. **Publishes 60 titles/year. Receives 25 queries and 200 mss/year. 25% of books from first-time authors; 98% from unagented writers. Pays royalty.** Accepts simultaneous submissions. Responds in 3 months on queries, 9 months on proposals and mss. Book catalog and ms guidelines free.

　　Oⁿ Teaching & Learning Company publishes teacher resources (supplementary activity/idea books) for grades pre K-8.

Nonfiction: Subjects include teacher resources: language arts, reading, math, science, social studies, arts and crafts, responsibility education. No picture books or storybooks. Submit table of contents, introduction, 3 sample chapters with SASE. Reviews artwork/photos as part of ms package. Send photocopies.

Recent Title(s): *Group Project Student Role Sheets*, by Christine Boardman Moen (nonfiction); *Poetry Writing Handbook*, by Greta Barclay Upson, Ed.D. (poetry).

Tips: "Our books are for teachers and parents of pre K-8th grade children."

TEMPLE UNIVERSITY PRESS, USB, 1601 N. Broad St., Philadelphia PA 19122-6099. (215)204-8787. Fax: (215)204-4719. E-mail: tempress@astro.ocis.temple.edu. Website: www.temple.edu/tempress/. **Acquisitions:** Michael Ames, consulting editor; Janet Francendese, editor-in-chief; Doris Braendel, senior acquisitions editor; Micah Kleit, senior acquisitions editor. Estab. 1969. **Publishes 60 titles/year. Pays up to 10% royalty on wholesale price.** Publishes book 10 months after acceptance. Responds in 2 months. Book catalog free.

  O— "Temple University Press has been publishing useful books on Asian-Americans, law, gender issues, film, women's studies and other interesting areas for nearly 30 years for the goal of social change."

Nonfiction: American history, sociology, women's studies, health care, ethics, labor studies, photography, urban studies, law, Latin American studies, African-American studies, Asian-American studies, public policy and regional (Philadelphia area). "No memoirs, fiction or poetry." Uses *Chicago Manual of Style*. Reviews artwork/photos. Query.

Recent Title(s): *Critical Race Theory: The Cutting Edge*, second edition, edited by Richard Delgado and Jean Stefancie.

TEN SPEED PRESS, P.O. Box 7123, Berkeley CA 94707. (510)559-1600. Fax: (510)524-1052. E-mail: info@tenspeed.com. Website: www.tenspeed.com. Publisher: Kirsty Melville. Editorial Director: Lorena Jones. **Acquisitions:** Address submissions to "Acquisitions Department." Estab. 1971. Publishes trade paperback originals and reprints. **Firm publishes 100 titles/year; imprints average 70 titles/year. 25% of books from first-time authors; 50% from unagented writers. Pays 15-20% royalty on net. Offers $2,500 average advance.** Publishes book 1 year after acceptance. Accepts simultaneous submissions. Responds in 3 months on queries. Book catalog for 9×12 SAE with 6 first-class stamps. Manuscript guidelines for #10 SASE.

  O— Ten Speed Press publishes authoritative books for an audience interested in innovative, proven ideas. Currently emphasizing cookbooks, food books, business.

Imprint(s): Celestial Arts, Tricycle Press.

Nonfiction: Cookbook, how-to, reference, self-help. Subjects include business and career, child guidance/parenting, cooking/foods/nutrition, gardening, health/medicine, money/finance, nature/environment, recreation, science. "We mainly publish innovative how-to books. We are always looking for cookbooks from proven, tested sources—successful restaurants, etc. *Not* 'Grandma's favorite recipes.' Books about the 'new science' interest us. No biographies or autobiographies, first-person travel narratives, fiction or humorous treatments of just about anything." Query or submit outline and sample chapters.

Recent Title(s): *Hiring Smart*, by Pierre Morrell.

Tips: "We like books from people who really know their subject, rather than people who think they've spotted a trend to capitalize on. We like books that will sell for a long time, rather than nine-day wonders. Our audience consists of a well-educated, slightly weird group of people who like food, the outdoors and take a light but serious approach to business and careers. Study the backlist of each publisher you're submitting to and tailor your proposal to what you perceive as their needs. Nothing gets a publisher's attention like someone who knows what he or she is talking about, and nothing falls flat like someone who obviously has no idea who he or she is submitting to."

TEXAS A&M UNIVERSITY PRESS, College Station TX 77843-4354. (409)845-1436. Fax: (409)847-8752. E-mail: fdl@tampress.tamu.edu. Website: www.tamu.edu/upress. **Acquisitions:** Noel Parsons, editor-in-chief (military, eastern Europe, natural history, agriculture, nautical archeaology); Mary Lenn Dixon, managing editor (political science, presidential studies, anthropology, borderlands, western history). Estab. 1974. **Publishes 50 titles/year. Nonauthor-subsidy publishes 25% of books. Pays in royalties.** Publishes book 1 year after acceptance. Responds in 1 month. *Writer's Market* recommends allowing 2 months for reply. Book catalog free.

  O— Texas A&M University Press publishes a wide range of nonfiction, scholarly trade and crossover books of regional and national interest, "reflecting the interests of the university, the broader scholarly community, and the people of our state and region."

Nonfiction: Books on Texas and the Southwest, military studies, American and western history, Texas and western literature, Mexican-US borderlands studies, nautical archaeology, women's studies, ethnic studies, natural history, the environment, presidential studies, economics, business history, architecture, Texas and western art and photography, agriculture and veterinary medicine. Query.

Recent Title(s): *Land of the Desert Sun: Texas' Big Bend Country*, by D. Gentry Steele.

Tips: Proposal requirements are posted on the website.

TEXAS STATE HISTORICAL ASSOCIATION, 2.306 Richardson Hall, University Station, Austin TX 78712. (512)471-1525. Website: www.tsha.utexas.edu. **Acquisitions:** George B. Ward, assistant director. Estab. 1897. Publishes hardcover and trade paperback originals and reprints. **Publishes 8 titles/year. Receives 50 queries and 50 mss/year. 10% of books from first-time authors; 95% from unagented writers. Pays 10% royalty on net cash proceeds.** Publishes book 1 year after acceptance. Responds in 2 months on mss. Catalog and ms guidelines free.

O⃨ "We are interested in scholarly historical articles and books on any aspect of Texas history and culture."
Nonfiction: Biography, coffee table book, illustrated book, reference. Historical subjects. Query. Reviews artwork/photos as part of ms package. Send photocopies.
Recent Title(s): *El Llano Estacado: Exploration and Imagination on the High Plains of Texas and New Mexico, 1536-1860*, by John Miller Morris (history).

TEXAS WESTERN PRESS, The University of Texas at El Paso, El Paso TX 79968-0633. (915)747-5688. Fax: (915)747-7515. E-mail: twp@utep.edu. Website: www.utep.edu/~twpress. Director: John Bristol. **Acquisitions:** Bobbi McConnaughey Gonzales. Estab. 1952. Publishes hardcover and paperback originals. **Publishes 7-8 titles/year. Pays standard 10% royalty.** Responds in 2 months. Catalog and ms guidelines free.
O⃨ Texas Western Press publishes books on the history and cultures of the American Southwest, especially historical and biographical works about West Texas, New Mexico, northern Mexico and the US-Mexico borderlands. Currently emphasizing developing border issues, economic issues of the border. De-emphasizing coffee table books.
Imprint(s): Southwestern Studies.
Nonfiction: Scholarly books. Historic and cultural accounts of the Southwest (West Texas, New Mexico, northern Mexico and Arizona). Also art, photographic books, Native American and limited regional fiction reprints. Occasional technical titles. "Our *Southwestern Studies* use manuscripts of up to 30,000 words. Our hardback books range from 30,000 words up. The writer should use good exposition in his work. Most of our work requires documentation. We favor a scholarly, but not overly pedantic, style. We specialize in superior book design." Query with outline. Follow *Chicago Manual of Style*.
Recent Title(s): *Frontier Cavalryman*, by Marcos Kinevan.
Tips: Texas Western Press is interested in books relating to the history of Hispanics in the US, will experiment with photo-documentary books, and is interested in seeing more 'popular' history and books on Southwestern culture/life. "We try to treat our authors professionally, produce handsome, long-lived books and aim for quality, rather than quantity of titles carrying our imprint."

N THIRD WORLD PRESS, P.O. Box 19730, Chicago IL 60619. (773)651-0700. Fax: (773)651-7286. E-mail: TWPress3@aol.com. Publisher: Haki R. Madhubuti. **Acquisitions:** Gwendolyn Mitchell, editor. Estab. 1967. Publishes hardcover and trade paperback originals and reprints. **Publishes 20 titles/year. Receives 200-300 queries and 200 mss/year. 20% of books from first-time authors; 80% from unagented writers. Pays 7% royalty on retail price.** Publishes book 18 months after acceptance of ms. Accepts simultaneous submissions. Responds in 6 months. Send $5 for book catalogue, SASE for ms guidelines.
● Third World Press is open to submissions in January and July.
Nonfiction: African-centered and African-American materials: illustrated book, children's/juvenile, reference, self-help, textbook. Subjects include anthropology/archaeology, Black studies, education, ethnic, government/politics, health/medicine, history, language/literature, literary criticism, philosophy, psychology, regional, religion, sociology, women's issues/studies. Query with outline and 5 sample chapters. Reviews artwork as part of ms package. Send photocopies.
Fiction: African-centered and African American materials: Ethnic, feminist, historical, juvenile, literary, mainstream/contemporary, picture books, plays, short story collections, young adult. Query with synopsis and 5 sample chapters.
Poetry: African-centered and African-American materials. Submit complete ms.
Recent Title(s): *Breaking Through the Wall: A Marathoner's Story*, by Delores E. Cross; *In the Shadow of the Son*, by Michael Simanga.

N ⭐ THORNDIKE PRESS, The Gale Group P.O Box 159, Thorndike ME 04986. (207)948-2962. Fax: (207)948-2863. E-mail: Hazel.Rumney@galegroup.com. **Acquisitions:** Hazel Rumney, editor (romance/western); Mary Smith, editor (western); Jamie Knobloch, senior editor (large print). Publishes hardcover originals, reprints and large print reprints. **Publishes 72 titles/year. Receives 1,000 queries and 1,000 mss/year. 60% of books from first-time authors; 90% from unagented writers. Pays royalty on wholesale or retail price. Offers $1,000-2,000 advance.** Publishes book 8 months after acceptance of ms. Accepts simultaneous submissions. Responds in 2 months to queries and proposals, 4 months to mss. Book catalog free. Manuscript guidelines for #10 SASE.
Imprints: Five Star (contact: Hazel Rumney).
Fiction: Mystery, romance, western. Submit proposal package, including synopsis and 3 sample chapters.
Recent Title(s): *The Last Enemy*, by Pauline Baird Jones (romantic suspense); *Doc Holliday's Gone*, by Jane Candia Coleman (western).
Tips: Audience is intelligent readers looking for something different and satisfying. "We want highly original material that contains believable motivation, with little repetitive introspection. Show us how a character feels, rather than tell us. Humor is good; clichés are not."

N THREE FORKS BOOKS, Falcon Publishing, Inc., P.O. Box 1718, Helena MT 59624. (406)442-6597. Fax: (406)442-0384. E-mail: falcon@falcon.com. Website: www.falcon.com. **Acquisitions:** Megan Hiller, senior editor. Publishes hardcover and trade paperback originals. **Publishes approximately 4 books/year. 80% of books from first-time authors; 80% from unagented writers. Pays variable royalty. Offers $0-5,000 advance.** Responds in 3 months. Book catalog and ms guidelines free.
O⃨ Three Forks specializes in regional cookbooks.

Nonfiction: Cookbook. Subjects include cooking/foods/nutrition. Query or submit proposal package. Reviews artwork/ photos as part of ms package. Send photocopies; do not send originals.

Recent Title(s): *Lipsmackin' Backpackin'*, by Tim & Christine Connors; *What's Cooking America*, by Linda Stradley & Andra Cook (cookbooks).

Tips: "Writers should review our catalog or website to gain a better understanding to our regional approach to selling books. Submit queries and proposals that are intelligent, well thought out, and seem to fit our publishing plan."

THUNDER'S MOUTH PRESS, Avalon Publishing Group, 841 Broadway, 4th Floor, New York NY 10003. (212)614-7880. Publisher: Neil Ortenberg. **Acquisitions:** Gayle Watkins, acquisitions editor. Estab. 1982. Publishes hardcover and trade paperback originals and reprints, almost exclusively nonfiction. **Publishes 70-80 titles/year. Receives 1,000 submissions/year. 15% of books from unagented writers. Pays 7-10% royalty on retail price. Offers $1,500 average advance.** Publishes book 8 months after acceptance. Responds in 2 months on queries.

Nonfiction: Biography, politics, popular culture. *No unsolicited mss.*

Recent Title(s): *Hindsight*, by Boris Vallejo.

[N] TIARE PUBLICATIONS, P.O. Box 493, Lake Geneva WI 53147-0493. Fax: (262)249-0299. E-mail: info@tiare.c om. Website: www.tiare.com. **Acquisitions:** Gerry L. Dexter, president. Estab. 1986. Publishes trade paperback originals. **Publishes 6-12 titles/year. Receives 25 queries and 10 mss/year. 40% of books from first-time authors; 100% from unagented writers. Pays 15% royalty on retail/wholesale price.** Publishes book 3 months after acceptance. Responds in 1 month on queries. Book catalog for $1.

  O— Tiare offers a wide selection of books for the radio communications enthusiast. LimeLight publishes general nonfiction on subjects ranging from crime to root beer. Balboa offers big band and jazz titles.

Imprint(s): LimeLight Books, Balboa Books.

Nonfiction: Technical, general nonfiction, mostly how-to, (Limelight); jazz/big bands (Balboa). Query.

Recent Title(s): *Air-Ways—The Insider's Guide to Air Travel.*

TIDEWATER PUBLISHERS, Cornell Maritime Press, Inc., P.O. Box 456, Centreville MD 21617-0456. (410)758-1075. Fax: (410)758-6849. **Acquisitions:** Charlotte Kurst, managing editor. Estab. 1938. Publishes hardcover and paperback originals. **Publishes 7-9 titles/year. Receives 150 submissions/year. 41% of books from first-time authors; 99% from unagented writers. Pays 7½-15% royalty on retail price.** Publishes book 1 year after acceptance. Responds in 2 months. Book catalog for 10 × 13 SAE with 5 first-class stamps.

  O— Tidewater Publishers issues adult nonfiction works related to the Chesapeake Bay area, Delmarva or Maryland in general. "The only fiction we handle is juvenile and must have a regional focus."

Nonfiction: Cookbook, history, illustrated book, juvenile, reference. Regional subjects only. Query or submit outline and sample chapters. Reviews artwork/photos as part of ms package.

Fiction: Regional juvenile fiction only. Query or submit outline/synopsis and sample chapters.

Recent Title(s): *Chesapeake Sails: A History of Yachting on the Bay*, by Richard Henderson.

Tips: "Our audience is made up of readers interested in works that are specific to the Chesapeake Bay and Delmarva Peninsula area. We do not publish personal narratives, adult fiction or poetry."

[N] [A] MEGAN TINGLEY BOOKS, Little, Brown & Co., Three Center Plaza, Boston MA 02108. (617)227-0730. Fax: (617)263-2864. Website: www.twbookmark.com. **Acquisitions:** Megan Tingley, editorial director; Alvina Ling, editorial assistant. Publishes hardcover and trade paperback originals. **Publishes 80-100 titles/year; imprint publishes 10-15 titles/year. Pays 0-15% royalty on retail price.**

  O— Megan Tingley Books is a new imprint of the children's book department of Little, Brown and Company.

Nonfiction: Children's/juvenile. Subjects include all juvenile interests. Query with SASE. *Agented submissions only.*

Fiction: Juvenile, picture books, young adult. *Agented submissions only.*

Recent Title(s): *The Girls' Guide to Life*, by Catherine Dee (nonfiction); *Just Like a Baby*, by Rebecca Bond (picture book).

TOR BOOKS, Tom Doherty Associates, LLC, 175 Fifth Ave., New York NY 10010. **Acquisitions**: Patrick Nielsen Hayden, senior editor. Estab. 1980. Publishes hardcover originals and trade and mass market paperback originals and reprints. **Publishes 150-200 books/year. 2-3% of books from first-time authors; 3-5% from unagented writers. Pays royalty on retail price.** Publishes book 1-2 years after acceptance. No simultaneous submissions. "No queries please." Responds in 2-6 months on proposals and mss. Book catalog for 9 × 12 SAE with 2 first-class stamps; ms guidelines for SASE.

  O— "Tor Books publishes what is arguably the largest and most diverse line of science fiction and fantasy ever produced by a single English-language publisher."

Fiction: Adventure, fantasy, historical, horror, science fiction. Submit synopsis and 3 sample chapters.

Recent Title(s): *Path of Daggers*, by Robert Jordan (fantasy).

Tips: "We're never short of good sf or fantasy, but we're always open to solid, technologically knowledgeable hard science fiction or thrillers by writers with solid expertise."

TORAH AURA PRODUCTIONS, 4423 Fruitland Ave., Los Angeles CA 90058. (213)585-7312. Website: www.tora haura.com. **Acquisitions:** Jane Golub. Estab. 1982. Publishes hardcover and trade paperback originals. **Publishes 25**

titles/year; imprint publishes 10 titles/year. **Receives 5 queries and 10 mss/year. 2% of books from first-time authors; 100% from unagented writers. Pays 10% royalty on wholesale price.** Publishes book 3 years after acceptance of ms. Accepts simultaneous submissions. Responds in 6 months on mss. Book catalog free.

○┅ Torah Aura publishes mostly educational materials for Jewish classrooms.

Nonfiction: Children's/juvenile, textbook. Subjects include language/literature (Hebrew), religion (Jewish). No picture books. Query with SASE. Reviews artwork/photos as part of ms package. Send photocopies.

Fiction: Juvenile, picture books, religious, young adult. All fiction must have Jewish interest. Query with SASE.

Recent Title(s): *The Bible from Alef to Tav*, by Penina V. Adelman.

TOTLINE PUBLICATIONS, Frank Schaffer Publications, Inc., 23740 Hawthorne Blvd., Torrance CA 90505-5906. (206)353-3100. E-mail: totline@gte.net. **Acquisitions:** Mina McMullin, managing editor (book mss); Submissions Editor (single activity ideas). Estab. 1975. Publishes educational activity books and parenting books for teachers and parents of 2-6-year-olds. **Publishes 50-60 titles/year. 100% from unagented writers. Makes outright purchase plus copies of book/newsletter author's material appears in.** Book catalog and ms guidelines free on written request.

○┅ Totline publishes educationally and developmentally appropriate books for 2-, 3-5-, and 6-year-olds.

Nonfiction: Illustrated activity books for parents and teachers of 2-6-year-olds. Subjects include animals, art, child guidance/parenting, cooking with kids, foods and nutrition, education, ethnic, gardening, hobbies, language/literature, music, nature/environment, science. Considers activity book and single activity submissions from early childhood education professionals. Considers parenting activity mss from parenting experts. Query with SASE. No children's storybooks, fiction or poetry.

Recent Title(s): *Multisensory Theme-A-Saurus*, edited by Gayle Bittinger.

Tips: "Our audience is teachers and parents who work with children ages 2-6. Write for submission requirements. We are especially interested in parent-child activities for 0- to 3-year-olds and teacher-child activities for toddler groups."

TOWER PUBLISHING, 588 Saco Rd., Standish ME 04084. (207)642-5400. Fax: (207)642-5463. E-mail: michael@t owerpublishingcompany.com. Website: www.towerpublishingcompany.com. **Acquisitions:** Michael Lyons, president. Estab. 1772. Publishes hardcover originals and reprints, trade paperback originals. **Publishes 15 titles/year. Receives 60 queries and 30 mss/year. 10% of books from first-time authors; 90% from unagented writers. Pays royalty on net receipts. No advance.** Publishes book 6 months after acceptance of ms. Accepts simultaneous submissions. Responds in 1 month on queries, 2 months on proposals and mss. Book catalog and guidelines free.

○┅ Tower Publishing specializes in business and professional directories and legal books.

Nonfiction: Reference. Business/economics subjects. Looking for legal books of a national stature. Query with outline.

▣ **TOWLEHOUSE PUBLISHING CO.**, 1312 Bell Grimes Lane, Nashville TN 37207. (615)612-3005. Fax: (615)612-0067. E-mail: vermonte@aol.com. Website: www.Towlehouse.com. **Acquisitions**: Mike Towle, president/publisher (nonfiction, sports, gift books, pop culture, cookbooks, Christianity). Publishes hardcover, trade paperback and mass market paperback originals, hardcover and trade paperback reprints. **Publishes 8-10 titles/year. Receives 100-250 mss/year. 75% of books from first-time authors; 80% from unagented writers. Pays 8-20% royalty on wholesale price. Offers $500-2,000 advance.** Publishes book 9 months after acceptance of ms. Accepts simultaneous submissions. Responds in 2 months.

○┅ "We publish nonfiction titles for adults with a fondness for news and popular culture."

Nonfiction: Biography, cookbook, gift book. Subjects include Americana, cooking/foods/nutrition, creative nonfiction, government/politics, history, military/war, regional, religion, sports, Insta-books dictated by headlines and milestone anniversaries of significant events. "I don't solicit children's books, poetry or non-Christian religious titles. Authors using profanity, obscenities or other vulgar or immoral language in their books need not contact me." Query with SASE or submit proposal package, including outline, 2 sample chapters, author bio and letter containing marketing plan. Reviews artwork/photos as part of ms package. Send photocopies.

Recent Title(s): *The Book of Landry*, by Jennifer Briggs Kaski (sports, nonfiction); *Two Sisters*, by Sheila Wade and Maureen Brown (gift book, nonficiton).

Tips: "Send one proposal for one book at a time. If you send me a query listing three, four or more 'ideas' for books, I will immediately know that you lack the commitment needed to author a book. Send a SASE for anything you send me. I don't accept fiction unless you're a bestselling fiction author."

TRAFALGAR SQUARE PUBLISHING, P.O. Box 257, N. Pomfret VT 05053-0257. (802)457-1911. Fax: (802)457-1913. E-mail: tsquare@sover.net. Website: www.horseandriderbooks.com. Publisher: Caroline Robbins. **Acquisitions:** Martha Cook, managing editor. Estab. 1987. Publishes hardcover and trade paperback originals and reprints. **Publishes 10 titles/year. Pays royalty.** Responds in 2 months.

○┅ "We publish high quality instructional books for horsemen and horsewomen, always with the horse's welfare in mind."

Nonfiction: Books about horses. "We publish books for intermediate to advanced riders and horsemen. No stories, children's books or horse biographies." Query with proposal package, including outline, 1-2 sample chapters, letter of writer's qualifications and audience for book's subject.

Recent Title(s): *Winning with Horse Power!*, by Rebekah Witter; *Taking Up the Reins*, by Priscilla Endicott; *Improve Your Horse's Well-Being*, by Linda Tellington-Jones.

TRANS-ATLANTIC PUBLICATIONS, INC., 311 Bainbridge St., Philadelphia PA 19147. Fax: (215)925-7412. E-mail: rsmolin@lx.netcom. com. Website: www.transatlanticpub.com. **Acquisitions:** Ron Smolin. Estab. 1984. Publishes hardcover, trade paperback and mass market paperback originals. **Publishes 100 titles/year. Imprint publishes 20 titles/year. Receives 500 queries and 500 mss/year. 15% of books from first-time authors; 20% from unagented writers. Pays 7½-12% royalty on retail price. Offers $2,000-10,000 advance.** Publishes book 11 months after acceptance of ms. Accepts simultaneous submissions.

    O–π Trans-Atlantic publishes a wide variety of nonfiction and fiction and distributes a wide variety of business books published in England.

Imprint(s): Bainbridge Books.

Nonfiction: Biography, coffee table book, illustrated book, reference. Subjects include animals, art/architecture, nutrition, creative nonfiction, gay/lesbian, government/politics, health/medicine, history, nature/environment, philosophy, photography, science, sex, sociology, sports. Query. Reviews artwork/photos as part of ms package. Send photocopies.

Fiction: Adventure, experimental, humor, literary, mainstream/contemporary, mystery, plays, science fiction, suspense, young adult. Query with 2 sample chapters. Materials are not returned.

Recent Title(s): *Pilates Method of Body Conditioning* (nonfiction); *The Methuselah Gene* (fiction).

TRANSNATIONAL PUBLISHERS, INC., 410 Saw Mill River Rd., Ardsley NY 10502. (914)693-5100. Fax: (914)693-4430. E-mail: transbooks@aol.com. Website: www.transnationalpubs.com. Publisher: Heike Fenton. **Acquisitions:** Senikha Ball, acquisitions editor. Estab. 1980. **Publishes 15-20 titles/year. Receives 40-50 queries and 30 mss/year. 60% of books from first-time authors; 95% from unagented writers. Pays 10% royalty of net revenue. Offers no advance.** Publishes book 6-9 months after acceptance of ms. Accepts simultaneous submissions. Responds in 1 month. Book catalog and ms guidelines free.

    O–π "We provide specialized international law publications for the teaching of law and law-related subjects in law school classroom, clinic and continuing legal education settings." Currently emphasizing any area of international law that is considered a current issue/event.

Nonfiction: Reference, technical, textbook. Subjects include international law, government/politics, women's issues/studies. Query or submit proposal package, including table of contents, introduction, sample chapter with SASE.

Recent Title(s): *The Practice of the International Criminal Tribunal for the Former Yugoslavia & Rwands,* by John R.W.D. Jones; *The Future of International Human Rights,* by Burns Weston & Stephen Marks.

:N: TRAVELERS' TALES, 330 Townsend St., Suite 208, San Francisco CA 94107. Phone/fax: (415)227-8600. E-mail: submit@travelerstales.com (submissions) or ttales@travelerstales.com (general inquiries). Website: www.travelers tales.com. **Acquisitions:** Lisa Bach, managing editor; James O'Reilly and Larry Habegger, series editors. Publishes anthologies, single author narratives, and consumer books. "We publish personal, nonfiction stories and anecdotes—funny, illuminating, adventurous, frightening or grim. Stories should reflect that unique alchemy that occurs when you enter unfamiliar territory and begin to see the world differently as a result. Stories that have already been published, including book excerpts, are welcome as long as the authors retain the copyright or can obtain permission from the copyright holder to reprint the material." **Publishes 12-14 titles/year.** Accepts simultaneous submissions. Book catalog and ms guidelines for SASE.

Imprints: Travelers' Tales Guides, Footsteps, Travelers' Tales Classics.

Nonfiction: Personal nonfiction travel anthologies, single author narratives and consumer books. **Pays 10¢/word for anthology pieces.**

Recent Title(s): *Kite Strings of the Southern Cross,* by Laurie Gough; *Take Me with You,* by Brad Newsham.

Tips: "We do not publish fiction."

TRICYCLE PRESS, Ten Speed Press, P.O. Box 7123, Berkeley CA 94707. (510)559-1600. Fax: (510)559-1637. Website: www.tenspeed.com. **Acquisitions:** Nicole Geiger, publisher. Publishes hardcover and trade paperback originals. **Publishes 14-16 titles/year. 20% of books from first-time authors; 60% from unagented authors. Pays 15-20% royalty on wholesale price (lower if book is illustrated). Offers $0-9,000 advance.** Publishes book 1 year after acceptance of ms. Accepts simultaneous submissions. Responds in 3 months on submissions (no query letters!) Book catalog for 9 × 12 SAE and 3 first-class stamps in postage; ms guidelines for #10 SASE; or one large envelope for both.

    O–π "Tricycle Press looks for something outside the mainstream; books that encourage children to look at the world from a possibly alternative angle."

Nonfiction: Children's/juvenile, how-to, self-help, picture books, activity books. Subjects include math, gardening, health/medicine, nature/environment, science, geography. Submit complete ms for activity books; 2-3 chapters or 20 pages for others. Reviews artwork/photos as part of ms package. Send photocopies.

Fiction: Picture books: Submit complete ms. Chapter books: Send complete outline and 2-3 sample chapters (ages 8-12). Query with synopsis and SASE for all others.

Recent Title(s): *Honest Pretzels,* by Mollie Katzen (nonfiction); *Never Let Your Cat Make Lunch for You,* by Lee Harris, illustrated by Debbie Tilley (fiction).

TRINITY PRESS INTERNATIONAL, 4775 Linglertown Rd., Harrisburg PA 17112. **Acquisitions:** Henry Carrigan, editorial director. Estab. 1989. Publishes trade paperback originals and reprints. **Publishes 40 titles/year. Pays 10% royalty on wholesale price.** Publishes book 9 months after acceptance of ms. Accepts simultaneous submissions. Book catalog free.

O-π Trinity Press International is an ecumenical publisher of serious books on theology and the Bible for the religious academic community, religious professionals, and serious book readers.

Nonfiction: Textbook, Christian/theological studies. Subjects include history (as relates to the Bible), translation (biblical/Christian texts). Submit outline and 1 sample chapter.

Recent Title(s): *God and Globalization*, by Max Stackhouse.

TROITSA BOOKS, Kroshka Books, 227 Main St., Suite 100, Huntington NY 11743. (631)424-6682. Fax: (631)424-4666. E-mail: novascience@earthlink.net. **Acquisitions:** Frank Columbus, editor-in-chief; Nadya Columbus, editor. Publishes hardcover and paperback originals. Publishes book up to 1 year after acceptance of ms. Accepts simultaneous submissions. Responds in 1 month.

O-π Troitsa Books is an imprint devoted to Christianity.

Nonfiction: Christianity. Subjects include biography, history, inspirational, sermons, prayer books, memoirs. Query with SASE. Reviews artwork/photos as part of ms package. Send photocopies.

Recent Title(s): *In His Own Words: The Beliefs and Teachings of Jesus*, by Albert Kirby Griffin.

TRUMAN STATE UNIVERSITY PRESS, (formerly Thomas Jefferson University Press), 100 E. Normal St., Kirksville MO 63501-4221. (660)785-7199. Fax: (660)785-4480. E-mail: tsup@truman.edu. Website: www2.truman.edu/tsup. **Acquisitions:** Paula Presley, director/editor-in-chief (reference works/bibliography/history); Nancy Reschly, poetry editor (contemporary narrative poetry); Raymond Mentzer, general editor (early modern history, literature, biography). **Publishes 8-10 titles/year. Pays 7% maximum royalty on net sales.**

O-π Truman State University Press publishes books in the humanities and social sciences with high standards of production quality. Currently emphasizing humanities, social sciences, early modern history, literature, church history. De-emphasizing theology.

Nonfiction: Biography, illustrated book, textbook and monographs on Americana, anthropology/archaeology, art/architecture, government/politics, history, language/literature, philosophy, religion and sociology.

Recent Title(s): *Frank Lloyd Wright's Taliesin Fellowship*, by Myron L. and Shirley Marty Bethsaida (nonfiction); *Rational Numbers*, by H.L. Hix; *The Naked Scarecrow*, by Richard Moore (poetry).

N TURTLE BOOKS, 866 United Nations Plaza, Suite #525, New York NY 10017. (212)644-2020. Fax: (212)223-4387. Website: www.turtlebooks.com. **Acquisitions:** John Whitman, publisher (children's picture books). Publishes hardcover and trade paperback originals. **Publishes 6-8 titles/year. Receives 1,000 mss/year. 25% of books from first-time authors; 50% from unagented writers. Pays royalty on retail price.** Publishes book 6 months after acceptance of ms. Accepts simultaneous submissions.

O-π Turtle Books publishes children's picture books.

Nonfiction: Children's/juvenile, illustrated book. Subjects include animals, education, history, language/literature, multicultural, nature/environment, regional, any suitable subject for a children's picture book. Submit completed ms. Do not send original art, only copies.

Fiction: Subjects suitable for children's picture books. Adventure, ethnic, fantasy, historical, multicultural, regional, sports, western. "We are looking for good stories which can be illustrated as children's picture books." Submit completed ms.

Poetry: Must be suitable for an illustrated children's book format. Submit complete ms.

Recent Title(s): *Keeper of the Swamp*, by Ann Garrett; *The Crab Man*, by Patricia Van West (children's picture books).

Tips: "Our preference is for stories rather than concept books. We will consider only children's picture book manuscripts."

TURTLE PRESS, S.K. Productions Inc., P.O. Box 290206, Wethersfield CT 06129-0206. (860)529-7770. Fax: (860)529-7775. E-mail: editorial@turtlepress.com. Website: www.turtlepress.com. **Acquisitions:** Cynthia Kim, editor. Publishes hardcover originals, trade paperback originals and reprints. **Publishes 4-6 titles/year. Pays 8-10% royalty. Offers $500-1,000 advance.** Responds in 1 month on queries. *Writer's Market* recommends allowing 2 months for reply.

O-π Turtle Press publishes sports and martial arts nonfiction for a specialty niche audience. Currently emphasizing martial arts, eastern philosophy. De-emphasizing self-help, juvenile fiction.

Nonfiction: How-to, martial arts, philosophy, self-help, sports. "We prefer tightly targeted topics on which there is little or no information available in the market, particularly for our sports and martial arts titles." Query with SASE

Fiction: "We have just begun a line of children's martial arts adventure stories and are very much interested in submissions to expand this line." Query with SASE.

Recent Title(s): *Martial Arts After 40*, by Sang H. Kim (nonfiction).

TUTTLE PUBLISHING, 153 Milk St., 5th Floor, Boston MA 02109. **Acquisitions:** Michael Lewis, acquisitions editor. Estab. 1832. Publishes hardcover and trade paperback originals and reprints. **Publishes 60 titles/year. Receives over 1,000 queries/year. 20% of books from first-time authors; 60% from unagented writers. Pays 5-10% royalty on net or retail price, depending on format and kind of book.** Publishes book 18 months after acceptance of ms. Accepts simultaneous submissions. Responds in 3 months on proposals.

O-π "Tuttle is America's leading publisher of books on Japan and Asia."

Nonfiction: Self-help, Eastern philosophy, alternative health. Subjects include cooking/foods/nutrition (Asian related), philosophy, Buddhist, Taoist, religion (Eastern). Submit query, outline and SASE. Cannot guarantee return of ms.
Recent Title(s): *The Rhythm of Compassion*, by Gail Straub; *Martial Arts Home Training*, by Mike Young.

TWENTY-FIRST CENTURY BOOKS, Millbrook Press, 2 Old New Milford Rd., Brookfield CT 06804. (203)740-2220. Editorial Director: Pat Culleton. Editor: Dominic Barth. **Acquisitions:** Editorial Department. Publishes hardcover originals. **Publishes 30 titles/year. Receives 200 queries and 50 mss/year. 20% of books from first-time writers; 75% from unagented writers. Pays 5-8% royalty on net price.** Publishes book 18 months after acceptance of ms. Accepts simultaneous submissions. Submit query letter first. Responds in 3 months on proposals.
○⇥ Twenty-First Century Books publishes nonfiction science, technology and social issues titles for children and young adults.
Nonfiction: Children's and young adult nonfiction. Subjects include government/politics, health/medicine, history, military/war, nature/environment, science, current events and social issues. "We publish primarily in series of four or more titles, for ages 12 and up, and single titles for grades 7 and up. No picture books, fiction or adult books." Submit proposal package including outline, sample chapter and SASE. Does not review artwork.
Recent Title(s): *The Glass Ceiling* (grades 7-up); *Confederate Ladies of Richmond*.
Tips: "We are now accepting single titles for young adult readers."

TWO DOT, Falcon Publishing Co. Inc., Box 1718, Helena MT 59624. (406)442-6597. Fax: (406)442-0384. E-mail: falcon@falcon.com. Website: www.twodotbooks.com. **Acquisitions:** Megan Hiller, editor; Charlene Patterson, editor (TwoDot series books, all). Publishes hardcover and trade paperback originals. **Publishes 10 titles/year. 30% of books from first-time authors; 100% from unagented writers. Pays 8-12½% on net. Offers minimal advance.** Publishes book 1 year after acceptance of ms. Accepts simultaneous submissions. Responds in 3 months. Book catalog for 9×12 SASE with 3 first-class stamps. Manuscript guidelines for SASE.
○⇥ "Two Dot looks for lively writing for a popular audience, well-researched, on regional themes." Currently emphasizing popular history, western history, regional history, western Americana. De-emphasizing scholarly writings, children's books, fiction, poetry.
Nonfiction: Subjects include Americana (western), history, regional. Two state by state series of interest: *More Than Petticoats*, on notable women; and *It Happened In . . .* state histories. Submit outline, 1 sample chapter and SASE. Reviews artwork/photos as part of the ms package. Send photocopies.
Recent Title(s): *Toward the Setting Sun: Pioneer Girls Traveling the Overland Trails*; *An Onery Bunch*; *More than Petticoats: Remarkable North Carolina Women*.

TYNDALE HOUSE PUBLISHERS, INC., 351 Executive Dr., Carol Stream IL 60188. (630)668-8300. Website: www.tyndale.com. **Acquisitions:** Manuscript Review Committee. Estab. 1962. Publishes hardcover and trade paperback originals and mass paperback reprints. **Publishes 125-150 titles/year. 5% of books from first-time authors. Average first print order for a first book is 5,000-10,000. Royalty and advance negotiable.** Publishes book 18 months after acceptance. Responds in up to 2 months. Manuscript guidelines for #10 SASE with 1 first-class stamp.
Nonfiction: Christian growth/self-help, devotional/inspirational, theology/Bible doctrine, children's nonfiction, contemporary/critical issues." Send query or synopsis with SASE. *No unsolicited mss.*
○⇥ Tyndale House publishes "practical, user-friendly Christian books for the home and family."
Fiction: "Biblical, historical and other Christian themes. No short story collections. Youth books: character building stories with Christian perspective. Especially interested in ages 10-14." Send query or synopsis with SASE. *No unsolicited mss.*
Recent Title(s): *How Now Shall We Live*, by Charles Colson (nonfiction); *Left Behind Series*, by Jerry Jenkins and Tim LaHaye (fiction).

N UCLA AMERICAN INDIAN STUDIES CENTER, 3220 Campbell Hall, Box 951548, UCLA, Los Angeles CA 90095-1548. (310)825-7315. Fax: (310)206-7060. E-mail: aisc@UCLA.edu. Website: www.sscnet.ucla.edu/indian/. **Acquisitions:** Duane Champagne, director/editor. Publishes hardcover and trade paperback originals. **Publishes 4 titles/year. Receives 10 queries and 8 mss/year. 60% of books from first-time authors; 100% from unagented writers. Pays 8% royalty on retail price.** No advance. Publishes book 7 months after acceptance of ms. Accepts simultaneous submissions. Responds in 2 months to queries, 3 months to mss. Book catalog and ms guidelines free on request.
○⇥ The American Indian Studies Center publishes books for people interested in Native American history, culture and contemporary issues.
Nonfiction: Reference. Subjects include government/politics, history, language/literature. Submit proposal package, including outline and 2 sample chapters. Reviews artwork/photos as part of the ms package. Send photocopies.
Fiction: Ethnic, plays, poetry, religious. Submit proposal package, including synopsis.
Poetry: Query or submit complete ms.
Recent Title(s): *American Indian Theater in Performance: A Reader*, (nonfiction); *Stories of Our Way: An Anthology of American Indian Plays* (fiction); *Migration Tears*, by Michael Kabotie (poetry).

N UNITED CHURCH PRESS, United Church of Christ, 700 Prospect Ave. E., Cleveland OH 44115-1100. (216)736-3715. Fax: (216)736-3703. E-mail: stavet@ucc.org. Website: www.pilgrimpress.com. **Acquisitions:** Kim

Sadler, editorial director. Estab. 1621. Publishes hardcover and trade paperback originals. **Publishes 12-15 titles/year. 30% of books from first-time authors; 80% from unagented writers. Pays standard royalties and advances where appropriate.** Publishes book an average of 18 months after acceptance. Responds in 3 months to queries. Book catalog and ms guidelines free.

• See also The Pilgrim Press.

Nonfiction: Worship, liturgy, music, Bible studies, prayer and devotional life, sermons. Send overview with statement of significance of project and potential market, table of contents, author bio, previously published works, sample chapters and SASE.

Recent Title(s): *Seeds of Racism in the Soul of America*, by Paul Griffin.

Tips: "We are concentrating more on academic and trade submissions. Writers should send books about contemporary social issues. Our audience is liberal, open-minded, socially aware, feminist, church members and clergy, teachers and seminary professors."

UNITY BOOKS, Unity School of Christianity, 1901 NW Blue Parkway, Unity Village MO 64065-0001. (816)524-3550 ext. 3190. Fax: (816)251-3552. E-mail: sprice@unityworldhq.org. Website: www.unityworldhq.org. **Acquisitions:** Michael Maday, editor; Raymond Teague, associate editor. Estab. 1889. Publishes hardcover and trade paperback originals and reprints. **Publishes 16 titles/year. Receives 100 queries and 500 mss/year. 30% of books from first-time authors; 95% from unagented writers. Pays 10-15% royalty on net receipts.** Publishes book 13 months after acceptance of final ms. Responds in 1 month on queries and proposals, 2 months on mss. Book catalog and ms guidelines free.

○ᴙ "Unity Books publishes metaphysical Christian books based on Unity principles, as well as inspirational books on metaphysics and practical spirituality. All manuscripts must reflect a spiritual foundation and express the Unity philosophy, practical Christianity, universal principles, and/or metaphysics."

Nonfiction: Inspirational, self-help, reference (spiritual/metaphysical). Subjects include health (holistic), philosophy (perennial/New Thought), psychology (transpersonal), religion (spiritual/metaphysical Bible interpretation/modern Biblical studies). "Writers should be familiar with principles of metaphysical Christianity but not feel bound by them. We are interested in works in the related fields of holistic health, spiritual psychology and the philosophy of other world religions." Query with book proposal, including cover letter, summarizing unique features and suggested sales and marketing strategies, toc or project outline and 1-3 sample chapters with SASE. Reviews artwork/photos as part of ms package. Send photocopies.

Recent Title(s): *Prayer Works*, by Rosemary Ellen Guiley.

[N] UNIVERSAL PUBLISHERS, 7525 NW 61 Terrace, Suite 2603, Parkland FL 33067-2421. (954)344-8203. Fax: (954)755-4059. E-mail: info@upublish.com. Website: www.upublish.com and www.dissertation.com. **Acquisitions:** Jeff Young, editor. Publishes trade paperback originals. **Publishes 100 titles/year; each imprint publishes 50 titles/year. Receives 1,000 queries/year. 20% of books from first-time authors; 90% from unagented writers. Pays 10-40% royalty on retail price.** Publishes book 2 months after acceptance of ms. Responds in 2 weeks. Book catalog and ms guidelines on website.

○ᴙ Universal publishes academic dissertations and other nonfiction.

Imprints: Dissertation.com, UPUBLISH.com.

Nonfiction: How-to, reference, self-help, technical, textbook. All subjects. Query with SASE or submit proposal package including outline via e-mail. All unsolicited mss returned unopened.

Recent Title(s): *Art of Information Warfare*, by Richard Furno (computer/business); *North Carolina Small Claims Court*, by Mary Ann Nixon (law).

THE UNIVERSITY OF AKRON PRESS, 374B Bierce Library, Akron OH 44325-1703. (330)972-5342. Fax: (330)972-5132. E-mail: press@uakron.edu. Website: www.uakron.edu/uapress. **Acquisitions:** Michael Carley, director. Estab. 1988. Publishes hardcover and trade paperback originals. **Publishes 4-5 titles/year. Receives 40-60 queries and over 500 mss/year** (because of poetry contest). **20% of books from first-time authors; 100% from unagented writers. Pays 4-10% royalty on wholesale price.** Publishes book 14 months after acceptance of ms. Accepts simultaneous submissions (only for poetry contest.) Responds in 1 month on queries, 2 months on proposals, 5 months on mss. Book catalog free. Manuscript guidelines for #10 SASE.

○ᴙ "The University of Akron Press strives to be the University's ambassador for scholarship and creative writing at the national and international levels." Currently emphasizing technology and the environment, Ohio history and culture, poetry. De-emphasizing fiction.

Nonfiction: Scholarly, Ohio history. Subjects include regional, technology and environment. "We publish mostly in our two nonfiction series: Technology and the Environment; Ohio history and culture. Writers often do not submit material suitable to our series books." Query. Reviews artwork/photos as part of ms package. Send photocopies.

Poetry: Follow the guidelines and submit manuscripts only for the contest.

Recent Title(s): *Mysteries of the Hopewell*, by William F. Romain; *Lake Erie Rehabilitated*, by William McGucken.

Tips: "We have mostly an audience of general educated readers, with a more specialized audience of public historians, sociologists and political scientists for the scholarly series."

UNIVERSITY OF ALABAMA PRESS, P.O. Box 870380, Tuscaloosa AL 35487-0380. Fax: (205)348-9201. Website: www.uapress.ua.edu. **Acquisitions:** Nicole Mitchell, director (history, political science, regional interest); Curtis Clark, assistant director/editor-in-chief (American literature, communications, Jewish studies, public administration); Judith Knight, acquisition editor (archaeology). Estab. 1945. Publishes nonfiction hardcover and paperbound originals and fiction paperback reprints. **Publishes 45-50 titles/year. Receives 300 submissions/year. 70% of books from first-time authors; 95% from unagented writers.** Publishes book 1 year after acceptance. Book catalog free. Manuscript guidelines for SASE.

Nonfiction: Considers upon merit almost any subject of scholarly interest, but specializes in communications, political science and public administration, literary criticism and biography, history, Jewish studies and archaeology of the Southeastern United States. Accepts nonfiction translations. Reviews artwork/photos as part of ms package.

Fiction: Reprints of works by contemporary Southern writers.

Tips: University of Alabama Press responds to an author within 2 weeks upon receiving the manuscript. If they think it is unsuitable for Alabama's program, they tell the author at once. If the manuscript warrants it, they begin the peer-review process, which may take two to four months to complete. During that process, they keep the author fully informed.

UNIVERSITY OF ALASKA PRESS, P.O. Box 756240, 1st Floor Gruening Bldg., UAF, Fairbanks AK 99775-6240. (907)474-5831 or (888)252-6657 (toll free in US). Fax: (907)474-5502. E-mail: fypress@uaf.edu. Website: www.uaf.edu/uapress. **Manager:** Debbie Gonzalez. **Acquisitions:** Pam Odom. Estab. 1967. Publishes hardcover originals, trade paperback originals and reprints. **Publishes 5-10 titles/year. Receives 100 submissions/year. Pays 7½-10% royalty on net sales.** Publishes book within 2 years after acceptance. Responds in 2 months. Book catalog free.

   O⊸ "The mission of the University of Alaska Press is to encourage, publish and disseminate works of scholarship that will enhance the store of knowledge about Alaska and the North Pacific Rim, with a special emphasis on the circumpolar regions."

Imprint(s): Classic Reprints, LanternLight Library, Oral Biographies, Rasmuson Library Historical Translation Series.

Nonfiction: Biography, reference, technical, textbook, scholarly nonfiction relating to Alaska-circumpolar regions. Subjects include agriculture/horticulture, Americana (Alaskana), animals, anthropology/archaeology, art/architecture, education, ethnic, government/politics, health/medicine, history, language, military/war, nature/environment, regional, science, translation. Nothing that isn't northern or circumpolar. Query or submit outline. Reviews copies of artwork/photos as part of ms package.

Recent Title(s): *The Iñupiaq Eskimo Nations of Northwest Alaska*, by Ernest S. Burch, Jr.

Tips: "Writers have the best chance with scholarly nonfiction relating to Alaska, the circumpolar regions and North Pacific Rim. Our audience is made up of scholars, historians, students, libraries, universities, individuals."

N UNIVERSITY OF ARIZONA PRESS, 1230 N. Park Ave., #102, Tucson AZ 85719-4140. (520)621-1441. Fax: (520)621-8899. E-mail: uapress@uapress.arizona.edu. Website: www.uapress.arizona.edu. **Acquisitions:** Christine Szuter, director; Cynthia Maude, editor-in-chief. Estab. 1959. Publishes hardcover and paperback originals and reprints. **Publishes 50 titles/year. Receives 300-400 submissions/year. 30% of books from first-time authors; 95% from unagented writers. Average print order is 1,500. Royalty terms vary; usual starting point for scholarly monograph is after sale of first 1,000 copies.** Publishes book 1 year after acceptance. Responds in 3 months. Book catalog and ms guidelines available via website or upon request.

   ● *Blue Horses Rush In*, by Luci Tapahonso was the winner of the 1998 MPBA Regional Poetry Award.

   O⊸ "University of Arizona is a publisher of scholarly books and books of the Southwest."

Nonfiction: Scholarly books about anthropology, Arizona, American West, archaeology, behavioral sciences, Chicano studies, environmental science, global change, Latin America, Native Americans, natural history, space sciences and women's studies. Query with outline, sample chapter and current curriculum vitae or résumé. Reviews artwork/photos as part of ms package.

Recent Title(s): *Speaking for the Generations*, edited by Simon Ortiz (Native American studies).

Tips: "Perhaps the most common mistake a writer might make is to offer a book manuscript or proposal to a house whose list he or she has not studied carefully. Editors rejoice in receiving material that is clearly targeted to the house's list, 'I have approached your firm because my books complement your past publications in . . . ,' presented in a straightforward, businesslike manner."

THE UNIVERSITY OF ARKANSAS PRESS, 201 Ozark Ave., Fayetteville AR 72701-1201. (501)575-3246. Fax: (501)575-6044. E-mail: uaprinfo@cavern.uark.edu. Website: www.uark.edu/~uaprinfo. **Acquisitions:** Lawrence J. Malley, director and editor-in-chief. Estab. 1980. Publishes hardcover and trade paperback originals and reprints. **Publishes 30 titles/year. Receives 1,000 submissions/year. 30% of books from first-time authors; 95% from unagented writers. Pays royalty on net receipts.** Publishes book 1 year after acceptance of ms. Accepted mss must be submitted on disk. Responds in up to 3 months. Book catalog for 9×12 SAE with 5 first-class stamps. Manuscript guidelines for #10 SASE.

   O⊸ The University of Arkansas Press publishes books on Ozark studies, Civil War in the West, black community studies, American music forms, literary studies and poetics, and sport and society.

Nonfiction: Arkansas and regional studies, African-American studies, Southern history and literature. "Our current needs include African-American studies and history. We won't consider manuscripts for general textbooks, juvenile or anything requiring a specialized or exotic vocabulary." Query or submit outline, sample chapters, and current résumé or cv.

Recent Title(s): *Arkansas Biography: A Collection of Notable Lives,* edited by Nancy A. Williams and Jeannie M. Whayne (nonfiction); *Finding the Princess,* by Thomas Hauser (fiction); *Flight from the Mother Stone,* by Laurence Lieberman (poetry).

UNIVERSITY OF CALIFORNIA PRESS, 2120 Berkeley Way, Berkeley CA 94720. (510)642-4247. Website: www.ucpress.edu. Director: James H. Clark. Associate Director: Lynne E. Withey. **Acquisitions:** Reed Malcolm, editor (religion); Doris Kretschmer, executive editor (natural history, biology); Deborah Kirshman, editor (art); Kate Toll, editor (classics); Sheila Levine, editorial director (Asian studies, history); Monica McCormick, editor (African studies, American history); Naomi Schneider, executive editor (sociology, politics, gender studies); Howard Boyer, executive editor (science); Linda Norton, editor (literature, poetry); Stephanie Fay, editor (art); Stan Holwitz, assistant director (anthropology, sociology); Eric Smoodin, editor (film, philosophy); Lynne Withey, associate director (music, Middle Eastern studies). Estab. 1893. Los Angeles office: 405 Hilgard Ave., Los Angeles CA 90024-1373. UK office: University Presses of California, Columbia, and Princeton, 1 Oldlands Way, Bognor Regis, W. Sussex PO22 9SA England. Publishes hardcover and paperback originals and reprints. **Publishes 180 titles/year. "On books likely to do more than return their costs, a standard royalty contract beginning at 7% on net receipts is paid; on paperbacks it is less."** Queries are always advisable, accompanied by outlines or sample material. Accepts nonfiction translations. Send to Berkeley address. Reports vary, depending on the subject. *Writer's Market* recommends allowing 2 months for reply. Enclose return postage.

    ○┬ University of California Press publishes mostly hardcover nonfiction written by scholars.
Nonfiction: Publishes scholarly books including history, art, literary studies, social sciences, natural sciences and some high-level popularizations. No length preferences. *Writer's Market* recommends query with SASE first.
Recent Title(s): *Los Angeles A to Z,* by Leonard and Dale Pitt (reference); *The Transformation of the Roman World,* edited by Leslie Webster and Michelle Brown; *Schubert: The Music and the Man,* by Brian Newbould.
Fiction and Poetry: Publishes fiction and poetry only in translation.

UNIVERSITY OF GEORGIA PRESS, 330 Research Dr., Athens GA 30602-4901. (706)369-6130. Fax: (706)369-6131. E-mail: books@ugapress@uga.edu. Website: www.uga.edu/ugapress. Executive Editor/Director: Barbara Ras. Estab. 1938. Publishes hardcover originals, trade paperback originals and reprints. **Publishes 85 titles/year; imprint publishes 10-15 titles/year. Receives 600 queries/year. 33% of books from first-time authors; 66% from unagented writers. Pays 7-10% royalty on net price. Rarely offers advance; amount varies.** Publishes book 1 year after acceptance of ms. Responds in 2 months on queries. Book catalog free. Manuscript guidelines for #10 SASE.
Nonfiction: Subjects include American history, art/architecture, government/politics, history, language/literature, nature/environment, regional. Query or submit outline with 1 sample chapter, author's bio with SASE. Reviews artwork/photos as part of ms package if essential to book.
Fiction: Short story collections published in Flannery O'Connor Award Competition. Query for guidelines and submission periods. $15 submission fee required.
Poetry: Published only through contemporary poetry series competition. Query first for guidelines and submission periods; $15 submission fee required.
Recent Title(s): *From Selma to Sorrow: The Life and Death of Viola Liuzzo,* by Mary Stanton (biography); *Apalachee,* by Joyce Hudson (novel); *Hotel Imperium,* by Rachel Loden (poetry).

UNIVERSITY OF IDAHO PRESS, 16 Brink Hall, Moscow ID 83844-1107. (208)885-6245. Fax: (208)885-9059. E-mail: uipress@uidaho.edu. Website: www.uidaho.edu/~uipress. **Acquisitions:** Ivar Nelson, director. Estab. 1972. Publishes hardcover and trade paperback originals and reprints. **Publishes 6-8 titles/year. Receives 150-250 queries and 25-50 mss/year. 100% of books from unagented writers. Pays up to 10% royalty on net sales.** Publishes book 1 year after acceptance of ms. Responds in 6 months. Book catalog free. Manuscript guidelines free.

    ○┬ The University of Idaho specializes in regional history and natural history, Native American studies, literature and Northwest folklore. Currently emphasizing wildlife, wild lands; de-emphasizing literary criticism.
Imprint(s): Northwest Folklife; Idaho Yesterdays; Northwest Naturalist Books; Living the West.
Nonfiction: Biography, reference, technical, textbook. Subjects include agriculture/horticulture, Americana, anthropology/archaeology, ethnic, folklore, history, language/literature, nature/environment, recreation, regional, women's issues/studies. "Writers should contact us to discuss projects in advance. Be aware of the constraints of scholarly publishing, and avoid submitting queries and manuscripts in areas in which the press doesn't publish." Query or submit proposal package, including sample chapter, contents, vita. Reviews artwork/photos as part of ms package. Send photocopies.
Recent Title(s): *For Wood River or Bust,* by Clark E. Spence (nonfiction); *Women on the Run,* by Janet Campbell Hale (fiction).

UNIVERSITY OF ILLINOIS PRESS, 1325 S. Oak St., Champaign IL 61820-6903. (217)333-0950. Fax: (217)244-8082. E-mail: uipress@uiuc.edu. Website: www.press.uillinois.edu. **Acquisitions:** Willis Regier, director/editor-in-chief. Estab. 1918. Publishes hardcover and trade paperback originals and reprints. **Publishes 100-110 titles/year. 50% of books from first-time authors; 95% from unagented writers. Nonauthor-subsidy publishes 10% of books. Pays 0-10% royalty on net sales. Offers $1,000-1,500 advance (rarely).** Publishes book 1 year after acceptance. Responds in 1 month. Book catalog for 9×12 SAE with 2 first-class stamps.

    ○┬ University of Illinois Press publishes "scholarly books and serious nonfiction" with a wide range of study interests.

Nonfiction: Biography, reference, scholarly books. Subjects include Americana, history (especially American history), music (especially American music), politics, sociology, philosophy, sports, literature. Always looking for "solid, scholarly books in American history, especially social history; books on American popular music, and books in the broad area of American studies." Query with outline.

Recent Title(s): *Rich Media, Poor Democracy*, by Robert McChesney.

Tips: "Serious scholarly books that are broad enough and well-written enough to appeal to nonspecialists are doing well for us in today's market."

UNIVERSITY OF IOWA PRESS, 119 W. Park Rd., Iowa City IA 52242-1000. (319)335-2000. Fax: (319)335-2055. Website: www.uiowa.edu/~uipress. **Acquisitions:** Holly Carver, director. Estab. 1969. Publishes hardcover and paperback originals. **Publishes 35 titles/year. Receives 300-400 submissions/year. 30% of books from first-time authors; 95% from unagented writers. Pays 7-10% royalty on net price.** Publishes book 1 year after acceptance. Reports within 6 months. Book catalog and ms guidelines free.

　　○☞ "We publish authoritative, original nonfiction that we market mostly by direct mail to groups with special interests in our titles and by advertising in trade and scholarly publications."

Nonfiction: Publishes anthropology, archaeology, British and American literary studies, U.S. history (autobiography), jazz studies, history of photography and natural history. Looks for evidence of original research; reliable sources; clarity of organization; complete development of theme with documentation, supportive footnotes and/or bibliography; and a substantive contribution to knowledge in the field treated. Query or submit outline. Use *Chicago Manual of Style*. Reviews artwork/photos as part of ms package.

Fiction and Poetry: Currently publishes the Iowa Short Fiction Award selections and winners of the Iowa Poetry Prize Competition. Query regarding poetry or fiction before sending ms.

Recent Title(s): *Memoirs of a Cold War Sun*, by Gaines Post, Jr.

Tips: "Developing a series in creative nonfiction."

UNIVERSITY OF MAINE PRESS, 5717 Corbett Hall, Orono ME 04469-5717. (207)581-1408. Fax: (207)581-1490. E-mail: umpress@umit.maine.edu. Website: umaine.edu/umpress. **Acquisitons:** Director. Publishes hardcover and trade paperback originals and reprints. **Publishes 4 titles/year. Receives 50 queries and 25 mss/year. 10% of mss from first-time authors; 90% from unagented writers.** Publishes book 1 year after acceptance of ms. *Writer's Market* recommends allowing 2 months for reply.

Nonfiction: "We are an academic book publisher, interested in scholarly works on regional history, regional life sciences, Franco-American studies. Authors should be able to articulate their ideas on the potential market for their work." Query.

Fiction: Rarely.

Recent Title(s): *Maine: The Pine Tree State*, by Judd, et.al. (history of Maine).

UNIVERSITY OF MISSOURI PRESS, 2910 LeMone Blvd., Columbia MO 65201. (573)882-7641. Fax: (573)884-4498. Website: www.system.missouri.edu/upress. Director: Beverly Jarrett. **Acquisitions:** (Mr.) Clair Willcox, acquisitions editor. Estab. 1958. Publishes hardcover and paperback originals and paperback reprints. **Publishes 55 titles/year. Receives 500 submissions/year. 25-30% of books from first-time authors; 90% from unagented writers. Pays up to 10% royalty on net receipts. No advance.** Publishes book 1 year after acceptance of ms. Responds in 6 months. Book catalog free.

　　○☞ University of Missouri Press publishes primarily scholarly nonfiction in the social sciences and also some short fiction collections.

Nonfiction: Scholarly publisher interested in history, literary criticism, political science, journalism, social science, some art history. Also regional books about Missouri and the Midwest. No mathematics or hard sciences. Query or submit outline and sample chapters. Consult *Chicago Manual of Style*.

Fiction: "Collections of short fiction are considered throughout the year; the press does not publish novels. Queries should include sample story, a table of contents and a brief description of the manuscript that notes its length."

Recent Title(s): *Brier Country*, Elaine Fowler Palencia; *Boxing the Kangaroo*, by Robert J. Donovan.

UNIVERSITY OF NEVADA PRESS, MS 166, Reno NV 89557. (775)784-6573. Fax: (775)784-6200. E-mail: dalrympl@scs.unr.edu. Director: Ronald E. Latimer. Editor-in-Chief: Margaret F. Dalrymple. **Acquisitions:** Trudy McMurrin, acquisitions editor. Estab. 1961. Publishes hardcover and paperback originals and reprints. **Publishes 35 titles/year. 20% of books from first-time authors; 99% from unagented writers. Pays average of 10% royalty on net price.** Publishes book 1 year after acceptance of ms. Preliminary report in 2 months. Book catalog and ms guidelines free.

　　○☞ "We are the first university press to sustain a sound series on Basque studies—New World and Old World."

Nonfiction: Specifically needs regional history and natural history, literature, current affairs, ethnonationalism, gambling and gaming, anthropology, biographies, Basque studies. No juvenile books. Submit complete ms. *Writer's Market* recommends a query with SASE first. Reviews photocopies of artwork/photos as part of ms package.

Recent Title(s): *Small Craft Warnings: Stories*, by Kate Braverman.

UNIVERSITY OF NEW MEXICO PRESS, 1720 Lomas Blvd. NE, Albuquerque NM 87131-1591. (505)277-2346. E-mail: unmpress@unm.edu. Director: Elizabeth Hadas. **Acquisitions:** Barbara Guth, managing editor (women's studies, chicano/a studies); Dana Asbury, editor (art, photography); Larry Durwood Ball, editor (western Americana, anthropology); David V. Holby, editor (Latin American studies, history). Estab. 1929. Publishes hardcover originals and trade paperback originals and reprints. **Publishes 70 titles/year. Receives 600 submissions/year. 12% of books from first-time authors; 90% from unagented writers. Royalty varies.** *Writer's Market* recommends allowing 2 months for reply. Book catalog free.

○━ "The Press is well known as a publisher in the fields of anthropology, archaeology, Latin American studies, photography, architecture and the history and culture of the American West, fiction, some poetry, Chicano/a studies and works by and about American Indians."

Nonfiction: Biography, illustrated book, scholarly books. Subjects include anthropology/archaeology, art/architecture, ethnic, history, photography. "No how-to, humor, juvenile, self-help, software, technical or textbooks." Query. Reviews artwork/photos as part of ms package. Send photocopies.

Recent Title(s): *Bone Voyage: A Journey in Forensic Anthropology*, by Stanley Rhine (nonfiction); *El Camino del Rio*, Jim Sanderson (fiction).

THE UNIVERSITY OF NORTH CAROLINA PRESS, P.O. Box 2288, Chapel Hill NC 27515-2288. (919)966-3561. Fax: (919)966-3829. E-mail: uncpress@unc.edu. Website: www.uncpress.edu. **Acquisitions:** Kate Torrey, director (women's history, gender studies); David Perry, editor-in-chief (regional trade, Civil War); Charles Grench, senior editor (American history); Elaine Maisner, editor (Latin American studies, religious studies, anthropology, regional); Sian Hunter, editor (literary studies, American studies, gender studies, social medicine). Estab. 1922. Publishes hardcover originals and trade paperback originals and reprints. **Publishes 90 titles/year. Receives 240 queries and 200 mss/year. 50% of books from first-time authors; 98% from unagented writers. Pays 5-15% royalty on wholesale price. Offers $1,000-10,000 advance.** Publishes book 1 year after acceptance of ms. Responds in 3 weeks on queries, 2 weeks on proposals and mss. Book catalog and ms guidelines free or on website.

○━ "UNC Press publishes nonfiction books for academic and general audiences. We have a special interest in trade and scholarly titles about our region. We do not, however, publish memoirs or Festshriften."

Nonfiction: Biography, cookbook, multimedia (CD-ROM format). Subjects include americana, anthropology/archaeology, art/architecture, cooking/foods/nutrition, gardening, government/politics, health/medicine, history, language/literature, military/war, multicultural, music/dance, nature/environment, philosophy, photography, regional, religion, translation, women's issues/studies, African-American studies, American studies, cultural studies, Latin-American studies, media studies, gender studies. Submit proposal package, including outline and résumé or cv, cover letter, abstract. Reviews artwork/photos as part of ms package. Send photocopies.

UNIVERSITY OF NORTH TEXAS PRESS, P.O. Box 311336, Denton TX 76203-1336. Fax: (940)565-4590. E-mail: vick@unt.edu or kdevinney@unt.edu. Website: www.unt.edu/untpress or www.tamu.edu/upress. **Acquisitions:** Frances B. Vick, director. Karen DeVinney, managing editor. Estab. 1987. Publishes hardcover and trade paperback originals and reprints. **Publishes 15-20 titles/year. Receives 500 queries and mss/year. 95% of books from unagented writers. Pays 7½-10% royalty of net.** Publishes book 2 years after acceptance of ms. Responds in 3 months on queries. Book catalog for 8½×11 SASE.

○━ UNT Press believes that university presses should be on the cutting edge and is not averse to the different or unusual. We are dedicated to producing the highest quality scholarly, academic and general interest books. We are committed to serving all peoples by publishing stories of their cultures and experiences that have been overlooked. Currently emphasizing folklore, multicultural topics, women's issues, history, Texana and western Americana.

Nonfiction: Biography, reference. Subjects include agriculture/horticulture, Americana, ethnic, government/politics, history, language/literature, military/war, regional. Query with SASE. Reviews artwork/photos as part of ms package. Send photocopies.

Poetry: Offers the Vassar Miller Prize in Poetry, an annual, national competition with a $1,000 prize and publication of the winning manuscript each fall. Query first with SASE.

Recent Title(s): *Stories from an Animal Sanctuary* , by Lynn Curry (natural science/natural history); *Panhandle Cowboy*, by John Erickson (fiction).

Tips: "We have series called War and the Southwest; Practical Guide Series; Texas Folklore Society Publications series; the Western Life Series; Literary Biographies of Texas Writers series."

UNIVERSITY OF OKLAHOMA PRESS, 1005 Asp Ave., Norman OK 73019-6051. (405)325-2000. Fax: (405)325-4000. E-mail: oupress@ou.edu. Website: www.ou.edu/oupress. **Acquisitions:** Jean Hurtado, acquisitions editor (political science, women's studies); Jeff Burnham, acquisitions editor (American Indian studies, Latin American studies, Mesoamerican studies); Ron Chrisman, acquisitions editor (paperbacks, military history). Estab. 1928. Publishes hardcover and paperback originals and reprints. **Publishes 100 titles/year. Pays standard royalty for comparable books.** Publishes book 18 months after acceptance. Responds in 3 months. Book catalog for $1 and 9×12 SAE with 6 first-class stamps.

○━ University of Oklahoma Press publishes books for both a scholarly and general audience.

Imprint(s): Oklahoma Paperbacks, Plains Reprints.

Nonfiction: Publishes American Indian studies, Western US history, political science, literary theory, natural history, women's studies, classical studies, Mesoamerican studies, military history. No unsolicited poetry or fiction. Query with outline, 1-2 sample chapters and author résumé. Use *Chicago Manual of Style* for ms guidelines. Reviews artwork/photos as part of ms package.

Recent Title(s): *Dark River: A Novel*, by Louis Owens (American Indian literature); *Frontier Children*, by Linda Peavy and Ursula Smith (western history).

UNIVERSITY OF PENNSYLVANIA PRESS, 4200 Pine St., Philadelphia PA 19104-4011. (215)898-6261. Fax: (215)898-0404. Website: www.upenn.edu/pennpress. Director: Eric Halpern. **Acquisitions:** Jerome Singerman, humanities editor; Patricia Smith, social sciences editor; Jo Joslyn, art and architecture editor; Robert Lockhart, history editor. Estab. 1890. Publishes hardcover and paperback originals and reprints. **Publishes 75 titles/year. Receives 650 submissions/year. 10-20% of books from first-time authors; 95% from unagented writers. Royalty determined on book-by-book basis.** Publishes book 10 months after delivery of final ms. Responds in 3 months or less. Book catalog available via website or with 9×12 SAE with 6 first-class stamps.
Nonfiction: Publishes American history, literary criticism, women's studies, cultural studies, ancient studies, medieval studies, business, anthropology, folklore, art history, architecture. "Serious books that serve the scholar and the professional, student and general reader." Follow the *Chicago Manual of Style*. Query with outline, résumé or vita. *No unsolicited mss.* Reviews artwork as part of ms package. Send photocopies.
Recent Title(s): *ABC of Architecture*, by James F. O'Gorman.

UNIVERSITY OF SOUTH CAROLINA PRESS, 937 Assembly St., 8th Floor, Columbia SC 29208. (803)777-5243. Fax: (803)777-0160. Website: www.sc.edu/uscpress. **Acquisitions:** Linda Fogle, assistant director (trade books); Barry Blose, acquisitions editor (literature, religious studies, rhetoric, social work); Alexander Moore, acquisitions editor (history, regional studies, culinary history). Estab. 1944. Publishes hardcover originals, trade paperback originals and reprints. **Publishes 50 titles/year. Receives 1,200 queries/year and 250 mss/year. 30% of books from first-time authors; 95% from unagented writers.** Publishes book 15 months after acceptance of ms. Accepts simultaneous submissions. Responds in 3 months on mss. Book catalog and ms guidelines free on request.
    ○━ "We focus on scholarly monographs and regional trade books of lasting merit."
Nonfiction: Biography, illustrated book, reference, monograph. Subjects include art/architecture, culinary history, language/literature, military/war, regional, rhetoric, religion, communication. "Do not submit entire unsolicited manuscripts or projects with limited scholarly value." Submit proposal package, including outline, 2 sample chapters, cv and résumé with SASE. Reviews artwork/photos as part of the ms package. Send photocopies.
Recent Title(s): *Who Is Jesus? History in Perfect Tense*, by Leander E. Keck; *Heaven Is a Beautiful Place: A Memoir of the South Carolina Coast*, by Genevieve C. Peterkin in conversation with William P. Baldwin.

THE UNIVERSITY OF TENNESSEE PRESS, 293 Communications Bldg., Knoxville TN 37996-0325. (865)974-3321. Fax: (865)974-3724. E-mail: utpress2@utk.edu. Website: www.sunsite.utk.edu/utpress/. **Acquisitions:** Joyce Harrison, acquisitions editor (scholarly books); Jennifer Siler, director (regional trades, fiction). Estab. 1940. **Publishes 30 titles/year. Receives 450 submissions/year. 35% of books from first-time authors; 99% from unagented writers. Nonauthor-subsidy publishes 10% of books. Pays negotiable royalty on net receipts.** Book catalog for 12×16 SASE with 2 first-class stamps. Manuscript guidelines for SASE.
    ○━ "Our mission is to stimulate scientific and scholarly research in all fields; to channel such studies, either in scholarly or popular form, to a larger number of people; and to extend the regional leadership of the University of Tennessee by stimulating research projects within the South and by non-university authors."
Nonfiction: American studies *only*, in the following areas: African-American studies; Appalachian studies, religion (history, sociology, anthropology, biography only), folklore/folklife, history, literary studies, vernacular architecture, historical archaeology, and material culture. Submissions in other fields, and submissions of poetry, textbooks, plays and translations, are not invited. Prefers "scholarly treatment and a readable style. Authors usually have Ph.D.s." Submit outline, author vita and 2 sample chapters. Reviews artwork/photos as part of ms package.
Fiction: Regional. Query with synopsis and author biographical information.
Recent Title(s): *Blood Feud*, by Annabel Thomas (fiction).
Tips: "Our market is in several groups: scholars; educated readers with special interests in given scholarly subjects; and the general educated public interested in Tennessee, Appalachia and the South. Not all our books appeal to all these groups, of course, but any given book must appeal to at least one of them."

UNIVERSITY OF TEXAS PRESS, P.O. Box 7819, Austin TX 78713-7819. (512)471-7233. Fax: (512)320-0668. E-mail: utpress@uts.cc.utexas.edu. Website: www.utexas.edu/utpress/. **Acquisitions:** Theresa May, assistant director/executive editor (social sciences, Latin American studies); James Burr, acquisition editor (humanities, classics); William Bishel (sciences). Estab. 1952. **Publishes 90 titles/year. Receives 1,000 submissions/year. 50% of books from first-time authors; 99% from unagented writers. Pays royalty usually based on net income. Offers advance occasionally.** Publishes book 18 months after acceptance of ms. Responds in up to 3 months. Book catalog and ms guidelines free.
    ○━ "In addition to publishing the results of advanced research for scholars worldwide, UT Press has a special obligation to the people of its state to publish authoritative books on Texas. We do not publish fiction or poetry, except for some Latin American and Middle Eastern literature in translation."
Nonfiction: General scholarly subjects: natural history, American, Latin American, Native American, Chicano and Middle Eastern studies, classics and the ancient world, film, contemporary regional architecture, archaeology, anthropology, geography, ornithology, environmental studies, biology, linguistics, women's literature, literary biography (Modern-

ist period). Also uses specialty titles related to Texas and the Southwest, national trade titles and regional trade titles. Accepts nonfiction translations related to above areas. Query or submit outline and 2 sample chapters. Reviews artwork/photos as part of ms package.

Fiction: Latin American and Middle Eastern fiction only in translation. No poetry.

Recent Title(s): *American Films of the '70s*, by Peter Lev (nonfiction); *Places for Dead Bodies*, by Gary Hausladen (nonfiction).

Tips: "It's difficult to make a manuscript over 400 double-spaced pages into a feasible book. Authors should take special care to edit out extraneous material. We look for sharply focused, in-depth treatments of important topics."

UNIVERSITY PRESS OF COLORADO, 5589 Arapahoe, Suite 206C, Boulder CO 80303. (720)406-8849. Fax: (720)406-3443. Director: Luther Wilson. **Acquisitions:** Darrin Pratt, acquisitions editor. Estab. 1965. Publishes hardcover and paperback originals. **Publishes 40 titles/year. Receives 1,000 submissions/year. 50% of books from first-time authors; 95% from unagented writers. Pays 5-15% royalty contract on net price.** Publishes book 2 years after acceptance of ms. Responds in 6 months. Book catalog free.

O➖ "We are a university press. Books should be solidly researched and from a reputable scholar."

Nonfiction: Scholarly, regional and environmental subjects. Length: 250-500 pages. Query first with table of contents, preface or opening chapter and SASE. Reviews artwork/photos as part of ms package.

Fiction: Limited fiction series; works of fiction on the trans-Mississippi West, by authors residing in the region. Query with SASE.

Recent Title(s): *Innocents on the Ice: A Memoir of Antarctic Exploration 1957*, by John C. Bohrendt (nonfiction); *October Revolution*, by Tom LaMarr (fiction); *Palma Cathedral*, by Michael White (poetry).

Tips: "We have series on the Women's West and on Mesoamerican worlds."

UNIVERSITY PRESS OF KANSAS, 2501 W. 15th St., Lawrence KS 66049-3905. (785)864-4154. Fax: (785)864-4586. E-mail: mail@newpress.upress.ukans.edu. Website: www.kansaspress.ku.edu. **Acquisitions:** Michael J. Briggs, editor-in-chief (military history, political science, law); Nancy Scott Jackson, acquisitions editor (western history, American studies, environmental studies, women's studies, philosophy); Fred M. Woodward, director, (political science, presidency, regional). Estab. 1946. Publishes hardcover originals, trade paperback originals and reprints. **Publishes 50 titles/year. Receives 600 queries/year. 20% of books from first-time authors; 98% from unagented writers. Pays 5-15% royalty on net price.** Publishes book 10 months after acceptance of ms. Responds in 1 month on proposals. Book catalog and ms guidelines free.

O➖ The University Press of Kansas publishes scholarly books that advance knowledge and regional books that contribute to the understanding of Kansas, the Great Plains and the Midwest.

Nonfiction: Biography. Subjects include Americana, anthropology/archaeology, government/politics, history, military/war, nature/environment, philosophy, regional, sociology, women's issues/studies. "We are looking for books on topics of wide interest based on solid scholarship and written for both specialists and informed general readers. Do not send unsolicited complete manuscripts." Submit cover letter, cv, and prospectus, outline or sample chapter. Reviews artwork/photos as part of the ms package. Send photocopies.

Recent Title(s): *Oliver Stone's USA: Film, History and Controversy*, edited by Robert Brent Toplin with commentary by Oliver Stone.

UNIVERSITY PRESS OF KENTUCKY, 663 S. Limestone, Lexington KY 40508-4008. (606)257-8150. Fax: (606)257-2984. Website: www.kentuckypress.com. **Acquisitions:** Kenneth Cherry, director and editor. Estab. 1943. Publishes hardcover and paperback originals and reprints. **Publishes 60 titles/year. Royalty varies. No advance.** Publishes ms 1 year after acceptance. Responds in 2 months on queries. Book catalog free.

O➖ "We are a scholarly publisher, publishing chiefly for an academic and professional audience, as well as books about Kentucky, the upper South, Appalachia, and the Ohio Valley."

Nonfiction: Biography, reference, monographs. "Strong areas are American history, biography, women's studies, film studies, American and African-American studies, folklore, Kentuckiana and regional books, Appalachian studies, Irish studies and military history. No textbooks, genealogical material, lightweight popular treatments, how-to books or books unrelated to our major areas of interest." The Press does not consider original works of fiction or poetry. Query.

Recent Title(s): *A Rose for Mrs. Miniver: The Life of Greer Garson*, by Michael Troyan; *Stroheim*, by Authur Lennig.

UNIVERSITY PRESS OF MISSISSIPPI, 3825 Ridgewood Rd., Jackson MS 39211-6492. (601)432-6205. Fax: (601)432-6217. E-mail: press@ihl.state.ms.us. Director/Editor-in-Chief: Seetha Srinivasan. **Acquisitions:** Craig Gill, senior editor (regional studies, anthropology, military history); Seetha Srinivasan, editor (art, literature). Estab. 1970. Publishes hardcover and paperback originals and reprints. **Publishes 55 titles/year. Receives 750 submissions/year. 20% of books from first-time authors; 90% from unagented writers. "Competitive royalties and terms."** Publishes book 1 year after acceptance. Responds in 3 months. Catalog for 9×12 SAE with 3 first-class stamps.

O➖ "University Press of Mississippi publishes scholarly and trade titles, as well as special series, including: American Made Music; Author and Artist; conversations with public intellectuals; interviews with filmmakers; Faulkner and Yoknapatawpha; Fiction Series; Folk Art and Artists; Folklife in the South; Literary Conversations; Natural History; Performance Studies in Culture; Studies in Popular Culture; Understanding Health and Sickness; Writers and Their Work."

Imprint(s): Muscadine Books (regional trade), Banner Books (literary reprints).

Nonfiction: Americana, biography, history, politics, folklife, literary criticism, ethnic/minority studies, art, photography, music, health, popular culture with scholarly emphasis. Interested in southern regional studies and literary studies. Submit outline, sample chapters and cv. "We prefer a proposal that describes the significance of the work and a chapter outline." Reviews artwork/photos as part of ms package.
Fiction: Commissioned trade editions by prominent writers.
Recent Title(s): *Dubose Heyward: A Charleston Gentleman and the World of Porgy and Bess*, by James Hutchisson.

UNIVERSITY PRESS OF NEW ENGLAND, (includes Wesleyan University Press), 23 S. Main St., Hanover NH 03755-2048. (603)643-7100. Fax: (603)643-1540. E-mail: university.press@dartmouth.edu. Website: www.dartmouth.edu/acad-inst/upne/. Director: Richard Abel. **Acquisitions:** Phil Pochoda, editorial director (American/northeastern studies, fiction, biography, cultural studies); Phyllis Deutsch, editor (Jewish studies, art, biography, American studies, French studies); April Ossmann, assistant editor (poetry, nature, performance studies, American/regional studies); Suzanna Tamminen, editor-in-chief (poetry [for Wesleyan], music, performance studies. Estab. 1970. Publishes hardcover and trade paperback originals, trade paperback reprints. **Publishes 75-80 titles/year. Pays standard royalty. Offers advance occasionally.** Responds in 2 months. Book catalog and guidelines for 9×12 SAE with 5 first-class stamps.

O─ "University Press of New England is a consortium of university presses. Some books—those published for one of the consortium members—carry the joint imprint of New England and the member: Wesleyan, Dartmouth, Brandeis, Tufts, University of New Hampshire and Middlebury College. We publish academic studies for an academic audience (mostly American studies and Jewish studies) as well as nonfiction aimed at the educated reader/intellectual. We also encourage regional (New England) work (academic, fiction, poetry or otherwise)." Currently emphasizing American studies, cultural studies. De-emphasizing fiction.
Nonfiction: Americana (New England), art, biography, music, nature, American studies, Jewish studies, performance studies, regional (New England). No festschriften, unrevised doctoral dissertations, or symposium collections. Submit outline, 1-2 sample chapters with SASE. *No electronic submissions.*
Fiction: *Only* New England novels and reprints.
Recent Title(s): *Mysteries of Paris: The Quest for Morton Fullerton*, by Marion Mainwaring (nonfiction); *Rainline*, by Anne Whitney Pierce (fiction); *The New American Poets: A Bread Loaf Anthology*, ed. Michael Collier (poetry).

THE URBAN LAND INSTITUTE, 1025 Thomas Jefferson St. N.W., Washington DC 20007-5201. (202)624-7000. Fax: (202)624-7140. E-mail: rlevit@uli.org. Website: www.uli.org. **Acquisitions**: Rachelle Levitt, senior vice president/publisher. Estab. 1936. Publishes hardcover and trade paperback originals. **Publishes 15-20 titles/year. Receives 20 submissions/year. 2% of books from first-time authors; 100% of books from unagented writers. Pays 10% royalty on gross sales. Offers $1,500-2,000 advance.** Publishes book 6 months after acceptance. Book catalog and ms guidelines available via website or for 9×12 SAE.

O─ The Urban Land Institute publishes technical books on real estate development and land planning.
Nonfiction: "The majority of manuscripts are created inhouse by research staff. We acquire two or three outside authors to fill schedule and subject areas where our list has gaps. We are not interested in real estate sales, brokerages, appraisal, making money in real estate, opinion, personal point of view, or manuscripts negative toward growth and development." Query. Reviews artwork/photos as part of ms package.
Recent Title(s): *Density by Design: Real Estate Development Principles and Process.*

UTAH STATE UNIVERSITY PRESS, 7800 Old Main Hill, Logan UT 84322-7800. (435)797-1362. Fax: (435)797-0313. Website: www.usu.edu/~usupress. **Acquisitions:** Michael Spooner, director (composition, poetry); John Alley, editor (history, folklore, fiction). Estab. 1972. Publishes hardcover and trade paperback originals and reprints. **Publishes 15 titles/year. Receives 170 submissions/year. 8% of books from first-time authors. Pays royalty on net price. No advance.** Publishes book 18 months after acceptance. Responds in 1 month on queries. Book catalog free. Manuscript guidelines for SASE.

O─ Utah State University Press publishes scholarly works in the academic areas noted below. Currently interested in book-length scholarly manuscripts dealing with folklore studies or composition studies.
Nonfiction: Biography, reference and textbooks on folklore, Americana and the West, history of the West, Native American studies, and studies in composition and rhetoric. Query with SASE. Reviews artwork/photos as part of ms package. Send photocopies.
Recent Title(s): *Wiring the Writing Center*, edited by Eric H. Hobson; *People of the West Desert*, by Craig Denton; *The Hammered Dulcimer*, by Lisa Williams (poetry).
Tips: Utah State University Press also sponsors the annual May Swenson Poetry Award.

VANDAMERE PRESS, AB Associates International, Inc., P.O. Box 5243, Arlington VA 22205. **Acquisitions:** Jerry Frank, editor. Estab. 1984. Publishes hardcover and trade paperback originals and reprints. **Publishes 8-15 titles/year. Receives 750 queries and 2,000 mss/year. 25% of books from first-time authors; 90% from unagented writers. Pays royalty on revenues generated.** Publishes book 1-3 years after acceptance of ms. Accepts simultaneous submissions. Responds in 6 months.

O─ Vandamere publishes general fiction as well as nonfiction of historical, biographical or regional interest. Currently emphasizing history and biography.

Nonfiction: Subjects include Americana, biography, disability/healthcare issues, education, history, military/war, regional (Washington D.C./Mid-Atlantic). Submit outline and 2-3 sample chapters. Reviews artwork/photos as part of ms package. Send photocopies.

Fiction: General fiction including adventure, erotica, humor, mystery, suspense. Submit synopsis and 5-10 sample chapters.

Recent Title(s): *Blackbird Fly Away*, by Hugh Gregory Gallagher (nonfiction); *Holy War*, by Alexander M. Grace.

Tips: "Authors who can provide endorsements from significant published writers, celebrities, etc., will *always* be given serious consideration. Clean, easy-to-read, *dark* copy is essential. Patience in waiting for replies is essential. All unsolicited work is looked at, but at certain times of the year our review schedule will stop." No response without SASE.

VANDERBILT UNIVERSITY PRESS, Box 1813, Station B, Nashville TN 37235. (615)322-3585. Fax: (615)343-8823. E-mail: vupress@vanderbilt.edu. Website: www.vanderbilt.edu/vupress. **Acquisitions:** Charles Backus, director. Among other titles, publishes Vanderbilt Library of American Philosophy (Herman J. Saatkamp, editor); Vanderbilt Issues in Higher Educations (John Braxton, editor) and Innovations in Applied Mathematics (Larry Schumacher, editor). Also distributes for and co-publishes with the Country Music Foundation. Estab. 1940. Publishes hardcover originals and trade paperback originals and reprints. **Publishes 15-20 titles/year. Receives 350-400 queries/year. 25% of books from first-time authors; 90% from unagented writers. Pays 10% maximum royalty on net income. Seldom offers advance.** Publishes book 10 months after acceptance of ms. No simultaneous submissions. Responds in 3 months on proposals. Book catalog and ms guidelines free. No fiction or poetry.

    O-π "Vanderbilt University Press, the publishing arm of the nation's leading research university, has maintained a strong reputation as a publisher of distinguished titles in the humanities, social sciences, education, medicine and regional studies, for both academic and general audiences, responding to rapid technological and cultural changes, while upholding high standards of scholarly publishing excellence."

Nonfiction: Biography, textbook, scholarly. Subjects include Americana, anthropology/archaeology, education, government/politics, health/medicine, history, language/literature, music and popular culture, nature/environment, philosophy, regional, religion, translation, women's issues/studies. Submit outline, 1 sample chapter and cv. Reviews artwork/photos as part of ms package. Send photocopies.

Recent Title(s): *Murder & Masculinity: Violent Fictions of 20th-Century Latin America*, by Rebecca E. Biron.

Tips: "Our audience consists of scholars and educated general readers."

VENTURE PUBLISHING, INC., 1999 Cato Ave., State College PA 16801. Fax: (814)234-4561. E-mail: vpublish@venturepublish.com. Website: www.venturepublish.com. **Acquisitions:** Geof Godbey, editor. Estab. 1979. Publishes hardcover and paperback originals and reprints. **Publishes 10-12 titles/year. Receives 50 queries and 20 mss/year. 40% of books from first-time authors; 100% from unagented writers. Pays royalty on wholesale price. Offers advance.** Publishes book 9 months after acceptance of ms. Responds in 1 month on queries; 2 months on proposals and mss. Book catalog and ms guidelines available via website or with SASE.

    O-π Venture Publishing produces quality educational publications, also workbooks for professionals, educators, and students in the fields of recreation, parks, leisure studies, therapeutic recreation and long term care.

Nonfiction: Textbook, college academic, professional. Subjects include nature/environment (outdoor recreation management and leadership texts), recreation, sociology (leisure studies), long-term care nursing homes, therapeutic recreation. "Textbooks and books for recreation activity leaders high priority." Submit outline and 1 sample chapter.

Recent Title(s): *Adventure Programming*, edited by John Miles and Simon Priest; *Leisure in Your Life*, by Geof Godbey.

VERSO, 180 Varick St., 10th Fl., New York NY 10014. (212)807-9680. Fax: (212)807-9152. E-mail: versoinc@aol.com. Website: www.versobooks.com. **Acquisitions:** Colin Robinson, managing director. Estab. 1970. Publishes hardcover and trade paperback originals. **Publishes 40-60 titles/year. Receives 300 queries and 150 mss/year. 10% of mss from first-time authors, 95% from unagented writers. Pays royalty.** Publishes book 1 year after acceptance of ms. Accepts simultaneous submissions. Responds in 5 months. Book catalog free.

    O-π "Our books cover politics, culture, and history (among other topics), but all come from a critical, Leftist viewpoint, on the border between trade and academic."

Nonfiction: Illustrated book. Subjects include economics, government/politics, history, philosophy, sociology and women's issues/studies. "We are loosely affiliated with *New Left Review* (London). We are not interested in academic monographs." Submit proposal package, including at least 1 sample chapter.

Recent Title(s): *No One Left to Lie to: The Triangulations of William Jefferson Clinton*, by Christopher Hitchens.

VGM CAREER HORIZONS, NTC/Contemporary Publishing Group, 4255 W. Touhy Ave., Lincolnwood IL 60646-1975. (847)679-5500. Fax: (847)679-2494. Vice President and Publisher: John T. Nolan (trade division). **Acquisitions:** Denise Betts, assistant editor. Estab. 1963. Publishes hardcover and paperback originals. **Publishes 50 titles/year. Receives 50-100 submissions/year. 15% of books from first-time authors; 95% from unagented writers. Pays royalty or makes outright purchase. Advance varies; $1,000-5,000.** Publishes book 1 year after acceptance of ms. Accepts simultaneous submissions. Responds in 3 months. Book catalog and ms guidelines for 9×12 SAE with 5 first-class stamps.

    O-π VGM publishes career-focused titles for job seekers, career planners, job changers, students and adults in education and trade markets.

Nonfiction: Textbook and general trade on careers in medicine, business, environment, etc. Query or submit outline and sample chapters.
Recent Title(s): *Career Change*, by Dr. David P. Helfand.
Tips: VGM also hires revision authors to handle rewrites and new editions of existing titles.

Ⓐ VIKING, Penguin Putnam Inc., 375 Hudson St., New York NY 10014. (212)366-2000. **Acquisitions:** Barbara Grossman, publisher. Publishes hardcover and trade paperback originals. **Pays 10-15% royalty on retail price. Advance negotiable.** Publishes book 1 year after acceptance of ms. Accepts simultaneous submissions. Report in 6 months on queries.
   ○┬ Viking publishes a mix of academic and popular fiction and nonfiction.
Nonfiction: Subjects include biography, business/economics, child guidance/parenting, cooking/foods/nutrition, health/medicine, history, language/literature, music/dance, philosophy, women's issues/studies. *Agented submissions only.*
Fiction: Literary, mainstream/contemporary, mystery, suspense. *Agented submissions only.*
Recent Title(s): *Without a Doubt*, by Marcia Clark (popular culture); *Out to Canaan*, by Jan Karon (novel).

VIKING CHILDREN'S BOOKS, Penguin Putnam Inc., 345 Hudson St., New York NY 10014. (212)366-2000. Editor-in-Chief: Elizabeth Law. **Acquisitions:** Regina Hayes, president/publisher. Publishes hardcover originals. **Publishes 80 books/year. Receives 7,500 queries and mss/year. 25% of books from first-time authors; 33% from unagented writers. Pays 10% royalty on retail price.** Advance negotiable. Publishes book 1 year after acceptance of ms. Report in 4 months on queries.
   ○┬ Viking Children's Books publishes high-quality trade books for children including fiction, nonfiction, picture
      books and novelty books for pre-schoolers through young adults.
Nonfiction: Children's books. Query with outline, 3 sample chapters and SASE.
Fiction: Juvenile, young adult. Submit complete ms for novels, picture books and chapter books with SASE.
Recent Title(s): *Joseph Had a Little Overcoat*, by Simms Taback; *Someone Like You*, by Sarah Dessen.

VIKING STUDIO, Penguin Putnam, Inc., 375 Hudson St., New York NY 10014. (212)366-2000. Fax: (212)366-2011. Website: www.penguinputnam.com. **Acquisitions:** Christopher Sweet, executive editor (art, music, history, photography, fashion, religion); Cyril Nelson, senior editor (arts & crafts, decorative arts); Marie Timell, senior editor (nonfiction general interest, astrology, New Age). Publishes hardcover originals. **Publishes 35-40 titles/year. Receives 300 submissions/year. Less than 10% of books are from first-time authors; less than 10% from unagented writers.** Publishes book 1 year after acceptance. Accepts simultaneous submissions. Responds in 2 months.
   ○┬ Viking publishes high production value, quality designed books on subjects of mainstream interest that allow
      a compelling visual treatment. Currently emphasizing reference, history, religion. De-emphasizing lifestyle,
      decorating, cookery.
Nonfiction: Subjects include Americana, architecture, photography, New Age/metaphysics, art, photography, popular culture, astrology, architecture, fashion. Reviews artwork as part of ms package. Send photocopies.
Recent Title(s): *David Bailey: Birth of the Cool*, by Martin Harrison; *The Pennyroyal Caxton Bible*, designed and illustrated by Barry Moser.

Ⓐ VILLARD BOOKS, Random House Inc., 201 E. 50th St., New York NY 10022. (212)572-2878. Publisher: Ann Godoff. Estab. 1983. Publishes hardcover and trade paperback originals. **Publishes 55-60 titles/year. 95% of books are agented submissions. Advances and royalties; negotiated separately.** Accepts simultaneous submissions.
   ○┬ "Villard Books is the publisher of savvy and sometimes quirky bestseller hardcovers and trade paperbacks."
Nonfiction and Fiction: Commercial nonfiction and fiction. *Agented submissions only.* Submit outline/synopsis and up to 50 pages in sample chapters. *No unsolicited submissions.*
Recent Title(s): *The Perfect Season*, by Tim McCarver; *I Ain't Got Time to Bleed*, by Jesse Ventura.

VINTAGE IMAGES, P.O. Box 4699, Silver Spring MD 20914. (301)879-6522. Fax: (301)879-6524. E-mail: vimages@erols.com. Website: www.vintageimages.com. **Acquisitions:** Brian Smolens, president. Publishes trade paperback originals. **Publishes 8 titles/year. Pays 4-8% royalty on wholesale price.** Publishes book 5 months after acceptance of ms. No simultaneous submissions. Manuscript guidelines for #10 SASE.
Nonfiction: Poster books. Photography subjects. Send for guidelines. Query with SASE. *All unsolicited mss returned unopened.*
Tips: "We are interested in creative writers who can weave a humorous/dramatic theme around 36 vintage photos (early 1900s)."

Ⓝ ⬛ VISIONS COMMUNICATIONS, 205 E. 10th St., 2D, New York NY 10003. Phone/fax: (212)529-4029. E-mail: bayeun@aol.com. **Acquisitions:** Beth Bay. Visions specializes in technical and reference titles. Estab. 1994. Publishes hardcover originals and trade paperback originals and reprints. **Publishes 5 titles/year. Receives 20 queries and 10 mss/year. 50% of books from first-time authors; 75% from unagented writers. Pays 5-20% royalty on retail price.** Publishes book 6 months after acceptance of ms. Accepts simultaneous submissions. Responds in 1 month on queries, 2 months on proposals, 3 months on mss. Manuscript guidelines free.

Nonfiction: Children's/juvenile, how-to, self-help, reference, technical, textbook. Subjects include art/architecture, business/economics, health/medicine, psychology, religion, science, women's issues/studies. Submit outline, 3 sample chapters and proposal package.
Recent Title(s): *Guide to Documented Essays.*

VISTA PUBLISHING, INC., 422 Morris Ave., Suite #1, Long Branch NJ 07740. (732)229-6500. Fax: (732)229-9647. E-mail: czagury@vistapubl.com. Website: www.vistapubl.com. **Acquisitions:** Carolyn Zagury, president. Estab. 1991. Publishes trade paperback originals. **Publishes 12 titles/year. Receives 200 queries and 125 mss/year. 75% of books from first-time authors; 100% from unagented writers. Pays 50% royalty on wholesale or retail price.** Publishes book 2-3 years after acceptance of ms. Accepts simultaneous submissions. Responds in 3 months on mss. Book catalog and ms guidelines free.
  O─┐ Vista publishes books by nurses and allied health professionals. Currently emphasizing clinical topics. De-emphasizing fiction.
Nonfiction: Nursing and career related. Subjects include business, child guidance/parenting, creative nonfiction, health/medicine, women's issues/studies, specific to nursing and allied health professionals. Submit full ms and SASE. *Writer's Market* recommends query with SASE first. Reviews artwork/photos as part of ms package. Send photocopies.
Fiction: Horror, multicultural, mystery, poetry, short story collections, nursing medical. "We specialize in nurse and allied health professional authors." Submit full ms and SASE.
Poetry: Nursing-related. Submit complete ms.
Recent Title(s): *Holistic Harmony*, by Dr. Arthur Brawer (nonfiction); *Nurses Notes*, by Linda Strangio, RN (fiction); *Drifting Among the Whales*, by Carol Battligia, RN (poetry).
Tips: "It's always worth the effort to submit your manuscript."

N̄ VOLCANO PRESS, INC., P.O. Box 270, Volcano CA 95689-0270. (209)296-4991. Fax: (209)296-4515. E-mail: ruth@volcanopress.com. Website: www.volcanopress.com. **Acquisitions:** Ruth Gottstein, publisher. Estab. 1969. Publishes trade paperback originals. **Publishes 4-6 titles/year. Pays royalties on net price. Offers $500-1,000 advance.** Responds in 1 month on queries. Book catalog free.
  O─┐ "We believe that the books we are producing today are of even greater value than the gold of yesteryear and that the sybolism of the term 'Mother Lode' is still relevant to our work."
Nonfiction: "We publish women's health and social issues, particularly in the field of domestic violence." Query with brief outline and SASE by mail; no e-mail or fax submissions.
Recent Title(s): *Journal and Letters from the Mines*, by John Doble.
Tips: "Look at our titles on the Web or in our catalog, and submit materials consistent with what we already publish."

VOYAGEUR PRESS, 123 N. Second St., Stillwater MN 55082. (651)430-2210. Fax: (651)430-2211. E-mail: mdregni @voyageurpress.com or tberger@voyageurpress.com. **Acquisitions:** Todd R. Berger (regional travel and photography. Michael Dregni, editorial director. Estab. 1972. Publishes hardcover and trade paperback originals. **Publishes 50 titles/ year. Receives 1,200 queries and 500 mss/year. 10% of books from first-time authors; 90% from unagented writers. Pays royalty.** Publishes book 1 year after acceptance of ms. Accepts simultaneous submissions. Responds in 3 months.
  O─┐ "Voyageur Press is internationally known as a leading publisher of quality natural history, wildlife and regional books."
Nonfiction: Coffee table book (and smaller format photographic essay books), cookbook. Subjects include natural history, nature/environment, Americana, collectibles, history, outdoor recreation, regional. Query or submit outline. Reviews artwork/photos. Send transparencies—duplicates and tearsheets only.
Recent Title(s): *This Old Tractor* (stories and photos about farm tractors); *Last Standing Woman* (Native American novel).
Tips: "We publish books for a sophisticated audience interested in natural history and cultural history of a variety of subjects. Please present as focused an idea as possible in a brief submission (one page cover letter; two page outline or proposal). Note your credentials for writing the book. Tell all you know about the market niche and marketing possibilities for proposed book."

WADSWORTH PUBLISHING COMPANY, 10 Davis Dr., Belmont CA 94002. (650)595-2350. Fax: (650)637-7544. Website: www.wadsworth.com. **Acquisitions:** Sean Wakely, editorial director; Peter Adams, editor (philosophy/religion); Karen Austin, editor (communications, radio/TV/film); Clark Baxter, publisher (history/political science/music); Deirdre Cavanaugh, executive editor (communications, speech and theater); Halee Dinsey, editor (sociology/anthropology [upper level]); Lisa Gebo, senior editor (psychology and helping professions); Sabra Horne, senior editor (criminal justice); Eve Howard, publisher (sociology and anthropology); Dianne Lindsay, editor (education/special education); Vicki Knight, executive editor (psychology); Peter Marshall, publisher (health/nutrition); Eileen Murphy, editor (counseling and social work); Edith Brady, editor (psychology); Marianne Tafliner, senior editor (psychology). Estab. 1956. Publishes hardcover and paperback originals and software. **Publishes 300 titles/year. 35% of books from first-time authors; 99% of books from unagented writers. Pays 5-15% royalty on net price. Advances not automatic policy.** Publishes ms 1 year after acceptance. Accepts simultaneous submissions. Book catalog and ms guidelines available via website or with SASE.
  O─┐ Wadsworth publishes college-level textbooks in social sciences, humanities, education and college success.

Nonfiction: Textbooks and multimedia products: higher education only. Subjects include anthropology, counseling, criminal justice, education, health, music, nutrition, philosophy, psychology, religious studies, sociology, speech and mass communications, broadcasting, TV and film productions, college success. Query or submit outline/synopsis and sample chapters.

Recent Title(s): *Production and Operations Management*, 7th edition, by Norman Gaither.

J. WESTON WALCH, PUBLISHER, P.O. Box 658, Portland ME 04104-0658. (207)772-2846. Fax: (207)774-7167. Website: www.walch.com. **Acquisitions:** Lisa French, editor-in-chief. Estab. 1927. **Publishes 100 titles/year. Receives 300 submissions/year. 10% of books from first-time authors; 95% from unagented writers. Offers 8-12% royalty on gross receipts. Advances negotiable.** Publishes book 18 months after acceptance of ms. Responds in 4 months. Book catalog for 9×12 SAE with 5 first-class stamps. Manuscript guidelines for #10 SASE.

○┳ "We publish only supplementary educational material for grades six to adult in the U.S. and Canada."

Nonfiction: Subjects include art, business, technology, economics, English, geography, government, history, literacy, mathematics, middle school, science, social studies, remdial and special education. Formats include books, reproducibles, posters and mixed packages. Most titles are assigned by us, though we occasionally accept an author's unsolicited submission. We have a great need for author/artist teams and for authors who can write at third- to seventh-grade levels. We do *not* want textbooks or anthologies. All authors should have educational experience at the secondary level. *Query first. No unsolicited mss.* Looks for sense of organization, writing ability, knowledge of subject, skill of communicating with intended audience." Reviews artwork/photos as part of ms package.

Recent Title(s): *Document-Based Assessment Activities for Global History*, by Theresa C. Noonan; *Bridges: Making the Transition from School to Work*, by Kathleen Zeien and Beverly Anderson.

WALKER AND CO., Walker Publishing Co., 435 Hudson St., New York NY 10014. Fax: (212)727-0984. Publisher: George Gibson. Editors: Jacqueline Johnson, Michael Seidman. Juvenile Publisher: Emily Easton. Juvenile Editor: Tim Travaglini. **Acquisitions:** Submissions Editor or Submisions Editor-Juvenile. Estab. 1959. Publishes hardcover and trade paperback originals. **Publishes 70 titles/year. Receives 3,500 submissions/year. Pays royalty on retail price, 7½-12% on paperback, 10-15% on hardcover. Offers competitive advances.** Material without SASE will not be returned. Responds in 3 months. Book catalog and ms guidelines for 9×12 SAE with 3 first-class stamps.

○┳ Walker publishes general nonfiction on a variety of subjects as well as mysteries, children's books and large print religious reprints. Currently emphasizing science, history, technology, math. De-emphasizing music, bio, self-help, sports.

Nonfiction: Biography, history, science and natural history, health, juvenile, music, nature and environment, reference, popular science, sports/baseball, and self-help books. Query with SASE. No phone calls.

Fiction: Adult mystery, juvenile fiction and picture books. Query with SASE.

Recent Title(s): *Galileo's Daughter*, by Dava Sobel (history/biography/science); *E=MC²*, by David Bodanis (history/science); *The Basque History of the World*, by Mark Kurlansky (history); *Captain's Command*, by Anna Myers (juvenile).

[N] [■] WALSWORTH PUBLISHING CO., Donning Co. Publishers, 306 N. Kansas Ave., Marceline MO 64658. (800)369-2646. Fax: (660)258-7798. E-mail: steve.mull@walsworth.com. Website: www.donning.com. **Acquisitions:** Steve Mull, general manager. Publishes hardcover originals and reprints. **Publishes 40-50 titles/year. Receives 25 queries and 50 mss/year. 70% of books from first-time authors; 99% from unagented writers. Pays 5-15% royalty on wholesale price.** Book catalog on website. Manuscript guidelines free on request.

○┳ Walsworth publishes coffee table books.

Nonfiction: Coffee table book. Subjects include community history, college history, agricultural history, business/economic history, ethnic, history, military/war, sports. Query with SASE.

[A] WARNER ASPECT, Warner Books, 1271 Avenue of the Americas, New York NY 10020. (212)522-7200. Website: twbookmark.com. Editor-in-Chief: Betsy Mitchell. Publishes hardcover, trade paperback, mass market paperback originals and mass market paperback reprints. **Publishes 30 titles/year. Receives 500 queries and 350 mss/year. 5-10% of books from first-time authors; 1% from unagented writers. Pays royalty on retail price. Offers $5,000-up advance.** Publishes book 1 year after acceptance of ms. Responds in 3 months on mss.

○┳ "We're looking for 'epic' stories in both fantasy and science fiction. Also seeking writers of color to add to what we've already published by Octavia E. Butler, Walter Mosley, etc."

Fiction: Fantasy, science fiction. "Sample our existing titles—we're a fairly new list and pretty strongly focused." Mistake writers often make is "hoping against hope that being unagented won't make a difference. We simply don't have the staff to look at unagented projects."

Recent Title(s): *The Naked God*, by Peter F. Hamilton (science fiction); *A Cavern of Black Ice*, by J.V. Jones (fantasy).

WARNER BOOKS, Time & Life Building, 1271 Avenue of the Americas, New York NY 10020. (212)522-7200. Website: www.twbookmark.com. President, Maureen Egen. **Acquisitions:** (Ms.) Jamie Raab, senior vice president/publisher (general nonfiction, commercial fiction); Rick Horgan, vice president/executive editor (popular culture, general nonfiction, thriller fiction); Amy Einhorn, executive editor, trade paperback (popular culture, business, fitness, self-help); Maggie Crawford, executive editor, mass market (women's fiction, spirituality and human potential); Rick Wolff, executive editor (business, humor, sports); Betsy Mitchell, executive editor (science fiction); Caryn Karmatz Rudy, senior editor (fiction, general nonfiction, popular culture); Rob McMahon (fiction, business, sports); Diana Baroni, editor (health, fitness, general nonfiction); Jessica Papin, associate editor (commercial fiction, general nonfiction); John Aherne, associate editor (popular culture, fiction, general nonfiction); William Malloy, editor-in-chief, Mysterious Press (mysteries, cookbooks); Sara Ann Freed, executive editor (mysteries, suspense). Estab. 1960. Publishes hardcover, trade paperback and mass market paperback originals and reprints. **Publishes 350 titles/year. Pays variable royalty. Advance varies.** Publishes book 2 years after acceptance of ms. Responds in 4 months.

○➜ Warner publishes general interest fiction and nonfiction.

Imprint(s): Mysterious Press (mystery/suspense), **Warner Aspect** (science fiction and fantasy), **Warner Vision**.

Nonfiction: Biography, business, cooking, current affairs, health, history, home, humor, popular culture, psychology, reference, self-help, sports, spirituality and human potential. Query with SASE.

Fiction: Fantasy, horror, mainsteam, mystery, romance, science fiction, suspense, thriller. Query with SASE.

Recent Title(s): *The Honk and Holler Opening Soon*, by Billie Letts; *Something More*, by Sarah Ban Breathnach; *Live Now, Age Later*, by Isadore Rosenfeld, M.D.

Tips: "We do not accept unsolicited manuscripts."

WASHINGTON STATE UNIVERSITY PRESS, Pullman WA 99164-5910. (800)354-7360. Fax: (509)335-8568. E-mail: wsupress@wsu.edu. Website: www.publications.wsu.edu/wsupress. Director: Thomas H. Sanders. **Acquisitions:** Glen Lindeman, editor. Estab. 1928. Publishes hardcover originals, trade paperback originals and reprints. **Publishes 10 titles/year. Receives 300-400 submissions/year. 50% of books from first-time writers; mostly unagented authors. Pays 5% minimum royalty, graduated according to sales.** Publishes book 18 months after acceptance of ms. Reports on queries in 2 months.

○➜ WSU Press publishes books on the history, pre-history, culture, and politics of the West, particularly the Pacific Northwest.

Nonfiction: Subjects include Americana, art, biography, environment, ethnic studies, history (especially of the American West and the Pacific Northwest), politics, essays. "We seek manuscripts that focus on the Pacific Northwest as a region. No romance novels, how-to books, gardening books or books used specifically as classroom texts. We welcome innovative and thought-provoking titles in a wide diversity of genres, from essays and memoirs to history, anthropology and political science." Submit outline and sample chapters. Reviews artwork/photos as part of ms package.

Recent Title(s): *Orphan Road: The Railroad Comes to Seattle, 1853-1911*, by Kurt Armbruster.

Tips: "We have developed our marketing in the direction of regional and local history and have attempted to use this as the base upon which to expand our publishing program. In regional history, the secret is to write a good narrative— a good story—that is substantiated factually. It should be told in an imaginative, clever way. Have visuals (photos, maps, etc.) available to help the reader envision what has happened. Tell the regional history story in a way that ties it to larger, national, and even international events. Weave it into the large pattern of history. We have published our first book of essays and a regional cookbook and will do more in these and other fields if we get the right manuscript."

[N] **WATSON-GUPTILL PUBLICATIONS**, Billboard Publications, Inc., 1515 Broadway, New York NY 10036. (212)764-7300. Fax: (212)382-6090. Website: www.watsonguptill.com. **Acquisitions:** Candace Raney, senior acquisitions editor (art); Bob Nirkind, senior editor (Billboard-music); Sylvia Warren, senior editor (Whitney-architecture); Victoria Craven, senior editor (Amphoto-photography). Publishes hardcover and trade paperback originals and reprints. **Receives 150 queries and 50 mss/year. 50% of books from first-time authors; 75% from unagented writers. Pays royalty on wholesale price.** Publishes book 9 months after acceptance of ms. Responds in 2 months on queries; 3 months on proposals. Book catalog and ms guidelines free.

○➜ Watson-Guptill is an arts book publisher.

Imprint(s): Watson-Guptill, Amphoto, Whitney Library of Design, Billboard Books, Back Stage Books.

Nonfiction: Coffee table book, gift book, how-to, illustrated book, reference, textbook. Subjects include art, photography, architecture, lifestyle, pop culture, music, theater. "Writers should be aware of the kinds of books (crafts, graphic design, mostly instructional) Watson-Guptill publishes before submitting. Although we are growing and will consider new ideas and approaches, we will not consider a book if it is clearly outside of our publishing schedule." Query or submit proposal package, including outline, 1-2 sample chapters. Reviews artwork/photos. Send photocopies or transparencies.

Recent Title(s): *The Tao of Watercolor*, by Jeanne Carbonetti; *American Impressionism*, by Elizabeth Prelinger.

FRANKLIN WATTS, Grolier Publishing, 90 Sherman Turnpike, Danbury CT 06816. (203)797-6802. Fax: (203)797-6986. Website: www.grolier.com. Publisher: John Selfridge. **Acquisitions:** Melissa Stewart, executive editor; Deborah Grahame, editor (young adult). Estab. 1942. Publishes hardcover and softcover originals. **Publishes 150 titles/year. 5% of books from first-time authors; 95% from unagented writers. Advance varies.** Publishes book 18 months after acceptance of ms. Accepts simultaneous submissions. Responds in 4 months on queries. Book catalog and author's guidelines available with SASE.

○➜ Franklin Watts publishes nonfiction books for the library market (K-12) to supplement textbooks.

Nonfiction: History, science, social issues, biography. Subjects include education, language/literature, American and world history, politics, natural and physical sciences, sociology. Multicultural, curriculum-based nonfiction lists published twice a year. Strong also in the area of contemporary problems and issues facing young people. No humor, coffee table books, fiction, picture books, poetry, cookbooks or gardening books. Query with outline, writing sample and SASE. *No unsolicited mss.* No phone calls. Prefers to work with unagented authors.

● Grolier was recently purchased by Scholastic, Inc.

Recent Title(s): *Look What Came From Mexico*, by Miles Harvey; *High School Hazing*, by Hank Nuwer.
Tips: Most of this publisher's books are developed inhouse; less than 5% come from unsolicited submissions. However, they publish several series for which they always need new books. Study catalogs to discover possible needs.

WEATHERHILL, INC., 41 Monroe Turnpike, Trumbull CT 06611. (203)459-5090. Fax: (203)459-5095. E-mail: weatherhill@weatherhill.com. Website: www.weatherhill.com. **Acqusitions:** Raymond Furse, editorial director. Estab. 1962. Publishes hardcover and trade paperback originals and reprints. **Publishes 36 titles/year. Receives 250 queries and 100 mss/year. 20% of books from first-time authors; 95% from unagented writers. Pays 12-18% royalty on wholesale price. Offers advances up to $10,000. Publishes books 8 months after acceptance of ms.** Accepts simultaneous submissions. Responds in 1 month on proposals. Book catalog and ms guidelines free.
　O─┮ Weatherhill publishes exclusively Asia-related nonfiction and Asian fiction and poetry in translation.
Imprint(s): Weatherhill, Tengu Books.
Nonfiction: Asia-related topics only. Biography, coffee table book, cookbook, gift book, how-to, humor, illustrated book, reference, self-help. Subjects include anthropology/archaeology, art/architecture, cooking/foods/nutrition, gardening, history, language/literature, music/dance, nature/environment, photography, regional, religion, sociology, translation, travel. Submit outline, 2 sample chapters and sample illustrations (if applicable). Reviews artwork/photos as part of ms package. Send photocopies.
Fiction: "We publish only important Asian writers in translation. Asian fiction is a hard sell. Authors should check funding possibilities from appropriate sources: Japan Foundation, Korea Foundation, etc." Query with synopsis.
Poetry: Only Asian poetry in translation. Query.
Recent Title(s): *The Jewelry of Nepal*; *Vegetarian Sushi Made Easy*.

WEIDNER & SONS PUBLISHING, P.O. Box 2178, Riverton NJ 08077. (609)486-1755. Fax: (609)486-7583. E-mail: weidner@waterw.com. Website: www.waterw.com/~weidner. **Acquisitions:** James H. Weidner, president. Estab. 1967. Publishes hardcover and trade paperback originals and reprints. **Publishes 10-20 titles/year; imprint publishes 10 titles/year. Receives hundreds of queries and 50 mss/year. 100% of books from first-time authors; 90% from unagented writers. Pays 10% maximum royalty on wholesale price.** Accepts simultaneous submissions. Responds in 1 month on queries.
　O─┮ Weidner & Sons publishes primarily science, text and reference books for scholars, college students and researchers.
Imprint(s): Bird Sci Books, Delaware Estuary Press, Hazlaw Books, Medlaw Books, Pulse Publications, Tycooly Publishing USA.
Nonfiction: Reference, technical, textbook. Subjects include agriculture/horticulture, animals, business/economics, child guidance/parenting, computers/electronics, education, gardening, health/medicine, hobbies (electronic), language/literature, nature/environment, psychology, science and ecology/environment. "We do not publish fiction; never poetry. No topics in the 'pseudosciences': occult, astrology, New Age and metaphysics, etc." Query or submit outline and sample chapters with return postage and SASE required. Include e-mail address for faster response. Reviews artwork/photos as part of ms package. Send photocopies. "Suggest 2 copies of ms, double spaced, along with PC disk in Word, Word Perfect, Write or Pagemaker."
Recent Title(s): *The Huntington Sexual Behavior Scale.*
Recent Title(s): *Barefoot Days* (children's poetry); *The Story of David* (board book); *Jolly Old Santa Claus.*

SAMUEL WEISER, INC., P.O. Box 612, York Beach ME 03910-0612. (207)363-4393. Fax: (207)363-5799. E-mail: email@weiserbooks.com. Website: www.weiserbooks.com. **Acquisitions:** Eliot Stearns, editor. Estab. 1956. Publishes hardcover originals and trade paperback originals and reprints. **Publishes 20-30 titles/year. Receives 200 submissions/year. 50% of books from first-time authors; 98% from unagented writers. Pays 10% royalty on wholesale and retail price. Offers $500 average advance.** Publishes book 18 months after acceptance of ms. Responds in 3 months. Book catalog free.
　O─┮ Samuel Weiser looks for strong books in Eastern philosophy, metaphysics, esoterica of all kinds (tarot, astrology, qabalah, magic, etc.) written by teachers and people who know the subject.
Nonfiction: How-to, self-help. Subjects include health, music, philosophy, psychology, religion. "We don't want a writer's rehash of all the astrology books in the library, only texts written by people with strong backgrounds in the field. No poetry or novels." Submit complete ms. *Writer's Market* recommends query with SASE first. Reviews artwork/photos as part of ms package.
Recent Title(s): *The Tao of Contemplation*, by Jasmin Lee Cori; *Yoga Self-Taught*, by André van Lysebeth.
Tips: "Most new authors do not check permissions, nor do they provide proper footnotes. If they did, it would help. We look at all manuscripts submitted to us. We are interested in seeing freelance art for book covers."

WESLEYAN UNIVERSITY PRESS, 110 Mount Vernon St., Middletown CT 06459. (860)685-2420. **Acquisitions:** Suzanna Tamminen, editor-in-chief. Estab. 1957. Publishes hardcover originals and paperbacks. **Publishes 25-30 titles/year. Receives 1,500 queries and 1,000 mss/year. 10% of books from first-time authors; 80% from unagented writers. Pays 0-10% royalty. Offers up to $3,000 advance.** Publishes book 1-3 years after acceptance of ms. Accepts simultaneous submissions. Responds in 1 month on queries, 2 months on proposals, 3 months on mss. Book catalog free. Manuscript guidelines for #10 SASE.
　O─┮ Wesleyan University Press is a scholarly press with a focus on cultural studies.

Nonfiction: Biography, textbook, scholarly. Subjects include art/architecture, ethnic, gay/lesbian, history, language/literature, music/dance, philosophy, sociology, theater, film. Submit outline, proposal package, including: introductory letter, curriculum vitae, table of contents. Reviews artwork/photos as part of ms package. Send photocopies.
Fiction: Science fiction. "We publish very little fiction, less than 3% of our entire list."
Poetry: "Writers should request a catalog and guidelines." Submit 5-10 sample poems.
Recent Title(s): *Thieves of Paradise*, by Yusef Kommunyakaa (poetry).

WESTCLIFFE PUBLISHERS, P.O. Box 1261, Englewood CO 80150. (303)935-0900. Fax: (303)935-0903. E-mail: westclif@westcliffepubishers.com. **Acquisitions:** Linda Doyle, associate publisher; Jenna Samelson, managing editor. Estab. 1981. Publishes hardcover originals, trade paperback originals and reprints. **Publishes 23 titles/year. Receives 100 queries and 60 mss/year. 75% of books from first-time authors; 100% from unagented writers. Pays royalty on retail price.** Publishes book 18 months after acceptance of ms. Accepts simultaneous submissions. Responds in 1 month. Book catalog free.
   O→ "Westcliffe Publishers produces the highest quality in regional photography and essays for our coffee table-style books and calendars. As an eco-publisher our mission is to foster environmental awareness by showing the beauty of the natural world." Strong concentration on color guide books.
Nonfiction: Coffee table book, gift book, illustrated book, reference. Subjects include Americana, animals, gardening, nature/environment, photography, regional, travel. "Writers need to do their market research to justify a need in the marketplace." Submit outline with proposal package. Westcliffe will contact you for photos, writing samples.
Recent Title(s): *Colorado's Best Wildflower Hikes*, by Pam Irwin; *New Mexico's Wilderness Areas*, by Bob Julyan.
Tips: Audience are nature and outdoors enthusiasts and photographers. "Just call us!"

WESTERNLORE PRESS, P.O. Box 35305, Tucson AZ 85740. (520)297-5491. Fax: (520)297-1722. **Acquisitions:** Lynn R. Bailey, editor. Estab. 1941. **Publishes 6-12 titles/year. Pays standard royalties on retail price "except in special cases."** Responds in 2 months.
   O→ WesternLore publishes Western Americana of a scholarly and semischolarly nature.
Nonfiction: Subjects include anthropology, history, biography, historic sites, restoration, and ethnohistory pertaining to the American West. Re-publication of rare and out-of-print books. Length: 25,000-100,000 words. Query with SASE.
Recent Title(s): *The Apache Kid*, by de la Gaza (western history).

WESTMINSTER JOHN KNOX PRESS, Presbyterian Publishing Corporation, 100 Witherspoon St., Louisville KY 40202-1396. (502)569-5342. Fax: (502)569-5113. E-mail: cnewman@ctr.pcusa.org. Website: www.wjk.org. Westminster John Knox is affiliated with the Presbyterian Church USA. **Acquisitions:** Stephanie Egnotovich, executive editor; G. Nick Street, editor; Carey Newman, editor. Publishes hardcover and trade paperback originals and reprints. **Publishes 100 titles/year. Receives 1,000 queries per year; 350 mss/year. 25% of books from first-time authors. Pays royalty on retail price.** Publishes book up to 18 months after acceptance of ms. Accepts simultaneous submissions. Book catalog and manuscript guidelines on request.
   O→ "All WJK books have a religious/spiritual angle, but are written for various markets—scholarly, professional, and the general reader."
Nonfiction: Biography, children's juvenile, coffee table book, humor, illustrated book, multimedia, reference, textbook. Subjects include anthropology/archaeology, child guidance/parenting, education, gay/lesbian, history, memoirs, multicultural, philosophy, psychology, religion, sociology, spirituality, women's issues/studies. Submit proposal according to WJK book proposal guidelines.
Fiction: Religious. Fiction must have spiritual/religious connection. Query with SASE or submit proposal package including synopsis, 1-2 sample chapters and SASE.
Recent Title(s): *Revolution and Renewal*, by Tony Campolo (nonfiction); *Sweet Summer*, by William Kelley (fiction).

WESTWIND PRESS, Graphic Arts Center Publishing, P.O. Box 10306, Portland OR 97296-0306. (503)226-2402. Fax: (503)223-1410. **Acquisitions:** Tricia Brown. Estab. 1999. **Publishes 5-7 titles/year. Receives hundreds of submissions/year. 10% of books from first-time authors; 90% from unagented authors. Pays 10-15% royalty on wholesale price. Buys mss outright rarely. Offers advance.** Publishes book an average of 1 year after acceptance. Accepts simultaneous submissions. Responds in 6 months to queries. Book catalog and ms guidelines for 9×12 SAE with 6 first-class stamps.
Nonfiction: Subjects from the western regional states, on nature, travel, cookbooks, Native American culture, adventure, outdoor recreation, sports, the arts and children's books.
Tips: See listing for Alaska Northwest Books.

WHAT'S INSIDE PRESS, P.O. Box 16965, Beverly Hills CA 90209. (800)269-7757. Fax: (800)856-2160. E-mail: marketing@whatsinsidepress.com. Website: www.whatsinsidepress.com. **Acquisitions:** Debbie Kirchen, president of creative affairs (all queries); Cheryl Stratford, acquisitions editor (all initial submissions); Christian Collingwood, editor-in-chief (by request only). Publishes hardcover and trade paperback originals. **Publishes 8-12 titles/year. Receives 250 queries/year. 50% of books from first-time authors; 100% from unagented writers. Pays 8-15% royalty. In addition to author royalty, 10% of net book sales goes to a children's charity of the author's choice. Offers $500 advance.** Publishes book 2 years after acceptance of ms. Accepts simultaneous submissions. Responds in 1 month on queries, 2 months on mss. Book catalog on website. Manuscript guidelines free on request or on website.

O⊸ Publisher of children's and YA fiction and picture books.

Fiction: Juvenile, picture books, young adult. Query with SASE. Submit completed ms.

Recent Title(s): *Kitty in the City*, by Kinsley Foster; *Kitty in the City, Mind Your Manners, S'il Vous Plait*, by Kinsley Foster (children's picture books).

Tips: "Please do not send a résumé of past publication or writing experience. A writer's manuscript should speak for itself. For the writer's convenience, a detailed explanation of submission procedures is available on our website."

WHISPERING COYOTE PRESS

● Whispering Coyote is now an imprint of Charlesbridge.

WHITE MANE BOOKS, White Mane Publishing Company Inc., 63 W. Burd St., P.O. Box 152, Shippensburg PA 17257. (717)532-2237. Fax: (717)532-6110. **Acquisitions:** Martin K. Gordon, president (White Mane Books); Harold Collier, vice president (other imprints). Estab. 1987. Publishes hardcover, and trade paperback originals and reprints. **Publishes 60 titles/year; each imprint publishes 12-18 titles/year. Receives 300 queries and 50 mss/year. 50% of books from first-time authors; 75% from unagented writers. Pays royalty on monies received.** Publishes book 18 months after acceptance of ms. Accepts simultaneous submissions. Responds in 1 month on queries and proposals, 3 months on mss. Book catalog and ms guidelines free.

O⊸ "White Mane Publishing Company, Inc., continues its tradition of publishing the finest military history, regional, religious and children's historical fiction books."

Imprints: Burd Street Press (military history, emphasis on American Civil War); Ragged Edge Press (religious); WMkids (historically based children's fiction).

Nonfiction: Adult/reference, children's/juvenile. Subjects include history, military/war. Query with SASE. Reviews artwork/photos as part of ms package. Send photocopies.

Fiction: Historical, juvenile. Query with SASE.

Recent Title(s): *Trial By Fire: Science, Technology and the Civil War*, by Charles Ross; *Confederate Retaliation: McCausland's 1864 Raid*, by Fritz Haselberger.

⚃ WHITE STONE CIRCLE PRESS, 5132 E. Pima St., Tucson AZ 85712. (877)424-7253. Fax: (520)322-6739. E-mail: wscpress@azstarnet.com. Website: www.blessingway.com. **Acquisitions:** Wayne A. Ewing, Ph.D., publisher (inspirational, devotional). Publishes hardcover originals. **Publishes 1-5 titles/year. Receives 25 queries and 10-15 mss/year. 100% of books from first-time authors; 100% from unagented writers. Pays 10-25% royalty on wholesale price.** Publishes book 18 months after acceptance of ms. Accepts simultaneous submissions. Responds in 2 months on queries, proposals and on mss. Book catalog on website. Manuscript guidelines for #10 SASE.

O⊸ White Stone Circle Press specializes in caregivers' literature.

Nonfiction: Devotional works. Subjects include religion, spirituality. Query with SASE. Reviews artwork/photos as part of ms package. Send photocopies.

Poetry: Interested in poetry of caregivers for future series. Query.

Recent Title(s): *Tears in God's Bottle: Reflections on Alzheimers Caregiving*, by W. Ewing (inspirational).

Tips: Audience is caregivers, hospice workers, clergy and chaplains. "We're interested only in work from the experienced heart; absolutely no schlock; not at all interested in ideological religious writing."

ALBERT WHITMAN AND CO., 6340 Oakton St., Morton Grove IL 60053-2723. (847)581-0033. **Acquisitions:** Kathleen Tucker, editor-in-chief. Estab. 1919. Publishes hardcover originals and paperback reprints. **Publishes 30 titles/year. Receives 5,000 submissions/year. 20% of books from first-time authors; 70% from unagented writers. Pays 10% royalty for novels; 5% for picture books.** Publishes book an average of 18 months after acceptance of ms. Accepts simultaneous submissions. Responds in 5 months. Book catalog for 8×10 SAE and 3 first-class stamps. Manuscript guidelines for #10 SASE.

O⊸ Albert Whitman publishes "good books for children ages 2-12."

Nonfiction: "All books are for ages 2-12." Concept books about special problems children have, easy science, social studies, math. Query.

Fiction: "All books are for ages 2-12." Adventure, ethnic, holiday, fantasy, historical, humor, mystery, picture books and concept books (to help children deal with problems). "We need easy historical fiction and picture books. No young adult and adult books." Submit outline/synopsis and sample chapters (novels) and complete ms (picture books).

Recent Title(s): *I Have a Weird Brother Who Digested a Fly*, by Joan Holub; *No Time for Mother's Day*, by Laurie Halse Anderson.

Tips: "There is a trend toward highly visual books. The writer can most easily sell us strong picture book text that has good illustration possibilities. We sell mostly to libraries, but our bookstore sales are growing."

WHITSTON PUBLISHING CO., INC., 1717 Central Ave., Suite 201, Albany NY 12205. Phone/fax: (518)452-1900. Fax: (518)452-1777. E-mail: whitson@capital.net. Website: www.whitston.com. **Acquisitions:** Michael Laddin, editorial director. Estab. 1969. Publishes hardcover originals. **Averages 12 titles/year. Receives 100 submissions/year. 50% of books from first-time authors; 100% from unagented writers. Pays 10% royalty on price of book (wholesale or retail) after sale of 500 copies.** Publishes book 1 year after acceptance. Responds in 6 months.

O⊸ Whitston focuses on Modern American and English literature and bibliographies.

Nonfiction: "We publish scholarly and critical books in the humanities, primarily pertaining to literature. We also publish bibliographies and indexes. We are interested in scholarly monographs and collections of essays." Query. Reviews artwork/photos as part of ms package.

Recent Title(s): *Understanding Toni Morrison's Beloved and Sula*, edited by Solomon and Marla Iyasere (nonfiction); *The Living Underground: Prose from America's Finest Unheralded Writers, 1970-1999*, edited by Hugh Fox (nonfiction).

MARKUS WIENER PUBLISHERS INC., 231 Nassau St., Princeton NJ 08542. (609)971-1141. **Acquisitions:** Shelley Frisch, editor-in-chief. Estab. 1981. Publishes hardcover originals and trade paperback originals and reprints. **Publishes 20-25 titles/year; imprint publishes 5 titles/year. Receives 50-150 queries and 50 mss/year. Pays 10% royalty on net sales.** Publishes book 1 year after acceptance. Responds in 2 months on queries and proposals. Book catalog free.

O→ Markus Wiener publishes textbooks in history subjects and regional world history.

Imprint(s): Princeton Series on the Middle East, Topics in World History.

Nonfiction: Textbook. History subjects, Caribbean studies, Middle East, Africa.

Recent Title(s): *Beauty in Arab Culture* (Middle East studies).

WILDCAT CANYON PRESS, Circulus Publishing Group, Inc., 2716 Ninth St., Berkeley CA 94710. (510)848-3600. Fax: (510)848-1326. E-mail: info@wildcatcanyon.com. Website: www.wildcatcanyon.com. **Acquisitions:** Tamara Traeder, publisher (relationships/gift books); Roy M. Carlisle, editorial director (psychology/relationships). Publishes trade paperback originals. **Publishes 15-20 titles/year. Receives 500 queries and 300 mss/year. Pays 10-16% royalty on wholesale price. Offers $1,000-3,000 advance.** Publishes book 9 months after acceptance of ms. Accepts simultaneous submissions. Responds in 3 months. Book catalog and ms guidelines free. Now accepting mss on behalf of Pagemill Press.

O→ Wildcat Canyon Press publishes books primarily for women that embrace and enhance such relationship subjects as friendship, spirituality, women's issues, and home and family, all with a focus on self-help and personal growth.

Nonfiction: Gift book, self-help. Subjects include psychology, women's issues/women's studies, relationships. Query with proposal package, including outline and SASE. Reviews artwork/photos as part of ms package. Send photocopies.

Recent Title(s): *40 over 40: 40 Things Every Woman Over 40 Needs to Know About Getting Dressed*, by Brenda Kinsel (fashion); *And What Do You Do? When Women Choose to Stay Home*, by Loretta Kaufman and Mary Quigley (women's issues/self-help).

Tips: "As a proactive publishing house we commission most of our titles and we are primarily interested in solicited queries and proposals."

WILDERNESS PRESS, 1200 Fifth St., Berkley CA 94710. (510)558-1666. Fax: (510)558-1696. E-mail: mail@wildernesspress.com. Website: www.wildernesspress.com. **Acquisitions:** Caroline Winnett, publisher. Mike Jones, associate publisher. Estab. 1967. Publishes paperback originals. **Publishes 10 titles/year. Receives 150 submissions/year. 20% of books from first-time authors; 95% from unagented writers. Pays 8-10% royalty on retail price. Offers $1,000 average advance.** Publishes book 8 months after acceptance of ms. Responds in 1 month. Book catalog and proposal guidelines available via website.

O→ "We seek to publish the most accurate, reliable and useful outdoor books and maps for self-propelled outdoor activities for hikers, kayakers, skiers, snowshoers, backpackers."

Nonfiction: "We publish books about the outdoors. Most are trail guides for hikers and backpackers, but we also publish how-to books about the outdoors. The manuscript must be accurate. The author must research an area in person. If writing a trail guide, you must walk all the trails in the area your book is about. Outlook must be strongly conservationist. Style must be appropriate for a highly literate audience." Request proposal guidelines.

Recent Title(s): *Day Hikes on the Pacific Coast Trail: California*, by George and Patricia Semb.

JOHN WILEY & SONS, INC., 605 Third Ave., New York NY 10158. Website: www.wiley.com. Publisher: G. Helferich. **Acquisitions:** Editorial Department. Estab. 1807. Publishes hardcover originals, trade paperback originals and reprints. **Pays "competitive royalty rates."** Accepts simultaneous submissions. Book catalog and ms guidelines free with #10 SASE.

O→ "The General Interest group publishes books for the consumer market."

Nonfiction: Biography, children's/juvenile, reference, self-help, narrative nonfiction. Subjects include parenting, health, history, popular science, African American interest. Query.

Recent Title(s): *Carl Sagan*, by Keay Davidson; *The Carbohydrate Addict's Cookbook*, by Dr. Richard F. Heller and Dr. Rachel F. Heller.

■ **WILLIAMSON PUBLISHING CO.**, P.O. Box 185, Church Hill Rd., Charlotte VT 05445. Website: www.williamsonbooks.com. **Acquisitions:** Susan Williamson, editorial director. Estab. 1983. Publishes trade paperback originals. **Publishes 15 titles/year. Receives 1,000 queries/year. 75% of books from first-time authors; 90% from unagented writers. Pays royalty or flat fee on retail price. Offers standard advance.** Publishes book 18 months after acceptance. Accepts simultaneous submissions, but prefers 6 months exclusivity. Responds in 4 months with SASE. Book catalog for 8½×11 SAE with 4 first-class stamps. Manuscript guidelines on website.

O→ "Our mission is to help every child fulfull his/her potential and experience personal growth through active learning. We want 'our kids' to be able to work toward a culturally rich, ethnically diverse, peaceful nation and global community." Currently emphasizing creataive approaches to specific areas of science, history, cultural experiences, diversity.

Nonfiction: Children's creative learning books on subjects ranging from science, art, history, geography, to early learning skills. Adult books include parenting, careers, psychology, cookbook, how-to, self-help. "Williamson has four very successful children's book series: *Little Hands®* (ages 2-6), *Kids Can!®* (ages 6-12), *Tales Alive®* (folktales plus activities, age 4-10) and *Kaleidoscope Kids®* (96-page, single subject, ages 7-12). They must incorporate learning through doing. *No picture books, story books, or fiction please!* Please don't call concerning your submission. It never helps your review, and it takes too much of our time. With an SASE, you'll hear from us." Submit outline, 2-3 sample chapters and SASE.

● Williamson's big success is its *Kids Can!®* and *Kaleidoscope Kids®*. *Pyramids, Knights & Castles* and *Mexico* were all chosen American Bookseller Pick of the Lists; *Pyramids* and *Knights & Castles* were selected as Children's Book Council Notable Books.

Recent Title(s): *Geology Rocks!*, by Cindy Blobaum; *ArtStarts for Little Hands*, by Judy Press.

Tips: "Our children's books are used by kids, their parents, and educators. They encourage self-discovery, creativity and personal growth. Our books are based on the philosophy that children learn best by doing, by being involved. Our authors need to be excited about their subject area and equally important, excited about kids."

WILLOW CREEK PRESS, P.O. Box 147, 9931 Highway 70 W., Minocqua WI 54548. (715)358-7010. Fax: (715)358-2807. E-mail: andread@newnorth.net. Website: www.willowcreekpress.com. **Acquisitions:** Andrea Donner, managing editor. Estab. 1986. Publishes hardcover and trade paperback originals and reprints. **Publishes 25 titles/year. Receives 400 queries and 150 mss/year. 15% of books from first-time authors; 50% from unagented writers. Pays 6-15% royalty on wholesale price. Offers $2,000-5,000 advance.** Publishes book 10 months after acceptance of ms. Accepts simultaneous submissions. Responds in 2 months.

○➔ "We specialize in nature, outdoor, and sporting topics, including gardening, wildlife and animal books. Pets, cookbooks, and a few humor books and essays round out our titles." Currently emphasizing pets, outdoor sports, hunting, fishing, gardening, cookbooks. De-emphasizing fiction, children's books.

Nonfiction: Coffee table book, cookbook, how-to, humor, illustrated book. Subjects include wildlife, pets, cooking/foods/nutrition, gardening, hobbies, nature/environment, photography, recreation, sports. Submit outline and 1 sample chapter with SASE for return of materials. Reviews artwork/photos as part of ms package. Send photocopies.

Fiction: Adventure, humor, short story collections, essays. Submit synopsis and 2 sample chapters.

Recent Title(s): *What Dogs Teach Us*, by Glenn Dromgoole; *North America's Greatest Fishing Lodges*, by John Ross.

[N] WILLOWGATE PRESS, P.O. Box 6529, Holliston MA 01746. (508)429-8774. E-mail: willowgatepress@yahoo.com. Website: www.willowgatepress.com. **Acquisitions:** Robert Tolins, editor. Publishes trade paperback and mass market paperback originals. **Publishes 3-5 titles/year. 50% of books from first-time authors; 100% from unagented writers. Pays 5-15% royalty on retail price. Offers $1,000-2,500 advance.** Publishes book 6 months after acceptance of ms. Accepts simultaneous submissions. Responds in 2 weeks on queries, 2 months on mss. Book catalog and manuscript guidelines on website.

○➔ Willowgate is a small, independent press established for the purpose of publishing good writing of the sort that the public is currently not receiving. Fundamentally, we seek to provide quality book length fiction in all categories, and to see our titles widely promoted and kept available for longer than the brief shelf life allowed by the traditional houses. We believe that there is a need for a press whose goal is to publish quality works by new and established writers, without regard for the "blockbuster" mentality that presently prevents more established houses from taking on such projects.

Fiction: Confession, erotica, ethnic, experimental, fantasy, feminist, gay/lesbian, gothic, hi-Lol, historical, horror, humor, literary, mainstream/contemporary, military/war, multicultural, multimedia, mystery, occult, regional, romance, science fiction, short story collections, sports. "Submit a complete, edited, revised, polished manuscript." Query with SASE or submit proposal package, including synopsis and chapter outline, first 10 pages and 10 consecutive pages of the author's choosing.

Tips: "If a manuscript is accepted for publication, we will make every effort to avoid lengthy delays in bringing the product to market. The writer will be given a voice in all aspects of publishing, promotion, advertising and marketing, including cover art, copy, promotional forums, etc. The writer will be expected to be an active and enthusiastic participant in all stages of the publication process. We hope to attract the finest writers of contemporary fiction and to help generate similar enthusiasm in them and in their readers."

◤◢ WILSHIRE BOOK CO., 12015 Sherman Rd., North Hollywood CA 91605-3781. (818)765-8579. Fax: (818)765-2922. E-mail: mpowers@mpowers.com. Website: www.mpowers.com. Publisher: Melvin Powers. **Acquisitions:** Marcia Grad, senior editor. Estab. 1947. Publishes trade paperback originals and reprints. **Publishes 25 titles/year. Receives 3,000 submissions/year. 80% of books from first-time authors; 75% from unagented writers. Pays standard royalty.** Publishes book 6 months after acceptance of ms. Responds in 2 months. Welcomes telephone calls to discuss mss or book concepts.

○➔ "We need personal stories about 1,000 words that describe significant or profound events that elicited strong emotions. Stories should be compelling accounts that included your thoughts and feelings."

Nonfiction: Self-help, motivation/inspiration/spiritual, psychology, recovery, how-to. Subjects include personal success, entrepreneurship, marketing on the Internet, mail order, horsemanship. Minimum 60,000 words. Requires detailed chapter outline, 3 sample chapters and SASE. Accepts queries and complete mss. Reviews artwork/photos as part of ms package. Send photocopies.

Fiction: Allegories that teach principles of psychological/spiritual growth or offer guidance in living. Minimum 30,000 words. Requires synopsis, 3 sample chapters and SASE. Accepts complete mss.

Recent Title(s): *Guide to Rational Living*, by Albert Ellis, Ph.D. and Robert Harper, Ph.D.; *The Princess Who Believed in Fairy Tales*, by Marcia Grad.

Tips: "We are vitally interested in all new material we receive. Just as you hopefully submit your manuscript for publication, we hopefully read every one submitted, searching for those that we believe will be successful in the marketplace. Writing and publishing must be a team effort. We need you to write what we can sell. We suggest that you read the successful books mentioned above or others that are similar to the manuscript you want to write. Analyze them to discover what elements make them winners. Duplicate those elements in your own style, using a creative new approach and fresh material, and you will have written a book we can catapult onto the bestseller list."

[N] WINDWARD PUBLISHING, INC., P.O. Box 371005, Miami FL 33137-1005. (305)576-6232. E-mail: windwar dfl@aol.com. **Acquisitions:** Jack Zinzow, vice president. Estab. 1973. Publishes trade paperback originals. **Publishes 6 titles/year. Receives 50 queries and 10 mss/year. 35% of books from first-time authors; 100% from unagented writers. Pays 10% royalty on wholesale price.** Publishes book 14 months after acceptance of ms. Accepts simultaneous submissions. Responds in 2 weeks. *Writer's Market* recommends allowing 2 months for reply.

    ○➔ Windward publishes illustrated natural history and recreation books.

Nonfiction: Illustrated books, natural history, handbooks. Subjects include agriculture/horticulture, animals, gardening, nature/environment, recreation (fishing, boating, diving, camping), science. Query with SASE. Reviews artwork/photos as part of the ms package.

Recent Title(s): *Mammals of Florida.*

WINSLOW PRESS, 115 E. 23rd St., 10th Floor, New York NY 10010. (212)254-2025. Fax: (212)254-2410. E-mail: winslow@winslowpress.com. Website: www.winslowpress.com. Publishes hardcover originals. **Publishes 20 titles/ year. Receives 2,000 mss/year. 20% of books from first-time authors; 30% from unagented writers. Pays royalty. Offers advance.** Accepts simultaneous submissions. Responds in 4 months. Book catalog for 8×10 SAE with 75¢ first-class stamps.

Nonfiction: Children's/juvenile. Query with SASE. Reviews artwork/photos as part of ms package. Send photocopies.

Fiction: Children's/juvenile only.

Poetry: Children's/juvenile only.

Tips: "We publish books for children, from pre-k to young adult. We have an innovative Web Program which all of our books are a part of."

WISDOM PUBLICATIONS, 199 Elm St., Somerville MA 02144. (617)776-7416, ext. 25. Fax: (617)776-7841. E-mail: editorial@wisdompubs.org. Website: www.widsompubs.org. Publisher: Timothy McNeill. **Acquisitions:** E. Gene Smith, acquisitions editor. Estab. 1976. Publishes hardcover originals, trade paperback originals and reprints. **Publishes 12-15 titles/year. Receives 240 queries/year. 50% of books from first-time authors; 95% from unagented writers. Pays 4-8% royalty on wholesale price (net).** Publishes book within 2 years after acceptance of ms. Book catalog and ms guidelines free on website.

    ○➔ Wisdom Publications is dedicated to making available authentic Buddhist works for the benefit of all. "We publish translations, commentaries and teachings of past and contemporary Buddhist masters and original works by leading Buddhist scholars." Currently emphasizing popular applied Buddhism, scholarly titles.

Nonfiction: Subjects include philosophy (Buddhist or comparative Buddhist/Western), Buddhism, Buddhist texts and Tibet. Query with SASE. Reviews artwork/photos as part of ms package. Send photocopies.

Poetry: Buddhist. Query with SASE.

Recent Title(s): *Engaged Buddhism in the West*, by Christopher S. Queen.

Tips: "We are basically a publisher of Buddhist books—all schools and traditions of Buddhism. Please see our catalog or our website *before* you send anything to us to get a sense of what we publish."

WIZARDS OF THE COAST, P.O. Box 707, Renton WA 98057-0707. (425)226-6500. Website: www.wizards.com. Executive Editor: Mary Kirchoff. **Acquisitions:** Novel Submissions Editor. Publishes hardcover and trade paperback originals and trade paperback reprints. **Publishes 50-60 titles/year. Receives 600 queries and 300 mss/year. 25% of books from first-time authors; 35% from unagented authors. Pays 4-8% royalty on retail price. Offers $4,000-6,000 average advance.** Publishes book 1 year after acceptance of ms. Accepts simultaneous submissions. Responds in 4 months on queries. Guidelines for #10 SASE.

    ○➔ TSR publishes science fiction and fantasy titles. Currently emphasizing solid fantasy writers. De-emphasizing gothic fiction.

Imprint(s): Dragonlance® Books; Forgotten Realms® Books; Greyhawk Novels; Magic: The Gathering® Books; Legend of the Five Rings Novels; Star*Drive Books.

Nonfiction: "All of our nonfiction books are generated inhouse."

Fiction: Fantasy, science fiction, short story collections. "We currently publish only work-for-hire novels set in our trademarked worlds. No violent or gory fantasy or science fiction." Request guidelines, then query with outline/synopsis and 3 sample chapters.

Recent Title(s): *Dragons of a Fallen Sun*, by Margaret Weis and Tracy Hickman.

Tips: "Our audience largely is comprised of highly imaginative 12-30 year-old males."

WOODBINE HOUSE, 6510 Bells Mill Rd., Bethesda MD 20817. (301)897-3570. Fax: (301)897-5838. E-mail: info@woodbinehouse.com. **Acquisitions**: Susan Stokes, editor. Estab. 1985. Publishes hardcover and trade paperback originals and reprints. **Publishes 10 titles/year. 90% of books from unagented writers. Pays 10-12% royalty.** Publishes book 18 months after acceptance of ms. Accepts simultaneous submissions. Responds in 2 months. Book catalog and ms guidelines for 6×9 SAE with 3 first-class stamps.

    ○┱ Woodbine House publishes books for or about individuals with disabilities to help those individuals and their families live fulfilling and satisfying lives in their communities.

Nonfiction: Publishes books for and about children and adults with disabilities. No personal accounts or general parenting guides. Submit outline and 3 sample chapters with SASE. Reviews artwork/photos as part of ms package.

Fiction: Children's picture books. Submit entire ms with SASE.

Recent Title(s): *Fine Motor Skills in Children with Down Syndrome*, by Maryanne Bruni.

Tips: "Do not send us a proposal on the basis of this description. Examine our catalog and a couple of our books to make sure you are on the right track. Put some thought into how your book could be marketed (aside from in bookstores). Keep cover letters concise and to the point; if it's a subject that interests us, we'll ask to see more."

WOODHOLME HOUSE PUBLISHERS, 131 Village Square 1, Village of Crose Keys, Baltimore MD 21210. (410)532-5018. Fax: (410)532-9741. E-mail: info@woodholmehouse.com. **Acquisitions**: Gregg A. Wilhelm, director. Estab. 1996. Publishes hardcover and trade paperback originals. **Publishes 5 titles/year. Receives 100 queries and 50 mss/year. 50% of books from first-time authors; 80% from unagented writers. Pays 5-15% royalty on retail price.** Publishes book 9 months after acceptance of ms. Accepts simultaneous submissions. Responds in 1 month on queries, 3 months on mss. Manuscript guidelines for #10 SASE.

    ○┱ Woodholme is a regional-interest publisher (mid-Atlantic/Chesapeake Bay area) covering a variety of genres.

Nonfiction: Biography, guidebooks, history, memoir. Regional subjects. Submit proposal package, including cover letter, outline/synopsis, author bio and SASE. Reviews artwork/photos as part of ms package. Send photocopies.

Fiction: Short story collections, regional interest. "Setting/people/place should have regional flavor. We are impressed with work that possesses a strong sense of place." Query or submit synopsis with 1 sample chapter and SASE.

Recent Title(s): *Maryland Lost and Found . . . Again!*, by Eugene L. Meyer.

Tips: "Audience is interested in the Chesapeake Bay and Mid-Atlantic area, radiating out from Baltimore, Maryland."

▓N▓ WOODLAND PUBLISHING INC., P.O. Box 160, Pleasant Grove UT 84062. (801)785-8100. Fax: (801)785-8511. Website: www.woodlandpublishing.com. Publisher: Trent Tenney. **Acquisitions**: Cord Udall, editor. Estab. 1974. Publishes perfect bound and trade paperback originals. **Publishes 20 titles/year. Receives 100 queries and 60 mss/year. 50% of books from first-time authors; 100% from unagented writers.** Publishes book 6 months after acceptance of ms. Accepts simultaneous submissions. Responds in 1 month on proposals. *Writer's Market* recommends allowing 2 months for reply. Book catalog and ms guidelines available via website or with SASE.

    ○┱ "Our readers are interested in herbs and other natural health topics. Most of our books are sold through health food stores."

Nonfiction: Health/alternative medicine subjects. Query.

Recent Title(s): *Soy Smart Health*, by Neil Soloman, M.D.

WORDWARE PUBLISHING, INC., 2320 Los Rios Blvd., Plano TX 75074. (972)423-0090. Fax: (972)881-9147. E-mail: jhill@wordware.com. Website: www.wordware.com. President: Russell A. Stultz. **Acquisitions:** J. Hill Parkleyter, publisher. Estab. 1983. Publishes trade paperback and mass market paperback originals. **Publishes 50-60 titles/year. Receives 100-150 queries and 50-75 mss/year. 40% of books from first-time authors; 95% from unagented writers. Pays 8% royalty on wholesale price. Offers advance.** Publishes book 6 months after acceptance of ms. Accepts simultaneous submissions. Responds in 2 months. Book catalog and ms guidelines free.

    ○┱ Wordware publishes computer/electronics books covering a broad range of technologies for professional programmers and developers.

Imprint(s): Republic of Texas Press.

Nonfiction: Reference, technical, textbook. Subjects include computers, electronics. "Wordware publishes advanced titles for developers and professional programmers." Submit proposal package, including table of contents, 2 sample chapters, target audience summation, competing books.

Recent Title(s): *Developers Guide to Delphi Troubleshooting*, by Clay Shannon.

◤◣ WORKMAN PUBLISHING CO., 708 Broadway, New York NY 10003. (212)254-5900. Fax: (212)254-8098. Website: www.workman.com. **Acquisitions:** Sally Kovalchik, editor-in-chief (gardening, popular reference, humor); Suzanne Rafer, executive editor (cookbook, child care, parenting, teen interest); Ruth Sullivan, senior editor (humor, fashion, health); Liz Carey, senior editor (crafts, children, humor). Estab. 1967. Publishes hardcover and trade paperback originals. **Publishes 40 titles/year. Receives thousands of queries/year. Open to first-time authors. Pays variable royalty on retail price. Advance varies.** Publishes book 1 year after acceptance of ms. Accepts simultaneous submissions. Responds in 5 months. Book catalog free.

> ☞ "We are a trade paperback house specializing in a wide range of popular nonfiction. We publish no adult fiction and very little children's fiction. We also publish a full range of full color wall and Page-A-Day® calendars."

Imprint(s): Algonquin Books of Chapel Hill, Artisan.
Nonfiction: Cookbooks, gift books, how-to, humor. Subjects include child guidance/parenting, gardening, health/medicine, sports, travel. Query with SASE first for guidelines. Reviews artwork/photos as part of ms package "if relevant to project. Don't send anything you can't afford to lose. No phone calls please. No fax or e-mail submissions."
Recent Title(s): *Antiques Roadshow Primer*, by Carol Prisant; *The Cake Mix Doctor*, by Anne Byrn.

WRITE WAY PUBLISHING, P.O. Box 441278, Aurora CO 80044. (303)617-0497. Fax: (303)617-1440. E-mail: staff@writewaypub.com. Website: www.writewaypub.com. **Acquisitions:** Dorrie O'Brien, owner/editor. Estab. 1993. Publishes hardcover and trade paperback originals. **Publishes 10-15 titles/year. Receives 1,000 queries and 350 mss/year. 50% of books from first-time authors; 5% from unagented writers. Pays 8-10% royalty on wholesale price. No advance.** Publishes book within 3 years after acceptance of ms. Accepts simultaneous submissions. Responds in 1 month on queries; 9 months on mss. Book brochure and ms guidelines for SASE.

> ☞ Write Way is a fiction-only small press concentrating on mysteries, soft science fiction and fairy tale/fantasys. Currently emphasizing adult (whodunit?) mysteries/science fiction/fantasy. De-emphasizing suspense, spy, adventure, literature, romance et al.

Fiction: Fantasy, horror, mystery, science fiction. Query with short synopsis, first 1-2 chapters and postage with proper-sized box or envelope. "We only consider completed works."
Recent Title(s): *The Music Box Mysteries*, by Larry Karp; *The Deadline*, by Ron Franscell.
Tips: "We find that lengthy outlines and/or synopsis are unnecessary and much too time-consuming for our editors to read. We prefer a very short plot review and one to two chapters to get a feel for the writer's style. If we like what we read, then we'll ask for the whole manuscript."

WRITER'S DIGEST BOOKS, F&W Publications, 1507 Dana Ave., Cincinnati OH 45207. (513)531-2690. Fax: (513)531-7107. Website: www.writersdigest.com. Editorial Director: Jack Heffron. **Acquisitions:** Acquisitions Coordinator. Estab. 1920. Publishes hardcover and paperback originals. **Publishes 28 titles/year. Receives 500 queries and 100 mss/year. No books from first-time authors; 20% unagented writers. Pays 10-20% royalty on net receipts. Offers average advance of $5,000 and up.** Accepts simultaneous submissions, if so noted. Publishes book 18 months after acceptance of ms. Responds in 2 months. Book catalog for 9×12 SAE with 6 first-class stamps.

> ☞ Writer's Digest is the premiere source for books about writing, with instructional and reference books for writers that concentrate on the creative technique and craft of writing rather than the marketing of writing.

Imprint: Walking Stick (journaling and self-discovery).
Nonfiction: Instructional, reference and creativity books for writers. "Our instruction books stress results and how specifically to achieve them. Should be well-researched, yet lively and readable. Our books concentrate on writing techniques over marketing techniques. We do *not* want to see books telling readers how to crack specific nonfiction markets: *Writing for the Computer Market* or *Writing for Trade Publications*, for instance. Concentrate on broader writing topics. We are continuing to grow our line of reference books for writers with our Howdunit series, and *A Writer's Guide to Everyday Life* series. References must be usable, accessible, and, of course, accurate." Query or submit outline and sample chapters with SASE. "Be prepared to explain how the proposed book differs from existing books on the subject." *No fiction or poetry.*
Recent Title(s): *Guerilla Marketing for Writers*, by Jay Conrad Levinson and Michael Larsen.
Tips: "Writer's Digest Books also publishes instructional books for photographers and songwriters, but the main thrust is on writing books. The same philosophy applies to songwriting and photography books: they must instruct about the creative craft, as opposed to instructing about marketing."

YALE UNIVERSITY PRESS, 302 Temple St., New Haven CT 06520. (203)432-0960. Fax: (203)432-0948. Website: www.yale.edu/yup. **Acquisitions:** Jonathan Brent, editorial director (literature, philosophy, poetry, Annals of Communism, Cold War studies); Susan C. Arellano (behavioral and social sciences, education); Jean E. Thomson Black (science and medicine); Otto Bohlmann (scholarly eidtions); John S. Covell (economics, law, political science); Robert T. Flynn (reference books); Charles Grench (anthropology, history, Judaic studies, religion, women's studies); Henning Gutmann (economics, business, political science, law); Harry Haskell (archaeology, classics, music and performing arts); Lara Heimert (English-language literary studies); Judy Metro (art and architectural history, geography, landscape studies); Mary Jane Peluso (languages); Nick Raposo (Yale Series of Younger Poets). Estab. 1908. Publishes hardcover and trade paperback originals. **Publishes 225 titles/year. Receives 8,000 queries and 400 mss/year. 15% of books from first-time authors; 85% from unagented writers. Pays 0-15% royalty on net price. Offers $500-50,000 advance (based on expected sales).** Publishes book 1 year after acceptance of ms. Accepts simultaneous submissions, if so noted. Responds in 1 month on queries, 2 months on proposals, 3 months on mss. Book catalog and ms guidelines for #10 SASE.

> ☞ Yale University Press publishes scholarly and general interest books.

Nonfiction: Biography, illustrated book, reference, textbook, scholarly works. Subjects include Americana, anthropology/archaeology, art/architecture, economics, education, history, language/literature, medicine, military/war, music/

dance, philosophy, psychology, religion, science, sociology, women's issues/studies. "Our nonfiction has to be at a very high level. Most of our books are written by professors or journalists, with a high level of expertise." Query by letter with SASE. "We'll ask if we want to see more. No unsolicited manuscripts. We won't return them." Reviews artwork/photos as part of ms package. Send photocopies, not originals.

Poetry: Publishes 1 book each year. Submit complete ms to Yale Series of Younger Poets Competition. Open to poets under 40 who have not had a book previously published. Submit ms of 48-64 pages in February. Entry fee: $15. Send SASE for rules and guidelines.

Recent Title(s): *Bill Evans: How My Heart Sings*, by Peter Pettinger.

YMAA PUBLICATION CENTER, 4354 Washington St., Roslindale MA 02131. (800)669-8892 or (617)323-7215. Fax: (617)323-7417. E-mail: ymaa@aol.com. Website: www.ymaa.com. **Acquisitions:** David Ripianzi, director. Estab. 1982. Publishes hardcover and trade paperback originals and reprints. **Publishes 10 titles/year. Pays royalty on retail price. No advance.** Responds in 3 months on proposals.

> O— "YMAA publishes books on Chinese Chi Kung (Qigong), Taijiquan and Asian martial arts. Our focus is expanding to include books on healing, wellness, meditation and subjects related to Asian culture and medicine."

Nonfiction: "We are most interested in Asian martial arts, Chinese medicine and Chinese Qigong. We publish Eastern thought, health, meditation, massage and East/West synthesis. We no longer publish or solicit books for children. We also produce instructional videos to accompany our books on traditional Chinese martial arts, meditation, massage and Chi Kung." Send proposal with outline, 1 sample chapter and SASE.

Recent Title(s): *Complete Cardiokickboxing*, by Tom Seabourne, Ph.D.

Tips: "If you are submitting fitness or health-related material, please refer to an Asian tradition."

ZEBRA BOOKS, Kensington, 850 Third Ave., 16th Floor, New York NY 10022. (212)407-1500. Website: www.kensingtonbooks.com. **Acquisitions**: Ann Lafarge, editor; Kate Duffy, senior editor (historical, regency, romance); John Scognamiglio, senior editor (romance, mystery, thrillers, pop culture); Hillary Sares (Precious Gem romances). Publishes hardcover originals, trade paperback and mass market paperback originals and reprints. **Publishes 140-170 titles/year. 5% of books from first-time authors; 30% from unagented writers. Pays variable royalty and advance.** Publishes book 18 months after acceptance of ms. Accepts simultaneous submissions. Responds in 1 month on queries, in 3 months on mss. Book catalog for #10 SASE.

> O— Zebra Books is dedicated to women's fiction, which includes, but is not limited to romance.

Fiction: Romance, women's fiction. Query with synopsis and SASE. *No unsolicited submissions.*

ZOLAND BOOKS, INC., 384 Huron Ave., Cambridge MA 02138. (617)864-6252. Fax: (617)661-4998. **Acquisitions:** Roland Pease, Jr., publisher/editor. Estab. 1987. Publishes hardcover and trade paperback originals. **Publishes 14 titles/year. Receives 700 submissions/year. 15% of books from first-time authors; 40% from unagented writers. Pays 7½% royalty on retail price.** Publishes book 18 months after acceptance of ms. Responds in 3 months. Book catalog for 6½×9½ SAE with 2 first-class stamps.

> O— Zoland Books is an independent publishing company producing fiction, poetry and art books of literary interest.

Nonfiction: Biography, art book. Subjects include art/architecture, language/literature, nature/environment, photography, regional, translation, travel, women's issues/studies. Query. Reviews artwork/photos as part of ms package.

Fiction: Literary, short story collections. Submit complete ms. *Writer's Market* recommends querying with SASE first.

Recent Title(s): *Glorie*, by Caryn James; *In the Pond*, by Ha Jin; *Camelot*, by Caryl Rivers.

Tips: "We are most likely to publish books which provide original, thought-provoking ideas, books which will captivate the reader and are evocative."

ZONDERVAN PUBLISHING HOUSE, HarperCollins Publishers, 5300 Patterson Ave. SE, Grand Rapids MI 49530-0002. (616)698-6900. E-mail: zpub@zph.com. Website: www.zondervan.com. Publisher: Scott Bolinder. **Acquisitions:** Manuscript Review Editor. Estab. 1931. Publishes hardcover and trade paperback originals and reprints. **Publishes 120 titles/year. Receives 3,000 submissions/year. 10% of books from first-time authors; 60% from unagented writers. Pays 14% royalty on net amount received on sales of cloth and softcover trade editions; 12% royalty on net amount received on sales of mass market paperbacks. Offers variable advance.** Responds in 3 months on proposals. SASE required. Guidelines for #10 SASE. Rarely publishes unsolicited mss.

> O— "Our mission is to be the leading Christian communications company meeting the needs of people with resources that glorify Jesus Christ and promote biblical principles."

Imprint(s): Zonderkidz.

Nonfiction and Fiction: Biography, autobiography, self-help, devotional, contemporary issues, Christian living, Bible study resources, references for lay audience; some adult fiction; youth and children's ministry, teens and children. Academic and Professional Books: college and seminary textbooks (biblical studies, theology, church history); preaching, counseling, discipleship, worship, and church renewal for pastors, professionals and lay leaders in ministry; theological and biblical reference books. All from religious perspective (evangelical). Submit outline/synopsis, 1 sample chapter, and SASE for return of materials.

Recent Title(s): *Soul Salsa*, by Leonard Sweet (nonfiction); *Blood of Heaven*, by Bill Myers (fiction).

Canadian & International Book Publishers

Canadian book publishers share the same mission as their U.S. counterparts—publishing timely books on subjects of concern and interest to a targetable audience. Most of the publishers listed in this section, however, differ from U.S. publishers in that their needs tend toward subjects that are specifically Canadian or intended for a Canadian audience. Some are interested in submissions from Canadian writers only. There are many regional Canadian publishers that concentrate on region-specific subjects, and many Quebec publishers will consider only works in French.

U.S. writers hoping to do business with Canadian publishers should take pains to find out as much about their intended markets as possible. The listings will inform you about what kinds of books the companies publish and tell you whether they are open to receiving submissions from nonCanadians. To further target your markets and see very specific examples of the books they are publishing, send for catalogs from publishers or check their websites.

There has always been more government subsidy of publishing in Canada than in the U.S. However, with continued cuts in such subsidies, government support is on the decline. There are a few author-subsidy publishers in Canada and writers should proceed with caution when they are made this offer.

Publishers offering author-subsidy arrangements (sometimes referred to as "joint venture," "co-publishing" or "cooperative publishing") are not listed in *Writer's Market*. If one of the publishers in this section offers you an author-subsidy arrangement or asks you to pay for all or part of the cost of any aspect of publishing (printing, marketing, etc.) or asks you to guarantee the purchase of a number of books yourself, please let us know about that company immediately.

Despite a healthy book publishing industry, Canada is still dominated by publishers from the U.S. Two out of every three books found in Canadian bookstores are published in the U.S. These odds have made some Canadian publishers even more determined to concentrate on Canadian authors and subjects. Canadian publishers that accept manuscripts only from Canadian authors are indicated by the ◪ symbol. Writers interested in additional Canadian book publishing markets should consult *Literary Market Place* (R.R. Bowker & Co.), and *The Canadian Writer's Market* (McClelland & Stewart).

INTERNATIONAL MAIL

U.S. postage stamps are useless on mailings originating outside of the U.S. When enclosing a self-addressed envelope for return of your query or manuscript from a publisher outside the U.S., you must include International Reply Coupons (IRCs) or postage stamps from that country. Canadian stamps are sold online at http://www.canadapost.ca. IRCs are available at your local post office and can be redeemed for stamps of any country. You can cut a substantial portion of your international mailing expenses by sending disposable proposals and manuscripts (i.e., photocopies or computer printouts which the recipient can recycle if she is not interested), instead of paying postage for the return of rejected material. Please note that the cost for items such as catalogs is expressed in the currency of the country in which the publisher is located.

For a list of publishers according to their subjects of interest, see the nonfiction and fiction

sections of the Book Publishers Subject Index. Information on book publishers and producers listed in the previous edition of *Writer's Market* but not included in this edition can be found in the General Index.

THE ALTHOUSE PRESS, University of Western Ontario, Faculty of Education, 1137 Western Rd., London, Ontario N6G 1G7 Canada. (519)661-2096. Fax: (519)661-3833. E-mail: press@julian.uwo.ca. Website: www.uwo.ca./edu/press. Director: Dr. David Radcliffe. **Acquisitions:** Katherine Butson, editorial assistant. Publishes trade paperback originals and reprints. **Publishes 1-5 titles/year. Receives 30 queries and 19 mss/year. 50% of books from first-time authors; 100% of books from unagented writers. Pays 10% royalty. Offers $300 advance.** Accepts simultaneous submissions. Publishes book 6 months after acceptance. Responds in 1 month to queries, 4 months to mss. Book catalog and manuscript guidelines free.

    Oₐ "The Althouse Press publishes both scholarly research monographs in education, and professional books and materials for educators in elementary schools, secondary schools and faculties of education." De-emphasizing curricular or instructional materials intended for use by elementary or secondary school students.

Nonfiction: Education (scholarly) subjects. Query. "Do not send incomplete manuscripts that are only marginally appropriate to our market and limited mandate." Reviews artwork/photos as part of ms package. Send photocopies.

Recent Title(s): *Sexual Idology and Schooling: Towards Democratic Sexuality Education*, by Alexander McKay; *For the Love of Teaching*, by Brent Kilbourn.

Tips: Audience is practicing teachers and graduate education students.

ⓝ ANNICK PRESS LTD., 15 Patricia Ave., Toronto, Ontario M2M 1H9 Canada. (416)221-4802. Fax: (416)221-8400. E-mail: annick@annickpress.com. Website: www.annickpress.com. **Acquisitions:** Rick Wilks, director (picture-books, nonfiction); Colleen MacMillan, associate publisher (YA, juvenile nonfiction). Publishes hardcover and trade paperback originals and mass market paperback reprints. **Publishes 25 titles/year. Receives 5,000 queries and 3,000 mss/year. 20% of books from first-time authors; 80-85% from unagented writers. Pays 10-12% royalty on retail price. Offers $2,000-4,000 advance.** Publishes book 2 years after acceptance of ms. Responds in 1 month to queries, 2 months to proposals, 3 months to mss. Book catalog free or on website. Manuscript guidelines free.

Nonfiction: Children's/juvenile. Query with SASE. Reviews artwork/photos as part of ms package. Send photocopies.

Fiction: Juvenile, young adult. Query with SASE.

Recent Title(s): *Create Millennium Time Capsule*, by Shapiro.

◆ ANVIL PRESS, 204-A 175 E. Broadway, Vancouver, British Columbia V5T 1W2 Canada. (604)876-8710. Fax: (604)879-2667. E.-mail: subter@portal.ca. Website: www.anvilpress.com. **Acquisitions:** Brian Kaufman. Publishes trade paperback originals. **Publishes 6 titles/year. Receives 300 queries/year. 80% of books from first-time authors; 70% from unagented writers. Pays 15% of net sales. Offers advance.** Publishes ms 8 months after acceptance of ms. Responds in 2 months to queries and proposals, 6 months to mss. Book catalog for 9×12 SAE with 2 first-class stamps. Manuscript guidelines for #10 SASE.

    Oₐ "Anvil Press publishes contemporary adult fiction, poetry and drama, giving voice to up-and-coming Canadian writers, exploring all literary genres, discovering, nurturing and promoting new Canadian literary talent."

Fiction: Contemporary, modern literature—no formulaic or genre. Query with 2 sample chapters and SASE.

    ● Anvil Press also sponsors the 3-Day Novel Writing Contest.

Poetry: "Get our catalog, look at our poetry. We publish maybe 1-2 titles per year." Query with 12 sample poems.

Recent Title(s): *White Lung*, by Grant Buday; *Touched*, by Jodi Lundgren.

Tips: Audience is young, informed, educated, aware, with an opinion, culturally active (films, books, the performing arts). "No U.S. authors, unless selected as the winner of our 3-Day Novel Contest. Research the appropriate publisher for your work."

ⓝ ◆ BEACH HOLME PUBLISHERS LTD., 226-2040 W. 12th Ave., Vancouver, British Columbia V6J 2G2 Canada. (604)773-4868. Fax: (604)733-4860. E-mail: bhp@beachholme.bc.ca. Website: www.beachholme.bc.ca. **Acquisitions:** Michael Carroll, managing editor (adult and young adult fiction, poetry); Jen Hamilton, production manager. Estab. 1971. Publishes trade paperback originals. **Publishes 14 titles/year. Receives 1,000 submissions/year. 40% of books from first-time authors; 75% of unagented writers. Pays 10% royalty on retail price. Offers $500 average advance.** Publishes ms 1 year after acceptance. Accepts simultaneous submissions, if so noted. Responds in 4 months. Manuscript guidelines free.

    Oₐ Beach Holme seeks "to publish excellent, emerging Canadian fiction and poetry and to contribute to Canadian materials for children with quality young adult historical novels."

Imprint(s): Porcepic Books (literary imprint); Sandcastle Book (children's/YA imprint).

    ● Beach Holme no longer publishes nonfiction.

Fiction: Adult literary fiction and poetry from authors published in Canadian literary magazines. Young adult (Canada historical/regional). "Interested in excellent quality, imaginative writing. *Accepting only Canadian submissions.* Send cover letter, SASE, outline and two chapters.

Recent Title(s): *The Allegra Series*, by Barbara Lambert; *Carrying the Shadow*, by Patrick Friesen.

Tips: "Make sure the manuscript is well written. We see so many that only the unique and excellent can't be put down. Prior publication is a must. This doesn't necessarily mean book-length manuscripts, but a writer should try to publish his or her short fiction."

BETWEEN THE LINES, 720 Bathurst St., Suite #404, Toronto, Ontario M5S 2R4 Canada. (416)535-9914. Fax: (416)535-1484. E-mail: btlbooks@web.net. Website: www.btlbooks.com. **Acquisitions:** Paul Eprile, editorial coordinator. Publishes trade paperback originals. **Publishes 8 titles/year. Receives 150 queries and 25 mss/year. 80% of books from first-time authors; 95% from unagented writers. Pays 8% royalty on retail price. No advance.** Publishes book 1 year after acceptance of ms. Accepts simultaneous submissions. Responds in 2 months to queries and proposals, 4 months to mss. Book catalog and ms guidelines for 8½×11 SAE and IRCs.

O— "We are a small independent house concentrating on politics and public policy issues, social issues, gender issues, international development, education and the environment. We mainly publish Canadian authors."

Nonfiction: Biography, reference, textbook. Subjects include education, gay/lesbian, government/politics, health, history, memoirs, sociology, women's issues/studies. Submit proposal package, including outline, 2-3 sample chapters and table of contents. Reviews artwork/photos as part of ms package.

Recent Title(s): *Sharing the Work, Sparing the Planet*, by Anders Hayden; *The Second Greatest Disappointment: Honeymooning and Tourism at Niagara Falls*, by Karen Dubinsky.

THE BOOKS COLLECTIVE, 214-21, 10405 Jasper Ave., Edmonton, Alberta T5J 3S2 Canada. (780)448-0590. Fax: (780)448-0640. Publishes hardcover and trade paperback originals. **Publishes 10-12 titles/year; imprint publishes 2-5 titles/year. 30-60% of books from first-time authors; 90% from unagented writers. Pays 6-12% royalty on retail price. Sometimes full royalties paid on sell through, especially to anthology contributors. Offers $250-500 (Canadian) advance.** Publishes book 1 year after acceptance of ms. Accepts simultaneous submissions in some circumstances. Responds in 1 month to queries and proposals, 6 months to mss. Book catalog for 9×12 SAE with 4 first-class Canadian stamps or on website. Manuscript guidelines on website.

O— "All nonfiction projects are developed from query letters or are developed inhouse. Always query first."

Imprints: Tesseract Books, River Books, Slipstream Books.

● This publisher is looking for Canadian authors only (expats or living abroad, landed immigrants OK). All non-Canadian submissions will be returned unread.

Nonfiction: Biography, multimedia. Subjects include creative nonfiction, language/literature, memoirs, multicultural, political issues. Query with SASE in Canadian stamps, or equivalent cost or submit proposal package, including outline, 1-3 sample chapters and author résumé (1-3 pages only). Reviews artwork/photos as part of ms package. Send photocopies of samples only with query.

Fiction: Experimental, fantasy, feminist, gay/lesbian, horror, literary, mainstream/contemporary, multicultural, multimedia, plays, poetry, regional, science fiction, short story collections, translation (Canadian languages only). Tesseract Books publishes an annual anthology of Canadian speculative short fiction and poetry. Query with SASE (in Canadian stamps or equivalent cost) or submit proposal package, including synopsis, 1-3 sample chapters and author résumé (1-3 pages only) or submit completed ms.

Poetry: Query, submit 5-10 sample poems or submit complete ms.

Recent Title(s): *The Edmonton Queen: Not A Riverboat Story*, by D. Hagen (contemporary memoir); and *Secrets In Water*, by Barbara Sapergia.

Tips: "Our books are geared for literate, intelligent readers of literary mainstream, cutting edge and speculative writing. If you do not know our titles, query first or write for guidelines. Look up our titles and study suitability of your manuscript. We are a writers' co-op—expect long timelines. Unless your manuscript is of surpassing excellence it will not survive omission of an SASE."

BOREALIS PRESS, LTD., 110 Bloomingdale St., Ottawa, Ontario K2C 4A4 Canada. (613)798-9299. Fax: (613)798-9747. E-mail: borealis@istar.ca. www.borealispress.com. Editorial Director: Frank Tierney. **Acquisitions:** Glenn Clever, senior editor. Estab. 1972. Publishes hardcover and paperback originals. **Publishes 10-12 titles/year. Receives 400-500 submissions/year. 80% of books from first-time authors; 95% from unagented writers. Pays 10% royalty on net price. No advance.** Publishes book 18 months after acceptance. No multiple submissions. Responds in 2 months. Book catalog for $3 and SASE.

Imprint(s): Tecumseh Press.

O— "Our mission is to publish work which will be of lasting interest in the Canadian book market." Currently emphasizing Canadian fiction, nonfiction, drama, poetry. De-emphasizing children's books.

Nonfiction: "Only material Canadian in content." Biography, children's/juvenile, reference. Subjects include government/politics, history, language/literature. Query with outline, 2 sample chapters and SASE. *No unsolicited mss.* Reviews artwork/photos as part of ms package. Looks for "style in tone and language, reader interest and maturity of outlook."

Fiction: "Only material Canadian in content and dealing with significant aspects of the human situation." Adventure, ethnic, historical, juvenile, literary, romance, short story collections, young adult. Query with synopsis, 1-2 sample chapters and SASE. *No unsolicited mss.*

Recent Title(s): *The Abbey at the Queen's: The History of the Irish National Theatre in Exile*, by Michael O'Neill (nonfiction); *An Answer for Pierre*, by Gretl Fischer (fiction); *Folds*, by Fred Cogswell (poetry).

THE BOSTON MILLS PRESS, Stoddart Publishing, 132 Main St., Erin, Ontario N0B 1T0 Canada. (519)833-2407. Fax: (519)833-2195. E-mail: books@boston-mills.on.ca. Website: www.boston-mills.on.ca. President: John Denison. **Acquisitions**: Noel Hudson, managing editor. Estab. 1974. Publishes hardcover and trade paperback originals. **Publishes 20 titles/year. Receives 100 submissions/year. 40% of books from first-time authors; 95% from unagented writers. Pays 8-15% royalty on retail price. No advance.** Publishes book 18 months after acceptance. Accepts simultaneous submissions. Responds in 2 months. Book catalog free.

    O➤ Boston Mills Press publishes specific market titles of Canadian and American interest including history, transportation and regional guidebooks.

Nonfiction: Coffee table book, gift book, illustrated books. Subjects include art/architecture, cooking/foods/nutrition, creative nonfiction, gardening, guidebooks, history, nature, recreation, regional. "We're interested in anything to do with Canadian or American history—especially transportation." No autobiographies. Query. Reviews artwork/photos as part of ms package. Send photocopies.

BPS BOOKS, The British Psychological Society, St. Andrews House, 48 Princess Rd. E, Leicester LE1 7DR United Kingdom. Phone: (+44)116 254 9568. Fax: (+44)116 247 0787. E-mail: books@bps.org.uk. Website: www.bps.org.uk. **Acquisitions**: Joyce Collins, publisher; Jon Reed, senior editor. Publishes trade paperback originals. **Publishes 12 titles/ year. Receives 30 queries and 15-20 mss/year. 25% of books from first-time authors; 95% from unagented writers. Pays 7-12% royalty on retail price. No advance.** Publishes book 1 year after acceptance of ms. Responds in 2 months. Book catalog free or on website. Manuscript guidelines free.

    O➤ "We publish psychology for managers, teachers, medical and healthcare professionals, students and practising psychologists."

Nonfiction: Multimedia (CD-ROM), reference, textbook, professional and educational. Subjects include education, psychology. Submit proposal package, including outline and 1 sample chapter and cv.

Recent Title(s): *Altruism and Aggression*, by Anne Campbell.

Tips: "We do not publish self-help or popular psychology or fiction. Please give us an indication of your qualifications for writing this particular book. We are a professional and learned society, and all submissions will go to an editorial board of practising psychologists."

N: BROADVIEW PRESS LTD., P.O. Box 1243, 71 Princess St., Peterborough, Ontario K9J 7H5 Canada. (705)743-8990. Fax: (705)743-8353. E-mail: 75322.44@compuserve.com. Website: www.broadviewpress.com. **Acquisitions**: Julia Gaunce, humanities editor (humanities—history, English, philosophy); Michael Harrison, vice president (social sciences—political science, sociology, anthropology). Estab. 1985. "We specialize in university/college supplementary textbooks which often have both a trade and academic market." Publishes trade paperback originals and reprints. **Publishes 40-50 titles/year. Receives 500 queries and 200 mss/year. 10% of books from first-time authors; 99% from unagented writers. Pays royalty.** Publishes book 1 year after acceptance. Accepts simultaneous submissions. Responds in 1 month to queries, 2 months to proposals, 4 months to mss. Book catalog free. Manuscript guidelines on website.

    O➤ "We publish in a broad variety of subject areas in the arts and social sciences. We are open to a broad range of political and philosophical viewpoints, from liberal and conservative to libertarian and Marxist, and including a wide range of feminist viewpoints."

Nonfiction: Biography, reference, textbook. Subjects include anthropology/archaeology, gay/lesbian, history, language/literature, philosophy, religion, sociology, women's issues/studies. "All titles must have some potential for university or college-level course use. Crossover titles are acceptable." Query or submit proposal package. Sometimes reviews artwork/photos as part of ms package. Send photocopies.

    ● Broadview Press has a significant presence in the U.S., with one third of its authors being American.

Recent Title(s): *In Search of Authority: An Introduction to Literary Theory*, by Stephen Bunnycastle.

Tips: "Our titles often appeal to a broad readership; we have many books that are as much of interest to the general reader as they are to academics and students."

BROKEN JAW PRESS, Box 596, Station A, Fredericton, New Brunswick E3B 5A6 Canada. Phone/fax: (506)454-5127. E-mail: jblades@nbnet.nb.ca. Website: www.brokenjaw.com. **Acquisitions**: Joe Blades, publisher. Publishes Canadian-authored trade paperback originals and reprints. **Publishes 8-12 titles/year. 50% of books from first-time authors; 100% from unagented writers. Pays 10% royalty on retail price. Offers $0-100 advance.** Publishes book 1-1½ years after acceptance of ms. Responds in 1 year to mss. Book catalog for 9×12 SAE with 2 first-class Canadian stamps in Canada. Manuscript guidelines for #10 SASE (Canadian postage or IRC).

    O➤ "We are a small mostly literary Canadian publishing house."

Imprint(s): Book Rat, SpareTime Editions, Dead Sea Physh Products, Maritimes Arts Projects Productions.

Nonfiction: Subjects include history, language/literature, nature/environment, regional, women's issues/studies, criticism, culture. Reviews artwork/photos as part of ms package. Send photocopies, transparencies. No query.

Fiction: Literary.

Recent Title(s): *What Was Always Hers*, by Uma Parameswaran (fiction); *New Power*, by Christine Lowther (poetry).

Tips: "We don't want unsolicited manuscripts or queries, except in the context of the New Muse Award and the Poet's Corner Award."

THE BRUCEDALE PRESS, P.O. Box 2259, Port Elgin, Ontario N0H 2C0 Canada. (519)832-6025. Website: www.bmts.com/~brucedale. **Acquisitions**: Anne Duke Judd, editor-in-chief. Publishes hardcover and trade paperback originals. **Publishes 3 titles/year. Receives 50 queries and 30 mss/year. 75% of books from first-time authors; 100% from unagented writers. Pays royalty.** No advance. Publishes book 1 year after acceptance of ms. Accepts simultaneous submissions "if identified as such." Book catalog and manuscript guidelines for #10 SASE or on website.
> The Brucedale Press publishes books and other materials of regional interest and merit as well as literary, historical and/or pictorial works.

Nonfiction: Biography, children's/juvenile, humor, illustrated book, reference. Subjects include history, language/literature, memoirs, military/war, nature/environment, photography. Submit proposal package, including outline and 3 sample chapters with writer's cv. "Invitations to submit are sent to writers and writers' groups on The Brucedale Press mailing list when projects are in progress. Send a #10 SASE to have your name added to the list. Unless responding to an invitation to submit, query first, with outline and sample chapter for book-length submissions. Submit full manuscript of work intended for children. A brief résumé of your writing efforts and successes is always of interest, and may bring future invitations, even if the present submission is not accepted for publication." Reviews artwork/photos as part of ms package.

Fiction: Fantasy, feminist, historical, humor, juvenile, literary, mainstream/contemporary, mystery, plays, poetry, romance, short story collections, young adult.

Recent Title(s): *Tales of the Unusual "True" Mysteries of Bruce and Grey*, by Diane Madden (nonfiction); *Barricade Summer*, by Nancy-Lou Patterson (young adult); *Strong in My Skin*, by Jennifer Frankum (contemporary).

Tips: "Our focus is very regional. In reading submissions, I look for quality writing with a strong connection to the Queen's Bush area of Ontario. Suggest all authors visit our website, get a catalogue and read our books before submitting."

BUTTERWORTHS CANADA, 75 Clegg Rd., Markham, Ontario L6G 1A1 Canada. (905)479-2665. Fax: (905)479-2826. E-mail: info@butterworths.ca. Website: www.butterworths.ca. **Acquisitions:** Caryl Young, publishing director. **Publishes 100 titles/year. Receives 100 queries and 10 mss/year. 50% of books from first-time authors; 100% from unagented writers. Pays 5-15% royalty on wholesale price; occasionally by fee. Offers $1,000-5,000 advance.** Publishes book 4 months after acceptance of ms. Accepts simultaneous submissions. Responds in 1 month. Book catalog free.
> Butterworths publishes professional reference material for the legal, business and accounting markets.

Nonfiction: Multimedia (disk and CD-ROM), reference, looseleaf. Subjects include health/medicine (medical law), legal and business reference. Query with SASE.

Recent Title(s): *The Law of Corporate Finance in Canada*, by Edmund Kwaw.

Tips: Audience is legal community, business, medical, accounting professions.

CAITLIN PRESS, INC., P.O. Box 2387 Station B, Prince George, British Columbia V2N 2S6 Canada. (250)964-4953. Fax: (250)964-4970. E-mail: caitlin_press@telus.net. Website: caitlinpress.com. **Acquisitions:** Cynthia Wilson. Estab. 1978. Publishes trade paperback and soft cover originals. **Publishes 6-7 titles/year. Receives 105-120 queries and 50 mss/year. 100% of books from unagented writers. Pays 15% royalty on wholesale price.** Publishes book 18 months after acceptance of ms. Accepts simultaneous submissions. Responds in 3 months to queries.
> "We publish books about Canada's middle north—that region between the far north of the territories and the heavily populated southern corridor."

Nonfiction: Biography, cookbook. Subjects include history, photography, regional. "We are not interested in manuscripts that do not reflect a British Columbia influence." Submit outline and proposal package. Reviews artwork/photos as part of ms package. Send photocopies.

Fiction: Adventure, historical, humor, mainstream/contemporary, short story collections, young adult. Query with SASE.

Poetry: Submit sample poems or complete ms.

Recent Title(s): *A Touch of Murder Now and Then*, by M. Robertson (nonfiction); *Paper Trees*, by R. Sinclair (fiction); *Rainbow Dancer*, by H. Harris (poetry).

Tips: "Our area of interest is British Columbia and northern Canada. Submissions should reflect our interest area."

CANADIAN EDUCATORS' PRESS, 100 City Centre Dr., P.O. Box 2094, Mississauga, Ontario L5B 3C6 Canada. Phone/fax: (905)826-0578. **Acquisitions:** S. Deonarine, manager. Publishes trade paperback originals. **Publishes 2 titles/year. Pays royalty. No advance.** Publishes book 1 year after acceptance of ms.

Nonfiction: Textbook. Subjects include education, government/politics, history, multicultural, philosophy, religion, sociology. Query with SASE. Inquire before submitting artwork/photos as part of the ms package.

 THE MAPLE LEAF symbol indicates publishers which consider book proposals by Canadian authors only.

Recent Title(s): *Adult Education: An Introductory Reader*, by Deo Poonwassie and Anne Poonwassie; *21st Century Canadian Diversity*, by Stephen E. Nancoo.

CARSWELL THOMSON PROFESSIONAL PUBLISHING, The Thomson Corp., One Corporate Plaza, 2075 Kennedy Rd., Scarborough, Ontario M1T 3V4 Canada. (416)298-5024. Fax: (416)298-5094. E-mail: robert.freeman@carswell.com. Website: www.carswell.com. **Acquisitions**: Robert Freeman, vice president, legal group. Publishes hardcover originals. **Publishes 150-200 titles/year. 30-50% of books from first-time authors. Pays 5-15% royalty on wholesale price. Offers $1,000-5,000 advance.** Publishes book 6 months after acceptance of ms. Accepts simultaneous submissions. Responds in 3 months. Book catalog and ms guidelines free.

　　O┳ Carswell Thomson is Canada's national resource of information and legal interpretations for law, accounting, tax and business professionals.

Nonfiction: Legal, tax and business reference. "Canadian information of a regulatory nature is our mandate." Submit proposal package, including résumé and outline.

Recent Title(s): *The Internet Handbook for Canadian Lawyers*, by M. Drew Jackson and Timothy L. Taylor.

Tips: Audience is Canada and persons interested in Canadian information; professionals in law, tax, accounting fields; business people interested in regulatory material.

CHA PRESS, Canadian Healthcare Association, 17 York St., Ottawa, Ontario K1N 9J6 Canada. (613)241-8005, ext. 264. Fax: (613)241-5055. E-mail: chapress@canadian-healthcare.org. Website: www.canadian-healthcare.org. **Acquisitions:** Eleanor Sawyer, director of publishing. Publishes softcover specialty textbooks. **Publishes 6-8 titles/year. Receives 7 queries and 3 mss/year. 60% from first-time authors, 90% from unagented writers. Pays 10-17% royalty on retail price or makes outright purchase of $250-1,000. Offers $500-1,500 advance.** Publishes book 10 months after acceptance of ms. Accepts simultaneous submissions. Responds in 3 months. Book catalog and ms guidelines free.

　　O┳ CHA Press strives to be Canada's health administration textbook publisher. We serve readers in our broad continuum of care in regional health authorities, hospitals and health care facilities and agencies, which are governed by trustees. Currently emphasizing leadership, tomorrow's leaders, aging, elderly home care, risk management, integration. De-emphasizing specific hospital issues—must be more broadly based.

Nonfiction: How-to, textbook. Subjects include health, history, management, healthcare policy, healthcare administration. Query with outline and with SASE.

Tips: "Audience is healthcare facility managers (senior/middle); policy analysts/researchers; nurse practitioners and other healthcare professionals; trustees. "CHA Press is looking to expand its frontlist for 2000-2001 on issues specific to Canadian healthcare system reform; continuum of care issues; integrated health delivery. Don't underestimate amount of time it will take to write or mistake generic 'how-to' health for mass media as appropriate for CHA's specialty press."

Recent Title(s): *Customized Manuals for Changing Times*, by Paula Cryderman; *Managing Missing Patient Incidents: Prevention and Response*, by James A. Hanna.

CHARLTON PRESS, 2040 Yonge St., Suite 208, Toronto, Ontario M4S 1Z9 Canada. Fax: (416)488-4656. E-mail: chpress@charltonpress.com. Website: www.charltonpress.com. **Acquisitions:** Jean Dale, managing editor. Publishes trade paperback originals and reprints. **Publishes 15 titles/year. Receives 30 queries and 5 mss/year. 10% of books from first-time authors; 100% from unagented writers. Pays 10% minimum royalty on wholesale price or makes variable outright purchase. Offers $1,000 advance.** Publishes book 6 months after acceptance of ms. Accepts simultaneous submissions. Responds in 1 month to queries and proposals, 2 months to mss. Book catalog free on request.

Nonfiction: Reference (price guides on collectibles). Subjects include numismatics, toys, military badges, ceramic collectibles, sport cards. Submit outline. Reviews artwork/photos as part of ms package. Send photocopies.

Recent Title(s): *Royal Doulton Figurines*, by J. Dale (reference guide).

CITRON PRESS PLC, 155 The Business Design Centre, 52 Upper St., Islington NI OQH United Kingdom. Phone: (44)2072886024. Fax: (44)2072886196. E-mail: citronpress@citronpress.co.uk. Website: www.citronpress.co.uk. **Acquisitions**: Fiona Stewart, editorial director (fiction). Publishes paperback originals. **Publishes 80 titles/year. Receives 9,000 queries and 1,500 mss/year. 80% of books from first-time authors; 100% from unagented writers. Pays 7½-15% royalty on retail price. No advance.** Publishes book 4 months after acceptance of ms. Accepts simultaneous submissions. Responds in 1 week to queries, 2 months to mss. Book catalog and ms guidelines free or on website.

　　O┳ "We are an authors' co-operative that publishes new fiction as paperback originals. We do not pay advances but operate as a profit share. We're looking for fresh, new, contemporary fiction."

Fiction: New fiction, mainly contemporary fiction, literary fiction, up-market thrillers and women's fiction, and short stories. Query with IRCs.

Recent Title(s): *Toilet Elephant*, by Nick Johnston-Jones.

N┇ COACH HOUSE BOOKS, 401 Huron St. on bpNichol Lane, Toronto, Ontario M5S 2G5 Canada. (416)979-2217. Fax: (416)977-1158. E-mail: mail@chbooks.com. Website: www.chbooks.com. **Acquisitions:** Darren Wershler-Henry, editor. Publishes hardcover and trade paperback originals. **Publishes 10 titles/year. 80% of books from first-time authors; 100% from unagented writers. Pays 10% royalty on retail price.** Publishes book 18 months after acceptance of ms. Responds in 6 months. Book catalog free or on website. Manuscript guidelines are on website.

Nonfiction: Multimedia. Subjects include art/architecture, language/literature. Query with SASE. All unsolicited mss returned unopened. Reviews artwork/photos as part of ms package. Send photocopies.

Fiction: Experimental, literary, multimedia, plays, poetry. "Consult website for submissions policy." All unsolicited mss returned unopened.
Poetry: Consult website for guidelines. Query.
Recent Title(s): *Lillian Lecture*, by W. Agnew (poetry); and *Outside the Hat*, by S. Barwin.

N **CORMORANT BOOKS INC.**, RR 1, Dunvegan, Ontario K0C 1J0 Canada. (613)527-3348. Fax: (613)527-2262. E-mail: cormorant@glen-net.ca. Website: www.cormorantbooks.com. **Acquisitions:** Jan Geddes, publisher (fiction). Publishes hardcover, trade paperback originals and reprints. **Publishes 7 titles/year. Receives 500-700 mss/year. 70% of books from first-time authors; 60% from unagented writers. Pays 10% royalty on retail price. Offers $500-10,000 advance.** Publishes book 1-2 years after acceptance of ms. Accepts simultaneous submissions. Responds in 2 months to queries, 6 months to mss. Book catalog free or on website.
○━ Cormorant publishes Canadian fiction and essay collections, occasional nonfiction titles, usually on literary themes.
Nonfiction: Essays, memoirs. Query with SASE.
Fiction: Literary, multicultural, short story collections, translation (French-Canadian authored). Query with SASE or submit synopsis with 3 sample chapters or submit completed ms.
Recent Title(s): *Living in The World As If It Were Home*, by Tim Lilburn (meditative essays); *The Good Body*, by Bill Gaston (novel).
Tips: "Writers should determine, from a study of our list, whether their fiction or essay collection would be appropriate. *Canadian authors only.*"

N **COTEAU BOOKS**, 2206 Dewdney Ave., Suite 401, Regina, Saskatchewan S4R 1H3 Canada. (306)777-0170. Fax: (306)522-5152. E-mail: coteau@coteau.unibase.com. Website: coteau.unibase.com. **Acquisitions:** Geoffrey Ursell, publisher. Estab. 1975. **Publishes 16 titles/year. Receives approximately 1,000 queries and mss/year. 10% of books from first-time authors; 95% from unagented writers. Pays 10% royalty on retail price or makes outright purchase of $50-200 for anthology contributors.** Publishes book 18 months after acceptance. Responds in 2 months to queries, 4 months to mss. Catalog for SASE.
Nonfiction: Reference, desk calendars. Subjects include language/literature, regional studies. *We publish only Canadian authors.* Query with SASE first.
○━ "Our mission is to publish the finest in Canadian fiction, nonfiction, poetry, drama and children's literature, with an emphasis on Saskatchewan and prairie writers." De-emphasizing science fiction, picture books.
Fiction: Ethnic, feminist, humor, juvenile, literary, mainstream/contemporary, plays, short story collections. Submit complete ms. Query with SASE first. "We publish fiction and poetry from Canadian authors only."
Recent Title(s): *Gold on Ice: The Story of the Sanora Schmirler Curling Team*, by Gary Schyolz (nonfiction); *The Walnut Tree*, by Martha Blum (fiction); *The Long Landscape*, by Paul Wilson (poetry); *Kalifax*, by Duncan Thornton (young adult).
Tips: "We do not publish picture books, but are interested in juvenile and YA fiction from Canadian authors."

ECRITS DES FORGES, C.P. 335, 1497 Laviolette, Trois-Rivieres, Quebec G9A 5G4 Canada. (819)379-9813. Fax: (819)376-0774. E-mail: ecrits.desforges@aiqnet.com. **Acquisitions:** Gaston Bellemare, president. Publishes hardcover originals. **Publishes 40 titles/year. Receives 30 queries and 1,000 mss/year. 10% of books from first-time authors; 90% from unagented writers. Pays 10-30% royalty. Offers 50% advance.** Publishes book 9 months after acceptance of ms. Accepts simultaneous submissions. Responds in 9 months. Book catalog free.
○━ Ecrits des Forges publishes only poetry written in French.
Poetry: Submit 20 sample poems.
Recent Title(s): *Poètes québécois*, by Louise Blouin/Bernard Pozier; *Corps et graphies*, by Gatien Lapointe.

ECW PRESS, 2120 Queen St. E., Suite 200, Toronto, Ontario M4E 1E2 Canada. (416)694-3348. Fax: (416)698-9906. E-mail: ecw@sympatico.ca. **Acquisitions:** Jack David, president (nonfiction); Michael Holmes, literary editor (fiction, poetry). Estab. 1979. Publishes hardcover and trade paperback originals. **Publishes 35 titles/year. Receives 400 submissions/year. 50% of books from first-time authors; 80% from unagented writers. Pays 10% royalty on net price.** Accepts simultaneous submissions. Responds in 1 month. Book catalog free.
○━ Currently emphasizing sports books and music biographies.
Nonfiction: Particularly interested in popular biography, sports books, popular culture, humor, music, and general trade books. Query. Reviews artwork/photos as part of ms package.
Recent Title(s): *Slammin': Wrestling's Greatest Heroes and Villains*; *Zipless Sex*; *Wedding Bell Hell*.

EDGE SCIENCE FICTION AND FANTASY PUBLISHING, Box 75064 Cambrian PO, Calgary, Alberta T2K 6J8 Canada. (403)282-5206. Fax: (403)254-0456. E-mail: editor@edgewebsite.com. Website: www.edgewebsite.com. **Acquisitions:** Jessie Tambay, Roxanne Bennett, Mike Bonde, Robyn Herrington, editors. Editorial Manager: Lynn Jennyc. Publishes hardcover and trade paperback originals. **Publishes 3-12 titles/year. Receives 40 queries and 400 mss/year. 50% of books from first-time authors; 75% from unagented writers. Pays 10% royalty on wholesale price. Offers $300-1,000 advance.** Publishes book 1 year after acceptance of ms. Accepts simultaneous submissions. Responds in 4 months to queries and proposals; 6 months to mss. Book catalog not available. Manuscript guidelines for #10 SASE (use IRCs from US).

O━ "Our goal is to publish quality science fiction and fantasy novels that attract a strong readership and generate interest within the industry."

Fiction: Fantasy, science fiction. "We are looking for all types of fantasy and science fiction, except juvenile/young adult." Submit synopsis and first sample chapter with SASE.

Recent Titles: *The Black Chalice*, by Marie Jakober (historical fantasy).

Tips: "Audience is anyone who enjoys a well written science fiction or fantasy novel. Polish your manuscript before you submit it. Get your manuscript critiqued by others before you submit it."

N: EDITIONS DU NOROÎT, 1835 Les Hauteurs, St. Hippolyte, Quebec J8A 2L7 Canada. (450)563-4260. Fax: (450)563-4622. **Acquisitions**: Paul Belanger, directors. Publishes trade paperback originals and reprints. **Publishes 27 titles/year. Receives 500 queries and 500 mss/year. 50% of books from first-time authors; 95% from unagented writers. Pays 10% royalty on retail price.** Publishes book 1 year after acceptance. Accepts simultaneous submissions. Responds in 3 months to mss. Book catalog SASE.

O━ Editions du Noiroît publishes poetry.

Poetry: Submit 40 sample poems.

Recent Poetry Title(s): *Transfiguration*, by Jacques Brault/E.D. Blodgett.

ÉDITIONS LOGIQUES/LOGICAL PUBLISHING, 7 Chemin Bates, Outremont, Quebec H2V 1A6 Canada. (514)490-2700. Fax: (514)270-3515. E-mail: logique@logique.com. Website: www.logique.com. **Acquisitions**: Louis-Philippe Hebert, president and general manager. Publishes hardcover, trade and mass market paperback originals and reprints. **Publishes 75 titles/year. Receives 200 queries and 100 mss/year. 40% of books from first-time authors; 100% from unagented writers. Pays 6-10% royalty on retail price. Offers advance up to $1,000.** Publishes book 6 months after acceptance of ms. Responds in 2 months. Book catalog free.

O━ "Les Éditions Logiques will only publish books translated or written in French."

Nonfiction: Biography, coffee table book, cookbook, how-to, humor, illustrated book, children's/juvenile, reference, self-help, technical, textbook and computer books. "We aim to the contemporary adult: technology, environment, learning, trying to cope and live a happy life. Writers should offer some insight on the reality of today." Submit outline, 2-3 sample chapters and pictures if required. Reviews artwork as part of the ms package. Send photocopies.

Fiction: Erotica, experimental, fantasy, literary, mainstream/contemporary and science fiction. "Be modern." Submit complete ms only.

Recent Title(s): *Relaxer*, (self-help, health); *L'ermite* (romance).

Tips: "Our audience consists of contemporary men and women. French manuscripts only, please, or a copy of English book if already published and French rights are available."

FERNWOOD PUBLISHING LTD., P.O. Box 9409, Station A, Halifax, Nova Scotia B3K 5S3 Canada. (902)422-3302. E-mail: Fernwood@HFX.EASTLINK.CA. Website: home.ISTAR.ca/~Fernwood. **Acquisitions**: Errol Sharpe, publisher (social science); Wayne Antony, editor (social science). Publishes trade paperback originals. **Publishes 12-15 titles/year. Receives 80 queries and 30 mss/year. 40% of books from first-time authors; 100% from unagented writers. Pays 7-10% royalty on wholesale price.** Publishes book 1 year after acceptance of ms. Accepts simultaneous submissions. Responds in 6 weeks to proposals. Book catalog and ms guidelines free.

O━ "Fernwood's objective is to publish critical works which challenge existing scholarship."

Nonfiction: Biography, reference, textbook. Subjects include anthropology/archaeology, education, ethnic, gay/lesbian, government/politics, health/medicine, history, language/literature, nature/environment, philosophy, sociology, sports, translation, women's issues/studies, Canadiana. "Our main focus is in the social sciences and humanities, emphasizing labor studies, women's studies, gender studies, critical theory and research, political economy, cultural studies and social work—for use in college and university courses." Submit proposal package, including outline, table of contents, sample chapters. Reviews artwork/photos as part of ms package. Send photocopies.

Recent Title(s): *The Skin I'm In: Racism, Sports and Education*, by Christopher Spence.

GOOSE LANE EDITIONS, 469 King St., Fredericton, New Brunswick E3B 1E5 Canada. (506)450-4251. **Acquisitions**: Laurel Boone, editorial director. Estab. 1956. **Publishes 12-14 titles/year. Receives 500 submissions/year. 20% of books from first-time authors; 75% from unagented writers. Pays royalty on retail price.** Responds in 6 months. Manuscript guidelines for SASE (Canadian stamps or IRCs).

O━ Goose Lane publishes fiction and nonfiction from well-read authors with finely crafted literary writing skills.

Nonfiction: Biography, illustrated book, literary history (Canadian). Subjects include art/architecture, history, language/literature, nature/environment, translation, women's issues/studies. No crime, confessional, how-to, self-help, medical, legal or cookbooks. Query first.

Fiction: Experimental, feminist, historical, literary, short story collections. "Our needs in fiction never change: substantial, character-centred literary fiction. No children's, YA, mainstream, mass market, genre, mystery, thriller, confessional or sci-fi fiction." Query with SASE first.

Recent Title(s): *English Lessons and Other Stories*, by Shauna Singh Baldwin; *Studio Rally: Art and Craft of Nova Scotia*, by Robin Metcalfe (nonfiction).

Tips: "Writers should send us outlines and samples of books that show a very well-read author who has thought long and deeply about the art of writing and, in either fiction or nonfiction, has something of Canadian relevance to offer. We almost never publish books by non-Canadian authors, and we seldom consider submissions from outside the country."

Our audience is literate, thoughtful and well-read. If I were a writer trying to market a book today, I would contact the targeted publisher with a query letter and synopsis, and request manuscript guidelines. Purchase a recent book from the publisher in a relevant area, if possible. Never send a complete manuscript blindly to a publisher. *Never* send a manuscript or sample without an SASE with IRC's or sufficient return postage in Canadian stamps."

GUERNICA EDITIONS, 27 Humewood Dr., Toronto, Ontario M6C 2W3 Canada. (416)658-9888. Fax: (416)657-8885. E-mail: guernicaeditions@cs.com. Website: www.guernicaeditions.com. **Acquisitions**: Antonio D'Alfonso, editor/publisher (poetry, nonfiction, novels); Pasquale Verdicchio, editor (Canadian reprints); Ken Scambray, editor (US reprints). Estab. 1978. Publishes trade paperback originals, reprints and software. **Publishes 20 titles/year. Receives 1,000 submissions/year. 5% of books from first-time authors. Pays 8-10% royalty on retail price or makes outright purchase of $200-5,000. Offers 10¢/word advance for translators.** IRCs required: "American stamps are of no use to us in Canada." Responds in 1 month to queries, 6 months to proposals, 1 year to mss. Book catalog for SASE/IRC.

> O-π Guernica Editions is an independent press dedicated to the bridging of cultures. "We do original and translations of fine works. We are seeking essays on authors and translations with less emphasis on poetry."

Nonfiction: Biography, art, film, history, music, philosophy, politics, psychology, religion, literary criticism, ethnic history, multicultural comparative literature, creative nonfiction, gay/lesbian, government/politics, sex, women's issues/studies. Query with SASE.

Fiction: Original works and translations. Subjects include ethnic, feminist, gay/lesbian, literary, multicultural, poetry, poetry in translation. "We wish to open up into the fiction world and focus less on poetry. Also specialize in European, especially Italian, translations." Query with SASE (IRCs).

Poetry: "We wish to have writers in translation. Any writer who has translated Italian poetry is welcomed. Full books only. Not single poems by different authors, unless modern, and used as an anthology. First books will have no place in the next couple of years." Submit samples.

Recent Title(s): *Embracing Serafina*, by Penny Petrone (nonfiction); *Lydia Trippe!*, by Daniel Sloate (fiction); *The Law of Return*, by Karen Shenfeld (poetry).

[N] [symbol] gynergy books, Ragweed Press, P.O. Box 2023, Charlottetown, Prince Edward Island C1A 7N7 Canada. (902)566-5750. Fax: (902)566-4473. E-mail: editor@gynergy.com. **Acquisitions**: Sibyl Frei, managing editor. Publishes trade paperback originals. **Publishes 3-5 titles/year; imprint publishes 3-5 titles/year. Receives 200 queries and 1,500-2,000 mss/year. 50% of books from first-time authors; 95% from unagented writers. Pays 8-10% royalty on wholesale or retail price. Advance amount confidential.** Publishes book 1-2 years after acceptance of ms. Accepts simultaneous submissions and unsolicited mss. Publishes only single-authored works by Canadians. Responds in 6 months to mss. Book catalog free. Manuscript guidelines for #10 SASE.

> O-π gynergy publishes lesbian fiction and nonfiction.

Nonfiction: Feminist, lesbian, gift book, humor, illustrated book. Subjects include child guidance/parenting, creative nonfiction, gay/lesbian, women's issues/studies. "For nonfiction, we prefer to review proposals and, if accepted, work with the author or editor on developing the book from concept through to final manuscript." Submit proposal package, including authority on subject and samples of writing, outline and SASE.

Fiction: Lesbian, mystery. "We are interested in series, looking to add line of feminist/lesbian fantasy or science fiction." Send complete ms and SASE.

Recent Title(s): *Fragment by Fragment: Feminist Perspectives in Memory and Child Sexual Abuse*, edited by Margo Rivera (feminist nonfiction anthology); *The Mennonite Madonna*, by Diane Drieger (poetry).

F.P. HENDRIKS PUBLISHING, 4806-53 St., Stettler, Alberta T0C 2L2 Canada. (403)742-6483. E-mail: editor@fphendriks.com. www.fphendrik.com. **Acquisitions**: Faye Boer, managing editor. **Publishes 2-5 titles/year. Receives 60 queries and 40 mss/year. 80% of books from first-time authors; 100% from unagented writers. Pays 10% royalty. Offers $250-1,000 advance depending on author.** Publishes book 2 years after acceptance of ms. Accepts simultaneous submissions. Responds in 4 months to queries, 4 months to proposals, 6 months to mss. Book catalog free.

> O-π F.P. Hendriks' primary focus is teacher's resources in English/language arts and sciences including lessons and activities with solid theoretical background. Currently emphasizing sports/health/literacy fiction. De-emphasizing science.

Nonfiction: Teacher's resources, self-help, textbook. Subjects include child guidance/parenting, education, health/medicine, language/literature, science, sports. Submit outline with SASE. Reviews artwork/photos as part of ms package. Send photocopies.

Fiction: Adventure, fantasy, humor, juvenile, mystery, science fiction, young adult. "We plan to begin publishing young adult fiction in the above categories to commence 2000-2001. Must include accompanying teacher resources or outline for same. Beware of lack of attention to intended audience; lack of attention to elements of plot." Submit synopsis with SASE. "Full length novels only."

Recent Title(s): *Hockey: The Technical, the Mental & the Physical Game*, by Dr. Randy Gregg.

Tips: "Primary audience is teachers of elementary, middle school, junior high in English/language arts and science."

[N] HERITAGE HOUSE PUBLISHING CO. LTD., 301-3555 Outrigger Rd., Nanoose Bay, British Columbia V9P 9K1 Canada. (250)468-5328. Fax: (250)468-5318. E-mail: publisher@heritagehouse.ca. Website: www.heritagehouse.

ca. **Acquisitions**: Rodger Touchie, publisher/president. Publishes trade paperback originals. **Publishes 10-12 titles/year. Receives 200 queries and 60 mss/year. 50% of books from first-time authors; 100% from unagented writers. Pays 9% royalty.** Publishes book 1 year after acceptance. Responds in 2 months. Book catalog for SASE.

> O— Heritage House is primarily a regional publisher of Western Canadiana and the Pacific Northwest. "We aim to publish and distribute good books that entertain and educate our readership regarding both historic and contemporary Western Canada and Pacific Northwest."

Nonfiction: Biography, how-to, illustrated book. Subjects include animals, anthropology/archaeology, history, nature/environment, recreation, regional, sports, western Canadiana. "Writers should include a sample of their writing, an overview sample of photos or illustrations to support the text and a brief letter describing who they are writing for." Query with outline, 2-3 sample chapters and SASE (Canadian postage or IRC). Reviews artwork/photos as part of ms package. Send photocopies.

Fiction: Very limited. Only author/illustrator collaboration.

Recent Title(s): *The Mulligan Affair*, by O'Keefe/Macdonald (police history); *Orca's Family & More Northwest Coast Stories*, by Jim Challenger (children's fiction).

Tips: "Our books appeal to residents and visitors to the northwest quadrant of the continent. Present your material only after you have done your best."

HORSDAL & SCHUBART PUBLISHERS LTD., 623-425 Simcoe St., Victoria, British Columbia V8V 4T3 Canada. (250)360-2031. Fax: (250)360-0829. **Acquisitions:** Marlyn Horsdal, editor. Publishes hardcover originals and trade paperback originals and reprints. **Publishes 8-10 titles/year. 50% of books from first-time authors; 100% from unagented writers. Pays 15% royalty on wholesale price. Negotiates advance.** Publishes books 6 months after acceptance of ms. Accepts simultaneous submissions. Responds in 1 month to queries. Book catalog free.

> O— "We concentrate on Western and Northern Canada and nautical subjects and offer useful information, to give readers pause for thought, to encourage action to help heal the Earth." Currently emphasizing environment, wider areas. De-emphasizing regional subjects.

Nonfiction: Subjects include anthropology/archaeology, art/architecture, biography, government/politics, history, nature/environment, recreation, regional. Query with outline, 2-3 sample chapters and SASE or SAE with IRCs. Reviews artwork/photos as part of ms package. Send photocopies.

Recent Title(s): *A Year on the Wild Side*, by Briony Penn (nonfiction); *Snow-Coming Moon*, by Stan Evans (fiction).

HOUSE OF ANANSI PRESS, 34 Lesmill Rd., Toronto, Ontario M3B 2T6 Canada. (416)445-3333. Fax: (416)445-5967. E-mail: info@anansi.ca. Website: www.anansi.ca. **Acquisitions:** Martha Sharpe, publisher. Publishes hardcover and trade paperback originals. **Publishes 10-15 titles/year. Receives 750 queries/year. 5% of books from first-time authors; 99% from unagented writers. Pays 8-15% royalty on retail price. Offers $500-2,000 advance.** Publishes book 9 months after acceptance of ms. Accepts simultaneous submissions. Responds in 2 months to queries, 3 months to proposals, 4 months to mss.

> O— "Our mission is to publish the best new literary writers in Canada and to continue to grow and adapt along with the Canadian literary community, while maintaining Anansi's rich history."

Nonfiction: Biography, critical thought, literary criticism. Subjects include anthropology, gay/lesbian, government/politics, history, language/literature, philosophy, science, sociology, women's issues/studies, *only Canadian writers*. "Our nonfiction list is literary, but not overly academic. Some writers submit academic work better suited for university presses or pop-psychology books, which we do not publish." Submit outline with 2 sample chapters and SASE. Send photocopies of artwork/photos.

Fiction: "We publish literary fiction by Canadian authors." Experimental, feminist, gay/lesbian, literary, short story collections. "Authors must have been published in established literary magazines and/or journals. We only want to consider sample chapters." Submit synopsis, 2 sample chapters with SASE.

Poetry: "We only publish book-length works by Canadian authors. Poets must have a substantial résumé of published poems in literary magazines or journals. We only want samples from a ms." Submit 10-15 sample poems or 15 pages.

Recent Title(s): *The Expanding Prison: The Crisis in Crime and Punishment and the Search for Alternatives*, by David Cayley (nonfiction); *The Plight of Happy People in an Ordinary World*, by Natalee Caple (fiction); *A Frame of the Book*, by Erin Mouré (poetry).

Tips: "Submit often to magazines and journals. Read and buy other writers' work. Know and be a part of your writing community."

INSTITUTE OF PSYCHOLOGICAL RESEARCH, INC./INSTITUT DE RECHERCHES PSYCHOLOGI-QUES, INC., 34 Fleury St. W., Montréal, Québec H3L 1S9 Canada. (514)382-3000. Fax: (514)382-3007. **Acquisitions:** Marie-Paule Chevrier, general director. Estab. 1958. Publishes hardcover and trade paperback originals and reprints. **Publishes 12 titles/year. Receives 15 submissions/year. 10% of books from first-time authors, 100% from unagented writers. Pays 10-12% royalty.** Publishes book 6 months after acceptance of ms. Responds in 2 months.

> O— Institute of Psychological Research publishes psychological tests and science textbooks for a varied professional audience.

Nonfiction: Textbooks, psychological tests. Subjects include philosophy, psychology, science, translation. "We are looking for psychological tests in French or English." Submit complete ms. *Writer's Market* recommends a query with SASE first.

Recent Title(s): *Épreuve individuelle d'habileté mentale*, by Jean-Marc Chevrier (intelligence test).

Tips: "Psychologists, guidance counselors, professionals, schools, school boards, hospitals, teachers, government agencies and industries comprise our audience."

ISER BOOKS, Institute of Social and Economic Research, Memorial University of Newfoundland, A 1044, St. John's A1K 1A9 Newfoundland. (709)737-8343. Fax: (709) 737-7560. E-mail: iser-books@morgan.ucs.mun.ca. Website: www. mun.ca/iser/. **Acquisitions:** Al Potter, manager. Publishes trade paperback originals. **Publishes 3-4 titles/year. Receives 10-20 queries and 10 mss/year. 45% of books published are from first-time authors; 85% from unagented writers. Pays 6-10% royalty on wholesale price. No advance.** Publishes book 6 months after acceptance of ms. Responds in 1 month to queries, 2 months to proposals; 3-4 months to mss. Book catalogue, ms guidelines free.
  ○→ Iser Books publishes research within such disciplines and in such parts of the world as are deemed of relevance to Newfoundland and Labrador.
Nonfiction: Biography, reference. Subjects include anthropology/archaeology, ethic, government/politics, history, multicultural, recreation, regional, sociology, translation, women's issues/studies. Query with SASE. Submit proposal package, including outline and 2-3 sample chapters.
Recent Title(s): *Remembering the Years of My Life: Journeys of a Labrador Inuit Hunter*, recounted by Paulus Maggo, edited by Carol Brice-Bennett.

JESPERSON PUBLISHING, LTD., Jesperson Press, 39 James Lane, St. John's, Newfoundland A1E 3H3 Canada. (709)753-0633. Fax: (709)753-5507. E-mail: jespersonpress@nf.aibn.com. Website: www.bcity.com/jesperson. **Acquisitions:** John Symonds, president; Cheryl Cofield, publishing assistant. Publishes trade paperback originals. **Publishes 10-12 titles/year. Receives 100 queries and 75 mss/year. 10% of books from first-time authors; 100% from unagented writers. Pays 10% royalty on retail price. No advance.** Publishes book 18 months after acceptance of ms. Accepts simultaneous submissions. Responds in 1 month to queries, 3 months to proposals and mss. Book catalog and ms guidelines free or to website.
  ○→ "We are interested in solid writing, a good grasp of the English language, and a Newfoundland angle." Currently emphasizing solid fiction, creative nonfiction. De-emphasizing poetry, children's books.
Nonfiction: Humor, historical/cultural. Subjects include creative nonfiction, education, history, military/war, women's issues/studies. Query with SASE. Reviews artwork/photos as part of ms package. Send photocopies.
Fiction: Experimental, feminist, historical, humor, literary, military/war, multicultural, poetry, regional, short story collections. Query with SASE.
Poetry: Query.
Recent Titles: *Flyfishing Tips & Tactics*, by Len Rich (nonfiction); *Tales From the Frozen Ocean*, by Dwain Campbell (fiction); *Christ in the Pizza Place*, by Clyde Rose (poetry).
Tips: "Do not send SASE with U.S. postage!!!"

[N] KINDRED PRODUCTIONS, 4-169 Riverton Ave., Winnipeg, Manitoba R2L 2E5 Canada. (204)669-6575. Fax: (204)654-1865. E-mail: kindred@mbconf.ca. Website: www.mbconf.org/mbc/kp/kindred.htm. **Acquisitions:** Marilyn Hudson, manager. Publishes trade paperback originals and reprints. **Publishes 3 titles/year. 1% of books from first-time authors; 100% from unagented writers. Non-author subsidy publishes 20% of books. Pays 10-15% royalty on net price.** Publishes book 18 months after acceptance of ms. Accepts simultaneous submissions. Responds in 3 months to queries, 5 months to proposals. Book catalog and ms guidelines free.
  ○→ "Kindred Productions publishes, promotes and markets print and nonprint resources that will shape our Christian faith and discipleship from a Mennonite Brethren perspective." Currently emphasizing inspirational with crossover potential. De-emphasizing personal experience, biographical. No longer publishing fiction.
Nonfiction: Biography (select) and Bible study. Religious subjects. "Our books cater primarily to our Mennonite Brethren denomination readers." Query with outline, 2-3 sample chapters and SASE.
Recent Title(s): *Rogues, Rascals, Rare Gems*, by Danny Unrau; *Remember Dad?*, by Lorlie Barbman; *It Takes Two to Tangle*, by Philip Wiebe..
Tips: "Most of our books are sold to churches, religious bookstores and schools. We are concentrating on devotional and inspirational books. We are accepting no children's manuscripts."

[N] LAMBRECHT PUBLICATIONS, 1763 Maple Bay Rd., Duncan, British Columbia V9L 5N6 Canada. (250)748-8722. Fax: (250)748-8723. E-mail: helgal@cowichan.com. **Acquisitions:** Helga Lambrecht, publisher. Publishes hardcover, trade paperback originals and reprints. **Publishes 2 titles/year. Receives 6 queries/year. 50% of books from first-time authors Pays 10% royalty on retail price. Book catalog free on request.**
  ○→ Lambrecht publishes local history books and cookbooks.
Nonfiction: Cookbook, local history. Subjects include cooking/foods/nutrition, regional. All unsolicited mss returned unopened.

LONE PINE PUBLISHING, 10145 81st Ave., #206, Edmonton, Alberta T6E 1W9 Canada. (403)433-9333. Fax: (403)433-9646. Website: www.lonepinepublishing.com. **Acquisitions:** Nancy Foulds, editorial director. Estab. 1980. Publishes trade paperback originals and reprints. **Publishes 12-20 titles/year. Receives 800 submissions/year. 75% of books from first-time authors; 95% from unagented writers. Pays royalty.** Responds in 2 months to queries. Book catalog free.

O─π Lone Pine publishes natural history and outdoor recreation—including gardening—titles, and some popular history.

Imprint(s): Lone Pine, Home World, Pine Candle and Pine Cone.

Nonfiction: Subjects include animals, anthropology/archaeology, botany/ethnobotany, gardening, nature/environment ("this is where most of our books fall"). The list is set for the next year and a half, but we are interested in seeing new material. Submit outline and sample chapters. Reviews artwork/photos as part of ms package. Do not send originals. Send SASE with sufficient international postage if you want your ms returned.

Recent Title(s): *Perennials for Washington and Oregon*, by Alison Beck and Marianne Binetti.

Tips: "Writers have their best chance with recreational or nature guidebooks. Most of our books are strongly regional in nature."

LYNX IMAGES, INC., 104 Scollard St., Toronto, Ontario M5R 1G2 Canada. (416)925-8422. Fax: (925)952-8352. E-mail: info@lynximages.com. Website: www.lynximages.com. **Acquisitions:** Russell Floren, president; Andrea Gutsche, director; Barbara Chesholm, producer. Publishes hardcover and trade paperback originals. **Publishes 6 titles/year. Receives 100 queries and 50 mss/year. 80% of books from first-time authors; 80% from unagented writers. Makes outright purchase of $6,000-15,000. Offers 40% advance.** Publishes book 6 months-1 year after acceptance of ms. Accepts simultaneous submissions. Responds in 6 months to mss. Book catalog free.

Profile: "Lynx Images specializes in high-quality projects on Great Lakes and Canadian history. Our approach is to actively search out and document vanishing pieces of our heritage, bringing history alive with gripping and engaging stories." Currently emphasizing Canadian history, Great Lakes, general history, travel.

O─π Lynx publishes historical tourism, travel, Canadian history, Great Lakes history. Currently emphasizing travel, history, nature. De-emphasizing boating, guides.

Nonfiction: Coffee table book, gift book, multimedia (video). Subjects include history, nature/environment, travel. Submit proposal package, including sample chapter. Reviews artwork/photos as part of ms package. Send photocopies or other formats.

Recent Title(s): *Mysterious Islands*, by Andrea Gutsche; *Palaces of the Night*, by John Lindsay; *Northern Lights*, by David Baird.

MARCUS BOOKS, P.O. Box 327, Queensville, Ontario L0G 1R0 Canada. (905)478-2201. Fax: (905)478-8338. **Acquisitions:** Tom Rieder, president. Publishes trade paperback originals and reprints. **Publishes 1 title/year. Receives 12 queries and 6 mss/year. 90% of books from first-time authors; 100% from unagented writers. Pays 10% royalty on retail price.** Publishes book 6 months after acceptance of ms. Responds in 4 months to mss. Book catalog for $1.

Nonfiction: "Interested in alternative health and esoteric topics." Submit outline and 3 sample chapters.

McGRAW-HILL RYERSON LIMITED, The McGraw-Hill Companies, 300 Water St., Whitby, Ontario L1N 9B6 Canada. (905)430-5116. Fax: (905)430-5044. E-mail: joanh@mcgrawhill.ca. Website: www.mcgrawhill.ca. **Acquisitions:** Joan Homewood, publisher. Publishes hardcover and trade paperback originals and revisions. **Publishes 20 new titles/year. 50% of books are revisions. 10% of books from first-time authors; 75% from unagented writers. Pays 7½-10% royalty on retail price. Offers $4,000 average advance.** Publishes book 1 year after acceptance. Accepts simultaneous submissions. Responds in 6 months to queries.

O─π McGraw-Hill Ryerson, Ltd., publishes books on Canadian business and personal finance for the Canadian market. Currently emphasizing business/management/financial planning/investing. De-emphasizing Canadian military history.

Nonfiction: How-to, reference, professional. Subjects include small business, management, personal finance, Canadian military history, training. "No books and proposals that are American in focus. We publish primarily for the Canadian market, but work with McGraw-Hill U.S. to distribute business, management and training titles in U.S. and internationally." Query. Submit proposal with outline.

Recent Title(s): *Make Sure It's Deductible*, by Evelyn Jacks.

Tips: "Writers have the best chance of selling us nonfiction business and personal finance books with a distinctly Canadian focus. Proposal guidelines are available. Thorough market research on competitive titles increases chances of your proposal getting serious consideration, as does endorsement by or references from relevant professionals."

NATURAL HERITAGE/NATURAL HERITAGE INC., P.O. Box 95, Station O, Toronto, Ontario M4A 2M8 Canada. (416)694-7907. Fax: (416)690-9907. E-mail: natherbooks@idirect.com. **Acquisitions:** Jane Gibson, editor-in-chief. "We are a Canadian publisher in the natural heritage and history fields." Publishes hardcover and trade paperback

---

ALWAYS SUBMIT unsolicited manuscripts or queries with a self-addressed, stamped envelope (SASE) within your country or a self-addressed envelope with International Reply Coupons (IRC) purchased from the post office for other countries.

originals. **Publishes 10-12 titles/year. 50% of books from first-time authors; 85% from unagented writers. Pays 8-10% royalty on retail price.** Publishes book 2 years after acceptance of ms. Responds in 4 months to queries; 6 months to proposals and mss. Book catalog free. Manuscript guidelines for #10 SAE and IRC.

Imprint(s): Natural Heritage.

⚷ Currently emphasizing heritage, history.

Nonfiction: Subjects include anthropology/archaeology, art/architecture, ethnic, history, military/war, nature/environment, photography, recreation, regional. Submit outline with *details* of visuals.

Recent Title(s): *The Canoe in Canadian Cultures*, (nonfiction essay collection); *Once Upon a Time Long, Long Ago*, by Henry Shykoff (fiction); *Bliss Pig and Other Poems*, by Charlene Jones & Linda Stitt (poetry).

Fiction: Historical, short story collections. Query.

PEDLAR PRESS, P.O. Box 26, Station P, Toronto, Ontario M5S 2S6 Canada. (416)534-2011. Fax: (416)535-9677. E-mail: feralgrl@interlog.com. **Acquisitions:** Beth Follett, editor (fiction, poetry). Publishes hardcover and trade paperback originals. **Publishes 4 titles/year. Receives 50-60 mss/year. 50% of books from first-time authors; 100% from unagented writers.** (Does not work with agents.) **Pays 10-15% royalty on retail price. Offers $400-800 advance.** Publishes book 1 year after acceptance of ms. Accepts simultaneous submissions. Responds in 1 month to queries, 6 months to mss. Book catalog and ms guidelines for #10 SASE.

⚷ Niche is marginal voices, experimental style and form. Please note: Pedlar will not consider USA authors until 2001. Currently emphasizing experimental fiction.

Nonfiction: Gift book, humor, illustrated book. Subjects include creative nonfiction, gay/lesbian, language/literature, sex, women's issues/studies. Query with SASE or submit proposal package, including outline and 5 sample chapters. Reviews artwork/photos as part of ms package. Send photocopies.

Fiction: Erotica, experimental, feminist, gay/lesbian, humor, literary, picture books, poetry, short story collections, translation. Query with SASE or submit proposal package, including synopsis and 5 sample chapters.

Recent Titles: *Mouthing the Words*, by Camilla Gibb (fiction); *Lake Where No One Swims*, by Chris Chambers (poetry).

Tips: "We select manuscripts according to our taste. Be familiar with some if not most of our recent titles."

PENGUIN BOOKS CANADA LTD., The Penguin Group, 10 Alcorn Ave., Suite 300, Toronto, Ontario M4V 3B2 Canada. (416)925-0068. **Acquisitions:** Jackie Kaiser, senior editor (literary nonfiction, biography, social issues); Barbara Berson, senior editor (literary fiction and nonfiction; children's and young adult fiction; history/current events); Cynthia Good, president/publisher.

Nonfiction: Any Canadian subject by Canadian authors. Query. *No unsolicited mss.*

Recent Title(s): *Titans*, by Peter C. Newman (business); *Home From the Vinyl Cafe*, by Stuart McLean (fiction); *Notes from the Hyena's Belly*, by Nega Mezlekia (memoir).

PICASSO PUBLICATIONS, INC., Picasso Entertainment Company, 10080 Jasper Ave., Suite 904, Edmonton, Alberta T5J 1V9 Canada. (780)420-1070. Fax: (780)420-0029. E-mail: Randolph@picassopublications.com. Website: www.picassopublications.com. **Acquisitions:** Randolph Ross Sr., director (new business development); Luis Chacon Sr., director (operations director). Publishes hardcover and trade paperback originals, mass market paperback originals. **Publishes 35 titles/year; imprint publishes 5 titles/year. Receives 50,000 queries and 10,000 mss/year. Less than 1% of books from first-time authors; less than 10% from unagented writers. Pays 10-12% royalty on retail price or makes outright purchase $500-20,000. Offers advance up to $1 million.** Publishes book 9 months after acceptance of ms. Accepts simultaneous submissions. Responds in 2 months to queries, 1 month to proposals, 3 months to mss. Book catalog and ms guidelines free on request or on website.

⚷ Picasso Publications publishes wide variety of books for mass market audience.

Imprints: Blink, Chronicle Fiction, Engima, Nebula, Mystic, Passion Enlightenment.

Nonfiction: Biography, children's/juvenile, coffee table book, cookbook, gift book, how-to, humor, illustrated book, multimedia, self-help. Subjects include Americana, animals, art/architecture, child guidance/parenting, cooking/foods/nutrition, creative nonviction, education, ethnic, gay/lesbian, government/politics, history, hobbies, language/literature, military/war, money/finance, multicultural, recreation, religion, sex, sports, women's issues/studies. Query with SASE. Reviews artwork/photos as part of ms package. Send photocopies.

Fiction: Adventure, comic books, erotica, ethnic, fantasy, feminist, gay/lesbian, gothic, historical, horror, humor, juvenile, literary, mainstream/contemporary, military/war, multicultural, multimedia, mystery, regional, religious, romance, science fiction, spiritual, sports, suspense, young adult. Query with SASE.

Recent Title(s): *Pain Behind the Smile*, by Leah Hulan (beauty queen memoir); *Shadowed Love*, by Martine Jardin (novel).

PLAYWRIGHTS CANADA PRESS, Playwrights Union of Canada, 54 Wolseley St., 2nd Floor, Toronto, Ontario M5T 1A5 Canada. (416)703-0201. Fax: (416)703-0059. E-mail: cdplays@interlog.com. Website: www.puc.ca. **Acquisitions:** Angela Rebeiro, publisher. Estab. 1972. Publishes paperback originals and reprints of plays *by Canadian citizens or landed immigrants*. **Receives 40 submissions/year. 50% of plays from first-time authors; 50% from unagented authors. Pays 10% royalty on list price.** Publishes 1 year after acceptance. Responds in up to 1 year. Play catalog for $5. Accepts children's plays.

⚷ Playwrights Canada Press publishes only drama which has received professional production.

Recent Title(s): *The Drawer Boy*, by Michael Healey; *Beating Heart Cadaver*, by Colleen Murphy; *Whyllah Falls*, by George Elliott Clarke.

PRODUCTIVE PUBLICATIONS, P.O. Box 7200 Station A, Toronto, Ontario M5W 1X8 Canada. (416)483-0634. Fax: (416)322-7434. **Acquisitions:** Iain Williamson, owner. Estab. 1985. Publishes trade paperback originals. **Publishes 24 titles/year. Receives 160 queries and 40 mss/year. 80% of books from first-time authors; 100% from unagented writers. Pays 10-15% royalty on wholesale price.** Publishes book 3 months after acceptance of ms. Responds in 1 month to queries and proposals, 3 months to mss. Accepts simultaneous submissions. Book catalog free.
- "Productive publishes books to help readers succeed and to help them meet the challenges of the new information age and global marketplace." Interested in books on business computer software, the Internet for business purposes, investment, stock market and mutual funds, etc. Currently emphasizing computers, software, personal finance. De-emphasizing jobs, how to get employment.

Nonfiction: How-to, reference, self-help, technical. Subjects include business and economics, computers and electronics, health/medicine, hobbies, money/finance, software (business). "We are interested in small business/entrepreneurship/employment/self-help (business)/how-to/health and wellness—100 to 300 pages." Submit outline. Reviews artwork as part of ms package. Send photocopies.

Recent Title(s): *Software for Small Business*, by Iain Williamson.

Tips: "We are looking for books written by *knowledgeable, experienced experts* who can express their ideas *clearly* and *simply.*"

PURICH PUBLISHING LTD., Box 23032, Market Mall Post Office, Saskatoon, Saskatchewan S7J 5H3 Canada. (306)373-5311. Fax: (306)373-5315. E-mail: purich@sk.sympatico.ca. Website: www3.sk.sympatico.ca/purich. **Acquisitions:** Donald Purich, publisher (law, Aboriginal issues); Karen Bolstad, publisher (history). Publishes trade paperback originals. **Publishes 3-5 titles/year. 20% of books from first-time authors. Pays 8-12% royalty on retail price or makes outright purchase. Offers $100-1,500 advance.** Publishes book 4 months after acceptance of ms. Accepts simultaneous submissions. Responds in 1 month to queries, 3 months to mss. Book catalog free.
- Purich publishes books on law, Aboriginal issues and Western Canadian history for the academic and professional trade reference market.

Nonfiction: Reference, technical, textbook. Subjects include agriculture/horticulture, government/politics, history, law, Aboriginal issues. "We are a specialized publisher and only consider work in our subject areas." Query.

Recent Title(s): *Education, Student Rights and the Charter*, by Ailsa M. Watkinson.

RAGWEED PRESS, P.O. Box 2023, Charlottetown, Prince Edward Island C1A 7N7 Canada. (902)566-5750. Fax: (902)566-4473. E-mail: editor@ragweed.com. **Acquisitions:** Sibyl Frei, managing editor. Publishes hardcover and trade paperback originals. **Publishes 3-5 titles/year; imprint publishes 3-5 titles/year. Receives 200 queries and 1,500-2,000 mss/year. 50% of books from first-time authors; 95% from unagented writers. Pays 8-10% royalty on wholesale or retail price. Offers advance.** Publishes book 1-2 years after acceptance of ms. Accepts simultaneous submissions and unsolicited mss. Responds in 6 months to mss. Book catalog free. Manuscript guidelines for #10 SASE.
- Ragweed publishes only single-authored works by Canadians.

Imprint(s): gynergy books.

Nonfiction: Biography, coffee table book, cookbook, gift book, humor, illustrated book. Subjects include feminist issues, government/politics, history, music/dance, nature/environment, photography, recreation, regional. "For nonfiction, we prefer to review proposals and, if accepted, work with the author or editor on developing the book from concept through to final manuscript." Submit proposal package, including draft of ms if available with SASE.

Fiction: Adventure, historical, juvenile, literary, multicultural, picture books, poetry, young adult. "Our children's, juvenile and young adult fiction features girl heroes (no rhyming stories for children). Our adult fiction must be written in or about the Atlantic Canada region." Submit complete ms and SASE.

Poetry: "Must be writers in the Atlantic Canada region." Submit complete ms.

Recent Title(s): *Sweeping the Earth: Women Taking Action for a Healthy Planet*, edited by Miriam Wyman (feminist nonfiction anthology); *The Dog Wizarrd*, by Anne Louise MacDonald, illustrated by Brenda Jones (children's fiction for ages 5-8).

RAINCOAST BOOK DISTRIBUTION LIMITED, 8680 Cambie St., Vancouver, British Columbia V6P 6M9 Canada. **Acquisitions:** Lyn Henry, managing editor. Publishes hardcover and trade paperback originals and reprints. **Publishes 20-25 titles/year. Receives 2,000 queries/year. 1% of books from first-time authors; 50% from unagented writers. Pays 8-12% royalty on retail price. Offers $1,000-6,000 advance.** Publishes book within 2 years after acceptance of ms. Responds in 1 month to queries and proposals. Book catalog and ms guidelines for #10 IRCs.

Imprint(s): Raincoast Books, Polestar Books (fiction).

Nonfiction: Children's, coffee table book, cookbook, gift book, illustrated book. Subjects include animals, art/architecture, cooking/foods/nutrition, history, nature/environment, photography, recreation, regional, sports, travel, business, Canadian subjects and native studies/issues. "We are expanding rapidly and plan on publishing a great deal more over the next two or three years, particularly nonfiction. Proposals should be focused and include background information on the author. Include a market study or examination of competition. We like to see proposals that cover all the bases and offer a new approach to the subjects we're interested in." Query first with SASE. *No unsolicited mss.*

Fiction: Literary novels, short fiction, young adult. "Our interest is high-quality children's picture books with Canadian themes." Query first with SASE. *No unsolicited mss.*

Recent Title(s): *Shocking Beauty*, by Thomas Hobbs (gardening); *The Dragon New Year*, by David Bouchard (children's picture book).

Tips: "We have very high standards. Our books are extremely well designed and the texts reflect that quality. Be focused in your submission. Know what you are trying to do and be able to communicate it. Make sure the submission is well organized, thorough, and original. We like to see that the author has done some homework on markets and competition, particularly for nonfiction."

REIDMORE BOOKS INC., 18228-102 Ave., Edmonton, Alberta T5S 1S7 Canada. (780)444-0912. Fax: (780)444-0933. E-mail: reidmore@compusmart.ab.ca. Website: www.reidmore.com. **Acquisitions:** Leah-Ann Lymer, senior editor. Estab. 1979. Publishes hardcover originals. **Publishes 10-12 titles/year. Receives 50 submissions/year. 60% of books from first-time authors; 100% from unagented writers. Nonauthor subsidy publishes 5% of books. Pays royalty.** Publishes book 1 year after acceptance. Responds in 8 months to queries. Book catalog free.

O—¬ Reidmore publishes social studies for kindergarten to grade 12.

Nonfiction: Textbook. Subjects include ethnic, government/politics, history, geography and social studies. Query. Most manuscripts are solicited by publisher from specific authors.

Recent Title(s): *Century of Change: Europe from 1789 to 1918*, by Mitchner and Tuffs (grades 10-12).

ROCKY MOUNTAIN BOOKS, #4 Spruce Centre SW, Calgary, Alberta T3C 3B3 Canada. (403)249-9490. Fax: (403)249-2968. E-mail: tonyd@rmbooks.com. Website: www.rmbooks.com. **Acquisitions:** Tony Daffern, publisher. Publishes trade paperback originals. **Publishes 5 titles/year. Receives 30 queries/year. 75% of books from first-time authors; 100% from unagented writers. Pays 10% royalty. Offers $1,000-2,000 advance.** Publishes book 1 year after acceptance. Responds in 1 month to queries. Book catalog and ms guidelines free.

O—¬ Rocky Mountain Books publishes on Western Canada and also mountaineering.

Nonfiction: How-to. Subjects include nature/environment, recreation, travel. "Our main area of publishing is outdoor recreation guides to Western and Northern Canada." Query.

Recent Title(s): *High on a Windy Hill: the Story of the Prince of Wales Hotel*, by Ray Djuff; *Not Won in a Day: Climbing Canada's Highpoints*, by Jack Bennett.

RONSDALE PRESS, 3350 W. 21st Ave., Vancouver, British Columbia V6S 1G7 Canada. Website: www.ronsdale press.com. **Acquisitions:** Ronald B. Hatch, director (fiction, poetry, social commentary); Veronica Hatch, managing director (children's literature). Publishes trade paperback originals. **Publishes 8 titles/year. Receives 100 queries and 200 mss/year. 60% of books from first-time authors; 95% from unagented writers. Pays 10% royalty on retail price.** Publishes book 1 year after acceptance of ms. Accepts simultaneous submissions. Responds in 1 week to queries, 1 month to proposals, 3 months to mss. Book catalog for #10 SASE. Writers *must* be Canadian citizens or landed immigrants.

O—¬ Ronsdale publishes fiction, poetry, regional history, biography and autobiography, books of ideas about Canada, as well as children's books. Currently emphasizing YA historical fiction.

Nonfiction: Biography, children's/juvenile. No picture books. Subjects include history, language/literature, nature/environment, regional.

Fiction: Novels, short story collections, children's literature. Query with at least 80 pages.

Poetry: "Poets should have published some poems in magazines/journals and should be well-read in contemporary masters." Submit complete ms.

Recent Title(s): *A Speaking Likeness*, by Joseph Plaskett (memoir); *Jackrabbit Moon*, by Sheila McLeod Arnopoulos (fiction); *Cobalt 3*, by Kevin Roberts (poetry).

Tips: "Ronsdale Press is a literary publishing house, based in Vancouver, and dedicated to publishing books from across Canada, books that give Canadians new insights into themselves and their country. We aim to publish the best Canadian writers."

SAXON HOUSE CANADA, P.O. Box 6947, Station A, Toronto, Ontario M5P 2H7 Canada. (416)488-7171. Fax: (416)488-2989. **Acquisitions:** Dietrich Hummell, editor-in-chief (poetry, legends); W.H. Wallace, general manager (history, philosophy); Carla Saxon, CEO (printed music). Publishes hardcover originals and trade paperback reprints. **Publishes 4 titles/year. Receives 6 queries and 20 mss/year. 20% of books from first-time authors; 80% from unagented writers. Pays royalty on wholesale price or makes outright purchase. "Each title assessed and negotiated."** Publishes book 15 months after acceptance of ms. Accepts simultaneous submissions. Responds in 4 months to mss.

Nonfiction: Illustrated book. Subjects include americana, history, music/dance, philosophy, religion. Submit proposal package, including 3 sample chapters and author résumé. Reviews artwork/photos as part of ms package. Send photocopies.

Fiction: Historical, literary, poetry. Submit proposal package, including 3 sample chapters and author résumé.

Poetry: Submit 8 sample poems.

Recent Title(s): *The Journey to Canada*, by David Mills (history); *Voices From the Lake*, by E.M. Watts (illustrated ancient American Indian legend); *The Wine of Babylon*, by David Mills (epic poem).

Tips: "We want books with literary integrity. Historical accuracy and fresh narrative skills."

[N] **SCHOLASTIC CANADA LTD.**, 175 Hillmount Rd., Markham, Ontario L6C 1Z7 Canada. (903)887-7323. Fax: (905)887-3643. Website: www.scholastic.ca. **Acquisitions:** Joanne Richter, Sandra Bogart Johnston, editors, children's books. Publishes hardcover and trade paperback originals. **Publishes 5 titles/year; imprint publishes 4 titles/year. 3% of books from first-time authors; 50% from unagented writers. Pays 5-10% royalty on retail price. Offers $1,000-5,000 (Canadian) advance.** Publishes book 1 year after acceptance of ms. Responds in 1 month to queries, 3 months to proposals. Book catalog for 8½×11 SAE with 2 first-class stamps (IRC or Canadian stamps only).
Imprint(s): North Winds Press; Les Éditions Scholastic (contact Sylvie Andrews, French editor).
  O┯ Scholastic Press focuses on books by Canadians and/or of special Canadian interest.
Nonfiction: Children's/juvenile. Subjects include animals, history, hobbies, nature, recreation, science, sports. Query with outline, 1-2 sample chapters and SASE. No unsolicited mss. Reviews artwork/photos as part of ms package. Send photocopies.
Fiction: Children's/juvenile, young adult. Query with synopsis, 3 sample chapters and SASE.
Recent Title(s): *Crazy for Horses*, by Karen Briggs (nonfiction); *The 6th Grade Nickname Game*, by Gordon Korman (fiction).

SHORELINE, 23 Ste-Anne, Ste-Anne-de-Bellevue, Quebec H9X 1L1 Canada. Phone/fax: (514)457-5733. E-mail: bookline@total.net. Website: www.total.net/~bookline. **Acquisitions:** Judy Isherwood, editor. Publishes trade paperback originals. **Publishes 3 titles/year. Pays 10% royalty on retail price.** Publishes book 1 year after acceptance. Responds in 1 month to queries, 4 months to ms. Book catalog for 50¢ postage.
  O┯ "Our mission is to support new authors by publishing literary works of considerable merit."
Nonfiction: Biography, essays, humour, illustrated book, reference. Subjects include: America, art, Canada, education, ethnic, health/mental health, history, mediation, regional, religion, Mexico, Spain, the Arctic, travel, women's studies.
Recent Title(s): *Girl in a CBC Studio*, by Mary Peate (nonfiction); *Tickets, A Play in One Act* (fiction); *The Prophet of the Plains*, by Robert Tessier (poetry).
Tips: Audience is "adults and young adults who like their nonfiction personal, different and special. Beginning writers welcome, agents unnecessary. Send your best draft (not the first!), make sure your heart is in it."

SIMON & PIERRE PUBLISHING CO. LTD., Dundurn Press, 8 Market St., Suite 200, Toronto, Ontario M5E 1M6 Canada. (416)214-5544. **Acquisitions:** Acquisitions Editor. Estab. 1972. Publishes hardcover and trade paperback originals and reprints. **Publishes 6-8 titles/year. Receives 300 submissions/year. 50% of books are from first-time authors; 85% from unagented writers. Pays 10-15% royalty on retail price for trade books. Pays 8% royalty of net for education books. Offers $500 average advance.** Publishes book an average of 1 year after acceptance. Accepts simultaneous submissions. Responds in 3 months to queries. Ms guidelines free.
  O┯ Simon & Pierre publishes Canadian themes by Canadian authors, literary fiction, drama theater.
Nonfiction: Reference, drama, language/literature, music/dance (drama). "We are looking for Canadian drama and drama related books." Query or submit outline and sample chapters. Sometimes reviews artwork/photos as part of ms package.
Fiction: Literary, mainstream/contemporary, mystery, plays (Canadian, must have had professional production). "No romance, sci-fi or experimental." Query or submit outline/synopsis and sample chapters.
Recent Fiction Title(s): *Found: A Body*, by Betsy Struthers (novel).
Tips: "We are looking for Canadian themes *by Canadian authors*. Special interest in drama and drama related topics. If I were a writer trying to market a book today, I would check carefully the types of books published by a publisher before submitting manuscript; books can be examined in bookstores, libraries, etc.; should look for a publisher publishing the type of book being marketed. Clean manuscripts essential; if work is on computer disk, give the publisher that information. Send information on markets for the book, and writer's résumé, or at least why the writer is an expert in the field. Covering letter is important first impression."

SKYFOOT TECHNICAL, 283 McAlpine Ave. S., Welland, Ontario L3B 1T8 Canada. (905)708-1784. E-mail: pboucher@skyfoot-technical.nu. Website: www.skyfoot-technical.nu. **Acquisitions:** Phillip Boucher, owner. Publishes trade paperback originals. **Publishes 2-5 titles/year. Pays 10% royalty on wholesale price.** Publishes book 1 year after acceptance of ms. Accepts simultaneous submissions. Responds within 1 month to queries, 2 months to proposals, 3 months to mss.
  O┯ Skyfoot is currently emphasizing technical how-to.
Nonfiction: How-to, reference, technical. Subjects include computers/electronics, hobbies, science, radio communications, amateur radio, scanner radio, customer service, Native, New Age. "We are a new, small technical publisher looking for quality manuscripts for niche book publication. We stress content quality, low price and interesting subject matter, rather than esthetics. All publications are 8½×11, side-stapled or loose-leaf format, depending on subject matter." Submit *very* short query about manuscript or proposal via e-mail or voice mail.
Tips: "Leave a voicemail or e-mail regarding your book or idea. We will get back to you and if interested, will tell you how to send the work to us. Please visit our website to get an understanding of what we are looking for. Our books are not mass market, so nobody is going to make a lot of money, if much at all. However, we do offer the chance of publication and some possible income from the product. As such, new or unpublished writers are most welcome."
Recent Title(s): *Skyfoot's Guide to Buying and Selling a Home*, by Ted Francis.

SNOWAPPLE PRESS, Box 66024, Heritage Postal Outlet, Edmonton, Alberta T6J 6T4 Canada. **Acquisitions**: Vanna Tessier, editor. Publishes hardcover originals, trade paperback originals and reprints, mass market paperback originals and reprints. **Publishes 5-6 titles/year. Receives 300 queries/year. 50% of books from first-time authors; 100% from unagented writers. Pays 10-50% royalty on retail price or makes outright purchase of $100 or pays in copies. Offers $100-200 advance.** Publishes book 2 years after acceptance. Accepts simultaneous submissions. Responds in 1 month to queries, 3 months to proposals and mss.

O─ "We focus on topics that are interesting, unusual and controversial."

Fiction: Adventure, ethnic, experimental, fantasy, feminist, historical, literary, mainstream/contemporary, mystery, picture books, short story collections, young adult. Query with SASE.

Poetry: Query with SASE or SAE and IRC.

Recent Title(s): *Thistle Creek*, by Vanna Tessier (fiction).

Tips: "We are a small press that will publish original, interesting and entertaining fiction and poetry."

SOUND AND VISION PUBLISHING LIMITED, 359 Riverdale Ave., Toronto, Ontario M4J 1A4 Canada. (416)465-2828. Fax: (416)465-0755. E-mail: musicbooks@soundandvision.com. Website: www.soundandvision.com. **Acquisitions:** Geoff Savage. Publishes trade paperback originals. **Publishes 3-5 titles/year. Receives 25 queries/year. 85% of books from first-time authors; 100% from unagented writers. Pays royalty on wholesale price. Offers $500-2,000 advance.** Responds in 1 month.

O─ Sound And Vision specializes in books on music with a humorous slant.

Nonfiction: Music/humor subjects. Query with SASE.

Recent Title(s): *Opera Antics and Anecdotes*, by Stephen Tanner, cartoons by Umberto Taccola.

[N] STELLER PRESS LTD., 13-4335 W. 10th Ave., Vancouver, British Columbia V6R 2H6 Canada. (604)222-2955. Fax: (604)222-2965. E-mail: harful@telus.net. **Acquisitions:** Guy Chadsey, publisher (outdoors/gardening). Publishes trade paperback originals. **Publishes 4 titles/year. 75% of books from first-time authors; 100% from unagented writers. Pays royalty on retail price.** Publishes book 6 months after acceptance of ms. Accepts simultaneous submissions. Responds in 6 months.

O─ "All titles are specific to the Pacific Northwest."

Nonfiction: Subjects include gardening, history, nature/environment, regional, travel. Query with SASE.

Recent Title(s): *Roses For the Pacific Northwest*, by Christine Allen; and *Herbs For the Pacific Northwest*, by Moira Carlson.

STODDART PUBLISHING CO., LTD., General Publishing Co., Ltd., 34 Lesmill Rd., Toronto, Ontario M3B 2T6 Canada. **Acquisitions:** Donald G. Bastian, managing editor. Publishes hardcover, trade paperback and mass market paperback originals and trade paperback reprints. **Publishes 100 titles/year. Receives 1,200 queries and mss/year. 10% of books from first-time authors; 50% from unagented writers. Pays 8-10% royalty on retail price.** Publishes book 1 year after acceptance of ms. Accepts simultaneous submissions. Responds in 2 months. Book catalog and ms guidelines for #10 SASE.

O─ Stoddart publishes "important Canadian books" for a general interest audience. Currently emphasizing money/finance, sports, business. De-emphasizing coffee table book, cookbook, gardening.

Imprint(s): Stoddart Kids (Kathryn Cole, publisher).

Nonfiction: Biography, how-to, humor, illustrated book, self-help. Subjects include art/architecture, business and economics, child guidance/parenting, computers and electronics, cooking/foods/nutrition, gardening, government/politics, health/medicine, history, language/literature, military/war, money/finance, nature/environment, psychology, science, sociology, sports. Submit outline, 2 sample chapters, résumé, with SASE.

Recent Title(s): *Water*, by Marq deVilliers (nonfiction); *Save Me, Joe Louis*, by M.T. Kelly (fiction); *Visible Amazement*, by Gale Zoë Garnett.

THOMPSON EDUCATIONAL PUBLISHING INC., 14 Ripley Ave., Suite 104, Toronto, Ontario M6S 3N9 Canada. (416)766-2763. Fax: (416)766-0398. E-mail: publisher@thompsonbooks.com. Website: www.thompsonbooks.com. **Acquisitions:** Keith Thompson, president. **Publishes 10 titles/year. Receives 15 queries and 10 mss/year. 80% of books from first-time authors; 100% from unagented writers. Pays 10% royalty on net price.** Publishes book 1 year after acceptance. Responds in 1 month. Book catalog free.

O─ Thompson Educational specializes in high-quality educational texts in the social sciences and humanities.

Nonfiction: Textbook. Subjects include business/economics, education, government/politics, sociology, women's issues/studies. Submit outline and 1 sample chapter and résumé.

Recent Title(s): *The Art of Evaluation*, by Tara Fenwick and Jim Parsons.

TITAN BOOKS LTD., 144 Southwark St., London SE1 OUP England. Fax: (0207)620-0032. E-mail: editorial@titanemail@com. **Acquisitions:** D. Barraclough, editorial manager. Publishes trade and mass market paperback originals and reprints. **Publishes 60-90 titles/year. Receives 1,000 queries and 500 mss/year. Less than 1% of books from first-time authors; 50% from unagented writers. Pays royalty of 6-8% on retail price. Advance varies.** Publishes books 1 year after acceptance of ms. Accepts simultaneous submissions. Responds in 1 month to queries, 3 months to proposals, 6 months to mss. Manuscript guidelines for SASE with IRC.

O─ Titan Books publishes film and TV titles.

Nonfiction: Film and TV subjects. Send synopsis and sample chapter with SASE.
Recent Title(s): *Millennium Movies*, by Ken Newman; *The Essential Monster Movie Guide*, by Stephen Jones.

N THE TOBY PRESS LTD., 146 New Cavendish St., London W1M 7FG United Kingdom. +44-20-7580-5440. Fax: +44-20-7580-5442. E-mail: toby@tobypress.com. Website: www.tobypress.com. **Acquisitions:** Matthew Miller, director (fiction, biography). Publishes hardcover originals. **Publishes 20-25 titles/year. Receives 300 queries/year. 50% of books from first-time authors; 10% from unagented writers. Pays 10-15% royalty on retail price or outright purchase $1,000 and up.** Publishes book up to 1 year after acceptance of ms. Accepts simultaneous submissions. Responds in 1 month on queries and proposals, 6 months on mss. Book catalog free or on website.
○━ The Toby Press publishes literary fiction.
Nonfiction: Biography. Submit proposal package, including outline and 1 sample chapter.
Fiction: Historical, literary, mainstream/contemporary, short story collections. Submit proposal package, including synopsis and 1-2 sample chapters.
Recent Title(s): *Failing Paris*, by Samantha Dunn (fiction); *Before Hiroshima*, by Josira Radman (fiction).

N TRADEWIND BOOKS, 2216 Stephens St., Vancouver, British Columbia V6K 3W6 Canada. (604)730-0153. Fax: (604)730-0154. E-mail: tradewindbooks@yahoo.com. Website: www.tradewindbooks.com. **Acquisitions:** Michael Katz, publisher (picturebooks); Carol Frank, art director (picturebooks); Leslie Owen (acquisitions editor). Publishes hardcover and trade paperback originals. **Publishes 3-4 titles/year. Receives 1,000 queries and mss/year. 10% of books from first-time authors; 50% from unagented writers. Pays 8% royalty on retail price. Advance varies.** Publishes book 3 years after acceptance of ms. Accepts simultaneous submissions. Responds in 1 month to mss. Book catalog and manuscript guidelines on website.
○━ Tradewind Books publishes juvenile picturebooks, young adult novels and a nonfiction natural history series. Currently emphasizing nonfiction YA novels.
Fiction: Juvenile. Query with SASE or submit proposal package, including synopsis, 2 sample chapters for YA novels. For picture books, include a letter showing you have read at least two of our published books.
Recent Title(s): *Mama God Papa God*, by Richardo Keens Douglass; *Wherever Bears Be*, by Sue Ann Alderson; *Mr. Belinsky's Bagels*, by Ellen Schwartz (all picturebooks).

TRILOBYTE PRESS & MULTIMEDIA, (formerly Trilobyte Press), 1486 Willowdown Rd., Oakville, Ontario L6L 1X3 Canada. (905)847-7366. Fax: (905)847-3258. E-mail: mail@successatschool.com. Website: www.successatschool.com. **Acquisitions:** Danton H. O'Day, Ph.D., publisher. Publishes trade paperback originals. **Publishes 3-4 titles/year. Receives 50 queries and 20 mss/year. 50% of books from first-time authors; 100% from unagented writers. Pays 10% royalty on wholesale price. No advance.** Publishes book 8 months after acceptance of ms. Accepts simultaneous submissions. Responds in 1 month to queries, 2 months to proposals, 3 months to mss. Book catalog and ms guidelines are available on website.
Nonfiction: How-to, reference, self-help, textbook. Subjects include education, health/medicine, science. "We are continually looking for guides to help students succeed in school and in their careers." Query with proposal package, including outline, 2 sample chapters, qualifications of author and SASE. Reviews artwork/photos as part of ms package. Send photocopies.
Recent Title(s): *Write on Track—The Teaching Kit*, by Philip Dimitroff.
Tips: Audience is "people from high school through college age who want to do their best in school. Think about your submission—why us and why is your book worth publishing? Who will read it and why?"

TURNSTONE PRESS, 607-100 Arthur St., Winnipeg, Manitoba R3B 1H3 Canada. (204)947-1555. Fax: (204)942-1555. E-mail: editor@turnstonepress.mb.ca. Website: www.turnstonepress.com. **Acquisitions:** Manuela Dias, managing editor. Estab. 1971. Publishes trade paperback originals. **Publishes 10-12 titles/year. Receives 1,000 mss/year. 25% of books from first-time authors; 75% from unagented writers. Pays 10% royalty on retail price.** Publishes book 1 year after acceptance of ms. Responds in 4 months. Book catalog free with SASE. *Publishes Canadians and permanent residents only.*
○━ Turnstone Press is a literary press that publishes Canadian writers with an emphasis on writers from, and writing on, the Canadian West. "We are interested in publishing experimental/literary works that mainstream publishers may not be willing to work with." Currently emphasizing nonfiction-travel, memoir, eclectic novels. De-emphasizing formula or mainstream work.
Imprint(s): Ravenstone (literary genre fiction).
Nonfiction: Turnstone Press would like to see more nonfiction books, particularly travel, nature, memoir, women's writing. Query with SASE.
Fiction: Adventure, ethnic, experimental, feminist, gothic, humor, literary, contemporary, mystery, short story collections, women's. Would like to see more novels. Query with SASE (Canadian postage) first.
Poetry: Submit complete ms.
Recent Title(s): *Island of the Human Heart: A Women's Travel Odyssey*, by Laurie Gough (nonfiction); *The Drum King*, by Richelle Kosar (fiction); *Elizabeth Went West*, by Jan Horner (poetry).
Tips: "Writers are encouraged to view our list and check if submissions are appropriate. Would like to see more women's writing, travel, memoir, life-writing as well as eclectic novels. Would like to see 'non-formula' genre writing, especially *literary* mystery, gothic and noir for our new imprint."

THE UNIVERSITY OF ALBERTA PRESS, Ring House 2, Edmonton, Alberta T6G 2E1 Canada. (780)492-3662. Fax: (780)492-0719. E-mail: uap@gpu.srv.ualberta.ca. Website: www.ualberta.ca/~uap. **Acquisitions**: Leslie Vermeer, managing editor. Estab. 1969. Publishes trade paperback originals and trade paperback reprints. **Publishes 18-25 titles/ year. Receives 400 submissions/year. 60% of books from first-time authors; majority from unagented writers. Pays 10% royalty on net price.** Publishes book within 18 months after acceptance. Responds in 3 months. Book catalog and ms guidelines free.

    O⟶ The University of Alberta publishes books on the Canadian West, the North, multicultural studies, health sciences, the environment, earth sciences, native studies, Canadian history, natural science and Canadian prairie literature. Currently emphasizing Canadian prairie literature.

Nonfiction: "Our interests include the Canadian West, the North, multicultural studies, health science and native studies." Submit table of contents, 1-2 chapters, sample illustrations and cv.

Recent Title(s): *The Alberta Elders' Cree Dictionary*, by Nancy LeClaire and George Cardinal, edited by Earle Waugh.

Tips: "Since 1969, the University of Alberta Press has earned recognition and awards from the Association of American University Presses, the Alcuin Society, the Book Publishers Association of Alberta and the Bibliographical Society of Canada, among others. Now we're growing—in the audiences we reach, the numbers of titles we publish, and our energy for new challenges. But we're still small enough to listen carefully, to work closely with our authors, to explore possibilities. Our list is strong in Canadian, western and northern topics, but it ranges widely."

N UNIVERSITY OF CALGARY PRESS, 2500 University Dr. NW, Calgary, Alberta T2N 1N4 Canada. (403)220-7578. Fax: (403)282-0085. E-mail: onn@ucalgary.ca. Website: www.ucalgary.ca/ucpress. **Acquisitions:** Walter Hildebrandt, acquisitions editor. "University of Calgary Press is committed to the advancement of scholarship through the publication of first-rate monographs and academic and scientific journals." Publishes hardcover and trade paperback originals and reprints. **Publishes 15-20 titles/year. Pays 4-6% royalty on wholesale price.** Publishes book 20 months after acceptance of ms. Responds in 1 month to queries, 2 months to proposals and mss. Book catalog and ms guidelines free.

Nonfiction: Subjects include art/architecture, business/economics, western history, women's issues/studies, Canadian studies, post-modern studies, international relations. Submit outline and 2 sample chapters with SASE. Reviews artwork/ photos of the ms package. Send photocopies.

Recent Title(s): *Greenwor(l)ds: Ecocritical Readings of Poetry by Canadian Women*, by Diana M.A. Relke.

N UNIVERSITY OF MANITOBA PRESS, 15 Gillson St., #423 University Cres., Winnipeg, Manitoba R3T 2N2 Canada. (204)474-9495. Fax: (204)474-7566. Website: www.umanitoba.ca/uofmpress. **Acquisitions**: David Carr, director. Estab. 1967. "Western Canadian focus or content is important." Publishes nonfiction hardcover and trade paperback originals. **Publishes 4-6 titles/year. Pays 5-15% royalty on wholesale price.** Responds in 3 months.

Nonfiction: Scholarly. Subjects include Western Canadian history, women's issues/studies, Native history. Query.

Recent Title(s): *A National Crime*, by John Milloy (native/history).

UNIVERSITY OF OTTAWA PRESS, 542 King Edward, Ottawa, Ontario K1N 6N5 Canada. (613)562-5246. Fax: (613)562-5247. E-mail: press@uottawa.ca. Website: www.uopress.uottawa.ca. **Acquisitions:** Vicki Bennett, editor-in-chief; Professor Jean Delisle, director translation collection (translation, history of translation, teaching translation); Chad Gaffield, Guy Leclaire, directors Institute Canadian Studies (Canadian studies); Gilles Paquet, director collection (governance). Estab. 1936. **Publishes 22 titles/year; 10 titles/year in English. Receives 250 submissions/year. 20% of books from first-time authors; 95% from unagented writers. Determines nonauthor subsidy by preliminary budget. Pays 5-10% royalty on net price.** Publishes book 6 months after acceptance. Responds in 1 month to queries, 6 months to mss. Book catalog and author's guide free.

    O⟶ The University Press publishes books for the scholarly and educated general audiences. They were "the first *officially* bilingual publishing house in Canada. Our goal is to help the publication of cutting edge research— books written to be useful to active researchers but accessible to an interested public." Currently emphasizing French in North America, language rights, social justice, translation, Canadian studies. De-emphasizing medieval studies, criminology.

Nonfiction: Reference, textbook, scholarly. Subjects include criminology, education, Canadian government/politics, Canadian history, language/literature, nature/environment, philosophy, religion, sociology, translation, women's issues/ studies. Submit outline/synopsis, sample chapters and cv.

Recent Title(s): *The Fallacy of Race & the Shoah*, by Naomi Kramer and Ronald Headland.

Tips: *No unrevised theses!* "Envision audience of academic specialists and (for some books) educated public."

UPNEY EDITIONS, 19 Appalachian Crescent, Kitchener, Ontario N2E 1A3 Canada. **Acquisitions:** Gary Brannon, publisher. Publishes trade paperback originals. **Publishes 2-4 titles/year. Receives 200 queries and 100 mss/year. 33% of books from first-time authors; 100% from unagented writers. Pays 10% royalty on wholesale price.** Publishes book 9 months after acceptance. Responds in 1 month. Book catalog for #10 SASE (Canadian).

    O⟶ Upney Editions is currently emphasizing foreign travel and lifestyle, also retirement topics. De-emphasizing nature/environment.

Nonfiction: Biography, reference. Subjects include Americana, art/architecture, history (with Canada/US connections or Canadian history), language/literature, military/war, retirement, travel. "Remember that we are a Canadian small press, and our readers are mostly Canadians! We are specifically interested in popular history with cross-border U.S.

Canada connection; also, popular travel literature (particularly Europe), but it must be witty and critically honest. No travel guides, cycling, hiking or driving tours! We prefer words to paint pictures rather than photographs, but line art will be considered. Queries or submissions that dictate publishing terms turn us right off. So do submissions with no SASE or submissions with return U.S. postage stamps. Enclose sufficient IRCs or we cannot return material." Length: 50,000 words maximum. Query with outline, 2 sample chapters and SASE for Canada. "We prefer to see manuscripts well thought out chapter by chapter, not just a first chapter and a vague idea of the rest." Reviews artwork/photos as part of ms package. Send photocopies.

Recent Title(s): *Walking the Skye Road to Skinidin*, by Ron M. Ritchie.

Tips: "We will consider any nonfiction topic with the exception of religion, politics and finance. City/regional/destination specific travel material expertly illustrated with pen and ink sketches will catch our attention. Although our titles are directed to a general audience, our sales and marketing are focused on libraries (public, high school, college) 70% and 30% on bookstores. We are dismayed by the 'pushy' attitude of some submissions. We will not even look at 'finished package, ready-to-print' submissions, which seem to be growing in number. The authors of these instant books clearly need a printer and/or investor and not a publisher. Electronic submissions on disk are welcome—we are a Mac, QuarkXPress environment."

VANWELL PUBLISHING LIMITED, 1 Northrup Crescent, P.O. Box 2131, St. Catharines, Ontario L2M 6P5 Canada. (905)937-3100. Fax: (905)937-1760. **Acquisitions:** Angela Dobler, general editor; Simon Kooter, military editor (collections, equipment, vehicles, uniforms, artifacts); Ben Kooter, publisher (general military). Estab. 1983. Publishes trade originals and reprints. **Publishes 5-7 titles/year. Receives 100 submissions/year. Publishes Canadian authors only. 85% of books from first-time authors; 100% from unagented writers. Pays 10% royalty on retail price. Offers $200 average advance.** Publishes book 1 year after acceptance of ms. Responds in 6 months to queries. Book catalog free.

○━ Vanwell is considered Canada's leading naval heritage publisher. Currently emphasizing military aviation, biography, WWI and WWII histories. Limited publishing in children's fiction and nonfiction, but not picture books. We are seeing an increased demand for biographical nonfiction for ages 10-14."

Nonfiction: All military/history related. Query with SASE. Reviews artwork/photos as part of ms package.

Recent Title(s): *A Great Fleet of Ships: Canada's Forts and Parks*, by S.C. Heal (merchant navy); *For Your Freedom and Ours: The Polish Armed Forces in the Second World War*, by Margaret Stowicki.

Tips: "The writer has the best chance of selling a manuscript to our firm which is in keeping with our publishing program, well written and organized. Our audience: older male, history buff, war veteran; regional tourist; students. *Canadian* only military/aviation, naval, military/history and children's nonfiction have the best chance with us. We see more interest in collective or cataloguing forms of history, also in modeling and recreating military historical artifacts."

[N] [symbol] VÉHICULE PRESS, Box 125, Place du Parc Station, Montreal, Quebec H2W 2M9 Canada. (514)844-6073. Fax: (514)844-7543. Website: www.vehiculepress.com. **Acquisitions:** Simon Dardick, president/publisher. Estab. 1973. Publishes trade paperback originals *by Canadian authors only.* **Publishes 15 titles/year. Receives 250 submissions/ year. 20% of books from first-time authors; 95% from unagented writers. Pays 10-15% royalty on retail price. Offers $200-500 advance.** Publishes book 1 year after acceptance. Responds in 4 months to queries. Book catalog for 9×12 SAE with IRCs.

○━ "Montreal's Véhicule Press has published the best of Canadian and Quebec literature—fiction, poetry, essays, translations and social history."

Imprint(s): Signal Editions (poetry), Dossier Quebec (history, memoirs).

Nonfiction: Biography, memoir. Subjects include Canadiana, feminism, history, politics, social history, literature. Especially looking for Canadian social history. Query. Reviews artwork/photos as part of ms package.

Recent Nonfiction Title(s): *Painting Friends: The Beaver Hall Women Painters*, by Barbara M. Jowcroft; *Stopping Time: Paul Bley and the Transformation of Jazz*, by Paul Bley with David Lee.

Poetry: Contact: Michael Harris. Not accepting new material before 1998.

Recent Poetry Title(s): *White Stone: The Alice Poems*, by Stephanie Bolster (winner 1998 Governor General's Award for Poetry).

Tips: "We are interested only in Canadian authors."

WALL & EMERSON, INC., 6 O'Connor Dr., Toronto, Ontario M4K 2K1 Canada. (416)467-8685. Fax: (416)352-5368. E-mail: wall@wallbooks.com. Website: www.wallbooks.com. **Acquisitions:** Byron E. Wall, president (history of science, mathematics). Estab. 1987. Publishes hardcover originals and reprints. **Publishes 3 titles/year. Receives 10 queries and 8 mss/year. 50% of books from first-time authors; 100% from unagented writers. Pays royalty of 5-12% on wholesale price.** Publishes book 1 year after acceptance. Accepts simultaneous submissions. Responds in 1 month to queries and proposals, 3 months to mss. Book catalog and ms guidelines free and on website.

○━ "We are most interested in textbooks for college courses that meet well-defined needs and are targeted to their audiences." Currently emphasizing adult education, engineering. De-emphasizing social work.

Nonfiction: Reference, textbook. Subjects include education, health/medicine, history, multicultural, psychology, science, sociology. "We are looking for any undergraduate college text that meets the needs of a well-defined course in colleges in the U.S. and Canada." Submit proposal package, including outline, 2 sample chapters and possible market.

Recent Title(s): *Principles of Engineering Economic Analysis*; *Voices Past and Present*.

Tips: "Our audience consists of college undergraduate students and college libraries. Our ideal writer is a college professor writing a text for a course he or she teaches regularly. If I were a writer trying to market a book today, I would identify the audience for the book and write directly to the audience throughout the book. I would then approach a publisher that publishes books specifically for that audience."

N WEIGL EDUCATIONAL PUBLISHERS LTD., 6325 Tenth St. SE, Calgary, Alberta T2H-2Z9 Canada. (403)233-7747. Fax: (403)233-7769. E-mail: calgary@weigl.com. Website: www.weigl.com. **Acquisitions:** Linda Weigl, president. Publishes hardcover originals and reprints, school library softcover. **Publishes 30 titles/year. Receives 40 queries and 20 mss/year. 5% of books from first-time authors; 100% from unagented writers. Makes outright purchase.** Accepts simultaneous submissions. Responds in 6 months. Book catalog and ms guidelines free on request.

○— Textbook publisher catering to juvenile and young adult audience (K-12).

Nonfiction: Children's/juvenile, textbook. Subjects include animals, education, government/politics, history, nature/environment, science. Query with SASE.

Recent Title(s): *The Science of Insects* (Living Science series); *Forgeries, Fingerprints and Forensics: The Science of Crime.*

WHITECAP BOOKS LTD., 351 Lynn Ave., North Vancouver, British Columbia V7J 2C4 Canada. (604)980-9852. Fax: (604)980-8197. E-mail: whitecap@whitecap.ca. Website: www.whitecap.ca. **Acquisitions:** Robin Rivers, editorial director. Publishes hardcover and trade paperback originals. **Publishes 24 titles/year. Receives 500 queries and 1,000 mss/year. 20% of books from first-time authors; 90% from unagented writers. Royalty and advance negotiated for each project.** Publishes book 18 months after acceptance. Accepts simultaneous submissions. Responds in 2 months to proposals.

○— Whitecap Books publishes a wide range of nonfiction with a Canadian and international focus. Currently emphasizing children's fiction, junior fiction. De-emphasizing memoirs.

Nonfiction: Coffee table book, cookbook, children's/juvenile. Subjects include animals, gardening, history, nature/environment, recreation, regional, travel. "We require an annotated outline. Writers should take the time to research our list. This is especially important for children's writers." Submit outline, 1 sample chapter, table of contents and SASE with international postal voucher for submission from the US. Send photocopies, not original material.

Recent Title(s): *Images of Our Inheritance*, by James Sidney, Sarah Stewart (nonfiction); *Cheese Louise*, by David Michael Slater (fiction).

Tips: "We want well-written, well-researched material that presents a fresh approach to a particular topic."

WOODHEAD PUBLISHING LTD., Abington Hall, Abington, Cambridge CB1 6AH United Kingdom. Phone: (+44)1223-891358. Fax: (+44)1223-893694. E-mail: wp@woodhead-publishing.com. Website: www.woodhead-publishing.com. **Acquisitions:** Francis Dodds (food science, technology and nutrition); Patricia Morrison (materials engineering, textile technology, welding and joining); Neil Wenborn (finance, investment). Publishes hardcover originals. **Publishes 40 titles/year. 75% of books from first-time authors; 99% from unagented writers. Pays 10% royalty on wholesale price. No advance.** Publishes book 6 months after acceptance of ms. Book catalog free or on website. Manuscript guidelines free.

Imprints: Woodhead Publishing, Abington Publishing, Gresham Books.

Nonfiction: Technical. Subjects include investment/finance, food science, technology and nutrition, engineering materials. Submit proposal package, including outline. Reviews artwork/photos as part of ms package. Send photocopies.

Recent Title(s): *Yoghurt: Science and Technology*; *Oil Trading Manual*; *The Welding Workplace.*

YORK PRESS LTD., 152 Boardwalk Dr., Toronto, Ontario M4L 3X4 Canada. E-mail: yorkpress@sympatico.ca. Website: www3.sympatico.ca/yorkpress. **Acquisitions:** Dr. S. Elkhadem, general manager/editor. Estab. 1975. Publishes trade paperback originals. **Publishes 10 titles/year. Receives 50 submissions/year. 10% of books from first-time authors; 100% from unagented writers. Pays 10-20% royalty on wholesale price.** Publishes book 6 months after acceptance. Responds in 2 weeks. *Writer's Market* recommends allowing 2 months for reply.

○— "We publish scholarly books and creative writing of an experimental nature."

Nonfiction and Fiction: Reference, textbook, scholarly. Especially needs literary criticism, comparative literature and linguistics and fiction of an experimental nature by well-established writers. Query.

Recent Title(s): *Herman Melville: Romantic & Prophet*, by C.S. Durer (scholarly literary criticism); *The Moonhare*, by Kirk Hampton (experimental novel).

Tips: "If I were a writer trying to market a book today, I would spend a considerable amount of time examining the needs of a publisher *before* sending my manuscript to him. The writer must adhere to our style manual and follow our guidelines exactly."

VISIT THE WRITER'S DIGEST WEBSITE at www.writersdigest.com for hot new markets, daily market updates, writers' guidelines and much more.

Small Presses

"Small press" is a relative term. Compared to the dozen or so conglomerates, the rest of the book publishing world may seem to be comprised of small presses. A number of the publishers listed in the Book Publishers section consider themselves small presses and cultivate the image. For our classification, small presses are those that publish three or fewer books per year.

The publishing opportunities are slightly more limited with the companies listed here than with those in the Book Publishers section. Not only are they publishing fewer books, but small presses are usually not able to market their books as effectively as larger publishers. Their print runs and royalty arrangements are usually smaller. It boils down to money, what a publisher can afford, and in that area, small presses simply can't compete with conglomerates.

However, realistic small press publishers don't try to compete with Penguin Putnam or Random House. They realize everything about their efforts operates on a smaller scale. Most small press publishers get into book publishing for the love of it, not solely for the profit. Of course, every publisher, small or large, wants successful books. But small press publishers often measure success in different ways.

Many writers actually prefer to work with small presses. Since small publishing houses are usually based on the publisher's commitment to the subject matter, and since they necessarily work with far fewer authors than the conglomerates, small press authors and their books usually receive more personal attention than the larger publishers can afford to give them. Promotional dollars at the big houses tend to be siphoned toward a few books each season that they have decided are likely to succeed, leaving hundreds of "midlist" books underpromoted, and, more likely than not, destined for failure. Since small presses only commit to a very small number of books every year, they are vitally interested in the promotion and distribution of each one.

Just because they publish three or fewer titles per year does not mean small press editors have the time to look at complete manuscripts on spec. In fact, the editors with smaller staffs often have even less time for submissions. The procedure for contacting a small press with your book idea is exactly the same as it is for a larger publisher. Send a one-page query with SASE first. If the press is interested in your proposal, be ready to send an outline or synopsis, and/or a sample chapter or two. Be patient with their reporting times; small presses can be slower to respond than larger companies. You might consider simultaneous queries, as long as you note this, to compensate for the waiting game.

For more information on small presses, see *Novel & Short Story Writer's Market* and *Poet's Market* (Writer's Digest Books), and *Small Press Review* and *The International Directory of Little Magazines and Small Presses* (Dustbooks).

For a list of publishers according to their subjects of interest, see the nonfiction and fiction sections of the Book Publishers Subject Index. Information on book publishers and producers listed in the previous edition of *Writer's Market* but not included in this edition can be found in the General Index.

N **aatec publications**, P.O. Box 7119, Ann Arbor MI 48107. (734)995-1470. Fax: (734)995-1471. E-mail: aatecpub @mindspring.com. **Acquisitions:** Christina Bych, publisher. Publishes hardcover and trade paperback originals. **Publishes 1-3 titles/year. Receives 20 queries and 10 mss/year. 75% of books from first-time authors; 100% from unagented writers. Pays 15% royalty. Offers no advance.** Publishes book 1 year after acceptance of ms. Responds in 1 month. Book catalog free.
Nonfiction: How-to, technical, history. Subjects include environment, renewable energies. "We publish—and update—the best basic books on the theory and practical use of solar electricity. Future publications should supplement or advance

on this in some way." Submit outline with 2-3 sample chapters, including introductory chapter, author biography, marketing prospects. Reviews artwork/photos as part of ms package. Send photocopies. Recent title: *From Space to Earth: The Story of Solar Electricity*, by John Perlin (history).

Tips: "Audience is nontechnical, potential users of renewable energies. Review existing publications (available at many libraries). Create a book a current or potential renewable energy user would want to read."

ACCENT BOOKS, Cheever Publishing, Inc., P.O. Box 700, Bloomington IL 61702. (309)378-2961. Fax: (309)378-4420. E-mail: acntlvng.@aol.com. Website: accentonliving.com. **Acquisitions:** Betty Garee, editor. **Publishes 2 titles/ year. Receives 50 queries and 150 mss/year. 90% of books from first-time authors; 90% from unagented writers. Makes outright purchase.** Publishes book 3 months after acceptance of ms. Accepts simultaneous submissions. Responds to queries in 1 month. Book catalog for 8×10 SAE with 2 first-class stamps. Manuscript guidelines for #10 SASE.

   ⚭ Accent Books publishes books pertaining to the physically disabled who are trying to live an independent life. Currently emphasizing housing accessibility, new technology. De-emphasizing personal books.

Nonfiction: How-to, humor, self-help. Subjects include business/economics, child guidance/parenting, cooking/foods/ nutrition, education, gardening, money/finance, recreation, religion, travel. All pertaining to physically disabled. Query. Reviews artwork/photos as part of ms package. Send snapshots or slides. Recent title: *Good Grief*, by Dee Bissell/ Michael Cruerer.

ADAMS-HALL PUBLISHING, P.O. Box 491002, Los Angeles CA 90049. (800)888-4452. **Acquisitions:** Sue Ann Bacon, editorial director. Publishes hardcover and trade paperback originals and reprints. **Publishes 3-4 titles/year. Pays 10% royalty on net receipts to publisher. Advance negotiable.** Responds in 1 month to queries. *Writer's Market* recommends allowing 2 months for reply. Accepts simultaneous submissions, if so noted.

Nonfiction: Quality business and personal finance books. Small, successful house that aggressively promotes select titles. Only interested in business or personal finance titles with broad appeal. Query first with proposed book idea, a listing of current, competitive books, author qualifications, how book is unique and the market(s) for book. Then submit outline and 2 sample chapters with SASE. Recent title: *Fail Proof Your Business*.

［N］ ALPINE PUBLICATIONS, 225 S. Madison Ave., Loveland CO 80537. (970)667-9317. Fax: (970)667-9157. E-mail: alpinepubl@aol.com. Website: alpinepub.com. **Acquisitions:** Ms. B.J. McKinney, publisher. Estab. 1975. Publishes hardcover and trade paperback originals and reprints. **Publishes 3 titles/year. 50% of books from first-time authors; 95% from unagented writers. Pays 8-15% royalty on wholesale price.** Publishes book 18 months after acceptance. Accepts simultaneous submissions. Responds in 4 month to queries; 3 months to proposals and mss. Book catalog and ms guidelines free.

Imprint(s): Blue Ribbon Books.

Nonfiction: Animal subjects. "Alpine specializes in books that promote the enjoyment of and responsibility for companion animals with emphasis on dogs and horses." Reviews artwork/photos as part of ms package. Send photocopies.

Recent Title(s): *Almost a Whisper*, by Sam Powell (horse); *Canine Nutrition*, Lowell Ackerman Dum (dog).

Tips: "Our audience is pet owners, breeders and exhibitors, veterinarians, animal trainers, animal care specialists and judges. Look up some of our titles before you submit. See what is unique about our books. Write your proposal to suit our guidelines."

AMERICAN CATHOLIC PRESS, 16565 S. State St., South Holland IL 60473. (312)331-5845. Fax: (708)331-5484. E-mail: acp@acpress.org. Website: www.acpress.org. **Acquisitions:** Rev. Michael Gilligan, Ph.D., editorial director. Estab. 1967. Publishes hardcover originals and hardcover and paperback reprints. **Publishes 4 titles/year. Makes outright purchase of $25-100. No advance.**

Nonfiction: "We publish books on the Roman Catholic liturgy—for the most part, books on religious music and educational books and pamphlets. We also publish religious songs for church use, including Psalms, as well as choral and instrumental arrangements. We are interested in new music, meant for use in church services. Books, or even pamphlets, on the Roman Catholic Mass are especially welcome. We have no interest in secular topics and are not interested in religious poetry of any kind."

Tips: "Most of our sales are by direct mail, although we do work through retail outlets."

ANHINGA PRESS, P.O. Box 10595, Tallahassee FL 32302. (850)521-9920. Fax: (850)442-6323. E-mail: info@anhinga.org. Website: www.anhinga.org. **Acquisitions:** Rick Campbell, Joann Gardner, Van Brock, editors. "We publish poetry only." Publishes hardcover and trade paperback originals. **Publishes 3-4 titles/year. Pays 10% royalty on retail price and offers Anhinga prize of $2,000. No advance.** Responds in 2 months.

Poetry: We like good poetry. Query or submit 10 sample poems. Recent title: *The Secret History of Water*, by Silvia Curbelo. Recent title: *Summer*, by Robert Dana.

BANDANNA BOOKS, 319-B Anacapa St., Santa Barbara CA 93101. (805)564-3559. Fax: (805)564-3559. E-mail: bandanna@bandannabooks.com. Website: www.bandannabooks.com. **Acquisitions:** Sasha Newborn, publisher. Pub-

lishes trade paperback originals and reprints. **Publishes 3 titles/year. Receives 300 queries and 100 mss/year. 25% of books from first-time authors; 100% from unagented writers. Pays negotiable royalty on net receipts. Offers up to $1,000 advance.** Accepts simultaneous submissions. Responds in 4 months to proposals.
Nonfiction: Textbooks for college students and self-learners, some illustrated. Subjects include literature, language, translations. "Bandanna Books seeks to humanize the classics, language in non-sexist, modernized translations, using direct and plain language." Submit query letter, table of contents and first chapter. Reviews artwork/photos as part of ms package. Send photocopies. Recent title: *Don't Panic: The Procrastinator's Guide to Writing an Effective Term Paper,* by Steven Posusta.
Tips: "Our readers have a liberal arts orientation. Inventive, professional, well-thought-out presentations, please. Always include a SASE for reply."

BLISS PUBLISHING CO., P.O. Box 920, Marlborough MA 01752. (508)779-2827. **Acquisitions:** Stephen H. Clouter, publisher. Publishes hardcover and trade paperback originals. **Publishes 2-4 titles/year. Pays 10-15% royalty on wholesale price. No advance.** Responds in 2 months.
Nonfiction: Biography, illustrated book, reference, textbook. Subjects include government/politics, history, music/dance, nature/environment, recreation, regional. Submit proposal package, including outline, table of contents, 3 sample chapters, brief author biography, table of contents, SASE. Recent title: *Ninnuock, The Algonkian People of New England,* by Steven F. Johnson.

BLUE SKY MARKETING, INC., P.O. Box 21583, St. Paul MN 55121. (612)456-5602. **Acquisitions:** Vic Spadaccini, president. Publishes hardcover and trade paperback originals. **Publishes 3 titles/year. Pays royalty on wholesale price.** Responds in 3 months.
Nonfiction: Gift book, how-to. Subjects include humor, regional, self-help, house and home. "Ideas must be unique. If it's been done, we're not interested!" Submit proposal package, including outline, 1 sample chapter, author bio, intended market, analysis comparison to competing books with SASE. Recent title: *Master Dating: How to Meet & Attract Quality Men* by Felicia Rose Adler.
Tips: "Our books are primarily 'giftbooks,' sold to women in specialty stores, gift shops and bookstores."

[N] BRIGHT MOUNTAIN BOOKS, INC., 138 Springside Rd., Asheville NC 28803. (828)684-8840. Fax: (828)681-1790. E-mail: BooksBMB@aol.com. **Acquisitions:** Cynthia F. Bright, editor. Imprint is Historical Images. Publishes hardcover originals and trade paperback originals and reprints. **Publishes 3 titles/year. Pays 5-10% royalty on retail price. No advance.** Responds in 1 month to queries; 3 months to mss.
Nonfiction: "Our current emphasis is on regional titles set in the Southern Appalachians and Carolinas, which can include nonfiction by local writers." Currently emphasizing history, biography. De-emphasizing humor, cookbooks. Query with SASE. Recent title: *The Witch Doctor's Dance,* by Dr. J.B. Wofford.

CALYX BOOKS, P.O. Box B, Corvallis OR 97339-0539. (541)753-9384. Also publishes *Calyx, A Journal of Art & Literature by Women.* **Acquisitions:** Margarita Donnelly, director. Managing Editor: Micki Reaman. Estab. 1986 for Calyx Books; 1976 for Calyx, Inc. Publishes fine literature by women, fiction, nonfiction and poetry. **Publishes 3 titles/year. Pays 10-15% royalty on net receipts; amount of advance depends on grant support.** Responds in 1 year.
● Next open submission period to be announced.
Nonfiction: Outline, 3 sample chapters and SASE. Recent title: *The Violet Shyness of Their Eyes,* by Barbara Scot.
Fiction: Literary fiction by women. "Please do not query." Send 3 sample chapters, bio, outline, synopsis and SASE during open book ms period only. Recent title: *The End of the Class War,* by Catherine Brady.
Poetry: "We only publish 1 poetry book a year." Submit 10 poems, table of contents, bio and SASE. Recent title: *Indian Singing,* by Gail Tremblay.
Tips: "Please be familiar with our publications."

CASSANDRA PRESS, P.O. Box 868, San Rafael CA 94915. (415)382-8507. **Acquisitions:** Gurudas, president. Estab. 1985. Publishes trade paperback originals. **Publishes 3 titles/year. Receives 200 submissions/year. 50% of books from first-time authors; 50% from unagented writers. Pays 6-8% maximum royalty on retail price. Advance rarely offered.** Publishes book 1 year after acceptance. Accepts simultaneous submissions. Responds in 3 weeks to queries, 3 months to mss. Book catalog and ms guidelines free.
Nonfiction: New Age, how-to, self-help. Subjects include cooking/foods/nutrition, health/medicine (holistic health), philosophy, psychology, religion (New Age), metaphysical, political tyranny. "We like to do around 3 titles a year in the general New Age, metaphysical and holistic health fields. No children's books or novels." Submit outline and sample chapters. Recent title: *Treason the New World Order,* by Gurudas (political).

CLARITY PRESS INC., 3277 Roswell Rd. NE, #469, Atlanta GA 30305. (877)613-1495. Fax: (404)231-3899 or (877)613-7868. E-mail: clarity@islandnet.com. Website: www.bookmasters.com/clarity. **Acquisitions:** Diana G. Collier, editorial director (contemporary justice issues). Estab. 1984. Publishes mss on contemporary issues in US, Middle East and Africa. Publishes hardcover and trade paperback originals. **Publishes 4 titles/year.** Responds in 3 months to queries only if interested.

Nonfiction: Human rights/socio-economic and minority issues. No fiction. Query with author's bio, synopsis and endorsements. Responds *only* if interested, so do *not* enclose SASE. Recent title: *Discovering America As It Is*, by Valdas Anelauskas.
Tips: "Check our titles on website."

N DISKOTECH, INC., 7930 State Line, Suite 210, Prairie Village KS 66208. (913)432-8606. Fax: (913)432-8606
* 51. **Acquisitions:** Jane Locke, submissions editor. Estab. 1989. Publishes multimedia nonfiction and fiction for PC's on CD-ROM. **Publishes 2 titles/year. Pays 10-15% royalty on wholesale price.** Responds in 2 months to queries. Query first.
● Diskotech, Inc. is publishing a new form of the novel, a CVN® (computerized video novel), that combines print, software and video for CD-ROM and the Internet.
Nonfiction: Considers most nonfiction subjects. Query first with SASE. Recent title: *The Martensville Nighmare CVN®*, by Karen Smith (true crime story on CD-Rom).
Fiction: Considers all fiction genres. Recent title: *Negative Space CVN®*, (computerized video novel) by Holly Franking.

EASTERN PRESS, P.O. Box 881, Bloomington IN 47402-0881. **Acquisitions:** Don Y. Lee, publisher. Estab. 1981. Publishes hardcover originals and reprints. **Publishes 3 titles/year. Pays by arrangement with author. No advance.** Responds in 3 months.
Oπ "Our publications are involved with English and Asian language(s) for higher academic works." Currently emphasizing Asian subjects, particularly East Asian.
Nonfiction: Academic books on Asian subjects and pedagogy on languages. Query with outline and SASE. Recent title: *Autohaiku*, by Don Y. Lee (6×9 hardcover).

ECOPRESS, 1029 NE Kirsten Place, Corvallis OR 97330. (541)758-7545. E-mail: ecopress@peak.org. **Acquisitions:** Christopher Beatty, editor-in-chief. Publishes trade paperback originals and reprints. **Publishes 2-4 titles/year. Pays 6-15% royalty on publisher's receipts. Offers $0-5,000 advance.** Responds in 1 month to queries and proposals, 3 months to mss. Manuscript guidelines for #10 SASE or submit electronically.
Nonfiction: How-to. Subjects include nature/environment, recreation (outdoor, hiking), sports (outdoor, fishing). "The work must have some aspect that enhances environmental awareness. Do a competitive analysis and create a marketing plan for your book or proposal." Query with SASE by electronic or regular mail. Recent title: *The Olympic Peninsula Rivers Guide*, by Steve Probasco.
Tips: "A major focus of Ecopress is outdoor guides, especially river and hiking guides. Other nonfiction will be considered. All Ecopress books must have an environmental perspective."

EMERALD WAVE, Box 969, Fayetteville AR 72702. **Acquisitions:** Maya Harrington. Publishes trade paperback originals. **Publishes 1-3 titles/year. Pays 7-10% royalty. No advance.** Responds in 1 month to queries, 3 months to mss.
Oπ "We publish thoughtful New Age books which relate to everyday life and/or the environment on this planet with enlightened attitudes. Nothing poorly written, tedious to read or too 'out there.' It's got to have style too."
Nonfiction: Spiritual/metaphysical New Age. Subjects include health, environment, philosophy, psychology. Submit outline and 3 sample chapters with SASE. Recent title: *Cao Dai, Faith of Unity*, by Hum Duc Bui, M.D..

N ENDLESS KNOT PRODUCTIONS, 59½ Amory St., Boston MA 02119. (617)445-4651. Fax: (603)452-3481. E-mail: editor@endless-knot.com. Website: www.endless-knot.com. **Acquisitions:** Alexander Dwinell. Publishes trade paperback originals and reprints. **Publishes 3-6 titles/year. Pays royalty.** Responds in 2 months.
Fiction: New publisher of fiction. "We are looking to publish cutting-edge fiction with a subversive kick."
Tips: "We are particularly interested in well-written stories which contain strong characters and plotting with a radical political subtext. The politics should be anti-authoritarian and anti-capitalist without being polemical."

N EQUILIBRIUM PRESS, INC., PMB 680, 10736 Jefferson Blvd., Culver City CA 90230. (310)204-3290. Fax: (310)204-3550. E-mail: equipress@mediaone.net. Website: www.equipress.com. Publishes trade paperback originals. **Publishes 1-2 titles/year. Pays 10-15% royalty on net. Advance varies.** Responds in 2 months.
Oπ "We're looking for books that inform and inspire—nonfiction related to women's health and wellness (physical, spiritual, financial, emotional, etc.), for an upscale, educated audience in a wide age range. No fiction, poetry, erotica."
Nonfiction: Biography, gift book, how-to, self-help. Subjects include business/economics, child guidance/parenting, health/medicine, memoirs, money/finance, spirituality. Query with SASE or submit proposal package, including outline, 1-3 sample chapters and a letter answering the following questions: how is the book unique (i.e., what are the competing books?); who is the audience?; how will you reach that audience? Recent title: *A Special Delivery: Mother-Daughter Letters from Afar*, by Mitchell & Mitchell (family/pregnancy).
Tips: "Do your homework—know what other books are similar and be able to say why yours is better and/or different. Know the audience and how you will reach them. What are you prepared to do to promote the book?"

THE FAMILY ALBUM, 4887 Newport Rd., Kinzers PA 17535. (717)442-0220. E-mail: rarebooks@pobox.com. **Acquisitions:** Ron Lieberman. Estab. 1969. Publishes hardcover originals and reprints and software. **Publishes 2 titles/year. Pays royalty on wholesale price.**

Nonfiction: "Significant works in the field of (nonfiction) bibliography. Worthy submissions in the field of Pennsylvania history, folk art and lore. We are also seeking materials relating to books, literacy, and national development. Special emphasis on Third World countries, and the role of printing in international development." No religious material or personal memoirs. Submit outline and sample chapters.

FIESTA CITY PUBLISHERS, ASCAP, P.O. Box 5861, Santa Barbara CA 93150-5861. (805)681-9199. E-mail: FCookE3924@aol.com. President: Frank E. Cooke. **Acquisitions:** Ann Cooke, secretary/treasurer (music); Johnny Harris, consultant (music). Publishes hardcover and mass market paperback originals. **Publishes 2-3 titles/year. Pays 5-20% royalty on retail price. No advance.** Responds in 1 month to queries, 2 months to proposals. Book catalog and ms guidelines for #10 SASE.

Nonfiction: "Seeking originality." Children's/juvenile, cookbook, how-to, humor and musical plays. Currently emphasizing musical plays for juvenile audience. De-emphasizing cookbooks. Query with outline and SASE. Recent title: *Break Point* (musical).

Plays: Musical plays only. "Must be original, commercially viable, preferably short, with eye-catching titles. Must be professionaly done and believable. Avoid too much detail." Query with 1 or 2 sample chapters and SASE. Recent title: *Break Point*, by Frank Cooke a.k.a. Eddie Franck (young people's musical).

Tips: "Looking for material which would appeal to young adolescents in the modern society. Prefer little or no violence with positive messages. Carefully-constructed musical plays always welcome for consideration."

[N] FOOTPRINT PRESS, P.O. Box 645, Fishers NY 14453-0645. Phone/fax: (716)421-9383. E-mail: rich@footprint press.com. Website: www.footprintpress.com. **Acquisitions:** Sue Freeman, publisher (NY state recreation). Publishes trade paperback originals. **Publishes 3 titles/year. Receives 15 queries and 5 mss/year. 100% of books from first-time authors; 100% from unagented writers. Pays 6-10% royalty on wholesale price.** Publishes book 1 year after acceptance of ms. Accepts simultaneous submissions. Responds in 1 month to queries and proposals, 2 months to mss. Book catalog and ms guidelines for #10 SASE or on website.

    O— "Topic should pertain to outdoor recreation in New York state."

Nonfiction: How-to. Subjects include recreation, regional, sports. Query with SASE. Recent titles: *Peak Experiences: Hiking the Highest Summits in New York State, County by County*, by Gary Fallesen; *Take Your Bike! Family Rides in the Finger Lakes and Genesee Valley Region*, by Rich and Sue Freeman.

GAMBLING TIMES, INC., 16140 Valerio St., Suite B, Van Nuys CA 91406-2916. (818)781-9355. Fax: (818)781-3125. E-mail: srs@gamblingtimes.com. Website: www.gamblingtimes.com. **Acquisitions:** Stanley R. Sludikoff, publisher. Publishes hardcover and trade paperback originals. **Publishes 2-4 titles/year. Pays 4-11% royalty on retail price.** Responds in 2 months to queries, 3 months to proposals, 6 months on mss.

Nonfiction: How-to and reference books on gambling. Submit proposal package, including ms and SASE. *Writer's Market* recommends sending a query with SASE first. Recent title: *Book of Tells*, by Caro (poker).

Tips: "All of our books serve to educate the public about some aspect of gambling."

HERBAL STUDIES LIBRARY, 219 Carl St., San Francisco CA 94117. (415)564-6785. Fax: (415)564-6799. **Acquisitions:** J. Rose, owner. Publishes trade paperback originals. **Publishes 3 titles/year. Pays 5-10% royalty on retail price. Offers $500 advance.** Responds in 1 month to mss with SASE. *Writer's Market* recommends allowing 2 months for reply.

Nonfiction: How-to, reference, self-help. Subjects include gardening, health/medicine, herbs and aromatherapy. No New Age. Query with sample chapter and SASE. Recent title: *The Aromatherapy Book: Applications and Inhalations*, by Jeanne Rose.

[N] THE HOFFMAN PRESS, P.O. Box 2996, Santa Rosa CA 95405. E-mail: hoffpress@worldnet.att.net. Website: http://foodandwinecookbooks.com. **Acquisitions:** R.P. Hoffman, publisher. Publishes mass market paperback originals. **Publishes 2-4 titles/year. Pays 5-10% royalty on wholesale price. No advance.** Publishes book 1 year after acceptance of ms. Responds in 2 months.

Nonfiction: "We publish cookbooks only." Query with 3 sample chapters and SASE. Reviews artwork/photos as part of ms package. Send photocopies. Recent title: *The California Wine Country Herbs & Spices Cookbook.*

ILLUMINATION ARTS, P.O. Box 1865, Bellevue WA 98009. (425)644-7185. Fax: (425)644-9274. E-mail: liteinfo@illumin.com. Website: www.illumin.com. **Acquisitions:** Ruth Thompson, editorial director. Publishes hardcover originals. **Publishes 1-3 titles/year. Receives 200-250 queries and 1,000 mss/year. 50% of books from first-time authors; 90% from unagented writers. Pays royalty.** Publishes book 1-2 years after acceptance of ms. Responds in 2 weeks to queries and proposals, 1 month to mss.

    O— Illumination Arts publishes inspirational/spiritual children's nonfiction and fiction. Currently emphasizing adventure, humorous stories with inspirational and spiritual values. De-emphasizing Bible based stories.

Nonfiction: Children's/juvenile. Child guidance/parenting subjects. "Our books are all high quality, inspirational/spiritual. Send for our guidelines. Stories need to be exciting and inspirational for children." Query with complete ms and SASE. Recent title: *The Right Touch*, by Sandy Kleven (book to help children avoid sexual abuse).
Fiction: Juvenile, picture books. "All are inspirational/spiritual. No full-length novels. Send for guidelines. Some writers do not include sufficient postage to return manuscripts. A few writers just do not have a grasp of correct grammar. Some are dull or uninteresting." Query with complete ms and SASE. Recent title: *The Bonsai Bear*.
Tips: "Audience is looking for a spiritual message and children who enjoy stories that make them feel self assured."

IN PRINT PUBLISHING, P.O. Box 20765, Sedona AZ 86336-9758. (520)284-5298. Fax: (520)284-5283. **Acquisitions:** Tomi Keitlen, publisher/editor. Estab. 1991. Publishes trade paperback originals. **Publishes 3-5 titles/year. Pays 6-10% royalty on retail price. Offers $250-500 advance.** Responds in 2 months to queries and proposals, 3 months to mss.
Nonfiction: "We are an eclectic publisher interested in books that have current impact: political, spiritual, financial, medical, environmental problems. We are interested in books that will leave a reader with hope. We are also interested in books that are metaphysical, books that give ideas and help for small business management and books that have impact in all general subjects. No violence, sex or poetry." Query with SASE. Recent title: *Voices of Awakening: Conversations Heart to Heart*, by Srajan Fothugill.
Tips: "We are interested in books about Angels. We are also interested in short books that will be part of a Living Wisdom Series™. These books must be no more than 18,000-20,000 words. We are not interested in any books that are over 300 pages—and are more likely interested in 75,000 words or less. Find areas that are not overdone and offer new insight to help others."

JELMAR PUBLISHING CO., INC., P.O. Box 488, Plainview NY 11803. (516)822-6861. **Acquisitions:** Joel J. Shulman, president. Publishes hardcover and trade paperback originals. **Publishes 2-5 titles/year. Pays 25% royalty after initial production and promotion expenses of first and successive printings.** Responds in 1 week. *Writer's Market* recommends allowing 2 months for reply.
Nonfiction: How-to and technical subjects on the packaging, package printing and printing fields. "The writer must be a specialist and recognized expert in the field." Query with SASE. Recent title: *Graphic Design for Corrugated Packaging*, by Donald G. McCaughey Jr. (graphic design).

JOHNSTON ASSOCIATES, INTERNATIONAL (JASI), P.O. Box 313, Medina WA 98039. (425)454-3490. Fax: (425)462-1355. E-mail: jasibooks@aol.com. Publisher: Priscilla Johnston. **Acquisitions:** Sarah Conroy, marketing director. Publishes trade paperback originals. **Publishes 3-5 titles/year. Receives 150 queries and 150 ms/year. Pays 12-17½% royalty on wholesale price. Offers $500-1,500 advance.** Publishes book 3-5 years after acceptance of ms. Accepts simultaneous submissions. Responds in 2 months. Book catalog and guidelines for #10 SASE.
Nonfiction: Recreation, regional (any region), gardening, travel and other nonfiction. "We are interested in books that hit unique niches or look at topics in new, unique ways." Query with proposal package, including outline, sample chapter, target market, competition, reason why the book is different and SASE. Recent title: *The Pitiful Gardener's Handbook* by C. Eden and T. Cheney.

KALI PRESS, P.O. Box 2169, Pagosa Springs CO 81147. (970)264-5200. E-mail: info@kalipress.com. **Acquisitions:** Cynthia Olsen. Publishes trade paperback originals. **Publishes 3 titles/year. Pays 8-10% royalty on net price. No advance.** Responds in 1 month to queries, 6 weeks to proposals, 2 months to mss.
   O→ "We specialize in complementary health which encompasses body, mind and spiritual topics." Currently emphasizing new alternative healing modalities.
Nonfiction: Natural health and spiritual nonfiction. Subjects include education on natural health issues. Query with 2 sample chapters and SASE. Reviews artwork/photos as part of ms package. Send photocopies. Recent title: *Australian Blue Cypress Oil: The Birth of the Blue*, by Cynthia Olsen.

LAHONTAN IMAGES, 210 S. Pine St., Susanville CA 96130. (530)257-6747. Fax: (530)251-4801. **Acquisitions:** Tim I. Purdy, owner. Estab. 1986. Publishes hardcover and trade paperback originals. **Publishes 2 titles/year. Pays 10-15% royalty on wholesale or retail price. No advance.** Responds in 2 months.
Nonfiction: Publishes nonfiction books pertaining to northeastern California and western Nevada. Query with outline and SASE. Recent title: *Maggie Greeno*, by George McDow Jr. (biography).

LAUREATE PRESS, 2710 Ohio St., Bangor ME 04401. **Acquisitions:** Robyn Beck, editor. Publishes trade paperback originals. **Publishes 3 titles/year.**
Nonfiction: Fencing subjects only—how-to, technical. Query letter only. Recent title: *The Science of Fencing*, by William Gaugler (fencing-technical); *On Fencing*, by Aldo Nadi.
Tips: Audience is recreational and competitive fencers worldwide, not martial arts or reenactment.

[N] LIFT EVERY VOICE, 16 Park Lane, Newton Centre MA 02459-1731. (617)244-9808. Fax: (617)964-5432. E-mail: liftever@qis.net. **Acquisitions:** Anna Dunwell Friedler. Publishes trade paperback originals. **Publishes 2 titles/year. Pays royalty or makes outright purchase for one-time usage.** Responds in 1 month. Book catalog for SAE with 1 first-class stamp.

Nonfiction: Children's/juvenile, reference. Subjects include animals, art/architecture, business/economics, child guidance/parenting, cooking/foods/nutrition, creative nonfiction, education, ethnic, gay/lesbian, history, language/literature, memoirs, multicultural, music/dance, religion, sex, spirituality, sports, women's issues. "We publish compendiums of resource materials." Query with SASE. Recent title: *Guide to the 400 Best Childrens & Adults Books of Religion*.

Tips: "We publish books for those interested in diversity and the under and misrepresented. Have a topic that depicts people with integrity and dignity."

[N] LIGHTHOUSE POINT PRESS, 100 First Ave., Suite 525, Pittsburgh PA 15222-1517. (412)323-9320. Fax: (412)323-9334. E-mail: cirons@yearick-millea.com. **Acquisitions:** Craig L. Irons, marketing director (business/career/ general nonfiction). Publishes hardcover and trade paperback originals and trade paperback reprints. **Publishes 2-3 titles/year. Receives 40-50 queries and 40-50 mss/year. 50% of books from first-time authors; 100% from un-agented writers. Pays 7-10% royalty on retail price. simultaneous submissions. Responds in 2 months.**

    O—¬ Lighthouse Point Press specializes in business/career nonfiction titles.

Nonfiction: Reference, business/career. Subjects include business/economics. "We are open to all types of submissions related to general nonfiction, but most interested in business/career manuscripts." Submit proposal package, including outline and minimum of 1-2 sample chapters or submit completed ms. Recent title: *Meetings: Do's, Don'ts and Donuts*, by Sharon M. Lippincott (reference/business).

Tips: "When submitting a manuscript or proposal, please tell us what you see as the target market/audience for the book. Also, be very specific about what you are willing to do to promote the book."

LINTEL, 24 Blake Lane, Middletown NY 10940. (914)344-1690. **Acquisitions:** Walter James Miller, editorial director. Estab. 1978. Publishes hardcover originals and reprints and trade paperback originals. **Publishes 2 titles/year. Authors get 100 copies originally, plus royalties after all expenses are cleared.** Responds in 2 months to queries, 4 months to proposals, 6 months to ms.

Nonfiction: "So far all our nonfiction titles have been textbooks. Query with SASE. Recent title: *Writing a Television Play, Second Edition*, by Michelle Cousin (textbook).

Fiction: Publishes experimental fiction, art poetry and selected nonfiction. Query with SASE. Recent title: *June*, by Mary Sanders Smith.

Poetry: Submit 5 sample poems. Recent title: *Mud River*, by Judy Aygildiz (hardcover with art work).

McGAVICK FIELD PUBLISHING, 118 N. Cherry, Olathe KS 66061. (913)780-1973. Fax: (913)781-1765. E-mail: fhernan@gateway.net. Website: www.abcnanny.com. **Acquisitions:** Phyllis McGavick, co-owner (children's issues), Frances Hernan, co-owner (human resource issues regarding all forms of child care). **Publishes 2 titles/1999; 6 planned for 2000. 75% of books from first-time authors; 75% from unagented writers. Pays 15-25% royalty on sliding scale on retail price. Advance varies.** Publishes book 1 year after acceptance of ms. Accepts simultaneous submissions. Fax or e-mail for ms guidelines.

    O—¬ McGavick Field publishes mostly personal self-help in parent care, child care and employment. "We are looking for books that can be published in the format of *The ABCs of Hiring a Nanny*, accompanied by a companion disk and website."

Nonfiction: How-to, humor, inspirational and guides for hiring childcare, parent care, international employees, employment, second careers and ways to turn volunteer activities into paid positions. Submit proposal package, including outline, 2 sample chapters, market research and competition or submit complete ms. "We are looking for short projects of 100 printed pages or under." Reviews artwork/photos as part of ms package. Send photocopies. Recent Title: *The ABCs of Hiring a Nanny*, by Frances Anne Hernan (handbook for hiring child care).

    • See the interview with Frances Hernan in the article "First Books."

Tips: "We are looking for manuscripts that deal with government agencies in trying to secure parent care or help for the disabled and that will help develop programs in this modern day society."

MENUS AND MUSIC, 1462 66th St., Emeryville CA 94608. (510)658-9100. Fax: (510)658-1605. E-mail: info@menusandmusic.com. Website: www.menusandmusic.com. **Acquisitions:** Sharon O'Connor, president (music, food, travel). Publishes trade paperback originals and reprints. **Publishes 2 titles/year. Receives 5 queries/year. Pays 7-10% royalty. No advance.** Accepts simultaneous submissions. Responds in 1 month to queries and proposals, 3 months to mss. Book catalog and ms guidelines free.

Nonfiction: Coffee table book, cookbook, gift book. Subjects include Americana, art/architecture, cooking/foods/ nutrition, gardening, hobbies, music/dance, photography, recreation, travel. Submit proposal package, including outline and 1 sample chapter. Reviews artwork/photos as part of ms package. Send photocopies. Recent title: *Bistro*, by Sharon O'Connor.

Fiction: Humor (women), multimedia, poetry, poetry in translation. "We are especially interested in proposals that will appeal to women, gift buyers, or books that can be paired with music." Submit proposal package, including synopsis and 1 sample chapter.

Poetry: Submit 3 sample poems.

Tips: "Our books are primarily bought by women who are interested in cooking, music and travel. We have excellent distribution in the gift industry and good distribution in the book trade. We are interested in high-quality work—we have completed books with New York's Metropolitan Opera and the San Francisco Ballet. Our books are beautiful and sell well for years."

MIDDLE ATLANTIC PRESS, 10 Twosome Dr., Box 600, Moorestown NJ 08057. (856)235-4444, ext. 321. Fax: (856)727-6914. E-mail: kdb@koen.com. Website: www.koen.com/midat/index.html. **Acquisitions:** Terence Doherty, associate publisher, acquisitions editor. Publishes trade paperback originals and reprints and mass market paperback originals. **Publishes 2-3 titles/year. Pays 6-10% royalty on wholesale price. Offers $500-3,000 advance.** Responds in 3 weeks. Book catalog for 9×6 SAE with 2 first-class stamps or on website.

Nonfiction: Biography, cookbook, reference. Subjects include Americana, history, memoirs, recreation, regional, sports, travel. "M.A.P. is a regional publisher specializing in nonfiction on varied subject matter. Most everything we publish, however, to a large degree, deals with some aspect of interest to the states of the mid-Atlantic region (NY, NJ, PA, DE and MD)." Query with SASE with general description. Recent nonfiction title: *Phantom of the Pines: More Tales of the Jersey Devil*, by James F. McCoy and Ray Miller Jr.

MISSOURI HISTORICAL SOCIETY PRESS, The Missouri Historical Society, P.O. Box 11940, St. Louis MO 63112-0040. (314)746-4557. Fax: (314)746-4548. E-mail: jstevens@mohistory.org. Website: www.mohistory.org. **Acquisitions:** Lee Sandweiss, director of publications (nonfiction with regional themes). Publishes hardcover originals and reprints and trade paperback originals and reprints. **Publishes 2-3 titles/year. Receives 40 queries and 20 mss/ year. 10% of books from first-time authors; 75% from unagented writers. Pays 5-10% royalty.** Responds in 1 month to queries and proposals, 2 months to mss.

Nonfiction: Biography, coffee table book, reference, textbook. Subjects include anthropology/archaeology, art/architecture, history, language/literature, multicultural, regional, sports, women's issues/studies. Query with SASE. Recent titles: *In Her Place: A Guide to St. Louis Women's History*, by Katharine Corbett (women's history); *A Century of St. Louis Sports*, by Bob Broels (sports).

Tips: "Our readers are scholars, academics and readers of regional history and related topics."

MOPAM PUBLISHING, Mopam Entertainment, Management & Publishing. 3600 South Harbor, Suite 126, Oxnard CA 93035. Phone/fax: (805)985-9907. E-mail: mopam@earthlink.net. Website: www.mopam.com. **Acquisitions:** Morris Heldt, editor (show business fiction); Jim Ed Morgans, editor (Civil War); Susan Sargent, editor (inspirational biographies). Publishes hardcover originals. **Publishes 2-3 titles/year. Negotiates contracts individually.** Publishes book 9 months after acceptance of ms. Accepts simultaneous submissions. Responds in 3 months to mss. Book catalog and ms guidelines on website.

○─ Mopam is a new publisher emphasizing show-business biographies with screen potential.

Nonfiction: Biography, show business. Subjects include show business bios. Submit completed ms.

Fiction: Sports, showbiz. "Very interested in inspirational showbiz, media and political stories." Query with SASE or submit completed ms.

Recent Title(s): *America Gonnif*, by E.M. Nolbay (autobiography); and *Hollywood Syrup*, by Morris Heldt.

Tips: "This is a new company with an open mind. We are looking for material that will translate to a movie or television screen."

MOUNT IDA PRESS, 152 Washington Ave., Albany NY 12210. (518)426-5935. Fax: (518)426-4116. **Acquisitions:** Diana S. Waite, publisher. Publishes trade paperback original illustrated books. "We specialize in high-quality publications on regional history, architecture and building technology." Currently focusing on historic structure reports and American history. Recent title: *Albany Architecture*, by Diana S. Waite.

NEW ENGLAND CARTOGRAPHICS, INC., P.O. Box 9369, North Amherst MA 01059. (413)549-4124. Fax: (413)549-3621. E-mail: geolopes@crocker.com. Website: www.necartographics.com. **Acquisitions:** Christopher Ryan, president. Editor: Valerie Vaughan. Publishes trade paperback originals and reprints. **Publishes 3 titles/year. Pays 5-10% royalty on retail price. No advance.** Responds in 2 months.

Nonfiction: Outdoor recreation nonfiction subjects include nature/environment, recreation, regional. "We are interested in specific 'where to' in the area of outdoor recreation guidebooks of the northeast U.S." Topics of interest are hiking/ backpacking, skiing, canoeing, rail-trails, etc. Query with outline, sample chapters and SASE. Reviews artwork/photos as part of ms package. Send photocopies. Recent title: *Steep Creeks of New England*, by Greg and Sue Hanlon.

NEXT DECADE, INC., 39 Old Farmstead Rd., Chester NJ 07930. (908)879-6625. Fax: (908)879-2920. E-mail: barbara@nextdecade.com. Website: www.nextdecade.com. **Acquisitions:** Barbara Kimmel, president (reference, self-help, how-to); Carol Rose, editor. Publishes trade paperback originals. **Publishes 2-4 titles/year. Receives 50 queries**

FOR EXPLANATIONS OF THESE SYMBOLS,
SEE THE INSIDE FRONT AND BACK COVERS OF THIS BOOK.

and 10 mss/year. **50% of books from first-time authors; most from unagented writers. Pays 10-15% royalty on wholesale price. Advances vary.** Publishes book 1 year after acceptance of ms. Accepts simultaneous submissions. Responds in 1 month. Catalog on website.

Nonfiction: How-to, reference, self-help. Subjects include business/economics, child guidance/parenting, cooking/foods/nutrition, health/medicine, hobbies, money/finance, multicultural, recreation. "We don't publish in all areas listed above, but would consider submissions." Currently emphasizing legal, finance, medicine, parenting, aging. Query with SASE. Recent title: *Immigration Made Simple*, by Barbara Brooks Kimmel and Alan M. Lubina.

Tips: "We publish books that simplify complex subjects. We are a small, award-winning press that successfully publishes a handful of books each year. Do not submit if you are looking for a large advance."

NICOLAS-HAYS, Box 612, York Beach ME 03910. (207)363-4393, ext. 12. Fax: (207)363-5799. E-mail: nhi@weiserbooks.com. Website: nhibooksonweiserbooks.com. **Acquisitions:** B. Lundsted, publisher. Publishes hardcover originals and trade paperback originals and reprints. **Publishes 2-4 titles/year. Pays 15% royalty on wholesale price. Offers $200-500 advance.** Responds in 2 months.

Nonfiction: Publishes self-help; nonfiction. Subjects include philosophy (Eastern), psychology (Jungian), religion (alternative), women's issues/studies. Query with outline, 3 sample chapters and SASE. Recent title: *Dancing in the Dragon's Den*, by Roseanne Bane.

Tips: "We publish only books that are the lifework of authors—our editorial plans change based on what the author writes."

OBERLIN COLLEGE PRESS, 10 N. Professor St., Oberlin College, Oberlin OH 44074. (440)775-8408. Fax: (440)775-8124. E-mail: oc.press@oberlin.edu. Website: www.oberlin.edu/~ocpress. **Acquisitions:** Linda Slocum, business manager. Editors: David Young, Pamela Alexander, Martha Collins, Alberta Turner, David Walker. Imprints are *Field Magazine: Contemporary Poetry & Poetics*, Field Translation Series, Field Poetry Series. Publishes hardcover and trade paperback originals. **Publishes 2-3 titles/year. Pays 7½-10% royalty on retail price.** Responds in 1 month to queries and proposals, 2 months to mss.

Poetry: *Field Magazine*—submit up to 5 poems with SASE for response; *Field* Translation Series—Query with SASE and sample poems; *Field* Poetry Series—no unsolicited mss, enter mss in *Field* Poetry Prize held annually in May. Send SASE for guidelines after February 1st. Recent title: *Stronger*, by Timothy Kelly.

OCEAN VIEW BOOKS, P.O. Box 9249, Denver CO 80209. **Acquisitions:** Lee Ballentine, editor. Publishes hardcover originals and trade paperback originals. **Publishes 2 titles/year. 100% from unagented writers. Pays negotiable royalty.** Responds in 2 months to queries, "if there is interest."

Fiction: Literary, science fiction, fiction about the 1960s. "Ocean View Books is an award-winning publisher of new speculative and slipstream fiction, poetry, criticism, surrealism and science fiction." Recent title: *All the Visions*, by Rudy Rucker.

N **OMEGA PUBLICATIONS**, 256 Darrow Rd., New Lebanon NY 12125-2615. (518)794-8183. Fax: (518)794-8187. E-mail: omegapub@wisdomschild.com. Website: www.omegapub.com. **Acquisitions:** Abi'l-Khayr. Estab. 1977. Publishes hardcover and trade paperback originals and reprints. **Publishes 2-3 titles/year. Pays 12-15% royalty on wholesale price. Offers $500-1,000 advance.** Responds in 3 months to mss.

Nonfiction: "We are interested in any material related to Sufism, and only that." Query with 2 sample chapters. Recent title: *The Drunken Universe*, by P.L. Wilson.

N **OUGHTEN HOUSE FOUNDATION, INC.**, 30950 Corrall Dr., P.O. Box 1059, Coarsegold CA 93614. (559)641-7950. Fax: (559)641-7952. E-mail: info@oughtenhouse.com. Website: www.oughtenhouse.com. **Acquisitions:** Anita Jarrett-Gerard, senior officer (feminine, spiritual); Dr. Robert J. Gerard, senior acquisitions editor (alternative health and self-help). Publishes trade paperback originals. **Publishes 2 titles/year. Pays 5-12% royalty on retail price. Offers $500-1,500 advance.** Responds in 1 month to queries, 3 months to proposals and mss. Book catalog on website.

Nonfiction: Self-help. Subjects include child guidance/parenting, education, philosophy, psychology, spirituality, women's issues/studies. "Currently we are extremely selective due to cutbacks. Please check our website." Query with SASE. All unsolicited mss returned unopened. Recent title: *Handling Verbal Confrontation*, by Dr. Robert Gerard.

Fiction: Spiritual, business humor. Recent title: *The Corporate Mule*, by Dr. Robert Gerard.

Tips: "We are oriented toward spirituality and alternative medicine/health. It must be unique and substantial."

OZARK MOUNTAIN PUBLISHING, INC., P.O. Box 754, Huntsville AR 72740. Phone/fax: (501)738-2348. Website: www.ozarkmt.com. **Acquisitions:** Nancy Garrison. Publishes hardcover and trade paperback originals and mass market paperback reprints. **Publishes 3-4 titles/year. Receives 100 queries and 100 mss/year. 25% of books from first-time authors; 90% from unagented writers. Pays 10% royalty on wholesale price. Offers $500 advance.** Publishes book 18 months after acceptance of ms. Accepts simultaneous submissions. Responds in 3 months. Book catalog free or on website.

Nonfiction: Biography. Subjects include spirituality, New Age/metaphysical. Query with SASE or submit proposal package, including outline and 2 sample chapters. "No phone calls, please." Recent nonfiction title: *Mankind-Child of the Stars*, by Max H. Flindt and Otto O. Binder.

N PACESETTER PUBLICATIONS, P.O. Box 101975, Denver CO 80250-1975. (303)722-7200. Fax: (303)733-2626. E-mail: jsabah@aol.com. Website: www.joesabah.com. **Acquisitions:** Joe Sabah, editor (how-to). Publishes trade paperback originals and reprints. **Publishes 3 titles/year. Pays 10-15% royalty on retail price. Offers $500-2,000 advance.** Responds in 1 month.
Nonfiction: How-to, self-help. Subjects include money/finance. Query with SASE or submit proposal package, including outline and 2 sample chapters. Recent title: *How to Get the Job You Really Want and Get Employers to Call You.*

PACIFIC VIEW PRESS, P.O. Box 2657, Berkeley CA 94702. (510)849-4213. **Acquisitions:** Pam Zumwalt, president. Publishes hardcover and trade paperback originals. **Publishes 3 titles/year. Pays 5-10% royalty on wholesale price. Offers $500-2,000 advance.** Responds in 2 months. Book catalog free.
Nonfiction: Subjects include Asia-related business and economics, Asian current affairs, Chinese medicine, nonfiction Asian-American multicultural children's books. "We are only interested in Pacific Rim related issues. Do not send proposals outside our area of interest." Query with proposal package, including outline, 1 sample chapter, author background, audience info and SASE. No unsolicited mss. Recent title: *The Great Taiwan Bubble: The Rise and Fall of an Emerging Stock Market*, by Steven R. Champion.

N PARABOLA BOOKS, Society for the Study of Myth & Tradition, 656 Broadway, New York NY 10012. (212)505-6200. Fax: (212)979-7325. E-mail: editors@parabola.org. Website: www.parabola.org. **Acquisitions:** David Appelbaum, editor; Natalie Baan, managing editor; Shanti Fader, assistant editor. Publishes hardcover and trade paperback originals and reprints. **Publishes 2 titles/year. Receives 10 queries and 8 mss/year. 10% of books from first-time authors; 100% from unagented writers. Pays 8-10% royalty on retail price.** Responds in 3 months.
    O-¬ Parabola Books is a small publisher specializing in spiritual, religious, and mythological subjects.
Nonfiction: Memoirs, explorations of the world's spiritual and religious traditions, essay collections. Subjects include multiculural, philosophy, psychology, religion, spirituality. Query with SASE. Recent title: *Such Stuff as Dreams Are Made On*, by Helen M. Luke (autobiography/journal).
Fiction: Multicultural, religious, spiritual. "We publish very little fiction: what we do print is based on the myths and religions of the word. No 'invented' mythology." Query with SASE.
Tips: "Our audience is the educated general public with an interest in spiritual growth. We are very small, and only publish a few books each year. The content of books we choose tends to echo that of *Parabola* Magazine, also published by SSMT. Familiarizing yourself with our magazine is a good first step."

POGO PRESS, INCORPORATED, 4 Cardinal Lane, St. Paul MN 55127-6406. E-mail: pogopres@minn.net. Website: www.pogopress.com. **Acquisitions:** Leo J. Harris, vice president. Publishes trade paperback originals. **Publishes 3 titles/year. Pays royalty on wholesale price.** Publishes book 6 months after acceptance. Responds in 2 months. Book catalog free.
Nonfiction: "We limit our publishing to Breweriana, history, art, popular culture and travel odysseys. Our books are heavily illustrated." No e-mail submissions. Query with SASE. Reviews artwork/photos as part of ms package. Send photocopies. Recent title: *The History of Beer and Brewing in Chicago—1833 to 1978*, by Bob Skilnik.

PRAKKEN PUBLICATIONS, INC., P.O. Box 8623, Ann Arbor MI 48107-8623. (313)975-2800. Fax: (313)975-2787. **Acquisitions:** George Kennedy, publisher. Book Editor: Susanne Peckham. Estab. 1934. Publishes educational hardcover and paperback originals as well as educational magazines. **Publishes 3 book titles/year. Pays 10% royalty on net sales** (negotiable with production costs). Responds in 2 months if reply requested and SASE furnished. Book catalog for #10 SASE.
Nonfiction: Industrial, vocational and technology education and related areas; general educational reference. "We are currently interested in manuscripts with broad appeal in any of the specific subject areas of industrial arts, technology education, vocational-technical education, and reference for the general education field." Submit outline and sample chapters. Recent title: *Workforce Education: Issues for the New Century*, edited by Albert J. Pautler, Jr.
Tips: "We have a continuing interest in magazine and book manuscripts which reflect emerging issues and trends in education, especially vocational, industrial and technological education."

PUCKERBRUSH PRESS, 76 Main St., Orono ME 04473-1430. (207)581-3832 or 866-4868. **Acquisitions:** Constance Hunting, publisher/editor. Estab. 1971. Publishes trade paperback originals and reprints of literary fiction and poetry. **Publishes 3-4 titles/year. Pays 10-15% royalty on wholesale price.** Responds in 1 month to queries; 2 months to proposals; 3 months to ms.
Nonfiction: Belles lettres, translations. Query with SASE. Recent title: *Art Notes*, by Farnham Blair.
Fiction: Literary and short story collections. Recent title: *The Crow in the Spruce*, by Chenoweth Hall.
Poetry: Highest literary quality. Submit complete ms with SASE. Recent title: *Settling*, by Patricia Ranzoni.
Tips: "No religious subjects, crime per se, tired prose. For sophisticated readers who retain love of literature. Maine writers continue to be featured." Currently emphasizing translations. De-emphasizing Maine back-to-the-land.

N QED PRESS, 155 Cypress St., Fort Bragg CA 95437. (707)964-9520. Fax: (707)964-7531. E-mail: qed@mcn.org. Website: www.cypresshouse.com. President: Cynthia Frank. **Acquisitions:** Joe Shaw. Publishes hardcover and trade paperback originals and hardcover reprints. **Publishes 3 titles/year. Pays 12-15% royalty on net price.** Responds in 3 months. Book catalog and ms guidelines free or on website.

Nonfiction: Subjects include health/medicine, paper airplanes. Publisher or books about health issues and books about paper airplanes. Submit completed ms. Recent nonfiction title(s): *Understanding Disease*, by G.A. Langes; *Exotic Paper Airplanes*, by Thay Yang.

Tips: "We're looking for well written, user friendly manuscripts, usually under 350 pages. Target market general public with specific health issues (for example, Parkinson Disease/Diabetes/Asthma)."

RED EYE PRESS, INC., P.O. Box 65751, Los Angeles CA 90065. **Acquisitions:** James Goodwin, president. Publishes trade paperback originals. **Publishes 2 titles/year. Pays 8-12% royalty on retail price. Offers $1-2,000 advance.** Responds in 1 month to queries, 3 months to mss. "We publish how-to and reference works that are the standard for their genre, authoritative, and able to remain in print for many years."

Nonfiction: How-to, gardening, reference books. Query with outline, 2 sample chapters and SASE. Recent title: *Great Labor Quotations—Sourcebook and Reader*, by Peter Bollen.

RISING STAR PRESS, P.O. Box BB, Los Altos CA 94023. (650)966-8920. Fax: (650)968-2658. E-mail: editor@rising starpress.com. Website: www.risingstarpress.com. **Contact:** Acquisitions Editor. Publishes hardcover originals and reprints, trade paperback originals and reprints. Rising Star publishes quality books that inform and inspire. **Publishes 2-4 titles/year. Pays 10-15% royalty on wholesale price. Offers $1,000-8,000 advance.** Publishes book 9 months after acceptance of ms. Accepts simultaneous submissions. Responds in 2 months to proposals.

   O→ "Rising Star selects manuscripts based on benefit to the reader. We are interested in a wide variety of nonfiction topics." Currently emphasizing social issues. De-emphasizing metaphysical, personal finance.

Nonfiction: Biography, humor, self-help. Subjects include education, health/medicine, language/literature, philosophy, regional, religion, social issues, sociology, spirituality. "Authors need to be able to answer these questions: Who will benefit from reading this? Why? Mistakes writers often make are not identifying their target market early and shaping the work to address it." Query with proposal package including outline, 2 sample chapters, target market, author's connection to market, author's credentials, e-mail address (required) and SASE. No fiction, children's books, or poetry. Recent title: *I'll Carry the Fork!—Recovering a Life After Brain Injury*, by Kara L. Swanson.

RUSSIAN INFORMATION SERVICES, 89 Main St., Suite 2, Montpelier VT 05602. (802)223-4955. Website: solar.ini.utk.edu/rispubs/ **Acquisitions:** Stephanie Ratmeyer, vice president. Publishes trade paperback originals and reprints. **Publishes 2-3 titles/year. Receives 20-30 queries and 10 mss/year. 50% of books from first-time authors; 100% from unagented writers. Pays 8-12% royalty on retail price.** Publishes book 8 months after acceptance of ms. Accepts simultaneous submissions. Responds in 2 months to mss. Book catalog free.

   O→ "Audience is business people and independent travelers to Russia and the former Soviet Union."

Nonfiction: Reference, travel, business. Subjects include business/economics, language/literature, travel. "Our editorial focus is on Russia and the former Soviet Union." Submit proposal package, including ms, summary and cv. Reviews artwork/photos as part of ms package. Send photocopies. Recent title: *Survival Russian*, by Ivanov (language).

SOUND VIEW PRESS, 859 Boston Post Rd., Madison CT 06443. (203)245-2246. Fax: (203)245-5116. E-mail: info@falkart.com. **Acquisitions:** Peter Hastings Falk, president. Estab. 1985. Publishes hardcover and trade paperback originals, dictionaries and exhibition records exclusive to fine art. All titles are related. Currently emphasizing American art history, conservation, exhibition. Recent title: *Who Was Who in American Art: 1564-1975*, by Peter Falk.

SPECTACLE LANE PRESS INC., P.O. Box 1237, Mt. Pleasant SC 29465-1237. Phone/fax: (843)971-9165 or (888)669-8114 (toll free). E-mail: jaskar@aol.com. **Acquisitions:** James A. Skardon, editor. Publishes nonfiction hardcover and trade paperback originals. **Publishes 2-3 titles/year. Pays 6-10% royalty on wholesale price. Offers $500-1,000 advance.** Responds in 1 month to queries, 2 months to mss.

Nonfiction: "More celebrity and TV-oriented humor and sports and family-oriented life-style subjects holding closely to current trends. "Query first. Then send outline and 3 chapters with SASE if we are interested." Recent title: *The Difference Between Cats & Dogs*, by Bob Zahn (cartoons).

N STORMLINE PRESS, P.O. Box 593, Urbana IL 61801. **Acquisitions:** Raymond Bial, publisher. Estab. 1985. Publishes hardcover and trade paperback originals. **Publishes 1-2 titles/year. Pays 10% royalty on retail price or "sometimes authors take a percentage of the print run in lieu of royalties.** Publishes fiction and nonfiction, generally with a Midwest connection. The Press considers queries (with SASE only) during November and December. We do not consider unsolicited manuscripts." Publishes mss by invitation only.

Nonfiction: Publishes photography and regional works of the highest literary quality, especially those having to do with rural and small town themes. Stormline prefers works which are rooted in a specific place and time, such as *When the Waters Recede: Rescue and Recovery During the Great Flood*, by Dan Guillory. Query with SASE.

Fiction: "We only publish books with rural, midwestern themes and very little fiction." Recent title: *Silent Friends*, by Margaret Lacey (short story collection).

Poetry: "We publish very little poetry." Recent title: *The Alligatory Inventions*, by Dan Guillory.

N STUDIO 4 PRODUCTIONS, P.O. Box 280400, Northridge CA 91328. (818)700-2522. Fax: (818)700-8666. E-mail: JoelTLeach@aol.com. Website: http://studio4productions.com. **Acquisitions:** Charlie Matthews, editor-in-chief (seniors/aging, character development); Karen Ervin-Pershing, associate editor (travel). Publishes trade paperback originals. **Publishes 2-5 titles/year. Pays 10% royalty on retail price. Advance negotiable depending on title and track record.** Responds in 1 month to queries and proposals, 3 months to mss.

Nonfiction: Subjects include character education (values, ethics and morals), parenting, travel, self-help. "We have also entered the area of Senior publications. We will continue to publish in previously established areas as well." Query with outline and SASE. Recent title: *Shadowdad*, by Richard Watrous.

TAMARACK BOOKS, INC., P.O. Box 190313, Boise ID 83719-0313. (800)962-6657. (208)387-2656. Fax: (208)387-2650. President/Owner. Kathy Gaudry. **Acquisitions:** Maggie Chenore, general editor. Publishes trade paperback originals and reprints. **Publishes 3-5 titles/year. Pays 5-15% royalty.** Responds in 4 months to queries, 6 months to mss.

    O⌐ "We publish nonfiction history of the American West and are avidly seeking women's books. Time period preference is for pre-1900s." Currently emphasizing "pioneer women who have made a difference, whether they have name recognition or not."

Nonfiction: History and illustrated books on West for people living in or interested in the American West. "We are looking for manuscripts for a popular audience, but based on solid research. We specialize in mountain man, women's issues and outlaw history prior to 1940 in the West, but will look at any good manuscript on Western history prior to 1940." Query with outline and SASE. Recent title: *Competitive Struggle, America's Western Fur Trading Posts, 1764-1865*, by R.G. Robertson.

Tips: "We look for authors who want to actively participate in the marketing of their books."

TECHNICAL BOOKS FOR THE LAYPERSON, INC., P.O. Box 391, Lake Grove NY 11755. (540)877-1477. **Acquisitions:** Mary Lewis. Publishes trade paperback originals. **Publishes 3 titles/year. Pays 10-40% royalty on actual earnings. No advance.** Responds in 2 months to mss. Book catalog and ms guidelines free.

Nonfiction: How-to, reference, self-help, technical, textbook. "Our primary goal is consumer-friendliness ('Books by consumers for consumers'). All topics are considered. There is a preference for completed work which equips an ordinary consumer to deal with a specialized or technical area." Submit 1 sample chapter. *Absolutely no phone calls.* Recent title: *Common Blood Tests*, by Gifford (medical reference).

Tips: "Our audience is the consumer who needs very explicit information to aid in making good purchasing decisions." Format chapter for camera-ready copy, with text enclosed in $4\frac{1}{2} \times 7$ area (including headers and footers).

⌶N⌶ THREE HAWKS PUBLISHING LC, 1300 Bishop Lane, Alexandria VA 22302. (703)823-9833. Fax: (703)823-9834. E-mail: kej@3hawks.com. Website: www.3hawks.com. **Acquisitions:** Kurt E. Johnson (medical/science/natural history/adventure travel). Publishes trade paperback originals. **Publishes 2 titles/year. Pays 10% royalty on wholesale price or makes outright purchase of $5,000-10,000. No advance.** Responds in 1 month.

Nonfiction: Adventure/travel. Subjects include animals, health/medicine, nature/environment, science. Query with SASE or submit completed ms. Recent title: *Out of Assa: Heart of the Congo*, by Glenn W. Geelhoed, M.D. (medical).

TIA CHUCHA PRESS, A Project of The Guild Complex, P.O. Box 476969, Chicago IL 60647. (773)377-2496. Fax: (773)252-5388. **Acquisitions:** Luis Rodriguez, director. Publishes trade paperback originals. **Publishes 2-4 titles/year. Receives 25-30 queries and 150 mss/year. Pays 10% royalty on wholesale price. Offers $500-1,000 advance.** Responds in 9 months to mss. Publishes book 1 year after acceptance. Book catalog and ms guidelines free.

Poetry: "No restrictions as to style or content. We do cross-cultural and performance-oriented poetry. It has to work on the page, however." Submit complete ms with SASE. Recent title: *Talisman*, by Afaa M. Weaver.

Tips: Audience is "those interested in strong, multicultural, urban poetry—the best of bar-cafe poetry. Annual manuscript deadline is June 30. Send your best work. No fillers. We read in the summer; we decide in the fall what books to publish for the following year."

VANDERWYK & BURNHAM, P.O. Box 2789, Acton MA 01720. (978)263-5906. Fax: (978)263-7553. **Acquisitions:** Meredith Rutter, president. Publishes hardcover and trade paperback originals. **Publishes 1-3 titles/year. Pays royalty on retail price. Offers $2,000-3,000 advance.** Responds in 3 months to queries. Book catalog and ms guidelines for #10 SASE.

    O⌐ "We publish books that make a difference in people's lives, including motivational books about admirable people and programs, and self-help books for people 50 and over."

Nonfiction: Self-help. Subjects include contemporary issues, education, psychology, creative nonfiction, aging. Query with proposal package, including résumé, publishing history, clips with SASE. Recent title: *As Parents Age: A Psychological and Practical Guide*.

VITESSE PRESS, 45 State St., Suite 367, Montpelier VT 05602. (802)229-4243. Fax: (802)229-6939. E-mail: dickmfield@aol.com. Website: www.Acornpub.com. **Acquisitions:** Richard H. Mansfield, editor. Estab. 1985. Publishes trade paperback originals. **Publishes 3 titles/year. Pays 7-10% royalty. No advance.** Responds in 1 month to queries.

Nonfiction: Regional mountain biking guides (Eastern), outdoor recreation books. Especially interested in cycling-related books. Recent title: *Cycling Along the Canals of New York*, by Louis Rossi.

WESTERN NEW YORK WARES INC., P.O. Box 733, Ellicott Station, Buffalo NY 14205. (716)832-6088. E-mail: waywares@gateway.net. Website: www.wnybooks.com. **Acquisitions:** Brian S. Meyer, publisher (regional history);

Tom Connolly, marketing manager (sports, regional travel). Publishes trade paperback originals. **Publishes 3 titles/year. Pays 50% of net profits on all runs. No advance.** Publishes book 1 year after acceptance on ms. Accepts simultaneous submissions. Responds in 6 weeks. Book catalog free or on website. Manuscript guidelines for #10 SASE.

Nonfiction: Regional history focusing on upstate Western New York (Buffalo, Niagara Falls, Chautauqua, Allegany). No fiction. Subjects include art/architecture, history, photography, travel. Currently emphasizing architectural history, regional tourism. De-emphasizing juvenile books. Query with SASE. No phone inquiries. Recent Titles: *Victorian Buffalo*, by Cynthia Van Ness.

N WHITEHORSE PRESS, P.O. Box 60, North Conway NH 03860-0060. (603)356-6556. Fax: (603)356-6590. **Acquisitions:** Dan Kennedy, publisher. Estab. 1988. Publishes trade paperback originals. **Publishes 3-4 titles/year. Pays 10% maximum royalty on wholesale price. No advance.** Responds in 1 month to queries.

Nonfiction: "We are actively seeking nonfiction books to aid motorcyclists in topics such as motorcycle safety, restoration, repair and touring. We are especially interested in technical subjects related to motorcycling." Query. Recent title: *How to Set Up Your Motorcycle Workshop*, by Charlie Masi (trade paperback).

Tips: "We like to discuss project ideas at an early stage and work with authors to develop those ideas to fit our market."

WHITFORD PRESS, Schiffer Publishing, Ltd., 4880 Lower Valley Rd., Atglen PA 19310. (610)593-1777. **Acquisitions:** Ellen Taylor, managing editor. Estab. 1985. Publishes trade paperback originals. **Publishes 1-3 titles/year. Pays royalty on wholesale price; no advances.** Responds within 2 months. Book catalog free. Guidelines for SASE.

Nonfiction: How-to, self-help, reference. Subjects include astrology, metaphysics, New Age topics. "We are looking for well written, well-organized, original books on all metaphysical subjects (except channeling and past lives). Books that empower the reader or show him/her ways to develop personal skills are preferred. New approaches, techniques, or concepts are best. No personal accounts unless they directly relate to a general audience. No moralistic, fatalistic, sexist or strictly philosophical books." Query first or send outline with SASE large enough to hold your submission.

Tips: "Our audience is knowledgeable in metaphysical fields, well-read and progressive in thinking. Please check bookstores to see if your subject has already been covered thoroughly. Expertise in the field is not enough; your book must be clean, well written and well organized. A specific and unique marketing angle is a plus. No Sun-sign material; we prefer more advanced work. Please don't send entire manuscript unless we request it, and be sure to include SASE. Let us know if the book is available on computer diskette and what type of hardware/software. Manuscripts should be between 60,000 and 110,000 words."

WOODBRIDGE PRESS, P.O. Box 209, Santa Barbara CA 93102. (805)965-7039. Fax: (805)963-0540. E-mail: woodpress@aol.com. Website: www.woodbridgepress.com. **Acquisitions:** Howard Weeks, editor. Estab. 1971. Publishes hardcover and trade paperback originals. **Publishes 2-3 titles/year. Pays 10-15% on wholesale price.** Accepts simultaneous submissions. Responds in 2 months with SASE. Book catalog free.

    ○━ "We publish books by expert authors on special forms of gardening, vegetarian cooking, very limited self-help psychology and humor." Currently emphasizing gardening. De-emphasizing humor, self-help.

Nonfiction: Cookbook (vegetarian), self-help. Subjects include agriculture/horticulture, cooking/foods/nutrition, gardening, health, psychology (popular). Query. Reviews artwork/photos as part of ms package. Recent title: *Hydroponics Questions and Answers*, by Howard M. Resh (gardening/horticulture).

N WYSTERIA PUBLISHING, P.O. Box 1250, Bellmore NY 11710. (516)377-9877. Fax: (516)867-3488. E-mail: wysteria@wysteria.com. Website: www.wysteria.com. Publishes hardcover, trade paperback and mass market paperback originals. **Publishes 3-5 titles/year. Pays 3-7% royalty on retail price. Offers negotiable advance.** Responds in 1 month to queries, 2 months to proposals, 2 months to mss.

Nonfiction: Biography, cookbook, how-to, illustrated book, reference, technical, textbook. Subjects include animals, art/architecture, cooking/foods/nutrition, education, health/medicine, memoirs, regional, science, sports, travel, law, house/home. "We prefer well written works that are concise, full of substance, well organized, and easy to understand." Submit proposal package, including outline, author biography, description of target market, or submit completed ms. Recent title: *Medical Acronyms, Eponyms, and Mnemonics*, by Kim N. Jones (medical reference).

Fiction: Adventure, historical, horror, humor, literary, mystery, poetry, regional, romance, science fiction, short story collections, suspense. "Please avoid vulgarity, pornography, and inappropriate violence." Submit completed ms. Recent fiction title: *The Red Witch*, by Roman Valdes (children's).

Poetry: Submit complete ms. Recent poetry title: *Medusa's Overbite*, by Peter V. Dugan (regional).

Tips: "We are looking for good quality work from new or experienced authors who are strongly committed to their work. We will consider all submissions; we encourage new authors."

Book Producers

Book producers provide services for book publishers, ranging from hiring writers to editing and delivering finished books. Most book producers possess expertise in certain areas and will specialize in producing books related to those subjects. They provide books to publishers who don't have the time or expertise to produce the books themselves (many produced books are highly illustrated and require intensive design and color-separation work). Some work with on-staff writers, but most contract writers on a per-project basis.

Most often a book producer starts with a proposal; contacts writers, editors and illustrators; assembles the book; and sends it back to the publisher. The level of involvement and the amount of work to be done on a book by the producer is negotiated in individual cases. A book publisher may simply require the specialized skill of a particular writer or editor, or a producer could put together the entire book, depending on the terms of the agreement.

Writers have a similar working relationship with book producers. Their involvement depends on how much writing the producer has been asked to provide. Writers are typically paid by the hour, by the word, or in some manner other than on a royalty basis. Writers working for book producers usually earn flat fees. Writers may not receive credit (a byline in the book, for example) for their work, either. Most of the contracts require work for hire, and writers must realize they do not own the rights to writing published under this arrangement.

The opportunities are good, though, especially for writing-related work, such as fact checking, research and editing. Writers don't have to worry about good sales. Their pay is secured under contract. Finally, writing for a book producer is a good way to broaden experience in publishing. Every book to be produced is different, and the chance to work on a range of books in a number of capacities may be the most interesting aspect of all.

Book producers most often want to see a query detailing writing experience. They keep this information on file and occasionally even share it with other producers. When they are contracted to develop a book that requires a particular writer's experience, they contact the writer. There are well over 100 book producers, but most prefer to seek writers on their own. The book producers listed in this section have expressed interest in being contacted by writers. For a list of more producers, contact the American Book Producers Association, 160 Fifth Ave., Suite 625, New York NY 10010, or look in *Literary Market Place* (R.R. Bowker).

For a list of publishers according to their subjects of interest, see the nonfiction and fiction sections of the Book Publishers Subject Index. Information on book publishers and producers listed in the previous edition of *Writer's Market* but not included in this edition can be found in the General Index.

N AMERICAN & WORLD GEOGRAPHIC PUBLISHING, P.O. Box 5630, Helena MT 59604. (406)443-2842. Fax: (406)443-5480. E-mail: bradhurd@montanamagazine.com. Website: http://montanamagazine.com. **Contact:** Brad Hurd, publisher. Publishes soft and hardcover books devoted to travel, tourism and outdoor recreation, with special emphasis on color photography. Mostly regional (northern Rockies, Pacific Northwest).
Nonfiction: Currently emphasizing Glacier and Yellowstone national parks, Lewis and Clark trail.
Recent Title(s): *Along the Trail with Lewis and Clark*, by Fifer; *Yellowstone Day Hikes*, by Anderson.

BOOKWRIGHTS PRESS, 2255 Westover Dr., Charlottesville VA 22901. Phone/fax: (804)823-8223. E-mail: editor@bookwrights.com. Website: www.bookwrights.com. Publisher: Mayapriya Long. **Contact:** Robin Field, editor. Produces hardcover and trade paperback originals. Averages 2 titles/year. 40% of books from first-time authors; 100% from unagented writers. Pays royalty. Responds in 2 months.

Nonfiction: How-to, self-help, technical, textbook. Subjects include regional, religion, Eastern religion. Query with résumé via e-mail or mail. "Do not send manuscripts."
Fiction: Historical, mainstream, Asian, Indian fiction. Query or submit proposal.
Recent Title(s): *Sentimental Journeys*, by Joe Lieberman (nonfiction); *Mandalay's Child*, by Prem Sharma (fiction).
Tips: "No unsolicited manuscripts. Query first. When requested, send manuscript on disk with accompanying hard copy."

ALISON BROWN CERIER BOOK DEVELOPMENT, INC., 815 Brockton Lane N., Plymouth MN 55410. (763)449-9668. Fax: (763)449-9674. "The vast majority of books start with our ideas or those of a publisher, not with proposals from writers. We do not act as authors' agents." Produces hardcover and trade paperback originals. Produces 4 titles/year. 50% of books from first-time authors; 90% from unagented writers. Payment varies with the project. Cannot respond to unsolicited proposals for original books but are looking for experienced health and business writers for existing projects.

O⌐ Currently emphasizing health, business self-help. De-emphasizing cookbooks.

Nonfiction: How-to, popular reference, self-help. Subjects include child guidance/parenting, cooking/foods/nutrition, health, sports, business self-help, women's interest. Query with SASE.
Recent Title(s): *AMA Complete Guide to Children's Health.*
Tips: "I often pair experts with writers and like to know about writers and journalists with co-writing experience."

COURSE CRAFTERS, INC., 44 Merrimac St., Newburyport MA 01950. (978)465-2040. Fax: (978)465-5027. E-mail: lise@coursecrafters.com. Website: www.coursecrafters.com. President: Lise B. Ragan. Produces textbooks, language materials (Spanish/ESL) and publishes packages for early childhood/family learning that feature storytelling and music. Makes outright purchase. Manuscript guidelines vary based upon project-specific requirements.
Nonfiction: Textbook. "We package materials that teach language. We are particularly looking for innovative approaches and visually appealing presentations." Subjects include language, education (preschool-adult), and early childhood. Submit résumé, publishing history and clips. Reviews artwork/photos as part of ms package.
Tips: "Mail (or fax) résumé with list of projects related to specific experience with ESL, bilingual and/or foreign language textbook development. Also interested in storytellers and musicians for our new audio/game packages."

N DESIGN PRESS, P.O. Box 3146, Savannah GA 31402-3146. (912)525-5212. Fax: (912)525-5211. E-mail: jshay@scad.edu. Website: www.designpress.com. **Contact:** Janice Shay, director. Produces hardcover and trade paperback originals. Produces 12-15 titles/year. 50% of books from first-time authors; 95% from unagented writers. Pays negotiable royalty (usually 3-7%) or makes outright purchase. Offers negotiable advance (usually $1,000 and up). Responds in 2 months. Book catalog and ms guidelines free on request.
Nonfiction: Children's/juvenile, coffee table book, cookbook, gift book, illustrated book. Subjects include art/architecture, cooking/foods/nutrition, photography, regional (Savannah, southeast coast). Query with résumé and publishing history or submit complete ms (for children's picture books). Accepts only text. No artwork please.
Fiction: Juvenile, picture books, young adult. Query with résumé and publishing history or submit complete ms (for picture books).
Recent Title(s): *Mrs. Wilkes Savannah Cookbook*, by John T. Edge (cookbook; Ten Speed Press); *My Mother's Pearls*, by Catherine Fruisen (picture book; Cedco Publishing).
Tips: "Design Press exists to produce books of exceptional quality showcasing the visual talent of the faculty and students of the Savannah College of Art and Design. A full-service book producer, Design Press takes both original and commissioned projects through the conceptual, visual, editorial and production stages that comprise the finished book. Design Press specializes in children's picture books, illustrated gift books, and other publications that emphasize the visual elements of art and design. We welcome inquiries from prospective authors, particularly in children's fiction and picture book genres."

N J.K. ECKERT & CO., INC., 4370 S. Tamiami Tr., Suite 106, Sarasota FL 34231-3400. (941)925-0468. Fax: (941)925-0272. E-mail: jkeckert@packet.net. Website: www.webbooks.net. **Contact:** William Marshall, acquisitions editor. "We handle only nonfiction, mostly in professional-level electrical/electronic engineering fields." Produces hardcover originals. Produces 12-18 titles/year. 80% of books from first-time authors; 100% from unagented writers. Pays 10-50% royalty on net receipts. Responds usually in 6 weeks. Manuscript guidelines free on request.
Nonfiction: Reference, software, technical, textbook. Subjects include telecommunications, circuit design, computer science and electronic engineering. Submit proposal. Reviews artwork/photos as part of ms package. Professional-level books only.
Recent Title(s): *Electronic Packaging Handbook*, (Harper); *Handbook of Commercial Catalysts* (Rase).
Tips: "1) Keep art and text separate—do not use page layout software. 2) Save any artwork as EPS or TIFF; use a real art program like Adobe Illustrator—not something built into a word processor. 3) Don't get creative with fonts—stick to Times and Helvetica. Avoid True-Type if humanly possible. 4) Send synopsis, TOC, and sample chapter (preferably not Chapter 1). Include bio if you want, but if the book is good, we don't care who you are."

GLEASON GROUP, INC., 6 Old Kings Hwy., Norwalk CT 06850. (203)847-6658. President: Gerald Gleason. Produces 4-8 titles/year. Work-for-hire.
Nonfiction: Textbooks about software with CD-ROMs. Submitt résumé. *No unsolicited mss.*
Recent Title(s): *Word 2000: A Professional Approach.*

Tips: "If writer is well versed in the most recent Microsoft Office software, and has written technical or software-related material before, he/she can send us their résumé."

[N] MARCH TENTH, INC., 4 Myrtle St., Haworth NJ 07641. (201)387-6551. Fax: (201)387-6552. E-mail: schoron @aol.com. **Contact:** Sandra Choron, president. Produces hardcover originals, trade paperback originals, mass market paperback originals. Produces 10 titles/year. 50% from first-time authors. Pays 10% royalty on retail price. Offers $10,000 advance. Responds in 2 weeks.
Nonfiction: Biography, coffee table book, gift book, how-to, illustrated book, reference, self-help. Subjects include Americana, art/architecture, ethnic, history, hobbies, language/literature, money/finance, music/dance, recreation, spirituality, women's issues/studies. Query. Reviews artwork/photos as part of the ms package. Writers should send photocopies.
Recent Title(s): *Songs*, by Bruce Springsteen (Avon); *Lynyrd Skynyrd*, by Lee Ballinger (Avon).
Tips: "Tell me as much as you can about your credentials."

McCLANAHAN BOOK COMPANY INC., 23 W. 26th St., New York NY 10010. (212)725-1515. Vice President, Managing Director: Jeanne Firestone. Produces 50-60 titles/year. 5% of books from first-time authors; 90% from unagented writers. Makes outright purchase. Responds within 3 months to submissions with SASE.
> ⚬┳ "Our goal is to provide entertaining books with an underlying educational value to the mass market—for children ages 2-10 years old." Currently emphasizing science topics. De-emphasizing story book topics.
Nonfiction: Juvenile. Submit proposal only. Reviews artwork/photos as part of ms package.
Recent Title(s): *Know-It-Alls*.

NEW ENGLAND PUBLISHING ASSOCIATES, INC., P.O. Box 5, Chester CT 06412. (860)345-READ. Fax: (860)345-3660. E-mail: nepa@nepa.com. Website: www.nepa.com. President: Elizabeth Frost-Knappman; Vice President/Treasurer: Edward W. Knappman. Staff: Victoria Harlow, Ron Formica and Kristine Schiavi. Estab. 1983. "Our mission is to provide personalized service to a select list of mainly nonfiction clients." NEPA develops adult and young adult reference and information titles and series for the domestic and international markets. Produces hardcover and trade paperback originals. 20% of books from first-time authors. Responds in 2 months.
> ● Elizabeth Frost-Knappman's *Women's Progress in America* was selected by *Choice* as Outstanding Reference Book of the Year.
Tips: "Revise, revise, revise."

NEWMARKET PRESS, 18 E. 48th St., Suite 1501, New York NY 10017. (212)832-3575. Fax: (212)832-3629. **Contact:** Esther Margolis, president. Managing Editor: John Jusino. Produces hardcover and trade paperback originals. Produces 25-30 titles/year. Pays royalty. Catalog for SAE 9×12 and $1.01 postage. Manuscript guidelines for #10 SASE.
> ⚬┳ Currently emphasizing movie tie-in/companion books, self-help, parenting/childcare. De-emphasizing fiction.
Nonfiction: General nonfiction, self-help. Subjects include child guidance/parenting, cooking/foods/nutrition, film, health, money/finance, psychology. Query with SASE or submit proposal.
Recent Title(s): *From Diapers to Dating: A Parents' Guide to Raising Sexually Healthy Children*, by Debra W. Haffner, M.P.H.; *Stuart Little: The Art, the Artists, and the Story Behind the Amazing Movie*, edited by Linda Sunshine.
Tips: "Check out other Newmarket titles before submitting to get a sense of the kind of books we publish. Be patient!"

[N] OTTENHEIMER PUBLISHERS, INC., 5 Park Center, Suite 300, Baltimore MD 21117-5001. (410)902-9100. Fax: (410)902-7210. E-mail: cignatowski@ottenheimerpub.com. Chairman of the Board: Allan T. Hirsh Jr. President: Allan T. Hirsh III. Publisher: Dan Wood. **Contact:** Laura Wallace. Estab. 1890. Produces hardcover and paperback originals and reprints and mass market paperback originals. Produces 200 titles/year. Receives 300 submissions/year. **20% of books from first-time authors; 85% of books from unagented writers. Pays flat fee.** Publishes book 9 months after acceptance. Responds in 2 months to queries, 4 months to proposals, mss. Guidelines free.
Nonfiction: Cookbooks, illustrated book, juvenile, gift book, reference. Subjects include cooking/foods/nutrition, health, religion, spirituality. Query with SASE. Reviews artwork/photos as part of ms package.
Recent Title(s): *Native American Healing Secrets*, by Porter Shimer (alternative healing, nonfiction).
Tips: "We are a book packager. Most projects are generated in-house and assigned to freelancers as work-for-hire. We're developing titles for children ages 0-3, 3-5 and early learning; also religious titles. For adults, we need generalist nonfiction for readers interested in health topics, religion, cooking and inspirational gift books."

PUBLICOM, INC., 411 Massachusetts Ave., Acton MA 01720-3739. (978)263-5773. Fax: (978)263-7553. E-mail: info@publicom1.com (textbooks), uburnham@publicom1.com (tradebooks). Website: www.VandB.com (tradebooks). Vice President (Publicom Textbook Services): Neil Sanders. Vice President (tradebooks): Patricia Moore. "We create and market leading-edge educational products and services, and we publish exemplary tradebooks that promote learning, compassion and self-reliance." Produces hardcover and trade paperback originals under the imprint VanderWyk & Burnham. Produces or publishes 100-200 titles/year. 50% of tradebooks from first-time authors; 90% from unagented writers. "Work for hire" for textbooks; pays 3-10% royalty or makes variable outright purchase. Offers up to $3,000 advance for trade publishing. Responds in 6 months.
Nonfiction: Biography, self-help, textbook. Subjects include school disciplines K-college, tradebook topics in social sciences, education, aging. Submit proposal, résumé, publishing history and clips.

Recent Title(s): *How to Feel Good As You Age*, by John Barnett (aging).

SACHEM PUBLISHING ASSOCIATES, INC., P.O. Box 412, Guilford CT 06437-0412. (203)453-4328. Fax: (203)453-4320. E-mail: sachempublishing@guilfordct.com. President: Stephen P. Elliott. Estab. 1974. Produces hardcover originals for publishers. Produces 3 titles/year. 5% of books from first-time authors; 100% from unagented writers. Pays royalty or works for hire. Responds in 1 month. *Writer's Market* recommends allowing 2 months for reply.
Nonfiction: Reference. Subjects include Americana, government/politics, history, military/war. Submit résumé and publishing history.
Recent Title(s): *American Heritage Encyclopedia of American History*, by John Mack Faragher, general editor.

N SETTEL ASSOCIATES INC., 11 Wimbledon Court, Jericho NY 11753. (516)681-1505. **Contact:** Trudy Settel. Produces hardcover, trade paperback, mass market paperback originals. Produces 3-10 titles/year. 15% of books from first-time authors; 10% from unagented writers. Pays 10-15% royalty on retail price. Responds in 1 month. *Writer's Market* recommends allowing 2 months for reply.
Nonfiction: Biography, cookbook, how-to, humor, illustrated book, juvenile, self-help. Subjects include Americana, business and economics, child guidance/parenting, cooking/foods/nutrition, health, history, hobbies, money/finance, philosophy, psychology, recreation, sociology, travel. Query.
Recent Title(s): *Low Fat Cooking*, by G. Schulman.
Fiction: Adventure, erotica, fantasy, historical, humor, juvenile, mystery, picture books, romance, suspense. Query.

N SOMERVILLE HOUSE BOOKS LIMITED, 3080 Yonge St., Suite 5000, Toronto Ontario M4N 3N1 Canada. **Contact:** Acquisition Department. Produces childrens nonfiction. Produces 15 titles/year. 5% of books from first-time authors. Responds in 4 months. Manuscript guidelines for #10 SASE with postage (Canadian or IRC).
Nonfiction: Query.
Recent Title(s): *The Holographic Night Sky Book & Kit*.
Tips: "We accept only children's nonfiction submissions."

2M COMMUNICATIONS LTD., 121 W. 27th St., New York NY 10001. (212)741-1509. Fax: (212)691-4460. Editorial Director: Madeleine Morel. Produces hardcover, trade paperback and mass market paperback originals. Produces 15 titles/year. 50% of books from first-time authors. Responds in 2 weeks. *Writer's Market* recommends allowing 2 months for reply.
Nonfiction: Biography, cookbook, how-to, humor. Subjects include child guidance/parenting, cooking/foods/nutrition, ethnic, gay/lesbian, health, psychology, women's studies. Query or submit proposal with résumé and publishing history.

VERNON PRESS, INC., 398 Columbus Ave., #355, Boston MA 02116-6008. (617)437-0388. Fax: (617)437-0894. E-mail: vpitwo@tiac.net. Website: www.vernonpress.com. **Contact:** Chris Dall, associate editor (art history, history, popular culture, travel). Book packager of hardcover and trade paperback originals. Produces 8-12 titles/year. 30% of books from first-time authors; 60% from unagented writers. Pays 50-60% royalty on net receipts or pays work-for-hire fee based on individual project. Responds in 6 weeks.
Nonfiction: Coffee table book, gift book, illustrated book. Subjects include Americana, art/architecture, gardening, history, language/literature, music/dance, photography, regional, translation, travel. Submit proposal. Reviews artwork/photos as part of ms package. Send photocopies or duplicate transparencies.
Recent Title(s): *Acadia: Visions and Verse*, by Jack Perkins (Down East Books, 1999).

THE WONDERLAND PRESS, 160 Fifth Ave., Suite 723, New York NY 10010. (212)989-2550. President: John Campbell. Produces hardcover and trade paperback originals and mass market paperback originals. Produces 50 titles/year. 80% of books from first-time authors; 90% from unagented writers. Payment depends on the book: sometimes royalty with advance, sometimes work-for-hire. Responds in 3 weeks.
Nonfiction: Biography, coffee table book, how-to, illustrated book, reference, self-help. Subjects include business and economics, education, gardening, gay/lesbian, history, money/finance, photography, psychology, art. Submit proposal with sample chapter(s). Reviews artwork/photos as part of ms package.
Recent Title(s): *The Essential Jackson Pollock* (Abrams).
Tips: "Always submit in writing, never by telephone. Know your market intimately. Study the competition and decide whether there is a genuine need for your book, with a market base that will justify publication. Send us an enthused, authoritative, passionately written proposal that shows your mastery of the subject and that makes us say, 'Wow, we want that!' "

MARKET CONDITIONS are constantly changing! If this is 2002 or later, buy the newest edition of *Writer's Market* at your favorite bookstore or order directly from Writer's Digest Books at (800)289-0963.

Consumer Magazines

Selling your writing to consumer magazines is as much an exercise of your marketing skills as it is of your writing abilities. Editors of consumer magazines are looking not simply for good writing, but for good writing which communicates pertinent information to a specific audience—their readers. Why are editors so particular about the readers they appeal to? Because it is only by establishing a core of faithful readers with identifiable and quantifiable traits that magazines attract advertisers. And with many magazines earning up to half their income from advertising, it is in their own best interests to know their readers' tastes and provide them with articles and features that will keep their readers coming back.

APPROACHING THE CONSUMER MAGAZINE MARKET

Marketing skills will help you successfully discern a magazine's editorial slant and write queries and articles that prove your knowledge of the magazine's readership to the editor. The one complaint we hear from magazine editors more than any other is that many writers don't take the time to become familiar with their magazine before sending a query or manuscript. Thus, editors' desks become cluttered with inappropriate submissions—ideas or articles that simply will not be of much interest to the magazine's readers.

You can gather clues about a magazine's readership—and thus establish your credibility with the magazine's editor—in a number of ways:

• Start with a careful reading of the magazine's listing in this section of *Writer's Market*. Most listings offer very straightforward information about their magazine's slant and audience.

• Study a magazine's writer's guidelines, if available. These are written by each particular magazine's editors and are usually quite specific about their needs and their readership.

• Check a magazine's website. Often writer's guidelines and a selection of articles are included in a publication's online version. A quick check of archived articles lets you know if ideas you want to propose have already been covered.

• Perhaps most important, read several current issues of the target magazine. Only in this way will you see firsthand the kind of stories the magazine actually buys.

• If possible, talk to an editor by phone. Many will not take phone queries, particularly those at the higher-profile magazines. But many editors of smaller publications will spend the time to help a writer over the phone.

Writers who can correctly and consistently discern a publication's audience and deliver stories that speak to that target readership will win out every time over writers who simply write what they write and send it where they will.

AREAS OF CURRENT INTEREST

Today's consumer magazines reflect societal trends and interests. As baby boomers age and the so-called "Generation X" comes along behind, magazines arise to address their concerns, covering topics of interest to various subsets of both of those wide-ranging demographic groups. Some areas of special interest now popular among consumer magazines include gardening, health & fitness, family leisure, computers, travel, fashion and cooking.

WHAT EDITORS WANT

In nonfiction, editors continue to look for short feature articles covering specialized topics. They want crisp writing and expertise. If you are not an expert in the area about which you are writing, make yourself one through research.

Always query before sending your manuscript. Don't e-mail or fax a query unless an editor specifically mentions an openness to this in the listing. Publishing, despite all the electronic advancements, is still a very paper-oriented industry. Once a piece has been accepted, however, many publishers now prefer to receive your submission via disk or modem so they can avoid re-keying the manuscript. Some magazines will even pay an additional amount for disk submission.

Fiction editors prefer to receive complete short story manuscripts. Writers must keep in mind that marketing fiction is competitive and editors receive far more material than they can publish. For this reason, they often do not respond to submissions unless they are interested in using the story. Before submitting material, check the market's listing for fiction requirements to ensure your story is appropriate for that market. More comprehensive information on fiction markets can be found in *Novel & Short Story Writer's Market* (Writer's Digest Books).

Many writers make their articles do double duty, selling first or one-time rights to one publisher and second serial or reprint rights to another noncompeting market. The heading, **Reprints**, offers details when a market indicates they accept previously published submissions, with submission form and payment information if available.

When considering magazine markets, be sure not to overlook opportunities with Canadian and international publications. Many such periodicals welcome submissions from U.S. writers and can offer writers an entirely new level of exposure for their work.

Regardless of the type of writing you do, keep current on trends and changes in the industry. Trade magazines such as *Writer's Digest*, *Folio:* and *Advertising Age* will keep you abreast of start-ups and shutdowns and other writing/business trends.

PAYMENT

Writers make their living by developing a good eye for detail. When it comes to marketing material, the one detail of interest to almost every writer is the question of payment. Most magazines listed here have indicated pay rates; some give very specific payment-per-word rates while others state a range. Any agreement you come to with a magazine, whether verbal or written, should specify the payment you are to receive and when you are to receive it. Some magazines pay writers only after the piece in question has been published. Others pay as soon as they have accepted a piece and are sure they are going to use it.

In *Writer's Market*, those magazines that pay on acceptance have been highlighted with the phrase **pays on acceptance** set in bold type. Payment from these markets should reach you faster than from markets who pay on publication. There is, however, some variance in the industry as to what constitutes payment "on acceptance"—some writers have told us of two- and three-month waits for checks from markets that supposedly pay on acceptance. It is never out of line to ask an editor when you might expect to receive payment for an accepted article.

So what is a good pay rate? There are no standards; the principle of supply and demand operates at full throttle in the business of writing and publishing. As long as there are more writers than opportunities for publication, wages for freelancers will never skyrocket. Rates vary widely from one market to the next, however, and the news is not entirely bleak. One magazine industry source puts the average pay rate for consumer magazine feature writing at $1.25 a word, with "stories that require extensive reporting . . . more likely to be priced at $2.50 a word." In our opinion, those estimates are on the high side of current pay standards. Smaller circulation magazines and some departments of the larger magazines will pay a lower rate.

Editors know that the listings in *Writer's Market* are read and used by writers with a wide range of experience, from those as-yet unpublished writers just starting out, to those with a successful, profitable freelance career. As a result, many magazines publicly report pay rates in the lower end of their actual pay ranges. Experienced writers will be able to successfully negotiate higher pay rates for their material. Newer writers should be encouraged that as your reputation grows (along with your clip file), you will be able to command higher rates. The article How Much Should I Charge? on page 61 gives you an idea of pay ranges for different freelance jobs.

WHAT'S NEW THIS YEAR?

We've added several features to make *Writer's Market* even more helpful in your search for the right magazine markets, features you won't find in any other writer's guide.

Many magazines are taking advantage of electronic media—and you should too. This year we've added information on whether a magazine accepts queries by e-mail or fax in addition to regular mail, and whether writers' guidelines are available online or by e-mail. We use a small computer icon to indicate that a magazine's website carries original online-only content and the online editor to address your query to.

Some areas of a magazine are more open to newer writers than others. Often writers unknown to the editor can break in with shorter features, columns or departments. This year we've added a key symbol (⚷) to identify the best ways to break in to *that* particular magazine.

Breaking into niche markets

Independent writers who blaze the freelance trails seem like free-spirited rebels. These highly energized professionals write hard and well for the highest bidder, but work largely for themselves. The best among their ranks are invaluable to editors, and they name their own terms. But while they are free to conduct business as they please, freelancers also face tough circumstances—cash flow issues, stiff competition and the endless need for self-promotion.

So how do these writers make a living without being "on staff?" Specialization in niche markets, answer many freelance experts. For the six writing renegades featured in this section, narrowing the field is the secret to real and lasting success. Focusing their writing to fit their respective niche markets—parenting, computers, health, food, travel and nature—has kept them a few steps ahead of the pack, with the comfort of a steady work flow and the luxury of writing in fields they love.

Throughout this Consumer Magazines section, you'll find the stories behind these freelancers' success in their niche markets: Child Care/Parenting, page 431; Food & Drink, page 470; Health & Fitness, page 494; Nature/Outdoors, page 594; Personal Computers, page 604; and Travel, page 779. Regardless of the subject matter, all freelancing requires perseverance, the ability to juggle several projects at one time, flexibility and resourcefulness. But for these niche markets, there are some other requirements as well. Throughout these six interviews, our freelance experts will share insights and advice from the trail: how to break in, what editors are looking for now, and how you can sidestep the pitfalls many rookies fall into.

—*Kelly Milner Halls*

—No slouch herself, Kelly Milner Halls has been a full-time freelance writer for nearly a decade, contributing frequently to the Chicago Tribune, The Atlanta Journal Constitution, FamilyFun, Highlights for Children, *and dozens of other publications. Her nonfiction title* I Bought a Baby Chick *was published by Boyds Mills Press in Spring 2000. She lives as a single mother in Spokane, with two daughters, four cats, two dogs and a ferret.*

Information at-a-glance

Last year we made some changes to help you access the information you need as efficiently as possible. Most immediately noticeable, we added a number of symbols at the beginning of each listing to quickly convey certain important information. In the Consumer Magazine section, symbols identify comparative payment rates (**$—$ $ $ $**); new listings (N); "opportunity" markets (⊠) that are at least 75% freelance written, appear quarterly or more frequently, and buy a high number of manuscripts; and magazines that do not accept freelance submissions (⊘). Different sections of *Writer's Market* include other symbols; check the front and back inside covers for an explanation of all the symbols used throughout the book.

We also highlighted important information in boldface, the "quick facts" you won't find in any other market book, but should know before you submit your work. To clearly identify the editorial "point person" at each magazine, the word "**Contact:**" identifies the appropriate person to query at each magazine. We also highlight what percentage of the magazine is freelance written, how many manuscripts a magazine buys per year of nonfiction, fiction, poetry and fillers and respective pay rates in each category.

Information on publications listed in the previous edition of *Writer's Market* but not included in this edition may be found in the General Index.

ANIMAL

The publications in this section deal with pets, racing and show horses, and other domestic animals and wildlife. Magazines about animals bred and raised for the market are classified in the Farm category of Trade, Technical & Professional Journals. Publications about horse racing can be found in the Sports section.

☆ $ ANIMALS, Massachusetts Society for the Prevention of Cruelty to Animals, 350 S. Huntington Ave., Boston MA 02130. (617)522-7400. Fax: (617)522-4885. Editor: Paula Abend. **90% freelance written.** Bimonthly magazine publishing "articles on wildlife (American and international), domestic animals, balanced treatments of controversies involving animals, conservation, animal welfare issues, pet health and pet care." Estab. 1868. Circ. 100,000. **Pays on acceptance.** Publishes ms an average of 5 months after acceptance. Byline given. Offers negotiable kill fee. Buys one-time rights or makes work-for-hire assignments. Submit seasonal material 6 months in advance. Responds in 6 weeks. Sample copy for $2.95 and 9×12 SAE with 4 first-class stamps. Writer's guidelines for #10 SASE.
Nonfiction: Exposé, general interest, how-to, opinion and photo feature on animal and environmental issues and controversies, plus practical pet-care topics. "*Animals* does not publish breed-specific domestic pet articles or 'favorite pet' stories. Poetry and fiction are also not used." **Buys 50 mss/year.** Query with published clips. Length: 2,200 words maximum. Sometimes pays the expenses of writers on assignment.
Photos: State availability of photos with submission, if applicable. Reviews contact sheets, 35mm transparencies and 5×7 or 8×10 prints. Payment depends on usage size and quality. Captions, model releases and identification of subjects required. Buys one-time rights.
Columns/Departments: Books (book reviews of books on animals and animal-related subjects). **Buys 18 mss/year.** Query with published clips. Length: 300 words maximum. Profile (women and men who've gone to extraordinary lengths to aid animals). Length: 800 words maximum. **Buys 6 mss/year.** Query with clips.
Tips: "Present a well-researched proposal. Be sure to include clips that demonstrate the quality of your writing. Stick to categories mentioned in *Animals'* editorial description. Combine well-researched facts with a lively, informative writing style. Feature stories are written almost exclusively by freelancers. We continue to seek proposals and articles that take a humane approach. Articles should concentrate on how issues affect animals, rather than humans."

$ $ APPALOOSA JOURNAL, Appaloosa Horse Club, 2728 West Pullmann, Moscow ID 83843-0903. (208)882-5578. Fax: (208)882-8150. E-mail: journal@appaloosa.com. **Contact:** Robin Hirzel, editor. **20-40% freelance written.** Monthly magazine covering Appaloosa horses. Estab. 1946. Circ. 25,000. Pays on publication. Publishes ms an average of 3 months after acceptance. Byline given. Buys first North American serial rights. Responds in 1 month to queries; 2 months to mss. Sample copy and writer's guidelines free.
• *Appaloosa Journal* no longer accepts material for columns.
Nonfiction: Historical, interview/profile, photo feature. **Buys 15-20 mss/year.** Query with or without published clips, or send complete ms. Length: 800-2,000 words. **Pays $100-400.** Sometimes pays expenses of writers on assignment.
Photos: Send photos with submission. Payment varies. Captions and identification of subjects required.
Tips: "Articles by writers with horse knowledge, news sense and photography skills are in great demand. If it's a strong article about an Appaloosa, the writer has a pretty good chance of publication. A good understanding of the breed and the industry is helpful. Make sure there's some substance and a unique twist."

$ $ ASPCA ANIMAL WATCH, The American Society for the Prevention of Cruelty to Animals, 315 E. 62nd St., New York NY 10021. (212)876-7700. Fax: (212)410-0087. E-mail: editor@aspca.org. Website: www.aspca.org. **Contact:** Marion Lane, editor. **40-50% freelance written.** Quarterly magazine covering animal welfare: companion animals, endangered species, farm animals, wildlife, animals in entertainment, laboratory animals and humane consumption, i.e., fur, ivory, etc. "The ASPCA's mission is to alleviate pain, fear and suffering in all animals. As the voice of the ASCPA, *Animal Watch* is our primary means of communicating with and informing our membership. In addition to in-depth, timely coverage and original reporting on important issues, *Animal Watch* provides practical advice on companion animal care. The ASCPA promotes the adoption and responsible care of pets, and through the magazine we encourage excellent stewardship in areas such as nutrition, training, exercise and veterinary care." Estab. 1980. Circ. 330,000. Pays on publication. Publishes ms an average of 4 months after acceptance. Byline given. Buys first North American serial and electronic rights. Editorial lead time 6 months. Submit seasonal material 6 months in advance. Accepts queries by mail, e-mail, fax. Accepts simultaneous submissions. Responds within 3 months. Sample copy for 10 × 13 SAE with 4 first-class stamps or on website. Writer's guidelines for #10 SASE or on website.

O→ Break in with a submission to the Animals Abroad column.

Nonfiction: Investigative, news, advocacy, historical/nostalgic, how-to, interview/profile, photo feature and respectful humor. No stories told from animals' point of view, religious stories, fiction or poetry, articles with strident animal rights messages or articles with graphic details. **Buys 25-30 mss/year.** Send formal query with published clips. Length: 650-3,000 words. **Pays $75-650.** Sometimes pays expenses of writers on assignment.

Photos: State availability of photos with submission. Reviews transparencies and prints. Offers $75-300/photo or negotiates payment individually. Captions, model releases and identification of subjects required. Buys one-time rights.

Columns/Departments: Last Looks (back page humor and light news), 150-300 words; Animals Abroad (first person by someone abroad), 650-700 words; Animals & the Law (balanced report on a legal or legislative subject), 650-700 words. **Buys 10 mss/year.** Query with or without published clips or send complete ms. **Pays $75-175.**

Tips: "The most important assets for an *Animal Watch* contributor are familiarity with the animal welfare movement in the U.S. and the ability to write lively, well-researched articles. We are always looking for positive stories about people and groups and businesses who are helping to protect animals in some way and may inspire others to do the same. We know the problems—share with us some solutions, some approaches that are working. Everything we publish includes 'How you can help. . . .' We are as likely to assign a feature as a short piece for one of the departments."

N $ $ THE BARK, the modern dog culture, The Bark, 2810 Eighth, Berkeley CA 94710. (510)704-0827. Fax: (510)704-0933. E-mail: editor@thebark.com. Website: www.thebark.com. **Contact:** Claudia Kawczynska, editor. **50% freelance written.** Quarterly magazine covering dogs in today's society. "*The Bark* brings a literate and entertaining approach to dog culture through essays, reviews, interviews and artwork. Our perspective is directed to the sophisticated reader. The point of view is topical, unsentimental and intelligent. We are smartly designed and stylish." Estab. 1997. Circ. 60,000. Pays on publication. Publishes ms an average of 6 months after acceptance. Byline given. Offers 20% kill fee. Buys first rights. Editorial lead time 3 months. Submit seasonal material 3 months in advance. Accepts queries by mail, phone. Sample copy for $3. Writer's guidelines free.

Nonfiction: Book excerpts, essays, exposé, historical/nostalgic, how-to, humor, interview/profile, opinion, personal experience, travel. Upcoming special issues include dogs in the visual arts and dogs in literature. No "death of a dog" pieces. **Buys 10 mss/year.** Query with published clips. Length: 600-1,700 words. **Pays $50-400.**

Reprints: Accepts previously published submissions.

Photos: State availability of photos with submission. Reviews contact sheets.

Columns/Departments: Health (holistic), 1,000 words; Training (non-aversive), 1,000 words; Behavior, 800 words. **Pays $50-300.**

Fiction: Adventure, humorous, mystery, novel excerpts, slice-of-life vignettes. No religious. **Buys 4 mss/year.** Query. Length: 400-1,200 words.

Poetry: Avant garde, free verse, haiku, light verse, traditional. **Buys 20 poems/year.**

Fillers: Anita Monga, associate editor. Anecdotes, facts, gags to be illustrated by cartoonist, newsbreaks, short humor. **Buys 20/year.** Length: 100-600 words. **Pays $25-150.**

Tips: "Have a true understanding of our editorial vision and have a true appreciation for dogs."

$ $ CAT FANCY, Fancy Publications, Inc., P.O. Box 6050, Mission Viejo CA 92690. (949)855-8822. Fax: 949-855-0654. E-mail: aluke@fancypubs.com Website: www.animalnetwork.com. **Contact:** Amanda Luke, editor. **80-90% freelance written.** Monthly magazine mainly for women ages 25-54 interested in all phases of cat ownership. Estab. 1965. Circ. 303,000. Pays on publication. Publishes ms an average of 6 months after acceptance. Buys first North American serial rights. Byline given. Absolutely no simultaneous submissions. Submit seasonal material 4 months in advance. Responds in 3 months. Sample copy for $5.50. Writer's guidelines for SASE.

Nonfiction: Behavior, health, lifestyle, how-to, humor, photo feature; must be cat oriented. **Buys 5-7 mss/issue.** Query by mail first with published clips. Length: 500-3,000 words. **Pays $35-400; special rates for photo/story packages.**

Photos: Photos purchased with or without accompanying ms. Pays $50 minimum for color prints; $50-200 for 35mm or 2¼ × 2¼ color transparencies; occasionally pays more for particularly outstanding or unusual work. Photo guidelines for SASE; then send prints and transparencies. Model release required.

Columns/Departments: Kids for Cats (short stories, how-to, crafts, puzzles for 10-16 year olds); Feline Friends (once or twice/year, readers' special cats).

Poetry: Short, cat-related poems. Submit any number but always with SASE.

Fiction: Not reviewing fiction at this time.

Fillers: Newsworthy or unusual; items with photos. Query first. **Buys 5/year.** Length: 500-1,000 words. **Pays $35-100.**

Tips: "Most of the articles we receive are profiles of the writers' own cats or profiles of cats that have recently died. We reject almost all of these stories. What we need are well-researched articles that will give our readers the information they need to better care for their cats or to help them fully enjoy cats. Please review past issues and notice the informative nature of articles before querying us with an idea. *Please query first.*"

$ $ CATS MAGAZINE, Primedia Special Interests, 260 Madison Ave., 8th Floor, New York NY 10016. E-mail: info@catsmag.com. Website: www.catsmag.com. **Contact:** Jane W. Reilly, editor-in-chief. **80% freelance written.** Monthly magazine for owners and lovers of cats. Estab. 1945. Circ. 127,000. **Pays on acceptance.** Byline given. Buys all rights. Editorial works 6 months in advance.

Nonfiction: General interest (concerning cats); how-to (care, etc. for cats); health-related; personal experience; travel. Query by mail. Length 1,500-2,500 words. **Pays $50-500.**

Photos: State availability of photos with submissions. Reviews color slides, 2¼ × 2¼ transparencies. Identification of subjects required. Buys all rights.

Columns/Departments: Cat Tales (true cat-theme short stories), 250-1,000 words. Buys Cat Tales on spec only. Do not query. **Pays $25.**

Tips: "Writer must show an affinity for cats. Extremely well-written, thoroughly researched, carefully thought-out articles have the best chance of being accepted. Innovative topics or a new twist on an old subject are always welcomed."

★ $ $ THE CHRONICLE OF THE HORSE, P.O. Box 46, Middleburg VA 20118-0046. (540)687-6341. Fax: (540)687-3937. Website: www.chronofhorse.com. Editor: John Strassburger. Managing Editor: Nancy Comer. **Contact:** Beth Rasin, assistant editor. **80% freelance written.** Weekly magazine about horses. "We cover English riding sports, including horse showing, grand prix jumping competitions, steeplechase racing, foxhunting, dressage, endurance riding, handicapped riding and combined training. We are the official publication for the national governing bodies of many of the above sports. We feature news, how-to articles on equitation and horse care and interviews with leaders in the various fields." Estab. 1937. Circ. 22,000. **Pays for features on acceptance**; news and other items on publication. Publishes ms an average of 4 months after acceptance. Byline given. Buys first North American rights and makes work-for-hire assignments. Submit seasonal material 3 months in advance. Accepts queries by mail, e-mail. Responds in 10 weeks. Sample copy for $2 and 9 × 12 SAE. Writer's guidelines for #10 SASE or on website.

Nonfiction: General interest; historical/nostalgic (history of breeds, use of horses in other countries and times, art, etc.); how-to (trailer, train, design a course, save money, etc.); humor (centered on living with horses or horse people); interview/profile (of nationally known horsemen or the very unusual); technical (horse care, articles on feeding, injuries, care of foals, shoeing, etc.). Length: 6-7 pages. **Pays $125-200.** News of major competitions, "clear assignment with us first." Length: 1,500 words. **Pays $150.** Small local competitions, 800 words. **Pays $50-75.** Special issues: Steeplechase Racing (January); American Horse in Sport and Grand Prix Jumping (February); Horse Show (March); Intercollegiate (April); Kentucky 4-Star Preview (April); Junior and Pony (April); Combined Training (May); Dressage (June); Endurance issue (July); Hunt Roster (September); Vaulting and Handicapped (November); Stallion (December). No Q&A interviews, clinic reports, Western riding articles, personal experience or wild horses. **Buys 300 mss/year.** Query or send complete ms. Length: 300-1,225 words. **Pays $25-200.**

Photos: State availability of photos. Accepts prints or color slides. Accepts color for b&w reproduction. Pays $25-30. Identification of subjects required. Buys one-time rights.

Columns/Departments: Dressage, Combined Training, Horse Show, Horse Care, Racing over Fences, Young Entry (about young riders, geared for youth), Horses and Humanities, Hunting. Query or send complete ms. Length: 300-1,225 words. **Pays $25-200.**

Poetry: Light verse, traditional. No free verse. **Buys 30/year.** Length: 5-25 lines. **Pays $15.**

Fillers: Anecdotes, short humor, newsbreaks, cartoons. **Buys 300/year.** Length: 50-175 lines. **Pays $10-20.**

■ The online magazine carries original content not found in the print edition and includes writer's guidelines. Contact Erin Harty, online editor.

Tips: "Get our guidelines. Our readers are sophisticated, competitive horsemen. Articles need to go beyond common knowledge. Freelancers often attempt too broad or too basic a subject. We welcome well-written news stories on major events, but clear the assignment with us."

★ $ $ DOG FANCY, Fancy Publications, Inc., P.O. Box 6050, Mission Viejo CA 92690-6050. Fax: (949)855-3045. E-mail: Sbiller@fancypubs.com. Website: www.dogfancy.com. Editor: Betty Liddick. **Contact:** Steven Biller, managing editor. **95% freelance written.** Monthly magazine for men and women of all ages interested in all phases of dog ownership. Estab. 1970. Circ. 286,000. Pays on publication. Publishes ms an average of 6 months after acceptance. Byline given. Offers $100 kill fee. Buys first North American serial and non-exclusive electronic and other rights. Submit seasonal material 6 months in advance. Accepts simultaneous submissions. Responds in 2 months. Sample copy for $5.50. Writer's guidelines for #10 SASE.

Nonfiction: Book excerpts, general interest, how-to, humor, inspirational, interview/profile, new product, personal experience, photo feature, travel. "No stories written from a dog's point of view, poetry, anything that advocates irresponsible dog care, tributes to dogs that have died or beloved family pets." **Buys 100 mss/year.** Query by mail. Length: 850-1,500 words. **Pays $200-500.**

Photos: State availability of photos with submission. Reviews contact sheets, transparencies and prints. Offers no additional payment for photos accepted with ms. Model release, identification of subjects required. Buys one-time and electronic rights.

Columns/Departments: Dogs on the Go (travel with dogs), 600-700 words; Dogs That Make a Difference (heroic dogs), 800 words. **Buys 24 mss/year.** Query by mail only. **Pays $300-400.**

Fiction: Occasionally publishes novel excerpts.

■ The online magazine contains original content not found in the print version. Contact: Stephanie Starr.

Tips: "We're looking for the unique experience that enhances the dog/owner relationship—with the dog as the focus of the story, not the owner. Medical articles are assigned to veterinarians. Note that we write for a lay audience (non-technical), but we do assume a certain level of intelligence. Read the magazine before making a pitch. Make sure your query is clear, concise and relevant."

⬛ $ $ DOG WORLD, The Authority on Dog Care, Primedia Special Interest Publications, 500 N. Dearborn, Suite 1100, Chicago IL 60610. (312)396-0600. Fax: (312)467-7118. E-mail: dogworld3@aol.com. Website: www.dogworldmag.com. **Contact:** Donna Marcel, editor. **95% freelance written.** Monthly magazine covering dogs. "We write for the serious dog enthusiasts, breeders, veterinarians, groomers, etc., as well as a general audience interested in in-depth information about dogs." Estab. 1915. Circ. 61,000. **Pays on acceptance.** Byline given. Buys first North American serial rights. Editorial lead time 10 weeks. Submit seasonal material 4 months in advance. Responds in 6 months. Writer's guidelines free.

Nonfiction: General interest on dogs including health care, veterinary medicine, grooming, legislation, responsible ownership, show awards, obedience training, show schedules, kennel operations, dog sports, breed spotlights and histories, new products, personal experience, travel. No fluffy poems or pieces about dogs. Special issues: July (breed standards); February (puppy). **Buys approximately 80 mss/year.** Query by mail only with SASE. Length: 3,000-3,500 words. **Payment negotiated.** Sometimes pays the expenses of writers on assignment.

Reprints: Rarely publishes reprints. Send tearsheet of article, typed ms with rights for sale noted, and information about when and where the article previously appeared. Payment negotiated on individual basis.

Photos: State availability of photos with submission. Offers no additional payment for photos accepted with ms; occasionally negotiates payment individually for professional photos. Current rate for a cover photo is $300; inside color photo $50-175; b&w $25-50, depending on size used. Payment on publication. Buys one-time rights.

■ The online magazine carries original content not found in the print edition. Contact: Peggy Moran.

Tips: "Get a copy of editorial calendar, stay away from 'fluffy' pieces—we run very few. Be able to translate technical/medical articles into what average readers can understand. Mention accompanying art—very important."

$ DOGGONE, The Newsletter About Fun Places to Go And Cool Stuff to Do With Your Dog, P.O. Box 651155, Vero Beach FL 32965-1155. Fax: (561)569-8434. E-mail: doggonel@aol.com. Website: www.doggonefun.com. **Contact:** Wendy Ballard, publisher. "*DogGone* is a bimonthly travel and activity newsletter for dog owners. All destination pieces are written with a dog slant, including lodgings that accept pets, dog-allowed tourist attractions, parks, hiking trails, walking tours, even restaurants with outdoor seating that don't mind a pooch on the porch." Estab. 1993. Circ. 3,000. Pays on publication. Publishes ms an average of 4 months after acceptance. Buys first rights and electronic rights. Editorial lead time 4 months. Submit seasonal material 4 months in advance. Accepts queriers by mail, e-mail. Responds in 1 month. Sample copy for 9 × 12 SAE and 3 first-class stamps. Writer's guidelines for #10 SASE.

Nonfiction: Travel, exposé, historical, how-to, personal experience. "No poetry or 'My dog is the best because . . .' articles." Query with published clips or send complete ms. Length: 300-1,000 words. **Pays $34-100.** Writers may opt to accept subscription to *DogGone* as partial payment.

Reprints: Send photocopy of article and information about when and where it previously appeared. **Pays $34-100.**

Photos: Send photos with submission. Reviews prints or slides. Offers no additional payment for photos accepted with ms. Captions required. Buys rights with ms.

Columns/Departments: Beyond Fetch (creative activities to enjoy with dogs), 300-900 words; Parks Department (dogs-allowed national, state, regional parks), 300 words; Visiting Vet (travel-related), 300 words; Touring (walking or driving tours with pets-allowed stops), 600-900 words; Worth a Paws (pet-friendly stops near highways/interstates). Query with published clips or send complete ms. **Pays $34-100.**

Fillers: Facts, dogs-allowed events. Length: 50-200 words. **Pays $15.**

Tip: "Submit an entertaining yet informative manuscript about a personal travel experience with your dog. Make me want to recreate your vacation for myself."

[N] ⬛ $ EQUINE JOURNAL, Turley Publications, 312 Marlboro St., Keene NH 03431. (603)357-4271. Fax: (603)357-7851. E-mail: equinejnl@monad.net. Website: www.equinejournal.com. **Contact:** Kathleen S. Lyons, managing editor. **90% freelance written.** Monthly tabloid covering horses—all breeds, all disciplines. "To educate, entertain and enable amateurs and professionals alike to stay on top of new developments in the field. Covers horse-related activities from all corners of New England, New York, New Jersey, Pennsylvania and the Midwest." Estab. 1988. Circ. 26,000. Pays on publication. Byline given. Buys first North American serial rights. Editorial lead time 2 months. Submit seasonal material 3 months in advance. Accepts queries by mail, e-mail, fax, phone. Responds in 1 month. Sample copy free. Writer's guidelines for #10 SASE.

Nonfiction: General interest, how-to, interview/profile. **Buys 100 mss/year.** Query with published clips or send complete ms. Length: 1,500-3,000 words. **Pays $95.**

Photos: Send photos with submission. Reviews prints. Offers $10/photo. Buys one-time rights.

Columns/Departments: Horse Health (health-related topics), 1,200-1,500 words; Driving (all types of driving), 1,200 words. **Buys 24 mss/year.** Query. **Pays $75.**

Fillers: Short humor. Length: 500-1,000 words. **Pays $40-75.**
Tips: "Submit samples and qualifications."

N ☆ $ $ FIELD TRIAL MAGAZINE, Androscoggin Publishing, Inc., P.O. Box 98, Milan NH 03588-0098. (617)449-6767. Fax: (603)449-2462. E-mail: birddog@ncia.net. Website: www.fielddog.com/ftm. **Contact:** Craig Doherty, editor. **75% freelance written.** Quarterly magazine covering field trials for pointing dogs. "Our readers are knowledgeable sports men and women who want interesting and informative articles about their sport." Estab. 1997. Circ. 6,000. Pays on publication. Publishes ms an average of 6 months after acceptance. Byline given. Buys first North American serial rights. Editorial lead time 3 months. Submit seasonal material 6 months in advance. Accepts queries by mail, e-mail, fax. Accepts simultaneous submissions. Responds in 2 weeks to queries; 2 months to mss. Sample copy and writer's guidelines free or on website.
Nonfiction: Book excerpts, essays, general interest, historical/nostalgic, how-to, opinion, personal experience. No hunting articles. **Buys 12-16 mss/year.** Query. Length: 1,000-3,000 words. **Pays $100-300.**
Photos: Send photos with submission. Offers no additional payment for photos accepted with ms. Captions and identification of subjects required. Buys one-time rights.
Fiction: Fiction that deals with bird dogs and field trials. **Buys 4 mss/year.** Send complete ms. Length: 1,000-2,500 words. **Pays $100-250.**
Tips: "Make sure you have correct and accurate information—we'll work with a writer who has good solid info even if the writing needs work."

■ $ GOOD DOG!, Consumer Magazine for Dog Owners, P.O. Box 10069, Austin TX 78766-1069. (512)454-6090. Fax: (512)454-3420. E-mail: judi@gooddogmagazine.com. Website: www.gooddogmagazine.com. Publisher: Ross Becker. **Contact:** Judi Becker, editor. **90% freelance written.** Bimonthly magazine for consumers/laypeople. "*Good Dog!* is a fun, easy, conversational read but the reader should also learn while enjoying the publication." Estab. 1988. Pays 30-90 days after publication. Byline given. Buys first North American serial rights. Editorial lead time 4 months. Submit seasonal material 4 months in advance. Accepts queriers by mail, e-mail, phone. Accepts simultaneous submissions. Sample copy and writer's guidelines for SAE.
   • *Good Dog!* has ceased print publication and is now an online-only magazine.
Nonfiction: General interest, humor, interview/profile, new product, opinion, personal experience. No fiction or poetry. **Buys 30 mss/year.** Send complete ms. Length: 700-1,200 words. Rates negotiable.
Photos: Send photos with submission. Reviews 4×6 or larger prints. Negotiates payment individually. Identification of subjects required with label of photo owner/address.
Tips: "E-mail a cover letter and manuscript (as an e-mail message not an attached file). It's faster this way."

$ THE GREYHOUND REVIEW, P.O. Box 543, Abilene KS 67410-0543. (785)263-4660. Fax: (785)263-4689. E-mail: nga@jc.net. Website: www.nga.jc.net. Editor: Gary Guccione. **Contact:** Tim Horan, managing editor. **20% freelance written.** Monthly magazine covering greyhound breeding, training and racing. Estab. 1911. Circ. 4,000. **Pays on acceptance.** Byline given. Buys first rights. Submit seasonal material 2 months in advance. Responds in 2 weeks to queries; 1 month to mss. Sample copy for $3. Writer's guidelines free.
Nonfiction: How-to, interview/profile, personal experience. "Articles must be targeted at the greyhound industry: from hard news, special events at racetracks to the latest medical discoveries. Do not submit gambling systems." **Buys 24 mss/year.** Query. Length: 1,000-10,000 words. **Pays $85-150.** Sometimes pays the expenses of writers on assignment.
Reprints: Send photocopy of article. Pays 100% of the amount paid for an original article.
Photos: State availability of photos with submission. Reviews 35mm transparencies and 8×10 prints. Offers $10-50/photo. Identification of subjects required. Buys one-time rights.

N $ HORSE & COUNTRY CANADA, Equine Publications Inc., Box 1051, Smiths Falls, Ontario K7A 5A5 Canada. (613)275-1684. Fax: (613)275-1686. **Contact:** Judith H. McCartney, editor. **40% freelance written.** Magazine published 7 times/year covering equestrian issues. "A celebration of equestrian sport and the country way of life." Estab. 1994. Circ. 14,000. Pays on publication. Publishes ms an average of 3 months after acceptance. Byline sometimes given. Buys one-time rights.
Nonfiction: Book excerpts, historical/nostalgic, how-to, inspirational, new product, travel. Query by mail only with published clips. Length: 1,200-1,700 words. **Pays $25-150 minimum for assigned articles; $25-100 for unsolicited articles.** Sometimes pays expenses of writers on assignment.
Photos: Send photos with submission. Reviews prints. Offers $15-125/photo or negotiates payment individually. Captions required. Buys one-time rights.
Columns/Departments: Back to Basics (care for horses); Ask the Experts (how to with horses); Nutrition (for horses), all 800 words. Query by mail only with published clips. **Pays $25-150.**

N $ $ $ HORSE & RIDER, The Magazine of Western Riding, Primedia, 1597 Cole Blvd., #350, Golden CO 80401. (719)445-4700. Fax: (719)445-4715. E-mail: hrsenrider@cowles.com. Managing Editor: Rene Riley. **Contact:** Kathy Kadash-Swan, editor. **25% freelance written.** Monthly magazine covering Western horse industry, competition, recreation. "*Horse & Rider's* mission is to educate, inform and entertain both competitive and recreational riders with tightly focused training articles, practical stable management techniques, hands-on healthcare tips, safe trail-riding practices, well-researched consumer advice and a behind-the-scenes, you-are-there approach to major equine events."

Estab. 1961. Circ. 170,000. **Pays on acceptance**. Publishes ms an average of 1 year after acceptance. Byline given. Offers $75 kill fee. Buys first North American serial rights. Editorial lead time 2 months. Submit seasonal material 6 months in advance. Accepts queries by mail, e-mail, fax. Responds in 2 weeks to queries; 2 months to mss. Sample copy and writer's guidelines free.

Nonfiction: General interest, how-to (horse training, horsemanship), interview/profile, personal experience, photo feature, travel. **Buys 12-15 mss/year.** Send complete ms. Length: 1,000-3,000 words. **Pays $150-1,000.**

Photos: State availability of photos with submission or send photos with submission. Negotiates payment individually. Captions, model releases and identification of subjects required. Buys rights on assignment or stock.

$ $ HORSE ILLUSTRATED, The Magazine for Responsible Horse Owners, Fancy Publications, Inc., P.O. Box 6050, Mission Viejo CA 92690-6050. (949)855-8822. Fax: (949)855-3045. E-mail: joltmann@fancypubs.com. Website: www.horseillustrated.com. Contact: Mora Harris, associate editor, ext 422. **90% freelance written.** Prefers to work with published/established writers but will work with new/unpublished writers. Monthly magazine covering all aspects of horse ownership. "Our readers are adults, mostly women, between the ages of 18 and 40; stories should be geared to that age group and reflect responsible horse care." Estab. 1976. Circ. 190,000. Pays on publication. Publishes ms an average of 8 months after acceptance. Byline given. Buys one-time rights; requires first North American rights among equine publications. Submit seasonal material 6 months in advance. Responds in 3 months. Sample copy for $3.50. Writer's guidelines for #10 SASE.

Nonfiction: How-to (horse care, training, veterinary care), photo feature. No "little girl" horse stories, "cowboy and Indian" stories or anything not *directly* relating to horses. "We are looking for longer, more authoritative, in-depth features on trends and issues in the horse industry. Such articles must be queried first with a detailed outline of the article and clips. We rarely have a need for fiction." **Buys 20 mss/year.** Query or send complete ms. Length: 1,000-2,000 words. **Pays $100-400 for assigned articles; $50-300 for unsolicited articles.**

Photos: Send photos with submission. Reviews 35mm transparencies, medium format transparencies and 5×7 prints.

Tips: "Freelancers can break in at this publication with feature articles on Western and English training methods; veterinary and general care how-to articles; and horse sports articles. We rarely use personal experience articles. Submit photos with training and how-to articles whenever possible. We have a very good record of developing new freelancers into regular contributors/columnists. We are always looking for fresh talent, but certainly enjoy working with established writers who 'know the ropes' as well. We are accepting less unsolicited freelance work—much is now assigned and contracted."

$ $ THE HORSE, Your Guide to Equine Health Care, P.O. Box 4680, Lexington KY 40544-4680. (859)276-6771. Fax: (859)276-4450. E-mail: kgraetz@thehorse.com. Website: www.thehorse.com. **Contact:** Kimberly S. Graetz, editor. **75% freelance written.** Monthly magazine covering equine health and care. *The Horse* is "an educational/news magazine geared toward the professional, hands-on horse owner." Estab. 1983. Circ. 40,000. **Pays on acceptance.** Publishes ms an average of 2 months after acceptance. Byline given. Buys first world and electronic rights, "depending on the writer." Accepts queries by mail, e-mail, fax. Responds in 2 months to queries. Sample copy for $2.95 or on website. Writer's guidelines free.

O─┐ Break in with short horse health news items.

Nonfiction: How-to, technical, topical interviews. "No first-person experiences not from professionals; this is a technical magazine to inform horse owners." **Buys 90 mss/year.** Query with published clips. Length: 500-5,000 words. **Pays $75-700.**

Photos: Send photos with submission. Reviews transparencies. Offers $35-350/photo. Captions and identification of subjects required.

Columns/Departments: Up Front (news on horse health), 100-500 words; Equinomics (economics of horse ownership), Step by Step (feet and leg care), Nutrition, Back to Basics, all 1,800-2,500 words. **Buys 50 mss/year.** Query with published clips. **Pays $50-400.**

▣ The online magazine carries original content not found in the print edition, mostly news items.

Tips: "We publish reliable horse health information from top industry professionals around the world. Manuscript must be submitted electronically or on disk."

$ HORSES ALL, North Hill Publications, 278-19 St. NE, Calgary, Alberta T2E 8P7 Canada. (403)248-9993. Fax: (403)248-8838. E-mail: nhpubs@cadvision.com **Contact:** Vanessa Peterelli, editor. **40% freelance written.** Eager to work with new/unpublished writers. Monthly tabloid for horse owners and the horse industry. Estab. 1977. Circ. 7,000. Pays on publication. Publishes ms an average of 3 months after acceptance. Byline given. Offers 30% kill fee. Buys first North American serial rights. Submit seasonal material 3 months in advance. Accepts queries by mail, e-mail, fax. Accepts simultaneous submissions. Sample copy and writer's guidelines for SAE.

Nonfiction: Book excerpts, essays, general interest, historical/nostalgic, how-to (training, horse care and maintenance), inspirational, interview/profile, personal experience, photo feature. "We would prefer more general stories, no specific local events or shows." **Buys 3 mss/year.** Query. Length: 800-1,400 words. **Pays $50-75 (Canadian) for solicited articles only.**

Reprints: Accepts previously published submissions.

Photos: Send photos with submission. Reviews prints 3×4 or larger. Negotiates payment individually. Captions, model releases, identification of subjects required. Buys one-time rights.

Tips: "Our writers must be knowledgeable about horses and the horse industry, and be able to write features in a readable, conversational manner, but in third person only, please. While we do include coverage of major events in our publication, we generally require that these events take place in Canada. Any exceptions to this general rule are evaluated on a case-by-case basis."

I LOVE CATS, I Love Cats Publishing, 450 Seventh Ave., Suite 1701, New York NY 10123. (212)244-2351. Fax: (212)244-2367. E-mail: yankee@izzy.net. Website: www.iluvcats.com. **Contact:** Lisa Allmendinger, editor. **100% freelance written.** Bimonthly magazine covering cats. "*I Love Cats* is a general interest cat magazine for the entire family. It caters to cat lovers of all ages. The stories in the magazine include fiction, nonfiction, how-to, humorous and columns for the cat lover." Estab. 1989. Circ. 100,000. Pays on publication. Publishes ms an average of 1 year after acceptance. Byline given. No kill fee. Buys all rights. Must sign copyright consent form. Editorial lead time 6 months. Submit seasonal material 9 months in advance. Accepts queries by mail, e-mail, phone. Responds in 3 months. Sample copy for $4. Writer's guidelines for #10 SASE, website or by e-mail.

Nonfiction: Essays, general interest, how-to, humor, inspirational, interview/profile, new product, opinion, personal experience, photo feature. No poetry. **Buys 100 mss/year.** Send complete ms. Length: 500-1,500 words. **Pays $50-150, contributor copies or other premiums "if requested."** Sometimes pays expenses of writers on assignment.

Photos: Send photos with submission. Offers no additional payment for photos accepted with ms. Identification of subjects required. Buys all rights. (Please send copies; art will no longer be returned.)

Fiction: Adventure, fantasy, historical, humorous, mainstream, mystery, novel excerpts, slice-of-life vignettes, suspense. "This is a family magazine. No graphic violence, pornography or other inappropriate material. *I Love Cats* is strictly 'G-rated.'" **Buys 100 mss/year.** Send complete ms. Length: 500-1,500 words. **Pays $50-150.**

Fillers: Anecdotes, facts, short humor. **Buys 25/year. Pays $25.**

Tips: "Please keep stories short and concise. Send complete ms with photos, if possible. I buy lots of first-time authors. Nonfiction pieces with color photos are always in short supply. With the exception of the standing columns, the rest of the magazine is open to freelancers. Be witty, humorous or take a different approach to writing."

MINIATURE DONKEY TALK, Miniature Donkey Talk, Inc., 1338 Hughes Shop Rd., Westminster MD 21158-2911. (410)875-0118. Fax: (410)857-9145. E-mail: minidonk@qis.net. Website: www.qis.net/~minidonk/mdt.htm. **Contact:** Bonnie Gross, editor. **65% freelance written.** Bimonthly magazine covering miniature donkeys or donkeys, with articles on healthcare, promotion and management of donkeys for owners, breeders or donkey lovers. Estab. 1987. Circ. 4,925. **Pays on acceptance.** Publishes ms an average of 4 months after acceptance. Byline given. Buys first and second serial (reprint) rights. Editorial lead time 2 months. Submit seasonal material 3 months in advance. Accepts queries by mail, e-mail, fax. Responds in 1 week to queries; 1 month to mss. Sample copy for $5. Writer's guidelines free.

Nonfiction: Book excerpts, humor, interview/profile, personal experience. **Buys 6 mss/year.** Send complete ms. Length: 700-7,000 words. **Pays $25-100.**

Reprints: Accepts previously published submissions.

Photos: State availability of photos with submission. Reviews 3×5 prints. Offers no additional payment for photos accepted with ms. Identification of subjects required. Buys one-time rights.

Columns/Departments: Humor, 2,000 words; Healthcare 2,000-5,000 words; Management, 2,000 words. **Buys 50 mss/year.** Query. **Pays $25-100.**

Fiction: Humorous only. **Buys 6 mss/year.** Query. Length: 3,000-7,000 words. **Pays $25-100.**

Fillers: Anecdotes, facts, gags to be illustrated by cartoonist, short humor. **Buys 12/year.** Length: 200-2,000 words. **Pays $15-35.**

Tips: "Simply send your manuscript. If on topic and appropriate, good possibility it will be published. We accept the following types of material: 1) Breeder profiles—either of yourself or another breeder. The full address and/or telephone number of the breeder will not appear in the article as this would constitute advertising; 2) Coverage of non-show events such as fairs, donkey gatherings, holiday events, etc. We do not pay for coverage of an event that you were involved in organizing; 3) Detailed or specific instructional or training material. We're always interested in people's training methods; 4) Relevant, informative equine health pieces. We much prefer they deal specifically with donkeys; however, we will consider articles specifically geared towards horses. If at all possible, substitute the word 'horse' for donkey. We reserve the right to edit, change, delete or add to health articles as we deem appropriate. Please be very careful in the accuracy of advice or treatment and review the material with a veterinarian; 5) Farm management articles; and 6) Fictional stories on donkeys."

MUSHING, Stellar Communications, Inc., P.O. Box 149, Ester AK 99725-0149. (907)479-0454. Fax: (907)479-3137. E-mail: editor@mushing.com. Website: www.mushing.com. Publisher: Todd Hoener. **Contact:** Enrico Sassi, managing editor. Bimonthly magazine on "all aspects of the growing sports of dogsledding, skijoring, carting, dog packing and weight pulling. *Mushing* promotes responsible dog care through feature articles and updates on working animal health care, safety, nutrition and training." Estab. 1987. Circ. 6,000. Pays within 60 days of publication. Publishes ms an average of 4 months after acceptance. Byline given. Buys first serial and second serial (reprint) rights. Submit seasonal material 4 months in advance. Accepts queries by mail, e-mail, fax, phone. Responds in 8 months. Sample copy for $5, $6 US to Canada. Writer's guidelines free (call or e-mail for information) or on website.

Nonfiction: "We consider articles on canine health and nutrition, sled dog behavior and training, musher profiles and interviews, equipment how-to's, trail tips, expedition and race accounts, innovations, sled dog history, current issues, personal experiences and humor." Themes: Iditarod and long-distance racing (January/February); Expeditions/Peak of Race Season (March/April); health and nutrition (May/June); musher and dog profiles, summer activities (July/August); equipment, fall training (September/October); races and places (November/December). Prefers query with or without published clips and SASE; considers complete ms with SASE. Length: 1,000-2,500 words. **Pays $50-250 for articles.** Payment depends on length and quality. Pays expenses of writers on assignment, if prearranged.

Photos: Send photos with submission. Reviews contact sheets, transparencies, prints. Prefers 8×10 glossy prints or negatives for b&w. Offers $20-165/photo. Captions, model releases, identification of subjects required. Buys one-time and second reprint rights. We look for good b&w and quality color for covers and specials.

Columns/Departments: Query with or without published clips and SASE or send complete ms with SASE. Length: 500-1,000 words.

Fiction: Considers short, well-written and relevant or timely fiction. Query or send complete ms with SASE. Pay varies.

Fillers: Anecdotes, facts, cartoons, newsbreaks, short humor, puzzles. Length: 100-250 words. **Pays $20-35.**

Tips: "Read our magazine. Know something about dog-driven, dog-powered sports."

N $ $ PETS MAGAZINE, Moorshead Magazines, Ltd., 505 Consumers Rd., Suite 500, Toronto, Ontario M2J 4V8 Canada. (416)491-3699. Fax: (416)491-3996. E-mail: pets@moorshead.com. Website: www.moorshead.com/pets. **Contact:** Edward Zapletal, editor. **40% freelance written.** Bimonthly magazine for "pet owners, primarily cat and dog owners, but we also cover rabbits, guinea pigs, hamsters, gerbils, birds and fish. Issues covered include: pet health care, nutrition, general interest, grooming, training humor, human-animal bond stories. No fiction! No poetry!" Estab. 1983. Circ. 51,000. Pays within 30 days of publication. Publishes ms an average of 2 months after acceptance. Byline given. Offers 50% kill fee. Buys first North American serial rights or other negotiable rights. Editorial lead time 3 months. Submit seasonal material 2 months in advance. Accepts queries by e-mail. Sample copy for #10 SAE with IRCs. Writer's guidelines for 9½×4 SAE with IRCs or on website. "Please no U.S. postage on return envelope."

Nonfiction: General interest, humor, new product, personal experience, veterinary medicine, human interest (i.e., working animal), training and obedience. No fiction. **Buys 10 mss/year.** Query. Length: 500-1,500 words. **Pays 12-18¢/word (Canadian funds).**

Reprints: Considers reprints of previously published submissions. **Pays 6-9¢/word.**

Photos: Prefers good color pictures or slides. Reviews photocopies. Identification of subjects required. Buys one-time rights.

Columns/Departments: Grooming Your Pet (mostly dogs and cats), 300-400 words. **Buys 6-12 mss/year.** Query.

Fillers: Facts. **Buys 5/year.** Length: 20-100 words. **Pays $10-20.**

Tips: "Always approach with a query letter first. E-mail is good if you've got it. We'll contact you if we like what we see. I like writing to be friendly, informative, well-balanced with pros and cons. Remember, we're catering to pet owners, and they are a discriminating audience."

$ $ THE QUARTER HORSE JOURNAL, P.O. Box 32470, Amarillo TX 79120. (806)376-4811. Fax: (806)349-6400. E-mail: aqhajrnl@aqha.org. Website: www.aqha.com. Editor-in-Chief: Jim Jennings. **Contact:** Jim Bret Campbell, editor. **20% freelance written.** Prefers to work with published/established writers. Monthly official publication of the American Quarter Horse Association. Estab. 1948. Circ. 78,000. **Pays on acceptance.** Publishes ms an average of 6 months after acceptance. Buys first North American serial rights. Submit seasonal material 6 months in advance. Accepts queries by mail, e-mail, fax. Responds in 2 months. Sample copy and writer's guidelines for SAE.

Nonfiction: How-to (fitting, grooming, showing, or anything that relates to owning, showing, or breeding); informational (educational clinics, current news); interview (feature-type stories—must be about established horses or people who have made a contribution to the business); personal opinion; and technical (equine updates, new surgery procedures, etc.). **Buys 20 mss/year.** Length: 800-1,800 words. **Pays $150-300.**

Photos: Purchased with accompanying ms. Captions required. Send prints or transparencies. Uses 4×6 color glossy prints, 2¼×2¼, 4×5 or 35mm color transparencies. No additional pay for photos accepted with accompanying ms.

Tips: "Writers must have a knowledge of the horse business."

$ $ REPTILE & AMPHIBIAN HOBBYIST, T.F.H. Publications, One TFH Plaza, Neptune NJ 07753. (732)988-8400, ext. 235. Fax: (732)988-9635. Website: www.tfh.com. **Contact:** Erica Ramus, editor. Editor-in-chief: Marilee Talman. **100% freelance written.** "Colorful, varied monthly covering reptiles and amphibians as pets aimed at beginning to intermediate hobbyists. Pet shop distribution. Writers must know their material, including scientific names, identification, general terrarium maintenance." Estab. 1995. Circ. 30,000. Pays 60 days after acceptance. Publishes ms 6 months after acceptance. Byline given. Buys all rights, multiple rights or non-exclusive rights. Editorial lead time 2 months. Responds in 1 month to queries; 2 months to mss. Sample copy for $4.50. Writer's guidelines free.

Nonfiction: General interest, interview/profile, personal experience, photo feature, technical, travel. **Buys 120 mss/year.** Query. Length: 1,500-2,000 words. **Pays $100-120.**

Photos: Send photos with submission. Reviews transparencies and prints. Offers $20/photo. Captions, model releases and identification of subjects required. Buys all rights.

Columns/Departments: Herp People (profiles herp-related personalities); In Review (book reviews); Invertebrate Corner (terrarium invertebrates), all 1,500 words. **Buys 45 mss/year.** Query. **Pays $75-100.**

Tips: "Talk to the editor before sending anything. A short telephone conversation tells more about knowledge of subject matter than a simple query. I'll read anything, but it is very easy to detect an uninformed author. Very willing to polish articles from new writers."

■ **$** ROCKY MOUNTAIN RIDER MAGAZINE, Regional All-Breed Horse Monthly, (formerly Rocky Mountain Rider Magazine, The Magazine About Horses, People & the West), Rocky Mountain Rider Magazine, P.O. Box 1011, Hamilton MT 59840. (406)363-4085. Fax: (406)363-1056. Website: http://rockymountainrider.com. **Contact:** Natalie Riehl, editor. **90% freelance written.** Monthly magazine "aiming to satisfy the interests of readers who enjoy horses."Estab. 1993. Circ. 14,000. Pays on publication. Publishes ms an average of 6 months after acceptance. Byline given. Buys one-time rights. Submit seasonal material 6 months in advance. Accepts simultaneous submissions. Responds in 1 month to queries; 2 months to mss. Sample copy free. Writer's guidelines for #10 SASE.

Nonfiction: Book excerpts, essays, general interest, historical/nostalgic, humor, interview/profile, new product, personal experience, photo feature, travel, cowboy poetry. **Buys 100 mss/year.** Send complete ms. Length: 500-2,000 words. **Pays $15-90.**

Photos: Send photos with submission. Reviews 3 × 5 prints. Pays $5/photo. Captions, identification of subjects required. Buys one-time rights.

Poetry: Light verse, traditional. **Buys 25 poems/year.** Submit maximum 10 poems. Length: 6-36 lines. **Pays $10.**

Fillers: Anecdotes, facts, gags to be illustrated by cartoonist, short humor. Length: 200-750 words. **Pays $15.**

Tips: "*RMR* is looking for positive, human interest stories that appeal to an audience of horsepeople. We accept profiles of unusual people or animals, history, humor, anecdotes, cowboy poetry, coverage of regional events and new products. We aren't looking for many 'how to' or training articles, and are not currently looking at any fiction."

N ■ **$ $** THE WESTERN HORSE, Adventure & Sport Out West, Fancy Publications, 3 Burroughs, Irvine CA 92618. (949)855-8822. Fax: (949)855-3045. E-mail: westernhorse@fancypubs.com. Website: www.animalnetwork.com. **Contact:** Jennifer Nice, editor. **90% freelance written.** Bimonthly magazine covering the Western horse industry. "*The Western Horse* is devoted to depicting the fun and excitement of western equine sports and pastimes, including showing, cutting, reining, timed events, rodeo, recreational riding and travel. *The Western Horse* also covers issues and industry news pertaining to western events; political, agricultural and ranching issues; current trends in fashion and art; and profiles of noted people and horses." Circ. 35,000. Pays on publication. Publishes ms an average of 6 months after acceptance. Byline given. Offers 30% kill fee. Buys first North American serial and electronic rights. Editorial lead time 3 months. Submit seasonal material 3 months in advance. Accepts queries by mail, e-mail, fax. Responds in 1 month. Sample copy for cover price. Writer's guidelines for #10 SASE.

Nonfiction: Interview/profile, photo feature, travel. Interested in seeing historical articles about horses. Upcoming theme issues: Quarter Horses USA Annual; Horses USA Annual. "No how-to, veterinary or training articles." **Buys 16 mss/year.** Query. Length: 700-2,500 words. **Pays $200-500.** Sometimes pays expenses of writers on assignment.

Columns/Departments: The News Trail (short, news-oriented articles), 600 words maximum. **Pays $50.** Sunset (short stories and personal experience essays), 800 words maximum. **Pays $125.**

Photos: State availability of photos with submission or send photos with submission. Negotiates payment individually. Captions, model releases and identification of subjects required. Buys one-time rights.

Tips: "Please review our issues of the magazine—it's easy to get a feel for the kind of writing I like. We are looking for quality, creative writing that can capture the heart and passion of the topic, whether it be the final go-round of the NCHA championships or a profile of a prominent western artist. Also, request the guidelines and include a SASE with all correspondence."

ART & ARCHITECTURE

Listed here are publications about art, art history, specific art forms and architecture written for art patrons, architects, artists and art enthusiasts. Publications addressing the business and management side of the art industry are listed in the Art, Design & Collectibles category of the Trade section. Trade publications for architecture can be found in Building Interiors, and Construction & Contracting sections.

$ $ THE AMERICAN ART JOURNAL, Kennedy Galleries, Inc., 730 Fifth Ave., New York NY 10019. (212)541-9600. Fax: (212)977-3833. **Contact:** Jayne A. Kuchna, editor-in-chief. Prefers to work with published/established writers; works with a small number of new/unpublished writers each year. "Annual scholarly magazine of American art history of the 17th, 18th, 19th and 20th centuries, including painting, sculpture, architecture, photography, cultural history, etc., for people with a serious interest in American art, and who are already knowledgeable about the subject. Readers are scholars, curators, collectors, students of American art, or persons with a strong interest in Americana." Circ. 2,000. **Pays on acceptance.** Publishes ms an average of 6 months after acceptance. Byline given. Buys all rights, but will reassign rights to writer. Responds in 2 months. Sample copy for $18.

Nonfiction: "All articles are about some phase or aspect of American art history. No how-to articles or reviews of exhibitions. No book reviews or opinion pieces. No human interest approaches to artists' lives. No articles written in a casual or 'folksy' style. *Writing style must be formal and serious.*" **Buys 10-15 mss/year.** Submit complete ms "with good cover letter." No queries. Length: 2,500-8,000 words. **Pays $400-600.**

Photos: Purchased with accompanying ms. Captions required. Uses b&w only. Offers no additional payment for photos accepted with accompanying ms.

Tips: "Articles *must be* scholarly, thoroughly documented, well-researched, well-written and illustrated. Whenever possible, all manuscripts must be accompanied by b&w photographs, which have been integrated into the text by the use of numbers."

$ $ $ AMERICAN STYLE, The Art of Living Creatively, The Rosen Group, 3000 Chestnut Ave., Suite 304, Baltimore MD 21211. (410)889-3093. Fax: (410)243-7089. E-mail: hoped@rosengrp.com. Website: www.americanstyle .com. **Contact:** Hope Daniels, editor. **50% freelance written.** Quarterly magazine covering handmade American Crafts. Estab. 1994. Circ. 50,000. Pays on publication. Publishes ms an average of 6 months after acceptance. Byline given. Buys first North American serial rights. Editorial lead time 9 months. Submit seasonal material 1 year in advance. Accepts queriers by mail, e-mail, fax. Sample copy for $3. Writer's guidelines for #10 SASE.
   • *American Style* is especially interested in travel articles on arts/resort destinations, profiles of contemporary craft collectors and studio artists.
Nonfiction: Specialized arts/crafts interests. Query with published clips. Length: 300-2,500 words. **Pays $500-800.** Sometimes pays expenses of writers on assignment.
Photos: Send color photos with submission. Reviews oversized transparencies and 35mm slides. Negotiates payment individually. Captions required.
Columns/Departments: Artist Profiles, Artful Dining, 700-1,000 words. Query with published clips. **Pays $300-500.**
Tips: "Contact editor about upcoming issues and article ideas or send clips. Concentrate on contemporary American craft art, such as ceramics, wood, fiber, glass, etc. No hobby crafts."

$ $ $ $ ART & ANTIQUES, Trans World Publishing, Inc., 2100 Powers Ferry Rd., Atlanta GA 30339. (770)955-5656. Fax: (770)952-0669. Editor: Barbara S. Tapp. **Contact:** Patti Verbanas, managing editor. **90% freelance written.** Magazine published 11 times/year covering fine art and antique collectibles and the people who collect them and/or create them. "*Art & Antiques* is the authoritative source for elegant, sophisticated coverage of the treasures collectors love, the places to discover them and the unique ways collectors use them to enrich their environments." Circ. 196,000. **Pays on acceptance.** Publishes ms an average of 6 months after acceptance. Byline given. Offers 25% kill fee or $250. Buys all rights. Editorial lead time 8 months. Submit seasonal material 8 months in advance. Responds in 6 weeks to queries, 2 months to mss. Sample copy and writer's guidelines free.
Nonfiction: Essays, how-to, interview/profile (especially interested in profiles featuring collectors outside the Northwest and Northern California areas), photo feature. Features are expanded, more in-depth articles that fit into any of the departments listed below. "We publish one 'interior design with art and antiques' focus feature a month. Special issues: Designing with art & antiques (September and April); Asian art & antiques (October); Contemporary art (December). **Buys 200 mss/year.** Query by mail only with or without published clips. Length: 200-2,000 words. **Pays $200-2,000.** Pays expenses of writers on assignment.
Photos: Send with submission. Reviews contact sheets, transparencies, prints. Captions, identification of subjects required. Scouting shots.
Columns/Departments: *Art & Antiques* Update (trend coverage and timely news of issues and personalities), 100-350 words; Review (thoughts and criticisms on a variety of worldwide art exhibitions throughout the year), 600-800 words; Value Judgments (experts highlight popular to undiscovered areas of collecting), 600-800 words; Emerging Artists (an artist on the cusp of discovery), 600-800 words; Collecting (profiles fascinating collectors, their collecting passions and the way they live with their treasures), 800-900 words; Discoveries (collections in lesser-known museums and homes open to the public), 800-900 words; Studio Session (peek into the studio of an artist who is currently hot or is a revered veteran allowing the reader to watch the artist in action), 800-900 words; Then & Now (the best reproductions being created today and the craftspeople behind the work), 800-900 words; World View (major art and antiques news worldwide; visuals preferred but not necessary), 600-800 words; Travelling Collector (hottest art and antiques destinations, dictated by those on editorial calendar; visuals preferred but not necessary), 800-900 words; Essay (first-person piece tackling a topic in a non-academic way; visuals preferred, but not necessary); Books (reviews of important books), 100-400 words; Profile (profiles those who are noteworthy and describes their interests and passions; very character-driven and should reveal their personalities), 600-800 words. **Buys 200 mss/year.** Query by mail only with or without published clips. **Pays $200-800.**
Fillers: Facts, newsbreaks. **Buys 22 mss/year.** Length: 150-350 words. **Pays $200.**
Tips: "Send scouting shots with your queries. We are a visual magazine and no idea will be considered without visuals. We are good about responding to writers in a timely fashion—excessive phone calls are not appreciated, but do check in if you haven't heard from us in two months. We like colorful, lively and creative writing. Have fun with your query. Multiple queries in a submission are allowed."

$ ART REVUE MAGAZINE, Innovative Artists, 302 W. 13th St., Loveland CO 80537. Phone/fax: (970)669-0625. E-mail: artrevue@aol.com. Website: http://artrevue.anthill.com. **Contact:** Jan McNutt, editor. **85% freelance written.** Quarterly magazine covering fine art of sculpture and painting. "Articles are focused on fine art: how to, business of art, profiles of artists, museums, galleries, art businesses, art shows and exhibitions. Light and breezy articles on artists, their personalities and their work. We are not particularly interested in an artist's philosophy or their 'art statements.'" Estab. 1990. Circ. 8,000. Pays on publication. Publishes ms an average of 3 months after acceptance. Byline given. Buys first rights. Editorial lead time 3 months. Submit seasonal material 6 months in advance. Accepts queries by mail, e-mail, phone. Responds in 1 month to queries, 3 months to mss. Sample copy for $3. Writer's guidelines for #10 SASE.

O→ Break in with articles on "regional (western) art or artists identified with Colorado fine art—sculpture and painting. Museums and galleries exhibiting this genre of art—could be in NYC or Pamona, CA."

Nonfiction: Essays, how-to, humor, interview/profile, new product, opinion, personal experience, photo feature, technical, travel. No crafts, pottery, doll-making, inspirational, religious, tie-dying. Special issues: Galleries and Gallery Owners (February); Artists in the West, North, South, East (May). **Buys 4-6 mss/year.** Query or preferably send complete ms. Length: 500-2,000 words. **Pays $100 and up.**

Photos: State availability of photos with submission. Reviews prints. Offers no additional payment for photos accepted with ms. Identification of subjects required. Acquires one-time rights.

Columns/Departments: Art Matters (interesting art happenings), 100-200 words; Meet . . . (short q&a with artist), 100-300 words; Frivolous Art (interesting, eclectic, fun), 50-100 words. **Buys 6 mss/year.** Query. **Pays $25-50.**

Tips: "Write about unusual, fun, interesting artists or art happenings, galleries or museums. Don't try to be too serious. Put in your personality as well as what you're writing about. We're more interested in style than formula."

N **⊠** **$ $** ART SPIRIT!, Art Spirit! Inc., P.O. Box 460669, Fort Lauderdale FL 33346. (954)763-3338. Fax: (954)763-4481. E-mail: sfbiz@mindspring.com. **Contact:** Sherry Friedlaw, editor. **90% freelance written.** Arts magazine published 3 times a year. "*Art Spirit!* covers music, art, drama, dance, special events." Estab. 1998. Circ. 20,000. Pays on publication. Publishes ms an average of 10 weeks after acceptance. Byline given. Buys first North American serial rights. Editorial lead time 3 months. Accepts queries by mail, e-mail, fax, phone. Responds in 2 weeks. Sample copy by e-mail. Writer's guidelines free.

Nonfiction: Interview/profile, photo feature. "Must be about the arts." Query with published clips. Length: 650-1,500 words. **Pays $100-200.**

Reprints: Accepts previously published submissions.

Photos: State availability of photos with submission or send photos with submission.

Tips: "Information should interest the arts group."

⊠ **$ $** THE ARTIST'S MAGAZINE, F&W Publications, Inc., 1507 Dana Ave., Cincinnati OH 45207-1005. (513)531-2690, ext. 467. Fax: (513)531-2902. E-mail: tamedit@aol.com. Website: www.artistsmagazine.com. Editor: Sandra Carpenter. **Contact:** Executive Editor. **80% freelance written.** Works with a large number of new/unpublished writers each year. Monthly magazine covering primarily two-dimensional art instruction for working artists. "Ours is a highly visual approach to teaching the serious amateur artist techniques that will help him improve his skills and market his work. The style should be crisp and immediately engaging." Circ. 250,000. Pays on publication. Publishes ms an average of 6 months after acceptance. Bionote given for feature material. Offers 25% kill fee. Buys first North American serial and second serial (reprint) rights. Responds in 3 months. Sample copy for $4.50. Writer's guidelines for #10 SASE.

● Writers must have working knowledge of art techniques. This magazine's most consistent need is for instructional feature articles written in the artist's voice.

Nonfiction: Instructional only—how an artist uses a particular technique, how he handles a particular subject or medium, or how he markets his work. "The emphasis must be on how the reader can learn some method of improving his artwork, or the marketing of it." No unillustrated articles; no seasonal material; no travel articles; no profiles. **Buys 60 mss/year.** Query first; all queries must be accompanied by slides, transparencies, prints or tearsheets of the artist's work as well as the artist's bio, and the writer's bio and clips. Length: 1,200-1,800 words. **Pays $200-350 and up.** Sometimes pays the expenses of writers on assignment.

Photos: "Transparencies—in 4×5 or 35mm slide format—are required with every accepted article since these are essential for our instructional format. Full captions must accompany these." Buys one-time rights.

Columns/Departments: "Two departments are open to freelance writers." Landscape Basics is a monthly column that explores the elements of landscape painting. Length: 1,000-1,200 words. Query first with slides of finished paintings. Drawing Board is a monthly column that covers basic art or drawing skills. Query first with illustrations. Length: 1,200 words. **Pays $250 and up.**

Tips: "Look at several current issues and read the author's guidelines carefully. Submissions must include artwork. Remember that our readers are fine artists and illustrators."

N **$ $** ARTNEWS, ABC, 48 W. 38th St., New York NY 10018. (212)398-1690. Fax: (212)768-4002. E-mail: goartnews@aol.com. Website: www.artnewsonline.com. **Contact:** Eric Gibson, executive editor. Monthly. "*Artnews* reports on the art, personalities, issues, trends and events that shape the international art world. Investigative features focus on art ranging from old masters to contemporary, including painting, sculpture, prints and photography. Regular columns offer exhibition and book reviews, travel destinations, investment and appreciation advice, design insights and updates on major art world figures." Estab. 1902. Circ. 9,877. Query before submitting. Accepts queries by mail, e-mail, fax, phone.

$ $ $ ART-TALK, Box 8508, Scottsdale AZ 85252. (480)948-1799. Fax: (480)994-9284. Editor: Bill Macomber. **Contact:** Thom Romeo. **30% freelance written.** Newspaper published 9 times/year covering fine art. "*Art-Talk* deals strictly with fine art, the emphasis being on the Southwest. National and international news is also covered. All editorial is of current interest/activities and written for the art collector." Estab. 1981. Circ. 42,000. **Pays on acceptance.** Publishes ms an average of 2 months after acceptance. Byline given. Buys first North American serial rights and makes work-for-hire assignments. Editorial lead time 3 months. Submit seasonal material 4 months in advance. Accepts simultaneous submissions. Responds in 2 weeks to queries; 1 month to mss. Sample copy free.

Nonfiction: Exposé, general interest, humor, interview/profile, opinion, personal experience, photo feature. No articles on non-professional artists (e.g., Sunday Painters) or about a single commercial art gallery. **Buys 12-15 mss/year.** Query with published clips. Length: 500-4,000 words. **Pays $75-800 for assigned articles; $50-750 for unsolicited articles.** Sometimes pays expenses of writers on assignment.

Photos: State availability of photos with submission. Reviews transparencies, prints. Offers no additional payment for photos accepted with ms. Captions, identification of subjects required. Buys one-time rights.

Columns/Departments: Maintains 9 freelance columnists in different cities. **Buys 38 mss/year.** Query with published clips. **Pays $100-175.**

Tips: "Good working knowledge of the art gallery/auction/artist interconnections. Should be a part of the 'art scene' in an area known for art."

[N] AZURE DESIGN, ARCHITECTURE AND ART, 20 Maud St., Suite 200, Toronto M5V 2M5 Canada. (416)203-9674. Fax: (416)522-2357. E-mail: azure@interlog.com. Website: www.azureonline.com. **Contact:** Nelda Rodger, editor. **50% freelance written.** Magazine covering design and architecture. Estab. 1985. Circ. 20,000. Pays on publication. Publishes ms an average of 1 month after acceptance. Kill fee varies. Buys first rights. Editorial lead time up to 45 days. Responds in 6 weeks.

Nonfiction: Buys 25-30 mss/year. Length: 350-2,000 words. **Payment varies.**

Columns/Departments: Rearview (essay/photo on something from a building environment); and Forms & Functions (coming exhibitions, happenings in world of design), both 300-350 words. **Payment varies.**

Tips: "Try to understand what the magazine is about. Writers must be well-versed in the field of architecture and design. It's very unusual to get something from someone I haven't worked quite closely with and gotten a sense of who the writer is. The best way to introduce yourself is by sending clips or writing samples and describe what your background is in the field."

[star] $ $C, international contemporary art, C The Visual Arts Foundation, P.O. Box 5, Station B, Toronto, Ontario M5T 2T2. (416)539-9495. Fax: (416)539-9903. E-mail: cmag@istar.ca. Website: www.CMagazine.com. **Contact:** Joyce Mason, editor/publisher. **80% freelance written.** Quarterly magazine covering international contemporary art. "*C* provides a vital and vibrant forum for the presentation of contemporary art and the discussion of issues surrounding art in our culture, including feature articles, dialogue, reviews and reports, as well as original artists' projects." Estab. 1983. Circ. 7,000. Pays on publication. Publishes ms an average of 4 months after acceptance. Byline given. Offers kill fee. Editorial lead time 3 months. Accepts queries by mail, e-mail, fax, phone. Accepts simultaneous submissions, if so noted. Responds in 6 weeks to queries; 4 months to mss. Sample copy for $10 (US). Writer's guidelines for #10 SASE.

Nonfiction: Essays, general interest, opinion, personal experience. **Buys 50 mss/year.** Query. Length: 1,000-3,000 words. **Pays $150-500 (Canadian), ($105-350 US).**

Columns/Departments: Reviews (review of art exhibitions), 500 words. **Buys 30 mss/year.** Query. **Pays $100 (Canadian) ($70 US).**

Photos: State availability of photos with submission or send photos with submission. Reviews 4×5 transparencies or 8×10 prints. Offers no additional payment for photos accepted with ms. Captions required. Buys one-time rights.

[star] $ $FUSE MAGAZINE, A magazine about issues of art & culture, ARTONS Publishing, 401 Richmond St. W., #454, Toronto, Ontario M5V 3A8 Canada. (416)340-8026. Fax: (416)340-0494. E-mail: fuse@interlog.com. Website: www.fusemagazine.org. **Contact:** Petra Chevrier, managing editor. **100% freelance written.** Quarterly magazine covering art and art criticism; analysis of cultural and political events as they impact on art production and exhibition. Estab. 1976. Circ. 3,000. Pays on publication. Publishes ms an average of 4 months after acceptance. Byline given. Offers 50% kill fee for commissioned pieces only. Buys first North American serial rights all languages. Editorial lead time 4 months. Submit seasonal material 2 months in advance. Accepts simultaneous submissions. Accepts queries by mail only. Sample copy for $5 (US funds if outside Canada). Writer's guidelines for #10 SAE with IRCs.

Nonfiction: Essays, interview/profile, opinion, art reviews. **Buys 50 mss/year.** Query with published clips and detailed proposal or send complete ms. Length: 800-6,000 words. **Pays 10¢/word; $100 for reviews (Canadian funds).**

Photos: State availability of photos with submission. Reviews 5×7 prints. Offers no additional payment for photos accepted with ms. Captions required.

Columns/Departments: Buys 10 mss/year. Pays 10¢/word.

Tips: Send detailed, but not lengthy, proposals or completed manuscripts for review by the editorial board.

[N] [star] $ $L.A. ARCHITECT, The Magazine of Design in Southern California, Balcony Press, 512 E. Wilson, Glendale CA 91206. (818)956-5313. Fax: (818)956-5904. E-mail: danette@balconypress.com. Website: www.LAArch.com. **Contact:** Danette Riddle, editor. **80% freelance written.** Bimonthly magazine covering architecture, interiors, landscape and other design disciplines. "*L.A. Architect* is interested in architectural, interiors, product, graphics and landscape design as well as news about the arts. We encourage designers to keep us informed on projects, techniques, and products that are innovative, new, or nationally newsworthy. We are especially interested in new and renovated projects that illustrate a high degree of design integrity and unique answers to typical problems in the urban cultural and physical environment." Estab. 1999. Circ. 5,000. Pays on publication. Publishes ms an average of 3 months after acceptance. Byline given. Makes work-for-hire assignments. Editorial lead time 4 months. Submit seasonal material 4 months in advance. Accepts queries by mail, e-mail, fax. Responds in 1 week to queries; 1 month to mss. Sample copy for $3. Writer's guidelines for #10 SASE or on website.

Nonfiction: Book excerpts, essays, historical/nostalgic, interview/profile, new product. "No technical; foo-foo interiors; non-Southern California subjects." **Buys 20 mss/year.** Query with published clips. Length: 500-2,000 words. **Pay negotiable.**

Photos: State availability of photos with submission. Offers no additional payment for photos accepted with ms. Captions, model releases and identification of subjects required. Buys one-time rights.

Tips: "Our magazine focuses on contemporary and cutting edge work either happening in Southern California or designed by a Southern California designer. We like to find little known talent which has not been widely published. We are not like *Architectural Digest* in flavor so avoid highly decorative subjects. Each project, product, or event should be accompanied by a story proposal or brief description and select images. Do not send original art without our written request; we make every effort to return materials we are unable to use, but this is sometimes difficult and we must make advance arrangements for original art."

$ $ THE MAGAZINE ANTIQUES, Brant Publications, 575 Broadway, New York NY 10012. (212)941-2800. Fax: (212)941-2819. **Contact:** Allison Ledes, editor. **75% freelance written.** Monthly. "Articles should present new information in a scholarly format (with footnotes) on the fine and decorative arts, architecture, historic preservation and landscape architecture." Estab. 1922. Circ. 65,835. Pays on publication. Publishes ms an average of 6 months after acceptance. Byline given. Buys all rights. Editorial lead time 6 months. Submit seasonal material 6 months in advance. Responds in 3 weeks to queries; 6 months to mss. Sample copy for $10.50.

Nonfiction: Historical/nostalgic, scholarly. **Buys 50 mss/year.** Query with cv. Length: 2,850-3,000 words. **Pays $250-500.** Sometimes pays expenses of writers on assignment.

Photos: State availability of photos with submission. Reviews contact sheets, negatives, transparencies and prints. Captions and identification of subjects required. Buys one-time rights.

⊠ $ $ $ METROPOLIS, The Magazine of Architecture and Design, Bellerophon Publications, 61 W. 23rd St., New York NY 10010. (212)722-5050. Fax: (212)627-9988. E-mail: edit@metropolismag.com. Website: www.metropolismag.com. Editor-in-Chief: Marissa Bartolucci. **Contact:** Jared Hohlt, managing editor. **80% freelance written.** Monthly magazine (combined issues February/March and August/September) for consumers interested in architecture and design. Estab. 1981. Circ. 48,000. **Pays on acceptance.** Publishes ms an average of 3 months after acceptance. Byline given. Makes work-for-hire assignments. Submit calendar material 6 weeks in advance. Responds in 8 months. Sample copy for $4.95.

Nonfiction: Contact: Susan Szenasy, editor-in-chief. Essays (design, architecture, urban planning issues and ideas), profiles (of multi-disciplinary designers/architects). No profiles on individual architectural practices, information from public relations firms, or fine arts. **Buys 30 mss/year.** Length: 500-2,000 words. **Pays $100-1,000.**

Photos: State availability of or send photos with submission. Reviews contact sheets, 35mm or 4×5 transparencies, or 8×10 b&w prints. Payment offered for certain photos. Captions required. Buys one-time rights.

Columns/Departments: Insites (short takes on design and architecture), 100-600 words; **pays $50-150.** In Print (book review essays: focus on issues covered in a group of 2-4 books), 2,500-3,000 words; The Metropolis Observed (architecture and city planning news features and opinion), 750-1,500 words; **pays $200-500.** Visible City (historical aspects of cities), 1,500-2,500 words; **pays $600-800;** direct queries to Kira Gould, managing editor. By Design (the process of design), 1,000-2,000 words; **pays $600-800;** direct queries to Janet Rumble, senior editor. **Buys approximately 40 mss/year.** Query with published clips.

Tips: "We're looking for ideas, what's new, the obscure or the wonderful. Keep in mind that we are interested *only* in the consumer end of architecture and design. Send query with examples of photos explaining how you see illustrations working with article. Also, be patient and don't expect an immediate answer after submission of query."

$ $ MIX, independent art and culture magazine, (formerly Mix: The Magazine of Independent Art and Culture), Parallélogramme Artist-Run Culture and Publishing, Inc., 401 Richmond St. #446, Toronto, Ontario M5V 3A8 Canada. (416)506-1012. Fax: (416)506-0141. E-mail: mix@web.net. Website: www.mix.web.net/mix/. Artist-Run Culture Editor: Kika Thorne. Prison Art Editor: Dañiel Rojas-Orrego. **Contact:** Karen Augustine, editor. **90% freelance written.** Quarterly magazine covering artist-run gallery activities. "*Mix* represents and investigates contemporary artistic practices and issues, especially in the progressive Canadian artist-run scene." Estab. 1973. Circ. 3,500. Pays on publication. Publishes ms an average of 6 months after acceptance. Byline given. Offers 40% kill fee. Buys first North American serial rights. Editorial lead time 6 months. Submit seasonal material 4 months in advance. Accepts queries by mail, e-mail, fax. Responds in 2 months to queries; 3 months to mss. Sample copy for $6.95, 8½×9¾ SASE and 6 first-class stamps. Writer's guidelines free or on website.

Nonfiction: Essays, interview/profile. **Buys 12-20 mss/year.** Query with published clips. Length: 750-3,500 words. **Pays $100-300.**

Reprints: Send photocopy of article and information about when and where the article previously appeared.

Photos: State availability of photos with submission. Captions and identification of subjects required. Buys one-time rights.

Columns/Departments: Prison Art, 1,000 words; Performances, Film, New Media, 1,000-2,000 words; Interviews, 2,000-3,000 words. Query with published clips. **Pays $50-300.**

▣ The online magazine carries original content not found in the print edition and includes writer's guidelines.
Tips: "Read the magazine and other contemporary art magazines. Understand the idea 'artist-run.' We're not interested in 'artsy-phartsy' editorial but rather pieces that are critical, dynamic and would be of interest to nonartists too."

$ $U.S. ART, MSP Communications, 220 S. Sixth St., Suite 500, Minneapolis MN 55402. (612)339-7571. Fax: (612)339-5806. E-mail: sgilbert@mspcommunications.com. Publisher: Frank Sisser. **Contact:** Tracy McCormick, managing editor. **40% freelance written.** Monthly magazine that reflects current events in the limited-edition-print market and educates collectors and the trade about the market's practices and trends. Circ. 50,000. Distributed primarily through a network of 900 galleries as a free service to their customers. **Pays on acceptance.** Publishes ms 4 months after acceptance. Byline given. Offers 25% kill fee. Buys all rights "for a period of 60 days following publication of article." Editorial lead time 4 months. Departments/columns are staff-written. Accepts queries by mail, e-mail, fax. Responds in 3 months. Sample copy and writer's guidelines for SASE.
Nonfiction: Two artist profiles per issue; an average of 6 features per issue including roundups of painters whose shared background of geographical region, heritage, or currently popular style illustrates a point; current events and exhibitions; educational topics on buying/selling practices and services available to help collectors purchase various print media. "Artists whose work is not available in print will *not* be considered for profiles." **Buys 4 mss/year.** Length: 1,000-2,000 words. **Pays $300-500 for features.**
Photos: Color transparencies are preferred. Returns materials after 2 months.
Tips: "We are open to writers whose backgrounds are not arts-specific. We generally do not look for art critics but prefer general-assignment reporters who can present factual material with flair in a magazine format. We also are open to opinion pieces from experts (gallery owners, publishers, consultants, show promoters) within the industry."

$WESTART, P.O. Box 6868, Auburn CA 95604. (530)885-0969. **Contact:** Martha Garcia, editor-in-chief. Semi-monthly 12-page tabloid emphasizing art for practicing artists and artists/craftsmen, students of art and art patrons. Estab. 1961. Circ. 4,000. Pays on publication. Byline given. Buys all rights. Sample copy and writer's guidelines free.
Nonfiction: Informational, photo feature, profile. No hobbies. **Buys 6-8 mss/year.** Query or submit complete ms with SASE for reply or return. Phone queries OK. Length: 700-800 words. **Pays 50¢/column inch.**
Photos: Purchased with or without accompanying ms. Send b&w prints. Pays 50¢/column inch.
Tips: "We publish information which is current—that is, we will use a review of an exhibition only if exhibition is still open on the date of publication. Therefore, reviewer must be familiar with our printing and news deadlines."

ASSOCIATIONS

Association publications allow writers to write for national audiences while covering local stories. If your town has a Kiwanis, Lions or Rotary Club chapter, one of its projects might merit a story in the club's magazine. If you are a member of the organization, find out before you write an article if the publication pays members for stories; some associations do not. In addition, some association publications gather their own club information and rely on freelancers solely for outside features. Be sure to find out what these policies are before you submit a manuscript. Club-financed magazines that carry material not directly related to the group's activities are classified by their subject matter in the Consumer and Trade sections.

$ $THE ELKS MAGAZINE, 425 W. Diversey, Chicago IL 60614-6196. (773)755-4740. E-mail: elksmag@elks.org. Website: www.elks.org/elksmag. **Contact:** Anna L. Idol, managing editor. Editor: Fred D. Oakes. **25% freelance written.** Will work with published or unpublished writers. Magazine published 10 times/year with basic mission of being the "voice of the Elks." All material concerning the news of the Elks is written in-house. Freelance, general interest articles are to be upbeat, wholesome, informative, with family appeal. Estab. 1922. Circ. 1,200,000. **Pays on acceptance.** Buys first North American serial rights, print only. Responds within 1 month. Sample copy and writer's guidelines for 9×12 SAE with 4 first-class stamps or on website.
Nonfiction: "We're really interested in seeing manuscripts on business, technology, history, or just intriguing topics, ranging from science to sports." No fiction, politics, religion, controversial issues, travel, first person, fillers or verse. **Buys 2-3 mss/issue.** Send complete ms. "No queries." Length: 1,500-2,500 words. **Pays 20¢ per word.**
Tips: "Check our website. Freelance articles are noted on the Table of Contents, but are not reproduced online, as we purchase only one-time print rights. If possible, please advise where photographs may be found. Photographs taken and submitted by the writer are paid for separately at $25 each. Please try us first. We'll get back to you soon."

$ $ $KIWANIS, 3636 Woodview Trace, Indianapolis IN 46268-3196. (317)875-8755. Fax: (317)879-0204. E-mail: cjonak@kiwanis.org. Website: www.kiwanis.org. Managing Editor: Chuck Jonak. **60-75% freelance written.** Magazine published 10 times/year for business and professional persons and their families. Estab. 1917. Circ. 260,000.

Pays on acceptance. Buys first serial rights. Offers 40% kill fee. Publishes ms an average of 3 months after acceptance. Byline given. Accepts queries by mail, e-mail, fax. Responds within 1 month. Sample copy and writer's guidelines for 9×12 SAE with 5 first-class stamps; writer's guidelines also on website.

Nonfiction: Articles about social and civic betterment, small-business concerns, children, science, education, religion, family, health, recreation, etc. Emphasis on objectivity, intelligent analysis and thorough research of contemporary issues. Positive tone preferred. Concise, lively writing, absence of clichés, and impartial presentation of controversy required. When applicable, include information and quotations from international sources. Avoid writing strictly to a US audience. "We have a continuing need for articles of international interest. In addition, we are very interested in proposals that concern helping youth, particularly prenatal through age five: day care, developmentally appropriate education, early intervention for at-risk children, parent education, safety and health." **Buys 40 mss/year.** Length: 1,500-2,500 words. **Pays $400-1,000.** "No fiction, personal essays, profiles, travel pieces, fillers or verse of any kind. A light or humorous approach is welcomed where the subject is appropriate and all other requirements are observed." Usually pays the expenses of writers on assignment. Query first. Must include SASE for response.

● Ranked as one of the best markets for freelance writers in *Writer's Yearbook* magazine's annual "Top 100 Markets," January 2000.

Photos: "We accept photos submitted with manuscripts. Our rate for a manuscript with good photos is higher than for one without." Model release and identification of subjects required. Buys one-time rights.

Tips: "We will work with any writer who presents a strong feature article idea applicable to our magazine's audience and who will prove he or she knows the craft of writing. First, obtain writer's guidelines and a sample copy. Study for general style and content. When querying, present detailed outline of proposed manuscript's focus and editorial intent. Indicate expert sources to be used, as well as article's tone and length. Present a well-researched, smoothly written manuscript that contains a 'human quality' with the use of anecdotes, practical examples, quotations, etc."

$ $ THE LION, 300 22nd St., Oak Brook IL 60523-8815. (630)571-5466. Fax: (630)571-8890. E-mail: lions@lions clubs.org. Website: www.lionsclubs.org. **Contact:** Robert Kleinfelder, senior editor. **35% freelance written.** Works with a small number of new/unpublished writers each year. Monthly magazine covering service club organization for Lions Club members and their families. Estab. 1918. Circ. 600,000. **Pays on acceptance.** Publishes ms an average of 5 months after acceptance. Buys all rights. Byline given. Accepts queries by mail, fax, phone. Responds in 6 weeks. Sample copy and writer's guidelines free.

Nonfiction: Informational (issues of interest to civic-minded individuals) and photo feature (must be of a Lions Club service project). No travel, biography or personal experiences. Welcomes humor, if sophisticated but clean; no sensationalism. Prefers anecdotes in articles. **Buys 4 mss/issue.** Query. Phone queries OK. Length: 500-2,200. **Pays $100-750.** Sometimes pays the expenses of writers on assignment.

Photos: Purchased with or without accompanying ms or on assignment. Captions required. Query for photos. B&w and color glossies at least 5×7 or 35mm color slides. Total purchase price for ms includes payment for photos accepted with ms. "Be sure photos are clear and as candid as possible."

Tips: "Send detailed description of proposed article. Query first and request writer's guidelines and sample copy. Incomplete details on how the Lions involved actually carried out a project and poor quality photos are the most frequent mistakes made by writers in completing an article assignment for us. We are geared increasingly to an international audience. Writers who travel internationally could query for possible assignments, although only locally related expenses could be paid."

$ $ $ THE ROTARIAN, Rotary International, 1560 Sherman Ave., Evanston IL 60201-4818. (847)866-3000. Fax: (847)866-9732. E-mail: prattc@rotaryintl.org. Website: www.rotary.org. **Contact:** Charles W. Pratt, editor; Cary Silver, managing editor. **40% freelance written.** Monthly magazine for Rotarian business and professional men and women and their families, schools, libraries, hospitals, etc. "Articles should appeal to an international audience and in some way help Rotarians help other people. The organization's rationale is one of hope, encouragement and belief in the power of individuals talking and working together." Estab. 1911. Circ. 514,565. **Pays on acceptance.** Byline usually given. Kill fee negotiable. Buys one-time or all rights. Accepts queries by mail, e-mail, fax. Responds in 3 weeks. Sample copy for 9×12 SAE with 6 first-class stamps. Writer's guidelines for #10 SASE.

Nonfiction: General interest, humor, sports, inspirational, photo feature, travel, business, environment. No fiction, religious or political articles. Query with published clips. Length: 1,500 words maximum. Payment negotiable.

Reprints: Send tearsheet or photocopy of article or typed ms with rights for sale noted and information about when and where the article previously appeared. Negotiates payment.

Photos: State availability of photos. Reviews contact sheets and transparencies. Usually buys one-time rights.

Columns/Departments: Manager's Memo (business), Database, Health Watch, Earth Diary, Travel Tips, Trends. Length: 800 words. Query.

Tips: "The chief aim of *The Rotarian* is to report Rotary International news. Most of this information comes through Rotary channels and is staff written or edited. The best field for freelance articles is in the general interest category. These run the gamut from humor pieces and 'how-to' stories to articles about such significant concerns as business management, technology, world health and the environment."

$ $ SCOUTING, Boy Scouts of America, 1325 W. Walnut Hill Lane, P.O. Box 152079, Irving TX 75015-2079. (972)580-2367. Fax: (972)580-2079. E-mail: 103064.3363@compuserve.com. Website: www.bsa.scouting.org/mags/scouting/index.html. Executive Editor: Scott Daniels. **Contact:** Jon C. Halter, editor. **80% freelance written.** Magazine published 6 times/year on Scouting activities for adult leaders of the Boy Scouts, Cub Scouts, Venture and BSA Learning for Life programs. Estab. 1913. Circ. 1,000,000. **Pays on acceptance**. Offers 25% kill fee. Publishes ms an average of 18 months after acceptance. Byline given. Buys first North American serial rights. Editorial lead time 12 months. Submit seasonal material 1 year in advance. Accepts queries by mail, fax. Accepts simultaneous submissions. Responds in 1 month to queries; 2 months to mss. Sample copy for $2.50 and 9×12 SAE with 4 first-class stamps or on website. Writer's guidelines for #10 SASE or on website.

   O→ Break in with "a profile of an outstanding Scout leader who has useful advice for new volunteer leaders (especially good if the situation involves urban Scouting or Scouts with disabilities or other extraordinary role)."

Nonfiction: Program activities; leadership techniques and styles; profiles; inspirational; occasional general interest for adults (humor, historical, nature, social issues, trends). **Buys 30-40 mss/year.** Query with published clips and SASE. Length: 600-1,200 words. **Pays $750-1,000 for assigned articles; $300-750 for unsolicited articles.** Pays expenses of writers on assignment.

   ● Ranked as one of the best markets for freelance writers in *Writer's Yearbook* magazine's annual "Top 100 Markets," January 2000.

Reprints: Send photocopy of article and information about where and when the article previously appeared. "First-person accounts of meaningful Scouting experiences (previously published in local newspapers, etc.) are a popular subject."

Photos: State availability of photos with submission. Reviews transparencies and prints. Identification of subjects required. Buys one-time rights.

Columns/Departments: Way it Was (Scouting history), 1,000 words; Family Talk (family—raising kids, etc.), 600-750 words. **Buys 8-12 mss/year.** Query. **Pays $300-500.**

Fillers: Anecdotes, short humor. **Buys 25-30/year.** Length: 50-150 words. **Pays $25 on publication.** "Limited to personal accounts of humorous or inspirational scouting experiences."

   ■ The online version carries original content not found in the print edition and includes writer's guidelines. Contact: Scott Daniels.

Tips: "*Scouting* magazine articles are mainly about successful program activities conducted by or for Cub Scout packs, Boy Scout troops, and Venturing crews. We also include features on winning leadership techniques and styles, profiles of outstanding individual leaders, and inspirational accounts (usually first person) of Scouting's impact on an individual, either as a youth or while serving as a volunteer adult leader. Because most volunteer Scout leaders are also parents of children of Scout age, *Scouting* is also considered a *family* magazine. We publish material we feel will help parents in strengthening families. (Because they often deal with communicating and interacting with young people, many of these features are useful to a reader in both roles as parent and Scout leader)."

$ $ THE TOASTMASTER, Toastmasters International, 23182 Arroyo Vista, Rancho Santa Margarita CA 92688 or P.O. Box 9052, Mission Viejo, CA 92690-7052. (949)858-8255. Fax: (949)858-1207. E-mail: sfrey@toastmasters.org. Website: www.toastmasters.org. **Contact:** Suzanne Frey, editor. **50% freelance written.** Monthly magazine on public speaking, leadership and club concerns. "This magazine is sent to members of Toastmasters International, a nonprofit educational association of men and women throughout the world who are interested in developing their communication and leadership skills. Members range from novice to professional speakers and come from a wide variety of ethnic and cultural backgrounds." Estab. 1932. Circ. 170,000. **Pays on acceptance.** Publishes ms an average of 10 months after acceptance. Byline given. Buys second serial (reprint), first-time or all rights. Submit seasonal material 3 months in advance. Accepts simultaneous submissions. Responds in 6 weeks to queries; 1 month to mss. Sample copy for 9×12 SAE with 4 first-class stamps. Writer's guidelines for #10 SASE or on website.

Nonfiction: How-to; humor; articles on topics related to communications and leadership; language use; profiles of well-known speakers and leaders. Especially looking for profiles of interesting leaders and speakers analyzing why they were effective. **Buys 50 mss/year.** Query by mail only. Length: 1,000-2,500 words. **Pays $100-250.** Sometimes pays expenses of writers on assignment. "Toastmasters members are requested to view their submissions as contributions to the organization. Sometimes asks for book excerpts and reprints without payment, but original contribution from individuals outside Toastmasters will be paid for at stated rates."

Reprints: Send typed ms with rights for sale noted and information about when and where the article previously appeared. Pays 50-70% of amount paid for an original article.

Photos: Reviews b&w prints. No additional payment for photos accepted with ms. Captions required. Buys all rights.

Tips: "We are looking primarily for 'how-to' articles on subjects from the broad fields of communications and leadership which can be directly applied by our readers in their self-improvement and club programming efforts. Concrete examples are useful. Avoid sexist or nationalist language and 'Americanisms' such as baseball examples, etc."

$ $ VFW MAGAZINE, Veterans of Foreign Wars of the United States, 406 W. 34th St., Kansas City MO 64111. (816)756-3390. Fax: (816)968-1169. Website: www.vfw.org. **Contact:** Rich Kolb, editor-in-chief. **40% freelance written.** Monthly magazine on veterans' affairs, military history, patriotism, defense and current events. "*VFW Magazine* goes to its members worldwide, all having served honorably in the armed forces overseas from World War II through Bosnia." Circ. 2,000,000. **Pays on acceptance.** Offers 50% kill fee on commissioned articles. Buys first rights. Submit seasonal material 6 months in advance. Accepts queries by mail, fax. Responds in 2 months. Sample copy for 9×12 SAE with 5 first-class stamps.

   O→ Break in with "fresh and innovative angles on veterans' rights; stories on little-known exploits in U.S. Military history. Will be particularly in the market for Korean War battle accounts during 2000-2003. Upbeat articles about severely disabled veterans who have overcome their disabilities; feel-good patriotism pieces; current events as they relate to defense policy; health and retirement pieces are always welcome."

Nonfiction: Veterans' and defense affairs, recognition of veterans and military service, current foreign policy, American armed forces abroad and international events affecting U.S. national security are in demand. **Buys 25-30 mss/year.** Query with 1-page outline, résumé and published clips. Length: 1,000 words. **Pays up to $500 maximum unless otherwise negotiated.**

Photos: Send photos with submission. Color transparencies (2¼×2¼) preferred; b&w prints (5×7, 8×10). Reviews contact sheets, negatives, transparencies and prints. Captions and identification of subjects required. Buys first North American rights.

Tips: "Absolute accuracy and quotes from relevant individuals are a must. Bibliographies useful if subject required extensive research and/or is open to dispute. Consult *The Associated Press Stylebook* for correct grammar and punctuation. Please enclose a 3-sentence biography describing your military service and your experience in the field in which you are writing. No phone queries."

ASTROLOGY, METAPHYSICAL & NEW AGE

Magazines in this section carry articles ranging from shamanism to extraterrestrial phenomena. With the coming millennium, there is increased interest in spirituality, angels, near death experiences, mind/body healing and other New Age concepts and figures. The following publications regard astrology, psychic phenomena, metaphysical experiences and related subjects as sciences or as objects of serious study. Each has an individual personality and approach to these phenomena. If you want to write for these publications, be sure to read them carefully before submitting.

$ $FATE, Llewellyn Worldwide, Ltd., P.O. Box 64383, St. Paul MN 55164-0383. Fax: (651)291-1908. E-mail: fate@llewellyn.com. Website: www.fatemag.com. **Contact:** Editor. **70% freelance written.** Estab. 1948. Circ. 65,000. Pays after publication. Byline given. Buys all rights. Query by mail, e-mail. Responds in 3 months or more. Sample copy and writer's guidelines for $3 and 9×12 SAE with 5 first-class stamps or on website.

Nonfiction: Personal psychic and mystical experiences, 350-500 words. **Pays $25.** Articles on parapsychology, Fortean phenomena, cryptozoology, spiritual healing, flying saucers, new frontiers of science, and mystical aspects of ancient civilizations, 500-3,000 words. Must include complete authenticating details. Prefers interesting accounts of single events rather than roundups. "We very frequently accept manuscripts from new writers; the majority are individual's first-person accounts of their own psychic/mystical/spiritual experiences. We do need to have all details, where, when, why, who and what, included for complete documentation. We ask for a notarized statement attesting to truth of the article." Query first. **Pays 10¢/word.**

Fillers: Fillers are especially welcomed and must be be fully authenticated also, and on similar topics. Length: 50-300 words.

Photos: Buys slides. prints, or digital photos/illustrations with mss. Pays $10.

Tips: "We would like more stories about *current* paranormal or unusual events."

N ☆ $FREE SPIRIT MAGAZINE, 107 Sterling Place, Brooklyn NY 11217. (718)638-3733. Fax: (718)230-3459. E-mail: fsny@fsmagazine.com. **Contact:** Paul English, editor. Bimonthly tabloid covering spirituality and personal growth and transformation. "We are a magazine that caters to the holistic health community in New York City." Circ. 50,000. **Pays on acceptance.** Publishes ms 3 months after acceptance. Byline given. Buys first rights. Editorial lead time 1 month. Accepts simultaneous submissions. Responds in 1 month. Sample copy for 8×10 SAE with 10 first-class stamps. Writer's guidelines free.

Nonfiction: Essays, how-to, humor, inspirational, interview/profile, new product, photo feature. **Buys 30 mss/year.** Query with or without published clips. Length: 1,000-3,500 words. **Pays $150 maximum.**

Reprints: Accepts previously published submissions.

Photos: State availability of photos with submission. Model releases required.

Columns/Departments: Fitness (new ideas in staying fit), 1,500 words (can be regional NY or LA); **Pays $150.**

Fiction: Humorous, inspirational, mainstream. **Buys 5 mss/year.** Query with published clips. Length: 1,000-3,500 words. **Pays $150.**

Tips: "Be vivid and descriptive. We are *very* interested in hearing from new writers."

$ $ $NEW AGE: The Journal for Holistic Living, 42 Pleasant St., Watertown MA 02472. (617)926-0200. Fax: (617)924-2967. E-mail: forum@newage.com. Website: www.newage.com. Managing Editor: Liz Phillips. Editor: Jennifer Cook. **Contact:** Liz Barker, editorial assistant. **35% freelance written.** Works with a small number of new/unpublished writers each year. Bimonthly magazine emphasizing "personal fulfillment and social change. The audience we reach is college-educated, social-service/hi-tech oriented, 25-55 years of age, concerned about social values, humanitarianism and balance in personal life." Estab. 1974. Cir. 275,000. Publishes ms 5 months after acceptance. Byline given. Offers 25% kill fee. Buys first North American serial and reprint rights. Submit seasonal material 6 months in advance. Accepts simultaneous submissions. Responds in 3 months to queries. Sample copy for $5 and 9×12 SAE. Guidelines for #10 SASE.

Nonfiction: Book excerpts, exposé, general interest, how-to (travel on business, select a computer, reclaim land, plant a garden), behavior, trend pieces, humor, inspirational, interview/profile, new product, food, sci-tech, music, media, nutrition, holistic health, education, personal experience. **Buys 60-80 mss/year.** Query with published clips. No phone calls. The process of decision making takes time and involves more than one editor. An answer cannot be given over the phone. Length: 200-4,000 words. **Pays $50-2,500.** Pays the expenses of writers on assignment.

Reprints: Send tearsheet or photocopy of article.

Photos: State availability of photos. Model releases, identification of subjects required. Buys one-time rights.

Columns/Departments: Body/Mind; Reflections; Upfront. **Buys 60-80 mss/year.** Query with published clips. Length: 250-1,500 words. **Pays $50-850.**

Tips: "Submit short, specific news items to the Upfront department. Query first with clips. A query is one to two paragraphs—if you need more space than that to *present* the idea, then you don't have a clear grip on it. The next open area is columns: Reflections often takes first-time contributors. Read the magazine and get a sense of type of writing run in column. In particular we are interested in seeing inspirational, first-person pieces that highlight an engaging idea, experience or issue. We are also looking for new cutting-edge thinking."

$ ⌧ PANGAIA, Creating an Earth Wise Spirituality, Blessed Bee, Inc., Box 641, Point Arena CA 95468. (707)882-2052. Fax: (707)882-2793. E-mail: dcdarling@saber.net. Website: www.pangaia.com. Editorial Assistant: Elizabeth Barrette. **Contact:** Diane Darling, editor. **95% freelance written.** Quarterly spirtual magazine covering the nature religion movement worldwide. "*PanGaia* is for all people who share a deep love and commitment to the earth. *PanGaia* is dedicated to helping explore our spiritual, emotional and mundane lives in a way which respects all persons, creatures, and the Earth, and which has immediate application to our everyday lives. We encourage folks of all paths to send their work, but our focus is on material which expresses an Earth-centered spirituality." Estab. 1997. Pays on publication. Publishes ms an average of 1 year after acceptance. Byline given. Buys first North American serial, one-time, second serial (reprint) or electronic rights. Editorial lead time 4 months. Submit seasonal material 6 months in advance. Accepts queries by mail, e-mail. Responds in 6 weeks to queries; 6 months to mss. Sample copy for $5. Writer's guidelines for #10 SASE or on website.

Nonfiction: Book excerpts, essays, historical/nostalgic, inspirational, interview/profile, personal experience, photo feature, religious, travel. No material on correlated topics, commercial promotion or personal diatribes. **Buys 20 mss/ year.** Send complete ms. Length: 500-3,000 words. **Pays $10-100.**

Reprints: Accepts previously published submissions.

Photos: State availability of photos with submission. Reviews prints. Negotiates payment individually. Captions and identification of subjects required. Buys one-time rights.

Columns/Departments: Sacred Place; Sacred Path; Scientific Mysticism and Worldwide Paganism. **Buys 16 mss/ year.** Send complete ms.

Fiction: Adventure, ethnic, fantasy, historical, humorous, religious, science fiction. No grim or abstract stories. **Buys 4 mss/year.** Send complete ms. Length: 1,000-3,000 words. **Pays $10-50.**

Poetry: Buys 2 poems/year. Submit maximum 4 poems.

Tips: 'Share a spiritual insight that can enlighten others. Back up your facts with citations where relevant, and make those facts sound like the neatest thing since self-lighting charcoal. Explain how to solve a problem; offer a new way to make the world a better place. We would also like to see serious scholarship on nature religion topics, material of interest to intermediate or advanced practitioners, which is both accurate and engaging."

$ $PARABOLA, The Magazine of Myth and Tradition, The Society for the Study of Myth and Tradition, 656 Broadway, New York NY 10012-2317. (212)505-9037. Fax: (212)979-7325. E-mail: parabola@panix.com. Website: www.parabola.org. **Contact:** Natalie Baan, managing editor. Quarterly magazine "devoted to the exploration of the quest for meaning as expressed in the myths, symbols, and tales of the religious traditions. Particular emphasis is on the relationship between this wisdom and contemporary life." Estab. 1976. Circ. 40,000. Pays on publication. Publishes ms 3 months after acceptance. Byline given. Offers kill fee for assigned articles only (usually $100). Buys first North American serial, first, one-time or second serial (reprint) rights. Editorial lead time 4 months. Accepts queries by mail, e-mail, fax. Accepts simultaneous submissions. Responds in 3 weeks to queries; to mss "variable—for articles directed to a particular theme, we usually respond the month after the deadline (so for an April 8 deadline, we are likely to respond in May). Articles not directed to themes may wait four months or more!" Sample copy for $6.95 current issue; $8.95 back issue. Writers guidelines and list of themes for SASE, via e-mail or on website.

Nonfiction: Book excerpts, essays, photo feature. Send for current list of themes. No articles not related to specific themes. **Buys 15-40 mss/year.** Query. Length: 1,500-3,000 words. **Pays $100 minimum.** Sometimes pays expenses of writers on assignment.

Reprints: Send photocopy of article or short story (must include copy of copyright page) and information about when and where the article or short story previously appeared.

Photos: State availability of photos with submission. Reviews contact sheets, any transparencies and prints. Identification of subjects required. Buys one-time rights.

Columns/Departments: Tangents (reviews of film, exhibits, dance, theater, video, music relating to theme of issue), 1,500-2,000 words; Book Reviews (reviews of current books in religion, spirituality, mythology and tradition), 500 words; Epicycles (retellings of myths and folk tales of all cultures—no fiction or made-up mythology!), under 2,000 words. **Buys 20-40 unsolicited mss/year.** Query. **Pays $75.**

Fiction: "We *very* rarely publish fiction; must relate to upcoming theme." Query. Publishes novel excerpts.

Tips: "Each issue of *Parabola* is organized around a theme. Examples of themes we have explored in the past include Rite of Passage, Sacred Space, The Child, Ceremonies, Addiction, The Sense of Humor, Hospitalilty, The Hunter and The Stranger. We are also looking for material relating to the cultures of Africa, Native Americans and other indigenous peoples. We do *not* publish poetry."

⊠ $ $ RECREATION NEWS, Official Publication of the ESM Association of the Capital Region 7339 D Hanover Pkwy., Greenbelt MD 20770. (301)474-4600. Fax: (301)474-6283. E-mail: editor@recreationnews.com. **Contact:** Karl Teel, publisher. **85% freelance written.** Monthly guide to leisure-time activities for federal and private industry workers covering outdoor recreation, travel, fitness and indoor pastimes. Estab. 1979. Circ. 104,000. Pays on publication. Publishes ms an average of 8 months after acceptance. Byline given. Buys first rights and second serial (reprint) rights. Submit seasonal material 10 months in advance. Accepts queries by mail, e-mail. Accepts simultaneous submissions. Responds in 2 months. Sample copy and writer's guidelines for 9×12 SAE with $1.05 in postage.

Nonfiction: Contact: Articles Editor. Leisure travel (mid-Atlantic travel only); sports; hobbies; historical/nostalgic (Washington-related); personal experience (with recreation, life in Washington). Special issues: skiing (December). **Buys 45 mss/year.** Query with published clips. Length: 800-2,000 words. **Pays from $50-300.**

Reprints: Send photocopy of article or typed ms with rights for sale noted, and information about where and when article previously appeared. **Pays $50.**

Photos: Contact: Photo Editor. State availability of photos with query letter or ms. Uses b&w prints. Pays $25. Uses color transparency on cover only. Pays $50-125 for transparency. Captions and identification of subjects required.

Tips: "Our writers generally have a few years of professional writing experience and their work runs to the lively and conversational. We like more manuscripts in a wide range of recreational topics, including the off-beat. The areas of our publication most open to freelancers are general articles on travel and sports, both participational and spectator, also historic in the DC area. In general, stories on sites visited need to include info on nearby places of interest and places to stop for lunch, to shop, etc."

$ SHAMAN'S DRUM, A Journal of Experiential Shamanism, Cross-Cultural Shamanism Network, P.O. Box 270, Williams OR 97544. (541)846-1313. Fax: (541)846-1204. **Contact:** Timothy White, editor. **75% freelance written.** Quarterly educational magazine of cross-cultural shamanism. "*Shaman's Drum* seeks contributions directed toward a general but well-informed audience. Our intent is to expand, challenge, and refine our readers' and our understanding of shamanism in practice. Topics include indigenous medicineway practices, contemporary shamanic healing practices, ecstatic spiritual practices, and contemporary shamanic psychotherapies. Our overall focus is cross-cultural, but our editorial approach is culture-specific—we prefer that authors focus on specific ethnic traditions or personal practices about which they have significant firsthand experience. We are looking for examples of not only how shamanism has transformed individual lives but also practical ways it can help ensure survival of life on the planet. We want material that captures the heart and feeling of shamanism and that can inspire people to direct action and participation, and to explore shamanism in greater depth." Estab. 1985. Circ. 14,000. Publishes ms 6 months after acceptance. Buys first North American serial and first rights. Editorial lead time 1 year. Responds in 3 months. Sample copy for $5. Writer's guidelines for #10 SASE.

Nonfiction: Book excerpts, essays, interview/profile (please query), opinion, personal experience, photo feature. *No fiction, poetry or fillers.* **Buys 16 mss/year.** Send complete ms. Length: 5,000-8,000 words. **"We pay 5-8¢/word,** depending on how much we have to edit. We also send two copies and tearsheets in addition to cash payment."

Reprints: Accepts rarely. Send typed ms with rights for sale noted and information about when and where the article previously appeared. Pays 50% of amount paid for an original article.

Photos: Send photos with submission. Reviews contact sheets, transparencies and all size prints. Offers $40-50/photo. Identification of subjects required. Buys one-time rights.

Columns/Departments: Earth Circles (news format, concerned with issues, events, organizations related to shamanism, indigenous peoples and caretaking Earth. Relevant clippings also sought. Clippings paid with copies and credit line), 500-1,500 words. **Buys 8 mss/year.** Send complete ms to Judy Wells, Earth Circles editor. **Pays 5-8¢/word.** Reviews (in-depth reviews of books about shamanism or closely related subjects such as indigenous lifestyles, ethnobotany, transpersonal healing and ecstatic spirituality), 500-1,500 words. Send query to Timothy White, Reviews editor. "Please query us first and we will send *Reviewer's Guidelines*." **Pays 5-8¢/word.**

Tips: "All articles must have a clear relationship to shamanism, but may be on topics which have not traditionally been defined as shamanic. We prefer original material that is based on, or illustrated with, first-hand knowledge and personal experience. Articles should be well documented with descriptive examples and pertinent background information. Photographs and illustrations of high quality are always welcome and can help sell articles."

$ WHOLE LIFE TIMES, P.O. Box 1187, Malibu CA 90265. (310)317-4200. Fax: (310)317-4206. E-mail: wholelifex @aol.com. Website: www.wholelifetimes.com. **Contact:** Kerri Hikida, associate editor. Monthly tabloid covering the holistic lifestyle. Estab. 1979. Circ. 58,000. Pays within 30 days after publication for feature stories only. Buys first North American serial rights. Accepts queries by mail, e-mail, fax. Sample copy for $3. Writer's guidelines for #10 SASE.

Nonfiction: Exposé, how-to, health, healing, inspirational, interview/profile, spiritual, food, travel, leading-edge information, revelant celebrity profiles. Special issues: Healing Arts (October), Food & Nutrition (November), Spirituality (December), New Beginnings (January), Relationships (February), Longevity (March), Travel (April), Arts and Cultures (May), Vitamins and Supplements (June), Women's (July), Men's (August). **Buys 45 mss/year.** Query with published clips or send complete ms. Length: up to 2,000 words. **Pays 5-10¢/word for feature stories only.**

Reprints: E-mail, fax or mail typed ms with rights for sale noted and information about when and where the article previously appeared. Pays 50% of amount paid for an original article.

Columns/Departments: Healing, Parenting, Finance, Food, Personal Growth, Relationships, Humor, Travel, Politics, Sexuality, Spirituality and Psychology. Length: 750-1,200 words.

Tips: "Queries should show an awareness of current topics of interest in our subject area. We welcome investigative reporting and are happy to see queries that address topics in a political context. We are especially looking for articles on health and nutrition."

AUTOMOTIVE & MOTORCYCLE

Publications in this section detail the maintenance, operation, performance, racing and judging of automobiles and recreational vehicles. Publications that treat vehicles as means of shelter instead of as a hobby or sport are classified in the Travel, Camping & Trailer category. Journals for service station operators and auto and motorcycle dealers are located in the Trade Auto & Truck section.

$ $AMERICAN IRON MAGAZINE, TAM Communications Inc., 1010 Summer St., Stamford CT 06905. (203)425-8777. Fax: (203)425-8775. **Contact:** Chris Maida, editor. **80% freelance written.** Thirteen issues/year, family-oriented magazine covering Harley-Davidson and other US brands with a definite emphasis on Harleys. Circ. 80,000. Pays on publication. Publishes ms an average of 6 months after acceptance. Byline given. Responds in 1 month to queries with SASE. Sample copy for $3.

Nonfiction: "Clean and non-offensive. Stories include bike features, touring stories, how-to tech stories with step-by-step photos, historical pieces, profiles, events, opinion and various topics of interest to the people who ride Harley-Davidsons." No fiction. **Buys 60 mss/year. Pays $250 for touring articles with slides to first-time writers.** Payment for other articles varies.

Photos: Submit color slides or large transparencies. No prints. Send SASE for return of photos.

Tips: "We're not looking for stories about the top ten biker bars or do-it-yourself tattoos. We're looking for articles about motorcycling, the people and the machines. If you understand the Harley mystique and can write well, you've got a good chance of being published."

$AMERICAN WOMAN ROAD & TRAVEL, (formerly *American Woman Motorscene*), American Woman Motorscene, 2424 Coolidge Rd., Suite 203, Troy, MI 48084. (248)614-0017. Fax: (248)614-8929. E-mail: courtney@americanwomanmag.com. Website: www.americanwomanmag.com. **Contact:** Jessica Moyer, communications manager. **80% freelance written.** Bimonthly automotive/adventure lifestyle and service-oriented magazine for women. Estab. 1988. Circ. 500,000. Pays on publication 3 months after acceptance. Byline always given. Buys first rights and second serial (reprint) rights or makes work-for-hire assignments. Submit seasonal material 4 months in advance. Responds in 3 months. For a sample copy send $1.50 and SASE. Writer's guidelines on website.

Nonfiction: Humor, inspirational, interview/profile, new product, photo feature, travel, lifestyle. No articles depicting women in motorsports or professions that are degrading, negative or not upscale. **Buys 30 mss/year.** Send complete ms. Length 250-1,500 words. **Pay depends on quantity, quality and content. Byline—$100.**

Reprints: Send photocopy of article and information about when and where the article previously appeared.

Photos: Send photos with submission. Reviews contact sheets. Black and white or Kodachrome 64 preferred. Captions, model releases and identification of subjects required. Buys all rights.

Fillers: Anecdotes, facts, gags to be illustrated by cartoonist, newsbreaks, short humor. **Buys 12/year.** Length: 25-100 words. Negotiable.

The online magazine contains material not found in the print edition and includes writer's guidelines.

Tips: "The *AW Road & Travel* reader is typically career and/or family oriented, independent, and adventurous. She demands literate, entertaining and useful information from a magazine enabling her to make educated buying decisions. It helps if the writer is into cars and trucks. We are a lifestyle type of publication more than a technical magazine. Positive attitudes wanted."

$ASPHALT ANGELS MAGAZINE, Thunder Press, Inc., Publications, 4865 Scotts Valley Dr., Suite 200, Scotts Valley CA 95066. (831)438-7882. Fax: (831)438-0993. E-mail: asphltmag@aol.com. Website: www.thunderpressinc.com. **Contact:** Genevieve Schmitt, editor. **50% freelance written.** Bimonthly magazine for motorcycle and Harley female enthusiasts. Estab. 1985. Circ. 60,000. Pays on publication. Publishes ms an average of 2 months after acceptance. Byline given. Buys first rights. Editorial lead time 2 months. Submit seasonal material 2 months in advance. Accepts queries by mail, e-mail, fax. Accepts simultaneous submissions. Writer's guidelines free.

Nonfiction: General interest, historical/nostalgic, how-to (technical motorcycle), humor, interview/profile, new product, personal experience, photo feature, technical. Looking for interesting profiles of people making a difference in the motorcycle industry. **Buys 35 mss/year.** Query with published clips. Length: 200-2,000 words. **Pay negotiable.** Sometimes pays expenses of writers on assignment.

Reprints: Send photocopy of article or typed ms with rights for sale noted and information about when and where the article previously appeared. **Pays 100% of amount paid for an original article.**

Photos: Send photos. Captions, model releases, identification of subjects required. Buys one-time rights.

$ $ AUTO RESTORER, Fancy Publications, Inc., P.O. Box 6050, Mission Viejo CA 92690-6050. (949)855-8822. Fax: (949)855-3045. E-mail: tkade@fancypubs.com. **Contact:** Ted Kade, editor. **85% freelance written.** Monthly magazine on auto restoration. "Our readers own old cars and they work on them. We help our readers by providing as much practical, how-to information as we can about restoration and old cars." Estab. 1989. Pays on publication. Publishes ms an average of 3 months after acceptance. Buys first North American serial or one-time rights. Submit seasonal material 4 months in advance. Accepts queries by mail, e-mail, fax. Responds in 2 months. Sample copy for $5.50. Writer's guidelines free.

Nonfiction: How-to (auto restoration), new product, photo feature, technical, product evaluation. **Buys 60 mss/year.** Query with or without published clips. Length: 200-2,500 words. **Pays $150/published page, including photos and illustrations.**

Photos: Send photos with submission. Reviews contact sheets, transparencies and 5×7 prints. Technical drawings that illustrate articles in black ink are welcome. Offers no additional payment for photos accepted with ms.

Tips: "Query first. Interview the owner of a restored car. Present advice to others on how to do a similar restoration. Seek advice from experts. Go light on history and non-specific details. Make it something that the magazine regularly uses. Do automotive how-tos."

$ $ AUTOMOBILE QUARTERLY, The Connoisseur's Magazine of Motoring Today, Yesterday, and Tomorrow, Kutztown Publishing Co., P.O. Box 348, 15076 Kutztown Rd., Kutztown PA 19530-0348. (610)683-3169. Fax: (610)683-3287. Publishing Director: Jonathan Stein. **Contact:** Karla Rosenbusch, senior editor. Assistant Editor: Stuart Wells. **85% freelance written.** Quarterly hardcover magazine covering "automotive history, with excellent photography." Estab. 1962. Circ. 13,000. **Pays on acceptance.** Publishes ms an average of 1 year after acceptance. Byline given. Buys first international serial rights. Editorial lead time 9 months. Responds in 2 weeks to queries; 2 months to mss. Sample copy for $19.95.

Nonfiction: Essays, historical/nostalgic, photo feature, technical. **Buys 25 mss/year.** Query by mail or fax. Length: 3,500-8,000 words. **Pays approximately 30¢/word.** Sometimes pays expenses of writers on assignment.

Photos: State availability of photos with submission. Reviews 4×5, 35mm and 120 transparencies and historical prints. Buys one-time rights.

Tips: "Study the publication, and stress original research."

$ $ $ $ AUTOWEEK, Crain Communications, 1400 Woodbridge, Detroit MI 48207. (313)446-6000. Fax: (313)446-0347. E-mail: letters@autoweek.com. Website: www.autoweek.com. Editor: Dutch Mandell. Managing Editor: Roger Hart. **Contact:** Todd Lassa, news editor. **33% freelance written.** "*AutoWeek* is the country's only weekly magazine for the auto enthusiast." Estab. 1958. Circ. 300,000. Pays on publication. Publishes ms an average of 1 month after acceptance. Byline given. Buys first North American serial rights. Accepts queries by mail, e-mail, phone, fax.

Nonfiction: Historical/nostalgic, interview/profile, new product, travel. **Buys 100 mss/year.** Query. Length: 700-3,000 words. **Pays $1/word.** Sometimes pays expenses of writers on assignment.

$ BACKROADS, The Local Source for Motorcycle Enthusiasts, Backroads Inc., P.O. Box 317, Branchville NJ 07826. (973)948-4176. Fax: (973)948-0823. E-mail: editor@backroadsusa.com. Website: www.backroadsusa.com. Managing Editor: Shira Kamil. **Contact:** Brian Rathjen, editor/publisher. **50% freelance written.** Monthly tabloid covering motorcycle touring. "*Backroads* is a motorcycle tour magazine geared toward getting motorcyclists on the road and traveling. We provide interesting destinations, unique roadside attractions and eateries plus Rip & Ride Route Sheefs®. We cater to all brands. If you really ride, you need *Backroads*." Estab. 1995. Circ. 40,000. Pays on publication. Publishes ms an average of 3 months after acceptance. Byline given. Buys one-time rights. Editorial lead time 1 month. Submit seasonal material 3 months in advance. Accepts queries by mail, e-mail, fax. Responds in 3 weeks. Sample copy and writer's guidelines free.

Nonfiction: Shira Kamil, editor/publisher. Essays (motorcycle/touring), how-to, humor, new product, opinion, personal experience, technical, travel. "No long diatribes on 'how I got into motorcycles.' " **Buys 2-4 mss/year.** Query. Length: 500-3,000 words. **Pays 4¢/word minimum for assigned articles; 2¢/word for unsolicited articles.** Pays writers with contributor copies or other premiums for short pieces on event recaps.

Reprints: Occasionally accepts previously published submissions.

Photos: Send photos with submission. Reviews contact sheets. Offers no additional payment for photos accepted with ms.

Columns/Departments: We're Outta Here (weekend destinations), 500-1,000 words; Great All American Diner Run (good eateries with great location), 300-800 words; Thoughts from the Road (personal opinion/insights), 250-500 words; Mysterious America (unique and obscure sights), 300-800 words; Big City Getaway (day trips), 500-1,000 words. **Buys 20-24 mss/year.** Query. **Pays 2¢/word-$50/article.**

Fiction: Adventure, humorous. **Buys 2-4 mss/year.** Query. Length: 500-1,500 words. **Pays 2-4¢/word..**

Fillers: Facts, newsbreaks. Length: 100-250 words. No payment for fillers.

Tips: "We prefer destination-oriented articles in a light, layman's format, with photos (not transparencies). Stay away from any name-dropping and first-person references."

[N] $ $ CANADIAN BIKER MAGAZINE, P.O. Box 4122, Victoria British Columbia V8X 3X4 Canada. (250)384-0333. Fax: (250)384-1832. E-mail: edit@canadianbiker.com. Website: http://canadianbiker.com. **Contact:** John Campbell, editor. **65% freelance written.** Magazine covers motorcycling. "A family-oriented motorcycle magazine whose purpose is to unite Canadian motorcyclists from coast to coast through the dissemination of information in a non-biased, open forum. The magazine reports on new product, events, touring, racing, vintage and custom motorcycling as well as new industry information." Estab. 1980. Circ. 20,000. Publishes non-time sensitive mss an average of 1 year after acceptance. Byline given. Buys first rights. Editorial lead time 3 months. Accepts queries by mail, e-mail, fax, phone. Responds in 6 weeks to queries; 6 months to mss. Sample copy for $5 or on website. Writer's guidelines free.

Nonfiction: General interest, historical/nostalgic, how-to, interview/profile (Canadian personalities preferred), new product, technical, travel. **Buys 12 mss/year.** All nonfiction must include photos and/or illustrations. Query with or without published clips, or send complete ms. Length: 500-1,500 words. **Pays $100-200 (Canadian) for assigned articles; $80-150 (Canadian) for unsolicited articles.**

Photos: State availability of or send photos with submission. Reviews 4×4 transparencies, 3×5 prints. Negotiates payment individually. Captions, model releases, identification of subjects required. Buys one-time rights.

   [■] The online version carries original content not found in the print edition. Contact: John Campbell.

Tips: "We're looking for more racing features, rider profiles, custom sport bikes, quality touring stories, 'extreme' riding articles. Contact editor first before writing anything. Have original ideas, an ability to write from an authoritative point of view, and an ability to supply quality photos to accompany text. Writers should be involved in the motorcycle industry and be intimately familiar with some aspect of the industry which would be of interest to readers. Observations of the industry should be current, timely and informative."

$ $ $ $ CAR AND DRIVER, Hachette Filipacchi Magazines, Inc., 2002 Hogback Rd., Ann Arbor MI 48105-9795. (734)971-3600. Fax: (734)971-9188. E-mail: spence1cd@aol.com. Website: www.caranddriver.com. **Contact:** Steve Spence, managing editor. Monthly magazine for auto enthusiasts; college-educated, professional, median 24-35 years of age. Estab. 1956. Circ. 1,300,000. **Pays on acceptance.** Byline given. Offers 25% kill fee. Buys first North American serial rights. Accepts queries by mail, e-mail, fax. Responds in 2 months.

Nonfiction: Articles about automobiles, new and old. Informational articles on cars and equipment, some satire and humor and personalities, past and present, auto-related. Informational, humor, historical, think articles and nostalgia. All road tests are staff-written. "Unsolicited manuscripts are not accepted. Query letters must be addressed to the Managing Editor. *Rates are generous, but few manuscripts are purchased from outside.*" **Buys 1 freelance ms/year. Pays maximum $3,000/feature; $750-1,500/short piece.** Pays expenses of writers on assignment.

Photos: Color slides and b&w photos sometimes purchased with accompanying mss.

   [■] The online magazine carries original content not found in the print edition. Contact: Brad Nevin, online editor.

Tips: "It is best to start off with an interesting query and to stay away from nuts-and-bolts ideas because that will be handled in-house or by an acknowledged expert. Our goal is to be absolutely without flaw in our presentation of automotive facts, but we strive to be every bit as entertaining as we are informative. We do not print this sort of story: 'My Dad's Wacky, Lovable Beetle.' "

[◆] $ $ CC MOTORCYCLE NEWSMAGAZINE, (formerly *CC Motorcycle Magazine*), Motomag Corp., P.O. Box 808, Nyack NY 10960. (914)353-MOTO. Fax: (914)353-5240. E-mail: info@motorcyclenewsmagazine.cc. Website: www.motorcyclenewsmagazine.cc. **Contact:** Mark Kalan, publisher/editor. **90% freelance written.** Monthly magazine featuring "positive coverage of motorcycling in America—riding, travel, racing and tech." Estab. 1989. Circ. 60,000. Pays on publication. Publishes ms 2 months after acceptance. Byline given. Buys one-time rights. Editorial lead time 3 months. Submit seasonal material 3 months in advance. Accepts simultaneous submissions. Responds in 1 month. Sample copy for $3. Writer's guidelines for #10 SASE.

Nonfiction: Essays, general interest, historical/nostalgic, how-to, humor, inspirational, interview/profile, new product, personal experience, photo feature, technical, travel. Daytona Beach Biketoberfest; Summer touring stories—travel. **Buys 12 mss/year.** Query with published clips. Length: 1,000-2,000 words. **Pays $50-250 for assigned articles; $25-125 for unsolicited articles.** Sometimes pays expenses of writers on assignment.

Reprints: Send tearsheet or photocopy of article or short story. No payment. Publishes novel excerpts.

Photos: State availability of photos with submission. Reviews contact sheets, transparencies. Negotiates payment individually. Captions, model releases, identification of subjects required. Buys one-time rights.

Fiction: Adventure, fantasy, historical, romance, slice-of-life vignettes. All fiction must be motorcycle related. **Buys 6 mss/year.** Query with published clips. Length: 1,500-2,500 words. **Pays $50-250.**

Poetry: Avant-garde, free verse, haiku, light verse, traditional. Must be motorcycle related. **Buys 6 poems/year.** Submit 12 maximum poems. Length: open. **Pays $10-50.**

Fillers: Anecdotes, cartoons. **Buys 12/year.** Length: 100-200 words. **Pays $10-50.**

Tips: "Ride a motorcycle and be able to construct a readable sentence!"

N $ $ CLASSIC TRUCKS, Primedia/McMullen Argus Publishing, 774 S. Placentia Ave., Placentia CA 92680. (714)572-2255. Fax: (714)572-1864. E-mail: classic.trucks@mcmullenargus.com. Website: www.mcmullenargus.com. **Contact:** James Rizzo, editor. Monthly magazine covering classic trucks from the 1930s to 1973. Estab. 1994. Circ. 60,000. Pays on publication. Byline given. Buys first North American serial rights. Editorial lead time 4 months. Submit seasonal material 4 months in advance. Writer's guidelines free.

Nonfiction: How-to, interview/profile, new product, technical, travel. Query. Length: 1,500-5,000 words. **Pays $75-200/page for assigned articles; $100/page maximum for unsolicited articles.**

Photos: Send photos with submission. Reviews transparencies and 5×7 prints. Negotiates payment individually. Captions, model releases, identification of subjects required. Buys one-time rights.

Columns/Departments: Buys 24 mss/year. Query.

N ⯐ $ $ MOTORCYCLE TOUR & CRUISER, TAM Communications, 1010 Summer St., Stamford CT 06905. (203)425-8777. Fax: (203)425-8775. E-mail: mtcmagazine@earthlink.net. **Contact:** Laura Brengelman, editor. **70% freelance written**. Magazine published 9 times/year covering motorcycling—tour and travel. Estab. 1993. Circ. 30,000. Pays on publication. Publishes ms an average of 6 months after acceptance. Byline given. Editorial lead time 4 months. Submit seasonal material 6 months in advance. Accepts simultaneous submissions. Accepts queries by mail, fax. Writer's guidelines free.

Nonfiction: How-to (motorcycle, camping, travel), interview/profile (motorcycle related), new product, photo feature (motorcycle events or gathering places with minimum of 1,000 words text), travel. No fiction. **Buys 100 mss/year.** Query with published clips or send complete ms with photos. Length: 1,000-3,500 words. **Pays $150-350.** Sometimes pays writers of product reviews with products.

Photos: Send photos with submission (slides preferred, prints accepted, b&w contact sheets for how-to). Offers no additional payment for photos accepted with ms. Captions required. Buys one-time rights.

Columns/Departments: Reviews (products, media, all motorcycle related), 600 words plus photo. Query with published clips or send complete ms. **Pays $50-150.**

Fillers: Facts.

N $ $ OUTLAW B:KER, Outlaw Biker Enterprises, Inc., 5 Marine View Plaza, Suite 207, Hoboken NJ 07030. (201)653-2700. Fax: (201)653-7892. E-mail: tattoo1@ix.netcom. Website: www.outlawbiker.com. **Contact:** Chris Miller, editor. **50% freelance written.** Magazine published 10 times per year covering bikers and their lifestyle. "All writers must be insiders of biker lifestyle. Features include coverage of biker events, profiles and humor." Estab. 1983. Circ. 150,000. Pays on publication. Publishes ms an average of 3 months after acceptance. Byline given. Buys first rights. Editorial lead time 3 months. Submit seasonal material 5 months in advance. Accepts queries by mail, e-mail, fax. Accepts simultaneous submissions. Responds in 2 weeks to queries; 2 months to mss. Sample copy for $4.99. Writer's guidelines for #10 SASE.

Nonfiction: Historical/nostalgic, humor, new product, personal experience, photo feature, travel. Special issues: Daytona Special, Sturgis Special (annual bike runs). No first time experiences—our readers already know. **Buys 10-12 mss/year.** Send complete ms with SASE. Length: 100-1,000 words. **Pays $50-200.**

Reprints: Accepts previously published submissions.

Photos: Send photos with submission. Reviews transparencies and prints. Offers $0-10/photo. Captions, model releases and identification of subjects required. Buys one-time rights.

Columns/Departments: Buys 10-12 mss/year. Send complete ms with SASE. **Pays $25-50.**

Fiction: Adventure, erotica, fantasy, historical, horror, humorous, romance, science fiction, slice-of-life vignettes, suspense. No racism. **Buys 10-12 mss/year.** Send complete ms. Length: 500-2,500 words. **Pays $50-200.**

Poetry: Avant garde, free verse, haiku, light verse, traditional. **Buys 10-12 poems/year.** Submit maximum 12 poems. Length: 2-1,000 lines. **Pays $10-25.**

Fillers: Anecdotes, facts, gags to be illustrated by cartoonist, newsbreaks, short humor. **Buys 10-12/year.** Length: 500-2,000 words. **Pays $10-25.**

■ The online version of *Outlaw Biker* carries original content not found in the print edition. Contact: Chris Miller.

Tips: "Writers must be insiders of the biker lifestyle. Manuscripts with accompanying photographs as art are given higher priority."

$ RIDER, TL Enterprises, Inc., 2575 Vista Del Mar Dr., Ventura CA 93001. (805)667-4100. Fax: (805)667-4378. E-mail: editor@ridermagazine.com. Managing Editor: Donya Carlson. **Contact:** Mark Tuttle, Jr., editor. **50% freelance written.** Monthly magazine on motorcycling. "*Rider* serves owners and enthusiasts of road and street motorcycling, focusing on touring, commuting, camping and general sport street riding." Estab. 1974. Circ. 140,000. Pays on publication. Publishes ms an average of 6-12 months after acceptance. Byline given. Offers 25% kill fee. Buys first North American serial rights. Editorial lead time 4 months. Submit seasonal material 6 months in advance. Responds in 2 months. Sample copy for $2.95. Writer's guidelines for #10 SASE.

o⊸ "The articles we do buy often share the following characteristics: 1. The writer queried us in advance by regular mail (not by telephone or e-mail) to see if we needed or wanted the story. 2. The story was well written and of proper length. 3. The story had sharp, uncluttered photos taken with the proper film—*Rider* does not buy stories without photos."

Nonfiction: General interest, historical/nostalgic, how-to (re: motorcycling), humor, interview/profile, personal experience. Does not want to see "fiction or articles on 'How I Began Motorcycling.'" **Buys 30 mss/year.** Query. Length: 500-1,500 words. **Pays $100 minimum for unsolicited articles.**

Photos: Send photos with submission. Reviews contact sheets, transparencies and 5×7 prints (b&w only). Offers no additional payment for photos accepted with ms. Captions required. Buys one-time rights.

Columns/Departments: Rides, Rallies & Clubs (favorite ride or rally), 800-1,000 words. **Buys 15 mss/year.** Query. **Pays $150.**

Tips: "We rarely accept manuscripts without photos (slides or b&w prints). Query first. Follow guidelines available on request. We are most open to feature stories (must include excellent photography) and material for 'Rides, Rallies and Clubs.' Include information on routes, local attractions, restaurants and scenery in favorite ride submissions."

$ $ $ ROAD & TRACK, Hachette Filipacchi Magazines Inc., P.O. Box 1757, 1499 Monrovia Ave., Newport Beach CA 92663. (949)720-5300. Fax: (949)631-2757. Editor: Thomas L. Bryant. **Contact:** Ellida Maki, managing editor. **25% freelance written.** Monthly automotive magazine. Estab. 1947. Circ. 740,000. Pays on publication. Publishes ms an average of 6 months after acceptance. Kill fee varies. Buys first rights. Editorial lead time 3 months. Responds in 1 month to queries; 2 months to mss.

Nonfiction: Automotive interest. No how-to. Query. Length: 2,000 words. Pay varies. Pays expenses of writers on assignment.

Photos: State availability of photos with submissions. Reviews transparencies, prints. Negotiates payment individually. Model releases required. Buys one-time rights.

Columns/Department: Reviews (automotive), 500 words. Query. Pay varies.

Fiction: Automotive. Query. Length: 2,000 words. Pay varies.

Tips: "Because mostly written by staff or assignment, we rarely purchase unsolicited manuscripts—but it can and does happen! Writers must be knowledgeable about enthusiast cars."

$ $ $ $ VIPER MAGAZINE, The Magazine for Dodge Viper Enthusiasts, J.R. Thompson Co., 31690 W. 12 Mile Rd., Farmington Hills MI 48334-4459. (248)553-4566. Fax: (248)553-2138. E-mail: jrt@jrthompson.com. **Contact:** Mark Giannatta, editor-in-chief. Editorial Director: John Thompson. **40% freelance written.** Quarterly magazine covering "all Vipers—all the time." Also the official magazine of the Viper Club of America. "Speak to *VM* readers from a basis of Viper knowledge and enthusiasm. We take an honest, journalistic approach to all stories, but we're demonstrably and understandably proud of the Dodge Viper sports car, its manufacturer and employees." Estab. 1995. Circ. 15,000. **Pays on acceptance.** Publishes ms an average of 4 months after acceptance. Byline given. Buys first rights or second serial (reprint) rights. Editorial lead time 5 months. Submit seasonal material 6 months in advance. Query by mail, e-mail, fax, phone. Responds in 1 week. Writer's guidelines for #10 SASE or by e-mail.

Nonfiction: Query. Length: 400-1,500 words. **Pays $1/word.** Sometimes pays expenses of writers on assignment.

Reprints: Send information about when and where the article previously appeared. Payment varies.

Photos: State availability or send photos with submission. Negotiates payment individually. Captions, model releases and identification of subjects required. Buys all rights.

Columns/Departments: SnakeBites (coverage of Viper Club of America events such as local chapter activities, fundraising, track days, etc.), under 200 words; Competition (competitive Viper events such as road-racing, drag-racing, etc.), under 200 words. **Pays $1/word.**

Fillers: Anecdotes, facts, gags to be illustrated by cartoonist, newsbreaks, short humor. Length: 25-100 words. **Pays $1/word.**

Tips: "Being a Viper owner is a good start, since you have been exposed to our 'culture' and probably receive the magazine. This is an even more specialized magazine than traditional auto-buff books, so knowing Vipers is essential."

AVIATION

Professional and private pilots and aviation enthusiasts read the publications in this section. Editors want material for audiences knowledgeable about commercial aviation. Magazines for passengers of commercial airlines are grouped in the Inflight category. Technical aviation and space journals and publications for airport operators, aircraft dealers and others in aviation businesses are listed under Aviation & Space in the Trade section.

$ $ $ $ AIR & SPACE/SMITHSONIAN MAGAZINE, 370 L'Enfant Promenade SW, 10th Floor, Washington DC 20024-2518. (202)287-3733. Fax: (202)287-3163. E-mail: editors@airspacemag.com. Website: www.airspacemag.com. Editor: George Larson. **Contact:** Linda Shiner, executive editor (features); Pat Trenner, senior editor (departments). **80% freelance written.** Prefers to work with published/established writers. Bimonthly magazine covering aviation and aerospace for a non-technical audience. "The emphasis is on the human rather than the technological, on the ideas behind the events. Features are slanted to a technically curious, but not necessarily technically knowledgeable audience.

We are looking for unique angles to aviation/aerospace stories, history, events, personalities, current and future technologies, that emphasize the human-interest aspect." Estab. 1985. Circ. 240,000. **Pays on acceptance.** Byline given. Offers kill fee. Buys first North American serial rights. Adapts from soon to be published books. Accepts queries by mail, e-mail, fax. Responds in 3 months. Sample copy for $5. Guidelines for #10 SASE or on website.

> **O→** "We're looking for 'reader service' articles—a collection of helpful hints and interviews with experts that would help our readers enjoy their interest in aviation. An example: An article telling readers how they could learn more about the space shuttle, where to visit, how to invite an astronaut to speak to their schools, what books are most informative, etc. A good place to break in is our 'Soundings' department."

Nonfiction: Book excerpts, essays, general interest (on aviation/aerospace), historical/nostalgic, humor, photo feature, technical. The editors are actively seeking stories covering space and general or business aviation. **Buys 50 mss/year.** Query with published clips. Length: 1,500-3,000 words. **Pays $1,500-3,000 average.** Pays expenses of writers on assignment.

> ● Ranked as one of the best markets for freelance writers in *Writer's Yearbook* magazine's annual "Top 100 Markets," January 2000.

Photos: State availability of illustrations with submission. Reviews 35mm transparencies. Refuses unsolicited material.
Columns/Departments: Above and Beyond (first person), 1,500-2,000 words; Flights and Fancy (whimsy), approximately 800 words. **Buys 25 mss/year.** Query with published clips. **Pays $1,000 maximum.** Soundings (brief items, timely but not breaking news), 500-700 words. **Pays $150-300.**

> ▣ The online version carries original content not found in the print edition. Contact: Linda Shiner, Pat Trenner.

Tips: "We continue to be interested in stories about space exploration. Also, writing should be clear, accurate, and engaging. It should be free of technical and insider jargon, and generous with explanation and background. The first step every aspiring contributor should take is to study recent issues of the magazine."

✭ $BALLOON LIFE, Balloon Life Magazine, Inc., 2336 47th Ave. SW, Seattle WA 98116-2331. (206)935-3649. Fax: (206)935-3326. E-mail: tom@balloonlife.com. Website: www.balloonlife.com. **Contact:** Tom Hamilton, editor-in-chief. **75% freelance written.** Monthly magazine for sport of hot air ballooning. Estab. 1986. Circ. 4,000. Pays on publication. Byline given. Offers 50-100% kill fee. Buys non-exclusive all rights. Submit seasonal material 4 months in advance. Responds in 3 weeks to queries; 1 month to mss. Sample copy for 9×12 SAE with $2 postage. Writer's guidelines for #10 SASE.
Nonfiction: Book excerpts, general interest, events/rallies, safety seminars, balloon clubs/organizations, how-to (flying hot air balloons, equipment techniques), interview/profile, new product, letters to the editor, technical. **Buys 150 mss/year.** Query with or without published clips, or send complete ms. Length: 1,000-1,500 words. **Pays $50-75 for assigned articles; $25-50 for unsolicited articles.** Sometimes pays expenses of writers on assignment.
Reprints: Send photocopy of article or short story or typed ms with rights for sale noted and information about when and where the article or story previously appeared. Pays 100% of amount paid for an original article or story.
Photos: Send photos with submission. Reviews transparencies, prints. Offers $15/inside photo, $50/cover. Identification of subjects required. Buys non-exclusive all rights.
Columns/Departments: Hangar Flying (real life flying experience that others can learn from), 800-1,500 words; Crew Quarters (devoted to some aspect of crewing), 900 words; Preflight (a news and information column), 100-500 words; **pays $50.** Logbook (recent balloon events—events that have taken place in last 3-4 months), 300-500 words; **pays $20. Buys 60 mss/year.** Send complete ms.
Fiction: Humorous. **Buys 3-5 mss/year.** Send complete ms. Length: 800-1,500 words. **Pays $50.**
Tips: "This magazine slants toward the technical side of ballooning. We are interested in articles that help to educate and provide safety information. Also stories with manufacturers, important individuals and/or of historic events and technological advances important to ballooning. The magazine attempts to present articles that show 'how-to' (fly, business opportunities, weather, equipment). Both our Feature Stories section and Logbook section are where most manuscripts are purchased."

$CESSNA OWNER MAGAZINE, Jones Publishing, Inc., N7450 Aanstad Rd., P.O. Box 5000, Iola WI 54945. (715)445-5000. Fax: (715)445-4053. E-mail: editor@cessnaowner.org. Website: www.cessnaowner.org. **Contact:** John Kronschnabl, senior editor. **50% freelance written.** Monthly magazine covering Cessna single and twin engine aircraft. "*Cessna Owner Magazine* is the official publication of the Cessna Owner Organization (C.O.O.). Therefore, our readers are Cessna aircraft owners, renters, pilots, and enthusiasts. Articles should deal with buying/selling, flying, maintaining, or modifying Cessnas. The purpose of our magazine is to promote safe, fun, and affordable flying." Estab. 1975. Circ. 6,000. Pays on publication. Publishes ms an average of 3 months after acceptance. Byline given. Buys first, one-time or second serial (reprint) rights or makes work-for-hire assignment on occasion. Editorial lead time 1 month. Submit seasonal material 3 months in advance. Accepts queries by mail, e-mail, fax, phone. Responds in 2 weeks to queries; 1 month to mss. Sample copy and writer's guidelines free or on website.
Nonfiction: Historical/nostalgic (of specific Cessna models), how-to (aircraft repairs and maintenance), new product, personal experience, photo feature, technical (aircraft engines and airframes). "We are always looking for articles about Cessna aircraft modifications. We also need articles on Cessna twin-engine aircraft. April, July, and October are always big issues for us, because we attend various airshows during these months and distribute free magazines. Feature articles on unusual, highly-modified, or vintage Cessnas are especially welcome during these months. Good photos are also a must." Special issues: Engines (maintenance, upgrades); Avionics (purchasing, new products). **Buys 24 mss/year.** Query. Length: 1,500-3,500 words. **Pays 7-11¢/word.**

Reprints: Send typed ms with rights for sale noted and information about when and where the article previously appeared.

Photos: Send photos with submission. Reviews 3 × 5 and larger prints. Captions and identification of subjects required.

Tips: "Always submit a hard copy or ASCII formatted computer disk. Color photos mean a lot to us, and manuscripts stand a much better chance of being published when accompanied by photos. Freelancers can best get published by submitting articles on aircraft modifications, vintage planes, restorations, flight reports, twin-engine Cessnas, etc."

$ FLYER, N.W. Flyer, Inc., P.O. Box 39099, Lakewood WA 98439-0099. (253)471-9888. Fax: (253)471-9911. E-mail: kirk.gormley@flyer-online.com. Website: www.flyer-online.com. **Contact:** Kirk Gormley, editor. **30% freelance written.** Prefers to work with published/established writers. Biweekly tabloid covering general, regional, national and international aviation stories of interest to pilots, aircraft owners and aviation enthusiasts. Estab. 1949. Circ. 35,000. Pays 1 month after publication. Publishes ms an average of 3 months after acceptance. Byline given. Buys one-time and first North American serial rights; on occasion second serial (reprint) rights. Submit seasonal material 2 months in advance. Accepts queries by mail, e-mail, fax, phone. Responds in 2 months. Sample copy for $3.50. Writer's and style guidelines for #10 SASE.

○→ Break in by having "an aviation background, being up to date on current events, and being able to write. A 1,000-word story with good photos is the best way to see your name in print.

Nonfiction: "We stress news. A controversy over an airport, a first flight of a new design, storm or flood damage to an airport, a new business opening at your local airport—those are the sort of projects that may get a new writer onto our pages, if they arrive here soon after they happen. We are especially interested in reviews of aircraft." Personality pieces involving someone who is using his or her airplane in an unusual way, and stories about aviation safety are of interest. Query first on historical, nostalgic features and profiles/interviews. Many special sections throughout the year; send SASE for list. **Buys 100 mss/year.** Query or send complete ms. Length: 500-2,000 words. **Pays up to $10/printed column inch maximum.** Rarely pays the expenses of writers on assignment.

Reprints: Accepts previously published submissions from noncompetitive publications, if so noted. Payment varies.

Photos: Shoot clear, up-close photos, preferably color prints or slides. Send photos with ms. Captions and photographer's ID required. Pays $10/b&w photo and $50/cover photo 1 month after publication.

Tips: "The longer the story, the less likely it is to be accepted. If you are covering controversy, send us both sides of the story. Most of our features and news stories are assigned in response to a query."

$ $ MOUNTAIN PILOT MAGAZINE, Wiesner Publishing Co. LLC, 7009 S. Potomac St., Suite 200, Englewood CO 80112. (303)397-7600. Fax: (303)397-7619. E-mail: ehuber@mountainpilot.p.com. Website: www.mountainpilot.c om. **Contact:** Edward Huber, editor. **50% freelance written.** Quarterly magazine covering mountain and high altitude flying. "*Mountain Pilot* is the only magazine that serves pilots operating or planning to operate in the mountainous states. Editorial material focuses on mountain performance—flying, safety and education." Considers anything on mountain flying or destination, also camping at mountain airstrips. Estab. 1985. Circ. 6,000. Pays on publication. Publishes ms an average of 3 months after acceptance. Offers $50 kill fee. Buys first North American and electronic rights. Editorial lead time 3 months. Submit seasonal material 6 months in advance. Accepts queries by mail, e-mail, fax. Responds in 2 weeks to queries; 1 month to mss. Sample articles available on website. Writer's guidelines for #10 SASE.

Nonfiction: Regular features include aviation experiences, technology, high-altitude maintenance and flying, cold-weather tips and pilot techniques. Also interested in how-to (fly in the mountains, make modifications to your aircraft or engine), new product, personal experience, photo feature, technical, travel. No fiction or articles not related to aviation. **Buys 18-35 manuscripts/year.** Query. Length: 250-1,000 words. **Pays $100/published page.** (includes text and photos).

Reprints: Send tearsheet or photocopy of article or short story and information about when and where the article previously appeared.

Photos: State availability of photos with submission (copies acceptable for evaluation). Reviews 3 × 5 transparencies and prints. Offers no additional payment for photos accepted with ms. Captions required. Credit line given. Buys all rights.

$ $ PIPERS MAGAZINE, Jones Publishing, Inc., N7450 Aanstad Rd., P.O. Box 5000, Iola WI 54945. (715)445-5000. Fax: (715)445-4053. E-mail: editor@piperowner.org. Website: www.piperowner.org. **Contact:** John Kronschnabl, senior editor. **50% freelance written.** Monthly magazine covering Piper single and twin engine aircraft. "*Pipers Magazine* is the official publication of the Piper Owner Society (P.O.S). Therefore, our readers are Piper aircraft owners, renters, pilots, mechanics and enthusiasts. Articles should deal with buying/selling, flying, maintaining or modifying Pipers. The purpose of our magazine is to promote safe, fun and affordable flying." Estab. 1988. Circ. 5,000. Pays on publication. Publishes ms an average of 3 months after acceptance. Buys first, one-time or second serial (reprint) rights or makes work-for-hire assignment on occasion. Editorial lead time 1 month. Submit seasonal material 3 months in advance. Accepts queries by mail, e-mail, fax, phone. Responds in 2 weeks to queries; 1 month to mss. Sample copy and writer's guidelines free.

Nonfiction: Historical/nostalgic (of specific models of Pipers), how-to (aircraft repairs & maintenance), new product, personal experience, photo feature, technical (aircraft engines and airframes). "We are always looking for articles about Piper aircraft modifications. We also are in need of articles on Piper twin engine aircraft, and late-model Pipers. April,

July, and October are always big issues for us, because we attend airshows during these months and distribute free magazines." Feature articles on unusual, highly-modified, vintage, late-model, or ski/float equipped Pipers are especially welcome. Good photos are a must. **Buys 24 mss/year.** Query. Length: 1,500-3,500 words. **Pays 7-11¢/word.**

Reprints: Send typed ms with rights for sale noted and information about when and where the article previously appeared.

Photos: Send photos with submissions. Reviews transparencies, 3×5 and larger prints. Offers no additional payment for photos accepted. Captions, identification of subjects required.

Tips: "Always submit a hard copy or ASCII formatted computer disk. Color photos mean a lot to us, and manuscripts stand a much greater chance of being published when accompanied by photos. Freelancers can best get published by submitting articles on aircraft modifications, vintage planes, late-model planes, restorations, twin-engine Pipers, etc."

$ $ PLANE AND PILOT, Werner Publishing Corp., 12121 Wilshire Blvd., Suite 1200, Los Angeles CA 90025. (310)820-1500. Fax: (310)826-5008. E-mail: editors@planeandpilot.com. Website: www.planeandpilotmag.com. Editor: Lyn Freeman. **Contact:** Jenny Shearer, managing editor. **100% freelance written.** Monthly magazine that covers general aviation. "We think a spirited, conversational writing style is most entertaining for our readers. We are read by private and corporate pilots, instructors, students, mechanics and technicians—everyone involved or interested in general aviation." Estab. 1964. Circ. 130,000. Pays on publication. Publishes ms an average of 3 months after acceptance. Byline given. Kill fee negotiable. Buys all rights. Submit seasonal material 4 months in advance. Responds in 2 months. Sample copy for $5.50. Writer's guidelines free or on website.

Nonfiction: How-to, new product, personal experience, technical, travel, pilot proficiency and pilot reports on aircraft. **Buys 75 mss/year.** Submit query with idea, length and the type of photography you expect to provide. Length: 1,000-1,800 words. **Pays $200-500.** Rates vary depending on the value of the material as judged by the editors. Pays expenses of writers on assignment.

Reprints: Send photocopy of article or typed ms with rights for sale noted with information about when and where the article previously appeared. Pays 50% of amount paid for original article.

Photos: Submit suggested heads, decks and captions for all photos with each story. Submit b&w photos in proof sheet form with negatives or 8×10 prints with glossy finish. Submit color photos in the form of 2¼×2¼ or 4×5 or 35mm transparencies in plastic sleeves. Offers $50-300/photo. Buys all rights.

Columns/Departments: Readback (any newsworthy items on aircraft and/or people in aviation), 100-300 words; Jobs & Schools (a feature or an interesting school or program in aviation), 1,000-1,500 words; and Travel (any traveling done in piston-engine aircraft), 1,000-2,500 words. **Buys 30 mss/year.** Send complete ms. **Pays $200-500.** Rates vary depending on the value of the material as judged by the editors.

Tips: "Pilot proficiency articles are our bread and butter. Manuscripts should be kept under 1,800 words."

$ $ $ PRIVATE PILOT, Y-Visionary, Inc., 265 S. Anita Dr., #120, Orange CA 92868. (714)939-9991, ext. 234. Fax: (714)939-9909. E-mail: bfedork@aol.com. Website: www.privatepilotmag.com. **Contact:** Bill Fedorko, editoral director or Amy Maclean, managing editor. **40% freelance written.** Monthly magazine covering general aviation. "*Private Pilot* is edited for owners and pilots of single and multi-engine aircraft." Estab. 1965. Circ. 85,000. Pays on publication. Publishes ms an average of 4 months after acceptance. Byline given. Offers 15% or $75 kill fee. Buys first North American serial rights. Editorial lead time 3 months. Submit seasonal material 6 months in advance. Accepts queries by mail, e-mail, fax. Responds in 2 months. Writer's guidelines for #10 SASE.

Nonfiction: General interest, how-to, humor, inspirational, interview/profile, new product, personal experience, travel, aircraft types. **Buys 12-15 mss/year.** Query. Length: 800-3,000 words. **Pays $350-650. Sometimes pays expenses of writers on assignment.**

Photos: State availability of photos with submission. Reviews 35mm transparencies. Negotiates payment individually. Captions, model releases, identification of subjects required. Buys one-time rights.

Fiction: Adventure, historical, humorous, slice-of-life vignettes, all aviation-related. **Buys 12-15 mss/year.** Query. Length: 800-3,500 words. **Pays $300-$600.**

Tips: "Send good queries. Readers are pilots who want to read about aircraft, places to go and ways to save money."

$ WOMAN PILOT, Aviatrix Publishing, Inc., P.O. Box 485, Arlington Heights IL 60006-0485. (847)797-0170. Fax: (847)797-0161. E-mail: womanpilot@womanpilot.com. Website: www.womanpilot.com. **Contact:** Editor. **80% freelance written.** Bimonthly magazine covering women who fly all types of aircraft and careers in all areas of aviation. Personal profiles, historical articles and current aviation events. Estab. 1993. Circ. 6,000. Pays on publication. Publishes ms an average of 5 months after acceptance. Byline given. Buys first North American serial rights. Editorial lead time 4 months. Accepts queries by mail, e-mail, phone. Sample copy for $3. Writer's guidelines for #10 SASE.

   O→ Break in with "interesting stories about women in aerospace with great photos."

Nonfiction: Book excerpts, historical/nostalgic, humor, interview/profile, new product, personal experience, photo feature. **Buys 35 mss/year.** Query with published clips or send complete ms. Length: 500-4,000 words. **Pays $20-55 for assigned articles; $20-40 for unsolicited articles; and contributor copies.**

Reprints: Send tearsheet or photocopy of article or short story or typed ms with rights for sale noted and information about when and where the article or short story previously appeared.

Photos: State availability or send photos/photocopies with submission. Negotiates payment individually. Captions, model releases, identification of subjects required. Buys one-time rights.

Fiction: Adventure, historical, humorous, slice-of-life vignettes. **Buys 4 mss/year.** Query with or without published clips. Length: 500-2,000 words. **Pays $20-35.**

Fillers: Cartoons. **Buys 6/year. Pays $10-20.**

■ The online version carries original content not found in the print edition. Contact: Editor.

Tips: "If a writer is interested in writing articles from our leads, she/he should send writing samples and explanation of any aviation background. Include any writing background."

BUSINESS & FINANCE

Business publications give executives and consumers a range of information from local business news and trends to national overviews and laws that affect them. National and regional publications are listed below in separate categories. Magazines that have a technical slant are in the Trade section under Business Management, Finance or Management & Supervision categories.

National

N ★ $ $ $ $ ACROSS THE BOARD, The Conference Board magazine, The Conference Board, 845 Third Ave., New York NY 10022-6679. (212)759-0900. Fax: (212)339-0214. E-mail: atb@conference-board.org. Website: www.conference-board.org. Editor: Al Vogl. Managing Editor: Matthew Budman. **Contact:** Kelley Allen, assistant to editor. **60% freelance written.** Monthly magazine covering business—focuses on higher management. *"Across the Board* is a nonprofit magazine of ideas and opinions for leaders in business, government, and other organizations. The editors present business perspectives on timely issues, including management practices, foreign policy, social issues, and science and technology. *Across the Board* is neither an academic business journal nor a 'popular' manual. That means we aren't interested in highly technical articles about business strategy. It also means we don't publish oversimple 'how-to' articles. We are an idea magazine, but the ideas should have practical overtones. We let *Forbes, Fortune,* and *Business Week* do most of the straight reporting, while we do some of the critical thinking; that is, we let writers explore the implications of the news in depth. *Across the Board* tries to provide different angles on important topics, and to bring to its readers' attention issues that they might otherwise not devote much thought to." Circ. 30,000. Pays on publication. Publishes ms an average of 4 months after acceptance. Byline given. Offers 20% kill fee. Buys all rights. Editorial lead time 6 months. Submit seasonal material 6 months in advance. Accepts queries by mail, e-mail, fax, phone. Accepts simultaneous submissions. Sample copy free. Writer's guidelines for #10 SASE or on website.

Nonfiction: Book excerpts, essays, humor, inspirational, interview/profile, opinion, personal experience. "No new product information." **Buys 50 mss/year.** Query with published clips or send complete ms. Length: 500-4,000 words. **Pays $50-2,500.** Sometimes pays expenses of writers on assignment.

Reprints: Accepts previously published submissions.

Photos: State availability of photos with submission. Reviews contact sheets. Negotiates payment individually. Captions and identification of subjects required. Buys one-time or all rights.

$ $ $ BUSINESS ASSET, BUSINESS SENSE, SMART BUSINESS, YOUR BUSINESS, Baumer Financial Publishing, 820 W. Jackson Blvd., #450, Chicago IL 60607. (312)627-1020. Fax: (312)627-1105. E-mail: baumerfpub@a ol.com. **Contact:** Elizabeth Seymour, editor. **50% freelance written.** Quarterly magazine covering small business and entrepreneurs. Estab. 1998. Circ. *Business Asset* 25,000; *Business Sense* 85,000; *Smart Business* 60,000; *Your Business* 15,000. Pays on publication. Publishes ms an average of 4 months after acceptance. Byline given. Offers 33% kill fee. Buys first North American serial rights. Editorial lead time 6 months. Submit seasonal material 6 months in advance. Accepts queries by mail, e-mail, fax.

Nonfiction: How-to (finance, legal, technology, marketing, management, HR, insurance), small business profiles. No humor, personal experience, religious, opinion, book excerpts, travel. **Buys 40 mss/year.** Query with published clips. Length: 800-2,000 words. **Pays 50¢/word.**

Photos: State availability of photos with submission. Offers no additional payment for photos accepted with ms. Identification of subjects required. Buys one-time rights.

Columns/Departments: Technology, Legal, Insurance, Marketing (for small business owners), 800-900 words. **Buys 20 mss/year.** Query with published clips. **Pays 50¢/word.**

N $ $ $ BUSINESS 2.0 MAGAZINE, Imagine Media, 150 N. Hill Dr., Brisbane CA 94005. Fax: (415)656-2483. E-mail: jdaly@business2.com. Website: www.business2.com. Managing Editor: Judy Lewenthal. **Contact:** James Daly, editor. Monthly magazine covering business in the Internet economy. Estab. 1998. Circ. 160,000. Pays on publication. Publishes ms an average of 3 months after acceptance. Byline given. Offers 20% kill fee. Buys all rights. Editorial lead time 2 months. Submit seasonal material 4 months in advance. Accepts queries by e-mail only. Accepts simultaneous submissions. Sample copy free.

Nonfiction: Essays, exposé, new product, opinion, technical, new business ideas for the Internet. **Buys 40-50 mss/ year.** Query with published clips. Length: 150-3,000 words. **Pays $1/word.** Pays expenses of writers on assignment.

🚫 **BUSINESS WEEK** does not accept freelance submissions.

$ $ ENTREPRENEUR MAGAZINE, 2445 McCabe Way, Irvine CA 92614. (949)261-2325. Fax: (714)755-4211. E-mail: entmag@entrepreneur.com. Website: www.entrepreneurmag.com. **Contact:** Peggy Reeves Bennett, articles editor. **60% freelance written.** "Readers are small business owners seeking information on running a better business. *Entrepreneur* readers already run their own businesses. They have been in business for several years and are seeking innovative methods and strategies to improve their business operations. They are also interested in new business ideas and opportunities, as well as current issues that affect their companies." **Pays on acceptance.** Publishes ms an average of 5 months after acceptance. Byline given. Buys first international rights. Submit seasonal material 6 months in advance of issue date. Accepts queries by mail, e-mail, fax. Responds in 3 months. Sample copy for $7 from Order Department or on website. Writer's guidelines for #10 SASE (please write "Attn: Writer's Guidelines" on envelope) or on website.

• *Entrepreneur* publishes the bimonthly *Entrepreneur International* which covers the latest in U.S. trends and franchising for an international audience. (This is not written for a U.S. audience.) They encourage writers with expertise in this area to please query with ideas. Sample copy $6.50 from Order Department.

Nonfiction: How-to (information on running a business, dealing with the psychological aspects of running a business, profiles of unique entrepreneurs), current news/trends and their effect on small business. **Buys 10-20 mss/year.** Query with clips of published work and SASE or query by fax. Length: 2,000 words. Payment varies. Columns not open to freelancers.

Photos: "We use color transparencies to illustrate articles. Please state availability with query." Uses standard color transparencies. Buys first rights.

▣ The online version carries original content not found in the print edition and includes writer's guidelines. Contact: Karen Axelton.

Tips: "Read several issues of the magazine! Study the feature articles versus the columns. Probably 75 percent of our freelance rejections are for article ideas covered in one of our regular columns. It's so exciting when a writer goes beyond the typical, flat 'business magazine query'—how to write a press release, how to negotiate with vendors, etc.— and instead investigates a current trend and then develops a story on how that trend affects small business. In your query, mention companies you'd like to use to illustrate examples and sources who will provide expertise on the topic."

$ $ ENTREPRENEUR'S BUSINESS START-UPS, Entrepreneur Media, Inc., 2445 McCabe Way, Irvine CA 92614. (949)261-2083. Fax: (949)755-4211. E-mail: bsumag@entrepreneur.com. Website: www.bizstartups.com. **Contact:** Karen E. Spaeder, managing editor. **65% freelance written.** Monthly magazine for young entrepreneurs (age 23 to 35). "We target tech-savvy, upscale and educated readers who are preparing to start a business within the next year or have started a business within the past 2 years. Articles cover ideas for hot businesses to start; how-to advice to help new entrepreneurs run and grow their businesses; cutting-edge technology, management and marketing trends; motivational topics and more." Estab. 1989. Circ. 250,000. **Pays on acceptance.** Byline given. Offers 20% kill fee. Buys first time international rights. Submit seasonal material 6 months in advance. Accepts queries by mail, e-mail. Responds in 3 months to queries. Sample copy for $3 and $3 shipping. Writer's guidelines for SASE (please write: "Attn: Writer's Guidelines" on envelope).

Nonfiction: "Our readers don't necessarily have tons of money, but they make up for it in attitude, energy and determination. They're seeking ideas for hot businesses to start; how-to advice to help them run and grow their businesses; cutting-edge articles to keep them on top of the latest business trends; and motivational articles to get (and keep) them psyched up. No matter what your topic, articles should be packed with real-life examples of exciting young entrepreneurs doing things in new and different ways, plus plenty of pull-outs, sidebars and tips that can be presented in an eye-catching style. Types of features we are seeking include: Psychological (staying motivated, sparking creativity, handling stress, overcoming fear, etc.); Profiles of successful young entrepreneurs with original, creative, outrageous ideas and strategies others can learn from; Operating articles (how-to advice for running a business, such as finding financing, choosing a partner, marketing on a shoestring, etc.); Issues (examination of how a current issue affects young entrepreneurs); Industry round-ups (articles covering a particular industry and highlighting several young entrepreneurs in that industry, for example, gourmet food entrepreneurs, cigar entrepreneurs, specialty travel entrepreneurs); Tech. We are always seeking people who can write interestingly and knowledgeably about technology." Feature length: 1,200-1,800 words. **Pays $500 and up for features, $100 for briefs.**

• Ranked as one of the best markets for freelance writers in *Writer's Yearbook* magazine's annual "Top 100 Markets," January 2000.

Reprints: Send tearsheet of article and info about when and where the article previously appeared. Pay varies.

Photos: Daryl Hoopes, art director. State availability of photos with submission. Identification of subjects required.

Columns/Departments: Biz 101 (management/operations topics such as management trends, legal issues, insuring your business and other things new entrepreneurs must know to run a successful business), 650-700 words; Hot Biz (spotlights a hot business to start. Examples include niche greeting cards, catering and personal coaching. The column explains why this industry is hot and its growth prospects, and spotlights several successful entrepreneurs who share their start-up secrets), 1,500 words.

Tips: "We are looking for irreverent, creative writers who can approach topics in new ways in terms of style, format and outlook. You must write in a way our audience can relate to. They want a lot of info, fast, with specifics on where to get more info and follow up. They're skeptical and don't believe everything they read. Tone should sound like a friend giving another friend the 'inside scoop'—not like a professor lecturing from an ivory tower. Humor helps a lot. How *not* to break in: Send a résumé without a query (I hate this!) or writing samples that are full of vague generalities."

■ $ $ $ $ **INDIVIDUAL INVESTOR**, Individual Investor Group, 125 Broad St., 14th Floor, New York NY 10004. (212)742-2277. Fax: (212)742-0747. Website: www.iionline.com. **Contact:** Paul Libassi, editor. **40% freelance written.** Monthly magazine covering stocks, mutual funds and personal finance. "Our readers range from novice to experienced investors. Our articles aim to be lively, informative, interesting, and to uncover 'undiscovered' investing opportunities." Circ. 500,000. **Pays on acceptance.** Publishes ms an average of 3 months after acceptance. Byline given. Buys all rights. Editorial lead time 2 months. Submit seasonal material 4 months in advance. Sample copy free.
Columns/Departments: Paul Libassi, editor. Educated Investor (investing basics and special topics), 1,500 words. **Buys 12 mss/year.** Query with published clips. **Pays up to $1/word.**
Tips: "Most ideas are generated inhouse and assigned to a stable of freelancers."

■ $ $ $ **INDUSTRYWEEK, The Management Resource**, Penton Media, Inc., 1100 Superior Ave., Cleveland OH 44114-2543. (216)696-7000. Fax: (216)696-7670. E-mail: ppanchak@industryweek.com. Website: www.industryweek.com. Editor-in-Chief: John R. Russell. **Contact:** Patricia Panchak, managing editor. **25% freelance written.** Biweekly magazine covering management issues. "*IndustryWeek* is a management magazine. It helps executives create more effective, more humane, and more profitable organizations. Every issue of *IndustryWeek* is edited for the management teams of today's most competitive manufacturing companies, as well as decision-makers in the service industries that support manufacturing growth and productivity." Estab. 1970. Circ. 233,000. **Pays on acceptance.** Publishes ms an average of 2 months after acceptance. Byline given. Offers 25% kill fee. Buys all rights. Editorial lead time varies. Accepts queries by mail, e-mail, fax, phone. "E-mail preferred, but all accepted." Responds in 1 month. Sample copy and writer's guidelines on website.
Nonfiction: Book excerpts, exposé, interview/profile. "No first person articles." **Buys 25 mss/year.** Query with published clips and résumé. Length: 1,800-3,000 words. **Pays average of $1/word for all articles; reserves right to negotiate.** Sometimes pays expenses of writers on assignment. Limit agreed upon in advance.
Photos: State availability of or send photos with submission. Reviews contact sheets, negatives, transparencies and prints. Negotiates payment individually. Captions and identification of subjects required. Buys one-time rights.
Tips: "Pitch wonderful ideas targeted precisely at our audience. Read, re-read, and understand the writer's guidelines. *IndustryWeek* readers are primarily senior executives—people with the title of vice president, executive vice president, senior vice president, chief executive officer, chief financial officer, chief information officer, chairman, managing director, and president. *IW*'s executive readers oversee global corporations. While *IW*'s primary target audience is a senior executive in a U.S. firm, your story should provide information that any executive anywhere in the world can use. *IW*'s audience is primarily in companies in manufacturing and manufacturing-related industries."

■ $ **THE NETWORK JOURNAL, Black Professional and Small Business News**, The Network Journal Communication, 139 Fulton St., Suite 407, New York, NY 10038. (212)962-3791. Fax: (212)962-3537. E-mail: tnj@obe1.com. Website: www.tnj.com. Editor: Njeru Waithaku. **Contact:** Cameron Brown, managing editor. **25% freelance written.** Monthly tabloid covering business and career articles. *The Network Journal* caters to Black professionals and small-business owners, providing quality coverage on business, financial, technology and career news germane to the Black community. Estab. 1993. Circ. 11,000. Pays on publication. Byline given. Buys all rights. Editorial lead time 2 months. Submit seasonal material 3 months in advance. Accepts queries by mail, e-mail, fax, phone. Accepts simultaneous submissions. Sample copy for $1 or on website. Writer's guidelines for SASE or on website.
Nonfiction: How-to, interview/profile. Send complete ms. Length: 1,200-1,500 words. **Pays $40.** Sometimes pays expenses of writers on assignment.
Reprints: Accepts previously published submissions.
Photos: Send photos with submission. Offers $20/photo. Identification of subjects required. Buys one-time rights.
Columns/Departments: Book reviews, 700-800 words; career management and small business development, 800 words. **Pays $25.**
　　　▣ The online magazine carries original content not found in the print version and includes writer's guidelines. Contact: Michael Prince, online editor.
Tips: "We are looking for vigorous writing and reporting for our cover stories and feature articles. Pieces should have gripping leads, quotes that actually say something and that come from several sources. Unless it is a column, please do not submit a one-source story. Always remember that your article must contain a nutgraph—that's usually the third paragraph telling the reader what the story is about and why you are telling it now. Editorializing should be kept to a minimum. If you're writing a column, make sure your opinions are well-supported."

■ $ $ **PERDIDO, Leadership with a Conscience**, High Tide Press, 3650 W. 183rd St., Homewood IL 60430-2603. (708)206-2054. Fax: (708)206-2044. E-mail: alex@hightidepress.com. Website: www.perdidomagazine.com. Managing Editor: Art Dykstra. **Contact:** Alex Lubertozzi, editor. **80% freelance written.** Quarterly magazine covering leadership and management as they relate to mission-oriented organizations. "We are concerned with what's happening in organizations that are mission-oriented—as opposed to merely profit-oriented. *Perdido* is focused on helping conscientious leaders put innovative ideas into practice. We seek pragmatic articles on management techniques as well as esoteric essays on social issues. The readership of *Perdido* is comprised mainly of CEOs, executive directors, vice presidents, and program directors of nonprofit and for-profit organizations. We try to make the content of *Perdido* accessible to all decision-makers, whether in the nonprofit or for-profit world, government, or academia. *Perdido* actively pursues diverse opinions and authors from many different fields." Estab. 1994. Circ. 6,000. Pays on publication. Publishes ms an average of 3 months after acceptance. Byline given. Buys first North American serial or second serial (reprint) rights. Editorial lead time 4 months. Submit seasonal material 6 months in advance. Accepts queries by mail, e-mail, fax. Accepts simultaneous submissions. Responds in 1 month. Sample copy for 6×9 SAE with 2 first-class stamps or on website. Writer's guidelines for #10 SASE or by e-mail.

Nonfiction: Book excerpts, essays, humor, inspirational, interview/profile. **Buys 12 mss/year.** Query with published clips. Length: 1,000-5,000 words. **Pays $70-350.**

Reprints: Accepts previously published submissions.

Photos: State availability of photos with submission. Reviews 5×7 prints. Negotiates payment individually. Captions, model releases and identification of subjects required. Buys one-time rights.

Columns/Departments: Book Review (new books on management/leadership), 800 words; Rewind, 750 words. **Buys 6 mss/year.** Send complete ms. **Pays $75.**

Tips: "Potential writers for *Perdido* should rely on the magazine's motto—Leadership with a Conscience—as a starting point for ideas. We're looking for thoughtful reflections or management that help people succeed. We're not asking for step-by-step recipes—'do this, do that.' In *Perdido*, we want readers to find thought-provoking, open-minded explorations of the moral dimensions of leadership from a socially aware, progressive perspective."

N $ $ $ $ SUCCESS, Success Publishing, Inc., 150 Fayetteville St. Mail, Suite 1110, Raleigh NC 27601. Fax: (919)807-1299. E-mail: info@successmagazine.com. Website: www.Successmagazine.com. Editor: Ripley Hotch. Managing Editor: Mike Foley. **Contact:** See website for specific sections. **30% freelance written.** Monthly magazine for business entrepreneurs. "We provide tools, advice, and encouragement to entrepreneurs in small and midsized businesses." Estab. 1891. Circ. 350,000. Publishes ms an average of 2 months after acceptance. Byline given. Offers 25% kill fee. Buys first North American serial or electronic rights. Editorial lead time 4 months. Submit seasonal material 4 months in advance. Accepts queries by mail, e-mail. Responds in 2 weeks to queries.

Nonfiction: Interview/profile, opinion, personal experience. **Buys 60 mss/year.** Query with published clips. Length: 100-1,400 words. **Pays $50-3,000.** Sometimes pays expenses of writers on assignment.

Photos: State availability of photos with submission. Reviews contact sheets and 35mm transparencies. Negotiates payment individually. Identification of subjects required. Buys one-time rights plus payment for electronic use.

Columns/Departments: Trends, tips, ideas, 100 words; Why I Love What I Do (first person from entrepreneur about how he/she started), 800 words; Mavericks (entrepreneurs who do things in an unusual way), 800 words; and Out Front (young, fast-rising companies worth watching), 300 words. **Buys 20 mss/year.** Query. **Pays $50-1,000.**

Tips: "We include lengthy guidelines on our website and encourage you to read them. We do not like phone queries; there's simply no way to respond to them. We prefer well-thought-out queries with evidence that you can provide what you say. We don't like to work with first-timers. We are looking for fresh approaches (who isn't?) and will accept pieces that surprise us with unusual approaches. We will, for example, accept humor pieces, including parodies and satire."

$ $ TECHNICAL ANALYSIS OF STOCKS & COMMODITIES, The Trader's Magazine, Technical Analysis, Inc., 4757 California Ave. SW, Seattle WA 98116-4499. (206)938-0570. Fax: (206)938-1307. E-mail: editor@traders.com. Website: www.traders.com. Publisher: Jack K. Hutson. **Contact:** John Sweeney, editor. **85% freelance written.** Eager to work with new/unpublished writers. Magazine covers methods of investing and trading stocks, bonds and commodities (futures), options, mutual funds, and precious metals. Estab. 1982. Circ. 65,000. Pays on publication. Publishes ms an average of 6 months after acceptance. Byline given. Buys all rights; however, second serial (reprint) rights revert to the author, provided copyright credit is given. Responds in 1 month. Sample copy for $5. Writer's guidelines for #10 SASE or on website.

Nonfiction: Reviews (new software or hardware that can make a trader's life easier, comparative reviews of software books, services, etc.); how-to (trade); technical (trading and software aids to trading); utilities (charting or computer programs, surveys, statistics or information to help the trader study or interpret market movements); humor (unusual incidents of market occurrences, cartoons). "No newsletter-type, buy-sell recommendations. The article subject must relate to trading psychology, technical analysis, charting or a numerical technique used to trade securities or futures. Virtually requires graphics with every article." **Buys 150 mss/year.** Query with published clips if available or send complete ms. Length: 1,000-4,000 words. **Pays $100-500.** (Applies per inch base rate and premium rate—write for information.) Sometimes pays expenses of writers on assignment.

Reprints: Send tearsheet or photocopy of article or typed ms with rights for sale noted and information about when and where the article appeared.

Photos: Christine M. Morrison, art director. State availability of art or photos. Pays $60-350 for b&w or color negatives with prints or positive slides. Captions, model releases and identification of subjects required. Buys one-time and reprint rights.

Columns/Departments: Buys 100 mss/year. Query. Length: 800-1,600 words. **Pays $50-300.**

Fillers: Karen Wasserman, fillers editor. Cartoons on investment humor. Must relate to trading stocks, bonds, options, mutual funds, commodities, or precious metals. **Buys 20/year.** Length: 500 words. **Pays $20-50.**

Tips: "Describe how to use technical analysis, charting or computer work in day-to-day trading of stocks, bonds, commodities, options, mutual funds or precious metals. A blow-by-blow account of how a trade was made, including the trader's thought processes, is the very best-received story by our subscribers. One of our primary considerations is to instruct in a manner that the layperson can comprehend. We are not hypercritical of writing style."

$ $ $ WORDS FOR SALE, 1149 Granada Ave., Salinas CA 93906. **Contact:** Lorna Gilbert, submission editor.

Nonfiction: "Since 1968, we have sold almost every kind of written material to a wide variety of individual and corporate clients. We deal in both the written as well as the spoken word, from humorous one liners and nightclub acts, to informative medical brochures, political speeches, and almost everything in between. We are not agents. We are a company that provides original written material created especially for the specific needs of our current clients. Therefore, do not send us a sample of your work. As good as it may be, it is almost certainly unrelated to our current needs. Instead begin by finding out what our clients want and write it for them. What could be simpler? It gets even better: *We buy sentences!* That's right. Forget conceiving, composing, editing and polishing endless drafts of magazine articles or book manuscripts. Simply create the type of sentence or sentences we're looking for and we'll buy one or more of them. We respond promptly. We pay promptly." **Pays $1 and up/sentence. Pays on acceptance.** All submissions must include SASE or they will not be returned.

Tips: "The key to your selling something to us, is to *first* find out *exactly* what we are currently buying. To do this simply mail us a #10 SASE and we will send you a list of what we are eager to buy at this time."

$ $ $ YOUR MONEY, Consumers Digest Inc., 8001 Lincoln Ave., 6th Floor, Skokie IL 60077-2403. (847)763-9200. Fax: (847)763-0200. E-mail: bhessel@consumersdigest.com. Website: www.consumersdigest.com. **Contact:** Brooke Hessel, assistant editor. **75% freelance written.** Bimonthly magazine on personal finance. "We cover the broad range of topics associated with personal finance—spending, saving, investing earning, etc." Estab. 1979. Circ. 500,000. **Pays on acceptance.** Publishes ms an average of 2 months after acceptance. Byline given. Offers 50% kill fee. Buys first rights and second serial (reprint) rights. Query by mail, e-mail, fax. Responds in 3 months (or longer) on queries. Do not send computer disks. Sample copy and writer's guidelines for 9×12 SAE with 4 first-class stamps. Writer's guidelines for #10 SASE.

- *Your Money* has been receiving more submissions and has less time to deal with them. Accordingly, they often need more than three months reporting time.

Nonfiction: How-to. "No first-person success stories or profiles of one company." Financial planning: debt management, retirement, funding education; investment: stocks and bonds, mutual funds, collectibles, treasuries, CDs; consumer-oriented topics: travel, car bargains, etc. **Buys 25 mss/year.** Send complete ms or query and clips. Include stamped, self-addressed postcard for more prompt response. Length: 1,500-2,500 words. **Pays 60¢/word.** Pays expenses of writers on assignment.

Tips: "Know the subject matter. Develop real sources in the investment community. Demonstrate a reader-friendly style that will help make the sometimes complicated subject of investing more accessible to the average person. Fill manuscripts with real-life examples of people who actually have done the kinds of things discussed—people we can later photograph. Although many of our readers are sophisticated investors, we provide jargon-free advice for people who may not be sophisticated. Articles must be thoroughly researched and professionally written. We ask writers to supply documentation: phone numbers of people interviewed, original sources of facts and figures, annual reports of recommended companies, etc. Sidebars, charts, tables, and graphs are frequently used, and these are expected from writers. Authors must be well-acquainted with the areas they discuss and should be prepared to render subjective and objective opinions about profit potential and risk."

Regional

$ $ ALASKA BUSINESS MONTHLY, Alaska Business Publishing, 501 W. Northern Lights Blvd., Suite 100, Anchorage AK 99503-2577. (907)276-4373. Fax: (907)279-2900. E-mail: info@akbizmag.com. Website: www.akbizmag.com. **Contact:** Debbie Cutler, editor. **90% freelance written.** Monthly magazine covering Alaska-oriented business and industry. "Our audience is Alaska businessmen and women who rely on us for timely features and up-to-date information about doing business in Alaska." Estab. 1985. Circ. 10,000. Pays on publication. Publishes ms an average of 4 months after acceptance. Byline given. Offers $50 kill fee. Buys first North American serial rights. Editorial lead time 5 months. Submit seasonal material 5 months in advance. Accepts queries by mail, e-mail, fax. Responds in 1 month. Sample copy for 9×12 SAE and 4 first-class stamps. Writer's guidelines free.

Nonfiction: General interest, how-to, interview/profile, new product (Alaska), opinion. No fiction, poetry or anything not pertinent to Alaska. **Buys approx. 130 mss/year.** Send complete ms. Length: 500-2,000 words. **Pays $150-300.** Sometimes pays expenses of writers on assignment. "Sometimes pays contributors in ad pay-cuts."

Reprints: Accepts previously published submissions.

Photos: State availability of photos with submission.

Columns/Departments: Required Reading (business book reviews), Right Moves, Alaska this Month, Monthly Calendars (all Alaska related), all 500-1,200 words. **Buys 12 mss/year.** Send complete ms. **Pays $50-75.**

Tips: "Send a well-written manuscript on a subject of importance to Alaska businesses. We seek informative, entertaining articles on everything from entrepreneurs to heavy industry. We cover all Alaska industry to include mining, tourism, timber, transportation, oil and gas, fisheries, finance, insurance, real estate, communications, medical services, technology and construction. We also cover Native and environmental issues, and occasionally feature Seattle and other communities in the Pacific Northwest."

◩ $ $ $ BC BUSINESS, Canada Wide Magazines & Communications Ltd., 4180 Lougheed Highway, 4th Floor, Burnaby, British Columbia V5C 6A7 Canada. (604)299-7311. Fax: (604)299-9188. **Contact:** Bonnie Irving,

editor. **80% freelance written.** Monthly magazine "reports on significant issues and trends shaping the province's business environment. Stories are lively, topical and extensively researched." Circ. 26,000. Pays 2 weeks prior to publication. Publishes ms an average of 2 months after acceptance. Byline given. Kill fee varies. Buys first Canadian rights. Editorial lead time 4 months. Submit seasonal material 4 months in advance. Accepts queries by mail, fax, phone. Accepts simultaneous submissions. Responds in 6 weeks. Writer's guidelines free.

Nonfiction: Query with published clips. Length: 800-3,000 words. **Pays 40-60¢/word,** depending on length of story (and complexity). Sometimes pays expenses of writers on assignment.

Photos: State availability of photos with submission.

N **⊠** **$BLUE RIDGE BUSINESS JOURNAL**, Landmark, Inc., 821 Franklin Rd. SW, Roanoke VA 24016. (540)985-0408. Fax: (540)343-7845. E-mail: dan@bizjournal.com. Website: www.roanokebiz.com. **Contact:** Dan Smith, editor. **75% freelance written.** Monthly regional business publication. "We take a regional slant on national business trends, products, methods, etc. Interested in localized features and news stories highlighting business activity." Estab. 1989. Circ. 15,000. **Pays on acceptance.** Publishes ms an average of 1 month after acceptance. Byline given. Buys all rights unless otherwise agreed. Editorial lead time 10 days. Accepts queries by mail, e-mail, fax. Responds immediately. Call the editor for sample copies and writer's guidelines.

Nonfiction: Regional business. Upcoming special issues include Health Care and Hospitals; Telecommunications; Building and Construction; Investments; Personal Finance and Retirement Planning; Guide to Architectural; Engineering and Construction Services; and Manufacturing and Industry. No columns or stories that are not pre-approved. **Buys 120-150 mss/year.** Query. Length: 500-2,000 words. **Pays $50-100.**

Reprints: Accepts previously published submissions.

Photos: State availability of photos with submission. Offers $10/photo. Captions and identification of subjects required. Buys all rights.

Tips: "Talk to the editor. Offer knowledgeable ideas (if accepted they will be assigned to that writer). We need fast turnaround, accurate reporting, neat dress, non-smokers. More interested in writing samples than educational background."

$BOULDER COUNTY BUSINESS REPORT, 3180 Sterling Circle, Suite 201, Boulder CO 80301-2338. (303)440-4950. Fax: (303)440-8954. E-mail: jwlewis@bcbr.com. Website: www.bcbr.com. **Contact:** Jerry W. Lewis, editor. **50% freelance written.** Prefers to work with local published/established writers; works with a small number of new/unpublished writers each year. Biweekly newspaper covering Boulder County business issues. Offers "news tailored to a monthly theme and read primarily by Colorado businesspeople and by some investors nationwide. Philosophy: Descriptive, well-written articles that reach behind the scene to examine area's business activity." Estab. 1982. Circ. 12,000. Pays on publication. Publishes ms an average of 1 month after acceptance. Byline given. Buys one-time rights and second serial (reprint) rights. Responds in 1 month to queries; 2 weeks to mss. Sample copy for $1.44.

Nonfiction: Interview/profile, new product, examination of competition in a particular line of business. "All our issues are written around three or four monthly themes. No articles are accepted in which the subject has not been pursued in depth and both sides of an issue presented in a writing style with flair." **Buys 120 mss/year.** Query with published clips. Length: 750-1,200 words. **Pays $50-150.**

Photos: State availability of photos with query letter. Reviews b&w contact sheets. Pays $10 maximum for b&w contact sheet. Identification of subjects required. Buys one-time rights and reprint rights.

Tips: "Must be able to localize a subject. In-depth articles are written by assignment. The freelancer located in the Colorado area has an excellent chance here."

N **BUSINESS JOURNAL OF CENTRAL NY**, CNY Business Review, Inc., 231 Wallton St., Syracuse NY 13202-1230. (315)472-3104. Fax: (315)478-8166. E-mail: editor@cnybusinessjournal.com. Website: www.cnybusinessjournal. com. **Contact:** Charles McChesney, editor. **35% freelance written.** Weekly newspaper covering "business news in a 16-county area surrounding Syracuse. The audience consists of owners and managers of businesses." Estab. 1985. Circ. 8,000. Pays on publication. Publishes ms an average of 2 months after acceptance. Byline given. Kill fee negotiable. Buys first rights. Editorial lead time 1 month. Accepts queries by mail, e-mail, fax. Sample copy and writer's guidelines free.

Nonfiction: Humor, opinion. Query. Length: 750-2,000 words. **Pay varies.** Sometimes pays in copies. Sometimes pays expenses of writers on assignment.

Photos: State availability of photos with submission. Reviews contact sheets. Negotiates payment individually. Captions, model releases, identification of subjects required.

Columns/Departments: Query with published clips.

▣ The online magazine carries original content not found in the print edition.

Fillers: Facts, newsbreaks, short humor. Length: 300-600 words. **Pay varies.**

Tips: "The audience is comprised of owners and managers. Focus on their needs. Call or send associate editor story ideas; be sure to have a Central New York 'hook.' "

$ $BUSINESS LIFE MAGAZINE, Business Life Magazine, Inc., 4101-A Piedmont Pkwy., Greensboro NC 27410-8110. (336)812-8801. Fax: (336)812-8832. E-mail: kmeekins@bizlife.com. Website: www.bizlife.com. **Contact:** Kay Meekins, editor-in-chief. **30% freelance written**. "*Business Life* is a monthly, full-color magazine profiling businesses and business people that have ties to the Piedmont Triad, are headquartered here, or have an impact on the lives

of local business people." Estab. 1989. Circ. 14,000. Pays on the 15th of the month of publication. Publishes ms 3 months after acceptance. Byline given. Offers ⅓ kill fee. Buys first rights and second serial (reprint) rights. Editorial lead time 2 months. Submit seasonal material 5 months in advance. Accepts queries by mail, e-mail, fax. Accepts simultaneous submissions. Responds in 3 weeks to queries. Sample copy for 9×12 SASE and $3 postage. Guidelines for SASE.

Nonfiction: Book excerpts, general interest, interview/profile, travel. No articles without ties to NC or the Piedmont Triad region (except travel). **Buys 45 mss/year.** Query with published clips. Length: 1,500-2,000 words. **Pays $250-300**.

Photos: State availability of photos with submission. Reviews transparencies (2×3). Negotiates payment individually. Captions and identification of subjects required. Buys one-time rights.

■ The online magazine carries original content not found in the print edition. Contact: Kay Meekins, online editor.

Tips: "Story should be of interest to readers in our area, either with a national angle that impacts people here or a more 'local' approach (a profile in the Piedmont Triad). We are primarily a regional publication."

N $ $BUSINESS NEW HAVEN, Second Wind Media Ltd., 1 Church St., New Haven CT 06510. Fax: (203)781-3482. E-mail: business@businessnewhaven.com. Website: www.businessnewhaven.com. **Contact:** Michael C. Bingham, editor. **33% freelance written.** Biweekly regional business publication covering the Connecticut business community. "*Business New Haven* is a business-to-business vehicle targeted to business owners and managers." Estab. 1993. Circ. 14,000. Pays on publication. Byline given. Buys one-time and all rights. Editorial lead time 1 month. Accepts queries by mail, e-mail, fax. Sample copy on website. Writer's guidelines by e-mail.

Nonfiction: Interview/profile, how-to, new product, technical. **Buys 40 mss/year.** Query with published clips. Length: 500-2,500 words. **Pays $25-200.** Sometimes pays expenses of writers on assignment.

Photos: State availability of photos with submission. Negotiates payment individually. Identification of subjects required. Buys all rights.

Tips: "We publish only stories specific to Connecticut business."

$ $BUSINESS NH MAGAZINE, 404 Chestnut St., Suite 201, Manchester NH 03101-1831. (603)626-6354. Fax: (603)626-6359. E-mail: bnhmag@aol.com. **Contact:** Matthew Mowry, editor. **50% freelance written.** Monthly magazine with focus on business, politics and people of New Hampshire. "Our audience consists of the owners and top managers of New Hampshire businesses." Estab. 1983. Circ. 13,000. Pays on publication. Publishes ms an average of 2 months after acceptance. Byline given. Query by e-mail, fax.

Nonfiction: Features—how-to, interview/profile. **Buys 24 mss/year.** Query with published clips and résumé. "No unsolicited manuscripts; interested in New Hampshire writers only." Length: 750-2,500 words. **Pays $75-350.**

Photos: Both b&w and color photos used. Pays $40-80. Buys one-time rights.

Tips: "I *always* want clips and résumé with queries. Freelance stories are almost always assigned. Stories *must* be local to New Hampshire."

$CHARLESTON REGIONAL BUSINESS JOURNAL, Setcom, Inc., P.O. Box 446, Charleston SC 29402. (843)723-7702. Fax: (843)723-7060. E-mail: info@crbj.com. Website: www.crbj.com. **Publisher:** William Settlemyer. **Contact:** Sheila Watson, associate editor. **60% freelance written.** Biweekly newspaper covering local business. "We publish articles of interest to small business owners, preferably with a local slant." Estab. 1994. Circ. 7,000. Pays on publication. Publishes ms an average of 1 month after acceptance. Byline given. Offers $40 kill fee. Buys all rights. Editorial lead time 1 month. Submit seasonal material 2 months in advance. Accepts queries by mail, e-mail, fax. Accepts simultaneous submissions. Responds in 2 weeks to queries. Sample copy on website.

Nonfiction: Interview/profile (business people), technical, other articles of interest to small business owners, women business owners. No how-to's. **Buys 100 mss/year.** Query with published clips. Length: 400-800 words. **Pays $40-145.**

Photos: State availability of photos with submission. Reviews e-mail photos (jpeg, 170 resolution minimum). Offers $30/photo. Identification of subjects required. Buys one-time rights.

$IN BUSINESS WINDSOR, Cornerstone Publications Inc., 1614 Lesperance Rd., Tecumseh, Ontario N8N 1Y3 Canada. (519)735-2080. Fax: (519)735-2082. E-mail: inbiz@mnsi.net. Website: www.inbizwin.com. **Contact:** Gordon Hillman, publisher. **70% freelance written.** Monthly magazine covering business. "We focus on issues/ideas which are of interest to businesses in and around Windsor and Essex County (Ontario). Most stories deal with business and finance; occasionally we will cover health and sports issues that affect our readers." Estab. 1988. Circ. 10,000. **Pays on acceptance.** Byline given. Buys first rights. Editorial lead time 3 months. Submit seasonal material 3 months in advance. Accepts queries by mail, e-mail, fax and phone. Responds in 2 weeks to queries; 1 month to mss. Sample copy for $3.50.

Nonfiction: General interest, how-to, interview/profile. **Buys 25 mss/year.** Query with published clips. Length: 800-1,500 words. **Pays $50-150.** Sometimes pays expenses of writers on assignment.

$ $INGRAM'S, Show-Me Publishing, Inc., 306 E. 12th St., Suite 1014, Kansas City MO 64106. (816)842-9994. Fax: (816)474-1111. **Contact:** Editor. **50% freelance written.** Monthly magazine covering Kansas City business/ executive lifestyle for "upscale, affluent business executives and professionals. Looking for sophisticated writing with style and humor when appropriate." Estab. 1975. Circ. 26,000. Pays 30 days from publication. Publishes ms an average of 2 months after acceptance. Byline given. Buys first rights and Internet rights. Editorial lead time 2 months. Submit seasonal material 3 months in advance. Responds in 6 weeks to queries. Sample copy for $3 current, $5 back.

Nonfiction: How-to (businesses and personal finance related), interview/profile (KC execs and politicians, celebrities), opinion. **Buys 30 mss/year.** Query with published clips. "All articles must have a Kansas City angle. We don't accept unsolicited manuscripts except for opinion column." Length: 500-3,000 words. **Pays $175-350 maximum.** Sometimes pays expenses of writers on assignment.

Columns/Departments: Say-So (opinion), 1,500 words. **Buys 12 mss/year. Pays $175 maximum.**

Tips: "Writers must understand the publication and the audience—knowing what appeals to a business executive, entrepreneur, or professional in Kansas City."

$ $ THE LANE REPORT, Lane Communications Group, 201 E. Main St., 14th Floor, Lexington KY 40507. (606)244-3522. Fax: (606)244-3555. E-mail: lanereport@aol.com. Website: www.lanereport.com. **Contact:** Adam Bruns, editorial director. **50% freelance written.** Monthly magazine covering statewide business. Estab. 1986. Circ. 14,000. Pays on publication. Byline given. Buys one-time rights. Editorial lead time 6 weeks. Submit seasonal material 3 months in advance. Accepts queries by mail, e-mail, fax. Accepts simultaneous submissions. Responds in 1 month. Sample copy and guidelines free.

Nonfiction: Essays, interview/profile, new product, photo feature. No fiction. **Buys 30-40 mss/year.** Query with published clips. Length: 500-2,000 words. **Pays $100-375.** Sometimes pays expenses of writers on assignment.

Reprints: Accepts previously published submissions.

Photos: State availability of photos with submission. Reviews contact sheets, negatives, transparencies, prints. Negotiates payment individually. Identification of subjects required. Buys one-time rights.

Columns/Departments: Copy Klatsch, Small Business Advisor, Financial Advisor, Exploring Kentucky, Perspective, Spotlight on the Arts. All less than 1,000 words.

   The online magazine carries original content not included in the print edition. Contact: Adam Bruns or Chris Taylor, online editors.

Tips: "As Kentucky's only business and economics publication with a *statewide* focus, we look for features that incorporate perspectives from the Commonwealth's various regions and prominent industries—tying it all into the national picture when appropriate. We also look for insightful profiles and interviews of entrepreneurs and business leaders."

N $ $ MASS HIGH TECH, Journal of New England Technology, American City Business Journals, 200 High St., Boston MA 02110. (617)478-0630. Fax: (617)478-0638. E-mail: editor@masshightech.com. Website: www.masshightech.com. Editor: Mark Pillsbury. Managing Editor: Rodney Brown. **Contact:** Matthew Kelly, special sections editor. **20% freelance written.** Weekly business newspaper covering New England-based technology companies. "*Mass High Tech* is a weekly newspaper about the business deals and products of New England technology companies, read by technology executives, engineers, professors and high-tech workers." Estab. 1983. Circ. 23,000 per week. Pays on publication. Publishes ms an average of 1 month after acceptance. Byline given. Offers $50 kill fee. Buys all rights. Editorial lead time 3 months. Accepts queries by mail, e-mail, phone. Sample copy and writer's guidelines free.

Nonfiction: Opinion, technical. "No product reviews." Query. Length: 700-900 words. **Pays $125-165.**

Reprints: Accepts previously published submissions.

Columns/Departments: E-commerce, Retailing, Stockwatch, Case Study, all 500 words. Query with published clips. **Pays 30¢/word.**

$ $ OKLAHOMA BUSINESS MONTHLY, (formerly Metro Journal), Langdon Publishing Co., 1603 S. Boulder, Tulsa OK 74119. (918)585-9924. Fax: (918)585-9926. E-mail: dayna@langdonpublishing.com. Website: www.okbusinessmonthly.com. **Contact:** Dayna Avery, associate editor. **10-20% freelance written.** Monthly business-to-business magazine covering all business topics and real estate. "*Oklahoma Business Monthly* is the only statewide business publication reaching the owner, president or CEO of virtually every Oklahoma business with annual revenue in excess of $1 million." Estab. 1999. Circ. 10,000. Pays on publication. Byline given. Offers 50% kill fee. Editorial lead time 2 months. Submit seasonal material 3 months in advance. Accepts queries by mail, e-mail, fax. Accepts simultaneous submissions. Sample copy free. Writer's guidelines by e-mail.

Nonfiction: Exposé, how-to (business related), interview/profile, new product, personal experience, photo feature. Query with published clips. Length: 500-1,000 words. **Pays 30¢/word. Pays expenses of writers on assignment.**

Reprints: Accepts previously published submissions.

Columns/Departments: E-commerce, retailing, stockwatch, case study. All 500 words. Query with published clips. **Pays 30¢/word.**

$ $ $ $ PROFIT, The Magazine for Canadian Entrepreneurs, Rogers Media, 777 Bay St., 5th Floor, Toronto, Ontario Canada M5W 1A7. (416)596-5016. Fax: (416)596-5111. E-mail: profit@cbmedia.ca. Website: www.profitguide.com. **Contact:** Ian Portsmouth, managing editor. **80% freelance written.** Magazine published 8 times/year covering small and medium business. "We specialize in specific, useful information that helps our readers manage their businesses better. We want Canadian stories only." Estab. 1982. Circ. 110,000. **Pays on acceptance.** Publishes ms an average of 2 months after acceptance. Byline given. Kill fee varies. Buys first North American serial rights and non-exclusive electronic rights. Submit seasonal material 6 months in advance. Accepts queries by mail, e-mail, fax, phone. Responds in 1 month to queries; 6 weeks to mss. Sample copy for 9×12 SAE with 84¢ postage (Canadian). Writer's guidelines free.

Nonfiction: How-to (business management tips), strategies and Canadian business profiles. **Buys 50 mss/year.** Query with published clips. Length: 800-2,000 words. **Pays $500-2,000 (Canadian).** Pays expenses of writers on assignment. State availability of photos with submission.

Columns/Departments: Finance (info on raising capital in Canada), 700 words; Marketing (marketing strategies for independent business), 700 words. **Buys 80 mss/year.** Query with published clips. Length: 200-800 words. **Pays $150-600 (Canadian).**

　　■ *Profit*'s online magazine carries original material not found in the print edition. Contact: Peter McDonald.

Tips: "We're wide open to freelancers with good ideas and some knowledge of business. Read the magazine and understand it before submitting your ideas—which should have a Canadian focus."

N $ $ TAMPA BAY BUSINESS JOURNAL, American City Business Journals, 4350 W. Cypress St., Suite 400, Tampa FL 33607. (813)873-8225. Fax: (813)876-1827. E-mail: tbbj@tbbj.com. Website: amcity.com. Mac McKerran, editor. **Contact:** Jackie McConnell, managing editor. **10% freelance written.** Weekly regional business newspaper. Estab. 1980. Circ. 13,000. Pays on publication. Publishes ms an average of 1 month after acceptance. Byline given. Offers $50 kill fee. Buys first North American serial rights. Editorial lead time 1 month. Responds in 1 week. Sample copy and writer's guidelines free.

Nonfiction: Interview/profile. **Buys 100 mss/year.** Query with published clips. Length: 1,500-3,000 words. **Pays $100-200.**

Photos: State availability of photos with submission. Reviews negatives. Negotiates payment individually. Identification of subjects required. Buys one-time rights.

Columns/Departments: Dave Szymanski, editor. Opinion (local issues), 1,000 words. Does not pay for opinion columns. Query.

N ★ $ $ TEXAS TECHNOLOGY, Power Media Group, 13490 TI Blvd., Suite 100, Dallas TX 75243. (972)690-6222, ext. 16. Fax: (972)690-6333. E-mail: editor@ttechnology.com. Website: www.ttechnology.com. **Contact:** Laurie Kline, editor. **95% freelance written.** Monthly magazine covering technology. "*Texas Technology* is a high-tech lifestyle magazine. We publish articles that discuss how technology affects our lives. Our audience is a mix of techies and mainstream consumers." Estab. 1997. Circ. 410,000. Pays on publication. Byline given. Offers $20 kill fee. Buys first North American serial, electronic, second serial (reprint) rights and makes work-for-hire assignments. Editorial lead time 3 months. Submit seasonal material 3 months in advance. Accepts queries by mail, e-mail. Accepts simultaneous submissions. Responds in 3 weeks to queries; 2 months to mss. Sample copy and writer's guidelines free.

Nonfiction: Essays, exposé, general interest, historical/nostalgic, humor, interview/profile, new product, technical. "No computer hardware articles." **Buys 50 mss/year.** Query with published clips. Length: 1,200-3,500 words. **Pays $75-350.**

Reprints: Accepts previously published submissions.

Photos: State availability of photos with submission. Reviews contact sheets. Negotiates payment individually. Captions, model releases and identification of subjects required. Buys all rights.

Columns/Departments: Tech Law (technology law), 800-2,000 words; New Online (new stuff on the Web/affecting the Web), 800-2,000 words; Career Monthly (high-tech/information tech career issues), 800-3,000 words; High Speed Notes (info on Internet connectivity), 800-2,000 words. **Buys 30 mss/year.** Query with published clips. **Pays $75-200.**

Tips: "Review the types of topics we cover. We are more mainstream and hip and less nitty-gritty technical. Our articles are fresh and sometimes off-beat, but they always address how technology is affecting our lives. We publish articles ranging from online shopping to wireless technology."

★ $ $ UTAH BUSINESS, The Magazine for Decision Makers, Olympus Publishing, 85 E. Fort Union Blvd., Midvale UT 84047-1531. (801)568-0114. E-mail: editor@utahbusiness.com. Website: www.utahbusiness.com. **Contact:** Oleah Clegg, editor. Associate Editor: Gail Anderson Newbold. **95% freelance written.** "*Utah Business* is a monthly magazine focusing on the people, practices, and principles that drive Utah's economy. Audience is business owners and executives." Estab. 1987. Circ. 35,000. Pays 2 weeks after publication. Byline given. Buys first, one-time, all rights and makes work-for-hire assignments. Editorial lead time 3 months. Submit seasonal material 5 months in advance. Accepts queries by mail, e-mail, fax. Accepts simultaneous submissions. Responds only if material is accepted. Sample copy for $5 and $8\frac{1}{2} \times 11$ SAE with 8 first-class stamps. Writer's guidelines for #10 SASE.

Nonfiction: How-to (business), interview/profile (business), new product, technical (business/technical), policy and politics. "No cake recipes. Nothing in first person. There is no self-only information." **Buys 50-70 mss/year.** Send complete ms. Length: 700-3,000 words. **Pays 20¢/word (cover story, other sections 16¢/word).** Sometimes pays expenses of writers on assignment.

Reprints: Accepts previously published submissions.

Photos: State availability of photos with submission. Reviews contact sheets, negatives, prints and transparencies. Offers no additional payment for photos accepted with ms. Captions, model releases and identification of subjects required. Buys one-time rights.

Columns/Departments: Query with published samples (unedited version requested as well). **Pays 20¢/word.**

Tips: "Use common sense; tailor your queries and stories to this market. Use AP style and colorful leads. Read the magazine first!"

CAREER, COLLEGE & ALUMNI

Three types of magazines are listed in this section: university publications written for students, alumni and friends of a specific institution; publications about college life for students; and publications on career and job opportunities. Literary magazines published by colleges and universities are listed in the Literary & "Little" section.

$ $ AMERICAN CAREERS, Career Communications, Inc., 6701 W. 64th St., Overland Park KS 66202. (913)362-7788. Fax: (913)362-4864. Website: www.carcom.com. **Contact:** Mary Pitchford, editor. **50% freelance written.** Quarterly high school and vocational/technical school student publication covering careers, career statistics, skills needed to get jobs. "*American Careers* provides career, salary and education information to middle school and high school students. Self-tests help them relate their interests and abilities to future careers. Articles on résumés, interviews, etc., help them develop employability skills." Estab. 1989. Circ. 500,000. **Pays on acceptance.** Byline given. Buys all rights and makes work-for-hire assignments. Editorial lead time varies. Submit seasonal material 6 months in advance. Accepts simultaneous submissions. Responds in 1 month. Sample copy for $3. Writer's guidelines for SASE.

O— Break in by "sending us query letters with samples and résumés. We want to 'meet' the writer before making an assignment."

Nonfiction: Career and education features related to 6 basic career paths: arts and communication; business, management and related technology; health services; human services; industrial and engineering technology; and natural resources and agriculture. "No preachy advice-to-teens articles that 'talk down' to students." **Buys 20 mss/year.** Query by mail only with published clips. Deadlines: June 1 (Fall); September 1 (Winter); December 1 (Spring). Length: 300-1,000 words. **Pay $100-$450.** Pays expenses of writers on assignment.

Photos: State availability of photos with submission. Reviews contact sheets, transparencies and prints. Negotiates payment individually. Captions, model releases and identification of subjects required. Buys all rights.

Tips: "Letters of introduction or query letters with samples and résumés are ways we get to know writers. Samples should include how-to articles and career-related articles. Articles written for teenagers also would make good samples. Short feature articles on careers, career-related how-to articles and self-assessment tools (10-20 point quizzes with scoring information) are primarily what we publish."

$ $ THE BLACK COLLEGIAN, The Career & Self Development Magazine for African-American Students, iMinorities.com, Inc., 140 Carondelet St., New Orleans LA 70130. (504)523-0154. Fax: (504)523-0271. E-mail: robert@black-collegiate.com. Website: www.black-collegian.com. Contact: Robert Miller, vice president/editor. **25% freelance written.** Magazine published biannually (October and February) during school year for African-American college students and recent graduates with an interest in career and job information, African-American cultural awareness, personalities, history, trends and current events. Estab. 1970. Circ. 109,000. Pays on publication. Buys one-time rights. Byline given. Submit seasonal and special interest material 2 months in advance of issue date. Accepts queries by mail, e-mail, fax. Responds in 6 months. Sample copy for $4 and 9×12 SAE. Writer's guidelines for #10 SAE.

Nonfiction: Material on careers, sports, black history, news analysis. Articles on problems and opportunities confronting African-American college students and recent graduates. Book excerpts, exposé, general interest, historical/nostalgic, how-to (develop employability), opinion, personal experience, profile, inspirational. Deadlines: June 1 (October issue) and September 1 (February issue). **Buys 40 mss/year** (6 unsolicited). Query with published clips or send complete ms. Length: 900-1,900 words. **Pays $100-500.**

Photos: State availability of or send photos with query or ms. Black & white photos or color transparencies purchased with or without ms. 8×10 prints preferred. Captions, model releases and identification of subjects required.

■ The online magazine carries original content not included in the print edition. Contact: Kathy De Joie, online editor.

Tips: Articles are published under primarily five broad categories: job hunting information, overviews of career opportunities and industry reports, self-development information, analyses and investigations of conditions and problems that affect African Americans, and celebrations of African-American success.

$ $ CAREER FOCUS, For Today's Rising Professional, Communications Publishing Group, Inc., 3100 Broadway, Suite 660, Kansas City MO 64111-2413. (816)960-1988. Fax: (816)960-1989. **Contact:** Jeanine Meiers, associate editor. **80% freelance written.** Bimonthly lifestyle magazine "devoted to career and business-minded Blacks and Hispanics (ages 21-54)." Estab. 1988. Circ. 250,000. Pays on publication. Byline often given. Buys first, one-time and second serial (reprint) rights. Submit seasonal material 6 months in advance. Accepts simultaneous submissions. Responds in 1 month. Sample copy for 9×12 SAE with 4 first-class stamps. Writer's guidelines for #10 SASE.

● The editor notes that if the writer can provide the manuscript on 3.25 disk, saved in generic ASCII, pay is $10 higher and chance of acceptance is greater.

Nonfiction: Business book excerpts, general interest, how-to, humor, inspirational, interview/profile, personal experience, photo feature, technical, travel. Looking for articles about changing careers as an adult, educational preparation for different careers, and up-and-coming professions. Length: 750-2,000 words. **Pays $150-400 for assigned articles; 12¢/word for unsolicited articles.** Sometimes pays expenses of writers on assignment.

Reprints: Send tearsheet of article or short story and information about when and where the article previously appeared. **Pays 10¢/word.**

Photos: State availability of photos with submission. Reviews transparencies. Pays $20-25/photo. Captions, model releases and identification of subjects required. Buys all rights.

Columns/Departments: Profiles (successful Black and Hispanic young adult, ages 21-40). **Buys 30 mss/year.** Send complete ms. Length: 500-1,000 words. **Pays $50-250.**

Fiction: Adventure, ethnic, historical, humorous, mainstream, slice-of-life vignettes. **Buys 3 mss/year.** Send complete ms. Length: 500-2,000 words. Pay varies.

Fillers: Anecdotes, facts, gags to be illustrated by cartoonist, newsbreaks, short humor. **Buys 10/year.** Length: 25-250 words. **Pays $25-100.**

Tips: For new writers: Submit full ms that is double-spaced; clean copy only. If available, send clips of previously published works and résumé. Should state when available to write. Most open to freelancers are profiles of successful persons including photos. Profile must be of a Black or Hispanic adult living in the US. Include on first page of ms name, address, phone number, Social Security number and number of words in article.

CHRISTIAN COLLEGE FOCUS, (formerly *Christian College Handbook*), Kipland Publishing House, P.O. Box 1357, Oak Park IL 60304. (708)524-5070. Fax: (708)524-5174. E-mail: kipland7@aol.com. Website: www.collegefocus.com. **Contact:** Phillip Huber, managing editor. **85% freelance written.** Annual magazine covering college planning. *"Christian College Focus* is a college planning guide for high school juniors and seniors and expresses the value of a Christian college or university education." Estab. 1994. Circ. 200,000. Pays on publication. Publishes ms 4 months after acceptance. Byline given. Buys all rights. Editorial lead time 4 months. Accepts queries by mail, e-mail, fax. Sample copy for $3. Writer's guidelines free.

    O⊶ Break in with "a well-written article that speaks the language of high school students without talking down to them."

Nonfiction: How-to, interview/profile, personal experience. First person and how-to features focus on all topics of interest to high schoolers planning for college. No fiction or poetry. **Buys 18-25 mss/year.** Query with published clips. Length: 800-1,200 words. **Pays 8-15¢/word.** Sometimes pays expenses of writers on assignment.

Photos: State availability of photos with submission. Negotiates payment individually. Captions, model releases, identification of subjects required.

Tips: "We are open to working with new, unpublished authors, especially college graduates, current college students, college professors, admissions personnel, career counselors, and financial aid officers. Visit our website to view articles previously published in *Christian College Focus.*"

$ $ CIRCLE K MAGAZINE, 3636 Woodview Trace, Indianapolis IN 46268-3196. (317)875-8755. Fax: (317)879-0204. E-mail: ckimagazine@kiwanis.org. Website: www.circlek.org. **Contact:** Shanna Mooney, executive editor. **60% freelance written.** Published 5 times/year. "Our readership consists almost entirely of above-average college students interested in voluntary community service and leadership development. They are politically and socially aware and have a wide range of interests." Circ. 15,000. **Pays on acceptance.** Buys first North American serial rights. Byline given. Accepts queries by mail, e-mail. Responds in 2 months. Sample copy and writer's guidelines for large SAE with 3 first-class stamps or on website.

Nonfiction: Articles published in *Circle K* are of 2 types—serious and light nonfiction. "We are interested in general interest articles on topics concerning college students and their lifestyles, as well as articles dealing with careers, community concerns and leadership development. No first person confessions, family histories or travel pieces." Query. Length: 1,500-2,000 words. **Pays $150-400.**

Photos: Purchased with accompanying ms. Captions required. Total purchase price for ms includes payment for photos.

Tips: "Query should indicate author's familiarity with the field and sources. Subject treatment must be objective and in-depth, and articles should include illustrative examples and quotes from persons involved in the subject or qualified to speak on it. We are open to working with new writers who present a good article idea and demonstrate that they've done their homework concerning the article subject itself, as well as concerning our magazine's style. We're interested in college-oriented trends, for example: entrepreneur schooling, high-tech classrooms, music, leisure and health issues."

◩ $ COLLEGE BOUND, The Magazine for High School Students By College Students, Ramholtz Publishing Inc., 2071 Clove Rd., Suite 206, Staten Island NY 10304-1643. (718)273-5700. Fax: (718)273-2539. E-mail: editorial@collegebound.net. Website: www.collegebound.net. **Contact:** Gina LaGuardia, editor-in-chief. **85% freelance written.** Bimonthly magazine "written by college students for high school students and is designed to provide an inside view of college life." Estab. 1987. Circ. 95,000. Pays on publication. Publishes ms an average of 4 months after acceptance. Byline given. Buys first and second rights; also buys electronic rights if an article is suitable to *The CollegeBound Network* (www.collegebound.net). Editorial lead time 4 months. Submit seasonal material 4 months in advance. Accepts queries by mail, e-mail. Accepts simultaneous submissions. Responds in 5 weeks. Sample copy and writer's guidelines for 9×12 SASE.

Nonfiction: How-to (apply for college, prepare for the interview, etc.), personal experience (college experiences). **Buys 30 mss/year.** Query with published clips. Length: 600-1,000 words. **Pays $70-100.**

Reprints: Send photocopy of article.

Photos: Send photos with submission. Reviews prints. Offers no additional payment for photos accepted with ms. Buys one time rights.

Columns/Departments: Passin' Notes (campus happenings, academic accolades, short profiles), 150-400 words; Cash Crunch (money-related tips, scholarship news, advice), 150-400 words; Personal Statement (first-person account of a college-related experience), 600-1,000 words; Show 'N Tell (a pictorial-based look at dynamite dorm rooms, on-campus activities, etc.; provide pictures with 25-150 word captions). **Buys 30 mss/year.** Query with published clips. **Pays $15-70.**

Fillers: Anecdotes, quick facts, short newsy items, short humor. **Buys 10/year.** Length: 50-200 words. **Pays $15-25.**

■ The online magazine carries original content not found in the print edition.

Tips: "College students from around the country (and those young at heart!) are welcome to serve as correspondents to provide our teen readership with both personal accounts and cutting edge, expert advice on the college admissions process and beyond. We're looking for well-researched articles packed with real-life student anecdotes and expert insight on everything from dealing with dorm-life, choosing the right college, and joining a fraternity or sorority, to college dating, cool campus happenings, scholarship scoring strategies, and other college issues."

■ **$ COLLEGE BOUND.NET, A Student's Interactive Guide to College Life**, Ramholtz Publishing, Inc., 2071 Clove Rd., Staten Island NY 10304. (718)273-5700. Fax: (718)273-2539. E-mail: editorial@collegebound.net. Website: www.collegebound.net. **Contact:** Gina LaGuardia, editor-in-chief. **60% freelance written.** "Online magazine for students making the transition from high school to college." Estab. 1996. Pays on publication. Publishes ms an average of 4 months after acceptance. Byline given. Buys first rights and second serial (reprint) rights. Editorial lead time 4 months. Submit seasonal material 4 months in advance. Responds in 2 months to queries. Writer's guidelines for #10 SASE.

Nonfiction: Query. Length: 300-700 words. **Pays $15-65.** Sometimes pays the expenses of writers on assignment.

Reprints: Send photocopy of article.

Photos: State availability of photos with submission. Reviews transparencies and prints. Offers no additional payment for photos accepted with ms. Captions and identification of subjects required.

Columns/Departments: Digital Details (technology), Money, Celeb 101 (campus success stories), Sports. Length: 300-500 words. **Buys 30 mss/year.** Query with published clips. **Pays $15-40.**

Fillers: Anecdotes, facts, newsbreaks, short humor. **Buys 10/year.** Length: 50 words.

Tips: "The tone of *The CollegeBound Network*'s content is light-hearted and informative. Imagine you're relating your experiences to a younger sibling or friend. You want to tell them 'how it really is' and give them helpful, expert pointers to make the transition between high school and college easier to handle. We recommend that you query us by structuring a proposal in the following manner: begin with the lead you expect to put on the article (make it catchy!); write a summary of your intended areas of coverage; give specifics about who you plan to interview, what types of real-life anecdotes you'll include, which resources you plan to utilize, and what conclusion the story might reach."

■ **$ $ COLLEGE PREVIEW, A Guide for College-Bound Students**, Communications Publishing Group, 3100 Broadway, Suite 660, Kansas City MO 64110. (816)960-1988. Fax: (816)960-1989. **Contact:** Jeanine Meiers, editor. **80% freelance written.** Quarterly educational and career source guide. "Contemporary guide designed to inform and motivate Black and Hispanic young adults, ages 16-21 years old about college preparation, career planning and life survival skills." Estab. 1985. Circ. 600,000. Pays on publication. Byline often given. Buys first serial and second serial (reprint) rights or makes work-for-hire assignments. Submit seasonal material 6 months in advance. Accepts simultaneous submissions. Responds in 1 month. Sample copy for 9×12 SAE with 4 first-class stamps. Writer's guidelines for #10 SASE.

● The editor notes that if the writer can provide the manuscript on 3.25 disk, saved in generic ASCII, pay is $10 higher and chance of acceptance is greater.

Nonfiction: Book excerpts or reviews, general interest, how-to (dealing with careers or education), humor, inspirational, interview/profile (celebrity or "up and coming" young adult), new product (as it relates to young adult market), personal experience, photo feature, technical, travel. Send complete ms. Length: 750-2,000 words. **Pays $150-400 for assigned articles; 12¢/word for unsolicited articles.** Sometimes pays expenses of writers on assignment.

Reprints: Send photocopy of article or short story or typed ms with rights for sale noted and information about when and where the article previously appeared. **Pays 10¢/word.**

Photos: State availability of photos with submission. Reviews transparencies. Offers $20-$25/photo. Captions, model releases and identification of subjects required. Will return photos—send SASE.

Columns/Departments: Profiles of Achievement (striving and successful minority young adults ages 16-35 in various careers). **Buys 30 mss/year.** Send complete ms. Length: 500-1,500. **Pays 10¢/word.**

Fiction: Adventure, ethnic, historical, humorous, mainstream, slice-of-life vignettes. **Buys 3 mss/year.** Send complete ms. Length: 500-2,000 words. Pay varies.

Fillers: Anecdotes, facts, gags to be illustrated by cartoonist, newsbreaks, short humor. **Buys 10/year.** Length: 25-250 words. **Pays $25-100.**

Tips: For new writers—send complete ms that is double spaced; clean copy only. If available, send clips of previously published works and résumé. Should state when available to write. Include on first page of ms name, address, phone, Social Security number, word count and SASE.

N ✪ **$ $ COMMUNITY COLLEGE WEEK**, CMA Publishing Inc., 10520 Warwick Ave., Suite B-8, Fairfax VA 22030. (703)385-2981. Fax: (703)385-1839. E-mail: scott@cmabiccw.com. Website: www.ccweek.com. Assistant Editor: Jamilah Evelyn. **Contact:** Scott W. Wright, editor. **80% freelance written.** Biweekly tabloid covering two-year colleges. "*Community College Week* is the nation's only independent newspaper covering news, features and trends at the country's 1,250 community, junior and technical colleges." Circ. 5,500. Pays on publication. Byline given. Offers $50 kill fee. Buys one-time rights. Editorial lead time 2 months. Submit seasonal material 2 months in advance. Accepts queries by mail, e-mail, fax. Responds in 2 weeks. Sample copy free. Writer's guidelines by e-mail.
Nonfiction: Book excerpts, interview/profile, opinion, photo feature. **Buys 260 mss/year.** Query with published clips. Length: 400-1,500 words. **Pays 25¢/word.** Sometimes pays expenses of writers on assignment.
Photos: State availability of photos with submission. Negotiates payment individually. Captions required. Buys one-time rights.
Columns/Departments: Pays 25¢/word.

✪ **$ $ DIRECT AIM, For Today's Career Strategies**, Communications Publishing Group, 3100 Broadway, Pen Tower, Suite 660, Kansas City MO 64110. (816)960-1988. Fax: (816)960-1989. **Contact:** Jeanine Meiers, editor. **80% freelance written.** Quarterly educational and career source guide for Black and Hispanic college students at traditional, non-traditional, vocational and technical institutions. "This magazine informs students about college survival skills and planning for a future in the professional world." Buys second serial (reprint) rights or makes work-for-hire assignments. Submit seasonal material 6 months in advance. Accepts simultaneous submissions. Responds in 1 month. Sample copy for 9×12 SAE with 4 first-class stamps. Writer's guidelines for #10 SASE.
• The editor notes that if the writer can provide the manuscript on 3.25 disk, saved in generic ASCII, pay is $10 higher and chance of acceptance is greater.
Nonfiction: Book excerpts or reviews, general interest, how-to (dealing with careers or education), humor, inspirational, interview/profile (celebrity or "up and coming" young adult), new product (as it relates to young adult market), personal experience, photo feature, technical, travel. Query or send complete ms. Length: 750-2,000 words. **Pays $150-400 for assigned articles; 12¢/word for unsolicited articles.** Sometimes pays expenses of writers on assignment.
Reprints: Send photocopy of article or typed ms with rights for sale noted and information about when and where the article previously appeared. **Pays 10¢/word.**
Photos: State availability of photos with submission. Reviews transparencies. Offers $20-25/photo. Captions, model releases and identification of subjects required. Will return photos.
Columns/Departments: Profiles of Achievement (striving and successful minority young adult age 18-35 in various technical careers). **Buys 25 mss/year.** Send complete ms. Length: 500-1,500. **Pays $50-250.**
Fiction: Publishes novel excerpts. Adventure, ethnic, historical, humorous, mainstream, slice-of-life vignettes. **Buys 3 mss/year.** Send complete ms. Length: 500-2,000 words. Pay varies.
Fillers: Anecdotes, facts, gags to be illustrated by cartoonist, newsbreaks, short humor. **Buys 30/year.** Length: 25-250 words. **Pays $25-100.**
Tips: For new writers—send complete ms that is double spaced; clean copy only. If available, send clips of previously published works and résumé. Should state when available to write. Include on first page of ms name, address, phone, Social Security number and word count. Photo availability is important."

✪ **$ $ DIVERSITY: CAREER OPPORTUNITIES & INSIGHTS**, CASS Recruitment Media/CASS Communications, Inc., 1800 Sherman Ave., Suite 404, Evanston IL 60201-3769. (847)448-1011. Fax: (847)424-9685. E-mail: pam.chwedyk@casscom.com. Website: www.casscom.com. **Contact:** Pam Chwedyk, editor. **75% freelance written.** Quarterly magazine covering "career planning and job-hunting for minorities, women and people with disabilities, who are college or university seniors preparing to enter the workforce or graduate school. Readers will be interested in white-collar professional positions in a variety of industries." Estab. 1967. Circ. 21,000. **Pays on acceptance.** Publishes ms an average of 3 months after acceptance. Byline given. Buys first North American serial rights. Editorial lead time 3 months. Accepts queries by mail, e-mail, fax. Responds in 3 weeks to queries; 1 month to mss. Sample copy for 10×12 SAE with 6 first-class stamps. Writer's guidelines for #10 SASE or by e-mail.
○┅ Break in with "a story targeted specifically to the concerns of women and minority college seniors who are getting ready to start their professional careers or go on to graduate school."
Nonfiction: How-to (job search and career management fundamentals), interview/profile, industry surveys, job/career/salary trends specific to minorities and women (e.g., workplace diversity). "We would like to see more articles *by* minority/women/disabled college students or recent grads." Special issues: Transitioning to Professional Life or Grad School (Summer 2001), Networking, Professional Associations and More (Fall 2001), Annual Industry Survey—Top Career Opportunities for Minorities and Women (Winter 2002). **Buys 20-30 mss/year.** Query with published clips. Length: 1,500-2,000 words. **Pays $400-550 for assigned articles; $350 for unsolicited articles.** Pays telephone interview expenses only.
Photos: State availability of photos with submission. Photo required for single-individual profiles. Offers no additional payment for photos accepted with ms. Identification of subjects required. Buys one-time rights. Contact editor for photo submission guidelines.

Columns/Departments: Columns are usually unpaid assignments.

Tips: "Remember our audience—college seniors who are minorities, women and persons with disabilities. Try to appeal to today's young, hip, Internet-savvy audience. Sources interviewed should reflect diversity."

$ $EQUAL OPPORTUNITY, The Nation's Only Multi-Ethnic Recruitment Magazine for Black, Hispanic, Native American & Asian American College Grads, Equal Opportunity Publications, Inc., 1160 E. Jericho Turnpike, Suite 200, Huntington NY 11743-5405. (516)421-9469. Fax: (516)421-0359. E-mail: info@aol.com. Website: http.//www.eop.com. **Contact:** James Schneider, editor. **70% freelance written.** Prefers to work with published/established writers. Triannual magazine covering career guidance for minorities. "Our audience is 90% college juniors and seniors; 10% working graduates. An understanding of educational and career problems of minorities is essential." Estab. 1967. Circ. 15,000, distributed through college guidance and placement offices. Pays on publication. Publishes ms an average of 6 months after acceptance. Byline given. Buys first rights. Editorial lead time 6 months. Submit seasonal material 6 months in advance. Accepts queries by mail, e-mail, fax, phone. Responds in 2 weeks to queries, 1 month to mss. Sample copy and writer's guidelines for 9×12 SAE with 5 first-class stamps.

Nonfiction: Book excerpts and articles (job search techniques, role models); general interest (specific minority concerns); how-to (job-hunting skills, personal finance, better living, coping with discrimination); humor (student or career related); interview/profile (minority role models); opinion (problems of minorities); personal experience (professional and student study and career experiences); technical (on career fields offering opportunities for minorities); travel (on overseas job opportunities); and coverage of Black, Hispanic, Native American and Asian American interests. **Buys 10 mss/year.** Query or send complete ms. Deadline dates: fall (June 10); winter (September 15); spring (January 1). Length: 1,000-2,000 words. **Pays 10¢/word.** Sometimes pays expenses of writers on assignment.

Reprints: Send information about when and where the article previously appeared. **Pays 10¢/word.**

Photos: Prefers 35mm color slides and b&w. Captions and identification of subjects required. Buys all rights. Pays $15/photo use.

Tips: "Articles must be geared toward questions and answers faced by minority and women students. We would like to see role-model profiles of professions."

$ $FIRST OPPORTUNITY, Today's Career Options, Communications Publishing Group, 3100 Broadway, Suite 660, Kansas City MO 64111. (816)960-1988. Fax: (816)960-1989. **Contact:** Jeanine Meiers, editor. **80% freelance written.** Resource publication focusing on advanced vocational/technical educational opportunities and career preparation for Black and Hispanic young adults, ages 16-21. Circ. 500,000. Pays on publication. Byline sometimes given. Buys first, one-time and second serial (reprint) rights or makes work-for-hire assignments. Submit seasonal material 6 months in advance. Accepts simultaneous submissions. Responds in 1 month. Sample copy for 9×12 SAE with 4 first-class stamps. Writer's guidelines for #10 SASE.

• The editor notes that if the writer can provide the manuscript on 3.25 disk, saved in generic ASCII, pay is $10 higher and chance of acceptance is greater.

Nonfiction: Book excerpts or reviews, general interest, how-to (dealing with careers or education), humor, inspirational, interview/profile (celebrity or "up and coming" young adult), new product (as it relates to young adult market), personal experience, photo feature, technical, travel. Looking for articles about volunteering (how it can prepare young adults for a career), education preparation for different careers, and management skills for young adults. Length: 750-2,000 words. **Pays $150-400 for assigned articles; 12¢/word for unsolicited articles.** Sometimes pays expenses of writers on assignment.

Reprints: Send photocopy of article or typed ms with rights for sale noted and information about when and where the article previously appeared. **Pays 10¢/word.**

Photos: State availability of photos with submission. Prefers transparencies. Offers $20-25/photo. Captions, model releases, identification of subjects required. Buys all rights.

Columns/Departments: Profiles of Achievement (successful minority young adult, age 16-35 in various vocational or technical careers). **Buys 30 mss/year.** Send complete ms. Length: 500-1,500. **Pays $50-250.**

Fiction: Adventure, ethnic, historical, humorous, mainstream, slice-of-life vignettes. **Buys 3 mss/year.** Send complete ms. Length: 500-5,000 words. Pay varies.

Fillers: Anecdotes, facts, gags to be illustrated by cartoonist, newsbreaks, short humor. **Buys 10/year.** Length: 25-250 words. **Pays $25-100.**

Tips: For new writers—send complete ms that is double spaced; clean copy only. If available, send clips of previously published works and résumé. Should state when available to write. Include on first page of ms name, address, phone, Social Security number and word count. Photo availability is important.

$I LOVE MY JOB!, Herbelin Publishing, P.O. Box 74, Riverbank CA 95367. Phone/fax: (209)869-6389. E-mail: herbelin@netfeed.com. Website: www.riverbankbooks.com. Managing Editor: Jocelyn Herbelin. **Contact:** Steve Herbelin, editor. **100% freelance written.** Online biweekly covering job- and workplace-related mini and short stories. Estab. 1997. Circ. 545. **Pays on acceptance.** Publishes ms an average of 1 month after acceptance. Byline given. Buys first North American serial or one-time rights. Editorial lead time 1 month. Submit seasonal material 1 month in advance. Accepts queries by mail, e-mail, fax. Accepts simultaneous submissions. Responds in 2 weeks to queries; 2 months to mss. Sample copy and writer's guidelines on website or by e-mail.

Nonfiction: Humor, inspirational. **Buys 50 mss/year.** Send complete ms. Length: 25-4,000 words. **Pays $25-100.**

Reprints: Accepts previously published submissions.

Fiction: Length: 2,000 words. **Pays $100.**
Tips: "Humorous, true anecdotes from the job and workplace are preferred."

N $ $ JOURNEY, A Success Guide for College and Career Bound Students, Communications Publishing Group, 3100 Broadway St., Suite 660, Kansas City MO 64111-2413. (816)960-1988. Fax: (816)960-1989. **Contact:** Jeanine Meiers, editor. **40% freelance written.** Biannual educational and career source guide for Asian-American high school and college students (ages 16-25) who have indicated a desire to pursue higher education through college, vocational and technical or proprietary schools. Estab. 1982. Circ. 200,000. Pays on publication. Byline sometimes given. Buys second serial (reprint) rights or makes work-for-hire assignments. Submit seasonal material 6 months in advance. Accepts simultaneous submissions. Responds in 2 months. Sample copy for 9×12 SAE with 4 first-class stamps. Writer's guidelines for #10 SASE.
   ● The editor notes that if the writer can provide the manuscript on 3.25 disk, saved in generic ASCII, pay is $10 higher and chance of acceptance is greater.
Nonfiction: Book excerpts or reviews, general interest, how-to (dealing with careers or education), humor, inspirational, interview/profile (celebrity or "up and coming" young adult), new product (as it relates to young adult market), personal experience, photo feature, sports, technical, travel. First time writers with *Journey* must submit complete ms for consideration. Length: 750-2,000 words. **Pays $150-400 for assigned articles; 12¢/word for unsolicited articles.** Sometimes pays expenses of writers on assignment.
Reprints: Send typed ms with rights for sale noted and information about when and where the article previously appeared. **Pays 10¢/word.**
Photos: State availability of photos with submission. Prefers transparencies. Offers $20-25/photo. Captions, model releases and identification of subjects required. Buys all or one-time rights.
Columns/Departments: Profiles of Achievement (striving and successful minority young adult, age 16-35 in various careers). **Buys 30 mss/year.** Send complete ms. Length: 500-1,500. **Pays $50-200.**
Fiction: Publishes novel exerpts. Adventure, ethnic, historical, humorous, mainstream, slice-of-life vignettes. **Buys 3 mss/year.** Send complete ms. Length: 1,000-3,000 words. **Pays $100-400.**
Fillers: Anecdotes, facts, gags to be illustrated by cartoonist, newsbreaks, short humor. **Buys 10/year.** Length: 25-250 words. **Pays $25-100.**
Tips: For new writers—must submit complete ms that is double spaced; clean copy only. If available, send clippings of previously published works and résumé. Should state when available to write. Include on first page your name, address, phone, Social Security number and word count. Availability of photos enhances your chances. "We desperately need more material dealing with concerns of Asian-American students."

N $ $ KANSAS ALUMNI, Kansas Alumni Association, 1266 Oread Ave., Lawrence KS 66044-3169. (785)864-4760. Fax: (785)864-5397. E-mail: ksalumni@kuaa.wpo.ukans.edu. Website: www.ukans.edu/~kualumni/. Editor: Jennifer Jackson Sanner. **Contact:** Chris Lazzarino, managing editor. **20% freelance written.** Alumni association magazine published bimonthly covering the University of Kansas alumni and related subjects. "Our mission is to keep members of the Kansas Alumni Association connected with the University of Kansas. We cover KU in a straightforward manner, presenting all manner of news and features about KU." Estab. 1902. Circ. 40,000. **Pays on acceptance.** Publishes ms an average of 2 months after acceptance. Byline given. Usually offers 50% kill fee. Buys first North American serial and electronic rights. Editorial lead time 4 months. Submit seasonal material 6 months in advance. Accepts queries by mail, e-mail. Responds in 4 weeks to queries; 2 months to mss. Sample copy and writer's guidelines free.
Nonfiction: Book excerpts, historical/nostalgic, humor, interview/profile, opinion, book reviews. **Buys 8-10 mss/year.** Query with published clips. Length: 500-2,000 words. **Pays $225-700.** Sometimes pays expenses of writers on assignment.
Photos: State availability of photos with submission. Reviews contact sheets and transparencies. Negotiates payment individually. Captions, model releases and identification of subjects required. Buys one-time rights.
Columns/Departments: Alumni profiles (interesting KU alumni), 500 words. **Buys 15 mss/year.** Query with published clips. **Pays $225.**
Tips: "We prefer first contact by mail, though e-mail or phone calls can be used. We usually start new writers with alumni profiles. We rarely assign material to new writers; we prefer to have them submit profile and article ideas."

$ $ $ NOTRE DAME MAGAZINE, University of Notre Dame, 538 Grace Hall, Notre Dame IN 46556-5612. (219)631-5335. Fax: (219)631-6767. E-mail: ndmag.1@nd.edu. Website: www.nd.edu/~ndmag. Managing Editor: Carol Schaal. **Contact:** Kerry Temple, editor. **75% freelance written.** Quarterly magazine covering news of Notre Dame and education and issues affecting contemporary society. "We are a university magazine with a scope as broad as that found at a university, but we place our discussion in a moral, ethical, spiritual context reflecting our Catholic heritage." Estab. 1972. Circ. 142,000. **Pays on acceptance.** Publishes ms an average of 1 year after acceptance. Byline given. Kill fee negotiable. Buys first serial and electronic rights. Accepts queries by mail, e-mail, fax. Responds in 2 months. Sample copy and writer's guidelines on website.
Nonfiction: Opinion, personal experience, religion. **Buys 35 mss/year.** Query with clips of published work. Length: 600-3,000 words. **Pays $250-1,500.** Sometimes pays expenses of writers on assignment.
Photos: State availability of photos. Reviews b&w contact sheets, transparencies and 8×10 prints. Model releases and identification of subjects required. Buys one-time and electronic rights.

Columns/Departments: Perspectives (essays, often written in first-person, deal with a wide array of issues—some topical, some personal, some serious, some light). Query with published clips or submit ms.

■ The online version carries original content not found in the print edition and includes writer's guidelines. Contact: Carol Schaal.

Tips: "The editors are always looking for new writers and fresh ideas. However, the caliber of the magazine and frequency of its publication dictate that the writing meet very high standards. The editors value articles strong in storytelling quality, journalistic technique, and substance. They do not encourage promotional or nostalgia pieces, stories on sports, or essays which are sentimentally religious."

$ $ OREGON QUARTERLY, The Magazine of the University of Oregon, 5228 University of Oregon, Chapman Hall, Eugene OR 97403-5228. (541)346-5048. Fax: (541)346-5571. E-mail: quarterly@oregon.uoregon.edu. Website: www.uoregon.edu/~oq. **Contact:** Guy Maynard. Assistant Editor: Kathleen Holt. **50% freelance written.** Quarterly university magazine of people and ideas at the University of Oregon and the Northwest. Estab. 1919. Circ. 100,000. **Pays on acceptance.** Publishes ms an average of 3 months after acceptance. Byline given. Buys first North American serial rights. Query by mail, e-mail. Responds in 2 months. Sample copy for 9×12 SAE with 4 first-class stamps or on website.

○─┐ Break in to the magazine with a profile (400 or 800 words) of a University of Oregon alumnus. Best to query first.

Nonfiction: Northwest issues and culture from the perspective of UO alumni and faculty. **Buys 30 mss/year.** Query with published clips. Length: 250-2,500 words. **Pays $100-750.** Sometimes pays expenses of writers on assignment.

Reprints: Send photocopy of article and information about when and where the article previously appeared. Pays 50% of the amount paid for an original article.

Photos: State availability of photos with submission. Reviews 8×10 prints. Offers $10-25/photo. Identification of subjects required. Buys one-time rights.

Fiction: Publishes novel excerpts.

Tips: "Query with strong, colorful lead; clips."

N $ $ $ OREGON STATER, Oregon State University Alumni Association, 204 CH2M Hill Alumni Center, Corvallis OR 97331-6303. (503)737-0780. E-mail: george.edmonston@orst.edu. **Contact:** George Edmonston Jr., editor. **20% freelance written.** Tabloid covering news of Oregon State University and its alumni. Estab. 1915. Circ. 111,000. **Pays on acceptance.** Byline given. Buys one-time rights. Editorial lead time 4 months. Submit seasonal material 3 months in advance. Responds in 2 weeks to queries; 3 months to mss. Sample copy and writer's guidelines free.

Nonfiction: General interest, historical/nostalgic, humor, inspirational, interview/profile, personal experience, photo feature. **Buys 40 mss/year.** Query with or without published clips. Length: 2,000 words maximum. **Pays $50-1,000.** Pays expenses of writers on assignment.

Photos: Send photos with submission. Offers no additional payment for photos accepted with ms. Captions, model releases and identification of subjects required. Buys one-time rights.

★ $ $ THE PENN STATER, Penn State Alumni Association, 141 W. Beaver Ave., Suite 15, University Park PA 16801. (814)865-2709. Fax: (814)863-5690. E-mail: pennstater@psu.edu. Website: www.alumni.psu.edu. **Contact:** Tina Hay, editor. **75% freelance written.** Bimonthly magazine covering Penn State and Penn Staters. Estab. 1910. Circ. 120,000. **Pays on acceptance.** Publishes ms an average of 4 months after acceptance. Byline given. Offers 50% kill fee. Buys first North American serial rights or second serial (reprint) rights. Web rights negotiable. Editorial lead time 3 months. Submit seasonal material 8 months in advance. Accepts simultaneous submissions. Accepts queries by mail, e-mail, fax. Responds in 3 months to queries. Sample copy and writer's guidelines free.

Nonfiction: Book excerpts (by Penn Staters), general interest, historical/nostalgic, humor (sometimes), interview/profile, personal essays, book reviews, photo feature, science/research. Stories must have Penn State connection. **Buys 20 mss/year.** Query with published clips and SASE. *No unsolicited mss.* Length: 200-3,000 words. Pays competitive rates. Pays expenses of writers on assignment.

Reprints: Send photocopy of article and information about when and where it previously appeared. Payment varies.

Photos: Send photos with submission. Reviews transparencies and prints. Negotiates payment individually. Captions required. Buys one-time rights.

Tips: "We are especially interested in attracting writers who are savvy in creative nonfiction/literary journalism. Most stories must have a Penn State tie-in."

$ $ THE PURDUE ALUMNUS, Purdue Alumni Association, Purdue Memorial Union 160, 101 N. Grant St., West Lafayette IN 47906-6212. (765)494-5182. Fax: (765)496-3778. E-mail: slmartin@purdue.edu. Website: www.purd ue.edu/PAA. **Contact:** Sharon Martin, editor. **50% freelance written.** Prefers to work with published/established writers; works with small number of new/unpublished writers each year. Bimonthly magazine covering subjects of interest to Purdue University alumni. Estab. 1912. Circ. 65,000. Pays on publication. Publishes ms an average of 2 months after acceptance. Byline given. Buys first rights and makes work-for-hire assignments. Submit seasonal material 6 months in advance. Accepts queries by mail, e-mail. Accepts simultaneous submissions. Responds in 2 weeks to queries; 1 month to mss. Sample copy for 9×12 SAE with 2 first-class stamps.

Nonfiction: Book excerpts, general interest, historical/nostalgic, humor, interview/profile, personal experience. Focus is on alumni, campus news, issues and opinions of interest to 65,000 members of the Alumni Association. Feature style, primarily university-oriented. Issues relevant to education. **Buys 12-20 mss/year.** Length: 1,500-2,500 words. **Pays $250-500.** Pays expenses of writers on assignment.

Reprints: Accepts previously published submissions.

Photos: State availability of photos. Reviews b&w contact sheet or 5×7 prints.

Tips: "We have more than 300,000 living, breathing Purdue alumni. If you can find a good story about one of them, we're interested. We use local freelancers to do campus pieces."

★ $ SUCCEED, The Magazine for Continuing Education, Ramholtz Publishing Inc., 2071 Clove Rd., Suite 206, Staten Island NY 10304-1643. (718)273-5700. Fax: (718)273-2539. E-mail: editorial@collegebound.net **Contact**: Gina LaGuardia, editor-in-chief. **85% freelance written.** Quarterly magazine. "*SUCCEED*'s readers are interested in continuing education, whether it be for changing careers or enhancing their current career." Estab. 1994. Circ. 155,000. Pays on publication. Publishes ms an average of 4 months after acceptance. Byline given. Buys first and second rights. Editorial lead time 4 months. Submit seasonal material 4 months in advance. Accepts queries by mail, e-mail. Accepts simultaneous submissions. Responds in 5 weeks. Sample copy for $1.50. Writer's guidelines for 9×12 SASE.

> O→ Break in with "an up-to-date, expert-driven article of interest to our audience with personal, real-life anecdotes as support—not basis—for exploration."

Nonfiction: Essays, exposé, general interest, how-to (change careers), interview/profile (interesting careers), new product, opinion, personal experience. **Buys 25 mss/year.** Query with published clips. Length: 1,000-1,500 words. **Pays $75-150.** Sometimes pays expenses of writers on assignment.

Reprints: Send photocopy of article.

Photos: Send photos with submission. Reviews negatives, prints. Offers no additional payment for photos accepted with ms. Captions and identification of subjects required. Buys one-time rights.

Columns/Departments: Tech Zone (new media/technology), 300-700 words; To Be... (personality/career profile), 600-800 words; Financial Fitness (finance, money management), 100-300 words; Memo Pad (short, newsworthy items that relate to today's changing job market and continuing education); Solo Success (how readers can "do it on their own," with recommended resources, books, and software). **Buys 10 mss/year.** Query with published clips. **Pays $50-75.**

Fillers: Facts, newsbreaks. **Buys 5/year.** Length: 50-200 words.

Tips: "Stay current and address issues of importance to our readers—lifelong learners and those in career transition. They're ambitious, hands-on and open to advice, new areas of opportunity, etc."

$ $ TOMORROW'S CHRISTIAN GRADUATE, WIN Press, P.O. Box 1357, Oak Park IL 60304. (708)524-5070. Fax: (708)524-5174. E-mail: WINPress7@aol.com. Website: www.christiangraduate.com. **Contact**: Phillip Huber, managing editor. **85% freelance written.** Annual magazine covering seminary and graduate school planning. "*Tomorrow's Christian Graduate* is a planning guide for adults pursuing a seminary or Christian graduate education and expresses the value of a seminary or Christian graduate education." Estab. 1998. Circ. 150,000. Pays on publication. Publishes ms 4 months after acceptance. Byline given. Buys all rights. Editorial lead time 4 months. Accepts queries by mail, e-mail. Sample copy for $3 or on website. Writer's guidelines free.

> O→ Break in with "a well-written, researched piece that shows how readers can get into a Christian graduate school or seminary or explains some program available at such schools."

Nonfiction: How-to, interview/profile, personal experience. First-person and how-to features focus on all topics of interest to adults pursuing graduate studies. No fiction or poetry. **Buys 10-15 mss/year.** Query with published clips. Length: 800-1,600 words. **Pays 8-15¢/word for assigned articles, 6-15¢/word for unsolicited articles.** Sometimes pays expenses of writers on assignment.

Photos: State availability of photos with submission. Negotiates payment individually. Captions, model releases, identification of subjects required.

Tips: "We are open to working with new/unpublished authors, especially current graduate students, graduate professors, admissions personnel, career counselors, and financial aid officers. Visit our website to view previously published articles."

$ WHAT MAKES PEOPLE SUCCESSFUL, The National Research Bureau, Inc., 320 Valley St., Burlington IA 52601. (319)752-5415. Fax: (319)752-3421. **Contact**: Nancy Heinzel, editor. **75% freelance written.** Quarterly magazine. Estab. 1948. Circ. 1,500. Pays on publication. Publishes ms an average of 1 year after acceptance. Buys all rights. Submit seasonal material 8 months in advance of issue date. Accepts queries by mail, phone, fax. Sample copy and writer's guidelines for #10 SAE with 2 first-class stamps. Eager to work with new/unpublished writers; works with a small number each year.

Nonfiction: How-to (be successful), general interest (personality, employee morale, guides to successful living, biographies of successful persons, etc.), experience, opinion. No material on health. **Buys 3-4 mss/issue.** Query with outline. Length: 500-700 words. **Pays 4¢/word.**

Tips: Short articles (rather than major features) have a better chance of acceptance because all articles are short.

$ $ WPI JOURNAL, Worcester Polytechnic Institute, 100 Institute Rd., Worcester MA 01609-2280. Fax: (508)831-5820. E-mail: wpi-journal@wpi.edu. Website: www.wpi.edu/+Journal. **Contact**: Michael Dorsey, editor. **50% freelance**

written. Quarterly alumni magazine covering science and engineering/education/business personalities for 25,000 alumni, primarily engineers, scientists, managers, national media. Estab. 1897. Circ. 28,000. Pays on publication. Publishes ms an average of 6 months after acceptance. Byline given. Buys one-time rights. Accepts queries by mail, e-mail, fax. Accepts simultaneous submissions. Query for electronic submissions. Requires hard copy also. Responds in 1 month to queries. Sample copy on website.

Nonfiction: Interview/profile (alumni in engineering, science, etc.), photo feature, features on people and programs at WPI. Query with published clips. Length: 1,000-4,000 words. Pays negotiable rate. Sometimes pays the expenses of writers on assignment.

Reprints: Accepts previously published submissions.

Photos: State availability of photos with query or ms. Reviews b&w contact sheets. Pays negotiable rate. Captions required.

■ The online magazine carries original content not found in the print edition.

Tips: "Submit outline of story and/or ms of story idea or published work. Features are most open to freelancers. Keep in mind that this is an alumni magazine, so most articles focus on the college and its graduates."

CHILD CARE & PARENTAL GUIDANCE

Magazines in this section address the needs and interests of families with children. Some publications are national in scope, others are geographically specific. Some offer general advice for parents, while magazines such as *Catholic Parent* answer the concerns of smaller groups. Other markets that buy articles about child care and the family are included in the Religious and Women's sections and in the Trade Education and Counseling section. Publications for children can be found in the Juvenile and Teen & Young sections.

$ $ $ AMERICAN BABY MAGAZINE, For Expectant and New Parents, Primedia Communications, 249 W. 17th St., New York NY 10011-5300. (212)462-3500. Fax: (212)367-8332. Website: www.americanbaby.com. **Contact:** Eilzabeth Haas, assistant editor. Editor-in-Chief: Judith Nolte. **70% freelance written.** Prefers to work with published/established writers; works with a small number of new/unpublished writers each year. Monthly magazine addressing health, medical and childcare concerns for expectant and new parents, particularly those having their first child or those whose child is between the ages of birth and 2 years old. Mothers are the primary readers, but fathers' issues are equally important. "A simple, straightforward, clear approach is mandatory." Estab. 1938. Circ. 1,650,000. **Pays on acceptance.** Publishes ms an average of 6 months after acceptance. Byline given. Offers 25% kill fee. Buys first North American serial rights. Editorial lead time 5 months. Submit seasonal material 6 months in advance. Accepts simultaneous submissions. Accepts queries by mail. Responds in 3 month to queries; 3 months to mss. Sample copy for 9×12 SAE with 6 first-class stamps. Writer's guidelines for #10 SASE.

Nonfiction: Book excerpts, essays, general interest, how-to (some aspect of pregnancy or baby care), humor, fitness, beauty, health, new product and personal experience. "No 'hearts and flowers' or fantasy pieces." Full-length articles should offer helpful expert information on some aspect of pregnancy or child care; should cover a common problem of child-raising, along with solutions; or should give expert advice on a psychological or practical subject. Articles about products, such as toys and nursery furniture, are not accepted, as these are covered by staff members. **Buys 60 mss/year.** Query with published clips or send complete ms. Length: 1,000-2,000 words. **Pays $750-1,200 for assigned articles; $600-800 for unsolicited articles.** Pays the expenses of writers on assignment.

● Ranked as one of the best markets for freelance writers in *Writer's Yearbook* magazine's annual "Top 100 Markets," January 2000.

Reprints: Send photocopy of article and information about when and where the article previously appeared. Pays 50% of amount paid for an original article.

Photos: State availability of photos with submission. Reviews transparencies and prints. Model release and identification of subjects required. Buys one-time rights.

Columns/Departments: Personal Experience, 700-1,000 words, **pays up to $1000**; Short Items, Crib Notes (news and feature items) and Medical Update, 50-250 words, **pays $200.**

Tips: "Get to know our style by thoroughly reading a recent issue of the magazine. Don't send something we recently published. Our readers want to feel connected to other parents, both to share experiences and to learn from one another. They want reassurance that the problems they are facing are solvable and not uncommon. They want to keep up with the latest issues affecting their new family, particularly health and medical news, but they don't have a lot of spare time to read. We forgo the theoretical approach to offer quick-to-read, hands-on information that can be put to use immediately."

◩ $ AT-HOME MOTHER, At-Home Mothers' Resource Center, 406 E. Buchanan Ave., Fairfield IA 52556-3810. E-mail: editor@athomemothers.com. Website: www.AtHomeMothers.com. **Contact:** Jeanette Lisefski, editor. **95% freelance written.** Quarterly magazine. "*At-Home Mother* provides support for at-home mothers and features up-beat articles that reinforce their choice to stay at home with their children, helping them to find maximum fulfillment in this most cherished profession. Through education and inspiration, we also help those mothers who want to stay at home

Parlay parenting experience into freelance work

Writer and mother Dana Nourie has worked as a freelancer for nine years. But slipping into the parenting niche four years ago helped kick her career into high gear. Publications like *Parenting*, *Family Life*, *Parents Press*, KBKids.com, *Woman's Day's Kids' Activities* and *Chicago Parent* pay top dollar for Nourie's proven expertise. That financial windfall helps Nourie explore other professional interests as well.

Dana Nourie

How does writing about parenting differ from freelance subjects?
Experience helps when covering parenting angles like no other writing field. My kids are the source of almost all my ideas. I get ideas from observing or hearing about other people's kids, too. But that is usually because I'm comparing them, in my head, with my own children.

Also, parenting editors are a bit different. They are very tolerant of having a call interrupted by a child needing something, or a cry in the background. They don't consider it unprofessional. On the contrary, they have all asked me right off the bat if I have kids. When I tell them yes, they always seem glad to hear it. That's not to say you can't write parenting articles without being a parent, but it's a huge plus.

What's the best way to break into parenting publications?
It's best to start with regionals and work your way up to nationals. They are easier to sell to, and you can gather a lot of clips to show editors at nationals. Regionals are also great just for the experience they provide writers.

What types of pieces can a parenting freelancer sell?
I've written a lot of articles about discovering the world through my children's eyes; sharing my knowledge with them while I'm at it. I've also written a lot of stage articles—what you can expect from your child at certain ages. For instance, I wrote about why children begin to lie and how it's important to their development. I also wrote one for *Parenting* about why kids talk to themselves and why it's important.

There are also care articles. I wrote one for *Parenting* on how to care for children's newly pierced ears. Another I wrote for *Family Life* on how to teach your kids to be better listeners by starting with yourself. And of course there are essays. That's how I broke into the parenting scene, and I think a few of them remain my best pieces of writing.

What is the pay scale for new, moderate and experienced freelancers writing about parenting?

Regionals' pay scales are low—anywhere from free (never have, never will) to around 30¢ a word. Nationals pay $1 a word and up. But keep in mind, judging an article by word worth is not always the best way to decide whether the assignment is worth it. I frequently write for Parent's Press, which only pays me $250-350 an article. That breaks down to about 25¢ a word. That stinks. On the other hand, those articles only took me three to four hours to research and write. So in reality I was getting paid a little over $50 an hour! Not bad. I did turn down an assignment that would have required a lot more hours.

Have you run into a "nightmare" assignment?

An assignment for *Parents*. The editor wanted a full feature based on a query I had sent, but with a slightly different focus. I worked hard on the article, but it wasn't what she wanted. The article did run as scheduled, but it was "by Dr. So and So." I got my kill fee, but the whole thing was so very disappointing. I've not queried them since.

What was your favorite assignment and why?

The first assignment I sold to *Parenting*, on why kids talk to themselves. It is the shortest one that's appeared, but it's my favorite because it was my first national parenting sale and because it led to my first psychology article for *Family Circle*, on why it's good for women to talk to themselves.

For interviews with the pros on more freelance niche markets see Food & Drink, page 470; Health & Fitness, page 494; Nature, page 594; Personal Computers, page 604; and Travel, page 779.
—Kelly Milner Halls

———◆◆◆———

TOP TIP: For beginning writers, the challenge is staying out of your own way. This is especially true if you're also a new mom or a new dad. We tend to "know" an awful lot about parenting in the beginning, but with each child you realize it's not all black and white. You relax in parenting in the same way you relax in writing over time. Each year of parenting that passes improves the quality of ideas for articles.

---

find ways to make this goal a reality." Estab. 1997. Circ. 8,000. Pays on publication. Publishes ms an average of 3 months after acceptance. Byline given. Buys first North American serial rights, second serial (reprint) rights and electronic rights. Editorial lead time 3 months. Accepts queries by mail, e-mail. Accepts simultaneous submissions. Responds in 1 month to queries; 3 months to mss. Sample copy for $4 or sample articles available on website. Writer's guidelines for #10 SASE.

   ○┅ Break in with upbeat, positive articles containing experiences by other mothers in answers to mother's concerns relating to all aspects of at-home mothering.

Nonfiction: Essays, how-to (managing home, parenting, etc.), humor, inspirational, interview/profile, personal experience, photo feature. **Buys 60-100 mss/year.** Query. Length: 500-2,500 words. **Pays $25-150.**

Reprints: Send photocopy of article or typed ms with rights for sale noted and information about when and where the article previously appeared. Pays 50% of amount paid for an original article.

Photos: State availability of photos with submission. Reviews contact sheets or prints. Offers $5-75/interior photo. Captions, model releases and identification of subjects required. Buys one-time rights.

Columns/Departments: Choosing Home (making the choice for at-home mothering); Making Money at Home (homework and home business); Saving Money at Home (money saving ideas); Parenting (several topics and philosophy); Mother's Self Esteem & Happiness (self-care); Celebrating Motherhood (essay, poetry, personal experience); Managing at Home (home management); Teaching at Home (home schooling & Children's activities); Learning at Home (home study), all 400-2,500 words. **Buys 60-100 mss/year.** Query. **Pays $10-150.**

Poetry: Avant-garde, free verse, haiku, light verse, traditional. **Buys 5-10 poems/year.** Length: 4-50 lines. **Pays $5-25.**

Fillers: Anecdotes, facts, short humor. **Buys 5-10/year.** Length: 20-500 words. **Pays $10-50.**

Tips: "Write specifically to at-home mothers. Articles must be uplifting and/or informative. Articles must show experience or insight into subject."

$ATLANTA PARENT/ATLANTA BABY, 2346 Perimeter Park Dr., Suite 101, Atlanta GA 30346. (770)454-7599. Fax: (770)454-7699. E-mail: atlparent@family.com. Website: www.atlantaparent.com. Editor: Liz White. **Contact:** Peggy Middendorf, managing editor. **50% freelance written.** Pays on publication. Publishes ms 3 months after acceptance. Byline given. Buys one-time rights. Submit seasonal material 6 months in advance. Accepts queries by mail, e-mail, fax. Responds in 4 months. Sample copy for $3.

Nonfiction: General interest, how-to, humor, interview/profile, travel. Special issues: Private school (January); Camp (February); Health and Fitness (March); Birthday Parties (April); Maternity and Mothering (May); Childcare (July); Back-to-school (August); Teens (October); Holidays (November/December). No first-person accounts or philosophical discussions. **Buys 60 mss/year.** Query with or without published clips, or send complete ms. Length: 800-2,100 words. **Pays $15-30.** Sometimes pays expenses of writers on assignment.

Reprints: Send tearsheet or photocopy of article or typed ms with rights for sale noted and information about when and where the article previously appeared. **Pays $15-30.**

Photos: State availability of photos with submission and send photocopies. Reviews 3×5 photos "color preferably." Offers $10/photo. Buys one-time rights.

Tips: "Articles should be geared to problems or situations of families and parents. Should include down-to-earth tips and be clearly written. No philosophical discussions or first-person narratives. We're also looking for well-written humor."

$ $ $ $BABY TALK, The Parenting Group, 1325 Avenue of the Americas, 27th Floor, New York NY 10019-6026. (212)522-8989. Fax: (212)522-8750. **Contact:** Susan Kane, editor-in-chief. **Mostly freelance written**. Magazine published 10 times/year. "*Baby Talk* is written primarily for women who are considering pregnancy or who are expecting a child, and parents of children from birth through 18 months, with the emphasis on pregnancy through first six months of life." Estab. 1935. Circ. 1,725,000. Responds in 2 months.

Nonfiction: Features cover pregnancy, the basics of baby care, infant/toddler health, growth and development, juvenile equipment and toys, work and day care, marriage and sex, "approached from a how-to, service perspective. The message—Here's what you need to know and why—is delivered with smart, crisp style. The tone is confident and reassuring (and, when appropriate, humorous and playful), with the backing of experts. In essence, *Baby Talk* is a training manual of parents facing the day-to-day dilemmas of new parenthood." Query in writing with SASE. No phone calls, please. Length: 1,000-2,000 words. **Pays $500-2,000,** depending on length, degree of difficulty, and the writer's previous experience.

Columns/Departments: Several departments are written by regular contributors. Length: 100-1,250 words. **Pays $100-$1,000.** Query in writing with SASE.

Tips: "Please familiarize yourself with the magazine before submitting a query. Take the time to focus your story idea; scattershot queries are a waste of everyone's time."

$BIG APPLE PARENT/QUEENS PARENT, Family Communications, Inc., 9 E. 38th St., 4th Floor, New York NY 10016. (212)889-6400. Fax: (212)689-4958. E-mail: hellonwheels@parentsknow.com. Website: www.parentsknow.com. **Contact:** Helen Freedman, managing editor. **70% freelance written.** Monthly tabloids covering New York City family life. "*BAP* readers live in high-rise Manhattan apartments; it is an educated, upscale audience. Often both parents are working full time in professional occupations. Child-care help tends to be one-on-one, in the home. Kids attend private schools for the most part. While not quite a suburban approach, some of our *QP* readers do have backyards (though most live in high-rise apartments). It is a more middle-class audience in Queens. More kids are in day care centers; majority of kids are in public schools." Estab. 1985. *Big Apple* circ. 70,000, *Queens* circ. 60,000. Pays end of month following publication. Byline given. Offers 50% kill fee. Buys first New York City rights. Reserves the right to publish an article in either or both the Manhattan and Queens editions and online. Submit seasonal material 3 months in advance. Accepts queries by mail, e-mail, fax. Accepts simultaneous submissions. Responds immediately; however, no submissions accepted during the summer months. Sample copy and writer's guidelines free.

Nonfiction: Essays, exposé, general interest, how-to, inspirational, interview/profile, opinion, family health, education. **Buys 60-70 mss/year.** Query or send complete ms. Length: 600-1,000 words. **Pays $35-50.** Sometimes pays expenses of writers on assignment. "We are not buying any more humor or personal parenting essays through end of 2001, but we're *always* looking for news and coverage of controversial issues."

Reprints: Send tearsheet or photocopy of article or typed ms with rights for sale noted and information about when and where the article previously appeared. Pays same as article rate.

Photos: State availability of or send photos with submission. Reviews contact sheets, prints. Offers $20/photo. Captions required. Buys one-time rights.

Columns/Departments: Dads; Education; Family Finance. **Buys 50-60 mss/year.** Send complete ms.

Tips: "We have a very local focus; our aim is to present articles our readers cannot find in national publications. To that end, news stories and human interest pieces must focus on New York and New Yorkers. Child-raising articles must include quotes from New York and Queens' experts and sources. We are always looking for news and newsy pieces; we keep on top of current events, frequently giving issues that may relate to parenting a local focus so that the idea will work for us as well."

$ $ CATHOLIC FAITH & FAMILY, Circle Media, 33 Rossotto Dr., Hamden CT 06514. (203)288-5600. Fax: (203)288-5157. E-mail: editor@twincircle.com. **Contact:** Loretta Seyer, editor. **95% freelance written.** Bi-weekly magazine. "We publish inspirational articles that focus on living/raising your children as Catholics. We look for articles on Catholic traditions, some travel pieces (usually to religious or educational family life), features on people living the Catholic life in a unique way." Estab. 1966. Circ. 16,000. Pays on publication. Byline given. Buys first rights. Accepts queries by mail, e-mail, fax.

Nonfiction: Inspirational, interview/profile, opinion, religious, travel. Send complete ms. Length: 1,000-2,000 words. **Pays $75-400.**

Photos: State availability of photos with submission or send photos with submission. Reviews prints. Identification of subjects required.

Columns/Departments: Hearth & Home (recipes, crafts, games, parties, traditions that celebrate/teach Catholic traditions/faith), 1,000 words. **Pays $75-175.**

$ $ CHICAGO PARENT, Connecting with Families, Wednesday Journal, Inc., 141 S. Oak Park Ave., Oak Park IL 60302-2972. (708)386-5555. Fax: (708)524-8360. E-mail: chiparent@aol.com. Website: chicagoparent.com. **Contact:** Sharon Bloyd-Peshkin, editor. **60% freelance written.** Monthly tabloid. "*Chicago Parent* has a distinctly local approach. We offer information, inspiration, perspective and empathy to Chicago-area parents. Our lively editorial mix has a 'we're all in this together' spirit, and articles are thoroughly researched and well written." Estab. 1988. Circ. 135,000 in three zones. Pays on publication. Publishes ms an average of 2 months after acceptance. Byline given. Offers 10-50% kill fee. Buys one-time rights; reprint rights at 20%, online at 10% of original ms payment. Editorial lead time 4 months. Submit seasonal material 4 months in advance. Query by mail, e-mail, fax. Responds in 6 weeks. Sample copy for $3.95 and 11×17 SASE with $1.65 postage. Writer's guidelines for #10 SASE.

O— Break in by "writing 'short stuff' items (front-of-the-book short items on local people, places and things of interest to families)."

Nonfiction: Exposé, local interest, how-to (parent-related), humor, investigative features, travel, interview/profile, essays. Special issues include Chicagoland's Healthy Woman, Chicago Baby, Healthy Child. "No pot-boiler parenting pieces, simultaneous submissions, previously published pieces or non-local writers (from outside the 6-county Chicago metropolitan area and northwest Indiana)." **Buys 40-50 mss/year.** Query with published clips. Length: 200-2,500 words. **Pays $25-300 for assigned articles, $25-100 for unsolicited articles.** Sometimes pays expenses of writers on assignment.

Photos: State availability of photos with submission. Reviews contact sheets, negatives and prints. Offers $0-40/photo. Negotiates payment individually. Captions and identification of subjects required. Buys one-time rights.

Columns/Departments: Healthy Child (kids' health issues), 850 words; Getaway (travel pieces), up to 1,200 words; other columns not open to freelancers. **Buys 30 mss/year.** Query with published clips or send complete ms. **Pays $100.**

Tips: "We don't like pot-boiler parenting topics and don't accept many personal essays unless they are truly compelling."

★ $ $ $ $ CHILD, Gruner + Jahr, 375 Lexington Ave., New York NY 10017-5514. (212)499-2000. Fax: (212)499-2038. E-mail: childmag@aol.com. Website: www.childmagazine.com. Editor-in-Chief: Miriam Arond. Managing Editor: Pamela Mitchell. **Contact:** Anna Attkisson, editorial assistant. **95% freelance written.** Monthly magazine for parenting. Estab. 1986. Circ. 930,000. **Pays on acceptance.** Byline given. Offers 25% kill fee. Buys first North American serial rights, first rights or one-time rights. Editorial lead time 3 months. Submit seasonal material 6 months in advance. Accepts queries by mail, fax. Responds in 2 months. Sample copy for $3.95. Writer's guidelines free.

Nonfiction: Book excerpts, general interest, interview/profile, new product, photo feature, travel. No poetry. **Buys 50 feature mss/year, 25-30 short pieces/year.** Query with published clips. Length: 650-2,500 words. **Pays $1/word.** Sometimes pays expenses of writers on assignment.

● Ranked as one of the best markets for freelance writers in *Writer's Yearbook* magazine's annual "Top 100 Markets," January 2000.

Photos: State availability of photos with submission. Reviews transparencies. Negotiates payment individually. Buys one-time rights.

Columns/Departments: First Person (mother's or father's perspective); Lesson Learned (experience mother or father learned from). Query with published clips. **Buys 100 mss/year.** Length: 1,500 words. **Pays $1/word.**

● *Child* receives too many inappropriate submissions. Please consider your work carefully before submitting.

Tips: "Stories should include opinions from experts as well as anecdotes from parents to illustrate the points being made. Service is key."

★ $ $ CHRISTIAN PARENTING TODAY, Christianity Today, Inc., 465 Gundersen Dr., Carol Stream IL 60188-2489. (630)260-6200. Fax: (630)260-0114. E-mail: cptmag@aol.com. Editor: Carala Barnhill. Associate Editor: Lisa Jack. **Contact:** Lori McCullough. **90% freelance written.** Bimonthly magazine "Strives to be a positive, practical magazine that targets real needs of today's family with authoritative articles based on real experience, fresh research and the timeless truths of the Bible. *CPT* provides parents information that spans birth to 14 years of age in the following areas of growth: spiritual, social, emotional, physical, academic." Estab. 1988. Circ. 90,000. **Pays on acceptance.** Byline given. Buys first North American serial or second serial (reprint) rights. Submit seasonal material 8 months in advance. Responds in 2 months. Sample copy for 9 × 12 SAE with $3 postage. Writer's guidelines for #10 SASE.

Nonfiction: Book excerpts, how-to, humor, inspirational, religious. Feature topics of greatest interest: practical guidance in spiritual/moral development and values transfer; practical solutions to everyday parenting issues; tips on how to enrich readers' marriages; ideas for nurturing healthy family ties; family activities that focus on parent/child interaction; humorous pieces about everyday family life. **Buys 50 mss/year.** Query only. Length: 750-2,000 words. **Pays 12-20¢/ word.**

Reprints: Send photocopy of article and typed ms with rights for sale noted and information about when and where the article previously appeared.

Photos: State availability of photos with submission. Do not submit photos without permission. Reviews transparencies. Model release required. Buys one-time rights.

Columns/Departments: Ideas That Work (family-tested parenting ideas from our readers), 25-100 words **(pays $25)**; Life In Our House (entertaining, true, humorous stories about your family), 25-100 words **(pays $25)**; Your Child Today (spiritual development topics from a Christian perspective), 420-520 words **(pays $150)**. Submissions become property of *CPT*. Submissions to *Life In Our House* and *Ideas That Work* are not acknowledged or returned.

Tips: "Tell it like it is. Readers have a 'get real' attitude that demands a down-to-earth, pragmatic take on topics. Don't sugar-coat things. Give direction without waffling. If you've 'been there,' tell us. The first-person, used appropriately, is OK. Don't distance yourself from readers. They trust people who have walked in their shoes. Get reader friendly. Fill your article with nuts and bolts: developmental information, age-specific angles, multiple resources, sound-bite sidebars, real-life people and anecdotes and realistic, vividly explained suggestions."

$ $ DALLAS FAMILY MAGAZINE, The Magazine for Today's Parents, Family Publications, Inc., 2501 Oak Lawn Ave., Suite 600, Dallas TX 75219. (214)521-2021. Fax: (214)522-9270. E-mail: dallasfam@aol.com. **Contact:** Susan Merkner, editor. **50% freelance written.** Monthly tabloid covering parenting/families. "It is our mission to provide information, resources, perspective and support to parents—to strengthen families and their communities." Estab. 1993. Circ. 80,000. Pays 30 days after publication. Byline given. Offers 25% kill fee. Buys first North American serial or all rights. Editorial lead time 2 months. Submit seasonal material 3 months in advance. Accepts queries by mail, e-mail, fax. Responds in 1 month. Sample copy and writer's guidelines free.

Nonfiction: Essays, how-to (parenting families), humor, interview/profile, new product, personal experience (only occasionally), photo feature, travel. **Buys 12-20 mss/year.** Query with published clips. Length: 750-2,500 words. **Pays $125-400 for assigned articles; $50-300 for unsolicited articles.**

Photos: State availability of photos with submission. Identification of subjects required. Buys one-time rights.

Tips: "Send a fully developed story idea that demonstrates reporting and writing skills and understanding of the parenting niche market."

★ $ $ FAMILY DIGEST, The Black Mom's Best Friend!, Family Digest Association, 696 San Ramon Valley Blvd., #349, Danville CA 94526. Fax: (925)838-4948. E-mail: editor@familydigest.com. **Contact:** Darryl Mobley, associate editor. **90% freelance written.** Quarterly magazine covering women's services. "Our mission: Help black moms/female heads-of-household get more out of their roles as wife, mother, homemaker. Editorial coverage includes parenting, health, love and marriage, travel, family finances, and beauty and style . . . All designed to appeal to black moms." Estab. 1997. Circ. 2,100,000. Pays on publication. Publishes ms an average of 6 months after acceptance. Byline sometimes given. Buys first North American serial rights, second serial (reprint) rights, or makes work-for-hire assignments. Editorial lead time 2 months. Submit seasonal material 3 months in advance. Accepts queries and submissions by e-mail *only*. Accepts simultaneous submissions. Responds in 1 month. Writer's guidelines free by e-mail.

Nonfiction: Book excerpts, general interest (dealing with relationships), historical/nostalgic, how-to, humor, inspirational, interview/profile, personal experience. "We are not political. We do not want articles that blame others. We do want articles that improve the lives of our readers." Query with published clips. Length: 1,000-3,000 words. **Pays $100-500.** Sometimes pays expenses of writers on assignment.

Reprints: Accepts previously published submissions.

Photos: State availability of or send photos with submission. Reviews negatives, transparencies, prints. Offers no additional payment for photos accepted with ms. Captions, model releases, identification of subjects required.

Columns/Departments: A Better You! (personal development), parenting, love and marriage, health, family finances, beauty and style. **Buys 100 mss/year.** Query with published clips. **Pays $100-500.**

Fiction: Erotica, ethnic, historical, humorous, novel excerpts, romance. Query with published clips.

Fillers: Anecdotes, facts, gags to be illustrated by cartoonist, short humor. **Buys 100 mss/year.** Length: 50-250 words.

★ $ THE FAMILY DIGEST, P.O. Box 40137, Fort Wayne IN 46804. **Contact:** Corine B. Erlandson, editor. **95% freelance written.** Bimonthly digest-sized magazine. "*The Family Digest* is dedicated to the joy and fulfillment of the Catholic family and its relationship to the Catholic parish." Estab. 1945. Circ. 150,000. Pays within 2 months of acceptance. Publishes ms usually within 1 year after acceptance. Byline given. Buys first North American rights. Submit seasonal material 7 months in advance. Responds in 2 months. Sample copy and writer's guidelines for 6 × 9 SAE with 2 first-class stamps.

Nonfiction: Family life, parish life, how-to, seasonal, inspirational, prayer life, Catholic traditions. Send ms with SASE. No poetry or fiction. **Buys 60 unsolicited mss/year.** Length: 750-1,200 words. **Pays $40-60/article.**

Reprints: Prefers previously unpublished articles. Send typed ms with rights for sale noted and information about when and where the article previously appeared. Pays 5¢/word.

Fillers: Anecdotes, tasteful humor based on personal experience. **Buys 3/issue.** Length: 25-100 words maximum. **Pays $25 on acceptance.** Cartoons: Publishes 5 cartoons/issue, related to family and Catholic parish life. **Pays $40/cartoon on acceptance.**

Tips: "Prospective freelance contributors should be familiar with the publication and the types of articles we accept and publish. We are especially looking for upbeat articles which affirm the simple ways in which the Catholic faith is expressed in daily life. Articles on family and parish life, including seasonal articles, how-to pieces, inspirational, prayer, spiritual life and Church traditions, will be gladly reviewed for possible acceptance and publication."

$ $ $ $ FAMILY LIFE, Time Inc., 1271 Avenue of the Americas, New York NY 10020. (212)522-6240. Fax: (212)467-1248. E-mail: family_life@timeinc.com. Website: www.parenting.com. **Contact:** Jacqueline Leigh Ross, editorial assistant. **60% freelance written.** Magazine published 10 times/year for parents of children ages 5-12. Estab. 1993. Circ. 500,000. **Pays on acceptance.** Publishes ms an average of 4 months after acceptance. Byline given. Offers 25% kill fee. Buys first worldwide rights. Editorial lead time 6 months. Submit seasonal material 8 months in advance. Accepts queries by mail, e-mail, fax. "No calls please." Accepts simultaneous submissions. Responds in 6 weeks to queries. Sample copy for $3, call (201)451-9420. Writer's guidelines for #10 SASE.

○π Break in through the Parent to Parent column ("We're always looking for new ideas here.") or Year by Year section.

Nonfiction: Parenting book excerpts, essays and articles on family topics, general interest, new product, photo feature, travel health. Does not want to see articles about children under 5, childbirth, expensive vacations or "my child's growing up too fast." Feature length: 2,000-3,500 words. Query with published clips. **Pays $1/word.** Pays expenses of writers on assignment.

• Ranked as one of the best markets for freelance writers in *Writer's Yearbook* magazine's annual "Top 100 Markets," January 2000.

Photos: State availability of photos with submission. Reviews transparencies. Negotiates payment individually. Buys one-time rights.

Columns/Departments: Family Matters section (newsy shorts on parenting topics, interesting travel destinations and the latest health issues), 150-250 words; Year by Year section (stories on child development specific to ages 5-7, 7-9 and 9-12), 150-250 words, 400 maximum. Individual columns: Parent to Parent (story by a parent about life with his or her child that epitomizes one issue in child-rearing); Motherhood (changes and challenges that being a mother brings to a woman's life); Family Affairs (personal issues parents face as their children grow up); School Smart (today's educational issues); House Calls (health); Chip Chat (the latest in family computing). Length: 1,000-1,500 words. Query with published clips.

▣ The online magazine carries original content not found in the print edition. Contact: Meg Seisfeld, online editor.

Tips: "Our readers are parents of children ages 5-12 who are interested in getting the most out of family life. Most are college educated and work hard at a full-time job. We want fresh articles dealing with the day-to-day issues that these families face, with personal insight and professional opinion on how to handle them."

N ✖ $ $ $ FAMILYFUN, Disney Magazine Publishing Inc., 244 Main St., Northampton MA 01060-3107. (413)585-0444. Fax: (413)586-5724. Website: www.familyfun.com. **Contact:** Fred Levine, features editor. Magazine published 10 times/year covering activities for families with kids ages 3-12. "*Family Fun* is about all the great things families can do together. Our writers are either parents or authorities in a covered field." Estab. 1991. Circ. 1,300,000. **Pays on acceptance.** Publishes ms an average of 4 months after acceptance. Byline sometimes given. Offers 25% kill fee. Buys simultaneous rights or makes work-for-hire assignments. Editorial lead time 4 months. Submit seasonal material 6 months in advance. Accepts simultaneous submissions. Responds in 2 months. Sample copy and writer's guidelines for $3 (call (800)289-4849) or on website.

Nonfiction: Features Editor. Book excerpts, essays, general interest, how-to (crafts, cooking, educational activities), humor, interview/profile, personal experience, photo feature, travel. Special issues: Crafts, Holidays, Back to School, Summer Vacations. **Buys hundreds mss/year.** Query by mail only with published clips. No unsolicited mss. Length: 850-3,000 words. **Pays $1.25/word.** Sometimes pays expenses of writers on assignment.

• Ranked as one of the best markets for freelance writers in *Writer's Yearbook* magazine's annual "Top 100 Markets," January 2000.

Photos: State availability of photos with submissions. Reviews contact sheets, negatives, transparencies. Offers $75-500/photo. Model releases, identification of subjects required. Buys all rights (simultaneous).

Columns/Departments: Family Almanac, Cindy Littlefield, senior editor (simple, quick, practical, inexpensive ideas and projects—outings, crafts, games, nature activities, learning projects, and cooking with children), 200-400 words; query or send ms; **pays $100-$200/article or $75 for ideas.** Family Traveler, Jodi Butler, (brief, newsy items about family travel, what's new, what's great, and especially, what's a good deal), 100-125 words; send ms; **pays $100, also pays $50 for ideas.** Family Ties, Jon Adolph, executive editor (first-person column that spotlights some aspect of family life that is humorous, inspirational, or interesting); 1,500 words; send ms; **pays $1,500.** My Great idea, Dawn Chipman, senior editor (explains fun and inventive ideas that have worked for writer's own family); 800-1,000 words; query or send letter letter or ms; **pays $750 on acceptance;** also publishes best letters from writers and readers following column, send to My Great Ideas editor, 100-150 words, **pays $25 on publication. Buys 20-25 mss/year.**

Tips: "Many of our writers break into *FF* by writing for Family Almanac or Family Traveler (front-of-the-book departments)."

$ $ $ GREAT EXPECTATIONS, Today's Parent Group, 269 Richmond St. W, Toronto, Ontario M5V 1X1 Canada. (416)569-8680. Fax: (416)496-1991. Website: www.todaysparent.com. **Contact:** Editor. **100% freelance written.** Magazine published 3 times a year. "*GE* helps, supports and encourages expectant and new parents with news and features related to pregnancy, birth, human sexuality and parenting." Estab. 1973. Circ. 200,000. **Pays on acceptance.** Publishes ms an average of 8 months after acceptance. Bylines given. Buys first North American serial rights. Editorial lead time 6 months. Responds in 6 weeks to queries. Sample copy and writer's guidelines for #10 SASE.
Nonfiction: Features about pregnancy, labor and delivery, post-partum issues. **Buys 12 mss/year.** Query with published clips. Length: 700-2,000 words. **Pays $400-1,200.** Sometimes pays expenses of writers on assignment.
Photos: State availability of photos with submission. Negotiates payment individually. Rights negotiated individually.
Tips: "Our writers are professional freelance writers with specific knowledge in the childbirth field. *GE* is written for a Canadian audience using Canadian research and sources."

$ $ GROWING PARENT, Dunn & Hargitt, Inc., P.O. Box 620, Lafayette IN 47902-0620. (765)423-2624. Fax: (765)742-8514. **Contact:** Nancy Kleckner, editor. **40-50% freelance written.** Works with a small number of new/unpublished writers each year. "We do receive a lot of unsolicited submissions but have had excellent results in working with some unpublished writers. So, we're always happy to look at material and hope to find one or two jewels each year." Monthly newsletter which focuses on parents—the issues, problems, and choices they face as their children grow. "We want to look at the parent as an adult and help encourage his or her growth not only as a parent but as an individual." Estab. 1973. Pays on publication. Publishes ms an average of 6 months after acceptance. Byline given. Buys first North American serial rights; maintains exclusive rights for three months. Submit seasonal material 6 months in advance. Responds in 2 weeks. Sample copy and writer's guidelines for 5×8 SAE with 2 first-class stamps.
Nonfiction: "We are looking for informational articles based on careful research and written in an easy-to-read, concise style. We would like to see articles that help parents deal with the stresses they face in everyday life—positive, upbeat, how-to-cope suggestions. In the past we have covered such topics as guilt, relating to aged parents, dealing with in-laws, crisis intervention, and time management. We rarely use humorous pieces, fiction or personal experience articles. Writers should keep in mind that most of our readers have children under two years of age." **Buys 15-20 mss/year.** Query. Length: 1,000-1,500 words; will look at shorter pieces. **Pays 10-15¢/word.**
Reprints: Send tearsheet of article and information about when and where it previously appeared.
Tips: "Submit a very specific query letter with samples."

⭐ $ $ $ $ HEALTHY KIDS, Primedia, 249 W. 17th St., New York NY 10011-5300. (212)462-3300. Fax: (212)367-8332. Website: www.healthykids.com. Editor: Laura Broadwell. **Contact:** Editorial assistant. **90% freelance written.** Bimonthly magazine that addresses all elements that go into the raising of a healthy, happy child, from basic health-care information to an analysis of a child's growing mind and behavior patterns. Extends the wisdom of the pediatrician into the home, and informs parents of young children (ages birth to 10 years) about proper health care. The only magazine produced for parents in association with the American Academy of Pediatrics, the nonprofit organization of more than 55,000 pediatricians dedicated to the betterment of children's health. To ensure accuracy, all articles are reviewed by an Editorial Advisory Board comprised of distinguished pediatricians. Estab. 1989. Circ. 1,550,000. **Pays on acceptance.** Byline given. Offers 33% kill fee. Buys first North American rights. Submit seasonal material at least 9 months in advance. Responds in 2 months. Writer's guidelines for #10 SASE.
Nonfiction: How to help your child develop as a person, keep safe, keep healthy. Each issue also includes one comprehensive Health Report (2,500 words) that focuses on a health topic such as asthma, colds and flu, back care and posture, and brain development. No poetry, fiction, travel or product endorsement. Special issues: Good Eating!—A complete guide to feeding your family (February/March); Summer Fun (June/July). Query by mail. No unsolicited mss. Length: 2,000-2,500 words. **Pays $1,500-2,500.** Pays expenses of writers on assignment.
Columns/Departments: Focus On . . . (an informal conversation with a pediatrician, in a question-and-answer format, about a timely health issue); Let's Eat (advice on how to keep mealtimes fun and nutritious, along with some child-friendly recipes); Behavior Basics (a helpful article on how to deal with some aspect of a child's behavior—from first friendships to temper tantrums). **Buys 20 mss/year.** Query. Length: 1,500-1,800 words. **Pays $1,200-1,500.**
   ▣ The online magazine carries original content not found in the print edition. Contact: Stephanie Portnoy, online editor.
Tips: "A simple, clear approach is mandatory. Articles should speak with the voice of medical authority in children's health issues, while being helpful and encouraging, cautionary but not critical, and responsible but not preachy. All articles should include interviews with appropriate Academy-member pediatricians and other health care professionals."

Ⓝ ⭐ $ HOME EDUCATION MAGAZINE, P.O. Box 1083, Tonasket WA 98855. (509)486-1351. E-mail: hem-editor@home-ed-magazine.com. Website: www.home-ed-magazine.com. **Contact:** Helen E. Hegener, managing editor. **80% freelance written.** Bimonthly magazine covering home-based education. "We feature articles which address the concerns of parents who want to take a direct involvement in the education of their children—concerns such as socialization, how to find curriculums and materials, testing and evaluation, how to tell when your child is ready to begin reading, what to do when homeschooling is difficult, teaching advanced subjects, etc." Estab. 1983. Circ. 32,000. **Pays on acceptance.** Publishes ms an average of 4 months after acceptance. Byline given. ("Please include a 30-50 word credit with your article.") Buys first North American electronic, serial, first, one-time rights. Submit seasonal material 6 months in advance. Accepts queries by mail, e-mail. Responds in 2 months. Sample copy for $6.50. Writer's guidelines for #10 SASE or via e-mail (write "Writers Guidelines" in the subject line).

O→ Break in by "reading our magazine, understanding how we communicate with our readers, having an understanding of homeschooling and being able to communicate that understanding clearly."

Nonfiction: Essays, how-to (related to home schooling), humor, interview/profile, personal experience, photo features, technical. **Buys 40-50 mss/year.** Query with or without published clips, or send complete ms. Length: 750-2,500 words. **Pays $50-100.** Sometimes pays expenses of writers on assignment.

Photos: Send photos with submission. Reviews enlargements, 35mm prints, b&w snapshots, CD-ROMs. Color transparencies for covers $50 each; inside b&w $10 each. Identification of subjects preferred. Buys one-time rights (print and electronic).

Tips: "We would like to see how-to articles (that don't preach, just present options); articles on testing, accountability, working with the public schools, socialization, learning disabilities, resources, support groups, legislation and humor. We need answers to the questions that homeschoolers ask. Please, no teachers telling parents how to teach. Personal experience with homeschooling is most preferred approach."

N ☒ $HOMESCHOOLING TODAY, S Squared Productions Inc., P.O. Box 1608, Ft. Collins CO 80524. Fax: (970)224-1824. E-mail: publisher@homeschooltoday.com. Website: www.homeschooltoday.com. **Contact:** Maureen McCaffrey, editor. **75% freelance written.** Bimonthly magazine covering homeschooling. "We are a practical magazine for homeschoolers with a broadly Christian perspective." Estab. 1992. Circ. 25,000. Pays on publication. Publishes ms an average of 1 year after acceptance. Byline given. Offers $50 kill fee. Buys first rights. Editorial lead time 6 months. Submit seasonal material 1 year in advance. Accepts queries by mail, e-mail, fax. Accepts simultaneous submissions. Responds in 1 month to queries; 2 months to mss. Sample copy and writer's guidelines free.

Nonfiction: Book excerpts, how-to, inspirational, interview/profile, new product. No fiction, poetry. **Buys 30 mss/ year.** Query. Length: 500-2,500 words. **Pays 8¢/word.**

Photos: State availability of photos with submission. Offers no additional payment for photos accepted with ms. Captions and identification of subjects required. Buys one-time rights.

N ☒ $ $LAS VEGAS FAMILY MAGAZINE, Churm Publishing, 6320 McLeod Dr., #3, Las Vegas NV 89120. (702)740-2260. Fax: (702)740-4299. E-mail: lvfamily@earthlink.net. Website: www.ocfamily.com. Executive Editor: Craig Reem. **Contact:** Greg Blake Miller, managing editor. **75% freelance written.** "*Las Vegas Family Magazine* is a monthly news magazine covering family issues for Clark County parents written in a journalistic style. Very good writing and a knowledge of Clark County and Las Vegas is required." Estab. 2000. Circ. 50,000. Pays on publication. Publishes ms an average of 2 months after acceptance. Byline given. Offers $50 kill fee. Buys electronic and one-time rights. Editorial lead time 2 months. Submit seasonal material 6 months in advance. Responds in 1 month to queries.

Nonfiction: How-to (how to raise multiple children, education options, coping with children who have growth problems, etc.), personal experience (especially for Dad on the Edge and Mother Knows columns), and topics related to family issues. Special issue: Annual Back to School issue (August). "Special interest area writers and physicians are encouraged to submit ideas: women's health (whole range, from physical to mental and spiritual). We prefer physicians and medical specialists write about women's health, but are open to ideas from all writers." No essays, exposé, historical, nostalgic, opinion, photo features or technical. **Buys 30 mss/year.** Query. "No unsolicited manuscripts." Length: 500-2,500 words. **Pays $100-350.**

Photos: Offers $80-200/photo assignment. Buys one-time and electronic rights.

Columns/Departments: ABCs (education column focuses on the ins and outs of local education, new learning methods, etc. This column must be written by local writer, runs 800-1,000 words and **pays $200**). Other columns are: Dad on the Edge (humorous discussion of the challenges of modern dadding); Mother Knows (more serious advice column); Passages (three-column series in every issue): The Early Years (ages 0-5, mostly health issues, psychology, habits and fun stuff); The Middle Years (ages 6-12, focuses on education, play, a social interaction); The Teen Years (ages 13-18, issues important to teens and parents of teens); Family Portrait (Q&A interview of a local family, usually prominent, but sometimes just an amazing and interesting family); In Shape (focuses on nutrition, exercise and family fitness activities); On the Field (focuses on youth sports); High Tech (focuses on educational software); Entertainment (focuses on special family in-town entertainment—must be written by local writer); all 550 words. **Buys 15 mss/year.** Query. **Pays $100-200.**

☒ $ $METRO PARENT MAGAZINE, Metro Parent Publishing Group, 24567 Northwestern Hwy., Suite 150, Southfield MI 48075. (248)352-0990. Fax: (248)352-5066. E-mail: metparent@aol.com. Website: www.family.com. **Contact:** Susan DeMaggio, editor. **75% freelance written.** Monthly magazine covering parenting, women's health, education. "We are a local magazine on parenting topics and issues of interest to Detroit-area parents. Related issues: Windsor, Ontario Parent; Ann Arbor Parent; African/American Parent; Metro Baby Magazine." Circ. 85,000. Pays on publication. Publishes ms an average of 3 months after acceptance. Byline given. Buys first rights. Editorial lead time 3 months. Submit seasonal material 3 months in advance. Accepts queries by mail, e-mail. Accepts simultaneous submissions. Responds in 2 weeks to queries; 3 months to mss. Sample copy for $2.50.

Nonfiction: Essays, humor, inspirational, personal experience. Upcoming special issues will cover Moms and Dads working from home; working in general. "No run-of-the-mill first-person baby experiences!" **Buys 100 mss/year.** Send complete ms. Length: 1,500-2,500 words. **Pays $30-300 for assigned articles.**
Reprints: Accepts previously published submissions.
Photos: State availability of photos with submission. Offers $100-200/photo or negotiates payment individually. Captions required. Buys one-time rights.
Columns/Departments: Boredom Busters (kids crafts, things to do), 750 words; Women's Health (latest issues of 20-40 year olds), 750-900 words; Home On The Range (recipes, food topics), 750 words; Tweens 'N Teens (handling teen "issues"), 750-800 words. **Buys 50 mss/year.** Send complete ms. **Pays $75-150.**

$ METROKIDS MAGAZINE, The Resource for Delaware Valley Families, Kidstuff Publications, Inc., 1080 N. Delaware Ave., #702, Philadelphia PA 19125-4330. (215)291-5560. Fax: (215)291-5563. E-mail: editor@metro kids.com. Website: www.localmom.com. **Contact:** Nancy Lisagor, editor-in-chief. **80% freelance written.** Monthly tabloid providing information for parents and kids in southeastern Pennsylvania, South Jersey and Delaware. Estab. 1990. Circ. 125,000. Pays on publication. Byline given. Buys one-time and electronic rights. Submit seasonal material 4 months in advance. Accepts queries by mail, e-mail, fax, phone. Responds in up to 8 months to queries. Guidelines for #10 SASE.
Nonfiction: General interest, how-to, new product, travel, parenting, health. Special issues: Baby First (April; pregnancy, childbirth, first baby); Camps (December-June); Special Kids (October; children with special needs); Vacations and Theme Parks (May, June); What's Happening (January; guide to events and activities); Kids 'N Care (July; guide to childcare). **Buys 40 mss/year.** Query with published clips. Prefers mss to queries. Length: 800-1,500 words maximum. **Pays $35-100.** Sometimes pays expenses of writers on assignment.
Reprints: Send photocopy of article and information about when and where it previously appeared. **Pays $20-40.**
Photos: State availability of photos with submission. Captions required. Buys one-time rights.
Columns/Departments: Book Beat (book reviews); Bytesize (CD-ROM and website reviews); Body Wise (health); Dollar Sense (finances); all 500-700 words. **Buys 25 mss/year.** Query. **Pays $1-50.**
Tips: "*MetroKids* is a resource guide, first and foremost. As such, we use very little 'column' or anecdotal writing that isn't a lead-in for practical parenting information and specific resources." Articles should cite expert sources and the most up-to-date theories and facts. We are looking for a journalistic-style of writing. Editorial calendar available on request. We are also interested in finding local writers for assignments."

$ $ NORTHWEST FAMILY MAGAZINE, MMB Publications, Inc., 1155 N. State St., #414, Bellingham WA 98225. (360)734-3025. Fax: (360)734-1550. E-mail: nwfamily@earthlink.net. Website: www.nwfamily.com. **Contact:** Lisa Laskey, editor. **50% freelance written.** Monthly parenting magazine providing information on parenting issues and helping local families to be in touch with resources, events and places in the Northwest and western Washington State. Estab. 1995. Circ. 50,000. Pays on publication. Publishes ms an average of 6 months after acceptance. Byline sometimes given. Buys one-time rights. Editorial lead time 3 months. Submit seasonal material 6 months in advance. Accepts queries by mail, e-mail. Accepts simultaneous submissions. Responds in 3 weeks to queries; 3 months to mss. Sample copy for $1.25. Writer's guidelines for #10 SASE.
Nonfiction: Essays, general interest, how-to relating to children and parenting, humor, inspirational, interview/profile, new product, personal experience, photo feature, travel with kids. **Buys 40-50 mss/year.** Send complete ms. Length: 300-1,600 words. **Pays 10¢/word for assigned articles; $25-45 for unsolicited articles** (depending on length). Sometimes pays expenses of writers on assignment.
Reprints: Accepts previously published submissions.
Photos: State availability of photos with submission. Reviews negatives and any size prints. Negotiates payment individually. Model releases required. Buys one-time rights.
Columns/Departments: School News (information about schools, especially local), 100-300 words; Community News (quick information for families in western Washington), 100-300 words; Reviews (videos/books/products for families), 100-300 words; Teen News (information of interest to parents of teens), 50-300 words. **Buys 8-10 mss/year.** Send complete ms. **Pays $10-20.**
Poetry: Lisa Laskey, editor. Avant garde, free verse, haiku, light verse, traditional. "No heavy or negative content." **Buys 6 poems/year.** Submit maximum 5 poems. Length: 6-25 lines. **Pays $5-20.**
Tips: "Send entire article with word count. Topic should apply to parents (regional focus increases our need for your article) and be addressed in a positive manner—'How to' not 'How not to.'"

$ $ $ $ PARENTING MAGAZINE, 1325 Avenue of the Americas, 27th Floor, New York NY 10019-6026. (212)522-8989. Fax: (212)522-8699. Editor-in-Chief: Janet Chan. Executive Editor: Lisa Bain. **Contact:** Articles Editor. Magazine published 10 times/year "for parents of children from birth to six and older, and covering both the psychological and practical aspects of parenting." Estab. 1987. **Pays on acceptance.** Byline given. Offers 25% kill fee. Buys first rights. Sample copy for $2.95 and 9×12 SAE with 5 first-class stamps. Writer's guidelines for #10 SASE.
Nonfiction: Articles editor. Book excerpts, child development/behavior/health, investigative reports, personal experience. **Buys 20-30 features/year.** Query with or without published clips. No phone queries, please. Length: 1,000-2,500 words. **Pays $1,000-3,000.** Usually pays expenses of writers on assignment.
• Ranked as one of the best markets for freelance writers in *Writer's Yearbook* magazine's annual "Top 100 Markets," January 2000.

Columns/Departments: Family Reporter (news items relating to children/family), 100-400 words; Ages and Stages (child development and behavior), 100-400 words; Children's Health, 100-350 words. **Buys 50-60 mss/year.** Query to the specific departmental editor. **Pays $50-400.**

Tips: "The best guide for writers is the magazine itself. Please familiarize yourself with it before submitting a query."

$ $ PARENTS' PRESS, The Monthly Newspaper for Bay Area Parents, 1454 Sixth St., Berkeley CA 94710-1431. (510)524-1602. Fax: (510)524-0912. E-mail: parentsprs@aol.com. Website: members.aol.com/parentsprs/index.html. **Contact**: Dixie M. Jordan, editor. **25% freelance written.** Monthly tabloid for parents. Estab. 1980. Circ. 75,000. Pays within 45 days of publication. Publishes ms an average of 4 months after acceptance. Kill fee varies (individually negotiated). Buys all rights, including electronic, second serial (reprint) and almost always Northern California Exclusive rights. Submit seasonal material 6 months in advance. Accepts queries by mail, e-mail. Responds in 3 months. Sample copy for $3. Writer's guidelines and editorial calendar for #10 SASE or on website. Rarely considers simultaneous submissions.

Nonfiction: Book excerpts, well-researched articles on children's health, development, education, family activities and travel. "We require a strong Bay Area focus in almost all articles. Use quotes from experts and Bay Area parents. Please, no child-rearing tips or advice based on personal experience." Special annual issues include Pregnancy, Birth & Baby, Family Travel, Back to School. **Buys 30-50 mss/year.** Query with or without published clips, or send complete ms. Length: 300-3,000 words; 1,500-2,000 average. **Pays $50-500 for assigned articles; $25-250 for unsolicited articles.** Will pay more if photos accompany article. Negotiable. Will negotiate fees for special projects written by Bay Area journalists.

Reprints: Send photocopy of article with rights for sale noted and information about when and where the article previously appeared and where else it is being submitted. Pays up to $50.

Photos: State availability of photos with submission. Reviews prints, any size, b&w only. Offers $10-15/photo. Model release and identification of subject required. Buys one-time rights.

Tips: "We're looking for more pieces on elementary education with a Bay-area focus."

$ $ PARENT.TEEN, The Magazine for Bay Area Families with Teens, Parents' Press, 1454 Sixth St., Berkeley CA 94710. (510)524-1602. Fax: (510)524-0912. E-mail: parentsprs@aol.com. Website: members.aol.com/parentsprs/index.html. **Contact**: Dixie M. Jordan, editor. **75% freelance written.** Monthly magazine for parents of teens. Estab. 1997. Circ. 80,000. Pays within 60 days of publication. Publishes ms an average of 3 months after acceptance. Kill fee varies (individually negotiated). Buys all rights, second serial (reprint) and almost always Northern California Exclusive rights. Submit seasonal material 6 months in advance. Accepts queries by mail, e-mail. Responds in 2 months. Sample copy for $3. Writer's guidelines and editorial calendar for #10 SASE or on website.

○┐ Break in with profiles of offbeat colleges or programs, especially California/West Coast and articles on innovative programs operated by teens in the Bay Area. Examples have been teenage members of Search & Rescue, a teen-run wildlife museum, teen-produced programs for National Public Radio.

Nonfiction: Regular features, open to all, cover adolescent medicine, teen psychology, youth culture and trends, education, college preparation, work, sports, sex, gender roles, family relationships, legal topics, financial issues and profiles of interesting teens, colleges and programs. "We require a strong Bay Area focus in most articles. Use quotes from experts and Bay Area teens." **Buys 40 mss/year.** Query with clips or send complete ms on spec. "We pay for lively, information-packed content, not length." Length: 500-1,200 words. **Pays $150-500.**

Reprints: Send a photocopy of article with rights for sale noted and information about when and where the article previously appeared. Pays up to $50.

Photos: State availability of photos with submission. Payment rates higher for mss with photos. Photos only: $15-50 for one-time rights (b&w). Reviews color slides for cover; contact art director Renee Benoit before sending. Photos returned only if accompanied by SASE. Model releases and subject identification required.

Columns/Departments: Pays $5-10 for "grab bag" items, ranging from one sentence to one paragraph on "weird facts about teens" or teen-related Bay Area news item. Submissions must cite sources of information.

Tips: "We do not commission stories by writers who are unknown to us, so your best bet is to send us original articles on spec or already published articles offered for reprint rights. We are looking for writers who can pack a lot of information in as few words as possible in lively prose. No first-person 'How I Got My Kid Through Teenhood.' "

N $ PEDIATRICS FOR PARENTS, Pediatrics for Parents, Inc., 747 53rd, #3, Philadelphia PA 19147-3321. Fax: (419)858-7221. E-mail: rich.sagall@pobox.com. **Contact:** Richard J. Sagall, editor. **10% freelance written.** Monthly newsletter covering children's health. "*Pediatrics For Parents* emphasizes an informed, common-sense approach to childhood health care. We stress preventative action, accident prevention, when to call the doctor and when and how to handle a situation at home. We are also looking for articles that describe general, medical and pediatric problems, advances, new treatments, etc. All articles must be medically accurate and useful to parents with children—prenatal to adolescence." Estab. 1981. Circ. 500. Pays on publication. Publishes ms an average of 4 months after acceptance. Byline given. Buys first North American serial and electronic rights. Accepts queries by mail, e-mail, fax. Accepts simultaneous submissions. Responds in 1 month. Sample copy for $3. Writer's guidelines for #10 SASE or by e-mail.

Nonfiction: Medical. No first person or experience. **Buys 10 mss/year.** Query or send complete ms. Length: 200-1,000 words. **Pays $10-50.**

Reprints: Accepts previously published submissions.

N $ $ $ $ **PREVENTION UPDATE, A Publication Devoted to Preventing the Exploitation of Children**, Committee for Children, 2203 Airport Way S, Suite 500, Seattle WA 98134-2035. (800)634-4449. Fax: (206)343-1445. E-mail: lwalls@cfchildren.org. Website: www.cfchildren.org. **Contact:** Lisa Walls, editor. **30% freelance written.** Education and counseling quarterly (during the school year) covering violence prevention, social and emotional skills education, and child sexual abuse prevention education. "Committee for Children is a not-for-profit organization whose mission is to promote the safety, well-being, and social development of children by creating quality educational programs for educators, families and communities. *Prevention Update* is Committee for Children's newsletter, mailed quarterly to our clients (those who've purchased our curricula—primarily school teachers and administrators and staff at youth organizations such as the Boys and Girls Clubs)." Estab. 1985. Circ. 17,000. ½ paid upon acceptance; ½ paid upon publication. Publishes ms an average of 5 months after acceptance. Byline given. Buys first and second serial (reprint) rights. Editorial lead time 8 months. Accepts queries by mail, e-mail, fax. Accepts simultaneous submissions. Responds in 1 month to queries; 3 months to mss. Sample copy and writer's guidelines free.

Nonfiction: Interview/profile, technical. "Nothing that does not deal with child sexual abuse prevention, violence prevention, or social and emotional skills education." **Buys varying number of mss/year.** Query with published clips. Length: 500-2,000 words. **Pays $250-1,125.**

Reprints: Accepts previously published submissions.

Photos: Send photos with submission. Reviews 8×10 prints. Offers no additional payment for photos accepted with ms. Model releases and identification of subjects required. Buys all rights.

Columns/Departments: Notes From the Field (volunteer experiences, classroom work), 500-1,000 words. **Buys 2 mss/year.** Query with published clips. **Payment varies.**

Tips: "Stories should strive to educate clients; convey practical information for use in the classroom; build relationships between CFC and its clients; assist clients in their work; and help clients convince their constituents of the programs' benefits."

$ **SAN DIEGO FAMILY MAGAZINE, San Diego County's Leading Resource for Parents & Educators Who Care!**, P.O. Box 23960, San Diego CA 92193-3960. (619)685-6970. Fax: (619)685-6978. E-mail: sandiegofamily.com. Website: http://family.disney.go.com/Local/sdfp/sdfp-about.html. **Contact:** Sharon Bay, editor-in-chief. **75% freelance written.** Monthly magazine for parenting and family issues. "*SDFM* strives to provide informative, educational articles emphasizing positive parenting for our typical readership of educated mothers, ages 25-45, with an upper-level income. Most articles are factual and practical, a few are humor and personal experience. Editorial emphasis is uplifting and positive." Estab. 1982. Circ. 120,000. Pays on publication. Byline given. Buys first, one-time or second serial (reprint) rights. Editorial lead time 2 months. Submit seasonal material 3 months in advance. Responds in 2 months to queries; 3 months to mss. Sample copy and writer's guidelines for $3.50 with 9×12 SAE.

Nonfiction: How-to, parenting, new baby help, enhancing education, family activities, interview/profile (influential or noted persons or experts included in parenting or the welfare of children) and articles of specific interest to or regarding San Diego (for California) families/children/parents/educators. "No rambling, personal experience pieces." **Buys 75 mss/year.** Send complete ms. Length: 800 words maximum. **Pays $1.25/column inch.** "Byline and contributor copies if writer prefers."

Reprints: Send typed ms with rights for sale noted and information about when and where the article previously appeared.

Photos: State availability of photos with submission. Reviews contact sheets and 3½×5 or 5×7 prints. Negotiates payment individually. Identification of subjects preferred. Buys one-time rights.

Columns/Departments: Kids' Books (topical book reviews), 800 words. **Buys 12 mss/year.** Query by mail only with published clips. **Pays $1.25/column inch minimum.**

Fillers: Facts and newsbreaks (specific to the family market). **Buys 10/year.** Length: 50-200 words. **Pays $1.25/column inch minimum.**

★ $ $ $ $ **SESAME STREET PARENTS**, Children's Television Workshop, 1 Lincoln Plaza, 2nd Floor, New York NY 10023-7129. (212)875-6470. Fax: (212)875-6105. Editor-in-Chief: Susan Lapinski. **Contact:** Patti Jones, associate editor. **80% freelance written.** Magazine published 10 times/year for parents of preschoolers that accompanies every issue of Sesame Street Magazine. Circ. 1,000,000. **Pays on acceptance.** Byline given. Offers 33% kill fee. Buys varying rights. Submit seasonal material 7 months in advance. Accepts queries by mail, fax. Responds in 3 months to queries. Sample copy for 9×12 SAE with 6 first-class stamps.

O─ Break in with a personal essay.

Nonfiction: Child development/parenting, how-to (practical tips for parents of preschoolers), interview/profile, personal experience, book excerpts, essays, photo feature, travel (with children). **Buys 100 mss/year.** Query with published clips or send complete ms. Length: 500-2,000 words. **Pays $300-2,000 for articles.**

● Ranked as one of the best markets for freelance writers in *Writer's Yearbook* magazine's annual "Top 100 Markets," January 2000.

Reprints: Send typed ms with rights for sale noted and information about when and where the article previously appeared. Negotiates payment.

Photos: State availability of photos with submission. Model releases, identification of subjects required. Buys one-time or all rights.

N ⭐ **$ $ SOUTH FLORIDA PARENTING**, 5555 Nob Hill Rd., Sunrise FL 33351. (954)747-3050. Fax: (954)747-3055. E-mail: vmccash@tribune.com. Website: www.sfparenting.com. **Contact:** Vicki McCash Brennan, managing editor. **90% freelance written.** Monthly magazine covering parenting, family. "*South Florida Parenting* provides news, information and a calendar of events for readers in Southeast Florida. The focus is on positive parenting and things to do or information about raising children in South Florida." Estab. 1990. Circ. 110,000. Pays on publication. Publishes ms an average of 2 months after acceptance. Byline given. Buys one-time rights, second serial (reprint) rights, simultaneous rights and electronic rights or makes work-for-hire assignments. Editorial lead time 4 months. Submit seasonal material 5 months in advance. Accepts queries by mail, e-mail, fax. Accepts simultaneous submissions. Responds in 1 month to queries; 6 months to mss. Sample copy for 9×12 SAE with $2.95 postage. Writer's guidelines for #10 SASE.

 O→ Break in with reviews of children's software. "We're looking for someone who is well-connected in the industry, devoted to reviewing software and can write."

Nonfiction: Family and children's issues, how-to, humor (preferably not first-person humor about kids and parents), interview/profile, personal experience. Special issues: Education Issue/Winter Health Issue (January); Birthday Party Issue (February); Summer Camp Issue (March); Maternity Issue (April); Florida/Vacation Guide (May); Kid Crown Awards (July); Back to School (August); Education (September); Holiday (December). **Buys 36-40 mss/year.** Query with published clips or send complete ms with SASE. Length: 500-2,000 words. **Pays $25-400 for articles.**

Reprints: Accepts previously published submissions "if not published in our circulation area." Send photocopy of article and information about when and where the article appeared. **Pays $25-50.**

Photos: State availability of photos with submission. Reviews negatives, transparencies, prints. Sometimes offers additional payment for ms with photos. Buys one-time rights.

Columns/Departments: Baby Basics (for parents of infants); Growing Concerns (child health); Preteen Power (for parents of preteens); Family Money (family finances), all 500-750 words. **Buys 30 mss/year.** Query with published clips or send complete ms. **Pays $40-150.**

Tips: "We want information targeted to the South Florida market. Multicultural and well-sourced is preferred. A unique approach to a universal parenting concern will be considered for publication. Profiles or interviews of courageous parents. Opinion pieces on child rearing should be supported by experts and research should be listed. First person stories should be fresh and insightful. All writing should be clear and concise. Submissions can be typewritten, double-spaced, but the preferred format is on diskette or by e-mail."

$ $ $ SUCCESSFUL STUDENT, Imagination Publishing, 820 W. Jackson Blvd., Suite 450, Chicago IL 60607. (312)627-1020. Fax: (312)627-1105. Website: www.imaginepub.com. **Contact:** Lisa Terry, editor. **30% freelance written.** Semiannual magazine published for customers of Sylvan Learning Centers covering education. "We focus on education-related issues and study habits and tips. We frequently use expert writers and/or sources." Circ. 550,000. Pays on publication. Publishes ms an average of 5 months after acceptance. Byline given. Offers 33% kill fee. Buys first North American serial rights. Editorial lead time 6 months. Accepts queries by mail, fax. Accepts simultaneous submissions.

Nonfiction: Book excerpts, essays, how-to (tips on studying, etc.), inspirational, interview/profile, new product. No parenting stories. Query with published clips and SASE. **Buys 2-4 mss/year.** Length: 300-1,700 words. **Pays 50¢/word.** Pays expenses of writers on assignment.

Reprints: Accepts previously published submissions.

Photos: State availability of photos with submission. Negotiates payment individually. Buys one-time rights.

Tips: "We're looking for writers with strong voices and an understanding of our editorial categories, who have the ability to write clearly and concisely. Because many of our stories include expert sources, our writers have enough of an education background to recognize these people. We frequently ask writers to pull short facts or tips into sidebars to complement the main stories. Stories are carefully reviewed for accuracy and appropriateness by the editorial staff and an advisory board from Sylvan Learning Systems."

N ⭐ **$ $ TIDEWATER PARENT**, Portfolio Publishing, 5700 Thurston Ave., Virginia Beach VA 23455. (757)363-7085. Fax: (757)363-1767. E-mail: tidewater@family.com. **Contact:** Jennifer O'Donnell, editor. **85% freelance written.** Monthly parenting tabloid. "All our readers are parents of children age 0-11. Our readers demand stories that will help them tackle the challenges and demands they face daily as parents." Estab. 1980. Circ. 40,000. Pays on publication. Byline given. Offers 10% kill fee. Buys first North American serial rights. Editorial lead time 2 months. Submit seasonal material 3 months in advance. Accepts queries by mail, e-mail, fax. Accepts simultaneous submissions. Responds in 1 week to queries; 4 months to mss. Sample copy and writer's guidelines free.

Nonfiction: Essays, general interest, historical/nostalgic, how-to, humor, interview/profile, personal experience, religious, travel. No poetry or fiction. **Buys 60 mss/year.** Query with published clips or send complete ms. Length: 500-3,000 words. **Pays $35-200.**

Reprints: Accepts previously published submissions.

Photos: State availability of photos with submission or send photos with submission. Negotiates payment individually. Captions required. Buys one-time rights.

Columns/Departments: Music and Video Software (reviews), both 600-800 words; also Where to Go, What to Do, Calendar Spotlight and Voices. **Buys 36 mss/year.** Send complete ms. **Pays $35-50.**

Tips: "Articles for *Tidewater Parent* should be informative and relative to parenting. An informal, familiar tone is preferable to a more formal style. Avoid difficult vocabulary and complicated sentence structure. A conversational tone works best. Gain your reader's interest by using real-life situations, people or examples to support what you're saying."

$ $ TOLEDO AREA PARENT NEWS, Toledo Area Parent News, Inc., 1120 Adams St., Toledo OH 43624-1509. (419)244-9859. Fax: (419)244-9871. E-mail: erin@toledocitypaper.com. Website: family.go.com/Local/tole. **Contact:** Erin Kramer, editor. **20% freelance written.** Monthly tabloid for Northwest Ohio/Southeast Michigan parents. Estab. 1992. Circ. 50,000. Pays on publication. Publishes ms an average of 1 month after acceptance. Byline given. Makes work-for-hire assignments. Editorial lead time 3 months. Accepts queries by mail, e-mail, fax. Responds in 1 month. Sample copy for $1.50.
Nonfiction: "We use only local writers, by assignment only." General interest, interview/profile, opinion. "We accept queries and opinion pieces only. Send cover letter and clips to be considered for assignments." **Buys 10 mss/year.** Length: 1,000-2,500 words. **Pays $75-125.**
Photos: State availability of photos with submission. Negotiates payment individually. Identification of subjects required. Buys all rights.
Tips: "We love humorous stories that deal with common parenting issues or features on cutting-edge issues."

★ $ $ TWINS, The Magazine for Parents of Multiples, The Business Word, Inc., 5350 S. Roslyn St., Suite 400, Englewood CO 80111-2125. (303)290-8500 or (888)55TWINS. Fax: (303)290-9025. E-mail: twins.editor@businessword.com. Website: www.twinsmagazine.com. Editor-in-Chief: Susan J. Alt. **Contact:** Marge D. Hansen, managing editor. **80% freelance written.** Bimonthly magazine covering parenting multiples. "*TWINS* is an international publication that provides informational and educational articles regarding the parenting of twins, triplets and more. All articles must be multiple specific and have an upbeat, hopeful and/or positive ending." Estab. 1984. Circ. 55,000. Pays on publication. Byline given. Buys first North American serial rights. Editorial lead time 3 months. Submit seasonal material 5 months in advance. Accepts queries by mail, e-mail, fax. Accepts simultaneous submissions. Response time varies. Sample copy for $5 or on website. Writer's guidelines for #10 SASE.
Nonfiction: Personal experience (first-person parenting experience) and professional experience as it relates to multiples. Interested in seeing twin-specific discipline articles. Nothing on cloning, pregnancy reduction or fertility issues. **Buys 12 mss/year.** Query with or without published clips or send complete ms. Length: 1,300 words. **Pays $25-250 for assigned articles; $25-75 for unsolicited articles.**
Photos: State availability of photos with submission. Offers no additional payment for photos accepted with ms. Identification of subjects required.
Columns/Departments: On Being Parents (parenting multiples/personal essay), 800-850 words; Special Miracles (miraculous stories about multiples with a happy ending), 800-850 words. **Buys 12-20 mss/year.** Query with or without published clips or send complete ms. **Pays $25-75.** "All department articles must have a happy ending, as well as teach a lesson that parents of multiples can learn from."

★ $ WESTERN NEW YORK FAMILY, Western New York Family Inc., P.O. Box 265, 287 Parkside Ave., Buffalo NY 14215-0265. (716)836-3486. Fax: (716)836-3680. E-mail: wnyfamily@aol.com. Website: www.westernnewyork.com. **Contact:** Michele Miller, editor/publisher. **90% freelance written.** Monthly magazine covering parenting in Western NY. "Readership is largely composed of families with children ages newborn to 12 years. Although most subscriptions are in the name of the mother, 91% of fathers also read the publication. Strong emphasis is placed on how and where to find family-oriented events, as well as goods and services for children, in Western New York." Estab. 1984. Circ. 22,500. Pays on publication. Publishes ms up to 18 months after acceptance. Byline given. Buys one-time, second serial (reprint) or simultaneous (non-local) rights. Editorial lead time 3 months. Submit seasonal material 3 months in advance. Accepts queries by mail, e-mail, fax. Accepts simultaneous submissions (non-local). Responds only if interested. Sample copy for $2.50 and 9×12 SAE with 3 first-class stamps. Guidelines for #10 SASE or by e-mail.
　　O— Break in with either a "cutting edge" topic that is new and different in its relevance to parenting in the 90s or a "timeless" topic which is "evergreen" and can be kept on file to fill last minute holes.
Nonfiction: How-to (craft projects for kids, holiday, costume, etc.), humor (as related to parenting), personal experience (parenting related), travel (family destinations). Special issues: Birthday Celebrations (January); Cabin Fever (February); Having A Baby (March); Education & Enrichment (April); Mother's Day (May); Father's Day (June); Summer Fun (July and August); Back to School (September); Halloween Happenings (October); Family Issues (November); and Holiday Happenings (December). **Buys 50 mss/year.** Send complete ms. Length: 750-3,000 words. **Pays $50-125 for assigned articles; $20-50 for unsolicited articles.** Sometimes pays expenses of writers on assignment.
Reprints: Accepts previously published submissions.
Photos: State availability of photos with submission. Reviews 3×5 prints. Offers no additional payment for photos accepted with ms. Captions, model releases and identification of subjects required. Buys one-time rights.
Fillers: Facts. **Buys 10/year.** Length: 450 words. **Pays $20.**
Tips: "We are interested in well-researched, nonfiction articles on surviving the newborn, preschool, school age and adolescent years. Our readers want practical information on places to go and things to do in the Buffalo area and nearby Canada. They enjoy humorous articles about the trials and tribulations of parenthood as well as 'how-to' articles (i.e., tips for finding a sitter, keeping your sanity while shopping with preschoolers, ideas for holidays and birthdays, etc.). Articles on making a working parent's life easier are of great interest as are articles written by fathers. We also need more material on pre-teen and young teen (13-15) issues. We prefer a warm, conversational style of writing."

$ $ $ $ WORKING MOTHER MAGAZINE, MacDonald Communications, 135 W. 50th St., 16th Floor, New York NY 10020-1201. (212)445-6100. Fax: (212)445-6174. E-mail: editors@workingmothers.com. **Contact**: Susie Rich-Brooke, senior editor. **90% freelance written.** Prefers to work with published/established writers; works with a small number of new/unpublished writers each year. Monthly magazine for women who balance a career with the concerns of parenting. Circ. 925,000. Publishes ms an average of 4 months after acceptance. Byline given. Buys all rights. Pays 20% kill fee. Submit seasonal material 6 months in advance. Accepts queries by mail. Sample copy for $4. Writer's guidelines for SASE.

Nonfiction: Service, humor, child development, material pertinent to the working mother's predicament. Query to *Working Mother Magazine.* **Buys 9-10 mss/issue.** Length: 1,500-2,000 words. Pays expenses of writers on assignment.

Tips: "We are looking for pieces that help the reader. In other words, we don't simply report on a trend without discussing how it specifically affects our readers' lives and how they can handle the effects. Where can they look for help if necessary?"

COMIC BOOKS

N $ $ COMICS SCENE, (formerly *Sci-Fi TV*), Starlog Group, 475 Park Ave. S, 8th Floor, New York NY 10016. (212)689-2839. Fax: (212)889-7933. E-mail: communications@starloggroup.com. Managing Editor: Keith Olexa. **Contact:** David McDonnell, editor. **90% freelance written.** Bimonthly magazine covering "current comic books, comic strips, the people who create them and TV/movie/animated adaptations of them. No nostalgia, no old favorites. Just the new stuff. It is a sister magazine to (and supplement to) *Starlog* (established 1976)." This is its third incarnation (previously published 1981-83, 1987-96). Pays on publication. Publishes ms an average of 4 months after acceptance. Byline given. Offers 25% kill fee. Buys all rights. Editorial lead time 3 months. Accepts queries by mail, e-mail, fax. Responds in 6 weeks. Sample copy for $7. Writer's guidelines for #10 SASE.

Nonfiction: Interview/profile, new product. "We basically run interviews with people—by the artists, writers, editors or animators." **Buys 100 mss/year.** Query with published clips. Length: 1,750-3,500 words. **Pays $150-275.** Sometimes pays expenses of writers on assignment.

Photos: State availability of photos with submission. Reviews prints. Offers $15-25/photo. Identification of subjects required. Buys all rights.

Columns/Departments: Columns devoted to comic book news, animation, movie/TV adaptations (mini-interviews), 35-350 words. **Buys 40 mss/year.** Query with published clips. **Pays $25-35.**

Fiction: "We do not publish fiction comic books or comic strips. Don't send it to us ever."

Tips: "Read the magazine and perhaps our sister magazine *Starlog.* Know that we only cover the current comics scene. Proposing something on an old comic is an automatic rejection. Do not call us ever. Only mail please—or if necessary, e-mail or fax queries."

$ $ WIZARD: THE COMICS MAGAZINE, Wizard Entertainment, 151 Wells Ave., Congers NY 10920-2036. (914)268-2000. Fax: (914)268-0053. E-mail: aekardon@aol.com. Website: www.wizardworld.com. Editor: Brian Cunningham. Senior Editor: Joe Yanarella. **Contact:** Andrew Kardon, managing editor. **50% freelance written.** Monthly magazine covering comic books, science fiction and action figures. Estab. 1991. Circ. 209,000. Pays on publication. Publishes ms an average of 3 months after acceptance. Byline given. Offers 50% kill fee. Buys all rights. Editorial lead time 4 months. Accepts queries by mail, e-mail, fax. Responds in 6 weeks. Sample copy and writer's guidelines free.

Nonfiction: Historical/nostalgic, how-to, humor, interview/profile, new product, personal experience, photo feature, first person diary. No columns or opinion pieces. **Buys 100 mss/year.** Query with or without published clips. Length: 250-4,000 words. **Pays 15-20¢/word.** Sometimes pays expenses of writers on assignment.

Photos: State availability of photos with submission. Negotiates payment individually. Identification of subjects required. Buys all rights.

Columns/Departments: Video Stuff (comic book, sci-fi and top-selling video games); Manga Mania (the latest news, anime, manga, toys, etc. from Japan); Coming Attractions (comic book-related movies and TV shows), 150-500 words. Query with published clips. **Pays $75-500.**

Tips: "Send plenty of samples showing the range of your writing styles. Have a good knowledge of comic books. Read a few issues to get the feel of the conversational 'Wizard Style.' "

CONSUMER SERVICE & BUSINESS OPPORTUNITY

Some of these magazines are geared to investing earnings or starting a new business; others show how to make economical purchases. Publications for business executives and consumers interested in business topics are listed under Business & Finance. Those on how to run specific businesses are classified by category in the Trade section.

■ $ ECONOMIC FACTS, The National Research Bureau, Inc., 320 Valley St., Burlington IA 52601. (319)752-5415. Fax: (319)752-3421. **Contact**: Nancy Heinzel, editor. **75% freelance written.** Quarterly magazine. Estab. 1948. Pays on publication. Publishes ms an average of 1 year after acceptance. Byline given. Buys all rights. Sample copy and writer's guidelines for #10 SAE with 2 first-class stamps.

 ● Eager to work with new/unpublished writers; works with a small number of new/unpublished writers each year.
Nonfiction: General interest (private enterprise, government data, graphs, taxes and health care). **Buys 10 mss/year.** Query with outline of article. Length: 500-700 words. **Pays 4¢/word.**

▦ $ FINANCIAL SENTINEL, Your beacon to the world of investing, Gulf/Atlantic Publishing, 1947 Lee Rd., Winter Park FL 32789. (407)628-5700. Fax: (407)628-3611. E-mail: mwonline@money-world.net. Website: www. worldmicrocap.com. Managing Editor: Michelle Berberet. **Contact:** Rebecca Ramsay, editor. **60% freelance written.** Monthly business/investing tabloid. "Our readers like to invest in small companies. 99% of the news in our publication is about publicly traded companies. Most *Sentinel* readers are experienced investors with an average knowledge of investing. Articles are intended to inform and dazzle the reader with news from the small-cap/OTCBB industries. All articles must mention at least two publicly traded companies. All quotes/stats must be referenced by a source." Estab. 1997. Circ. 100,000. **Pays on acceptance.** Publishes ms an average of 3 months after acceptance. Byline given. Buys one-time and electronic rights. Editorial lead time 3 months. Submit seasonal material 4 months in advance. Accepts queries by mail, e-mail, fax. Accepts simultaneous submissions. Responds in 2 weeks to queries; 2 months to mss. Sample copy for $2.50. Writer's guidelines by e-mail.
Nonfiction: Exposé, how-to (invest), interview/profile, opinion, book reviews, health. **Buys 12 mss/year.** Query with published clips. Length: 400-1,300 words. **Pays $10-100.** Sometimes pays writers with contributor copies or other premiums with a published bio acknowledging author's business.
Reprints: Accepts previously published submissions.
Photos: State availability of photos with submission. Offers no additional payment for photos accepted with ms. Identification of subjects required. Buys one-time rights.
Columns/Departments: For Sale (all about real estate, retail, franchising), 500-900 words; Hidden Gems (mining, diamonds, oil, gas, etc.), 500-900 words; Health Alert (public health companies to invest in), 500-900 words; Global Profits (international industrial mergers/acquisitions), 900-1,300 words. **Buys 36 mss/year.** Query with published clips. **Pays $10-100.**
Tips: "Writers must have knowledge of the stock market. Previous business writing experience preferred."

■ $ $ HOME BUSINESS MAGAZINE, United Marketing & Research Company, Inc., 9582 Hamilton Ave. PMB 368, Huntington Beach CA 92646. Fax: (714)962-7722. E-mail: henderso@ix.netcom.com. Website: www.homebu sinessmag.com. **Contact**: Stacy Ann Henderson, editor-in-chief. **75% freelance written.** "*Home Business Magazine* covers every angle of the home-based business market including: cutting edge editorial by well-known authorities on sales and marketing, business operations, the home office, franchising, business opportunities, network marketing, mail order and other subjects to help readers choose, manage and prosper in a home-based business; display advertising, classified ads and a directory of home-based businesses; technology, the Internet, computers and the future of home-based business; home-office editorial including management advice, office set-up, and product descriptions; business opportunities, franchising and work-from-home success stories." Estab. 1993. Circ. 84,000. Pays on publication. Publishes ms an average of 6 months after acceptance. Byline given. Buys first, one-time, second serial (reprint) rights or makes work-for-hire assignments. Editorial lead time 2 months. Submit seasonal material 3 months in advance. Accepts queries by mail, e-mail, fax. Accepts simultaneous submissions. Sample copy for 9 × 12 SAE with 8 first-class stamps or on website. Writer's guidelines for #10 SASE.
Nonfiction: Book excerpts, general interest, how-to (home business), inspirational, interview/profile, new product, personal experience, photo feature, technical, mail order, franchise, business management, Internet, finance network marketing. No non-home business related topics. **Buys 40 mss/year.** Send complete ms with 9 × 12 SAE with 8 first-class stamps. Length: 200-1,000 words. **Pays 20¢/word for assigned articles; $0-100 for unsolicited articles.** Pays with contributor copies or other premiums on request or per pre-discussed arrangement with magazine.
Reprints: Accepts previously published submissions.
Photos: Send photos with submission. Offers no additional payment for photos accepted with ms. Identification of subjects required. Buys one-time rights.
Columns/Departments: Marketing & Sales; Money Corner; Home Office; Management; Technology; Working Smarter; Franchising; Network Marketing, all 200-1,000 words. Send complete ms. **Pays $0-100.**
 ▣ The online magazine carries original content not found in the print edition. Contact: Stacy Henderson, online editor.
Tips: "Send complete information by mail as per our writer's guidelines and e-mail if possible. We encourage writers to submit Feature Articles (1-2 pages) and Departmental Articles (⅓-1½ pages). Please submit polished, well-written, organized material. It helps to provide subheadings within the article. Boxes, lists and bullets are encouraged because they make your article easier to read, use and reference by the reader. A primary problem in the past is that articles do not stick to the subject of the title. Please pay attention to the focus of your article and to your title. Please don't call to get the status of your submission. We will call if we're interested in publishing the submission."

$ $ $ KIPLINGER'S PERSONAL FINANCE, 1729 H St. NW, Washington DC 20006. (202)887-6400. Fax: (202)331-1206. Website: www.kiplinger.com. Editor: Ted Miller. **Contact:** Dale Sanders. **Less than 10% freelance**

written. Prefers to work with published/established writers. Monthly magazine for general, adult audience interested in personal finance and consumer information. "*Kiplinger's* is a highly trustworthy source of information on saving and investing, taxes, credit, home ownership, paying for college, retirement planning, automobile buying and many other personal finance topics." Estab. 1947. Circ. 1,300,000. **Pays on acceptance.** Publishes ms an average of 2 months after acceptance. Buys all rights. Responds in 1 month.

Nonfiction: "Most material is staff-written, but we accept some freelance. Thorough documentation is required for fact-checking." Query with clips of published work. Pays expenses of writers on assignment.

Tips: "We are looking for a heavy emphasis on personal finance topics."

N LIVING SAFETY, A Canada Safety Council publication for safety in the home, traffic and recreational environments, 1020 Thomas Spratt Place, Ottawa, Ontario K1G 5L5 Canada. (613)739-1535. Fax (613)739-1566. E-mail: csc@safety-council.org. Website: www.safety-council.org. Editor: Jack Smith. **65% freelance written.** Quarterly magazine covering off-the-job safety. "Off-the job health and safety magazine covering topics in the home, traffic and recreational environments. Audience is the Canadian employee and his/her family." Estab. 1983. Circ. 25,000. **Pays on acceptance.** Publishes ms an average of 2 months after acceptance. Byline given. Buys all rights. Editorial lead time 4 months. Submit seasonal material 6 months in advance. Accepts simultaneous submissions. Responds in 1 month to queries. Sample copy and writer's guidelines free.

Nonfiction: General interest, how-to (safety tips, health tips), personal experience. **Buys 24 mss/year.** Query with published clips. "Send intro letter, query, résumé and published clips (magazine preferable). Editor will call if interested." Length: 1,000-2,500 words. **Pays $500 maximum.** Sometimes pays expenses of writers on assignment.

Reprints: Send tearsheet of article or short story.

Photos: State availability of photos with submission. Reviews contact sheet, negatives, transparencies, prints. Offers no additional payment for photos accepted with ms. Identification of subjects required.

$ MONEY SAVING IDEAS, The National Research Bureau, 320 Valley St., Burlington IA 52601. (319)752-5415. Fax: (319)752-3421. **Contact:** Nancy Heinzel, editor. **75% freelance written**. Quarterly magazine that features money saving strategies. "We are interested in money saving tips on various subjects (insurance, travel, heating/cooling, buying a house, ways to cut costs and balance checkbooks). Our audience is mainly industrial and office workers." Estab. 1948. Circ. 1,000. Pays on publication. Publishes ms an average of 1 year after acceptance. Byline given. Buys all rights. Sample copy and writers guidelines for #10 SAE with 2 first-class stamps. Writer's guidelines for #10 SASE.

Nonfiction: How-to (save on grocery bills, heating/cooling bills, car expenses, insurance, travel). Query with or without published clips, or send complete ms. Length: 500-700 words. **Pays 4¢/word.**

Tips: "Follow our guidelines. Keep articles to stated length, double-spaced, neatly typed. If writer wishes rejected manuscript returned include SASE. Name, address and word length should appear on first page."

★ $ $ SPARE TIME MAGAZINE, The Magazine of Money Making Opportunities, Kipen Publishing Corp., 2400 S. Commerce Dr., New Berlin WI 53151. (262)780-1070. Fax: (262)780-1071. E-mail: editor@spare-time.com. Website: www.spare-time.com. **Contact:** Peter Abbott, editor. **75% freelance written.** Magazine published monthly except July covering affordable money-making opportunities. "We publish information the average person can use to begin and operate a spare-time business or extra income venture, with the possible goal of making it fulltime." Estab. 1955. Circ. 300,000. Pays on publication. Publishes ms an average of 3 months after acceptance. Byline given. Buys first North American serial rights. Editorial lead time 2 months. Submit seasonal material 3 months in advance. Accepts queries by mail, e-mail, fax, phone. Accepts simultaneous submissions, query first. Responds in 1 month to queries; 2 months to mss. Sample copy for $2.50. Writer's guidelines and editorial calendar for #10 SASE or via e-mail.

Nonfiction: Book excerpts and reviews (small business related), how-to (market, keep records, stay motivated, choose opportunity), interview/profile and personal experience (small business related). "No comparative or negative product reviews; political, philosophical or religious viewpoints; or controversial subjects." **Buys 22-33 mss/year.** Query with SASE. Length: up to 1,100 words (cover story: 1,500-2,000 words; installment series, three parts up to 1,100 words each). **Pays 15¢/word upon publication.**

Reprints: Send photocopy of article or typed ms with information about when and where the article previously appeared. Pays 50% of amount paid for an original article.

Photos: State availability of photos with submission. Reviews contact sheets, 3×5 or larger prints. Pays $15/published photo. Captions, identification of subjects required. Buys one-time rights.

Tips: "We look for articles that are unusual or unique; include examples of successful people whose experiences illustrate the points you're trying to make and inspire our readers with the hope that they, too, can succeed; quote experts rather than read like essays (if you're the expert, give some examples from your own experiences, but try to include comments from at least one other expert and one other person's real-life experience); add sidebars with check-off or to-do lists, tips, examples or additional resources; and include art or photos—especially action photos—to 'dress up' your piece. It is always best to query. At all times keep in mind that the audience is the average person, not over-educated in terms of business techniques. The best pieces are written in lay language and relate to that type of person."

$ THE UNDERGROUND SHOPPER, Talk Productions, 1508 E. Belt Line Rd., Carrollton TX 75006. (972)245-1144. E-mail: queries@undergroundshopper.com. **Contact:** Kit King, senior editor. Eager to work with new/unpublished writers. Monthly magazine focused on showing consumers how and where to find a useful and pleasant shopping experience. Articles must emphasize value—in time, money and service. **Pays on acceptance.** Byline given. Buys first rights, some second rights. Submit seasonal/holiday material 4 months in advance. Query by mail, e-mail. Responds in 1 month. Sample copy and writer's guidelines for $1.50 postage and SASE.

Nonfiction: How-to, new product, personal experience, consumer tips. Query. Length 400-1,000 words. **Pays $150-300** for first-time freelancers.

Photos: State availability of photos with query. Offers $25-50 per photo to freelance photographers. Buys first rights and reprint rights.

Fillers: Anecdotes, facts and consumer information. Length: 50 words maximum. **Pays $10-20.**

Tips: "Interested in articles focused on shopping for goods and services. Submissions should give consumers information on how and where to find the best value, regardless of price and should explain how to recognize good workmanship and quality in merchandise."

CONTEMPORARY CULTURE

These magazines often combine politics, current events and cultural elements such as art, literature, film and music, to examine contemporary society. Their approach to institutions is typically irreverent and investigative. Some, like *Madison*, report on alternative culture and appeal to a young adult "Generation X" audience. Others treat mainstream culture for a baby boomer generation audience.

$ $ $ $ A&U, America's AIDS Magazine, Art & Understanding, Inc., 25 Monroe St., Albany NY 12210. (518)426-9010. Fax: (518)436-5354. E-mail: mailbox@aumag.org. Website: www.aumag.org. **Contact:** David Waggoner, editor-in-chief. **50% freelance written.** Monthly magazine covering cultural responses to AIDS/HIV. Estab. 1991. Circ. 175,000. Pays on publication. Publishes ms an average of 3 months after acceptance. Byline given. Offers 20% kill fee. Buys first North American serial rights. Editorial lead time 6 months. Accepts queries by mail, e-mail. Accepts simultaneous submissions. Responds in 1 month to queries; 2 months to mss. Sample copy for $5. Writer's guidelines for #10 SASE.

Nonfiction: Book excerpts, essays, general interest, how-to, humor, interview/profile, new product, opinion, personal experience, photo feature, reviews (film, theater, art exhibits, video, music, other media), travel, medical news. **Buys 120 mss/year.** Query with published clips. Length: 800-4,800 words. **Pays $250-2,500 for feature articles and cover stories; $50-150 for reviews.** Sometimes pays expenses of writers on assignment.

Photos: State availability of photos with submission. Reviews contact sheets, transparencies (up to 4×5), prints (5×7 to 8×10) Offers $50-500/photo. Captions, model releases, identification of subjects required. Buys one-time rights.

Columns/Departments: The Culture of AIDS (reviews of books, music, film), 800 words; Viewpoint (personal opinion), 900-1,500 words; MediaWatch (mass media opinion), 800-1,200 words. **Buys 100 mss/year.** Send complete ms. **Pays $100-250.**

Fiction: Unpublished work only. Send complete ms. Length: 5,000 words maximum (2,500-4,000 words preferred). **Pays $150-750.**

Poetry: Any length/style (shorter works preferred). **Pays $75-150.**

Tips: "We're looking for more articles on youth and HIV/AIDS; more international coverage; more small-town America coverage."

N ⊠ $ $ AFTERIMAGE, The Journal of Media Arts & Cultural Criticism, Visual Studies Workshop, 31 Prince St., Rochester NY 14607. E-mail: afterimg@servtech.com. Website: www.vsw.org. **Contact:** Karen van-Meenen, editor. **75% freelance written.** Bimonthly tabloid covering photography, independent film and video, artists' books, related cultural studies. "We publish news briefs and reports as well as in-depth reviews and research-based scholarly feature articles on photography, video, independent film, artists' books, new technologies." Estab. 1972. Circ. 10,000. Pays 6 weeks after publication. Publishes ms an average of 4 months after acceptance. Byline given. No kill fee. Holds joint copyright with full permission for authors to reprint with appropriate publication citation line. Editorial lead time 6 months. Submit seasonal material 6 months in advance. Responds in 2 weeks to queries; 1 month to mss. Sample copy and writer's guidelines free.

Nonfiction: Essays, historical, interview/profile, opinion, personal experience, scholarly features, film, books, festival and exhibition reviews (especially from regions such as Florida, the Midwest and the desert Southwest). "No Hollywood film, no historical photo research unless new scholarship, and no queries about writing about your work or that of your organization/employer." **Buys 65-70 mss/year.** Query by mail only with published clips. Length: 1,000-10,000 words depending on type of article. **Pays 5¢/word up to maximum of $100 for news, reports, reviews; $150 for essays; $300 for features.** Includes free copies and a half-price subscription in pay.

Photos: State availability of photos with submission or send photos with submission. Reviews transparencies and prints. Offers no additional payment for photos accepted with ms. Captions and identification of subjects required. Requests one-time rights with no royalty payments necessary.

Tips: "Query with specific idea and timeline by mail, as in advance of event (for reports and reviews) as possible. Expect 4 month turnaround time at longest. Expect 2 rounds of editorial input."

[N] **BOOKPAGE**, Promotion, Inc., 2501 21st Ave. S., Suite 5, Nashville TN 37212. (615)292-8926. Fax: (615)292-8249. E-mail: katherine_wyrick@bookpage.com. Website: www.bookpage.com. **Contact:** Katherine H. Wyrick, editor. **95% freelance written.** Monthly newspaper covering new book releases. "*BookPage* is a general interest consumer publication which covers a broad range of books. Bookstores and libraries buy *BookPage* in quantity to use as a way to communicate with their regular customers/patrons and keep them up to date on new releases. We rarely review backlist books. In terms of categories, we review just about anything: fiction, biography, history, pop culture, romance, gardening, cooking. Just let me know what your tastes are." Estab. 1988. Circ. 650,000. **Pays on acceptance.** Byline given. Editorial lead time 2 months. Submit seasonal material 2 months in advance. Accepts queries by mail, e-mail, fax, phone. Sample copy on website. Writer's guidelines free.

Columns/Departments: Romance: Love, Exciting and New, 1,000 words; Business, 1,500 words; New and Good, 800 words; Mystery/Audio, 800-1,000 words. Query with published clips.

Tips: "All *BookPage* reviews are positive. Because we don't run negative reviews, it's essential that your review be heartfelt and genuine. I am not looking for catalog copy or a simple summary, nor do I want insincere puffery. Saying that you like the book is not enough; the fact that it's being reviewed in *BookPage* means that you liked it. More interesting to the reader is your reaction to the book: Why do you like the book? What in particular makes you like it?"

[N] **$ $ $ $** **BOOK®, The Magazine for the Reading Life**, West Egg Communications LLC, 4645 N. Rockwell St., Chicago IL 60625. (773)267-4300. Fax: (773)267-5496. E-mail: alanger@bookmagazine.com. Website: www.bookmagazine.com. Editor: Jerome Kramer. **Contact:** Adam Langer. **80% freelance written.** Bimonthly magazine covering books and reading. Estab. 1998. Circ. 100,000. Pays 30 days after publication. Byline sometimes given. Kill fee varies. Buys first and electronic rights or makes work-for-hire assignments (most of the time). Editorial lead time 3 months. Submit seasonal material 4 months in advance. Accepts queries by mail, e-mail, fax. Sample copy on website.

Nonfiction: Book excerpts, essays, interview/profile. Query with published clips. Length: 1,000-4,000 words. **Pays 50¢-$1.50/word.**

• Ranked as one of the best markets for freelance writers in *Writer's Yearbook* magazine's annual "Top 100 Markets," January 2000.

Photos: Send photos with submission. Identification of subjects required. Buys one-time rights.

Columns/Departments: Shop Watch (bookstore profiles); Locations (literary travel); Group Dynamics (book-group tips, stories); Web Catches (related to books online), all 1,500 words. **Buys 36 mss/year.** Query with published clips. **Pays $500-750.**

Fiction: Literary short stories. **Buys 6 mss/year.** Send complete ms. Length: 1,000-10,000 words. **Pays $300-5,000.**

BOSTON REVIEW, E53-407, M.I.T., Cambridge MA 02139. (617)253-3642. E-mail: bostonreview@mit.edu. Website: http://bostonreview.mit.edu. Editor: Josh Cohen. **Contact:** Jefferson Decker, managing editor. **90% freelance written.** Bimonthly magazine of cultural and political analysis, reviews, fiction and poetry. "The editors are committed to a society and culture that foster human diversity and a democracy in which we seek common grounds of principle amidst our many differences. In the hope of advancing these ideals, the *Review* acts as a forum that seeks to enrich the language of public debate." Estab. 1975. Circ. 20,000. Publishes ms an average of 3 months after acceptance. Byline given. Buys first American serial rights. Responds in 6 months. Sample copy $5 or on website. Writer's guidelines for #10 SASE or on website.

• The Boston Review also offers a poetry contest. See Contests & Awards/Poetry section.

Nonfiction: Critical essays and reviews. Query with clips. "We do not accept unsolicited book reviews: if you would like to be considered for review assignments, please send your résumé along with several published clips." **Buys 125 mss/year.**

Fiction: Jodi Daynard, fiction editor. "I'm looking for stories that are emotionally and intellectually substantive and also interesting on the level of language. Things that are shocking, dark, lewd, comic, or even insane are fine so long as the fiction is *controlled* and purposeful in a masterly way. Subtlety, delicacy and lyricism are attractive too." **Buys 8 mss/year.** Length: 1,200-5,000 words.

Poetry: Mary Jo Bang and Timothy Donnelly, poetry editors.

$ CANADIAN DIMENSION, Dimension Publications Inc., 91 Albert St., Room 2-B, Winnipeg, Manitoba, R3B 1G5 Canada. Fax: (204)957-1519. E-mail: info@canadiandimension.mb.ca. Website: www.canadiandimension.mb.ca/~edol/. **80% freelance written. Contact:** Ed Janzen. Bimonthly magazine "that makes sense of the world. We bring a socialist perspective to bear on events across Canada and around the world. Our contributors provide in-depth coverage on popular movements, peace, labour, women, aboriginal justice, environment, third world and eastern Europe." Estab. 1963. Circ. 4,000. Pays on publication. Publishes ms an average of 6 months after acceptance. Copyrighted by *CD* after publication. Accepts simultaneous submissions. Responds in 6 weeks to queries. Sample copy for $2. Writer's guidelines for #10 SAE with IRC.

Nonfiction: Interview/profile, opinion, reviews, political commentary and analysis, journalistic style. **Buys 8 mss/year.** Length: 500-2,000 words. **Pays $25-100.**

Reprints: Sometimes accepts previously published submissions. Send typed ms with rights for sale noted (electronic copies when possible) and information about when and where the article previously appeared.

☆ **$ $ $ FIRST THINGS**, Institute on Religion & Public Life, 156 Fifth Ave., Suite 400, New York NY 10010. (212)627-1985. Fax: (212)627-2184. E-mail: ft@firstthings.com. Website: www.firstthings.com. Editor-in-Chief: Richard John Neuhaus. Managing Editor: Matthew Berke. Associate Editor: Daniel Moloney. **Contact:** James Nuechterlein, editor. **70% freelance written.** "Intellectual journal published 10 times/year containing social and ethical commentary in broad sense, religious and ethical perspectives on society, culture, law, medicine, church and state, morality and mores." Estab. 1990. Circ. 32,000. Pays on publication. Publishes ms an average of 4 months after acceptance. Byline given. Kill fee varies. Buys all rights. Editorial lead time 2 months. Submit seasonal material 5 months in advance. Responds in 3 weeks to mss. Sample copy and writer's guidelines for SAE.
Nonfiction: Essays, opinion. **Buys 60 mss/year.** Send complete double-spaced ms. Length: 1,500 words for Opinion; 4,000-6,000 words for long articles. **Pays $300-800.** Sometimes pays expenses of writers on assignment.
Poetry: Traditional. **Buys 25-30 poems/year.** Length: 4-40 lines. **Pays $50.**
Tips: "We prefer complete manuscripts (hard copy, double-spaced) to queries, but will reply if unsure."

$ $ FRANCE TODAY, FrancePress Inc., 1051 Divisadero St., San Francisco CA 94115. (415)921-5100. Fax: (415)921-0213. E-mail: mail@francentral.com. Website: www.francepress.com. **Contact:** Lisel Fay, editor. **90% freelance written.** Bimonthly tabloid covering contemporary France. "*France Today* is a feature publication on contemporary France including sociocultural analysis, business, trends, current events and travel." Estab. 1989. Circ. 25,000. Pays on publication. Publishes ms an average of 5 months after acceptance. Byline given. Buys first North American and second serial (reprint) rights. Submit seasonal material 4 months in advance. Accepts queries by mail, e-mail, fax. Responds in 3 months. Sample copy for 10×13 SAE with 5 first-class stamps.
Nonfiction: Essays, exposé, general interest, historical, humor, interview/profile, personal experience, travel. "No travel pieces about well-known tourist attractions." Special issues: Paris, France on the Move, France On a Budget, Summer Travel, The French Palate, French Around the World, France Adventure. **Buys 50 mss/year.** Query with or without published clips, or send complete ms. Length: 500-2,000 words. **Pays $150-300.**
Reprints: Send typed ms with rights for sale noted and information about when and where the article previously appeared. Pay varies.
Photos: Offers $25/photo. Identification of subjects required. Buys one-time rights.

$ $ $ HIGH TIMES, Trans High Corp., 235 Park Ave. S., 5th Floor, New York NY 10003-1405. (212)387-0500. Fax: (212)475-7684. E-mail: hteditor@hightimes.com. Website: www.hightimes.com. Publisher: Mike Edison. News Editor: Dean Latimer. **Contact:** Steven Hager, editorial director. **30% freelance written.** Monthly magazine covering marijuana and the counterculture. Estab. 1974. Circ. 250,000. Pays on publication. Byline given. Offers 20% kill fee. Buys one-time or all rights or makes work-for-hire assignments. Submit seasonal material 6 months in advance. Accepts queries by mail, e-mail, fax. Responds in 1 month to queries; 4 months to mss. Sample copy for $5 and #10 SASE. Writer's guidelines for SASE or on website.
Nonfiction: Book excerpts, exposé, humor, interview/profile, new product, personal experience, photo feature, travel. **Buys 30 mss/year.** Send complete ms. Length: 2,000-7,000 words. **Pays $300-1,000.** Sometimes pays expenses of writers on assignment.
Reprints: Send tearsheet of article or typed ms with rights for sale noted. Pays in ad trade.
Photos: Shirley Halperin, photo editor. Send photos with submission. Pays $25-400, $400 for cover photos, $350 for centerfold. Captions, model release, identification of subjects required. Buys all rights or one-time use.
Columns/Departments: Steve Bloom, music editor; Chris Simunek, cultivation editor; Steve Wishnia, views editor. Drug related books, news. **Buys 10 mss/year.** Query with published clips. Length: 100-2,000 words. **Pays $25-300.**
Fillers: Frank Max, cartoon editor. Gags to be illustrated by cartoonist, newsbreaks, short humor. **Buys 10 mss/year.** Length: 100-500 words. **Pays $10-50.**
Tips: "Although promoting the legalization and cultivation of medicinal plants, primarily cannabis, is central to our mission, *High Times* does not promote the indiscriminate use of such plants. We are most interested in articles on cannabis cultivation, the history of hemp, the rise of the modern hemp industry, the history of the counterculture and countercultural trends and events. The best way for new writers to break in is through our news section. We are always looking for regional stories involving the Drug War that have national significance. This includes coverage of local legal battles, political controversies, drug testing updates and legalization rally reports. All sections are open to good, professional writers."

N ☆ $ $ $ MOTHER JONES, Foundation for National Progress, 731 Market St., Suite 600, San Francisco CA 94103. (415)665-6637. Fax: (415)665-6696. E-mail: query@motherjones.com. Website: www.motherjones.com. Editor: Jeffrey Klein. **Contact:** Eric Bates, investigative editor; Roger Cohn, editor-in-chief; Monika Bauerlein, features editor; Tim Dickenson, assistant editor. **80% freelance written.** Bimonthly national magazine covering politics, investigative reporting, social issues and pop culture. "*Mother Jones* is a 'progressive' magazine—but the core of its editorial well is reporting (i.e., fact-based). No slant required. MoJo Wire is an online sister publication." Estab. 1976. Circ. 150,000. Pays on publication. Publishes ms an average of 4 months after acceptance. Byline given. Offers 33% kill fee. Buys first North American serial rights, first rights, one-time rights or online rights (limited). Editorial lead time 4 months. Submit seasonal material 6 months in advance. Responds in 2 months. Sample copy for $6 and 9×12 SAE. Writer's guidelines for #10 SASE and on website.

Nonfiction: Book excerpts, essays, exposé, humor, interview/profile, opinion, personal experience, photo feature, current issues, policy. **Buys 70-100 mss/year.** Query with 2-3 published clips and SASE. Length: 2,000-5,000 words. **Pays 80¢/word.** Sometimes pays expenses of writers on assignment.

● Ranked as one of the best markets for freelance writers in *Writer's Yearbook* magazine's annual "Top 100 Markets, January 2000.

Columns/Departments: Tim Dickenson. Outfront (short, newsy and/or outrageous and/or humorous items), 200-500 words; Profiles of "Hellraisers," "Visionaries" (short interviews), 250 words. **Pays 80¢/word.**

Tips: "We're looking for hard-hitting, investigative reports exposing government cover-ups, corporate malfeasance, scientific myopia, institutional fraud or hypocrisy; thoughtful, provocative articles which challenge the conventional wisdom (on the right or the left) concerning issues of national importance; and timely, people-oriented stories on issues such as the environment, labor, the media, health care, consumer protection, and cultural trends. Send a great, short query and establish your credibility as a reporter. Explain what you plan to cover and how you will proceed with the reporting. The query should convey your approach, tone and style, and should answer the following: What are your specific qualifications to write on this topic? What 'ins' do you have with your sources? Can you provide full documentation so that your story can be fact-checked?"

N $ $ PAPER MAGAZINE, Paper Publishing Co., Inc., 365 Broadway, 6th Floor, New York NY 10013. (212)226-4405. Fax: (212)226-5929/0002. E-mail: davidh@papermag.com. Website: www.papermag.com. **Contact:** David Hershkovits, editor/publisher. **30% freelance written.** Monthly magazine covering pop culture, fashion, entertainment. "The underground alternative for hip 18-35 year olds who like to know what's on the cutting edge now or tomorrow." Estab. 1984. Circ. 100,000. Pays on publication. Publishes ms an average of 2 months after acceptance. Byline given. Offers kill fee. Buys one-time rights. Editorial lead time 6 weeks. Submit seasonal material 6 weeks in advance. Accepts queries by mail, e-mail, fax. Writer's guidelines free.

Nonfiction: Book excerpts, exposé, general interest, interview/profile. Does not want to see fiction. **Buys 60 mss/ year.** Query with published clips. Length: 3,000 words. **Pays $5-500.** Sometimes pays expenses of writers on assignment.

Columns/Departments: Music, Stage, Film. Query with published clips. **Pays $5-500.**

Tips: "If you would like to write for us, please pitch you story idea in one or two paragraphs. We do not routinely assign stories to new writers. Send us two or three clips or writing samples. Briefly tell us why you're qualified to write the story you propose. We are not necessarily interested in work experience—*PAPER* prides itself on publishing stories by people with a unique perspective who are truly involved in their subject.

N ✪ $ $ STAGEBILL, Stagebill Inc., 144 E. 44 St., New York NY 10017. Fax: (212)949-0518. Website: www.stagebill.com. Editor: John Istel. **Contact:** Ben Mattison, associate editor. **80% freelance written.** Program distributed free to performing arts audiences covering dance, theater, opera, classical music, jazz and some film. "Our editorial is geared toward an educated and sophisticated arts audience. We suggest to writers that the closest analogous publication is the *New York Times'* Sunday Arts & Leisure section." Estab. 1924. Circ. 20,000,000/year. Pays on publication. Publishes ms an average of 2 months after acceptance. Byline given. Offers 50% kill fee. Buys 90-day exclusive rights; non-exclusive thereafter. Editorial lead time 2 months. Submit seasonal material 3 months in advance. Accepts queries by mail, e-mail. Responds in 2 weeks to queries; 1 month to mss. Sample copy on website.

Nonfiction: Book excerpts, essays (on arts or cultural trends), humor, opinion. **Buys 200 mss/year.** Query with published clips. Length: 350-1,200 words. **Pays $400 for assigned articles; $300 for unsolicited articles.** Sometimes pays expenses of writers on assignment.

Reprints: Sometimes accepts previously published submissions.

Photos: State availability of photos with submission. Offers no additional payment for photos accepted with ms.

Columns/Departments: See/Hear (book/CD reviews), 200 words; By Design (art, design and fashion), 600-750 words; Critical Slant (opinions on culture), 350-400 words. **Buys 75 mss/year.** Query with published clips. **Pays $50-350.**

UTNE READER, 1624 Harmon Place, Suite 330, Minneapolis MN 55403. (612)338-5040. Fax: (612)338-6043. E-mail: editor@utne.com. Website: www.utne.com. **Contact:** Craig Cox, managing editor. Accepts queries by mail, e-mail, phone, fax.

● The *Utne Reader* has been a finalist three times for the National Magazine Award for general excellence.

Reprints: Accepts previously published submissions. Send tearsheet or photocopy of article or typed ms with rights for sale noted and information about when and where the article previously appeared.

O—π Break in with submissions for 'New Planet.'

Tips: "State the theme(s) clearly, let the narrative flow, and build the story around strong characters and a vivid sense of place. Give us rounded episodes, logically arranged."

$ YES! A Journal of Positive Futures, Positive Futures Network, P.O. Box 10818, Bainbridge Island WA 98110. (206)842-0216. Fax: (206)842-5208. E-mail: editors@futurenet.org. Website: www.futurenet.org. Editor: Sarah van Gelder. **Contact**: Carol Estes, associate editor. Quarterly magazine emphasizing sustainability and community. "Interested in stories on building a positive future: sustainability, overcoming divisiveness, ethical business practices, etc." Estab. 1996. Circ. 14,000. Pays on publication. Byline given. Buys various rights. Editorial lead time 4 months. Accepts queries by mail, e-mail, fax. Accepts simultaneous submissions. Responds in 6 months to mss; 1 month to queries. Writer's guidelines and sample copy on website.

Nonfiction: Book excerpts, essays, how-to, humor, interview/profile, personal experience, photo feature, technical, environmental. "No negativity or blanket prescriptions for changing the world." Query with published clips. "Please check website for a detailed call for submission before each issue." Length: 200-3,500 words. Pays writers with 1-year subscription and 2 contributor copies. **Pays $20-50 (negotiable).** Sometimes pays expenses of writers on assignment.
Reprints: Send photocopy of article or typed ms with rights for sale noted and information about when and where the article previously appeared. Pays 100% of amount paid for an original article.
Photos: State availability of photos with submission. Reviews contact sheets, negatives, transparencies and prints. Offers $20-75/photo. Identification of subjects required. Buys one-time rights.
Columns/Departments: Query with published clips. **Pays $20-60.**
Poetry: Avant-garde, free verse, haiku, light verse, traditional. **Buys 2-3 poems/year.** Submit maximum 10 poems.
Tips: "Read and become familiar with the publication's purpose, tone and quality. We are about facilitating the creation of a better world. We are looking for writers who want to participate in that process. *Yes!* is less interested in bemoaning the state of our problems and more interested in highlighting promising solutions. We are highly unlikely to accept submissions that simply state the author's opinion on what needs to be fixed and why. Our readers know *why* we need to move towards sustainability; they are interested in *how* to do so."

DETECTIVE & CRIME

Fans of detective stories want to read accounts of actual criminal cases, detective work and espionage. Markets specializing in crime fiction are listed under Mystery publications.

$ P. I. MAGAZINE, America's Private Investigation Journal, 755 Bronx, Toledo OH 43609. (419)382-0967. Fax: (419)382-0967. E-mail: pimag1@aol.com. Website: www.PIMAG.com. **Contact:** Bob Mackowiak, editor/publisher. **75% freelance written.** "Audience includes professional investigators, attorneys, paralegals and law enforcement personnel." Estab. 1988. Circ. 5,200. Pays on publication. Publishes ms an average of 3 months after acceptance. Buys one-time rights. Submit seasonal material 3 months in advance. Accepts simultaneous submissions. Responds in 3 months to queries; 4 months to mss. Sample copy for $6.75.
Nonfiction: Interview/profile, personal experience and accounts of real cases. **Buys 4-10 mss/year.** Send complete ms. Length: 1,000 words and up. **Pays $75 minimum for unsolicited articles.**
Photos: Send photos with submission. May offer additional payment for photos accepted with ms. Model releases, identification of subjects required. Buys one-time rights.
Tips: "The best way to get published in *P. I.* is to write a detailed story about a professional P.I.'s true-life case. No fiction, please. Unsolicited fiction manuscripts will not be returned."

DISABILITIES

These magazines are geared toward disabled persons and those who care for or teach them. A knowledge of disabilities and lifestyles is important for writers trying to break in to this field; editors regularly discard material that does not have a realistic focus. Some of these magazines will accept manuscripts only from disabled persons or those with a background in caring for disabled persons.

✪ $ $ ACCENT ON LIVING, P.O. Box 700, Bloomington IL 61702-0700. (309)378-2961. Fax: (309)378-4420. E-mail: acntlvng@aol.com. Website: www.accentonliving.com. **Contact:** Betty Garee, editor. **75% freelance written.** Eager to work with new/unpublished writers. Quarterly magazine for physically disabled persons and rehabilitation professionals. Estab. 1956. Circ. 20,000. Buys first and second (reprint) rights. Byline usually given. Pays on publication. Publishes ms an average of 6 months after acceptance. Accepts queries by mail, e-mail, fax, phone. Responds in 1 month. Sample copy and writer's guidelines for $3.50 and #10 SAE with 7 first-class stamps. Writer's guidelines for #10 SASE.
Nonfiction: Articles about new devices that would make a disabled person with limited physical mobility more independent; should include description, availability and photos. Medical breakthroughs for disabled people. Intelligent discussion articles on acceptance of physically disabled persons in normal living situations; topics may be architectural barriers, housing, transportation, educational or job opportunities, organizations, or other areas. How-to articles concerning everyday living, giving specific, helpful information so the reader can carry out the idea himself/herself. News articles about active disabled persons or groups. Good strong interviews. Vacations, accessible places to go, sports, organizations, humorous incidents, self-improvement and sexual or personal adjustment—all related to physically handicapped persons. "We are looking for upbeat material." **Buys 50-60 unsolicited mss/year.** Query with SASE. Length: 250-1,000 words. **Pays 10¢/word for published articles** (after editing and/or condensing by staff).
Reprints: Send tearsheet and information about when and where the article previously appeared. **Pays 10¢/word.**
Photos: Pays $10 minimum for b&w photos purchased with accompanying captions. Amount will depend on quality of photos and subject matter. Pays $50 and up for four-color cover photos. "We need good-quality color or b&w photos (or slides and transparencies)."

Tips: "Ask a friend who is disabled to read your article before sending it to *Accent*. Make sure that he/she understands your major points and the sequence or procedure."

N **$ $ ALLERGY AND ASTHMA HEALTH**, Signature Health Publications, 11030 Ables Lane, Dallas TX 75229-4593. (974)406-4664. Fax: (972)484-6010. E-mail: griffiths@aarc.org. Editor: Dale Griffiths. **Contact:** Sherry Milligan, managing editor. **10% freelance written.** Quarterly magazine covering allergies and asthma. "*Allergy and Asthma Health* is a practical guide for people living with asthma or allergies. Scientifically valid articles written in a conversational, layperson's style will be reviewed by medical personnel before publication." Estab. 1999. Circ. 12,000. **Pays on acceptance.** Publishes ms an average of 6 months after acceptance. Byline given. Buys first rights or makes work-for-hire assignments. Editorial lead time 6 months. Submit seasonal material 6 months in advance. Accepts queries by mail, fax. Responds in 1 month to queries; 2 months to mss. Sample copy for 9 × 12 SAE and 4 first-class stamps. Writer's guidelines for #10 SASE.
Nonfiction: General interest, how-to, humor, inspirational, interview/profile, personal experience. **Buys 10 mss/year.** Query with published clips. Length: 500-2,000 words. **Pays $100-800 minimum for assigned articles; $50-500 for unsolicited articles.** Sometimes pays expenses of writers on assignment.
Photos: State availability of photos with submission. Negotiates payment individually. Captions, model releases and identification of subjects required. Buys one-time rights.
Tips: "Articles by people living with asthma and allergies will be reviewed most favorably."

$ $ $ $ ARTHRITIS TODAY, Arthritis Foundation. 1330 W. Peachtree St., Atlanta GA 30309. (404)872-7100. Fax: (404)872-9559. E-mail: atmail@arthritis.org. Website: www.arthritis.org. Editor: Cindy T. McDaniel. Managing Editor: Shannon Wilder. Executive Editor: Marcy O'Koon. **Contact**: Michele Taylor, assistant editor. **50% freelance written.** Bimonthly magazine about living with arthritis; latest in research/treatment. "*Arthritis Today* is written for the more than 43 million Americans who have arthritis and for the millions of others whose lives are touched by an arthritis-related disease. The editorial content is designed to help the person with arthritis live a more productive, independent and painfree life. The articles are upbeat and provide practical advice, information and inspiration." Estab. 1987. Circ. 700,000. **Pays on acceptance.** Offers 25% kill fee. Buys first North American serial rights but requires unlimited reprint rights in any Arthritis Foundation-affiliated endeavor. Editorial lead time 6 months. Submit seasonal material 6 months in advance. Accepts queries by mail, e-mail, fax. Considers simultaneous submissions. Responds in 2 months. Sample copy for 9 × 11 SAE with 4 first-class stamps. Writer's guidelines for #10 SASE.
Nonfiction: General interest, how-to (tips on any aspect of living with arthritis), service, inspirational, opinion, personal experience, photo feature, technical, nutrition, general health and lifestyle. **Buys 60-70 unsolicited mss/year.** Query with published clips or send complete ms. Length: 150-2,000 words. **Pays $150-2,000.** Pays expenses of writers on assignment.
  ● Ranked as one of the best markets for freelance writers in *Writer's Yearbook* magazine's annual "Top 100 Markets," January 2000.
Photos: Send photos with submission. Reviews prints. Negotiates payment individually. Identification of subjects required. Buys one-time rights.
Columns/Departments: Research Spotlight (research news about arthritis); LifeStyle (travel, leisure), 100-300 words; Well Being (arthritis-specific medical news), 100-300 words; Hero (personal profile of people with arthritis), 100-300 words. **Buys 10 mss/year.** Query with published clips. **Pays $150-300.**
Fillers: Facts, gags to be illustrated by cartoonist, short humor. **Buys 10/year.** Length: 40-100 words. **Pays $80-150.**
Tips: "Our readers are already well-informed. We need ideas and writers that give in-depth, fresh, interesting information that truly adds to their understanding of their condition and their quality of life. Quality writers are more important than good ideas. The staff generates many of our ideas but needs experienced, talented writers who are good reporters to execute them. Please provide published clips. In addition to articles specifically about living with arthritis, we look for articles to appeal to an older audience on subjects such as hobbies, general health, lifestyle, etc."

$ $ ASTHMA MAGAZINE, Strategies For Taking Control, Lifelong Publications, 3 Bridge St., Newton MA 02158. (617)964-4910. Fax: (617)964-8095. E-mail: asthmamag@aol.com. **Contact:** Rachel Butler, editor-in-chief. **50% freelance written.** Bimonthly. "*Asthma Magazine* offers unbiased education for people with asthma. We are an independent publication (not sponsored by any drug company) and we provide indepth education to help the asthmatic manage his/her disease and live an active and healthy life." Estab. 1995. Circ. 100,000. Pays on publication. Publishes ms an average of 1 month after acceptance. Byline given. Offers 25% kill fee. Buys all rights. Editorial lead time 6 weeks. Submit seasonal material 3 months in advance. Accepts queries by mail, e-mail, fax, phone. Sample copy and writer's guidelines free.
Nonfiction: Buys 4 features/issue. How-to, inspirational, interview/profile, new product (usually a news blurb, not a full article), personal experience, technical, travel—all related to the subject matter. **Buys 12-15 mss/year.** Query with published clips. Length: 800-1,200 words. **Pays $200-500.**
Photos: State availability of photos with submission. Reviews prints. Offers no additional payment for photos accepted with ms. Buys all rights.
Columns/Departments: Hear My Story (personal experience of a person with asthma or article about someone who has accomplished something significant despite their asthma, or someone in the asthma/medical field); 900 words. Query with published clips. **Pays $250.**

Tips: "We look for writers who have had experience writing for the medical community for either clinicians or patients. Writing must be clear, concise and easy to understand (7th-9th grade reading level), as well as thoroughly researched and medically accurate."

\$ \$ CAREERS & the disABLED, Equal Opportunity Publications, 1160 E. Jericho Turnpike, Suite 200, Huntington NY 11743. (516)421-9421. Fax: (516)421-0359. E-mail: info@aol.com. Website: www.eop.com. **Contact:** James Schneider, editor. **60% freelance written.** Quarterly magazine "offers role-model profiles and career guidance articles geared toward disabled college students and professionals and promotes personal and professional growth." Pays on publication. Publishes ms an average of 6 months after acceptance. Estab. 1967. Circ. 10,000. Byline given. Buys first North American serial rights. Editorial lead time 6 months. Submit seasonal material 6 months in advance. Accepts queries by mail, e-mail, fax, phone. Accepts simultaneous submissions. Responds in 3 weeks. Sample copy and writer's guidelines for 9×12 SAE with 5 first-class stamps.
Nonfiction: Essays, general interest, how-to, interview/profile, new product, opinion, personal experience. **Buys 30 mss/year.** Query. Length: 1,000-2,500 words. **Pays 10¢/word, $350 maximum.** Sometimes pays the expenses of writers on assignment.
Reprints: Send information about when and where the article previously appeared.
Photos: State availability of or send photos with submission. Reviews transparencies, prints. Offers $15-50/photo. Captions, identification of subjects required. Buys one-time rights.
Tips: "Be as targeted as possible. Role model profiles and specific career guidance strategies that offer advice to disabled college students are most needed."

\$ \$ DIABETES SELF-MANAGEMENT, R.A. Rapaport Publishing, Inc., 150 W. 22nd St., Suite 800, New York NY 10011-2421. (212)989-0200. Fax: (212)989-4786. E-mail: editor@diabetes-self-mgmt.com. Website: www.diabetes-self-mgmt.com. **Contact:** Ingrid Strauch, managing editor. **20% freelance written.** Bimonthly. "We publish how-to health care articles for motivated, intelligent readers who have diabetes and who are actively involved in their own health care management. All articles must have immediate application to their daily living." Estab. 1983. Circ. 480,000. Pays on publication. Publishes ms an average of 3 months after acceptance. Byline given. Offers 20% kill fee. Buys all rights ("We are extremely generous regarding permission to republish.") Submit seasonal material 6 months in advance. Accepts queries by mail, e-mail, fax, phone. Responds in 6 weeks. Sample copy for $4 and 9×12 SAE with 6 first-class stamps or on website. Writer's guidelines for #10 SASE.
Nonfiction: How-to (exercise, nutrition, diabetes self-care, product surveys), technical (reviews of products available, foods sold by brand name, pharmacology), travel (considerations and prep for people with diabetes). No personal experiences, personality profiles, exposés or research breakthroughs. **Buys 10-12 mss/year.** Query with published clips. Length: 1,500-2,500 words. **Pays $400-700 for assigned articles; $200-700 for unsolicited articles.**
Tips: "The rule of thumb for any article we publish is that it must be clear, concise, useful, and instructive, and it must have immediate application to the lives of our readers. If your query is accepted, expect heavy editorial supervision."

\$ DIALOGUE, Blindskills, Inc., P.O. Box 5181, Salem OR 97301-0181. (800)860-4224; (503)581-4224. Fax: (503)581-0178. E-mail: blindskl@teleport.com. Website: www.blindskills.com. **Contact:** Carol M. McCarl, editor. **85% freelance written.** Quarterly journal covering the visually impaired. Estab. 1961. Circ. 1,100. Pays on publication. Publishes ms an average of 8 months after acceptance. Byline given. Buys first rights. Editorial lead time 3 months. Submit seasonal material 3 months in advance. Accepts queries by mail, e-mail, fax. Sample copy $6. Writer's guidelines for #10 SASE.
Nonfiction: Essays, general interest, historical/nostalgic, how-to, humor, interview/profile, new product, personal experience. Prefer material by visually impaired writers. No controversial, explicit sex or religious or political topics. **Buys 20 mss/year.** Send complete ms. Length: 500-1,200 words. **Pays $10-35 for assigned articles; $10-25 for unsolicited articles.**
Reprints: Send tearsheet or photocopy of article or short story or typed ms with rights for sale noted and information about when and where the article or story previously appeared.
Columns/Departments: All material should be relative to blind and visually impaired readers. Careers, 1,000 words; What's New & Where to Get It (resources, new product), 2,500 words; What Do You Do When . . . ? (dealing with sight loss), 1,000 words. **Buys 40 mss/year.** Send complete ms. **Pays $10-25.**
Fiction: Adventure, humorous, science fiction, slice-of-life vignettes, first person experiences. Prefer material by visually impaired writers. No controversial, explicit sex. No religious or political. **Buys 6-8 mss/year.** Query with complete ms. Length: 800-1,200 words. **Pays $15-25.**
Poetry: Free verse, light verse, traditional. Prefer material by visually impaired writers. No controversial, explicit sex or religious or political topics. **Buys 15-20 poems/year.** Submit maximum 5 poems. Length: 20 lines maximum. **Pays $10-15.**
Fillers: Anecdotes, facts, newsbreaks, short humor. Length: 50-150 words. No payment.
Tips: Send SASE for free writers guidelines, $6 for sample in Braille, cassette or large print.

\$ \$ HEARING HEALTH, Voice International Publications, Inc., P.O. Drawer V, Ingleside TX 78362-0500. (361)776-7240. Fax: (361)776-3278. E-mail: ears2u@hearinghealthmag.com. Website: www.hearinghealthmag.com. **Contact:** Paula Bonillas, editor. **20% freelance written.** Bimonthly magazine covering issues and concerns pertaining to hearing and hearing loss. Estab. 1984. Circ. 20,000. Pays on publication. Byline given. Buys one-time rights. Editorial lead time 2 months. Submit seasonal material 4 months in advance. Accepts queries by mail, fax. Accepts simultaneous submissions. Responds in 6 weeks to queries; 2 months to mss. Sample copy for $2 or on website. Writer's guidelines for #10 SASE or on website.

O— "Break in with a fresh approach—positive, a splash of humor—or well-researched biographical or historical pieces about people with hearing loss."

Nonfiction: Books excerpts, essays, exposé, general interest, historical/nostalgic, humor, inspirational, interview/profile, new product, opinion, personal experience, photo feature, technical, travel. No self-pitying over loss of hearing. Query with published clips. Length: 500-2,000 words. **Pays $75-200.** Sometimes pays expenses of writers on assignment.

Reprints: Accepts previously published submissions, if so noted.

Photos: State availability of photos with submission. Reviews contact sheets. Negotiates payment individually. Captions, model releases, identification of subjects required. Buys one-time rights.

Columns/Departments: Kidink (written by kids with hearing loss), 300 words; People (shares stories of successful, everyday people who have loss of hearing), 300-400 words. **Buys 2 mss/year.** Query with published clips.

Fiction: Fantasy, historical, humorous, novel excerpts, science fiction. **Buys 2 mss/year.** Query with published clips. Length: 400-1,500 words.

Poetry: Avant-garde, free verse, light verse, traditional. **Buys 2/year.** Submit 2 poems max. Length: 4-50 lines.

Fillers: Anecdotes, facts, gags to be illustrated, newsbreaks, short humor. **Buys 6/year.** Length: 25-1,500 words.

Tips: "We look for fresh stories, usually factual but occasionally fictitious, about coping with hearing loss. A positive attitude is a must for *Hearing Health*. Unless one has some experience with deafness or hearing loss—whether their own or a loved one's—it's very difficult to 'break in' to our publication. Experience brings about the empathy and understanding—the sensitivity—and the freedom to write humorously about any handicap or disability."

$ KALEIDOSCOPE: International Magazine of Literature, Fine Arts, and Disability, Kaleidoscope Press, 701 S. Main St., Akron OH 44311-1019. (330)762-9755. Fax: (330)762-0912. E-mail: mshiplett@udsakron.org. **Contact:** Gail Willmott, senior editor. **75% freelance written.** Semiannual. Subscribers include individuals, agencies and organizations that assist people with disabilities and many university and public libraries. Estab. 1979. Circ. 1,000. Byline given. Rights return to author upon publication. Eager to work with new/unpublished writers; appreciates work by established writers as well. Especially interested in work by writers with a disability, but features writers both with and without disabilities. "Writers without a disability must limit themselves to our focus, while those with a disability may explore any topic (although we prefer original perspectives about experiences with disability)." Accepts queries by mail, fax. Responds in 3 weeks, acceptance or rejection may take 6 months. Sample copy for $4 prepaid. Guidelines free for SASE.

Nonfiction: Personal experience essays, book reviews and articles related to disability. Special issues: Disability Studies (January 2001, deadline August 2000); International Fiction (July 2001, deadline March 2001). Submit photocopies with SASE for return of work. Please type submissions. All submissions should be accompanied by an autobiographical sketch. May include art or photos that enhance works, prefer b&w with high contrast. **Publishes 8-14 mss/year.** Maximum 5,000 words. **Pays $10-125 plus 2 copies.**

Reprints: Send typed ms with rights for sale noted and information about when and where the article previously appeared. Publishes novel excerpts.

Fiction: Short stories, novel excerpts. Traditional and experimental styles. Works should explore experiences with disability. Use people-first language. Maximum 5,000 words.

Poetry: Limit 5 poems/submission. **Publishes 12-20 poems/year.** Do not get caught up in rhyme scheme. High quality with strong imagery and evocative language. Reviews any style.

Tips: "Inquire about future themes of upcoming issues. Sample copy very helpful. Works should not use stereotyping, patronizing or offending language about disability. We seek fresh imagery and thought-provoking language."

$ SILENT NEWS, World's Most Popular Newspaper of the Deaf and Hard of Hearing People, Silent News, Inc., 135 Gaither Dr., Suite F, Mt. Laurel NJ 08054-1710. (856)802-1977 (voice) or (856)802-1978 (TTY). Fax: (609)802-1979. E-mail: silentnews@aol.com. **Contact:** Editorial staff. **50% freelance written.** Monthly newspaper covering news of deaf, hard of hearing and deaf-blind concerns, the "World's Most Popular Newspaper of the Deaf and Hard of Hearing." Estab. 1969. Circ. 15,000. Pays on publication. Byline given. Editorial lead time 2 months. Submit seasonal material 3 months in advance. Accepts simultaneous submissions. Responds in 2 weeks to queries; 2 months to mss.

Nonfiction: General interest, historical/nostalgic, humor, inspirational, interview/profile, new product, opinion, personal experience, photo feature, religious, technical, travel. All articles must concern deaf and hard of hearing or deaf-blind people. Special issues: Deaf Awareness (September); Holiday Shoppers Guide (November); Assistive Technology (March); Hard of Hearing Issues (May). **Buys 60 mss/year.** Query with published clips. Length: 100-500 words. **Pays $50.** Sometimes pays expenses of writers on assignment.

Reprints: Accepts previously published submissions.

Photos: Send photos with submission. Reviews negatives, 5×7 transparencies and prints. Negotiates payment individually. Identification of subjects required. Buys all rights.

Columns/Departments: National News, International News (both regarding hard of hearing and deaf); Sports (for the blind); all 500 words. **Buys 60 mss/year.** Query with published clips.

Fiction: "Presently we don't use fiction, but we would be interested in reviewing subject-appropriate material." Query.

Poetry: Light verse. "Nothing too deep!" **Buys 12 poems/year.** Submit maximum 2 poems. Length: 10-20 lines.

Fillers: Anecdotes, facts, gags to be illustrated, newsbreaks, short humor. **Buys 100/year.** Length: 50-100 words.
Tips: "Writers must have understanding of issues confronting deaf, hard of hearing, and deaf-blind people."

ENTERTAINMENT

This category's publications cover live, filmed or videotaped entertainment, including home video, TV, dance, theater and adult entertainment. In addition to celebrity interviews, most publications want solid reporting on trends and upcoming productions. Magazines in the Contemporary Culture and General Interest sections also use articles on entertainment. For those publications with an emphasis on music and musicians, see the Music section.

$ CINEASTE, America's Leading Magazine on the Art and Politics of the Cinema, Cineaste Publishers, Inc., 200 Park Ave. S., #1601, New York NY 10003. Phone/fax: (212)982-1241. E-mail: cineaste@cineaste.com. **Contact:** Gary Crowdus, editor-in-chief. **30% freelance written.** Quarterly magazine covering motion pictures with an emphasis on social and political perspective on cinema. Estab. 1967. Circ. 10,000. Pays on publication. Publishes ms an average of 4 months after acceptance. Byline given. Offers 50% kill fee. Buys first North American serial rights. Editorial lead time 3 months. Submit seasonal material 4 months in advance. Accepts queries by mail, e-mail, fax. Responds in 1 month. Sample copy $5. Writer's guidelines for #10 SASE.
Nonfiction: Essays, historical/nostalgic, humor, interview/profile, opinion. **Buys 20-30 mss/year.** Query with published clips. Length: 2,000-5,000 words. **Pays $30-100.** Pays in contributor copies at author's request.
Photos: State availability of photos with submission. Reviews transparencies and 8×10 prints. Offers no additional payment for photos accepted with ms. Identification of subjects required. Buys one-time rights.
Columns/Departments: Homevideo (topics of general interest or a related group of films); A Second Look (new interpretation of a film classic or a reevaluation of an unjustly neglected release of more recent vintage); Lost and Found (film that may or may not be released or otherwise seen in the US but which is important enough to be brought to the attention of our readers); all 1,000-1,500 words. Query with published clips. **Pays $50 minimum.**
Tips: "We dislike academic jargon, obtuse Marxist teminology, film buff trivia, trendy 'buzz' phrases, and show biz references. We do not want our writers to speak of how they have 'read' or 'decoded' a film, but to view, analyze and interpret same. The author's processes and quirks should be secondary to the interests of the reader. Warning the reader of problems with specific films is more important to us than artificially 'puffing' a film because its producers or politics are agreeable. One article format we encourage is an omnibus review of several current films, preferably those not reviewed in a previous issue. Such an article would focus on films that perhaps share a certain political perspective, subject matter or generic concerns (e.g., films on suburban life, or urban violence, or revisionist Westerns). Like individual Film Reviews, these articles should incorporate a very brief synopsis of plots for those who haven't seen the films. The main focus, however, should be on the social issues manifested in each film and how it may reflect something about the current political/social/esthetic climate."

$ DANCE INTERNATIONAL, 601 Cambie St., Suite 302, Vancouver, British Columbia V6B 2P1 Canada. (604)681-1525. Fax: (604)681-7732. E-mail: danceint@direct.ca. **Contact:** Maureen Riches, editor. **100% freelance written.** Quarterly magazine covering dance arts. "Articles and reviews on current activities in world dance, with occasional historical essays; reviews of dance films, video and books." Estab. 1973. Circ. 3,500. Pays on publication. Publishes ms an average of 3 months after acceptance. Byline given. Offers 50% kill fee. Buys one-time rights. Editorial lead time 3 months. Submit seasonal material 6 weeks in advance. Accepts queries by mail, e-mail, fax, phone. Responds in 2 weeks to queries; 1 month to mss. Sample copy and guidelines for SAE.
Nonfiction: Book excerpts, essays, historical/nostalgic, interview/profile, personal experience, photo feature. **Buys 100 mss/year.** Query. Length: 1,200-2,200 words. **Pays $40-150.**
Reprints: Accepts previously published submissions.
Photos: Send photos with submission. Reviews prints. Offers no additional payment for photos accepted with ms. Identification of subjects required.
Columns/Departments: Kaija Pepper, copy editor. Dance Bookshelf (recent books reviewed), 1,200 words; Regional Reports (events in each region), 1,200-2,000 words. **Buys 100 mss/year.** Query. **Pays $60-70.**
Tips: "Send résumé and samples of recent writings."

$ $ DANCE SPIRIT, Lifestyle Ventures, LLC, 250 W. 57th St., Suite 420, New York NY 10107. (212)265-8890. Fax: (212)265-8908. E-mail: editor@lifestyleventures.com. Website: www.dancespirit.com. **Contact:** Sheila Noone, managing editor. Editorial Director: Julie Davis. **50% freelance written.** Monthly magazine covering all dance disciplines. "*Dance Spirit* is a special interest teen magazine for girls and guys who study and perform either through a studio or a school dance performance group." Estab. 1997. Circ. 150,000. Pays on publication. Publishes ms an average of 4 months after acceptance. Byline given. Offers 25% kill fee. Buys all rights. Editorial lead time 4 months. Submit seasonal material 6 months in advance. Accepts queries by mail, e-mail, fax. Responds in 3 months to queries; 4 months to mss. Sample copy for $4.95.

Nonfiction: Personal experience, photo feature, dance-related articles only. **Buys 100 mss/year.** Query with published clips. Length: 100-500 words. **Pays $100-600.** Pays writers with contributor copies or other premiums if writer is not a published author, but rather an educator. Sometimes pays expenses of writers on assignment.

Photos: Reviews transparencies. Negotiates payment individualy. Captions, model releases, identification of subjects required. Buys all rights.

Columns/Departments: 8-counts (music selection); Star Turns (dance celebrity profile); both 300 words. **Buys 50 mss/year.** Query with published clips. **Pays $100-200.**

　　▣ The online magazine carries original content not found in the print edition. Contact: Sheila Noone.

Tips: "Reading the magazine can't be stressed enough. We are looking for experienced dancers/choreographers to contribute succinct writing style and hip outlook."

N $ $ DANCE SPIRITS IN MOTION, Lifestyle Ventures, LLC, 250 W. 57th St., Suite 420, New York NY 10107. (212)265-8890. Fax: (212)265-8908. **Contact:** Lynn Singer, editor. **100% freelance written.** Quarterly magazine covering dance teams, color guards and other performing groups. (Formerly *Dance Drill.*) "Our audience is high school and college dance team and color guard members and their directors, coaches and choreographers." Circ. 50,000. **Pays on acceptance.** Publishes ms an average of 2 months after acceptance. Byline given. Offers 25% kill fee. Buys all rights or makes work-for-hire assignments. Editorial lead time 2 months. Submit seasonal material 2 months in advance. Accepts queries by mail, e-mail, fax. Accepts simultaneous submissions. Responds in 3 weeks to queries; 1 month to mss. Sample copy for cover price ($3.95 US, $4.95 Canada).

Nonfiction: Exposé, general interest (pertaining to the industry), historical/nostalgic, how-to (skill execution, preparation for camps and competitions), inspirational, interview/profile, personal experience. **Buys many mss/year.** Query. Length: 300-1,000 words. **Pays $0-200.** Sometimes pays expenses of writers on assignment.

Photos: Send photos with submission. Reviews transparencies and prints. Negotiates payment individually. Captions, model releases and identification of subjects required.

Columns/Departments: Team and individual profiles, skill how-to's, fundraising, costuming, makeup, health & fitness, industry news. Query. **Pays $200.**

Fillers: Anecdotes, facts, newsbreaks. **Buys many/year.** Length: 50-100 words. **Pays $25.**

Tips: "Have at least a working knowledge of dance and color guard industry—experience a plus. Keep queries brief. The writing style of the publication is casual, teen-oriented. Articles take a fun, yet educational approach on performing and training."

$ $ DRAMATICS MAGAZINE, Educational Theatre Association, 2343 Auburn Ave., Cincinnati OH 45219-2815. (513)421-3900. Fax: (513)421-7077. E-mail: dcorathers@etassoc.org. Website: www.etassoc.org. **Contact:** Donald Corathers, editor-in-chief. **70% freelance written.** Works with small number of new/unpublished writers. For theater arts students, teachers and others interested in theater arts education. "*Dramatics* is designed to provide serious, committed young theatre students and their teachers with the skills and knowledge they need to make better theatre; to be a resource that will help high school juniors and seniors make an informed decision about whether to pursue a career in theatre, and about how to do so; and to prepare high school students to be knowledgeable, appreciative audience members for the rest of their lives." Magazine published monthly, September-May. Estab. 1929. Circ. 40,000. **Pays on acceptance.** Publishes ms an average of 3 months after acceptance. Buys first North American serial rights. Byline given. Submit seasonal material 3 months in advance. Accepts queries by mail, e-mail, fax. Accepts simultaneous submissions. Responds in 3 months; longer to unsolicited mss. Sample copy for 9 × 12 SAE with 5 first-class stamps. Guidelines free or on website.

　　O— "The best way to break in is to know our audience—drama students, teachers and others interested in theater—and to write for them."

Nonfiction: How-to (technical theater, directing, acting, etc.), informational, interview, photo feature, humorous, profile, technical. **Buys 30 mss/year.** Submit complete ms. Length: 750-3,000 words. **Pays $50-400.** Rarely pays expenses of writers on assignment.

Reprints: Send tearsheet or photocopy of article or play, or typed ms with rights for sale noted and information about when and where it previously appeared. Pays up to 75% of amount paid for an original article.

Photos: Purchased with accompanying ms. Uses b&w photos and transparencies. Query. Total purchase price for ms usually includes payment for photos.

Fiction: Drama (one-act and full-length plays). "No plays for children, Christmas plays or plays written with no attention paid to the conventions of theater." Prefers unpublished scripts that have been produced at least once. **Buys 5-9 mss/year.** Send complete ms. **Pays $100-400.**

Tips: "Writers who have some practical experience in theater, especially in technical areas, have a leg-up here, but we'll work with anybody who has a good idea. Some freelancers have become regular contributors. Others ignore style suggestions included in our writer's guidelines."

⊠ $ $ EAST END LIGHTS, The Quarterly Magazine for Elton John Fans, P.O. Box 636, New Baltimore MI 48047. (810)725-8200. Fax: (810)725-7077. E-mail: eastendlts@aol.com. **Contact:** Tom Stanton, editor. **90% freelance written.** Quarterly magazine covering Elton John. "In one way or another, a story must relate to Elton John, his activities or associates (past and present). We appeal to discriminating Elton fans. No gushing fanzine material. No current concert reviews." Estab. 1990. Circ. 1,700. Pays 3 weeks after publication. Publishes ms an average of 3 months after acceptance. Byline given. Offers 100% kill fee. Buys first rights and second serial (reprint) rights. Submit seasonal material 6 months in advance. Accepts queries by mail, e-mail, fax. Responds in 2 months. Sample copy $2.

Nonfiction: Book excerpts, essays, exposé, general interest, historical/nostalgic, humor and interview/profile. **Buys 20 mss/year.** Query with or without published clips or send complete ms. Length: 400-1,000 words. **Pays $75-250 for assigned articles; $75-150 for unsolicited articles.** Pays with contributor copies only if the writer requests.

Reprints: Send tearsheet or photocopy of article or typed ms with rights for sale noted and information about when and where the article previously appeared. Pays 50% of amount paid for an original article.

Photos: State availability of photos with submission. Reviews negatives and 5×7 prints. Offers $40-75/photo. Buys one-time rights and all rights.

Columns/Departments: Clippings (non-wire references to Elton John in other publications), maximum 200 words. **Buys 12 mss/year.** Send complete ms. Length: 50-200 words. **Pays $20-50.**

Tips: "Approach us with a well-thought-out story idea. We prefer interviews with Elton-related personalities—past or present; try to land an interview we haven't done. We are particularly interested in music/memorabilia collecting of Elton material."

N **□** **ENTERTAINMENT TODAY, L.A.'s Entertainment Weekly Since 1967**, Best Publishing Inc., 2325 W. Victory Blvd., Burbank CA 91506. (818)566-4030. Fax: (818)566-4295. E-mail: jsalazar@artnet.net. Website: www.entertainment-today.com. Editor: Brent Simon. Managing Editor: Eric Layton. **Contact:** Ginny Zoraster, editorial assistant. **40% freelance written.** Weekly print and online newspaper covering entertainment. Estab. 1967. Circ. 210,000. Pays on publication. Publishes ms an average of 3 months after acceptance. Byline given. Offers 25% kill fee. Buys one-time rights. Editorial lead time 2 months. Submit seasonal material 2 months in advance. Accepts queries by mail, e-mail, fax, phone. Accepts simultaneous submissions. Responds in 2 months to queries. Sample copy and writer's guidelines free.

Nonfiction: General interest, humor, interview/profile, opinion, photo feature, travel, any entertainment-related material. **Buys 6-12 mss/year.** Query with published clips. Length: 675-1,850 words.

Reprints: Accepts previously published submissions.

Photos: State availability of photos with submission. Offers no additional payment for photos accepted with ms. Negotiates payment individually. Identification of subjects required.

Columns/Departments: Book Report (book review, often entertainment-related), 415-500 words; Film Reviews, 300-600 words; Disc Domain (CD reviews), 250-400 words. **Buys 6-12 mss/year.** Query with published clips.

Fillers: Short humor.

$ $FANGORIA: Horror in Entertainment, Starlog Communications, Inc., 475 Park Ave. S., 8th Floor, New York NY 10016. (212)689-2830. Fax: (212)889-7933. Website: www.fangoria2000.com. **Contact:** Anthony Timpone, editor. **95% freelance written.** Works with a small number of new/unpublished writers each year. Magazine published 10 times/year covering horror films, TV projects, comics, videos and literature and those who create them. "We emphasize the personalities and behind-the-scenes angles of horror filmmaking." Estab. 1979. Pays on publication. Publishes ms an average of 3 months after acceptance. Byline given. Buys all rights. Submit seasonal material 4 months in advance. Responds in 6 weeks. "We provide an assignment sheet (deadlines, info) to writers, thus authorizing queried stories that we're buying." Sample copy for $7 and 10×13 SAE with 4 first-class stamps. Writer's guidelines for #10 SASE.

● *Fangoria* is looking for more articles and profiles on independent filmmakers and better-known horror novelists. The magazine is not looking for interviews with current, mainstream filmmakers and actors.

Nonfiction: Book excerpts; interview/profile of movie directors, makeup FX artists, screenwriters, producers, actors, noted horror/thriller novelists and others—with genre credits; special FX and special makeup FX how-it-was-dones (on filmmaking only). Occasional "think" pieces, opinion pieces, reviews, or sub-theme overviews by industry professionals. **Buys 100 mss/year.** Query by mail (never by phone) with ideas and published clips. Length: 1,000-3,500 words. **Pays $100-250.** Rarely pays expenses of writers on assignment. Avoids most articles on science fiction films—see listing for sister magazine *Starlog* in *Writer's Market* Science Fiction consumer magazine section.

Photos: State availability of photos. Reviews b&w and color prints and transparencies. "No separate payment for photos provided by film studios." Captions, identification of subjects required. Photo credit given.

Columns/Departments: Monster Invasion (exclusive, early information about new film productions; also mini-interviews with filmmakers and novelists). Query by mail only with published clips. Length: 300-500 words. **Pays $45-75.**

● *Fangoria* emphasizes that it does not publish fiction or poetry.

Tips: "Other than recommending that you study one or several copies of *Fangoria*, we can only describe it as a horror film magazine consisting primarily of interviews with technicians and filmmakers in the field. Be sure to stress the interview subjects' words—not your own opinions as much. We're very interested in small, independent filmmakers working outside of Hollywood. These people are usually more accessible to writers, and more cooperative. *Fangoria* is also sort of a *de facto* bible for youngsters interested in movie makeup careers and for young filmmakers. We are devoted only to *reel* horrors—the fakery of films, the imagery of the horror fiction of a Stephen King or a Clive Barker— *we do not* want nor would we *ever* publish articles on real-life horrors, murders, etc. A writer must *like* and *enjoy* horror films and horror fiction to work for us. If the photos in *Fangoria* disgust you, if the sight of *(stage)* blood repels you, if you feel 'superior' to horror (and its fans), you aren't a writer for us and we certainly aren't the market for you. We love giving new writers their *first* chance to break into print in a national magazine. We are currently looking for Vancouver-, Arizona- and Las Vegas-based correspondents."

N $ $ MAD RHYTHMS, College Entertainment Inc., P.O. Box 5328, Suffolk VA 23435. Fax: (757)638-9551. E-mail: madrhythms@aol.com. **Contact:** Yasmin Shiraz, editor-in-chief. **50% freelance written.** "Quarterly magazine covering entertainment of interest to the urban market and college market. Most of our readers are African American—92%. Most of our readers are female—69%. This publication discusses entertainment with an educational and informative slant. It writes for a knowledgeable audience." Estab. 1994. Circ. 70,000. Pays on publication. Publishes ms an average of 3 months after acceptance. Byline given. Buys first rights and one-time rights. Editorial lead time 3 months. Submit seasonal material 4 months in advance. Accepts simultaneous submissions. Responds in 3 weeks to queries. Sample copy for SAE with 4 first-class stamps. Writer's guidelines for #10 SASE.

Nonfiction: Essays, interview/profile, opinion, personal experience, music. Special issue: End of the Entertainment Year: highlights; profiles on entertainers who have grown the most. No erotic, historical, how-to, technical. Query with published clips. Length: 500-1,500 words. **Pays $100-200 for assigned articles, $25-75 for unsolicited articles.** Pays writers with contributor copies or other premiums for music or concert reviews.

Photos: State availability of photos with submission or send photos with submission. Negotiates payment individually. Captions and identification of subjects required. Buys one-time rights.

Columns/Departments: Features on Entertainers (in film, fashion, music), 500 words; Macks in the Back (profile of behind the scenes entertainer), 500 words; Thoughts (issues in the media affecting the urban population), 500 words. **Buys 12 mss/year.** Query with published clips. **Pays $100-200.**

Fillers: Facts, newsbreaks, short humor. **Buys 3/year.** Length: 100-300 words. **Pays $10.**

Tips: "Write on a relatively unknown entertainer and make it so interesting that everyone wants to know them."

$ $ NATIONAL EXAMINER, America's Favorite Family Weekly, Globe Communications Corp., 5401 Broken Sound Blvd., Boca Raton FL 33487. (561)997-7733. Fax: (561)997-5595. E-mail: examtab@aol.com or examtab@gate.net. Editor: Brian Williams. **Contact:** Roger Capettini (ext. 1106), news editor. Weekly magazine covering entertainment, general interest, crime, health, celebrity reporting. "*The National Examiner* is a general interest magazine that specializes in celebrity reporting, Hollywood gossip, human interest stories and cutting edge health reporting." Estab. 1972. Circ. 500,000. Pays on publication. Byline given. Buys all rights. Editorial lead time 5 days. Submit seasonal material 2 months in advance. Accepts queries by mail, e-mail, fax. Responds in 2 weeks.

Nonfiction: How-to, humor, inspirational, crime, celebrity. **Pays $200** for leads for page 1 **plus $200** if writing story. **Pays $40** for shorts **plus $20** if writing story.

Photos: State availability of photos with submission or send photos with submission. Captions, model releases and identification of subjects required. Buys one-time and all rights.

$ THE NEWFOUNDLAND HERALD, Sunday Herald Ltd., Box 2015, St. John's, Newfoundland A1C 5R7 Canada. (709)726-7060. Fax: (709)726-8227/6971. E-mail: kdawe@nfldherald.com. Website: www.nfldherald.com. **Contact:** Karen Dawe, managing editor. **25% freelance written.** Weekly entertainment magazine. "We prefer Newfoundland and Labrador-related items." Estab. 1946. Circ. 30,000. Pays on publication. Publishes ms an average of 2 months after acceptance. Byline given. Buys first North American serial, one-time or all rights. Editorial lead time 4 months. Submit seasonal material 3 months in advance. Accepts queries by mail, e-mail, fax. Sample copy for $5. Guidelines on website or free via fax ($1 by mail).

Nonfiction: General interest, investigative news, how-to, interview/profile, travel. No opinion, humor, poetry, fiction, satire. **Buys 500 mss/year.** Query with published clips. Length: 700-2,500 words. **Pays $20 minimum.** Sometimes pays expenses of writers on assignment.

Reprints: Send typed ms with rights for sale noted (Mac disk or e-mail attachment of text preferred).

Photos: Send photos with submission. Offers $7.50-25/photo. Captions required. Buys one-time or all rights.

Columns/Departments: Music (current artists), Video/Movies (recent releases/themes), TV shows (Top 20); all 1,500-2,500 words. **Buys 500 mss/year.** Query with published clips.

Tips: "Know something about Newfoundlanders and Labradorians—for example, travel writers should know where we like to travel. Query first. No opinion pieces, satire, humor or poetry is purchased; fiction is not accepted. Original cartoons which focus on local politics will be considered. Photos should be submitted with all articles. Please use color 35mm print or slide film. No b&w photos unless otherwise requested. Please read several issues of the magazine before submitting any material to the *Herald*."

N ☆ $ $ $ PERFORMING ARTS MAGAZINE, Performing Arts Network, 10350 Santa Monica Blvd., #350, Los Angeles CA 90025. (310)551-1115. Fax: (310)551-2769. Website: www.performingartsmagazine.com. **Contact:** David Bowman, editor. **95% freelance written.** Monthly magazine covering arts and performing arts. "We cover performing arts events throughout the state of California only. Theatre-going audience." Estab. 1963. Circ. 570,000. Pays on publication. Byline given. Offers 50% kill fee. Buys all rights or makes work-for-hire assignments. Editorial lead time 3 months. Submit seasonal material 6 months in advance. Responds in 6 weeks to queries; do not send mss. Sample copy for 10×12 SAE with 5 first-class stamps.

Nonfiction: Interview/profile, new productions. **Buys 75 mss/year.** Query by mail only with published clips. Length: 800-1,200 words. **Pays $500-1,000.** "Do not send unsolicited articles." Sometimes pays expenses of writers on assignment.

Photos: State availability of photos with submission. Negotiates payment individually. Captions and identification of subjects required. Buys all rights.

✖ $ $ THE READERS SHOWCASE, Suggitt Group Ltd., 950 Canada Trust Tower, 10104-103 Ave., Edmonton, Alberta T5J 0H8 Canada. (780)413-6163. Fax: (780)413-6185. E-mail: readers@suggitt.com. Website: www.readers showcase.com. **Contact:** Maureen Hutchison, senior editor. **80-100% freelance written.** Bimonthly magazine covering books available at the Canadian SmithBooks and Coles bookstores. "*The Readers Showcase* consists of author interviews, book reviews, lifestyle pieces, industry news, contests, book-related editorials, etc." Estab. 1993. Circ. 400,000 (1.4 million in November/December). Pays within 30 days of publication. Publishes ms an average of 1 month after acceptance. Byline given. Offers 50% kill fee. Editorial lead time 2 months. Submit seasonal material 2 months in advance. Accepts queries by mail, e-mail, fax. Accepts simultaneous submissions. Sample copy and writer's guidelines free.

Nonfiction: Book excerpts, lifestyle issues, interview/profile, book reviews. **Buys 300 mss/year.** Query with published clips. Length: 300-2,000 words. **Pay rates vary, starting at 25¢/word.**

Tips: Writer's best bet to break in is to "provide writer samples, along with a résumé and covering letter, indicating what you could offer to the magazine. Indicate your areas of interest. Writers should be prepared to be flexible regarding deadlines and assignment choices. Most importantly, writers' articles must be informative, yet inviting to the reader."

✖ $ $ SCI-FI ENTERTAINMENT, Sovereign Media, 11305 Sunset Hills Rd., Reston VA 20190. (703)471-1556. E-mail: sormedia@erols.com. **Contact:** Dan Perez, editor. **100% freelance written.** Published 6 times/year. Magazine covering science fiction movies and television—old, new, upcoming sci-fi. Estab. 1994. Circ. 70,000. Pays 1-2 months after acceptance. Publishes ms an average of 1 month after acceptance. Byline given. Offers 10% kill fee. Buys first world rights. Editorial lead time 1 month. Submit seasonal material 3 months in advance. Accepts simultaneous submissions. Responds in 2 weeks to queries; 1 month to mss. Sample copy for $4.95. Guidelines for #10 SASE.

Nonfiction: General interest, historical/nostalgic, interview/profile, new product (games), opinion, personal experience. photo feature. **Buys 100 mss/year.** Query. Length: 2,000-3,000 words. **Pays $200-500.** Sometimes pays expenses of writers on assignment.

Photos: State availability of photos with submissions. Offers no additional payment for photos accepted with ms. Identification of subjects required. Buys one-time rights.

Columns/Departments: Infinite Channels (games), 2,300 words; Video (video reviews), 2,400 words; Books (books on movies), 2,500 words. **Buys 6 mss/year.** Query with published clips.

$ $ SOAP OPERA UPDATE, Bauer Publishing, 270 Sylvan Ave., Englewood Cliffs NJ 07632. (201)569-6699. Fax: (201)569-2510. **Contact:** Richard Spencer, editor-in-chief. **25% freelance written.** Biweekly. "We cover daytime and prime time soap operas with preview information, in-depth interviews and exclusive photos, history, character sketches, events where soap stars are seen and participate." Estab. 1988. Circ. 288,000. Pays on publication. Byline given. Buys first North American serial rights. Submit seasonal material 3 months in advance. Accepts queries by mail, fax. Responds in 1 month.

Nonfiction: Humor, interview/profile. "Only articles directly about actors, shows or history of a show." **Buys 100 mss/year.** Query with published clips. Length: 750-2,200 words. **Pays $400.** Sometimes pays expenses of writers on assignment.

Photos: State availability of photos with submission. Reviews transparencies. Offers $25. Captions and identification of subjects required. Buys all rights.

Tips: "Come up with fresh, new approaches to stories about soap operas and their people. Submit ideas and clips. Take a serious approach; don't talk down to the reader. All articles must be well written and the writer must be knowledgeable about his subject matter."

Ⓝ $ $ $ STEREO REVIEW'S SOUND & VISION, Hachette Filipacchi Magazines, Inc. 1633 Broadway, New York NY 10019. (212)767-6000. Fax: (212)767-5615. E-mail: bfenton@hfmag.com. Website: www.soundandvisio nmag.com. Editor-in-Chief: Bob Ankosko. Entertainment Editor: Ken Richardson. **Contact:** Mike Gaughn, senior editor. **50% freelance written**, almost entirely by established contributing editors, and on assignment. Published 10 times a year. Estab. 1958. Circ. 450,000. **Pays on acceptance.** Publishes ms an average of 4 months after acceptance. Byline given. Buys first North American serial plus electronic rights. Accepts queries by mail, e-mail, fax. Sample copy for 9×12 SAE with 11 first-class stamps.

Nonfiction: Home theater, audio, video and multimedia equipment plus movie and music reviews, how-to-buy and how-to-use A/V gear, interview/profile. **Buys 25 mss/year.** Query with published clips. Length: 1,500-3,000 words. **Pays $800-1,200.**

Tips: "Send proposals or outlines, rather than complete articles, along with published clips to establish writing ability. Publisher assumes no responsibility for return or safety of unsolicited art, photos or manuscripts."

Ⓝ ✖ $ TELE REVISTA, Su Mejor Amiga, Teve Latino Publishing, Inc., P.O. Box 145179, Coral Gables FL 33114-5179. (305)445-1755. Fax: (305)445-3907. E-mail: telerevista@aol.com. Website: www.telerevista.com. **Con-**

tact: Ana Pereiro, editor. **100% freelance written.** Monthly magazine covering Hispanic entertainment (US and Puerto Rico). "We feature interviews, gossip, breaking stories, behind-the-scenes happenings, etc." Estab. 1986. Pays on publication. Publishes ms an average of 3 months after acceptance. Byline sometimes given. Buys all rights. Editorial lead time 2 months. Submit seasonal material 3 months in advance. Accepts queries by mail, e-mail, fax. Sample copy free.

Nonfiction: Exposé, interview/profile, opinion, photo feature. **Buys 200 mss/year.** Query. **Pays $25-75.**

Photos: State availability of or send photos with submission. Negotiates payment individually. Captions required. Buys all rights.

Columns/Departments: Buys 60 mss/year. Query. **Pays $25-75.**

Fillers: Anecdotes, facts, gags to be illustrated by cartoonist, newsbreaks, short humor.

$ THEATREFORUM, International Theatre Journal, UCSD Department of Theatre, 9500 Gilman Dr., La Jolla CA 92093-0344. (858)534-6598. Fax: (858)534-1080. E-mail: theatreforum@ucsd.edu. Website: www-theatre.ucsd.edu/ TF. **Contact:** Jim Carmody, editor. **75% freelance written.** Semiannual magazine covering performance, theatrical and otherwise. "*TheatreForum* is an international journal of theater, performance art, dance theater, music theater and forms yet to be devised. We publish performance texts, interviews with artists on their creative process, and articles about innovative productions and groups. Written by and for members of both the academic and artistic community, we represent a wide variety of aesthetic and cultural interests." Estab. 1992. Circ. 2,000. Pays on publication. Byline given. Buys one-time rights or anthology rights for scripts. Editorial lead time 4 months. Accepts queries by e-mail only. Responds in 1 month to queries; 2 months to mss. Sample copy for $5. Writer's guidelines for #10 SASE or on website.

   O— Break in with "a sophisticated, insightful piece on a new, innovative and not widely known performance. We do not publish any articles not related to a specific performance or play."

Nonfiction: Essays, interview/profile, photo feature, performance criticism. **Buys 10-12 mss/year.** Query by e-mail only. Length: 1,000-5,000 words. **Pays 5¢/word.**

Photos: State availability of photos with submission. Negotiates payment individually. Identification of subjects required. Buys one-time rights.

Scripts: Previously published plays are not considered. **Buys 4-6 mss/year.** Query with published clips. **Pays $200.**

Tips: "We want material on contemporary performance only—from 1997 on. We are interested in documenting, discussing, and disseminating innovative and provocative theaterworks. Non-traditional and inventive texts (plays) are welcome. We also publish in-depth analyses of innovative theatrical productions. We are interested in finding artists who want to write about other artists."

N $ $ $ $ US WEEKLY, Wenner Media LLC, 1290 Avenue of the Americas, New York NY 10104. (212)484-1761. Fax: (212)767-8204. Website: www.usmagazine.com. Editor: Charlie Leerhsen. Managing Editor: Maura Fritz. **Contact:** Lucia Ware, editorial manager. Weekly magazine covering entertainment. "We will cover more opinion or personal perspective on stories rather than real, hard-breaking news reporting." Estab. 2000. Pays on publication. Buys exclusive rights for 120 days. Accepts queries by mail, fax. Responds in 1 month to queries.

Nonfiction: Interview/profile, photo feature, reviews for film, TV, book, music, websites. Query with published clips. Length: 3,500-4,000 words. **Pays $1.50/word.**

Columns/Departments: Spotlight (photo-driven short story to accompany picture), 300 words; Q&A's (interview with celeb or up and coming person), 100-200 words. Query with published clips. **Pays $1.50/word.**

Tips: "Best way to break in: reviews (150-200 words) on film, books, TV, music, websites."

ETHNIC & MINORITY

Ideas and concerns of interest to specific nationalities and religions are covered by publications in this category. General interest lifestyle magazines for these groups are also included. Many ethnic publications are locally oriented or highly specialized and do not wish to be listed in a national publication such as *Writer's Market*. Query the editor of an ethnic publication with which you're familiar before submitting a manuscript, but do not consider these markets closed because they are not listed in this section. Additional markets for writing with an ethnic orientation are located in the following sections: Career, College & Alumni; Juvenile; Literary & "Little"; Men's; Women's; and Teen & Young Adult.

$ $ AFRICAN ACCESS MAGAZINE, Mainstreaming Africa, 44 Dalhurst Way NW, Calgary, Alberta T3A 1N7 Canada. (403)210-2726. Fax: (403)210-2484. E-mail: editor@africanaccess.com. Website: www.africanaccess.com. **Contact:** Chris Roberts, editor. **50% freelance written.** A quarterly consumer/trade hybrid magazine covering business, investment and travel in Africa. "*AfriCan Access Magazine* is Canada's guide to the African Renaissance. Our audience is internationally oriented: business, investment and travel interest in Africa. Articles should have a North American-African connection." Estab. 1998. Circ. 5,000. Pays on publication. Publishes ms an average of 2 months after acceptance. Byline given. Offers 20% kill fee. Buys first North American serial, one-time or electronic rights. Editorial lead time 2 months. Accepts queries by mail, e-mail, fax, phone. Accepts simultaneous submissions. Responds in 2 weeks to queries; 1 month to mss. Sample copy for $5. Writer's guidelines on website.

Nonfiction: Book excerpts/reviews, essays, exposé, general interest, how-to (do business, case studies, travel, invest), interview/profile, opinion, personal experience, photo feature, travel, investment/political analysis. "If Africa isn't part of the story, we aren't interested." **Buys 20 mss/year.** Query with published clips. Length: 600-2,000 words. **Pays $100-400 for assigned articles; $50-300 for unsolicited articles (Canadian).** Pays sometimes in copies and/or advertising.

Reprints: Accepts previously published submissions.

Photos: State availability of photos with submission. Negotiates payment individually. Captions and identification of subjects required. Buys one-time rights.

Columns/Departments: Recommended Reading: Reviews (book, film, TV, video, art reviews), 100-300 words; NGO Profile (work of an NGO active in Africa), 500-750 words; Travel Stories (humorous/adventure first person), 200-400 words; Business Profiles (detailed how-to look at SMEs active overseas), 400-750 words; Cyber Africa (Africa on the Internet, best sites), 200-350 words. **Buys 8-12 mss/year.** Query with published clips or send complete ms. **Pays $100.**

⬛ The online magazine carries original content not found in the print edition.

Tips: "If a writer has first hand experience in Africa, has studied Africa, or is African, that helps! We want practical stories our readers can use."

★ $ **AIM MAGAZINE**, AIM Publishing Company, 7308 S. Eberhart Ave., Chicago IL 60619-0554. (708)344-4414. Fax: (206)543-2746. E-mail: ruthone@earthlink.net. Website: http://aimmagazine.org. **Contact:** Dr. Myron Apilado, editor. **75% freelance written.** Works with a small number of new/unpublished writers each year. Quarterly magazine on social betterment that promotes racial harmony and peace for high school, college and general audience. Estab. 1975. Circ. 10,000. Pays on publication. Publishes ms an average of 3 months after acceptance. Offers 60% kill fee. Not copyrighted. Buys one-time rights. Submit seasonal material 6 months in advance. Accepts queries by mail, e-mail. Accepts simultaneous submissions. Responds in 2 months to queries. Sample copy and writer's guidelines for $4 and 9×12 SAE with $1.70 postage or on website.

Nonfiction: Exposé (education); general interest (social significance); historical/nostalgic (Black or Indian); how-to (create a more equitable society); profile (one who is making social contributions to community); book reviews and reviews of plays "that reflect our ethnic/minority orientation." No religious material. **Buys 16 mss/year.** Send complete ms. Length: 500-800 words. **Pays $25-35.**

Photos: Reviews b&w prints. Captions, identification of subjects required.

Fiction: Ethnic, historical, mainstream, suspense. "Fiction that teaches the brotherhood of man." **Buys 20 mss/year.** Send complete ms. Length: 1,000-1,500 words. **Pays $25-35.**

Poetry: Avant-garde, free verse, light verse. No "preachy" poetry. **Buys 20 poems/year.** Submit maximum 5 poems. Length: 15-30 lines. **Pays $3-5.**

Fillers: Jokes, anecdotes, newsbreaks. **Buys 30/year.** Length: 50-100 words. **Pays $5.**

Tips: "Interview anyone of any age who unselfishly is making an unusual contribution to the lives of less fortunate individuals. Include photo and background of person. We look at the nations of the world as part of one family. Short stories and historical pieces about Blacks and Indians are the areas most open to freelancers. Subject matter of submission is of paramount concern for us rather than writing style. Articles and stories showing the similarity in the lives of people with different racial backgrounds are desired."

$ **ALBERTA SWEETGRASS**, Aboriginal Multi-Media Society of Alberta, 15001 112th Ave., Edmonton, Alberta T5M 2V6 Canada. (800)661-5469. Fax: (780)455-7639. E-mail: edwind@ammsa.com. Website: www.ammsa.com. **Contact:** Debora Lockyer Steel, managing editor. Monthly tabloid newspaper. **50% freelance written.** "*Alberta Sweetgrass* is a community paper that focuses on people from within Alberta's First Nations, Métis and non-status Aboriginal communities." Estab. 1993. Circ. 7,500. Pays 10th of month following publication. Accepts queries by mail, e-mail, fax, phone. Sample copy free. Writer's guidelines available on website and production schedule available upon request.

Nonfiction: Features, general interest, interview/profile, opinion, photo feature, travel, community-based stories, all with an Alberta angle (no exceptions). **Usually runs 2-3 focus sections/month.** Query. Length: 400-1,200 words. **Pays $3/published inch for one-source stories; $3.60 for multiple sources** (less for excess editorial work).

Reprints: Pays 50% of amount paid for an original article.

Photos: State availability of photos with submission. Offers $15/b&w photo; $50/color cover; $15/inside color.

Columns/Departments: Book/Film/Art Reviews (Alberta Aboriginal), 450-500 words; Briefs (community news shorts), 150-200 words.

Tips: "Aboriginal knowledge is definitely an asset in order to send us usable stories, but even if you aren't familiar with Aboriginal culture, but are still a good writer, bounce a story idea off the editor."

N $ $ **AMBASSADOR MAGAZINE**, National Italian American Foundation, 1860-19 St. NW, Washington DC 20009. Fax: (202)387-0800. E-mail: dona@niaf.org. Website: www.niaf.org. **Contact:** Dona De Sanctis, editor. **50% freelance written.** Cultural magazine for Italian Americans covering Italian-American history and culture. "We publish nonfiction articles on little-known events in Italian-American history, and articles on Italian-American culture, traditions and personalities living and dead." Estab. 1989. Circ. 20,000. Pays on approval of final draft. Byline given. Offers 50% or $100 kill fee. Buys second serial (reprint) rights. Editorial lead time 3 months. Accepts queries by mail, e-mail. Accepts simultaneous submissions. Responds in 1 month to queries. Sample copy and writer's guidelines free.

Nonfiction: Historical/nostalgic, interview/profile, personal experience, photo feature. **Buys 12 mss/year.** Send complete ms. Length: 1,500-2,500 words. **Pays $200.**
Reprints: Accepts previously published submissions.
Photos: Send photos with submission. Reviews contact sheets and prints. Offers no additional payment for photos accepted with ms. Captions and identification of subjects required. Buys one-time rights.
Tips: "Good photos, clear prose and a good story-telling ability are all prerequisites."

[N] [⊠] $ $ AMERICAN VISIONS, The Magazine of Afro-American Culture, 1101 Pennsylvania Ave. NW, Suite 820, Washington DC 20004. (202)347-3820. Fax: (202)347-4096. E-mail: editor@avs.americanvisions.com. Website: www.americanvisions.com. **Contact:** Joanne Harris, editor. **75% freelance written.** Bimonthly. "Editorial is reportorial, current, objective, 'pop-scholarly.' Audience is ages 25-54, mostly black, college educated. The scope of the magazine includes the arts, history, literature, cuisine, genealogy and travel—all filtered through the prism of the African-American experience." Estab. 1986. Circ. 125,000. Pays 30 days after publication. Publishes ms an average of 2 months after acceptance. Byline given. Offers 25% kill fee. Buys all and second serial (reprint) rights. Submit seasonal material 5 months in advance. Accepts simultaneous submissions. Responds in 3 months. Sample copy and writer's guidelines with SASE.
Nonfiction: Book excerpts, general interest, historical, interview/profile, literature, photo feature, travel. Publishes travel supplements—domestic, Africa, Europe, Canada, Mexico. No fiction, poetry, personal experience or opinion. **Buys about 60-70 mss/year.** Query by mail only with or without published clips, or send complete ms. Accepts queries by mail, fax and e-mail. Length: 500-2,500 words. **Pays $100-600 for assigned articles; $100-400 for unsolicited articles.** Sometimes pays expenses of writers on assignment.
Reprints: Send tearsheet of article or short story or typed ms with rights for sale noted and information about when and where the article or story previously appeared. **Pays $100.**
Photos: State availability of photos with submission. Reviews contact sheets, 3×5 transparencies, and 3×5 or 8×10 prints. Offers $15 minimum. Identification of subjects required. Buys one-time rights.
Columns/Departments: Arts Scene, Books, Cuisine, Film, Music, Profile, Genealogy, Computers & Technology, Travel, 750-1,750 words. **Buys about 40 mss/year.** Query or send complete ms. **Pays $100-400.**
Fiction: Publishes novel excerpts.
Tips: "Little-known but terribly interesting information about black history and culture is desired. Aim at an upscale audience. Send ms with credentials. Looking for writers who are enthusiastic about their topics."

[N] $ ASIAN PAGES, Kita Associates, Inc., P.O. Box 11932, St. Paul MN 55111-1932. (612)884-3265. Fax: (612)888-9373. E-mail: asianpages@att.net. Website: www.asianpages.com. **Contact:** Cheryl Weiberg, editor-in-chief. **40% freelance written.** Biweekly (ethnic) newspaper covering the Asian community in the Midwest. "*Asian Pages* serves an audience of over twenty different Asian groups, including Cambodian, Chinese, Filipino, Hmong, Indian, Indonesian, Japanese, Korean, Laotian, Malaysian, Sri Lankan, Thai, Tibetan, and Vietnamese. In addition, *Asian Pages* has many non-Asian readers who, for many different reasons, have an interest in the vibrant Asian community. *Asian Pages* celebrates the achievements of the Asian community in the Midwest and promotes a cultural bridge among the many different Asian groups that the newspaper serves." Estab. 1990. Circ. 75,000. Pays on publication. Publishes ms an average of 8 months after acceptance. Byline given. Offers 50% kill fee. Buys first North American serial rights. Editorial lead time 4 months. Submit seasonal material 6 months in advance. Accepts simultaneous submissions. Responds in 1 month to queries; 2 months to mss. Sample copy for 9×12 SAE and 3 first-class stamps. Writer's guidelines for #10 SASE.
Nonfiction: Essays, general interest, humor, inspirational, interview/profile, personal experience, travel. "All articles must have an Asian slant. We're interested in articles on the Asian New Years, banking, business, finance, sports/leisure, home and garden, education and career planning. No culturally insensitive material." **Buys 50-60 mss/year.** Send complete ms. Length: 500-750 words. **Pays $40.**
Photos: State availability of photos with submission. Reviews transparencies and prints. Offers no additional payment for photos accepted with ms. Captions and identification of subjects required. Buys one-time rights.
Columns/Departments: "Query with exceptional ideas for our market and provide 1-2 sample columns." **Buys 100 mss/year. Pays $40.**
Fiction: Adventure, Ethnic (Asian), humorous, stories based on personal experiences. No culturally insensitive material. **Buys 8 mss/year.** Send complete ms. Length: 750-1,000 words. **Pays $40.**
Tips: "We look for articles that reflect a direct insight into Asian culture or being an Asian-American in today's society."

[N] [⊠] $ $ THE B'NAI B'RITH INTERNATIONAL JEWISH MONTHLY, B'nai B'rith International, 1640 Rhode Island Ave. NW, Washington DC 20036. Fax: (202)296-1092. E-mail: ijm@bnaibrith.org. Website: bnaibrith.org. Editor: Eric Rozenman. **Contact:** Stacey Freed, managing editor. **90% freelance written.** Bimonthly magazine covering Jewish affairs in the US and abroad. Estab. 1886. Circ. 110,000. Pays on publication. Publishes ms an average of 6 months after acceptance. Byline given. Offers 25% kill fee. Buys first rights. Editorial lead time 3 months. Submit seasonal material 5 months in advance. Accepts queries by mail, e-mail, fax. Accepts simultaneous submissions. Responds in 2 weeks to queries; 6 weeks to mss. Sample copy for $2. Writer's guidelines for #10 SASE or by e-mail.

Nonfiction: General interest pieces of relevance to the Jewish community of US and abroad; interview/profile, photo feature, religious, travel. "No Holocaust memoirs, no first-person essays/memoirs." **Buys 18-20 mss/year.** Query with published clips. Length: 1,000-2,500 words. **Pays $300-750 for assigned articles; $300-600 for unsolicited articles.** Sometimes pays expenses of writers on assignment.

Photos: "Rarely assigned." Buys one-time rights.

Columns/Departments: Carla Lancit, assistant editor. Up Front (book, CD reviews; small/short items with Jewish interest), 150-200 words. **Buys 3 mss/year.** Query. **Pays $50.**

Tips: "Know what's going on in the Jewish world. Look at other Jewish publications also. Writers should submit clips with their queries. Read our guidelines carefully and present a good idea expressed well. Proofread your query letter"

[N] COLORLINES, Center for Third World Organizing and Applied Research Center, 3871 Broadway, Oakland CA 94611. (510)653-3415. Fax: (510)653-3427. E-mail: colorlines@arc.org. Website: www.colorlines.com. **Contact:** Bob Wing, executive editor. **65% freelance written.** Bimonthly magazine covering communities of color, grassroots organizing, low-income communities. "Must reflect knowledge and understanding of issues in various communities of color. Writers of color are especially encouraged to submit queries." Estab. 1998. Circ. 20,000. Publishes ms an average of 3 months after acceptance. Byline given. Editorial lead time 3 months. Submit seasonal material 4 months in advance. Accepts queries by mail, e-mail. Responds in 6 weeks to queries; 2 months to mss. Sample copy and writer's guidelines free or on website.

Nonfiction: Essays, exposé, general interest, culture (pop music, film, book reviews and critiques), historical, interview/profile, opinion, photo feature. Query with published clips or writing samples. Length: 700-3,000 words.

Reprints: Send photocopy of article and information about when and where the article previously appeared. No pay.

Photos: State availability of photos with submissions. Negotiates payment individually. Captions, identification of subjects required. Buys one-time rights.

Columns/Departments: Editorial/Commentary (political, cultural, social), 800 words; Historical (histories of organizing or other issues in communities of color), 1,000 words. **Buys 6 mss/year.** Query with published clips or send complete ms. Pay negotiable.

Fillers: Timely political/social cartoons (strip or single panel) or illustrations. **Buys 6/year.** Pay negotiable.

■ The online magazine carries original content not found in the print edition and includes writer's guidelines.

Tips: "The best way for writers to break in is to write or propose a short feature about a particular political struggle or grassroots campaign that the writer is familiar with. Authors of short features are often assigned longer features. Queries should be concise and clear and should include information on the writer's experience and expertise." The tag line for this magazine is 'Race, Culture and Organizing in communities of color.' Our general editorial vision is of a publication that examines issues, problems and events from the point of view of people of color; is concerned primarily with struggles and circumstances of low-income, working class and poor communities of color; takes a deliberately multicultural approach; and frames the subject matter in terms of grassroots community and/or labor organizing. In other words, the analytical perspective should pay particular respect to efforts (or lack thereof) to develop organizations capable of building power in the community or workplace and the kinds of campaigns these organizations are conducting (or could conduct). We are interested in writing that is passionate and vigorous, that takes command of the subject matter and holds the reader's interest, that has personality and rhythm. The style we are looking for is more popular than academic, more controversial than polite, and certainly more interested in figuring out what's really going on than in being 'politically correct.' Avoid editorializing, jargon and linguistic clutter as much as possisble."

$ CONGRESS MONTHLY, American Jewish Congress, 15 E. 84th St., New York NY 10028. (212)879-4500. **Contact:** Jack Fischel, managing editor. **90% freelance written.** Bimonthly magazine. "*Congress Monthly*'s readership is popular, but well-informed; the magazine covers political, social, economic and cultural issues of concern to the Jewish community in general and to the American Jewish Congress in particular." Estab. 1933. Circ. 35,000. Pays on publication. Publishes ms an average of 3 months after acceptance. Byline given. Buys one-time rights. Submit seasonal material 2 months in advance. No simultaneous submissions. Responds in 2 months.

Nonfiction: General interest ("current topical issues geared toward our audience"). No technical material. Query only. *No unsolicited mss.* Length: 2,000-2,500 words. Book reviews, 1,000-1,500 words; author profiles, film and theater reviews, travel. Payment amount determined by author experience and article length.

Photos: State availability of photos. Reviews b&w prints. "Photos are paid for with payment for ms."

⚡ $ $ $ EMERGE, Black America's Newsmagazine, BET Holdings, Inc., 1 BET Plaza, 1900 W Place NE, Washington DC 20018. (202)608-2093. Fax: (202)608-2598. E-mail: emergemag@msbet.com. Website: www.emergemag.com. Managing Editor: Florestine Purnell. **Contact:** George E. Curry, editor. **80% freelance written.** African-American news monthly. "*Emerge* is a general interest publication reporting on a wide variety of issues from health to sports to politics, almost anything that affects Black Americans. Our audience is comprised primarily of African-Americans 25-49, individual income of $55,000, professional and college educated." Estab. 1989. Circ. 200,000. **Pays on acceptance.** Publishes ms an average of 3 months after acceptance. Byline given. Offers 25% kill fee. Buys first North American serial rights. Submit seasonal material 6 months in advance. Accepts queries by mail, e-mail, fax. Responds in 2 months only if SAE is enclosed with query or ms. Sample copy for $3 and 9×12 SAE or on website. Writer's guidelines for #10 SAE with 2 first-class stamps or on website.

Nonfiction: Essays, exposé, general interest, historical/nostalgic, humor, interview/profile, technical, travel. "We are not interested in standard celebrity pieces that lack indepth reporting, as well as analysis, or pieces dealing with interpersonal relationships." Query with published clips. Length: 600-2,000 words. **Pays 60-75¢/word.**

Photos: State availability of photos with submission. Reviews contact sheets. Negotiated payment. Captions, model releases, indentification of subjects required. Buys one-time rights.

Columns/Departments: Cover to Cover (review and news on new books or magazines), 650-750 words; Destinations (experiences, culture and adventure in far-off places or unique approaches to familiar destinations), 650-750 words; Dialogue (short-formed Q&A with African-American newsmakers and scholars), 2,000 words; Education (news and trends), 650-750 words; Etcetera (stories or insights—often humorous), 750 words; Film (what's new and of interest to African-American moviegoers and home videos), 750-1,800 words; Gallery (critical perspective and news about visual arts and artists), 650-750 words; International (covers all corners of the globe from an Afrocentric perspective), 650-1,200 words; Media (behind the scenes insight on television and radio shows, their stars and creators) 650-750 words; Perspective (personal thought and experience) 1,200-2,000 words; Religion, 650-750 words; Speaking Volumes (interview with new authors or publishers), 650-750 words; Theatre (spotlight on the world of theatre and dance), 650-750 words; Take Note (musical artists, new releases and trends), 650-750 words; and The Last Word (full-page opinion piece), 650-750 words. Query.

Tips: "If a writer doesn't have a completed manuscript, then he should mail a query letter with clips. No phone calls. First-time authors should be extremely sensitive to the *Emerge* style and fit within these guidelines as closely as possible. We do re-write and re-edit pieces. We are a news monthly so articles must be written with a 3-month lead time in mind. Writers must assist our research department during fact checking process and closing. Read at least six issues of the publication before submitting ideas."

⭐ **$ $ ESTYLO MAGAZINE**, Latina Lifestyle, Mandalay Publishing, 3600 Wilshire Blvd., Suite 1903, Los Angeles CA 90010. (213)383-6300. Fax: (213)383-6499. E-mail: Estylo@aol.com. Editor: Linda Cauthen **50% freelance written.** "Bimonthly fashion, beauty and entertainment magazine for the affluent and mobile Latina. It contains a variety of features and departments devoted to cuisine, health, fitness, beauty, fashion and entertainment topics." Estab. 1997. Circ. 50,000. Pays on publication. Publishes ms an average of 2 months after acceptance. Byline given. Buys first rights. Editorial lead time 3 months. Submit seasonal material 3 months in advance. Query by mail, e-mail. Accepts simultaneous submissions.

Reprints: Send photocopy of article.

Photos: State availability of photos with submission. Reviews contact sheets. Negotiates payment individually. Captions, model releases, identificiation of subjects required. Buys all rights.

[N] **$ FILIPINAS, A magazine for All Filipinos**, Filipinas Publishing, Inc., 363 El Camino Read 1, Suite 100, South San Francisco CA 94080. (650)872-8650. Fax: (650)872-8651. E-mail: filmagazin@aol.com. Website: www.filipinasmag.com. **Contact:** Laarni C. Almendrala, assistant editor. Monthly magazine focused on Filipino American affairs. "*Filipinas* answers the lack of mainstream media coverage of Filipinos in America. It targets both Filipino immigrants and American-born Filipinos, gives in-depth coverage of political, social, cultural events in The Philippines and in the Filipino American community. Features role models, history, travel, food and leisure, issues and controversies." Estab. 1992. Circ. 40,000. Pays on publication. Publishes ms an average of 3 months after acceptance. Byline given. Offers $10 kill fee. Buys first rights or all rights. Editorial lead time 2 months. Submit seasonal material 4 months in advance. Accepts queries by mail, e-mail, fax. Responds in 5 weeks to queries; 18 months to mss. Sample copy for $5. Writer's guidelines for 9½×4 SASE or on website.

○→ Break in with "a good idea outlined well in the query letter. Also, tenacity is key. If one idea is shot down, come up with another."

Nonfiction: Exposé, general interest, historical/nostalgic, how-to, humor, interview/profile, personal experience, travel. Interested in seeing "more issue-oriented pieces, unusual topics regarding Filipino Americans and stories from the Midwest and other parts of the country other than the coasts." No academic papers. **Buys 80-100 mss/year.** Query with published clips. Length: 800-1,500 words. **Pays $50-100.** Sometimes pays writers other than cash payment agreement.

Photos: State availability of photos with submission. Reviews 2¼×2¼ and 4×5 transparencies. Offers $15-35/photo. Captions and model releases required. Buys one-time rights.

Columns/Departments: Entree (reviews of Filipino restaurants), 1,200 words; Cultural Currents (Filipino traditions, beliefs), 1,500 words. Query with published clips. **Pays $50-75.**

▣ The online version contains material not found in the print edition. Contact: Laarni C. Almardrala.

$ $ GERMAN LIFE, Zeitgeist Publishing Inc., 1068 National Hwy., LaVale MD 21502. (301)729-6012. Fax: (301)729-1720. E-mail: editor@GermanLife.com. Website: www.GermanLife.com. **Contact:** Carolyn Cook, editor. **50% freelance written.** Bimonthly magazine covering German-speaking Europe. "*German Life* is for all interested in the diversity of German-speaking culture, past and present, and in the various ways that the United States (and North America in general) has been shaped by its German immigrants. The magazine is dedicated to solid reporting on cultural, historical, social and political events." Estab. 1994. Circ. 40,000. Pays on publication. Publishes ms an average of 6 months after acceptance. Byline given. Buys first North American serial rights. Editorial lead time 4 months. Submit seasonal material 6 months in advance. Accepts queries by mail, e-mail. Responds in 2 months to queries; 3 months to mss. Sample copy for $4.95 and SAE with 4 first-class stamps. Writer's guidelines free.

Nonfiction: Exposé, general interest, historical/nostalgic, how-to (German crafts, recipes, gardening), interview/profile, opinion (only for final column), photo feature, travel. Special issues: Oktoberfest-related (October); seasonal relative to Germany, Switzerland or Austria (December); travel to German-speaking Europe (April); education or politics in German-speaking Europe (August). **Buys 50 mss/year.** Query with published clips. Length: 1,000-2,000 words. **Pays $200-500 for assigned articles; $200-350 for unsolicited articles.** Sometimes pays expenses of writers on assignment.
Photos: State availability of photos with submission. Reviews color transparencies, 5×7 color or b&w prints. Offers no additional payment for photos accepted with ms. Identification of subjects required. Buys one-time rights.
Columns/Departments: German-Americana (regards specific German-American communities, organizations and/or events past or present), 1,500 words; Profile (portrays prominent Germans, Americans, or German-Americans), 1,000 words; At Home (cuisine, home design, gardening, crafts, etc. relating to German-speaking Europe), 800 words; Library (reviews of books, videos, CDs, etc.), 300 words. **Buys 30 mss/year.** Query with published clips. **Pays $130-300.**
Fillers: Anecdotes, facts, newsbreaks, short humor. Length: 100-300 words. **Pays $50-150.**
Tips: "The best queries include several informative proposals. Ideally, clips show a background in a German-related topic, but more importantly, a flair for 'telling stories.' Majority of articles present a human interest angle. Even though *German Life* is a special interest magazine, writers should avoid overemphasizing autobiographical experiences/stories."

$ $ HADASSAH MAGAZINE, 50 W. 58th St., New York NY 10019. (212)688-0937. Fax: (212)446-9521. **Contact:** Joan Michel, associate editor. **90% freelance written.** Works with small number of new/unpublished writers each year. Monthly (except combined issues June/July and August/September). "*Hadassah* is a general interest, Jewish feature and literary magazine. We speak to our readers on a vast array of subjects ranging from politics to parenting, to midlife crisis to Mideast crisis. Our readers want coverage on social and economic issues, Jewish women's (feminist) issues, the arts, travel and health." Circ. 334,000. Buys first rights (with travel and family articles, buys all rights). Sample copy and writer's guidelines for 9×13 SASE.
Nonfiction: Primarily concerned with Israel, Jewish communities around the world and American civic affairs as relates to the Jewish community. "We are also open to art stories that explore trends in Jewish art, literature, theater, etc. Will not assign/commission a story to a first-time writer for Hadassah." **Buys 10 unsolicited mss/year.** Send queries to hadamag8@aol.com or send query and writing samples by mail. *No phone queries.* Length: 1,500-2,000 words. **Pays $350 minimum, $75 for reviews.** Sometimes pays expenses of writers on assignment.
Photos: "We buy photos only to illustrate articles, with the exception of outstanding color photos from Israel which we use on our covers. We pay $175 and up for a suitable cover photo." Offers $50 for first photo; $35 for each additional. "Always interested in striking cover (color) photos, especially of Israel and Jerusalem."
Columns/Departments: "We have a Family column and a Travel column, but a query for topic or destination should be submitted first to make sure the area is of interest and the story follows our format."
Fiction: Short stories with strong plots and positive Jewish values. No personal memoirs, "schmaltzy" or shelter magazine fiction. "We continue to buy very little fiction because of a backlog." Length: 1,500 words maximum. **Pays $300 minimum.** "Require proper size SASE."
Tips: "We are interested in reading articles that offer an American perspective on Jewish affairs (1,500 words). For example, a look at the presidential candidates from a Jewish perspective. Send query of topic first."

$ HERITAGE FLORIDA JEWISH NEWS, P.O. Box 300742, Fern Park FL 32730-0742. (407)834-8787. Fax: (407)831-0507. E-mail: heritagefl@aol.com. Publisher/Editor: Jeffrey Gaeser. **20% freelance written.** Weekly tabloid on Jewish subjects of local, national and international scope, except for special issues. "Covers news of local, national and international scope of interest to Jewish readers and not likely to be found in other publications." Estab. 1976. Circ. 3,500. Pays on publication. Publishes ms an average of 2 months after acceptance. Byline given. Buys first North American serial, first, one-time, second serial (reprint) or simultaneous rights. Submit seasonal material 3 months in advance. Accepts queries by mail, e-mail, fax. Responds in 1 month. Sample copy for $1 and 9×12 SASE.
Nonfiction: General interest, interview/profile, opinion, photo feature, religious, travel. "Especially needs articles for these annual issues: Rosh Hashanah, Financial, Chanukah, Celebration (wedding and bar mitzvah), Passover, Health and Fitness, Education, Travel and Savvy Seniors. No fiction, poems, first-person experiences." **Buys 50 mss/year.** Send complete ms. Length: 500-1,000 words. **Pays 50¢/column inch.**
Reprints: Send typed ms with rights for sale noted.
Photos: State availability of photos with submission. Reviews b&w prints up to 8×10. Offers $5/photo. Captions, identification of subjects required. Buys one-time rights.

N $ INDIAN LIFE, News from Across Native North America, Indian Life Ministries, P.O. Box 3765, RPO Redwood Centre, Winnipeg, Manitoba R2W 3R6 Canada. (204)661-9333. Fax: (204)661-3982. E-mail: il.edit@home.com. Website: www.indianlife.org. **Contact:** Jim Uttley, editor. **5% freelance written.** Bimonthly newspaper designed to help the Native North American church speak to the social, cultural and spiritual needs of her people and reaches every province and state of English-speaking North America. Its purpose is to bring hope, healing and honor through the presentation of positive news, role models and a Christian message." Estab. 1979. Circ. 32,000. Pays on publication. Byline given. Buys first North American serial rights and requests permission to publish material online. Editorial lead time 2 months. Submit seasonal material 3 months in advance. Accepts queries by mail, e-mail, fax. Responds in 1 month. Sample copy for $1 or on website. Writer's guidelines free.
    O→ Break in with good personality pieces of people currently in the news, such as entertainers and newsmakers.

Nonfiction: Book excerpts, general interest, historical/nostalgic, inspirational, interview/profile, personal experience, photo feature, religious. **Buys 10 mss/year.** Query. Length: 300-1,500 words. **Pays $25-100.** Sometimes pays in contributor copies.

Photos: State availability of photos with submission. Offers $20-50/photo. Captions and identification of subjects required. Buys all rights.

Fiction: Adventure, ethnic, historical, religious, slice-of-life vignettes. **Buys 2 mss/year.** Query. Length: 500-2,000 words. **Pays $25-100.**

Poetry: Free verse, light verse, traditional. No avant-garde or erotic. **Buys 1-2 poems/year.** Submit maximum 5 poems. Length: 25 lines. **Pays $25.**

Fillers: Anecdotes, facts, newsbreaks. **Buys 6/year.** Length: 100 words. **Pays $10-20.**

$ $ $ ITALIAN AMERICA, Official Publication of the Order Sons of Italy in America, Order Sons of Italy in America, 219 E St. NE, Washington DC 20002. (401)277-5306. Fax: (401)277-5100. Website: www.uri.edu/prov/italian/italian.html. **Contact**: C.B. Albright, editor. **50% freelance written.** Quarterly magazine. "*Italian America* strives to provide timely information about OSIA, while reporting on individuals, institutions, issues and events of current or historical significance in the Italian-American community." Estab. 1996. Circ. 65,000. Pays on publication. Publishes ms an average of 3 months after acceptance. Byline given. Offers 50% kill fee. Buys first North American serial rights. Editorial lead time 3 months. Accepts simultaneous submissions. Sample copy and writer's guidelines free.

Nonfiction: Essays, exposé, historical, current events, nostalgic, interview/profile, opinion, personal experience, travel. **Buys 10 mss/year.** Query with published clips. Length: 500-2,500 words. **Pays $150-1,000.** Sometimes pays expenses of writers on assignment.

Photos: State availability of photos with submission. Reviews contact sheets. Negotiates payment individually. Identification of subjects required. Buys one-time rights.

Columns/Departments: Community Notebook (Italian American life), 500 words; Postcard from Italy (life in Italy today), 750 words; Reviews (books, films by or about Italian Americans), 500 words. **Buys 5 mss/year.** Send complete ms. **Pays $100-500.**

$ $ JEWISH ACTION, Union of Orthodox Jewish Congregations of America, 11 Broadway, 14th Floor, New York NY 10004-1302. (212)613-8146. Fax: (212)613-0646. E-mail: mashiben@ou.org. Website: www.ou.org. Editor: Charlotte Friedland. **Contact**: Mashi Benzaquen, assistant editor. **80% freelance written.** "Quarterly magazine offering a vibrant approach to Jewish issues, Orthodox lifestyle and values." Circ. 30,000. Pays 2 months after publication. Byline given. Submit seasonal material 4 months in advance. Accepts queries by mail, e-mail, fax. Responds in 3 months. Sample copy and guidelines for 9×12 SAE with 5 stamps; sample articles available on website.

　　O— Break in with a query for "Just Between Us" column.

Nonfiction: Current Jewish issues, history, biography, art, inspirational, humor, music and book reviews. "We are not looking for Holocaust or personal memoir." Query with published clips. **Buys 30-40 mss/year.** Length: 1,000-3,000 words, including footnotes. **Pays $100-400 for assigned articles; $75-150 for unsolicited articles.**

Photos: Send photos with submission. Identification of subjects required.

Fiction: Must have relevance to Orthodox reader. Length: 1,000-2,000 words.

Poetry: Limited number accepted. **Pays $25-75.**

Columns/Departments: Just Between Us (personal opinion on current Jewish life and issues), 1,000 words. **Buys 4 mss/year.**

Tips: "Remember that your reader is well educated and has a strong commitment to Orthodox Judaism. Articles on the Holocaust, holidays, Israel and other common topics should offer a fresh insight. Because the magazine is a quarterly, we do not generally publish articles which concern specific timely events."

$ $ $ MOMENT, The Magazine of Jewish Culture, Politics and Religion, 4710 41st St. NW, Washington DC 20016. (202)364-3300. Fax: (202)364-2636. E-mail: editor@momentmag.com. Publisher/Editor: Hershel Shanks. **Contact**: Joshua Rolnick, managing editor. **90% freelance written.** "*Moment* is an independent Jewish bimonthly general interest magazine that specializes in cultural, political, historical, religious and 'lifestyle' articles relating chiefly to the North American Jewish community and Israel." Estab. 1975. Circ. 65,000. Pays on publication. Publishes ms an average of 6 months after acceptance. Byline given. Buys first North American serial rights. Editorial lead time 3 months. Submit seasonal material 6 months in advance. Accepts queries by mail, e-mail, fax. Accepts simultaneous submissions. Responds within 1 month to queries; 3 months to mss. Sample copy for $4.50 and SAE. Writer's guidelines free.

Nonfiction: "We look for meaty, colorful, thought-provoking features and essays on Jewish trends and Israel. We occasionally publish book excerpts, memoirs and profiles." **Buys 25-30 mss/year.** Query with published clips. Length: 2,500-4,000 words. **Pays $200-1,200 for assigned articles; $40-500 for unsolicited articles.**

Photos: State availability of photos with submission. Negotiates payment individually. Identification of subjects required. Buys one-time rights.

Columns/Departments: 5760—snappy pieces of not more than 250 words about quirky events in Jewish communities, news and ideas to improve Jewish living; Olam (The Jewish World)—first-person pieces, humor and colorful reportage of 600-1,500 words; Book reviews (fiction and nonfiction) are accepted but generally assigned, 400-800 words. **Buys 30 mss/year.** Query with published clips. **Pays $50-250.**

Tips: "Stories for *Moment* are usually assigned, but unsolicited manuscripts are often selected for publication. Successful features offer readers an in-depth journalistic treatment of an issue, phenomenon, institution, or individual. The more the writer can follow the principle of 'show, don't tell,' the better. The majority of the submissions we receive are about The Holocaust and Israel. A writer has a better chance of having an idea accepted if it is not on these subjects."

$ $ NA'AMAT WOMAN, Magazine of NA'AMAT USA, the Women's Labor Zionist Organization of America, NA'AMAT USA, 350 Fifth Ave., Suite 4700, New York NY 10118. (212)239-2828. Fax: (212)239-2833. Website: www.naamatusa@naamat.org. **Contact:** Judith A. Sokoloff, editor. **80% freelance written.** Magazine published 4 times/year covering Jewish themes and issues; Israel; women's issues; and social and political issues. Estab. 1926. Circ. 25,000. Pays on publication. Byline given. Not copyrighted. Buys first North American serial, one-time, first serial and second serial (reprint) rights to book excerpts and makes work-for-hire assignments. Accepts queries by mail, fax. Responds in 3 months. Writer's guidelines for SASE.
Nonfiction: Exposé, general interest (Jewish), historical/nostalgic, interview/profile, opinion, personal experience, photo feature, travel, art and music. "All articles must be of particular interest to the Jewish community." **Buys 20 mss/year.** Query with clips of published work or send complete ms. **Pays 10¢/word.**
Photos: State availability of photos. Pays $25-45 for 4×5 or 5×7 prints. Captions, identification of subjects required. Buys one-time rights.
Columns/Departments: Film and book reviews with Jewish themes. **Buys 20 mss/year.** Query with clips of published work or send complete ms. **Pays 10¢/word.**
Fiction: Historical/nostalgic, humorous, women-oriented and novel excerpts. "Intelligent fiction with Jewish slant. No maudlin nostalgia or trite humor." **Buys 3 mss/year.** Send complete ms. Length: 1,200-3,000 words. **Pays 10¢/word.**

$ $ NATIVE PEOPLES MAGAZINE, The Arts and Lifeways, 5333 N. Seventh St., Suite C-224, Phoenix AZ 85014-2804. (602)265-4855. Fax: (602)265-3113. E-mail: editorial@nativepeoples.com. Website: www.nativepeoples.com. **Contact**: Ben Winton, editor. Quarterly full-color magazine on Native Americans. "Extremely high-quality reproduction with full color throughout. The primary purpose of this magazine is to offer a sensitive portrayal of the arts and lifeways of native peoples of the Americas." Estab. 1987. Circ. 95,000. Pays on publication. Byline given. Buys one-time rights. Accepts queries by mail, e-mail, fax. Responds in 2 months to queries; 4 months to mss. Writer's guidelines sent or on website.
Nonfiction: Book excerpts (pre-publication only), historical/nostalgic, interview/profile, personal experience, photo feature. **Buys 35 mss/year.** Query with published clips. Length: 1,500-3,000 words. **Pays 25¢/word.**
Photos: State availability of photos with submission. Reviews transparencies (all formats) but prefers 35mm slides. Offers $45-150/page rates. Pays $250 for cover photos. Identification of subjects required. Buys one-time rights.
Columns/Departments: On The Wind (current news, people and events). Length: 300 words accompanied by b&w photo of individual. Byline given.
Tips: "We are extremely focused upon authenticity and a positive portrayal of present-day traditional and cultural practices. Our readership has been expanded to include Native American students in schools throughout the country. This is being done for the purpose of giving young people a sense of pride in their heritage and culture, to offer role models and potential career considerations. Therefore, it is extremely important that the Native American point of view be incorporated in each story."

$ NJEMA MAGAZINE, Sesh Communications, 354 Hearne Ave., Cincinnati OH 45229. (513)961-3331. Fax: (513)961-0304. E-mail: sesh@fuse.net. **Contact:** Jan-Michele Lemon Kearney. **25% freelance written.** Monthly magazine for African-Americans. Estab. 1955. Circ. 50,000. Pays on publication for pre-approved feature. Byline given. Accepts queries by mail, e-mail, fax, phone.
Nonfiction: Book excerpts, essays, exposé, general interest, historical/nostalgic, how-to, humor, inspirational, interview/profile, new product, opinion, personal experience, photo feature, religious, technical, travel. **Buys 4 mss/year.** Query with published clips. Length: 500-1,000 words. **Pays $25-75.**
Photos: Send photos with submission. Offers no additional payment for photos accepted with ms. Captions, model releases and identification of subjects required. Buys one-time rights.

$ $ RUSSIAN LIFE, RIS Publications, 89 Main St., #2, Montpelier VT 05602. Phone/fax: (802)223-4955. E-mail: sales@rispubs.com. Website: www.rispubs.com. Editor: Mikhail Ivanov. **Contact:** Paul Richardson, publisher. **40% freelance written.** Bimonthly magazine covering Russian culture, history, travel and business. "Our readers are informed Russophiles with an avid interest in all things Russian. But we do not publish personal travel journals or the like." Estab. 1956. Circ. 15,000. Pays on publication. Publishes ms 2 months after acceptance. Byline given. Offers $25 kill fee. Buys first rights. Editorial lead time 2 months. Submit seasonal material 3 months in advance. Responds in 1 month: Sample copy for 9×12 SAE with 6 first-class stamps. Writer's guidelines for #10 SASE.
Nonfiction: General interest, photo feature, travel. No personal stories, i.e., "How I came to love Russia." **Buys 15-20 mss/year.** Query. Length: 1,000-6,000 words. **Pays $100-300.**
Reprints: Accepts previously published submissions.
Photos: Send photos with submission. Reviews contact sheets. Negotiates payment individually. Captions required. Buys one-time rights.
Tips: "A straightforward query letter with writing sample or manuscript (not returnable) enclosed."

$ $ SCANDINAVIAN REVIEW, The American-Scandinavian Foundation, 15 E. 65th St., New York NY 10021. (212)879-9779. Fax: (212)249-3444. Website: www.amscan.org. **Contact:** Adrienne Gyongy, editor. **75% freelance written.** Triannual magazine for contemporary Scandinavia. Audience: members, embassies, consulates, libraries. Slant: popular coverage of contemporary affairs in Scandinavia. Estab. 1913. Circ. 4,000. Pays on publication. Publishes ms 2 months after acceptance. Byline given. Buys first North American serial and second serial (reprint) rights. Editorial lead time 3 months. Submit seasonal material 3 months in advance. Responds in 6 weeks to queries. Sample copy on website and writer's guidelines free.
Nonfiction: General interest, interview/profile, photo feature, travel (must have Scandinavia as topic focus). Special issue: Scandinavian travel. *No pornography.* **Buys 30 mss/year.** Query with published clips. Length: 1,500-2,000 words. **Pays $300 maximum.**
Reprints: Accepts previously published submissions, though unpublished mss are preferred.
Photos: State availability or send photos with submission. Reviews 3×5 transparencies or prints. Pays $25-50/photo; negotiates payment individually. Captions required. Buys one-time rights.

$ TAKE PRIDE! COMMUNITY, Topaz Realty, Inc., 1014 Franklin St. SE, Grand Rapids MI 49507-1327. (616)243-1919. Fax: (616)243-6844. E-mail: wmathis@triton.net. Website: www.takepride.com. President/CEO: Walter L. Mathis. **Contact:** Pat Mathis, editor. **50% freelance written.** Bimonthly magazine and weekly tabloid covering education and economic empowerment for all people especially African-Americans. Estab. 1991. Circ. 5,000. Pays on publication. Publishes ms an average of 1 month after acceptance. Byline given. Buys one-time rights and makes work-for-hire assignments. Editorial lead time 1 month. Submit seasonal material 1 month in advance. Accepts queries by mail, e-mail, fax, phone. Accepts simultaneous submissions. Responds in 2 weeks to queries; 1 month to mss. Sample copy and writer's guidelines on website.
Nonfiction: Exposé, general interest, historical/nostalgic, how-to, humor, inspirational, interview/profile, opinion, religious, technical. Special issue: MLK Day (January). **Buys 4 mss/year.** Query by mail with or without published clips or send complete ms. Length: 200-1,500 words. **Pays $25-35.**
Photos: State availability of photos or send photos with submission. Reviews 3×5 prints. Negotiates payment individually. Model releases and identification of subjects required. Buys one-time rights.
Columns/Departments: Inspirational (religious, advice); Education; Economics; all 350 words. Query by mail with or without published clips or send complete ms. **Pays $25-35.**
Fillers: Myron Stankey, graphic designer. Facts, gags to be illustrated by cartoonist, newsbreaks, short humor, book reviews. Length: 50 words. **Pays $15.**
The online magazine carries original content not found in the print edition. Contact: Patricia E. Grier.
Tips: "Get in touch with our target audience and write about what is important to them. A writer's best bet to break in to this magazine is to present issues and facts relevant to all aspects of the African-American community. Dare to say what needs to be said and to tell it like it is whether it is 'popular' or not."

$ $ UPSCALE MAGAZINE, Exposure to the World's Finest, Upscale Communications, Inc., 600 Bronner Brothers Way SW, Atlanta, GA 30310. (404)758-7467. Fax: (404)755-9892. E-mail: upscale8@mindspring.com. Website: www.upscalemagazine.com. Editor-in-Chief: Sheila Bronner. **Contact:** Leslie E. Royal, assignment editor. **75-80% freelance written.** Monthly magazine covering topics that inspire, inform or entertain African-Americans. "*Upscale* is a general interest publication featuring a variety of topics—beauty, health and fitness, business news, travel, arts, relationships, entertainment and other issues that affect day-to-day lives of African-Americans." Estab. 1989. Circ. 242,000. Byline given. Offers 25% kill fee. Buys all rights in published form. Editorial lead time 4 months. Submit seasonal material 6 months in advance. Accepts queries by mail, e-mail, fax. Sample copy for $2 or on website. Writer's guidelines for #10 SASE
Nonfiction: Book excerpts/reviews, general interest, historical/nostalgic, inspirational, interview/profile, personal experience, religious, travel. **Buys 135 mss/year.** Query. Length varies. **Pays $100 minimum.**
• *Upscale Magazine* is interested in seeing relationships articles written by men and articles about excursions in Europe, Asia, Hong Kong and Russia. It is not interested in articles about how to rekindle a romance or travels to the islands and Africa.
Photos: State availability of photos with submission. Reviews contact sheets, transparencies, prints. Negotiates payment individually. Captions, model releases, identification of subjects required. Buys one-time or reprint rights.
Columns/Departments: Kim Hamilton, Body & Soul/Living editor. Positively You, Viewpoint (personal inspiration/ perspective). **Buys 25 mss/year.** Query.
Fiction: Publishes novel excerpts.
Tips: "No unsolicited fiction, poetry or essays. Unsolicited nonfiction is accepted for our Positively You and Viewpoint sections. Queries for exciting and informative nonfiction story ideas are welcomed."

$ $ VISTA MAGAZINE, The Magazine for all Hispanics, Hispanic Publishing Corporation, 999 Ponce de Leon Blvd., Suite 600, Coral Gables FL 33134. (305)442-2462. Fax: (305)443-7650. E-mail: jlobaco@aol.com. Website: www.vistamagazine.com. **Contact:** Julia Bencomo Lobaco, editor. **50% freelance written.** Monthly "Sunday supplement style magazine targeting Hispanic audience. Dual-language, Spanish/English, 50/50%. Stories appear in one language or another, not both. Topics of general interest, but with a Hispanic angle." Estab. 1985. Circ. 1,100,000. Pays on publication. Publishes ms an average of 2 months after acceptance. Byline given. Offers 25% kill fee. Buys all rights, title and interest. Editorial lead time 2 months. Submit seasonal material 4 months in advance. Accepts queries by mail, e-mail, fax, phone. Sample copy free or on website.

Nonfiction: Exposé, general interest, historical/nostalgic, how-to (home improvement), inspirational, interview/profile, new product, opinion, personal experience, photo feature, travel. "No creative writing, poems, etc." **Buys 40-50 mss/ year.** Query with published clips. Length: 500-1,600 words. **Pays $250-450.** Sometimes pays expenses of writers on assignment.

Photos: State availability of photos with submission.

Columns/Departments: Voices (personal opinion re: Hispanic-related theme), 500 words. **Pays $100.**

Tips: "Query by phone is usually best. Articles must be related to Hispanic, be of national interest, timely and, unless assigned by VISTA, should be 850-1,200 words—not longer."

FOOD & DRINK

Magazines appealing to gourmets, health-conscious consumers and vegetarians are classified here. Some publications emphasize "the art and craft" of cooking for food enthusiasts who enjoy developing these skills as a leisure activity. Another popular trend stresses healthy eating and food choices. Many magazines in the Health & Fitness category present a holistic approach to well-being through nutrition and fitness for healthful living. Magazines in General Interest and Women's categories also buy articles on food topics. Journals aimed at food processing, manufacturing and retailing are in the Trade section.

$ $ $ $ BON APPETIT, America's Food and Entertaining Magazine, Condé Nast Publications, Inc., 6300 Wilshire Blvd., Los Angeles CA 90048. (323)965-3600. Fax: (323)937-1206. Editor-in-Chief: William J. Garry. **Contact:** Barbara Fairchild, executive editor. **90% freelance written.** Monthly magazine that covers fine food, restaurants and home entertaining. "*Bon Appetit* readers are upscale food enthusiasts and sophisticated travelers. They eat out often and entertain four to six times a month." Estab. 1975. Circ. 1,331,853. **Pays on acceptance.** Byline given. Buys all rights. Submit seasonal material 1 year in advance. Responds in 6 weeks. Guidelines for #10 SASE.

 • *Bon Appetit* reports it is looking for food-related humor essays, profiles, etc. of less than 1,000 words. It is not interested in material about three-star dining in France or celebrity chefs.

Nonfiction: Travel (restaurant or food-related), food feature, dessert feature. "No cartoons, quizzes, poetry, historic food features or obscure food subjects." **Buys 80-120 mss/year.** Query by mail with published clips. Length: 750-2,000 words. **Pays $500-1,800.** Pays expenses of writers on assignment.

 • Ranked as one of the best markets for freelance writers in *Writer's Yearbook* magazine's annual "Top 100 Markets," January 2000.

Photos: Never send photos.

Tips: "We are not interested in receiving specific queries per se, but we are always looking for new good writers. They must have a good knowledge of the *Bon Appetit*-related topic (as shown in accompanying clips) and a light, lively style with humor. Nothing long and pedantic please."

N ☆ $ $ CHILE PEPPER, The Magazine of Spicy Foods, River Plaza, 1701 River Run #702, Ft. Worth TX 76102. (817)877-1048. Fax: (817)877-8870. E-mail: rwalsh@chilepepperhq.com. **70-80% freelance written.** Bimonthly magazine on spicy foods. "The magazine is devoted to spicy foods, and most articles include recipes. We have a very devoted readership who love their food hot!" Estab. 1986. Circ. 85,000. Pays on publication. Buys first and second rights and first electronic rights. Submit seasonal material 6 months in advance. Sample copy for 9 × 12 SAE with 5 first-class stamps. Writer's guidelines for #10 SASE.

Nonfiction: Book excerpts (cookbooks), how-to (cooking and gardening with spicy foods), humor (having to do with spicy foods), new product (hot products), travel (having to do with spicy foods). **Buys 50 mss/year.** Query by mail only. Length: 1,000-3,000 words. **Pays $300 minimum for feature article.**

Reprints: Send tearsheet or photocopy of article and information about when and where the article previously appeared.

Photos: State availability of photos with submission. Reviews contact sheets, negatives, transparencies, prints. Offers $25/photo minimum. Captions, identification of subjects required. Buys one-time rights.

Tips: "We're always interested in queries from *food* writers. Articles about spicy foods with six to eight recipes are just right. No fillers. Need location travel/food pieces from inside the U.S. and Mexico."

N $ $ COME & EAT!, Great Food for Busy Families, (formerly *Fast and Healthy Magazine*), Pillsbury Co., 200 S. Sixth St., M.S. 28M7, Minneapolis MN 55402. (612)330-5401. Fax: (612)330-4875. Website: www.come&eat.c om. **Contact:** Maureen Rosener, editor. **50% freelance written.** "*C&E* is a family-oriented quarterly food magazine with healthful recipes for families with children living at home. All recipes can be prepared in 30 minutes or less and meet the U.S. Dietary guidelines for healthful eating. The magazine's emphasis is on Monday through Friday cooking. Our readers are busy people who are looking for information and recipes that help them prepare healthy meals quickly."

Freelancing food writers must bring knowledge and personality to the table

Orlando writer Joseph Hayes has freelanced fulltime for only four years. But he's struck Florida gold in the realm of good taste. "Make that 'tastes good,'" he says with a chuckle. Whether it's for *Orlando Magazine*, the *Orlando Sentinel* or the Greater Orlando Chamber of Commerce, Hayes has established himself as a knowledgeable food writer in his regional market. "Writing about food is very personal," Hayes says. "You can't synthesize it." But in a freelance field that's a bit more subjective than technical, Hayes knows whether he's writing restaurant reviews or interviewing star chefs, he still has to know his facts. And while the pay in regional markets isn't terribly high, he's not going to starve.

Joseph Hayes

How does freelancing for food-related issues differ from freelancing for other topics?
It doesn't. I would say it takes as much skill and knowledge to write about food as it does to write about any other specific topic. In fact, anytime you're dealing with "first person" journalism—where you're laying out your own ideas and preferences—even more intensive homework is required to establish your credibility.

I went to a culinary institute when I was young, though I had no intention of becoming a professional chef. That experience gave me a substantial food background. But it's the same in any specialty. You've got to know what you're talking about if you want to relay critical information to your readers. If you don't have that background, it immediately shows.

What special challenges present themselves when writing about food?
Again, you've got to know your stuff. That is the ultimate challenge. If you don't know the specifics about a cuisine when you go into a restaurant, you better have core knowledge when you leave. Don't just walk into the restaurant. Talk to the chef. Don't just find out what he's cooking and how—find out why.

Are all food assignments recipe or restaurant reviews? If not, what else can a food freelancer sell?
Some of them are, of course. But the really good food pieces, the articles you love reading, such as Janet Maslin at *New York Magazine*, go far beyond a simple recipe write-up. The best food writers get involved. They know the history of a cuisine, the background of the foods employed, how a dish is prepared and why.

Where would you begin, if you wanted to add food specialties to your freelance résumé?

My first stop would be the local weekly newspaper. In all but the smallest towns, they are desperate for local information. They pick up a lot of content from syndicates. But to maintain a local flavor, they have to include community-based material. That means there is always room for a review of a new local restaurant or a new fad in food.

The pay rate at local weeklies is terrible, if they pay at all. And I hate the concept of giving work away. But if you're just getting started, sometimes you have very little choice. Just use those clips to build toward others.

What can a new, moderately experienced and experienced food writer expect to make per assignment?

A new writer should plan on making zero, zilch, nothing. Moderately experienced food writers can expect to earn between $25 and $100 per assignment. An experienced food writer working for magazines should plan on $300 per assignment and up.

What common mistakes do food freelancers make?

When the piece is about the writer, not the food, that's a mistake. That's true with any type of critical writing, but particularly so with food, since it's so immediate, so personal. Writers tend to get very snippy about food. They go in thinking, "I'm going to be smart and witty and critical, just because I can." And that's a big mistake when writing food pieces.

What three tips would you offer a writer just getting started as a food freelancer?

First, know your territory. You're not going to start out as a national food writer, so you have to know your local restaurants, local chefs, and other local food writers. Second, do your homework, as far as the foods themselves are concerned. Third, read experienced food writers like Calvin Trillin, who pioneered the travel cookbook. Read *New York Magazine* or *Esquire* so you'll understand the sensuality of writing about food.

For interviews with the pros on more freelance niche markets see Child Care, page 431; Health & Fitness, page 494; Nature, page 594; Personal Computers, page 604; and Travel, page 779.
—Kelly Milner Halls

TOP TIP: "I've found that good chefs are extremely welcoming. I've never had any problem picking up a telephone and asking a chef for an interview. They adore it. They never seem to get enough praise. They have their secrets (and they like to keep them secret), but they like people to know they have them. Remember, when you are talking about four- and five-star chefs, they're "stars." They love the attention that goes with it."

Estab. 1992. Circ. 200,000. **Pays on acceptance.** Publishes ms an average of 8 months after acceptance. Byline given. Offers 20% kill fee. Buys all rights. Editorial lead time 1 year. Submit seasonal material 18 months in advance. Responds in 6 weeks to queries. Sample copy for $3. Writer's guidelines for #10 SASE.

Nonfiction: Food topics related to health, nutrition, convenience. **Buys 6 mss/year.** Query by mail only with résumé and published clips. Length: 100-1,500 words. **Pays $50-500.**

Columns/Departments: Living Better (health, nutrition, healthy lifestyle news), 25-200 words. **Buys 25 mss/year.** Query with published clips. **Pays $25-200.**

◾ The online magazine carries original content not found in the print edition.

⊠ **$ $ $ $ COOKING LIGHT, The Magazine of Food and Fitness**, P.O. Box 1748, Birmingham AL 35201-1681. (205)877-6000. Fax: (205)877-6600. Website: cookinglight.com. Editor: Douglas Crichton. **Contact:** Rod Davis, executive editor (food and fitness). **75% freelance written.** Magazine published 11 times/year on healthy recipes and fitness information. *"Cooking Light* is a positive approach to a healthier lifestyle. It's written for healthy people on regular diets who are counting calories or trying to make calories count toward better nutrition. Moderation, balance and variety are emphasized. The writing style is fresh, upbeat and encouraging, emphasizing that eating a balanced, varied, lower-calorie diet and exercising regularly do not have to be boring." Estab. 1987. Circ. 1,600,000. **Pays on acceptance.** Publishes ms an average of 1 year after acceptance. Byline sometimes given. Offers 33% kill fee. Submit seasonal material 1 year in advance. Responds in 1 year.

Nonfiction: Service approaches to nutrition, healthy recipes, fitness/exercise. Back up material a must. **Buys 150 mss/ year.** Must query with résumé and published clips; no unsolicited mss. Response guaranteed with SASE. Length: 400-2,000 words. **Pays $250-2,000.** Pays expenses of writers on assignment.

◾ The online magazine contains original content not found in the print edition. Contact: Lisa DeLaney, online editor.

Tips: "Emphasis should be on achieving a healthier lifestyle through food, nutrition, fitness, exercise information. In submitting queries, include information on professional background. Food writers should include examples of healthy recipes which meet the guidelines of *Cooking Light.*"

$ $ HOME COOKING, House of White Birches, Publishers, 306 E. Parr Rd., Berne IN 46711. (219)589-4000, ext. 396. Fax: (219)589-8093. E-mail: home_cooking@whitebirches.com. Website: www.whitebirches.com. Project Supervisor: Barb Sprunger. **Contact:** Shelly Vaughan James, editor. **60% freelance written.** *"Home Cooking* delivers dozens of kitchen-tested recipes from home cooks every month. Special monthly features offer recipes, tips for today's busy cooks, techniques for food preparation, nutritional hints and more. Departments cover topics to round out the cooking experience." Circ. 75,000. **Pays within 45 days after acceptance.** Publishes ms an average of 8 months after acceptance. Byline given. Buys all or first rights, occasionally one-time rights. Editorial lead time 6 months. Submit seasonal material 8 months in advance. Accepts queries by mail, e-mail. Accepts simultaneous submissions. Responds in 1 month to queries; 2 months to mss. Sample copy for 6×9 SAE and 3 first-class stamps. Editorial calendar for #10 SASE.

○┐ Break in with a submission or query to one of *Home Cooking*'s departments.

Nonfiction: How-to, humor, new product, personal experience, recipes, book reviews, all in food/cooking area. No health/fitness or travel articles. **Buys 72 mss/year.** Query or send complete ms. Length: 250-750 words plus 6-8 recipes. **Pays $50-300 for assigned articles; $50-175 for unsolicited articles.** Sometimes pays expenses of writers on assignment.

Reprints: Accepts previously published submissions.

Photos: State availability of photos with submission. Reviews prints. Negotiates payment individually. Model releases and identification of subjects required. Buys one-time rights.

Columns/Departments: Dinner Tonight (complete 30-minute meal with preparation guide), 500 words; Stirring Comments (book and product reviews), 100 words; Pinch of Sage (hints for the home cook), 200-500 words. **Buys 48 mss/year.** Query or send complete ms. **Pays $50-100.**

Fillers: Anecdotes, facts, newsbreaks, short humor. **Buys 15/year.** Length: 10-150 words. **Pays $15-25.**

Tips: "Departments are most open to new writers. All submissions should be written specifically for our publication. Be sure to check spelling, grammar and punctuation before mailing. If that means setting aside your manuscript for two weeks to regain your objectivity, do it. A sale two weeks later beats a rejection earlier. If you follow our style in your manuscript, we know you've read our magazine."

$ $ KASHRUS MAGAZINE, The Bimonthly for the Kosher Consumer and the Trade, Yeshiva Birkas Reuven, P.O. Box 204, Parkville Station, Brooklyn NY 11204. (718)336-8544. **Contact:** Rabbi Yosef Wikler, editor. **25% freelance written.** Prefers to work with published/established writers, but will work with new/unpublished writers. Bimonthly magazine covering kosher food industry and food production. Estab. 1980. Circ. 10,000. Pays on publication. Publishes ms an average of 2 months after acceptance. Byline given. Offers 50% kill fee. Buys first or second serial (reprint) rights. Submit seasonal material 2 months in advance. Accepts queries by mail, phone. Accepts simultaneous submissions. Responds in 1 week to queries, 2 weeks to mss. Sample copy for $3.

Nonfiction: General interest, interview/profile, new product, personal experience, photo feature, religious, technical and travel. Special issues feature: International Kosher Travel (October); Passover (March). **Buys 8-12 mss/year.** Query with published clips. Length: 1,000-1,500 words. **Pays $100-250 for assigned articles; up to $100 for unsolicited articles.** Sometimes pays expenses of writers on assignment.

Reprints: Send tearsheet or photocopy of article and information about when and where the article previously appeared. Pays 25-50% of amount paid for an original article.

Photos: State availability of photos with submission. Offers no additional payment for photos accepted with ms. Acquires one-time rights.

Columns/Departments: Book Review (cook books, food technology, kosher food), 250-500 words; People in the News (interviews with kosher personalities), 1,000-1,500 words; Regional Kosher Supervision (report on kosher supervision in a city or community), 1,000-1,500 words; Food Technology (new technology or current technology with accompanying pictures), 1,000-1,500 words; Travel (international, national), must include Kosher information and Jewish communities, 1,000-1,500 words; Regional Kosher Cooking, 1,000-1,500 words. **Buys 8-12 mss/year.** Query with published clips. **Pays $50-250.**

Tips: "*Kashrus Magazine* will do more writing on general food technology, production, and merchandising as well as human interest travelogs and regional writing in 2001 than we have done in the past. Areas most open to freelancers are interviews, food technology, cooking and food preparation, dining, regional reporting and travel. We welcome stories on the availability and quality of Kosher foods and services in communities across the U.S. and throughout the world. Some of our best stories have been by non-Jewish writers about kosher observance in their region. We also enjoy humorous articles. Just send a query with clips and we'll try to find a storyline that's right for you, or better yet, call us to discuss a storyline."

$ $RISTORANTE, Foley Publishing, P.O. Box 73, Liberty Corner NJ 07938. (908)766-6006. Fax: (908)766-6607. E-mail: barmag@aol.com. Website: www.bartender.com. **Contact:** Raymond Foley, publisher or Jaclyn Foley, editor. **75% freelance written.** Bimonthly magazine covering "Italian anything! *Ristorante—The magazine for the Italian Connoisseur.* For Italian restaurants and those who love Italian food, travel, wine and all things Italian!" Estab. 1994. Circ. 40,000. Pays on publication. Publishes ms an average of 3 months after acceptance. Byline sometimes given. Buys first North American and one-time rights. Editorial lead time 3 months. Submit seasonal material 3 months in advance. Responds in 1 month to queries; 2 months to mss. Sample copy and writer's guidelines for 9×12 SAE and 4 first-class stamps.

Nonfiction: Book excerpts, general interest, historical/nostalgic, how-to (prepare Italian foods), humor, new product, opinion, personal experience, travel. **Buys 25 mss/year.** Send complete ms. Length: 100-1,000 words. **Pays $100-350 for assigned articles; $75-300 for unsolicited articles.** Sometimes pays expenses of writers on assignment.

Reprints: Send tearsheet or photocopy of article and information about when and where the article previously appeared. Pays 25% of amount paid for an original article.

Photos: Send photos with submission. Reviews 3×5 prints. Negotiates payment individually. Captions, model releases required. Buys one-time rights.

Columns/Departments: Send complete ms. **Pays $50-200.**

Fillers: Anecdotes, facts, short humor. **Buys 10/year. Pays $10-50.**

$ $ $TV GUIDE CELEBRITY DISH, TV Guide Magazine Group, 1211 Avenue of the Americas, 4th Floor, New York NY 10036-8701. (212)626-2515. Fax: (212)852-7470. E-mail: catherine.cavender@tvguide.com. Website: www.tvguide.com. **Contact:** Catherine Cavender, editor. Monthly digest-sized magazine covering anything having to do with celebrities and food. "The magazine will not only focus on TV celebrities, nor only on recipes. Yet, each issue will contain 35-40 recipes, usually with some accompanying text. All articles will have a food angle. Other avenues might be restaurants or spas that are hot celebrity hangouts or celebrity parties. The January issue will include an article about prop men and how they arrange food on the set. Think celebrities and food. Read the gossip columns." Estab. 1999. **Pays on acceptance.** Byline given. Buys exclusive first North American serial rights. Accepts queries by mail, e-mail, fax. Accepts simultaneous submissions. Responds in 2 months.

Nonfiction: General interest, humor, interview/profile. No recipes alone. Query with published clips. Length: 200-1,500 words. **Pays $2/word.**

Tips: "Think food and celebrities and see what comes up. Watch gossip columns about celebrities and good events. I want articles to be event-, news- and trend-driven."

$ $WINE X MAGAZINE, Wine, Food and an Intelligent Slice of Vice, X Publishing, Inc., 880 Second St., Santa Rosa CA 95404-4611. (707)545-0992. Fax: (707)542-7062. E-mail: winex@sonic.net. Website: www.winexwired.com. **Contact:** Darryl Roberts, editor/publisher. **100% freelance written.** Bimonthly magazine covering wine and other beverages. "*Wine X* is a lifestyle magazine for young adults featuring wine, beer, spirits, music, movies, fashion, food, coffee, celebrity interviews, health/fitness." Estab. 1997. Circ. 35,000. Pays on publication. Published ms 3 months after acceptance. Byline given. Not copyrighted. Buys first North American serial and electronic rights. Editorial lead time 3 months. Submit seasonal material 4 months in advance. Accepts queries by mail, e-mail, fax. Responds in 3 weeks to queries; 3 months to mss. Sample copy for $5. Guidelines online at website.

Nonfiction: Essays, personal experience, photo feature. No restaurant reviews, wine collector profiles. **Buys 6 mss/ year.** Query. Length: 500-1,500 words. **Pays $50-250 for assigned articles; $50-150 for unsolicited articles.** Sometimes pays expenses of writers on assignment.

Photos: Reviews transparencies. Offers no additional payment for photos accepted with ms. Model releases and identification of subjects required. Buys one-time rights.

Columns/Departments: Wine, Other Beverages, Lifestyle, all 1,000 words. **Buys 72 mss/year.** Query.

Fiction: Buys 6 mss/year. Query. Length: 1,000-1,500 words. **No pay for fiction.**

Poetry: Avant garde, free verse, haiku, light verse, traditional. **Buys 2 poems/year.** Submit maximum 3 poems. Length: 10-1,500 lines.

Fillers: Short humor. **Buys 6/year.** Length: 100-500 words. **Pays $0-50.**

Tips: "See our website."

GAMES & PUZZLES

These publications are written by and for game enthusiasts interested in both traditional games and word puzzles and newer role-playing adventure, computer and video games. Other puzzle markets may be found in the Juvenile section.

[N] $ THE BRIDGE BULLETIN, American Contract Bridge League, 2990 Airways Blvd., Memphis TN 38116-3847. Fax: (901)398-7754. E-mail: acbl@acbl.org. Website: www.acbl.org. Managing Editor: Paul Linxwiler. **Contact:** Brent Manley, editor. **20% freelance written.** Monthly membership magazine covering duplicate (tournament) bridge. Estab. 1938. Circ. 155,000. Pays on publication. Publishes ms an average of 3 months after acceptance. Byline given. Buys first or second serial (reprint) rights. Editorial lead time 2 months. Accepts queries by mail, e-mail, fax, phone. Accepts simultaneous submissions.
Nonfiction: Book excerpts, essays, how-to (play better bridge), humor, interview/profile, new product, personal experience, photo feature, technical, travel. **Buys 6 mss/year.** Query. Length: 500-2,000 words. **Pays $50/page.**
Reprints: Accepts previously published submissions.
Photos: State availability of photos with submission. Negotiates payment individually. Identification of subjects required. Buys all rights.
Tips: "Articles must relate to contract bridge in some way. Cartoons on bridge welcome."

$ $ $ $ GAMES MAGAZINE, Games Publications, Inc., 7002 W. Butler Pike, Suite 210, Ambler PA 19002. (215)643-6385. Fax: (215)628-3571. E-mail: gamepub@tidalwave.com. **Contact:** R. Wayne Schmittberger, editor-in-chief. **50% freelance written.** Magazine published 9 times/year covering puzzles and games. "*Games* is a magazine of puzzles, contests, and features pertaining to games and ingenuity. It is aimed primarily at adults and has an emphasis on pop culture." Estab. 1977. Circ. 175,000. Pays on publication. Publishes ms an average of 4 months after acceptance. Byline given. Offers 25% kill fee. Buys first North American serial rights, first rights, one-time rights, second serial (reprint) rights, all rights or makes work-for-hire assignments. Editorial lead time 3 months. Submit seasonal material 6 months in advance. Accepts queries by mail, e-mail. Accepts simultaneous submissions. Responds in 6 weeks to queries; 3 months to mss. Sample copy for $5. Writer's guidelines for #10 SASE.
Nonfiction: Photo features, puzzles, games. **Buys 3 mss/year; 100 puzzles/year.** Query. Length: 1,500-2,500 words. **Pays $1,000-1,750.** Sometimes pays expenses of writers on assignment.
Reprints: Accepts previously published submissions.
Photos: State availability of photos with submission. Reviews contact sheets, negatives, transparencies and prints. Negotiates payment individually. Captions, model releases and identification of subjects required. Buys one-time rights.
Columns/Departments: Gamebits (game/puzzle news), 250 words; Games & Books (product reviews), 350 words; Wild Cards (short text puzzles), 100 words. **Buys 50 mss/year.** Query. **Pays $25-250.**
Fiction: Interactive adventure and mystery stories. **Buys 1-2 mss/year.** Query. Length: 1,500-2,500 words. **Pays $1,000-1,750.**
Tips: "Look for real-life people, places, or things that might in some way be the basis for a puzzle."

[N] $ GIANT CROSSWORDS, Scrambl-Gram, Inc., Puzzle Buffs International, 41 Park Dr., Port Clinton OH 43452. (216)923-2397. **Contact:** C.R. Elum, editor. Submissions Editor: S. Bowers. **40% freelance written.** Eager to work with new/unpublished writers. Quarterly crossword puzzle and word game magazine. Estab. 1970. **Pays on acceptance.** Publishes ms an average of 1 month after acceptance. No byline given. Buys all rights. Responds in 1 month.
Nonfiction: Crosswords and word games only. Query. Pays according to size of puzzle and/or clues.
Reprints: Send information about when and where material previously appeared.
Tips: "We are expanding our syndication of original crosswords and our publishing schedule to include new titles and extra issues of current puzzle books."

GAY & LESBIAN INTEREST

The magazines listed here cover a wide range of politics, culture, news, art, literature and issues of general interest to gay and lesbian communities. Magazines of a strictly sexual content are listed in the Sex section.

$ $ THE ADVOCATE, Liberation Publications, Inc., 6922 Hollywood Blvd., 10th Floor, Suite 1000, Los Angeles CA 90028-6148. (213)871-1225. Fax: (213)467-6805. E-mail: newsroom@advocate.com. **Contact:** Judy Wieder, editor-in-chief. Biweekly magazine covering national news events with a gay and lesbian perspective on the issues. Estab. 1967. Circ. 80,000. Pays on publication. Byline given. Buys first North American serial rights. Responds in 1 month. Sample copy for $3.95. Writer's guidelines for #10 SASE.
Nonfiction: Exposé, interview/profile, news reporting and investigating. "Here are elements we look for in all articles: *Angling:* An angle is the one editorial tool we have to attract a reader's attention. An *Advocate* editor won't make an assignment unless he or she has worked out a very specific angle with you. Once you've worked out the angle with an

editor, don't deviate from it without letting the editor know. Some of the elements we look for in angles are: a news hook; an open question or controversy; a 'why' or 'how' element or novel twist; national appeal; and tight focus. *Content*: Lesbian and gay news stories in all areas of life: arts, sciences, financial, medical, cyberspace, etc. *Tone*: Tone is the element that makes an emotional connection. Some characteristics we look for: toughness; edginess; fairness and evenhandedness; multiple perspectives." Special issues: gays on campus, coming out interviews with celebrities, HIV and health. Query. Length: 1,200 words. **Pays $550.**

- Ranked as one of the best markets for freelance writers in *Writer's Yearbook* magazine's annual "Top 100 Market," January 2000.

Columns/Departments: Arts & Media (news and profiles of well-known gay or lesbians in entertainment) is most open to freelancers. Query. Length: 750 words. **Pays $100-500.**

Fiction: Publishes novel excerpts.

Tips: "*The Advocate* is a unique newsmagazine. While we report on gay and lesbian issues and are published by one of the country's oldest and most established gay-owned companies, we also play by the rules of mainstream-not gay-community-journalism."

⚡ $ $ALTERNATIVE FAMILY MAGAZINE, AFM Publishing, P.O. Box 7179, Van Nuys CA 91409. (818)909-0314. Fax: (818)909-3792. E-mail: altfammag@aol.com. Website: www.altfammag.com. Assistant Editor: Michael Watters. **Contact:** Kelly Taylor, editor-in-chief. **90% freelance written.** Bimonthly magazine covering general parenting and topics more specific to gay and lesbian parenting. "Editorial content must be diverse to reflect gay and lesbian parenting. Topics might also include product information, nutrition, safety, medicine, general health, financial information and children's interest. Also publishes articles of interest to parents-to-be." Estab. 1998. Circ. 8,000. Pays on publication. Publishes ms an average of 3 months after acceptance. Byline given. Offers 25% kill fee. Buys first North American serial rights. Editorial lead time 2 months. Submit seasonal material 3 months in advance. Accepts simultaneous submissions. Responds in 6 weeks to queries; 2 months to mss. Sample copy for $3.95 and 9 × 12 SAE with 6 first-class stamps. Writer's guidelines for #10 SASE.

Nonfiction: Book excerpts, essays, general interest, how-to, humor, inspirational, interview/profile, new product, opinion, personal experience, photo feature, travel. "No articles that focus on heterosexual parents or interests." **Buys 20 mss/year.** Send complete ms. Length: 200-3,000 words. **Pays $25-300 for assigned articles; $25-300 for unsolicited articles.**

Reprints: Accepts previously published submissions.

Photos: Send photos with submission. Reviews contact sheets, transparencies and prints. Negotiates payment individually. Captions, model releases and identification of subjects required. Buys one-time rights.

Columns/Departments: Gadgets (product information), 150 words; Your Health (health topics for entire family), 200 words; Baby Tips, 25 words and up. **Buys 15 mss/year.** Send complete ms. **Pays $10-200.**

Fillers: Facts, gags to be illustrated by cartoonist, newsbreaks, short humor. **Buys 5-10/year.** Length: 75-300 words. **Pays $5-30.**

Tips: "We're looking for general parenting articles, tips and topics for our audience of gay, lesbian, bisexual, transgendered audience of parents and expectant parents—keeping in mind that our reader audience also includes single GLBT parents."

$ BAY WINDOWS, New England's Largest Gay and Lesbian Newspaper, Bay Windows, Inc., 631 Tremont St., Boston MA 02118-2034. (617)266-6670. Fax: (617)266-5973. E-mail: news@baywindows.com. Website: www.bay windows.com. Editor: Jeff Epperly. Arts Editor: Rudy Kikel. **Contact:** Loren King, assistant editor. **30-40% freelance written.** Weekly newspaper of gay news and concerns. "*Bay Windows* covers predominantly news of New England, but will print non-local news and features depending on the newsworthiness of the story. We feature hard news, opinion, news analysis, arts reviews and interviews." Estab. 1983. Publishes ms within 2 months of acceptance, pays within 2 months of publication. Byline given. Offers 50% kill fee. Rights obtained vary, usually first serial rights. Simultaneous submissions accepted if other submissions are outside of New England. Submit seasonal material 3 months in advance. Accepts queries by mail, e-mail, fax, phone. Responds in 3 months. Sample copy for $5. Writer's guidelines for #10 SASE.

Nonfiction: Hard news, general interest with a gay slant, interview/profile, opinion, photo features. **Publishes 200 mss/year.** Query with published clips or send complete ms. Length: 500-1,500 words. **Pay varies: $25-100 news, arts.**

Reprints: Send tearsheet or photocopy of article and information about when and where the article previously appeared. Pays 75% of amount paid for an original article.

Photos: Pays $25/published photo. Model releases and identification of subjects required.

Columns/Departments: Film, music, dance, books, art. Length: 500-1,500 words. **Buys 200 mss/year. Pays $25-100.** Letters, opinion to Jeff Epperly, editor; news, features to Loren King, assistant editor; arts, reviews to Rudy Kikel, arts editor.

Poetry: All varieties. **Publishes 50 poems/year.** Length: 10-30 lines. No payment. **Contact:** Rudy Kikel.

Tips: "Too much gay-oriented writing is laden with the clichés and catch phrases of the movement. Writers must have intimate knowledge of gay community; however, this doesn't mean that standard English usage isn't required. We look for writers with new, even controversial perspectives on the lives of gay men and lesbians. While we assume gay is good, we'll print stories which examine problems within the community and movement. No pornography or erotica."

$ $ CURVE MAGAZINE, Outspoken Enterprises, Inc., 1 Haight St., #B, San Francisco CA 94102. Fax: (415)863-1609. E-mail: editor@curvemag.com. Editor-in-chief: Frances Stevens. **Contact:** Gretchen Lee, managing editor. **40% freelance written.** Magazine published 8 times/year covering lesbian general interest categories. "We want dynamic and provocative articles written by, about and for lesbians." Estab. 1991. Circ. 68,000. Pays on publication. Byline given. Offers 25% kill fee. Buys first North American serial rights. Editorial lead time 3 months. Submit seasonal material 3 months in advance. Accepts queries by mail, e-mail, fax. Sample copy for $3.95 with $2 postage. Writer's guidelines free.

Nonfiction: Book excerpts, exposé, general interest, interview/profile, photo feature, travel. Special issues: Pride issue (June); Music issue (July/August). No fiction or poetry. **Buys 25 mss/year.** Query. Length: 200-2,500 words. **Pays $40-300.** Sometimes pays expenses of writers on assignment.

Photos: Send photos with submission. Offers $50-100/photo; negotiates payment individually. Captions, model releases, identification of subjects required. Buys one-time rights.

Columns/Departments: Buys 72 mss/year. Query. **Pays $75-300.**

Tips: "Feature articles generally fit into one of the following categories: Celebrity profiles (lesbian, bisexual or straight women who are icons for the lesbian community or actively involved in coalition-building with the lesbian community). Community segment profiles—e.g., lesbian firefighters, drag kings, sports teams (multiple interviews with a variety of women in different parts of the country representing a diversity of backgrounds). Non-celebrity profiles (activities of unknown or low-profile lesbian and bisexual activists/political leaders, athletes, filmmakers, dancers, writers, musicians, etc.). Controversial issues (spark a dialogue about issues that divide us as a community, and the ways in which lesbians of different backgrounds fail to understand and support one another. We are not interested in inflammatory articles that incite or enrage readers without offering a channel for action). Trends (community trends in a variety of areas, including sports, fashion, image, health, music, spirituality and identity). Visual essays (most of our fashion and travel pieces are developed and produced in-house. However, we welcome input from freelancers and from time to time publish outside work)."

N $ $ $ GENRE, Genre Publishing, 7080 Hollywood Blvd., #818, Hollywood CA 90028. (323)467-8300. Fax: (323)467-8365. E-mail: genre@aol.com. Website: www.genremagazine.com. Editor: Morris Weissinger. **Contact:** Bryan Buss, managing editor. **60% freelance written.** Magazine published 11 times/year. "*Genre*, America's best-selling gay men's lifestyle magazine, covers entertainment, fashion, travel and relationships in a hip, upbeat, upscale voice." Estab. 1991. Circ. 50,000. Pays on publication. Publishes ms an average of 3 months after acceptance. Byline given. Offers 25% kill fee. Buys first North American serial rights and electronic rights. Editorial lead time 10 weeks. Submit seasonal material 10 weeks in advance. Accepts queries by mail, e-mail, fax. Sample copy for $6.95 ($5 plus $1.95 postage). Guidelines for #10 SASE.

Nonfiction: Essays, exposé, general interest, historical/nostalgic, how-to, humor, inspirational, interview/profile, new product, opinion, personal experience, photo feature, religious, travel, relationships, fashion. Not interested in articles on 2 males negotiating a sexual situation or coming out stories. **Buys variable number of mss/year.** Query with published clips. Length: 500-1,500 words. **Pays $150-1,000.** Pays writer with contributor copies or other premiums rather than a cash payment if so negotiated.

Photos: State availability of photos with submission. Reviews contact sheets or prints (3×5 or 5×7). Negotiates payment individually. Model releases required. Buys one-time rights.

Columns/Departments: Body (how to better the body); Mind (how to better the mind); Spirit (how to better the spirit), all 700 words; Reviews (books, movies, music, travel, etc.), 500 words. **Buys variable number of mss/year.** Query with published clips or send complete ms. **Pays $200 maximum.**

Fiction: Adventure, experimental, horror, humorous, mainstream, mystery, novel excerpts, religious, romance, science fiction, slice-of-life vignettes, suspense. **Buys 10 mss/year.** Send complete ms. Length: 2,000-4,000 words.

Tips: "Like you, we take our journalistic responsibilities and ethics very seriously, and we subscribe to the highest standards of the profession. We expect our writers to represent original work that is not libelous and does not infringe upon the copyright or violate the right of privacy of any other person, firm or corporation."

$ $ GIRLFRIENDS MAGAZINE, Lesbian culture, politics and entertainment, 3415 Cesar Chavez, Suite 101, San Francisco CA 94110. (415)648-9464. Fax: (415)648-4705. E-mail: editorial@girlfriendsmag.com. Website: www.girlfriendsmag.com. **Contact**: Heather Findlay, editor-in-chief. Monthly lesbian magazine. "*Girlfriends* provides its readers with intelligent, entertaining and visually-pleasing coverage of culture, politics and entertainment—all from an informed and critical lesbian perspective." Estab. 1994. Circ. 75,000. Pays on publication. Publishes ms an average of 6 months after acceptance. Byline given. Offers 25% kill fee. Buys first rights, use for advertising/promoting *Girlfriends*. Editorial lead time 3 months. Submit seasonal material 6 months in advance. Accepts queries by mail, e-mail. Accepts simultaneous submissions. Responds in 3 weeks to queries; 2 months to mss. Sample copy for $4.95 plus $1.50 s/h or on website. Writer's guidelines for #10 SASE or on website.

Nonfiction: Investigative features, celebrity profiles, exposé, humor, interviews, photo feature, travel. Special features: best lesbian restaurants in the US; best places to live. Special issues: sex issue, gay pride issue, breast cancer issue. **Buys 20-25 mss/year.** Query with published clips. Length: 1,000-3,500 words. **Pays 10-25¢/word.**

Reprints: Send photocopy of article or typed ms with rights for sale noted and information about when and where the article previously appeared. Negotiable payment.

Photos: Send photos with submissions. Reviews contact sheets, 4×5 or $2\frac{1}{4} \times 2\frac{1}{4}$ transparencies, prints. Offers $30-250/photo. Captions, model releases, identification of subjects required. Buys one-time rights, use for advertising/promoting *GF*.

Columns/Departments: Book reviews, 900 words; Music reviews, 600 words; Travel, 600 words. Query with published clips. **Pays 10-25¢/word.**

  • *Girlfriends* is not accepting fiction, poetry or fillers.

Tips: "Be unafraid of controversy—articles should focus on problems and debates raised around lesbian culture, politics, and sexuality. Avoid being 'politically correct.' We don't want just to know what's happening in the lesbian world, we want to know how what's happening in the world affects lesbians."

$ $ THE GUIDE, To Gay Travel, Entertainment, Politics and Sex, Fidelity Publishing, P.O. Box 990593, Boston MA 02199-0593. (617)266-8557. Fax: (617)266-1125. E-mail: theguide@guidemag.com. Website: www.guidemag.com. **Contact**: French Wall, editor. **25% freelance written.** Monthly magazine on the gay and lesbian community. Estab. 1981. Circ. 30,000. **Pays on acceptance.** Publishes ms an average of 2 months after acceptance. Kill fee negotiable. Buys first-time rights. Submit seasonal material 2 months in advance. Accepts queries by mail, e-mail. Accepts simultaneous submissions. Responds in 3 months. Sample copy for 9×12 SAE with 8 first-class stamps. Writer's guidelines for #10 SASE.

Nonfiction: Book excerpts (if yet unpublished), essays, exposé, general interest, historical/nostalgic, humor, interview/profile, opinion, personal experience, photo feature, religious. **Buys 24 mss/year.** Query with or without published clips or send complete ms. Length: 500-5,000 words. **Pays $75-220.**

Reprints: Occasionally buys previously published submissions. Pays 100% of amount paid for an original article.

Photos: Send photos with submission. Reviews contact sheets. **Pays $15 per image used.** Captions, model releases, identification of subjects preferred; releases required sometimes. Buys one-time rights.

Tips: "Brevity, humor and militancy appreciated. Writing on sex, political analysis and humor are particularly appreciated. We purchase very few freelance travel pieces; those that we do buy are usually on less commercial destinations."

$ $ HERO MAGAZINE, 451 N. La Cienega Blvd., Suite One, Los Angeles CA 90048. (310)360-8022. E-mail: editor@heromag.com. Website: www.heromag.com. **Contact:** Paul Horne, editorial director. **90% freelance written.** Award-winning monthly general interest/service magazine for gay men. Estab. 1996. Circ. 100,000. Pays on publication. Publishes ms an average of 2 months after acceptance. Byline given. Buys one-time rights. Editorial lead time 2 months. Submit seasonal material 4 months in advance. Responds in 1 month to queries. Sample copy for $4.95. Writer's guidelines on website.

Nonfiction: Book excerpts, essays, general interest, how-to, humor, inspirational, interview/profile, opinion, personal experience, photo feature, technology, travel. "*HERO* selects articles which challenge and broaden the current depiction of gay men in the media. Therefore, erotic material and overtly sexual submissions will likely be overlooked." Query by mail with published clips. No queries by fax or e-mail. **Buys 30 mss/year.** Length: 300-4,000 words. **Pays 10-50¢/word for print publication only**, not for online publication.

Reprints: Accepts previously published submissions.

Photos: Send photos with submission. Reviews contact sheets. Offers no additional payment for photos accepted with ms. Model releases required. Buys one-time rights.

Columns/Departments: Book (book features and reviews), 300-1,000 words. Family (profiles of gay fathers, children of gay parents), Youth (out gay kids making a difference); Boy Toys (technology, high-tech gadgets); Music and Theatre (interviews and reviews); Spirituality, all 500-1,000 words. **Buys 20 mss/year.** Query by mail with published clips. **Pays 10-50¢/word**.

Tips: "*HERO* brings gay readers and a gay sensibility into the mainstream. We feature relationships and romance, spirituality, families, and health & fitness, in addition to fashion, entertainment, travel, and general how-to/better living articles. Successful freelancers will have read the magazine before querying. Please keep maximum one-page query letters brief and to the point."

N $ IN STEP, In Step, Inc., 1661 N. Water St., #411, Milwaukee WI 53202. (414)278-7840. Fax: (414)278-5868. E-mail: editor@instepnews.com. Website: www.instepnews.com. Managing Editor: Jorge Cabal. **Contact:** William Attewell, editor. **30% freelance written.** Consumer tabloid published biweekly for gay and lesbian readers. Estab. 1984. Circ. 15,000. Buys first North American serial and second serial (reprint) rights. Submit seasonal material 2 months in advance. Accepts queries by mail, e-mail. Accepts simultaneous submissions. Responds in 3 weeks to queries; 1 month to mss. Sample copy for $3. Writer's guidelines for #10 SASE.

Nonfiction: Book excerpts, interview/profile, new product, travel. Query. Length: 500-2,000 words. **Pays $15-100.**

Photos: State availability of photos with submission. Reviews 5×7 prints. Negotiates payment individually. Captions, model releases and identification of subjects required. Buys one-time rights.

N $ $ IN THE FAMILY, The Magazine for Lesbians, Gays, Bisexuals and Their Relations, Family Magazine, Inc., P.O. Box 5387, Takoma Park MD 20913. (301)270-4771. Fax: (301)270-4660. E-mail: lmarkowitz@aol.com. Website: www.inthefamily.com. **Contact:** Laura Markowitz, editor. **20% freelance written.** Quarterly magazine covering lesbian, gay and bisexual family relationships. "Using the lens of psychotherapy, our magazine looks at the complexities of L/G/B family relationships as well as professional issues for L/G/B therapists." Estab. 1995. Circ.

3,000. Pays on publication. Publishes ms 3 months after acceptance. Byline given. Offers 25% kill fee. Buys first rights. Editorial lead time 6 months. Submit seasonal material 4 months in advance. Responds in 1 month to queries; 3 months to mss. Sample copy for $5.50. Writer's guidelines free or on website.

Nonfiction: Essays, exposé, humor, opinion, personal experience, photo feature. "No autobiography or erotica." **Buys 4 mss/year.** Send complete ms. Length: 2,500-4,000 words. **Pays $100-300 for assigned articles; $50-200 for unsolicited articles.** Sometimes pays expenses of writers on assignment.

Photos: State availability of photos with submission. Reviews contact sheets. Negotiates payment individually. Captions, model releases, identification of subjects required. Buys one-time rights.

Columns/Departments: Karen Sundquist, senior editor. Family Album (aspects of Queer family life), 1,500 words; In the Therapy Room (clinical case presentations), 2,000 words; A Look at Research (relevant social science findings), 1,500 words; The Last Word (gentle humor), 800 words. **Buys 4 mss/year.** Send complete ms. **Pays $50-150.**

Fiction: Helena Lipstadt, fiction editor. Confession, ethnic, humorous, slice-of-life vignettes, family life theme for g/l/bs. No erotica, sci-fi, horror, romance, serialized novels or western. **Buys 4 mss/year.** Send complete ms. Length: 1,000-2,500 words. **Pays $50-100.**

Poetry: Helena Lipstadt, fiction editor. Avant-garde, free verse, haiku, light verse, traditional. **Buys 4 poems/year.** Submit maximum 6 poems. Length: 10-35 lines. **Pays $50-75.**

Tips: "*In the Family* takes an in-depth look at the complexities of lesbian, gay and bisexual family relationships, including couples and intimacy, money, sex, extended family, parenting and more. Readers include therapists of all sexual orientations as well as family members of lesbian, gay and bisexuals, and also queer people who are interested in what therapists have to say about such themes as how to recover from a gay bashing; how to navigate single life; how to have a good divorce; how to understand bisexuality; how to come out to children; how to understand fringe sexual practices; how to reconcile homosexuality and religion. Therapists read it to learn the latest research about working with queer families, to learn from the regular case studies and clinical advice columns. Family members appreciate the multiple viewpoints in the magazine. We look for writers who know something about these issues and who have an engaging, intelligent, narrative style. We are allergic to therapy jargon and political rhetoric."

$ LAMBDA BOOK REPORT, A Review of Contemporary Gay and Lesbian Bisexual & Transgender Literature, Lambda Literary Foundation, P.O. Box 73910, Washington DC 20056-3910. (202)462-7924. Fax: (202)462-5264. E-mail: lbreditor@lambdalit.com. **Contact:** Shelley Bindon, senior editor. **90% freelance written.** Monthly magazine that covers gay/lesbian literature. "*Lambda Book Report* devotes its entire contents to the discussion of gay, lesbian bisexual and transgender books and authors. Any other submissions would be inappropriate." Estab. 1987. Circ. 11,000. Pays 90 days after publication. Byline given. Buys first rights and first electronic rights. Responds in 2 months. Sample copy for $4.95. Guidelines free.

● This editor sees an increasing need for writers familiar with economic and science/medical-related topics.

Nonfiction: Book excerpts, essays (on gay literature), interview/profile (of authors), book reviews. "No historical essays, fiction or poetry." Query with published clips. Length: 200-2,000 words. **Pays $15-125 for assigned articles; $5-25 for unsolicited articles.**

Photos: Send photos with submission. Reviews contact sheets. Offers $10-25/photo. Model releases required. Buys one-time rights.

Tips: "Assignments go to writers who query with 2-3 published book reviews and/or interviews. It is helpful if the writer is familiar with gay and lesbian literature and can write intelligently and objectively on the field. Review section is most open. Clips should demonstrate writers' knowledge, ability and interest in reviewing gay books."

$ $ METROSOURCE, MetroSource Publishing Inc., 180 Varick St., 5th Floor, New York NY 10014. (212)691-5127. Fax: (212)741-2978. E-mail: metrosource@aol.com. Website: www.metrosource.com. **Contact:** Eva Leonard, editor. **70% freelance written.** Quarterly magazine. "*MetroSource* is a celebration and exploration of urban gay and lesbian life. *MetroSource* is an upscale, glossy, four-color lifestyle magazine targeted to an urban, professional gay and lesbian readership." Estab. 1990. Circ. 80,000. Pays on publication. Publishes ms an average of 6 months after acceptance. Byline given. Buys all rights. Editorial lead time 6 months. Submit seasonal material 4 months in advance. Accepts queries by mail, e-mail, fax, phone. Accepts simultaneous submissions. Sample copy for $5.

Nonfiction: Exposé, interview/profile, photo feature, travel, opinion pieces. **Buys 20 mss/year.** Query with published clips. Length: 1,000-2,500 words. **Pays $100-900.**

Photos: State availability of photos with submission. Negotiates payment individually. Captions and model releases required.

Columns/Departments: Book reviews and health columns (both of interest to gay and lesbian audience), word lengths vary. Query with published clips. **Pays $100-850.**

$ MOM GUESS WHAT NEWSPAPER, 1725 L St., Sacramento CA 95814. (916)441-6397. Fax: (916)441-6422. E-mail: info@mgwnew.com. Website: www.mgwnews.com. **Contact:** Linda Birner, editor. **80% freelance written.** Works with small number of new/unpublished writers each year. Biweekly tabloid covering gay rights and gay lifestyles. A newspaper for gay men, lesbians and their straight friends in the State Capitol and the Sacramento Valley area. First and oldest gay newspaper in Sacramento. Estab. 1977. Circ. 21,000. Publishes ms an average of 3 months after acceptance. Byline given. Buys all rights. Submit seasonal material 3 months in advance. Responds in 2 months. Sample copy for $1. Writer's guidelines for 10×13 SAE with 4 first-class stamps or on website.

Nonfiction: Interview/profile and photo feature of international, national or local scope. **Buys 8 mss/year.** Query. Length: 200-1,500 words. Payment depends on article. Pays expenses of writers on special assignment.

Reprints: Send tearsheet or photocopy and information about when and where previously appeared. Pay varies.

Photos: Send photos with submission. Reviews 5×7 prints. Offers no additional payment for photos accepted with ms. Captions and identification of subjects required. Buys one-time rights.

Columns/Departments: News, Restaurants, Political, Health, Film, Video, Book Reviews. **Buys 12 mss/year.** Query. Payment depends on article.

Tips: "*MGW* is published primarily from volunteers. With some freelancers payment is made. Put requirements in your cover letter. Byline appears with each published article; photos credited. Editors reserve right to edit, crop, touch up, revise, or otherwise alter manuscripts, and photos, but not to change theme or intent of the work. Enclose SASE postcard for acceptance or rejection. We will not assume responsibility for returning unsolicited material lacking sufficient return postage or lost in the mail."

$ OUTSMART, Up & Out Communications, 3406 Audubon Place, Houston TX 77006. (713)520-7237. Fax: (713)522-3275. E-mail: ann@outsmartmagazine.com. Website: www.outsmartmagazine.com. **Contact:** Ann Walton Sieber, editor. **70% freelance written.** Monthly magazine covering gay and lesbian issues. "*OutSmart* provides positive information to gay men, lesbians and their associates to enhance and improve the quality of our lives." Estab. 1994. Circ. 20,000. Pays on publication. Publishes ms an average of 2 months after acceptance. Byline given. Buys one-time rights, simultaneous rights and permission to publish on website. Editorial lead time 2 months. Submit seasonal material 2 months in advance. Accepts queries by mail, e-mail, fax. Accepts simultaneous submissions. Responds in 6 weeks to queries; 2 months to mss. Sample copy and writer's guidelines for SASE or on website.

Nonfiction: Historical/nostalgic, interview/profile, opinion, personal experience, photo feature, travel, health/wellness, local/national news. **Buys 10 mss/year.** Send complete ms. Length: 450-2,300 words. **Pays $20-100.**

Reprints: Send photocopy of article.

Photos: State availability of photos with submission. Reviews 4×6 prints. Negotiates payment individually. Identification of subjects required. Buys one-time rights.

The online magazine carries original content not found in the print edition and includes writer's guidelines.

Tips: "*OutSmart* is a mainstream publication that covers culture, politics, personalities, entertainment and health/wellness as well as local and national news and events. It is our goal to address the diversity of the lesbian and gay community, fostering understanding among all Houston's citizens."

$ THE JAMES WHITE REVIEW, A Gay Men's Literary Quarterly, P.O. Box 73910, Washington DC 20056-3910. (202)462-7924. E-mail: merlapatrick@aol.com. Website: www.lambdalit.org. Publisher: Jim Marks. **Contact:** Patrick Merla, editor. **100% freelance written.** Quarterly tabloid covering gay men. Estab. 1983. Circ. 6,000. Byline given. Buys first North American serial rights. Editorial lead time 3 months. Submit seasonal material 9 months in advance. Sample copy for $4.95. Writer's guidelines for #10 SASE.

Nonfiction: Book excerpts and essays. **Buys 4 mss/year.** Send complete ms. Length: 2,000 words maximum. **Pays $20-50 minimum.**

Photos: Send photos with submission. Reviews prints. Negotiates payment individually. Buys one-time rights.

Fiction: Confession, erotica, experimental, fantasy, historical, novel excerpts and serialized novels. **Buys 20 mss/year.** Send complete ms. Length: 2,000 words maximum. **Pays $100 maximum.**

Poetry: Avant-garde, free verse and traditional. **Buys 80 poems/year.** Submit no more than 8 poems, or no more than 250 lines of verse (whichever is less). **Pays $20.**

GENERAL INTEREST

General interest magazines need writers who can appeal to a broad audience—teens and senior citizens, wealthy readers and the unemployed. Each magazine still has a personality that suits its audience—one that a writer should study before sending material to an editor. Other markets for general interest material are in these Consumer categories: Contemporary Culture, Ethnic/Minority, Inflight, Men's, Regional and Women's.

N $ AFRICAN AMERICAN MAGAZINE, Everyone Learns by Reading, Topaz Marketing & Distributing, 1014 Franklin SE, Grand Rapids MI 49507-1327. (616)243-6759. Fax: (616)243-6844. E-mail: wmathis@triton.net. Website: www.africanamericanmag.com. President & CEO: Walter Mathis. **Contact:** Pat Mathis, editor-in-chief. **50% freelance written.** Bimonthly magazine covering African Americans and other ethnic groups. "We are guided by the principles of fine press and are open to everyone regardless of their race, gender or religion." Estab. 1998. Circ. 5,000. Pays on publication. Publishes ms an average of 1 month after acceptance. Byline given. Buys one-time rights. Editorial lead time 1 month. Submit seasonal material 1 month in advance. Accepts queries by mail, e-mail, fax. Responds in 2 weeks to queries; 1 month to mss. Sample copy and writer's guidelines online at website.

Nonfiction: Book excerpts, essays, exposé, general interest, historical/nostalgic, how-to, humor, inspirational, interview/profile, new product, opinion, personal experience, photo feature, religious, technical, travel, book reviews (ethnic). **Buys 10 mss/year.** Query with published clips or send complete ms. Length: 200-1,500 words. Pays writers with contributor copies or other premiums rather than a cash payment. Sometimes pays expenses of writers on assignment.

Photos: State availability of photos with submission or send photos with submission. Reviews 3×5 prints. Negotiates payment individually. Model releases and identification of subjects required. Buys one-time rights.

Columns/Departments: Looking Within; Economic Focus; Positive Notes; Pastor's Perspective; Classified. **Buys 10 mss/year.** Query with published clips or send complete ms. **Pays $25-35.**

Fillers: Anecdotes, facts, newsbreaks. **Buys 10/year.** Length: 10-100 words. **Pays $15-25.**

Tips: "Dare to say what needs to be said, and to tell it like it is—whether it is 'popular' or not. Read a sample copy first and query if you have any further questions."

$ $ THE AMERICAN LEGION MAGAZINE, P.O. Box 1055, Indianapolis IN 46206-1055. (317)630-1200. Fax: (317)630-1280. E-mail: tal@legion.org. Website: www.legion.org. Editorial Administrator: Patricia Marschand. **Contact:** John Raughter, executive editor. **70% freelance written.** Monthly magazine. "Working through 15,000 community-level posts, the honorably discharged wartime veterans of The American Legion dedicate themselves to God, country and traditional American values. They believe in a strong defense; adequate and compassionate care for veterans and their families; community service; and the wholesome development of our nation's youth. We publish articles that reflect these values. We inform our readers and their families of significant trends and issues affecting our nation, the world and the way we live. Our major features focus on the American flag, national security, foreign affairs, business trends, social issues, health, education, ethics and the arts. We also publish selected general feature articles, articles of special interest to veterans, and question-and-answer interviews with prominent national and world figures." Prefers to work with published/established writers, but works with a small number of new/unpublished writers each year. Estab. 1919. Circ. 2,800,000. Buys first North American serial rights. Responds in 6 weeks on submissions. **Pays on acceptance.** Publishes ms an average of 6 months after acceptance. Byline given. Accepts queries by mail, e-mail, fax. Responds in 2 months. Sample copy for $3.50 and 9×12 SAE with 6 first-class stamps. Writer's guidelines for #10 SASE.

Nonfiction: Query with SASE first, will only consider unsolicited mss that are of interest to military veterans. Query should explain the subject or issue, article's angle and organization, writer's qualifications and experts to be interviewed. Well-reported articles or expert commentaries cover issues/trends in world/national affairs, contemporary problems, general interest, sharply-focused feature subjects. Monthly Q&A with national figures/experts. Few personality profiles. No regional topics or promotion of partisan political agendas. **Buys 50-60 mss/year.** Length: 500-2,000 words. **Pays 40¢/word and up.** Pays phone expenses of writers on assignment.

Photos: On assignment.

Tips: "Queries by new writers should include clips/background/expertise; no longer than 1½ pages. Submit suitable material showing you have read several issues. *The American Legion Magazine* considers itself 'the magazine for a strong America.' Reflect this theme (which includes economy, educational system, moral fiber, social issues, infrastructure, technology and national defense/security). We are a general interest, national magazine, not a strictly military magazine. We are widely read by members of the Washington establishment and other policy makers. No unsolicited jokes. No phone queries."

■ $ $ THE AMERICAN SCHOLAR, The Phi Beta Kappa Society, 1785 Massachusetts Ave., NW, 4th Floor, Washington DC 20036. (202)265-3808. Fax: (202)265-0083. E-mail: scholar@pbk.org. Editor: Anne Fadiman. **Contact:** Jean Stipicevic, managing editor. **100% freelance written.** Quarterly magazine. "Our articles are written by scholars and experts but written in nontechnical language for an intelligent audience. Material covers a wide range in the arts, sciences, current affairs, history and literature." Estab. 1932. Circ. 25,000. Pays publication. Byline given. Offers 50% kill fee. Buys first rights. Editorial lead time 6 months. Submit seasonal material 6 months in advance. Accepts queries by mail, e-mail, fax. Responds in 2 weeks to queries; 2 months to ms. Sample copy for $6.95. Writer's guidelines for #10 SASE.

Nonfiction: Book excerpts (prior to publication only), essays, historical/nostalgic, humor. **Buys 40 mss/year.** Query. Length: 3,000-5,000 words. **Pays $500.**

Columns/Departments: **Buys 16 mss/year.** Query. Length: 3,000-5,000 words. **Pays $500.**

Poetry: Rob Farnsworth, poetry editor. **Buys 20/year.** Submit maximum 3 poems. Length: 34-75 lines. **Pays $50.** "Write for guidelines."

Tips: "The section most open to freelancers is the book review section. Query and send samples of reviews written. No phone queries."

$ $ $ $ THE ATLANTIC MONTHLY, 77 N. Washington St., Boston MA 02114. Fax: (617)854-7877. Editor: Michael Kelly. Managing Editor: Cullen Murphy. **Contact:** C. Michael Curtis, senior editor. Monthly magazine of arts and public affairs. Circ. 500,000. **Pays on acceptance.** Byline given. Buys first North American serial rights. Accepts queries by mail, e-mail, fax. Simultaneous submissions discouraged. Response time varies.

Nonfiction: Book excerpts, essays, general interest, humor, personal experience, religious, travel. Reportage preferred. Query with or without published clips or send complete ms with SASE. All unsolicited mss must be accompanied by SASE. Length: 1,000-6,000 words. Payment varies. Sometimes pays expenses of writers on assignment.

Fiction: Literary and contemporary fiction. "Seeks fiction that is clear, tightly written with strong sense of 'story' and well-defined characters." **Buys 12-15 mss/year.** Send complete ms. Length: 2,000-6,000 words preferred. **Pays $3,000.**

● Ranked as one of the best markets for fiction writers in *Writer's Digest* magazine's "Fiction 50," June 2000.

Poetry: Peter Davison, poetry editor. **Buys 40-60 poems/year.**

▣ The online magazine carries original content not found in the print edition. Contact: Wen Stephenson, online editor.

Tips: Writers should be aware that this is not a market for beginner's work (nonfiction and fiction), nor is it truly for intermediate work. Study this magazine before sending only your best, most professional work. When making first contact, "cover letters are sometimes helpful, particularly if they cite prior publications or involvement in writing programs. Common mistakes: melodrama, inconclusiveness, lack of development, unpersuasive characters and/or dialogue."

N **$ BIBLIOPHILOS, A Journal of History, Literature, and the Liberal Arts**, The Bibliophile Publishing Co., Inc., 200 Security Building, Fairmont WV 26554. **Contact:** Dr. Gerald J. Bobango, editor. **65-70% freelance written.** Quarterly literary magazine concentrating on 19th century American and European history. "We see ourself as a forum for new and unpublished writers, historians, philosophers, literary critics and reviewers, and those who love animals. Audience is academic-oriented, college graduate, who believes in traditional Aristotelian-Thomistic thought and education, and has a fair streak of the Luddite in him/her. Our ideal reader owns no television, has never sent nor received e-mail, and avoids shopping malls at any cost. He loves books." Estab. 1981. Circ. 400. Pays on publication. Publishes ms an average of 4 months after acceptance. Byline given. Buys first North American serial rights. Editorial lead time 4 months. Submit seasonal material 4 months in advance. Accepts simultaneous submissions. Responds in 2 weeks to queries; 1 month to mss. Sample copy for $5. Writer's guidelines for 9½×4 SAE with 2 first-class stamps.

○─ Break in with "either prose or poetry which is illustrative of man triumphing over and doing without technology, pure Ludditism, if need be. Send material critical of the socialist welfare state, constantly expanding federal government (or government at all levels), or exposing the inequities of affirmative action, political correctness, and the mass media packaging of political candidates. We want to see a pre-1960 world view."

Nonfiction: Book excerpts, essays, general interest, historical/nostalgic, humor, interview/profile, opinion, personal experience, photo feature, travel, book review-essay literary criticism. Upcoming theme issues include an annual all book-review issue, containing 10-15 reviews and review-essays, or poetry about books and reading. Does not want to see "anything that Oprah would recommend, or that Erma Bombeck or Ann Landers would think humorous or interesting. No 'I found Jesus and it changed my life' material." **Buys 8-12 mss/year.** Query by mail only. Length: 1,500-3,000 words. **Pays $5-50.**

Reprints: Accepts previously published submissions.

Photos: State availability of photos with submission. Reviews 4×6 prints. Negotiates payment individually. Identification of subjects required. Buys one-time rights.

Columns/Departments: "Features" (fiction and nonfiction, short stories), 1,500-3,000 words; "Poetry" (batches of 5, preferably thematically related), 3-150 lines; "Reviews" (book reviews or review essays on new books or individual authors, current and past), 1,000-1,500 words; "Opinion" (man triumphing over technology and technocrats, the facade of modern education, computer fetishism), 1,000-1,500 words. **Buys 4 mss/year.** Query by mail only. **Pays $25-50.**

Fiction: Adventure, condensed novels, ethnic, experimental, historical, humorous, mainstream, mystery, novel excerpts, romance, slice-of-life vignettes, suspense, Utopian, Orwellian. "No 'I found Jesus and it turned my life around'; no 'I remember Mama, who was a saint and I miss her terribly'; no gay or lesbian topics; anything harping on political correctness; anything to do with healthy living, HMOs, medical programs, or the welfare state, unless it is against statism in these areas." **Buys 8-12 mss/year.** Query by mail only. Length: 1,500-3,000 words. **Pays $25-50.**

Poetry: Avant-garde, free verse, light verse, traditional, political satire, doggerel. "No inspirational verse, or poems about grandchildren and the cute things they do." **Buys 20-25 poems/year.** Submit maximum 5 poems. Length: 3-150 lines. **Pays $5-50.**

Fillers: Anecdotes, short humor. **Buys 5-6/year.** Length: 25-100 words. **Pays $5-10.**

Tips: "Query first, and include a large SASE and $5 for sample issues and guidelines. Tell us of your academic expertise, what kinds of books you can review, and swear that you will follow Turabian's bibliographic form as set forth in the guidelines and no other. Do not call us, nor fax us, nor try e-mailing, which wouldn't work anyway. Avoid the cult of relevantism and contemporaneity. Send us perfect copy, no misspellings, no grammatical errors, no trendy, PC language."

$ $ CAPPER'S, Ogden Publications, Inc., 1503 SW 42nd St., Topeka KS 66609-1265. (913)274-4345. Fax: (913)274-4305. E-mail: cappers@cjnetworks.com. Website: www.cappers.com. Associate Editors: Cheryl Ptacek, Kandy Hopkins, Vicki Parks. Senior Editor: Jean Teller. **Contact:** Ann T. Crahan, editor. **25% freelance written.** Works with a small number of new/unpublished writers each year. Biweekly tabloid emphasizing home and family for readers who live in small towns and on farms. "*Capper's* is upbeat, focusing on the homey feelings people like to share, as well as hopes and dreams." Estab. 1879. Circ. 250,000. **Pays for poetry and fiction on acceptance;** articles on publication. Publishes ms an average of 8 months after acceptance. Byline given. Buys first North American and one-time serial rights. Editorial lead time 6 months. Submit seasonal material at least 3 months in advance. Responds in 6 weeks to queries; 6 months to mss; 10 months for serialized novels. Sample copy for $1.95 or on website. Writer's guidelines for #10 SASE or on website.

Nonfiction: General interest, historical (local museums, etc.), inspirational, interview/profile, nostalgia, budget travel (Midwest slants), people stories (accomplishments, collections, etc.). **Buys 50 mss/year.** Submit complete ms. Length: 750 words maximum. **Pays $2.50/inch. Pays additional $5 if used on website.**

Reprints: Send typed ms with rights for sale noted and information about when and where the article previously appeared.

Photos: Purchased with accompanying ms. Submit prints. Pays $5-40 for b&w glossy prints. Purchase price for ms includes payment for photos. Limited market for color photos (35mm color slides); pays $10-30 for color photos, $40 for covers. Additional payment of $5 if used on website. Captions and identification of subjects required. Buys one-time rights.

Columns/Departments: Heart of the Home (homemakers' letters, recipes, hints); Community Heartbeat (volunteerism). Submit complete ms. Length: 300 words maximum. **Pays approximately $2 per printed inch.**

Fiction: "We buy very few fiction pieces—longer than short stories, shorter than novels." Adventure, historical, humorous, mainstream, mystery, romance, serialized novels, western. No explicit sex, violence or profanity. **Buys 4-5 mss/year.** Query. Length: 7,500-40,000 words. **Pays $100-300.**

Poetry: Free verse, haiku, light verse, traditional, nature, inspiration. "The poems that appear in *Capper's* are not too difficult to read. They're easy to grasp. We're looking for everyday events and down-to-earth themes." **Buys 150/year.** Limit submissions to batches of 5. Length: 4-16 lines. **Pays $10-15.**

Tips: "Study a few issues of our publication. Most rejections are for material that is too long, unsuitable or out of character for our magazine (too sexy, too much profanity, wrong kind of topic, etc.). On occasion, we must cut material to fit column space."

$ $ THE CHRISTIAN SCIENCE MONITOR, 1 Norway St., Boston MA 02115. (617)450-2000. Website: www. csmonitor.com. **Contact:** Scott Armstrong (National), David Scott (International), Amelia Newcomb (Learning), Jim Bencivenga (Ideas), Gregory Lamb (Arts & Leisure), April Austin (Home Front), Clay Collins (Work & Money). International newspaper issued daily except Saturdays, Sundays and holidays in North America; weekly international edition. Estab. 1908. Circ. 95,000. Pays on publication. Buys all newspaper rights worldwide for 3 months following publication. Accepts queries by mail, e-mail. Responds in 1 month. Writer's guidelines for #10 SASE.

Nonfiction: In-depth features and essays. The newspaper includes 5 sections: Learning (education and life-long learning), Arts & Leisure, Ideas (religion, ethics, science and technology, environment, book reviews), Home Front (home and community issues) and Work & Money. Buys limited number of mss, "top quality only." Publishes original (exclusive) material only. Query to the appropriate section editor. **Pays $200 average.** Home Forum page buys essays of 400-900 words. **Pays $150 average.**

Poetry: Traditional, blank and free verse. Seeks non-religious poetry of high quality and of all lengths up to 75 lines. **Pays $35-75 average.**

Tips: "Style should be bright but not cute, concise but thoroughly researched. Try to humanize news or feature writing so reader identifies with it. Avoid sensationalism. Accent constructive, solution-oriented treatment of subjects."

$ $ $ $ CIVILIZATION, Worth Media LLC, 575 Lexington Ave., New York NY 10022. (212)230-3790. Fax: (212)238-8560. **Contact:** Regan Solmo, managing/senior editor. Bimonthly magazine. "*Civilization* is the membership magazine of the Library of Congress covering contemporary culture. Well-known writers contribute articles on the arts, travel, religion, economics, social issues, government, history, education and social issues." Estab. 1994. Circ. 200,000. **Pays on acceptance.** Buys all rights.

Nonfiction: *Civilization*'s departments and columns are often staff-written, but virtually all features come from freelancers. **Pays $1.50/word.** (Pay depends on subject matter, quality and the amount of time a writer has put into a piece.)

Tips: "*Civilization* is not a history magazine. We are a magazine of contemporary American culture. The key thing for us is that when we do look into the past, we connect it to the present. The magazine is now giving more emphasis to contemporary subjects. We take relatively few over-the-transom pieces. But we do look at everything that comes in, and sometimes we pick up something that looks really impressive. We put an enormous stress on good writing. Subject is important, but unless a writer can show us a sheaf of clips, we won't get started with them. There is a *Civilization* sensibility that we try to maintain. If you don't know the magazine well, you won't really understand what we're trying to do." To break in, look to contemporary subjects and the arts—including fine arts, contemporary culture, the lively arts and book reviews.

$ $ $ DIVERSION, 1790 Broadway, New York NY 10019. (212)969-7500. Fax: (212)969-7557. Contact: Tom Passavant, editor-in-chief. Monthly magazine covering travel and lifestyle, edited for physicians. "*Diversion* offers an eclectic mix of interests beyond medicine. Regular features include stories on domestic and foreign travel destinations, discussions of food and wine, sports columns, guidance on gardening and photography, and information on investments and finance. The editorial reflects its readers' affluent lifestyles and diverse personal interests. Although *Diversion* doesn't cover health subjects, it does feature profiles of doctors who excel at nonmedical pursuits." Estab. 1973. Circ. 176,000. Pays 3 months after acceptance. Offers 25% kill fee. Editorial lead time 4 months. Responds in 1 month. Sample copy $4.50. Guidelines available.

Nonfiction: "We get loads of travel and food queries, but not enough in culture, the arts, sports, personal finance, etc." **Buys 70 ms/year.** Length: 1,800-2,000 words. **Pays $50-1,200.** Query with proposal, published clips and author's credentials.

● Ranked as one of the best markets for freelance writers in *Writer's Yearbook* magazine's annual "Top 100 Markets," January 2000.

Columns/Departments: Travel, food & wine, photography, gardening, finance. Length: 1,200 words. **Pays $500-750.** Query with proposal, published clips and author's credentials.

N $ EDUCATION IN FOCUS, Books for All Times, Inc., P.O. Box 2, Alexandria VA 22313. (703)548-0457. E-mail: staff@bfat.com. Website: www.bfat.com. **Contact:** Joe David, editor. **80% freelance written.** Semiannual newsletter for public interested in education issues at all levels. "We are always looking for intelligent articles that provide educationally sound ideas that enhance the understanding of what is happening or what should be happening in our schools today. We are not looking for material that might be published by the Department of Education. Instead we want material from liberated and mature thinkers and writers, tamed by reason and humanitarianism." Estab. 1989. Circ. 1,000. **Pays on acceptance.** Publishes ms an average of 2 months after acceptance. Byline given. Buys first, one-time, second serial (reprint) rights and book, newsletter and Internet rights. Editorial lead time 2 months. Accepts queries by mail, e-mail. Accepts simultaneous submissions. Responds in 1 month to queries. Sample copy for #10 SASE.
Nonfiction: Book excerpts, exposé, general interest. "We prefer documented, intelligent articles that deeply inform. The best way to be quickly rejected is to send articles that defend the public school system as it is today, or was!" **Buys 4-6 mss/year.** Query or send complete ms. Length: 3,000 words. Some longer articles can be broken into 2 articles—one for each issue. **Pays $25-75.** Pays writers contributor copies or other premiums "for any published news clippings we print that they submit to us."
Reprints: Accepts previously published submissions.
Tips: "Maintain an honest voice and a clear focus on the subject."

$ $ $ $ EQUINOX: Canada's Magazine of Discovery, Malcolm Publishing, 11450 Albert-Hudon Blvd., Montreal North, Quebec H1G 3J9 Canada. (514)327-4464. Fax: (514)327-0514. E-mail: eqxmag@globetrotter.net. **Contact:** Martin Silverstone, editor. Bimonthly magazine "encompassing the worlds of human cultures and communities, the natural world and science and technology. *Equinox* is Canada's world-class magazine of discovery. It serves a large readership of intelligent Canadians who share a desire to learn more about themselves, their country, and the world around them. Its editorial range is eclectic, with a special emphasis on biology, ecology, wildlife, the earth sciences, astronomy, medicine, geography, natural history, the arts, travel and adventure. Throughout the theme is that of discovery and, in many cases, rediscovery. While exploring the unfamiliar, *Equinox* also provides fresh insights into the familiar." Estab. 1982. Circ. 120,000. **Pays on acceptance.** Byline given. Offers 50% kill fee. Buys first North American serial rights only. Submit seasonal queries 1 year in advance. Accepts queries by mail, e-mail, fax. Responds in 2 months. Sample copy for $5 and SAE with Canadian postage or IRCs. Writer's guidelines for #10 SASE (U.S. writers must send IRCs, not American stamps).
Nonfiction: Book excerpts (occasionally). No travel articles. Should have Canadian focus. Query with SAE including Canadian postage or IRCs. Length: 1,500-5,000 words. **Pays $1,500-3,500 (Canadian) negotiated.**
Reprints: Accepts previously published submissions. Send tearsheet of article and information about when and where the article previously appeared. Pays 30% of amount paid for an original article.
Photos: Send photos with ms. Reviews color transparencies—must be of professional quality; no prints or negatives. Captions and identification of subjects required. Pays $110-350. Pays $500 for covers. Sometimes pays package fees.
Columns/Departments: Nexus (current science that isn't covered by daily media), 250-350 words. **Pays $250 (Canadian).** Pursuits (service section for active living), 200-1,000 words. **Pays $900 (Canadian).** Query with published clips.
Tips: "Submit ideas for short photo essays as well as longer features. We welcome queries by mail and e-mail."

N $ $ $ FRIENDLY EXCHANGE, C-E Publishers: Publishers, Friendly Exchange Business Office, P.O. Box 2120, Warren MI 48090-2120. Publication Office: (810)753-8326. Fax: (248)447-7566. Website: www.friendlyexchange .com. **Contact:** Dan Grantham, editor. **80% freelance written.** Works with a small number of new/unpublished writers each year. Quarterly magazine for policyholders of Farmers Insurance Group of Companies exploring travel, lifestyle and leisure topics of interest to active families. "These are traditional families (median adult age 39) who live primarily in the area bounded by Ohio on the east and the Pacific Ocean on the west, along with Tennessee, Alabama, and Virginia." Estab. 1981. Circ. 6,200,000. **Pays on acceptance.** Publishes ms an average of 5 months after acceptance. Offers 25% kill fee. Buys all rights. Submit seasonal material 1 year in advance. Accepts simultaneous queries. Responds in 2 months. Sample copy for 9 × 12 SAE with 5 first-class stamps. Writer's guidelines for #10 SASE.
Nonfiction: "We provide readers with 'news they can use' through articles that help them make smart choices about lifestyle issues. We focus on home, auto, health, personal finance, travel and other lifestyle/consumer issues of interest to today's families. Readers should get a sense of the issues involved, and information that could help them make those decisions. Style is warm and colorful, making liberal use of anecdotes and quotes." **Buys 8 mss/issue.** Query. Length: 200-1,200 words. **Pays $500-$1,000/article including expenses.**
Columns/Departments: Consumer issues, health and leisure are topics of regular columns.
Tips: "We concentrate on providing readers information relating to current trends. Don't focus on destination-based travel, but on travel trends. We prefer tightly targeted stories that provide new information to help readers make decisions about their lives. We don't take query or MS on first-person essays or humorous articles."

■ $ $ **GRIT: American Life and Traditions**, Ogden Publications, 1503 SW 42nd St., Topeka KS 66609-1265. (785)274-4300. Fax: (785)274-4305. E-mail: grit@cjnetworks.com. Website: www.grit.com. **Contact:** Donna Doyle, editor-in-chief. **90% freelance written.** Open to new writers. "*Grit* is Good News. As a wholesome, family-oriented magazine published for more than a century and distributed nationally, *Grit* features articles about family lifestyles, traditions, values and pastimes. *Grit* accents the best of American life and traditions—past and present. Our readers cherish family values and appreciate practical and innovative ideas. Many of them live in small towns and rural areas across the country; others live in cities but share many of the values typical of small-town America." Estab. 1882. Circ. 200,000. Pays on publication. Byline given. Buys all and first rights. Submit seasonal material 6 months in advance. Sample copy and writer's guidelines for $4 and 11 × 14 SASE with 4 first-class stamps. Sample articles on website.

　　○━ How to break in: Departments such as Readers True Stories, Pet Tales, Looking Back, Profile, Seasonal Readers Memories (Easter, Christmas, Mother's Day), Poetry.

Nonfiction: Need features (timely, newsworthy, touching but with a *Grit* angle), profiles, humor, readers' true stories, outdoor hobbies, collectibles, gardening, crafts, hobbies and leisure pastimes. The best way to sell work is by reading each issue cover to cover. Special issues: Gardening (January-October); Health (twice a year); Travel (spring and fall); Collectibles; Pet issue; Canning Contest (essays and entries); Christmas. **Query by mail only. Features pay up to 22¢/ word plus $25-200 each for photos depending on quality and placement.** Main features run 1,200 to 1,500 words. Department features average 800-1,000 words and pay varies on placement and length. Departments are paid a flat rate for photo and article.

　　● *Grit* reports it is looking for articles about how soon-to-retire baby boomers are planning for retirement and how children are coping with aging parents.

Fiction: Short stories, 1,500-2,000 words; may also purchase accompanying art if of high quality and appropriate. Need serials (romance, westerns, mysteries) 3,500-10,000 words. Send ms with SASE to Fiction Dept.

Photos: Professional quality photos (b&w prints or color slides) increase acceptability of articles. Photos: $25-200 each in features according to quality, placement and color/b&w.

Tips: "Articles should be directed to a national audience, mostly 40 years and older. Sources identified fully. Our readers are warm and loving. They want to read about others with heart. Tell us stories about someone unusual, an unsung hero, an artist of the backroads, an interesting trip with an emotional twist, a memory with a message, an ordinary person accomplishing extraordinary things. Tell us stories that will make us cry with joy." Send complete ms with photos for consideration.

$ $ $ $ **HARPER'S MAGAZINE**, 666 Broadway, 11th Floor, New York NY 10012. (212)614-6500. Fax: (212)228-5889. Editor: Lewis H. Lapham. **Contact:** Ann Gollin, editor's assistant. **90% freelance written.** Monthly magazine for well-educated, socially concerned, widely read men and women who value ideas and good writing. "*Harper's Magazine* encourages national discussion on current and significant issues in a format that offers arresting facts and intelligent opinions. By means of its several shorter journalistic forms—Harper's index, Readings, Forum, and Annotation—as well as with its acclaimed essays, fiction, and reporting, *Harper's* continues the tradition begun with its first issue in 1850: to inform readers across the whole spectrum of political, literary, cultural, and scientific affairs." Estab. 1850. Circ. 216,000. Rights purchased vary with author and material. Pays negotiable kill fee. **Pays on acceptance.** Publishes ms an average of 3 months after acceptance. Responds in 1 month. Sample copy for $3.95.

　　● *Harper's Magazine* won the 1998 National Magazine Award for Feature Writing and the 1999 NMA for fiction writing.

Nonfiction: "For writers working with agents or who will query first only, our requirements are: public affairs, literary, international and local reporting and humor." No interviews; no profiles. Complete ms and query must include SASE. No unsolicited poems will be accepted. Publishes one major report per issue. Length: 4,000-6,000 words. Publishes one major essay/issue. Length: 4,000-6,000 words. "These should be construed as topical essays on all manner of subjects (politics, the arts, crime, business, etc.) to which the author can bring the force of passionate and informed statement."

Reprints: Accepts previously published material for its "Readings" section. Send typed ms with rights for sale noted and information about when and where the article previously appeared.

Fiction: Publishes 1 short story/month. Generally pays 50¢-$1/word.

Photos: Contact: Angela Riechers, art director. Occasionally purchased with mss; others by assignment. Pays $50-500.

Tips: "Some readers expect their magazines to clothe them with opinions in the way that Bloomingdale's dresses them for the opera. The readers of *Harper's Magazine* belong to a different crowd. They strike me as the kind of people who would rather think in their own voices and come to their own conclusions."

■ $ $ $ $ **HOPE MAGAZINE, How to be Part of the Solution**, Hope Publishing, Inc., P.O. Box 160, Brooklin ME 04616. (207)359-4651. Fax: (207)359-8920. E-mail: info@hopemag.com. Website: www.hopemag.com. Editor-in-Chief/Publisher: Jon Wilson. Editor: Kimberly Ridley. Associate Editor: Amy Rawe. Assistant Editor: Lane Fisher. **Contact:** Adrienne Ricci, editorial assistant. **90% freelance written.** Quarterly magazine covering humanity at its best and worst. "*Hope* is a solutions-oriented journal focused on people addressing personal and societal challenges with uncommon courage and integrity. A magazine free of religious, political, or new age affiliation, *Hope* awakens the impulse we all have—however hidden or distant—to make our world more liveable, humane, and genuinely loving. We strive to evoke empathy among readers." Estab. 1996. Circ. 22,000. Pays on publication. Publishes ms an average of 6 months after acceptance. Byline given. Offers 20% kill fee. Buys first, one-time or second serial (reprint) rights. Editorial lead time 4 months. Submit seasonal material 6 months in advance. Accepts queries by mail, e-mail, fax. Accepts simultaneous submissions. Responds in 6 months. Sample copy for $5. Writer's guidelines for #10 SASE.

Nonfiction: Book excerpts, essays, general interest, interview/profile, personal experience, photo feature. Nothing explicitly religious, political or New Age. **Buys 50-75 mss/year.** Query with published clips or writing samples and SASE. Length: 250-4,000 words. **Pays $50-2,000.** Sometimes pays expenses of writers on assignment.

Photos: State availability of or send photos with submission. "We are very interested in and committed to the photo essay form, and enthusiastically encourage photographers and photojournalists to query us with ideas, or to submit images for thematic photo essays." Reviews contact sheets and 5×7 prints. Negotiates payment individually. Captions and identification of subjects required. Buys one-time rights.

Columns/Departments: Contact Departments Editor. Signs of Hope (inspiring dispatches/news), 250-500 words; Aspirations (reports on individuals or groups in their teens—or younger—who are engaged in works worthy of our recognition), 1,000-1,500 words; Arts of Hope (reviews and discussions of music, art, and literature related to hope), 1,000-2,000 words; Book Reviews (devoted primarily to nonfiction works in widely diverse subjects areas related to struggle and triumph), 500-800 words. **Buys 50-60 mss/year.** Query with published clips or send complete ms and SASE. **Pays $50-150.**

Tips: "Write very personally, and very deeply. We're not looking for shallow 'feel-good' pieces. Approach uncommon subjects. Cover the ordinary in extraordinary ways. Go to the heart. Surprise us. Many stories we receive are too 'soft.' Absolutely no phone queries."

N **★** **$ $ IDEALS MAGAZINE**, Ideals Publications Inc., 535 Metroplex Dr., Suite 250, Nashville TN 37211. (615)333-0478. Website: www.idealspublications.com. Publisher: Patricia Pingry. **Contact:** Michelle Prater Burke. **95% freelance written.** Seasonal magazine published 6 times/year. "Our readers are generally conservative, educated women over 50. The magazine is mainly light poetry and short articles with a nostalgic theme. Issues are seasonally oriented and thematic." Estab. 1944. Circ. 180,000. Pays on publication. Byline given. Buys one-time, worldwide serial and subsidiary rights. Submit seasonal material 8 months in advance. Does not accept queries. Accepts simultaneous submissions. Responds in 2 months. Sample copy for $4. Writer's and photographer's guidelines for #10 SASE.

O— "Poetry is the area of our publication most open to freelancers. It must be oriented around a season or theme."

Nonfiction: Essays, historical/nostalgic, humor, inspirational, personal experience. "No depressing articles." Themes include: Easter, Mother's Day, Country, Friendship, Thanksgiving and Christmas. **Buys 20 mss/year.** Send complete ms. Length: 800-1,000 words. **Pays 10¢/word.**

Reprints: Send tearsheet or photocopy of article or short story and information about when and where the article previously appeared. **Pays 10¢/word.**

Photos: Guidelines for SASE. Reviews tearsheets. Offers no additional payment for photos accepted with ms. Captions, model releases, identification of subjects required. Buys one-time rights. Payment varies.

Fiction: Slice-of-life vignettes. **Buys 10 mss/year.** Length: 800-1,000 words. **Pays 10¢/word.**

Poetry: Light verse, traditional. "No erotica or depressing poetry." **Buys 250 poems/year.** Submit maximum 10 poems, 20-30 lines. **Pays $10/poem.**

Tips: "Nostalgia is an underlying theme of every issue. Poetry must be optimistic. We prefer that you submit complete ms instead of a query. No phone queries, please."

N **▣** **$ $ LEADER GUIDE MAGAZINE, Practical Ways to do the Right Things Right**, Leadership, 113 First Ave., Mt. Pleasant TN 38474. (931)379-3799. Fax: (931)379-3791. E-mail: lmhatcher@hotmail.com. Website: www.leadershipdevelopment.com. **Contact:** Linda Hatcher, editor. **25-50% freelance written.** Monthly online leadership development guide covering ethical leadership. "Our slogan sums up our focus on ethical, effective leadership: Practical Ways to Do the Right Things Right." Estab. 1999. Pays on publication. Byline given. Offers 50% kill fee. Buys first rights. Editorial lead time 3 months. Submit seasonal material 5 months in advance. Accepts queries by mail, e-mail, fax, phone. Accepts simultaneous submissions. Responds in 1 month to queries; 2 months to mss. Sample copy on website. Writer's guidelines free or on website.

Nonfiction: Book excerpts, how-to, humor, inspirational, interview/profile (ethical leadership). Query or send complete ms. Length: 500-1,000 words. **Pays $100-500.** Sometimes pays expenses of writers on assignment.

Reprints: Accepts previously published submissions.

Photos: State availability of photos with submission. Offers no additional payment for photos accepted with ms. Captions, model releases and identification of subjects required. Buys all rights.

Columns/Departments: 500-1,000 words. Query. **Pays $100-500.**

Fillers: Anecdotes, facts, gags to be illustrated by cartoonist, newsbreaks, short humor. Length: 50-150 words. **Pays $10-50.**

Tips: "We want stories that will help people become more effective leaders all from a practical, ethical foundation write along those lines and we're interested!"

N **★** **$ LIVING, For the Whole Family**, Shalom Publishers, Route 2, Box 656, Grottoes VA 24441. E-mail: tgether@aol.com. **Contact:** Melodie M. Davis, editor. Managing Editor: Eugene Souder. **90% freelance written.** "*Living* is a quarterly 'good news' paper published to encourage and strengthen family life at all stages, directed to the general newspaper-reading public." Estab. 1992. Circ. 250,000. Pays on publication. Publishes ms an average of 9 months after acceptance. Byline given. Buys one-time or second serial (reprint) rights. Editorial lead time 6 months. Submit seasonal material 6 months in advance. Accepts simultaneous submissions. Responds in 2 months to queries; 6 months to mss. Sample copy for 9×12 SAE with 4 first-class stamps. Writer's guidelines for #10 SASE or by e-mail.

Nonfiction: General interest, humor, inspirational, personal experience. **Buys 40-50 mss/year.** Send complete ms. Length: 300-1,000 words. **Pays $35-50.**

Reprints: Accepts previously published submissions.

Photos: State availability of photos with submission or send photos with submission. Reviews 3×5 or larger prints. Offers $25/photo. Identification of subjects required. Buys one-time rights.

Fiction: Slice-of-life vignettes, emotionally grabbing stories of interest to all. No dog stories. **Buys 4 mss/year.** Send complete ms. Length: 500-1,000 words. **Pays $50.**

Tips: "This paper is for a general audience in the community, but written from a Christian-value perspective. It seems to be difficult for some writers to understand our niche—*Living* is not a 'religious' periodical but handles an array of general interest family topics and mentioning Christian values or truths as appropriate. Writing is extremely competitive and we attempt to publish only high quality writing."

$ $ $ $ NATIONAL GEOGRAPHIC MAGAZINE, 1145 17th St. NW, Washington DC 20036. (202)775-7868. Fax: (202)857-7252. Website: www.nationalgeographic.com. Editor: William Allen. **Contact:** Oliver Payne, senior assistant editor, manuscripts. **60% freelance written.** Prefers to work with published/established writers. Monthly magazine for members of the National Geographic Society. "Timely articles written in a compelling, 'eyewitness' style. Arresting photographs that speak to us of the beauty, mystery, and harsh realities of life on earth. Maps of unprecedented detail and accuracy. These are the hallmarks of *National Geographic* magazine. Since 1888, the *Geographic* has been educating readers about the world." Circ. 10,300,000.

Nonfiction: *National Geographic* publishes general interest, illustrated articles on science, natural history, exploration, cultures and geographical regions. Of the freelance writers assigned, a few are experts in their fields; the remainder are established professionals. Fewer than 1% of unsolicited queries result in assignments. Query (500 words with clips of published magazine articles by mail to Senior Assistant Editor Oliver Payne). Do not send mss. Before querying, study recent issues and check a *Geographic Index* at a library since the magazine seldom returns to regions or subjects covered within the past 10 years. Length: 2,000-8,000 words. Pays expenses of writers on assignment.

Photos: Photographers should query in care of the Photographic Division.

■ The online magazine carries original content not included in the print edition. Contact: Valerie May, online editor.

Tips: "State the theme(s) clearly, let the narrative flow, and build the story around strong characters and a vivid sense of place. Give us rounded episodes, logically arranged."

$ $ $ NEWSWEEK, 251 W. 57th St., New York NY 10019. (212)445-4000. Circ. 3,180,000. Contact: Pam Hamer. "*Newsweek* is edited to report the week's developments on the newsfront of the world and the nation through news, commentary and analysis." Accepts unsolicited mss for My Turn, a column of personal opinion. The 850-900 word essays for the column must be original, not published elsewhere and contain verifiable facts. **Payment is $1,000, on publication.** Buys non-exclusive world-wide rights. Responds in 2 months only on submissions with SASE.

N ◪ OPEN SPACES, Open Spaces Publications, Inc. PMB 134, 6327-C SW Capitol Hwy., Portland OR 97201-1937. (503)227-5764. Fax: (503)227-3401. E-mail: info@open-spaces.com. Website: www.open-spaces.com. President: Penny Harrison. Managing Editor: James Bradley. **Contact:** Elizabeth Arthur, editor. **95% freelance written.** Quarterly general interest magazine. "*Open Spaces* is a forum for informed writing and intelligent thought. Articles are written by experts in various fields. Audience is varied (CEOs and rock climbers, politicos and university presidents, etc.) but is highly educated and loves to read good writing." Estab. 1997. Pays on publication. Publishes ms an average of 6 months after acceptance. Byline given. Offers 20% kill fee. Rights vary with author and material. Editorial lead time 9 months. Accepts queries by mail, fax. Accepts simultaneous submissions. Sample copy for $10 or on website. Writer's guidelines for #10 SASE or on website.

Nonfiction: Major articles. Length: 2,500-6,000 words. Essays, general interest, historical, how-to (if clever), humor, interview/profile, personal experience, travel. **Buys 35 mss/year.** Query with published clips. Length: 1,500-2,500 words. **Pay varies.**

Photos: State availability of photos with submission. Captions and identification of subjects required. Buys one-time rights.

Columns/Departments: David Williams, departments editor. Books (substantial topics such as the Booker Prize, The Newbery, etc.); Travel (must reveal insight); Sports (past subjects include rowing, swing dancing and ultimate); Unintended Consequences, all 2,500 words. **Buys 20-25 mss/year.** Query with published clips or send complete ms. **Pay varies.**

Fiction: Ellen Teicher, fiction editor. "Quality is far more important than type. Read the magazine." **Buys 8 mss/year.** Send complete ms with credits. **Pay varies.**

Poetry: Susan Juve-Hu, poetry editor. "Again, quality is far more important than type."

Fillers: Anecdotes, facts, short humor.

Tips: "*Open Spaces* reviews all manuscripts submitted in hopes of finding writing of the highest quality. We present a Northwest perspective as well as a national and international one. Best advice is read the magazine."

$ $ $ THE OXFORD AMERICAN, The Southern Magazine of Good Writing, The Oxford American, Inc., P.O. Drawer 1156, Oxford MS 38655. (662)236-1836. Fax: (662)236-3141. E-mail: oxam@watervalley.net. Website: www.oxfordamericanmag.com. Editor: Marc Smirnoff. **Contact:** Annie Wedekind, associate editor. **50-65% freelance**

written. Bimonthly magazine covering the South. "*The Oxford American* is a general-interest literary magazine about the South." Estab. 1992. Circ. 30,000. Pays on publication. Publishes ms an average of 6 months after acceptance. Byline given. Offers 25% kill fee. Buys first North American serial rights and one-time rights. Editorial lead time 2 months. Submit seasonal material 4 months in advance. Accepts queries by mail, e-mail, fax. Responds in 3 weeks to queries; 3 months to mss. Sample copy for $6.50. Writer's guidelines for #10 SASE.

O→ Break in with "a brief, focused query highlighting the unusual, fresh aspects to your pitch, and clips. All pitches must have some Southern connection."

Nonfiction: Essays, general interest, humor, personal experience, reporting, profiles, memoirs concerning the South. **Buys 6 mss/year.** Query with published clips or send complete ms. Pay varies. Sometimes pays expenses of writers on assignment.

Photos: Negotiates payment individually. Captions required. Buys one-time rights.

Columns/Departments: Send complete ms. Pay varies.

Fiction: Publishes novel excerpts and short stories. **Buys 10 mss/year.** Send complete ms. Pay varies.

Tips: "Like other editors, I stress the importance of being familiar with the magazine. Those submitters who know the magazine always send in better work because they know what we're looking for. To those who don't bother to at least flip through the magazine, let me point out we only publish articles with some sort of Southern connection."

★ **$ $ $ $ PARADE,** *The Sunday Magazine,* Parade Publications, Inc., 711 Third Ave., New York NY 10017. (212)450-7000. Fax: (212)450-7284. Website: www.parade.com. Editor: Walter Anderson. Managing Editor: Larry Smith. **Contact:** Paula Silverman, articles editor. Weekly magazine for a general interest audience. **95% freelance written.** Estab. 1941. Circ. 81,000,000. **Pays on acceptance.** Publishes ms an average of 5 months after acceptance. Kill fee varies in amount. Buys one-time or all rights. Editorial lead time 1 month. Accepts queries by mail, e-mail, fax. Accepts simultaneous submissions. Sample copy free on website. Writer's guidelines free by e-mail.

Nonfiction: General interest (on health, trends, social issues or anything of interest to a broad general audience); interview/profile (of news figures, celebrities and people of national significance); and "provocative topical pieces of news value." Spot news events are not accepted, as *Parade* has a 1 month lead time. No fiction, fashion, travel, poetry, cartoons, nostalgia, regular columns, quizzes or fillers. Unsolicited queries concerning celebrities, politicians, sports figures, or technical are rarely assigned. **Buys 150 mss/year.** Query with published clips. Length of published articles: 1,000-1,200 words. **Pays $2,500 minimum.** Pays expenses of writers on assignment.

Tips: "Send a well-researched, well-written one-page proposal and enclose a SASE. Do not submit completed manuscripts."

N ★ $ PRESENCE SENSE MAGAZINE, The Horstman Teed Corp., P.O. Box 547, Rancocas NJ 08073. E-mail: presencesensemag@jersey.net. Website: www.jerseynet/~presensesensemag. **Contact:** Kimberly Teed, editor. **70% freelance written.** Bimonthly magazine covering etiquette, social customs and lifestyle. "*Presence Sense,* an art deco styled print publication that educates, guides and entertains its savvy readers through the world of etiquette, social customs, lifestyle, life's pleasures and mysteries." Estab. 2000. Circ. 5,000. Pays on publication. Publishes ms an average of 9 months after acceptance. Byline sometimes given. Buys one-time and second serial (reprint) rights. Editorial lead time 6 months. Submit seasonal material 6 months in advance. Accepts queries by mail, e-mail. Accepts simultaneous submissions. Responds in 3 months to queries. Sample copy for $4.50. Writer's guidelines free for #10 SASE, online at website or by e-mail.

Nonfiction: Book excerpts, essays, exposé, general interest, historical/nostalgic, how-to, humor, interview/profile, new product, opinion, personal experience, travel. Upcoming special issues will cover jazz, tap, blues, wedding. "No negative articles—do not want anti-TV, Howard Stern, etc." **Buys 100 mss/year.** Query or send complete ms. Length: 250-1,500 words. **Pays $25-45.** Sometimes pays expenses of writers on assignment.

Reprints: Accepts previously published submissions.

Photos: State availability of photos with submission. Negotiates payment individually. Identification of subjects required. Buys one-time rights.

Fillers: Anecdotes, facts, gags to be illustrated by cartoonist, short humor. **Buys 100/year.** Length: 5-250 words. **Pays $25-45.**

Tips: "Articles should offer specific information on etiquette, social customs and lifestyle; introduce the reader to a custom or lifestyle issue; or inform the reader about current trends. We publish articles on manners, celebrities, entertainment, travel, people and places, politics, art and science . . . just about anything, as long as it relates to the many different aspects of life. Articles must entertain and/or educate, and above all, must never be 'preachy' nor prejudiced."

N ★ $ RANDOM LENGTHS, Harbor Independent News, P.O. Box 731, San Pedro CA 90733-0731. (310)519-1016. Editor: James Elmendorf. **30% freelance written.** Biweekly tabloid covering alternative news/features. "*Random Lengths* follows Twain's dictum of printing news 'to make people mad enough to do something about it.' Our writers do exposés, scientific, environmental, political reporting and fun, goofy, insightful, arts and entertainment coverage, for a lefty, labor-oriented, youngish crowd." Estab. 1979. Circ. 30,000. Pays in 60 days. Byline given. Offers 50% kill fee. Buys all rights. Editorial lead time 1 month. Submit seasonal material 2 months in advance. Accepts simultaneous submissions. Responds in 6 weeks to queries. Sample copy for 9×13 SAE with 3 first-class stamps. Writer's guidelines free.

Nonfiction: Exposé, general interest, historical/nostalgic, interview/profile, opinion. Special issues: Labor Day, triannual book edition; women and black history months. **Buys 150 mss/year.** Query. Length: 300-2,000 words. **Pays 5¢/word.** Sometimes pays expenses of writers on assignment.

Reprints: Accepts previously published submissions.

Photos: State availability of photos with submissions. Reviews prints. Offers $10/photo. Captions, identification of subjects required. Buys all rights.

Columns/Departments: Community News (local angle), 300-600 words; Commentary (national/world/opinion), 600-800 words; Feature (books/music/local events), 300-600 words. **Buys 75 mss/year.** Query. **Pays 5¢/word.**

Tips: "We use mostly local material and local writers, but we are open to current-event, boffo entertaining writing. Read other alternative weeklies for reference. We need local news most. Next, entertainment stuff with a local pitch."

$ $ $ $ READER'S DIGEST, Reader's Digest Rd., Pleasantville NY 10570-7000. Website: www.readersdigest. com. **Contact:** Editorial Correspondence. Monthly general interest magazine. "We are looking for contemporary stories of lasting interest that give the magazine variety, freshness and originality." Estab. 1922. Circ. 15,000,000. **Pays on acceptance.** Byline given. Buys exclusive world periodical rights, electronic rights, among others. Editorial lead time 3 months. Submit seasonal material 6 months in advance. Accepts queries by mail, e-mail, fax. Address article queries and tearsheets of published articles to the editors.

Nonfiction: Book excerpts, essays, exposé, general interest, historical/nostalgic, humor, inspirational, interview/profile, opinion, personal experience. **Buys 100 mss/year.** Query with published clips. Does not read or return unsolicited mss. Length: 2,500-4,000 words. **Original article rates generally begin at $5,000.**

• Ranked as one of the best markets for freelance writers in *Writer's Yearbook* magazine's annual "Top 100 Markets," January 2000.

Reprints: Send tearsheet or photocopy with rights for sale noted and information about where and when the article appeared. **Pays $1,200/*Reader's Digest* page** for World Digest rights (usually split 50/50 between original publisher and writer).

Columns/Departments: "Original contributions become the property of *Reader's Digest* upon acceptance and payment. Life's Like That contributions must be true, unpublished stories from one's own experience, revealing adult human nature, and providing appealing or humorous sidelights on the American scene." Length: 300 words maximum. **Pays $400 on publication.** True, unpublished stories are also solicited for Humor in Uniform, Campus Comedy, Virtual Hilarity and All in a Day's Work. Length: 300 words maximum. **Pays $400 on publication.** Towards More Picturesque Speech—the first contributor of each item used in this department is paid $50 for original material, $35 for reprints. For items used in Laughter, the Best Medicine, Personal Glimpses, Quotable Quotes, Notes From All Over, Points to Ponder and elsewhere in the magazine payment is as follows; to the *first* contributor of each from a published source, $35. For original material, $30/*Reader's Digest* two-column line. Previously published material must have source's name, date and page number. Contributions cannot be acknowledged or returned. Send complete anecdotes to *Reader's Digest*, Box 100, Pleasantville NY 10572-0100, fax to (914)238-6390 or e-mail laughlines@readersdigest.com. CompuServe address is notes:readersdigest or use readersdigest@notes.compuserve.com from other online services and the Internet."

Tips: "Roughly half the 30-odd articles we publish every month are reprinted from magazines, newspapers, books and other sources. The remaining 15 or so articles are original—most of them assigned, some submitted on speculation. While many of these are written by regular contributors—on salary or on contract—we're always looking for new talent and for offbeat subjects that help give our magazine variety, freshness and originality. Above all, in the writing we publish, *The Digest* demands accuracy—down to the smallest detail. Our worldwide team of 60 researchers scrutinizes every line of type, checking every fact and examining every opinion. For an average issue, they will check some 3500 facts with 1300 sources. So watch your accuracy. There's nothing worse than having an article fall apart in our research checking because an author was a little careless with his reporting. We make this commitment routinely, as it guarantees that the millions of readers who believe something simply because they saw it in *Reader's Digest* have not misplaced their trust."

Ⓝ $ $ $ $ READER'S DIGEST (CANADA), 1100, boul. René-Lévesque Blvd., West Montreal, Quebec H3B 5H5 Canada. (514)940-0751. Website: www.readersdigest.com. Editor-in-Chief: Murray Lewis. **Contact:** Ron Starr, senior associate editor. **10-25% freelance written.** Monthly magazine of general interest articles and subjects. Estab. 1948. Circ. 1.3 million. **Pays on acceptance** for original works. Pays on publication for "pickups." Byline given. Offers $500 (Canadian) kill fee. Buys one-time rights (for reprints), all rights (for original articles). Submit seasonal material 5 months in advance. Accepts queries by mail, e-mail. Responds in 5 weeks to queries. Writer's guidelines for #10 SASE with Canadian postage or #10 SAE with 1 IRC.

Nonfiction: General interest, how-to (general interest), inspirational, personal experience. "We're looking for true stories that depend on emotion and reveal the power of our relationships to help us overcome adversity; also looking for true first-person accounts of an event that changed a life for the better or led to new insight. No fiction, poetry or articles too specialized, technical or esoteric—read *Reader's Digest* to see what kind of articles we want." Query with published clips to Associate Editor: Ron Starr. Length: 3,000-5,000 words. **Pays a minimum of $2,700.** Pays expenses of writers on assignment.

Reprints: Send photocopy of article. Reprint payment is negotiable.

Photos: State availability of photos with submission.

   ◧ The online magazine carries original content not found in the print edition. Contact: Peter Des Lauriers.

Tips: "*Reader's Digest* usually finds its freelance writers through other well-known publications in which they have previously been published. There are guidelines available and writers should read *Reader's Digest* to see what kind of stories we look for and how they are written. We do not accept unsolicited manuscripts."

$ READERS REVIEW, The National Research Bureau, Inc., 320 Valley St., Burlington IA 52601. (319)752-5415. Fax: (319)752-3421. **Contact:** Nancy Heinzel, editor. **75% freelance written.** Quarterly magazine. Estab. 1948. Pays on publication. Publishes ms an average of 1 year after acceptance. Buys all rights. Submit seasonal material 7 months in advance of issue date. Sample copy and writers guidelines for #10 SAE with 2 first-class stamps.

• The *Readers Review* works with a small number of new/unpublished writers each year, and is eager to work with new/unpublished writers.

Nonfiction: General interest (steps to better health, attitudes on the job); how-to (perform better on the job, do home repairs, car maintenance); travel. **Buys 10-12 mss/year.** Query with outline or submit complete ms. Length: 500-700 words. **Pays 4¢/word.**

Tips: "Writers have a better chance of breaking in our publication with short articles."

$ $ REAL PEOPLE, The Magazine of Celebrities and Interesting People, Main Street Publishing Co., Inc., 450 Seventh Ave., Suite 1701, New York NY 10123. (212)244-2351. Fax: (212)244-2367. E-mail: mrs-2@idt.net. **Contact:** Alex Polner, editor. **75% freelance written.** Bimonthly magazine for ages 30 and up focusing on celebs and show business, but also interesting people who might appeal to a national audience. Estab. 1988. Circ. 75,000. Pays on publication. Byline given. Pays 33% kill fee. Buys all rights. Submit seasonal material 6 months in advance. Accepts queries by mail, e-mail. Responds to queries in 6 weeks. Sample copy for $4 and 8×11 SAE with 3 first-class stamps. Guidelines for #10 SASE.

Nonfiction: Interview/profile. Q&A formats are not encouraged. "We do a fall preview of TV and film in September. Material must be in by June. Other seasonal stories are 3-6 months in advance." **Buys 80 mss/year.** Query with published clips and SASE. Length: 200-1,500 words. **Pays $200-500 for assigned articles; $100-250 for unsolicited articles.**

Columns/Departments: Psst (gossip), 100 words; Follow-up (humor), 100 words. **Pays $25-50.** Stolen Moments (topics on new media, Internet and popular culture), 1,000 words. **Pays up to $300.**

Photos: State availability of photos with submissions. Reviews 5×7 prints and/or slides or hi-res photos on disk. Offers no additional payment for photos accepted with ms. Captions, model releases and identification of subjects required. Buys one-time rights.

Tips: "We are mainly interested in articles/interviews with celebrities of national prominence (Hollywood, music, authors, politicians, businesspeople in the media). Profiles must be based on personal interviews. As a rule, profiles should be tough, revealing, exciting and entertaining."

$ REUNIONS MAGAZINE, P.O. Box 11727, Milwaukee WI 53211-0727. (414)263-4567. Fax: (414)263-6331. E-mail: reunions@execpc.com. Website: www.reunionsmag.com. **Contact:** Edith Wagner, editor. **75% freelance written.** Quarterly magazine covering reunions—all aspects, all types. "*Reunions Magazine* is primarily for people actively involved with family, class, military and other reunions. We want easy, practical ideas about organizing, planning, researching/searching, attending or promoting reunions." Estab. 1990. Circ. 18,000. Pays on publication. Publishes ms an average of 1 year after acceptance (but often pulls a particularly hot submission ahead of the pack!). Byline given. Buys one-time rights. Editorial lead time minimum 6 months. Submit seasonal material 1 year in advance. Accepts queries by mail, e-mail, fax; appreciates e-mail submissions. Responds in 1 year. "We're so swamped we get years behind. We appreciate patience!" Sample copy free or on website. Writer's guidelines for #10 SASE or on website.

Nonfiction: How-to, travel—all must be reunion-related, historical/nostalgic, humor, interview/profile, new product, personal experience, reunion recipes with reunion anecdote, photo feature. "We can never get enough about activities at reunions, particularly family reunions with multigenerational activities. We would also like more reunion food-related material." Needs reviewers for books, videos, software (include your requirements). Special issues: Ethnic/African-American family reunions (Winter); Food, Kids stuff, theme parks, small venues (bed & breakfasts, dormitories, condos) (Summer); Golf, Travel and Gaming features (Autumn); Themes, cruises, ranch reunions and reunions in various sections of the US (Spring). **Buys 25 mss/year.** Query with published clips. Length: 500-2,500 words. **Pays $25.** Often rewards with generous copies.

Reprints: Send tearsheet or photocopy of article or typed ms with rights for sale noted and information about when and where the article previously appeared. **Usually pays $10.**

Photos: State availability of photos with submission. Reviews contact sheets, negatives, 35mm transparencies and prints. Offers no additional payment for photos accepted with ms. Captions, model releases and identification of individuals or small groups required. Buys one-time rights. Always looking for vertical cover photos that scream: "Reunion!"

Fillers: Anecdotes, facts, news, short humor—must be reunion-related. **Buys 20/year.** Length: 50-250 words. **Pays $5.**

▣ The online magazine carries original content and includes writer's guidelines and articles. Contact: Edith Wagner, online editor.

Tips: "All copy must be reunion-related with strong reunion examples and experiences. Write a lively account of an interesting or unusual reunion, either upcoming or soon afterward while it's hot. Tell readers why reunion is special, what went into planning it and how attendees reacted. Our *Masterplan* section is a great place for a freelancer to start. Send us how-tos or tips on any aspect of reunion organizing. Open your minds to different types of reunions—they're all around!"

$ $ $ $ ROBB REPORT, The Magazine for the Luxury Lifestyle, 1 Acton Place, Acton MA 01720. (978)795-3000. Fax: (978)795-3266. E-mail: robb@robbreport.com. Website: www.robbreport.com. **Contact:** Steven Castle, editor. **60% freelance written.** Monthly magazine. "We are a lifestyle magazine geared toward active, affluent readers. Addresses upscale autos, luxury travel, boating, technology, lifestyles, watches, fashion, sports, investments, collectibles." Estab. 1976. Circ. 111,000. Pays on publication. Byline given. Offers 50% kill fee. Buys all rights or first North American serial rights. Submit seasonal material 5 months in advance. Accepts queries by mail, fax. Responds in 2 months to queries; 1 month to mss. Sample copy for $10.95 plus shipping and handling. Writer's guidelines for #10 SASE.

Nonfiction: General interest (autos, lifestyle, etc.), interview/profile (prominent personalities/entrepreneurs), new product (autos, boats, consumer electronics), travel (international and domestic). Special issues: Home issue (October); Recreation (March). **Buys 60 mss/year.** Query with published clips if available. Length: 500-3,500 words. **Pays $150-2,000.** Sometimes pays expenses of writers on assignment.

Photos: State availability of photos with submission. Payment depends on article. Buys one-time rights.

■ The online magazine carries original content not found in the print edition. Contact: Steven Castle.

Tips: "Show zest in your writing, immaculate research and strong thematic structure, and you can handle most any assignment. We want to put the reader there, whether the article is about test driving a car, fishing for marlin, touring a luxury home or profiling a celebrity. The best articles will be those that tell compelling stories. Anecdotes should be used liberally, especially for leads, and the fun should show in your writing."

$ $ THE SATURDAY EVENING POST, The Saturday Evening Post Society, 1100 Waterway Blvd., Indianapolis IN 46202. (317)636-8881. Fax: (317)637-0126. E-mail: satevepst@aol.com. Website: www.satevepost.org. **Contact:** Patricia Perry, managing editor. Travel Editor: Holly Miller. **30% freelance written.** Bimonthly general interest, family-oriented magazine focusing on physical fitness, preventive medicine. "Ask almost any American if he or she has heard of *The Saturday Evening Post*, and you will find that many have fond recollections of the magazine from their childhood days. Many readers recall sitting with their families on Saturdays awaiting delivery of their *Post* subscription in the mail. *The Saturday Evening Post* has forged a tradition of 'forefront journalism.' *The Saturday Evening Post* continues to stand at the journalistic forefront with its coverage of health, nutrition, and preventive medicine." Estab. 1728. Circ. 400,000. Pays on publication. Publishes ms an average of 3 months after acceptance. Byline given. Buys second serial (reprint) and all rights. Submit seasonal material 4 months in advance. Accepts queries by mail, fax. Accepts simultaneous submissions. Responds in 1 month to queries; 6 weeks to mss. Writer's guidelines for #10 SASE or on website.

Nonfiction: Book excerpts, general interest, how-to (gardening, home improvement), humor, interview/profile, travel. "No political articles or articles containing sexual innuendo or hypersophistication." **Buys 25 mss/year.** Query with or without published clips, or send complete ms. Length: 750-2,500 words. **Pays $150 minimum**, negotiable maximum for assigned articles. Sometimes pays expenses of writers on assignment.

Photos: State availability of photos with submission. Reviews negatives and transparencies. Offers $50 minimum, negotiable maximum per photo. Model release, identification required. Buys one-time or all rights.

Columns/Departments: Travel (destinations); Post Scripts (well-known humorists); Post People (activities of celebrities). **Buys 16 mss/year.** Query with published clips or send complete ms. Length: 750-1,500 words. **Pays $150 minimum,** negotiable maximum.

Poetry: Light verse.

Fillers: Post Scripts Editor: Steve Pettinga. Anecdotes, short humor. **Buys 200/year.** Length: 300 words. **Pays $15.**

Tips: "Areas most open to freelancers are Health, Fitness, Research Breakthroughs, Nutrition, Post Scripts and Travel. For travel we like text-photo packages, pragmatic tips, side bars and safe rather than exotic destinations. Query by mail, not phone. Send clips."

$ $ $ $ SMITHSONIAN MAGAZINE, 900 Jefferson Dr., Washington DC 20560-0406. (202)786-2900. E-mail: siarticles@aol.com. Website: http://www.smithsonianmag.si.edu. **Contact:** Marlane A. Liddell, articles editor. **90% freelance written.** Prefers to work with published/established writers. Monthly magazine for associate members of the Smithsonian Institution; 85% with college education. "*Smithsonian Magazine*'s mission is to inspire fascination with all the world has to offer by featuring unexpected and entertaining editorial that explores different lifestyles, cultures and peoples, the arts, the wonders of nature and technology, and much more. The highly educated, innovative readers of *Smithsonian* share a unique desire to celebrate life, seeking out the timely as well as the timeless, the artistic as well as the academic and the thought-provoking as well as the humorous." Circ. 2,300,000. Buys first North American serial rights. "Payment for each article to be negotiated depending on our needs and the article's length and excellence." **Pays on acceptance.** Publishes ms an average of 6 months after acceptance. Editorial leadtime 2 months. Submit seasonal material 3 months in advance. Responds in 2 months. Sample copy for $5, % Judy Smith. Writer's guidelines for #10 SASE or on website.

○⊸ "We consider focused subjects that fall within the general range of Smithsonian Institution interests, such as: cultural history, physical science, art and natural history. We are always looking for offbeat subjects and profiles. We do not consider fiction, poetry, travel features, political and news events, or previously published articles. We publish only twelve issues a year, so it is difficult to place an article in *Smithsonian*, but please be assured that all proposals are considered."

Nonfiction: "Our mandate from the Smithsonian Institution says we are to be interested in the same things which now interest or should interest the Institution: cultural and fine arts, history, natural sciences, hard sciences, etc." Query with clips. **Buys 120-130 feature articles** (up to 5,000 words) **and 12 short pieces** (500-650 words)/year. **Pays various rates per feature, $1,500 per short piece.** Pays expenses of writers on assignment.
   ● Ranked as one of the best markets for freelance writers in *Writer's Yearbook* magazine's annual "Top 100 Markets," January 2000.
Photos: Purchased with or without ms and on assignment. Captions required. Pays $400/full color page. "Illustrations are not the responsibility of authors, but if you do have photographs or illustration materials, please include a selection of them with your submission. In general, 35mm color transparencies or black-and-white prints are perfectly acceptable. Photographs published in the magazine are usually obtained through assignments, stock agencies or specialized sources. No photo library is maintained and photographs should be submitted only to accompany a specific article proposal."
Columns/Departments: Buys 12-15 department articles/year. Length: 1,000-2,000 words. Back Page humor, 500-650 words. **Pays $1,000 per department article.**
Tips: "We prefer a written proposal of one or two pages as a preliminary query. The proposal should convince us that we should cover the subject, offer descriptive information on how you, the writer, would treat the subject and offer us an opportunity to judge your writing ability. Background information and writing credentials and samples are helpful. All unsolicited proposals are sent to us on speculation and you should receive a reply within eight weeks. Please include a self-addressed stamped envelope. We also accept proposals via electronic mail at siarticles@aol.com. If we decide to commission an article, the writer receives full payment on acceptance of the manuscript. If the article is found unsuitable, one-third of the payment serves as a kill fee."

$ $ $ THE SUN, A Magazine of Ideas, The Sun Publishing Company, 107 N. Roberson St., Chapel Hill NC 27516. (919)942-5282. Website: www.thesunmagazine.org. **Contact:** Sy Safransky, editor. **90% freelance written.** Monthly general interest magazine. "We are open to all kinds of writing, though we favor work of a personal nature." Estab. 1974. Circ. 50,000. Pays on publication. Publishes ms an average of 6 months after acceptance. Byline given. Buys first or one-time rights. Responds in 1 month to queries; 3 months to mss. Sample copy for $5. Send SASE for writer's guidelines or see website.
Nonfiction: Book excerpts, essays, general interest, interview, opinion, personal experience, spiritual. **Buys 36 mss/year.** Send complete ms. Length: 7,000 words maximum. **Pays $300-1,000.** "Complimentary subscription is given in addition to payment (applies to payment for *all* works, not just nonfiction)."
Reprints: Send photocopy of article or short story and information about when and where the article or story previously appeared. Pays 50% of amount paid for an original article or story.
Photos: Send b&w photos with submission. Offers $50-200/photo. Model releases preferred. Buys one-time rights.
Fiction: Literary. "We avoid stereotypical genre pieces like sci-fi, romance, western and horror. Read an issue before submitting." **Buys 30 mss/year.** Send complete ms. Length: 7,000 words maximum. **Pays $300-500 for original fiction.**
   ● Ranked as one of the best markets for fiction writers in *Writer's Digest* magazine's last "Fiction 50."
Poetry: Free verse, prose poems, short and long poems. **Buys 24 poems/year.** Submit maximum 6 poems. **Pays $50-200.**

$ $ $ $ TOWN & COUNTRY, The Hearst Corp., 1700 Broadway, New York NY 10019. (212)903-5000. Fax: (212)765-8308. **Contact:** John Cantrell, deputy editor. **40% freelance written.** Monthly lifestyle magazine. "*Town & Country* is a lifestyle magazine for the affluent market. Features focus on fashion, beauty, travel, interior design, and the arts as well as individuals' accomplishments and contributions to society." Estab. 1846. Circ. 488,000. Pays on acceptance. Offers 25% kill fee. Buys first North American serial and electronic rights. Responds in 1 month to queries.
Nonfiction: "We're looking for engaging service articles for a high income, well-educated audience, in numerous categories: travel, personalities, interior design, fashion, beauty, jewelry, health, city news, country life news, the arts, philanthropy." **Buys 25 mss/year.** Length: column items, 100-300 words; feature stories, 800-2,000 words. **Pays $2/word.** Query by mail only with clips before submitting.
   ● Ranked as one of the best markets for freelance writers in *Writer's Yearbook* magazine's annual "Top 100 Markets," January 2000.
Tips: "We have served the affluent market for over 150 years, and our writers need to be expert in the needs and interests of that market. Most of our freelance writers start by doing short pieces for our front-of-book columns, then progress from there."

$ $ $ TROIKA; Wit, Wisdom & Wherewithal, Lone Tout Publications, Inc., P.O. Box 1006, Weston CT 06883. (203)319-0873. Fax: (203)319-0755. E-mail: etroika@aol.com. Website: www.troikamagazine.com. **Contact:** Celia Meadow, editor. **80% freelance written.** Quarterly magazine covering general interest, lifestyle. "A magazine for men and women seeking a balanced, three-dimensional lifestyle: personal achievement, family commitment, community involvement. Readers are upscale, educated, 30-50 age bracket. The *Troika* generation is a mix of what is called the X generation and the baby boomers. We are that generation. We grew up with sex, drugs and rock 'n roll, but now it really is our turn to make a difference, if we so choose." Estab. 1993. Circ. 120,000. Pays on publication. Publishes ms an average of 6 months after acceptance. Byline given. Buys first North American and Internet rights. Editorial lead time 3 months. Submit seasonal material 6 months in advance. Accepts queries by mail, e-mail. Accepts simultaneous submissions. Responds in 2 months. Sample copy for $5 or on website. Guidelines for #10 SASE or on website.

Nonfiction: Essays, exposé, general interest, international affairs, environment, how-to (leisure activities, pro bono, finance), parenting, culture, humor, inspirational, interview/profile (music-related), personal experience. No celebrity profiles. **Buys 60-80 mss/year.** Query or send complete ms. Length:800-3,000 words. **Pays $200-1,000 for assigned articles; $250-400 for first appearance of unsolicited articles.**

Reprints: Send photocopy with information about when and where the article or story previously appeared.

Photos: State availability of photos with submission. Reviews negatives, transparencies. Offers no additional payment for photos accepted with ms. Captions, model releases, identification of subjects required.

Columns/Departments: Literati; Pub Performances (literary, theater, arts, culture); Blueprints (architecture, interior design, fashion); Body of Facts (science); Hippocratic Horizons (health); Home Technology; Capital Commitments (personal finance); Athletics; Leisure; Mondiale (international affairs); all 750-1,200 words. **Buys 40-60 mss/year.** Query or send complete ms. **Pays $200 maximum.**

Fiction: Adventure, confession, contemporary, historical, mainstream, mystery, novel excerpts, slice-of-life vignettes, suspense. **Buys 4-8 mss/year.** Send complete ms. Length: 3,000 words maximum. **Pays $200 maximum**; $20 for Internet version only.

■ The online magazine carries original content not found in the print edition and includes writer's guidelines.

⚂ $ $ THE WORLD & I, The Magazine for Lifelong Learners, News World Communications, Inc., 3600 New York Ave. NE, Washington DC 20002. (202)635-4000. Fax: (202)269-9353. E-mail: theworldandi@mcimail.com. Website: www.worldandi.com. Editor: Morton A. Kaplan. Executive Editor: Michael Marshall. **Contact:** Gary Rowe, editorial office coordinator. **90% freelance written.** Monthly magazine. "A broad interest magazine for the thinking, educated person." Estab. 1986. Circ. 30,000. Pays on publication. Publishes ms an average of 6 months after acceptance. Byline given. Offers 20% kill fee. Buys all rights. Submit seasonal material 5 months in advance. Responds in 6 weeks to queries; 10 weeks to mss. Sample copy for $5 and 9×12 SASE. Guidelines for #10 SASE.

Nonfiction: "Description of Sections: Current Issues: Politics, economics and strategic trends covered in a variety of approaches, including special report, analysis, commentary and photo essay. The Arts: International coverage of music, dance, theater, film, television, craft, design, architecture, photography, poetry, painting and sculpture—through reviews, features, essays, opinion pieces and a 6-page Gallery of full-color reproductions. Life: Surveys all aspects of life in 22 rotating subsections which include: Travel and Adventure (first person reflections, preference given to authors who provide photographic images), Profile (people or organizations that are 'making a difference'), Food and Garden (must be accompanied by photos), Education, Humor, Hobby, Family, Consumer, Trends, and Health. Send SASE for complete list of subsections. Natural Science: Covers the latest in science and technology, relating it to the social and historical context, under these headings: At the Edge, Impacts, Nature Walk, Science and Spirit, Science and Values, Scientists: Past and Present, Crucibles of Science and Science Essay. Book World: Excerpts from important, timely books (followed by commentaries) and 10-12 scholarly reviews of significant new books each month, including untranslated works from abroad. Covers current affairs, intellectual issues, contemporary fiction, history, moral/religious issues and the social sciences. Currents in Modern Thought: Examines scholarly research and theoretical debate across the wide range of disciplines in the humanities and social sciences. Featured themes are explored by several contributors. Investigates theoretical issues raised by certain current events, and offers contemporary reflection on issues drawn from the whole history of human thought. Culture: Surveys the world's people in these subsections: Peoples (their unique characteristics and cultural symbols), Crossroads (changes brought by the meeting of cultures), Patterns (photo essay depicting the daily life of a distinct culture), Folk Wisdom (folklore and practical wisdom and their present forms), and Heritage (multicultural backgrounds of the American people and how they are bound to the world). Photo Essay: Patterns, a 6- or 8-page photo essay, appears monthly in the Culture section. Emphasis is placed on comprehensive photographic coverage of a people or group, their private or public lifestyle, in a given situation or context. Accompanying word count: 300-500 words. Photos must be from existing stock, no travel subsidy. Life & Ideals, a 6- or 8-page photo essay, occasionally appears in the Life section. First priority is given to those focused on individuals or organizations that are 'making a difference.' Accompanying word count: 700-1,000 words. 'No *National Enquirer*-type articles.' " **Buys 1,200 mss/year.** Query with published clips and SASE. Length: 1,000-5,000 words. Pays on a per-article basis that varies according to the length of the article, the complexity of special research required, and the experience of the author. Seldom pays expenses of writers on assignment.

Reprints: Send typed ms with rights for sale noted and information about when and where the article previously appeared.

Fiction: Publishes novel excerpts.

Poetry: Contact: Arts Editor. Avant-garde, free verse, haiku, light verse, traditional. **Buys 4-6 poems/year.** Query with maximum 5 poems. **Pays $30-75.**

Photos: State availability of photos with submission. Reviews contact sheets, transparencies and prints. Payment negotiable. Model releases and identification of subjects required. Buys one-time rights.

Tips: "We accept articles from journalists, but also place special emphasis on scholarly contributions. It is our hope that the magazine will enable the best of contemporary thought, presented in accessible language, to reach a wider audience than would normally be possible through the academic journals appropriate to any given discipline."

HEALTH & FITNESS

The magazines listed here specialize in covering health and fitness topics for a general audience. Health and fitness magazines have experienced a real boom lately. Most emphasize developing healthy lifestyle choices in exercise, nutrition and general fitness. Many magazines offer alternative healing and therapies that are becoming more mainstream, such as medicinal herbs, health foods and a holistic mind/body approach to well-being. As wellness is a concern to all demographic groups, publishers have developed editorial geared to specific audiences: African-American women, older readers, men, women. Also see the Sports/Miscellaneous section where publications dealing with health and particular sports may be listed. For magazines that cover healthy eating, refer to the Food & Drink section. Many general interest publications are also potential markets for health or fitness articles. ring health topics from a medical perspective are listed in the Medical category of Trade.

N **$ $**ACTION (CANADA) MAGAZINE, Action Communications, Box 577, Porcupine Plain, SK S0E 1H0 Canada. (306)278-3291. Fax: (306)278-3251. E-mail: actionwest@sk.sympatico.ca. Website: www.actioncanada.ca. Editor: Edward Danneberg. **Contact:** Shannon Hill, senior editor. **60% freelance written.** Bimonthly magazine covering health, nutrition and the active lifestyle. "Easy going and straightforward information on nutrition, health, diet, active lifestyle, travel (adventure) in an easy, fun style." Estab. 1994. Circ. 60,000. Pays 90 days after "off sale" date. Publishes ms an average of 9 months after acceptance. Byline given. Offers 10% kill fee. Buys first North American serial or one-time rights. Editorial lead time 3 months. Submit seasonal material 6 months in advance. Accepts queries by mail, e-mail. Responds in 2 weeks to queries. Sample copy for 9×11 SAE with $2 (US) for postage. Writer's guidelines for #10 SASE.

Nonfiction: How-to (active lifestyle, sports, recreation, health, nutrition), interview/profile (Canadian athletes), new product, personal experience, photo feature, travel (adventure). **Buys 8-12 mss/year.** Query. Length: 300-3,000 words. **Pays 10-20¢/word.** Sometimes pays expenses of writers on assignment.

Reprints: Accepts previously published submissions.

Photos: State availability of photos with submission. Reviews 4×6 prints. Negotiates payment individually. Captions, model releases and identification of subjects required. Buys one-time rights.

Columns/Departments: Health Q&A (questions/answers), 200-300 words; Move of the Month (exercise and description), 50-70 words; Book reviews (health, nutrition, active lifestyle), 100-200 words. Query. **Pays 10-20¢/word.**

Tips: "Writers should have qualifications on the subject queried. E-mail with short query and qualifications."

$ $AMERICAN FITNESS, 15250 Ventura Blvd., Suite 200, Sherman Oaks CA 91403. (818)905-0040. Fax: (818)990-5468. Website: http://www.afaa.com. Publisher: Roscoe Fawcett. **Contact:** Raymond Horowitz, senior editor. **75% freelance written.** Eager to work with new/unpublished writers. Bimonthly magazine covering exercise and fitness, health and nutrition. "We need timely, in-depth, informative articles on health, fitness, aerobic exercise, sports nutrition, age-specific fitness and outdoor activity." Circ. 40,000. Pays 6 weeks after publication. Publishes ms an average of 6 months after acceptance. Byline given. Buys all rights. Submit seasonal material 4 months in advance. Accepts queries by mail, fax. Accepts simultaneous submissions. Responds in 6 weeks. Sample copy for $3 and SAE with 6 first-class stamps. Writer's guidelines for SAE.

Nonfiction: Health and fitness, including women's issues (pregnancy, family, pre- and post-natal, menopause and eating disorders); new research findings on exercise techniques and equipment; aerobic exercise; sports nutrition; sports medicine; innovations and trends in aerobic sports; tips on teaching exercise and humorous accounts of fitness motivation; physiology; exposé (on nutritional gimmickry); historical/nostalgic (history of various athletic events); inspirational (sports leader's motivational pieces); interview/profile (fitness figures); new product (plus equipment review); personal experience (successful fitness story); photo feature (on exercise, fitness, new sport); youth and senior fitness; travel (activity adventures). No articles on unsound nutritional practices, popular trends or unsafe exercise gimmicks. **Buys 18-25 mss/year.** Query with published clips or send complete ms. Length: 800-1,200 words. **Pays $200 for features, $80 for news.** Sometimes pays expenses of writers on assignment.

Reprints: Accepts previously published submissions.

Photos: Sports, action, fitness, aquatic aerobics, aerobics competitions and exercise classes. "We are especially interested in photos of high-adrenalin sports like rock climbing and mountain biking." Pays $0 for b&w prints; $35 for transparencies. Captions, model release and identification of subjects required. Usually buys all rights; other rights purchased depend on use of photo.

Columns/Departments: Research (latest exercise and fitness findings); Alternative paths (non-mainstream approaches to health, wellness and fitness); Strength (latest breakthroughs in weight training); Clubscene (profiles and highlights of fitness club industry); Adventure (treks, trails and global challenges); Food (low-fat/non-fat, high-flavor dishes); Homescene (home workout alternatives); Clip 'n' Post (concise exercise research to post in health clubs, offices or on refrigerators). Query with published clips or send complete ms. Length: 800-1,000 words. **Pays $100-140.**

Tips: "Make sure to quote scientific literature or good research studies and several experts with good credentials to validate exercise trend, technique, or issue. Cover a unique aerobics or fitness angle, provide accurate and interesting findings, and write in a lively, intelligent manner. Please, no first person accouts of 'how I lost weight or discovered running.' *AF* is a good place for first-time authors or regularly published authors who want to sell spin-offs or reprints."

insider report

Health & fitness freelancing: a lucrative and diverse market

From free weights to carbohydrates, Chicago-based lawyer-turned-freelance-writer Kelly James-Enger knows her fitness facts. Solid dedication to accuracy and keeping current on health and lifestyle trends has made James-Enger invaluable to editors at more than a dozen magazines, including *Woman's Day*, *Family Circle*, *Marie Claire*, *Cosmopolitan*, *Fitness*, *Fit*, *Good Housekeeping*, and *Shape*.

Kelly James-Enger

How does freelancing for the health & fitness arena differ from freelancing for other topics?
The basics are the same—you need to have good research and interviewing skills, be able to juggle multiple projects, meet deadlines, and come up with story ideas. But because most health and fitness stories tend to reflect current trends, writers have to keep up on the latest trends to be able to pitch timely story ideas.

Are nutrition and exercise the only subjects of interest to the fitness market?
Health and fitness articles encompass a wide variety of subject areas. In addition to the "traditional" stories (e.g., how to reduce your risk of osteoporosis, how to lose those holiday pounds), magazines run stories about mental health issues, alternative health therapies, therapeutic diets, health care techniques, exercise programs, etc.

Some magazines focus on the fitness aspects of exercise, and others focus more on the health benefits. To give you an idea of the breadth of the market, in the past three years I've written about hidden causes of fatigue in women and how to combat them; easy ways to eat healthier; what contraceptive option is right for you; how to maintain your workout routine when you move; how to use a heart rate monitor to get (and stay) fit; the emotional consequences of continual dieting; how to use your brain to get more out of your workouts; and a slew of "typical" workout and diet stories.

What pay scale can new, somewhat experienced and seasoned freelancers expect to face when covering this subject?
Most national consumer magazines start at about one dollar a word for new writers (meaning you haven't worked with the editor before), and will pay more after you've written a couple of stories for the magazine. It really depends on the magazine and the writer, but experienced freelancers can make $1.50-2 a word, and probably more, for health and fitness stories.

What are the most common mistakes health and fitness writers make when writing assignments?

One is not getting enough experts and research to back up your claims. Another mistake is focusing too much on your personal experience instead of reporting the story. If you lost fifty pounds on a low-carb diet, for example, that's great, but unless it's a first person story about your weight loss success, you'll need some other expert sources' anecdotes to flesh out a story on the benefits and dangers of low-carb diets.

What are the easiest sales in the realm of health and fitness?

Most magazines have front-of-the-book sections filled with short, news-driven items. The editors of these sections are nearly always looking for material to fill these, and it's a good place for writers new to the magazine to break in.

What is your best tip for writers just getting started in this genre?

Pick one or two target markets and focus on the types of stories the magazine publishes instead of trying to pitch to a dozen markets at the same time. I've had much more success targeting specific magazines rather than what I call the "saturation-bombing technique," which is based on the theory that if you send out enough queries, you'll sell a story eventually.

What was your favorite assignment, and why was it your favorite?

I really don't have favorite stories, other than those that pay well and get accepted after turning in the first draft! Nearly every story is interesting to me—I enjoy researching and putting the pieces together, and always wind up learning something.

What was your nightmare assignment?

I haven't really had any health and fitness nightmares. I did work on one story for eight months—including the query, a revised and re-slanted query, a first draft and two revisions—that wound up being killed. That was painful, but it helped me develop a thicker skin, which every freelancer needs to have.

For interviews with the pros on more freelance niche markets, see Child Care, page 431; Food & Drink, page 470; Nature, page 594; Personal Computers, page 604; and Travel, page 779.
—*Kelly Milner Halls*

TOP TIP: "The ability to track down experts, well known and respected in their fields, is critical for health and fitness writers. With most stories, you need an expert or a study to back up any claims you're making. Even if the background material doesn't make it into the story, you'll have to turn in the material for fact checking."

$ $ BETTER HEALTH, Better Health Magazine, 1450 Chapel St., New Haven CT 06511-4440. (203)789-3972. Fax: (203)789-4053. **Contact:** Cynthia Wolfe Boynton, editor/publishing director. **90% freelance written.** Prefers to work with published/established writers; will consider new/unpublished writers. Bimonthly magazine devoted to health, wellness and medical issues. Estab. 1979. Circ. 500,000. **Pays on acceptance.** Byline given. Offers 20% kill fee. Buys first rights. Query first; do not send article. Sample copy for $2.50. Writer's guidelines for #10 SASE.

Nonfiction: Wellness/prevention issues are of prime interest. New medical techniques or nonmainstream practices are not considered. No fillers, poems, quizzes, seasonal, heavy humor, inspirational or personal experience. Length: 1,500-3,000 words. **Pays $300-700.**

$ $BETTER NUTRITION, SABOT Publishing, 4 High Ridge Park, Stamford CT 06905. (203)321-1722. Fax: (203)322-0302. E-mail: jamesg@cowles.com. Website: www.betternutrition.com. **Contact:** James J. Gormley, editor-in-chief. **57% freelance written.** Monthly magazine covering nutritional news and approaches to optimal health. "Since 1938, *Better Nutrition*'s mission has been to inform our readers about the latest breakthroughs in nutritional (and lifestyle) approaches to optimal health and ongoing research into supplementation with vitamins, botanicals, minerals and other natural products." Estab. 1938. Circ. 480,000. Pays on publication. Publishes ms an average of 2 months after acceptance. Byline given. Offers 50% kill fee. Rights purchased vary. Editorial lead time 3 months. Accepts queries by mail, e-mail, fax. Sample copy free.

Nonfiction: Clinical research crystallized into accessible articles on nutrition, health, alternative medicine, disease prevention, FDA exposés. Each issue has a featured article (e.g., February, Healthy Heart; April, Organic). **Buys 120-180 mss/year.** Query. Length: 630-1,500 words. **Pays $300-500.** Sometimes pays expenses of writers on assignment.

Photos: State availability of photos with query. Reviews 4×5 transparencies and 3×5 prints. Negotiates payment individually. Captions, model releases, identification of subjects required if applicable. Buys one-time rights or non-exclusive reprint rights.

Columns/Departments: Health Watch; Nutrition News; Women's Health; Earth Medicine; Healing Herbs; Better Hair, Skin & Nails; Herb Update; Health in Balance; Book Zone; Supplement Update; Natural Energy; Children's Health; Sports Nutrition; Earth Watch; Homeopathy; Botanical Medicine; Meatless Meals; Trim Time; Healthier Pets; Ayurvedic Medicine; Longevity; Healing Herbs; Frontiers of Science.

Fillers: Nutrition-related crossword puzzles, sidebars, charts and lists.

Tips: "Be on top of what's newsbreaking in nutrition and supplementation. Interview experts. Be available for one-week-assignment/in-our-hands turnarounds. Fact-check, fact-check, fact-check. Find out what distinguishes us from other consumer-directed industry publications. Send in a résumé (including Social Security/IRS number), a couple of clips and a list of article possibilities."

N ✗ $ $ $COUNTRY LIVING'S HEALTHY LIVING, Hearst Magazines, 1790 Broadway, New York NY 10019. (212)492-1350. Fax: (212)246-3952. Website: www.healthylivingmag.com. Executive Editor: Kathryn Keller. Editor: Rachel Newman. **Contact:** Cheryl Krementz, managing editor. **80% freelance written.** Bimonthly magazine. "*Country Living's Healthy Living* covers alternative health for a mainstream audience. Subjects include nutrition, fitness, beauty, profiles, news, recipes. Most readers are baby boomer women." Estab. 1996. Circ. 350,000. **Pays on acceptance.** Byline given. Offers 15% kill fee. Editorial lead time 3 months. Submit seasonal material 6 months in advance. Accepts simultaneous submissions. Responds in 3 months.

Nonfiction: Book excerpts, essays, general interest, humor, inspirational, interview/profile, new product, opinion, personal experience, photo feature, travel. **Buys 60 mss/year.** Query with published clips or send complete ms on spec. Length: 200-1,500 words. **Pays $75-1,000 for assigned articles; $75-500 for unsolicited articles.** Sometimes pays expenses of writers on assignment.

Reprints: Accepts previously published submissions.

Photos: State availability of photos with submission. Reviews transparencies. Negotiates payment individually. Identification of subjects required. Buys all rights.

Columns/Departments: "Our columnists are already chosen, and departments make up most of the magazine. See the nonfiction list of topics." **Pays $75-800.**

📧 The online magazine carries original content not found in the print edition.

Tips: "Have some knowledge of the world of alternative health. We love it if a writer is reading the journals and attending the conferences, so the ideas are timely."

$ $DELICIOUS!, Your Magazine of Natural Living, New Hope Natural Media, 1401 Pearl St., Suite 200, Boulder CO 80302. E-mail: delicious@newhope.com. Editor Director: Karen Raterman. **Contact:** Debra Bokur, managing editor. **85% freelance written.** Monthly magazine covering natural products, nutrition, alternative medicines, herbal medicines. "*Delicious!* magazine empowers natural foods store shoppers to make health-conscious choices in their lives. Our goal is to improve consumers' perception of the value of natural methods in achieving health. To do this, we educate consumers on nutrition, disease prevention, botanical medicines and natural personal care products." Estab. 1985. Circ. 420,000. **Pays on acceptance.** Publishes ms an average of 6 months after acceptance. Byline given. Offers 20% kill fee. Editorial lead time 4 months. Submit seasonal material 8 months in advance. Accepts simultaneous submissions. Responds in 3 months. Sample copy and writer's guidelines free.

Nonfiction: Book excerpts, how-to, personal experience (regarding natural or alternative health), health nutrition, herbal medicines, alternative medicine. **Buys 150 mss/year.** Query with published clips. Length: 500-2,000 words. **Pays $100-700 for assigned articles; $50-300 for unsolicited articles.**

Photos: State availability of photos with submission. Reviews 3×5 prints. Offers no additional payment for photos accepted with ms. Identification of subjects required. Buys one-time rights.

Columns/Departments: Herbal Kingdom (scientific evidence supporting herbal medicines) 1,500 words; Nutrition (new research on diet for good health) 1,200 words; Dietary Supplements (new research on vitamins/minerals, etc.) 1,200 words. Query with published clips. **Pays $100-500.**

Tips: "Highlight any previous health/nutrition/medical writing experience. Demonstrate a knowledge of natural medicine, nutrition, or natural products. Health practitioners who demonstrate writing ability are ideal freelancers."

$ $ FIT, Goodman Media Group, Inc., 1700 Broadway, 34th Floor, New York NY 10019. (212)541-7100. Fax: (212)245-1241. **Contact:** Lisa Klugman, editor. **50% freelance written.** Works with a small number of new/unpublished writers each year. Bimonthly magazine covering fitness and health for active, young women. Circ. 125,000. Pays on publication. Publishes ms an average of 5 months after acceptance. Byline given. Offers 20% kill fee. Buys all rights. Submit seasonal material 6 months in advance. Accepts queries by mail, e-mail. Responds in 1 month if rejecting ms, longer if considering for publication.

    ⌐ Break in by sending writing samples (preferably published) and a long list of queries/article ideas. The magazine reports it is looking for first-person accounts of new and interesting sports, adventures, etc.

Nonfiction: Health, fitness, sports, beauty, psychology, relationships, athletes and nutrition. "We get many queries on how to treat/handle many physical and mental ailments—we wouldn't do an entire article on an illness that only 5% or less of the population suffers from." **Buys 20 mss/year.** Query with published clips. No phone queries. Length: 1,000-1,500 words.

Photos: Reviews contact sheets, transparencies, prints. Model releases, identification of subjects required. Buys all rights.

Columns/Departments: Finally Fit Contest. Readers can submit "before and after" success stories along with color slides or photos. **Pays $100.**

Tips: "We strive to provide the latest health and fitness news in an entertaining way—that means coverage of real people (athletes, regular women, etc.) and/or events (fitness shows, marathons, etc.), combined with factual information. First-person is okay. Looking for stories that are fun to read, revealing, motivational and informative."

$ $ $ $ FITNESS MAGAZINE, 375 Lexington Ave., New York NY 10017-5514. (212)499-2000. Fax: (212)499-1568. **Contact**: Carla Levy, executive editor. "Do not call." Monthly magazine for women in their twenties and thirties who are interested in fitness and living a healthy life. **Pays on acceptance**. Byline given. Offers 20% kill fee. Buys first North American serial rights. Responds in 2 months to queries. Writer's guidelines for #10 SASE.

Nonfiction: "We need timely, well-written nonfiction articles on exercise and fitness, beauty, health, diet/nutrition, and psychology. We always include boxes and sidebars in our stories." **Buys 60-80 mss/year.** Query. Length: 1,500-2,500 words. **Pays $1,500-2,500.** Pays expenses of writers on assignment.

    ● Ranked as one of the best markets for freelance writers in *Writer's Yearbook* magazine's annual "Top 100 Markets," January 2000.

Reprints: Accepts previously published submissions. Send photocopy of article. Negotiates fee.

Columns/Departments: Buys 30 mss/year. Query. Length: 600-1,200 words. **Pays $800-1,500.**

Tips: "Our pieces must get inside the mind of the reader and address her needs, hopes, fears and desires. *Fitness* acknowledges that getting and staying fit is difficult in an era when we are all time-pressured."

Ⓝ ✪ ▣ $ $ FITNESSLINK, FitnessLink Inc., 113 Circle Dr. S., Lambertville NJ 08530. Fax: (609)397-7347. E-mail: shannon@fitnesslink.com. Website: www.fitnesslink.com. **Contact:** Shannon Entin, publisher and editor. **90% freelance written**. Daily consumer website covering fitness, sports, exercise and nutrition. "*FitnessLink* is an online fitness ezine, publishing the truth about fitness, sports training, and nutrition in our irreverent, 'tell it like it is' style. We dig beneath the sound bites to reveal the truth behind health and fitness fads." Estab. 1996. Circ. 800,000. Pays on publication. Publishes ms an average of 1 month after acceptance. Byline given. Buys first serial rights. Editorial lead time 1 month. Submit seasonal material 2 months in advance. Accepts queries by mail, e-mail, fax. Responds in 2 weeks. Writer's guidelines available at www.fitnesslink.com/info/guide.shtml.

Nonfiction: How-to (exercise, sports, nutrition), workout programs, personal experience of extreme sport adventures or fitness makeovers, interview/profile, new product reviews. **Buys 200 mss/year.** Length: 200-1,200 words. **Pays $40-400.**

Photos: State availability of photos with submission. Reviews prints. Offers payment for photos in some cases. Identification of subject required.

Tips: "We're looking for specific workouts for sports and 'adventure' activities. Since our publication is online, we archive all of our articles. It's important for writers to be aware of what we have already published and not duplicate the idea."

$ $ $ $ HEALTH, Time, Inc., Two Embarcadero Center, Suite 600, San Francisco CA 94111. (415)248-2700. Fax: (415)248-2779. Website: www.healthmag.com. Editor-in-Chief: Barbara Paulsen. **Contact**: Tiffinie P. McEntire, assistant to the editor. Magazine published 9 times/year on health, fitness and nutrition. "Our readers are predominantly college-educated women in their 30s, 40s and 50s. Edited to focus not on illness, but on events, ideas and people." Estab. 1987. Circ. 1,050,000. **Pays on acceptance**. Byline given. Offers 25% kill fee. Buys first North American serial rights. Accepts queries by mail, fax. Accepts simultaneous submissions. Responds in 2 months to queries. Sample copy for $5 to "Back Issues." Writer's guidelines for #10 SASE. "No phone calls, please."

    ● *Health* stresses that writers must send for guidelines before sending a query, and that only queries that closely follow the guidelines get passed on to editors.

Nonfiction: Buys 25 mss/year. No unsolicited mss. Query with published clips and SASE. Length: 1,200 words. **Pays $1,800.** Pays the expenses of writers on assignment.

Columns/Departments: Food, Mind, Healthy Looks, Fitness, Mind, Relationships.

Tips: "We look for well-articulated ideas with a narrow focus and broad appeal. A query that starts with an unusual local event and hooks it legitimately to some national trend or concern is bound to get our attention. Use quotes, examples and statistics to show why the topic is important and why the approach is workable. We need to see clear evidence of credible research findings pointing to meaningful options for our readers. Stories should offer practical advice and give clear explanations."

\$ \$ \$ \$ HEART & SOUL, Health, Fitness and Beauty for African-American Women, Black Entertainment Television (BET), One BET Plaza, 1900 W. Place NE, Washington DC 20018. (202)608-2241. Fax: (202)608-2598. E-mail: heartandsoul@BET.net. Website: www.BET.com. Editorial Director: Yanick Rice Lamb. **Contact:** Barbranda Lumpkins Walls, managing editor. Bimonthly magazine covering how-to health, fitness, nutrition, beauty, travel, weight loss, parenting, relationships, spirituality; information researched and edited specifically for African-Americans. Estab. 1993. Circ. 300,000. **Pays on acceptance**. Byline given. Offers 25% kill fee. Buys all rights or first North American serial rights. Editorial lead time 9 months. Submit seasonal material 6 months in advance. Accepts queries by mail, fax. Writer's guidelines available upon request.

Nonfiction: Book excerpts, how-to (health, fitness, beauty), relationships, interview/profile, humor, spiritual health. Query with published clips. Length: 1,200-1,800 words. **Pays 75¢-$1/word for assigned articles.** Pays itemized expenses of writers on assignment.

Columns/Departments: My Body (personal experience, healthy weight loss); Livin' Healthy (health news); Well-Being (mind, body and spirit); Healthy Vacations; Family Health; Male Call (male relationships column); Sanctuary (relaxing environments); Natural Healing; Natural Beauty; Nutrition; Soul Kitchen; Best Medicine (humor).

■ The online magazine carries original content not found in the print edition. Contact: Tanishia Harvey, online editor.

Tips: "Writers should be experienced in health and service writing and knowledgeable about issues important to African-American women. Please query; no phone calls."

\$ \$ \$ LET'S LIVE MAGAZINE, Franklin Publications, Inc., 320 N. Larchmont Blvd., P.O. Box 74908, Los Angeles CA 90004-3030. (323)469-3901. Fax: (323)469-9597. E-mail: info@letslivemag.com. Website: www.letsliveonline.com. Editor-in-Chief: Beth Salmon. **Contact:** Nicole Brechka, assistant editor or Laura Barnaby, managing editor. Monthly magazine emphasizing health and preventive medicine. "Our editorial mission at *Let's Live* is to encourage readers to manage and promote their own health and well-being by providing well-researched, authoritative and practical information on preventive and complementary medicine, natural health products and the importance of an active lifestyle." **95% freelance written.** Works with a small number of new/unpublished writers each year; expertise in health field helpful. Estab. 1933. Circ. 1,700,000. Pays within 30 days. Publishes ms an average of 4 months after acceptance. Buys all rights. Byline given. Submit seasonal material 6 months in advance. Accepts queries by mail, e-mail, fax. Responds in 2 months to queries; 3 months to mss. Sample copy for $5 and 10×13 SAE with 6 first-class stamps or on website. Writer's guidelines for #10 SASE.

● The editors are looking for more cutting-edge, well-researched natural health information that is substantiated by experts and well-respected scientific research literature.

Nonfiction: General interest (effects of vitamins, minerals, herbs and nutrients in improvement of health or afflictions); historical (documentation of experiments or treatment establishing value of nutrients as boon to health); how-to (enhance natural beauty, exercise/bodybuilding, acquire strength and vitality, improve health of adults and/or children and prepare tasty, healthy meals); interview (benefits of research in establishing prevention as key to good health); personal opinion (views of orthomolecular doctors or their patients on value of health foods toward maintaining good health); profile (background and/or medical history of preventive medicine, M.D.s or Ph.D.s, in advancement of nutrition). Manuscripts must be well-researched, reliably documented and written in a clear, readable style. "No pre-written articles or mainstream medicine pieces such as articles on drugs or surgery". **Buys 2-4 mss/issue.** Query with published clips and SASE. Length: 1,200-1,400 words. **Pays $850-1,200 for features.**

Columns/Departments: Sports Nutrition (Expert Column, Your Personal Trainer), Natural Medicine Chest, Herbs for Health, Millennium Medicine. Query with published clips and SASE. Length: 1,200-1,400 words. **Pays $700.**

Photos: Send photos. Pays $50 for 8×10 color prints, 35mm transparencies. Captions, model releases required.

Tips: "We want writers with experience in researching nonsurgical medical subjects and interviewing experts with the ability to simplify technical and clinical information for the layman. A captivating lead and structural flow are essential. The most frequent mistakes made by writers are in writing articles that are too technical, in poor style, written for the wrong audience (publication not thoroughly studied), or have unreliable documentation or overzealous faith in the topic reflected by flimsy research and inappropriate tone."

N ⊠ \$ \$ \$ LIFE EXTENSION MAGAZINE, 1881 N.E. 26th St., #221, Fort Lauderdale FL 33305. (954)561-7909. Fax: (954)561-8335. E-mail: lemagazine@lef.com. Website: www.lef.org. **Contact:** Rocio Paola Yaffar, editor-in-chief. **80% freelance written.** Monthly magazine covering "health care, scientific findings, medical research, alternative medicines, natural therapies. *Life Extension* covers all aspects of health and longevity, with particular emphasis on alternative therapies, dietary supplements, and anti-aging research. Rigorous medical/science articles are complemented by articles on healthy people." Estab. 1994. Circ. 101,000. **Pays on acceptance**. Publishes ms an average of 2 months after acceptance. Byline given. Buys first North American serial rights. Editorial lead time 3 months. Accepts simultaneous submissions. Accepts queries by mail, e-mail. Responds in 1 month.

Nonfiction: Book excerpts, general interest, interview/profile, opinion, personal experience, company profiles, case histories. **Buys 60 mss/year.** Query or query with published clips. Length: 2,000-4,000 words. **Pays 50¢/word.** Pays expenses of writers on assignment.

Reprints: Send typed ms with rights for sale noted and information about when and where the article appeared.

Photos: State availability of photos with submission. Reviews transparencies. Negotiates payment individually. Identification of subjects required. Buys all rights.

Columns/Departments: Point of view (opinion of aspects of the alternative medicine/medical/health care world), 1,500-2,000 words. **Buys 12 mss/year.** Query with published clips. **Pays 50¢/word.**

▣ The online magazine carries original content found in the print edition.

Tips: "A working knowledge of how to access medical research/abstracts essential (online or otherwise). Important to understand how latest research affects real people with therapies they can use now."

N ✫ $ $ $ MAMM MAGAZINE, Courage, Respect & Survival, Poz Publishing L.L.C., 349 W. 12th St., New York NY 10014. (212)242-2163. Fax: (212)675-8505. E-mail: elsieh@mamm.com. Website: www.mamm.com. Managing Editor: Craig Moskowitz. **Contact:** Gwen Darien, editor. **100% freelance written.** Monthly women's magazine focusing on cancer prevention, treatment and survival. "*MAMM* gives its readers the essential tools and emotional support they need before, during and after diagnosis of breast, ovarian and other female reproductive cancers. We offer a mix of survivor profiles, conventional and alternative treatment information, investigative features, essays and cutting-edge news." Estab. 1997. Circ. 91,000. Pays within 45 days of acceptance. Publishes ms an average of 5 months after acceptance. Byline given. Offers 20% kill fee. Buys exclusive rights up to 90 days after publishing, first rights after that. Editorial lead time 4 months. Submit seasonal material 4 months in advance. Accepts simultaneous submissions. Sample copy and writers guidelines free on request.

Nonfiction: Book excerpts, essays, exposé, historical/nostalgic, how-to, humor, inspirational, interview/profile, opinion, personal experience, photo features. **Buys 90 mss/year.** Query with published clips. Length: 200-3,000 words. **Pays $50-1,000.** Sometimes pays expenses of writers on assignment.

● Ranked as one of the best markets for freelance writers in *Writer's Yearbook* magazine's "Top 100 Markets," January 2000.

Photos: Send photos with submission. Reviews contact sheets and negatives. Negotiates payment individually. Identification of subjects required. Buys first rights.

Columns/Departments: Cancer Girl (humor/experience); Opinion (cultural/political); International Dispatch (experience); all 600 words. **Buys 30 mss/year.** Query with published clips. **Pays $200-250.**

Fiction: Adventure, confession, historical, humorous, mainstream, novel excerpts, romance, science fiction, slice-of-life vignettes, must relate to women's health issues. **Buys 6 mss/year.** Query with published clips. Please inquire for word length and payment.

Poetry: Avant-garde, free verse, haiku, light verse, traditional. **Buys 6 poems/year.** Submit maximum 3 poems. Length: 10-40 lines. **Pays $100-150.**

Fillers: Anecdotes, facts, gags to be illustrated, newsbreaks. **Buys 30/year.** Length: 50-150 words. **Pays $50-75.**

$ $ MASSAGE MAGAZINE, Keeping Those Who Touch—In Touch, 200 Seventh Ave. #240, Santa Cruz CA 95062. (408)477-1176. Fax: (408)477-2918. E-mail: edit@massagemag.com. Website: www.massagemag.com. **Contact:** Karen Menehan, editor. **40% freelance written.** Prefers to work with published/established writers. Bimonthly magazine on massage-bodywork and related healing arts. Estab. 1985. Circ. 45,000. Pays on publication. Publishes ms an average of 1 year after acceptance. Byline given. Buys first North American rights. Accepts queries by mail, e-mail. Responds in 2 months to queries; 3 months to mss. Sample copy and writer's guidelines free.

Nonfiction: General interest, how-to, experiential, inspirational, interview/profile, photo feature, technical. Length: 600-2,000 words. **Pays $50-300 for articles.**

Reprints: Send tearsheet of article and typed ms with rights for sale noted and information about when and where the article previously appeared. Pays 50-75% of amount paid for an original article.

Photos: Send photos with submission. Offers $10-25/photo. Identification of subjects and photographer required. Buys one-time rights.

Columns/Departments: Touching Tales (experiential); Profiles; Table Talk (news briefs); Practice Building (business); Technique; Body/mind. Length: 800-1,200 words. **Pays $50-300** for most of these columns.

Fillers: Facts, news briefs. Length: 100-800 words. **Pays $125 maximum.**

Tips: "In-depth feature articles that detail the benefits of massage are a high priority."

$ $ $ $ MEN'S HEALTH, Rodale, 33 E. Minor St., Emmaus PA 18098. (610)967-5171. Fax: (610)967-7725. E-mail: tmcgrat1@rodalepress.com. Website: www.menshealth.com. Editor: Greg Gutfeld. Executive Editor: Peter Moore. **Contact:** Tom McGrath, deputy editor. **50% freelance written.** Prefers to work with established/published writers. Magazine published 10 times/year covering men's health and fitness. "*Men's Health* is a lifestyle magazine showing men the practical and positive actions that make their lives better, with articles covering fitness, nutrition, relationships, travel, careers, grooming and health issues." Estab. 1986. Circ. 1.6 million. **Pays on acceptance.** Offers 25% kill fee. Buys all rights. Accepts queries by mail, fax. Responds in 3 weeks. Writer's guidelines for SASE.

○━ Freelancers have the best chance with the front-of-the-book piece, Malegrams.

Nonfiction: "Authoritative information on all aspects of men's physical and emotional health. We rely on writers to seek out the right experts and to either tell a story from a first-person vantage or get good anecdotes." **Buys 30 features/year, 360 short pieces/year.** Query with published clips and SASE. Length: 1,200-4,000 words for features, 100-300 words for short pieces. **Pays $1,000-5,000 for features, $100-500 for short pieces.**

● Ranked as one of the best markets for freelance writers in *Writer's Yearbook* magazine's annual "Top 100 Markets," January 2000.

Columns/Departments: Buys 80 mss/year. Length: 750-1,500 words. **Pays $750-2,000.**

▣ The online magazine carries original content not included in the print edition. Contact: Fred Zahradnick, online associate.

Tips: "We have a wide definition of health. We believe that being successful in every area of your life is being healthy. The magazine focuses on all aspects of health, from stress issues to nutrition to exercise to sex. It is 50% staff written, 50% from freelancers. The best way to break in is not by covering a particular subject, but by covering it within the magazine's style. There is a very particular tone and voice to the magazine. A writer has to be a good humor writer as well as a good service writer. Prefers mail queries. No phone calls, please."

$ $ $ MUSCLE & FITNESS, The Science of Living Super-Fit, Weider Health & Fitness, 21100 Erwin St., Woodland Hills, CA 91367. (818)884-6800. Fax: (818)595-0463. Website: www.muscle-fitness.com. Editor: Bill Geiger. **Contact:** Vincent Scalisi, editorial director; Bill Geiger, editor (training and other articles); Jo Ellen Krumm, managing editor (nutrition and food articles). **50% freelance written.** Monthly magazine covering bodybuilding and fitness for healthy, active men and women. It contains a wide range of features and monthly departments devoted to all areas of bodybuilding, health, fitness, injury prevention and treatment, and nutrition. Editorial fulfills two functions: information and entertainment. Special attention is devoted to how-to advice and accuracy. Estab. 1950. Circ. 500,000. **Pays on acceptance.** Publishes ms an average of 2 months after acceptance. Offers 25-40% kill fee. Buys all rights and second serial (reprint) rights. Editorial lead time 5 months. Submit seasonal material 6 months in advance. Accepts queries by mail, fax. Accepts simultaneous submissions. Responds in 2 weeks to queries.

Nonfiction: Bill Geiger, editor. Book excerpts, how-to (training), humor, interview/profile, photo feature. **Buys 120 mss/year.** "All features and departments are written on assignment." Query with published clips. Length: 800-1,800 words. **Pays $250-800.** Pays expenses of writers on assignment.

Reprints: Send photocopy of article or typed ms with rights for sale noted and information about when and where the article previously appeared. Payment varies.

Photos: State availability of photos with submission.

Tips: "Know bodybuilders and bodybuilding. Read our magazine regularly (or at least several issues), come up with new information or a new angle on our subject matter (bodybuilding training, psychology, nutrition, diets, fitness, etc.), then pitch us in terms of providing useful, unique, how-to information for our readers. Send a one-page query letter (as described in *Writer's Market*) to sell us on your idea and on you as the best writer for that article. Send a sample of your published work. If we like your idea and assign the article, be sure to research and fact-check it thoroughly, write and edit it carefully and turn it in on time. Act like a professional even if you're just beginning your freelance career."

★ $ $ MUSCLE MAG INTERNATIONAL, 6465 Airport Rd., Mississauga, Ontario L4V 1E4 Canada. (905)678-7311. Fax: (905)678-9236. **Contact:** Johnny Fitness, editor. **80% freelance written.** "We do not care if a writer is known or unknown; published or unpublished. We simply want good instructional articles on bodybuilding." Monthly magazine for 16- to 60-year-old men and women interested in physical fitness and overall body improvement. Estab. 1972. Circ. 300,000. **Pays on acceptance.** Publishes ms an average of 4 months after acceptance. Byline given. Buys all rights. Sample copy for $5 and 9 × 12 SAE. Accepts queries by mail, fax, phone. Submit complete ms with IRCs. Responds in 2 months.

Nonfiction: Articles on ideal physical proportions and importance of supplements in the diet, training for muscle size. Should be helpful and instructional and appeal to young men and women who want to live life in a vigorous and healthy style. "We would like to see articles for the physical culturist on new muscle building techniques or an article on fitness testing." Informational, how-to, personal experience, interview, profile, inspirational, humor, historical, expose, nostalgia, personal opinion, photo, spot news, new product, merchandising technique. "Also now actively looking for good instructional articles on Hardcore Fitness." **Buys 200 mss/year.** Length: 1,200-1,600 words. **Pays 20¢/word.** Sometimes pays the expenses of writers on assignment.

Columns/Departments: Nutrition Talk (eating for top results), Shaping Up (improving fitness and stamina). Length: 1,300 words. **Pays 20¢/word.**

Photos: Color and b&w photos are purchased with or without ms. Pays $50 for 8 × 10 glossy exercise photos; $50 for 8 × 10 b&w posing shots. Pays $200-1,000 for color cover and $50 for color used inside magazine (transparencies). More for "special" or "outstanding" work.

Fillers: Newsbreaks, puzzles, quotes of the champs. Length: open. **Pays $10 minimum.**

Tips: "The best way to break in is to seek out the muscle-building 'stars' and do in-depth interviews with biography in mind. Color training picture support essential. Writers have to make their articles informative in that readers can apply them to help gain bodybuilding success. Specific fitness articles should quote experts and/or use scientific studies to strengthen their theories. Write strong articles full of 'how-to' information. We want to genuinely help our readers build better, fitter, stronger bodies."

$ $ $ $ NATURAL HEALTH, Weider Publications, Inc., 70 Lincoln St., 5th Floor, Boston MA 02111. (617)753-8900. Fax: (617)457-0966. E-mail: naturalhealth@weiderpub.com. Website: www.naturalhealthmag.com. Editor: Rachel Streit. **Contact:** Clare Horn, research editor. **50% freelance written.** Magazine published 9 times/year covering alternative health and natural living. "We are an authoritative guide to the best in mind, body and spirit self-care." Estab. 1971. Circ. 425,000. **Pays on acceptance**. Publishes ms an average of 3 months after acceptance. Byline given. Offers 33% kill fee. Buys first rights and reprint rights. Editorial lead time 6 months. Submit seasonal material 6 months in advance. Accepts simultaneous submissions. Responds in 3 months to queries. Sample articles on website.

　O➤ Break in with a well-researched News & Notes piece.

Nonfiction: Book excerpts, exposé, how-to, inspirational, personal experience. No fiction, reprints from other publications or event coverage. **Buys 20 mss/year.** Query by mail with published clips. Length: 150-3,000 words. **Pays $75-2,000.** Sometimes pays the expenses of writers on assignment.

　• Ranked as one of the best markets for freelance writers in *Writer's Yearbook* magazine's annual "Top 100 Markets," January 2000.

Photos: State availability of photos with submission. Buys one-time rights.

Columns/Departments: My Story (personal account of illness or condition treated naturally), 1,500 words. **Buys 9 mss/year. Pays $100.** New & Notes (health, fitness, body care news briefs), 125 words. **Buys 20 mss/year. Pays $75.** Readers On (personal reflections on selected topics; see latest issue for topic), 100-500 words. Query.

Tips: "Read the magazine. The recipes are always vegan. The products are non-chemical. Read books written by the advisory board members: Andrew Weil, James Gordon, Joseph Pizzorno, Jennifer Jacobs, etc."

$ $ $ $ NEW CHOICES, Living Even Better After 50, Reader's Digest Publications, Inc., Reader's Digest Rd., Plesantville NY 10570. Fax: (914)244-5888. E-mail: newchoices@readersdigest.com. **Contact:** Elaine Rubino, editorial administrative assistant. Magazine published 10 times/year. "*New Choices* is a lifestyle service magazine for adults 50 and over. Editorial focuses on health, money, food and travel." Estab. 1960. Circ. 600,000.

Nonfiction: Planning for retirement, personal health and fitness, financial strategies, housing options, travel, relationships, leisure pursuits. **Buys 60 mss/year.** Length: 500-2,000 words. **Pays $1/word,** negotiable. Query with 2-3 published clips and SASE. No phone calls.

Columns/Departments: Personal essays, online, bargains, taxes, cooking, travel, style. **Buys 84 mss/year.** Pay varies. Query with 2-3 published clips. No phone calls.

$ $ $ OXYGEN!, Serious Fitness for Serious Women, Muscle Mag International, 6465 Airport Rd., Mississauga, Ontario L4V 1E4 Canada. (905)678-7311. Fax: (905)678-9236. **Contact:** Pamela Cottrell, editor. **70% freelance written.** Bimonthly magazine covering women's health and fitness. "*Oxygen* encourages various exercise, good nutrition to shape and condition the body." Estab. 1997. Circ. 200,000. **Pays on acceptance**. Publishes ms an average of 4 months after acceptance. Byline given. Offers 25% kill fee. Buys all rights. Editorial lead time 3 months. Submit seasonal material 6 months in advance. Accepts queries by mail, fax. Responds in 5 weeks to queries; 2 months to mss. Sample copy for $5.

Nonfiction: Exposé, how-to (training and nutrition), humor, inspirational, interview/profile, new product, personal experience, photo feature. No "poorly researched articles that do not genuinely help the readers towards physical fitness, health and physique." **Buys 100 mss/year.** Send complete ms. Length: 1,400-1,800 words. **Pays $250-1,000.** Sometimes pays expenses of writers on assignment.

　• Ranked as one of the best markets for freelance writers in *Writer's Yearbook* magazine's annual "Top 100 Markets," January 2000.

Reprints: Send tearsheet, photocopy or typed manuscript with rights for sale noted and information about when and where the article previously appeared. Pay varies.

Photos: State availability of or send photos with submission. Reviews contact sheets, 35mm transparencies, prints. Offers $35-500. Identification of subjects required. Buys all rights.

Columns/Departments: Nutrition (low fat recipes), 1,700 words; Weight Training (routines and techniques), 1,800 words; Aerobics (how-tos), 1,700 words. **Buys 50 mss/year.** Send complete ms. **Pays $150-500.**

Tips: "Every editor of every magazine is looking, waiting, hoping and praying for the magic article. The beauty of the writing has to spring from the page; the edge imparted has to excite the reader because of its unbelievable information."

N $ $ $ REMEDY MAGAZINE, Prescriptions for a Healthy Life, Remedy, Inc., 120 Post Rd. W., Westport CT 06880. Editor-in-chief: Valorie G. Weaver. **Contact:** Shari Miller Sims, editor. **95% freelance written.** Bimonthly magazine covering health for people age 50 and over. "*REMEDY* covers everything that affects and improves the health of people 50 and up—nutrition and exercise, medicine and medications, mainstream and alternative approaches, hormones and hair loss, you name it—and does it in an in-depth but reader-friendly way." Estab. 1992. Circ. 2,200,000 households. **Pays on acceptance**. Publishes ms an average of 4 months after acceptance. Byline given. Offers 20% kill fee. Buys first North American serial rights. Editorial lead time 3 months. Submit seasonal material 6 months in advance. Accepts simultaneous submissions. Responds in 6 weeks to queries; 2 months to mss. Samples for $3 and SAE with 4 first-class stamps. Writer's guidelines free.

Nonfiction: Book excerpts, exposé (medical), how-to (exercise and nutrition for people age 50 and over), interview/profile (health); medical journalism/reporting for lay readers. **Buys 30 mss/year.** Query by mail only with published clips. Length: 600-2,500 words. **Pays $1-1.25/word.** Pays pre-approved expenses of writers on assignment.

Photos: State availability of photos with submission. Negotiates payment individually. Model releases, identification of subjects required. Buys one-time rights.

Columns/Departments: The Nutrition Prescription (how-to research), The Fitness Prescription (how-to research), Housecall (interviews with top specialists), Mediview (overviews of topical subjects, e.g., "endless" menopause, seebetter surgery), all 600-900 words. **Buys 15 mss/year.** Query by mail only. **Pays $1-1.25/word.**

Tips: "Query should include specific doctors/practitioners likely to be interviewed for the piece, and at least one clip showing writing/reporting familiarity with topic of query. Also, an ability to write in a casual, friendly way about often complex material is essential."

$ $ $ $ SHAPE MAGAZINE, Weider Health & Fitness, 21100 Erwin St., Woodland Hills CA 91367. (818)595-0593. Fax: (818)992-6895. Website: www.shapemag.com. Editor-in-Chief: Barbara Harris. **Contact:** Peg Moline, editorial director. **70% freelance written.** Prefers to work with published/established writers. Monthly magazine covering women's health and fitness. "*Shape* reaches women who are committed to the healthful, active lifestyles. Our readers are participating in a variety of sports and fitness related activities, in the gym, at home and outdoors, and they are also proactive about their health and are nutrition conscious." Estab. 1981. Circ. 900,000. **Pays on acceptance**. Offers 33% kill fee. Buys all rights and reprint rights. Submit seasonal material 8 months in advance. Responds in 2 months. Sample copy for 9 × 12 SAE and 4 first-class stamps.
 • Weider also publishes *Fit Pregnancy* (for pregnant and postpartum women); and *Jump* (for teenage girls).
Nonfiction: Book excerpts; exposé (health, fitness, nutrition related); how-to (get fit); interview/profile (of fit women); health/fitness, recipes. "We use some health and fitness articles written by professionals in their specific fields. No articles that haven't been queried first." Special issues: every September is an anniversary issue. **Buys 27 features/ year, 36-54 short pieces/year.** Query by mail only with clips of published work. Length: 3,000 words for features, 1,000 words for short pieces. **Pays $1/word.**
 • Ranked as one of the best markets for freelance writers in *Writer's Yearbook* magazine's annual "Top 100 Markets," January 2000.
Photos: Submit slides or photos with photographer's name or institution to be credited. Provide necessary captions and all model releases.
Tips: "Review a recent issue of the magazine. Provide source verification materials and sources for items readers may buy, including 800 numbers. Not responsible for unsolicited material. We reserve the right to edit any article."

$ $ VIBRANT LIFE, A Magazine for Healthful Living, Review and Herald Publishing Assn., 55 W. Oak Ridge Dr., Hagerstown MD 21740-7390. (301)393-4019. Fax: (301)393-4055. E-mail: vibrantlife@rhpa.org. Website: www.vibrantlife.com. **Contact:** Larry Becker, editor. **80% freelance written.** Enjoys working with published/established writers; works with a small number of new/unpublished writers each year. Bimonthly magazine covering health articles (especially from a prevention angle and with a Christian slant). Estab. 1885. Circ. 50,000. **Pays on acceptance.** "The average length of time between acceptance of a freelance-written manuscript and publication of the material depends upon the topics: some immediately used; others up to 2 years." Byline always given. Offers 50% kill fee. Buys first serial, first world serial, or sometimes second serial (reprint) rights. Submit seasonal material 9 months in advance. Accepts queries by mail, e-mail, fax. Responds in 2 months. Sample copy for $1. Guidelines for #10 SASE or on website.
Nonfiction: Interview/profile (with personalities on health). "We seek practical articles promoting better health and a more fulfilled life. We especially like features on breakthroughs in medicine, and most aspects of health. We need articles on how to integrate a person's spiritual life with their health. We'd like more in the areas of exercise, nutrition, water, avoiding addictions of all types and rest—all done from a wellness perspective." **Buys 50-60 feature articles/ year, 6-12 short pieces/year.** Send complete ms. Length: 500-1,500 words for features, 25-250 words for short pieces. **Pays $75-300 for features, $50-75 for short pieces.**
 • Ranked as one of the best markets for freelance writers in *Writer's Yearbook* magazine's annual "Top 100 Markets," January 2000.
Reprints: Send tearsheet of article and information about when and where the article previously appeared. Pays 50% of amount paid for an original article.
Photos: Send photos with ms. Needs 35mm transparencies. Not interested in b&w photos.
Columns/Departments: Buys 12-18 department artices/year. Length: 500-650 words. **Pays $75-175.**
Tips: "*Vibrant Life* is published for baby boomers, particularly young professionals, age 35-50. Articles must be written in an interesting, easy-to-read style. Information must be reliable; no faddism. We are more conservative than other magazines in our field. Request a sample copy, and study the magazine and writer's guidelines."

$ $ VIM & VIGOR, America's Family Health Magazine, 1010 E. Missouri Ave., Phoenix AZ 85014-2601. (602)395-5850. Fax: (602)395-5853. E-mail: jennw@mcpub.com. Website: www.vigormagazine.com **Contact:** Sally Clasen , associate publisher/editor. **75% freelance written.** Quarterly magazine covering health and healthcare. Estab. 1985. Circ. 1,100,000. **Pays on acceptance.** Publishes an average of 3 months after acceptance. Byline given. Buys all rights. Sample copy for 9 × 12 SAE with 8 first-class stamps or on website. Writer's guidelines for #10 SASE.
Nonfiction: Health, diseases, medical breakthroughs, exercise/fitness trends, wellness, and healthcare. "Absolutely no complete manuscripts will be accepted. All articles are assigned. Send samples of your style. Any queries regarding story ideas will be placed on the following year's conference agenda and will be addressed on a topic-by-topic basis." **Buys 12 mss/year.** Send published clips by mail or e-mail. Length: 2,000 words. **Pays $500.** Pays expenses of writers on assignment.
 ▣ The online magazine carries original content not included in the print edition.

$ $ $ $ THE WALKING MAGAZINE, Walking Inc., 45 Bromfield St., Boston MA 02108. (617)574-0076. Fax: (617)338-7433. **Contact:** Lori Lundberg. **60% freelance written.** Bimonthly magazine covering health and fitness.

"The Walking Magazine is written for healthy, active adults who are committed to fitness walking as an integral part of their lifestyle. Each issue offers advice on exercise techniques, diet, nutrition, personal care and contemporary health issues. It also covers information on gear and equipment, competition and travel, including foreign and domestic destinations for walkers." Estab. 1986. Circ. 650,000. **Pays on acceptance.** Offers 25% kill fee. Editorial lead time 3 months. Accepts simultaneous submissions. Responds in 2 months. Sample copy for $3.95. SASE for guidelines.

Nonfiction: Walks for travel and adventure, fitness, health, nutrition, fashion, equipment, famous walkers, and other walking-related topics. **Buys 35-42 mss/year.** Query with published clips (no more than 3). Length: 1,500-2,500 words. **Pays $750-2,500.**

Columns/Departments: Walking Shorts, Your Self, Health, Nutrition, Active Beauty, Weight Loss, Events, Shopping (gear and equipment), Escapes (travel), Ramblings (back page essay), 300-1,200 words. Query with clips. **Pays $150-1,500.**

⊠ **$ $ $ WEIGHT WATCHERS MAGAZINE**, W/W Twentyfirst Corp., 360 Lexington Ave., 11th floor, New York NY 10017. (212)370-0644. Fax: (212)687-4398. Editor-in-Chief: Nancy Gagliarch. Senior Editor: GeriAnne Fennessey. Food Editor: Rebecca Adams. Publishing Assistant: Jerry Laboy-Bruce. **Approximately 70% freelance written.** Magazine published 6 times/year mostly for women interested in weight loss, including healthy lifestyle/behavior information/advice, news on health, nutrition, fitness, beauty, fashion, psychology and food/recipes. Weight loss success and before-and-after stories also welcome. Estab. 1968. Circ. 500,000. **Pays on acceptance**. Offers 25% kill fee. Buys first North American rights. Editorial lead time 3-12 months. Accepts queries by mail.

Nonfiction: Covers diet, nutrition, motivation/psychology, food, spas, beauty, fashion and products for both the kitchen and an active lifestyle. Articles have an authoritative yet friendly tone. How-to and service information crucial for all stories. Send detailed queries with published clips and SASE. Average article length: 700-1,500 words.

• Ranked as one of the best markets for freelance writers in *Writer's Yearbook* magazine's annual "Top 100 Markets," January 2000.

Columns/Departments: Accepts editorial in health, fitness, diet, inspiration, nutrition.

Tips: "Well developed, tightly written queries always a plus, as are trend pieces. We're always on the lookout for a fresh angle on an old topic. Sources must be reputable; we prefer subjects to be medical professionals with university affiliations who are published in their field of expertise. Lead times require stories to be seasonal, long-range and forward-looking. We're looking for fresh, innovative stories that yield worthwhile information for women interested in losing weight—the latest exercise alternatives, a suggestion of how they can reduce stress, nutritional information that may not be common knowledge, reassurance about their lifestyle or health concerns, etc. Familiarity with the Weight Watchers philosophy/program is a plus."

⊠ **$ $ $ $ YOGA JOURNAL**, 2054 University Ave., Berkeley CA 94704. (510)841-9200. Website: www.yogajournal.com. **Contact:** Kathryn Arnold, editor in chief; Jeanne Ricci, managing editor. **75% freelance written.** Bimonthly magazine covering yoga, holistic health, conscious living, spiritual practices, ecology and nutrition. Estab. 1975. Circ. 130,000. Publishes mss an average of 10 months after acceptance. Byline given. Offers kill fee on assigned articles. Buys first North American serial rights. Submit seasonal material minimum 4 months in advance. Responds in approx. 3 months. Sample copy $4.99. Writer's guidelines free.

Nonfiction: Book excerpts; how-to (yoga, exercise, etc.); inspirational (yoga or related); profile/interview; opinion; photo feature; yoga-related travel. "Yoga is a main concern, but we also highlight other conscious living/New Age personalities and endeavors (nothing too 'woo-woo')." **Buys 50-60 mss/year.** Query with SASE. Length: 2,500-6,000 words. **Pays $1,000-3,000.**

Reprints: Submit tearsheet or photocopy of article with information about when and where the article previously appeared and rights for sale noted.

Columns/Departments: Health (self-care; well-being); Body-Mind (hatha Yoga; other body-mind modalities; meditation; yoga philosophy; Western mysticism); Community (service; profiles; organizations; events). Length: 1,500-2,000 words. **Pays $600-800.** Living (books; video; arts; music), 800 words. **Pays $250-300.** World of Yoga, Spectrum (brief yoga and healthy living news/events/fillers), 150-600 words. **Pays $50-150.**

Tips: "Please read our writer's guidelines before submission. Do not e-mail or fax unsolicited manuscripts."

⊠ **$ $ YOUR HEALTH & FITNESS**, General Learning Communications, 900 Skokie Blvd., Northbrook IL 60062-1574. (847)205-3000. Fax: (847)564-8197. **Contact:** Deb Bastian, executive editor. **90-95% freelance written.** Prefers to work with published/established writers. Quarterly magazine covering health and fitness. Needs "general, educational material on health, fitness and safety that can be read and understood easily by the layman." Estab. 1969. Circ. 1,000,000. Pays after publication. Publishes ms an average of 6 months after acceptance. No byline given (contributing editor status given in masthead). Offers 50% kill fee. Buys all rights.

Nonfiction: Health-related general interest. No alternative medicine. "All article topics assigned. No queries; if you're interested in writing for the magazine, send a cover letter, résumé, curriculum vitae and writing samples. All topics are determined a year in advance of publication by editors. No unsolicited manuscripts." **Buys approximately 65 mss/year.** Length: 350-850 words. Pay varies, commensurate with experience and quality of ms.

Tips: "Write to a general audience with only a surface knowledge of health and fitness topics. Possible subjects include exercise and fitness, psychology, nutrition, safety, disease, drug data, and health concerns. No phone queries."

HISTORY

Listed here are magazines and other periodicals written for historical collectors, genealogy enthusiasts, historic preservationists and researchers. Editors of history magazines look for fresh accounts of past events in a readable style. Some publications cover an era, while others may cover a region or subject area, such as aviation history.

◪ AMERICAN HERITAGE, 60 Fifth Ave., New York NY 10011. (212)206-5500. Fax: (212)620-2332. E-mail: mail@americanheritage.com. Website: www.americanheritage.com. **Contact:** Richard Snow, editor. **70% freelance written.** Magazine published 8 times/year. "*American Heritage* writes from a historical point of view on politics, business, art, current and international affairs, and our changing lifestyles. The articles are written with the intent to enrich the reader's appreciation of the sometimes nostalgic, sometimes funny, always stirring panorama of the American experience." Circ. 300,000. Usually buys first North American rights or all rights. Byline given. **Pays on acceptance.** Publishes ms an average of 6-12 months after acceptance. Before submitting material, "check our index to see whether we have already treated the subject." Submit seasonal material 1 year in advance. Responds in 2 months. Writer's guidelines for #10 SASE.
Nonfiction: Wants "historical articles by scholars or journalists intended for intelligent lay readers rather than for professional historians." Emphasis is on authenticity, accuracy and verve. "Interesting documents, photographs and drawings are always welcome. Query. Style should stress readability and accuracy." **Buys 30 unsolicited mss/year.** Length: 1,500-6,000 words. Pay varies. Sometimes pays the expenses of writers on assignment.
Tips: "We have over the years published quite a few 'firsts' from young writers whose historical knowledge, research methods and writing skills met our standards. The scope and ambition of a new writer tell us a lot about his or her future usefulness to us. A major article gives us a better idea of the writer's value. Everything depends on the quality of the material. We don't really care whether the author is 20 and unknown, or 80 and famous, or vice versa. No phone calls, please."

$ $ $ AMERICAN HISTORY, 6405 Flank Dr., Harrisburg PA 17112-2750. (717)657-9555. Website: www.thehis torynet.com. **Contact:** Tom Huntington, editor. **60% freelance written.** Bimonthly magazine of cultural, social, military and political history published for a general audience. Estab. 1966. Circ. 100,000. **Pays on acceptance.** Byline given. Buys first rights. Responds in 10 weeks to queries. Writer's guidelines for #10 SASE or online. Sample copy and guidelines for $5 (includes 3rd class postage) or $4 and 9×12 SAE with 4 first-class stamps.
Nonfiction: Features biographies of noteworthy historical figures and accounts of important events in American history. Also includes pictorial features on artists, photographers and graphic subjects. "Material is presented on a popular rather than a scholarly level." Query by mail only with published clips and SASE. "Query letters should be limited to a concise 1 page proposal defining your article with an emphasis on its unique qualities." **Buys 20 mss/year.** Length: 2,000-4,000 words depending on type of article. **Pays $500-800.**
Photos: Welcomes suggestions for illustrations.
◪ The online magazine carries some original content not included in the print edition. Contact: Christine Techky, managing editor.
Tips: "Key prerequisites for publication are thorough research and accurate presentation, precise English usage and sound organization, a lively style, and a high level of human interest. Unsolicited manuscripts not considered. Inappropriate materials include: fiction, book reviews, travelogues, personal/family narratives not of national significance, articles about collectibles/antiques, living artists, local/individual historic buildings/landmarks and articles of a current editorial nature. Currently seeking articles on significant Civil War subjects. No phone, fax or e-mail queries, please."

◪ $ $ AMERICA'S CIVIL WAR, Primedia History Group, 741 Miller Dr., SE, Suite D-2, Leesburg VA 20175-8920. (703)771-9400. Fax: (703)779-8345. E-mail: cheryls@cowles.com. Website: www.thehistorynet.com. **Contact:** Roy Morris, Jr., editor. Managing Editor: Carl Von Wodtke. **95% freelance written.** Bimonthly magazine of "popular history and straight historical narrative for both the general reader and the Civil War buff covering strategy, tactics, personalities, arms and equipment." Estab. 1988. Circ. 125,000. Pays on publication. Publishes ms up to 2 years after acceptance. Byline given. Buys all rights. Accepts queries by mail, e-mail, fax. Responds in 3 months to queries; 6 months to mss. Sample copy for $5. Writer's guidelines for #10 SASE or online.
Nonfiction: Book excerpts, historical, travel. No fiction or poetry. **Buys 24 mss/year.** Query. Length: 3,500-4,000 words and should include a 500-word sidebar. **Pays $300 maximum.**
Photos: Send photos with submission or cite sources. "We'll order." Captions and identification of subjects required.
Columns/Departments: Personality (probes); Ordnance (about weapons used); Commands (about units); Eyewitness to War (about appropriate historical sites). **Buys 24 mss/year.** Query. Length: 2,000 words. **Pays up to $150.**
◪ The online magazine carries original content not found in the print edition. Contact: Roger Vance. Includes writer's guidelines.
Tips: "All stories must be true. We do not publish fiction or poetry. Write an entertaining, informative and unusual story that grabs the reader's attention and holds it. Include suggested readings in a standard format at the end of your piece. Manuscript must be typed, double-spaced on one side of standard white 8½×11, 16 to 30 pound paper—no onion skin paper or dot matrix printouts. All submissions are on speculation. Prefer subjects to be on disk (IBM- or Macintosh-compatible floppy disk) as well as a hard copy. Choose stories with strong art possibilities."

$ THE ARTILLERYMAN, Historical Publications, Inc., 234 Monarch Hill Rd., Tunbridge VT 05077. (802)889-3500. Fax: (802)889-5627. E-mail: mail@civilwarnews.com. ("attention: the Artilleryman"). **Contact:** Kathryn Jorgensen, editor. **60% freelance written.** Quarterly magazine covering antique artillery, fortifications and crew-served weapons 1750-1900 for competition shooters, collectors and living history reenactors using artillery. "Emphasis on Revolutionary War and Civil War but includes everyone interested in pre-1900 artillery and fortifications, preservation, construction of replicas, etc." Estab. 1979. Circ. 2,000. Pays on publication. Publishes ms an average of 6 months after acceptance. Byline given. Not copyrighted. Buys one-time rights. Accepts queries by mail, e-mail, fax. Accepts simultaneous submissions. Responds in 3 weeks. Sample copy and writer's guidelines for 9×12 SAE with 4 first-class stamps.

O⟶ Break in with an historical or travel piece featuring artillery—the types and history of guns and their use.
Nonfiction: Historical; how-to (reproduce ordnance equipment/sights/implements/tools/accessories, etc.); interview/profile; new product; opinion (must be accompanied by detailed background of writer and include references); personal experience; photo feature; technical (must have footnotes); travel (where to find interesting antique cannon). Interested in "artillery *only*, for sophisticated readers. Not interested in other weapons, battles in general." **Buys 24-30 mss/year.** Send complete ms. Length: 300 words minimum. **Pays $20-60.** Sometimes pays the expenses of writers on assignment.
Reprints: Send tearsheet or photocopy of article and information about when and where the article previously appeared. Pays 100% of amount paid for an original article.
Photos: Send photos with ms. Pays $5 for 5×7 and larger b&w prints. Captions, identification of subjects required.
Tips: "We regularly use freelance contributions for Places-to-Visit, Cannon Safety, The Workshop and Unit Profiles departments. Also need pieces on unusual cannon or cannon with a known and unique history. To judge whether writing style and/or expertise will suit our needs, writers should ask themselves if they could knowledgeably talk *artillery* with an expert. Subject matter is of more concern than writer's background."

⬧ $ $ CIVIL WAR TIMES ILLUSTRATED, 6405 Flank Dr., Harrisburg PA 17112. (717)657-9555. Fax: (717)657-9552. E-mail: cwt@cowles.com. Website: www.thehistorynet.com. Editor: Jim Kushlan. **90% freelance written.** Works with a small number of new/unpublished writers each year. Magazine published 7 times/year. "*Civil War Times* is the full-spectrum magazine of the Civil War. Specifically, we look for non-partisan coverage of battles, prominent military and civilian figures, the home front, politics, military technology, common soldier life, collectible artifacts, prisoners and escapes, art and photography, the naval war, blockade-running, specific regiments and much more." Estab. 1962. Circ. 170,000. **Pays on acceptance.** Publishes ms an average of 18 months after acceptance. Buys all rights. Submit seasonal material 1 year in advance. Responds in 8 months to mss. Sample copy for $5.50. Writer's guidelines for SASE.
Nonfiction: Profile, photo feature, Civil War historical material. "Don't send us a comprehensive article on a well-known major battle. Instead, focus on some part or aspect of such a battle, or some group of soldiers in the battle. Similar advice applies to major historical figures like Lincoln and Lee. Positively no fiction or poetry." **Buys 20 freelance mss/year. Send complete ms.** Send complete ms. Length: 2,500-5,000 words. **Pays $75-600.**
Photos: Jeff King, art director.
Tips: "We're very open to new submissions. Send submissions after examining writer's guidelines and several recent issues. Include photocopies of photos that could feasibly accompany the article. Confederate soldiers' diaries and letters are welcome."

$ $ GATEWAY HERITAGE, Missouri Historical Society, P.O. Box 11940, St. Louis MO 63112-0040. Fax: (314)746-4548. E-mail: books@mohistory.org. Website: www.mohistory.org. **Contact:** Katherine Douglass, editor. **75% freelance written.** Quarterly magazine covering Missouri history. "*Gateway Heritage* is a popular history magazine which is sent to members of the Missouri Historical Society. Thus, we have a general audience with an interest in history." Estab. 1980. Circ. 6,200. Pays on publication. Publishes ms an average of 6 months after acceptance. Byline given. Offers $75 kill fee. Buys first North American serial rights. Editorial lead time 6 months. Submit seasonal material 1 year in advance. Accepts queries by mail, e-mail, fax. Responds in 2 weeks to queries; 2 months to mss. Sample copy for 9×12 SAE with 7 first-class stamps. Writer's guidelines for #10 SASE.
Nonfiction: Book excerpts, historical/nostalgic, interview/profile, personal experience, photo feature. No genealogies. **Buys 12-15 mss/year.** Query with published clips. Length: 3,500-5,000 words. **Pays $200 (average).**
Photos: State availability of photos with submission.
Columns/Departments: Literary Landmarks (biographical sketches and interviews of famous Missouri literary figures) 1,500-2,500 words; Missouri Biographies (biographical sketches of famous and interesting Missourians) 1,500-2,500 words; Gateway Album (excerpts from diaries and journals) 1,500-2,500 words. **Buys 6-8 mss/year.** Query with published clips. **Pays $100 (average).**
Tips: "Ideas for our departments are a good way to break into *Gateway Heritage*."

⬧ $ GOOD OLD DAYS, America's Premier Nostalgia Magazine, House of White Birches, 306 E. Parr Rd., Berne IN 46711. (219)589-4000. **Contact:** Ken Tate, editor. **75% freelance written.** Monthly magazine of first person nostalgia, 1900-1955. "We look for strong narratives showing life as it was in the first half of this century. Our readership is comprised of nostalgia buffs, history enthusiasts and the people who actually lived and grew up in this era." Pays on publication. Publishes ms an average of 8 months after acceptance. Byline given. Buys all, first North American serial or one-time rights. Submit seasonal material 10 months in advance. Responds in 2 months. Sample copy for $2. Writer's guidelines for #10 SASE.

Nonfiction: Historical/nostalgic, humor, interview/profile, personal experience, favorite food/recipes and photo features, year-round seasonal material, biography, memorable events, fads, fashion, sports, music, literature, entertainment. Regular features: Good Old Days on Wheels (transportation auto, plane, horse-drawn, tram, bicycle, trolley, etc.); Good Old Days In the Kitchen (favorite foods, appliances, ways of cooking, recipes); Home Remedies (herbs and poultices, hometown doctors, harrowing kitchen table operations). **Buys 350 mss/year.** Query or send complete ms. Preferred length: 500-1,500 words. **Pays $15-75, depending on quality and photos.** No fiction accepted.
Photos: Send photos or photocopies of photos alone or with submission. Offers $5/photo. Identification of subjects required. Buys one-time or all rights.
Tips: "Most of our writers are not professionals. We prefer the author's individual voice, warmth, humor and honesty over technical ability."

$ $PERSIMMON HILL, National Cowboy Hall of Fame and Western Heritage Center, 1700 NE 63rd St., Oklahoma City OK 73111. (405)478-6404. Fax: (405)478-4714. E-mail: editor@cowboyhalloffame.org. Website: www.cowboyhalloffame.org. **Contact:** M.J. Van Deventer, editor. **70% freelance written.** Prefers to work with published/established writers; works with a small number of new/unpublished writers each year. Quarterly magazine for an audience interested in Western art, Western history, ranching and rodeo, including historians, artists, ranchers, art galleries, schools, and libraries. Estab. 1970. Circ. 15,000. Pays on publication. Publishes ms up to 2 years after acceptance. Buys first rights. Byline given. Responds in 3 months. Sample copy for $10.50, including postage. Writer's guidelines for #10 SASE or on website.
Nonfiction: Historical and contemporary articles on famous Western figures connected with pioneering the American West, Western art, rodeo, cowboys, etc. (or biographies of such people), stories of Western flora and animal life and environmental subjects. "We want thoroughly researched and historically authentic material written in a popular style. May have a humorous approach to subject. No broad, sweeping, superficial pieces; i.e., the California Gold Rush or rehashed pieces on Billy the Kid, etc." Length: 1,500 words. **Buys 35-50 mss/year.** Query by mail only with clips. **Pays $150-250.**
   ● The editor of *Persimmon Hill* reports: "We need more material on rodeo, both contemporary and historical. And we need more profiles on contemporary working ranches in the West."
Photos: Glossy b&w prints or color transparencies purchased with ms, or on assignment. Pays according to quality and importance for b&w and color photos. Suggested captions required.
Tips: "Send us a story that captures the spirit of adventure and individualism that typifies the Old West or reveals a facet of the Western lifestyle in contemporary society. Excellent illustrations for articles are essential! We lean toward scholarly, historical, well-researched articles. We're less focused on western celebrities than some of the other contemporary Western magazines."

$ $ $ $PRESERVATION MAGAZINE, National Trust for Historic Preservation, 1785 Massachusetts Ave. NW, Washington DC 20036. (202)588-6388. **Contact:** Robert Wilson, editor. **75% freelance written.** Prefers to work with published/established writers. Bimonthly covering preservation of historic buildings in the US. "We cover subjects related in some way to place. Most entries are features, department or opinion pieces." Circ. 250,000. Pays on publication. Publishes ms an average of 1 month after acceptance. Byline given. Offers variable kill fee. Buys one-time rights. Responds in 2 months to queries. No writer's guidelines.
Nonfiction: Features, news, profiles, opinion, photo feature, travel. **Buys 30 mss/year.** Query with published clips. Length: 500-3,500 words. Sometimes pays expenses of writers on assignment, but not long-distance travel.
   ● Ranked as one of the best markets for freelance writers in *Writer's Yearbook* magazine's annual "Top 100 Markets," January 2000.
Tips: "Do not send or propose histories of buildings, descriptive accounts of cities or towns or long-winded treatises."

$ $ $TIMELINE, Ohio Historical Society, 1982 Velma Ave., Columbus OH 43211-2497. (614)297-2360. Fax: (614)297-2367. E-mail: cduckworth@ohiohistory.org. **Contact:** Christopher S. Duckworth, editor. **90% freelance written.** Works with a small number of new/unpublished writers each year. Bimonthly magazine covering history, prehistory and the natural sciences, directed toward readers in the Midwest. Estab. 1885. Circ. 19,000. **Pays on acceptance.** Publishes ms an average of 1 year after acceptance. Byline given. Offers $75 minimum kill fee. Buys first North American serial or all rights. Submit seasonal material 6 months in advance. Responds in 3 weeks to queries; 6 weeks to mss. Sample copy for $6 and 9 × 12 SAE. Writer's guidelines for #10 SASE.
Nonfiction: Book excerpts, essays, historical, profile (of individuals), photo feature. Topics include the traditional fields of political, economic, military, and social history; biography; the history of science and technology; archaeology and anthropology; architecture; the fine and decorative arts; and the natural sciences including botany, geology, zoology, ecology, and paleontology. **Buys 22 mss/year.** Query by mail only. Length: 1,500-6,000 words. Also vignettes of 500-1,000 words. **Pays $100-900.**
Photos: Send photos with submission. Submissions should include ideas for illustration. Reviews contact sheets, transparencies, 8 × 10 prints. Captions, model releases, identification of subjects required. Buys one-time rights.
Tips: "We want crisply written, authoritative narratives for the intelligent lay reader. An Ohio slant may strengthen a submission, but it is not indispensable. Contributors must know enough about their subject to explain it clearly and in an interesting fashion. We use high-quality illustration with all features. If appropriate illustration is unavailable, we can't use the feature. The writer who sends illustration ideas with a manuscript has an advantage, but an often-published illustration won't attract us."

$ $ TRACES OF INDIANA AND MIDWESTERN HISTORY, Indiana Historical Society, 450 W. Ohio St., Indianapolis IN 46202-3269. (317)232-1877. Fax: (317)233-0857. E-mail: rboomhower@indianahistory.org. Website: www.indianahistory.org/traces.htm. Executive Editor: Thomas A. Mason. **Contact:** Ray E. Boomhower, managing editor. **80% freelance written.** Quarterly magazine on Indiana and Midwestern history. "Conceived as a vehicle to bring to the public good narrative and analytical history about Indiana in its broader contexts of region and nation, *Traces* explores the lives of artists, writers, performers, soldiers, politicians, entrepreneurs, homemakers, reformers, and naturalists. It has traced the impact of Hoosiers on the nation and the world. In this vein, the editors seek nonfiction articles that are solidly researched, attractively written, and amenable to illustration, and they encourage scholars, journalists, and freelance writers to contribute to the magazine." Estab. 1989. Circ. 11,000. **Pays on acceptance.** Publishes ms an average of 6 months after acceptance. Byline given. Buys one-time rights. Submit seasonal material 1 year in advance. Responds in 3 months to mss. Sample copy and writer's guidelines for $5.25 (make checks payable to Indiana Historical Society) and 9×12 SAE with 7 first-class stamps or on website. Writer's guidelines only for #10 SASE.

Nonfiction: Book excerpts, historical essays, historical photographic features on topics of biography, literature, folklore, music, visual arts, politics, economics, industry, transportation and sports. **Buys 20 mss/year.** Send complete ms. Length: 2,000-4,000 words. **Pays $100-500.**

Photos: Send photos with submission. Reviews contact sheets, photocopies, transparencies and prints. Pays "reasonable photographic expenses." Captions, permissions and identification of subjects required. Buys one-time rights.

Tips: "Freelancers should be aware of prerequisites for writing history for a broad audience. Should have some awareness of this magazine and other magazines of this type published by midwestern and western historical societies. Preference is given to subjects with an Indiana connection and authors who are familiar with *Traces*. Quality of potential illustration is also important."

✦ $ TRUE WEST, True West Publishing, Inc., P.O. Box 8008, Cave Creek AZ 85327. (888)587-1881. Fax: (480)575-1903. E-mail: mail@truewestmagazine.com. Website: www.truewestmagazine.com. Executive Editor: Bob Boze Bell. **Contact:** Marcus Huff, editor. **80% freelance written.** Works with a small number of new/unpublished writers each year. *True West* (monthly) covers Western American history from prehistory to 1930. "We want reliable research on significant historical topics written in lively prose for an informed general audience. More recent topics may be used if they have a historical angle or retain the Old West flavor of trail dust and saddle leather." Estab. 1953. Circ. 50,000. **Pays on acceptance.** Publishes ms an average of 6 months after acceptance. Byline given. Buys first North American serial rights. Editorial lead time 3 months. Submit seasonal material 6 months in advance. Responds in 6 weeks to queries; 2 months to mss. Sample copy for $2 and 9×12 SAE. Writer's guidelines for #10 SASE.

> ⊶ "Do not think you can break in with us easily. We have published the best historians in Western history for 47 years. We take established authors and researchers first. It is wise to publish a book on your subject before approaching us. Writers can also break in with reviews and fillers."

Nonfiction: Book excerpts, historical/nostalgic, humor, interview/profile, travel. No fiction or unsupported, undocumented tales. **Buys 110 mss/year.** Query by mail only. Length: 1,200-5,000 words. **Pays $50-800.**

Photos: State availability of photos with submission. Reviews contact sheets, negatives, 4×5 transparencies and 4×5 prints. Offers $10-75/photo. Captions, model releases and identification of subjects required. Buys one-time rights.

Columns/Departments: Bob Boze Bell, executive editor. True Reviews (book reviews), 300-800 words. **Buys 50 mss/year.** Query by mail only with published clips. **Pays $50-200.**

Fillers: Bob Boze Bell, executive editor. Anecdotes, facts, gags to be illustrated by cartoonist, newsbreaks, short humor. **Buys 30/year.** Length: 50-600 words. **Pays $30-250.**

Tips: "Do original research on fresh topics. Stay away from controversial subjects unless you are truly knowledgeable in the field. Read our magazines and follow our guidelines. A freelancer is most likely to break in with us by submitting thoroughly researched, lively prose on relatively obscure topics. First-person accounts rarely fill our needs. Historical accuracy and strict adherence to the facts are essential. We much prefer material based on primary sources (archives, court records, documents, contemporary newspapers and first-person accounts) to those that rely mainly on secondary sources (published books, magazines, and journals). Note: We are currently trying to take *True West* and *Old West* back to their 'roots' by publishing shorter pieces. Ideal length is between 1,500-3,000 words."

HOBBY & CRAFT

Magazines in this category range from home video to cross-stitch. Craftspeople and hobbyists who read these magazines want new ideas while collectors need to know what is most valuable and why. Collectors, do-it-yourselfers and craftspeople look to these magazines for inspiration and information. Publications covering antiques and miniatures are also listed here. Publications covering the business side of antiques and collectibles are listed in the Trade Art, Design & Collectibles section.

⊞ $ THE AMERICAN MATCHCOVER COLLECTORS CLUB, The Retskin Report, P.O. Box 18481, Asheville NC 28814-0481. (828)254-4487. Fax: (828)254-1066. E-mail: bill@matchcovers.com. **Contact:** Bill Retskin, editor. **10% freelance written.** Quarterly newsletter for matchcover collectors and historical enthusiasts. Estab. 1986.

Circ. 550. Pays on publication. Publishes ms an average of 3 months after acceptance. Byline given. Offers 20% kill fee. Buys first North American serial rights. Submit seasonal material 6 months in advance. Sample copy for 9×12 SAE with 2 first-class stamps. Writer's guidelines for #10 SASE.

Nonfiction: General interest, historical/nostalgic, how-to (collecting techniques), humor, personal experience, photo feature; all relating to match industry, matchcover collecting hobby or ephemera. **Buys 2 mss/year.** Query with published clips. Length: 200-1,200 words. **Pays $25-50 for assigned articles; $10-25 for unsolicited articles.**

Photos: Send photos with submission. Reviews b&w contact sheets and 5×7 prints. Offers $2-5/photo. Captions and identification of subjects required.

Fiction: Historical (matchcover collecting and match industry related only). **Buys 2 mss/year.** Query with published clips. Length: 200-1,200 words. **Pays $25-50.**

Tips: "We are interested in clean, direct style with the collector audience in mind."

$ $ANTIQUE REVIEW, P.O. Box 538, Worthington OH 43085-0538. (614)885-9757. Fax: (614)885-9762. E-mail: editor@antiquereview.net. Website: www.antiquereview.net. **Contact:** Charles Muller, editor. **60% freelance written.** Eager to work with new/unpublished writers. Monthly tabloid for an antique-oriented readership, "generally well-educated, interested in Early American furniture and decorative arts, as well as folk art." Estab. 1975. Circ. 10,000. Pays on publication date assigned at time of purchase. Publishes ms an average of 2 months after acceptance. Byline given. Buys first North American serial and second (reprint) rights. Accepts queries by mail, e-mail, fax, phone. Responds in 3 months. Free sample copy and writer's guidelines for #10 SASE.

• *Antique Review* has added a new section focusing on trends and collectibles.

Nonfiction: "The articles we desire concern history and production of furniture, pottery, china, and other quality Americana. In some cases, contemporary folk art items are acceptable. We are also interested in reporting on antiques shows and auctions with statements on conditions and prices." **Buys 5-8 mss/issue.** Query with clips of published work. Query should show "author's familiarity with antiques, an interest in the historical development of artifacts relating to early America and an awareness of antiques market." Length: 200-2,000 words. **Pays $100-200.** Sometimes pays expenses of writers on assignment.

Reprints: Accepts previously published submissions if not first printed in competitive publications. Send tearsheet or photocopy of article or typed ms with rights for sale noted and information about when and where the article previously appeared. Pays 100% of amount paid for an original article.

Photos: Send photos with query. Payment included in ms price. Uses 3×5 or larger glossy b&w or color prints. Captions required. Articles with photographs receive preference.

Tips: "Give us a call and let us know of specific interests. We are more concerned with the background in antiques than in writing abilities. The writing can be edited, but the knowledge imparted is of primary interest. A frequent mistake is being too general, not becoming deeply involved in the topic and its research. We are interested in primary research into America's historic material culture."

▧ $AUTOGRAPH COLLECTOR, Odyssey Publications, 510-A South Corona Mall, Corona CA 92879-1420. (909)734-9636. Fax: (909)371-7139. E-mail: DBTOGI@aol.com. Website: www.AutographCollector.com. **Contact:** Ev Phillips, editor. **80% freelance written.** Monthly magazine covering the autograph collecting hobby. "The focus of *Autograph Collector* is on documents, photographs or any collectible item that has been signed by a famous person, whether a current celebrity or historical figure. Articles stress how and where to locate celebrities and autograph material, authenticity of signatures and what they are worth." Byline given. Negotiable kill fee. Buys all rights. Editorial lead time 2 months. Submit seasonal material 3 months in advance. Accepts queries by mail, e-mail, fax, phone. Responds in 2 weeks to queries; 1 month to mss. Sample copy and writer's guidelines free.

Nonfiction: Historical/nostalgic, how-to, interview/profile, personal experience. "Articles must address subjects that appeal to autograph collectors and should answer six basic questions: Who is this celebrity/famous person? How do I go about collecting this person's autograph? Where can I find it? How scarce or available is it? How can I tell if it's real? What is it worth?" **Buys 25-35 mss/year.** Query. Length: 1,600-2,000 words. **Pays 5¢/word.** Sometimes pays expenses of writers on assignment.

Photos: State availability of photos with submission. Reviews transparencies, prints. Offers $3/photo. Captions, identification of subjects required. Buys one-time rights.

Columns/Departments: "*Autograph Collector* buys 8-10 columns per month written by regular contributors. Send query for more information." **Buys 90-100 mss/year.** Query. **Pays $50 or as determined on a per case basis.**

Fillers: Anecdotes, facts. **Buys 20-25/year.** Length: 200-300 words. **Pays $15.**

Tips: "Ideally writers should be autograph collectors themselves and know their topics thoroughly. Articles must be well-researched and clearly written. Writers should remember that *Autograph Collector* is a celebrity-driven magazine and name recognition of the subject is important."

$ $BECKETT BASEBALL CARD MONTHLY, Statabase, Inc., 15850 Dallas Pkwy., Dallas TX 75248. (972)991-6657. Fax: (972)233-6488. E-mail: JKelley@beckett.com. Website: www.beckett.com. **Contact:** Margaret Steele, vice president of publishing. **60% freelance written.** Monthly magazine on baseball card and sports memorabilia collecting. "Our readers expect our publication to be entertaining and informative. Our slant is that hobbies are fun and rewarding. Especially wanted are how-to-collect articles." Estab. 1984. **Pays on acceptance.** Publishes ms an average of 4 months after acceptance. Byline given. Pays $50 kill fee. Buys all rights. Submit seasonal material 6 months in advance. Responds in 1 month. Sample copy for $3.95. Writer's guidelines free.

Nonfiction: How-to, humor, interview/profile, new product, opinion, personal experience, photo feature, technical. Special issues: Spring training (February); season preview (April); All-Star game (July); Hobby Awards (August); World Series (October). No articles that emphasize speculative prices and investments. **Buys 50 mss/year.** Send complete ms. Length: 300-1,500 words. **Pays $100-400 for assigned articles; $50-200 for unsolicited articles.** Sometimes pays expenses of writers on assignment.

Photos: Send photos with submission. Reviews 35mm transparencies, 5×7 or larger prints. Offers $10-300/photo. Captions, model releases and identification of subjects required. Buys one-time rights.

Fiction: Humorous only.

Tips: "A writer for *Beckett Baseball Card Monthly* should be an avid baseball fan and card collector with passion for the hobby and an enthusiasm for sharing his/her interests with others. Articles must be factual, but not overly statistic-laden. First person (not research) articles presenting the writer's personal experiences told with wit and humor, and emphasizing the stars of the game, are *always* wanted. Acceptable articles must be of interest to our two basic reader segments: teenaged boys and their middle-aged fathers who are re-experiencing an interest in baseball card collecting. Prospective writers should not write down to either group!"

$ $ BECKETT HOCKEY COLLECTOR, Statabase, Inc., 15850 Dallas Pkwy., Dallas TX 75248. (972)991-6657. Fax: (972)233-6488. Website: www.beckett.com. **Contact:** Al Muir, senior editor. **75% freelance written.** Monthly magazine on hockey, hockey card and memorabilia collecting. "Our readers expect our publication to be entertaining and informative, with intense coverage of the hockey collectibles market. Our slant is that the hobby is fun and rewarding. Especially wanted are how-to-collect articles." Estab. 1990. **Pays on acceptance.** Publishes ms an average of 2 months after acceptance. Byline given. Pays $50 kill fee. Buys all rights. Submit seasonal material 6 months in advance. Responds in 1 month. Sample copy for $3.95. Writer's guidelines free.

Nonfiction: New collecting ideas, great collections in North America, interview/profile, new product, opinion, personal experience, photo feature, technical. Special issues: All-Star game (February); Hobby Awards (August); draft (June); season preview (October). No articles that emphasize speculative prices and investments. **Buys 50 mss/year.** Send complete ms. Length: 300-1,500 words. **Pays $100-400 for assigned articles.** Sometimes pays expenses of writers on assignment.

Photos: Send photos with submission. Reviews 35mm transparencies, 5×7 or larger prints. Offers $10-300/photo. Captions, model releases and identification of subjects required. Buys one-time rights.

Tips: "A writer for *Beckett Hockey Collector* should be an avid sports fan and/or a collector with an enthusiasm for sharing his/her interests with others. Articles must be factual, but not overly statistic-laden. Acceptable articles must be of interest to our two basic reader segments: teenaged boys and their middle-aged fathers who are re-experiencing a nostalgic renaissance of their own childhoods. Prospective writers should write down to neither group!"

$ $ BECKETT POKÉMON COLLECTOR, (formerly *Hot Toys*), Beckett Publications, 15850 Dallas Pkwy., Dallas TX 75248. (972)991-6657. Fax: (972)991-8930. E-mail: dkale@beckett.com. Website: www.beckett.com. Publisher: Claire Backus. **Contact:** Doug Kale, editor. **80% freelance written.** Monthly magazine covering Pokémon, Digimon, Dragon Ball Z, and other popular kids' animated TV shows. "We're reaching the consumer of toys and trading cards, toy enthusiasts, as well as collectors." Estab. 1999. Circ. 560,000. **Pays on acceptance.** Byline given. Buys all rights. Editorial lead time 3 months. Submit seasonal material 3 months in advance. Accepts simultaneous submissions. Sample copy for $4.95, writer's guidelines for #10 SASE.

Nonfiction: General interest, historical/nostalgic, how-to, humor, interview/profile, new product, personal experience, photo feature. "We're also looking for authors for book publishing." **Pays $100-250.**

Photos: State availability of photos with submission. Reviews contact sheets, negatives, transparencies and prints. Negotiates payment individually. Buys all rights.

N ⊠ $ $ BLADE MAGAZINE. The World's #1 Knife Publication, Krause Publications, 700 E. State St., Iola WI 54990. (715)445-2214. Fax: (715)445-4087. E-mail: blade@krause.com. Website: www.krause.com. Editor: Steve Shackleford. **Contact:** Joe Kertzman, associate editor. **60% freelance written.** Monthly magazine for knife enthusiasts who want to know as much as possible about quality knives and edged tools, hand-made and factory knife industries, antique knife collecting, etc. "*Blade* is designed to highlight the romance and history of man's oldest tool, the knife. Our readers are into any and all knives used as tool/collectibles." Estab. 1973. Circ. 75,000. Pays on publication. Publishes ms an average of 1 year after acceptance. Byline given. Pays $20 kill fee. Buys all rights. Editorial lead time 4 months. Submit seasonal material 4 months in advance. Accepts queries by mail, e-mail, fax, phone. Responds in 3 months. Writer's guidelines for #10 SASE.

Nonfiction: Book excerpts, exposé, general interest, how-to, historical (on knives), humor, adventure (on a knife theme), celebrities who own knives, knives featured in movies with shots from the movie, etc., new product, personal experience, photo feature, technical, travel. "We would also like to receive articles on knives in adventuresome life-saving situations." No articles on how to use knives as weapons. No poetry. **Buys 50 mss/year.** Query. Length: 1,000-1,500 words, longer if content warrants it. **Pays $125-300.** "We will pay top dollar in the knife market." Sometimes pays the expenses of writers on assignment.

Photos: State availability of photos with submission, or send photos with ms. Offers no additional payment for photos accepted with ms. Captions and identification of subjects required.

Columns/Departments: Buys 60 mss/year. Query. **Pays $150-250.**

Fillers: Anecdotes, facts, newsbreaks. **Buys 1-2/year.** Length: 50-200 words. **Pays $25-50.**

Tips: "We are always willing to read submissions from anyone who has read a few copies and studied the market. The ideal article for us is a piece bringing out the romance, legend, and love of man's oldest tool—the knife. We like articles that place knives in peoples' hands—in life saving situations, adventure modes, etc. (Nothing gory or with the knife as the villain.) People and knives are good copy. We are getting more and better written articles from writers who are reading the publication beforehand. That makes for a harder sell for the quickie writer not willing to do his homework. Go to knife shows and talk to the makers and collectors. Visit knifemakers' shops and knife factories. Read anything and everything you can find on knives and knifemaking."

⚔ **$ BREW YOUR OWN, The How-to Homebrew Beer Magazine**, Battenkill Communications, 5053 Main St., Suite A, Manchester Center VT 05255. (802)362-3981. Fax: (802)362-2377. E-mail: edit@byo.com. Website: www.byo.com. **Contact:** Kathleen Ring, editor. **85% freelance written.** Monthly magazine covering home brewing. "Our mission is to provide practical information in an entertaining format. We try to capture the spirit and challenge of brewing while helping our readers brew the best beer they can." Estab. 1995. Circ. 42,000. **Pays on acceptance.** Publishes ms 4 months after acceptance. Byline given. Offers 25% kill fee. Buys all rights. Editorial lead time 3 months. Submit seasonal material 3 months in advance. Accepts queries by mail, e-mail, fax. Responds in 2 months. Writer's guidelines for #10 SASE.

    O─ Break in by "sending a detailed query in one of two key areas: how to brew a specific, interesting style of beer or how to build your own specific piece of brewing equipment."

    ● *Brew Your Own* was purchased by Battenkill Communications in December 1999; the company also owns *Winemaker*.

Nonfiction: How-to (home brewing), informational pieces on equipment, ingredients and brewing methods. Length: 1,500-3,000 words. Humor (related to home brewing), interview/profile of professional brewers, personal experience, historical, trends. Length: 800-2,000 words. **Buys 75 mss/year.** Query with published clips and SASE. **Pays $50-150** depending on length, complexity of article and experience of writer. Sometimes pays expenses of writers on assignment.
Photos: State availability of photos with submission. Reviews contact sheets, transparencies, 5×7 prints. Negotiates payment individually. Captions required. Buys all rights.
Columns/Departments: News (humorous, unusual news about homebrewing), 50-250 words; Last Call (humorous stories about homebrewing), 700 words. **Buys 12 mss/year.** Query with or without published clips. **Pays $50.**
Tips: "*Brew Your Own* is for anyone who is interested in brewing beer, from beginners to advanced all-grain brewers. We seek articles that are straightforward and factual, not full of esoteric theories or complex calculations. Our readers tend to be intelligent, upscale, and literate."

$ CERAMICS MONTHLY, The American Ceramic Society, P.O. Box 6102, Westerville OH 43086. (614)523-1660. Fax: (614)891-8960. E-mail: editorial@ceramicsmonthly.org. Website: www.ceramicsmonthly.org. **Contact:** Renée Fairchild, editorial assistant. **50% freelance written**. Monthly magazine, except July and August, covering the ceramic art and craft field. "Technical and business information for potters and ceramic artists." Estab. 1953. Circ. 39,000. Pays on publication. Byline given. Editorial lead time 3 months. Submit seasonal material 6 months in advance. Accepts queries by mail, e-mail, fax, phone. Responds in 6 weeks to queries; 2 months to mss. Writer's guidelines for #10 SASE or on website.
Nonfiction: Essays, how-to, interview/profile, opinion, personal experience, technical. **Buys 100 mss/year**. Send complete ms. Length: 500-3,000 words. **Pays 7¢/word.**
Photos: Send photos with submission. Reviews transparencies (2 ¼×2¼ or 4×5). Offers $15 for black and white; $25 for color photos. Captions required.
Columns/Departments: Up Front (workshop/exhibition review), 500-1,000 words. **Buys 20 mss/year**. Send complete ms. **Pays 7¢/word.**

⚔ **$ $ CLASSIC TOY TRAINS**, Kalmbach Publishing Co., 21027 Crossroads Circle, Waukesha WI 53187. (262)796-8776. Fax: (262)796-1142. E-mail: editor@classtrain.com. Website: www.kalmbach.com/ctt/toytrains.html. **Contact:** Neil Besougloff, editor. **75-80% freelance written.** Magazine published 9 times/year covering collectible toy trains (O, S, Standard, G scale, etc.) like Lionel, American Flyer, Marx, Dorfan, etc. "For the collector and operator of toy trains, *CTT* offers full-color photos of layouts and collections of toy trains, restoration tips, operating information, new product reviews and information, and insights into the history of toy trains." Estab. 1987. Circ. 72,000. **Pays on acceptance**. Publishes ms an average of 1 year after acceptance. Byline given. Buys all rights. Editorial lead time 3 months. Submit seasonal material 6 months in advance. Accepts queries by mail, e-mail, fax, phone. Responds in 3 weeks to queries; 1 month to mss. Sample copy for $4.95 plus s&h. Writer's guidelines for #10 SASE or on website.
Nonfiction: General interest, historical/nostalgic, how-to (restore toy trains; design a layout; build accessories; fix broken toy trains), interview/profile, personal experience, photo feature, technical. **Buys 90 mss/year.** Query. Length: 500-5,000 words. **Pays $75-500.** Sometimes pays expenses of writers on assignment.
Photos: Send photos with submission. Reviews 4×5 transparencies; 5×7 prints preferred. Offers no additional payment for photos accepted with ms or $15-75/photo. Captions required. Buys all rights.
Fillers: Uses cartoons. **Buys 6 fillers/year. Pays $30.**

    ▣ The online magazine carries original content not found in the print edition and includes writer's guidelines. Contact: Neil Besougloff, online editor.
Tips: "It's important to have a thorough understanding of the toy train hobby; most of our freelancers are hobbyists themselves. One-half to two-thirds of *CTT*'s editorial space is devoted to photographs; superior photography is critical."

$ COLLECTIBLES CANADA, Your National Guide to Limited Edition Collectible Art, Trajan Publishing, 103 Lakeshore Rd., Suite 202, St. Catharines, Ontario L2N 2T6 Canada. (905)646-7744. Fax: (905)646-0995. E-mail: newsroom@trajan.com. Website: www.trajan.com. **Contact:** Joanne Keogh, editor. **60% freelance written.** Bimonthly publication covering modern day collectible art. "We provide news and profiles of limited edition collectible art from a positive perspective. We are an informational tool for collectors who want to read about the products they love." Circ. 20,000. Pays 2 months after publication. Publishes ms an average of 1 month after acceptance. Byline given. Buys first North American serial rights. Editorial lead time 4 months. Submit seasonal material 5 months in advance. Accepts queries by mail, e-mail, fax, phone. Responds in 1 month. Sample copy free.

Nonfiction: Interview/profile, new product. "We publish both a Christmas issue and a nature issue (Jan-Feb)." No articles on antique related subjects (we are modern day collectibles). **Buys 30 mss/year.** Query with published clips. Length: 1,000-2,000 words. **Pays $100.** Sometimes pays expenses of writers on assignment.

Photos: State availability of photos with submission. Reviews negatives, any size transparencies and prints. Offers no additional payment for photos accepted with ms. Identification of subjects required. Buys one-time rights.

Columns/Departments: Book reviews (positive slant, primarily informational), 500-800 words. **Buys 2 mss/year.** Query with published clips. **Pays $50-75.**

Tips: "Freelancers should become familiar with the collectibles market. Always query first and send samples of your writing."

$ $ COLLECTOR EDITIONS, Collector Communications Corp., 170 Fifth Ave., New York NY 10010-5911. (212)989-8700. Fax: (212)645-8976. **Contact:** James van Maanen, editor. **40% freelance written.** Works with a small number of new/unpublished writers each year. Published 7 times/year, it covers collectible plates, figurines, cottages, prints, etc. "We specialize in contemporary (post-war ceramic, resin and glass) collectibles, including reproductions, but also publish articles about antiques, if they are being reproduced today and are generally available." Estab. 1973. Circ. 96,000. Pays within 30 days of acceptance. Publishes ms an average of 6 months after acceptance. Buys first North American serial rights. "First assignments are always done on a speculative basis." Responds in 2 months. Sample copy for $2. Writer's guidelines for #10 SASE.

Nonfiction: "Short features about collecting, written in tight, newsy style. We specialize in contemporary (postwar) collectibles. Values for pieces being written about should be included." Informational, interview, profile, nostalgia. Special issues: Christmas Collectibles (December). **Buys 15-20 mss/year.** Query with samples. Length: 800-1,200 words. **Pays $250-400.** Sometimes pays expenses of writers on assignment.

Photos: B&w and color photos purchased with accompanying ms with no additional payment. Captions are required. "We want clear, distinct, full-frame images that say something."

Tips: "Unfamiliarity with the field is the most frequent mistake made by writers in completing an article for us."

$ $ COLLECTOR'S MART, Contemporary Collectibles, Limited Edition Art & Gifts, Krause Publications, 700 E. State St., Iola WI 54990. (715)445-2214. Fax: (715)445-4087. E-mail: sieberm@krause.com. Website: www.collectorsmart.net. **Contact:** Mary L. Sieber, editor. **50% freelance written.** Bimonthly magazine covering contemporary collectibles, for collectors of all types. Estab. 1976. Circ. 170,000. Pays on publication. Publishes ms an average of 6 months after acceptance. Byline given. Buys perpetual but non-exclusive rights. Editorial lead time 2 months. Submit seasonal material 4 months in advance. Accepts queries by mail, e-mail, fax, phone. Responds in 1 month to mss. Writer's guidelines available.

O— Break in with "exciting, interesting theme topics for collections, i.e., seaside, fun and functional, patio decor, etc."

Nonfiction: Buys 35-50 mss/year. Send complete ms. Length: 1,000-2,000 words. **Pays $50-300.**

Photos: Send only color photos with submission. Reviews transparencies, prints, electronic images. Offers no additional payment for photos accepted with ms. Captions required. Buys one-time rights.

■ The online magazine carries original content not found in the print edition. Contact: Lisa Wilson.

Tips: "We're looking for more pieces on unique Christmas theme collectibles, i.e., tree toppers. No more Christmas themes of santas, angels, ornaments."

$ $ COLLECTORS NEWS & THE ANTIQUE REPORTER, P.O. Box 306, Grundy Center IA 50638-0156. (319)824-6981. Fax: (319)824-3414. E-mail: collectors@collectors-news.com. Website: collectors-news.com. **Contact:** Linda Kruger, editor. **20% freelance written.** Works with a small number of new/unpublished writers each year. Monthly magazine-size publication on newsprint covering antiques, collectibles and nostalgic memorabilia. Estab. 1959. Circ. 13,000. Pays on publication. Publishes ms an average of 1 year after acceptance. Byline given. Buys first rights and makes work-for-hire assignments. Submit seasonal material 3 months in advance. Accepts queries by mail, e-mail, fax, phone. Responds in 2 weeks to queries; 6 weeks to mss. Sample copy for $4 and 9×12 SAE. Writer's guidelines free.

O— Break in with articles on internet/computers and collecting; celebrity collectors; collectors with unique and/or extensive collections; music collectibles; transportation collectibles; advertising collectibles; bottles; glass, china and silver; primitives; furniture; jewelry; lamps; western; textiles; toys; black memorabilia; political collectibles; movie memorabilia and any 20th century and timely subjects.

Nonfiction: General interest (any subject re: collectibles, antique to modern); historical/nostalgic (relating to collections or collectors); how-to (display your collection, care for, restore, appraise, locate, add to, etc.); interview/profile (covering individual collectors and their hobbies, unique or extensive; celebrity collectors, and limited edition artists); technical (in-depth analysis of a particular antique, collectible or collecting field); and travel (coverage of special interest or regional shows, seminars, conventions—or major antique shows, flea markets; places collectors can visit, tours they can take, museums, etc.). Special issues: 12-month listing of antique and collectible shows, flea markets and conventions, (January includes events January-December; June includes events June-May); Care & Display of Collectibles (September); holidays (October-December). **Buys 70 mss/year.** Query with sample of writing. Length: 800-1,000 words. **Pays $1.10/column inch.**

Photos: "Articles must be accompanied by photographs for illustration." A selection of 2-8 prints is suggested. "Articles are eligible for full-color front page consideration when accompanied by quality color prints, color slides, and/or color transparencies. Only one article is highlighted on the cover per month. Any article providing a color photo selected for front page use receives an additional $25." Reviews color or b&w prints. Payment for photos included in payment for ms. Captions required. Buys first rights.

Tips: "Present a professionally written article with quality illustrations—well researched and documented information."

$ $ CRAFTS MAGAZINE, 2 News Plaza, Peoria IL 61656. Fax: (309)679-5454. E-mail: crafts@primediasi.com. **Contact:** Miriam Olson, editor. Magazine published 10 times/year covering crafts and needlecrafts, mostly how-to projects using products found in a craft, needlework or fabric store. Estab. 1978. Circ. 300,000. **Pays on acceptance.** Byline given. Buys all rights. Editorial lead time 6 months. Accepts queries by mail, e-mail, fax. Responds in 1 month to queries. Writer's guidelines for #10 SASE.

Nonfiction: All how-to articles. "We also publish a quarterly scrapbooking (memory-album-making) issue called *Snapshot Memories*." **Buys 400 mss/year.** Query with photo or sketch of how-to project. **Pays $150-400.**

Tips: "Project should use readily-available supplies. Project needs to be easily duplicated by reader. Most projects are made for gifts, home decorating accents, wearables and holidays, especially Christmas. Include a photo of the project; second best is a clear, labeled sketch. Must know likes, dislikes and needs of today's crafter and have in-depth knowledge of craft products. *Crafts* is a mix of traditional techniques plus all the latest trends and fads."

[N] [■] $ $ CRITICAL CERAMICS, 13 Flying Point Rd., Freeport ME 04032. (207)805-0845. E-mail: editor@criticalceramics.org. Website: www.criticalceramics.org. **Contact:** Forrest Snyder, editor. **100% freelance written.** Non-profit online magazine covering contemporary ceramic art. Estab. 1997. Circ. 5,000. Pays on publication. Publishes ms an average of 1 month after acceptance. Byline given. Buys non-exclusive rights in perpetuity. Editorial lead time 1 month. Submit seasonal material 1 month in advance. Accepts queries by mail, e-mail. Accepts simultaneous submissions. Responds in 1 week to queries; 1 month to mss. Sample copy on website. Writer's guidelines on website or by e-mail.

Nonfiction: Book excerpts, essays, exposé, interview/profile, opinion, personal experience, photo feature, travel, cross-cultural dialog. **Buys 12-24 mss/year.** Query. Length: 750-1,500 words. **Pays $75-500 for assigned articles; $50-350 for unsolicited articles.** Sometimes pays expenses of writers on assignment.

Reprints: Accepts previously published submissions.

Photos: State availability of photos with submission. Reviews transparencies and 4×6 prints. Negotiates payment individually. Captions and identification of subjects required. Buys non-exclusive electronic rights in perpetuity.

Columns/Departments: Exhibition (reviews), 500-750 words; Book reviews, 500 words; Video reviews, 500 words. **Buys 12-24 mss/year.** Query. **Pays $20-150.**

Tips: "Show enthusiasm for contemporary art with a unique view of subject area. This is a publication for professional contemporary ceramic artists."

$ $ CROCHET WORLD, House of White Birches, P.O. Box 776, Henniker NH 03242. Fax: (219)589-8093. Website: www.whitebirches.com. **Contact:** Susan Hankins, editor. **100% freelance written.** Bimonthly magazine covering crochet patterns. "*Crochet World* is a pattern magazine devoted to the art of crochet. We also feature a Q&A column, letters (swap shop) column and occasionally non-pattern manuscripts, but it must be devoted to crochet." Estab. 1978. Circ. 75,000. Pays on publication. Byline given. Buys all rights. Editorial lead time 4 months. Submit seasonal material 6 months in advance. Responds in 1 month. Sample copy for $2. Writer's guidelines free.

Nonfiction: How-to (crochet). **Buys 0-2 mss/year.** Send complete ms. Length: 500-1,500 words. **Pays $50.**

Columns/Departments: Touch of Style (crocheted clothing); It's a Snap! (quick one-night simple patterns); Pattern of the Month, first and second prize each issue. **Buys dozens of patterns/year.** Send complete pattern. **Pays $40-300.**

Poetry: Strictly crochet-related. **Buys 0-5 poems/year.** Submit maximum 2 poems. Length: 6-20 lines. **Pays $10-20.**

Fillers: Anecdotes, facts, short humor. **Buys 0-10/year.** Length: 25-200 words. **Pays $5-30.**

Tips: "Be aware that this is a pattern generated magazine for crochet designs. I prefer the actual item sent along with complete directions/graphs etc., over queries. In some cases a photo submission or good sketch will do. Crocheted designs must be well-made and original and directions must be complete. Write for Designer's Guidelines which detail how to submit designs. Non-crochet items, such as fillers, poetry *must* be crochet-related, not knit, not sewing, etc."

[N] $ DARK SKIN ART, Tattoos For All Tones, Art & Ink Enterprises, 5 Marine View Plaza, #207, Hoboken NJ 07030. (201)653-2700. Fax: (201)653-7892. E-mail: tattoo1@ix.netcom.com. Website: www.darkskinart.com. Managing Editor: Scot Rienecker. **Contact:** Jean-Chris Miller, editorial director. **50% freelance written.** Quarterly magazine covering tattoos for dark-skinned people. "*Dark Skin Art* features information on tattoos for dark-skinned people and design and historical information on tattoo traditions for dark-skinned people." Estab. 1998. Pays on publication.

Publishes ms an average of 3 months after acceptance. Byline given. Buys first rights. Editorial lead time 3 months. Submit seasonal material 3 months in advance. Accepts queries by mail, e-mail, fax. Accepts simultaneous submissions. Responds in 2 weeks to queries; 1 month to mss. Sample copy for $6. Writer's guidelines free.

O— Break in with "articles specifically geared towards tattoo collectors with dark skin."

Nonfiction: Essays, historical/nostalgic, humor, interview/profile, opinion, personal experience, photo feature. No "My first tattoo" or "A tattoo turned into some sort of monster" stories. **Buys 10 mss/year.** Send complete ms. Length: 200-2,500 words. **Pays $25-100.** Sometimes pays expenses of writers on assignment.

Photos: Send photos with submission. Reviews transparencies and 3×5 prints. Offers $10-20/photo. Identification of subjects required. Buys one-time rights.

Fiction: Erotica, ethnic, fantasy, historical, horror, humorous, science fiction. **Buys 5 mss/year.** Send complete ms. Length: 500-2,500 words. **Pays $25-50.**

Poetry: Avant garde, free verse, light verse, traditional. **Buys 2 poems/year. Pays $20-40.**

Fillers: Facts, short humor. **Buys 2/year.** Length: 50-200 words. **Pays $10-40.**

▣ The online version contains material not found in the print edition. Contact: Jean-Chris Miller.

$ $ DECORATIVE ARTIST'S WORKBOOK, F&W Publications, Inc., 1507 Dana Ave., Cincinnati OH 45207-1005. (513)531-2690, ext. 461. Fax: (513)531-2902. E-mail: dawedit@fwpubs.com. Website: www.decorativeartist.com. **Contact:** Anne Hevener, editor. **75% freelance written.** Bimonthly magazine covering decorative painting projects and products of all sorts. Offers "straightforward, personal instruction in the techniques of decorative painting." Estab. 1987. Circ. 90,000. **Pays on acceptance.** Byline given. Offers 25% kill fee. Buys first North American serial rights. Submit seasonal material 8 months in advance. Accepts queries by mail, e-mail. Responds in 1 month. Sample copy for $4.65 and 9×12 SAE with 5 first-class stamps.

Nonfiction: How-to (related to decorative painting projects), new products, techniques. **Buys 30 mss/year.** Query with slides or photos. Length: 1,200-1,800 words. **Pays 15-25¢/word.**

Photos: Send photos with submission. Reviews 35mm, 4×5 transparencies and quality photos. Offers no additional payment for photos accepted with ms. Captions required. Buys one-time rights.

▣ The online magazine carries original content not found in the print edition and includes writer's guidelines. Contact: Michelle Taute, online editor.

Tips: "Find a design, surface or technique that is fresh and new to decorative painting. The more you know—and can prove you know—about decorative painting the better your chances. I'm looking for experts in the field who, through their own experience, can artfully describe the techniques involved. How-to articles are most open to freelancers. Be sure to query with photo/slides, and show that you understand the extensive graphic requirements for these pieces and can provide painted progressives—slides or illustrations that show works in progress."

▨ $ DOLL WORLD The Magazine for Doll Lovers, House of White Birches, 306 E. Parr Rd., Berne IN 46711. (219)589-4000. Fax: (219)589-8093. E-mail: doll_world@whitebirches.com. Website: www.dollworld-magazine.com. **Contact:** Vicki Steensma, editor. **90% freelance written.** Bimonthly magazine covering doll collecting, restoration. "Interested in informative articles about doll history, interviews with doll artists and collectors, and how-to articles." Estab. 1976. Circ. 65,000. Pays pre-publication. Byline given. Buys all rights. Submit material 9 months in advance. Accepts queries by mail, e-mail, fax. Responds in 2 months. Writer's guidelines and editorial calendar for SASE.

Nonfiction: "Subjects with broad appeal to the 'boomer' generation." The editor reports an interest in seeing features on dolls of the 1930s-1960s. **Buys 50 mss/year.** Send complete ms. **Pays $50 and up.**

Photos: Send top-quality photos (transparencies preferred). Captions and identification of subjects required.

Tips: "Choose a specific manufacturer or artist and talk about his dolls or a specific doll—modern or antique—and explore its history and styles made. Be descriptive, but do not overuse adjectives. Use personal conversational tone."

$ $ DOLLHOUSE MINIATURES, Kalmbach Publishing Co., 21027 Crossroads Circle, Waukesha WI 53187-9951. (262)798-6618. Fax: (262)796-1383. E-mail: cstjacques@dhminiatures.com. Website: www.dhminiatures.com. Editor: Jane D. Lange. **Contact:** Candice St. Jacques, managing editor. **50% freelance written.** Monthly magazine covering dollhouse scale miniatures. "*Dollhouse Miniatures* is aimed at passionate miniatures hobbyists. Our readers take their miniatures seriously and do not regard them as toys. We avoid 'cutesiness' and treat our subject as a serious art form and/or an engaging leisure interest." Estab. 1971. Circ. 40,000. **Pays on acceptance.** Byline given. Buys all rights but will revert rights by agreement. Submit seasonal material 1 year in advance. Responds in 3 weeks to queries; 2 months to mss. Sample copy for $4.50. Writer's guidelines for #10 SASE.

Nonfiction: How-to miniature projects in 1″, ½″, ¼″ scales, interview/profile (artisans or collectors), photo feature (dollhouses, collections, museums). No articles on miniature shops or essays. **Buys 120 mss/year.** Query with few sample photos. Length: 1,000-1,500 words for features, how-to's may be longer. **"Payment varies, but averages $150."**

Photos: Send photos with submission. Requires 35mm slides and larger, 3×5 prints. "Photos are paid for with manuscript. Seldom buy individual photos." Captions preferred; identification of subjects required. Buys all rights.

Tips: "It is essential that writers for *Dollhouse Miniatures* be active miniaturists, or at least very knowledgeable about the hobby. Our readership is intensely interested in miniatures and will discern lack of knowledge or enthusiasm on the part of an author. A writer can best break in to magazine by sending photos of work, credentials and a story outline. Photographs must be sharp and properly exposed to reveal details. Photos showing scale are especially appreciated. For articles about subjects in the Chicago/Milwaukee area, we can usually send our staff photographer."

$ DOLLMAKING, Your Resource for Creating & Costuming Modern Porcelain Dolls, Jones Publishing, N7450 Aanstad Rd., P.O. Box 5000, Iola WI 54945. (715)445-5000. Fax: (715)445-4053. E-mail: editor@dollmakingarti san.com. Website: www.dollmakingartisan.com. **Contact:** Stacy D. Carlson, editor. **50% freelance written.** Bimonthly magazine covering porcelain dollmaking. "*Dollmaking*'s intent is to entertain and inform porcelain and sculpted modern doll artists and costumers with the newest projects and techniques. It is meant to be a resource for hobby enthusiasts." Estab. 1985. Circ. 15,000. Pays on publication. Byline sometimes given. Buys all rights. Editorial lead time 4 months. Submit seasonal material 4 months in advance. Accepts queries by mail, e-mail, fax, phone. Sample copy online at website. Writer's guidelines free.
Nonfiction: Inspirational, interview/profile, personal experience. **Buys 12 mss/year.** Query. Length: 800 words. **Pays $75-150.**
Photos: State availability of photos with submission. Reviews 2½ × 2½ transparencies. Negotiates payment individually. Buys all rights.
Columns/Departments: Sewing Q&A (readers write in with sewing questions), 1,600 words. **Buys 2-3 mss/year.** Query. **Pays $75.**
Fillers: Anecdotes. **Buys 6/year.** Length: 500-800 words. **Pays $55-75.**
Tips: "The best way to break in is to send a manuscript of something the author has written concerning porcelain dollmaking and costuming. The article may be a personal story, a special technique used when making a doll, a successful doll fundraiser, sewing tips for dolls, or anything that would be of interest to a serious doll artisan. If no manuscript is available, at least send a letter of interest."

N ✄ $ $ DOLLS, Collector Communications, 170 Fifth Ave., Suite 1200, New York NY 10010. Fax: (212)645-8976. E-mail: nr@collector-online.com. Managing Editor: Bessie Nestoras. **Contact:** Nayda Rondon, editor. **75% freelance written.** Special interest magazine published 10 times/year covering dolls, doll artists and related topics of interest to doll collectors and enthusiasts." "*Dolls* enhances the joy of collecting by introducing readers to the best new dolls from around the world, along with the artists and designers who create them. It keeps readers up-to-date on shows, sales and special events in the doll world. With beautiful color photography, *Dolls* offers an array of easy-to-read, informative articles that help our collectors select the best buys." Estab. 1982. Circ. 100,000. Pays on publication. Byline given. Buys first North American serial rights. Accepts queries by mail, e-mail, fax. Accepts simultaneous submissions. Responds in 1 month.
Nonfiction: Book reviews, historical/nostalgic, how-to, interview/profile, new product, photo feature. **Buys 55 mss/year.** Query with published clips or send complete ms. Length: 750-1,200 words. **Pays $100-400.** Sometimes pays expenses of writers on assignment.
Photos: Send photos with submission. Reviews transparencies. Offers no additional payment for photos accepted with ms. Captions, model releases and identification of subjects required. Buys one-time rights.
Tips: "Know the subject matter and artists. Having quality artwork and access to doll artists for interviews are big pluses. We need original ideas of interest to doll lovers."

$ $ $ FAMILY TREE MAGAZINE, Discover, Preserve & Celebrate Your Family's History, F&W Publi-cations, 1507 Dana Ave., Cincinnati OH 45207. (513)531-2690. Fax: (513)531-2902. E-mail: ftmedit@fwpubs. com. Website: www.familytreemagazine.com. **Contact:** David A. Fryxell, editorial director. **75% freelance written.** Bimonthly magazine covering family history, heritage and genealogy. "*Family Tree Magazine* is a general-interest consumer magazine that helps readers discover, preserve and celebrate their family's history. We cover genealogy, ethnic heritage, personal history, genealogy Web sites and software, scrapbooking, photography and photo preservation, and other ways that families connect with their past." Estab. 1999. Circ. 130,000. **Pays on acceptance.** Publishes ms an average of 6 months after acceptance. Byline given. Offers 25% kill fee. Buys first rights and electronic rights. Editorial lead time 8 months. Submit seasonal material 8 months in advance. Accepts queries by mail, e-mail. Accepts simultane-ous submissions. Responds in 1 month to queries. Sample copy for $5.25 or on website. Writer's guidelines for #10 SASE or on website.
Nonfiction: Book excerpts, historical/nostalgic, how-to (genealogy), new product (photography, computer), technical (genealogy software, photography equipment), travel (with ethnic heritage slant). "Articles are geared to beginners but never talk down to the audience. We emphasize sidebars, tips and other reader-friendly 'packaging,' and each article aims to give the reader the resources necessary to take the next step in his or her quest for their personal past." **Buys 60 mss/year.** Query with published clips. Length: 1,000-3,500 words. **Pays $250-800.** Sometimes pays expenses of writers on assignment.
Reprints: Accepts previously published submissions.
Photos: State availability of photos with submission. Reviews transparencies and 8 × 10 prints. Negotiates payment individually. Captions required. Buys one-time rights.
   ▪ The online magazine carries original content not found in the print edition and includes writer's guidelines.
Tips: "We see too many broad, general stories on genealogy or records, and personal accounts of 'how I found great-aunt Sally' without how-to value."

$ $ FIBERARTS, The Magazine of Textiles, Altamont Press, 50 College St., Asheville NC 28801. (828)253-0467. Fax: (828)253-7952. E-mail: fiberarts@larkbooks.com. Website: www.larkbooks.com/fiberarts. **Contact:** Ann Batchelder, editor. **100% freelance written.** Eager to work with new writers. Magazine published 5 times/year covering textiles as art and craft (contemporary trends in fiber sculpture, weaving, quilting, surface design, stitchery, papermaking, basketry, felting, wearable art, knitting, fashion, crochet, mixed textile techniques, ethnic dying, fashion, eccentric tidbits, etc.) for textile artists, craftspeople, hobbyists, teachers, museum and gallery staffs, collectors and enthusiasts. Estab. 1975. Circ. 25,250. Pays 30 days after publication. Publishes ms an average of 4 months after acceptance. Byline given. Buys first rights. Sample copy for $5 and 10×12 SAE with 2 first-class stamps. Writer's guidelines for #10 SAE with 2 first-class stamps. Editorial guidelines and style sheet available.

Nonfiction: Historical, artist interview/profile, opinion, photo feature, technical, education, trends, exhibition reviews, textile news. Query with brief outline prose synopsis and SASE. Include a few visuals that might accompany the article. No phone queries. "Please be very specific about your proposal. Also an important consideration in accepting an article is the kind of photos—35mm slides and/or b&w glossies—that you can provide as illustration. We like to see photos in advance." Length: 250-2,000 words plus 4-5 photos. **Pays $100-400,** depending on article. Rarely pays the expenses of writers on assignment or for photos.

Photos: B&w photos or color slides must accompany every article. The more photos to choose from, the better. Full photo captions are essential. Please include a separate, number-keyed caption sheet. The names and addresses of those mentioned in the article or to whom the visuals are to be returned are necessary.

Columns/Departments: Swatches (new ideas for fiber, unusual or offbeat subjects, work spaces, resources and marketing, techniques, materials, equipment, design and trends), 400 words. **Pays $100.** Profile (focuses on one artist), 400 words and one photo. **Pays $100.** Reviews (exhibits and shows; summarize quality, significance, focus and atmosphere, then evaluate selected pieces for aesthetic quality, content and technique—because we have an international readership, brief biographical notes or quotes might be pertinent for locally or regionally known artists), 400 words and 3-5 photos. (Do not cite works for which visuals are unavailable; you are not eligible to review a show in which you have participated as an artist, organizer, curator or juror.) **Pays $100.**

Tips: "Our writers are very familiar with the textile field, and this is what we look for in a new writer. Familiarity with textile techniques, history or events determines clarity of an article more than a particular style of writing. The writer should also be familiar with *Fiberarts*, the magazine. While the professional is essential to the editorial depth of *Fiberarts*, and must find timely information in the pages of the magazine, this is not our greatest audience. Our editorial philosophy is that the magazine must provide the non-professional textile enthusiast with the inspiration, support, useful information, and direction to keep him or her excited, interested, and committed. No phone queries."

N **$** **FIBRE FOCUS, Magazine of the Ontario Handweavers and Spinners**, (formerly *Bulletin*), 450 Westheights Dr., P.O. Box 44009, Kitchener, Ontario N2N 3G7 Canada. E-mail: dburns@golden.net. Website: www.OHS .on.ca. **Contact:** Dianne Burns, editor. **80-90% freelance written.** Quarterly magazine covering handweaving, spinning, basketry, beading and other fibre arts. "Our readers are weavers and spinners. All articles deal with some aspect of these crafts." Estab. 1957. Circ. 1,000. Pays within 30 days after publication. Buys one-time rights. Editorial lead time 6 months. Submit seasonal material 6 months in advance. Responds in 1 month to mss. Sample copy for $5 (Canadian).

Nonfiction: How-to, interview/profile, new production, opinion, personal experiences, technical. **Buys 40-60 mss/ year.** Length varies, "however, articles over 5,000 words may be split and published in two consecutive issues." **Pays $25 (Canadian) per published page.**

Reprints: Accepts previously published submissions.

Photos: Send photos with submission. Reviews 4×6 color prints. Offers additional payment for photos accepted with ms. Captions, identification of subjects required. Buys one-time rights.

Fiction: Humorous, slice-of-life vignettes, if they deal with weaving, spinning or other related crafts. **Pays $25 (Canadian) per published page.**

Tips: "Submissions from men and women who love the fibre arts as much as we do are always welcome."

$ $ FINE TOOL JOURNAL, Antique & Collectible Tools, Inc., 27 Fickett Rd., Pownal ME 04069. (207)688-4962. Fax: (207)688-4831. E-mail: ceb@finetoolj.com. Website: www.finetoolj.com. **Contact:** Clarence Blanchard, editor. **90% freelance written.** "The *Fine Tool Journal* is a quarterly magazine specializing in older or antique hand tools from all traditional trades. Readers are primarily interested in woodworking tools, but some subscribers have interests in such areas as leatherworking, wrenches, kitchen and machinist tools. Readers range from beginners just getting into the hobby to advanced collectors and organizations." Estab. 1970. Circ. 2,500. Pays on publication. Publishes ms an average of 6 months after acceptance. Byline given. Offers $50 kill fee. Buys first and second serial (reprint) rights. Editorial lead time 9 months. Submit seasonal material 6 months in advance. Accepts queries by mail, e-mail, fax. Responds in 2 months to queries; 3 months to mss. Sample copy for $5. Guidelines for SASE.

Nonfiction: General interest, historical/nostalgic, how-to (make, use, fix and tune tools), interview/profile, personal experience, photo feature, technical. "We're looking for articles about tools from all trades. Interests include collecting, preservation, history, values and price trends, traditional methods and uses, interviews with collectors/users/makers, etc. Most articles published will deal with vintage, pre-1950, hand tools. Also seeking articles on how to use specific tools or how a specific trade was carried out. However, how-to articles must be detailed and not just of general interest. We do on occasion run articles on modern toolmakers who produce traditional hand tools." **Buys 24 mss/year.** Send complete ms. Length: 400-2,000 words. **Pays $50-200.** Sometimes pays expenses of writers on assignment.

Reprints: Accepts previously published submissions.

Photos: Send photos with submission. Reviews 4×5 prints. Negotiates payment individually. Model releases, identification of subjects required. Buys all rights.

Columns/Departments: Stanley Tools (new finds and odd types), 300-400 words; Tips of the Trade (how to use tools), 100-200 words. **Buys 12 mss/year.** Send complete ms. **Pays $30-60.**

Tips: "The easiest way to get published in the *Journal* is to have personal experience or know someone who can supply the detailed information. We are seeking articles that go deeper than general interest and that knowledge requires experience and/or research. Short of personal experience find a subject that fits our needs and that interests you. Spend some time learning the ins and outs of the subject and with hard work and a little luck you will earn the right to write about it."

$ $ FINE WOODWORKING, The Taunton Press, P.O. Box 5506, Newtown CT 06470-5506. (203)426-8171. Fax: (203)270-6751. E-mail: fw@taunton.com. Website: www.taunton.com. Editor: Tim Schreiner. **Contact:** Anatole Burkin, managing editor. Bimonthly magazine on woodworking in the small shop. "All writers are also skilled woodworkers. It's more important that a contributor be a woodworker than a writer. Our editors (also woodworkers) will fix the words." Estab. 1975. Circ. 270,000. **Pays on acceptance.** Byline given. Kill fee varies; "editorial discretion." Buys first rights and rights to republish in anthologies and use in promo pieces. Submit seasonal material 6 months in advance. Accepts simultaneous submissions. Responds in 2 months. Writer's guidelines free and on website.

> O—ᵣ "We're looking for good articles on almost all aspects of woodworking from the basics of tool use, stock preparation and joinery to specialized techniques and finishing. We're especially keen on articles about shop-built tools, jigs and fixtures or any stage of design, construction, finishing and installation of cabinetry and furniture. Whether the subject involves fundamental methods or advanced techniques, we look for high-quality workmanship, thoughtful designs, safe and proper procedures."

Nonfiction: How-to (woodworking). **Buys 120 mss/year.** Query with proposal letter. "No specs—our editors would rather see more than less." **Pays $150/magazine page.** Sometimes pays expenses of writers on assignment.

Photos: Send photos with submission. Reviews contact sheets, negatives, transparencies, prints. Captions, model releases, identification of subjects required. Buys one-time rights.

Columns/Departments: Notes & Comment (topics of interest to woodworkers); Question & Answer (woodworking Q & A); Methods of Work (shop tips); Tools & Materials (short reviews of new tools). **Buys 400 items/year.** Length varies. **Pays $10-150/published page.**

The online magazine carries original content not found in the print edition. Contact: Tim Sams, online editor.

Tips: "Send for authors guidelines and follow them. Stories about woodworking reported by non-woodworkers are *not* used. Our magazine is essentially reader-written by woodworkers."

✪ $ $ FINESCALE MODELER, Kalmbach Publishing Co., 21027 Crossroads Circle, P.O. Box 1612, Waukesha WI 53187. (414)796-8776. Fax: (414)796-1383. E-mail: tthompson@finescale.com. Website: www.finescale.com. Editor: Terry Thompson. **80% freelance written.** Eager to work with new/unpublished writers. Magazine published 10 times/year "devoted to how-to-do-it modeling information for scale model builders who build non-operating aircraft, tanks, boats, automobiles, figures, dioramas, and science fiction and fantasy models." Circ. 80,000. **Pays on acceptance.** Publishes ms an average of 14 months after acceptance. Byline given. Buys all rights. Responds in 6 weeks to queries; 3 months to mss. Sample copy for 9×12 SAE with 3 first-class stamps. Writer's guidelines free.

Nonfiction: How-to (build scale models); technical (research information for building models). Query or send complete ms. Length: 750-3,000 words. **Pays $55/published page minimum.**

• *Finescale Modeler* is especially looking for how-to articles for car modelers.

Photos: Send color photos with ms. Pays $7.50 minimum for transparencies and $5 minimum for color prints. Captions and identification of subjects required. Buys one-time rights.

Columns/Departments: *FSM* Showcase (photos plus description of model); *FSM* Tips and Techniques (model building hints and tips). **Buys 25-50 Tips and Techniques/year.** Query or send complete ms. Length: 100-1,000 words. **Pays $25-50.**

Tips: "A freelancer can best break in first through hints and tips, then through feature articles. Most people who write for *FSM* are modelers first, writers second. This is a specialty magazine for a special, quite expert audience. Essentially, 99% of our writers will come from that audience."

$ $ GENEALOGICAL COMPUTING, Ancestry Inc., 266 W. Center St., Orem UT 84057. (801)426-3500. Fax: (734)354-6442. E-mail: liz@ancestordetective.com. Website: www.ancestry.com. **Contact:** Elizabeth Kelley Kerstens, managing editor. **85% freelance written.** Quarterly magazine covering genealogy and computers. Estab. 1980. Circ. 13,500. Pays on publication. Publishes ms an average of 4 months after acceptance. Byline given. Buys all rights. Editorial lead time 4 months. Submit seasonal material 4 months in advance.

Nonfiction: How-to, interview/profile, new product, technical. **Buys 40 mss/year.** Query by mail. Length: 1,500-2,500 words. **Pays $40-200.**

Reprints: Accepts previously published submissions. Pays 75% of amount paid for an original article.

✪ $ $ GREAT AMERICAN CRAFTS, Krause Publications, 700 E. State St., Iola WI 54990-0001. (715)445-2214. Fax: (715)445-4087. Website: www.krause.com. Editor: Julie Stephani. **Contact:** Sandra Sparks, managing editor. **75% freelance written.** Bimonthly magazine covering general crafts. "*Great American Crafts* contains projects using needlework, knitting, crocheting, sewing, quilting, clay, painting and general projects for beginning and intermediate crafters. Subscribers get book discounts and other special benefits." Estab. 1998. Pays on publication. Publishes ms an average of 6 months after acceptance. Byline given. Buys all rights and occasional second serial (reprint) or makes work-for-hire assignments. Editorial lead time 4 months. Submit seasonal material 6 months in advance. Accepts queries by mail, e-mail. Writer's guidelines free or on website.

Nonfiction: How-to (craft project directions), new product, photo feature. **Buys 300 mss/year for craft projects.** Query. **Pays $50-250.**

Photos: Send photos with submission. Offers no additional payment for photos accepted with ms. Model releases and identification of subjects required. Buys all rights.

Columns/Departments: Pays $50-250.

Tips: "To submit an original design to *Great American Crafts* magazine, please include the following: designer's name, address, daytime phone number, clear photo or detailed sketch, brief paragraph describing the project. If your design is accepted for publication, we will call you to discuss the contract, fee, and deadlines. You will be asked to send us the project and instructions at this time. Instructions must be typed. We prefer to receive them on disk along with a hard copy. Include the following: complete materials list, detailed step-by-step instructions, full-size patterns if needed, illustrations and charts if needed."

$ $ THE HOME SHOP MACHINIST, 2779 Aero Park Dr., P.O. Box 1810, Traverse City MI 49685. (616)946-3712. Fax: (616)946-3289. E-mail: jrice@villagepress.com. Website: www.villagepress.com. **Contact:** Joe D. Rice, editor. **95% freelance written.** Bimonthly magazine covering machining and metalworking for the hobbyist. Circ. 34,000. Pays on publication. Publishes ms an average of 2 years after acceptance. Byline given. Buys first North American serial rights only. Responds in 2 months. Free sample copy and writer's guidelines for 9×12 SASE.

Nonfiction: How-to (projects designed to upgrade present shop equipment or hobby model projects that require machining), technical (should pertain to metalworking, machining, drafting, layout, welding or foundry work for the hobbyist). No fiction or "people" features. **Buys 40 mss/year.** Query or send complete ms. Length: open—"whatever it takes to do a thorough job." **Pays $40/published page, plus $9/published photo.**

Photos: Send photos with ms. Pays $9-40 for 5×7 b&w prints; $70/page for camera-ready art; $40 for b&w cover photo. Captions and identification of subjects required.

Columns/Departments: Book Reviews; New Product Reviews; Micro-Machining; Foundry. "Become familiar with our magazine before submitting." Query first. **Buys 25-30 mss/year.** Length: 600-1,500 words. **Pays $40-70/page.**

Fillers: Machining tips/shortcuts. No news clippings. **Buys 12-15/year.** Length: 100-300 words. **Pays $30-48.**

Tips: "The writer should be experienced in the area of metalworking and machining; should be extremely thorough in explanations of methods, processes—always with an eye to safety; and should provide good quality b&w photos and/ or clear dimensioned drawings to aid in description. Visuals are of increasing importance to our readers. Carefully planned photos, drawings and charts will carry a submission to our magazine much farther along the path to publication."

N $ $ $ INTERNATIONAL WRISTWATCH MAGAZINE, International Wristwatch Magazine, Inc., 979 Summer St., Stamford CT 06905. (203)352-1818. Fax: (203)352-1820. E-mail: wristwatch@snet.net. Website: www.intl wristwatch.com. **Contact:** Gary George, editor. **50% freelance written.** Magazine covering wristwatches. "We're interested in all information about wristwatches—collecting, modern production, historical, etc." Estab. 1989. Circ. 25,000. Pays on publication. Publishes ms an average of 2 months after acceptance. Byline given. Offers 50% kill fee. Buys first rights. Editorial lead time 4 months. Accepts queries by mail, e-mail, fax, phone. Accepts simultaneous submissions.

Nonfiction: General interest, historical/nostalgic, interview/profile, new product, technical. No trade-related wristwatch matter. Query. Length: 500-3,000 words. **Pays 10¢-$1/word.** "Watch trade is possible option for payment."

Reprints: Accepts previously published submissions.

Photos: State availability of photos with submission. Negotiates payment individually. Captions required. Buys one-time rights.

Columns/Departments: News (events sponsored by watch companies), 50 words; Market (new product section), 50-75 words; Auction (auction reports and analysis), 100-150 words; Collecting (collecting vintage watches), 1,000 words. Query. **Pays 10-50¢/word.**

JOY OF COLLECTING, Publications International, 7373 N. Cicero, Lincolnwood IL 60712. (847)329-5318. Fax: (847)329-5387. E-mail: akahlenberg@pubint.com. Editor: Sara Hauber. **Contact:** Ann Kahlenberg, acquisitions editor. **100% freelance written.** Bimonthly magazine covering contemporary limited edition and open edition collectibles. We cover only "new" collectibles such as dolls, figurines, ornaments, coins, crystal, plush, sports, miniatures, prints, plates and bears—no secondary market or antiques. Estab. 1997. Circ. 175,000. **Pays on acceptance.** Publishes ms an average of 4 months after acceptance. Byline given. Buys all rights. Editorial lead time 6 months. Submit seasonal material 6 months in advance. Accepts queries by mail, e-mail, fax. Responds in 1 month to queries; 2 months to mss. Sample copy and writer's guidelines for SAE.

　　O─ Break in by "demonstrating a strong knowledge of the collectibles industry. Send previously published clips on the collectibles industry. Have a fun, conversational tone in your writing."

Nonfiction: How-to, interview/profile, new product, personal experience, photo feature. No antiques, memorabilia or secondary market coverage. **Buys 50 mss/year.** Query with published clips. Length varies per assignment.

Photos: Send photos with submission. Reviews transparencies and prints. Negotiates payment individually. Captions, model releases and identification of subjects required. Buys one-time rights.

Tips: "Our target audience is mostly middle-aged women in a lower- to middle- income bracket. Prices should be mentioned, but they should never be the focus of an article. When covering a general theme, skew the coverage toward the more affordable items. It's not necessary to avoid the more expensive manufacturers entirely, but reserve more space for the lower end of the price range. Our goal is to portray collecting as accessible and fun for everyone. Send a query with clips and a solid cover letter that allows us to evaluate your background. Do not send manuscript."

$ $ KITPLANES, For designers, builders and pilots of experimental aircraft, A Primedia Publication, 8745 Arrow Dr., Suite 105, San Diego CA 92123. (619)694-0491. Fax: (619)694-8147. E-mail: dave@kitplanes.com. Website: www.kitplanes.com. Managing Editor: Keith Beveridge. **Contact:** Dave Martin, editor. **70% freelance written.** Eager to work with new/unpublished writers. Monthly magazine covering self-construction of private aircraft for pilots and builders. Estab. 1984. Circ. 83,000. Pays on publication. Publishes ms an average of 3 months after acceptance. Byline given. Buys exclusive complete serial rights. Submit seasonal material 6 months in advance. Accepts queries by mail, e-mail. Responds in 2 weeks to queries; 6 weeks to mss. Sample copy for $5. Writer's guidelines free.
Nonfiction: How-to, interview/profile, new product, personal experience, photo feature, technical, general interest. "We are looking for articles on specific construction techniques, the use of tools, both hand and power, in aircraft building, the relative merits of various materials, conversions of engines from automobiles for aviation use, installation of instruments and electronics." No general-interest aviation articles, or "My First Solo" type of articles. **Buys 80 mss/ year.** Query. Length: 500-3,000 words. **Pays $70-600,** including story photos.
Photos: State availability of or send photos with query or ms. Pays $300 for cover photos. Captions and identification of subjects required. Buys one-time rights.
Tips: "*Kitplanes* contains very specific information—a writer must be extremely knowledgeable in the field. Major features are entrusted only to known writers. I cannot emphasize enough that articles must be directed at the individual aircraft builder. We need more 'how-to' photo features in all areas of homebuilt aircraft."

$ $ KNIVES ILLUSTRATED, The Premier Cutlery Magazine, 265 S. Anita Dr., Suite 120, Orange CA 92868-3310. (714)939-9991, ext. 201. Fax: (714)939-9909. E-mail: budlang@pacbell.net. Website: www.knivesillustrated.com. **Contact:** Bud Lang, editor. **40-50% freelance written.** Bimonthly magazine covering high-quality factory and custom knives. "We publish articles on different types of factory and custom knives, how-to-make knives, technical articles, shop tours, articles on knife makers and artists. Must have knowledge about knives and the people who use and make them. We feature the full range of custom and high tech production knives, from miniatures to swords, leaving nothing untouched. We're also known for our outstanding how-to articles and technical features on equipment, materials and knife making supplies. We do not feature knife maker profiles as such, although we do spotlight some makers by featuring a variety of their knives and insight into their background and philosophy." Estab. 1987. Circ. 35,000. Pays on publication. Byline given. Editorial lead time 3 months. Accepts queries by mail, e-mail, fax, phone. Responds in 2 weeks to queries. Sample copy available. Writer's guidelines for #10 SASE.
Nonfiction: How-to, interview/profile, photo features, technical. **Buys 35-40 mss/year.** Query first. Length: 400-2,000 words. **Pays $100-500 minimum.**
Photos: Send photos with submission. Reviews 35mm, 2¼×2¼, 4×5 transparencies, 5×7 prints. Negotiates payment individually. Captions, model releases, identification of subjects required.
Tips: "Most of our contributors are involved with knives, either as collectors, makers, engravers, etc. To write about this subject requires knowledge. A 'good' writer can do OK if they study some recent issues. If you are interested in submitting work to *Knives Illustrated* magazine, it is suggested you analyze at least two or three different editions to get a feel for the magazine. It is also recommended that you call or mail in your query to determine if we are interested in the topic you have in mind. While verbal or written approval may be given, all articles are still received on a speculation basis. We cannot approve any article until we have it in hand, whereupon we will make a final decision as to its suitability for our use. Bear in mind we do not suggest you go to the trouble to write an article if there is doubt we can use it promptly."

$ $ THE LEATHER CRAFTERS & SADDLERS JOURNAL, 331 Annette Court, Rhinelander WI 54501-2902. (715)362-5393. Fax: (715)362-5391. Managing Editor: Dorothea Reis. **Contact:** William R. Reis, publisher. **100% freelance written.** Bimonthly magazine. "A leather-working publication with how-to, step-by-step instructional articles using full-size patterns for leathercraft, leather art, custom saddle, boot and harness making, etc. A complete resource for leather, tools, machinery and allied materials plus leather industry news." Estab. 1990. Circ. 9,000. Pays on publication. Publishes ms an average of 2 months after acceptance. Byline given. Buys first North American serial and second serial (reprint) rights. Submit seasonal material 6 months in advance. Accepts queries by mail, fax, phone. Accepts simultaneous submissions. Responds in 1 month. Sample copy for $5. Writer's guidelines for #10 SASE.
Oⲧ Break in with a how-to, step-by-step leather item article from beginner through masters and saddlemaking.
Nonfiction: How-to (crafts and arts and any other projects using leather). "I want only articles that include hands-on, step-by-step, how-to information." **Buys 75 mss/year.** Send complete ms. Length: 500-2,500 words. **Pays $20-250 for assigned articles; $20-150 for unsolicited articles.**
Reprints: Send tearsheet or photocopy of article. Pays 50% of amount paid for an original article.
Columns/Departments: Beginners, Intermediate, Artists, Western Design, Saddlemakers, International Design and Letters (the open exchange of information between all peoples). Length: 500-2,500 words on all. **Buys 75 mss/year.** Send complete ms. **Pays 5¢/word.**
Photos: Send good contrast color print photos and full-size patterns and/or full-size photo-carve patterns with submission. Lack of these reduces payment amount. Captions required.
Fillers: Anecdotes, facts, gags illustrated by cartoonist, newsbreaks. Length: 25-200 words. **Pays $5-20.**

Tips: "We want to work with people who understand and know leathercraft and are interested in passing on their knowledge to others. We would prefer to interview people who have achieved a high level in leathercraft skill."

LINN'S STAMP NEWS, Amos Press, 911 Vandemark Rd., P.O. Box 29, Sidney OH 45365. (937)498-0801. Fax: (800)340-9501. E-mail: linns@linns.com. Website: www.linns.com. Editor: Michael Laurence. **Contact:** Michael Schreiber, managing editor. **50% freelance written.** Weekly tabloid on the stamp collecting hobby. "All articles must be about philatelic collectibles. Our goal at *Linn's* is to create a weekly publication that is indispensable to stamp collectors." Estab. 1928. Circ. 60,000. Pays within one month of publication. Publishes ms an average of 1 month after acceptance. Byline given. Buys first worldwide serial rights. Submit seasonal material 2 months in advance. Responds in 6 weeks to mss. Free sample copy. Writer's guidelines for #10 SAE with 2 first-class stamps.

Nonfiction: General interest, historical/nostalgic, how-to, interview/profile, technical, club and show news, current issues, auction realization and recent discoveries. "No articles merely giving information on background of stamp subject. Must have philatelic information included." **Buys 300 mss/year.** Send complete ms. Length: 500 words maximum. **Pays $20-50.** Rarely pays expenses of writers on assignment.

Photos: Good illustrations a must. Send photos with submission. Provide captions on separate sheet of paper. Prefers crisp, sharp focus, high-contrast glossy b&w prints. Offers no additional payment for photos accepted with ms. Captions required. Buys all rights.

Tips: "Check and double check all facts. Footnotes and bibliographies are not appropriate to our newspaper style. Work citation into the text. Even though your subject might be specialized, write understandably. Explain terms. *Linn's* features are aimed at a broad audience of relatively novice collectors. Keep this audience in mind. Do not write down to the reader but provide information in such a way to make stamp collecting more interesting to more people. Embrace readers without condescending to them."

$ LOST TREASURE, INC., P.O. Box 451589, Grove OK 74345. Fax: (918)786-2192. E-mail: managingeditor @losttreasure.com. Website: www.losttreasure.com. **Contact:** Patsy Beyerl, managing editor. **75% freelance written.** Monthly and annual magazines covering lost treasure. Estab. 1966. Circ. 55,000. Pays on publication. Byline given. Buys all rights. Accepts queries by mail, e-mail, fax. Responds in 1 month to queries, 2 months to ms. Writers guidelines for #10 SASE. Sample copy and guidelines for 10×13 SAE with $1.47 postage or on website. Editorial calendar for *Lost Treasure* for SASE.

Nonfiction: *Lost Treasure*, a monthly, is composed of lost treasure stories, legends, folklore, how-to articles, treasure hunting club news, who's who in treasure hunting, tips. Length: 500-1,500 words. *Treasure Cache*, an annual, contains stories about documented treasure caches with a sidebar from the author telling the reader how to search for the cache highlighted in the story. **Buys 225 mss/year.** Length: 1,000-2,000 words. Query on *Treasure Cache* only. **Pays 4¢/word.**

Photos: Black & white or color prints, hand-drawn or copied maps, art with source credit with mss will help sell your story. Pays $5/published photo. We are always looking for cover photos with or without accompanying ms. Pays $100/published photo. Must be 35mm color slides, vertical. Captions required.

Tips: "We are only interested in treasures that can be found with metal detectors. Queries welcome but not required. If you write about famous treasures and lost mines, be sure we haven't used your selected topic recently and story must have a new slant or new information. Source documentation required. How-tos should cover some aspect of treasure hunting and how-to steps should be clearly defined. If you have a *Treasure Cache* story we will, if necessary, help the author with the sidebar telling how to search for the cache in the story. *Lost Treasure* articles should coordinate with theme issues when possible."

$ $ MEMORY MAKERS, The First Source for Scrapbooking Ideas, Satellite Press, 475 W. 115th Ave., #6, Denver CO 80234. (303)452-1968. Fax: (303)452-2164. E-mail: editorial@memorymakersmagazine.com. Website: www.memorymakersmagazine.com. **Contact:** Deborah Mock, editor. **25% freelance written.** Bimonthly magazine covering scrapbooking, hobbies and crafts. "*Memory Makers* is an international magazine that showcases ideas and stories of scrapbookers. It includes articles with information, instructions, and products that apply to men and women who make creative scrapbooks." Estab. 1996. Circ. 200,000. Pays on project completion. Publishes ms 4 months after acceptance. Byline given. Buys all rights. Editorial lead time 6 months after acceptance. Submit seasonal material 6 months in advance. Accepts queries by mail, e-mail, fax. Accepts simultaneous submissions. Responds in 1 month to queries. Guidelines for #10 SASE.

○→ Break in with articles on "unique craft techniques that can apply to scrapbooking and personal stories of how scrapbooking has impacted someone's life."

Nonfiction: Historical/nostalgic, how-to (scrapbooking techniques), inspirational, interview/profile, new product, personal experience, travel (all related to scrapbooking). No "all-encompassing how-to scrapbook" articles. **Buys 6-10 mss/year.** Query with published clips. Length: 1,000-1,500 words. Pays **$100-750.**

Columns/Departments: Keeping It Safe (issues surrounding the safe preservation of scrapbooks), Scrapbooking 101 (how-to scrapbooking techniques for beginners), Photojournaling (new and useful ideas for improving scrapbook journaling), Sure Shots (photography and camera usage tips), Modern Memories (computer and modern technology scrapbooking issues), all 500-700 words. Query with published clips. **Pays $150-300.**

N $ $ MERCATOR'S WORLD, The magazine of maps, exploration and discovery, Aster Publishing Corp., 845 Willamette St., Eugene OR 97401. (541)345-3800. Fax: (541)302-9872. E-mail: gturley@asterpub.com. Website: www.mercatormag.com. **Contact:** Gary Turley, managing editor. **90% freelance written.** Bimonthly magazine covering antique map trade, collecting. "*Mercator's World* is a lively and informative consumer magazine designed for map enthusiasts and collectors. Each issue presents provocative and authoritative stories that examine the art and science of cartography and the political and cultural influences of ancient and modern maps." Estab. 1996. Circ. 20,000. Pays on publication. Publishes ms an average of 4 months after acceptance. Byline given. Offers 20% kill fee. Buys first North American serial, electronic and future anthology rights. Editorial lead time 6 months. Submit seasonal material 4 months in advance. Accepts queries by mail, e-mail, fax. Responds in 6 weeks to queries; 3 months to mss. Sample copy for 10×12 SAE with 7 first-class stamps or on website. Writer's guidelines free.

Nonfiction: Book excerpts, essays, historical/nostalgic, how-to, interview/profile, new product, personal experience, photo feature, technical, travel, biography. **Buys 35 mss/year.** Query with published clips. Length: 300-3,500 words. **Pays $400-600.** Sometimes pays expenses of writers on assignment.

Reprints: Occasionally accepts previously published submissions.

Photos: State availability of photos with submission. Reviews contact sheets, transparencies and 8×10 prints. Negotiates payment individually. Identification of subjects required. Buys one-time rights.

Columns/Departments: Cheri Brooks, senior editor (cbrooks@asterpub.com). Mercator's Log (cartographic news from around the world), 300 words; Aficionado (profiles map collector or scholar), 2,000 words; Multimedia (review of website or digital product), 1,000 words; Destination (carto-curiosity), 300 words. **Buys 18 mss/year.** Query with published clips. **Pays $100-500.**

Tips: "We want articles that will appeal to knowledgeable, sophisticated, well-educated readers. Feature articles focus on the following, or related, topics: The art and science of mapmaking; discoveries of rare or unusual maps; map collecting stories; cartographic curiosities; profiles of noteworthy cartographers, explorers, and map collectors; high and low spots in the history of exploration and discovery; news from the map trade; cartography-related auctions and sales; galleries, libraries, and special collections of maps, globes, atlases, and exploration journals; specialty maps; indigenous maps and mapmaking; cultural and political geography; geographic, political, social and religious roots of cartography; celebrated and unsung cartographers: individuals, companies, 'schools;' how maps have aided in scientific discoveries; how maps have perpetuated misconceptions and myths."

N $ MINIATURE QUILTS, Chitra Publications, 2 Public Ave., Montrose PA 18801. (570)278-1984. Fax: (570)278-2223. E-mail: chitraed@epix.net. Website: www.quilttownusa.com. **Contact:** Joyce Libal, senior editor. **40% freelance written.** Bimonthly magazine on miniature quilts. "We seek articles of an instructional nature (all techniques), profiles of talented quiltmakers and informational articles on all aspects of miniature quilts. Miniature is defined as quilts made up of blocks smaller than five inches." Estab. 1990. Circ. 70,000. Pays on publication. Publishes ms an average of 6 months after acceptance. Byline given. Buys second serial (reprint) rights. Submit seasonal material 8 months in advance. Accepts queries by mail, fax. Responds in 2 months. Writer's guidelines for SASE or on website.

○→ "Best bet—a quilter writing about a new or unusual quilting technique."

Nonfiction: How-to, profile articles about quilters who make small quilts, photo features about noteworthy miniature quilts or exhibits. Query with ideas. Length: 1,500 words maximum. **Pays $75/published page of text.**

Photos: Send photos with submission. Reviews 35mm slides and larger transparencies. Offers $20/photo. Captions, model releases and identification of subjects required.

Tips: "We're looking for articles (with slides or transparencies) on quilts in museum collections."

N $ $ MODEL RAILROADER, P.O. Box 1612, Waukesha WI 53187. Fax: (262)796-1142. E-mail: mrmag@mr mag.com. Website: www.modelrailroader.com/. **Contact:** Andy Sperandeo, editor. Monthly for hobbyists interested in scale model railroading. "We publish articles on all aspects of model-railroading and on prototype (real) railroading as a subject for modeling." Buys exclusive rights. Reports on submissions within 60 days.

Nonfiction: Wants construction articles on specific model railroad projects (structures, cars, locomotives, scenery, benchwork, etc.). Also photo stories showing model railroads. Query. "Study publication before submitting material." First-hand knowledge of subject almost always necessary for acceptable slant. **Pays base rate of $90/page.**

Photos: Buys photos with detailed descriptive captions only. Pays $15 and up, depending on size and use. Pays double b&w rate for color; full color cover earns $200.

Tips: "Before you prepare and submit any article, you should write us a short letter of inquiry describing what you want to do. We can then tell you if it fits our needs and save you from working on something we don't want."

$ $ MONITORING TIMES, Grove Enterprises Inc., P.O. Box 98, Brasstown NC 28902-0098. (828)837-9200. Fax: (828)837-2216. E-mail: mteditor@grove-ent.com. Website: www.grove-ent.com. Publisher: Robert Grove. **Contact:** Rachel Baughn, editor. **20% freelance written.** Monthly magazine for radio hobbyists. Estab. 1982. Circ. 30,000. Pays on publication. Publishes ms an average of 4 months after acceptance. Byline given. Buys first North American serial rights and limited reprint rights. Submit seasonal material 4 months in advance. Accepts queries by mail, e-mail, phone. Responds in 1 month. Sample copy and writer's guidelines for 9×12 SAE and 9 first-class stamps.

○→ Break in with a shortwave station profile or topic, or scanning topics of broad interest.

Nonfiction: General interest, how-to, humor, interview/profile, personal experience, photo feature, technical. **Buys 72 mss/year.** Query. Length: 1,500-3,000 words. **Pays $50/published page average.**

Reprints: Send photocopy of article and information about when and where the article previously appeared. Pays 25% of amount paid for an original article.

Photos: Send photos with submission. Captions required. Buys one-time rights.

Columns/Departments: "Query managing editor."

Tips: "Need articles on radio communications systems and shortwave broadcasters. We are accepting more technical projects."

★ **PACK-O-FUN, Projects For Kids & Families**, Clapper Communications, 2400 Devon Ave., Des Plaines IL 60018-4618. (847)635-5800. Fax: (847)635-6311. Website: www.craftideas.com. Editor: Billie Ciancio. **Contact:** Irene Mueller, managing editor. **85% freelance written.** Bimonthly magazine covering crafts and activities for kids and those working with kids. Estab. 1951. Circ. 102,000. Pays 45 days after signed contract. Byline given. Buys all rights. Editorial lead time 6 months. Submit seasonal material 8 months in advance. Accepts simultaneous submissions. Accepts queries by mail, fax. Responds in 2 months. Sample copy for $3.50 or on website.

Nonfiction: "We request quick and easy, inexpensive crafts and activities. Projects must be original, and complete instructions are required upon acceptance." Pay is negotiable.

Reprints: Send tearsheet of article and information about when and where the article previously appeared.

Photos: Photos of project may be submitted in place of project at query stage.

Tips: "*Pack-O-Fun* is looking for original how-to projects for kids and those working with kids. Write simple instructions for crafts to be done by children ages 5-13 years. We're looking for recyclable ideas for throwaways. We seldom accept fiction unless accompanied by a craft. It would be helpful to check out our magazine before submitting."

Ⓝ ★ $ $ **PIECEWORK MAGAZINE**, Interweave Press, Inc., 201 E. Fourth St., Loveland CO 80537-5655. (970)669-7672. Fax: (970)667-8317. E-mail: piecework@interweave.com. Website: www.interweave.com. Editor: Jeane Hutchins. **Contact:** Jake Rexus, assistant editor. **90% freelance written.** Bimonthly magazine covering needlework history. "*PieceWork* celebrates the rich tradition of needlework and the history of the people behind it. Stories and projects on embroidery, cross-stitch, knitting, crocheting and quilting, along with other textile arts, are featured in each issue." Estab. 1993. Circ. 60,000. Pays on publication. Byline given. Offers 30% kill fee. Buys first North American serial rights. Editorial lead time 6 months. Submit seasonal material 6 months in advance. Accepts queries by mail, e-mail, fax, phone. Responds in 6 months. Sample copy and writer's guidelines free.

Nonfiction: Book excerpts, historical/nostalgic, how-to, interview/profile, new product. No contemporary needlework articles. **Buys 25-30 mss/year.** Send complete ms. Length: 1,000-2,000 words. **Pays $100/printed page.**

Photos: State availability of photos with submission or send photos with submission. Reviews transparencies and prints. Captions, model releases and identification of subjects required. Buys one-time rights.

Tips: Submit a "well-researched article on a historical aspect of needlework complete with information on visuals and suggestion for accompanying project."

$ **POP CULTURE COLLECTING**, Odyssey Publications, Inc., 510-A South Corona Mall, Corona CA 92879-1420. (909)734-9636. Fax: (909)371-7139. E-mail: DBTOGI@aol.com. **Contact:** Ev Phillips, general manager. **80% freelance written.** Monthly magazine for people interested in collecting celebrity or pop culture-related memorabilia. "Focus is on movie and TV props, costumes, movie posters, rock 'n' roll memorabilia, animation art, space or sports memorabilia, even vintage comic books, newspapers and magazines. Any collectible item that has a celebrity or pop culture connection and evokes memories. *Pop Culture Collecting* likes to profile people or institutions with interesting and unusual collections and tell why they are meaningful or memorable. Articles stress how to find and collect memorabilia, how to preserve and display it, and determine what it is worth." Estab. 1995. Circ. 15,000. Pays on publication. Publishes ms 3 months after acceptance. Byline given. Offers negotiable kill fee. Buys all rights. Editorial lead time 2 months. Submit seasonal material 3 months in advance. Accepts queries by mail, e-mail, fax, phone. Responds in 2 weeks to queries; 1 month to mss. Sample copy and writer's guidelines free.

Nonfiction: Historical/nostalgic, how-to, interview/profile, personal experience, description of celebrity memorabilia collections. "No material not related to celebrity memorabilia, such as antiques. Articles must address subjects that appeal to collectors of celebrity or pop culture memorabilia and answer the following: What are these items? How do I go about collecting them? Where can I find them? How scarce or available are they? How can I tell if they're real? What are they worth?" **Buys 25-35 mss/year.** Query. Length: 1,400-1,600 words. **Pays 5¢/word.** Sometimes pays expenses of writers on assignment.

Photos: State availability of photos with submission. Reviews transparencies and prints. Offers $3/photo. Captions and identification of subjects required. Buys one-time rights.

Columns/Departments: "We print 8-10 columns a month written by regular contributors." Send query for more information. **Buys 90-100 mss/year. Pays $50 or as determined on a per case basis.**

Tips: "Writers ideally should be collectors of celebrity or pop culture memorabilia and know their topics thoroughly. Feature articles must be well-researched and clearly written. Writers should remember that *Pop Culture Collecting* is a celebrity/pop culture/nostalgia magazine. For this reason topics dealing with antiques or other non-related items are not suitable for publication."

★ $ $ $ **POPTRONIS**, (formerly *Electronics Now*), Gernsback Publications, Inc., 275-G Marcus Blvd., Hauppauge NY 11788. (631)592-6720. Fax: (631)592-6723. E-mail Jsuda@gernsback.com or popeditor@gernsback.com. Website: www.gernsback.com. **Contact:** Carl Laron, editor. **75% freelance written.** Monthly magazine on electronics technology and electronics construction, such as communications, computers, test equipment, components, video and audio. Estab. January 2000 (92 year history in electronic publications. The new magazine *Poptronis* is a combination of 2 older publications, one of which began in 1929). Circ. 104,000. **Pays on acceptance.** Publishes ms an average of

6 months after acceptance. Byline given. Buys all rights. Submit seasonal material 6 months in advance. Accepts queries by mail, e-mail. Responds in 2 months to queries; 4 months to mss. Sample copy and writer's guidelines free or on website.

Nonfiction: How-to (electronic project construction), humor (cartoons), new product. **Buys 150-200 mss/year.** Send complete ms. Length: 1,000-10,000 words. **Pays $200-800 for assigned articles; $100-800 for unsolicited articles.**

Photos: Send photos with submission. Offers no additional payment for photos accepted with ms. Captions, model releases and identification of subjects required. Buys all rights.

$ POPULAR COMMUNICATIONS, CQ Communications, Inc., 25 Newbridge Rd., Hicksville NY 11801. (516)681-2922. Fax: (516)681-2926. E-mail: popularcom.@aol.com. Website: www.popular-communications.com. **Contact:** Harold Ort, editor. **25% freelance written.** Monthly magazine covering the radio communications hobby. Estab. 1982. Circ. 50,000. Pays on publication. Publishes ms an average of 6 months after acceptance. Buys first North American serial rights. Editorial lead time 3 months. Submit seasonal material 6 months in advance. Accepts queries by mail, e-mail, fax. Responds in 1 month to queries; 2 months to mss. Sample copy free. Writer's guidelines for #10 SASE.

Nonfiction: General interest, how-to, new product, photo feature, technical. **Buys 6-10 mss/year.** Query. Length: 1,800-3,000 words. **Pays $35/printed page.**

Photos: State availability of photos with submission. Negotiates payment individually. Captions, model releases, identification of subjects required.

Tips: "Be a radio enthusiast with a keen interest in ham, shortwave, amateur, scanning or CB radio."

$ $ $ $ POPULAR MECHANICS, Hearst Corp., 224 W. 57th St., 3rd Floor, New York NY 10019. (212)649-2000. Fax: (212)586-5562. E-mail: popularmechanics@hearst.com. Website: www.popularmechanics.com. **Contact:** Joe Oldham, editor-in-chief. Managing Editor: Sarah Deem. **Up to 50% freelance written.** Monthly magazine on automotive, home improvement, science, boating, outdoors, electronics. "We are a men's service magazine that tries to address the diverse interests of today's male, providing him with information to improve the way he lives. We cover stories from do-it-yourself projects to technological advances in aerospace, military, automotive and so on." Estab. 1902. Circ. 1,400,000. **Pays on acceptance.** Publishes ms an average of 6 months after acceptance. Byline given. Offers 25% kill fee. Buys all rights. Submit seasonal material 6 months in advance. Responds in 3 weeks to queries; 1 month to mss. Writer's guidelines for SASE or on website.

Nonfiction: General interest, how-to (shop projects, car fix-its), new product, technical. Special issues: Boating Guide (February); Home Improvement Guide (April); Consumer Electronics Guide (May); New Cars Guide (October); Woodworking Guide (November). No historical, editorial or critique pieces. **Buys 2 mss/year.** Query with or without published clips or send complete ms. Length: 500-1,500 words. **Pays $500-1,500 for assigned articles; $300-1,000 for unsolicited articles.** Sometimes pays expenses of writers on assignment.

Photos: Usually assigns a photographer. "If you have photos, send with submission." Reviews slides and prints. Offers no additional payment for photos accepted with ms. Captions, model releases and identification of subjects required. Buys all rights.

Columns/Departments: New Cars (latest and hottest cars out of Detroit and Europe), Car Care (Maintenance basics, How It Works, Fix-Its and New products: send to Don Chaikin. Electronics, Audio, Home Video, Computers, Photography: send to Toby Grumet. Boating (new equipment, how-tos, fishing tips), Outdoors (gear, vehicles, outdoor adventures): send to Sarah Deem. Home & Shop Journal: send to Steve Willson. Science (latest developments), Tech Update (breakthroughs) and Aviation (sport aviation, homebuilt aircraft, new commercial aircraft, civil aeronautics): send to Jim Wilson. All columns are about 800 words.

The online magazine contains material not found in the print edition. Contact: Bill Rhodes, online editor.

$ $ POPULAR WOODWORKING, F&W Publications, 1507 Dana Ave., Cincinnati OH 45207. (513)531-2690, ext 407. Fax: (513)531-0919. E-mail: popwood@fwpubs.com. Website: www.popularwoodworking.com. Editor: Steve Shanesy. **Contact:** Christopher Schwarz, senior editor. **45% freelance written.** "*Popular Woodworking* is published 7 times a year and invites woodworkers of all levels into a community of professionals who share their hard-won shop experience through in-depth projects and technique articles, which help the readers hone their existing skills and develop new ones. Related stories increase the readers' understanding and enjoyment of their craft. Any project submitted must be aesthetically pleasing, of sound construction and offer a challenge to readers. On the average, we use four freelance features per issue. Our primary needs are 'how-to' articles on woodworking projects. Our secondary need is for articles that will inspire discussion concerning woodworking. Tone of articles should be conversational and informal, as if the writer is speaking directly to the reader. Our readers are the woodworking hobbyist and small woodshop owner. Writers should have an extensive knowledge of woodworking, or be able to communicate information gained from woodworkers." Estab. 1981. Circ. 215,000. **Pays on acceptance.** Publishes ms an average of 10 months after acceptance. Byline given. Buys first world rights. Submit seasonal material 6 months in advance. Accepts queries by mail, e-mail, fax, phone. Responds in 2 months. Sample copy and writer's guidelines for $4.50 and 9×12 SAE with 6 first-class stamps or on website.

Nonfiction: How-to (on woodworking projects, with plans); humor (woodworking anecdotes); technical (woodworking techniques). No tool reviews. Special issues: Shop issue, Outdoor Projects issue, Tool issue, Holiday Projects issue.

Buys 20 mss/year. Query with or without published clips or send complete ms. **Pay starts at $150/published page.** "The project must be well designed, well constructed, well built and well finished. Technique pieces must have practical application."

Reprints: Send photocopy of article or typed ms with rights for sale noted and information about when and where the article previously appeared. Pays 25% of amount paid for an original article.

Photos: Send photos with submission. Reviews color only, slides and transparencies, 3×5 glossies acceptable. Photographic quality may affect acceptance. Need sharp close-up color photos of step-by-step construction process. Captions and identification of subjects required.

Columns/Departments: Tricks of the Trade (helpful techniques), Out of the Woodwork (thoughts on woodworking as a profession or hobby, can be humorous or serious), 500-1,500 words. **Buys 6 mss/year.** Query.

■ The online version of this publication contains material not found in the print edition. Contact: Christopher Schwarz.

Tips: "Write an 'Out of the Woodwork' column for us and then follow up with photos of your projects. Submissions should include materials list, complete diagrams (blueprints not necessary), and discussion of the step-by-step process. We have become more selective on accepting only practical, attractive projects with quality construction. We are also looking for more original topics for our other articles."

◪ **$ $ QUILTING TODAY MAGAZINE**, Chitra Publications, 2 Public Ave., Montrose PA 18801. (570)278-1984. Fax: (570)278-2223. E-mail: chitraed@epix.net. Website: www.quilttownusa.com. **Contact:** Joyce Libal, senior editor. **50% freelance written.** Bimonthly magazine on quilting, traditional and contemporary. "We seek articles that will cover one or two full pages (800 words each); informative to the general quilting public, present new ideas, interviews, instructional, etc." Estab. 1986. Circ. 70,000. Pays on publication. Publishes ms an average of 6 months after acceptance. Byline given. Buys second serial (reprint) rights. Submit seasonal material 8 months in advance. Accepts queries by mail, fax. Responds in 1 month to queries; 2 months to mss. Writer's guidelines for SASE or on website.

○┐ "Best bet—a quilter writing about a new or unusual quilting technique."

Nonfiction: Book excerpts, essays, how-to (for various quilting techniques), humor, interview/profile, new product, opinion, personal experience, photo feature. **Buys 20-30 mss/year.** Query or send complete ms. Length: 800-1,600 words. **Pays $75/full page of published text.**

Reprints: Occasionally accepts previously published submissions. Send photocopy of article or typed ms with rights for sale noted and information about when and where the article previously appeared. **Pays $75/published page.**

Photos: Send photos with submission. Reviews 35mm slides and larger transparencies. Offers $20/photo. Captions, identification of subjects required.

Tips: "Our publications appeal to traditional quilters. We're interested in articles (with slides or transparencies) on quilts in museum collections."

$ $ $ RAILMODEL JOURNAL, Golden Bell Press, 2403 Champa St., Denver CO 80205. **Contact:** Robert Schleicher, editor. **80% freelance written.** "Monthly magazine for advanced model railroaders. 100% photo journalism. We use step-by-step how-to articles with photos of realistic and authentic models." Estab. 1989. Circ. 16,000. Pays on publication. Byline given. Offers 100% kill fee. Buys first and second serial (reprint) rights. Editorial lead time 6 months. Submit seasonal material 6 months in advance. Responds in 4 months to queries; 8 months to mss. Sample copy for $5.50. Writer's guidelines free.

Nonfiction: Historical/nostalgic, how-to, photo feature, technical. "No beginner articles or anything that could even be mistaken for a toy train." **Buys 70-100 mss/year.** Query. Length: 200-5,000 words. **Pays $60-800.** Sometimes pays expenses of writers on assignment.

Photos: Send photos with submission. Reviews contact sheets, 35mm transparencies and 5×7 prints. Captions, model releases and identification of subjects required. Buys one-time and reprint rights.

Tips: "Writers must understand dedicated model railroaders who recreate 100% of their model cars, locomotives, buildings and scenes from specific real-life prototypes. Close-up photos a must."

$ RENAISSANCE MAGAZINE, Phantom Press, 13 Appleton Rd., Nantucket MA 02554. Fax: (508)325-5992. E-mail: renzine@aol.com. Website: www.renaissancemagazine.com. **Contact:** Kim Guarnaccia, managing editor. **90% freelance written.** Quarterly magazine covering the history of the Middle Ages and the Renaissance. "Our readers include historians, reenactors, roleplayers, medievalists and Renaissance Faire enthusiasts." Estab. 1996. Circ. 30,000. Pays on publication. Publishes ms an average of 1 year after acceptance. Byline given. Buys North American serial rights. Editorial lead time 6 months. Submit seasonal material 4 months in advance. Accepts queries by mail, e-mail, fax, phone. Responds in 3 weeks to queries; 2 months to mss. Sample copy for $6. Writer's guidelines for #10 SASE or on website.

○┐ Break in by submitting short (500-1,000 word) articles as fillers or querying on upcoming theme issues.

Nonfiction: Essays, exposé, historical/nostalgic, how-to, interview/profile, new product, opinion, photo feature, religious, travel. No fiction. **Buys 25 mss/year.** Query or send ms with SASE. Length: 1,000-5,000 words. **Pays 5¢/word.** Pays writers with 2 contributor copies or other premiums upon request.

● The editor reports an interest in seeing costuming "how-to" articles; good, comprehensive period website reviews; and Renaissance Festival "insider" articles.

Reprints: Accepts previously published submissions.

Photos: State availability of photos with submission. Reviews contact sheets, any size negatives, transparencies and prints. Offers no additional payment for photos accepted with ms or negotiates payment individually. Captions, model releases and identification of subjects required. Buys all rights.

Columns/Departments: Book reviews, 500 words. Include original or good copy of book cover. "For interested reviewers, books can be supplied for review; query first." **Pays 5¢/word.**

Tips: "Send in all articles in the standard manuscript format with photos/slides or illustrations for suggested use. Writers *must* be open to critique and all historical articles should also include a recommended reading list. An SASE must be included to receive a response to any submission."

N ⊠ $ $ ROCK & GEM, The Earth's Treasures, Minerals and Jewelry, Miller Magazines, Inc., 4880 Market St., Ventura CA 93003-7783. Fax: (805)644-3875. E-mail: rockgemmag@aol.com. Website: www.rockhounds.c om. **Contact:** Bonnie-Jane Mason, managing editor. **99% freelance written.** Monthly magazine covering rockhounding field trips, how-to lapidiary projects, minerals, fossils, gold prospecting, mining, etc. "This is not a scientific journal. Its articles appeal to amateurs, beginners and experts, but its tone is conversational and casual, not stuffy. It's for hobbyists." Estab. 1971. Circ. 55,000. Pays on publication. Byline given. Buys first North American serial rights. Editorial lead time 4 months. Submit seasonal material 6 months in advance. Sample copy for 9×12 SAE with $1.75 postage. Writer's guidelines free, on website or by e-mail.

Nonfiction: General interest, how-to, humor, personal experience, photo feature, travel. Does not want to see "The 25th Anniversary of the Pet Rock" or anything so scientific that it could be a thesis. **Buys 156-200 mss/year.** Send complete ms; "queries *not* welcome!" Length: 1,575-4,000 words. **Pays $100-250.**

Photos: Send photos with submission. Reviews transparencies, graphic files and prints. Offers no additional payment for photos accepted with ms. Captions required.

Tips: "We're looking for more how-to articles and field trips with maps. Read writers guidelines very carefully and follow all instructions in them. Then be patient. Your manuscript may be published within a month or even three years from date of submission."

$ $ RUG HOOKING MAGAZINE, Stackpole Magazines, 500 Vaughn St., Harrisburg PA 17110-2220. (717)234-5091. Fax: (717)234-1359. E-mail: rughook@paonline.com. Website: www.rughookingonline.com. Editor: Patrice Crowley. **Contact:** Brenda Wilt, assistant editor. **75% freelance written.** Magazine published 5 times/year covering the craft of rug hooking. "This is the only magazine in the world devoted exclusively to rug hooking. Our readers are both novices and experts. They seek how-to pieces, features on fellow artisans and stories on beautiful rugs new and old." Estab. 1989. Circ. 10,000. **Pays on acceptance.** Publishes ms an average of 1 year after acceptance. Byline given. Buys all rights. Editorial lead time 6 months. Submit seasonal material 6 months in advance. Accepts queries by mail, e-mail, fax. Responds in 2 months. Sample copy for $5.

Nonfiction: How-to (hook a rug or a specific aspect of hooking), personal experience. **Buys 30 mss/year.** Query with published clips. Length: 825-2,475 words. **Pays $74.25-222.75.** Sometimes pays expenses of writers on assignment.

Reprints: Send photocopy of article and information about when and where the article previously appeared.

Photos: Send photos with submission. Reviews 2×2 transparencies, 3×5 prints. Negotiates payment individually. Identification of subjects required. Buys all rights.

⊠ $ $ SCALE AUTO ENTHUSIAST, Kalmbach Publishing Co., 21027 Crossroads Circle, P.O. Box 1612, Waukesha WI 53187-1612. (262)796-8776. Fax: (262)796-1383. E-mail: editor@scaleautomag.com. Website: www.kal mbach.com/scaleauto/scaleauto.html. **Contact:** Kirk Bell, editor. **70% freelance written.** Magazine published 8 times/year covering model car building. "We are looking for model builders, collectors and enthusiasts who feel their models and/or modeling techniques and experiences would be of interest and benefit to our readership." Estab. 1979. Circ. 75,000. Pays on publication. Publishes ms an average of 1 year after acceptance. Byline given. Buys all rights. Editorial lead time 4 months. Submit seasonal material 4 months in advance. Accepts queries by mail, e-mail, fax. Responds in 2 months to queries; 3 months to mss. Sample copy and writer's guidelines free or on website.

Nonfiction: Book excerpts, historical/nostalgic, how-to (build models, do different techniques), interview/profile, personal experience, photo feature, technical. Query or send complete ms. Length: 750-3,000 words. **Pays $75-100/ published page.**

Photos: Send photos and negatives with submission. Prefers color glossy prints and 35mm color transparencies. When writing how-to articles be sure to take photos *during* project. Negotiates payment individually. Captions, model releases, identification of subjects required. Buys all rights.

Columns/Departments: Buys 50 mss/year. Query. **Pays $75-100/published page.**

Tips: "First and foremost, our readers like how-to material: how-to paint, how-to scratchbuild, how-to chop a roof, etc. Basically, our readers want to know how to make their own models better. Therefore, any help or advice you can offer is what modelers want to read. Also, the more photos you send, taken from a variety of views, the better choice we have in putting together an outstanding article layout. Send us more photos than you would ever possibly imagine we could use. This permits us to pick and choose the best of the bunch."

$ SHUTTLE SPINDLE & DYEPOT, Handweavers Guild of America, Inc., 3327 Duluth Highway, Two Executive Concourse, Suite 201, Duluth GA 30096. (770)495-7702. Fax: (770)495-7703. E-mail: weavespindye@compuserve.c om. Website: www.weavespindye.org. Publications Manager: Pat King. **Contact:** Sandra Bowles, editor-in-chief. **60% freelance written.** "Quarterly membership publication of the Handweavers Guild of America, Inc., *Shuttle Spindle &*

Dyepot magazine seeks to encourage excellence in contemporary fiber arts and to support the preservation of techniques and traditions in fiber arts. It also provides inspiration for fiber artists of all levels and develops public awareness and appreciation of the fiber arts. *Shuttle Spindle & Dyepot* appeals to a highly educated, creative and very knowledgeable audience of fiber artists and craftsmen—weavers, spinners, dyers and basket makers." Estab. 1969. Circ. 30,000. Pays on publication. Publishes ms 6 months after acceptance. Byline given. Buys first North American serial, reprint and electronic rights. Editorial lead time 8 months. Submit seasonal material 8 months in advance. Accepts queries by mail, e-mail, fax, phone. Sample copy for $7.50 plus shipping. Writer's guidelines on website.

O→ Articles featuring up-and-coming artists, new techniques, cutting-edge ideas and designs, fascinating children's activities, and comprehensive fiber collections are a few examples of "best bet" topics.

Nonfiction: Inspirational, interview/profile, new product, personal experience, photo feature, technical, travel. "No self-promotional and no articles from those without knowledge of area/art/artists." **Buys 40 mss/year.** Query with published clips. Length: 1,000-2,000 words. **Pays $75-150.**

Photos: State availability of photos with query. Offers no additional payment for photos accepted with ms. Captions, model releases and identification of subjects required.

Columns/Departments: Books and Videos, News and Information, Calendar and Conference, Travel and Workshop, Guildview (all fiber/art related). **Buys 8 mss/year.** Query with published clips. **Pays $50-75.**

Tips: "Become knowledgeable about the fiber arts and artists. The writer should provide an article of importance to the weaving, spinning, dyeing and basket making community. Query by telephone (once familiar with publication) by appointment helps editor and writer.

$ SPORTS COLLECTORS DIGEST, Krause Publications, 700 E. State St., Iola WI 54990. (715)445-2214. Fax: (715)445-4087. E-mail: kpsports@aol.com. Website: www.krause.com. **Contact:** Tom Mortenson, editor. Estab. 1952. **50% freelance written.** Works with a small number of new/unpublished writers each year. Weekly sports memorabilia magazine. "We serve collectors of sports memorabilia—baseball cards, yearbooks, programs, autographs, jerseys, bats, balls, books, magazines, ticket stubs, etc." Circ. 52,000. Pays after publication. Publishes ms an average of 3 months after acceptance. Byline given. Buys first North American serial rights only. Submit seasonal material 3 months in advance. Responds in 5 weeks to queries; 2 months to mss. Free sample copy. Writer's guidelines for #10 SASE.

Nonfiction: General interest (new card issues, research on older sets); historical/nostalgic (old stadiums, old collectibles, etc.); how-to (buy cards, sell cards and other collectibles, display collectibles, ways to get autographs, jerseys and other memorabilia); interview/profile (well-known collectors, ball players—but must focus on collectibles); new product (new card sets); personal experience ("what I collect and why"-type stories). No sports stories. "We are not competing with *The Sporting News*, *Sports Illustrated* or your daily paper. Sports collectibles only." **Buys 100-200 mss/year.** Query. Length: 300-3,000 words; prefers 1,000 words. **Pays $100-150.**

Reprints: Send tearsheet of article. Pays 100% of amount paid for an original article.

Photos: Unusual collectibles. Send photos. Pays $25-150 for b&w prints. Identification of subjects required. Buys all rights.

Columns/Departments: "We have all the columnists we need but welcome ideas for new columns." **Buys 100-150 mss/year.** Query. Length: 600-3,000 words. **Pays $90-150.**

Tips: "If you are a collector, you know what collectors are interested in. Write about it. No shallow, puff pieces; our readers are too smart for that. Only well-researched articles about sports memorabilia and collecting. Some sports nostalgia pieces are OK. Write only about the areas you know about."

[N] $ STAMP COLLECTOR, Krause Publications, 700 E. State St., Iola WI 54990-0001. (715)445-2214. Fax: (715)445-4612. E-mail: youngbloodw@krause.com. Website: www.stampcollector.net. **Contact:** Wayne L. Youngblood, editor/publisher. **10% freelance written.** Biweekly tabloid covering philately (stamp collecting). "For stamp collectors of all ages and experience levels." Estab. 1931. Circ. 17,941. Pays on publication. Publishes ms an average of 6 months after acceptance. Byline given. Buys first North American serial rights. Editorial lead time 1 month. Submit seasonal material 3 months in advance. Accepts queries by mail, e-mail, fax, phone. Accepts simultaneous submissions. Responds in 1 week to queries; 1 month to mss. Sample copy free.

Nonfiction: How-to (collecting stamps). Upcoming specialty guides include World and US stamps, postal history, holiday gift guide, topical stamps, other specialty areas. Send complete ms. Length: 150-950 words. **Pays $25-100.** Sometimes pays writers with subscriptions and hobby books. Sometimes pays expenses of writers on assignment.

Photos: State availability of photos with submission. Reviews prints. Offers no additional payment for photos accepted with ms. Captions and identification of subjects required. Buys one-time rights.

Columns/Departments: Postal History (a detailed look at how a particular stamp or cover played a role in moving the mail), 500-950 words. **Buys 6-10 mss/year.** Query. **Pays $25-75.**

Tips: "Submissions are pretty much limited to writers with stamp collecting experience and/or interest."

[N] $ $ TATTOO REVUE, Art & Ink Enterprises, Inc., 5 Marine View Plaza, Suite 207, Hoboken NJ 07030. (201)653-2700. Fax: (201)653-7892. E-mail: tattoo2@ix.netcom.com. Website: tattoorevue.com. Editor: Jean Chris Miller. **Contact:** Scot Rienecker, managing editor. **25% freelance written.** Interview and profile magazine published 10 times/year covering tattoo artists, their art and lifestyle. "All writers must have knowledge of tattoos. Features include interviews with tattoo artists and collectors." Estab. 1990. Circ. 100,000. Pays on publication. Publishes ms an average of 3 months after acceptance. Byline given. Buys one-time rights. Editorial lead time 3 months. Submit seasonal material 5 months in advance. Accepts queries by mail, e-mail, fax. Accepts simultaneous submissions. Responds in 2 weeks to queries; 2 months to mss. Sample copy for $5.95. Writer's guidelines for #10 SASE.

Nonfiction: Book excerpts, historical/nostalgic, humor, interview/profile, photo feature. Publishes special convention issues—dates and locations provided upon request. "No first time experiences—our readers already know." **Buys 10-30 mss/year.** Query with published clips or send complete ms. Length: 500-2,500 words. **Pays $50-200.**

Reprints: Accepts previously published submissions.

Photos: Send photos with submission. Reviews transparencies and prints. Offers $0-10/photo. Captions, model releases and identification of subjects required. Buys one-time rights.

Columns/Departments: Buys 10-30 mss/year. Query with published clips or send complete ms. **Pays $25-50.**

Fiction: Adventure, erotica, fantasy, historical, horror, humorous, science fiction, suspense. "No stories featuring someone's tattoo coming to life!" **Buys 10-30 mss/year.** Query with published clips or send complete ms. Length: 500-2,500 words. **Pays $50-100.**

Poetry: Avant garde, free verse, haiku, light verse, traditional. **Buys 10-30 poems/year.** Submit maximum 12 poems. Length: 2-1,000 lines. **Pays $10-25.**

Fillers: Anecdotes, facts, gags to be illustrated by cartoonist, newsbreaks, short humor. **Buys 10-20/year.** Length: 50-2,000 words. **Pays $10-25.**

The online magazine carries original content not found in the print edition. Contact: Chris Miller.

Tips: "All writers must have knowledge of tattoos! Either giving or receiving."

TEDDY BEAR REVIEW, Collector Communications Corp., 170 Fifth Ave., New York NY 10010. (212)989-8700. E-mail: gg@teddybearreview.com. Website: www.teddybearreview.com. **Contact:** Eugene Gilligan, editor. **65% freelance written.** Works with a small number of new/unpublished writers each year. Bimonthly magazine on teddy bears for collectors, enthusiasts and bearmakers. Estab. 1985. Pays 30 days after acceptance. Byline given. Buys first North American serial rights. Submit seasonal material 6 months in advance. Sample copy and writer's guidelines for $2 and 9×12 SAE.

Nonfiction: Book excerpts, historical, how-to, interview/profile. No nostalgia on childhood teddy bears. **Buys 30-40 mss/year.** Query with photos and published clips. Length: 900-1,500 words. **Pays $100-350.** Sometimes pays the expenses of writers on assignment "if approved ahead of time."

Photos: Send photos with submission. Reviews transparencies and b&w prints. Offers no additional payment for photos accepted with ms. Captions required. Buys one-time rights.

Tips: "We are interested in good, professional writers around the country with a strong knowledge of teddy bears. Historical profile of bear companies, profiles of contemporary artists and knowledgeable reports on museum collections are of interest. We are looking for humorous, offbeat stories about teddy bears in general."

$ $ THREADS, Taunton Press, 63 S. Main St., P.O. Box 5506, Newtown CT 06470. (203)426-8171. **Contact:** Chris Timmons, editor. Bimonthly magazine covering sewing, garment construction, home decor and embellishments (quilting and embroidery). "We're seeking proposals from hands-on authors who first and foremost have a skill. Being an experienced writer is of secondary consideration." Estab. 1985. Circ. 176,000. Pays $150/page. Byline given. Offers $150 kill fee. Buys one-time rights or reprint rights in article collections. Editorial lead time 4 months minimum. Query for electronic submissions. Responds in 1-2 months. Writer's guidelines free.

Nonfiction: "We prefer first-person experience."

Columns/Departments: Notes (current events, new products, opinions); Book reviews; Tips; Closures (stories of a humorous nature). Query. **Pays $150/page.**

Tips: "Send us a proposal (outline) with photos of your own work (garments, samplers, etc.)."

$ $ TODAY'S COLLECTOR, The Nation's Antiques and Collectibles Marketplace, Krause Publications, 700 E. State St., Iola WI 54990-0001. (715)445-2214. Fax: (715)445-4087. E-mail: korbeck@krause.com. Website: www.krause.com. **Contact:** Sharon Korbeck, editor. **90% freelance written.** Monthly magazine covering antiques and collectibles. "*Today's Collector* is for serious collectors of all types of antiques and collectibles." Estab. 1993. Circ. 60,000. Pays on publication. Publishes ms an average of 1 year after acceptance. Byline given. Offers 50% kill fee. Buys perpetual but non-exclusive rights. Editorial lead time 2 months. Submit seasonal material 8 months in advance. Accepts queries by mail, e-mail, fax. Accepts simultaneous submissions. Responds in 3 weeks to queries; 3 months to mss. Sample copy for $3.95. Writer's guidelines free or on website.

Nonfiction: How-to (antiques and collectibles), interview/profile, personal experience. No articles that are too general—specific collecting areas only. **Buys 60-80 mss/year.** Query or send complete ms. Length: 500-1,200 words. **Pays $50-200.** Sometimes pays expenses of writers on assignment.

Reprints: Send typed ms with rights for sale noted and information about when and where the article previously appeared. Pays 50% of amount paid for an original article.

Photos: State availability of photos with submission. Reviews transparencies, prints. Offers no additional payment for photos accepted with ms. Captions and identification of subjects required. Buys one-time rights.

Columns/Departments: Collector profiles of prominent collections, auction/show highlights. Query. **Pays $50-200.**

Tips: "I want detailed articles about specific collecting areas—nothing too broad or general. Our articles need to inform readers of diverse collecting areas—from vintage to more 'modern' antiques and collectibles. I need lots of information about pricing and values, along with brief history and background."

■ ★ $**TOY CARS & VEHICLES**, Krause Publications, 700 E. State St., Iola WI 54990-0001. (715)445-2214. Fax: (715)445-4087. E-mail: dudleym@krause.com. Website: www.toycarsmag.com. **Contact:** Merry Dudley, associate editor. **85-90% freelance written.** Monthly 4-color, glossy magazine covering collectible toy vehicles/models. "We cover the hobby market for collectors of die-cast models, model kit builders and fans of all types of vehicle toys." Estab. 1998. Circ. 20,000. Pays on publication. Publishes ms an average of 1 year after acceptance. Byline given. Buys perpetual, non-exclusive rights. Editorial lead time 4 months. Submit seasonal material 6 months in advance. Accepts queries by mail, e-mail, fax. Accepts simultaneous submissions. Responds in 2 weeks to queries; 2 months to mss. Sample copy for $2.99 or on website. Writer's guidelines for SASE or on website.
Nonfiction: How-to, interview/profile, new product. Interested in seeing histories of obscure companies/toy lines/scale model/kits. No Hot Wheels history ("We would much rather see coverage of new Hot Wheels"). **Buys 25 mss/year.** Query with published clips. Length: 800-1,500 words. **Pays $30-100.** Sometimes pays expenses of writers on assignment.
Photos: Send photos with submission. Reviews negatives, 3×5 transparencies and 3×5 prints. No additional payment for photos accepted with ms. Captions, model releases and identification of subjects required. Buys one-time rights.
Columns/Departments: The Checkered Flag (nostalgic essays about favorite toys), 500-800 words; Helpful Hints (tips about model kit buildings, etc.), 25-35 words; model reviews (reviews of new die-cast and model kits), 100-350 words. **Buys 25 mss/year.** Query with published clips. **Pays $30-100.**
Tips: "Our magazine is for serious hobbyists looking for info about kit building, model quality, new product info and collectible value."

$ $**TOY FARMER**, Toy Farmer Publications, 7496 106 Ave. SE, LaMoure ND 58458-9404. (701)883-5206. Fax: (701)883-5209. E-mail: zekesez@aol.com. Website: www.toyfarmer.com. President: Claire D. Scheibe. Publisher: Cathy Scheibe. **Contact:** Delanee Fox, editorial assistant. **65% freelance written.** Monthly magazine covering farm toys. Youth involvement is strongly encouraged. Estab. 1978. Circ. 27,000. Pays on publication. Publishes ms an average of 1 month after acceptance. Byline given. Buys first North American serial rights. Editorial lead time 3 months. Submit seasonal material 3 months in advance. Accepts queries by mail, e-mail, phone, fax. Responds in 1 month to queries; 2 months to mss. Sample copy for $4. Writer's guidelines for #10 SASE.
Nonfiction: General interest, historical/nostalgic, humor, new product, technical. **Buys 100 mss/year.** Query with published clips. 800-1,500 words. **Pays 10¢/word.** Sometimes pays expenses of writers on assignment.
Reprints: Accepts previously published submissions.
Photos: State availability of photos with submission. Reviews transparencies. Offers no additional payment for photos accepted with ms. Buys one-time rights.
Columns/Departments: **Buys 36 mss/year.** Query with published clips. **Pays 10¢/word.**

■ $ $**TOY SHOP**, Krause Publications, 700 E. State St., Iola WI 54990. (715)445-2214. Fax: (715)445-4087. E-mail: korbecks@krause.com. Website: www.krause.com. **Contact:** Sharon Korbeck, editor. **85-90% freelance written.** Biweekly tabloid covering toy collecting. "We cover primarily vintage collectible toys from the 1930s-present. Stories focus on historical toy companies, the collectibility of toys and features on prominent collections." Estab. 1988. Circ. 40,000. Pays on publication. Publishes ms an average of 8-30 months after acceptance. Byline given. Buys "perpetual, nonexclusive rights." Editorial lead time 4 months. Submit seasonal material 6 months in advance. Accepts queries by mail, e-mail. Accepts simultaneous submissions. Responds in 2 months. Sample copy for $3.98. Writer's guidelines on website.
Nonfiction: Historical/nostalgic (toys, toy companies), interview/profile (toy collectors), new products (toys), photo feature (toys), features on old toys. No opinion, broad topics or poorly researched pieces. **Buys 100 mss/year.** Query. Length: 500-1,500 words. **Pays $50-200.** Contributor's copies included with payment. Sometimes pays expenses of writers on assignment.
Reprints: Send photocopy of article and information about when and where the article previously appeared.
Photos: State availability of or send photos with submission. Reviews negatives, transparencies, 3×5 prints and electronic photos. Negotiates payment individually. Captions, model releases, identification of subjects required. Rights purchased with ms rights.
Columns/Departments: Collector Profile (profile of toy collectors), 700-1,000 words. **Buys 25 mss/year.** Query. **Pays $50-150.**
Tips: "Articles must be specific. Include historical info, quotes, values of toys and photos with story. Talk with toy dealers and get to know how big the market is."

$ $**TOY TRUCKER & CONTRACTOR**, Toy Farmer Publications, 7496 106th Ave. SE, LaMoure ND 58458-9404. (701)883-5206. Fax: (701)883-5209. E-mail: zekesez@aol.com. Website: www.toytrucker.com. President: Claire Scheibe. Publisher: Cathy Scheibe. **Contact:** Delanee Fox, editorial assistant. **75% freelance written.** Monthly magazine covering collectible toys. "We are a magazine on hobby and collectible toy trucks and construction pieces." Estab. 1990. Circ. 6,500. Pays on publication. Publishes ms an average of 3 months after acceptance. Byline given. Buys first North American serial rights. Editorial lead time 3 months. Submit seasonal material 3 months in advance. Accepts queries by mail, e-mail, fax, phone. Responds in 1 month to queries; 2 months to mss. Sample copy for $4. Writer's guidelines free on request.
Nonfiction: Historical/nostalgic, interview/profile, new product, technical. **Buys 35 mss/year.** Query. Length: 800-2,400. **Pays 10¢/word. Sometimes pays expenses of writers on assignment.**
Reprints: Accepts previously published submissions.

Photos: Send photos with submission. Offers no additional payment for photos accepted with ms. Captions, model releases and identification of subjects required.

Tips: "Send sample work that would apply to our magazine. Also, we need more articles on collectors or builders. We have regular columns, so a feature should not repeat what our columns do."

$ $ TOYFARE, The Toy Magazine, Wizard Entertainment Group, 151 Wells Ave., Congers NY 10920. (914)268-2000. Fax: (914)268-0053. E-mail: fanfare@toyfare.com. Website: www.toyfare.com. Managing Editor: Joe Yanarella. **Contact:** Tom Palmer, editor. **70% freelance written.** Monthly magazine covering action figures and collectible toys. Estab. 1997. Pays on publication. Byline given. Offers 50% kill fee. Buys all rights. Editorial lead time 4 months. Submit seasonal material 4 months in advance. Accepts queries by mail, e-mail, fax. Responds in 6 weeks. Sample copy and writer's guidelines for SAE.

Nonfiction: Historical/nostalgic, how-to, humor, interview/profile, new product, personal experience, photo feature, technical. No column or opinion pieces. **Buys 75-100 mss/year.** Query with published clips. Length: 250-4,000 words. **Pays 15¢/word.**

Photos: State availability of photos with submission. Negotiates payment individually. Identification of subjects required. Buys all rights.

  ■ The online magazine carries original content not found in the print version and includes writer's guidelines. Contact: Buddy Scalera.

Columns/Departments: Toy Story (profile of past toy line), Sneak Peek (profile of new action figure); both 750-900 words. Query with published clips. **Pays $75-100.**

Tips: "Knowledge of action figures is a must. We'd also like to see more well-done humorous writing. We've got too much in the way of retrospective histories of toy lines."

$ $ TRADITIONAL QUILTER, All American Crafts, Inc., 243 Newton-Sparta Rd., Newton NJ 07860. (973)383-8080. Fax: (973)383-8133. E-mail: craftpub@aol.com. **Contact:** Laurette Koserowski, editor. **45% freelance written.** Bimonthly magazine on quilting. Estab. 1988. Pays on publication. Byline given. Buys first or all rights. Submit seasonal material 6 months in advance. Responds in 2 months. Sample copy for 9×12 SAE with 4 first-class stamps. Writer's guidelines for #10 SASE.

Nonfiction: Quilts and quilt patterns with instructions, quilt-related projects, guild news, interview/profile, photo feature—all quilt related. Query with published clips. Length: 350-1,000 words. **Pays 10-12¢/word.**

Photos: Send photos with submission. Reviews all size transparencies and prints. Offers $10-15/photo. Captions and identification of subjects required. Buys one-time or all rights.

Columns/Departments: Feature Teacher (qualified quilt teachers with teaching involved—with slides); Profile (award-winning and interesting quilters); The Guilded Newsletter (reports on quilting guild activities, shows, workshops, and retreats). Length: 1,000 words maximum. **Pays 10¢/word, $15/photo.**

$ $ TRADITIONAL QUILTWORKS, The Pattern Magazine for Traditional Quilters, Chitra Publications, 2 Public Ave., Montrose PA 18801. (570)278-1984. Fax: (570)278-2223. E-mail: chitraed@epix.net. Website: www.quiltownusa.com. **Contact:** Joyce Libal, senior editor. **50% freelance written.** Bimonthly magazine on quilting. "We seek articles of an instructional nature, profiles of talented teachers, articles on the history of specific areas of quiltmaking (patterns, fiber, regional, etc.)." Estab. 1988. Circ. 70,000. Pays on publication. Publishes ms an average of 6 months after acceptance. Byline given. Buys second serial (reprint) rights. Submit seasonal material 8 months in advance. Accepts queries by mail, fax. Responds in 2 months. Writer's guidelines for SASE or on website.

  ○┐ "Best bet—a quilter writing about a new or unusual quilting technique."

Nonfiction: Historical, instructional, quilting education. **Buys 12-18 mss/year.** Query or send complete ms. Length: 1,500 words maximum. **Pays $75/published page of text.**

Reprints: Send photcopy of article and information about when and where the article previously appeared.

Photos: Send photos with submission. Reviews 35mm slides and larger transparencies (color). Offers $20/photo. Captions, model releases and identification of subjects required.

Tips: "Our publications appeal to traditional quilters."

N $ TREASURE CHEST, The Information Source & Marketplace for Collectors and Dealers of Antiques and Collectibles, Treasure Chest Publishing Inc., 564 Eddy St., #326, Providence RI 02903. (401)272-9444. **Contact:** David F. Donnelly, publisher. **100% freelance written.** Monthly newspaper on antiques and collectibles. Estab. 1988. Circ. 50,000. Pays on publication. Publishes ms an average of 3 months after acceptance. Byline given. Buys first rights and second serial (reprint) rights. Responds in 2 months to mss. Sample copy for 9×12 SAE with $2. Writer's guidelines for #10 SASE.

Nonfiction: Primarily interested in feature articles on a specific field of antiques or collectibles with reproducible photographs. **Buys 40 mss/year.** Send complete ms. Articles on diskette preferred. Length: 750-1,000 words. **Pays $30-40 with photos.**

Reprints: Send tearsheet or photocopy of article and information about when and where the article previously appeared.

Tips: "Learn about your subject by interviewing experts—appraisers, curators, dealers."

$ $ WOODSHOP NEWS, Soundings Publications Inc., 35 Pratt St., Essex CT 06426-1185. (860)767-8227. Fax: (860)767-0645. E-mail: woodshopnews@worldnet.att.net. Website: www.woodshopnews.com. Editor: Thomas K.

Clark. **Contact:** A.J. Hamler, associate editor. **20% freelance written.** Monthly tabloid "covering woodworking for professionals and hobbyists. Solid business news and features about woodworking companies. Feature stories about interesting professional and amateur woodworkers. Some how-to articles." Estab. 1986. Circ. 100,000. Pays on publication. Publishes ms an average of 6 months after acceptance. Byline given. Offers 25% kill fee. Buys first North American serial rights. Submit seasonal material 4 months in advance. Accepts queries by mail, e-mail, fax. Responds in 1 month. Sample copy on website and writer's guidelines free.

• *Woodshop News* needs writers in major cities in all regions except the Northeast. Also looking for more editorial opinion pieces.

Nonfiction: How-to (query first), interview/profile, new product, opinion, personal experience, photo feature. Key word is "newsworthy." No general interest profiles of "folksy" woodworkers. **Buys 12-15 mss/year.** Query with published clips or submit ms. Length: 100-1,200 words. **Pays $50-400 for assigned articles; $40-250 for unsolicited articles; $40-100 for workshop tips.** Pays expenses of writers on assignment.

Photos: Send photos with submission. Reviews contact sheets and prints. Offers $20-35/b&w photo; $250/4-color cover, usually with story. Captions and identification of subjects required. Buys one-time rights.

Columns/Departments: Pro Shop (business advice, marketing, employee relations, taxes etc. for the professional written by an established professional in the field), 1,200-1,500 words. **Buys 12 mss/year.** Query. **Pays $200-250.**

Fillers: Small filler items, briefs, or news tips that are followed up by staff reporters. **Pays $10.**

Tips: "The best way to start is a profile of a business or hobbyist woodworker in your area. Find a unique angle about the person or business and stress this as the theme of your article. Avoid a broad, general-interest theme that would be more appropriate to a daily newspaper. Our readers are woodworkers who want more depth and more specifics than would a general readership. If you are profiling a business, we need standard business information such as gross annual earnings/sales, customer base, product line and prices, marketing strategy, etc. Black and white 35 mm photos are a must. We need more freelance writers from the Mid-Atlantic, Midwest and West Coast."

$ $ WOODWORK, A Magazine For All Woodworkers, Ross Periodicals, P.O. Box 1529, Ross CA 94957-1529. (415)382-0580. Fax: (415)382-0587. E-mail: woodwrkmag@aol.com. Publisher: Tom Toldrian. **Contact:** John Lavine, editor. **90% freelance written.** Bimonthly magazine covering woodworking. "We are aiming at a broad audience of woodworkers, from the hobbyist to professional. Articles run the range from the simple to the complex. We cover such subjects as carving, turning, furniture, tools old and new, design, techniques, projects and more. We also feature profiles of woodworkers, with the emphasis being always on communicating woodworking methods, practices, theories and techniques. Suggestions for articles are always welcome." Estab. 1986. Circ. 80,000. Pays on publication. Byline given. Buys first North American serial and second serial (reprint) rights. Accepts queries by mail, e-mail, fax. Sample copy for $5 and 9×12 SAE with 6 first-class stamps. Writer's guidelines for #10 SASE.

Nonfiction: How-to (simple or complex, making attractive furniture), interview/profile (of established woodworkers that make attractive furniture), photo feature (of interest to woodworkers), technical (tools, techniques). "Do not send a how-to unless you are a woodworker." Query first. Length: 1,500-2,000 words. **Pays $150/published page.**

Photos: Send photos with submission. Reviews 35mm slides. Pays higher page rate for photos accepted with ms. Captions and identification of subjects required. Buys one-time rights. Photo guidelines available on request.

Columns/Departments: Tips and Techniques column **pays $35-75.** Interview/profiles of established woodworkers. Bring out woodworker's philosophy about the craft, opinions about what is happening currently. Good photos of attractive furniture a must. Section on how-to desirable. Query with published clips. **Pays $150/published page.**

Tips: "Our main requirement is that each article must directly concern woodworking. If you are not a woodworker, the interview/profile is your best, really only chance. Good writing is essential as are good photos. The interview must be entertaining, but informative and pertinent to woodworkers' interests. Include sidebar written by the profile subject."

HOME & GARDEN

The baby boomers' turn inward, or "cocooning," has caused an explosion of publications in this category. Gardening magazines in particular have blossomed, as more people are developing leisure interests at home. Some magazines here concentrate on gardens; others on the how-to of interior design. Still others focus on homes and gardens in specific regions of the country. Be sure to read the publication to determine its focus before submitting a manuscript or query.

[N] $ THE ALMANAC FOR FARMERS & CITY FOLK, Greentree Publishing, Inc., 850 S. Rancho, #2319, Las Vegas NV 89106. (702)387-6777. **Contact:** Stephanie Doucette, editor. **40% freelance written.** Annual almanac of "down-home, folksy material pertaining to farming, gardening, animals, etc." Estab. 1983. Circ. 800,000. Pays on publication. Publishes ms 6 months after acceptance. Byline given. Buys first North American serial rights. Accepts queries by mail, fax, phone. Deadline: January 31. Sample copy for $4.95.

O→ Break in with short, humorous, gardening, or how-to pieces.

Nonfiction: Essays, general interest, how-to, humor. No fiction or controversial topics. "Please, no first-person pieces!" **Buys 30 mss/year.** Send complete ms. No queries please. Length: 350-1,400 words. **Pays $45/page.**

Poetry: **Buys 1-4 poems/year. Pays $45 for full pages**, otherwise proportionate share thereof.

Fillers: Anecdotes, facts, short humor, gardening hints. **Buys 60/year.** Length 125 words maximum. **Pays $10-45.**

Tips: "Typed submissions essential as we scan in manuscript. Short, succinct material is preferred. Material should appeal to a wide range of people and should be on the 'folksy' side, preferably with a thread of humor woven in. No first-person pieces."

$ $ THE AMERICAN GARDENER, A Publication of the American Horticultural Society, 7931 E. Boulevard. Dr., Alexandria VA 22308-1300. (703)768-5700. Fax: (703)768-7533. E-mail: editor@ahs.org. Website: www.ahs.org. Managing Editor: Mary Yee. **Contact**: David J. Ellis, editor. **90% freelance written.** Bimonthly magazine covering gardening and horticulture. "*The American Gardener* is the official publication of the American Horticultural Society (AHS), a national, nonprofit, membership organization for gardeners, founded in 1922. AHS is dedicated to educating and inspiring people of all ages to become successful, environmentally responsible gardeners by advancing the art and science of horticulture. Readers of *The American Gardener* are avid amateur gardeners; about 22% are professionals. Most prefer not to use synthetic pesticides." Estab. 1922. Circ. 26,000. Pays on publication. Publishes ms an average of 6 months after acceptance. Byline given. Offers 25% kill fee. Buys first North American serial rights and limited time rights to run brief excerpts on website; negotiates full electronic rights separately. Editorial lead time 3 months. Submit seasonal material 1 year in advance. Responds in 3 months to queries if SASE included. Sample copy for $4. Writer's guidelines for #10 SASE.
Nonfiction: "Feature-length articles include in-depth profiles of individual plant groups, profiles of prominent American horticulturists and gardeners (living and dead), profiles of unusual public or private gardens, descriptions of historical developments in American gardening, descriptions of innovative landscape design projects (especially relating to use of regionally native plants or naturalistic gardening), and descriptions of important plant breeding and research programs tailored to a lay audience. We run relatively few how-to articles; these should address relatively complex or unusual topics that most other gardening magazines won't tackle—photography needs to be provided." **Buys 30 mss/year.** Query by mail only with published clips. Length: 1,500-2,000 words. **Pays $250-500** depending on article's length, complexity, author's horticultural background, and publishing experience. Pays with contributor copies or other premiums when other horticultural organizations contribute articles.
Reprints: Rarely purchases second rights. Send photocopy of article with information about when and where the article previously appeared. Pay varies.
Photos: State availability of photos with submission. Reviews transparencies, prints; these must be accompanied by postage-paid return mailer. Pays $50-200/photo. Identification of subjects required. Buys one-time rights. Sometimes pays expenses of writers on assignment.
Columns/Departments: Offshoots (humorous, sentimental or expresses an unusual viewpoint), 650-800 words; Conservationist's Notebook (articles about individuals or organizations attempting to save endangered species or protect natural areas), 750-1,200 words; Natural Connections (explains a natural phenomenon—plant and pollinator relationships, plant and fungus relationships, parasites—that may be observed in nature or in the garden), 750-1,200 words; Habitat Gardening (focuses on gardens designed to replicate regional plant communities and ecosystems, or landscape designers who specialize in such projects), 1,000-1,200 words; Urban Gardener (looks at a successful small space garden—indoor, patio, less than a quarter-acre; a program that successfully brings plants to city streets or public spaces; or a problem of particular concern to city dwellers), 750-1,200 words; Planting the Future (children and youth gardening programs), 750 words; Regional Happenings (events that directly affect gardeners only in 1 area, but are of interest to others: an expansion of a botanical garden, a serious new garden pest, the launching of a regional flower show, a hot new gardening trend), 250-300 words. **Buys 20 mss/year.** Query by mail only with published clips. **Pays $50-250.**
Tips: "Our readers are advanced, passionate amateur gardeners; about 20 percent are horticultural professionals. Our articles are intended to bring this knowledgeable group new information, ranging from the latest scientific findings that affect plants, to the history of gardening and gardens in America."

$ $ $ $ AMERICAN HOMESTYLE & GARDENING MAGAZINE, Gruner & Jahr USA Publishing, 375 Lexington Ave., New York NY 10017. (212)499-2000. Fax: (212)499-1536. Editor-in-Chief: Kathleen Madden. **Contact:** Paulie Chevalier, managing editor. Magazine published 10 times/year. "*American Homestyle & Gardening* is a guide to complete home design. It is edited for homeowners interested in decorating, building and remodeling products. It focuses on a blend of style, substance and service." Estab. 1986. Circ. 1,000,000. **Pays on acceptance.** Byline given. Offers 25% kill fee. Buys first North American serial rights. Writer's guidelines for #10 SASE.
Nonfiction: Writers with expertise in design, decorating, building or gardening. "Because stories begin with visual elements, queries without scouting photos rarely lead to assignments." Length: 750-2,000 words. **Pays $750-2,500.** Pays expenses of writers on assignment.
Tips: "Writers must have knowledge of interior design, remodeling or gardening."

$ $ ATLANTA HOMES AND LIFESTYLES, Weisner Publishing LLC, 1100 Johnson Ferry Rd., Suite 595, Atlanta GA 30342. Fax: (404)252-6673. Website: www.atlantahomesmag.com. **Contact:** Oma Blaise, editor. **65% freelance written.** Magazine published 8 times/year. "*Atlanta Homes and Lifestyles* is designed for the action-oriented, well-educated reader who enjoys his/her shelter, its design and construction, its environment, and living and entertaining in it." Estab. 1983. Circ. 33,091. Pays on publication. Byline given. Publishes ms an average of 6 months after acceptance. Buys all rights. Responds in 3 months. Sample copy for $3.95. Writer's guidelines on website.
Nonfiction: Interview/profile, new products, well-designed homes, photo features, gardens, local art, remodeling, food, preservation, entertaining. "We do not want articles outside respective market area, not written for magazine format,

or that are excessively controversial, investigative or that cannot be appropriately illustrated with attractive photography." **Buys 35 mss/year.** Query with published clips. Length: 500-1,200 words. **Pays $400 for features.** Sometimes pays expenses of writers on assignment "if agreed upon in advance of assignment."

Photos: State availability of photos with submission; most photography is assigned. Reviews transparencies. Offers $40-50/photo. Captions, model releases and identification of subjects required. Buys one-time rights.

Columns/Departments: Short Takes (newsy items on home and garden topics); Quick Fix (simple remodeling ideas); Cheap Chic (stylish decorating that is easy on the wallet); Digging In (outdoor solutions from Atlanta's gardeners); Big Fix (more extensive remodeling projects); Real Estate News. Query by mail only with published clips. Length: 350-500 words. **Pays $50-200.**

◪ **$ BACKHOME: Your Hands-On Guide to Sustainable Living**, Wordsworth Communications, Inc., P.O. Box 70, Hendersonville NC 28793. (828)696-3838. Fax: (828)696-0700. E-mail: backhome@ioa.com. Website: www.BackHomemagazine.com. **Contact:** Lorna K. Loveless, editor. **80% freelance written.** Bimonthly magazine. "*BackHome* encourages readers to take more control over their lives by doing more for themselves: productive organic gardening; building and repairing their homes; utilizing alternative energy systems; raising crops and livestock; building furniture; toys and games and other projects; creative cooking. *BackHome* promotes respect for family activities, community programs and the environment." Estab. 1990. Circ. 26,000. Pays on publication. Publishes ms an average of 1 year after acceptance. Byline given. Offers $25 kill fee at publisher's discretion. Buys first North American serial rights. Editorial lead time 3 months. Submit seasonal material 6 months in advance. Accepts queries by mail, e-mail, fax, phone. Responds in 6 weeks to queries; 2 months to mss. Sample copy for $4 or on website. Writer's guidelines for SASE or on website.

    ○╼ Break in by writing about personal experience (expecially in overcoming challenges) in fields in which *Backhome* focuses.

Nonfiction: How-to (gardening, construction, energy, home business), interview/profile, personal experience, technical, self-sufficiency. No essays or old-timey reminiscences. **Buys 80 mss/year.** Query. Length: 750-5,000 words. **Pays $25** (approximately)/printed page.

    ● The editor reports an interest in seeing "more alternative energy experiences, *good* small houses, workshop projects (for handy persons, not experts) and community action others can copy."

Reprints: Send photocopy of article and information about when and where the article previously appeared. **Pays $25/printed page.**

Photos: Send photos with submission: 35mm slides and color prints. Offers additional payment for photos published. Identification of subjects required. Buys one-time rights.

Tips: "Very specific in relating personal experiences in the areas of gardening, energy, and homebuilding how-to. Third-person approaches to others' experiences are also acceptable but somewhat less desirable. Clear color photo prints, especially those in which people are prominent, help immensely when deciding upon what is accepted."

$ $ $ $ BETTER HOMES AND GARDENS, 1716 Locust St., Des Moines IA 50309-3023. (515)284-3044. Fax: (515)284-3763. Website: www.bhg.com. Editor-in-Chief: Jean LemMon. Editor (Building): Joan McCloskey. Editor (Food & Nutrition): Nancy Byal. Editor (Garden/Outdoor Living): Mark Kane. Editor (Health): Martha Miller. Editor (Education & Parenting): Richard Sowienski. Editor (Money Management, Automotive, Electronics): Lamont Olson. Editor (Features & Travel): Nina Elder. Editor (Interior Design): Sandy Soria. **10-15% freelance written.** "*Better Homes and Gardens* provides home service information for people who have a serious interest in their homes." Estab. 1922. Circ. 7,605,000. **Pays on acceptance.** Buys all rights. "We read all freelance articles, but much prefer to see a letter of query rather than a finished manuscript."

Nonfiction: Travel, education, gardening, health, cars, home entertainment. "We do not deal with political subjects or with areas not connected with the home, community, and family." Pays rates "based on estimate of length, quality and importance." No poetry or fiction.

    ● Most stories published by this magazine go through a lengthy process of development involving both editor and writer. Some editors will consider *only* query letters, not unsolicited manuscripts.

Tips: Direct queries to the department that best suits your story line.

▨ ◪ **$ $ $ CANADIAN HOME WORKSHOP, The Do-It-Yourself Magazine**, Avid Media Inc., 340 Ferrier St., Suite 210, Markham, Ontario L3R 2Z5 Canada. (416)475-8440. Fax: (905)475-4856. E-mail: letters@canadianworkshop.ca. Website: www.canadianworkshop.ca. **Contact:** Douglas Thomson, editor. **90% freelance written;** half of these are assigned. Monthly magazine covering the "do-it-yourself" market including woodworking projects, renovation, restoration and maintenance. Circ. 100,000. Payment in two installments: half when received, half the month following. Byline given. Offers 50% kill fee. Rights are negotiated with the author. Submit seasonal material 6 months in advance. Responds in 6 weeks. Sample copy for 9×12 SASE. Writer's guidelines for #10 SASE.

Nonfiction: How-to (home maintenance, renovation and woodworking projects and features). **Buys 40-60 mss/year.** Query with published clips. Length: 1,500-2,500 words. **Pays $800-1,200.** Pays expenses of writers on assignment.

Photos: Send photos with ms. Payment for photos, transparencies negotiated with the author. Captions, model releases, identification of subjects required.

Tips: "Freelancers must be aware of our magazine format. Products used in how-to articles must be readily available across Canada. Deadlines for articles are four months in advance of cover date. How-tos should be detailed enough for the amateur but appealing to the experienced. Articles must have Canadian content: sources, locations, etc."

⭐ **$ $ $ $ COTTAGE LIFE**, Quarto Communications, 54 St. Patrick St., Toronto, Ontario M5T 1V1 Canada. (416)599-2000. Fax: (416)599-0708. E-mail: dzimmer@cottagelife.com. Managing Editor: Penny Caldwell. **Contact:** David Zimmer, editor. **80% freelance written.** Bimonthly magazine. "*Cottage Life* is written and designed for the people who own and spend time at waterfront cottages throughout Canada and bordering U.S. states. The magazine has a strong service slant, combining useful 'how-to' journalism with coverage of the people, trends, and issues in cottage country. Regular columns are devoted to boating, fishing, watersports, projects, real estate, cooking, nature, personal cottage experience, and environmental, political, and financial issues of concern to cottagers." Estab. 1988. Circ. 70,000. **Pays on acceptance.** Publishes ms an average of 2 months after acceptance. Byline given. Offers 50-100% kill fee. Buys first North American serial rights.
Nonfiction: Book excerpts, exposé, historical/nostalgic, how-to, humor, interview/profile, personal experience, photo feature, technical. **Buys 90 mss/year.** Query with published clips and SAE with Canadian postage or IRCs. Length: 1,500-3,500 words. **Pays $100-2,200 for assigned articles; $50-1,000 for unsolicited articles.** Sometimes pays expenses of writers on assignment. Query first.
Columns/Departments: On the Waterfront (front department featuring short news, humor, human interest, and service items). Length: 400 words maximum. **Pays $100.** Cooking, Real Estate, Fishing, Nature, Watersports, Personal Experience and Issues. Length: 150-1,200 words. Query with published clips and SAE with Canadian postage or IRCs. **Pays $100-750.**
Tips: "If you have not previously written for the magazine, the 'On the Waterfront' section is an excellent place to break in."

N $ $ $ COUNTRY HOME, Meredith Corp., 1716 Locust St., Des Moines IA 50309-3023. (515)284-2015. Fax: (515)284-2552. E-mail: countryh@mdp.com. Editor-in-Chief: Carol Sama Sheehan. **Contact:** Lori Blachford, managing editor. Magazine published 8 times/year "for people interested in the country way of life." Estab. 1979. Circ. 1,000,000. "*Country Home* magazine is a lifestyle publication created for readers who share passions for American history, style, craftsmanship, tradition, and cuisine. These people, with a desire to find a simpler, more meaningful lifestyle, live their lives and design their living spaces in ways that reflect those passions." **Pays on acceptance.** Publishes ms an average of 5 months after acceptance. Byline given. Submit seasonal material 6 months in advance. Responds in 6 weeks. Sample copy for $4.95.
Nonfiction: Architecture and Design, Families at Home, Travel, Food and Entertaining, Art and Antiques, Gardens and Outdoor Living, Personal Reflections. Query by mail only with writing samples and SASE. "We are not responsible for unsolicited manuscripts, and we do not encourage telephone queries." Length: features, 750-1,500 words; columns or departments, 500-750 words. **Pays $500-1,500 for features, $300-500 for columns or departments.** Pays on completion of assignment.

$ $ $ COUNTRY JOURNAL, 98 North Washington Street, Boston MA 02114. (617)788-9300. Fax: (617)367-6364. E-mail: cntryjournal@primediasi.com. Executive Editor: Toby Lester. Managing Editor: robert Ostergaard. Bimonthly magazine "designed to be a lively, practical and intellectual companion for those interested in life in the American countryside. Publishes essays, reports, profiles of issues and people of interest in rural America, and runs many how-to and lifestyle pieces on such topics as gardening, food, outdoor recreation, and home design and maintenance." Estab. 1974. Circ. 150,000. Pays on publication. Byline given. Buys all rights. Editorial lead time 1 year. Responds in 3 months.
Nonfiction: Essays, reports, profiles, how-to and lifestyles covering gardening, food, health, the natural world, small-scale farming, land conservation, the environment, energy and other issues affecting country life. **Buys 50 mss/year.** Query by mail with published clips, a list of sources and details as to why you are an authority on the subject, as well as your qualifications for writing the piece. Length: 2,500 words. **Pay varies.** Pays some expenses of writers on assignment.
Columns/Departments: "Rubrics include, but are not limited to: Amateur Farmer (how-to pieces on home farming), Field Guide (examinations of both animals and plants), Fruits and Vegetables, In the Garden, The General Store (short essays, reports, stories, and general information on and from the country—an excellent venue for new writers), Handtools (advice on the use and maintenance of tools), Housesmith (home maintenance and repair), The Country Life (essays specifically on country matters), The Back Porch (whimsical illustrations and essays appearing on the magazine's last page)."

$ $ $ COUNTRY LIVING, The Hearst Corp., 224 W. 57th St., New York NY 10019. (212)649-3509. **Contact:** Marjorie Gage, senior editor. Monthly magazine covering home design and interior decorating with an emphasis on "country" style. "A lifestyle magazine for readers who appreciate the warmth and traditions associated with American home and family life. Each monthly issue embraces American country decorating and includes features on furniture, antiques, gardening, home building, real estate, cooking, entertaining and travel." Estab. 1978. Circ. 1,816,000.
Nonfiction: Most open to freelancers: antiques articles from authorities, personal essay. **Buys 20-30 mss/year.** Send complete ms and SASE. **Pay varies.**
Columns/Departments: Most open to freelancers: Readers Corner. Send complete ms and SASE. Pay varies.
Tips: "Know the magazine, know the market and know how to write a good story that will interest *our* readers."

$ $ DESIGN TIMES, The Art of Interiors, Regis Publishing Co., Inc., 1 Design Center Place, Suite 249, Boston MA 02210. (617)443-0636. Fax: (617)443-0637. E-mail: dtimes@aol.com. Website: www.designtimes.com. **Contact:**

S. Jill Thompson, managing editor. **75% freelance written.** Bimonthly magazine covering high-end residential interior design nationwide. "Show, don't tell. Readers want to look over the shoulders of professional interior designers. Avoid cliché. Love design." Estab. 1988. Circ. 20,000. Pays on publication. Publishes ms an average of 4 months after acceptance. Byline given. Offers 10% kill fee. Buys all rights. Editorial lead time 3 months. Submit seasonal material 6 months in advance. Accepts queries by mail, e-mail, fax. Accepts simultaneous submissions. Responds in 1 month. Sample copy for 10×13 SAE with 10 first-class stamps or on website.

Nonfiction: Residential interiors. **Buys 25 mss/year.** Query with published clips. Length: 1,200-3,000 words. Pay varies. Sometimes pays the expenses of writers on assignment.

Photos: State availability of photos with submission. Reviews 4×5 transparencies, 9×10 prints. Negotiates payment individually. Caption, model releases, identification of subject required. Buys one-time rights.

Columns/Departments: Pays $100-150.

Tips: "A home owned by a well-known personality or designer would be a good feature query. Since the magazine is so visual, great photographs are a big help. We're also looking for before/after 'design emergency' stories."

$ $ EARLY AMERICAN HOMES, Celtic Moon Publishing, Inc., 207 House Ave., Suite 103, Camp Hill PA 17011. Fax: (717)730-6263. **Contact:** Mimi Handler, editor. **20% freelance written.** Bimonthly magazine for "people who are interested in capturing the warmth and beauty of the 1600 to 1840 period and using it in their homes and lives today. They are interested in antiques, traditional crafts, architecture, restoration and collecting." Estab. 1970. Circ. 130,000. **Pays on acceptance.** Publishes ms an average of 1 year after acceptance. Buys worldwide rights. Accepts queries by mail, fax. Responds in 3 months. Sample copy and writer's guidelines for 9×12 SAE with 4 first-class stamps.

    O→ Break in "by offering highly descriptive, entertaining, yet informational articles on social culture, decorative arts, antiques or well-restored and appropriately furnished homes that reflect middle-class American life prior to 1850."

Nonfiction: "Social history (the story of the people, not epic heroes and battles), travel to historic sites, antiques and reproductions, restoration, architecture and decorating. We try to entertain as we inform. We're always on the lookout for good pieces on any of our subjects. Would like to see more on how real people did something great to their homes." **Buys 40 mss/year.** Query or submit complete ms. Length: 750-3,000 words. **Pays $100-600.** Pays expenses of writers on assignment.

Tips: "Our readers are eager for ideas on how to bring early America into their lives. Conceive a new approach to satisfy their related interests in arts, crafts, travel to historic sites, and especially in houses decorated in the early American style. Write to entertain and inform at the same time. Be prepared to help us with sources for illustrations."

N $ $ $ FINE GARDENING, Taunton Press, 63 S. Main St., P.O. Box 5506, Newtown CT 06470-5506. (203)426-8171. Fax: (203)426-3434. E-mail: fg@taunton.com. Website: www.finegardening.com. **Contact:** Marc Vassallo, editor. Bimonthly "high-value magazine on landscape and ornamental gardening. Articles written by avid gardeners—first person, hands-on gardening experiences." Estab. 1988. Circ. 200,000. **Pays on acceptance.** Publishes ms an average of 6 months after acceptance. Byline given. Buys all rights. Editorial lead time 1 year. Submit seasonal material 1 year in advance. Accepts queries by mail, e-mail, fax. Writer's guidelines free.

Nonfiction: Book review, how-to, personal experience, photo feature. **Buys 60 mss/year.** Query. Length: 1,000-3,000 words. **Pays $300-1,200.**

    ● Ranked as one of the best markets for freelance writers in *Writer's Yearbook* magazine's annual "Top 100 Markets," January 2000.

Photos: Send photos with submission. Reviews 35mm transparencies. Buys serial rights.

Columns/Department: Book, video and software reviews (on gardening); Last Word (essays/serious, humorous, fact or fiction). **Buys 30 mss/year.** Length: 250-500 words. Query. **Pays $50-200.**

    ▣ The online magazine carries original content not found in the print edition. **Contact:** Marc Vassallo, online editor.

Tips: "It's most important to have solid first-hand experience as a gardener. Tell us what you've done with your own landscape and plants."

$ $ FINE HOMEBUILDING, The Taunton Press, 63 S. Main St., P.O. Box 5506, Newtown CT 06470-5506. (800) 283-7252. Fax: (203) 270-6751. E-mail: fh@taunton.com. Website: www.taunton.com. **Contact:** Kevin Ireton, editor. "*Fine Homebuilding* is a bimonthly magazine for builders, architects, contractors, owner/builders and others who are seriously involved in building new houses or reviving old ones." Estab. 1981. Circ. 247,712. Pays half on acceptance, half on publication. Publishes ms 1 year after acceptance. Byline given. Offers on acceptance payment as kill fee. Buys first and reprint rights. Responds in 1 month. Writer's guidelines for SASE and on website.

Nonfiction: "We're interested in almost all aspects of home building, from laying out foundations to capping cupolas." Query with outline, description, photographs, sketches and SASE. **Pays $150/published page** with "a possible bonus on publication for an unusually good manuscript."

Photos: "Take lots of work-in-progress photos. Color print film, ASA 400, from either Kodak or Fuji works best. If you prefer to use slide film, use ASA 100. Keep track of the negatives; we will need them for publication. If you're not sure what to use or how to go about it, feel free to call for advice."

Columns/Departments: Tools & Materials, Reviews, Questions & Answers, Tips & Techniques, Cross Section, What's the Difference?, Finishing Touches, Great Moments, Breaktime, Drawing Board (design column). Query with outline, description, photographs, sketches and SASE. **Pays $150/published page.**
Tips: "Our chief contributors are home builders, architects and other professionals. We're more interested in your point of view and technical expertise than your prose style. Adopt an easy, conversational style and define any obscure terms for non-specialists. We try to visit all our contributors and rarely publish building projects we haven't seen, or authors we haven't met."

$ $ FLOWER AND GARDEN MAGAZINE, 4645 Belleview, Kansas City MO 64112. (816)531-5730. Fax: (816)531-3873. E-mail: kcpublishing@earthlink.net. **Contact:** senior editor. **80% freelance written.** Works with a small number of new/unpublished writers each year. Bimonthly picture magazine. "*Flower & Garden* focuses on ideas that can be applied to the home garden and outdoor environs, primarily how-to, but also historical and background articles are considered if a specific adaptation can be obviously related to home gardening." Estab. 1957. Circ. 300,000. **Pays on acceptance.** Publishes ms an average of 1 year after acceptance. Buys first-time nonexclusive reprint rights. Byline given. Accepts queries by mail, e-mail, fax. Responds in 2 months. Sample copy for $3. Writer's guidelines for #10 SASE.
Nonfiction: Interested in illustrated articles on how to do certain types of gardening and descriptive articles about individual plants. Flower arranging, landscape design, house plants and patio gardening are other aspects covered. "The approach we stress is practical (how-to-do-it, what-to-do-it-with). We emphasize plain talk, clarity and economy of words. An article should be tailored for a national audience." **Buys 20-30 mss/year.** Query. Length: 500-1,000 words. Rates vary depending on quality and kind of material and author's credentials, **$200-500.**
Reprints: Sometimes accepts previously published articles. Send typed ms with rights for sale noted, including information about when and where the article previously appeared.
  • The editor tells us good quality photos accompanying articles are more important than ever.
Photos: Color slides and transparencies preferred, 35mm and larger but 35mm slides or prints not suitable for cover. Submit cover photos as 2¼ × 2¼ or larger transparencies. An accurate packing list with appropriately labeled photographs and numbered slides with description sheet (including Latin botanical and common names) must accompany submissions. In plant or flower shots, indicate which end is up on each photo. Photos are paid for on publication, $60-175 inside, $300 for covers.
Tips: "The prospective author needs good grounding in gardening practice and literature. Offer well-researched and well-written material appropriate to the experience level of our audience. Photographs help sell the story. Describe special qualifications for writing the particular proposed subject."

$ $ $ GARDEN DESIGN, 100 Avenue of the Americas, New York NY 10013. (212)334-1212. Fax: (212)334-1260. E-mail: gardendesign@meigher.com. Website: www.gardendesignmag.com. Editor: Michael Boobro. **Contact:** Julia Morrill, assistant editor. Magazine published 8 times/year devoted to the fine art of garden design. Circ. 400,000. Pays 2 months after acceptance. Byline given. Buys first North American rights. Submit seasonal material 6 months in advance. Sample copy for $5. Writer's guidelines for #10 SASE.
Nonfiction: "We look for literate writing on a wide variety of garden-related topics—history, architecture, the environment, furniture, decorating, travel, personalities." Query by mail with outline, published clips and SASE. Length: 200-1,200 words. Sometimes pays expenses of writer or photographer on assignment.
  • Ranked as one of the best markets for freelance writers in *Writer's Yearbook* magazine's annual "Top 100 Markets," January 2000.
Photos: Submit scouting photos when proposing article on a specific garden.
Tips: "Our greatest need is for extraordinary private gardens. Scouting locations is a valuable service freelancers can perform, by contacting designers and garden clubs in the area, visiting gardens and taking snapshots for our review. All departments of the magazine are open to freelancers. Familiarize yourself with our departments and pitch stories accordingly. Writing should be as stylish as the gardens we feature."

$ $ THE HERB COMPANION, Interweave Press, 201 E. Fourth St., Loveland CO 80537-5655. (970)669-7672. Fax: (970)669-6117. E-mail: HerbCompanion@HCPress.com. Website: www.discoverherbs.com. **Contact:** Robyn Griggs Lawrence, editor. **80% freelance written.** Bimonthly magazine about herbs: culture, history, culinary, crafts and some medicinal use for both experienced and novice herb enthusiasts. Circ. 180,000. Pays on publication. Byline given. Buys all rights. Editorial lead time 4 months. Responds in 2 months. Sample copy for $4. Guidelines for #10 SASE.
Nonfiction: Practical horticultural, original recipes, historical, how-to, herbal crafts, profiles, helpful hints and book reviews. Submit by mail only detailed query or ms. Length: 4 pages or 1,000 words. **Pays 33¢/word.**
Photos: Send photos with submission. Transparencies preferred. Returns photos and artwork.
Tips: "New approaches to familiar topics are especially welcome. If you aren't already familiar with the content, style and tone of the magazine, we suggest you read a few issues. Technical accuracy is essential. Please use scientific as well as popular names for plants and cover the subject in depth while avoiding overly academic presentation. Information should be made accessible to the reader, and we find this is best accomplished by writing from direct personal experience where possible and always in an informal style."

N: $ $ HERB QUARTERLY, P.O. Box 689, San Anselmo CA 94960-0689. Fax: (415)455-9541. E-mail: herbquart@aol.com. Website: www.HerbQuarterly.com. Publisher: James Keough. **Contact:** Heather K. Scott, associate editor.

80% freelance written. Quarterly magazine for herb enthusiasts. Estab. 1979. Circ. 35,000. Pays on publication. Publishes ms an average of 6 months after acceptance. Buys first North American serial and second (reprint) rights. Query letters recommended. Accepts queries by mail, e-mail, fax. Responds in 2 months. Sample copy for $5 and 9×12 SASE. Writer's guidelines for #10 SASE.

Nonfiction: Gardening (landscaping, herb garden design, propagation, harvesting), medicinal and cosmetic use of herbs, crafts, cooking, historical (folklore, focused piece on particular period—*not* general survey), interview of a famous person involved with herbs or folksy herbalist, personal experience, photo essay ("cover quality" 8×10 b&w or color prints). "We are particularly interested in herb garden design, contemporary or historical." No fiction. Query. Length: 1,000-3,500 words. **Pays $75-250.**

Tips: "We're looking for more articles on interesting, obscure herbs, good book reviews and articles on plant-based cultures and/or folklore. Our best submissions are narrowly focused on herbs with much practical information on cultivation and use for the experienced gardener."

$ HOME DIGEST, The Homeowner's Family Resource Guide, Home Digest International Inc., 268 Lakeshore Rd. E, Unit 604, Oakville, Ontario L6J 7S4 Canada. (905)844-3361. Fax: (905)849-4618. E-mail: homedigest@canada.com. **Contact:** William Roebuck, editor. **25% freelance written.** Quarterly magazine covering house, home and life management for families in stand-alone houses in the greater Toronto region. "*Home Digest* has a strong service slant, combining useful how-to journalism with coverage of the trends and issues of home ownership and family life. In essence, our focus is on the concerns of families living in their own homes." Estab. 1995. Circ. 522,000. Pays on publication. Publishes ms an average of 3 months after acceptance. Byline given. Buys first North American serial rights. Editorial lead time 3 months. Submit seasonal material 5 months in advance. Accepts queries by mail, e-mail, fax. Accepts simultaneous submissions. Responds in 1 month. Sample copy for 9×6 SASE and 2 Canadian stamps. Writer's guidelines for #10 SASE.

Nonfiction: General interest, how-to (household hints, basic home renovation, decorating), humor (living in Toronto), inspirational. No travel, opinion, puff pieces. **Buys 8 mss/year.** Query. Length: 350-700 words. **Pays $50-125** (Canadian).

Reprints: Accepts previously published submission.

Photos: Send photos with submission. Reviews transparencies and prints. Offers $10-20 per photo. Captions, model releases, and identification of subjects required. Buys one-time rights.

Columns/Departments: Household Hints (tested tips that work); Healthy Living (significant health/body/fitness news); both 300-350 words. **Buys 4-6 mss/year.** Query. **Pays $40-75** (Canadian).

Tips: "Base your ideas on practical experiences. We're looking for 'uncommon' advice that works."

$ $ HOMES & COTTAGES, The In-Home Show Ltd., 6557 Mississauga Rd., Suite D, Mississauga, Ontario L5N 1A6 Canada. (905)567-1440. Fax: (905)567-1442. E-mail: jadair@homesandcottages.com. Website: www.homesandcottages.com. Editor: Janice Naisby. **Contact:** Jim Adair, editor-in-chief. **50% freelance written.** Magazine published 8 times/year covering building and renovating; "technically comprehensive articles." Estab. 1987. Circ. 64,000. Pays on publication. Publishes ms an average of 2 months after acceptance. Byline given. Offers 10% kill fee. Buys first North American serial rights. Editorial lead time 3 months. Submit seasonal material 3 months in advance. Sample copy for SAE. Writer's guidelines for SASE.

Nonfiction: Humor (building and renovation related), new product, technical. Looking for how-to projects and simple home improvement ideas. **Buys 32 mss/year.** Query by mail only. Length: 1,000-2,000 words. **Pays $300-750.** Sometimes pays expenses of writers on assignment.

Photos: Send photos with submission. Reviews transparencies and prints. Negotiates payment individually. Captions and identification of subjects required. Buys one-time rights.

Tips: "Read our magazine before sending in a query. Remember that you are writing to a Canadian audience."

$ $ $ HORTICULTURE, Gardening at Its Best, 98 N. Washington St., Boston MA 02114. (617) 742-5600. Fax: (617) 367-6364. E-mail: tfischer@primediasi.com. Website: www.hortmag.com. **Contact:** Thomas Fischer, executive editor. Magazine published 8 times/year. "*Horticulture*, the country's oldest gardening magazine, is designed for active amateur gardeners. Our goal is to offer a blend of text, photographs and illustrations that will both instruct and inspire readers." Circ. 300,000. Byline given. Offers kill fee. Buys one-time or first North American serial rights. Submit seasonal material 10 months in advance. Accepts queries by mail, e-mail, fax. Responds in 3 months. Writer's guidelines for SASE or e-mail.

Nonfiction: "We look for an encouraging personal experience, anecdote and opinion. At the same time, a thorough article should to some degree place its subject in the broader context of horticulture." **Buys 15 mss/year.** Query with published clips, subject background material and SASE. Include disk where possible. Length: 1,000-2,000 words. **Pays $600-1,500.** Pays expenses of writers on assignment if previously arranged with editor.

- Ranked as one of the best markets for freelance writers in *Writer's Yearbook* magazine's annual "Top 100 Markets," January 2000.

Columns/Departments: Query with published clips, subject background material and SASE. Include disk where possible. Length: 100-1,500 words. **Pays $50-750.**

Tips: "We believe every article must offer ideas or illustrate principles that our readers might apply on their own gardens. No matter what the subject, we want our readers to become better, more creative gardeners."

$ $LOG HOME LIVING, Home Buyer Publications Inc., 4200-T Lafayette Center Dr., Chantilly VA 20151. (703)222-9411. Fax: (703)222-3209. E-mail: jbrewster@homebuyerpubs.com. Website: www.loghomeliving.com. **Contact:** Janice Brewster, editor. **50% freelance written.** Monthly magazine for enthusiasts who are dreaming of, planning for, or actively building a log home. Estab. 1989. Circ. 132,000. **Pays on acceptance.** Publishes ms an average of 6 months after acceptance. Byline given. Offers $100 kill fee. Buys first or second serial (reprint) rights. Editorial lead time 6 months. Submit seasonal material 6 months in advance. Responds in 6 weeks. Sample copy for $4. Writer's guidelines for #10 SASE.

Nonfiction: Book excerpts, how-to (build or maintain log home), interview/profile (log home owners), personal experience, photo feature (log homes), technical (design/decor topics), travel. "We do not want historical/nostalgic material." **Buys 6 mss/year.** Query by mail only. Length: 1,000-2,000 words. **Pays $250-500.** Pays expenses of writers on assignment.

Reprints: Send tearsheet or photocopy of article and information about when and where the article previously appeared. Pays 50% of amount paid for an original article.

Photos: State availability of photos with submission. Reviews contact sheets, 4×5 transparencies and 4×6 prints. Negotiates payment individually. Buys one-time rights.

Tips: "*Log Home Living* is devoted almost exclusively to modern manufactured and handcrafted kit log homes. Our interest in historical or nostalgic stories of very old log cabins, reconstructed log homes, or one-of-a-kind owner-built homes is secondary and should be queried first."

$ $LOG HOMES ILLUSTRATED, Goodman Media Group, Inc., 419 Park Ave. South, New York NY 10016. (212)541-7100. Fax: (212)245-1241. Website: www.goodmanmediagroup.com. Editor: Roland Sweet. **Contact:** Stacy Durr Albert, managing editor. **30-40% freelance written.** Bimonthly magazine. "*Log Homes Illustrated* presents full-color photo features and inspirational stories of people who have fulfilled their dream of living in a log home. We show readers how they can make it happen too." Estab. 1994. Circ. 126,000. Pays on publication. Publishes ms within a year of acceptance. Byline given. Buys first rights or second serial (reprint) rights. Editorial lead time 4 months. Submit seasonal material 6 months in advance. Accepts queries by mail, fax. Accepts simultaneous submissions. Sample copy for $3.99.

O— To break in "include photos with queries if possible. Offer hands-on tips for our readers. Include sidebar ideas."

Nonfiction: Book excerpts, how-to (gardening, building), profile (architects), new product, personal experience, photo feature, technical, travel. Special issues: Annual Buyer's Guide; PLANS issue. "We tend to stay away from articles that focus on just one craftsman, promotional pieces." **Buys 20-25 mss/year.** Query with published clips or send complete ms. Length: 1,200-3,000 words. **Pays $300-900.** Pays expenses of writers on assignment with limit agreed upon in advance.

Reprints: Accepts previously published submissions.

Photos: Send photos with submission. Reviews 4×5 transparencies, slides or prints. Negotiates payment individually. Captions required. Buys one-time rights.

Columns/Departments: Diary (personal glimpses of log experience), 1,200-2,000 words; Going Places (visiting a log B&B, lodge, etc.), 1,200-2,000 words; Worth a Look (log churches, landmarks, etc.), 1,200-2,000 words; Gardening (rock gardens, water gardens, etc.), 2,000-3,000 words. **Buys 15 mss/year.** Query with published clips or send complete ms. **Pays $300-600.**

Tips: "Professional photos frequently make the difference between articles we accept and those we don't. Look for unique log structures in your travels, something we may not have seen before. We also consider carefully researched articles pertaining to insuring a log home, financing, contracting, etc."

[N] MIDWEST HOME AND GARDEN, 10 S. Fifth St., Suite 1000, Minneapolis MN 55402. Fax: (612)371-5801. E-mail: editor@mnmo.com. Website: www.mnmo.com. **Contact:** Jan Senn, editor, or Pamela Hill Nettleton, editorial director. **50% freelance written.** "*Midwest Home and Garden* is an upscale shelter magazine showcasing innovative architecture, interesting interior design, and beautiful gardens of the Midwest." Estab. 1997. Circ. 80,000. **Pays on acceptance.** Accepts queries by mail, e-mail, fax. Writer's guidelines for SASE.

Nonfiction: Profiles of regional designers, architects, craftspeople related to home and garden. Photo-driven articles on home décor and design, and gardens. "We like exclusive or first-time rights to showcase a home or garden, and are always looking for fresh designs in any style." Query with resume, published clips, and SASE. Length: 300-1,000 words. Pay negotiable.

Columns/Departments: Designing People (profiles of dealers, craftspeople, designers, garden designers, etc.), 500 words; Design Directions (trends in garden and home design), 1,000 words; Open House (home interview with regional celebrity about their home), 500 words.

Tips: "We are always looking for great new interior design, architecture, and gardens—in Minnesota and in the Midwest."

$ $MOUNTAIN LIVING, Wiesner Publishing, 7009 S. Potomac St., Englewood CO 80112. (303)397-7600. Fax: (303)397-7619. E-mail: rawlings@winc.usa.com. Website: www.mtnliving.com. **Contact:** Irene Rawlings, editor. **90% freelance written.** Bimonthly magazine covering "shelter and lifestyle issues for people who live in, visit or hope to live in the mountains." Estab. 1994. Circ. 35,000. **Pays on acceptance.** Publishes ms an average of 4 months after acceptance. Byline given. Offers 15% kill fee. Buys first North American serial rights. Editorial lead time 6 months. Submit seasonal material 6 months in advance. Accepts queries by mail, e-mail. Accepts simultaneous submissions. Responds in 6 weeks to queries; 2 months to mss. Sample copy for $5 or on website. Writer's guidelines for #10 SASE.

Nonfiction: Book excerpts, essays, historical/nostalgic, interview/profile, personal experience, photo feature, travel, home features. **Buys 30 mss/year.** Query with published clips. Length: 1,200-2,000 words. **Pays $50-400.** Sometimes pays expenses of writers on assignment.

Reprints: Send photocopy of article or typed ms with rights for sale noted. Payment varies.

Photos: State availability of photos with submission. Negotiates payment individually. Buys one-time rights.

Columns/Departments: Architecture, Art, Gardening, Sporting Life, Travel (often international), Off the Beaten Path (out-of-the-way mountain areas in U.S.), History, Health, Cuisine, Environment, Destinations (an art-driven department featuring a beautiful mountain destination in U.S.—must be accompanied by quality photograph), Trail's End (mountain-related essays). **Buys 35 mss/year.** Query with published clips. Length: 300-1,500 words. **Pays $50-300.**

Tips: "A deep understanding of and respect for the mountain environment is essential. Think out of the box. We love to be surprised. Write a brilliant, short query and always send clips."

[N] [▪] $ $ NATIONAL NEIGHBORHOOD NEWS, Neighborhood America.com, 4380 Gulfshore Blvd. N., Suite 808, Naples FL 34103. (941)403-4305. Fax: (941)403-4835. E-mail: hot issues@neighborhoodamerica.com. Website: www.neighborhoodamerica.com. **Contact:** Christina Morrow, content coordinator. **50% freelance written.** Online e-zine covering land use planning/environment/neighborhood. **Pays on acceptance** within 30 days of signed contract/edited article. No byline. Not copyrighted. Buys electronic and archival rights. Editorial lead time 1 month. Accepts queries by e-mail. Accepts simultaneous submissions. Responds in 2 weeks to queries. Sample copy on website. Writer's guidelines and sample contract free, on website or by e-mail.

Nonfiction: Interview/profile, news. No opinion/fiction. Query with published clips or send complete ms. Length: 500-1,000 words. **Pays $300.**

Photos: State availability of or send photos with submission. Reviews digital prints. Offers no additional payment for photos accepted with ms. Minimum of one photo required with accepted article.

$ $ ROMANTIC HOMES, Y-Visionary Publishing, 265 Anita Dr., Suite 120, Orange CA 92868. (714)939-9991. Fax: (714)939-9909. Website: www.romantichomesmag.com. Editor: Eileen Paulin. **Contact:** Catherine Yarnovich, executive managing editor. **60% freelance written.** Bimonthly magazine covering home decor. "*Romantic Homes* is the magazine for women who want to create a warm, intimate, and casually elegant home—a haven that is both a gathering place for family and friends and a private refuge from the pressures of the outside world. The *Romantic Homes* reader is personally involved in the decor of her home. Features offer unique ideas and how-to advice on decorating, home furnishings, and gardening. Departments focus on floor and wall coverings, paint, textiles, refinishing, architectural elements, artwork, travel and entertaining. Every article responds to the reader's need to create a beautiful, attainable environment, providing her with the style ideas and resources to achieve her own romantic home." Estab. 1994. Circ. 140,000. **Pays on acceptance.** Publishes ms an average of 2 months after acceptance. Byline given. Buys all rights. Editorial lead time 5 months. Submit seasonal material 6 months in advance. Accepts queries by mail, fax. Accepts simultaneous submissions. Responds in 2 weeks to queries; 2 months to mss. Writer's guidelines for SASE.

Nonfiction: How-to. "Not just for dreaming, *Romantic Homes* combines unique ideas and inspirations with practical how-to advice on decorating, home furnishings, remodeling and gardening for readers who are actively involved in improving their homes. Every article responds to the reader's need to know how to do it and where to find it." **Buys 150 mss/year.** Query with published clips. Length: 1,000-1,200 words. **Pays $500.**

Photos: State availability of photos or send photos with submission. Reviews transparencies. Captions, model releases and identification of subjects required. Buys all rights.

Columns/Departments: Departments cover antiques, collectibles, artwork, shopping, travel, refinishing, architectural elements, flower arranging, entertaining and decorating. Length: 400-500 words. **Pays $250.**

$ $ SAN DIEGO HOME/GARDEN LIFESTYLES, Mckinnon Enterprises, Box 719001, San Diego CA 92171-9001. (619)571-1818. Fax: (619)571-1889. E-mail: sdhg@sen.rr.com. Senior Editor: Phyllis Van Doren. **Contact:** Eva Ditler, managing editor. **50% freelance written.** Monthly magazine covering homes, gardens, food, intriguing people, real estate, art, culture, and local travel for residents of San Diego city and county. Estab. 1979. Circ. 50,000. Pays on publication. Publishes ms an average of 3 months after acceptance. Byline given. Buys first North American serial rights only. Submit seasonal material 3 months in advance. Accepts queries by mail, e-mail, fax, phone. Responds in 3 months. Sample copy for $4.

Nonfiction: Residential architecture and interior design (San Diego-area homes only), remodeling (must be well-designed—little do-it-yourself), residential landscape design, furniture, other features oriented towards upscale readers interested in living the cultured good life in San Diego. Articles must have local angle. Query with published clips. Length: 700-2,000 words. **Pays $50-350.**

Tips: "No out-of-town, out-of-state subject material. Most freelance work is accepted from local writers. Gear stories to the unique quality of San Diego. We try to offer only information unique to San Diego—people, places, shops, resources, etc. We plan more food and entertaining-at-home articles and more articles on garden products. We also need more in-depth reports on major architecture, environmental, and social aspects of life in San Diego and the border area."

N ✉ $ $ **SEATTLE HOMES AND LIFESTYLES**, Wiesner Publishing LLC, 1221 East Pike St., Suite 204, Seattle WA 98122-3930. (206)322-6699. Fax: (206)322-2799. E-mail: falbert@seattlehomesmag.com. Website: www.se attlehomesmag.com. **Contact:** Fred Albert, editor. **75% freelance written.** Magazine published 7 times/year covering home design and lifestyles. "*Seattle Homes and Lifestyles* showcases the finest homes and gardens in the Northwest, and the personalities and lifestyles that make this region special. We try to help our readers take full advantage of the resources the region has to offer with in-depth coverage of events, travel, entertaining, shopping, food and wine. And we write about it with a warm, personal approach that underscores our local perspective." Estab. 1996. Circ. 30,000. **Pays on acceptance.** Publishes ms an average of 2 months after acceptance. Byline given. Offers 25% kill fee. Buys first and electronic rights. Editorial lead time 3 months. Submit seasonal material 4 months in advance. Accepts simultaneous submissions. Responds in 2 months. Writer's guidelines for SAE with 1 first-class stamp, on website or by e-mail.
Nonfiction: General interest, how-to (decorating, cooking), interview/profile, photo feature, travel. "No essays, journal entries, sports coverage." **Buys 75 mss/year.** Query by mail only with published clips. Length: 300-1,500 words. **Pays $100-350.**
Reprints: Accepts previously published submissions.
Photos: State availability of photos with submission. Reviews contact sheets, transparencies and prints. Negotiates payment individually. Captions, model releases and identification of subjects required. Buys one-time rights.
Columns/Departments: Profiles (human interest/people making contribution to community), 300 words; Design Watch (consumer pieces related to home design), 1,200 words; Taking Off (travel to a region—not one sole destination), 1,500 words; Artisan's Touch (craftsperson producing work for the home), 400 words. **Buys 50 mss/year.** Query by mail only ewith published clips. **Pays $100-250.**
Tips: "We're always looking for experienced journalists with clips that demonstrate a knack for writing engaging, informative features. We're also looking for writers knowledgeable about architecture and decorating who can communicate a home's flavor and spirit through the written word. Since all stories are assigned by the editor, please do not submit manuscripts. Send a résumé and three published samples of your work. Story pitches are not encouraged. Please mail all submissions—do not e-mail or fax. Please don't call—we'll call you if we have an assignment. Writers from the Northwest preferred."

$ $ $ **SOUTHERN ACCENTS**, Southern Progress Corp., 2100 Lakeshore Dr., Birmingham AL 35209. (205)877-6000. Fax: (205)877-6990. E-mail: candace_schlosser@spc.com. Website: www.southernaccents.com. **Contact:** Candace Schlosser, managing editor. "*Southern Accents* celebrates the best of the South." Estab. 1977. Circ. 370,000. Responds in 2 months.
Nonfiction: "Each issue features the finest homes and gardens along with a balance of features that reflect the affluent lifestyles of its readers, including architecture, antiques, entertaining, collecting and travel." Query by mail with SASE, clips and photos.
■ The online magazine carries original content not found in the print edition. Contact: Lynn Carter, online editor.
Tips: "Query us only with specific ideas targeted to our current columns."

$ $ $ **STYLE AT HOME**, Telemedia Publishing, Inc., 25 Sheppard Ave. W., Suite 100, Toronto, Ontario M2N 6S7 Canada. (416)733-7600. Fax: (416)218-3632. E-mail: letters@styleathome.com. Managing Editor: Laurie Grassi. **Contact:** Gail Johnston Habs, editor. **85% freelance written.** Home decor magazine published 8 times/year. "The number one magazine choice of Canadian women aged 25 to 54 who own a home and have a serious interest in decorating. Provides an authoritative, stylish collection of inspiring and accessible interiors, decor projects; reports on style design trends." Estab. 1997. Circ. 205,000. **Pays on acceptance.** Publishes manuscript an average of 4 months after acceptance. Byline given. Offers 50% kill fee. Buys first rights and electronic rights. Editorial lead time 4 months. Submit seasonal material 6 months in advance. Accepts queries by mail, e-mail. Responds in 1 month to queries, 2 weeks to mss. Writer's guidelines by e-mail.
O─ Break in by "familiarizing yourself with the type of interiors we show. Be very up-to-date with the design and home decor market in Canada. Provide a lead to a fabulous home or garden."
Nonfiction: Interview/new product. "No how-to; these are planned in-house." **Buys 80 mss/year.** Query with published clips; include scouting shots with interior story queries. Length: 300-700 words. **Pays $100-1,000.** Sometimes pays expenses of writers on assignment.
● Ranked as one of the best markets for freelance writers in *Writer's Yearbook* magazine's annual "Top 100 Markets," January 2000.
Columns/Departments: Humor (fun home decor/renovating experiences), 500 words. Query with published clips. **Pays $250-500.**

$ $ **TEXAS GARDENER, The Magazine for Texas Gardeners, by Texas Gardeners**, Suntex Communications, Inc., P.O. Box 9005, Waco TX 76714-9005. (254)848-9393. Fax: (254)848-9779. E-mail: suntex@calpha.com. **Contact:** Chris Corby, editor. **80% freelance written.** Works with a small number of new/unpublished writers each year. Bimonthly magazine covering vegetable and fruit production, ornamentals and home landscape information for home gardeners in Texas. Estab. 1981. Circ. 30,000. Pays on publication. Publishes ms an average of 4 months after acceptance. Byline given. Buys first North American serial and all rights. Submit seasonal material 6 months in advance. Accepts queries by mail, e-mail, fax. Responds in 2 months. Sample copy for $2.95 and SAE with 5 first-class stamps. Writer's guidelines for #10 SASE.

Nonfiction: How-to, humor, interview/profile, photo feature. "We use feature articles that relate to Texas gardeners. We also like personality profiles on hobby gardeners and professional horticulturists who are doing something unique." **Buys 50-60 mss/year.** Query with clips of published work. Length: 800-2,400 words. **Pays $50-200.**

Photos: "We prefer superb color and b&w photos; 90% of photos used are color." Send photos. Pays negotiable rates for 2¼ or 35mm color transparencies and 8×10 b&w prints and contact sheets. Model release and identification of subjects required.

Columns/Departments: Between Neighbors. **Pays $25.**

Tips: "First, be a Texan. Then come up with a good idea of interest to home gardeners in this state. Be specific. Stick to feature topics like 'How Alley Gardening Became a Texas Tradition.' Leave topics like 'How to Control Fire Blight' to the experts. High quality photos could make the difference. We would like to add several writers to our group of regular contributors and would make assignments on a regular basis. Fillers are easy to come up with in-house. We want good writers who can produce accurate and interesting copy. Frequent mistakes made by writers in completing an article assignment for us are that articles are not slanted toward Texas gardening, show inaccurate or too little gardening information or lack good writing style."

$ $ TIMBER HOMES ILLUSTRATED, Goodman Media Group, Inc., 419 Park Ave. South, New York NY 10016. (212)541-7100. Fax: (212)245-1241. Website: www.goodmanmediagroup.com. Editor: Roland Sweet. **Contact:** Stacy Durr Albert, managing editor. **30% freelance written.** "*Timber Homes Illustrated* (published 6 times/year) presents full-color photo features and stories about timber-frame, log, post-and-beam and other classic wood homes. We feature stories of homeowners who've achieved their dream and encouragement for those who dream of owning a timber home." Estab. 1996. Circ. 75,000. Pays on publication. Byline given. Buys first North American serial rights or second serial (reprint) rights. Editorial lead time 4 months. Submit seasonal material 6 months in advance. Accepts queries by mail, fax. Accepts simultaneous submissions. Sample copy for $3.99.

   O→ To break in "find a historical timber structure that we may not have discovered. Both U.S. and foreign examples will be considered. Always provide photos."

Nonfiction: Book excerpts, historical/nostalgic, how-to (building), interview/profile (architects), personal experience, photo feature, travel. Special issue: Annual Buyer's Directory. No self-promotion pieces about furniture designers, etc. **Buys 15 mss/year.** Query with published clips or send complete ms. Length: 1,200-3,000 words. **Pays $300-600.** Pays expenses of writers on assignment with limit agreed upon in advance.

Reprints: Accepts previously published submissions.

Photos: Send photos with submission. Reviews 4×5 transparencies, slides or prints. Negotiates payment individually. Captions required. Buys one-time rights.

Columns/Departments: Traditions (history of timber-framing), 1,200-3,000 words; Interior Motives (decorating timber homes), 1,200-2,200 words; Space & Place (decor ideas, timber-frame components), 1,200-2,000 words. **Buys 10 mss/year.** Query with published clips or send complete ms. **Pays $300-600.**

Tips: "We suggest including photos with your submission. Present a clear idea of where and how your story will fit into our magazine. We are always interested in seeing timber structures other than homes, such as wine vineyards or barns. Look for something unique—including unique homes."

$ $ $ TODAY'S HOMEOWNER, 2 Park Ave., New York NY 10016. (212)779-5000. Fax: (212)725-3281. Website: www.todayshomeowner.com. Editor: Paul Spring. Managing Editor: Steven Saltzman. **Contact:** Fran Donegan, executive editor. **10% freelance written.** Prefers to work with published/established writers. "If it's good, and it fits the type of material we're currently publishing, we're interested, whether writer is new or experienced." Magazine published 10 times/year for the active home owner. "Articles emphasize an active, home-oriented lifestyle. Includes information useful for maintenance, repair and renovation to the home. Information on how to buy, how to select products useful to homeowners. Emphasis in home-oriented articles is on good design, inventive solutions to styling and space problems, useful home-workshop projects." Estab. 1928. Circ. 950,000. **Pays on acceptance.** Publishes ms an average of 4 months after acceptance. Byline given. Buys first North American serial rights. Accepts queries by mail, fax. Responds in 3 months.

   O→ Break in with a submission to the Homeowner's Digest department.

Nonfiction: Feature articles relating to homeowner, 1,200-2,500 words. "This may include personal home-renovation projects, professional advice on interior design, reports on different or unusual construction methods, energy-related subjects, outdoor/backyard projects, etc. No high-tech subjects such as aerospace, electronics, photography or military hardware. Articles on construction, tool use, refinishing techniques, etc., are also sought." **Pays $1,000 minimum for features;** fees based on number of printed pages, photos accompanying mss., etc. Query only; *no unsolicited mss.* Pays expenses of writers on assignment.

Photos: Photos should accompany mss. Pays $600 and up for transparencies for cover. Inside color: $300/1 page, $500/2, $700/3, etc. Captions and model releases required.

Tips: "The most frequent mistake made by writers in completing an article assignment for *Today's Homeowner* is not taking the time to understand its editorial focus and special needs."

$ $ VICTORIAN HOMES, Y-Visionary Publishing L.P., 265 S. Anita Dr., Suite 120, Orange CA 92868-3310. (714)939-9991, ext. 332. Fax: (714)939-9909. E-mail: ekotite@pacbell.net. Managing Editor: Cathy Yarnovich. **Contact:** Erika Kotite, editor. **90% freelance written.** Bimonthly magazine covering Victorian home restoration and decoration. "*Victorian Homes* is read by Victorian home owners, restorers, house museum management and others interested in the Victorian revival. Feature articles cover home architecture, interior design, furnishings and the home's history. Photography is *very* important to the feature." Estab. 1981. Circ. 100,000. **Pays on acceptance**. Publishes ms an average of 1 year after acceptance. Byline given. Offers $50 kill fee. Buys first North American serial and one-time rights. Editorial lead time 4 months. Submit seasonal material 1 year in advance. Accepts queries by mail, e-mail, fax. Accepts simultaneous submissions. Responds in 6 weeks to queries; 2 months to mss. Sample copy and writer's guidelines for SAE.

Nonfiction: How-to (create period style curtains, wall treatments, bathrooms, kitchens, etc.), photo feature. "Article must deal with structures—no historical articles on Victorian people or lifestyles." **Buys 30-35 mss/year.** Query. Length: 800-1,800 words. **Pays $300-500.** Sometimes pays expenses of writers on assignment.

Photos: State availability of photos with submission. Reviews 2¼ × 2¼ transparencies. Negotiates payment individually. Captions required. Buys one-time rights.

HUMOR

Publications listed here specialize in gaglines or prose humor, some for readers and others for performers or speakers. Other publications that use humor can be found in nearly every category in this book. Some have special needs for major humor pieces; some use humor as fillers; many others are interested in material that meets their ordinary fiction or nonfiction requirements but also has a humorous slant. The majority of humor articles must be submitted as complete manuscripts on speculation because editors usually can't know from a query whether or not the piece will be right for them.

⊠ $ $ MAD MAGAZINE, 1700 Broadway, New York NY 10019. (212)506-4850. Website: www.madmag.com. **Contact:** Editorial Dept. **100% freelance written.** Monthly magazine "always on the lookout for new ways to spoof and to poke fun at hot trends." Estab. 1952. **Pays on acceptance.** Publishes ms an average of 6 months after acceptance. Byline given. Buys all rights. Submit seasonal material 6 months in advance. Responds in 10 weeks. Sample articles on website. Writer's guidelines for #10 SASE.

Nonfiction: Satire, parody. "We're *not* interested in formats we're already doing or have done to death like 'what they say and what they really mean.' " **Buys 400 mss/year.** "Submit a premise with three or four examples of how you intend to carry it through, describing the action and visual content. Rough sketches desired but not necessary. One-page gags: two- to eight- panel cartoon continuities at minimum very funny, maximum hilarious!" **Pays minimum of $400/*MAD* page.** "*Don't* send previously published submissions, riddles, advice columns, TV or movie satires, book manuscripts, top ten lists, articles about Alfred E. Neuman, poetry, essays, short stories or other text pieces."

Tips: "Have fun! Remember to think visually! Surprise us! Freelancers can best break in with satirical nontopical material. Include SASE with each submission. Originality is prized. We like outrageous, silly and/or satirical humor."

$ $ $ $ WORDS FOR SALE, 1149 Granada Ave., Salinas CA 93906. **Contact:** Lorna Gilbert, submission editor.

Nonfiction: "Since 1968, we have sold almost every kind of written material to a wide variety of individual and corporate clients. We deal in both the written as well as the spoken word, from humorous one liners and nightclub acts, to informative medical brochures, political speeches, and almost everything in between. We are not agents. We are a company that provides original written material created especially for the specific needs of our current clients. Therefore, do not send us a sample of your work. As good as it may be, it is almost certainly unrelated to our current needs. Instead begin by finding out what our clients want and write it for them. What could be simpler? It gets even better: *We buy sentences!* That's right. Forget conceiving, composing, editing and polishing endless drafts of magazine articles or book manuscripts. Simply create the type of sentence or sentences we're looking for and we'll buy one or more of them. We respond promptly. We pay promptly." **Pays $1 and up/sentence. Pays on acceptance.** All submissions must include SASE or they will not be returned.

Tips: "The key to your selling something to us, is to *first* find out *exactly* what we are currently buying. To do this simply mail us a #10 SASE and we will send you a list of what we are anxious to buy at this time."

INFLIGHT

Most major inflight magazines cater to business travelers and vacationers who will be reading, during the flight, about the airline's destinations and other items of general interest.

$ ABOARD MAGAZINE, 100 Almeria Ave., Suite 220, Coral Gables FL 33134. (305)441-9738. Fax: (305)441-9739. E-mail: aboard@worldnet.att.net. Website: www.aboardmagazines.com. **Contact:** Sarah Múnoz, managing editor. **40% freelance written.** Bilingual inflight magazines designed to reach travelers to and from Latin America, carried on 7 major Latin-American airlines. Estab. 1976. Circ. 180,000. Pays on publication. Byline given. Buys one-time or simultaneous rights. Accepts queries by mail, e-mail. Accepts simultaneous submissions. Responds in 3 months.

Nonfiction: General interest, new product, business, science, art, fashion, photo feature, technical, travel. "No controversial or political material." Query with SASE. **Buys 50 mss/year.** Length: 750 words. **Pays $100-150.**

Reprints: Send photocopy of article or typed ms with rights for sale noted and information about when and where the article previously appeared. Pays 0-50% of amount paid for an original article.

Photos: Send photos with submission. Reviews 35mm slides or transparencies only. Offers no additional payment for photos accepted with ms. Offers $20/photo minimum. Identification of subjects required. Buys one-time rights.

Fillers: Facts. **Buys 6/year.** Length: 800-1,000 words. **Pays $100.**

Tips: "Send article with photos. We need travel material on Chile, Ecuador, Bolivia, El Salvador, Honduras, Guatemala, Uruguay, Nicaragua, Venezuela."

$ $AIRWAVES, CONNECTIONS, The Magazines of ASA and Logan Airport, (formerly *Wingtips*), Graf/X Publishing, 3000 N. 2nd St., Minneapolis MN 55411. (612)520-2348. Fax: (610)588-2265. E-mail: mquach@graf-x.net. **Contact:** Molly Quach, managing editor. Bimonthly inflight magazine for ASA and Logan Airport. "*Airwaves* and *Connections* cover travel, business, sports and profiles." Estab. 1995. Circ. 32,000. Pays 60 days after publication. Byline given. Offers 50% kill fee. Buys first North American serial rights, second serial rights and makes work-for-hire assignments. Editorial lead time 4 months. Submit seasonal material 4 months in advance. Accepts simultaneous submissions. Responds in 6 weeks to queries, 2 months to mss. Sample copy for 8×11 SAE with 3 first-class stamps. Writer's guidelines for #10 SASE.

Nonfiction: Book excerpts, general interest, how-to, humor, interview/profile, personal experience, travel. **Buys 20-30 mss/year.** Query by mail only with published clips. Length: 750-2,500 words. **Pays $50-500 for assigned articles; $10-250 for unsolicited articles.** Sometimes pays expenses of writers on assignment.

Reprints: State availability of photos with submission. Negotiates payment individually.

Tips: "Since this publication doubles as an airline marketing tool, the writers with the best chance are the ones who can write a piece with a positive slant, that is still informative and stylistic. Work published here needs to be ultimately positive but not sterile. Also, we need more e-commerce and business-related pieces."

$ $ $AMERICA WEST AIRLINES MAGAZINE, Skyword Marketing Inc., 4636 E. Elwood St., Suite 5, Phoenix AZ 85040-1963. (602)997-7200. Fax: (602)997-9875. **Contact:** Michael Derr, editor. **80% freelance written.** Monthly general interest magazine covering business, the arts, science, cuisine, travel, culture, lifestyle, sports. "We look for thoughtful writing, full of detail, and a writer's ability to create a sense of place." Estab. 1986. Circ. 135,000. Pays on publication. Publishes ms an average of 6 months after acceptance. Byline given. Offers 15% kill fee. Buys first North American serial rights. Editorial lead time 6 months. Submit seasonal material 6 months in advance. Accepts queries by mail, fax. Accepts simultaneous submissions. Responds in 1 month. Sample copy for $3. Writer's guidelines for #10 SASE.

Nonfiction: Essays, general interest, historical/nostalgic, humor, interview/profile, personal experience, photo feature. "Ours is not a traditional feature well, but a mix of short, medium and long articles, specialty subjects and special-format features, but all still with the graphic appeal of a traditional feature." No how-to, poetry or flying articles. Query with published clips. Length: 500-2,000 words. **Pays $150-1,000.** Sometimes pays expenses of writers on assignment.

Photos: State availability of photos with submission. Reviews transparencies. Offers $25-100/photo. Identification of subjects required. Buys one-time rights.

Columns/Departments: This and That (a wide-ranging mix of timely, newsy and entertaining short articles), 150-400 words. Query with published clips.

Fiction: Adventure, historical, humorous, mainstream, mystery, slice-of-life vignettes. Nothing of a sexual or potentially controversial or offensive nature. **Buys 12 mss/year.** Send completed ms. Length: 200-2,000 words. **Pays $200-500.**

Fillers: Short humor.

Tips: "In general, we prefer an informal yet polished style with personal, intimate storytelling. We especially appreciate visual, robust and passionate writing—a literary flair is never out of place. Be creative and capture a sense of the people and places you write about."

$ $ $ $AMERICAN WAY, P.O. Box 619640, Mail Drop 5598, Dallas/Fort Worth Airport TX 75261-9640. (817)967-1804. Fax: (817)967-1571. E-mail: tiffany_franke@amrcorp.com. Website: www.AA.com/away. Editorial Director: John Clark. Executive Editor: Elaine Srnka. **Contact:** Tiffany Franke, associate editor. **98% freelance written.** Works exclusively with published/established writers. Biweekly inflight magazine for passengers flying with American Airlines and American Eagle. Estab. 1966. **Pays on acceptance.** Publishes ms an average of 4 months after acceptance. Buys first serial rights. Accepts queries by mail, e-mail, fax. Request sample copy by calling (817)967-1784; sample articles are available on website.

• *American Way* no longer publishes fiction and does not accept first-person travelogues.

Nonfiction: Travel, business, arts/culture, sports, law, fashion and computer/technology. "Present story ideas that are timely, relevant, heavy on service, and appealing to a mostly male audience that travels often." Feature articles. Query with résumé, pertinent clips and SASE. Length: 2,000-2,500 words. **Pays $2,000.**

Columns/Departments: Sojourns, 200 words; 1-page departments, 400 words; departments, 800-1,000 words. **Pays $1/word.**

Tips: "We do not respond to queries sent without an SASE unless we plan to pursue them. All stories are by assignment only. If your suggestion is accepted, you will be contacted by an editor who will assign the story and negotiate the deadline and your payment."

⚐ **$ $ $ $** ATTACHÉ MAGAZINE, Pace Communications, 1301 Carolina St., Greensboro NC 27401. (336)378-6065. Fax: (336)378-8278. E-mail: AttacheAir@aol.com. Website: www.attachemag.com. Editor: Lance Elko. **Contact:** Abigail Seymour, managing editor. **75% freelance written.** Monthly magazine for travelers on U.S. Airways. "We focus on 'the best of the world' and use a humorous view." Estab. 1997. Circ. 441,000. **Pays on acceptance.** Publishes ms an average of 4 months after acceptance. Byline given. Offers 25% kill fee. Buys first global serial rights for most articles. Editorial lead time 3 months. Accepts queries by mail, e-mail. Responds in 6 weeks to queries; 1 month to mss. Sample copy for $7.50 or on website. Writer's guidelines for #10 SASE or on website.

Nonfiction: Book excerpts, essays, food, general interest, lifestyle, personal experience, sports, travel. Features are highly visual, focusing on some unusual or unique angle of travel, food, business, or other topic approved by an *Attaché* editor." **Buys 50-75 mss/year.** Query with published clips. Length: 350-2,500 words. **Pays $350-2,500.** Sometimes pays expenses of writers on assignment.

● Ranked as one of the best markets for freelance writers in *Writer's Yearbook* magazine's annual "Top 100 Markets," January 2000.

Photos: State availability of photos with submission. Reviews contact sheets, negatives, transparencies. Negotiates payment individually. Model releases, identification of subjects required. Buys one-time rights.

Columns/Departments: Passions includes several topics such as "Vices," "Food," "Golf," "Sporting," "Shelf Life," and "Things That Go;" Paragons features short lists of the best in a particular field or category, as well as 400-word pieces describing the best of something—for example, the best home tool, the best ice cream in Paris, and the best reading library. Each piece should lend itself to highly visual art. Informed Sources are departments of expertise and first-person accounts; they include "How It Works," "Home Front," "Improvement," and "Genius at Work." **Buys 50-75 mss/year.** Query with published clips. **Pays $500-2,000.**

Tips: "We look for cleverly written, entertaining articles with a unique angle, particularly pieces that focus on 'the best of' something. Study the magazine for content, style and tone. Queries for story ideas should be to the point and presented clearly. Any correspondence should include SASE."

⚐ **$ $ $** HEMISPHERES, **Pace Communications for United Airlines**, 1301 Carolina St., Greensboro NC 27401. (336)378-6065. **Contact:** Randy Johnson, editor. **95% freelance written.** Monthly magazine for the educated, sophisticated business and recreational frequent traveler on an airline that spans the globe. Estab. 1992. Circ. 500,000. **Pays on acceptance.** Publishes ms 3 months after acceptance. Byline given. Offers 20% kill fee. Usually buys first, worldwide rights. Editorial lead time 8 months. Submit seasonal material 8 months in advance. Responds in 2 months to queries; 4 months to mss. Sample copy for $5. Writer's guidelines for #10 SASE.

Nonfiction: General interest, humor, personal experience. "Keeping 'global' in mind, we look for topics that reflect a modern appreciation of the world's cultures and environment. No 'What I did (or am going to do) on a trip to. . . .' " Query with published clips. Length: 500-3,000 words. **Pays 50¢/word and up.**

Photo: State availability of photos with submission. Reviews transparencies "only when we request them." Negotiates payment individually. Captions, model releases, identification of subjects required. Buys one-time rights.

Columns/Departments: Making a Difference (Q&A format interview with world leaders, movers, and shakers. A 500-600 word introduction anchors the interview. We want to profile an international mix of men and women representing a variety of topics or issues, but all must truly be making a difference. No puffy celebrity profiles.); On Location (A snappy selection of one or two sentences, "15 Fascinating Facts" that are obscure, intriguing, or travel-service-oriented items that the reader never knew about a city, state, country or destination.); Executive Secrets (Things that top executives know); Case Study (Business strategies of international companies or organizations. No lionizations of CEOs. Strategies should be the emphasis. "We want international candidates."); Weekend Breakway (Takes us just outside a major city after a week of business for several activities for a physically active, action-packed weekend. This isn't a sedentary "getaway" at a "property."); Roving Gourmet (Insider's guide to interesting eating in major city, resort area, or region. The slant can be anything from ethnic to expensive; not just "best." The four featured eateries span a spectrum from "hole in the wall," to "expense account lunch" and on to "big deal dining."); Collecting (Occasional 800-word story on collections and collecting that can emphasize travel); Eye on Sports (Global look at anything of interest in sports); Vintage Traveler (Options for mature, experienced travelers); Savvy Shopper (Insider's tour of best places in the world to shop. Savvy Shopper steps beyond all those stories that just mention the great shopping at a particular destination. A shop-by-shop, gallery-by-gallery tour of the best places in the world."); Science and Technology (Substantive, insightful stories on how technology is changing our lives and the business world. Not just another column on audio components or software. No gift guides!); Aviation Journal (For those fascinated with aviation. Aviation Journal is an opportunity to enthrall all of those fliers who are fascinated with aviation. Topics range widely. A fall 1998 redesign of the magazine ushered in a reader-service-oriented "Terminal Bliss," a great airports guide series.); Grape And Grain (Wine and spirits with emphasis on education, not one-upmanship); Show Business (Films, music and entertainment); Musings (Humor or just curious musings); Quick Quiz (Tests to amuse and educate); Travel News (Brief, practical, invaluable, trend-oriented tips); Book Beat (Tackles topics like the Wodehouse Society, the birth of a book, the competition between local bookshops and national chains. Please, no review proposals. Slant—what the world's reading—residents explore how current best sellers tell us what their country is thinking.). Length: 1,400 words. Query with published clips. **Pays 50¢/word and up.**

Fiction: Adventure, humorous, mainstream, slice-of-life vignettes. **Buys 8 mss/year.** Query. Length: 500-2,000 words. **Pays 50¢/word and up.**

Tips: "We increasingly require writers of 'destination' pieces or departments to 'live whereof they write.' Increasingly want to hear from U.S., U.K. or other English speaking/writing journalists (business & travel) who reside outside the

U.S. in Europe, South America, Central America and the Pacific Rim—all areas that United flies. We're not looking for writers who aim at the inflight market. *Hemispheres* broke the fluffy mold of that tired domestic genre. Our monthly readers are a global mix on the cutting edge of the global economy and culture. They don't need to have the world filtered by US writers. We want a Hong Kong restaurant writer to speak for that city's eateries, so we need English speaking writers around the globe. That's the 'insider' story our reader's respect. We use resident writers for departments such as Roving Gourmet, Savvy Shopper, On Location, 3 Perfect Days and Weekend Breakaway, but authoritative writers can roam in features. Sure we cover the US, but with a global view: No 'in this country' phraseology. 'Too American' is a frequent complaint for queries. We use UK English spellings in articles that speak from that tradition and we specify costs in local currency first before US dollars. Basically, all of above serves the realization that today, 'global' begins with respect for 'local.' That approach permits a wealth of ways to present culture, travel and business for a wide readership. We anchor that with a reader service mission that grounds everything in 'how to do it.' "

N ⚝ $ $ HORIZON AIR MAGAZINE, Paradigm Communications Group, 2701 First Ave., Suite 250, Seattle WA 98121. Fax: (206)448-6939. **Contact:** Michele Andrus Dill, editor. **90% freelance written.** Monthly in-flight magazine covering travel, business and leisure in the Pacific Northwest. *"Horizon Air Magazine* serves a sophisticated audience of business and leisure travelers. Stories must have a Northwest slant." Estab. 1990. Circ. 1,000,000. Pays on publication. Publishes within 1 year of acceptance. Byline given. Offers 33% kill fee. Buys first North American series and electronic rights (nonexclusive). Editorial lead time 6 months. Submit seasonal material 5 months in advance. Accepts queries by mail, fax. Sample copy for 10×12 SASE. Writer's guidelines for #10 SASE.
Nonfiction: Essays (personal), general interest, historical/nostalgic, how-to, humor, interview/profile, personal experience, photo feature, travel, business. Upcoming special issues include meeting planners' guide, golf, gift guide. No material unrelated to the Pacific Northwest. **Buys approximately 50 mss/year.** Query with published clips or current mss. Length: 1,500-3,000 words. **Pays $300-700.** Sometimes pays expenses of writers on assignment.
Photos: State availability of photos with submission. Reviews transparencies and prints. Negotiates payment individually. Captions, model releases and identification of subjects required. Buys one-time rights.
Columns/Departments: Region (Northwest news/profiles), 200-400 words; Air Time (personal essays), 700 words. **Buys 15 mss/year.** Query with published clips. **Pays $100 (region)-250 (air time).**

$ $ $ KWIHI, The In-Flight Magazine of Air Aruba, ABARTA Metro Publishing, 11900 Biscayne Blvd., Suite 300, Miami FL 33181-2726. (305)892-6644. Fax: (305)892-1005. **Contact:** Jenny Bronson, editor. **50-75% freelance written.** Quarterly magazine covering Aruba. *"Kwihi* is written for vacationing passengers of Air Aruba. Articles focus on activities, sports, entertainment, dining and other subjects of interest to visitors of the island of Aruba." Estab. 1995. Circ. 10,000. **Pays on acceptance**. Publishes ms an average of 2 months after acceptance. Byline given. Buys all rights. Editorial lead time 3 months. Submit seasonal material 3 months in advance. Accepts queries by mail, e-mail, fax.
Nonfiction: Interview/profile (locals), travel (Aruba only). **Buys 12 mss/year.** Query with published clips. Length: 500-3,000 words. **Pays $250-1,500.**
Photos: State availability of photos with submission. Negotiates payment individually. Identification of subjects required.
Columns/Departments: On the Island & Off the Cuff (island news, travel tidbits, book reviews), 150-200 words each, total column is around 2,500; Personality Profile (profile of interesting Arubans—artists, business owners, etc.), 1,000 words. Query with published clips. **Pays $100-500.**

N ⚝ $ MIDWEST EXPRESS MAGAZINE, Paradigm Communications Group, 2701 First Ave., Suite 250, Seattle WA 98121. **Contact:** Steve Hansen, managing editor. **90% freelance written.** Bimonthly magazine for Midwest Express Airlines. "Positive depiction of the changing economy and culture of the US, plus travel and leisure features." Estab. 1993. Circ. 35,000. Pays on publication. Byline given. Buys first North American serial rights. Editorial lead time 9 months. Responds in 6 weeks to queries. Do not phone or fax. Sample copy for 9×12 SASE. Writer's guidelines free.
● *Midwest Express* continues to look for *sophisticated* travel and golf writing.
Nonfiction: Business, travel, sports and leisure. No humor or how-to. "Need good ideas for golf articles in spring." **Buys 20-25 mss/year.** Query by mail only with published clips and résumé. Length: 250-3,000 words. **Pays $100 minimum.** Sometimes pays expenses of writers on assignment.
Columns/Department: Preview (arts and events), 200-400 words; Portfolio (business), 200-500 words. **Buys 12-15 mss/year.** Query by mail only with published clips. **Pays $100-150.**
Tips: "Article ideas *must* encompass areas within the airline's route system. We buy quality writing from reliable writers. Editorial philosophy emphasizes innovation and positive outlook. Do not send manuscripts unless you have no clips."

$ $ $ $ SOUTHWEST AIRLINES SPIRIT, 4333 Amon Carter Blvd., Fort Worth TX 76155-9616. (817)967-1804. Fax: (817)967-1571. E-mail: 102615.376@compuserve.com. Website: www.spiritmag.com. **Contact:** John Clark, editorial director. Monthly magazine for passengers on Southwest Airlines. Estab. 1992. Circ. 300,000. **Pays on acceptance**. Byline given. Buys first North American serial and electronic rights. Responds in 1 month to queries.
Nonfiction: "Seeking accessible, entertaining, relevant and timely glimpses of people, places, products and trends in the regions Southwest Airlines serves. Newsworthy/noteworthy topics; well-researched and multiple source only.

Experienced magazine professionals only. Business, travel, technology, sports and lifestyle (food, fitness and culture) are some of the topics covered in *Spirit*." **Buys 48 features/year.** Query by mail only with published clips. Length: 2,000 words. **Pays $2,000.** Pays expenses of writers on assignment.

Columns/Departments: Buys 21 mss/year. Query by mail only with published clips. Length: 1,000-1,200 words. Pay varies.

Fillers: Buys 12/year. Length: 250 words. Pay varies.

Tips: *Southwest Airlines Spirit* magazine reaches nearly 1.6 million readers every month aboard Southwest Airlines. Our median reader is a college-educated, 44-year-old business person with a household income of nearly $115,000. Our stories tap the vitality of life through accessible, entertaining and oftentimes unconventional glimpses of people, places, products and trends in the regions that Southwest Airlines serves. Business, travel, technology, sports and lifestyle (food, fitness and culture) are some of the topics covered in *Spirit*."

[N] $ $ SPIRIT OF ALOHA, The Inflight Magazine of Aloha Airlines and Island Air, Honolulu Publishing Co. Ltd., 36 Merchant St., Honolulu HI 96701. (808)524-7400. Fax: (808)531-2306. E-mail: jotaguro@honpub.com. **Contact:** Janice Otaguro, editor. **50% freelance written.** Monthly magazine covering visitor activities/destinations and Hawaii culture and history. "Although we are an inflight magazine for an inter-island airline, we try to keep our editorial as fresh and lively for residents as much as for visitors." Estab. 1978. Circ. 60,000. **Pays on acceptance.** Publishes ms an average of 2 months after acceptance. Byline given. Buys first (one-time) rights. Editorial lead time 2 months. Submit seasonal material 2 months in advance. Responds in 2 months. Sample copy and writer's guidelines free.

Nonfiction: Book excerpts, general interest, historical/nostalgic, interview/profile, photo feature, travel. All must be related to Hawaii. No poetry or "How I spent my vacation in Hawaii" type pieces. **Buys 24 mss/year.** Query with published clips. Length: 1,500-2,500 words. **Pays $500.** Sometimes pay expenses of writers on assignment.

Photos: State availability of photos with submission. Reviews transparencies. Negotiates payment individually. Captions, model releases and identification of subjects required. Buys one-time rights.

$ $ $ $ TWA AMBASSADOR, 27 Melcher St., 2nd Floor, Boston MA 02210. (617)451-1700, ext. 955. Fax: (617)338-7767. **Contact:** Michael Buller, editor. Monthly magazine for foreign and domestic TWA passengers. Estab. 1968. Circ. 223,000. **Pays on acceptance.** Byline given. Offers 25% kill fee. Buys first rights. Accepts queries by mail, fax. Responds in 3 weeks to queries. Sample copy for 9×12 SASE plus $2.17 postage (no checks or postal coupons—US postage only). Writer's guidelines for #10 SASE, attn. Charlotte.

Nonfiction: "We need solid journalism stylishly rendered. We look for first-rate reporting by professionals with a track record. Stories cover a range of general interest topics with a strong emphasis on relevant business and travel stories. For travel stories, we need pieces that place the reader in the destination, which should be a city to which TWA flies." **Buys 25-30 mss/year.** Query with published clips. Length: 1,000-2,000 words. **Pays 75¢-$1/word.** Pays expenses of writers on assignment.

• Ranked as one of the best markets for freelance writers in *Writer's Yearbook* magazine's annual "Top 100 Markets," January 2000.

Columns/Departments: Buys 45-50 mss/year. "Most columns are written by regular columnists." Query with published clips. Length: 500-1,200 words. **Pays 75¢-$1/word.**

Fiction: "We accept fiction but buy very little."

Tips: "We have a small staff and a huge volume of mail—please query with SASE."

[N] $ $ ZOOM! MAGAZINE, Valley Media, LLC, 5383 South 900 East, Salt Lake City UT 84117. (801)267-5921. Fax: (801)267-5822. E-mail: mevans@murdocktravel.com. **Contact:** Mildred Evans, editor. **75% freelance written.** Bimonthly magazine covering general interest, places and events in cities on Vanguard Airlines' schedules. Estab. 1996. Circ. 15,000; issue readership 200,000. Pays on publication. Publishes ms an average of 6 months after acceptance. Byline given. Offers $50 kill fee. Buys one-time rights. Editorial lead time 3 months. Submit seasonal material 3 months in advance. Accepts queries by mail, e-mail. Responds in 1 month to queries; 3 months to mss. Sample copy for $2. Writer's guidelines free.

Nonfiction: General interest, historical/nostalgic, interview/profile, new product, travel. No articles on business, humor, Internet or health. **Buys 12 mss/year.** Query with or without published clips. Length: 1,000-2,500 words. **Pays $100-250.**

Reprints: Accepts previously published submissions.

Tips: "Submit previously published clips with a specific idea."

JUVENILE

Just as children change and grow, so do juvenile magazines. Children's magazine editors stress that writers must read recent issues. A wide variety of issues are addressed in the numerous magazines for the baby boom echo. Respecting nature, developing girls' self-esteem and establishing good healthy habits all find an editorial niche. This section lists publications for children up to age 12. Magazines for young people 13-19 appear in the Teen and Young Adult category.

Many of the following publications are produced by religious groups and, where possible, the specific denomination is given. A directory for juvenile markets, *Children's Writer's & Illustrator's Market*, is available from Writer's Digest Books.

$ BABYBUG, Carus Corporation, P.O. Box 300, Peru IL 61354. (815)224-6656. Editor-in-Chief: Marianne Carus. **Contact:** Paula Morrow, editor. **50% freelance written.** Board-book magazine published monthly except for combined May/June and July/August issues. "*Babybug* is 'the listening and looking magazine for infants and toddlers,' intended to be read aloud by a loving adult to foster a love of books and reading in young children ages 6 months-2 years." Estab. 1994. Circ. 45,000. Pays on publication. Publishes ms an average of 18 months after acceptance. Byline given. Buys first, second serial (reprint) or all rights. Editorial lead time 10 months. Submit seasonal material 1 year in advance. Accepts simultaneous submissions, if so noted. Sample copy for $5. Writer's guidelines for #10 SASE.
Nonfiction: General interest and "World Around You" for infants and toddlers. **Buys 5-10 mss/year.** Send complete ms. Length: 1-10 words. **Pays $25.**
Fiction: Adventure, humorous and anything for infants and toddlers. **Buys 5-10 mss/year.** Send complete ms. Length: 2-8 short sentences. **Pays $25.**
Poetry: Buys 8-10 poems/year. Submit maximum 5 poems. Length: 2-8 lines. **Pays $25.**
Tips: "Imagine having to read your story or poem—out loud—fifty times or more! That's what parents will have to do. Babies and toddlers demand, 'Read it again!' Your material must hold up under repetition."

N ★ $ $ $ BOYS' LIFE, Boy Scouts of America, P.O. Box 152079, Irving TX 75015-2079. Fax: (972)580-2079. Website: www.bsa.scouting.org. **Contact:** Michael Goldman, senior editor. **75% freelance written.** Prefers to work with published/established writers; works with small number of new/unpublished writers each year. Monthly magazine covering activities of interest to all boys ages 6-18. Most readers are Scouts or Cub Scouts. Estab. 1911. Circ. 1,300,000. **Pays on acceptance.** Publishes ms an average of 1 year after acceptance. Buys one-time rights. Accepts queries by mail, fax. Responds in 2 months. Sample copy for $3 and 9 × 12 SAE. Writer's guidelines for #10 SASE.
Nonfiction: Mike Goldman, senior editor. Subject matter is broad, everything from professional sports to American history to how to pack a canoe. Look at a current list of the BSA's more than 100 merit badge pamphlets for an idea of the wide range of subjects possible. Major articles run 500-1,500 words; preferred length is about 1,000 words including sidebars and boxes. **Pays $400-1,500.** Uses strong photo features with about 500 words of text. Separate payment or assignment for photos. **Buys 60 major articles/year.** Also needs how-to features and hobby and crafts ideas. Query in writing with SASE. No phone queries. Pays expenses of writers on assignment.
● Ranked as one of the best markets for freelance writers by *Writer's Yearbook* magazine's "Top 100 Markets," January 2000.
Columns: Contact: Rich Haddaway, associate editor. "Science, nature, earth, health, sports, space and aviation, cars, computers, entertainment, pets, history, music are some of the columns for which we use 300-750 words of text. This is a good place to show us what you can do." **Buys 75-80 columns/year.** Query first in writing. **Pays $250-300.**
Fiction: Contact: fiction editor. Humor, mystery, science fiction and adventure. Short stories 1,000-1,500 words; rarely longer. **Buys 12-15 short stories/year.** Send complete ms with SASE. **Pays $750 minimum.**
Fillers: Also buys freelance comics pages and scripts.
Tips: "We strongly recommend reading at least 12 issues of the magazine before you submit queries. We are a good market for any writer willing to do the necessary homework."

★ $ BOYS QUEST, Bluffton News Publishing, 103 N. Main, P.O. Box 227, Bluffton OH 45817. (419)358-4610. E-mail: hsbq@wcoil.com. Website: www.boysquest.com. Editor: Marilyn Edwards. **Contact:** Virginia Edwards, associate editor. **70% freelance written.** Bimonthly magazine covering boys ages 6-12, with a mission to inspire boys to read, maintain traditional family values, and emphasize wholesome, innocent childhood interests. Estab. 1995. Circ. 7,000. Pays on publication. Byline given. Buys first North American serial rights. Editorial lead time 1 year. Submit seasonal material 1 year in advance. Accepts simultaneous submissions. Responds in 1 month to queries; 2 months to mss. Sample copy for $4. Writer's guidelines for #10 SASE.
Nonfiction: General interest, historical/nostalgic, how-to (building), humor, interview/profile, personal experience. Send complete ms. Length: 300-700 words with photos. **Pays 5¢/word.**
Reprints: Send photocopy of article or short story or typed ms with rights for sale noted. **Pays 5¢/word.**
Photos: State availability of photos or send with submission. Offers $10/photo. Model releases required. Buys one-time rights.
Columns/Departments: Send complete ms. **Pays 5¢/word.**
Fiction: Adventure, historical, humorous. Send complete ms. Length: 300-700 words. **Pays 5¢/word.**
Poetry: Traditional. **Buys 25-30 poems/year.** Length: 10-30 lines. **Pays $10-15.**
Tips: "We are looking for lively writing, most of it from a young boy's point of view—with the boy or boys directly involved in an activity that is both wholesome and unusual. We need nonfiction with photos and fiction stories—around 500 words—puzzle, poems, cooking, carpentry projects, jokes and riddles. Nonfiction pieces that are accompanied by black and white photos are far more likely to be accepted than those that need illustrations."

$ $ CALLIOPE: The World History Magazine for Young People, Cobblestone Publishing Co., 30 Grove St., Suite C, Peterborough NH 03458-1454. (603)924-7209. Fax: (603)924-7380. E-mail: editorial@cobblestone.mv.com. Website: www.cobblestonepub.com. Editors: Rosalie and Charles Baker. **Contact:** Rosalie F. Baker. **50% freelance written.** Magazine published 9 times/year covering world history (East and West) through 1800 AD for 8- to 14-year-olds. Articles must relate to the issue's theme. Circ. 10,000. Pays on publication. Byline given. Buys all rights. Prefers not to accept simultaneous submissions. Sample copy for $4.50 and 7½×10½ SASE with 4 first-class stamps or on website. Writer's guidelines for SASE or on website.

Nonfiction: Essays, general interest, historical/nostalgic, how-to (activities), recipes, humor, interview/profile, personal experience, photo feature, technical, travel. Articles must relate to the theme. No religious, pornographic, biased or sophisticated submissions. **Buys 30-40 mss/year.** Query with published clips. Length: feature articles 700-800 words. Supplemental nonfiction 300-600 words. **Pays 20-25¢/printed word.**

Photos: State availability of photos with submission. Reviews contact sheets, color slides and b&w prints. Buys one-time rights. Pays $15-100 (color cover negotiated).

Fiction: All fiction must be theme-related. **Buys 10 mss/year.** Query with published clips. Length: up to 800 words. **Pays 20-25¢/printed word.**

Columns/Departments: Activities (crafts, recipes, projects); up to 700 words. Pays on an individual basis.

Fillers: Puzzles and Games (no word finds). Crossword and other word puzzles using the vocabulary of the issue's theme. Mazes and picture puzzles that relate to the theme. Pays on an individual basis.

Tips: "A query must consist of all of the following to be considered (please use non-erasable paper): a brief cover letter stating the subject and word length of the proposed article; a detailed one-page outline explaining the information to be presented in the article; an extensive bibliography of materials the author intends to use in preparing the article; a self-addressed stamped envelope. (Authors are urged to use primary resources and up-to-date scholarly resources in their bibliography.) Writers new to *Calliope* should send a writing sample with the query. If you would like to know if your query has been received, please also include a stamped postcard that requests acknowledgement of receipt. In all correspondence, please include your complete address as well as a telephone number where you can be reached."

$ $ CHICKADEE MAGAZINE, Discover a World of Fun, The Owl Group, Bayard Press Canada, 179 John St., Suite 500, Toronto, Ontario M5T 3G5 Canada. (416)340-2700. Fax: (416)340-9769. E-mail: owl@owlkids.com. Website: www.owlkids.com. **Contact:** Angela Keenlyside, managing editor. **25% freelance written.** Magazine published 9 times/year for 6- to 9-year-olds. "We aim to interest children in the world around them in an entertaining and lively way." Estab. 1979. Circ. 110,000 Canada and US. Pays on publication. Byline given. Buys all rights. Accepts queries by mail, e-mail, fax. Responds in 3 months. Sample copy for $4 and SAE ($2 money order or IRCs). Writer's guidelines for SAE ($2 money order or IRCs).

Nonfiction: How-to (easy and unusual arts and crafts), personal experience (real children in real situations). No articles for older children; no religious or moralistic features.

Photos: Send photos with ms. Reviews 35mm transparencies. Identification of subjects required.

Fiction: Adventure (relating to the 6-9-year-old), humor. No talking animal stories or religious articles. Send complete ms with $2 money order or IRCs for handling and return postage. **Pays $200** (US).

Tips: "A frequent mistake made by writers is trying to teach too much—not enough entertainment and fun."

⊘ CHILD LIFE does not accept freelance submissions.

CHILDREN'S DIGEST does not accept freelance submissions. "The publisher wishes to concentrate only on in-house material at this time."

★ $ $ CHILDREN'S PLAYMATE, Children's Better Health Institute, P.O. Box 567, Indianapolis IN 46206-0567. (317)636-8881, ext. 267. Fax: (317)684-8094. Website: www.childrensplaymatemag.org. **Contact:** (Ms.) Terry Harshman, editor. **70% freelance written.** Eager to work with new/unpublished writers. Magazine published 8 times/year for children ages 6-8. "We are looking for articles, stories, poems, and activities with a health, sports, fitness or nutritionally oriented theme. We also publish general interest fiction and nonfiction. We try to present our material in a positive light, and we try to incorporate humor and a light approach wherever possible without minimizing the seriousness of what we are saying." Estab. 1929. Buys all rights. Byline given. Pays on publication. Submit seasonal material 8 months in advance. Responds in 3 months; may hold mss for up to 1 year before acceptance/publication. Sample copy for $1.75. Writer's guidelines for #10 SASE.

Nonfiction: "A feature may be an interesting presentation on good health, exercise, proper nutrition and safety as well as science and historical breakthrough in medicine." **Buys 25 mss/year.** Include word count. Length: 500 words maximum. Submit complete ms; no queries. Material will not be returned unless accompanied by a SASE." **Pays up to 17¢/word.**

Fiction: Short stories for beginning readers, not over 500 words. Seasonal stories with holiday themes. Humorous stories, unusual plots. Also uses rebus stories of 100-300 words. Vocabulary suitable for ages 6-8. Submit complete ms. Include word count with stories. **Pays up to 17¢/word.**

Fillers: Recipes, crafts, puzzles, dot-to-dots, color-ins, hidden pictures, mazes. **Buys 30 fillers/year.** Payment varies. Prefers camera-ready activities. Activity guidelines for #10 SASE.

Tips: "We need more historical nonfiction on medicine, medical breakthroughs (vaccines, etc.) and simple science articles with occasional experiments. We're especially interested in features, stories, poems and articles about health, nutrition, science, medicine, fitness, and fun."

$ $CLUBHOUSE MAGAZINE, Focus on the Family, 8605 Explorer Dr., Colorado Springs CO 80920. Fax: (719)531-3499. Website: www.family.org. Editor: Jesse Florea. **Contact:** Annette Bourland, associate editor. **25% freelance written.** Monthly magazine geared for Christian kids ages 8-12. Estab. 1987. Circ. 123,000. **Pays on acceptance.** Byline given. Buys one-time rights. Editorial lead time 5 months. Submit seasonal material 7 months in advance. Sample copy for $1.50 with 9×12 SASE. Writer's guidelines for #10 SASE.

Nonfiction: Essays, general interest, historical/nostalgic, how-to, humor, inspirational, interview/profile, personal experience, photo feature, religious experience. **Buys 3 mss/year.** Send complete ms. Length: 800-1,200 words. **Pays $25-450 for assigned articles; 10-25¢/word for unsolicited articles.** Sometimes pays expenses of writers on assignment.

Photos: Send photos with submission. Reviews contact sheets, transparencies. Negotiates payment individually. Captions, model releases, identification of subjects required. Buys negotiable rights.

Columns/Departments: Lookout (news/kids in community), 50 words. **Buys 2 mss/year.** Send complete ms. **Pays $25-150.**

Fiction: Adventure, fantasy, holiday, humor, historical, religious (Christian), mystery, western, children's literature (Christian), novel excerpts. **Buys 10 mss/year.** Send complete ms. Length: 400-2,000 words. **Pays $200-450.**

Fillers: Buys 2 facts, newsbreaks/year. Length: 40-100 words. **Pays $25-150.**

$ $COUNSELOR, Scripture Press Publications, 4050 Lee Vance View, Colorado Springs CO 80918. (719)536-0100. Fax: (719)533-3045. E-mail: BurtonJ@Cookministries.org. **Contact:** Janice K. Burton, editor. **60% freelance written.** Quarterly Sunday School take-home paper with 13 weekly parts. "Our readers are 8-10 years old. All materials attempt to show God's working in the lives of children. Must have a true Christian slant, not just a moral implication." **Pays on acceptance.** Publishes ms an average of 2 years after acceptance. Byline given. Buys all or one-time rights with permission to reprint. Editorial lead time 1 year. Submit seasonal material 1 year in advance. Responds in 2 months to mss. Sample copy and writer's guidelines for #10 SASE.

O— Break in by sending age-appropriate, well-written material that follows guidelines as outlined in tips. We're looking for more stories relating to home-schoolers.

Nonfiction: Inspirational (stories), interview/profile, personal experience, religious. All stories must have a spiritual perspective. Show God at work in a child's life. **Buys 10-20 mss/year.** Send complete ms with SASE. Length: 800-850 words. **Pays 10¢/word.**

Reprints: Send typed ms with rights for sale noted and information about when and where the article previously appeared.

Columns/Departments: God's Wonders (seeing God through creation and the wonders of science), Kids in Action (kids doing unusual activities to benefit others), Around the World (missions stories from child's perspective), all 300-350 words. Send complete ms. **Pays 10¢/word.**

Fiction: Adventure, ethnic, religious. **Buys 10-15 mss/year.** Send complete ms. Length: 800-850 words. **Pays 10¢/word.**

Fillers: Buys 8-12 puzzles, games, fun activities/year. Length: 150 words maximum. **Pays 10¢/word.**

Tips: "Show a real feel for the age level. Know your readers and what is age appropriate in terms of concepts and vocabulary. Submit only best quality manuscripts. We're looking for lively, interesting, true stories that show children how biblical principles can be applied to their everyday lives; stories that are Christ centered, not merely moral and true-to-life fiction with lots of action and dialogue that shows the Holy Spirit at work in the lives of children. Stories that reveal inner attitudes, spiritual conflicts, good decision-making, effects of prayer, issues of Christian character, salvation. If submitting nonfiction, you must include permission from story's subject."

$ $CRICKET, Carus Publishing Co., P.O. Box 300, Peru IL 61354-0300. (815)224-6656. **Contact:** Marianne Carus, editor-in-chief. Monthly general interest literary magazine for children ages 9-14. Estab. 1973. Circ. 73,000. Pays on publication. Byline given. Buys first publication rights in the English language. Submit seasonal material 1 year in advance. Responds in 3 months. Sample copy and writer's guidelines for $5 and 9×12 SAE. Writer's guidelines only for #10 SASE.

● *Cricket* is looking for more fiction and nonfiction for the older end of its 9-14 age range. It also seeks humorous stories and mysteries (*not* detective spoofs) fantasy and original fairy tales, stand-alone excerpts from unpublished novels and well-written/researched science articles.

Nonfiction: Adventure, biography, foreign culture, geography, history, natural science, science, social science, sports, technology, travel. (A short bibliography is required for *all* nonfiction articles.) Send complete ms. Length: 200-1,500 words. **Pays up to 25¢/word.**

Reprints: Send typed ms with rights for sale noted and information about when and where the article previously appeared. Pays 50% of amount paid for an original article.

Fiction: Adventure, ethnic, fairy tales, fantasy, historical, humorous, mystery, novel excerpts, science fiction, suspense, western. No didactic, sex, religious or horror stories. **Buys 75-100 mss/year.** Send complete ms. Length: 200-2,000 words. **Pays up to 25¢/word.**

● Ranked as one of the best markets for fiction writers in *Writer's Digest* magazine's "Fiction 50," June 2000.

Poetry: Buys 20-30 poems/year. Length: 25 lines maximum. **Pays up to $3/line.**

$ CRUSADER MAGAZINE, P.O. Box 7259, Grand Rapids MI 49510-7259. (616)241-5616. Fax: (616)241-5558. Website: www.gospelcom.net/cadets/. **Contact:** G. Richard Broene, editor. **40% freelance written.** Works with a small number of new/unpublished writers each year. Magazine published 7 times/year. "*Crusader Magazine* shows boys 9-14 how God is at work in their lives and in the world around them." Estab. 1958. Circ. 13,000. **Pays on acceptance.** Byline given. Publishes ms an average of 8 months after acceptance. Rights purchased vary with author and material; buys first serial, one-time, second serial (reprint) and simultaneous rights. Accepts simultaneous submissions. Responds in 2 months. Sample copy and writer's guidelines for 9×12 SAE with $1.01 in postage.

Nonfiction: Articles about young boys' interests: sports, outdoor activities, bike riding, science, crafts, etc., and problems. Emphasis is on a Christian multi-racial perspective, but no simplistic moralisms. Informational, how-to, personal experience, interview, profile, inspirational, humor. Upcoming themes: The Rock, My Rock (September/October 2000); Choices and Consequences (November 2000); What Would Jesus Do? (December 2000); Sportsmanship (January 2001); Anger (February 2001); Generosity (March 2001); and Free Time (April/May 2001). **Buys 20-25 mss/year.** Submit complete ms. Length: 500-1,500 words. **Pays 2-5¢/word.**

Reprints: Send typed ms with rights for sale noted. Pay varies.

Photos: Pays $4-25 for photos purchased with mss.

Columns/Departments: Project Page—uses simple projects boys 9-14 can do on their own.

Fiction: "Considerable fiction is used. Fast-moving stories that appeal to a boy's sense of adventure or sense of humor are welcome. Avoid preachiness. Avoid simplistic answers to complicated problems. Avoid long dialogue and little action." Length: 900-1,500 words. **Pays 2¢/word minimum.**

Fillers: Uses short humor and any type of puzzles as fillers.

Tips: "Best time to submit stories/articles is early in calendar year—in March or April. Also remember readers are boys ages 9-14. Stories must reflect or add to the theme of the issue."

$ DISCOVERIES, Word Action Publishing Co., 6401 The Paseo, Kansas City MO 64131. Fax: (816)333-4439. Editor: Virginia Folsom. **Contact:** Emily J. Freeburg, editorial assistant. **75% freelance written.** Weekly Sunday school take-home paper. "Our audience is third and fourth graders. We require that the stories relate to the Sunday school lesson for that week." Circ. 5,000. Pays on publication. Publishes ms an average of 1 year after acceptance. Byline given. Buys multi-use rights. Accepts simultaneous submissions. Responds in 6 weeks to queries; 2 months to mss. Sample copy and writer's guidelines for #10 SASE.

Reprints: Send typed ms with rights for sale noted and information about when and where the article previously appeared.

Fiction: Religious. Must relate to our theme list. **Buys 45 mss/year.** Send complete ms. Length: 400-500 words. **Pays 5¢/word.**

Fillers: Gags to be illustrated by cartoonist, puzzles, Bible trivia (need bibliography documentation). **Buys 100/year.** Length: 50-200 words. **Pays $15.**

Tips: "Follow our theme list, read the Bible verses that relate to the theme. September 2002 begins our new curriculum."

$ DISCOVERY TRAILS, Gospel Publishing House, 1445 Boonville Ave., Springfield MO 65802-1894. (417)862-2781. Fax: (417)862-6059. E-mail: discoverytrails@gph.org. **Contact:** Sinda S. Zinn, editor. **98% freelance written.** Weekly 4-page Sunday school take-home paper. *Discovery Trails* is written for boys and girls 10-12 (slanted toward older group). Fiction, adventure and mystery stories showing children applying Christian principles in everyday living are used in the paper. **Pays on acceptance.** Publishes ms an average of 18 months after acceptance. Byline given. Buys one-time, second serial (reprint) and simultaneous rights. Editorial lead time 18 months. Submit seasonal material 18 months in advance. Accepts simultaneous submissions. Responds in 4 weeks. Sample copy and writer's guidelines for #10 SASE.

Nonfiction: Wants articles with reader appeal, emphasizing some phase of Christian living or historical, scientific or natural material with a spiritual lesson. Submissions should include a bibliography of facts. **Buys 15-20 mss/quarter.** Send complete ms. Length: 500 words maximum. **Pays 7-10¢/word.**

Reprints: Send typed ms with rights for sale noted and information about when and where the article previously appeared. Pays 7¢/word for second rights.

Fiction: Adventure, historical, humorous, mystery. No Bible fiction, "Halloween" or "Santa Claus" stories. Wants fiction that presents realistic characters working out their problems according to Bible principles, presenting Christianity in action without being preachy. Serial stories acceptable. **Buys 80-90 mss/year.** Send complete ms. Length: 1,000 words (except for serial stories). **Pays 7-10¢/word.**

Poetry: Light verse, traditional. **Buys 10 poems/year.** Submit maximum 2-3 poems. **Pays $5-15.**

Fillers: Bits & Bytes of quirky facts, puzzles, interactive activities, quizzes, word games, and fun activities that address social skills on a focused topic with accurate research, vivid writing, and spiritual emphasis. Crafts, how-to articles, recipes should be age appropriate, safe and cheap, express newness/originality and accuracy, a clear focus, and an opening that makes kids want to read and do it. Length: 300 words maximum.

Tips: "Follow the guidelines, remember the story should be interesting—carried by dialogue and action rather than narration—and appropriate for a Sunday school take-home paper. Don't send groups of stories in one submission."

$ $ THE FRIEND, 50 E. North Temple, Salt Lake City UT 84150-3226. Fax: (801)240-5732. **Contact:** Vivian Paulsen, managing editor. **50% freelance written.** Eager to work with new/unpublished writers as well as established writers. Monthly publication of The Church of Jesus Christ of Latter-Day Saints for children ages 3-11. Circ. 350,000. **Pays on acceptance.** Buys all rights. Submit seasonal material 8 months in advance. Responds in 2 months. Sample copy and writer's guidelines for $1.50 and 9×12 SAE with 4 first-class stamps.

Nonfiction: Subjects of current interest, science, nature, pets, sports, foreign countries, things to make and do. "*The Friend* is particularly interested in stories based on true experiences." Special issues: Christmas, Easter. "Submit only complete manuscript with SASE—no queries, please." Length: 1,000 words maximum. **Pays 10¢/word minimum.**

Fiction: Seasonal and holiday stories, stories about other countries and their children. Wholesome and optimistic; high motive, plot and action. Character-building stories preferred. Length: 1,200 words maximum. Stories for younger children should not exceed 250 words. Submit complete ms. **Pays 10¢/word minimum.**

Poetry: Serious, humorous, holiday. Any form with child appeal. **Pays $25 minimum.**

Tips: "Do you remember how it feels to be a child? Can you write stories that appeal to children ages 3-11 in today's world? We're interested in stories with an international flavor and those that focus on present-day problems. Send material of high literary quality slanted to our editorial requirements. Let the child solve the problem—not some helpful, all-wise adult. No overt moralizing. Nonfiction should be creatively presented—not an array of facts strung together. Beware of being cutesy."

$ $ $ GIRL'S LIFE, Monarch Publishing, 4517 Harford Rd., Baltimore MD 21214. Fax: (410)254-0991. Website: www.girlslife.com. Editor: Karen Bokram. **Contact:** Kelly A. White, senior editor. Bimonthly magazine covering girls ages 8-15. Estab. 1994. Circ. 980,000. Pays on publication. Publishes ms an average of 3 months after acceptance. Byline given. Buys first exclusive North American serial rights. Editorial lead time 5 months. Submit seasonal material 6 months in advance. Responds in 3 months. Sample copy for $5 or on website. Writer's guidelines for #10 SASE.

Nonfiction: Beauty, book excerpts, essays, general interest, how-to, humor, inspirational, interview/profile, new product, relationship, sports, travel. Special issues: Back to School (August/September); Fall, Halloween (October/November); Holidays, Winter (December/January); Valentine's Day, Crushes (February/March); Spring, Mother's Day (April/May); and Summer, Father's Day (June/July). **Buys 20 mss/year.** Query by mail with published clips. Submit complete mss on spec only. Length: 700-2,000 words. **Pays $150-800.**

Photos: State availability of photos with submission. Reviews contact sheets, negatives, transparencies. Negotiates payment individually. Captions, model releases, identification of subjects required.

Columns/Departments: Sports; Try It! (new stuff to try); both 1,200 words. **Buys 20 mss/year.** Query with published clips. **Pays $150-450.**

■ The online magazine carries original content not found in the print edition. Contact: Miki Hicks, online editor.

Tips: Send queries with published writing samples and detailed résumé. "Have new ideas, a voice that speaks to our audience—not *down* to our audience, and supply artwork (i.e. color slides)."

$ $ GUIDEPOSTS FOR KIDS, P.O. Box 638, Chesterton IN 46304. Fax: (219)926-3839. Website: www.gp4k.com. Editor-in-Chief: Mary Lou Carney. **Contact:** Rosanne Tolin, managing editor. **30% freelance written.** Bimonthly magazine for kids. "*Guideposts for Kids* is a value-centered, fun-to-read kids magazine for 7-12-year-olds (with an emphasis on the upper end of this age bracket). Issue-oriented, thought-provoking. No preachy stories." *Guideposts For Kids* is very interested in seasonal stories, especially Thanksgiving and Christmas. Estab. 1990. Circ. 200,000. **Pays on acceptance.** Byline given. Offers 25% kill fee. Buys all rights. Editorial lead time 6 months. Submit seasonal material 6 months in advance. Accepts queries by mail, fax. Responds in 6 weeks. Sample copy for $3.25. Writer's guidelines for #10 SASE.

⊙┓ Break in with short nonfiction on topics of general interest, under 500 words, and "The Buzz," profiles of interesting kids 7-12 as lead-ins to topical subjects, like BMX biking, 250 words plus sidebars.

Nonfiction: Issue-oriented, thought-provoking features, general interest, humor, interview/profile, photo essays, technical (technology). No articles with adult voice/frame of reference or Sunday-School-type articles. **Buys 20 mss/year.** Query with SASE. Length: 150-1,500 words. **Pays $125-400.** Sometimes pays expenses of writers on assignment.

Photos: State availability of or send photos with submission. Negotiates payment individually. Identification of subjects required. Buys one-time rights.

Columns/Departments: Tips from the Top (Christian athletes and celebrities), 650 words; "The Buzz." **Buys 15 mss/year.** Query or send complete ms with SASE. **Pays $100-350.**

Fiction: Adventure, fantasy, historical, humorous, mystery, suspense. **Buys 8 mss/year.** Send complete ms and SASE. Length: 500-1,300 words. **Pays $175-350.**

Fillers: Facts, short humor, puzzles, mazes, jokes. **Buys 8-10/year.** Length: 300 words maximum. **Pays $25-175.** Finders fee ($20-25) for news clippings used.

Tips: "Before you submit to one of our departments, study the magazine. In most of our pieces, we look for a strong kid voice/viewpoint. We do not want preachy or overtly religious material. Looking for value-driven stories and profiles. In the fiction arena, we are very interested in historical and mysteries. In nonfiction, we welcome tough themes and current issues. This is not a beginner's market."

N ✖ $ GUIDE®, Stories Pointing to Jesus, Review and Herald Publishing Association, 55 W. Oak Ridge Dr., Hagerstown MD 21740. (301)393-4037. Fax: (301)393-4055. E-mail: guide@rhpa.org. Website: www.guidemagazine.org. **Contact:** Randy Fishell, editor or Helen Lee, assistant editor. **90% freelance written.** Weekly magazine featuring all-true stories showing God's involvement in 10-14-year-olds' lives. Estab. 1953. Circ. 33,000. **Pays on acceptance.**

Publishes ms an average of 6 months after acceptance. Byline given. Buys first North American serial rights. Editorial lead time 8 months. Submit seasonal material 8 months in advance. Accepts queries by mail, e-mail, fax. Responds in 1 month. Sample copy for SAE with 2 first-class stamps. Writer's guidelines for #10 SASE or on website.

O— Break in with "a true story that shows in a clear way that God is involved in a 10- 14-year-old's life."

Nonfiction: Religious. "No fiction. Non-fiction should set forth a clearly-evident spiritual application." **Buys 300 mss/year.** Send complete ms. Length: 750-1,500 words. **Pays $25-125.**

Reprints: Send photocopy of article. **Pays 50% of usual rates.**

Fillers: Games, puzzles, religious. **Buys 75/year. Pays $25-40.**

Tips: "The majority of 'misses' are due to the lack of a clearly-evident (not 'preachy') spiritual application."

HIGHLIGHTS FOR CHILDREN, 803 Church St., Honesdale PA 18431-1824. (570)253-1080. Managing Editor: Christine French Clark. **Contact:** Beth Troop, manuscript coordinator. **80% freelance written.** Monthly magazine for children ages 2-12. Estab. 1946. Circ. 3,000,000. **Pays on acceptance.** Buys all rights. Accepts queries by mail. Responds in about 2 months. Sample copy free. Writer's guidelines for #10 SASE.

Nonfiction: "We need articles on science, technology and nature written by persons with strong backgrounds in those fields. Contributions always welcomed from new writers, especially engineers, scientists, historians, teachers, etc., who can make useful, interesting facts accessible to children. Also writers who have lived abroad and can interpret the ways of life, especially of children, in other countries in ways that will foster world brotherhood. Sports material, biographies and articles of general interest to children. Direct, original approach, simple style, interesting content, not rewritten from encyclopedias. State background and qualifications for writing factual articles submitted. Include references or sources of information." Query by mail only. Length: 900 words maximum. **Pays $100 minimum.** Articles geared toward our younger readers (3-7) especially welcome, up to 400 words. Also buys original party plans for children ages 4-12, clearly described in 300-600 words, including drawings or samples of items to be illustrated. Also, novel but tested ideas in crafts, with clear directions and made-up models. Projects must require only free or inexpensive, easy-to-obtain materials. Especially desirable if easy enough for early primary grades. Also, fingerplays with lots of action, easy for very young children to grasp and to dramatize. Avoid wordiness. We need creative-thinking puzzles that can be illustrated, optical illusions, brain teasers, games of physical agility and other 'fun' activities." **Pays minimum $50 for party plans; $25 for crafts ideas; $25 for fingerplays.**

● Ranked as one of the best markets for freelance writers in *Writer's Yearbook* magazine's annual "Top 100 Markets," January 2000.

Photos: Color 35mm slides, photos or art reference materials are helpful and sometimes crucial in evaluating mss.

Fiction: Unusual, meaningful stories appealing to both girls and boys, ages 2-12. "Vivid, full of action. Engaging plot, strong characterization, lively language." Prefers stories in which a child protagonist solves a dilemma through his or her own resources. Seeks stories that the child ages 8-12 will eagerly read, and the child ages 2-7 will begin to read and/or will like to hear when read aloud (400-900 words). "We publish stories in the suspense/adventure/mystery, fantasy and humor category, all requiring interesting plot and a number of illustration possibilities. Also need rebuses (picture stories 125 words or under), stories with urban settings, stories for beginning readers (100-400 words), sports and horse stories and retold folk tales. We also would like to see more material of 1-page length (300-500 words), both fiction and factual. War, crime and violence are taboo." **Pays $100 minimum.**

● Ranked as one of the best markets for fiction writers in *Writer's Digest* magazine's "Fiction 50," June 2000.

Tips: "We are pleased that many authors of children's literature report that their first published work was in the pages of *Highlights*. It is not our policy to consider fiction on the strength of the reputation of the author. We judge each submission on its own merits. With factual material, however, we do prefer that writers be authorities in their field or people with first-hand experience. In this manner we can avoid the encyclopedic article that merely restates information readily available elsewhere. We don't make assignments. Query with simple letter to establish whether the nonfiction subject is likely to be of interest. A beginning writer should first become familiar with the type of material that *Highlights* publishes. Include special qualifications, if any, of author. Write for the child, not the editor. Write in a voice that children understand and relate to. Speak to today's kids, avoiding didactic, overt messages. Even though our general principles haven't changed over the years, we are contemporary in our approach to issues. Avoid worn themes."

HOPSCOTCH, The Magazine for Girls, Bluffton News Publishing & Printing Co., P.O. Box 164, Bluffton OH 45817-0164. (419)358-4610. E-mail: hsbq@wcoil.com. Website: www.hopscotchmagazine.com. Editor: Marilyn B. Edwards. **Contact:** Virginia Edwards, associate editor. **90% freelance written.** Bimonthly magazine on basic subjects of interest to young girls. "*Hopscotch* is a digest-size magazine with a four-color cover and two-color format inside. It is designed for girls ages 6-12, with youngsters 8, 9 and 10 the specific target age; it features pets, crafts, hobbies, games, science, fiction, history, puzzles, careers, etc." Estab. 1989. Pays on publication. Byline given. Buys first or second rights. Submit seasonal material 8 months in advance. Accepts simultaneous submissions. Responds in 3 weeks to queries; 2 months to mss. Sample copy for $4. Writer's guidelines, current theme list and needs for #10 SASE.

● *Hopscotch* has a sibling magazine, *Boys' Quest*, for ages 6-13, with the same old-fashioned values as *Hopscotch*.

Nonfiction: General interest, historical/nostalgic, how-to (crafts), humor, inspirational, interview/profile, personal experience, pets, games, fiction, careers, sports, cooking. "No fashion, hairstyles, sex or dating articles." **Buys 60 mss/year.** Send complete ms. Length: 400-1,000 words. **Pays 5¢/word.**

Reprints: Send tearsheet or photocopy of article or typed ms with rights for sale noted. **Pays 5¢/word.**

Photos: Send photos with submission. Prefers b&w photos, but color photos accepted. Offers $5-10/photo. Captions, model releases and identification of subjects required. Buys one-time rights.

Columns/Departments: Science—nature, crafts, pets, cooking (basic), 400-700 words. Send complete ms. **Pays $10-35/column.**

Fiction: Adventure, historical, humorous, mainstream, mystery, suspense. **Buys 15 mss/year.** Send complete ms. Length: 600-900 words. **Pays 5¢/word.**

Poetry: Free and light verse, traditional. "No experimental or obscure poetry." Send 6 poems max. **Pays $10-30.**

Tips: "Almost all sections are open to freelancers. Freelancers should remember that *Hopscotch* is a bit old-fashioned, appealing to *young* girls (6-12). We cherish nonfiction pieces that have a young girl or young girls directly involved in unusual and/or worthwhile activities. Any piece accompanied by decent photos stands an even better chance of being accepted. *Hopscotch* uses more nonfiction than fiction."

$ $HUMPTY DUMPTY'S MAGAZINE, Children's Better Health Institute, P.O. Box 567, Indianapolis IN 46206-0567. (317)636-8881. **Contact:** Nancy S. Axelrad, editor. **75% freelance written.** Magazine published 8 times/year covering health, nutrition, hygiene, fitness and safety for children ages 4-6. "Our publication is designed to entertain and to educate young readers in healthy lifestyle habits. Fiction, poetry, pencil activities should have an element of good nutrition or fitness." Estab. 1948. Circ. 350,000. Pays on publication. Publishes ms 8 months after acceptance. Byline given. Buys all rights. Editorial lead time 8 months. Submit seasonal material 10 months in advance. Accepts simultaneous submissions. Responds in 3 months. Sample copy for $1.75. Writer's guidelines for #10 SASE.

Nonfiction: "Material must have a health theme—nutrition, safety, exercise, hygiene. We're looking for articles that encourage readers to develop better health habits without preaching. Very simple factual articles that creatively teach readers about their bodies. We use several puzzles and activities in each issue—dot-to-dot, hidden pictures and other activities that promote following instructions, developing finger dexterity and working with numbers and letters." **Buys 3-4 mss/year.** Submit complete ms with word count. Length: 500 words maximum. **Pays 22¢/word.**

Photos: Send photos with submission. Offers no additional payment for photos accepted with ms. Buys all rights.

Columns/Departments: Mix & Fix (no-cook recipes), 100 words. **Buys 8 mss/year.** Send complete ms. Pay varies.

Fiction: "We use some stories in rhyme and a few easy-to-read stories for the beginning reader. All stories should work well as read-alouds. Currently we need health/sports/fitness stories. We try to present our health material in a positive light, incorporating humor and a light approach wherever possible. Avoid stereotyping. Characters in contemporary stories should be realistic and reflect good, wholesome values." **Buys 4-6 mss/year.** Submit complete ms with word count. Length: 350 words maximum. **Pays 22¢/word.**

Poetry: Free verse, light verse, traditional. Short, simple poems. **Buys 6-8 poems/year.** Submit 2-3 poems at one time. **Pays $20 minimum.**

Tips: "Get to know the magazine before submitting work—remember, we are only buying material with a health or fitness slant. Be creative about it."

$ $JACK AND JILL, Children's Better Health Institute, P.O. Box 567, Indianapolis IN 46206-0567. (317)636-8881. Fax: (317)684-8094. **Contact:** Daniel Lee, editor. **50% freelance written.** Magazine published 8 times/year for children ages 7-10. Estab. 1938. Circ. 200,000. Pays on publication. Publishes ms an average of 8 months after acceptance. Buys all rights. Byline given. Submit seasonal material 8 months in advance. No queries. Responds in 10 weeks. May hold material being seriously considered for up to 1 year. "Material will not be returned unless accompanied by SASE with sufficient postage." Sample copy for $1.25. Writer's guidelines for #10 SASE.

⊶ Break in with nonfiction about ordinary kids with a news hook—something that ties in with current events, matters the kids are seeing on television and in mainstream news—i.e., space exploration, scientific advances, sports, etc.

Nonfiction: "Because we want to encourage youngsters to read for pleasure and for information, we are interested in material that will challenge a young child's intelligence *and* be enjoyable reading. Our emphasis is on good health, and we are in particular need of articles, stories, and activities with health, safety, exercise and nutrition themes. We try to present our health material in a positive light—incorporating humor and a light approach wherever possible without minimizing the seriousness of what we are saying." Straight factual articles are OK if they are short and interestingly written. "We would rather see, however, more creative alternatives to the straight factual article. Items with a news hook will get extra attention. We'd like to see articles about interesting kids involved in out-of-the-ordinary activities. We're also interested in articles about people with unusual hobbies for our Hobby Shop department." **Buys 10-15 nonfiction mss/year.** Length: 500-800 words. **Pays 17¢/word minimum.**

Photos: When appropriate, photos should accompany ms. Reviews sharp, contrasting b&w glossy prints. Sometimes uses color slides, transparencies or good color prints. Pays $15 for photos. Buys one-time rights.

Fiction: May include, but is not limited to, realistic stories, fantasy adventure—set in past, present or future. "All stories need a well-developed plot, action and incident. Humor is highly desirable. Stories that deal with a health theme need not have health as the primary subject." **Buys 20-25 mss/year.** Length: 500-800 words (short stories). **Pays 15¢/word minimum.**

Fillers: Puzzles (including various kinds of word and crossword puzzles), poems, games, science projects, and creative craft projects. We get a lot of these. To be selected, an item needs a little extra spark and originality. Instructions for activities should be clearly and simply written and accompanied by models or diagram sketches. "We also have a need for recipes. Ingredients should be healthful; avoid sugar, salt, chocolate, red meat and fats as much as possible. In all material, avoid references to eating sugary foods, such as candy, cakes, cookies and soft drinks."

Tips: "We are constantly looking for new writers who can tell good stories with interesting slants—stories that are not full of out-dated and time-worn expressions. We like to see stories about kids who are smart and capable, but not sarcastic or smug. Problem-solving skills, personal responsibility and integrity are good topics for us. Obtain *current* issues of the magazine and *study* them to determine our present needs and editorial style."

$ $ LADYBUG, the Magazine for Young Children, Carus Publishing Co., P.O. Box 300, Peru IL 61354-0300. (815)224-6656. Editor-in-Chief: Marianne Carus. **Contact:** Paula Morrow, editor. Monthly general interest magazine for children ages 2-6. "We look for quality writing—quality literature, no matter the subject." Estab. 1990. Circ. 134,000. Pays on publication. Byline given. Buys first publication rights in the English language. Submit seasonal material 1 year in advance. Responds in 3 months. Sample copy and guidelines for $4 and 9 × 12 SAE. Guidelines only for #10 SASE.

● *Ladybug* needs even more activities based on concepts (size, color, sequence, comparison, etc.) and interesting, appropriate nonfiction. Also needs articles and parent-child activities for its parents' section. See sample issues.

Nonfiction: Can You Do This?, 1-2 pages; The World Around You, 2-4 pages; activities based on concepts (size, color, sequence, comparison, etc.), 1-2 pages. **Buys 35 mss/year.** Send complete ms; no queries. "Most *Ladybug* nonfiction is in the form of illustration. We'd like more simple science, how-things-work and behind-the-scenes on a preschool level." Length: 250-300 words maximum. **Pays up to 25¢/word.**

Fiction: Adventure, ethnic, fantasy, folklore, humorous, mainstream, mystery. **Buys 30 mss/year.** Send complete ms. Length: 850 words maximum. **Pays up to 25¢/word.**

● Ranked as one of the best markets for fiction writers in *Writer's Digest* magazine's "Fiction 50," June 2000.

Poetry: Light verse, traditional, humorous. **Buys 20 poems/year.** Submit *maximum* 5 poems. Length: 20 lines maximum. **Pays up to $3/line.**

Fillers: Anecdotes, facts, short humor. **Buys 10/year.** Length: 250 words maximum. **Pays up to 25¢/word.** "We welcome interactive activities: rebuses, up to 100 words; *original* fingerplays and action rhymes (up to 8 lines)."

Tips: "Reread manuscript *before* sending in. Keep within specified word limits. Study back issues before submitting to learn about the types of material we're looking for. Writing style is paramount. We look for rich, evocative language and a sense of joy or wonder. Remember that you're writing for preschoolers—be age-appropriate but not condescending. A story must hold enjoyment for both parent and child through repeated read-aloud sessions. Remember that people come in all colors, sizes, physical conditions and have special needs. Be inclusive!"

$ $ $ MUSE, The Cricket Magazine Group, Carus Publishing, 332 S. Michigan, Suite 1100, Chicago IL 60604. (312)939-1500. Fax: (312)939-8150. E-mail: muse@caruspub.com. Website: www.musemag.com. Editor: Diana Lutz. Managing Editor: Agnieszka Biskup. **Contact:** Tina Coleman, administrative assistant. **100% freelance written.** Nonfiction magazine for children ages 8-14 published 10 times/year. Estab. 1996. Pays 60 days after acceptance or upon acceptance. Offers 50% kill fee. Buys first English rights or all rights. Responds in 3 months. Sample copy for $5 or on website. Guidelines for #10 SASE.

Nonfiction: Children's: art, historical, photo feature, science, technical. "The goal of *MUSE* is to give as many children as possible access to the most important ideas and concepts underlying the principle areas of human knowledge. It will take children seriously as developing intellects by assuming that, if explained clearly, the ideas and concepts of an article will be of interest to them. Articles should meet the highest possible standard of clarity and transparency aided, wherever possible, by a tone of skepticism and humor." Please send SASE for writer's guidelines first. Query with published clips, résumé and possible topics. Length: 1,000-2,500 words. **Pays 50¢/word for assigned articles; 25¢/word for unsolicited articles** plus 3 free copies of issue in which article appears; negotiates higher rates for experienced writers.

● Ranked as one of the best markets for freelance writers in *Writer's Yearbook* magazine's annual "Top 100 Markets," January 2000.

Tips: "Each article must be about a topic that children can understand. The topic must be a large one that somehow connects with a fundamental tenet of some discipline or area of practical knowledge. The treatment of the topic must be of the competence one would expect of an expert in the field. On the other hand, *MUSE* does not want articles that could be mistaken for chapters in a textbook. Instead we prefer the author visit the scientist or research site and report on what he or she sees or hears there. An article must be interesting to children, who are under no obligation to read it."

$ MY FRIEND, The Catholic Magazine for Kids, Pauline Books & Media/Daughters of St. Paul, 50 St. Paul's Ave., Jamaica Plain, Boston MA 02130-3495. (617)522-8911. Fax: (617)541-9805. E-mail: myfriend@pauline.org. Website: www.pauline.org. (click on Kidstuff). Editor-in-Chief: Donna Williams, fsp. **Contact:** Sister Kathryn James Hermes, fsp, managing editor. **40% freelance written.** Magazine published 10 times/year for children ages 6-12. "*My Friend* is a 32-page monthly Catholic magazine for boys and girls. Its goal is to celebrate the Catholic Faith—as it is lived by today's children and as it has been lived for centuries." Circ. 12,000. Pays on editorial completion of the issue (five months ahead of publication date). Buys serial rights. Accepts queries by mail, e-mail, fax. Responds in 2 months. Sample copy for $2.95. Writer's guidelines for #10 SASE. No theme lists.

○─ Break in with "well-written fiction that grabs imagination and gently teaches a lesson."

Nonfiction: How-to, religious, technical, media-related articles, real-life features. "This year we are emphasizing cultural and ecumenical themes. We prefer authors who have a rich background and mastery in these areas. We are looking for fresh perspectives into a child's world that are imaginative, unique, challenging, informative, current and fun. We prefer articles that are visual, not necessarily text-based—articles written in 'windows' style with multiple points of entry." Send complete ms. Length: 150-800 words. **Pays $35-100.** Pays in contributor copies by prior agreement with an author "who wishes to write as a form of sharing our ministry."

Photos: Send photos with submission.

Fiction: "We are looking for stories that immediately grab the imagination of the reader. Good dialogue, realistic character development, current lingo are necessary. A child protagonist must resolve a dilemma through his or her own resources. We prefer seeing a sample or submission of a story. Often we may not be able to use a particular story but the author will be asked to write another for a specific issue based on his or her experience, writing ability, etc. At this time we are especially analyzing submissions for the following: intercultural relations, periodic appearance of a child living with a disability or a sibling of a child or adult with a disability, realistic and current issues kids face today and computer literacy."

Fillers: Puzzles and jokes. "We need new creative ideas, small-size puzzles, picture puzzles, clean jokes." **Jokes pay $7. Puzzles pay $10-15.**

Tips: "We have a strong commitment to working with our authors to produce material that is factual, contemporary and inspiring. We prefer those authors who write well and are able to work as a team with us. We need stories that are relevant, have substance, include detail, and are original. Try science fiction for moral issues, etc."

$ NATURE FRIEND, Carlisle Press, 2727 TR 421, Sugarcreek OH 44681. (330)852-1900. Fax: (330)852-3285. Managing Editor: Elaine Troyer. **Contact:** Marvin Wengerd, owner/editor. **80% freelance written.** Monthly Christian nature magazine. "*Nature Friend* includes stories, puzzles, science experiments, nature experiments—all submissions need to honor God as creator." Estab. 1983. Circ. 9,000. Pays on publication. Publishes ms an average of 10 months after acceptance. Byline given. Buys first or one-time rights. Editorial lead time 4 months. Submit seasonal material 2 months in advance. Accepts queries by mail, fax. Accepts simultaneous submissions. Responds in 4 weeks to queries; 4 months to mss. Sample copy for $2.50 postage paid. Writer's guidelines for $4 postage paid.

　　○➔ Break in with a "conversational story about a nature subject that imparts knowledge and instills Christian values."

Nonfiction: How-to (nature, science experiments), photo feature, religious, articles about interesting/unusual animals. No poetry, evolution, animals depicted in captivity. **Buys 50 mss/year.** Send complete ms. Length: 250-1,200 words. **Pays 5¢/word.**

Photos: Send photos with submission. Reviews any transparencies and prints. Offers $35-50/photo. Captions and identification of subjects required. Buys one-time rights.

Columns/Departments: Learning By Doing, Hands on! Hands on! Hands on (anything about nature), 500-1,000 words. **Buys 20 mss/year.** Send complete ms.

Fillers: Facts, puzzles, and short essays on something current in nature. **Buys 35/year.** Length: 150-250 words. **Pays 5¢/word.**

Tips: "We want to bring joy to children by opening the world of God's creation to them. We endeavor to educate with science experiments, stories, etc. We endeavor to create a sense of awe about nature's creator and a respect for His creation. I'd like to see more submissions on hands-on things to do with a nature theme (not collecting rocks or leaves—real stuff!). Also looking for good stories that are accompanied by good photography."

$ $ NEW MOON: THE MAGAZINE FOR GIRLS & THEIR DREAMS, New Moon Publishing, Inc., P.O. Box 3620, Duluth MN 55803-3620. (218)728-5507. Fax: (218)728-0314. E-mail: girl@newmoon.org. Website: www.newmoon.org. **Contact:** Bridget Grosser or Deb Mylin, managing editors. **25% freelance written.** Bimonthly magazine covering girls ages 8-14, edited by girls aged 8-14. "In general, all material should be pro-girl and feature girls and women as the primary focus. *New Moon* is for every girl who wants her voice heard and her dreams taken seriously. *New Moon* celebrates girls, explores the passage from girl to woman and builds healthy resistance to gender inequities. The *New Moon* girl is true to herself and *New Moon* helps her as she pursues her unique path in life, moving confidently into the world." Estab. 1992. Circ. 35,000. Pays on publication. Publishes ms within a year of acceptance. Byline given. Buys all rights. Editorial lead time 6 months. Submit seasonal material 8 months in advance. Accepts queries by mail, e-mail. Accepts simultaneous submissions. Responds in 8 months. Sample copy for $6.50 or on website. Guidelines for SASE or on website.

　　○➔ Adult writers can break in with "*Herstory* articles about less well-known women from all over the world, especially if it relates to one of our themes. Same as *Women's Work* articles. Girls can break in with essays and articles (non-fiction) that relate to a theme."

Nonfiction: Essays, general interest, humor, inspirational, interview/profile, opinion, personal experience written by girls, photo feature, religious, travel, multicultural/girls from other countries. No fashion, beauty, or dating. **Buys 20 mss/year (mainly from girls).** Query or send complete ms. Length: 600 words. **Pays 6-12¢/word.**

Reprints: Send typed ms with rights for sale noted and information about when and where the article previously appeared. Negotiates fee.

Photos: State availability of photos with submission. Negotiates payment individually. Captions and identification of subjects required. Buys one-time rights.

Columns/Departments: Global Village (girl's life in a non-North American country, usually but not always written by a girl), 800 words; Women's Work (profile of a woman and her job(s) relating the the theme), 600 words; Herstory (historical woman relating to theme), 600 words. **Buys 10 mss/year.** Query. **Pays 6-12¢/word.**

Fiction: Adventure, fantasy, historical, humorous, slice-of-life vignettes, all girl-centered. **Buys 6 mss/year.** Send complete ms. Length: 900-1,200 words. **Pays 6-12¢/word.** Prefers girl-written material.

Poetry: No poetry by adults.

Tips: "We'd like to see more girl-written feature articles that relate to a theme. These can be about anything the girl has done personally, or she can write about something she's studied. Please read *New Moon* before submitting to get a sense of our style. Writers and artists who comprehend our goals have the best chance of publication. We love creative articles—both nonfiction and fiction—that are not condescending to our readers. Keep articles to suggested word lengths; avoid stereotypes. Refer to our guidelines and upcoming themes."

N ⚡ $ ON THE LINE, Mennonite Publishing House, 616 Walnut Ave., Scottdale PA 15683-1999. (724)887-8500. Fax: (724)887-3111. E-mail: mary@mph.org. **Contact:** Mary Clemens Meyer, editor. **90% freelance written.** Works with a small number of new/unpublished writers each year. Monthly Christian magazine for children ages 9-14. "*On the Line* helps upper elementary and junior high children understand and appreciate God, the created world, themselves and others." Estab. 1908. Circ. 6,000. **Pays on acceptance.** Publishes ms an average of 1 year after acceptance. Byline given. Buys one-time rights. Submit seasonal material 6 months in advance. Accepts simultaneous submissions. Responds in 1 month. Sample copy for 9 × 12 SAE with 2 first-class stamps.

Nonfiction: How-to (things to make with easy-to-get materials including food recipes); informational (300-500 word articles on wonders of nature, people who have made outstanding contributions). **Buys 95 unsolicited mss/year.** Send complete ms. **Pays $15-35.**

Reprints: Send typed ms with rights for sale noted and information about when and where the article previously appeared. Pays 75% of amount paid for an original article.

Photos: Limited number of photos purchased with or without ms. Pays $25-50 for 8 × 10 b&w photos. Total purchase price for ms includes payment for photos.

Fiction: Adventure, everday problems, humorous, religious. **Buys 50 mss/year.** Send complete ms. Length: 1,000-1,500 words. **Pays 3-5¢/word.**

Poetry: Light verse, religious. Length: 3-12 lines. **Pays $10-25.**

Fillers: Appropriate puzzles, cartoons, quizzes.

Tips: "Study the publication first. We need short well-written how-to and craft articles; also more puzzles. Don't send query; we prefer to see the complete manuscript."

$ $ OWL MAGAZINE, The Discovery Magazine for Children, Owl Group (owned by Bayard Press), 179 John St., Suite 500, Toronto, Ontario M5T 3G5 Canada. (416)340-2700. Fax: (416)340-9769. E-mail: owl@owlkids.com. Website: www.owlkids.com. **Contact:** Elizabeth Siegel, editor. **25% freelance written.** Works with small number of new writers each year. Magazine published 9 times/year covering science and nature. Aims to interest children in their environment through accurate, factual information about the world presented in an easy, lively style. Estab. 1976. Circ. 75,000. Pays on publication. Byline given. Buys all rights. Submit seasonal material 1 year in advance. Accepts queries by mail, e-mail. Responds in 3 months. Sample copy for $4.28. Writer's guidelines for SAE (large envelope if requesting sample copy) and money order for $1 postage (no stamps please).

Nonfiction: Personal experience (real life children in real situations); photo feature (natural science, international wildlife, and outdoor features); science, nature and environmental features. No problem stories with drugs, sex or moralistic views, or talking animal stories. **Buys 6 mss/year.** Query with clips of published work. Length: 500-1,500 words. **Pays $200-500** (Canadian).

Photos: State availability of photos. Reviews 35mm transparencies. Identification of subjects required. Send for photo package before submitting material.

Tips: "Write for editorial guidelines first. Review back issues of the magazine for content and style. Know your topic and approach it from an unusual perspective. Our magazine never talks down to children. Our articles have a very light conversational tone and this must be reflected in any writing that we accept. We would like to see more articles about science and technology that aren't too academic."

$ $ POCKETS, The Upper Room, 1908 Grand Ave., P.O. Box 340004, Nashville TN 37203-0004. (615)340-7333. Fax: (615)340-7267. E-mail: pockets@upperroom.org. Website: www.upperroom.org. Editor: Janet R. Knight. **Contact:** Lynn Gilliam, associate editor. **60% freelance written.** Eager to work with new/unpublished writers. Monthly magazine (except February) covering children's and families' spiritual formation. "We are a Christian, inter-denominational publication for children 6-11 years of age. Each issue reflects a specific theme." Estab. 1981. Circ. 94,000. **Pays on acceptance.** Byline given. Buys first North American serial rights. Submit seasonal material (both secular and liturgical) 1 year in advance. Responds in 6 weeks to mss. Sample copy for 7½ × 10½ or larger SASE with 4 first-class stamps. Writer's guidelines and themes for #10 SASE or on website.

• *Pockets* publishes fiction and poetry, as well as short, short stories (no more than 600 words) for children 4-7. They publish one of these stories per issue.

Nonfiction: Interview/profile, religious (retold scripture stories), personal experience. Each issue reflects a specific theme; themes available for #10 SASE. No violence or romance. **Buys 5 mss/year.** Length: 400-1,000 words. **Pays 14¢/word.**

Reprints: Accepts one-time previously published submissions. Send typed ms with rights for sale noted and information about when and where the article previously appeared.

Photos: Send photos with submission. No photos unless they accompany an article. Reviews contact sheets, transparencies or prints. $25/photo. Buys one-time rights.

Columns/Departments: Refrigerator Door (poetry and prayer related to themes), maximum of 24 lines; Pocketsful of Love (family communications activities), 300 words; Peacemakers at Work (profiles of children working for peace, justice and ecological concerns), 300-800 words. **Buys 20 mss/year. Pays 14¢/word.** Activities/Games (related to themes). **Pays $25 and up.** Kids Cook (simple recipes children can make alone or with minimal help from an adult). **Pays $25.**

Fiction: Adventure, ethnic, slice-of-life. "Submissions do not need to be overtly religious. They should reflect daily living, lifestyle and problem-solving based on living as faithful disciples. They should help children experience the Christian life that is not always a neatly wrapped moral package but is open to the continuing revelation of God's will for their lives." **Buys 44 mss/year.** Length: 600-1,400 words. **Pays 14¢/word.**

Poetry: **Buys 22 poems/year.** Length: 4-24 lines. **Pays $2/line. Pays $25 minimum.**

▣ The online magazine carries original content not found in the print edition and includes writer's guidelines, themes and fiction-writing contest guidelines. Contact: Lynn Gilliam, associate editor.

Tips: "Theme stories, role models and retold scripture stories are most open to freelancers. We are also looking for nonfiction stories about children involved in peace/justice/ecology efforts. Poetry is also open. It is very helpful if writers send for themes. These are *not* the same as writer's guidelines. We have an annual Fiction Writing Contest. Contest guidelines available with #10 SASE or on our website. Writer's guidelines, themes, and contest guidelines, are all available on our website."

🏁 **$ $** **SPIDER, The Magazine for Children**, Cricket Magazine Group, P.O. Box 300, Peru IL 61354. (815)224-6656. Fax: (815)224-6615. Editor-in-Chief: Marianne Carus. Editor: Laura Tillotson. **Contact:** Submissions Editor. **80% freelance written.** Monthly magazine covering literary, general interest. "*Spider* introduces 6- to 9-year-old children to the highest quality stories, poems, illustrations, articles and activities. It was created to foster in beginning readers a love of reading and discovery that will last a lifetime. We're looking for writers who respect children's intelligence." Estab. 1994. Circ. 87,000. Pays on publication. Publishes ms an average of 4 years after acceptance. Byline given. Buys first North American serial rights (for stories, poems, articles), second serial (reprint) rights or all rights (for crafts, recipes, puzzles). Editorial lead time 9 months. Accepts simultaneous submissions. Responds in 4 months to mss. Sample copy for $5. Writer's guidelines for #10 SASE.

Nonfiction: Adventure, biography, geography, history, science, social science, sports, technology, travel. A bibliography is required with all nonfiction submissions. **Buys 6-8 mss/year.** Send complete ms. Length: 300-800 words. **Pays 25¢/word.**

Reprints: Note rights for sale and information about when and where article previously appeared.

Photos: Send photos with submission (prints or slide dupes OK). Reviews contact sheets, 35mm to 4×4 transparencies, 8×10 maximum prints. Offers $35-50/photo. Captions, model releases, identification of subjects required. Buys one-time rights.

Fiction: Adventure, ethnic, fantasy, historical, humorous, mystery, science fiction, suspense, realistic fiction, folk tales, fairy tales. No romance, horror, religious. **Buys 15-20 mss/year.** Send complete ms. Length: 300-1,000 words. **Pays 25¢/word.**

Poetry: Free verse, traditional, nonsense, humorous, serious. No forced rhymes, didactic. **Buys 10-20 poems/year.** Submit maximum 5 poems. Length: 20 lines maximum. **Pays $3/line maximum.**

Fillers: Puzzles, mazes, games, brainteasers, math and word activities. **Buys 15-20/year.** Payment depends on type of filler.

Tips: "We'd like to see more of the following: nonfiction, particularly photoessays, that focuses on an angle rather than providing an overview; fillers, puzzles, and 'takeout page' activities; folktales and humorous stories. Most importantly, do not write down to children."

$ $ $ **SPORTS ILLUSTRATED FOR KIDS**, Time-Warner, Time & Life Building, 1271 Sixth Ave., New York NY 10020. (212)522-1212. Fax: (212)522-0120. Website: wwwsikids.com. Managing Editor: Neil Cohen. **Contact:** Editorial Administrator. **20% freelance written.** Monthly magazine on sports for children 8 years old and up. Content is divided 20/80 between sports as played by kids, and sports as played by professionals. Estab. 1989. **Pays on acceptance.** Publishes ms an average of 3 months after acceptance. Byline given. Offers 25% kill fee. Buys all rights. Accepts queries by mail, fax. For sample copy call (800)992-0196. Writer's guidelines for #10 SASE.

Nonfiction: Games, general interest, how-to, humor, inspirational, interview/profile, photo feature, puzzles. **Buys 15 mss/year.** Query with published clips. Length: 100-1,500 words. **Pays $75-1,000 for assigned articles; $75-800 for unsolicited articles.** Pays expenses of writers on assignment.

Photos: State availability of photos with submission. Buys one-time rights.

Columns/Departments: The Worst Day I Ever Had (tells about day in pro athlete's life when all seemed hopeless), 150 words.

▣ The online magazine carries original content not found in the print edition. Contact: Peter Kay, Director of New Media.

$ **STONE SOUP, The Magazine by Young Writers and Artists**, Children's Art Foundation, P.O. Box 83, Santa Cruz CA 95063-0083. (831)426-5557. Fax: (831)426-1161. E-mail: editor@stonesoup.com. Website: www.stonesoup.com. **Contact:** Ms. Gerry Mandel, editor. **100% freelance written.** Bimonthly magazine of writing and art by children, including fiction, poetry, book reviews, and art by children through age 13. Estab. 1973. Audience is children, teachers, parents, writers, artists. "We have a preference for writing and art based on real-life experiences; no formula stories or poems." Pays on publication. Publishes ms an average of 3 months after acceptance. Buys all rights. Submit seasonal material 6 months in advance. Responds in 1 month. Sample copy for $4 or on website. Writer's guidelines for SASE or on website.

Nonfiction: Book reviews. **Buys 12 mss/year.** Query with SASE. **Pays $25.**

Reprints: Send photocopy of article or story and information about when and where the article or story previously appeared. Pays 100% of amount paid for an original article or story.

Fiction: Adventure, ethnic, experimental, fantasy, historical, humorous, mystery, science fiction, slice-of-life vignettes, suspense. "We do not like assignments or formula stories of any kind." **Accepts 60 mss/year.** Send complete ms with SASE. **Pays $25 for stories.** Authors also receive 2 copies and discounts on additional copies and on subscriptions.

Poetry: Avant-garde, free verse. **Accepts 12 poems/year. Pays $25/poem.** (Same discounts apply.)

Tips: "All writing we publish is by young people ages 13 and under. We do not publish any writing by adults. We can't emphasize enough how important it is to read a couple of issues of the magazine. We have a strong preference for writing on subjects that mean a lot to the author. If you feel strongly about something that happened to you or something you observed, use that feeling as the basis for your story or poem. Stories should have good descriptions, realistic dialogue and a point to make. In a poem, each word must be chosen carefully. Your poem should present a view of your subject and a way of using words that are special and all your own."

Ⓝ $ STORY FRIENDS, Mennonite Publishing House, 616 Walnut Ave., Scottdale PA 15683-1999. (724)887-3753. Fax: (724)887-3111. **Contact:** Rose Mary Stutzman, editor. **80% freelance written.** Monthly magazine for children ages 4-9. "*Story Friends* is planned to provide wholesome Christian reading for the 4-9-year-old. Practical life stories are included to teach moral values and remind the children that God is at work today. Activities introduce children to the Bible and its message for them." Estab. 1905. Circ. 7,000. **Pays on acceptance.** Publishes ms an average of 1 year after acceptance. Byline given. Publication not copyrighted. Buys one-time and second serial (reprint) rights. Submit seasonal material 6 months in advance. Accepts simultaneous submissions. Responds in 2 months. Sample copy for 9×12 SAE with 2 first-class stamps. Writer's guidelines for #10 SASE.

Nonfiction: How-to (craft ideas for young children), photo feature. **Buys 20 mss/year.** Send complete ms. Length: 300-500 words. **Pays 3-5¢/word.**

Reprints: Send photocopy or typed ms with rights for sale noted and information about when and where the article previously appeared. Pays 100% of amount paid for an original article.

Photos: Send photos with submission. Reviews 8½×11 b&w prints. Offers $20-25/photo. Model releases required. Buys one-time rights.

Fiction: Buys 50 mss/year. Send complete ms. Length: 300-800 words. **Pays 3-5¢/word.**

Poetry: Traditional. **Buys 20 poems/year.** Length: 4-16 lines. **Pays $10/poem.**

Tips: "Send stories that children from a variety of ethnic backgrounds can relate to; stories that deal with experiences similar to all children. For example, all children have fears but their fears may vary depending on where they live. Send stories with a humorous twist. We're also looking for well-planned puzzles that challenge and promote reading readiness."

$ TOGETHER TIME, WordAction Publishing Company, 6401 The Paseo, Kansas City MO 64131. Website: www.nazarene.org. Editor: Melissa Hammer. **Contact:** Kathleen Johnson, assistant editor. Weekly children's story paper featuring a children's Sunday school theme. "*Together Time* is a full-color story paper for three and four year olds which correlates directly with the WordAction Sunday school curriculum. It is designed to connect Sunday school learning with the daily living experiences and growth of the child." Circ. 5,000. Pays on publication. Publishes ms an average of 1 year after acceptance. Byline given. Buys multi-use rights. Editorial lead time 1 year. Submit seasonal material 1 year in advance. Accepts simultaneous submissions. Accepts queries by mail, e-mail. Responds in 2 weeks to queries; 1 month to mss. Sample copy and writer's guidelines for #10 SASE.

Nonfiction: Religious. "We do not want to see anything that does not match our theme-list." **Buys 30 mss/year.** Send complete ms. Length: 200-350 words. **Pays $10-25.**

Reprints: Accepts previously published submissions.

Columns/Departments: Crafts/activities and finger plays (both simple, 3-4 year old level of understanding). **Buys 30 mss/year.** Send complete ms. **Pays 25¢/line-$15.**

Fiction: Religious. "We do not want to see anything that does not match our theme-list." **Buys 30 mss/year.** Send complete ms. Length: 200-350 words. **Pays $10-25.**

Poetry: Free verse. "Avoid portrayals of extremely precocious, abnormally mature children." **Buys 20 poems/year.** Submit maximum 5 poems. Length: 4-12 lines. **Pays 25¢/line.**

Tips: "We're looking for stories and poems on specific Bible characters like Daniel, Ruth and Naomi, David, Samuel, Paul. We do not need creation stories or stories on 'the golden rule.' Write on a three- and four-year-old level of understanding. We prefer rhythmic, pattern poems, but will accept free-verse if thought and 'read aloud' effect flow smoothly. Include word pictures of subject matter relating to everyday experiences."

$ TOUCH, Touching Girls' Hearts with God's Love, GEMS Girls' Clubs, P.O. Box 7259, Grand Rapids MI 49510. (616)241-5616. Fax: (616)241-5558. E-mail: carol@gemsgc.org. Website: www.gospelcom.net/gems. Editor: Jan Boone. **Contact:** Carol Smith, managing editor. **80% freelance written.** Works with new and published/established writers. Monthly magazine "to show girls ages 9-14 how God is at work in their lives and in the world around them. Our readers are mainly girls from Christian homes who belong to GEMS Girls' Clubs, a relationship-building club program available through churches. The May/June issue annually features material written by our readers." Estab. 1971. Circ. 13,000. Pays on publication. Publishes ms an average of 1 year after acceptance. Byline given. Buys second serial (reprint) and first North American serial rights. Submit seasonal material 1 year in advance. Accepts simultaneous submissions. Responds in 2 months. Sample copy for 9×12 SAE with 3 first-class stamps and $1. Writer's guidelines for #10 SASE.

Nonfiction: Biographies and autobiographies of "heroes of the faith," informational (write for issue themes), humor (need much more), inspirational (seasonal and holiday), interview, multicultural materials, travel, personal experience (avoid the testimony approach), photo feature (query first), religious. "Because our magazine is published around a monthly theme, requesting the letter we send out twice a year to our established freelancers would be most helpful. We do not want easy solutions or quick character changes from bad to good. No pietistic characters. No 'new girl at school starting over after parents' divorce' stories. Constant mention of God is not necessary if the moral tone of the story is positive. We do not want stories that always have a happy ending." Special issues: School Skills Needed (September); Danger Ahead! Join the Rescue Squad (October); Lost and Found (November); Rescuing Christmas (December); Dial 9-1-1 (January); I'm Lonely . . . Rescue Me! (February); Danger . . . Beware!(March); Team Up With Mother Earth (April); You Want Me to Join What? (May/June). **Buys 10 unsolicited mss/year.** Submit complete ms. Length: 200-800 words. **Pays $10-20** plus 2 copies.

Reprints: Send typed ms with rights for sale noted and information about when and where the article previously appeared.

Photos: Purchased with or without ms. Reviews 5×7 or 8×10 clear color glossy prints. Appreciate multicultural subjects. Pays $25-50 on publication.

Columns/Departments: How-to (crafts); puzzles and jokes; quizzes. Length: 200-400 words. Submit complete ms. Pay varies.

Fiction: Adventure (that girls could experience in their hometowns or places they might realistically visit), historical, humorous, mystery (believable only), romance (stories that deal with awakening awareness of boys are appreciated), slice-of-life vignettes, suspense (can be serialized), religious (nothing preachy). **Buys 20 mss/year.** Submit complete ms. Length: 400-1,000 words. **Pays $20-50.**

Poetry: Free verse, haiku, light verse, traditional. **Buys 5/year.** Length: 15 lines maximum. **Pays $5-15 minimum.**

Tips: "Prefers not to see anything on the adult level, secular material or violence. Writers frequently over-simplify the articles and often write with a Pollyanna attitude. An author should be able to see his/her writing style as exciting and appealing to girls ages 9-14. The style can be fun, but also teach a truth. Subjects should be current and important to *Touch* readers. Use our theme update as a guide. We would like to receive material with a multicultural slant."

⊠ $ $ TURTLE MAGAZINE FOR PRESCHOOL KIDS, Children's Better Health Institute, P.O. Box 567, Indianapolis IN 46206-0567. (317)636-8881. Fax: (317)684-8094. Website: www.turtlemag.com. **Contact:** (Ms.) Terry Harshman, editor. **70% freelance written.** Bimonthly magazine (monthly March, June, September, December). General interest, interactive magazine with the purpose of helping preschoolers develop healthy minds and bodies. Circ. 300,000. Pays on publication. May hold mss for up to 1 year before acceptance/publication. Byline given. Buys all rights. Submit seasonal material 8 months in advance. Responds in 3 months. Sample copy for $1.75. Writer's guidelines for #10 SASE.

Nonfiction: "We use very simple science experiments. These should be pretested. We also publish simple, healthful recipes." **Buys 24 mss/year.** Length: 100-300 words. **Pays up to 22¢/word.**

Fiction: All should have single-focus story lines and work well as read-alouds. "Most of the stories we use have a character-building bent, but are not preachy or overly moralistic. We are in constant need of stories to help a preschooler appreciate his/her body and what it can do; stories encouraging active, vigorous play; stories about good health. We are also in need of short (50-150 words) rebus stories. We no longer buy stories about 'generic' turtles because we now have PokeyToes, our own trade-marked turtle character. All should 'move along' and lend themselves well to illustration. Writing should be energetic, enthusiastic and creative—like preschoolers themselves. No queries, please." **Buys 25 mss/year.** Length: 150-300 words. **Pays up to 22¢/word.**

Poetry: "We're especially looking for action rhymes to foster creative movement in preschoolers. We also use short verse on our inside front cover and back cover."

Tips: "We are looking for more easy science experiments and simple, nonfiction health articles. We are trying to include more material for our youngest readers. Stories must be age-appropriate for two- to five-year-olds, entertaining and written from a healthy lifestyle perspective."

$ $U.S. KIDS, A Weekly Reader Magazine, Children's Better Health Institute, P.O. Box 567, Indianapolis IN 46206-0567. (317)636-8881. Webstie: www.satevepost.org/kidsonline. **Contact:** Nancy S. Axelrad, editor. **50% freelance written.** Published 8 times/year featuring "kids doing extraordinary things, especially activities related to heatlh, sports, the arts, interesting hobbies, the environment, computers, etc." Reading level appropriate for 1st to 3rd grade readers. Estab. 1987. Circ. 230,000. Pays on publication. Publishes ms an average of 4 months after acceptance. Byline given. Buys all rights. Editorial lead time 6 months. Submit seasonal material 6 months in advance. Responds in 4 months to mss. Sample copy for $2.95 or on website. Writer's guidelines for #10 SASE.

• *U.S. Kids* is being re-targeted for a younger audience.

Nonfiction: Especially interested in articles with a health/fitness angle. Also general interest, how-to, interview/profile, science, kids using computers, multicultural. **Buys 16-24 mss/year.** Send complete ms. Length: 400 words maximum. **Pays up to 25¢/word.**

Photos: State availability of photos with submission. Reviews contact sheets or color photocopies, negatives, transparencies, prints. Negotiates payment individually. Captions, model releases, identification of subjects required. Buys one-time rights.

Columns/Departments: Real Kids (kids doing interesting things); Fit Kids (sports, healthy activities); Computer Zone. Length: 300-400 words. Send complete ms. **Pays up to 25¢/word.**

Fiction: Buys very little fictional material. **Buys 1-2 mss/year.** Send complete ms. Length: 400 words. **Pays up to 25¢/word.**

Poetry: Light verse, traditional, kid's humorous, health/fitness angle. **Buys 6-8 poems/year.** Submit maximum 6 poems. Length: 8-24 lines. **Pays $25-50.**

Fillers: Facts, newsbreaks (related to kids, especially kids' health), short humor, puzzles, games, activities. Length: 200-500 words. **Pays 25¢/word.**

Tips: "We are re-targeting magazine for first-, second-, and third-graders and looking for fun and informative articles on activities and hobbies of interest to younger kids. Special emphasis on fitness, sports and health. Availability of good photos a plus."

$ WONDER TIME, 6401 The Paseo Blvd., Kansas City MO 64131-1213. (816)333-7000. Fax: (816)333-4439. E-mail: dfillmore@nazarene.org. or pcraft@nazarene.org. **Contact:** Patty Craft, associate editor. **75% freelance written.** "Willing to read and consider appropriate freelance submissions." Published weekly by WordAction for children ages 6-8. Correlates to the Bible Truth in the weekly Sunday School lesson. Pays on publication. Publishes ms an average of 1 year after acceptance. Byline given. Buys rights to reuse and all rights for curriculum assignments. Accepts queries by mail, e-mail, fax. Responds in 2 months. Sample copy and writer's guidelines for 9×12 SAE with 2 first-class stamps.

Fiction: Buys stories portraying Christian attitudes without being preachy. Uses true-to-life stories teaching honesty, truthfulness, kindness, helpfulness or other important spiritual truths, and avoiding symbolism. Also, stories about real life problems children face today. "God should be spoken of as our Father who loves and cares for us; Jesus, as our Lord and Savior." **Buys 40 mss/year.** Length: 250-350 words. **Pays $25 on publication.**

Tips: "Any stories that allude to church doctrine must be in keeping with Wesleyan beliefs. Avoid fantasy, precocious children or personification of animals. Write on a first to second grade readability level."

LITERARY & "LITTLE"

Fiction, poetry, essays, book reviews and scholarly criticism comprise the content of the magazines listed in this section. Some are published by colleges and universities, and many are regional in focus.

Everything about "little" literary magazines is different than other consumer magazines. Most carry few or no ads, and many do not seek them. Circulations under 1,000 are common. And sales often come more from the purchase of sample copies than from the newsstand.

The magazines listed in this section cannot compete with the pay rates and exposure of the high-circulation general interest magazines also publishing fiction and poetry. But most "little" literary magazines don't try. They are more apt to specialize in publishing certain kinds of fiction or poetry: traditional, experimental, works with a regional sensibility, or the fiction and poetry of new and younger writers. For that reason, and because fiction and poetry vary so widely in style, writers should *always* invest in the most recent copies of the magazines they aspire to publish in.

Many "little" literary magazines pay contributors only in copies of the issues in which their works appear. *Writer's Market* lists only those that pay their contributors in cash. However, *Novel & Short Story Writer's Market* includes nonpaying fiction markets, and has in-depth information about fiction techniques and markets. The same is true of *Poet's Market* for nonpaying poetry markets (both books are published by Writer's Digest Books). Many literary agents and book editors regularly read these magazines in search of literary voices not found in mainstream writing. There are also more literary opportunities listed in the Contests and Awards section.

$ AFRICAN AMERICAN REVIEW, Indiana State University, Department of English, ISU, Terre Haute IN 47809. (812)237-2968. Fax: (812)237-4382. E-mail: asleco@isugw.indstate.edu. Website: web.indstate.edu/Artsci/AAR. Managing Editor: Connie LeComte. **Contact:** Joe Weixlmann, editor. **65% freelance written.** Quarterly magazine covering African-American literature and culture. "Essays on African-American literature, theater, film, art and culture generally; interviews; poetry and fiction by African-American authors; book reviews." Estab. 1967. Circ. 3,137. Pays on publication. Publishes ms an average of 1 year after acceptance. Byline given. Buys first North American serial rights. Editorial lead time 1 year. Responds in 1 month to queries; 3 months to mss. Sample copy for $6. Writer's guidelines for #10 SASE.

Nonfiction: Essays, interview/profile. **Buys 30 mss/year.** Query. Length: 3,500-6,000 words. **Pays $50-150.** Pays in contributor copies upon request.

Photos: State availability of photos with submission. Offers no additional payment for photos accepted with ms. Captions required.

Fiction: Ethnic. **Buys 4 mss/year.** Send complete ms. Length: 2,500-5,000 words. **Pays $50-150.**

$ AGNI, Dept. WM, Boston University, 236 Bay State Rd., Boston, MA 02215. (617)353-7135. Fax: (617)353-7134. E-mail: agni@bu.edu. Website: www.bu.edu/AGNI. **Contact:** Askold Melnyczuk, editor; Eric Grunwald, managing editor. Biannual literary magazine. "*AGNI* publishes poetry, fiction and essays. Also regularly publishes translations and is committed to featuring the work of emerging writers. We have published Derek Walcott, Joyce Carol Oates, Sharon Olds, John Updike, Ha Jin, John Keene, Jhumpa Lahiri, Robert Pinsky, and many others. Estab. 1972. Circ. 2,000. Pays on publication. Publishes ms an average of 6 months after acceptance. Byline given. Buys first North American serial rights and rights to reprint in *AGNI* anthology (with author's consent). Editorial lead time 6 months. Reading period Oct. 1-Jan 31. Accepts simultaneous submissions. Responds in 2 weeks to queries; 6 months to mss. Sample copy for $9 or on website. Writer's guidelines for #10 SASE.

Fiction: Short stories. **Buys 6-12 mss/year.** Send complete ms with SASE. **Pays $20-150.**

● Ranked as one of the best markets for fiction writers in Writer's Digest magazine's "Fiction 50," June 2000.

Poetry: Buys more than 140/year. Submit maximum 5 poems with SASE. **Pays $20-150.**

Tips: "We're looking for extraordinary translations from little-translated languages. It is important to look at a copy of *AGNI* before submitting, to see if your work might be compatible. Please write for guidelines or a sample."

$ $ ALASKA QUARTERLY REVIEW, ESB 208, University of Alaska-Anchorage, 3211 Providence Dr., Anchorage AK 99508. (907)786-6916. E-mail: ayaqr@uaa.alaska.edu. Website: www.uaa.alaska.edu/aqr. **Contact:** Ronald Spatz, executive editor. **95% freelance written.** Prefers to work with published/established writers; eager to work with new/unpublished writers. Semiannual magazine publishing fiction, poetry, literary nonfiction and short plays in traditional and experimental styles. Estab. 1982. Circ. 2,200. Pays honorariums on publication when funding permits. Publishes ms an average of 6 months after acceptance. Byline given. Buys first North American serial rights. Upon request, rights will be transferred back to author after publication. Responds in 4 months. Sample copy for $6. Writer's guidelines for SASE or on website.

● *Alaska Quarterly* reports they are always looking for freelance material and new writers.

Nonfiction: Literary nonfiction: essays and memoirs. **Buys 0-5 mss/year.** Query. Length: 1,000-20,000 words. **Pays $50-200** subject to funding; pays in contributor's copies and subscriptions when funding is limited.

Reprints: Accepts previously published submissions under special circumstances (special anthologies or translations). Send photocopy of article or short story or typed ms with rights for sale noted and information about when and where the article previously appeared.

Fiction: Experimental and traditional literary forms. No romance, children's or inspirational/religious. Publishes novel excerpts. **Buys 20-30 mss/year.** Send complete ms. Length: Up to 20,000 words. **Pays $50-200** subject to funding; pays in contributor's copies and subscriptions when funding is limited.

Drama: Experimental and traditional one-act plays. **Buys 0-2 mss/year.** Query. Length: Up to 20,000 words but prefers short plays. **Pays $50-200** subject to funding; contributor's copies and subscriptions when funding is limited.

Poetry: Avant-garde, free verse, traditional. No light verse. **Buys 20-65 poems/year.** Submit maximum 10 poems. **Pays $10-50** subject to availability of funds; pays in contributor's copies and subscriptions when funding is limited.

▣ The online magazine carries original content not found in the print edition and includes writer's guidelines.

Tips: "All sections are open to freelancers. We rely almost exclusively on unsolicited manuscripts. *AQR* is a nonprofit literary magazine and does not always have funds to pay authors."

$ AMELIA MAGAZINE, Amelia Press, 329 E St., Bakersfield CA 93304. (661)323-4064. Fax: (661)323-5326. E-mail: amelia@lightspeed.net. **Contact:** Frederick A. Raborg, Jr., editor. **100% freelance written.** Eager to work with new/unpublished writers. "*Amelia* is a quarterly international magazine publishing the finest poetry and fiction available, along with expert criticism and reviews intended for all interested in contemporary literature. *Amelia* also publishes two separate magazines each year: *Cicada* and *SPSM&H*." Estab. 1983. Circ. 1,750. **Pays on acceptance.** Publishes ms an average of 6 months after acceptance. Byline given. Offers 50% kill fee. Buys first North American serial rights. Submit seasonal material 2 months in advance. Responds in 3 months to mss. Sample copy for $10.95 (includes postage). Writer's guidelines for #10 SASE.

● An eclectic magazine, open to greater variety of styles—especially genre and mainstream stories unsuitable for other literary magazines. Receptive to new writers.

Nonfiction: Historical/nostalgic (in the form of belles lettres), humor (in fiction or belles lettres), interview/profile (poets and fiction writers), opinion (on poetry and fiction only), personal experience (as it pertains to poetry or fiction in the form of belles lettres), travel (in the form of belles lettres only), criticism and book reviews of poetry and small press fiction titles. "Nothing overtly slick in approach. Criticism pieces must have depth; belles lettres must offer important insights into the human scene." **Buys 8 mss/year.** Send complete ms and SASE. Length: 1,000-2,000 words. **Pays $25** or by arrangement. Sometimes pays the expenses of writers on assignment.

Fiction: Adventure, book excerpts (original novel excerpts only), erotica (of a quality seen in Anais Nin or Henry Miller only), ethnic, experimental, fantasy, historical, horror, humorous, mainstream, mystery, novel excerpts, science fiction, suspense, western. "We would consider slick fiction of the quality seen in *Esquire* or *Vanity Fair* and more excellent submissions in the genres—science fiction, wit, Gothic horror, traditional romance, stories with complex *raisons d'être*; avant-garde ought to be truly avant-garde." No pornography ("good erotica is not the same thing"). **Buys 24-36 mss/year.** Send complete ms. Length: 1,000-5,000 words, sometimes longer. "Longer stories really have to sparkle." **Pays $35** or by arrangement for exceptional work.

Poetry: Avant-garde, free verse, haiku, light verse, traditional. "No patently religious or stereotypical newspaper poetry." **Buys 100-240 poems**/year depending on lengths. Prefers submission of at least 3 poems. Length: 3-100 lines. "Shorter poems stand the best chance." **Pays $2-25.**

Tips: "*Have something to say* and say it well. If you insist on waving flags or pushing your religion, then do it with subtlety and class. We enjoy a good cry from time to time, too, but sentimentality does not mean we want to see mush. Read our fiction carefully for depth of plot and characterization, then try very hard to improve on it. With the growth of quality in short fiction, we expect to find stories of lasting merit. I also hope to begin seeing more critical essays which, without sacrificing research, demonstrate a more entertaining obliqueness to the style sheets, more 'new journalism' than MLA. In poetry, we also often look for a good 'storyline' so to speak. Above all we want to feel a sense of honesty and value in every piece. No e-mail or fax manuscript submissions."

$ THE ANTIGONISH REVIEW, St. Francis Xavier University, P.O. Box 5000, Antigonish, Nova Scotia B2G 2W5 Canada. (902)867-3962. Fax: (902)867-5563. E-mail: tar@stfx.ca. Website: www.antigonish.com/review/. Managing Editor: Gertrude Sanderson. **Contact:** George Sanderson, editor. **100% freelance written.** Quarterly literary magazine. Estab. 1970. Circ. 850. Pays on publication. Publishes ms an average of 4 months after acceptance. Byline given. Offers variable kill fee. Rights retained by author. Editorial lead time 4 months. Submit seasonal material 4 months in advance. Accepts queries by mail, e-mail, fax. Responds in 4 months to mss; 1 month to queries. Sample copy for $4 or on website. Writer's guidelines for #10 SASE or on website.

Nonfiction: Essays, interview/profile, book reviews/articles. No academic pieces. **Buys 15-20 mss/year.** Query. Length: 1,500-5,000 words. **Pays $50-150.**

Fiction: Literary. No erotica. **Buys 35-40 mss/year.** Send complete ms. Length: 500-5,000 words. **Pays in copies.**

Poetry: Buys 100-125 poems/year. Submit maximum 5 poems. **Pays in copies.**

Tips: "Send for guidelines and/or sample copy. Send ms with cover letter and SASE with submission."

$ ANTIOCH REVIEW, P.O. Box 148, Yellow Springs OH 45387-0148. **Contact:** Robert S. Fogarty, editor. Quarterly magazine for general, literary and academic audience. Estab. 1941. Circ. 5,100. Byline given. Pays on publication. Publishes ms an average of 10 months after acceptance. Rights revert to author upon publication. Responds in 2 months. Sample copy for $6. Writer's guidelines for #10 SASE.

Nonfiction: "Contemporary articles in the humanities and social sciences, politics, economics, literature and all areas of broad intellectual concern. Somewhat scholarly, but never pedantic in style, eschewing all professional jargon. Lively, distinctive prose insisted upon." Length: 2,000-8,000 words. **Pays $10/published page.**

Fiction: "Quality fiction only, distinctive in style with fresh insights into the human condition." No science fiction, fantasy or confessions. **Pays $10/published page.**

Poetry: No light or inspirational verse. "We do not read poetry May 1-September 1."

⊠ $ ARC, Canada's National Poetry Magazine, Arc Poetry Society, Box 7368, Ottawa, Ontario K1L 8E4 Canada. **Contact:** John Barton, Rita Donovan, co-editors. Semiannual literary magazine featuring poetry, poetry-related articles and criticism. "Our focus is poetry, and Canadian poetry in general, although we do publish writers from elsewhere. We are looking for the best poetry from new and established writers. We often have special issues. SASE for upcoming special issues and contests." Estab. 1978. Circ. 1,000. Pays on publication. Publishes ms an average of 6 months after acceptance. Byline given. Buys one-time rights. Responds in 4 months. Sample copy for $4 with 10 first-class stamps.

Nonfiction: Essays, interview/profile, photo feature, book reviews. Query. Length: 1,000 words. **Pays $30/printed page** plus 2 copies.

Photos: Query with samples. Pays $25/photo. Buys one-time rights.

Poetry: Avant-garde, free verse. **Buys 40/year.** Submit maximum 6 poems. **Pays $30/printed page** (Canadian).

Tips: "SASE for guidelines. Please include brief biographical note with submission."

$ BLACK WARRIOR REVIEW, P.O. Box 862936, Tuscaloosa AL 35486-0027. (205)348-4518. Website: www.sa.ua.edu/osm/bwr. **90% freelance written.** Semiannual magazine of fiction, poetry, essays and reviews. Estab. 1974. Circ. 2,000. Pays on publication. Publishes ms an average of 6 months after acceptance. Byline given. Buys first rights. Responds in 2 weeks to queries; 3 months to mss. Sample copy for $8. Writer's guidelines for #10 SASE.

● Consistently excellent magazine. Placed stories and poems in recent *Best American Short Stories*, *Best American Poetry* and *Pushcart Prize* anthologies.

Nonfiction: Interview/profile, book reviews and literary/personal essays. **Buys 5 mss/year.** No queries; send complete ms. **Pays up to $100** and 2 contributor's copies.

Fiction: Jennifer Davis, fiction editor. **Buys 10 mss/year.** Publishes novel excerpts if under contract to be published. One story/chapter per envelope, please. **Pays up to $150** and 2 contributor's copies.

Poetry: Mark Neely, poetry editor. Submit 3-6 poems. **Buys 50 poems/year. Pays up to $75** and 2 copies.

Tips: "Read the *BWR* before submitting; editors change each year. Send us your best work. Submissions of photos and/or artwork is encouraged. We sometimes choose unsolicited photos/artwork for the cover. Address all submissions to the appropriate genre editor."

⚒ $ $ BOULEVARD, Opojaz, Inc., 4579 Laclede Ave., #332, St. Louis MO 63108-2103. (314)361-2986. **Contact:** Richard Burgin, editor. **100% freelance written.** Triannual literary magazine covering fiction, poetry and essays. "*Boulevard* is a diverse literary magazine presenting original creative work by well-known authors, as well as by writers of exciting promise." Estab. 1985. Circ. 3,500. Pays on publication. Publishes ms an average of 9 months after acceptance. Byline given. No kill fee. Buys first North American serial rights. Accepts queries by mail, phone. Accepts simultaneous submissions. Responds in 2 weeks to queries; 2 months to mss. Sample copy for $7. Writer's guidelines for #10 SASE.

Nonfiction: Book excerpts, essays, interview/profile. "No pornography, science fiction, children's stories or westerns." **Buys 8 mss/year.** Send complete ms. Length: 8,000 words maximum. **Pays $50-250** (sometimes higher).

Fiction: Confession, experimental, mainstream, novel excerpts. "We do not want erotica, science fiction, romance, western or children's stories." **Buys 20 mss/year.** Send complete ms. Length: 8,000 words maximum. **Pays $50-250** (sometimes higher). Publishes novel excerpts.

● Ranked as one of the best markets for fiction writers in *Writer's Digest* magazine's "Fiction 50," June 2000.

Poetry: Avant-garde, free verse, haiku, traditional. "Do not send us light verse." **Buys 80 poems/year.** Submit maximum 5 poems. Length: up to 200 lines. **Pays $25-250** (sometimes higher).

Tips: "Read the magazine first. The work *Boulevard* publishes is generally recognized as among the finest in the country. We continue to seek more good literary or cultural essays. Send only your best work."

$ $ THE CAPILANO REVIEW, The Capilano Press Society, 2055 Purcell Way, North Vancouver, British Columbia V7J 3H5 Canada. Fax: (604)990-7837. E-mail: tcr@capcollege.bc.ca. Website: www.capcollege.bc.ca/dept/TCR/tcr. **Contact:** Ryan Knighton, editor. **100% freelance written.** "Triannual visual and literary arts magazine that publishes only what the editors consider to be the very best fiction, poetry, drama or visual art being produced. *TCR* editors are interested in fresh, original work that stimulates and challenges readers. Over the years, the magazine has developed a reputation for pushing beyond the boundaries of traditional art and writing. We are interested in work that is new in concept and in execution." Estab. 1972. Circ. 1,000. Pays on publication. Byline given. Buys first North American serial rights. No e-mail or fax submissions. No simultaneous submissions please. Responds in 1 month to queries; 5 months to mss. Sample copy for $9 or on website. Writer's guidelines for #10 SASE with IRC or Canadian stamps or on website.

Fiction: Literary. **Buys 10-15 mss/year.** Length: 6,000 words maximum. Query by mail only or send complete ms with SASE and Canadian postage or IRCs. **Pays $50-200.** Publishes previously unpublished novel excerpts.

Poetry: Avant-garde, free verse. **Buys 40 poems/year.** Submit 5-10 unpublished poems with SASE. **Pays $50-200.**

$ THE CHARITON REVIEW, Truman State University, Kirksville MO 63501-9915. (660)785-4499. Fax: (660)785-7486. **Contact:** Jim Barnes, editor. **100% freelance written.** Semiannual (fall and spring) magazine covering contemporary fiction, poetry, translation and book reviews. Circ. 600. Pays on publication. Publishes ms an average of 6 months after acceptance. Byline given. Buys first North American serial rights. Responds in 1 week to queries; 1 month to mss. Sample copy for $5 and 7×10 SAE with 4 first-class stamps.

Nonfiction: Essays, essay reviews of books. **Buys 2-5 mss/year.** Send complete ms. Length: 1,000-5,000. **Pays $15.**

Fiction: Ethnic, experimental, mainstream, novel excerpts, traditional. Publishes novel excerpts if they can stand alone. "We are not interested in slick or sick material." **Buys 6-10 mss/year.** Query by mail only or send complete ms. Length: 1,000-6,000 words. **Pays $5/page (up to $50).**

Poetry: Avant-garde, traditional. **Buys 50-55 poems/year.** Submit maximum 5 poems. Length: open. **Pays $5/page.**

Tips: "Read *Chariton*. Know the difference between good literature and bad. Know what magazine might be interested in your work. We are not a trendy magazine. We publish only the best. All sections are open to freelancers. Know your market or you are wasting your time—and mine. Do *not* write for guidelines; the only guideline is excellence."

N: $ CHELSEA, Chelsea Associates, P.O. Box 773, Cooper Station, New York NY 10276. **Contact:** Richard Foerster, editor. **70% freelance written.** Semiannual literary magazine. "We stress style, variety, originality. No special biases or requirements. Flexible attitudes, eclectic material. We take an active interest, as always, in cross-cultural exchanges, superior translations, and are leaning toward cosmopolitan, interdisciplinary techniques, but maintain no strictures against traditional modes." Estab. 1958. Circ. 1,800. Pays on publication. Publishes ms an average of 6 months after acceptance. Byline given. Buys first North American serial rights. Responds in 6 months to mss. Sample copy for $6.

● *Chelsea* also sponsors fiction and poetry contests. Send SASE for guidelines.

Nonfiction: Essays, book reviews (query first with sample). **Buys 6 mss/year.** Send complete ms with SASE. Length: 6,000 words. **Pays $15/page.**

Fiction: Mainstream, literary, novel excerpts. **Buys 12 mss/year.** Send complete ms with SASE. Length: 5-6,000 words. **Pays $15/page.** Publishes novel excerpts.

Poetry: Avant-garde, free verse, traditional. **Buys 60-75 poems/year. Pays $15/page.**

Tips: "We only accept written correspondence. We are looking for more super translations, first-rate fiction and work by writers of color. No need to query; submit complete manuscript. We suggest writers look at a recent issue of *Chelsea*."

$ CICADA, *Amelia Magazine*, 329 E St., Bakersfield CA 93304. (661)323-4064. **Contact:** Frederick A. Raborg, Jr., editor. **100% freelance written.** Quarterly magazine covering Oriental fiction and poetry (haiku, etc.). "Our readers expect the best haiku and related poetry forms we can find. Our readers circle the globe and know their subjects. We include fiction, book reviews and articles related to the forms or to the Orient." Estab. 1984. Circ. 800. Pays on publication. Publishes ms an average of 6 months after acceptance. Byline given. Offers 50% kill fee. Buys first North American serial rights. Editorial lead time 2 months. Submit seasonal material 3 months in advance. Accepts simultaneous submissions. Responds in 2 weeks to queries, 3 months to mss. Sample copy for $6.. Guidelines for #10 SASE.

Nonfiction: Essays, general interest, historical/nostalgic, humor, interview/profile, opinion, personal experience, travel. **Buys 1-3 mss/year.** Send complete ms. Length: 500-2,500 words. **Pays $10.**

Photos: Send photos with submission. Reviews 5×7 or 8×10 b/w prints. Offers $10-25/photo. Model releases required. Buys one-time rights.

Fiction: Adventure, erotica, ethnic, experimental, fantasy, historical, horror, humorous, mainstream, mystery, romance, science fiction, slice-of-life vignettes, suspense. **Buys 4 mss/year.** Send complete ms. Length: 500-2,500 words. **Pays $10-20.**

Poetry: Buys 400 poems/year. Submit maximum 12 poems. Length: 1-50 lines. **Pays 3 "best of issue" poets $10.**

Fillers: Anecdotes, short humor. **Buys 1-4/year.** Length: 25-500 words. No payment for fillers.

Tips: "Writers should understand the limitations of contemporary Japanese forms particularly. We also use poetry based on other Asian ethnicities and on the South Seas ethnicities. Don't be afraid to experiment within the forms. Be professional in approach and presentation."

$ $ CONFRONTATION, A Literary Journal, Long Island University, Brookville NY 11548. (516)299-2720. Fax: (516)299-2735. Assistant to Editor: Michael Hartnett.**Contact:** Martin Tucker, editor-in-chief. **75% freelance written.** Semiannual literary magazine. "We are eclectic in our taste. Excellence of style is our dominant concern." Estab. 1968. Circ. 2,000. Pays on publication. Publishes ms an average of 1 year after acceptance. Byline given. "Rarely offers kill fee." Buys first North American serial, first, one-time or all rights. Accepts simultaneous submissions. Responds in 3 weeks to queries; 2 months to mss. Sample copy for $3.

Nonfiction: Essays, personal experience. **Buys 15 mss/year.** Send complete ms. Length: 1,500-5,000 words. **Pays $100-300 for assigned articles; $15-300 for unsolicited articles.**

Photos: State availability of photos with submission. Offers no additional payment for photos accepted with ms. Buys one-time rights.

Fiction: Jonna Semeiks. Experimental, mainstream, slice-of-life vignettes, novel excerpts (if they are self-contained stories). "We judge on quality, so genre is open." **Buys 60-75 mss/year.** Send complete ms. Length 6,000 words maximum. **Pays $25-250.**

Poetry: Katherine Hill-Miller. Avant-garde, free verse, haiku, light verse, traditional. **Buys 60-75 poems/year.** Submit maximum 6 poems. Length open. **Pays $10-100.**

Tips: "Most open to fiction and poetry."

$ $ $ DOUBLETAKE, 55 Davis Square, Somerville MA 02144. (617)591-9389. Fax: (617)625-6478. Website: www.doubletakemagazine.org. **Contact:** Fiction Editor. **Pays on acceptance.** Byline given. Buys first North American serial rights. Accepts simultaneous submissions. Responds in 3 months to mss. Sample copy for $12. Writer's guidelines for #10 SASE or on website.

Fiction: "We accept realistic fiction in all of its variety. We look for stories with a strong, narrative voice and an urgency in the writing." **Buys 12 mss/year.** Send complete ms with cover letter. No preferred length. **Pays competitively.**

The online magazine carries original content not found in the print edition and includes writer's guidelines.

Tips: "Be careful of stories that are too leisurely paced. Also, the essential conflict of the story should be discernible to the reader. We're interested in how a character is changed in some way be the end of the story."

$ DREAMS & VISIONS, New Frontiers in Christian Fiction, Skysong Press, 35 Peter St. S., Orillia, Ontario L3V 5A8 Canada. Phone/fax: (705)329-1770. E-mail: skysong@bconnex.net. Website: www.bconnex.net/~skysong. **Contact:** Steve Stanton, editor. **100% freelance written.** Semiannual magazine covering Christian fiction. "Innovative literary fiction for adult Christian readers." Estab. 1988. Circ. 200. Pays on publication. Publishes ms an average of 1 year after acceptance. Byline given. Buys first North American serial and second serial (reprint) rights. Editorial lead time 1 year. Accepts queries by mail, e-mail. Accepts simultaneous submissions. Responds in 6 weeks to queries; 6 months to mss. Sample copy for $4.95. Writer's guidelines for #10 SASE or on website.

Fiction: Experimental, fantasy, humorous, mainstream, mystery, novel excerpts, religious, science fiction, slice-of-life vignettes. "We do not publish stories that glorify violence or perversity." **Buys 10 mss/year.** Send complete ms. Length: 2,000-6,000 words. **Pays ½¢/word.**

$ DREAMS OF DECADENCE, P.O. Box 2988, Radford VA 24143-2988. (540)763-2925. Fax: (540)763-2924. E-mail: dnapublications@iname.com. Website: sfsite.com/dnaweb/home.htm. **Contact:** Angela Kessler, editor. Quarterly literary magazine featuring vampire fiction and poetry. Pays on publication. Publishes ms an average of 6 months after acceptance. Buys first North American serial rights. Accepts simultaneous submissions. Responds in 1 month. Sample copy for $5. Writer's guidelines for #10 SASE or on website.
Fiction: "I like elegant prose with a Gothic feel. The emphasis is on dark fantasy rather than horror. No vampire feeds, vampire has sex, someone becomes a vampire pieces." **Buys 30-40 mss/year.** Send complete ms. Length: 1,000-15,000 words. **Pays 1-5¢/word.**
Poetry: "Looking for all forms; however, the less horrific and the more explicitly vampiric a poem is, the more likely it is to be accepted." Pays in copies.
Tips: "We look for atmospheric, well-written stories with original ideas, not rehashes."

N $ ▣ 1812, A Magazine of New Writing & the Arts, New Writing, Box 1812, Amherst NY 14226-7812. E-mail: 1812@newwriting.com. Website: www.newwriting.com. Managing Editor: Richard Lynch. **Contact:** Sam Meade, co-editor. **98% freelance written.** Annual online literary magazine. "*1812* is a magazine for new writers, new writing and new ways. Hopefully a war of sorts, a revolution and attempt to change the old guard." Estab. 1989. Pays on publication. Publishes ms an average of 6 months after acceptance. Byline given. Not copyrighted. Buys electronic rights. Editorial lead time 4 months. Accepts queries by mail, e-mail. Accepts simultaneous submissions. Responds in 1 month to queries; 4 months to mss. Sample copy and writer's guidelines free or online at website.
Nonfiction: Essays, how-to, interview/profile (unusual/philosophy writing associated). "No static prose." **Buys 1 ms/year.** Send complete ms. Length: 500 words. **Pays $50.**
Reprints: Accepts previously published submissions.
Photos: State availability of photos with submission. Reviews 35mm transparencies. Offers no additional payment for photos accepted with ms. Captions, model releases and identification of subjects required.
Fiction: Richard Lynch, co-editor. Experimental, mainstream, slice-of-life vignettes, contemporary, literary, new forms. "No death-from-cancer stories, I woke up stories, stories about cars and family trips, stories the writer never read over to edit." **Buys 5 mss/year.** Send complete ms. **Pays $50.**
Poetry: Avant garde, free verse. "No light verse, love poems, kiss poems, musty poems, poems that rhyme so fluently that they don't mean anything." **Buys 5-10 poems/year.** Submit maximum 4 poems. Length: 3 lines. **Pays $25.**
Tips: "E-mail submissions are becoming popular and they are easy to respond to. Don't send attachments—cut and paste the text. We are looking for interesting, not a résumé or list of publications."

$ $ EVENT, Douglas College, P.O. Box 2503, New Westminster, British Columbia V3L 5B2 Canada. (604)527-5293. Fax: (604)527-5095. E-mail: event@douglas.bc.ca. **Contact:** Ian Cockfield, assistant editor. **100% freelance written.** Triannual magazine containing fiction, poetry, creative nonfiction and reviews. "We are eclectic and always open to content that invites involvement. Generally, we like strong narrative." Estab. 1971. Circ. 1,100. Pays on publication. Publishes ms an average of 8 months after acceptance. Byline given. Buys first North American serial rights. Accepts queries by mail, fax, phone. No e-mail submissions. All submissions must include SASE (Canadian postage or international reply coupons only). Accepts simultaneous submissions. Responds in 1 month to queries; 4 months to mss. Sample copy for $5. Guidelines for #10 SASE.
• *Event* does not read manuscripts in July.
Fiction: Christine Dewar, fiction editor. "We look for readability, style and writing that invites involvement." **Buys 12-15 mss/year.** Send complete ms. Length: 5,000 words. Submit maximum 2 stories. **Pays $22/page to $500.**
Poetry: Gillian Harding-Russell, poetry editor. Free verse and prose poems. No light verse. "In poetry, we tend to appreciate the narrative and sometimes the confessional modes." **Buys 30-40 poems/year.** Submit maximum 10 poems. **Pays $25-500.**

$ FIELD MAGAZINE, Contemporary Poetry & Poetics, 10 N. Professor St., Oberlin College, Oberlin OH 44074-1095. (440)775-8408. Fax: (440)775-8124. E-mail: ocpress@oberlin.edu. Website: www.oberlin.edu/~ocpress. Business Manager: Linda Slocum. **Contact:** David Young, David Walker, Pamela Alexander, Martha Collins, Alberta Turner, editors. **60% freelance written.** Semiannual magazine of poetry, poetry in translation, and essays on contemporary poetry by poets. Estab. 1969. Circ. 2,300. Pays on publication. Byline given. Buys first rights. Editorial lead time 4 months. Accepts queries by mail, e-mail, fax, phone. No electronic submissions. Responds in 1 month to mss. Sample copy for $7. Writer's guidelines on website.
Poetry: Buys 100 poems/year. Submit maximum 10 poems. **Pays $20/page.**

$ FRANK, An International Journal of Contemporary Writing & Art, Association Frank, 32 rue Edouard Vaillant, Montreuil France. Phone: (33)(1)48596658. Fax: (31)(1)48596668. E-mail: david@paris-anglo.com. Website: www.paris-anglo.com/frank. **Contact:** David Applefield, editor. **80% freelance written.** Bilingual magazine covering contemporary writing of all genres. "Writing that takes risks and isn't ethnocentric is looked upon favorably." Estab. 1983. Circ. 4,000. Pays on publication. Publishes ms an average of 1 year after acceptance. Byline given. Buys one-time rights. Editorial lead time 6 months. Responds in 1 month to queries; 2 months to mss. Sample copy for $10. Writer's guidelines for #10 SASE or on website.
Nonfiction: Interview/profile, travel. **Buys 2 mss/year.** Query. **Pays $100.** Pays in contributor copies by agreement.
Photos: State availability of photos with submission. Negotiates payment individually. Buys one-time rights.

Fiction: Experimental, international, novel excerpts. **Buys 8 mss/year.** Send complete ms. Length: 1-3,000 words. **Pays $10/printed page.**

Poetry: Avant-garde, translations. **Buys 20 poems/year.** Submit maximum 10 poems. **Pays $20.**

Tips: "Suggest what you do or know best. Avoid query form letters—we won't read the ms. Looking for excellent literary/cultural interviews with leading American writers or cultural figures."

N. $ FUTURES MAGAZINE, 3039 38th Ave., Minneapolis MN 55406-2140. (612)724-4023. E-mail: barbl@tele. com. Website: www.firetowrite.com. Editor: Barbara (Babs) Lakey. **Contact:** Kit Sloane, associate editor. **98% freelance written.** Bimonthly literary magazine. "We nourish writers and artists; attempt to throw out the net so they can fly without fear! The futures in commodities is a good analog for writers and artists. Their work, in many cases, is greatly undervalued. Their future market value will be higher than can be imagined. In the writing community there is a tremendous amount of energy; a rolling boil. It takes the form of many people with talent and motivation anxious to unleash their creative juices." Estab. 1998. Circ. 2,000. Pays on publication. Publishes ms an average of 8 months after acceptance. Byline given. Editorial lead time 8 months. Submit seasonal material 6 months in advance. Accepts queries by e-mail. Accepts simultaneous submissions. Responds in 1 week to queries; 1 month to mss. Sample copy for $3.75 includes shipping. Writer's guidelines for #10 SASE, on website or by e-mail.

Nonfiction: Babs Lakey, editor. Essays, exposé, general interest, historical/nostalgic, how-to (craft screenwriting), humor, inspirational on writing, interview/profile, new product, opinion, personal experience, photo feature, technical, success stories with a point. "No political ranting or sappy memoirs." **Buys 50 mss/year.** Query. Length: 250-2,000 words. **Pays $10-50.**

Columns/Departments: Marcia Rendon, editor. Starting Line (fiction from first time publications), 1,000-4,000 words; Writers Share (comments on life of a writer), 100 words. **Buys 60 mss/year.** Send complete ms. **Pays $5-25.**

Fiction: Adventure, ethnic, experimental, fantasy, historical, horror, humorous, mainstream, mystery, romance, science fiction, suspense, western. **Buys 120-150 mss/year.** Send complete ms. Length: 4,500 words. **Pays $5-25.**

Poetry: RC Hildebrandt, editor. Avant garde, free verse, light verse, traditional, narrative. **Buys 40-80 poems/year.** Submit maximum 5 poems. **Pays $2-5.**

Fillers: Illustrations with humor. **Pays $5-25.**

Tips: "Reading what we have published is still the best but we do love to see excitement and enthusiasm for the craft, and those who care enough to self-edit. Send SASE for anything you want returned and do not send mail that requires a signature on arrival. Give us a try. We want to see you succeed."

$ THE GETTYSBURG REVIEW, Gettysburg College, Gettysburg PA 17325. (717)337-6770. Managing Editor: Cara Diaconoff. **Contact:** Peter Stitt, editor. Quarterly literary magazine. "Our concern is quality. Manuscripts submitted here should be extremely well-written." Estab. 1988. Circ. 4,000. Pays on publication. Byline given. Buys first North American serial rights. Editorial lead time 1 year. Submit seasonal material 9 months in advance. Accepts queries by mail, fax. No simultaneous submissions. Responds in 1 month to queries; 3 months to mss. Sample copy for $7. Writer's guidelines for #10 SASE. Reading period September-May.

Nonfiction: Essays. **Buys 20/year.** Send complete ms. Length: 3,000-7,000. **Pays $25/page.**

Fiction: High quality, literary. Publishes novel excerpts. **Buys 20 ms/year.** Send complete ms. Length: 2,000-7,000. **Pays $25/page.**

Poetry: **Buys 50 poems/year.** Submit maximum 3 poems. **Pays $2/line.**

⊠ $ $ GLIMMER TRAIN STORIES, Glimmer Train Press, Inc., 710 SW Madison St., #504, Portland OR 97205. (503)221-0836. Fax: (503)221-0837. Website: www.glimmertrain.com. Co-editor: Susan Burmeister-Brown. **Contact:** Linda Burmeister Davies, co-editor. **90% freelance written.** Quarterly magazine covering short fiction. "We are interested in well-written, emotionally-moving short stories published by unknown, as well as known, writers." Estab. 1991. Circ. 16,000. **Pays on acceptance.** Byline given. Buys first rights. Accepts simultaneous submissions. Responds in 3 months to mss. Sample copy for $9.95 or on website. Writer's guidelines for #10 SASE or on website.

Fiction: "We are not restricted to any types. We don't see enough well-written humor." **Buys 32 mss/year.** Send complete ms. Length: 1,200-8,000 words. **Pays $500.**

● Ranked as one of the best markets for fiction writers in *Writer's Digest* magazine's "Fiction 50," June 2000.

Tips: "Manuscripts should be sent to us in the months of January, April, July and October. Be sure to include a sufficiently-stamped SASE. We are particularly interested in receiving work from new writers." See *Glimmer Train's* contest listings in Contest and Awards section.

$ GRAIN LITERARY MAGAZINE, Saskatchewan Writers Guild, P.O. Box 1154, Regina, Saskatchewan S4P 3B4 Canada. (306)244-2828. Fax: (306)244-0255. E-mail: grain.mag@sk.sympatico.ca. Website: www.skwriter.com. Business Administrator: Jennifer Still. **Contact:** Elizabeth Philips, editor. **100% freelance written.** Quarterly literary magazine covering poetry, fiction, creative nonfiction, drama. "*Grain* publishes writing of the highest quality, both traditional and innovative in nature. The *Grain* editors' aim: To publish work that challenges readers; to encourage promising new writers; and to produce a well-designed, visually interesting magazine." Estab. 1973. Circ. 1,500. Pays on publication. Publishes ms an average of 11 months after acceptance. Byline given. Buys first, Canadian, serial rights. Editorial lead time 6 months. Accepts queries by mail, e-mail, fax, phone. Responds in 1 month to queries; 4 months to mss. Sample copy for $8 or on website. Writer's guidelines for #10 SASE or on website.

Nonfiction: Interested in creative nonfiction.

Photos: Review transparencies and prints. Submit 12-20 slides and b&w prints, short statement (200 words) and brief resume. Pays $100 for front cover art, $30/photo.

Fiction: Literary fiction of all types. "No romance, confession, science fiction, vignettes, mystery." **Buys 40 mss/year.** Query or send 2 stories maximum or 30 pages of novel-in-progress and SAE with postage or IRCs. Does not accept e-mail submissions, but will respond by e-mail—save on stamps. **Pays $40-175.**

• Ranked as one of the best markets for fiction writers in *Writer's Digest* magazine's "Fiction 50," June 2000.

Poetry: Avant-garde, free verse, haiku, traditional. "High quality, imaginative, well-crafted poetry. No sentimental, end-line rhyme, mundane." **Buys 78 poems/year.** Submit maximum 10 poems and SASE with postage or IRCs. **Pays $40-175.**

Tips: "Sweat the small stuff. Pay attention to detail, credibility. Make sure you have researched your piece and that the literal and metaphorical support on another."

$ $ $ $ GRANTA, The Magazine of New Writing, 2-3 Hanover Yard, Noel Rd., London NI 8BE England. Phone: 0701 704 9776. Fax: 0701 704 0474. E-mail: editorial@grantamag.co.uk. **Contact:** Ian Jack, editor. Quarterly magazine. "*Granta* magazine publishes fiction, reportage, biography and autobiography, travel and documentary photography. It rarely publishes 'writing about writing.' The realistic narrative—the story—is its primary form." *Granta* has been called "the most impressive literary magazine of its time" by the *London Daily Telegraph*, and has published Salman Rushdie, Martin Amis, Saul Bellow and Paul Theroux, among others. Estab. 1979. Circ. 90,000. Pays on publication. Rights purchased vary. Responds in 1 month to queries; up to 4 months to mss.

Nonfiction: Reportage, biography, autobiography, travel.

Fiction: Literary. No fantasy, science fiction, romance, historical, occult or other genre fiction. **Buys 1-2 mss/year.** Query by mail. Length: varies. **Pays £75-5,000** (British pounds).

Tips: "We're looking for the best in realistic narrative or stories—originality of voice or subject, without jargon, contrivance or self-conscious 'performance.' Either the story or your treatment of it should be, in some way, unique. If it's a nonfiction piece, it must have a story and yet not neglect facts entirely. If it's fiction, originality and personality certainly count." No poetry and no e-mail submissions.

$ HAPPY, 240 E. 35th St., Suite 11A, New York NY 10016. E-mail: bayardx@aol.com. **Contact:** Bayard, editor. Pays on publication. Byline given. Buys one-time rights. Accepts queries by mail, e-mail. Accepts simultaneous submissions. Responds in 1 month to mss. Sample copy for $12. Writer's guidelines for #10 SASE.

Reprints: Accepts previously published submissions.

Fiction: Novel excerpts, short stories. "We accept anything that's beautifully written. Genre isn't important. It just has to be incredible writing." **Buys 100-130 mss/year.** Send complete ms with cover letter. Length: 250-5,000 words. **Pays $5/1,000 words.**

• Ranked as one of the best markets for fiction writers in *Writer's Digest* magazine's "Fiction 50," June 2000.

Tips: "Don't bore us with the mundane—blast us out of the water with the extreme!"

$ HIGH PLAINS LITERARY REVIEW, 180 Adams St., Suite 250, Denver CO 80206. (303)320-6828. Fax: (303)320-0463. Managing Editor: Phyllis A. Harwell. **Contact:** Robert O. Greer, Jr., editor-in-chief. **80% freelance written.** Triannual literary magazine. "The *High Plains Literary Review* publishes short stories, essays, poetry, reviews and interviews, bridging the gap between commercial quarterlies and academic reviews." Estab. 1986. Circ. 1,200. Pays on publication. Byline given. Buys first North American serial rights. Accepts simultaneous submissions. Responds in 3 months. Sample copy for $4. Writer's guidelines for #10 SASE.

• Its unique editorial format—between commercial and academic—makes for lively reading. Could be good market for that "in between" story.

Nonfiction: Essays, reviews. **Buys 20 mss/year.** Send complete ms. Length: 10,000 words maximum. **Pays $5/page.**

Fiction: Ethnic, historical, humorous, mainstream. **Buys 12 mss/year.** Send complete ms. Length: 10,000 words maximum. **Pays $5/page.**

Poetry: **Buys 45 poems/year. Pays $10/page.**

N $ ▣ HOTREAD.COM, Quality Literature for Discerning Readers, HotRead.com, P.O. Box 2833, Iowa City IA 52244. E-mail: HotReadQ@Yahoo.com. Website: www.HotRead.com. **Contact:** Susan Benton, editor/co-founder or Brett Williams. **100% freelance written.** Online site selling short fiction and nonfiction. "We have no particular slant or philosophy. Nonfiction should read more like fiction with some detail setting, characterization as well as facts. We want all kinds of pieces that will appeal to a variety of age groups and audiences." Estab. 1999. Pays quarterly for sales during the previous 3 months—within 30 days of end of quarter. Publishes ms an average of 1 month after acceptance. Byline given. "Uses contract including minimum exclusive posting time of one quarter. Authors maintain copyright throughout." Submit seasonal material 3 months in advance. Accepts queries by e-mail. Accepts simultaneous submissions. Responds in 1 month. Writer's guidelines online at website.

Nonfiction: Essays, personal experience, memoirs. **Buys unlimited mss/year.** Send complete ms. Length: 1,000-10,000 words. **Pays 40¢ per story purchased during the previous quarter.** We sometimes offer a premium in addition to payment.

Reprints: Accepts previously published submissions.

Fiction: Adventure, fantasy, historical, horror, humorous, mainstream, mystery, romance, science fiction, slice-of-life vignettes, suspense, western, inspirational. "No erotica, pornography, extreme violence, graphic sex." **Buys unlimited mss/year.** Send complete ms. Length: 1,000-10,000 words. **Pays 40¢ per story sold during the previous quarter.**
Tips: "If you are previously unpublished, please solicit critique from a writer's group first, if possible. Do not send early drafts. A story that has been re-written is always improved. We want clean, tight writing and well-told stories that readers can relate to. Promising stories will be edited for free if changes are minor. We rarely publish without suggesting some edits."

$ INDIANA REVIEW, Indiana University, Ballantine Hall 465, 1020 E. Kirkwood, Bloomington IN 47405-7103. (812)855-3439. Website: www.indiana.edu/~inreview/ir.html. Editors change yearly. **100% freelance written.** Biannual magazine. "*Indiana Review*, a non-profit organization run by IU graduate students, is a journal of previously unpublished poetry and fiction. Literary interviews and essays also considered. We publish innovative fiction and poetry. We're interested in energy, originality and careful attention to craft. While we publish many well-known writers, we also welcome new and emerging poets and fiction writers." Estab. 1982. Pays on publication. Byline given. Buys first North American serial rights. Responds within 3 months. Sample copy for $8. Writer's guidelines for SASE or on website.
 O⤳ Break in with 500-1,000 word book reviews of fiction, poetry, nonfiction and literary criticism published within the last 2 years, "since this is the area in which there's the least amount of competition."
Nonfiction: Essays. No strictly academic articles dealing with the traditional canon. Length: 9,000 maximum. **Pays $5/page.**
Fiction: Experimental, mainstream, novel excerpts. "We look for daring stories which integrate theme, language, character and form. We like polished writing, humor and fiction which has consequence beyond the world of its narrator." **Buys 12 mss/year.** Send complete ms. Length: 250-15,000. **Pays $5/page.**
Poetry: Avant-garde, free verse. Looks for inventive and skillful writing. **Buys 80 mss/year.** Submit up to 5 poems at one time only. Length: 5 lines minimum. **Pays $5/page.**
Tips: "We're always looking for non-fiction essays that go beyond merely autobiographical revelation and utilize sophisticated organization and slightly radical narrative strategies. We want essays that are both lyrical and analytical where confession does not mean nostalgia. Read us before you submit. Often reading is slower in summer and holiday months. Only submit work to journals you would proudly subscribe to, then subscribe to a few. Take care to read the latest two issues and specifically mention work you identify with and why. Submit work that 'stacks up' with the work we've published."

$ INDIGENOUS FICTION, I.F. Publishing, P.O. Box 2078, Redmond WA 98073-2078. E-mail: deckr@earthlink.net. **Contact:** Sherry Decker, managing editor. **98% freelance written**. Triannual magazine covering short fiction, poetry and art. "We want literary—fantasy, dark fantasy, science fiction, horror, mystery and mainstream. We enjoy elements of the supernatural or the unexplained, odd, intriguing characters and beautiful writing. Most accepted stories will be between 2,500-4,500 words in length." Estab. 1998. Circ. 300. Pays on publication. Publishes ms an average of 6 months after acceptance. Byline given. Buys first North American serial and second serial (reprint) rights. Editorial lead time 6 months. Submit seasonal material 6 months in advance. Accepts simultaneous submissions. Responds in 2 weeks to queries; 1 month to mss. Sample copy for $6. Writer's guidelines for SASE.
Fiction: Adventure, experimental, fantasy, dark fantasy, horror, humorous, mainstream, mystery, science fiction, suspense, odd, bizarre, supernatural and the unexplained. "No porn, abuse of children, gore; no it was all a dream, evil cat, unicorn or sweet nostalgic tales. No vignettes or slice-of-life (without beginning, middle and end)." **Buys 30 mss/year.** Send complete ms, cover letter, SASE and credits. Length: 500-8,000 words, usually 2,000-4,500 words. **Pays $5-20 and one contributor's copy.**
Poetry: Free verse, haiku, light verse, traditional. No poetry that neither tells a story nor evokes an image. **Buys 20 poems/year.** Submit maximum 5 poems. Length: 3-30 lines. **Pays $5.**
Fillers: Short humor. **Buys 6/year.** Length: 100-500 words. **Pays $5.**
Tips: "Proper manuscript format; no e-mail or fax submissions. No disks unless asked. We like beautiful, literary writing where something happens in the story. By literary we don't mean a long, rambling piece of beautiful writing for the sake of beauty—we mean characters and situations, fully developed, beautifully. Ghosts, time travel, parallel words, 'the bizarre'—fine! Vampires? Well, okay, but no clichés or media tie-ins. Vampire tales should be bone-chillingly dark, beautiful, erotic or humorous. Everything else has been done. Also, no deals with devil; revenge stories; gullible fool meets sexy vampire, ghost or disguised ghoul in a bar; gratuitous sex; traditional mysteries. Writers we admire: Joyce Carol Oates, Ray Bradbury, Pat Conroy, Dale Bailey, Tanith Lee."

⊠ $ THE IOWA REVIEW, 369 EPB, The University of Iowa, Iowa City IA 52242. (319)335-0462. Fax: (319)335-2535. E-mail: iareview@blue.weeg.uiowa.edu. Website: www.uiowa.edu/~iareview/. Editor: David Hamilton. Triannual magazine. Estab. 1970. Buys first North American and non-exclusive anthology, classroom and online serial rights. Responds in 3 months. Sample copy and writer's guidelines for $6 or on website.
 • This magazine uses the help of colleagues and graduate assistants. Its reading period is September-January 31.
Nonfiction, Fiction and Poetry: "We publish essays, reviews, novel excerpts, stories and poems and would like for our essays not always to be works of academic criticism. We have no set guidelines as to content or length." **Buys 65-85 unsolicited mss/year.** Submit complete ms with SASE. **Pays $1/line for verse; $10/page for prose.**
 • Ranked as one of the best markets for fiction writers in *Writer's Digest* magazine's annual "Fiction 50," June 2000.

$ JAPANOPHILE PRESS, P.O. Box 7977, 415 N. Main St., Ann Arbor MI 48107. E-mail: jpnhand@japanophile.c om. Website: www.japanophile.com. **Contact:** Susan Aitken, editor or Ashby Kinch, associate editor. **80% freelance written.** Works with a small number of new/unpublished writers each year. Quarterly magazine for literate people interested in Japanese culture anywhere in the world. Estab. 1974. Pays on publication. Publishes ms an average of 3 months after acceptance. Buys first North American serial rights. Accepts queries by mail, e-mail. Responds in 3 months. Sample copy for $5, postpaid or on website. Writer's guidelines for #10 SASE or on website.

    O→ Break in with "nonfiction articles or short personal essays. We're also looking for nonfiction with photos, movie reviews, short short stories and Japan-related illustration.

Nonfiction: "We want material on Japanese culture in *North America or anywhere in the world*, even Japan. We want articles, preferably with pictures, about persons engaged in arts of Japanese origin: a Virginia naturalist who is a haiku poet, a potter who learned raku in Japan, a vivid 'I was there' account of a Go tournament in California. We would like to hear more about what it's like to be a Japanese in the U.S. Our particular slant is a certain kind of culture wherever it is in the world: Canada, the U.S., Europe, Japan. The culture includes flower arranging, haiku, sports, religion, travel, art, photography, fiction, etc. It is important to study the magazine." **Buys 8 mss/issue.** Query preferred but not required. Length: 1,800 words maximum. **Pays $8-25.**

Reprints: Send information about when and where the article was previously published. Pays up to 100% of amount paid for original article.

Photos: Pays $10-50 for glossy prints. "We prefer b&w people pictures."

Columns/Departments: Regular columns and features are Tokyo Topics and Japan in North America. "We also need columns about Japanese culture in various American cities." Query. Length: 1,000 words. **Pays $1-20.**

Fiction: Experimental, mainstream, mystery, adventure, humorous, romance, historical. Themes should relate to Japan or Japanese culture. Length: 1,000-4,000 words. Annual contest pays $100 to best short story (contest reading fee $5). Should include 1 or more Japanese and non-Japanese characters in each story.

Poetry: Traditional, avant-garde and light verse related to Japanese culture or any subject in a Japanese form such as haiku. Length: 3-50 lines. **Pays $1-20.**

Fillers: Newsbreaks, clippings and short humor of up to 200 words. **Pays $1-5.**

Tips: "We want to see more articles about Japanese culture worldwide, including unexpected places, but especially U.S., Canada and Europe. Lack of convincing fact and detail is a frequent mistake."

$ THE JOURNAL, Ohio State University, 421 Denney Hall, 164 W. 17th Ave., Columbus OH 43210. (614)292-4076. Fax: (614)292-7816. E-mail: thejournal05@postbox.acs.ohio-state.edu. Website: www.cohums.ohio-state.edu/english/ journals/the_journal/homepage.htm. **Contact:** Kathy Fagan, Michelle Herman, editors. **100% freelance written.** Semi-annual literary magazine. "We're open to all forms; we tend to favor work that gives evidence of a mature and sophisticated sense of the language." Estab. 1972. Circ. 1,500. Pays on publication. Byline given. Buys first North American serial rights. Responds in 2 weeks to queries; 2 months to mss. Sample copy for $7 or on website. Writer's guidelines for #10 SASE or on website.

Nonfiction: Essays, interview/profile. **Buys 2 mss/year.** Query by mail only. Length: 2,000-4,000 words. **Pays $25 maximum**.

Columns/Departments: Reviews of contemporary poetry, 2,000-4,000 words. **Buys 2 mss/year.** Query by mail only. **Pays $25.**

Fiction: Novel excerpts, literary short stories. **Pays $25 minimum.**

Poetry: Avant-garde, free verse, traditional. **Buys 100 poems/year.** Submit maximum 5 poems/year. **Pays $25.**

$ KALLIOPE, a journal of women's literature & art, Florida Community College at Jacksonville, 3939 Roosevelt Blvd., Jacksonville FL 32205. (904)381-3511. Website: www.fccj.org/kalliope. **Contact:** Mary Sue Koeppel, editor. **100% freelance written.** Triannual magazine. "*Kalliope* publishes poetry, short fiction, reviews, and b&w art, usually by women artists. We look for artistic excellence." Estab. 1978. Circ. 1,600. Pays on publication. Publishes ms an average of 3 months after acceptance. Buys first rights. Responds in 1 week to queries. Sample copy for $7 (recent issue) or $4 (back copy) or see sample articles on website. Writer's guidelines for #10 SASE or on website.

Nonfiction: Q&A/interview/profile, reviews of new works of poetry and fiction. **Buys 6 mss/year.** Send complete ms. Length: 500-2,000 words. **Pays $10 honorarium if funds are available**.

    ● *Kalliope's* reading period is September through May.

Fiction: Ethnic, experimental, literay, novel excerpts. **Buys 12 mss/year.** Send complete ms. Length: 100-2,000 words. **Pays $10 if funds are available.**

Photos: Visual art should be sent in groups of 4-10 works. We require b&w professional quality, glossy prints made from negatives. Please supply photo credits, date of work, title, medium, and size on the back of each photo submitted. Include artist's resume and model releases where applicable. We welcome an artist's statement of 50-75 words.

Poetry: Avant-garde, free verse, haiku, traditional. **Buys 75 poems/year.** Submit 3-5 poems. Length: 2-120 lines. **Pays $10** if finances permit.

Tips: "We publish the best of the material submitted to us each issue. (We don't build a huge backlog and then publish from that backlog for years.) Although we look for new writers and usually publish several with each issue alongside already established writers, we love it when established writers send us their work. We've recently published Tess Gallagher, Enid Shomer and one of the last poems by Denise Levertov. Send a bio with all submissions."

$ THE KENYON REVIEW, Kenyon College, Gambier OH 43022. (740)427-5208. Fax: (740)427-5417. E-mail: kenyonreview@kenyon.edu. Website: www.kenyonreview.org. **Contact:** David H. Lynn, editor. **100% freelance written.** Triannual magazine covering contemporary literature and criticism. "An international journal of literature, culture and the arts dedicated to an inclusive representation of the best in new writing, interviews and criticism from established and emerging writers." Estab. 1939. Circ. 4,500. Pays on publication. Publishes ms 1 year after acceptance. Byline given. Buys first rights. Editorial lead time 1 year. Submit seasonal material 1 year in advance. Sample copy for $8 or on website. Writer's guidelines for 4×9 SASE or on website.

$ THE KIT-CAT REVIEW, 244 Halstead Ave., Harrison NY 10528. (914)835-4833. **Contact:** Claudia Fletcher, editor. **100% freelance written.** Quarterly literary magazine. "*The Kit-Cat Review* is named after the 18th Century Kit-Cat Club, whose members included Addison, Steele, Congreve, Vanbrugh and Garth. Its purpose is to promote/discover excellence and originality. Some issues are part anthology." Estab. 1998. Circ. 200. **Pays on acceptance.** Byline given. Buys one-time rights. Accepts queries by mail, phone. Responds in 1 week to queries, 1 month to mss. Sample copy $7, payable to Claudia Fletcher.

Nonfiction: Book excerpts, essays, general interest, historical/nostalgic, humor, interview/profile, personal experience, travel. **Buys 2 mss/year.** Send complete ms. Length: up to 6,000 words. **Pays $25-100.**

Fiction: Experimental, novel excerpts, slice-of-life vignettes. No stories with "O. Henry-type formula endings." **Buys 20 mss/year.** Send complete ms. Length: up to 6,000 words. **Pays $25-100.**

Poetry: Free verse, traditional. No excessively obscure poetry. **Buys 100 poems/year.** Two issues (spring, autumn) include a poetry award of $1000. **Pays $10-100.**

Tips: "Obtaining a sample copy is strongly suggested."

N $ KRATER QUARTERLY, Block M Press, P.O. Box 1371, Lincoln Park MI 48146. E-mail: kraterquarterly@aol. com. Website: www.kraterquarterly.com. **Contact:** Leonard D. Fritz, editor. **80% freelance written.** "Quarterly literary and arts magazine of outstanding short fiction, creative non-fiction and poetry. Open to working with beginning writers as well as established writers. Estab. 1999. Circ. 4,000. Pays on publication. Publishes ms an average of 6 months after acceptance. Byline given. No kill fee. Buys first rights; rights revert to author upon publication. Accepts queries by mail, e-mail. Accepts simultaneous submissions. Responds in 1 month to queries; 2 months to mss. Sample copy for $5. Writer's guidelines for #10 SASE.

Photos: State availability of photos with submission. Reviews 5×7 or 8×10 b&w prints only. Offers no additional payment for photos accepted with ms. Offers $10-25/photo. Model releases required. Buys one-time rights.

Fiction: Mainstream, literary. "No genre fiction, unless innovative in style and language. Novel excerpts, book reviews, plays and literary criticism are *never* considered." **Buys 25 mss/year.** Send complete ms. Length: 750-5,000 words. **Pays $50-150.**

Poetry: Avant garde, free verse, traditional, prose poems. **Buys 15 poems/year.** Submit 5 poems maximum. Length: 10-75 lines. **Pays $10-25.**

Tips: "Obviously, read us before submitting so that material is appropriate. Don't send submissions on disk; let's stick with paper. Include brief cover letter about author and priors. Submit one stylish, high-quality story (in professional format) per mailing, please. We cannot respond to submissions without enclosed SASE. New writers welcome. We will not accept submissions from April 1 through September 1."

★ $ LEGIONS OF LIGHT, Box 874, Margaretville, NY 12455. Phone/fax: (914)586-2759. E-mail: dancing_hawk @yahoo.com. Website: www.stepahead.net/~lol/legions.htm. **Contact:** Elizabeth Mami, editor, or Shirley Brown, assistant editor. **100% freelance written.** Bimonthly magazine. "*Legions of Light* accepts all material except graphic violence or sex. All ages read the magazine, all subjects welcomed." Estab. 1990. Circ. 2,000. Pays on publication. Publishes ms an average of 2 years after acceptance. Byline sometimes given. Buys one-time rights. Editorial lead time 4 months. Submit seasonal material 6 months in advance. Accepts queries by mail, e-mail, phone. Accepts simultaneous submissions. Responds in 6 weeks to queries. Sample copy for $3 or on website. Guidelines for #10 SASE or on website.

Nonfiction: Historical/nostalgic, humor, inspirational, humor/profile, personal experience, religious. No graphic violence or adult material. **Buys 10-20 mss/year.** Send complete ms. Length: 500-1,500 words. **Pays $5-10.**

Reprints: Accepts previously published submissions. Send photocopy of article or short story. Publishes novel excerpts.

Photos: State availability of photos with submission. Reviews 3×5 prints. Offers no additional payment for photos accepted with ms. Identification of subjects required. Buys one-time rights.

Fiction: Adventure, ethnic, experimental, fantasy, historical, horror, humorous, mainstream, mystery, religious, romance, science fiction, slice-of-life vignettes, suspense, western. No adult or graphic violence. **Buys 20-30 mss/year.** Query or send complete ms. Length: 1,500 words maximum. **Pays $5-10.**

Poetry: Avant-garde, free verse, haiku, light verse, traditional. No erotica. **Buys 15-20 poems/year. Pays $5-10.**

▣ The online magazine carries original content not found in the print edition and includes writer's guidelines.

Fillers: Anecdotes, facts, newsbreaks, short humor. **Buys 5-15/year. Pays $5-10.**

Tips: "*Legions of Light* caters to unpublished talent, especially children. Subscribers are used first, but subscribing is *not* a requirement to be accepted for publication. All are accepted, but due to overload, it does take time to actually get published. *All will though.* Calls and reminders are encouraged. I eventually get every one in."

$ LIBIDO, The Journal of Sex & Sensibility, Libido, Inc., 5318 N. Paulina St., Chicago IL 60640. (773)275-0842. Fax: (773)275-0752. E-mail: rune@mcs.com. Website: www.Libidomag.com. Co-editors: Marianna Beck and Jack Hafferkamp. **Contact:** J.L. Beck, submissions editor. **50% freelance written.** Quarterly magazine covering literate erotica. "*Libido* is about sexuality. Orientation is not an issue, writing ability is. The aim is to enlighten as often as it is to arouse. Humor—sharp and smart—is important, so are safer sex contexts." Estab. 1988. Circ. 10,000. Pays on publication. Byline given. Kill fee "rare, but negotiable." Buys one-time or second serial (reprint) rights. Editorial lead time 3 months. Submit seasonal material 4 months in advance. Responds in 6 months. Sample copy for $8. Writer's guidelines for #10 SASE.

Nonfiction: Book excerpts, essays, historical/nostalgic, humor, photo feature, travel. "No violence, sexism or misty memoirs." **Buys 10-20 mss/year.** Send complete ms. Length: 300-2,500 words. **Pays $50 minimum for assigned articles; $15 minimum for unsolicited articles.** Pays contributor copies "when money isn't an issue and copies or other considerations have equal or higher value." Sometimes pays expenses of writers on assignment.

Reprints: Send photocopy of article or short story or typed ms with rights for sale noted and information about when and where the material previously appeared. Pays 100% of amount paid for an original article.

Photos: Reviews contact sheets and 5×7 and 8×10 prints. Negotiates payment individually. Model releases required. Buys one-time rights.

Fiction: Erotica, short novel excerpts. **Buys 20 mss/year.** Send complete ms. Length: 800-2,500 words. **Pays $50-100.**

Poetry: Uses humorous short erotic poetry. No limericks. **Buys 10 poems/year.** Submit maximum 3 poems. **Pays $25.**

Tips: "*Libido*'s guidelines are purposely simple and loose. All sexual orientations are appreciated. The only taboos are exploitative and violent sex. Send us a manuscript—make it short, sharp and with a lead that makes us want to read. If we're not hooked by paragraph three, we reject the manuscript."

[N] $ LITERARY MAGAZINE REVIEW, Department of English Language and Literature, University of Northern Iowa, Cedar Falls IA 50614-0502. (319)273-2821. Fax: (319)273-5807. E-mail: grant.tracey@uni.edu. **Contact:** Grant Tracey, editor. **98% freelance written.** Quarterly magazine devoted almost exclusively to reviews of the current contents of small circulation serials publishing some fiction or poetry. "Most of our reviewers are recommended to us by third parties." Estab. 1981. Circ. 500. Pays on publication. Publishes ms an average of 1 month after acceptance. Byline given. Buys first rights. Accepts queries by mail, e-mail. Responds in 2 weeks. *Writer's Market* recommends allowing 2 months for reply. Sample copy for $5.

Nonfiction: **Buys 60 mss/year.** Query. Length: 1,500 words. **Pays $25 maximum** and 2 contributor's copies for assigned articles. Sometimes pays expenses of writers on assignment.

Photos: State availability of photos with submission. Identification of subjects required.

Tips: "Interested in omnibus reviews of magazines sharing some quality, editorial philosophy, or place of origin and in articles about literary magazine editing and the literary magazine scene."

$ $ THE MALAHAT REVIEW, The University of Victoria, P.O. Box 1700, STN CSC, Victoria, British Columbia V8W 2Y2 Canada. (250)721-8524. E-mail: malahat@uvic.ca (for queries only). Website: web.uvic.ca/malahat. **Contact:** Marlene Cookshaw editor. **100% freelance written.** Eager to work with new/unpublished writers. Quarterly covering poetry, fiction, drama and reviews. Estab. 1967. Circ. 1,000. **Pays on acceptance.** Publishes ms up to 6 months after acceptance. Byline given. Offers 100% kill fee. Buys first world rights. Accepts queries by mail, e-mail, phone. Responds in 2 weeks to queries; 3 months to mss. Sample copy for $10 U.S. Sample articles and guidelines on website.

Nonfiction: "Query first about review articles, critical essays, interviews and visual art which we generally solicit." Include SASE with Canadian postage or IRCs. **Pays $30/magazine page.**

Photos: Pays $30 for b&w prints. Captions required.

Fiction: **Buys 20 mss/year.** Send complete ms up to 20 pages. **Pays $30/magazine page.**

Poetry: Avant-garde, free verse, traditional. Length: 5-10 pages. **Buys 100/year. Pays $30/magazine page.**

Tips: "Please do not send more than one manuscript (the one you consider your best) at a time. See the *Malahat Review's* long poem and novella contests in Contest & Awards section."

$ $ MANOA, A Pacific Journal of International Writing, University of Hawaii Press, 1733 Donaghho Rd., Honolulu HI 96822. (808)956-3070. Fax: (808)956-7808. E-mail: fstewart@hawaii.edu. Website: www2.hawaii.edu/mjournal. Managing Editor: Patricia Matsueda. **Contact:** Frank Stewart, editor. Semiannual literary magazine. "High quality literary fiction, poetry, essays, personal narrative, reviews. About half of each issue devoted to U.S. writing, and half new work from Pacific and Asian nations. Our audience is primarily in the U.S., although expanding in Pacific countries. U.S. writing need not be confined to Pacific settings or subjects." Estab. 1989. Circ. 2,500. Pays on publication. Byline given. Buys first North American serial or non-exclusive, one-time reprint rights. Editorial lead time 6 months. Submit seasonal material 8 months in advance. Responds in 3 weeks to queries; 2 months to poetry mss, 4 months to fiction. Sample copy for $10. Writer's guidelines free with SASE.

Nonfiction: Frank Stewart, editor. Book excerpts, essays, interview/profile, creative nonfiction or personal narrative related to literature or nature. Book reviews on recent books in arts, humanities and natural sciences, usually related to Asia, the Pacific or Hawaii or published in these places. No Pacific exotica. **Buys 3-4 mss/year,** excluding reviews. Query or send complete ms. Length: 1,000-5,000 words. **Pays $25/printed page.**

Fiction: Ian MacMillan, fiction editor. "We're potentially open to anything of literary quality, though usually not genre fiction as such." Publishes novel excerpts. No Pacific exotica. **Buys 12-18 mss/year** in the US (excluding translation). Send complete ms. Length: 1,000-7,500. **Pays $100-500** normally ($25/printed page).

Poetry: Frank Stewart, editor. No light verse. **Buys 40-50 poems/year.** Send 5-6 poems minimum. **Pays $25.**
Tips: "Although we are a Pacific journal, we are a general interest U.S. literary journal, not limited to Pacific settings or subjects."

$ THE MASSACHUSETTS REVIEW, South College, University of Massachusetts, Amherst MA 01003-9934. (413)545-2689. Fax: (413)577-0740. E-mail: massrev@external.umass.edu. Website: www.litline.org/html/massreview. html. Editors: Mary Heath, Jules Chametzky, Paul Jenkins. Quarterly magazine. Estab. 1959. Pays on publication. Publishes ms within 18 months of acceptance. Buys first North American serial rights. Accepts queries by mail, e-mail, fax. Responds in 3 months. Does not return mss without SASE. Sample copy for $7 with 3 first-class stamps. Sample articles and writer's guidelines on website.
Nonfiction: Articles on literary criticism, women, public affairs, art, philosophy, music and dance. No reviews of single books. Send complete ms or query with SASE. Length: 6,500 words average. **Pays $50.**
Fiction: Publishes 2-3 short stories per issue. One story per submission. Length: 25-30 pages maximum. **Pays $50.**
Poetry: Submit 6 poems maximum. **Pays 35¢/line** to **$10 minimum.**
Tips: "No manuscripts are considered June-October. No fax or e-mail submissions."

$ $ MERLYN'S PEN, Fiction, Essays and Poems by America's Teens, Merlyn's Pen Inc., 4 King St., East Greenwich RI 02818. (401)885-5175. Fax: (401)885-5222. E-mail: merlynspen@aol.com. Website: www.merlynspen.c om. Editor: R. James Stahl. **Contact:** Naomi Mead-Ward, project coordinator. **100% freelance written.** Annual. "We publish fiction, essays and poems by America's teen writers, age 11-19 exclusively." Estab. 1985. Circ. 5,000. Pays on publication. Publishes ms an average of 6 months after acceptance. Byline given. Buys all rights. Editorial lead time up to 10 months. Accepts queries by mail, e-mail, fax, phone. Responds in 3 months. Sample articles and writer's guidelines on website.
Nonfiction: Essays, exposé, general interest, historical/nostalgic, how-to, humor, opinion, personal experience, travel. **Buys 10 mss/year.** Send complete ms. Length: 100-5,000 words. **Pays $25-200.**
Fiction: Adventure, experimental, fantasy, historical, horror, humorous, mainstream, mystery, romance, science fiction, slice-of-life vignettes, suspense. **Buys 40 mss/year.** Send complete ms. Length: 100-5,000 words. **Pays $20-250.**
Poetry: Avant garde, free verse, haiku, light verse, traditional. **Buys 25 poems/year.** Submit 3 poems maximum. Length: 3-250 lines. **Pays $20-250.**
Tips: "**Contributors must be between ages 11-19.** We select about 50 pieces out of 10,000 received and we do respond. Writers *must* use *our* cover sheet, which is on our website or free by calling (800)247-2027."

$ MICHIGAN QUARTERLY REVIEW, 3032 Rackham Bldg., University of Michigan, Ann Arbor MI 48109-1070. E-mail: dorisk@umich.edu. Website: www.umich.edu/~mqr. **Contact:** Laurence Goldstein, editor. **75% freelance written.** Prefers to work with published/established writers. Quarterly. Estab. 1962. Circ. 1,500. Publishes ms an average of 1 year after acceptance. Pays on publication. Buys first serial rights. Responds in 2 months. Sample copy for $2.50 with 2 first-class stamps.
    ● The Lawrence Foundation Prize is a $1,000 annual award to the best short story published in the *Michigan Quarterly Review* during the previous year.
Nonfiction: "*MQR* is open to general articles directed at an intellectual audience. Essays ought to have a personal voice and engage a significant subject. Scholarship must be present as a foundation, but we are not interested in specialized essays directed only at professionals in the field. We prefer ruminative essays, written in a fresh style and which reach interesting conclusions. We also like memoirs and interviews with significant historical or cultural resonance." **Buys 35 mss/year.** Query by mail. Length: 2,000-5,000 words. **Pays $100-150.**
Fiction and Poetry: No restrictions on subject matter or language. **Buys 10 mss/year.** "We are very selective. We like stories which are unusual in tone and structure, and innovative in language." Send complete ms. **Pays $10/published page.**
Tips: "Read the journal and assess the range of contents and the level of writing. We have no guidelines to offer or set expectations; every manuscript is judged on its unique qualities. On essays—query with a very thorough description of the argument and a copy of the first page. Watch for announcements of special issues which are usually expanded issues and draw upon a lot of freelance writing. Be aware that this is a university quarterly that publishes a limited amount of fiction and poetry; that it is directed at an educated audience, one that has done a great deal of reading in all types of literature."

[N] $ miller's pond, H&H Press, RR 2, Box 241, Middlebury Center PA 16935. (570)376-3361. E-mail: cjhoughtalin g@usa.net. Website: millerspond.tripod.com or handhpress.bizland.com. **Contact:** C.J. Houghtaling, editor. **100% freelance written.** Annual magazine featuring poetry with poetry reviews and interviews of poets. Estab. 1998. Circ. 200. Pays on publication. Publishes ms an average of 1 year after acceptance. Byline given. Buys one-time rights. Editorial lead time 12 months. Accepts queries by mail, e-mail (e-mail submissions **must** come from the form on the website millerspond.tripod.com). Accepts simultaneous submissions. Responds in 10 months. Sample copy for $5 plus $3 p&h or on website. Writer's guidelines for #10 SASE or on website.
Nonfiction: Interview/profile, poetry chapbook reviews. **Buys 1-2 mss/year.** Query or send complete ms. Length: 100-500 words. **Pays $5.**
Reprints: Accepts previously published submissions.

Poetry: Free verse. No religious, horror, vulgar, rhymed, preachy, lofty, trite, overly sentimental. **Buys 20-25 poems/ year.** Submit maximum 3-5 poems. Length: 40 lines maximum. **Pays $2.**

■ The online magazine carries original content not found in the print edition and includes writer's guidelines. Contact: C.J. Houghtaling, online editor.

Tips: "View our website to see what we like. Study the contemporary masters: Billy Collins, Maxine Kumin, Colette Inez, Hayden Carruth."

$ $ THE MISSOURI REVIEW, 1507 Hillcrest Hall, University of Missouri, Columbia MO 65211. (573)882-4474. Fax: (573)884-4671. E-mail: missouri_@missouri.edu. Website: www.missourireview.org. **Contacts:** Speer Morgan, editor; Greg Michalson, poetry editor; Evelyn Somers, nonfiction editor. **90% freelance written.** Triannual literary magazine. "We publish contemporary fiction, poetry, interviews, personal essays, cartoons, special features—such as 'History as Literature' series and 'Found Text' series—for the literary and the general reader interested in a wide range of subjects." Estab. 1978. Circ. 6,500. Pays on signed contract. Byline given. Buys first rights. Editorial lead time 4-6 months. Accepts queries by mail, e-mail, phone. Responds in 2 weeks to queries; 3 months to mss. Sample copy for $7 or on website. Writer's guidelines for #10 SASE or on website.

Nonfiction: Evelyn Somers, nonfiction editor. Book excerpts, essays. No literary criticism. **Buys 10 mss/year.** Send complete ms. **Pays $15-20/printed page up to $750.**

Fiction: Mainstream, literary, novel excerpts. No genre fiction. **Buys 25 mss/year.** Send complete ms. **Pays $15-20/ printed page up to $750.**

● Ranked as one of the best markets for fiction writers in *Writer's Digest* magazine's "Fiction 50," June 2000.

Poetry: Greg Michalson, poetry editor. Publishes 3-5 poetry features of 6-12 pages each per issue. "Please familiarize yourself with the magazine before submitting poetry." **Buys 50 poems/year. Pays $125-250.**

■ The online magazine carries original content not found in the print edition and includes writer's guidelines. Contact: Speer Morgan, online editor.

Tips: "Send your best work. We'd especially like to see more personal essays."

$ NEW ENGLAND REVIEW, Middlebury College, Middlebury VT 05753. (802)443-5075. E-mail: nereview@mid dlebury.edu. Website: www.middlebury.edu/~nereview/. Editor: Stephen Donadio. Managing Editor: Jodee Stanley Rubins. **Contact** on envelope: Poetry, Fiction, or Nonfiction Editor; on letter: Stephen Donadio. Quarterly magazine. Serious literary only. Estab. 1978. Circ. 2,000. Pays on publication. Publishes ms an average of 6 months after acceptance. Byline given. Buys first North American serial rights. Accepts simultaneous submissions. Reads September 1 to May 31 (postmark dates). Responds in 2 weeks to queries; 3 months to mss. Sample copy for $7. Writer's guidelines for #10 SASE.

Nonfiction: Serious literary only. **Buys 20-25 mss/year.** Send complete ms. Length: 7,500 words maximum, though exceptions may be made. **Pays $10/page, $20 minimum** plus 2 copies.

Reprints: Rarely accepts previously published submissions, (if out of print or previously published abroad only.)

Fiction: Serious literary only, novel excerpts. **Buys 25 mss/year.** Send complete ms. Send 1 story at a time. **Pays $10/ page, minimum $20** plus 2 copies.

Poetry: Serious literary only. **Buys 75-90 poems/year.** Submit 6 poems max. **Pays $10/page or $20** and 2 copies.

Tips: "We consider short fiction, including shorts, short-shorts, novellas, and self-contained extracts from novels. We consider a variety of general and literary, but not narrowly scholarly, nonfiction; long and short poems; speculative, interpretive, and personal essays; book reviews; screenplays; graphics; translations; critical reassessments; statements by artists working in various media; interviews; testimonies; and letters from abroad. We are committed to exploration of all forms of contemporary cultural expression in the United States and abroad. With few exceptions, we print only work not published previously elsewhere."

$ NEW LETTERS, University of Missouri-Kansas City, University House, 5101 Rockhill Rd., Kansas City MO 64110-2499. (816)235-1168. Fax: (816)235-2611. E-mail: newletters@umkc.edu. Website: umkc.edu/newletters. Managing Editor: Robert Stewart. **Contact:** James McKinley, editor. **100% freelance written.** Quarterly magazine. "*New Letters* is intended for the general literate reader. We publish literary fiction, nonfiction, essays, poetry. We also publish art." Estab. 1934. Circ. 1,800. Pays on publication. Publishes ms an average of 5 months after acceptance. Byline given. Buys first North American serial rights. Editorial lead time 6 months. Submit seasonal material 6 months in advance. Accepts queries by mail, e-mail. Accepts simultaneous submissions. Responds in 1 month to queries; 3 months to mss. Sample copy for $5.50 (current issue) or sample articles on website. Writer's guidelines for #10 SASE or on website.

● Submissions are not read between May 15 and October 15.

Nonfiction: Essays. No self-help, how-to or non-literary work. **Buys 6-8 mss/year.** Send complete ms. Length: 5,000 words maximum. **Pays $40-100.**

Photos: Send photos with submission. Reviews contact sheets, 2×4 transparencies, prints. Offers $10-40/photo. Buys one-time rights.

Fiction: No genre fiction. **Buys 12 mss/year.** Send complete ms. Length: 5,000 words maximum. **Pays $30-75.**

Poetry: Avant-garde, free verse, haiku, traditional. No light verse. **Buys 40 poems/year.** Submit maximum 3 poems. Length: open. **Pays $10-25.**

[N] $ THE NORTH AMERICAN REVIEW, University of Northern Iowa, Cedar Falls IA 50614-0516. (319)273-6455. **Contact:** Robley Wilson, editor. **50% freelance written.** Bimonthly. Circ. 4,000. Pays on publication. Publishes ms an average of 9 months after acceptance. Buys first rights. Responds in 10 weeks. Sample copy for $4.

● This is one of the oldest and most prestigious literary magazines in the country. Also one of the most entertaining— and a tough market for the young writer.

Nonfiction: No restrictions, but most nonfiction is commissioned. Query. Rate of payment arranged.

Fiction: No restrictions; highest quality only. Length: open. **Pays $15/published page minimum.**

Poetry: Peter Cooley. No restrictions; highest quality only. Length: open. **Pays $1/line; $20 minimum.**

$ NOSTALGIA, A Sentimental State of Mind, Nostalgia Publications, P.O. Box 2224, Orangeburg SC 29116. Website: www.nospub.com. **Contact:** Connie L. Martin, editor. **100% freelance written.** Semiannual magazine for "true, personal experiences that relate faith, struggle, hope, success, failure and rising above problems common to all." Estab. 1986. Circ. 1,000. Pays on publication. Publishes ms an average of 1 year after acceptance. Byline given. Buys one-time rights. Submit seasonal material 6 months in advance. Responds in 6 weeks to queries. Sample copy for $5. Writer's guidelines for #10 SASE or on website.

Nonfiction: General interest, historical/nostalgic, humor, inspirational, opinion, personal experience, photo feature, religious and travel. Does not want to see anything with profanity or sexual references. **Buys 20 mss/year.** Send complete ms. Length: 1,500 words. **Pays $25 minimum.** Pays contributor copies if preferred. Short Story Awards $300 annually.

O⇥ The editor reports an interest in seeing "more humorous, funny experiences in life; need heartwarming more than sad. I would appreciate **not** receiving material all about Mom, Dad, Uncle, Aunt or siblings or pets. I need true personal experience."

Reprints: Send tearsheet, typed ms or photocopy of article or short story and information about when and where the article previously appeared. Payment varies.

Photos: State availability of photos with submission. Offers no additional payment for photos with ms.

Poetry: Free verse, haiku, light verse, traditional and modern prose. "No ballads; no profanity; no sexual references." Submit 3 poems maximum. Length: no longer than 45-50 lines preferably. Poetry Awards $600 annually.

Tips: Write for guidelines before entering contests. Short Story Award (deadline March 31); Poetry Award (deadlines June 30 and December 31). Entry fees reserve future edition.

[N] $ $ ON SPEC MAGAZINE, Copper Pig Writers Society, Box 4727, Edmonton, Alberta T6E 5G6 Canada. (780)413-0215. Fax: (780)413-1538. E-mail: onspec@earthlink.net. Website: www.icomm.ca/onspec. **Contact:** Jena Snyder, general editor. **100% freelance written.** Literary quarterly. "*On Spec Magazine* was launched in 1989 by the nonprofit Copper Pig Writers' Society to provide a voice and a paying market for Canadian writers working in the speculative genre. Aside from the then-biannual *Tesseracts* anthology, there were almost no speculative fiction markets in Canada for Canadian writers. *On Spec* was created to provide this market. *On Spec* is published quarterly by the Copper Pig Writers Society, a collective whose members all writers themselves donate their professional services and their time. Our readers have told us what they want is fiction, fiction and more fiction, and that's what we give them: each 112-page issue of the digest-size magazine typically contains one or two poems and nonfiction pieces, some illustrations, and at least ten short stories, all in the speculative genre." **Pays on acceptance**. Byline given. Buys first rights. Accepts queries by mail. Writer's guidelines free.

Fiction: Fantasy, horror, science fiction. **Buys 40-50 mss/year.** Send complete ms. Length: 1,000-6,000 words. **Pays $50-180 (Canadian).**

Tips: "The *On Spec* editors are looking for original, unpublished science fiction—fantasy, horror, ghost stories, fairy stories, magic realism, or any other speculative material. Since our mandate is to provide a market for the Canadian viewpoint, strong preference is given to submissions by Canadians."

$ $ PARNASSUS, Poetry in Review, Poetry in Review Foundation, 205 W. 89th St., #8-F, New York NY 10024. (212)362-3492. Fax: (212)875-0148. E-mail: parnew@aol.com. Managing Editor: Ben Downing. **Contact:** Herbert Leibowitz, editor. Semiannual trade paperback-size magazine covering poetry and criticism. Estab. 1972. Circ. 1,500. Pays on publication. Publishes ms an average of 5 months after acceptance. Byline given. Buys one-time rights. Accepts queries by mail, e-mail. Sample copy for $15.

Nonfiction: Essays. **Buys 30 mss/year.** Query with published clips. Length: 1,500-7,500 words. **Pays $50-300.** Sometimes pays writers in contributor copies or other premiums rather than a cash payment upon request.

Poetry: Accepts most types of poetry including avant-garde, free verse, traditional. **Buys 3-4 unsolicited poems/year.**

Tips: "Be certain you have read the magazine and are aware of the editor's taste. Blind submissions are a waste of everybody's time. We'd like to see more poems that display intellectual acumen and curiosity about history, science, music, etc. and fewer trivial lyrical poems about the self, or critical prose that's academic and dull. Prose should sing."

$ PLEIADES, Pleiades Press, Dept. of English & Philosophy, Central Missouri State University, Warrensburg MO 64093. (660)543-4425. Fax: (660)543-8544. E-mail: kdp8106@cmsu2.cmsu.edu. **Contact:** R.M. Kinder, editor (fiction, essays); Kevin Prufer, editor (poetry, reviews). **100% freelance written.** Semiannual journal (5½ × 8½ perfect bound). "We publish contemporary fiction, poetry, interviews, literary essays, special-interest personal essays, reviews for a general and literary audience." Estab. 1991. Circ. 3,000. Pays on publication. Publishes ms an average of 9 months after acceptance. Byline given. Buys first North American and second serial (reprint) rights (occasionally requests rights for WordBeat, TV, radio reading, website). Editorial lead time 9 months. Accepts queries by mail, e-mail, phone. Accepts simultaneous submissions. Responds in 2 months. Sample copy for $5 (back issue), $6 (current issue). Writer's guidelines for #10 SASE.

O➔ Break in with book reviews: "We're always looking for reviews of small-press books, but receive few that are well-written and interesting."

Nonfiction: Book excerpts, essays, interview/profile, reviews. "Nothing pedantic, slick or shallow." **Buys 4-6 mss/year.** Send complete ms. Length: 2,000-4,000 words. **Pays $10.**

Fiction: R.M. Kinder, editor. Ethnic, experimental, humorous, mainstream, novel excerpts, magic realism. No science fiction, fantasy, confession, erotica. **Buys 16-20 mss/year.** Send complete ms. Length: 2,000-6,000 words. **Pays $10.**

Poetry: Kevin Prufer, editor. Avant-garde, free verse, haiku, light verse, traditional. "Nothing didactic, pretentious, or overly sentimental." **Buys 40-50 poems/year.** Submit maximum 6 poems. **Pays $3/poem "or one year subscription, poets choice.** We also sponsor the Lena-Miles Wever Todd Poetry Series competition, a contest for the best book manuscript by an American poet. The winner receives $1,000, publication by Pleiades Press and distribution by Louisiana State University Press. Deadline March 30. Send SASE for guidelines."

Tips: "We're always looking for book reviews. We're most interested in insightful, articulate reviews of small-press books of poetry and fiction. Show care for your material and your readers—submit quality work in a professional format. Include cover letter with brief bio and list of publications. Include SASE."

$ $ PLOUGHSHARES, Emerson College, Dept. M, 100 Beacon St., Boston MA 02116. Website: www.emerson.edu/ploughshares/. **Contact:** Don Lee, editor. Triquarterly magazine for "readers of serious contemporary literature." Circ. 6,000. Pays on publication. Publishes ms an average of 6 months after acceptance. Buys first North American serial rights. Accepts simultaneous submissions, if so noted. Responds in 5 months. Sample copy for $8 (back issue). Writer's guidelines for SASE.

• A competitive and highly prestigious market. Rotating and guest editors make cracking the line-up even tougher, since it's difficult to know what is appropriate to send. The reading period is August 1 through March 31.

Nonfiction: Personal and literary essays (accepted only occasionally). Length: 6,000 words maximum. **Pays $25/printed page, $50-$250.**

Fiction: Literary, mainstream. **Buys 25-35 mss/year.** Length: 300-6,000 words. **Pays $25/printed page, $50-250.**

• Ranked as one of the best markets for fiction writers in *Writer's Digest* magazine's "Fiction 50," June 2000.

Poetry: Traditional forms, blank verse, free verse and avant-garde. Length: open. **Pays $25/printed page, $50-$250.**

Tips: "We no longer structure issues around preconceived themes. If you believe your work is in keeping with our general standards of literary quality and value, submit at any time during our reading period."

$ POTTERSFIELD PORTFOLIO, Stork and Press, P.O. Box 40, Station A, Sydney, Nova Scotia B1P 6G9 Canada. Website: www.pportfolio.com. Managing Editor: Douglas Arthur Brown. Literary magazine published 3 times a year. "*Pottersfield Portfolio* is always looking for poetry and fiction that provides fresh insights and delivers the unexpected. The stories and poems that capture our attention will be the ones that most effectively blend an intriguing voice with imaginative language. Our readers expect to be challenged, enlightened and entertained." Estab. 1979. Circ. 1,000. Pays on publication. Publishes ms an average of 6 months after acceptance. Byline given. Buys first North American serial rights. Editorial lead time 3 months. Responds in 3 weeks to queries; 3 months to mss. Writer's guidelines for #10 SASE, Canadian postage or IRC only, or on website.

Nonfiction: Book excerpts, essays, interview/profile, photo feature. **Buys 6 mss/year.** Query by mail. Length: 500-5,000 words. **Pays $5-25 (Canadian).**

Fiction: Contact fiction editor. Experimental, novel excerpts, short fiction. No fantasy, horror, mystery, religious, romance, science fiction, western. **Buys 12-15 mss/year.** Send complete ms. Length: 500-5,000 words. **Pays $5-25.**

Poetry: Contact poetry editor. Avant garde, free verse, traditional. **Buys 20-30 poems/year.** Submit maximum 10 poems. **Pays $5-25.**

Tips: Looking for creative nonfiction, essays.

$ THE PRAIRIE JOURNAL of Canadian Literature, P.O. Box 61203, Brentwood Postal Services, 217K-3630 Brentwood Rd. NW, Calgary, Alberta T2L 2K6 Canada. E-mail: prairiejournal@iname.com. Website: www.geocities.com/Athens/Ithaca/r4336/. **Contact:** A. Burke, editor. **100% freelance written.** Semiannual magazine of Canadian literature. "Since 1983, *The Prairie Journal* has been publishing quality poetry, short fiction, drama, literary criticism, reviews, bibliography, interviews, profiles and artwork." Estab. 1983. Circ. 600. Pays on publication; "honorarium depends on grant." Byline given. Buys first North American serial rights. Responds in 6 months. Sample copy for $6 and IRC (Canadian stamps) or 50¢ payment for postage. Writer's guidelines on website.

Nonfiction: Interview/profile, scholarly, literary. **Buys 5 mss/year.** Query first. Include IRCs. **Pays $25-100.**

Photos: Send photocopies of photos with submission. Offers additional payment for photos accepted with ms. Identification of subjects required. Buys first North American rights.

Fiction: Literary. **Buys 10 mss/year.** Send complete ms. Pays contributor copies or honoraria for literary work.

Poetry: Avant-garde, free verse. **Buys 10 poems/year.** Submit maximum 6-10 poems.

Tips: "Commercial writers are advised to submit elsewhere. Art needed, black and white pen and ink drawings or good-quality photocopy. Do not send originals. We are strictly small press editors interested in highly talented, serious artists. We are oversupplied with fiction but seek more high-quality poetry, especially the contemporary long poem or sequences from longer works. We welcome freelancers."

$ PRISM INTERNATIONAL, Department of Creative Writing, Buch E462-1866 Main Mall, University of British Columbia, Vancouver, British Columbia V6T 1Z1 Canada. (604)822-2514. Fax: (604)822-3616. E-mail: prism@intercha nge.ubc.ca. Website: www.arts.ubc.ca/prism. Executive Editor: Laisha Rosnau. **Contact:** Jennica Harper, Kiera Miller, editors. **100% freelance written.** Eager to work with new/unpublished writers. Quarterly magazine emphasizing contemporary literature, including translations, for university and public libraries, and private subscribers. Estab. 1959. Circ. 1,200. Pays on publication. Publishes ms an average of 4 months after acceptance. Buys first North American serial rights. Accepts queries by mail, e-mail, fax, phone. Responds in 6 months. Sample copy for $5 or on website. Writer's guidelines for #10 SAE with 1 first-class Canadian stamp (Canadian entries) or 1 IRC (US entries) or on website.

> **O—** Break in by "sending unusual or experimental work (we get mostly traditional submissions) and playing with forms (e.g., nonfiction, prose poetry, etc.)"

Nonfiction: "*Creative* nonfiction that reads like fiction. Nonfiction pieces should be creative, exploratory, or experimental in tone rather than rhetorical, academic, or journalistic." No reviews, tracts or scholarly essays.

Fiction: Experimental, traditional, novel excerpts. **Buys 3-5 mss/issue.** Send complete ms. Length: 5,000 words maximum. **Pays $20/printed page** and 1-year subscription. Publishes novel excerpts up to 25 double-spaced pages.

Poetry: Avant-garde, traditional. **Buys 20 poems/issue.** Submit maximum 6 poems. **Pays $20/printed page** and 1-year subscription.

Drama: One-acts preferred. Also interested in seeing dramatic monologues. **Pays $20/printed page** and 1-year subscription.

Tips: "We are looking for new and exciting fiction. Excellence is still our number one criterion. As well as poetry, imaginative nonfiction and fiction, we are especially open to translations of all kinds, very short fiction pieces and drama which work well on the page. Translations must come with a copy of the original language work. Work may be submitted through e-mail or our website. We pay an additional $10/printed page to selected authors whose work we place on our on-line version of *Prism*."

$ $ QUARTERLY WEST, University of Utah, 200 S. Central Campus Dr., Rm. 317, Salt Lake City UT 84112-9109. (801)581-3938. Website: chronicle.utah.edu/QW. **Contact:** Margot Schilpp, editor. Semiannual magazine. "We publish fiction, poetry, and nonfiction in long and short formats, and will consider experimental as well as traditional works." Estab. 1976. Circ. 1,900. Pays on publication. Publishes ms an average of 6 months after acceptance. Buys first North American serial and all rights. Accepts simultaneous submissions, if so noted. Responds in 6 months to mss. Sample copy for $7.50 or on website. Writer's guidelines for #10 SASE or on website.

Nonfiction: Essays, interview/profile, book reviews. **Buys 6-7 mss/year.** Send complete ms with SASE. Length: 10,000 words maximum. **Pays $25.**

Fiction: Contact: Rebekah Lindberg. Ethnic, experimental, humorous, mainstream, novel excerpts, short shorts, slice-of-life vignettes, translations. **Buys 20-30 mss/year.** Send complete ms with SASE. Pays $25-500. No preferred lengths; interested in longer, fuller short stories and short shorts. Length: 50-125 pages. **Pays $25-500.**

> ● Ranked as one of the best markets for fiction writers in *Writer's Digest* magazine's "Fiction 50," June 2000.

Poetry: Contact: Heidi Blitch. Avant-garde, free verse, traditional. **Buys 70-80 poems/year.** Submit 5 poems maximum. **Pays $15-100.**

Tips: "We publish a special section or short shorts every issue, and we also sponsor a biennial novella contest. We are open to experimental work—potential contributors should read the magazine! Don't send more than one story per submission, but submit as often as you like. Biennial novella competition guidelines available upon request with SASE."

$ $ QUEEN'S QUARTERLY, A Canadian Review, Queen's University, Kingston, Ontario K7L 3N6 Canada. (613)533-2667. Fax: (613)533-6822. E-mail: qquarter@post.queensu.ca. Website: info.queensu.ca/quarterly. **Contact:** Joan Harcourt, literary editor. Quarterly magazine covering a wide variety of subjects, including science, humanities, arts and letters, politics and history for the educated reader. **95% freelance written.** Estab. 1893. Circ. 3,000. Pays on publication. Publishes ms an average of 6 months after acceptance. Byline given. Buys first North American serial rights. Accepts queries by mail, e-mail, fax. Responds in 1 month to mss. *Writer's Market* recommends allowing 2 months for reply. Sample copy $6.50 or on website. Writer's guidelines on website. No reply/return without IRC.

Fiction: Publishes novel excerpts. **Buys 8-12 mss/year.** Send complete ms. Length: 2,000 words maximum. **Pays $150-250.**

Poetry: **Buys 25/year.** Submit maximum 6 poems. Length: open. Three year subscription in lieu of payment.

Tips: No multiple submissions. No more than six poems or two stories per submission

[N] $ RAIN CROW, Rain Crow Publishing, 2127 W. Pierce Ave., Apt. 2B, Chicago IL 60622-1824. Fax: (503)214-6615. E-mail: msm@manley.org. Website: www.rain-crow.com/. **Contact:** Michael S. Manley, editor. Literary magazine published 3 times/year featuring well-crafted, original, entertaining fiction. "We publish new and established writers in many styles and genres. We are a publication for people passionate about the short story form." Estab. 1995. Circ. 1,000. Pays on publication. Publishes ms an average of 4 months after acceptance. Byline given. Buys one-time and electronic rights. Editorial lead time 4 months. Submit seasonal material 8 months in advance. Accepts queries by mail, e-mail. Accepts simultaneous submissions. Responds in 3 weeks to queries; 4 months to mss. Sample copy for $5. Writer's guidelines for #10 SASE, on website or by e-mail.

Reprints: Accepts previously published submissions.

Fiction: Erotica, experimental, mainstream, science fiction, literary. "No propaganda, pornography, juvenile, formulaic." **Buys 30 mss/year.** Send complete ms. Length: 250-8,000 words. **Pays $5-150.**

Tips: "Write to the best of your abilities, submit your best work. Present yourself and your work professionally. When we evaluate a submission, we ask, 'Is this something we would like to read again? Is this something we would give to someone else to read?' A good manuscript makes the reader forget they are reading a manuscript. We look for attention to craft: voice, language, character and plot working together to maximum effect. Unique yet credible settings and situations that entertain get the most attention."

$RARITAN, A Quarterly Review, 31 Mine St., New Brunswick NJ 08903. (732)932-7887. Fax: (732)932-7855. Editor: Richard Poirier. **Contact:** Stephanie Volmer, managing editor. Quarterly magazine covering literature, general culture. Estab. 1981. Circ. 3,500. Pays on publication. Publishes ms 1 year after acceptance. Byline given. Buys first North American serial rights. Editorial lead time 5 months. Accepts simultaneous submissions.
Nonfiction: Book excerpts, essays. **Buys 50 mss/year.** Send complete ms. Length 15-30 pages. **Pays $100.**
• Raritan no longer accepts previously published submissions.

$RIVER STYX, Big River Association, 634 N. Grand Blvd., 12th Floor, St. Louis MO 63103. (314)533-4541. Fax: (314)533-3345. Website: www.riverstyx.org. Senior Editors: Quincy Troupe and Michael Castro. **Contact:** Richard Newman, editor. Triannual literary magazine. "*River Styx* publishes the highest quality fiction, poetry, interviews, essays and visual art. We are an internationally distributed multicultural literary magazine." Estab. 1975. Pays on publication. Publishes ms an average of 12 months after acceptance. Byline given. Buys one-time rights. Manuscripts read May-November. Accepts simultaneous submissions, if so noted. Responds in 4 months to mss. Sample copy for $7. Writer's guidelines for #10 SASE or on website.
Nonfiction: Essays, interviews. **Buys 2-5 mss/year.** Send complete ms. Pays 2 contributor copies, plus one-year subscription; **$8/page** if funds are available.
• River Styx has won several prizes, including Best American Poetry 1998; Pushcart Prize; and Stanley Hanks Prizes.
Photos/Art: Send with submission. Reviews 5×7 or 8×10 b&w prints or color. Also slides. Pays 2 contributor copies, plus one-year subscription; $8/page if funds are available. Buys one-time rights.
Fiction: Literary, novel excerpts. **Buys 6-9 mss/year.** Send complete ms. Pays 2 contributor copies, plus one-year subscription; **$8/page** if funds are available.
Poetry: Traditional, free verse, avant-garde. No religious. **Buys 40-50 poems/year.** Submit 3-5 poems. Pays 2 contributor copies, plus one-year subscription. **$8/page** if funds are available.

$ROOM OF ONE'S OWN, A Canadian Quarterly of Women's Literature and Criticism, West Coast Feminist Literary Magazine Society, P.O. Box 46160, Station D, Vancouver, British Columbia V6J 5G5 Canada. Website: www.islandnet.com/Room/enter. **Contact:** Growing Room Collective. **100% freelance written.** Quarterly literary journal of feminist literature. Estab. 1975. Circ. 1,000. Pays on publication. Publishes ms an average of 8 months after acceptance. Byline given. Buys first North American serial rights. Editorial lead time 9 months. Responds in 3 months to queries; 6 months to mss. Sample copy for $7 or on website. Writer's guidelines for #10 SAE with 2 IRCs (US postage not valid in Canada) or on website.
Nonfiction: Reviews. **Buys 1-2 mss/year.** Send complete ms. Length: 1,000-2,500 words. **Pays $35 (Canadian)** and 1-year subscription.
Photos: Send photos with submission. Reviews prints. Offers no additional payment for photos accepted with ms. Buys one-time rights.
Fiction: "By, for and about women: adventure, ethnic, experimental, fantasy, humorous, mainstream, slice-of-life vignettes, science fiction, feminist literature. **Buys 80 mss/year.** Length: 2,000-5,000 words. **Pays $35 (Canadian) and 1-year subscription .**
Poetry: Avant-garde, free verse. "Nothing light, undeveloped." **Buys 20 poems/year.** Submit maximum 8 poems. Length: 3-80 lines. **Pays $35 (Canadian) and 1-year subscription.**

$ $ROSEBUD, The Magazine For People Who Enjoy Good Writing, Rosebud, Inc., P.O. Box 459, Cambridge WI 53523. (608)423-9609. (800)786-5669. Website: www.rsbd.net. **Contact:** Rod Clark, editor. **100% freelance written.** Quarterly magazine "for people who love to read and write. Our readers like good storytelling, real emotion, a sense of place and authentic voice." Estab. 1993. Circ. 9,000. Pays on publication. Publishes ms an average of 2 months after acceptance. Byline given. Buys one-time or second serial (reprint) rights. Editorial lead time 3 months. Submit seasonal material 3 months in advance. Accepts simultaneous submissions. Sends acknowledgment postcard upon receipt of submission and responds within 5 months. Sample copy for $5.95 or sample articles on website. Writer's guidelines for SASE or on website.
Nonfiction: Book excerpt, essays, general interest, historical/nostalgic, humor, interview/profile, personal experience, travel. "No editorializing." Send complete ms and SASE. Length: 1,200-1,800 words. **Pays $45-195** plus 3 copies.
Reprints: Send tearsheet, photocopy or typed ms with rights for sale noted. Pays 100% of amount paid for an original article.
Photos: State availability of photos with submission. Offers no additional payment for photos accepted with ms. Captions, model releases and identification of subjects required. Buys one-time rights.
Fiction: Ethnic, experimental, historical, humorous, mainstream, novel excerpts, slice-of-life vignettes, suspense. "No formula pieces." **Buys 80 mss/year.** Send complete ms and SASE. Length: 1,200-1,800 words. **Pays $45-195** plus 3 copies.

• Ranked as one of the best markets for fiction writers in *Writer's Digest* magazine's "Fiction 50," June 2000.

Poetry: Avant-garde, free verse, traditional. No inspirational poetry. **Buys 36 poems/year.** Submit maximum 5 poems. Length: open. **Pays $45-195** and 3 contributor's copies.

■ The online magazine carries original content not found in the print edition.

Tips: "Something has to 'happen' in the pieces we choose, but what happens inside characters is much more interesting to us than plot manipulation. We prefer to respond with an individualized letter (send SASE for this) and recycle submitted manuscripts. We will return your manuscript only if you send sufficient postage. We can only give detailed editorial feedback on pieces we are going to buy."

[N:] $ SHENANDOAH, The Washington and Lee University Review, Washington and Lee University, Troubadour Theater, 2nd Floor, Lexington VA 24450-0303. (540)463-8765. Website: www.w/u.edu/~shenando. Managing Editor: Lynn Leech. **Contact:** R.T. Smith, editor. Literary quarterly magazine. Estab. 1950. Circ. 2,000. Pays on publication. Publishes ms an average of 10 months after acceptance. Byline given. Buys first North American serial and one-time rights. Responds in 2 months to mss. Sample copy for $5. Writer's guidelines on website.

Nonfiction: Book excerpts, essays. **Buys 6 mss/year.** Send complete ms. **Pays $25/page.**

Fiction: Mainstream, novel excerpts. No sloppy, hasty, slight fiction. **Buys 15 mss/year.** Send complete ms. **Pays $25/page.**

Poetry: No inspirational, confessional poetry. **Buys 70 poems/year.** Submit maximum 6 poems. Length open. **Pays $2.50/line.**

$ SHORT STUFF, for Grown-ups, Bowman Publications, 712 W. 10th St., Loveland CO 80537. (970)669-9139. E-mail: Shortstuf@oneimage.com. **Contact:** Donnalee Bowman, editor. **98% freelance written.** Bimonthly magazine. "We are perhaps an enigma in that we publish only clean stories in any genre. We'll tackle any subject, but don't allow obscene language or pornographic description. Our magazine is for grown-ups, *not* X-rated 'adult' fare." Estab. 1989. Circ. 10,400. Payment and contract on publication. Byline given. Buys first North American serial rights. Editorial lead time 3 months. Submit seasonal material 3 months in advance. Responds in 6 months to mss. Sample copy for $1.50 and 9×12 SAE with 5 first-class stamps. Writer's guidelines for #10 SASE.

○→ Break in with "*real* short stories, not essays."

Nonfiction: Humor. Special issues: "We are holiday oriented and each issue reflects the appropriate holidays." **Buys 20 mss/year.** Most nonfiction is staff written. Send complete ms. Length: 500-1,500 words. **Pays $10-50.**

Photos: Send photos with submission. Offers no additional payment for photos accepted with ms. Identification of subjects required. Buys one-time rights.

Fiction: Adventure, historical, humorous, mainstream, mystery, romance, science fiction (seldom), suspense, western. **Buys 144 mss/year.** Send complete ms. Length: 500-1,500 words. **Pays $10-50.**

Fillers: Anecdotes, short humor. **Buys 200/year.** Length: 20-500 words. **Pays $1-5.**

Tips: "Don't send floppy disks or cartridges. Do include cover letter about the author, not a synopsis of the story. We are holiday oriented; mark on *outside* of envelope if story is for Easter, Mother's Day, etc. We receive 500 manuscripts each month. This is up about 200%. Because of this, I implore writers to send one manuscript at a time. I would not use stories from the same author more than once an issue and this means I might keep the others too long."

$ THE SOUTHERN REVIEW, 43 Allen Hall, Louisiana State University, Baton Rouge LA 70803-5001. (225)388-5108. Fax: (225)388-5098. E-mail: bmacon@unix1.sncc.lsu.edu. Website: www.LSU.edu/guests/wwwtsm. **Contact:** Michael Griffith, associate editor. **100% freelance written.** Works with a moderate number of new/unpublished writers each year. Quarterly magazine "with emphasis on contemporary literature in the United States and abroad, and with special interest in Southern culture and history." Estab. 1935. Circ. 3,100. Pays on publication. Publishes ms an average of 6 months after acceptance. Byline given. Buys first serial rights only. No queries. Responds in 2 months. Sample copy for $8. Writer's guidelines for #10 SASE or on website. Reading period: September through May.

Nonfiction: Essays with careful attention to craftsmanship, technique and seriousness of subject matter. "Willing to publish experimental writing if it has a valid artistic purpose. Avoid extremism and sensationalism. Essays should exhibit thoughtful and sometimes severe awareness of the necessity of literary standards in our time." Emphasis on contemporary literature, especially southern culture and history. No footnotes. **Buys 25 mss/year.** Length: 4,000-10,000 words. **Pays $12/page.**

Fiction and Poetry: Short stories of lasting literary merit, with emphasis on style and technique, also novel excerpts. Length: 4,000-8,000 words. **Pays $12/page.**

• Ranked as one of the best markets for fiction writers in *Writer's Digest* magazine's "Fiction 50," June 2000.

Poetry: Length: 1-4 pages. **Pays $20/page.**

$ SPORT LITERATE, Honest Reflections on Life's Leisurely Diversions, Pint-Size Publications, P.O. Box 577166, Chicago IL 60657-7166. E-mail: avalon.net/~librarian/sportliterate/. Website: www.sportliterate.org. **Contact:** William Meiners, editor-in-chief and Gina Vozenilek, managing editor. **95% freelance written**. Semi-annual literary journal covering leisure/sport . . . life outside the daily grind of making a living. "*Sport Literate* publishes the highest quality creative nonfiction and poetry on themes of leisure and sport. Our writers use a leisure activity to explore a larger theme. This creative allegorical writing serves a broad audience." Estab. 1995. Circ. 1,500. Pays on publication.

Publishes ms an average of 3 months after acceptance. Byline given. Buys first North American serial rights. Editorial lead time 3 months. Submit seasonal material 4 months in advance. Accepts queries by mail, e-mail. Responds in 3 weeks to queries; 2 months to mss. Sample copy for $7.75. Writer's guidelines for #10 SASE or on website.

Nonfiction: Essays, historical/nostalgic, humor, interview/profile, personal experience, travel, creative nonfiction. No book reviews, straight reporting on sports. **Buys 28 mss/year**. Send complete ms. Length: 250-5,000 words. **Pays up to $20.**

Photos: Steve Mend (contact through website). Accepts b&w photo essays "that tell a deeper story of folks passing their time."

Poetry: Frank Van Zant, poetry editor. Avant-garde, free verse, haiku, light verse, traditional. **Buys 25 poems/year**. Submit maximum 5 poems. Length: 30 lines maximum. **Pays up to $20.**

Tips: "We like to explore all the avenues of the creative nonfiction form—personal essays, literary journalism, travel pieces, historical, humor and interviews—as they relate to our broad definition of sport. We don't publish fiction. Read any publication that you're submitting to. It can be a great time saver."

$ SPSM&H, *Amelia Magazine*, 329 E St., Bakersfield CA 93304. (661)323-4064. **Contact:** Frederick A. Raborg, Jr., editor. **100% freelance written**. Quarterly magazine featuring fiction and poetry with Romantic or Gothic theme. "*SPSM&H* (Shakespeare, Petrarch, Sidney, Milton and Hopkins) uses one short story in each issue and 20-36 sonnets, plus reviews of books and anthologies containing the sonnet form and occasional articles about the sonnet form or about some romantic or Gothic figure or movement. We look for contemporary aspects of the sonnet form." Estab. 1984. Circ. 600. Pays on publication. Publishes ms an average of 6 months after acceptance. Byline given. Offers 50% kill fee. Buys first North American serial rights. Editorial lead time 2 months. Submit seasonal material 3 months in advance. Accepts simultaneous submissions. Responds in 2 weeks to queries; 3 months to mss. Sample copy for $6. Writer's guidelines for #10 SASE.

Nonfiction: Essays, general interest, historical/nostalgic, humor, interview/profile, opinion and anything related to sonnets or to romance. **Buys 1-4 mss/year**. Send complete ms. Length: 500-2,000 words. **Pays $10.**

Photos: Send photos with submission. Reviews 8×10 or 5×7 b&w prints. Offers $10-25/photo. Model releases required. Buys one-time rights.

Fiction: Confession, erotica, experimental, fantasy, historical, humor, humorous, mainstream, mystery, romance, slice-of-life vignettes. **Buys 4 mss/year**. Send complete ms. Length: 500-2,500 words. **Pays $10-20.**

Poetry: Sonnets, sonnet sequences. **Buys 140 poems/year**. Submit maximum 10 poems. Length: 14 lines. Two "best of issue" poets each receive $14.

Fillers: Anecdotes, short humor. **Buys 2-4/year**. Length: 25-500 words. No payment for fillers.

Tips: "Read a copy certainly. Understand the limitations of the sonnet form and, in the case of fiction, the requirements of the romantic or Gothic genres. Be professional in presentation, and realize that neatness does count. Be contemporary and avoid Victorian verse forms and techniques. Avoid convolution and forced rhyme. Idiomatics ought to be contemporary. Don't be afraid to experiment. We consider John Updike's 'Love Sonnet' to be the extreme to which poets may experiment."

N: $ STAND MAGAZINE, Dept. of English, VCU, Richmond VA 23284-2005. (804)828-1331. E-mail: dlatane@vcu.edu. Website: saturn.vcu.edu/~dlatane/stand.html. Editors: Michael Hulse and John Kinsella. **Contact:** David Latané, U.S. editor. **99% freelance written**. Quarterly magazine covering short fiction, poetry, criticism and reviews. "*Stand Magazine* is concerned with what happens when cultures and literatures meet, with translation in its many guises, with the mechanics of language, with the processes by which the polity receives or disables its cultural makers. *Stand* promotes debate of issues that are of radical concern to the intellectual community worldwide." Estab. 1952. Circ. 3,000 worldwide. Pays on publication. Publishes ms 10 months after acceptance. Byline given. Buys first world rights. Editorial lead time 2 months. Accepts queries by mial. Responds in 6 weeks to queries, 3 months to mss. Sample copy for $11. Writer's guidelines for #10 SASE with sufficient number of IRCs or on website.

Nonfiction: Reviews of poetry/fiction. "Reviews are commissioned from known freelancers." **Buys 8 mss/year**. Query. Length: 200-5,000 words. **Pays $30/1,000 words.**

Fiction: Adventure, ethnic, experimental, historical, mainstream. "No genre fiction." **Buys 12-14 mss/year**. Send complete ms. Length: 8,000 words maximum. **Pays $37.50/1,000 words.**

Poetry: Avant-garde, free verse, traditional. **Buys 100-120 poems/year**. Submit maximum 6 poems. **Pays $37.50/poem.**

Tips: "Poetry/fiction areas are most open to freelancers. *Stand* is published in England and reaches an international audience. North American writers should submit work to the U.S. address. While the topic or nature of submissions does not have to be 'international,' writers may do well to keep in mind the range of *Stand*'s audience."

$ THE STRAIN, Interactive Arts Magazine, 1307 Diablo, Houston TX 77532-3004. **Contact:** Norman Clark Stewart Jr., editor. **80% freelance written**. Monthly literary magazine. Estab. 1987. Circ. 100. Pays on publication. Publishes ms up to 3 years after acceptance. Byline given. Buys first, one-time or second serial rights. Makes work-for-hire assignments. Responds in up to 2 years.

Nonfiction: Alicia Alder, articles editor. Essays, exposé, how-to, humor, photo feature, technical. **Buys 2-20 mss/year**. Send complete ms. **Pays $5 minimum.**

Reprints: Send typed ms with rights for sale noted and information about when and where article previously appeared.

Photos: Send photos with submissions. Reviews transparencies and prints. Model releases and identification of subjects required. Buys one-time rights.

Columns/Departments: Charlie Mainze, editor. Multi-media performance art. Send complete ms. **Pays $5 minimum.**

Fiction: Michael Bond, editor. **Buys 1-35 mss/year.** Send complete ms. **Pays $5 minimum.**

Poetry: Annas Kinder, editor. Avant-garde, free verse, light verse, traditional. **Buys 100/year.** Submit maximum 5 poems. **Pays $5 minimum.**

$ THE STRAND MAGAZINE, P.O. Box 1418, Birmingham MI 48012-1418. (800)300-6652. Fax: (248)874-1046. E-mail: strandmag@worldnet.att.net. **Contact:** A.F. Gulli, managing editor. Quarterly magazine covering mysteries, short stories, essays, book reviews. "Mysteries and short stories written in the classic tradition of this century's great authors." Estab. 1998. Pays on publication. Publishes ms an average of 4 months after acceptance. Byline given. Buys first North American serial rights. Responds in 1 month to queries; 4 months to mss. Guidelines for #10 SASE.

Fiction: Horror, humorous, mystery, suspense. Send complete ms. Length: 2,000-6,000 words. **Pays $25-150.**

$ THEMA, Box 8747, Metairie LA 70011-8747. (504)887-1263. E-mail: thema@mindspring.com. Website: www.litline.org/html/THEMA.html. **Contact:** Virginia Howard, editor. **100% freelance written.** Triannual literary magazine covering a different theme for each issue. "*Thema* is designed to stimulate creative thinking by challenging writers with unusual themes, such as 'laughter on the steps' and 'jogging on ice.' Appeals to writers, teachers of creative writing and general reading audience." Estab. 1988. Circ. 350. **Pays on acceptance.** Byline given. Buys one-time rights. Accepts queries by mail, e-mail. Responds in 5 months to mss (after deadline for particular issue). Sample copy for $8. Writer's guidelines for #10 SASE or on website. Upcoming themes for SASE.

Fiction: Adventure, ethnic, experimental, fantasy, historical, humorous, mainstream, mystery, religious, science fiction, slice-of-life vignettes, suspense, western, novel excerpts. "No erotica." Special issues: Safety in Numbers (November 1, 2000); What Sarah (or Edward) Remembered (March 1, 2001); The Third One (July 1, 2001). **Buys 30 mss/year.** Send complete ms and *specify theme* for which it is intended. **Pays $10-25.**

● Ranked as one of the best markets for fiction writers in *Writer's Digest* magazine's "Fiction 50," June 2000.

Reprints: Send typed ms with rights for sale noted and information about when and where the article previously appeared. Pays same amount paid for original story or poem.

Poetry: Avant-garde, free verse, haiku, light verse, traditional. No erotica. **Buys 27 poems/year.** Submit maximum 3 poems. Length: 4-50 lines. **Pays $10.**

Tips: "Be familiar with the themes. *Don't submit* unless you have an upcoming theme in mind. Specify the target theme on the first page of your manuscript or in a cover letter. Put your name on *first* page of manuscript only. (All submissions are judged in blind review after the deadline for a specified issue.) Most open to fiction and poetry. Don't be hasty when you consider a theme—mull it over and let it ferment in your mind. We appreciate interpretations that are carefully constructed, clever, subtle, well thought out."

■ $ $ THE THREEPENNY REVIEW, P.O. Box 9131, Berkeley CA 94709. (510)849-4545. Website: www.threepennyreview.com. **Contact:** Wendy Lesser, editor. **100% freelance written.** Works with small number of new/unpublished writers each year. Quarterly literary tabloid. "We are a general interest, national literary magazine with coverage of politics, the visual arts and the performing arts as well." Estab. 1980. Circ. 9,000. **Pays on acceptance.** Publishes ms an average of 1 year after acceptance. Byline given. Buys first North American serial rights. Responds in 1 month to queries; 2 months to mss. Does *not* read mss in summer months. Sample copy for $10 or on website. Writer's guidelines for SASE or on website.

Nonfiction: Essays, exposé, historical, personal experience, book, film, theater, dance, music and art reviews. **Buys 40 mss/year.** Query with or without published clips by mail only or send complete ms. Length: 1,500-4,000 words. **Pays $200.**

Fiction: No fragmentary, sentimental fiction. **Buys 10 mss/year.** Send complete ms. Length: 800-4,000 words. **Pays $200.**

● Ranked as one of the best markets for fiction writers in *Writer's Digest* magazine's annual "Fiction 50," June 2000.

Poetry: Free verse, traditional. No poems "without capital letters or poems without a discernible subject." **Buys 30 poems/year.** Submit 5 poems maximum. **Pays $100.**

Tips: "Nonfiction (political articles, memoirs, reviews) is most open to freelancers."

$ TICKLED BY THUNDER, Helping Writers Get Published, Tickled by Thunder, 14076-86A Ave., Surrey, British Columbia V3W 0V9 Canada. (604)591-6095. E-mail: thunder@istar.ca. Website: www.home.istar.ca/~thunder. **Contact:** L. Lindner, publisher/editor. **100% freelance written.** Quarterly literary magazine on writing. "Our readers are generally writers hoping to improve their craft and gain writing experience/credits." Estab. 1990. Circ. 1,000. Pays on publication. Publishes ms an average of 4 months after acceptance. Byline given. Buys one-time rights. Editorial lead time 4 months. Submit seasonal material 6 months in advance. Accepts simultaneous submissions. Responds in 6 weeks to queries; 4 months to mss. Sample copy for $2.50 or sample articles on website. Writer's guidelines for #10 SASE or on website.

Nonfiction: Interview/profile, opinion, personal experience (must relate to writing). Does not want to see articles not slanted to writing. **Buys 4 mss/year.** Send complete ms. Length: 300-2,000 words. **Pays 5¢/line-$5.**

Photos: State availability of photos with submission. Model releases and identification of subjects required. Buys one-time rights.
Fiction: Experimental, fantasy, humorous, mainstream, mystery, religious, science fiction, slice-of-life vignettes, suspense, western. No bad language—not even "damn" or "hell." **Buys 8-12 mss/year.** Send complete ms. Length: 300-2,000 words. **Pays 10¢/line-$5.**
Poetry: Avant-garde, free verse, haiku, light verse, traditional. "Nothing that requires a manual to understand." **Buys 12-20 poems/year.** Submit maximum 7 poems. Length: 50 lines. **Pays 2¢/line-$2.**

$ $ $TIN HOUSE, McCormack Communications. 2601 NW Thurman St., Portland OR 97210. (503)274-4393. Fax: (503)222-1154. E-mail: tinhouse@aol.com. Editor-in-Chief: Win McCormack. Managing Editor: Holly Macarthur. Editors: Rob Spillman, Elissa Schappell. **Contact:** Serena Crawford, assistant editor. **90% freelance written.** Quarterly literary magazine. "We are a general interest literary quarterly. Our watchword is quality. Our audience is people interested in literature in all its aspects, from the mundane to the exalted." Estab. 1998. Circ. 5,000. Pays on publication. Publishes ms up to 1 year after acceptance. Byline given. Offers 25-50% kill fee. Buys first North American serial rights and anthology rights. Editorial lead time 6 months. Submit seasonal material 6 months in advance. Accepts simultaneous submissions. Responds in 6 weeks to queries, 3 months to mss. Sample copy $12.50.
Nonfiction: Book excerpts, essays, general interest, interview/profile, personal experience. Query or send complete ms. Length: up to 2,000 words. **Pays $50-800 for assigned articles; $50-500 for unsolicited articles.** Sometimes pays expenses of writers on assignment.
Photos: State availability of photos with submission. Reviews prints. Offers no additional payment for photos accepted with ms. Buys one-time rights.
Columns/Departments: Lost and Found (mini-reviews of forgotten or under appreciated books), up to 500 words; Readable Feasts (fiction or nonfiction literature with recipes), 2,000-3,000 words; Pilgrimmage (journey to a personally significant place, especially literary), 2,000-3,000 words. **Buys 15-20 mss/year.** Query or send complete ms. **Pays $50-500.**
Fiction: Literary, experimental, mainstream, novel excerpts. **Buys 15-20 mss/year.** Send complete ms. Length: up to 5,000 words. **Pays $200-800.**
Poetry: Amy Bartlett, poetry editor. Avant-garde, free verse, traditional. No prose masquerading as poetry. **Buys 40-80 poems/year.** Submit 5 poems/batch. **Pays $50-150.**
Fillers: Tucker Malarkey, senior editor. Interesting literary facts or anecdotes with citations. Length: up to 100 lines. **Pays $0-10.**
Tips: "We seek: boldness of concept, intense level of energy and emotion, precision of observation, deployment of imagination, grace of style. We require both an investment of strong feeling and great professional care from the writer."

$ TRIQUARTERLY, 2020 Ridge Ave., Northwestern University, Evanston IL 60208-4302. (847)491-3490. Fax: (847)467-2096. Website: triquarterly.nwu.edu. **Contact:** Susan Firestone Hahn, editor. **70% freelance written.** Eager to work with new/unpublished writers. Triannual magazine of fiction, poetry and essays, as well as artwork. Estab. 1964. Pays on publication. Publishes ms an average of 1 year after acceptance. Buys first serial and nonexclusive reprint rights. Responds in 3 months. Study magazine before submitting. Sample copy for $5. Writer's guidelines for #10 SASE.
  • *TriQuarterly* has had several stories published in the *O. Henry Prize* anthology and *Best American Short Stories* as well as poetry in *Best American Poetry.*
Nonfiction: Query before sending essays (no scholarly or critical essays except in special issues).
Fiction and Poetry: No prejudice against style or length of work; only seriousness and excellence are required. Publishes novel excerpts. **Buys 20-50 unsolicited mss/year.** Payment varies depending on grant support. Does not accept or read mss between April 1 and September 30.

$ VIRGINIA QUARTERLY REVIEW, University of Virginia, One West Range, PO Box 400223, Charlottesville VA 22904-4223. (804)924-3124. Fax: (804)924-1397. Website: www.virginia.edu/vqr. **Contact:** Staige D. Blackford, editor. Quarterly magazine. "A national journal of literature and thought." Estab. 1925. Circ. 4,000. Pays on publication. Publishes ms an average of 1 year after acceptance. Byline given. Buys first rights. Editorial lead time 6 months. Submit seasonal material 6 months in advance. Responds in 2 weeks to queries; 2 months to mss. Sample copy $5. Guidelines for #10 SASE or on website.
Nonfiction: Book excerpts, essays, general interest, historical/nostalgic, humor, inspirational, personal experience, travel. Send complete ms. Length: 2,000-4,000 words. **Pays $10/page maximum.**
Fiction: Adventure, ethnic, historical, humorous, mainstream, mystery, novel excerpts, romance. Send complete ms. Length: 2,000-4,000 words. **Pays $10/page maximum.**
Poetry: Gregory Orr, poetry editor. All types. Submit maximum 5 poems. **Pays $1/line.**

$ WESTERN HUMANITIES REVIEW, University of Utah, English Dept., 255 S. Central Campus Dr. Room 3500, Salt Lake City UT 84112-0494. (801)581-6070. Fax: (801)585-5167. E-mail: whr@lists.utah.edu. **Contact:** Jenny Mueller, managing editor. Semi-annual magazine for educated readers. Estab. 1947. Circ. 1,000. Pays on publication. Publishes ms up to 1 year after acceptance. Buys all rights. Accepts queries by mail, phone. Accepts simultaneous submissions. Responds in 5 months.

Nonfiction: Barry Weller, editor-in-chief. Authoritative, readable articles on literature, art, philosophy, current events, history, religion and anything in the humanities. Interdisciplinary articles encouraged. Departments on film and books. **Buys 4-5 unsolicited mss/year. Pays $5/published page.**

Fiction: Karen Brennan, fiction editor. Any type, including experimental. **Buys 8-12 mss/year.** Send complete ms. **Pays $5/published page.**

Poetry: Richard Howard, poetry editor.

Tips: "Because of changes in our editorial staff, we urge familiarity with *recent* issues of the magazine. Inappropriate material will be returned without comment. We do not publish writer's guidelines because we think that the magazine itself conveys an accurate picture of our requirements. Please, *no* e-mail submissions."

$WHETSTONE, Barrington Area Arts Council, Box 1266, Barrington IL 60011. (847)382-5626. Fax: (847)382-3685. **Contact:** S. Berris, M. Portnoy, J. Tolle, editors. **100% freelance written.** Annual literary magazine featuring fiction, creative nonfiction and poetry. "We publish work by emerging and established authors for readers hungry for poetry and prose of substance." Estab. 1982. Circ. 800. Pays on publication. Publishes ms up to 14 months after acceptance. Byline given. Not copyrighted. Buys first North American serial rights. Accepts simultaneous submissions. Responds in 5 months to mss. Sample copy and writer's guidelines for $5.

    Oᴙ To break in, "send us your best work after it has rested long enough for you to forget it and therefore can look at it objectively to fine-tune before submitting."

Nonfiction: Creative essay. "No articles." **Buys 0-3 mss/year.** Send complete ms. Length: 500-5,000 words. Pays with 2 copies and variable cash payment.

Fiction: Novel excerpts (literary) and short stories. **Buys 10-12 mss/year.** Send complete ms. Length: 500-5,000 words. Pays with 2 copies and variable cash payment.

Poetry: Free verse, traditional. "No light verse, for children, political poems." **Buys 10-20 poems/year.** Submit maximum 7 poems. Pays with 2 copies and variable cash payment.

Tips: "We look for fresh approaches to material. We appreciate careful work. Send us your best. We welcome unpublished authors. Though we pay in copies and small monetary amounts that depend on the generosity of our patrons and subscribers, we offer prizes for work published in *Whetstone*. These prizes totaled $1,000, and are given to three or more writers. The editors make their decisions at the time of publication. This is not a contest. In addition, we nominate authors for *Pushcart*; *Best American Short Stories*; *Poetry and Essays*; *O. Henry Awards*; *Best of the South*; Illinois Arts Council Awards; and other prizes and anthologies as they come to our attention. Though our press run is moderate, we work for our authors and offer a prestigious vehicle for their work."

$WILLOW SPRINGS, 705 W. First Ave., Eastern Washington University, Spokane WA 99201. (509)623-4349. **Contact:** Christopher Howell, editor. **100% freelance written.** Semiannual literary magazine. "We publish quality contemporary poetry, fiction, nonfiction and works in translation." Estab. 1977. Circ. 1,500. Publishes ms an average of 4 months after acceptance. Byline given. Acquires first publication rights. Editorial lead time 2 months. Responds in 2 months. Sample copy for $5.50. Writer's guidelines for #10 SASE.

    ● A magazine of growing reputation. Takes part in the AWP Intro Award program.

Nonfiction: Essays. **Accepts 4 mss/year.** Send complete ms. Pays 2 contributor copies.

Fiction: Literary fiction only. "No genre fiction, please." **Accepts 5-8 mss/year.** Send complete ms.

Poetry: Avant-garde, free verse. "No haiku, light verse or religious." **Accepts 50-80 poems/year.** Submit maximum 6 poems. Length: 12 pages maximum.

Tips: "We do not read manuscripts in June, July and August."

$WRITER'S BLOCK MAGAZINE, Canada's Leading Literary Digest, Box 32, 9944-33 Ave., Edmonton, Alberta T6N 1E8 Canada. **Contact:** Shaun Donnelly, publisher/editor. **100% freelance written.** Semiannual magazine covering genre fiction. "We look for outstanding genre fiction and poetry (i.e., horror, mystery, romance, science fiction and western). Estab. 1994. Circ. 5,000. Pays on publication. Publishes ms an average of 6 months after acceptance. Byline given. Offers 50% kill fee. Buys first North American serial rights. Editorial lead time 6 months. Submit seasonal material 6 months in advance. Accepts simultaneous submissions. Responds in 2 weeks to queries; 3 months to mss. Sample copy for $5. Writer's guidelines for #10 SASE.

    Oᴙ "New writers have a better chance via the contest rather than regular submission because they aren't competing with writers like Koontz!"

Nonfiction: Humor (the editor reports an interest in seeing more submissions in this area), photo feature, book reviews. **Buys 4-8 mss/year.** Send complete ms. Length: 250-5,000 words. **Pays 2-5¢/word.**

Reprints: Accepts previously published submissions.

Photos: Send photos with submission. Reviews prints. Negotiates payment individually. Buys one-time rights.

Columns/Departments: Book reviews (genre fiction), 250-1,000 words. **Buys 2-4 mss/year.** Send complete ms. **Pays 2-5¢/word.**

Fiction: Adventure, fantasy, horror, humorous, mainstream, mystery, romance, science fiction, suspense, western. "No sex or profanity." **Buys 8-12 mss/year.** Send complete ms. Length: 500-5,000 words. **Pays 2-5¢/word.**

Poetry: Krista Fisher, associate editor. Avant-garde, free verse, haiku, light verse, traditional. **Buys 8-12 poems/year.** Submit maximum 5 poems. **Pays $5-25.**

N **$ $** THE YALE REVIEW, Yale University, P.O. Box 208243, New Haven CT 06520-8243. (203)432-0499. **Contact:** J.D. McClatchy, editor. Managing Editor: Susan Bianconi. **20% freelance written.** Buys one-time rights. Estab. 1911. Pays prior to publication. Publishes ms within 1 year of acceptance. Responds in 2 months. "No writer's guidelines available. Consult back issues."
- *The Yale Review* has published work chosen for the Pushcart anthology, *The Best American Poetry*, and the O. Henry Award.

Nonfiction and Fiction: Authoritative discussions of politics, literature and the arts. Buys quality fiction. No previously published submissions. Send complete ms with cover letter and SASE. Length: 3,000-5,000 words. **Pays $100-500.**

$ $ $ ZOETROPE: ALL STORY, AZX Publications, 1350 Avenue of the Americas, 24th Floor, New York NY 10019-4801. (212)708-0400. Fax: (212)708-0475. E-mail: info@all-story.com. Website: www.zoetrope-stories.com. **Contact:** Adrienne Brodeur, editor-in-chief. Quarterly literary magazine specializing in high caliber short fiction. "*Zoetrope: All Story* bridges the worlds of fiction and film by publishing stories alongside essays and reprints of classic stories that were adapted for the screen." Open to outstanding work by beginning and established writers. Estab. 1997. Circ. 40,000. Publishes ms 6 months after acceptance. Byline given. Buys first serial rights and 2 year film option. Accepts simultaneous submissions. Responds in 5 months. Sample copy on website. Guidelines for SASE or on website.
- *Zoetrope: All Story* does not accept submissions from June 1 through August 31.

Fiction: Literary, mainstream/contemporary, one act plays. 7,000 words maximum. No short shorts or reprints. Receives 10,000 submissions/year. **Buys 32-40 ms/year.** Query with SASE and complete ms (1 story maximum). **Pays $1,400.**
- Ranked as one of the best markets for fiction writers in *Writer's Digest* magazine's "Fiction 50," June 2000.
- The online magazine carries original content not found in the print edition and includes writer's guidelines. "We have an online supplement to our writers' workshop that publishes stories from the online workshop. It is guest edited by workshop members."

Tips: "We're always looking for tightly written stories that have a compelling narrative arc. Most of the stories that capture our attention have classic elements, such as strong characters and compelling themes, and illuminate the human condition with acute perception. *Zoetrope* considers unsolicited submissions of short stories no longer than 7,000 words. Excerpts from larger works, screenplays, treatments and poetry will be returned unread. We are unable to respond to submissions without SASE."

$ ZYZZYVA, The Last Word: West Coast Writers & Artists, P.O. Box 590069, San Francisco CA 94159-0069. (415)752-4393. Fax: (415)752-4391. E-mail: editor@zyzzyva.org. Website: www.zyzzyva.org. **Contact:** Howard Junker, editor. **100% freelance written.** Works with a small number of new/unpublished writers each year. "We feature work by West Coast writers only. We are essentially a literary magazine, but of wide-ranging interests and a strong commitment to nonfiction." Estab. 1985. Circ. 3,500. **Pays on acceptance.** Publishes ms an average of 3 months after acceptance. Byline given. Buys first North American serial rights and one-time anthology rights. Accepts queries by mail, e-mail, fax. Responds in 1 week to queries; 1 month to mss. Sample copy and writer's guidelines for $7 or on website.

Nonfiction: Book excerpts, general interest, historical/nostalgic, humor, personal experience. **Buys 15 mss/year.** Query by mail or e-mail. Length: open. **Pays $50.**

Photos: Copies or slides only.

Fiction: Ethnic, experimental, humorous, mainstream. **Buys 20 mss/year.** Send complete ms. Length: open. **Pays $50.**
- Ranked as one of the best markets for fiction writers in *Writer's Digest* magazine's "Fiction 50," June 2000.

Poetry: **Buys 20 poems/year.** Submit maximum 5 poems. Length: 3-200 lines. **Pays $50.**

Tips: "West Coast writers means those currently living in California, Alaska, Washington, Oregon or Hawaii."

MEN'S

Magazines in this section offer features on topics of general interest primarily to men. Magazines that also use material slanted toward men can be found in Business & Finance, Child Care & Parental Guidance, Ethnic/Minority, Gay & Lesbian Interest, General Interest, Health & Fitness, Military, Relationships and Sports sections. Magazines featuring pictorial layouts accompanied by stories and articles of a sexual nature, both gay and straight, appear in the Sex section.

$ $ $ CIGAR AFICIONADO, M. Shanken Communications, Inc., 387 Park Ave. S., New York NY 10016. (212)684-4224. Fax: (212)684-5424. Website: www.cigaraficionado.com. Editor: Marvin Shanken. **Contact:** Gordon Mott, executive editor. **75% freelance written.** Bimonthly magazine covering cigars and men's lifestyle. Estab. 1992. Circ. 400,000. **Pays on acceptance.** Publishes ms an average of 9 months after acceptance. Byline given. Offers 25% kill fee. Buys all rights. Editorial lead time 3 months. Submit seasonal material 3 months in advance. Accepts queries by mail, fax. Responds in 2 months. Sample copy and writer's guidelines for SASE.

Nonfiction: **Buys 80-100 features/year.** Query. Length: 2,000 words. Pay varies. Sometimes pays expenses of writers on assignment.

Columns/Departments: **Buys 20 short pieces year.** Length: 1,000 words. Pay varies.

■ The online magazine carries original content not found in the print edition. Contact: Jason Sheftell, online editor.

[N] [✕] $ COWBOY MAGAZINE, Range Writer, Inc., P.O. Box 126, La Veta CO 81055. Fax: (719)742-3041. **Contact:** Darrell Arnold, publisher/editor. **85% freelance written.** Quarterly magazine covering the world of the working ranch cowboy. "You probably can't write for us unless you have a first-hand knowledge of cowboying and ranching. Our writers need to know exactly what ranch life is like. If you've been out there horseback, and know which end of the cow gets up first, you might be right for us. No gunfighters or rodeo or trail rides or dude stories. We want to know how the working ranch cowboy, historical or contemporary, gets the job done." Estab. 1990. Circ. 12,000. Pays on publication. Publishes ms an average of 9 months after acceptance. Byline given. Buys first rights or makes work-for-hire assignments. Editorial lead time 2 months. Submit seasonal material 3 months in advance. Sample copy for $5.50. Writer's guidelines for #10 SASE.

Nonfiction: Essays, exposé, general interest, historical/nostalgic, how-to (do a cowboy's work), humor, interview/profile, opinion, personal experience, photo feature, technical. "No dude stories, no trailrides, no veterinarian articles, horse articles (unless ranch horses), gunfighters, no stories from phonies—we can spot you." **Buys 30 mss/year.** Send complete ms, with photos if possible. Length: 800-1,500 words. **Pays $2/column inch.** Sometimes pays expenses of writers on assignment.

Photos: Send photos with submission. Reviews transparencies and glossy prints. Offers $10/photo maximum; $100 for covers. Captions and identification of subjects required. Buys one-time rights.

Columns/Departments: Legacy (the heritage of ranching and ranching issues), 1,500 words. **Buys 3 mss/year.** Send complete ms. **Pays $2/column inch.**

Fiction: Authentic working cowboy stories. Nothing that is not true to ranch cowboy life. No gunfighters, gambling, drinking, whores, Hollywood westerns. **Buys 2 mss/year.** Send complete ms. Length: 1,200 words. **Pays $2/column inch.**

Poetry: Traditional. Nothing that doesn't pertain to working ranch cowboys or isn't precisely rhymed and metered. **Buys 2 poems/year.** Submit maximum 4 poems. Length: 20 lines maximum. **Pays $25.**

Tips: "Go live the cowboy life for a year, if you haven't already had that ranch experience."

[N] $ $ $ ESQUIRE, 250 W. 55th St., New York NY 10019. (212)649-4020. Editor-in-Chief: David Granger. Monthly magazine for smart, well-off men. Estab. 1933. General readership is college educated and sophisticated, between ages 30 and 45. Written mostly by contributing editors on contract. Rarely accepts unsolicited mss. **Pays on acceptance.** Offers 20% kill fee. Publishes ms an average of 2 months after acceptance. Retains first worldwide periodical publication rights for 90 days from cover date.

Nonfiction: Columns average 1,500 words; features average 5,000 words; short front-of-book pieces average 200-400 words. Focus is on the ever-changing trends in American culture. Topics include current events and politics, social criticism, sports, celebrity profiles, the media, art and music, men's fashion. Queries must be sent by letter. **Buys 4 features and 12 short pieces. Pays $1/word.**

Photos: Marianne Butler, photo editor. Uses mostly commissioned photography. Payment depends on size and number of photos.

Fiction: Contact: literary editor. "Literary excellence is our only criterion." Accepts work chiefly from literary agencies. Publishes short stories, some poetry, and excerpts from novels, memoirs and plays.

Tips: "A writer has the best chance of breaking in at *Esquire* by querying with a specific idea that requires special contacts and expertise. Ideas must be timely and national in scope."

$ $ $ HEARTLAND USA, UST Publishing, 1 Sound Shore Dr., Greenwich CT 06830-7251. (203)622-3456. Fax: (203)863-5393. E-mail: husaedit@ustnet.com. **Contact:** Brad Pearson, editor. **95% freelance written.** Bimonthly magazine for working men. "*HUSA* is a general interest lifestyle magazine for adult males—active outdoorsmen. The editorial mix includes hunting, fishing, sports, automotive, how-to, country music, human interest and wildlife." Estab. 1991. Circ. 901,000. **Pays on acceptance.** Byline given. Offers 20% kill fee. Buys first North American serial and second serial (reprint) rights. Submit seasonal material 1 year in advance. Accepts queries by mail, e-mail, fax. Accepts simultaneous submissions. Responds in 1 month to queries. Sample copy on request. Writer's guidelines for #10 SASE.

Nonfiction: Book excerpts, general interest, historical/nostalgic, how-to, humor, inspirational, interview/profile, new product, personal experience, photo feature, technical, travel. "No fiction or dry expository pieces." **Buys 30 mss/year.** Query with or without published clips or send complete ms. Length: 350-1,200 words. **Pays 50-80¢/word for assigned articles; 25-80¢/word for unsolicited articles.** Sometimes pays expenses of writers on assignment.

● Ranked as one of the best markets for freelance writers in *Writer's Yearbook* magazine's annual "Top 100 Markets," January 2000.

Reprints: Send photocopy of article and information about when and where the article previously appeared. Pays 25% of amount paid for an original article.

Photos: Send photos with submission. Reviews transparencies. Identification of subjects required. Buys one-time rights.

Tips: "Features with the possibility of strong photographic support are open to freelancers, as are our departments. We look for a relaxed, jocular, easy-to-read style, and look favorably on the liberal use of anecdote or interesting quotations. Our average reader sees himself as hardworking, traditional, rugged, confident, uncompromising and daring."

$ $ $ $ THE INTERNATIONAL, The Magazine of Adventure and Pleasure for Men, Tomorrow Enterprises, 2228 E. 20th St., Oakland CA 94606. (510)532-6501. Fax: (510)536-5886. E-mail: tonyattomr@aol.com. **Con-**

tact: Mr. Anthony L. Williams, managing editor. **70% freelance written.** Monthly magazine covering "bush and seaplane flying, seafaring, pleasure touring, etc. with adventure stories from all men who travel on sexual tours to Asia, Latin America, The Caribbean and the Pacific." Estab. 1997. Circ. 5,000. Pays on publication. Publishes ms 2 months after acceptance. Buys first rights. Editorial lead time 2 months. Submit seasonal material 3 months in advance. Accepts queries by mail, e-mail. Accepts simultaneous submissions. Responds in 2 weeks to queries; 2 months to mss. Writer's guidelines free.

Nonfiction: Exposé, general interest, historical/nostalgic, humor, interview/profile, opinion, personal experience, photo feature, travel. Seafaring stories of all types published with photos. Military and veteran stories also sought, as well as ex-pats living abroad. Especially interested in airplane flying stories with photos. No pornography, no family or "honeymoon" type travel. **Buys 40-50 mss/year.** Query or send complete ms. Length: 700 words max. **Pays $100-2,000 for assigned articles, $25-1,000 for unsolicited articles.** Sometimes pays expenses of writers on assignment.

- Ranked as one of the best markets for freelance writers in *Writer's Yearbook* magazine's annual "Top 100 Markets," January 2000.

Photos: Send photos with submission. Reviews negatives and 5×6 prints. Offers no additional payment for photos accepted with ms. Identification of subjects required. Buys one-time rights or all rights.

Columns/Departments: Asia/Pacific Beat; Latin America/Caribbean Beat (Nightlife, Adventure, Air & Sea), 450 words; Lifestyles Abroad (Expatriate Men's Doings Overseas), 600-1,000 words. **Buys 25 mss/year.** Query or send complete ms. **Pays $25-1,000.**

Fillers: Anecdotes, facts, gags to be illustrated by cartoonist, newsbreaks, short humor. **Buys 25/year.** Length: 200-600 words. **Pays $25-100.**

Tips: "If a single male lives in those parts of the world covered, and is either a pleasure tourist, pilot or seafarer, we are interested in his submissions. He can visit our upcoming website or contact us directly. Stories from female escorts or party girls are also welcomed."

N $ $ $ MEN'S JOURNAL, Wenner Media Inc., 1290 Avenue of the Americas, New York NY 10104-0298. (212)484-1616. Fax: (212)767-8213. Editor: Mark Bryant. **Contact:** Taylor A. Plimpton, editorial assistant. Magazine published 10 times/year covering general lifestyle for men, ages 25-49. "*Men's Journal* is for active men with an interest in participatory sports, travel, fitness and adventure. It provides practical, informative articles on how to spend quality leisure time." Estab. 1992. Circ. 550,000. Accepts queries by mail, fax.

- *Men's Journal* won the National Magazine Award for Personal Science.

Nonfiction: Features and profiles. 2,000-7,000 words; shorter features of 400-1,200 words; equipment and fitness stories 400-1,800 words. Query with SASE. "No phone queries, please." Pay varies.

N ▢ $ SHARPMAN.COM, The Ultimate Guide's to Men's Living, SharpMan Media LLC, 11718 Barrington Court, No. 702, Los Angeles CA 90049-2930. (310)446-7915. Fax: (310)446-7965. E-mail: NewWriters@SharpMan .com. Website: www.sharpman.com. Editor: Y.M. Reiss. **Contact:** Elizabeth Felicetti, managing editor. **50% freelance written.** Weekly online publication. "*SharpMan.com* is an online community for professional men, ages 18-35. The *SharpMan.com* magazine is designed to be 'the Ultimate Men's Guide to SharpLiving.' In articles on wardrobe, work, grooming, dating, health, toys and more, *SharpMan.com* attempts to provide meaningful instruction on where to go, what to do, how to dress, and what to buy." Estab. 1998. Circ. approximately 60,000. Pays on publication. Byline given. Buys exclusive rights to version posted, negotiable on excerpts from existing ms published for promotional purposes and all rights. Editorial lead time 1 month. Submit seasonal material 4 months in advance. Accepts queries by mail, e-mail. Responds in 1 month to queries; 2 months to mss. Sample copy online at website. Writer's guidelines by e-mail.

Nonfiction: Book excerpts, exposé, how-to, interview/profile, new product, technical, travel, men's interest: SharpDating, SharpWork, SharpTravel, SharpHealth, SharpGrooming, SharpToys (all in "how-to" form). **Buys 100 mss/year.** Query with published clips. Length: 600-2,000 words. **Pays $25-50.** "*SharpMan.com* frequently features writers who publish for the purpose of gaining professional recognition or promotion for published manuscripts and other services. Where a writer seeks to promote a product, remuneration is provided by way of a link to their desired URL, in lieu of cash." Sometimes pays expenses of writers on assignment.

Reprints: Accepts previously published submissions in a modified form with SharpMan Media, LLC retaining rights to modified product.

Photos: State availability of photos with submission. Negotiates payment individually. Captions, model releases and identification of subjects required. "Must be a "legal" use of the photo provided."

Columns/Departments: SharpTravel (for business and leisure travelers); SharpWork (oriented towards young professionals); and SharpDating (slanted towards men in their 20s-30s), all 600-2,000 words; SharpToysm 300-1,500 words; SharpHealth, 600-1,500 words; and Sharp Grooming. We also publish a "Tip of the Week," generally 100-300 words. **Buys 100 mss/year.** Query with published clips. **Pays $25-50.**

Fillers: Facts. Length: 25-100 words. **Pays $5.**

Tips: "Familiarize yourself with our magazine's topics and tone. We write for a very specific audience. The Editorial Team prefers content written in the 'SharpMan Tone,' a fast, male-oriented tone that provides specific information on the subject at hand. Ideally, each articles features 'top tips' or step-by-step 'how-to' language delivering specific information that can be easily and immediately implemented by the reader. SharpMan.com content is non-erotic in nature and article may not include any inappropriate language."

$ $ $SMOKE MAGAZINE, Life's Burning Desires, Lockwood Publications, 130 W. 42nd St., New York NY 10036. (212)391-2060. Fax: (212)827-0945. E-mail: cigarbar@aol.com. Website: www.smokemag.com. Editor: Alyson Boxman. Senior Editor: Michael Malone. **Contact:** Michael Jessee, assistant editor. **75% freelance written**. Quarterly magazine covering cigars and men's lifestyle issues. "A large majority of *Smoke's* readers are affluent men, ages 28-40; active, educated and adventurous." Estab. 1995. Circ. 175,000. Pays 2 months after publication. Publishes ms an average of 3 months after acceptance. Byline given. Offers 25% kill fee. Buys first rights. Editorial lead time 2 months. Submit seasonal material 6 months in advance. Accepts simultaneous submissions. Responds in 6 weeks to queries; 3 months to mss. Sample copy for $4.95; writer's guidelines for #10 SASE.

    O→ Break in with "good nonfiction that interests guys—beer, cuisine, true-crime, sports, cigars, of course. Be original."

Nonfiction: Essays, exposé, general interest, historical/nostalgic, how-to, humor, interview/profile, opinion, true-crime, personal experience, photo feature, travel. **Buys 25 mss/year.** Query by mail only with published clips. Length: 1,500-3,000 words. **Pays $500-1,500.** Sometimes pays expenses of writers on assignment.

Photos: State availability of photos with submission. Reviews transparencies (2¼×2¼). Negotiates payment individually. Identification of subjects required.

Columns/Departments: Smoke Undercover, Smoke Slant (humor); What Lew Says (cigar industry news); Workin' Stiffs (world's best jobs), all 1,500 words. **Buys 20 mss/year.** Query by mail only with published clips. **Pays $500-1,500.**

Fillers: Anecdotes, facts, gags to be illustrated by cartoonist, newsbreaks, short humor. **Buys 12/year.** Length: 200-500 words. **Pays $200-500.**

    ▣ The online magazine carries original content not found in the print edition. Contact: Mike Malone.

Tips: "Send a short, clear query with clips. Go with your field of expertise: cigars, sports, music, true crime, etc."

MILITARY

These publications emphasize military or paramilitary subjects or other aspects of military life. Technical and semitechnical publications for military commanders, personnel and planners, as well as those for military families and civilians interested in Armed Forces activities are listed here. Publications covering military history can be found in the History section.

$ $AIR FORCE TIMES, Army Times Publishing Co., 6883 Commercial Dr., Springfield VA 22159. (703)750-9000. Fax: (703)750-8622. Websites: www.armytimes.com; www.navytimes.com; www.airforcetimes.com; www.marinecorpstimes.com. **Contact:** Chris Lawson, managing editor, *Army Times*; Alex Neill, managing editor, *Navy Times*; Julie Bird, managing editor, *Air Force Times*; Phillip Thompson, managing editor, *Marine Corps Times*. Weeklies edited separately for Army, Navy, Marine Corps, and Air Force military personnel and their families. They contain career information such as pay raises, promotions, news of legislation affecting the military, housing, base activities and features of interest to military people. Estab. 1940. Circ. 230,000. **Pays on acceptance.** Byline given. Offers kill fee. Buys first rights. Accepts queries by mail, e-mail, phone. Accepts simultaneous submissions. Responds in 1 month to queries. Sample copy and writer's guidelines for SASE.

Nonfiction: Features of interest to career military personnel and their families. No advice pieces. Query. **Buys 150-175 mss/year.** Length: 750-2,000 words. **Pays $100-500.**

    ● Ranked as one of the best markets for freelance writers in *Writer's Yearbook* magazine's annual "Top 100 Markets," January 2000.

Columns/Departments: Buys 75 mss/year. Length: 500-900 words. **Pays $75-125.**

    ▣ The online magazine carries original content not found in the print editions. Contact: Neff Hudson, online editor.

Tips: Looking for "stories on active duty, reserve and retired military personnel; stories on military matters and localized military issues; stories on successful civilian careers after military service."

$ $AMERICAN SURVIVAL GUIDE, Y-Visionary Publishing, 265 S. Anita Dr., Suite 120, Orange CA 92868-3310. (714)939-9991, ext. 204. Fax: (714)939-9909. E-mail: jim4asg@aol.com. **Contact:** Jim Benson, editor. **60% freelance written.** Monthly magazine covering "self-reliance, defense, meeting day-to-day and possible future threats—survivalism for survivalists." Circ. 65,000. Pays on publication. Publishes ms up to 1 year after acceptance. Byline given. Submit seasonal material 5 months in advance. Sample copy for $6. Writer's guidelines for SASE.

    ● *American Survival Guide* is always looking for more good material with quality artwork (photos). They want articles on recent events and new techniques, etc. giving the latest available information to their readers.

Nonfiction: How-to, interview/profile, personal experience (how I survived), photo feature (equipment and techniques related to survival in all possible situations), emergency medical, health and fitness, communications, transportation, food preservation, water purification, nutrition, tools, shelter, etc. "No general articles about how to survive. We want specifics and single subjects." **Buys 60-100 mss/year.** Query or send complete ms. Length: 1,500-3,000 words. **Pays $160-500.** Sometimes pays some expenses of writers on assignment.

Photos: Send photos with ms. "One of the most frequent mistakes made by writers in completing an article assignment for us is sending photo submissions that are inadequate." Captions, model releases and identification of subjects mandatory. Buys exclusive one-time rights.

Tips: "We need hard copy with computer disk and photos or other artwork. Prepare material of value to individuals who wish to sustain human life no matter what the circumstance. This magazine is a text and reference."

$ $ARMY MAGAZINE, Box 1560, Arlington VA 22210. (703)841-4300. Fax: (703)841-3505. E-mail: armymag@ ausa.org. Website: www.ausa.org/armyzine/. **Contact:** Mary Blake French, editor. **70% freelance written.** Prefers to work with published/established writers. Monthly magazine emphasizing military interests. Estab. 1904. Circ. 90,000. Pays on publication. Publishes ms an average of 5 months after acceptance. Byline given except for back-up research. Buys all rights. Submit seasonal material 3 months in advance. Accepts queries by mail, fax. Sample copy and writer's guidelines for 9 × 12 SAE with $1 postage or on website.
   • *Army Magazine* looks for shorter articles.
Nonfiction: Historical (military and original); humor (military feature-length articles and anecdotes); interview; new product; nostalgia; personal experience dealing especially with the most recent conflicts in which the US Army has been involved (Desert Storm, Panama, Grenada); photo feature; profile; technical. No rehashed history. "We would like to see more pieces about little-known episodes involving interesting military personalities. We especially want material lending itself to heavy, contributor-supplied photographic treatment. The first thing a contributor should recognize is that our readership is very savvy militarily. 'Gee-whiz' personal reminiscences get short shrift, unless they hold their own in a company in which long military service, heroism and unusual experiences are commonplace. At the same time, Army readers like a well-written story with a fresh slant, whether it is about an experience in a foxhole or the fortunes of a corps in battle." **Buys 8 mss/issue.** Submit complete ms (hard copy and disk). Length: 1,500 words, but shorter items, especially in 1,000 to 1,500 range, often have better chance of getting published. **Pays 12-18¢/word.** No unsolicited book reviews.
Photos: Submit photo material with accompanying ms. Pays $25-50 for 8 × 10 b&w glossy prints; $50-350 for 8 × 10 color glossy prints or 2¼ × 2¼ transparencies; will also accept 35mm. Captions preferred. Buys all rights. Pays $35-50 for cartoon with strong military slant.
Columns/Departments: Military news, books, comment (*New Yorker*-type "Talk of the Town" items). **Buys 8/issue.** Submit complete ms. Length: 1,000 words. **Pays $40-150.**

$ $ARMY TIMES, Army Times Publishing Co., 6883 Commercial Dr., Springfield VA 22159. (703)750-9000. Fax: (703)750-8622. Websites: www.armytimes.com; www.navytimes.com; www.airforcetimes.com; www.marinecorps times.com. **Contact:** Chris Lawson, managing editor, *Army Times*; Alex Neill, managing editor, *Navy Times*; Julie Bird, managing editor, *Air Force Times*; Phillip Thompson, managing editor, *Marine Corps Times*. Weeklies edited separately for Army, Navy, Marine Corps, and Air Force military personnel and their families. They contain career information such as pay raises, promotions, news of legislation affecting the military, housing, base activities and features of interest to military people. Estab. 1940. Circ. 230,000. **Pays on acceptance.** Byline given. Offers kill fee. Buys first rights. Accepts queries by mail, e-mail, phone. Accepts simultaneous submissions. Responds in 1 month to queries. Sample copy and writer's guidelines for SASE.
Nonfiction: Features of interest to career military personnel and their families. No advice pieces. Query. **Buys 150-175 mss/year.** Length: 750-2,000 words. **Pays $100-500.**
   • Ranked as one of the best markets for freelance writers in *Writer's Yearbook* magazine's annual "Top 100 Markets," January 2000.
Columns/Departments: Buys 75 mss/year. Length: 500-900 words. **Pays $75-125.**
   ▣ The online magazine carries original content not found in the print editions. Contact: Neff Hudson, online editor.
Tips: Looking for "stories on active duty, reserve and retired military personnel; stories on military matters and localized military issues; stories on successful civilian careers after military service."

[N] $ $LIFELINES SECTION/MILITARY TIMES, Army Times Publishing Co. (subsidiary of Gannett Corp.), 6883 Commercial Dr., Springfield VA 22159. Fax: (703)750-8781. E-mail: features@atpco.com. Website: www.military city.com. Managing Editor: David Craig. **Contact:** G.E. Willis, editor. **25% freelance written.** Weekly tabloid covering lifestyle topics for active, retired and reserve military members and their families." "Features need to have real military people in them, and appeal to readers in all the armed services. Our target audience is 90% male, young, fit and adventurous, mostly married and often with young children. They move frequently. Writer queries should approach ideas with those demographics and facts firmly in mind." Circ. 300,000. **Pays on acceptance.** Publishes ms an average of 2 months after acceptance. Byline given. Offers 25% kill fee. Buys first (worldwide) and electronic rights. Editorial lead time 2 months. Submit seasonal material 3 months in advance. Accepts queries by mail, e-mail, fax. Accepts simultaneous submissions. Responds in 6 weeks. Sample copy for $2.25 or on website. Writer's guidelines for SAE with 1 first-class stamp or by e-mail.
   ⊙━ "Greatest need is in the adventure categories of sports, recreation, outdoor, personal fitness and running. Personal finance features are especially needed, but they must be specifically tailored to our military audience's needs and interests."
Nonfiction: Book excerpts, how-to, interview/profile, new product, photo feature, technical, travel, sports, recreation, entertainment, health, personal fitness, self-image (fashion, trends), relationships, personal finance, food. "No poems, war memoirs or nostalgia, fiction, travel pieces that are too upscale (luxury cruises) or too focused on military monuments/museums." **Buys 110 mss/year.** Query with published clips. Length: 300-1,500 words. **Pays $100-350.** Sometimes pays expenses of writers on assignment.

Photos: State availability of photos with submission. Reviews transparencies. Offers $35/photo. Captions and identification of subjects required. Buys one-time rights.

Columns/Departments: Slices of Life (human-interest shorts), 300 words; Running (how-to for experienced runners, tips, techniques, problem-solving), 500 words; Personal Fitness (how-to, tips, techniques for working out, improving fitness), 500 words. **Buys 40 mss/year.** Query. **Pays $100-200.**

Tips: "New writers have a great opportunity to sell to *Lifelines* if they do their homework. Pitch us stories we need, not just the ones you want to sell us. Our *Lifelines* section appears every week with a variety of services, information and entertainment articles on topics that relate to readers' off-duty lives; or to personal dimensions of their on-duty lives. Topics include food, relationships, parenting, education, retirement, shelter, health and fitness, sports, personal appearances, community, recreation, personal finance and entertainment. We are looking for articles about military life, its problems and how to handle them, as well as interesting things people are doing, on the job and in their leisure. Keep in mind that our readers come from all of the military services. For instance, a story can focus on an Army family, but may need to include families or sources from other services as well. The editorial 'voice' of the section is familiar and conversational; good-humored without being flippant; sincere without being sentimental; savvy about military life but in a relevant and subtle way, never forgetting that our readers are individuals first, spouses or parents or children second, and service members third."

$ $ MARINE CORPS TIMES, Army Times Publishing Co., 6883 Commercial Dr., Springfield VA 22159. (703)750-9000. Fax: (703)750-8622. Websites: www.armytimes.com; www.navytimes.com; www.airforcetimes.com; www.marinecorpstimes.com. **Contact:** Chris Lawson, managing editor, *Army Times*; Alex Neill, managing editor, *Navy Times*; Julie Bird, managing editor, *Air Force Times*; Phillip Thompson, managing editor, *Marine Corps Times*. Weeklies edited separately for Army, Navy, Marine Corps, and Air Force military personnel and their families. They contain career information such as pay raises, promotions, news of legislation affecting the military, housing, base activities and features of interest to military people. Estab. 1940. Circ. 230,000. **Pays on acceptance.** Byline given. Offers kill fee. Buys first rights. Accepts queries by mail, e-mail, phone. Accepts simultaneous submissions. Responds in 1 month to queries. Sample copy and writer's guidelines for SASE.

Nonfiction: Features of interest to career military personnel and their families. No advice pieces. Query. **Buys 150-175 mss/year.** Length: 750-2,000 words. **Pays $100-500.**

● Ranked as one of the best markets for freelance writers in *Writer's Yearbook* magazine's annual "Top 100 Markets," January 2000.

Columns/Departments: Buys 75 mss/year. Length: 500-900 words. **Pays $75-125.**

■ The online magazine carries original content not found in the print editions. Contact: Neff Hudson, online editor.

Tips: Looking for "stories on active duty, reserve and retired military personnel; stories on military matters and localized military issues; stories on successful civilian careers after military service."

N ■ $ MILITARY.COM, The Web portal for the military community, Military.com, 1235 Jefferson Davis Hwy., #304, Arlington VA 22202. (703)414-3035. Fax: (703)414-3095. E-mail: submissions@military.com. Website: www.military.com. **Contact:** Bradley Peniston, editor. **50% freelance written.** Daily online magazine covering the military-operations, career, family, history. "We serve and salute those who serve and served in uniform and those who support them. We are the Web portal for active-duty, reserve, retired, veteran, family and buffs." Estab. 1999. **Pays on acceptance.** Publishes ms an average of 1 month after acceptance. Byline given. Offers ⅓% kill fee. Buys first North American serial and electronic rights. Accepts queries by e-mail. Responds in 2 weeks to queries; 1 month to mss. Writer's guidelines free, on website or by e-mail.

Nonfiction: General interest, historical/nostalgic, how-to, humor, interview/profile, personal experience. **Buys hundreds mss/year.** Query with published clips. Length: 200-500 words. **Pays $100-300 minimum for assigned articles; $50-300 for unsolicited articles.** Sometimes pays expenses of writers on assignment.

Photos: Send photos with submission. Negotiates payment individually. Captions, model releases and identification of subjects required. Buys all rights.

Columns/Departments: Query with published clips.

Fillers: Anecdotes, newsbreaks, short humor. **Buys hundreds/year.** Length: 50-200 words. **Pays $10-25.**

Tips: "Write to appeal to a general military audience and write tight and punchy."

$ $ NAVAL HISTORY, US Naval Institute, 291 Wood Rd., Annapolis MD 21402-5034. (410)295-1079. Fax: (410)269-7940. E-mail: fschultz@usni.org. Website: www.usni.org. Associate Editors: Colin Babb and Giles Roblyer. **Contact:** Fred L. Schultz, editor-in-chief. **90% freelance written.** Bimonthly magazine covering naval and maritime history, worldwide. "We are committed, as a publication of the 126-year-old US Naval Institute, to presenting the best and most accurate short works in international naval and maritime history. We do find a place for academicians, but they should be advised that a good story generally wins against a dull topic, no matter how well researched." Estab. 1988. Circ. 40,000. **Pays on acceptance.** Publishes ms an average of 2 years after acceptance. Byline given. Buys first North American serial rights; occasionally allows rights to revert to authors. Editorial lead time 6 months. Submit seasonal material 6 months in advance. Accepts queries by mail, e-mail, fax, phone. Responds in 1 month to queries; 2 months to mss. Sample copy for $3.95 and SASE or on website. Writer's guidelines for #10 SASE or on website.

Nonfiction: Book excerpts, essays, historical/nostalgic, humor, inspirational, interview/profile, personal experience, photo feature, technical. **Buys 50 mss/year.** Query. Length: 1,000-3,000 words. **Pays $300-500 for assigned articles; $75-400 for unsolicited articles.**

Photos: State availability of photos with submission. Reviews contact sheets, transparencies, 4×6 or larger prints and digital submissions or CD-ROM. Offers $10 minimum. Captions, model releases, identification of subjects required. Buys one-time rights.

Fillers: Anecdotes, news breaks (naval-related), short humor. **Buys 40-50/year.** Length: 50-1,000 words. **Pays $10-50.**

Tips: "A good way to break in is to write a good, concise, exciting story supported by primary sources and substantial illustrations. Naval history-related news items (ship decommissionings, underwater archaeology, etc.) are also welcome. Because our story bank is substantial, competition is severe. Tying a topic to an anniversary many times is an advantage. We still are in need of Korean and Vietnam War-era material."

N **$ $** **NAVY TIMES**, Army Times Publishing Co., 6883 Commercial Dr., Springfield VA 22159. (703)750-8636. Fax: (703)750-8767. E-mail: navylet@atpco.com. Website: www.navytimes.com. **Contact:** Alex Neil, editor. Weekly newspaper covering sea services. News and features of men and women in the Navy, Coast Guard and Marine Corps. Estab. 1950. Circ. 90,000. **Pays on acceptance.** Byline given. Buys first North American serial or second serial (reprint) rights. Submit seasonal material 2 months in advance. Responds in 2 months. Guidelines free.

Nonfiction: Historical/nostalgic, opinion. No poetry. **Buys 100 mss/year.** Query. Length: 500-1,000 words. **Pays $50-500.** Sometimes pays expenses of writers on assignment.

Reprints: Send tearsheet of article or short story.

Photos: Send photos with submission. Offers $20-100/photo. Captions and identification of subjects required. Buys one-time rights.

$ **PARAMETERS: U.S. Army War College Quarterly**, US Army War College, Carlisle Barracks PA 17013-5050. (717)245-4943. E-mail: parameters@awc.carlisle.army.mil. Website: carlisle-www.army.mil/usawc/Parameters/. **Contact:** Editor, *Parameters*. **100% freelance written.** Prefers to work with published/established writers or experts in the field. Readership consists of senior leadership of US defense establishment, both uniformed and civilian, plus members of the media, government, industry and academia interested in national and international security affairs, military strategy, military leadership and management, art and science of warfare, and military history (provided it has contemporary relevance). Estab. 1971. Circ. 13,500. Pays on publication. Publishes ms an average of 6 months after acceptance. Byline given. Not copyrighted; unless copyrighted by author, articles may be reprinted with appropriate credits. Buys first serial rights. Accepts queries by mail, e-mail, fax, phone. Responds in 6 weeks. Sample copy and writer's guidelines for SASE or on website.

Nonfiction: Articles are preferred that deal with current security issues, employ critical analysis and provide solutions or recommendations. Liveliness and verve, consistent with scholarly integrity, appreciated. Theses, studies and academic course papers should be adapted to article form prior to submission. Documentation in complete endnotes. Submit complete ms. Length: 4,500 words average, preferably less. **Pays $150 average (including visuals).**

Tips: "Make it short; keep it interesting; get criticism and revise accordingly. Write on a contemporary topic. Tackle a subject only if you are an authority. No fax submissions."

★ **$ $** **PROCEEDINGS**, U.S. Naval Institute, 291 Wood Rd., Annapolis MD 21402-5034. (410)268-6110. Fax: (410)295-1049. Website: www.usni.org. Editor: Fred H. Rainbow. **Contact:** John G. Miller, managing editor. **80% freelance written.** Monthly magazine covering Navy, Marine Corps, Coast Guard. Estab. 1873. Circ. 100,000. **Pays on acceptance.** Publishes ms an average of 9 months after acceptance. Byline given. Buys all rights. Editorial lead time 3 months. Responds in 2 months to submissions. Sample copy for $3.95. Writer's guidelines free.

Nonfiction: Essays, historical/nostalgic, interview/profile, photo feature, technical. **Buys 100-125 mss/year.** Query or send complete ms. Length: 3,000 words. **Pays $60-150/printed page** for unsolicited articles.

Photos: State availability of or send photos with submission. Reviews transparencies and prints. Offers $25/photo maximum. Buys one-time rights.

Columns/Departments: Comment & Discussion (letters to editor), 750 words; Commentary (opinion), 1,000 words; Nobody Asked Me, But . . . (opinion), less than 1,000 words. **Buys 150-200 mss/year.** Query or send complete ms. **Pays $32-150.**

Fillers: Anecdotes. **Buys 20/year.** Length: 100 words. **Pays $25.**

$ $ $ $ **THE RETIRED OFFICER MAGAZINE**, 201 N. Washington St., Alexandria VA 22314-2539. (800)245-8762. Fax: (703)838-8179. E-mail: editor@troa.org. Website: www.troa.org. Editor: Col. Warren S. Lacy, USA-Ret. Managing Editor: Heather Lyons. **Contact:** Molly Wyman. **60% freelance written.** Prefers to work with published/established writers. Monthly magazine for officers of the 7 uniformed services and their families. "*The Retired Officer Magazine* covers topics such as current military/political affairs, military history, travel, finance, hobbies, health and fitness, and military family and retirement lifestyles." Estab. 1945. Circ. 395,000. **Pays on acceptance.** Publishes ms an average of 1 year after acceptance. Byline given. Buys first North American serial rights. Accepts queries by mail, e-mail, fax. Responds to material accepted for publication within 3 months. Sample copy and writer's guidelines for 9×12 SASE with 6 first-class stamps or on website.

Nonfiction: Current military/political affairs, health and wellness, recent military history, travel, military family lifestyle. Emphasis now on current military and defense issues. "We rarely accept unsolicited manuscripts. We look for detailed query letters with résumé, sample clips and SASE attached. We do not publish poetry or fillers." **Buys 48 mss/year.** Length: 800-2,500 words. **Pays up to $1,700.**

• Ranked as one of the best markets for freelance writers in *Writer's Yearbook* magazine's "Top 100 Markets," January 2000.

Photos: Query with list of stock photo subjects. Pays $20 for each 8×10 b&w photo (normal halftone) used. Original slides or transparencies must be suitable for color separation. Pays $75-200 for inside color; $300 for cover.

▣ The online magazine carries original content not found in the print edition and includes writer's guidelines. Contact: Ronda Reid, online editor.

MUSIC

Music fans follow the latest industry news in these publications that range from opera to hip hop. Types of music and musicians or specific instruments are the sole focus of some magazines. Publications geared to the music industry and professionals can be found in the Trade Music section. Additional music and dance markets are found in the Contemporary Culture and Entertainment sections.

N $ AMERICAN COUNTRY, Music Monthly, Publishing Services Inc., 820 Monroe NW, Suite 211A, Grand Rapids MI 49503. (616)458-1011. Fax: (616)458-2285. E-mail: cookparr@iserv.net. **Contact:** Bruce L. Parrott, editor. **50% freelance written.** Monthly tabloid covering country music. "*American Country* is a country music publication syndicated to radio stations around the country and featuring articles on country artists, album reviews, outdoor life, recipes, etc." Estab. 1992. Circ. 300,000. Pays on publication. Publishes ms an average of 2 months after acceptance. Byline given. Buys one-time rights or makes work-for-hire assignments. Editorial lead time 2 months. Accepts queries by mail, e-mail, fax, phone. Accepts simultaneous submissions. Responds in 1 week. Sample copy and writer's guidelines free.

Nonfiction: Interview/profile, new product (all pertaining to country music). No country music news. **Buys 40-50 mss/year.** Query with published clips. Length: 1,000-2,000 words. **Pays $10-50.**

• The editor reports an interest in seeing articles about outdoor life—camping, hiking, hunting, fishing, etc.

Columns/Departments: CD Jukebox (album reviews), 50-100 words. **Buys 35-50 mss/year.** Query with published clips. **Pays $10.**

Tips: "Call and tell me the kind of stuff you're doing and send some copies. Have existing contacts within the Nashville music scene."

$ AMERICAN SONGWRITER, 1009 17th Ave. S., Nashville TN 37212-2201. (615)321-6096. Fax: (615)321-6097. E-mail: asongmag@aol.com. Website: www.americansongwriter.com. **Contact:** Vernell Hackett, editor. **30% freelance written.** Bimonthly magazine about songwriters and the craft of songwriting for many types of music, including pop, country, rock, metal, jazz, gospel, and r&b. Estab. 1984. Circ. 5,000. Pays on publication. Publishes ms an average of 2 months after acceptance. Offers 25% kill fee. Buys first North American serial rights. Responds in 2 months. Sample copy for $4. Writer's guidelines for SASE.

Nonfiction: General interest, interview/profile, new product, technical, home demo studios, movie and TV scores, performance rights organizations. No fiction. **Buys 20 mss/year.** Query with published clips. Length: 300-1,200 words. **Pays $25-60.**

Reprints: Send tearsheet or photocopy of article and information about when and where the article previously appeared. Pays same amount as paid for an original article.

Photos: Send photos with submission. Reviews 3×5 prints. Offers no additional payment for photos accepted with ms. Identification of subjects required. Buys one-time rights.

Tips: "*American Songwriter* strives to present articles which can be read a year or two after they were written and still be pertinent to the songwriter reading them."

⊠ $ $ BLUEGRASS UNLIMITED, Bluegrass Unlimited, Inc., P.O. Box 111, Broad Run VA 20137-0111. (540)349-8181 or (800)BLU-GRAS. Fax: (540)341-0011. E-mail: editor@bluegrassmusic.com. Website: www.bluegrass music.com. Editor: Peter V. Kuykendall. **Contact:** Sharon Watts, managing editor. **70% freelance written.** Prefers to work with published/established writers. Monthly magazine on bluegrass, acoustic and old-time country music. Estab. 1966. Circ. 27,000. Pays on publication. Publishes ms an average of 4 months after acceptance. Byline given. Kill fee negotiated. Buys first North American serial, one-time, all rights and second serial (reprint) rights. Submit seasonal material 4 months in advance. Accepts queries by mail, e-mail, fax. Responds in 2 weeks to queries; 2 months to mss. Sample copy free. Writer's guidelines for #10 SASE.

Nonfiction: General interest, historical/nostalgic, how-to, interview/profile, personal experience, photo feature, travel. No "fan"-style articles. **Buys 60-70 mss/year.** Query with or without published clips. Length: open. **Pays 8-10¢/word.**

Reprints: Send photocopy or typed ms with rights for sale noted and information about when and where the article previously appeared. Payment is negotiable.

Photos: State availability of or send photos with query. Reviews 35mm transparencies and 3×5, 5×7 and 8×10 b&w and color prints. Pays $50-175 for transparencies; $25-60 for b&w prints; $50-250 for color prints. Identification of subjects required. Buys one-time and all rights.

Fiction: Ethnic, humorous. **Buys 3-5 mss/year.** Query. Length: negotiable. **Pays 8-10¢/word.**

Tips: "We would prefer that articles be informational, based on personal experience or an interview with lots of quotes from subject, profile, humor, etc."

$ $ CHAMBER MUSIC, Chamber Music America, 305 Seventh Ave., New York NY 10001-6008. (212)242-2022. Website: www.chamber-music.org. **Contact:** Johanna B. Keller, editor or Karissa Krenz, assistant editor. Bimonthly magazine covering chamber music. Estab. 1977. Circ. 13,000. Pays on publication. Publishes ms an average of 5 months after acceptance. Byline given. Offers kill fee. Buys first publication rights. Editorial lead time 8 months.

Nonfiction: Issue-oriented stories of relevance to the chamber music field written by top music journalists and critics, or music practitioners. No artist profiles, no stories about opera or symphonic work. **Buys 35 mss/year.** Query with clips by mail only. Length: 2,500-3,500 words. **Pays $500 minimum.** Sometimes pays expenses of writers on assignment.

Photos: State availability of photos with submission. Offers no additional payment for photos accepted with ms.

★ $ $ $ $ GUITAR MAGAZINE, Cherry Lane Music, 6 E. 32nd St., New York NY 10016. Fax: (212)251-0840. E-mail: editors@guitarmag.com. Website: www.guitarmag.com. **Contact:** Jon Chappell, editor-in-chief. **75% freelance written.** Monthly magazine covering guitars, music, technology. Estab. 1983. Circ. 175,000. Pays on publication. Publishes ms an average of 1 month after acceptance. Byline given. Offers 50% kill fee. Buys one-time rights. Editorial lead time 3 months. Accepts queries by mail, e-mail, fax. Accepts simultaneous submissions. Sample copy on website.

Nonfiction: Book excerpts, essays, exposé, general interest, historical/nostalgic, how-to, humor, interview/profile, new product, opinion, personal experience, photo feature, technical. **Buys 48 mss/year.** Send complete ms. Length: 700-4,000 words. **Pays $75-2,000.** Sometimes pays expenses of writers on assignment.

Reprints: Accepts previously published submissions.

Photos: State availability of photos with submission. Offers $25-500/photo. Captions and identification of subjects required. Buys one-time rights.

Columns/Departments: Groundwire (newsy items on guitars and music), 250 words; Encore (humor on guitar and music experience), 800 words. **Buys 12 mss/year.** Send complete ms. **Pays $75-2,000.**

　　■ The online magazine carries original content not found in the print edition. Contact: Jon Chappell, online editor.

Tips: "E-mail pitches with sample heads and subheads, a brief synopsis and mock lead."

$ $ $ GUITAR ONE, The Magazine You Can Play, Cherry Lane Magazines, 6 E. 32nd St., 11th Floor, New York NY 10016. Fax: (212)561-3000. E-mail: guitarone@cherrylane.com. Website: www.guitar-one.com. Managing Editor: Jeff Bauer. **Contact:** Jeff Schroedl (jschroedl@halleonard.com), editor-in-chief. **50% freelance written.** Magazine published 9 times/year covering music and guitar. Estab. 1995. Circ. 100,000. **Pays on acceptance.** Byline given. Offers 100% kill fee. Makes work-for-hire assignments. Editorial lead time up to 6 months. Submit seasonal material 5 months in advance. Accepts queries by e-mail. Accepts simultaneous submissions. Responds in 2 months to mss. Sample copy by e-mail.

Nonfiction: Interview/profile (with guitarists). **Buys 15 mss/year.** Query with published clips. Length: 2,000-5,000 words. **Pays $300-1,200 for assigned articles; $150-800 for unsolicited articles.** Sometimes pays expenses of writers on assignment.

Photos: State availability of photos with submission. Reviews negatives, transparencies and prints. Negotiates payment individually. Buys one-time rights.

Tips: "Find an interesting feature with a nice angle that pertains to guitar enthusiasts. Submit a well-written draft or samples of work."

$ $ MODERN DRUMMER, 12 Old Bridge Rd., Cedar Grove NJ 07009. (201)239-4140. Fax: (201)239-7139. Editorial Director: William F. Miller. Senior Editor: Rick Van Horn. **Contact:** Ronald Spagnardi, editor-in-chief. Monthly magazine for "student, semi-pro and professional drummers at all ages and levels of playing ability, with varied specialized interests within the field." **60% freelance written.** Circ. 102,000. Pays on publication. Publishes ms an average of 3 months after acceptance. Buys all rights. Responds in 2 weeks. Sample copy for $4.99. Guidelines for #10 SASE.

Nonfiction: How-to, informational, interview, new product, personal experience, technical. "All submissions must appeal to the specialized interests of drummers." **Buys 40-50 mss/year.** Query or submit complete ms. Length: 5,000-8,000 words. **Pays $200-500.**

Reprints: Accepts previously published submissions.

Photos: Purchased with accompanying ms. Reviews 8×10 b&w prints and color transparencies.

Columns/Departments: Music columns: Jazz Drummers Workshop, Rock Perspectives, Rock 'N' Jazz Clinic, Driver's Seat (Big Band), In The Studio, Show Drummers Seminar, Teachers Forum, Drum Soloist, The Jobbing Drummer, Strictly Technique, Shop Talk, Latin Symposium. Profile columns: Portraits, Up & Coming, From the Past. Book Reviews, Record Reviews, Video Reviews. "Technical knowledge of area required for most columns." **Buys 40-50 mss/year.** Query or submit complete ms. Length: 500-1,000 words. **Pays $50-150.**

Tips: "*MD* is looking for music journalists rather than music critics. Our aim is to provide information, not to make value judgments. Therefore, keep all articles as objective as possible. We are interested in how and why a drummer plays a certain way; the readers can make their own decisions about whether or not they like it."

[N] [image] **$ MUSIC FOR THE LOVE OF IT**, 67 Parkside Dr., Berkeley CA 94705. (510)656-9134. Fax: (510)654-4656. E-mail: tedrust@home.com. Website: www.music.holowww.com. **Contact:** Ted Rust, editor. **20% freelance written.** Bimonthly online newsletter covering amateur musicianship. "A lively, intelligent source of ideas and enthusiasm for a musically literate audience of adult amateur musicians." Estab. 1988. Circ. 600. Pays on publication. Publishes ms an average of 2 months after acceptance. Byline given. Buys one-time rights. Editorial lead time 1 month. Submit seasonal material 1 month in advance. Accepts queries by mail, e-mail, fax, phone. Responds in 1 week to queries; 1 month to mss. Sample copy for $6. Writer's guidelines free, online at website or by e-mail.

○⇥ Break in with "a good article, written from a musician's point of view, with at least one photo."

Nonfiction: Essays, historical/nostalgic, how-to, personal experience, photo feature. No concert reviews, star interviews, CD reviews. **Buys 6 mss/year.** Query. Length: 500-1,500 words. **Pays $50** or gift subscriptions.

Photos: State availability of photos with submission. Reviews 4×6 prints or larger. Offers no additional payment for photos accepted with ms. Identification of subjects required. Buys one-time rights.

Tips: "We're looking for more good how-to articles on musical styles. Love making music. Know something about it."

$ RELEASE MAGAZINE, Christian Music Covered in Style, Vox Publishing, 3670 Central Pike, Suite J, Hermitage TN 37076. (615)872-8080. Fax: (615)872-9786. E-mail: editorial@voxcorp.com. Website: www.releasemagazine.com. Editor: Chris Well. **50% freelance written.** Bimonthly magazine covering Christian pop music/artists. "*Release* is the most widely-circulated magazine in the Christian music industry, reaching its fans through retail stores and individual subscriptions. Its core audience is the 12- to 30-year-old pop or mainstream music fan." Estab. 1991. Circ. 110,000. Pays 30 days after publication. Publishes ms an average of 2 months after acceptance. Byline given. Buys first North American serial rights and electronic rights. Editorial lead time 6 months. Submit seasonal material 4 months in advance. Sample copy for $5.

Nonfiction: Artist interview/profile, new product reviews. "We have an annual 'year in review' issue that features the newsmakers of the year and the winners of the Readers' Choice poll." No essays, non-Christian music-related articles. **Buys 45 mss/year.** Query with published clips. Length: 500-2,500 words. **Pays 6-10¢/word.**

Tips: "We're looking for people who can exhibit working knowledge of the music and artists we cover, and can convince us that they've read our magazine."

$ RELIX MAGAZINE, Music for the Mind, P.O. Box 94, Brooklyn NY 11229. (718)258-0009. E-mail: relixedit@aol.com. Website: www.relix.com. **Contact:** Toni A. Brown, editor. **60% freelance written.** Eager to work with new/unpublished writers. Bimonthly magazine covering classic rock 'n' roll music and specializing in Grateful Dead and other San Francisco and 60s-related groups, but also offering new music alternatives, such as "Roots Rock" and "Jam Bands." Estab. 1974. Circ. 70,000. Pays on publication. Publishes ms an average of 6 months after acceptance. Byline given. Buys all rights. Accepts queries by mail. Responds in 1 year. Sample copy for $5.

Nonfiction: Historical/nostalgic, interview/profile, new product, personal experience, photo feature, technical. Feature topics include blues, bluegrass, rock, jazz and world music; also deals with environmental and cultural issues. Special issue: year-end special. Query by mail with published clips if available or send complete ms. Length: 1,200-3,000 words. **Pays $2/column inch.**

Reprints: Send photocopy of article and information about when and where the article previously appeared.

Photos: "Whenever possible, submit promotional photos with articles."

Columns/Departments: Query with published clips, if available, or send complete ms. Pays variable rates.

Tips: "The most rewarding aspects of working with freelance writers are fresh writing and new outlooks."

[image] **$ 7BALL MAGAZINE, Modern Music on Cue**, Vox Publishing, 3670 Central Pike, Suite J, Hermitage TN 37076. (615)872-8080. Fax: (615)872-9786. E-mail: 7ball@7ball.com. Website: www.7ball.com. Editor: Chris Well. **Contact:** Cameron Strang, managing editor. **70% freelance written.** Bimonthly magazine covering Christian modern rock/alternative music. "*7ball*—the fastest growing magazine in Christian music—captivates the teenage and young adult music lover whose tastes include modern rock, alternative, hip-hop and other styles of music with an edge." Estab. 1995. Circ. 60,000. Pays within 30 days after publication. Publishes ms an average of 2 months after acceptance. Byline given. Buys first North American serial rights and electronic rights. Editorial lead time 6 months. Submit seasonal material 4 months in advance. Accepts queries by mail, e-mail. Sample copy for $5 or on website.

Nonfiction: Artist interview/profile, media that is of interest to Christian modern music fans (extreme sports, video, etc.). **Buys 20 mss/year.** Query with published clips. Length: 500-2,500 words. **Pays 6-10¢/word.** Sometimes pays expenses of writers on assignment.

Photos: State availability of photos with submission. Offers no additional payment for photos accepted with ms. Identification of subjects required. Buys one-time rights.

Columns/Departments: Bankshots (brief artist profiles), 400-800 words; Reviews (new music/product reviews), 200-300 words. **Buys 80 mss/year.** Query with published clips. **Pays 6-10¢/word.**

[image] The online magazine carries original content not found in the print edition. Contact: Cameron Strang, online editor.

Tips: "We're looking for people who can exhibit working knowledge of the music and artists we cover and can convince us that they've actually read our magazine."

N: SPIN, 205 Lexington Ave., 3rd Floor, New York NY 10016. (212)231-7400. Fax: (212)231-7300. Publisher: Malcolm Campbell. **Contact:** Allan Light, editor-in-chief. Monthly magazine covering music and popular culture. "*Spin* covers progressive rock as well as investigative reporting on issues from politics, to pop culture. Editorial includes reviews, essays, profiles and interviews on a wide range of music from rock to jazz. It also covers sports, movies, politics, humor, fashion and issues—from AIDS research to the environment. The editorial focuses on the progressive new music scene and young adult culture more from an 'alternative' perspective as opposed to mainstream pop music. The magazine discovers new bands as well as angles for the familiar stars." Estab. 1985. Circ. 413,000.

Nonfiction: Cultural, political or social issues. New writers: submit complete ms with SASE. Established writers: query specific editor with published clips. Features are not assigned to writers who have not established a prior relationship with *Spin.*

    ● Ranked as one of the best markets for freelancers in *Writer's Yearbook* magazine's annual "Top 100 Markets," January 2000.

Columns/Departments: Most open to freelancers: Exposure (short articles on music and popular culture), 300-600 words, query Maureen Callahan, associate editor; Reviews (record reviews), 150 or 400 words, queries/mss to Jon Dolan, senior editor; Noise (music and new artists), query Tracey Pepper, senior associate editor. Query before submitting.

Tips: "The best way to break into the magazine is the Exposure and Reviews sections. We primarily work with seasoned, professional writers who have extensive national magazine experience and very rarely make assignments based on unsolicited queries."

$ $ SYMPHONY, American Symphony Orchestra League, 33 W. 60th St., Fifth Floor, New York NY 10023-7905. (212)262-5161. Fax: (212)262-5198. E-mail: editor@symphony.org. **Contact:** Melinda Whiting, editor. **50% freelance written.** Bimonthly magazine for the orchestra industry and classical music enthusiasts covering classical music, orchestra industry, musicians. "Writers should be knowledgeable about classical music and have critical or journalistic/repertorial approach." Circ. 20,000. **Pays on acceptance.** Publishes ms an average of 2 months after acceptance. Byline given. Buys first and one-time rights. Editorial lead time 6 months. Submit seasonal material 8 months in advance. Accepts simultaneous submissions "but we must be first to publish." Sample copy and writer's guidelines for SAE.

Nonfiction: Book excerpts, essays/commentary, profile, opinion, personal experience (rare), photo feature (rare), issue features, trend pieces (by assignment only; pitches welcome). Does not want to see reviews, interviews. **Buys 30 mss/year.** Query with published clips. Length: 900-3,500 words. **Pays $150-600 for assigned articles; $0-400 for unsolicited articles.** Sometimes pays expenses of writers on assignment.

Photos: State availability of photos or send photos with submission. Reviews contact sheets, negatives, transparencies and prints. Offers no additional payment for photos accepted with ms. Captions and identification of subjects required. Buys one-time rights.

Columns/Departments: Repertoire (orchestral music—essays), 1,000 words. **Buys 4 mss/year.** Query with published clips.

Tips: "We need writing samples before assigning pieces. We prefer to craft the angle with the writer, rather than adapt an existing piece. Pitches and queries should demonstrate a clear relevance to the American orchestra industry and should be timely."

N: $ $ $ $ VIBE, 215 Lexington Ave., 6th Floor, New York NY 10016. (212)448-7300. Fax: (212)448-7400. Managing editor: Jacquline Monk. **Contact:** individual editors as noted below. Magazine published 10 times/year covering urban music and culture. "*Vibe* chronicles and celebrates urban music and the youth culture that inspires and consumes it." Estab. 1993. Circ. 750,000. Pays on publication. Buys all rights. Editorial lead time 4 months. Responds in 2 months. Sample copy available on newsstands. Writer's guidelines for #10 SASE.

Nonfiction: Jeanine Amber, features editor. Cultural, political or social issues. Contact Tiarra Mukherju, music editor, for music features. Query with published clips, resume and SASE. Length: 800-3,000 words. **Pays $1/word.**

Columns/Departments: Start (introductory news-based section), 75-400 words, contact Brett Johnson, senior editor; Revolutions (music reviews), 100-800 words, contact Karen Good, assistant editor; Book reviews, contact Tiarra Mukherju. **Pays $1/word.** Query with published clips, resume and SASE.

Tips: "A writer's best chance to be published in *Vibe* is through the Start or Revolutions Sections. Keep in mind that *Vibe* is a national magazine, so ideas should have a national scope. People in Cali should care as much about the story as people in NYC. Also, *Vibe* has a four-month lead time. What we work on today will appear in the magazine four or more months later. Stories must be timely with respect to this fact."

MYSTERY

These magazines buy fictional accounts of crime, detective work, mystery and suspense. Skim through other sections to identify markets for fiction; some will consider mysteries. Markets for true crime accounts are listed under Detective & Crime.

$ HARDBOILED, Gryphon Publications, P.O. Box 209, Brooklyn NY 11228. **Contact:** Gary Lovisi, editor. **100% freelance written.** Quarterly magazine covering crime/mystery fiction and nonfiction. "Hard-hitting crime fiction and columns/articles and reviews on hardboiled crime writing and private-eye stories—the newest and most cutting-edge work and classic reprints." Estab. 1988. Circ. 1,000. Pays on publication. Publishes ms an average of 18 months after acceptance. Byline given. Offers 100% kill fee. Buys one-time rights. Editorial lead time 6 months. Submit seasonal material 6 months in advance. Responds in 2 weeks to queries; 1 month to mss. Sample copy for $8. New double issue: $16.Writer's guidelines for #10 SASE.

Nonfiction: Book excerpts, essays, exposé. Query first. **Buys 4-6 mss/year.** Length: 500-3,000 words. **Pays 1 copy.**
Reprints: Query first.
Photos: State availability of photos with submission.
Columns/Departments: Various review columns/articles on hardboiled writers. Query first. **Buys 2-4 mss/year.**
Fiction: Mystery, hardboiled crime and private-eye stories *all* on the cutting-edge. **Buys 40 mss/year.** Send complete ms. Length: 500-3,000 words. **Pays $5-50,** depending on length and quality.

⊠ $ALFRED HITCHCOCK'S MYSTERY MAGAZINE, Dell Magazines, 475 Park Ave. S, New York NY 10016. Website: www.mysterypages.com. Editor: Cathleen Jordan. **100% freelance written.** Monthly magazine featuring new mystery short stories. Circ. 615,000 readers. **Pays on acceptance.** Byline given. Buys first and foreign rights. Submit seasonal material 7 months in advance. Responds in 2 months. Sample issue for $4. Writer's guidelines for SASE.

Fiction: Original and well-written mystery and crime fiction. "Because this is a mystery magazine, the stories we buy must fall into that genre in some sense or another. We are interested in nearly every kind of mystery, however: stories of detection of the classic kind, police procedurals, private eye tales, suspense, courtroom dramas, stories of espionage, and so on. We ask only that the story be about crime (or the threat or fear of one). We sometimes accept ghost stories or supernatural tales, but those also should involve a crime." Length: up to 14,000 words. Send complete ms with SASE. **Pays 8¢/word.**

● Ranked as one of the best markets for fiction writers in *Writer's Digest* magazine's annual "Fiction 50," June 2000.

Tips: "No simultaneous submissions, please. Submissions sent to *Alfred Hitchcock's Mystery Magazine* are not considered for or read by *Ellery Queen's Mystery Magazine*, and vice versa."

$MURDEROUS INTENT, Mystery Magazine, Deadly Alibi Press Ltd., P.O. Box 5947, Vancouver WA 98668-5947. (360)695-9004. Fax: (360)693-3354. E-mail: madison@teleport.com. Website: www.murderousintent.com. **Contact:** Margo Power, editor. **90% freelance written.** Quarterly magazine covering mystery. "Everything in *Murderous Intent* is mystery/suspense related. We bring you quality nonfiction articles, columns, interviews and 10-12 (or more) pieces of short mystery fiction per issue. You'll find stories and interviews by Carolyn Hart, Ed Gorman, Barbara Paul, Jerimiah Healy and many more excellent authors." Estab. 1994. Circ. 5,000. **Pays on acceptance.** Publishes ms an average of 18 months after acceptance. Byline given. Offers 100% kill fee or $10. Buys first North American serial rights. Submit seasonal material 6 months in advance. Accepts queries by e-mail only with brief synopsis and word count. "No hard copy submissions." Responds in 1 week. Sample copy for $5.95, 9×12 SAE and 4 first-class stamps or on website. Writer's guidelines for #10 SASE or on website.

O⌐ Break in with very short, 500-700 nonfiction mystery related fillers and 4-8 line mystery verse.

Nonfiction: Humor (mystery); interview/profile (mystery authors), 500-700 words. **Buys 4-8 mss./issue.** Mystery-related nonfiction, 2,000-4,000 words. **Pays $10.** Sometimes pays expenses of writers on assignment. **Buys 8-12 mss/year.** Query by e-mail with published clips.
Photos: State availability of photos and artwork with submission. Offers no additional payment for photos accepted with ms or negotiates payment individually. Captions, model releases, identification of subjects required. Buys one-time rights.
Fiction: Humorous (mystery), mystery. "Please don't send anything that is not mystery/suspense-related in some way." **Buys 48-52 mss/year.** Query by e-mail. Preferred length: 2,000-4,000 words. **Pays $10.**
Poetry: Free verse, haiku, light verse, limerick, traditional. Nothing that is not mystery/suspense-related. **Buys 12-36 poems/year.** Length: 4-16 lines. **Pays $2-5.**
Fillers: Anecdotes, facts, cartoons, jokes. All fillers must be mystery related. Length: 25-200 words. **Pays $2-5.**
Tips: "Send us mysteries like the ones you love to read—as long as they fit within our guidelines. We love humorous mysteries, mysteries and suspense with exotic settings (kitchens, bathrooms, islands, etc.), good puzzles, all around good stories with characters we can't forget. We also seek permission to include select stories and articles on the website. There is no additional payment at this time."

$THE MYSTERY REVIEW, A Quarterly Publication for Mystery Readers, C. von Hessert & Associates, P.O. Box 233, Colborne, Ontario K0K 1S0 Canada. US: P.O. Box 488, Wellesley Island NY 13640-0488. (613)475-4440. Fax: (613)475-3400. E-mail: mystrev@reach.net. Website: www.inline-online.com/mystery/. **Contact:** Barbara Davey, editor. **80% freelance written.** Quarterly magazine covering mystery and suspense. "Our readers are interested in mystery and suspense books, films. All topics related to mystery—including real life unsolved mysteries." Estab. 1992. Circ. 5,000 (80% of distribution is in US). Pays on publication. Publishes ms an average of 6 months after acceptance. Byline given. Buys first North American serial rights. Editorial lead time 6 months. Submit seasonal material 6 months in advance. Accepts queries by mail, e-mail, fax. Responds in 6 weeks to queries; 1 month to mss. Does not assume responsibility for unsolicited manuscripts. Sample copy for $5. Writer's guidelines for #10 SASE or on website.
Nonfiction: Interview/profile, true life mysteries. Query. Length: 2,000-5,000 words. **Pays $30 maximum.**

Photos: Send photos with submission. Offers no additional payment for photos accepted with ms. Model releases, identification of subjects required. Buys all rights.

Columns/Departments: Book reviews (mystery/suspense titles only), 500 words; Truly Mysterious ("unsolved," less-generally-known, historical or contemporary cases; photos/illustrations required), 2,000-5,000 words; Book Shop Beat (bookstore profiles; questionnaire covering required information available from editor), 500 words. **Buys 50 mss/ year.** Query with published clips. **Pays $10-30.**

Fillers: Puzzles, trivia, shorts (items related to mystery/suspense). **Buys 4/year.** Length: 100-500 words. **Pays $10-20.**

★ $ **ELLERY QUEEN'S MYSTERY MAGAZINE,** Dell Magazine Fiction Group, 475 Park Ave. S., 11th Floor, New York NY 10016. (212)686-7188. Fax: (212)686-7414. **Contact:** Janet Hutchings, editor. **100% freelance written.** Magazine published 11 times/year featuring mystery fiction. Estab. 1941. Circ. 500,000 readers. **Pays on acceptance.** Publishes ms an average of 6 months after acceptance. Byline given. Buys first serial or second serial (reprint) rights. Accepts simultaneous submissions. Responds in 3 months. Writer's guidelines for #10 SASE.

• Ranked as one of the best markets for fiction writers in *Writer's Digest* magazine's "Fiction 50," June 2000.

Fiction: Special consideration given to "anything timely and original. We publish every type of mystery: the suspense story, the psychological study, the private-eye story, the deductive puzzle—the gamut of crime and detection from the realistic (including stories of police procedure) to the more imaginative (including 'locked rooms' and impossible crimes). We always need detective stories. No sex, sadism or sensationalism-for-the-sake-of-sensationalism, no gore or horror. Seldom publishes parodies or pastiches. **Buys up to 13 mss/issue.** Length: 10,000 words maximum; occasionally higher but not often. Also buys 2-3 short novels/year of up to 20,000 words, by established authors and minute mysteries of 250 words. Short shorts of 1,500 words welcome. **Pays 3-8¢/word,** occasionally higher for established authors. Send complete ms with SASE.

Poetry: Short mystery verses, limericks. Length: 1 page, double-spaced maximum.

Tips: "We have a Department of First Stories to encourage writers whose fiction has never before been in print. We publish an average of 11 first stories every year."

NATURE, CONSERVATION & ECOLOGY

These publications promote reader awareness of the natural environment, wildlife, nature preserves and ecosystems. Many of these "green magazines" also concentrate on recycling and related issues, and a few focus on environmentally-conscious sustainable living. They do not publish recreation or travel articles except as they relate to conservation or nature. Other markets for this kind of material can be found in the Regional; Sports (Hiking & Backpacking in particular); and Travel, Camping & Trailer categories, although magazines listed there require that nature or conservation articles be slanted to their specialized subject matter and audience. Some publications listed in Juvenile and Teen, such as *Wild Outdoor World* or *Owl*, focus on nature-related material for young audiences, while others occasionally purchase such material.

★ $ $ $ **AMC OUTDOORS, The Magazine of the Appalachian Mountain Club,** Appalachian Mountain Club, 5 Joy St., Boston MA 02108. (617)523-0655. Fax: (617)523-0722. E-mail: meno@amcinfo.org. Website: www.out doors.org. **Contact:** Madeleine Eno, editor/publisher. **90% freelance written.** Monthly magazine covering outdoor recreation and conservation issues in the Northeast. Estab. 1907. Circ. 85,000. Pays on publication. Publishes ms an average of 3 months after acceptance. Byline given. Offers 25% kill fee. Buys all rights. Editorial lead time 3 months. Submit seasonal material 4 months in advance. Accepts queries by mail, e-mail. Responds in 1 month to queries; 2 months to mss. Sample copy for 9×12 SASE. Writer's guidelines free or on website.

Nonfiction: Book excerpts, essays, exposé, general interest, historical/nostalgic, how-to, interview/profile, opinion, personal experience, photo feature, technical, travel. Looking for writing familiar to particularities of Northeast— landscape and conservation issues. No "how hiking changed my life" or first-person outdoor adventure without a hook. Special issues: Northern Forest Report (April) featuring the northern areas of New York, New Hampshire, Vermont, and Maine, and protection efforts for these areas. **Buys 10 mss/year.** Query with or without published clips. Length: 500-3,000 words. Sometimes pays expenses of writers on assignment.

Photos: State availability of photos with submission. Reviews contact sheets, transparencies and prints. Model releases and identification of subjects required.

Columns/Departments: Jane Roy Brown. News (environmental/outdoor recreation coverage of Northeast), 1,300 words. **Buys 40 mss/year.** Query. **Pays $250-1,200.**

$ $ $ **AMERICAN FORESTS,** American Forests, P.O. Box 2000, Washington DC 20013. (202)955-4500. Fax: (202)887-1075. E-mail: mrobbins@amfor.org. Website: www.americanforests.org. **Contact:** Michelle Robbins, editor. **75% freelance written** (mostly assigned). Quarterly magazine "of trees and forests, published by a nonprofit citizens' organization that strives to help people plant and care for trees for ecosystem restoration and healthier communities."

insider report

Naturalists' interests open freelance doors in print, online

Lone Star journalist Wendee Holtcamp has a Texas-sized passion for nature and the great outdoors. By selling her work to *Audubon*, *Animals Magazine*, *Texas Parks & Wildlife*, Discovery Channel Online, the online publication Freelance Success (www.freelancesuccess.com) and the American College of Journalism, Holtcamp has turned her passion into cash flow. With an M.S. in wildlife ecology, Holtcamp began freelancing on ecological issues, and has five years' experience under her belt covering everything from leatherback sea turtles to stream channelization for print, online and television markets.

Wendee Holtcamp

Can you define what you do as a "nature" and "outdoors" writer?
Writing about nature and the outdoors falls into two broad categories: personal essay nature writing, and journalistic reporting on nature and the environment. I have done both.

Like science journalism, writing about the environment requires a writer to dig into technical jargon and yet deliver polished prose that is understandable—and interesting—to the general public. Environmental journalism should also be free from bias, so writers have to make sure to get different perspectives from interviewees. To write quality essays about nature is more similar to creative nonfiction than journalism. Writers should learn excellent outdoor observation skills and be able to describe things in creative and intriguing ways.

What are the special challenges that go along with freelancing about nature and the outdoors?
Interviewing scientists can sometimes be a challenge. Writers have to go into interviews prepared and well-read on the subject matter. We have to be prepared to elicit anecdotes as well as factual information from interviewees. And in nature writing, a journal is essential! Whenever I travel, I observe the types of plants, birds, rocks, the weather, and I write the sights, sounds, and textures in my journal. That way, when I'm writing an article related to that place I don't have to rely on memory.

Do all nature stories fall into the "ahhh, animals" category?
Not at all. Nature writers can sell news briefs to any number of outdoor sports, recreation, nature and science magazines or e-zines, as well as personal essays or journalistic pieces on the environment or conservation efforts.

What is the pay scale for freelancers within this specialty?

Experienced freelancers can make upwards of $5,000 per article, or $1-2/word, for the top-paying magazines or websites. This usually comes when you've already established a relationship with a publication. Experienced/moderate freelancers that are new to a particular publication can make 50¢ cents to one dollar per word with good clips and solid queries. Beginners with good writing skills should aim for 20¢ per word, but may have to write for less than that to get a few good clips. A lot of payment issues depend on the particular publication's budget.

What is the most common mistake freelancers make?

Sending queries that aren't matched to the publication—either in tone, content, or angle. An article on Baja sea turtles would have very different slants for *Scuba Times*, *Natural History*, *Amicus Journal*, or *Wildlife Conservation*.

How can aspiring nature writers improve their odds of success?

First, keep up with the latest science/environment news and controversies. Secondly, travel as much as you can and keep a journal. Practice observing nature through all your senses and writing about it. Lastly, don't give up if you get rejections! Just keep on trying, and constantly work to improve your writing skills.

Do you have a favorite assignment? And a nightmare?

Assignments for Discovery Channel Online have always been my favorite. The topics are fun, you get to use a unique voice, and the pay is great. They sent me to Costa Rica to cover a live expedition with leatherback sea turtles.

My nightmare assignment was my first article for *Texas Parks & Wildlife* magazine, a journalistic piece on a proposed stream channelization project. It involved a lot more research and time than I had expected, and being my first article for them, I wanted to do a really great job. I had to turn what could be a very dry and biased article into something lively, interesting and balanced. It had me stressed out, but it ended up being the article I am the most proud of! ("Turbulence Over Clear Creek," Feb. 1999). It turned out really well and the editors were also very pleased.

For interviews with the pros on more freelance niche markets see Child Care, page 431; Food & Drink, page 470; Health & Fitness, page 494; Personal Computers, page 604; and Travel, page 779.
—*Kelly Milner Halls*

TOP TIP: "There are over 35 magazines dedicated to nature/environment, but increasingly writers can sell such articles to general interest, travel, in-flight, outdoor sports, children's, parenting, and natural health/lifestyle magazines. The Internet is also a rapidly growing market for nature/environment articles. Websites like Great Outdoor Recreation Places (www.gorp.com) specialize in covering outdoor recreation and include environmental news. And broadcast markets are also opening up: Discovery Online and ScienceNow run daily news stories."

Estab. 1895. Circ. 25,000. **Pays on acceptance.** Publishes ms an average of 8 months after acceptance. Byline given. Buys one-time rights. Submit seasonal material 5 months in advance. Accepts queries by mail, e-mail. Responds in 2 months. Sample copy for $2. Writer's guidelines for SASE or online.

> **O—** Break in with "stories that resonate with city dwellers who love trees, or small, forestland owners (private). This magazine is looking for more urban and suburban-oriented pieces.

Nonfiction: General interest, historical, how-to, humor, inspirational. All articles should emphasize trees, forests, forestry and related issues. **Buys 2-3 mss/issue.** Query by mail or send résumé and clips to be considered for assignment. Length: 1,200-2,000 words. **Pays $250-800.**

Reprints: Send tearsheet of article or typed ms with rights for sale noted and information about when and where the article previously appeared. Pays 50% of amount paid for an original article.

Photos: Send photos. Offers no additional payment for photos accompanying ms. Uses glossy color prints; 35mm or larger transparencies, originals only. Captions required. Buys one-time rights.

Tips: "We're looking for more good urban forestry stories, and stories that show cooperation among disparate elements to protect/restore an ecosystem. Query should have honesty and information on photo support. We *do not* accept fiction or poetry at this time."

⊠ $ $ $ THE AMICUS JOURNAL, 40 W. 20th St., New York NY 10011. (212)727-2700. Fax: (212)727-1773. E-mail: amicus@nrdc.org. Website: /www.nrdc.org/eamicus/index.html. **Contact:** Kathrin Day Lassila, editor. **80% freelance written.** Quarterly magazine covering national and international environmental issues. "*The Amicus Journal* is intended to provide the general public with a journal of thought and opinion on environmental affairs, particularly those relating to policies of national and international significance." Estab. 1979. Circ. 250,000. Pays on publication. Publishes ms an average of 6 months after acceptance. Offers 25% kill fee. Buys first North American serial rights (and print/electronic reprint rights). Submit seasonal material 6 months in advance. Responds in 3 months to queries. Sample copy for $4 with 9×12 SAE or on website. Writer's guidelines for SASE.

> ● Submissions must be of the highest writing quality only and must be grounded in thorough knowledge of subject.

Nonfiction: Exposé, interview/profile, essays, reviews. Query by mail with published clips. **Buys 35 mss/year.** Length: 200-3,500 words. Pay negotiable. Sometimes pays expenses of writers on assignment.

Photos: State availability of photos with submission. Reviews contact sheets, color transparencies, 8×10 b&w prints. Negotiates payment individually. Captions, model releases, identification of subjects required. Buys one-time rights.

Columns/Departments: News & Comment (summary reporting of environmental issues, tied to topical items), 700-2,000 words; International Notebook (new or unusual international environmental stories), 700-2,000 words; People, 2,000 words; Reviews (in-depth reporting on issues and personalities, well-informed essays on books of general interest to environmentalists interested in policy and history), 500-1,000 words. Query with published clips. Pay negotiable.

Poetry: Brian Swann. Avant-garde, free verse, haiku, others. All poetry should be rooted in nature. Must submit with SASE. **Buys 16 poems/year.** Length: 1 ms page. **Pays $50** plus a year's subscription.

Tips: "Please stay up to date on environmental issues, and review *The Amicus Journal* before submitting queries. Except for editorials all departments are open to freelance writers. Queries should precede manuscripts, and manuscripts should conform to the *Chicago Manual of Style*. *Amicus* needs interesting environmental stories—of local, regional or national import—from writers who can offer an on-the-ground perspective. Accuracy, high-quality writing, and thorough knowledge of the environmental subject are vital."

⊞ $ $ APPALACHIAN TRAILWAY NEWS, Appalachian Trail Conference, P.O. Box 807, Harpers Ferry WV 25425-0807. (304)535-6331. Fax: (304)535-2667. E-mail: rrubin@atconf.org. **Contact:** Robert A. Rubin, editor. **50% freelance written.** Bimonthly magazine. Estab. 1925. Circ. 26,000. **Pays on acceptance.** Byline given. Buys first North American serial or second serial (reprint) rights. Responds in 2 months. Sample copy, guidelines for $2.50. Writer's guidelines only for SASE.

> ● Articles must relate to Appalachian Trail.

Nonfiction: Essays, general interest, historical/nostalgic, how-to, humor, inspirational, interview/profile, photo feature, technical, travel. **Buys 15-20 mss/year.** Query with or without published clips, or send complete ms. Length: 250-3,000 words. **Pays $25-300.** Pays expenses of writers on assignment. Publishes, but does not pay for "hiking reflections."

Reprints: Send photocopy of article or typed ms with rights for sale noted and information about when and where the article previously appeared.

Photos: State availability of photos with submission. Reviews contact sheets, negatives, 5×7 prints. Offers $25-125/photo. Identification of subjects required. Negotiates future use by Appalachian Trail Conference.

Tips: "Contributors should display a knowledge of or interest in the Appalachian Trail. Those who live in the vicinity of the Trail may opt for an assigned story and should present credentials and subject of interest to the editor."

⊞ $ $ THE ATLANTIC SALMON JOURNAL, The Atlantic Salmon Federation, P.O. Box 429, St. Andrews, New Brunswick E0G 2X0 Canada. Fax: (506)529-4985. E-mail: asfpub@nbnet.nb.ca. Website: www.asf.ca. **Contact:** Jim Gourlay, editor. **50-68% freelance written.** Quarterly magazine covering conservation efforts for the Atlantic salmon, catering to "affluent and responsive audience—the dedicated angler and conservationist." Circ. 10,000. Pays on publication. Publishes ms an average of 6 months after acceptance. Byline given. Buys first serial rights to articles and one-time rights to photos. Submit seasonal material 3 months in advance. Accepts simultaneous submissions. Responds in 2 months. Sample copy for 9×12 SAE with $1 (Canadian), or IRC. Writer's guidelines free.

Nonfiction: Exposé, historical/nostalgic, how-to, humor, interview/profile, new product, opinion, personal experience, photo feature, technical, travel, conservation, science, research and management. "We are seeking articles that are pertinent to the focus and purpose of our magazine, which is to inform and entertain our membership on all aspects of the Atlantic salmon and its environment, preservation and conservation." **Buys 15-20 mss/year.** Query with published clips and state availability of photos. Length: 1,500-2,500 words. **Pays $200-400.** Sometimes pays the expenses of writers on assignment.

Columns/Departments: Conservation issues and salmon research; the design, construction and success of specific flies (*Fit To Be Tied*); interesting characters in the sport; opinion pieces by knowledgeable writers, 900 words, **pays $150-250;** *Casting Around* (short, informative, entertaining reports, book reviews and quotes from the world of Atlantic salmon angling and conservation), **pays $50.** Query.

Photos: Send photos with query. Pays $50 for 3×5 or 5×7 b&w prints; $50-100 for 2¼×3¼ or 35mm color slides. Captions and identification of subjects required.

Tips: "Articles must reflect informed and up-to-date knowledge of Atlantic salmon. Writers need not be authorities, but research must be impeccable. Clear, concise writing is essential, and submissions must be typed. The odds are that a writer without a background in outdoor writing and wildlife reporting will not have the 'informed' angle I'm looking for. Our readership is well read and critical of simplification and generalization."

$ $ $ $ AUDUBON, The Magazine of the National Audubon Society, National Audubon Society, 700 Broadway, New York NY 10003-9501. Fax: (212)477-9069. E-mail: writersqueries@audubon.com. Website: www.audu bon.com. Lisa Gosselin, editor in chief. **Contact:** Sydney Horton, assistant editor. **85% freelance written.** Bimonthly magazine "reflecting nature with joy and reverence and reporting the issues that affect and endanger the delicate balance and life on this planet." Estab. 1887. Circ. 460,000. **Pays on acceptance.** Byline given. Buys all rights. Accepts queries by mail, e-mail. "No phone calls, please." Responds in 3 months. Sample copy for $5 and postage or on website. Writer's guidelines for #10 SASE or on website.

Nonfiction: Essays, investigative, historical, humor, interview/profile, opinion, photo feature, book excerpts (well in advance of publication). Query before submission. "No fax queries, please." Length: 150-3,000 words. **Pays $100-3,000.** Pays expenses of writers on assignment.

Tips: "*Audubon* articles deal with the natural and human environment. They cover the remote as well as the familiar. What they all have in common, however, is that they have a story to tell, one that will not only interest *Audubon* readers, but that will interest everyone with a concern for the affairs of humans and nature. We want good solid journalism. We want stories of people and places, good news and bad: humans and nature in conflict, humans and nature working together, humans attempting to comprehend, restore and renew the natural world. We are looking for new voices and fresh ideas. Among the types of stories we seek: profiles of individuals whose life and work illuminate some issues relating to natural history, the environment, conservation, etc.; balanced reporting on environmental issues and events here in North America and abroad; analyses of events, policies, and issues from fresh points of view. We do not publish fiction or poetry. We're not seeking first-person meditations on 'nature,' accounts of wild animal rescue or taming, or birdwatching articles."

$ THE BEAR DELUXE MAGAZINE, P.O. Box 10342, Portland OR 97296. (503)242-1047. Fax: (503)243-2645. E-mail: bear@orlo.org. Website: www.orlo.org. **Contact:** Tom Webb, editor. **80% freelance written.** Quarterly magazine. "*The Bear Deluxe Magazine* provides a fresh voice amid often strident and polarized environmental discourse. Street level, solution-oriented and non-dogmatic, *The Bear Deluxe* presents lively creative discussion to a diverse readership." Estab. 1993. Circ. 17,000. Pays on publication. Publishes ms 2 months after acceptance. Byline given. Offers 25% kill fee. Buys first rights. Editorial lead time 3 months. Submit seasonal material 4 months in advance. Query by mail, e-mail. Accepts simultaneous and previously published submissions. Responds in 1 month to queries; 2 months to mss. Sample copy for $3. Writer's guidelines for #10 SASE or on website.

Nonfiction: Book excerpts, essays, exposé, general interest, humor, interview/profile, new product, opinion, personal experience, photo feature, travel, artist profiles. Publishes 1 theme/year. Send #10 SASE for theme. **Buys 40 mss/year.** Query with published clips. Length: 250-4,500 words. **Pays 5¢/word.** Sometimes pays expenses of writers on assignment.

Photos: State availability of photos with submission. Reviews contact sheets, transparencies and 8×10 prints. Offers $30/photo. Model releases and identification of subjects required. Buys one-time rights.

Columns/Departments: Reviews (almost anything), 300 words; Hands-On (individuals or groups working on eco-issues, getting their hands dirty), 1,200 words; Talking Heads (creative first person), 500 words; News Bites (quirk of eco-news), 300 words; Portrait of an Artist (artist profiles), 1,200 words. **Buys 16 mss/year.** Query with published clips. **Pays 5¢/word, subscription and copies.**

Fiction: Adventure, condensed novels, historical, horror, humorous, mystery, novel excerpts, science fiction, western. "Stories must have some environmental context." **Buys 8 mss/year.** Send complete ms. Length: 750-4,500 words. **Pays 5¢/word.**

Poetry: Avant-garde, free verse, Haiku, light verse, traditional. **Buys 16-20 poems/year.** Submit 5 poems maximum. Length: 50 lines maximum. **Pays $10, subscription and copies.**

Fillers: Facts, newsbreaks, short humor and "found writing." **Buys 10/year.** Length: 100-750 words. **Pays 5¢/word, subscription and copies.**

Tips: "Offer to be stringer for future ideas. Get a copy of the magazine and guidelines, and query us with specific nonfiction ideas and clips. We're looking for original, magazine-style stories, not fluff or PR. Fiction, essay and poetry writers should know we have an open and blind review policy and should keep sending their best work even if rejected once. Be as specific as possible in queries."

$ $ BIRD WATCHER'S DIGEST, Pardson Corp., P.O. Box 110, Marietta OH 45750. (740)373-5285. E-mail: editor@birdwatchersdigest.com. Website: www.birdwatchersdigest.com. **Contact:** William H. Thompson III, editor. **60% freelance written.** Works with a small number of new/unpublished writers each year. Bimonthly magazine covering natural history—birds and bird watching. "*BWD* is a nontechnical magazine interpreting ornithological material for amateur observers, including the knowledgeable birder, the serious novice and the backyard bird watcher; we strive to provide good reading and good ornithology." Estab. 1978. Circ. 90,000. Pays on publication. Publishes ms 2 years after acceptance. Byline given. Buys one-time, first serial and second serial (reprint) rights. Submit seasonal material 6 months in advance. Responds in 2 months. Sample copy for $3.99 or on website. Writer's guidelines for #10 SASE or on website.
Nonfiction: Book excerpts, how-to (relating to birds, feeding and attracting, etc.), humor, personal experience, travel (limited—we get many). "We are especially interested in fresh, lively accounts of closely observed bird behavior and displays and of bird-watching experiences and expeditions. We often need material on less common species or on unusual or previously unreported behavior of common species." No articles on pet or caged birds; none on raising a baby bird. **Buys 75-90 mss/year.** Send complete ms. All submissions must be accompanied by SASE. Length: 600-3,500 words. **Pays from $50.**
Reprints: Accepts previously published submissions.
Photos: Send photos with ms. Pays $10 minimum for b&w prints; $50 minimum for transparencies. Buys one-time rights.
☐ The online magazine carries content not found in the print edition and includes writer's guidelines.
Tips: "We are aimed at an audience ranging from the backyard bird watcher to the very knowledgeable birder; we include in each issue material that will appeal at various levels. We always strive for a good geographical spread, with material from every section of the country. We leave very technical matters to others, but we want facts and accuracy, depth and quality, directed at the veteran bird watcher and at the enthusiastic novice. We stress the joys and pleasures of bird watching, its environmental contribution, and its value for the individual and society."

$ $ $ CALIFORNIA WILD, Natural Science for Thinking Animals, California Academy of Sciences, Golden Gate Park, San Francisco CA 94118. (415)750-7116. Fax: (415)221-4853. Website: www.calacademy.org/calwi ld. **Contact:** Keith Howell, editor. **75% freelance written.** Quarterly magazine covering natural sciences and the environment. "Our readers' interests range widely from ecology to geology, from endangered species to anthropology, from field identification of plants and birds to armchair understanding of complex scientific issues." Estab. 1948. Circ. 32,000. Pays prior to publication. Publishes ms an average of 3 months after acceptance. Byline given. Offers 50% kill fee (maximum $200). Buys first North American serial or one-time rights. Editorial lead time 3 months. Submit seasonal material 6 months in advance. Query by mail, fax. Responds in 6 weeks to queries; 6 months to mss. Sample copy for 9×12 SASE or on website. Writer's guidelines for #10 SASE or on website.
Nonfiction: Personal experience, photo feature, biological and earth sciences. No travel pieces. Mostly California stories, but also from Pacific Ocean countries. **Buys 20 mss/year.** Query with published clips. Length: 1,000-3,000 words. **Pays $250-1,000 for assigned articles; $200-800 for unsolicited articles.** Sometimes pays expenses of writers on assignment.
Photos: State availability of photos with submission. Reviews transparencies. Offers $75-150/photo. Model releases and identification of subjects required. Buys one-time rights.
Columns/Departments: Trail Less Traveled (unusual places); Wild Lives (description of unusual plant or animal); Science Track (innovative student, teacher, young scientist), all 1,000-1,500 words; Skywatcher (research in astronomy), 2,000-3,000 words. **Buys 12 mss/year.** Query with published clips. **Pays $200-400.**
Fillers: Facts. **Pays $25-50.**
Tips: "We are looking for unusual and/or timely stories about California environment or biodiversity."

▨ $ $ E THE ENVIRONMENTAL MAGAZINE, Earth Action Network, P.O. Box 5098, Westport CT 06881-5098. (203)854-5559. Fax: (203)866-0602. E-mail: info@emagazine.com. Website: www.emagazine.com. **Contact:** Jim Motavalli, editor. **60% freelance written.** Bimonthly magazine. "*E Magazine* was formed for the purpose of acting as a clearinghouse of information, news and commentary on environmental issues." Estab. 1990. Circ. 50,000. Pays on publication. Byline given. Buys first North American serial rights. Editorial lead time 3 months. Submit seasonal material 6 months in advance. Query by mail, e-mail, fax. Accepts simultaneous submissions. Sample copy for $5 or on website. Writer's guidelines for #10 SASE or on website.
Nonfiction: Exposé (environmental), how-to (the "Green Living" section), interview/profile, new products and book reviews. No fiction or poetry. **Buys 100 mss/year.** Query with published clips. Length: 100-4,200 words. **Pays 20¢/ word.** On spec or free contributions welcome.
● The editor reports an interest in seeing more investigative reporting.
Photos: State availability of photos. Reviews printed samples, e.g., magazine tearsheets, postcards, etc. to be kept on file. Negotiates payment individually. Identification of subjects required. Buys one-time rights.

Columns/Departments: In Brief/Currents (environmental news stories/trends), 400-1,000 words; Interviews (environmental leaders), 2,200 words; Green Living; Your Health; Going Green (travel); Eco-home; Eating Right; Green Business; Consumer News; New & Different Products (each 700-1,200 words). Query with published clips. **Pays 20¢/word.** On spec or free contributions welcome.

▣ The online magazine carries original content not found in the print edition and includes writer's guidelines. Contact: Jim Motavalli, online editor.

Tips: "Contact us to obtain writer's guidelines and back issues of our magazine. Tailor your query according to the department/section you feel it would be best suited for. Articles must be lively, well-researched, fair-sided and relevant to a mainstream, national readership."

$ $ HIGH COUNTRY NEWS, High Country Foundation, P.O. Box 1090, Paonia CO 81428-1090. (303)527-4898. E-mail: betsym@HCN.org. Website: www.hcn.org. **Contact:** Betsy Marston, editor. **80% freelance written.** Works with a small number of new/unpublished writers each year. Biweekly tabloid covering Rocky Mountain West, the Great Basin and Pacific Northwest environment, rural communities and natural resource issues in 10 western states for environmentalists, politicians, companies, college classes, government agencies, grass roots activists, public land managers, etc. Estab. 1970. Circ. 20,000. Pays on publication. Publishes ms an average of 2 months after acceptance. Byline given. Buys one-time rights. Query by mail. Responds in 1 month. Sample copy and writer's guidelines for SAE or on website.

Nonfiction: Reporting (local issues with regional importance); exposé (government, corporate); interview/profile; personal experience; centerspread photo feature. **Buys 100 mss/year.** Query. Length: up to 3,000 words. **Pays 20¢/word minimum.** Sometimes pays expenses of writers on assignment for lead stories.

Reprints: Send tearsheet of article and info about when and where the article previously appeared. **Pays 15¢/word.**

Photos: Send photos with ms. Prefers b&w prints. Captions and identification of subjects required.

Columns/Departments: Roundups (topical stories), 800 words; opinion pieces, 1,000 words.

Tips: "We use a lot of freelance material, though very little from outside the Rockies. Familiarity with the newspaper is a must. Start by writing a query letter. We define 'resources' broadly to include people, culture and aesthetic values, not just coal, oil and timber."

$ $ $ $ INTERNATIONAL WILDLIFE, National Wildlife Federation, 8925 Leesburg Pike, Vienna VA 22184-0001. (703)790-4510. Fax: (703)790-4544. E-mail: pubs@nwf.org. Website: www.nwf.org/nwf. **Contact:** Jonathan Fisher, editor. **85% freelance written.** Prefers to work with published/established writers. Bimonthly magazine for persons interested in natural history and the environment in countries outside the US. Estab. 1971. Circ. 200,000. **Pays on acceptance.** Publishes ms an average of 4 months after acceptance. Buys exclusive first time worldwide rights and nonexclusive worldwide rights after publication. "We are now assigning most articles but will consider detailed proposals for quality feature material of interest to a broad audience." Accepts queries by mail, e-mail, fax. Responds in 6 weeks. Writer's guidelines for #10 SASE.

Nonfiction: Focuses on world wildlife, environmental problems and peoples' relationship to the natural world as reflected in such issues as population growth, pollution, resource utilization, food production, etc. Stories deal with non-US subjects. Especially interested in articles on animal behavior and other natural history, first-person experiences by scientists in the field, well-reported coverage of wildlife-status case studies which also raise broader themes about international conservation and timely issues. Query. Length: 2,000 words. Examine past issues for style and subject matter. **Pays $2,000 minimum** for long features. Sometimes pays expenses of writers on assignment.

● Ranked as one of the best markets for freelance writers in *Writer's Yearbook* magazine's annual "Top 100 Markets," January 2000.

Photos: Purchases top-quality color photos; prefers packages of related photos and text, but single shots of exceptional interest and sequences also considered. Prefers Kodachrome or Fujichrome transparencies. Buys one-time rights.

Tips: "*International Wildlife* readers include conservationists, biologists, wildlife managers and other wildlife professionals, but the majority are not wildlife professionals. In fact, *International Wildlife* caters to the unconverted—those people who may have only a passing interest in wildlife. Consequently, our writers should avoid a common pitfall: talking only to an 'in group.' *International Wildlife* is in competition with television and hundreds of other periodicals for the limited time and attention of busy people. So our functions include attracting readers with engaging subjects, pictures and layouts; then holding them with interesting and entertaining, as well as instructional, text."

$ $ MOUNTAINFREAK, for freaks like us, Lungta, LLC, P.O. Box 4149, 122½ N. Oak St., Telluride CO 81435. (970)728-9731. Fax: (970)728-9821. E-mail: freaks@mountainfreak.com. Website: www.mountainfreak.com. **Contact:** Suzanne Cheavens, senior editor. **50% freelance written.** "Quarterly magazine. Our magazine is one that aims for entertainment, enlightenment, pulse-pounding adventure, conscientious living, spiritual awakening and healing of both the soul and the body. *Mountainfreak* is the magazine for those who cannot accept the status quo and who believe that life is how you script it for yourself." Estab. 1996. Circ. 25,000. Pays on publication. Publishes ms an average of 1 year after acceptance. Byline given. Offers 33% kill fee. Buys first rights or makes work-for-hire assignments. Editorial lead time 1 year. Submit seasonal material 1 year in advance. Accepts simultaneous submissions. Sample copy for $5 or on website. Writer's guidelines for SASE or on website.

Nonfiction: Book excerpts, essays, exposé, general interest, how-to, humor, inspirational, interview/profile, new product, personal experience, technical, travel. "Our readers are interested in the how-tos of alternative living. Some topics that have appeared in our pages include cob building, permaculture and solar energy. Organic gardening, soapmaking, and herbal remedies for the common cold have also been featured in *Mountainfreak*. Think about preserving a healthy, sustainable environment for our children's children and submit accordingly. Nothing preachy and don't be afraid to interview the naysayers of your topics." **Buys 100 mss/year.** Query by mail with published clips. Length: 250-3,000 words. **Pays 10-25¢/word.**

Photos: Send photos with submission. Reviews original transparencies. Offers $25-400/photo or negotiates payment individually. Captions required.

Columns/Departments: Smoke Signals (environmental and political news), 300-500 words; Grooves 'N' Such (new, mainstream music), 500-700 words; Be Well (alternative health, i.e., yerba maté, fire, walking, etc.), 750-1,000 words; Art Beat (interesting art news and features. Think beyond mainstream. Send queries to Karen Metzger, Art Beat editor, same address); Playground (fun adventure and treading lightly); Good Biz (a profile of companies creating quality products while maintaining conscientious business ethnics); Yummy Grub (good healthy food and recipes); Touch the Earth (living sustainably); Profile (interesting, dynamic people who have made a difference). Query with published clips. **Pays 10-25¢/word.**

Fiction: Query with published clips. Length: 500-3,000 words. **Pays 10-25¢/word.** "Outdoor-oriented fiction is good but writers should not be limited to the genre."

Poetry: Avant-garde, free verse, haiku, light verse, traditional. **Buys 4-5 poems/year.** Submit maximum 5 poems. **Pays $25.**

▣ The online magazine carries content not found in the print edition. Contact: Suzanne Cheavens.

Tips: "If a writer is talking about an outdoor adventure, remember that many readers have done that, too. Write from a spiritual perspective. We're not about peak bagging or first ascents: we're about worshipping the outdoors, the mountains, the air, the water. We'd like to hear from gentle travelers that are not out to conquer, but to understand. Excellent, thoughtful, original queries are a good start. Though *Mountainfreak* is slicker and more professional than our seminal, black and white publications, we are still 'freaky' compared to the mainstream media. Know our magazine well. We have a lot of departments so finding a fit may not be as difficult as one might think. Our mission statement and writer's guidelines will either make sense to you or not. If they make sense, give it a try. Writers that supply captioned, excellent photos have a huge leg-up on those who do not. An exception to this would be fiction submissions. And, I must see writing samples. If you are a yet-to-be-published writer, send your favorite work."

$ $ $ NATIONAL PARKS, 1300 19th St. NW, Washington DC 20036. (202)223-6722. Fax: (202)659-0650. E-mail: npmag@npca.org. Website: www.npca.org/. Editor-in-Chief: Linda Rancourt. **Contact:** William Updike, editorial assistant. **85% freelance written.** Prefers to work with published/established writers. Bimonthly magazine for a largely unscientific but highly educated audience interested in preservation of National Park System units, natural areas and protection of wildlife habitat. Estab. 1919. Circ. 400,000. **Pays on acceptance.** Publishes ms an average of 2 months after acceptance. Offers 33% kill fee. Buys first North American serial and second serial (reprint) rights. Responds in 5 months. Sample copy for $3 and 9×12 SAE or on website. Writer's guidelines for #10 SASE.

Nonfiction: Exposé (on threats, wildlife problems in national parks); descriptive articles about new or proposed national parks and wilderness parks; natural history pieces describing park geology, wildlife or plants; new trends in park use; legislative issues. All material must relate to national parks. No poetry, philosophical essays or first-person narratives. No unsolicited mss. Length: 2,000-2,500 words. **Pays $1,200 for full-length features; $500 for service articles.**

Photos: Send photos with submission. No color prints or negatives. Prefers color slides and transparencies. Pays $125-325 inside; $500 for covers. Captions required. Buys first North American serial rights. Send for guidelines first. Not responsible for unsolicited photos.

Tips: "Articles should have an original slant or news hook and cover a limited subject, rather than attempt to treat a broad subject superficially. Specific examples, descriptive details and quotes are always preferable to generalized information. The writer must be able to document factual claims, and statements should be clearly substantiated with evidence within the article. *National Parks* does not publish fiction, poetry, personal essays or 'My trip to . . .' stories."

$ $ $ $ NATIONAL WILDLIFE, National Wildlife Federation, 8925 Leesburg Pike, Vienna VA 22184-0001. (703)790-4524. Fax: (703)790-4544. E-mail: pubs@nwf.org. Website: www.nwf.org/natlwild. **Contact:** Bob Strohm, editor-in-chief; Mark Wexler, editor. **75% freelance written,** "but assigns almost all material based on staff ideas. Assigns few unsolicited queries." Bimonthly magazine. "Our purpose is to promote wise use of the nation's natural resources and to conserve and protect wildlife and its habitat. We reach a broad audience that is largely interested in wildlife conservation and nature photography." Estab. 1963. Circ. 660,000. **Pays on acceptance.** Publishes ms an average of 1 year after acceptance. Offers 25% kill fee. Buys all rights. Submit seasonal material 8 months in advance. Accepts queries by mail, e-mail, fax. Responds in 6 weeks. Writer's guidelines for #10 SASE.

Nonfiction: General interest (2,500-word features on wildlife, new discoveries, behavior, or the environment); how-to (an outdoor or nature related activity); personal experience (outdoor adventure); photo feature (wildlife); profiles (people who have gone beyond the call of duty to protect wildlife and its habitat, or to prevent environmental contamination and people who have been involved in the environment or conservation in interesting ways); short 700-word features on an unusual individual or new scientific discovery relating to nature. "Avoid too much scientific detail. We prefer anecdotal, natural history material." **Buys 50 mss/year.** Query with or without published clips. Length: 750-2,500 words. **Pays $500-2,000.** Sometimes pays expenses of writers on assignment.

● Ranked as one of the best markets for freelance writers in *Writer's Yearbook* magazine's annual "Top 100 Markets," January 2000.

Photos: John Nuhn, photo editor. Send photos or send photos with query. Prefers Kodachrome or Fujichrome transparencies. Buys one-time rights.

Tips: "Writers can break in with us more readily by proposing subjects (initially) that will take only one or two pages in the magazine (short features)."

\$ \$ \$ \$ NATURAL HISTORY, Natural History Magazine, Central Park W. at 79th St., New York NY 10024. (212)769-5500. Fax: (212)769-5511. E-mail: nhmag@amnh.org. **Contact:** Ellen Goldensohn, editor-in-chief. **15% freelance written.** Published 10 times a year for well-educated audience: professional people, scientists and scholars. Circ. 400,000. **Pays on acceptance.** Publishes ms an average of 3 months after acceptance. Byline given. Buys first serial rights and becomes agent for second serial (reprint) rights. Submit seasonal material at least 6 months in advance.

Nonfiction: Uses all types of scientific articles except chemistry and physics—emphasis is on the biological sciences and anthropology. "We always want to see new research findings in almost all branches of the natural sciences—anthropology, archeology, zoology and ornithology. We find it is particularly difficult to get something new in herpetology (amphibians and reptiles) or entomology (insects), and would like to see material in those fields." **Buys 60 mss/year.** Query by mail or submit complete ms. Length: 1,500-3,000 words. **Pays \$500-2,500,** additional payment for photos used.

• Ranked as one of the best markets for freelance writers in *Writer's Yearbook* magazine's annual "Top 100 Markets," January 2000.

Photos: Rarely uses 8×10 b&w glossy prints; pays \$125/page maximum. Much color is used; pays \$300 for inside and up to \$600 for cover. Buys one-time rights.

Columns/Departments: Journal (reporting from the field); Findings (summary of new or ongoing research); Naturalist At Large; The Living Museum (relates to the American Museum of Natural History); Discovery (natural or cultural history of a specific place).

Tips: "We expect high standards of writing and research. We do not lobby for causes, environmental or other. The writer should have a deep knowledge of his subject, then submit original ideas either in query or by manuscript."

\$ \$ NATURE CANADA, Canadian Nature Federation, 1 Nicholas St., Suite 606, Ottawa, Ontario K1N 7B7 Canada. Fax: (613)562-3371. E-mail: cnf@cnf.ca. Website: www.cnf.ca. **Contact:** Barbara Stevenson, editor. Quarterly membership magazine covering conservation, natural history and environmental/naturalist community. "*Nature Canada* is written for an audience interested in nature. Its content supports the Canadian Nature Federation's philosophy that all species have a right to exist regardless of their usefulness to humans. We promote the awareness, understanding and enjoyment of nature." Estab. 1971. Circ. 16,000. Pays on publication. Publishes ms an average of 3 months after acceptance. Byline given. Offers \$100 kill fee. Buys one-time rights. Editorial lead time 3 months. Submit seasonal material 6 months in advance. Responds in 3 months to mss. Sample copy for \$5. Writer's guidelines for SASE or on website.

Nonfiction: Canadian environmental issues and natural history. **Buys 20 mss/year.** Query by mail with published clips. Length: 2,000-4,000 words. **Pays 25¢/word (Canadian).**

Photos: State availability of photos with submission. Offers \$40-100/photo (Canadian). Identification of subjects required. Buys one-time rights.

Columns/Departments: The Green Gardener (naturalizing your backyard), 1,200 words; Small Wonder (on less well-known species such as invertebrates, nonvascular plants, etc.), 800-1,500 words; Connections (Canadians making a difference for the environment), 1,000-1,500 words; Pathways (about natural places to visit). **Buys 16 mss/year.** Query with published clips. **Pays 25¢/word (Canadian).**

Tips: "Our readers are knowledgeable about nature and the environment so contributors should have a good understanding of the subject. We also deal exclusively with Canadian issues and species."

N \$ \$ \$ \$ OUTDOOR AMERICA, Izaak Walton League of America, 707 Conservation Lane, Gaithersburg MD 20878. (301)548-0150. Fax: (301)548-0146. Website: www.iwla.org. **Contact:** Zachary Hoskins, editor. Company quarterly covering national conservation efforts/issues. "*Outdoor America*, one of the nation's most established conservation magazines, has been published by the Izaak Walton League, a national conservation organization, since 1922. A quarterly 4-color publication, *Outdoor America* is received by approximately 40,000 League members, as well as representatives of Congress and the media. Our audience, located predominantly in the midwestern and mid-Atlantic states, enjoys traditional recreational pursuits, such as fishing, hiking, hunting and boating. All have a keen interest in protecting the future of our natural resources and outdoor recreation heritage." Estab. 1922. Circ. 50,000. Pays on publication. Publishes ms an average of 2 months after acceptance. Accepts queries by mail. Sample copy for \$2.50. Writer's guidelines free.

Nonfiction: Conservation. Send complete ms. Length: 1,500-3,000 words. **Pays \$1,000.**

\$ \$ \$ \$ SIERRA, 85 Second St., 2nd Floor, San Francisco CA 94105-3441. (415)977-5656. Fax: (415)977-5794. E-mail: sierra.letters@sierraclub.org. Website: www.sierraclub.org. Editor-in-Chief: Joan Hamilton. Senior Editors: Reed McManus, Paul Rauber. **Contact:** Robert Schildgen, managing editor. Works with a small number of new/unpublished writers each year. Bimonthly magazine emphasizing conservation and environmental politics for people who are well educated, activist, outdoor-oriented and politically well informed with a dedication to conservation. Estab. 1893. Circ.

550,000. **Pays on acceptance.** Publishes ms an average of 4 months after acceptance. Byline given. Kill fees negotiable when a story is assigned. Buys first North American serial rights. Responds in 2 months. Sample copy for $3 and SASE or on website. Writer's guidlines on website.

- The editor reports an interest in seeing pieces on environmental "heroes," thoughtful features on environmental issues in the Midwest and South (except Florida) and engaging stories about achievements of local activists.

Nonfiction: Exposé (well-documented articles on environmental issues of national importance such as energy, wilderness, forests, etc.); general interest (well-researched nontechnical pieces on areas of particular environmental concern); photo feature (photo essays on threatened or scenic areas); journalistic treatments of semi-technical topics (energy sources, wildlife management, land use, waste management, etc.). No "My trip to . . . " or "why we must save wildlife/ nature" articles; no poetry or general superficial essays on environmentalism; no reporting on purely local environmental issues. Special issues: Travel (March/April 2001). **Buys 5-6 mss/issue.** Query with published clips by mail only. Length: 800-3,000 words. **Pays $450-4,000.** Pays limited expenses of writers on assignment.

- Ranked as one of the best markets for freelance writers in *Writer's Yearbook* magazine's annual "Top 100 Markets," January 2000.

Reprints: Send photocopy or typed ms with rights for sale noted and information about when and where the article previously appeared. Pay negotiable.

Photos: Tanuja Mehrotra, art and production manager. Send photos. Pays $300 maximum for transparencies; more for cover photos. Buys one-time rights.

Columns/Departments: Food for Thought (food's connection to environment); Good Going (adventure journey); Hearth & Home (advice for environmentally sound living); Body Politics (health and the environment); Way to Go (wilderness trips), 750 words. **Pays $500.** Lay of the Land (national/international concerns), 500-700 words. Pay varies. Mixed Media (book reviews), 200-300 words. **Pays $50.**

Tips: "Queries should include an outline of how the topic would be covered and a mention of the political appropriateness and timeliness of the article. Statements of the writer's qualifications should be included."

N $ SNOWY EGRET, The Fair Press, P.O. Box 9, Bowling Green IN 47833. **Contact:** Philip Repp, editor. Managing Editor: Ruth C. Acker. **95% freelance written.** Semiannual literary magazine featuring nature writing. "We publish works which celebrate the abundance and beauty of nature and examine the variety of ways in which human beings interact with landscapes and living things. Nature writing from literary, artistic, psychological, philosophical and historical perspectives." Estab. 1922. Circ. 400. Pays on publication. Publishes ms an average of 6 months after acceptance. Byline given. Buys first North American serial and one-time anthology or reprint rights. Editorial lead time 2 months. Accepts queries by mail, e-mail. Accepts simultaneous submissions. Responds in 1 month to queries; 2 months to mss. Sample copy for 9 × 12 SASE and $8. Writer's guidelines free for #10 SASE.

Nonfiction: Essays, general interest, interview/profile, personal experience, travel. **Buys 10 mss/year.** Send complete ms. Length: 500-10,000 words. **Pays $2/page for unsolicited articles.**

Columns/Departments: Jane Robertson, Woodnotes editor. Woodnotes (short descriptions of personal encounters with wildlife or natural settings), 200-2,000 words. **Buys 12 mss/year. Pays $2/page.**

Fiction: Nature-oriented works (in which natural settings, wildlife or other organisms, and/or characters who identify with the natural world are significant components). "No genre fiction, e.g., horror, western romance, etc." **Buys 4 mss/ year.** Send complete ms. Length: 500-10,000 words. **Pays $2/page.**

Poetry: Avant-garde, free verse, traditional. **Buys 30 poems/year.** Submit maximum 5 poems. **Pays $4/poem or page.**

Tips: "The writers we publish invariably have a strong personal identification with the natural world, have examined their subjects thoroughly, and write about them sincerely. They know what they're talking about and show their subjects in detail, using, where appropriate, detailed description and dialogue."

$ WHOLE EARTH, Point Foundation, 1408 Mission Ave., San Rafael CA 94901. (415)256-2800. Fax: (415)256-2808. E-mail: editor@wholeearthmag.com. Website: www.wholeearthmag.com. Editor: Peter Warshall. Managing Editor: Michael Stone. Senior Editor: Nicole Parizeau. **Contact:** Attn. Submissions. **80% freelance written.** "Quarterly periodical, descendent of the Whole Earth Catalog. Evaluates tools, ideas, and practices to sow the seeds for a long-term, viable planet." Estab. 1971. Circ. 30,000. Pays on publication. Publishes ms an average of 6 months after acceptance. Byline given. Buys one-time rights to articles; all rights for reviews. Editorial lead time 3 months. Accepts simultaneous submissions. Responds in 1 month (no promises). Sample copy on website. Writer's guidelines for SASE or on website.

Nonfiction: Book reviews, essays, exposé, general interest, historical/nostalgic, how-to, humor, interview/profile, new product, personal experience, photo feature, religious, travel. "No dull repeats of old ideas or material; no 'goddess' material, spiritual, New Age or 'Paths to . . .' " Send complete ms (queries are discouraged). Length: 500-3,000 words.

Reprints: Accepts previously published submissions.

Photos: State availability of photos with submission. Negotiates payment individually. Buys one-time rights.

Fiction: Rarely publishes fiction. **Buys 2-4 mss/year.**

Poetry: Avant-garde, free verse, haiku, light verse, traditional. No long works. **Buys 1-4 poems/year.** Length: 100 lines maximum. Pay negotiable.

Tips: "We like your personal voice: intimate, a lively conversation with an attentive friend. We like ideas, thoughts and events to appear to stand independent and clear of the narrator. Don't send a variation on an old idea. Show us you did your homework."

PERSONAL COMPUTERS

Personal computer magazines continue to evolve. The most successful have a strong focus on a particular family of computers or widely-used applications and carefully target a specific type of computer use, although as technology evolves, some computers and applications fall by the wayside. Be sure you see the most recent issue of a magazine before submitting material.

N ✕ $ $ $ $ ACCESS INTERNET MAGAZINE, Access Media Inc., 35 Highland Circle, Needham MA 02494-3032. (781)453-3990. Fax: (781)453-3988. Website: www.accessmagazine.com. Editor: Stephanie Chang. Managing Editor: Dennis Barker. **Contact:** Douglas McDaniel, senior editor. **90% freelance written.** Weekly Sunday newspaper magazine insert covering the Internet. "*Access* is a plain-speak magazine for the average PC and Mac user. We cover the Web and how people interact with the new medium." Estab. 1998. Circ. 7,000,000. **Pays on acceptance.** Publishes ms an average of 2 months after acceptance. Byline given. Offers 25% kill fee. Buys first North American serial and electronic rights. Editorial lead time 3 months. Submit seasonal material 3 months in advance. Accepts queries by e-mail. Responds in 2 weeks. Sample copy online at website. Writer's guidelines by e-mail.

Nonfiction: General interest, how-to, humor, new product. **Buys 200 mss/year.** Query with published clips. Length: 750-1,500 words. **Pays $1/word.** Sometimes pays expenses of writers on assignment.

Photos: State availability of photos with submission. Reviews transparencies. Negotiates payment individually. Captions, model releases and identification of subjects required. Buys one-time rights.

✕ $ $ $ COMPUTER CURRENTS, Real World Solutions for Business Computing, Computer Currents Publishing, 1250 Ninth St., Berkeley CA 94710. (510)527-0333. Fax: (510)527-4106. E-mail: editorial@currents.net. Website: www.computercurrents.com. **Contact:** Robert Luhn, editor-in-chief. **90% freelance written.** Biweekly magazine "for fairly experienced PC and Mac business users. We provide where to buy, how to buy and how to use information. That includes buyers guides, reviews, tutorials and more." Estab. 1983. Circ. 700,000. **Pays on acceptance.** Byline given. Offers 20% kill fee. Buys all rights. Editorial lead time 2 months. Submit seasonal material 2 months in advance. Accepts queries by mail, e-mail, fax. Responds in 2 weeks to queries; 2 months to mss. Sample copy for 10 × 12 SAE with $5 postage or on website. Writer's guidelines for #10 SASE or via e-mail.

Nonfiction: Book excerpts, exposé, how-to (using PC or Mac products), new product, opinion, technical. Special issues: Holiday Gift Guide (November). "No fiction, poetry or 'I just discovered PCs' essays." **Buys 40 mss/year.** Query with published clips and SASE. Length: 1,000-2,500 words. **Pays $700-2,000.** Sometimes pays expenses of writers on assignment.

Reprints: Send tearsheet or typed ms with rights for sale noted and information about when and where the article previously appeared. Pays 10-40% of amount paid for an original article.

Photos: State availability of photos with submission. Reviews 35mm transparencies, 8 × 10 prints. Offers no additional payment for photos accepted with ms. Buys first North American and nonexclusive reprint rights.

Columns/Departments: Robert Luhn. "Previews & Reviews" of new and beta hardware, software and services, 300-600 words; Features (PC, Mac, hardware, software, investigative pieces), 1,000-2,500 words. **Buys 60 mss/year.** Query with published clips and SASE. **Pays $50-500.**

■ The online magazine carries original content not found in the print edition. Contact Robert Luhn, online editor.

Tips: "Writers must know PC or Mac technology and major software and peripherals. Know how to write, evaluate products critically, and make a case for or against a product under review. *Computer Currents* is the magazine for the rest of us. We don't torture test 500 printers or devote space to industry chit-chat. Instead, we provide PC and Mac users with real-world editorial they can use every day when determining what to buy, where to buy it, and how to use it. Along with supplying this kind of nitty-gritty advice to both small and large business users alike, we also demystify the latest technologies and act as a consumer advocate. We're also not afraid to poke fun at the industry, as our annual 'Year in Review' issue and biweekly 'Gigglebytes' column demonstrate."

$ COMPUTERCREDIBLE MAGAZINE, Assimilations, Inc., 1249 W. Jordan River Dr., South Jordan UT 84095-8250. (801)254-5432. Fax: (801)253-0914. E-mail: computer@credible.com. Website: www.credible.com. Editor: Rick Simi. **Contact:** Kerry Simi, managing editor. **100% freelance written.** Monthly magazine covering computers. Estab. 1995. Circ. 35,000. **Pays on acceptance.** Publishes ms an average of 1 month after acceptance. Byline given. Buys first North American serial rights, electronic rights, and second serial (reprint) rights. Accepts queries by mail, e-mail. Sample copy for $1. Writer's guidelines for #10 SASE or on website.

Nonfiction: General interest, how-to, humor, interview/profile, new product, opinion, technical. **Buys 40 mss/year.** Length: 650-1,500 words. **Pays 5-10¢/word.**

Reprints: Accepts previously published submissions.

Photos: State availability of photos with submission.

Columns/Departments: **Buys 40 mss/year.** Send complete ms. **Pays 5-10¢/word.**

Fiction: Humorous. **Buys 6 mss/year.** Send complete ms. Length: 650-1,000 words. **Pays 5-10¢/word.**

Fillers: Facts, short humor. Length: 250-650 words. **Pays 5-10¢/word.**

insider report

Computer freelancing: Keeping pace with the field pays off in tech writing

Writer Joe Hutsko considers himself a novelist first. But freelancing about computers and technology for publications including *The New York Times* 'Circuits' section, *Time Digital*, *PC World* and *Macworld*, *Popular Science*, *Wired*, and *Gamepro* yielded success long before Forge agreed to publish Hutsko's novel, *The Deal*. Tech writing pays the bills, Hutsko admits, and makes it possible for him to pursue his more literary ambitions.

Joe Hutsko

How does computer freelancing differ from freelancing for other topics?
I've pretty much always done tech-bent stories, in one way or another. In a lot of ways I expect the process is the same as any other story, be it a movie review, political intrigue expose, or travel piece.

What special challenges are associated with writing about computers and technology?
Knowledge is power. I tend to think anyone can write the reviews I write, but then I realize I have so many years of knowledge—from age sixteen with my first Apple II and video game systems. That's where the value to my editors comes in—I am able to compare and contrast products, and evaluate new concepts in relation to old ways of thinking. In a way, having seen so much over so many years, I can try to predict how a certain new product may pan out over the short then long term.

Staying up on the goings-on is a challenge. I start every morning with a cup of coffee and generally two or more hours browsing *The New York Times* site first, then ZD Net, CNET, *Wired*, and other tech-bent sites, to see if anything interests me. If I hear about a new product coming up, I'll contact an editor at one magazine or another to pitch it. For the most part I've been assigned just about every product review pitch I've ever suggested. But clearly, staying up on the latest-everything is essential to my kind of freelance writing.

Are all electronics and computer articles updates or review write-ups?
There's definitely more to high-tech writing and reporting than products. For instance, *Vanity Fair* had a feature on Silicon Valley's IPO madness. *The New Yorker* regularly covers high-tech topics, as do so many of the mainstream magazines. The Time Warner and AOL merger is a good (Steve) Case in point. As technology becomes more integrated into daily life, it makes total sense that we'll start seeing more and more coverage that is high-tech based.

Where would you turn to expand your freelance base when it comes to computers and electronics-centered writing?

I'd try for the more mainstream magazines like *Vanity Fair* or *The New Yorker*, two of my favorites. If and when I'm ready to branch out with a wider-reaching general interest story, something along the lines of the kind of fiction I write, those would be my first two choices. And possibly *Talk*. Ideally, though, I'd wish any of those magazines would excerpt my fiction rather than have me write nonfiction stories. The truth is, I pretty much only write non-fiction to pay the rent, whereas my heart lies in my fiction.

What is the pay scale a new, moderate and experienced freelancer can expect when writing about computers and technology?

Tricky to say. Newspapers are notoriously low on the pay scale, but the visibility is good. *Time* magazine, for instance, pays double or more than *The New York Times*. Some of the online sites pay very well, by reviewer standards. If you're a good writer I'd say $1 a word is pretty much the going rate at many of the online review sites like ZD Net, CNET, etc.

What are the easiest sales in this market?

Straightforward reviews. There are new computers and programs released every day, and keeping up with it means reviews. A good writer can keep busy constantly.

What tips would you offer a writer just getting started in the computer freelancing niche?

Send out lots and lots of e-mail queries. Short, and right to the point. You can almost always find out whom to send a query to on any of the more popular computer and product review sites. It helps to have written about the topic before, which is always a chicken-and-egg thing. You need some clips, which ideally you can include in the e-mail or point to on other sites you've written for, so the editor can see you can write. On the other hand, how do you get your first assignment without any clips at all? My first assignments were lucky breaks, but they came mostly through persistence.

For interviews with the pros on more freelance niche markets see Child Care, page 431; Food & Drink, page 470; Health & Fitness, page 494; Nature, page 594; and Travel, page 779.
—*Kelly Milner Halls*

➤◆◆◆

TOP TIP: "Being out of the loop and missing a product or update is a common mistake new tech freelancers make. The tech business moves so fast, and it is really important to be up on the very latest products, software versions, and updates. It can make or break a review: for instance, you say a product has a problem with its modem, then find out that the company has released a new update that fixes the error."

Tips: "Our diverse readership allows us to print articles in varying styles (technical, light-hearted, instructional). We are looking for fiction and non-fiction writers who can explain technical information to our experienced readers without confusing the novice reader. We look for writers who can provide interesting points of view, solutions, and humorous anecdotes on issues facing the computer user."

N ⚑ $ $ **COMPUTOREDGE, San Diego, Denver and Albuquerque's Computer Magazine,** The Byte Buyer, Inc., P.O. Box 83086, San Diego CA 92138. (619)573-0315. Fax: (619)573-0205. E-mail: submissions@computor edge.com (accepts electronic submissions only). Website: www.computoredge.com. Executive Editor: Leah Steward. Senior Editor: Patricia Smith. **Contact:** John San Filippo, editor. **90% freelance written.** "We are the nation's largest regional computer weekly, providing San Diego, Denver and Albuquerque with entertaining articles on all aspects of computers. We cater to the novice/beginner/first-time computer buyer. Humor is welcome." Estab. 1983. Circ. 175,000. Pays on publication. Net 30 day payment after publication. Byline given. Offers $15 kill fee. Buys first North American serial rights, plus one-week exclusive and 90-day non-exclusive Web rights. Submit seasonal material 2 months in advance. Responds in 2 months. Download writer's guidelines and editorial calendar from website. Read sample issue online." Sample issue for SAE with 7 first-class stamps.

• Published as *ComputorEdge* in San Diego and Denver; published as *ComputerScene* in Albuquerque.

Nonfiction: General interest (computer), how-to, humor, personal experience. **Buys 80 mss/year.** Send query or complete ms. Length: 900-1,200 words. **Pays $100-200.**

Columns/Departments: Beyond Personal Computing (a reader's personal experience); Mac Madness (Macintosh-related), I Don't Do Windows (alternative operating systems). **Buys 80 mss/year.** Send query or complete ms. Length: 500-1,000 words. **Pays $50-145.**

Fiction: Confession, fantasy, slice-of-life vignettes. No poetry. **Buys 20 mss/year.** Send complete ms. Length: 900-1,200 words. **Pays $100-200.**

Tips: "Be relentless. Convey technical information in an understandable, interesting way. We like light material, but not fluff. Write as if you're speaking with a friend. Avoid the typical 'Love at First Byte' and the 'How My Grandmother Loves Her New Computer' article. We do not accept poetry. Avoid sexual innuendoes/metaphors. Reading a sample issue is advised."

$ $ $ $ MACADDICT, Imagine Media, 150 North Hill Dr., Suite 40, Brisbane CA 94005. (415)468-4684. Fax: (415)468-4686. E-mail: dreynolds@macaddict.com. Managing Editor: Jeff T. Herton. **Contact:** David Reynolds, editor. **25% freelance written.** Monthly magazine covering Macintosh computers. "*MacAddict* is a magazine for Macintosh computer enthusiasts of all levels. Writers must know, love and own Macintosh computers." Estab. 1996. Circ. 160,000. Pays on publication. Publishes ms an average of 3 months after acceptance. Byline given. Buys all rights. Editorial lead time 3 months. Submit seasonal material 5 months in advance. Accepts queries by mail, e-mail. Accepts simultaneous submissions. Responds in 1 month.

Nonfiction: General interest, how-to, new product, photo feature, technical. No humor, case studies, personal experiences, essays. **Buys 30 mss/year.** Query with or without published clips and SASE. Length: 750-5,000 words. **Pays $50-2,500.** Sometimes pays expenses of writers on asssignment.

Photos: State availability of photos with submission. Negotiates payment individually. Captions, model releases, identification of subjects required. Buys one-time rights.

Columns/Departments: Reviews (always assigned), 300-750 words; How-to's (detailed, step-by-step), 500-4,000 words; features, 1,000-4,000 words. **Buys 30 mss/year.** Query with or without published clips. **Pays $50-2,500.**

Fillers: Mark Simmons, senior editor. Get Info. **Buys 20/year.** Length: 50-500 words. **Pays $25-200.**

■ The online magazine carries original content not found in the print edition. Contact: David Reynolds, online editor.

Tips: "Send us an idea for a short one to two page how-to and/or send us a letter outlining your publishing experience and areas of Mac expertise so we can assign a review to you (reviews editor is Jennifer Ho). Your submission should have great practical hands-on benefit to a reader, be fun to read in the author's natural voice, and include lots of screenshot graphics. We require electronic submissions. Impress our reviews editor with well-written reviews of Mac products and then move up to bigger articles from there."

Ⓝ $ $ $ $ MACWEEK, Mac Publishing LLC, 301 Howard St., 15th Floor, San Francisco CA 94105. (415)243-3500. Fax: (415)243-3535. E-mail: catherine_lacroix@macweek.com. Website: www.macweek.com. **Contact:** Catherine LaCroix, executive editor/features. **35% freelance written.** Weekly tabloid "reaching sophisticated buyers of Macintosh-related products for large organizations." Estab. 1986. Circ. 85,000. **Pays on acceptance.** Publishes ms an average of 1 month after acceptance. Byline given. Offers 25% kill fee. Buys all worldwide rights. Editorial lead time: news, 10 days; reviews, 2 months; features, 1 month. Responds in 1 month to mss. Writer's guidelines free.

Columns/Departments: David Morgenstern and Joanna Pearlstein (news); Missy Roback (reviews); Catherine LaCroix (features and special reports). Reviews (new product testing), 500-1,200 words; Solutions (case histories), 1,600 words. **Buys 30 mss/year.** Query with published clips. **Pays 65¢-$1/word.** *No unsolicited mss.*

Tips: "We do not accept unsolicited material. If a writer would like to pitch a story to me by e-mail, I'm open to that. Knowledge of the Macintosh market is essential. Know which section you would like to write for and submit to the appropriate editor."

$ $ $ SMART COMPUTING, Sandhills Publishing, 131 W. Grand Dr., Lincoln NE 68521. (800)544-1264. Fax: (402)479-2104. E-mail: editor@smartcomputing.com. Website: www.smartcomputing.com. Managing Editor: Trevor Meers. **Contact:** Ron Kobler, editor-in-chief. **45% freelance written.** Monthly. "We focus on plain-English computing articles with an emphasis on tutorials that improve productivity without the purchase of new hardware." Estab. 1990. Circ. 300,000. **Pays on acceptance.** Publishes ms 2 months after acceptance. Byline given. Offers 25% kill fee. Buys all rights. Editorial lead time 4 months. Submit seasonal material 4 months in advance. Accepts queries by mail, e-mail. Accepts simultaneous submissions. Responds in 1 month. Sample copy for $7.99. Writer's guidelines for SASE.

○━ Break in with "any article containing little-known tips for improving software and hardware performance and Web use. We're also seeking clear reporting on key trends changing personal technology."

Nonfiction: How-to, new product, technical. No humor, opinion, personal experience. **Buys 250 mss/year.** Query with published clips. Length: 800-3,200 words. **Pays $240-960.** Pays the expenses of writers on assignment up to $75.

Photos: Send photos with submission. Offers no additional payment for photos accepted with ms. Captions required. Buys all rights.

▣ The online magazine carries original content not found in the print edition. Contact: Meredith Witulski, online editor.

Tips: "Focus on practical, how-to computing articles. Our readers are intensely productivity-driven. Carefully review recent issues. We receive many ideas for stories printed in the last six months."

⚔ **$ $ $ WIRED MAGAZINE,** Condé Nast Publications, 520 Third St., 3rd Floor, San Francisco CA 94107-1815. (415)276-5000. Fax: (415)276-5150. E-mail: submit@wired.com. Website: www.wired.com. Publisher: Dean Shutte. Editor-in-Chief: Katrina Heron. **Contact:** Valerie Cover, editorial assistant. **95% freelance written.** Monthly magazine covering technology and digital culture. "We cover the digital revolution and related advances in computers, communications and lifestyles." Estab. 1993. Circ. 500,000. **Pays on acceptance.** Publishes ms an average of 3 months after acceptance. Byline given. Offers 25% kill fee. Buys all rights for items less than 1,000 words, first North American serial rights for pieces over 1,000 words. Editorial lead time 3 months. Responds in 3 weeks. Sample copy for $4.95. Guidelines for #10 SASE or e-mail to guidelines@wired.com.

Nonfiction: Essays, interview/profile, opinion. "No poetry or trade articles." **Buys 85 features, 130 short pieces, 200 reviews, 36 essays and 50 other mss/year.** Query. Pays expenses of writers on assignment.

● Ranked as one of the best markets for freelance writers in *Writer's Yearbook* magazine's "Top 100 Markets," January 2000.

PHOTOGRAPHY

Readers of these magazines use their cameras as a hobby and for weekend assignments. To write for these publications, you should have expertise in photography. Magazines geared to the professional photographer can be found in the Professional Photography section.

$ $ BALIAN'S OUTDOOR & NATURE PHOTOGRAPHY, 1042 N. Camino Real, Suite B-123, Encinitas CA 92024. (760)436-8811. Fax: (760)436-8822. Website: www.outdoorandnature.com. **Contact:** Edward Balian, editorial director. Quarterly. "Primarily a how-to magazine for outdoor photo enthusiasts. We buy only illustrated articles." Estab. 1995. Circ. 40,000. Pays on publication. Publishes ms an average of 6 months after acceptance. Byline given. Buys first North American serial rights. Editorial lead time 12 months. Submit seasonal material 24 months in advance. Accepts queries by mail. Accepts simultaneous submissions. Responds in 6 weeks to queries; 3 months to mss. Sample copy for 11 × 14 SAE and 3 first-class stamps. Writer's guidelines for #10 SASE (required before any submission).

○━ Break in with "great, outstanding, *fantastic* photos!"

Nonfiction: How-to, technical. "No vacation photography; destination-oriented travel stories." **Buys 40 mss/year.** Query by mail with published clips. Length: 1,500-2,500 words. **Pay varies.**

Photos: State availability of photos with submission. Reviews contact sheets and any prints. Offers no additional payment for photos accepted with ms. Captions required. Buys one-time rights.

Columns/Departments: Pro Tips (pro photographer's tips on some topic) and So What's New? (survey of photo equipment), both 1,800 words. **Buys 16 mss/year.** Query with published clips. **Pay varies.**

Tips: "Above all, *ONP* is a 'how-to' magazine. Hence, we seek a strong educational component, in a conversational style, i.e., 'Here's how I do it . . . here's how you can too.' Specifics as to technique and equipment (including brands, models, distributors) will be expected by our readers. Submit query with non-returnable samples of photos and previously published articles. Preference is given to pro and semi-pro photographers with proven expertise on any one topic."

$ NATURE PHOTOGRAPHER, Nature Photographer Publishing Co., Inc., P.O. Box 690518, Quincy MA 02269. (617)847-0091. Fax: (617)847-0952. E-mail: nature_photographer@yahoo.com. Website: www.naturephotographermag.com. **Contact:** Helen Longest-Saccone and Evamarie Mathaey, co-editors-in-chief/photo editors. **65% freelance written.** Bimonthly magazine "emphasizing nature photography that uses low-impact and local less-known locations, techniques and ethics. Articles include how-to, travel to world-wide wilderness locations, and how nature photography can be used to benefit the environment and environmental education of the public." Estab. 1990. Circ. 25,000. Pays on publication. Buys one-time rights. Submit seasonal material 8 months in advance. Accepts queries by mail, e-mail. Accepts simultaneous submissions. Responds in 2 months. Sample copy for 9 × 12 SAE with 6 first-class stamps. Writer's guidelines for #10 SASE or on website.

Nonfiction: How-to (underwater, exposure, creative techniques, techniques to make photography easier, low-impact techniques, macro photography, large-format, wildlife), photo feature, technical, travel. No articles about photographing in zoos or on game farms. **Buys 12-18 mss/year.** Query with published clips or writing samples. Length: 750-2,500 words. **Pays $75-150.**

Reprints: Send photocopy of article and information about when and where the article previously appeared. Pays 75% of amount *Nature Photographer* pays for an original article.

Photos: Send photos upon request. Do not send with submission. Reviews 35mm, 2¼×2¼ and 4×5 transparencies. Offers no additional payment for photos accepted with ms. Identification of subjects required. Buys one-time rights.

Tips: "Query with original, well-thought-out ideas and good writing samples. Make sure you send SASE. Areas most open to freelancers are travel, how-to and conservation articles with dramatic slides to illustrate the articles. Must have good, solid research and knowledge of subject. Be sure to obtain guidelines by sending SASE with request before submitting query. If you have not requested guidelines within the last year, request an updated version of guidelines."

[N] $ $ PHOTO LIFE, Canada's Photography Magazine, Apex Publications Inc., One Dundas St. W, Suite 2500, P.O. Box 84, Toronto, Ontario M5G 1Z3 Canada. (800)905-7468. Fax: (800)664-2739. E-mail: editor@photolife. com or subscription@photolife.com. Website: www.photolife.com. **Contact:** Suzie Ketene, editor. **15% freelance written.** Bimonthly magazine covering photography. "*Photo Life* is geared to a Canadian and U.S. audience of advanced amateur photographers. *Photo Life* is not a technical magazine per se, but techniques should be explained in enough depth to make them clear." Estab. 1976. Circ. 73,500. Pays on publication. Publishes ms an average of 1 year after acceptance. Byline given. Buys one-time rights. Editorial lead time 4 months. Submit seasonal material 6 months in advance. Accepts queries by mail, e-mail. Accepts simultaneous submissions. Responds in 3 months. Sample copy for $5.50. Writer's guidelines free by e-mail.

Nonfiction: How-to (photo tips, technique), inspirational, photo feature, technical, travel. **Buys 10 mss/year.** Query with published clips or send complete ms. Length: 250-1,300 words. **Pays $100-600 (Canadian).**

Photos: Reviews transparencies and prints. Negotiates payment individually. Captions and model releases required. Buys one-time rights.

Tips: "We will review any relevant submissions that include a full text or a detailed outline of an article proposal. Accompanying photographs are necessary as the first decision of acceptance will be based upon images. Most of the space available in the magazine is devoted to our regular contributors. Therefore, we cannot guarantee publication of other articles within any particular period of time. Currently, we are overflowing with travel nature articles. You are still welcome to submit to this category, but the waiting period may be longer than expected (up to 1½ years). You may however, use your travel photography to explain photo techniques. A short biography is optional."

$ $ $ PHOTO TECHNIQUES, Preston Publications, Inc., 6600 W. Touhy Ave., Niles IL 60714. (847)647-2900. Fax: (847)647-1155. E-mail: michaeljohnston@ameritech.net. Publisher: S. Tinsley Preston III. Managing Editor: Nancy Getz. **Contact:** Mike Johnston, editor. **50% freelance written.** Bimonthly publication covering photochemistry, lighting, optics, processing and printing, Zone System, special effects, sensitometry, etc. Aimed at advanced workers. Prefers to work with experienced photographer-writers; happy to work with excellent photographers whose writing skills are lacking. "Article conclusions often require experimental support." Estab. 1979. Circ. 35,000. Pays within 2 weeks of publication. Publishes ms an average of 8 months after acceptance. Byline given. Buys one-time rights. Sample copy for $5. Writer's guidelines with #10 SASE.

Nonfiction: Special interest articles within above listed topics; how-to, technical product reviews, photo features. Query or send complete ms. Length open, but most features run approximately 2,500 words or 3-4 magazine pages. **Pays $200-1,000** for well-researched technical articles.

Photos: Photographers have a much better chance of having their photos published if the photos accompany a written article. Manuscript payment includes payment for photos. Prefers 8×10 b&w and color prints. Captions, technical information required. Buys one-time rights.

Tips: "Study the magazine! Virtually all writers we publish are readers of the magazine. We are now more receptive than ever to articles about photographers, history, aesthetics and informative backgrounders about specific areas of the photo industry or specific techniques. Successful writers for our magazine are doing what they write about."

[N] $ TODAY'S PHOTOGRAPHER INTERNATIONAL, The Make Money With Your Camera Magazine, P.O. Box 777, Lewisville NC 27023. (336)945-9867. Fax: (336)945-3711. Website: www.aipress.com. Editor: Vonda H. Blackburn. **Contact:** Sarah Hinshaw, associate editor. **100% freelance written.** Bimonthly magazine addressing "how to make money—no matter where you live—with the equipment that you currently own." Estab. 1986. Circ. 85,000. Editor's sweepstakes pays $500 for the best story in each issue. Publishes ms an average of 6 months after acceptance.. Byline given. Buys one-time rights. Editorial lead time 6 months. Submit seasonal material 6 months in advance. Accepts simultaneous submissions. Responds in 3 weeks to queries; 3 months to mss. Sample copy for $2, 9×12 SAE and 4 first-class stamps or for $3. Writer's guidelines free.

Nonfiction: How-to, new product, opinion, personal experience, photo feature, technical, travel. No "What I did on my summer vacation" stories.

Reprints: Accepts previously published submissions.

Photos: Reviews transparencies and prints. Offers no additional payment for photos accepted with ms. Captions, model releases, identification of subjects required.

Columns/Departments: Vonda Blackburn, editor. Books (how-to photography), 200-400 words; Sports (how-to photograph sports), 1,000 words. **Buys 40 mss/year.** Query. Pay negotiable.

Tips: Present a complete submission package containing: your manuscript, photos (with captions, model releases and technical data) and an inventory list of the submission package.

POLITICS & WORLD AFFAIRS

These publications cover politics for the reader interested in current events. Other publications that will consider articles about politics and world affairs are listed under Business & Finance, Contemporary Culture, Regional and General Interest. For listings of publications geared toward the professional, see Government & Public Service in the Trade section.

N **$ $ $ AMERICAN SPECTATOR**, 2020 N. 14th St., #750, Arlington VA 22201. (703)243-3733. Fax: (703)243-6814. Editor-in-Chief: R. Emmett Tyrrell. Monthly magazine. "For many years, one ideological viewpoint dominated American print and broadcast journalism. Today, that viewpoint still controls the entertainment and news divisions of the television networks, the mass-circulation news magazines, and the daily newspapers. *American Spectator* has attempted to balance the Left's domination of the media by debunking its perceived wisdom and advancing alternative ideas through spirited writing, insightful essays, humor and, most recently, through well-researched investigative articles that have themselves become news." Estab. 1967. Circ. 200,011. Send queries and mss to Attn: Manuscripts.
Nonfiction: "Topics include politics, the press, foreign relations, the economy, culture. Stories most suited for publication are timely articles on previously unreported topics with national appeal. Articles should be thoroughly researched with a heavy emphasis on interviewing and reporting, and the facts of the article should be verifiable. We prefer articles in which the facts speak for themselves and shy away from editorial and first person commentary. No unsolicited poetry, fiction, satire or crossword puzzles." Query with resume, clips and SASE.
Columns/Departments: The Continuing Crisis and Current Wisdom (humor); On the Prowl ("Washington insider news"). Query with résumé, clips and SASE.

N **$ $ $ CALIFORNIA JOURNAL**, 2101 K St., Sacramento CA 95816. (916)444-2840. Fax: (916)444-2339. E-mail: edit@statenet.com. Editor: Cindy Craft. **Contact:** Cladiu Buck, managing editor. **20% freelance written.** Prefers to work with published/established writers. Monthly magazine "with non-partisan coverage aimed at a literate, well-informed, well-educated readership with strong involvement in issues, politics or government." Estab. 1970. Circ. 17,000. Pays on publication. Publishes ms an average of 3 months after acceptance. Byline given. Buys all rights. Responds in 2 weeks to queries, 2 months to mss. Writer's guidelines and sample copy for #10 SASE.
Nonfiction: Profiles of state and local government officials and political analysis. No outright advocacy pieces, fiction, poetry, product pieces. **Buys 25 unsolicited mss/year.** Query. Length: 900-3,000 words. **Pays $300-1,000.** Sometimes pays the expenses of writers on assignment.
Photos: State availability of photos with submission. Reviews contact sheets. Negotiates payment individually. Identification of subjects required. Buys all rights.
Columns/Departments: Soapbox (opinion on current affairs), 800 words. Does not pay.
Tips: "Be well versed in political and environmental affairs as they relate to California."

N **$ COMMONWEAL, A Review of Public Affairs, Religion, Literature and the Arts**, Commonweal Foundation, 475 Riverside Dr., Room 405, New York NY 10115. (212)662-4200. Fax: (212)662-4183. E-mail: commonweal@msn.com. Website: www.commonwealmagazine.org. Editor: Margaret O'Brien Steinfels. **Contact:** Patrick Jordan, managing editor. Biweekly journal of opinion edited by Catholic lay people, dealing with topical issues of the day on public affairs, religion, literature and the arts. Estab. 1924. Circ. 19,000. **Pays on acceptance** or publication. Byline given. Buys all rights. Submit seasonal material 2 months in advance. Responds in 2 months. Free sample copy.
Nonfiction: Essays, general interest, interview/profile, personal experience, religious. **Buys 20 mss/year.** Query with published clips. Length: 1,200-3,000 words. **Pays $75-100.**
Columns/Departments: Upfronts (brief, newsy reportorials, giving facts, information, and some interpretation behind the headlines of the day), 750-1,000 words; Last Word (usually of a personal nature, on some aspect of the human condition: spiritual, individual, political or social), 800 words.
Poetry: Rosemary Deen, poetry editor. Free verse, traditional. **Buys 25-30 poems/year. Pays 75¢/line.**
Tips: "Articles should be written for a general but well-educated audience. While religious articles are always topical, we are less interested in devotional and churchy pieces than in articles which examine the links between 'worldly' concerns and religious beliefs."

N **$ DISASTER NEWS NETWORK**, Villagelife.org Inc., 7855 Rappahannock Ave., Suite 200, Jessup MD 20794. (443)755-9999. Fax: (443)755-9995. E-mail: susank@disasternews.net. Website: www.disasternews.net. **Contact:** Susan Kim, managing editor. **100% freelance written.** Online daily news magazine. "The Disaster News Network is a comprehensive Internet site of timely news and information about U.S. disaster response and volunteer opportunities. In addition to home page articles about breaking disasters, a unique section of individual disaster news sections continues to provide up-to-date information about each disaster as long as response activity continues. In addition, 'Hot Topic' reporting looks at Y2K, Public Violence and Farm Disasters from the perspective of people helping others make a difference. DNN has been designed to be the primary first source of public information about U.S. disaster response efforts. Its news content is unusual because 100% of our content is original—DNN does not subscribe to any wire services or syndicates. The DNN news staff is located across the country, but meet regularly by telephone. All of the writers have previous daily news experience." Estab. 1998. Pays at the end of the month. Publishes ms an average of 1 day after acceptance. Byline given. Buys all rights or makes work-for-hire assignments. Accepts queries by e-mail. Writer's guidelines free online at website or by e-mail.

Nonfiction: Religious, disaster response features. **Buys 600 mss/year.** Query with published clips. Length: 750-1,500 words. **Pays $85-100.** Pays expenses of writers on assignment.

Photos: Send photos with submission. Reviews prints. Negotiates payment individually. Captions required. Buys all rights.

Columns/Departments: Query. **Pays $85-100.**

Tips: "Daily news background/experience is helpful."

$ $ EMPIRE STATE REPORT, The Independent Magazine of Politics, Policy and the Business of Government, (formerly Empire State Report, the Magazine of Politics and Public Policy in New York State), P.O. Box 9001, Mount Vernon NY 10552. Fed-Ex/UPS address: 25-25 Beechwood Ave., Mount Vernon NY 10553. (914)699-2020. Fax: (914)699-2025. E-mail: bobfois@westnet.com. Website: www.empirestatereport.com. **Contact:** Robert A. Fois, editor. Monthly magazine providing "timely and independent information on politics, policy and governance for local and state officials throughout New York State." Estab. 1974. Circ. 16,000. Pays 2 months after publication. Byline given. Buys first North American serial rights. Accepts queries by mail, e-mail, fax, phone. Responds in 1 month to queries; 2 months to mss. Sample copy for $4.50 with 9×12 SASE or on website.

Nonfiction: Essays, analysis, exposé, interview/profile and opinion. Editorial calendar available. **Buys 48 mss/year.** Query with published clips. Length: 500-4,500 words. **Pays $100-700.** Sometimes pays expenses of writers on assignment.

Photos: Send photos with submission. Reviews any size prints. Identification of subjects required.

Columns/Departments: Empire State Notebook (short news stories about state politics), 300-900 words; Perspective (opinion pieces), 900-950 words. Perspectives do not carry remuneration.

■ The online magazine carries original content not found in the print edition and includes writer's guidelines. Contact: Robert A. Fois, online editor.

Tips: "We are seeking journalists and non-journalists from throughout New York State who can bring a new perspective and/or forecast on politics, policy and the business of government."

$ $ EUROPE, Delegation of the European Commission, 2300 M St. NW, 3rd Floor, Washington DC 20037. (202)862-9555. Fax: (202)429-1766. Website: www.eurunion.org. Managing Editor: Peter Gwin. **Contact:** Robert Guttman, editor-in-chief. **50% freelance written.** Monthly magazine for anyone with a professional or personal interest in Europe and European/US relations. Estab. 1963. Circ. 75,000. Pays on publication. Publishes ms an average of 3 months after acceptance. Byline given. Offers 50% kill fee. Buys first serial and all rights. Editorial lead time 2 months. Submit seasonal material 4 months in advance. Accepts queries by mail, e-mail, fax, phone. Responds in 6 months. Sample articles and writer's guidelines on website.

Nonfiction: General interest, historical/nostalgic, interview/profile. Interested in current affairs (with emphasis on economics, business and politics), the Single Market and Europe's relations with the rest of the world. Publishes monthly cultural travel pieces, with European angle. "High quality writing a must. We publish articles that might be useful to people (primarily American readers) with a professional interest in Europe." Query or submit complete ms or article outline. Include résumé of author's background and qualifications. **Buys 20 mss/year.** Length: 600-1,500 words. **Pays $50-500 for assigned articles; $50-400 for unsolicited articles.**

Columns/Departments: Arts & Leisure (book, art, movie reviews, etc.), 200-800 words. **Pays $50-250.**

Photos: Photos purchased with or without accompanying mss. Buys b&w and color. Pays $25-35 for b&w print, any size; $100 for inside use of transparencies; $450 for color used on cover; per job negotiable.

Tips: "We are always interested in stories that connect Europe to the U.S.—especially business stories. Company profiles, a U.S. company having success or vice versa, are a good bet. Also interested in articles on the 'euro' and good, new and different travel pieces."

N ⚐ $ $ IDEAS ON LIBERTY, (formerly *The Freeman*), 30 S. Broadway, Irvington-on-Hudson NY 10533. (914)591-7230. Fax: (914)591-8910. E-mail: iol@fee.org. Website: www.fee.org. **Contact:** Sheldon Richman, editor. **85% freelance written.** Eager to work with new/unpublished writers. Monthly publication for "the layman and fairly advanced students of liberty." Buys all rights, including reprint rights. Estab. 1946. Pays on publication. Byline given. Publishes ms an average of 5 months after acceptance. Sample copy for 7½×10½ SASE with 4 first-class stamps.

Nonfiction: "We want nonfiction clearly analyzing and explaining various aspects of the free market, private property, limited-government philosophy. Though a necessary part of the literature of freedom is the exposure of collectivistic cliches and fallacies, our aim is to emphasize and explain the positive case for individual responsibility and choice in a free economy. We avoid name-calling and personality clashes. Ours is an intelligent analysis of the principles underlying a free-market economy. No political strategy or tactics." **Buys 100 mss/year.** Query with SASE. Length: 3,500 words maximum. **Pays 10¢/word.** Sometimes pays expenses of writers on assignment.

Tips: "It's most rewarding to find freelancers with new insights, fresh points of view. Facts, figures and quotations cited should be fully documented, to their original source, if possible."

N $ $ THE NATION, 33 Irving Place, 8th Floor, New York NY 10003. (212)209-5400. Fax: (212)982-9000. E-mail: submissions@thenation.com. Website: www.thenation.com. Editor: Katrina Vanden Heuvel. **Contact:** Peggy

Suttle, assistant to editor. **75% freelance written.** Estab. 1865. Works with a small number of new/unpublished writers each year. Weekly magazine "firmly committed to reporting on the issues of labor, national politics, business, consumer affairs, environmental politics, civil liberties, foreign affairs and the role and future of the Democratic Party." Buys first serial rights. Accepts queries by mail, e-mail, fax. Free sample copy and writer's guidelines for 6×9 SASE.

Nonfiction: "We welcome all articles dealing with the social scene, from an independent perspective." Queries encouraged. **Buys 100 mss/year.** Length: 2,000 words maximum. **Pays $225-300.** Sometimes pays expenses of writers on assignment.

Columns/Departments: Editorial, 500-700 words. **Pays $75.**

Poetry: Contact: Grace Schulman, poetry editor. Send poems with SASE. *The Nation* publishes poetry of outstanding aesthetic quality. **Pays $1/line.**

▪ The online magazine carries original content not found in the print edition and includes writer's guidelines. Contact: Katrina Vanden Heuvel, editor.

N $ $ **THE NATIONAL VOTER**, League of Women Voters, 1730 M St. NW, #1000, Washington DC 20036. (202)429-1965. Fax: (202)429-0854. E-mail: megd@lwv.org. Website: www.lwv.org. **Contact:** Meg S. Dusken, editor. Quarterly magazine covering public policy. "*The National Voter* provides background, perspective and commentary on public policy issues confronting citizens and their leaders at all levels of government. And it empowers people to make a difference in their communities by offering guidance, maturation and models for action." Estab. 1951. Circ. 100,000. Pays on publication. Byline given. Makes work-for-hire assignments. Editorial lead time 2 months. Accepts queries by mail, e-mail, fax, phone. Sample copy free.

Nonfiction: Exposé, general interest, interview/profile. No essays, personal experience, religious, opinion. **Buys 6 mss/year.** Query with published clips. Length: 200-4,000 words. Payment always negotiated. Pays expenses of writers on assignment.

Reprints: Accepts previously published submissions.

Photos: State availability of photos with submission. Reviews contact sheets. Offers no additional payment for photos accepted with ms. Captions and identification of subjects required. Buys one-time rights.

$ $ **NEW JERSEY REPORTER, A Journal of Public Issues**, The Center for Analysis of Public Issues, 64 Nassau St., Princeton NJ 08542. (609)924-9750. Fax: (609)924-0363. E-mail: njreporter@rcn.com. Website: njreporter.org. **Contact:** Mark Magyar, editor. Managing Editor: Barbara Fitzgerald. **90% freelance written.** Prefers to work with published/established writers but will consider proposals from others. Bimonthly magazine covering New Jersey politics, public affairs and public issues. "*New Jersey Reporter* is a hard-hitting and highly respected magazine published for people who take an active interest in New Jersey politics and public affairs, and who want to know more about what's going on than what newspapers and television newscasts are able to tell them. We publish a great variety of stories ranging from analysis to exposé." Estab. 1970. Circ. 3,200. Pays on publication. Byline given. Buys all rights. Accepts queries by mail, e-mail, fax, phone. Responds in 1 month. Sample copy available on request or on website.

⊶ Break in with a piece with a strong polcy focus on New Jersey issues.

Nonfiction: Book excerpts, exposé, interview/profile, opinion. "We like articles from specialists (in planning, politics, economics, corruption, etc.)—particularly if written by professional journalists—but we reject stories that do not read well because of jargon or too little attention to the actual writing of the piece. Our magazine is interesting as well as informative." **Buys 18-25 mss/year.** Query with published clips. Length: 1,000-4,000 words. **Pays $100-800.**

Tips: "Queries should be specific about how the prospective story is an issue that affects or will affect the people of New Jersey and its government. The writer's résumé should be included. Stories—unless they are specifically meant to be opinion—should come to a conclusion but avoid a 'holier than thou' or preachy tone. Allegations should be scrupulously substantiated. Our magazine represents a good opportunity for freelancers to acquire great clips. Our publication specializes in longer, more detailed, analytical features. The most frequent mistake made by writers in completing an article for us is too much personal opinion versus reasoned advocacy. We are less interested in opinion than in analysis based on sound reasoning and fact. *New Jersey Reporter* is a well-respected publication, and many of our writers go on to nationally respected newspapers and magazines."

N $ $ **POLICY REVIEW**, The Heritage Foundation, (formerly *Policy Review: The Journal of American Citizenship*), 214 Massachusetts Ave. NE, Washington DC 20002. (202)546-4400. **Contact:** Tod Lindberg, editor. Bimonthly magazine. "We have been described as 'the most thoughtful, the most influential and the most provocative publication of the intellectual right.' *Policy Review* is a journal of essays and articles of general intellectual interest, with a particular emphasis on politics and social criticism." Estab. 1977. Circ. 20,000. Pays on publication. Byline given.

Nonfiction: **Buys 4 mss/year.** Send complete ms. Length: 2,000-6,000 words. **Pays average $500.**

$ $ **THE PROGRESSIVE**, 409 E. Main St., Madison WI 53703-2899. (608)257-4626. Fax: (608)257-3373. E-mail: editorial@progressive.org. Website: www.progressive.org. **Contact:** Matthew Rothschild, editor. **75% freelance written.** Monthly. Estab. 1909. Pays on publication. Publishes ms an average of 6 weeks after acceptance. Byline given. Buys all rights. Responds in 1 month. Sample copy for 9×12 SAE with 4 first-class stamps or sample articles on website. Guidelines for #10 SASE.

⊶ Break in through the "On the Line" section.

Nonfiction: Primarily interested in articles which interpret, from a progressive point of view, domestic and world affairs. Occasional lighter features. "*The Progressive* is a *political* publication. General-interest material is inappropriate." Query by mail. Length: 500-4,000 words maximum. **Pays $100-500.**

Tips: "*The Progressive* is always looking for writers who can describe and explain political, social and economic developments in a way that will interest non-specialists. We like articles that recount specific experiences of real people to illustrate larger points. We're looking for writing that is thoughtful, clear and graceful, conversational and non-academic. Display some familiarity with our magazine, its interests and concerns, its format and style. We want query letters that fully describe the proposed article without attempting to sell it—and that give an indication of the writer's competence to deal with the subject."

N $ $PUBLIC CITIZEN NEWS, Public Citizen, 1600 20th St. NW, Washington DC 20009-1001. (202)588-1000. E-mail: pcmail@citizen.org. Website: www.citizen.org. **Contact:** Bob Mentzinger, editor. **15% freelance written.** Bimonthly consumer tabloid "protecting health, safety and democracy since 1971." "We're the membership newsletter of Public Citizen, Washington's leading pro-consumer lobby, founded by Ralph Nader in 1971. Submissions should address issues we are working on currently (in current session of Congress or at state level)." Estab. 1971. Circ. 100,000. Pays on publication. Publishes ms an average of 2 months after acceptance. Byline given. Buys first North American serial, one-time and second serial (reprint) rights. Editorial lead time 4 months. Submit seasonal material 6 months in advance. Accepts queries by mail, e-mail. Responds in 2 weeks to queries; 1 month to mss. Sample copy for $2. Writer's guidelines for #10 SASE.

   O→ " 'Activist Ally' department is the best place to start, and we are always looking for 'Money in Politics' pieces that are well-researched."

Nonfiction: Exposé, general interest, interview/profile. No poetry, fiction, personal experience. **Buys 1-2 mss/year.** Query with published clips. Length: 500-1,000 words. **Pays $100-500.** "Will sometimes 'swap' articles if by pre-arrangement." Sometimes pays expenses of writers on assignment.

Reprints: Accepts previously published submissions.

Photos: State availability of photos with submission. Reviews contact sheets and 3×5 prints or larger. Offers $50-150/photo. Model releases and identification of subjects required. Buys one-time rights.

Columns/Departments: Meet the CEO (profile of a CEO whose company commits anti-consumer behavior), 300 words; various investigative (local angles on national legislation), 500-1,500 words; Activist Ally (people who overcome corporations to bolster the health, safety of their communities), 500 words. **Buys 1-2 mss/year.** Query. **Pays $50-150.**

Tips: "Your best bet is to know what consumer protection or anti-consumer bills are being considered—in Congress or at the state level—and write either human interest or investigative fact-finding bits that help illuminate the issues surrounding the legislation."

$ $ $ $REASON, (formerly *Reason, Free Minds and Free Markets*), Reason Foundation, 3415 S. Sepulveda Blvd., Suite 400, Los Angeles CA 90034. (310)391-2245. Fax: (310)391-4395. E-mail: editor@reason.com. Website: www.reason.com. Editor: Nick Gillespie. **Contact:** Jesse Walker, associate editor. **30% freelance written.** Monthly magazine covering politics, current events, culture, ideas. "*Reason* covers politics, culture and ideas from a dynamic libertarian perspective. It features reported works, opinion pieces, and book reviews." Estab. 1968. Circ. 55,000. **Pays on acceptance.** Byline given. Offers kill fee. Buys first North American serial rights, first rights or all rights. Editorial lead time 2 months. Submit seasonal material 3 months in advance. Accepts queries by mail, e-mail. Responds in 6 weeks to queries; 2 months to mss. Sample copy for $4. Writer's guidelines for #10 SASE.

Nonfiction: Book excerpts, essays, exposé, general interest, humor, interview/profile, opinion. No products, personal experience, how-to, travel. **Buys 50-60 mss/year.** Query with published clips. Length: 1,000-5,000 words. **Pays $300-2,000.** Sometimes pays expenses of writers on assignment.

   ◼ The online magazine carries original context not found in the print edition and includes writer's guidelines. Contact: Nick Gillespie.

Tips: "We prefer queries of no more than one or two pages with specifically developed ideas about a given topic rather than more general areas of interest. Enclosing a few published clips also helps."

$ $TOWARD FREEDOM, A progressive perspective on world events, Toward Freedom Inc., P.O. Box 468, Burlington VT 05422-0468. (802)658-2523. E-mail: tfmag@aol.com. Website: www.towardfreedom.com. **Contact:** Greg Guma, editor. **75% freelance written.** Political magazine published 8 times/year covering politics/culture, focus on Third World, Europe and global trends. "*Toward Freedom* is an internationalist journal with a progressive perspective on political, cultural, human rights and environmental issues around the world. Also covers the United Nations, the post-nationalist movements and U.S. foreign policy." Estab. 1952. Circ. 3,500. Pays on publication. Byline given. Kill fee "rare–negotiable." Buys first North American serial and one-time rights. Editorial lead time 1 month. Accepts queries by mail, e-mail. Responds in 3 months. Sample copy for $3. Writer's guidelines for #10 SASE or on website.

   O→ Break in with "a clear, knowledgeable and brief query, either by e-mail or U.S. mail, along with the basis of your knowledge about the subject. We're also looking for a new hook for covering subjects we follow, as well as comparisons between us and other places. We're also eager to break stories that are being 'censored' in mainstream media."

Nonfiction: Features, essays, book reviews, interview/profile, opinion, personal experience, travel, foreign, political analysis. Special issues: Women's Visions (March); Global Media (December/January). No how-to, fiction. **Buys 80-100 mss/year.** Query. Length: 700-2,500 words. **Pays up to 10¢/word.**

Photos: Send photos with submission, if available. Reviews any prints. Offers $35 maximum/photo. Identification of subjects required. Buys one-time rights.

Columns/Departments: *TF* Reports (from foreign correspondents), UN, Beyond Nationalism, Art and Book Reviews, 800-1,200 words. **Buys 20-30 mss/year.** Query. **Pays up to 10¢/word.** Last Word (creative commentary), 900 words. **Buys 8/year.** Query. **Pays $100.**

   ■ The online magazine carries original content not found in the print edition and includes guidelines. Contact: Greg Guma.

Tips: "We're looking for articles linking politics and culture; effective first-person storytelling; proposals for global solutions with realistic basis and solid background; provocative viewpoints within the progressive tradition; political humor. We receive too many horror stories about human rights violations, lacking constructive suggestions and solutions; knee-jerk attacks on imperialism."

N **$** **$** **WASHINGTON MONTHLY**, The Washington Monthly Company, 1611 Connecticut Ave. NW, Suite 4A, Washington DC 20009. (202)462-0128. Fax: (202)332-8413. E-mail: editors@washingtonmonthly.com. Website: www.washingtonmonthly.com. Editor: Charles Peters. **Contact:** Stephen Pomper, editor or Nicholas Thompson, editor. **50% freelance written.** Monthly magazine covering politics, policy, media. "We are a neo-liberal publication with a long history and specific views—please read our magazine before submitting." Estab. 1969. Circ. 30,000. Pays on publication. Publishes ms an average of 2 months after acceptance. Byline given. Buys all rights. Editorial lead time 2 months. Submit seasonal material 4 months in advance. Accepts queries by mail, e-mail, fax, phone. Responds in 3 weeks to queries; 2 months to mss. Sample copy for 11×17 SAE with 5 first-class stamps or by e-mail. Writer's guidelines for #10 SASE, online at website or by e-mail.

Nonfiction: Book excerpts, essays, exposé, general interest, historical/nostalgic, interview/profile, opinion, personal experience, technical, 1st person political. "No humor, how-to or generalized articles. Know our publication before you submit a manuscript." **Buys 10 mss/year.** Query with or without published clips or send complete ms. Length: 1,500-5,000 words. **Pays 10¢/word.**

Photos: State availability of photos with submission. Reviews contact sheets and prints. Negotiates payment individually. Buys one-time rights.

Columns/Departments: Nicholas Thompson, book review editor. Memo of the Month (memos); On Political Books, Booknotes (both reviews of current political books), 1,500-3,000 words. **Buys 10 mss/year.** Query with or without published clips or send complete ms. **Pays 10¢/word.**

Tips: "Call our editors to talk about ideas. Always pitch articles showing background research. We're particularly looking for first-hand accounts of working in government. We also like original work showing that the government is or is not doing something important. We do not have writer's guidelines, so do your research."

PSYCHOLOGY & SELF-IMPROVEMENT

These publications focus on psychological topics, how and why readers can improve their own outlooks, and how to understand people in general. Many General Interest, Men's and Women's publications also publish articles in these areas. Magazines treating spiritual development appear in the Astrology, Metaphysical & New Age section, as well as in Religion, while markets for holistic mind/body healing strategies are listed in Health & Fitness.

$ ROSICRUCIAN DIGEST, Rosicrucian Order, AMORC, 1342 Naglee Ave., San Jose CA 95191-0001. (408)947-3600. Website: www.rosicrucian.org. **Contact:** Robin M. Thompson, editor-in-chief. **50% freelance written.** Works with a small number of new/unpublished writers each year. Quarterly magazine (international) emphasizing mysticism, science, philosophy and the arts for educated men and women of all ages seeking alternative answers to life's questions. **Pays on acceptance.** Publishes ms an average of 6 months after acceptance. Buys first serial and second serial (reprint) rights. Byline given. Submit seasonal material 5 months in advance. Accepts queries by mail, phone. Responds in 2 months. Free sample copy. Writer's guidelines for #10 SASE.

Nonfiction: How to deal with life—and all it brings us—in a positive and constructive way. Informational articles—new ideas and developments in science, the arts, philosophy and thought. Historical sketches, biographies, human interest, psychology, philosophical and inspirational articles. "We are always looking for good articles on the contributions of ancient civilizations to today's civilizations, the environment, ecology, inspirational (non-religious) subjects." No religious, astrological or political material or articles promoting a particular group or system of thought. Buys variable amount of mss/year. Query by mail. Length: 1,000-1,500 words. **Pays 6¢/word.**

Reprints: Prefers typed ms with rights for sale noted and information about when and where the article previously appeared, but tearsheet or photocopy acceptable. Pays 50% of amount paid for an original article; 100% "if article is really good and author has rights."

Photos: Purchased with accompanying ms. Send prints. Pays $10/8×10 b&w glossy print.

Fillers: Short inspirational or uplifting (not religious) anecdotes or experiences. **Buys 6/year.** Query. Length: 22-250 words. **Pays 2¢/word.**

Tips: "We're looking for more pieces on these subjects: our connection with the past—the important contributions of ancient civilizations to today's world and culture and the relevance of this wisdom to now; how to channel teenage energy/angst into positive, creative, constructive results (preferably written by teachers or others who work with young people—written for frustrated parents); and the vital necessity of raising our environmental consciousness if we are going to survive the coming millennium or even century."

$ SCIENCE OF MIND MAGAZINE, 3251 W. Sixth St., P.O. Box 75127, Los Angeles CA 90075-0127. (213)388-2181. Fax: (213)388-1926. E-mail: sdelgado@scienceofmind.com. Website: www.scienceofmind.com. Editor-in-Chief: Kenneth Lind. **Contact:** Sylvia Delgado, editorial associate. **30% freelance written.** Monthly magazine that features articles on spirituality, self-help and inspiration. "Our publication centers on oneness of all life and spiritual empowerment through the application of Science of Mind principles." Pays on publication. Publishes ms an average of 5 months after acceptance. Byline given. Buys first North American serial rights. Submit seasonal material 6 months in advance. No queries. Only accepts will be notified. Manuscripts cannot be returned. Writer's guidelines for SASE or go to website.

Nonfiction: Book excerpts, inspirational, personal experience of Science of Mind, spiritual. **Buys 35-45 mss/year.** Length: 750-2,000 words. **Pays $25/printed page.** Pays copies for some features written by readers.

Photos: Reviews 35mm transparencies and 5×7 or 8×10 b&w prints. Buys one-time rights.

Poetry: Inspirational and Science of Mind oriented. "We are not interested in poetry not related to Science of Mind principles." **Buys 1-3 poems/year.** Length: 7-25 lines. Send 3 poems maximum. **Pays $25.** Publishes poetry 2-3 times a year.

▣ The online version contains material not found in the print edition. Contact: Sylvia Delgado.

Tips: "We are interested in first-person experiences of a spiritual nature having to do with the Science of Mind."

REGIONAL

Many regional publications rely on staff-written material, but others accept work from freelance writers who live in or know the region. The best regional publication to target with your submissions is usually the one in your hometown, whether it's a city or state magazine or a Sunday supplement in a newspaper. Since you are familiar with the region, it is easier to propose suitable story ideas.

Listed first are general interest magazines slanted toward residents of and visitors to a particular region. Next, regional publications are categorized alphabetically by state, followed by Canada. Publications that report on the business climate of a region are grouped in the regional division of the Business & Finance category. Recreation and travel publications specific to a geographical area are listed in the Travel, Camping & Trailer section. Keep in mind also that many regional publications specialize in specific areas, and are listed according to those sections. Regional publications are not listed if they only accept material from a select group of freelancers in their area or if they did not want to receive the number of queries and manuscripts a national listing would attract. If you know of a regional magazine that is not listed, approach it by asking for writer's guidelines before you send unsolicited material.

General

◩ **$ $ BLUE RIDGE COUNTRY**, Leisure Publishing, P.O. Box 21535, Roanoke VA 24018-9900. (703)989-6138. Fax: (703)989-7603. E-mail: info@leisurepublishing.com. Website: www.blueridgecountry.com. **Contact:** Kurt Rheinheimer, editor-in-chief. **75% freelance written.** Bimonthly magazine. "The magazine is designed to celebrate the history, heritage and beauty of the Blue Ridge region. It is aimed at the adult, upscale readers who enjoy living or traveling in the mountain regions of Virginia, North Carolina, West Virginia, Maryland, Kentucky, Tennessee, South Carolina and Georgia." Estab. 1988. Circ. 75,000. Pays on publication. Publishes ms an average of 8 months after acceptance. Byline given. Offers $50 kill fee for commissioned pieces only. Buys first and second serial (reprint) rights. Submit seasonal material 6 months in advance. Query by mail, e-mail, fax. Responds in 2 months. Sample copy for 9×12 SAE with 6 first-class stamps or on website. Writer's guidelines for #10 SASE.

Nonfiction: General interest, historical/nostalgic, personal experience, photo feature, travel, history. "Looking for more backroads travel, history and legend/lore pieces." **Buys 25-30 mss/year.** Query with or without published clips or send complete ms. Length: 500-1,800 words. **Pays $50-250 for assigned articles; $25-250 for unsolicited articles.**

Photos: Send photos with submission. Prefers transparencies. Offers $10-25/photo and $100 for cover photo. Identification of subjects required. Buys one-time rights.

Columns/Departments: Country Roads (shorts on people, events, travel, ecology, history, antiques, books). **Buys 12-24 mss/year.** Query. **Pays $10-40.**

Tips: "Would like to see more pieces dealing with contemporary history (1940s-70s). Freelancers needed for regional departmental shorts and 'macro' issues affecting whole region. Need field reporters from all areas of Blue Ridge region. Also, we need updates on the Blue Ridge Parkway, Appalachian Trail, national forests, ecological issues, preservation movements."

N **$** **CHRONOGRAM,** Luminary Publishing, P.O. Box 459, New Paltz NY 12561. Fax: (914)256-0349. E-mail: info@chronogram.com. Website: www.chronogram.com. **Contact:** Brian K. Mahoney, editor. **50% freelance written.** Monthly regional arts and cultural magazine. "*Chronogram* features accomplished, literary writing on issues of cultural, spiritual and idea-oriented interest." Estab. 1994. Circ. 20,000. Pays on publication. Publishes ms an average of 3 months after acceptance. Byline given. Buys one-time rights. Editorial lead time 2 months. Submit seasonal material 3 months in advance. Accepts queries by mail, e-mail. Accepts simultaneous submissions. Responds in 2 weeks to queries; 1 month to mss. Sample copy and writer's guidelines online at website.

Nonfiction: Book excerpts, essays, exposé, general interest, historical/nostalgic, humor, interview/profile, opinion, personal experience, photo feature, religious, travel. "No health practitioners writing about their own healing modality." **Buys 24 mss/year.** Query with published clips. Length: 1,000-3,500 words. **Pays $75-150.**

Photos: State availability of photos with submission. Reviews contact sheets. Negotiates payment individually. Captions required. Buys one-time rights.

Poetry: Lee Anne Albritton, poetry editor. Avant-garde, free verse, haiku, traditional. "We do not pay contributors for poetry."

Tips: "The editor's ears are always open for new voices and all story ideas are invited for pitching. *Chronogram* welcomes all voices and viewpoints as long as they are expressed well. We descriminate solely based on the quality of the writing, nothing else. Clear, thoughtful writing on any subject will be considered for publication in *Chronogram*. We publish a good deal of introspective first-person narratives and find that in the absence of objectivity, subjectivity at least is a quantifiable middle ground between ranting opinion and useless facts."

$** **$ **GUESTLIFE, Monterey Bay/New Mexico/El Paso/St. Petersburg/Clearwater,** Desert Publications, Inc., 303 N. Indian Canyon Dr., Palm Springs CA 92262. Fax: (760)325-7008. E-mail: edit@desert-resorts.com. Website: www.guestlife.com. **Contact:** Jaime Cannon, managing editor. **95% freelance written.** Annual prestige hotel room magazine covering history, highlights and activities of the area named (ex. *Monterey Bay GuestLife*). "*GuestLife* focuses on its respective area and is placed in hotel rooms in that area for the affluent vacationer." Estab. 1979. Pays on publication. Publishes ms an average of 9 months after acceptance. Byline given. Offers 25% kill fee. Buys electronic and all rights. Editorial lead time 4 months. Submit seasonal material 3 months in advance. Accepts queries by mail, e-mail. Responds in 1 month. Sample copy for $10.

Nonfiction: General interest (regional), historical/nostalgic, photo feature, travel. **Buys 3 mss/year.** Query with published clips. Length: 300-1,500 words. **Pays $100-500.**

Photos: State availability of photos with submission. Reviews contact sheets. Negotiates payment individually. Identification of subjects required. Buys all rights.

Fillers: Facts. **Buys 3/year.** Length: 50-100 words. **Pays $50-100.**

$** **$ **NOW AND THEN, The Appalachian Magazine,** Center for Appalachian Studies and Services, P.O. Box 70556-ETSU, Johnson City TN 37614-0556. (423)439-6173. Fax: (423)439-6340. E-mail: woodsidj@etsu.edu. Website: http://cass.etsu.edu/n&t/guidelin.html. Managing Editor: Nancy Fischman. **Contact:** Jane Harris Woodside, editor-in-chief. **80% freelance written.** Magazine published 3 times/year covering Appalachian region from Southern New York to Northern Mississippi. "*Now & Then* accepts a variety of writing genres: fiction, poetry, nonfiction, essays, interviews, memoirs and book reviews. All submissions must relate to Appalachia and to the issue's specific theme. Our readership is educated and interested in the region." Estab. 1984. Circ. 1,000. Pays on publication. Publishes ms an average of 4 months after acceptance. Byline given. Buys all rights. Editorial lead time 6 months. Query by mail, e-mail, fax. Accepts simultaneous submissions. Responds in 5 months. Sample copy for $5. Writer's guidelines for #10 SASE or on website.

Nonfiction: Book excerpts, essays, general interest, historical/nostalgic, humor, interview/profile, opinion, personal experience, photo feature, book reviews of books from and about Appalachia. "We don't consider articles which have nothing to do with Appalachia; articles which blindly accept and employ regional stereotypes (dumb hillbillies, poor and downtrodden hillfolk and miners)." Special issues: Appalachian Museums and Archives (July 1 deadline); Appalachian Rivers and Valleys (November 1 deadline). Query with published clips. Length: 1,000-2,500 words. **Pays $15-250 for assigned articles; $15-100 for unsolicited articles.** Sometimes pays expenses of writers on assignment.

Reprints: Send typed ms with rights for sale noted and information about when and where the article previously appeared. Pays 100% of amount paid for an original article. Typically $15-60.

Photos: State availability of photos with submission. Offers no additional payment for photos accepted with ms. Captions and identification of subjects required. Buys one-time rights.

Fiction: Adventure, ethnic, experimental, fantasy, historical, humorous, mainstream, slice-of-life vignettes. "Fiction has to relate to Appalachia and to the issue's theme in some way." **Buys 3-4 mss/year.** Send complete ms. Length: 750-2,500 words. **Pays $15-100.**

Poetry: Free verse, haiku, light verse, traditional. "No stereotypical work about the region. I want to be surprised and embraced by the language, the ideas, even the form." **Buys 25-30 poems/year.** Submit 5 poems maximum. **Pays $10.**

Tips: "Get the Writers' Guidelines and read them carefully. Show in your cover letter that you know what the theme of the upcoming issue is and how your submission fits the theme."

$ $ $ $ SUNSET MAGAZINE, Sunset Publishing Corp., 80 Willow Rd., Menlo Park CA 94025-3691. (650)321-3600. Fax: (650)327-7537. Website: www.sunset.com. Editor-in-Chief: Rosalie Muller Wright. **Contact:** P. Fish, senior travel editor; K. Brenzel, senior garden editor. Monthly magazine covering the lifestyle of the Western states. "*Sunset* is a Western lifestyle publication for educated, active consumers. Editorial provides localized information on gardening and travel, food and entertainment, home building and remodeling." Freelance articles should be timely and only about the 13 Western states. Pays on acceptance. Byline given. Accepts queries by mail. Guidelines for freelance travel items for #10 SASE addressed to Editorial Services.
  • Ranked as one of the best markets for freelancers in *Writer's Yearbook* magazine's annual "Top 100 Markets," January 2000.
Nonfiction: "Travel items account for the vast majority of *Sunset*'s freelance assignments, although we also contract out some short garden items. However, *Sunset* is largely staff-written." Travel in the West. **Buys 50-75 mss/year.** Length: 550-750 words. **Pays $1/word.** Query before submitting.
Columns/Departments: Departments open to freelancers are: Building & Crafts, Food, Garden, Travel. *Travel Guide* length: 300-350 words. Direct queries to the specific editorial department.
Tips: "Here are some subjects regularly treated in *Sunset*'s stories and Travel Guide items: outdoor recreation (i.e., bike tours, bird-watching spots, walking or driving tours of historic districts); indoor adventures (i.e., new museums and displays, hands-on science programs at aquariums or planetariums, specialty shopping); special events (i.e., festivals that celebrate a region's unique social, cultural, or agricultural heritage). Also looking for great weekend getaways, backroad drives, urban adventures and culinary discoveries such as ethnic dining enclaves. Planning and assigning begins a year before publication date."

$ $ VILLAGE PROFILE, Progressive Publishing, Inc., 33 N. Geneva, Elgin IL 60120. (800)600-0134. E-mail: almanac123@earthlink.net. Website: www.villageprofile.com. Managing Editor: Laura Otto. **Contact:** Juli Bridgers, editor. **90% freelance written.** Annual local community guides covering over 30 states. "We publish community guides and maps for (primarily) chambers of commerce across the U.S. and Canada. Editorial takes on a factual, yet upbeat, positive view of communities. Writers need to be able to make facts and figures 'friendly,' to present information to be used by residents as well as businesses as guides are used for economic development." Estab. 1988. Publishes 350 projects/year. **Pays on acceptance.** Publishes ms 4 months after acceptance. Byline given. Offers 100% kill fee on completed projects. Buys all rights, electronic rights, and makes work-for-hire assignments. Editorial lead time 2 months. Accepts queries by mail, e-mail, fax. Sample copy for 9×12 SASE. Writer's guidelines free.
Nonfiction: **Buys 200 mss/year** Query with published clips and geographic availability. Length: 1,000-4,000 words. **Pays $200-500.** Sometimes pays expenses of writers on assignment.
Photos: State availability of photos. Negotiates payment individually. Identification of subjects required.
Tips: "Writers must meet deadlines, know how to present a positive image of a community without going overboard with adjectives and adverbs! Know how to find the info you need if our contact (typically a busy chamber executive) needs your help doing so. Availability to 'cover' a region/area is a plus."

$ $ $ YANKEE, Yankee Publishing Inc., P.O. Box 520, Dublin NH 03444-0520. (603)563-8111. Fax: (603)563-8252. E-mail: queries@yankeepub.com. Website: www.newengland.com. Editor: Jim Collins. **Contact:** Sam Darley, editorial assistant. **50% freelance written.** Monthly magazine covering New England. "Our mission is to express and perhaps, indirectly, preserve the New England culture—and to do so in an entertaining way. Our audience is national and has one thing in common—they love New England." Estab. 1935. Circ. 500,000. Pays within 30 days of acceptance. Publishes ms an average of 10 months after acceptance. Byline given. Offers 33% kill fee. Buys first rights. Submit seasonal material 6 months in advance. Accepts simultaneous submissions. Responds in 2 months to queries. Writer's guidelines for #10 SASE.
Nonfiction: Essays, general interest, historical/nostalgic, humor, interview/profile, personal experience. "No 'good old days' pieces, no dialect humor and nothing outside New England!" **Buys 30 mss/year.** Query with published clips and SASE. Length: 250-2,500 words. **Pays $100-1,500.** Pays expenses of writers on assignment.
  • Ranked as one of the best markets for freelance writers in *Writer's Yearbook* magazine's annual "Top 100 Markets," January 2000, and as one of the best markets for fiction writers in *Writer's Digest* magazine's annual "Fiction 50," June 2000.
Photos: Send photos with submission. Reviews contact sheets and transparencies. Offers $50-150/photo. Identification of subjects required. Buys one-time rights.
Columns/Departments: New England Sampler (short bits on interesting people, anecdotes, historical oddities), 100-400 words, **pays $50-200.** Great New England Cooks (profile recipes), 500 words, **pays $800.** Recipe with a History (family favorites that have a story behind them), 100-200 words plus recipe, **pays $50.** I Remember (nostalgia focused on specific incidents), 400-500 words, **pays $200.** Travel, 25-200 words, query first, **pays $25-250. Buys 80 mss/year.** Query with published clips and SASE.
Fiction: Edie Clark, fiction editor. "We publish high-quality literary fiction that explores human issues and concerns in a specific place—New England." Publishes novel excerpts. **Buys 4 mss/year.** Send complete ms. Length: 500-2,500 words. **Pays $1,000.**

Poetry: Jean Burden, poetry editor. "We don't choose poetry by type. We look for the best. No inspirational, holiday-oriented, epic, limericks, etc." **Buys 40 poems/year.** Submit maximum 3 poems. Length: 2-20 lines. **Pays $50.**

Tips: "Submit lots of ideas. Don't censor yourself—let *us* decide whether an idea is good or bad. We might surprise you. Remember we've been publishing for 65 years, so chances are we've already done every 'classic' New England subject. Try to surprise us—it isn't easy. These departments are most open to freelancers: New England Sampler; I Remember; Recipe with a History. Study the ones we publish—the format should be apparent. It is to your advantage to read several issues of the magazine before sending us a query or a manuscript."

Alabama

$ $ ALABAMA HERITAGE, University of Alabama, Box 870342, Tuscaloosa AL 35487-0342. (205)348-7467. Fax: (205)348-7473. **Contact:** Suzanne Wolfe, editor. **50% freelance written.** "*Alabama Heritage* is a nonprofit historical quarterly published by the University of Alabama and the University of Alabama at Birmingham for the intelligent lay reader. We are interested in lively, well-written and thoroughly researched articles on Alabama/Southern history and culture. Readability and accuracy are essential." Estab. 1986. Pays on publication. Byline given. Buys first rights and second serial (reprint) rights. Responds in 1 month. Sample copy for $6. Writer's guidelines for #10 SASE.

Nonfiction: Historical. "We do not want fiction, poetry, book reviews, articles on current events or living artists or personal/family reminiscences." **Buys 10 mss/year.** Query. Length: 1,500-5,000 words. **Pays $100 minimum.** Also sends 10 copies to each author plus 1-year subscription.

Photos: Reviews contact sheets. Identification of subjects required. Buys one-time rights.

Tips: "Authors need to remember that we regard history as a fascinating subject, not as a dry recounting of dates and facts. Articles that are lively and engaging, in addition to being well researched, will find interested readers among our editors. No term papers, please. All areas are open to freelance writers. Best approach is a written query."

$ $ BIRMINGHAM WEEKLY, Birmingham Weekly Publishing Co., Inc., 2101 Magnolia Ave. S., Suite 404, Birmingham AL 35205. (205)322-2426. E-mail: editor@bhamweekly.com. **Contact:** Darin Powell, editor. **40% freelance written.** "We are an alternative newsweekly; alternative in the sense that we're an alternative to daily papers and TV news. We are edgy, hip, well written but based in solid journalism. Our audience is 18-54, educated with disposable income and an irreverant but intelligent point of view." Estab. 1997. Circ. 30,000. Pays on publication. Publishes ms an average of 2 weeks after acceptance. Byline given. Editorial lead time 3 weeks. Submit seasonal material 2 months in advance. Accepts queries by mail, e-mail. Accepts simultaneous submissions. Responds in 2 weeks to queries. Sample copy free.

Nonfiction: Essays, exposé, general interest, historical/nostalgic, humor, interview/profile. "No opinion columns, i.e., op-ed stuff. We are strictly interested in stories that have a Birmingham connection, except in reviews, where the requirement is for readers to be able to buy the CD or book or see the film in Birmingham." Query with or without published clips. Length: 100-1,000 words. **Pays 10¢/word.** Sometimes pays expenses of writers on assignment.

Columns/Departments: Sound Advice (CD reviews), 100 words; Between the Covers (book reviews), 300 words. Query with or without published clips. **Pays 10¢/word.**

$ $ BLACK & WHITE, Birmingham's City Paper, Black & White, Inc., 1312 20th St. S, Birmingham AL 35205. (205)933-0460. E-mail: blkwhite@aol.com. Managing Editor: Kerry Echols. **Contact:** Alison Nichols, editor. **25% freelance written.** Free biweekly city paper covering arts, entertainment news, film, music in Birmingham and anything that strikes our fancy. Audience covers the spectrum. Estab. 1992. Circ. 35,000. Pays 21 days after publication. Publishes ms an average of 1 month after acceptance. Byline given. Offers $50-100 kill fee. Buys one-time rights and local rights in market area. Editorial lead time 3 weeks. Submit seasonal material 1 month in advance. Accepts simultaneous submissions. Responds in 2 weeks to queries; 2 months to mss. Sample copy for 10×12 with 4 first-class stamps. Writer's guidelines for #10 SASE.

Nonfiction: Alison Nichols, editor. Essays, general interest, interview/profile, opinion, photo feature, travel. Special issues: Music; restaurants. No fiction, poetry. **Buys 10 mss/year.** Query. Length: 200-8,000 words. **Pays $50-600.** Sometimes pays expenses of writers on assignment.

Reprints: Accepts previously published submissions.

Photos: State availability of photos with submission. Reviews contact sheets. Negotiates payment individually. Identification of subjects required. Buys one-time rights.

Columns/Departments: Kerry Echols, managing editor. Record/CD reviews (music), 200 words; In Print (book reviews), 600-800 words; Cinema (film revision), 400-1,000 words. **Buys 100 mss/year.** Query with published clips. **Pays $50-125.**

Fillers: Kerry Echols, managing editor. Cartoons. **Buys 90/year. Pays $10-20.**

Tips: "Send a simple, short e-mail pitch/query and/or sample of your work."

N $ $ MOBILE BAY MONTHLY, PMT Publishing, P.O. Box 66200, Mobile AL 36660. (334)473-6269. Fax: (334)479-8822. **Contact:** Michelle Roberts, editor. **25% freelance written.** "*Mobile Bay Monthly* is a monthly lifestyle magazine for the South Alabama/Gulf Coast region focusing on the people, ideas, issues, arts, homes, food, culture and businesses that make Mobile Bay an interesting place." Estab. 1990. Circ. 10,000. Pays on publication. Publishes ms an average of 4 months after acceptance. Byline given. Buys first rights. Editorial lead time 4 months. Submit seasonal material 6 months in advance. Sample copy for $2.

Nonfiction: Historical/nostalgic, interview/profile, personal experience, photo feature, travel. **Buys 10 mss/year.** Query with published clips. Length: 1,200-3,000 words. **Pays $100-300.**

Photos: State availability of photos with submission. Negotiates payment individually. Identification of subjects required. Buys one-time rights.

Tips: "We use mostly local writers. Strong familiarity with the Mobile area is a must. No phone calls; please send query letters with writing samples."

Alaska

⊠ $ $ $ ALASKA, Exploring Life on the Last Frontier, 619 E. Ship Creek Ave., Suite 329, Anchorage AK 99501. (907)272-6070. Fax: (907)258-5360. E-mail: bwwoods@alaskamagazine.com. Editor: Bruce Woods. **Contact:** Donna Rae Thompson, editorial assistant. **70% freelance written.** Eager to work with new/unpublished writers. Monthly magazine covering topics "uniquely Alaskan." Estab. 1935. Circ. 205,000. Pays on publication. Publishes ms an average of 6 months after acceptance. Byline given. Buys first or one-time rights. Submit seasonal material 1 year in advance. Responds in 2 months. Sample copy for $3 and 9×12 SAE with 7 first-class stamps. Writer's guidelines for #10 SASE.

Nonfiction: Historical/nostalgic, adventure, how-to (on anything Alaskan), outdoor recreation (including hunting, fishing), humor, interview/profile, personal experience, photo feature. Also travel articles and Alaska destination stories. No fiction or poetry. **Buys 40 mss/year.** Query by mail. Length: 100-2,500 words. **Pays $100-1,250.**

Photos: Send photos. Reviews 35mm or larger transparencies. Captions and identification of subjects required.

Tips: "We're looking for top-notch writing—original, well-researched, lively. Subjects must be distinctly Alaskan. A story on a mall in Alaska, for example, won't work for us; every state has malls. If you've got a story about a Juneau mall run by someone who is also a bush pilot and part-time trapper, maybe we'd be interested. The point is *Alaska* stories need to be vivid, focused and unique. Alaska is like nowhere else—we need our stories to be the same way."

Arizona

$ $ ARIZONA FOOTHILLS MAGAZINE, Media That Deelivers, Inc. P.O. Box 93014, Phoenix AZ 85070-3014. (480)460-5203. Fax: (480)460-5776. E-mail: reneedee@azfoothillsmag.com. Website: www.azfoothillsmagazine.com. Editor: Renee Dee. **Contact:** Shannon Bartlett, departments editor. **50% freelance written.** Monthly magazine covering lifestyle. Estab. 1996. Circ. 50,000. Pays on publication. Publishes ms an average of 6 months after acceptance. Byline given. Buys first North American serial rights. Editorial lead time 6 months. Submit seasonal material 4 months in advance. Responds in 1 month. Sample copy and writer's guidelines for #10 SASE.

Nonfiction: Renee Dee, publisher. General interest, how-to (decorate, plant, outdoor recreation), humor, inspirational, interview/profile, new product, personal experience, photo feature, travel, fashion, decor, arts. **Buys 30 mss/year.** Query with published clips. Length: 900-2,000 words. **Pays 15¢/word for assigned articles; 10¢/word for unsolicited articles.** Sometimes pays in ads, contributor copies. Sometimes pays expenses of writers on assignment.

Reprints: Accepts previously published material.

Photos: Send photos with submission. Reviews contact sheets and transparencies. Negotiates payment individually. Captions, model releases and identification of subjects required. Buys one-time rights.

Columns/Departments: Road-Tested Travel (in-state AZ travel); Great Escapes (outside AZ); Live Well (health and fitness); Your Money (finance). **Buys 21 mss/year.** Query with published clips. **Pays 10¢/word.**

Tips: "We prefer stories that appeal to my audience written with an upbeat, contemporary approach and reader service in mind."

$ $ $ ARIZONA HIGHWAYS, 2039 W. Lewis Ave., Phoenix AZ 85009-9988. (602)271-5900. Fax: (602)254-4505. Website: www.arizonahighways.com. **Contact:** Rebecca Mong, senior editor. **100% freelance written.** State-owned magazine designed to help attract tourists into and through Arizona. Estab. 1925. Circ. 425,000. **Pays on acceptance.** Buys first serial rights. Responds in 1 month. Writer's guidelines for SASE.

Oⁿ Break in with "a concise query written with flair, backed by impressive clips that reflect the kind of writing that appears in *Arizona Highways*."

Nonfiction: Feature subjects include narratives and exposition dealing with history, anthropology, nature, wildlife, armchair travel, out of the way places, small towns, Old West history, Indian arts and crafts, travel, etc. Travel articles are experience-based. All must be oriented toward Arizona. **Buys 6 mss/issue.** Query with a lead paragraph and brief outline of story. "We deal with professionals only, so include list of current credits." Length: 600-2,000 words. **Pays 55¢/word.** Pays expenses of writers on assignment.

Photos: Peter Ensenberger, photo editor. "We use transparencies of medium format, 4×5, and 35mm when appropriate to the subject matter, or they display exceptional quality or content. We prefer 35mm at 100 ISO or slower. Each transparency *must* be accompanied by information attached to each photograph: where, when, what. No photography will be reviewed by the editors unless the photographer's name appears on *each* and *every* transparency." Pays $100-600 for "selected" transparencies. Buys one-time rights.

Columns/Departments: Departments include Focus on Nature (short feature in first or third person dealing with the unique aspects of a single species of wildlife). Length: 800 words. Along the Way (short essay dealing with life in Arizona or a personal experience keyed to Arizona). Length: 800 words. Back Road Adventure (personal back-road trips, preferably off the beaten path and outside major metro areas). Length: 1,000 words. Great Weekends (focus on a town or area's tourist attractions and include insider tips on places to spend the night, eat, and shop. Length: 1,200 words. Hike of the Month (personal experiences on trails anywhere in Arizona). Length: 500 words. Arizona Humor (amusing short anecdotes about Arizona). Length: 200 words maximum **Pays $75.**

Tips: "Writing must be of professional quality, warm, sincere, in-depth, well-peopled and accurate. Avoid themes that describe first trips to Arizona, the Grand Canyon, the desert, Colorado River running, etc. Emphasis is to be on Arizona adventure and romance as well as flora and fauna, when appropriate, and themes that can be photographed. Double check your manuscript for accuracy. Our typical reader is a 50-something person with the time, the inclination and the means to travel."

$ CAREFREE ENTERPRISE MAGAZINE, Arizona's Second-Oldest Magazine, Carefree Enterprise Magazine, Inc., P.O. Box 1145, Carefree AZ 85377. (480)488-3098. E-mail: staff@carefreeenterprise.com. Website: www.care freeenterprise.com. Editor: Fran Barbano. **Contact:** Susan Smyth, assistant editor. **50% freelance written.** Magazine published 11 times year. "CEM is a good news publication. We dwell on the positive, uplifting, and inspiring influences of life. We promote our areas and people. (We have readers across the country and overseas.)" Estab. 1963. Circ. 3,200. Pays within 3 months after publication. Publishes ms up to 1 year after acceptance. Byline given. Buys first North American serial, first, one-time and second serial rights. Editorial lead time 3 months. Submit seasonal material 6 months in advance. Accepts queries by mail, e-mail. Responds in 4 months. Sample copy for $2 with 12 × 15 SAE with $1.93 postage or $4, includes postage. Writer's guidelines for #10 SASE.

Nonfiction: Book excerpts, general interest, historical/nostalgic, humor, inspirational, interview/profile, personal experience, photo feature, travel, health, alternative medicine. "Nothing negative or controversial." **Buys 50 mss/year.** Query with published clips or send complete ms. Length: 800-3,000 words. **Pays $50 for assigned articles; $5-50 for unsolicited articles.**

Reprints: Accepts previously published submissions.

Photos: State availability of photos with submission or send photos with submission. Reviews transparencies and prints (up to 8 × 10). Offers $5/photo. Captions, model releases and identification of subjects required. Buys one-time rights.

Columns/Departments: Stephanie Bradley, assistant editor. Health, new column (no hot topics—general interest), 300-600 words; golf (profile a course or pro), 300-500 words. **Buys 18 mss/year.** Query with published clips or send complete ms. **Pays $20-35.**

Fiction: General interest, historical, inspirational, humorous. **Pays up to $50 for feature**. Serial pays up to $50 for each part.

Poetry: Avant-garde, free verse, haiku, light verse, traditional. "Nothing negative, controversial or unacceptable to families." **Buys 4-12 poems/year.** Submit maximum 3 poems. **Pays $5-25.**

Fillers: Anecdotes, facts, short humor. **Buys 12-50/year.** Length: 100-500 words. **Pays $15-35.**

Tips: "We are particularly easy to work with. New and established writers should be familiar with our publication and audience (upscale, affluent, world-travelers, multiple home-owners). Our youngest columnist is a 15-year-old blind girl who writes from a teen's point of view and often touches on blindness, and how others interact with handicapped individuals. We are open and receptive to any/all good news, upbeat, family-oriented material. We could use more humor, inspiration, travel (regional and worldwide) and positive solutions to everyday challenges. We like to feature profiles of outstanding people (no politics) who are role model material. Be familiar with this publication."

N $ $ CITY AZ, City AZ Publishing LLC, 2525 E. Camelback Rd., #120, Phoenix AZ 85016. (602)667-9798. Fax: (602)508-9454. E-mail: cityaz@aol.com. Website: www.cityaz.com. **Contact:** Michelle Savoy, executive editor. **100% freelance written.** Bimonthly magazine covering lifestyle and culture. "Lifestyle and culture magazine with an emphasis on modern design, culinary trends, cultural trends, fashion, great thinkers of our time and entertainment." Estab. 1997. Circ. 40,000. Pays 30 days after publication. Byline given. Offers 50% kill fee. Buys first and electronic rights. Editorial lead time 3 months. Submit seasonal material 3 months in advance. Accepts queries by mail, e-mail, fax, phone. Responds in 3 weeks to queries; 2 months to mss. Sample copy for $2 or online at website.

Nonfiction: General interest, interview/profile, new product, photo feature, travel, architecture. Query with published clips. Length: 600-4,000 words. **Pays $40-400.**

Photos: State availability of photos with submission. Reviews contact sheets, negatives, transparencies and prints. Negotiates payment individually. Model releases and identification of subjects required. Buys one-time rights or electronic rights.

Columns/Departments: Design (articles on industrial/product design and firms), 2,000 words; Music (articles on artists and industry leaders), 1,500 words. **Buys 100 mss/year.** Query with published clips.

$ $ $ PHOENIX, Cities West Publishing, Inc., 4041 N. Central Ave., Suite 530, Phoenix AZ 85012. (602)234-0840. Fax: (602)604-0169. **Contact:** Kathy Khoury, managing editor. **70% freelance written.** Monthly magazine covering regional issues, personalities, events, customs and history of the Southwest, state of Arizona and metro Phoenix.

Estab. 1966. Circ. 50,000. Pays on publication. Publishes ms an average of 5 months after acceptance. Byline given. Buys first North American serial rights and one-time rights. Submit seasonal material 6 months in advance. Accepts simultaneous submissions. Responds in 2 months. Sample copy for $3 and 9×12 SAE with 5 first-class stamps. Writer's guidelines for #10 SASE.

> **O—π** Break in with "short pieces of 150-400 words for the PHX-files highlighting local trends and personalities or with other short features of 750-1,000 words on same topics. Avoid the obvious. Look for the little-known, funky and offbeat."

Nonfiction: Investigative, general interest, historical, how-to, interview/profile, photo feature. "No material dealing with travel outside the region or other subjects that don't have an effect on the area. No sports, politics, business, fiction or personal essays, please." **Buys 50 mss/year.** Query with published clips. Length: 150-2,000 words. **Pays $50-1,500.**
Reprints: Send tearsheet or photocopy of article and/or typed ms with rights for sale noted and information about when and where the article previously appeared.
Fillers: Buys 6/year. Length: 1,000 words. **Pays $400.**
Tips: "Our audience is well-educated, upper middle-class Phoenicians. Articles must have strong local connection, vivid, lively writing to put the reader in the story and present new information or a new way of looking at things."

[N] SCOTTSDALE LIFE, The City Magazine, CitiesWest, 4041 N. Central, #A-100, Phoenix AZ 85012. (602)234-0840. Fax: (602)277-7857. E-mail: sdalelife@aol.com. **Contact:** Karlin McCarthy, editor. **50% freelance written.** Monthly magazine covering city and lifestyle, fashion, entertaining, people, business, society, dining. Estab. 1998. Circ. 40,000. **Pays on acceptance.** Byline given. Offers 10% kill fee. Buys all rights and electronic rights. Editorial lead time 2 months. Submit seasonal material 4 months in advance. Accepts queries by mail, e-mail. Responds in 1 month to queries. Sample copy free.
Nonfiction: Essays, expose, general interest, historical/nostalgic, how-to, humor, inspirational, interview/profile, new product, personal experience, photo feature, travel—all relating to the Arizona reader. Special issues: Real Estate, Beauty & Health, Art, Golf, Lifestyle. **Buys 20 mss/year** Query with or without published clips. Length: 1,000-2,000 words. **Pay varies.**
Photos: State availability of photos with submission. Reviews transparencies, prints. Negotiates payment individually. Captions, model releases, identification of subjects required. Buys all rights.
Columns/Departments: City (briefs, mini-profiles); Artful Diversions (gallery reviews), both 300-500 words; Good Taste (dining reviews), 700 words. **Buys 50 mss/year.** Query with published clips. **Pay varies.**
Fiction: Adventure, historical, humorous, novel excerpts, lsice-of-life vignettes, Western. **Buys 2 mss/year.** Query with published clips. Length: 500-1,000 words. **Pay varies.**
Poetry: Cowboy poetry. **Buys 2-5 poems/year.**
Tips: "No idea is a bad idea. Do not fax or phone unless you have written first. Look for the local angle or a way to make the idea relevant to the Phoenix/Scottsdale reader. Suggest photo possibilities."

$ $ TUCSON LIFESTYLE, Conley Publishing Group, Ltd., Suite 12, 7000 E. Tanque Verde Rd., Tucson AZ 85715-5318. (520)721-2929. Fax: (520)733-6110. E-mail: tucsonlife@aol.com. **Contact:** Scott Barker, executive editor. **90% freelance written.** Prefers to work with published/established writers. Monthly magazine covering Tucson-related events and topics. Estab. 1982. Circ. 32,000. **Pays on acceptance.** Publishes ms an average of 6 months after acceptance. Byline given. Buys first Arizona rights. Submit seasonal material 1 year in advance. Accepts queries by mail, e-mail, fax. Responds in 2 months to queries; 3 months to mss. Sample copy for $2.95 plus $3 postage. Writer's guidelines free.

> **O—π** Features are not open to freelancers.

Nonfiction: All stories need a Tucson angle. "Avoid obvious tourist attractions and information that most residents of the Southwest are likely to know. No anecdotes masquerading as articles. Not interested in fish-out-of-water, Easterner-visiting-the-Old-West pieces." **Buys 20 mss/year. Pays $50-500.**
Photos: Reviews contact sheets, 2¼×2¼ transparencies and 5×7 prints. Query about electronic formats. Offers $25-100/photo. Identification of subjects required. Buys one-time rights.
Columns/Departments: In Business (articles on Tucson businesses and business people); Lifestylers (profiles of interesting Tucsonans). Query. **Pays $100-200.**
Tips: "Style is not of paramount importance; good, clean copy with interesting lead is a must."

California

$ ANGELENO, The Toast of Los Angeles, 5670 Wilshire Blvd., Suite 700, Los Angeles CA 90036. (323)930-9402 ext. 2316. Fax: (323)930-9402. **50% freelance written.** Bimonthly luxury lifestyle magazine. "We cover the good things in life—fashion, fine dining, home design, the arts—from a sophisticated, cosmopolitan, well-to-do perspective." Estab. 1999. Circ. 50,000. Pays 2 months after receipt of invoice. Byline given. Offers 50% kill fee. Buys first and all rights in this market. Editorial lead time 6 months. Submit seasonal material 6 months in advance. Responds in 1 month. Sample copy $7.15 for current issue; $8.20 for back issue. Writer's guidelines for #10 SASE.

Nonfiction: General interest, how-to (culinary, home design), interview/profile, photo feature (occasional), travel. No fiction; *no unsolicited mss.* Query with published clips only. Length: 500-4,500 words. Pays expenses of writers on assignment.

Photos: State availability of photos with submission. Reviews transparencies and prints. Buys one-time first rights.

$ $ BRNTWD MAGAZINE, PTL Productions, 2118 Wilshire Blvd., #1060, Santa Monica CA 90403. (310)390-0251. Fax: (310)390-0261. E-mail: brntwdmag@aol.com. Website: www.brntwdmagazine.com. **Contact:** Dylan Nugent, editor. **100% freelance written.** Bi-monthly magazine covering entertainment, business, lifestyles, reviews. "Wanting in-depth interviews with top entertainers, politicians and similar individuals. Also travel, sports, adventure." Estab. 1995. Circ. 70,000. Pays on publication. Byline given. Editorial lead time 2-3 months. Submit seasonal material 3 months in advance. Accepts queries by mail, fax, phone. Accepts simultaneous submissions. Sample copy for $2. Writer's guidelines available.

Nonfiction: Book excerpts, exposé, general interest, historical/nostalgic, humor, interview/profile, new product, opinion, personal experience, photo feature, travel. **Buys 80 mss/year.** Query with published clips. Length: 1,000-2,500 words. **Pays 10-15¢/word.**

Photos: State availability of photos with submission. Reviews contact sheets, negatives, transparencies, prints. Offers no additional payment for photos accepted with ms. Captions and identification of subjects required.

Columns/Departments: Reviews (film/books/theater/museum), 100-500 words; Sports (Southern California angle), 200-600 words. **Buys 20 mss/year.** Query with published clips or send complete ms. **Pays 10-15¢/word.**

Tips: "Los Angeles-based writers preferred for most articles."

N ★ $ $ THE EAST BAY MONTHLY, The Berkeley Monthly, Inc., 1301 59th St., Emeryville CA 94608. (510)658-9811. Fax: (510)658-9902. E-mail: themonthly@aol.com. **Contact:** Tim Devaney, editor. **95% freelance written.** Monthly tabloid. "We like stories about local people and issues, but we also accept ideas for articles about topics that range beyond the East Bay's borders or have little or nothing to do with the region." Estab. 1970. Circ. 75,000. Pays on publication. Byline given. Buys first rights or second serial (reprint) rights. Editorial lead time 2 months. Submit seasonal material 2 months in advance. Accepts simultaneous submissions. Responds in 1 month. Sample copy for $1. Writer's guidelines for #10 SASE.

Nonfiction: Essays, exposé, general interest, historical/nostalgic, humor, interview/profile, opinion, personal experience, photo feature, travel. **Buys 55 mss/year.** Query with published clips. Length: 1,500-3,000 words. **Pays $350-700,** depending on length.

Reprints: Send tearsheet of article and information about when and where the article previously appeared.

Photos: State availability of photos with submission. Reviews contact sheets, 4×5 transparencies, 8×10 prints. Negotiates payment individually. Identification of subjects required. Buys one-time rights.

Fiction: Publishes novel excerpts.

Columns/Departments: Shopping Around (local retail news), 2,000 words; Food for Thought (local food news), 2,000 words; First Person, 2,000 words. **Buys 15 mss/year.** Query with published clips. **Pays 10¢/word.**

$ $ L.A. WEEKLY, 6715 Sunset Blvd., Los Angeles CA 90020. (323)465-9909. Fax: (323)465-3220. Website: www.laweekly.com. **Editor:** Sue Horton. **Managing Editor:** Kateri Butler. **Contact:** Janet Duckworth, features editor; Tom Christie, arts editor; Alan Mittelstaedt, news editor. **40% freelance written.** Weekly newspaper. "*L.A. Weekly* provides a fresh, alternative look at Los Angeles. We have arts coverage, news analysis and investigative reporting and a comprehensive calendar section." Estab. 1978. Circ. 225,000. Pays on publication. Byline given. Offers 33% kill fee. Buys first North American serial and electronic rights. Accepts queries by mail, e-mail, fax. Responds in 1 month to queries; 4 months to mss. Sample copy on website.

Nonfiction: Essays, exposé, interview/profile, personal experience. "No fashion, health, religion, fiction or poetry. We buy hundreds of assigned articles from freelancers but very few unsolicited manuscripts." Query with published clips. **Pays 34¢/word.**

Photos: State availability of photos with submission.

Columns/Departments: First Person (essays drawn from personal experiences), 1,400 words; Real Gone (travel column), 800 words. Query with published clips. **Pays 34¢/word basic rate.**

N $ $ $ $ LOS ANGELES MAGAZINE, ABC, 11100 Santa Monica Blvd., 7th Floor, Los Angeles CA 90025. (310)312-2200. Fax: (310)312-2285. **Contact:** Spencer Beck, editor-in-chief. **60% freelance written.** Monthly magazine about southern California. "Our editorial mission is to provide an authentic, compelling voice that engages and entertains one of the most media-savvy audiences in the world. Showcasing the diversity and vitality of the city, *Los Angeles*' quest is to deliver a timely, vibrant, must-read magazine that is witty, funny, sophisticated and skeptical but not cynical—a book that has regional resonance and national import." Estab. 1963. Circ. 183,373. Pays on publication. Publishes ms an average of 4 months after acceptance. Byline given. Offers 30% kill fee. Buys first North American serial rights. Submit seasonal material 6 months in advance. Accepts queries by mail, fax. Responds in 3 months. Sample copy for $6.50. Writer's guidelines for #10 SASE.

   ०⊷ Break in with "a piece for the L.A. Buzz section. We're also looking for more breaking city (L.A. specific) stories on politics, business and education."

   • *Los Angeles Magazine* continues to do stories with local angles, but it is expanding its coverage to include topics of interest on a national level.

Nonfiction: "Coverage includes both high and low culture—people, places, politics, the Industry and lifestyle trends." Book excerpts (about L.A. or by famous L.A. author); exposé (any local issue); general interest; historical/nostalgic (about L.A. or Hollywood); interview/profile (about L.A. person). **Buys 100 mss/year.** Query with published clips. Length: 250-6,000 words. **Pays $50-6,000.** Sometimes pays expenses of writers on assignment.
 ● Ranked as one of the best markets for freelance writers in *Writer's Yearbook* magazine's annual "Top 100 Markets," January 2000.
Photos: Lisa Thackaberry, photo editor. Send photos.
Columns/Departments: Buys 170 mss/year. Query with published clips. Length: 250-1,200 words. **Pays $100-2,000.**
Tips: "*Los Angeles* magazine seeks a stimulating mix of timely journalism, eye-catching design and useful service pieces that will appeal to the broadest possible audience."

N LOS ANGELES TIMES MAGAZINE, *Los Angeles Times*, Times Mirror Sq., Los Angeles CA 90053. (213)237-7000. Fax: (213)237-7386. **Contact:** Alice Short, editor. **50% freelance written.** Weekly magazine of regional general interest. Circ. 1,164,388. Payment schedule varies. Publishes ms an average of 2 months after acceptance. Byline given. Buys first North American serial rights. Submit seasonal material 3 months in advance. Accepts simultaneous submissions. Responds in 2 months. Sample copy and writer's guidelines free.
Nonfiction: General interest, investigative and narrative journalism, interview/profiles and reported essays. Covers California, the West, the nation and the world. Query with published clips only. Length: 2,500-4,500 words. Payment agreed upon expenses.
Photos: Query first; prefers to assign photos. Reviews color transparencies and b&w prints. Payment varies. Captions, model releases and identification of subjects required. Buys one-time rights.
Tips: "Prospective contributors should know their subject well and be able to explain why a story merits publication. Previous national magazine writing experience preferred."

N $ $ METRO, Metro Newspapers, 550 S. 1st St., San Jose CA 95113-2806. (408)298-8000. Website: www.metro active.com. Editor: Dan Pulcrano. Managing Editor: Corinne Asturias. **20-30% freelance written.** Weekly alternative newspaper. "*Metro* is for a sophisticated urban audience—stories must be more in-depth with an unusual slant not covered in daily newspapers. Subjects with local, Silicon Valley-angle preferred." Estab. 1985. Circ. 212,000. Pays on publication from one week to two months. Publishes ms after acceptance. Byline given. Offers kill fee only with assignment memorandum signed by editor. Buys first North American serial and second serial (reprint) rights—non-exclusive. Submit seasonal material 3 months in advance. Responds in 2 months to queries; 4 months to mss. Sample copy for $4. Writer's guidelines for #10 SASE.
Nonfiction: Book excerpt, exposé and interview/profile (particularly entertainment oriented), personal essay. Some sort of local angle needed. **Buys 75 mss/year.** Query with published clips. Length: 500-4,000 words. **Pays $50-1,000.** Sometimes pays expenses of writers on assignment.
Reprints: Send photocopy of article including information about when and where it previously appeared. **Pays $25-200.**
Photos: Send photos with submission. Reviews contact sheets, negatives, any size transparencies and prints. Offers $25-50/photo, more if used on cover. Captions, model releases, identification of subjects required. Buys one-time rights.
Columns/Departments: MetroMenu (food, dining out), 500-1,000 words; MetroGuide (entertainment features, interviews), 500-1,500 words. **Buys 75 mss/year.** Query with published clips. **Pays $25-200.**
Tips: "Seasonal features are most likely to be published, but we take only the best stuff. Local stories or national news events with a local angle will also be considered. Preferred submission format is Macintosh disk with printout. We are enthusiastic about receiving freelance inquiries. What impresses us most is newsworthy writing, compellingly presented. We define news broadly and consider it to include new information about old subjects as well as a new interpretation of old information. We like stories which illustrate broad trends by focusing in detail on specific examples."

N $ $ METRO SANTA CRUZ, Metro Newspapers, 115 Cooper St., Santa Cruz CA 95060. (831)457-9000. Fax: (831)457-5829. E-mail: buz@metcruz.com. Website: www.metroactive.com. **Contact:** Buz Bezore, editor. **20-30% freelance written.** Weekly alternative newspaper. "*Metro* is for a sophisticated coastal university town audience—stories must be more in-depth with an unusual slant not covered in daily newspapers." Estab. 1994. Circ. 50,000. Pays on publication from 2-3 weeks. Publishes ms after acceptance. Byline given. Offers kill fee only with assignment memorandum signed by editor. Buys first North American serial and second serial (reprint) rights—nonexclusive. Submit seasonal material 3 months in advance. Responds in 2 months to queries; 4 months to mss.
Nonfiction: Features include a cover story of 3,000-3,500 words and a hometown story of 1,000-1,200 words about an interesting character. Book excerpt, exposé and interview/profile (particularly entertainment oriented), personal essay. Some local angle needed. **Buys 75 mss/year.** Query with published clips. Length: 500-4,000 words. **Pays $50-500.**
Reprints: Send photocopy of article including information about when and where it previously appeared. **Pays $25-200.**
Photos: Send photos with submission. Reviews contact sheets, negatives, any size transparencies and prints. Offers $25-50/photo, more if used on cover. Captions, model releases, identification of subjects required. Buys one-time rights.
Columns/Departments: MetroMenu (food, dining out), 500-1,000 words; MetroGuide (entertainment features, interviews), 500-3,000 words; Taste (quarterly), 3,000 words. **Buys 75 mss/year.** Query with published clips. **Pays $25-200.**

Tips: "Seasonal features are most likely to be published, but we take only the best stuff. Local stories or national news events with a local angle will also be considered. Preferred submission format is Macintosh disk with printout. We are enthusiastic about receiving freelance inquiries. What impresses us most is newsworthy writing, compellingly presented. We define news broadly and consider it to include new information about old subjects as well as a new interpretation of old information. We like stories which illustrate broad trends by focusing in detail on specific examples."

N **$ $ $ $** NEW TIMES LOS ANGELES, 1950 Sawtelle Blvd., Suite 200, Los Angeles CA 90025. (310)954-2037. Fax: (310)478-9873. E-mail: editor@newtimesla.com. Website: www.newtimesla.com. **Contact:** Marnye Oppenheim, editorial administrator. **85% freelance written.** Weekly magazine of features and reviews for "intelligent young Los Angelenos interested in politics, the arts and popular culture." Estab. 1996. Circ. 100,000. Pays on publication. Publishes ms an average of 60 days after acceptance. Byline given. Buys first North American serial rights. Accepts simultaneous submissions. Accepts queries by mail, e-mail, fax.

> "Break in with submissions for our Cityside pages which use short (400-800 words) news items on Los Angeles happenings, personalities and trends. Try to have some conflict in submissions: 'x exists' is not as good a story as 'x is struggling with y over z.' "

Nonfiction: General interest, journalism, interview/profile, personal experience, photo features—all with strong local slant. Buys "scores" of mss/year. Query, send complete ms. Length: 200-5,000 words. **Pays $25-2,500.**

■ The online version of this publication contains material not found in the print edition. Contact: Dan Reines.
Tips: "Stories must have Los Angeles angle. We much prefer submissions in electronic form."

$ $ $ ORANGE COAST MAGAZINE, The Magazine of Orange County, Orange Coast Kommunications Inc., 3701 Birch St., Suite 100, Newport Beach CA 92660-2618. (949)862-1133. Fax: (949)862-0133. E-mail: ocmag@aol.com. Website: www.orangecoast.com. **Contact:** Patrick Mott, editor. **95% freelance written.** Monthly magazine "designed to inform and enlighten the educated, upscale residents of Orange County, California; highly graphic and well researched." Estab. 1974. Circ. 40,000. **Pays on acceptance.** Publishes ms an average of 4 months after acceptance. Byline given. Offers 20% kill fee. Buys one-time rights. Submit seasonal material at least 6 months in advance. Accepts queries by mail, e-mail, fax. Accepts simultaneous submissions. Responds in 2 months. Sample copy for $2.95 and 10×12 SAE with 8 first-class stamps. Writer's guidelines for SASE.

> Break in with Short Cuts (topical briefs of about 200 words), pays $50; Close Up (short 600-word profiles of Orange County people), pays $200.

Nonfiction: Exposé (Orange County government, politics, business, crime), general interest (with Orange County focus); historical/nostalgic, guides to activities and services, interview/profile (prominent Orange County citizens), local sports, travel. Special issues: Health and Fitness (January); Dining and Entertainment (March); Home and Garden (June); Resort Guide (November); Holiday (December). **Buys 100 mss/year.** Query or send complete ms. Absolutely no phone queries. Length: 2,000-3,000 words. **Pays $400-800.**

● Ranked as one of the best markets for freelance writers in *Writer's Yearbook* magazine's annual "Top 100 Markets," January 2000.

Reprints: Send tearsheet or photocopy of article or typed ms with rights for sale noted and information about when and where the article previously appeared.

Columns/Departments: Most departments are not open to freelancers. **Buys 200 mss/year.** Query or send complete ms. Length: 1,000-2,000 words. **Pays $200 maximum.**

Fiction: Buys only under rare circumstances. Send complete ms. Length: 1,000-5,000 words. **Pays $250.**

Tips: "We're looking for more local personality profiles, analysis of current local issues, local takes on national issues. Most features are assigned to writers we've worked with before. Don't try to sell us 'generic' journalism. *Orange Coast* prefers articles with specific and unusual angles focused on Orange County. A lot of freelance writers ignore our Orange County focus. We get far too many generalized manuscripts."

$ $ ORANGE COUNTY WOMAN, Orange Coast Publishing, 3701 Birch, Suite 100, Newport Beach CA 92660. (949)862-1133. Fax: (949)862-0133. E-mail: ocmag@aol.com. Website: www.orangecoast.com. **Contact:** Carroll Lachnit, editor. **90% freelance written.** "*Orange County Woman* is published monthly for the educated and affluent woman of Orange County, California." Estab. 1997. Circ. 40,000. **Pays on acceptance.** Publishes ms an average of 2 months after acceptance. Byline given. Offers 20% kill fee. Buys first North American serial and electronic rights. Editorial lead time 2 months. Submit seasonal material 4 months in advance. Accepts queries by mail, e-mail, fax. Accepts simultaneous submissions. Sample copy and writer's guidelines for SASE.

Nonfiction: General interest, how-to, humor, interview/profile, new product, personal experience. No fiction or poetry. Query with published clips or send complete ms and SASE. Length: 100-1,500 words. **Pays $50-300.**

Reprints: Send information about when and where the article previously appeared.

Photos: State availability of photos with submission or send photos with submission. Reviews contact sheets, negatives, transparencies, prints. Negotiates payment individually. Captions, model releases and identification of subjects required. Buys one-time rights.

Tips: "We are looking for profiles or trends related to women in Orange County. Read previous issues to gauge the range of story ideas and how they were handled. Write about real women in real situations; let their stories crystallize the broader issues. Remember that you are writing for an audience that generally is literate, affluent and sophisticated, but avoid dry intellectual discourse. All stories must have a strong Orange County angle. Our readers are busy women."

[N] $ $ PALM SPRINGS LIFE, The California Prestige Magazine, Desert Publications, Inc., 303 N. Indian Canyon, Palm Springs CA 92262. (760)325-2333. Fax: (760)325-7008. Editor: Stewart Weiner. Contact: Sarah Hagerty, executive editor. **75% freelance written.** Monthly magazine covering "affluent resort/southern California/Palm Springs desert resorts. *Palm Springs Life* is a luxurious magazine aimed at the affluent market." Estab. 1958. Circ. 20,000. Pays on publication. Publishes ms an average of 3 months after acceptance. Byline given. Offers 25% kill fee. Buys all rights (negotiable). Submit seasonal material 6 months in advance. Responds in 3 weeks to queries. Sample copy for $3.95.
Nonfiction: Book excerpts, essays, interview/profile. Query with published clips. Length: 500-2,500 words. **Pays $50-750 for assigned articles; $25-500 for unsolicited articles.**
   • Increased focus on desert region and business writing opportunities.
Photos: State availability of photos with submissions. Reviews contact sheets. Offers $5-125/photo. Captions, model releases, identification of subjects required. Buys all rights.
Columns/Departments: Around Town (local news), 50-250 words. **Buys 12 mss/year.** Query with or without published clips. **Pays $5-200.**

$ $ SACRAMENTO MAGAZINE, 4471 D St., Sacramento CA 95819. (916)452-6200. Fax: (916)452-6061. Managing Editor: Darlena Belushin McKay. **Contact:** Krista Minard, editor. **100% freelance written.** Works with a small number of new/unpublished writers each year. Monthly magazine with a strong local angle on politics, local issues, human interest and consumer items for readers in the middle to high income brackets. Estab. 1975. Circ. 29,000. Pays on publication. Publishes ms 3 months after acceptance. Rights vary; generally buys first North American serial rights and electronic rights, rarely second serial (reprint) rights. Responds in 2 months. Sample copy for $4.50. Writer's guidelines for #10 SASE.
   O━ Break in with submissions to City Lights.
Nonfiction: Local issues vital to Sacramento quality of life. **Buys 5 unsolicited feature mss/year.** Query first in writing ("no e-mail, fax or phone queries will be answered"). Length: 1,500-3,000 words, depending on author, subject matter and treatment. **Pays minimum $250.** Sometimes pays expenses of writers on assignment.
Photos: Send photos. Payment varies depending on photographer, subject matter and treatment. Captions (including IDs, location and date) required. Buys one-time rights.
Columns/Departments: Business, home and garden, media, parenting, first person essays, regional travel, gourmet, profile, sports, city arts (1,000-1,800 words); City Lights (250-300 words). **Pays $50-400.**

$ $ SACRAMENTO NEWS & REVIEW, Chico Community Publishing, 1015 20th St., Sacramento CA 95814. (916)498-1234. Fax: (916)498-7920. E-mail: melindaw@newsreview.com. Website: www.newsreview.com. **Contact:** Melinda Welsh, executive editor. **25% freelance written.** News and entertainment published weekly. "We are an alternative news and entertainment weekly. We maintain a high literary standard for submissions; unique or alternative slant. Publication aimed at a young, intellectual audience; submissions should have an edge and strong voice." Estab. 1989. Circ. 90,000. Pays on publication. Publishes ms an average of 1-2 months after acceptance. Byline given. Offers 10% kill fee. Buys first rights. Editorial lead time 1-2 months. Submit seasonal material 2 months in advance. Accepts queries by mail, e-mail, fax. Accepts simultaneous submissions. Responds in 1 month to queries; 2 months to mss. Sample copy for 50¢. Writer's guidelines for #10 SASE.
Nonfiction: Essays, exposé, general interest, humor, interview/profile, personal experience. Publishes holiday gift guides (November/December). Does not want to see travel, product stories, business profile. **Buys 6-10 mss/year.** Query with published clips. Length: 750-2,800 words. **Pays $40-300.** Sometimes pays expenses of writers on assignment.
Photos: State availability of photos with submission. Reviews 8 × 10 prints. Negotiates payment individually. Identification of subjects required. Buys one-time rights.
Columns/Departments: In the Mix (CD/TV/book reviews), 150-750 words. **Buys 10-15 mss/year.** Query with published clips. **Pays $10-300.**

[N] $ $ SAN DIEGO MAGAZINE, San Diego Magazine Publishing Co., 401 W. A St., Suite 250, San Diego CA 92101. (619)230-9292. Fax: (619)230-9220. E-mail: rdonoho@sandiego-online.com. Editor: Tom Blair. **Contact:** Ron Donoho, managing editor. **30% freelance written.** Monthly magazine. "We produce informative and entertaining features about politics, community and neighborhood issues, sports, design and other facets of life in San Diego." Estab. 1948. Circ. 55,000. Pays on publication. Publishes ms an average of 2 months after acceptance. Byline given. Offers 25% kill fee. Buys first North American serial rights and second serial (reprint) rights. Editorial lead time 2 months. Submit seasonal material 4 months in advance. Accepts simultaneous submissions. Sample copy and writer's guidelines not available.
Nonfiction: Exposé, general interest, historical/nostalgic, how-to, humor, interview/profile, travel. **Buys 12-24 mss/year.** Query with published clips or send complete ms. Length: 1,000-3,000 words. **Pays $250-750.** Sometimes pays expenses of writers on assignment.
Photos: State availability of photos with submission. Offers no additional payment for photos accepted with ms. Buys one-time rights.

$ $ $ $ SAN FRANCISCO, Focus on the Bay Area, 243 Vallejo St., San Francisco CA 94111. (415)398-2800. Fax: (415)398-6777. E-mail: melanie@sanfran.com. Website: www.sanfran.com. **Contact:** Lisa Trotter, managing editor. **50% freelance written.** Prefers to work with published/established writers. Monthly city/regional magazine.

Estab. 1968. Circ. 180,000. Pays on publication. Publishes ms an average of 2 months after acceptance. Byline given. Offers 25% kill fee. Submit seasonal material 5 months in advance. Responds in 2 months. Sample copy for $2.95. Writer's guidelines for SASE.

Nonfiction: Exposé, interview/profile, the arts, politics, public issues, sports, consumer affairs and travel. All stories should relate in some way to the San Francisco Bay Area (travel excepted). Query with published clips. Length: 400-4,000 words. **Pays $100-2,000** plus some expenses.

● Ranked as one of the best markets for freelance writers in *Writer's Yearbook* magazine's annual "Top 100 Markets," January 2000.

✗ $ $ $ SAN JOSE, The Magazine for Silicon Valley, Renaissance Publications, Inc., 4 N. Second St., Suite 550, San Jose CA 95113. (408)975-9300. Fax: (408)975-9900. E-mail: alastair@sanjosemagazine.com. Website: www.sanjosemagazine.com. Editor: Gilbert Sangari. **Contact:** Alastair Goldfisher, managing editor. **80% freelance written.** Switching from a bimonthly to a monthly magazine as of January 2001. "As the lifestyle magazine for those living at center of the technological revolution, we cover the people and places that make Silicon Valley the place to be for the new millenium. All stories must have a local angle, though they should be of national relevance." Estab. 1997. Circ. 60,000. Pays on publication. Publishes ms an average of 3 months after acceptance. Byline given. Offers 25% or $100 kill fee. Buys first North American serial rights and pays an additional electronic fee. Editorial lead time 18 weeks. Submit seasonal material 6 months in advance. Accepts queries by mail, e-mail, fax. Accepts simultaneous submissions. Responds in 1 month. Sample copy for $5. Writer's guidelines for #10 SASE.

○─ "Get your feet wet by writing smaller pieces, (200-500 words). Writers can get into my good graces by agreeing to write some of our unsigned pieces. What impresses the editor the most is meeting the assigned length and meeting deadlines."

Nonfiction: General interest, interview/profile, photo feature, travel. "No technical, trade or articles without a tie-in to Silicon Valley". **Buys 120 mss/year.** Query with published clips. Length: 1,000-2,000 words. **Pays 35¢/word.** Pays some expenses of writers on assignment.

Photos: State availability of photos with submission. Offers no additional payment for photos accepted with ms. Captions, model releases and identification of subjects required.

Columns/Departments: Fast Forward (a roundup of trends and personalities and news that has Silicon Valley buzzing; topics include health, history, politics, nonprofits, education, Q&As, business, technology, dining, wine and fashion). **Pays up to 50 mss/yr.** Query. **Pays 35¢/word.**

Tips: "Study our magazine for style and content. Nothing is as exciting as reading a tightly written query and discovering a new writer."

Colorado

Ñ $ $ $ ASPEN MAGAZINE, Ridge Publications, 720 E. Durant Ave., Suite E-8, Aspen CO 81612. (970)920-4040. Fax: (970)920-4044. E-mail: aspenmag@rof.net. Editor: Janet C. O'Grady. **Contact:** Jamie Miller, managing editor. **30% freelance written.** Bimonthly magazine covering Aspen and the Roaring Fork Valley. "All things Aspen, written in a sophisticated, insider-oriented tone." Estab. 1974. Circ. 20,000. Pays within 30 days of publication. Byline sometimes given. Offers 10% kill fee. Buys first North American serial rights and electronic rights. Editorial lead time 2 months. Responds in 6 months. Accepts queries by mail, e-mail, fax. Accepts simultaneous submissions. Responds in 2 months to queries. Sample copy for 9×12 SAE with 10 first-class stamps. Writer's guidelines for #10 SASE.

Nonfiction: Essay, historical, interview/profile, new product, photo feature, enrivonmental and local issues, architecture and design, sports and outdoors, arts. "We do not publish general interest articles without a strong Aspen hook. We do not publish 'theme' (skiing in Aspen) or anniversary (40th year of Aspen Music Festival)." **Buys 30-60 mss/year.** Query with published clips. Length: 50-4,000 words. **Pays $50-1,000.**

Photos: Send photos with submission. Reviews contact sheets, negatives, transparencies, prints. Model release and identification of subjects required.

Ñ $ $ STEAMBOAT MAGAZINE, Sundance Plaza, 1250 S. Lincoln Ave., P.O. Box 881659, Steamboat Springs CO 80488. (970)871-9413. Fax: (970)871-1922. E-mail: deb@steamboatmagazine.com. Website: www.steamboatmagazine.com. **Contact:** Deborah Olsen, editor. **80% freelance written.** Semiannual magazine "showcases the history, people, lifestyles and interests of Northwest Colorado. Our readers are generally well-educated, well-traveled, upscale, active people visiting our region to ski in winter and recreate in summer. They come from all 50 states and many foreign countries. Writing should be fresh, entertaining and informative." Estab. 1978. Circ. 30,000. Pays on publication. Publishes ms an average of 6 months after acceptance. Byline given. Buys exclusive rights. Editorial lead time 1 year. Submit seasonal material 1 year in advance. Accepts queries by mail, e-mail, fax, phone. Responds in 3 months to queries. Sample copy for $3.95 and SAE with 10 first-class stamps. Writer's guidelines free.

Nonfiction: Essays, general interest, historical/nostalgic, humor, interview/profile, personal experience, photo feature. **Buys 10-15 mss/year.** Query with published clips. Length: 150-1,500 words. **Pays $100-300 for assigned articles; $50-300 for unsolicited articles.** Sometimes pays expenses of writers on assignment.

Photos: State availability of photos with submission. Reviews transparencies. Offers $50-250/photo. Captions, model releases, identification of subjects required. Buys one-time rights.

Tips: "Western lifestyles, regional history, nature (including environmental subjects), sports and recreation are very popular topics for our readers. We're looking for new angles on ski/snowboard stories and activity-related stories. Please query first with ideas to make sure subjects are fresh and appropriate. We try to make subjects and treatments 'timeless' in nature because our magazine is a 'keeper' with a multi-year shelf life."

Connecticut

$ $ $ CONNECTICUT MAGAZINE, Journal Register Company, 35 Nutmeg Dr., Trumbull CT 06611. (203)380-6600. Fax: (203)380-6610. E-mail: cmonagan@connecticutmag.com. Website: http://www.connecticutmag.com. Editor: Charles Monagan. **Contact:** Dale Salm, managing editor. **80% freelance written.** Prefers to work with published/established writers who know the state and live/have lived here. Monthly magazine "for an affluent, sophisticated, suburban audience. We want only articles that pertain to living in Connecticut." Estab. 1971. Circ. 93,000. Pays on publication. Publishes ms an average of 4 months after acceptance. Byline given. Offers 20% kill fee. Buys first North American serial rights. Submit seasonal material 4 months in advance. Accepts queries by mail, e-mail. Responds in 6 weeks to queries. Writer's guidelines for #10 SASE.

○━ Freelancers can best break in with "First" (short, trendy pieces with a strong Connecticut angle); find a story that is offbeat and write it in a lighthearted, interesting manner.

Nonfiction: Book excerpts, exposé, general interest, interview/profile, other topics of service to Connecticut readers. Interested in seeing hard-hitting investigative pieces and strong business pieces (not advertorial). No personal essays. **Buys 50 mss/year.** Query with published clips. Length: 3,000 words maximum. **Pays $600-1,200.** Sometimes pays the expenses of writers on assignment.

Photos: Send photos with submission. Reviews contact sheets and transparencies. Offers $50 minimum/photo. Model releases and identification of subjects required. Buys one-time rights.

Columns/Departments: Business, Health, Politics, Connecticut Guide, Arts, Gardening, Environment, Education, People, Sports, Media. **Buys 50 mss/year.** Query with published clips. Length: 1,500-2,500 words. **Pays $400-700.**

Fillers: Short pieces about Connecticut trends, curiosities, interesting short subjects, etc. **Buys 50/year.** Length: 150-400 words. **Pays $75.**

▣ The online magazine carries original content not found in the print edition. Contact: Charles Monagan, online editor.

Tips: "Make certain your idea has not been covered to death by the local press and can withstand a time lag of a few months. Again, we don't want something that has already received a lot of press."

$ $ $ $ NORTHEAST MAGAZINE, *The Hartford Courant*, 285 Broad St., Hartford CT 06115-2510. (860)241-3700. Fax: (860)241-3853. E-mail: northeast@courant.com. Website: http://www.ctnow.com. Editor: Lary Bloom. **Contact**: Jane Bronfman, editorial assistant. **5% freelance written.** Weekly Sunday magazine for a Connecticut audience. Estab. 1982. Circ. 316,000. **Pays on acceptance.** Publishes ms an average of 5 months after acceptance. Byline given. Buys one-time rights. Accepts queries by mail. Responds in 3 months.

Nonfiction: "We are primarily interested in hard-hitting nonfiction articles spun off the news and compelling personal stories, as well as humor, fashion, style and home. We have a strong emphasis on Connecticut subject matter." General interest (has to have strong Connecticut tie-in); in-depth investigation of stories behind news (has to have strong Connecticut tie-in); historical/nostalgic; personal essays (humorous or anecdotal). No poetry. **Buys 10 mss/year.** Query by mail. Length: 750-2,500 words. **Pays $200-1,500.**

Photos: Most assigned; state availability of photos. "Do not send originals."

Fiction: Well-written, original short stories and (rarely) novel excerpts. Length: 750-1,500 words.

Tips: "Less space available for all types of writing means our standards for acceptance will be much higher. We can only print three to four short stories a year recently confined to a yearly fiction issue. It is to your advantage to read several issues of the magazine before submitting a manuscript or query. Virtually all our pieces are solicited and assigned by us, with about two percent of what we publish coming in 'over the transom.' "

District of Columbia

$ $ WASHINGTON CITY PAPER, 2390 Champlain St., Washington DC 20009. (202)332-2100. Fax: (202)462-8323. E-mail: mschaffer@washcp.com. Website: www.washcp.com. Editor: Michael Schaffer. **50% freelance written.** "Relentlessly local alternative weekly in nation's capital covering city politics, media and arts. No national stories." Estab. 1981. Circ. 98,000. Pays on publication. Publishes ms an average of 1 month after acceptance. Byline given. Offers 10% kill fee. Buys first rights. Editorial lead time 1 week. Responds in 1 month. Writer's guidelines for #10 SASE.

Nonfiction: "The paper's greatest single need is for well-reported stories about the city, which includes (but is not limited to) profiles, investigative pieces, 'Talk of the Town'-type articles and stories about local institutions. We're not interested in op-ed material, fiction, poetry, stories about news conferences or demonstrations, or service journalism.

Nor are we much interested in celebrity-worshipping journalism." No national politics. **Buys 100 mss/year.** Length: 2,500-10,000 words, feature stories; 200-2,000 words, shorter stories. **Pays 10-20¢/word.** Query with published clips or submit complete ms. Sometimes pays expenses of writers on assignment.

Photos: Pays minimum of $75. Make appointment to show portfolio to Jandos Rothstein, art director.

Columns/Departments: Contact: Brad McKee. Music Writing (eclectic), 1,200 words. **Buys 30 mss/year.** Query with published clips or submit complete ms. **Pays 10-20¢/word.**

Tips: "Send local stories that describe the city in new ways. A great idea is the best leverage. We will work with anyone who has a strong idea, regardless of vita."

N $ $ $ THE WASHINGTON POST, 1150 15th St. NW, Washington DC 20071. (202)334-7750. Fax: (202)334-1069. **Contact:** K.C. Summers, travel editor. **60% freelance written.** Prefers to work with published/established writers. Weekly newspaper travel section (Sunday). Pays on publication. Publishes ms an average of 6 months after acceptance. Byline given. "We are now emphasizing staff-written articles as well as quality writing from other sources. Stories are rarely assigned; all material comes in on speculation; there is no fixed kill fee." Buys only first North American serial rights. Travel must not be subsidized in any way. Usually responds in 1 month.

Nonfiction: Emphasis is on travel writing with a strong sense of place, color, anecdote and history. Query with published clips. Length: 1,500-2,500 words, plus sidebar for practical information.

Photos: State availability of photos with ms.

$ $ $ THE WASHINGTONIAN, 1828 L St. NW, #200, Washington DC 20036. (202)296-3600. Website: www.washingtonian.com. Editor: Jack Limpert. **Contact:** Brooke Foster, communications director. **20-25% freelance written.** Monthly magazine. "Writers should keep in mind that we are a general interest city-and-regional magazine. Nearly all our articles have a hard Washington connection. And, please, no political satire." Estab. 1965. Circ. 160,000. Pays on publication. Publishes ms an average of 3 months after acceptance. Byline given. Buys first North American serial rights, limited, non-exclusive electronic rights. Editorial lead time 6 weeks. Writer's guidelines for #10 SASE.

Nonfiction: Book excerpts, general interest, historical/nostalgic (with specific Washington, DC focus), interview/profile, personal experience, photo feature, travel. **Buys 15-30 mss/year.** Query by mail with published clips. **Pays 50¢/word.** Sometimes pays expenses of writers on assignment.

●	Ranked as one of the best markets for freelance writers in *Writer's Yearbook* magazine's annual "Top 100 Markets," January 2000.

Columns/Departments: Howard Means, senior editor. First Person (personal experience that somehow illuminates life in Washington area), 650-700 words. **Buys 9-12 mss/year.** Query. **Pays $325.**

Tips: "The types of articles we publish include service pieces; profiles of people; investigative articles; rating pieces; institutional profiles; first-person articles; stories that cut across the grain of conventional thinking; articles that tell the reader how Washington got to be the way it is; light or satirical pieces (send the complete manuscript, not the idea, because in this case execution is everything); and fiction that tells readers how a part of Washington works or reveals something about the character or mood or people of Washington. Subjects of articles include the federal government, local government, dining out, sports, business, education, medicine, fashion, environment, how to make money, how to spend money, real estate, performing arts, visual arts, travel, health, nightlife, home and garden, self-improvement, places to go, things to do, and more. Again, we are interested in almost anything as long as it relates to the Washington area. We don't like puff pieces or what we call 'isn't-it-interesting' pieces. In general, we try to help our readers understand Washington better, to help our readers live better, and to make Washington a better place to live. Also, remember—a magazine article is different from a newspaper story. Newspaper stories start with the most important facts, are written in short paragraphs with a lot of transitions, and usually can be cut from the bottom up. A magazine article usually is divided into sections that are like 400-word chapters of a very short book. The introductory section is very important—it captures the reader's interest and sets the tone for the article. Scenes or anecdotes often are used to draw the reader into the subject matter. The next section then might foreshadow what the article is about without trying to summarize it—you want to make the reader curious. Each succeeding section develops the subject. Any evaluations or conclusions come in the closing section."

Florida

N $ $ BOCA RATON MAGAZINE, JES Publishing, 6413 Congress Ave., Suite 100, Boca Raton FL 33487. (561)997-8683. Fax: (561)997-8909. E-mail: bocamag@aol.com. Website: www.bocamag.com. **Contact:** Marie Speed, editor. Associate Editor: Gail Friedman. **70% freelance written.** Bimonthly lifestyle magazine "devoted to the residents of South Florida, featuring fashion, interior design, food, people, places and issues that shape the affluent South Florida market." Estab. 1981. Circ. 20,000. **Pays on acceptance.** Publishes ms an average of 3 months after acceptance. Byline given. Buys second serial (reprint) rights. Submit seasonal material 7 months in advance. Accepts simultaneous submissions. Responds in 1 month. Sample copy for $4.95 for 10×13 SAE with 10 first-class stamps. Writer's guidelines for #10 SASE.

Nonfiction: General interest, historical/nostalgic, humor, interview/profile, photo feature, travel. Special issues: Interior Design (September-October); Beauty (January-February); Health (July-August). Query with published clips, or send complete ms. Length: 800-2,500 words. **Pays $50-600 for assigned articles; $50-300 for unsolicited articles.**

Reprints: Send tearsheet of article. Payment varies.

Photos: Send photos with submission.

Columns/Departments: Body & Soul (health, fitness and beauty column, general interest), 1,000 words; Hitting Home (family and social interactions), 1,000 words. Query with published clips or send complete ms. **Pays $50-250.**

Tips: "We prefer shorter manuscripts, highly localized articles, excellent art/photography."

$ $ FLORIDA LIVING MAGAZINE, Florida Media, Inc., 3235 Duff Rd., Lakeland FL 33810. (863)858-7244. Fax: (863)859-3197. E-mail: flliving@earthlink.net. Website: www.flaliving.com. Publisher: E. Douglas Cifers. **Contact:** Roberta Deakins, managing editor. Monthly lifestyle magazine covering Florida travel, food and dining, heritage, homes and gardens and all aspects of Florida lifestyle. Full calendar of events each month. Estab. 1981. Circ. 170,000. Pays on publication. Publishes ms an average of 6 months after acceptance. Byline given. No kill fee. Buys first rights. Editorial lead time 3 months. Submit seasonal material 6 months in advance. Accepts queries by mail, e-mail. Responds in 2 months. Sample copy $5. Writer's guidelines for SASE.

　　O→ Break in with stories specific to Florida showcasing the people, places, events and things that are examples of Florida's rich history and culture.

Nonfiction: General Florida interest, historical/nostalgic, interview/profile, travel, out-of-the-way Florida places, dining, attractions, festivals, shopping, resorts, bed & breakfast reviews, retirement, real estate, business, finance, health, recreation and sports. **Buys 50-60 mss/year.** Query with published clips. Length: 500-2,500 words. **Pays $100-400 for assigned articles; $50-250 for unsolicited articles.**

　　● Interested in material on areas outside of the larger cities.

Columns/Departments: Golf, Homes & Gardenings, Heritage, all Florida-related; 750 words. **Buys 24 mss/year.** Query with published clips. **Pays $75-250.**

Photos: Send photos with submission. Reviews 3×5 color prints and slides. Offers $6/photo. Captions required.

N ✗ $ $ $ GULFSHORE LIFE, 2975 S. Horseshoe Dr., Suite 100, Naples FL 34104. (941)643-3933. Fax: (941)643-5017. E-mail: gsledit@olsusa.com. **Contact:** Janeen Costello, editor. **75% freelance written.** Magazine published 9 times/year for "southwest Florida, the workings of its natural systems, its history, personalities, culture and lifestyle." Estab. 1970. Circ. 35,000. Pays on publication. Publishes ms an average of 4 months after acceptance. Byline given. Offers 25% kill fee. Buys first North American serial rights. Submit seasonal material 8 months in advance. Accepts simultaneous submissions. Accepts queries by mail, e-mail, fax. Sample copy for 9×12 SAE with 10 first-class stamps.

Nonfiction: Historical/nostalgic, interview/profile, issue/trend. All articles must be related to southwest Florida. **Buys 100 mss/year.** Query with published clips. Length: 500-3,000 words. **Pays $100-1,000.**

Photos: Send photos with submission, if available. Reviews 35mm transparencies and 5×7 prints. Pays $25-50. Model releases and identification of subjects required. Buys one-time rights.

Tips: "We buy superbly written stories that illuminate southwest Florida personalities, places and issues. Surprise us!"

N ✗ $ $ JACKSONVILLE, White Publishing Co., 1032 Hendricks Ave., Jacksonville FL 32207. (904)396-8666. Fax: (904)396-0926. **Contact:** Joseph White, managing editor. **80% freelance written.** Monthly magazine covering life and business in northeast Florida "for upwardly mobile residents of Jacksonville and the Beaches, Orange Park, St. Augustine and Amelia Island, Florida." Estab. 1985. Circ. 25,000. Pays on publication. Byline given. Offers 25-33% kill fee to writers on assignment. Buys first North American serial rights or second serial (reprint) rights. Editorial lead time 3 months. Submit seasonal 4 months in advance. Responds in 6 weeks to queries; 1 month to mss. Sample copy for $5 (includes postage). Writer's guidelines free.

Nonfiction: Book excerpts, exposé, general interest, historical, how-to (service articles), humor, interview/profile, personal experience, commentary, photo feature, travel, local business successes, trends, personalities, community issues, how institutions work. All articles *must* have relevance to Jacksonville and Florida's First Coast (Duval, Clay, St. Johns, Nassau, Baker counties). **Buys 50 mss/year.** Query with published clips. Length: 1,200-3,000 words. **Pays $50-500 for feature-length pieces.** Sometimes pays expenses of writers on assignment.

Reprints: Accepts reprints of previously published submissions. Send photocopy of article. Pay varies.

Photos: State availability of photos with submission. Reviews contact sheets, transparencies. Negotiates payment individually. Captions, model releases required. Buys one-time rights.

Columns/Departments: Business (trends, success stories, personalities), 1,000-1,200 words; Health (trends, emphasis on people, hopeful outlooks), 1,000-1,200 words; Smart Money (practical personal financial/advice using local people, anecdotes and examples), 1,000-1,200 words; Real Estate/Home (service, trends, home photo features), 1,000-1,200 words; Technology (local people and trends concerning electronics and computers), 1,000-1,200 words; Travel (weekends; daytrips; excursions locally and regionally, 1,000-1,200 words; occasional departments and columns covering local history, sports, family issues, etc. **Buys 40 mss/year. Pays $150-250.**

Tips: "We are a writer's magazine and demand writing that tells a story with flair."

N $ SENIOR VOICE OF FLORIDA, Florida's Leading Newspaper for Active Mature Adults, L&M Media, 18860 US Hwy. 19N, Suite 151, Clearwater FL 33764-3168. (727)536-1827. Fax: (727)536-1721. Publisher: LoRee Russell. **Contact:** Brendan Fitzsimons, editor. **25% freelance written.** Prefers to work with published/established writers. Monthly newspaper serving the needs of mature adults 50 years of age and over on the Florida Gulf Coast. Estab. 1981. Circ. 120,000. Pays on publication. Publishes ms an average of 3 months after acceptance. Byline given.

Buys one-time rights. Submit seasonal material 6 months in advance. Accepts simultaneous submissions. Responds in 2 months. Sample copy for $1 and 10×13 SAE with 6 first-class stamps. Writer's guidelines for SAE with 1 first-class stamp.

Nonfiction: General interest, historical, how-to, humor, inspirational, interview/profile, opinion, photo feature, travel, health, finance, all slanted to a senior audience. **Buys 10 mss/year.** Send complete ms. Length: 300-600 words. **Pays $5-15.**

Reprints: Send typed ms with rights for sale noted and information about when and where the article previously appeared. Pays 50% of amount paid for an original article. Pays flat fee.

Photos: Send photos with submission. Reviews 4×6 color and 5×7 b&w prints. Identification of subjects required.

Columns/Departments: Travel (senior slant) and V.I.P. Profiles (mature adults). **Buys 3 mss/year.** Send complete ms. Length: 300-600 words. **Pays $5-15.**

Fillers: Anecdotes, facts, cartoons, short humor. **Buys 3/year.** Length: 150-250 words. **Pays $5.**

Tips: "Our service area is the Florida Gulf Coast, an area with a high population of resident retirees and repeat visitors who are 50 plus. In writing for that readership, keep their interests in mind; what they are interested in, we are interested in. We like a clean, concise writing style. Photos are important."

$ $ TALLAHASSEE MAGAZINE, Rowland Publishing Inc., 1932 Miccosokee Rd., P.O. Box 1837, Tallahassee FL 32308. (850)878-0554. Fax: (850)656-1871. E-mail: tazzcat@yahoo.com. Website: www.talmag.talstar.com. **Contact:** Kathleen M. Grobe, managing editor. **60-75% freelance written.** Bimonthly magazine covering Tallahassee area—North Florida and South Georgia. "*Tallahassee Magazine* is dedicated to reflecting the changing needs of a capital city challenged by growth and increasing economic, political and social diversity." Estab. 1979. Circ. 17,300. **Pays on acceptance.** Publishes ms an average of 3 months after acceptance. Byline given. Buys one-time rights. Editorial lead time 3 months. Submit seasonal material 4 months in advance. Accepts queries by mail, e-mail, fax, phone. Accepts simultaneous submissions. Responds in 1 month. Sample copy for $2.95 and #10 SASE with 4 first-class stamps; sample articles on website. Writer's guidelines for #10 SASE.

Nonfiction: General interest, historical/nostalgic, how-to, humor, inspirational, interview/profile, personal experience, photo feature, travel, politics, sports, lifestyles. **Buys 10 mss/year.** Query or submit ms with SASE. Length: 1,000-1,500 words. **Pays $100-250.**

Reprints: Send typed ms with rights for sale noted and information about when and where the article previously appeared. **Pays $100-350.**

Photos: State availability of photos with submission. Reviews 35mm transparencies, 3×5 prints. Offers no additional payment for photos accepted with ms. Model releases and identification of subjects required. Buys one-time rights.

Columns/Departments: Humor; Cooking; People and Social, all 850 words or less. **Buys 12-18 mss/year.** Query with published clips. **Pays $100.**

Tips: "Know the area we cover. This area is unusual in terms of the geography and the people. We are a Southern city, not a Florida city, in many ways. Know what we have published recently and don't try to sell us on an idea that we have published within three years of your query. Be lucid and concise and take enough time to get your facts straight. Make submissions on disk, either in Microsoft Word or Word Perfect."

Georgia

$ $ $ $ ATLANTA, 1330 Peachtree St., Suite 450, Atlanta GA 30309. (404)872-3100. Fax: (404)870-6219. E-mail: hlalli@atlantamag.emmis.com. Website: www.atlantamagazine.com. Executive Director: Howard Lalli. **Contact:** Jennifer McLaine, managing editor. Monthly magazine that explores people, pleasures, useful information, regional happenings, restaurants, shopping, etc. for a general adult audience in Atlanta, including subjects in government, sports, pop culture, urban affairs, arts and entertainment. "*Atlanta* magazine articulates the special nature of Atlanta and appeals to an audience that wants to understand and celebrate the uniqueness of the region. The magazine's mission is to serve as a tastemaker by virtue of in-depth information and authoritative, provocative explorations of issues, personalities and lifestyles." Circ. 65,000. **Pays on acceptance.** Byline given. Offers 25% kill fee. Buys first North American serial rights. Accepts queries by mail, e-mail, fax, phone. Responds in 2 months to queries. Sample copy on website.

Nonfiction: Buys 36-40 mss/year. Query with published clips. Length: 1,500-5,000 words. **Pays $300-2,000.** Pays expenses of writer on assignment.

● Ranked as one of the best markets for freelance writers in *Writer's Yearbook* magazine's "Top 100 Markets," January 2000.

Columns/Departments: Essay, travel. **Buys 30 mss/year.** Query with published clips. **Pays $500.** Length: 1,000-1,500 words.

Fiction: Publishes novel excerpts.

Fillers: Buys 80/year. Length: 75-175 words. **Pays $50-100.**

Tips: "Writers must know what makes their piece a story rather than just a subject."

[N] $ $ ATLANTA TRIBUNE: THE MAGAZINE, Black Atlanta's Number One Resource for Business, Careers, Technology and Wealth-Building, L&L Communications, 875 Old Roswell Rd, Suite C-100, Roswell GA 30076. Fax: (770)642-6501. E-mail: rsherrell@atlantatribune.com. Website: www.atlantatribune.com. **Contact:**

Rick Sherrell, editor. **90% freelance written.** Monthly magazine covering African-American business, careers, technology and wealth-building. "*The Atlanta Tribune* is written for Atlanta's Black executives, professionals and entrepreneurs with a primary focus of business, careers, technology and wealth-building. Our publication serves as an advisor that offers helpful information and direction to the Black entrepreneur." Estab. 1987. Circ. 30,000. **Pays on acceptance.** Byline given. Offers 10% kill fee. Buys electronic and all rights. Editorial lead time 4 months. Submit seasonal material 4 months in advance. Accepts queries by e-mail. Responds in 6 weeks to queries. Writer's guidelines online. Sample copy online or mail a request.

　　　Oπ Break in with "the ability to write feature stories that give insight into Black Atlanta's business community, technology, businesses and career and wealth-building opportunities. Also, stories with real social, political or economic impact."

Nonfiction: How-to (business, careers, technology), interview/profile, new product, technical. "Our special sections include Black history, real estate, Scholarship Roundup and Health & Wellness." **Buys 100 mss/year.** Query with published clips. Length: 1,400-2,500 words. **Pays $250-600.** Sometimes pays expenses of writers on assignment.

Photos: State availability of photos with submission. Reviews 2¼ × 2¼ transparencies. Negotiates payment individually. Model releases and identification of subjects required. Buys one-time rights.

Columns/Departments: Business, Careers, Technology and Wealth-Building, all 700 words. **Buys 100 mss/year.** Query with published clips. **Pays $100-200.**

　　　■ The online version contains material not found in the print edition. Contact: Rick Sherrell.

Tips: "Send a well-written, convincing query by e-mail that demonstrates that you have thoroughly read previous issues and reviewed our online writer's guidelines."

$ $ GEORGIA MAGAZINE, Georgia Electric Membership Corp., P.O. Box 1707, Tucker GA 30085. (770)270-6950. Fax: (770)270-6995. E-mail: ann.orowski@georgiaemc.com. Website: www.Georgiamagazine.org. **Contact**: Ann Orowski, editor. **50% freelance written.** "We are a monthly magazine for and about Georgians, with a friendly, conversational tone and human interest topics." Estab. 1945. Circ. 325,000. Pays on publication. Publishes ms an average of 4 months after acceptance. Byline given. Buys first North American serial rights and website rights. Editorial lead time 2 months. Submit seasonal material 6 months in advance. Accepts simultaneous submissions. Responds in 1 month to subjects of interest. Sample copy for $2 each. Writer's guidelines for #10 SASE.

Nonfiction: Georgia-focused general interest, historical/nostalgic, how-to (in the home and garden), humor, inspirational, interview/profile, photo feature, travel. **Buys 8 mss/year.** Query with published clips. Length: 800-1,000 words; 500 words for smaller features and departments. **Pays $50-300.** Pays contributor copies upon negotiation. Sometimes pays expenses of writers on assignment.

Photos: State availability of photos with submission. Reviews contact sheets, transparencies, prints. Negotiates payment individually. Model releases, identification of subjects required. Buy one-time rights.

$ $ KNOW ATLANTA MAGAZINE, New South Publishing, 1303 Hightower Trail, Suite 101, Atlanta GA 30350. (770)650-1102. Fax: (770)650-2848. E-mail: editor1@knowatlanta.com. Website: www.knowatlanta.com/. **Contact:** Geoff Kohl, editor. **80% freelance written.** Quarterly magazine covering the Atlanta area. "Our articles offer information on Atlanta that would be useful to newcomers—homes, schools, hospitals, fun things to do, anything that makes their move more comfortable." Estab. 1986. Circ. 192,000. Pays on publication. Byline given. Offers 100% kill fee. Buys first North American serial rights. Editorial lead time 2 months. Submit seasonal material 2 months in advance. Accepts queries by mail or fax. Sample copy free.

　　　Oπ "Know the metro Atlanta area, especially hot trends in real estate. Writers who know about international relocation trends and commercial real estate topics are hot."

Nonfiction: General interest, how-to, personal experience, photo feature. No fiction. **Buys 10 mss/year.** Query with clips by mail or fax. Length: 1,000-2,000 words. **Pays $100-500 for assigned articles; $100-300 for unsolicited articles.** Sometimes pays expenses of writers on assignment.

Reprints: Accepts previously published submissions.

Photos: Send photos with submission. Reviews contact sheets. Negotiates payment individually. Captions and identification of subjects required. Buys one-time rights.

$ $ NORTH GEORGIA JOURNAL, Legacy Communications, Inc., P.O. Box 127, Roswell GA 30077. (770)642-5569. Fax: (770)642-1415. E-mail: sumail@mindspring.com. Website: mindspring.com/~north.ga.travel. **Contact:** Olin Jackson, publisher. **70% freelance written.** Quarterly magazine "for readers interested in travel, history, and mountain lifestyles of north Georgia." Estab. 1984. Circ. 18,450. Pays on publication. Publishes ms an average of 5 months after acceptance. Byline given. Offers 25% kill fee. Buys first and all rights. Editorial lead time 6 months. Submit seasonal material 6 months in advance. Accepts queries by mail, e-mail, fax. Sample copy for 9 × 12 SAE and 8 first-class stamps or on website. Writer's guidelines for #10 SASE.

Nonfiction: Historical/nostalgic, how-to (survival techniques; mountain living; do-it-yourself home construction and repairs, etc.), interview/profile (celebrity), personal experience (anything unique or unusual pertaining to north Georgia mountains), photo feature (any subject of a historic nature which can be photographed in a seasonal context, i.e.—old mill with brilliant yellow jonquils in foreground), travel (subjects highlighting travel opportunities in North Georgia). Query with published clips. **Pays $75-350.**

Photos: Send photos with submission. Reviews contact sheets, transparencies. Negotiates payment individually. Captions, model releases, identification of subjects required. Buys all rights.

Fiction: Publishes novel excerpts.
Tips: "Good photography is crucial to acceptance of all articles. Send written queries then *wait* for a response. *No telephone calls please.* The most useful material involves a first-person experience of an individual who has explored a historic site or scenic locale and *interviewed* a person or persons who were involved with or have first hand knowledge of a historic site/event. Interviews and quotations are crucial. Articles should be told in writer's own words."

Hawaii

\$ \$ HONOLULU, Honolulu Publishing Co., Ltd., 36 Merchant St., Honolulu HI 96813. (808)524-7400. Fax: (808)531-2306. E-mail: honmag@pixi.com. Publisher: John Alves. **Contact:** John Heckathorn, editor. **50% freelance written.** Prefers to work with published/established writers. Monthly magazine covering general interest topics relating to Hawaii residents. Estab. 1888. Circ. 30,000. **Pays on acceptance.** Publishes ms an average of 4 months after acceptance. Byline given. Buys first-time rights. Submit seasonal material 5 months in advance. Accepts simultaneous submissions. Responds in 2 months. Sample copy for \$2 and 9 × 12 SAE with 8 first-class stamps. Writer's guidelines for #10 SASE.
Nonfiction: Exposé, general interest, historical/nostalgic, photo feature—all Hawaii-related. "We write for Hawaii residents, so travel articles about Hawaii are not appropriate." **Buys 30 mss/year.** Query with published clips if available. Length: 2,000-3,000 words. **Pays \$100-700.** Sometimes pays expenses of writers on assignment.
Photos: Michel Lê, art director. Send photos. Pays \$75-175 for single image inside; \$500 maximum for cover. Captions and identification of subjects required as well as model release. Buys one-time rights.
Columns/Departments: Calabash ("newsy," timely, humorous department on any Hawaii-related subject). **Buys 15 mss/year.** Query with published clips or send complete ms. Length: 50-750 words. **Pays \$35-100.** First Person (personal experience or humor). **Buys 10 mss/year.** Length: 1,500 words. **Pays \$200-300.**

Idaho

⭐ \$ \$ BOISE MAGAZINE, Earls Communications, 4619 Emerald, Suite D-1, Boise ID 83701. (208)338-5454. Fax: (208)338-0006. E-mail: colleen@boisemag.com. **Contact:** Colleen Birch Maile, managing editor. **90% freelance written.** "*Boise Magazine* is a city/regional quarterly devoted to Idaho's capital and its environs. We publish profiles, articles, reviews and features on business, sports, the arts, politics, community development and have regular departments that cover travel, design, books, food and wine as well as a calendar of events and a section entitled About Idaho." Estab. 1997. Circ. 12,000. Pays on publication. Byline given. Buys first rights. Editorial lead time 3 months. Submit seasonal material 6 months in advance. Accepts queries by mail, e-mail, fax. Responds in 6 weeks to queries; 3 months to mss. Sample copy \$3.50. Guidelines for #10 SASE.
Nonfiction: Book excerpts, essays, general interest, humor, photo feature, travel. **Buys 12 mss/year.** Query by mail with published clip. Length: 500-3,500 words. **Pays \$500.** Sometimes pays expenses of writers on assignment.
Photos: State availability of photos with submission. Negotiates payment individually. Model releases and identification of subjects required. Buys one-time rights.
Columns/Departments: About Idaho (short pieces on life around Boise); Out of Town; Book Reviews, all 500-1,250 words. **Buys 30 mss/year.** Query with published clips. **Pays \$150-200.**
Fiction: Idaho or regional themes. No romance, science fiction, western, erotica, adventure, religious. **Buys 2-3 mss/ year.** Query. Length: 1,000-2,500 words. **Pays \$200.**
Tips: "About Idaho and Book Reviews are the best entry-levels for freelance writers. Profiles and other departments are not as easy, and features are virtually all done by local writers. All submissions should have an Idaho or northwest/ intermountain theme. We prefer regional writers—former Idahoans or folks with a tie to the state have a good chance too."

Illinois

⭐ \$ CHICAGO LIFE, P.O. Box 11311, Chicago IL 60611-0311. (773)880-1360. E-mail: chgolife@mcs.com. Publisher: Pam Berns. **Contact:** Joan Black, editor. **95% freelance written.** Bimonthly magazine on Chicago life for educated, affluent professionals, 25-50 years old. Estab. 1984. Circ. 50,000. Pays on publication. Byline given. Kill fee varies. Submit seasonal material 8 months in advance. Accepts simultaneous submissions. Responds in 3 months. Sample copy for 9 × 12 SAE with 7 first-class stamps.
Nonfiction: Environment, health, interior design, exposé, how-to, photo feature, travel. **Buys 50 mss/year.** Send complete ms. Length: 400-1,200 words. **Pays \$30.** Sometimes pays the expenses of writers on assignment.
Reprints: Send photocopy of article and information about when and where the article previously appeared.
Photos: Send photos with submission. Reviews contact sheets, negatives, transparencies, prints. Offers \$15-30/photo. Buys one-time rights.

Columns/Departments: Law, Book Reviews, Travel, Health, Environment, Home Decorating. Send complete ms. Length: 500 words. **Pays $30.**

Fillers: Facts. **Pays $15-30.**

Tips: "Please send finished work with visuals (photos, if possible). Topics open include environmental concerns, health, interior design, travel, self improvement, how-to-do almost anything, entrepreneurs."

$ $ $ $ CHICAGO MAGAZINE, 500 N. Dearborn, Suite 1200, Chicago IL 60610-4901. Fax: (312)222-0699. E-mail: chimagst@aol.com. Website: www.chicagomagazine.com. **Contact:** Shane Tritsch, managing editor. **50% freelance written.** Prefers to work with published/established writers. Monthly magazine for an audience which is "95% from Chicago area; 90% college educated; upper income, overriding interests in the arts, politics, dining, good life in the city and suburbs. Most are in 25-50 age bracket, well-read and articulate." Estab. 1968. Circ. 175,000. **Pays on acceptance.** Publishes ms an average of 3 months after acceptance. Buys first serial rights. Submit seasonal material 4 months in advance. Accepts queries by mail, e-mail. Responds in 1 month. For sample copy, send $3 to Circulation Dept. Writer's guidelines for #10 SASE.

Nonfiction: "On themes relating to the quality of life in Chicago: past, present, and future." Writers should have "a general awareness that the readers will be concerned, influential, longtime Chicagoans. We generally publish material too comprehensive for daily newspapers." Personal experience and think pieces, profiles, humor, spot news, historical articles, exposés. **Buys 100 mss/year.** Query; indicate "specifics, knowledge of city and market, and demonstrable access to sources." Length: 200-6,000 words. **Pays $100-3,000 and up, depending on the story.** Pays expenses of writers on assignment.

Photos: Reviews b&w glossy prints, 35mm color transparencies or color prints. Usually assigned separately, not acquired from writers.

■ The online magazine carries content not found in the print edition. Contact: Tara Croft, online editor.

Tips: "Submit detailed queries, be business-like and avoid clichéd ideas."

N $ $ $ $ CHICAGO READER, Chicago's Free Weekly, Chicago Reader, Inc., 11 E. Illinois, Chicago IL 60611. (312)828-0350. Fax: (312)828-9926. E-mail: mail@chicagoreader.com. Website: www.chicagoreader.com. Editor: Alison True. **Contact:** Patrick Arden, managing editor. **50% freelance written.** Alternative weekly tabloid for Chicago. Estab. 1971. Circ. 136,000. Pays on publication. Publishes ms an average of 3 months after acceptance. Byline given. No kill fee. Buys one-time rights. Editorial lead time up to 6 months. Accepts queries by mail, e-mail, fax. Accepts simultaneous submissions. Responds if interested. Sample copy free. Writer's guidelines free or on website.

Nonfiction: Book excerpts, essays, exposé, general interest, historical/nostalgic, humor, interview/profile, opinion, personal experience, photo feature. No celebrity interviews, national news or issues. **Buys 500 mss/year.** Send complete ms. Length: 4,000-50,000 words. **Pays $100-2,000.** Sometimes pays expenses of writers on assignment.

Reprints: Accepts previously published submissions.

Columns/Departments: Reading, First Person, Cityscape, Neighborhood News, all 1,500-2,500 words; arts and entertainment reviews, up to 1,200 words; calendar items, 400-1,000 words. **Pays $100-2,000.**

Tips: "Our greatest need is for full-length magazine-style feature stories on Chicago topics. We're *not* looking for: hard news (What the Mayor Said About the Schools Yesterday); commentary and opinion (What I Think About What the Mayor Said About the Schools Yesterday); fiction; poetry. We are not particularly interested in stories of national (as opposed to local) scope, or in celebrity for celebrity's sake (a la *Rolling Stone, Interview,* etc.). More than half the articles published in the *Reader* each week come from freelancers, and once or twice a month we publish one that's come in 'over the transom'—from a writer we've never heard of and may never hear from again. We think that keeping the *Reader* open to the greatest possible number of contributors makes a fresher, less predictable, more interesting paper. We not only publish unsolicited freelance writing, we depend on it."

$ $ $ CHICAGO SOCIAL, Chicago's Monthly Social Magazine, Prairie City Media, 727 N. Hudson Ave., #001, Chicago IL 60610. (312)787-4600. Fax: (312)787-4628. Editor: Michael Blaise Kong. Editor-in-Chief: Royaa G. Silver. **Contact:** Gina Fridland, senior editor. **70% freelance written.** Monthly luxury lifestyle magazine. "We cover the good things in life—fashion, fine dining, the arts, etc.—from a sophisticated, cosmopolitan, well-to-do perspective." Circ. 75,000. Pays 2 months after receipt of invoice. Byline given. Offers 50% kill fee. Buys first rights and all rights in this market. Editorial lead time 6 months. Submit seasonal material 6 months in advance. Responds in 1 month. Sample copy for $7.15 for current issue; $8.20 for back issue. Writer's guidelines for #10 SASE.

Nonfiction: General interest, how-to (gardening, culinary, home design), interview/profile, photo feature (occasional), travel. No fiction; *no unsolicited mss.* Query with published clips only. Length: 500-4,500 words. **Pays $50-900.** Pays expenses of writers on assignment.

Photos: State availability of photos with submission. Reviews transparencies and prints. "We pay for film and processing only." Buys one-time rights.

Columns/Departments: Few Minutes With (Q&A), 800 words; City Art, Home Design, Gold List, Sporting Life (feature), 2,000 words. Query with published clips only. **Pays $150-400.**

Tips: "Send résumé, clips and story ideas. Mention interest and expertise in cover letter. We need writers who are knowledgeable about home design, architecture, art, culinary arts, entertainment, fashion and retail."

N ★ $ ILLINOIS ENTERTAINER, Chicago's Music Monthly, Roberts Publishing, Inc., 124 W. Polk, #103, Chicago IL 60605. (312)922-9333. E-mail: ieeditors@aol.com. Website: www.illinoisentertainer.com or www.ieweekly.

net. Contact: Michael C. Harris, editor. **80% freelance written.** Free monthly magazine covering "popular and alternative music, as well as other entertainment: film, theater, media. We're more interested in new, unknown artists than the usual Madonna/Prince fare. Also, we cover lots of Chicago-area artists." Estab. 1974. Circ. 75,000. Pays on publication. Publishes ms an average of 2 months after acceptance. Byline given. Offers 50% kill fee. Buys first North American serial rights. Editorial lead time 2 months. Submit seasonal material 2 months in advance. Accepts simultaneous submissions. Accepts queries by mail, e-mail. Responds in 2 months. Sample copy for $5.

Nonfiction: Exposé, how-to, humor, interview/profile, new product, reviews. No personal, confessional, inspirational articles. **Buys 75 mss/year.** Query with published clips. Length: 600-2,600 words. **Pays $15-160.** Sometimes pays expenses of writers on assignment.

Reprints: Send typed ms with rights for sale noted and information about when and where the article previously appeared. Pays 100% of amount paid for an original article.

Photos: Send photos with submission. Reviews contact sheets, transparencies and 5×7 prints. Offers $20-200/photo. Captions, model releases, identification of subjects required. Buys one-time rights.

Columns/Departments: Spins (LP reviews), 250-300 words. **Buys 200-300 mss/year.** Query with published clips. **Pays $15.**

☐ The online version contains material not found in the print edition. Contact: Michael C. Harris.

Tips: "Send clips, résumé, etc. and be patient. Also, sending queries that show you've seen our magazine and have a feel for it greatly increases your publication chances."

Indiana

$ $INDIANAPOLIS MONTHLY, Emmis Publishing Corp., 40 Monument Circle, Suite 100, Indianapolis IN 46204. (317)237-9288. Fax: (317)684-2080. E-mail: freelance@indymonthly.emmis.com. Website: www.indianapolism onthly.com. Editor-in-Chief: Deborah Paul. Senior Editor: Brian D. Smith. **Contact**: Rebecca Poynor Burns, editor. **50% freelance written.** Prefers to work with published/established writers. Monthly. "*Indianapolis Monthly* attracts and enlightens its upscale, well-educated readership with bright, lively editorial on subjects ranging from personalities to social issues, fashion to food. Its diverse content and attention to service make it the ultimate source by which the Indianapolis area lives." Estab. 1977. Circ. 45,000. Pays on publication. Publishes ms an average of 2 months after acceptance. Byline given. Offers negotiable kill fee. Buys first North American serial rights or one-time rights. Editorial lead time 3 months. Submit seasonal material 3 months in advance. Accepts queries by mail, e-mail. Accepts simultaneous submissions. Responds in 3 weeks. Sample copy for $6.10. Guidelines for #10 SASE.

● This magazine is using more first-person essays, but they must have a strong Indianapolis or Indiana tie. It will consider nonfiction book excerpts of material relevant to its readers.

Nonfiction: Book excerpts (by Indiana authors or with strong Indiana ties), essays, exposé, general interest, interview/profile, photo feature. Must have a strong Indianapolis or Indiana angle. No poetry, fiction or domestic humor; no "How Indy Has Changed Since I Left Town," "An Outsider's View of the 500," or generic material with no or little tie to Indianapolis/Indiana. **Buys 50 mss/year.** Query with published clips by mail or e-mail, or send complete ms. Length: 200-3,000 words. **Pays $50-600.**

Reprints: Accepts reprints only from non-competing markets. Send typed ms with rights for sale noted and information about when and where the article previously appeared. Pays 100% of the amount paid for an original article.

Photos: State availability of photos with submission. Reviews upon request. Negotiates payment individually. Captions, model releases and identification of subjects required. Buys one-time rights.

Columns/Departments: Sport; Health; First Person; Hoosiers at Large (essays by Indiana natives); Business; Coping; Controversy; Books, all 2,000-2,500 words. **Buys 35 mss/year. Pays $300.**

Tips: "Our standards are simultaneously broad and narrow: broad in that we're a general interest magazine spanning a wide spectrum of topics, narrow in that we buy only stories with a heavy emphasis on Indianapolis (and, to a lesser extent, Indiana). Simply inserting an Indy-oriented paragraph into a generic national article won't get it: all stories must pertain primarily to things Hoosier. Once you've cleared that hurdle, however, it's a wide-open field. We've done features on national celebrities—Indianapolis native David Letterman and *Mir* astronaut David Wolf of Indianapolis, to name two—and we've published two-paragraph items on such quirky topics as an Indiana gardening supply house that sells insects by mail. We also like local pieces on national celebs: one of our most popular cover stories was titled 'Oprah's Indiana Home.' Probably the easiest place to break in is our front-of-the-book section, IndyScene, a collection of short takes on trendy topics (including Homegrown, spotlighting Hoosiers making it big elsewhere). Query with clips showing lively writing and solid reporting. E-mail queries are OK, and snail mail queries should include SASE. No phone queries please."

Kansas

$ $KANSAS!, Kansas Department of Commerce and Housing, 700 SW Harrison, Suite 1300, Topeka KS 66603-3957. (785)296-3479. Fax: (785)296-6988. **Contact**: Andrea Glenn, editor. **90% freelance written.** Quarterly magazine emphasizing Kansas travel attractions and events. Estab. 1945. Circ. 52,000. **Pays on acceptance.** Publishes ms an average of 1 year after acceptance. Byline given. Buys one-time rights. Submit seasonal material 8 months in advance. Responds in 2 months. Sample copy and writer's guidelines available.

Nonfiction: General interest, photo feature, travel. "Material must be Kansas-oriented and have good potential for color photographs. The focus is on travel with articles about places and events that can be enjoyed by the general public. In other words, events must be open to the public, places also. Query letter should clearly outline story. I'm especially interested in Kansas freelancers who can supply their own quality photos." Query by mail. Length: 750-1,250 words. **Pays $200-400.**

Photos: "We are a full-color photo/manuscript publication." Send photos (original transparencies only) with query. Pays $50-75 (generally included in ms rate) for 35mm or larger format transparencies. Captions required.

Tips: "History and nostalgia stories do not fit into our format because they can't be illustrated well with color photos. Submit a query letter describing one appropriate idea with outline for possible article and suggestions for photos."

Kentucky

$ BACK HOME IN KENTUCKY, Greysmith Publishing Inc., P.O. Box 681629, Franklin TN 37068-1629. (615)790-0790. Fax: (615)790-6188. **Contact**: Nanci P. Gregg, managing editor. **50% freelance written.** "Bimonthly magazine covering Kentucky heritage, people, places, events. We reach Kentuckians and 'displaced' Kentuckians living outside the state." Estab. 1977. Circ. 8,163. Pays on publication. Publishes ms an average of 6 months after acceptance. Byline given. Buys first North American serial rights. Submit seasonal material 8 months in advance. Responds in 2 months. Sample copy for $3 and 9×12 SAE with 5 first-class stamps. Writer's guidelines for #10 SASE.

● This magazine is increasing its emphasis on the "Back Home." It is interested in profiles of Kentucky gardeners, Kentucky cooks, Kentucky craftspeople.

Nonfiction: Historical (Kentucky-related eras or profiles), profiles (Kentucky cooks, gardeners and craftspersons), memories (Kentucky related), photo feature (Kentucky places and events), travel (unusual/little known Kentucky places). No inspirational or religion. **Buys 25 mss/year.** Query with or without published clips, or send complete ms. Length: 500-2,000 words. **Pays $50-150 for assigned articles; $15-75 for unsolicited articles.** "In addition to normal payment, writers receive 4 copies of issue containing their article." Sometimes pays expenses of writers on assignment.

Reprints: Occasionally accepts previously published submissions. Send tearsheet of article and information about when and where the article previously appeared. Pays 50% of amount paid for an original article.

Photos: Send photos with submission. Reviews transparencies and 4×6 prints. Offers no additional payment for photos accepted with ms. Model releases and identification of subjects required. Rights purchased depends on situation. Also looking for color transparencies for covers. Vertical format. Pays $50-150.

Columns/Departments: Kentucky travel, Kentucky crafts, Kentucky gardeners. **Buys 10-12 mss/year.** Query with published clips. Length: 500-750 words. **Pays $15-40.**

Tips: "We work mostly with unpublished writers who have a feel for Kentucky's people, places and events. Areas most open are little known places in Kentucky, unusual history and profiles of interesting, unusual Kentuckians."

$ $ KENTUCKY LIVING, P.O. Box 32170, Louisville KY 40232-0170. (502)451-2430. Fax: (502)459-1611. **Contact**: Paul Wesslund, editor. **Mostly freelance written.** Prefers to work with published/established writers. Monthly feature magazine primarily for Kentucky residents. Estab. 1948. Circ. 450,000. **Pays on acceptance.** Publishes ms on average of 4-12 months after acceptance. Byline given. Buys first serial rights for Kentucky. Submit seasonal material at least 6 months in advance. Accepts simultaneous submissions (if previously published and/or submitted outside Kentucky). Responds in 1 month. Sample copy for 9×12 SAE with 4 first-class stamps.

Nonfiction: Kentucky-related profiles (people, places or events), recreation, travel, leisure, lifestyle articles, book excerpts. **Buys 18-24 mss/year.** Query or send complete ms. **Pays $75-125** for "short" features (600-800 words) used in section known as "Commonwealths." For major articles (750-1,500 words) **pays $150-350**. Sometimes pays the expenses of writers on assignment.

● Ranked as one of the best markets for freelancers in *Writer's Yearbook* magazine's annual "Top 100 Markets," January 2000.

Reprints: Considers previously published submissions (if published outside Kentucky).

Photos: State availability of or send photos with submission or advise as to availability. Reviews color slides and prints. Identification of subjects required. Payment for photos included in payment for ms.

Tips: "The quality of writing and reporting (factual, objective, thorough) is considered in setting payment price. We prefer general interest pieces filled with quotes and anecdotes. Avoid boosterism. Well-researched, well-written feature articles are preferred. All articles must have a strong Kentucky connection."

N $ $ KENTUCKY MONTHLY, Vested Interest Publications, 213 St. Clair St., Frankfort KY 40601. (502)227-0053. Fax: (502)227-5009. E-mail: smvest@kentuckymonthly.com or membry@kentuckymonthly.com. Website: www.kentuckymonthly.com. Editor: Stephen M. Vest. **Contact**: Michael Embry, executive editor. **75% freelance written.** Monthly magazine. "We publish stories about Kentucky and Kentuckians, including those who live elsewhere." Estab. 1998. Circ. 30,000. Pays within 90 days of publication. Publishes ms an average of 3 months after acceptance. Byline given. Buys first North American serial rights. Editorial lead time 3 months. Submit seasonal material 4 months in advance. Accepts queries by mail, e-mail, fax. Accepts simultaneous submissions. Responds in 2 weeks to queries; 1 month to mss. Sample copy and writer's guidelines online at website.

Nonfiction: Book excerpts, general interest, historical/nostalgic, how-to, humor, interview/profile, photo feature, religious, travel, all with a Kentucky angle. **Buys 60 mss/year.** Query with or without published clips. Length: 300-2,000 words. **Pays $25-350 for assigned articles; $20-100 for unsolicited articles.**

Photos: State availability of photos with submission. Reviews negatives. Captions required. Buys all rights.

Fiction: Adventure, historical, mainstream, novel excerpts, all Kentucky-related stories. **Buys 4 mss/year.** Query with published clips. Length: 1,000-5,000 words. **Pays $50-100.**

Tips: "We're looking for more fashion, home and garden, first-person experience, mystery. Please read the magazine to get the flavor of what we're publishing each month. We accept articles via e-mail, fax and mail."

$ $ LOUISVILLE MAGAZINE, 137 W. Muhammad Ali Blvd., Suite 101, Louisville KY 40202-1438. (502)625-0100. Fax: (502)625-0109. E-mail: loumag@loumag.com. Website: www.louisville.com. **Contact:** Geri Miller, associate editor. **67% freelance written.** Monthly magazine "for and generally about people of the Louisville Metro area. Routinely covers arts, entertainment, business, sports, dining and fashion. Features range from news analysis/exposé to silly/funny commentary. We like lean, clean prose, crisp leads." Estab. 1950. Circ. 20,000. Publishes ms an average of 3 months after acceptance. Byline given. Offers 50% kill fee. Buys first North American serial rights. Editorial lead time 6 weeks. Submit seasonal material 6 months in advance. Accepts queries by mail, e-mail, fax. Responds in 3 months. Sample copy for $2.95 or on website.

Nonfiction: Essays, exposé, general interest, historical, interview/profile, photo feature. Special issues: City Guide (January); Kentucky Derby (April); EATS (September); Louisville Bride (December). **Buys 75 mss/year.** Query. Length: 500-3,500 words. **Pays $50-500 for assigned articles; $50-400 for unsolicited articles.**

Photos: State availability of photos with submissions. Reviews transparencies. Offers $25-50/photo. Identification of subjects required. Buys one-time rights.

Columns/Departments: End Insight (essays), 750 words. **Buys 10 mss/year.** Send complete ms. **Pays $100-150.**

Maine

[N] $ MAINE MAGAZINE, The Magazine of Maine's Treasures, County Wide Communications, Inc., 78 River St., Dover-Foxcroft ME 04426. (207)564-7548. Website: www.mainemagazine.com. Editor: Bob Bertu. **Contact:** Lester J. Reynolds, managing editor. **30% freelance written.** Monthly magazine and online covering Maine and its people. Estab. 1977. Circ. 16,000. **Pays on acceptance** or publication (negotiable). Byline sometimes given. Offers 100% kill fee. Buys electronic and all rights. Editorial lead time 9 months. Submit seasonal material 9 months in advance. Accepts queries by mail. Accepts simultaneous submissions. Responds in 30 days. Sample copy and writer's guidelines for $4 or online at website.

Nonfiction: Book excerpts, essays, how-to, humor, inspirational, interview/profile, new product, personal experience, photo feature, religious, travel. "First-person not interesting unless you're related to a rich and famous or unique Mainer." Query. Length: 1,000-2,000 words. **Pays $25-50.** Sometimes pays expenses of writers on assignment.

Reprints: Sometimes accepts previously published submissions.

Photos: State availability of photos with submission or send photos with submission. Reviews contact sheets, negatives and transparencies. Offers $15/photo or negotiates payment individually. Captions and identification of subjects required. Buys one-time or all rights.

Columns/Departments: "We are usually set here with Maine writers." **Buys 10 or fewer mss/year.** Query. **Pays $10-20.**

Poetry: **Buys 10 or fewer poems/year.** "Many are submitted by readers who love Maine." **Pays $5.**

Tips: "We're looking for work that is unique and about Maine—unusual people, places. We always want Stephen King interviews—good luck. We can give you his office address."

Maryland

[N] $ BALTIMORE ALTERNATIVE, Maryland's Award Winning Newsmagazine, 11 West Media, P.O. Box 2351, Baltimore MD 21203. Fax: (410)889-5665. E-mail: baltalt@aol.com. Website: www.baltalt.com. **Contact:** Paula Langguth Ryan, editor. **55% freelance written.** Biweekly tabloid covering gay, lesbian, bisexual, transgendered and the arts. "We cover national, local and international news, features, profiles of local artists, people involved with community, and queer musicians, actors, directors, dancers, artists, authors, etc. All stories must have a local angle—our well-read readers want in-depth, pithy articles." Estab. 1986. Circ. 40,000. **Pays on acceptance.** Publishes ms an average of 2 months after acceptance. Byline given. Offers 50% kill fee. Buys first or one-time rights. Editorial lead time 2 months. Submit seasonal material 3 months in advance. Accepts queries by mail, e-mail, fax. Accepts simultaneous submissions. Responds in 2 weeks to queries; 2 months to mss. Sample copy for $2 or on website. Writer's guidelines for #10 SASE.

Nonfiction: Exposé, general interest, interview/profile, opinion, personal experience, photo feature, religious, travel. Upcoming special issues include a holiday shopping guide. "No fiction, poetry, book reviews." **Buys 120 mss/year.** Query with published clips or send complete ms. Length: 300-4,000 words. **Pays $10-50.** Sometimes pays expenses of writers on assignment.
Reprints: Accepts previously published submissions (as long as not published in Baltimore area or D.C.).
Photos: Send photos with submission. Reviews contact sheets and negatives. Offers $20/photo. Captions, model releases and identification of subjects required. Buys one-time rights.
Columns/Departments: Viewpoints (opinion pieces), 900-1,000 words; Roundup (regional: MD, PA, DC), 300-600 words. **Buys 60 mss/year.** Send complete ms. **Pays $10-25.**
Fillers: Newsbreaks. **Buys 10/year.** Length: 100-500 words. **Pays $10-15.**
Tips: "Submit a strong query for a cover feature with clips; or send complete manuscript via e-mail or mail, with disc for columns. Be straightforward and to the point. Send a SASE. I'll call if I'm interested; follow up with a phone call in two weeks to make sure I received your material. It gets hectic here!"

$ $ $ $ BALTIMORE MAGAZINE, Inner Harbor East, 1000 Lancaster St., Suite 400, Baltimore MD 21202. (410)752-4200. Fax: (410)625-0280. E-mail: smarge@baltimoremag.com. Website: www.baltimoremag.com. **Contact:** Margaret Guroff, managing editor. **50-60% freelance written.** Monthly magazine. "Pieces must address an educated, active, affluent reader and must have a very strong Baltimore angle." Estab. 1907. Circ. 57,000. Pays within 60 days of acceptance. Byline given. Offers 30% kill fee. Buys first rights in all media. Submit seasonal material 4 months in advance. Accepts queries by mail, e-mail. Responds in 2 months to queries; 2 weeks to assigned mss; 3 months to unsolicited mss. Sample copy for $4.45. Writer's guidelines for #10 SASE.
Nonfiction: Book excerpt (Baltimore subject or author), essays, exposé, humor, interview/profile (w/Baltimorean), personal experience, photo feature, travel (local and regional to Maryland *only*). "Nothing that lacks a strong Baltimore focus or angle." Query by mail with published clips or send complete ms. Length: 1,000-3,000 words. **Pays $25-2,500 for assigned articles; $25-500 for unsolicited articles.** Sometimes pays expenses of writers on assignment.
Columns/Departments: Hot Shot, Health, Education, Sports. Length: 1,000-1,500 words. Query with published clips. "These shorter pieces are the best places to break into the magazine."
Tips: "Writers who live in the Baltimore area can send résumé and published clips to be considered for first assignment. Must show an understanding of writing that is suitable to an educated magazine reader and show ability to write with authority, describe scenes, help reader experience the subject. Too many writers send us newspaper-style articles. We are seeking: 1) *Human interest features*—strong, even dramatic profiles of Baltimoreans of interest to our readers. 2) *First-person accounts* of experience in Baltimore, or experiences of a Baltimore resident. 3) *Consumer*—according to our editorial needs, and with Baltimore sources. Writers new to us have most success with small humorous stories and 1,000-word personal essays that exhibit risky, original thought."

N CHESAPEAKE LIFE MAGAZINE, Lund Media Ventures, Ltd., 8258 Veterans Highway, Suite 19B, Millersville MD 21108. (410)729-9908. Fax: (410)729-8870. E-mail: cheslife@toad.net. Website: www.chesapeakelifemag.com. **Contact:** Kessler Burnett, editor. **99% freelance written.** Bimonthly magazine covering restaurant reviews, travel, book reviews, health, business, regional calendar of events, feature articles, gardening, sailing. "*Chesapeake Life* is a regional magazine covering the Chesapeake regions of Maryland, Virginia and Southern Delaware." Estab. 1995. Circ. 85,000. Pays on publication. Byline given. Buys North American serial rights. Editorial lead time 2 months. Accepts queries by mail, e-mail, fax, phone. Writer's guidelines free.
Nonfiction: Book excerpts, essays, general interest, historical/nostalgic, how-to, humor, interview/profile, personal experience, photo feature, travel. Query with published clips. Length: open.
Photos: Send photos with submission. Negotiates payment individually. Buys one-time rights.

Massachusetts

N BOSTON GLOBE MAGAZINE, *Boston Globe*, P.O. Box 2378, Boston MA 02107. (617)929-2955. Website: www.globe.com/globe/magazine. **Contact:** Nick King, editor-in-chief. Assistant Editors: Cathe Foster, Jan Freeman. **50% freelance written.** Weekly magazine. Circ. 805,099. Pays on publication. Publishes ms an average of 2 months after acceptance. Buys first serial rights. Editorial lead time 2 months. Submit seasonal material 3 months in advance. Responds in 2 months. Sample copy for 9×12 SAE with 2 first-class stamps.
Nonfiction: Exposé (variety of issues including political, economic, scientific, medical and the arts), interview (not Q&A), profile, book excerpts (first serial rights only). No travelogs or poetry. **Buys up to 100 mss/year.** Query; SASE must be included with ms or queries for return. Length: 2,500-5,000 words. Payment negotiable.
Photos: Purchased with accompanying ms or on assignment. Reviews contact sheets. Pays standard rates according to size used. Captions required.

$ $ $ $ BOSTON MAGAZINE, 300 Massachusetts Ave., Boston MA 02115. (617)262-9700. Fax: (617)267-1774. Website: www.bostonmagazine.com. Editor: Craig Unger. **Contact:** Erika Blauck, editorial assistant. **10% freelance written.** Monthly magazine covering the city of Boston. Estab. 1972. Circ. 125,000. Pays on publication. Publishes ms an average of 3 months after acceptance. Byline given. Offers 20% kill fee. Buys first North American serial rights. Editorial lead time 2 months. Submit seasonal material 4 months in advance. Accepts queries by mail, fax. Responds in 6 weeks to queries. Writer's guidelines for SASE.

Nonfiction: Book excerpts, exposé, general interest, interview/profile, politics, crime, trends, fashion. **Buys 20 mss/year.** Query. *No unsolicited mss.* Length: 1,200-12,000 words. Sometimes pays expenses of writers on assignment.

Photos: State availability of photos with submissions. Negotiates payment individually. Buys one-time rights.

Columns/Departments: Dining, Finance, City Life, Personal Style, Politics, Ivory Tower, Media, Wine, Boston Inc., Books, Theatre, Music. Query.

Tips: "Read *Boston*, and pay attention to the types of stories we use. Suggest which column/department your story might best fit, and keep you focus on the city and its environs. We like a strong narrative style, with a slightly 'edgy' feel—we rarely do 'remember when' stories. Think *city* magazine."

$ $ PROVINCETOWN ARTS, Provincetown Arts, Inc., 650 Commercial St., Provincetown MA 02657. (508)487-3167. Fax: (508)487-8634. Website: www.capecodaccess.com. **Contact:** Christopher Busa, editor. **90% freelance written.** Annual magazine for contemporary art and writing. "*Provincetown Arts* focuses broadly on the artists and writers who inhabit or visit the Lower Cape, and seeks to stimulate creative activity and enhance public awareness of the cultural life of the nation's oldest continuous art colony. Drawing upon a 75-year tradition rich in visual art, literature and theater, *Provincetown Arts* offers a unique blend of interviews, fiction, visual features, reviews, reporting and poetry." Estab. 1985. Circ. 8,000. Pays on publication. Publishes ms an average of 4 months after acceptance. Offers 50% kill fee. Buys one-time and second serial (reprint) rights. Editorial lead time 6 months. Submit seasonal material 6 months in advance. Responds in 3 weeks to queries; 2 months to mss. Sample copy for $10. Writer's guidelines for #10 SASE.

Nonfiction: Book excerpts, essays, humor, interview/profile. **Buys 40 mss/year.** Send complete ms. Length: 1,500-4,000 words. **Pays $150 minimum for assigned articles; $125 minimum for unsolicited articles.**

Photos: Send photos with submission. Reviews 8×10 prints. Offers $20-100/photo. Identification of subjects required. Buys one-time rights.

Fiction: Mainstream. Also publishes novel excerpts. **Buys 7 mss/year.** Send complete ms. Length: 500-5,000 words. **Pays $75-300.**

Poetry: Buys 25 poems/year. Submit maximum 3 poems. **Pays $25-150.**

N $ $ WORCESTER MAGAZINE, 172 Shrewsbury St., Worcester MA 01604-4636. (508)755-8004. Fax: (508)755-4734. E-mail: 75662.1176@compuserve.com. **Contact:** Martha M. Akstin, managing editor. **10% freelance written.** Weekly tabloid emphasizing the central Massachusetts region. Estab. 1976. Circ. 40,000. Pays on publication. Publishes ms an average of 3 weeks after acceptance. Byline given. Buys all rights. Submit seasonal material 2 months in advance. Does not respond to unsolicited material.

Nonfiction: Exposé (area government, corporate), how-to (concerning the area, homes, vacations), interview (local), personal experience, opinion (local), photo feature. "We are interested in any piece with a local angle." **Buys 75 mss/year.** Length: 500-1,500 words. **Pays $35-250.**

Michigan

$ $ $ ANN ARBOR OBSERVER, Ann Arbor Observer Company, 201 E. Catherine, Ann Arbor MI 48104. Fax: (734)769-3375. E-mail: hilton@aaobserver.com. Website: www.arborweb.com. **Contact:** John Hilton, editor. **50% freelance written.** Works with a small number of new/unpublished writers each year. Monthly magazine featuring people and events in Ann Arbor. "We depend heavily on freelancers and we're always glad to talk to new ones. We look for the intelligence and judgment to fully explore complex people and situations, and the ability to convey what makes them interesting. We've found that professional writing experience is not a good predictor of success in writing for the *Observer*. So don't let lack of experience deter you. Writing for the *Observer* is, however, a demanding job. Our readers range from U-M faculty members to hourly workers at GT Products. That means articles have to be both accurate and accessible." Estab. 1976. Circ. 62,000. Pays on publication. Publishes ms an average of 2 months after acceptance. Byline given. Accepts queries by mail, e-mail. Responds in 3 weeks to queries; several months to mss. Sample copy for 12½×15 SAE with $3 postage. Writer's guidelines for #10 SASE.

Nonfiction: Historical, investigative features, profiles, brief vignettes. Must pertain to Ann Arbor. **Buys 75 mss/year.** Length: 100-7,000 words. **Pays up to $1,000/article.** Sometimes pays expenses of writers on assignment.

Columns/Departments: Inside Ann Arbor (short, interesting tidbits), 300-500 words. **Pays $125.** Around Town (unusual, compelling ancedotes), 750-1,500 words. **Pays $150-200.**

Tips: "If you have an idea for a story, write a 100-200-word description telling us why the story is interesting. We are open most to intelligent, insightful features of up to 5,000 words about interesting aspects of life in Ann Arbor."

$ HOUR DETROIT, Hour Media LLC, 117 W. Third St., Royal Oak MI 48067. (248)691-1800. Fax: (248)691-4531. E-mail: rbohy@hourdetroit.com Managing Editor: George Bulanda. Senior Editor: Rebecca Powers. **Contact:** Ric Bohy, editor. **50% freelance written.** Monthly "general interest/lifestyle magazine aimed at a middle- to upper-

income readership aged 17-70." Estab. 1996. Circ. 45,000. **Pays on acceptance**. Publishes ms an average of 2 months after acceptance. Byline given. Offers 30% kill fee. Buys first North American serial rights. Editorial lead time minimum 1½ months. Submit seasonal material 12 months in advance. Accepts queries by mail, e-mail, fax. Sample copy for $6.
Nonfiction: Book excerpts, exposé, general interest, historical/nostalgic, interview/profile, new product, photo feature, technical, travel. **Buys 150 mss/year**. Query with published clips. Length: 300-2,500 words. Sometimes pays expenses of writers on assignment.
Photos: State availability of photos with submission.

N $ $ TRAVERSE, Northern Michigan's Magazine, Prism Publications, 148 E. Front St., Traverse City MI 49684. Fax: (231)941-8391. E-mail: traverse@traversemagazine.com. Website: www.traversemagazine.com. **Contact:** Jeff Smith, editor. **20% freelance written.** Monthly magazine covering northern Michigan life. "*Traverse* is a celebration of the life and environment of northern Michigan." Estab. 1981. Circ. 30,000. **Pays on acceptance.** Byline given. Offers 10% kill fee. Buys first North American serial rights. Editorial lead time 1 year. Submit seasonal material 1 year in advance. Accepts queries by mail, e-mail. Accepts simultaneous submissions. Responds in 2 months. Sample copy for $3. Writer's guidelines for #10 SASE.
Nonfiction: Book excerpts, essays, general interest, historical/nostalgic, humor, interview/profile, personal experience, photo feature, travel. No fiction or poetry. **Buys 24 mss/year.** Query with published clips or send complete ms. Length: 1,000-3,200 words. **Pays $150-500.** Sometimes pays expenses of writers on assignment.
Reprints: Accepts previously published submissions.
Photos: State availability of photos with submission. Negotiates payment individually. Buys one-time rights.
Columns/Departments: Up in Michigan Reflection (essays about northern Michigan); Reflection on Home (essays about northern homes), both 700 words. **Buys 18 mss/year.** Query with published clips or send complete ms. **Pays $100-200.**
Tips: "When shaping an article for us, consider first that it must be strongly rooted in our region. The lack of this foundation element is one of the biggest reasons for our rejecting material. If you send us a piece about peaches, even if it does an admirable job of relaying the history of peaches, their medicinal qualities, their nutritional magnificence and so on, we are likely to reject if it doesn't include local farms as a reference point. We want sidebars and extended captions designed to bring in a reader not enticed by the main subject. Primarily we cover the Northwest Michigan counties of Antrim, Benzie, Charlevoix, Crawford, Emmet, Grand Traverse, Leelanau, Manistee, Otsego, Cheboygan and Mackinac. We have begun to venture beyond our traditional turf, however, and are periodically running pieces based in the eastern Lower Peninsula and the eastern Upper Peninsula. We are willing to look farther west in the Upper Peninsula if the topic has broad appeal. General categories of interest include nature and the environment, regional culture, personalities, the arts (visual, performing, literary), crafts, food & dining, homes, history and outdoor activities (e.g., fishing, golf, skiing, boating, biking, hiking, birding, gardening). We are keenly interested in environmental and land-use issues but seldom use material dealing with such issues as health care, education, social services, criminal justice and local politics. We use service pieces and a small number of how-to pieces, mostly focused on small projects for the home or yard. Also, we value research. We need articles built with information. Many of the pieces we reject use writing style to fill in for information voids. Style and voice are strongest when used as vehicles for sound research."

Minnesota

N ☆ $ $ LAKE COUNTRY JOURNAL MAGAZINE, Evergreen Press of Brainerd, 1863 Design Dr., Baxter MN 56425. Fax: (218)825-7816. E-mail: info@lakecountryjournal.com. Website: www.lakecountryjournal.com. Contributing Editor: Linda Henry. **Contact:** Jodi Schwen, editor. **90% freelance written.** Bimonthly magazine covering central Minnesota's lake country. "We target a specific geographical niche in central Minnesota. The writer must be familiar with our area. We promote positive family values, foster a sense of community, increase appreciation for our natural and cultural environments, and provide ideas for enhancing the quality of our lives." Estab. 1996. Circ. 14,500. Pays on publication. Publishes ms an average of 6 months after acceptance. Byline given. Offers 25% kill fee. Buys first North American serial, second serial (reprint) and electronic rights. Editorial lead time 1 year. Submit seasonal material 1 year in advance. Accepts queries by mail, e-mail. Responds in 2 months to queries; 3 months to mss. Sample copy for $5.
Nonfiction: Essays, general interest, how-to, humor, interview/profile, personal experience, photo feature. "No articles that come from writers who are not familiar with our target geographical location." **Buys 30 mss/year.** Query with or without published clips. Length: 1,000-1,500 words. **Pays $100-175.** Sometimes pays expenses of writers on assignment.
Reprints: Accepts previously published submissions.
Photos: State availability of photos with submission. Reviews transparencies. Negotiates payment individually. Model releases and identification of subjects required. Buys one-time rights.
Columns/Departments: Profile-People from Lake Country, 800 words; Essay, 800 words; Health (topics pertinent to central Minnesota living), 500 words; Family Fun, 500 words. **Buys 40 mss/year.** Query with published clips. **Pays $50-75.**
Fiction: Adventure, humorous, mainstream, slice-of-life vignettes, literary, also family fiction appropriate to Lake Country and seasonal fiction. **Buys 6 mss/year.** Send complete ms. Length: 1,500 words. **Pays $100-175.**

Poetry: Free verse. "Never use rhyming verse, avant-garde, experimental, etc." **Buys 20 poems/year.** Submit maximum 4 poems. Length: 8-32 lines. **Pays $25.**

Fillers: Anecdotes, short humor. **Buys 20/year.** Length: 100-500 words. **Pays $25.**

Tips: "Most of the people who will read your articles live in the north central Minnesota lakes area. All have some significant attachment to the area. We have readers of various ages, backgrounds, and lifestyles. After reading your article, we hope to have a deeper understanding of some aspect of our community, our environment, ourselves, or humanity in general. Tell us something new. Show us something we didn't see before. Help us grasp the significance of your topic. Use analogies, allusions, and other literary techniques to add color to your writing. Add breadth by making the subject relevant to all readers—especially those who aren't already interested in your subject. Add depth by connecting your subject with timeless insights. If you can do this without getting sappy or didactic or wordy or dull, we're looking for you."

$ $LAKE SUPERIOR MAGAZINE, Lake Superior Port Cities, Inc., P.O. Box 16417, Duluth MN 55816-0417. (218)722-5002. Fax: (218)722-4096. E-mail: edit@lakesuperior.com. Website: www.lakesuperior.com. Editor: Paul L. Hayden. **Contact:** Konnie LeMay, managing editor. **60% freelance written.** Works with a small number of new/unpublished writers each year. Bimonthly regional magazine covering contemporary and historic people, places and current events around Lake Superior. Estab. 1979. Circ. 20,000. Pays on publication. Publishes ms an average of 10 months after acceptance. Byline given. Offers $25 kill fee. Buys first North American serial and some second rights. Submit seasonal material 1 year in advance. Accepts queries by mail, e-mail (please include phone number and address with e-mail queries.) Responds in 3 months. Sample copy for $3.95 and 5 first-class stamps. Writer's guidelines for #10 SASE.

Nonfiction: Book excerpts, general interest, historic/nostalgic, humor, interview/profile (local), personal experience, photo feature (local), travel (local), city profiles, regional business, some investigative. **Buys 45 mss/year.** Query with published clips. Length: 300-2,200 words. **Pays $60-600.** Sometimes pays the expenses of writers on assignment.

Photos: "Quality photography is our hallmark." Send photos with submission. Reviews contact sheets, 2×2 and larger transparencies, 4×5 prints. Offers $20 for b&w and $40 for color; $125 for covers. Captions, model releases, identification of subjects required.

Columns/Departments: Current events and things to do (for Events Calendar section), less than 300 words; Around The Circle (media reviews; short pieces on Lake Superior; Great Lakes environmental issues; themes, letters and short pieces on events and highlights of the Lake Superior Region); I Remember (nostalgic lake-specific pieces), up to 1,100 words; Life Lines (single personality profile with photography), up to 900 words. Other headings include Destinations, Nature, Wilderness Living, Heritage, Shipwreck, Chronicle, Lake Superior's Own, House for Sale. **Buys 20 mss/year.** Query with published clips. **Pays $60-90.**

Fiction: Ethnic, historic, humorous, mainstream, novel excerpts, slice-of-life vignettes, ghost stories. Must be targeted regionally. **Buys 2-3 mss/year.** Query with published clips. Length: 300-2,500 words. **Pays $1-125.**

Tips: "Well-researched queries are attended to. We actively seek queries from writers in Lake Superior communities. We prefer manuscripts to queries. Provide enough information on why the subject is important to the region and our readers, or why and how something is unique. We want details. The writer must have a thorough knowledge of the subject and how it relates to our region. We prefer a fresh, unused approach to the subject which provides the reader with an emotional involvement. Almost all of our articles feature quality photography, color or black and white. It is a prerequisite of all nonfiction. All submissions should include a *short* biography of author/photographer; mug shot sometimes used. Blanket submissions need not apply."

$ $MINNESOTA MONTHLY, 10 S. Fifth St., Suite 1000, Minneapolis MN 55402. Fax: (612)371-5801. E-mail: phnettleton@mnmo.com. Website: www.mnmo.com. **Contact:** Pamela Hill Nettleton, editor. **50% freelance written.** "*Minnesota Monthly* is a regional lifestyle publication written for a sophisticated, well-educated audience living in the Twin Cities area and in greater Minnesota." Estab. 1967. Circ. 80,000. **Pays on acceptance.** Accepts queries by mail, e-mail, fax. Writer's guidelines for SASE.

Nonfiction: Regional news and events, issues, services, places, people. "We want exciting, excellent, compelling writing." Query with résumé, published clips and SASE. Length: 1,000-4,000 words. Pay negotiable.

Columns/Departments: Portrait (photo-driven profile), 360 words; Just Asking (interview), 900 words; Midwest Traveler, 950-2,000 words; Diversions (travel piece on a day trip), 275 words; Postcards (chatty notes from Midwest towns), 300 words; Journey (diary/journal of a life-changing experience), 2,000 words. Query with résumé, published clips and SASE. Pay negotiable.

Tips: "Our readers are bright, artsy and involved in their communities. Writing should reflect that. Stories must all have a Minnesota angle. If you can write well, try us!"

Mississippi

$COAST MAGAZINE, Ship Island Holding Co., P.O. Box 1209, Gulfport MS 39502. (228)594-0004. Fax: (228)594-0074. **Contact:** Carla Arsaga, editor. **20% freelance written.** Bimonthly magazine. "We describe ourselves as a lifestyle magazine." Estab. 1993. Circ. 15,000. Pays on publication. Publishes ms an average of 4 months after acceptance. Byline given. Offers $25 kill fee. Buys first North American serial rights. Editorial lead time 6 months. Writer's guidelines for #10 SASE.

Nonfiction: General interest, historical/nostalgic, interview/profile, photo feature. All content is related to the Mississippi gulf coast. **Buys 6 mss/year.** Query by mail only with published clips. **Pays $25-150.**

Photos: Transparencies preferred. Negotiates payment individually. Captions, model releases, identification of subjects required. Buys all rights. Does not return unsolicited material.

Columns/Departments: Hot Shots (interesting people), 400 words; Art Scene (local artists), 750 words; Reflections (historical), 1,200 words. **Buys 6 mss/year.** Query with published clips. **Pays $25-75.**

Tips: "Being familiar with *Coast Magazine* and its readership is a must. Freelancers should send the editor a cover letter that is indicative of his or her writing style along with strong writing samples."

$ $ MISSISSIPPI MAGAZINE, DownHome Publications, 5 Lakeland Circle, Jackson MS 39216. Fax: (601)982-8447. **Contact:** Jane Alexander, editor. **90% freelance written.** Bimonthly magazine covering Mississippi—the state and its lifestyles. "We are interested in positive stories reflecting Mississippi's rich traditions and heritage, and focusing on the contributions the state and its natives have made to the arts, literature and culture. In each issue we showcase homes and gardens, lifestyle issues, food, business, design, art and more." Estab. 1981. Circ. 30,000. Pays on publication. Publishes ms an average of 6 months after acceptance. Byline given. Offers 50% kill fee. Buys first North American serial rights. Editorial lead time 6 months. Submit seasonal material 1 year in advance. Accepts queries by mail, fax. Accepts simultaneous submissions. Responds in 3 months. Sample copy and writer's guidelines for SASE.

Nonfiction: General interest, historical/nostalgic, how-to (home decor), interview/profile, personal experience, travel. "No opinion, political, essay, book reviews, exposé." **Buys 15 mss/year.** Query. Length: 900-1,800 words. **Pays $150-350 for assigned articles; $75-200 for unsolicited articles.**

Photos: Send photos with submission. Reviews transparencies and prints. Negotiates payment individually. Captions, model releases and identification of subjects preferred. Buys one-time rights.

Columns/Departments: Business (positive stories about old, new or innovative people or products), 1,000 words; People (interviews and profiles of famous Mississippi natives or residents), 1,200 words. **Buys 6 mss/year.** Query. **Pays $150-300.**

Missouri

$ $ FOCUS/KANSAS CITY, Communications Publishing Group, 3100 Broadway, #660, Kansas City MO 64111. (816)960-1988. Fax: (816)960-1989. **Contact:** Jeanine Meiers, editor. **80% freelance written.** Quarterly magazine covering professional and business development. "Positive how-to, motivational profiles." Estab. 1994. Circ. 30,000. Pays on publication. Publishes ms an average of 6 months after acceptance. Byline given. Buys first rights. Accepts simultaneous submissions. Responds in 1 month. Sample copy for $3. Writer's guidelines for #10 SASE.

Nonfiction: Book excerpts, general interest, how-to, humor, inspirational, interview/profile, personal experience, photo feature, technical, travel. **Buys 15 mss/year.** Length: 750-2,000 words. **Pays $150-400 for assigned articles; 12¢/word for unsolicited articles.** Sometimes pays expenses of writers on assignment.

Photos: State availability of photos with submission. Reviews transparencies. Offers $20-25/photo. Captions, model releases and identification of subjects required. Buys all rights.

Columns/Departments: Profiles of Achievement (regional Kansas Citians), 500-1,500 words. **Buys 30 mss/year. Pays 10¢/word.**

Fiction: Adventure, ethnic, historical, humorous, mainstream, slice-of-life vignettes. **Buys 3 mss/year.** Length: 25-250 words. **Pays $25-100.**

Fillers: Anecdotes, facts, gags to be illustrated by cartoonist, newsbreaks, short humor. **Buys 10/year.** Length: 25-250 words. **Pays $25-100.**

Tips: "For new writers—send complete manuscript, double-spaced; clean copy only. If available, send clips of previously published work and résumé. Should state when available to write. Include on first page of manuscript: name, address, phone, social security number, word count and include SASE."

$ $ $ KANSAS CITY MAGAZINE, 118 Southwest Blvd., 3rd Floor, Kansas City MO 64108. (816)421-4111. Fax: (816)936-0509. Website: www.kcmag.com. **Contact:** Zim Loy, editor. **75% freelance written.** Magazine published 10 times/year. "Our mission is to celebrate living in Kansas City. We are a consumer lifestyle/general interest magazine focused on Kansas City, its people and places." Estab. 1994. Circ. 31,000. **Pays on acceptance.** Publishes ms an average of 3 months after acceptance. Byline given. Offers 10% kill fee. Buys first North American serial rights. Editorial lead time 4 months. Submit seasonal material 6 months in advance. Accepts queries by mail, e-mail, fax. Accepts simultaneous submissions. Sample copy for 8½×11 SAE or on website.

Nonfiction: Exposé, general interest, interview/profile, photo feature. **Buys 15-20 mss/year.** Query with published clips. Length: 250-3,000 words.

Photos: Negotiates payment individually. Buys one-time rights.

Columns/Departments: Entertainment (Kansas City only), 1,000 words; Food (Kansas City food and restaurants only), 1,000 words. **Buys 10 mss/year.** Query with published clips. **Pays $200-500.**

$ RIVER HILLS TRAVELER, Todd Publishing, Route 4, Box 4396, Piedmont MO 63957. (573)223-7143. Fax: (573)223-2117. E-mail: btodd@semo.net. Website: www.deepozarks.com. **Contact**: Bob Todd, editor. **50% freelance written.** Monthly tabloid covering "outdoor sports and nature in the southeast quarter of Missouri, the east and central Ozarks. Topics like those in *Field & Stream* and *National Geographic*." Estab. 1973. Circ. 7,500. Pays on publication. Publishes ms an average of 2 months after acceptance. Byline given. Buys one-time rights. Editorial lead time 2 months. Submit seasonal material 1 year in advance. Accepts queries by mail, e-mail, fax. Accepts simultaneous submissions. Responds in 2 months. Sample copy and writer's guidelines for SAE or on website.

Nonfiction: Historical/nostalgic, how-to, humor, opinion, personal experience ("Me and Joe"), photo feature, technical, travel. "No stories about other geographic areas." **Buys 80 mss/year.** Query with writing samples. Length: 1,500 word maximum. **Pays $15-50.** Sometimes pays expenses of writers on assignment.

Reprints: Send typed ms with rights for sale noted and information about when and where the article previously appeared.

Photos: Send photos with submission. Negotiates payment individually. Pays $25 for covers. Buys one-time rights.

■ The online magazine carries original content not found in the print edition and includes writer's guidelines. Contact: Bob Todd, online editor.

Tips: "We are a 'poor man's' *Field & Stream* and *National Geographic*—about the eastern Missouri Ozarks. We prefer stories that relate an adventure that causes a reader to relive an adventure of his own or consider embarking on a similar adventure. Think of an adventure in camping or cooking, not just fishing and hunting. How-to is great, but not simple instructions. We encourage good first-person reporting."

$ $ SPRINGFIELD! MAGAZINE, Springfield Communications Inc., P.O. Box 4749, Springfield MO 65808-4749. (417)882-4917. **Contact**: Robert C. Glazier, editor. **85% freelance written.** Eager to work with a small number of new/unpublished writers each year. "This is an extremely local and provincial monthly magazine. No *general* interest articles." Estab. 1979. Circ. 10,000. Pays on publication. Publishes ms from 3 months to 3 years after acceptance. Byline given. Buys first serial rights. Submit seasonal material 1 year in advance. Responds in 3 months to queries; 2 weeks to queries with Springfield hook; 6 months to mss. Sample copy for $5.30 and 9½×12½ SAE.

O— Break in with short humorous pieces with a local angle.

Nonfiction: Book excerpts (Springfield authors only), exposé (local topics only), historical/nostalgic (top priority but must be local history), how-to, humor, interview/profile (needs more of females than males), personal experience, photo feature, travel (1 page/month). Local interest *only*; no material that could appeal to other magazines elsewhere. **Buys 150 mss/year.** Query with published clips by mail only or send complete ms with SASE. Length: 500-3,000 words. **Pays $35-250.**

Photos: Send photos with query or ms. Reviews b&w and color contact sheets, 4×6 color prints, 5×7 b&w prints. Pays $5-35 for b&w, $10-50 for color. Captions, model releases, identification of subjects required. Buys one-time rights. "Needs more photo features of a nostalgic bent."

Columns/Departments: Buys 250 mss/year. Query by mail only or send complete ms. Length varies, usually 500-2,500 words.

Tips: "We prefer writers read eight or ten copies of our magazine prior to submitting any material for our consideration. The magazine's greatest need is for features which comment on these times in Springfield. We are overstocked with nostalgic pieces right now. We also need profiles about young women and men of distinction."

Montana

$ $ MONTANA MAGAZINE, Lee Enterprises, P.O. Box 5630, Helena MT 59604-5630. (406)443-2842. Fax: (406)443-5480. E-mail: editor@montanamagazine.com. Website: www.montanamagazine.com. **Contact**: Beverly R. Magley, editor. **90% freelance written.** Bimonthly "strictly Montana-oriented magazine that features community profiles, contemporary issues, wildlife and natural history, travel pieces." Estab. 1970. Circ. 40,000. Publishes ms an average of 1 year after acceptance. Byline given. Offers $50-100 kill fee on assigned stories only. Buys one-time rights. Submit seasonal material at least 12 months in advance. Accepts queries by mail, e-mail, fax. Accepts simultaneous submissions. Responds in 6 months. Sample copy for $5 or on website. Guidelines for #10 SAE or on website.

Nonfiction: Essays, general interest, interview/profile, photo feature, travel. Special features on summer and winter destination points. Query by September for summer material; March for winter material. No 'me and Joe' hiking and hunting tales; no blood-and-guts hunting stories; no poetry; no fiction; no sentimental essays. **Buys 30 mss/year.** Query with samples and SASE. Length: 300-3,000 words. **Pays 15¢/word for articles.** Sometimes pays the expenses of writers on assignment.

Reprints: Send information about when and where the article previously appeared. Pays 50% of amount paid for an original article.

Photos: Send photos with submission. Reviews contact sheets, 35mm or larger format transparencies, 5×7 prints. Offers additional payment for photos accepted with ms. Captions, model releases, identification of subjects required. Buys one-time rights.

Columns/Departments: Memories (reminisces of early-day Montana life), 800-1,000 words; Outdoor Recreation, 1,500-2,000 words; Community Festivals, 500 words plus b&w or color photo. Humor, 800-1,000 words. Query with samples and SASE.

Tips: "We avoid commonly known topics so Montanans won't ho-hum through more of what they already know. If it's time to revisit a topic, we look for a unique slant."

Nevada

$ $ NEVADA MAGAZINE, 401 N. Carson St., Carson City NV 89701-4291. (775)687-5416. Fax: (775)687-6159. E-mail: editor@nevadamagazine.com. Website: www.nevadamagazine.com. Editor: David Moore. **Contact:** Carolyn Graham, associate editor. **50% freelance written.** Works with a small number of new/unpublished writers each year. Bimonthly magazine published by the state of Nevada to promote tourism. Estab. 1936. Circ. 90,000. Pays on publication. Publishes ms an average of 8 months after acceptance. Byline given. Buys first North American serial rights. Submit seasonal material at least 6 months in advance. Accepts queries by mail, e-mail, fax, phone. Responds in 1 month. Sample copy for $1. Writer's guidelines for SASE.

O— Break in with shorter departments, rather than trying to tackle a big feature. Good bets are Dining Out, Recreation, Casinoland, Side Trips, and Roadside Attractions.

Nonfiction: Nevada topics only. Historical, nostalgia, photo feature, people profile, recreational, travel, think pieces. "We welcome stories and photos on speculation." Publishes nonfiction book excerpts. **Buys 40 unsolicited mss/year.** Submit complete ms or query. Length: 500-1,800 words. **Pays $50-500.**

Photos: Denise Barr, art director. Send photo material with accompanying ms. Pays $20-100 for color transparencies and glossy prints. Name, address and caption should appear on each photo or slide. Buys one-time rights.

Tips: "Keep in mind the magazine's purpose is to promote Nevada tourism. Keys to higher payments are quality and editing effort (more than length). Send cover letter; no photocopies. We look for a light, enthusiastic tone of voice without being too cute; articles bolstered by facts and thorough research; and unique angles on Nevada subjects."

New Hampshire

$ $ NEW HAMPSHIRE MAGAZINE, Network Publications, Inc., 100 Main St., Nashua NH 03060. Fax: (603)889-5557. E-mail: editor@nhmagazine.com. Website: www.nhmagazine.com. **Contact:** Rick Broussard, editor. **50% freelance written.** Monthly magazine devoted to New Hampshire. "We want stories written for, by and about the people of New Hampshire with emphasis on qualities that set us apart from other states. We promote business and economic development." Estab. 1986. Circ. 24,000. Pays on publication. Byline given. Offers 25% kill fee. Buys all rights. Editorial lead time 3 months. Submit seasonal material 3 months in advance. Query by mail, e-mail, fax. Accepts simultaneous submissions. Responds in 2 months to queries; 3 months to mss.

Nonfiction: Essays, general interest, historical/nostalgic, photo feature, business. **Buys 30 mss/year.** Query with published clips. Length: 800-2,000 words. **Pays $25-175.** Sometimes pays expenses of writers on assignment.

Photos: State availability of photos with submission. Offers no additional payment for photos accepted with ms. Captions, model releases, identification of subjects required. Rights purchased vary.

■ The online magazine carries original content not found in the print edition. Contact: Rick Broussard, online editor.

Tips: Network Publications publishes 1 monthly magazine entitled *New Hampshire Magazine* and a "specialty" publication called *Destination New Hampshire*. "In general, our articles deal with the people of New Hampshire—their lifestyles and interests. We also present localized stories about national and international issues, ideas and trends. We will only use stories that show our readers how these issues have an impact on their daily lives. We cover a wide range of topics, including healthcare, politics, law, real-life dramas, regional history, medical issues, business, careers, environmental issues, the arts, the outdoors, education, food, recreation, etc. Many of our readers are what we call 'The New Traditionalists'—aging Baby Boomers who have embraced solid American values and contemporary New Hampshire lifestyles."

New Jersey

$ $ ATLANTIC CITY MAGAZINE, P.O. Box 2100, Pleasantville NJ 08232-1924. (609)272-7900. Fax: (609)272-7910. E-mail: bergen@pressplus.com. **Contact:** Doug Bergen, editor. **80% freelance written.** Works with small number of new/unpublished writers each year. Monthly regional magazine covering issues pertinent to the Jersey Shore area. Estab. 1978. Circ. 50,000. Pays on publication. Publishes ms an average of 4 months after acceptance. Byline given. Buys one-time rights. Offers variable kill fee. Submit seasonal material 6 months in advance. Responds in 6 weeks. Sample copy for $3 and 9 × 12 SAE with 6 first-class stamps. Writer's guidelines for SASE.

Nonfiction: Entertainment, general interest, recreation, history, lifestyle, interview/profile, photo feature, trends. "No hard news or investigative pieces. No travel pieces or any article without a south Jersey shore area/Atlantic City slant." Query. Length: 100-3,000 words. **Pays $50-500 for assigned articles; $50-350 for unsolicited articles.** Sometimes pays the expenses of writers on assignment.

Photos: Send photos. Reviews contact sheets, negatives, 2¼ × 2¼ transparencies, 8 × 10 prints. Pay varies. Captions, model releases, identification of subjects required. Buys one-time rights.

Columns/Departments: Art, Gambling, Entertainment, Sports, Dining, History, Style, Real Estate. Query with published clips. Length: 500-2,000 words. **Pays $150-400.**

Tips: "Our readers are a broad base of local residents and visiting tourists. We need stories that will appeal to both audiences."

$ $ MONTAGE MAGAZINE, The Write Approach, P.O. Box 2, Allamuchy NJ 07820. (908)979-0400. Fax: (908)813-3201. E-mail: approach@goes.com. Website: www.montagemagazine.com. Executive Director: L.A. Popp. **Contact:** Candace Botha Popp, editor. **60% freelance written.** Quarterly magazine covering New Jersey living. "We are a lifestyle publication covering all aspects of living in New Jersey—travel, medical, dining, antiques, photography, health, fitness, pet care, celebrity profiles, and timely topics of interest to our readers." Estab. 1995. Circ. 30,000. Pays on publication. Publishes ms an average of 4 months after acceptance. Byline given. Offers 25% kill fee. Buys first, electronic or all rights. Editorial lead time 6 weeks. Submit seasonal material 4 months in advance. Accepts queries by mail, e-mail, fax. Accepts simultaneous submissions. Responds in 3 weeks to queries; 2 months to mss. Sample copy for $3.50 or on website. Writer's guidelines for #10 SASE or by e-mail.

   O➨ Break in by "focusing on interesting topics about northern New Jersey. Have contacts with New Jersey celebrities.

Nonfiction: General interest, historical/nostalgic, humor, inspirational, interview/profile, travel, medical, dining. No fiction, poetry, how to and anything morbid or sexually slanted. **Buys 40-50 mss/year.** Query with published clips. Length: 750-2,500 words. **Pays $275-450.**

Photos: State availability of or send photos with submission. Reviews 2×2 transparencies and 4×6 prints. Negotiates payment individually. Captions, model releases and identification of subjects required. Buys one-time or all rights (if assigned).

Columns/Departments: Susan Paulits, associate editor. "We currently have writers for all our columns. However, we are always open to queries and good ideas for future columns." **Buys 40-60 mss/year.** Query with published clips. **Pays $225-350.**

Fillers: Susan Paulits, associate editor. Facts, gags to be illustrated by cartoonist, short humor. **Buys 10/year.** Length: 100-250 words. **Pays $50-100.**

Tips: "Great grammar, proper punctuation and a sincere appreciation of the advantages of living in New Jersey will always interest the editorial staff. We are always looking for that unusual slant that spotlights a unique individual, a celebrity, an event or a topic of interest that is specific to New Jersey."

N $ $ $ $ NEW JERSEY MONTHLY, The Magazine of the Garden State, New Jersey Monthly LLC, 55 Park Place, P.O. Box 920, Morristown NJ 07963-0920. (973)539-8230. Fax: (973)538-2953. E-mail: editor@njmonthly.com. Website: www.njmonthly.com. Editor: Nancy Nusser. **Contact: Christopher Hann, senior editor. 75-80% freelance written.** Monthly magazine covering "almost anything that's New Jersey-related. We cover just about anything to do with New Jersey, from news, politics and sports to decorating trends and lifestyle issues. Our readership is well-educated, affluent, and on average our readers have lived in New Jersey twenty years or more." Estab. 1976. Circ. 95,000. Pays on completion of fact-checking. Publishes ms an average of 3 months after acceptance. Byline given. Offers 20% kill fee. Buys first North American serial rights. Editorial lead time 3 months. Submit seasonal material 6 months in advance. Accepts queries by mail, e-mail, fax, phone. Accepts simultaneous submissions. Responds in 2 months to queries; 1 month to mss. Writer's guidelines for $2.95.

   ● This magazine continues to look for strong investigative reporters with novelistic style and solid knowledge of New Jersey issues.

Nonfiction: Book excerpts, essays, exposé, general interest, historical, humor, interview/profile, personal experience, photo feature, travel (within New Jersey). "No experience pieces from people who used to live in New Jersey or general pieces that have no New Jersey angle." **Buys 90-100 mss/year.** Query with published magazine clips and SASE. Length: 1,200-3,500 words. **Pays $750-2,000.** Pays reasonable expenses of writers on assignment with prior approval.

Photos: State availability of photos with submission. Reviews transparencies and prints. Payment negotiated. Model releases and identification of subjects required. Buys one-time rights.

Columns/Departments: Exit Ramp (back page essay usually originating from personal experience but told in such a way that it tells a broader story of statewide interest), 1,200-1,400 words. **Buys 12 mss/year.** Query with published clips. **Pays $200-400.**

Fillers: Anecdotes. **Buys 12-15/year.** Length: 200-250 words. **Pays $100.**

Tips: "The best approach: Do your homework! Read the past year's issues to get an understanding of our well-written, well-researched articles that tell a tale from a well-established point of view."

$ $ NEW JERSEY OUTDOORS, New Jersey Department of Environmental Protection, P.O. Box 402, Trenton NJ 08625. (609)777-4182. Fax: (609)984-0583. E-mail: njo@dep.state.nj.us. Website: www.state.nj.us/dep/njo. **Contact:** Denise Damiano Mikics, editor. **75% freelance written.** Quarterly magazine highlighting New Jersey's natural and historic resources and activities related to them. Estab. 1950. Circ. 13,000. Pays on publication. Byline given. Buys one-time rights. Editorial lead time 1 year. Submit seasonal material 1 year in advance. Accepts queries by mail, e-mail, fax. Responds in 6 months. Sample copy for $4.25. Writer's guidelines for #10 SASE or on website.

Nonfiction: How-to, personal experience and general interest articles and photo features about the conservation and enjoyment of natural and historic resources (e.g., fishing, hunting, hiking, camping, skiing, boating, gardening, trips to/

activities in specific New Jersey locations). "*New Jersey Outdoors* is not interested in articles showing disregard for the environment or in items demonstrating unskilled people taking extraordinary risks." **Buys 30-40 mss/year.** Query with published clips. Length: 600-2,000 words. **Pays $100-450.** Sometimes pays expenses of writers on assignment.

Reprints: Rarely accepts previously published submissions. Send typed ms with rights for sale noted and information about when and where the article previously appeared. Pays up to 100% of amount paid for the original article.

Photos: State availability of photos with submission. Reviews duplicate transparencies and prints. Offers $20-125/photo. Buys one-time rights.

Tips: "*New Jersey Outdoors* generally publishes season-specific articles, planned a year in advance. Topics should be fresh, and stories should be accompanied by *great* photography. Articles and photos *must* relate to New Jersey. Also, we'd like to see more personal experience stories of enjoying New Jersey's outdoor and historic resources."

New Mexico

$ $ NEW MEXICO MAGAZINE, Lew Wallace Bldg., 495 Old Santa Fe Trail, Santa Fe NM 87501. (505)827-7447. Editor-in-Chief: Emily Drabanski. Editor: Jon Bowman. Senior Editor: Walter K. Lopez. Associate editor: Steve Larese. **Contact any editor. 70% freelance written.** Monthly magazine emphasizing New Mexico for a college-educated readership with above average income and interest in the Southwest. Estab. 1923. Circ. 125,000. **Pays on acceptance.** Publishes ms an average of 8 months to a year after acceptance. Buys first North American serial rights. Submit seasonal material 1 year in advance. Responds in 2 months. Sample copy for $3.95. Writer's guidelines for SASE.

Nonfiction: New Mexico subjects of interest to travelers. Historical, cultural, informational articles. "We are looking for more short, light and bright stories for the 'Asi Es Nuevo Mexico' section. Also, we are buying 12 mss per year for our Makin' Tracks series. No columns, cartoons, poetry or non-New Mexico subjects." **Buys 7-10 mss/issue.** Query by mail. with 3 published writing samples. No phone or fax queries. Length: 250-1,500 words. **Pays $100-600.**

Reprints: Rarely publishes reprints but sometimes publishes excerpts from novels and nonfiction books.

Photos: Purchased as portfolio or on assignment. Query or send contact sheet or transparencies to Art Director John Vaughan. Pays $50-80 for 8×10 b&w glossy prints; $50-150 for 35mm—prefers Kodachrome. Photos should be in plastic-pocketed viewing sheets. Captions and model releases required. Buys one-time rights.

Tips: "Your best bet is to write a fun, lively short feature (200-350 words) for our Asi Es Nuevo Mexico section or send a superb short (300 words) manuscript on a little-known person, event, aspect of history or place to see in New Mexico. Faulty research will ruin a writer's chances for the future. Good style, good grammar. No generalized odes to the state or the Southwest. No sentimentalized, paternalistic views of Indians or Hispanics. No glib, gimmicky 'travel brochure' writing. No first-person vacation stories. We're always looking for well-researched pieces on unusual aspects of New Mexico and lively writing."

New York

$ $ ADIRONDACK LIFE, P.O. Box 410, Jay NY 12941-0410. (518)946-2191. Fax: (518)946-7461. E-mail: aledit@primelink1.net. Website: www.adirondacklife.com. **Contact:** Elizabeth Folwell, editor or Galen Crane, managing editor. **70% freelance written.** Prefers to work with published/established writers. Emphasizes the Adirondack region and the North Country of New York State in articles concerning outdoor activities, history and natural history directly related to the Adirondacks. Publishes 8 issues/year, including special Annual Outdoor Guide. Estab. 1970. Circ. 50,000. Pays 45 days after acceptance. Publishes ms an average of 6 months after acceptance. Byline given. Buys first North American serial rights. Submit seasonal material 1 year in advance. Accepts queries by mail, e-mail, fax. Responds in 45 days. Sample copy for $3 and 9×12 SAE. Writer's guidelines for #10 SASE or on website.

○┐ "For new writers, the best way to break into the magazine is through departments."

Nonfiction: "*Adirondack Life* attempts to capture the unique flavor and ethos of the Adirondack mountains and North Country region through feature articles directly pertaining to the qualities of the area ." Special issues: Outdoors (May); Single-topic Collector's issue (September). **Buys 20-25 unsolicited mss/year.** Query with published clips. Length: 2,500-5,000 words. **Pays 25¢/word.** Sometimes pays expenses of writers on assignment.

Photos: All photos must have been taken in the Adirondacks. Each issue contains a photo feature. Purchased with or without ms or on assignment. All photos must be individually identified as to subject or locale and must bear photographer's name. Submit color transparencies or b&w prints. Pays $125 for full page, b&w or color; $300 for cover (color only, vertical in format). Credit line given.

Columns/Departments: Special Places (unique spots in the Adirondack Park); Watercraft; Barkeater (personal to political); Wilderness (environmental issues); Working (careers in the Adirondacks); Home; Yesteryears; Kitchen; Profile; Historic Preservation; Sporting Scene. Query with published clips. Length: 1,200-2,400 words. **Pays 25¢/word.**

Fiction: Considers first-serial novel excerpts in its subject matter and region.

Tips: "Do not send a personal essay about your meaningful moment in the mountains. We need factual pieces about regional history, sports, culture and business. We are looking for clear, concise, well-organized manuscripts that are strictly Adirondack in subject. Check back issues to be sure we haven't already covered your topic. Please do not send unsolicited manuscripts via e-mail."

N **$ $ $** AVENUE, 950 Third Ave., New York NY 10022. (212)758-9516. Fax: (212)758-7395. Editor-in-Chief: David Patrick Columbia. **Contact:** Stan Ballen, managing editor. **25% freelance written.** Monthly magazine covering New York art, fashion, restaurants; business, design and travel. "As *Avenue* is intended for readers on Manhattan's Upper East Side our subject matter is generally high end, and most pieces focus on a New York personality." Estab. 1976. Circ. 80,000. Pays 60 days after publication. Publishes ms an average of 2 months after acceptance. Byline given. Offers 15% kill fee. Buys all rights. Editorial lead time 3 months. Submit seasonal material 3 months in advance. Accepts queries by mail, fax. Sample copy free.

O⇥ Break in with memoir of life in New York or profiles of leading socialities.

Nonfiction: Essays, general interest, historical/nostalgic, humor, interview/profile, personal experience, travel. **Buys 30 mss/year.** Query with published clips. Length: 150-1,800 words. **Pays $150-1,500.** Sometimes pays expenses of writers on assignment.

Photos: State availability of photos with submission. Reviews prints. Negotiates payment individually. Model releases, identification of subjects required. Buys one-time rights.

Columns/Departments: Buys 30 mss/year. Query with published clips. **Pays $150.**

Tips: "Send submission by mail or fax after looking over a recent issue to familiarize yourself with our format."

$ $ $ BROOKLYN BRIDGE MAGAZINE, 388 Atlantic Ave., Brooklyn NY 11217-1703. (718)596-7400. E-mail: bbridge@mennen.tiac.net. Website: www.brooklynbridgemag.com. Editor: Melissa Ennen. **Contact:** Joe Fodor, senior editor. **50% freelance written.** Bimonthly magazine covering Brooklyn. Estab. 1995. Circ. 40,000. Pays on publication. Byline given. Offers 25% kill fee. Buys first North American serial rights. Editorial lead time 2 months. Submit seasonal material 3 months in advance. Accepts queries by mail, e-mail, phone. Responds in 1 week to queries; 1 month to mss. Sample copy for 9×11 SAE and $2.39 postage or on website.

O⇥ Break in with health and education stories, short items about arresting Brooklyn characters, investigative pieces and crime stories.

Nonfiction Essays, exposé, general interest, historical/nostalgic, interview/profile, personal experience, photo feature, Brooklyn's health, home and education. Must be related to Brooklyn. **Buys 100 mss/year.** Query with published clips. Length: 200-3,000 words. **Pays $100-1,000.** Sometimes pays expenses of writers on assignment.

Photos: Offers no additional payment for photos accepted with ms. Identification of subjects required. Acquires one-time rights.

Columns/Departments: Family, 1,250 words; Last Exit, 850 words; Street, 1,100 words. **Buys 24 mss/year.** Query with published clips or send complete ms. **Pays $250-500.**

N **$** BUFFALO SPREE MAGAZINE, David Laurence Publications, Inc., 5678 Main St., Buffalo NY 14221. (716)634-0820. Fax: (716)810-0075. E-mail: info@buffalospree.com. Website: www.buffalospree.com. Editor: Johanna Hall Van De Mark. **Contact:** Elizabeth Licata, editor. **90% freelance written.** Quarterly, consumer-oriented, city magazine. Estab. 1967. Circ. 25,000. Pays on publication. Publishes ms an average of 2 months after acceptance. Byline given. Buys first North American serial rights. Submit seasonal material 1 year in advance. Accepts queries by mail, e-mail, fax. Responds in 6 months to mss. Sample copy for $3.95 and 9×12 SAE with 9 first-class stamps.

Nonfiction: Interview/profile, issue-oriented features, humor, personal experience, arts, living, food, regional, travel. **Buys 5-10 mss/year.** Query with clips or send complete ms. Length: 1,000-2,000 words. **Pays $125-250.** "Most articles are assigned not unsolicited."

Tips: "Send a well-written, compelling query or an interesting topic, and *great* clips. We no longer regularly publish fiction or poetry."

N **$ $** CITY LIMITS, New York's Urban Affairs News Magazine, City Limits Community Information Service, 120 Wall St., 20th Floor, New York NY 10005. (212)479-3344. Fax: (212)344-6457. E-mail: cl@citylimits.org. Website: www.citylimits.org. **Contact:** Alyssa Katz, editor. **50% freelance written.** Monthly magazine covering urban politics and policy. "*City Limits* is a 25-year-old nonprofit magazine focusing on issues facing New York City and its neighborhoods, particularly low-income communities. The magazine is strongly committed to investigative journalism, in-depth policy analysis and hard-hitting profiles." Estab. 1976. Circ. 4,000. Pays on publication. Publishes ms an average of 3 months after acceptance. Byline given. Offers 50% kill fee. Buys first North American serial and second serial (reprint) rights. Editorial lead time 2 months. Accepts queries by mail, e-mail, fax. Accepts simultaneous submissions. Sample copy for $2.95. Writer's guidelines free.

Nonfiction: Book excerpts, exposé, humor, interview/profile, opinion, photo feature. No essays, polemics. **Buys 25 mss/year.** Query with published clips. Length: 400-3,500 words. **Pays $100-1,200 for assigned articles; $100-800 for unsolicited articles.** Sometimes pays expenses of writers on assignment.

Photos: State availability of photos with submission. Reviews contact sheets, negatives and transparencies. Offers $50-100/photo.

Columns/Departments: Cityview (opinion); Spare Change (humor); Book Review, all 800 words. **Buys 15 mss/year.** Query with published clips. **Pays $100-200.**

Tips: "*City Limits*' specialty is covering low-income communities. We want to know how the news of the day is going to affect neighborhoods—at the grassroots. Among the issues we're looking for stories about housing, health care, criminal justice, child welfare, education, economic development, welfare reform, politics and government."

$ $ $ $ NEW YORK MAGAZINE, Primedia Magazines, 444 Madison Ave., New York NY 10022. (212)508-0700. Website: www.newyorkmag.com. Editor: Caroline Miller. Managing Editor: Sarah Jewler. **Contact:** John Homans, executive editor. **25% freelance written.** Weekly magazine focusing on current events in the New York metropolitan area. Circ. 433,813. **Pays on acceptance.** Offers 25% kill fee. Buys first world serial and electronic rights. Submit seasonal material 2 months in advance. Responds in 1 month. Sample copy for $3.50 or on website. Writer's guidelines for SASE.
Nonfiction: New York-related journalism that covers lifestyle, politics and business. Query by mail. **Pays $1/word.** Pays expenses of writers on assignment.
■ The online magazine carries original content not found in the print edition. Contact: Marion Mannekar, online editor.
Tips: "Submit a detailed query to John Homans, *New York*'s executive editor. If there is sufficient interest in the proposed piece, the article will be assigned."

★ $ NEW YORK NIGHTLIFE, MM&B Publishers, 990 Motor Pkwy., Central Islip NY 11722. (516)435-8890. Fax: (516)435-8925. E-mail: nynl@aol.com. **Contact:** Fran Petito, editor-in-chief. **75% freelance written.** Monthly magazine. "*Nightlife* features stories on topics concerning New Yorkers, from local events to new products. We also cover entertainment on both the local level and Hollywood." Estab. 1990. Circ. 56,000. Pays on publication. Publishes ms an average of 3 months after acceptance. Byline given. Buys first rights. Editorial lead time 2 months. Submit seasonal material 3 months in advance. Accepts queries by mail, e-mail, fax, phone. Responds in 2 weeks. Sample copy for 11×14 SAE with 8 first-class stamps. Writer's guidelines for #10 SASE.
Nonfiction: General interest, how-to (home remodeling, decorating, etc.), humor, interview/profile, new product, travel. Special issues: Bridal Guide (April 1999). **Buys 100-120 mss/year.** Query with published clips. Length: 200-1,700 words. **Pays $50-125.**
Photos: State availability of photos with submission. Reviews 3×5 transparencies, 5×7 prints. Offers no additional payment for photos accepted with ms. Buys one-time rights. Sometimes pays $15 per photo used.
Columns/Departments: Business (money matters, personal finance); Gourmet (recipes, new products); Health (medical news, exercise, etc.); all 600-750 words. Query with published clips. **Pays $50.**
Fiction: Humorous. **Buys 8-10 mss/year.** Query with published clips. Length: 600-750 words. **Pays $50.**
Tips: "We're looking for a flair for creative writing and an interest in celebrities, film, food and entertainment in general. No techies! Queries are happily reviewed and responded to. Feel free to follow up with a phone call 2-3 weeks later."

$ $ NEWSDAY, Melville NY 11747-4250. (516)843-2900. Fax: (516)843-2313. Website: www.newsday.com. **Contact:** Noel Rubinton, viewpoints editor. Opinion section of daily newspaper. Byline given. Estab. 1940. Circ. 555,203.
Nonfiction: Seeks "opinion on current events, trends, issues—whether national or local, government or lifestyle. Must be timely, pertinent, articulate and opinionated. Preference for authors within the circulation area including New York City." Length: 700-800 words. **Pays $150-200.**
Tips: "It helps for prospective authors to be familiar with our paper and section."

$ $ SPOTLIGHT MAGAZINE, Meadow Publications Inc., 126 Library Lane, Mamaroneck NY 10543. (914)381-4740. Fax: (914)381-4641. E-mail: meadowpub@aol.com. Website: www.spotlightpub.com. **Contact:** Dana B. Asher, editor-in-chief. **30% freelance written.** Monthly lifestyle magazine for the "upscale, educated, adult audience in the New York-New Jersey-Connecticut tri-state area. We try to appeal to a broad audience throughout our publication area." Estab. 1977. Circ. 75,000. **Pays on acceptance.** Byline given. Editorial lead time 3 months. Submit seasonal material 5 months in advance. Responds in 1 month. Sample copy for $2.95.
● *Spotlight* is looking for human interest articles and issue-related features woven around New York, New Jersey and Connecticut. Also, interesting profiles of well-known people and investigative pieces.
Nonfiction: Book excerpts, exposé, general human interest, how-to, humor, interview/profile, new product, photo feature, illustrations. Annual special-interest guides: Wedding (February, June, September); Dining (December, July); Home Design (March, April, October); Health (July, January); Education (January, August); Holiday Gifts (November); Senior Living (May, November). No fiction or poetry. **Buys 30 mss/year.** Query. **Pays $150 minimum.**
● Ranked as one of the best markets for freelance writers in *Writer's Digest* magazine's annual "Top 100 Markets," January 2000.
Photos: State availability of or send photos with submission. Reviews transparencies and prints. Negotiates payment individually. Captions, model releases, identification of subjects required (when appropriate). Buys one-time rights.

$ $ SYRACUSE NEW TIMES, A. Zimmer, Ltd., 1415 W. Genesee St., Syracuse NY 13204. Fax: (315)422-1721. E-mail: editorial@syracusenewtimes.com. Website: www.newtimes.rway.com. **Contact:** Christina Schwab, editor. **50% freelance written.** Weekly tabloid covering news, sports, arts and entertainment. "*Syracuse New Times* is an alternative weekly that can be topical, provocative, irreverent and intensely local." Estab. 1969. Circ. 43,000. Pays on publication. Publishes ms an average of 1 month after acceptance. Byline given. Buys one-time rights. Editorial lead time 3 months. Submit seasonal material 3 months in advance. Accepts simultaneous submissions. Responds in 2 weeks to queries; 1 month to mss. Sample copy for 9×11 SAE with 2 first-class stamps. Writer's guidelines for #10 SASE.

Nonfiction: Essays, general interest. **Buys 200 mss/year.** Query by mail with published clips. Length: 250-2,500 words. **Pays $25-200.**

Reprints: Accepts previously published submissions.

Photos: State availability of photos or send photos with submission. Reviews 8×10 prints and color slides. Offers $10-25/photo or negotiates payment individually. Identification of subjects required. Buys one-time rights.

Tips: "Move to Syracuse and query with strong idea."

$ $ TIME OUT NEW YORK, Time Out New York Partners, LP, 627 Broadway, 7th Floor, New York NY 10012. (212)539-4444. Fax: (212)253-1174. E-mail: letters@timeoutny.com. Website: www.timeoutny.com. President/Editor-in-Chief: Cyndi Stivers. **Contact:** Sunny Lee, editorial assistant. **20% freelance written.** Weekly magazine covering entertainment in New York City. "Those who want to contribute to *Time Out New York* must be intimate with New York City and its environs." Estab. 1995. Circ. 102,000. Pays on publication. Publishes ms an average of 1 month after acceptance. Byline sometimes given. Offers 25% kill fee. Accepts queries by mail, e-mail, fax. Makes work-for-hire assignments. Responds in 2 months.

Oₜ Pitch ideas to the editor of the section to which you would like to contribute (i.e., film, music, dance, etc.). Be sure to include clips or writing samples with your query letter.

Nonfiction: General interest, interview/profile, travel (primarily within NYC area), reviews of various entertainment topics. No essays, articles about trends, unpegged articles. Query with published clips. Length: 250-1,500. **Pays 20¢/word for b&w features and $300/page for color features.**

Columns/Departments: Around Town (Billy Cohen); Art (Tim Griffin); Books & Poetry (Janet Steen); Technology (Michael Freidson); Cabaret (H. Scott Jolley); Check Out (Milena Damjanov); Clubs (Adam Goldstone); Comedy (Greg Emmanuel); Dance (Gia Kourlas); Eat Out (Adam Rapoport); Film; Gay & Lesbian (Les Simpson); Kids (Barbara Aria); Music: Classical & Opera (Susan Jackson); Music: Rock, Jazz, etc. (Gail O'Hara); Radio (Ian Landau); Sports (Brett Martin); Television (Greg Emmanuel); Theater (Sam Whitehead); Video (Michael Freidson).

Tips: "We're always looking for quirky, less-known news about what's going on in New York City."

North Carolina

N $ $ AAA CAROLINAS GO MAGAZINE, 6600 AAA Dr., Charlotte NC 28212. Fax: (704)569-7815. Website: www.aaacarolinas.com. Managing Editor: Kristy Tolley. **Contact:** Tom Crosby, editor. **20% freelance written.** Member publication for the American Automobile Association covering travel, auto-related issues. "We prefer stories that focus on travel and auto safety in North and South Carolina and surrounding states." Estab. 1922. Circ. 670,000. Pays on publication. Byline given. Buys all rights. Editorial lead time 2 months. Accepts queries by mail. Sample copy and writer's guidelines for #10 SASE.

Nonfiction: Travel (auto-related). Length: 750 words. **Pays 15¢/word.**

Photos: Send photos with submission (slides preferred). Offers no additional payment for photos accepted with ms. Identification of subjects required. Buys all rights.

N $ $ $ CHARLOTTE MAGAZINE, Abarta Media, 127 W. Worthington Ave., Suite 208, Charlotte NC 28203. (704)335-7181. Fax: (704)335-3739. E-mail: editor@charlottemag.com. Website: www.charlottemag.com. **Contact:** Richard H. Thurmond, editorial director. **75% freelance written.** Consumer magazine published monthly covering Charlotte life. "This magazine tells its readers things they didn't know about Charlotte, in an interesting, entertaining and sometimes provocative style." Circ. 30,000. **Pays within 30 days of acceptance.** Publishes ms an average of 3 months after acceptance. Byline given. Offers 25% kill fee. Buys first North American serial rights. Editorial lead time 3 months. Submit seasonal material 6 months in advance. Accepts queries by mail, e-mail. Accepts simultaneous submissions. Responds in 6 weeks to mss. Sample copy for 8½×11 SAE and $2.09.

Nonfiction: Book excerpts, exposé, general interest, historical/nostalgic, interview/profile, photo feature, travel. **Buys 90-100 mss/year.** Query with published clips. Length: 200-3,000 words. **Pays 25-50¢/word.** Sometimes pays expenses of writers on assignment.

Photos: State availability of photos with submission. Negotiates payment individually. Identification of subjects required. Buys one-time rights.

Columns/Departments: Buys 35-50 mss/year. **Pays 25-50¢/word.**

Tips: "A story for *Charlotte* magazine could only appear in *Charlotte* magazine. That is, the story and its treatment are particularly germane to this area."

◆ $ $ OUR STATE, Down Home in North Carolina, Mann Media, P.O. Box 4552, Greensboro NC 27404. (336)286-0600. Fax: (336)286-0100. Website: www.ourstate.com. **Contact:** Mary Ellis, editor. **95% freelance written.** Monthly magazine covering North Carolina. "*Our State* is dedicated to providing editorial about the history, destinations, out-of-the-way places and culture of North Carolina." Estab. 1933. Circ. 65,000. Pays on publication. Publishes ms 6-24 months after acceptance. Byline given. Buys first North American serial rights. Editorial lead time 4 months. Submit seasonal material 4 months in advance. Accepts queries by mail, e-mail, fax. Responds in 6 weeks to queries; 2 months to mss. Sample copy for $3.95. Guidelines for #10 SASE.

Nonfiction: Historical/nostalgic, humor, personal experience, photo feature, travel. **Buys 60 mss/year.** Send complete ms. Length: 1,000-1,500 words. **Pays $125-250 for assigned articles; $50-125 for unsolicited articles.** Sometimes pays expenses of writers on assignment.

Photos: State availability of photos with submission. Reviews 35mm or 4×5 transparencies. Negotiates payment individually. Identification of subjects required. Buys one-time rights.

Columns/Departments: Tar Heel Memories (remembering something specific about NC), 1,200 words; Tar Heel Profile (profile of interesting North Carolinian), 1,500 words; Tar Heel Literature (review of books by NC writers and about NC), 300 words. **Buys 40 mss/year.** Send complete ms. **Pays $50-150.**

Tips: "We are developing a style for travel stories that is distinctly *Our State*. That style starts with outstanding photographs, which not only depict an area, but interpret it and thus become an integral part of the presentation. Our stories need not dwell on listings of what can be seen. Concentrate instead on the experience of being there, whether the destination is a hiking trail, a bed and breakfast, a forest or an urban area. What thoughts and feelings did the experience evoke? We want to know why you went there, what you experienced, and what impressions you came away with. With at least one travel story an issue, we run a short sidebar called "If you're going." It explains how to get to the destination; rates or admission costs if there are any; a schedule of when the attraction is open or list of relevant dates; and an address and phone number for readers to write or call for more information. This sidebar eliminates the need for general-service information in the story."

North Dakota

$ $ NORTH DAKOTA REC/RTC MAGAZINE, North Dakota Association of Rural Electric Cooperatives, 3201 Nygren Dr. NW, P.O. Box 727, Mandan ND 58554-0727. (701)663-6501. Fax: (701)663-3745. E-mail: kbrick@ndarec.com. Website: www.ndarec.com. **Contact:** Kent Brick, editor. **40% freelance written.** Consumer publication published monthly covering information of interest to memberships of electric cooperatives and telephone cooperatives. "We publish a general interest magazine for North Dakotans. We treat subjects pertaining to living and working in the northern Great Plains. We provide progress reporting on electric cooperatives and telephone cooperatives." Estab. 1954. Circ. 80,000. **Pays on acceptance.** Publishes ms an average of 6 months after acceptance. Byline given. Buys one-time rights or makes work-for-hire assignments. Editorial lead time 6 months. Submit seasonal material 6 months in advance. Accepts queries by mail, e-mail, fax. Accepts simultaneous submissions.

Nonfiction: General interest, historical/nostalgic, interview/profile, new product, travel. Upcoming theme issues include farm equipment sales show, home improvement and healthcare. **Buys 20 mss/year.** Query with published clips. Length: 1,500-2,000 words. **Pays $100-500 minimum for assigned articles; $300-600 for unsolicited articles.** Sometimes pays expenses of writers on assignment.

Reprints: Accepts previously published submissions.

Photos: State availability of photos with submission. Reviews contact sheets. Negotiates payment individually. Identification of subjects required. Buys one-time rights.

Columns/Departments: Energy use and financial planning, both 750 words. **Buys 6 mss/year.** Query with published clips. **Pays $100-300.**

Fiction: Historical, humorous, slice-of-life vignettes, western. **Buys 1 ms/year.** Query with published clips. Length: 1,000-2,500 words. **Pays $100-400.**

Tips: "Deal with what's real: real data, real people, real experiences, real history, etc."

Ohio

$ BEND OF THE RIVER MAGAZINE, P.O. Box 859, Maumee OH 43537. (419)893-0022. **Contact:** R. Lee Raizk, publisher. **90% freelance written.** Monthly magazine for readers interested in northwestern Ohio history, antiques, etc. Estab. 1972. Circ. 6,500. Pays on publication. Publishes ms an average of 6 months after acceptance. Byline given. Buys one-time rights. Submit seasonal material 2 months in advance; deadline for holiday issue is November 1. Responds in up to 6 months. Sample copy for $1.25.

● This magazine reports that it is eager to work with new/unpublished writers. "We buy material that we like whether it is by an experienced writer or not."

Nonfiction: "We deal heavily in Northwestern Ohio history and nostalgia. We are looking for old snapshots of the Toledo area to accompany articles, personal reflection, etc." **Buys 75 unsolicited mss/year.** Submit complete ms or send query. Length: 1,500 words. **Pays $10-75.**

Reprints: Accepts previously published submissions. Send tearsheet of article and information about when and where the article previously appeared. Pays 100% of the amount paid for an original article.

Photos: Purchases b&w or color photos with accompanying ms. Pays $1 minimum. Captions required.

Tips: "Any Toledo area, well-researched nostalgia, local history will be put on top of the heap. If you send a picture with manuscript, it gets an A+! We pay a small amount but usually use our writers often and through the years. We're loyal."

N **$ $ $** CINCINNATI MAGAZINE, One Centennial Plaza, 705 Central Ave., Suite 370, Cincinnati OH 45202. (513)421-4300. Fax: (513)562-2746. Contact: Kitty Morgan, editor. Monthly magazine emphasizing Cincinnati living. Circ. 25,000. Pays on publication. Byline given. Buys first time rights.

Nonfiction: Articles on personalities, business, sports, lifestyles, history relating to Cincinnati. Query. Feature length: 2,500-3,500 words. **Pays $500-1,000.**

Columns/Departments: Cincinnati dining, media, arts and entertainment, people, homes, politics, sports. **Buys 2-4 mss/issue.** Query. Length: 1,000-2,000 words. **Pays $300-400.**

Reprints: Rarely accepts reprints of previously published submissions. Send photocopy of article. Pays 50% of amount paid for an original article.

Tips: "Freelancers may find a market in At Home section (bimonthly), special advertising sections on varying topics from golf to cardiac care (query Special Projects Editor Doug Uhlenbrock). Always query in writing, with clips. All articles have a Cincinnati base. No generics, please. Also: no movie, book, theater reviews, poetry or fiction."

N **$ $** COLUMBUS MONTHLY, P.O. Box 29913, Columbus OH 43229-7513. (614)888-4567. Editor: Lenore E. Brown. **20-40% freelance written.** Prefers to work with published/established writers. Monthly magazine emphasizing subjects specifically related to Columbus and central Ohio. Pays on publication. Publishes ms an average of 2 months after acceptance. Byline given. Buys all rights. Responds in 1 month. Sample copy for $4.89.

Nonfiction: No humor, essays or first person material. "I like query letters which are well-written, indicate the author has some familiarity with *Columbus Monthly*, give me enough detail to make a decision and include at least a basic biography of the writer." **Buys 4-5 unsolicited mss/year.** Query. Length: 400-4,500 words. **Pays $50-400.** Sometimes pays the expenses of writers on assignment.

Photos: Send photos. Pay varies for b&w or color prints. Model release required.

Columns/Departments: Art, business, food and drink, politics, sports and theatre. **Buys 2-3 columns/issue.** Query. Length: 1,000-2,000 words. **Pays $100-175.**

Tips: "It makes sense to start small—something for our City Journal section, perhaps. Stories for that section run between 400-1,000 words."

$ $ NORTHERN OHIO LIVE, LIVE Publishing Co., 11320 Juniper Rd., Cleveland OH 44106. (216)721-1800. Fax: (216)721-2525. E-mail: bgleisser@livepub.com. **Contact:** David Budin, editor. Managing Editor: Benjamin Gleisser. **70% freelance written.** Monthly magazine covering Northern Ohio news, politics, business, arts, entertainment, education and dining. "Reader demographic is mid-30s to 50s, though we're working to bring in the late 20s. Our readers are well educated, many with advanced degrees. They're interested in Northern Ohio's cultural scene and support it." Estab. 1980. Circ. 32,000. Pays 20th of publication month. Publishes ms an average of 1 month after acceptance. Byline given. Offers 50% kill fee. Buys first North American serial rights. Editorial lead time 3 months. Submit seasonal material 4 months in advance. Responds in 3 weeks to queries; 2 months to mss. Sample copy for $3.

Nonfiction: Essays, exposé, general interest, humor, interview/profile, photo feature, travel. All should have a Northern Ohio slant. Special issues: Gourmet Guide (restaurants) (May). "No business/corporate articles." **Buys 100 mss/year.** Query with published clips. Length: 1,000-3,500 words. **Pays $100-1,000.** Sometimes pays expenses of writers on assignment.

Reprints: Send photocopy of article and information about when and where the article previously appeared.

Photos: State availability of photos with submission. Reviews contact sheets, 4×5 transparencies and 3×5 prints. Negotiates payment individually. Identification of subjects required. Buys one-time rights.

Columns/Departments: News & Reviews (arts previews, personality profiles, general interest), 800-1,800 words. **Buys 60-70 mss/year.** Query with published clips. **Pays $200-300.** Timed Place (essay), 400-450 words. **Pays $100.**

Fiction: Publishes novel excerpts.

$ $ $ OHIO MAGAZINE, Ohio Magazine, Inc., Subsidiary of Dispatch Printing Co., 62 E. Broad St., Columbus OH 43215-3522. (614)461-5083. Fax: (614)461-7648. E-mail: editorial@ohiomagazine.com. Website: www.ohiomagazine.com. **Contact:** Alyson Borgerding, managing editor. **70% freelance written.** Works with a small number of new/unpublished writers/year. Magazine published 10 times/year emphasizing Ohio-based travel, news and feature material that highlights what's special and unique about the state. Estab. 1978. Circ. 95,000. **Pays on acceptance.** Publishes ms an average of 6 months after acceptance. Buys all, second serial (reprint), one-time, first North American serial or first serial rights. Byline given except on short articles appearing in sections. Submit seasonal material minimum 6 months in advance. Accepts queries by mail, e-mail, fax. Responds in 3 months. Sample copy for $3 and 9×12 SAE or on website. Writer's guidelines for #10 SASE.

O— Break in by "knowing the magazine—read it thoroughly for several issues. Send good clips—that show your ability to write on topics we cover. We're looking for thoughtful stories on topics that are more contextual and less shallow. I want queries that show the writer has some passion for the subject."

Nonfiction: Features: 1,000-3,000 words. **Pays $800-1,800.** Sometimes pays expenses of writers on assignment.

• Ranked as one of the best markets for freelance writers in *Writer's Yearbook* magazine's annual "Top 100 Markets," January 2000.

Columns/Departments: Buys minimum 20 unsolicited mss/year. Length: 100-1,500 words. **Pays $50-500.**

Reprints: Accepts previously published submissions. Send tearsheet or photocopy of article and information about when and where the article previously appeared. Pays 50% of amount paid for an original article.

Photos: Brooke Wenstrup, art director. Rate negotiable.

Tips: "Freelancers should send all queries in writing, not by telephone. Successful queries demonstrate an intimate knowledge of the publication. The magazine has undergone a reformatting recently, placing an emphasis on Ohio travel, history and people that will appeal to a wide audience. We are looking to increase our circle of writers who can write about the state in an informative and upbeat style."

$ $ OVER THE BACK FENCE, Southern and Northern Ohio's Own Magazine, Back Fence Publishing, Inc., P.O. Box 756, Chillicothe OH 45601. (740)772-2165. Fax: (740)773-9273. E-mail: backfenc@bright.net. Website: www.backfence.com. **Contact:** Sarah Williamson, managing editor. Quarterly magazine. "We are a regional magazine serving 20 counties in Southern Ohio and 10 counties in Northern Ohio. *Over The Back Fence* has a wholesome, neighborly style. It appeals to readers from young adults to seniors, showcasing art and travel opportunities in the area." Estab. 1994. Circ. 15,000. Pays on publication. Publishes ms an average of 2 years after acceptance. Byline given. Buys one-time North American print publication rights, making some work-for-hire assignments. Editorial lead time 6-12 months. Submit seasonal material 6-12 months in advance. Accepts queries by mail, e-mail. Accepts simultaneous submissions, if so noted. Responds in 3 months. Sample copy for $4 or on website. Writer's guidelines for #10 SASE or on website.

➤ Break in with personality profiles (1,000-2,000 words), short features, columns and food essays/features (100-400 words); and features (1,000-3,000 words).

Nonfiction: General interest, historical/nostalgic, humor, inspirational, interview/profile, personal exprience, photo feature, travel. **Buys 9-12 mss/year.** Query with or without published clips or send complete ms. Length: 750-1,000 words. **Pays 10¢/word minimum,** negotiable depending on experience.

Reprints: Send photocopy of article or short story and typed ms with rights for sale noted and information about when and where the article or story previously appeared. Pay negotiable.

Photos: State availability of photos or send photos with submission. Reviews color transparencies (35mm or larger), 3⅓×5 prints. Offers $25-100/photo. Captions, model releases and identification of subjects required. Buys one-time usage rights. "If sending photos as part of a text/photo package, please request our photo guidelines and submit color transparencies."

Columns/Departments: The Arts, 750-1,000 words; History (relevant to a designated county), 750-1,000 words; Inspirational (poetry or short story), short story 600-850 words; Recipes, 750-1,000 words; Profiles From Our Past, 300-600 words; Sport & Hobby, 750-1,000 words; Our Neighbors (i.e., people helping others), 750-1,000 words. All must be relevant to Southern or Northern Ohio. **Buys 24 mss/year.** Query with or without published clips or send complete ms. **Pays 10¢/word minimum,** negotiable depending on experience.

Fiction: Humorous. **Buys 4 mss/year.** Query with published clips. Length: 300-850 words. **Pays 10¢/word minimum,** negotiable depending on experience.

Poetry: Wholesome, traditional free verse, light verse and rhyming. **Buys 4 poems/year.** Submit maximum 4 poems. Length: 4-32 lines preferred. **Pays 10¢/word or $25 minimum.**

Tips: "Our approach can be equated to a friendly and informative conversation with a neighbor about interesting people, places and events in Southern Ohio (counties: Adams, Athens, Clinton, Fayette, Fairfield, Gallia, Greene, Highland, Hocking, Jackson, Lawrence, Meigs, Perry, Pickaway, Pike, Ross, Scioto, Vinton, Warren and Washington) and Northern Ohio (counties: Ashland, Erie, Western Cuyahoga, Huron, Lorain, Medina, Ottawa, Richland, Sandusky and Wayne)."

Oklahoma

$ $ OKLAHOMA TODAY, P.O. Box 53384, Oklahoma City OK 73152-9971. Fax: (405)522-4588. E-mail: mccune@oklahomatoday.com. Website: www.oklahomatoday.com. **Contact:** Louisa McCune, editor-in-chief. **70% freelance written.** Works with a small number of new/unpublished writers each year. Bimonthly magazine covering people, places and things Oklahoman. "We are interested in showing off the best Oklahoma has to offer; we're pretty serious about our travel slant but regularly run history, nature and personality profiles." Estab. 1956. Circ. 50,000. Pays on publication. Publishes ms an average of 6 months after acceptance. Byline given. Buys first serial rights. Submit seasonal material 1 year in advance "depending on photographic requirements." Responds in 4 months. Sample copy for $3.95 and 9×12 SASE or on website. Writer's guidelines for #10 SASE or on website.

● *Oklahoma Today* has won Magazine of the Year, awarded by the International Regional Magazine Association, four out of the last eight years, and in 1999 won *Folio* magazine's Editorial Excellence Award for Best Regional Magazine.

Nonfiction: Book excerpts (on Oklahoma topics); photo feature and travel (in Oklahoma). Special issue: Art issue (Summer 2000). **Buys 20-40 mss/year.** Query by mail with published clips; no phone queries. Length: 250-3,000 words. **Pays $25-750.**

Photos: High-quality transparencies, slides, and b&w prints. "We are especially interested in developing contacts with photographers who live in Oklahoma or have shot here. Send samples and price range." Photo guidelines for SASE. Pays $50-100 for b&w and $50-750 for color; reviews 2¼ and 35mm color transparencies. Model releases, identification of subjects, other information for captions required. Buys one-time rights plus right to use photos for promotional purposes.

Fiction: Publishes novel excerpts and occasional short fiction.

Tips: "The best way to become a regular contributor to *Oklahoma Today* is to query us with one or more story ideas, each developed to give us an idea of your proposed slant. We're looking for *lively*, concise, well-researched and reported stories, stories that don't need to be heavily edited and are not newspaper style. We have a three-person full-time editorial staff, and freelancers who can write and have done their homework get called again and again."

Oregon

⭐ $ $ CASCADES EAST, P.O. Box 5784, Bend OR 97708-5784. (541)382-0127. Fax: (541)382-7057. E-mail: sunpub@sun-pub.com. Website: www.sunpub.com. **Contact:** Geoff Hill,publisher/editor. **90% freelance written.** Prefers to work with published/established writers. Quarterly magazine for "all ages as long as they are interested in outdoor recreation, history, people and arts and entertainment in central Oregon: fishing, hunting, sight-seeing, golf, tennis, hiking, bicycling, mountain climbing, backpacking, rockhounding, skiing, snowmobiling, etc." Estab. 1972. Circ. 10,000 (distributed throughout area resorts and motels and to subscribers). Pays on publication. Publishes ms an average of 6 months after acceptance. Byline given. Buys all rights. Submit seasonal material at least 6 months in advance. Accepts queries by mail, e-mail, fax, phone. Responds in 3 months. Sample copy and writer's guidelines for $5 and 9×12 SAE.
- *Cascades East* now accepts and prefers manuscripts along with a 3.5 disk. They can translate most word processing programs. You can also send electronic submissions.

Nonfiction: General interest (first person experiences in outdoor central Oregon—with photos, can be dramatic, humorous or factual), historical (for feature, "Little Known Tales from Oregon History," with b&w photos), personal experience (needed on outdoor subjects: dramatic, humorous or factual). Art feature (on recognized Central Oregon artists of any medium, with color photos/transparencies and b&w photos). Homes & Living (unique custom/"dream" homes, architectural styles, alternative energy designs, interior designs, building locations, etc. in central Oregon); 1,000-2,500 words with color photos/transparencies. "No articles that are too general, sight-seeing articles that come from a travel folder, or outdoor articles without the first-person approach." **Buys 20-30 unsolicited mss/year.** Query. Length: 1,000-2,000 words. **Pays 5-15¢/word.**
Reprints: Send photocopy of article and information about when and where the article previously appeared.
Photos: "Old photos will greatly enhance chances of selling a historical feature. First-person articles need b&w photos also." Pays $10-25 for b&w; $15-100 for transparencies. Captions preferred. Buys one-time rights.
Columns/Departments: Short features on a successful Central Oregon businessperson making an impact on the community or excelling in the business market: local, national, or worldwide, with color/b&w photo. Query preferred. Length: 1,000-1,500 words.
Tips: "Submit stories a year or so in advance of publication. We are seasonal and must plan editorials for summer 2002 in the spring of 2001, etc., in case seasonal photos are needed."

$ $ OREGON COAST, P.O. Box 18000, 1525 12th St., Florence OR 97439-0130. (541)997-8401 ext. 15 or (800)348-8401 ext. 15. Fax: (541)997-1124. E-mail: judy@ohwy.com. Website: www.ohwy.com. Editor: Jim Forst. **Contact:** Judy Fleagle, managing editor. **65% freelance written.** Bimonthly regional magazine covering the Oregon Coast. Estab. 1982. Circ. 70,000. Pays after publication. Publishes ms an average of 1 year after acceptance. Byline given. Offers 33% kill fee. Buys first North American serial rights. Submit seasonal material 6 months in advance. Accepts queries by mail, e-mail. Responds in 1 month to queries; 3 months to mss. Sample copy for $4.50. Writer's guidelines for #10 SASE.
- This company also publishes *Northwest Travel* and *Oregon Outside*.
- ⊶ Break in with "good slides to go with a story that is about the Oregon Coast—anything to do with the coast, its people, its towns, its events, its beaches, its parks, etc. Keep story focused and lively and grammatically correct."

Nonfiction: "A true regional with general interest, historical/nostalgic, humor, interview/profile, personal experience, photo feature, travel and nature as pertains to Oregon Coast." **Buys 55 mss/year.** Query with published clips. Length: 500-2,000 words. **Pays $75-350** plus 2-5 contributor copies.
Reprints: Sometimes accepts previously published submissions. Enclose clips. Send tearsheet or photocopy of article and information about when and where the article previously appeared. Pays an average of 60% of the amount paid for an original article.
Photos: Send photos with submission. Reviews 35mm or larger transparencies. Photo submissions with no ms or stand alone or cover photos. Captions, model releases (for covers), photo credits, identification of subjects required. Buys one-time rights.
Fillers: Newsbreaks (no-fee basis).
Tips: "Slant article for readers who do not live at the Oregon Coast. At least one historical article is used in each issue. Manuscript/photo packages are preferred over mss with no photos. List photo credits and captions for each historic print or color slide. Check all facts, proper names and numbers carefully in photo/ms packages. Need stories with great color photos—could be photo essays. Must pertain to Oregon Coast somehow."

$ $ OREGON OUTSIDE, Educational Publications Foundation, P.O. Box 18000, 1525 12th St., Suite C, Florence OR 97439-0130. (800)348-8401. Fax: (541)997-1124. E:mail judy@ohwy.com. Website: www.ohwy.com. **Contact:**

Judy Fleagle, managing editor. **70% freelance written.** Quarterly magazine covering "outdoor activities for experts as well as for families and older folks, from easy hikes to extreme skiing. We like first person, lively accounts with quotes, anecdotes, compelling leads and satisfying endings. Nitty-gritty info can be in sidebars. Send a rough map if needed." Estab. 1993. Circ. 20,000. Publishes ms an average of 1 year after acceptance. Byline given. Offers 33% kill fee. Buys first North American serial (stories and story/photo packages) and one-time rights (stand alone photos, covers and calendars). Editorial lead time 4 months. Submit seasonal material 6 months in advance. Accepts queries by mail, e-mail. Responds in 2 months to queries; 3 months to mss. Sample copy for $4.50. Writer's guidelines for #10 SASE.

Nonfiction: Book excerpts, how-to, interview/profile, personal experience, photo feature. "Nothing overdone. We like understatement." Query with published clips. Length: 800-1,750 words. **Pays $75-350 plus 2-5 contributor copies.**

Reprints: Send photocopy of article and information about when and where the article previously appeared. Pays 60% of amount paid for an original article.

Photos: Send photos with submission. "We need more photos showing human involvement in the outdoors." Reviews 35mm up to 4×5 transparencies. Offers $25-75 with story, $350/cover photo, $75/stand alone, $100/calendar. Captions, model releases, identification of subjects required for cover consideration. Buys one-time rights.

Columns/Departments: Back Page (unusual outdoor photo with technical information), 80-100 words. Query with photo. **Pays $75.**

Fillers: Newsbreaks, events. **Uses 10/year.** Length: 200-400 words. Does not pay for fillers.

Tips: "A short piece with a couple super photos for a 1- or 2-page article" is a freelancer's best chance for publication.

Pennsylvania

$ $ CENTRAL PA, WITF, Inc., P.O. Box 2954, Harrisburg PA 17105-2954. (717)221-2800. Fax: (717)221-2630. E-mail: centralpa@centralpa.org. Website: www.centralpa.org. **Contact:** Steve Kennedy, senior editor. **90% freelance written.** Monthly magazine covering life in Central Pennsylvania. Estab. 1982. Circ. 42,000. Pays on publication. Publishes ms 4 months after acceptance. Offers 20% kill fee. Buys first North American serial rights. Editorial lead time 3 months. Submit seasonal material 6 months in advance. Accepts queries by mail, e-mail, fax. Accepts simultaneous submissions. Responds in 6 weeks. Sample copy for $3.50 and SASE. Writer's guidelines for #10 SASE.

 ☞ Break in through Central Stories, Thinking Aloud, blurbs and accompanying events calendar.

Nonfiction: Essays, general interest, historical/nostalgic, how-to, humor, interview/profile, opinion, personal experience, photo feature, travel. Special issues: Dining/Food (January); Regional Insider's Guide (July). **Buys 50 mss/year.** Query with published clips or send complete ms. Length: 800-3,000 words. **Pays $200-750 for assigned articles; $50-500 for unsolicited articles.** Sometimes pays expenses of writers on assignment.

Photos: State availability of photos with submission. Reviews contact sheets, transparencies, prints. Negotiates payment individually. Identification of subjects required. Buys one-time rights.

Columns/Departments: Central Stories (quirky, newsy, regional), 300 words; Thinking Aloud (essay), 1,200 words; Cameo (interview), 800 words. **Buys 90 mss/year.** Query with published clips or send complete ms. **Pays $50-100.**

Tips: "Wow us with something you wrote, either a clip or a manuscript on spec. If it's off target but shows you can write well and know the region, we'll ask for more. We're looking for creative nonfiction, with an emphasis on conveying valuable information through near literary-quality narrative."

N ⛨ $ $ PENNSYLVANIA, Pennsylvania Magazine Co., P.O. Box 755, Camp Hill PA 17001-0755. (717)697-4660. E-mail: pamag@aol.com. Publisher: Albert E. Holliday. **Contact:** Matt Holliday, editor. **90% freelance written.** Bimonthly magazine covering people, places, events and history in Pennsylvania. Estab. 1981. Circ. 33,000. **Pays on acceptance** except for articles (by authors unknown to us) sent on speculation. Publishes ms an average of 9 months after acceptance. Byline given. Offers 25% kill fee for assigned articles. Buys first North American serial or one-time rights. Submit seasonal queries 9 months in advance. Accepts queries by mail. Responds in 1 month. Sample copy for $2.95. Writer's guidelines for #10 SASE.

 ☞ To break in, "be able to submit a text/photo package—learn to take photos or hook up with a photographer who will shoot for our rates."

Nonfiction: Features include general interest, historical, photo feature, vacations and travel, people/family success stories, consumer-related inventions, serious statewide issues—all dealing with or related to Pennsylvania. Nothing on Amish topics, hunting or skiing. **Buys 75-120 mss/year.** Query with SASE. Length: 750-2,500 words. **Pays 10-15¢/word.** *Will not consider without illustrations*; send photocopies of possible illustrations with query or mss.

Reprints: Send photocopy of article, typed ms with rights for sale noted and information about when and where the article previously appeared. **Pays 5¢/word.**

Photos: Reviews 35mm and 2¼ color transparencies (no originals) and 5×7 to 8×10 color and b&w prints. Do not send original slides. Americana Photo Journal includes 1-4 interesting photos and a 250-word caption; Photography Essay highlights annual photo contest entries. Pays $15-25 for inside photos; up to $100 for covers. Captions required. Buys one-time rights.

Columns/Departments: Panorama (short items about people, unusual events, family and individually owned consumer-related businesses), 250-900 words; Almanac (short historical items), 1,000-2,500 words; Museums, 400-500 words. All must be illustrated. Query with SASE. **Pays 10-15¢/word.**

Tips: "Our publication depends upon freelance work—send queries."

$ $PENNSYLVANIA HERITAGE, Pennsylvania Historical and Museum Commission and the Pennsylvania Heritage Society, P.O. Box 1026, Harrisburg PA 17108-1026. (717)787-7522. Fax: (717)787-8312. E-mail: momalley@p hmc.state.pa.us. Website: www.paheritage.org. **Contact:** Michael J. O'Malley III, editor. **90% freelance written.** Prefers to work with published/established writers. Quarterly magazine. "*Pennsylvania Heritage* introduces readers to Pennsylvania's rich culture and historic legacy, educates and sensitizes them to the value of preserving that heritage and entertains and involves them in such a way as to ensure that Pennsylvania's past has a future. The magazine is intended for intelligent lay readers." Estab. 1974. Circ. 13,000. **Pays on acceptance.** Publishes ms an average of 1 year after acceptance. Byline given. Buys all rights. Accepts queries by mail, e-mail. Accepts simultaneous queries and submissions. Responds in 10 weeks to queries; 8 months to mss. Sample copy for $5 and 9 × 12 SAE or on website. Writer's guidelines for #10 SASE or on website.

- *Pennsylvania Heritage* is now considering freelance submissions that are shorter in length (2,000 to 3,000 words), pictorial/photographic essays, biographies of famous (and not-so-famous) Pennsylvanians and interviews with individuals who have helped shape, make, preserve the Keystone State's history and heritage.

Nonfiction: Art, science, biographies, industry, business, politics, transportation, military, historic preservation, archaeology, photography, etc. No articles which in no way relate to Pennsylvania history or culture. "Our format requires feature-length articles. Manuscripts with illustrations are especially sought for publication. We are now looking for shorter (2,000 words) manuscripts that are heavily illustrated with *publication-quality* photographs or artwork. We are eager to work with experienced travel writers for destination pieces on historical sites and museums that make up 'The Pennsylvania Trail of History.' " **Buys 20-24 mss/year.** Prefers to see mss with suggested illustrations. Length: 2,000-3,500 words. **Pays $100-500.**

Photos: State availability of, or send photos with ms. Pays $25-200 for transparencies; $5-50 for b&w photos. Captions and identification of subjects required. Buys one-time rights.

Tips: "We are looking for well-written, interesting material that pertains to any aspect of Pennsylvania history or culture. Potential contributors should realize that, although our articles are popularly styled, they are not light, puffy or breezy; in fact they demand strident documentation and substantiation (sans footnotes). The most frequent mistake made by writers in completing articles for us is making them either too scholarly or too sentimental or nostalgic. We want material which educates, but also entertains. Authors should make history readable and enjoyable. Our goal is to make the Keystone State's history come to life in a meaningful, memorable way."

N $ $PHILADELPHIA MAGAZINE, 1818 Market St., 36th Floor, Philadelphia PA 19103. (215) 564-7700. Fax: (215) 656-3500. Website: www.phillymag.com. President/Publisher: David R. Lipson. **Contact:** Stephen Fried, editor. Monthly magazine. "*Philadelphia* is edited for the area's community leaders and their families. It provides in-depth reports on crucial and controversial issues confronting the region—business trends, political analysis, metropolitan planning, sociological trends—plus critical reviews of the cultural, sports and entertainment scene." Estab. 1908. Circ. 133,083. Accepts queries by mail.

- Break in by sending queries along with clips. "Remember that we are a general interest magazine that focuses exclusively on topics of interest in the Delaware Valley."

Nonfiction: "Articles range from law enforcement to fashion, voting trends to travel, transportation to theater, also includes background studies of the area newsmakers." Query with clips and SASE.

Tips: "*Philadelphia Magazine* readers are an affluent, interested and influential group who can afford the best the region has to offer. They're the greater Philadelphia area residents who care about the city and its politics, lifestyles, business and culture."

$ $ $PITTSBURGH MAGAZINE, WQED Pittsburgh, 4802 5th Ave., Pittsburgh PA 15213. (412)622-1360. Website: www.pittsburghmag.com. **Contact:** Michelle Pilecki, managing editor. **60% freelance written.** "*Pittsburgh* presents issues, analyzes problems and strives to encourage a better understanding of the community. Our region is western Pennsylvania, eastern Ohio, northern West Virginia and western Maryland." Prefers to work with published/established writers. The monthly magazine is purchased on newsstands and by subscription, and is given to those who contribute $40 or more/year to public TV in western Pennsylvania. Estab. 1970. Circ. 75,000. Pays on publication. Publishes ms an average of 2 months after acceptance. Byline given. Buys first North American serial rights and second serial (reprint) rights. Offers kill fee. Submit seasonal material and travel ideas at least 6 months in advance. Responds in 2 months. Sample copy for $2 (old back issues).

- The editor reports a need for more hard news and stories targeting readers in their 30s and 40s, especially those with young families.

Nonfiction: "Without exception—whether the topic is business, travel, the arts or lifestyle—each story is clearly oriented to Pittsburghers and the greater Pittsburgh region of today. We have minimal interest in historical articles and do not publish fiction, poetry, advocacy or personal reminiscence pieces." Exposé, lifestyle, sports, informational, service, business, medical, profile. Must have greater Pittsburgh angle. Query in writing with outline and clips. No fax, phone or e-mail queries. *No complete mss.* Length: 3,500 words or less. **Pays $300-1,500.**

Columns/Departments: The Front (short, front-of-the-book items). Length: 300 words maximum. **Pays $50-150.**

Photos: Query for photos. Model releases required. Pays pre-negotiated expenses of writers on assignment.

Tips: "Best bet to break in is through hard news with a region-wide impact or service pieces or profiles with a regional interest. The point is that we want more stories that reflect our region, not just a tiny part. And we *never* consider any story without a strong regional focus."

[N] $ $ WESTSYLVANIA, Allegheny Heritage Development Corporation, P.O. Box 565, 105 Zee Plaza, Hollidaysburg PA 16648-0565. (814)696-9380. Fax: (814)696-9569. E-mail: westsylvania@allegheny.org. Website: www.westsylvania.com. **Contact:** Dave Hurst, editor. **90% freelance written.** Quarterly magazine covering regional heritage in southwestern Pennsylvania. "*Westsylvania* magazine celebrates the heritage and lifestyles of south-central and southwestern Pennsylvania. Articles must reflect the region's natural and/or cultural heritage in some fashion. This is not a history magazine, but articles should show how the region's history has influenced the contemporary scene." Estab. 1997. Circ. 15,000. **Pays on acceptance.** Publishes ms an average of 4 months after acceptance. Byline given. Offers $50 kill fee. Buys first North American serial rights. Editorial lead time 2 months. Submit seasonal material 2 months in advance. Accepts queries by mail, e-mail, fax, phone. Accepts simultaneous submissions. Responds in 1 month. Sample copy for 9×12 SAE and 6 first-class stamps. Writer's guidelines for #10 SASE or by e-mail.

　O⌐ Break in with "a query with a strong Southwestern Pennsylvania heritage angle—the broader the angle, the better. I like features that have region-wide perspectives."

Nonfiction: Book excerpts, essays, general interest, historical/nostalgic, humor, inspirational, interview/profile, personal experience, photo feature, religious, travel (regional pieces only). **Buys 30 mss/year.** Query with published clips. "No unsolicited manuscripts." Length: 1,000-2,500 words. **Pays $100-250.** Sometimes pays writers with contributor copies or other premiums rather than a cash payment by personal arrangement.

Reprints: Accepts previously published submissions.

Photos: State availability of photos with submission. Reviews contact sheets and transparencies. Negotiates payment individually. Captions, model releases and identification of subjects required. Buys one-time rights.

Columns/Departments: First-Person (oral histories), 1,000 words; Foodways (recipes), Book Reviews (informational), both 500 words. **Buys 15 mss/year.** Query with published clips. **Pays $50-100.**

Fillers: Anecdotes, facts, short humor. Length: 50-500 words. **Pays $25-100.**

Tips: "Be familiar with south-central/southwestern Pennsylvania, its history, lifestyle, cultures, themes and attributes. Understand the difference between heritage and history. Provide published clips/writing samples with queries. No unsolicited manuscripts—prefer e-mail queries. Write as a storyteller, combining information and entertainment."

[N] $ $ WHERE & WHEN, Pennsylvania Travel Group, The Barash Group, 403 S. Allen St., State College PA 16801. (800)326-9584. Fax: (814)238-3415. E-mail: akris@barashgroup.com. Website: www.whereandwhen.com. **Contact:** Amy Krisay, editor. **75% freelance written.** Bimonthly magazine covering travel and tourism in Pennsylvania. "*Where & When* presents things to see and do in Pennsylvania." Circ. 100,000. Pays on publication. Byline given. Offers 50% kill fee. Buys first North American serial rights. Editorial lead time 6 months. Submit seasonal material 6 months in advance. Responds in 1 month. Sample copy and writer's guidelines free.

Nonfiction: Travel. **Buys 20-30 mss/year.** Query. Length: 800-2,500 words. **Pays $150-400.**

Photos: State availability of photos with submission. Reviews transparencies, slides and prints. Negotiates payment individually. Captions, identification of subjects required. Buys one-time rights.

Columns/Departments: Bring the Kids (children's attractions); Heritage Traveler (state heritage parks); Small Town PA (villages and hamlets in Pennsylvania); On the Road Again (attractions along a particular road); all 800-1,200 words. **Buys 10 mss/year.** Query. **Pays $100-250.**

Rhode Island

$ $ $ RHODE ISLAND MONTHLY, The Providence Journal Company, 280 Kinsley Ave., Providence RI 02903. (401)421-2552. Fax: (401)831-5624. E-mail: rimonthly.com. Website: www.rimonthly.com. Editor: Paula M. Bodah. **Contact:** Sarah Francis, managing editor. **80% freelance written.** Monthly magazine. "*Rhode Island Monthly* is a general interest consumer magazine with a strict Rhode Island focus." Estab. 1988. Circ. 41,000. **Pays on acceptance.** Publishes ms an average of 3 months after acceptance. Byline given. Offers 20% kill fee. Buys all rights for 90 days from date of publication. Editorial lead time 3 months. Submit seasonal material 6 months in advance. Accepts queries by mail, e-mail, fax. Responds in 6 weeks to queries; 1 month to mss. Sample copy on website.

Nonfiction: Exposé, general interest, interview/profile, photo feature. **Buys 40 mss/year.** Query with published clips. Length: 1,800-3,000 words. **Pays $600-1,200.** Sometimes pays expenses of writers on assignment.

South Carolina

[★] $ $ CHARLESTON MAGAZINE, P.O. Box 1794, Mt. Pleasant SC 29465-1794. (843)971-9811. Fax: (843)971-0121. E-mail: dberry@charlestonmag.com. **Contact:** David Berry, editor. **80% freelance written.** Bimonthly magazine covering current issues, events, arts and culture, leisure pursuits, travel, personalities as they pertain to the city of Charleston. "Each issue reflects an essential element of Charleston life and Lowcountry living." Estab. 1976. Circ. 20,000. Pays 30 days after publication. Publishes ms an average of 3 months after acceptance. Byline given. Buys one-time rights. Submit seasonal material 4 months in advance. Accepts queries by mail, fax. Responds in 1 month. Sample copies for 9×12 SAE with 5 first-class stamps. Writer's guidelines for #10 SASE.

Nonfiction: General interest, humor, food, architecture, sports, interview/profile, opinion, photo feature, travel, current events/issues, art. "Not interested in 'Southern nostalgia' articles or gratuitous history pieces. Must pertain to the Charleston area and its present culture." **Buys 40 mss/year.** Query with published clips with SASE. Length: 150-1,500 words. Payment negotiated. Sometimes pays expenses of writers on assignment.

Reprints: Send photocopy of article and information about when and where the article previously appeared. Pay negotiable.

Photos: Send photos with submission if available. Reviews contact sheets, transparencies, slides. Offers $35/photo maximum. Identification of subjects required. Buys one-time rights.

Columns/Departments: Channel Markers (general local interest), 50-400 words; Spotlight (profile of local interest), 250-300 words; The Home Front (interiors, renovations and gardens), 1,000-1,200 words; Sporting Life (humorous, adventurous tales of life outdoors), 850-1,200 words; In Good Taste (restaurants and culinary trends in the city), 1,000-1,200 words; On the Road (travel opportunities near Charleston), 1,000-1,200 words; Southern View (personal experience about Charleston life), 750 words; The Marketplace (profiles of exceptional local businesses), 1,000-1,200 words; The Good Fight (worthwhile battles fought locally and statewide), 1,000-1,200 words; To Your Health (medicine, nutrition, exercise, healthcare), 1,000-1,200 words; The Arts (in Charleston and surrounding communities), 700 words.

Tips: "Charleston, although a city with a 300-year history, is a vibrant, modern community with a tremendous dedication to the arts and no shortage of newsworthy subjects. Don't bother submitting coffee-table-magazine-style pieces. Areas most open to freelancers are Columns/Departments and features. Should be of local interest. We're looking for the freshest stories about Charleston—and those don't always come from insiders, but outsiders who are keenly observant. Offer a fresh perspective on issues and events. Write a story (non-fiction) that's not been told before. Profile intriguing Lowcountry residents."

N $ $ HILTON HEAD MONTHLY, Voice of the Community, Frey Media, Inc., P.O. Box 5926, Hilton Head Island SC 29938. Fax: (843)842-5743. E-mail: kperkins34@hotmail.com. **Contact:** Kim Perkins Moore, editor. **75% freelance written.** Monthly magazine covering the business, people and lifestyle of Hilton Head, SC. "Our mission is to provide fresh, upbeat reading about the residents, lifestyle and community affairs of Hilton Head Island, an upscale, intensely pro-active resort community on the Eastern seaboard. We are not even remotely 'trendy,' but we like to see how national trends/issues play out on a local level. Especially interested in: home design and maintenance, entrepreneurship, nature, area history, golf/tennis/boating, volunteerism." Circ. 28,000. **Pays on acceptance.** Publishes ms an average of 6 months after acceptance. Byline given. Offers 50% kill fee. Buys first North American serial rights or makes work-for-hire assignments. Editorial lead time 3 months. Submit seasonal material 4 months in advance. Accepts queries by mail, e-mail, fax, phone. Accepts simultaneous submissions. Responds in 1 week to queries; 4 months to mss. Sample copy for $3. Writer's guidelines for #10 SAE and 1 first-class stamp.

Nonfiction: Historical/nostalgic, how-to (home related), interview/profile (Hilton Head Island residents only), opinion (general humor or Hilton Head Island community affairs), travel. Does not want to see "exposé; interviews with people who are not Hilton Head Island residents; profiles of people, events or businesses in Beaufort, SC, Savannah, GA, Charleston or other surrounding cities, unless it's within a travel piece." **Buys 225-250 mss/year (including departments).** Query with published clips. Length: 800-2,000 words. **Pays 10¢/word.**

Reprints: Accepts previously published submissions.

Photos: State availability of photos with submission. Reviews contact sheets, any size prints or slides. Negotiates payment individually. Buys one-time rights.

Columns/Departments: Wellness (any general healthcare topic, especially for older audience), 800-1,100 words; Entrepreneur (profile of Hilton Head Island-based business, no franchises/chains), 800-1,000 words; Focus (profile of Hilton Head Island personality/community leader), 1,000-1,300 words; Community (profile of Hilton Head Island volunteer organization), 800-1,100 words. Query with published clips. **Pays 10¢/word ($100 minimum).**

Tips: "Give us concise, bullet-style descriptions of what the article covers (in the query letter); choose upbeat, pro-active topics; delight us with your fresh (not trendy) description and word choice."

$ $ SANDLAPPER, The Magazine of South Carolina, The Sandlapper Society, Inc., P.O. Box 1108, Lexington SC 29071-1108. (803)359-9941. Fax: (803)359-0629. E-mail: aida@sandlapper.org. Website: www.sandlapper.org. Editor: Robert P. Wilkins. **Contact:** Aida Rogers, managing editor. **35% freelance written.** Quarterly feature magazine focusing on the positive aspects of South Carolina. "*Sandlapper* is intended to be read at those times when people want to relax with an attractive, high-quality magazine that entertains and informs them about their state." Estab. 1989. Circ. 10,000. Pays during the dateline period. Publishes ms an average of 1 year after acceptance. Byline given. Buys first North American serial rights and the right to reprint. Submit seasonal material 6 months in advance. Accepts queries by mail, e-mail, fax. Sample copy on website. Writer's guidelines for SASE.

Nonfiction: Feature articles and photo essays about South Carolina's interesting people, places, cuisine, things to do. Occasional history articles. Query with clips and SASE. Length: 800-3,000 words. **Pays $50-500.** Sometimes pays the expenses of writers on assignment.

Photos: "*Sandlapper* buys black-and-white prints, color transparencies and art. Photographers should submit working cutlines for each photograph." Pays $25-75, $100 for cover or centerspread photo.

  The online version contains material not found in the print edition. Contact: Dan Harmon.

Tips: "We're not interested in articles about topical issues, politics, crime or commercial ventures. Avoid first-person nostalgia and remembrances of places that no longer exist. We look for top-quality literature. Humor is encouraged. Good taste is a standard. Unique angles are critical for acceptance. Dare to be bold, but not too bold."

South Dakota

$ DAKOTA OUTDOORS, South Dakota, Hipple Publishing Co., P.O. Box 669, 333 W. Dakota Ave., Pierre SD 57501-0669. (605)224-7301. Fax: (605)224-9210. E-mail: dakdoor@aol.com. Website: www.capjournal.com\dakotaoutdoors. Editor: Kevin Hipple. **Contact:** Rachel Engbrecht, managing editor. **85% freelance written.** Monthly magazine on Dakota outdoor life, focusing on hunting and fishing. Estab. 1974. Circ. 7,000. Pays on publication. Publishes ms an average of 2 months after acceptance. Byline given. Submit seasonal material 3 months in advance. Accepts simultaneous submissions. Responds in 3 months. Sample copy for 9×12 SAE with 3 first-class stamps.

Nonfiction: General interest, how-to, humor, interview/profile, personal experience, technical (all on outdoor topics—prefer in Dakotas). "Topics should center on fishing and hunting experiences and advice. Other topics, such as boating, camping, hiking, environmental concerns and general nature, will be considered as well." **Buys 120 mss/year.** Send complete ms. Length: 500-2,000 words. **Pays $5-50.** Sometimes pays in contributor copies or other premiums (inquire).

Reprints: Send typed ms with rights for sale noted and information about when and where the article previously appeared. Pays 50% of amount paid for an original article.

Photos: Send photos with submission. Reviews 3×5 or 5×7 prints. Offers no additional payment for photos accepted with ms or negotiates payment individually. Identification of subjects preferred. Buys one-time rights.

Columns/Departments: Kids Korner (outdoors column addressing kids from 12 to 16 years of age). Length: 50-500 words. **Pays $5-15.**

Fiction: Adventure, humorous. **Buys 15 mss/year.** Send complete ms.

Fillers: Anecdotes, facts, gags to be illustrated by cartoonist, newsbreaks, short humor. **Buys 10/year.** Also publishes line drawings of fish and game. Prefers 5×7 prints.

Tips: "Submit samples of manuscript or previous works for consideration; photos or illustrations with manuscript are helpful."

Tennessee

$ $ MEMPHIS, Contemporary Media, 460 Tennessee St., Memphis TN 38103. (901)521-9000. Fax: (901)521-0129. E-mail: memmag@mem.net. Website: www.memphismagazine.com. Managing Editor: Frank Murtaugh. **Contact:** Michael Finger, senior editor. **30% freelance written.** Monthly general interest magazine covering Memphis and the local region. "Our mission is to provide Memphis with a colorful and informative look at the people, places, lifestyles and businesses that make the Bluff City unique." Works with a small number of new/unpublished writers. Estab. 1976. Circ. 24,000. Pays on publication. Publishes ms an average of 2 months after acceptance. Byline given. Offers 25% kill fee. Buys first North American serial rights. Editorial lead time 2 months. Submit seasonal material 3 months in advance. Accepts queries by mail, e-mail, fax. Accepts simultaneous submissions. Responds in 2 months. Sample copy free or on website. Writer's guidelines free.

Nonfiction: Essays, general interest, historical, interview/profile, photo feature, travel, interiors/exteriors. Special issues include Restaurant Guide and City Guide. "Virtually all of our material has strong Memphis area connections." **Buys 20 mss/year.** Query with published clips. Length: 500-3,000 words. **Pays 10-30¢/word.** Sometimes pays expenses of writers on assignment.

Photos: State availability of photos with submission. Reviews contact sheets, transparencies. Buys one-time rights.

Columns/Departments: IntroSpective (personal experiences/relationships), 1,000-1,500 words; CityScape (local events/issues), 1,500-2,000 words; City Beat (people, places and things—some quirky), 200-400 words. **Buys 10 mss/year.** Query. **Pays 10-20¢/word.**

Fiction: One story published annually as part of contest. Send complete ms. Contact: Marilyn Sadler, associate editor. Length: 1,500-3,000 words.

Tips: "Send a query letter with specific ideas that apply to our short columns and departments. Good ideas that apply specifically to these sections will often get published."

Texas

$ $ $ HOUSTON PRESS, New Times, Inc., 1621 Milam, Houston TX 77002. (713)280-2400. Fax: (713)280-2496. Website: www.houstonpress.com. Editor: Margaret Downing. Managing Editor: Tim Carmen. Associate Editor: George Flynn. **Contact:** Kirsten Bubier, editorial administrator. **40% freelance written.** Alternative weekly tabloid covering "news and arts stories of interest to a Houston audience. If the same story could run in Seattle, then it's not for us." Estab. 1989. Pays on publication. Publishes ms an average of 2 weeks after acceptance. Byline given. Buys first North American serial and website rights. Editorial lead time 2 months. Submit seasonal material 3 months in advance. Sample copy for $3.

Nonfiction: Contact Lisa Gray, managing editor. Expose, general interest, interview/profile, arts reviews, music. Query with published clips. Length: 300-4,500 words. **Pays $10-1,000.** Sometimes pays expenses of writers on assignment.

Photos: State availability of photos with submission. Negotiates payment individually. Identification of subjects required. Buys all rights.

$ $ $ **TEXAS HIGHWAYS, The Travel Magazine of Texas**, Box 141009, Austin TX 78714-1009. (512)486-5858. Fax: (512)486-5879. E-mail: editors@texashighways.com. Website: www.texashighways.com. **Contact:** Jill Lawless, managing editor. **80% freelance written.** Monthly magazine "encourages travel within the state and tells the Texas story to readers around the world." Estab. 1974. Circ. 300,000. **Pays on acceptance.** Publishes ms up to 1 year after acceptance. Buys first North American serial and electronic rights. Accepts queries by mail. Responds in 2 months. Writer's guidelines for SASE or on website.

Nonfiction: "Subjects should focus on things to do or places to see in Texas. Include historical, cultural and geographic aspects if appropriate. Text should be meticulously researched. Include anecdotes, historical references, quotations and, where relevant, geologic, botanical and zoological information." Query with description, published clips, additional background materials (charts, maps, etc.) and SASE. Story length: 1,200-1,800 words. **Pays 40-50¢/word.** Send SASE for copy of writer's guidelines.

Columns/Departments: Contact: Ann Gallaway. Speaking of Texas (history, folklore, facts), 50-200 words. **Prints 3-5 items/month.** Send complete ms with reference sources. **Pays 40¢/word.**

Tips: "We like strong leads that draw in the reader immediately and clear, concise writing. Be specific and avoid superlatives. Avoid overused words. Don't forget the basics—who, what, where, why and how."

⊠ $ $ $ **TEXAS PARKS & WILDLIFE**, 3000 South I.H. 35, Suite 120, Austin TX 78704. (512)912-7000. Fax: (512)707-1913. E-mail: richard.zelace@tpwd.state.tx.us. Website: www.tpwmagazine.com. Managing Editor: Mary-Love Bigony. **Contact:** Executive Editor. **80% freelance written.** Monthly magazine featuring articles about Texas hunting, fishing, birding, outdoor recreation, game and nongame wildlife, state parks, environmental issues. All articles must be about Texas. Estab. 1942. Circ. 150,000. **Pays on acceptance.** Publishes ms an average of 6 months after acceptance. Byline given. Kill fee determined by contract, usually $200-250. Buys first rights. Submit seasonal material 6 months in advance. Accepts queries by mail, e-mail. Responds in 1 month to queries; 3 months to mss. Sample copy and writer's guidelines on website.

• *Texas Parks & Wildlife* needs more hunting and fishing material.

Nonfiction: General interest (Texas only), how-to (outdoor activities), photo feature, travel (state parks). **Buys 60 mss/year.** Query with published clips. Length: 500-2,500 words.

Photos: Send photos with submission. Reviews transparencies. Offers $65-350/photo. Captions and identification of subjects required. Buys one-time rights.

Tips: "Read outdoor pages of statewide newspapers to keep abreast of news items that can lead to story ideas. Feel free to include more than one story idea in one query letter. All areas are open to freelancers. All articles must have a Texas focus."

$ $ **WHERE DALLAS MAGAZINE**, Abarta Media, 4809 Cole Ave., Suite 165, Dallas TX 75205. (214)522-0050. Fax: (214)522-0504. E-mail: cchwhere@abartapub.com. **Contact:** Charmaine Cooper Hussain, editor. Website: www.travelfacts.com. **75% freelance written.** Monthly visitor's magazine. "*WHERE Dallas* is part of the *WHERE Magazine International* network, the world's largest publisher of travel magazines. Published in more than 46 cities around the world, travelers trust *WHERE* to guide them to the best in shopping, dining, nightlife and entertainment." Estab. 1996. Circ. 45,000. Pays on publication. Publishes ms an average of 2 months after acceptance. Byline given. Buys all rights. Editorial lead time 2 months. Submit seasonal material 2 months in advance. Accept queries by mail, e-mail. Accepts simultaneous submissions. Sample copy for $3.

○┅ Break in with "a solid idea—solid meaning the local Dallas angle is *everything*. We're looking for advice and tips that would/could only come from those living in the area."

Nonfiction: General interest, historical/nostalgic, photo feature, travel, special events. **Buys 30 mss/year.** Query with published clips, preferably by e-mail. Length: 650-1,200 words. **Pays $100-450.** Sometimes pays expenses of writers on assignment.

Photos: Send photos with submission. Reviews transparencies. Negotiates payment individually. Captions, model releases and identification of subjects required. Buys one-time rights, all rights on cover photos.

Columns/Departments: Pays $100-450.

Tips: "To get our attention, send clips with clever, punchy writing, like you might find in a society or insider column in the newspaper. We're also looking for writers with an expertise in shopping, with knowledge of fashion/art/antiques/collectibles."

Vermont

⊠ $ $ **VERMONT LIFE MAGAZINE**, 6 Baldwin St., Montpelier VT 05602-2109. (802)828-3241. Fax: (802)828-3366. E-mail: vtlife@life.state.vt.us. Website: www.vtlife.com. **Contact:** Thomas K. Slayton, editor-in-chief. **90% freelance written.** Prefers to work with published/established writers. Quarterly magazine. "*Vermont Life* is interested in any article, query, story idea, photograph or photo essay that has to do with Vermont. As the state magazine, we are most favorably impressed with pieces that present positive aspects of life within the state's borders." Estab. 1946. Circ. 85,000. Publishes ms an average of 9 months after acceptance. Byline given. Offers kill fee. Buys first serial rights. Submit seasonal material 1 year in advance. Responds in 1 month. Writer's guidelines for #10 SASE.

○┅ Break in with "short humorous Vermont anecdotes for our 'Postboy' column."

Nonfiction: Wants articles on today's Vermont, those which portray a typical or, if possible, unique aspect of the state or its people. Style should be literate, clear and concise. Subtle humor favored. No "Vermont clichés"—maple syrup, town meetings or stereotyped natives. **Buys 60 mss/year.** Query by letter essential. Length: 1,500 words average. **Pays 25¢/word.** Seldom pays expenses of writers on assignment.

• Ranked as one of the best markets for freelance writers in *Writer's Yearbook* magazine's annual "Top 100 Markets," January 2000.

Photos: Buys photographs with mss; buys seasonal photographs alone. Prefers b&w contact sheets to look at first on assigned material. Color submissions must be 4×5 or 35mm transparencies. Pays $75-250 inside color; $500 for cover. Gives assignments but only with experienced photographers. Query in writing. Captions, model releases, identification of subjects required. Buys one-time rights, but often negotiates for re-use rights.

Fiction: Publishes novel excerpts.

◻ The online version contains material not found in the print edition. Contact: Andrew Jackson.

Tips: "Writers who read our magazine are given more consideration because they understand that we want authentic articles about Vermont. If a writer has a genuine working knowledge of Vermont, his or her work usually shows it. Vermont is changing and there is much concern here about what this state will be like in years ahead. It is a beautiful, environmentally sound place now and the vast majority of residents want to keep it so. Articles reflecting such concerns in an intelligent, authoritative, non-hysterical way will be given very careful consideration. The growth of tourism makes us interested in intelligent articles about specific places in Vermont, their history and attractions to the traveling public."

Virginia

N **$ $** **ALBEMARLE, Living in Jefferson's Virginia**, Carden Jennings Publishing, 1224 W. Main St., Suite 200, Charlottesville VA 22903-2858. (804)817-2000. Fax: (804)817-2020. E-mail: kvalenzi@cjp.com. Website: www.cjp.com. **Contact:** Kathleen D. Valenzi, editor. **80% freelance written.** Bimonthly magazine. "Lifestyle magazine for central Virginia." Estab. 1987. Circ. 10,000. Pays on publication. Publishes ms an average of 4 months after acceptance. Byline given. Offers 30% kill fee. Buys first North American serial rights. Editorial lead time 6 months. Submit seasonal material 6 months in advance. Accepts queries by mail, e-mail, fax. Accepts simultaneous submissions. Responds in 1 month to queries; 2 months to mss. Sample copy for 10×12 SAE with 5 first-class stamps. Writer's guidelines for #10 SASE.

○─ Break in with "a strong idea backed by good clips to prove abilities. Ideas should be targeted to central Virginia and lifestyle, which can be very broad—a renaissance man or woman approach to living."

Nonfiction: Essays, historical/nostalgic, interview/profile, photo feature, travel. "No fiction, poetry or anything without a direct tie to central Virginia." **Buys 30-35 mss/year.** Query with published clips. Length: 900-3,500 words. **Pays $75-225 for assigned articles; $75-175 for unsolicited articles.** Sometimes pays expenses of writers on assignment.

Photos: State availability of photos with submission. Reviews transparencies. Negotiates payment individually. Captions, model releases and identification of subjects required. Buys one-time rights.

Columns/Departments: Etcetera (personal essay), 900-1,200 words; Good Taste (food, recipes), 2,500 words; Good Spirits (wine & spirits), 2,000 words; Leisure (travel, sports), 3,000 words. **Buys 20 mss/year.** Query with published clips. **Pays $75-150.**

Tips: "Be familiar with the central Virginia area and lifestyle. Without a regional slant, you won't be accepted for publication. We're a very traditional market, so don't try to reinvent the wheel."

⊠ **$ $** **THE ROANOKER**, Leisure Publishing Co., 3424 Brambleton Ave., P.O. Box 21535, Roanoke VA 24018-9900. (540)989-6138. Fax: (540)989-7603. E-mail: info@leisurepublishing.com. Website: www.theroanoker.com. **Contact:** Kurt Rheinheimer, editor. **75% freelance written.** Works with a small number of new/unpublished writers each year. Magazine published 6 times/year. "*The Roanoker* is a general interest city magazine for the people of Roanoke, Virginia and the surrounding area. Our readers are primarily upper-income, well-educated professionals between the ages of 35 and 60. Coverage ranges from hard news and consumer information to restaurant reviews and local history." Estab. 1974. Circ. 14,000. Pays on publication. Publishes ms an average of 4 months after acceptance. Byline given. Buys all rights; makes work-for-hire assignments. Submit seasonal material 4 months in advance. Accepts queries by mail, e-mail, fax. Responds in 2 months. Sample copy for $2 and 9×12 SAE with 5 first-class stamps or on website.

Nonfiction: Exposé, historical/nostalgic, how-to (live better in western Virginia), interview/profile (of well-known area personalities), photo feature, travel (Virginia and surrounding states). "We're looking for more photo feature stories based in western Virginia. We place special emphasis on investigative and exposé articles." Periodic special sections on fashion, real estate, media, banking, investing. **Buys 30 mss/year.** Query with published clips or send complete ms. Length: 1,400 words maximum. **Pays $35-200.**

Reprints: Occasionally accepts previously published submissions. Send tearsheet of article. Pays 50% of amount paid for an original article.

Photos: Send photos with ms. Reviews color transparencies. Pays $5-10 for 5×7 or 8×10 b&w prints; $10-50 for color transparencies. Captions and model releases required. Rights purchased vary.

Tips: "We're looking for more pieces on contemporary history (1930s-70s). It helps if freelancer lives in the area. The most frequent mistake made by writers in completing an article for us is not having enough Roanoke-area focus: use of area experts, sources, slants, etc."

Washington

$ $SEATTLE MAGAZINE, Oak Publications Inc., 423 Third Ave., W., Seattle WA 98119. (206)284-1750. Fax: (206)284-2550. E-mail: jkp@seattlemag.com. Website: www.seattlemag.com. Editor: Rachel Hart. **Contact:** J. Kingston Pierce, managing editor. **80% freelance written**. "Monthly magazine serving the Seattle metropolitan area. Articles should be written with our readers in mind. They are interested in social issues, the arts, politics, homes and gardens, travel and maintaining the region's high quality of life." Estab. 1992. Circ. 45,000. Pays on or about 30 days after publication. Publishes ms an average of 3 months after acceptance. Byline given. Offers 25% kill fee. Buys first print rights. Editorial lead time 6 months. Submit seasonal material 6 months in advance. Accepts queries by mail, e-mail, fax. Responds in 2 months. Sample copy and writer's guidelines for SASE; guidelines also on website.
Nonfiction: General interest, interview/profile, photo feature, local and regional interest, local book excerpts. Query with published clips. Length: 100-3,000 words. **Pays $50 minimum for unsolicited articles**. Rarely pays expenses of writers on assignment.
Reprints: Rarely accepts previously published submissions. Send photocopy of article and information about when and where the article previously appeared. Pay varies.
Photos: State availability of photos with submission. Negotiates payment individually. Buys one-time rights.
Columns/Departments: Scoop, Urban Safari, Voice, Daytrips/Travel, People, Environment, Politics, Fitness, Shelter, Style, Eat and Drink. Query with published clips. Pays $100-300.
Tips: "The best queries include some idea of a lead and sources of information, plus compelling reasons why the article belongs specifically in *Seattle Magazine*. In addition, queries should demonstrate the writer's familiarity with the magazine. New writers are often assigned front- or back-of-the-book contents, rather than features. However, the editors do not discourage writers from querying for longer articles and are especially interested in receiving trend pieces, in-depth stories with a news hook and cultural criticism with a local angle."

N $ $SEATTLE WEEKLY, Village Voice, 1008 Western Ave., Suite 300, Seattle WA 98104. (206)623-0500. Fax: (206)467-4377. E-mail: editorial@seattleweekly.com. **Contact:** Knute Berger. **20% freelance written.** Eager to work with writers in the region. Weekly tabloid covering arts, politics, food, business and books with local and regional emphasis. Estab. 1976. Circ. 75,000. Pays on publication. Publishes ms an average of 1 month after acceptance. Byline given. Offers variable kill fee. Buys first North American serial rights. Submit seasonal material minimum 2 months in advance. Responds in 1 month. Sample copy for $3. Writer's guidelines for #10 SASE.
Nonfiction: Book excerpts, exposé, general interest, historical/nostalgic (Northwest), humor, interview/profile, opinion, arts-related essays. **Buys 6-8 cover stories/year.** Query with cover letter, résumé, published clips and SASE. Length: 700-2,000 words. **Pays $75-500.** Sometimes pays expenses of writers on assignment.
Reprints: Send tearsheet of article. Pay varies.
Tips: "The *Seattle Weekly* publishes stories on Northwest politics and art, usually written by regional and local writers, for a mostly upscale, urban audience; writing is high-quality magazine style."

Wisconsin

$ $ $MILWAUKEE MAGAZINE, 417 E. Chicago St., Milwaukee WI 53202. (414)273-1101. Fax: (414)273-0016. E-mail: jfennell@qgraph.com. **Contact:** John Fennell, editor. **40% freelance written.** Monthly magazine. "We publish stories about Milwaukee, of service to Milwaukee-area residents and exploring the area's changing lifestyle, business, arts, politics and dining." Circ. 42,000. Pays on publication. Publishes ms an average of 2 months after acceptance. Byline given. Offers 20% kill fee. Buys first rights. Submit seasonal material 6 months in advance. Accepts queries by mail, e-mail. Responds in 6 weeks. Sample copy for $4.
Nonfiction: Essays, exposé, general interest, historical, interview/profile, photo feature, travel, food and dining and other services. "No articles without a strong Milwaukee or Wisconsin angle." **Buys 30-50 mss/year.** Query with published clips and SASE. Full-length features: 2,500-6,000 words. **Pays $400-1,000.** Two-page "breaker" features (short on copy, long on visuals), 1,800 words. Query. **Pays $150-400.** Sometimes pays expenses of writers on assignment.
Photos: Send photos with submission. Reviews contact sheets, negatives, any transparencies and any prints. Offers no set rate per photo. Identification of subjects required. Buys one-time rights.
Columns/Departments: Insider (inside information on Milwaukee, exposé, slice-of-life, unconventional angles on current scene), up to 500 words; Mini reviews for Insider, 125 words; Endgame column (commentary), 850 words. Query with published clips. **Pays $25-125.**
Tips: "Pitch something for the Insider, or suggest a compelling profile we haven't already done. Submit clips that prove you can do the job. The department most open is Insider. Think short, lively, offbeat, fresh, people-oriented. We are actively seeking freelance writers who can deliver lively, readable copy that helps our readers make the most out of the Milwaukee area. Because we're only human, we'd like writers who can deliver copy on deadline that fits the specifications of our assignment. If you fit this description, we'd love to work with you."

N $ $WISCONSIN OUTDOOR JOURNAL, Krause Publications, 700 E. State St., Iola WI 54990-0001. (715)445-2214. Fax: (715)445-4087. Website: www.krause.com/outdoors. **Contact:** Brian Lovett, editor. **95% freelance written.** Magazine published 8 times/year. "*Wisconsin Outdoor Journal* is more than a straight hook-and-bullet magazine. Though *WOJ* carries how-to and where-to information, it also prints narratives, nature features and state history pieces to give our readers a better appreciation of Wisconsin's outdoors." Estab. 1987. Circ. 48,000. **Pays on acceptance.** Byline given. Buys first North American serial rights. Submit seasonal material 1 year in advance. Responds in 6 weeks. *Writer's Market* recommends allowing 2 months for reply. Sample copy for 9×12 SAE with 7 first-class stamps. Writer's guidelines for #10 SASE.

Nonfiction: Book excerpts, essays, historical/nostalgic, how-to, humor, interview/profile, personal experience, photo feature. No articles outside of the geographic boundaries of Wisconsin. **Buys 80 mss/year.** Query. Send complete ms. "Established writers may query, send the complete ms." Length: 1,500-2,000 words. **Pays $100-250.**

Photos: Send photos with submission. Reviews 35mm transparencies. Offers no additional payment. Captions required. Buys one-time rights. Photos without mss pay from $10-150. Credit line given.

Fiction: Adventure, historical, humorous, novel excerpts. "No eulogies of a good hunting dog." **Buys 10 mss/year.** Send complete ms. Length: 1,500-2,000 words. **Pays $100-250.**

Tips: "Writers need to know Wisconsin intimately—stories that appear as regionals in other magazines probably won't be printed within *WOJ*'s pages."

$ $WISCONSIN TRAILS, P.O. Box 5650, Madison WI 53705-1056. (608)231-2444. Fax: (608)231-1557. E-mail: kbast@wistrails.com. Website: www.wistrails.com/guide. **Contact:** Kate Bast, editor. **40% freelance written.** Works with published/established writers. Bimonthly magazine for readers interested in Wisconsin and its contemporary issues, personalities, recreation, history, natural beauty and arts. Estab. 1960. Circ. 55,000. Buys first serial rights, one-time rights occasionally. Pays on publication. Submit seasonal material at least 1 year in advance. Publishes ms an average of 6 months after acceptance. Byline given. Responds in 4 months. Sample copy for $4.95. Writer's guidelines for #10 SASE.

○ "We're looking for active articles about people, places, events and outdoor adventures in Wisconsin. We want to publish one in-depth article of state-wide interest or concern per issue, and several short (600-1,500 words) articles about short trips, recreational opportunities, personalities, restaurants, inns, history and cultural activities. We're looking for more articles about out-of-the-way Wisconsin places that are exceptional in some way and engaging pieces on Wisconsin's little-known and unique aspects."

Nonfiction: "Our articles focus on some aspect of Wisconsin life: an interesting town or event, a person or industry, history or the arts, and especially outdoor recreation. We do not use first-person essays or biographies about people who were born in Wisconsin but made their fortunes elsewhere. No poetry. No articles that are too local for our regional audience, or articles about obvious places to visit in Wisconsin. We need more articles about the new and little-known." **Buys 3 unsolicited mss/year.** Query or send outline. "Queries accepted only in written form." Length: 1,000-3,000 words. **Pays 25¢/word.** Sometimes pays expenses of writers on assignment.

Photos: Purchased with or without mss or on assignment. Uses 35mm transparencies; larger format OK. Color photos usually illustrate an activity, event, region or striking scenery. Prefer photos with people in scenery. Black-and-white photos usually illustrate a given article. Pays $50 each for b&w on publication. Pays $50-75 for inside color; $100-200 for covers. Caption information and releases required. All submitted images must be labeled with photographer's name.

Tips: "When querying, submit well-thought-out ideas about stories specific to people, places, events, arts, outdoor adventures, etc. in Wisconsin. Include published clips with queries. Do some research—many queries we receive are pitching ideas for stories we recently have published. Know the tone, content and audience of the magazine. Refer to our writers' guidelines, or request them, if necessary."

Canada/International

N $ $ABACO LIFE, Caribe Communications, P.O. Box 37487, Raleigh NC 27627. (919)859-6782. Fax: (919)859-6769. E-mail: jimkerr@mindspring.com. Website: www.abacolife.com. Managing Editor: Cathy Kerr. **Contact:** Jim Kerr, editor/publisher. **50% freelance written.** Consumer quarterly covering Abaco, an island group in the Northeast Bahamas. "*Abaco Life* editorial focuses entirely on activities, history, wildlife, resorts, people and other subjects pertaining to the Abacos. Readers include locals, vacationers, second home owners and other visitors whose interests range from real estate and resorts to scuba, sailing, fishing and beaches. The tone is upbeat, adventurous, humorous. No fluff writing for an audience already familiar with the area." Estab. 1979. Circ. 10,000. Pays on publication. Publishes ms an average of 2 months after acceptance. Byline given. Offers 40% kill fee. Buys one-time rights. Editorial lead time 2 months. Submit seasonal material 4 months in advance. Accepts queries by mail, e-mail. Accepts simultaneous submissions. Responds in 2 weeks to queries; 2 months to mss. Sample copy for $2. Writer's guidelines free.

Nonfiction: General interest, historical/nostalgic, how-to, interview/profile, personal experience, photo feature, travel. "No general first-time impressions. Articles must be specific, show knowledge and research of the subject and area—'Abaco's Sponge Industry'; 'Diving Abaco Wrecks'; 'The Hurricane of '36.' " **Buys 8-10 mss/year.** Query or send complete ms. Length: 400-2,000 words. **Pays $150-350.**

Reprints: Accepts previously published submissions.

Photos: State availability of photos or send photos with submission. Reviews transparencies and prints. Offers $25-100/photo. Negotiates payment individually. Captions, model releases and identification of subjects required. Buys one-time rights.

Tips: "Travel writers must look deeper than a usual destination piece, and the only real way to do that is spend time in Abaco. Beyond good writing, which is a must, we like submissions on Microsoft Word or Works, but that's optional. Color slides are also preferred over prints, and good ones go a long way in selling the story."

N **$ $ $ ALBERTAVIEWS, The Magazine About Alberta for Albertans,** Local Perspectives Publishing, Inc., 520 23rd Ave. S.W., Calgary, Alberta T2S 0J5 Canada. (403)243-5334. Fax: (403)243-8599. E-mail: contactus@albertaviews.ab.ca. Website: www.albertaviews.ab.ca. Publisher/Editor: Jackie Flanagan. **Contact:** John McDermid, associate publisher. **50% freelance written.** Bimonthly magazine covering Alberta culture: politics, economy, social issues and art. "We are a regional magazine providing thoughtful commentary and background information on issues of concern to Albertans. Most of our writers are Albertans." Estab. 1997. Circ. 20,000. Pays on publication. Publishes ms an average of 3 months after acceptance. Byline given. Offers 50% kill fee. Buys first North American serial and electronic rights. Editorial lead time 3 months. Submit seasonal material 3 months in advance. Accepts queries by mail, e-mail. Responds in 6 weeks to queries; 2 months to mss. Sample copy free. Back issues $5. Writer's guidelines free or on website or by e-mail.

Nonfiction: Essays. Does not want anything not directly related to Alberta. **Buys 18 mss/year.** Query with published clips. Length: 3,000-5,000 words. **Pays $1,000-1,500 for assigned articles; $350-750 for unsolicited articles.** Sometimes pays expenses of writers on assignment.

Photos: State availability of photos with submission. Negotiates payment individually. Buys one-time rights, web rights.

Fiction: Only fiction by Alberta writers. **Buys 6 mss/year.** Send complete ms. Length: 2,500-4,000 words. **Pays $1,000 maximum.**

$ ATLANTIC BOOKS TODAY, Atlantic Provinces Book Review Society, 1657 Barrington St., #502, Halifax, Nova Scotia B3J 2A1 Canada. (902)429-4454. E-mail: booksatl@istar.ca. **Contact:** Elizabeth Eve, managing editor. **50% freelance written.** Quarterly tabloid covering books and writers in Atlantic Canada. "We only accept written inquiries for stories pertaining to promoting interest in the culture of the Atlantic region." Estab. 1992. Circ. 20,000. Pays on publication. Byline given. Offers $25 kill fee. Buys one-time rights. Editorial lead time 6 months. Submit seasonal material 3 months in advance. Accepts simultaneous submissions. Responds in 1 month. Sample copy and writer's guidelines for SASE.

Nonfiction: Book excerpts, general interest. Query with published clips. Length: 1,000 words maximum. **Pays $120 maximum.** Sometimes pays expenses of writers on assignment.

$ $ $ THE BEAVER, Canada's History Magazine, Canada's National History Society, 478-167 Lombard Ave., Winnipeg, Manitoba R3B 0T6 Canada. (204)988-9300. Fax: (204)988-9309. E-mail: cnhs@historysociety.ca. Website: www.historysociety.ca. Associate Editor: Doug Whiteway. **Contact:** Annalee Greenberg, editor. **65% freelance written.** Bimonthly history magazine covering Canadian history. Estab. 1920. Circ. 41,000. **Pays on acceptance.** Byline given. Offers $200 kill fee. Buys first North American serial rights and subsidiary electronic rights. Editorial lead time 4 months. Submit seasonal material 8 months in advance. Accepts queries by mail, e-mail, fax. Accepts simultaneous submissions. Responds in 6 weeks to queries; 2 months to mss. Sample copy for 9×12 SAE and 2 first-class stamps or on website. Writer's guidelines for #10 SASE or on website.

Nonfiction: Historical (Canadian focus), photo feature (historical). Does not want anything unrelated to Canadian history. **Buys 30 mss/year.** Query with published clips and SASE. Length: 600-4,000 words. **Pays $400-1,000 for assigned articles; $300-600 for unsolicited articles.** Sometimes pays expenses of writers on assignment.

Photos: State availability of photos with submission. Offers no additional payment for photos accepted with ms. Model releases and identification of subjects required. Buys one-time rights.

Columns/Departments: Book and other media reviews and Canadian history subjects, 600 words ("These are assigned to freelancers with particular areas of expertise, i.e., women's history, labour history, French regime, etc.") **Buys 15 mss/year. Pays $125.**

Tips: "*The Beaver* is directed toward a general audience of educated readers, as well as to historians and scholars. We are in the market for lively, well-written, well-researched, and informative articles about Canadian history that focus on all parts of the country and all areas of human activity. Subject matter covers the whole range of Canadian history, with particular emphasis on social history, politics, exploration, discovery and settlement, aboriginal peoples, business and trade, war, culture and sport. Articles are obtained through direct commission and by submission. Queries should be accompanied by a stamped, self-addressed envelope. *The Beaver* publishes articles of various lengths, including long features (from 1,500-4,000 words) that provide an in-depth look at an event, person or era; short, more narrowly focused features (from 600-1,500 words). Longer articles may be considered if their importance warrants publication. Articles should be written in an expository or interpretive style and present the principal themes of Canadian history in an original, interesting and informative way."

$ BRAZZIL, Brazzil, P.O. Box 50536, Los Angeles CA 90050. (323)255-8062. Fax: (323)257-3487. E-mail: brazzil@brazzil.com. Website: www.brazzil.com. **Contact:** Rodney Mello, assistant editor. **60% freelance written.** Monthly magazine covering Brazilian culture. Estab. 1989. Circ. 12,000. Pays on publication. Publishes ms an average of 2 months after acceptance. Byline given. Offers 10% kill fee. Buys one-time rights. Editorial lead time 2 months. Submit seasonal material 2 months in advance. Accepts queries by mail, e-mail. Accepts simultaneous submissions. Responds in 2 weeks. Sample copy free or on website.

Nonfiction: Book excerpts, essays, exposé, general interest, historical/nostalgic, interview/profile, personal experience, travel. "All subjects have to deal in some way with Brazil and its culture. We assume our readers know very little or nothing about Brazil, so we explain everything." **Buys 15 mss/year.** Query. Length: 800-5,000 words. **Pays $20-50.** Pays writers with contributor copies or other premiums by mutual agreement.

Reprints: Accepts reprints of previously published submissions. Include information about when and where the article previously appeared. Pays 50% of amount paid for an original article.

Photos: State availability of photos with submission. Reviews prints. Offers no additional payment for photos accepted with ms. Identification of subjects required. Buys one-time rights.

■ The online version of *Brazzil* contains content not included in the print edition. Contact: Rodney Mello, online editor.

Tips: "We are interested in anything related to Brazil: politics, economy, music, behavior, profiles. Please document material with interviews and statistical data if applicable. Controversial pieces are welcome."

★ $ $ $**CANADIAN GEOGRAPHIC**, 39 McArthur Ave., Ottawa, Ontario K1L 8L7 Canada. (613)745-4629. Fax: (613)744-0947. E-mail: editorial@cangeo.ca. Website: www.cangeo.ca/. **Contact:** Rick Boychuk, editor. **90% freelance written.** Works with a small number of new/unpublished writers each year. Estab. 1930. Circ. 240,000. Bimonthly magazine. "*Canadian Geographic*'s colorful portraits of our ever-changing population show readers just how important the relationship between the people and the land really is." **Pays on acceptance.** Publishes ms an average of 3 months after acceptance. Buys first Canadian rights; interested only in first-time publication. Accepts queries by mail, e-mail, fax. Responds in 1 month. Sample copy for $4.25 (Canadian.) and 9×12 SAE or on website.

Nonfiction: Buys authoritative geographical articles, in the broad geographical sense, written for the average person, not for a scientific audience. Predominantly Canadian subjects by Canadian authors. **Buys 30-45 mss/year.** *Always query first in writing and enclose SASE.* Cannot reply personally to all unsolicited proposals. Length: 1,500-3,000 words. **Pays 80¢/word minimum. Usual payment for articles ranges between $1,000-3,000.** Higher fees reserved for commissioned articles. Sometimes pays the expenses of writers on assignment.

• *Canadian Geographic* reports a need for more articles on earth sciences.

Photos: Pays $75-400 for color photos, depending on published size.

$ $**THE COTTAGE MAGAZINE, Country Living in Western Canada**, Greenheart Publications, Ltd., 322 John St., Victoria, British Columbia V8T 1T3 Canada. (250)360-0709. Fax: (250)360-1709. E-mail: cottagemag@home.com. **Contact:** Caryl Worden, editor. **80% freelance written**. Bimonthly magazine covering recreational property in Western Canada. Estab. 1992. Circ. 10,000. Pays on publication. Publishes ms an average of 1 month after acceptance. Byline given. Offers 50% kill fee. Buys first North American serial rights. Editorial lead time 2 months. Submit seasonal material 6 months in advance. Accepts simultaneous submissions. Accepts queries by e-mail, fax. Responds in 1 month to queries; 2 months to mss. Sample copy for $2. Writer's guidelines for #10 SASE (Canadian stamps only).

O─ Break in through practical "how-to" with good photos/diagrams on topics ranging from utilities (wells, septic, power, etc.) to building projects (sheds, docks, etc.) to recreational (boats, games, etc.); feature cottages from interior BC, Alberta and Saskatchewan.

Nonfiction: General interest, historical/nostalgic, how-to, humor, interview/profile, new product, personal experience, technical. **Buys 30 mss/year.** Query. Length: 200-2,000 words. **Pays $50-300.** Sometimes pays expenses of writers on assignment (telephone expenses mostly).

Photos: State availability of photos with submission. Reviews contact sheets, transparencies, prints and slides. Offers no additional payment for photos accepted with ms. Buys one-time rights. Cover Photo, $100 (Canadian).

Columns/Departments: Utilities (solar and/or wind power), 650-700 words; Maintenance/Repairs; Getting Around (boats, bikes, etc.) Weekend Projects; Recycling. **Buys 10 mss/year.** Query. **Pays $100-200.**

Fillers: Anecdotes, facts, seasonal tips, newsbreaks. **Buys 12/year.** Length: 50-200 words. **Pays 20¢/word.**

Tips: "We're looking for practical info that allows readers to DIY or at least gives enough info to pursue topic further. Emphasis on alternative energy, water waste systems and innovative buildings/techniques/materials in Western Canada."

★ $ $**OUTDOOR CANADA MAGAZINE**, 340 Ferrier St., Suite 210, Markham, Ontario L3R 2Z5 Canada. (905)475-8440. Fax: (905)475-9560. E-mail: jameslittle@outdoorcanadamagazine.com. **Contact:** James Little, editor-in-chief. **90% freelance written.** Works with a small number of new/unpublished writers each year. Magazine published 8 times/year emphasizing noncompetitive outdoor recreation in Canada *only.* Estab. 1972. Circ. 95,000. Pays on publication. Publishes ms an average of 8 months after acceptance. Buys first rights. Submit seasonal material 1 year in advance of issue date. Byline given. *Enclose SASE or IRCs or material will not be returned.* Accepts queries by mail, e-mail, fax. Responds in 1 month. Mention *Writer's Market* in request for editorial guidelines.

Nonfiction: Fishing, canoeing, hunting, outdoor issues, outdoor destinations in Canada, some how-to. **Buys 35-40 mss/year, usually with photos.** Length: 2,500 words. **Pays $500 and up.**

Reprints: Send information about when and where the article previously appeared. Pay varies. Publishes book excerpts.

Photos: Emphasize people in the Canadian outdoors. Pays $100-250 for 35mm transparencies; and $400/cover. Captions and model releases required.

Fillers: Short news pieces. **Buys 30-40/year.** Length: 100-500 words. **Pays $50 and up.**

★ $ $**THIS MAGAZINE**, Red Maple Foundation, 401 Richmond St. W. #396, Toronto, Ontario M5V 3A8 Canada. (416)979-8400. Fax: (416)979-1143. E-mail: thismag@web.net. Website: www.thismag.org. **Contact:** Sarmishta Subramanian, editor. **80% freelance written.** Bimonthly publication covering Canadian politics and culture. "*This* is Canada's leading alternative magazine. We publish stories on politics, culture and the arts that mainstream media won't touch." Estab. 1966. Circ. 6,000. Pays 1 month after publication. Publishes ms an average of 2 months after acceptance. Byline given. Buys first North American serial and electronic rights. Editorial lead time 6 weeks. Accepts queries by mail, e-mail, fax. Sample copy for $5 or on website. Writer's guidelines for #10 SASE or on website.

    ○┓ "If unpublished or little-published, break in with shorter pieces tailored to the magazine's content. If published, pitch an unusual, under-reported idea."

Nonfiction: Exposé, personal experience, literary nonfiction/journalistic essays on cultural, political issues, trends. **Buys 60 mss/year.** Query with published clips. Length: 2,000-5,000 words. **Pays $250-500.**

Columns/Departments: Shorter essays, journalistic pieces; stylish interpretive front-section items. Length: 500-2,000. **Pays $50-200.**

Tips: "We'd love to see more literary nonfiction with a strong voice and a political bent (no rants), strong cultural analysis that is au courant and suitable for a journalistic format, arts/literary criticism that is reasonally accessible."

N ★ $ $ $ TORONTO LIFE, 59 Front St. E., Toronto, Ontario M5E 1B3 Canada. (416)364-3333. Fax: (416)861-1169. E-mail: editorial@torontolife.com. Website: www.tor-lifeline.com. **Contact:** John Macfarlane, editor. **95% freelance written.** Prefers to work with published/established writers. Monthly magazine emphasizing local issues and social trends, short humor/satire, and service features for upper income, well-educated and, for the most part, young Torontonians. Circ. 92,438. **Pays on acceptance.** Publishes ms an average of 4 months after acceptance. Byline given. Buys first North American serial rights. Pays 50% kill fee for commissioned articles only. Responds in 3 weeks. Sample copy for $3.95 with SAE and IRCs.

Nonfiction: Uses most types of articles. Buys 17 mss/issue. Query with published clips and SASE. Phone queries OK. **Buys about 40 unsolicited mss/year.** Length: 1,000-6,000 words. **Pays $500-5,000.**

Columns/Departments: "We run about five columns an issue. They are all freelanced, though most are from regular contributors. They are mostly local in concern and cover politics, money, fine art, performing arts, movies and sports." Length: 1,800 words. **Pays $1,500.** Query with SASE.

Tips: "Submissions should have strong Toronto orientation."

$ $ UP HERE, Life at the Top of the World, OUTCROP: The Northern Publishers, P.O. Box 1350, Yellowknife, Northwest Territories X1A 2N9 Canada. (867)920-4652. Fax: (867)873-2844. E-mail: uphere@outcrop.com. Website: www.uphere.ca. **Contact:** Cooper Langford, editor. **70% freelance written.** Magazine published 8 times/year, covering general interest about Canada's North. "We publish features, columns and shorts about people, wildlife, native cultures, travel and adventure in Yukon and Northwest Territory, with an occasional swing into Alaska. Be informative, but entertaining." Estab. 1984. Circ. 35,000. Pays on publication. Byline given. Offers 50% kill fee. Buys first North American serial rights. Editorial lead time 6 months. Submit seasonal material 1 year in advance. Responds in 4 months. Sample copy for $3.50 (Canadian) and 9×12 SASE with $1.45 Canadian postage. Writer's guidelines for legal-sized SASE and 45¢ Canadian postage.

Nonfiction: Essays, general interest, historical/nostalgic, how-to, humor, interview/profile, lifestyle/culture, new product, personal experience, photo feature, technical, travel. No poetry or fiction. **Buys 25-30 mss/year.** Query. Length: 1,500-3,000 words. **Pays $250-750 or 15-25¢/word.** Pays with advertising space where appropriate.

Photos: Send photos with submission. "*Please* do not sent unsolicited original photos, slides. Photocopies are sufficient." Reviews transparencies and prints. Offers $25-350/photo (Canadian). Captions and identification of subjects required. Buys one-time rights.

Columns/Departments: Write for updated guidelines, visit website or e-mail. **Buys 25-30 mss/year.** Query with published clips. **Pays $150-250 or 15-25¢/word.**

Tips: "We like well-researched, concrete adventure pieces, insights about Northern people and lifestyles, readable natural history. Features are most open to freelancers—travel, adventure and so on. Outer Edge (a shorter, newsy, gee-whiz section) is a good place to break in with a 50-500 word piece. We don't want a comprehensive 'How I spent my summer vacation' hour-by-hour account. We want stories with angles, articles that look at the North through a different set of glasses. Photos are important; you greatly increase your chances with top-notch images."

$ $ WESTERN PEOPLE, Supplement to the Western Producer, Western Producer Publications, Box 2500, Saskatoon, Saskatchewan S7K 2C4 Canada. (306)665-3500. E-mail: people@producer.com. Website: www.producer.com. **Contact:** Karen Morrison or Sheila Robertson, features editors. Weekly farm newspaper supplement "reflecting the life and people of rural Western Canada both in the present and historically." Estab. 1978. Circ. 90,000. **Pays on acceptance.** Publishes ms an average of 3 months after acceptance. Byline given. Buys first rights. Submit seasonal material 3 months in advance. Accepts queries by mail, e-mail, fax. Responds in 3 weeks. Sample copy for 9×12 SAE and 3 IRCs. Guidelines for #10 SAE and 2 IRCs.

Nonfiction: General interest, historical/nostalgic, humor, interview/profile, personal experience, photo feature. **Buys 225 mss/year.** Send complete ms. Length: 500-1,800 words. **Pays $100-275.**

Photos: Send photos with submission. Reviews transparencies and prints. Captions and identification of subjects required. No stand-alone photos.

Fiction: Adventure, historical, humorous, mainstream, mystery, romance, suspense, western stories reflecting life in rural Western Canada. **Buys 15 mss/year.** Send complete ms. Length: 1,000-2,000 words. **Pays $150-200.**

Poetry: Free verse, traditional, haiku, light verse. **Buys 75 poems/year.** Submit maximum 3 poems. Length: 4-50 lines. **Pays $15-50.**

Tips: "Western Canada is geographically very large. The approach for writing about an interesting individual is to introduce that person *neighbor-to-neighbor* to our readers."

⊠ $ $ $ WESTWORLD MAGAZINE, Canada Wide Magazines and Communications, 4180 Lougheed Hwy., 4th floor, Burnaby, British Columbia V5C 6A7 Canada. Fax: (604)299-9188. E-mail: acollette@canadawide.com. **Contact:** Ann Collette, editor. **80% freelance written.** Quarterly association magazine distributed to members of The Canadian Automobile Association, with a focus on local (British Columbia), regional and international travel. Estab. 1983. Circ. 500,000. Pays on publication. Byline given. Offers 50% kill fee. Buys first North American serial rights; second serial (reprint) rights at reduced rate. Editorial lead time 6 months. Submit seasonal material 1 year in advance. Accepts simultaneous submissions. Writer's guidelines currently under revision. Editorial lineup for following year determined in June; queries held for consideration at that time. No phone calls.

Nonfiction: Domestic and international travel. "No purple prose." **Buys 6 mss/year.** Query with published clips only. Length: 800-1,500 words. **Pays 35-50¢/word.**

Reprints: Submit photocopy of article and information about when and where the article previously appeared. Pays 50% of amount paid for an original article.

Photos: State availability of photos with submission, do not send photos until requested. Offers $35-75/photo. Captions, model releases and identification of subjects required. Buys one-time rights.

Columns/Departments: Query with published clips only. **Pays 35-50¢/word.**

Tips: "Don't send gushy, travelogue articles. We prefer stories that are informative with practical, useful tips that are well written and researched. Approach an old topic/destination in a fresh/original way."

RELATIONSHIPS

These publications focus on lifestyles and relationships of single adults. Other markets for this type of material can be found in the Women's category. Magazines of a primarily sexual nature, gay or straight, are listed under the Sex category. Gay & Lesbian Interest contains general interest editorial targeted to that audience.

⊠ ✖ ▣ $ $ CONVERSELY, Conversely, Inc., PMB #121, 3053 Fillmore St., San Francisco CA 94123-4009. E-mail: writers@conversely.com. Website: www.conversely.com. **Contact:** Alejandro Gutierrez, editor. **60-80% freelance written.** Monthly online literary magazine (some sections will be published weekly) covering relationships between women and men. "*Conversely* is dedicated to exploring relationships between women and men—every stage, every aspect—through different forms of writing: essays, memoirs, fiction. Our audience is both female and male, mostly in the 18-35 year age range. We look for writing that is intelligent, provocative and witty; we look for topics that are original and appealing to our readers." Estab. 2000. Pays on publication. Publishes ms an average of 3 months after acceptance. Byline given. Negotiable kill fee. Buys electronic rights (60 days exclusive, non-exclusive thereafter). Editorial lead time 3 months. Submit seasonal material 3 months in advance. Accepts queries by e-mail only. Accepts simultaneous submissions (please note on cover letter). Responds in 2 weeks to queries; 2 months to mss. Sample copy and writer's guidelines on website.

Nonfiction: Essays, opinion, personal experience. "No how-to or anything that very overtly tries to teach or tell readers what to do or how to behave. No explicit sex." **Buys 30-36 mss/year.** Send complete ms. Length: 500-3,000 words. **Pays $50-150 for assigned articles; $50-100 for unsolicited articles.** Sometimes pays expenses of writers on assignment.

Reprints: Accepts previously published submissions, if so noted.

Photos: State availability of photos with submission. Negotiates payment individually.

Fiction: Mainstream. No erotica, science-fiction, gothic, romance. **Buys 5-10 mss/year.** Send complete ms. Length: 500-3,000 words. **Pays $50-100.**

Tips: "We value writing that is original in its choice of subject and/or its approach to it. We prefer work that explores different and/or unconventional, yet engaging, aspects of relationships. We seek writing that achieves a balance between 'intelligent,' 'provocative' and 'witty.' Intelligent as in complex and sophisticated. Provocative as in it challenges the reader by presenting unexpected or non-traditional viewpoints. Witty as in it uses clever humor, and the writing doesn't take itself too seriously. We turn down many otherwise fine submissions that discuss clichéd topics. We also turn down many well-written pieces in which the 'voice' is not right for us."

$ $ $ $ COUPLES, Couples Magazine, LLC, 17117 W. Nine Mile Rd., Suite 1211, Southfield MI 48075. (248)559-5707. **Contact:** Ivie Jonathan Shelton, editor. **90% freelance written.** Monthly magazine designed solely to nurture, build and enhance a loving relationship between a man and a woman. **Pays on acceptance.** Byline given. Offers 10-15% kill fee. Buys all magazine rights. Accepts queries by mail. Responds in 3 weeks to queries; 2 months to mss. Accepts simultaneous submissions. Send $2.50 and #10 SASE for writer's guidelines. Publishes ms an average of 5 months after acceptance.

Nonfiction: *Couples* is a source of information for men and women who want to have or enhance a loving and exciting relationship with their significant other. Consequently, we need articles that address lovers etiquette, interior design ideas for creating a more seductive and romantic home environment, finding that special someone, fashion, beauty, romantic getaways, communication ideas and techniques, imaginative means and ways to spice up your sex lives, going for the gold, etc. These articles must be lively, well researched and well written with references to those experts supporting the articles. Length: 1,500-3,000 words. **Pays $1/word.**

Photos: State availability of photos with submission. Reviews contact sheets, negatives, prints. Negotiates payment individually. Model releases, identification of subjects required.

Tips: "Our feature subjects include Etiquette for Lovers; Good Grooming and Glamour; What About . . . Sex?; Creating a Romantic Environment at Home; Romantic Getaways; Finding the Right Someone; Working Pairs; and Loving Your Children."

N **$ $** **DIVORCE MAGAZINE**, Segue Esprit Inc., 145 Front St., Suite 301, Toronto, Ontario M4K 1G3 Canada. E-mail: editors@divorcemag.com. Website: www.DivorceMagazine.com. **Contact:** Diana Shepherd, editor. **20% freelance written.** Quarterly magazine covering separation and divorce. "We have four quarterly editions: New York/New Jersey, Illinois, Southern California and Ontario. "*Divorce Magazine* is designed to help people cope with the difficult transition of separation and divorce. Our mandate is to provide a unique, friendly resource of vital information and timely advice to help our readers survive—even thrive—during their divorce." Estab. 1996. Circ. 100,000. Pays on publication. Publishes ms an average of 6 months after acceptance. Byline given. Offers 25% kill fee. Buys all rights. Editorial lead time 2-3 months. Submit seasonal material 6 months in advance. Accepts simultaneous submissions. Accepts queries by mail, e-mail, fax. Responds in 6 months to queries. Sample copy for $3.95 with SASE (note to Americans: Must use International postage not US postage). Writer's guidelines free.

Oπ Break in with "an article that will help people survive and thrive through separation and divorce."

Nonfiction: Book excerpts, how-to (see our website for previous examples), humor, family law. No first-person narrative stories (except for the humor column), poetry, fiction, celebrity gossip, "The Divorce from Hell" stories. **Buys 10-15 mss/year.** Query with published clips. Length: 1,000-3,000 words. **Pays 10-30¢/word.**

Reprints: Accepts previously published submissions.

Columns/Departments: Last Word (humor). Length: 750 words. **Buys 4 mss/year.** Query with published clips. **Pays 10-20¢/word.**

▣ The online version contains material not found in the print edition. Contact: Diana Shepherd.

Tips: "We accept submissions in writing only. To get an idea of the types of articles we publish, visit our website."

$ $ **LOVING MORE MAGAZINE**, PEP, P.O. Box 4358, Boulder CO 80306. Phone/fax: (303)543-7540. E-mail: lmm@lovemore.com. Website: www.lovemore.com. **Contacts:** Ryam Nearing/Brett Hill, editors. **80% freelance written.** "*Loving More* is a quarterly publication whose mission is to support, explore and enhance the many beautiful forms which families and loving relationships can take. We affirm that loving more than one can be a natural expression of health, exuberance, joy and intimacy. We view the shift from enforced monogamy and isolated families to polyamory and intentional families or tribes in the context of a larger shift toward a more balanced, peaceful and sustainable way of life." Estab. 1984. Circ. 3,000. Pays on publication. Publishes ms 6 months after acceptance. Byline given. Buys one-time rights or all rights. Editorial lead time 3 months. Submit seasonal material 6 months in advance. Accepts queries by mail, e-mail, fax. Responds in 1 month to queries. Sample copy for $6. Writer's guidelines for #10 SASE or via e-mail at writers@lovemore.com.

Nonfiction: Book excerpts, essays, exposé, how-to, humor, interview/profile, opinion, personal experience, photo feature. "No swinging sex, hardcore." **Buys 12-20 mss/year.** Query with published clips. Length: 750-3,000 words. **Pays $25-200.**

Reprints: Send information about when and where the article previously appeared. Pays 50% of amount paid for an original article.

Photos: Send photos with submission. Negotiates payment individually. Model releases required. Buys one-time rights.

Poetry: "We publish select poetry relevant to our theme."

$ **THE ROMANTIC, Hundreds of Creative Tips to Enrich Your Relationship**, Sterling Publications, P.O. Box 1567, Cary NC 27512-1567. (919)462-0900. Fax: (919)461-8333. E-mail: writer@TheRomantic.com. Website: www.TheRomantic.com. **Contact:** Michael Webb. **20% freelance written**. Bimonthly newsletter covering the art of romance. "*The RoMANtic* aims to inspire its readers to continually improve their relationships by providing them with creative ideas, practical advice and lots of fun suggestions." Estab. 1996. Circ. 10,000. Pays on publication. Publishes ms 4 months after acceptance. Byline given. Buys first North American serial rights or second serial (reprint) rights. Editorial lead time 3 months. Submit seasonal material 4 months in advance. Accepts simultaneous submissions. Responds in 3 months to mss. Sample copy for $3.

Nonfiction: Inspirational, personal experience. No sex, erotica or romance novels. Send complete ms. Length: 500 words maximum. **Pays 2¢/word.**

Tips: "Read one or more back issues on the website to see the types of romantic ideas and stories that are printed."

N **$** **SINGLES LIFESTYLE & ENTERTAINMENT MAGAZINE**, Single Lifestyle Publishing Group, 7611 S. Orange Blossom Trail, #190, Orlando FL 32809. **Contact:** Michael Orlando, editor. **50% freelance written.** Bimonthly tabloid "for single, divorced and widowed persons ages 25-50." Estab. 1997. Circ. 25,000. **Pays on acceptance.**

Publishes ms 1 month after acceptance. Byline given. Offers 100% kill fee. Buys one-time rights. Editorial lead time 2 months. Submit seasonal material 2 months in advance. Responds in 3 weeks to queries. Sample copy and writer's guidelines free.

Nonfiction: General interest, humor, interview/profile, travel, single life, lifestyles, relationships, single parenting, trends, health, fitness. **Buys 20 mss/year.** Query with published clips. Length: 500-1,500 words. **Pays 10¢/word.** Sometimes pays expenses of writers on assignment (limit agreed upon in advance).

Photos: State availability of photos with submission. Reviews contact sheets. Negotiates payment individually. Model releases required. Buys one-time rights.

Columns/Departments: Single Lifestyles; Single Parenting; Coping with Divorce. Length: 250-1,000 words. **Buys 25 mss/year.** Query with published clips. **Pays 10¢/word.**

Fiction: Humor, romance. **Buys 12 mss/year.** Query with published clips. Length: 1,000-2,000 words. **Pays 10¢/word.**

Reprints: Send tearsheet or photocopy of article and information about when and where the article previously appeared. Payment negotiable.

Fillers: Anecdotes, facts, gags to be illustrated by cartoonist, newsbreaks, short humor. **Buys 50/year.** Length: 50-150 words. **Pays 10¢/word.**

Tips: "Freelance writers must review our writer's guidelines in depth, plus thoroughly read our issues for a true feel for what we look for in articles and features. Query first with past published clips (any subject). Be creative in your query. Think Single Lifestyle!"

RELIGIOUS

Religious magazines focus on a variety of subjects, styles and beliefs. Most are sectarian, but a number approach topics such as public policy, international affairs and contemporary society from a non-denominational perspective. Fewer religious publications are considering poems and personal experience articles, but many emphasize special ministries to singles, seniors or other special interest groups. Such diversity makes reading each magazine essential for the writer hoping to break in. Educational and inspirational material of interest to church members, workers and leaders within a denomination or religion is needed by the publications in this category. Religious magazines for children and teenagers can be found in the Juvenile and Teen & Young Adult classifications. Other religious publications can be found in the Contemporary Culture and Ethnic/Minority sections as well. Spiritual topics are also addressed in Astrology, Metaphysical and New Age as well as Health & Fitness. Publications intended to assist professional religious workers in teaching and managing church affairs are classified in Church Administration & Ministry in the Trade section.

$ AMERICA, 106 W. 56th St., New York NY 10019. (212)581-4640. Fax: (212)399-3596. E-mail: articles@americapress.org. Website: wwwamericapress.org. **Contact:** Rev. Thomas J. Reese, editor. Published weekly for adult, educated, largely Roman Catholic audience. Estab. 1909. **Pays on acceptance.** Byline given. Usually buys all rights. Responds in 3 weeks. Free writer's guidelines by mail or on website.

Nonfiction: "We publish a wide variety of material on politics, economics, ecology and so forth. We are not a parochial publication, but almost all pieces make some moral or religious point. We are not interested in purely informational pieces or personal narratives which are self-contained and have no larger moral interest." Articles on literature, current political, social events. Length: 1,500-2,000 words. **Pays $50-200.**

Poetry: Contact Paul Mariani, poetry editor. Length: 15-30 lines. Only 10-12 poems published a year, thousands turned down.

N ✕ $ $ ANGELS ON EARTH, Guideposts, Inc., 16 E. 34th St., New York NY 10016. (212)251-8100. E-mail: angelsedtr@guideposts.org. **Contact:** Colleen Hughes, editor-in-chief. **90% freelance written.** Bimonthly. "*Angels on Earth* publishes true stories about God's messengers at work in today's world. We are interested in stories of heavenly angels and stories involving humans who have played angelic roles in daily life." Estab. 1995. Circ. 800,000. Pays on publication. Byline given. Buys all rights. Editorial lead time 6 months. Submit seasonal material 6 months in advance. Accepts queries by mail, e-mail. Responds in 3 months. Sample copy for 6½ × 9½ SAE with $1.01 postage. Writer's guidelines for SASE.

Nonfiction: True, inspirational, personal experience, religious (most stories are first-person experiences but can be ghost-written). Nothing that directly preaches, no how-to's. **Buys 80-100 mss/year.** Send complete ms. Length: 100-2,000 words. **Pays $25-400.**

Photos: State availability of photos or send photos with submission. Offers no additional payment for photos accepted with ms. Buys one-time rights.

Columns/Departments: Catherine Scott, departments editor. Earning Their Wings (unusual stories of good deeds worth imitating); Only Human? (Is the angelic character a human being? The narrator is pleasantly unsure and so is the reader), both 500 words. **Buys 25 mss/year.** Send complete ms. **Pays $50-100.** Messages (brief, mysterious happenings, or letters describing how a specific article helped you). **Pays $25.** Short angel incidents, attributed quotes about angels. **Buys 20-30/year.**

$ THE ANNALS OF SAINT ANNE DE BEAUPRÉ, Redemptorist Fathers, P.O. Box 1000, St. Anne De Beaupré, Quebec G0A 3C0 Canada. (418)827-4538. Fax: (418)827-4530. Editor: Father Bernard Mercier, CSs.R. **Contact:** Father Roch Achard, managing editor. **80% freelance written.** Monthly religious magazine. "Our mission statement includes a dedication to Christian family values and a devotion to St. Anne." Estab. 1885. Circ. 45,000. **Pays on acceptance.** Buys first North American rights. Editorial lead time 6 months. Submit seasonal material 4 months in advance. "Please, no reprints or simultaneous submissions." Responds in 3 weeks. Sample copy and writer's guidelines for 8½ × 11 SAE and IRCs.

Nonfiction: Inspirational, religious. **Buys 350 mss/year.** Send complete ms. Length: 500-1,500 words. **Pays 3-4¢/word,** plus 3 copies.

Photos: Send photos with submission. Negotiates payment individually. Identification of subjects required. Buys one-time rights.

Fiction: Religious, inspirational. "No senseless, mockery." **Buys 200 mss/year.** Send complete ms. Length: 500-1,500 words. **Pays 3-4¢/word.**

Tips: "Write something inspirational with spiritual thrust. Reporting rather than analysis is simply not remarkable. Each article must have a spiritual theme. Please only submit first North American rights mss with the rights clearly stated. We maintain an article bank and pick from it for each month's needs which loosely follow the religious themes for each month. Right now, our needs lean towards nonfiction of approximately 1,100 words."

$ BIBLE ADVOCATE, Bible Advocate Press, Church of God (Seventh Day), P.O. Box 33677, Denver CO 80233. (303)452-7973. E-mail: BibleAdvocate@cog7.org/BA/. Website: www.cog7.org/BA/. Editor: Calvin Burrell. **Contact**: Sherri Langton, associate editor. **25% freelance written.** Religious magazine published 10 times/year. "Our purpose is to advocate the Bible and represent the Church of God (Seventh Day) to a Christian audience." Estab. 1863. Circ. 13,500. Pays on publication. Publishes ms an average of 9 months after acceptance. Byline given. Offers 50% kill fee. Buys first and second serial (reprint) rights, plus electronic rights. Editorial lead time 3 months. Submit seasonal material 6 months in advance. Accepts queries by mail, e-mail. Accepts simultaneous submissions. Responds in 2 months. Sample copy for 9 × 12 SASE with 3 first-class stamps. Writer's guidelines for #10 SASE.

Nonfiction: Inspirational, opinion, personal experience, religious, biblical studies. No articles on Christmas or Easter. **Buys 20-25 mss/year.** Send complete ms and SASE. Length: 1,500 words. **Pays $10-35.**

Reprints: Send typed ms with rights for sale noted.

Photos: Send photos with submission. Reviews prints. Offers payment for photos accepted with ms. Identification of subjects required.

Columns/Departments: Viewpoint (opinion), 500-700 words. **Buys 3 mss/year.** Send complete ms and SASE. No payment for opinion pieces.

Poetry: Free verse, traditional. No avant-garde. **Buys 10-12 poems/year.** Submit maximum 5 poems. Length: 5-20 lines. **Pays $10.**

Fillers: Anecdotes, facts. **Buys 5/year.** Length: 50-400 words. **Pays $5-10.**

   ■ See the listing for Bible Advocate Online.

Tips: "Be fresh, not preachy! We're trying to reach a younger audience now, so think how you can cover contemporary and biblical topics with this audience in mind. Articles must be in keeping with the doctrinal understanding of the Church of God (Seventh Day). Therefore, the writer should become familiar with what the Church generally accepts as truth as set forth in its doctrinal beliefs. We reserve the right to edit manuscripts to fit our space requirements, doctrinal stands and church terminology. Significant changes are referred to writers for approval. No fax or handwritten submissions, please."

$ ■ BIBLE ADVOCATE ONLINE, Bible Advocate Press/Church of God (Seventh Day), P.O. Box 33677, Denver CO 80233. (303)452-7973. Fax: (303)452-0657. E-mail: BibleAdvocate@cog7.org. Website: www.cog7.org/BA/. Editor: Calvin Burrell. **Contact**: Sherri Langton, associate editor. **75% freelance written.** "Online religious publication covering social and religious topics; more inclusive of non-Christians." Estab. 1996. Pays on publication. Publishes ms an average of 3 months after acceptance. Byline given. Offers 50% kill fee. Buys first rights and second serial (reprint) rights. Editorial lead time 3 months. Submit seasonal material 6 months in advance. Accepts queries by mail, e-mail. Accepts simultaneous submissions. Responds in 6 weeks to queries. Sample copy for 9 × 12 SAE and 2 first-class stamps. Writer's guidelines for #10 SASE and on website.

   ○┐ "For the online magazine, write for the 'felt needs' of the reader and come up with creative ways for communicating to the unchurched."

Nonfiction: Inspirational, personal experience, religious. No Christmas or Easter pieces. **Buys 20-25 mss/year.** Send complete ms and SASE. Length: 1,500-1,800 words. **Pays $15-35.**

Reprints: Accepts previously published submissions. Send typed ms with rights for sale noted and information about when and where the article previously appeared. **Pays $15-35.**

Photos: Send photos with submission. Reviews prints. Offers additional payment for photos accepted with ms. Identification of subjects required. Buys one-time rights.

Fillers: Anecdotes, facts, resources. **Buys 6-10/year.** Length: 50-250 words. **Pays $5-10.**

Tips: "Be vulnerable in your personal experiences. Show, don't tell! Delete Christian jargon and write from perspective of a non-Christian. Articles must be in keeping with the doctrinal understanding of the Church of God (Seventh Day). Therefore, the writer should become familiar with what the Church generally accepts as truth as set forth in their doctrinal beliefs. We reserve the right to edit manuscripts to fit our space requirements, doctrinal stands and church terminology. Significant changes are referred to writers for approval. No fax or handwritten submissions, please."

N $ $CATHOLIC DIGEST, University of St. Thomas, 2115 Summit Ave., St. Paul MN 55105. (651)962-6739. Fax: (651)962-6758. E-mail: cdigest@stthomas.edu. Website: www.CatholicDigest.org. Editor: Richard J. Reece, **Contact:** Kathleen Stauffer, managing editor. **15% freelance written.** Monthly magazine "publishes features and advice on topics ranging from health, psychology, humor, adventure and family, to ethics, spirituality and Catholics, from modern-day heroes to saints through the ages. Helpful and relevant reading culled from secular and religious periodicals." Estab. 1936. Circ. 509,385. **Pays on acceptance** for articles. Publishes ms an average of 4 months after acceptance. Byline given. Buys first rights, one-time rights or second serial (reprint) rights. Editorial lead time 4 months. Submit seasonal material 5 months in advance. Responds in 2 months to mss. Sample copy and writer's guidelines free.

Nonfiction: Book excerpts, essays, general interest, historical/nostalgic, how-to, humor, inspirational, interview/profile, personal experience, religious, travel. **Buys 60 mss/year.** Send complete ms. Length: 1.000-5,000 words. **Pays $200-400.**

Reprints: "Most articles we use are reprinted." Send tearsheet of article or typed ms with rights for sale noted and information about when and where the article previously appeared. **Pays $100.**

Photos: State availability of photos with submission. Reviews contact sheets, transparencies, prints. Negotiates payment individually. Captions, model releases, identification of subjects required.

Columns/Departments: Buys 75 mss/year. Send complete ms. **Pays $4-50.**

　　▣ The online magazine carries original content not found in the print edition and includes writer's guidelines. Contact: Kathleen Stauffer, editor.

Fillers: Contact: Filler Editor. Anecdotes, short humor. **Buys 200/year.** Length: 1 line minimum, 500 words maximum. **Pays $2/per published line upon publication.**

Tips: "We're a lot more aggressive with inspirational/pop psychology/how-to articles these days. Spiritual and all other wellness self-help is a good bet for us. We would also like to see material with an innovative approach to traditional religion, articles that show new ways of looking at old ideas, problems."

$ $CATHOLIC FORESTER, Catholic Order of Foresters, 355 Shuman Blvd., P.O. Box 3012, Naperville IL 60566-7012. Fax: (630)983-3384. E-mail: cofpr@aol.com. Website: www.catholicforester.com. Associate Editor: Patricia Baron. **Contact:** Mary Ann File, editor. **20% freelance written.** Bimonthly magazine for members of the Catholic Order of Foresters. "*Catholic Forester* articles cover varied topics to create a balanced issue for the purpose of informing, educating and entertaining our readers." Circ. 100,000. **Pays on acceptance.** Publishes ms within 1 year after acceptance. Byline given. Offers $25 kill fee. Buys first North American serial rights. Editorial lead time 6 months. Submit seasonal material 6 months in advance. Accepts queries by mail. Responds in 3 months. Sample copy for 9 × 12 SAE and 4 first-class stamps. Writer's guidelines for #10 SASE.

Nonfiction: Humor, inspirational, religious, health, parenting, financial. **Buys 12-16 mss/year.** Send complete ms. Length: 500-1,500 words. **Pays 20-25¢/word.**

Photos: State availability of photos with submission. Reviews transparencies. Negotiates payment individually. Buys one-time rights.

Fiction: Humorous, religious. **Buys 12-16 mss/year.** Send complete ms. Length: 500-1,500 words. **Pays 20-25¢/word.**

Poetry: Light verse, traditional. **Buys 1 poem/year.** Submit maximum 5 poems. Length: 5-15 lines. **Pays 20-25¢/word.**

Tips: "Our audience covers a broad age spectrum, ranging from youth to seniors. Nonfiction topics that appeal to our members include health and wellness, money management and budgeting, parenting and family life, interesting travels, historical or contemporary personalities, nostalgia and humor pieces. Although we are more interested in nonfiction topics, we also like to entertain our readers with humor, light fiction and short inspirational pieces. A good children's story would rate high on our list."

$ $CATHOLIC NEAR EAST MAGAZINE, Catholic Near East Welfare Association, 1011 First Ave., New York NY 10022-4195. (212)826-1480. Fax: (212)826-8979. Website: www.cnewa.org. Executive Editor: Michael La Cività. **Contact:** Helen C. Packard, assistant editor. **50% freelance written.** Bimonthly magazine for a Catholic audience with interest in the Near East, particularly its current religious, cultural and political aspects. Estab. 1974. Circ. 100,000. Pays on publication. Publishes ms an average of 6 months after acceptance. Byline given. Buys all rights. Accepts queries by mail, fax. Responds in 2 months. Sample copy and writer's guidelines for 7½ × 10½ SAE with 2 first-class stamps.

Nonfiction: "Cultural, devotional, political, historical material on the Near East, with an emphasis on the Eastern Christian churches. Style should be simple, factual, concise. Articles must stem from personal acquaintance with subject matter, or thorough up-to-date research." Length: 1,200-1,800 words. **Pays 20¢/edited word.**

Photos: "Photographs to accompany manuscript are welcome; they should illustrate the people, places, ceremonies, etc. which are described in the article. We prefer color transparencies but occasionally use b&w. Pay varies depending on use—scale from $50-300."

Tips: "We are interested in current events in the Near East as they affect the cultural, political and religious lives of the people."

$ $ CELEBRATE LIFE, American Life League, P.O. Box 1350, Stafford VA 22555. (540)659-4171. Fax: (540)659-2586. E-mail: clmag@all.org. Website: www.all.org/. Editor: Anne Tinsdale. **Contact:** Cathy Kenyon, associate editor. **50% freelance written.** Bimonthly educational magazine covering pro-life education and human interest. "We are a religious-based publication specializing in pro-life education through human-interest stories and investigative exposés. Our purpose is to inspire, encourage, motivate and educate pro-life individuals and activists." Estab. 1979. Circ. 70,000. Pays on publication. Publishes ms an average of 8 months after acceptance. Byline given. Offers 25% kill fee. Buys first, second serial (reprint) rights or makes work-for-hire assignments. Editorial lead time 6 months. Submit seasonal material 4 months in advance. Accepts queries by mail, e-mail, fax. Accepts simultaneous submissions. Responds in 6 months to mss. Sample copy for 9×12 SAE and 4 first-class stamps. Writer's guidelines free by mail or e-mail.

    ⊶ Break in with "interview-based human interest or investigative exposés."

Nonfiction: "No fiction, book reviews, poetry, allegory, devotionals." **Buys 40 mss/year.** Query with published clips or send complete ms. Length: 300-1,500 words. **Pays 20¢/word for assigned articles; 5-10¢/word for unsolicited articles.** Pays expenses of writers on assignment.

Reprints: Accepts previously published submissions.

Photos: State availability of photos with submission. Reviews 4×6 prints. Identification of subjects required. Buys one-time rights.

Fillers: Newsbreaks. **Buys 5/year.** Length: 75-200 words. **Pays $10.**

    ▣ Online version of magazine: www.all.org/celebrate_life/indexht.

Tips: "We look for inspiring, educational or motivational human-interest stories. We are religious based and no exceptions pro-life. All articles must have agreement with the principles expressed in Pope John Paul II's encyclical *Evangelium Vitae*. Our common themes include: abortion, post-abortion healing, sidewalk counseling, adoption and contraception."

$ $ THE CHRISTIAN CENTURY, Christian Century Foundation, 104 S. Michigan Ave., Suite 700, Chicago IL 60605-1150. (312)263-7510. Fax: (312)263-7540. Website: www.christiancentury.org. Editor/Publisher: John M. Buchanan. **Contact**: David Heim, executive editor. **90% freelance written.** Eager to work with new/unpublished writers. Weekly magazine for ecumenically-minded, progressive Protestant church people, both clergy and lay. "Authors must have a critical and analytical perspective on the church and be familiar with contemporary theological discussion." Estab. 1884. Circ. 30,000. Pays on publication. Publishes ms an average of 3 months after acceptance. Buys all rights. Editorial lead time 1 month. Submit seasonal material 4 months in advance. Accepts queries by mail, e-mail, fax. Accepts simultaneous submissions. Responds in 1 week to queries; 2 months to mss. Sample copy for $3. Writer's guidelines on website.

Nonfiction: Essays, humor, interview/profile, opinion, religious. "We use articles dealing with social problems, ethical dilemmas, political issues, international affairs and the arts, as well as with theological and ecclesiastical matters. We focus on concerns that arise at the juncture between church and society, or church and culture." No inspirational. **Buys 150 mss/year.** Send complete ms; query appreciated, but not essential. All queries, mss should be accompanied by 9×12 SASE. Length: 1,000-3,000 words. **Pays $75-200 for assigned articles; $75-150 for unsolicited articles.**

Photos: State availability of photos. Reviews any size prints. Offers $25-100/photo. Buys one-time rights.

Fiction: Humorous, religious, slice-of-life vignettes. No moralistic, unrealistic fiction. **Buys 4 mss/year.** Send complete ms. Length: 1,000-3,000 words. **Pays $75-200.**

Poetry: Jill Peláez Baumgaertner, poetry editor. Avant-garde, free verse, haiku, traditional. No sentimental or didactic poetry. **Buys 50 poems/year.** Length: 20 lines. **Pays $50.**

    ▣ The online magazine carries original content not found in the print edition and includes writer's guidelines.

Tips: "We seek manuscripts that articulate the public meaning of faith, bringing the resources of religious tradition to bear on such topics as poverty, human rights, economic justice, international relations, national priorities and popular culture. We are also interested in articles that examine or critique the theology and ethos of individual religious communities. We welcome articles that find fresh meaning in old traditions and which adapt or apply religious traditions to new circumstances. Authors should assume that readers are familiar with main themes in Christian history and theology; are unthreatened by the historical-critical study of the Bible; and are already engaged in relating faith to social and political issues. Many of our readers are ministers or teachers of religion at the college level."

ℕ $ CHRISTIAN COURIER, Calvinist Contact Publishing, 4-261 Martindale Rd., St. Catharines, Ontario L2W 1A1 Canada. (905)682-8311. Fax: (905)682-8313. E-mail: cceditor@aol.com. **Contact:** Harry Der Nederlanden, editor. **20% freelance written.** Weekly newspaper covering news of importance to Christians, comments and features. "We assume a Christian perspective which acknowledges that this world belongs to God and that human beings are invited to serve God in every area of society." Estab. 1945. Circ. 4,000. Pays 30 days after publication. Publishes ms an average of 2 months after acceptance. Byline given. Offers 50% kill fee. Editorial lead time 1 month. Submit seasonal material 6 months in advance. Accepts simultaneous submissions. Responds only if material is accepted.

Nonfiction: Interview/profile, opinion. **Buys 40 mss/year.** Send complete ms. Length: 500-1,200 words. **Pays $35-60 for assigned articles; $25-50 for unsolicited articles.** Sometimes pays expenses of writers on assignment.

Reprints: Accepts previously published submissions.

Photos: State availability of photos with submission.

N $ CHRISTIAN EDUCATION COUNSELOR, General Council of the Assemblies of God, 1445 Boonville, Springfield MO 65802-1894. (417)862-2781. Fax: (417)862-0503. E-mail: ceeditor@ag.org. Website: www.we-build-people.org. Editor: Sylvia Lee. **20% freelance written.** Works with small number of new/unpublished writers each year. Bimonthly magazine on religious education in the local church—the official Sunday school voice of the Assemblies of God channeling programs and help to local, primarily lay, leadership. Estab. 1939. Circ. 20,000. **Pays on acceptance.** Publishes ms an average of 9 months after acceptance. Byline given. Offers variable kill fee. Buys first North American serial, one-time, all, simultaneous, first serial or second serial (reprint) rights or makes work-for-hire assignments. Submit seasonal material 7 months in advance. Accepts simultaneous submissions. Responds in 1 month. Sample copy and writer's guidelines for SASE.

Nonfiction: How-to, inspirational, interview/profile, personal experience, photo feature. All related to religious education in the local church. **Buys 100 mss/year.** Send complete ms. Length: 300-700 words. **Pays $25-150.**

Reprints: Send tearsheet of article or typed ms with rights for sale noted and information about when and where the article previously appeared. Pays 50% of amount paid for an original article.

Photos: Send photos with ms. Reviews b&w and color prints. Model releases and identification of subjects required. Buys one-time rights.

  • Looking for more photo-illustrated mss.

$ $ CHRISTIAN HOME & SCHOOL, Christian Schools International, 3350 E. Paris Ave. SE, Grand Rapids MI 49512. (616)957-1070, ext. 239. Fax: (616)957-5022. E-mail: rogers@csionline.org. Website: www.csionline.org/csi/chs. Executive Editor: Gordon L. Bordewyk. **Contact:** Roger Schmurr, senior editor. **30% freelance written.** Circ. 65,000. Works with a small number of new/unpublished writers each year. Bimonthly magazine covering family life and Christian education. "*Christian Home & School* is designed for parents in the United States and Canada who send their children to Christian schools and are concerned about the challenges facing Christian families today. These readers expect a mature, biblical perspective in the articles, not just a bible verse tacked onto the end." Estab. 1922. Pays on publication. Publishes ms an average of 4 months after acceptance. Byline given. Buys first North American serial rights. Submit seasonal material 4 months in advance. Accepts queries by mail, e-mail. Responds in 1 month. Sample copy and writer's guidelines for 9×12 SAE with 4 first-class stamps. Writer's guidelines only for #10 SASE or on website.

  ☛ Break in by picking a contemporary parenting situation/problem, and writing to Christian parents.

Nonfiction: Book excerpts, interview/profile, opinion, personal experience, articles on parenting and school life. "We publish features on issues that affect the home and school and profiles on interesting individuals, providing that the profile appeals to our readers and is not a tribute or eulogy of that person." **Buys 40 mss/year.** Send complete ms. Length: 1,000-2,000 words. **Pays $125-200.**

  • The editor reports an interest in seeing articles on how to raise polite kids in a rude world and good educational practices in Christian schools.

Photos: "If you have any color photos appropriate for your article, send them along."

Tips: "Features are the area most open to freelancers. We are publishing articles that deal with contemporary issues that affect parents. Use an informal easy-to-read style rather than a philosophical, academic tone. Try to incorporate vivid imagery and concrete, practical examples from real life. We look for manuscripts with a mature Christian perspective."

N $ $ CHRISTIAN READER, Stories of Faith, Hope and God's Love, Christianity Today, 465 Gundersen Dr., Carol Stream IL 60188. (630)260-6200. Fax: (630)260-0114. E-mail: creditoria@aol.com. Website: www.Christianreader.net. Editor: Bonne Steffen. **Contact:** Randy Bishop, assistant editor. **25% freelance written.** Bimonthly magazine for adult evangelical Christian audience. Estab. 1963. Circ. 185,000. **Pays on acceptance**; on publication for humor pieces. Byline given. Editorial lead time 5 months. Submit seasonal material 8 months in advance. Accepts queries by mail, e-mail, fax, phone. Accepts simultaneous submissions. Responds in 1 month. Sample copy for 5×8 SAE with 4 first-class stamps. Writer's guidelines for #10 SASE.

Nonfiction: Book excerpts, general interest, historical/nostalgic, humor, inspirational, interview/profile, personal experience, photo feature, religious. **Buys 100-125 mss/year.** Query or send complete ms. Length: 250-1,500 words. **Pays $125-600** depending on length. Pays expenses of writers on assignment.

Reprints: Accepts previously published submissions. Send tearsheet or photocopy of article or typed manuscript with rights for sale noted and information about when and where the article previously appeared. Pays 35-50% of amount paid for an original article on publication.

Photos: Send photos with submission. Reviews transparencies, prints. Negotiates payment individually. Identification of subjects required. Buys one-time rights.

Columns/Departments: Cynthia Thomas, editorial coordinator. Lite Fare (adult church humor), 50-200 words; Kids of the Kingdom (kids say and do funny things), 50-200 words; Rolling Down the Aisle (humorous wedding tales), 50-200 words. **Buys 50-75 mss/year.** Send complete ms. **Pays $25-35.**

Fillers: Anecdotes, short fillers, 100-250 words. **Buys 10-20 mss/year.** Send complete ms. **Pays $35.**

Tips: "Most of our articles are reprints or staff-written. Freelance competition is keen, so tailor submissions to meet our needs by observing the following: The *Christian Reader* audience is truly a general interest one, including men and women, urban professionals and rural homemakers, adults of every age and marital status, and Christians of every church affiliation. We seek to publish a magazine that people from the variety of ethnic groups in North America will find interesting and relevant."

$ CHRISTIAN SOCIAL ACTION, 100 Maryland Ave. NE, Washington DC 20002. (202)488-5631. Fax: (202)488-1617. E-mail: ealsgaard@umc-gbcs.org. **Contact:** Erik Alsgaard, editor. **10% freelance written.** Works with a small number of new/unpublished writers each year. Bimonthly for "United Methodist clergy and lay people interested in in-depth analysis of social issues, with emphasis on the church's role or involvement in these issues." Circ. 2,500. May buy all rights. Pays on publication. Publishes ms an average of 2 months after acceptance. Rights purchased vary with author and material. Accepts queries by mail, e-mail, fax. Returns rejected material in 5 weeks. Reports on material accepted for publication in a month. Sample copy and writer's guidelines for #10 SASE.

Nonfiction: "This is the social action publication of The United Methodist Church published by the denomination's General Board of Church and Society. Our publication tries to relate social issues to the church—what the church can do, is doing; why the church should be involved. We only accept articles relating to social issues, e.g., war, draft, peace, race relations, welfare, police/community relations, labor, population problems, drug and alcohol problems. No devotional, 'religious,' superficial material, highly technical articles, personal experiences or poetry." **Buys 25-30 mss/year.** "Query to show that writer has expertise on a particular social issue, give credentials, and reflect a readable writing style." Length: 2,000 words maximum. **Pays $75-125.** Sometimes pays the expenses of writers on assignment.

Reprints: Send tearsheet of article and information about where and when the article previously appeared. Payment negotiable.

Tips: "Write on social issues, but not superficially; we're more interested in finding an expert who can write (e.g., on human rights, alcohol problems, peace issues) than a writer who attempts to research a complex issue."

N □ $ $ CHRISTIANITY ONLINE MAG, Your Guide to the Internet, Christianity Today Inc., 465 Gunderson Dr., Carol Stream IL 60188. (630)260-6200. Fax: (630)260-0114. E-mail: comagazine@aol.com. Website: www.christianityonline.com/comag/current. **Contact:** Mark Moring, managing editor or Matt Donnelly, assistant editor. **15-20% freelance written.** Quarterly magazine providing a Christian guide to the Internet. "Our writers must have an understanding of the evangelical Christian audience." Estab. 1999. Circ. 100,000. **Pays on acceptance.** Publishes ms an average of 6 months after acceptance. Byline given. Offers 50% kill fee. Buys first or electronic rights. Editorial lead time 8 months. Submit seasonal material at least 8 months in advance. Accepts queries by mail, e-mail, fax. Accepts simultaneous submissions. Responds in 1 month to queries; 2 months to mss. Sample copy for 9×11 SAE and $3. Writer's guidelines for #10 SASE or online at website.

Nonfiction: Book excerpts, general interest, how-to, humor, interview/profile, personal experience, technical, trends. "No highly technical stuff; keep it simple." **Buys 2-4 mss/year.** Query with published clips. Length: 500-2,000 words. **Pays 15-20¢/word.**

Tips: "Know the evangelical culture. Know trends on the Internet. We're always looking for Net-related human interest stories/profiles."

$ $ CHRISTIANITY TODAY, 465 Gundersen Dr., Carol Stream IL 60188-2498. (630)260-6200. Fax: (630)260-0114. E-mail: CTEdit@aol.com Website: www.christianitytoday.com. **Contact:** Editor. **80% freelance written.** Works with a small number of new/unpublished writers each year. Semimonthly magazine emphasizing orthodox, evangelical religion; "covers Christian doctrine, issues, trends and current events and news from a Christian perspective. It provides a forum for the expression of evangelical conviction in theology, evangelism, church life, cultural life, and society. Special features include issues of the day, books, films, missions, schools, music and services available to the Christian market." Estab. 1956. Circ. 187,000. Publishes ms an average of 6 months after acceptance. Usually buys first serial rights. Submit seasonal material at least 8 months in advance. Accepts queries by mail, e-mail, fax, phone. Responds in 3 months. Sample copy and writer's guidelines for 9×12 SAE with 3 first-class stamps.

Nonfiction: Theological, ethical, historical, informational (not merely inspirational). **Buys 4 mss/issue.** *Query only.* Unsolicited mss not accepted and not returned. Length: 1,000-4,000 words. Pays negotiable rates. Sometimes pays the expenses of writers on assignment.

Reprints: Pays 25% of amount paid for an original article.

Columns/Departments: Church in Action (profiles of not-so-well-known Christians involved in significant or offbeat services). **Buys 7 mss/year.** Query only. Length: 900-1,000 words.

□ The online magazine carries original content not found in the print edition. Contact: Ted Olsen, online editor.

Tips: "We are developing more of our own manuscripts and requiring a much more professional quality from others. Queries without SASE will not be answered and manuscripts not containing SASE will not be returned."

$ $ CHRYSALIS READER, R.R. 1, Box 4510, Dillwyn VA 23936. E-mail for themes and guidelines (no mss will be accepted by e-mail): chrysalis@hovac.com. Website: www.swedenborg.com. Managing Editor: Susanna van Rensselaer. **Contact:** Richard Butterworth, associate editor. **90% freelance written.** Biannual literary magazine on spiritually related topics. *"It is very important to send for writer's guidelines and sample copies before submitting.* Content of fiction, articles, reviews, poetry, etc., should be directly focused on that issue's theme and directed to the educated, intellectually curious reader." Estab. 1985. Circ. 3,000. Pays at page-proof stage. Publishes ms an average of 9 months after acceptance. Byline given. Buys first rights and makes work-for-hire assignments. Accepts queries by mail, e-mail. Responds in 1 month to queries; 3 months to mss. Sample copy for $10 and 8½×11 SAE. Writer's guidelines and copy deadlines for SASE or by e-mail.

Nonfiction: Essays and interview/profile. Upcoming themes: Autumn (2001); Serendipity (2002). **Buys 20 mss/year.** Query. Length: 2,500-3,500 words. **Pays $50-250 for assigned articles; $50-150 for unsolicited articles.**

Photos and Illustrations: Send suggestions for illustrations with submission. Offers no additional payment for photos accepted with ms. Captions and identification of subjects required. Buys original artwork for cover and inside copy; b&w illustrations related to theme; pays $25-150. Buys one-time rights.
Fiction: Robert Tucker, fiction editor. Adventure, experimental, historical, mainstream, mystery, science fiction, related to theme of issue. **Buys 10 mss/year.** Query. Length: 2,500-3,500 words. Short fiction more likely to be published. **Pays $50-150.**
Poetry: Rob Lawson, senior editor. Avant-garde and traditional *but not religious.* **Buys 15 poems/year.** Submit maximum 6. **Pays $25.**

$ $COLUMBIA, 1 Columbus Plaza, New Haven CT 06510. (203)772-2130. Fax: (203)777-0114. E-mail: thickey @kofcsupreme.com. Website: www.kofc.org. **Contact:** Tim S. Hickey, editor. Monthly magazine for Catholic families. Caters particularly to members of the Knights of Columbus. Estab. 1921. Circ. 1,500,000. **Pays on acceptance.** Buys first serial rights. Accepts queries by mail, e-mail, fax. Free sample copy and writer's guidelines.
Nonfiction: Fact articles directed to the Catholic layman and his family dealing with current events, social problems, Catholic apostolic activities, education, ecumenism, rearing a family, literature, science, arts, sports and leisure. No reprints, poetry or cartoons. **Pays $300-600.** Query with SASE. Length: 1,000-1,500 words. **Buys 20 mss/year.**
  ● Ranked as one of the best markets for freelance writers in *Writer's Yearbook* magazine's annual "Top 100 Markets," January 2000.
  ◪ The online magazine carries original content not found in the print edition. Contact: Tim S. Hickey, online editor.
Tips: "Few unsolicited manuscripts are accepted."

$CONSCIENCE, A Newsjournal of Prochoice Catholic Opinion, Catholics for a Free Choice, 1436 U St. NW, Suite 301, Washington DC 20009-3997. (202)986-6093. E-mail: conscience@catholicsforchoice.org. Website: www.catholicsforchoice.org. **Contact:** Editor. **80% freelance written.** Sometimes works with new/unpublished writers. Quarterly newsjournal covering reproductive health and rights, including but not limited to abortion rights in the church, and church-state issues in US and worldwide. "A feminist, pro-choice perspective is a must, and knowledge of Christianity and specifically Catholicism is helpful." Estab. 1980. Circ. 12,000. Pays on publication. Publishes ms an average of 4 months after acceptance. Byline given. Buys first North American serial rights or makes work-for-hire assignments. Accepts queries by mail, e-mail. Responds in 4 months. Sample copy for 9×12 SAE with 4 first-class stamps. Writer's guidelines for #10 SASE.
Nonfiction: Book excerpts, interview/profile, opinion, issue anaylsis, a small amount of personal experience. Especially needs material that recognizes the complexity of reproductive issues and decisions, and offers original, honest insight. **Buys 8-12 mss/year.** Query with published clips or send complete ms. Length: 1,000-3,500 words. **Pays $25-150.** "Writers should be aware that we are a nonprofit organization."
Reprints: Sometimes accepts previously published submissions. Send typed ms with rights for sale noted and information about when and where the article previously appeared. Pays 20-30% of amount paid for an original article.
Photos: State availability of photos with query or ms. Prefers b&w prints. Identification of subjects required.
Columns/Departments: Book reviews. **Buys 6-10 mss/year.** Length: 600-1,200 words. **Pays $25-50.**
Tips: "Say something new on the issue of abortion, or sexuality, or the role of religion or the Catholic church, or women's status in the church. Thoughtful, well-researched and well-argued articles needed. The most frequent mistakes made by writers in submitting an article to us are lack of originality and wordiness."

Ⓝ $ $CORNERSTONE, Cornerstone Communications, Inc., 939 W. Wilson, Chicago IL 60640-5718. (773)561-2450, ext. 2080. Fax: (773)989-2076. E-mail: fiction@cornerstonemag.com, poetry@cornerstonemag.com, nonfiction@ cornerstonemag.com. Editor: Jon Trott. **Contact:** Tara Anderson, submissions editor. **10% freelance written.** Eager to work with new/unpublished writers. Irregularly published magazine covering contemporary issues in the light of Evangelical Christianity. Estab. 1972. Pays after publication. Byline given. Buys first serial rights. Submit seasonal material 6 months in advance. Accepts simultaneous submissions. Does not return mss. "We will contact you *only* if your work is accepted for possible publication. We *encourage* simultaneous submissions because we take so long to get back to people! E-mail all submissions to appropriate address. Send no queries." Sample copy and writer's guidelines for 8½×11 envelope with 5 first-class stamps.
Nonfiction: Essays, personal experience, religious. **Buys 1-2 mss/year.** E-mail complete ms. Length: 2,700 words maximum. **Pays 8-10¢/word.** Sometimes pays expenses of writers on assignment.
Reprints: Accepts previously published submissions. Send typed ms with rights for sale noted and information about when and where the article previously appeared. **Pays 8-10¢/word.**
Columns/Departments: Music (interview with artists, mainly rock, focusing on artist's world view and value system as expressed in his/her music), Current Events, Personalities, Film and Book Reviews (focuses on meaning as compared and contrasted to biblical values). **Buys 1-4 mss/year.** Query. Length: 100-2,500 words (negotiable). **Pays 8-10¢/word.**
Fiction: "Articles may express Christian world view but should not be unrealistic or 'syrupy.' Other than porn, the sky's the limit. We want fiction as creative as the Creator." **Buys 1-4 mss/year.** E-mail complete ms. Length: 250-2,500 words (negotiable). **Pays negotiable rate, 8-10¢/word.**
Poetry: Avant-garde, free verse, haiku, light verse, traditional. No limits *except* for epic poetry ("We've not the room!"). **Buys 10-50 poems/year.** Submit maximum 5 poems. **Payment negotiated. 1-15 lines: $10. Over 15 lines: $25.**

Tips: "A display of creativity which expresses a biblical world view without clichés or cheap shots at non-Christians is the ideal. We are known as one of the most avant-garde magazines in the Christian market, yet attempt to express orthodox beliefs in today's language. *Any* writer who does this may well be published by *Cornerstone*. Creative fiction is begging for more Christian participation. We anticipate such contributions gladly. Interviews where well-known personalities respond to the gospel are also strong publication possibilities."

$ $ DECISION, Billy Graham Evangelistic Association, 1300 Harmon Place, Minneapolis MN 55403-1988. (612)338-0500. Fax: (612)335-1299. E-mail: submissions@bgea.org. Website: www.decisionmag.org. Editor: Kersten Beckstrom. **Contact**: Bob Paulson, associate editor. **25-40% freelance written.** Works each year with small number of new/unpublished writers, as well as a solid stable of experienced writers. Monthly magazine with a mission "to set forth to every reader the Good News of salvation in Jesus Christ with such vividness and clarity that he or she will be drawn to make a commitment to Christ; to encourage, teach and strengthen Christians." Estab. 1960. Circ. 1,700,000. Pays on publication. Byline given. Buys first rights and assigns work-for-hire manuscripts, articles, projects. Include telephone number with submission. Submit seasonal material 10 months in advance; other mss published up to 18 months after acceptance. Responds in 3 months to mss. Sample copy for 9×12 SAE with 4 first-class stamps. Writer's guidelines for #10 SASE.

Nonfiction: How-to, motivational, personal experience and religious. "No personality-centered articles or articles that are issue-oriented or critical of denominations." **Buys approximately 75 mss/year.** Send complete ms. Length: 400-1,000 words. **Pays $30-260.** Pays expenses of writers on assignment.

Photos: State availability of photos with submission. Reviews prints. Captions, model releases and identification of subjects required. Buys one-time rights.

Poetry: Accepting submissions. No queries.

Tips: "We are seeking personal conversion testimonies and personal experience articles that show how God intervened in a person's daily life and the way in which Scripture was applied to the experience in helping to solve the problem. The conversion testimonies describe in first person what author's life was like before he/she became a Christian, how he/she committed his/her life to Christ and what difference Christ has made in the author's life. We also are looking for vignettes on various aspects of personal evangelism. SASE required with submissions."

$ $ DISCIPLESHIP JOURNAL, NavPress, a division of The Navigators, P.O. Box 35004, Colorado Springs CO 80935-0004. (719)531-3571. Fax: (719)598-7128. E-mail: adam.holz@navpress.com. Website: www.discipleshipjournal.com. **Contact:** Adam Holz, associate editor. **90% freelance written.** Works with a small number of new/unpublished writers each year. Bimonthly magazine. "The mission of *Discipleship Journal* is to help believers develop a deeper relationship with Jesus Christ, and to provide practical help in understanding the scriptures and applying them to daily life and ministry. We prefer those who have not written for us before begin with non-theme articles about almost any aspect of Christian living. We'd like more articles that explain a Bible passage and show how to apply it to everyday life, as well as articles about developing a relationship with Jesus; reaching the world; or specific issues related to leadership and helping other believers grow." Estab. 1981. Circ. 115,000. **Pays on acceptance.** Publishes ms an average of 6 months after acceptance. Byline given. Buys first North American serial rights and second serial (reprint) rights. Submit seasonal material 6 months in advance. Accepts queries by mail, e-mail, fax. Responds in 6 weeks. Sample copy and writer's guidelines for $2.56 and 9×12 SAE or on website.

    O┐ Break in through departments (On the Home Front, Getting into God's Word, DJ Plus) and with non-theme feature articles.

Nonfiction: Book excerpts (rarely); how-to (grow in Christian faith and disciplines; help others grow as Christians; serve people in need; understand and apply the Bible); inspirational; interview/profile (focusing on one aspect of discipleship); and interpretation/application of the Bible. "We'd like to see more articles that encourage involvement in world missions; help readers in personal evangelism, follow-up, and Christian leadership; or show how to develop a real relationship with Jesus." No personal testimony; humor; anything not directly related to Christian life and faith; politically partisan articles. **Buys 80 mss/year.** Query with published clips and SASE only. Length: 500-2,500 words. **Pays 25¢/word for first rights.** Sometimes pays the expenses of writers on assignment.

    ● Ranked as one of the best markets for freelance writers in *Writer's Yearbook* magazine's annual "Top 100 Markets," January 2000.

Reprints: Send tearsheet of article and information about when and where the article previously appeared. **Pays 5¢/word for reprints.**

Tips: "Our articles are meaty, not fluffy. Study writer's guidelines and back issues and try to use similar approaches. Don't preach. Polish before submitting. About half of the articles in each issue are related to one theme. Freelancers should write to request theme list. We are looking for more practical articles on ministering to others and more articles dealing with world missions. Be vulnerable. Show the reader that you have wrestled with the subject matter in your own life. We can no longer accept unsolicited manuscripts. Query first."

$ DOVETAIL, A Journal By and For Jewish/Christian Families, Dovetail Institute for Interfaith Family Resources, 775 Simon Greenwell Ln., Boston, KY 40107. Fax: (502)549-3543. E-mail: dif-ifr@bardstown.com. Website: www.dovetailpublishing.com. **Contact:** Mary Heléne Rosenbaum. **75% freelance written.** Bimonthly newsletter for interfaith families. "All articles must pertain to life in an interfaith (Jewish/Christian) family. We accept all kinds of opinions related to this topic." Estab. 1992. Circ. 1,500. Pays on publication. Publishes ms an average of 9 months after acceptance. Byline given. Buys first, one-time or second serial (reprint) rights. Editorial lead time 6 months. Submit seasonal material 6 months in advance. Accepts simultaneous submissions. Accepts queries by mail, e-mail, fax, phone. Electronic submissions preferred (unformatted text). Responds in 3 months. Sample copy for 9×12 SAE with 3 first-class stamps. Writer's guidelines free.

O—π Break in with "a fresh approach to standard interfaith marriage situations."

Nonfiction: Interview/profile, opinion, personal experience. No fiction. **Buys 5-8 mss/year.** Send complete ms. Length: 800-1,000 words. **Pays $20** plus 2 copies. Book reviews: 500 words. **Pays $10** plus 2 copies.

Reprints: Accepts previously published submissions.

Photos: Send photos with submission. Reviews 5×7 prints. Offers no additional payment for photos accepted with ms. Model releases and identification of subjects required. Buys one-time rights.

Fillers: Anecdotes, short humor. **Buys 1-2/year.** Length: 25-100 words. **Pays $10.**

Tips: "Write on concrete, specific topics related to Jewish/Christian intermarriage: no proselytizing, sermonizing, or general religious commentary. Successful freelancers are part of an interfaith family themselves, or have done solid research/interviews with members of interfaith families. We look for honest, reflective personal experience. We're looking for more on alternative or nontraditional families, e.g., interfaith gay/lesbian, single parent raising child in departed partner's faith."

⊠ $ EVANGEL, Free Methodist Publishing House, P.O. Box 535002, Indianapolis IN 46253-5002. (317)244-3660. **Contact:** Julie Innes, editor. **100% freelance written.** Weekly take-home paper for adults. Estab. 1897. Circ. 20,000. Pays on publication. Publishes ms an average of 1 year after acceptance. Buys simultaneous, second serial (reprint) or one-time rights. Submit seasonal material 9 months in advance. Accepts queries by mail. Responds in 1 month. Sample copy and writer's guidelines for #10 SASE.

Nonfiction: Interview (with ordinary person who is doing something extraordinary in his community, in service to others), profile (of missionary or one from similar service profession who is contributing significantly to society), personal experience (finding a solution to a problem common to young adults; coping with handicapped child, for instance, or with a neighborhood problem. Story of how God-given strength or insight saved a situation). **Buys 125 mss/year.** Submit complete ms. Length: 300-1,000 words. **Pays 4¢/word.**

Reprints: Send typed ms with rights for sale noted and information about when and where the article previously appeared.

Photos: Purchased with accompanying ms. Captions required.

Fiction: Religious themes dealing with contemporary issues dealt with from a Christian frame of reference. Story must "go somewhere." **Buys 50 mss/year.** Submit complete ms.

Poetry: Free verse, light verse, traditional, religious. **Buys 20 poems/year.** Submit maximum 5 poems. Length: 4-24 lines. **Pays $10.**

Tips: "Seasonal material will get a second look. Write an attention-grabbing lead followed by an article that says something worthwhile. Relate the lead to some of the universal needs of the reader—promise in that lead to help the reader in some way. Lack of SASE brands author as a nonprofessional."

⌖ $ THE EVANGELICAL BAPTIST, Fellowship of Evangelical Baptist Churches in Canada, 18 Louvigny, Lorraine, Quebec J6Z 1T7 Canada. (450)621-3248. Fax: (450)621-0253. E-mail: eb@fellowship.ca. Website: www.fellowship.ca. **Contact:** Ginette Cotnoir, managing editor. **30% freelance written.** Magazine published 5 times/year covering religious, spiritual, Christian living, denominational and missionary news. "We exist to enhance the life and ministry of the church leaders of our association of churches—including pastors, elders, deacons and all the men and women doing the work of the ministry in local churches." Estab. 1953. Circ. 3,000. Pays on publication. Publishes ms an average of 6 months after acceptance. Byline given. Buys one-time or second serial (reprint) rights. Editorial lead time 4 months. Accepts queries by mail, e-mail. Accepts simultaneous submissions. Responds in 6 weeks to queries; 2 months to mss. Sample copy for 9×12 SAE with $1.50 in first-class stamps. Writer's guidelines for #10 SASE.

O—π Break in with items for "Church Life (how-to and how-we articles about church ministries, e.g., small groups, worship, missions) or Columns (Joy in the Journey, View from the Pew)."

Nonfiction: Religious. No poetry, fiction, puzzles. **Buys 12-15 mss/year.** Send complete ms. Length: 500-2,400 words. **Pays $25-50.** Pays in copies for small church news items. Sometimes pays expenses of writers on assignment.

Reprints: Accepts previously published submissions.

Photos: State availability of photos with submission. Reviews prints. Offers no additional payment for photos accepted with ms. Captions required. Buys one-time rights.

Columns/Departments: Church Life (practical articles about various church ministries, e.g., worship, Sunday school, missions, seniors, youth, discipleship); Joy in the Journey (devotional article re: a lesson learned from God in everyday life); View from the Pew (light, humorous piece with spiritual value on some aspect of Christian living), all 600-800 words. **Buys 10 mss/year.** Send complete ms. **Pays $25-50.**

Tips: "Columns and departments are the best places for freelancers. Especially looking for practical articles for Church Life from writers who are themselves involved in a church ministry. Looking for 'how-to' and 'how-we' approach."

⌖ $ EVANGELICAL MISSIONS QUARTERLY, A Professional Journal Serving the Missions Community, Billy Graham Center/Wheaton College, P.O. Box 794, Wheaton IL 60189. (630)752-7158. Fax: (630)752-7155. E-mail: emqjournal@aol.com. Website: www.wheaton.edu/bgc/emis. Editor: Gary Corwin. **Contact:** Stan Guthrie, managing editor. **67% freelance written.** Quarterly magazine covering evangelical missions. "This is a professional journal for evangelical missionaries, agency executives and church members who support global missions ministries." Estab.

1964. Circ. 7,000. Pays on publication. Publishes ms an average of 18 months after acceptance. Byline given. Offers negotiable kill fee. Buys electronic and all rights. Editorial lead time 1 year. Accepts queries by mail, e-mail, fax. Responds in 2 weeks to queries. Sample copy and writer's guidelines free.

Nonfiction: Essays, interview/profile, opinion, personal experience, religious. No sermons, poetry, straight news. **Buys 24 mss/year.** Query. Length: 800-3,000 words. **Pays $50-100.**

Reprints: Accepts previously published submissions.

Photos: Send photos with submission. Reviews prints. Offers no additional payment for photos accepted with ms. Identification of subjects required. Buys all rights.

Columns/Departments: In the Workshop (practical how to's), 800-2,000 words; Perspectives (opinion), 800 words. **Buys 8 mss/year.** Query. **Pays $50-100.**

$ $ EVANGELIZING TODAY'S CHILD, Child Evangelism Fellowship Inc., Box 348, Warrenton MO 63383-0348. (636)456-4321. Fax: (636)456-2078. E-mail: etceditor@cefinc.org. Website: www.cefing.org/etcmag/. **Contact:** Elsie Lippy, editor. **50% freelance written.** Prefers to work with published/established writers. Bimonthly magazine. "Our purpose is to equip Christians to win the world's children to Christ and disciple them. Our readership is Sunday school teachers, Christian education leaders and children's workers in every phase of Christian ministry to children up to 12 years old." Estab. 1942. Circ. 20,000. Pays within 90 days of acceptance. Publishes ms an average of 6 months after acceptance. Byline given. Offers kill fee if assigned. Buys first serial rights. Submit seasonal material 6 months in advance. Accepts queries by mail, e-mail, fax. Responds in 2 months. Sample copy for $2. Writer's guidelines for SASE.

Nonfiction: Unsolicited articles welcomed from writers with Christian education training or current experience in working with children. **Buys 35 mss/year.** Query. Length: 1,200 words. **Pays 10-14¢/word.**

Reprints: Send photocopy of article and information about when and where the article previously appeared. Pays 35% of amount paid for an original article.

$ $ FAITH TODAY, Informing Canadian Evangelicals On Thoughts, Trends, Issues and Events, Evangelical Fellowship of Canada, MIP Box 3745, Markham, Ontario L3R 0Y4 Canada. (905)479-5885. Fax: (905)479-4742. E-mail: ft@efc-canada.com. Website: www.efc-canada.com. **Contact:** Larry Matthews, managing editor. "*FT* is a bimonthly interdenominational, evangelical news/feature magazine that informs Canadian Christians on issues facing church and society, and on events within the church community. It focuses on corporate faith interacting with society rather than on personal spiritual life. Writers should have a thorough understanding of the *Canadian evangelical* community." Estab. 1983. Circ. 18,000. Pays on publication. Publishes ms an average of 6 months after acceptance. Byline given. Offers 30-50% kill fee. Buys first rights. Editorial lead time 4 months. Accepts queries by mail, e-mail, fax. Responds in 6 weeks. Sample copy and writer's guidelines free with SASE in Canadian postage.

Nonfiction: Religious, news feature. **Buys 75 mss/year.** Query. Length: 400-2,000 words. **Pays $100-500 Canadian,** more for cover topic material. Sometimes pays expenses of writers on assignment.

Reprints: Send photocopy of article. Pays 50% of amount paid for an original article. Rarely used.

Photos: State availability of photos with submission. Reviews contact sheets, prints. Identification of subjects required. Buys one-time rights.

Tips: "Query should include brief outline and names of the sources you plan to interview in your research. Use Canadian postage on SASE."

N $ THE FIVE STONES, Newsletter for Small Churches, 69 Weymouth St., Providence RI 02906. (401)861-9405. E-mail: pappas@ma.ultranet.com. **Contact:** Tony Pappas, editor. **33% freelance written.** Quarterly newsletter covering issues related to small church life. "*The Five Stones* is the only journal for the issues small congregations face. First-person articles and accounts of positive experiences best." Circ. 750. Pays on publication. Byline given. Not copyrighted. Editorial lead time 1 year. Submit seasonal material 1 year in advance. Accepts queries by mail, e-mail, fax, phone. Accepts simultaneous submissions. Responds in 1 month to queries; 4 months to mss. Sample copy for 9 × 12 SAE and 3 first-class stamps. Writer's guidelines for #10 SASE.

Nonfiction: Book excerpts, essays, general interest, historical/nostalgic, how-to, humor, inspirational, interview/profile, new product, personal experience, religious. **Buys 8-12 mss/year.** Send complete ms. Length: 1,500 words maximum. **Pays $5.**

Reprints: Accepts previously published submissions.

$ $ GROUP MAGAZINE, Group Publishing Inc., P.O. Box 481, Loveland CO 80539. (970)669-3836. Fax: (970)669-1994. E-mail: rlawrence@grouppublishing.com. Website: www.grouppublishing.com. Publisher: Tim Gilmour. **Contact:** Rick Lawrence, editor. Departments Editor: Kathy Dieterich. **60% freelance written.** Bimonthly magazine covering youth ministry. "Writers must be actively involved in youth ministry. Articles we accept are practical, not theoretical, and focused for local church youth workers." Estab. 1974. Circ. 57,000. **Pays on acceptance.** Publishes ms an average of 6 months after acceptance. Byline given. Offers $20 kill fee. Buys all rights. Submit seasonal material 7 months in advance. Responds in 2 months. Sample copy for $2 and 9 × 12 SAE. Writer's guidelines for SASE or on website.

Nonfiction: How-to (youth ministry issues). No personal testimony, theological or lecture-style articles. **Buys 50-60 mss/year.** Query. Length: 250-2,200 words. **Pays $40-250.** Sometimes pays for phone calls on agreement.

Tips: "Submit a youth ministry idea to one of our mini-article sections—we look for tried-and-true ideas youth ministers have used with kids."

\$ \$ GUIDEPOSTS MAGAZINE, 16 E. 34th St., New York NY 10016-4397. (212)251-8100. Website: www.guide posts.org. **Contact:** Mary Ann O'Roark, executive editor. **30% freelance written.** Works with a small number of new/ unpublished writers each year. "*Guideposts* is an inspirational monthly magazine for people of all faiths, in which men and women from all walks of life tell in true first-person narrative how they overcame obstacles, rose above failures, handled sorrow, gained new spiritual insight and became more effective people through faith in God." Estab. 1945. Publishes ms an "indefinite" number of months after acceptance. Pays 20% kill fee for assigned articles. "Many of our stories are ghosted articles, so the writer would not get a byline unless it was his/her own story." Buys all rights and second serial (reprint) rights. Responds in 2 months.

Nonfiction and Fillers: Articles and features should be true stories written in simple, anecdotal style with an emphasis on human interest. Short mss of approximately 250-750 words **(pays \$100-250)** considered for such features as "Angels Among Us," "His Mysterious Ways" and general one-page stories. Address short items to Celeste McCauley. For full-length mss, 750-1,500 words, **pays \$250-500.** All mss should be typed, double-spaced and accompanied by SASE. Annually awards scholarships to high school juniors and seniors in writing contest. **Buys 40-60 unsolicited mss/year.** Pays expenses of writers on assignment.

Tips: "Study the magazine before you try to write for it. Each story must make a single spiritual point that readers can apply to their own daily lives. And it may be easier to just sit down and write them than to have to go through the process of preparing a query. They should be warm, well written, intelligent and upbeat. We require personal narratives that are true and have some spiritual aspect, but the religious element can be subtle and should *not* be sermonic. A writer succeeds with us if he or she can write a true article using short-story techniques with scenes, drama, tension and a resolution of the problem presented."

\$ HOME TIMES, "A Good Little Newspaper for God & Country," Neighbor News, Inc., 3676 Collin Dr., #12, West Palm Beach FL 33406. (561)439-3509. E-mail: hometimes2@aol.com. **Contact:** Dennis Lombard, publisher/ editor. **50% freelance written.** Monthly tabloid of conservative, pro-Christian news and views. "*Home Times* is a conservative newspaper written for the general public but with a Biblical worldview and family-values slant. It is not religious or preachy. We are going on the Internet in 2000. We want to place our best writers on there too." Estab. 1988. Circ. 5,000. Pays on publication. Publishes ms an average of 3 months after acceptance. Byline given. No kill fee. Buys one-time rights. Editorial lead time 1 month. Submit seasonal material 2 months in advance. Accepts simultaneous submissions. Responds in 1 month. Sample copy for \$3. Writer's guidelines for #10 SASE.

• *Home Times* is developing extended guidelines in 2000 for local stringers and freelancers, and a new editorial menu and map.

Nonfiction: Current events, essays, general interest, historical/nostalgic, how-to, humor, inspirational, interview/profile, opinion, personal experience, photo feature, religious, travel. "Nothing preachy, moralistic or with churchy slant." **Buys 25 mss/year.** Send complete ms. Length: 500-900 words. **Pays \$5 minimum.** Pays contributor's copies or subscriptions on mutual agreement.

Reprints: Send tearsheet or photocopy of article or short story and information about when and where the material previously appeared. **Pays \$5-10.**

Photos: Send photos with submission. Reviews any size prints. Offers \$5/photo used. Captions, model releases (when legally needed), identification of subjects required. Buys one-time rights.

Columns/Departments: Buys 50 mss/year. Send complete ms, maximum of 3 samples. **Pays \$5-15.**

Fiction: Historical, humorous, mainstream, religious, issue-oriented contemporary. "Nothing preachy, moralistic." **Buys 5 mss/year.** Send complete ms. Length: 500-700 words. **Pays \$5-25.**

Poetry: Free verse, light verse, traditional. **Buys 12 poems/year.** Submit 3 poems maximum, 2-24 lines. **Pays \$5.**

Fillers: Anecdotes, facts, good quotes, short humor. **Uses 25/year.** Length: to 100 words. Pays 6 issues on acceptance.

Tips: "We encourage new writers. We are different from ordinary news or religious publications. We strongly suggest you read guidelines and sample issues. (Writer's subscription 12 issues for \$12, regularly \$16.) We are most open to material for new columns; journalists covering hard news in major news centers—with conservative slant. Also, lots of letters and short op-eds though we pay only in issues (6) for them. We're also looking for good creative nonfiction, especially historical, conservative and/or humorous."

[N] \$ \$ INSIDE JOURNAL, The Hometown Newspaper of America's Prisoners, Prison Fellowship Ministries, P.O. Box 17429, Washington DC 20041-0429. (703)478-0100. Fax: (703)318-0235. E-mail: jpeck@pfm.org. Editor: Terry White. **Contact:** Jeff Peck, managing editor. **5% freelance written.** Bimonthly newspaper covering prisons, prison life, surviving prison. "*IJ* is a Christian newspaper written exclusively for prisoners. All content is passed through a Christian worldview to inspire hope and aid inmates in their present circumstances. Material must have direct influence on prison life with practical takeaway value for the readers." Estab. 1990. Circ. 400,000. Pays on publication. Publishes ms an average of 2 months after acceptance. Byline given. Buys first, second serial (reprint) and simultaneous rights. Editorial lead time 2 months. Submit seasonal material 2 months in advance. Accepts queries by mail, e-mail. Accepts simultaneous submissions. Responds in 2 months to queries; 8 months to mss. Sample copy and writer's guidelines free.

Nonfiction: How-to (survive prison, find a job, fight depression), humor, inspirational, interview/profile, religious. No fiction, stories that have nothing to do with prison or ex-prisoners, or Bible studies. **Buys 5 mss/year.** Send complete ms. Length: 500-1,500 words. **Pays $50-200.** Pays prisoners in contributor copies.

Reprints: Accepts previously published submissions.

Photos: State availability of or send photos with submission. Reviews contact sheets, transparencies and prints. Negotiates payment individually. Identification of subjects required. Buys one-time rights.

Columns/Departments: Shortimer (preparing for release from prison); Especially for Women (how women cope with prison); Fatherly Advice (how to be a father in prison), all 500 words. **Buys 3 mss/year.** Send complete ms.

Tips: "Visit a prison, find out firsthand what inmates are dealing with. Or find an ex-prisoner who is making it on the outside. Interview person for 'How are you successful' tips. What are they doing differently to avoid returning to prison. Also, we need more celebrity interviews with people of Christian faith."

N ✄ $LIFEGLOW, Christian Record Services, P.O. Box 6097, Lincoln NE 68506. (402)488-0981. Fax: (402)488-7582. **Contact:** Gaylena Gibson, editor. **95% freelance written.** Large print Christian publication for sight-impaired over 25 covering health, handicapped people, uplifting articles. Estab. 1984. Circ. 32,700. **Pays on acceptance.** Publishes ms an average of 3 years after acceptance. Byline given. Buys one-time rights. Submit seasonal material "anytime—if accepted, we will drop in the proper month." Accepts queries by mail. Accepts simultaneous submissions. Responds in 5 weeks to queries; 4 months to mss. "Prefer manuscripts." Sample copy for 7×10 SAE and 5 first-class stamps. Writer's guidelines for #10 SASE (or included with sample copy in 7×10).

   O→ "Write for an interdenominational Christian audience."

Nonfiction: Adventure, biography, careers, essays, general interest, handicapped, health, historical/nostalgic, hobbies, humor, inspirational, marriage, nature, personal experience, travel. "No 'hot' issues: gun control, abortion, etc." **Buys 40 mss/year.** Send complete ms. Length: 200-1,400 words. **Pays 4-5¢/word.** "We do send complimentary copies in addition to payment."

Reprints: Accepts previously published submissions.

Photos: Send photos with submission. Reviews prints. Negotiates payment individually. Buys one-time rights.

Columns/Departments: Baffle U! (puzzle), 150 words; Vitality Plus (current health topics), length varies. **Buys 10 mss/year.** Send complete ms. **Pays 4¢/word** for "Vitality." "Baffle U!" is a flat rate $15-25 per puzzle.

Poetry: Light verse. **Buys very few poems/year.** Length: 12 lines. **Pays $10-20.**

Fillers: Anecdotes, facts, short humor. **Buys very few/year.** Length: 300 words maximum. **Pays 4¢/word.**

Tips: "Make sure manuscript has a strong ending that ties everything together and doesn't leave us dangling. Pretend someone else wrote it—would it hold your interest? Draw your readers into the story by being specific rather than abstract or general."

$ $LIGUORIAN, One Liguori Dr., Liguori MO 63057-9999. (636)464-2500. Fax: (636)464-8449. E-mail: aweinert@liguori.com. Website: www.liguori.org. Managing Editor: Cheryl Plass. **Contact:** Fr. Allen Weinert, CSSR, editor-in-chief. **25% freelance written.** Prefers to work with published/established writers. Magazine published 10 times/year for Catholics. "Our purpose is to lead our readers to a fuller Christian life by helping them better understand the teachings of the gospel and the church and by illustrating how these teachings apply to life and the problems confronting them as members of families, the church and society." Estab. 1913. Circ. 260,000. **Pays on acceptance.** Buys all rights but will reassign rights to author *after* publication upon written request. Submit seasonal material 8 months in advance. Accepts queries by mail, e-mail, fax, phone. Responds in 6 months. Sample copy and writer's guidelines for 6×9 SAE with 3 first-class stamps or on website.

Nonfiction: "Pastoral, practical and personal approach to the problems and challenges of people today. No travelogue approach or unresearched ventures into controversial areas. Also, no material found in secular publications—fad subjects that already get enough press, pop psychology, negative or put-down articles." **Buys 60 unsolicited mss/year.** Length: 400-2,000 words. **Pays 10-12¢/word.** Sometimes pays expenses of writers on assignment.

Photos: Photographs on assignment only unless submitted with and specific to article.

N ✄ $LIVE WIRE, Standard Publishing, 8121 Hamilton Ave., Cincinnati OH 45231. Fax: (513)931-0950. Website: www.standardpub.com. **Contact:** Carla J. Crane, editor. **100% freelance written.** Sunday school take-home paper. "A weekly Sunday school take-home newspaper geared to preteens (10-12-year-olds) who want to live a godly life and connect with Christ." Estab. 1997. Circ. 40,000. **Pays on acceptance.** Publishes ms an average of 1 year after acceptance. Byline given. Buys first, one-time, second serial (reprint) and all rights. Editorial lead time 1 year. Submit seasonal material 1 year in advance. Accepts simultaneous submissions. Responds in 2 months. Sample copy and writer's guidelines for #10 SASE.

Nonfiction: General interest, historical/nostalgic, interview/profile, personal experience, religious. **Buys 60-90 mss/year.** Send complete ms. Length: 200-350 words. **Pays 3-7¢/word.**

Reprints: Accepts previously published submissions.

Photos: State availability of photos with submission.

$THE LIVING CHURCH, Living Church Foundation, 816 E. Juneau Ave., P.O. Box 514036, Milwaukee WI 53203. (414)276-5420. Fax: (414)276-7483. E-mail: tlc@livingchurch.org. Managing Editor: John Schuessler. **Contact:** David Kalvelage, editor. **50% freelance written.** Weekly religious magazine on the Episcopal church. News or articles of interest to members of the Episcopal church. Estab. 1878. Circ. 9,000. Does not pay unless article is requested.

Publishes ms an average of 3 months after acceptance. Byline given. Buys one-time rights. Editorial lead time 3 weeks. Submit seasonal material 1 month in advance. Accepts queries by mail, e-mail, fax. Responds in 2 weeks to queries; 1 month to mss. Sample copy free. Writer's guidelines on website.

Nonfiction: Opinion, personal experience, photo feature, religious. **Buys 10 mss/year.** Send complete ms. Length: 1,000 words. **Pays $25-100.** Sometimes pays expenses of writers on assignment.

Photos: Send photos with submission. Reviews any size prints. Offers $15-50/photo. Buys one-time rights.

Columns/Departments: Benediction (devotional) 250 words; Viewpoint (opinion) under 1,000 words. Send complete ms. **Pays $50 maximum.**

Poetry: Light verse, traditional.

$ LIVING LIGHT NEWS, Living Light Ministries, 5304 89th St., #200, Edmonton, Alberta T6E 5P9 Canada. (780)468-6397. Fax: (780)468-6872. E-mail: shine@livinglightnews.org. Website: www.livinglightnews.org. **Contact:** Jeff Caporale, editor. **75% freelance written.** Bimonthly tabloid covering Christianity. "We are an evangelical Christian newspaper slanted towards proclaiming the gospel and encouraging Christians." Estab. 1995. Circ. 20,000. Pays on publication. Publishes ms an average of 4 months after acceptance. Byline sometimes given. Offers 100% kill fee. Buys first North American serial rights, first rights, one-time rights, second serial (reprint) rights and makes work-for-hire assignments. Editorial lead time 3 months. Submit seasonal material 3 months in advance. Accepts queries by mail, e-mail, fax. Accepts simultaneous submissions. Sample copy for 9×12 SAE with 2 IRCs. Writer's guidelines free or on website.

O— Break in with "a story about a well-known Christian in sports or entertainment."

Nonfiction: General interest, humor, inspirational, interview/profile, religious. "We have a special Christmas issue focused on the traditional meaning of Christmas." No issue-oriented, controversial stories. **Buys 5-10 mss/year.** Query. Length: 300-1,200 words. **Pays $20-125 for assigned articles; $10-70 for unsolicited articles.** Sometimes pays expenses of writers on assignment.

Reprints: Send photocopy of article or short story or typed ms with rights for sale noted and information about when and where it previously appeared. **Pays 5¢/word.**

Photos: State availability of photos with submission. Reviews 3×5 prints. Offers $10-50/photo. Identification of subjects required. Buys one-time rights.

Columns/Departments: Relationships (Christian perspective), 500 words; Finance (Christian perspective), 500 words; Book, music, video reviews (Christian perspective parenting), 250-350 words. **Buys 5-10 mss/year.** Query with published clips. **Pays $15-40.**

Fiction: Christmas. "We only want to see Christmas-related fiction." **Buys 2-3 mss/year.** Query with published clips. Length: 500-2,000 words. **Pays $20-100.**

Tips: "It is very helpful if the person is a Bible believing Christian interested in proclaiming the gospel through positive, uplifting and timely stories of interest to Christians and non-Christians."

[N] $ $ THE LOOKOUT, For Today's Growing Christian, Standard Publishing, 8121 Hamilton Ave., Cincinnati OH 45231-9981. (513)931-4050. Fax: (513)931-0950. E-mail: lookout@standardpub.com. Website: www.standardpub.com. Editor: David Faust. Managing Editor: Alvalee Harley. **Contact:** Pat McCarty, assistant editor. **50% freelance written.** Weekly magazine for Christian adults, with emphasis on spiritual growth, family life, and topical issues. "Our purpose is to provide Christian adults with practical, biblical teaching and current information that will help them mature as believers." Audience is mainly conservative Christians. Estab. 1894. Circ. 100,000. **Pays on acceptance.** Publishes ms an average of 1 year after acceptance. Byline given. Pays 33% kill fee. Buys first rights or one-time rights. Editorial lead time 6 months. Submit seasonal material 6 months in advance. Accepts queries by mail, e-mail, fax. Accepts simultaneous submissions. Responds in 3 weeks to queries; 2 months to mss. Sample copy and writer's guidelines for 75¢. Guidelines for #10 SASE.

Nonfiction: Inspirational, interview/profile, opinion, personal experience, religious. "Writers need to send for current theme list. No fiction or poetry." **Buys 100 mss/year.** Query or send complete ms. Length: 350-800 words. **Pays 5-12¢/word.** "We also use inspirational short pieces." Sometimes pays expenses of writers on assignment.

Reprints: Accepts previously published submissions. Pays 60% of amount paid for an original article.

Photos: State availability of photos with submission. Offers no additional payment for photos accepted with ms. Identification of subjects required. Buys one-time rights.

Tips: "*The Lookout* publishes from a theologically conservative, nondenominational, and noncharismatic perspective. It is a member of the Evangelical Press Association. We have readers in every adult age group, but we aim primarily for those aged 35 to 55. Most readers are married and have older elementary to young adult children. But a large number come from other home situations as well. Our emphasis is on the needs of ordinary Christians who want to grow in their faith, rather than on trained theologians or church leaders. As a Christian general-interest magazine, we cover a wide variety of topics—from individual discipleship to family concerns to social involvement. We value well-informed articles that offer lively and clear writing as well as strong application. We often address tough issues and seek to explore fresh ideas or recent developments affecting today's Christians."

$ $ $ THE LUTHERAN, Magazine of the Evangelical Lutheran Church in America, 8765 W. Higgins Rd., Chicago IL 60631-4183. (773)380-2540. Fax: (773)380-2751. E-mail: lutheran@elca.org. Website: www.TheLutheran.org. Managing Editor: Sonia Solomonson. **Contact:** David L. Miller, editor. **15% freelance written.** Monthly magazine for "lay people in church. News and activities of the Evangelical Lutheran Church in America, news of the world of religion, ethical reflections on issues in society, personal Christian experience." Estab. 1988. Circ. 620,000. **Pays on acceptance.** Publishes ms an average of 6 months after acceptance. Byline given. Offers 50% kill fee. Buys first rights. Submit seasonal material 4 months in advance. Accepts queries by mail, e-mail. Responds in 6 weeks. Sample copy and writer's guidelines free.

O→ Break in by checking out the theme list on the website and querying with ideas related to these themes.

Nonfiction: Inspirational, interview/profile, personal experience, photo feature, religious. "No articles unrelated to the world of religion." **Buys 40 mss/year.** Query with published clips. Length: 500-1,500 words. **Pays $400-700 for assigned articles; $100-500 for unsolicited articles.** Pays expenses of writers on assignment.

Photos: Send photos with submission. Reviews contact sheets, transparencies, prints. Offers $50-175/photo. Captions and identification of subjects required. Buys one-time rights.

▣ The online magazine carries original content not found in the print edition. Contact: Lorel Fox, online editor.

Columns/Departments: Lite Side (humor—church, religious), In Focus, Living the Faith, Values & Society, In Our Churches, Our Church at Work, 25-100 words. Send complete ms. **Pays $10.**

Tips: "Writers have the best chance selling us feature articles."

THE LUTHERAN DIGEST, The Lutheran Digest, Inc., P.O. Box 4250, Hopkins MN 55343. (612)933-2820. Fax: (612)933-5708. **Contact:** David L. Tank, editor. **95% freelance written.** Quarterly magazine covering Christianity from a Lutheran perspective. "Articles frequently reflect a Lutheran Christian perspective, but are not intended to be sermonettes. Popular stories show how God has intervened in a person's life to help solve a problem." Estab. 1953. Circ. 125,000. **Pays on acceptance.** Publishes ms an average of 6 months after acceptance. Byline given. Buys first (original articles) or second serial rights. Editorial lead time 9 months. Submit seasonal material 9 months in advance. Accepts queries by mail. Accepts simultaneous submissions. Responds in 1 month to queries; 4 months to mss. Sample copy for $3. Writer's guidelines free.

O→ Break in with "reprints from other publications that will fill less than three pages of *TLD*. Articles of one or two pages are even better. As a digest, we primarily look for previously published articles to reprint, however, we do publish about twenty to thirty percent original material. Articles from new writers are always welcomed and seriously considered."

Nonfiction: Historical/nostalgic, how-to (personal or spiritual growth), humor, inspirational, personal experience, religious. Does not want to see "personal tributes to deceased relatives or friends. They are seldom used unless the subject of the article is well-known. We also avoid articles about the moment a person finds Christ as his or her personal savior." **Buys 50-60 mss/year.** Send complete ms. Length: 1,500 words. **Pays $25-50.** "For some reprint permissions and for poetry, pays writers in contributor copies or other premiums."

Reprints: Accepts previously published submissions. "We prefer this as we are a digest and 70-80% of our articles are reprints."

Photos: State availability of photos with submission. Buys one-time rights.

Tips: "An article that tugs on the 'heart strings' just a little and closes leaving the reader with a sense of hope is a writer's best bet to breaking into *The Lutheran Digest*."

THE LUTHERAN JOURNAL, 7317 Cahill Rd., Suite 201, Minneapolis MN 55439-2081. (952)562-1234. Fax: (952)941-3010. Publisher: Michael L. Beard. Editor: Rev. Armin U. Deye. **Contact:** Jessica Person, editorial assistant. Published 3 times/year. Family magazine for Lutheran Church members, middle age and older. Estab. 1938. Circ. 130,000. Pays on publication. Byline given. Buys one-time rights. Accepts simultaneous submissions. Responds in 4 months. Sample copy for 9×12 SAE with 78¢ postage.

Nonfiction: Inspirational, religious, human interest, historical articles. Interesting or unusual church projects. Informational, how-to, personal experience, interview, humor, think articles. **Buys 25-30 mss/year.** Submit complete ms. Length: 1,500 words maximum; occasionally 2,000 words. **Pays 1-4¢/word.**

Reprints: Send tearsheet or photocopy of article or typed ms with rights for sale noted and information about when and where the article previously appeared. Pays up to 50% of amount paid for an original article.

Photos: Send photocopies of b&w and color photos with accompanying ms. Please do not send original photos.

Poetry: Publishes 2-3 poems/issue, as space allows. **Pays $5-30.**

Tips: "Send submissions with SASE so we may respond."

LUTHERAN PARTNERS, Augsburg Fortress, Publishers, ELCA (DM), 8765 W. Higgins Rd., Chicago IL 60631-4195. (773)380-2875. Fax: (773)380-2829. E-mail: lpartmag@elca.org. Website: www.elca.org/dm/lp. Managing Editor: William A. Decker. **Contact:** Carl E. Linder, editor. **15-20% freelance written.** Bimonthly magazine covering issues of religious leadership. "We are a leadership magazine for the ordained and rostered lay ministers of the Evangelical Lutheran Church in America (ELCA), fostering an exchange of opinions on matters involving theology, leadership, mission and service to Jesus Christ. Know your audience: ELCA congregations and the various kinds of leaders who make up this church and their prevalent issues of leadership." Estab. 1979. Circ. 20,000. Pays on publication. Publishes ms an average of 6 months after acceptance. Byline given. Buys first, one-time (including electronic), second serial (reprint) or archival rights. Editorial lead time 6 months. Submit seasonal material 6 months in advance. Accepts queries by mail, e-mail, fax, phone. Accepts simultaneous submissions. Responds in 1 month to queries; 6 months to mss. Sample copy for $2 or on website. Writer's guidelines free or on website.

O→ Break in through "Jottings" (practical how-to articles involving congregational ministry ideas; 500 words maximum)."

Nonfiction: Historical/nostalgic, how-to (leadership in faith communities), humor (religious cartoon), inspirational, opinion (religious leadership issues), religious, book reviews (query book review editor). "No exposés, no articles primarily promoting products/services; no anti-religion." **Buys 15-20 mss/year.** Query with published clips or send complete ms. Length: 500-2,000 words. **Pays $25-170.** Pays in copies for book reviews.
  • The editor reports an interest in seeing articles on various facets of ministry from the perspectives of ethnic authors (Hispanic, African-American, Asian, Native American, Arab-American).
Reprints: Accepts previously published submissions.
Photos: State availability of photos with submission. Offers no additional payment for photos accepted with ms. Captions and identification of subjects required. Buys one-time rights.
Columns/Departments: Thelma Megill Cobbler, review editor. Partners Review (book reviews), 700 words. Query. **Pays in copies.**
Fiction: Religious. Rarely accepts fiction. Query.
Poetry: Free verse, haiku, light verse, traditional, hymn. **Buys 6-10 poems/year.** Submit maximum 10 poems. **Pays $50-75.**
Fillers: Practical ministry (education, music, youth, social service, administration, worship, etc.) in congregation. **Buys 3-6/year.** Length: 500 words. **Pays $25.**
Tips: "Understand ELCA congregational life. Think current and future leadership needs. Know congregational life, especially from the perspective of leadership, including both ordained pastor and lay staff. It would be good to be familiar with ELCA rostered pastors, lay ministers, and congregations."

N $ $ THE LUTHERAN WITNESS, The Lutheran Church—Missouri Synod, 1333 S. Kirkwood Rd., St. Louis MO 63122. (314)965-9000. Fax: (314)965-3396. E-mail: ic_mahsmadl@lcms.org. Editor: Rev. David Mahsman. **Contact:** Don Folkemer, managing editor. **50% freelance written.** Monthly magazine. "*The Lutheran Witness* provides Missouri Synod laypeople with stories and information that complement congregational life, foster personal growth in faith, and help interpret the contemporary world from a Christian perspective." Estab. 1882. Circ. 325,000. **Pays on acceptance.** Publishes ms an average of 6 months after acceptance. Byline given. Offers 50% kill fee. Buys first rights. Editorial lead time 4 months. Submit seasonal material 6 months in advance. Accepts queries by mail, e-mail, fax. Accepts simultaneous submissions. Responds in 2 months. Sample copy and writer's guidelines free or on website.
Nonfiction: General interest, humor, inspirational, interview/profile, opinion, personal experience, religious. **Buys 40-50 mss/year.** Send complete ms. Length: 250-1,600 words. **Pays $100-300.** Pays expenses of writers on assignment.
Reprints: Accepts previously published submissions.
Photos: Send photos with submission. Offers $50-200/photo. Captions required. Buys one-time rights.
Columns/Departments: Humor, Opinion, Bible Studies. **Buys 60 mss/year.** Send complete ms. **Pays $50-100.**

$ MENNONITE BRETHREN HERALD, 3-169 Riverton Ave., Winnipeg, Manitoba R2L 2E5 Canada. (204)669-6575. Fax: (204)654-1865. E-mail: mbherald@mbconf.ca. Website: www.herald.com. **Contact:** Jim Coggins, editor or Susan Brandt, managing editor. **25% freelance written.** Biweekly family publication "read mainly by people of the Mennonite faith, reaching a wide cross section of professional and occupational groups, including many homemakers. Readership includes people from both urban and rural communities. It is intended to inform members of events in the church and the world, serve personal and corporate spiritual needs, serve as a vehicle of communication within the church, serve conference agencies and reflect the history and theology of the Mennonite Brethren Church." Estab. 1962. Circ. 15,500. Pays on publication. Publishes ms 6 months after acceptance. Not copyrighted. Byline given. Buys one-time rights. Accepts queries by e-mail, fax. Responds in 6 months. Sample copy for $1 and 9×12 SAE with 2 IRCs.
Nonfiction: Articles with a Christian family orientation; youth directed, Christian faith and life, and current issues. Wants articles critiquing the values of a secular society, attempting to relate Christian living to the practical situations of daily living; showing how people have related their faith to their vocations. Send complete ms. "Articles and manuscripts not accepted for publication will be returned if a SASE (Canadian stamps or IRCs) is provided by the writer." Length: 250-1,500 words. **Pays $30-40.** Pays the expenses of writers on assignment.
Reprints: Send tearsheet or photocopy of article or typed ms with rights for sale noted and information about when and where the article previously appeared. Pays 70% of amount paid for an original article.
Photos: Photos purchased with ms.
Columns/Departments: Viewpoint (Christian opinion on current topics), 850 words. Crosscurrent (Christian opinion on music, books, art, TV, movies), 350 words.
Poetry: Length: 25 lines maximum.
Tips: "We like simple style, contemporary language and fresh ideas. Writers should take care to avoid religious clichés."

$ $ MESSAGE MAGAZINE, Review and Herald Publishing, 55 West Oak Ridge Dr., Hagerstown MD 21740. (301)393-4099 ext. 2565. Fax: (301)393-4103. E-mail: message@rhpa.org. Website: www.messagemagazine.org. Editor: Ron Smith. Associate Editor: Dwain Esmond. **Contact:** Rhoda K. Johnson, editorial assistant. **10-20% freelance written.** Bimonthly magazine. "*Message* is the oldest religious journal addressing ethnic issues in the country. Our audience is predominantly black and Seventh-day Adventist; however, *Message* is an outreach magazine geared to the unchurched." Estab. 1898. Circ. 120,000. **Pays on acceptance.** Publishes ms an average of 12 months after acceptance.

Byline given. Buys first North American serial rights; "the exception to this rule is for supplemental issues, for which we usually purchase all rights." Editorial lead time 6 months. Submit seasonal material 6 months in advance. Send complete ms. Responds in 9 months. Sample copy and writer's guidelines free.

Nonfiction: General interest to a Christian audience, how-to (overcome depression; overcome defeat; get closer to God; learn from failure, etc.), inspirational, interview/profile (profiles of famous African-Americans), personal experience (testimonies), religious. **Buys 10 mss/year.** Send complete ms. Length: 800-1,300 words. **Pays $50-300.**

Photos: State availability of photos with submission. Identification of subjects preferred. Buys one-time rights.

Columns/Departments: Voices in the Wind (community involvement/service/events/health info); Message, Jr. (stories for children with a moral, explain a biblical or moral principle); Recipes (no meat or dairy products—12-15 recipes and an intro); Healthspan (health issues); all 500 words. **Buys 12-15 mss/year.** Send complete ms for Message, Jr. and Healthspan. Query editorial assistant with published clips for Voices in the Wind and Recipes. **Pays $50-300.**

Fiction: "We do not generally accept fiction, but when we do it's for Message, Jr. and/or has a religious theme. We buy about 3 (if that many) fiction manuscripts a year." Send complete ms. Length: 500-700 words. **Pays $50-125.**

Fillers: Anecdotes, facts, newsbreaks. **Buys 1-5 fillers/year.** Length: 200-500 words. **Pays $50-125.**

▣ The online version contains material not found in the print edition.

Tips: "Please look at the magazine before submitting manuscripts. *Message* publishes a variety of writing styles as long as the writing style is easy to read and flows—please avoid highly technical writing styles."

$ THE MESSENGER OF THE SACRED HEART, Apostleship of Prayer, 661 Greenwood Ave., Toronto, Ontario M4J 4B3 Canada. (416)466-1195. **Contact:** Rev. F.J. Power, S.J., editor. Monthly magazine for "Canadian and U.S. Catholics interested in developing a life of prayer and spirituality; stresses the great value of our ordinary actions and lives." **20% freelance written.** Estab. 1891. Circ. 15,000. Buys first rights only. Byline given. **Pays on acceptance.** Submit seasonal material 5 months in advance. Responds in 1 month. Sample copy for $1 and 7½×10½ SAE. Writer's guidelines for SASE.

Fiction: Religious/inspirational. Stories about people, adventure, heroism, humor, drama. **Buys 12 mss/year.** Send complete ms with SAE and IRCs. Does not return mss without SASE. Length: 750-1,500 words. **Pays 4¢/word.**

Tips: "Develop a story that sustains interest to the end. Do not preach, but use plot and characters to convey the message or theme. Aim to move the heart as well as the mind. Before sending, cut out unnecessary or unrelated words or sentences. If you can, add a light touch or a sense of humor to the story. Your ending should have impact, leaving a moral or faith message for the reader."

Ⓝ $ $ MINNESOTA CHRISTIAN CHRONICLE, Beard Communications, 7317 Cahill Rd., Suite 201, Minneapolis MN 55439. Fax: (612)941-3010. E-mail: chronicle@myhometown.net. **Contact:** Doug Trouten, editor. **10% freelance written.** Biweekly newspaper covering Christian community in Minnesota. "Our readers tend to be conservative evangelicals with orthodox Christian beliefs and conservative social and political views." Estab. 1978. Circ. 8,000. Pays 1 month following publication. Publishes ms an average of 2 months after acceptance. Byline given. Buys one-time rights. Editorial lead time 1 month. Submit seasonal material 2 months in advance. Accepts simultaneous submissions. Responds in 1 month. Sample copy for $2. Writer's guidelines for #10 SASE.

Nonfiction: Exposé, general interest, historical/nostalgic, how-to, humor, inspirational, interview/profile, new product, photo feature, religious. Special issues: Higher education guide, Christmas section, Christian school directory. **Buys 36 mss/year.** Query. Length: 500-2,000 words. **Pays $20-200.** Sometimes pays expenses of writers on assignment.

Reprints: Send typed ms with rights for sale noted. Pays 50% of amount paid for an original article.

Photos: State availability of photos with submission. Reviews contact sheets. Negotiates payment individually. Captions preferred. Buys one-time rights.

Columns/Departments: Lis Trouten, associate editor. Family Gatherings (home and family), 200-500 words. **Buys 6 mss/year.** Query. **Pays $10-50.**

Tips: "Stories for the Minnesota Christian Chronicle must have a strong Minnesota connection and a clear hook for the Christian community. We do not publish general nonreligious stories or devotionals. We rarely buy from writers who are not in Minnesota."

$ THE MIRACULOUS MEDAL, 475 E. Chelten Ave., Philadelphia PA 19144-5785. (215)848-1010. **Contact:** Rev. William J. O'Brien, C.M., editor. **40% freelance written.** Quarterly. Estab. 1915. **Pays on acceptance.** Publishes ms an average of 2 years after acceptance. Buys first North American serial rights. Buys articles only on special assignment. Accepts queries by mail. Responds in 3 months. Sample copy for 6×9 SAE with 2 first-class stamps.

MARKET CONDITIONS are constantly changing! If this is 2002 or later, buy the newest edition of *Writer's Market* at your favorite bookstore or order directly from Writer's Digest Books at (800)289-0963.

Fiction: Should not be pious or sermon-like. Wants good general fiction—not necessarily religious, but if religion is basic to the story, the writer should be sure of his facts. Only restriction is that subject matter and treatment must not conflict with Catholic teaching and practice. Can use seasonal material, Christmas stories. Length: 2,000 words maximum. Occasionally uses short-shorts from 1,000-1,250 words. **Pays 2¢/word minimum.**

Poetry: Maximum of 20 lines, preferably about the Virgin Mary or at least with religious slant. **Pays 50¢/line minimum.**

$ $ MOODY MAGAZINE, Moody Bible Institute, 820 N. LaSalle Blvd., Chicago IL 60610. (312)329-2164. Fax: (312)329-2149. E-mail: moodyedit@moody.edu. Website: www.moody.edu. **Contact:** Andrew Scheer, managing editor. **62% freelance written.** Bimonthly magazine for evangelical Christianity (6 issues/year). "Our readers are conservative, evangelical Christians highly active in their churches and concerned about applying their faith in daily living." Estab. 1900. Circ. 112,000. **Pays on acceptance.** Publishes ms an average of 9 months after acceptance. Byline given. Buys first North American serial rights. Submit seasonal material 9 months in advance. Query first for all submissions by mail, but not by phone. Unsolicited mss will be returned unread. Responds in 2 months. Sample copy for 9×12 SAE with $2 first-class postage. Writer's guidelines for #10 SASE.

    O— Break in with "non-cover, freestanding narrative articles."

Nonfiction: Personal narratives (on living the Christian life), a few reporting articles. **Buys 55 mss/year.** "No biographies, historical articles, or studies of Bible figures." Query. Length: 1,200-2,200 words. **Pays 15¢/word for queried articles; 20¢/word for assigned articles.** Sometimes pays the expenses of writers on assignment.

    ● Ranked as one of the best markets for freelance writers in *Writer's Yearbook* magazine's annual "Top 100 Markets," January 2000.

Columns/Departments: First Person (the only article written for non-Christians; a personal conversion testimony written by the author [will accept "as told to's"]; the objective is to tell a person's testimony in such a way that the reader will understand the gospel and want to receive Christ as Savior), 800-900 words; News Focus (in-depth, researched account of current news or trend), 1,000-1,400 words. **Buys 12 mss/year.** May query by fax or e-mail for News Focus only. **Pays 15¢/word.**

Fiction: Will consider well-written contemporary stories that are directed toward scriptural application. Avoid clichéd salvation accounts, biblical fiction, parables, and allegories. Length: 1,200-2,000 words. **Pays 15¢/word.**

Tips: "We want articles that cover a broad range of topics, but with one common goal: to foster application by a broad readership of specific biblical principles. *Moody* especially seeks narrative accounts showing one's realization and application of specific, scriptural principles in daily life. In generating ideas for such articles, we recommend a writer consider: what has God been 'working on' in your life in the past few years? How have you been learning to apply a new realization of what Scripture is commanding you to do? What difference has this made for you and those around you? By publishing accounts of people's spiritual struggles, growth and discipleship, our aim is to encourage readers in their own obedience to Christ. We're also looking for some pieces that use an anecdotal reporting approach."

$ $ MY DAILY VISITOR, Our Sunday Visitor, Inc., 200 Noll Plaza, Huntington IN 46750. (219)356-8400. E-mail: mdvisitor@osv.com. **Contact:** Catherine M. Odell, editor. **99% freelance written.** Bimonthly magazine of Scripture meditations based on the day's Catholic mass readings. Circ. 30,000. **Pays on acceptance.** Publishes ms an average of 6 months after acceptance. Byline given. Not copyrighted. Buys one-time rights. Accepts queries by mail, e-mail. Responds in 2 months. Sample copy and writer's guidelines for #10 SAE with 2 first-class stamps. "Guest editors write on assignment basis only."

Nonfiction: Inspirational, personal experience, religious. **Buys 12 mss/year.** Query with published clips. Length: 150-160 words times number of days in month. **Pays $500** for 1 month (28-31) of meditations and 5 free copies.

$ OBLATES, Missionary Association of Mary Immaculate, 9480 N. De Mazenod Dr., Belleville IL 62223-1160. (618)398-4848. Fax: (618)398-8788. Managing Editor: Christine Portell. **Contact:** Mary Mohrman, manuscripts editor. **30% freelance written.** Prefers to work with published writers. Bimonthly inspirational magazine for Christians; audience mainly older Catholic adults. Circ. 500,000. **Pays on acceptance.** Usually publishes ms within 2 years after acceptance. Byline given. Buys first North American serial rights. Submit seasonal material 6 months in advance. Accepts queries by phone only. Responds in 2 months. Sample copy and writer's guidelines for 6×9 or larger SAE with 2 first-class stamps.

Nonfiction: Inspirational and personal experience with positive spiritual insights. No preachy, theological or research articles. Avoid current events and controversial topics. Send complete ms; 500-600 words. **Pays $80.**

    ● "We no longer accept Christmas season material. Our November/December issue is all inhouse."

Poetry: Light verse—reverent, well-written, perceptive, with traditional rhythm and rhyme. "Emphasis should be on inspiration, insight and relationship with God." Submit maximum 2 poems. Length: 8-16 lines. **Pays $30.**

Tips: "Our readership is made up mostly of mature Americans who are looking for comfort, encouragement, and a positive sense of applicable Christian direction to their lives. Focus on sharing of personal insight to problem (i.e., death or change), but must be positive, uplifting. We have well-defined needs for an established market but are always on the lookout for exceptional work."

N $ $ ON MISSION, North American Mission Board, SBC, 4200 North Point Pkwy., Alpharetta GA 30022-4176. Fax: (770)410-6105. E-mail: onmission@namb.net. Website: www.onmission.com. Managing Editor: Joe Conway. **Contact:** Carolyn Curtis, editor. **20% freelance written.** Religious bimonthly covering evangelism and church planting. "*On Mission*'s primary purpose is to help readers and churches become more *on mission* in the area of personal evangelism. Effective articles will always include elements that move readers toward spiritual growth and evangelism. Each article should move readers toward a deeper walk with God and a commitment to sharing Christ with others. *On Mission* articles must maintain an eternal, 'big picture' perspective." Estab. 1997. Circ. 300,000. Pays on publication. Publishes ms an average of 6 months after acceptance. Byline given. Offers 10-50% kill fee. Buys first North American serial, first and electronic rights. Editorial lead time 9 months. Submit seasonal material 9 months in advance. Accepts queries by mail, e-mail. Responds in 1 month to queries; 2 months to mss. Sample copy free or on website. Writer's guidelines free, on website or by e-mail.

Nonfiction: Book excerpts, personal experience, religious. **Buys 2-4 mss/year.** Query with published clips. Length: 350-1,500 words. **Pays 25¢/word.** Pays expenses of writers on assignment.

Photos: State availability of photos with submission. Reviews contact sheets, transparencies and prints. Offers $25/photo. Captions and identification of subjects required. Buys one-time rights.

Columns/Departments: My Mission (personal evangelism), 700 words. **Buys 2 mss/year.** Query. **Pays 25¢/word.**

Tips: "Readers might be intimidated if those featured appear to be 'super Christians' who seem to live on a higher spiritual plane. Try to introduce subjects as three-dimensional, real people. Include anecdotes or examples of their fears and failures, including ways they overcame obstacles. In other words, take the reader inside the heart of the *on mission* Christian and reveal the inevitable humanness that makes that person not only believable, but also approachable. We want the reader to feel encouraged to become *on mission* by identifying with people like them who are featured in the magazine."

$ $ THE OTHER SIDE, 300 W. Apsley St., Philadelphia PA 19144-4285. (215)849-2178. Website: www.theothersi de.com. **Contact:** Dee Dee Risher and Doug Davidson, coeditors. **80% freelance written.** Prefers to work with published/established writers. Bimonthly magazine emphasizing "spiritual nurture, prophetic reflection, forgotten voices and artistic visions from a progressive Christian perspective." Estab. 1965. Circ. 14,000. **Pays on acceptance.** Publishes ms an average of 6 months after acceptance. Byline given. Buys all or first serial rights. Responds in 3 months. Sample copy for $4.50. Writer's guidelines for #10 SASE or on website.

Nonfiction: Doug Davidson, coeditor. Current social, political and economic issues in the US and around the world: personality profiles, interpretative essays, interviews, how-to's, personal experiences, spiritual reflections, biblical interpretation. "Articles must be lively, vivid and down-to-earth, with a radical faith-based Christian perspective." Length: 500-3,500 words. **Pays $25-300.**

Fiction: Monica Day, fiction editor. "Short stories, humor and satire conveying insights and situations that will be helpful to Christians with a radical commitment to peace and justice." Length: 300-4,000 words. **Pays $25-250.**

Poetry: Jean Minahan, poetry editor. "Short, creative poetry that will be thought-provoking and appealing to radical Christians who have a strong commitment to spirituality, peace and justice." Length: 3-50 lines. No more than 4 poems may be submitted at one time by any one author. **Pays $15-20.**

Tips: "We're looking for tightly written pieces (1,000-1,500 words) on interesting and unusual Christians (or Christian groups) who are putting their commitment to peace and social justice into action in creative and useful ways. We're also looking for provocative analytical and reflective pieces (1,000-4,000 words) dealing with contemporary social issues in the U.S. and abroad."

$ $ OUR FAMILY, Missionary Oblates of St. Mary's Province, P.O. Box 249, Battleford, Saskatchewan S0M 0E0 Canada. (306)937-7771. Fax: (306)937-7644. E-mail: editor@ourfamilymagazine.com. Website: www.ourfamilymagazi ne.com. **Contact:** Marie-Louise Ternier-Gommers, editor. **80% freelance written.** Prefers to work with published/established writers. Monthly magazine for Canadian Catholics. Estab. 1949. Circ. 8,000. **Pays on acceptance.** Publishes ms an average of 6 months after acceptance. Byline given. Offers 100% kill fee. Generally purchases first North American serial rights; also buys all, simultaneous, second serial (reprint) or one-time rights. Submit seasonal material 4 months in advance. Accepts queries by mail, e-mail, fax, phone. Accepts simultaneous submissions. Responds in 6 weeks. Sample copy for 9×12 SAE with $2.50 postage. Only Canadian postage or IRC useful in Canada. Writer's guidelines, editorial policy and themes for upcoming issues on website.

Nonfiction: Humor (related to family life or husband/wife relations), inspirational (anything that depicts people responding to adverse conditions with courage, hope and love), personal experience (with religious dimensions), photo feature (particularly in search of photo essays on human/religious themes and on persons whose lives are an inspiration to others). Accepts phone queries. **Buys 88-100 unsolicited mss/year.** Length: 1,000-3,000 words. **Pays 7¢/word.**

Reprints: Send tearsheet or photocopy of article or typed ms with rights for sale noted and information about when and where the article previously appeared.

Photos: Photos purchased with or without accompanying ms. Pays $35 for 5×7 or larger b&w glossy prints and color photos (which are converted into b&w). Offers additional payment for photos accepted with ms (payment for these photos varies according to their quality). Free photo spec sheet for SASE.

Poetry: Avant-garde, free verse, haiku, light verse, traditional. **Buys 3-6 poems/issue.** Length: 3-30 lines. **Pays 75¢-$1/line.** Must have a religious dimension.

Fillers: Jokes, gags, anecdotes, short humor. **Buys 2-10/issue.**

Tips: "Writers should ask themselves whether this is the kind of an article, poem, etc. that a busy person would pick up and read in a few moments of leisure. We look for articles on the spirituality of marriage. We concentrate on recent movements and developments in the church to help make people aware of the new church of which they are a part. We invite reflections on ecumenical experiences."

N OUR SUNDAY VISITOR, Our Sunday Visitor, Inc., 200 Noll Plaza, Huntington IN 46750. (800)348-2440. Fax: (219)356-8472. E-mail: oursunvis@osv.com. Website: www.osv.com. Managing Editor: Richard G. Beemer. **Contact:** David Scott, editor. **90% freelance written (mostly assigned).** Weekly tabloid covering world events and culture from a Catholic perspective. Estab. 1912. Circ. 87,000. **Pays on acceptance.** Publishes ms an average of 1 month after acceptance. Byline given. Accepts queries by mail, e-mail, fax, phone.

N $ PANGAIA, Creating an EarthWise Spirituality, Blessed Bee, Inc., Box 641, Point Arena CA 95468. (707)882-2052. Fax: (707)882-2793. E-mail: dcdarling@saber.net. **Contact:** Diane Conn Darling, editor. **100% freelance written.** Quarterly journal of Earth spirituality covering Earth-based religions. "We publish articles pertinent to an Earth-loving readership. Mysticism, science, humor, tools all are described." Estab. 1997. Circ. 5,000. Pays on publication. Publishes ms an average of 1 year after acceptance. Byline given. Buys first North American serial rights. Editorial lead time 3 months. Submit seasonal material 3 months in advance. Accepts queries by mail, e-mail. Accepts simultaneous submissions. Responds in 2 weeks to queries; 6 months to mss. Sample copy and writer's guidelines free.
Nonfiction: Essays, historical/nostalgic, how-to, humor, inspirational, interview/profile, opinion, personal experience, photo feature, religious, travel. "Nothing unrelated to Earth-loving activity/thought." **Buys 20 mss/year.** Send complete ms. Length: 1,000-3,500 words. **Pays $10-50.** Sometimes pays with contributor copies or other premiums rather than a cash payment if negotiated/requested by writer.
Reprints: Accepts previously published submissions.
Photos: State availability of photos with submission. Reviews 5×7 prints or scans. Offers $15/photo. Captions required. Buys one-time rights.
Columns/Departments: Scientific Mysticism (factual discussions/world); Ritual World (worldwide polytheism); Sacred Places (experiences of place); Pathfinders (practices), all 2,000 words. **Buys 12 mss/year.** Send complete ms. **Pays $20-50.**
Fiction: Adventure, erotica, fantasy, historical, horror, humorous, religious, romance, science fiction. **Buys 4 mss/year.** Send complete ms. Length: 3,000-4,000 words. **Pays $50-100.**
Poetry: Free verse, haiku, light verse, traditional. **Buys 4 poems/year.** Submit maximum 4 poems. Length: 1 word-1 line. **Pays $15-25.**
Fillers: Short humor. **Buys 2/year.** Length: 500-700 words. **Pays $10.**
Tips: "*PanGaia* is a magazine for all people who share a deep love and commitment to the Earth. This includes both religious Pagans (Wiccans, Neo-Pagans, Druids, etc.) as well as people on other spiritual paths. We are pleased to accept contributions of essays, fiction, poetry, ritual scripts, plays, interviews, editorial pieces, factual articles, cartoons and black-and-white art and photographs pertaining to the topics and themes of *PanGaia*. We're looking for pieces on ecology, activism, magic, personal development, shamanism, prayer, ritual, insight experiences, fiction (including fantasy), scholarly research, history, legends, mythology, God and Goddess lore, gardening, herbs, recipes, health, political concerns, celebrations of Nature, Love, Birth, Death and other transitions, humor, interpersonal relations, sexuality, interviews and profiles of individuals and groups. Send hard copy and disk or submit by e-mail. Include SASE for prompt reply. Include short bio, offer photos."

$ PENTECOSTAL EVANGEL, The General Council of the Assemblies of God, 1445 Boonville, Springfield MO 65802-1894. (417)862-2781. Fax: (417)862-0416. E-mail: pevangel@ag.org. Website: www.ag.org/evangel. Editor: Hal Donaldson. **Contact:** Ann Floyd, associate editor. **10% freelance written.** Works with a small number of new/unpublished writers each year. Weekly magazine emphasizing news of the Assemblies of God for members of the Assemblies and other Pentecostal and charismatic Christians. Estab. 1913. Circ. 265,000. **Pays on acceptance.** Publishes ms an average of 6 months after acceptance. Byline given. Buys first serial rights, electronic rights and second serial (reprint) rights. Submit seasonal material 6 months in advance. Accepts queries by mail, e-mail, fax. Responds in 3 months. Sample copy and writer's guidelines available for $1 or on website.
Nonfiction: Informational (articles on homelife that convey Christian teachings), inspirational, personal experience, news, human interest, evangelical, current issues, seasonal. **Buys 3 mss/issue.** Send complete ms. Length: 500-1,200 words. **Pays $25-150.** Pays expenses of writers on assignment.
Reprints: Send typed ms with rights for sale noted and information about when and where the article previously appeared. Pays 30% of amount paid for an original article.
Photos: Photos purchased without accompanying ms. Pays $30 for 8×10 b&w glossy prints; $50 for 35mm or larger color transparencies. Total purchase price for ms includes payment for photos.
Tips: "We publish first-person articles concerning spiritual experiences; that is, answers to prayer for help in a particular situation, of unusual conversions or healings through faith in Christ. All articles submitted to us should be related to religious life. We are Protestant, evangelical, Pentecostal, and any doctrines or practices portrayed should be in harmony with the official position of our denomination (Assemblies of God)."

N $ THE PENTECOSTAL MESSENGER, Messenger Publishing House, P.O. Box 850, Joplin MO 64802-0850. (417)624-7050. Fax: (417)624-7102. E-mail: aaronw@pcg.org. Website: www.pcg.org. **Contact:** Kevin Risner, editor. **10% or less freelance written.** Works with small number of new/unpublished writers each year. Monthly magazine covering Pentecostal Christianity. "*The Pentecostal Messenger* is the official organ of the Pentecostal Church of God. It goes to ministers and church members." Estab. 1919. Circ. 12,000. Pays on publication. Publishes ms an average of

6 months after acceptance. Byline given. Buys second serial (reprint) or simultaneous rights. Submit seasonal material 4 months in advance. Accepts queries by mail, e-mail, phone. Accepts simultaneous submissions. Responds in 2 months. Sample copy for 6×9 SAE with 2 first-class stamps. Writer's guidelines free.

Nonfiction: Spiritual solutions to life's problems, preferably through human experience; testimony; family-strengthening ideas; financial advice; inspirational, religious. Send complete ms. Length: 400-1,200 words. **Pays 2¢/word.**

Reprints: Send tearsheet or photocopy of article or typed ms with rights for sale noted and information about when and where the article previously appeared. Pays 100% of amount paid for an original article.

Tips: "Articles need to be inspirational, informative, written from a positive viewpoint, and not extremely controversial. No blatant use of theology or sermonizing."

⊠ **$ $ THE PLAIN TRUTH, Renewing faith & values**, Plain Truth Ministries, 300 W. Green St., Pasadena CA 91129. Fax: (626)304-8172. E-mail: Phyllis_Duke@ptm.org. Website: www.ptm.org. Editor: Greg Albrecht. **Contact**: Phyllis Duke, assistant editor. **90% freelance written.** Bimonthly religious magazine. "We seek to reignite the flame of shattered lives by illustrating the joy of a new life in Christ." Estab. 1935. Circ. 70,000. Pays on publication. Publishes ms an average of 8 months after acceptance. Byline given. Offers $50 kill fee. Buys all-language, world, one-time nonexclusive, first or reprint rights. Editorial lead time 6 months. Submit seasonal material 6 months in advance. Accepts queries by mail, e-mail. Accepts simultaneous submissions. Sample copy for 9×12 SAE with 4 first-class stamps. Guidelines for #10 SASE or on website.

Nonfiction: Inspirational, interview/profile, personal experience, religious. **Buys 48-50 mss/year.** Query with published clips and SASE. *No unsolicited mss.* Length: 750-2,500 words. **Pays 25¢/word.**

Reprints: Send tearsheet or photocopy of article or typed ms with rights for sale noted and information about when and where the article previously appeared with SASE for response. **Pays 15¢/word.**

Photos: State availability of photos with submission. Reviews transparencies, prints. Negotiates payment individually. Captions required. Buys one-time rights.

Columns/Departments: Christian People (interviews with Christian leaders), 1,500 words. **Buys 6-12 mss/year.** Send complete ms. **Pays 15-25¢/word.**

Fillers: Anecdotes. **Buys 0-20/year.** Length: 25-200 words. **Pays 15-25¢/word.**

▣ The online magazine carries original content not found in the print edition and includes writer's guidelines.

Tips: "Material should offer biblical solutions to real-life problems. Both first-person and third-person illustrations are encouraged. Articles should take a unique twist on a subject. Material must be insightful and practical for the Christain reader. All articles must be well researched and biblically accurate without becoming overly scholastic. Use convincing arguments to support your Christian platform. Use vivid word pictures, simple and compelling language, and avoid stuffy academic jargon. Captivating anecdotes are vital."

Ⓝ $ $ POWER FOR LIVING, Scripture Press Publications Inc., P.O. Box 36640, Colorado Springs CO 80936. Fax: (719)536-3243. Editor: Donald H. Alban, Jr. **10% freelance written.** Quarterly Sunday School take-home paper with 13 weekly parts. "*Power*'s mission is twofold: to show Christian adults how the Lord can work in their lives, and to convince non-Christians of their need to receive Christ as Saviour." Circ. 250,000 weekly. **Pays on acceptance.** Publishes ms an average of 1 year after acceptance. Byline given. Buys one-time and second serial (reprint) rights. Editorial lead time 1 year. Submit seasonal material 1 year in advance. Accepts simultaneous submissions. Sample copy and writer's guidelines for #10 SASE.

Nonfiction: Inspirational profiles of prominent Christians or ministries (Evangelical). **Buys 50 mss/year.** Send complete ms. Length: 1,500 words. **Pays to 15¢/word.**

Reprints: Send photocopy of article or typed ms with rights for sale noted and information about when and where the article previously appeared. Pays 50% of amount paid for an original article.

Photos: State availability of photos with submission. Negotiates payment individually. Model releases, identification of subjects required. Buys one-time rights.

$ PRESBYTERIAN RECORD, 50 Wynford Dr., North York, Ontario M3C 1J7 Canada. (416)444-1111. Fax: (416)441-2825. E-mail: pcrecord@presbyterian.ca. Website: www.presbycan.ca/record. **Contact:** Rev. John Congram, editor. **50% freelance written.** Eager to work with new/unpublished writers. Monthly magazine for a church-oriented, family audience. Circ. 55,000. Pays on publication. Publishes ms an average of 4 months after acceptance. Buys first serial, one-time or simultaneous rights. Submit seasonal material 3 months in advance. Accepts queries by mail, e-mail, fax, phone. Responds in 2 months to accepted ms; returns rejected material in 3 months. Sample copy and guidelines for 9×12 SAE with $1 Canadian postage or IRCs or on website.

Nonfiction: Material on religious themes. Check a copy of the magazine for style. Also personal experience, interview, inspirational material. No material solely or mainly American in context. No sermons, accounts of ordinations, inductions, baptisms, receptions, church anniversaries or term papers. When possible, photos should accompany manuscript; e.g., current events, historical events and biographies. Special upcoming themes: small groups in the church; conflict in the church; lay leadership. **Buys 15-20 unsolicited mss/year.** Query. Length: 600-1,500 words. **Pays $50 (Canadian).** Sometimes pays expenses of writers on assignment.

Reprints: Send tearsheet, photocopy of article or typed ms with rights for sale noted and information about when and where the article previously appeared.

Photos: Pays $15-20 for glossy photos. Uses positive transparencies for cover. Pays $50 plus. Captions required.

Columns/Departments: Vox Populi (items of contemporary and often controversial nature), 700 words; Mission Knocks (new ideas for congregational mission and service), 700 words.

■ The online magazine carries original content not found in the print edition and includes writer's guidelines. Contact: Tom Dickey, online editor.

Tips: "There is a trend away from maudlin, first-person pieces redolent with tragedy and dripping with simplistic, pietistic conclusions. Writers often leave out those parts which would likely attract readers, such as anecdotes and direct quotes. Using active rather than passive verbs also helps most manuscripts."

$ $ PRESBYTERIANS TODAY, Presbyterian Church (U.S.A.), 100 Witherspoon St., Louisville KY 40202-1396. (502)569-5637. Fax: (502)569-8632. E-mail: today@pcusa.org. Website: www.pcusa.org/today. **Contact:** Eva Stimson, editor. Estab. 1867. **45% freelance written.** Prefers to work with published/established writers. Denominational magazine published 10 times/year covering religion, denominational activities and public issues for members of the Presbyterian Church (U.S.A.). "The magazine's puspose is to increase understanding and appreciation of what the church and its members are doing to live out their Christian faith." Estab. 1867. Circ. 70,000. **Pays on acceptance.** Publishes ms an average of 6 months after acceptance. Byline given. Offers 50% kill fee. Buys first North American serial rights. Editorial lead time 3 months. Submit seasonal material 3 months in advance. Accepts queries by mail, e-mail, fax, phone. Responds in 2 weeks to queries; 1 month to mss. Sample copy and writer's guidelines free.

Nonfiction: How-to (everyday Christian living), inspirational, Presbyterian programs, issues, peoples. "Most articles have some direct relevance to a Presbyterian audience; however, *Presbyterians Today* also seeks well-informed articles written for a general audience that help readers deal with the stresses of daily living from a Christian perspective." **Buys 20 mss/year.** Send complete ms. Length: 1,000-1,800 words. **Pays $300 maximum for assigned articles; $75-200 for unsolicited articles.**

Photos: State availability of photos. Reviews contact sheets, transparencies, b&w prints. Negotiates payment individually. Identification of subjects required. Buys one-time rights.

$ PRESERVING CHRISTIAN HOMES, General Youth Division, 8855 Dunn Rd., Hazelwood MO 63042. (314)837-7304. Fax: (314)837-4503. E-mail: tgaddy@upci.org. Website: www.upci.org/youth. **Contact:** Todd Gaddy, editor and general youth director of promotions. **40% freelance written.** Bimonthly magazine covering Christian home and family. "All submissions must conform to Christian perspective." Estab. 1970. Circ. 4,500. Pays on publication. Publishes ms an average of 9 months after acceptance. Byline sometimes given. Buys one-time or simultaneous rights. Editorial lead time 6 months. Submit seasonal material 6 months in advance. Accepts queries by mail, fax. Accepts simultaneous submissions. Responds in 2 weeks to queries; 2 months to mss. Sample copy for 10×13 SAE with 2 first-class stamps.

Nonfiction: General interest, humor, inspirational, personal experience, religious. Special issues: Mothers Day/Fathers Day. No "editorial or political." **Buys 15 mss/year.** Send complete ms. Length: 500-1,500 words. **Pays $30-40.**

Photos: State availability of photos with submission. Negotiates payment individually. Buys all rights.

Fiction: Humorous, religious, slice-of-life vignettes. **Buys 6 mss/year.** Send complete ms. Length: 500-1,500 words. **Pays $30-40.**

Poetry: Free verse, light verse, traditional. **Buys 3 poems/year.** Submit maximum 5 poems. Length: 10-40 lines. **Pays $20-25.**

Fillers: Anecdotes, facts, short humor. **Buys 2/year.** Length: 50-200 words. **Pays $10-20.**

Tips: "Be relevant to today's Christian families!"

ℕ $ $ PRISM MAGAZINE, America's Alternative Evangelical Voice, Evangelicals for Social Action, 10 E. Lancaster Ave., Wynnewood PA 19096. (610)645-9390. Fax: (610)649-8090. E-mail: prism@esa-online.org. Website: www.esa-online.org. Editor: Rodney Clapp. **Contact:** Fred Clark, managing editor. **25% freelance written.** Bimonthly magazine covering Christianity and social justice. For holistic, biblical, socially-concerned, progressive Christians. Estab. 1993. Circ. 5,500. Pays on publication. Publishes ms an average of 3 months after acceptance. Byline given. Offers 50% kill fee. Buys first North American serial rights. Editorial lead time 3 months. Submit seasonal material 4 months in advance. Accepts queries by mail, e-mail, fax, phone. Responds in 2 weeks to queries; 2 months to mss. Sample copy for $3. Writer's guidelines free.

Nonfiction: Book excerpts, essays, humor, inspirational, opinion, personal experience, religious. **Buys 10-12 mss/year.** Send complete ms. Length: 500-3,000 words. **Pays $50-200 for assigned articles; $25-200 for unsolicited articles.** "We're a nonprofit, some writers are pro bono."

Reprints: Accepts previously published submissions.

Photos: Send photos with submission. Reviews 5×7 prints. Negotiates payment individually. Buys one-time rights.

Tips: "Short book reviews (150-400 words) are often the easiest way to introduce your work to *Prism*'s readers. We always look closely at stories of holistic ministry."

✪ $ PURPOSE, 616 Walnut Ave., Scottdale PA 15683-1999. (724)887-8500. Fax: (724)887-3111. E-mail: horsch@mph@org. Website: www.mph.org. **Contact:** James E. Horsch, editor. **95% freelance written.** Weekly magazine "for adults, young and old, general audience with varied interests. My readership is interested in seeing how Christianity works in difficult situations." Estab. 1968. Circ. 13,000. **Pays on acceptance.** Publishes ms an average of 8 months after acceptance. Byline given, including city, state/province. Buys one-time rights. Submit seasonal material 6 months in advance. Accepts simultaneous submissions. Responds in 3 months. Sample copy and writer's guidelines for 6×9 SAE with 2 first-class stamps.

Nonfiction: Inspirational stories from a Christian perspective. "I want upbeat stories that deal with issues faced by believers in family, business, politics, religion, gender and any other areas—and show how the Christian faith resolves them. *Purpose* conveys truth through quality fiction or true life stories. Our magazine accents Christian discipleship. Christianity affects all of life, and we expect our material to demonstrate this. I would like story-type articles about individuals, groups and organizations who are intelligently and effectively working at such problems as hunger, poverty, international understanding, peace, justice, etc., because of their faith. Essays and how-to-do-it pieces must include a lot of anecdotal, life exposure examples." **Buys 130 mss/year.** Submit complete ms. Length: 750 words maximum. **Pays 5¢/word maximum.** Buys one-time rights only.

Reprints: Send tearsheet or photocopy of article or short story, or typed ms with rights for sale noted and information about when and where the material previously appeared.

Photos: Photos purchased with ms. Pays $5-15 for b&w (less for color), depending on quality. Must be sharp enough for reproduction; requires prints in all cases. Captions desired.

Fiction: Humorous, religious, historical fiction related to discipleship theme. "Produce the story with specificity so that it appears to take place somewhere and with real people."

Poetry: Traditional poetry, blank verse, free verse, light verse. **Buys 130 poems/year.** Length: 12 lines maximum. **Pays $7.50-20/poem** depending on length and quality. Buys one-time rights only.

Fillers: Anecdotal items up to 599 words. **Pays 4¢/word maximum.**

Tips: "We are looking for articles which show the Christian faith working at issues where people hurt; stories need to be told and presented professionally. Good photographs help place material with us."

$ QUEEN OF ALL HEARTS, Montfort Missionaries, 26 S. Saxon Ave., Bay Shore NY 11706-8993. (516)665-0726. Fax: (516)665-4349. **Contact:** Roger Charest, S.M.M., managing editor. **50% freelance written.** Bimonthly magazine. "Subject: Mary, Mother of Jesus, as seen in the sacred scriptures, tradition, history of the church, the early Christian writers, lives of the saints, poetry, art, music, spiritual writers, apparitions, shrines, ecumenism, etc." Estab. 1950. Circ. 2,000. **Pays on acceptance.** Publishes ms an average of 6 months after acceptance. Byline given. Not copyrighted. Submit seasonal material 6 months in advance. Accepts queries by mail, e-mail, fax, phone. Responds in 2 months. Sample copy for $2.50.

Nonfiction: Essays, inspirational, personal experience, religious. **Buys 25 ms/year.** Send complete ms. Length: 750-2,500 words. **Pays $40-60.** Sometimes pays writers in contributor copies or other premiums "by mutual agreement."

Photos: Send photos with submission. Reviews transparencies, prints. Pay varies. Buys one-time rights.

Fiction: Religious. **Buys 6 mss/year.** Send complete ms. Length: 1,500-2,500 words. **Pays $40-60.**

Poetry: Joseph Tusiani, poetry editor. Free verse. **Buys approximately 10 poems/year.** Submit maximum of 2 poems at one time. Pays in contributor copies.

$ THE QUIET HOUR, Cook Communications Ministries, 4050 Lee Vance View, Colorado Springs CO 80918. (719)536-0100. Fax: (407)359-2850. E-mail: gwilde@mac.com. Managing Editor: Doug Schmidt. **Contact:** Gary Wilde, editor. **100% freelance written.** Devotional booklet published quarterly featuring daily devotions. "*The Quiet Hour* is the adult-level quarterly devotional booklet published by David C. Cook. The purpose of *The Quiet Hour* is to provide Bible-based devotional readings for Christians who are in the process of growing toward Christlikeness. Most often, *The Quiet Hour* is used at home, either in the morning or evening, as part of a devotional period. It may be used by individuals, couples or families. For those studying with our Bible-in-Life curriculum, it also helps them prepare for the upcoming Sunday school lesson." **Pays on acceptance.** Publishes ms an average of 14 months after acceptance. Byline given. Makes work-for-hire assignments. Editorial lead time 14 months. Responds in 3 months. Writer's guidelines free.

Nonfiction: Daily devotionals. **Buys 52 mss/year.** Query by mail only with résumé and/or list of credits. **Pays $15-35 per devotional.**

Tips: "Send list of credits with query—especially other devotional writing. Do not send samples. We will assign the scripture passages to use."

$ $ REFORM JUDAISM, Union of American Hebrew Congregations, 633 3rd Ave., New York NY 10017-6778. (212)650-4240. Website: www.uahc.org/rjmag/. Editor: Aron Hirt-Manheimer. **Contact:** Joy Weinberg, managing editor. **30% freelance written.** Quarterly magazine of Reform Jewish issues. "*Reform Judaism* is the official voice of the Union of American Hebrew Congregations, linking the institutions and affiliates of Reform Judaism with every Reform Jew. *RJ* covers developments within the Movement while interpreting events and Jewish tradition from a Reform perspective." Pays on publication. Publishes ms an average of 3 months after acceptance. Byline given. Offers kill fee for commissioned articles. Buys first North American serial rights. Submit seasonal material 6 months in advance. Responds in 2 months to queries and mss. Writer's guidelines for SASE or on website. Sample copy for $3.50.

Nonfiction: Book excerpts, exposé, general interest, historical/nostalgic, inspirational, interview/profile, opinion, personal experience, photo feature, travel. **Buys 30 mss/year.** Submit complete ms with SASE. Length: cover stories: 2,500-3,500 words; major feature: 1,800-2,500 words; secondary feature: 1,200-1,500 words; department (e.g., Travel): 1,200 words; letters: 200 words maximum; opinion: 630 words maximum. **Pays 30¢/word.** Sometimes pays expenses of writers on assignment.

Reprints: Send tearsheet or photocopy of article or short story or typed ms with rights for sale noted and information about when and where the material previously appeared. Usually does not publish reprints.

Photos: Send photos with ms. Prefers 8×10/color or slides and b&w prints. Pays $25-75. Identification of subjects required. Buys one-time rights.

Fiction: Sophisticated, cutting-edge, superb writing. **Buys 4 mss/year.** Send complete ms. Length: 600-2,500 words. **Pays 30¢/word.** Publishes novel excerpts.

■ The online magazine carries original content not found in the print edition and includes writer's guidelines.

Tips: "We prefer a stamped postcard including the following information/checklist: _yes we are interested in publishing; _no, unfortunately the submission doesn't meet our needs; _maybe, we'd like to hold on to the article for now. Submissions sent this way will receive a faster response."

$ $ THE REPORTER, Women's American ORT, Inc., 315 Park Ave. S., 17th Floor, New York NY 10010. (800)51-WAORT, ext. 265. Fax: (212)674-3057. E-mail: rhayman@waort.org. **Contact:** Randy Hayman, associate director of publications. **85% freelance written.** Quarterly nonprofit journal published by Jewish women's organization covering Jewish women celebrities, issues of contemporary Jewish culture, Israel, anti-semitism, women's rights, Jewish travel and the international Jewish community. Estab. 1966. Circ. 65,000. Payment time varies. Publishes ms within a year of acceptance. Byline given. Buys first North American serial rights. Submit query for seasonal material 6 months in advance. Accepts queries by mail, e-mail, phone. Responds in 3 months. Free sample copy for 9×12 SAE with 3 first-class stamps. Writer's guidelines for SASE.

Nonfiction: Cover feature profiles a dynamic Jewish woman making a difference in Judaism, women's issues, education, entertainment, profiles, business, journalism, sports or the arts. Query. Length varies; no more than 1,800 words. **Pays $200 and up.**

Photos: Send photos with submission. Identification of subjects required.

Columns/Departments: Education Horizon; Destination (Jewish sites/travel); Inside Out (Advocacy); Women's Business; Art Scene (interviews, books, films); Mind/body/spirit (uplifting/inspirational).

Fiction: Publishes novel excerpts and short stories as part of "Last Impressions." **Buys 4 ms/year.** Length: 800 words. **Pays $150-300.**

Tips: "Send query only by e-mail or postal mail."

$ REVIEW FOR RELIGIOUS, 3601 Lindell Blvd., Room 428, St. Louis MO 63108-3393. (314)977-7363. Fax: (314)977-7362. E-mail: foppema@slu.edu. **Contact:** David L. Fleming, S.J., editor. **100% freelance written.** Bimonthly magazine for Roman Catholic priests, brothers and sisters. Estab. 1942. Pays on publication. Publishes ms an average of 9 months after acceptance. Byline given. Buys first North American serial rights; rarely buys second serial (reprint) rights. Accepts queries by mail, fax, phone. Responds in 2 months.

Nonfiction: Articles on spiritual, liturgical, canonical matters only; not for general audience. Length: 1,500-5,000 words. **Pays $6/page.**

Tips: "The writer must know about religious life in the Catholic Church and be familiar with prayer, vows, community life and ministry."

$ $ ST. ANTHONY MESSENGER, 1615 Republic St., Cincinnati OH 45210-1298. Fax: (513)241-0399. E-mail: stanthony@americancatholic.org. Website: www.AmericanCatholic.org. **Contact:** Jack Wintz, O.F.M., editor. **55% freelance written.** "Willing to work with new/unpublished writers if their writing is of a professional caliber." Monthly general interest magazine for a national readership of Catholic families, most of which have children or grandchildren in grade school, high school or college. Circ. 330,000. **Pays on acceptance.** Publishes ms an average of 9 months after acceptance. Byline given. Buys first worldwide serial and all electronic rights. Submit seasonal material 6 months in advance. Accepts queries by mail, e-mail, fax. Responds in 2 months. Sample copy and writer's guidelines for 9×12 SAE with 4 first-class stamps.

Nonfiction: How-to (on psychological and spiritual growth, problems of parenting/better parenting, marriage problems/marriage enrichment), humor, informational, inspirational, interview, personal experience (if pertinent to our purpose), social issues, personal opinion (limited use; writer must have special qualifications for topic), profile. **Buys 35-50 mss/year.** Length: 1,500-2,500 words. **Pays 16¢/word.** Sometimes pays the expenses of writers on assignment.

Fiction: Mainstream, religious. **Buys 12 mss/year.** Submit complete ms. Length: 2,000-2,500 words. **Pays 16¢/word.**

Poetry: *"Our poetry needs are very limited."* Submit 4-5 poems maximum. Up to 20-25 lines, "the shorter, the better." **Pays $2/line; $20 minimum.**

■ The online magazine carries original content not found in the print edition. Contact: John Bookser Feister, online editor.

Tips: "The freelancer should consider why his or her proposed article would be appropriate for us, rather than for *Redbook* or *Saturday Review.* We treat human problems of all kinds, but from a religious perspective. Articles should reflect Catholic theology, spirituality and employ a Catholic terminology and vocabulary. We need more articles on prayer, scripture, Catholic worship. Get authoritative information (not merely library research); we want interviews with experts. Write in popular style; use lots of examples, stories and personal quotes. Word length is an important consideration."

$ ST. JOSEPH'S MESSENGER & ADVOCATE OF THE BLIND, Sisters of St. Joseph of Peace, St. Joseph's Home, P.O. Box 288, Jersey City NJ 07303-0288. **Contact:** Sister Mary Kuiken, CSJP, editor. **30% freelance written.**

Eager to work with new/unpublished writers. Semiannual magazine. Estab. 1898. Circ. 15,500. **Pays on acceptance.** Publishes ms an average of 6 months after acceptance. Buys first serial and second serial (reprint) rights; reassigns rights back to author after publication in return for credit line in next publication. Submit seasonal material 3 months in advance (no Christmas issue). Accepts simultaneous submissions. Responds in 1 month. Sample copy and writer's guidelines for 9×12 SAE with 2 first-class stamps.

Nonfiction: Humor, inspirational, nostalgia, personal opinion, personal experience. **Buys 10 mss/year.** Submit complete ms. Length: 800-1,500 words. **Pays $35-50.**

Reprints: Send typed ms with rights for sale noted and information about when and where the article previously appeared. Pays 100% of amount paid for an original article.

Fiction: Romance, suspense, contemporary, mainstream, religious. **Buys 10 mss/year.** Submit complete ms. Length: 800-1,500 words. **Pays $35-50.**

Poetry: Light verse, traditional. **Buys 10 poems/year.** Submit 10 poems maximum. Length: 50-300 words. **Pays $10-25.**

Tips: "It's rewarding to know that someone is waiting to see freelancers' efforts rewarded by 'print.' It's annoying, however, to receive poor copy, shallow material or inane submissions. Human interest fiction, touching on current happenings, is what is most needed. We look for social issues woven into story form. We also seek non-preaching articles that carry a message that is positive."

N: $ $ SAY AMEN MAGAZINE, The Magazine for Living in Christian Authority, Word Communications, P.O. Box 360658, Decatur GA 30036-0658. (770)808-4595. Fax: (770)808-0046. E-mail: vconwell@sayamen.com. Website: www.sayamen.com. **Contact:** Vikki Conwell, editor-in-chief. **80-90% freelance written.** Quarterly magazine covering Christian lifestyles. "*Say Amen* dialogues through innovative content targeted to, but not limited to, the urban community of faith. Our content is thought-provoking and entertaining, not preachy and lecturing. We consider our magazine to be a lifestyles magazine." Estab. 1994. Circ. 50,000. Pays on publication. Publishes ms an average of 3 months after acceptance. Byline given. Buys first North American serial rights. Editorial lead time 2 months. Submit seasonal material 4 months in advance. Accepts queries by mail, e-mail, fax. Responds in 1 month to queries; 2 months to mss. Sample copy and writer's guidelines free.

Nonfiction: General interest, inspirational, interview/profile, photo feature, religious. **Buys 16-20 mss/year.** Query with published clips. Length: 500-2,000 words. **Pays $50-250 for assigned articles; $50-150 for unsolicited articles.** Sometimes pays expenses of writers on assignment.

Reprints: Accepts previously published submissions.

Photos: State availability of photos with submission. Reviews contact sheets and 4×6 prints. Negotiates payment individually. Model releases and identification of subjects required. Buys one-time rights.

Columns/Departments: Our Community (community issues and concerns), 1,000 words; Doing Good (profile of positive ministry, organization or activity), 1,000 words; Relationships (personal relationships—friends, family, couples), 1,500 words; Wealthwise (financial/business concerns), 1,000 words. **Pays $50-250.**

Tips: "The best content for *Say Amen* is lighthearted yet thought-provoking about basic concerns and issues pertaining to anyone. The slant should address how members of the Christian community of faith handle the situation or respond to it or how it impacts their lives."

$ THE SECRET PLACE, Educational Ministries, ABC/USA, P.O. Box 851, Valley Forge PA 19482-0851. (610)768-2240. **Contact:** Kathleen Hayes, senior editor. **100% freelance written.** Devotional published quarterly covering Christian daily devotions. Estab. 1938. Circ. 150,000. **Pays on acceptance.** Byline given. Buys first rights. Editorial lead time 1 year. Submit seasonal material 9 months in advance. Sample copy free. Writer's guidelines for #10 SASE.

Nonfiction: Inspirational. **Buys about 400 mss/year.** Send complete ms. Length: 100-200 words. **Pays $15.**

Poetry: Avant-garde, free verse, light verse, traditional. **Buys 12-15 poems/year.** Submit maximum 6 poems. Length: 4-30 lines. **Pays $15.**

$ SEEK, Standard Publishing, 8121 Hamilton Ave., Cincinnati OH 45231. (513)931-4050, ext. 365. Fax: (513)931-0950. Website: www.standardpub.com. **Contact:** Eileen H. Wilmoth, editor. **98% freelance written.** Prefers to work with published/established writers. Quarterly Sunday school paper, in weekly issues for young and middle-aged adults who attend church and Bible classes. Circ. 45,000. **Pays on acceptance.** Publishes ms an average of 1 year after acceptance. Byline given. Buys first serial and second serial (reprint) rights. Submit seasonal material 1 year in advance. Responds in 3 months. Sample copy and writer's guidelines for 6×9 SAE with 2 first-class stamps.

Nonfiction: "We look for articles that are warm, inspirational, devotional, of personal or human interest; that deal with controversial matters, timely issues of religious, ethical or moral nature, or first-person testimonies, true-to-life happenings, vignettes, emotional situations or problems; communication problems and examples of answered prayers. Article must deliver its point in a convincing manner but not be patronizing or preachy. It must appeal to either men or women, must be alive, vibrant, sparkling and have a title that demands the article be read. We always need stories about families, marriages, problems on campus and life testimonies." **Buys 150-200 mss/year.** Submit complete ms. Length: 400-1,200 words. **Pays 5¢/word.**

Reprints: Accepts previously published submissions. Send tearsheet or photocopy of article or typed ms with rights for sale noted and information about when and where the article previously appeared. Pays 50% of amount paid for an original article.

Photos: B&w photos purchased with or without mss. Pays $20 minimum for good 8×10 glossy prints.

Fiction: Religious fiction and religiously slanted historical and humorous fiction. No poetry. Length: 400-1,200 words. **Pays 5¢/word.**

Tips: "Submit manuscripts which tell of faith in action or victorious Christian living as central theme. We select manuscripts as far as one year in advance of publication. Complimentary copies are sent to our published writers immediately following printing."

N **$ $ SHARING THE VICTORY**, Fellowship of Christian Athletes, 8701 Leeds Rd., Kansas City MO 64129. (816)921-0909. Fax: (816)921-8755. E-mail: stu@fca.org. Website: www.fca.org. Assistant Editor: Allen Palmeri. **Contact:** David Smale, editor. **50% freelance written.** Prefers to work with published/established writers, but works with a growing number of new/unpublished writers each year. Published 9 times/year. "We seek to encourage and enable athletes and coaches at all levels to take their faith seriously on and off the 'field'." Estab. 1959. Circ. 75,000. Pays on publication. Publishes ms an average of 4 months after acceptance. Byline given. Buys first rights. Submit seasonal material 3 months in advance. Responds in 3 months to queries; 3 months to mss. Sample copy for $1 and 9 × 12 SAE with 3 first-class stamps. Free writer's guidelines for #10 SASE.

Nonfiction: Humor, inspirational, interview/profile (with "name" athletes and coaches solid in their faith), personal experience, photo feature. No "sappy articles on 'I became a Christian and now I'm a winner.' " **Buys 5-20 mss/year.** Query. Length: 500-1,000 words. **Pays $100-200** for unsolicited articles, more for the exceptional profile.

Reprints: Send typed ms with rights for sale noted. Pays 50% of amount paid for an original article.

Photos: State availability of photos with submission. Reviews contact sheets. Pay depends on quality of photo but usually a minimum $50. Model releases required for "name" individuals. Buys one-time rights.

Poetry: Free verse. Buys 9 poems/year. Pays $25.

Tips: "Profiles and interviews of particular interest to coed athlete, primarily high school and college age. Our graphics and editorial content appeal to youth. The area most open to freelancers is profiles on or interviews with well-known athletes or coaches (male, female, minorities) and offbeat but interscholastic team sports."

$ $ SIGNS OF THE TIMES, Pacific Press Publishing Association, P.O. Box 5353, Nampa ID 83653-5353. (208)465-2579. Fax: (208)465-2531. E-mail: mmoore@pacificpress.com. **Contact:** Marvin Moore, editor. **40% freelance written.** Works with a small number of new/unpublished writers each year. "We are a monthly Seventh-day Adventist magazine encouraging the general public to practice the principles of the Bible." Estab. 1874. Circ. 225,000. **Pays on acceptance.** Publishes ms an average of 6 months after acceptance. Byline given. Offers kill fee. Buys first North American serial rights, one-time rights, or second serial reprint rights. Editorial lead time 1 year. Submit seasonal material 1 year in advance. Responds in 1 month to queries; 2 months to mss. Sample copy and writer's guidelines for 9 × 12 SAE with 3 first-class stamps. Writer's guidelines on website.

Nonfiction: General interest, how-to, humor, inspirational, interview/profile, personal experience, religious. "We want writers with a desire to share the good news of reconciliation with God. Articles should be people-oriented, well-researched and should have a sharp focus. Gospel articles deal with salvation and how to experience it. While most of our gospel articles are assigned or picked up from reprints, we do occasionally accept unsolicited manuscripts in this area. Gospel articles should be 1,000 to 1,200 words. Christian lifestyle articles deal with the practical problems of everyday life from a biblical and Christian perspective. These are typically 1,000 to 1,200 words. We request that authors include sidebars that give additional information on the topic wherever possible. First-person stories must illuminate a spiritual or moral truth that the individual in the story learned. We especially like stories that hold the reader in suspense or that have an unusual twist at the end. First-person stories are typically 600 to 1,000 words long." **Buys 75 mss/year.** Query by mail only with or without published clips or send complete ms. Length: 500-1,500 words. **Pays 10-20¢/word.** Sometimes pays the expenses of writers on assignment.

Reprints: Send tearsheet or photocopy of article or typed ms with rights for sale noted and information about when and where the article previously appeared. Pays 50% of amount paid for an original article.

Photos: Merwin Stewart, photo editor. Reviews b&w contact sheets, 35mm color transparencies, 5 × 7 or 8 × 10 b&w prints. Pays $35-300 for transparencies; $20-50 for prints. Model releases and identification of subjects required (captions helpful). Buys one-time rights.

Columns/Departments: Send complete ms. **Pays $25-150.**

Fillers: "Short fillers can be inspirational/devotional, Christian lifestyle, stories, comments that illuminate a biblical text—in short, anything that might fit in a general Christian magazine. Fillers should be 500 to 600 words."

Tips: "The audience for *Signs of the Times* includes both Christians and non-Christians of all ages. However, we recommend that our authors write with the non-Christian in mind, since most Christians can easily relate to articles that are written from a non-Christian perspective, whereas many non-Christians will have no interest in an article that is written from a Christian perspective. While *Signs* is published by Seventh-day Adventists, we mention even our own denominational name in the magazine rather infrequently. The purpose is not to hide who we are but to make the magazine as attractive to non-Christian readers as possible. We are especially interested in articles that respond to the questions of everyday life that people are asking and the problems they are facing. Since these questions and problems nearly always have a spiritual component, articles that provide a biblical and spiritual response are especially welcome. Any time you can provide us with one or more sidebars that add information to the topic of your article, you enhance your chance of getting our attention. Two kinds of sidebars seem to be especially popular with readers: Those that give information in lists, with each item in the list consisting of only a few words or at the most a sentence or two; and technical information or long explanations that in the main article might get the reader too bogged down in detail."

Whatever their length, sidebars need to be part of the total word count of the article. We like the articles in *Signs of the Times* to have interest-grabbing introductions. One of the best ways to do this is with anecdotes, particularly those that have a bit of suspense or conflict."

$ SISTERS TODAY, The Liturgical Press, St. John's Abbey, Collegeville MN 56321-2099. Fax: (320)363-7130. E-mail: mwagner@csbsju.edu. Website: www.csbsju/osb.sisters/public.html. **Contact:** Sister Mary Anthony Wagner, O.S.B., editor-in-chief. **30% freelance written.** Prefers to work with published/established writers. Bimonthly magazine exploring the role of women and the Church, primarily. Circ. 3,500. Pays on publication. Publishes ms several months after acceptance probably. Byline given. Buys first rights. Submit seasonal material 4 months in advance. Accepts queries by mail, fax. Sample copy for $4.50.

> "Plug into our goal: exploring the role of women and the Church."

Nonfiction: How-to (pray, live in a religious community, exercise faith, hope, charity etc.), informational, inspirational. Also articles concerning religious renewal, community life, worship, the role of women in the Church and in the world today. **Buys 50-60 unsolicited mss/year.** Query. Length: 500-2,500 words. **Pays $5/printed page.** Send book reviews to Sister Stephanie Weisgram, O.S.B.

Poetry: Sister Mary Virginia Micka, C.S.J. Free verse, haiku, light verse, traditional. **Buys 5-6 poems/issue.** Submit maximum 4 poems. **Pays $10.**

Tips: "Some of the freelance material evidences the lack of familiarity with *Sisters Today*. We would prefer submitted articles not to exceed eight or nine pages."

$ SOCIAL JUSTICE REVIEW, 3835 Westminster Place, St. Louis MO 63108-3472. (314)371-1653. **Contact:** Rev. John H. Miller, C.S.C., editor. **25% freelance written.** Works with a small number of new/unpublished writers each year. Bimonthly. Estab. 1908. Publishes ms an average of 1 year after acceptance. Not copyrighted; "however special articles within the magazine may be copyrighted, or an occasional special issue has been copyrighted due to author's request." Buys first serial rights. Sample copy for 9×12 SAE with 3 first-class stamps.

Nonfiction: Scholarly articles on society's economic, religious, social, intellectual, political problems with the aim of bringing Catholic social thinking to bear upon these problems. Query by mail only with SASE. Length: 2,500-3,000 words. **Pays about 2¢/word.**

Reprints: Send typed ms with rights for sale noted and information about when and where the article previously appeared. **Pays about 2¢/word.**

N $ SPIRIT, Messenger Publishing House, P.O. Box 850, Joplin MO 64802-0850. (417)624-7050. Fax: (417)624-7102. E-mail: aaronw@pcg.org. Website: www.pcg.org. **Contact:** Aaron M. Wilson, editor. **80% freelance written.** Monthly magazine covering Pentecostal Christianity. "*Spirit* offers testimonials about the workings of the Holy Spirit in the lives of believers." Estab. 1919. Circ. 12,000. Pays on publication. Publishes ms an average of 6 months after acceptance. Byline given. Buys second serial (reprint) or simultaneous rights. Submit seasonal material 4 months in advance. Accepts queries by mail, e-mail, fax. Accepts simultaneous submissions. Responds in 2 months. Sample copy for 6×9 SAE with 2 first-class stamps. Writer's guidelines free.

> Break in with good short inspirational material, particularly in the healing of relationships and marriages. Always need more personal testimonials of answered prayer.

Nonfiction: Spiritual solutions to life's problems, preferably through human experience; testimony; family-strengthening ideas; financial advice; inspirational, religious. Send complete ms. Length: 400-1,200 words. **Pays 2¢/word.**

Reprints: Send tearsheet or photocopy of article or typed ms with rights for sale noted and information about when and where the article previously appeared. Pays 100% of amount paid for an original article.

Tips: "Articles need to be inspirational, informative, written from a positive viewpoint, and not extremely controversial. No blatant use of theology or sermonizing."

$ SPIRITUAL LIFE, 2131 Lincoln Rd. NE, Washington DC 20002-1199. (202)832-8489. Fax: (202)832-8967. E-mail: edodonnell@aol.com. Website: www.Spiritual-Life.org. **Contact:** Br. Edward O'Donnell, O.C.D., editor. **80% freelance written.** Prefers to work with published/established writers. Quarterly magazine for "largely Catholic, well-educated, serious readers. A few are non-Catholic or non-Christian." Circ. 12,000. **Pays on acceptance.** Publishes ms an average of 1 year after acceptance. Buys first North American serial rights. Responds in 2 months. Sample copy and writer's guidelines for 7×10 or larger SASE with 5 first-class stamps.

Nonfiction: Serious articles of contemporary spirituality and its pastoral application to everyday life. High quality articles about our encounter with God in the present day world. Language of articles should be college level. Technical terminology, if used, should be clearly explained. Material should be presented in a positive manner. Sentimental articles or those dealing with specific devotional practices not accepted. Buys inspirational and think pieces. "Brief autobiographical information (present occupation, past occupations, books and articles published, etc.) should accompany article." No fiction or poetry. **Buys 20 mss/year.** Length: 3,000-5,000 words. **Pays $50 minimum** and 2 contributor's copies. Book reviews should be sent to Br. Edward O'Donnell, O.C.D.

N $ $ SPORTS SPECTRUM, Discovery House Publishers, P.O. Box 3566, Grand Rapids MI 49501-3566. (616)974-2711. Fax: (616)957-5741. E-mail: ssmag@sport.org. Website: www.sport.org/. **Contact:** Dave Branon, managing editor. "*Sports Spectrum* is produced 6 times/year as a way of presenting the Christian faith through the lives of Christian athletes. Writers should share our love for sports and our interest in telling readers about Jesus Christ." Estab.

1987. Circ. 50,000. **Pays on acceptance.** Publishes ms an average of 2 months after acceptance. Byline given. Offers 40% kill fee. Not copyrighted. Buys first all print rights. Editorial lead time 4 months. Responds in 1 month to queries. Sample copy for 8½×11 SAE and 4 first-class stamps. Writer's guidelines free.

Nonfiction: Interview/profile. No poems, reprints, fiction, profiles of sports ministries or unsolicited mss. **Buys 40 mss/year.** Query with published clips. Length: 225-2,000 words. **Pays $40-360.** Sometimes pays expenses of writers on assignment.

Photos: State availability of photos. Reviews transparencies and prints. Negotiates payment individually.

Columns/Departments: Champions (stories of lesser-known athletes), 225 words. **Buys 15 mss/year.** Query with published clips. **Pays $40-145.**

Tips: "Make sure you understand our unique purpose and can write articles that contribute to the purpose. Send a query letter and clips. Tell why your story idea fits and how you propose to research the article."

$ STANDARD, Nazarene International Headquarters, 6401 The Paseo, Kansas City MO 64131. (816)333-7000. **Contact:** Everett Leadingham, editor. **100% freelance written.** Works with a small number of new/unpublished writers each year. Weekly inspirational paper with Christian reading for adults. Estab. 1936. Circ. 160,000. **Pays on acceptance.** Publishes ms an average of 18 months after acceptance. Byline given. Buys one-time rights and second serial (reprint) rights. Submit seasonal material 6 months in advance. Responds in 10 weeks. Sample copy free. Writer's guidelines for SAE with 2 first-class stamps.

Reprints: Send tearsheet of short story.

Fiction: Prefers fiction-type stories *showing* Christianity in action. Send complete ms; no queries. Length: 500-1,200 words. **Pays 3½¢/word for first rights; 2¢/word for reprint rights.**

● Ranked as one of the best markets for fiction writers in *Writer's Digest* magazine's "Fiction 50," June 2000.

Poetry: Free verse, haiku, light verse, traditional. Buys 50 poems/year. Submit maximum 5 poems. Length: 50 lines maximum. **Pays 25¢/line.**

Tips: "Stories should express Christian principles without being preachy. Setting, plot and characterization must be realistic."

$ THESE DAYS, Presbyterian Publishing Corp., 100 Witherspoon St., Louisville KY 40202-1396. (502)569-5102. Fax: (502)569-5113. E-mail: kaysno@worldnet.att.net **Contact:** Kay Snodgrass, editor. **95% freelance written.** Bi-monthly magazine covering religious devotionals. "*These Days* is published especially for the Cumberland Presbyterian Church, The Presbyterian Church in Canada, The Presbyterian Church (U.S.A.), The United Churches of Canada, and The United Church of Christ as a personal, family and group devotional guide." Estab. 1970. Circ. 200,000. **Pays on acceptance.** Publishes ms an average of 8 months after acceptance. Byline given. Buys all rights and makes work-for-hire assignments. Editorial lead time 10 months. Submit seasonal material 1 year in advance. Accepts queries by mail, e-mail. Responds in 1 month to queries; 6 months to mss. Sample copy for 6×9 SAE and 2 first-class stamps. Writer's guidelines for #10 SASE.

Nonfiction: Devotions and devotional aids in our format. "Use freelance in all issues. Only devotional material will be accepted. Send for issue themes and scripture references. Enclose #10 SASE." **Buys 365 mss/year.** Query or query with published clips. Length: 200 words. **Pays $14.25 for devotions, $30 for devotional aids: "These Moments" and "These Times."**

Poetry: Buys 2-6 poems/year. Submit maximum 5 poems. Length: 3-20 lines. **Pays $10.**

Tips: "The best way to be considered is to send a one-page query that includes your religious affiliation and your religious, writing-related experience plus a sample devotion in our format and/or published clips of similar material. Read a current issue devotionally to get a feel for the magazine. We would also like to see more minority and Canadian writers."

N ⊠ $ TOGETHER, Shalom Publishers, Box 656, Route 2, Grottoes VA 24441. E-mail: tgether@aol.com. Managing Editor: Eugene Souder. **Contact:** Melodie M. Davis, editor. **95% freelance written.** "*Together* is used quarterly by churches as an outreach paper to encourage readers to faith in Christ and God and participation in a local church. In addition to testimonies of spiritual conversion or journey, we publish general inspirational or family-related articles." Estab. 1987. Circ. 150,000. Pays on publication. Publishes ms an average of 9 months after acceptance. Byline given. Buys one-time or second serial (reprint) rights. Editorial lead time 6 months. Submit seasonal material 9 months in advance. Accepts simultaneous submissions. Responds in 2 months to queries; 6 months to mss. Sample copy for 9×12 SAE and 4 first-class stamps. Writer's guidelines for #10 SASE or e-mail.

Nonfiction: Inspirational, personal experience/testimony, religious. **Buys 22-24 mss/year.** Send complete ms. Length: 300-1,000 words. **Pays $35-50.**

Reprints: Accepts previously published submissions.

Photos: State availability of photos with submission. Reviews 3×5 prints. Offers $25/photo. Identification of subjects required. Buys one-time rights.

Tips: "We can use good contemporary conversion stories (to Christian faith) including as-told-to's. Read other stuff that is being published and then ask if your writing up to the level of what is being published today."

N $ $ $ TRICYCLE: THE BUDDHIST REVIEW, The Buddhist Ray, Inc., 92 Vandam St., New York NY 10013. Fax: (212)645-1493. E-mail: editorial@tricycle.com. Website: www.tricycle.com. Editor: Helen Tworkov. Managing Editor: Philip Ryan. **Contact:** Peter Alsop, editorial assistant. **80% freelance written.** Quarterly magazine covering the impact of Buddhism on Western culture. "*Tricycle* readers tend to be well-educated and open-minded." Estab. 1991. Circ. 65,000. Pays on publication. Publishes ms an average of 3 months after acceptance. Byline given. Offers 25% kill fee. Buys one-time rights. Editorial lead time 3 months. Submit seasonal material 3 months in advance. Accepts queries by mail, e-mail, fax. Accepts simultaneous submissions. Responds in 1 month to queries; 3 months to mss. Sample copy for $7.50 or online at website. Writer's guidelines free.

Nonfiction: Book excerpts, essays, general interest, historical/nostalgic, humor, inspirational, interview/profile, personal experience, photo feature, religious, travel. **Buys 10-15 mss/year.** Send complete ms. Length: 1,000-5,000 words. **Pays $300-5,000.**

Photos: State availability of photos with submission. Reviews contact sheets. Negotiates payment individually. Captions and identification of subjects required. Buys one-time rights.

Columns/Departments: Reviews (film, books, tapes), 600 words; Science and Gen Next, both 700 words. **Buys 12 mss/year.** Query. **Pays $0-300.**

Poetry: Joel Whitney, poetry editor. Free verse, haiku, traditional. **Buys 5-20 poems/year.** Submit maximum 5 poems.

Tips: "*Tricycle* is a Buddhist magazine, and nearly every unsolicited manuscript that interests us is Buddhist-related."

⚔ $ $U.S. CATHOLIC, Claretian Publications, 205 W. Monroe St., Chicago IL 60606. (312)236-7782. Fax: (312)236-8207. E-mail: editors@uscatholic.org. Website: www.uscatholic.org. Editor: Rev. Mark J. Brummel, CMF. Managing Editor: Meinrad Scherer-Emunds. **Contact:** Fran Hurst, editorial assistant. **100% freelance written.** Monthly magazine covering Roman Catholic spirituality. "*U.S. Catholic* is dedicated to the belief that it makes a difference whether you're Catholic. We invite and help our readers explore the wisdom of their faith tradition and apply their faith to the challenges of the 21st century." Estab. 1935. Circ. 50,000. **Pays on acceptance.** Publishes ms an average of 3 months after acceptance. Byline given. Buys first North American serial rights. Editorial lead time 8 months. Submit seasonal material 6 months in advance. Accepts queries by mail, e-mail, fax, phone. Responds in 1 month to queries; 2 months to mss. Sample copy free. Writer's guidelines for #10 SASE.

Nonfiction: Essays, inspirational, opinion, personal experience, religious. **Buys 100 mss/year.** Send complete ms. Length: 2,500-3,500 words (depends on type of article). **Pays $250-600.** Sometimes pays expenses of writers on assignment.

Photos: State availability of photos with submission.

Columns/Departments: Pays $250-600.

Fiction: Maureen Abood, literary editor. Mainstream, religious, slice-of-life vignettes. **Buys 4-6 mss/year.** Send complete ms. Length: 2,500-3,000 words. **Pays $300.**

Poetry: Maureen Abood, literary editor. Free verse. "No light verse." **Buys 12 poems/year.** Submit maximum 5 poems. Length: 50 lines. **Pays $75.**

THE UNITED CHURCH OBSERVER, 478 Huron St., Toronto, Ontario M5R 2R3 Canada. (416)960-8500. Fax: (416)960-8477. E-mail: general@ucobserver.org. Website: www.ucobserver.org. **Contact:** Muriel Duncan, editor. **20% freelance written.** Prefers to work with published/established writers. Monthly newsmagazine for people associated with The United Church of Canada. Deals primarily with events, trends and policies having religious significance. Most coverage is Canadian, but reports on international or world concerns will be considered. Pays on publication. Publishes ms an average of 4 months after acceptance. Byline usually given. Buys first serial rights and occasionally all rights. Accepts queries by mail, e-mail, fax.

Nonfiction: Occasional opinion features only. Extended coverage of major issues usually assigned to known writers. No opinion pieces or poetry. Submissions should be written as news, no more than 1,200 words length, accurate and well-researched. Queries preferred. Rates depend on subject, author and work involved. Pays expenses of writers on assignment "as negotiated."

Reprints: Send tearsheet or photocopy of article with information about when and where the article previously appeared. Payment negotiated.

Photos: Buys photographs with mss. B&w should be 5×7 minimum; color 35mm or larger format. Payment varies.

Tips: "The writer has a better chance of breaking in at our publication with short articles; this also allows us to try more freelancers. Include samples of previous *news* writing with query. Indicate ability and willingness to do research, and to evaluate that research. The most frequent mistakes made by writers in completing an article for us are organizational problems, lack of polished style, short on research, and a lack of inclusive language."

⚔ $THE UPPER ROOM, Daily Devotional Guide, P.O. Box 340004, Nashville TN 37203-0004. (615)340-7252. Fax: (615)340-7267. E-mail: TheUpperRoomMagazine@upperroom.org. Website: www.upperroom.org. Editor and Publisher: Stephen D. Bryant. **Contact:** Office of the Managing Editor. **95% freelance written.** Eager to work with new/unpublished writers. Bimonthly magazine "offering a daily inspirational message which includes a Bible reading, text, prayer, 'Thought for the Day,' and suggestion for further prayer. Each day's meditation is written by a different person and is usually a personal witness about discovering meaning and power for Christian living through scripture study which illuminates daily life." Circ. 2.2 million (US); 385,000 outside US. Pays on publication. Publishes ms an average of 1 year after acceptance. Byline given. Buys first North American serial rights and translation rights. Submit seasonal material 14 months in advance. "Manuscripts are not returned. If writers include a stamped, self-addressed postcard, we will notify them that their writing has reached us. This does not imply acceptance or interest in purchase. Does not respond unless material is accepted for publication." Sample copy and writer's guidelines with a 4 × SAE and 2 first-class stamps. Guidelines only for #10 SASE or on website.

Nonfiction: Inspirational, personal experience, Bible-study insights. No poetry, lengthy "spiritual journey" stories. Special issues: Lent and Easter 2001; Advent 2000. **Buys 365 unsolicited mss/year.** Send complete ms by mail or e-mail. Length: 300 words maximum. **Pays $50.**

Tips: "The best way to break into our magazine is to send a well-written manuscript that looks at the Christian faith in a fresh way. Standard stories and sermon illustrations are immediately rejected. We very much want to find new writers and welcome good material. We are particularly interested in meditations based on Old Testament characters and stories. Good repeat meditations can lead to work on longer assignments for our other publications, which pay more. A writer who can deal concretely with everyday situations, relate them to the Bible and spiritual truths, and write clear, direct prose should be able to write for *The Upper Room.* We want material that provides for more interaction on the part of the reader—meditation suggestions, journaling suggestions, space to reflect and link personal experience with the meditation for the day. Meditations that are personal, authentic, exploratory and full of sensory detail make good devotional writing."

$ $ THE WAR CRY, The Salvation Army, 615 Slaters Lane, Alexandria VA 22313. Fax: (703)684-5539. E-mail: warcry@usn.salvationarmy.org. Website: publications.salvationarmyusa.org. Managing Editor: Jeff McDonald. **Contact:** Lt. Colonel Marlene Chase, editor. **10% freelance written.** Biweekly magazine covering army news and Christian devotional writing. Estab. 1881. Circ. 400,000. **Pays on acceptance.** Publishes ms an average of 1 year after acceptance. Byline given. Buys one-time rights. Editorial lead time 6 weeks. Submit seasonal material 1 year in advance. Accepts queries by mail, e-mail. Responds in 1 month. Sample copy and writer's guidelines free or on website.

    O→ "A best bet would be a well-written profile of an exemplary Christian or a recounting of a person's experiences that deepened the subject's faith and showed God in action. Most popular profiles are of Salvation Army programs and personnel."

Nonfiction: Humor, inspirational, interview/profile, personal experience, religious. No missionary stories, confessions. **Buys 40 mss/year.** Send complete ms. **Pays up to 20¢/word for assigned articles; 15-20¢/word for unsolicited articles.** Sometimes pays expenses of writers on assignment.

Reprints: Send typed ms with rights for sale noted and information about when and where the article previously appeared. **Pays 12¢/word.**

Photos: Offers $35-200/photo. Identification of subjects required. Buys one-time rights.

Fiction: Religious. **Buys 5-10 mss/year.** Send complete ms. Length: 1,200-1,500 words maximum. **Pays up to 20¢/word.**

Poetry: Free verse. Inspirational only. **Buys 10-20 poems/year.** Submit maximum 5 poems. Length: 16 lines maximum. **Pays $20-50.**

Fillers: Anecdotes (inspirational). **Buys 10-20/year.** Length: 200-500 words. **Pays 15-20¢/word.**

Tips: "We are soliciting more short fiction, inspirational articles and poetry, interviews with Christian athletes, evangelical leaders and celebrities, and theme-focused articles."

$ THE WESLEYAN ADVOCATE, The Wesleyan Publishing House, P.O. Box 50434, Indianapolis IN 46250-0434. (317)576-8156. Fax: (317)842-1649. E-mail: communications@wesleyan.org. Executive Editor: Dr. Norman G. Wilson. **Contact:** Jerry Brecheisen, managing editor. **50% freelance written.** Monthly magazine of The Wesleyan Church. Estab. 1842. Circ. 20,000. Pays on publication. Byline given. Buys first rights or simultaneous rights (prefers first rights). Submit seasonal material 6 months in advance. Accepts simultaneous submissions. Responds in 2 weeks. Sample copy for $2. Writer's guidelines for #10 SASE.

Nonfiction: Humor, inspirational, religious. Send complete ms. Length: 500-700 words. **Pays $10-40 for assigned articles; $5-25 for unsolicited articles.**

Reprints: Send photocopy of article and typed ms with rights for sale noted and information about when and where the article previously appeared.

Photos: Send photos with submission. Buys one-time rights.

Tips: "Write for a guide."

$ THE WESLEYAN WOMAN, Wesleyan Publishing House, P.O. Box 50434, Indianapolis IN 46250. (317)570-5164. Fax: (317)570-5254. E-mail: wwi@wesleyan.org. Website: www.wesleyan.org. Editor: Nancy Heer. **Contact:** Martha Blackburn, managing editor. **60-70% freelance written.** "Quarterly instruction and inspiration magazine for women 20-80. It is read by believers mainly." Estab. 1980. Circ. 4,000. Pays on publication. Byline given. Buys one-time and second serial (reprint) rights. Editorial lead time 3 months. Submit seasonal material 6 months in advance. Accepts simultaneous submissions. Sample copy and writer's guidelines free or on website.

Nonfiction: General interest, how-to (ideas for service and ministry), humor, inspirational, personal experience, religious. "We look for interesting, easy-to-read articles about the Christian life that capture the readers' interest. We look for uplifting articles that grab your attention; that inspire you to reach up to God with devotion, and out to those around us with unconditional love. No 'preaching' articles that tell others what to do." **Buys 60 mss/year.** Query by mail only or send complete ms. Length: 200-700 words. **Pays 2-4¢/word.**

Reprints: Send photocopy of article or typed ms with rights for sale noted and information about when and where the article previously appeared. Pays 50-75% of amount paid for an original article.

Photos: Send photos with submission. Offers $30/photo. Captions and identification of subjects required. Buys one-time rights.

Fillers: Anecdotes, facts, newsbreaks, short humor. **Buys 20/year.** Length: 150-350 words. **Pays 2-4¢/word.**

Tips: "Send a complete article after seeing our guidelines. Articles that are of your personal journey are welcomed. We go for the nerve endings—touching the spots where women are hurting, perplexed or troubled. Every article must pass the text question. 'Why would today's busy, media-blitzed Christian woman want to read this article?' We seldom publish sermons and Bible studies. Our denomination has other magazines which do these."

⭐ **\$ \$ WHISPERS FROM HEAVEN**, Publications International, Ltd., 7373 N. Cicero, Lincolnwood IL 60712. (847)329-5656. Fax: (847)329-5387. E-mail: tgavin@pubint.com. Editor: Julie Greene. Managing Editor: Becky Bell. **Contact:** Theresa Gavin, associate acquisitions editor. **100% freelance written.** Bimonthly magazine covering inspirational human-interest. "We're looking for real-life experiences (personal and otherwise) that lift the human spirit and illuminate positive human traits and values: though many stories may deal with (the overcoming of) tragedy and/or difficult times, descriptions shouldn't be too visceral and the emphasis should be on adversity overcome a positive result. *Whispers*, though inspiring, is not overtly religious." Estab. 1999. Circ. 120,000. **Pays on acceptance.** Publishes ms an average of 5 months after acceptance. Byline given. Offers 25% kill fee. Buys all rights. Editorial lead time 5 months. Submit seasonal material 5 months in advance. Accepts queries by mail, e-mail, fax, phone. Accepts simultaneous submissions. Writer's guidelines free.
Nonfiction: General interest, inspirational, personal experience. "Nothing overtly religious or anything that explores negative human characteristics." **Buys 150 mss/year.** Query with or without published clips. Length: 1,000-1,500 words. **Pays \$100-300 for assigned articles; \$100-225 for unsolicited articles.** Pays expenses of writers on assignment.
Reprints: Accepts previously published submissions.
Photos: State availability of photos with submission. Reviews negatives. Negotiates payment individually. Acquires negotiable rights.
Tips: "We are particularly fond of stories (when they warrant it) that have a 'twist' at the end—an extra bit of surprising information that adds meaning and provides an emotional connecting point to the story itself."

\$ WOMAN'S TOUCH, Assemblies of God Women's Ministries Department (GPH), 1445 Boonville Ave., Springfield MO 65802-1894. (417)862-2781. Fax: (417)862-0503. E-mail: womanstouch@ag.org. Website: www.ag.org/womans touch. **Contact:** Lillian Sparks, editor. Managing Editor: Darla Knoth. **50% freelance written.** Willing to work with new/unpublished writers. Bimonthly inspirational magazine for women. "Articles and contents of the magazine should be compatible with Christian teachings as well as human interests. The audience is women, both homemakers and those who are career-oriented." Estab. 1977. Circ. 15,000. Pays on publication. Publishes ms an average of 10 months after acceptance. Byline given. Buys first, second or one-time and electronic rights. Editorial lead time 10 months. Submit seasonal material 10 months in advance. Accepts queries by mail, e-mail, fax. Responds in 3 months. Sample copy for 9½×11 SAE with 3 first-class stamps or on website. Writer's guidelines for #10 SASE or on website.
Nonfiction: Book excerpts, general interest, inspirational, personal experience, religious, health. No fiction, poetry. **Buys 30 mss/year.** Send complete ms. Length: 200-1,000 words. **Pays \$10-50 for assigned articles; \$10-35 for unsolicited articles.**
Reprints: Send photocopy of article and information about when and where the article previously appeared. Pays 50-75% of amount paid for an original article.
Columns/Departments: A Final Touch (inspirational/human interest), 400 words; A Better You (health/wellness), 400 words; A Lighter Touch (true, unpublished anecdotes), 100 words. **Buys 8-10 mss/year. Pays \$10-35.**
Tips: "Submit manuscripts on current issues of interest to women."

⭐ **\$ WORLD CHRISTIAN**, Global Activists for the Cause of Christ, WinPress, P.O. Box 1357, Oak Park IL 60304. (708)524-5070. Fax: (708)524-5174. E-mail: WINPress7@aol.com. **Contact:** Phillip Huber, managing editor. Quarterly magazine covering religious missions. "*World Christian* exists to inform, encourage, provoke and mobilize this generation in obedience to the Great Commission." Estab. 1982. Circ. 30,000 (March, June, September), 150,000 (December). Pays on publication. Publishes ms 6 months after acceptance. Byline given. Buys all rights. Editorial lead time up to 6 months. Accepts queries by mail, e-mail, fax. Sample copy for \$4. Writer's guidelines free.
● The editor reports an interest in seeing good profiles of average Christians making a difference around the world.
Nonfiction: Book excerpts, essays, general interest, how-to, inspirational, interview/profile, opinion, personal experience, photo feature, religious, travel, some sidebars. No fiction, poetry or feel-good, warm, fuzzy stories about how God is important in a person's life. **Buys 50-60 mss/year.** Query with published clips. Length: 600-2,000 words. **Pays 6-15¢/word.** Sometimes pays expenses of writers on assignment.
⌐ Break in with well-written articles that show evidence of careful research from multiple sources, about interesting or unusual aspects of missions and evangelism.
Photos: State availability of photos with submission. Negotiates payment individually. Captions, model releases, identification of subjects required.

🅽 ⭐ **\$ WORLD PULSE**, Billy Graham Center at Wheaton College, P.O. Box 794, Wheaton IL 60189. (630)752-7158. Fax: (630)752-7155. E-mail: pulsenews@aol.com. Website: www.wheaton.edu/bgc/emis. **Contact:** Stan Guthrie, editor. **50% freelance written.** Biweekly newsletter covering evangelical missions. "News and features on world evangelization written from an evangelical position." Estab. 1965. Circ. 5,000. Pays on publication. Byline given. Offers negotiable kill fee. Buys first North American serial rights. Editorial lead time varies. Accepts queries by mail, e-mail, fax. Responds in 2 weeks to queries; 1 month to mss. Sample copy and writer's guidelines free.

Nonfiction: Interview/profile, personal experience, photo feature, religious. No poetry, sermons or humor. **Buys 50 mss/year.** Query. Length: 500-1,000 words. **Pays $30-100.** Sometimes pays expenses of writers on assignment.

Photos: State availability of photos with submission. Reviews prints. Offers $25/photo. Identification of subjects required. Buys one-time rights.

Columns/Departments: InterView (Q&A with newsmakers), 300-500 words. **Pays 10¢/word up to $50.**

Tips: "*Pulse* is not a daily newspaper. Don't write a vanilla news story (with just the 5 Ws and an H). Sprinkle human interest and memorable facts throughout the story. Try to inform *and* entertain."

RETIREMENT

January 1, 1996 the first baby boomer turned 50. With peak earning power and increased leisure time, this generation is able to pursue varied interests while maintaining active lives. More people are retiring in their 50s, while others are starting a business or traveling and pursuing hobbies. These publications give readers specialized information on health and fitness, medical research, finances and other topics of interest, as well as general articles on travel destinations and recreational activities.

■ $ $ $ ACTIVETIMES MAGAZINE, 417 Main St., Carbondale CO 81623. **Contact:** Chris Kelly, editor. **80% freelance written.** Monthly newspaper magazine covering over 50 market. "We target active, adults over 50. We emphasize the positive, enjoyable aspects of aging." Estab. 1992. Circ. 4,000,000. Pays on publication. Publishes ms an average of 4 months after acceptance. Byline given. Offers 50% kill fee. Buys all print and electronic rights. Editorial lead time 3 months. Submit seasonal material 9 months in advance. Responds in 2 months. Sample copy and guidelines for 9×12 SAE with 3 first-class stamps. Writer's guidelines only for #10 SASE.

Nonfiction: General interest, how-to, interview/profile, travel round-ups (not destination stories), outdoor, business, careers, education, housing, entertainment, books, celebrities, food, nutrition, health, products, relationships, sex, volunteerism, community service, sports/recreation. No personal essays, first person narratives or nostalgia. **Buys 120 mss/year.** Query with published clips and SASE or postcard. No SASE, no reply. Length: 400-750 words. **Pays $75-400 for assigned articles; $50-250 for unsolicited articles.**

Photos: State availability of photos with submission. Reviews contact sheets, 35mm transparencies, prints. Negotiates payment individually. Identification of subjects required.

Columns/Departments: Profile (interesting over-50), 500-600 words. **Buys 8 mss/year.** Query with published clips. **Pays $75-250.** Never-Evers (over-50 doing something never, ever did including b&w photo), 150 words. Send complete ms. **Pays $35.**

Tips: "Write a detailed query, with substantiating clips. Show how story will appeal to active over-50 reader. Not interested in pain, death, suffering, loss, illness and other similarly depressing subjects."

$ ALIVE! A Magazine for Christian Senior Adults, Christian Seniors Fellowship, P.O. Box 46464, Cincinnati OH 45246-0464. (513)825-3681. Editor: J. David Lang. **Contact:** A. June Lang, office editor. **60% freelance written.** Bimonthly magazine for senior adults ages 50 and older. "We need timely articles about Christian seniors in vital, productive lifestyles, travels or ministries." Estab. 1988. Pays on publication. Byline given. Buys first or second serial (reprint) rights. Submit seasonal material 6 months in advance. Accepts queries by mail. Responds in 2 months. Membership $15/year. Sample copy for 9×12 SAE with 3 first-class stamps. Writer's guidelines for #10 SASE.

Nonfiction: General interest, humor, inspirational, interview/profile, photo feature, religious, travel. **Buys 25-50 mss/year.** Send complete ms and SASE. Length: 600-1,200 words. **Pays $18-75.** Organization membership may be deducted from payment at writer's request.

Reprints: Send tearsheet, photocopy of article or typed ms with rights for sale noted and information about when and where the article previously appeared. Pays 60-75% of amount paid for an original article.

Photos: State availability of photos with submission. Offers $10-25. Model releases and identification of subjects required. Buys one-time rights.

Columns/Departments: Heart Medicine (humorous personal anecdotes; prefer grandparent/grandchild stories or anecdotes re: over-55 persons), 10-100 words; Games n' Stuff (word games, puzzles, word search), 200-500 words. **Buys 50 mss/year.** Send complete ms and SASE. **Pays $2-25.**

Fiction: Adventure, humorous, religious, romance (if it fits age group), slice-of-life vignettes, motivational/inspirational. **Buys 12 mss/year.** Send complete ms. Length: 600-1,500 words. **Pays $20-60.**

Fillers: Anecdotes, facts, gags to be illustrated, short humor. **Buys 15/year.** Length: 50-500 words. **Pays $2-15.**

Tips: "Include SASE and whether manuscript is to be returned or tossed."

Ⓝ ■ $ $ FIFTY-FIVE PLUS, Promoting An Active Mature Lifestyle, Valley Publishers Inc., 95 Abbeyhill Dr., Kanata, Ontario K2L 2M8 Canada. (613)592-3578. Fax: (613)592-9033. **Contact:** Pat den Boer, editor. **95% freelance written.** Bimonthly magazine. "We focus on the health, financial, nutrition and travel interests of active retirees." Circ. 40,000. Pays on publication. Publishes ms an average of 1 year after acceptance. Byline given. Offers 50% kill fee. Buys first North American serial rights. Editorial lead time 3 months. Submit seasonal material 6 months in advance. Sample copy for 9×12 SAE and 3 first-class stamps. Writer's guidelines for #10 SASE.

Nonfiction: How-to, inspirational, travel. **Buys 70 mss/year.** Send complete ms. Length: 500-1,000 words. **Pays $60-300.** Pays writers with contributor copies or other premiums for travel promotional pieces. Sometimes pays expenses of writer on assignment.

Photos: Send photos with submission. Reviews 2×3 and 4×5 transparencies. Offers no additional payment for photos accepted with ms or negotiates payment individually. Buys one-time rights.

Columns/Departments: Health; Backyard Heroes (people giving back to community); Personal Finance; Nutrition; Great Mature Getaways. Length: 600 words. **Buys 6 mss/year.** Send complete ms. **Pays $60.**

$ MATURE LIVING, A Magazine for Christian Senior Adults, LifeWay Press of the Southern Baptist Convention, 127 Ninth Ave. N., Nashville TN 37234-0140. (615)251-2274. Fax: (615)251-5008. E-mail: matureliving@lifeway. com. Editor: Al Shackleford. **Contact:** Judy Pregel, managing editor. **70% freelance written.** Monthly leisure reading magazine for senior adults 50 and older. Estab. 1977. Circ. 350,000. **Pays on acceptance.** Byline given. Prefers to purchase all rights if writer agrees. Submit seasonal material 1 year in advance. Responds in 3 months. Sample copy for 9×12 SAE with 4 first-class stamps. Writer's guidelines for #10 SASE.

Nonfiction: General interest, historical/nostalgic, how-to, humor, inspirational, interview/profile, personal experience, photo feature, crafts, travel. No pornography, profanity, occult, liquor, dancing, drugs, gambling. **Buys 100 mss/year.** Send complete ms. Length: 600-1,200 words maximum. **Pays 5½¢/word (accepted); $75 minimum.**

Photos: State availability of photos with submission. Offers $10-25/photo. Pays on publication. Buys one-time rights.

Columns/Departments: Cracker Barrel (brief, humorous, original quips and verses), **pays $15**; Grandparents' Brag Board (something humorous or insightful said or done by your grandchild or great-grandchild), **pays $15**; Inspirational (devotional items), **pays $25**; Food (introduction and 4-6 recipes), **pays $50**; Over the Garden Fence (vegetable or flower gardening), **pays $40**; Crafts (step-by-step procedures), **pays $40**; Game Page (crossword or word-search puzzles and quizzes), **pays $40.**

Fiction: Humorous, mainstream, slice-of-life vignettes. No reference to liquor, dancing, drugs, gambling; no pornography, profanity or occult. **Buys 12 mss/year.** Send complete ms. Length: 900-1,200 words. **Pays 5½¢/word; $75 minimum.**

Poetry: Light verse, traditional, seasonal, inspirational. **Buys 30 poems/year.** Submit maximum 5 poems. Length: open. **Pays $25.**

★ $ $ $ $ MATURE OUTLOOK, Meredith Corp., 1716 Locust St., Des Moines IA 50309-3023. E-mail: outlook@mdp.com. **Contact:** Peggy Person, editor. **80% freelance written.** Bimonthly magazine on travel, health, nutrition, food, money and people for over-50 audience. "*Mature Outlook* is for the 50+ reader who is discovering new possibilities for a new time of life. It provides information for establishing a secure base of health and financial well-being, as well as stories of travel, hobbies, volunteerism and more. They may or may *not* be retired." Circ. 725,000. **Pays on acceptance.** Publishes ms an average of 7 months after acceptance. Byline given. Offers 25% kill fee. Buys all rights or makes work-for-hire assignments. Submit all material 9 months in advance. Responds in 2 weeks. Sample copy for $3 and 9×12 SAE. Writer's guidelines for #10 SASE.

Nonfiction: How-to, travel, health, fitness, financial, people profiles. No poetry, celebrities or reprints. **Buys 50-60 mss/year.** Query with published clips. Length: 75-2,500 words. **Pays $50-2,000.** Pays telephone expenses of writers on assignment.

Photos: State availability of photos with submission. Pays for photos on publication.

Tips: "Please query. Please don't call. Reviews manuscripts for short articles or department briefs of 500 words or less."

$ MATURE YEARS, The United Methodist Publishing House, 201 Eighth Ave. S., Nashville TN 37202-0801. Fax: (615)749-6512. E-mail: mcropsey@umpublishing.org. **Contact:** Marvin W. Cropsey, editor. **50% freelance written.** Prefers to work with published/established writers. Quarterly magazine "designed to help persons in and nearing the retirement years understand and appropriate the resources of the Christian faith in dealing with specific problems and opportunities related to aging." Estab. 1954. Circ. 70,000. **Pays on acceptance.** Publishes ms an average of 1 year after acceptance. Buys one-time North American serial rights. Submit seasonal material 14 months in advance. Responds in 2 weeks to queries; 2 months to mss. Sample copy for $5 and 9×12 SAE. Writer's guidelines for #10 SASE.

Nonfiction: How-to (hobbies), inspirational, religious, travel (special guidelines), older adult health, finance issues. Especially important are opportunities for older adults to read about service, adventure, fulfillment and fun. **Buys 75-80 mss/year.** Send complete ms. Length: 900-2,000 words. **Pays $45-125.** Sometimes pays expenses of writers on assignment.

Reprints: Send photocopy or typed ms with rights for sale noted and information about when and where the article previously appeared. Pays 100% of amount paid for an original article.

Photos: Send photos with submission. Negotiates payment individually. Captions, model releases required. Buys one-time rights.

Columns/Departments: Health Hints (retirement, health), 900-1,500 words; Going Places (travel, pilgrimage), 1,000-1,500 words; Fragments of Life (personal inspiration), 250-600 words; Modern Revelations (religious/inspirational),

900-1,500 words; Money Matters (personal finance), 1,200-1,800 words; Merry-Go-Round (cartoons, jokes, 4-6 line humorous verse); Puzzle Time (religious puzzles, crosswords). **Buys 4 mss/year each.** Send complete ms. **Pays $25-45.**

Fiction: Religious, slice-of-life vignettes, retirement years. **Buys 4 mss/year.** Send complete ms. Length: 1,000-2,000 words. **Pays $60-125.**

Poetry: Free verse, haiku, light verse, traditional. **Buys 24 poems/year.** Submit 6 poems maximum. Length: 3-16 lines. **Pays $5-20.**

$ $ $ $ MODERN MATURITY, American Association of Retired Persons, 601 E St., NW, Washington DC 20049. (202)434-6880. Website: www.aarp.org. **Contact:** Hugh Delehanty, editor. **50% freelance written.** Prefers to work with published/established writers. Bimonthly magazine. "*Modern Maturity* is devoted to the varied needs and active life interests of AARP members, age 50 and over, covering such topics as financial planning, travel, health, careers, retirement, relationships and social and cultural change. Its editorial content serves the mission of AARP seeking through education, advocacy and service to enhance the quality of life for all by promoting independence, dignity and purpose." Circ. 20,500,000. **Pays on acceptance.** Publishes ms an average of 6 months after acceptance. Byline given. Buys exclusive first worldwide publication rights. Submit seasonal material 6 months in advance. Responds in 3 months. Free sample copy and writer's guidelines.

Nonfiction: Careers, workplace, practical information in living, financial and legal matters, personal relationships, consumerism. Query first by mail only. *No unsolicited mss.* Length: up to 2,000 words. **Pays up to $3,000.** Sometimes pays expenses of writers on assignment.

Photos: Photos purchased with or without accompanying ms. Pays $250 and up for color; $150 and up for b&w.

Fiction: Very occasional short fiction.

Tips: "The most frequent mistake made by writers in completing an article for us is poor follow-through with basic research. The outline is often more interesting than the finished piece. We do not accept unsolicited manuscripts."

★ $ PLUS, (formerly *Senior Magazine*), 3565 S. Higuera St., San Luis Obispo CA 93401. (805)544-8711. Fax: (805)544-4450. Publisher: Gary D. Suggs. **Contact:** George Brand, editor. **60% freelance written.** Monthly magazine covering seniors to inform and entertain the "over-50" but young-at-heart audience. Estab. 1981. Circ. 140,000. Pays on publication. Publishes ms an average of 2 months after acceptance. Byline given. Buys one-time rights. Editorial lead time 2 months. Submit seasonal material 2 months in advance. Accepts queries by mail, fax, phone. Accepts simultaneous submissions. Responds in 2 weeks to queries; 1 month to mss. Sample copy for 9×12 SAE with $1.50 postage. Writer's guidelines for SASE.

Nonfiction: Historical/nostalgic, humor, interview/profile, book reviews, entertainment, health, personal experience, travel. "We favor upbeat articles." Special issues: Second Careers; Going Back to School; Christmas (December); Travel (October, April). No finance, automotive, heavy humor, poetry or fiction. **Buys 60-70 mss/year.** Query with SASE or send complete ms. Length: 900-1,200 words. **Pays $1.50/inch.**

Photos: Send photos with submission. Reviews 5×7 prints, transparencies. Offers $5-15/photo. Captions and identification of subjects required. Buys one-time rights. Uses mostly well-known personalities.

Tips: "Request and read a sample copy before submitting."

★ $ $ PRIME TIMES, Members Prime Club, P.O. Box 391, Madison WI 53701-0391. (608)231-7188. Fax: (608)231-7229. E-mail: philp.tschudy@cunamutual.com. **Contact:** Philip Tschudy, managing editor. **75% freelance written.** Bimonthly membership magazine for MEMBERS Prime Club, formerly the National Association for Retired Credit Union People (NARCUP). "*Prime Times* is a topical magazine of broad appeal to a general adult audience, emphasizing issues relevant to people over age 50. It offers timely articles on health, fitness, finance, travel, outdoor sports, consumer issues, lifestyle, home arts and family relationships. Estab. 1979. Circ. 35,000. **Pays on acceptance.** Publishes ms an average of 6 months after acceptance. Byline given. Buys first North American serial rights, one-time rights and second serial (reprint) rights. Editorial lead time 7 months. Submit seasonal material 8 months in advance. Accepts queries by mail, e-mail, fax, phone. Responds in 2 months to queries; 2 months to mss. Sample copy for $3.75 and 9×12 SAE with 4 first-class stamps. Writer's guidelines for #10 SASE.

Nonfiction: Book excerpts, general interest, health/fitness, travel, historical, humor, recipes, photo features. "No nostalgia pieces, medical or financial pieces based solely on personal anecdotes, personal opinion essays, fiction or poetry." **Buys 8-12 mss/year.** Prefers to see complete ms. Length: 1,000-2,000 words. **Pays $250 minimum for full-length assigned articles; $100 minimum for unsolicited full-length articles.**

Reprints: Buys 8-16 reprints/year. Send photocopy or typed ms with rights for sale noted and info about when and where the article previously appeared. **Pays $50-125,** depending on length, quality and number of times published.

Photos: Needs professional-quality photos. State availability of or send photos with submission. Welcomes text-photo packages. Reviews contact sheets, transparencies and prints. Negotiates payment individually. Model releases and identification of subjects required. Buys one-time rights.

Tips: "Articles that contain useful, well-documented, up-to-date information have the best chance of publication. Don't send personal essays, or articles that repeat information readily available in mainstream media. Articles on health and medical issues *must* be founded in sound scientific method and include current data. Quotes from experts add to an article's validity. You must be able to document your research. Make it easy for us to make a decision on your submission."

If the article is written, submit the entire thing—manuscript with professional-quality photos. If you query, be specific. Write part of it in the style in which you would write the article. Be sure to enclose clips. With every article we publish, something about the story must lend itself to strong graphic representation."

$ SENIOR LIVING NEWSPAPERS, Smith III Publications, Inc., 318 E. Pershing St., Springfield MO 65806. (417)862-0852. Fax: (417)862-9079. E-mail: elefantwalk@msn.com. Website: www.seniorlivingnewspaper.com. Editor: Robert Smith. **Contact:** Joyce Yonker O'Neal, managing editor. **25-50% freelance written.** Monthly newspaper covering active seniors in retirement. "For people 55+. Positive and upbeat attitude on aging, prime of life times. Slant is directed to mid-life and retirement lifestyles. Readers are primarily well-educated and affluent retirees, homemakers and career professionals. *Senior Living* informs; health, fitness-entertains; essays, nostalgia, humor, etc." Estab. 1995. Circ. 40,000. Pays 30 days after publication. Publishes ms an average of 2 months after acceptance. Byline given. Offers 25% kill fee. Buys first and second serial (reprint) rights and electronic rights. Editorial lead time 3 months. Submit seasonal material 4 months in advance. Accepts queries by mail, e-mail. Responds in 2 weeks to queries; 1 month to mss. Sample copy for 9×12 SAE with 5 first-class stamps. Writer's guidelines for #10 SASE.
Nonfiction: Essays, general interest, health-related, historical/nostalgic, humor, inspirational, personal experience, photo feature, travel. No youth-oriented, preachy, sugar-coated, technical articles. **Buys 65 mss/year.** Send complete ms. Length: 600-700 words. **Pays $20-35 for assigned articles; $5-35 for unsolicited articles.**
Reprints: Accepts previously published submissions.
Photos: Send photos with submission. Offers $5/photo. Captions, model releases and identification of subjects required. Buys one-time rights.
Fillers: Anecdotes, facts, short humor. **Buys 15/year.** Length: 150-250 words. **Pays $5-10.**
Tips: "Beginning writers who are in need of byline clips stand a good chance if they indicate that they do not require payment for article. A query letter is not necessary, but a cover letter telling a bit about yourself is nice."

ROMANCE & CONFESSION

Listed here are publications that need stories of romance ranging from ethnic and adventure to romantic intrigue and confession. Each magazine has a particular slant; some are written for young adults, others to family-oriented women. Some magazines also are interested in general interest nonfiction on related subjects.

$ THE BLACK ROMANCE GROUP, Black Confessions, Black Intimacy, Black Romance, Black Secrets, Bronze Thrills, Jive, Sizzling Black Love Stories, True Black Experience, Sterling/McFadden Partnership, 233 Park Ave. S., 5th Floor, New York NY 10003. (212)979-4800. Fax: (212)780-3555. E-mail: jpestaina@sterling macfadden.com. **Contact:** Janet Pestaina, editor. **100% freelance written.** Eager to work with new/unpublished writers. Bimonthly magazines of romance and love. Pays on publication. Publishes ms an average of 2 months after acceptance. Byline given on special feature articles only but not short stories. Company maintains all property rights or stories. Accepts queries by mail, e-mail, fax. Allow 2 months for review of ms. Sample copy for 9×12 SAE with 5 first-class stamps. Writer's guidelines free.
Nonfiction: How-to (relating to romance and love) and feature articles on any aspect of relationships. "We like our articles to have a down-to-earth flavor. They should be written in the spirit of sisterhood, fun and creativity. Come up with an original idea that our readers may not have thought of but will be dying to try out." Query with published clips or send complete ms. Length: 3-5 typed pages. **Pays $125.**
Fiction: Romantic confessional stories told from an African-American female perspective. Stories should include two love scenes, alluding to sex. Include spicy, sexual topics of forbidden love, but not graphic detail. Send complete ms (5,300-5,800 words). **Pays $100-125.** Stories must include a conflict between the heroine and her love interest. The age of characters can range from mid-teenage years through late thirties. Make stories exciting, passionate (uninhibited sexual fantasies) and romantic.
Tips: "Follow our writer's guidelines and read a few sample copies before submitting your manuscript. Use a romance writer's phrase book as a guide when writing stories, especially love scenes. Submit stories with original, modern conflicts. Incorporate romance and sex in manuscripts, uninhibiatedly—making the stories an exciting, passionate escape for readers to imagine fulfilling their secret desires."

$ TRUE CONFESSIONS, Macfadden Women's Group, 233 Park Ave. S., New York NY 10003. (212)979-4800. Fax: (212)979-7342. E-mail: trueconfessionsmail@yahoo.com. **Contact:** Pat Byrdsong, editor. **100% freelance written.** Eager to work with new/unpublished writers. Monthly magazine for high-school-educated, working class women, teens through maturity. Circ. 200,000. Buys all rights. Byline given on featured columns. Pays during the last week of month of issue. Publishes ms an average of 4 months after acceptance. Submit seasonal material 8 months in advance. Responds in 15 months.
  ○━ "If you have a strong story to tell, tell it simply and convincingly. We always have a need for 4,000-word stories with dramatic impact about dramatic events." Asian-, Latina-, Native- and African-American stories are encouraged.

Nonfiction: Timely, exciting, true emotional first-person stories on the problems that face today's women. The narrators should be sympathetic, and the situations they find themselves in should be intriguing, yet realistic. Many stories may have a strong romantic interest and a high moral tone; however, personal accounts or "confessions," no matter how controversial the topic, are encouraged and accepted. Careful study of a current issue is suggested. Length: 4,000-7,000 words and mini stories 1,000-1,500 words; also book lengths of 8,000-9,000 words. **Pays 5¢/word.** Submit complete ms. No simultaneous submissions. SASE required. Buys all rights.

Columns/Departments: Family Zoo (pet feature), 50 words or less, **pays $50 for pet photo and story.** All other features are 200-300 words: My Moment With God (a short prayer); Incredible But True (an incredible/mystical/spiritual experience); My Man (a man who has been special in your life); Woman to Woman (a point of view about a contemporary subject matter or a woman overcoming odds). Send complete ms and SASE. **Pays $65** for all features; **$75** for My Moment with God.

Poetry: Poetry should rhyme. Length: 4-20 lines. **Pays $10 minimum.**

Tips: "Our magazine is almost 100% freelance. We purchase all stories that appear in our magazine. Read 3-4 issues before sending submissions. Do not talk down to our readers. We prefer manuscripts on disk as well as hard copy."

◩ $ TRUE ROMANCE, Sterling/Macfadden Partnership, 233 Park Ave. S., New York NY 10003. (212)979-4800. Fax: (212)979-7342. E-mail: pvitucci@sterlingmacfadden.com. Website: www.truestory.com. **Contact:** Pat Vitucci, editor. **100% freelance written.** Monthly magazine for women, teens through retired, offering compelling confession stories based on true happenings, with reader identification and strong emotional tone. No third-person material. Estab. 1923. Circ. 225,000. Pays 1 month after publication. Buys all rights. Submit seasonal material at least 6 months in advance. Accepts queries by mail. Responds within 8 months.

Nonfiction: Confessions, true love stories; mini-adventures: problems and solutions; dating and marital and child-rearing difficulties. Realistic yet unique stories dealing with current problems, everyday events; strong emotional appeal. **Buys 12 stories/issue.** Submit ms. Length: 3,000-8,000 words. **Pays 3¢/word;** slightly higher rates for short-shorts.

Columns/Departments: That's My Child (photo and 50 words); Loving Pets (photo and 50 words), **both pay $50;** Cupid's Corner (photo and 500 words about you and spouse), **pays $100;** That Precious Moment (1,000 words about a unique experience), **pays $50.**

Poetry: Light romantic poetry. Length: 24 lines maximum. **Pays $10-30.**

Tips: "A timely, well-written story that is told by a sympathetic narrator who sees the central problem through to a satisfying resolution is *all* important to break into *True Romance*. We are always looking for interesting, emotional, identifiable stories."

◩ $ TRUE STORY, Sterling/Macfadden Partnership, 233 Park Ave. S., New York NY 10003. (212)979-4800. Fax: (212)979-7342. E-mail: tpappalardo@sterlingmacfadden.com. Website: www.truestorymail.com. **Contact:** Tina Pappalardo, editor. **80% freelance written.** Monthly magazine for young married, blue-collar women, 20-35; high school education; increasingly broad interests; home-oriented, but looking beyond the home for personal fulfillment. Circ. 580,000. Buys all rights. Byline given "on articles only." Pays 1 month after publication. Submit seasonal material 1 year in advance. Responds in 1 year. Guidelines on website.

    ○━ Subject matter can range from light romances to sizzling passion, from all-out tearjerkers to happily-ever-after endings, and everything in between.

Nonfiction: "First-person stories covering all aspects of women's interests: love, marriage, family life, careers, social problems, etc. The best direction a new writer can be given is to carefully study several issues of the magazine; then submit a fresh, exciting, well-written true story. We have no taboos. It's the handling and believability that make the difference between a rejection and an acceptance." **Buys about 125 full-length mss/year.** Submit only complete mss and disk for stories. Length: 2,000-10,000 words. **Pays 5¢/word; $100 minimum.** Pays a flat rate for columns or departments, as announced in the magazine.

Tips: "*True Story* is unique because all of our stories are written from the hearts of real people, and deal with all of the issues that affect us today—parenthood, relationships, careers, family affairs, and social concerns. All of our stories are written in first person, and should be no less than 2,000 words and no more than 10,000 words. If you have access to a computer, we require you to send your submission on a disk, along with a clean hard copy of the story. Please keep in mind, all files must be saved as rich text format (RTF)."

RURAL

These publications draw readers interested in rural lifestyles. Surprisingly, many readers are from urban centers who dream of or plan to build a house in the country. Magazines featuring design, construction, log homes and "country" style interior decorating appear in Home & Garden.

$ $ THE COUNTRY CONNECTION, Ontario's Pro-Nature Magazine, Pinecone Publishing, P.O. Box 100, Boulter, Ontario K0L 1G0 Canada. Fax: (613)332-5183. E-mail: pinecone@northcom.net. Website: web.northcom.net/pinecone. **Contact:** Gus Zylstra, editor. **75% freelance written.** Semiannual magazine covering country life and tourism. "*The Country Connection* is a magazine for true nature lovers and the rural adventurer. Building on our commitment to heritage, cultural, artistic, and outdoor themes, we continually add new topics to illuminate the country experience of people living within nature. Our goal is to chronicle rural life in its many aspects, giving 'voice' to the countryside." Estab. 1989. Circ. 10,000. Pays on publication. Publishes ms an average of 6 months after acceptance. Byline given. Buys first rights. Editorial lead time 4 months. Submit seasonal material 4 months in advance. Accepts queries by mail, e-mail. Sample copy $4.55. Writer's guidelines for #10 SASE (in Canada) or SAE and IRC (in US) or on website.

Nonfiction: General interest, historical/nostalgic, humor, personal experience, photo feature, lifestyle, leisure, art and culture, travel, vegan recipes only. No hunting, fishing, animal husbandry or pet articles. **Buys 20 mss/year.** Send complete ms. Length: 500-2,000 words. **Pays 7-10¢/word.** Sometimes pays expenses of writers on assignment.

Photos: Send photos with submission. Reviews transparencies and prints. Offers $10-50/photo. Captions required. Buys one-time rights.

Columns/Departments: Pays 7-10¢/word.

Fiction: Adventure, fantasy, historical, humorous, slice-of-life vignettes, country living. **Buys 4 mss/year.** Send complete ms. Length: 500-1,500 words. **Pays 7-10¢/word.**

Tips: "Canadian content only. Send (original content) manuscript with appropriate support material such as photos, illustrations, maps, etc. Do not send American stamps. They have no value in Canada!"

$ COUNTRY FOLK, Salaki Publishing & Design, HC77, Box 608, Pittsburg MO 65724. Phone/fax: (417)993-5944. **Contact:** Susan Salaki, editor. **100% freelance written.** Bimonthly magazine. "*Country Folk* publishes true stories and history of the Ozarks." Estab. 1994. Circ. 5,000. Pays on publication. Publishes ms an average of 3 months after acceptance. Byline given. Buys first rights. Editorial lead time 2 months. Submit seasonal material 3 months in advance. Accepts queries by mail, fax, phone. Responds in 1 month to queries; 2 months to mss. Sample copy for $4. Writer's guidelines for #10 SASE.

• *Country Folk* has increased from quarterly to bimonthly and doubled its circulation.

Nonfiction: Historical/nostalgic, how-to, humor, inspirational, personal experience, photo feature, true ghost stories of the Ozarks. **Buys 10 mss/year.** Send complete ms and SASE. Length: 750-1,000 words. **Pays $5-20.** Pays writers with contributor copies or other premiums if we must do considerable editing to the work.

Photos: Send photos with submission. Buys one-time rights.

Fiction: Historical, humorous, mystery, novel excerpts. **Buys 10 mss/year.** Send complete ms. Length: 750-800 words. **Pays $5-50.**

Poetry: Haiku, light verse, traditional. **Buys 25 poems/year.** Submit maximum 3 poems. **Pays $1-5.**

Fillers: Anecdotes, facts, gags to be illustrated by cartoonist, newsbreaks, short humor. **Buys 25/year. Pays $1-5.**

Tips: "We want material from people who are born and raised in the country, especially the Ozark region. We accept submissions in any form, handwritten or typed. Many of the writers and poets whose work we publish are first-time submissions. Most of the work we publish is written by older men and women who have heard stories from their parents and grandparents about how the Ozark region was settled in the 1800s. Almost any writer who writes from the heart about a true experience from his or her youth will get published. Our staff edits for grammar and spelling errors. All the writer has to be concerned about is conveying the story."

$ $ FARM & RANCH LIVING, Reiman Publications, 5925 Country Lane, Greendale WI 53129. (414)423-0100. Fax: (414)423-8463. E-mail: editors@farmandranchliving.com. Website: www.farmandranchliving.com or www.reiman pub.com. **Contact:** Nick Pabst, editor. **30% freelance written.** Eager to work with new/unpublished writers. Bimonthly lifestyle magazine aimed at families that farm or ranch full time. "*F&RL* is *not* a 'how-to' magazine—it focuses on people rather than products and profits." Estab. 1978. Circ. 480,000. Pays on publication. Publishes ms an average of 6 months after acceptance. Byline given. Buys first serial rights and one-time rights. Submit seasonal material 6 months in advance. Responds in 6 weeks. Accepts queries by mail, e-mail, fax. Sample copy for $2. Writer's guidelines for #10 SASE.

Nonfiction: Interview/profile, photo feature, nostalgia, humor, inspirational, personal experience, "Prettiest Place in the Country" (photo/text tour of ranch or farm). No how-to articles or stories about "hobby farmers" (doctors or lawyers with weekend farms); no issue-oriented stories (pollution, animal rights, etc.). **Buys 30 mss/year.** Query or send ms. Length: 600-1,200 words. **Pays up to $200 for text/photos package.** Payment for "Prettiest Place" negotiable.

Reprints: Send photocopy of article with rights for sale noted. Payment negotiable.

Photos: Scenic. State availability of photos with query. Pays $75-200 for 35mm color slides. Buys one-time rights.

Fillers: Jokes, anecdotes, short humor with farm or ranch slant. **Buys 50/year.** Length: 50-150 words. **Pays $10-25.**

Tips: "Our readers enjoy stories and features that are upbeat and positive. A freelancer must see *F&RL* to fully appreciate how different it is from other farm publications—ordering a sample is strongly advised (not available on newsstands). Photo features (about interesting farm or ranch families) and personality profiles are most open to freelancers."

$ FARM TIMES, 504 Sixth St., Rupert ID 83350. (208)436-1111. Fax: (208)436-9455. E-mail: farmtimes@safelink.n et. Website: www.farmtimes.com. **Contact:** Robyn Maxfield, managing editor. **50% freelance written.** Monthly regional tabloid for agriculture-farming/ranching. "*Farm Times* is dedicated to rural living in the Intermountain and Pacific Northwest. Stories related to farming and ranching in the states of Idaho, Montana, Nevada, Oregon, Utah, Washington and Wyoming are our mainstay, but farmers and ranchers do more than just work. Human interest articles that appeal to rural readers are used on occasion." Estab. 1987. Pays on publication. Byline given. Editorial lead time 1 month. Submit seasonal material 3 months in advance. Accepts queries by mail, e-mail. Responds in 2 months to queries. Writer's guidelines for #10 SASE. Sample copy for $2.50 or on website.

O→ Break in by writing tight and including photos, charts or graphs if possible.

Nonfiction: Farm or ranch issues, exposé, general interest, how-to, interview/profile, new product (few), opinion, late breaking ag news. Always runs one feature article of interest to women. No humor, essay, first person, personal experience or book excerpts. Special issues: Irrigation, Chemical/Fertilizer, Potato Production. **Buys 200 mss/year.** Query with published clips. Send complete ms. Length: 500-800 words. **Pays $1.50/column inch.**

● The editor reports an interest in seeing articles about global agriculture issues and trends that affect the Pacific Northwest and Intermountain West agriculture producer, rural health care and Western water issues.

Reprints: Send typed ms with rights for sale noted and information about when and where the article previously appeared. Pays 100% of amount paid for an original article.

Photos: Send photocopy of article and photos with submission. Reviews contact sheets with negatives, 35mm or larger transparencies and 3×5 or larger prints. Offers $7/b&w inside, $35/color front page cover. Captions, model releases, identification of subjects required. Buys one-time rights.

Column/Departments: Horse (horse care/technical), 500-600 words; Rural Religion (interesting churches/missions/religious activities) 600-800 words; Dairy (articles of interest to dairy farmers) 600-800 words. **Buys 12 mss/year.** Query. Send complete ms. **Pays $1.50/column inch.**

Tips: "Ag industry-related articles should have a Pacific Northwest and Intermountain West slant (crops, production techniques, etc.), or how they pertain to the global market. Write tight, observe desired word counts. Feature articles can vary between agriculture and rural living. Good quality photos included with manuscript increase publication chances. Articles should have farm/ranch/rural slant on various topics: health, travel (farmers vacation, too), financial, gardening/landscape, etc."

$ $MOTHER EARTH NEWS, Sussex Publishers, 49 E. 21st St., 11th Floor, New York NY 10010. (212)260-7210. Fax: (212)260-7445. E-mail: letters@motherearthnews.com. Website: www.motherearthnews.com. Editor: Matthew Scanlon. Managing Editor: Michael Seeber. **Contact:** Marguerite Lamb, senior editor. **Mostly freelance written.** Bimonthly magazine emphasizing "country living and country skills, for both long-time and would-be ruralites. *Mother Earth News* is dedicated to presenting information that will help readers become more self-sufficient, financially independent, and environmentally aware." Circ. 450,000. Pays on publication. Byline given. Submit seasonal material 5 months in advance. No handwritten mss. Responds within 6 months. Sample copy for $5. Writer's guidelines for #10 SASE with 1 first-class stamp.

Nonfiction: How-to, home business, alternative energy systems, home building, home retrofit and home maintenance, energy-efficient structures, seasonal cooking, gardening. **Buys 35-50 mss/year.** Query. "A short, to-the-point paragraph is often enough. If it's a subject we don't need at all, we can answer immediately. If it tickles our imagination, we'll ask to take a look at the whole piece. No phone queries, please." Length: 300-3,000 words. Payment negotiated. Publishes nonfiction book excerpts.

Photos: Purchased with accompanying ms. Send prints or transparencies. Uses 8×10 b&w glossies or any size color transparencies. Include type of film, speed and lighting used. Total purchase price for ms includes payment for photos. Captions and credits required.

Columns/Departments: Country Lore (down-home solutions to everyday problems); Bits & Pieces (snippets of news, events and silly happenings); Herbs & Remedies (home healing, natural medicine); Energy & Environment (ways to conserve energy while saving money; also alternative energy).

Tips: "Probably the best way to break in is to study our magazine, digest our writer's guidelines, and send us a concise article illustrated with color transparencies that we can't resist. When folks query and we give a go-ahead on speculation, we often offer some suggestions. Failure to follow those suggestions can lose the sale for the author. We want articles that tell what real people are doing to take charge of their own lives. Articles should be well-documented and tightly written treatments of topics we haven't already covered. The critical thing is length, and our payment is by space, not word count. *No phone queries.*"

◧ $RURAL HERITAGE, 281 Dean Ridge Lane, Gainesboro TN 38562-5039. (931)268-0655. E-mail: editor@ruralheritage.com. Website: www.ruralheritage.com. Publisher: Allan Damerow. **Contact:** Gail Damerow, editor. **98% freelance written.** Willing to work with a small number of new/unpublished writers. Bimonthly magazine devoted to the training and care of draft animals and other traditional country skills. Estab. 1976. Circ. 4,500. Pays on publication. Publishes ms an average of 6 months after acceptance. Byline given. Buys first English language rights. Submit seasonal material 6 months in advance. Accepts queries by mail, e-mail. Responds in 3 months. Sample copy for $7. Writer's guidelines for #10 SASE or on website.

Nonfiction: How-to (crafting and farming); interview/profile (people using draft animals); photo feature. No articles on *mechanized* farming. **Buys 100 mss/year.** Query or send complete ms. Length: 1,200-1,500 words. **Pays 5¢/word.**

Reprints: Accepts previously published submissions, but only if notified in advance *and* previous publication had limited or regional circulation. Send tearsheet or photocopy of article, typed ms with rights for sale noted and information about when and where the article previously appeared. Pays 100% of amount paid for an original article.

Photos: Send photos with ms. Pays $10. Captions and identification of subjects required. Buys one-time rights. Six covers/year (color transparency or 5×7 horizontal print), animals in harness $75. Photo guidelines for #10 SASE.

Columns/Departments: Drafter's Features (draft animals used for farming, logging or pulling—their training and care), Crafting (horse-drawn implement designs and patterns), both 750-1,500 words; Humor, 750-900 words. **Pays 5¢/ word.**

Poetry: Traditional. **Pays $5-25.**

Tips: "Thoroughly understand our subject: working draft animals in harness. We'd like more pieces on plans and instructions for constructing various horse-drawn implements and vehicles. Always welcome are: 1) Detailed descriptions and photos of horse-drawn implements, 2) Prices and other details of draft animal and implement auctions and sales."

$ $ RURALITE, P.O. Box 558, Forest Grove OR 97116-0558. (503)357-2105. Fax: (503)357-8615. E-mail: ruralite @ruralite.org. Website: www.ruralite.org. **Contact:** Curtis Condon, editor-in-chief. **80% freelance written.** Works with new, unpublished writers "who have mastered the basics of good writing." Monthly magazine aimed at members of consumer-owned electric utilities throughout 10 western states, including Alaska. Publishes 48 regional editions. Estab. 1954. Circ. 320,000. Buys first rights, sometimes reprint rights. **Pays on acceptance.** Byline given. Accepts queries by mail, e-mail, fax. Responds in 1 month. Sample copy and writer's guidelines for 10×13 SAE with 4 first-class stamps; guidelines also on website.

Nonfiction: Looking for well-written nonfiction, dealing primarily with human interest topics. Must have strong Northwest perspective and be sensitive to Northwest issues and attitudes. Wide range of topics possible, from energy-related subjects to little-known travel destinations to interesting people living in areas served by consumer-owned electric utilities. Family-related issues, Northwest history (no encyclopedia rewrites), people and events, unusual tidbits that tell the Northwest experience are best chances for a sale. Special issue: Gardening (February 2001). Query first; unsolicited manuscripts submitted without request rarely read by editors. **Buys 50-60 mss/yr.** Length 300-2,000 words. **Pays $50-450.**

Reprints: Send typed ms with rights for sale noted and information about when and where the article previously appeared. For reprints, pays 50% of "*our* regular freelance rates."

Photos: "Illustrated stories are the key to a sale. Stories without art rarely make it. Black-and-white prints, color slides, all formats, accepted with 'razor-sharp' focus."

Tips: "Study recent issues. Follow directions when given an assignment. Be able to deliver a complete package (story and photos). We're looking for regular contributors to whom we can assign topics from our story list after they've proven their ability to deliver quality mss."

SCIENCE

These publications are published for laymen interested in technical and scientific developments and discoveries, applied science and technical or scientific hobbies. Publications of interest to the personal computer owner/user are listed in the Personal Computers section. Journals for scientists and engineers are listed in Trade in various sections.

$ $ AD ASTRA, The Magazine of the National Space Society, 600 Pennsylvania Ave. SE, Suite 201, Washington DC 20003-4316. (202)543-1900. Fax: (202)546-4189. E-mail: adastraed@aol.com. Website: www.nss.org/adast ra. **Contact:** Frank Sietzen, Jr., editor-in-chief. **80% freelance written.** Bimonthly magazine covering the space program. "We publish non-technical, lively articles about all aspects of international space programs, from shuttle missions to planetary probes to plans for the future." Estab. 1989. Circ. 30,000. Pays on publication. Byline given. Buys first North American serial rights. Responds to queries when interested. Sample copy for 9×12 SASE. Writer's guidelines for #10 SASE.

Nonfiction: Book excerpts, essays, expose, general interest, interview/profile, opinion, photo feature, technical. No science fiction or UFO stories. Query with published clips. Length: 1,500-3,000 words. **Pays $150-250 for features.**

Photos: State availability of photos with submission. Reviews 35mm slides, 3×5 color transparencies and b&w prints. Negotiates payment. Identification of subjects required. Buys one-time rights.

Columns/Departments: Reviews, editorials, education. Length: 750 words. Query. **Pays $75-100.**

The online magazine carries original content not found in the print edition. Contact: Rob Pearlman, online editor.

Tips: "We require manuscripts to be accompanied by ASCII or Word or Word Perfect 7.0 floppy disk. Know the field of space technology, programs and policy. Know the players. Look for fresh angles. And, please, know how to write!"

N $ $ $ AMERICAN ARCHAEOLOGY, The Archaeological Conservancy, 5301 Central Ave. NE, #1218, Albuquerque NM 87108-1517. Fax: (505)266-0311. E-mail: archcons@nm.net. Website: www.americanarchaeology.c om. Assistant Editor: Tamara Stewart. **Contact:** Michael Bawaya, editor. **60% freelance written.** Archaeology magazine published quarterly. "We're a popular archaeology magazine. Our readers are very interested in this science. Our features cover important digs, prominent archaeologists and most any aspect of the science. We only cover North America." Estab. 1997. Circ. 35,000. **Pays on acceptance.** Publishes ms an average of 3 months after acceptance. Byline given. Offers 20% kill fee. Buys one-time and electronic rights. Editorial lead time 3 months. Accepts queries by mail, e-mail, fax. Responds in 3 weeks to queries; 1 month to mss.

Nonfiction: Archaeology. No fiction, poetry, humor. **Buys 12 mss/year.** Query with published clips. Length: 2,000-2,500 words. **Pays $700-1,000.** Sometimes pays expenses of writers on assignment.

Photos: State availability of photos with submission. Reviews transparencies and prints. Offers $300-1,000/photo. Negotiates payment individually. Identification of subjects required. Buys one-time rights.

Tips: "Read the magazine. Features must have a considerable amount of archaeological detail."

▲ $ $ ASTRONOMY, Kalmbach Publishing, P.O. Box 1612, Waukesha WI 53187-1612. (262)796-8776. Fax: (262)798-6468. E-mail: astro@astronomy.com. Managing Editor: David J. Eicher. **Contact:** Bonnie Gordon, editor. **75% freelance written.** Monthly magazine covering the science and hobby of astronomy. "Half of our magazine is for hobbyists (who may have little interest in the heavens in a scientific way); the other half is directed toward armchair astronomers who may be intrigued by the science." Estab. 1973. Circ. 185,000. **Pays on acceptance.** "We are governed by what is happening in the space program and the heavens. It can be up to a year before we publish a manuscript." Byline given. Buys first North American serial, one-time and all rights. Query for electronic submissions. Responds in 1 month to queries; 2 months to mss. Writer's guidelines for SASE.

Nonfiction: Book excerpts, space and astronomy, how-to for astro hobbyists, humor (in the viewpoints column and about astro), new product, photo feature, technical. **Buys 100-200 mss/year.** Query. Length: 500-4,500 words. **Pays $50-500.**

Photos: Send photos with submission. Reviews transparencies and prints. Pays $25/photo. Captions, model releases and identification of subjects required.

Tips: "Submitting to *Astronomy* could be tough. (Take a look at how technical astronomy is.) But if someone is a physics teacher (or math or astronomy), he or she might want to study the magazine for a year to see the sorts of subjects and approaches we use and then submit a proposal."

N $ $ THE ELECTRON, 1776 E. 17th St., Cleveland OH 44114-3679. (216)781-9400. Fax: (216)781-0331. Website: www.cie.wc.edu. Managing Editor: Michael Manning. **Contact:** Ted Sheroke, advertising manager. **80% freelance written.** Bimonthly tabloid on development and trends in electronics and high technology. Estab. 1934. Circ. 25,000. Pays on publication. Publishes ms an average of 2 months after acceptance. Byline given. Buys all rights. Responds as soon as possible. Sample copy and writer's guidelines for 8½×11 SASE.

Nonfiction: Technical (tutorial and how-to), technology news and feature, photo feature, career/educational. All submissions must be electronics/technology-related. Special issue: Electronics into the Year 2001 (October, November, December). Query with letter/proposal and published clips. Length: 800 words. **Pays $50-500.**

Reprints: Send photocopy of article or typed ms with rights for sale noted and information about when and where the article previously appeared. Does not pay for reprints.

Photos: State availability of photos. Reviews 8×10 and 5×7 b&w prints. Captions and identification of subjects required.

Tips: "We would like to receive educational electronics/technical articles. They must be written in a manner understandable to the beginning-intermediate electronics student. We are also seeking news/feature-type articles covering timely developments in high technology."

N $ $ $ POPULAR SCIENCE, *The What's New Magazine*, Times Mirror Magazines, 2 Park Ave., New York NY 10016. (212)779-5000. Fax: (212)481-8062. E-mail: mariette.dichristina@tmm.com. Website: www.popsci.com. Editor: Cecelia Wessner. **Contact:** Mariette DiChristina, executive editor. **50% freelance written.** Prefers to work with published/established writers. Monthly magazine for the well-educated adult, interested in science, technology, new products. "*Popular Science* is devoted to exploring (and explaining) to a nontechnical but knowledgeable readership the technical world around us. We cover all of the sciences, engineering and technology, and above all, products. We are largely a 'thing'-oriented publication: things that fly or travel down a turnpike, or go on or under the sea, or cut wood, or reproduce music, or build buildings, or make pictures. We are especially focused on the new, the ingenious and the useful. Contributors should be as alert to the possibility of selling us pictures and short features as they are to major articles. Freelancers should study the magazine to see what we want and avoid irrelevant submissions." Estab. 1872. Circ. 1,550,000. **Pays on acceptance.** Publishes ms an average of 4 months after acceptance. Byline given. Offers 25% kill fee. Buys first North American serial rights and second serial (reprint) rights. Editorial lead time 3 months. Accepts queries by mail, e-mail, fax. Responds in 1 month. Writer's guidelines for #10 SASE or on website.

Tips: "Probably the easiest way to break in here is by covering a news story in science and technology that we haven't heard about yet. We need people to be acting as scouts for us out there and we are willing to give the most leeway on these performances. We are interested in good, sharply focused ideas in all areas we cover. We prefer a vivid, journalistic style of writing, with the writer taking the reader along with him, showing the reader what he saw, through words."

$ $ THE SCIENCES, 655 Madison Ave., 16th Floor, New York NY 10021. (212)838-6727. Fax: (212)355-3795. E-mail: sciences@nyas.org. Website: www.nyas.org. **Contact:** Peter Brown, editor-in-chief. **50% freelance written.**

ALWAYS ENCLOSE a self-addressed, stamped envelope (SASE) with all your queries and correspondence.

Bimonthly magazine. "*The Sciences* is the cultural magazine of science. This is the kind of magazine that scientists would come to after work, that they can talk about to a friend, a spouse, a colleague in another discipline." Pays on publication. Byline given. Query with SASE. Accepts queries by mail, e-mail, fax.

   O→ Break in by offering an intimate knowledge of the scientific subject matter you want to write about. Though hard science is needed, a story must emerge from the hard science.

Nonfiction: Profiles, opinion, book or product reviews, features. Every piece must have "lots of science in it. It's important for writers to remember that many of our readers are members of the New York Academy of Science." Length: 3,000 words. **Pays $750.** Query with SASE.

Columns/Departments: Opinion, sciences news. Length: 1,000 words. Opinion pieces are always worth trying but that absolutely must include "significant scientific content." Query with SASE.

$ $ $ $ SCIENTIFIC AMERICAN, 415 Madison Ave., New York NY 10017. (212)754-0550. Fax: (212)755-1976. E-mail: editors@sciam.com. Website: www.sciam.com. **Contact:** Philip Yam, news editor. Monthly publication covering developments and topics of interest in the world of science. "*Scientific American* brings its readers directly to the wellspring of exploration and technological innovation. The magazine specializes in first-hand accounts by the people who actually do the work. Their personal experience provides an authoritative perspective on future growth. Over 100 of our authors have won Nobel Prizes. Complementing those articles are regular departments written by *Scientific American*'s staff of professional journalists, all specialists in their fields. . . . *Scientific American* is the authoritative source of advance information. Authors are the first to report on important breakthroughs, because they're the people who make them. . . . It all goes back to *Scientific American*'s corporate mission: to link those who use knowledge with those who create it." Estab. 1845. Circ. 666,630. Query before submitting.

   ● Ranked as one of the best markets for freelancers in *Writer's Yearbook* "Top 100 Markets," January 2000.

Nonfiction: Freelance opportunities limited to news and analysis section. **Pays $1/word average.**

$ $ SKY & TELESCOPE, The Essential Magazine of Astronomy, Sky Publishing Corp., P.O. Box 9111, Belmont MA 02748. (617)864-7360. Fax: (617)576-0336. E-mail: skytel@skypub.com. Website: www.skypub.com. Editor: Leif J. Robinson. **Contact:** Bud Sadler, managing editor. **15% freelance written.** Monthly magazine covering astronomy. "*Sky & Telescope* is the magazine of record for astronomy. We cover amateur activities, research news, equipment, book and software reviews. Our audience is the amateur astronomer who wants to learn more about the night sky." Estab. 1941. Circ. 125,000. Pays on publication. Publishes ms an average of 6 months after acceptance. Byline given. Buys first rights. Editorial lead time 4 months. Submit seasonal material 6-12 months in advance. Accepts queries by mail, e-mail, fax, phone. Responds in 3 weeks to queries; 1 month to mss. Sample copy for $3.99. Guidelines free by e-mail request to auguide@skypub.com, on website or for #10 SASE.

Nonfiction: Essays, historical/nostalgic, how-to, opinion, personal experience, photo feature, technical. No poetry, crosswords, new age or alternative cosmologies. **Buys 10 mss/year.** Query. Length: 1,500-4,000 words. **Pays at least 20¢/word**. Sometimes pays expenses of writers on assignment.

Photos: Send photos with submission. Reviews contact sheets. Negotiates payment individually. Identification of subjects required. Buys one-time rights.

Columns/Departments: Focal Point (opinion), 1,000 words; Books & Beyond (reviews), 800 words; Amateur Astronomers (profiles), 1,500 words. **Buys 20 mss/year.** Query. **Pays 20¢/word.**

Tips: "Good artwork is key. Keep the text lively and provide captions."

N $ $ $ STAR DATE, University of Texas McDonald Observatory, 2609 University Ave., #3.118, Austin TX 78712. Fax: (512)471-5060. E-mail: harrison@astro.as.utexas.edu. Website: www.stardate.utexas.edu. Executive Editor: Damond Benningfield. **Contact:** Gary Harrison, editor. **80% freelance written.** Bimonthly magazine covering astronomy. "*StarDate* is written for people with an interest in astronomy and what they see in the night sky, but no special astronomy training or background." Estab. 1975. Circ. 12,000. **Pays on acceptance.** Publishes ms an average of 4 months after acceptance. Byline given. Offers 25% kill fee. Buys first North American serial and electronic rights. Editorial lead time 6 months. Submit seasonal material 6 months in advance. Accepts queries by mail, e-mail, fax. Responds in 6 weeks to queries; 2 months to mss. Sample copy and writer's guidelines free.

   O→ "*StarDate* magazine covers a wide range of topics related to the science of astronomy, space exploration, skylore, and skywatching. Many of our readers rely on the magazine for most of their astronomy information, so articles may cover recent discoveries or serve as a primer on basic astronomy or astrophysics. We also introduce our readers to historical people and events in astronomy and space exploration, as well as look forward to what will make history next year or fifty years from now. *StarDate* topics should appeal to a wide audience, not just professional or amateur astronomers. Topics are not limited to hard-core science. When considering topics, look for undercovered subjects, or give a familiar topic a unique spin. Research findings don't have to make the front page of every newspaper in the country to be interesting. Also, if you'd like to write an historical piece, look for offbeat items and events; we've already covered Copernicus, Kepler, Tycho, Newton and the like pretty well."

Nonfiction: General interest, historical/nostalgic, interview/profile, photo feature, technical, travel. "No first-person; first stargazing experiences; paranormal." **Buys 8 mss/year.** Query with published clips. Length: 1,500-3,000 words. **Pays $500-1,500.** Sometimes pays expenses of writers on assignment.

Photos: Send photos with submission. Reviews transparencies and prints. Negotiates payment individually. Identification of subjects required. Buys one-time rights.

Columns/Departments: Astro News (short astronomy news items), 250 words. **Buys 6 mss/year.** Query with published clips. **Pays $100-200.**
Tips: "Keep up to date with current astronomy news and space missions. No technical jargon."

☒ **$ $** WEATHERWISE, The Magazine About the Weather, Heldref Publications, 1319 18th St. NW, Washington DC 20036. (202)296-6267. Fax: (202)296-5149. E-mail: ww@heldref.org. Website: www.weatherwise.org. Associate Editor: Kimbra Cutlip. Editorial Assistant: Ellen Fast. **Contact:** Doyle Rice, managing editor. **75% freelance written.** Bimonthly magazine covering weather and meteorology. "*Weatherwise* is America's only magazine about the weather. Our readers range from professional weathercasters and scientists to basement-bound hobbyists, but all share a common craving for information about weather as it relates to technology, history, culture, society, art, etc." Estab. 1948. Circ. 32,000. Pays on publication. Publishes ms an average of 6 months after acceptance. Byline given. Offers 25% kill fee. Buys all rights or first North American serial or second (reprint) serial rights. Editorial lead time 6 months. Submit seasonal material 6 months in advance. Accepts queries by mail, e-mail, phone, fax. Responds in 2 months to queries. Sample copy for $4 and a 9×12 SAE with 10 first-class stamps. Writer's guidelines for #10 SASE or on website.

    O→ "First, familiarize yourself with the magazine by taking a close look at the most recent six issues. (You can also visit our website, which features the full text of many recent articles.) This will give you an idea of the style of writing we prefer in *Weatherwise*. Then, read through our writer's guidelines (available from our office or on our website) which detail the process for submitting a query letter. As for the subject matter, keep your eyes and ears open for the latest research and/or current trends in meteorology and climatology that you feel would be appropriate for the general readership of *Weatherwise*. And always keep in mind weather's awesome power and beauty—its 'fun, fury, and fascination' that so many of our readers enjoy."

Nonfiction: Book excerpts, essays, general interest, historical/nostalgic, how-to, humor, interview/profile, new product, opinion, personal experience, photo feature, technical, travel. Special issue: Photo Contest (September/October deadline June 1). Special issue: 2000 Weather in Review (March/April 2001). "No blow-by-blow accounts of the biggest storm to ever hit your backyard." **Buys 15-18 mss/year.** Query with published clips. Length: 1,500-2,500 words. **Pays $200-500 for assigned articles; $0-300 for unsolicited articles.** Sometimes pays expenses of writers on assignment.
Reprints: Send photocopy of article and information about when and where the article previously appeared. Pays 25% of amount paid for an original article. Publishes book excerpts.
Photos: State availability of or send photos with submission. Reviews contact sheets, negatives, transparencies, prints and electronic files. Negotiates payment individually. Captions, identification of subjects required. Buys one-time rights.
Columns/Departments: Front & Center (news, trends, opinion), 300-400 words; Weather Talk (folklore and humor), 1,000 words; The Lee Word (humorous first-person accounts of adventures with weather), 1,000 words. **Buys 12-15 mss/year.** Query with published clips. **Pays $0-200.**
Tips: "Don't query us wanting to write about broad types like the Greenhouse Effect, the Ozone Hole, El Niño, etc. If it's capitalized, you can bet you won't be able to cover it all in 2,000 words. With these topics and all others, find the story within the story. And whether you're writing about a historical storm or new technology, be sure to focus on the human element—the struggles, triumphs, and other anecdotes of individuals."

SCIENCE FICTION, FANTASY & HORROR

These publications often publish experimental fiction and many are open to new writers. More information on these markets can be found in the Contests & Awards section under the Fiction heading.

N ☒ **$ $** ABORIGINAL SCIENCE FICTION, The 2nd Renaissance Foundation Inc., P.O. Box 2449, Woburn MA 01888-0849. Website: www.AboriginalSF.com. **Contact:** Charles C. Ryan, editor. **99% freelance written.** Quarterly science fiction magazine. "We publish short, lively and entertaining science fiction short stories and poems, accompanied by b&w illustrations." Estab. 1986. Circ. 6,000. Pays on publication. Publishes ms an average of 2 years after acceptance. Byline given. Buys first North American serial rights, non-exclusive options on other rights. Accepts queries by mail. Responds in 3 months. Sample copy for $5.95 and 9×12 SAE with 4 first-class stamps. Writer's guidelines for #10 SASE or on website.
Fiction: Science fiction of all types. "We do not use fantasy, horror, sword and sorcery or *Twilight Zone*-type stories." **Buys 40-48 mss/year.** Send complete ms. Length: 2,000-6,500 words. **Pays $200.** Publishes novel excerpts only if they can stand by themselves as a short story.
Poetry: Science and science fiction. **Buys 4-8 poems/year.** Length: 1-2 pages, typewritten.
Tips: "Read science fiction novels and all the science fiction magazines. Do not rely on science fiction movies or TV. We are open to new fiction writers who are making a sincere effort. We are now looking at short articles on cutting-edge science, 1,000-1,500 words. **Pays $100 on publication.**"

☒ **$** ABSOLUTE MAGNITUDE, Science Fiction Adventures, DNA Publications, P.O. Box 2988, Radford VA 24143. E-mail: dnapublications@iname.com. Website: www.sfsite/dnaweb/home.htm. **Contact:** Warren Lapine, editor-in-chief. **95% freelance written.** Quarterly science fiction magazine covering science fiction short stories. "We specialize in action/adventure science fiction with an emphasis on hard science. Interested in tightly-plotted, character-driven stories." Estab. 1993. Circ. 6,000. Pays on publication. Publishes ms an average of 6 months after acceptance. Byline given. Buys first English language serial rights, first rights. Editorial lead time 6 months. Accepts simultaneous submissions. "Do not query—send completed ms." Responds in 1 month to mss. Sample copy for $5. Writer's guidelines for #10 SASE.

● This editor is still looking for tightly plotted stories that are character driven. He is now purchasing more short stories than before.

Fiction: Science fiction. **Buys 40 mss/year.** Send complete ms. Length: 1,000-25,000 words. **Pays 1-5¢/word.**

● Ranked as one of the best markets for fiction writers in *Writer's Digest* magazine's annual "Fiction 50," June 2000.

Poetry: Any form. **Buys 4 poems/issue.** Submit maximum 5 poems. Length: up to 25,000 words. **Pays $10/poem.** Best chance with light verse.

Tips: "We are very interested in working with new writers but we are not interested in 'drawer-cleaning' exercises. There is no point in sending less than your best effort if you are interested in a career in writing. We do not use fantasy, horror, satire, or funny science fiction. We're looking for character-driven, action/adventure based Technical Science Fiction. We want tightly plotted stories with memorable characters. Characters should be the driving force behind the action of the story; they should not be thrown in as an afterthought. We need to see both plot development and character growth. Stories which are resolved without action on the protagonist's part do not work for us; characters should not be spectators in situations completely beyond their control or immune to their influence. Some of our favorite writers are Roger Zelazny, Frank Herbert, Robert Silverberg, and Fred Saberhagen."

⊠ $AMAZING STORIES, Wizards of the Coast, Inc., P.O. Box 707, Renton WA 98057-0707. (425)254-2263. Fax: (425)204-5928. E-mail: amazing@wizards.com. Website: www.wizards.com/amazing. Editor-in-chief: Mr. Kim Mohan. **Contact:** Pamela Mohan, associate editor; Sue Weinlein Cook, managing editor. **100% freelance written.** Quarterly magazine featuring quality science fiction short stories. Estab. 1926. Circ. 35,000. **Pays on acceptance.** Publishes ms 4 months after acceptance. Byline given. Offers 33% kill fee. Buys first or all rights. Editorial lead time 6 months. Submit seasonal material 6 months in advance. Responds in 2 months to queries; 3 months to mss. Sample copy can be ordered at http://store.wizards.com/magazines. Writer's guidelines for #10 SASE or on website.

Nonfiction: Sue Weinlein Cook, managing editor. Essays, interview/profile, opinion, personal experience, all relating to science fiction genre. **Buys 16 mss/year.** Query with published clips. Length: 2,000-3,000 words. **Pays 8-10¢/word.** Sometimes pays expenses of writers on assignment.

Columns/Departments: Sue Weinlein Cook, managing editor. Observatory (essay/opinion), 2,500 words; Silver Screen (film reviews/essays), 2,200 words; Scientifiction (book reviews), 3,000 words; Game Space (game reviews/essays), 2,000 words; all relating to science fiction. **Buys 16 mss/year.** Query with published clips. **Pays 8-10¢/word.**

Fiction: Science fiction. Published authors only, please. No fantasy or horror. **Buys 32 mss/year.** Query. Length: 2,000-8,000 words. **Pays 6-8¢/word.**

● Ranked as one of the best markets for fiction writers in *Writer's Digest* magazine's annual "Fiction 50," June 2000.

Tips: "Read writer's guidelines. Write a good, short query letter. Your manuscript should look professional. We are not likely to publish sword-and-sorcery fantasy; ethnic fantasy that is a rehash or an interpretation of a myth or legend; and horror that relies on gratuitous vulgarity or excessive gore to make the story work."

N ⊠ ▣ $ANOTHEREALM, 287 Gano Ave., Orange Park FL 32073. (904)269-5429. E-mail: goldstrm@tu.infi.net or jgoldstrom@WorldSpy.net or anotherealm@mailcity.com. Website: http://anotherealm.com. **Contact:** Jean Goldstrom, editor. **100% freelance written.** Weekly online magazine covering science fiction, fantasy and horror. "An e-zine of short (5,000 words and under) science fiction, fantasy and horror." Estab. 1998. Circ. 5,000/week. **Pays on acceptance.** Byline given. Buys first Internet rights. Editorial lead time 3 months. Submit seasonal material 3 months in advance. Accepts queries by mail, e-mail. Responds in 2 weeks to queries; 2 months to mss. Sample copy and writer's guidelines on website.

Fiction: Fantasy, horror, science fiction. No experimental, stream-of-consciousness, avante-garde or vampire stories. **Buys 104 mss/year.** Send complete ms. Length: 5,000 words. **Pays $10.**

Tips: "At least half of our writers made their first sale to *Anotherealm*."

N $ARTEMIS MAGAZINE, Science and Fiction for a Space-Faring Age, LRC Publications, Inc., 1380 E. 17th St., Suite 201, Brooklyn NY 11230-6011. E-mail: magazine@lrcpubs.com. Website: www.LRCPublications.com. **Contact:** Ian Randal Strock, editor. **90% freelance written.** Quarterly magazine covering the Artemis Project and manned space flight/colonization in general. "As part of the Artemis Project, we present lunar and space development in a positive light." Estab. 1999. **Pays on acceptance.** Publishes ms an average of 1 year after acceptance. Byline given. Buys first world English serial rights. Editorial lead time 3 months. Accepts queries by mail. Responds in 2 months. Sample copy for $5. Writer's guidelines for #10 SASE or online at website.

Nonfiction: Essays, general interest, how-to (get to, build, or live in a lunar colony), humor, interview/profile, new product, opinion, technical, travel. **Buys 12-16 mss/year.** Send complete ms. Length: 5,000 words maximum. **Pays 3-5¢/word.**

Photos: State availability of or send photos with submission. Reviews transparencies and prints. Negotiates payment individually. Captions, model releases and identification of subjects required. Buys one-time rights.

Columns/Departments: News Notes (news of interest regarding the moon and manned space flight), under 300 words. **Buys 15-20 mss/year.** Send complete ms. **Pays 3-5¢/word.**

Fiction: Science fiction. "We publish near-term, new-Earth, hard sf. We don't want to see non-that." **Buys 12-16 mss/year.** Send complete ms. Length: 15,000 words maximum (shorter is better). **Pays 3-5¢/word.**

Fillers: Newsbreaks, short humor, cartoons. **Buys 4-12/year.** Length: 100 words maximum. **Pays 3-5¢/word.**

Tips: "Know your material, and write me the best possible article/story you can. You want me to read your manuscript, so show me the courtesy of reading my magazine. Also, the Artemis Project website (www.asi.org) may be a good source of inspiration."

$ ASIMOV'S SCIENCE FICTION, Dell Magazine Fiction Group, 475 Park Avenue S., 11th Floor, New York NY 10016. (212)686-7188. Fax: (212)686-7414 (for correspondence only, no submissions). E-mail: asimovs@dellmagazines .com. Website: www.asimovs.com. Executive Editor: Sheila Williams. **Contact:** Gardner Dozois, editor. **98% freelance written.** Works with a small number of new/unpublished writers each year. Published 11 times a year, including 1 double issue. Estab. 1977. Circ. 50,000. **Pays on acceptance.** Buys first North American serial and nonexclusive foreign serial rights; reprint rights occasionally. No simultaneous submissions. Accepts queries by mail. Responds in 2 months. Sample copy for $5 and 6½×9½ SAE or on website. Writer's guidelines for #10 SASE or on website.

Reprints: Send typed ms with rights for sale noted and information about when and where the story previously appeared.

Fiction: Science fiction primarily. Some fantasy and humor but no "Sword and Sorcery." No explicit sex or violence that isn't integral to the story. Publishes novel excerpts; doesn't serialize novels. "It's best to read a great deal of material in the genre to avoid the use of some *very* old ideas." **Buys 10 mss/issue.** Submit complete ms and SASE with *all* submissions. Length: 750-15,000 words. **Pays 5-8¢/word.**

● Ranked as one of the best markets for fiction writers in *Writer's Digest* magazine's "Fiction 50," June 2000.

Poetry: Length should not exceed 40 lines; **pays $1/line.**

Tips: "In general, we're looking for 'character-oriented' stories, those in which the characters, rather than the science, provide the main focus for the reader's interest. Serious, thoughtful, yet accessible fiction will constitute the majority of our purchases, but there's always room for the humorous as well. Borderline fantasy is fine, but no Sword & Sorcery, please. A good overview would be to consider that all fiction is written to examine or illuminate some aspect of human existence, but that in science fiction the backdrop you work against is the size of the Universe. Please do not send us submissions on disk. We've bought some of our best stories from people who have never sold a story before."

[N] [▲] $ CENTURY, Century Publishing, Inc., P.O. Box 150510, Brooklyn NY 11215. E-mail: editor@centurymag .com. Website: www.centurymag.com. **Contact:** Robert K.J. Killheffer, editor. **100% freelance written.** Quarterly 6×9 magazine covering speculative fiction (science fiction, fantasy, horror). "We're looking for speculative fiction with a high degree of literary accomplishment—ambitious work which can appeal not only to the genre's regular audience but to readers outside the genre as well." Estab. 1994. Circ. 2,500. **Pays on acceptance.** Publishes ms an average of 6 months after acceptance. Byline given. Buys first world English rights, non-exclusive reprint rights. Responds in 3 months to mss. Sample copy for $7. Writer's guidelines for #10 SASE or on website.

Fiction: Experimental, fantasy, horror, science fiction. **Buys 24-28 mss/year.** Send complete ms. Length: 250-20,000 words. **Pays 4¢/word.**

[N] [▲] $ CHALLENGING DESTINY, New Fantasy & Science Fiction, Crystalline Sphere Publishing, RR #6, St. Marys, Ontario N4X 1C8 Canada. (519)584-7556. E-mail: csp@golden.net. Website: home.golden.net/~csp/. **Contact:** Dave Switzer and Bob Switzer, editors. **80% freelance written.** Quarterly magazine covering science fiction and fantasy. Estab. 1997. Circ. 200. Pays on publication. Publishes ms an average of 5 months after acceptance. Byline given. Buys first North American serial rights. Accepts queries by mail, e-mail. Accepts simultaneous submissions. Responds in 1 week to queries; 1 month to mss. Sample copy for $7.50 (Canadian), $6.50 (US). Writer's guidelines for #10 SASE or on website.

Fiction: Fantasy, science fiction. **Buys 24 mss/year.** Send complete ms. Length: 2,000-10,000 words. **Pays 1¢/word (Canadian).**

Tips: "We're interested in stories where violence is rejected as a means for solving problems. We're also interested in stories with philosophical, political or religious themes. We're not interested in stories where the good guys kill the bad guys and then live happily ever after."

$ $ THE CRYSTAL BALL, The Starwind Press, P.O. Box 98, Ripley OH 45167. (937)392-4549. **Contact:** Marlena Powell, editor. **90% freelance written.** Quarterly magazine covering science fiction and fantasy for young adult readers. *"We are especially targeting readers of middle school age."* Estab. 1997. **Pays on acceptance.** Publishes ms an average of 6 months after acceptance. Byline given. Offers 100% kill fee. Buys first or second serial (reprint) rights. Editorial lead time 4 months. Accepts queries by mail, phone. Sample copy for 9×12 SASE and $3. Writer's guidelines for #10 SASE.

Nonfiction: How-to (science), interview/profile, personal experience, book reviews, science information. **Buys 4-6 mss/year.** Query. Length: 900-3,000 words. **Pays ¼¢/word.**

Reprints: Send typed ms with rights for sale noted and information and when and where the article previously appeared. Pays 100% of amount paid for an original article.

Photos: Send photos with submission. Negotiates payment individually. Captions, identification of subjects required.

Columns/Departments: Book reviews (science fiction and fantasy), 100-200 words or less; museum reviews (science & technology, museums & centers, children's museums), 900 words. **Buys 10-15 mss/year.** Query. **Pays ¼¢/word.**
Fiction: Fantasy, science fiction. **Buys 10-12 mss/year.** Send complete ms. Length: 1,000-5,000 words. **Pays ¼¢/word.**
Tips: "Have a good feel for writing for kids. Don't 'write down' to your audience because they're kids. We look for articles of scientific and technological interest."

■ **$** DEEP OUTSIDE SFFH, (formerly *Outside*), C&C Clocktower Fiction, Box 260, 6549 Mission Gorge Rd., San Diego CA 92120. E-mail: outside@clocktowerfiction.com. Website: http://outside.clocktowerfiction.com. **Contact:** Editorial. Editors: Brian Callahan and John Cullen. **100% freelance written.** Online magazine offering science fiction and dark imaginative and horror. "*Deep Outside SFFH* is a paying professional magazine of science fiction and dark imaginative fiction, aimed at people who love to read well-plotted character-driven genre fiction." Estab. 1998. **Pays on acceptance.** Publishes ms an average of 3 months after acceptance. Byline given. Buys first serial and first electronic serial rights. Responds in 3 months to mss. Sample copy and writer's guidelines on website.
  ○━ "Write the story we couldn't see coming. Get us excited about your characters and slammed by your unexpected, but inevitable ending. Our favorite stories are original and exciting—the aren't rehashes of overdone monster movie themes. We love stories that take us to exotic locales."
Fiction: Horror, science fiction. "We seek well-written, character-driven fiction that is tightly plotted. Professionally executed, with attention to basics—grammar, punctuation, usage. No sword and sorcery, shared worlds, porno of any kind, excessive violence or gore beyond the legitimate needs of a story, no vulgarity unless it furthers the story (sparingly at that). No derivative works emulating TV shows or movies (e.g., *Star Trek*)." **Buys 12 mss/year.** Send complete ms. Length: 1,500-5,000 words. **Pays 3¢/word.**
Tips: "Please read the tips and guidelines on the magazine's website for further and up-to-the-moment details. *Submissions by mail only.* Traditional format, #10 SASE minimum for reply. E-mail submissions will be deleted unread."

$ FLESH AND BLOOD, 121 Joseph St., Bayville NJ 08721. E-mail: ahhh@webtv.net. Website: www.geocities.com/soho/lofts/3459/fnb.html. **Contact:** Jack Fisher, editor. **90% freelance written.** Small press horror magazine published tri-annually covering horror/dark fantasy. Estab. 1997. Circ. 500. **Pays within 3 months from acceptance.** Publishes ms an average of 10 months after acceptance. Editorial lead time 1 month. Accepts queries by mail, e-mail. Responds in 2 weeks to queries; 2 months to mss. Sample copy for $4 (check payable to John Fisher). Writer's guidelines for #10 SASE or on website.
  ● The editor reports an interest in seeing powerful vignettes/stories with surrealism-avante-garde(ism) to them and original, unique ghost stories.
Reprints: Accepts previously published submissions.
Fiction: Horror, slice-of-life vignettes, dark fantasy. "No garden-variety work, or work where the main character is a 'nut,' killer, etc." **Buys 18-24 mss/year.** Length: 500-4,000 words. **Pays ½-2¢/word.**
Poetry: Avant-garde, free verse, horror/dark fantasy surreal, bizarre. "No rhyming, love pieces." **Buys 15-20 poems/year.** Submit maximum 5 poems. Length: 3-25 lines. **Pays $5.**
Tips: "We like light horror over gore. Don't let the title deceive you. Surreal, bizarre, eccentric tales have a good chance. We especially like dark fantasy pieces and vignettes."

✖ **$** THE MAGAZINE OF FANTASY & SCIENCE FICTION, Mercury Press, P.O. Box 1806, Madison Square Station, New York NY 10159-1806. Fax: (212)982-2676. E-mail: gordonfsf@aol.com. Website: www.fsfmag.com/. **Contact:** Gordon Van Gelder, editor. **100% freelance written.** Monthly fantasy fiction and science fiction magazine. "*The Magazine of Fantasy and Science Fiction* publishes various types of science fiction and fantasy short stories and novellas, making up about 80% of each issue. The balance of each issue is devoted to articles about science fiction, a science column, book and film reviews, cartoons and competitions." Estab. 1949. Circ. 80,000. **Pays on acceptance.** Byline given. Buys first North American and foreign serial rights. Submit seasonal material 8 months in advance. Responds in 2 months. Sample copy for $5. Writer's guidelines for #10 SASE or on website.
Reprints: Accepts previously published submissions.
Columns/Departments: Curiosities (forgotten books), 250 words. **Buys 11 mss/year. Pays $50.**
Fiction: Fantasy, horror, science fiction. Prefers character-oriented stories. **Buys 70-100 mss/year.** Send complete ms. No electronic submissions. Length: 2,000-25,000 words. **Pays 5-8¢/word.**
  ● Ranked as one of the best markets for fiction writers in *Writer's Digest* magazine's "Fiction 50," June 2000.
Tips: "We need more hard science fiction and humor."

N ■ MILLENNIUM SCIENCE FICTION & FANTASY, Jo Pop Publications, P.O. Box 8118, Roswell NM 88202-8118. E-mail: jopoppub@jopoppub.com. Website: www.jopoppub.com. Managing Editor: S. Joan Popek. **Contact:** D.S. Moreland, editor. **90% freelance written.** Science fiction and fantasy monthly covering science fiction, fantasy, horror. "Think 'Twilight Zone.' " Estab. 1993. Circ. 1,000. **Pays on acceptance.** Publishes ms an average of 4 months after acceptance. Byline given. Buys one-time rights and other rights (with option to print in yearly anthology as "Best.") Editorial lead time 4 months. Submit seasonal material 6 months in advance. Accepts queries by mail, e-mail. Responds in 2 months. Sample copy for $6.50 (print issue) or online at website. Writer's guidelines for #10 SASE, online at website or by e-mail.

Nonfiction: S. Joan Popek, review and poetry editor. Reviews of related books/stories. Special issues: Science fiction (Spring, 2000); fantasy (Summer, 2000); Halloween issue (October, 2000), featuring all the traditional monsters in a new setting. No excessive violence, explicit sex. **Buys 12-16 mss/year.** Query. Length: 50-300 words. Sometimes pays in contributor copies or other premiums rather than a cash payment for reviews and poetry.

Reprints: Accepts previously published submissions.

Columns/Departments: S. Joan Popek, review editor. Reviews (science fiction, fantasy, horror, books/stories), 50-300 words. **Buys 12-16 mss/year.** Send complete ms. **Pays sample copy.**

Fiction: Fantasy, horror, humorous, science fiction. **Buys 40-50 mss/year.** Send complete ms. Length: 50-2,500 words. **Pays $5-10.**

Poetry: S. Joan Popek, editor. Free verse, light verse, traditional. No haiku, and "please no 'bare my soul' poetry." **Buys 24-30 poems/year.** Submit maximum 3 poems. Length: 5-40 lines. **Pays contributor copy.**

Tips: "Read us to see what we publish, then contact us and talk to us. We love author contact."

⚡ $ ON SPEC, The Copper Pig Writers Society, P.O. Box 4727, Edmonton, Alberta T6E 5G6 Canada. E-mail: onspec@earthling.net. Website: www.icomm.ca/onspec/. **Contact:** Editorial Collective. General Editor: Jena Snyder. Fiction Editors: Barry Hammond, Susan MacGregor, Hazel Sangster, Jena Snyder, Diane L. Walton. **95% freelance written.** Quarterly literary magazine covering Canadian science fiction, fantasy and horror. Estab. 1989. Circ. 2,000. **Pays on acceptance.** Publishes ms an average of 1 year after acceptance. Byline given. Buys first North American serial rights. Editorial lead time 6 months. Accepts queries by mail, e-mail, phone, fax. Responds in 2 weeks to queries, in 2 months after deadline to mss. Sample copy for $6. Writer's guidelines available on website.

Nonfiction: Commissioned only. Yearly theme issue. 2000 theme is "Future Crime." "Each year we offer $100 prize to best story by a young and upcoming author published in *On Spec* in the past year."

Fiction: Science fiction, fantasy, horror, magic realism. No media tie-in or shaggy-alien stories. **Buys 50 mss/year.** Send complete ms only. Length: 6,000 words maximum. **Pays $50-180 (Canadian); 3¢/word.**

Poetry: Barry Hammond, poetry editor. Avant-garde, free verse. "We rarely buy rhyming or religious material." **Buys 6 poems/year.** Submit maximum 10 poems. Length: 4-100 lines. **Pays $20.**

Tips: "We want to see stories with plausible characters, a well-constructed, consistent, and vividly described setting, a strong plot and believable emotions; characters must show us (not tell us) their emotional responses to each other and to the situation and/or challenge they face. Also: don't send us stories written for television. We don't like media tie-ins, so don't watch TV for inspiration! Read, instead! Absolutely no e-mailed or faxed submissions. Strong preference given to submissions by Canadians."

N ▢ $ PULP ETERNITY ONLINE, Eternity Press, P.O. Box 930068, Norcross GA 30003. Phone/fax: (770)577-7445. E-mail: pulpeternity@hotmail.com. Website: www.pulpeternity.com. **Contact:** Steve Algieri, editor. **100% freelance written.** Monthly online magazine covering speculative fiction. "*Pulp Eternity* features edge genre fiction from new and established writers. We publish science fiction, fantasy, horror, mystery and fantastic romance, or any combination of the above." Estab. 1996. Circ. 10,000. Pays on publication. Publishes ms an average of 6 months after acceptance. Byline given. Offers 100% kill fee. Buys second serial (reprint) and electronic rights. Editorial lead time 2 months. Submit seasonal material 6 months in advance. Accepts queries by mail, e-mail. Accepts simultaneous submissions. Responds in 1 week to queries; 2 months to mss. Sample copy and writer's guidelines online at website.

Reprints: Accepts previously published submissions.

Fiction: Erotica, experimental, fantasy, historical, horror, mystery, romance, science fiction, suspense. No young adult, suicide stories, child abuse or vignettes. **Buys 15-25 mss/year.** Send complete ms. Length: 1-3,000 words. **Pays $20-150 (5¢/word).**

Tips: "We're different and proud of it. Stories must have a defined setting, plot, conflict/resolution and characters we care about *and* change. We like exotic and ethnic settings/characters, alternative sexuality, sly or cerebral humor, controversial topics, hybrids and stories with attitude. It's not enough to write well; you must say something."

$ THE SILVER WEB, A Magazine of the Surreal, Buzzcity Press, P.O. Box 38190, Tallahassee FL 32315. (850)385-8948. Fax: (850)385-4063. E-mail: annk19@mail.idt.net. **Contact:** Ann Kennedy, publisher/editor. **100% freelance written.** Semiannual literary magazine. "*The Silver Web* is a semi-annual publication featuring science fiction, dark fantasy and horror, fiction, poetry, art, and thought-provoking articles. The editor is looking for works ranging from speculative fiction to dark tales and all weirdness in between; specifically works of the surreal." Estab. 1988. Circ. 2,000. **Pays on acceptance.** Byline given. Offers 100% kill fee. Buys first North American serial, one-time or second serial (reprint) rights. Editorial lead time 2 months. Accepts simultaneous submissions. Accepts queries by mail, e-mail. Responds in 1 week to queries; 2 months to mss. Sample copy for $7.20; subscription: $12. Writer's guidelines for #10 SASE or via e-mail.

Nonfiction: Book excerpts, essays, interview/profile, opinion. **Buys 6 mss/year.** Query. Length: 500-8,000 words. **Pays $20-250.**

Reprints: Send information before submitting ms about when and where material previously appeared. Pays 100% of amount paid for an original article.

Photos: State availability of photos with submission. Reviews prints. Negotiates payment individually. Identification of subjects required. Buys one-time rights.

Columns/Departments: Book Reviews, Movie Reviews, TV Reviews, all 3,000 words. **Buys 6 mss/year.** Send complete ms. **Pays $20-250.**

Fiction: Experimental, horror, science fiction, dark fantasy, surreal. "We do not want to see typical storylines, endings or predictable revenge stories." **Buys 20-25 mss/year.** Send complete ms. Length: 500-8,000 words. **Pays $10-320.** Publishes novel excerpts but query first. Open to submissions January 1 to September 30.
Poetry: Avant-garde, free verse, haiku, light verse, traditional. **Buys 18-30/year.** Submit maximum 5 poems. **Pays $10-50.**
Fillers: Art fillers. **Buys 10/year. Pays $5-10.**
Tips: "Give us an unusual unpredictable story with strong, believable characters we care about. Surprise us with something unique. We do look for interviews with people in the field (writers, artists, filmmakers)."

$ SPACE AND TIME, 138 W. 70th St., 4B, New York NY 10023-4468. Website: www.cith.org/space&time.html. Editor-in-Chief: Gordon Linzner. **Contacts:** Gerard Houarner, fiction editor; Linda D. Addison, poetry editor. **99% freelance written.** Semiannual magazine of science fiction and fantasy. "We feature a mix of fiction and poetry in all aspects of the fantasy genre—science fiction, supernatural horror, sword & sorcery, mixed genre, unclassifiable. Its variety makes it stand out from more narrowly focused magazines. Our readers enjoy quality material that surprises and provokes." Estab. 1966. Circ. 2,000. **Pays on acceptance.** Publishes ms an average of 9 months after acceptance. Byline given. Buys first North American serial rights. Editorial lead time 1 year. Accepts queries by mail. Responds in 3 months to mss. Sample copy $6.50. Writer's guidelines for #10 SASE or on website.
Photos/Artwork: Art director. Artwork (could include photos). Send nonreturnable photocopies. Reviews prints. Pays $10 for interior illustration, $25 for cover, plus 2 contributor copies. Model releases required. Buys one-time rights.
Fiction: Gerard Houarner, fiction editor. Fantasy, horror, science fiction, mixed genre (i.e., science-fiction-mystery, western-horror, etc.) and unclassifiable; "Do not want anything that falls outside of fantasy/science fiction (but that leaves a lot). No fiction set in a franchised universe, i.e., *Star Trek*." **Buys 20-24 mss/year.** Send complete ms. Length: 10,000 words maximum. **Pays 1¢/word plus 2 contributor copies, $5 minimum.**
Poetry: Linda D. Addison, poetry editor. Avant-garde, free verse, haiku, light verse, traditional. "Do not send poetry without a solid connection to the genres we publish. Imaginative metaphors alone do not make it fantasy." **Buys 20 poems/year.** Submit maximum 5 poems. Length: no limits. **Pays 1¢/word ($5 minimum) plus 2 contributor copies.**
Tips: "Avoid clichés and standard plots unless you have something new to add."

$ $ STARLOG MAGAZINE, The Science Fiction Universe, Starlog Group, 475 Park Ave. S., 8th Floor, New York NY 10016-1689. Fax: (212)889-7933. E-mail: communications@starloggroup.com. Website: http://starlog.com. **Contact:** David McDonnell, editor. **90% freelance written.** "We are now somewhat hesitant to work with unpublished writers." Monthly magazine covering "the science fiction-fantasy genre: its films, TV, books, art and personalities." Estab. 1976. "We concentrate on interviews with actors, directors, writers, producers, special effects technicians and others. Be aware that 'sci-fi' and 'Trekkie' are seen as derogatory terms by our readers and by us." Pays on publication. Publishes ms an average of 4 months after acceptance. Byline given. Offers kill fee "only to manuscripts *written* or interviews *done for us.*" Buys all rights. No simultaneous submissions. Responds in 6 weeks or less. "We provide an assignment sheet to *all* writers with deadline and other info, authorizing a queried piece. No such sheets provided for already completed stories sent in on speculation. Manuscripts *must* be submitted on computer disk or by e-mail. Printouts helpful." Sample copy for $7. Writer's guidelines for #10 SASE.
   Oⁿ Break in by "doing something fresh, imaginative or innovative—or all three. Or by getting an interview we can't get. The writers who sell to us try *hard* and manage to meet one or both challenges."
Nonfiction: Interview/profile (actors, directors, screenwriters who've done science fiction films and science fiction novelists); coverage of science fiction fandom, etc. "We also sometimes cover science fiction/fantasy animation." No personal opinion think pieces/essays. *No* first person. Avoids articles on horror films/creators. "We prefer article format as opposed to Q&A interviews." **Buys 200 mss/year.** Query first with published clips. "We accept queries by regular mail *only*, by fax if there's a critical time factor or by e-mail. No phone calls. Ever! Unsolicited phone calls *won't* be returned." Length: 500-3,000 words. **Pays $35 (500-word or less items); $50-75 (sidebars); $150-275 (1,000-4,000 word pieces).**
Reprints: Pays $50 for *each* reprint in each foreign edition or such.
Photos: State availability of photos. Pays $10-25 for color slide transparencies depending on quality. "No separate payment for photos provided by film studios." Captions, model releases, identification of subjects and credit line on photos required. Photo credit given. Buys all rights.
Columns/Departments: Booklog (book reviews, **$15 each,** by assignment only). **Buys 150 reviews/year.** Query with published clips. Book review, 125 words maximum. No kill fee.
   ■ The online magazine carries original content not found in the print edition. Contact: Keith Olexa, online editor.
Tips: "Absolutely *no fiction.* We do *not* publish it and we throw away fiction manuscripts from writers who *can't* be bothered to include SASE. Nonfiction only please! We are always looking for *fresh* angles on the various *Star Trek* shows, *The X-Files,* and *Star Wars.* Know your subject before you try us. Most full-length major assignments go to freelancers with whom we're already dealing. But if we like your clips and ideas, it's possible we'll give *you* a chance. No phone calls for *any* reason please—we *mean* that!"

$ THE URBANITE, Surreal & Lively & Bizarre, Urban Legend Press, P.O. Box 4737, Davenport IA 52808. Website: members.tripod.com/theurbanite/. **Contact:** Mark McLaughlin, editor. **95% freelance written.** Triannual magazine covering surreal fiction and poetry. "We look for quality fiction with a surrealistic tone. . . We prefer character-driven storylines. Our audience is urbane, culture-oriented, and hard to please!" Estab. 1991. Circ. 1,000. **Pays on**

acceptance. Contributors to recent issues include Thomas Ligotti, Basil Copper, Alexa deMonterice, Rain Graves and Pamela Briggs. Publishes ms an average of 6 months after acceptance. Byline given. Buys first North American serial rights or second serial (reprint) rights and non-exclusive rights for public readings. "We hold readings of the magazine at various venues—like arts centers, literary conventions and libraries." Editorial leadtime 6 months. Responds in 1 month to queries; 2 months to mss. Sample copy for $5. Writer's guidelines for #10 SASE.

● Fiction from the magazine has been reprinted in *The Year's Best Fantasy and Horror* and England's *Best New Horror,* and a poem in *The Year's Best Fantastic Fiction.* The magazine has been nominated for the International Horror Guild Award.

Nonfiction: Essays, humor, interview/profile. Each issue has a theme. We don't publish recipes, fishing tips or music/CD reviews." **Buys up to 6 mss/year.** Query. Length: 500-3,000 words. **Pays $15-90 for assigned articles; $10-60 for unsolicited articles.**

Reprints: Accepts previously published submissions (but query first). Send typed ms with rights for sale noted and information about when and where the article previously appeared. Pays 100% of amount paid for an original article.

Columns/Departments: "We haven't run any columns, but would like to. Unfortunately, we haven't seen any queries that really thrill us." **Pays $15-90.**

Fiction: Experimental, fantasy (contemporary), horror, humorous, science fiction (but not "high-tech"), slipstream/cross genre, surrealism of all sorts. Upcoming theme: No. 12: The Zodiac; No. 13: the All-Horror Issue. **Buys 54 mss/year.** Send complete ms. Length: 500-3,000 words. We do publish longer works, up to 10,000 words—but query first. **Pays $10-300 (2-3¢/word).** Publishes novel excerpts. Each issue has a Featured Writer, who receives 3¢/word, 10 contributor copies, and a lifetime subscription to the magazine.

● Ranked as one of the best markets for fiction writers in *Writer's Digest* magazine's "Fiction 50," June 2000.

Poetry: Avant-garde, free verse, traditional, narrative poetry. No haiku or light verse. **Buys 18 poems/year.** Submit maximum 3 poems. Length: up to 2 ms pages. **Pays $10/poem.** Each issue has a featured poet who receives 10 contributor copies.

Tips: "Writers should familiarize themselves with surrealism in literature: too often, we receive stories filled with genre clichés. Also: we prefer character-driven stories. Don't just write because you want to see your name in print. Write because you have something to say."

SEX

Magazines featuring pictorial layouts accompanied by stories and articles of a sexual nature, both gay and straight, are listed in this section. Dating and single lifestyle magazines appear in the Relationships section. Other markets for articles relating to sex can be found in the Men's and Women's sections.

$ BUMP & GRIND, Full Deck Productions, P.O. Box 893, Hudson PQ J0P 1H0 Canada. (450)458-1934. Fax: (203)794-0008. Send submissions to: Full Deck Productions, P.O. Box 893, Hudson PQ J0P 1H0 Canada. Editor: John Todds. **Contact:** Robert Lafave, publisher/managing editor. **100% freelance written.** Monthly men's magazine covering "hard-core, anything goes (not an anal title), very dirty and lusty. All Full Deck Productions titles deal with hardcore sex." Estab. 1996. Circ. 40,000. Pays on 60 day terms. Publishes ms an average of 3 months after acceptance. Byline sometimes given. Buys all rights. Editorial lead time 3 months. Accepts queries by mail, e-mail, fax, phone. Accepts simultaneous submissions. Sample copy for $5 US per issue. Writer's guidelines for #10 SASE or by e-mail.

Fiction: "We will not accept anything to do with violence, children, non-consenting sex or degradation." **Buys 64 mss/year.** Send complete ms. Length: 1,300-2,000 words. **Pays $15-20.**

Tips: See *Sticky Buns.*

$ BUTTIME STORIES, Full Deck Productions, P.O. Box 893, Hudson PQ J0P 1H0 Canada. (450)458-1934. Fax: (203)794-0008. Send submissions to: Full Deck Productions, P.O. Box 893, Hudson PQ J0P 1H0 Canada. Website: www.fulldeck@total.net. Editor: John Todds. **Contact:** Robert Lafave, publisher/managing editor. **100% freelance written.** Monthly men's magazine covering anal adventure. "All Full Deck Productions titles deal with hardcore sex." Estab. 1996. Circ. 40,000. Pays on 60 day terms. Publishes ms an average of 3 months after acceptance. Byline sometimes given. Buys all rights. Editorial lead time 3 months. Accepts queries by mail, e-mail, fax, phone. Accepts simultaneous submissions. Sample copy for $5 US per issue. Writer's guidelines for #10 SASE or by e-mail.

Fiction: "We will not accept anything to do with violence, children, non-consenting sex or degradation." **Buys 64 mss/year.** Send complete ms. Length: 1,300-2,000 words. **Pays $15-20.**

Tips: See *Sticky Buns.*

$ CHEATERS CLUB, Full Deck Productions, P.O. Box 893, Hudson PQ J0P 1H0 Canada. (450)458-1934. Fax: (203)794-0008. Send submissions to: Full Deck Productions, P.O. Box 893, Hudson PQ J0P 1H0 Canada. Website: www.fulldeck@total.net. Editor: John Todds. **Contact:** Robert Lafave, publisher/managing editor. **100% freelance written.** Monthly men's magazine covering "swingers, lesbians, couples who invite others to join them; threesomes, foursomes and moresomes." "All Full Deck Productions titles deal with hardcore sex." Estab. 1996. Circ. 40,000. Pays on 60 day terms. Publishes ms an average of 3 months after acceptance. Byline sometimes given. Buys all rights. Editorial lead time 3 months. Accepts queries by mail, e-mail, fax, phone. Accepts simultaneous submissions. Sample copy for $5 US per issue. Writer's guidelines for #10 SASE or by e-mail.

Fiction: "We will not accept anything to do with violence, children, non-consenting sex or degradation." **Buys 64 mss/year.** Send complete ms. Length: 1,300-2,000 words. **Pays $15-20.**

Tips: See *Sticky Buns.*

$ $ EXOTIC MAGAZINE, X Publishing, 625 SW 10th Ave. #324, Portland OR 97205. Fax: (503)241-7239. E-mail: xmag@teleport.com. Website: www.xmag.com. **Contact:** Gary Aker, editor. Monthly magazine covering adult entertainment, sexuality. "*Exotic* is pro-sex, informative, amusing, mature, intelligent. Our readers rent and/or buy adult videos, visit strip clubs and are interested in topics related to the adult entertainment industry and sexuality/culture. Don't talk down to them or fire too far over their heads. Many readers are computer literate and well-traveled. We're also interested in insightful fetish material. We are not a 'hard core' publication." Estab. 1993. Circ. 120,000. Pays 30 days after publication. Byline given. Buys first North American serial rights; and on-line rights; may negotiate second serial (reprint) rights. Accepts queries by e-mail, fax. Accepts simultaneous submissions. Responds in 2 weeks to queries; 2 months to mss. Sample copy for 9 × 12 SASE and 5 first-class stamps. Writer's guidelines for #10 SASE.

Nonfiction: Exposé, general interest, historical/nostalgic, how-to, humor, interview/profile, travel, news. Interested in seeing articles about Viagra, auto racing, gambling, insider porn industry and real sex worker stories. No "men writing as women, articles about being a horny guy, opinion pieces pretending to be fact pieces." **Buys 36 mss/year.** Send complete ms. Length: 1,000-1,800 words. **Pays 10¢/word up to $150.**

Reprints: Send typed ms with rights for sale noted and information about when and where the article previously appeared. Pays 100% of amount paid for an original article.

Photos: Rarely buys photos. Most provided by staff. Reviews prints. Negotiates payment individually. Model releases required.

Fiction: "We are currently overwhelmed with fiction submissions. Please only send fiction if it's really amazing." Erotica, slice-of-life vignettes. (Must present either erotic element or some "vice" of modern culture, such as gambling, music, dancing). Send complete ms. Length: 1,000-1,800 words. **Pays 10¢/word up to $150.**

Tips: "Read adult publications, spend time in the clubs doing more than just tipping and drinking. Look for new insights in adult topics. For the industry to continue to improve, those who cover it must also be educated consumers and affiliates. Please type, spell-check and be realistic about how much time the editor can take 'fixing' your manuscript."

$ $ $ FOX MAGAZINE, Montcalm Publishing, 401 Park Ave. S., New York NY 10016-8802. (212)779-8900. Fax: (212)725-7215. Website: www.gallerymagazine.com. Managing Editor: Rich Friedman. **Contact:** Harry Montana, senior editor. **50% freelance written.** Prefers to work with published/established writers. Monthly magazine "focusing on features of interest to the young American man." Estab. 1982. Circ. 300,000. Pays on publication. Byline given. Offers 25% kill fee. Buys first North American serial rights or makes work-for-hire assignments. Submit seasonal material 6 months in advance. Responds in 1 month to queries; 2 months to mss. Sample copy for $8.95 (add $2 for Canadian and foreign orders). Writers' guidelines for #10 SASE.

Nonfiction: Investigative pieces of notable figures in adult entertainment, sex advice, porn star/stripper profiles, video reviews, on the set stories for adult movies, swinger convention news. **Buys 10-12 mss/year.** Query by mail only or send complete ms. Length: 1,500-2,500 words. **Pays $300-1,500.** "Special prices negotiated." Sometimes pays expenses of writers on assignment.

Reprints: Send tearsheet or photocopy of article or typed ms with rights for sale noted and information about when and where the article previously appeared. Pays 25% of amount paid for an original article.

Photos: Send photos with accompanying ms. Pay varies. Reviews b&w or color contact sheets and negatives. Buys one-time rights. Captions preferred; model releases and photo IDs required.

Fiction: Erotic letters only (special guidelines available). **Buys 3-4 letters/issue.** Send complete ms. Length: 250-1,500 words. **Pays $40/letter.**

$ $ $ $ GALLERY MAGAZINE, Montcalm Publishing Corp., 401 Park Ave. S., New York NY 10016-8802. (212)779-8900. Fax: (212)725-7215. E-mail: csobrien@gallerymagazine.com. Website: www.gallerymagazine.com. Managing Editor: Rich Friedman. **Contact:** C.S. O'Brien, editorial director. **50% freelance written.** Prefers to work with published/established writers. Monthly magazine "focusing on features of interest to the young American man. *Gallery* is a magazine aimed at entertaining and educating the contemporary man. *Gallery* covers political, cultural, and social trends on a national and global level through serious and provocative investigative reports, candid interviews, human-interest features, fiction, erotica, humor and photographic portfolios of beautiful women. Estab. 1972. Circ. 500,000. Pays on publication. Byline given. Pays 10-25% kill fee. Buys first North American serial rights or makes work-for-hire assignments. Submit seasonal material 6 months in advance. Accepts queries by mail, e-mail, fax, phone. Responds in 1 month to queries; 2 months to mss. Back issue for $8.95 (add $2 for Canadian and foreign orders). Writer's guidelines for SASE.

Oℸ Break in with "well-written, cutting-edge journalism, focusing on interesting subject matter (news, crime, sports, popular arts, etc.). No basic how-to's, introductory essays on tired subjects, or lame humor."

● *Gallery* works on Macintosh, so it accepts material on Mac or compatible disks if accompanied by hard copy.

Nonfiction: Investigative pieces, general interest, sports, the popular arts, interview, new products, profile. **Buys 4-5 mss/issue.** Query or send complete mss. Length: 1,500-3,500 words. **Pays $1,500-2,500.** "Special prices negotiated." Sometimes pays expenses of writers on assignment.

Reprints: Send tearsheet, photocopy or typed ms of article or story with rights for sale noted and information about when and where the article previously appeared. Pays 25% of amount paid for an original article or story.

Photos: Send photos with accompanying mss. Pay varies for b&w or color contact sheets and negatives. Buys one-time rights. Captions preferred; model release, photo ID required.

Fiction: Erotica only (special guidelines available). **Buys 1 ms/issue.** Send complete ms. Length: 1,000-3,000 words. **Pays $350-500.**

Tips: "*Gallery* needs more up-to-the-moment celebrity interviews and is always interested in quirky, innovative writing, whether fiction or non-fiction."

$ $ GENESIS, Magna Publications, 210 Route 4 E., Suite 401, Paramus NJ 07652. (201)843-4004. Fax: (201)843-8636. E-mail: genesismag@aol.com. Website: www.genesismagazine.com. Editor: Paul Gambino. **Contact:** Dan Davis, managing editor. **85% freelance written.** "Monthly men's sophisticate with celebrity interviews, erotic and non-erotic fiction, exposé, product and media reviews, lifestyle pieces." Estab. 1974. Circ. 450,000. Pays on publication. Publishes ms an average of 3 months after acceptance. Byline given. Offers 50% kill fee. Buys first or second serial (reprint) rights. Editorial lead time 4 months. Submit seasonal material 6 months in advance. Accepts simultaneous submissions. Responds in 1 month to queries; 2 months to mss. Sample copy for $6.99. Writer's guidelines for #10 SASE.

Nonfiction: Exposé, general interest, how-to, humor, interview/profile, new product, personal experience, photo feature, film, music, book, etc., reviews, lifestyle pieces. "No investigative articles not backed up by facts." **Buys 24 mss/yr.** Send complete ms. Length: 150-2,500 words. **Pays 22¢/word.** Sometimes pays expenses of writers on assignment.

Reprints: Send tearsheet, photocopy of article or typed ms with rights for sale noted with information about when and where the article previously appeared. Pays 50% of amount paid for an original article.

Photos: State availability of photos with submission. Reviews 4×5 transparencies, 8×10 prints, slides. Negotiates payment individually. Captions, model releases and identification of subjects required. Buys first/exclusive rights.

Columns/Departments: Film/video/B movies (interviews, sidebars), music, books, consumer products, all 150-500 words. **Buys 30 mss/year.** Query with published clips or send complete ms. Length: 2,500-3,500. **Pays 22¢/word.**

Fiction: Adventure, confession, erotica, fantasy, horror, humorous, mainstream, mystery, romance, science fiction, slice of life vignettes, suspense. Publishes novel excerpts. **Buys 24 mss/year.** Query or send complete ms. Length: 2,500-3,500 words. **Pays $500.**

Fillers: Anecdotes, facts, newsbreaks, short humor. **Buys 24/year.** Length: 25-500 words. **Pays 22¢/word, $50 minimum.**

Tips: "Be patient, original and detail-oriented."

$ $ GENT, "Home of the D-Cups," Dugent Corp., 14411 Commerce Way, Suite 420, Miami Lakes FL 33016. Fax: (305)362-3120. E-mail: jack@dugent.com. Website: www.sexmags.com. **Contact:** Fritz Bailey, articles editor. **50% freelance written.** Monthly men's sophisticate magazine with emphasis on big breasts. Estab. 1960. Circ. 150,000. Pays on publication. Byline given. Buys first North American serial and electronic rights. Editorial turnaround time 6 months. Submit seasonal material 6 months in advance. Sample copy for $7. Writer's guidelines for #10 SASE.

Photos: Send photos with submission. Reviews 35mm transparencies. Negotiates payment individually. Model releases and identification of subjects required. Buys first North American and second rights.

Fiction: Erotica, fantasy. **Buys 13 mss/year.** Send complete ms. Length: 2,500 words. **Pays $200.**

Tips: "An easy, smooth read full of graphic sexual content involving women with big breasts. Fiction and letters!"

$ $ $ HUSTLER, HG Inc., 8484 Wilshire Blvd., Suite 900, Beverly Hills CA 90211. Fax: (213)651-2741. E-mail: dbuchbinder@lfp.com. Website: www.hustler.com. Editor: Allan MacDonell. **Contact:** David Buchbinder, features editor. **60% freelance written.** Magazine published 13 times/year. "*Hustler* is the no-nonsense men's magazine, one that is willing to speak frankly about society's sacred cows and expose its hypocrites. The *Hustler* reader expects honest, unflinching looks at hard topics—sexual, social, political, personality profile, true crime." Estab. 1974. Circ. 750,000. Pays as boards ship to printer. Publishes ms an average of 3 months after acceptance. Byline given. Offers 20% kill fee. Buys all rights. Editorial lead time 4 months. Submit seasonal material 6 months in advance. Accepts queries by mail, e-mail, fax. Responds in 2 weeks to queries; 1 month to mss. Writer's guidelines for #10 SASE.

 • *Hustler* is most interested in well-researched nonfiction reportage focused on sexual practices and subcultures.

Nonfiction: Book excerpts, exposé, general interest, how-to, interview/profile, personal experience, trends. **Buys 30 mss/year.** Query. Length: 3,500-4,000 words. **Pays $1,500.** Sometimes pays expenses of writers on assignment.

Columns/Departments: Sex Play (some aspect of sex that can be encapsulated in a limited space), 2,500 words. **Buys 13 mss/year.** Send complete ms. **Pays $750.**

Fiction: "Difficult fiction market. While sex is a required element in *Hustler* fiction, we are not a market for traditional erotica—do not write a 'Hot Letter.' A successful fiction submission will both arouse the reader and take him into a world he may not be able to visit on his own. What an author is able to dream up in front of a computer is rarely as compelling as the product of first-hand experience and keen observation." Publishes novels and excerpts. **Buys 2 mss/year.** Send complete ms. Length: 3,000-3,500. **Pays $1,000.**

Fillers: Pays $50-100. Jokes and "Graffilthy," bathroom-wall humor.

Tips: "Don't try and mimic the *Hustler* style. If a writer needs to be molded into our voice, we'll do a better job of it than he or she will. Avoid first- and second-person voice. The ideal manuscript is quote-rich, visual and is narratively driven by events and viewpoints that push one another forward."

$HUSTLER BUSTY BEAUTIES, America's Breast Magazine, HG Publications, Inc., 8484 Wilshire Blvd., Suite 900, Beverly Hills CA 90211. (213)651-5400. Fax: (213)651-2741. E-mail: busty@lfp.com. Website: www.bustybeauty.com. **Contact:** N. Morgen Hagen, associate publisher. **40% freelance written.** Men's monthly sophisticate magazine. "*Hustler Busty Beauties* is an adult title that showcases attractive large-breasted women with accompanying erotic fiction, reader letters, humor." Estab. 1974. Circ. 180,000. Pays on publication. Publishes ms an average of 6 months after acceptance. Byline given. Buys all rights. Accepts queries by mail, e-mail, fax. Responds in 1 month. Sample copy for $6 and 9 × 12 SAE. Free writer's guidelines.
Columns/Departments: LewDDD Letters (erotic experiences involving large-breasted women from first-person point-of-view), 500-1,000 words. **Buys 24-36 mss year.** Send complete ms. **Pays $50-75.**
Fiction: Adventure, erotica, fantasy, humorous, mystery, science fiction, suspense. "No violent stories or stories without a bosomy female character." **Buys 13 mss year.** Send complete ms. Length: 750-2,500 words. **Pays $250-500.**
Jokes: Appropriate for audience. **Pays $10-25.**

⚃ $IN TOUCH/INDULGE FOR MEN, In Touch International, Inc., 13122 Saticoy St., North Hollywood CA 91605-3402. (818)764-2288. Fax: (818)764-2307. E-mail: alan@intouchformen.com. Website: www.intouchformen.com. **Contact:** Alan W. Mills, editor. **80% freelance written.** Works with a small number of new/unpublished writers each year. Monthly magazine covering the gay male lifestyle, gay male humor and erotica. Estab. 1973. Circ. 70,000. Pays on publication. Byline given, pseudonym OK. Buys one-time rights. Accepts simultaneous submissions. Accepts queries by mail, e-mail, fax. Responds in 2 months. Sample copy for $6.95. Writer's guidelines for #10 SASE or on website.
Nonfiction: Rarely buys nonfiction. Send complete ms. Length: 3,000-3,500 words. **Pays $25-75.**
Photos: Send photos with submission. Reviews contact sheets, transparencies, prints. Offers $25/photo. Captions, model releases, identification of subjects required. Buys one-time rights.
Fiction: Gay male erotica. **Buys 82 mss/year.** Send complete ms. Length: 3,000-3,500 words. **Pays $75 maximum.**
Fillers: Buys 12/year. Length: 1,500-2,500 words. **Pays $25-50.**
   ▣ The online magazine carries original content not found in the print edition and includes writer's guidelines.
Tips: "Our publications feature male nude photos plus three fiction pieces, several articles, cartoons, humorous comments on items from the media, photo features. We try to present positive aspects of the gay lifestyle, with an emphasis on humor. Humorous pieces may be erotic in nature. We are open to all submissions that fit our gay male format; the emphasis, however, is on humor and the upbeat. We receive many fiction manuscripts but not nearly enough unique, innovative, or even experimental material."

$KEY CLUB, Full Deck Productions, P.O. Box 893, Hudson PQ J0P 1H0 Canada. (450)458-1934. Fax: (203)794-0008. Send submissions to: Full Deck Productions, P.O. Box 893, Hudson PQ J0P 1H0 Canada. Editor: John Todds. **Contact:** Robert Lafave, publisher, managing editor. **100% freelance written.** Monthly mens magazine covering "first time anal virgins, new partners, new toys, new experiences. All Full Deck Productions titles deal with hardcore sex." Estab. 1996. Circ. 40,000. Pays on 60 day terms. Publishes ms an average of 3 months after acceptance. Byline sometimes given. Buys all rights. Editorial lead time 3 months. Accepts queries by mail, e-mail, fax, phone. Accepts simultaneous submissions. Sample copy for $5 US per issue. Writer's guidelines for #10 SASE.
Fiction: Erotica. "We will not accept anything to do with violence, children, non-consenting sex or degradation." **Buys 64 mss/year.** Send complete ms. Length: 1,300-2,000 words. **Pays $15-20.**
Tips: See *Sticky Buns*.

$ $NUGGET, Dugent Corp., 14411 Commerce Way, Suite 420, Miami Lakes FL 33016-1598. Fax: (305)362-3120. E-mail: editor-nugget@dugent.com. Website: www.dugent.com/nug/. **Contact:** Christopher James, editor-in-chief. **100% freelance written.** Monthly magazine covering fetish and kink. "*Nugget* is a one-of-a-kind publication which appeals to daring, open-minded adults who enjoy all forms of both kinky, alternative sex (S/M, B&D, golden showers, infantalism, amputeeism, catfighting, transvestism, fetishism, bisexuality, etc.) and conventional sex." Estab. 1960. Circ. 100,000. Pays on publication. Publishes ms an average of 1 year after acceptance. Byline given. Buys first North American serial rights. Editorial lead time 5 months. Submit seasonal material 1 year in advance. Accepts simultaneous submissions. Responds in 2 weeks to queries; 2 months to mss. Sample copy for $5. Writer's guidelines free.
Nonfiction: Interview/profile, sexual matters/trends (fetish and kink angle). **Buys 8 mss/year.** Query. Length: 2,000-3,000 words. **Pays $200 minimum.**
Photos: Send photos with submission. Reviews transparencies. Offers no additional payment for photos accepted with ms. Model releases required. Buys one-time second rights.
Fiction: Erotica, fantasy. **Buys 20 mss/year.** Send complete ms. Length: 2,000-3,000 words. **Pays $200-250.**
Tips: Most open to fiction submissions. (Follow guidelines for suitable topics.)

$OPTIONS, AJA Publishing, P.O. Box 170, Irvington NY 10533. E-mail: dianaeditr@aol.com. Editor: Don Stone. **Contact:** Diana Sheridan, associate editor. Mostly freelance written. Sexually explicit magazine for and about bisexuals and to a lesser extent homosexuals, published 10 times/year. "Articles, stories and letters about bisexuality. Positive approach. Safe-sex encounters unless the story clearly pre-dates the AIDS situation." Estab. 1977. Circ. 100,000. Pays on publication. Publishes mss an average of 10 months after acceptance. Byline given, usually pseudonymous. Buys all rights. Buys almost no seasonal material. Accepts queries by mail, e-mail. Responds in 3 weeks. Sample copy for $2.95 and 6×9 SAE with 5 first-class stamps. Writer's guidelines for SASE.

Nonfiction: Essays (occasional), how-to, humor, interview/profile, opinion, personal experience (especially). All must be bisexually or gay related. Does not want "anything not bisexually/gay related, anything negative, anything opposed to safe sex, anything dry/boring/ponderous/pedantic. Write even serious topics informally if not lightly." **Buys 10 mss/year.** Send complete ms. Length: 2,000-3,000 words. **Pays $100.**

Photos: Reviews transparencies and prints. Pays $20 for b&w photos; $200 for full color. Color or b&w sets $150. Previously published photos acceptable.

Fiction: "We don't usually get enough true first-person stories and need to buy some from writers. They must be bisexual, usually man/man, hot and believable. They must not read like fiction." **Buys 70 fiction mss/year.** Send complete ms. Length: 2,000-3,000 words. **Pays $100.**

Tips: "We use many more male/male pieces than female/female. Use only one serious article per issue. A serious/humorous approach is good here, but only if it's natural to you; don't make an effort for it. No longer buying 'letters'. We get enough real ones."

[N] $ $ $ $ PENTHOUSE, General Media, 11 Penn Plaza, 12th floor, New York NY 10001. (212)702-6000. Fax: (212)702-6279. Website: www.penthousemag.com. Editor: Peter Bloch. Monthly magazine. "*Penthouse* is for the sophisticated male. Its editorial scope ranges from outspoken contemporary comment to photography essays of beautiful women. *Penthouse* features interviews with personalities, sociological studies, humor, travel, food and wines, and fashion and grooming for men." Estab. 1969. Circ. 1,100,000. **Pays 2 months after acceptance.** Byline given. Offers 25% kill fee. Buys all rights. Editorial lead time 3 months. Accepts simultaneous submissions. Guidelines for #10 SASE.

Nonfiction: Exposé, general interest (to men), interview/profile. **Buys 50 mss/year.** Query with published clips or send complete ms. Length: 4,000-6,000 words. **Pays $3,000.**

Columns/Departments: Length: 1,000 words. **Buys 25 mss/year.** Query with published clips or send complete ms. **Pays $500.**

Tips: "Because of our long lead time, writers should think at least 6 months ahead. We take chances. Go against the grain; we like writers who look under rocks and see what hides there."

$ STICKY BUNS, Full Deck Productions, P.O. Box 893, Hudson PQ J0P 1H0 Canada. (450)458-1934. Fax: (203)794-0008. Send submissions to: Full Deck Productions, P.O. Box 893, Hudson PQ J0P 1H0 Canada. Editor: John Todds. **Contact:** Robert Lafave, publisher, managing editor. **100% freelance written.** Monthly men's magazine covering "the anal fetish as well as S&M and bondage. All Full Deck Productions titles deal with hardcore sex." Estab. 1996. Circ. 40,000. Pays on 60 day terms. Publishes ms an average of 3 months after acceptance. Byline sometimes given. Buys all rights. Editorial lead time 3 months. Accepts queries by mail, e-mail, fax, phone. Accepts simultaneous submissions. Sample copy for $5 US per issue. Writer's guidelines for #10 SASE.

Fiction: Looking for "anal adventures; very sticky, lots of wet descriptions, oils, etc. We will not accept anything to do with violence, children, non-consenting sex or degradation." **Buys 64 mss/year.** Send complete ms. Length: 1,300-2,000 words. **Pays $15-20.**

Tips: "Story length should not exceed 2,000 words. Cut the introduction—get straight to the sex. Stories of 800-1,200 words are needed; send three of these stories to each one longer title. Open with a bang—is it interesting? Does it excite the reader? Be very descriptive and very graphic, but not violent. Be explicitly descriptive. We want to smell leather, taste the skin, and feel the action as it takes place. But the sex must be enjoyable for all participants; nobody does anything in these stories against their will."

[X] $ $ SWANK, Swank Publications, 210 Route 4 E., Suite 211, Paramus NJ 07652. (201)843-4004. Fax: (201)843-8636. E-mail: genesismag@aol.com. Website: www.swankmag.com. Editor: Paul Gambino. **Contact:** D.J. Zuzio, associate editor. **75% freelance written.** Works with new/unpublished writers. Monthly magazine on "sex and sensationalism, lurid. High quality adult erotic entertainment." Audience of men ages 18-38, high school and some college education, medium income, skilled blue-collar professionals, union men, some white-collar. Estab. 1954. Circ. 400,000. Pays on publication. Publishes ms an average of 4 months after acceptance. Byline given, pseudonym if wanted. Buys first North American serial rights. Submit seasonal material 6 months in advance. Accepts queries by mail. Responds in 3 weeks to queries; 1 month to mss. Sample copy for $6.95. Writer's guidelines for SASE.

• *Swank* reports a need for more nonfiction, non-sex-related articles.

Nonfiction: Exposé (researched), adventure must be accompanied by color photographs. "We buy articles on sex-related topics, which don't need to be accompanied by photos." Interested in unusual lifestyle pieces. How-to, interviews with entertainment, sports and sex industry celebrities. Buys photo pieces on autos, action, adventure. **Buys 34 mss/year.** Query with or without published clips. **Pays $350-500.** Sometimes pays the expenses of writers on assignment. "It is strongly recommended that a sample copy is reviewed before submitting material."

Reprints: Send photocopy of article or short story or typed ms with rights for sale noted and information on when and where the article or story previously appeared. Pays 50% of amount paid for an original article or story.

Photos: Alex Suarez, art director. "Articles have a much better chance of being purchased if you have accompanying photos." Model releases required.

Fiction: Publishes novel excerpts. "All of the fiction used by *Swank* is erotic in some sense—that is, both theme and content are sexual. New angles are always welcome. We will consider stories that are not strictly sexual in theme (humor, adventure, detective stories, etc.). However, these types of stories are much more likely to be considered if they portray some sexual element, or scene, within their context."

Tips: "All erotic fiction currently being used by *Swank* must follow certain legal guidelines."

N ⊠ $ $VARIATIONS, For Liberated Lovers, General Media Inc., 11 Penn Plaza, 12th Floor, New York NY 10001. (212)702-6000. E-mail: variationsmag@generalmedia.com. Website: www.variationsmag.com. **Contact:** Victor King, editorial director. **100% freelance written.** Monthly men's magazine. "*Variations* is a pleasure guide for the 21st century. It offers today's liberated lovers a window into the erotic sexstyles of America's most exciting couples. Each issue is an elegantly erotic package of healthy sexual fact and fantasy reflecting the rich color in the rainbow of human delight." Estab. 1978. Circ. 300,000. **Pays on acceptance.** Publishes ms an average of 14 months after acceptance. No byline. Buys all rights. Editorial lead time 7 months. Submit seasonal material 10 months in advance. Responds in 1 month to queries; 2 months to mss. Sample copy from 888-312-BACK. Writer's guidelines for #10 SASE or by e-mail.

Nonfiction: Book excerpts, interview/profile, personal experience. "No humor, no poetry, no children, no one under 21, no relatives, no pets, no coercion." **Buys 50 mss/year.** Query by mail only or send complete ms. Length: 2,500-3,200 words. **Pays $0-400.**

Fiction: Erotica. "Although *Variations* does not publish short stories or fiction style per se, we do run narrative pieces in which a couple fully describe their favorite sex scenes squarely focused within one of our pleasure categories, in highly explicit erotic detail, using their best language skills." Query by mail only or send complete ms. Length: 2,500-3,200 words. **Pays $400 maximum.**

Tips: "While we are seldom able to place pre-existing erotic fiction, and the competition here even for excellent writers is rather high, we are always glad to work with newcomers who choose to go the distance to write successful pieces for us. Remember to use standard professional manuscript style, with name and address on first page and material double-spaced on white paper—and SASE."

⊠ $WICKED FETISHES, Full Deck Productions, P.O. Box 893, Hudson PQ J0P 1H0 Canada. (450)458-1934. Fax: (203)794-0008. Send submissions to: Full Deck Productions, P.O. Box 893, Hudson PQ J0P 1H0 Canada. Editor: John Todds. **Contact:** Robert Lafave, publisher/managing editor. **100% freelance written.** "Monthly men's sophisticate" digest covering "fetish, domination/submission, feet, etc.—within the law. All Full Deck Productions titles deal with hardcore sex." Estab. 1996. Circ. 40,000. Pays on 60 day terms. Publishes ms an average of 3 months after acceptance. Byline sometimes given. Buys all rights. Editorial lead time 3 months. Accepts queries by mail, e-mail, fax, phone. Accepts simultaneous submissions. Sample copy for $5 US per issue. Writer's guidelines for #10 SASE.

Fiction: "We will not accept anything to do with violence, children, non-consenting sex or degradation." **Buys 64 mss/year.** Send complete ms. Length: 1,300-2,000 words. **Pays $15-20.**

Tips: See *Sticky Buns.*

SPORTS

A variety of sports magazines, from general interest to sports medicine, are covered in this section. For the convenience of writers who specialize in one or two areas of sport and outdoor writing, the publications are subcategorized by the sport or subject matter they emphasize. Publications in related categories (for example, Hunting & Fishing; Archery & Bowhunting) often buy similar material. Writers should read through this entire section to become familiar with the subcategories. Publications on horse breeding and hunting dogs are classified in the Animal section, while horse racing is listed here. Publications dealing with automobile or motorcycle racing can be found in the Automotive & Motorcycle category. Markets interested in articles on exercise and fitness are listed in the Health & Fitness section. Outdoor publications that promote the preservation of nature, placing only secondary emphasis on nature as a setting for sport, are in the Nature, Conservation & Ecology category. Regional magazines are frequently interested in sports material with a local angle. Camping publications are classified in the Travel, Camping & Trailer category.

Archery & Bowhunting

N ⊠ $ $BOW & ARROW HUNTING, Y-Visionary Publishing, LP, 265 S. Anita Dr., Suite 120, Orange CA 92868-3310. (714)939-9991. Fax: (714)939-9909. Website: www.bowandarrowhunting.com. **Contact:** Joe Bell, editor. **70% freelance written.** Consumer magazine covering bowhunting; published 9 times annually. "Dedicated to serve the serious bowhunting enthusiast. Writers must be willing to share their secrets so our readers can become better bowhunters." Estab. 1962. Circ. 100,000. Pays on publication. Publishes ms an average of 2 months after acceptance. Byline given. Kill fee varies. Buys first North American serial or second serial (reprint) rights. Submit seasonal material 6 months in advance. Accepts queries by mail. Accepts simultaneous submissions. Responds in 1 month to queries; 6 weeks to mss. Sample copy and writer's guidelines free.

Nonfiction: How-to, humor, interview/profile, opinion, personal experience, technical. **Buys 60 mss/year.** Send complete ms. Length: 1,700-3,000 words. **Pays $200-450.**

Photos: Send photos with submission. Reviews contact sheets, 35mm and 2¼ × 2¼ transparencies and 5 × 7 prints. Offers no additional payment for photos accepted with ms. Captions required. Buys one-time rights.

Fillers: Facts, newsbreaks. **Buys 12/year.** Length: 500 words. **Pays $20-100.**

Tips: "Inform readers how they can become better at the sport, but don't forget to keep it fun! Sidebars are recommended with every submission."

$ $ BOWHUNTER, The Number One Bowhunting Magazine, Primedia Enthusiast Publications, 6405 Flank Dr., Harrisburg PA 17112-8200. (717)657-9555. Fax: (717)657-9552. E-mail: bowhunter@cowles.com. Website: www.bowhunter.com. Founder/Editor-in-Chief: M.R. James. **Contact:** Jeff Waring, managing editor. **50% freelance written.** Bimonthly magazine (with three special issues) on hunting big and small game with bow and arrow. "We are a special interest publication, produced by bowhunters for bowhunters, covering all aspects of the sport. Material included in each issue is designed to entertain and inform readers, making them better bowhunters." Estab. 1971. Circ. 185,000. **Pays on acceptance.** Publishes ms an average of 1 year after acceptance. Byline given. Kill fee varies. Buys first North American serial and one-time rights. Submit seasonal material 8 months in advance. Accepts queries by mail, e-mail. Responds in 1 month to queries; 5 weeks to mss. Sample copy for $2. Free writer's guidelines.

Nonfiction: General interest, how-to, interview/profile, opinion, personal experience, photo feature. "We publish a special 'Big Game' issue each Fall (September) but need all material by mid-March. Another annual publication, *Whitetail Bowhunter*, is staff written or by assignment only. Our latest special issue is the *Gear Guide*, which highlights the latest in equipment. We don't want articles that graphically deal with an animal's death. And, please, no articles written from the animal's viewpoint." **Buys 60 plus mss/year.** Query. Length: 250-2,000 words. **Pays $500 maximum for assigned articles; $100-400 for unsolicited articles.** Sometimes pays expenses of writers on assignment.

Photos: Send photos with submission. Reviews 35mm and 2¼ × 2¼ transparencies and 5 × 7 and 8 × 10 prints. Offers $75-250/photo. Captions required. Buys one-time rights.

Tips: "A writer must know bowhunting and be willing to share that knowledge. Writers should anticipate *all* questions a reader might ask, then answer them in the article itself or in an appropriate sidebar. Articles should be written with the reader foremost in mind; we won't be impressed by writers seeking to prove how good they are—either as writers or bowhunters. We care about the reader and don't need writers with 'I' trouble. Features are a good bet because most of our material comes from freelancers. The best advice is: Be yourself. Tell your story the same as if sharing the experience around a campfire. Don't try to write like you think a writer writes."

$ $ BOWHUNTING WORLD, Ehlert Publishing Group, Suite 600, 601 Lakeshore Parkway, Minnetonka MN 55305-5215. (612)476-2200. Fax: (612)476-8065. E-mail: mike-s@mail.epginc.com. **Contact:** Mike Strandlund, editor. **50% freelance written.** Bimonthly magazine with three additional special issues for bowhunting and archery enthusiasts who participate in the sport year-round. Estab. 1951. Circ. 130,000. **Pays on acceptance.** Publishes ms an average of 5 months after acceptance. Byline given. Buys first rights and reprint rights. Accepts queries by mail, e-mail; prefers e-mail queries. *No calls, please!* Responds in 3 weeks to queries, 6 weeks to mss. Sample copy for $3 and 9 × 12 SAE with 10 first-class stamps. Writer's and photographers guidelines for SASE.

Nonfiction: How-to articles with creative slants on knowledgeable selection and use of bowhunting equipment and bowhunting methods. Articles must emphasize knowledgeable use of archery or hunting equipment, and/or specific bowhunting techniques. Straight hunting adventure narratives and other types of articles now appear only in special issues. Equipment-oriented articles must demonstrate wise and insightful selection and use of archery equipment and other gear related to the archery sports. Some product-review, field-test, equipment how-to and technical pieces will be purchased. We are not interested in articles whose equipment focuses on random mentioning of brands. Technique-oriented articles most sought are those that briefly cover fundamentals and delve into leading-edge bowhunting or recreational archery methods. Primarily focusing on retail archery and tournament coverage." **Buys 60 mss/year.** Query or send complete ms. Length: 1,500-3,000 words. **Pays $350 to over $500.**

Photos: "We are seeking cover photos that depict specific behavioral traits of the more common big game animals (scraping whitetails, bugling elk, etc.) and well-equipped bowhunters in action. Must include return postage."

Tips: "Writers are strongly advised to adhere to guidelines and become familiar with our format, as our needs are very specific. Writers are urged to query before sending packages. We prefer detailed outlines of six or so article ideas per query. Assignments are made for the next 18 months."

$ $ PETERSEN'S BOWHUNTING, Petersen Publishing Company, L.L.C., 6420 Wilshire Blvd., Los Angeles CA 90048-5515. (323)782-2180. Fax: (323)782-2477. Editor: Jay Michael Strangis. **Contact:** David Dolhee, associate editor. **70% freelance written.** Magazine published 8 times/year covering bowhunting. "Very equipment oriented. Our readers are 'superenthusiasts,' therefore our writers must have an advanced knowledge of hunting archery." Circ.

155,000. **Pays on acceptance.** Byline given. Buys all rights. Editorial lead time 6 months. Submit seasonal material 6 months in advance. Accepts queries by mail. Responds in 1 month. Sample copy for #10 SASE. Writer's guidelines free on request.

Nonfiction: How-to, humor, interview/profile, new product, opinion, personal experience, photo feature. **Buys 40 mss/year.** Send complete ms. Length: 2,000 words. **Pays $300.**

Photos: Send photos with submission. Reviews contact sheets, 35mm transparencies, 5×7 prints. Offers $35-250/photo. Captions and model releases required. Buys one-time rights.

Columns/Departments: Query. **Pays $200-300.**

Fillers: Facts, newsbreaks. Buys 12/year. Length: 150-400 words. **Pays $25-75.**

Tips: Feature articles must be supplied in either 3.50 IBM (or compatible) or 3.50 Mac floppy disks.

Baseball

[N] **$ $ BASEBALL AMERICA**, Baseball America Inc., P.O. Box 2089, Durham NC 27702. (919)682-9635. Fax: (919)682-2880. E-mail: allansimpson@baseballamerica.com.. Editor: Allan Simpson. Managing Editor: Will Lingo. Senior Editor: John Rocoster. **10% freelance written.** Biweekly tabloid covering baseball. "*Baseball America* is read by industry insiders and passionate, knowledgeable fans. Writing should go beyond routine baseball stories to include more depth or a unique angle." Estab. 1981. Circ. 80,000. Pays on publication. Publishes ms an average of 2 months after acceptance. Byline given. Buys one-time rights. Editorial lead time 1 month. Submit seasonal material 2 months in advance. Accepts simultaneous submissions. Sample copy for $3.25.

Nonfiction: Historical/nostalgic, interview/profile, theme or issue-oriented baseball features. "No major league player features that don't cover new ground; superficial treatments of baseball subjects." **Buys 10 mss/year.** Send complete ms. Length: 100-2,000 words. **Pays $10-500 for assigned articles; $10-250 for unsolicited articles.**

Reprints: Accepts previously published submissions.

Photos: State availability of photos with submission. Negotiates payment individually. Identification of subjects required. Buys one-time rights.

Tips: "We use little freelance material, in part because we have a large roster of excellent correspondents and because much of what we receive is too basic or superficial for our readership. Sometimes writers stray too far the other way and get too arcane. But we're always interested in great stories that baseball fans haven't heard yet."

$ $ JUNIOR BASEBALL, America's Youth Baseball Magazine, 2D Publishing, P.O. Box 9099, Canoga Park CA 91309. (818)710-1234. E-mail: dave@juniorbaseball.com. Website: www.juniorbaseball.com. **Contact:** Dave Destler, editor. **25% freelance written.** Bimonthly magazine covering youth baseball. "Focused on youth baseball players ages 7-17 (including high school) and their parents/coaches. Edited to various reading levels, depending upon age/skill level of feature." Estab. 1996. Circ. 60,000. Pays on publication. Publishes ms an average of 4 months after acceptance. Byline given. Buys all rights. Editorial lead time 3 months. Submit seasonal material 3 months in advance. Accepts simultaneous submissions. Responds in 2 weeks to queries; 1 month to mss. Sample copy for $5 (also online). Writer's guidelines for #10 SASE.

Nonfiction: How-to (skills, tips, features, how to play better baseball, etc.), interview/profile (with major league players; only on assignment), personal experience (from coaches' or parents' perspective). When I Was a Kid (a current Major League Baseball player profile); Leagues, Tournaments (spotlighting a particular youth baseball league, organization, event, tournament); Industry (featuring businesses involved in baseball, e.g., how bats are made); Parents Feature (topics of interest to parents of youth ball players); all 1,000-1,500 words. In the Spotlight (news, events, new products), 50-100 words; League Notebook (news, events, new ideas or tips geared to the parent or league volunteer, adult level), 250-500 words; Hot Prospect (written for the 14 and older competitive player. High school baseball is included, and the focus is on improving the finer points of the game to make the high school team, earn a college scholarship, or attract scouts, written to an adult level), 500-1,000 words. **Buys 8-12 mss/year.** Query. **Pays $50-100.** "No trite first-person articles about your kid."

Photos: State availability of or send photos with submission. Reviews 35mm transparencies, 3×5 prints. Offers $10-100/photo; negotiates payment individually. Captions and identification of subjects required.

Tips: "Must be well-versed in baseball! Having a child who is very involved in the sport, or have extensive hands-on experience in coaching baseball, at the youth, high school or higher level. We can always use accurate, authoritative skills information and good photos to accompany is a big advantage! This magazine is read by experts."

Bicycling

[icon] **$ $ $ ADVENTURE CYCLIST**, Adventure Cycling Assn., Box 8308, Missoula MT 59807. (406)721-1776. Fax: (406)721-8754. E-mail: ddambrosio@adv-cycling.org. Website: www.adv-cycling.org. **Contact:** Daniel D'Ambrosio, editor. **75% freelance written.** Bicycle touring magazine for Adventure Cycling Association members published 9 times/year. Estab. 1975. Circ. 30,000. Pays on publication. Byline given. Buys first serial rights. Submit seasonal material 3 months in advance. Sample copy and guidelines for 9×12 SAE with 4 first-class stamps.

Nonfiction: Features include: U.S. or foreign tour accounts; special focus (on tour experience); how-to; humor; interview/profile; photo feature; technical; travel. **Buys 20-25 mss/year.** Query with published clips or send complete ms; include short bio with ms. Length: 800-2,500 words. **Pays $450-1,200.**

Reprints: Send photocopy of article.

Photos: Color transparencies should accompany tour accounts and profiles. Bicycle, scenery, portraits. State availability of photos. Model releases, identification of subjects required.

N $ $ $ BICYCLING, Rodale Press, Inc., 135 N. 6th St., Emmaus PA 18098. (610)967-5171. Fax: (610)967-8960. E-mail: bicycling@rodale.com. Website: www.bicycling.com. Publisher: Nelson Peña. **Contact:** Doug Donaldson, associate editor. **20-25% freelance written.** Prefers to work with published/established writers. Magazine published 11 times/year. "*Bicycling* features articles about fitness, training, nutrition, touring, racing, equipment, clothing, maintenance, new technology, industry developments, and other topics of interest to committed bicycle riders. Editorially, we advocate for the sport, industry, and the cycling consumer." Estab. 1961. Circ. 280,000. **Pays on acceptance.** Byline given. Buys all rights. Submit seasonal material 6 months in advance. Responds in 2 months. Sample copy for $3.50. Writer's guidelines for #10 SASE.

Nonfiction: How-to (on all phases of bicycle touring, repair, maintenance, commuting, new products, clothing, riding technique, nutrition for cyclists, conditioning); fitness is more important than ever; also travel (bicycling must be central here); photo feature (on cycling events of national significance); and technical (component review—query). "We are strictly a bicycling magazine. We seek readable, clear, well-informed pieces. We sometimes run articles that are inspirational and inspiration might flavor even our most technical pieces. No poetry or fiction." **Buys 6 unsolicited mss/year.** Query. "We will contact you." **Payment varies.** Sometimes pays expenses of writers on assignment.

Reprints: Occasionally accepts previously published submissions. Send photocopy or typed ms with information about when and where the article previously appeared.

Photos: State availability of photos with query letter or send photo material with ms. Pays $15-50 for b&w prints and $35-250 for transparencies. Captions preferred; model release required.

Fillers: Anecdotes.

Tips: "Our focus is narrowed to the how-to of cycling, how to be a better rider, and bicycling experiences."

N $ $ BIKE MAGAZINE, Surfer Publications, 33046 Calle Aviador, San Juan Capistrano CA 92675. (949)496-5922. Fax: (714)496-7849. **Contact:** Vernon Filton, editor. **35% freelance written.** Magazine published 10 times/year covering mountain biking. Estab. 1993. Circ. 85,000. **Pays on acceptance.** Publishes ms an average of 2 months after acceptance. Byline given. Offers 25% kill fee. Buys first North American serial rights. Editorial lead time 4 months. Submit seasonal material 6 months in advance. Responds in 2 months. Sample copy for $8. Guidelines for #10 SASE.

Nonfiction: Humor, interview/profile, new product, personal experience, photo feature, technical, travel. No fiction. **Buys 20 mss/year.** Send complete ms. Length: 1,000-2,500 words. **Pays 40¢/word.** Sometimes pays expenses of writers on assignment.

Photos: Send photos with submission. Negotiates payment individually. Captions and identification of subjects required. Buys one-time rights.

Columns/Departments: Splatter (news), 600 words. **Buys 10 mss/year.** Send complete ms. **Pays 40¢/word.**

Tips: "Remember that we focus on hard core mountain biking, not beginners. We're looking for ideas that deliver the excitement and passion of the sport in ways that aren't common or predictable. Ideas should be vivid, unbiased, irreverent, probing, fun, humorous, funky, quirky, smart, good. Great feature ideas are always welcome, especially features on cultural matters or issues in the sport. However, you're much more likely to get published in *Bike* if you send us great ideas for short articles. In particular we need stories for our Splatter, a front-of-the-book section devoted to news, funny anecdotes, quotes, and odds and ends. These stories range from 50 to 700 words. We also need personality profiles of 600 words or so for our People Who Ride section. Racers are OK but we're more interested in grassroots people with interesting personalities—it doesn't matter if they're Mother Theresas or scumbags, so long as they make mountain biking a little more interesting. Short descriptions of great rides are very welcome for our travel column; the length should be from 700 to 900 words."

$ CRANKMAIL, Cycling in Northeastern Ohio, P.O. Box 33249, Cleveland OH 44133-0249. Fax: (440)877-0373. E-mail: editor@crankmail.com. Website: www.crankmail.com. **Contact:** James Guilford, editor. Monthly magazine covering bicycling in all aspects. "Our publication serves the interests of bicycle enthusiasts . . . established, accomplished adult cyclists. These individuals are interested in reading about the sport of cycling, bicycles as transportation, ecological tie-ins, sports nutrition, the history and future of bicycles and bicycling." Estab. 1977. Circ. 1,000. Pays on publication. Byline given. Not copyrighted. Buys one-time or second serial (reprint) rights. Editorial lead time 1 month. Submit seasonal material 3 months in advance. Sample copy for $1. Writer's guidelines for #10 SASE.

Nonfiction: Essays, historical/nostalgic, how-to, humor, interview/profile, personal experience, technical. "No articles encouraging folks to start or get involved in bicycling—our readers are already cyclists." Send complete ms; no queries. Length: 600-1,800 words. **Pays $10 minimum for unsolicited articles.**

Reprints: Send typed ms with rights for sale noted and info about when and where it previously appeared.

Fiction: Publishes very short novel excerpts.

Fillers: Cartoons. **Pays $5-10.**

$ $ CYCLE CALIFORNIA!, Advanced Project Management, P.O. Box 189, Mountain View CA 94042. (650)961-2663. Fax: (650)968-9030. E-mail: cycleca@cyclecalifornia.com. Website: www.cyclecalifornia.com. **Contact:** Tracy L. Corral, editor/publisher. **75% freelance written.** Magazine published 11 times/year "covering Northern California bicycling events, races, people. Issues (topics) covered include bicycle commuting, bicycle politics, touring, racing, nostalgia, history, anything at all to do with riding a bike." Estab. 1995. Circ. 25,500. Pays on publication. Publishes ms 3 months after acceptance. Byline given. Buys first North American serial rights. Editorial lead time 6 weeks. Submit seasonal material 6 weeks in advance. Accepts queries by mail, e-mail, phone. Accepts simultaneous submissions. Responds in 1 month. Sample copy for 10×13 SAE with 3 first-class stamps. Writer's guidelines for #10 SASE.

Nonfiction: Historical/nostalgic, interview/profile, opinion, personal experience, technical, travel. Special issue: Bicycle Tour & Travel (January/February). No articles about any sport that doesn't relate to bicycling, no product reviews. **Buys 36 mss/year.** Query with or without published clips. Length: 500-1,500 words. **Pays 3-10¢/word.** Sometimes pays expenses of writers on assignment.

Photos: Send photos with submission. Reviews 3×5 prints. Negotiates payment individually. Identification of subjects required. Buys one-time rights.

Columns/Departments: Buys 2-3 mss/year. Query with published clips. **Pays 3-10¢/word.**

■ The online magazine carries original content not found in the print edition. Contact: Tracy L. Corral, online editor.

Tips: "E-mail or call editor with good ideas. While we don't exclude writers from other parts of the country, articles really should reflect a Northern California slant, or be of general interest to bicyclists. We prefer stories written by people who like and use their bikes."

$ USA CYCLING MAGAZINE, One Olympic Plaza, Colorado Springs CO 80909. (719)578-4581. Fax: (719)578-4596. E-mail: media@usacycling.org or joe@tpgsports.com. Website: www.usacycling.org or www.tpgsports.com. Editor: B.J. Hoeptner. **Contact:** Joseph Oberle, publications manager, (763)595-0808, ext. 114. **25% freelance written.** Bimonthly magazine covering reportage and commentary on American bicycle racing, personalities and sports physiology for USAC licensed cyclists. Estab. 1980. Circ. 52,000. Pays on publication. Publishes ms an average of 2 months after acceptance. Byline given. Accepts queries by mail, e-mail, fax, phone. Responds in 2 weeks. Sample copy for 10×12 SAE with 2 first-class stamps.

● *USAC Magazine* is looking for longer, more in-depth features (800-1,200 words).

Nonfiction: How-to (train, prepare for a bike race), interview/profile, photo feature. No comparative product evaluations. Length: 800-1,200 words. **Pays $50-75/article** depending on type and length of article.

Reprints: Send photocopy of article.

Photos: State availability of photos. Captions required. Buys one-time rights.

■ The online magazine carries original content not found in the print edition. Contact: B.J. Hoeptner, online editor.

Tips: "We do not want race reports. We want features from 800-1,200 words on USA Cycling members and their activities. Our focus is on personalities, not opinions or competition."

$ $ VELONEWS, The Journal of Competitive Cycling, 1830 55th St., Boulder CO 80301-2700. (303)440-0601. Fax: (303)444-6788. E-mail: vnedit@7dogs.com. Website: www.VeloNews.com. **Contact:** Kip Mickler, senior editor. **40% freelance written.** Monthly tabloid September-February, biweekly March-August covering bicycle racing. Estab. 1972. Circ. 48,000. Pays on publication. Publishes ms an average of 1 month after acceptance. Byline given. Buys one-time worldwide rights. Accepts simultaneous submissions. Responds in 3 weeks.

Nonfiction: Freelance opportunities include race coverage, reviews (book and videos), health-and-fitness departments. **Buys 100 mss/year.** Query. Length: 300-1,200 words.

Reprints: Send typed ms with rights for sale noted and info about when and where it previously appeared.

Photos: State availability of photos. Pays $16.50 for b&w prints. Pays $200 for color used on cover. Captions and identification of subjects required. Buys one-time rights.

Boating

$ $ BASS & WALLEYE BOATS, The Magazine of Performance Fishing Boats, Poole Publications, Inc., 20700 Belshaw Ave., Carson CA 90746. (310)537-6322. Fax: (310)537-8735. E-mail: bassboats@aol.com. Editor: Steve Quinlan. **Contact:** Debbie Rosenkrantz, managing editor. **50% freelance written.** "*Bass & Walleye Boats* is published 9 times/year for the bass and walleye fisherman/boater. Directed to give priority to the boats, the tech, the how-to, the after-market add-ons and the devices that help anglers enjoy their boating experience." Estab. 1994. Circ. 65,000. **Pays on acceptance.** Publishes ms 3 months after acceptance. Byline given. Offers 25% kill fee. Buys all rights. Editorial lead time 2 months. Submit seasonal material 3 months in advance. Accepts queries by mail, e-mail, fax. Responds "A.S.A.P." Sample copy for $3.95 and 9×12 SAE with 7 first-class stamps. Writer's guidelines free.

○→ Break in by writing as an expert on using, modifying and tuning bass and walleye boats/engines for performance fishing use. Writer must be knowledgeable and able to back up document articles with hard sources. Also, your photography skills need to be honed for a marine environment.

Nonfiction: General interest, how-to, interview/profile, personal experience, photo feature, technical, travel. Special issues: Annual towing guide and new boats. No fiction. **Buys about 120 mss/year.** Query. Length: 1,000-3,000 words. **Pays $300-700.** Sometimes pays expenses of writers on assignment.
Photos: State availability of photos with submission. Reviews 2¼×2¼ transparencies and 35mm slides. Negotiates payment individually. Captions and identification of subjects required. Buys one-time rights.
Tips: "Write from and for the bass and walleye boaters' perspective."

$ $ BOATING LIFE, World Publications Inc., 330 W. Canton Ave., Winter Park FL 32789. (407)628-4802. Fax: (407)628-7061. E-mail: boatlife@worldzine.com. Website: www.boatinglifemag.com. Editor: Pierce Hoover. **Contact:** Brett Becker, managing editor. **20% freelance written.** Bimonthly magazine covering powerboats under 30 feet, lifestyle, news, technology, maneuvers, operation, travel. "We are a product-related and lifestyle title. As such, we focus on people, fun, boating skills and technical subjects or product reviews. We demand a higher caliber of writing than has been the norm in the boating industry. In other words, we try not to use established 'boating writers,' and instead prefer qualified generalists who can bring color and excitement to the water." Estab. 1997. Circ. 103,000. Pays on publication. Publishes ms an average of 4 months after acceptance. Byline given. Offers 15% kill fee. Editorial lead time 6 months. Submit seasonal material 6 months in advance. Accepts queries by mail, e-mail, fax. Accepts simultaneous submissions. Responds in 2 weeks to queries; 1 month to mss. Sample copy and writer's guidelines free.
Nonfiction: How-to, humor, interview/profile, new product, photo feature, technical, travel. "No stories on sailing or sailboats." **Buys 12 mss/year.** Query. Length: 400-2,500 words. **Pays $125-750.**
Photos: State availability of photos with submission. Offers $50-500/photo. Identification of subjects required. Buys one-time rights.
Columns/Departments: On Maneuvers (tips on operating a powerboat); Family Boating (tips for family boating); Owner's Manual (tips on everything from buying to selling), all 500-600 words. **Buys 12 mss/year.** Query. **Pays $125-350.**
Fillers: Facts, newsbreaks. **Buys 6/year.** Length: 50-125 words. **Pays $50-100.**
  O— Break in with 200-500 word travel stories involving great places to take your boat and buying, maintenance and handling tips.
Tips: "Our focus is ninety percent fresh water, ten percent coastal. We avoid straight travelogues and instead favor activity or personality-based stories. The general tone is light and conversational, but all articles should in some way help the reader through the boat buying or owning process, and/or promote some aspect of the "boating lifestyle."

⚑ $ $ CANOE & KAYAK MAGAZINE, Canoe America Associates, 10526 NE 68th St., Suite 3, Kirkland WA 98033. (425)827-6363. Fax: (425)827-1893. E-mail: jan@canoekayak.com. Website: www.canoekayak.com. Editor-in-Chief: Jan Nesset. **Contact:** Robin Stanton, managing editor. **75% freelance written.** Bimonthly magazine. "*Canoe & Kayak Magazine* is North America's #1 paddlesports resource. Our readers include flatwater and whitewater canoeists and kayakers of all skill levels. We provide comprehensive information on destinations, technique and equipment. Beyond that, we cover canoe and kayak camping, safety, the environment, and the history of boats and sport." Estab. 1972. Circ. 90,000. Pays on publication. Publishes ms an average of 6 months after acceptance. Byline given. Offers 50% kill fee. Buys first North American serial rights or one-time rights. Editorial lead time 4 months. Submit seasonal material 6 months in advance. Accepts queries by mail, e-mail. Responds in 2 months. Sample copy and writer's guidelines for 9×12 SAE with 7 first-class stamps.
  O— Break in with "a good destination or Put-In (news) pieces with excellent photos. "Take a good look at the types of articles we publish before sending us any sort of query."
Nonfiction: Historical/nostalgic, how-to (canoe, kayak camp; load boats; paddle whitewater, etc.), personal experience, photo feature, technical, travel. Annuals: Whitewater Paddling; Beginner's Guide; Kayak Touring; Canoe Journal. "No cartoons, poems, stories in which bad judgment is portrayed or 'Me and Molly' articles." **Buys 20 mss/year.** Query with or without published clips or send complete ms. Length: 400-2,500 words. **Pays $25-800 for assigned articles; $25-450 for unsolicited articles.** Sometimes pays the expenses of writers on assignment.
Photos: State availability of or send photos with submission. "Good photos help sell a story." Reviews 35mm transparencies and 4×6 prints. "Some activities we cover are canoeing, kayaking, canoe fishing, camping, canoe sailing or poling, backpacking (when compatible with the main activity) and occasionally inflatable boats. We are not interested in groups of people in rafts, photos showing disregard for the environment, gasoline-powered, multi-horsepower engines unless appropriate to the discussion, or unskilled persons taking extraordinary risks." Offers $25-350/photo. Captions, model releases and identification of subjects required. Buys one-time rights.
Columns/Departments: Put In (environment, conservation, events), 650 words; Destinations (canoe and kayak destinations in US, Canada), 1,500 words; Traditions (essays: traditional paddling), 750 words. **Buys 40 mss/year.** Query with or without published clips or send complete ms. **Pays $175-350.**
Fillers: Anecdotes, facts, newsbreaks. **Buys 20/year.** Length: 500-1,000 words. **Pays $5/column inch.**
Tips: "Start with Put-In articles (short featurettes), book reviews, or short, unique equipment reviews. Or give us the best, most exciting article we've ever seen—with great photos. Short Strokes is also a good entry forum focusing on short trips on good waterways accessible to lots of people. Focusing more on technique and how-to articles."

$ $ $ CHESAPEAKE BAY MAGAZINE, Boating at Its Best, Chesapeake Bay Communications, 1819 Bay Ridge Ave., Annapolis MD 24403. (410)263-2662. Fax: (410)267-6924. E-mail: editor@cbmmag.net. Managing Editor: Jane Meneely. **Contact:** Tim Sayles, editor. **60% freelance written.** Monthly magazine covering boating and the

Chesapeake Bay. "Our readers are boaters. Our writers should know boats and boating. Read the magazine before submitting." Estab. 1972. Circ. 42,000. **Pays within 60 days of acceptance.** Publishes ms 2-12 months after acceptance. Byline given. Buys first North American serial rights. Editorial lead time 1 year. Submit seasonal material 1 year in advance. Accepts queries by mail, e-mail. Accepts simultaneous submissions. Responds in 2 months to queries; 3 months to mss. Sample copy for $5.19 prepaid.

Nonfiction: Destinations, boating adventures, how-to, marina reviews, history, nature, environment, lifestyles, personal and institutional profiles, boat-type profiles, boatbuilding, boat restoration, boating anecdotes, boating news. **Buys 30 mss/year.** Query with unedited writing samples. Length: 300-3,000 words. **Pays $100-1,000.** Pays expenses of writers on assignment.

Photos: Offers $45-150/photo, $350 day rate for assignment photography. Captions and identification of subjects required. Buys one-time rights.

Tips: "Send us unedited writing samples (not clips) that show the writer can write, not just string words together. We look for well-organized, lucid, lively, intelligent writing."

N **$ CURRENTS, Voice of the National Organization for Rivers**, 212 W. Cheyenne Mountain Blvd., Colorado Springs CO 80906. (719)579-8759. Fax: (719)576-6238. E-mail: nors@rmi.net. Website: www.nors.org. **Contact:** Eric Leaper, editor. **25% freelance written.** Quarterly magazine covering river running (kayaking, rafting, river canoeing). Estab. 1979. Circ. 5,000. Pays on publication. Publishes ms an average of 6 months after acceptance. Byline given. Offers 25% kill fee. Buys first North American serial, first and one-time rights. Submit seasonal material 4 months in advance. Responds in 2 weeks to queries; 1 month to mss. Sample copy for $1 and 9×12 SAE with 3 first-class stamps. Writer's guidelines for #10 SASE.

Nonfiction: How-to (run rivers and fix equipment), in-depth reporting on river conservation and access issues and problems, humor (related to rivers), interview/profile (any interesting river runner), opinion, personal experience, technical, travel (rivers in other countries). "We tell river runners about river conservation, river access, river equipment, how to do it, when, where, etc." No trip accounts without originality; no stories about "my first river trip." **Buys 20 mss/ year.** Query with or without clips. Length: 500-2,500 words. **Pays $35-150.**

Reprints: Accepts previously published submissions, if so noted.

Photos: State availability of photos. Pays $35-50. Reviews color prints or photos on disk. Captions and identification of subjects (if racing) required. Buys one-time rights. Captions must include names of the river and rapid.

Columns/Departments: Book and film reviews (river-related). **Buys 5 mss/year.** Query with or without clips, or send complete ms. Length: 100-500 words. **Pays $25.**

Fiction: Adventure (river). **Buys 2 mss/year.** Query. Length: 1,000-2,500 words. **Pays $35-75.** "Must be well-written, on well-known river and beyond the realm of possibility."

Fillers: Clippings, jokes, gags, anecdotes, short humor, newsbreaks. Must be related to river running. **Buys 5/year.** Length: 25-100 words. **Pays $5-10.**

Tips: "We need more material on river news—proposed dams, wild and scenic river studies, accidents, etc. If you can provide brief (300-500 words) on these subjects, you will have a good chance of being published. Material must be on rivers. Go to a famous river and investigate it; find out something we don't know—especially about rivers that are *not* in Colorado or adjacent states—we already know about those."

$ $ GO BOATING MAGAZINE, America's Family Boating Magazine, Duncan McIntosh Co., 17782 Cowan, Suite C, Irvine CA 92614. (949)660-6150. Fax: (949)660-6172. E-mail: editorial@goboatingamerica.com. Website: http://www.goboatingmag.com.. **Contact:** Eston Ellis, managing editor. **60% freelance written.** Published 6 times/year covering family power boating. Typical reader "owns a power boat between 14-25 feet long and has for 3-9 years. Boat reports that appear in *Go Boating* are designed to give readers a quick look at a new model. They must be lively, entertaining and interesting to our savvy boat-owning readership." Estab. 1997. Circ. 100,000. Pays on publication. Publishes ms an average of 3-6 months after acceptance. Byline given. Buys first North American serial rights. Editorial lead time 3 months. Submit seasonal material 4 months in advance. Accepts simultaneous submissions. Responds in 3 months. Sample copy free. Writer's guidelines for #10 SASE.

Nonfiction: General interest, how-to, humor, new product, personal experience, travel. **Buys 10-15 mss/year.** Query. Length: 1,000-1,200 words. **Pays $150-400.** Sometimes pays expenses of writers on assignment.

Photos: State availability of photos with submission. Reviews transparencies and prints. Offers $50-250/photo. Model releases and identification of subjects required. Buys one-time rights.

Columns/Departments: Buys 10 mss/year. Query. **Pays $150-350.**

Fillers: Anecdotes, facts and newsbreaks. **Buys 10/year.** Length: 250-500 words. **Pays $50-100.**

Tips: "Every vessel has something about it that makes it stand apart from all the others. Tell us what makes this boat different from all the rest on the market today. Include specifications and builder's address and phone number. See past issues for format."

N **$ GULF COAST & TEXAS BOATING**, Gulf Coast Boating, P.O. Box 1199, Boutte LA 70039. (504)758-7217. Fax: (504)758-7000. E-mail: boating@acadiacom.net. Editor: Todd Masson. **Contact:** Andy Crawford, managing editor. **90% freelance written.** Monthly magazine covering boating on the Gulf Coast and Texas. "We place emphasis on destinations, care of boats and boat reviews." Estab. 1992. Circ. 40,000. Pays on publication. Publishes ms an average of 2 months after acceptance. Byline given. Kill fee negotiable. Buys one-time and electronic rights. Editorial lead time 2 months. Submit seasonal material 4 months in advance. Accepts queries by mail, e-mail. Responds in 2 weeks to queries; 1 month to mss. Sample copy for $7. Writer's guidelines free.

Nonfiction: General interest, historical/nostalgic, how-to (boat care, winterizing, etc.), interview/profile, technical, travel, fishing on Gulf Coast/Texas. No material on national boating destinations (unless approved in advance). **Buys 50-75 mss/year.** Query with published clips. Length: 1,000-1,500 words. **Pays $100-200.** Sometimes pays expenses of writers on assignment.

Photos: Send photos with submission. Reviews transparencies. Offers $10-100/photo. Captions required. Buys one-time rights.

Columns/Departments: Along the Waterfront (news briefs/issues), 200 words. **Buys 12 mss/year.** Query. **Pays $40-75.**

Fillers: Newsbreaks. **Buys 12/year.** Length: 100-200 words. **Pays $40-75.**

Tips: "Submit material on subjects you are knowledgeable about, provide helpful tips or information not easily found elsewhere, and include good, publishable photo support."

⚏ $ $HEARTLAND BOATING, The Waterways Journal, Inc., 319 N. Fourth St., Suite 650, St. Louis MO 63102. (314)241-4310. Fax: (314)241-4207. E-mail: hlb@socket.net. Website: www.heartlandboating.com. **Contact:** H. Nelson Spencer, editor/publisher. **70% freelance written.** Magazine published 9 times/year covering recreational boating on the inland waterways of mid-America, from the Great Lakes south to the Gulf of Mexico and over to the east. "Our writers must have experience with and a great interest in boating, particularly in the area described above. *Heartland Boating*'s content is both informative and humorous—describing boating life as the heartland boater knows it. We are boating and enjoying the outdoor, water-oriented way of life. The content reflects the challenge, joy and excitement of our way of life afloat. We are devoted to both power and sailboating enthusiasts throughout middle America; houseboats are included. The focus is on the freshwater inland rivers and lakes of the Heartland, primarily the waters of the Tennessee, Cumberland, Ohio, Missouri and Mississippi rivers, the Tennessee-Tombigbee Waterway and the lakes along these rivers." Estab. 1989. Circ. 16,000. Pays on publication. Publishes ms an average of 3 months after acceptance. Byline given. Buys first North American serial or one-time rights; electronic rights always included. Editorial lead time 3 months. Submit seasonal material 6 months in advance. Accepts queries by mail, e-mail, fax, phone. Responds in 1 month. Sample copy and writer's guidelines free.

Nonfiction: How-to (articles about navigation information and making time spent aboard easier and more comfortable), personal experience (sharing experiences aboard and on cruises in our coverage area), technical (boat upkeep and maintenance), travel (along the rivers and on the lakes in our coverage area and on-land stops along the way). Special issues: Annual Boat Show/New Products issue in December looks at what is coming out on the market for the coming year. Annual Houseboat Issue in May highlights new houseboat models for the year. No articles on waterways that are not within our coverage area or places, attractions and events that are not easily accessible by water. **Buys 110 mss/ year.** Query with published clips or send complete ms. Length: 850-1,500 words. **Pays $100-300.**

Reprints: Accepts previously published submissions. Send photocopy of article or typed ms and information about where and when it previously appeared. Pays 50% of amount paid for an original article.

Photos: Send photos with submission. Reviews transparencies and prints. Offers no additional payment for photos accepted with ms. Buys first North American serial rights.

Columns/Departments: Food Afloat (recipes easy to make when aboard), Books Aboard (book reviews), Handy Hints (small boat improvement projects), Waterways History (on-water history tidbits), all 850 words. **Buys 45 mss/ year.** Query with published clips or send complete ms. **Pays $75-150.**

Tips: "We usually plan an editorial schedule for the coming year in August. Submitting material between May and July will be most helpful for the planning process, although we accept submissions year-round."

⚏ $ $HOT BOAT, LFP Publishing, 8484 Wilshire Blvd., Suite 900, Beverly Hills CA 90211. (323)651-5400. Fax: (323)951-0384. **Contact:** Brett Bayne, executive editor. **50% freelance written.** Monthly magazine on performance boating (16-35 feet), water skiing and water sports in general. "We're looking for concise, technically oriented 'how-to' articles on performance modifications; personality features on interesting boating-oriented personalities, and occasional event coverage." Circ. 30,000. Pays upon publication. Publishes ms an average of 2 months after acceptance. Byline given. Offers 40% kill fee. Buys all rights; also reprint rights occasionally. Submit seasonal material 3 months in advance. Responds in 3 weeks to queries; 1 month to mss. Sample copy for $3 and 9 × 12 SAE with $1.35 postage.

Nonfiction: How-to (increase horsepower, perform simple boat related maintenance), humor, interview/profile (racers and manufacturers), new product, personal experience, photo feature, technical. "Absolutely no sailing—we deal strictly in powerboating." **Buys 30 mss/year.** Query with published clips. Length: 500-2,000 words. **Pays $75-450.** Sometimes pays expenses of writers on assignment.

Reprints: Pays $150-200/printed page.

Photos: Send photos with submission. Reviews transparencies. Captions, model releases, identification of subjects required. Buys all rights.

Tips: "We're always open to new writers. If you query with published clips and we like your writing, we can keep you on file even if we reject the particular query. It may be more important to simply establish contact. Once we work together there will be much more work to follow."

$ NORTHERN BREEZES, SAILING MAGAZINE, Northern Breezes, Inc., 245 Brunswick Ave. S., Golden Valley MN 55416. (612)542-9707. Fax: (612)542-8998. E-mail: thomnbreez@aol.com. Managing Editor: Thom Burns. **Contact:** Gloria Peck, editor. **70% freelance written.** Regional monthly sailing magazine for the Upper Midwest. Estab. 1989. Circ. 22,300. Pays on publication. Byline given. Buys first North American serial rights. Editorial lead time 1 month. Submit seasonal material 3 months in advance. Accepts queries by mail, e-mail, fax, phone. Responds in 1 month to queries; 2 months to mss. Sample copy and writer's guidelines free or on website.

Nonfiction: Book excerpts, how-to (sailing topics), humor, inspirational, interview/profile, new product, personal experience, photo feature, technical, travel. Interested in seeing good sailboat restoration articles and youth in sailing (empowerment from learning to sail, race, etc.). No boat reviews. **Buys 24 mss/year.** Query with published clips. Length: 300-2,000 words. **Pays $50-150.**

Reprints: Accepts previously published submissions.

Photos: Send photos with submission. Reviews negatives, 35mm slides, 3×5 or 4×6 prints. Offers no additional payment for photos accepted with ms or negotiates payment individually. Captions required. Buys one-time rights.

Columns/Departments: This Old Boat (sailboat), 500-1,000 words; Surveyor's Notebook, 500-800 words. **Buys 8 mss/year.** Query with published clips. **Pays $50-150.**

    ◼ The online magazine carries original content not found in the print edition and includes writer's guidelines. Contact: Thom Burns, online editor.

Tips: "Query with a regional connection already in mind."

N ⭐ $ $ OFFSHORE, Northeast Boating at its Best, Offshore Communications, Inc., 220 Reservoir St., Suite 9, Needham MA 02494. (781)449-6204. Fax: (781)449-9702. E-mail: editor@offshoremag.net. **Contact:** Betsy Frawley Haggerty, editor. Estab. 1976. **80% freelance written.** Monthly magazine covering power and sail boating and the coast from Maine to New Jersey. Circ. 35,000. Publishes ms an average of 5 months after acceptance. Byline given. Offers negotiable kill fee. Buys first North American serial rights. Submit seasonal material 6 months in advance. Accepts simultaneous submissions. *Writer's Market* recommends allowing 2 months for reply. Sample copy for 10×13 SAE with 8 first-class stamps. Writer's guidelines for #10 SASE.

Nonfiction: Articles on boats, boating, New York, New Jersey and New England coastal places and people, Northeast coastal history. Thumbnail and/or outline of topic will elicit response. **Buys 90 mss/year.** Query with writing sample or send complete ms. Length: 1,200-2,500 words. **Pays approximately $350-500 for features depending on length.**

Photos: Reviews 35mm slides only. For covers, pays $300. Pays $150 for last-page photos—humorous or whimsical nautical subjects. Identification of subjects required. Buys one-time rights.

Tips: "Writers must demonstrate a familiarity with boats and with the Northeast coast. Specifically we are looking for articles on boating destinations, boating events (such as races, rendezvous and boat parades), on-the-water boating adventures, boating culture, maritime museums, maritime history, boating issues (such as safety and the environment), seamanship, fishing, how-to stories and essays. Note: Since *Offshore* is a regional magazine, all stories must focus on the area from New Jersey to Maine. We are always open to new people, the best of whom may gradually work their way into regular writing assignments. Important to ask for (and follow) our writer's guidelines if you're not familiar with our magazine."

⭐ $ $ PACIFIC YACHTING, Western Canada's Premier Boating Magazine, OP Publishing Ltd., 780 Beatty St., Suite 300, Vancouver, British Columbia V6B 2M1 Canada. (604)606-4644. Fax: (604)687-1925. E-mail: oppubl@istar.ca. Website: www.oppub.com. **Contact:** Duart Snow, editor. **90% freelance written.** Monthly magazine covering all aspects of recreational boating on British Columbia coast. "The bulk of our writers and photographers not only come from the local boating community, many of them were long-time PY readers before coming aboard as a contributor. The PY reader buys the magazine to read about new destinations or changes to old haunts on the B.C. coast and to learn the latest about boats and gear." Circ. 19,000. Pays on publication. Publishes ms an average of 6 months after acceptance. Byline given. Buys first North American serial and simultaneous rights. Editorial lead time 4 months. Submit seasonal material 6 months in advance. Accepts queries mail, e-mail, fax. Sample copy for $2 plus postage charged to VISA credit card. Writer's guidelines free.

Nonfiction: Historical/nostalgic, how-to, humor, interview/profile, personal experience, travel, cruising and destinations on the B.C. coast. "No articles from writers who are obviously not boaters!" Length: 1,500-2,000 words. Query with SAE and IRCs or by e-mail or phone. **Pays $150-500.** Pays expenses of writers on assignment if arranged in advance.

Photos: Send sample photos with query. Reviews transparencies, 4×6 prints and slides. Offers no additional payment for photos accepted with ms and $25-300/photo not accepted with ms. Identification of subjects required. Buys one-time rights. Covers: (transparencies): $300.

Columns/Departments: Currents (current events, trade and people news, boat gatherings and festivities), 50-250 words. Other departments: Reflections, Cruising, 800-1,000 words. Query. **Pay varies.**

Tips: "We strongly encourage queries before submission (written with SAE and IRCs, or by phone or e-mail). While precise nautical information is important, colorful anecdotes bring your cruise to life. Both are important. In other words, our reader wants you to balance important navigation details with first-person observations, blending the practical with the romantic. Write tight, write short, write with the reader in mind, write to inform, write to entertain. Be specific, accurate and historic."

N **$ $PONTOON & DECK BOAT**, Harris Publishing, Inc., 520 Park Ave., Idaho Falls ID 83402. (208)524-7000. Fax: (208)522-5241. E-mail: scott@pdbworld.com. Website: www.pdbworld.com **Contact:** Scott Springer, editor. **15% freelance written.** Published 8 times/year. "We are a boating niche publication geared towards the pontoon and deck boating lifestyle and consumer market. Our audience is comprised of people who utilize these boats for varied family activities and fishing. Our magazine is promotional of the PDB industry and its major players. We seek to give the reader a two-fold reason to read our publication: to celebrate the lifestyle and to do it aboard a first-class craft." Estab. 1995. Circ. 82,000. Pays on publication. Byline given. Buys one-time rights. Editorial lead time 2 months. Submit seasonal material 3 months in advance. Accepts simultaneous submissions. Responds in 6 weeks to queries; 3 months to mss. Sample copy and writer's guidelines free.

Nonfiction: How-to, personal experience, technical, remodeling, rebuilding. "We are saturated with travel pieces, no general boating, no humor, no fiction, poetry." **Buys 15 mss/year.** Query or send complete ms. Length: 600-2,000 words. **Pays $50-300.** Sometimes pays expenses of writers on assignment.

Photos: State availability of photos. Reviews transparencies. Captions, model releases required. Rights negotiable.

Columns/Departments: No Wake Zone (short, fun quips); Better Boater (how-to). **Buys 6-12 mss/year.** Query with published clips. **Pays $50-150.**

Tips: "Be specific to pontoon and deck boats. Any general boating material goes to the slush pile. The more you can tie together the lifestyle, attitudes and the PDB industry, the more interest we'll take in what you send us."

$ $ $POWER & MOTORYACHT, Primedia, 260 Madison Ave., 8th Floor, New York NY 10016. (917)256-2200. Fax: (917)256-2282. E-mail: dbyrne@primediasi.com. Editor: Richard Thiel. Managing Editor: Jeanine Detz. **Contact:** Diane M. Byrne, exectuve editor. **20% freelance written.** Monthly magazine covering powerboating. "*Power & Motoryacht* is devoted exclusively to the high-end powerboat market, those boats 24 feet or larger. Every reader owns at least one powerboat in this size range. Our magazine reaches virtually every U.S. owner of a 40-foot or larger powerboat—the only publication that does so. For our readers, boating is not a hobby, it's a lifestyle." Estab. 1985. Circ. 157,000. **Pays on acceptance.** Publishes ms an average of 6 months after acceptance. Byline given. Offers 33% kill fee. Buys first North American serial and electronic rights. Editorial lead time up to 1 year. Submit seasonal material 6 months in advance. Accepts queries by mail, e-mail, fax. *No unsolicited mss.* Accepts simultaneous submissions. Responds in 1 month to queries. Sample copy for 10×12 SASE. Writer's guidelines for #10 SASE or by e-mail.

    O− Break in by "knowing the boat business—know which manufacturers specialize in cruising boats vs. sportfishing boats, for example, and know the difference between production-built and semi-custom vessels—and being an authority on the subject you're pitching—our readers can spot uninformed writers!"

Nonfiction: Book excerpts, how-to (how to fix things, install things, shop for boats and accessories smarter, etc.), humor, interview/profile, personal experience, technical, travel. Coming themes: custom yachts; maintenance; US cruising. "Nothing sailing-related! This includes motorsailers!" **Buys 10-15 mss/year.** Query with published clips. *No unsolicited mss.* Length: 800-1,400 words. **Pays $500-1,200.** Sometimes pays expenses of writers on assignment.

Photos: State availability of photos with submission. Reviews 4×5 transparencies; "Slides OK, too." Offers no additional payment for photos accepted with ms. Captions and identification of subjects required. Buys one-time rights.

Tips: "Writers must be authorities on the subject matter they write about—our readers have an average of 31 years' experience on the water, so they want experts to provide advice and information. Some of our regular feature themes are seamanship (rules of the road and boating protocol techniques); cruising (places readers can take their own boats for a few days' enjoyment); maintenance (tips on upkeep and repair); engines (innovations that improve efficiency and/or lessen environmental impact)."

$ $POWER BOATING CANADA, 2585 Skymark Ave., Unit 306, Mississauga, Ontario L4W 4L5 Canada. (905)624-8218. Fax: (905)624-6764. **Contact:** Karen Hill, editor. **70% freelance written.** Bimonthly magazine covering recreational power boating. "*Power Boating Canada* offers boating destinations, how-to features, boat tests (usually staff written), lifestyle pieces—with a Canadian slant—and appeal to recreational power boaters across the country." Estab. 1984. Circ. 50,000. Pays on publication. Publishes ms an average of 3 months after acceptance. Byline given. Buys first North American serial rights. Editorial lead time 2 months. Submit seasonal material 3 months in advance. Responds in 1 month to queries, 2 months to mss. Sample copy free.

Nonfiction: "Any articles related to the sport of power boating, especially boat tests." Historical/nostalgic, how-to, interview/profile, personal experience, travel (boating destinations). No general boating articles or personal anecdotes. **Buys 40-50 mss/year.** Query. Length: 1,200-2,500 words. **Pays $150-300.** Sometimes pays expenses of writers on assignment.

Reprints: Send photocopy of article or typed ms with rights for sale noted and information about when and where the article previously appeared.

Photos: Send photos with submission. Reviews contact sheets, negatives, transparencies, prints. No additional payment for photos accepted with ms. Captions, identification of subjects required. Buys one-time rights. Pay varies.

$ $ $SAIL, 84 State St., Boston MA 02109-2262. (617)720-8600. Fax: (617)723-0912. E-mail: primediasi.com. Website: www.sailmag.com. Editor: Patience Wales. **Contact:** Amy Ullrich, managing editor. **50% freelance written.** Works with a small number of new/unpublished writers each year. Monthly magazine "written and edited for everyone who sails—aboard a coastal or bluewater cruiser, trailerable, one-design or offshore racer, or daysailer. How-to and technical articles concentrate on techniques of sailing and aspects of design and construction, boat systems, and gear; the feature section emphasizes the fun and rewards of sailing in a practical and instructive way." Estab. 1970. Circ.

180,000. **Pays on acceptance.** Byline given. Publishes ms an average of 10 months after acceptance. Buys first North American rights. Submit seasonal or special material at least 6 months in advance. Accepts queries by mail, e-mail, fax. Responds in 10 weeks. Writer's guidelines for SASE or on website.

Nonfiction: Technical, techniques, how-to, personal experience, distance cruising, destinations. "Generally emphasize the excitement of sail and the human, personal aspect. No day-by-day logs." Length: 1,500-3,000 words. Examples of shorter features are: vignettes of day sailing, cruising and racing life (at home or abroad, straight or humorous); maritime history; astronomy; marine life; cooking; nautical love; fishing; boat owning, boat building and outfitting; regatta reports. Length: 1,000-1,500 words. Special issues: "Cruising, chartering, fitting-out, special race (e.g., America's Cup), boat show." **Buys 100 mss/year** (freelance and commissioned). Query with SASE. **Pays $200-800.** Sometimes pays the expenses of writers on assignment.

Reprints: Send photocopy of article or typed ms with rights for sale noted and information about when and where the article previously appeared. Pays 33-50% of amount paid for an original article.

Photos: Offers additional payment for photos. Uses 50-100 ASA transparencies. Identification of subjects, captions and credits required. Pay varies, on publication. Pays $600 if photo is used on the cover.

Columns/Departments: Sailing Memories (short essay); Sailing News (cruising, racing, legal, political, environmental). Query. **Pays $25-400.**

▣ The online magazine carries original content not found in the print edition and includes writer's guidelines. Contact: Amy Ullrich or Josh Adams, online editors.

Tips: "Request an articles specification sheet. We look for unique ways of viewing sailing. Skim old issues of *Sail* for ideas about the types of articles we publish. Always remember that *Sail* is a sailing magazine. Stay away from gloomy articles detailing all the things that went wrong on your boat. Think constructively and write about how to avoid certain problems. You should focus on a theme or choose some aspect of sailing and discuss a personal attitude or new philosophical approach to the subject. Notice that we have certain issues devoted to special themes—for example, chartering, electronics, commissioning, and the like. Stay away from pieces that chronicle your journey in the day-by-day style of a logbook. These are generally dull and uninteresting. Select specific actions or events (preferably sailing events, not shorebound activities), and build your articles around them. Emphasize the sailing."

$ $ $ SAILING MAGAZINE, 125 E. Main St., Port Washington WI 53074-0249. (262)284-3494. Fax: (262)284-7764. E-mail: sailing@execpc.com. Website: www.sailingonline.com. **Contact:** Gregory O. Jones, editor. Publisher: William F. Schanen, III. Monthly magazine for the experienced sailor. Estab. 1966. Circ. 52,000. Pays on publication. Buys one-time rights. Accepts queries by mail, e-mail, fax. Responds in 2 months.

○┐ "Let us get to know your writing with short newsy, sailing-oriented pieces with good slides for our Splashes section. Query for upcoming theme issues; read the magazine; writing must show the writer loves sailing as much as our readers. We are always looking for fresh stories on new destinations with vibrant writing and top-notch photography. Always looking for short (100-1,500 word) articles or newsy items."

Nonfiction: "Experiences of sailing, cruising and racing or cruising to interesting locations, whether a small lake near you or islands in the Southern Ocean, with first-hand knowledge and tips for our readers. Top-notch photos (transparencies only), with maps, charts, cruising information complete the package. No regatta sports unless there is a story involved." Must be written to AP Stylebook. **Buys 15-20 mss/year.** Length: 750-2,500 words. Must be accompanied by photos, and maps if applicable. **Pays $100-800.**

Photos: Color photos (transparencies) purchased with or without accompanying text. Captions required. Pays $50-300.

Tips: Prefers text in Word on disk for Mac or to e-mail address. "No attached files, please."

$ $ SAILING WORLD, Miller Sports Group, LLC, 5 John Clarke Rd., Box 3400, Newport RI 02840-0992. Fax: (401)848-5048. E-mail: editorial@sailingworld.com. Website: www.sailingworld.com. Editor: John Burnham. **Contact:** Kristan McClintock, managing editor. **40% freelance written.** Monthly magazine emphasizing performance sailing. Estab. 1962. Circ. 66,000. Pays on publication. Publishes ms an average of 4 months after acceptance. Buys first North American and world serial rights. Byline given. Responds in 3 months. Sample copy for $5.

○┐ Break in with short articles and fillers such as regatta news reports from your own area.

Nonfiction: How-to for racing and performance-oriented sailors, photo feature, profile, regatta reports and charter. No travelogs. **Buys 5-10 unsolicited mss/year.** Query. Length: 500-1,500 words. **Pays $600 for up to 2,000 words.**

Tips: "Send query with outline and include your experience. Prospective contributors should study recent issues of the magazine to determine appropriate subject matter. The emphasis here is on performance sailing: keep in mind that the *Sailing World* readership is relatively educated about the sport. Unless you are dealing with a totally new aspect of sailing, you can and should discuss ideas on an advanced technical level. 'Gee-whiz' impressions from beginning sailors are generally not accepted."

✪ $ $ SEA KAYAKER, Sea Kayaker, Inc., P.O. Box 17170, Seattle WA 98107-0870. (206)789-1326. Fax: (206)781-1141. E-mail: mail@seakayakermag.com. Website: www.seakayakermag.com. **Contact:** Leslie Forsberg, executive editor. Editor: Christopher Cunningham. **95% freelance written.** Works frequently with new/unpublished writers each year. "*Sea Kayaker* is a bimonthly publication with a worldwide readership that covers all aspects of kayak touring. It is well-known as an important source of continuing education by the most experienced paddlers." Estab. 1984. Circ. 25,000. Pays on publication. Publishes ms an average of 6 months after acceptance. Byline given. Offers 10% kill fee.

Buys first North American serial or second serial (reprint) rights. Editorial lead time 4 months. Submit seasonal material 4 months in advance. Accepts queries by mail, e-mail, fax, phone. Responds in 2 months. Sample copy for $5.75. Writer's guidelines for SASE or on website.

Nonfiction: Essays, historical, how-to (on making equipment), humor, new product, profile, opinion, personal experience, technical, travel. **Buys 50 mss/year.** Query or send complete ms. Length: 1,500-5,000 words. **Pays 18-20¢/word for assigned articles; 12-15¢/word for unassigned articles.**

Photos: Send photos with submission. Reviews transparencies and prints. Offers $15-400. Captions and identification of subjects required. Buys one-time rights.

Columns/Departments: Technique, Equipment, Do-It-Yourself, Food, Safety, Health, Environment, Book Reviews. Length: 1,000-2,500 words. **Buys 40-45 mss/year.** Query. **Pays 18-20¢/word for assigned articles; 12-15¢/word for unassigned articles.**

Tips: "We consider unsolicited manuscripts that include a SASE, but we give greater priority to brief descriptions (several paragraphs) of proposed articles accompanied by at least two samples—published or unpublished—of your writing. Enclose a statement as to why you're qualified to write the piece and indicate whether photographs or illustrations are available to accompany the piece."

$ $ SOUTHERN BOATING MAGAZINE, The South's Largest Boating Magazine, Southern Boating & Yachting Inc., 330 N. Andrews Ave., Ft. Lauderdale FL 33301. (954)522-5575. Fax: (954)522-2260. E-mail: sboating@southernboating.com. Editor: Skip Allen. Executive Editor: David Strickland. **50% freelance written.** "Upscale monthly yachting magazine focusing on SE U.S., Bahamas, Caribbean and Gulf of Mexico." Estab. 1972. Circ. 40,000. Pays on publication. Publishes ms an average of 2 months after acceptance. Byline given. Buys one-time rights. Editorial lead time 6 weeks. Submit seasonal material 2 months in advance. Accepts queries by mail, e-mail, fax, phone. Sample copy free.

 O→ Break in with destination, how-to and technical articles.

Nonfiction: How-to (boat maintenance), travel (boating related and destination pieces). **Buys 100 mss/year.** Query. Length: 600-3,000 words. **Pays $200.**

Reprints: Accepts previously published submissions.

Photos: State availability of or send photos. Reviews transparencies, prints. Offers $50/photo maximum; negotiates payment individually. Captions, model releases and identification of subjects required. Buys one-time rights.

Columns/Departments: Weekend Workshop (how to/maintenance), 600 words; What's New in Electronics (electronics), 1,000 words; Engine Room (new developments), 1,000 words. **Buys 24 mss/year.** Query. **Pays $150.**

$ $ TRAILER BOATS MAGAZINE, Poole Publications, Inc., 20700 Belshaw Ave., Carson CA 90746-3510. (310)537-6322. Fax: (310)537-8735. E-mail: editors@trailerboats.com. Website: www.trailerboats.com. Executive Editor: Ron Eldridge. **Contact:** Jim Henricks, editor. **50% freelance written.** Works with a small number of new/unpublished writers each year. Monthly magazine (November/December issue combined) covering legally trailerable power boats and related powerboating activities. Estab. 1971. Circ. 85,000. **Pays on acceptance.** Publishes ms 3 months after acceptance. Byline given. Buys all rights. Editorial lead time 4 months. Submit seasonal material 5 months in advance. Responds in 1 month. Sample copy for 9 × 12 SAE with 7 first-class stamps.

Nonfiction: General interest (trailer boating activities); historical (places, events, boats); how-to (repair boats, installation, etc.); humor (almost any power boating-related subject); personal experience; photo feature; profile; technical; travel (boating travel on water or highways); product evaluations. Annual new boat review. No "How I Spent My Summer Vacation" stories, or stories not directly connected to trailerable boats and related activities. **Buys 70-80 unsolicited mss/year.** Query by mail only. Length: 1,000-2,500 words. **Pays $150-1,000.** Sometimes pays expenses of writers on assignment.

Photos: Send photos with ms. Reviews transparencies (2¼ × 2¼) and 35mm slides. Captions, model releases and identification of subjects required. Buys one-time rights, reprint rights and Internet rights.

Columns/Departments: Over the Transom (funny or strange boating photos); Watersports (boat-related); Marine Electronics (what and how to use); Back to Basics (elementary boating tips), all 1,000-1,500 words. **Buys 60-70/year.** Query by mail only. **Pays $250-450.** Open to suggestions for new columns/departments.

Tips: "Query should contain short general outline of the intended material; what kind of photos; how the photos illustrate the piece. Write with authority, covering the subject with quotes from experts. Frequent mistakes are not knowing the subject matter or the audience. The writer may have a better chance of breaking in at our publication with short articles and fillers if they are typically hard-to-find articles. We do most major features inhouse, but try how-to stories dealing with smaller boats, installation and towing tips, boat trailer repair. Good color photos will win our hearts every time."

[N] $ $ WATERWAY GUIDE, Intertec Publishing Corp., a Primedia Co., 6151 Powers Ferry Rd. NW, Atlanta GA 30339-2941. (770)618-0320. Fax: (770)618-0347. E-mail: emily_pike@intertec.com. Website: www.waterwayguide.com. **Contact:** Judith Powers, editor. **90% freelance written.** Triannual magazine on intracoastal waterway travel for recreational boats. "Writer must be knowledgeable about navigation and the areas covered by the guide." Estab. 1947. Circ. 30,000. Pays on publication. Publishes ms 3 months after acceptance. Byline given. Buys first North American serial rights, electronic rights and makes work-for-hire assignments. Editorial lead time 4 months. Submit seasonal material 3 months in advance. Accepts queries by mail, e-mail, fax, phone. Responds in 6 weeks to queries; 2 months to mss. Sample copy for $39.95 with $3 postage.

Nonfiction: Essays, historical/nostalgic, how-to, photo feature, technical, travel. **Buys 6 mss/year.** Query with or without published clips, or send complete ms. Length: 250-5,000 words. **Pays $50-500.** Pays in contributor copies or other premiums for helpful tips and useful information.

Photos: Send photos with submission. Reviews transparencies and 3×5 prints. Offers $25-50/photo. Captions and identification of subjects required. Buys all rights.

Tips: "Must have on-the-water experience and be able to provide new and accurate information on geographic areas covered by *Waterway Guide*."

$ WAVE-LENGTH PADDLING MAGAZINE, Wave-Length Communications, Inc., R.R. 1, Site 17, C-49, Gabriola Island, British Columbia V0R 1X0 Canada. Phone/fax: (250)247-9789. E-mail: wavenet@island.net. Website: www. wavelengthmagazine.com. **Contact:** Alan Wilson, editor. **75% freelance written.** Bimonthly magazine covering sea kayaking. "We promote safe paddling, guide paddlers to useful products and services and explore coastal environmental issues." Estab. 1991. Circ. 20,000 plus Internet readers. Pays on publication. Publishes ms an average of 4 months after acceptance. Byline given. Offers 10% kill fee. Buys first North American serial and electronic reprint rights. Editorial lead time 2 months. Submit seasonal material 2 months in advance. Accepts queries by mail, e-mail. Responds in 2 months. Sample copy and writer's guidelines for $2 or on website.

○━ "Sea kayaking content, even if from a beginner's perspective, is essential. We like a light approach to personal experiences and humor is appreciated. Good detail (with maps and pics) for destinations material. Write to our feature focus."

Nonfiction: Personal experience, trips, advice, book excerpts, how-to (paddle, travel), humor, interview/profile, new product, opinion, technical. **Buys 25 mss/year.** Query. Length: 1,000-2,000 words. **Pays $50-75.** Pays businesses with advertising.

Photos: State availability of photos with query. Reviews 4×6 prints. Offers $25/photo; $50 for covers (must be vertical). Captions and identification of subjects required. Buys first and electronic rights. Query.

Fillers: Anecdotes, facts, gags to be illustrated by cartoonist, newsbreaks and short humor. **Buys 8-10/year.** Length: 25-250 words. **Pays $10-25.**

▣ The online magazine contains original content not found in the print edition and includes writer's guidelines.

Tips: "You must know paddling—although novice paddlers are welcome. A strong environmental or wilderness appreciation component is advisable. We are willing to help refine work with flexible people. E-mail queries preferred. Check out our Editorial Calendar for our upcoming features."

$ $ WOODENBOAT MAGAZINE, The Magazine for Wooden Boat Owners, Builders, and Designers, WoodenBoat Publications, Inc., P.O. Box 78, Brooklin ME 04616. (207)359-4651. Fax: (207)359-8920. Website: www.m edia4.hypernet.com/~WOODENBOAT/wb.htm. Editor-in-Chief: Jonathan A. Wilson. Senior Editor: Mike O'Brien. Associate Editor: Tom Jackson. **Contact:** Matthew P. Murphy, editor. **50% freelance written.** Works with a small number of new/unpublished writers each year. Bimonthly magazine for wooden boat owners, builders and designers. "We are devoted exclusively to the design, building, care, preservation, and use of wooden boats, both commercial and pleasure, old and new, sail and power. We work to convey quality, integrity and involvement in the creation and care of these craft, to entertain, inform, inspire, and to provide our varied readers with access to individuals who are deeply experienced in the world of wooden boats." Estab. 1974. Circ. 106,000. Pays on publication. Publishes ms an average of 1 year after acceptance. Byline given. Offers variable kill fee. Buys first North American serial rights. Accepts simultaneous submissions. Responds in 3 weeks to queries; 2 months to mss. Sample copy for $4.50. Writer's guidelines for SASE.

Nonfiction: Technical (repair, restoration, maintenance, use, design and building wooden boats). No poetry, fiction. **Buys 50 mss/year.** Query with published clips. Length: 1,500-5,000 words. **Pays $200-250/1,000 words.** Sometimes pays expenses of writers on assignment.

Reprints: Send tearsheet or photocopy of article or typed ms with rights for sale noted information about when and where the article previously appeared.

Photos: Send photos with query. Negatives must be available. Pays $15-75 for b&w; $25-350 for color. Identification of subjects required. Buys one-time rights.

Columns/Departments: On the Waterfront pays for information on wooden boat-related events, projects, boatshop activities, etc. **Buys 25/year.** "We use the same columnists for each issue." Send complete information. Length: 250-1,000 words. **Pays $5-50 for information.**

Tips: "We appreciate a detailed, articulate query letter, accompanied by photos, that will give us a clear idea of what the author is proposing. We appreciate samples of previously published work. It is important for a prospective author to become familiar with our magazine first. It is extremely rare for us to make an assignment with a writer with whom we have not worked before. Most work is submitted on speculation. The most common failure is not exploring the subject material in enough depth."

$ $ $ YACHTING, Times Mirror Magazines Inc., 20 E. Elm St., Greenwich CT 06830. (203)625-4480. Fax: (203)625-4481. Publisher: Peter Beckenbach. Editor-in-Chief: Kenny Wooton. **30-40% freelance written.** "Monthly magazine written and edited for experienced, knowledgeable yachtsmen." Estab. 1907. Circ. 132,000. **Pays on acceptance.** Byline given. Buys first North American serial rights and electronic rights. Editorial lead time 2 months. Submit seasonal material 6 months in advance. Accepts queries by mail, e-mail, fax. Responds in 1 month to queries, 3 months to mss. Sample copy free. Writer's guidelines on website.

Nonfiction: Personal experience, technical. **Buys 50 mss/year.** Query with published clips. Length: 750-800 words. **Pays $150-1,500.** Pays expenses of writers on assignment.

- Ranked as one of the best markets for freelance writer's in *Writer's Yearbook* magazine's annual "Top 100 Markets," January 2000.

Photos: Send photos with submission. Reviews transparencies. Negotiates payment individually. Captions, model releases and identification of subjects required.

Tips: "We require considerable expertise in our writing because our audience is experienced and knowledgeable. Vivid descriptions of quaint anchorages and quainter natives are fine, but our readers want to know how the yachtsmen got there, too. They also want to know how their boats work. *Yachting* is edited for experienced, affluent boatowners—power and sail—who don't have the time or the inclination to read sub-standard stories. They love carefully crafted stories about places they've never been or a different spin on places they have, meticulously reported pieces on issues that affect their yachting lives, personal accounts of yachting experiences from which they can learn, engaging profiles of people who share their passion for boats, insightful essays that evoke the history and traditions of the sport and compelling photographs of others enjoying the game as much as they do. They love to know what to buy and how things work. They love to be surprised. They don't mind getting their hands dirty or saving a buck here and there, but they're not interested in learning how to make a masthead light out of a mayonnaise jar. If you love what they love and can communicate like a pro (that means meeting deadlines, writing tight, being obsessively accurate and never misspelling a proper name), we'd love to hear from you."

Gambling

N $ $ CHANCE MAGAZINE, The Best of Gaming, ARC Publishing, LLC, 16 E. 41st St., 2nd Floor, New York NY 10017. Fax: (212)889-3630. E-mail: bphillips@chancemag.com. Website: www.chancemag.com. **Contact:** Buster Phillips, managing editor. **50% freelance written.** Magazine published bimonthly covering gambling lifestyle, upscale resorts, food, wine, spas, etc. "*Chance* is an upscale magazine for readers interested in getting the most out of a gambling vacation. From travel, resorts and spas, to tips and advice on gaming, *Chance* is a smartly written and fun guide for the gaming connoisseur." Circ. 165,000. Pays on publication. Publishes ms an average of 3 months after acceptance. Byline given. Offers 25% kill fee. Buys first North American serial rights. Editorial lead time 6 months. Submit seasonal material 6 months in advance. Accepts queries by mail, e-mail, fax. Sample copy on website.

Nonfiction: General interest, how-to, interview/profile, personal experience, photo feature, anything gambling related. No systems or self-promotion. **Buys 50 mss/year.** Query with published clips or send complete ms. Length: 1,200-3,500 words. **Pays $150-650 for assigned articles; $75-500 for unsolicited articles.** Sometimes pays expenses of writers on assignment.

Photos: State availability of photos with submission or send photos with submission. Negotiates payment individually. Rights negotiated.

Columns/Departments: The Intelligent Player (advanced advice for the serious gambler), 2,000 words; Ante (short, quick upfront pieces), 300-600 words; Ramblin' Gambler (fun stories on out-of-the-way casinos), 2,000 words. **Buys 12 mss/year.** Query with published clips or send complete ms. **Pays $150-500.**

Tips: "Either be a gambling fan with specific knowledge or be familiar with the life of a high roller—luxuries that somehow tie in to casinos and gaming. Above all, be a good writer with experience."

General Interest

$ ALL-STATER SPORTS, America's High School Sports Magazine, All-Stater Publishing, LLC, 1373 Grandview Ave., Suite 206, Columbus OH 43212. (614)487-1280. Fax: (614)487-1283. E-mail: jvaughn@all-statersport s.com. Website: www.all-statersports.com. **Contact:** Jessica Vaughn, associate editor. **80% freelance written.** Bi-monthly magazine. "The mission of *All-Stater Sports* is to inform, inspire and recognize today's high school student-athlete. Our audience consists of student-athletes, coaches and athletic directors, but our intention is to speak primarily to student-athletes." Estab. 1995. Circ. 100,000. Pays on publication. Publishes ms an average of 1 month after acceptance. Byline given. Editorial lead time 2 weeks. Submit seasonal material 1 month in advance. Accepts simultaneous submissions. Accepts queries by mail, e-mail, fax, phone. Responds in 1 month. Sample copy $5 for writers only.

FOR EXPLANATIONS OF THESE SYMBOLS, SEE THE INSIDE FRONT AND BACK COVERS OF THIS BOOK.

O→ Break in with profiles of nationally ranked high school athletes or teams, tournaments with regional or national interest.

Nonfiction: How-to (training, cross-training, strength building, etc.), humor, inspirational, interview/profile, new product, opinion, personal experience, photo feature, technical (sports issues, skill building). **Pay is negotiable on a per story basis.** "Profiles writers in our contributor's column, provides extra copies of issue, plugs product, institution, company, etc." Only stories will be printed with photos.

Reprints: Send typed ms with rights for sale noted and information about when and where it previously appeared.

Photos: State availability of photos with submission. Reviews 5×7 minimum prints. Negotiates payment individually. Model release (if deemed necessary) and identification of subjects required. Buys one-time rights.

Columns/Departments: Getting The Edge (sports training/skill building), 1,200 words; Next Step articles about college sports, 1,200 words; Winning with Heart (overcoming the odds to play high school sports), 1,000 words; In Recognition of Sportsmanship (specific act of sportsmanship in high school sports—real incidents), 1,000 words. Profiles (short articles on outstanding current student athletes). **Buys 10-15 unsolicited mss/year.** Query. Pay negotiable.

Fillers: Anecdotes, facts, gags to be illustrated, newsbreaks, embarrassing sports moments, college signings (300-500 words), short humor. Length: 50-300 words. **Pays $15-30.**

▣ The online version contains material not found in the print edition. Contact: Matt Booher.

Tips: "We are happy to consider any material that would be of interest to high school athletes—even something that is not already included in our issues printed to date. No fiction or poetry. We profile outstanding achievers, but would also like to have human interest stories of accomplishment, satisfaction, sportsmanship, obsessive fans, original coaching methods, team bonding, unusually fine coaches, etc., from non-blue chipper's perspective as well."

$ $ROCKY MOUNTAIN SPORTS MAGAZINE, Rocky Mountain Sports, Inc., 1521 Central St., Suite 1C, Denver CO 80211. (303)477-9770. Fax: (303)477-9747. E-mail: editorial@rockymountainsports.com. Website: www.rockymountainsports.com. Publisher: Mary Thorne. **Contact:** Kellee Katagi, editor. **50% freelance written.** Monthly magazine of sports in Colorado. "*Rocky* is a magazine for sports-related lifestyles and activities. Our mission is to reflect and inspire the active lifestyle of Rocky Mountain residents." Estab. 1986. Circ. 80,000. Pays on publication. Publishes ms an average of 2 months after acceptance. Byline given. Offers kill fee. Buys second serial (reprint) rights. Editorial lead time 3 months. Submit seasonal material 2 months in advance. Accepts queries by mail, e-mail, fax. Responds in 3 weeks to queries; 2 months to mss. Sample copy and writer's guidelines for #10 SASE.

● The editor says she wants to see mountain outdoor sports writing *only*. No ball sports, hunting or fishing.

Nonfiction: Book excerpts, essays, exposé, how-to, humor, inspirational, interview/profile, new product, opinion, personal experience, photo feature, travel. Interested in seeing good nutrition or sports medicine articles. Special issues: Snowboarding (December); Alpine and Nordic (January and February); Running (March); Adventure Travel (April), Triathlon (May), Paddling and Climbing (July), Mountain Biking (June), Women's Sports (September). No articles on football, baseball, basketball or other sports covered in-depth by newspapers. **Buys 24 mss/year.** Query with published clips. Length: 2,500 words maximum. **Pays $150 minimum.** Also publishes short articles on active outdoor sports, catch-all topics that are seasonably targeted. Query with idea first by mail or e-mail. Sometimes pays expenses of writers on assignment.

Reprints: Send photocopy of article and information about when and where the article previously appeared. Pays 20-25% of amount paid for an original article.

Photos: State availability of photos with submission. Reviews transparencies and prints. Captions and identification of subjects required. Buys one-time rights.

Columns/Departments: Starting Lines (short newsy items); Running, Cycling, Fitness, Nutrition, Sports Medicine, Off the Beaten Path (sports we don't usually cover). **Buys 20 mss/year.** Query. **Pays $25-200.**

Tips: "Have a Colorado angle to the story, a catchy cover letter, good clips and demonstrate that you've read and understand our magazine and its readers."

$SILENT SPORTS, Waupaca Publishing Co., P.O. Box 152, Waupaca WI 54981-9990. (715)258-5546. Fax: (715)258-8162. E-mail: info@silentsports.net. Website: www.silentsports.net. **Contact:** Greg Marr, editor. **75% freelance written.** Eager to work with new/unpublished writers. Monthly magazine on running, cycling, cross-country skiing, canoeing, kayaking, snowshoeing, in-line skating, camping, backpacking and hiking aimed at people in Wisconsin, Minnesota, northern Illinois and portions of Michigan and Iowa. "Not a coffee table magazine. Our readers are participants from rank amateur weekend athletes to highly competitive racers." Estab. 1984. Circ. 10,000. Pays on publication. Publishes ms an average of 3 months after acceptance. Byline given. Offers 20% kill fee. Buys one-time rights. Submit seasonal material 4 months in advance. Responds in 3 months. Sample copy and writer's guidelines for 10×13 SAE with 6 first-class stamps.

● The editor needs local angles on in-line skating, recreation bicycling and snowshoeing.

Nonfiction: General interest, how-to, interview/profile, opinion, technical, travel. All stories/articles must focus on the Upper Midwest. First-person articles discouraged. **Buys 25 mss/year.** Query. Length: 2,500 words maximum. **Pays $15-100.** Sometimes pays expenses of writers on assignment.

Reprints: Send typed ms with rights for sale noted and information about when and where the article previously appeared. Pays 50% of amount paid for an original article.

Photos: State availability of photos with submission. Reviews transparencies. Pays $5-15 for b&w story photos; $50 for color covers. Buys one-time rights.

Tips: "Where-to-go and personality profiles are areas most open to freelancers. Writers should keep in mind that this is a regional, Midwest-based publication. We want only stories/articles with a focus on our region."

$ $ $ SPIKE, The Magazine from Finish Line, Emmis Publishing, One Emmis Plaza, 40 Monument Circle, Suite 100, Indianapolis IN 46204. E-mail: jbt@indymonthly.emmis.com. **Contact:** John Thomas, special projects editor. **100% freelance written.** Quarterly. "*Spike* goes to customers of Finish Line, a chain of more than 300 athletic shoe and apparel stores. Most readers are young males with an interest in sports and pop culture. Writing should be bright, hip and tight." Estab. 1997. Circ. 1 million. Pays on publication. Publishes ms 3 months after acceptance. Byline given. Buys first North American serial rights and one-time rights. Editorial lead time 4 months. Submit seasonal material 6 months in advance. Accepts queries by mail, e-mail. Sample copy for 9×12 SAE and 5 first-class stamps.

Nonfiction: General interest, how-to (fitness), interview/profile, new product. *No unsolicited mss.* No first-person essays. **Buys 12-15 mss/year.** Query with published clips. Length: 750-2,000 words. **Pays $250-1,000.** Sometimes pays expenses of writers on assignment.

• Ranked as one of the best markets for freelance writers in *Writer's Yearbook* magazine's annual "Top 100 Markets," January 2000.

Columns/Departments: Fitness (for ages 15-20); Music (hot new groups); High Tech (games, web pages, etc. that are sports related), all 500-750 words. **Buys 12 mss/year.** Query with published clips. **Pays $50-500.**

Tips: "Demonstrated access to and ability to work with top athletes and pop-culture figures is a plus."

⊠ $ $ $ SPORT, EMAP USA, 110 Fifth Ave., 3rd Floor, New York NY 10011. (212)886-3600. Fax: (212)229-4838. E-mail: sport@emapusa.com. Website: www.emapusa.com. Managing Editor: Steve Gordon. Editor: Norb Garrett. **Contact:** John Roach, executive editor. **10% freelance written.** Monthly magazine "for the active adult sports fan. *Sport* offers profiles of the players and the people behind the scenes in the world of sports. *Sport* magazine is the oldest, largest, monthly sports feature publication reaching over 4.3 million young, active, sports-minded enthusiasts each issue. Not a recap of what happened last week, but previews and predictions of what will happen this month, next month, next year. In-depth profiles, investigative reporting, lively features about the action on and off the field! *Sport* magazine is the complete sports magazine written and edited for the ultimate sports fan!" Estab. 1946. Circ. 1 million. Pays on publication. Publishes ms an average of 2 months after acceptance. Offers ⅓% kill fee. Buys first North American serial and electronic rights. Editorial lead time 6 weeks. Submit seasonal material 6 months in advance. Responds in 2 months.

Nonfiction: Book excerpts, exposé, historic/nostalgic, humor, interview/profile, photo feature, travel. "Prefers to see articles on professional, big-time sports: basketball, football, baseball, hockey, some boxing. Articles must be contemporary pieces, not a history of sports or a particular sport." **Pays $1/word.**

Columns/Departments: Scott Burton, sections editor. Business (how sports affect fans), 800 words; Media (features on top broadcast talent), 1,200 words; Raw Sport (photo-driven look at emerging sports), 400 words. **Buys 40 ms/year.** Query with published clips. **Pays $1/word.**

Fiction: Norb Garret, editor. Sports. **Buys 1 ms/year.** Query with published clips. Send complete ms. Length: 1,200-3,600 words. **Pays $1/word.**

Tips: "Do not query. We accept no unsolicited work without phone calls or e-mail contact."

N $ $ $ THE SPORTING LIFE, TSL, TSL Publications Inc., 21 E. 40th St., New York NY 10016. (212)696-2484. Fax: (212)696-1678. E-mail: racquet@walrus.com. **Contact:** Stephen Weiss, editor. **50% freelance written.** Bimonthly magazine covering sports and lifestyle. Estab. 1998. Circ. 150,000. Pays on publication. Publishes ms an average of 3 months after acceptance. Byline given. Offers 50% kill fee. Buys first North American serial rights. Editorial lead time 3 months. Submit seasonal material 3 months in advance. Accepts queries by mail, e-mail, fax. Accepts simultaneous submissions. Responds in 1 month to queries; 6 months to mss. Sample copy for $4.95. Writer's guidelines free.

Nonfiction: Book excerpts, essays, exposé, general interest, historical/nostalgic, how-to, humor, interview/profile, new product, personal experience, photo feature, technical, travel. **Buys 20 mss/year.** Send complete ms. Length: 400-3,000 words. **Pays $125-1,000 for assigned articles; $125-750 for unsolicited articles.** Sometimes pays expenses of writers on assignment.

Reprints: Accepts previously published submissions.

Photos: State availability of photos with submission. Reviews transparencies. Negotiates payment individually. Captions required. Buys one-time rights.

Columns/Departments: Essentials (an element of style), 500 words. **Buys 6 mss/year.** Send complete ms. **Pays $150-400.**

Tips: "Read the magazine to get a sense of our style."

$ SPORTS ETC, The Northwest's Outdoor Magazine, Sports Etc, P.O. Box 9272, Seattle WA 98109. (206)286-8566. Fax: (206)286-1330. E-mail: staff@sportsetc.com. Website: www.sportsetc.com. **Contact:** Carolyn Price, editor. **80% freelance written.** Monthly magazine covering outdoor recreation in the Pacific Northwest. "Writers must have a solid knowledge of the sport they are writing about. They must be doers." Estab. 1988. Circ. 50,000. Pays on publication. Publishes ms an average of 3 months after acceptance. Byline given. Buys first rights. Editorial lead time 2 months. Submit seasonal material 4 months in advance. Accepts queries by mail, e-mail, fax. Accepts simultaneous submissions. Sample copy and writer's guidelines $3.

Nonfiction: Interview/profile, new product, travel. Query with published clips. Length: 750-1,500 words. **Pays $10-50.** Sometimes pays expenses of writers on assignment.

Reprints: Accepts previously published submissions.

Photos: Send photos with submission. Reviews negatives and transparencies. Captions, model releases and identification of subjects required. Buys all rights.

Columns/Departments: Your Health (health and wellness), 750 words. **Buys 10-12 mss/year.** Query with published clips. **Pays $40-50.**

▣ The online magazine carries original content not found in the print edition.

Tips: "*Sports Etc* is written for the serious Pacific Northwest outdoor recreationalist. The magazine's look, style and editorial content actively engage the reader, delivering insightful perspectives on the sports it has come to be known for—alpine skiing, bicycling, hiking, in-line skating, kayaking, marathons, mountain climbing, Nordic skiing, running and snowboarding. *Sports Etc* magazine wants vivid writing, telling images and original perspectives to produce its smart, entertaining monthly."

$ $ $ $ SPORTS ILLUSTRATED, Time Inc. Magazine Co., Time & Life Bldg., Rockefeller Center, New York NY 10020. (212)522-1212. **Contact:** Myra Gelband. Weekly. "*Sports Illustrated* reports and interprets the world of sport, recreation and active leisure. It previews, analyzes and comments upon major games and events, as well as those noteworthy for character and spirit alone. It features individuals connected to sport and evaluates trends concerning the part sport plays in contemporary life. In addition, the magazine has articles on such subjects as fashion, physical fitness and conservation. Special departments deal with sports equipment, books and statistics." Estab. 1954. Circ. 3,339,000. Query only by mail before submitting.

$ $ TSL, TSL Publications, 21 E. 40th St., 13th Floor, New York NY 10016. (212)696-2484. Fax: (212)696-1678. E-mail: racquet@walrus.com. **Contact:** Stephen Weiss, managing editor. **30% freelance written.** Bimonthly sports/lifestyle magazine. "*TSL* celebrates the lifestyle of the game." Estab. 1978. Circ. 145,000. Pays on publication. Publishes ms an average of 3 months after acceptance. Byline given. Offers negotiable kill fee. Rights purchased negotiable. Submit seasonal material 5 months in advance. Accepts simultaneous submissions. Accepts queries by mail, e-mail, fax. Responds in 1 month. Sample copy for $4.

● *TSL*, formerly *Racquet*, has enlarged its focus from tennis to general sporting lifestyle.

Nonfiction: Regular Features: Gear (the best new equipment); TSL Journal (a guide for the sophisticated traveler); Fashion (sporting looks for the season); Essentials (style, travel and trends); Personal Best (health and fitness); Passions (celebrities and the sports they love); Destinations (top sporting resorts around the world); Traditions (the classic sporting events). **Buys 15-20 mss/year.** Query. Length: 1,000-4,000 words. **Pays $200-750 for assigned articles; $100-300 for unsolicited articles.** Sometime pays expenses of writers on assignment.

Reprints: Send tearsheet or photocopy of article and information about when and where the article previously appeared.

Photos: State availability of photos with submission. Offers no additional payment for photos accepted with ms. Rights negotiable.

Columns/Departments: Buys 5-10 mss/year. Query. **Pays $100-300.**

Fiction: Publishes novel excerpts.

Fillers: Anecdotes, short humor. **Buys 5/year.** Length: 250-750 words. **Pays $50-150.**

Tips: "Get a copy, understand how we approach sports, submit article written to style and follow up. We are always looking for innovative or humorous ideas."

Golf

N $ $ ARIZONA, THE STATE OF GOLF, TPG Sports Inc., 1710 Douglas Dr. N., Golden Valley MN 55422. (763)595-0808. Fax: (763)595-0016. E-mail: joe@tpgsports.com or rchrist@azgolf.org. Website: www.tpgsports.com or www.azgolf.org. Editor: Russ Christ. (603)944-3035. **Contact:** Joseph Oberle, publications manager, (763)595-0808, ext. 114. **50% freelance written.** Bimonthly magazine covering golf in Arizona, the official publication of the Arizona Golf Association. Estab. 1999. Circ. 45,000. **Pays on acceptance** or publication. Byline given. Buys all rights. Editorial lead time 6 months. Submit seasonal material 3 months in advance. Accepts queries by mail. Accepts simultaneous submissions. Sample copy and writer's guidelines free.

Nonfiction: Book excerpts, essays, historical/nostalgic, how-to (golf), humor, inspirational, interview/profile, new product, opinion, personal experience, photo feature. **Buys 20-30 mss/year.** Query with or without published clips. Length: 500-2,000 words. **Pays $50-500.** Sometimes pays expenses of writers on assignment.

Reprints: Accepts previously published submissions.

Photos: State availability of photos with submission. Reviews contact sheets. Negotiates payment individually. Captions, identification of subjects required. Negotiates payment individually. Rights purchased varies.

Columns/Departments: Short Strokes (golf news and notes), Improving your game (golf tips), Out of Bounds (guest editorial—800 words). Query.

$ $ CHICAGO DISTRICT GOLFER, TPG Sports Inc., 1710 Douglas Dr. N., Golden Valley MN 55422. (763)595-0808. Fax: (763)595-0016. E-mail: joe@tpgsports.com or rdoyle@cdga.org. Website: www.tpgsports.com or www.cdga.org. Editor: Ryan Doyle (630)954-2180. **Contact:** Joseph Oberle, publications manager, (763)595-0808, ext. 114. **90% freelance written.** Bimonthly magazine covering golf in Illinois, the official publication of the Chicago District Golf Association and Golf Association of Illinois. Estab. 1922. Circ. 71,000. Pays on acceptance or publication. Byline given. Buys all rights. Editorial lead time 2 months. Submit seasonal material 3 months in advance. Accepts queries by mail, e-mail. Accepts simultaneous submissions. Sample copy and writer's guidelines free.

Nonfiction: Book excerpts, general interest, historical/nostalgic, how-to (golf), humor, interview/profile, new product, opinion, personal experience, photo feature, technical, travel. **Buys 25-35 mss/year**. Query with or without published clips. Length: 500-5,000 words. **Pays $50-500**. Sometimes pays expenses of writers on assignment.

Reprints: Accepts previously published submissions.

Photos: State availability of photos with submission. Reviews contact sheets. Negotiates payment individually. Captions, identification of subjects required.

Columns/Departments: CDGA/GAI Update (news and notes), Club Profile, The Rules of Golf (golf rules explanations and discussions); and Turfgrass Update (course maintenance issues). Query.

$ $ $ GOLF CANADA, Official Magazine of the Royal Canadian Golf Association, RCGA/Laurel Oak Marketing, 1333 Dorval Dr., Oakville, Ontario L6J 4Z3 Canada. (905)849-9700. Fax: (905)845-7040. E-mail: golfcanada @rcga.org. Website: www.rcga.org. Managing Editor: Joe Romagnolo. **Contact:** Bill Steinburg, editor. **80% freelance written.** Magazine published 4 times/year April-November covering Canadian golf. "*Golf Canada* is the official magazine of the Royal Canadian Golf Association, published to entertain and enlighten members about RCGA-related activities and to generally support and promote amateur golf in Canada." Estab. 1994. Circ. 135,000. **Pays on acceptance**. Byline given. Offers 100% kill fee. Buys first translation rights and electronic rights (occasionally). Editorial lead time 3 months. Submit seasonal material 6 months in advance. Accepts queries by mail, e-mail, fax, phone. Sample copy free.

Nonfiction: Historical/nostalgic, interview/profile, new product, opinion, photo feature, travel. No professional golf-related articles. **Buys 42 mss/year.** Query with published clips. Length: 750-3,000 words. **Pays 50¢/word.** Sometimes pays expenses of writers on assignment.

Reprints: Accepts previously published submissions.

Photos: State availability of photos with submission. Reviews contact sheets, negatives, transparencies and prints. Negotiates payment individually. Captions required. Buys all rights.

Columns/Departments: Guest Column (focus on issues surrounding the Canadian golf community), 700 words. **Buys 4 mss/year.** Query. **Pays 50¢/word.**

Tips: "Keep story ideas focused on Canadian competitive golf."

N ⊠ $ $ $ $ GOLF DIGEST WOMAN, The New York Times Company Magazine Group, Inc., 1120 Avenue of the Americas, New York NY 10036. (212)789-3000. Fax: (212)789-3112. E-mail: gdwoman@golfdigest.com. Website: www.gdwoman.com. Managing Editor: John Stoltenberg. **Contact:** Rona Cherry, editor-in-chief. **70% freelance written.** Quarterly magazine covering golf lifestyle. "Our magazine celebrates the game, sense of style, way of life enjoyed by sophisticated boomer women with a passion for golf." Circ. 250,000. **Pays on acceptance**. Byline given. Offers 20% kill fee. Buys all rights. Accepts queries by mail, e-mail, fax. Responds in 3 weeks to queries; 1 month to mss.

Nonfiction: Book excerpts, essays, general interest, historical/nostalgic, how-to (golf related), humor, inspirational, interview/profile, new product, personal experience, photo feature, travel. "As they relate to golf and interests of mid-life, sophisticated boomers." **Buys 75 mss/year.** Query. Length: 250-2,500 words. **Pays $1/word.** Sometimes pays expenses of writers on assignment.

Photos: State availability of photos with submission. Negotiates payment individually. Model releases required. Buys one-time rights.

Columns/Departments: Playing Through (first person/inspirational piece related to golf experiences); Body/Health (staying healthy—mid life active woman health issues), both 600 words; and At the Turn (humor/games). **Pays $1-2/word.**

$ GOLF NEWS MAGAZINE, Premier Golf Magazine Since 1984, Golf News Magazine, 73-280 El Paseo, Suite 6, Palm Desert CA 92260. (760)836-3700. Fax: (760)836-3703. E-mail: golfnews@aol.com. Website: www.golfne wsmag.com. **Contact:** Dan Poppers, editor/publisher. **70% freelance written.** Monthly magazine covering golf. "Our publication specializes in the creative treatment of the sport of golf, offering a variety of themes and slants as related to golf. If it's good writing and relates to golf, we're interested." Estab. 1984. Circ. 18,000. **Pays on acceptance**. Publishes ms an average of 2 months after acceptance. Byline given. Offers negotiable kill fee. Buys first rights and makes work-for-hire assignments. Editorial lead time 2 months. Submit seasonal material 2 months in advance. Accepts queries by mail, e-mail, fax. Accepts simultaneous submissions. Responds in 1 month to queries; 2 months to mss. Sample copy for $2 and 9 × 12 SAE with 4 first-class stamps.

Nonfiction: Book excerpts, essays, exposé, general interest, historical/nostalgic, how-to, humor, inspirational, interview/profile, opinion, personal experience, photo feature, technical, travel, real estate. "We will consider any topic related to golf that is written well with high standards. **Buys 20 mss/year.** Query with published clips. Length: "Whatever it takes to get the job done." **Pays $25-125.**

Reprints: Accepts previously published submissions.

Photos: State availability of photos with submission. Negotiates payment individually. Identification of subjects required. Buys one-time rights.

Columns/Departments: Submit ideas. **Buys 10 mss/year.** Query with published clips. **Pays $25-100.**

▣ The online magazine carries content not found in the print edition.

Tips: "Solid, creative, good, professional writing. Stay away from clichés and the hackneyed. Only good writers need apply. We are a national award-winning magazine looking for the most creative writers we can find."

$ $ $ GOLF TIPS, The Game's Most In-Depth Instruction & Equipment Magazine, Werner Publishing Corp., 12121 Wilshire Blvd., Suite 1200, Los Angeles CA 90025. (310)820-1500. Fax: (310)826-5008. E-mail: editors@ golftipsmag.com. Website: www.golftipsmag.com. Senior Editor: Mike Chwasky. Editor: David DeNunzio. Editor at Large: Tom Ferrell. **Contact:** Loren Colin, managing editor. **95% freelance written.** Magazine published 9 times/year covering golf instruction and equipment. "We provide mostly concise, very clear golf instruction pieces for the serious golfer." Estab. 1986. Pays on publication. Publishes ms an average of 2 months after acceptance. Byline given. Offers 33% kill fee. Buys first rights and second serial (reprint) rights. Editorial lead time 3 months. Submit seasonal material 4 months in advance. Responds in 1 month. Sample copy and writer's guidelines free.

Nonfiction: Book excerpts, how-to, interview/profile, new product, photo feature, technical, travel: all golf related. "General golf essays rarely make it." **Buys 125 mss/year.** Send complete ms. Length: 250-2,000 words. **Pays $300-1,000 for assigned articles; $300-800 unsolicited articles.** Occasionally negotiates other forms of payment. Sometimes pays expenses of writers on assignment.

Reprint(s): Accepts previously published submissions.

Photos: State availability of photos with submission. Reviews 2×2 transparencies. Negotiates payment individually. Captions and identification of subjects required. Buys all rights.

Columns/Departments: Stroke Saver (very clear, concise instruction), 350 words; Lesson Library (book excerpts—usually in a series), 1,000 words; Travel Tips (formated golf travel), 2,500 words. **Buys 40 mss/year.** Query with published clips or send complete ms. **Pays $300-850.**

▣ The online magazine carries original content not found in the print edition. Contact: Tom Ferrell, online editor.

Tips: "Contact a respected PGA Professional and find out if they're interested in being published. A good writer can turn an interview into a decent instruction piece."

◩ $ $ GOLF TRAVELER, Official Publication of Golf Card International, Affinity Group, Inc., 2575 Vista del Mar, Ventura CA 93001. Fax: (805)667-4217. Website: www.golfcard.com. **Contact:** Valerie Law, editorial director. **50% freelance written.** Bimonthly magazine "is the membership magazine for the Golf Card, an organization that offers its members reduced or waived greens fees at 3,500 affiliated golf courses in North America." Estab. 1976. Circ. 130,000. **Pays on acceptance.** Byline given. Offers 33% kill fee. Buys first North American serial rights and electronic rights. Editorial lead time 3 months. Submit seasonal material 5 months in advance. Accepts simultaneous submissions. Responds in 1 month. Sample copy for $2.50 plus 9×12 SASE.

Nonfiction: Book excerpts, essays, how-to, interview/profile, new product, personal experience, photo feature, technical. No poetry or cartoons. **Buys 12 mss/year.** Query with published clips or send complete ms. Length: 500-2,500 words. **Pays $75-500.** Sometimes pays expenses of writers on assignment.

Reprints: Accepts previously published submissions.

Photos: Send photos with submission. Reviews transparencies. Negotiates payment individually. Model releases and identification of subjects required. Buys one-time rights.

$ $ THE GOLFER, Heather & Pine Publishing, 21 E. 40th St., New York NY 10016. (212)696-2484. Fax: (212)696-1678. E-mail: racquet@walrus.com. Editor: H.K. Pickens. **Contact:** Colin Sheehan, features editor. **40% freelance written.** Bimonthly magazine covering golf. "A sophisticated, controversational tone for a lifestyle-oriented magazine." Estab. 1994. Circ. 253,000. Pays on publication. Publishes ms an average of 2 months after acceptance. Byline given. Offers negotiable kill fee. Buys all rights. Editorial lead time 2 months. Submit seasonal material 4 months in advance. Accepts queries by mail, e-mail, fax. Accepts simultaneous submissions. Sample copy free.

Nonfiction: Book excerpts, essays, general interest, historical/nostalgic, how-to, humor, inspirational, interview/profile, new product, opinion, personal experience, photo feature, technical, travel. Send complete ms. Length: 300-2,000 words. **Pays $150-600.**

Reprints: Accepts previously published submissions.

Photos: Send photos with submission. Reviews any size transparencies. Buys one-time rights.

N $ $ GULF COAST GOLFER, Golfer Magazines, Inc., 10301 Northwest Freeway, Suite 418, Houston TX 77092. (713)680-1680. Fax: (713)680-0138. Editor: Bob Gray. **Contact:** David Widener, managing editor. **30% freelance written.** Monthly tabloid covering golf in Texas. Estab. 1984. Circ. 35,000. Pays on publication. Publishes ms an average of 2 months after acceptance. Byline given. Buys first, one-time or second serial (reprint) rights. Editorial lead time 2 months. Submit seasonal material 3 months in advance. Responds in 2 weeks to queries; 1 month to mss. Sample copy free. Prefers direct phone discussion for writer's guidelines.

Nonfiction: Book excerpts, humor, personal experience, all golf-related. No stories about golf outside of Texas. **Buys 40 mss/year.** Query. **Pays $50-425.**

Photos: State availability of photos. Reviews contact sheets and prints. No additional payment for photos accepted with ms, but pays $125 for cover photo. Captions and identification of subjects required. Buys one-time rights.

Tips: "Most of our purchases are in how-to area, so writers must know golf quite well and play the game."

$ $MICHIGAN LINKS, TPG Sports Inc., 1710 Douglas Dr. N., Golden Valley MN 55422. (763)595-0808. Fax: (763)595-0016. E-mail: joe@tpgsports.com or tbranch@gam.org. Website: www.tpgsports.com or www.gam.org. Managing Editor: Tonia Branch. **Contact:** Joseph Oberle, publications manager, (763)595-0808, ext. 114. **80% freelance written**. Bimonthly magazine covering golf in Michigan, the official publication of the Golf Association of Michigan. Estab. 1997. Circ. 40,000. Pays on acceptance or publication. Byline sometimes given. Buys all rights. Editorial lead time 6 months. Submit seasonal material 3 months in advance. Accepts queries by mail, e-mail. Accepts simultaneous submissions. Sample copy and guidelines free.

Nonfiction: Book excerpts, essays, historical/nostalgic, how-to (golf), humor, inspirational, interview/profile, new product, opinion, personal experience, photo feature, technical (golf equipment). **Buys 30-40 mss/year**. Query with or without published clips or send complete ms. Length: 500-5,000 words. **Pays $50-500**. Sometimes pays expenses of writers on assignment.

Reprints: Accepts previously published submissions on a case-by-case basis.

Photos: State availability of photos with submission. Reviews contact sheets. Negotiates payment individually. Captions, identification of subjects required. Rights purchased varies.

Columns/Departments: Forecaddie (news and notes), Playing by the Rules (golf rules explanations and discussion); and Turf Talk (course maintenance issues). Query.

$ $MINNESOTA GOLFER, 6550 York Ave. S, Suite 211, Edina MN 55435. (952)927-4643. Fax: (952)927-9642. Website: www.mngolf.org. Editor: W.P. Ryan, (952) 927-4643. **Contact:** Joseph Oberle, publications manager, (763) 595-0808, ext. 114. **75% freelance written**. Bimonthly magazine covering golf in Minnesota, the official publication of the Minnesota Golf Association. Estab. 1975. Circ. 72,500. Pays on acceptance or publication. Byline given. Buys all rights. Editorial lead time 6 months. Submit seasonal material 3 months in advance. Accepts simultaneous submissions. Sample copy and writer's guidelines free.

Nonfiction: Book excerpts, essays, historical/nostalgic, how-to (golf), humor, inspirational, interview/profile, new product, opinion, personal experience, photo feature. **Buys 20-30 mss/year**. Query by mail only with published clips. Length: 500-2,500 words. **Pays $50-500**. Sometimes pays expenses of writers on assignment.

Photos: State availability of photos with submission. Reviews contact sheets. Negotiates payment individually. Captions, identification of subjects required. Negotiates payment individually. Rights purchased varies.

Columns/Departments: Punch shots (golf news and notes). Query.

N $ $NORTH TEXAS GOLFER, Golfer Magazines, Inc., 10301 N.W. Freeway, Suite 418, Houston TX 77092. (713)680-1680. Fax: (713)680-0138. Editor: Bob Gray. **Contact:** David Widener, managing editor. **30% freelance written.** Monthly tabloid covering golf in Texas. Estab. 1986. Circ. 31,000. Pays on publication. Publishes ms an average of 2 months after acceptance. Byline given. Buys first rights or second serial (reprint) rights. Editorial lead time 2 months. Submit seasonal material 3 months in advance. Responds in 2 weeks to queries; 1 month to mss. Sample copy free. Prefers direct phone discussion for writer's guidelines.

Nonfiction: Book excerpts, humor, personal experience, all golf related. **Buys 40 mss/year**. Query. **Pays $50-425.**

Photos: State availability of photos with submission. Reviews contact sheets and prints. Offers no additional payment for photos accepted with ms, but offers $125 for cover photo. Captions and identification of subjects required. Buys one-time rights.

Tips: "Most of our purchases are in how-to area, so writers must know golf quite well and play the game."

N $ $ $ $SCORE, Golf Magazine, Canadian Controlled Media Communications, 287 MacPherson Ave., Toronto, Ontario M4V 1A4 Canada. (416)928-2909. Fax: (416)928-1357. E-mail: weeksy@idirect.com. Website: www.s coregolf.com. Publisher: (Mr.) Kim Locke. Managing Editor: Bob Weeks. **70% freelance written.** Works with a small number of new/unpublished writers each year. Magazine published 6 times/year covering golf. "*Score Golf Magazine* provides seasonal coverage of the Canadian golf scene, professional, amateur, senior and junior golf for men and women golfers in Canada, the US and Europe through profiles, history, travel, editorial comment and instruction." Estab. 1980. Circ. 150,000 audited. **Pays on acceptance.** Byline given. Offers negotiable kill fee. Buys all rights and second serial (reprint) rights. Submit seasonal material 8 months in advance. Responds in 8 months. Sample copy for $3.50 (Canadian) and 9×12 SAE with IRCs. Writer's guidelines for #10 SAE and IRC.

Nonfiction: Book excerpts (golf); historical/nostalgic (golf and golf characters); interview/profile (prominent golf professionals); photo feature (golf); travel (golf destinations only). No personal experience, technical, opinion or general-interest material. Most articles are by assignment only. **Buys 25-30 mss/year**. Query with published clips. Length: 700-3,500 words. **Pays $200-1,500.**

Photos: Send photos with query or ms. Pays $50-100 for 35mm color transparencies (positives) or $30 for 8×10 or 5×7 b&w prints. Captions, model release (if necessary), identification of subjects required. Buys all rights.

Columns/Departments: Profile (historical or current golf personalities or characters); Great Moments ("Great Moments in Canadian Golf"—description of great single moments, usually game triumphs); New Equipment (Canadian availability only); Travel (golf destinations, including "hard" information such as greens fees, hotel accommodations, etc.); Instruction (by special assignment only; usually from teaching golf professionals); The Mental Game (psychology of the game, by special assignment only); History (golf equipment collections and collectors, development of the game, legendary figures and events). **Buys 17-20 mss/year.** Query with published clips or send complete ms. Length: 700-1,700 words. **Pays $140-400.**

Tips: "Only writers with an extensive knowledge of golf and familiarity with the Canadian golf scene should query or submit in-depth work to *Score Golf*. Many of our features are written by professional people who play the game for a living or work in the industry. All areas mentioned under Columns/Departments are open to freelancers. Most of our *major* features are done on assignment only."

$ $ VIRGINIA GOLFER, TPG Sports Inc., 1710 Douglas Dr. N., Golden Valley MN 55422. (763)595-0808. Fax: (763)595-0016. E-mail: joe@tpgsports.com. or hdpearson@aol.com for editorial and info@vsga.org for general information. Website: www.tpgsports.com or www.vsga.org. Editor: Harold Pearson. **Contact:** Joseph Oberle, publications manager (763)595-0808, ext 114. **65% freelance written.** Bimonthly magazine covering golf in Virginia, the official publication of the Virginia Golf Association. Estab. 1983. Circ. 33,000. Pays on publication. Byline given. Buys all rights. Editorial lead time 6 months. Submit seasonal material 3 months in advance. Accepts queries by mail, e-mail. Accepts simultaneous submissions. Sample copy and writer's guidelines free.

Nonfiction: Book excerpts, essays, historical/nostalgic, how-to (golf), humor, inspirational, interview/profile, personal experience, where to play, golf business, photo feature, technical (golf equipment). **Buys 30-40 mss/year.** Query with or without published clips or send complete ms. Length: 500-2,500 words. **Pays $50-500.** Sometimes pays expenses of writers on assignment.

Reprints: Accepts previously published submissions.

Photos: State availability of photos with submission. Reviews contact sheets. Negotiates payment individually. Captions, identification of subjects required. Negotiates payment individually. Rights purchased varies.

Columns/Departments: Chip ins & Three Putts (news and notes), Rules Corner (golf rules explanations and discussion) and Pro Tips, plus Golf Travel (where to play), Golf Business (what's happening?). Query.

Guns

$ $ GUN DIGEST, DBI Books, Inc., Division of Krause Publications, 700 E. State St., Iola WI 54990. (888)457-2873. Fax: (715)445-4087. **Contact:** Ken Ramage, editor-in-chief. **50% freelance written.** Prefers to work with published/established writers but works with a small number of new/unpublished writers each year. Annual journal covering guns and shooting. Estab. 1944. **Pays on acceptance.** Publishes ms an average of 20 months after acceptance. Byline given. Buys all rights. Responds in 1 month.

Nonfiction: Buys 50 mss/issue. Query. Length: 500-5,000 words. **Pays $100-600** for text/art package.

Photos: State availability of photos with query letter. Reviews 8×10 b&w prints. Payment for photos included in payment for ms. Captions required.

Tips: Award of $1,000 to author of best article (juried) in each issue.

N $ $ GUNS MAGAZINE, Suite 200, 591 Camino de la Reina, San Diego CA 92108. (619)297-5352. Fax: (619)297-5353. **Contact:** Scott Ferrell, editor. **100% freelance written.** Monthly magazine for firearms enthusiasts covering firearms, reviews, tactics and related products. Circ. 200,000. Pays on publication. Publishes manuscripts 4-6 months after acceptance. Buys all world rights. Offers $50 kill fee. Responds in 2 weeks. Writer's guidelines for SASE.

Nonfiction: Test reports on new firearms; round-up articles on firearms types; guns for specific purposes (hunting, target shooting, self-defense); custom gunmakers; and history of modern guns. **Buys approximately 10 ms/year.** Query. Length: 1,000-2,500 words. **Pays $300-500.**

Photos: Major emphasis on quality photography. Additional payment of $50-200 for color, 4×5 or 2¼×2¼ preferred.

Columns/Departments: Buys 5-10 columns. Query. Length: 1,000 words. **Pays $400.**

$ $ MUZZLE BLASTS, National Muzzle Loading Rifle Association, P.O. Box 67, Friendship IN 47021. (812)667-5131. Fax: (812)667-5137. E-mail: nmlra@nmlra.org. Website: www.nmlra.org. Editor: Eric A. Bye. **Contact:** Terri Trowbridge, director of publications. **65% freelance written.** Monthly association magazine. "Articles must relate to muzzleloading or the muzzleloading era of American history." Estab. 1939. Circ. 25,000. Pays on publication. Publishes ms an average of 6 months after acceptance. Byline given. Offers $50 kill fee. Buys first North American serial rights, one-time rights and second serial (reprint) rights. Editorial lead time 4 months. Submit seasonal material 6 months in advance. Responds in 1 month to mss. Sample copy and writer's guidelines free.

   ● *Muzzle Blasts* now accepts manuscripts on 5.25 or 3.5 DOS diskettes in most major word processing programs; they prefer any of the Word Perfect™ formats.

Nonfiction: Book excerpts, general interest, historical/nostalgic, how-to, humor, interview/profile, new product, personal experience, photo feature, technical, travel. "No subjects that do not pertain to muzzleloading." **Buys 80 mss/year.** Query. Length: 2,500 words. **Pays $200 minimum for assigned articles; $50 minimum for unsolicited articles.**

Photos: Send photos with submission. Reviews 5×7 prints. Negotiates payment individually. Captions and model releases required. Buys one-time rights.

Columns/Departments: Buys 96 mss/year. Query. **Pays $50-200.**

Fiction: Adventure, historical, humorous. Must pertain to muzzleloading. **Buys 6 mss/year.** Query. Length: 2,500 words. **Pays $50-300.**

Fillers: Facts. **Pays $50.**

◼ The online magazine carries original content not found in the print edition.

Tips: The National Muzzle Loading Rifle Association also publishes *Muzzle Blasts Online* on the World Wide Web. This electronic magazine is focused primarily for a nonmember audience. Writers and photographers are free to accept or reject this use of their work, and statements regarding this issue can be enclosed with your submission. (No additional payment will be made for use on *Muzzle Blasts Online*. The only time payment will be made for electronic use is when your article is used exclusively on the Web and has not been printed on the paper version of the magazine.) Please contact the NMLRA for writer's guidelines.

Hiking/Backpacking

$ $ $ $ BACKPACKER, Rodale, 33 E. Minor St., Emmaus PA 18098-0099. (610)967-8296. Fax: (610)967-8181. E-mail: bpeditor@rodalepress.com. Website: www.backpacker.com. Executive Editor: Thom Hogan. Editor: Tom Shealey. **Contact:** Matt Purdue, senior editor. **50% freelance written.** Magazine published 9 times/year covering wilderness travel for backpackers. Estab. 1973. Circ. 280,000. **Pays on acceptance.** Byline given. Buys one-time rights or all rights. Accepts queries by phone, e-mail, fax. Responds in 2 months. Writer's guidelines for #10 SASE.

Nonfiction: Essays, exposé, historical/nostalgic, how-to (expedition planner), humor, inspirational, interview/profile, new product, opinion, personal experience, technical, travel. No step-by-step accounts of what you did on your summer vacation—stories that chronicle every rest stop and gulp of water. Query with published clips and SASE. Length: 750-3,000 words. **Pays $400-2,000.** Sometimes pays (pre-determined) expenses of writers on assignment. "What we want are features that let us and the readers 'feel' the place, and experience your wonderment, excitement, disappointment or other emotions encountered 'out there.' If we feel like we've been there after reading your story, you've succeeded."

● Ranked as one of the best markets for freelancers in *Writer's Yearbook* magazine's annual "Top 100 Markets," January 2000.

Photos: State availability of photos with submission. Pay varies. Buys one-time rights.

Columns/Departments: Signpost, "News From All Over" (adventure, environment, wildlife, trails, techniques, organizations, special interests—well-written, entertaining, short, newsy item), 50-500 words; Body Language (in-the-field health column), 750-1,200 words; Moveable Feast (food-related aspects of wilderness: nutrition, cooking techniques, recipes, products and gear), 500-750 words; Weekend Wilderness (brief but detailed guides to wilderness areas, providing thorough trip-planning information, only enough anecdote to give a hint, then the where/when/hows), 500-750 words; Know How (ranging from beginner to expert focus, written by people with solid expertise, details ways to improve performance, how-to-do-it instructions, information on equipment manufacturers and places readers can go), 750-1,500 words; and Backcountry (personal perspectives, quirky and idiosyncratic, humorous critiques, manifestos and misadventures, interesting angle, lesson, revelation or moral), 750-1,200 words. **Buys 50-75 mss/year.** Query with published clips. **Pays $200-1,000.** No phone calls regarding story ideas. Written queries only.

◼ The online magazine carries original content not found in the print edition.

Tips: "Our best advice is to read the publication—most freelancers don't know the magazine at all. The best way to break in is with an article for the Backcountry, Weekend Wilderness or Signpost Department."

▨ $ $ $ $ OUTSIDE, Mariah Media Inc., Outside Plaza, 400 Market St., Santa Fe NM 87501. (505)989-7100. Editor: Hal Espen. **Contact:** Sharon Parker, assistant to the editor. **90% freelance written.** "*Outside* is a monthly national magazine for active, educated, upscale adults who love the outdoors and are concerned about its preservation." Estab. 1977. Circ. 500,000. **Pays on acceptance.** Publishes ms an average of 3 months after acceptance. Byline given. Offers 25% kill fee. Buys first North American serial rights. Submit seasonal material 5 months in advance. Responds in 2 months. Sample copy for $5 and 9×12 SAE with 9 first-class stamps. Writer's guidelines for SASE.

● *Outside* won the 1998 National Magazine Award for General Excellence for magazines with circulation of 100,000-400,000.

Nonfiction: Book excerpts; essays; reports on the environment; outdoor sports and expeditions; general interest; how-to; humor; inspirational; interview/profile (major figures associated with sports, travel, environment, outdoor); opinion; personal experience (expeditions; trying out new sports); photo feature (outdoor photography); technical (reviews of equipment, how-to); travel (adventure, sports-oriented travel). All should pertain to the outdoors: Bike section; Downhill Skiing; Cross-country Skiing; Adventure Travel. Do not want to see articles about sports that we don't cover (basketball, tennis, golf, etc.). **Buys 40 mss/year.** Query with published clips and SASE. Length: 1,500-4,000 words. **Pays $1/word.** Pays expenses of writers on assignment.

Photos: "Do not send photos; if we decide to use a story, we may ask to see the writer's photos." Reviews transparencies. Offers $180/photo minimum. Captions, identification of subjects required. Buys one-time rights.

Columns/Departments: Dispatches, contact Kevin Fedanko (news, events, short profiles relevant to outdoors), 200-1,000 words; Destinations, contact Susan Enfield (places to explore, news, and tips for adventure travelers), 250-400 words; Review, contact Eric Hagerman (evaluations of products), 200-1,500 words. **Buys 180 mss/year.** Query with published clips. Length: 200-2,000 words. **Pays $1/word.**

◼ The online magazine carries original content not found in the print edition. Contact: Amy Marr, online editor.

Tips: "Prospective writers should study the magazine before querying. Look at the magazine for our style, subject matter and standards." The departments are the best areas for freelancers to break in.

Hockey

N $ $ $ AMERICAN HOCKEY INC., Official Publication of USA Hockey, % TPG Sports, Inc., 1710 Douglas Dr. N., #201, Golden Valley MN 55422. (763)595-0808. Fax: (763)595-0016. E-mail: joe@tpgsports.com. or hthompson@usahockey.org. Website: www.tpgsports.com or www.usahockey.com. Editor: Harry Thompson. **Contact:** Joseph Oberle, publications manager. **60% freelance written.** Magazine published 10 times/year covering amateur hockey in the US. "The world's largest hockey magazine, *AHM* is the official magazine of USA Hockey, Inc., the national governing body of hockey." Estab. 1980. Circ. 422,000. Pays on acceptance or publication. Byline given. Buys all rights. Editorial lead time 6 months. Submit seasonal material 4 months in advance. Accepts simultaneous submissions. Sample copy and writer's guidelines free.
Nonfiction: Essays, general interest, historical/nostalgic, how-to (play hockey), humor, inspirational, interview/profile, new product, opinion, personal experience, photo feature, travel, hockey camps, pro hockey, juniors, college, NCAA hockey championships, Olympics and youth, etc. **Buys 20-30 mss/year.** Query. Length: 500-5,000 words. **Pays $50-1,000.** Sometimes pays expenses of writers on assignment.
Reprints: Accepts previously published submissions.
Photos: State availability of photos. Reviews contact sheets. Negotiates payment individually. Captions, identification of subjects required. Rights purchased varies.
Columns/Departments: Short Cuts (news and notes), Coaches' Corner (teaching tips), USA Hockey Inline Notebook (news and notes). **Pays $150-250.**
Fiction: Adventure, humorous, slice-of-life vignettes. **Buys 10-20 mss/year. Pays $150-1,000.**
Fillers: Anecdotes, facts, gags to be illustrated by cartoonist, newsbreaks, short humor. **Buys 20-30/year.** Length: 10-100 words. **Pays $25-250.**
Tips: Writers must have a general knowledge and enthusiasm for hockey, including ice, inline, street and other. The primary audience is youth players in the US.

N $ $ MINNESOTA HOCKEY JOURNAL, Official Publication of Minnesota Hockey, Inc., % TPG Sports, Inc., 1710 Douglas Dr. N., Golden Valley MN 55422. (763)595-0808. Fax: (763)595-0016. E-mail: joe@tpgsports .com. Website: www.tpgsports.com. Editor: Ross Bernstein. **Contact:** Joseph Oberle, publications manager. **50% freelance written.** Published 4 times/year. *MJH* covers hockey in ths state of Minnesota. Estab. 2000. Circ. 40,000. Pays on acceptance or publication. Byline given. Buys all rights. Editorial lead time 6 months. Submit seasonal material 4 months in advance. Accepts simultaneous submissions. Sample copy and writer's guidelines free.
Nonfiction: Essays, general interest, historical/nostalgic, how-to (play hockey), humor, inspirational, interview/profile, new product, opinion, personal experience, photo feature, travel, hockey camps, pro hockey, juniors, college, Olympics and youth, etc. **Buys 5-10 mss/year.** Query. Length: 500-5,000 words. **Pays $100-500.** Sometimes pays expenses of writers on assignment.
Reprints: Accepts previously published submissions.
Photos: State availability of photos. Reviews contact sheets. Negotiates payment individually. Captions, identification of subjects required. Rights purchased varies.
Columns/Departments: Hot Shots (news and notes), Open Ice (opinion). **Pays $50-250.**
Fillers: Anecdotes, facts, gags to be illustrated by cartoonist, newsbreaks, short humor. **Buys 5-10 mss/year.** Length: 10-100 words. **Pays $25-250.**

Horse Racing

N ⊠ $ $ AMERICAN TURF MONTHLY, Star Sports Corp., 306 Broadway, Lynbrook NY 11563. (516)599-2121. Fax: (516)599-0451. E-mail: webmaster@winsports.com. Website: www.americanturf.com. **Contact:** Ian C. Blair, editor-in-chief. **90% freelance written.** Monthly magazine covering Thoroughbred racing, handicapping and wagering. "Squarely focused on Thoroughbred handicapping and wagering. *ATM* is a magazine for horseplayers, not owners, breeders or 12-year-old girls enthralled with ponies." Estab. 1946. Circ. 28,000. Pays on publication. Publishes ms an average of 4 months after acceptance. Byline given. Makes works-for-hire assignments. Editorial lead time 2 months. Submit seasonal material 2 months in advance. Accepts queries by mail, e-mail, fax. Responds in 1 month to queries. Sample copy and writer's guidelines free.
Nonfiction: Handicapping and wagering features. Special issues: Triple Crown/Kentucky Derby (May); Saratoga/Del Mar (August); Breeder's Cup (November). No historical essays, bilious 'guest editorials,' saccharine poetry, fiction. **Buys 50 mss/year.** Query. Length: 800-2,000 words. **Pays $75-300 for assigned articles; $100-500 for unsolicited articles.**
Photos: Send photos with submission. Reviews 3×5 transparencies and prints. Offers $25 interior b&w; $150 for cover. Identification of subjects required. Buys one-time rights.

Fillers: Newsbreaks, short humor. **Buys 5/year.** Length: 400 words. **Pays $25.**

Tips: "Send a good query letter specifically targeted at explaining how this contribution will help our readers to cash a bet at the track!"

$ $ THE BACKSTRETCH, United Thoroughbred Trainers of America, Inc., P.O. Box 7065, Louisville KY 40257-0065. (800)325-3487. Fax: (502)893-0026. E-mail: bstretch@couriernet.infi.net. Website: www.thebackstretch.com. **Contact:** Kevin Baker, copy editor and designer. **90% freelance written.** Estab. 1962. Circ. 10,000. Uses mostly established turf writers, but works with a few less experienced writers each year. Bimonthly magazine directed chiefly to Thoroughbred trainers but also to owners, fans and others working in or involved with the racing industry. Accepts queries by mail, e-mail, fax, phone. Pays on publication. Publishes ms 3 months after acceptance, often longer. Sample copy on request.

　　O→ Break in with "an outline and samples with your query; be available for questions regarding manuscript; try to provide photos and adhere to electronic format for submissions."

Nonfiction: Profiles of trainers, owners, jockeys, horses and other personalities who make up the world of racing; analysis of industry issues; articles on particular tracks or races, veterinary topics; information on legal or business aspects of owning, training or racing horses; and historical perspectives. Opinions should be informed by expertise on the subject treated. Non-commissioned articles are accepted on a speculation basis. Pays on publication. If not suitable, articles are returned only if a SASE is included. Length: 1,500-2,500 words. **Pays $150-450.**

　　● Looking for "features that relate other topics and fields of interest to the racing industry, e.g., art, science, unusual profiles, well-researched historical pieces (series)."

Reprints: Occasionally accepts previously published material, especially if it has appeared only in a regional or specialized publication. Send typed ms with rights for sale noted and information about when and where the article previously appeared. Payment negotiable.

Photos: It is advisable to include photo illustrations when possible, or these can be arranged for separately.

　　▣ The online magazine carries original content not found in the print edition.

Tips: "If an article is a simultaneous submission, this must be stated and we must be advised if it is accepted elsewhere. Articles should be double spaced and may be submitted by mail, fax or e-mail on 3½-inch disk saved in text or in program compatible with QuarkXPress for Macintosh."

$ $ THE QUARTER RACING JOURNAL, American Quarter Horse Association, P.O. Box 32470, Amarillo TX 79120. (806)376-4888. Fax: (806)349-6400. E-mail: aowens@aqha.org. Website: www.aqha.com/racing. Executive Editor: Jim Jennings. **Contact:** Amy Owens, editor. **10% freelance written.** Monthly magazine. "The official racing publication of the American Quarter Horse Association. We promote quarter horse racing. Articles include training, breeding, nutrition, sports medicine, health, history, etc." Estab. 1988. Circ. 9,000. **Pays on acceptance.** Publishes ms an average of 3 months after acceptance. Buys first North American serial rights. Submit seasonal material 3 months in advance. Accepts queries by mail, e-mail, fax, phone. Responds in 1 month to queries. Free sample copy and writer's guidelines.

Nonfiction: Historical (must be on quarter horses or people associated with them), how-to (training), nutrition, health, breeding and opinion. "We welcome submissions year-round." Special issues: Yearlings (August), subject to negotiation. Stallions (December). Query. Length: 700-1,500 words. **Pays $150-300.**

Reprints: Send photocopy of article and information about when and where the article previously appeared.

Photos: Send photos with submission. Additional payment for photos accepted with ms might be offered. Captions and identification of subjects required.

Fiction: Publishes novel excerpts.

　　▣ The online magazine carries original content not found in the print edition.

Tips: "Query first—must be familiar with quarter horse racing and be knowledgeable of the sport. The *Journal* directs its articles to those who own, train and breed racing quarter horses, as well as fans and handicappers. Most open to features covering training, nutrition, health care. Use a knowledgeable source with credentials."

Hunting & Fishing

◩ $ $ ALABAMA GAME & FISH, Game & Fish Publications, P.O. Box 741, Marietta GA 30061. **Contact:** Jimmy Jacobs, editor. See *Game & Fish Publications.*

◩ $ $ AMERICAN ANGLER, the Magazine of Fly Fishing & Fly Tying, Abenaki Publishers, Inc., 160 Benmont Ave., Bennington VT 05201. Fax: (802)447-2471. **Contact:** Philip Monahan, editor. **95% freelance written.** Bimonthly magazine covering fly fishing. "*American Angler* is dedicated to giving fly fishers practical information they can use—wherever they fish, whatever they fish for." Estab. 1976. Circ. 60,000. Pays on publication. Publishes ms an average of 6 months after acceptance. Byline given. Buys first North American serial rights (articles) or one-time rights (photos). Editorial lead time over 3 months. Submit seasonal material 5 months in advance. Reluctantly accepts simultaneous submissions, if so noted. Accepts queries by mail, fax. Responds in 6 weeks to queries; 2 months to mss. Sample copy for $6. Writer's guidelines for SASE.

Nonfiction: How-to (most important), personal experience ("but tired of the 'me 'n' Joe' stories"), photo feature (seldom), technical. No promotional flack to pay back free trips or freebies, no superficial, broad-brush coverage of subjects. **Buys 45-60 mss/year.** Query with published clips and SASE. Length: 800-2,200 words. **Pays $200-400.**
Reprints: Send information about when and where the article previously appeared. Pay negotiable.
Photos: Send photos with submission. Reviews contact sheets, transparencies. Offers no additional payment for photos accepted with ms. Captions, identification of subjects required. Acquires one-time rights. "Photographs are important. A fly-tying submission should always include samples of flies to send to our staff photographer, even if photos of the flies are included."
Columns/Departments: One-page shorts (problem solvers), 350-750 words. Query with clips. **Pays $100-300.**
Tips: "If you are new to this editor, please submit complete queries."

$ $AMERICAN HUNTER, 11250 Waples Mill Rd., Fairfax VA 22030-9400. (703)267-1335. Fax: (703)267-3971. E-mail: lfaulk@nrahq.org. Website: www.nra.org. Editor: John Zent. **Contact:** Scott Olmsted, associate editor. For hunters who are members of the National Rifle Association. "*American Hunter* contains articles dealing with various sport hunting and related activities both at home and abroad. With the encouragment of the sport as a prime game management tool, emphasis is on technique, sportsmanship and safety. In each issue hunting equipment and firearms are evaluated, legislative happenings affecting the sport are reported, lore and legend are retold and the business of the Association is recorded in the Official Journal section." Circ. 1,000,000. **Pays on acceptance** for articles and on publication for photos. Buys first North American serial rights and subsequent reprint rights for NRA publications. Byline given. Responds in 1 month. Writer's guidelines for #10 SASE.
Nonfiction: Factual material on all phases of hunting: expository how-to, where-to, and general interest pieces; humor: personal narratives; and semi-technical articles on firearms, wildlife management or hunting. "Subject matter for feature articles falls into five general categories that run in each issue: deer, upland birds, waterfowl, big game and varmints/small game. Special issues: pheasants, whitetail tactics, black bear feed areas, mule deer, duck hunters' transport by land and sea, tech topics to be decided; rut strategies, muzzleloader moose and elk, fall turkeys, staying warm, goose talk, long-range muzzleloading. Not interested in material on fishing, camping or firearms legislation." Prefers queries by mail only. Length: 1,800-2,000 words. **Pays $250-600.**
Reprints: Send typed ms with rights for sale noted and info about when and where it previously appeared.
Photos: No additional payment made for photos used with mss. Pays $25 for b&w photos purchased without accompanying mss. Pays $50-175 for color.
Columns/Departments: Hunting Guns, Hunting Loads and Public Hunting Grounds. Study back issues for appropriate subject matter and style. Length: 1,200-1,500 words. **Pays $300-350.**
Tips: "Although unsolicited manuscripts are welcomed, detailed query letters outlining the proposed topic and approach are appreciated and will save both writers and editors a considerable amount of time. If we like your story idea, you will be contacted by mail or phone and given direction on how we'd like the topic covered. NRA Publications accept all manuscripts and photographs for consideration on a specualtion basis only. Story angles should be narrow, but coverage must have depth. How-to articles are popular with readers and might range from methods for hunting to techniques on making gear used on successful hunts. Where-to articles should contain contacts and information needed to arrange a similar hunt. All submissions are judged on three criteria: story angle (it should be fresh, interesting, and informative); quality of writing (clear and lively—capable of holding the readers' attention throughout); and quality and quantity of accompanying photos (sharpness, reproduceability, and connection to text are most important.)"

$ $ARKANSAS SPORTSMAN, Game & Fish Publications, P.O. Box 741, Marietta GA 30061. (770)953-9222. **Contact:** Ken Duke. See *Game & Fish Publications*.

$BAIT FISHERMAN, Beaver Pond Publishing, P.O. Box 224, Greenville PA 16125. (724)588-3492. Fax: (724)588-2486. E-mail: beaverpond@pathway.net. Website: www.beaverpondpublishing.com. **Contact:** Rich Faler, editor. **80% freelance written.** Bimonthly magazine covering natural bait fishing, fresh and saltwater. "We are slanted exclusively toward bait fishing of all species of fresh and saltwater fish." Estab. 1995. Circ. 5,000. Pays on publication. Publishes ms an average of 6 months after acceptance. Byline given. Buys first rights, one-time rights or second serial (reprint) rights. Editorial lead time 4 months. Submit seasonal material 4-6 months in advance. Accepts simultaneous submissions. Accepts electronic submissions by disk but hard copy preferred. Responds in 2 months to queries; 3 months to mss. Writer's guidelines free.
Nonfiction: General interest, how-to (bait collection, presentation, maintenance, etc.), interview/profile, personal experience (with bait fishing-specific slant), travel ("hot spot" locations). **Buys 30-40 mss/year.** Query. Length: 1,000-2,000 words. **Pays $30-100** plus 3 copies.
Reprints: Send ms and information about when and where the article previously appeared. Pays 50-70% of amount paid for an original article.
Photos: Send photos with submission. Reviews contact sheets, negatives, 35mm transparencies, 5×7 prints (preferred). No additional payment for photos accepted with ms. Captions, identification of subjects required. Buys one-time rights.
Fillers: Anecdotes, facts, newsbreaks, bait-specific legislation pieces, how-tos and hints. **Buys 10-20/year.** Length: 50-500 words. **Pays $10-30.**
Tips: "Query with detailed description of what you can provide our readers. State availability of photos, graphics and sidebars. We want detailed how-to, where-to and natural history pieces regarding all facets of bait fishing. We are most in need of articles on bait shops, the bait business and catching, raising and maintaining bait."

N ⭐ **$ $BASSMASTER MAGAZINE**, B.A.S.S. Publications, 5845 Carmichael Pkwy., Montgomery AL 36117. (334)272-9530. Fax: (334)279-7148. E-mail: bassmag@mindspring.com. Website: www.bassmaster.com. **Contact**: Catherine VanHerrin, editorial assistant. Editor: Dave Precht. **80% freelance written.** Prefers to work with published/established writers. Magazine published 10 issues/year about largemouth, smallmouth and spotted bass, offering "how-to" articles for dedicated beginning and advanced bass fishermen, including destinations and new product reviews. Estab. 1968. Circ. 600,000. **Pays on acceptance.** Publishes ms an average of 6-12 months after acceptance. Byline given. Buys all rights, including electronic rights. Editorial lead time 2 months. Submit seasonal material 6 months in advance. Responds in 2 months. Sample copy for $2. Writer's guidelines for #10 SASE.

Nonfiction: Historical, how-to (patterns, lures, etc.), interview (of knowledgeable people in the sport), profile (outstanding fishermen), travel (where to go to fish for bass), how-to (catch bass and enjoy the outdoors), new product (reels, rods and bass boats), conservation related to bass fishing. "No first person, personal experience 'Me and Joe go fishing' type articles." **Buys 100 mss/year.** Query. Length: 500-2,500 words. **Pays $100-500.**

● Needs destination stories (how to fish a certain area) for the Northwest and Northeast.

Photos: Send photos with submission. Reviews transparencies. Offers no additional payment for photos accepted with ms. Pays $700 for color cover transparencies. Captions required; model releases preferred. Buys all rights.

Columns/Departments: Short Cast/News/Views/Notes/Briefs (upfront regular feature covering news-related events such as new state bass records, unusual bass fishing happenings, conservation, new products and editorial viewpoints); 250-400 words. **Pays $100-3,000.**

Fillers: Anecdotes, newsbreaks. **Buys 4-5 mss/issue.** Length: 250-500 words. **Pays $50-100.**

Tips: "Editorial direction continues in the short, more direct how-to article. Compact, easy-to-read information is our objective. Shorter articles with good graphics, such as how-to diagrams, step-by-step instruction, etc., will enhance a writer's articles submitted to *Bassmaster Magazine*. The most frequent mistakes made by writers in completing an article for us are poor grammar, poor writing, poor organization and superficial research. Send in detailed queries outlining specific objectives of article, obtain writer's guidelines. Be as concise as possible."

N ⭐ **$ $BC OUTDOORS**, OP Publishing, 780 Beatty St., Suite 300, Vancouver, British Columbia V6B 2M1 Canada. (604)606-4644. Fax: (604)687-1925. E-mail: oppubl@istar.ca. Managing Editor: Roegan Lloydd. Editor: G. Gruenefeld. **80% freelance written.** Works with a small number of new/unpublished writers each year in BC. Magazine published 8 times/year covering fishing, camping, hunting and the environment of outdoor recreation. Estab. 1945. Circ. 42,000. Pays on publication. Publishes ms an average of 3 months after acceptance. Byline given. Offers negotiable kill fee. Buys first North American serial rights. Responds in 1 month (approximately). Sample copy and writer's guidelines for 8×10 SAE with 7 Canadian first-class stamps or International equivalent.

Nonfiction: How-to (new or innovative articles on fishing/hunting subjects), personal experience (outdoor adventure), outdoor topics specific to British Columbia. "We would like to receive how-to, where-to features dealing with hunting and fishing in British Columbia." **Buys 80-90 mss/year.** Query. Length: 1,500-2,000 words. **Pays $300-500.** Sometimes pays the expenses of writers on assignment.

● Wants in-depth, informative, professional writing only.

Photos: State availability of photos with query. Pays $25-75 on publication for 5×7 b&w prints; $35-150 for color contact sheets and 35mm transparencies. Captions and identification of subjects required. Buys one-time rights.

Tips: "Emphasis on environmental issues. Those pieces with a conservation component have a better chance of being published. Subject must be specific to British Columbia. We receive many manuscripts written by people who obviously do not know the magazine or market. The writer has a better chance of breaking in with short, lesser-paying articles and fillers, because we have a stable of regular writers who produce most main features."

$ $BUGLE, Journal of Elk and the Hunt, Rocky Mountain Elk Foundation, 2291 W. Broadway, Missoula MT 59802. (406)523-4570. Fax: (406)523-4550. E-mail: bugle@rmef.org. Website: www.rmef.org. Editor: Dan Crockett. **Contact:** Lee Cromrich, assistant editor; David Stalling, conservation editor; Don Burgess, hunting editor; Jan Brocci, managing editor. **50% freelance written.** Bimonthly magazine covering conservation and hunting. "*Bugle* is the membership publication of the Rocky Mountain Elk Foundation, a nonprofit wildlife conservation group; it also sells on newsstands. Our readers are predominantly hunters, many of them naturalists who care deeply about protecting wildlife habitat. Hunting stories and essays should celebrate the hunting experience, demonstrating respect for wildlife, the land and the hunt. Articles on elk behavior or elk habitat should include personal observations and entertain as well as educate." Estab. 1984. Circ. 195,000. **Pays on acceptance.** Publishes ms 9 months after acceptance. Byline given. Offers variable kill fee. Buys one-time rights. Editorial lead time 6 months. Submit seasonal material 6 months in advance. Accepts queries by mail, e-mail, fax, phone. Responds in 1 month to queries; 2 months to mss. Sample copy $5. Writer's guidelines for #10 SASE.

○┱ Preparation: "read as many issues of *Bugle* as possible to know what the Elk Foundation and magazine are about. Then write a strong query with those things in mind. Send it with clips of other published or unpublished pieces representative of story being proposed."

Nonfiction: Book excerpts, essays, general interest (elk related), historical/nostalgic, humor, opinion, personal experience, photo feature. No how-to, where-to. **Buys 20 mss/year.** Query with or without published clips, or send complete ms. Length: 1,500-4,500 words. **Pays 20¢/word** and 3 contributor copies; more issues at cost.

Reprints: Send typed ms with information about when and where the article previously appeared and rights for sale noted. Pays 75% of amount paid for an original article.

Columns/Departments: Situation Ethics, 1,000-2,000 words; Thoughts & Theories, 1,500-4,000 words; Women in the Outdoors, 1,000-2,500 words. **Buys 13 mss/year.** Query with or without published clips or send complete ms. **Pays 20¢/word.**

Fiction: Adventure, historical, humorous, slice-of-life vignettes, western, novel excerpts. No fiction that doesn't pertain to elk or elk hunting. **Buys 4 mss/year.** Query with or without published clips or send complete ms. Length: 1,500-4,500 words. **Pays 20¢/word.**

Poetry: Free verse, haiku, light verse, traditional. **Buys 6 poems/year.** Submit maximum 6 poems.

Tips: "Creative queries (250-500 words) that showcase your concept and your style remain the most effective approach. We're hungry for submissions for three specific columns: Situation Ethics, Thoughts & Theories, and Women in the Outdoors. Send a SASE for guidelines. We also welcome strong, well-reasoned opinion pieces on topics pertinent to hunting and wildlife conservation, and humorous pieces about elk behavior or encounters with elk (hunting or otherwise). We'd also like to see more humor; more natural history pertaining to elk and elk country; more good, thoughtful writing from women."

⊠ $ $ CALIFORNIA GAME & FISH, Game & Fish Publications, Box 741, Marietta GA 30061. **Contact:** Burt Carey, editor. See *Game & Fish Publications.*

$ $ CANADIAN SPORTFISHING MAGAZINE, Canada's Fishing Authority, Canadian Sportfishing Productions, 937 Centre Rd., Dept. 2020, Waterdown, Ontario L0R 2H0 Canada. (905)689-1112, ext. 202. Fax: (905)689-2065. E-mail: editor@canadian-sportfishing.com. **Contact:** Randy Lucenti, editor. **70% freelance written.** Bimonthly magazine covering sport fishing. Estab. 1988. Circ. 30,000. Pays on publication. Publishes ms an average of 3 months after acceptance. Byline given. Offers 50% kill fee. Buys all rights. Editorial lead time 6 months. Submit seasonal material 8 months in advance. Accepts queries by mail, e-mail, fax. Responds in 2 months to queries; 6 months to mss. Sample copy for $4. Writer's guidelines for #10 SASE.

Nonfiction: How-to, humor, new product. **Buys 40 mss/year.** Query. Length: 1,500-4,000 words. **Pays 15¢/word minimum (Canadian funds).** Sometimes pays expenses of writers on assignment.

Photos: Send photos with submission. Reviews contact sheets, transparencies and prints. Offers no additional payment for photos accepted with ms. Captions, model releases and identification of subjects required. Buys all rights.

⊠ $ $ DEER & DEER HUNTING, Krause Publications, 700 E. State St., Iola WI 54990-0001. Fax: (715)445-4087. Editor: Patrick Durkin. Website: www.deeranddeerhunting.com. **Contact:** Dan Schmidt, managing editor. **95% freelance written.** Published 9 times/year covering white-tailed deer and deer hunting. "Readers include a cross section of the deer hunting population—individuals who hunt with bow, gun or camera. The editorial content of the magazine focuses on white-tailed deer biology and behavior, management principle and practices, habitat requirements, natural history of deer, hunting techniques, and hunting ethics. We also publish a wide range of 'how-to' articles designed to help hunters locate and get close to deer at all times of the year. The majority of our readership consists of two-season hunters (bow and gun) and approximately one-third camera hunt." Estab. 1977. Circ. 140,000. **Pays on acceptance.** Byline given. Editorial lead time 6 months. Submit seasonal material 6 months in advance. Accepts queries by mail. Responds in 3 months. Sample copy for 9×12 SASE. Writer's guidelines free.

Nonfiction: General interest, how-to, inspirational, photo feature. No "Me and Joe" articles. **Buys 30-50 mss/year.** Query. Length: 750-3,000 words. **Pays $150-525 for assigned articles; $150-325 for unsolicited articles.** Sometimes pays expenses of writers on assignment.

Photos: Send photos with submission. Reviews transparencies. Negotiates payment individually. Captions, model releases and identification of subjects required.

Fiction: "Mood" deer hunting pieces. **Buys 9 mss/year.** Send complete ms.

Fillers: Facts, newsbreaks. **Buys 40-50/year.** Length: 100-500 words. **Pays $15-150.**

Tips: "Feature articles dealing with deer biology or behavior should be documented by scientific research (the author's or that of others) as opposed to a limited number of personal observations."

$ $ DISCOVERING AND EXPLORING NEW JERSEY'S FISHING STREAMS AND THE DELAWARE RIVER, New Jersey Sportsmen's Guides, P.O. Box 100, Somerdale NJ 08083. Fax: (856)665-8656. Website: www.njsportsmensguide.com. **Contact:** Steve Perrone, editor. **60-70% freelance written.** Annual magazine covering freshwater stream and river fishing. Estab. 1993. Circ. 4,500. **Pays on acceptance.** Publishes ms an average of 6 months after acceptance. Byline given. Buys first rights and makes work-for-hire assignments. Editorial lead time 6 months. Accepts queries by mail, e-mail. Sample copy for $14.50 postage paid.

Nonfiction: How-to fishing and freshwater fishing. **Buys 6-8 mss/year.** Query with published clips. Length: 500-2,000 words. **Pays $75-250.**

Photos: State availability of photos with submission. Reviews 4×5 transparencies and prints. Negotiates payment individually. Captions, model releases, identification of subjects required. Buys one-time rights.

Tips: "We want queries with published clips of articles describing fishing experiences on New Jersey streams and the Delaware River."

Ⓝ $ $ DRAKE MAGAZINE, For People Who Fish, Paddlesport Publishing, P.O. Box 5450, Steamboat SPrings CO 80477-5450. (970)879-1450. Fax: (970)870-1404. E-mail: bieline@paddlermagazine.com. Website: www.drakemag.com. **Contact:** Tom Bie, editor. **70% freelance written.** Annual magazine for people who love fishing. Pays

30 days after publication. Publishes ms an average of 1 year after acceptance. Byline given. Buys first North American serial and one-time electronic rights. Editorial lead time 1 year. Submit seasonal material 1 year in advance. Accepts queries by mail, e-mail, fax. Responds in 6 months to mss.

Nonfiction: Book excerpts, essays, general interest, historical/nostalgic, how-to, humor, inspirational, interview/profile, new product, opinion, personal experience, photo feature, technical, travel (fishing related). **Buys 18 mss/year.** Query. Length: 250-3,000 words. **Pays 10-20¢/word "depending on the amount of work we have to put into the piece."**

Photos: State availability of photos with submission. Reviews contact sheets, negatives and transparencies. Offers $25-250/photo. Buys one-time rights.

$ $ $ $ FIELD & STREAM, 2 Park Ave., New York NY 10016-5695. Editor: Slaton White. **Contact:** David E. Petzal, executive editor. **50% freelance written.** Willing to work with new/unpublished writers. Monthly. "Broad-based service magazine for the hunter and fisherman. Editorial content ranges from very basic how-to stories detailing a useful technique or a device that sportsmen can make, to articles of penetrating depth about national hunting, fishing, and related activities. Also humor and personal essays, nostalgia and 'mood pieces' on the hunting or fishing experience and profiles on outdoor people." Estab. 1895. Circ. 1,790,400. **Pays on acceptance.** Byline given. Buys first rights. Responds in 2 weeks. Writer's guidelines for #10 SASE.

Nonfiction: Length: 1,500 words for features. Payment varies depending on the quality of work, importance of the article. **Pays $800 and up to $1,000 and more on a sliding scale for major features.** *Field & Stream* also publishes regional sections with feature articles on hunting and fishing in specific areas of the country. The sections are geographically divided into East, Midwest, West and South, and appear 12 months/year. Query by mail only: regional articles and ideas by mail to Regionals Editor. Length: 100-600 words. **Pays $100-400.**

Photos: Prefers color slides to b&w. Query first with photos. When photos purchased separately, pays $450 minimum for color. Buys first rights to photos.

Columns/Departments: Personal essays suitable for the "Finally . . ." department. Length: 750-800 words.

Fillers: Buys short "how it's done" fillers, 75 to 150 words, on unusual or helpful subjects. Also buys short (up to 500 words) pieces on tactics or techniques for specific hunting or fishing situations; short "Field Guide" pieces on natural phenomena as related to hunting and fishing; "Myths and Misconceptions," short pieces debunking a commonly held belief about hunting and fishing; short "Outdoor Basics"; and short pieces for the "Up Front" section that run the gamut from natural history to conservation news, anecdotal humor, short tips, and carefully crafted opinion pieces (word length: 25-400).

Tips: "Writers are encouraged to submit queries on article ideas. These should be no more than a paragraph or two, and should include a summary of the idea, including the angle you will hang the story on, and a sense of what makes this piece different from all others on the same or a similar subject. Many queries are turned down because we have no idea what the writer is getting at. Be sure that your letter is absolutely clear. We've found that if you can't sum up the point of the article in a sentence or two, the article doesn't have a point. Pieces that depend on writing style, such as humor, mood, and nostalgia or essays often can't be queried and may be submitted in manuscript form. The same is true of short tips. All submissions to *Field & Stream* are on an on-spec basis. Before submitting anything, however, we encourage you to *study*, not simply read, the magazine. Many pieces are rejected because they do not fit the tone or style of the magazine, or fail to match the subject of the article with the overall subject matter of *Field & Stream*. Above all, study the magazine before submitting anything."

$ $ THE FISHERMAN, LIF Publishing Corp., 14 Ramsey Rd., Shirley NY 11967-4704. (516)345-5200. Fax: (516)345-5304. Publisher: Fred Golofaro. Associate Publisher: Pete Barrett. Senior Editor: Tim Coleman. 4 regional editions: *Long Island, Metropolitan New York*, Tom Melton, editor; *New England*, Tim Coleman, editor; *New Jersey*, Pete Barrett, editor; *Delaware-Maryland-Virginia*, Keith Kaufman, editor. **75% freelance written.** A weekly magazine covering fishing with an emphasis on saltwater. Combined circ. 100,000. Pays on publication. Byline given. Offers variable kill fee. Buys all rights. Articles may be run in one or more regional editions by choice of the editors. Submit seasonal material 2 months in advance. Responds in 6 weeks. Free sample copy and writer's guidelines.

Nonfiction: Send submission to regional editor. General interest, historical/nostalgic, how-to, interview/profile, personal experience, photo feature, technical, travel. Special issues: Boat & Motor Buyer's Guide and Winter Workbench (January); Tackle, Trout (March); Inshore Fishing (April); Saltwater Fly, Party Boat, Black Bass (May); Offshore Fishing (June); Surf Fishing (August); Striped Bass (October); Travel (December). "No 'me and Joe' tales. We stress how, where, when, why." **Buys 300 mss/year, each edition.** Length: 1,000-1,500 words. **Pays $110-150.**

Photos: Send photos with submission; also buys single color photos for cover use (pays $50-$100). Offers no additional payment for photos accepted with ms. Identification of subjects required.

Tips: "Focus on specific how-to and where-to subjects within each region."

$ $ FLORIDA GAME & FISH, Game & Fish Publications, Box 741, Marietta GA 30061. (770)953-9222. **Contact:** Jimmy Jacobs, editor. See *Game & Fish Publications*.

$ $ FLORIDA SPORTSMAN, Wickstrom Communications Division of PRIMEDIA Special Interest Publications, 2700 S. Kanner Hwy., Stuart FL 34994. (561)219-7400. Fax: (561)219-6900. E-mail: editor@floridasportsman.com. Website: www.floridasportsman.com. **Contact:** Jeff Weakley, editor. **70% freelance written.** Works with new/unpublished writers. Monthly magazine covering fishing, boating and related sports—Florida and Caribbean only. "*Florida Sportsman* is edited for the boatowner and offshore, coastal and fresh water fisherman. It provides a how, when and where approach in its articles, which also include occasional camping, diving and hunting stories—plus ecology; in-depth articles and editorials attempting to protect Florida's wilderness, wetlands and natural beauty." Circ. 115,000. **Pays on acceptance.** Publishes ms an average of 6 months after acceptance. Byline given. Offers 50% kill fee. Buys first North American serial rights. Submit seasonal material 6 months in advance. Accepts queries by mail. Responds in 2 months to queries; 1 month to mss. Sample copy free. Writer's guidelines for #10 SASE or on website.

Nonfiction: Essays (environment or nature), how-to (fishing, hunting, boating), humor (outdoors angle), personal experience (in fishing, etc.), technical (boats, tackle, etc., as particularly suitable for Florida specialties). "We use reader service pieces almost entirely—how-to, where-to, etc. One or two environmental pieces per issue as well. Writers *must* be Florida based, or have lengthy experience in Florida outdoors. All articles must have strong Florida emphasis. We do not want to see general how-to-fish-or-boat pieces which might well appear in a national or wide-regional magazine." **Buys 40-60 mss/year.** Query; no e-mail queries. Length: 2,000-3,000 words. **Pays $450.** Sometimes pays expenses of writers on assignment.

Photos: Send photos with submission. Reviews 35mm transparencies and 4×5 and larger prints. Offers no additional payment for photos accepted with ms. Pays up to $1,000 for cover photos. Buys one-time rights.

Tips: "Feature articles are most open to freelancers; however there is little chance of acceptance unless contributor is an accomplished and avid outdoorsman *and* a competent writer-photographer with considerable experience in Florida."

N $ FLORIDA WILDLIFE, Florida Game & Fresh Water Fish Commission, 620 S. Meridian St., Tallahassee FL 32399-1600. (850)488-5563. Fax: (850)488-8974. E-mail: subletd@gfc.state.fl. Website: www.state.fl.us/fwc/. **Contact:** Dick Sublette, editor. **50% freelance written.** Noncommercial bimonthly state magazine covering hunting, natural history, fishing, endangered species and wildlife conservation. "In outdoor sporting articles we seek themes of wholesome recreation. In nature articles we seek accuracy and conservation purpose." Estab. 1947. Circ. 26,000. Pays on publication. Byline given. Buys first North American serial and occasionally second serial (reprint) rights. Submit seasonal material 6 months in advance. Accepts simultaneous submissions. Responds in 2 months (acknowledgement of receipt of materials); up to 2 years for acceptance, usually less for rejections. Prefers photo/ms packages. Sample copy for $2.95. Writer's/photographer's guidelines for SASE.

Nonfiction: Florida saltwater features, general interest (bird watching, hiking, camping, boating), how-to (hunting and fishing), humor (wildlife related; no anthropomorphism), inspirational (conservation oriented), personal experience (wildlife, hunting, fishing, outdoors), photo feature (Florida species: game, nongame, botany), technical (rarely purchased, but open to experts), nature appreciation and outdoor ethics. "We buy general interest hunting, fishing and nature stories. No stories that humanize animals, or opinionated stories not based on confirmable facts." Special issues: Annual Florida Fishing edition (March/April); Hunting season (September/October and November/December). **Buys 40-50 mss/year.** Send slides/ms. Length: 500-1,500 words. **Generally pays $55/published page plus a per-photo disbursement.**

Photos: State availability of photos with story query. Accepts transparencies only (slides) of hunting, fishing, and natural science series of Florida wildlife species. Pays $35-80 for inside photos; $150 for front cover photos, $90 for back cover. "We like short, specific captions." Buys one-time rights.

Fiction: "We rarely buy fiction, and then only if it is true to life and directly related to good sportsmanship and conservation. No fairy tales, erotica, profanity or obscenity." **Buys 1-2 mss/year.** Send complete mss and label "fiction." Length: 500-1,200 words. **Generally pays $55/published page.**

Tips: "Read and study recent issues for subject matter, style and examples of our viewpoint, philosophy and treatment. We look for wholesome recreation, ethics, safety, and good outdoor experience more than bagging the game in our stories. We usually need well-written hunting, saltwater and freshwater fishing articles that are entertaining and informative and that describe places to hunt and fish in Florida. We do not publish articles that feature a commercial interest or a specific brand name product. Use the active rather than the passive voice. Our readership varies from schoolchildren to senior citizens, and a large number of subscribers reside in urban areas and in all 50 states."

$$ FLY FISHING IN SALT WATERS, World Publications, Inc., 460 N. Orlando Ave,. Suite 200, Winter Park FL 32789-7061. (407)628-4802. Fax: (407)628-7061. E-mail: flyfishinsalt@flyfishinsalt.com. Website: www.flyfishinsalt.com. **Contact:** David Ritchie, editor. **90% freelance written.** Bimonthly magazine covering fly fishing in salt waters anywhere in the world. Estab. 1994. Circ. 44,000. Pays on publication. Publishes ms an average of 1 year after acceptance. Byline given. Buys first North American serial rights and electronic rights. Editorial lead time 3 months. Submit seasonal material at least 2 months in advance. Accepts queries by mail, e-mail, phone. Responds in 1 month to queries; 2 months to mss. Sample copy for $3, back issues $6, plus $1 S&H. Writer's guidelines for #10 SASE.

Nonfiction: Book excerpts, essays, historical/nostalgic, how-to, interview/profile, new product, personal experience, photo feature, technical, travel, resource issues (conservation); all on flyfishing. **Buys 40-50 mss/year.** Query with or without published clips. Length: 1,500-2,500 words. **Pays $400-500.**

Photos: Send photos with submission. Reviews transparencies (35mm color only). Negotiates payment individually: offers no additional payment for photos accepted with ms; pays $80-300/photo if purchased separately. Captions, identification of subjects required. Buys one-time rights.

Columns/Departments: Legends/Reminiscences (history-profiles-nostalgia), 2,000-2,500 words; Resource (conservation issues), 1,000-1,500 words; Fly Tier's Bench (how to tie saltwater flies), 1,000-1,200 words, photos critical; Tackle & Technique (technical how-to), 1,000-1,500 words, photos or illustrations critical; Boating (technical how-to), 2,000-2,500 words; Saltwater 101 (for beginners, tackle tips and techniques), 1,000-2,000 words. (Other departments are mostly staff written or by assignment only.) **Buys 25-30 mss/year.** Query. **Pays $400-500.**

Fiction: Adventure, humorous, mainstream; all dealing with flyfishing. **Buys 2-3 mss/year.** Send complete ms. Length: 2,000-3,000 words. **Pays $500.**

Fillers: Most fillers are staff-written.

■ The online magazine carries content not found in the print edition.

Tips: "Follow up on your inquiry with a phone call."

N ☒ $ $ FLY FISHING QUARTERLY, Aqua-Field Publishing, 39 Avenue-At-The-Common, Shrewsbury NJ 07702. (732)224-9288. Fax: (732)224-8944. **Contact:** Steve Ferber, editor/publisher. **90% freelance written.** Quarterly magazine directed to the intermediate-to-expert fly fisherman. Estab. 1989. Circ. 54,000. **Often pays on acceptance,** sometimes on publication. Publishes ms an average of 6 months after acceptance. Byline given. Offers $100 kill fee. Buys first North American serial rights. Editorial lead time 9 months. Submit seasonal material 6 months in advance. Responds in 3 weeks to queries; 2 months to mss. Sample copy and writer's guidelines free.

Nonfiction: How-to, interview/profile, new product, photo feature, travel. Special issues: Fly Fishing Made Easy, Fly Fishing For Trout, Saltwater Flyfishing. No worn out ideas. **Buys 250 mss/year.** Query. Length; 1,000-2,500 words. **Pays $200-350 for assigned articles; $150-300 for unsolicited articles.**

Photos: Send photos with submission. Reviews transparencies and 4×5 prints. Offers no additional payment for photos accepted with ms. Captions and identification of subjects required. Buys one-time rights.

Columns/Departments: Fly Tying (how-to), 500 words; Travel, 1,000 words; New Products, 500 words. All with pictures. **Buys 50 mss/year.** Query or send complete ms. **Pays $100.**

Tips: "Send clear queries, good pictures and original material."

FLYFISHING & TYING JOURNAL, A Compendium for the Complete Fly Fisher, Frank Amato Publications, P.O. Box 82112, Portland OR 97282. (503)653-8108. Fax: (503)653-2766. E-mail: fap eleport.com. Website: www.ama-tobooks.com. **Contact:** Kim Koch. **60% freelance written.** Quarterly magazine covering flyfishing and fly tying for both new and veteran anglers. Every issue is seasonally focused: spring, summer, fall and winter. Estab. 1980. Circ. 60,000. Pays on publication. Publishes ms 6 months after acceptance. Byline given. Buys first rights. Editorial lead time 6 months. Submit seasonal material 6 months in advance. Accepts queries by mail, e-mail, fax. Responds in 1 month to queries, 2 months to mss. Writer's guidelines for #10 SASE.

Nonfiction: How-to, new product, personal experience, travel. **Buys 55-60 mss/year.** Query. Length: 800-3,000 words. **Pays $200-600.**

Photos: State availability of photos with submission. Reviews transparencies. Offers no additional payment for photos accepted with ms. Captions, model releases, identification of subjects required. Buys one-time rights.

$ FUR-FISH-GAME, 2878 E. Main, Columbus OH 43209-9947. **Contact:** Mitch Cox, editor. **65% freelance written.** Works with a small number of new/unpublished writers each year. Monthly magazine for outdoorsmen of all ages who are interested in hunting, fishing, trapping, dogs, camping, conservation and related topics. Estab. 1900. Circ. 111,000. **Pays on acceptance.** Publishes ms an average of 7 months after acceptance. Byline given. Buys first serial rights or all rights. Responds in 2 months. Sample copy for $1 and 9×12 SAE. Writer's guidelines for #10 SASE.

Nonfiction: "We are looking for informative, down-to-earth stories about hunting, fishing, trapping, dogs, camping, boating, conservation and related subjects. Nostalgic articles are also used. Many of our stories are 'how-to' and should appeal to small-town and rural readers who are true outdoorsmen. Some recent articles have told how to train a gun dog, catch big-water catfish, outfit a bowhunter and trap late-season muskrat. We also use personal experience stories and an occasional profile, such as an article about an old-time trapper. 'Where-to' stories are used occasionally if they have broad appeal." Query with SASE. Length: 500-3,000 words. **Pays $150 or more** for features depending upon quality, photo support, and importance to magazine. **Short filler stories pay $75-125.**

Photos: Send photos with ms. Photos are part of ms package and receive no additional payment. Prefers color prints or transparencies. Prints can be 5×7 or 8×10. Pays $25 for separate freelance photos. Captions and credits required.

Tips: "We are always looking for quality how-to articles about fish, game animals or birds that are popular with everyday outdoorsmen but often overlooked in other publications, such as catfish, bluegill, crappie, squirrel, rabbit, crows, etc. We also use articles on standard seasonal subjects such as deer and pheasant, but like to see a fresh approach or new technique. Instructional trapping articles are useful all year. Articles on gun dogs, ginseng and do-it-yourself projects are also popular with our readers. An assortment of photos and/or sketches greatly enhances any manuscript, and sidebars, where applicable, can also help. No phone queries, please."

☒ $ $ GAME & FISH PUBLICATIONS, 2250 Newmarket Pkwy., Suite 110, Marietta GA 30067. (770)953-9222. Fax: (770)933-9510. **Contact:** Ken Dunwoody, editorial director. Publishes 30 different monthly outdoor magazines, each one covering the fishing and hunting opportunities in a particular state or region (see individual titles and editors). **90% freelance written.** Estab. 1975. Circ. 575,000. Pays 75 days prior to cover date of issue. Publishes ms an average of 7 months after acceptance. Byline given. Offers negotiable kill fee. Buys first North American serial rights. Submit seasonal material at least 8 months in advance. Editors prefer to hold queries until that season's material is assigned. Responds in 3 months to mss. Sample copy for $2.99 and 9×12 SASE. Writer's guidelines for #10 SASE.

Nonfiction: Prefer queries over unsolicited ms. Article lengths either 1,500 or 2,400 words. Pays separately for articles and accompanying photos. **Manuscripts pay $125-300,** cover photos $250, inside color $75 and b&w $25. Reviews transparencies and b&w prints. Prefers captions and identification of species/subjects. Buys one-time rights to photos.

Fiction: Buys some humor, nostalgia and adventure pertaining to hunting and fishing. **Pays $125-250.** Length 1,100-2,500 words.

Tips: "Our readers are experienced anglers and hunters, and we try to provide them with useful, specific articles about where, when and how to enjoy the best hunting and fishing in their state or region. We also cover topics concerning game and fish management. Most articles should be tightly focused and aimed at outdoorsmen in one particular state. After familiarizing themselves with our magazine(s), writers should query the appropriate state editor (see individual listings) or send to Ken Dunwoody."

$ $ GEORGIA SPORTSMAN, Game & Fish Publications, Box 741, Marietta GA 30061. (770)953-9222. **Contact:** Jimmy Jacobs, editor. See *Game & Fish Publications.*

$ $ GREAT PLAINS GAME & FISH, Game & Fish Publications, Box 741, Marietta GA 30061. (770)953-9222. **Contact:** Nick Gilmore, editor. See *Game & Fish Publications.*

$ $ ILLINOIS GAME & FISH, Game & Fish Publications, Box 741, Marietta GA 30061. (770)953-9222. **Contact:** Dennis Schmidt, editor. See *Game & Fish Publications.*

$ $ INDIANA GAME & FISH, Game & Fish Publications, Box 741, Marietta GA 30061. (770)953-9222. **Contact:** Ken Freel, editor. See *Game & Fish Publications.*

$ $ IOWA GAME & FISH, Game & Fish Publications, Box 741, Marietta GA 30061. (770)953-9222. **Contact:** Nick Gilmore, editor. See *Game & Fish Publications.*

$ $ KENTUCKY GAME & FISH, Game & Fish Publications, Box 741, Marietta GA 30061. (770)953-9222. **Contact:** Ken Freel, editor. See *Game & Fish Publications.*

$ $ LOUISIANA GAME & FISH, Game & Fish Publications, Box 741, Marietta GA 30061. (770)953-9222. **Contact:** Ken Duke. See *Game & Fish Publications.*

$ $ THE MAINE SPORTSMAN, P.O. Box 365, Augusta ME 04330. (207)626-3315. E-mail: ursushpv@mint.net. Website: www.mainesportsman.com. **Contact:** Harry Vanderweide, editor. **80% freelance written.** "Eager to work with new/unpublished writers, but because we run over 30 regular columns, it's hard to get into *The Maine Sportsman* as a beginner." Monthly tabloid. Estab. 1972. Circ. 30,000. Pays during month of publication. Buys first rights. Publishes ms 3 months after acceptance. Byline given. Accepts queries by mail, e-mail. Responds in 2 weeks.

Nonfiction: "We publish only articles about Maine hunting and fishing activities. Any well-written, researched, knowledgeable article about that subject area is likely to be accepted by us." **Buys 25-40 mss/issue.** Submit complete ms. Length: 200-2,000 words. **Pays $20-300.** Sometimes pays the expenses of writers on assignment.

Reprints: Send typed ms with rights for sale. Pays 100% of amount paid for an original article.

Photos: "We can have illustrations drawn, but prefer 1-3 b&w photos." Submit photos with accompanying ms. Pays $5-50 for b&w print.

The online magazine carries original content not found in the print edition.

Tips: "We publish numerous special sections each year and are eager to buy Maine-oriented articles on snowmobiling, ice fishing, boating, salt water and deer hunting. Send articles or queries. You can e-mail us at ursushpv@mint.net."

N $ $ MARLIN, The International Sportfishing Magazine, Marlin Magazine, a division of World Publications, Inc., P.O. Box 2456, Winter Park FL 32790. (407)628-4802. Fax: (407)628-7061. E-mail: marlin@worldzine.com. **Contact:** David Ritchie, editor. **90% freelance written.** Bimonthly magazine on big game fishing. "*Marlin* covers the sport of big game fishing (billfish, tuna, dorado and wahoo). Our readers are sophisticated, affluent and serious about their sport—they expect a high-class, well-written magazine that provides information and practical advice." Estab. 1982. Circ. 40,000. **Pays on acceptance for text**, on publication for photos. Publishes ms an average of 3 months after acceptance. Byline given. Buys first North American serial rights. Submit seasonal material 2-3 months in advance. Query for electronic submissions. Sample copy and writer's guidelines for $3.20 and SAE.

Nonfiction: General interest, how-to (bait-rigging, tackle maintenance, etc.), new product, personal experience, photo feature, technical, travel. "No freshwater fishing stories. No 'me & Joe went fishing' stories." **Buys 30-50 mss/year.** Query with published clips. Length: 800-3,000 words. **Pays $250-500.**

Photos: State availability of photos with submission. Original slides, please. Offers $25-300/photo. $1,000 for a cover. Buys one-time rights.

Columns/Departments: Tournament Reports (reports on winners of major big game fishing tournaments), 200-400 words; Blue Water Currents (news features), 100-400 words. **Buys 25 mss/year.** Query. **Pays $75-250.**

Reprints: Accepts previously published articles in news section only. Send photocopy of article, including information about when and where the article previously appeared. Pays 50-75% of the amount paid for an original article.

Tips: "Tournament reports are a good way to break in to *Marlin*. Make them short but accurate, and provide photos of fishing action or winners' award shots (*not* dead fish hanging up at the docks!). We always need how-tos and news items. Our destination pieces (travel stories) emphasize where and when to fish, but include information on where to stay also. For features: crisp, high action stories with emphasis on exotic nature, adventure, personality, etc.—nothing flowery or academic. Technical/how-to: concise and informational—specific details. News: Again, concise with good details—watch for legislation affecting big game fishing, outstanding catches, new clubs and organizations, new trends and conservation issues."

$ MICHIGAN OUT-OF-DOORS, P.O. Box 30235, Lansing MI 48909. (517)371-1041. Fax: (517)371-1505. E-mail: mucc@mucc.org. Website: www.mucc.org. **Contact:** Dennis C. Knickerbocker, editor. **75% freelance written.** Works with a small number of new/unpublished writers each year. Monthly magazine emphasizing Michigan outdoor recreation, especially hunting and fishing, conservation, nature and environmental affairs. Estab. 1947. Circ. 100,000. **Pays on acceptance.** Publishes ms an average of 6 months after acceptance. Byline given. Buys first North American serial rights. Submit seasonal material 6 months in advance. Accepts queries by mail, phone. Responds in 1 month. Sample copy for $3.50. Writer's guidelines free or on website.
　　O⊸ Break in by "writing interestingly about an *unusual* aspect of Michigan natural resources and/or outdoor recreation.

Nonfiction: Exposé, historical, how-to, informational, interview, nostalgia, personal experience, personal opinion, photo feature, profile. No humor or poetry. "Stories *must* have a Michigan slant unless they treat a subject of universal interest to our readers." Special issues: Archery Deer Hunting (October); Firearm Deer Hunting (November); Cross-country Skiing and Early-ice Lake Fishing (December). **Buys 8 mss/issue.** Send complete ms. Length: 1,000-2,000 words. **Pays $90 minimum for feature stories.** Pays expenses of writers on assignment.
　　● Interested in seeing "family participation articles about somewhat unusual outdoor activities, such as snorkeling, snowshoeing, etc."

Photos: Purchased with or without accompanying ms. Pays $20 minimum for any size b&w glossy prints; $175 maximum for color (for cover). Offers no additional payment for photos accepted with accompanying ms. Buys one-time rights. Captions preferred.

Tips: "Top priority is placed on true accounts of personal adventures in the out-of-doors—well-written tales of very unusual incidents encountered while hunting, fishing, camping, hiking, etc. The most rewarding aspect of working with freelancers is playing a part in their development. But it's annoying to respond to queries that never produce a manuscript."

⊠ $ $ MICHIGAN SPORTSMAN, Game & Fish Publications, Box 741, Marietta GA 30061. (770)953-9222. **Contact:** Dennis Schmidt, editor. See *Game & Fish Publications*.

⊠ $ $ MID-ATLANTIC GAME & FISH, Game & Fish Publications, Box 741, Marietta GA 30061. (770)953-9222. **Contact:** Ken Freel, editor. See *Game & Fish Publications*.

⊠ $ MID WEST OUTDOORS, Mid West Outdoors, Ltd., 111 Shore Drive, Hinsdale (Burr Ridge) IL 60521-5885. (630)887-7722. Fax: (630)887-1958. E-mail: mwdmagtv30@aol.com. Website: www.MidWestOutdoors.com. **Contact:** Gene Laulunen, editor. **100% freelance written.** Monthly tabloid emphasizing fishing, hunting, camping and boating. Estab. 1967. Circ. 45,000. Pays on publication. Buys simultaneous rights. Byline given. Submit seasonal material 2 months in advance. Accepts simultaneous submissions. Responds in 3 weeks. Publishes ms an average of 3 months after acceptance. Sample copy for $1 or on website. Writer's guidelines for #10 SASE or on website.

Nonfiction: How-to (fishing, hunting, camping in the Midwest) and where-to-go (fishing, hunting, camping within 500 miles of Chicago). "We do not want to see any articles on 'my first fishing, hunting or camping experiences,' 'cleaning my tackle box,' 'tackle tune-up,' or 'catch and release.' " **Buys 1,800 unsolicited mss/year.** Send complete ms and 1 or 2 photos on 3.5 diskette with ms included. Length: 1,000-1,500 words. **Pays $15-30.**

Reprints: Send tearsheet of article.

Photos: Offers no additional payment for photos accompanying ms; uses slides and b&w prints. Buys all rights. Captions required.

Columns/Departments: Fishing, Hunting. Open to column/department suggestions. Send complete ms. **Pays $25.**

Tips: "Break in with a great unknown fishing hole or new technique within 500 miles of Chicago. Where, how, when and why. Know the type of publication you are sending material to."

⊠ $ $ MINNESOTA SPORTSMAN, Game & Fish Publications, Box 741, Marietta GA 30061. (770)953-9222. **Contact:** Dennis Schmidt, editor. See *Game & Fish Publications*.

⊠ $ $ MISSISSIPPI GAME & FISH, Game & Fish Publications, Box 741, Marietta GA 30061. (770)953-9222. **Contact:** Ken Dukes, editor. See *Game & Fish Publications*.

⊠ $ $ MISSOURI GAME & FISH, Game & Fish Publications, Box 741, Marietta GA 30061. (770)953-9222. **Contact:** Ken Duke. See *Game & Fish Publications*.

Ⓝ ⊠ $ $ MUSKY HUNTER MAGAZINE, Willow Creek Press, P.O. Box 340, St. Germain WI 54558. (715)477-2178. Fax: (715)477-8858. Editor: Jim Saric. **90% freelance written.** Bimonthly magazine on musky fishing. "Serves the vertical market of musky fishing enthusiasts. We're interested in how-to where-to articles." Estab. 1988.

Circ. 34,000. Pays on publication. Publishes ms an average of 4 months after acceptance. Byline given. Buys first or one-time rights. Submit seasonal material 4 months in advance. Responds in 2 months. Sample copy for 9 × 12 SAE with $1.93 postage. Writer's guidelines for #10 SASE.

Nonfiction: Historical/nostalgic (related only to musky fishing), how-to (modify lures, boats and tackle for musky fishing), personal experience (must be musky fishing experience), technical (fishing equipment), travel (to lakes and areas for musky fishing). **Buys 50 mss/year.** Send complete ms. Length: 1,000-2,500 words. **Pays $100-300 for assigned articles; $50-300 for unsolicited articles.** Payment of contributor copies or other premiums negotiable.

Photos: Send photos with submission. Reviews 35mm transparencies and 3 × 5 prints. Offers no additional payment for photos accepted with ms. Identification of subjects required. Buys one-time rights.

⚑ $ $ NEW ENGLAND GAME & FISH, Game & Fish Publications, Box 741, Marietta GA 30061. (770)953-9222. **Contact:** Steve Carpenteri, editor. See *Game & Fish Publications.*

$ $ NEW JERSEY LAKE SURVEY FISHING MAPS GUIDE, New Jersey Sportsmen's Guides, P.O. Box 100, Somerdale NJ 08083. (609)783-1271. (856)665-8350. Fax: (856)665-8656. Website: www.njsportsmensguide.com. **Contact:** Steve Perrone, editor. **30-40% freelance written.** Annual magazine covering freshwater lake fishing. "*New Jersey Lake Survey Fishing Maps Guide* is edited for freshwater fishing for trout, bass, perch, catfish and other species. It contains 140 pages and approximately 100 full-page maps of the surveyed lakes that illustrate contours, depths, bottom characteristics, shorelines and vegetation present at each location. The guide includes a 10-page chart which describes over 250 fishing lakes in New Jersey. It also includes more than 125 fishing tips and 'Bass'n Notes.'" Estab. 1989. Circ. 4,500. **Pays on acceptance.** Publishes ms an average of 6 months after acceptance. Byline given. Buys first rights and makes work-for-hire assignments. Editorial lead time 6 months. Accepts queries by mail, fax. Sample copy for $14.50 postage paid.

Nonfiction: How-to fishing, freshwater fishing. Length: 500-2,000 words. **Pays $75-250.**

Photos: State availability of photos with submission. Reviews transparencies, 4 × 5 slides or 4 × 6 prints. Captions, model releases, identification of subjects required. Buys one-time rights.

Tips: "We want queries with published clips of articles describing fishing experiences on New Jersey lakes and ponds."

⚑ $ $ NEW YORK GAME & FISH, Game & Fish Publications, Box 741, Marietta GA 30061. (770)953-9222. **Contact:** Steve Carpenteri, editor. See *Game & Fish Publications.*

$ $ NORTH AMERICAN WHITETAIL, The Magazine Devoted to the Serious Trophy Deer Hunter, Game & Fish Publications, 2250 Newmarket Pkwy., Suite 110, Marietta GA 30067. (770)953-9222. Fax: (770)933-9510. **Contact:** Gordon Whittington, editor. **70% freelance written.** Magazine published 8 times/year about hunting trophy-class white-tailed deer in North America, primarily the US. "We provide the serious hunter with highly sophisticated information about trophy-class whitetails and how, when and where to hunt them. We are not a general hunting magazine or a magazine for the very occasional deer hunter." Estab. 1982. Circ. 130,000. Pays 75 days prior to cover date of issue. Publishes ms an average of 6 months after acceptance. Byline given. Offers negotiable kill fee. Buys first North American serial rights. Submit seasonal material 10 months in advance. Responds in 3 months to mss. Editor prefers to keep queries on file, without notification, until the article can be assigned or author informs of prior sale. Sample copy for $3 and 9 × 12 SAE with 7 first-class stamps. Writer's guidelines for #10 SASE.

Nonfiction: How-to, interview/profile. **Buys 50 mss/year.** Query. Length: 1,000-3,000 words. **Pays $150-400.**

Photos: Send photos with submission. Reviews 2 × 2 transparencies and 8 × 10 prints. Offers no additional payment for photos accepted with ms. Captions and identification of subjects required. Buys one-time rights.

Columns/Departments: Trails and Tails (nostalgic, humorous or other entertaining styles of deer-hunting material, fictional or nonfictional), 1,400 words. **Buys 8 mss/year.** Send complete ms. **Pays $150.**

Tips: "Our articles are written by persons who are deer hunters first, writers second. Our hard-core hunting audience can see through material produced by non-hunters or those with only marginal deer-hunting expertise. We have a continual need for expert profiles/interviews. Study the magazine to see what type of hunting expert it takes to qualify for our use, and look at how those articles have been directed by the writers. Good photography of the interviewee and his hunting results must accompany such pieces."

⚑ $ $ NORTH CAROLINA GAME & FISH, Game & Fish Publications, Box 741, Marietta GA 30061. (770)953-9222. Fax: (770)933-9510. **Contact:** Editor. See *Game & Fish Publications.*

⚑ $ $ OHIO GAME & FISH, Game & Fish Publications, Box 741, Marietta GA 30061. (770)953-9222. **Contact:** Steve Carpenteri, editor. See *Game & Fish Publications.*

⚑ $ $ OKLAHOMA GAME & FISH, Game & Fish Publications, Box 741, Marietta GA 30061. (770)953-9222. Fax: (770)933-9510. **Contact:** Nick Gilmore, editor. See *Game & Fish Publications.*

⚑ $ $ ONTARIO OUT OF DOORS, Rogeis Media, 777 Bay St., 6th Floor, Toronto, Ontario M5W 1A7 Canada. (416)596-5815. Fax: (416)596-2517. E-mail: jkerr@mhpublishing.com. Website: www.fishontario.com. Editor: Burt Myers. **Contact:** John Kerr, managing editor. **90% freelance written.** Magazine published 10 times/year covering the outdoors (hunting, fishing, camping). Estab. 1968. **Pays on acceptance.** Circ. 93,865. Publishes ms an average of

6 months after acceptance. Byline given. Offers 100% kill fee. Buys first and electronic rights. Editorial lead time 6 months. Submit seasonal material 6 months in advance. Accepts queries by mail, fax, phone. Responds in 3 months to queries. Sample copy and writer's guidelines free.

● Editor notes that *Ontario Out of Doors* needs more articles on camping, boating, recreational vehicles, photography, target shooting and archery as they relate to angling and hunting.

Nonfiction: Book excerpts, essays, exposé, how-to and where-to (fishing and hunting), humor, inspirational, interview/profile, new product, opinion, personal experience, photo feature, technical, travel, wildlife management and environmental concerns. "No Me and Joe features or articles written from a women's point of view on how to catch a bass." Special issues: Travel (March); Trout (April). **Buys 100 mss/year.** Query with SASE. Length: 500-2,500 words maximum. **Pays $750 maximum for assigned articles; $700 maximum for unsolicited articles.** Sometimes pays expenses of writers on assignment.

Photos: Send photos with submission. Reviews transparencies. Offers no additonal payment for photos accepted with ms except for cover and contents use. Pays $450-750 for covers. Captions required. Buys one-time rights and electronic rights.

Columns/Departments: Trips & Tips (travel pieces), 50-150 words; Short News, 50-500 words. **Buys 30-40 mss/year.** Query. **Pays $50-250.**

Fiction: Humorous. **Buys 6 mss/year.** Send complete ms. Length: 1,000 words maximum. **Pays $500 maximum.** Occasionally publishes novel excerpts.

Fillers: Facts, newsbreaks. **Buys 40/year.** Length: 25-100 words. **Pays $15-50.**

Tips: "With the exception of short news stories, it is suggested that writers query prior to submission."

N $ $ $ $ OUTDOOR LIFE, The Sportsman's Authority Since 1898, Times Mirror Magazines, 2 Park Ave., New York NY 10016. (212)779-5000. Fax: (212)779-5366. E-mail: olmagazine@aol.com. Website: www.outdoorlife.com. Editor: Todd W. Smith. Managing Editor: Camille Cozzone Rankin. **Contact:** Ed Scheff, executive editor. **60% freelance written.** Magazine published 10 times/year (2 double issues) covering hunting and fishing in North America. "*Outdoor Life* is a major national source of information for American and Canadian hunters and anglers. It offers news, regional reports, adventure stories, how-to, regular advice from experts, profiles and equipment tests." Estab. 1898. Circ. 1,350,000. **Pays on acceptance.** Publishes ms an average of 6 months after acceptance. Byline given. Buys first North American serial and electronic rights. Editorial lead time 4 months. Submit seasonal material 5 months in advance. Accepts queries by mail, e-mail, fax. Responds in 1 month to queries; 2 months to mss. Sample copy for 9×12 SAE plus proper postage. Writer's guidelines for #10 SASE.

Nonfiction: Essays, exposé, how-to, interview/profile, personal experience, travel, interesting/weird news stories. All articles must pertain to hunting and fishing pursuits. *OL* does not publish poetry or fiction; no freelance photo essays." Query with published clips. Length: 100-500 words for small articles; 1,000-2,000 for larger articles. **Pays $1,500-3,000 for major stories.** No set minimums or maximums—negotiated with individual writers. Sometimes pays expenses of writers on assignment.

● Ranked as one of the best markets for freelance writers in *Writer's Yearbook* magazine's annual "Top 100 Markets," January 2000.

Photos: State availability of photos with submission. Reviews contact sheets and transparencies. Model releases and identification of subjects required.

Columns/Departments: Frank Miniter, associate editor (Regionals); Scott Bowen, assistant editor (Compass) or Ed Scheff, executive editor (Private Lessons). Regionals (state-by-state news/destinations), 150-300 words; Compass (national news stories), 250-500 words; Snap Shots (part of Compass, news/fact blurbs), 150 words; Private Lessons (outdoor/hunting/fishing how-to), 500-700 words. **Buys 500 mss/year. Query with published clips. Pays $75-500.** "Most sections open to freelancers pay 50¢/word and most stories average 300 words."

Fillers: Scott Bowen, Compass assistant editor. Facts, newsbreaks. (See Snap Shots in Compass.) Must be timely, short newsbreaks or small items of particular interest. Look at a recent issue. **Buys 40-50/year.** Length: 150 words. **Pays $75.**

Tips: "If someone catches a record fish or takes a record game animal, or has a great adventure/survival story, they may try to submit a full-sized feature, but the story must be exceptional."

✪ $ $ PENNSYLVANIA ANGLER & BOATER, Pennsylvania Fish and Boat Commission, P.O. Box 67000, Harrisburg PA 17106-7000. (717)657-4520. E-mail: amichaels@fish.state.pa.us. Website: www.fish.state.pa.us. **Contact:** Art Michaels, editor. **80% freelance written.** Prefers to work with published/established writers but works with a few unpublished writers every year. Bimonthly magazine covering fishing, boating and related conservation topics in Pennsylvania. Circ. 35,000. Pays 2 months after acceptance. Publishes ms an average of 8 months after acceptance. Byline given. Rights purchased vary. Submit seasonal material 8 months in advance. Responds in 1 month to queries; 2 months to mss. Sample copy for 9×12 SAE with 9 first-class stamps. Guidelines for #10 SASE.

Nonfiction: How-to, where-to, technical. No saltwater or hunting material. **Buys 100 mss/year.** Query. Length: 500-3,500 words. **Pays $25-300.**

Photos: Send photos with submission. Reviews 35mm and larger transparencies. Offers no additional payment for photos accepted with ms. Captions, model releases and identification of subjects required. Also reviews photos separately. Rights purchased and rates vary.

Tips: "Our mainstays are how-tos, where-tos and conservation pieces. Articles are occasionally aimed at novice anglers and boaters, and some material is directed toward the most skilled fishermen and boaters. Most articles cater to people between these extremes."

◻ **$ $ PENNSYLVANIA GAME & FISH**, Game & Fish Publications, Box 741, Marietta GA 30061. (770)953-9222. **Contact:** Steve Carpenteri, editor. See *Game & Fish Publications*.

▣ **$ $ PETERSEN'S HUNTING**, Petersen Publishing Co., 6420 Wilshire Blvd., Los Angeles CA 90048. (323)782-2180. Fax: (323)782-2477. Editor: J. Scott Rupp. Executive Editor: Lee J. Hoots. **40% freelance written.** Works with a small number of new/unpublished writers each year. Monthly magazine covering sport hunting. "We are a 'how-to' magazine devoted to all facets of sport hunting, with the intent to make our readers more knowledgeable, more successful and safer hunters." Circ. 325,000. **Pays on acceptance.** Publishes ms an average of 9 months after acceptance. Byline given. Buys all rights. Submit seasonal queries 1 year in advance. Responds in 1 month. Free sample copy and writer's guidelines covering format, sidebars and computer disks available on request.
Nonfiction: General interest, historical/nostalgic, how-to (on hunting techniques), travel. Special issues: Hunting Annual (August). **Buys 30 mss/year.** Query. Length: 2,400 words. **Pays $350 minimum.**
Photos: Send photos with submission. Reviews 35mm transparencies. Captions, model releases, identification of subjects required. Buys one-time rights.

◻ **$ $ ROCKY MOUNTAIN GAME & FISH**, Game & Fish Publications, Box 741, Marietta GA 30061. Fax: (770)933-9510. **Contact:** Burt Carey, editor. See *Game & Fish Publications*.

◻ **$ $ SAFARI MAGAZINE, The Journal of Big Game Hunting**, Safari Club International, 4800 W. Gates Pass Rd., Tucson AZ 85745. (520)620-1220. Fax: (520)617-3555. E-mail: sskinner@safariclub.org. Website: www.safariclub.org. Director of Publications/Editor: Steve Comus. **Contact:** Stan Skinner, managing editor. **90% freelance written.** Bimonthly club journal covering international big game hunting and wildlife conservation. Circ. 30,000. Pays on publication. Publishes ms an average of 18 months after acceptance. Byline given. Buys all rights on story; first rights on photos. Submit seasonal material 1 year in advance. Accepts queries by mail, e-mail. Responds in 2 weeks to queries; 6 weeks to mss. Sample copy for $4. Guidelines for SASE.
○━ Break in with "engaging, suspenseful, first-person stories of big-game hunts that involve unique circumstances or unusual regions and animals. Conservation stories should include reputable, known sources in the field, plenty of facts and be supported by scientific data."
Nonfiction: Photo feature (wildlife), technical (firearms, hunting techniques, etc.). **Buys 72 mss/year.** Query or send complete ms. Length: 2,000-2,500 words. **Pays $300 for professional writers, lower rates if not professional.**
Photos: State availability of photos with query; or send photos with ms. Payment depends on size in magazine. Pays up to $45 for b&w; $100 color. Captions, model releases, identification of subjects required. Buys first rights.
Tips: "Study the magazine. Send complete manuscript and photo package. Make it appeal to knowledgeable, world-traveled big game hunters. Features on conservation contributions from big game hunters around the world are open to freelancers. We have enough stories on first-time African safaris. We need North and South American, European and Asian hunting stories, plus stories dealing with wildlife conservation, especially as it applies to our organization and members."

◻ **$ $ SALT WATER SPORTSMAN MAGAZINE**, 263 Summer St., Boston MA 02210. (617)790-5400. Fax: (617)790-5455. E-mail: editor@saltwatersportsman.com. Website: www.saltwatersportsman.com. **Contact:** Barry Gibson, editor. **85% freelance written.** Works with a small number of new/unpublished writers each year. Monthly magazine. "*Salt Water Sportsman* is edited for serious marine sport fishermen whose lifestyle includes the pursuit of game fish in US waters and around the world. It provides information on fishing trends, techniques and destinations, both local and international. Each issue reviews offshore and inshore fishing boats, high-tech electronics, innovative tackle, engines and other new products. Coverage also focuses on sound fisheries management and conservation." Circ. 150,000. **Pays on acceptance.** Publishes ms an average of 5 months after acceptance. Byline given. Buys first North American serial rights. Offers 100% kill fee. Submit seasonal material 8 months in advance. Accepts queries by mail, e-mail, fax. Responds in 1 month. Sample copy and writer's guidelines available for SASE.
Nonfiction: How-to, personal experience, technical, travel (to fishing areas). "Readers want solid how-to, where-to information written in an enjoyable, easy-to-read style. Personal anecdotes help the reader identify with the writer." Prefers new slants and specific information. Query. "It is helpful if the writer states experience in salt water fishing and any previous related articles. We want one, possibly two well-explained ideas per query letter—not merely a listing. Good pictures with query often help sell the idea." **Buys 100 mss/year.** Length: 1,200-2,000 words. **Pays $350 and up.** Also seeking short feature articles (500-1,000 words) on regional hot spots, species, special rigs, fishing methods, etc. **Pays $200-500,** depending on the quality of writing and accompanying photos. Query.
● Ranked as one of the best markets for freelance writers in *Writer's Yearbook* magazine's annual "Top 100 Markets," January 2000.
Reprints: Occasionally accepts reprints of previously published submissions. Send tearsheet of article. Pays up to 50% of amount paid for an original article.
Photos: Purchased with or without accompanying ms. Captions required. Uses color slides. Pays $1,000 minimum for 35mm, 2¼×2¼ or 8×10 transparencies for cover. Offers additional payment for photos accepted with ms.
Columns/Departments: Sportsman's Tips (short, how-to tips and techniques on salt water fishing, emphasis is on building, repairing, or reconditioning specific items or gear). Send ms. Length: 100-300 words.
Tips: "There are a lot of knowledgeable fishermen/budding writers out there who could be valuable to us with a little coaching. Many don't think they can write a story for us, but they'd be surprised. We work with writers. Shorter articles

that get to the point which are accompanied by good, sharp photos are hard for us to turn down. Having to delete unnecessary wordage—conversation, clichés, etc.—that writers feel is mandatory is annoying. Often they don't devote enough attention to specific fishing information."

N ▨ $ $ SHOTGUN SPORTS MAGAZINE, America's leading shotgun magazine, Shotgun Sports, Inc., P.O. Box 6810, Auburn CA 95604. (530)889-2220. Fax: (530)889-9106. E-mail: shotgun@shotgunsportsmagazine. com. Website: www.shotgunsportsmagazine.com. **Contact:** Frank Kodl, editorial director. **100% freelance written.** Magazine published 11/year (Jan/Feb combined) covering shotgun sports and shotgun hunting. "We cover any and all activities performed with a shotgun—sporting clays, trapshooting, skeet, hunting, gunsmithing, shotshell patterning, shotshell reloading, mental exercises to improve performance, equipment tests—anything that has a shotgun approach to the subject." Estab. 1978. Circ. 120,000. Pays on publication. Publishes ms an average of 6 months after acceptance. Byline given. Buys first North American serial or all rights. Editorial lead time 4 months. Submit seasonal material 5 months in advance. Accepts queries by mail, e-mail, fax, phone. Responds in 3 weeks to queries; 3 months to mss. Sample copy and writer's guidelines free.

Nonfiction: Book excerpts, exposé, general interest, historical/nostalgic, how-to, humor, interview/profile, opinion, personal experience, photo feature, technical. "No stories that invite going to a specific club or sponsored hunting trip that appear to be payback pieces." **Buys 50-75 mss/year.** Query with or without published clips or send complete ms. Length: 1,000-5,000 words. **Pays $50-200.** Sometimes pays expenses of writers on assignment.

Photos: State availability of photos with submission. Reviews contact sheets, transparencies and prints. Offers no additional payment for photos accepted with ms. Captions and identification of subjects required. Buys all rights.

Fillers: Anecdotes, facts, newsbreaks, short humor. **Buys 10/year.** Length: 100-1,000 words. **Pays $15-50.**

Tips: "Take a fresh approach. Writers for *Shotgun Sports* should have firsthand knowledge of hunting, trapshooting, skeet or sporting clays or be knowledgeable in other areas of shotgunning such as collecting, repairing or reloading. Current issues of *Shotgun Sports* are the best guide to our style. Try to create a professional, yet friendly article. Quality is the key. I would rather see 1,000 well-written words than 5,000 which have to be edited and rewritten before they become readable. Photographs of high quality are almost always required with any submission. In some cases, we can provide additional photographs from our files."

▨ $ $ SOUTH CAROLINA GAME & FISH, Game & Fish Publications, Box 741, Marietta GA 30061. (770)953-9222. **Contact:** Editor. See *Game & Fish Publications*.

▨ $ $ SOUTH CAROLINA WILDLIFE, P.O. Box 167, Rembert Dennis Bldg., Columbia SC 29202-0167. (803)734-3972. E-mail: scwmed@scdnr.state.sc.us. Editor: John Davis. **Contact:** Linda Renshaw, managing editor. Bimonthly magazine for South Carolinians interested in wildlife and outdoor activities. **75% freelance written.** Estab. 1954. Circ. 60,000. Byline given. **Pays on acceptance.** Publishes ms an average of 6 months after acceptance. Buys first rights. Free sample copy. Responds in 2 months.

Nonfiction: Articles on outdoor South Carolina with an emphasis on preserving and protecting our natural resources. "Realize that the topic must be of interest to South Carolinians and that we must be able to justify using it in a publication published by the state department of natural resources—so if it isn't directly about outdoor recreation, a certain plant or animal, it must be somehow related to the environment and conservation. Readers prefer a broad mix of outdoor related topics (articles that illustrate the beauty of South Carolina's outdoors and those that help the reader get more for his/her time, effort, and money spent in outdoor recreation). These two general areas are the ones we most need. Subjects vary a great deal in topic, area and style, but must all have a common ground in the outdoor resources and heritage of South Carolina. Review back issues and query with a one-page outline citing sources, giving ideas for photographs, explaining justification and giving an example of the first two paragraphs." Does not need any column material. Generally does not seek photographs. The publisher assumes no responsibility for unsolicited material. **Buys 25-30 mss/year.** Length: 1,000-3,000 words. **Pays $200-400** depending upon length and subject matter.

Tips: "We need more writers in the outdoor field who take pride in the craft of writing and put a real effort toward originality and preciseness in their work. Query on a topic we haven't recently done. Frequent mistakes made by writers in completing an article are failure to check details and go in-depth on a subject."

$ $ $ SPORT FISHING, The Magazine of Saltwater Fishing, 460 N Orlando Ave., Suite 200, Winter Park FL 32789-7061. (407)628-4802. Fax: (407)628-7061. E-mail: doug.orlander@worldpub.net. Managing Editor: Jason Cannon. **Contact:** Doug Olander, editor-in-chief. **60% freelance written.** Magazine covering saltwater sport fishing. Estab. 1986. Circ. 150,000. Pays within 6 weeks of acceptance. Byline given. Offers $100 kill fee. Buys first North American serial or one-time rights. Submit seasonal material 5 months in advance. Accepts queries by mail, e-mail, fax. Accepts simultaneous submission. Responds in 2 weeks. Sample copy and writer's guidelines for SASE.

↝ Break in with freelance pieces for the *Tips & Techniques News* and *Fish Tales* departments.

Nonfiction: How-to (rigging & techniques tips), technical, conservation, and where-to (all on sport fishing). **Buys 32-40 mss/year.** Query with or without clips, e-mail preferred; fax, letter acceptable. Length: 1,500-2,500 words. **Pays $800-1,200 with photos.**

Photos: Send photos with submission. Reviews transparencies and returns within 1 week. Pays $75-300 inside; $1,000 cover. Buys one-time rights.

Columns/Departments: Fish Tales (humorous sport fishing anecdotes); Rigging (how-to rigging for sport fishing); Technique (how-to technique for sport fishing). Length: 800-1,200 words. **Buys 8-24 mss/year.** Send complete ms. **Pays $250 for Fish Tales.**

Tips: "Don't query unless you are familiar with the magazine; note—*salt water only.* Find a fresh idea or angle to an old idea. We welcome the chance to work with new/unestablished writers who know their stuff—and how to say it."

$ $TENNESSEE SPORTSMAN, Game & Fish Publications, Box 741, Marietta GA 30061. (770)953-9222. **Contact:** Editor. See *Game & Fish Publications.*

$ $TEXAS SPORTSMAN, Game & Fish Publications, Box 741, Marietta GA 30061. (770)953-9222. **Contact:** Nick Gilmore, editor. See *Game & Fish Publications.*

$ $TIDE MAGAZINE, Coastal Conservation Association, 220W, 4801 Woodway, Houston TX 77056. (713)626-4222. Fax: (713)961-3801. E-mail: tide@joincca.org. **Contact:** Doug Pike, editor. Bimonthly magazine on saltwater fishing and conservation of marine resources. Estab. 1977. Circ. 60,000. Pays on publication. Byline given. Buys one-time rights. Submit seasonal material 6 months in advance. Responds in 1 month.

Nonfiction: Essays, exposé, general interest, historical/nostalgic, humor, opinion, personal experience and travel, related to saltwater fishing and Gulf/Atlantic coastal habits. **Buys 30 mss/year.** Query with published clips. Length: 1,200-1,500 words. **Pays $250-350 for ms/photo package.**

Photos: Reviews 35mm transparencies and color negs/prints. Offers no additional payment for photos accepted with ms. Captions required. Buys one-time rights. Pays $25 for b&w, $50 for color inside.

$ $TRAPPER & PREDATOR CALLER, Krause Publications Inc., 700 E. State St., Iola WI 54990. (715)445-2214. Fax: (715)445-4087. E-mail: waitp@krause.com. Website: www.trapperpredatorcaller.com. **Contact:** Paul Wait, editor. **90% freelance written.** Monthly tabloid covers trapping, predator calling and muzzleloading. "Our editorial goal is to entertain and educate our readers with national and regional articles that promote trapping and predator calling." Estab. 1975. Circ. 41,000. Pays on publication. Buys first North American serial rights. Submit seasonal material 6 months in advance. Free sample copy and writer's guidelines.

Nonfiction: How-to, humor, interview/profile, new product, opinion and personal experience. **Buys 100 mss/year.** Query with or without published clips, or send complete ms. Length: 1,200-2,500 words. **Pays $80-250 for assigned articles; $40-200 for unsolicited articles.**

Photos: Send photos with submission. Reviews prints. Offers no additional payment for photos accepted with ms. Captions and identification of subjects required. Buys one-time rights.

The online version contains material not found in the print edition. Contact: Paul Wait.

Tips: "Detailed how-to articles receive strongest consideration. How-to and adventure stories about trapping wolves, lynx, mountain lions, wolverines, arctic foxes and nutria wanted."

$ $TURKEY & TURKEY HUNTING, Krause Publications, 700 E. State St., Iola WI 54990-0001. (715)445-2214, ext. 484. Fax: (715)445-4087. E-mail: lovettb@krause.com. Website: www.turkeyandturkeyhunting.com. **Contact:** Brian Lovett, editor. **90% freelance written.** Magazine published 6 times/year (4 spring, 1 fall, 1 winter) covering turkey hunting and turkey biology. "*Turkey & Turkey Hunting* is for serious, experienced turkey hunters." Estab. 1983. Circ. 28,000. **Pays on acceptance.** Publishes ms an average of 1 year after acceptance. Byline given. Offers 50% kill fee. Buys first North American serial rights. Editorial lead time 1 year. Submit seasonal material 1 year in advance. Responds in 2 months. Sample copy and writer's guidelines free.

Nonfiction: How-to, personal experience. **Buys 45 mss/year.** Query with published clips. Length: 2,000 words. **Pays $275-300.** Sometimes pays expenses of writers on assignment.

Photos: Send photos with submission. Reviews transparencies. Offers $75-300/photo, depending on size. Pays on publication for photos. Buys one-time rights.

Tips: "Have a thorough knowledge of turkey hunting and the hunting industry. Send fresh, informative queries, and indicate topics you'd feel comfortable covering on assignment."

$ $TURKEY CALL, Wild Turkey Center, P.O. Box 530, Edgefield SC 29824-0530. (803)637-3106. Fax: (803)637-0034. E-mail: dhowlett@nwtf.net. Editor: Jay Langston. **Contact:** Doug Howlett, managing editor. **50-60% freelance written.** Eager to work with new/unpublished writers and photographers. Bimonthly educational magazine for members of the National Wild Turkey Federation. Estab. 1973. Circ. 145,000. Buys one-time rights. Byline given. **Pays on acceptance for assigned articles,** on publication for unsolicited articles. Publishes ms an average of 6 months after acceptance. Responds in 1 month. Queries required. Submit complete package if article is assigned. Wants original mss only. Sample copy for $3 and 9×12 SAE. Writer's guidelines for #10 SASE or on website.

Nonfiction: Feature articles dealing with the hunting and management of the American wild turkey. Must be accurate information and must appeal to national readership of turkey hunters and wildlife management experts. No poetry or first-person accounts of unremarkable hunting trips. May use some fiction that educates or entertains in a special way. Length: up to 2,500 words. **Pays $100 for short fillers of 600-700 words, $200-500 for features.**

Reprints: Send photocopy of article and information about when and where the article previously appeared. Pays 50% of amount paid for an original article.

Photos: "We want quality photos submitted with features." Art illustrations also acceptable. "We are using more and more inside color illustrations." Transparencies of any size are acceptable. No typical hunter-holding-dead-turkey photos or setups using mounted birds or domestic turkeys. Photos with how-to stories must make the techniques clear (example: how to make a turkey call; how to sculpt or carve a bird in wood). Pays $35 minimum for one-time rights on b&w photos and simple art illustrations; up to $100 for inside color, reproduced any size; $200-400 for covers.

Tips: "The writer should simply keep in mind that the audience is 'expert' on wild turkey management, hunting, life history and restoration/conservation history. He/she *must know the subject*. We are buying more third-person, more fiction, more humor—in an attempt to avoid the 'predictability trap' of a single subject magazine."

■ **$ $ VIRGINIA GAME & FISH**, Game & Fish Publications, Box 741, Marietta GA 30061. (770)953-9222. **Contact:** Editor. See *Game & Fish Publications*.

■ **$ $ WARMWATER FLY FISHING**, Abenaki Publishers, Inc., 160 Benmont Ave., P.O. Box 4100, Bennington VT 05201. (802)447-1518. Website: www.flyfishmags.com. **Contact:** John M. Likakis, editor. **95% freelance written.** Quarterly magazine covering fly fishing for bass, panfish, and other warmwater fish. "*Warmwater Fly Fishing* specializes in how-to, where-to, and when-to stories about fly fishing for warmwater species of fish. The emphasis is on nuts-and-bolts articles that tell the reader about specific techniques, places, equipment, etc." Estab. 1997. Pays on publication. Publishes ms an average of 6 months after acceptance. Byline given. Buys first North American and one-time rights. Editorial lead time 6 months. Submit seasonal material 6 months in advance. Accepts queries by mail, phone. Responds in 6 weeks to queries; 3 months to mss. Sample copy for $4.99. Writer's guidelines for $3 and #10 SASE.

Nonfiction: Historical/nostalgic, how-to, technical. No 'Me and Joe' fishing stories, exotic destinations, product reviews or puff pieces. **Buys 70 mss/year.** Query. Length: 1,000-2,500 words. **Pays $250-350.**

Photos: Send photos with submission. Reviews transparencies. Offers no additional payment for photos accepted with ms. "Unless otherwise specified, photos are considered part of the submission." Captions, model releases, identification of subjects required. Buys one-time rights.

Columns/Departments: Tech Tackle (innovative rigging); The Deep (fly fishing in deep water); Basic Techniques; The Tier (tying warmwater flies); all 1,500 words. **Buys 54 mss/year.** Query. **Pays $250-350.**

Tips: "Brief but complete query letters detailing what the article intends to cover. Neatness counts! Check your letter carefully for typos, misspellings, proper address and so forth."

■ **$ $ WASHINGTON-OREGON GAME & FISH**, Game & Fish Publications, Box 741, Marietta GA 30061. **Contact:** Burt Carey, editor. See *Game & Fish Publications*.

■ **$ $ WEST VIRGINIA GAME & FISH**, Game & Fish Publications, Box 741, Marietta GA 30061. (770)953-9222. **Contact:** Ken Freel, editor. See *Game & Fish Publications*.

$ $ WESTERN OUTDOORS, 3197-E Airport Loop, Costa Mesa CA 92626. (714)546-4370. Fax: (714)662-3486. E-mail: woutdoors@aol.com. **Contact:** Lew Carpenter, editor. **60% freelance written.** Works with a small number of new/unpublished writers each year. Emphasizes fishing, boating for California, Oregon, Washington, Baja California, and Alaska. "We are the West's leading authority on fishing techniques, tackle and destinations, and all reports present the latest and most reliable information." Publishes 9 issues/year. Estab. 1961. Circ. 100,000. **Pays on acceptance.** Publishes ms an average of 6 months after acceptance. Buys first North American serial rights. Submit seasonal material 6 months in advance. Accepts queries by mail, e-mail, fax. Responds in 2 weeks. Sample copy free. Writer's guidelines for #10 SASE.

• *Western Outdoors* now emphasizes freshwater and saltwater fishing and boating exclusively. Area of coverage is limited to far west states and Baja California.

Nonfiction: Where-to (catch more fish, improve equipment, etc.), how-to informational, photo feature. "We do not accept fiction, poetry." **Buys 36-40 assigned mss/year.** Query with SASE. *No simultaneous queries.* Length: 1,500-2,000 words. **Pays $450-600.**

Photos: Purchased with accompanying ms. Captions required. Prefers professional quality 35mm slides. Offers no additional payment for photos accepted with accompanying ms. **Pays $350-500 for covers.**

Tips: "Provide a complete package of photos, map, trip facts and manuscript written according to our news feature format. Excellence of color photo selections make a sale more likely. Include sketches of fishing patterns and techniques to guide our illustrators. Graphics are important. The most frequent mistake made by writers in completing an article for us is that they don't follow our style. Our guidelines are quite clear. One query at a time via mail, e-mail, fax. No phone calls. You can become a regular *Western Outdoors* byliner by submitting professional quality packages of fine writing accompanied by excellent photography. Pros anticipate what is needed, and immediately provide whatever else we request. Furthermore, they meet deadlines!"

$ $WISCONSIN OUTDOOR JOURNAL, Krause Publications, 700 E. State St., Iola WI 54990. (715)445-2214, ext. 484. Fax: (715)445-4087. E-mail: lovettb@krause.com. Website: www.wisoutdoorjournal.com. **Contact:** Brian Lovett, editor. **90% freelance written.** Magazine published 8 times/year covering Wisconsin hunting, fishing, trapping, wildlife and related issues. *"Wisconsin Outdoor Journal* is for people interested in state-specific hunting, fishing, trapping and wildlife. We mix how-to features with area profiles and state outdoor issues." Estab. 1987. Circ. 26,000. **Pays on acceptance.** Publishes ms an average of 8-12 months after acceptance. Byline given. Offers 50% kill fee. Buys first North American serial rights. Editorial lead time 1 year. Submit seasonal material 1 year in advance. Responds in 2 months. Sample copy and writer's guidelines for SASE.
Nonfiction: General interest, historical/nostalgic, how-to. No stories focusing on out-of-state topics; no general recreation (hiking, biking, skiing) features. **Buys 65 mss/year.** Query with published clips. Length: 1,600-2,000 words. **Pays $150-250.** Sometimes pays expenses of writers on assignment.
Photos: Send photos with submission. Reviews transparencies. Offers $75-275/photo. Buys one-time rights.
Columns/Departments: Wisconsin Field Notes (anecdotes, outdoor news items not extensively covered by newspapers, interesting outdoor occurrences, all relevant to Wisconsin; may include photos), 50-750 words. **Pays $5-75 on publication.** "Include SASE with photos only. Submissions other than photos for Field Notes will not be returned.
Tips: "Don't submit personal hunting and fishing stories. Seek fresh, new topics, such as an analysis of long-term outdoor issues."

$ $WISCONSIN SPORTSMAN, Game & Fish Publications, Box 741, Marietta GA 30061. (770)953-9222. **Contact:** Dennis Schmidt, editor. See *Game & Fish Publications*.

Martial Arts

$ $BLACK BELT, Black Belt Communications, Inc., 24715 Ave. Rockefeller, Valencia CA 91355. (661)257-4066. Fax: (661)257-3028. E-mail: bobyounged@earthlink.net. Website: www.blackbeltmag.com. **Contact:** Robert Young, executive editor. **80% freelance written.** Works with a small number of new/unpublished writers each year. Monthly magazine emphasizing martial arts for both experienced practitioner and layman. Estab. 1961. Circ. 100,000. Pays on publication. Publishes ms an average of 1 year months after acceptance. Buys all rights, retains right to republish. Submit seasonal material 6 months in advance. Accepts simultaneous submissions if notified. Accepts queries by mail, e-mail, phone, fax. Responds in 3 weeks.
Nonfiction: Exposé, how-to, informational, health/fitness, interview, new product, personal experience, technical, training, travel. "We never use personality profiles." **Buys 8-9 mss/issue.** Query with outline. Length: 1,200 words minimum. **Pays $100-300.**
Photos: Very seldom buys photos without accompanying ms. Captions required. Total purchase price for ms includes payment for photos. Model releases required.
Tips: "We also publish an annual yearbook and special issues periodically. The yearbook includes our annual 'Black Belt Hall of Fame' inductees."

$ $INSIDE KUNG-FU, The Ultimate In Martial Arts Coverage!, CFW Enterprises, 4201 Vanowen Place, Burbank CA 91505. (818)845-2656. Fax: (818)845-7761. E-mail: davecater@cfwenterprises.com. **Contact:** Dave Cater, editor. **90% freelance written.** Monthly magazine for those with "traditional, modern, athletic and intellectual tastes. The magazine slants toward little-known martial arts, and little-known aspects of established martial arts." Estab. 1973. Circ. 125,000. Pays on publication date on magazine cover. Publishes ms an average of 6 months after acceptance. Byline given. Offers 20% kill fee. Buys first North American serial rights. Editorial lead time 6 months. Submit seasonal material 6 months in advance. Accepts simultaneous submissions. Responds in 1 month to queries; 2 months to mss. Sample copy for $2.95 and 9×12 SAE with 5 first-class stamps. Writer's guidelines for #10 SASE.
Nonfiction: Book excerpts, essays, exposé (topics relating to the martial arts), general interest, historical/nostalgic, how-to (primarily technical materials), cultural/philosophical, inspirational, interview/profile, new product, personal experience, photo feature, technical, travel. "Articles must be technically or historically accurate." *Inside Kung-Fu* is looking for external-type articles (fighting, weapons, multiple hackers). No "sports coverage, first-person articles or articles which constitute personal aggrandizement." **Buys 120 mss/year.** Query or send complete ms. Length: 1,500-3,000 words (8-10 pages, typewritten and double-spaced). **Pays $125-175.**
Reprints: Send tearsheet of article or short story or typed ms with rights for sale noted and information about when and where the article or story previously appeared. No payment.
Photos: State availability or send photos with ms. Reviews contact sheets, negatives, 5×7 or 8×10 color prints. No additional payment for photos. Captions, model release and identification of subjects required. Buys all rights.
Fiction: Adventure, historical, humorous, mystery, novel excerpts, suspense. "Fiction must be short (1,000-2,000 words) and relate to the martial arts. We buy very few fiction pieces." Publishes novel excerpts. **Buys 2-3 mss/year.**

Tips: "See what interests the writer. May have a better chance of breaking in at our publication with short articles and fillers since smaller pieces allow us to gauge individual ability, but we're flexible—quality writers get published, period. The most frequent mistakes made by writers in completing an article for us are ignoring photo requirements and model releases (always number one—and who knows why? All requirements are spelled out in writer's guidelines)."

N ✪ $ $ JOURNAL OF ASIAN MARTIAL ARTS, Via Media Publishing Co., 821 W. 24th St., Erie PA 16502-2523. (814)455-9517. Fax: (814)838-7811. E-mail: viamedia@ncinter.net. Website: www.ncinter.net/~viamedia. **Contact:** Michael A. DeMarco, editor. **90% freelance written.** Quarterly magazine covering "all historical and cultural aspects related to Asian martial arts, offering a mature, well-rounded view of this uniquely fascinating subject. Although the journal treats the subject with academic accuracy (references at end), writing need not lose the reader!" Estab. 1991. Pays on publication. Publishes ms an average of 1 year after acceptance. Byline given. Buys first world rights and second serial (reprint) rights. Submit seasonal material 6 months in advance. Responds in 1 month to queries; 2 months to mss. Sample copy for $10. Writer's guidelines for #10 SASE.

Nonfiction: Essays, exposé, historical/nostalgic, how-to (martial art techniques and materials, e.g., weapons, symbols), interview/profile, personal experience, photo feature (place or person), religious, technical, travel. "All articles should be backed with solid, reliable reference material. No articles overburdened with technical/foreign/scholarly vocabulary, or material slanted as indirect advertising or for personal aggrandizement." **Buys 30 mss/year.** Query with short background and martial arts experience. Length: 2,000-10,000 words. **Pays $150-500 for unsolicited articles.**

Reprints: Send information about when and where the article previously appeared. Pays 50% of amount paid for an original article.

Photos: State availability of photos with submission. Reviews contact sheets, negatives, transparencies, prints. Offers no additional payment for photos accepted with ms. Model releases and identification of subjects required. Buys one-time and reprint rights.

Columns/Departments: Location (city, area, specific site, Asian or Non-Asian, showing value for martial arts, researchers, history); Media Review (film, book, video, museum for aspects of academic and artistic interest). **Buys 16 mss/year.** Query. Length: 1,000-2,500 words. **Pays $50-200.**

Fiction: Adventure, historical, humorous, slice-of-life vignettes, translation. No material that does not focus on martial arts culture. **Buys 1 mss/year.** Query. Length: 1,000-10,000 words. **Pays $50-500 or copies.**

Poetry: Avant-garde, free verse, haiku, light verse, traditional, translation. "No poetry that does not focus on martial art culture." **Buys 2 poems/year.** Submit maximum 10 poems. Pays **$10-100 or in copies.**

Fillers: Anecdotes, facts, gags to be illustrated by cartoonist, newsbreaks, short humor. **Buys 2/year.** Length: 25-500 words. **Pays $1-50 or copies.**

Tips: "Always query before sending a manuscript. We are open to varied types of articles; most however require a strong academic grasp of Asian culture. For those not having this background, we suggest trying a museum review, or interview, where authorities can be questioned, quoted and provide supportive illustrations. We especially desire articles/reports from Asia, with photo illustrations, particularly of a martial art style, so readers can visually understand the unique attributes of that style, its applications, evolution, etc. 'Location' and media reports are special areas that writers may consider, especially if they live in a location of martial art significance."

$ KARATE/KUNG FU ILLUSTRATED, Rainbow Publications, Inc., P.O. Box 918, Santa Clarita CA 91380. (805)257-4066. Fax: (805)257-3028. E-mail: rainbow@rsabbs.com. Website: www.blackbeltmag.com. **Contact:** Douglas Jeffrey, executive editor. **40% freelance written.** Bimonthly magazine. "KKI presents factual historical accounts of the development of the martial arts, along with technical pieces on self-defense. We use only material from which readers can learn." Estab. 1969. Circ. 35,000. Pays on publication. Publishes ms an average of 8 months after acceptance. Byline given. Buys all rights. Editorial lead time 3 months. Submit seasonal material 4 months in advance. Accepts queries by mail, e-mail, fax, phone. Accepts simultaneous submissions. Responds in 2 weeks to queries; 1 month to mss. Sample copy for 9×12 SAE and 5 first-class stamps. Writer's guidelines free.

• *Karate/Kung Fu Illustrated* now publishes "Black Belt for Kids," a separate section currently attached to the main magazine. Query with article ideas for young martial artists.

Nonfiction: Book excerpts, general interest (martial arts), historical/nostalgic (martial arts development), how-to (technical articles on specific kicks, punches, etc.), interview/profile (only with *major* martial artist), new products (for annual product review), travel (to Asian countries for martial arts training/research), comparisons of various styles and techniques. "No self-promotional pieces." **Buys 30 mss/year.** Query. Length: 1,000-3,000 words. **Pays $100-200.**

• "We are now focusing heavily on competition results, profiles, training tips, etc."

Reprints: Send tearsheet, photocopy or typed ms with rights for sale noted and information about when and where the article previously appeared. Pays 75-100% of amount paid for an original article.

Photos: Freelancers should send photos with submission. Reviews contact sheets, negatives and 5×7 prints. Offers no additional payment for photos accepted with ms. Captions, model releases and identification of subjects required.

Columns/Departments: Traditional Passages (importance of tradition); Counterkicks (letters to the editor). **Buys 12 mss/year.** Query. **Pays $50-100.**

Fiction: Publishes novel excerpts.

Tips: "You need not be an expert in a specific martial art to write about it. But if you are not an expert, find one and use his knowledge to support your statements. Also, references to well-known books can help lend credence to the work of unknown writers. Inexperienced writers should begin by writing about a subject they know well. For example, if you study karate, start by writing about karate. Don't study karate for one year, then try to break in to a martial arts magazine by writing about Kung fu, because we already have Kung fu practitioners who write about that."

\$ \$ MARTIAL ARTS TRAINING, Rainbow Publications, P.O. Box 918, Santa Clarita CA 91380-9018. (805)257-4066. Fax: (805)257-3028. E-mail: rainbow@rsabbs.com. Website: www.blackbeltmag.com. **Contact:** Douglas Jeffrey, executive editor. **40% freelance written.** Works with many new/unpublished writers each year. Bimonthly magazine about martial arts training. Estab. 1973. Circ. 35,000. Pays on publication. Publishes ms an average of 6 months after acceptance. Buys all rights. Submit seasonal material 4 months in advance. Accepts queries by mail, e-mail, fax, phone. Responds in 1 month. Writer's guidelines for #10 SASE.
Nonfiction: How-to (training related features). **Buys 30-40 unsolicited mss/year.** Query. Length: 1,500-2,500 words. **Pays $125-200.**
Reprints: Send tearsheet, photocopy or typed ms of article with rights for sale noted and information about when and where the article previously appeared. Pays 75-100% of amount paid for an original article.
Photos: "We prefer color prints. Please include the negatives." Model releases required. Buys all rights.
Tips: "I'm looking for how-to, nuts-and-bolts training stories that are martial arts related. Weight training, plyometrics, speed drills, cardiovascular workouts, agility drills, etc. Our magazine covers fitness and conditioning, not the martial arts techniques themselves. We're interested in traditional training and state-of-the-art, cutting-edge training."

⊠ \$ \$ T'AI CHI, Leading International Magazine of T'ai Chi Ch'uan, Wayfarer Publications, P.O. Box 39938, Los Angeles CA 90039. (323)665-7773. Fax: (323)665-1627. E-mail: taichi@tai-chi.com. Website: www.tai-chi.com. **Contact:** Marvin Smalheiser, editor. **90% freelance written.** Bimonthly consumer magazine covering T'ai Chi Ch'uan as a martial art and for health and fitness. "Covers T'ai Chi Ch'uan and other internal martial arts, plus qigong and Chinese health, nutrition and philosophical disciplines. Readers are practitioners or laymen interested in developing skills and insight for self-defense, health and self-improvement." Estab. 1977. Circ. 30,000. Pays on publication. Publishes ms an average of 3 months after acceptance. Byline given. Buys first North American serial rights. Editorial lead time 3 months. Submit seasonal material 6 months in advance. Accepts queries by mail, e-mail, fax. Responds in 3 weeks to queries; 3 months to mss. Sample copy for $3.95. Writer's guidelines for #10 SASE or on website.
    O▬ Break in by "understanding the problems our readers have to deal with learning and practicing T'ai Chi, and developing an article that deals with one or more of those problems.
Nonfiction: Book excerpts, essays, how-to (on T'ai Chi Ch'uan, qigong and related Chinese disciplines), interview, personal experience. "Do not want articles promoting an individual, system or school." **Buys 50-60 mss/year.** Query or send complete ms. Length: 1,200-4,500 words. **Pays $75-500.** Sometimes pays expenses of writers on assignment.
Photos: Send photos with submission. Reviews color transparencies and color or b&w 4×6 or 5×7 prints. Offers no additional payment for photos accepted with ms but overall payment takes into consideration the number and quality of photos. Captions, model releases and identification of subjects required. Buys one-time and reprint rights.
Tips: "Think and write for practitioners and laymen who want information and insight and who are trying to work through problems to improve skills and their health. No promotional material."

Miscellaneous

\$ \$ AMERICAN CHEERLEADER, Lifestyle Ventures, 250 W. 57th St., Suite 420, New York NY 10107. (212)265-8890. Fax: (212)265-8908. E-mail: editors@americancheerleader.com. Website: www.americancheerleader.com. Editorial Director: Julie Davis. **Contact:** Meredith Cristiano, managing editor. **50% freelance written.** Bimonthly magazine covering high school and college cheerleading. Estab. 1995. Circ. 200,000. Pays on publication. Publishes ms 2 months after acceptance. Byline given. Buys all rights. Editorial lead time 4 months. Submit seasonal material 4 months in advance. Accepts queries by mail, e-mail, fax. Responds in 3 weeks to queries; 2 months to mss. Writer's guidelines for #10 SASE.
Nonfiction: How-to (cheering techniques, routines, pep songs, etc.), interview/profile (sports personalities), new product, personal experience. **Buys 20 mss/year.** Query with published clips. Length: 750-2,000 words. **Pays $75-300.** Sometimes pays expenses of writers on assignment.
Columns/Departments: All Yours (advice on relationships, peer pressure, fitting in, and other teen problems); Ask Us (expert advice on readers' cheer, stunt and tumble questions); Cheer-O-Scope (cheer-y horoscope forecasts); Coach to Coach (helpful hints from experienced cheer coaches); College Spotlight (the lowdown on great college cheer programs); Cool Stuff (product picks, usually with cheerleading/sports themes); Eating Smart (nutritious tidbits for the active cheerleader); Fab Fundraising (fundraising ideas with originality and pizzazz to keep the cash rolling in); Gameday Beauty (makeovers, cosmetics, hair products, beauty tips); Healthy Athlete (anything from PMS to how to buy running shoes to athletic training tips); Squad of the Month (highlighting the country's coolest high school and all-star cheer squads); Star Struck (celebs who cheered, and what cheering has brought to their current careers); Stunt School (technical know-how and step-by-step instruction on tumbling, jumping, stunting, and more); What's Going On (cheer news in bite-size newsy paragraphs).
    ▣ The online magazine carries original content not found in the print edition.

Photos: State availability of photos with submission. Reviews transparencies and 5×7 prints. Offers no additional payment for photos accepted with ms. Captions, model releases and identification of subjects required. Buys all rights.
Tips: "We invite proposals from freelance writers who are involved in or have been involved in cheerleading—i.e. coaches, sponsors or cheerleaders. Our writing style is upbeat and 'sporty' to catch and hold the attention of our teenaged readers. Articles should be broken down into lots of sidebars, bulleted lists, Q&As, etc."

$ CANADIAN RODEO NEWS, Canadian Rodeo News, Ltd., #223, 2116 27th Ave. NE, Calgary, Alberta T2E 7A6 Canada. (403)250-7292. Fax: (403)250-6926. E-mail: rodeonews@iul-ccs.com. Website: www.rodeocanada.com. **Contact:** Vicki Mowat, editor. **60% freelance written.** Monthly tabloid covering "Canada's professional rodeo (CPRA) personalities and livestock. Read by rodeo participants and fans." Estab. 1964. Circ. 4,800. Pays on publication. Publishes ms an average of 1 month after acceptance. Byline given. Buys first and second serial (reprint) rights. Editorial lead time 1 month. Submit seasonal material 1 month in advance. Accepts simultaneous submissions. Accepts queries by mail, e-mail, fax, phone. Responds in 1 month to queries; 2 months to mss. Sample copy and writer's guidelines free.
Nonfiction: General interest, historical/nostalgic, interview/profile. **Buys 70-80 mss/year.** Query. Length: 500-1,200 words. **Pays $30-60.**
Reprints: Send photocopy of article or typed ms with rights for sale noted, and information about when and where the article previously appeared. Pays 100% of amount paid for an original article.
Photos: Send photos with submission. Reviews 4×6 prints. Offers $15-25/cover photo. Buys one-time rights.
Tips: "Best to call first with the story idea to inquire if it is suitable for publication. Readers are very knowledgeable of the sport, so writers need to be as well."

N ⊠ $ FENCERS QUARTERLY MAGAZINE, 6751 CR 3850, Peace Valley MO 65788. (417)256-0432. E-mail: ale@townsqr.com/ale/vfq.htm. Editor-in-Chief: Nick Evangelista. **Contact:** Anita Evangelista, managing editor. **60% freelance written.** Quarterly magazine covering fencing, fencers, history of sword/fencing/dueling, modern techniques and systems, controversies, personalities of fencing, personal experience. "This is a publication for all fencers and those interested in fencing; we favor the grassroots level rather than the highly-promoted elite. Readers will have a grasp of terminology of the sword and refined fencing skills—writers must be familiar with fencing and current changes and controversies. We are happy to air any point of view on any fencing subject, but the material must be well-researched and logically presented." Estab. 1996. Circ. 5,000. Pays prior to or at publication. Publishes ms 6 months after acceptance. Byline given. Offers 25% kill fee. Buys first North American serial rights, electronic rights, reprint rights and makes work-for-hire assignments. Editorial lead time: 3 months. Submit seasonal material 6 months in advance. Accepts queries by mail, e-mail only (no phone queries). Accepts simultaneous submissions, if so noted. Responds in 1 week or less for e-mail; 1 month for snail mail if SASE; no reply if no SASE and material not useable. Sample copy for $3 and 8×10 SASE with 2 first-class stamps. Writer's guidelines for #10 SASE.
Nonfiction: "All article types acceptable—however, we have never used fiction or poetry (though will consider if has special relationship to fencing)." How-to should reflect some aspect of fencing or gear. Personal experience welcome. No articles "that lack logical progression of thought, articles that rant, 'my weapon is better than your weapon' emotionalism, puff pieces, or public relations stuff." **Buys 100 mss/year.** Query or send complete mss. Length: 100-4,000 words. **Pays $100-200 (rarely) maximum for assigned articles; $10-60 for unsolicited articles.**
Photos: Send photos by mail or as e-mail attachment. Prefers prints, all sizes. Negotiates payment individually. Captions, model releases, identification of subjects required. Buys all rights.
Columns/Departments: Cutting-edge news (sword or fencing related), 100 words; reviews of books/films, 300 words; fencing generations (profile), 200-300 words; tournament results (veteran events only please), 200 words. **Buys 40 mss/year.** Send complete ms. **Pays $10-20.**
Fiction: Will consider all as long as strong fencing/sword slant is major element. No erotica. Query or send ms. Length: 1,500 words maximum. **Pays $25-100.**
Poetry: Will consider all which have distinct fencing/sword element as central. No erotica. Submit maximum 10 poems. Length: up to 100 lines. **Pays $10.**
Fillers: Anecdotes, facts, gags, cartoons, newsbreaks. **Buys 30/year.** Length: 100 words maximum. **Pays $5.**
Tips: "We love new writers! Professionally presented work impresses us. We prefer complete submissions, and e-mail or disk (Win 3.x/MS Works 3.0/ASCII) are our favorites. Ask for our writer's guidelines. Always aim your writing to knowledgeable fencers who are fascinated by this subject, take their fencing seriously, and want to know more about its history, current events and controversies. Action photos should show proper form—no flailing or tangled-up images, please. We want to know what the "real" fencer is up to these days, not just what the Olympic contenders are doing. If we don't use your piece, we'll tell you why not."

N $ $ POLO PLAYERS' EDITION, Rizzo Management Corp., 3500 Fairlane Farms Rd., Suite 9, Wellington FL 33414. (561)793-9524. Fax: (561)793-9576. E-mail: info@poloplayersedition.com Website: www.poloplayersedition.com. **Contact:** Gwen Rizzo, editor. Monthly magazine on polo—the sport and lifestyle. "Our readers are affluent, well-educated, well-read and highly sophisticated." Circ. 6,500. **Pays on acceptance.** Publishes ms an average of 2 months after acceptance. Kill fee varies. Buys first North American serial rights and makes work-for-hire assignments. Submit seasonal material 3 months in advance. Accepts simultaneous submissions. Accepts queries by mail, e-mail, fax, phone. Responds in 3 months. Writer's guidelines for #10 SAE with 2 stamps.

Nonfiction: Historical/nostalgic, interview/profile, personal experience, photo feature, technical, travel. Special issues: Annual Art Issue/Gift Buying Guide; Winter Preview/Florida Supplement. **Buys 20 mss/year.** Query with published clips or send complete ms. Length: 800-3,000 words. **Pays $150-400 for assigned articles; $100-300 for unsolicited articles.** Sometimes pays expenses of writers on assignment.

Reprints: Send tearsheet of article or typed ms with rights for sale noted and information about when and where the article previously appeared. Pays 50% of amount paid for an original article.

Fiction: Publishes novel excerpts.

Photos: State availability of photos or send photos with submission. Reviews contact sheets, transparencies, prints. Offers $20-150/photo. Captions required. Buys one-time rights.

Columns/Departments: Yesteryears (historical pieces), 500 words; Profiles (clubs and players), 800-1,000 words. **Buys 15 mss/year.** Query with published clips. **Pays $100-300.**

Tips: "Query us on a personality or club profile or historic piece or, if you know the game, state availability to cover a tournament. Keep in mind that ours is a sophisticated, well-educated audience."

$ PRIME TIME SPORTS & FITNESS, GND Prime Time Publishing, P.O. Box 6097, Evanston IL 60204. (847)784-1195. Fax: (847)784-1194. E-mail: dennisdorner@bowldtalk.com. Website: www.bowldtalk.com. **Contact:** Dennis A. Dorner, editor. Managing Editor: Steven Ury. **80% freelance written.** Eager to work with new/unpublished writers. Monthly magazine covering seasonal pro sports and racquet and health club sports and fitness. Estab. 1974. Circ. 35,000. Pays on publication. Publishes ms an average of 6 months after acceptance. Byline given. Buys all rights; will assign back to author in 85% of cases. Submit seasonal material 6 months in advance. Accepts queries by mail, e-mail, fax. Accepts simultaneous submissions. Responds in 6 months. Sample copy on request. Writer's guidelines on website.

Nonfiction: Book excerpts (fitness and health), exposé (in tennis, fitness, racquetball, health clubs, diets), adult (slightly risqué and racy fitness), how-to (expert instructional pieces on any area of coverage), humor (large market for funny pieces on health clubs and fitness), inspirational (on how diet and exercise combine to bring you a better body, self), interview/profile, new product, opinion (only from recognized sources who know what they are talking about), personal experience (definitely—humor), photo feature (on related subjects); technical (on exercise and sport), travel (related to fitness, tennis camps, etc.), news reports (on racquetball, handball, tennis, running events). Special issues: Swimwear (March); Baseball Preview (April); Summer Fashion (July); Pro Football Preview (August); Aerobic Wear (September); Fall Fashion (October); Ski Issue (November); Workout and Diet Routines (December/January). "We love short articles that get to the point. Nationally oriented big events and national championships. No articles on local only tennis and racquetball tournaments without national appeal." **Buys 150 mss/year.** Length: 2,000 words maximum. **Pays $20-150.** Sometimes pays the expenses of writers on assignment.

Reprints: Send tearsheet or photocopy of article or short story or typed ms with rights for sale noted and information about when and where the article or story previously appeared. Pays 20% of amount paid for an original article or story.

Photos: Nancy Thomas, photo editor. Specifically looking for fashion photo features. Send photos with ms. Pays $5-75 for b&w prints. Captions, model releases, identification of subjects required. Buys all rights, "but returns 75% of photos to submitter."

Columns/Departments: George Thomas, column/department editor. New Products; Fitness Newsletter; Handball Newsletter; Racquetball Newsletter; Tennis Newsletter; News & Capsule Summaries; Fashion Spot (photos of new fitness and bathing suits and ski equipment); related subjects. **Buys 100 mss/year.** Send complete ms. Length: 50-250 words ("more if author has good handle to cover complete columns"). "We want more articles with photos and we are searching for one woman columnist, Diet and Nutrition." **Pays $5-25.**

Fiction: Judy Johnson, fiction editor. Erotica (if related to fitness club), fantasy (related to subjects), humorous, religious ("no God-is-my shepherd, but Body-is-God's-temple"), romance (related subjects), novel excerpts. "Upbeat stories are needed." **Buys 20 mss/year.** Send complete ms. Length: 500-2,500 words maximum. **Pays $20-150.**

Poetry: Free verse, haiku, light verse, traditional on related subjects. Length: up to 150 words. **Pays $10-25.**

The online magazine contains original content not found in the print edition and includes writer's guidelines.

Tips: "Send us articles dealing with court club sports, exercise and nutrition that exemplify an upbeat 'you can do it' attitude. Pro sports previews 3-4 months ahead of their seasons are also needed. Good short fiction and humorous articles can break in. Expert knowledge of any related subject can bring assignments; any area is open. We consider everything as a potential article, but are turned off by credits, past work and degrees. We have a constant demand for well-written articles on instruction, health and trends in both. Other articles needed are professional sports training techniques, fad diets, tennis and fitness resorts, photo features with aerobic routines. A frequent mistake made by writers is in length—articles are too long. When we assign an article, we want it newsy if it's news and opinion if opinion."

$ $ RACQUETBALL MAGAZINE, United States Racquetball Association, 1685 W. Uintah, Colorado Springs CO 80904. (719)635-5396. Fax: (719)635-0685. E-mail: lmojer@racqmag.com. Website: www.racqmag.com. **Contact:** Linda Mojer, director of communications. **20-30% freelance written.** Bimonthly magazine "geared toward a readership of informed, active enthusiasts who seek entertainment, instruction and accurate reporting of events." Estab. 1990. Circ. 45,000. Pays on publication. Publishes ms an average of 2 months after acceptance. Buys one-time rights. Editorial lead time 3 months. Submit seasonal material 3 months in advance. Accepts simultaneous submissions. Responds in 2 months. Sample copy for $4. Writer's guidelines free.

Nonfiction: How-to (instructional racquetball tips), humor, interview/profile (personalities who play racquetball). **Buys 2-3 mss/year.** Send complete ms. Length: 1,500-3,000 words. **Pays $100.** Sometimes pays expenses of writers on assignment.

Reprints: Send typed ms with rights for sale noted and info about when and where it previously appeared.

Photos: Send photos with submission. Reviews 3×5 prints. Negotiates payment individually. Model releases, identification of subjects required. Buys one-time rights.

Fiction: Humorous (racquetball related). **Buys 1-2 mss/year.** Send complete ms. Length: 1,500-3,000 words. **Pays $100-250.**

🖽 $RUGBY MAGAZINE, Rugby Press Limited, 2350 Broadway, New York NY 10024. (212)787-1160. Fax: (212)595-0934. E-mail: rugbymag@aol.com. Website: www.inch.com/~rugby. Editor: Ed Hagerty. **75% freelance written.** Monthly tabloid. "*Rugby Magazine* is the journal of record for the sport of rugby in the U.S. Our demographics are among the best in the country." Estab. 1975. Circ. 10,000. Pays on publication. Publishes ms 2 months after acceptance. Byline given. Buys all rights. Editorial lead time 1 month. Submit seasonal material 2 months in advance. Accepts simultaneous submissions. Accepts queries by mail, e-mail, fax, phone. Responds in 2 weeks to queries; 1 month to mss. Sample copy for $3. Writer's guidelines free.

Nonfiction: Book excerpts, essays, general interest, historical/nostalgic, how-to, humor, interview/profile, new product, opinion, personal experience, photo feature, technical, travel. **Buys 15 mss/year.** Send complete ms. Length: 600-2,000 words. **Pays $50 minimum.** Pays expenses of writers on assignment.

Reprints: Send tearsheet of article or short story or typed ms with rights for sale noted and information about when and where the article or story previously appeared. Pay varies.

Photos: Send photos with submission. Reviews negatives, transparencies and prints. Offers no additional payment for photos accepted with ms. Buys all rights.

Columns/Departments: Nutrition, athletic nutrition, 900 words; Referees' Corner, 1,200 words. **Buys 2-3 mss/year.** Query with published clips. **Pays $50 maximum.**

Fiction: Condensed novels, humorous, novel excerpts, slice-of-life vignettes. **Buys 1-3 mss/year.** Query with published clips. Length: 1,000-2,500 words. **Pays $100.**

Tips: "Give us a call. Send along your stories or photos; we're happy to take a look. Tournament stories are a good way to get yourself published in *Rugby Magazine.*"

$SKYDIVING, 1725 N. Lexington Ave., DeLand FL 32724. (904)736-4793. Fax: (904)736-9786. E-mail: editor@skydivingmagazine.com. **Contact:** Sue Clifton, editor. **25% freelance written.** Works with a small number of new/unpublished writers each year. Monthly tabloid featuring skydiving for sport parachutists, worldwide dealers and equipment manufacturers. "*Skydiving* is a news magazine. Its purpose is to deliver timely, useful and interesting information about the equipment, techniques, events, people and places of parachuting. Our scope is national. *Skydiving*'s audience spans the entire spectrum of jumpers, from first-jump students to veterans with thousands of skydives. Some readers are riggers with a keen interest in the technical aspects of parachutes, while others are weekend 'fun' jumpers who want information to help them make travel plans and equipment purchases." Circ. 14,200. Pays on publication. Publishes ms an average of 3 months after acceptance. Byline given. Buys one-time rights. Accepts simultaneous submissions, if so noted. Responds in 1 month. Sample copy for $2. Writer's guidelines for 9×12 SAE with 4 first-class stamps.

Nonfiction: Average issue includes 3 feature articles and 3 columns of technical information. "Send us news and information on how-to, where-to, equipment, techniques, events and outstanding personalities who skydive. We want articles written by people who have a solid knowledge of parachuting." No personal experience or human-interest articles. Query. Length: 500-1,000 words. **Pays $25-100.** Sometimes pays the expenses of writers on assignment.

Reprints: Accepts previously published submissions.

Photos: State availability of photos. Reviews 5×7 and larger b&w glossy prints. Offers no additional payment for photos accepted with ms. Captions required.

Fillers: Newsbreaks. Length: 100-200 words. **Pays $25 minimum.**

Tips: "The most frequent mistake made by writers in completing articles for us is that the writer isn't knowledgeable about the sport of parachuting. Articles about events are especially time-sensitive so yours must be submitted quickly. We welcome contributions about equipment. Even short, 'quick look' articles about new products are appropriate for *Skydiving.* If you know of a drop zone or other place that jumpers would like to visit, write an article describing its features and tell them why you liked it and what they can expect to find if they visit it. Avoid first-person articles."

Motor Sports

🅽 🖽 $ $AUTO RACING DIGEST, Century Publishing, 990 Grove St., Evanston IL 60207-4370. (847)491-6440. Fax: (847)491-6203. Editor: Ken Leiker. **Contact:** James O'Connor, managing editor. **100% freelance written.** "Bimonthly digest focusing on American stock-car racing. Occasionally features F1, Indy car style." Estab. 1974. Circ. 50,000. Pays on publication. Publishes ms an average of 1 months after acceptance. Byline given. Offers 50% kill fee. Buys all rights. Editorial lead time 6 weeks. Submit seasonal material 6 weeks in advance. Accepts simultaneous submission. Responds in 1 month. Sample copy for $5.

Nonfiction: Essays, exposé, general interest, opinion, technical. No "remember when" pieces. No personal experience unless extraordinary. **Buys 70 mss/year.** Query. Length: 1,200-2,000 words. **Pays $50-200.** Sometimes pays the expenses of writers on assignment.

Photos: State availability of photos with submission. Reviews negatives, 35mm, 4×6 transparencies, 8×10 prints. Offers $10-30 per photo, $100 for cover. Identification of subjects required. Buys one-time rights.

Columns/Departments: Circuit No Circuit (racing roundup), 1,000 words; Biz (business), 500-1,000 words; Notes & Quotes (racing filler), 1,000 words. **Buys 25 mss/year.** Query. **Pays $50-150.**

Tips: "Query by mail. Clips should reflect subject matter you're trying to sell me."

$ $ DRAG RACING USA, (formerly *Bracket Racing USA*), McMullen/Argus Publishing, 774 S. Placentia Ave., Placentia CA 92870. (714)939-2400. Website: www.cskpub.com. Managing Editor: Debra Wentz. **Contact:** Steve Collison, editor. Monthly magazine covering bracket cars and drag racing. Estab. 1989. Circ. 45,000. Pays on publication. Publishes ms 6 months after acceptance. Byline given. Buys first North American serial rights. Accepts queries by mail. Sample copy for $3 and 9×12 SAE with 5 first-class stamps.

Nonfiction: Automotive how-to and technical. **Buys 35 mss/year.** Query by mail only. Length: 500-4,000 words. **Pays $150/page.** Sometimes pays expenses of writers on assignment.

Photos: Send photos with submission.

$ $ SAND SPORTS MAGAZINE, Wright Publishing Co. Inc., P.O. Box 2260, Costa Mesa CA 92628. (714)979-2560 ext. 107. Fax: (714)979-3998. Website: www.sandsports.net. **Contact:** Michael Sommer, editor. **20% freelance written.** Bimonthly magazine covering vehicles for off-road and sand dunes. Estab. 1995. Circ. 25,000. Pays on publication. Byline given. Buys first rights and one-time rights. Editorial lead time 3 months. Submit seasonal material 6 months in advance. Accepts queries by mail. Sample copy and writer's guidelines free.

Nonfiction: How-to technical-mechanical, photo feature, technical. **Buys 20 mss/year.** Query. Length: 1,500 words minimum. **Pays $125-175/page.** Sometimes pays expenses of writers on assignment.

Photos: Send photos with submission. Reviews contact sheets, transparencies, 5×7 prints. Negotiates payment individually. Captions, model releases, identification of subjects required. Buys one-time rights.

N ✕ $ $ SPEEDWAY ILLUSTRATED, Performance Media, LLC, 107 Elm St., Salisbury MA 01952. (978)465-9099. Fax: (978)465-9033. Executive Editor: Dick Berggren. **Contact:** Rob Sneddon, editor. **80% freelance written.** Monthly magazine covering stock car racing. "We are a new magazine focusing on stock car racing. We are especially searching for interesting features on local short track personalities as well as stories about trends, human interest items and technical material." Estab. 2000. Circ. 95,000. Pays on publication. Byline given. Buys first rights. Editorial lead time 6 weeks. Accepts queries by mail, fax. Responds in 2 weeks to queries; 1 month to mss. Sample copy and writer's guidelines free.

Nonfiction: Book excerpts, exposé, humor, interview/profile, new product, opinion, personal experience, photo feature, technical. **Buys 300 mss/year.** Query. **Pay varies.**

Photos: Send photos with submission. Reviews transparencies and prints. Offers $25/photo. Captions, model releases and identification of subjects required. Buys all rights.

Columns/Departments: We seek short, high interest items with photos. **Buys 300 mss/year.** Query. **Pays $25-1,000.**

Tips: "We pay for everything that is published and aggressively seek short, high-interest value pieces that are accompanied by strong photography."

Running

$ INSIDE TEXAS RUNNING, 9514 Bristlebrook Dr., Houston TX 77083. (281)498-3208. Fax: (281)879-9980. E-mail: insideTx@aol.com. Website: www.RunningNetwork.com/TexasRunning. **Contact:** Joanne Schmidt, editor. **70% freelance written.** Monthly (except June and August) tabloid covering running and running-related events. "Our audience is made up of Texas runners who may also be interested in cross training." Estab. 1977. Circ. 10,000. **Pays on acceptance.** Publishes ms an average of 2 months after acceptance. Byline given. Buys one-time rights, exclusive Texas. Submit seasonal material 2 months in advance. Responds in 1 month to mss. Sample copy for $1.50. Writer's guidelines for #10 SASE.

    O⟶ "The best way to break in to our publication is to submit brief (2 or 3 paragraphs) fillers for our 'Texas Roundup' section."

Nonfiction: Various topics of interest to runners: profiles of newsworthy Texas runners of all abilities; unusual events; training interviews. Special issues: Fall Race Review (September); Marathon Focus (October); Shoe Review (March); Resource Guide (December). **Buys 20 mss/year.** Send complete ms. Length: 500-1,500 words. **Pays $100 maximum for assigned articles; $50 maximum for unsolicited articles.**

Reprints: Send tearsheet, photocopy or typed ms with rights for sale noted and information about when and where the article previously appeared.

Photos: Send photos with submission. Offers $25 maximum/photo. Captions required. Buys one-time rights.

    🖥 The online magazine carries original content not found in the print edition.

Tips: "Writers should be familiar with the sport and the publication."

$ $ NEW YORK RUNNER, New York Road Runners Club, 9 E. 89th St., New York NY 10128. (212)423-2260. Fax: (212)423-0879. E-mail: newyorkrun@nyrrc.org. Website: www.nyrrc.org. **Contact:** Lisa Schwartz, associate editor. Bimonthly regional sports magazine covering running, racewalking, nutrition and fitness. Material should be of interest to members of the New York Road Runners Club. Estab. 1958. Circ. 45,000. Pays on publication. Time to publication varies. Byline given. Offers 33% kill fee. Buys first North American serial rights. Submit seasonal material 4 months in advance. Accepts simultaneous submissions. Accepts queries by mail, e-mail. Responds in 2 months. Sample copy for $3. Writer's guidelines for #10 SASE.

O─• Break in through departments *Runner's Diary* (essay); *Footnote* (humor); or *On the Roads* (interesting places to run).

Nonfiction: Running and marathon articles. Special issues: N.Y.C. Marathon (submissions in by August 1). No non-running stories. **Buys 25 mss/year.** Query. Length: 750-1,000 words. **Pays $50-250.**

Reprints: Send photocopy of article with information about when and where it previously appeared. Pays 25-50% of amount paid for an original article.

Photos: Send photos with submission. Reviews 8×10 b&w prints. Offers $35-300/photo. Captions, model releases, identification of subjects required. Buys one-time rights.

Tips: "Be knowledgeable about the sport of running. Write like a runner."

$ $ $ $ RUNNER'S WORLD, Rodale, 33 E. Minor St., Emmaus PA 18098. (610)967-5171. Deputy Editor: Bob Wischnia. **Contact:** Adam Bean, managing editor. **5% freelance written.** Monthly magazine on running, mainly long-distance running. "The magazine for and about distance running, training, health and fitness, injury precaution, race coverage, personalities of the sport." Estab. 1966. Circ. 500,000. Pays on publication. Publishes ms an average of 6 months after acceptance. Byline given. Buys all rights. Submit seasonal material 6 months in advance. Accepts queries by mail, e-mail. Responds in 2 months. Writer's guidelines for #10 SASE.

O─• Break in through columns *Women's Running*, *Human Race* and *Finish Line*. Also *Warmups*, which mixes international running news with human interest stories. If you can send us a unique human interest story from your region, we will give it serious consideration.

Nonfiction: How-to (train, prevent injuries), interview/profile, personal experience. No "my first marathon" stories. No poetry. **Buys 10 mss/year.** Query. **Pays $1,500-2,000.** Pays expenses of writers on assignment.

Photos: State availability of photos with submission. Identification of subjects required. Buys one-time rights.

Columns/Departments: Finish Line (back-of-the-magazine essay, personal experience—humor); Women's Running (essay page written by and for women). **Buys 15 mss/year.** Query. **Pays $50 for departments, $300 for essays.**

▣ The online version contains material not found in the print edition. Contact: Marty Post.

Tips: "We are always looking for 'Adventure Runs' from readers—runs in wild, remote, beautiful and interesting places. These are rarely race stories but more like backtracking/running adventures. Great color slides are crucial,"

Ⓝ $ $ TRAIL RUNNER, The Magazine of Running Adventure, North South Publications, 603 S. Broadway, Suite A, Boulder CO 80303. (303)499-8410. Fax: (303)499-4131. E-mail: trailedit@aol.com. Website: www.trailrunner mag.com. **Contact:** Brian Metzler, editor. **65% freelance written.** Bimonthly magazine covering all aspects of off-road running. "The only nationally circulated four-color glossy magazine dedicated to covering trail running." Estab. 1999. Circ. 40,000. Pays on publication. Publishes ms an average of 2 months after acceptance. Byline given. Offers $50 kill fee. Buys first North American serial and electronic rights. Editorial lead time 3 months. Submit seasonal material 5 months in advance. Accepts queries by mail, e-mail. Accepts simultaneous submissions. Responds in 3 weeks to queries; 2 months to mss. Sample copy for $3. Writer's guidelines free, online at website or by e-mail.

Nonfiction: Essays, exposé, general interest, historical/nostalgic, how-to, humor, inspirational, interview/profile, new product, opinion, personal experience, photo feature, technical, travel, racing. No gear reviews, race results. **Buys 30-40 mss/year.** Query with published clips. Length: 800-2,000 words. **Pays 30-40¢/word.** Sometimes pays expenses of writers on assignment.

Photos: Send photos with submission. Reviews 35mm transparencies and prints. Offers $50-250/photo. Model releases and identification of subjects required. Buys one-time rights.

Columns/Departments: Monique Cole, senior editor. Training (race training, altitude training, etc.), 800 words; Adventure (off-beat aspects of trail running), 600-800 words; Wanderings (personal essay on any topic related to trail running), 600 words; Urban Escapes (urban trails accessible in and around major US sites), 800 words; Personalities (profile of a trail running personality), 1,000 words. **Buys 5-10 mss/year.** Query with published clips. **Pays 30-40¢/word.**

Fiction: Adventure, fantasy, slice-of-life vignettes. **Buys 1-2 mss/year.** Query with published clips. Length: 1,000-1,500 words. **Pays 25-35¢/word.**

Fillers: Anecdotes, facts, gags to be illustrated by cartoonist, newsbreaks, short humor. **Buys 50-60/year.** Length: 75-400 words. **Pays 25-35¢/word.**

▣ The online version contains material not found in the print edition. Contact: Brian Metzler.

Tips: "Best way to break in is with interesting and unique trail running news, notes and nonsense from around the world. Also, check the website for more info."

$ $ TRIATHLETE MAGAZINE, The World's Largest Triathlon Magazine, Triathlon Group of North America, 2037 San Elijo, Cardiff CA 92007. (760)634-4100. Fax: (760)634-4110. E-mail: cgandolfo@triathletemag.c om. Website: www.triathletemag.com. Editor: T.J. Murphy. **Contact:** Christina Gandolfo, managing editor. **50% free-**

lance written. Monthly magazine. "In general, articles should appeal to seasoned triathletes, as well as eager newcomers to the sport. Our audience includes everyone from competitive athletes to people considering their first event." Estab. 1983. Circ. 50,000. Pays on publication. Byline given. Buys second serial (reprint) and all rights. Editorial lead time 3 months. Submit seasonal material 6 months in advance. Accepts queries by mail, e-mail. Accepts simultaneous submissions. Sample copy for $5.

Nonfiction: How-to, interview/profile, new product, photo feature, technical. "No first-person pieces about your experience in triathlon or my-first-triathlon stories." **Buys 36 mss/year.** Query with published clips. Length: 1,000-3,000 words. **Pays $200-600.** Sometimes pays expenses of writers on assignment.

Photos: State availability of photos with submission. Reviews transparencies. Offers $50-300/photo. Buys first North American rights.

Tips: "Writers should know the sport and be familiar with the nuances and history. Training-specific articles that focus on new, but scientifically based, methods are good, as are seasonal training pieces."

Skiing & Snow Sports

$ AMERICAN SKATING WORLD, Independent Newsmonthly of American Ice Skating, American Skating World Inc., 1105-07 E. Carson St., #2, Pittsburgh PA 15203-1123. (412)431-4380. Fax: (412)431-4365. E-mail: editorial@americansk8world.com. Website: americansk8world.com. Editor: Robert A. Mock. **Contact:** H. Kermit Jackson, executive editor. **70% freelance written.** Eager to work with new/unpublished writers. Monthly magtab on figure skating. Estab. 1979. Circ. 15,000. Pays following publication. Publishes ms an average of 3 months after acceptance. Byline given. Buys first North American serial rights and occasionally second serial (reprint) rights. Submit seasonal material 3 months in advance. Responds in 3 months. Sample copy and writer's guidelines for $3.50.

● The increased activity and interest in figure skating have increased demands on *American Skating World*'s contributor network. New writers from nontraditional areas (i.e., outside of East Coast, Upper Midwest, California) are particularly welcome.

Nonfiction: Competition coverage (both technical and human interest), exposé, historical/nostalgic, how-to (technique in figure skating), humor, inspirational, interview/profile and overview (leading current or past individuals in the field, whether they are skaters, coaches, choreographers, arrangers or parents), new product, opinion, performance coverage (review or human interest), personal experience, photo feature, technical, travel. Also interested in amateur recreational skating (overseen by the Ice Skating Institute); "eligible" competitive skating (overseen by the USFSA, the CFSA and other bodies associated with the Olympics) and professional skating (overseen by the Professional Skaters Association. Rarely accepts fiction. "AP Style Guidelines are the basic style source, but we are not bound by that convention. Short, snappy paragraphs desired." **Buys 150 mss/year.** Send complete ms. "Include phone number; response time longer without it." Length: 600-1,000 words. **Pays $25-100.**

Reprints: Occasionally accepts previously published submissions. Send tearsheet of article or typed ms with rights for sale noted and information about when and where the article previously appeared. Pays 50% of amount paid for an original article.

Photos: Send photos with query or ms. Reviews transparencies and b&w prints. Pays $5 for b&w; $10 for color. Identification of subjects required. Buys all rights for b&w; one-time rights for color.

Columns/Departments: Buys 30 mss/year. Send complete ms. Length: 500-750 words. **Pays $25-50.**

Fillers: Clippings, anecdotes. No payment for fillers.

Tips: "Event coverage is most open to freelancers; confirm with executive editor to ensure event has not been assigned. We are drawing more extensively from non-U.S. based writers. Questions are welcome; call executive editor EST, 10-4, Monday-Friday."

N $ $ AMERICAN SNOWMOBILER, The Enthusiast Magazine, Recreational Publications, Inc., 7582 Currell Blvd., #212, St. Paul MN 55125. (651)738-1953. Fax: (651)738-2302. E-mail: editor@amsnow.com. Website: www.amsnow.com. **Contact:** Anna Boisjoli, assistant editor. **30% freelance written.** Magazine published 6 times seasonally covering snowmobiling. Estab. 1985. Circ. 90,000. **Pays on acceptance.** Publishes ms an average of 4 months after acceptance. Byline given. Buys all rights including electronic. Editorial lead time 4 months. Submit seasonal material 6 months in advance. Accepts queries by mail, e-mail, fax. Responds in 1 month to queries; 2 months to mss. Guidelines for SASE.

O─ Break in with "a packet complete with résumé, published clips and photos (or color copies of available photos) and a complete query with a few paragraphs to get me interested and to give an idea of the angle the writer will be taking. When sending an e-mail, do not attach anything."

Nonfiction: General interest, historical/nostalgic, how-to, interview/profile, new product, personal experience, photo feature, travel. **Buys 10 mss/year.** Query with published clips. Length: 1,000-2,000 words. Pay varies for assigned articles; **$100 minimum for unsolicited articles.**

Photos: State availability of photos with submission. Offers no additional payment for photos accepted with ms. Captions, model releases and identification of subjects required. Buys all rights.

■ The online version contains material not found in the print edition. Contact: Anna Boisjoli or Wade West.

$ $POWDER, The Skier's Magazine, Emap USA, P.O. Box 1028, Dana Point CA 92629. (949)496-5922. Fax: (949)496-7849. E-mail: powdermag@emapUSA.com. **Contact:** Keith Carlson, editor. **40% freelance written.** Magazine published 7 times/year covering skiing for expert skiers. Estab. 1972. Circ. 110,000. **Pays on acceptance.** Byline given. Buys first North American serial rights. Editorial lead time 3 months. Submit seasonal material 3 months in advance. Accepts queries by mail, e-mail, fax. Responds in 2 months. Sample copy for $8. Writer's guidelines free.
Photos: If available, send photos with submission. Reviews 35mm transparencies. Negotiates payment individually. Identification of subjects required. Buys one-time rights.

[N] $SKATING, United States Figure Skating Association, 20 First St., Colorado Springs CO 80906-3697. (719)635-5200. Fax: (719)635-9548. E-mail: lfawcett@usfsa.org. **Contact:** Laura Fawcett, editor. Official publication of the USFSA, published 10 times/year. "*Skating* magazine is the official publication of U.S. Figure Skating and thus we cover skating at both the championship and grass roots level." Estab. 1923. Circ. 48,000. Pays on publication. Publishes ms an average of 3 months after acceptance. Buys all rights. Byline given. Accepts queries by mail, e-mail, fax, phone.

  O➤ The best way for a writer to break in is through the "Ice Time with . . ." department, which features USFSA members (skaters, coaches, volunteers, etc.) who have unique or interesting stories to tell. This is a feature that highlights members and their accomplishments and stories on and off the ice (800-1,500 words).

Nonfiction: Historical, informational, interview, photo feature, historical biographies, profile (background and interests of skaters, coaches, volunteers or other USFSA members, technical and competition reports, figure skating issues and trends. **Buys 4 mss/issue.** All work by assignment. Length: 500-2,000 words. **Pay varies.**
Reprints: Send photocopy of article and information about when and where the article previously appeared. Pay varies.
Photos: Photos purchased with or without accompanying ms. Pays $15 for 8×10 or 5×7 b&w glossy prints and $35 for color prints or transparencies. Query.
Columns/Departments: Ice Breaker (news briefs), Foreign Competition Reports, Ice Time with. . . (features on USFSA members), Sports Medicine, In Synch (synchronized skating news). **Buys 4 mss/issue.** All work by assignment. Length: 500-2,000 words.
Tips: "We want writing by experienced persons knowledgeable in the technical and artistic aspects of figure skating with a new outlook on the development of the sport. Knowledge and background in technical aspects of figure skating is helpful, but not necessary to the quality of writing expected. We would also like to receive articles on former competitive skaters, and more short features on coaches, volunteers, skaters who normally wouldn't get recognized, as opposed to features on championship-level athletes, which are usually assigned to regular contributors. Good quality color photos are a must with submissions. Also would be interested in seeing figure skating "issues and trends" articles, instead of just profiles. No professional skater material."

$ $ $SKI MAGAZINE, Times Mirror Magazines, 929 Pearl St., Suite 200, Boulder CO 80302. (303)448-7600. Fax: (303)448-7638. Website: www.skinet.com. Editor-in-Chief: Andy Bigford. **Contact:** Natalie Kurylko, managing editor. **15% freelance written.** Monthly. "*Ski* is a ski-lifestyle publication written and edited for recreational skiers. Its content is intended to help them ski better (technique), buy better (equipment and skiwear), and introduce them to new experiences, people and adventures." Estab. 1936. Circ. 430,000. **Pays on acceptance.** Publishes ms 3 months after acceptance. Byline given. Offers 15% kill fee. Buys first North American serial rights. Submit seasonal material 8 months in advance. Responds in 1 month. Sample copy for 9×12 SAE with 5 first-class stamps.
Nonfiction: Essays, historical/nostalgic, how-to, humor, interview/profile and personal experience. **Buys 5-10 mss/year.** Send complete ms. Length: 1,000-3,500 words. **Pays $500-1,000 for assigned articles; $300-700 for unsolicited articles.** Pays the expenses of writers on assignment.

  ● Ranked as one of the best markets for freelancers in *Writer's Yearbook* magazine's annual "Top 100 Markets," January 2000.

Photos: Send photos with submission. Offers $75-300/photo. Captions, model releases and identification of subjects required. Buys one-time rights.
Columns/Departments: Ski Life (interesting people, events, oddities in skiing), 150-300 words; Going Places (items on new or unique places, deals or services available to skiers); and Take It From Us (special products or services available to skiers that are real values or out of the ordinary), 25-50 words.
Fillers: Facts and short humor. **Buys 10/year.** Length: 60-75 words. **Pays $50-75.**
Tips: "Writers must have an extensive familiarity with the sport and know what concerns, interests and amuses skiers. Columns are most open to freelancers."

$ $ $ $SKIING, Times Mirror Magazines, Inc., 929 Pearl St., Suite 200, Boulder CO 80302. (303)448-7600. Fax: (303)448-7676. E-mail: helen_olsson@tmm.com. Website: www.skinet.com. Editor-in-Chief: Rick Kahl. **Contact:** Helen Olsson, executive editor. Magazine published 7 times/year for skiers who deeply love winter, who live for travel, adventure, instruction, gear, and news. "*Skiing*, is the user's guide to winter adventure. It is equal parts jaw-dropping inspiration and practical information, action and utility, attitude and advice. It relates the lifestyles of dedicated skiers and captures their spirit of daring and exploration. Dramatic photography transports readers to spine-tingling mountains with breathtaking immediacy. Reading *Skiing* is almost as much fun as being there." Estab. 1948. Circ. 400,000. Byline given. Offers 40% kill fee. Query. No previously published articles or poetry.
Nonfiction: Buys 10-15 features (1,500-2,000 words) and **12-24 short pieces** (100-500 words). **Pays $1,000-2,500/feature; $100-500/short piece.**

• Ranked as one of the best markets for freelancers in *Writer's Yearbook* magazine's annual "Top 100 Markets," January 2000.
Columns/Departments: Buys 2-3 articles/year. Length: 200-1,200 words. **Pays $150-1,000.**

■ The online magazine carries original content not found in the print edition. Contact: Sarah Woodberry, online editor.

Tips: "Consider less obvious subjects: smaller ski areas, specific local ski cultures, unknown aspects of popular resorts. Be expressive, not merely descriptive! We want readers to feel the adventure in your writing—to tingle with the excitement of skiing steep powder, of meeting intriguing people, of reaching new goals or achieving dramatic new insights. We want readers to have fun, to see the humor in and the lighter side of skiing and their fellow skiers."

N **$ $ SNOW GOER**, Ehlert Publishing Group, 6420 Sycamore Lane, Maple Grove MN 55369. Fax: (612)476-8065. E-mail: john-p@mail.epginc.com. Website: www.ehlertpowersports.com. **Contact:** John T. Prusak, editor. **5% freelance written.** Magazine published 6 times/year covering snowmobiling. "*Snow Goer* is a hard-hitting, tell-it-like-it-is magazine designed for the ultra-active snowmobile enthusiast. It is fun, exciting, innovative and on the cutting edge of technology and trends." Estab. 1967. Circ. 76,000. Pays on publication. Publishes ms an average of 5 months after acceptance. Byline given. Buys first and one-time rights. Editorial lead time 5 months. Submit seasonal material 6 months in advance. Accepts queries by mail, e-mail, fax. Accepts simultaneous submissions. Responds in 3 months to queries. Sample copy for 8×10 SAE with 4 first-class stamps.
Nonfiction: General interest, how-to, interview/profile, new product, personal experience, photo feature, technical, travel. **Buys 6 mss/year.** Query. Length: 500-4,000 words. **Pays $50-500.** Sometimes pays expenses of writers on assignment.
Photos: State availability of photos with submission. Reviews contact sheets, negatives and prints. Negotiates payment individually. Captions and identification of subjects required. Buys one-time rights or all rights.

N **$ $ SNOW WEEK, The Snowmobile Racing Authority**, Ehlert Publishing Group, 6420 Sycamore Lane N., Maple Grove MN 55369. Fax: (612)476-8065. E-mail: john-p@mail.epginc.com. Website: www.ehlertpowersports.com. **Contact:** John Prusak, editor. **15% freelance written.** Magazine published 18 times/year covering snowmobile racing. "We cover snowmobile racing from coast to coast for hard core fans. We get in the pits, inside the race trailers and pepper our race coverage with behind the scenes details." Estab. 1973. Circ. 26,000. Pays on publication. Publishes ms an average of 2 months after acceptance. Byline given. Buys first, one-time and simultaneous rights. Editorial lead time 2 weeks. Accepts queries by mail, e-mail, fax. Sample copy for 8×11 SAE with 4 first-class stamps.
Nonfiction: Technical, race coverage. **Buys 20 mss/year.** Query. Length: 500-4,000 words. **Pays $50-450.** Sometimes pays expenses of writers on assignment.
Photos: State availability of photos with submission. Reviews contact sheets, prints. Offers no additional payment for photos accepted with ms. Captions and identification of subjects required. Buys one-time rights.

N **$ $ SNOWEST MAGAZINE**, Harris Publishing, 520 Park Ave., Idaho Falls ID 83402. (208)524-7000. Fax: (208)522-5241. E-mail: lindstrm@snowest.com. **Contact:** Lane Lindstrom. editor. Managing Editor: Steve Janes. **10-25% freelance written.** Magazine published 11 times/year. "*SnoWest* covers the sport of snowmobiling, products and personalities in the western states. This includes mountain riding, deep powder and trail riding as well as destination pieces, tech tips and new model reviews." Estab. 1972. Circ. 172,000. Pays on publication. Publishes ms an average of 2 months after acceptance. Byline given. Buys first North American serial rights. Editorial lead time 6 months. Submit seasonal material 3 months in advance. Sample copy and writer's guidelines free.
Nonfiction: How-to (fix a snowmobile, make it high performance), new product, technical, travel. **Buys 3-5 mss/year.** Query with published clips. Length: 500-1,500 words. **Pays $150-300.**
Photos: Send photos with submission. Negotiates payment individually. Captions and identification of subjects required. Buys one-time rights.

N **$ $ TRANSWORLD STANCE**, Transworld Media, 353 Airport Rd., Oceanside CA 92054. (760)722-7777. Fax: (760)722-0653. **Contact:** Warren Salas, editor or Kevin Imamura, managing editor. **50-75% freelance written.** Bimonthly consumer magazine geared toward teen males. "*Stance* is a lifestyle magazine written from the perspective of skateboarders and snowboarders. The main focus is celebrities (from our world as well as everywhere else), products, music, and fashion. Estab. 2000. Circ. 100,000. Pays on publication. Publishes ms an average of 4 months after acceptance. Byline given. Offers 50% kill fee. Makes work-for-hire assignments. Editorial lead time 4 months. Submit seasonal material 6 months in advance. Accepts queries by mail, e-mail, fax. Sample copy for 8×11 SAE and 4 first-class stamps.
Nonfiction: Historical, how-to (customize cars, buy a car), humor, interview/profile, new product, technical, travel (how to travel cross country and through Europe for cheap). Length: 25-1,500 words. **Pays 25¢/word minimum for assigned articles; 15-25¢/word for unsolicited articles.** Sometimes pays expenses of writers on assignment.
Photos: Send photos with submission. Reviews contact sheets. Negotiates payment individually. Model releases and identification of subjects required. Buys one-time rights.
Columns/Departments: Jason Stein, associate editor. Prodi Dogs (product reviews); Cover Girl (cover feature), 300-500 words; Now Playing (video game reviews), 100-150 words; Media Injection (book/video/magazine reviews), 100 words. Query. **Pays 25¢/word.**
Fillers: Jason Stein, associate editor. Facts, gags to be illustrated by cartoonist.

Tips: "We like to include as many how-to's and service-oriented pieces as possible."

Soccer

N ☆ $ $ SOCCER DIGEST, Century Publishing, 990 Grove St., Evanston IL 60207-4370. (847)491-6440. Fax: (847)491-6203. Editor: Ken Leiker. **Contact:** James O'Connor, managing editor. **80% freelance written.** "Bimonthly digest featuring investigative reportage on national and international soccer. Writers must be well-established and previously published." Estab. 1977. Circ. 40,000. Pays on publication. Publishes ms 1 month after acceptance. Byline given. Offers 50% kill fee. Buys all rights. Editorial lead time 6 weeks. Submit seasonal material 2 months in advance. Accepts simultaneous submissions. Responds in 1 month. Sample copy for $5. Guidelines free.

Nonfiction: Essays, exposé, general interest, interview/profile, opinion. No how-to, nostalgic, humor, personal experience. **Buys 60 mss/year.** Query. Length: 1,200-2,000 words. **Pays $75-500 for assigned articles; $75-200 for unsolicited articles.** Sometimes pays expenses of writers on assignment.

Photos: State availability of photos with submission. Reviews negatives, 35mm transparencies, 8×10 prints. Offers $10-30/photo, $100 for cover. Captions required. Buys one-time rights.

Columns/Departments: Touch Line (opinion), 1,000-1,200 words; Biz (business-related), 500-1,000 words. **Buys 12 mss/year.** Query. **Pays $75-200.**

Tips: "Send query by mail. Include related clips—do not deluge us with cooking clips (for example) if you're trying to sell me a sports story!"

N $ $ SOCCER JR., Scholastic Inc., 27 Unquowa Rd., Fairfield CT 06430-5015. (203)259-5766. Fax: (203)256-1119. E-mail: ischoff@soccerjr.com. Website: www.soccerjr.com. **Contact:** Jill Schoff, associate editor. Covers soccer as it relates to children. "The editorial focus of *Soccer Jr.* is on the fun and challenge of soccer, and is aimed at boys and girls, ages 8-14, who live in the U.S. and love soccer." Estab. 1992. Circ. 112,000. **Pays on acceptance.** Accepts queries by mail, e-mail. Accepts simultaneous submissions. Responds in 6 weeks to queries. Sample copy for $4; $8 (US) for non-US residents.

Nonfiction: Coverage of major soccer events, also action photos, comics, games, puzzles and contests. Special issues: Publishes coach's edition (once a year); soccer parents edition (twice a year). **Buys 10-20 mss/year.** Length: 1,000-2,000 words. **Pays $50-600.**

Reprints: Accepts previously published submissions.

Fiction: Short fiction stories with a soccer focus. **Pays $50-600.**

N $ $ SOCCER NOW, Official Publication of the American Youth Soccer Organization, American Youth Soccer Organization, 12501 S. Isis Ave., Hawthorne CA 90250. (800)USA-AYSO or (310)643-6455. Fax: (310)643-5310. E-mail: soccernow@ayso.org. Website: www.soccer.org. Editor: Amber Avines. Quarterly magazine covering soccer (AYSO and professional). "For AYSO members, both players (age 5-18) and their parents. Human interest about AYSO players and adult volunteers, or professional players (especially if they played in AYSO as kids)." Estab. 1976. Circ. 470,000. Pays on publication. Publishes ms an average of 3 months after acceptance. Byline given. Makes work-for-hire assignments. Editorial lead time 3 months. Accepts queries by mail, e-mail, fax, phone. Responds in 1 month to queries. Sample copy free on request.

Nonfiction: General interest (soccer), historical/nostalgic, how-to (playing tips subject to approval by Director of Coaching), interview/profile, personal experience, photo feature. Query. Length: 400-2,000 words. **Pays $50-200.** Sometimes pays expenses of writers on assignment.

Photos: Send photos with submission. Reviews contact sheets, transparencies, prints. Offers $0-50/photo. Identification of subjects required. Buys one-time rights.

Columns/Departments: Heroes & Hotshots (profile of AYSO players or volunteers who stand out in something *other* than soccer), 750 words; On The Spot (interview [Q&A format] with pro player), 1,300 words; Ask the Experts (soccer experts answer questions). Query. **Pays $100-200.**

Tennis

N $ $ TENNIS WEEK, Tennis News, Inc., 341 Madison Ave., 6th Floor, New York NY 10017. (212)808-4750. Fax: (212)983-6302. Managing Editors: Heather H. Holland, Kim Kodl. 10% freelance written. Biweekly magazine covering tennis. "For readers who are either tennis fanatics or involved in the business of tennis." Estab. 1974. Circ. 80,000. Pays on publication. Byline given. Buys all rights. Editorial lead time 1 month. Submit seasonal material 1 month in advance. Responds in 1 month to queries. Sample copy for $3.

Nonfiction: Buys 15 mss/year. Query with or without published clips. Length: 1,000-2,000 words. **Pays $300.**

Water Sports

$ $ DIVER, Seagraphic Publications, Ltd., Box 1312, Station A, Delta, British Columbia V4M 3Y8 Canada. (604)274-4333. Fax: (604)274-4366. E-mail: divermag@axion.net. Website: www.divermag.com. Publisher: Peter Vassilopoulos. **Contact:** Stephanie Bold, editor. Magazine published 9 times/year emphasizing scuba diving, ocean science and technology for a well-educated, outdoor-oriented readership. Circ. 17,500. Payment "follows publication." Buys first North American serial rights. Byline given. Travel features considered only August through October for use following year. Accepts queries by mail, e-mail, fax, phone. Responds in up to 3 months. Publishes ms up to 1 year after acceptance. "Articles are subject to being accepted for use in supplement issues on tabloid."
Nonfiction: How-to (underwater activities such as photography, etc.), general interest (underwater oriented), humor, historical (shipwrecks, treasure artifacts, archeological), interview (underwater personalities in all spheres—military, sports, scientific or commercial), personal experience (related to diving), photo feature (marine life), technical (related to oceanography, commercial/military diving, etc.), travel (dive resorts). No subjective product reports. **Buys 25 mss/ year. Buys 6 freelance travel items/year.** Submit complete ms. Send SAE with IRCs. Length: 800-1,000 words. **Pays $2.50/column inch.**
Photos: "Features are mostly those describing dive sites, experiences, etc. Photo features are reserved more as specials, while almost all articles must be well illustrated with color or b&w prints supplemented by color transparencies." Submit original photo material with accompanying ms. Pays $15 minimum for 5×7 or 8×10 b&w glossy prints; $20 minimum for 35mm color transparencies. Captions and model releases required. Buys one-time rights.
Columns/Departments: Book reviews. Submit complete ms. Length: 200 words maximum. No payment.
Fillers: Anecdotes, newsbreaks, short humor. **Buys 8-10/year.** Length: 50-150 words. No payment for news items.
Tips: "No phone calls about status of manuscript. Write if no response within reasonable time. Only brief, to-the-point correspondence will be answered. Lengthy communications will probably result in return of work unused. Publisher assumes no liability to use material even after lengthy waiting period. Acceptances subject to final and actual use."

$ THE DIVER, P.O. Box 28, Saint Petersburg FL 33731-0028. (813)866-9856. Fax: (813)866-9740. E-mail: boxer55270@aol.com. **Contact:** Bob Taylor, publisher/editor. **50% freelance written.** Magazine published 6 times/year for divers, coaches and officials. Estab. 1978. Circ. 1,500. Pays on publication. Byline given. Submit material at least 2 months in advance. Accepts simultaneous submissions. Accepts queries by mail, e-mail, fax, phone. Responds in 2 weeks to queries; 1 month to mss. Sample copy for 9×12 SAE with 3 first-class stamps.
Nonfiction: Interview/profile (of divers, coaches, officials), results, tournament coverage, any stories connected with platform and springboard diving, photo features, technical. **Buys 35 mss/year.** Query. Length: 500-2,500 words. **Pays $25-50.**
Reprints: Send tearsheet of article. Pays 50% of amount paid for an original article.
Photos: Pays $5-10 for b&w prints. Captions and identification of subjects required. Buys one-time rights.
Tips: "We're very receptive to new writers."

$ $ HOT WATER, Taylor Publishing Group, 2585 Skymark Ave., Unit 306, Mississauga, Ontario L4W 4L5 Canada. (905)624-8218. Fax: (905)624-6764. **Contact:** Karen Hill, editor. **50% freelance written.** Quarterly magazine covering personal watercraft market (jet skis, sea-doo's). "Focused on fun-loving watersports enthusiasts, *Hot Water* contains features on new personal watercraft and accessories, places to ride, racing, and profiles on people in the industry. Technical and handling tips are also included." Estab. 1993. Circ. 18,000 Pays on publication. Publishes ms an average of 4 months after acceptance. Byline given. Buys first North American serial rights. Editorial lead time 2 months. Submit seasonal material 3 months in advance. Accepts queries by mail, e-mail, fax, phone. Sample copy and writer's guidelines free.
Nonfiction: Historical/nostalgic, how-to (anything technical or handling etc.), humor, interview/profile, personal experience, photo feature, technical, travel. Send complete ms. Length: 1,000-3,000 words. **Pays $300 maximum.** Sometimes pays expenses of writers on assignment.
Reprints: Send photocopy of article or typed ms with rights for sale noted and information about when and where the article previously appeared. Pay negotiable.
Photos: Send photos with submission. Reviews transparencies, 4×6 prints. Offers no additional payment for photos accepted with ms. Captions, model releases, identification of subjects required.
Columns/Departments: Workbench (technical tips); Hot Waterways (riding adventures); all 1,000 words. **Buys 6 mss/year.** Send complete ms. **Pays $200 maximum.**
Fillers: Facts, newsbreaks. Length: 500-1,000 words. **Pays $150 maximum.**
Tips: "Make sure your idea has a Canadian angle. If you have a story idea you feel is appropriate, feel free to contact the editor to discuss. Or, if you're familiar with watercraft but need some direction, call the editor who will gladly assign a feature."

$ $ IMMERSED MAGAZINE, The International Technical Diving Magazine, Immersed LLC, FDR Station, P.O. Box 947, New York NY 10150-0947. (201)792-1331. Fax: (212)259-9310. E-mail: bsterner@prodigy.net or immersed@njscuba.com. Website: www.immersed.com. **Contact:** Bob Sterner, publisher/editor. **40% freelance written.** Quarterly magazine covering scuba diving. "Advances on the frontier of scuba diving are covered in theme-oriented issues that examine archeology, biology, history, gear and sciences related to diving. We emphasize training, education and safety." Estab. 1996. Circ. 25,000. Pays on publication. Byline given. Offers kill fee. Buys one-time and electronic rights. Editorial lead time 6 months. Accepts queries by mail, e-mail, fax, phone. Sample copy online at website. Writer's guidelines for #10 SASE.

O-¬ Break in with "how-to equipment rigging stories or travel stories on unusual but accessible destinations."

Nonfiction: Historical/nostalgic, how-to, interview/profile, new product, personal experience, photo feature, technical, travel. No poetry, opinion diatribes, axe-grinding exposés. **Buys 30 mss/year.** Query. Length: 500-2,000 words. **Pays $150-250.** Sometimes pays expenses of writers on assignment.

Photos: Send photos with submission. Reviews transparencies and prints. Offers no additional payment for photos accepted with ms. Captions required. Buys one-time and promotional website rights.

Columns/Departments: Technically Destined (travel), 1,200 words; Rigging for Success (how-to), few words/illustration; Explorer (personality profile), 2,000 words; Tech Spec (product descriptions), 1,000 words; New Products (product press releases), 200 words; Book Review (book review), 800 words. **Buys 12 mss/year.** Query. **Pays $150-250.**

Fillers: Newsbreaks. **Pays 35¢/word.**

Tips: "Query first with a short, punchy paragraph that describes your story and why it would be of interest to our readers. There's bonus points for citing which feature or department would be most appropriate for your story."

$ $ PADDLER MAGAZINE, World's No. 1 Canoeing, Kayaking and Rafting Magazine, Paddlesport Publishing, P.O. Box 5450, Steamboat Springs CO 80477-5450. (970)879-1450. Fax: (970)870-1404. E-mail: editor@aca-paddler.org. Website: www.aca-paddler.org/paddler. Editor: Eugene Buchanan. **Contact:** Tom Bie, managing editor. **70% freelance written.** Bimonthly magazine covering paddle sports. "*Paddler* magazine is written by and for those knowledgeable above river running, flatwater tripping and sea kayaking. Our core audience is the intermediate to advanced paddler, yet we strive to cover the entire range from beginners to experts. Our editorial coverage is divided between whitewater rafting, whitewater kayaking, canoeing and sea kayaking. We strive for balance between the Eastern and Western U.S. paddling scenes and regularly cover international expeditions. We also try to integrate the Canadian paddling community into each publication." Estab. 1991. Circ. 80,000. Pays on publication. Publishes ms an average of 6 months after acceptance. Byline given. Buys first North American serial and one-time electronic rights. Editorial lead time 3 months. Submit seasonal material 6 months in advance. Accepts queries by mail, e-mail, fax. Responds in 6 months. Sample copy $3 with 8½×11 SASE. Writer's guidelines for #10 SASE.

Nonfiction: Book excerpts, essays, general interest, historical/nostalgic, how-to, humor, inspirational, interview/profile, new product, opinion, personal experience, photo feature, technical, travel (must be paddlesport related). **Buys 75 mss/year.** Query. Length: 100-3,000 words. **Pays 10-25¢/word for assigned articles (more for established writers); 10-20¢/word for unsolicited articles.** Sometimes pays expenses of writers on assignment.

Photos: State availability of photos with submission. Reviews contact sheets, negatives and transparencies. Offers $25-250/photo. Buys one-time rights.

Columns/Departments: Submissions should include photos or other art. Consider submitting to Departments, especially as a first-time contributor, and be creative. Hotline (timely news and exciting developments relating to the paddling community. Stories should be lively and newsworthy), 150-750 words; Paddle People (unique people involved in the sport and industry leaders), 600-800 words; Destinations (informs paddlers of unique places to paddle), we often follow regional themes and cover all paddling disciplines. Submissions should include map and photo, 800 words; Marketplace (gear reviews, gadgets and new products and is about equipment paddlers use, from boats and paddles to collapsible chairs, bivy sacks and other accessories), 250-800 words; Paddle Tales (short, humorous anecdotes), 75-300 words; Skills (a "How-to" forum for experts to share tricks of the trade, from playboating techniques to cooking in the backcountry), 250-1,000 words. Query. **Pays 10-20¢/word.**

Tips: "We prefer queries, but will look at manuscripts on speculation. No phone queries please. Be familiar with the magazine and offer us unique, exciting ideas. Most positive responses to queries are on spec, but we will occasionally make assignments."

SEA MAGAZINE, America's Western Boating Magazine, Duncan McIntosh Co., 17782 Cowan, Suite C, Irvine CA 92614. (949)660-6150. Fax: (949)660-6172. Website: www.goboatingamerica.com. Managing editor: Eston Ellis. **70% freelance written.** Monthly magazine covering West Coast power boating. Estab. 1908. Circ. 50,000. Pays on publication. Publishes ms an average of 3 months after acceptance. Byline given. Buys first North American serial rights. Editorial lead time 3 months. Submit seasonal material 5 months in advance. Accepts simultaneous submissions. Responds in 6 weeks to queries.

Nonfiction: Exposé, how-to, new product, personal experience, technical, travel. **Buys 36 mss/year.** Query or send complete ms. Length: 300-1,200 words. **Pay varies.** Sometimes pays expenses of writers on assignment.

Photos: State availability of photos with submission. Reviews transparencies. Offers $50-250/photo. Captions, model releases and identification of subjects required. Buys one-time rights.

■ $ $ SPORT DIVER, World Publications, 330 W. Canton Ave., Winter Park FL 32789. (407)628-5662. Fax: (407)628-7061. E-mail: kirk.brown@worldpub.net. Website: www.sportdiver.com. **Contact:** Kirk Brown, managing editor. **75% freelance written.** Bimonthly magazine covering scuba diving. "We portray the adventure and fun of diving—the reasons we all started diving in the first place." Estab. 1993. Circ. 120,000. Pays on publication, sometimes on acceptance. Byline given. Offers 50% kill fee. Buys first North American serial rights. Editorial lead time 3 months. Submit seasonal material 4 months in advance. Accepts queries by mail, e-mail. Responds in 2 weeks to queries; 3 months to mss. Writer's guidelines for #10 SASE.

Nonfiction: Personal experience, travel, diving. No non-diving related articles. **Buys 150 mss/year.** Query with SASE. Length: 800-2,000 words. **Pays $300-500.**

Photos: State availability of photos with submission. Reviews transparencies. Offers $50-200/photo. Offers $500 for covers. Captions required. Buys one-time rights.

Columns/Departments: Divebriefs (shorts), 150-450 words. Query. **Pays $50-250.**

▪ The online version contains material not found in the print edition. Contact: Brian Courtney.

Tips: "Know diving, and even more importantly, know how to write. It's getting much more difficult to break into the market due to a recent series of takeovers."

$ $ SWIM MAGAZINE, The Official Magazine of U.S. Masters Swimming, Sports Publications, Inc., 90 Bell Rock Plaza, Suite 200, Sedona AZ 86351. (520)284-4005. Fax: (520)284-2477. E-mail: swimworld@aol.com. Website: www.swimworld.com. **Contact:** Dr. Phillip Whitten, editor. **50% freelance written.** Prefers to work with published/selected writers. Bimonthly magazine for adults interested in swimming for fun, fitness and competition. Readers are fitness-oriented adults from varied social and professional backgrounds who share swimming as part of their lifestyle. Readers are well-educated, affluent and range in age from 20-100 with most in the 30-49 age group; about 50% female, 50% male." Estab. 1984. Circ. 46,000. Pays 1 month after publication. Publishes ms an average of 3 months after acceptance. Byline given. Buys all rights. Editorial lead time 3 months. Submit seasonal material 3 months in advance. Accepts simultaneous submissions. Responds in 1 month to queries; 4 months to mss. Sample copy for $5 (prepaid) and 9×12 SAE with 4 first-class stamps. Writer's guidelines for #10 SASE.

Nonfiction: Book excerpts, essays, exposé, general health, general interest, historical, how-to (training plans and techniques), humor, inspirational, interview/profile (people associated with fitness and competitive swimming), new product (articles describing new products for fitness and competitive training), personal experience, photo feature, technical, travel. "Articles need to be informative as well as interesting. In addition to fitness and health articles, we are interested in exploring fascinating topics dealing with swimming for the adult reader." **Buys 12-18 mss/year.** Query with or without published clips. Length: 250-2,500 words. **Pays 12¢/word minimum.**

Photos: Send photos with ms. Negotiates payment individually. Captions, model releases, identification of subjects required.

Tips: "*Always* query first. Writers should be familiar with or an expert in adult fitness and/or adult swimming. Our how-to and profile articles best typify *Swim Magazine*'s style for fitness and competitive swimmers. *Swim Magazine* accepts medical guidelines and exercise physiology articles primarily by M.D.s and Ph.Ds."

$ $ SWIMMING TECHNIQUE, Sports Publications, Inc., 90 Bell Rock Plaza, Suite 200, Sedona AZ 86351. (520)284-4005. Fax: (520)284-2477. E-mail: swimworld@aol.com. Website: www.swiminfo.com. Managing Editor: Mr. Bob Engram. **Contact:** Dr. Phillip Whitten, editor. **75% freelance written.** Quarterly magazine for professional swim coaches covering swimming techniques. "Covers all aspects of swimming technique and training." Estab. 1963. Circ. 9,000. Pays on publication. Publishes ms an average of 4 months after acceptance. Byline given. Buys first and all rights. Editorial lead time 4 months. Submit seasonal material 4 months in advance. Accepts queries by mail, e-mail, fax, phone. Responds in 1 month. Sample copy for $5. Writer's guidelines free.

Nonfiction: Book excerpts, essays, how-to (swim & technique), interview/profile, opinion, personal experience, technical. **Buys 16-20 mss/year.** Query with published clips. Length: 500-4,000 words. **Pays 12-15¢/word.** Sometimes pays expenses of writers on assignment.

Reprints: Accepts previously published submissions.

Photos: Send photos with submission. Negotiates payment individually. Captions and identification of subjects required. Buys all rights.

$ $ SWIMMING WORLD, Sports Publications, Inc., 90 Bell Rock Plaza, Suite 200, Sedona AZ 86351. (520)284-4005. Fax: (520)284-2477. E-mail: swimworld@aol.com. Website: www.swiminfo.com. **Contact:** Dr. Phillip Whitten, editor-in-chief. Managing Editor: Bob Ingram. **25-50% freelance written.** Monthly magazine. "*Swimming World* is recognized as the authoritative source in the sport of swimming. It publishes articles about all aspects of competitive swimming." Estab. 1959. Circ. 39,700. Pays on publication. Byline given. Kill fee negotiated. Buys all rights. Editorial lead time 2 months. Submit seasonal material 3 months in advance. Accepts queries by mail, e-mail, fax, phone. Accepts simultaneous submissions. Responds in 1 month. Sample copy for $5 and SAE with 4 first-class stamps. Writer's guidelines free.

Nonfiction: Book excerpts, essays, exposé, general interest, historical/nostalgic, how-to, humor, inspirational, interview/profile, new product, opinion, personal experience, photo feature, technical, travel. **Buys 30 mss/year.** Query. Length: 300-3,000 words. **Pays $75-400.** Sometimes pays expenses of writers on assignment.

Photos: State availability of photos with submission. Reviews prints. Negotiates payment individually. Captions, model releases and identification of subjects required. Buys negotiable rights.

Columns/Departments: Buys 18 mss/year. Query with published clips. **Pays $75-200.**

▪ The online magazine carries original content not found in the print edition.

$ THE WATER SKIER, American Water Ski Association, 799 Overlook Dr., Winter Haven FL 33884. (941)324-4341. Fax: (914)325-8259. E-mail: satkinson@usawaterski.org. Website: www.usawaterski.org. **Contact:** Scott Atkinson, editor. **10-20% freelance written.** Magazine published 9 times/year. "*The Water Skier* is the membership magazine of USA Water Ski, the national governing body for organized water skiing in the United States. The magazine has a controlled circulation and is available only to USA Water Skis membership, which is made up of 20,000 active competitive water skiers and 10,000 members who are supporting the sport. These supporting members may participate in the sport but they don't compete. The editorial content of the magazine features distinctive and informative writing about the sport of water skiing only." Estab. 1951. Circ. 30,000. Byline given. Offers 30% kill fee. Buys all rights (no exceptions). Editorial lead time 4 months. Submit seasonal material 6 months in advance. Responds in 2 weeks. Sample copy for $1.25. Writer's guidelines for #10 SASE.

O→ Most open to material for feature articles (query editor with your idea).

Nonfiction: Historical/nostalgic (has to pertain to water skiing), interview/profile (call for assignment), new product (boating and water ski equipment), travel (water ski vacation destinations). **Buys 10-15 mss/year.** Query. Length: 1,500-3,000 words. **Pays $100-150 for assigned feature articles.**

Reprints: Send photocopy of article. Pay negotiable.

Photos: State availability of photos with submission. Reviews contact sheets. Negotiates payment individually. Captions and identification of subjects required. Buys all rights.

Columns/Departments: The Water Skier News (small news items about people and events in the sport), 400-500 words. Other topics include safety, training (3-event, barefoot, disabled, show ski, ski race, kneeboard and wakeboard); champions on their way; new products. Query. **Pays $50-100.** Pay for columns negotiated individually with each writer.

▣ The online magazine carries original content not found in the print edition. Contact: Scott Atkinson, online editor.

Tips: "Contact the editor through a query letter (please no phone calls) with an idea. Avoid instruction, these articles are written by professionals. Concentrate on articles about the people of the sport. We are always looking for interesting stories about people in the sport. Also, short news features which will make a reader say to himself, 'Hey, I didn't know that.' Keep in mind that the publication is highly specialized about the sport of water skiing."

Wrestling

◩ $ WRESTLING WORLD, Sterling/MacFadden, 233 Park Ave. S., New York NY 10003. (212)780-3500. Fax: (212)780-3555. E-mail: sterlingsports@yahoo.com. **Contact:** Stephen Ciacciarelli, editor. **100% freelance written.** Monthly magazine for professional wrestling fans. "We run profiles of top wrestlers and managers and articles on current topics of interest on the mat scene." Circ. 100,000. **Pays on acceptance.** Byline given. Buys first North American serial rights. Responds in 2 weeks. Sample copy for $4 and SAE with 3 first-class stamps.

• *Wrestling World* has increased its frequency from a bimonthly to a monthly.

Nonfiction: Interview/profile and photo feature. "No general think pieces." **Buys 100 mss/year.** Query with or without published clips or send complete ms. Length: 1,500-2,500 words. **Pays $75-125.**

Photos: State availability of photos with submission. Reviews 35mm transparencies and prints. Offers $25-50/photo package. Pays $50-150 for transparencies. Identification of subjects required. Buys one-time rights.

Tips: "Anything topical has the best chance of acceptance. Articles on those hard-to-reach wrestlers stand an excellent chance of acceptance."

TEEN & YOUNG ADULT

Publications in this category are for teens (13-19). Publications for college students are in Career, College & Alumni. Those for younger children are in Juvenile.

$ $ ALL ABOUT YOU, Emap USA, 6420 Wilshire Blvd., 15th Floor, Los Angeles CA 90048-5515. Fax: (323)782-2660. E-mail: fortj@emapusa.com. **Contact:** Jane Fort, editor. **50% freelance written.** Quarterly magazine covering fashion/beauty/lifestyle for girls age 9-14. "We strive to promote self-esteem in our girls. We look for fun quizzes, self-help pieces and articles on dating and friends that are geared toward the younger segment of the teen market." Estab. 1994. **Pays on acceptance.** Publishes ms 4 months after acceptance. Byline given. Buys all rights. Editorial lead time 4 months. Submit seasonal material 5 months in advance. Accepts simultaneous submissions. Responds in 1 month. Sample copy for a fee. Call 800-482-0957.

Nonfiction: How-to (examples: throw a party, talk to your crush, overcome shyness), inspirational, personal experience. "No fiction, profiles on teens or businesspeople; no articles that are preachy, stiff or sexual." **Buys 100-140 mss/year.** Query with published clips or send complete ms. Length: 700-7,000 words. **Pays $150-700.**

Photos: "We buy paparazzi/celeb photos only." Send photos with submission. Negotiates payment individually. Model releases and identification of subjects required. Buys one-time rights.

Tips: "Submit a list of quiz ideas and we'll select one for you to write on spec. Have fun with the writing, but don't force the teen lingo."

$ $ CAMPUS LIFE, Christianity Today, Inc., 465 Gundersen Dr., Carol Stream IL 60188. (630)260-6200. Fax: (630)260-0114. E-mail: cledit@aol.com. Website: www.campuslife.net. **Contact:** Amber Penney, assistant editor. **35% freelance written.** Magazine published 9 times/year for the Christian life as it relates to today's teen. "*Campus Life* is a magazine for high-school and early college-age teenagers. Our editorial slant is not overtly religious. The indirect style is intended to create a safety zone with our readers and to reflect our philosophy that God is interested in all of life. Therefore, we publish 'message stories' side by side with general interest, humor, etc." Estab. 1942. Circ. 100,000. **Pays on acceptance.** Publishes ms an average of 5 months after acceptance. Byline given. Offers 50% kill fee. Buys first and one-time rights. Editorial lead time 4 months. Accepts queries by mail, e-mail, fax. Responds in 5 weeks to queries. Sample copy for $3 and 8×10 SAE with 3 first-class stamps. Writer's guidelines for #10 SASE or on website.
Nonfiction: Humor, personal experience, photo feature. **Buys 15-20 mss/year.** Query with published clips. Length: 750-1,500 words. **Pays 15-20¢/word minimum.**
Reprints: Send tearsheet or photocopy of article or short story or typed ms with rights for sale noted and information about when and where the article or story previously appeared. **Pays $50.**
Photos: State availability of photos with submission. Reviews contact sheets, transparencies, 5×7 prints. Negotiates payment individually. Model release required. Buys one-time rights.
Fiction: Buys 1-5 mss/year. Query. Length: 1,000-2,000 words. **Pays 15-20¢/word.**
Tips: "The best way to break in to *Campus Life* is through writing first-person or as-told-to first-person stories. We want stories that capture a teen's everyday 'life lesson' experience. A first-person story must be highly descriptive and incorporate fictional technique. While avoiding simplistic religious answers, the story should demonstrate that Christian values or beliefs brought about a change in the young person's life. But query first with theme information telling the way this story would work for our audience."

$ THE CONQUEROR, United Pentecostal Church International, 8855 Dunn Rd., Hazelwood MO 63042-2299. (314)837-7300. Fax: (314)837-4503. E-mail: gyouth8855@aol.com. Website: www.upci.org/youth. **Contact:** Travis Miller, editor. **80% freelance written.** Literary magazine published bimonthly covering Christian youth. "*The Conqueror* addresses the social, intellectual and spiritual concerns of youth aged 12-21 years from a Christian viewpoint." Estab. 1957. Circ. 6,000. Pays on publication. Publishes ms an average of 4 months after acceptance. No byline. Buys one-time rights. Editorial lead time 4 months. Submit seasonal material 4 months in advance. Accepts queries by mail, e-mail, fax, phone. Accepts simultaneous submissions. Responds in 2 months. Sample copy for 9×12 SAE with 3 first-class stamps. Writer's guidelines free.
Nonfiction: Essays, general interest, historical/nostalgic, inspirational, personal experience, religious. **Buys 18 mss/year.** Send complete ms. Length: 250-1,250 words. **Pays $15-30.**
Reprints: Accepts previously published submissions.
Photos: State availability of photos with submission. Offers no additional payment for photos accepted with ms.
Columns/Departments: Time Out for Truth (applying Biblical truth to everyday living), 750 words. **Buys 6-10 mss/year.** Send complete ms. **Pays $30 maximum.**
Fiction: Adventure, ethnic, historical, humorous, mainstream, religious, slice-of-life vignettes. **Buys 4-6 mss/year.** Send complete ms. Length: 250-1,250 words. **Pays $15-30.**
Poetry: Traditional. **Buys 2-4 poems/year.** Submit maximum 5 poems. **Pays $15.**
Fillers: Anecdotes, gags to be illustrated by cartoonist, short humor. **Buys 4/year.** Length: 100 words. **Pays $15.**
Tips: "Choose subjects relevant to single youth. Most subjects *are* relevant if properly handled. Today's youth are interested in more than clothes, fashion, careers and dating. Remember our primary objective: inspiration—to portray happy, victorious living through faith in God."

$ ENCOUNTER, (formerly *Straight*), Standard Publishing Co., 8121 Hamilton Ave., Cincinnati OH 45231-2323. (513)931-4050. Fax: (513)931-0950. Website: www.standardpub.com. **Contact:** Kelly Carr, editor. **90% freelance written.** Estab. 1950. Weekly magazine (published quarterly) for "teens, age 13-19, from Christian backgrounds who generally receive this publication in their Sunday School classes or through subscriptions." **Pays on acceptance.** Publishes ms an average of 1 year after acceptance. Buys first rights and second serial (reprint) rights. Byline given. Submit seasonal material 9-12 months in advance. Accepts queries by mail. Responds in 2 months. Sample copy and writer's guidelines for 9×12 SAE with 2 first-class stamps. "We use freelance material in every issue. Our theme list is available on a quarterly basis. Writers need only give us their name and address in order to be added to our mailing list."
Nonfiction: Religious-oriented topics, teen interest (school, church, family, dating, sports, part-time jobs), humor, inspirational, personal experience. "We want articles that promote Christian values and ideals." No puzzles. Query or submit complete ms. Include Social Security number on ms. "We're buying more short pieces these days; 8 pages fill up much too quickly." Length: 800-1,100 words. **Pays 5-6¢/word.**
Reprints: Send tearsheet of article or story or typed ms with rights for sale noted. **Pays 5¢/word.**
Fiction: Adventure, humorous, religious, suspense. "All fiction should have some message for the modern Christian teen. Fiction should deal with all subjects in a forthright manner, without being preachy and without talking down to teens. No tasteless manuscripts that promote anything adverse to the Bible's teachings." Submit complete ms. Length: 900-1,100 words. **Pays 5-6¢/word.**
Photos: Submit photos with ms. Pays $75-125 for color slides. Model releases required. Buys one-time rights.
Tips: "Don't be trite. Use unusual settings or problems. Use a lot of illustrations, a good balance of conversation, narration, and action. Style must be clear, fresh—no sermonettes or sickly-sweet fiction. Take a realistic approach to

problems. Be willing to submit to editorial policies on doctrine; knowledge of the *Bible* a must. Also, be aware of teens today, and what they do. Language, clothing, and activities included in manuscripts should be contemporary. We are also looking for articles for a monthly feature entitled 'Spotlight,' which is about real teens who are making a difference in their school, community or church. Articles for this feature should be approx. 900 words in length. We would also like a picture of the teen or group of teens to run with the article."

$ $ GUIDEPOSTS FOR TEENS, Guideposts, P.O. Box 638, Chesterton IN 46304. (219)929-4429. Fax: (219)926-3839. E-mail: gp4t@guideposts.org. Editor-in-Chief: Mary Lou Carney. **Contact:** Betsy Kohn, editor. **90% freelance written**. Bimonthly teen inspirational magazine. "*Guideposts for Teens* is published for teenagers ages 12-18. It is a 48 +-page, 4-color, value-centered magazine that offers teens advice, humor, and true stories—lots of true stories." Estab. 1998. Circ. 200,000. **Pays on acceptance**. Byline sometimes given. Offers 25% kill fee. Buys all rights. Editorial lead time 6 months. Submit seasonal material 6 months in advance. Accepts simultaneous submissions. Responds in 1 month to queries, 2 months to mss. Sample copy for $4.50. Writer's guidelines for #10 SASE.
Nonfiction: How-to, humor, inspirational, interview/profile, personal experience, religious. Nothing written from an adult point of view. **Buys 80 mss/year** Query. Length: 700-1,500 words. **Pays $175-500 for assigned articles; $150-400 for unsolicited articles**. Pays expenses of writers on assignment.
Photos: State availability of photos with submission. Negotiates payment individually. Identification of subjects required. Buys one-time rights.
Columns/Departments: Quiz (teen-relevant topics, teen language), 1,000 words; How-to (strong teen voice/quotes, teen topics), 750-1,000 words; Profiles/Poster (teens who initiate change/develop service projects), 300-500 words; Humor (essays teens can relate to), 750 words; embarassing celebrity moments (celebrity/athlete), 300-500 words. **Buys 40 mss/year**. Query with published clips. **Pays $175-400**.
Fillers: Short humor (cartoons, jokes, short humor, quotes). **Buys 20/year**. Length: 100-300 words. **Pays $25-100**.
Tips: "We are new and eagerly looking for a number of things: teen how-to pieces, celebrity and embarassing moments for quizzes, humor. Most of all, though, we are about TRUE STORIES in the *Guideposts* tradition. Teens in dangerous, inspiring, miraculous situations. These first-person (ghostwritten) true narratives are the backbone of *GP4T*—and what sets us apart from other publications."

$ INSIGHT, A Spiritual Lift for Teens, The Review and Herald Publishing Association, 55 W. Oak Ridge Dr., Hagerstown MD 21740. E-mail: insight@rhpa.org. Website: www.insightmagazine.org. **Contact:** Lori Peckham, editor. **80% freelance written.** Weekly magazine covering spiritual life of teenagers. "*Insight* publishes true dramatic stories, interviews, and community and mission service features that relate directly to the lives of Christian teenagers, particularly those with a Seventh-day Adventist background." Estab. 1970. Circ. 20,000. Pays on publication. Publishes ms an average of 4 months after acceptance. Byline given. Buys first rights and second serial (reprint) rights. Editorial lead time 6 months. Submit seasonal material 6 months in advance. Accepts queries by mail, e-mail, fax. Responds in 1 month. Sample copy for $2 and #10 SASE. Guidelines for #10 SASE or on website.
Nonfiction: How-to (teen relationships and experiences), humor, interview/profile, personal teen experience, photo feature, religious. **Buys 120 mss/year.** Send complete ms. Length: 500-2,000 words. **Pays $25-150 for assigned articles; $25-125 for unsolicited articles.**
Reprints: Send typed ms with rights for sale noted and information about when and where the article previously appeared. **Pays $50.**
Photos: State availability of photos with submission. Reviews contact sheets, negatives, transparencies, prints. Negotiates payment individually. Model releases required. Buys one-time rights.
Columns/Departments: Big Deal (topic of importance to teens) 1,200-1,700 words; Interviews (Christian culture figures, esp. musicians), 2,000 words; It Happened to Me (1st person teen experiences containing spiritual insights), 1,000 words; On the Edge (dramatic true stories about Christians), 2,000 words; So I Said . . . (true short stories in the 1st person of common, everyday events and experiences that taught the writer something), 300-500 words. Send complete ms. **Pays $25-125.**
  ● "*Big Deal*" appears in *Insight* often, covering a topic of importance to teens. Each feature contains: an opening story involving real teens (can be written in first-person), "Scripture Picture" (a sidebar that discusses what the Bible says about the topic) and another sidebar (optional) that adds more perspective and help.
Tips: "Skim two months of *Insight*. Write about your teen experiences. Use informed, contemporary style and vocabulary. Become a Christian if you haven't already."

$ $ $ JUMP, For Girls Who Dare to be Real, Weider, 21100 Erwin St., Woodland Hills CA 91367. Fax: (818)594-0972. E-mail: letters@jumponline.com. Website: www.jumponline.com. Editor: Lori Berger. Managing Editor: Maureen Meyers. **Contact:** Jennifer Howell, assistant to the editor-in-chief. **50% freelance written.** Monthly magazine for a female teen market. Estab. 1997. Circ. 350,000. Pays on publication. Publishes ms 4 months after acceptance. Byline given. Offers 33% kill fee. Buys all rights. Editorial lead time 4 months. Submit seasonal material 5 months in advance. Accepts simultaneous submissions. Responds in 1 month.
Nonfiction: General interest, how-to, interview/profile, new product, personal experience. Query with published clips. Length: 1,500-2,000 words. **Pays 50¢-$1/word.**
Columns/Departments: Busted! (quirky, bizarre and outrageous trends, news, quotes), 6 items, 50 words each; The Dish (food and nutrition for teens), 1,500 words; Jump On . . . In, Music, Sports, Body & Soul (small news and trend items on sports, health, music, etc.), 6 items per page, 75 words each. Query with published clips. **Pays 50¢-$1/word.**

Tips: "Writers must read magazine before submitting queries. Will turn away queries that clearly show the writer is not familiar with the content of the magazine."

$ $ KEYNOTER, Key Club International, 3636 Woodview Trace, Indianapolis IN 46268-3196. E-mail: Keynoter@ Kiwanis.org. Website: www.Keyclub.org. **Contact:** Amy L. Wiser, executive editor. **65% freelance written.** Works with a small number of new writers each year, but is eager to work with new/unpublished writers willing to adjust their writing styles. Monthly youth magazine (December/January combined issue), distributed to members of Key Club International, a high school service organization for young men and women. Estab. 1946. Circ. 171,000. **Pays on acceptance.** Publishes ms an average of 5 months after acceptance. Byline given. Buys first North American serial rights. Submit seasonal material 7 months in advance. Accepts queries by mail, e-mail. Accepts simultaneous submissions. Responds in 2 months. Sample copy for 65¢ and 8½×11 SAE. Guidelines for SASE.

Nonfiction: Book excerpts (included in articles), general interest (for intelligent teen audience), academic, self-help, historical/nostalgic (generally not accepted), how-to (advice on how teens can enhance the quality of lives or communities), humor (accepted if adds to story), interview/profile (rarely purchased, "would have to be on/with an irresistible subject"), new product (affecting teens), photo feature (if subject is right), technical (understandable and interesting to teen audience), travel (must apply to club travel schedule), subjects that entertain and inform teens on topics that relate directly to their lives. "We would also like to receive self-help and school-related nonfiction on leadership, community service, and teen issues. *Please, no first-person confessions, fiction or articles that are written down to our teen readers. No filler, or book, movie or music reviews.*" **Buys 10-15 mss/year.** Query with SASE. Length: 1,200-1,500 words. **Pays $150-350.** Sometimes pays the expenses of writers on assignment.

Reprints: Send tearsheet or photocopy of article and information about when and where the article previously appeared.
Photos: State availability of photos. Reviews color contact sheets and negatives. Identification of subjects required. Buys one-time rights. Payment for photos included in payment for ms.
Tips: "We want to see articles written with attention to style and detail that will enrich the world of teens. Articles must be thoroughly researched and must draw on interviews with nationally and internationally respected sources. Our readers are 13-18, mature and dedicated to community service. We are very committed to working with good writers, and if we see something we like in a well-written query, we'll try to work it through to publication."

$ LISTEN MAGAZINE, Review & Herald Publishing Association, 55 W. Oak Ridge Dr., Hagerstown MD 21740. (301)393-4019. Fax: (301)393-4055. E-mail: listen@healthconnection.org. Editor: Lincoln Steed. **Contact:** Anita Jacobs, assistant editor. **75% freelance written.** Works with a small number of new/unpublished writers each year. Monthly magazine specializing in drug and alcohol prevention, presenting positive alternatives to various drug and alcohol dependencies. "*Listen* is used in many high school classes and by professionals: medical personnel, counselors, law enforcement officers, educators, youth workers, etc." Circ. 40,000. Buys first rights for use in *Listen*, reprints and associated material. Byline given. **Pays on acceptance.** Publishes ms 6 months after acceptance. Accepts simultaneous submissions if notified. Accepts queries by mail, e-mail, fax. Responds in 2 months. Sample copy for $1 and 9×12 SASE. Guidelines for SASE.

Nonfiction: Seeks articles that deal with causes of drug use such as poor self-concept, family relations, social skills or peer pressure. Especially interested in youth-slanted articles or personality interviews encouraging non-alcoholic and non-drug ways of life and showing positive alternatives. Also interested in good activity articles of interest to teens. an activity that teens would want to do instead of taking abusive substances because they're bored. Teenage point of view is essential. Popularized medical, legal and educational articles. Also seeks narratives which portray teens dealing with youth conflicts, especially those related to the use of or temptation to use harmful substances. Growth of the main character should be shown. "Submit an article with an ending that catches you by surprise. We don't want typical alcoholic story/skid-row bum, AA stories. We are also being inundated with drunk-driving accident stories. Unless yours is unique, consider another topic." **Buys 30-50 unsolicited mss/year.** Query. Length: 1,000-1,200 words. **Pays 5-10¢/ word.** Sometimes pays the expenses of writers on assignment.
Reprints: Send photocopy of article or typed ms with rights for sale noted and information about when and where it previously appeared. Pays their regular rates.
Photos: Purchased with accompanying ms. Captions required. Color photos preferred, but b&w acceptable.
Fillers: Word square/general puzzles are also considered. **Pays $15.**
Tips: "True stories are good, especially if they have a unique angle. Other authoritative articles need a fresh approach. In query, briefly summarize article idea and logic of why you feel it's good. Make sure you've read the magazine to understand our approach."

$ LIVE, A Weekly Journal of Practical Christian Living, Gospel Publishing House, 1445 Boonville Ave., Springfield MO 65802-1894. (417)862-2781. Fax: (417)862-6059. E-mail: rl-live@gph.org. Website: www.radiantlife.o rg. **Contact**: Paul W. Smith, adult curriculum editor. **100% freelance written.** Quarterly magazine for weekly distribution covering practical Christian living. "*LIVE* is a take-home paper distributed weekly in young adult and adult Sunday school classes. We seek to encourage Christians in living for God through fiction and true stories which apply biblical principles to everyday problems." Estab. 1928. Circ. 100,000. **Pays on acceptance.** Publishes ms an average of 18 months after acceptance. Byline given. Buys first rights or second serial (reprint) rights. Editorial lead time 12 months. Submit seasonal material 18 months in advance. Accepts queries by mail, e-mail, fax, phone. Accepts simultaneous submissions. Responds in 2 weeks to queries; 2 months to mss. Sample copy and writer's guidelines for #10 SASE or writer's guidelines *only* on website.

O→ Break in with "true stories that demonstrate how the principles in the Bible work in every day circumstances as well as crises."

Nonfiction: Inspirational, religious. No preachy articles or stories that refer to religious myths (e.g. Santa Claus, Easter bunny, etc.) **Buys 50-100 mss/year.** Send complete ms. Length: 400-1,500 words. **Pays 7-10¢/word.**

Reprints: Send tearsheet, photocopy or typed ms with rights for sale noted and information about when and where the article previously appeared. Pays 7¢/word.

Photos: Send photos with submission. Reviews 35mm transparencies and 3×4 prints or larger. Offers $35-60/photo. Identification of subjects required. Buys one-time rights.

Fiction: Religious, inspirational. No preachy fiction, fiction about Bible characters or stories that refer to religious myths (e.g. Santa Claus, Easter bunny, etc.). No science or Bible fiction. **Buys 50-100 mss/year.** Send complete ms. Length: 800-1,600 words. **Pays 7-10¢/word.**

Poetry: Free verse, haiku, light verse, traditional. **Buys 15-24 poems/year.** Submit maximum 3 poems. Length: 12-25 lines. **Pays $35-60.**

Fillers: Anecdotes, short humor. **Buys 12-36/year.** Length: 300-600 words. **Pays 7-10¢/word.**

Tips: "Don't moralize or be preachy. Provide human interest articles with Biblical life application. Stories should consist of action, not just thought-life; interaction, not just insight. Heroes and heroines should rise above failures, take risks for God, prove that scriptural principles meet their needs. Conflict and suspense should increase to a climax! Avoid pious conclusions. Characters should be interesting, believable and realistic. Avoid stereotypes. Characters should be active, not just pawns to move the plot along. They should confront conflict and change in believable ways. Describe the character's looks and reveal his personality through his actions to such an extent that the reader feels he has met that person. Readers should care about the character enough to finish the story. Feature racial, ethnic and regional characters in rural and urban settings."

[N] $ $ $ MH-18, Fitness, Sports, Girls, Gear, Life, Rodale Inc., 400 S. 10th St., Emmaus PA 18049. Fax: (610)967-7725. Website: www.mh-18.com. Editor: Jeff Csatari. Senior Editor: Stan Zukowski. **Contact:** Jenny Everett, editorial assistant. **80% freelance written.** Bimonthly magazine covering sports, fitness, girls, gear, life. "Men's health for teenage boys, ages 13-18." Estab. 2000. **Pays on acceptance.** Byline sometimes given. Offers 25% kill fee. Buys all rights. Editorial lead time 4 months. Submit seasonal material 5 months in advance. Accepts queries by mail with clips. Responds in 1 month to queries.

Nonfiction: General interest, how-to, humor, interview/profile, new product. No fiction. **Buys 150 mss/year.** Query with published clips. Length: 100-2,000 words. **Pays $1/word.** Pays expenses of writers on assignment.

Photos: State availability of photos with submission.

Columns/Departments: Stan Zukowski, senior editor/web editor. Playbook (fitness, sports, gear, girls), 100 words. **Buys 500 mss/year.** Query with published clips. **Pays 50¢-$1/word.**

Fillers: Anecdotes, facts, newsbreaks, short humor. **Buys 100/year.** Length: 10-300 words. **Pays 50¢-$1/word.**

$ $ THE NEW ERA, 50 E. North Temple, Salt Lake City UT 84150. (801)240-2951. Fax: (801)240-5997. E-mail: cur-editorial-newera@ldschurch.org. **Contact:** Larry A. Hiller, managing editor. **20% freelance written.** "We work with both established writers and newcomers." Monthly magazine for young people (ages 12-18) of the Church of Jesus Christ of Latter-day Saints (Mormon), their church leaders and teachers. Estab. 1971. Circ. 230,000. **Pays on acceptance.** Publishes ms an average of 1 year after acceptance. Byline given. Buys all rights. Rights reassigned upon written request. Submit seasonal material 1 year in advance. Accepts queries by mail, e-mail, fax. Responds in 2 months. Sample copy for $1.50 and 9×12 SAE with 2 first-class stamps. Guidelines for SASE.

Nonfiction: Material that shows how the Church of Jesus Christ of Latter-day Saints is relevant in the lives of young people today. Must capture the excitement of being a young Latter-day Saint. Special interest in the experiences of young Mormons in other countries. No general library research or formula pieces without the *New Era* slant and feel. Uses informational, how-to, personal experience, interview, profile, inspirational, humor. Query preferred. Length: 150-1,200 words. **Pays 3-12¢/word.** Pays expenses of writers on assignment.

Photos: Uses b&w photos and transparencies with mss. Payment depends on use, $10-125 per photo. Individual photos used for *Photo of the Month.*

Columns/Departments: Bulletin Board (news of young Mormons around the world); How I Know; Scripture Lifeline. **Pays 3-12¢/word.**

Fiction: Adventure, relationships, humorous. Must relate to young Mormon audience. **Pays minimum 3¢/word.**

Poetry: Traditional forms, blank verse, free verse, light verse, all other forms. Must relate to editorial viewpoint. **Pays 25¢/line minimum.**

Tips: "The writer must be able to write from a Mormon point of view. We're especially looking for stories about successful family relationships and personal growth. We anticipate using more staff-produced material. This means freelance quality will have to improve. Try breaking in with a department piece for 'How I Know' or 'Scripture Lifeline.' Well-written, personal experiences are always in demand."

$ $ $ REACT, The Magazine That Raises Voices, Parade Publications, 711 Third Ave., New York NY 10017. (212)450-0900. Fax: (212)450-0978. E-mail: srgarvey@react.com. Website: www.react.com. Editor: Lee Kravitz. **Contact:** Marga Christopher, managing editor. **90% freelance written.** "*react* is a weekly news, sports and entertainment magazine for teens." Estab. 1995. Circ. 3,300,000. **Pays on acceptance.** Publishes ms an average of 2 months after acceptance. Editorial lead time 2 months. Submit seasonal material 4 months in advance. Accepts queries by mail, fax. Sample copy for 10½ × 12 SAE and 80¢ postage. Writer's guidelines for #10 SASE.

Nonfiction: No articles written for adults from adult points of view. Query with published clips. **Pays $250-1,500.** Pays expenses of writers on assignment.

● Ranked as one of the best markets for freelance writers in *Writer's Yearbook magazine's "Top 100 Markets,"* January 2000.

Photos: All photos by assignment only; others purchased from stock houses. Model releases and identification of subjects required. Buys all rights.

Columns/Departments: Query with published clips.

■ The online magazine carries original content not found in the print edition. Contact: Ann Lien, online editor.

Tips: "Before you write, keep in mind: Young Americans in the first throes of teenhood want you to write with clarity and come to them free of any preconceived ideas of who and what they are. When writing for them: Walk their walk. See events through their eyes. Let their world be your world. Let their questions be your questions. Don't talk down. Do not preach. Be as professional and rigorous in reporting as you would be writing for adults. Be honest. They have a built-in 'phony' detector. Report long but write short. Write with style. To put readers at ease, be personal in your writing tone."

★ **$ $ $** SEVENTEEN, 850 Third Ave., New York NY 10022. (212)407-9700. Fax: (212)407-9899. Website: www.seventeen.com. Editor-in-Chief: Patrice G. Aderoft. **Contact:** Tamara Glenny, deputy editor; Melanie Mannarino, senior editor; Andrea Chambers, sex and body issues. **50% freelance written.** Works with a small number of new/unpublished writers each year. Monthly. *"Seventeen* is a young women's first fashion and beauty magazine. Tailored for young women in their teens and early twenties, *Seventeen* covers fashion, beauty, health, fitness, food, cars, college, entertainment, fiction, plus crucial personal and global issues." Circ. 2,400,000. Buys one-time rights. Pays 25% kill fee. **Pays on acceptance.** Publishes ms an average of 6 months after acceptance. Byline given. Accepts queries by mail, fax. Responds in up to 3 months.

○┐ Break in with The Who Knew section, which contains shorter items, or *Quiz.*

Nonfiction: Articles and features of general interest to young women who are concerned with intimate relationships and how to realize their potential in the world; strong emphasis on topicality and service. Send brief outline and query, including a typical lead paragraph, summing up basic idea of article with clips of previously published works. Length: 1,200-3,000 words. Articles are commissioned after outlines are submitted and approved. Pays the expenses of writers on assignment. **Pays $1/word, occasionally more.**

Photos: Georgia Paralemos, art director. Photos usually by assignment only.

Fiction: Melanie Mannarino, fiction editor. Thoughtful, well-written stories on subjects of interest to young women between the ages of 13 and 21. Avoid formula stories—"She's blonde and pretty; I'm not,"—no heavy moralizing or condescension of any sort. Length: 1,000-3,000 words. **Pays $500-1,500.** We also have an annual fiction contest.

● Ranked as one of the best markets for fiction writers in *Writer's Digest* magazine's "Fiction 50," June 2000.

■ The online magazine carries original content not found in the print edition. Contact: Katherine Raymond, online editor.

Tips: "Writers have to ask themselves whether or not they feel they can find the right tone for a *Seventeen* article—a tone which is empathetic yet never patronizing; lively yet not superficial. Not all writers feel comfortable with, understand or like teenagers. If you don't like them, *Seventeen* is the wrong market for you. An excellent way to break in to the magazine is by contributing ideas for quizzes or the Voice (personal essay) column."

$ $ SPIRIT, Lectionary-based Weekly for Catholic Teens, Good Ground Press, 1884 Randolph Ave., St. Paul MN 55105-1700. (651)690-7010. Fax: (651)690-7039. E-mail: jmcsj9@mail.idt.net. **Contact:** Joan Mitchell, CSJ, editor. Managing Editor: Therese Sherlock, CSJ. **50% freelance written.** Weekly newsletter for religious education of Catholic high schoolers. "We want realistic fiction and nonfiction that raises current ethical and religious questions and that deals with conflicts that teens face in multi-racial contexts. The fact we are a religious publication does *not* mean we want pious, moralistic fiction." Estab. 1981. Circ. 26,000. Pays on publication. Publishes ms an average of 3 months after acceptance. Byline given. Buys all rights. Editorial lead time 6 months. Submit seasonal material 6 months in advance. Accepts simultaneous submissions. Accepts queries by mail, e-mail, fax. Responds in 1 month to queries; 6 months to mss. Sample copy and writer's guidelines free.

Nonfiction: Interview/profile, personal experience, photo feature (homelessness, illiteracy), religious, Roman Catholic leaders, human interest features, social justice leaders, projects, humanitarians. "No Christian confessional, born-again pieces." Buys 4 mss/year. Query with published clips or send complete ms. Length: 1,000-1,200 words. **Pays $150-250 for assigned articles; $150 for unsolicited articles.**

Photos: State availability of photos with submission. Reviews 8 × 10 prints. Offers $40-80/photo. Identification of subjects required. Buys one-time rights.

Fiction: Conflict vignettes. "We want realistic pieces for and about teens—non-pedantic, non-pious. We need good Christmas stories that show spirit of the season, and stories about teen relationship conflicts (boy/girl, parent/teen)." **Buys 10 mss/year.** Query with published clips, or send complete ms. Length: 1,000-1,200 words. **Pays $150-200.**

Tips: "Writers must be able to write from and for teen point of view rather than adult or moralistic point of view. In nonfiction, interviewed teens must speak for themselves. Query to receive call for stories, spec sheet, sample issues."

$TODAY'S CHRISTIAN TEEN, Marketing Partners, Inc., P.O. Box 100, Morgantown PA 19543. (610)913-0796. Fax: (610)913-0797. E-mail: tcpubs@mkpt.com. Editor: Jerry Thacker. **Contact:** Elaine Williams, assistant editor. **75% freelance written.** Quarterly magazine covering teen issues from a Biblical perspective. "*Today's Christian Teen* is designed to deal with issues in the life of Christian teenagers from a conservative perspective." Estab. 1990. Circ. 100,000. Pays on publication. Publishes ms an average of 1 year after acceptance. Byline sometimes given. Buys simultaneous rights. Editorial lead time 1 year. Submit seasonal material 1 year in advance. Accepts simultaneous submissions. Accepts queries by mail, e-mail, fax. Responds in 1 month to queries; 3 months to mss. Sample copy for 9×12 SAE with 4 first-class stamps. Writer's guidelines for #10 SASE.

⊙┱ "Make your article practical, using principles from KJV Bible. We are not accepting articles for review before January 2001."

Nonfiction: Inspirational, personal experience, religious. **Buys 10 mss/year.** Send complete ms. Length: 800-1,200 words. **Pays $150.**

• Interested in seeing material against gambling.

Reprints: Accepts previously published submissions.

Photos: Offers no additional payment for photos accepted with ms.

$$$$TWIST, Bauer Publishing, 270 Sylvan Ave., Englewood Cliffs NJ 07632. Fax: (201)569-4458. E-mail: twistmail@aol.com. Editor: Lisa Lombardi. Managing Editor: Christine Summer. **Contact:** Jeannie Kim, articles editor or Kathleen Renda, senior editor. **20% freelance written.** "Monthly magazine targeting 14-19 year old girls, with an emphasis on using the words, viewpoints and faces of real teenagers. Estab. 1997. Circ. 700,000. **Pays on acceptance.** Publishes ms an average of 3 months after acceptance. Byline given. Offers 20% kill fee. Buys first North American serial rights. Editorial lead time 3 months. Submit seasonal material 4 months in advance. Accepts simultaneous submissions. Responds in 1 month to queries. Writer's guidelines for #10 SASE.

Nonfiction: Personal experience (real teens' experiences, preferably in first person), relationships, health, sex, quizzes. "No articles written from an adult point of view about teens—i.e., a mother's or teacher's personal account." **Buys 60 mss/year.** Query with published clips. Length: 100-1,800 words. **Pays minimum $50 for short item; up to $1/word for longer pieces.** Pays expenses of writers on assignment.

Photos: State availability of photos with submission. "We generally prefer to provide/shoot our own art." Negotiates payment individually. Model releases and identification of subjects required.

Columns/Departments: Pop Life (reviews, short celebrity/media items); Body Buzz (health news/tips), all 75-200 words. **Buys 15 mss/year.** Query with published clips. **Pays minimum $50 for short item; up to $1/word for longer pieces.**

Tips: "*Tone* must be conversational, neither condescending to teens nor trying to be too slangy. If possible, send clips that show an ability to write for the teen market. We are in search of real-life stories, and writers who can find teens with compelling real-life experiences (who are willing to use their full names and be photographed for the magazine). Please refer to a current issue to see examples of tone and content. No e-mail queries or submissions, please."

$$WHAT MAGAZINE, What! Publishers Inc., 108-93 Lombard Ave., Winnipeg, Manitoba R3B 3B1 Canada. (204)985-8160. Fax: (204)957-5638. E-mail: l.malkin@m2ci.mb.ca. **Contact:** Leslie Malkin, editor. **40% freelance written.** Magazine covering teen issues and pop culture published 5 times during the school year. "*What magazine* is distributed to high school students across Canada. We produce a mag that is empowering, interactive and entertaining. We respect the reader—today's teens are smart and creative (and critical)." Estab. 1987. Circ. 250,000. Pays 30 days after publication. Publishes ms an average of 3 months after acceptance. Byline given. Offers negotiable kill fee. Buys first North American serial rights. Editorial lead time 5 months. Submit seasonal material 5 months in advance. Accepts queries by mail, e-mail, fax. Responds in 2 months to queries; 1 month to mss. Sample copy for 9×12 SAE with Canadian postage. Writer's guidelines for #10 SAE with Canadian postage.

Nonfiction: General interest, interview/profile, issue-oriented features. No cliché teen material. **Buys 6-10 mss/year.** Query with published clips. Length: 700-1,900 words. **Pays $100-300 (Canadian).** Sometimes pays expenses of writers on assignment.

Photos: Send photos with submission. Reviews transparencies, 4×6 prints. Negotiates payment individually. Identification of subjects required.

Tips: "We're looking for more coverage of issues that affect Canadian teens in particular. Because *What magazine* is distributed through schools (with the consent of school officials), it's important that each issue find the delicate balance between very cool and very responsible. We target very motivated young women and men. Pitches should stray from cliché and stories should challenge readers with depth, insight and color. All stories must be meaningful to a Canadian readership."

$WITH, The Magazine for Radical Christian Youth, Faith and Life Press, 722 Main St., P.O. Box 347, Newton KS 67114-0347. (316)283-5100. Fax: (316)283-0454. E-mail: deliag@gcmc.org. Editor: Carol Duerksen. **60% freelance written.** Magazine for teenagers published 8 times/year. "We are the magazine for Mennonite, Brethren, and Mennonite Brethren youth. Our purpose is to disciple youth within congregations." Circ. 6,100. **Pays on acceptance.** Byline given. Buys one-time rights. Submit seasonal material 6 months in advance. Accepts simultaneous submissions. Accepts queries by mail. Responds in 1 month to queries; 2 months to mss. Sample copy for 9×12 SAE with 4 first-class stamps. Writer's guidelines and theme list for #10 SASE. Additional detailed guidelines for first person stories, how-to articles and/or fiction available for #10 SASE.

Nonfiction: Humor, personal experience, religious, how-to, youth. **Buys 15 mss/year.** Send complete ms. Length: 400-1,800 words. **Pays 5¢/word for simultaneous rights; 3¢/word for reprint rights for unsolicited articles.** Higher rates for first-person stories and how-to articles written on assignment. (Query on these.)

Reprints: Send typed ms with rights for sale noted, including information about when and where the material previously appeared. Pays 60% of amount paid for an original article. Sometimes pays the expenses of writers on assignment.

Photos: Send photos with submission. Reviews 8×10 b&w prints. Offers $10-50/photo. Identification of subjects required. Buys one-time rights.

Fiction: Humorous, religious, youth, parables. **Buys 15 mss/year.** Send complete ms. Length: 500-2,000 words. Payment same as nonfiction.

● Ranked as one of the best markets for fiction writers in *Writer's Digest* magazine's "Fiction 50," June 2000.

Poetry: Avant-garde, free verse, haiku, light verse, traditional. **Buys 0-2 poems. Pays $10-25.**

Tips: "We're looking for more wholesome humor, not necessarily religious—fiction, nonfiction, cartoons, light verse. Christmas and Easter material has a good chance with us because we receive so little of it."

$ $ $YM, Gruner & Jahr, 375 Lexington Ave, 8th Floor, New York NY 10017-5514. (212)499-2000. Editor: Diane Salvatore. **Contact:** Chandra Czape, senior editor. **75% freelance written.** Magazine covering teenage girls/dating. "We are a national magazine for young women ages 13-24. They're bright, enthusiastic and inquisitive. Our goal is to guide them—in effect, to be a 'best friend' and help them through the many exciting, yet often challenging, experiences of young adulthood." Estab. 1940s. Circ. 2,200,000. **Pays on acceptance.** Byline given. Offers 25% kill fee. Buys all rights. Editorial lead time 4 months. Submit seasonal material 5 months in advance. Accepts simultaneous submissions. Responds in 1 month. Writer's guidelines free.

Nonfiction: How-to, interview/profile, personal experience, first-person stories. "*YM* publishes three special issues a year. One is a self-discovery issue, the second is a prom issue, and the third is a love issue filled with articles on relationships." Query with published clips (mark "Query" on the envelope). Length: 2,000 words maximum. Pays expenses of writers on assignment.

Tips: "Our relationship articles are loaded with advice from psychologists and real teenagers. Areas most open to freelancers are: 2,000 word first-person stories covering a personal triumph over adversity—incorporating a topical social/political problem; 2,000 word relationship stories; 1,200 word relationship articles; 800 word local hangouts; and 800 word quizzes. All articles should be lively and informative, but not academic in tone, and any 'expert' opinions (psychologists, authors and teachers) should be included as a supplement to the feelings and experiences of young women. Do not call our offices."

N ⊠ $YOUNG & ALIVE, Christian Record Services, P.O. Box 6097, Lincoln NE 68506. Website: www.christianrecord.org. **Contact:** Gaylena Gibson, editor. **95% freelance written.** Large-print Christian material for sight-impaired people age 12-25 (also in braille), covering health, handicapped people, uplifting articles. "Write for an interdenominational Christian audience—we also like to portray handicapped individuals living normal lives or their positive impact on those around them." Estab. 1976. Circ. 25,000 large print; 3,000 braille. **Pays on acceptance.** Publishes ms an average of 3 years after acceptance. Byline given. Buys one-time rights. Submit seasonal material "anytime—if accepted, we will drop in the proper month." Accepts queries by mail. Accepts simultaneous submissions. Responds in 5 weeks to queries; 4 months to mss. Sample copy for 7×10 SAE with 5 first-class stamps. Writer's guidelines for #10 SASE or included with sample copy.

Nonfiction: Adventure (true), biography, camping, careers, essays, general interest, handicapped, health, historical/nostalgic, hobbies, holidays, humor, inspirational, nature, personal experience, sports, travel. "No 'hot' issues: gun control, abortion, etc." **Buys 40 mss/year.** Send complete ms. Length: 200-1,400 words. **Pays 4-5¢/word.** "We do provide complimentary copies in addition to payment."

Reprints: Accepts previously published submissions.

Photos: Send photos with submission. Reviews 3×5 to 10×12 prints. Negotiates payment individually. Model releases required. Buys one-time rights.

Poetry: Light verse. "Poetry should follow same guidelines as other material in content." Length: 12 words. **Pays $10-20.**

Fillers: Anecdotes, facts, short humor. Length: 300 words maximum. **Pays 4¢/word.**

Tips: "Make sure article has a strong ending that ties everything together. Pretend someone else wrote it—would it hold your interest? Draw your readers into the story by being specific rather than abstract or general."

⊠ $ $YOUNG SALVATIONIST, The Salvation Army, P.O. Box 269, Alexandria VA 22313-0269. (703)684-5500. Fax: (703)684-5539. E-mail: ys@usn.salvationarmy.org. Website: publications.salvationarmyusa.org. **Contact:** Tim Clark, managing editor. **80% freelance written.** Works with a small number of new/unpublished writers each year. Monthly magazine for high school teens. "Only material with Christian perspective with practical real-life application will be considered." Circ. 48,000. **Pays on acceptance.** Publishes ms an average of 6 months after acceptance. Byline

---

FOR INFORMATION on setting your freelance fees, see How Much Should I Charge?

given. Buys first North American serial, first, one-time or second serial (reprint) rights. Submit seasonal material 6 months in advance. Accepts queries by mail, e-mail. Responds in 2 months. Sample copy for 9×12 SAE with 3 first-class stamps or on website. Writer's guidelines and theme list for #10 SASE or on website.

O━ "Our greatest need is for nonfiction pieces based in real life rather than theory or theology. Practical living articles are especially needed. We receive many fiction submissions but few good nonfiction."

Nonfiction: Inspirational, how-to, humor, interview/profile, personal experience, photo feature, religious. "Articles should deal with issues of relevance to teens (high school students) today; avoid 'preachiness' or moralizing." **Buys 60 mss/year.** Send complete ms. Length: 1,000-1,500 words. **Pays 15¢/word for first rights.**

Reprints: Send tearsheet, photocopy of article or typed ms with rights for sale noted and information about when and where the article previously appeared. **Pays 10¢/word for reprints.**

Fiction: Only a small amount is used. Adventure, fantasy, humorous, religious, romance, science fiction—all from a Christian perspective. **Buys few mss/year. Length: 500-1,200 words. Pays 15¢/word.**

Tips: "Study magazine, familiarize yourself with the unique 'Salvationist' perspective of *Young Salvationist*; learn a little about the Salvation Army; media, sports, sex and dating are strongest appeal."

⊠ $ $ YOUTH UPDATE, St. Anthony Messenger Press, 1615 Republic St., Cincinnati OH 45210-1298. (513)241-5615. Fax: (513)241-0399. E-mail: CarolAnn@americancatholic.org. Website: www.AmericanCatholic.org. **Contact:** Carol Ann Morrow, editor. **90% freelance written.** Monthly 4-page newsletter of faith life for teenagers, "designed to attract, instruct, guide and challenge Catholics of high school age by applying the Gospel to modern problems/situations." Circ. 24,000. **Pays on acceptance.** Publishes ms an average of 6 months after acceptance. Byline given. Responds in 3 months. Sample copy and writer's guidelines for #10 SASE.

Nonfiction: Inspirational, practical self-help, spiritual. "Adults who pay for teen subs want more church-related and curriculum-related topics." **Buys 12 mss/year.** Query or send outline. Length: 2,200-2,300 words. **Pays $375-400.** Sometimes pays expenses of writers on assignment.

▣ The online magazine carries original content not found in the print edition. Contact: Carol Ann Morrow.

Tips: "Write for a 15-year-old with a C+ average."

TRAVEL, CAMPING & TRAILER

Travel magazines give travelers indepth information about destinations, detailing the best places to go, attractions in the area and sites to see—but they also keep them up to date about potential negative aspects of these destinations. Publications in this category tell tourists and campers the where-tos and how-tos of travel. This category is extremely competitive, demanding quality writing, background information and professional photography. Each publication has its own slant. Sample copies should be studied carefully before sending submissions.

$ AAA GOING PLACES, Magazine for Today's Traveler, AAA Auto Club South, 1515 N. Westshore Blvd., Tampa FL 33607. (813)289-5923. Fax: (813)289-6245. **Contact:** Phyllis Zeno, editor-in-chief. **50% freelance written.** Bimonthly magazine on auto news, driving trips, cruise travel, tours. Estab. 1982. Circ. 2,300,000. Pays on publication. Publishes ms an average of 6 months after acceptance. Byline given. Buys one-time rights. Submit seasonal material 9 months in advance. Accepts simultaneous submissions. Responds in 2 months. Writer's guidelines for SAE.

Nonfiction: Historical/nostalgic, how-to, humor, interview/profile, personal experience, photo feature, travel. Travel stories feature domestic and international destinations with practical information and where to stay, dine and shop, as well as personal anecdotes and historical background; they generally relate to tours currently offered by AAA Travel Agency. Special issues include Cruise Guide and Europe Issue. **Buys 15 mss/year.** Send complete ms. Length: 500-1,500 words. **Pays $50/printed page.**

Photos: State availability of photos with submission. Reviews 2×2 transparencies. Offers no additional payment for photos accepted with ms. Captions required.

Columns/Departments: AAAway We Go (local attractions in Florida, Georgia or Tennessee).

Tips: "We prefer lively, upbeat stories that appeal to a well-traveled, sophisticated audience, bearing in mind that AAA is a conservative company."

$ $ AAA MIDWEST TRAVELER, (formerly *The Midwest Motorist*), AAA Auto Club of Missouri, 12901 N. 40 Dr., St. Louis MO 63141. (314)523-7350. Fax: (314)523-6982. Editor: Michael J. Right. **Contact:** Deborah Klein, managing editor. **80% freelance written.** Bimonthly magazine. "We feature articles on regional and world travel, area history, auto safety, highway and transportation news." Estab. 1971. Circ. 435,000. **Pays on acceptance.** Byline given. Offers 50% kill fee. Not copyrighted. Buys first North American serial rights, second serial (reprint) rights or electronic rights. Accepts simultaneous submissions. Responds in 18 months with SASE enclosed. Submit seasonal material 18 months in advance. Sample copy or media kit for $12\frac{1}{2} \times 9\frac{1}{2}$ SAE with 3 first-class stamps. Writer's guidelines for #10 SASE.

Nonfiction: Travel. No humor. **Buys 40 mss/year.** Query. Length: 800-1,600 words. **Pays $250-350.**

insider report

Travel freelancing: Take your writing on the road

Imagine traveling to exotic destinations—for money—and you've imagined the freelancing life of Terry Miller Shannon. From her Oregon home, Shannon writes about travel and related themes for dozens of publications that include *Sunset Magazine*, *Reader's Digest* and the *Christian Science Monitor*. Freelancers who find travel writing appealing should consider that these articles do not always involve trips to the Champs Elysees or the Great Wall of China. A good number will take you no farther than a local winery tour, or a museum day trip. But despite the implied vacation-like atmosphere, Shannon insists, travel writing is not all fun and games.

Terry Miller Shannon

What special challenges set freelancing for the travel industry apart from other specialties?
Things seem to change rapidly. Ownership changes, resorts quit serving lunches to tour groups, telephone numbers change, businesses relocate or go out of business—all before the article is published. That can be a problem. You can also be limited by how far you want to travel. And should you accept freebies? Will gratis trips, tours, etc,, sway your article? I've chosen to say "No, thanks," to passes.

Are most travel assignments resort reviews?
No. My first big article for *Sunset* was about a day trip in one area of Oregon's southern coast. It concentrated on a tiny family-owned brandy distillery, but I talked about the drive through the mountains and along the coast—where to stop and what to look for. It was written in first person and had an almost personal essay feeling to it.

How would you try to break into travel writing, if you were a beginner?
I think new writers should be aware that travel writing can be applied to many different magazines: "Ten Fun Spots for Kids on the Oregon Coast" for family magazines; "Hiking the Oregon Coast" for fitness magazines; "Southern Oregon's Best Seafood Festivals" for cooking magazines. Travel has a broad reach.

What pay scale can a freelancer expect when writing about travel?
There is no easy answer to this one. *Sunset* pays $1 a word. But I think you can write for free or pennies—I see some websites not paying much—and the sky is the limit for upper-end magazines. Like all freelancing, it varies.

What common mistakes do freelancers make when writing their travel assignments?

I can speak from personal experience. I wrote the day trip/brandy distillery story as a straight travel piece: "Heading up 101 ten miles from Brookings, turn right onto Carpenterville . . . ." The editor wrote back, saying, "Inject *your* personality into this piece. It sounds like you're writing public relations copy."

What tips would you offer a writer just getting started in this area of freelance writing?

First, start at the top and work down. Query the big magazines first. Next, include clips of your best work, even if it isn't in the realm of travel when you query. Third, watch for unusual happenings, one-of-a-kind events, such as a tall-tale competition I recently wrote up for *Sunset*. Also, remember to think local: what's happening in your own area that no one who doesn't live there would know about? Submit that to local and national publications. Sell what you know best.

Have you had a favorite travel assignment?

Yes, I loved the Oregon day trip piece, just because it was longer. Rewriting it was a true joy because of the editor's plea to put more of "me" into it.

Have you experienced a nightmare assignment?

I had one piece turned in, but when the editor called me to check on a few last minute items, I called and found the tour was moving to another city. The contact information was no longer current—my entire article was worthless! That piece ended up being pulled.

For interviews with the pros on more freelance niche markets see Child Care, page 431; Food & Drink, page 470; Health & Fitness, page 494; Nature, page 594; and Personal Computers, page 604.
—Kelly Milner Halls

Reprints: Send typed ms with rights for sale noted and information about when and where the article previously appeared. **Pays $150-250.**

Photos: State availability of photos with submission. Reviews transparencies. Offers no additional payment for photos accepted with ms. Captions required. Buys one-time rights.

Tips: "Send queries between December and February, as we plan our calendar for the following year. Request a copy. Serious writers ask for media kit to help them target their piece. Travel destinations and tips are most open to freelancers; all departments and auto-related news handled by staff. We see too many 'Here's a recount of our family vacation' manuscripts. Go easy on first-person accounts."

$ $AAA TODAY, 1515 N. Westshore Blvd., Tampa FL 33607. (813)289-1391. Fax: (813)288-7935. E-mail: sklim@aaasouth.com. **Contact:** Sandy Klim, editor. **25% freelance written.** Bimonthly AAA Club magazine covering travel destinations. Estab. 1960. Circ. 4,000,000. Pays on publication. Publishes ms an average of 6 months after acceptance. Byline given. Editorial lead time 1 year. Submit seasonal material 1 year in advance. Accepts queries by mail. Sample copy and writer's guidelines free.

Nonfiction: Travel. **Buys 18 mss/year.** Query with published clips or send complete ms. Length: 500-1,000 words. **Pays $250.**

Photos: State availability or send photos with submission.

$ $ARUBA NIGHTS, Nights Publications, 1831 Rene Levesque Blvd. W., Montreal, Quebec H3H 1R4 Canada. (514)931-1987. Fax: (514)931-6273. E-mail: editor@nightspublications.com. Website: www.nightspublications .com. Managing Editor: Zelly Zuskin. **Contact:** Stephen Trotter, editor. **90% freelance written.** Annual magazine covering the Aruban vacation lifestyle experience with an upscale, upbeat touch. Estab. 1988. Circ. 225,000. **Pays on**

acceptance. Publishes ms an average of 9 months after acceptance. Byline given. Buys first North American serial and first Caribbean rights. Editorial lead time 1 month. Accepts queries by mail, e-mail, fax. Responds in 2 weeks to queries; 1 month to mss. Sample copy for $5 (make checks payable to "Nights Publications Inc."). Writer's guidelines free.

O— *Aruba Nights* is looking for more articles on nightlife experiences.

Nonfiction: General interest, historical/nostalgic, how-to features relative to Aruba vacationers, humor, inspirational, interview/profile, eco-tourism, opinion, personal experience, photo feature, travel, Aruban culture, art, activities, entertainment, topics relative to vacationers in Aruba. "No negative pieces or stale rewrites." **Buys 5-10 mss/year.** Submit ms and SAE with Canadian postage or IRC. Length: 250-750 words. **Pays $100-250.**

Photos: State availability with submission. Offers $50/photo. Captions, model releases, identification of subjects required. Buys one-time rights.

Tips: "Demonstrate your voice in your query letter. Be descriptive, employ vivid metaphors. Stories should immerse the reader in a sensory adventure. Focus on individual aspects of the Aruban lifestyle and vacation experience (e.g., art, gambling tips, windsurfing, a colorful local character, a personal experience, etc.), rather than generalized overviews. Provide an angle that will be entertaining to vacationers who are already there. E-mail submissions accepted."

$ $ ASU TRAVEL GUIDE, ASU Travel Guide, Inc., 1525 Francisco Blvd. E., San Rafael CA 94901. (415)459-0300. Fax: (415)459-0494. E-mail: chris@asuguide.com. Website: www.ASUguide.com. **Contact:** Christopher Gil, managing editor. **80% freelance written.** Quarterly guidebook covering international travel features and travel discounts for well-traveled airline employees. Estab. 1970. Circ. 50,000. Publishes ms an average of 4 months after acceptance. Byline given. Buys first North American serial rights, first and second rights to the same material, and second serial (reprint) rights. Also makes work-for-hire assignments. Submit seasonal material 6 months in advance. Accepts simultaneous submissions. Responds in 1 year. Sample copy available for 6×9 SAE with 5 first-class stamps. Writer's guidelines for #10 SASE.

Nonfiction: International travel articles "similar to those run in consumer magazines. Not interested in amateur efforts from inexperienced travelers or personal experience articles that don't give useful information to other travelers." **Buys 16 ms/year.** Destination pieces only; no "Tips On Luggage" articles. Unsolicited mss or queries without SASE will not be acknowledged. No telephone queries. Length: 1,800 words. **Pays $200.**

Reprints: Send tearsheet of article with information about when and where the article previously appeared. Pays 100% of amount paid for an original article.

Photos: "Interested in clear, high-contrast photos." Reviews 5×7 and 8×10 b&w or color prints. "Payment for photos is included in article price; photos from tourist offices are acceptable."

Tips: "Query with samples of travel writing and a list of places you've recently visited. We appreciate clean and simple style. Keep verbs in the active tense and involve the reader in what you write. Avoid 'cute' writing, coined words and stale clichés. The most frequent mistakes made by writers in completing an article for us are: 1) Lazy writing—using words to describe a place that could describe any destination such as 'there is so much to do in (fill in destination) that whole guidebooks have been written about it'; 2) Including fare and tour package information—our readers make arrangements through their own airline."

$ BIG WORLD, Big World Publishing, P.O. Box 8743-G, Lancaster PA 17604. E-mail: subs@bigworld.com. Website: www.bigworld.com. **Contact:** Jim Fortney, editor. **85% freelance written.** Quarterly magazine covering independent travel. "Big World is a magazine for people who like their travel on the cheap and down-to-earth. And not necessarily because they have to—but because they want to. It's for people who prefer to spend their travelling time responsibly discovering, exploring, and learning, in touch with local people and their traditions, and in harmony with the environment. We're looking for casual, first-person narratives that take into account the cultural/sociological/political side of travel." Estab. 1995. Circ. 5,000. Pays on publication. Publishes ms an average of 3 months after acceptance. Byline given. Buys one-time rights. Editorial lead time 2 months. Submit seasonal material 4 months in advance. Accepts queries by mail, e-mail. Responds in 1 month to queries; 2 months to mss. Sample copy for $4. Writer's guidelines for #10 SASE or on website.

Nonfiction: New product, opinion, personal experience, photo feature, travel, how-to, tips on transportation bargains and adventuring, overseas work study advice. **Buys 32-40 mss/year.** Length: 500-4,000 words. Query. Pay varies. Sometimes pays with subscriptions.

Reprints: Send photocopy of article. Pays 50% of amount paid for an original article.

Photos: Reviews prints. Negotiates payment individually. Captions required. Buys one-time rights.

Columns/Departments: Readers Writes (book reviews by subscribers), 400-500 words; Dispatches (slice-of-life pieces), 200-800 words; Hostel Intentions, My Town, Bike World, Better Adventuring. Pay varies.

Tips: "Take a look at the glossy, fluffy travel mags in the bookstore. They're *not* what we're about. We're *not* looking for romantic getaway pieces or lap-of-luxury bits. Our readers are decidedly downbeat and are looking for similarly-minded on-the-cheap and down-to-earth, first-person articles. Be breezy. Be yourself. First-time writers especially encouraged. You can submit your story to us on paper or 3.5 disc."

$ $ BONAIRE NIGHTS, Nights Publications, 1831 René Lévesque Blvd. W., Montreal, Quebec H3H 1R4 Canada. (514)931-1987. Fax: (514)931-6273. E-mail: editor@nightspublications.com. **Contact:** Stephen Trotter, editor. **90% freelance written.** Annual magazine covering Bonaire vacation experience. "Upbeat entertaining lifestyle articles: colorful profiles of locals, eco-tourism; lively features on culture, activities (particularly scuba and snorkeling), special events, historical attractions, how-to features. Audience is North American tourist." Estab. 1993. Circ. 60,000. **Pays on acceptance.** Publishes ms an average of 9 months after acceptance. Byline given. Buys first North American serial rights and first Caribbean rights. Editorial lead time 1 month. Accepts queries by mail, e-mail, fax. Responds in 2 weeks to queries; 1 month to mss. Sample copy for $5 (make check payable to Nights Publications, Inc). Writer's guidelines for #10 SAE.

Nonfiction: Lifestyle, general interest, historical/nostalgic, how-to, humor, inspirational, interview/profile, opinion, personal experience, photo feature, travel, local culture, art, activities, especially scuba diving, snorkeling, eco-tourism. **Buys 6-9 mss/ year.** Length: 250-750 words. Query or submit ms and SAE with Canadian postage or IRC. **Pays $100-250.**

Photos: State availability of photos with submission. Reviews transparencies. Offers $50/slide. Captions, model releases, identification of subjects required. Buys one-time or first rights.

Tips: "Demonstrate your voice in your query letter. Focus on the Bonaire lifestyle, what sets it apart from other islands. We want personal experience, not generalized overviews. Be positive and provide an angle that will appeal to vacationers who are already there. Our style is upbeat, friendly, fluid and descriptive."

CAMPERWAYS, CAMP-ORAMA, CAROLINA RV TRAVELER, SOUTHERN RV, TEXAS RV, Woodall Publications Corp., P.O. Box 8686, Ventura CA 93002. (800)323-9076. Fax: (805)667-4122. E-mail: mbaccanari@affinit ygroup.com. Website: www.woodalls.com. **Contact**: Melinda Baccanari. **75% freelance written**. Monthly tabloid covering RV lifestyle. "We're looking for articles of interest to RVers. Lifestyle articles, destinations, technical tips, interesting events and the like make up the bulk of our publications." Circ. 30,000. **Pays on acceptance.** Byline given. Offers 50% kill fee. Buys first North American serial rights. Submit seasonal material 4 months in advance. Accepts queries by mail, e-mail. Responds in 3 weeks to queries, 1 month on ms. Sample copy free. Writer's guidelines for #10 SASE.

Nonfiction: How-to, humor, inspirational, interview/profile, new product, opinion, personal experience, technical, travel. Special issues: Checkered Flag (relationship between RVs and racing), Northeast Summers (destinations of interest to RVers in the Northeast), Discover RVing (guide to new RVers about how-to get started). No "Camping From Hell" articles. **Buys 1,000 mss/year.** Query with published clips. Length: 500-1,500 words. **Pay varies.** Sometimes pays expenses of writers on assignment.

Photos: State availability of or send photos with submission. Prefers slides. Reviews negatives, 4×5 transparencies, 4×5 prints. Offers $5/photo. Captions, identification of subjects required. Buys one-time rights.

Columns/Departments: Gadgets, Gears & Gizmos (new product reviews), 600 words. RV Renovations (how-to building/renovations project), 1,000 words; Stopping Points (campground reviews), 1,000 words. **Buys 100 mss/year.** Query with published clips. Pay negotiable.

Tips: "Be an expert in RVing. Make your work readable to a wide variety of readers, from novices to full-timers."

$ $ CAMPING CANADA'S RV LIFESTYLES, 2585 Skymark Ave., Unit 306, Mississauga, Ontario L4W 4L5 Canada. (905)624-8436. Fax: (905)624-8486. Website: www.rvlifemag.com. **Contact:** Howard Elmer, editor. **50% freelance written.** Magazine published 7 times/year (monthly January-June and November). "*Camping Canada's RV Lifestyles* is geared to readers who enjoy travel/camping. Upbeat pieces only. Readers vary from owners of towable campers or motorhomes to young families and entry-level campers (RV only)." Estab. 1971. Circ. 45,000. Pays on publication. Byline given. Buys first North American serial rights. Editorial lead time 6 months. Responds in 2 months to queries; 3 months to mss. Sample copy free.

Nonfiction: How-to, personal experience, travel, practical, technical RV experience. No inexperienced, unresearched or too general pieces. **Buys 20-30 mss/year.** Query. Length: 1,200-2,000 words. **Pay varies.** Sometimes pays expenses of writers on assignment.

Reprints: Occasionally accepts previously published submissions, if so noted.

Photos: Send photos with submission. Offers no additional payment for photos accepted with ms. Buys one-time rights. No original photos.

Tips: "Pieces should be slanted toward RV living. All articles must have an RV slant."

$ CAMPING TODAY, Official Publication of the Family Campers & RVers, 126 Hermitage Rd., Butler PA 16001-8509. (724)283-7401. **Contact:** DeWayne Johnston and June Johnston, editors. **30% freelance written.** Prefers to work with published/established writers. Monthly official membership publication of the FCRV, "the largest nonprofit family camping and RV organization in the United States and Canada. Members are heavily oriented toward RV travel, both weekend and extended vacations. Concentration is on member activities in chapters. Group is also interested in conservation and wildlife. The majority of members are retired." Estab. 1983. Circ. 25,000. Pays on publication. Publishes ms an average of 6 months after acceptance. Byline given. Buys one-time rights. Submit seasonal material 3 months in advance. Accepts simultaneous submissions. Responds in 2 months. Sample copy and guidelines for 4 first-class stamps. Writer's guidelines only for #10 SASE.

Nonfiction: Travel (interesting places to visit by RV, camping), humor (camping or travel related, please, no "our first campout stories"), interview/profile (interesting campers), new products, technical (RVs related). **Buys 10-15 mss/year.** Query by mail only or send complete ms with photos. Length: 750-2,000 words. **Pays $50-150.**

Reprints: Send typed ms with rights for sale noted and information about when and where the article previously appeared. Pays 35-50% of amount paid for an original article.

Photos: Send photos with ms. Need b&w or sharp color prints inside (we can make prints from slides) and vertical transparencies for cover. Captions required.

Tips: "Freelance material on RV travel, RV maintenance/safety, and items of general camping interest throughout the United States and Canada will receive special attention. Good photos increase your chances."

⬛ **\$ \$CARIBBEAN TRAVEL AND LIFE**, 460 N. Orlando Ave., Suite 200, Winter Park FL 32789. (407)628-4802. Fax: (407)628-7061. E-mail: editor@caribbeantravelmag.com. Website: www.caribbeantravelmag.com. Editor: Bob Morris. Managing Editor: Sue Whitney. **Contact:** Bob Friel, executive editor. **80% freelance written.** Prefers to work with published/established writers. Magazine covering travel to the Caribbean, Bahamas and Bermuda for sophisticated, upscale audience, published 8 times/year. Estab. 1985. Circ. 135,000. **Pays on acceptance.** Publishes ms an average of 2 months after acceptance. Byline given. Offers 25% kill fee. Buys first North American serial rights. Submit seasonal material 4 months in advance. Accepts queries by mail, e-mail (from writers we know). Responds in 2 months. Sample copy for 9 × 12 SAE with 9 first-class stamps. Writer's guidelines for #10 SASE.

Nonfiction: General interest, how-to, interview/profile, culture, personal experience, travel. No guidebook rehashing, superficial destination pieces or critical exposes. **Buys 50-60 mss/year.** Query. Length: 1,150-3,000 words. **Pays \$200-2,000 for assigned articles.**

● Ranked as one of the best markets for freelance writers in *Writer's Yearbook* magazine's annual "Top 100 Markets," January 2000.

Photos: State availability of photos with submission. Reviews 35mm transparencies and prints. Offers \$100-1,000/photo. Captions and identification of subjects required. Buys one-time rights. Pays \$75-400.

○➥ Break in through columns and departments. "We are in the process of redesigning and editorially restructuring the magazine, so read recent issues and know where we have visited. Be prepared to contribute short items for departments before getting a feature assignment."

Columns/Departments: Gazette (news, humor); Travel Desk (hotels, cruises, airlines); Day Trip (island excursions); Caribbean Life (people, arts, culture, music); Caribbean Kitchen (restaurants, chefs, food). Query with published clips and SASE. Length: 500-1,250 words. **Pays \$250-500.** Buys one-time rights.

▣ The online version contains material not found in the print edition. Contact: Jay Kohn.

Tips: "We're always looking for new takes on the oft-visited places we must return to again and again—Virgin Islands, Bahamas, etc. Our only requirements are that the writing be superb, the subject be something unique and interesting, and the writer must know his/her subject. We are NOT interested in stories about the well-known, over-publicized and commonly visited places of the Caribbean. Our readers have likely already 'been there, done that.' We want to guide them to the new, the unusual and the interesting. Please do not call and do not send a complete manuscript unless requested by an editor. E-mail queries OK from writers we know. Newcomers should send writing samples by snail mail."

\$ \$CHICAGO TRIBUNE, Travel Section, 435 N. Michigan Ave., Chicago IL 60611. (312)222-3999. Fax: (312)222-0234. E-mail: rcurwen@tribune.com. **Travel Contact:** Randy Curwen, editor. Weekly Sunday newspaper leisure travel section averaging 22 pages aimed at vacation travelers. Circ. 1,100,000. Pays on publication. Publishes ms an average of 6 weeks after acceptance. Byline given. Buys one-time rights (which includes microfilm, online and CD/ROM usage). Accepts ms by mail, e-mail. Submit seasonal material 2 months in advance. Accepts simultaneous submissions. Responds in 1 month. Sample copy for large SAE with \$1.50 postage. Writer's guidelines for #10 SASE.

Nonfiction: Essays, general interest, historical/nostalgic, how-to (travel, pack), humor, opinion, personal experience, photo feature, travel. "There will be 16 special issues in the next 18 months." **Buys 150 mss/year.** Send complete ms. Length: 500-2,000 words. **Pays \$150-500.**

Photos: State availability of photos with submission. Reviews 35mm transparencies, 8 × 10 or 5 × 7 prints. Offers \$100/color photo; \$25/b&w; \$100 for cover. Captions required. Buys one-time rights.

▣ The online magazine carries original content not found in the print edition. Contact: Elise Bittner, online editor.

Tips: "Be professional. Use a word processor. Make the reader want to go to the area being written about. Only 1% of manuscripts make it."

⬚ ⬛ \$CLUBMEX, 660 Bay Blvd., Suite 214, Chula Vista CA 91910-5200. (619)585-3033. Fax: (619)420-8133. **Contact:** Chuck Stein, publisher/editor. **75% freelance written.** Bimonthly newsletter. "Our readers are travelers to Baja California and Mexico, and are interested in retirement, RV news, fishing and tours. They are knowledgeable but are always looking for new places to see." Estab. 1975. Circ. 5,000. Pays on publication. Publishes an average of 2 months after acceptance. Byline given. Buys first North American serial rights. Submit seasonal material at least 3 months in advance. Responds in 1 month. Writer's guidelines and free sample for 9 × 12 SAE with 2 first-class stamps.

● *Clubmex* accepts articles dealing with all of Mexico. They want upbeat, positive articles about Mexico which motivate readers to travel there by car.

Nonfiction: Historical, humor, interview, personal experience, travel. **Buys 36-50 mss/year.** Send complete ms. Length: 900-1,500 words. **Pays \$65 for the cover story, \$50 for other articles used, and \$25 for informative short pieces** in Letter to the Editor format.

Reprints: Send photocopy or tearsheet of article or typed ms with rights for sale noted and information about when and where the article previously appeared, what rights were sold and what releases are needed. Pays 100% of amount paid for an original article.

Photos: State availability of photos with submission. Reviews 3 × 5 prints. Offers no additional payment for photos accepted with ms. Captions required. Buys one-time rights.

⬛ \$ \$COAST TO COAST MAGAZINE, Affinity Group, Inc., 2575 Vista Del Mar Dr., Ventura CA 93001-3920. Fax: (805)667-4217. Website: www.coastresorts.com. **Contact:** Valerie Law, editorial director. **80% freelance written.** Club magazine published 8 times/year for members of Coast to Coast Resorts. "*Coast to Coast* focuses on travel, recreation and good times, with most stories targeted to recreational vehicle owners." Estab. 1982. Circ. 200,000.

Pays on acceptance. Publishes ms an average of 5 months after acceptance. Byline given. Offers 33% kill fee. Buys first North American serial and electronic rights. Submit seasonal material 5 months in advance. Responds in 1 month to queries; 2 months to mss. Sample copy for $4 and 9 × 12 SASE.

Nonfiction: Book excerpts, essays, general interest, historical/nostalgic, how-to, humor, inspirational, interview/profile, new product, opinion, personal experience, photo feature, technical, travel. No poetry, cartoons. **Buys 50 mss/year.** Query with published clips. Length: 500-2,500 words. **Pays $75-600.**

• Ranked as one of the best markets for freelance Writers in *Writer's Yearbook* magazine's annual "Top 100 Markets," January 2000.

Reprints: Send photocopy of article, information about when and where the article previously appeared. Pays approximately 50% of the amount paid for an original article.

Photos: Send photos with submission. Reviews transparencies. Offers $50-600/photo. Identification of subjects required. Buys one-time rights.

Tips: "Send published clips with queries, or story ideas will not be considered."

$ $ $ $ CONDÉ NAST TRAVELER, The Condé Nast Publications, 4 Times Square, New York NY 10036. (212)286-2101. Fax: (212)286-2190. Website: www.condenet.com. Editor: Thomas J. Wallace. **Contact:** Dee Aldrich, managing editor. **75% freelance written.** Monthly. "Our motto, Truth in Travel, sums up our editorial philosophy: to present travel destinations, news and features in a candid, journalistic style. Our writers do not accept complimentary tickets, hotel rooms, gifts, or the like. While our departments present service information in a tipsheet or newsletter manner, our destination stories are literary in tone. Our readers are affluent, well-educated, and sophisticated about travel." Estab. 1987. Circ. 850,000. "Please keep in mind that we very rarely assign stories based on unsolicited queries because (1) our inventory of unused stories (features and departments) is very large, and (2) most story ideas are generated inhouse by the editors, as it is very difficult for outsiders to anticipate the needs of our inventory. To submit story ideas, send a brief (one paragraph) description of the idea(s) to the appropriate editor (by mail or fax). Please do not send clips, résumés, photographs, itineraries, or abridged or full-length manuscripts. Due to our editorial policy, we *do not* purchase completed manuscripts. Telephone calls are not accepted."

Tips: *Condé Nast Traveler* tells us that they are no longer accepting unsolicited submissions. Research this market carefully before submitting your best work.

$ $ CURAÇAO NIGHTS, Nights Publications, 1831 Rene Levesque Blvd. West, Montreal, Quebec H3H 1R4 Canada. (514)931-1987. Fax: (514)931-6273. E-mail: editor@nightspublications.com. **Contact:** Stephen Trotter, editor. Managing Editor: Zelly Zuskin. **90% freelance written.** Annual magazine covering the Curaçao vacation experience. "We are seeking upbeat, entertaining lifestyle articles; colorful profiles of locals; lively features on culture, activities, night life, eco-tourism, special events, gambling; how-to features; humor. Our audience is the North American vacationer." Estab. 1989. Circ. 155,000. **Pays on acceptance.** Publishes ms 9 months after acceptance. Byline given. Buys first North American serial and first Caribbean rights. Editorial lead time 1 month. Accepts queries by mail, e-mail, fax. Responds in 2 weeks to queries; 1 month to mss. Sample copy for $5 (check payable to Nights Publications Inc.). Guidelines free.

Nonfiction: General interest, historical/nostalgic, how-to help a vacationer get the most from their vacation, eco-tourism, humor, inspirational, interview/profile, lifestyle, opinion, personal experience, photo feature, travel, local culture, art, activities, night life, topics relative to vacationers in Curaçao. "No negative pieces, generic copy or stale rewrites." **Buys 5-10 mss/year.** Query with published clips and SASE that includes Canadian postage or IRC. Length: 250-750 words. **Pays $100-250.**

Photos: State availability of photos with submission. Reviews transparencies. Offers $50/photo. Captions, model releases, identification of subjects required. Buys one-time rights.

Tips: "Demonstrate your voice in your query letter. Focus on individual aspects of the island lifestyle and vacation experience (e.g., art, gambling tips, windsurfing, a colorful local character, a personal experience, etc.), rather than generalized overviews. Provide an angle that will be entertaining to vacationers who are already on island. Our style is upbeat, friendly, fluid and descriptive."

$ THE EDUCATED TRAVELER, The Educated Traveler, P.O. Box 220822, Chantilly VA 20153. (703)471-1063. Fax: (703)471-4807. E-mail: edtrav@aol.com. Website: www.educated-traveler.com. Editor: Ann Waigand. **Contact:** Joanne Cosker, managing editor. **10% freelance written.** Bimonthly newsletter covering special interest travel, with "specific, unique, extreme travel experiences and/or destinations." Estab. 1989. Circ. 2,000. Pays on publication. No byline. Buys first rights. Editorial lead time 4 months. Accepts queries by mail, e-mail, fax. Sample copy for $8 or on website. Writer's guidelines free or on website.

Nonfiction: Travel. Special interest travel only. **Buys 3 mss/year.** Query with published clips or send complete ms. Length: 250-800 words. Longer articles (learning vacations, cover feature—travel program profile, an ET Find), 800 words, including sidebar with contact information. For shorter articles (theme tours, inside knowledge), 250-300 words. **Pays $50-150.**

Fillers: Length: 50 words. **Pays $15.**

Tips: "An ET Find is something relatively obscure that may not be adequately publicized but is a delightful, upscale, in-depth travel experience. Travel Program Profiles require a chart as sidebar detailing different types of programs/tours available (contact information, tour size, price, typical destinations and dates, leadership, amenities, etc.) Theme Tours focuses on one particular type of tour (in one specific destination or are of the world usually). A few paragraphs describe the type of tour or why that type of tour is particularly suited for that destination. The main purpose of the column however, is to list operators (with addresses and phone numbers) that serve that market, so that readers can request, and compare, itineraries. Inside Knowledge asks one specific question (of interest to readers) of an insider in the travel industry (for example, asking Lars Linblad, the travel pioneer, what is the next destination he expects to open up to U.S. travelers."

N **$ $ $ENDLESS VACATION**, Endless Vacation, P.O. 80260, Indianapolis IN 46280-0260. (317)871-9504. Fax: (317)871-9507. **Contact:** Jackson Mahaney, managing editor. Prefers to work with published/established writers. Bimonthly magazine. "*Endless Vacation* is the vacation-idea magazine edited for people who love to travel. Each issue offers articles for America's dedicated and frequent leisure travelers—time-share owners. Articles and features explore the world through a variety of vacation opportunities and options for travelers who average 4 weeks of leisure travel each year." Estab. 1974. Circ. 1,024,287. **Pays on acceptance.** Publishes ms an average of 6 months after acceptance. Byline given. Buys first North American serial rights. Accepts simultaneous submissions. Responds in 2 months. Sample copy for $5 and 9×12 SAE with 3 first-class stamps. Writer's guidelines for #10 SASE.
Nonfiction: Contact: Managing Editor. **Buys 24 mss/year** (approximately). Most are from established writers already published in *Endless Vacation. Accepts very few unsolicited pieces.* Query with published clips. Length: 1,000-2,000 words. **Pays $500-1,000 for assigned articles; $250-800 for unsolicited articles.** Sometimes pays the expenses of writers on assignment.
Photos: Reviews 4×5 transparencies and 35mm slides. Offers $100-500/photo. Model releases and identification of subjects required. Buys one-time rights.
Columns/Departments: Complete Traveler (on travel news and service-related information); Weekender (on domestic weekend vacation travel). Query with published clips. Length: 800-1,000 words. **Pays $150-600.** Sometimes pays the expenses of writers on assignment. Also news items for Facts, Fads and Fun Stuff column on travel news, products or problems. Length: 100-200 words. **Pays $100/item.**
Tips: "We will continue to focus on travel trends and timeshare resort destinations. Articles must be packed with pertinent facts and applicable how-tos. Information—addresses, phone numbers, dates of events, costs—must be current and accurate. We like to see a variety of stylistic approaches, but in all cases the lead must be strong. A writer should realize that we require first-hand knowledge of the subject and plenty of practical information. For further understanding of *Endless Vacation*'s direction, the writer should study the magazine and guidelines for writers."

$ $FAMILY MOTOR COACHING, Official Publication of the Family Motor Coach Association, 8291 Clough Pike, Cincinnati OH 45244-2796. (513)474-3622. Fax: (513)388-5286. E-mail: magazine@fmca.com. Website: www.fmca.com. Publishing Director: Pamela Wisby Kay. **Contact:** Robbin Gould, editor. **80% freelance written.** "We prefer that writers be experienced RVers." Monthly magazine emphasizing travel by motorhome, motorhome mechanics, maintenance and other technical information. "*Family Motor Coaching* magazine is edited for the members and prospective members of the Family Motor Coach Association who own or are about to purchase recreational vehicles of the motor coach style and use them exclusively for pleasure. Featured are articles on travel and recreation, association news, meetings, activities, and conventions plus articles on new products. Approximately ⅓ of editorial content is devoted to travel and entertainment, ⅓ to association news, and ⅓ to new products and industry news." Estab. 1963. Circ. 130,000. **Pays on acceptance.** Publishes ms an average of 8 months after acceptance. Buys first North American serial rights. Byline given. Submit seasonal material 4 months in advance. Responds in 4 months. Sample copy for $3.99. Writer's guidelines for #10 SASE.
Nonfiction: Motorhome travel (various areas of country accessible by motor coach), how-to (do-it-yourself motor home projects and modifications), bus conversions, humor, interview/profile, new product, technical, nostalgia. **Buys 8-10 mss/issue.** Query with published clips. Length: 1,000-2,000 words. **Pays $100-500.**
Photos: State availability of photos with query. Offers no additional payment for b&w contact sheets, 35mm or 2¼×2¼ color transparencies. Captions, photo credits, model releases required. Prefers first North American serial rights but will consider one-time rights on photos only.
Tips: "The greatest number of contributions we receive are travel; therefore, that area is the most competitive. However, it also represents the easiest way to break in to our publication. Articles should be written for those traveling by self-contained motor home. The destinations must be accessible to motor home travelers and any peculiar road conditions should be mentioned."

$ $FRONTIER MAGAZINE, Adventure Media, 650 S. Orcas St., Suite 103, Seattle WA 98108. (206)762-1922. Fax: (206)762-1886. E-mail: lauras@adventuremedia.com. **Contact:** Laura Slavik, managing editor. **60% freelance written.** In-flight magazine published bimonthly covering travel, with special emphasis on the Rocky Mountain states. "*Frontier Magazine* is a sophisticated yet fun-to-read magazine that celebrates the Rocky Mountain lifestyle. It celebrates those attitudes, traditions and issues that define the modern west." Estab. 1998. Circ. 250,000. Pays on publication. Publishes ms an average of 4 months after acceptance. Byline given. Offers 25% kill fee. Buys first North American serial rights. Editorial lead time 4 months. Submit seasonal material 4 months in advance. Accepts queries by mail, e-mail. Responds in 2 months. Sample copy for $2 (shipping and handling). Writer's guidelines for #10 SASE.
Nonfiction: Essays, general interest, historical/nostalgic, interview/profile, photo feature, travel, children's stories (8-12 years old). Special issues: Golf guide (June); and Ski guide (November). "We do not accept fiction, religious or how-to articles." **Buys 15 mss/year.** Query with published clips. Length: 350-1,500 words. **Pays 30-35¢/word for assigned articles; $75-600 for unsolicited articles.** Occasionally pays in cash and airline tickets.

written. Bimonthly newspaper covering travel, automotive, safety (traffic) and insurance. "Consumer-oriented membership publication providing information on complex or expensive subjects—car buying, vacations, traffic safety problems, etc." Estab. 1928. Circ. 650,000. Pays on publication. Publishes ms an average of 2 months after acceptance. Buys second serial (reprint) rights, simultaneous rights or makes work-for-hire assignments. Editorial lead time 6 weeks. Submit seasonal material 6 weeks in advance. Accepts queries by mail, fax. Responds in 2 weeks to queries; 2 months to mss. Sample copy for SAE with 4 first-class stamps. Writer's guidelines for #10 SASE.

Nonfiction: How-to (fix auto, travel safety, etc.), travel, automotive insurance, traffic safety. **Buys 12-14 mss/year.** Query with published clips. Length: 600-900 words. **Pays 15¢/published word.**

     Go Magazine's condensed online version contains some of the same material as the print magazine. Contact: Tom Crosby, editor.

Photos: Send photos with submission. Offers no additional payment for photos accepted with ms. Buys one-time rights.

$ HEALING RETREATS & SPAS, 24 E. Cota St., Suite 101, Santa Barbara CA 93101. (805)962-7107. Fax: (805)962-1337. E-mail: editorial@healingretreats.com. Website: www.healingretreats.com. Editor: Anthony Carroccio. **Contact:** Eden Marriott Kennedy, managing editor. **90% freelance written.** Bimonthly magazine covering retreats, spas, health and lifestyle issues. "We try to present healing and nurturing *alternatives* for the global community, and provide a bridge between travel, health, and New Age magazine material." Estab. 1996. Circ. 45,000. Pays on publication. Publishes ms within 1 year after acceptance. Byline given. Buys one-time rights. Editorial lead time 6 months. Submit seasonal material 6 months in advance. Accepts queries by mail, e-mail, fax. Responds in 6 months to queries; 6 months to mss. Sample copy for $6.95. Writer's guidelines for #10 SASE.

Nonfiction: Book excerpts, general interest, how-to (at-home therapies), interview/profile, new product, photo feature, travel (spas and retreats only), health alternatives. **Buys 50 mss/year.** Query with published clips. Length: 700-3,000 words. **Pays $25-75.** Pays writers with contributor copies or other premiums if they want 20 or more copies for self-promotion.

Photos: Send photos with submission. Reviews transparencies. Offers no additional payment for photos accepted with ms. Captions required. Buys one-time rights.

Columns/Departments: Buys 40 mss/year. Send complete ms. **Pays $25-50.**

Tips: "Writers can break in with well-written, first-hand knowledge of an alternative health issue or therapy. Even our travel pieces require this type of knowledge. Once a writer proves capable, other assignments can follow. We're particularly looking for stories on religious retreats—ashrams, monasteries, zen centers. Please, no more 'I was stressed out from my life, I went to a spa, now I feel great, the end.'"

N $ $ HIGHROADS MAGAZINE, AAA Arizona, 3144 N. 7th Ave., Phoenix AZ 85013. (602)274-1116, ext. 2239. Fax: (602)277-1194. E-mail: rantioco@arizona.aaa.com. **Contact:** Rebecca Antiocco, interim editor. **25% freelance written.** Bimonthly magazine covering travel. "*Highroads* is sent to AAA members in Arizona, and provides information about local, national and international travel destinations. It also provides membership-related information." Estab. 1931. Circ. 325,000. Pays on publication. Publishes ms an average of 3 months after acceptance. Byline given. Buys one-time rights or makes work-for-hire assignments. Editorial lead time 3 months. Submit seasonal material 3 months in advance. Accepts queries by mail, e-mail, fax. Accepts simultaneous submissions. Sample copy and writer's guidelines free.

Nonfiction: Interview/profile (local), personal experience (travel related), photo feature (travel related), travel. **Buys 15 mss/year.** Query with published clips. Length: 1,000-1,500 words. **Pays 25-40¢/word for assigned articles; $25-35¢/word for unsolicited articles.**

Reprints: Accepts previously published submissions.

Photos: State availability of photos with submission. Reviews transparencies. Offers $50-500/photo. Identification of subjects required. Buys one-time rights.

Columns/Departments: En Route Arizona (Arizona destinations); Calendar (Arizona), both 500 words. **Buys 5-10 mss/year.** Query with or without published clips. **Pays 25-35¢/word.**

Tips: "We encourage writers to submit concise queries, not more than one page, outlining one story idea. We prefer stories that have a well-defined, third-person voice. Articles should convey the magic and wonder of a destination. Facts must be fully researched and accurate."

$ $ HIGHWAYS, The Official Publication of the Good Sam Club, TL Enterprises Inc., 2575 Vista Del Mar, Ventura CA 93001. (805)667-4100. Fax: (805)667-4454. E-mail: goodsam@goodsamclub.com. Website: www.goodsamclub.com/highways. **Contact:** Ronald H. Epstein, editorial director. **40% freelance written.** Monthly magazine (November/December issues combined) covering recreational vehicle lifestyle. "All of our readers—since we're a membership publication—own or have a motorhome, trailer, camper or van conversion. Thus, our stories include road-travel conditions and terms and information about campgrounds and locations. Estab. 1966. Circ. 950,000. **Pays on acceptance.** Publishes ms an average of 6 months after acceptance. Byline given. Offers 50% kill fee. Buys first North American serial and electronic rights. Editorial lead time 15 weeks. Submit seasonal material 5 months in advance. Accepts queries by mail, e-mail, fax. Responds in 3 weeks to queries; 2 months to mss. Sample copy and writer's guidelines free or on website.

Nonfiction: How-to (repair/replace something on an RV); humor; technical; travel; (all RV related). **Buys 15-25 mss/year.** Query. Length: 1,500-2,500 words.

Photos: Send photos with submission. Reviews contact sheets, negatives, transparencies, prints. No additional payment for photos accepted with ms. Captions, model releases, identification of subjects required. Buys one-time rights.

Columns/Departments: Beginners (people buying an RV for the first time), 1,200 words; View Points (issue-related, 750 words. Query. **Pays $200-250.**

Tips: "Understand RVs and RVing. It's a unique lifestyle and different than typical traveling. Aside from that, we welcome good writers!"

N **$ $** **INTERLINE ADVENTURES**, Grand Adventures Tour and Travel Publishing Corporation, 211 E. 7th St., Suite 1100, Austin TX 78701. (512)391-2050. Fax: (512)391-2092. E-mail: ckosta@perx.com. Website: www.perx.com. Editor: Mr. In Churl Yo. **Contact:** Christina Kosta, senior editor. **75% freelance written.** Bimonthly magazine covering airline employee travel. "This bimonthly publication features destinations worldwide. In-depth features explore a destination's sights, cost, shopping, cuisine and nightlife for well-traveled airline employees." Circ. 100,000. Pays on publication. Publishes ms an average of 1 month after acceptance. Byline given. Buys one-time, second serial (reprint) rights or makes work-for-hire assignments. Editorial lead time 4 months. Accepts queries by mail, e-mail, fax. Accepts simultaneous submissions. Responds in 1 month. Sample copy and writer's guidelines free.

Nonfiction: Interview/profile, new product, travel. Does not want to see fiction. **Buys 60 mss/year.** Query. Length: 800-2,000 words. **Pays $350-600 for assigned articles; $150-450 for unsolicited articles.** Sometimes pays expenses of writers on assignment.

Reprints: Accepts previously published submissions.

Photos: State availability of photos with submission. Offers $50-250/photo. Identification of subjects required. Buys one-time rights.

Columns/Departments: Weekender (domestic weekend destinations); Cuisine (different types/recipes); Great Outdoors (sports or outdoors); all 900 words. Query.

Tips: "Stories must appeal to active and retired airline employees predominantly from the U.S., but from other parts of the world as well. We like solidly researched, fun and informative feature articles on all types of destinations and cruise vacations."

$ **THE INTERNATIONAL RAILWAY TRAVELER**, Hardy Publishing Co., Inc., Editorial offices: P.O. Box 3747, San Diego CA 92163. (619)260-1332. Fax: (619)296-4220. E-mail: irt.trs@worldnet.att.net. Website: www.irtsociety.com. **Contact:** Gena Holle, editor. **100% freelance written.** Monthly newsletter covering rail travel. Estab. 1983. Circ. 3,500. Pays within 3 months of publication date. Byline given. Offers 25% kill fee. Buys first North American serial, one-time and all electronic rights. Editorial lead time 4 months. Submit seasonal material 6 months in advance. Query for electronic submissions. Responds in 1 month to queries; 2 months to mss. Sample copy for $6. Writer's guidelines for #10 SASE.

Nonfiction: Book reviews, general interest, how-to, interview/profile, new product, opinion, personal experience, travel. **Buys 24-30 mss/year.** Query with published clips or send complete ms. Include SASE for return of ms. Length: 800-1,200 words. **Pays 3¢/word.**

Photos: Send photos with submission. Include SASE for return of photos. Reviews contact sheets, negatives, transparencies, prints (8×10 preferred; will accept 5×7). Offers $10 b&w; $20 cover photo. Costs of converting slides and negatives to prints are deducted from payment. Captions and identification of subjects required. Buys one-time, first North American serial rights and all electronic rights.

Tips: "We want factual articles concerning world rail travel which would not appear in the mass-market travel magazines. IRT readers and editors love stories and photos on off-beat train trips as well as more conventional train trips covered in unconventional ways. With IRT, the focus is on the train travel experience, not a blow-by-blow description of the view from the train window. Be sure to include details (prices, passes, schedule info, etc.) for readers who might want to take the trip."

$ $ $ $ **ISLANDS, An International Magazine**, Islands Media Corp., P.O. Box 4728, Santa Barbara CA 93140-4728. (805)745-7100. Fax: (805)745-7102. E-mail: editorial@islands.com. Website: www.islandsmag.com. **Contact:** Joan Tapper, editor. **95% freelance written.** Works with established writers. Published 8 times/year magazine covering "accessible and once-in-a-lifetime islands from many different perspectives: travel, culture, lifestyle. We ask our authors to give us the essence of the island and do it with literary flair." Estab. 1981. Circ. 200,000. **Pays on acceptance.** Publishes ms an average of 8 months after acceptance. Byline given. Offers 25% kill fee. Buys all rights. Query by mail, e-mail, fax. Responds in 2 months to queries; 6 weeks on ms. Sample copy for $6. Writer's guidelines for #10 SASE or on website.

Nonfiction: General interest, personal experience, photo feature, any island-related material. No service stories. "Each issue contains 5-6 feature articles and 6-7 departments. Any authors who wish to be commissioned should send a detailed proposal for an article, an estimate of costs (if applicable) and samples of previously published work." **Buys 25 feature mss/year.** "The majority of our feature manuscripts are commissioned." Query with published clips or send complete ms. Feature length: 2,000-4,000 words. **Pays $1,000-4,000.** Pays expenses of writers on assignment.

● Ranked as one of the best markets for freelance writers in *Writer's Yearbook* magazine's annual "Top 100 Markets," January 2000.

Photos: State availability of or send photos with query or ms. Pays $75-300 for 35mm transparencies. "Fine color photography is a special attraction of *Islands*, and we look for superb composition, technical quality and editorial applicability." Label slides with name and address, include captions, and submit in protective plastic sleeves. Identification of subjects required. Buys one-time rights.

Columns/Departments: Arts, Profiles, Nature, Sports, Lifestyle, Encounters, Island Hopping featurettes—all island related, 750-1,500 words; Brief Logbook (highly-focused item on some specific aspect of islands), 500 words. **Buys 50 mss/year.** Query with published clips. **Pays $100-700.**

Tips: "A freelancer can best break in to our publication with short (500-1,000 word) departments or Logbooks that are highly focused on some aspect of island life, history, people, etc. Stay away from general, sweeping articles. We are always looking for topics for our Islanders and Logbook pieces. We will be using big name writers for major features; will continue to use newcomers and regulars for columns and departments."

N $ ▣ KAFENIO, Where Europe is only a mouseclick away, Meier & Jacobson, Box 142, Karpathos, Greece 85700. Phone: (+30)245 31716. Fax: (+30)245 31716. E-mail: editor@kafeniocom.com. Website: www.kafeni ocom.com. Publisher: Alf B. Meier. **Contact:** Roberta Beach Jacobson, editor. **60-65% freelance written.** Monthly magazine covering European life and culture. "*Kafenio*, focusing on European life and culture, has adult readers in North America, Europe and Australia." Estab. 2000. Circ. 25,300. **Pays on acceptance.** Publishes ms an average of 2 months after acceptance. Byline given. Buys electronic rights (one-time 1 month—we do not post archives. Editorial lead time 2 months. Submit seasonal material 2 months in advance. Responds in 3 days. Sample copy and writer's guidelines free or online at website.

Nonfiction: Contact: essay@kafeniocom.com. Essays, humor, opinion, personal experience, travel (all first person only). Nonfiction for speakers table department only. Send complete ms. Length: open. **Pays $100.**

Reprints: Accepts previously published submissions.

Tips: "Know something about Europe. Have a little fun with your writing. If you don't enjoy it, others won't either. Remember, our readers either live in or travel to Europe."

$ $ LEISURE WORLD, Formula Publications, 447 Speers Rd., Suite 4, Oakville, Ontario L6K 357 Canada. (905)842-6591. Fax: (905)842-6843. E-mail: formmags@cgocable.net. **Contact:** Diane Tierney, editor. **20% freelance written.** Bimonthly magazine distributed to members of the Canadian Automobile Association in southwestern and midwestern Ontario, the Niagara Peninsula and the maritime provinces. Editorial content is focused on travel, entertainment and leisure time pursuits of interest to CAA members." Estab. 1988. Circ. 345,000. Pays on publication. Publishes ms an average of 2 months after acceptance. Buys first rights only. Submit seasonal material 4 months in advance. Accepts queries by e-mail. Responds in 2 months. Sample copy for $2. Writer's guidelines for SASE or on website.

Nonfiction: Lifestyle, humor, travel. **Buys 20 mss/year.** Send complete ms. Length: 800-1,200 words. **Pays $50-200.**

Photos: Reviews slides only. Offers $60/photo. Captions, model releases required. Buys one-time rights.

Tips: "We are most interested in travel destination articles that offer a personal, subjective and positive point of view on international (including U.S.) destinations. Good quality color slides are a must."

$ $ MICHIGAN LIVING, AAA Michigan, 2865 Waterloo, Troy MI 48084. (248)816-9265. Fax: (248)816-2251. E-mail: michliving@aol.com. **Contact:** Ron Garbinski, editor. **50% freelance written.** Monthly magazine. "*Michigan Living* is edited for the residents of Michigan and contains information about travel and lifestyle activities in Michigan, the U.S. and around the world. Articles also cover automotive developments, highway safety. Regular features include a car care column, a calendar of coming events, restaurant and overnight accomodations reviews and news of special interest to Auto Club members." Estab. 1922. Circ. 1,099,000. Pays on publication. Publishes ms an average of 6 months after acceptance. Buys first North American serial rights. Offers 20% kill fee. Byline given. Submit seasonal material 9 months in advance. Accepts queries by mail, e-mail. Responds in 6 weeks. Free sample copy and writer's guidelines.

   ● For writers and photographers to reecive a monthly e-mail message sent by *Michigan Living*'s editor, please send your e-mail address to michliving@aol.com.

Nonfiction: Travel articles on US and Canadian topics. **Buys few unsolicited mss/year.** Query. Length: 200-1,000 words. **Pays $75-600.**

Photos: Photos purchased with accompanying ms. Captions required. Pays $450 for cover photos; $50-400 for color transparencies.

Tips: "In addition to descriptions of things to see and do, articles should contain accurate, current information on costs the traveler would encounter on his trip. Items such as lodging, meal and entertainment expenses should be included, not in the form of a balance sheet but as an integral part of the piece. We want the sounds, sights, tastes, smells of a place or experience so one will feel he has been there and knows if he wants to go back. Prefers most travel-related queries via e-mail rather than mail."

$ $ MOTORHOME, TL Enterprises, 2575 Vista Del Mar Dr., Ventura CA 93001. (805)667-4100. Fax: (805)667-4484. Website: www.motorhomemagazine.com. Editorial Director: Barbara Leonard. **Contact:** Sherry McBride, senior managing editor. **60% freelance written.** Monthly. "*MotorHome* is a magazine for owners and prospective buyers of self-propelled recreational vehicles who are active outdoorsmen and wide-ranging travelers. We cover all aspects of the RV lifestyle; editorial material is both technical and non-technical in nature. Regular features include tests and descriptions of various models of motorhomes and mini-motorhomes, travel adventures and hobbies pursued in such vehicles, objective analysis of equipment and supplies for such vehicles and do-it-yourself articles. Guides within the magazine provide listings of manufacturers, rentals and other sources of equipment and accessories of interest to enthusiasts. Articles must have an RV slant and excellent transparencies accompanying text." Estab. 1968. Circ. 144,000. **Pays on acceptance.** Publishes ms within 1 year of acceptance. Byline given. Offers 30% kill fee. Buys first North American and electronic rights. Editorial lead time 4 months. Submit seasonal material 6 months in advance. Query by mail, fax. Responds in 3 weeks to queries; 2 months to mss. Sample copy free. Guidelines for #10 SASE.

O━ Break in with *Crossroads* items.

Nonfiction: How-to, humor, new product, personal experience, photo feature, technical, travel, profiles, recreation, lifestyle, legislation, all RV related. No diaries of RV trips or negative RV experiences. **Buys 120 mss/year.** Query with or without published clips. Length: 250-2,500 words. **Pays $300-600.**

Photos: Send 35mm transparencies with submission. Offers no additional payment for art accepted with ms. Pays $500 + for covers. Captions, model releases and identification of subjects required. Buys one-time rights.

Columns/Departments: Crossroads (offbeat briefs of people, places of interest to travelers), 100-200 words; Keepers (tips, resources). Query or send complete ms. **Pays $100-200.**

Tips: "If a freelancer has an idea for a good article, it's best to send a query and include possible photo locations to illustrate the article. We prefer to assign articles and work with the author in developing a piece suitable to our audience. We are in a specialized field with very enthusiastic readers who appreciate articles by authors who actually enjoy motorhomes. The following areas are most open: Crossroads—(brief descriptions of places to see or special events, with one photo/slide, 100-200 words; travel—places to go with a motorhome, where to stay, what to see, etc.; we prefer not to use travel articles where the motorhome is secondary; and how-to—personal projects on author's motorhomes to make travel easier, etc., unique projects, accessories. Also articles on unique personalities, motorhomes, humorous experiences. Be sure to submit appropriate photography (35mm slides) with at least one good motorhome shot to illustrate travel articles. No phone queries, please."

$ $ $ $ NATIONAL GEOGRAPHIC TRAVELER, National Geographic Society, 1145 17th St. N.W., Washington DC 20036. Website: nationalgeographic.com/traveler. Editor: Keith Bellows. Executive Editor: Paul Martin. **Contact:** Scott Stuckey, or Jonathan Tourtellot, senior editors. **90% freelance written.** Published 8 times/year. "*National Geographic Traveler* is filled with practical information and detailed maps designed to encourage readers to explore and travel. Features domestic and foreign destinations, photography, the economics of travel, adventure trips, and weekend getaways to help readers plan a variety of excursions. Our writers need to equip our readers with inspiration to travel. We want lively writing—personal anecdotes with telling details, not an A to Z account of a destination." Estab. 1984. Circ. 720,000. **Pays on acceptance.** Publishes ms up to 1 year after acceptance. Byline given. Offers 30% kill fee. Buys one-time and electronic rights. Editorial lead time 3-12 months. Submit seasonal material 1 year in advance with SASE. Accepts queries by mail. Responds in 6 weeks. Sample copy and writer's guidelines free with SASE.

Nonfiction: Essays, general interest, historical/nostalgic, how-to, humor, inspirational (destinations), new product (travel oriented), opinion, personal experience, photo feature, travel. "We do not want to see general, impersonal, fact-clogged articles. We do not want to see any articles similar to those we, or our competitors, have run recently." **Buys 80-100 mss/year.** Query with published clips. Length: 250-2,500 words. **Pays 50¢/word and up.** Pays expenses of writers on assignment.

Columns/Departments: Smart Traveler—Norie Danyliw, editor (travel trends, sources, strategies and solutions); 48 Hours—Susan O'Keefe, editor (the best of a city); Room Check (unique and special places to stay). **Buys 150-200 mss/ year.** Query with published clips and SASE. **Pays 50¢/word and up.**

▣ The online magazine carries original content not found in the print. Contact: Tom Giovanni, online editor.

Tips: "Familiarize yourself with our magazine—not only the types of stories we run, but the types of stories we've run in the past. Formulate a story idea, and then send a detailed query, recent clips and contact information to the editor responsible for the section you'd like to be published in." No unsolicited photographs. Will accept unsolicited mss with SASE.

$ NATURALLY, Nude Recreation Travel, Events Unlimited Publishing Co., P.O. Box 317, Newfoundland NJ 07435-0317. (973)697-3552. Fax: (973)697-8313. E-mail: naturally@nac.net. Website: www.internaturally.com. **Contact:** Bernard Loibl, editor. **90% freelance written.** Quarterly magazine covering wholesome family nude recreation and travel locations. "*Naturally* nude recreation looks at why millions of people believe that removing clothes in public is a good idea, and at places specifically created for that purpose—with good humor, but also in earnest. *Naturally* nude recreation takes you to places where your personal freedom is the only agenda, and to places where textile-free living is a serious commitment." Estab. 1981. Circ. 35,000. Pays on publication. Byline given. Buys first rights and one-time rights. Editorial lead time 4 months. Submit seasonal material 4 months in advance. Accepts queries by mail, e-mail, fax. Accepts simultaneous submissions. Sample copy for $9. Writer's guidelines free.

Nonfiction: General interest, interview/profile, personal experience, photo feature, travel. **Buys 12 mss/year.** Send complete ms. Length: 2 pages. **Pays $70/published page including photos.** Frequent contributors and regular columnists, who develop a following through *Naturally*, are paid from the Frequent Contributors Budget. Payments increase on the basis of frequency of participation

Reprints: Accepts previously published submissions.

Photos: Send photos with submission. Reviews contact sheets, negatives, transparencies and prints. Payment for photos included in payment forms. Buys one-time rights.

Fillers: Cheryl Hanenberg, associate editor. Anecdotes, facts, gags to be illustrated by cartoonist, newsbreaks, short humor.

Tips: "*Naturally* nude recreation invokes the philosophies of naturism and nudism, but also activities and beliefs in the mainstream that express themselves, barely: spiritual awareness, New Age customs, pagan and religious rites, alternative and fringe lifestyle beliefs, artistic expressions and many individual nude interests. Our higher purpose is simply to help restore our sense of self. Although the term 'nude recreation' may, for some, conjure up visions of sexual frivolities inappropriate for youngsters—because that can also be technically true—these topics are outside the scope of *Naturally* magazine. Here the emphasis is on the many varieties of human beings, of all ages and backgrounds, recreating in their most natural state, at extraordinary places, their reasons for doing so, and the benefits they derive."

$ $ NORTHEAST OUTDOORS, Woodall's Publications, 2575 Vista Del Mar, Ventura CA 93001. (800)323-9078. Fax: (805)667-4122. E-mail: mbaccanari@affinitygroup.com. Website: www.woodalls.com. **Contact:** Melinda Baccanari, senior managing editor. **50% freelance written.** Works with a small number of new/unpublished writers each year. Monthly tabloid covering family camping in the Northeastern US. Estab. 1968. Circ. 30,000. Pays on publication. Publishes ms an average of 4 months after acceptance. Byline given. Offers 50% kill fee. Buys first rights and regional rights. Submit seasonal material 5 months in advance. Accepts queries by mail, e-mail. Responds in 2 weeks. Sample copy for 9×12 SAE with 4 first-class stamps. Writer's guidelines for #10 SASE.

○─ Break in with regional articles showcasing the RV lifestyle. Local destinations, camp ground news and the like are the best ways to get published.

Nonfiction: How-to (camping), new product (company and RV releases only), recreation vehicle and camping experiences in the Northeast, features about private (only) campgrounds and places to visit in the Northeast while RVing, personal experience, photo feature, travel. "No diaries of trips, dog or fishing-only stories, or anything not camping and RV related." Query. Length: 300-1,500 words. **Pays 10¢/word.**

Reprints: Send typed ms with rights for sale noted and info about when and where it previously appeared.

Photos: Send photos with submission. Reviews contact sheets and 5×7 prints or larger. Captions and identification of subjects required. Pays $5/photo. Buys one-time rights.

Columns/Departments: Northeast News (500-1,000 words), Going Places (800-1,000 words). **Pays 10¢/word.**

Tips: "We most often need material on private campgrounds and attractions in New England. We are looking for upbeat, first-person stories about where to camp, what to do or see, and how to enjoy camping."

N $ $ NORTHWEST TRAVEL, Northwest Regional Magazines, 4969 Hwy 101N #2, P.O. Box 18000, Florence OR 97439. (541)997-8401. (800)348-8401. Fax: (541)997-1124. E-mail: judy@ohwy.com. Website: www.ohwy.com. Co-editor: Jim Forst.**Contact:** Judy Fleagle, co-editor. **60% freelance written.** Bimonthly magazine. "We like energetic writing about popular activities and destinations in the Pacific Northwest. *Northwest Travel* aims to give readers practical ideas on where to go in the region. Magazine covers Oregon, Washington, Idaho and British Columbia; occasionally Alaska and Western Montana." Estab. 1991. Circ. 50,000. Pays after publication. Publishes ms an average of 8 months after acceptance. Buys first North American serial rights. Submit seasonal material 6 months in advance. Accepts queries by mail, e-mail. Responds in 1 month to queries; 3 months to mss. Sample copy for $4.50. Writer's guidelines for #10 SASE.

● Have good slides to go with a story that is lively with compelling leads, quotes, anecdotes, and no grammar problems.

Nonfiction: Book excerpts, general interest, historical/nostalgic, interview/profile (rarely), photo feature, travel (only in Northwest region). "No cliché-ridden pieces on places that everyone covers." **Buys 40 mss/year.** Query with or without published clips. Length: 1,250-2,000 words. **Pays $100-350** for feature articles and 2-5 contributor copies.

Reprints: Rarely accepts reprints of previously published submissions. Send photocopy of article and information about when and where the article previously appeared. Pays 60% of amount paid for an original article.

Photos: State availability of photos with submission. Uses transparencies (prefers dupes). Captions, model releases (cover photos), credits and identification of subjects required. Buys one-time rights.

Columns/Departments: Restaurant Features, 1,000 words. **Pays $125.** Worth a Stop (brief items describing places "worth a stop"), 300-350 words. **Buys 25-30 mss/year.** Send complete ms. **Pays $50.** Back Page (photo and text package on a specific activity, season or festival with some technical photo info), 80 words and 1 slide. **Pays $75.**

Tips: "Write fresh, lively copy (avoid clichés) and cover exciting travel topics in the region that haven't been covered in other magazines. A story with stunning photos will get serious consideration. The department most open to freelancers is the Worth a Stop department. Take us to fascinating and interesting places we might not otherwise discover."

$ PATHFINDERS, Travel Information for People of Color, 6424 N. 13th St., Philadelphia PA 19126. (215)927-9950. Fax: (215)927-3359. E-mail: blaktravel@aol.com. Website: www.Pathfinderstravel.com. **Contact:** Joseph P. Blake, managing editor. **99% freelance written.** Quarterly magazine covering travel for people of color, primarily African-Americans. "We look for lively, original, well-written stories that provide a good sense of place, with useful information and fresh ideas about travel and the travel industry. Our main audience is African-Americans, though we do look for articles relating to other persons of color: Native Americans, Hispanics and Asians." Estab. 1997. Circ. 50,000. Pays on publication. Byline given. Buys first North American serial rights and electronic rights. Accepts queries by mail, e-mail. Responds in 2 months. Sample copy at bookstores (Barnes & Noble, Borders, Waldenbooks). Writer's guidelines on website.

O➔ Break in through *Looking Back*, 600-word essay on travel from personal experience that provides a historical perspective.

Nonfiction: Essays, historical/nostalgic, how-to, personal experience, photo feature, travel, all vacation travel oriented. Interested in seeing more Native American stories, places that our readers can visit and rodeos (be sure to tie-in African-American cowboys). "No more pitches on Jamaica." **Buys 16-20 mss/year**. Send complete ms. Length: 1,200-1,400 words for cover stories, 1,000-1,200 words features. **Pays $100.**

Photos: State availability of photos with submission.

Columns/Departments: Chef's Table, Post Cards from Home, 500-600 words. Send complete ms. **Pays $50.**

Tips: "We prefer seeing finished articles rather than queries. All articles are submitted on spec. Articles should be saved in either WordPerfect of Microsoft Word, double-spaced and saved as a text-only file. Include a hard copy. E-mail articles are accepted only by request of the editor."

⭐ **$ $ $ $** PORTHOLE CRUISE MAGAZINE, A View of the Sea and Beyond, Panoff Publishing, 7100 W. Commercial Blvd., Suite 106, Ft. Lauderdale FL 33319. (954)746-5554. Fax: (954)746-5244. E-mail: cruisemag @aol.com. Website: www.porthole.com. Editorial Director: Dale Rim. **Contact**: Lesley Abravanel, managing editor. **90% freelance written**. Bimonthly magazine covering the cruise industry. "*Porthole Cruise Magazine* entices its readers into taking a cruise vacation by delivering information that is timely, accurate, colorful and entertaining." Estab. 1992. Circ. 35,000. Pays on publication. Publishes ms an average of 6 months after acceptance. Byline given. Offers 35% kill fee. Buys first international serial rights, second serial (reprint) rights and electronic rights. Editorial lead time 8 months. Submit seasonal material 5 months in advance. Accepts queries by mail, e-mail, fax. Accepts simultaneous submissions. Responds in 2 months to queries; 6 months to mss. Sample copy for 8×11 SAE with $3 postage. Writer's guidelines for #10 SASE.

Nonfiction: Book excerpts, essays (your cruise experience), exposé, general interest (cruise-related), historical/nostalgic, how-to (i.e., pick a cruise, not get seasick, travel tips), humor, interview/profile (crew on board or industry executives), new product, personal experience, photo features, travel (off-the-beaten path, adventure, ports, destinations, cruises), onboard fashion, spa articles, duty-free shopping, port shopping, ship reviews. No articles on destinations that can't be reached by ship. Special issues: Cuba, Europe. "Please, please do not send us accounts of your lovely, spectacular or breathtaking family cruise vacations from point of embarkation or debarkation. Concentrate on vivid details, personal experiences and go above and beyond the normal, 'We cruised to. . . .' Include out-of-the-ordinary subject matter. Try to transport the reader from the pages to the places you traveled rather than simply giving a laundry list of what you saw. Please don't write asking for a cruise so that you can do an article! You must be an experienced cruise writer to do a ship review." **Buys 75 mss/year**. Query with published clips or send letter with complete ms. Length: 1,000-3,000 words, average 1,100. **Pays $400-1,600 for assigned articles; $250-1,000 for unsolicited articles.** Pays expenses of writers on assignment.

Reprints: Send photocopy of article or typed ms with rights for sale noted and information about when and where the article previously appeared. Negotiates payment.

Photos: Contact: Linda Douthat, creative director. State availability of photos with submission. Reviews transparencies and prints. Negotiates payment individually. Captions, model releases, identification of subjects required. Buys one-time rights.

Columns/Departments: Deckadence (luxury); Ombudsman (investigative), "My" Port City (personal accounts of experiences in certain destination), 1,200 words; Beautiful Thing (spa service on board), 700 words; Brass Tacks (consumer-oriented travel tips, short bits); Personality Plus (intriguing travel-oriented profiles), 400 words; Fashion File (onboard fashion), 400 words. Also humor, cruise cuisine, shopping, photo essays. **Buys 50 mss/year.** Query with published clips or send letter with complete ms. **Pays $400-1,600.**

Fillers: Facts, gags to be illustrated by cartoonist, newsbreaks, short humor. **Buys 30/year.** Length: 25-200 words. **Pays 25¢/word.**

📧 The online magazine carries original content not found in the print edition and includes writer's guidelines. Contact: Lesley Abravanel, online editor.

Tips: "We prefer to be queried via e-mail. Submit an outline showing how you will incorporate anecdotes and dialogue. Clips are not necessary. Offbeat, original travel stories are preferred. Tie-ins to celebrity culture, pop culture, arts/entertainment, politics, cuisine, architecture, are highly regarded."

🅽 **$ $** ROADS TO ADVENTURE, The Magazine of Family Camping, Affinity Group, Inc., 2575 Vista Del Mar Dr., Ventura CA 93001. (805)667-4100. Fax: (805)667-4484. E-mail: www.rv.net. Senior Editors: Jim Brightly and Sherry McBride. **Contact:** Barbara Leonard, associate editorial director. **60% freelance written.** Annual magazine. "Articles must be slanted toward campers and their families, either with an RV or tents. Adventure is the primary focus of this publication, which is aimed at ages 35-50." Estab. 1996. **Pays on acceptance.** Publishes ms an average of 1 year after acceptance. Byline given. Buys first North American and electronic rights. Editorial lead time 6 months. Submit seasonal material 1 year in advance. Accepts queries by mail. Responds in 3 weeks to queries; 3 months to mss.

O➔ Break in with a "heartwarming, informative or unusual article on a family camping/RVing trip, which piques the interest of like individuals to do the same."

Nonfiction: Essays, humor, inspirational, interview/profile, opinion, personal experience, photo feature, travel, family reunions, health and children on the road. All camping related. **Buys 20 mss/year.** Query with published clips. Length: 250-1,500 words. **Pays $100-600 for assigned articles; $100-400 for unsolicited articles.**

Photos: Send photos with submission. Reviews transparencies. Offers no additional payment for photos accepted with ms. Captions, model releases and identification of subjects required. Buys one-time and electronic rights.

■ The online version contains material not found in the print edition. Contact: Barbara Leonard.

Tips: "Have first-hand outdoor recreational experience. Enjoy adventure on the road. We'd like to see more hands-on, true togetherness travel/adventure with children ranging in age from 5-18."

⊠ $ $ ST. MAARTEN NIGHTS, Nights Publications Inc., 1831 Rene Levesque Blvd. West, Montreal, Quebec H3H 1R4 Canada. (514)931-1987. Fax: (514)931-6273. E-mail: editor@nightspublications.com. Website: www.nightspublications.com. Managing Editor: Zelly Zuskin. **Contact**: Stephen Trotter, editor. **90% freelance written.** Annual magazine covering the St. Maarten/St. Martin vacation experience seeking "upbeat entertaining lifestyle articles. Our audience is the North American vacationer." Estab. 1981. Circ. 225,000. **Pays on acceptance.** Publishes ms an average of 9 months after acceptance. Byline given. Buys first North American serial and first Caribbean rights. Editorial lead time 1 month. Accepts queries by mail, e-mail, fax. Responds in 2 weeks to queries; 1 month to mss. Sample copy for $5 (make check payable to Nights Publications Inc.). Writer's guidelines free.

Nonfiction: Lifestyle with a lively, upscale touch. General interest, colorful profiles of islanders, historical/nostalgia, how-to (gamble), sailing, humor, inspirational, interview/profile, opinion, ecological (eco-tourism), personal experience, photo feature, travel, local culture, art, activities, entertainment, night life, special events, topics relative to vacationers in St. Maarten/St. Martin. "No negative pieces or stale rewrites or cliché copy." **Buys 8-10 mss/year.** Query with published clips and SASE with Canadian postage or IRC. Length: 250-750 words. **Pays $100-250.**

Photos: State availability of photos with submission. Reviews transparencies. Offers $50/photo. Captions, model releases, identification of subjects required. Buys one-time rights.

Tips: "Our style is upbeat, friendly, fluid and descriptive. Our magazines cater to tourists who are already at the destination, so ensure your story is of interest to this particular audience. We welcome stories that offer fresh angles to familiar tourist-related topics."

Ⓝ ⊠ $ $ THE SOUTHERN TRAVELER, AAA Auto Club of Missouri, 12901 N. Forty Dr., St. Louis MO 63141. (314)523-7350. Fax: (314)523-6982. Editor: Michael J. Right. **Contact:** Deborah Klein, managing editor. **80% freelance written.** Bimonthly magazine. Estab. 1997. Circ. 130,000. **Pays on acceptance**. Byline given. Not copyrighted. Buys first North American print serial, second serial (reprint) rights. Accepts simultaneous submissions. Responds in 1 month with SASE enclosed. Sample copy for 12½×9½ SAE with 3 first-class stamps. Guidelines for SASE.

Nonfiction: "We feature articles on regional and world travel, area history, auto safety, highway and transportation news." **Buys 30 mss/year.** Query, with best chance for good reception January-March for inclusion in following year's editorial calendar. Length: 2,000 words maximum. **Pays $250 (maximum).**

Reprints: Send typed ms with rights for sale noted and information about when and where the article previously appeared. **Pays $125-150.**

Photos: State availability of photos with submission. Reviews transparencies. Offers no additional payment for photos accepted with ms. Captions required. Buys one-time photo reprint rights.

Tips: "Editorial schedule is set 18 months in advance. Request a copy. Serious writers ask for media kit to help them target their story. Some stories available throughout the year, but most are assigned early. Travel destinations and tips are most open to freelancers; auto-related topics handled by staff. Make story bright and quick to read. We see too many 'Here's what I did on my vacation' manuscripts. Go easy on first-person accounts."

⊠ $ $ TIMES OF THE ISLANDS, The International Magazine of the Turks & Caicos Islands, Times Publications Ltd., P.O. Box 234, Caribbean Place, Providenciales, Turks & Caicos Islands, British West Indies. (649)946-4788. Fax: (649)941-3402. E-mail: timespub@tciway.tc. Website: www.timespub.tc. **Contact**: Kathy Borsuk, editor. **80% freelance written.** Quarterly magazine covering The Turks & Caicos Islands. "*Times of the Islands* is used by the public and private sector to attract visitors and potential investors/developers to the Islands. It goes beyond a superficial overview of tourist attractions with in-depth articles about natural history, island heritage, local personalities, new development, offshore finance, sporting activities, visitors' experiences and Caribbean fiction." Estab. 1988. Circ. 6,000-9,000. Pays on publication. Publishes ms an average of 6 months after acceptance. Byline given. Buys second serial (reprint) rights and publication rights for 6 months with respect to other publications distributed in Caribbean. Editorial lead time 4 months. Submit seasonal material 4 months in advance. Accepts simultaneous submissions. Accepts queries by mail, e-mail, fax. Responds in 6 weeks to queries; 2 months to mss. "Keep in mind, mail to Islands is SLOW. Faxing can speed response time." Sample copy for $4 and postage between Miami and your destination. Writer's guidelines for #10 SASE.

Nonfiction: Book excerpts or reviews, essays, general interest (Caribbean art, culture, cooking, crafts), historical/nostalgic, humor, interview/profile (locals), personal experience (trips to the Islands), photo feature, technical (island businesses), travel, nature, ecology, business (offshore finance), watersports. **Buys 30 mss/year.** Query. Length: 500-3,000 words. **Pays $200-600.**

Reprints: Send photocopy of article along with information about when and where the article previously appeared. Pay varies.

Photos: Send photos with submission. Reviews slides, prints or digital photos. Offers no additional payment for photos accepted with ms. Pays $15-100/photo. Identification of subjects required.

Columns/Departments: On Holiday (unique experiences of visitors to Turks & Caicos), 500-1,500 words. **Buys 4 mss/year.** Query. **Pays $200-300.**

Fiction: Adventure (sailing, diving), ethnic (Caribbean), historical (Caribbean), humorous (travel-related), mystery, novel excerpts. **Buys 2-3 mss/year.** Query. Length: 1,000-2,000 words. **Pays $250-400.**

Tips: "Make sure that the query/article specifically relates to the Turks and Caicos Islands. The theme can be general (ecotourism, for instance), but the manuscript should contain specific and current references to the Islands. We're a high-quality magazine, with a small budget and staff and are very open-minded to ideas (and manuscripts). Writers who have visited the Islands at least once would probably have a better perspective from which to write."

N **$ $ TRAILER LIFE, RVing At Its Best,** Affinity Group, Inc., 2575 Vista Del Mar Dr., Ventura CA 93001. (805)667-4100. Fax: (805)667-4184. Website: www.rv.net. Managing Editor: Jim Brightly. **Contact:** Barbara Leonard, editorial director. **40% freelance written.** Monthly magazine. *"Trailer Life* magazine is written specifically for active people whose overall lifestyle is based on travel and recreation in their RV. Every issue includes product tests, travel articles, and other features—ranging from lifestyle to vehicle maintenance." Estab. 1941. Circ. 290,000. **Pays on acceptance.** Publishes ms an average of 6 months after acceptance. Byline given. Offers 30% kill fee for assigned articles that are not acceptable. Buys first North American rights. Editorial lead time 4 months. Submit seasonal material 6 months in advance. Accepts queries by mail, e-mail. Responds in 2 months. Sample copy free. Writer's guidelines for #10 SASE.

　　O➤ Break in with a "small piece for the Campground Spotlight or Etc. section; a short article on an interesting RV trip."

Nonfiction: Historical/nostalgic, how-to (technical), new product, opinion, humor, personal experience, travel. No vehicle tests, product evaluations or road tests; tech material is strictly assigned. No diaries or trip logs, no non-RV trips; nothing without an RV-hook. **Buys 75 mss/year.** Query with or without published clips. Length: 250-2,500 words. **Pays $125-700.** Sometimes pays expenses of writers on assignment.

Photos: Send photos with submission. Reviews b&w contact sheets, transparencies (which should be labeled). Offers no additional payment for photos accepted with ms. Model releases, identification of subjects required. Buys one-time and occasionally electronic rights.

Columns/Departments: Campground Spotlight (report with 1 photo of campground recommended for RVers), 250 words; Bulletin Board (news, trends of interest to RVers), 100 words; Etcetera (useful tips and information affecting RVers), 240 words. **Buys 70 mss/year.** Query or send complete ms. **Pays $75-250.**

　　▣ The online version of this publication contains material not found in the print edition. Contact: Barbara Leonard.

Tips: "Prerequisite: must have RV focus. Photos must be magazine quality. These are the two biggest reasons why manuscripts are rejected. Our readers are travel enthusiasts who own all types of RVs (travel trailers, truck campers, van conversions, motorhomes, tent trailers, fifth-wheels) in which they explore North America and beyond, embrace the great outdoors in national, state and private parks. They're very active and very adventurous."

⬛ $ TRANSITIONS ABROAD, P.O. Box 1300, Amherst MA 01004-1300. (413)256-3414. Fax: (413)256-0373. E-mail: editor@transitionsabroad.com. Website: www.TransitionsAbroad.com. Editor/Publisher: Clay Hubbs. **Contact:** Nicole Roxenleaf Ritter, managing editor. **80-90% freelance written.** Eager to work with new/unpublished writers. Magazine resource for low-budget international travel, often with an educational or work component. Focus is on the alternatives to mass tourism. Estab. 1977. Circ. 20,000. Pays on publication. Buys first rights and second (reprint) rights. Byline given. Accepts queries by mail, e-mail, fax. Responds in 1 month. Sample copy for $6.45. Writer's guidelines and topics schedule for #10 SASE or on website.

Nonfiction: Lead articles (up to 1,500 words) provide first-hand practical information on independent travel to featured country or region (see topics schedule). **Pays $75-150.** Also, how to find educational and specialty travel opportunities, practical information (evaluation of courses, special interest and study tours, economy travel), travel (new learning and cultural travel ideas). Foreign travel only. Few destination ("tourist") pieces or first-person narratives. *Transitions Abroad* is a resource magazine for independent, educated, and adventurous travelers, not for armchair travelers or those addicted to packaged tours or cruises. Emphasis on information—which must be usable by readers—and on interaction with people in host country. **Buys 20 unsolicited mss/issue.** Query with credentials and SASE. Length: 500-1,500 words. **Pays $25-150.** Include author's bio with submissions.

Photos: Send photos with ms. Pays $10-45 for prints (color acceptable, b&w preferred), $125 for covers (b&w only). Photos increase likelihood of acceptance. Buys one-time rights. Captions and ID on photos required.

Columns/Departments: Worldwide Travel Bargains (destinations, activities and accomodations for budget travelers—featured in every issue); Tour and Program Notes (new courses or travel programs); Travel Resources (new information and ideas for independent travel); Working Traveler (how to find jobs and what to expect); Activity Vacations (travel opportunities that involve action and learning, usually by direct involvement in host culture); Responsible Travel (information on community-organized tours). **Buys 10/issue.** Send complete ms. Length: 1,000 words maximum. **Pays $20-50.**

Fillers: Info Exchange (information, preferably first-hand—having to do with travel, particularly offbeat educational travel and work or study abroad). **Buys 10/issue.** Length: 750 words maximum. **Pays $20.**

　　▣ The online magazine carries original content not found in the print edition and includes writer's guidelines.

Tips: "We like nuts and bolts stuff, practical information, especially on how to work, live, and cut costs abroad. Our readers want usable information on planning a travel itinerary. Be specific: names, addresses, current costs. We are very interested in educational and long-stay travel and study abroad for adults and senior citizens. *Overseas Travel Planner* published each year in July provides best information sources on work, study, and independent travel abroad. Each bimonthly issue contains a worldwide directory of educational and specialty travel programs."

⭐ **$ $ TRAVEL AMERICA, The U.S. Vacation Magazine**, World Publishing Co., 990 Grove St., Evanston IL 60201-4370. (847)491-6440. Editor-in-Chief/Associate Publisher: Bob Meyers. **Contact**: Randy Mink, managing editor. **80% freelance written.** Bimonthly magazine covering US vacation travel. Estab. 1985. Circ. 400,000. Byline given. Buys first North American serial rights. Submit seasonal material 6 months in advance. Responds in 1 month to queries; 6 weeks on ms. Sample copy for $5 and 9 × 12 SASE with $1.65 postage.

Nonfiction: Primarily destination-oriented travel articles and resort/hotel profiles and roundups, but will consider essays, how-to, humor, nostalgia, Americana. "U.S. destination travel features must have personality and strong sense of place, developed through personal experiences, quotes, humor, human interest, local color. We prefer people-oriented writing, not dry guidebook accounts and brochure-style fluff. Always in the market for nationwide roundup stories— past roundups have included U.S. Gambling Meccas and Top 10 Amusement Parks. Also short slices of Americana focusing on nostalgia, collectibles and crafts, ethnic communities and celebrations, special events, special individuals. It is best to study current contents and query by mail only first." **Buys 60 mss/year.** Average length: 1,000 words. **Pays $150-300.**

Reprints: Send typed ms with rights for sale noted. Pay varies.

Photos: Top-quality original color slides preferred. Captions required. Buys one-time rights. Prefers photo feature package (ms plus slides), but will purchase slides only to support a work in progress.

Tips: "Because we are heavily photo-oriented, superb slides are our foremost concern. The most successful approach is to send 2-3 sheets of slides with the query or complete ms. Include a list of other subjects you can provide as a photo feature package."

$ TRAVEL IMPULSE, Sun Tracker Enterprises Ltd., 9336 117th St., Delta, British Columbia V4C 6B8 Canada. (604)951-3238. Fax: (604)951-8732. E-mail: smboyce@suntrackercafe.com. Website: www.suntrackercafe.com. **Contact**: Susan M. Boyce, editor/publisher. **95% freelance written.** "We work with at least one new writer each issue and are always looking for new voices. *Travel Impulse* is a quarterly magazine for people who love to travel—in fact, they find travel irresistible. Appeal to their sense of adventure and the playfulness of travel. Many of our readers like to 'pick up and go' at short notice and are looking for inexpensive, unique ways to accomplish that." Estab. 1984. Circ. 1,000. Pays 2 weeks after publication. Publishes an average of 8 months after acceptance. Byline given. Buys first North American serial rights and second serial (reprint) rights. Editorial lead time 8 months. Submit seasonal material 8 months in advance. Responds in 2 months to queries; 4 months to mss. Sample copy for $6 or on website. Writer's guidelines for #10 SASE or on website.

○► "Write in first person and tell me about *your* experience. I'm not looking for another advertisement—I want stories about real places and real people."

Nonfiction: Humor, interview/profile, new product (travel gadgets and gear), personal experience, photo feature. No political commentary. **Buys 20-25 mss/year.** Query by mail only or send complete ms with Canadian postage or IRCs only. Length: 1,000-1,500 words. **Pays $20-30 for features.**

Reprints: Accepts previously published submissions.

Photos: State availability of photos with submission or send photocopies. No originals until requested. Reviews 4 × 6 prints (preferred size). Offers no additional payment for photos accepted with ms, but photos greatly enhance your chances of acceptance. Captions, model releases, identification of subjects required. Buys rights with ms.

Tips: "Our readers find travel irresistible. Entice them with unusual destinations and unique ways to travel inexpensively. Show us the playful side of travel."

⭐ **$ $ $ $ TRAVEL + LEISURE**, American Express Publishing Corp., 1120 Avenue of the Americas, New York NY 10036. (212)382-5600. E-mail: tlquery@travelandleisure.com. Website: www.travelandleisure.com. Editor-in-Chief: Nancy Novogrod. Executive Editor: Barbara Peck. Managing Editor: Mark Orwoll. **95% freelance written.** "*Travel + Leisure* is a monthly magazine edited for affluent travelers. It explores the latest resorts, hotels, fashions, foods and drinks." Circ. 1,000,000. **Pays on acceptance.** Byline given. Offers 25% kill fee. Buys first world rights. Responds in 6 weeks. Sample copy for $5.50 from (800)888-8728 or P.O. Box 2094, Harlan IA 51537-4094. Writer's guidelines for #10 SASE.

● There is no single editorial contact for *Travel + Leisure*. It is best to find the name of the editor of each section, as appropriate for your submission.

Nonfiction: Travel. **Buys 40-50 features** (3,000-5,000 words) **and 200 short pieces** (125-500 words). Query by e-mail preferred. **Pays $4,000-6,000/feature; $100-500/short piece.** Pays the expenses of writers on assignment.

● Ranked as one of the best markets for freelance writers in *Writer's Yearbook* magazine's annual "Top 100 Markets," January 2000.

Columns/Departments: Buys 125-150 mss. Length: 1,200-2,500 words. **Pays $1,000-2,500.**

Photos: Discourages submission of unsolicited transparencies. Payment varies. Captions required. Buys one-time rights.

Tips: "Read the magazine. There are two regional editions: East and West. Short-takes sections (e.g., "T&L Reports" and "Smart Going") are best places to start."

N ⚔ $ TRAVEL WORLD INTERNATIONAL, East-West News Bureau, 75-784 Via Allegre, Indian Wells CA 92210. (760)346-2777. Fax: (760)346-6788. E-mail: bureau@east-west-news.com. Website: www.east-west-news.com. Editor: Lee Stanley. **Contact:** Cecil Beare, associate publisher/editor, at bearecub@aol.com. **90% freelance written.** Bimonthly newsletter covering travel, food, wine and photos. "We run 10-12 pages on the web directed to the consumer of travel, food and wine." Estab. 1986. Circ. 3,500,000. Pays on publication. Byline given. Makes work-for-hire assignments. Editorial lead time 15 days. Submit seasonal material 15 days in advance. Accepts queries by e-mail. Responds in 2 weeks. Sample copy and writer's guidelines by e-mail.

Nonfiction: Lee Stanley, senior bureau chief (leeandpita@aol.com). General interest, photo feature, travel, food & wine and hospitality industry. **Buys 1,200 mss/year.** Query. Length: 600-1,200 words. **Pay varies.**

Reprints: Accepts previously published submissions.

Photos: Send photos with submission. Reviews 2×3 prints. Offers $5/photo. Identification of subjects required.

Columns/Departments: Travel; Food; Wine, all 600-1,200 words. Query. **Pay varies.**

   📰 The online version contains material not found in the print edition. Contact: Cecil Beare.

Tips: "Read our web page. Contact Lee by e-mail only (leeandpita@aol.com)."

N TRAVELER'S TALES 330 Townsend St., Suite 208, San Francisco CA 94107.

   • See the listing for *Traveler's Tales* in the Book Publisher section.

$ $ TREKS & JOURNEYS, The Student International Travel Journal, Treks & Journeys Press, 715 Canyon Rd., Tuscaloosa AL 35406. (205)348-8247. Fax: (205)366-9866. E-mail: GFrangou@sa.ua.edu. Editor: George Frangoulis. **85% freelance written.** Quarterly magazine. "*Treks & Journeys* is for a different kind of traveller. Directed towards students and young adults ages 20-35, it is for a person who is independent, adventurous, interested in spreading their wings and discovering new places of cultural interest and enrichment. It encompasses all aspects of travel, as well as study and working abroad." Estab. 1995. Circ. 127,000. **Pays on acceptance.** Byline given. Offers 50% kill fee. Editorial lead time 6 months. Submit seasonal material 6 months in advance. Responds in 2 weeks to queries; 3 months to mss. Sample copy and writer's guidelines free.

Nonfiction Book excerpts, essays, general interest, historical/nostalgic, how-to, humor, inspirational, interview/profile, new product, opinion, personal experience, photo feature, travel. **Buys 15-20 mss/year.** Query. Length: 500-3,500 words. **Pays $50-350 for assigned articles; $25-250 for unsolicited articles.**

Reprints: Send tearsheet or photocopy of article or typed ms with rights for sale noted and information about when and where the article previously appeared. Pays 100% of amount paid for an original article.

Photos: State availability of photos with submission. Reviews contact sheets, transparencies, 5×7 prints. Offers $5-25/photo. Captions, model releases, identification of subjects required.

Tips: "*Treks & Journeys* is particularly interested in articles on new destinations that are 'off the beaten path,' recreational opportunities, budget travel for both short-term and long-term stays, and environmentally responsible tourism experiences."

⚔ $ $ $ trips, a travel journal, 155 Filbert St., Suite 245, Oakland CA 94607. (510)834-3433. Fax: (510)834-2663. E-mail: office@tripsmag.com. Website: www.tripsmag.com. **Contact:** Tony Stucker, editor. **90% freelance written.** Bimonthly magazine. "*trips magazine* is the travel journal for active travelers looking for travel information in an unusual, offbeat, irreverent voice. We are looking for travel articles that would not, or could not, appear anywhere else. We want the exotic, unusual destinations, but we are also looking for traditional sites viewed in unconventional ways. All editorial should be as interesting and entertaining to someone whether they're planning on visiting a destination, have just returned from the destination or never plan on going there. It should educate and inform, but also entertain. Travel is fun—travel writing should be as well." Estab. 1997. Circ. 100,000. Pays on publication. Publishes ms 3 months after acceptance. Byline given. Buys first North American serial rights. Editorial lead time 6 months. Submit seasonal material 6 months in advance. Accepts queries by mail, e-mail. Accepts simultaneous submissions. Responds in 6 weeks to queries; 3 months to mss. Sample copy for 10×13 SAE with 7 first-class stamps. Writer's guidelines for #10 SASE.

   ○⊸ Break in through well-developed, informative or offbeat pieces for our smaller sections, i.e., "Tips," "A Travel Journal," "Lessons In" and "Vice."

Nonfiction: Book excerpts, essays, exposé, general interest, how-to, humor, interview/profile, new product, personal experience, photo feature, travel. Especially looking for "how-to" tips and advice, reader service pieces and funny/goofy filler for "Customs" section. No "run-of-the-mill travel stories that would appear in Sunday travel sections." **Buys 40 mss/year.** Query with published clips. Length: 450-6,000 words. **Pays $100-1,500.** Sometimes pays expenses of writers on assignment.

Reprints: Send photocopy of article and information about when and where the article previously appeared.

Photos: State availability of photos with submission. Reviews contact sheets, negatives. Negotiates payment individually. Identification of subjects required. Buys one-time rights.

Columns/Departments: "Lessons In . . ." (travel reader service); "Vice" (unusual vices from around the world); "A Travel Journal" (first person essays), all 800-1,000 words. **Buys 30 mss/year.** Query. **Pays $100-500.**

   📰 The online magazine carries original content not found in the print edition and includes writer's guidelines.

Tips: "We want to develop relationships with writers around the world. If you don't have a piece that works now, perhaps a future trip will yield something that's right. E-mail queries encouraged."

$ $ $ VOYAGEUR, The Magazine of Carlson Hospitality Worldwide, Pace Communications, 1301 Carolina St., Greensboro NC 27401. (336)378-6065. Fax: (336)383-5690. Editor: Jaci H. Ponzoni. **Contact:** Sarah Lindsay, senior editor. **90% freelance written.** In-room magazine for Radisson hotels and affiliates. "*Voyageur* is an international magazine published quarterly for Carlson Hospitality Worldwide and distributed in the rooms of Radisson Hotels & Resorts Worldwide, Radisson SAS Hotels, Carlson Cruises Worldwide, and Country Inns & Suites By Carlson throughout North and South America, Europe, Australia, Africa, Asia and the Middle East. All travel-related stories must be in destinations where Radisson or Country Inns & Suites have hotels." Estab. 1992. Circ. 160,000. **Pays on acceptance.** Publishes ms an average of 2 months after acceptance. Offers 25% kill fee. Buys first North American serial rights. Editorial lead time 4 months. Submit seasonal material 6 months in advance. Responds in 2 months. Sample for $5. Writer's guidelines for #10 SASE.

> O→ Break in with a "well-thought-out, well-written, well-researched query on a city or area the writer lives in or knows well—one where Carlson has a presence (Radisson or Country Inns)."

Nonfiction: Travel. The *Cover Story* is an authoritative yet personal profile of a destination where Radisson has a major presence, featuring a mix of standard and off-the-beaten-path activities and sites including sightseeing, recreation, restaurants, shopping and cultural attractions. Length: 1,000 words including one sidebar, plus At a Glance, a roundup of useful and intriguing facts for travelers. *Our World* brings to life the spectrum of a country's or region's arts and culture, including performing, culinary, visual and folk arts. The successful article combines a timely sample of cultural activities for travelers with a sense of the destination's unique spirit or personality as reflected in the arts. Must be a region where Radisson has a major presence. Length: 1,000 words plus one 200-word sidebar. Query with published clips. **Pays $800-1,000.** Sometimes pays expenses of writers on assignment.

Photos: State availability of photos with submission. Reviews contact sheets, transparencies, prints. Negotiates payment individually. Model releases and identification of subjects required. Buys one-time rights.

Columns/Departments: In The Bag (place-specific shopping story with cultural context and upscale attitude), 600-800 words and 50-word mini-sidebar; Good Sport (action-oriented, first person focusing on travel involving sports such as biking, kayaking, scuba diving, hiking or sailing), 600-800 words plus 50-word mini-sidebar; Business Wise (insights into conducting business and traveling for business internationally), 350-400 words with 50-word mini-sidebar. **Buys 24 mss/year.** Query with published clips. **Pays $300-700.**

Tips: "We look for authoritative, energetic and vivid writing to inform and entertain business and leisure travelers, and we are actively seeking writers with an authentic European, Asian, Latin American, African or Australian perspective. Travel stories should be authoritative yet personal."

$ WESTERN RV NEWS, 64470 Sylvan Loop, Bend OR 97701. (541)318-8089. Fax: (541)318-0849. E-mail: editor@westernrvnews.com. Website: www.westernrvnews.com. **Contact:** Terie Snyder, editor. **75% freelance written.** Monthly magazine for owners of recreational vehicles and those interested in the RV lifestyle. Estab. 1966. Pays on publication. Publishes ms an average of 6 months after acceptance. Byline given. Buys first rights and second serial (reprint) rights. Accepts simultaneous submissions. Accepts queries by mail, e-mail, fax. Responds in 2 months. Sample copy and writer's guidelines for 9 × 12 SAE with 5 first-class stamps. Guidelines for #10 SASE.

Nonfiction: How-to (RV oriented, purchasing considerations, maintenance), humor (RV experiences), new product (with ancillary interest to RV lifestyle), personal experiences (varying or unique RV lifestyles), technical (RV systems or hardware), travel. "No articles without an RV slant." **Buys 100 mss/year.** Submit complete ms on paper or diskette. Length: 250-1,200 words. **Pays $20-100.**

Reprints: Send photocopy of article or typed ms with rights for sale noted and information about when and where the article previously appeared. Pays 60% of *Western RV News* first rights.

Photos: Send photos with submission. Accepts b&w or color slides or photos. Can submit on 3.5″ IBM-compatible disk. Offers $5/photo. Captions, model releases, identification of subjects required. Buys one-time rights.

Fillers: Encourage anecdotes, RV related tips and short humor. Length: 50-250 words. **Pays $5-25.**

Tips: "Highlight the RV lifestyle! Western travel articles should include information about the availability of RV sites, dump stations, RV parking and accessibility. Thorough research and a pleasant, informative writing style are paramount. Technical, how-to, and new product writing is also of great interest. Photos enhance the possibility of article acceptance."

WOMEN'S

Women have an incredible variety of publications available to them. A number of titles in this area have been redesigned to compete in the crowded marketplace. Many have stopped publishing fiction and are focusing more on short, human interest nonfiction articles. Magazines that also use material slanted to women's interests can also be found in the following categories: Business and Finance; Child Care and Parental Guidance; Contemporary Culture; Food & Drink; Gay & Lesbian Interest; Health & Fitness; Hobby & Craft; Home & Garden; Relationships; Religious; Romance & Confession; and Sports.

$ $ $ AMERICAN WOMAN, Goodman Publishing, 1700 Broadway, 34th Floor, New York NY 10019-5905. (212)541-7100. Fax: (212)245-1241. Managing Editor: Sandy Kosherick. **50% freelance written.** Magazine published

7 times/year for "women in their 20s, 30s, 40s, single and married, dealing with relationships and self-help." Estab. 1990. Circ. 138,000. Pays on publication. Publishes ms an average of 2 months after acceptance. Byline given. Offers 25% kill fee. Buys one-time and second serial (reprint) rights. Submit seasonal material 5 months in advance. Accepts simultaneous submissions. Responds in 2 months. Sample copy for $2.99. Writer's guidelines for #10 SASE.

Nonfiction: Book excerpts, self-help, inspirational, interview/profile, personal experience, true life drama. "No poetry, recipes or fiction." **Buys 40 mss/year.** Query with published clips. Length: 750-1,900 words. **Pays $300-900 for assigned articles; $200-500 for unsolicited articles.** Pays for phone, mailings, faxes, transportation costs of writers on assignment.

Reprints: Send photocopy of article and information about when and where the article previously appeared. **Pays $200-400.**

Photos: State availability of photos with submission. Reviews contact sheets, transparencies, prints. Offers $100-175/photo. Captions, model releases, identification of subjects required. Buys one-time rights.

Tips: "We are always interested in true-life stories and stories of inspiration—women who have overcome obstacles in their lives, trends (new ideas in dating, relationships, places to go, new ways to meet men), articles about health, beauty, diet, self-esteem, fun careers, and money-saving articles (on clothes, beauty, vacations, mail order, entertainment)."

N $ $ $ $B. SMITH STYLE, 1120 Avenue of the Americas, New York NY 10036. (212)827-6410. Website: www.bsmithstyle.com. **Contact:** Dan Gasby, publisher. Director of Planning: Frene Wong. **95% freelance written,** will decrease as staff is hired. Bimonthly magazine covering entertaining/lifestyles/recipes. "Named for B. Smith, African-American TV show host, *B. Smith Style* covers entertaining and lifestyle with an ethnic flair." Estab. 1999. Circ. 135,000. Pays on publication. Buys first North American serial rights. Editorial lead time 2 months. Accepts queries by mail, e-mail. Responds in 2 months. For sample copy call (877)339-0508 or on newsstand.

Nonfiction: General interest, how-to (cooking, entertaining, crafts), interview, profile, travel, recipes, book reviews. Query with published clips. Length: 1,000-1,500 words. **Pays $1,000-1,500.**

N $ $BBW, Real Women, Real Beauty, Aeon Publishing Group, Inc., P.O. Box 1297, Elk Grove CA 95759-1297. Fax: (916)684-7628. E-mail: sesmith@bbwmagazine.com. Website: www.bbwmagazine.com. **Contact:** Sally E. Smith, editor-in-chief. **50% freelance written.** Bimonthly magazine covering fashion and lifestyle for women size 16+. "*BBW* strives to inspire women all sizes of large to celebrate their beauty and enrich their lives by providing them with affirming information and resources in the areas of fashion and beauty, health and well-being, entertainment and romance, and work and leisure." Estab. 1979. Circ. 100,000. Pays on publication. Publishes ms an average of 2 months after acceptance. Byline given. Offers 20% kill fee. Buys all rights. Editorial lead time 4 months. Accepts queries by mail, e-mail, fax. Responds in 1 month. Sample copy for $5. Writer's guidelines for #10 SASE, online at website or by e-mail.

Nonfiction: Book excerpts, essays, exposé, general interest, how-to (beauty/style), humor, new product, opinion, photo feature, travel. "No first-person narratives, poetry, fiction." **Buys 18 mss/year.** Query with published clips. Length: 800-2,500 words. **Pays $125-500.**

Photos: State availability of photos with submission. Reviews contact sheets, negatives, 2¼×2¼ transparencies or slides. Offers no additional payment for photos accepted with ms. Captions and model releases required. Buys all rights.

Columns/Departments: Personal Best (improve well-being), 1,200 words; Careers (tools to manage/enhance careers), 1,500 words; Finance (increase financial security), 1,200 words; Perspectives (male perspective), 800 words; Last Word (humorous end page), 700 words; Destinations (travel within US), 1,200 words; Entertaining, 1,000 words. **Buys 30 mss/year.** Query with published clips. **Pays $125-250.**

Fillers: Anecdotes, facts (products, trends, style, fashion, reviews). **Buys 12/year.** Length: 100-200 words. **Pays $25.**

Tips: "Pitch specific articles/topics—2-3 sentences summarizing your proposed topic, and communicating how the piece will be written, i.e., interviews, sidebars, etc."

$ $ $BRIDAL GUIDE, Globe Communications Corp., 3 E. 54th St., 15th Floor, New York NY 10022. (212)838-7733. Fax: (212)308-7165. Editor-in-Chief: Diane Forden. **Contact:** Denise Schipani, executive editor; Laurie Bain Wilson, travel editor for travel features. **50% freelance written.** Prefers to work with experienced/published writers. Bimonthly magazine covering relationships, sexuality, fitness, wedding planning, psychology, finance, travel. **Pays on acceptance.** Responds in 3 months. Sample copy for $4.95 and SAE with 4 first-class stamps.

Nonfiction: Accepts queries by mail only, accompanied by published clips. "Please do not send queries concerning beauty and fashion, since we produce them in-house. We do not accept personal wedding essays, fiction, or poetry. Address travel queries to travel editor." All correspondence accompanied by an SASE will be answered (response time is within 3 months). **Buys 100 mss/year.** Length: 1,000-2,000 words. **Pays 50¢/word.**

● Ranked as one of the best markets for freelance writers in *Writer's Yearbook* magazine's annual "Top 100 Markets," January 2000.

Photos: Robin Zachary, art director; Catherine Diaz, associate art director. Photography and illustration submissions should be sent to the art department.

Columns/Departments: The only columns written by freelancers cover finance and wedding-planning issues. Welcome queries from men who are engaged or married for Groom with a View essay.

Tips: "We are looking for service-oriented, well-researched pieces that are journalistically written. Writers we work with use at least three expert sources, such as physicians, book authors, and business people in the appropriate field. Our tone is conversational yet authoritative. Features are also generally filled with real-life anecdotes. We also do features that are completely real-person based—such as roundtables of bridesmaids discussing their experiences, or grooms-to-be talking about their feelings about getting married. In queries, we are looking for a well thought-out idea, the specific angle of focus the writer intends to take, and the sources he or she intends to use. Queries should be brief and snappy—and titles should be supplied to give the editor an even better idea of the direction the writer is going in."

$ $ BRIDE AGAIN, The Only Magazine Designed for Second Time Brides, 1240 N. Jefferson Ave., Suite G, Anaheim CA 92807. (714)632-7000. Fax: (714)632-5405. E-mail: editor@brideagain.com. Website: www.brideagain. com. **Contact:** Beth Reed Ramirez, editor. Quarterly magazine for the encore bride. "*Bride Again* is targeted primarily to women ages 35-45 and secondarily to those 45 and over. They have been married at least once before, and most likely have children from a previous marriage or will be marrying someone with children. They have a career and income of over $45,000 per year, and are more mature and sophisticated than the 26-year-old first-time bride." Estab. 1997. Circ. 125,000. Pays on publication. Byline given. Buys all rights. Writer's guidelines for #10 SASE.

Nonfiction: How-to, humor, inspirational, interview/profile, personal experience. "Topics can be on, but not limited to: remarriage, blending families, becoming a stepmother, combining households, dealing with children in the wedding party, children—his, mine and ours; joint custody, dealing with difficult ex-spouses, real dresses for real women, legal aspects of remarriage, pre- and post-nuptial agreements, alternatives to the wedding veil, unusual wedding and/or honeymoon locations." Interfaith marriages; Handling extended step families; Having another child together. Send complete ms. Does not return mss. *No queries, please.* Length: 1,000 words. **Pays 35¢/word.**

Photos: Does not purchase photos.

Columns/Departments: Finances, Blending Families, Religion, Groom's Viewpoint, Unusual Honeymoon Locations, Beauty for Ages 30+/40+/50+, Remarriage, Fashion; all 800-1,000 words. Book reviews (on the feature topics listed above), 250 words. Send complete ms. **Pays 35¢/word.**

Tips: "All articles must be specific to encore brides."

$ $ $ $ CHATELAINE, 777 Bay St., #800, Toronto, Ontario M5W 1A7 Canada. (416)596-5000. Fax: (416)596-5516. E-mail: editors@chatelaine.com. Website: www.chatelaine.com. **Contact:** Caroline Connell, Managing Editor. Monthly magazine. "*Chatelaine* is edited for Canadian women ages 25-49, their changing attitudes and lifestyles. Key editorial ingredients include health, finance, social issues and trends, high profile personalities and politics, as well as fashion, beauty, food and home decor. Regular departments include Health pages, entertainment, Laugh Lines, How-to. **Pays on acceptance.** Byline given. Offers 25-100% kill fee. Buys first and electronic rights. Accepts queries by mail, e-mail, fax. Writer's guidelines for #10 SASE with postage.

○━ Break in with one-page columns or up-front items.

Nonfiction: Seeks "agenda-setting reports on national issues and trends as well as pieces on health, careers, personal finance and other facts of Canadian life." **Buys 50 mss/year.** Query with published clips. Length: 1,000-2,500 words. **Pays $1,000-2,500.** Pays expenses of writers on assignment.

Columns/Departments: Length: 500-1,000 words. Query with published clips. **Pays $500-750.**

■ The online magazine carries original content not found in the print edition. Contact: Pamela Chan, online editor.

N ✦ $ CINCINNATI WOMAN MAGAZINE, Niche Publishing and Media L.L.C., P.O. Box 8170, West Chester OH 45069-8170. Phone/fax: (513)851-8916. E-mail: alicia@cincinnatiwoman.com. **Contact:** Alicia Wiehe, co-publisher. Editor: Cathy Habes. **90% freelance written.** Monthly magazine covering women's issues and needs. "Dedicated exclusively to capturing the spirit of Cincinnati-area women, we are committed to providing our readers with information as well as inspiration. Estab. 1998. Circ. 35,000. Pays on publication. Publishes ms 4 months after acceptance. Byline given. Buys one-time rights. Editorial lead time 2 months. Submit seasonal material 3 months in advance. Accepts simultaneous submissions. Accepts queries by mail, e-mail, fax. Prefers e-mail. Responds in 2 weeks to queries. Sample copy for 8 × 10 SAE with 3 first-class stamps. Writer's guidelines for #10 SASE.

Nonfiction: Book excerpts, essays, general interest, how-to, humor, inspirational, interview/profile, new product, opinion, personal experience, photo feature, health/beauty. **Buys 50 mss/year.** Query with published clips or send complete ms. Length: 500-1,000 words. **Pays $80 max. for assigned articles; $30 max. for unsolicited articles.**

Reprints: Accepts previously published submissions. Send photocopy of article or typed ms with rights for sale noted and information about when and where the article previously appeared.

Photos: State availability of photos with submission. Reviews transparencies and 4 × 6 prints. Offers no additional payment for photos accepted with ms. Captions and identification of subjects required. Buys one-time rights.

Columns/Departments: Body Shop (health/beauty nuggets), 700 words; CWM Cooks (entertaining and recipes), 700 words; CWM Style (women's fashion), 700 words; CWM Travel, 700 words. **Buys 30 mss/year.** Query with published clips or send complete ms. **Pays $30.**

Fiction: Adventure, confession, horror, humorous, mainstream, mystery, religious, romance, slice-of-life vignettes. **Buys 20 mss/year.** Query with published clips or send complete ms. Length: 700-1,200 words. **Pays $30.**

Poetry: Avant-garde, free verse, light verse, traditional. **Buys 5 poems/year.** Submit maximum 3 poems. Length: 5-60 lines. **Pays $20.**

Fillers: Anecdotes, facts, newsbreaks, short humor. **Buys 5/year.** Length: 50-100 words. **Pays $15.**

Tips: "We're looking for material on 20-something, dating, fashion, first-time mom experiences, holistic health, cooking, short personal essays."

$ $COMPLETE WOMAN, For All The Women You Are, Associated Publications, Inc., 875 N. Michigan Ave., Suite 3434, Chicago IL 60611-1901. (312)266-8680. Editor: Bonnie L. Krueger. **Contact**: Lora Wintz, executive editor. **90% freelance written.** Bimonthly. "Manuscripts should be written for today's busy women, in a concise, clear format with useful information. Our readers want to know about the important things: sex, love, relationships, career and self-discovery. Examples of true-life anecdotes incorporated into articles work well for our readers, who are always interested in how other women are dealing with life's ups and downs." Estab. 1980. Circ. 350,000. Pays 45 days after acceptance. Publishes ms an average of 6 months after acceptance. Byline given. Buys first North American serial, second serial (reprint) or simultaneous rights. Editorial lead time 6 months. Submit seasonal material 5 months in advance. Accepts simultaneous submissions. Responds in 2 months. Writer's guidelines for #10 SASE.

　　○⊸ "Break in with writing samples that relate to the magazine. We need more relationship stories."

Nonfiction: Book excerpts, exposé (of interest to women), general interest, how-to (beauty/diet-related), humor, inspirational, interview/profile (celebrities), new product, personal experience, photo feature, sex, love and relationship advice. "We want self-help articles written for today's woman. Articles that address dating, romance, sexuality and relationships are an integral part of our editorial mix, as well as inspirational and motivational pieces." **Buys 60-100 mss/year.** Query with published clips, or send complete ms. Length: 800-2,000 words. **Pays $160-400.** Sometimes pays expenses of writers on assignment.

Reprints: Send tearsheet or photocopy of article or send typed ms with rights for sale noted and information about when and where the article previously appeared.

Photos: Photo features with little or no copy should be sent to Gail Mitchell. Send photos with submission. Reviews 2¼ or 35mm transparencies and 5×7 prints. Offers $35-100/photo. Captions, model releases, identification of subjects required. Buys one-time rights.

Tips: "Freelance writers should review publication, review writer's guidelines, then submit their articles for review. We're looking for new ways to explore the usual topics, written in a format that will be easy for our readers (24-40+ women) to understand. We also like sidebar information that readers can review quickly before or after reading the article. Our focus is relationship-driven, with an editorial blend of beauty, health and career."

$ $ $ $CONDÉ NAST BRIDE'S, Condé Nast, 4 Times Square, 6th Floor, New York NY 10036. (212)286-2518. Fax: (212)286-8331. E-mail: letters@brides.com. Managing Editor: Sally Kilbridge. Editor-in-Chief: Millie Martini-Bratten. **Contact:** Nancy Mattia, features editor. Bimonthly magazine for the first- and second-time bride, the groom and their families and friends. Circ. 400,000. **Pays on acceptance.** Byline given. Offers 25% kill fee. Buys all rights. Editorial lead time 8 months. Accepts simultaneous submissions. Responds in 2 months to queries. Writer's guidelines for #10 SASE.

Nonfiction: Topic (1) Personal essays on wedding planning, aspects of weddings or marriage. Length: 800 words. Written by brides, grooms, attendants, family members, friends in the first person. The writer's unique experience qualifies them to tell this story. (2) Articles on specific relationship and lifestyle issues. Length: 800 words. Select a specialized topic in the areas of relationships, religion, in-laws, second marriage, finances, careers, health, fitness, nutrition, sex, decorating, or entertaining. Written either by experts (attorneys, doctors, financial planners, marriage counselors, etc) or freelancers who interview and quote experts and real couples. (3) In-depth explorations of relationship and lifestyle issues. Length: 2,000-3,000 words. Well-researched articles on finances, health, sex, wedding and marriage trends. Should include statistics, quotes from experts and real couples, a resolution of the issues raised by each couple. **Buys 100 mss/year.** Query with published clips. Length: 2,000 words. **Pays 50¢-$1/word.** Pays expenses of writers on assignment.

　　● Ranked as one of the best markets for freelance writers in *Writer's Yearbook* magazine's annual "Top 100 Markets," January 2000.

Columns/Departments: Length: 750 words. **Buys 100 mss/year.** Query with published clips. **Pays 50¢-$1/word.**

Tips: "We look for good, helpful relationship pieces that will help a newlywed couple adjust to marriage. Wedding planning articles are usually written by experts or depend on a lot of interviews with experts. Writers must have a good idea of what we would and would not do: Read the 3 or 4 most current issues. What separates us from the competition is quality—writing, photographs, amount of information."

$COUNTRY WOMAN, Reiman Publications, P.O. Box 643, Milwaukee WI 53201. (414)423-0100. **Contact:** Kathy Pohl, executive editor. **75-85% written by readers.** Willing to work with new/unpublished writers. Bimonthly magazine. "*Country Woman* is for contemporary rural women of all ages and backgrounds and from all over the U.S. and Canada. It includes a sampling of the diversity that makes up rural women's lives—love of home, family, farm, ranch, community, hobbies, enduring values, humor, attaining new skills and appreciating present, past and future all within the context of the lifestyle that surrounds country living." Estab. 1970. **Pays on acceptance.** Byline given. Buys first North American serial, one-time and second serial (reprint) rights. Submit seasonal material 5 months in advance. Responds in 2 months to queries; 3 months to mss. Sample copy for $2. Writer's guidelines for #10 SASE.

Nonfiction: General interest, historical/nostalgic, how-to (crafts, community projects, decorative, antiquing, etc.), humor, inspirational, interview/profile, personal experience, photo/feature packages profiling interesting country women—all pertaining to a rural woman's interest. Articles must be written in a positive, light and entertaining manner. Query. Length: 1,000 words maximum. **Pays $35-150.**

Reprints: Send typed ms with rights for sale noted and information about when and where the material previously appeared. Payment varies.

Photos: Send color photos with query or ms. Reviews 35mm or 2¼ transparencies or excellent-quality color prints. Uses only excellent quality color photos. No b&w. "We pay for photo/feature packages." Captions, model releases and identification of subjects required. Buys one-time rights.

Columns/Departments: Why Farm Wives Age Fast (humor), I Remember When (nostalgia) and Country Decorating. **Buys 10-12 mss/year** (maximum). Query or send complete ms. Length: 500-1,000 words. **Pays $50-125.**

Fiction: Main character *must* be a country woman. All fiction must have a country setting. Fiction must have a positive, upbeat message. Includes fiction in every issue. Would buy more fiction if stories suitable for our audience were sent our way. Send complete ms. Length: 750-1,000 words. **Pays $90-125.**

Poetry: Traditional, light verse. "Poetry must have rhythm and rhyme! It must be country-related, positive and upbeat. Always looking for seasonal poetry." **Buys 6-12/year.** Submit 6 poems maximum. Length: 4-24 lines. **Pays $10-25.**

Tips: "We have broadened our focus to include 'country' women, not just women on farms and ranches but also women who live in a small town or country home and/or simply have an interest in country-oriented topics. This allows freelancers a wider scope in material. Write as clearly and with as much zest and enthusiasm as possible. We love good quotes, supporting materials (names, places, etc.) and strong leads and closings. Readers relate strongly to where they live and the lifestyle they've chosen. They want to be informed and entertained, and that's just exactly why they subscribe. Readers are busy—not too busy to read—but when they do sit down, they want good writing, reliable information and something that feels like a reward. How-to, humor, personal experience and nostalgia are areas most open to freelancers. Profiles, to a certain degree, are also open. Be accurate and fresh in approach."

$ $ ESSENCE, 1500 Broadway, New York NY 10036. (212)642-0600. Fax: (212)921-5173. Website: www.essence. com. Publication Director: Susan L. Taylor. **Contact:** Monique Greenwood, editor-in-chief. Monthly. "*Essence* is the magazine for today's Black women. Edited for career-minded, sophisticated and independent achievers, *Essence's* editorial is dedicated to helping its readers attain their maximum potential in various lifestyles and roles. The editorial content includes career and educational opportunities; fashion and beauty; investing and money management; health and fitness; parenting; information on home decorating and food; travel; cultural reviews; fiction; and profiles of achievers and celebrities." Estab. 1970. Circ. 1 million. **Pays on acceptance.** Makes assignments on one-time serial rights basis. 3 month lead time. Pays 25% kill fee. Byline given. Submit seasonal material 6 months in advance. Accepts queries by mail, fax. Responds in 2 months. Sample copy for $3.25. Guidelines for #10 SASE.

Nonfiction: Buys 200 mss/year. Query only; word length will be given upon assignment. **Pays $500 minimum.** Also publishes novel and nonfiction book excerpts.

Reprints: Send tearsheet of article, information about when and where the article previously appeared. Pays 50% of the amount paid for an original article.

Photos: Jan de Chabert, creative director. State availability of photos with query. Pays $100 for b&w page; $300 for color page. Captions and model release required. "We particularly would like to see photographs for our travel section that feature Black travelers."

Columns/Departments: Query department editors: Lifestyle (food, lifestyle, travel, parenting, consumer information): Amy Barnett; Entertainment: Elayue Fluker; Health & Fitness: Tamara Jefferies. Query only, word length will be given upon assignment. **Pays $100 minimum.**

Fiction: Martha Southgate, editor. Publishes novel excerpts.

🔲 The online magazine carries original content not found in the print edition.

Tips: "Please note that *Essence* no longer accepts unsolicited mss for fiction, poetry or nonfiction, except for the Brothers, Windows, Back Talk and Interiors columns. So please only send query letters for nonfiction story ideas."

$ $ $ $ FAMILY CIRCLE MAGAZINE, Gruner & Jahr, 375 Lexington Ave., New York NY 10017-5514. (212)499-2000. Fax: (212)499-1987. E-mail: nclark@familycircle.com. Website: www.familycircle.com. Editor-in-Chief: Susan Ungaro. **Contact:** Nancy Clark, deputy editor. **80% freelance written.** Magazine published every 3 weeks. "We are a national women's service magazine which covers many stages of a woman's life, along with her everyday concerns about social, family and health issues. Estab. 1932. Circ. 5,000,000. Byline given. Offers 20% kill fee. Buys one-time rights or all rights. Editorial lead time 4 months. Submit seasonal material 4 months in advance. Responds in 2 months. Writer's guidelines for #10 SASE.

🔾 Break in with "Women Who Make A Difference." Send queries to Marilyn Balamaci, senior editor.

Nonfiction: Essays, humor, opinion, personal experience. Women's interest subjects such as family and personal relationships, children, physical and mental health, nutrition and self-improvement. "We look for well-written, well-reported stories told through interesting anecdotes and insightful writing. We want well-researched service journalism on all subjects." Special issues: Computers Made Easy (3 times/year). No fiction or poetry. **Buys 200 mss/year.** Query with SASE. "Query should stress the unique aspects of an article and expert sources; we want articles that will help our readers or make a difference in how they live." Length: 1,000-2,500 words. **Pays $1/word.** Pays expenses of writers on assignment.

● Ranked as one of the best markets for freelance writers in *Writer's Yearbook* magazine's annual "Top 100 Markets," January 2000.

Columns/Departments: Women Who Make a Difference (profiles of volunteers who have made a significant impact on their community), 1,500 words; Profiles in Courage/Love (dramatic narratives about women and families overcoming adversity), 2,000 words; Full Circle (opinion/point of view on current issue/topic of general interest to our readers), 750 words; Humor, 750 words. **Buys 200 mss/year.** Query with published clips and SASE. **Pays $1/word.**

Tips: "Query letters should be concise and to the point. Also, writers should keep close tabs on *Family Circle* and other women's magazines to avoid submitting recently run subject matter."

$ $ $ $ GOOD HOUSEKEEPING, Hearst Corp., 959 Eighth Ave., New York NY 10019. (212)649-2000. Fax: (212) 265-3307. Editor-in-Chief: Ellen Levine. **Contact:** Executive Editor. Prefers to work with published/established writers. Monthly magazine. "*Good Housekeeping* is edited for the 'New Traditionalist.' Articles which focus on food, fitness, beauty, and child care draw upon the resources of the Good Housekeeping Institute. Editorial includes human interest stories, articles that focus on social issues, money management, health news, travel, and 'The Better Way,' an 8-page hard-fact guide to better living." Circ. 5,000,000. **Pays on acceptance.** Buys first North American serial rights. Pays 25% kill fee. Byline given. Submit seasonal material 6 months in advance. Responds in 2 months. For sample copy, call (800)925-0485. Writer's guidelines for #10 SASE.
Nonfiction: Contact: Executive editor. Toni Hope, news director. Consumer, social issues, dramatic narrative, nutrition, work, relationships, psychology, trends. **Buys 4-6 mss/issue.** Query. Length: 1,500-2,500 words. **Pays $1,500+** on acceptance for full articles from new writers. **Pays $250-350** for local interest and travel pieces of 2,000 words. Pays expenses of writers on assignment.
  • Ranked as one of the best markets for freelance writers in *Writer's Yearbook* magazine's annual "Top 100 Markets," January 2000.
Photos: Gina Davis, art director. Gail Tolvanen, photo editor. Photos purchased on assignment mostly. Pays $100-350 for b&w; $200-400 for color photos. Query. Model releases required.
Columns/Departments: The Better Way, editor: Mary Kate Hogan (consumer advice, how-to, shopping strategies, money savers, health). Profiles editor: Kathy Powers (inspirational, activist or heroic women), 300-600 words. My Problem and How I Solved It, My Problem editor (as told-to format), 2,000 words. Query. **Pays $1/word** for items 300-600 words.
Fiction: Lee Quarfoot, fiction editor. Uses original short fiction and condensations of novels that can appear in one issue. Looks for reader identification. "We get 1,500 unsolicited mss/month. A freelancer's odds are overwhelming, but we do look at all submissions." Send complete mss. Manuscripts will not be returned. Responds only on acceptance. Length: 1,500 words (short-shorts); novel according to merit of material; average 5,000-word short stories. **Pays $1,000** minimum for fiction from new writers.
Tips: "Always send a SASE and clips. We prefer to see a query first. Do not send material on subjects already covered in-house by the Good Housekeeping Institute—these include food, beauty, needlework and crafts."

[N] $ GRACE, A Companion For Women on Their Spiritual Journey, Grace Press Inc., 301 S. Bedford St., #213, Madison WI 53703-3695. (608)294-9008. Fax: (608)294-9010. E-mail: gracemag1@aol.com. **Contact:** Norine Conroy, editor/publisher. **70% freelance written.** Bimonthly magazine covering women's spirituality. "*Grace* celebrates women's lives, empowers women's voices, and provides a forum to honor and exchange ideas that will enrich women's spiritual journeys. Also, *Grace* inspires women to seek the Divine within themselves and in relationship." Circ. 1,000. Pays on publication. Byline given. Offers 50% kill fee. Buys first North American serial rights. Editorial lead time 3 months. Accepts queries by mail, e-mail, fax, phone. Accepts simultaneous submissions. Responds in 1 month to queries; 2 months to mss. Sample copy and writer's guidelines free.
Nonfiction: Book excerpts, essays, general interest, humor, inspirational, interview/profile, personal experience, photo feature, spiritual. Call or write for upcoming issue focus. Upcoming themes include Love, Bodies, Abundance, Forgiveness, Truth. "Please do not send any articles of an evangelical nature, or personal witness material." **Buys 10 mss/year.** Query. Length: 1,500-3,000 words. **Pays $50 and up.** Sometimes pays expenses of writers on assignment.
Reprints: Accepts previously published submissions.
Photos: State availability of photos with submission. Reviews 4×5 transparencies. Negotiates payment individually. Model releases and identification of subjects required. Buys one-time rights.
Fiction: Adventure, ethnic, slice-of-life, spiritual. **Buys 15 mss/year.** Query with or without published clips. Length: 1,500-3,000 words. **Pays $50 and up.**
Poetry: Avant-garde, free verse, haiku, light verse, traditional. **Buys 5 poems/year.** Submit maximum 5 poems. **Pays $50 and up.**
Fillers: Anecdotes, facts, newsbreaks, short humor. **Buys 5/year.** Length: 50-300 words. **Pays $50 and up.**
Tips: "Since each issue of *Grace* explores a certain topic, focus your writing on a subject which best highlights your interest and gifts. Spirituality honors all religious traditions and your work should embrace women's quest for spirit in everyday life."

$ $ $ $ HARPER'S BAZAAR, The Hearst Corp., 1700 Broadway, New York, NY 10019. (212)903-5000. Publisher: Jeannette Chang. **Contact:** Barbara O'Dair, executive editor. "*Harper's Bazaar* is a monthly specialist magazine for women who love fashion and beauty, sophisticated women with exceptional taste. *Bazaar* offers ideas in fashion and beauty, and reports on issues and interests relevant to the lives of modern women." Estab. 1867. Circ. 711,000. Pays on publication. Byline given. Offers 25% kill fee. Buys worldwide rights. Responds in 2 months.
Nonfiction: Buys 36 mss/year. Query with published clips. Length: 2,000-3,000 words. Payment negotiable.
Columns/Departments: Length: 500-700 words. Payment negotiable.

$ $ INDIANAPOLIS WOMAN MAGAZINE, Weiss Communications, 6081 E. 82nd St., Suite 401, Indianapolis IN 46250. (317)585-5858. Fax: (317)585-5855. E-mail: dmullinix@indianapoliswoman.com. Website: www.indianapoli

swoman.com. Editor: Donna S. Mullinix. **Contact:** Tamara Aubuchon, managing editor. **65% freelance written.** Monthly regional women's magazine. "*Indianapolis Woman* aims to capture the spirit of Indianapolis-area women who are committed to maximizing their potential at home, in the community and in the workplace. *IW* strives to provide its readers with information as well as inspiration in a proactive arena." Estab. 1992. Circ. 53,000. Pays on publication. Publishes ms an average of 4 months after acceptance. Byline given. Buys first rights. Editorial lead time 5 months. Submit seasonal material 4 months in advance. Accepts simultaneous submissions. Responds in 3 weeks to queries; 1 month to mss. Sample copy online at website. Writer's guidelines for #10 SASE.

Nonfiction: General interest, how-to, inspirational, interview/profile. "No poetry, first-person accounts, book reviews, cooking reviews, historical pieces, humor, articles about a single organization, building or business." Query by mail only with published clips. Length: 2,500-3,000 words. **Pays $100-300.**

Photos: State availability of photos with submission. Offers no additional payment for photos accepted with ms. Identification of subjects required. Buys one-time rights.

Tips: "Send queries by mail only. Before submitting story ideas, writers are encouraged to read the magazine and understand its mission. In general, articles should focus on Central Indiana women who are making a difference—and current issues of special relevance to women in this area."

$ $ $ $ LADIES' HOME JOURNAL, Meredith Corporation, 125 Park Ave., 20th Floor, New York NY 10017-5516. (212)557-6600. Fax: (212)455-1313. Publishing Director/Editor-in-Chief: Myrna Blyth. **50% freelance written.** Monthly magazine focusing on issues of concern to women 30-45. They cover a broader range of news and political issues than many other women's magazines. "*Ladies' Home Journal* is for active, empowered women who are evolving in new directions. It addresses informational needs with highly focused features and articles on a variety of topics including beauty and fashion, food and nutrition, health and medicine, home decorating and design, parenting and self-help, personalities and current events." Circ. 5,000,000. **Pays on acceptance.** Offers 25% kill fee. Rights bought vary with submission. Accepts queries by mail. Responds to queries within 3 months with SASE. Writer's guidelines for #10 SASE, Attention: Writer's Guidelines on envelope.

Nonfiction: Submissions on the following subjects should be directed to the editor listed for each: investigative reports, news-related features, psychology/relationships/sex (Pam O'Brien, articles editor); medical/health (Elena Rover, health editor); celebrities/entertainment (Melina Gerosa, entertainment editor); travel stories (Karyn Dabaghian, associate editor). Query with published clips. Length: 2,000-3,000 words. **Pays $2,000-4,000.** Pays expenses of writers on assignment.

● Ranked as one of the best markets for freelancers in *Writer's Yearbook* magazine's annual "Top 100 Markets," January 2000.

Photos: State availability of photos with submission. Offers variable payment for photos accepted with ms. Captions, model releases and identification of subjects required. Rights bought vary with submission. (*LHJ* arranges for its own photography almost all the time.)

Columns/Departments: Query the following editor or box for column ideas. First Person (Karyn Dabaghian, associate editor). **Pays $750-2,000.**

Fiction: Shana Aborn, senior editor, books. Only short stories and novels submitted by an agent or publisher will be considered. **Buys 12 mss/year.** No poetry of any kind.

◫ The online magazine carries original content not found in the print edition. Contact: Carolyn Noyes, managing editor.

$ THE LINK & VISITOR, Baptist Women's Missionary Society of Ontario and Quebec, 414-195 The West Mall, Etobicoke, Ontario M9C 5K1 Canada. (416)622-8600. Fax: (416)695-0938. **Contact:** Interim Editor. **50% freelance written.** "Magazine published 9 times/year designed to help Baptist women grow their world, faith, relationships, creativity, and mission vision-evangelical, egalitarian, Canadian." Estab. 1878. Circ. 4,300. Pays on publication. Publishes ms 6 months after acceptance. Byline given. Buys one-time, second serial (reprint) or simultaneous rights and makes work-for-hire assignments. Editorial lead time 2 months. Submit seasonal material 3 months in advance. Accepts simultaneous submissions. Sample copy for 9 × 12 SAE with 2 first-class Canadian stamps. Writer's guidelines free.

Nonfiction: Inspirational, interview/profile, religious. "Articles must be Biblically literate. No easy answers, American mindset or U.S. focus, retelling of Bible stories, sermons." **Buys 30-35 mss/year.** Send complete ms. Length: 750-2,000 words. **Pays 5¢/word (Canadian).** Sometimes pays expenses of writers on assignment.

Photos: State availability of photos with submission. Reviews any prints. Offers no additional payment for photos accepted with ms. Captions required. Buys one-time rights.

Tips: "Canadian women writers preferred. Don't send little stories with a moral attached. Show some thought, research, depth of insight. We're looking for material on praise."

$ $ $ MADEMOISELLE, Condé Nast, 350 Madison Ave., New York NY 10017. (212)880-8800. **Contact:** Faye Haun, managing editor. **95% freelance written.** Prefers to work with published/established writers. Columns are written by contributing editors Monthly magazine for women age 18-31. "*Mademoiselle* is edited for a woman in her twenties. It focuses on the decade when she is starting out in life as an independent adult and experiencing being on her own for the first time. Editorial offers advice on fashion, beauty, relationships, work and self-discovery." Circ. 1,200,000. Buys first North American serial rights. **Pays on acceptance;** rates vary.

Nonfiction: Particular concentration on articles of interest to the intelligent young woman 18-31, including personal relationships, health, careers, trends, and current social problems. Send entertainment queries to Jeanie Pyun. Query with published clips and SASE. Length: 800-3,000 words. Rates vary.

Photos: Cindy Searight, creative director. Commissioned work assigned according to needs. Photos of fashion, beauty, travel. Payment ranges from no-charge to an agreed rate of payment per shot, job series or page rate. Buys all rights. Pays on publication for photos.

Tips: "We are looking for timely, well-researched manuscripts that address the particular needs of our readers."

⊠ $ $ $ $ McCALL'S, Gruner & Jahr, 375 Lexington Ave., New York NY 10017-5514. (212)499-2000. Fax: (212)499-1778. Editor: Sally Koslow. **Contact:** Emily Listfield, executive editor. **90% freelance written.** Monthly. "Our constantly evolving publication carefully and conscientiously serves the needs of the woman reader—concentrating on matters that directly affect her life and offering information and understanding on subjects of personal importance to her." Circ. 4,200,000. **Pays on acceptance.** Publishes ms an average of 6 months after acceptance. Offers 20% kill fee. Byline given. Buys exclusive or First North American rights. Responds in 2 months. Guidelines for SASE.

Nonfiction: The editors are seeking meaningful stories of personal experience, fresh slants for self-help and relationship pieces, and well-researched action-oriented articles and narratives dealing with social problems concerning readers. Topics must have broad appeal, but they must be approached in a fresh, new, you-haven't-read-this-elsewhere way. **Buys 200-300 mss/year,** many in the 1,500-2,000-word length. **Pays $1/word.** These are on subjects of interest to women: health, personal narratives, celebrity biographies and autobiographies, etc. Almost all features on food, fashion, beauty and decorating are staff-written. Sometimes pays expenses of writers on assignment.

● Ranked as one of the best markets for freelance writers in *Writer's Yearbook* magazine's annual "Top 100 Markets," January 2000.

Columns/Departments: Real Life (stories of women who have lived through or accomplished something extraordinary), 1,800 words; Inspirations (first-person stories of women who have changed their lives or accomplished a goal or dream—not stories about overcoming odds), 600 words; Couples (how to make marriages work better), 1,200 words; Consumer Watch (how to spend and save wisely, avoid scams and shop smarter), 600 words; Health Alert, 600 words; Medical Report, 2,000 words; Mind and Body, 1,800 words; Staying Fit, 1,200 words; Prime Time (special bimonthly section featuring articles on health, finance and self-help for readers over 50), 800-1,000 words; Mind & Body (psychological and emotional aspects of good health from overcoming fears to improving one's outlook on life), 1,200 words. Query. **Pays $1/word.**

▣ The online magazine carries original content not found in the print edition. Contact: Rachel Hager, online editor.

Tips: "Query first with clips (preferably from major national magazine). We're looking for amazine real-life stories involving babies. Articles about food, fashion, beauty, home decorating and travel are staff-written. Read our writer's guidelines and know the type of women we are looking to profile. Use the tone and format of our most recent issues as your guide. Address submissions to executive editor unless otherwise specified. We do make outside assignments for our department categories."

$ $ $ MODERN BRIDE, Primedia, 249 W. 17th St., New York NY 10011. (212)462-3472. Fax: (212)367-8342. Website: www.modernbride.com. Editor: Stacy Morrison. **Contact:** Antonia VanderMeer, editor. "*Modern Bride* is designed as the bride-to-be's guide to planning her wedding, honeymoon, and first home or apartment. Issues cover: (1) bridal fashion (including attendants and mother-of-the-bride), travel trousseau and lingerie; (2) home furnishings (tableware, furniture, linens, appliances, housewares, coverings, accessories, etc.); (3) honeymoon travel (covering the United States, Canada, Mexico, the Bahamas, the Caribbean, Europe and Asia). Additional regular features include personal and beauty care, wedding gifts, etiquette, marital relations, financial advice, and shopping information." Estab. 1949. Circ. 406,000. Byline given. **Pays on acceptance.** Offers 25% kill fee. Publishes ms 6 months after acceptance. Editorial lead time 6 months. Buys first periodical rights. Responds in 6 weeks.

Nonfiction: Book excerpts, general interest, how-to, personal experience. **Buys 60 mss/year.** Query with published clips. Length: 500-2,000 words. **Pays $600-1,200.**

Reprints: Send tearsheet of article or short story. Pays 50% of amount paid for an original article.

Columns/Departments: Contact: Geri Bain, editor for travel. Voices and On His Mind (personal experiences of bride and groom).

▣ The online magazine carries original content not found in the print edition. Contact: Nancy Davis, online editor.

⊠ $ $ MORE MAGAZINE, Meredith Corp. (Ladies Home Journal), 125 Park Ave., New York NY 10017. Fax: (212)455-1433. **Contact:** Stephanie Woodard, articles editor. Editor-in-Chief: Myrna Blyth. **90% freelance written.** Bimonthly consumer magazine covering smart, sophisticated 40+ women. Estab. 1998. Circ. 525,000. **Pays on acceptance.** Publishes ms an average of 3 months after acceptance. Byline given. Offers 25% kill fee. Buys first North American serial, first, all rights. Editorial lead time 4 months. Submit seasonal material 6 months in advance. Accepts simultaneous submissions. Accepts queries by mail, e-mail, fax. Responds in 3 months. Guidelines for #10 SASE.

Nonfiction: Essays, exposé, general interest, interview/profile, personal experience, travel. **Buys 50 mss/year.** Query with published clips. Length: 300-3,000 words. Payment depending on writer/story length. Pays expenses of writers on assignment.

● Ranked as one of the best markets for freelance writers in *Writer's Yearbook* magazine's annual "Top 100 Markets," January 2000.

Photos: State availability of photos with submission. Negotiates payment individually. Captions, model releases and identification of subjects required.

Columns/Departments: Buys 20 mss/year. Query with published clips. **Pays $300.**

▣ The online magazine carries content from the print edition. Contact: Eve Golden, copy editor.

N ☆ $ MOXIE MAGAZINE, For the Woman Who Dares, 1230 Glen Ave., Berkeley CA 94708. (510)540-5510. E-mail: emily@moxiemag.com. Website: www.moxiemag.com. **Contact:** Emily Hancock, editor. **95% freelance written.** Quarterly magazine covering women who are putting together lives that work. "*Moxie* is filled with positive, upbeat, first-person accounts aimed at women who do not need a quiz to figure out what to do in bed. *Moxie* provides vibrant, often feisty examples of real women doing real things in the real world." Estab. 1998. Circ. 10,000. Pays on publication. Publishes ms an average of 3 months after acceptance. Byline given. Buys one-time, second serial (reprint), simultaneous rights and makes work-for-hire assignments. Editorial lead time 3 months. Submit seasonal material 3 months in advance. Accepts queries by e-mail only. Accepts simultaneous submissions. Responds in 2 weeks to queries; 2 months to mss. Sample copy for $5. Writer's guidelines for #10 SASE, online at website or by e-mail.

Nonfiction: Book excerpts, essays, exposé, interview/profile, opinion, personal experience, photo feature. Interested in seeing feminist theory woven into first-person stories. No " 'confessional', whining or poor-me articles." **Buys 50 mss/year.** Send complete ms. Length: 800-4,000 words. **Pays $25-50.** Sometimes pays expenses of writers on assignment.

Reprints: Accepts previously published submissions.

Photos: State availability of photos with submission. Reviews contact sheets and prints. Offers no additional payment for photos accepted with ms. Offers $25-50/photo. Negotiates payment individually. Model releases and identification of subjects required. Rights belong to photographer.

Columns/Departments: News Flash (news items of pressing interest to women in their 20s and 30s); Maverick Women (women who stand out—historical and contemporary). **Buys 4-6 mss/year.** Query. **Pays $25-50.**

Fiction: Adventure, ethnic, humorous, slice-of-life vignettes. No erotic, fantasy, confessional, mystery, horror, historical, sci-fi, suspense. **Buys 4-8 mss/year.** Send complete ms. Length: 800-4,000 words. **Pays $25-50.**

Poetry: Avant-garde, free verse, haiku, light verse, traditional. **Buys 4-6 poems/year.** Submit maximum 4 poems. Length: 10-50 lines. **Pays $25-50.**

Fillers: Anecdotes, facts, newsbreaks, short humor. **Buys 12/year.** Length: 15-100 words. **Pays $10.**

▣ The online magazine carries original content not found in the print edition and includes writer's guidelines.

Tips: "E-mail submissions please."

☆ $ $ $ $ MS. MAGAZINE, Liberty Media for Women, UC, 20 Exchange Place, 22nd Floor, New York NY 10005. (212)509-2092. Fax: (212)509-2407. E-mail: info@msmagazine.com. Website: www.msmagazine.com. Editor-in-Chief: Marcia Gillespie. Executive Editors: Barbara Findlen, Gloria Jacobs. **Contact:** Manuscripts Editor. **85% freelance written.** Bimonthly magazine on women's issues and news. Estab. 1972. Circ. 200,000. Byline given. Offers 20% kill fee. Buys first North American serial rights. Responds in 2 months. Sample copy for $9. Guidelines for #10 SASE.

● At press time, *Ms.* had just returned after a 6-month hiatus in publication. New publisher Fayne Erickson has plans for changes to the publication—be sure to request updated guidelines before submitting.

Nonfiction: International and national (US) news, the arts, books, popular culture, feminist theory and scholarship, ecofeminism, women's health, spirituality, political and economic affairs. Photo essays. **Buys 4-5 features** (3,000 words) and **4-5 short pieces** (500 words)/year. **Pays $1/word.** Query with published clips. Length: 300-3,000 words. Pays expenses of writers on assignment.

Reprints: Send tearsheets of article or typed ms with rights for sale noted and information about when and where the article previously appeared. Pays 50% of amount paid for an original article.

Photos: State availability of photos with submission. Model releases and identification of subjects required. Buys one-time rights.

Columns/Departments: **Buys 4-5 mss/year.** Length: up to 3,000 words. **Pays $1/word.**

Tips: Needs "international and national women's news, investigative reporting, personal narratives, humor, world-class fiction and poetry, and prize-winning journalists and feminist thinkers."

☆ $ $ GRACE ORMONDE WEDDING STYLE, Elegant Publishing Inc., P.O. Box 89, Barrington RI 02806. (401)245-9726. Fax: (401)245-5371. E-mail: yanni@bridalpromotions.com. Website: www.Bridalpromotions.com. Editor: Grace Ormonde. **Contact:** Yannis Tzoumas, editorial director/publisher. **90% freelance written**. Annual magazine covering wedding and special event planning resource. "*Grace Ormonde Wedding Style* is a wedding and special event planning magazine with editorial covering home and home decorating, women's health issues, cooking, beauty and travel." Estab. 1997. Circ. 60,000. Pays on publication. Publishes ms 4 months after acceptance. Accepts queries by mail, e-mail, fax.

Nonfiction: General interest, how-to, interview/profile, personal experience, travel. **Buys 35 mss/year.** Query. Length: 300-3,500 words. **Pays $100-300.** Sometimes pays expenses of writers on assignment.

Photos: State availability of photos with submission. Reviews transparencies. Negotiates payment individually.

Columns/Departments: Wedding related (flowers, beauty, etc.), 450 words, **buys 25 mss**; Women's Health, 3,000 words, **buys 1 ms**; Home Decorating/Cooking, 400 words, **buys 5 mss**; Travel, 350 words, **buys 3 mss**. Query. **Pays $100-300.**

Poetry: Avant-garde, free verse, light verse, traditional. **Buys 10 poems/year.** Length: 4-28 lines. **Pays $50-100.**

Fillers: Anecdotes, facts.

Tips: "Be well informed about the wedding planning industry. Most editorial is a 'how-to.' In a constantly changing industry with new styles, techniques, etc. it is important for the writer to keep up to date with trends, ideas, etc."

insider report

Emily Hancock: Real women reading, real women writing

There is no denying the market for women's magazines is expansive—bookstores and magazine stands are forever stocked with a heavy supply. But to the eye of Emily Hancock, most of those magazines do not reflect what she calls "real women." The founder, publisher, and editor of *Moxie*, Hancock started the magazine out of a concern about the media's negative effect on young women's self-esteem. She has succeeded in creating a publication far different from typical women's magazines, that tend to be filled with tips on how to lose weight, bake a cake, get a man and buy the perfect lipstick.

© Art Bacon

Emily Hancock

Based in Berkeley, California, *Moxie* is distributed nationally and in Canada. *Moxie* is also accessible worldwide as an online magazine that tallies some thirty-thousand visits each month. The magazine is 95 percent freelance written, and welcomes previously unpublished writers. From an article on inspirational female super heroes to a lesson on how to write a successful résumé, *Moxie* encourages women to be both adventurous and responsible. First-person narratives are a vital ingredient in the magazine, allowing women to share their life experiences with others. In Hancock's words, "*Moxie* is simply providing a resource for women who are putting together lives that work, women who want to learn about other women's lives in the process."

WHAT WOMEN WANT

Hancock's interest in women's issues prompted her to pursue a doctorate in human development at Harvard, where she wrote her dissertation on women's development. In narratives collected for her doctoral dissertation, Hancock found that women pointed to age nine as "a very strong age in girlhood that had a lot to do with who they became as women." After that age, Hancock's subjects showed a downward plunge in their self-esteem.

This study became the premise for her book, *The Girl Within* (Fawcett Columbine, 1990), now in its tenth printing. In this book, Hancock studies the loss of confidence that most women suffer when their surrounding culture pressures them to change from girls with agency into women who fit into an idealized mold. "Self-confidence yields to self-consciousness," Hancock writes, "as a girl judges herself as others judge her—against an impossible feminine ideal. To match that ideal, she must stash away a great many parts of herself. She gives up being childlike in order to be ladylike. She loses her self-possession." *The Girl Within* calls for a woman to remember the confident girl she used to be, and to reclaim that girl's strong sense of identity.

After writing *The Girl Within*, Hancock performed further research on college women. It was in these interviews that Hancock found "how dependent they were on the media to figure out how to make a life that works, but all they were getting was how to play into the hands of a man." Hancock also discovered many of the college women she interviewed could picture where they wanted to be ten years down the road, but had a blank space in their imaginations between graduation and age thirty. In mainstream women's magazines, they were not finding the material and encouragement they needed to start building their lives as independent women.

From her findings it became obvious to Hancock that women needed more in a magazine than fashion, sex and beauty. Unfortunately, not everyone was receptive to her idea to start a magazine written for and by strong young women. One publishing executive responded to her proposal, she says, with the comment, "It's a magazine the world needs, but not a magazine the world wants."

Dissatisfied with this response and unwilling to give up, Hancock established *Moxie* on the Internet, asking in an online survey what women wanted in a magazine. Thousands of responses told her that women did need and want a new type of magazine—one about "real women doing real things in the real world." So that is exactly what she gave them.

WHAT *MOXIE* WANTS

Moxie's website (www.moxiemag.com) gives potential writers a good idea of the type of material the magazine wants to publish. *Moxie* seeks to address the interests of college-educated women and recent graduates, covering everything from careers to friends, and from sexuality to multiculturalism, with travel, technology and sports thrown in for good measure. Anything is game, especially the topics that make most national magazines shy away.

When asked what freelance writers should know before querying, Hancock says, "Potential writers should know that we follow the first-person format, although we are not at all opposed to essays. Writers need to know we have themed issues, and that it's important to avoid shameless self-promotion, something that's very easy to fall into if you're writing a first-person account."

Unlike some other contemporary feminist magazines, Hancock says, "We don't focus on ordeals. We think people have had enough of ordeals. We want to focus on women's strengths and reflect them, mirror them." Even if a serious subject is addressed in a piece of writing, Hancock likes writers to stay "upbeat and positive."

What makes *Moxie* nontraditional is the position from which the topics it includes are approached. In *Moxie's* issue on identity, for example, traditional women's topics are addressed in a more personal way: a short story about breast cancer details one woman's emotional healing after a mastectomy; a professional woman writes about the anxiety and joy that her unplanned pregnancy has brought her; and an interview with a sex therapist who practices in Cairo sheds light on the courage it takes to practice her profession in an area of the world where discussion of sex is taboo.

The same personal angle can be found in *Moxie's* companion online magazine, which also has a quarterly theme. Although both versions of the magazine deal with the same topics, there is no overlapping material between the two. *Moxie's* online magazine "probably reaches a different audience," Hancock says. "And of course the articles are shorter. You're not going to put a 4,000-word article on the website."

Moxie's printed and online magazines are part of a rapidly growing market that portrays real people rather than idealized prototypes. Hancock explains: "It's not just our magazine. You see it in other magazines, in advertising on the radio, TV, and also in print. We're part of that, and we're also part of a new force in media that includes other alternative magazines starting for women, like *Bitch, Bust, Skirt!* and *Fabula.* We're all in this together, trying to make a forum for a voice that can be heard."

Although the magazine's writers are as diverse as its readers, Hancock does ask the same question of every manuscript: "The main criterion we have for whether we accept a piece is 'will this article matter to women who are putting together lives that work?' That matters more than whether it's air-brushed writing, glossy or flippant, or written according to a style you learn in a class."

The life affirming and self-esteem strengthening mood of the magazine distinguishes *Moxie* from other publications for women, and so does the type of writing it features. "I think that's what sets *Moxie* apart," Hancock says, "That, and the fact that we publish so many profiles, fiction, and poetry. Those forms have very few venues." In order to reach *Moxie*'s audience of "real women," writers should know that far more important than following a formula is writing from the heart. This is what makes the writing appearing in *Moxie* simultaneously professional and personal.

—*Clara Ellertson*

✖ $ RADIANCE, The Magazine for Large Women, Box 30246, Oakland CA 94604. (510)482-0680. Fax: (510)482-1576. E-mail: alice@radiancemagazine.com. Website: www.radiancemagazine.com. Editor: Alice Ansfield. **95% freelance written.** Quarterly magazine "that encourages and supports *all* sizes of large to live fully now, to stop putting their lives on hold until they lose weight." Estab. 1984. Circ. 15,000. Pays on publication. Publishes ms an average of 30 months after acceptance. Byline given. Offers $25 kill fee. Buys one-time and second serial (reprint) rights. Submit seasonal material at least 1 year in advance. Accepts previously published submissions. Responds in 4 months. Sample copy for $3.50. Writer's guidelines for #10 SASE and on website.

● *Radiance* welcomes participation in their new Kids Project! They've expanded to include essays from girls and boys about *their* lives, specifically on issues of body size, self-esteem, self-acceptance, and will provide information for those who work with (or parent) kids on how to raise children to feel seen, loved, and valued for the person they are.

Nonfiction: Book excerpts (related to large women), essays, exposé, general interest, historical/nostalgic, how-to (on health/well-being/fashion/fitness, etc.), humor, inspirational, interview/profile, opinion, personal experience, photo feature, travel. "No diet successes or articles condemning people for being fat." Query with published clips. Length: 1,000-2,500 words. **Pays $35-100** and contributor copy.

Photos: State availability of photos with submission. Offers $15-50/photo. Captions and identification of subjects preferred. Buys one-time rights.

Columns/Departments: Up Front and Personal (personal profiles of women from all areas of life); Health and Well-Being (physical/emotional well-being, self care, research); Expressions (features on artists who celebrate the full female figure); Images (designer interviews, color/style/fashion, features); Inner Journeys (spirituality, personal experiences, interviews); Perspectives (cultural and political aspects of being in a larger body); On the Move (women active in all kinds of sports, physical activities); Young Activists (bringing size awareness and esteem to the younger generation); Getaways (vacation spots and world travel, with tips specifically for people of size); Women and Mid-Life, Aging (articles on all important passages in a woman's life); Book reviews (nonfiction and fiction, related to size issue). **Buys 60 mss/year.** Query with published clips. Length: 1,000-3,500 words. **Pays $50-100; book reviews $35-75.**

Fiction: Condensed novels, ethnic, fantasy, historical, humorous, mainstream, novel excerpts, romance, science fiction, serialized novels, slice-of-life vignettes relating somehow to large women. "No woman-hates-self-till-meets-man-type fiction!" **Buys 15 mss/year.** Query with published clips. Length: 800-2,500 words. **Pays $35-100.**

Poetry: Reflective, empowering, experiential. Related to women's feelings and experience, re: their bodies, self-esteem, acceptance. "We want well-crafted poems; prefer unrhymed; not preachy poetry." **Buys 30 poems/year.** Length: 4-45 lines. **Pays $10-15.**

Tips: "We welcome talented, sensitive, responsible, open-minded writers. We profile women from all walks of life who are all sizes of large, of all ages and from all ethnic groups and lifestyles. We welcome writers' ideas on interesting large women the world over. We're an open, size-positive magazine that documents and celebrates body acceptance. *Radiance* is one of the major forces working for size acceptance. We want articles to address all areas of vital importance in women's lives. Please read a copy of *Radiance* before writing for us."

Ⓝ ✖ REAL YOU, Redwood Custom Communications, 65 Front St. E, 2nd Floor, Toronto, Ontario M5R 1L9 Canada. (416)360-7339. Fax: (416)360-8846. E-mail: erin@redwood-cmp.com. **Contact:** Erin McLaughlin, senior editor, features. **80% freelance written.** Covers fashion, women's lifestyles. "*Real You* is a magazine for real women with real lives and real issues. It's inspirational, approachable, fun, readable and solutions oriented." Estab. 2000. Circ. 4 million. Publishes ms an average of 1 year after acceptance. Offers 25-50% kill fee. Buys 6 month world-wide license. Editorial lead time 6 months. Submit seasonal material 6 months. Responds in 1 month to queries; 4 months to mss. Sample copy free.

Nonfiction: "No fiction." **Buys 60 mss/year.** Length: 1,200-2,100 words. **Pay varies.**

Tips: "Writing must be upbeat, sophisticated, intelligent, and entertaining. People who submit ideas should really know our market well."

N $ $ $ REDBOOK MAGAZINE, 224 W. 57th St., New York NY 10019. Senior Editor: Andrea Bauman. Book and Fiction Editor: Debra Birnbaum. **Contact:** Julia Dahl. **90% freelance written.** Monthly magazine. "*Redbook* addresses young married women between the ages of 25 and 44. Most of our readers are married with children 12 and under; over 60 percent work outside the home. The articles entertain, educate and inspire our readers to confront challenging issues. Each article must be timely and relevant to *Redbook* readers' lives." Estab. 1903. Circ. 3,200,000. **Pays on acceptance.** Publishes ms an average of 6 months after acceptance. Rights purchased vary with author and material. Responds in 3 months. Writer's guidelines for #10 SASE.

Nonfiction: Contact: Articles Department. Subjects of interest: social issues, parenting, sex, marriage, news profiles, true crime, dramatic narratives, money, psychology, health. Query with published clips. Length: articles, 2,500-3,000 words; short articles, 1,000-1,500 words. "Please review at least the past six issues of *Redbook* to better understand subject matter and treatment." Enclose SASE for response.

● Ranked as one of the best markets for freelance writers in *Writer's Yearbook* magazine's annual "Top 100 Markets," January 2000.

Fiction: Contact: Fiction Department. "Of the 20,000 unsolicited manuscripts that we receive annually, **we buy less than five.** We also find many more stories that are not necessarily suited to our needs but are good enough to warrant our encouraging the author to send others. *Redbook* looks for fresh, well-crafted stories that reflect some aspect of the experiences and interests of our readers; it's a good idea to read several issues to get a feel for what we buy. No unsolicited novels or novellas, please." **Payment begins at $1,000 for short stories.** Include SASE with all stories.

Tips: "Most *Redbook* articles require solid research, well-developed anecdotes from on-the-record sources, and fresh, insightful quotes from established experts in a field that pass our 'reality check' test."

$ $ $ $ SELF, 4 Times Square, 5th Floor, New York NY 10036. (212)286-2860. Fax: (212)286-8110. **Contact:** Dana Points, executive editor. Monthly magazine for women ages 20-45. "Self-confidence, self-assurance, and a healthy, happy lifestyle are pivotal to *Self* readers. This healthy lifestyle magazine delivers by addressing real-life issues from the inside out, with unparalleled energy and authority. From beauty, fitness, health and nutrition to personal style, finance, and happiness, the path to total well-being begins with *Self*." **Pays on acceptance.** Byline given on features and most short items. Buys one-time rights. Accepts simultaneous submissions. Responds in 1 month to queries. Writer's guidelines for #10 SASE.

Nonfiction: Considers proposals for major pieces on health, nutrition, psychology, fitness, family relationships and sociological issues. **Buys 40 mss/year.** Query with published clips. Length: 1,500-5,000 words. **Pays $1-2/word.**

Columns/Departments: Uses short, news-driven items on health, fitness, nutrition, money, jobs, love/sex, psychology and happiness, travel. Length: 300-1,000 words. **Buys 50 mss/year.** Query with published clips. **Pays $1-2/word.**

◾ The online version contains material not found in the print edition. Contact: Catherine Winters.

$ $ TODAY'S CHRISTIAN WOMAN, 465 Gundersen Dr., Carol Stream IL 60188-2498. (630)260-6200. Fax: (630)260-0114. E-mail: tcwedit@aol.com. Website: www.todayschristianwoman.net. Managing Editor: Jane Johnson Struck. Associate Editor: Camerin Courtney. **Contact:** Ginger McFarland, assistant editor. **25% freelance written.** Works with a small number of new/unpublished writers each year. Bimonthly magazine for Christian women of all ages, single and married, homemakers and career women. "*Today's Christian Woman* seeks to help women deal with the contemporary issues and hot topics that impact their lives, as well as provide depth, balance, and a biblical perspective to the relationships they grapple with daily in the following arenas: family, friendship, faith, marriage, single life, self, work, and health." Estab. 1979. Circ. 330,000. **Pays on acceptance.** Publishes ms an average of 6 months after acceptance. Byline given. Buys first rights only. Submit seasonal material 9 months in advance. Accepts queries by mail, e-mail, fax. Responds in 2 months. Sample copy for $5. Writer's guidelines for #10 SASE or on website.

Nonfiction: How-to, narrative, inspirational. *Practical* spiritual living articles, 1,500-1,800 words. Humor (light, first-person pieces that include some spiritual distinctive), 1,000-1,500 words. Issues (first-person, true-life stories that give a personal perspective on a current hot topic), 1,500-1,800 words. Query only; *no unsolicited mss*. "The query should include article summary, purpose and reader value, author's qualifications, suggested length, date to send and SASE for reply." **Pays 20-25¢/word.**

Columns/Departments: Faith @ Work (recent true story of how you shared your faith with someone on the job), 100-200 words. **Pays $25.** My Favorite Web Site (a short description of a web site you've found particularly helpful or interesting), 100 words. **Pays $25.** Readers' Picks (a short review of your current favorite CD or book, and why), 200 words. **Pays $25.** My Story (1st person, true-life dramatic story of how you solved a problem or overcame a difficult situation), 1,500-1,800 words. **Pays $300.** Small Talk (true humorous or inspirational anecdotes about children), 50-100 words. **Pays $25.** Does not return or acknowledge submissions to these departments.

Tips: "Articles should be practical and contain a distinct evangelical Christian perspective. While *TCW* adheres strictly to this underlying perspective in all its editorial content, articles should refrain from using language that assumes a reader's familiarity with Christian or church-oriented terminology. Bible quotes and references should be used selectively. All Bible quotes should be taken from the New International Version if possible. All articles should be highly anecdotal, personal in tone, and universal in appeal."

$ $ $ $ VOGUE, Condé Nast, 4 Times Square, New York NY 10036. (212)286-2600. E-mail: voguemail@aol.com. **Contact:** Laurie Jones, managing editor. Monthly magazine. "*Vogue* mirrors the changing roles and concerns of women, covering not only evolutions in fashion, beauty and style, but the important issues and ideas of the arts, health care, politics and world affairs." Estab. 1892. Circ. 1,136,000. **Pays on acceptance.** Byline sometimes given. Offers 25% kill fee. Responds in 3 months to queries. Writer's guidelines for #10 SASE.
Nonfiction: "Needs fresh voices on unexpected topics." **Buys 5 unsolicited mss/year.** Query with published clips. Length: 2,500 words maximum. **Pays $1-2/word.**
Tips: "Sophisticated, surprising and compelling writing a must." Please note: *Vogue* accepts *very* few unsolicited manuscripts. Most stories are generated in-house and are written by staff.

N $ $ WOMAN'S LIFE, A Publication of Woman's Life Insurance Society, 1338 Military St., P.O. Box 5020, Port Huron MI 48061-5020. (810)985-5191, ext. 181. Fax: (810)985-6970. E-mail: wkrabach@womanslifeins.com. Website: www.womanslifeins.com. Editor: Janice U. Whipple. **Contact:** Wendy L. Krabach, director of communications and fraternal services. **30% freelance written.** Works only with published/established writers. Quarterly magazine published for a primarily female-membership to help them care for themselves and their families. Estab. 1892. Circ. 32,000. Pays on publication. Publishes ms an average of 1 year after acceptance. Byline given. Not copyrighted. Buys one-time, simultaneous and second serial (reprint) rights. Submit seasonal material 6 months in advance. Accepts queries by mail, e-mail, fax. Accepts simultaneous submissions. Responds in 1 year (usually less). Sample copy for 9×12 SASE with 4 first-class stamps. Writer's guidelines for #10 SASE.
Nonfiction: Looking primarily for general interest stories for women aged 25-55 regarding physical, mental and emotional health and fitness; and financial/fiscal health and fitness. "We would like to see more creative financial pieces that are directed at women." **Buys 4-10 mss/year.** Send complete ms. Length: 1,000-2,000 words. **Pays $150-500.**
Reprints: Send tearsheet or photocopy of article or send typed ms with rights for sale noted and information about when and where ms previously appeared. Pays 15% of amount paid for an original article.
Photos: Only interested in photos included with ms. Model release and identification of subjects required.

$ $ $ WOMAN'S OWN, Harris Publications, Inc., 1115 Broadway, 8th Floor, New York NY 10010. (212)807-7100. Fax: (212)627-4678. E-mail: womansown@aol.com. Website: womansown.com. **Contact:** Lynn Varacalli, editor-in-chief. **40% freelance written.** Consumer magazine published 8 times a year. "Woman's Own is a self-improvement/lifestyle magazine for women 25-45. It is a service publication which offers advice, inspiration and tips on relationships, self esteem, beauty, health and jobs." Estab. 1993. Circ. 200,000. Pays on publication. Publishes ms an average of 2 months after acceptance. Bylines given. Offers 25% kill fee. Buys first North American serial rights, one-time rights, and second serial (reprint) rights. Editorial lead time 4 months. Submit seasonal material 5 months in advance. Accepts simultaneous submissions. Responds in 3 weeks to queries; 1 month to mss. Sample copy $4.00. Writer's guidelines for #10 SASE.
Nonfiction: Book excerpts, inspirational, interview/profile, personal experience, travel. No fiction, poetry, recipes or humor. **Buys 30 mss/year.** Query with published clips or send complete ms. Length: 900-2,000 words. **Pays $350-900 for assigned articles; $250 for unsolicited articles.** Pays expenses of writers on assignment.
Reprints: Accepts previously published submissions.
Photos: State availability of or send photo with submission. Reviews transparencies and prints. Negotiates payment individually. Captions, model releases required. Buys one-time rights.
Columns/Departments: Women Doing It Their Way (real women entrepreneurs or women who overcome obstacles to find success), 100-250 words; Money Matters (saving money, ideas, best ideas), 900-1,200 words. **Buys 10 mss/year.** Query with published clips or send complete ms. **Pays $200-400.**
Tips: "Be very specific, very narrowly focused about what you want to write about. Keep queries concise. Do not try to oversell an idea. If it's good, it'll sell itself."

$ $ $ WOMAN'S WORLD, The Woman's Weekly, Heinrich Bauer North America Inc., 270 Sylvan Ave., Englewood Cliffs NJ 07632. Fax: (201)569-3584. Editor-in-Chief: Stephanie Saible. **Contact:** Kathy Fitzpatrick. **95% freelance written.** Weekly magazine covering "human interest and service pieces of interest to family-oriented women across the nation. *Woman's World* is a women's service magazine. It offers a blend of Fashion, Food, Parenting, Beauty and Relationship features coupled with the true-life human interest stories." **Pays on acceptance.** Publishes ms an average of 4 months after acceptance. Buys first North American serial rights for 6 months. Submit seasonal material 4 months in advance. Responds in 6 weeks to queries; 2 months to mss. Writer's guidelines for #10 SASE.
Nonfiction: Dramatic personal women's stories and articles on self-improvement, medicine and health topics; **pays $500 for 1,000 words.** Features include Emergency (real life drama); My Story; Medical Miracle; Triumph; Courage; My Guardian Angel; Happy Ending (queries to Kathy Fitzpatrick). Also service stories on parenting, marriage, and work (queries to Irene Daria).

Fiction: Johnene Granger, fiction editor. Short story, romance and mainstream of 1,000 words and mini-mysteries of 1,000 words. "Each of our stories has a light romantic theme and can be written from either a masculine or feminine point of view. Women characters may be single, married or divorced. Plots must be fast moving with vivid dialogue and action. The problems and dilemmas inherent in them should be contemporary and realistic, handled with warmth and feeling. The stories must have a positive resolution." Not interested in science fiction, fantasy, historical romance or foreign locales. No explicit sex, graphic language or seamy settings. Specify "short story" on envelope. Always enclose SASE. Responds in 4 months. No phone queries. **Pays $1,000** for romances on acceptance for North American serial rights for 6 months. "The 1,000 word mini-mysteries may feature either a 'whodunnit' or 'howdunnit' theme. The mystery may revolve around anything from a theft to murder. However, we are not interested in sordid or grotesque crimes. Emphasis should be on intricacies of plot rather than gratuitous violence. The story must include a resolution that clearly states the villain is getting his or her come-uppance." Submit complete mss. Specify "mini mystery" on envelope. Enclose SASE. Stories slanted for a particular holiday should be sent at least 6 months in advance. No phone queries. **Pays $500.**

Tips: "Come up with good queries. Short queries are best. We have a strong emphasis on well-researched material. Writers must send research with ms including book references and phone numbers for double checking. The most frequent mistakes made by writers in completing an article for us are sloppy, incomplete research, not writing to the format, and not studying the magazine carefully enough beforehand."

N **$ $ WOMEN IN BUSINESS**, American Business Women's Association (The ABWA Company Inc.), 9100 Ward Pkwy. P.O. Box 8728, Kansas City MO 64114-0728. (816)361-6621. Fax: (816)361-4991. E-mail: abwa@abwahq. org. Editor: Rachel Warbington. **30% freelance written.** Bimonthly association magazine covering issues affecting working women. "How-to features for career women on business trends, small-business ownership, self-improvement and retirement issues. Profiles of ABWA members only." Estab. 1949. Circ. 90,000. **Pays on acceptance.** Publishes ms an average of 3 months after acceptance. Byline given. Buys first North American serial rights. Editorial lead time 3 months. Accepts queries by mail, e-mail, fax. Accepts simultaneous submissions. Responds in 3 weeks to queries; 2 months to mss. Sample copy for 9×12 SAE and 4 first-class stamps. Writer's guidelines for #10 SASE.

Nonfiction: How-to, interview/profile (ABWA members only), computer/Internet. No fiction or poetry. Buys 3% of submitted mss/year. Query. Length: 1,000-1,500 words. Pay varies.

Photos: State availability of photos with submission. Reviews 3×5 prints. Offers no additional payment for photos accepted with ms. Identification of subjects required. Buys all rights.

Columns/Departments: Life After Business (concerns of retired business women); It's Your Business (entrepreneurial advice for business owners); Career Smarts (career advice for every woman). Length: 315-700 words. Query. Pay varies.

Tips: "All articles must feature ABWA members as sources."

$ $ $ WORKING WOMAN, A Working Woman Network, Inc. Publication, 135 W. 50th St., 16th Floor, New York NY 10020. (212)445-6100. Fax:(212)445-6197. E-mail: editors@workingwoman.com. Website: www.workingwo man.com. Publisher: Jayne Young. Editor-in-Chief: Bernadette Grey. **Contact:** Articles Department. **80% freelance written.** Magazine published 10 times a year. "*Working Woman* reports on news, trends, information, people and ideas as they impact women in business. Professional/managerial women turn to *Working Women* as their key resource for managing the complexities of business today, from small business to the new corporate structure." Estab. 1978. Circ. 625,000. **Pays on acceptance.** Offers 25% kill fee. Buys all rights. Editorial lead time 5 months. Responds in 2 months. Guidelines for SASE or on website.

O— Break in with "our Fast Forward and Been There departments."

Nonfiction: Articles on all aspects of the career woman's professional life. "Our readers are managers, professionals and business owners at midcareer and up." **Buys 50 mss/year.** Query with published clips. Length: 2,000-3,000 words. Pay varies.

Columns/Departments: Length: 200-800 words. **Buys 70 mss/year.** Pay varies.

■ The online magazine carries original content not found in the print edition. Contact: Bernadette Grey.

Tips: "The Fast Forward section is the best entry point into the magazine. We welcome queries from experienced writers with mastery of the subject matter they wish to cover."

Trade, Technical & Professional Journals

Many writers who pick up a *Writer's Market* for the first time do so with the hope of selling an article or story to one of the popular, high-profile consumer magazines found on newsstands and in bookstores. Many of those writers are surprised to find an entire world of magazine publishing that exists outside the realm of commercial magazines and that they may have never known about—trade journals. Writers who *have* discovered trade journals have found a market that offers the chance to publish regularly in subject areas they find interesting, editors who are typically more accessible than their commercial counterparts and pay rates that rival those of the big-name magazines.

Trade journal is the general term for any publication focusing on a particular occupation or industry. Other terms used to describe the different types of trade publications are business, technical and professional journals. They are read by truck drivers, brick layers, farmers, fishermen, heart surgeons—let's not forget butchers, bakers, and candlestick makers—and just about everyone else working in a trade or profession. Trade periodicals are sharply angled to the specifics of the professions they report on. They offer business-related news, features and service articles that will foster their readers' professional development. A beautician reads *American Salon* to keep up with developments in hair care and cosmetics as well as business management. Readers of *Wine Business Monthly* find the latest news and information about viticulture.

Trade magazine editors tell us their readers are a knowledgeable and highly interested audience. Writers for trade magazines have to either possess knowledge about the field in question or be able to report it accurately from interviews with those who do. Writers who have or can develop a good grasp of a specialized body of knowledge will find trade magazine editors who are eager to hear from them. And since good writers with specialized knowledge are a somewhat rare commodity, trade editors tend, more than typical consumer magazine editors, to cultivate ongoing relationships with writers. If you can prove yourself as a writer who "delivers," you will be paid back with frequent assignments and regular paychecks.

An ideal way to begin your foray into trade journals is to write for those that report on your present profession. Whether you've been teaching dance, farming or working as a paralegal, begin by familiarizing yourself with the magazines that serve your occupation. After you've read enough issues to have a feel for the kinds of pieces they run, approach the editors with your own article ideas. If you don't have experience in a profession but can demonstrate an ability to understand (and write about) the intricacies and issues of a particular trade that interests you, editors will still be willing to hear from you.

Photographs help increase the value of most stories for trade journals. If you can provide photos, mention that in your query or send copies. Since selling photos with a story usually means a bigger paycheck, it is worth any freelancer's time to develop basic camera skills.

Query a trade journal as you would a consumer magazine. Most trade editors like to discuss an article with a writer first and will sometimes offer names of helpful sources. Mention any direct experience you may have in the industry in your cover letter. Send a resume and clips if they show you have some background or related experience in the subject area. Read each listing carefully for additional submission guidelines.

To stay abreast of new trade magazines starting up, watch for news in *Folio:* and *Advertising Age* magazines. Another source for information about trade publications is the *Business Publica-*

tion Advertising Source, published by Standard Rate and Data Service (SRDS) and available in most libraries. Designed primarily for people who buy ad space, the volume provides names and addresses of thousands of trade journals, listed by subject matter.

Information on trade publications listed in the previous edition of *Writer's Market* but not included in this edition can be found in the General Index.

ADVERTISING, MARKETING & PR

Trade journals for advertising executives, copywriters and marketing and public relations professionals are listed in this category. Those whose main focus is the advertising and marketing of specific products, such as home furnishings, are classified under individual product categories. Journals for sales personnel and general merchandisers can be found in the Selling & Merchandising category.

N **$ $ $ BRAND PACKAGING**, Independent Publishing Co., 210 S. Fifth St., St. Charles IL 60174. (630)377-0100. Fax: (630)377-1688. E-mail: jpeters@brandpackaging.com. Website: www.brandpackaging.com. **Contact:** James W. Peters, editor. Managing Editor: Lisa Joerin. **15% freelance written.** Bimonthly magazine about how packaging can be a marketing tool. "We publish strategies and tactics to make products stand out on the shelf. Our market is brand managers who are marketers but need to know something about packaging." Estab. 1997. Circ. 35,000. **Pays on acceptance.** Publishes ms an average of 2 months after acceptance. Byline given. Makes work-for-hire assignments. Editorial lead time 3 months. Accepts queries by mail, fax. Submit seasonal material 3 months in advance. Sample copy and writer's guidelines free.
Nonfiction: How-to, interview/profile, new product. **Buys 30 mss/year.** Send complete ms. Length: 600-2,400 words. **Pays $150-1,200.**
Photos: State availability of photos with submission. Reviews contact sheets, 35mm transparencies and 4×5 prints. Negotiates payment individually. Identification of subjects required. Buys one-time rights.
Columns/Departments: Whatever happened to . . . (packaging failures); New Technology (new packaging technology), both 600 words. **Buys 20 mss/year.** Query. **Pays $150-400.**
■ The online version of this publication contains material not found in the print edition.
Tips: "Be knowledgeable on marketing techniques and be able to grasp packaging techniques. Be sure you focus on packaging as a marketing tool. Use concrete examples. We are not seeking case histories at this time."

$ DECA DIMENSIONS, 1908 Association Dr., Reston VA 20191. (703)860-5000. Fax: (703)860-4013. E-mail: carol_lund@deca.org. Website: www.DECA.org. **Contact:** Carol Lund, editor. **30% freelance written.** Bimonthly magazine covering professional development, business, career training. "*Deca Dimensions* is the membership magazine for the Association of Marketing Students—primarily ages 16-20 in all 50 states and Canada. The magazine is delivered through the classroom. Students are interested in developing professional, leadership and career skills." Estab. 1947. Circ. 160,000. Pays on publication. Byline given. Buys first rights and second serial (reprint) rights. Editorial lead time 3 months. Submit seasonal material 4 months in advance. Accepts queries by mail, e-mail, fax, phone. Accepts simultaneous submissions. Sample copy free.
Nonfiction: Essays, general interest, how-to (get jobs, start business, plan for college, etc.), leadership development, interview/profile (business leads), personal experience (working). "Interested in seeing trends/forecast information of interest to audience (how do you forecast? why? What are the trends for the next 5 years in fashion or retail?" **Buys 10 mss/year.** Send complete ms. Length: 800-1,000 words. **Pays $125 for assigned articles; $100 for unsolicited articles.**
Reprints: Send photocopy of article and information about when and where the article previously appeared. Pays 85% of amount paid for an original article.
Photos: State availability of photos with submission. Reviews negatives, transparencies, prints. Offers $15-25/photo. Captions required. Buys one-time rights.
Columns/Departments: Professional Development, leadership. **Buys 6 mss/year.** Send complete ms. Length: 350-500 words. **Pays $75-100.**
Fillers: Anecdotes, facts, short humor. Length: 50-200 words. **Pays $25-50.**

N **MEDIA INC., Pacific Northwest Media, Marketing and Creative Services News**, P.O. Box 24365, Seattle WA 98124-0365. (206)382-9220. Fax: (206)382-9437. E-mail: media@media-inc.com. Website: www.media-inc.com. Publisher: James Baker. **Contact:** Betsy Model, executive editor. **70% freelance written.** Quarterly magazine covering Northwest media, advertising, marketing and creative-service industries. Audience is Northwest ad agencies, marketing professionals, media and creative-service professionals. Estab. 1987. Circ. 10,000. Byline given. Responds in 1 month. Sample copy for 9×12 SAE with 6 first-class stamps.

Tips: "It is best if writers live in the Pacific Northwest and can report on local news and events in Media Inc.'s areas of business coverage."

N $ $ SIGN BUILDER ILLUSTRATED, America's How-To Sign Magazine, Journalistic Inc., 4905 Pine Cone Dr., Suite 2, Durham NC 27707. (919)489-1916. Fax: (919)489-4767. E-mail: jeff@journalistic.com. Website: www.signshop.com. **Contact:** Jeff Wooten, editor. **40% freelance written.** Bimonthly trade magazine covering sign and graphic industry. *"Sign Builder Illustrated* targets sign professionals where they work: on the shop floor. Our topics cover the broadest spectrum of the sign industry, from design to fabrication, installation, maintenance and repair. Our readers own a similarly wide range of shops, including commercial, vinyl, sign erection and maintenance, electrical and neon, architectural, and awnings." Estab. 1974. Circ. 14,500. **Pays on acceptance.** Publishes ms an average of 3 months after acceptance. Byline given. Offers 25% kill fee. Buys all rights. Editorial lead time 3 months. Submit seasonal material 4 months in advance. Accepts queries by mail, e-mail, fax, phone. Accepts simultaneous submissions. Responds in 1 month. Sample copy, writer's guidelines free.
Nonfiction: Historic/nostalgic, how-to, humor, interview/profile, photo feature, technical. **Buys 50-60 mss/year.** Query. Length: 1,500-2,500 words. **Pays $250-550.** Sometimes pays expenses of writers on assignment.
Photos: Send photos with submission. Reviews 3×5 prints. Negotiates payment individually. Captions and identification of subjects required. Buys all rights.
Tips: "Be very knowledgeable about a portion of the sign industry you are coverint. We want our readers to come away from each article with at least one good idea, one new technique, or one more 'trick of the trade.' At the same time, we don't want a purely textbook listing of 'do this, do that.' Our readers enjoy *Sign Builder Illustrated* because the publication speaks to them in a clear and lively fashion, from one sign professional to another. We want to engage the reader who has been in the business for some time. While there might be a place for basic instruction in new techniques, our average paid subscriber has been in business over twenty years, employs over seven people, and averages of $800,000 in annual sales. These people aren't neophytes content with retread articles they can find anywhere. It's important for our writers to use anecdotes and examples drawn from the daily sign business. We also ask for at least one sidebar per feature article."

$ $ SIGNCRAFT, The Magazine for Today's Sign Maker, SignCraft Publishing Co., Inc., P.O. Box 60031, Fort Myers FL 33906. (941)939-4644. Fax: (941)939-0607. E-mail: signcraft@signcraft.com. Website: www.signcraft.com. **Contact:** Tom McIltrot, editor. **10% freelance written.** Bimonthly magazine of the sign industry. "Like any trade magazine, we need material of direct benefit to our readers. We can't afford space for material of marginal interest." Estab. 1980. Circ. 18,500. Pays on publication. Publishes ms an average of 6 months after acceptance. Byline given. Offers negotiable kill fee. Buys first North American serial or all rights. Accepts queries by mail, e-mail, fax. Responds in 1 month. Sample copy and writer's guidelines for $3.
Nonfiction: Interviews, profiles. "All articles should be directly related to quality commercial signs. If you are familiar with the sign trade, we'd like to hear from you." **Buys 10 mss/year.** Query with or without published clips. Length: 500-2,000 words. **Pays up to $350.**
Reprints: Accepts previously published submissions.

$ $ SIGNS OF THE TIMES, The Industry Journal Since 1906, ST Publications, Dept. WM, 407 Gilbert Ave., Cincinnati OH 45202-2285. (513)421-2050. Fax: (513)421-5144. E-mail: sconner@stpubs.com. Website: www.signweb. com. **Contact:** Susan Conner, managing editor. **15-30% freelance written.** Monthly magazine covering the sign and outdoor advertising industries. Estab. 1906. Circ. 17,000. Pays on publication. Publishes ms an average of 3 months after acceptance. Byline given. Buys variable rights. Accepts queries by mail, e-mail, fax, phone. Responds in 3 months. Sample copy and writer's guidelines for 9×12 SAE with 10 first-class stamps.
Nonfiction: Historical/nostalgic (regarding the sign industry); how-to (carved signs, goldleaf, etc.); interview/profile (focusing on either a signshop or a specific project); photo feature (query first); technical (sign engineering, etc.). Nothing "nonspecific on signs, an example being a photo essay on 'signs I've seen.' We are a trade journal with specific audience interests." **Buys 15-20 mss/year.** Query with clips. **Pays $150-500.**
Reprints: Send tearsheet of article or typed ms with rights for sale noted and information about when and where the article previously appeared. Payment is negotiated.
Photos: Send photos with ms. "Sign industry-related photos only. We sometimes accept photos with funny twists or misspellings."
   ▣ The online version contains material not found in the print edition.
Fillers: Open to queries; request rates.
Tips: "Be thoroughly familiar with the sign industry, especially in the CAS-related area. Have an insider's knowledge plus an insider's contacts."

ART, DESIGN & COLLECTIBLES

The businesses of art, art administration, architecture, environmental/package design and antiques/collectibles are covered in these listings. Art-related topics for the general public are located in the Consumer Art & Architecture category. Antiques and collectibles magazines for enthusiasts are listed in Consumer Hobby & Craft. (Listings of markets looking for freelance artists to do artwork can be found in *Artist's and Graphic Designer's Market*, Writer's Digest Books.)

$AIRBRUSH ACTION MAGAZINE, Airbrush Action, Inc., 1985 Swarthmore Ave., Lakewood NJ 08701. (732)364-2111. Fax: (732)367-5908. E-mail: cstieglitz@monmouth.com. Website: www.airbrushaction.com. **Contact:** Jennifer L. Bohanan, editor. **80% freelance written.** Bimonthly magazine covering the spectrum of airbrush applications: illustration, t-shirt airbrushing, fine art, automotive and sign painting, hobby/craft applications, wall murals, fingernails, body airbrushing, artist profiles, reviews and more. Estab. 1985. Circ. 60,000. Pays in 30 days. Publishes ms an average of 6 months after acceptance. Byline given. Offers 50% kill fee. Buys all rights. Editorial lead time 6 months. Submit seasonal material 6 months in advance. Accepts queries by mail, e-mail, fax, phone. Accepts simultaneous submissions. Sample copy and writer's guidelines free.
Nonfiction: How-to, humor, inspirational, interview/profile, new product, personal experience, technical. Nothing unrelated to airbrush. Query by mail with published clips. **Pays 10¢/word.** Sometimes pays expenses of writers on assignment.
Photos: Send photos with submission. Negotiates payment individually. Captions, model releases and identification of subjects required. Buys all rights.
Columns/Departments: Query with published clips.
    ◘ The online version contains material not found in the print edition. Contact: Cliff Stieglitz.
Tips: "Send bio and writing samples. Send well-written technical information pertaining to airbrush art. We publish a lot of artist profiles—they all sound the same. Looking for new pizzazz!"

N $ $ANTIQUEWEEK, Mayhill Publications Inc., P.O. Box 90, Knightstown IN 46148-0090. (765)345-5133. Fax: (800)695-8153. E-mail: antiquewk@aol.com. Website: www.antiqueweek.com. **Contact:** Tom Hoepf, central edition editor. Eastern Edition Editor: Connie Swaim. Genealogy Editor: Shirley Richardson. **80% freelance written.** Weekly tabloid on antiques, collectibles and genealogy with 2 editions: Eastern and Central. "*AntiqueWeek* has a wide range of readership from dealers and auctioneers to collectors, both advanced and novice. Our readers demand accurate information presented in an entertaining style." Estab. 1968. Circ. 64,000. Pays on publication. Byline given. Buys first and second serial (reprint) rights. Submit seasonal material 1 month in advance. Accepts queries by mail, e-mail, fax. Free sample copy. Writer's guidelines for #10 SASE.
Nonfiction: Historical/nostalgic, how-to, interview/profile, opinion, personal experience, antique show and auction reports, feature articles on particular types of antiques and collectibles. **Buys 400-500 mss/year.** Query with or without published clips, or send complete ms. Length: 1,000-2,000 words. **Pays $50-250.**
Reprints: Send typed ms with rights for sale noted and information about when and where the article previously appeared.
Photos: Send photos with submission. Identification of subjects required.
Columns/Departments: Insights (opinions on buying, selling and collecting antiques), 500-1,000 words; Your Ancestors (advice, information on locating sources for genealogists). **Buys 150 mss/year.** Query. Length: 500-1,500 words. **Pays $25-50.**
    ◘ The online magazine carries original content not found in the print edition. **Contact:** Connie Swaim, online editor.
Tips: "Writers should know their topics thoroughly. Feature articles must be well-researched and clearly written. An interview and profile article with a knowledgeable collector might be the break for a first-time contributor. We seek a balanced mix of information on traditional antiques and 20th century collectibles."

N $ $ $CRITIQUE MAGAZINE, The magazine of graphic design thinking, Neumeier Design Team, 120 Hawthorne Ave., Suite 102, Palo Alto CA 94301. Fax: (650)323-3298. E-mail: editor@critiquemag.com. Website: www.critiquemag.com. Editor: Marty Neumeier. **Contact:** Nancy E. Bernard, managing editor. **75% freelance written.** Quarterly magazine covering graphic design; best practices, ideas. "Other graphic design magazines publish profiles, portfolios, technical tips, or academic speculation. *Critique* cuts to the heart of graphic design: the thinking that goes into it. Articles cover concepting, aesthetics, management, etc." Estab. 1996. Circ. 10,000. Pays 30 days after publication. Publishes ms an average of 3 months after acceptance. Byline given. "We either cancel at first draft, or pay for completed ms, regardless of publication." Buys one-time rights. Editorial lead time 6 months. Accepts queries by mail, e-mail, fax. Responds in 1 week to queries; 1 month to mss. "Try to respond to all submissions within days of receipt." Writer's guidelines free online at website.
Nonfiction: Book excerpts, essays, historical/nostalgic, humor, interview. "No famous designer profiles; unsubstantiated opinions; self-promo or production tips. **Buys 24-30 mss/year.** Query with published clips or send complete ms. Length: 500-2,500 words. **Pays $250-1,250.** Pays writers with contributor copies or other premiums "when author initiates request." Sometimes pays expenses of writers on assignment.
Photos: State availability of photos with submission. Reviews transparencies and prints. Negotiates payment individually. Captions, model releases and identification of subjects required. Buys one-time rights.
Columns/Departments: "Columns are negotiated directly with writers, usually after writing several pieces and developing a relationship with the material and with the editors." Query with published clips or send complete ms.

Fillers: Facts, gags to be illustrated by cartoonist, short humor. **Buys variable number of mss/year.** Length: 250-700 words. **Pays $215-350.**

Tips: "Start by reading back issues and being familiar with other publications in graphic design. Then identify your area of best knowledge and greatest interest in the graphic design profession."

[N] **$ $ $ HOW, Design Ideas at Work**, F&W Publications, Inc., 1507 Dana Ave., Cincinnati OH 45207-1005. (513)531-2222. Fax: (513)531-2902. E-mail: editorial@howdesign.com. Website: www.howdesign.com. **Contact:** Bryn Mooth, editor. **75% freelance written.** Bimonthly graphic design and illustration business journal. "*HOW: Design Ideas at Work* strives to serve the business, technological and creative needs of graphic design professionals. The magazine provides a practical mix of essential business information, up-to-date technological tips, the creative whys and hows behind noteworthy projects, and profiles of professionals who are impacting design. The ultimate goal of *HOW* is to help designers, whether they work for a design firm or for an inhouse design department, run successful, creative, profitable studios." Estab. 1985. Circ. 38,000. **Pays on acceptance.** Byline given. Buys first North American serial rights. Responds in 6 weeks. Sample copy for cover price plus $1.50 (cover price varies per issue). Writer's guidelines for #10 SASE.

Nonfiction: Features: interview/profile, business tips, new products, environmental graphics, digital design, hot design markets. Special issues: Self-Promotion Annual (September/October); Business Annual (November/December); International Annual of Design (March/April); Creativity/Paper/Stock Photography (May/June); Digital Design Annual (July/August). No how-to articles for beginning artists or fine-art-oriented articles. **Buys 40 mss/year.** Query with published clips and samples of subject's work (artwork or design). Length: 1,500-2,000 words. **Pays $700-900.** Sometimes pays expenses of writers on assignment.

Photos: State availability of artwork with submission. Reviews 35mm or larger transparencies (dupes only) or digital files. Captions are required. Buys one-time rights.

Columns/Departments: Marketplace (focuses on lucrative fields for designers/illustrators); Production (ins, outs and tips on production); Interactivity (behind the scenes of electronically produced design projects); Software Review and Workspace (takes an inside look at the design of creatives' studios). Other columns include Web Workshop (examines the web-design process) and Bottomline (business issues that impact design studios). **Buys 35 mss/year.** Query with published clips. Length: 1,200-1,500 words. **Pays $250-400.**

Tips: "We look for writers who can recognize graphic designers on the cutting-edge of their industry, both creatively and business-wise. Writers must have an eye for detail, and be able to relay *HOW*'s step-by-step approach in an interesting, concise manner—without omitting any details. Showing you've done your homework on a subject—and that you can go beyond asking 'those same old questions'—will give you a big advantage."

[N] **$ INTERIOR BUSINESS MAGAZINE**, The Lawn & Landscape Media Group, 4012 Bridge Ave., Cleveland OH 44113. (800)456-0707. Fax: (216)961-0364. E-mail: bwest@lawnandlandscape.com. Website: www.interiorbusinessonline.com. Publisher: Cindy Cole. **Contact:** Bob West, editor. **5-10% freelance written.** Covers interior landscaping. "*Interior Business* addresses the concerns of the professional interior landscape contractor. It's devoted to the business management needs of interior landscape professionals." Estab. 2000. Circ. 6,000. Publishes ms an average of 3 months after acceptance. Editorial lead time 3 months. Submit seasonal material 5 months in advance. Responds in 1 week.

Nonfiction: Interior landscaping. "No articles oriented to the consumer or homeowner." **Buys 2 mss/year.** Length: 1,000-2,500 words. **Pays $250-500.**

Tips: "Know the audience. It's the professional business person, not the consumer."

$ $ LETTER ARTS REVIEW, P.O. Box 9986, Greensboro NC 27429. (336)272-6139. Fax: (336)272-9015. E-mail: info@JohnNealBooks.com. Website: www.letterarts.com. **Contact:** Karyn L. Gilman, editor. **98% freelance written.** Eager to work with new/unpublished writers with calligraphic expertise and language skills. Quarterly magazine on lettering and related book arts, both historical and contemporary in nature. Estab. 1982. Circ. 5,500. Pays on publication. Publishes ms an average of 9 months after acceptance. Byline given. Offers 20% kill fee. Buys first rights. Accepts queries by mail, e-mail, fax, phone. Responds in 3 months. Sample copy for 9 × 12 SAE with 8 first-class stamps. Writer's guidelines for SASE.

Nonfiction: Interview/profile, opinion, contemporary, historical. **Buys 50 mss/year.** Query with or without published clips, or send complete ms. Length: 1,000-2,000 words. **Pays $50-250 for assigned articles; $25-200 for unsolicited articles.** Sometimes pays the expenses of writers on assignment.

Photos: State availability of photos with submission. Reviews contact sheets, negatives, transparencies and prints. Pays agreed upon cost. Captions and identification of subjects required. Buys one-time rights.

Columns/Departments: Book Reviews, Viewpoint (critical), 500-1,500 words; Ms. (discussion of manuscripts in collections), 1,000-2,000 words; Profile (contemporary calligraphic figure), 1,000-2,000 words; exhibition reviews; font reviews. Query. **Pays $50-200.**

Tips: "*Letter Arts Review*'s primary objective is to encourage the exchange of ideas on calligraphy and the lettering arts—its past and present as well as trends for the future. Historical research, typography, graphic design, fine press and artists' books, and other related aspects of the lettering arts are welcomed. Third person is preferred, however first person will be considered if appropriate. Writer should realize that this is a specialized audience."

[N] **$ MANHATTAN ARTS INTERNATIONAL MAGAZINE**, Manhattan Arts International, 200 E. 72nd St., Suite 26L, New York NY 10021. (212)472-1660. Fax: (212)794-0324. E-mail: ManArts@aol.com. Website: ManhattanA rts.com. Editor-in-Chief: Renée Phillips. **Contact:** Michael Jason, managing editor. Bimonthly magazine covering fine art. Audience is comprised of art professionals, artists and collectors. Educational, informative, easy-to-read style, making art more accessible. Highly promotional of new artists. Estab. 1983. Circ. 50,000. Pays on publication. Publishes ms an average of 1 month after acceptance. Byline given. Makes work-for-hire assignments. Submit seasonal material 3 months in advance. Accepts simultaneous submissions. Accepts queries by mail, e-mail. Responds in 3 months. Sample copy for $5, payable to Manhattan Arts International (no postage or envelope required).

Nonfiction: Book excerpts (art), essays (art world), general interest (collecting art), inspirational (artists success stories), interview/profile (major art leaders), new product (art supplies), technical (art business). **Buys 30 mss/year.** New writers receive byline and promotion, art books. Sometimes pays expenses of writers on assignment.

Photos: Send photos with submission. Offers no additional payment for photos accepted with ms. Captions, model releases and identification of subjects required.

Tips: "A knowledge of the current, contemporary art scene is a must. We are not actively seeking new writers at this time."

AUTO & TRUCK

These publications are geared to automobile, motorcycle and truck dealers; professional truck drivers; service department personnel; or fleet operators. Publications for highway planners and traffic control experts are listed in the Government & Public Service category.

N $ AUTO & FLAT GLASS JOURNAL, Grawin Publications, Inc., 303 Harvard E., Suite 101, P.O. Box 12099, Seattle WA 98102-0099. (206)322-5120. **Contact:** Jeff Martin, editor. **10% freelance written.** Prefers to work with published/established writers. Monthly magazine for the auto glass replacement industry. Includes step-by-step glass replacement procedures for current model cars and business management, industry news and trends. Estab. 1953. Circ. 5,700. **Pays on acceptance.** Publishes ms an average of 5 months after acceptance. No byline given. Buys all rights. Responds in 5 months. Sample copy for 6×9 SAE with 3 first-class stamps. Writer's guidelines for #10 SASE.

Nonfiction: Articles relating to auto glass and general business management. **Buys 12-20 mss/year.** Query with published clips. Length: 1,000-1,500 words. **Pays $50-200**, with photos.

Photos: State availability of photos. Reviews b&w contact sheets and negatives. Payment included with ms. Captions required. Buys all rights.

N $ $ AUTO RENTAL NEWS, Bobit Publishing Co., 21061 S. Western Ave., Torrance CA 90501. (310)533-2470. Fax: (310)533-2503. E-mail: dstepner@bobit.com. Website: www.fleet-central.com. **Contact:** David Stepner, managing editor. **33% freelance written.** Bimonthly magazine covering auto rental. Estab. 1986. Circ. 17,000. Pays on publication. Publishes ms an average of 4 months after acceptance. Byline given. Buys first and electronic rights. Editorial lead time 2 months. Submit seasonal material 1 month in advance. Accepts queries by mail, e-mail, fax, phone. Sample copy and writer's guidelines free.

Nonfiction: How-to, new product, travel. **Buys 10 mss/year.** Query with published clips. Length: 1,800-2,500 words. **Pays $100-400.** Sometimes pays expenses of writers on assignment.

Photos: Send photos with submission. Reviews prints. Offers no additional payment for photos accepted with ms. Identification of subjects required. Buys one-time rights.

N $ $ BUSINESS FLEET, Managing 10-50 Company Vehicles, Bobit Publishing, 21061 S. Western Ave., Torrance CA 90501-1711. (310)533-2592. Fax: (310)533-2503. E-mail: selliott@bobit.com. Website: www.fleet-central.com. **Contact:** Steve Elliott, senior editor. **50% freelance written.** Quarterly magazine covering businesses which operate 10-50 company vehicles. "While it's a trade publication aimed at a business audience, *Business Fleet* has a lively, conversational style. The best way to get a feel for our 'slant' is to read the magazine." Estab. 2000. Circ. 100,000. **Pays on acceptance.** Publishes ms an average of 2 months after acceptance. Byline given. Offers 25% kill fee. Buys first rights, second serial (reprint) rights and electronic rights. Editorial lead time 2 months. Submit seasonal material 2 months in advance. Accepts queries by mail, e-mail, fax. Responds in 2 weeks to queries; 2 months to mss. Sample copy free. Writer's guidelines free.

Nonfiction: How-to, interview/profile, new product, personal experience, photo feature, technical. **Buys 16 mss/year.** Query with published clips. Length: 500-2,000 words. **Pays $50-400.** Pays with contributor copies or other premiums by prior arrangement. Sometimes pays expenses of writers on assignment.

Photos: State availability of photos with submission. Reviews 3×5 prints. Negotiates payment individually. Captions required. Buys one-time rights, reprint rights, electronic rights.

Columns/Departments: Hot Products (automotive and fleet-oriented), 125-250 words. **Buys 4-6 mss/year.** Query with published clips. **Pays $25-75.**

Tips: Our mission is to educate our target audience on more economical and efficient ways of operating small fleets, and to inform the audience of the latest vehicles, products, and services available to small commercial companies. Be knowledgeable about automotive and fleet-oriented subjects."

N: CALTRUX, Moving the Industry That Moves California, California Trucking Association, 3251 Beacon Blvd., West Sacramento CA 95691. Fax: (916)373-3664. E-mail: mriley@caltrux.org. Website: www.caltrux.org. **Contact:** Michael Riley, editor. **10% freelance written.** Monthly magazine covering the trucking industry in California. "We feature news and information impacting the second-largest industry in the state, which provides jobs for one in twelve working Californians. Readership: 2,500 association member companies, state legislature, highway patrol, regulatory agencies." Estab. 1949. Circ. 4,400. Pays on publication. Publishes ms an average of 3 months after acceptance. Byline given. Buys first North American serial and negotiable rights. Editorial lead time 3 months. Submit seasonal material 6 months in advance. Accepts queries by mail, e-mail, fax. Accepts simultaneous submissions. Sample copy for 9×12 SAE and 2 first-class stamps. Writer's guidelines for #10 SASE.
Nonfiction: Interview/profile, photo feature, technical. "We look for feature material of high interest to the decision-makers of California's trucking industry." **Buys 10-15 mss/year.** Query with published clips. Length: 500-1,500 words. Sometimes pays writers in endorsements.
Reprints: Accepts previously published submissions.
Photos: State availability of or send photos with submission. Reviews contact sheets. Negotiates payment individually. Captions, model releases and identification of subjects required. Buys negotiable rights.
Columns/Departments: Query with published clips.
Tips: "Material must be of immediate importance to the California trucking company decision-maker, or of long-term interest."

N: $CARLINK NEWS, Northwest Automotive Publishing Company, P.O. Box 46937, Seattle WA 98146-0937. (206)935-3336. Fax: (206)937-9732. E-mail: nwautopub@galaxy-7.net. **Contact:** J.B. Smith, editor-in-chief. **5% freelance written.** Monthly newspaper covering automobile news and reviews. "*Carlink* features news for Northwest Car enthusiasts. Industry, local and general news about cars, trucks, vans and SUVs. Includes vehicle test reviews." Estab. 1999. Circ. 15,000. Pays on publication. Byline given. Offers 10% kill fee or $25. Buys simultaneous rights. Editorial lead time 1 month. Submit seasonal material 3 months in advance. Accepts queries by e-mail. Accepts simultaneous submissions. Sample copy for $1.50. Writer's guidelines free.
Nonfiction: How-to, humor, new product, photo feature, technical, test reviews-vehicles. Query with published clips. **Pays $25-175.**
Photos: State availability of photos with submission. Negotiates payment individually. Buys one-time rights.
Columns/Departments: Query.

N: $ $FLEET EXECUTIVE, The Magazine of Vehicle Management, The National Association of Fleet Administrators, Inc., 100 Ave. S, Suite 310, Iselin NJ 08830-2716. (732)494-8100. Fax: (732)494-6789. E-mail: jsyp@nafa.org. Website: www.nafa.org. Managing Editor: Jessica Sypniewski. **50% freelance written.** Monthly magazine covering automotive fleet management. "*NAFA Fleet Executive* focuses on car, van and light-duty truck management in U.S. and Canadian corporations, government agencies and utilities. Editorial emphasis is on general automotive issues; improving jobs skills, productivity and professionalism; legislation and regulation; alternative fuels; safety; interviews with prominent industry personalities; technology; Association news; public service fleet management; and light-duty truck fleet management." Estab. 1957. Circ. 4,000. Pays on publication. Publishes ms an average of 4 months after acceptance. No byline. Buys all rights. Editorial lead time 2 months. Accepts queries by mail, e-mail, fax. Accepts simultaneous submissions. Responds in 1 month to queries. Sample copy online at website. Writer's guidelines free.
Nonfiction: Interview/profile, technical. "NAFA hosts its Fleet Management Institute, an educational conference and trade show, which is held in a different city in the U.S. and Canada each year. *Fleet Executive* would consider articles on regional attractions, particularly those that might be of interest to those in the automotive industry, for use in a conference preview issue of the magazine. The preview issue is published one month prior to the conference. Information about the conference, its host city, and conference dates in a given year may be found on NAFA's Web site, www.nafa.org, or by calling the association at (732)494-8100." **Buys 12 mss/year.** Query with published clips. Length: 500-3,000 words. **Pays $500 maximum.**
Photos: State availability of photos with submission. Reviews electronic.
Tips: "The sample articles online at www.nafa.org/admenu.htm should help writers get a feel of the journalistic style we require. However, an important thing to remember about our audience is they do not have the time to sift through extraneous information to get to the facts they need."

N: $ $GLASS DIGEST, Ashlee Publishing, 18 E. 41st St., New York NY 10017. (212)376-7722. Fax: (212)376-7723. E-mail: glassdigest@iname.com. Website: www.ashlee.com. Editor: Julian Phillips. **Contact:** Cataya Dunn, associate editor. **15% freelance written.** Monthly magazine covering flat glass, glazing, auto glass. Estab. 1921. Pays on publication. Publishes ms an average of 2 months after acceptance. Byline given. Buys first and all rights or makes work-for-hire assignments. Editorial lead time 3 months. Accepts queries by mail, e-mail, fax. Accepts simultaneous submissions.
Nonfiction: Photo feature, technical. "No reports on stained glass hobbyists or art glass." **Buys 16-20 mss/year.** Query. Length: 1,000-2,000 words. **Pays $100-400.** Sometimes pays expenses of writers on assignment.
Photos: State availability of photos with submission. Negotiates payment individually. Identification of subjects required.
Tips: "Architecturally interesting projects with good photography make excellent features for *Glass Digest*."

[N] NORTHWEST MOTOR, Journal for the Automotive Industry, Northwest Automotive Publishing Co., P.O. Box 46937, Seattle WA 98146-0937. (206)935-3336. Fax: (206)937-9732. E-mail: nwautopub@galaxy-7.net. **Contact:** J.B. Smith, editor. **5% freelance written.** Monthly magazine covering the automotive industry. Estab. 1909. Circ. 6,000. Pays on publication. Byline given. Offers 10% kill fee. Buys all rights. Editorial lead time 1 month. Submit seasonal material 2 months in advance. Accepts queries by mail, e-mail. Accepts simultaneous submissions. Sample copy $2. Guidelines for #10 SASE.

Break in by sending a listing of available articles.

Nonfiction: Book excerpts, general interest, how-to, new product, photo feature, technical. Interested in seeing automotive environmental articles. **Buys 6 mss/year.** Query. Length: 250-1,200 words. **Pay varies.** Sometimes pays expenses of writers on assignment.

Photos: Send photos with submission. Reviews 3×5 prints. Negotiates payment individually. Buys all rights.

Columns/Departments: Buys 4-6 mss/year. Query. **Pay varies.**

Fillers: Anecdotes, facts. **Buys 4-9/year.** Length: 15-100 words. **Pay varies.**

[N] O&A MARKETING NEWS, KAL Publications Inc., 532 El Dorado St., Suite 200, Pasadena CA 91101. Fax: (626)683-0969. **Contact:** Kathy Laderman, editor. **10% freelance written.** Bimonthly tabloid. "*O&A Marketing News* is editorially directed to people engaged in the distribution, merchandising, installation and servicing of gasoline, oil, TBA, quick lube, carwash, convenience store, alternative fuel and automotive aftermarket products in the 13 Western states." Estab. 1966. Circ. 8,000. Pays on publication. Publishes ms an average of 3 months after acceptance. Byline sometimes given. Not copyrighted. Buys one-time rights. Editorial lead time 1 month. Accepts simultaneous submissions. Responds in 1 month to mss. Sample copy for $3.

Nonfiction: Exposé, interview/profile, photo feature, industry news. **Buys 20 mss/year.** Send complete ms. Length: 100-10,000 words. **Pays per column-inch typeset.**

Photos: State availability of photos with submission. Reviews contact sheets, prints (5×7 preferred). Offers $5/photo. Identification of subjects required. Buys one-time rights.

Fillers: Gags to be illustrated by cartoonist, short humor. **Buys 7 mss/year.** Length: 1-200 words. **Pays per column-inch.**

Tips: "Seeking Western industry news. We're always seeking more stories covering the more remote states such as Montana, Idaho, and Hawaii—but any timely, topical *news*-oriented stories will be considered."

$ OLD CARS WEEKLY, News & Marketplace, Krause Publications, 700 E. State St., Iola WI 54945. (715)445-2214. Fax: (715)445-4087. E-mail: gunnelj@krause.com. Website: www.krause.com. Editor: John A. Gunnell. **Contact:** Chad Elmore, associate editor. **50% freelance written.** Weekly tabloid covering old cars. Estab. 1971. Circ. 65,000. Pays in the month after publication date. Publishes ms an average of 6 months after acceptance. Byline given. Buys perpetual but non-exclusive rights. For sample copy call circulation department. Writer's guidelines for #10 SASE.

Nonfiction: How-to, technical, auction prices realized lists. No "Grandpa's Car," "My First Car" or "My Car" themes. **Buys 1,600 mss/year.** Send complete ms. Length: 400-1,600 words. **Pays 3¢/word.**

Photos: Send photos with submission. Pays $5/photo. Captions and identification of subjects required. Offers no additional payment for photos accepted with ms. Buys perpetual but non-exclusive rights.

Tips: "Ninety percent of our material is done by a small group of regular contributors. Many new writers break in here, but we are *usually overstocked* with material and *never* seek nostalgic or historical pieces from new authors. Our big need is for well-written items that fit odd pieces in a tabloid page layout. Budding authors should try some short, catchy items that help us fill odd-ball 'news holes' with interesting writing. Authors with good skills can work up to longer stories. A weekly keeps us too busy to answer mail and phone calls. The best queries are 'checklists' where we can quickly mark a 'yes' or 'no' to article ideas."

[N] $ $ OVERDRIVE, The Magazine for the American Trucker, Randall Publishing Co./Overdrive, Inc., 3200 Rice Mine Rd., Tuscaloosa AL 35406. (205)349-2990. Fax: (205)750-8070. E-mail: mheine@randallpub.com. Website: www.etrucker.net. Editorial Director: Linda Longton. **Contact:** Max Heine, senior editor. **10% freelance written.** Monthly magazine for independent truckers. Estab. 1961. Circ. 140,000. Pays on publication. Publishes ms an average of 2 months after acceptance. Byline given. 10% kill fee. Buys all North American rights, including electronic rights. Responds in 2 months. Sample copy and writers' guidelines for 9×12 SASE.

Nonfiction: Essays, exposé, how-to (truck maintenance and operation), interview/profile (successful independent truckers), personal experience, photo feature, technical. All must be related to independent trucker interest. Query with or without published clips, or send complete ms. Length: 500-2,000 words. **Pays $200-1,000 for assigned articles; $50-500 for unsolicited articles.**

Photos: Send photos with submission. Reviews transparencies and 5×7 prints. Offers $25-50/photo. Identification of subjects required. Buys all rights.

Tips: "Talk to independent truckers. Develop a good knowledge of their concerns as small-business owners, truck drivers and individuals. We prefer articles that quote experts, people in the industry and truckers to first-person expositions on a subject. Get straight facts. Look for good material on truck safety, on effects of government regulations, and on rates and business relationships between independent truckers, brokers, carriers and shippers."

[N] $ $ PARTS & PEOPLE, Automotive Counseling & Publishing Co., 450 Lincoln St., Suite 110, Denver CO 80203. Fax: (303)765-4664. E-mail: info@partsandpeople.com. Website: www.partsandpeople.com. **Contact:** Kevin

Loewen, managing editor. **15% freelance written.** Monthly trade newspaper covering automotive parts and service industry. "This is a publication for the owners and managers of businesses which repair automobiles. We are interested in stories about successful businesses within our circulation area (Central U.S.) that illustrate ways to run them more efficiently, profitably and with better customer satisfaction. Amateur mechanics need not apply." Estab. 1985. Circ. 32,000. Pays on publication. Publishes ms an average of 2 months after acceptance. Byline given. Makes work-for-hire assignments. Editorial lead time 2 months. Accepts queries by mail, e-mail. Accepts simultaneous submissions. Responds in 2 weeks to queries; 1 month to mss. Sample copy and writer's guidelines online at website.

Nonfiction: Interview/profile. "No car-enthusiast pieces. This is a high-tech field with sophisticated management issues. Writers without industry experience will not be considered." **Buys 50-60 mss/year.** Query with published clips. Length: 500-1,500 words. **Pays $50-200.** Pays expenses of writers on assignment.

Reprints: Accepts previously published submissions.

Photos: State availability of photos with submission. Offers $25/photo. Captions and identification of subjects required. Buys one-time rights.

$ PML, The Market Letter for Porsche Automobiles, PML Consulting, P.O. Box 6010, Oceanside CA 92058. (760)940-9170. Fax: (760)940-9170. E-mail: pmletter@aol.com. Website: www.pmletter.com. **Contact:** Pat Van Buskirk, publisher/editor. **100% freelance written.** Monthly magazine covering technical tips, personality profiles and race coverage of Porsche automobiles. Estab. 1981. Circ. 1,500. Pays on publication. Publishes ms an average of 2 months after acceptance. Byline given. Buys one-time rights. Editorial lead time 2 months. Submit seasonal material 2 months in advance. Accepts simultaneous and previously published submissions. Accepts queries by mail, e-mail, fax. Responds in 2 weeks to queries; 1 month to mss. Sample copy for $5. Writer's guidelines for #10 SASE.

Nonfiction: General interest, historical/nostalgic, how-to, humor, interview/profile, new product, personal experience, photo feature, technical, travel, race results. **Buys 30-40 mss/year.** Query with published clips. Length: 500-2,000 words. **Pays $30-50 and up**, depending on length and topic. Sometimes pays expenses of writers on assignment.

Reprints: Accepts previously published submissions.

Photos: Send photos with submission. Reviews 8×10 b&w prints. Negotiates payment individually. Captions, model releases and identification of subjects required. Buys one-time rights.

Fillers: Anecdotes, facts, gags to be illustrated by cartoonist, newsbreaks, short humor. Pay negotiable.

Tips: "Check any auto-related magazine for types, styles of articles. We are looking for people doing anything unusual or interesting in the Porsche world. Submit well-prepared, thoroughly-edited articles with photos."

$ $ ROAD KING MAGAZINE, For the Professional Driver, Hammock Publishing, Inc., 3322 West End Ave. #700, Nashville TN 37203. (615)385-9745. Fax: (615)386-9349. E-mail: roadking@hammock.com. Website: www.road king.com. Editor: Tom Berg. **Contact:** Bill Hudgins, editorial director. **80% freelance written.** "*Road King* is published bimonthly for long-haul truckers. It celebrates the lifestyle and work and profiles interesting and/or successful drivers. It also reports on subjects of interest to our audience, including outdoors, vehicles, music and trade issues." Estab. 1963. Circ. 229,900. **Pays on acceptance.** Publishes ms an average of 4 months after acceptance. Byline given. Offers 25% kill fee. Buys first North American serial rights or electronic rights. Editorial lead time 3 months. Submit seasonal material 4 months in advance. Accepts queries by mail, e-mail, fax. Responds in 2 months to queries. Sample copy for 9×12 SAE and 5 first-class stamps. Writer's guidelines for #10 SASE.

Nonfiction: How-to (trucking-related), humor, interview/profile, new product, photo feature, technical, travel. Road-Runner Tools (the latest tools, techniques and industry developments to help them run a smarter, more efficient trucking business; Haul of Fame (salutes drivers whose work or type of rig makes them unique); At Home on the Road ("creature comfort" products, services and information for the road life, including what's new, useful, interesting or fun for cyber-trucking drivers); Fleet Focus (asks fleet management about what their companies offer, and drivers about why they like it there); Weekend Wheels (from Harleys to Hondas, most drivers have a passion for their "other" set of wheels. This section looks at this aspect of drivers' lives)."No fiction, poetry." **Buys 20 mss/year.** Query with published clips. Length: 850-2,000 words. Pay is negotiable. Sometimes pays expenses of writers on assignment.

Photos: State availability of photos with submission. Reviews contact sheets. Negotiates payment individually. Model releases and identification of subjects required. Buys negotiable rights.

Columns/Departments: Lead Driver (profile of outstanding trucker), 250-500 words; Roadrunner (new products, services suited to the business of trucking or to truckers' lifestyles). **Buys 6-10 mss/year.** Query. Pay is negotiable.

Fillers: Anecdotes, facts, gags to be illustrated by cartoonist, short humor. Length: 100-250 words. **Pays $50.**

The online magazine of *Road King* carries original content not found in the print edition. Contact: Bill Hudgins.

N $ $ RV TRADE DIGEST, The Marketplace of the RV Industry, Cygnus Business Media Inc., 58025 C.R. 9, Elkhart IN 46517. (219)295-1962. Fax: (219)295-7574. **Contact:** Lee C. Keyser, editor. **25% freelance written.** "Controlled-circulation monthly magazine for manufacturers, suppliers, dealers, campground and other service providers to the recreational vehicle industry. Company and industry news, dealer profiles, manufacturer profiles, sales and marketing articles, technical articles." Estab. 1980. Circ. 17,000. Pays 30 days after acceptance. Publishes ms an average of 3 months after acceptance. Byline given. Buys first North American serial rights. Editorial lead time 3 months. Submit seasonal material 4 months in advance. Accepts simultaneous submissions. Responds in 2 months. Sample copy and writer's guidelines free.

Nonfiction: How-to (install, service parts, accessories), interview/profile, new product, technical, business subjects, mobile electronics. No sales and marketing subjects. **Buys 24-36 mss/year.** Length: 1,000-2,000 words. **Pays $100-500.**

Photos: Send photos with submission. Reviews transparencies and prints. Negotiates payment individually. Model releases required. Buys one-time rights.

Tips: "Send complete manuscript. Queries must include background/experience and published clips."

N $ $ SPORT TRUCK & SUV ACCESSORY BUSINESS, Covering the Light Truck-Van-SUV After-market, Cygnus Business Media, 1233 Janesville Ave., Ft. Atkinson WI 53533. (920)563-6388. Fax: (920)563-1702. E-mail: peter.hubbard@cygnuspub.com. **Contact:** Peter A. Hubbard, editor. **25% freelance written.** "Published bi-monthly for manufacturers and retailers of accessories ranging from caps and bedliners and towing equipment for pickup trucks, vans and sport utility vehicles, controlled circulation. Balanced between news, how-to, trade shows, product trends, etc." Estab. 1996. Circ. 15,000. Pays 30 days after acceptance. Publishes ms an average of 6 months after acceptance. Byline given. Buys first North American serial rights. Editorial lead time 3 months. Submit seasonal material 6 months in advance. Accepts simultaneous submissions. Responds in 1 month. Sample copy and writer's guidelines free.

   O— Break in with "a feature on a top truck or SUV retailer in your area."

Nonfiction: General interest, how-to (installation, service), interview/profile, new product, technical; considers car-toons. No travel, sales and marketing advice. **Buys 20-30 mss/year.** Query. Length: 1,000-2,000 words. **Pays $300-500.**

Photos: Send photos with submission. Reviews transparencies and prints. Negotiates payment individually. Model releases required. Buys one-time rights.

Tips: "Send query with or without completed manuscripts. Background/experience and published clips are required."

N $ $ TODAY'S TRUCKING, New Communications Group, 130 Belfield Rd., Toronto, Ontario M9W 1G1 Canada. (416)614-2200. Fax: (416)614-8861. E-mail: editors@todaystrucking.com. Website: www.todaystrucking.com. Editor: Stephen Petit. **15% freelance written.** Monthly magazine covering the trucking industry in Canada. "We reach nearly 30,000 fleet owners, managers, owner-operators, shop supervisors, equipment dealers, and parts distributors across Canada. Our magazine has a strong service slant, combining useful how-to journalism with analysis of news, business issues, and heavy-duty equipment trends. Before you sit down to write, please take time to become familiar with *Today's Trucking.* Read a few recent issues." Estab. 1987. Circ. 30,000. **Pays on acceptance.** Byline given. Buys first North American rights and second serial (reprint) rights. Editorial lead time 2 months. Submit seasonal material 3 months in advance. Accepts queries by mail, e-mail, fax. Sample copy free. Writer's guidelines free.

Nonfiction: How-to, interview/profile, technical. **Buys 20 mss/year.** Query with published clips. Length: 500-2,000 words. **Pays 40¢/word.** Sometimes pays expenses of writers on assignment.

Photos: State availability of photos with submission.

Columns/Departments: Pays 40¢/word.

$ TOWING & RECOVERY PHOOTNOTES, Trader Publishing Co., 100 W. Plume St., Norfolk VA 23510. (877)219-7734. Fax: (757)314-2508. E-mail: pnotes@ix.netcom.com. **Contact:** Rick Porter, general manager. **100% freelance written.** Monthly trade tabloid newspaper covering the towing business. "*Phootnotes*' mission is increasing profits through education and knowledge." Estab. 1991. Circ. 46,000. Pays on publication. Publishes ms an average of 2 months after acceptance. Byline given. Buys industry rights. Editorial lead time 1 month. Submit seasonal material 2 months in advance. Accepts queries and submissions by e-mail only. Sample copy free.

   O— Break in by sending us first-hand experiences in the towing and recovery field with practical advice for the towing business operator or color photos of unusual recoveries or tow trucks."

Nonfiction: Technical, business management. Query. Length: 800-1,200 words. **Pays $50-100.**

Reprints: Accepts previously published submissions not in same industry.

Columns and Departments: Business Management (related to towing industry), 500-800 words. **Buys 12-18 mss/ month.** Query. **Pays $50-100.**

   • *Towing & Recovery Phootnotes is under new ownership as of December 1999.*

N $ $ $ TRUCKING TIMES & SPORT UTILITY, Wiesner Publishing LLC, 7009 S. Potomac St., Suite 200, Englewood CO 80112. (303)397-7600. Fax: (303)397-7619. E-mail: ed@truckingtimes.com. Website: www.Trucki ngTimes.com. **Contact:** Dave Herrmeyer, editor. **30% freelance written.** Bimonthly magazine covering light trucks, SUVs and van aftermarket products. "Our publication is geared to the light-truck aftermarket: every issue features industry news, marketing techniques, installation procedures, business issues and new products." Estab. 1988. Circ. 13,800. Pays on publication. Publishes ms an average of 4 months after acceptance. Byline given. Offers $50 kill fee. Buys first North American serial rights and electronic rights. Editorial lead time 4 months. Submit seasonal material 6 months in advance. Accepts queries by mail, e-mail, fax. Responds in 2 weeks to queries; 1 month to mss. Sample copy for #10 SASE. Writer's guidelines for #10 SASE.

Nonfiction: General interest, how-to (installation of aftermarket products), interview/profile, new product, technical. No fiction. **Buys 20 mss/year.** Query. Length: 500-2,000 words. **Pays $50-800.**

Photos: State availability of photos with submission. Reviews 3×5 transparencies and 3×5 prints or anything close. Offers no additional payment for photos accepted with ms. Captions and identification of subjects required.

Columns/Departments: Buys 3 mss/year. Query. **Pays $50-500.**

Tips: "Know the industry/trade—light trucks, vans and SUVs aftermarket products."

$ $ WESTERN CANADA HIGHWAY NEWS, Craig Kelman & Associates, 3C-2020 Portage Ave., Winnipeg, Manitoba R3J 0K4 Canada. (204)985-9785. Fax: (204)985-9795. E-mail: kelman@escape.com. **Contact:** Terry Ross, managing editor. **30% freelance written.** Quarterly magazine covering trucking. "The official magazine of the Alberta, Saskatchewan and Manitoba trucking associations." Estab. 1995. Circ. 4,000. Pays on publication. Publishes ms an average of 2 months after acceptance. Byline given. Buys one-time rights. Editorial lead time 3 months. Submit seasonal material 3 months in advance. Accepts simultaneous submissions. Responds in 2 months to queries; 4 months to mss. Sample copy for 10×13 SAE with 1 IRC. Writer's guidelines free.

Nonfiction: Essays, general interest, how-to (run a trucking business), interview/profile, new product, opinion, personal experience, photo feature, technical, profiles in excellence (bios of trucking or associate firms enjoying success). **Buys 8-10 mss/year.** Query. Length: 500-3,000 words. **Pays 18-25¢/word.** Sometimes pays expenses of writers.

Reprints: Send photocopy of article or short story and information about when and where the article previously appeared. Pays 60% of amount paid for an original article.

Photos: State availability of photos with submission. Reviews 4×6 prints. Identification of subjects required. Buys one-time rights.

Columns/Departments: Safety (new safety innovation/products), 500 words; Trade Talk (new products), 300 words. Query. **Pays 18-25¢/word.**

Tips: "Our publication is fairly time-sensitive re: issues affecting the trucking industry in Western Canada. Current 'hot' topics are international trucking (NAFTA-induced changes), deregulation, driver fatigue, health and safety, emissions control and national/international highway systems."

AVIATION & SPACE

In this section are journals for aviation business executives, airport operators and aviation technicians. Publications for professional and private pilots are in the Consumer Aviation section.

N $ $ AG-PILOT INTERNATIONAL MAGAZINE, Graphics Plus, P.O. Box 1607, Mt. Vernon WA 98273-1607. (360)336-6129. Fax: (360)336-2506. E-mail: agpilot@cnw.com. Editor/Publisher: Tom J. Wood. **Contact:** Krista Madlung. Monthly magazine emphasizing agricultural aviation, aerial fire fighting, forestry spraying. **10% freelance written.** Estab. 1978. Pays on publication. Publishes ms an average of 2 months after acceptance. Buys all rights. Byline given. Responds in 1 month. Sample copy for $3 and 9×12 SAE. Writer's guidelines for #10 SASE.

Nonfiction: Exposé (of EPA, OSHA, FAA, NTSB or any government function concerned with this industry), general interest, historical, humor, interview (of well-known ag/aviation person), new product, personal experience, photo feature. Sometimes pays expenses of writers on assignment. **Buys 20 mss/year.** Send complete ms. Length: 500-15,000 words. **Pays $100-200.**

Reprints: Accepts previously published submissions.

Photos: Send photos with submission. Reviews 4×5 transparencies, 5×7 prints. Offers no additional payment for photos accepted with ms. Captions required.

Columns/Departments: Good Old Days (ag/aviation history), 500-700 words. **Buys 10 mss/year.** Send complete ms. **Pays $50-150.**

Poetry: Interested in all ag-aviation-related poetry. **Buys 1 poem/issue.** Submit maximum 2 at one time. Length: 24-72 lines. **Pays $25-50.**

Fillers: Short jokes, short humor and industry-related newsbreaks. Length: 40-100 words. **Pays $15-20.**

Tips: "Writers should be witty and knowledgeable about the crop dusting aviation world and aerial fire fighting. Material *must* be agricultural/aviation-oriented."

$ $ AVIATION INTERNATIONAL NEWS, The Newsmagazine of Corporate, Business and Regional Aviation, The Convention News Co., P.O. Box 277, 214 Franklin Ave., Midland Park NJ 07432. (201)444-5075. Fax: (201)444-4647. E-mail: editor@ainonline.com. Website: www.ainonline.com. Managing Editor: Nigel Moll. **Contact:** R. Randall Padfield, editor-in-chief. **30-40% freelance written.** Monthly magazine (with onsite issues published at two conventions and two air shows each year) covering business and commercial aviation with news features, special reports, aircraft evaluations and surveys on business aviation worldwide, written for business pilots. "While the heartbeat of *AIN* is driven by the news it carries, the human touch is not neglected. We pride ourselves on our people stories about the industry's 'movers and shakers' and others in aviation who make a difference." Estab. 1972. Circ. 35,000. **Pays on acceptance** or upon receipt of writer's invoice. Publishes ms an average of 2 months after acceptance. Byline given. Kill fee varies. Buys first North American serial, second serial (reprint) rights and makes work-for-hire assignments. Editorial lead time 2 months. Submit seasonal material 3 months in advance. Accepts queries by mail, fax. Responds in 6 weeks to queries; 2 months to mss. Sample copy for $10. Writer's guidelines for 9×12 SAE with 3 first-class stamps or on website.

Nonfiction: How-to (aviation), interview/profile, new product, opinion, personal experience, photo feature, technical. "We hire freelancers to work on our staff at two aviation conventions and two international airshows each year. Must have strong reporting and writing skills and knowledge of aviation." No puff pieces. "Our readers expect serious, real news." **Buys 150-200 mss/year.** Query with published clips. Length: 200-3,000 words. **Pays 30¢/word.** Pays expenses of writers on assignment.

Photos: Send photos with submission. Reviews contact sheets, transparencies and prints. Negotiates payment individually. Captions required. Buys one-time rights.

■ The online newsletter carries original content not found in the print version. This subscription-based newsletter requires 45-50 news items of about 100 words each week. Contact: Gordon Gilbert, ggilbert@ainonline.com.

Tips: "Our core freelancers are professional pilots with good writing skills, good journalists and reporters with an interest in aviation (some with pilot licenses) or technical experts in the aviation industry. Hit me with a strong news story relating to business avaiation that takes me by surprise—something from your local area or area of expertise. Make it readable, fact-filled and in the inverted-pyramid style. Double-check facts and names. Interview the right people. Send me good, clear photos and illustrations. Send me well-written, logically ordered copy. Do this for me consistently and we may take you along on our staff to one of the conventions in the U.S. or an airshow in Paris, Singapore, London or Dubai."

$ $ GSE TODAY, P.O. Box 480, Hatch NM 87937. Fax: (505)267-1920. **Contact:** Dixie Binning, managing editor. **50% freelance written.** Magazine published 8 times/year. "Our readers are those aviation professionals who are involved in ground support—the equipment manufacturers, the suppliers, the ramp operators, ground handlers, airport and airline managers. We cover issues of interest to this community—deicing, ramp safety, equipment technology, pollution, etc." Estab. 1993. Circ. 15,000. Pays on publication. Publishes ms an average of 2 months after acceptance. Buys all rights. Editorial lead time 2 months. Responds in 3 weeks to queries; 3 months to mss. Sample copy for 9×11 SAE with 5 first-class stamps.

Nonfiction: How-to (use or maintain certain equipment), interview/profile, new products, personal experience (from ramp operators), technical aspects of ground support equipment and issues, industry events, meetings, new rules and regulations. **Buys 12-20 mss/year.** Send complete ms. Length: 400-3,000 words. **Pays 25¢/published word.**

Reprints: Send photocopy or typed ms with rights for sale noted and information about when and where the article previously appeared. Pays 50% of the amount paid for an original article.

Photos: Send photos with submissions. Reviews 5×7 prints. Offers no additional payment for photos accepted with ms. Identification of subjects required. Buys all rights.

Tips: "Write about subjects that relate to ground services. Write in clear and simple terms—personal experience is always welcome. If you have an aviation background or ground support experience, let us know."

★ $ $ $ PROFESSIONAL PILOT, Queensmith Communications, 3014 Colvin St., Alexandria VA 22314. (703)370-0606. Fax: (703)370-7082. E-mail: editorial@propilotmag.com. Website: www.propilotmag.com. **Contact:** Justin Marchand, managing editor. **75% freelance written.** Monthly magazine on regional airline, corporate and various other types of professional aviation. "The typical reader has a sophisticated grasp of piloting/aviation knowledge and is interested in articles that help him/her do the job better or more efficiently." Estab. 1967. Circ. 38,000. **Pays on acceptance.** Publishes ms an average of 2-3 months after acceptance. Byline given. Kill fee negotiable. Buys all rights. Accepts queries by mail, e-mail, fax, phone.

○═ "Affiliation with an active flight department, weather activity of Air Traffic Control (ATC) is helpful. Our readers want tool tech stuff from qualified writers with credentials. We have been looking for good weather articles, air traffic controller viewpoints, articles on future aircraft."

Nonfiction: "Typical subjects include new aircraft design, new product reviews (especially avionics), pilot techniques, profiles of regional airlines, fixed base operations, profiles of corporate flight departments and technological advances." All issues have a theme such as regional airline operations, maintenance, avionics, helicopters, etc. Special issues: Salary Study and Paris Show (June); FBO/Flight Support Directory and Contest Awards (July); Regional Aircraft Product Support (August); Corporate Aircraft Product Support (September); NBAA Convention Issue (October); Post NBAA Issue and Powerplant Product Support and Air Traffic Control & CAT3 (November); FBO Contest Ballot and Awards (December). **Buys 40 mss/year.** Query. Length: 750-2,500 words. **Pays $200-1,000**, depending on length. A fee for the article will be established at the time of assignment. Sometimes pays expenses of writers on assignment.

Photos: Send photos with submission. Prefers transparencies or slides. Additional payment for photos negotiable. Captions and identification of subjects required. Buys all rights.

Tips: Query first. "Freelancer should be a professional pilot or have background in aviation. Authors should indicate relevant aviation experience and pilot credentials (certificates, ratings and hours). We place a greater emphasis on corporate operations and pilot concerns."

BEAUTY & SALON

N $ $ BEAUTY STORE BUSINESS, Serving Open-Line and Professional-Only Stores and Distributors, Creative Age Communications, 7628 Densmore Ave., Van Nuys CA 91406-2042. (818)782-7328. Fax: (818)782-7450. E-mail: mbirenbaum@creativeage.com. **Contact:** Marc Birenbaum, editor. **75% freelance written.** Magazine published 7 times/year covering beauty store business management. "The publication is read by beauty store owners and managers—professional-only stores of salon industry distributors, open-to-the public stores, salon stores and ethnic stores." Estab. 1994. Circ. 15,000. **Pays on acceptance**. Publishes ms an average of 3 months after acceptance. Byline given. Offers negotiable kill fee. Buys all rights. Editorial lead time 3 months. Submit seasonal material 4 months in advance. Accepts queries by mail, e-mail, fax. Responds in 2 weeks to queries; 1 month to mss. Sample copy free.

Nonfiction: How-to (business management, merchandising, retailing), interview/profile (industry leaders). "No business articles available in general-circulation publications." **Buys 2-3 mss/year.** Query. Length: 1,250-2,500 words. **Pays $250-475 for assigned articles.** Sometimes pays expenses of writers on assignment.

Photos: State availability of photos with submission. Reviews transparencies and computer art. Negotiates payment individually. Captions and identification of subjects required. Buys all rights.

Columns/Departments: Ethnic Spotlight (beauty trends and news that ethnic beauty stores can use), 1,000 words. **Buys 7 mss/year.** Query with published clips. **Pays $250-375.**

N **$ $ COSMETICS, Canada's Business Magazine for the Cosmetics, Fragrance, Toiletry and Personal Care Industry**, Maclean Hunter Publishing Ltd., 777 Bay St., Suite 405, Toronto, Ontario M5W 1A7 Canada. (416)596-5817. Fax: (416)596-5179. E-mail: rowood@mhpublishing.com. Website: www.mhbizlink.com/cosmetics. **Contact:** Ronald A. Wood, editor. **35% freelance written**; "99.9% of freelance articles are assigned by the editor to writers whose work he is familiar with and who have a broad knowledge of this industry as well as contacts, etc." Bimonthly magazine. "Our main reader segment is the retail trade—department stores, drugstores, salons, estheticians—owners and cosmeticians/beauty advisors; plus manufacturers, distributors, agents and suppliers to the industry." Estab. 1972. Circ. 13,000. **Pays on acceptance.** Publishes ms an average of 3 months after acceptance. Byline given. Offers 50% kill fee. Buys all rights. Editorial lead time 4 months. Submit seasonal material 4 months in advance. Accepts queries by mail, e-mail, fax, phone. Responds in 1 month. Sample copy for $6 (Canadian) and 8% GST.

Nonfiction: General interest, interview/profile, photo feature. **Buys 60 mss/year.** Query. Length: 250-1,200 words. **Pays 25¢/word.** Sometimes pays expenses of writers on assignment.

Photos: Send photos with submission. Reviews transparencies (2½ up to 8×10) and prints (4×6 up to 8×10). Offers no additional payment for photos accepted with ms. Captions, model releases and identification of subjects required. Buys all rights.

Columns/Departments: Behind the Scenes (brief profile of person not directly involved with major industry firms), 300 words and portrait photo. **Buys 28 mss/year,** "all assigned on a regular basis from correspondents and columnists that we know personally from the industry." **Pays 25¢/word.**

Tips: "Must have broad knowledge of the Canadian cosmetics, fragrance and toiletries industry and retail business."

$ $ DAYSPA, For the Salon of the Future, Creative Age Publications, 7628 Densmore Ave., Van Nuys CA 91406. (818)782-7328. Fax: (818)782-7450. E-mail: dayspamag@aol.com. Website: wwwdayspamagazine.com. **Contact:** Linda Lewis, executive editor. Managing Editor: Linda Kossoff. **60% freelance written.** "Bimonthly magazine covering the business of day spas, skincare salons, wellness centers. "Dayspa includes only well targeted business articles directed at the owners and managers of high-end, multi-service salons, day spas, resort spas and destination spas." Estab. 1996. Circ. 31,000. **Pays on acceptance.** Publishes ms an average of 4 months after acceptance. Byline given. Buys first or one-time rights. Editorial lead time 4 months. Submit seasonal material 4 months in advance. Accepts queries by mail, e-mail, fax, phone. Responds in 2 months. Sample copy for $5.

Nonfiction: Book excerpts, how-to, interview/profile, photo feature. **Buys 40 mss/year.** Query. Length: 1,200-3,000 words. **Pays $150-500.**

Photos: Send photos with submission. Negotiates payment individually. Model releases and identification of subjects required. Buys one-time rights.

Columns/Departments: Legal Pad (legal issues affecting salons/spas); Money Matters (financial issues), all 1,200-1,500 words. Buys 20 mss/year. Query. Pays $150-300.

N **$ $ DERMASCOPE MAGAZINE, The Encyclopedia of Aesthetics & Spa Therapy**, Geneva Corporation, 2611 N. Belt Line Rd., Suite 140, Sunnyvale TX 75182. (972)226-2309. Fax: (972)226-2339. E-mail: dermascope@aol.com. Website: www.dermascope.com. **Contact:** Saundra Wallens, editor-in-chief. Monthly magazine covering aesthetics (skin care) and body and spa therapy. "Our magazine is a source of practical advice and continuing education for skin care, body and spa therapy professionals. Our main readers are salon, day spa and destination spa owners, managers or technicians." Estab. 1976. Circ. 15,000. Pays on publication. Publishes ms an average of 6 months after acceptance. Byline given. Buys all rights. Editorial lead time 3 months. Submit seasonal material 6 months in advance. Accepts queries by mail, e-mail, fax. Responds in 1 month to queries; 6 months to mss. Sample copy on website.

Nonfiction: Book excerpts, general interest, historical/nostalgic, how-to, inspirational, personal experience, photo feature, technical. Interested in seeing non-product specific how-to articles with photographs. **Buys 6 mss/year.** Query with published clips. Length: 1,500-2,500 words. **Pays $50-250.**

Photos: State availability of photos with submission. Reviews 4×5 prints. Offers no additional payment for photos accepted with ms. Captions, model releases and identification of subjects required. Buys all rights.

Tips: "Write from the practitioner's point of view. Step-by-step how to's that show the skin care and body and spa therapist practical methodology are a plus. Would like more business and finance ideas, applicable to the industry."

X **$ $ NAILPRO, The Magazine for Nail Professionals**, Creative Age Publications, 7628 Densmore Ave., Van Nuys CA 91406. (818)782-7328. Fax: (818)782-7450. E-mail: nailpro@aol.com. Website: www.nailpro.com. **Contact:** Kathy Kirkland, executive editor. **75% freelance written.** Monthly magazine written for manicurists and nail technicians working in full-service salons or nails-only salons. It covers technical and business aspects of working in and operating a nail-care service, as well as the nail-care industry in general. Estab. 1989. Circ. 65,000. **Pays on acceptance.** Publishes ms 6 months after acceptance. Byline given. Offers 50% kill fee. Buys first North American serial rights. Editorial lead time 3 months. Submit seasonal material 3 months in advance. Accepts simultaneous submissions. Accepts queries by mail, e-mail, fax. Responds in 6 weeks. Sample copy for $2 and 8½×11 SASE.

Nonfiction: Book excerpts, how-to, humor, inspirational, interview/profile, personal experience, photo feature, technical. No general interest articles or business articles not geared to the nail-care industry. **Buys 50 mss/year.** Query. Length: 1,000-3,000 words. **Pays $150-450.**

Reprints: Send typed ms with rights for sale noted and information about when and where the article previously appeared. Pays 25-50% of amount paid for an original article.

Photos: Send photos with submission. Reviews transparencies and prints. Negotiates payment individually. Model releases and identification of subjects required. Buys one-time rights.

Columns/Departments: Building Business (articles on marketing nail services/products), 1,200-2,000 words; Shop Talk (aspects of operating a nail salon), 1,200-2,000 words. **Buys 50 mss/year.** Query. **Pays $200-300.**

▣ The online magazine carries original content not found in the print edition. Contact Kathy Kirkland.

$ $ NAILS, Bobit Publishing, 21061 S. Western Ave., Torrance CA 90501-1711. (310)533-2400. Fax: (310)533-2504. E-mail: nailsmag@bobit.com. Website: www.nailsmag.com. **Contact:** Cyndy Drummey, editor. **10% freelance written.** Monthly magazine. "*NAILS* seeks to educate its readers on new techniques and products, nail anatomy and health, customer relations, working safely with chemicals, salon sanitation, and the business aspects of running a salon." Estab. 1983. Circ. 55,000. **Pays on acceptance.** Byline given. Buys all rights. Submit seasonal material 4 months in advance. Accepts queries by mail, e-mail, fax. Responds in 3 months to queries. Sample copy and writer's guidelines free for #10 SASE.

Nonfiction: Historical/nostalgic, how-to, inspirational, interview/profile, personal experience, photo feature, technical. "No articles on one particular product, company profiles or articles slanted toward a particular company or manufacturer." **Buys 20 mss/year.** Query with published clips. Length: 1,200-3,000 words. **Pays $200-500.** Sometimes pays expenses of writers on assignment.

Photos: State availability of photos with submission. Reviews contact sheets, transparencies and prints (any standard size acceptable). Offers $50-200/photo. Captions, model releases and identification of subjects required. Buys all rights.

▣ The online version contains material not found in the print edition. Contact: Hannah Lee.

Tips: "Send clips and query; *do not send unsolicited manscripts.* We would like to see ideas for articles on a unique salon or a business article that focuses on a specific aspect or problem encountered when working in a salon. The Modern Nail Salon section, which profiles nail salons and full-service salons, is most open to freelancers. Focus on an innovative business idea or unique point of view. Articles from experts on specific business issues—insurance, handling difficult employees, cultivating clients—are encouraged."

$ $ SKIN INC. MAGAZINE, The Complete Business Guide for Face & Body Care, Allured Publishing Corp., 362 S. Schmale Rd., Carol Stream IL 60188. (630)653-2155. Fax: (630)665-2699. E-mail: taschetta-millane@allured.com. Website: www.skininc.com. Publisher: Marian Raney. **Contact:** Melinda Taschetta-Millane, editor. **30% freelance written.** Magazine published 12 times/year. "Manuscripts considered for publication that contain original and new information in the general fields of skin care and makeup, dermatological and esthetician-assisted surgical techniques. The subject may cover the science of skin, the business of skin care and makeup, and plastic surgeons on healthy (i.e. non-diseased) skin. Subjects may also deal with raw materials, formulations and regulations concerning claims for products and equipment." Estab. 1988. Circ. 16,000. Pays on publication. Publishes ms an average of 6 months after acceptance. Byline given. No kill fee. Buys all rights. Editorial lead time 6 months. Submit seasonal material 1 year in advance. Accepts queries by mail, e-mail, fax, phone. Responds in 2 weeks to queries; 1 month to mss. Sample copy and writer's guidelines free.

Nonfiction: General interest, how-to, interview/profile, personal experience, technical. **Buys 6 mss/year.** Query with published clips. Length: 2,000 words. **Pays $100-300 for assigned articles; $50-200 for unsolicited articles.**

Photos: State availability of photos with submission. Reviews 3×5 prints. Offers no additional payment for photos accepted with ms. Captions, model releases, identification of subjects required. Buys one-time rights.

Columns/Departments: Finance (tips and solutions for managing money), 2,000-2,500 words; Personnel (managing personnel), 2,000-2,500 words; Marketing (marketing tips for salon owners), 2,000-2,500 words; Retail (retailing products and services in the salon environment), 2,000-2,500 words. Query with published clips. **Pays $50-200.**

Fillers: Facts, newsbreaks. **Buys 6 mss/year.** Length: 250-500 words. **Pays $50-100.**

Tips: Have an understanding of the skin care industry.

BEVERAGES & BOTTLING

Manufacturers, distributors and retailers of soft drinks and alcoholic beverages read these publications. Publications for bar and tavern operators and managers of restaurants are classified in the Hotels, Motels, Clubs, Resorts & Restaurants category.

N $ $ THE BEVERAGE JOURNAL, Michigan Edition, MI Licensed Beverage Association, 920 N. Fairview Ave., Lansing MI 48912. (518)374-9611. Fax: (517)374-1165. E-mail: ktuinstra@mlba.org. Website: www.mlba.org. Editor: Richard Allen. **Contact:** Kristen Tuinstra, assistant editor. **40-50% freelance written.** Monthly magazine covering hospitality industry. "A monthly trade magazine devoted to the beer, wine and spirits industry in Michigan. It is dedicated to serving those who make their living serving the public and the state through the orderly and responsible sale of beverages." Estab. 1983. Circ. 4,200. Pays on publication. Buys one-time rights, second serial (reprint) rights, makes work-for-hire assignments. Editorial lead time 3 months. Submit seasonal material 3 months in advance. Accepts queries by mail, e-mail, fax. Responds in 1 month to queries; 2 months to mss. Sample copy for 9×12 SAE and 9 first-class stamps. Writer's guidelines for #10 SASE.

Nonfiction: Essays, general interest, how-to (make a drink, human resources, tips, etc.) humor, interview/profile, new product, opinion, personal experience, photo feature, technical. **Buys 24 mss/year.** Send complete ms. Length: 1,000 words maximum. **Pays $20-200.**

Reprints: Accepts previously published submissions.

Columns/Departments: Interviews (legislators, others), 750-1,000 words; Personal experience (waitstaff, customer, bartenders), 500 words. "Open to essay content ideas." **Buys 12 mss/year.** Send complete ms. **Pays $25-100.**

Tips: "We are particularly interested in nonfiction concerning responsible consumption/serving of alcohol. We are looking for reviews, company profiles, personal experiences that would benefit our audience. Our audience is a busy group of business owners and hospitality professionals striving to obtain pertinent information that is not too wordy."

$ $ BREWPUB, Successful Brewpub Management Strategies, 216 F St., Davis CA 95616. (530)758-4596. Fax: (530)758-7477. E-mail: bp@brewpubmag.com. Website: www.brewpubmag.com. **Contact:** Erika Ehmsen, managing editor. **100% freelance written.** Bimonthly trade magazine aimed at brewpub general managers, restaurant managers, brewers, and other personnel. Estab. 1996. Circ. 5,000. Pays on publication. Publishes ms an average of 4 months after acceptance. Byline given. Offers 25% kill fee. Buys all rights. Editorial lead time 3 months. Submit seasonal material 3 months in advance. Accepts queries by: mail, e-mail. Responds in 2 months. Writer's guidelines for #10 SASE.

Nonfiction: General interest (brewpub business), how-to (market and brew beer, manage restaurants, run a brewpub business). "Be certain that your article is targeted specifically at our magazine/audience (make sure articles are brewpub-specific; we don't print general-business articles)." **Buys 50 mss/year.** Query with published clips. Length: 1,200-3,000 words. **Pays $50-250.**

Photos: State availability of photos with submission. Negotiates payment individually.

Columns/Departments: Marketing; Start-ups (brewpub startup issues); Craft Brewer (technical beer brewing tips); After Hours (funny brewpub business stories), Pub news (news stories that relate to brewpub industry), all 750-1,500 words. **Buys 25 mss/year.** Query with or without published clips. **Pays $50-150.**

The online magazine carries original content not found in the print edition and includes writer's guidelines.

Tips "Start by submitting query for Pub News or After Hours."

N $ $ PATTERSON'S CALIFORNIA BEVERAGE JOURNAL, Interactive Color, Inc., 4910 San Fernando Rd., Glendale CA 91204. (818)547-4507. Fax: (818)547-4607. E-mail: nswords@interactivecolor.com. Website: www. beveragelink.com. Managing Editor: Natasha Swords. **50% freelance written.** Monthly magazine covering the alcohol, beverage and wine industries. "Patterson's reports on the latest news in product information, merchandising, company appointments, developments in the wine industry and consumer trends. Our readers can be informed, up-to-date and confident in their purchasing decisions." Estab. 1962. Circ. 20,000. Byline given. Offers 50% kill fee. Editorial lead time 1 month. Submit seasonal material 1 month in advance. Accepts queries by mail, e-mail, fax. Accepts simultaneous submissions. Sample copy free. Writer's guidelines free.

Nonfiction: Interview/profile, new product, market reports. "No consumer-oriented articles or negative slants on industry as a whole." **Buys 200 mss/year.** Query with published clips. Length: 600-1,800 words. **Pays $60-200.**

Photos: State availability of photos with submission. Reviews transparencies. Offers no additional payment for photos accepted with ms. Captions and identification of subjects required. Buys all rights.

Columns/Departments: Query with published clips.

$ $ VINEYARD & WINERY MANAGEMENT, P.O. Box 231, Watkins Glen NY 14891-0231. (607)535-7133. Fax: (607)535-2998. E-mail: gparnell@vwm.online.com. Website: www.vwm-online.com. **Contact:** J. William Moffett, editor. **80% freelance written.** Bimonthly trade magazine of professional importance to grape growers, winemakers and winery sales and business people. Estab. 1975. Circ. 4,500. Pays on publication. Byline given. Buys first North American serial rights and occasionally simultaneous rights. Responds in 3 weeks to queries; 1 month to mss. Sample copy free. Writer's guidelines for #10 SASE.

Nonfiction: How-to, interview/profile, technical. Subjects are technical in nature and explore the various methods people in these career paths use to succeed, and also the equipment and techniques they use successfully. Business articles and management topics are also featured. The audience is national with western dominance. **Buys 30 mss/year.** Query. Length: 300-5,000 words. **Pays $30-1,000.** Pays some expenses of writers on some assignments.

Photos: State availability of photos with submission. Reviews contact sheets, negatives and transparencies. Identification of subjects required. Black and white often purchased for $20 each to accompany story material; 35mm and/or 4×5 transparencies for $50 and up; 6/year of vineyard and/or winery scene related to story. Query.

Tips: "We're looking for long-term relationships with authors who know the business and write well. Electronic submissions required; query for formats."

BOOK & BOOKSTORE

Publications for book trade professionals from publishers to bookstore operators are found in this section. Journals for professional writers are classified in the Journalism & Writing category.

$ BLOOMSBURY REVIEW, A Book Magazine, Dept. WM, Owaissa Communications Co., Inc., P.O. Box 8928, Denver CO 80201. (303)455-3123. Fax: (303)455-7039. E-mail: bloomsb@aol.com. Publisher/Editor-in-Chief: Tom Auer. Editor/Associate Publisher: Marilyn Auer. **Contact:** Lori Kranz, associate editor. **75% freelance written.** Bimonthly tabloid covering books and book-related matters. "We publish book reviews, interviews with writers and poets, literary essays and original poetry. Our audience consists of educated, literate, *non-specialized* readers." Estab. 1980. Circ. 50,000. Pays on publication. Publishes ms an average of 4 months after acceptance. Byline given. Buys first or one-time rights. Responds in 4 months. Sample copy for $4 and 9×12 SASE. Writer's guidelines for #10 SASE.
Nonfiction: Essays, interview/profile, book reviews. "Summer issue features reviews, etc., about the American West. *We do not publish fiction.*" **Buys 60 mss/year.** Query with published clips or send complete ms. Length 800-1,500 words. **Pays $10-20.** Sometimes pays writers with contributor copies or other premiums "if writer agrees."
Reprints: Considered but not encouraged. Send photocopy of article and information about when and where the article previously appeared. Pays 100% of amount paid for an original article.
Photos: State availability of photos with submissions. Reviews prints. Offers no additional payment for photos accepted with ms. Buys one-time rights.
Columns/Departments: Book reviews and essays. **Buys 6 mss/year.** Query with published clips or send complete ms. Length: 500-1,500 words. **Pays $10-20.**
Poetry: Ray Gonzalez, poetry editor. Avant-garde, free verse, haiku, light verse, traditional. **Buys 20 poems/year.** Submit up to 5 poems at one time. **Pays $5-10.**
Tips: "We appreciate receiving published clips and/or completed manuscripts. Please—no rough drafts. Book reviews should be of new books (within 6 months of publication)."

$ $ FOREWORD MAGAZINE, ForeWord Magazine Inc., 129 E. Front St., Traverse City MI 49684. (231)933-3699. Fax: (231)933-3899. E-mail: mlink@forewordmagazine.com. Website: www.forewordmagazine.com. **Contact:** Mardi Link, editor-in-chief. **35% freelance written.** Monthly review magazine covering independent and university presses for booksellers and librarians with articles, news, book reviews. Estab. 1998. Circ. 15,000. Pays on publication. Publishes ms an average of 1 month after acceptance. Byline given. Buys all rights. Editorial lead time 3 months. Submit seasonal material 5 months in advance. Accepts queries by mail, e-mail, fax. Responds in 2 weeks to queries; 1 month to mss. Sample copy for 8×10 SASE.
Nonfiction: Book excerpts, essays, exposé, interview/profile, opinion. **Buys 20 mss/year.** Query with published clips or send complete ms. Length: 600-4,000 words. **Pays $45-400 for assigned articles; $45-250 for unsolicited articles.** Sometimes pays expenses of writers on assignment.
Photos: State availability of photos with submission. Reviews prints. Offers no additional payment for photos accepted with ms. Captions required. Buys all rights.
Columns/Departments: Pays $45-400.
Tips: "Be knowledgeable about the needs of booksellers and librarians—remember we are an industry trade journal, not a how-to or consumer publication. We review books prior to publication, so book reviews are always assigned."

$ THE HORN BOOK MAGAZINE, The Horn Book, Inc., 56 Roland St., Suite 200, Boston MA 02129. (617)628-0225. Fax: (617)628-0882. E-mail: magazine@hbook.com. Website: www.hbook.com. **Contact:** Roger Sutton, editor-in-chief. **10% freelance written.** Prefers to work with published/established writers. Bimonthly magazine covering children's literature for librarians, booksellers, professors, teachers and students of children's literature. Estab. 1924. Circ. 21,500. Pays on publication. Publishes ms an average of 4 months after acceptance. Byline given. Submit seasonal material 6 months in advance. Accepts queries by mail, e-mail, fax. Accepts simultaneous submissions. Responds in 2 months. Sample copy on website. Writer's guidelines available upon request or on website.
Nonfiction: Interview/profile (children's book authors and illustrators); topics of interest to the children's bookworld. Interested in seeing strong, authoritative pieces about children's books and contemporary culture. Writers should be familiar with the magazine and its contents. **Buys 20 mss/year.** Query or send complete ms. Length: 1,000-2,800 words. Honorarium paid upon publication.
   ▣ The online magazine carries original content not found in the print edition and includes writer's guidelines.
Tips: "Writers have a better chance of breaking into our publication with a query letter on a specific article they want to write."

▣ $ INDEPENDENT PUBLISHER, The Jenkins Group, 121 E. Front St., 4th Floor, Traverse City MI 49684. (231)933-0445. Fax: (231)933-0448. E-mail: jimb@bookpublishing.com. Website: www.independentpublisher.com. **Contact:** Jim Barnes, managing editor. **25% freelance written.** "*Independent Publisher* is a monthly online trade journal for small and independent publishing companies. We focus on marketing, promoting and producing books and how independent publishers can compete in this competitive industry. We also run profiles of successful publishers, an awards section and book reviews." Estab. 1983. Circ. 10,000. Pays on publication. Publishes ms an average of 1 month after acceptance. Byline given. Editorial lead time 2 months. Submit seasonal material 4 months in advance. Accepts simultaneous submissions. Accepts queries by mail, e-mail. Responds in 3 weeks to queries; 1 month to mss. Sample guidelines and writer's guidelines free.

Nonfiction: Book excerpts, essays, exposé, how-to, interview/profile, opinion, travel. "No consumer-oriented stories. We are a trade magazine for publishers." **Buys 12 mss/year.** Query with published clips. Length: 1,000-4,000 words.

Photos: State availability of photos with submission. Reviews transparencies and prints. Offers no additional payment for photos accepted with ms. Identification of subjects required. Buys one-time rights.

Columns/Departments: Book Biz; Advice from the Bar (legal advice); Industry Update; The Travel Directory. Passageways to Profit (distribution strategies), all 1,200-1,600 words. **Buys 6 mss/year.** Query with published clips. **Pays $50-100.**

Tips: "We're looking for in-depth publisher profiles."

$ $ LOS ANGELES TIMES BOOK REVIEW, Times Mirror, Times Mirror Square, Los Angeles CA 90053. (213)237-7778. Fax: (213)237-4712. Website: www.LATIMES.com. Editor: Steve Wasserman. **Contact:** Tom Curwen, deputy editor. **90% freelance written.** Weekly tabloid reviewing current books. Estab. 1881. Circ. 1,500,000. Pays on publication. Byline given. Offers variable kill fee. Buys first North American serial rights.

Nonfiction: No unsolicited book reviews or requests for specific titles to review. "Query with published samples—book reviews or literary features." **Buys 500 mss/year.** Length: 200-1,500 words. **Pay varies; approximately 35¢/word.**

BRICK, GLASS & CERAMICS

These publications are read by manufacturers, dealers and managers of brick, glass and ceramic retail businesses. Other publications related to glass and ceramics are listed in the Consumer Art & Architecture and Consumer Hobby & Craft sections.

$ STAINED GLASS, Stained Glass Association of America, 6 S.W. Second St., #7, Lee's Summit MO 64063. (800)438-9581. Fax: (816)524-9405. E-mail: sgmagaz@kcnet.com. Website: www.stainedglass.org. **Contact:** Richard Gross, editor. **70% freelance written.** Quarterly magazine. "Since 1906, *Stained Glass* has been the official voice of the Stained Glass Association of America. As the oldest, most respected stained glass publication in North America, *Stained Glass* preserves the techniques of the past as well as illustrates the trends of the future. This vital information, of significant value to the professional stained glass studio, is also of interest to those for whom stained glass is an avocation or hobby." Estab. 1906. Circ. 5,000. Pays on publication. Publishes ms an average of 6 months after acceptance. Byline given. Buys one-time rights. Editorial lead time 3 months. Submit seasonal material 6 months in advance. Accepts queries by mail, e-mail, fax. Responds in 3 months. Sample copy and writer's guidelines free.

○━ Break in with "excellent photography and in-depth stained glass architectural knowledge."

Nonfiction: How-to, humor, interview/profile, new product, opinion, photo feature, technical. Strong need for technical and how to create architectural type stained glass. Glass etching, use of etched glass in stained glass compositions, framing. **Buys 9 mss/year.** Query or send complete ms but must include photos or slides—very heavy on photos. **Pays $125/illustrated article; $75 for non-illustrated.**

Reprints: Accepts previously published submissions from non-stained glass publications only. Send tearsheet of article. Pay negotiable.

Photos: Send slides with submission. Reviews 4×5 transparencies. Pays $75 for non-illustrated. Pays $125 plus 3 copies for line art or photography. Identification of subjects required. Buys one-time rights.

Columns/Departments: Teknixs (technical, how-to, stained and glass art), word length varies by subject. **Buys 4 mss/year.** Query or send complete ms, but must be illustrated.

Tips: "We need more technical articles. Writers should be extremely well versed in the glass arts. Photographs are extremely important and must be of very high quality. Submissions without photographs or illustrations are seldom considered unless something special and writer states that photos are available. However, prefer to see with submission."

$ $ US GLASS, METAL & GLAZING, Key Communications Inc., P.O. Box 569, Garrisonville VA 22463. (540)720-5584. Fax: (540)720-5687. E-mail: ttaffera@glass.com. Website: www.uglassmag.com. **Contact:** Tara Taffera, editor. **25% freelance written.** Monthly magazine for companies involved in the auto glass and flat glass trades. Estab. 1966. Circ. 23,000. Pays on publication. Publishes ms an average of 3 months after acceptance. Byline given. Buys all rights. Editorial lead time 3 months. Submit seasonal material 2 months in advance. Accepts simultaneous submissions. Responds in 1 month to queries; 2 months to mss. Sample copy and writer's guidelines free on website. **Buys 12 mss/year.** Query with published clips. **Pays $300-600 for assigned articles.** Sometimes pays expenses of writers on assignment.

Photos: State availability of photos with submission. Reviews contact sheets. Offers no additional payment for photos accepted with ms. Captions, identification of subjects required. Buys first North American rights.

■ The online magazine carries original content not found in the print edition. Contact: Melissa Light.

BUILDING INTERIORS

Owners, managers and sales personnel of floor covering, wall covering and remodeling businesses read the journals listed in this category. Interior design and architecture publications may be found in the Consumer Art, Design & Collectibles category. For journals aimed at other construction trades see the Construction & Contracting section.

$ $ PWC, Painting & Wallcovering Contractor, Finan Publishing Co. Inc., 107 W. Pacific Ave., St. Louis MO 63119-2323. (314)961-6644. Fax: (314)961-4809. E-mail: jbeckner@finan.com. Website: www.paintstore.com. **Contact:** Jeffery Beckner, editor. **90% freelance written.** Bimonthly magazine *"PWC* provides news you can use: information helpful to the painting and wallcovering contractor in the here and now." Estab. 1928. Circ. 30,000. Pays 30 days after acceptance. Publishes ms an average of 1 month after acceptance. Byline given. Kill fee determined on individual basis. Buys first North American serial rights. Editorial lead time 2 months. Submit seasonal material 2 months in advance. Accepts simultaneous submissions. Responds in 2 weeks. Sample copy free.
Nonfiction: Essays, exposé, how-to (painting and wallcovering), interview/profile, new product, opinion personal experience. **Buys 40 mss/year.** Query with published clips. Length: 1,500-2,500 words. **Pays $300 minimum.** Pays expenses of writers on assignment.
Reprints: Send photocopy of article and information about when and where previously appeared. Negotiates payment.
Photos: State availability of or send photos with submission. Reviews contact sheets, negatives, transparencies and digital prints. Offers no additional payment for photos accepted with ms. Identification of subjects required. Buys one-time and all rights.
Columns/Departments: Anything of interest to the small businessman, 1,250 words. **Buys 2 mss/year.** Query with published clips. **Pays $50-100.**
Tips: "We almost always buy on an assignment basis. The way to break in is to send good clips, and I'll try and give you work."

$ $ QUALIFIED REMODELER, The Business Management Tool for Professional Remodelers, Cygnus Publishing, 1233 Janesville Ave., Fort Atkinson WI 53538. Website: www.qrmagazine.com. Editor: Roger Stanley. Managing Editor: Shanin Pepple. **15% freelance written.** Monthly trade journal covering residential remodeling. Estab. 1975. Circ. 92,500. **Pays on acceptance.** Publishes ms an average of 1 month after acceptance. Byline given. Buys all rights. Editorial lead time 2-3 months. Submit seasonal material 2 months in advance. Accepts queries by mail, e-mail, fax, phone. Sample copy online at website.
Nonfiction: How-to (business management), new product, photo feature. "We review remodeling websites every spring." **Buys 12 mss/year.** Query with published clips. Length: 1,200-2,500 words. **Pays $300-600; $200-400 for unsolicited articles.** Sometimes pays expenses of writers on assignment.
Photos: Send photos with submission. Reviews negatives and transparencies. Negotiates payment individually. Buys one-time rights.
Columns/Departments: Query with published clips. **Pays $200-400.**
   ■ The online version contains material not found in the print edition.
Tips: "We focus on business management issues faced by remodeling contractors. For example, sales, marketing, liability, taxes and just about any matter addressing small business operation."

BUSINESS MANAGEMENT

These publications cover trends, general theory and management practices for business owners and top-level business executives. Publications that use similar material but have a less technical slant are listed in the Consumer Business & Finance section. Journals for middle management, including supervisors and office managers, appear in the Management & Supervision section. Those for industrial plant managers are listed under Industrial Operations and under sections for specific industries, such as Machinery & Metal. Publications for office supply store operators are included in the Office Environment & Equipment section.

N $ $ ACCOUNTING TODAY, Faulkner & Gray, 11 Penn Plaza, New York NY 10001. (212)967-7000. **Contact:** Rick Telberg, editor. Biweekly newspaper. *"Accounting Today* is the newspaper of record for the accounting industry." Estab. 1987. Circ. 35,000. Pays on publication. Publishes ms an average of 1 month after acceptance. Byline given. Buys all rights. Editorial lead time 2 weeks. Responds in 1 month. Sample copy for $5.
Nonfiction: Book excerpts, essays, exposé, how-to, interview/profile, new product, technical. **Buys 35 mss/year.** Query with published clips. Length: 500-1,500 words. **Pays 25-50¢/word for assigned articles.** Pays expenses of writers on assignment.

Photos: State availability of photos with submission. Negotiates payment individually.

$ $ $ ACROSS THE BOARD, The Conference Board Magazine, The Conference Board, 845 Third Ave., New York NY 10022. (212)339-0451. Fax: (212)980-7014. E-mail: atb@conference-board.org. Website: www.confere nce-board.org. **Contact:** Al Vogl, editor. Managing Editor: Matthew Budman. **60% freelance written.** Monthly magazine covering business issues of interest to senior executives of Fortune 500 companies. "For leaders in business, government, and other organizations. It is published by The Conference Board, America's preeminent business research and forecasting organization, and most of its readers are top-level managers in the United States and abroad—many of them CEOs." Estab. 1976. Circ. 30,000. Pays on publication. Publishes ms an average of 6 months after acceptance. Byline given. Offers 33% kill fee. Buys first North American serial rights. Editorial lead time 3 months. Accepts simultaneous submissions. Accepts queries by mail, e-mail, fax, phone. Responds in 3 weeks. Sample copy and writer's guidelines for 8½×11 SASE or on website.

Nonfiction: Book excerpts, essays, interview/profile, opinion, personal experience. Business perspectives on timely issues, including management practices, foreign policy, social issues, and science and technology. No interest in highly technical articles about business strategy and "how-to" articles. **Buys 75-100 mss/year.** Query with published clips, or send complete ms. Length: 2,500-3,500 words. **Pays $500-1,000.** Sometimes pays expenses of writers on assignment.

Reprints: Send tearsheet, photocopy or typed ms of article or short story with rights for sale noted and information about when and where the article previously appeared.

Photos: State availability of photos with submission.

Columns/Departments: Soundings (strong opinions on subjects of pertinence to our readers), 400-800 words. **Buys 75 mss/year.** Query. **Pays $200-400.**

Tips: "We let *Forbes*, *Fortune* and *Business Week* do most of the straight reporting, while we do some of the critical thinking; that is, we let writers explore the implications of the news in depth. *Across the Board* tries to provide different angles on important topics, and to bring to its readers' attention issues that they might otherwise not devote much thought to. A few examples from past issues: ethics overseas; how and why a company should set up shop on the Internet; and business lessons learned from the art world. We emphasize the human side of organizational life at all levels. We're as concerned with helping managers who are 'lonely at the top' as with motivating workers and enhancing job satisfaction."

N $ $ AMERICAN DRYCLEANER/COIN-OP/CLEAN CAR/AMERICAN LAUNDRY NEWS, American Trade Magazines/Crain Communications Inc., 500 N. Dearborn, Chicago IL 60610. (312)337-7700. Fax: (312)337-8654. E-mail: atmpub@aol.com. Managing Editor: Ian Murphy. **Contact:** Earl Fischer, editor. **20% freelance written.** Monthly tabloid covering drycleaning, coin laundry, coin car cleaning, institutional laundry. "Freelancers need professional drycleaning or business writing experience." Estab. 1934. Circ. 25,000. Pays on publication. Publishes ms an average of 1 month after acceptance. Byline given. Offers 10% kill fee. Buys first, second serial (reprint) and all rights. Editorial lead time 2 months. Submit seasonal material 2 months in advance. Accepts queries by mail, e-mail, fax, phone. Accepts simultaneous submissions. Responds in 1 month to queries; 4 months to mss. Sample copy for 6×9 SAE and 2 first-class stamps.

Nonfiction: Ian P. Murphy, managing editor. How-to (general biz, industry-specific), interview/profile, new product, personal experience, technical. No inspirational, consumer-geared. **Buys 12-15 mss/year.** Query. Length: 600-2,000 words. **Pays $50-500 minimum for assigned articles; $25-250 for unsolicited articles.** Sometimes pays expenses of writers on assignment.

Reprints: Accepts previously published submissions.

Photos: State availability of photos with submission. Reviews contact sheets, negatives, 4×5 or slide transparencies and 3×5-5×7 prints. Negotiates payment individually. Identification of subjects required. Buys one-time rights.

Columns/Departments: Ian P. Murphy, managing editor. General Business, 1,200 words. **Buys 72 mss/year.** Send complete ms. **Pays $50-150.**

Tips: "Each magazine is geared toward small-business owners in these specific industries. Writers will find professional experience in the industry is a plus; general small-business articles are often used, but tailored to each magazine's audience."

N $ $ BEDTIMES, The Business Journal for the Sleep Products Industry, International Sleep Products Association, 501 Wythe St., Alexandria VA 22304-1917. (703)683-8371. Fax: (703)683-4503. Website: www.sleepprodu cts.org. **Contact:** Kathleen Burns, editor. Managing Editor: Kathleen Smith. **20-40% freelance written.** Monthly magazine covering the mattress manufacturing industry. "Our news and features are straight forward—we are not a lobbying vehicle for our association. No special slant or philosophy." Estab. 1917. Circ. 4,000. **Pays on acceptance.** Publishes ms an average of 4 months after acceptance. Byline sometimes given. "Always on a cover story, a sidebar or a major feature." Buys first North American serial rights. Editorial lead time 2 months. Accepts queries by mail, e-mail, fax. Accepts simultaneous submissions. Responds in 1 month. Sample copy for $4. Writer's guidelines free for #10 SASE or by e-mail.

    O→ Break in with stories on "interesting promotions by bedding manufacturers or retailers (i.e., retailer bought some of Princess Diana's jewels to display in his store to generate traffic); the scientific or health aspect of sleep research; ergonomic aspects of the workplace (i.e., manufacturing); flammability and bedding results.

Nonfiction: Interview/profile. Special issue: Philanthropy in the workplace (November). "No pieces that do not relate to business in general or mattress industry in particular." **Buys 15-25 mss/year.** Query with published clips. Length: 500-3,500 words. **Pays 35-50¢/word.** "Negotiates separately for cover stories." Sometimes pays expenses of writers on assignment.

Photos: State availability of photos with submission. Negotiates payment individually. Identification of subjects required. Buys one-time rights.

Columns/Departments: Millennium Milestones (companies marking anniversaries from 25 to 150 years), 1,000 words. **Buys 10-12 mss/year.** Query with 3 published clips. **Pays 35-50¢/word.**

Tips: "Cover stories are a major outlet for freelance submissions. Once a story is written and accepted, the author is encouraged to submit suggestions to the graphic designer of the magazine regarding ideas for the cover illustration as well as possible photos/graphs/charts, etc. to be used with the story itself. Topics have included annual industry forecast; physical expansion of industry facilities; e-commerce; flammability and home furnishings; the risks and rewards of marketing overseas; the evolving family business; the shifting workplace environment; and what do consumers really want?"

$ $ CBA MARKETPLACE, CBA Service Corp., P.O. Box 62000, Colorado Springs CO 80962. E-mail: publication s@cbaonline.org. Website: www.cbaonline.org. **Contact:** Debby Weaver, managing editor. **20% freelance written.** Monthly magazine covering the Christian retail industry. "Writers must have knowledge of and direct experience in the Christian retail industry. Subject matter must specifically pertain to the Christian retail audience." Estab. 1968. Pays on publication. Publishes ms an average of 3 months after acceptance. Byline given. Buys all rights in all media. Editorial lead time 5 months. Submit seasonal material 6 months in advance. Accepts queries by mail, e-mail. Responds in 2 months. Sample copy for $7.50 or on website.

Nonfiction: Christian retail. **Buys 24 mss/year.** Query. Length: 750-1,500 words. **Pays 15-25¢/word.**

Fillers: Contact: Graphic designer. Cartoons. **Buys 12/year. Pays $150.**

  The online magazine carries original news content not found in the print edition. Contact: Debby Weaver.

Tips: "Only experts on Christian retail industry, completely familiar with retail audience and their needs and considerations, should submit a query. Do not submit articles unless requested."

N $ $ $ CONSUMER GOODS MANUFACTURER, Improving Business Performance Using Technology, Edgell Communications, 4 Middlebury Blvd., Suite 107, Randolph NJ 07869. (973)252-0100. E-mail: mfrantz@ edgellmail.com. Website: www.consumergoods.com. **Contact:** Mark Frantz, editor. **60% freelance written.** Monthly tabloid covering suppliers to retailers. "Readers are the functional managers/executives in all types of retail and consumer goods firms. They are making major improvements in company operations and in alliances with customers/suppliers." Estab. 1991. Circ. 26,000. Pays on publication. Byline sometimes given. Buys first rights, Internet, and second serial (reprint) rights. Editorial lead time 3 months. Accepts queries by mail, e-mail, phone. Sample copy for 11×15 SAE with 6 first-class stamps. Writer's guidelines for #10 SASE.

Nonfiction: How-to, interview/profile, technical. **Buys 100 mss/year.** Query with published clips. Length: 1,200-2,400 words. **Pays $900 maximum for assigned articles.** Sometimes pays contributor copies as negotiated. Sometimes pays expenses of writers on assignment.

Photos: Send photos with submission. Reviews contact sheets, negatives, transparencies and prints. Offers no additional payment for photos accepted with ms. Identification of subjects required. Buys one-time rights plus reprint and Internet, if applicable.

Tips: "Case histories about companies achieving substantial results using advanced management practices and/or advanced technology are best."

$ $ CONSUMER GOODS TECHNOLOGY, Improving Business Performance Through Technology, Edgell Communications, 4 Middleburg Blvd., Randolph NJ 07869-4214. (973)252-0100. Fax: (973)252-9020. E-mail: Apantages@edgellmail.com. Website: www.consumergoods.com. Editor: Mark Frantz. **Contact:** Angeline Pantages, managing editor. **80% freelance written.** Bimonthly trade journal covering how marketers and manufacturers use technology to improve business performance. "*CGT* is a how-to publication to help marketers and manufacturers improve business performance through technology. Readers learn how technology helps them achieve financial returns from investments in technology; implement supply/demand chain strategies; integrate technology enterprisewide, use logistics techniques; improve forecasting, replenishment, and customer service; form alliances with suppliers and customers; commit to core competencies; and outsource successfully. *CG* helps its readers actively move the supply/demand chain." Estab. 1992. Circ. 25,000. **Pays on acceptance.** Publishes ms an average of 2 months after acceptance. Byline given. Buys first and electronic rights. Editorial lead time 3 months. Accepts queries by mail, fax, phone, e-mail. Sample copy and writer's guidelines free.

Nonfiction: How-to (case histories of technology implementations), interview/profile, new product, technical. "No personal experience/view opinion." **Buys 25 mss/year.** Send complete ms. Length: 700-2,000 words. **Pays $500-700.** Sometimes pays expenses of writers on assignment.

Photos: Send photos with submission. Reviews 5×7 prints. Model releases and identification of subjects required.

  The online magazine carries original content not found in the print edition.

Tips: "Showing quantified business benefits of technology implementation is key to a successful submission. Pitfalls and success factors are valuable, as is showing the next steps for improvement in the future."

N **$ $** **CONTINGENCY PLANNING & MANAGEMENT**, Witter Publishing, 84 Park Ave. Flemington NJ 08822. (908)788-0343. Fax: (908)788-3782. E-mail: cpmmagazine@witterpublishing.com. Website: ContingencyPlanni ng.com. **Contact:** Vanessa Van Gilson, editor. Managing Editor: Michelle Simonelli. Monthly magazine covering business continuity/contingency planning. *"Contingency Planning & Management* magazine is the comprehensive information source for business continuity. We go out to decision-makers for the Fortune 1000 interested in risk management, contingency planning and disaster recovery." Estab. 1996. Circ. 35,000 qualified. Pays on publication. Publishes ms an average of 2 months after acceptance. Byline given. Buys all rights. Editorial lead time 3 months. Accepts queries by mail, e-mail, fax, phone. Responds in 1 week to queries. Sample copy free. Writer's guidelines free.
Nonfiction: How-to, interview/profile, technical. "No personal material." **Buys 2 mss/year.** Query with published clips. Length: 1,500-3,500 words. **Pays up to $200.**
Photos: State availability of photos with submission. Reviews negatives, transparencies and prints. Negotiates payment individually. Captions required, model releases and identification of subjects required. Buys all rights.

N **$ $** **CONTRACTING PROFITS**, Trade Press Publishing, 2100 W. Florist Ave., Milwaukee WI 53209. (414)228-7701. E-mail: dianna.b@tradepress.com. Website: www.cleanlink.com/cp. **Contact:** Dianna Bisswurm, editor. **40% freelance written.** Magazine published 9 times/year covering "building service contracting, business management advice. We are the pocket MBA for this industry—focusing not only on cleaning-specific topics, but also discussing how to run businesses better and increase profits through a variety of management articles." Estab. 1995. Circ. 32,000. Pays within 30 days of submission. Byline given. Buys all rights. Editorial lead time 2 months. Submit seasonal material 3 months in advance. Accepts queries by mail, e-mail. Responds in 3 weeks to queries. Sample copy online at website. Writer's guidelines free.
Nonfiction: Exposé, how-to, interview/profile, technical. "No product-related reviews or testimonials." **Buys 30 mss/ year.** Query with published clips. Length: 1,200-3,000 words. **Pays $100-500.** Sometimes pays expenses of writers on assignment.
Columns/Departments: Query with published clips.
Tips: "Read back issues on our website and be able to understand some of those topics prior to calling."

$ **CONVENTION SOUTH**, Covey Communications Corp., 2001 W. First St., P.O. Box 2267, Gulf Shores AL 36547-2267. (334)968-5300. Fax: (334)968-4532. E-mail: info@conventionsouth.com. Website: www.conventionsouth. com. **Contact:** Kristen McIntosh, executive editor. Editor: J. Talty O'Connor. **50% freelance written.** Monthly tabloid for meeting planners who plan events in the South. Topics relate to the meetings industry—how-to articles, industry news, destination spotlights. Estab. 1983. Circ. 11,800. Pays on publication. Publishes ms an average of 2 months after acceptance. Byline given. Buys first rights or second serial (reprint) rights. Editorial lead time 3 months. Submit seasonal/ holiday material 4 months in advance. Accepts simultaneous submissions. Responds in 2 months to queries. Sample copy free. Writer's guidelines for #10 SASE.
Nonfiction: How-to (relative to meeting planning/travel), interview/profile, photo feature, technical, travel. **Buys 50 mss/year.** Query. Length: 1,250-3,000 words. **Pays $75-150.** Pays in contributor copies or other premiums if arranged in advance. Sometimes pays expenses of writers on assignment.
Reprints: Accepts previously published submissions. Send photocopy of article and information about when and where the article previously appeared. Pay negotiable.
Photos: Send photos with submission. Reviews 5×7 prints. Offers no additional payment for photos accepted with ms. Captions and identification of subjects required. Buys one-time rights.
Columns/Departments: How-tos (related to meetings), 700 words. **Buys 12 mss/year.** Query with published clips. Payment negotiable.
Tips: "Know who our audience is and make sure articles are appropriate for them."

N **$ $ $** **EXPO**, Atwood Publishing LLC, 11600 College Blvd., Overland Park KS 66210. (913)469-1185. Fax: (913)469-0806. E-mail: dvasos@expoweb.com. Website: www.expoweb.com. Managing Editor: Janine Taylor. **Contact:** Danica Vasos, editor-in-chief. **80% freelance written.** Magazine covering expositions. *"EXPO* is the information and education resource for the exposition industry. It is the only magazine dedicated exclusively to the people with direct responsibility for planning, promoting and operating trade and consumer shows. Our readers are show managers and their staff, association executives, independent show producers and industry suppliers. Every issue of *EXPO* contains in-depth, how-to features and departments that focus on the practical aspects of exposition management, including administration, promotion and operations." Pays on publication. Byline given. Offers 50% kill fee. Buys first North American serial rights. Editorial lead time 3 months. Accepts queries by mail, e-mail, fax. Responds in 3 weeks to queries. Sample copy free. Writer's guidelines free or online at website.
Nonfiction: How-to, interview/profile. Query with published clips. Length: 600-2,400 words. **Pays 50¢/word.** Pays expenses of writers on assignment.
Photos: State availability of photos with submission.
Columns/Departments: Profile (personality profile), 650 words; Exhibitor Matters (exhibitor issues) and EXPOTech (technology), both 600-1,300 words. **Buys 10 mss/year.** Query with published clips.
Tips: *"EXPO* now offers shorter features and departments, while continuing to offer in-depth reporting. Editorial is more concise, using synopsis, bullets and tidbits whenever possible. Every article needs sidebars, call-outs, graphs, charts, etc., to create entry points for readers. Headlines and leads are more provocative. And writers should elevate the level of shop talk, demonstrating that *EXPO* is the leader in the industry. We plan our editorial calendar about one year

in advance, but we are always open to new ideas. Please query before submitting a story to *EXPO*—tell us about your idea and what our readers would learn. Include your qualifications to write about the subject and the sources you plan to contact."

$ $EXECUTIVE UPDATE, Greater Washington Society of Association Executives, 1426 21st St. NW, Washington DC 20036. Fax: (202)429-0553. E-mail: jschultz@gwsae.org. Website: www.executiveupdate.com. **Contact:** Jane Schultz, editor-in-chief. **60% freelance written.** "Monthly magazine exploring a broad range of association management issues and for introducing and discussing management and leadership philosophies. It is written for individuals at all levels of association management, with emphasis on senior staff and CEOs." Estab. 1979. Circ. 14,000. **Pays on acceptance.** Publishes ms an average of 6 months after acceptance. Byline given. Offers 20% kill fee. Buys first rights. Editorial lead time 3 months. Submit seasonal material 6 months in advance. Accepts simultaneous submissions. Accepts queries by mail, e-mail, fax, phone. Responds in 2 weeks to queries; 2 months to mss. Sample copy and writer's guidelines free.
Nonfiction: How-to, humor, interview/profile, opinion, personal experience, travel, management and workplace issues. **Buys 24-36 mss/year.** Query with published clips. Length: 2,500-3,500 words. **Pays $500-700.** Pays expenses of writers on assignment.
Reprints: Accepts previously published submissions.
Columns/Departments: Intelligence (new ways to tackle day-to-day issues), 500-700 words; Off the Cuff (guest column for association executives). Query. **Pays $100-200.**

N $ $ $ $GLOBAL TECHNOLOGY BUSINESS, Dasar, Inc., 1157 San Antonio Rd., Mountain View CA 94043. (650)934-2300. Fax: (650)934-2306. Website: www.gtbusiness.com. Editor: Laurence Scott. **Contact:** Assignment Editor. **5-10% freelance written.** Monthly magazine covering global IT and e-business for high-tech executives. "*GTB* focuses on information technology from a global perspective. In the US, over 60,000 executives in the high-tech industry rely on *GTP* to follow the global integration of technologies and the strategies, products and alliances of global IT provides." Estab. 1998. Circ. 60,000. Pays on billing cycle. Publishes ms 4 months after acceptance. Byline sometimes given. Buys all rights. Editorial lead time 3 months. Submit seasonal material 2 months in advance. Accepts queries by mail, phone. Sample copy online at website.
Nonfiction: Book excerpts, exposé, general interest, how-to, new product, technical. **Buys 50 mss/year.** Query with published clips. Length: 500-3,000 words. **Pays $500-2,500.** Sometimes pays expenses of writers on assignment.
Columns/Departments: Pays $500-2,500.

$ $MEETINGS IN THE WEST, Stamats Communications, 550 Montgomery St., #750, San Francisco CA 94111. (415)788-2005. Fax: (415)788-0301. E-mail: sandi-garza@stamats.com. Website: www.meetingsweb.com. **Contact:** Christa Palmer, editor. Managing Editor: Sandi Garza. **75% freelance written.** Monthly tabloid covering meeting, event and conference planning. Estab. 1986. Circ. 25,000. Pays 1 month after acceptance. Publishes ms an average of 1 month after acceptance. Byline given. Buys first North American serial rights and electronic rights. Editorial lead time 3 months. Submit seasonal material 3 months in advance. Accepts queries by mail, e-mail, fax. Responds in 3 weeks. Sample copy for 9 × 13 SAE and 5 first-class stamps. Writer's guidelines for #10 SASE or on website.
   O— "Break in with travel experience and destination knowledge, strong clips, meetings and event planning knowledge and experience. Our magazine is heavy on travel destinations. We are always looking for area experts."
Nonfiction: How-to (save money, theme party ideas, plan interesting meetings, etc.), travel (as it pertains to meetings and conventions, what to do after the convention, etc.). "No first-person fluff. We are a business magazine." **Buys 30 mss/year.** Query with published clips. Length: 1,200-2,000 words. **Pays 16¢/word.**
Photos: State availability of photos with submission. Offers no additional payment for photos accepted with ms. Identification of subjects required. Buys one-time rights.
Tips: "We're looking for more technology featuare articles (1,200) words) regarding meeting planning."

N $ $MINORITY BUSINESS ENTREPRENEUR (MBE), 3528 Torrance Blvd., Suite 101, Torrance CA 90503. (310)540-9398. Fax: (310)792-8263. E-mail: mbewbe@ix.netcom.com. Website: www.mbemag.com. **Contact:** Angela Cranon, editor-in-chief. **50% freelance written.** Bimonthly magazine covering minority and women business ownership and development. "*MBE* magazine examines programs in the public and private sectors designed to develop minority and women owned businesses into viable enterprises. *MBE* magazine covers a broad range of industries, from construction and banking to telecommunications and high tech." Estab. 1984. Circ. 40,000. Pays on publication. Byline given. Buys first North American serial rights. Editorial lead time 3 months. Responds in 3 weeks to queries. Sample copy for 9½ × 12½ SASE and 7 first-class stamps. Writer's guidelines free.
Nonfiction: Interview/profile. Nothing unrelated to minority or women's business. **Buys 4-6 mss/year.** Query with published clips. Length: 750-1,000 words. **Pays $0-300.** Sometimes pays expenses of writers on assignment.
Tips: Every issue features a Cover Story (spotlighting the achievements of an individual entrepreneur); Corporate View (highlighting corporate minority and women supplier programs); and Different Drummers (profiling innovators, risk takers, visionaries).

$ $NORTHEAST EXPORT, A Magazine for New England Companies Engaged in International Trade, Laurentian Business Publishing, 404 Chestnut St., Suite 201, Manchester NH 03101-1831. (603)626-6354. Fax: (603)626-6359. E-mail: neexport@aol.com. **Contact:** Hope Jordan, editor. **30% freelance written.** Bimonthly business-to-business magazine. "*Northeast Export* is the only publication directly targeted at New England's international trade community. All stories relate to issues affecting New England companies and feature only New England-based profiles and examples. No unsolicited material." Estab. 1997. Circ. 13,500. **Pays on acceptance**. Byline given. Offers 10% kill fee. Buys all rights. Editorial lead time 2 months. Accepts queries by mail, e-mail, fax. Sample copy free.

Nonfiction: Interview/profile, how-to, industry trends/analysis. "We will not take unsolicited articles. Query first with clips." **Buys 10-12 mss/year.** Query with published clips and SASE. Length: 800-2,000 words. Pay varies.

Photos: State availability of photos with submission or send photos with submission. Reviews 2¼ transparencies and 5×7 prints. Negotiates payment individually. Captions, model releases and identification of subjects required. Buys one-time rights.

Tips: "We're looking for writers with availability; the ability to write clearly about tough, sometimes very technical subjects; the fortitude to slog through industry jargon to get the story straight; a knowledge of international trade issues and/or New England transportation infrastructure. We're interested in freelancers with business writing and magazine experience, especially those with contacts in the New England manufacturing, finance and transportation communities."

N $ $ PORTABLE RESTROOM OPERATOR, Rangoon Moon Inc., P.O. Box 904, Dahlonega GA 30533. (877)766-1629. Fax: (706)864-6838. E-mail: sesails@yahoo.com. Managing Editor: M.A. Watson. **Contact:** K.M. Gralton, editor. **50% freelance written.** Magazine published 9 times/year covering portable sanitation. Estab. 1998. **Pays on acceptance**. Publishes ms an average of 2 months after acceptance. Byline given. Editorial lead time 1 month. Submit seasonal material 2 months in advance. Accepts queries by mail, e-mail, fax.

Nonfiction: Expose (government regulations, OSHA, EPS associated, trends, public attitudes etc.); general interest (state portable restroom associations, conventions, etc.); new products; personal experience; technical; quality articles that will be of interest to our readers. Studies on governmental changes, OSHA regulations, and sanitation articles that deal with portable restrooms are of strong interest. Length is not important. Query or send complete ms. **Pays 15¢/word.**

Reprints: Send photos with query or ms. Pays $15 for b&w and color prints that are used. No negatives. "We need good contrast." Captions, model release required. Buys one-time rights.

Tips: "Material must pertain to portable sanitation industry."

$ $ $ $ PROFESSIONAL COLLECTOR, Pohly & Partners, 27 Melcher St., 2nd Floor, Boston MA 02210-1516. (617)451-1700. Fax: (617)338-7767. E-mail: procollector@pohlypartners.com. Website: www.pohlypartners.com. **Contact:** Karen English, editor. **90% freelance written.** Quarterly magazine published for Western Union's Financial Services Inc.'s Quick Collect Service, covering debt collection business/lifestyle issues. "We gear our articles directly to the debt collectors, not their managers. Each issue offers features covering the trends and players, the latest technology, legislation and other issues affecting the collections industry. It's all designed to help collectors be more productive and improve their performance." Estab. 1993. Circ. 161,000. Pays on publication. Byline given. Buys first North American serial rights. Editorial lead time 9 months. Submit seasonal material 9 months in advance. Accepts query by mail, e-mail, fax. Sample copy and writer's guidelines free.

Nonfiction: Book excerpts, general interest, how-to (tips on good collecting), humor, interview/profile, new product, legal issues for collectors/FDCPA, business/industry issues dealing with debt collectors. **Buys 10-15 mss/year.** Query with published clips. Length: 400-2,000 words. Pay negotiable for assigned articles. Sometimes pays expenses of writers on assignment.

Photos: State availability of photos with submission. Reviews contact sheets and 3×5 prints. Negotiates payment individually. Captions, model releases and identification of subjects required. Buys one-time rights.

Columns/Departments: Industry Roundup (issues within industry), 500-1,000 words; Tips, 750-1,000 words; Q&A (questions & answers for collectors), 1,500 words. **Buys 15-20 mss/year.** Query with published clips. Pay negotiable.

Tips: "Writers should be aware that *Professional Collector* is a promotional publication, and that its content must support the overall marketing goals of Western Union. It helps to have extensive insider knowledge about the debt collection industry."

N $ $ PROGRESSIVE RENTALS, The Voice of the Rental-Purchase Industry, Association of Progressive Rental Organizations, 9015 Mountain Ridge Dr., #220, Austin TX 78759. (800)204-2776. Fax: (512)794-0097. E-mail: jsherrier@apro-rto.com. Website: www.apro-rto.com. **Contact:** Julie Stephen Sherrier, editor. **50% freelance written.** Bimonthly magazine covering the rent-to-own industry. *Progressive Rentals* is the only publication representing the rent-to-own industry and members of APRO. The magazine covers timely news and features affecting the industry, association activities and member profiles. Awarded best 4-color magazine by the American Society of Association Executives in 1999." Estab. 1980. Circ. 5,500. **Pays on acceptance**. Publishes ms an average of 2 months after acceptance. Byline given. Offers 25% kill fee. Buys first North American serial rights. Editorial lead time 2 months. Submit seasonal material 4 months in advance. Accepts queries by mail, e-mail, fax, phone. Accepts simultaneous submissions. Responds in 1 month to queries; 2 months to mss. Sample copy free.

Nonfiction: Exposé, general interest, how-to, inspirational, interview/profile, technical, industry features. **Buys 12 mss/year.** Query with published clips. Length: 1,200-2,500 words. **Pays $150-500.** Sometimes pays expenses of writers on assignment.

$ $ RENTAL MANAGEMENT, American Rental Association, 1900 19th St., Moline IL 61265. (309)764-2475. Fax: (309)764-1533. E-mail: brian.alm@ararental.org. Website: www.ararental.org. Editor: Brian R. Alm. Managing

Editor: Tamera Dawson. **30% freelance written.** Monthly business magazine for the equipment rental industry world-wide (*not* property, real estate, appliances, furniture or cars), emphasizing management topics in particular but also marketing, merchandising, technology, etc. Estab. 1970. Circ. 17,000. **Pays on acceptance.** Publishes ms an average of 3 months after acceptance. Byline sometimes given. Buys first North American serial rights. Editorial lead time 2 months. Submit seasonal material 3 months in advance. Does not report on unsolicited work unless being considered for publication. Accepts queries by mail, e-mail, fax. Sample copy for 9 × 12 SAE and 6 first-class stamps.

Nonfiction: Small-business management and marketing. **Buys 20-25 mss/year.** Query with published clips. Length: 600-1,500 words. Pay is negotiated. Sometimes pays expenses of writers on assignment.

Reprints: Sometimes accepts previously published submissions. Send tearsheet or typed ms with rights for sale noted and information about when and where the article previously appeared.

Photos: State availability of photos with submission. Reviews contact sheets, negatives, 35mm or 2¼ transparencies and any size prints. Negotiates payment individually. Identification of subjects required. Buys one-time rights.

Columns/Departments: "We are adequately served by existing columnists and have a long waiting list of others to use pending need." **Buys 20 mss/year.** Query with published clips. Pay is negotiated.

Tips: "Show me you can write maturely, cogently and fluently on management matters of direct and compelling interest to the small-business owner or manager in a larger operation; no sloppiness, no unexamined thoughts, no stiffness or affectation—genuine, direct and worthwhile English."

$ $ RETAIL INFO SYSTEMS NEWS, Where Retail Management Shops for Technology, Edgell Communications, 4 Middlebury Blvd., Suite 107, Randolph NJ 07869. (973)252-0100. Fax: (973)252-9020. Website: www.consumergoods.com. **Contact:** Mark Frantz, editor. **65% freelance written.** Monthly magazine. "Readers are functional managers/executives in all types of retail and consumer goods firms. They are making major improvements in company operations and in alliances with customers/suppliers." Estab. 1988. Circ. 20,000. Pays on publication. Publishes ms an average of 2 months after acceptance. Byline sometimes given. Buys first North American serial rights, electronic rights, second serial (reprint) rights, all rights. Editorial lead time 3 months. Accepts queries by mail. Submit seasonal material 3 months in advance. Sample copy online at website.

Nonfiction: Essays, exposé, how-to, humor, interview/profile, technical. **Buys 80 mss/year.** Query with published clips. Length: 700-1,900 words. **Pays $600-1,200 for assigned articles.** Sometimes pays in contributor copies as negotiated. Sometimes pays expenses of writers on assignment.

Photos: State availability of photos with submission, or send photos with submission. Negotiates payment individually. Identification of subjects required. Buys one-time rights plus reprint, if applicable.

Columns: News/trends (analysis of current events), 150-300 words. **Buys 4 mss/year.** Query with published clips. **Pays $100-300.**

Tips: "Case histories about companies achieving substantial results using advanced management practices and/or advanced technology are best."

$ $ SECURITY DEALER, Cygnus Publishing, 445 Broad Hollow Rd., Melville NY 11747. (516)845-2700. Fax: (516)845-7109. E-mail: susan.brady@cygnuspub.com. **Contact:** Susan A. Brady, editor. **25% freelance written.** Monthly magazine for electronic alarm dealers, burglary and fire installers, with technical, business, sales and marketing information. Circ. 25,000. Pays 3 weeks after publication. Publishes ms an average of 4 months after acceptance. Byline sometimes given. Buys first North American serial rights. Accepts simultaneous submissions.

Nonfiction: How-to, interview/profile, technical. No consumer pieces. Query by mail only. Length: 1,000-3,000 words. **Pays $300 for assigned articles; $100-200 for unsolicited articles.** Sometimes pays the expenses of writers on assignment.

Photos: State availability of photos with submission. Reviews contact sheets and transparencies. Offers $25 additional payment for photos accepted with ms. Captions and identification of subjects required.

Columns/Departments: Closed Circuit TV, Access Control (both on application, installation, new products), 500-1,000 words. **Buys 25 mss/year.** Query by mail only. **Pays $100-150.**

Tips: "The areas of our publication most open to freelancers are technical innovations, trends in the alarm industry and crime patterns as related to the business as well as business finance and management pieces."

$ THE STATE JOURNAL, The State Journal Corp., 904 Virginia St. E., Charleston WV 25301. (304)344-1630. Fax: (304)345-2721. E-mail: sjeditor@aol.com. Website: www.statejournal.com. **Contact:** Jack Bailey, editor. **30% freelance written.** "We are a weekly journal dedicated to providing stories of interest to the business community in West Virginia." Estab. 1984. Circ. 12,000. Pays on publication. Publishes ms an average of 2 months after acceptance. Byline given. Buys first rights. Editorial lead time 2 months. Submit seasonal material 4 months in advance. Accepts queries by mail, e-mail, fax. Responds in 3 weeks to queries; 2 months to mss. Sample copy and writer's guidelines for #10 SASE.

Nonfiction: General interest, interview/profile, new product, opinion, all business related. **Buys 150 mss/year.** Query. Length: 250-1,500 words. **Pays $50.** Sometimes pays expenses of writers on assignment.

Photos: State availability of photos with submission. Reviews contact sheets. Offers $15/photo. Captions required. Buys one-time rights.

Columns/Departments: Business related, especially slanted toward WV. **Buys 25 mss/year.** Query. **Pays $50.**

Tips: "Localize your work—mention West Virginia specifically in the article; or talk to business people in West Virginia.

N $ $ $ TEXTILE RENTAL, Uniform and Linen Service Management Trends, Textile Rental Services Association of America, 1130 E. Hallandale Beach Blvd., Suite B, Hallandale FL 33009. (954)457-7555. Fax: (954)457-3890. Website: www.trsa.org. Executive Editor: David Schmitt. **Contact:** John D. Adams, managing editor. **30% freelance written.** Monthly magazine. **Pays on acceptance.** Publishes ms an average of 1 month after acceptance. Byline given. Buys first North American serial and electronic rights. Editorial lead time 2 months. Submit seasonal material 3 months in advance. Accepts queries by mail, e-mail, fax. Accepts simultaneous submissions. Responds in 2 months. Sample copy free or online at website. Writer's guidelines free.
Nonfiction: How-to, interview/profile, new product, personal experience, photo feature, technical, travel. **Buys 50 mss/year.** Query with published clips or send complete ms. Length: 500-3,000 words. **Pays $200-800 minimum for assigned articles; $50-500 for unsolicited articles.** Members get free copies. Sometimes pays expenses of writers on assignment.
Photos: Send photos with submission. Reviews negatives and transparencies. Offers no additional payment for photos accepted with ms. Negotiates payment individually. Identification of subjects required. Buys all rights.
Columns/Departments: Query. **Pays $50-350.**
Tips: "The content of what you write is more important than your prose. As a professional working in the textile rental industry, you have valuable insight into industry concerns. Your association magazine is an excellent forum for exchanging perspectives with your peers about issues such as new technology, experiences with workers' compensation, consolidation in the industry, and new market opportunities."

N $ $ UDM, Upholstery Design & Management, Chartwell Communications, 380 E. Northwest Hwy., Suite 300, Des Plaines IL 60016-2208. Fax: (847)390-7100. E-mail: mchazin@chartcomm.com. Website: www.udm.com. **Contact:** Michael Chazin, editor/associate publisher. **10-20% freelance written.** Monthly business-to-business magazine covering upholstered furniture/industry management. "*UDM* targets suppliers, manufacturers and retailers/resellers of upholstered furniture for the home, office, institution. Because we are highly specialized, we need writers with a knowledge of the furniture industry and familiarity and ability to identify new style trends." Estab. 1989. Circ. 9,500. Pays on publication. Publishes ms an average of 2 months after acceptance. Byline usually given. Buys first North American serial rights. Accepts queries by mail, e-mail. Responds in 2 weeks to queries; 2 months to mss. Sample copy free.
Nonfiction: Interview/profile. **Buys 15 mss/year.** Query. Length: 500-2,500 words. **Pays $250-700.** Sometimes pays expenses of writers on assignment.
Photos: State availability of photos with submission. Send photos with submission. Reviews transparencies and prints. Offers no additional payment for photos accepted with ms. Captions and identification of subjects required. Prefers buying all rights.
Columns/Departments: "Open to suggestions." **Buys 15 mss/year. Pays $250-500.**
Tips: "Writers must have inside knowledge of furniture/upholstery or be privy to knowledge. We try to stay on the leading edge of color and style trends—12-18 months before they hit retail stores!"

N $ $ $ WORLD TRADE, "For the Executive with Global Vision", BNP, 27130-A Paseo Espada, #1427, San Juan Capistrano CA 92675. Fax: (949)234-1701. Website: www.worldtrademag.com. Editor: Davis Goodman. **Contact:** Sherrie E. Zhan, managing editor. **50% freelance written.** Monthly magazine covering international business. Estab. 1988. Circ. 85,000. Pays on publication. Publishes ms an average of 1 month after acceptance. Byline given. Buys all rights. Editorial lead time 3 months. Accepts queries by mail, fax.
Nonfiction: Historical/nostalgic, interview/profile, technical, travel, market reports, finance, logistics. "See our editorial calendar online at www.worldtrademag.com." **Buys 40-50 mss/year.** Query with published clips. Length: 650-3,500 words. **Pays 55¢/word.**
Photos: State availability of photos with submission. Reviews transparencies and prints. Negotiates payment individually. Identification of subjects required. Buys all rights.
Columns/Departments: International Business Services, 1,000 words; Shipping, Supply Chain Management, Logistics, 1,200 words; Software & Technology, 1,200 words; Economic Development (US, International), 1,200 words. **Buys 40-50 mss/year. Pays 55¢/word.**
Tips: "We seek writers with expertise in their subject areas, as well as solid researching and writing skills. We want analysts more than reporters. We don't accept unsolicited manuscripts, and we don't want phone calls! Please read *World Trade* before sending a query."

CHURCH ADMINISTRATION & MINISTRY

Publications in this section are written for clergy members, church leaders and teachers. Magazines for lay members and the general public are listed in the Consumer Religious section.

N $ THE AFRICAN AMERICAN PULPIT, Judson Press, 588 N. Gulph Rd., King of Prussia PA 19406. (610)768-2128. Fax: (610)768-2441. E-mail: Victoria.McGoey@abc-usa.org. Website: www.judsonpress.com/TAAP. Editors: Martha Simmons and Frank A. Thomas. **Contact:** Victoria McGoey, managing editor. **100% freelance written.** Quarterly magazine covering African American preaching. "*The African American Pulpit* is the only journal devoted exclusively to the art of black preaching. Ecumenical in outlook and theologically diverse in style, *TAAP* covers many topics relevant to today's African American pastor." Estab. 1997. Circ. 1,300. Pays on publication. Publishes ms an average of 6 months after acceptance. Byline always given. Buys first rights. Editorial lead time 9 months. Submit seasonal material 9-12 months in advance. Accepts queries by mail, e-mail, fax, phone. Accepts simultaneous submissions. "The editor contacts only those whose work was chosen." Writer's guidelines free online at website or by e-mail.

Nonfiction: Book excerpts, essays, how-to (craft a sermon), inspirational, interview/profile, opinion, religious, sermons/articles relating to African American preaching and the African American Church. **Buys 60 mss/year.** Send complete ms. Length: 1,500-3,000 words. **Pays $50** and complimentary contributor's copy.

$CE CONNECTION COMMUNIQUE, Creative Christian Ministries, P.O. Box 12624, Roanoke VA 24027. Fax: (540)342-7511. E-mail: ccmbbr@juno.com. **Contact:** Betty Robertson, editor. **25% freelance written.** Monthly e-newsletter, "a vehicle of communication for pastors, local church Christian education leaders and volunteer teachers." Estab. 1995. **Pays on acceptance.** Publishes ms an average of 6 months after acceptance. Byline given. Buys one-time rights. Editorial lead time 6 months. Submit seasonal material 6 months in advance. Accepts simultaneous submissions. Responds in 6 months. Writer's guidelines for #10 SASE.

Nonfiction: How-to, new product. **Buys 12 mss/year.** Send complete ms. Length: 100-600 words. **Pays $5-10.**
Reprints: Accepts previously published submissions.

$THE CHRISTIAN COMMUNICATOR, ACW, 9731 N. Fox Glen Dr., #6F, Niles IL 60714-5861. (847)296-3964. Fax: (847)296-0754. E-mail: linjohnson@compuserve.com. **Contact:** Lin Johnson, editor. **90% freelance written.** Monthly trade magazine covering Christian writing and speaking. "We look for good articles about all aspects of Christian writing and speaking." Circ. 4,000. Pays on publication. Publishes ms an average of 2 months after acceptance. Byline given. Buys first or one-time rights. Editorial lead time 3 months. Submit seasonal material 3 months in advance. Accepts queries by mail, e-mail. Accepts simultaneous submissions. Responds in 2 months to queries; 3 months to mss. Sample copy for $10 with SAE and 3 first-class stamps. Writer's guidelines free or by e-mail.

Nonfiction: Book excerpts, essays, general interest, how-to, humor, inspirational, interview/profile, opinion, personal experience, religious, technical. "Nothing preachy, angry or strongly denominational." **Buys 150 mss/year.** Query or send complete ms. Length: 500-1,500 words. **Pays $10.**
Reprints: Accepts previously published submissions.
Photos: Send photos with submission. Reviews contact sheets. Offers no additional payment for photos accepted with ms. Identification of subjects required.
Columns/Departments: Speaker's Corner (speaking), 500-1,500 words. **Buys 11 mss/year.** Query. **Pays $10.**
Poetry: Free verse, light verse, traditional. "Must be about writing." **Buys 10-20 poems/year.** Submit maximum 3 poems. Length: 8-32 lines. **Pays $10.**
Fillers: Anecdotes, facts, newsbreaks, short humor. **Buys 10-30/year.** Length: 50-300 words. **Pays $10.**
Tips: "We're looking for upbeat, fun, informative, non-preachy articles. We primarily use 'how to' articles, personal experience articles, and personality features on experienced writers and editors. However, we're willing to look at any other pieces or fillers geared to the writing life. *TCC* does operate on a theme list. If you're interested in being part of the *TCC* assignment team, please send a résumé of your experiences, information on your interests, and clips of your work. Because *TCC* pays minimal right now, we try to match article writers with topics that they are very familiar with, are interested in learning about, or are in an area in which the writer wants to make contacts."

$CHRISTIAN EDUCATION LEADERSHIP, Pathway Press, P.O. Box 2250, Cleveland TN 37320-2250. (423)478-7599. Fax: (423)478-7616. E-mail: TPLane@extremegen.org (editor) or Ann.Steely@PathwayPress.org (editorial assistant). Editor: Tony P. Lane. **Contact:** Ann Steely, editorial assistant. **25% freelance written.** Quarterly magazine covering Christian education. "*Leadership* is written for teachers, youth pastors, children's pastors, and other local church Christian education leaders." Estab. 1976. Circ. 10,000. **Pays on acceptance.** Publishes ms an average of 6 months after acceptance. Not copyrighted. Buys first North American serial, first, one-time, second serial (reprint) or simultaneous rights. Editorial lead time 6 months. Submit seasonal material 6 months in advance. Accepts queries by mail, e-mail. Accepts simultaneous submissions. Responds in 3 months to mss. Sample copy for $1 and 9×12 SASE. Writer's guidelines free.

Nonfiction: How-to (for church teachers), inspirational, interview/profile. **Buys 16 mss/year.** Send complete ms; include SSN. Send SASE. Length: 400-1,200 words. **Pays $25-55 for assigned articles; $25-45 for unsolicited articles.**
Reprints: Accepts previously published submissions. Send typed ms with rights for sale noted and information about when and where the article previously appeared. Pays 80% of amount paid for an original article.
Photos: State availability of photos with submission. Reviews contact sheets, transparencies. Negotiates payment individually. Buys one-time rights.
Columns/Departments: Sunday School Leadership, Reaching Out (creative evangelism), The Pastor and Christian Education, Preschool, Elementary, Teen, Adult, Drawing Closer, Kids Church; all 500 words. Send complete ms with SASE. Pays $25-45.

$CHURCH EDUCATOR, Educational Ministries, Inc., 165 Plaza Dr., Prescott AZ 86303. (520)771-8601. Fax: (520)771-8621. E-mail: edmin2@aol.com. **Contact:** Linda Davidson, editor. **95% freelance written.** Monthly magazine covering resources for Christian educators. "*Church Educator* has programming ideas for the Christian educator in the mainline Protestant church. We are *not* on the conservative, fundamental side theologically, so slant articles to the liberal side. Programs should offer lots of questions and not give pat answers." Estab. 1978. Circ. 4,500. Pays 60 days after publication. Publishes ms an average of 2 months after acceptance. Byline given. Buys first rights. Editorial lead time 3 months. Submit seasonal material 7 months in advance. Accepts simultaneous submissions. Responds in 2 weeks to queries; 4 months to mss. Sample copy for 9 × 12 SAE with 4 first-class stamps. Writer's guidelines free on request.

Nonfiction: How-to, religous. Special issues: How to recruit volunteers; Nurturing faith development of children. No testimonials. **Buys 200 mss/year.** Send complete ms. Length: 500-2,000 words. **Pays 3¢/word.**

Fiction: Religious. "No 'How God Saved My Life' or 'How God Answers Prayers.' " **Buys 10 mss/year.** Send complete ms. Length: 500-1,500 words. **Pays 3¢/word.**

Tips: "We are always looking for material on the seasons of the church year: Advent, Lent, Pentecost, Epiphany. Write up a program for one of those seasons directed toward children, youth, adults or intergenerational."

$ CREATOR MAGAZINE, Bimonthly Magazine of Balanced Music Ministries, 735 Industrial, San Carlos CA 94070. (650)598-0785. Fax: (650)593-0423. E-mail: creator@creatormagazine.com. **Contact:** Rod Ellis, editor. **35% freelance written.** Bimonthly magazine. "Most readers are church music directors and worship leaders. Content focuses on the spectrum of worship styles from praise and worship to traditional to liturgical. All denominations subscribe. Articles on worship, choir rehearsal, handbells, children's/youth choirs, technique, relationships, etc." Estab. 1978. Circ. 6,000. Pays on publication. Publishes ms an average of 3 months after acceptance. Byline given. Buys first rights, one-time rights or second serial (reprint) rights; occasionally buys no rights. Editorial lead time 3 months. Submit seasonal material 4 months in advance. Accepts simultaneous submissions, if so noted. Accepts queries by mail. Sample copy for 9 × 12 SAE with 5 first-class stamps. Guidelines free.

Nonfiction: Essays, how-to (be a better church musician, choir director, rehearsal technician, etc.), humor (short personal perspectives), inspirational, interview/profile (call first), new product (call first), opinion, personal experience, photo feature, religious, technical (choral technique). Special issues: July/August is directed toward adult choir members, rather than directors. **Buys 20 mss/year.** Query or send complete ms. Length: 1,000-10,000 words. **Pays $30-75 for assigned articles; $30-60 for unsolicited articles.** Pays expenses of writers on assignment.

Reprints: Accepts previously published submissions.

Photos: State availability of or send photos with submission. Reviews negatives, 8 × 10 prints. Offers no additional payment for photos accepted with ms. Captions appreciated. Buys one-time rights.

Columns/Departments: Hints & Humor (music ministry short ideas, anecdotes [cute] ministry experience), 75-250 words; Inspiration (motivational ministry stories), 200-500 words; Children/Youth (articles about specific choirs), 1,000-5,000 words. **Buys 15 mss/year.** Query or send complete ms. **Pays $20-60.**

■ The online magazine carries original content not found in the print edition.

Tips: "Request guidelines and stick to them. If theme is relevant and guidelines are followed, we'll probably publish."

N $ CROSS & QUILL, The Christian Writers Newsletter, Christian Writers Fellowship International, 1624 Jefferson Davis Rd., Clinton SC 29325-6401. (864)697-6035. E-mail: cwfi@cwfi-online.org. Website: www.cwfi-online. org. **Contact:** Sandy Brooks, editor/publisher. **75% freelance written.** Bimonthly trade journal featuring information and encouragement for writers. "We serve Christian writers and others in Christian publishing. We like informational and how-to articles." Estab. 1976. Circ. 1,000. Pays on publication. Publishes ms an average of 6 months after acceptance. Byline given. Buys first and second serial (reprint) rights. Editorial lead time 6 months. Submit seasonal material 6 months in advance. Accepts queries by mail. Responds in 2 weeks to queries; 2 months to mss. Sample copy for $2 with 9 × 11 SAE and 2 first-class stamps. Writer's guidelines free for #10 SASE.

○━ Break in with "solid how-to, nuts and bolts articles. We're also looking for substantial articles on juvenile writing, drama, speech writing, television scripts, how to get on television/radio talk shows for interviews, do video-conferencing."

Nonfiction: How-to, humor, inspirational, interview/profile, new product, technical. **Buys 25 mss/year.** Send complete ms. Length: 300-800 words. **Pays $10-25.** Sometimes pays in contributor copies or other premiums for fillers, poetry.

Reprints: Accepts previously published submissions.

Photos: State availability of photos with submission.

Poetry: Free verse, haiku, light verse, traditional. **Buys 6 poems/year.** Submit maximum 3 poems. Length: 12 lines. **Pays $5.**

Fillers: Buys 6/year. Length: 100 words. **Pays $5.**

Tips: "Study guidelines and follow them. No philosophical, personal reflection or personal experiences."

N $ $ GROUP MAGAZINE, Group Publishing, Inc., 1515 Cascade Ave., Loveland CO 80538. (970)669-3836. Fax: (970)679-4372. E-mail: greditor@grouppublishing.com. Website: www.grouppublishing.com. Editor: Rick Lawrence. **Contact:** Kathy Dieterich, assistant editor. **50% freelance written.** Bimonthly magazine for Christian youth workers. "*Group* is the interdenominational magazine for leaders of Christian youth groups. *Group*'s purpose is to supply ideas, practical help, inspiration and training for youth leaders." Estab. 1974. Circ. 55,000. **Pays on acceptance.** Byline sometimes given. Buys all rights. Editorial lead time 4 months. Submit seasonal material 5 months in advance. Accepts queries by mail, e-mail, fax. Responds in 6 weeks to queries; 2 months to mss. Sample copy for $2 plus 10 × 12 SAE and 3 first-class stamps. Writer's guidelines for #10 SASE.

Nonfiction: Inspirational, personal experience, religious. No fiction. **Buys 30 mss/year.** Query. Length: 175-2,000 words. **Pays $125-225 for assigned articles; $35-125 for unsolicited articles.** Sometimes pays expenses of writers on assignment.

Columns/Departments: Try This One (short ideas for group use), 300 words; Hands-On-Help (tips for youth leaders), 175 words; Strange But True (profiles remarkable youth ministry experience), 500 words. **Pays $35-40.**

$ THE JOURNAL OF ADVENTIST EDUCATION, General Conference of SDA, 12501 Old Columbia Pike, Silver Spring MD 20904-6600. (301)680-5075. Fax: (301)622-9627. E-mail: 74617.1231@compuserve.com. **Contact:** Beverly J. Rumble, editor. Bimonthly (except skips issue in summer) professional journal covering teachers and administrators in Seventh Day Adventist school systems. Estab. 1939. Circ. 7,500. Pays on publication. Publishes ms 1 year after acceptance. Byline given. Buys first rights. Editorial lead time 3 months. Accepts queries by mail, e-mail, fax, phone. Responds in 6 weeks to queries; 4 months to mss. Sample copy for 10×12 SAE with 5 first-class stamps. Writer's guidelines free.

Nonfiction: Book excerpts, essays, how-to, personal experience, photo feature, religious, education. Theme issues have assigned authors. "No brief first-person stories about Sunday Schools." Query. Length: 1,000-1,500 words. **Pays $25-150.**

Reprints: Send tearsheet or photocopy of article and information about when and where the article previously appeared.

Photos: State availability of photos or send photos with submission. Reviews prints. Negotiates payment individually. Captions required. Buys one-time rights.

Tips: "Articles may deal with educational theory or practice, although the *Journal* seeks to emphasize the practical. Articles dealing with the creative and effective use of methods to enhance teaching skills or learning in the classroom are especially welcome. Whether theoretical or practical, such essays should demonstrate the skillful integration of Seventh-day Adventist faith/values and learning."

$ KIDS' MINISTRY IDEAS, Review and Herald Publishing Association, 55 W. Oak Ridge Dr., Hagerstown MD 21740. (301)393-4115. Fax: (301)393-4055. E-mail: kidsmin@rhpa.org. **Contact:** Patricia Fritz, editor. Managing Editor: Tamara Michelenko Terry. **95% freelance written.** "A quarterly resource for those leading children to Jesus, *Kids' Ministry Ideas* provides affirmation, pertinent and informative articles, program ideas, resource suggestions, and answers to questions from a Seventh-day Adventist Christian perspective." Estab. 1991. Circ. 5,000. **Pays on acceptance.** Publishes ms an average of 3 months after acceptance. Byline given. Kill fee varies. Buys first North American serial and electronic rights. Editorial lead time 3 months. Submit seasonal material 3 months in advance. Accepts queries by mail, e-mail, fax. Responds in 3 weeks to queries; 3 months to mss. Sample copy and writer's guidelines free.

Nonfiction: Inspirational, new product (related to children's ministry), articles fitting the mission of *Kids' Ministry Ideas*. **Buys 40-60 mss/year.** Send complete ms. Length: 500-1,500 words. **Pays $120 for assigned articles; $80 for unsolicited articles.**

Photos: State availability of photos with submission. Captions required. Buys one-time rights.

Columns/Departments: Buys 20-30 mss/year. Query. **Pays $60-120.**

Tips: "Request writers' guidelines and a sample issue."

$ $ LEADERSHIP, A Practical Journal for Church Leaders, Christianity Today, Inc., 465 Gundersen Dr., Carol Stream IL 60188. (630)260-6200. Fax: (630)260-0114. E-mail: leaderj@aol.com. Website: www.LeadershipJournal.net. Editor: Marshall Shelley. Associate Editor: Eric Reed. **Contact:** Dawn Zemke, editorial coordinator. **75% freelance written.** Works with a small number of new/unpublished writers each year. Quarterly magazine. Writers must have a "knowledge of and sympathy for the unique expectations placed on pastors and local church leaders. Each article must support points by illustrating from real life experiences in local churches." Estab. 1980. Circ. 65,000. **Pays on acceptance.** Publishes ms an average of 6 months after acceptance. Byline given. Pays 33% kill fee. Buys first rights and electronic rights. Editorial lead time 6 months. Submit seasonal material 6 months in advance. Accepts queries by mail, e-mail, fax. Responds in 3 weeks to queries; 2 months to mss. Sample copy for $5 or online at website. Free writer's guidelines with SASE or on website.

Nonfiction: How-to, humor, interview/profile, personal experience, sermon illustrations. "No articles from writers who have never read our journal." **Buys 60 mss/year.** Query. Length: 300-3,000 words. **Pays $35-400.** Sometimes pays expenses of writers.

Photos: Send photos with submission. Reviews contact sheets. Offers $25-250/photo. Captions, model releases and identification of subjects required. Buys one-time rights.

Columns/Departments: Eric Reed, associate editor. Growing Edge (book/software reviews); Ministry Staff (stories from church staffers), both 500 words. **Buys 8 mss/year.** Query. **Pays $100-200.**

Tips: "Every article in *Leadership* must provide practical help for problems that church leaders face. *Leadership* articles are not essays expounding a topic or editorials arguing a position or homilies explaining biblical principles. They are how-to articles, based on first-person accounts of real-life experiences in ministry. They allow our readers to see 'over the shoulder' of a colleague in ministry who then reflects on those experiences and identifies the lessons learned. As you know, a magazine's slant is a specific personality that readers expect (and it's what they've sent us their subscription money to provide). Our style is that of friendly conversation rather than directive discourse—what I learned about local church ministry rather than what you need to do."

N $ MOMENTUM, Official Journal of the National Catholic Educational Association, National Catholic Educational Association, 1077 30th St. NW, Suite 100, Washington DC 20007-3852. (202)337-6232. Fax: (202)333-6706. E-mail: momentum@ncea.org. Website: www.ncea.org. **Contact:** Margaret Anderson, editor. **50% freelance written.** Quarterly educational journal covering educational issues in Catholic schools, parishes and private schools. "*Momentum* is a membership journal of the National Catholic Educational Association. The audience is educators and administrators in Catholic and private schools K-12, and parish programs." Estab. 1970. Circ. 28,000. Pays on publication. Publishes ms an average of 3 months after acceptance. Byline given. Buys first rights. Sample copy for $5 SASE and 8 first-class stamps; writer's guidelines free.
Nonfiction: Educational trends, issues, research. "Do not want to see articles unrelated to educational and catechesis issues." **Buys 25-30 mss/year.** Query and send complete ms. Length: 1,500 words. **Pays $75 maximum.**
Photos: State availability of photos with submission. Reviews prints. Offers no additional payment for photos accepted with ms. Captions and identification of subjects required.
Columns and Departments: From the Field (practical application in classroom), 500 words; Justice and Peace Education (examples); DRE Direction (parish catechesis), all 900 words. **Buys 10 mss/year.** Query and send complete ms. **Pays $50.**

N $ PASTORAL LIFE, Society of St. Paul, P.O. Box 595, Canfield OH 44406-0595. (330)533-5503. Fax: (330)533-1076. E-mail: bro_joshua@hotmail.com. Website: www.albahouse.org. **Contact:** Rev. Matthew Roehrig or Brother Joshua Seidl. **66% freelance written.** Works with new/unpublished writers. "Monthly magazine designed to focus on the current problems, needs, issues and all important activities related to all phases of Catholic pastoral work and life." Estab. 1953. Circ. 2,000. Buys first rights only. Byline given. Pays on publication. Publishes ms an average of 4 months after acceptance. Responds in 1 month. Sample copy and writer's guidelines for 6×9 SAE with 4 first-class stamps.
Nonfiction: "*Pastoral Life* is a professional review, principally designed to focus attention on current problems, needs, issues and important activities related to all phases of pastoral work and life." Query with outline before submitting ms. "New contributors are expected to include, in addition, a few lines of personal data that indicate academic and professional background." **Buys 30 unsolicited mss/year.** Length: 2,000-3,000 words. **Pays 4¢/word minimum.**

$ $ THE PRIEST, Our Sunday Visitor, Inc., 200 Noll Plaza, Huntington IN 46750-4304. (219)356-8400. Fax: (219)359-9117. Editor: Msg. Owen F. Campion. **Contact:** George P. Foster, associate editor. **80% freelance written.** Monthly magazine. "We run articles that will aid priests in their day-to-day ministry. Includes items on spirituality, counseling, administration, theology, personalities, the saints, etc." **Pays on acceptance.** Byline given. Not copyrighted. Buys first North American serial rights. Editorial lead time 3 months. Submit seasonal material at least 4 months in advance. Responds in 5 weeks to queries; 3 months to mss. Sample copy and writer's guidelines free.
Nonfiction: Essays, historical/nostalgic, humor, inspirational, interview/profile, opinion, personal experience, photo feature, religious. **Buys 96 mss/year.** Send complete ms. Length: 1,500-5,000 words. **Pays $200 minimum for assigned articles; $50 minimum for unsolicited articles.**
Photos: Send photos with submission. Reviews transparencies and prints. Negotiates payment individually. Captions and identification of subjects required. Buys one-time rights.
Columns/Departments: Viewpoint (whatever applies to priests and the Church), 1,000 words. **Buys 36 mss/year.** Send complete ms. **Pays $50-100.**
Tips: "Say what you have to say in an interesting and informative manner and stop. Freelancers are most often published in 'Viewpoints.' Please do not stray from the magisterium of the Catholic Church."

$ PULSE, Evangelism and Missions Information Service/Wheaton College, 500 College Ave., 3rd Floor, Billy Graham Center, Wheaton IL 60187. (630)752-7158. Fax: (630)752-7155. E-mail: pulsenews@aol.com. **Contact:** Stan Guthrie, editor. **60% freelance written.** Semimonthly newsletter covering mission news and trends. "We provide current information about evangelical Christian missions and churches around the world. Most articles are news-oriented, although we do publish some features and interviews." Estab. 1964. Circ. 5,000. Pays on publication. Publishes ms an average of 2 months after acceptance. Byline given. Offers 50% kill fee. Buys first or all rights. Editorial lead time 2 months. Accepts queries by mail, e-mail, fax, phone. Responds in 2 weeks to queries; 1 month to mss. Sample copy and writer's guidelines free.
○━ Break in with "coverage of the subjects requested, bringing to the task both the topic's essential components, but with a dash of style, as well."
Nonfiction: Interview/profile, photo feature, religious, travel. Does not want anything that does not cover the world of evangelical missions. **Buys 50-60 mss/year.** Query with published clips. Length: 300-1,000 words. **Pays $25-100.** Sometimes pays expenses of writers on assignment.
Reprints: Accepts previously published submissions.
Photos: Send photos with submission. Reviews contact sheets. Negotiates payment individually. Identification of subjects required. Buys all rights.
Tips: "Have a knowledge of and appreciation for the evangelical missions community, as well as for cross-cultural issues. Writing must be economical, with a judicious use of quotes and examples."

$ $ REV., (formerly *Vital Ministry*), Group Publishing, Inc., 1515 Cascade Ave., Loveland CO 80538-8681. (970)669-3836. Fax: (970)669-1994. E-mail: TheRev@Rev-magazine.com. Editor: Paul Allen. **Contact:** Kristi Rector, assistant editor. **25% freelance written.** Bimonthly magazine for pastors. "We offer practical solutions to revolutionize and revitalize ministry. Our audience is pastors." Estab. 1997. Circ. 25,000. **Pays on acceptance.** Publishes ms an average of 6 months after acceptance. Byline given. Buys all rights and makes work-for-hire assignments. Editorial lead time 6 months. Submit seasonal material 8 months in advance. Accepts queries by mail, e-mail. Responds in 2 months. Writer's guidelines for #10 SASE or online.

O─┐ Break in with short, practical department pieces.

Nonfiction: Ministry, leadership and personal articles with practical application. "No devotions, articles for church members, theological pieces." **Buys 18-24 mss/year.** Query or send complete ms. Length: 1,500-1,800 words. **Pays $300-400.**

Columns/Departments: Preaching & Teaching (preparation & techniques); Worship (all aspects of the worship service); Personal Growth (personal or spiritual growth); Team Work (working with staff and volunteer leaders); Family Ministry (helping families including singles and elderly); Outreach (local and missions); Discipleship (small groups and one-on-one); Current Trends (trends that affect the church), Home Front (pastor's family), Church Biz (leadership and administration), all 250-300 words. **Buys 25 mss/year.** Send complete ms. **Pays $35-50.**

Fillers: Cartoons. **Buys 12/year. Pays $50.**

Tips: "We're most open to submissions for our departments. Remember that we focus on practical articles with an edgy tone."

$ TEACHERS INTERACTION, Concordia Publishing House, 3558 S. Jefferson Ave., St. Louis MO 63118-3968. (314)268-1083. Fax: (314)268-1329. E-mail: NummelaTA@cphnet.org. Jean Muser, editorial associate. **Contact:** Tom Nummela, editor. **20% freelance written.** Quarterly magazine of practical, inspirational, theological articles for volunteer church school teachers. Material must be true to the doctrines of the Lutheran Church—Missouri Synod. Estab. 1960. Circ. 16,000. Pays on publication. Publishes ms an average of 1 year after acceptance. Byline given. Buys all rights. Submit seasonal material 1 year in advance. Query by mail, e-mail, fax. Responds in 3 months to mss. Sample copy for $2.75. Writer's guidelines for #10 SASE.

Nonfiction: How-to (practical help/ideas used successfully in own classroom), inspirational (to the church school worker—must be in accordance with LCMS doctrine), personal experience (of a Sunday school classroom nature—growth). No theological articles. **Buys 6 mss/year.** Send complete ms. Length: 1,200 words. **Pays up to $100.**

Fillers: "*Teachers Interaction* buys short Interchange items—activities and ideas planned and used successfully in a church school classroom." **Buys 48/year.** Length: 200 words maximum. **Pays $20.**

Tips: "Practical or 'it happened to me' experiences articles would have the best chance. Also short items—ideas used in classrooms; seasonal and in conjunction with our Sunday school material, Our Life in Christ. Our format includes *all* volunteer church school teachers, Sunday school teachers, Vacation Bible School, and midweek teachers, as well as teachers of adult Bible studies."

N $ $ TEAM NYI MAGAZINE, Resourcing Nazarene Youth Workers, Nazarene Publishing House, 6401 The Paseo, Kansas City MO 64131. Fax: (816)333-4315. E-mail: TeamNYI@nazarene.org. Website: www.nazarene.org/nyi. **Contact:** Jeff Edmondson, editor. **85% freelance written.** Quarterly magazine covering youth ministry. "Published as a resource for the youth pastor or lay youth worker on the business and philosophical work of youth ministry." Estab. 1997. Circ. 10,000. **Pays on acceptance.** Publishes ms an average of 9 months after acceptance. Byline given. Buys first rights, second serial (reprint) rights. Editorial lead time 6 months Submit seasonal material 6 months in advance. Accepts queries by mail, e-mail, fax. Responds in 1 month to queries; 6 months to mss. Sample copy free for 9 × 12 SASE and 4 first-class stamps. Writer's guidelines free online at website.

Nonfiction: Essays, how-to, humor, inspirational, interview/profile, opinion, personal experience, religious, technical. "Please do not send fiction, poetry, historical or exposé." **Buys 15 mss/year.** Query, send complete ms. Length: 1,000-1,500 words. **Pays $25-100.**

Reprints: Accepts previously published submissions.

Photos: State availability of photos with submission. Offers no additional payment for photos accepted with ms.

Columns/Departments: Query, send complete ms.

Fillers: Anecdotes, facts, short humor. Length: 50-100 words. "No pay."

Tips: "E-mail query is the fastest way to get our attention. Cover letter with an attached article is fine too. Make sure your ideas are timely. No ministry ideas that worked in the '70s and '80s. Teens in the 21st century are a whole different animal."

$ $ TODAY'S CATHOLIC TEACHER, The Voice of Catholic Education, Peter Li Education Group, 330 Progress Rd., Dayton OH 45449. (937)847-5900. Fax: (937)847-5910. E-mail: mnoschang@peterli.com. Website: www. catholicteacher.com. **Contact:** Mary C. Noschang, editor. **60% freelance written.** Magazine published 6 times/year during school year covering Catholic education for grades K-12. "We look for topics of interest and practical help to teachers in Catholic elementary schools in all curriculum areas including religion technology, discipline, motivation." Estab. 1972. Circ. 50,000. Pays on publication. Publishes ms an average of 2 months after acceptance. Byline given. Buys first rights, all rights or makes work-for-hire assignments. Editorial lead time 3 months. Submit seasonal material 6 months in advance. Accepts queries by mail, e-mail, fax. Accepts simultaneous submissions. Responds in 1 month to queries; 3 months to mss. Sample copy for $3 or on website. Writer's guidelines website.

Nonfiction: Essays, how-to, humor, interview/profile, personal experience. Interested in articles detailing ways to incorporate Catholic values into academic subjects other than religion class. "No articles pertaining to public education." **Buys 15 mss/year.** Query or send complete ms. Length: 1,500-3,000 words. **Pays $150-300.** Pays in contributor copies if author prefers copies. Sometimes pays expenses of writers on assignment.

Photos: State availability of photos with submission. Reviews transparencies and prints. Offers $20-50/photo. Captions required, model releases and identification of subjects required. Buys one-time rights.

Tips: "Although our readership is primarily classroom teachers, *Today's Catholic Teacher* is read also by principals, supervisors, superintendents, boards of education, pastors, and parents. *Today's Catholic Teacher* aims to be for Catholic educators a source of information not available elsewhere. The focus of articles should span the interests of teachers from early childhood through junior high. Articles may be directed to just one age group yet have wider implications. Preference is given to material directed to teachers in grades four through eight. The desired magazine style is direct, concise, informative and accurate. Writing should be enjoyable to read, informal rather than scholarly, lively, and free of educational jargon."

N $ VISION, Christian Educators Association International, P.O. Box 41300, Pasadena CA 91114. (626)798-1124. Fax: (626)798-2346. E-mail: ceaieduca@aol.com. Website: www.ceai.org. **Contact:** Denise Jones, managing editor. Editor: Forrest Turpen. **50% freelance written.** Published 9 times/year. "*Vision* is the official publication of CEAI, focusing on education issues pertinent to the Christian educator in public education. Topics include prayer in public schools, union activities, religious expression and activity in public schools and legal rights of Christian educators." Estab. 1953. Circ. 7,500. Pays on publication. Publishes ms an average of 6 months after acceptance. Byline given. Buys first rights. Editorial lead time 4 months. Submit seasonal material 6 months in advance. Accepts simultaneous submissions. Responds in 6 weeks to queries; 3 months to mss. Sample copy for 9 × 12 SAE and 4 first-class stamps. Writer's guidelines free.

Nonfiction: Humor, inspirational, interview/profile, opinion, personal experience, religious, book review, curriculum review, how-to. **Buys several mss/year.** Query. Length: 300-1,000 words. **Pays $30-40.** Pays in contributor copies for non-main features (book reviews, etc.).

Reprints: Accepts previously published submissions. Send information about when and where the article previously appeared. Pays our standard rate.

Photos: Send photos with submission. Offers no additional payment for photos accepted with ms. Identification of subjects required. Buys one-time rights.

Columns/Departments: Direct to You (informational column from Director).

Fiction: Ethnic, historical, humorous, religious. **Buys very few mss/year.** Send complete ms. Length: 600-1,200 words. **Pays $30-40.**

Poetry: Avant-garde, free verse, haiku, light verse, traditional. Buys 1-4 poems/year. Submit maximum 1-2 poems. Pays in copies.

Fillers: Anecdotes, facts, newsbreaks, book reviews of interest to educators. Buys 1-5/year. Pays in copies..

$ $ WORSHIP LEADER MAGAZINE, CCM Communications, 104 Woodmont Blvd., 3rd Floor, Nashville TN 37205-2245. (615)386-3011. Fax: (615)385-4112. E-mail: ddisabatino@ccmcom.com. Website: www.worshipleader.org. Executive Editor: Chuck Fromm. **Contact:** David Di Sabatino, managing editor. **80% freelance written.** Bimonthly magazine covering all aspects of Christian worship. "*Worship Leader Magazine* exists to challenge, serve, equip and train those involved in leading the 21st century Church in worship. The intended readership is the worship team (all those who plan and lead) of the local church." Estab. 1992. Circ. 50,000. Pays on publication. Byline given. Offers 50% kill fee. Buys first North American serial or all rights. Editorial lead time 3 months. Submit seasonal material 6 months in advance. Responds in 6 weeks to queries; 3 months to mss. Sample copy for $5. Writer's guidelines for #10 SASE.

Nonfiction: General interest, how-to (related to purpose/audience), inspirational, interview/profile, opinion. **Buys 15-30 mss/year.** Query with published clips. Length: 1,200-2,000 words. **Pays $200-800 for assigned articles; $200-500 for unsolicited articles.** Sometimes pays expenses of writers on assignment.

Photos: State availability of photos with submission. Negotiates payment individually. Identification of subjects required. Buys one-time rights.

Tips: "Our goal has been and is to provide the tools and information pastors, worship leaders, and ministers of music, youth, and the arts need to facilitate and enhance worship in their churches. In achieving this goal, we strive to maintain high journalistic standards, biblical soundness, and theological neutrality. Our intent is to present the philosophical, scholarly insight on worship, as well as the day-to-day, 'putting it all together' side of worship, while celebrating our unity and diversity."

$ $ YOUR CHURCH, Helping You With the Business of Ministry, Christianity Today, Inc., 465 Gundersen Dr., Carol Stream IL 60188. (630)260-6200. Fax: (630)260-0114. E-mail: yceditor@aol.com. Website: www.christianity. net/yc. **Contact:** Phyllis Ten Elshof, editor. **70% freelance written.** Bimonthly magazine. "Articles pertain to the business aspects of ministry pastors are called upon to perform: administration, purchasing, management, technology, building, etc." Estab. 1955. Circ. 150,000. **Pays on acceptance.** Publishes ms an average of 4 months after acceptance. Byline given. Buys one-time rights. Submit seasonal material 5 months in advance. Accepts simultaneous submissions. Accepts queries by mail, fax. Responds in 1 month to queries; 2 months to mss. Sample copy and writer's guidelines for 9 × 12 SAE with 5 first-class stamps.

Nonfiction: How-to, new product, technical. Special issues: Church Management, Construction. **Buys 25 mss/year.** Send complete ms. Length: 900-1,500 words. **Pays about 15¢/word.**

Reprints: Send photocopy of article and information about when and where the article previously appeared. Pays 30% of the amount paid for an original article.

Photos: State availability of photos with submission. Reviews 4×5 transparencies and 5×7 or 8×10 prints. Offers no additional payment for photos accepted with ms. Captions, model releases and identification of subjects required. Buys one-time rights.

Tips: "The editorial is generally geared toward brief and helpful articles dealing with some form of church business. Concise, bulleted points from experts in the field are typical for our articles."

CLOTHING

N: BOBBIN, Bobbin Publishing, 1110 Shop Rd., P.O. Box 1986, Columbia SC 29202-1986. (803)771-7500. Fax: (803)799-1461. Website: www.bobbin.com. Editor-in-Chief: Lisa Rabon. 25% freelance written. Monthly magazine for CEO's and top management in apparel and sewn products manufacturing companies. Circ. 18,000. Pays on publication. Byline given. Buys all rights. Responds in 6 weeks. Free sample copy and writer's guidelines.

Columns/Departments: Trade View, R&D, Information Strategies, Personnel Management, Labor Forum, NON-Apparel Highlights, Fabric Notables, West Coast Report.

Tips: "Articles should be written in a style appealing to busy top managers and should in some way foster thought or new ideas, or present solutions/alternatives to common industry problems/concerns. CEOs are most interested in quick read pieces that are also informative and substantive. Articles should not be based on opinions but should be developed through interviews with industry manufacturers, retailers or other experts, etc. Sidebars may be included to expand upon certain aspects within the article. If available, illustrations, graphs/charts, or photographs should accompany the article."

$ $ MADE TO MEASURE, Halper Publishing Company, 600 Central Ave., Suite 226, Highland Park IL 60035. (847)433-1114. Fax: (847)433-6602. E-mail: mtm@halper.com. Website: www.halper.com. **Contact:** Rick Levine, editor/publisher. **10% freelance written.** Semiannual magazine covering uniforms and career apparel. "A semi-annual magazine/buyers' reference containing leading sources of supply, equipment and services of every description related to the Uniform, Career Apparel, Tailoring and allied trades, throughout the entire U.S." Estab. 1930. Circ. 25,000. **Pays on acceptance.** Publishes ms an average of 2 months after acceptance. Byline given. Buys first North American serial rights. Editorial lead time 4 months. Submit seasonal material 4 months in advance. Accepts queries by mail, e-mail. Accepts simultaneous submissions. Responds in 3 weeks. Sample copy free or online at website.

Nonfiction: Historical/nostalgic, interview/profile, new product, personal experience, photo feature, technical. "Please only consider sending queries related to stories to companies that wear or make uniforms, career apparel or identifying apparel. **Buys 5 mss/year.** Query with published clips. Length: 1,000-3,000 words. **Pays $300-600.** Sometimes pays expenses of writers on assignment.

Photos: State availability of photos with submission. Reviews contact sheets and any prints. Negotiates payment individually. Buys one-time rights.

Tips: "We look for features about large and small companies who wear uniforms (restaurants, hotels, industrial, medical, public safety, etc.)."

CONFECTIONERY & SNACK FOODS

These publications focus on the bakery, snack and candy industries. Journals for grocers, wholesalers and other food industry personnel are listed in Groceries & Food Products.

$ $ PACIFIC BAKERS NEWS, 3155 Lynde St., Oakland CA 94601 (510)532-5513. **Contact:** C.W. Soward, publisher. **30% freelance written.** Eager to work with new/unpublished writers. Monthly business newsletter for commercial bakeries in the western states. Estab. 1961. Pays on publication. No byline given; uses only 1-paragraph news items.

Nonfiction: Uses bakery business reports and news about bakers. Buys only brief "boiled-down news items about bakers and bakeries operating only in Alaska, Hawaii, Pacific Coast and Rocky Mountain states. We welcome clippings. We need monthly news reports and clippings about the baking industry and the donut business. No pictures, jokes, poetry or cartoons." Length: 10-200 words. **Pays 10¢/word for news and 6¢ for clips (words used).**

CONSTRUCTION & CONTRACTING

Builders, architects and contractors learn the latest industry news in these publications. Journals targeted to architects are also included in the Consumer Art & Architecture category. Those for specialists in the interior aspects of construction are listed under Building Interiors.

$ $CONCRETE CONSTRUCTION, (formerly *Aberdeen's Concrete Construction*), The Aberdeen Group, a division of Hanley-Wood, LLC., 426 S. Westgate St., Addison IL 60101. (630)543-0870. Fax: (630)543-5399. E-mail: cceditor@wocnet.com. Website: www.worldofconcrete.com. **Contact:** Anne Balogh, managing editor. Editor: Ward Malisch. **20% freelance written.** Monthly how-to magazine for concrete contractors, engineers, architects, specifiers and others who design and build residential, commercial, industrial and public works, cast-in-place concrete structures. It also covers job stories and new equipment in the industry. Estab. 1956. Circ. 80,000. **Pays on acceptance.** Publishes ms an average of 4 months after acceptance. Byline given. Editorial lead time 4 months. Submit seasonal material 4 months in advance. Accepts queries by mail, e-mail, fax, phone. Responds in 2 weeks to queries; 1 month to mss. Sample copy and writer's guidelines free.

Nonfiction: How-to, new product, personal experience, photo feature, technical, job stories. Buys 7-10 mss/year. Query with published clips. Length: 2,000 words maximum. **Pays $250 or more for assigned articles; $200 minimum for unsolicited articles.** Pays expenses of writers on assignment.

Photos: Send photos with submission. Reviews contact sheets, negatives, transparencies, prints. Offers no additional payment for photos accepted with ms. Captions required. Buys one-time rights.

Tips: "Have a good understanding of the concrete construction industry. How-to stories only accepted from industry experts. Job stories must cover procedures, materials, and equipment used as well as the project's scope."

N $ $ $THE CONCRETE PRODUCER, The Aberdeen Group, 426 S. Westgate St., Addison IL 60101. (630)705-2623. Fax: (630)543-3112. E-mail: dtalend@wocnet.com. Website: www.worldofconcrete.com. Editor: Rick Yelton. **Contact:** Don Talend, managing editor. **30% freelance written.** Monthly trade magazine covering concrete production. "Our audience consists of producers who have succeeded in making concrete the preferred building material through management, operating, quality control, use of the latest technology, or use of superior materials." Estab. 1982. Circ. 18,000. Pays on publication. Publishes ms an average of 2 months after acceptance. Byline given. Buys second serial (reprint) rights or makes work-for-hire assignments. Editorial lead time 4 months. Accepts queries by mail, e-mail, fax, phone. Responds in 1 week to queries; 2 months to mss. Sample copy for $4. Writer's guidelines free.

Nonfiction: How-to promote concrete, new product, technical. **Buys 5 mss/year.** Send complete ms. Length: 500-2,000 words. **Pays $200-1,000.** Sometimes pays expenses of writers on assignment.

Photos: State availability of photos with submission. Reviews 2×2 transparencies and 3×5 prints. Offers no additional payment for photos accepted with ms. Captions and identification of subjects required.

Columns/Departments: Management (successful marketing), Operations (improving efficiency), and Technology (using new technology), all 1,200 words. **Buys 5 mss/year. Pays $200-1,000.**

$CONSTRUCTION EQUIPMENT GUIDE, 470 Maryland St., Ft. Washington PA 19034. (800)523-2200. Fax: (215)885-2910. E-mail: editorial@constructionequipguide.com. **Contact:** Melissa Buchanan, Managing Editor. **30% freelance written.** Biweekly newspaper. "We are looked at as the primary source of information in the construction industry by equipment manufacturers, sellers and users. We cover the Midwest, Northeast, Southwest and Southeast states with our 4 editions published biweekly. We give the latest news on current construction projects, legislative actions, political issues, mergers and acquisitions, new unique applications of equipment and in-depth features." Estab. 1957. Circ. 120,000. Pays on publication. Publishes ms an average of 1 month after acceptance. Byline given. Offers 100% kill fee. Buys all rights. Editorial lead time varies. Accepts queries by: mail, e-mail, fax, phone. Sample copy and writer's guidelines free.

Nonfiction: General interest, historical/nostalgic, how-to (winterizing construction equipment, new methods of construction applications), interview/profile, new product, personal experience, photo feature, technical. **Buys 200-600 mss/year.** Query with published clips. Length: 150-1,200 words. Negotiates payment individually. Pays most expenses of writers on assignment.

Photos: Send photos with submission. Negotiates payment individually. Captions, identification of subjects required.

Columns/Departments: Equipment Auctions (photo coverage only with captions). Query. Pays $60 and expenses.

Tips: "Keep an eye out for commercial construction in your area. Take note of the name of the contractors on site. Then give us a call to see if you should follow up with a full story and photos. Pay attention to large and small jobs right around you. Read articles in *Construction Equipment Guide* to learn what information is important to our readers, who are equipment users, sellers and makers."

N $ $EQUIPMENT JOURNAL, Canada's National Equipment Newspaper, Economic Affairs Bureau, 5160 Explorer Dr., Unit 6, Mississauga, Ontario L4W 4T7 Canada. (800)667-8541. Fax: (905)629-7988. E-mail: equipmentjournal@globalserve.net. Website: www.equipmentjournal.com. **Contact:** Michael Anderson, editor. **10% freelance written.** Trade journal published 17 times/year covering heavy equipment used in construction, mining and forestry industries." Estab. 1966. Circ. 25,000. Pays on publication. Byline given. Buys all rights, makes work-for-hire assignments. Editorial lead time 1 month. Submit seasonal material 1 month in advance. Accepts queries by mail, e-mail, fax. Accepts simultaneous submissions. Sample copy free.

Nonfiction: Interview/profile, new product, technical. "No material that falls outside of *EJ*'s mandate—the Canadian equipment industry." **Buys 10 mss/year.** Query. Length: 500-1,000 words. **Pays $100-200.** Sometimes pays expenses of writers on assignment.

Reprints: Accepts previously published submissions.

Photos: State availability of photos with submission. Reviews 4×6 prints. Negotiates payment individually. Identification of subjects required. Buys all rights.

$ $ $ HARD HAT NEWS, Lee Publications, Inc., 6113 State Highway 5, Palatine Bridge NY 13428. (518)673-3237. Fax: (518)673-2381. E-mail: ffanning@LeePub.com. Website: www.LeePub.com. **Contact:** Fred Fanning, editor. **80% freelance written.** Biweekly tabloid covering heavy construction, equipment, road and bridge work. "Our readers are contractors and heavy construction workers involved in excavation, highways, bridges, utility construction and underground construction." Estab. 1980. Circ. 24,000. Byline given. Not copyrighted. Editorial lead time 2 weeks. Submit seasonal material 2 weeks in advance. Does not accept simultaneous submissions. Sample copy and writer's guidelines free. Accepts queries by: mail, e-mail, fax, phone.

    O⊓ "We especially need writers with some knowledge of heavy construction, although anyone with good composition and interviewing skills is welcome. Focus on major construction in progress in your area."

Nonfiction: Interview/profile, new product, opinion, photo feature, technical. Also 'Job Stories,' (a brief overall description of the project, the names and addresses of the companies and contractors involved, and a description of the equipment used, including manufacturers' names and model numbers. Quotes from the people in charge, as well as photos, are important). Send complete ms. Length: 50-1,400 words. **Pays $2.50/inch.** Sometimes pays expenses of writers on assignment.

Photos: Send photos. Reviews prints and slides. Offers $5/photo. Captions and identification of subjects required.

Departments: New Products; Association News; Parts and Repairs; Attachments; Trucks and Trailers; People on the Move.

Fillers: Cartoons. Pays $10/cartoon.

Tips: "Every issue has a focus—see our editorial calender. Special consideration is given to a story that coincides with the focus. A color photo is necessary for the front page. Vertical shots work best. We need more writers in Maryland, Delaware and the Washington, DC area. Also, we are expanding our distribution into the Mid-Atlantic states and need writers in Virginia, Tennessee, North Carolina and South Carolina."

N⃞ $ $ HEAVY EQUIPMENT NEWS, Vulcan Publications, 1 Chase Corporate Dr., Suite 300, Birmingham AL 35242. Fax: (205)987-2880. E-mail: aboatright@vulcanpub.com. Website: www.heavyequipmentnews.com. **Contact:** Ashley Boatright, senior editor. **40-50% freelance written.** Monthly magazine covering construction equipment and construction industry. "*Heavy Equipment News* is an editorial-driven publication for the construction contractor, focusing on job sites, asphalt-road building, concrete, business management, equipment selection and material handling." Estab. 1995. Circ. 50,000. **Pays on acceptance.** Publishes ms an average of 3 months after acceptance. Byline given. Offers 10% kill fee. Buys first North American serial, second serial (reprint) and electronic rights. Editorial lead time 6 months. Submit seasonal material 6 months in advance. Accepts queries by mail, e-mail, fax. Responds in 2 weeks to queries; 1 month to mss. Sample copy for #10 SASE. Writer's guidelines free.

Nonfiction: How-to, interview/profile, new product, personal experience, technical. **Buys 24 mss/year.** Query with published clips. Length: 1,200-1,500 words. **Pays $500.**

Photos: Reviews transparencies and prints. Offers no additional payment for photos accepted with ms. Captions and identification of subjects required. Buys all rights.

Columns/Departments: Asphalt Road, Concrete Batch, Material Handling Advances, Truck Stop. Query with published clips. **Pays $200.**

$ $ JOINERS' QUARTERLY, Journal of Timber Framing & Traditional Building, Fox Maple Press, Inc., P.O. Box 249, Brownfield ME 04010. (207)935-3720. Fax: (207)935-4575. E-mail: foxmaple@nxi.com. Website: www.nxi.com/WWW/joinersquarterly/Welcome.html. **Contact:** Steve K. Chappell, editor. **75% freelance written.** Quarterly magazine covering traditional building, timber framing, natural and sustainable construction. Estab. 1982. Circ. 10,000. Pays on publication. Publishes ms an average of 9 months after acceptance. Byline given. Buys all rights. Editorial lead time 9 months. Submit seasonal material 6 months in advance. Accepts simultaneous submissions. Accepts queries by mail. Responds in 1 month to queries; 2 months to mss. Sample copy for $4.50. Writer's guidelines for #10 SASE.

Nonfiction: Historical/nostalgic (building techniques), how-to (timber frame, log build, sustainable materials, straw building), inspirational (craftsmanship), new product, technical (alternative building techniques). **Buys 12 mss/year.** Query. Length: 500-2,500 words. **Pays $50/published page.** Sometimes pays expenses of writers on assignment.

Reprints: Send photocopy of article or short story and information about when and where the article previously appeared. **Pays 50-100% of amount paid for an original article.**

Photos: Send photos with submission. Reviews transparencies and prints. Offers no additional payment for photos accepted with ms. Identification of subjects required. Buys all rights.

Tips: "We're looking for articles on sustainable construction, especially from a timber framing aspect. Architects, builders and owner/builders are our primary readers and writers. We also like to feature natural and historical home building techniques such as straw/clay, roof thatching, sod home, etc. We need clean and concise articles with photos and/or artwork."

$ $ MC MAGAZINE, The Voice of the Manufactured Concrete Products Industry, National Precast Concrete Association, 10333 N. Meridian St., Suite 272, Indianapolis IN 46290. (317)571-9500. Fax: (317)571-0041. E-mail: pmanning@precast.org. Website: www.precast.org. **Contact:** Pam Manning, managing editor. **75% freelance written.** Quarterly magazine covering manufactured concrete products. "*MC Magazine* is a publication for owners and managers of factories that produce concrete materials used in construction. We publish business articles, technical articles, company profiles, safety articles and project profiles with the intent of educating our readers in order to increase the quality and use of precast concrete." Estab. 1995. Circ. 8,500. **Pays on acceptance.** Publishes ms an average of 6 months after acceptance. Byline given. Buys first North American serial, second serial or all rights. Editorial lead time 3 months. Accepts queries by mail, e-mail, fax. Accepts simultaneous submissions. Responds in 1 month to queries; 2 months to mss. Sample copy for 9×12 SAE and 8 first-class stamps or online at website. Writer's guidelines for #10 SASE, online at website or by e-mail.

Nonfiction: How-to (business), interview/profile, technical (concrete manufacturing). "No humor, essays, fiction or fillers." **Buys 16-20 mss/year.** Query or send complete ms. Length: 2,000-3,500 words. **Pays $250-750.** Sometimes pays expenses of writers on assignment.

Photos: State availability of photos with submission. Offers no additional payment for photos accepted with ms. Captions required. Buys all rights.

Tips: "Understand the audience and the purpose of the magazine. We have an ongoing need for business-related articles that would be pertinent to small- to mid-sized manufacturers. Understanding audience interests and needs is important and expressing a willingness to tailor a subject to get the right slant is critical. Our primary freelance needs are about general business or technology topics. Of course, if you are an engineer or a writer specializing in industry, construction or manufacturing technology, other possibilities would certainly exist. Writing style should be concise, yet lively and entertaining. Avoid clichés. We require a third-person perspective, encourage a positive tone and active voice, and welcome a humorous tone where appropriate. For stylistic matters, follow the *Chicago Manual of Style*."

N MICHIGAN CONTRACTOR & BUILDER, CMD Group, 40000 Grand River, Suite 404, 1 Hovi MI 48375-2147. (248)471-5811. Fax: (248)471-6103. E-mail: aram.kalousdian@cndg.com. **Contact:** Adam Kalousdian. **25% freelance written.** Weekly magazine covering the commercial construction industry in Michigan (no home building). "*Michigan Contractor & Builder's* audience is contractors, equipment suppliers, engineers and architects. The magazine reports on construction projects in Michigan. It does not cover homebuilding. Stories should focus on news or innovative techniques or materials in construction." Estab. 1967. Circ. 3,700. Pays 30 days after publication. Byline given. Buys all rights. Accepts queries by mail, e-mail, fax, phone. Sample copy free.

Nonfiction: Michigan construction projects. **Buys 52 mss/year.** Query with published clips. Length: 1,500 words with 3-5 photos. **Pay negotiable.**

Photos: Send photos with submission. Reviews 4×7 transparencies and 5×6 prints. Offers no additional payment for photos accepted with ms. Captions required. Buys all rights.

$ $ PERMANENT BUILDINGS & FOUNDATIONS (PBF), R.W. Nielsen Co., 4321 NE Vivion Rd. Ste. 101, P.O. Box 11067, Kansas City MO 64119. (816)453-0590. Fax: (816)453-0591. E-mail: rnielsen@pbf.org. Website: www.pbf.org. Managing Editor: Carolyn R. Nielsen. **Contact:** Roger W. Nielsen, editor. **15% freelance written.** Magazine published 8 times/year. "*PBF* readers are contractors who build residential, commercial and industrial buildings. Editorial focus is on materials that last: concrete and new technologies to build solid, energy efficient structures, insulated concrete and tilt-up, waterproofing, underpinning, roofing and the business of contracting and construction." Estab. 1989. Circ. 30,000. Pays on publication. Byline given. Buys first North American serial rights. Editorial lead time 1 month. Submit seasonal material 2 months in advance. Accepts queries by mail, e-mail, fax, phone. Responds in 2 weeks to queries; 1 month to mss. Sample copy for 9×12 SASE or on website. Writer's guidelines free or on website.

Nonfiction: How-to (construction methods, management techniques), humor, interview/profile, new product, technical, book reviews, tool reviews. Special issues: Water proofing (February); Insulated Concrete Forming supplement (April). **Buys 15 mss/year.** Query. Length: 500-1,500 words. **Pays $150-750 for assigned articles; $50-500 for unsolicited articles.** Sometimes pays expenses of writers on assignment.

Photos: State availability of photos with submission. Reviews contact sheets. Offers no additional payment for photos accepted with ms. Captions and identification of subjects required. Buys one-time rights.

Columns/Departments: Marketing Tips, 250-500 words; Q&A (solutions to contractor problems), 200-500 words. Query. **Pays $50-500.**

The online magazine carries original content not found in its print edition and includes writer's guidelines. Contact: Roger Nielsen.

$ $ ST. LOUIS CONSTRUCTION NEWS & REVIEW, Finan Publishing Co., 107 W. Pacific, St. Louis MO 63119-2323. (314)961-6644. Fax: (314)961-4809. E-mail: pdowns@finan.com. Website: www.stlconstruction.com. **Contact:** Peter Downs, editor. **50% freelance written.** Bimonthly regional magazine covering projects, products, processes that affect the local industry. Estab. 1969. Circ. 35,000. Pays 30 days after acceptance. Publishes ms an average of 2 months after acceptance. Byline given. Pays 100% kill fee. Buys first North American serial rights and electronic rights. Editorial lead time 2 months. Submit seasonal material 3 months in advance. Accepts queries by mail. Sample copy $5.

Nonfiction: Exposé, interview/profile, news, product features, as they relate to local construction. **Buys 30 mss/year.** Query with published clips. Length: 800-2,000 words. **Pays $100-400.** Sometimes pays expenses of writers on assignment.

Photos: State availability of photos with submission. Offers $50/photo. Captions, identification of subjects required. Buys non-exclusive unlimited use in publication rights.

Tips: "We are a regional magazine covering eastern Missouri and southwestern Illinois. Be familiar with issues affecting the construction industry in that region and use sources relevant to the region."

DRUGS, HEALTHCARE & MEDICAL PRODUCTS

[N] CANADIAN PHARMACEUTICAL JOURNAL, 21 Concourse, Gate #13, Nepean, Ontario K2E 754 Canada. (613)727-1364. Fax: (613)727-3757. E-mail: cpj@cyberus.ca. Website: www.keithhealthcare.com. **Contact:** Andrew Reinboldt, editor. Works with a small number of new/unpublished writers each year. Monthly journal for pharmacists. Estab. 1868. Circ. 13,038. Pays after editing. Publishes ms an average of 6 months after acceptance. Buys first serial rights. Accepts queries by mail, e-mail, fax, phone. Responds in 2 months. Free sample copy and writer's guidelines.
Nonfiction: Relevant to Canadian pharmacy. Publishes continuing education, pharmacy practice, education and legislation, how-to; historical. Length: 200-400 words (for news notices); 800-1,500 words (for articles). Query. **Payment varies.** Sometimes pays expenses of writers on assignment.
Photos: Color and b&w 5×7 glossies purchased with mss. Captions, model releases required.
Tips: "Query with complete description of proposed article, including topic, sources (in general), length, payment requested, suggested submission date, and whether photographs will be included. It is helpful if the writer has read a *recent* copy of the journal; we are glad to send one if required. References should be included where appropriate (this is vital where medical and scientific information is included). Send three copies of each manuscript. Author's degree and affiliations (if any) and writing background should be listed."

$ $ FRAMESDATA.COM, Optical Technology for the 21st Century, (formerly *Optical Technology 21st Century*), Frames Data, 16269 Laguna Canyon Rd., Suite 100, Irvine CA 92618. (949)788-0150. Fax: (949)788-0130. E-mail: cwalker@framesdata.com. Website: www.framesdata.com. **Contact:** Christie Walker, editor. **20% freelance written.** Magazine for the eye wear industry. "*FRAMESdata.com*, published six times a year, features articles for information-aware professionals who are looking for the newest and best means to improve their practices and increase profits through technology." Estab. 1970. Circ. 18,000. Pays on publication. Publishes ms an average of 3 months after acceptance. Byline given. Buys first North American serial rights. Editorial lead time 3 months. Submit seasonal material 3 months in advance. Accepts simultaneous submissions. Accepts queries by mail, e-mail. Responds in 2 weeks to queries; 1 month to mss. Sample copy for 8×10 SAE with 2 first-class stamps.
Nonfiction: How-to, new products. **Buys 10 mss/year.** Query with published clips. Length: 800-1,600 words. **Pays $300-500.** Sometimes pays expenses of writers on assignment.
Reprints: Accepts previously published submissions.
Photos: Send photos with submission. Offers no additional payment for photos accepted with ms. Captions and identification of subjects required. Buys one-time rights.
Tips: "Write on how technology can help optometrists to sell more product."

[N] $ $ $ HOME CARE MAGAZINE, For Business Leaders in Home Health Care, Intertec Publishing Corp., 23815 Stuart Ranch Rd., Malibu CA 90265-8987. Fax: (310)317-0264. E-mail: marie_blakey@intertec.com. Website: www.homecaremag.com. Managing Editor: Susanne Hopkins. **Contact:** Marie Blakey, editor. **20% freelance written.** Trade journal published monthly covering the needs of home medical equipment retailers. "We provide product and business advice and market analysis to small family-held companies that offer medical equipment and related services to patients in a home setting." Estab. 1979. Circ. 17,000. Pays on publication. Publishes ms an average of 3 months after acceptance. Byline given. Buys first and second serial (reprint) rights. Editorial lead time 3 months. Accepts queries by mail, e-mail, fax. Accepts simultaneous submissions. Responds in 3 weeks to queries and mss. Sample copy online at website.
Nonfiction: How-to (by assignment). **Buys 2 mss/year.** Query with published clips. Length: 500-2,500 words. **Pays 50¢/word.** Sometimes pays expenses of writers on assignment.
Photos: State availability of photos with submission. Captions, model releases and identification of subjects required. Buys all rights.
Tips: "Contributors should have knowledge of health industry."

[N] MASSAGE & BODYWORK, Associated Bodywork & Massage Professionals, 28677 Buffalo Park Rd., Evergreen CO 80439-7347. (303)674-8478. Fax: (303)674-0859. E-mail: editor@abmp.com. Website: www.abmp.com. **Contact:** Karrie Mowen, editor. **85% freelance written.** Bimonthly trade magazine covering therapeutic massage/bodywork. "A trade publication for the massage therapist, bodyworker and esthetician. An all-inclusive publication encompassing everything from traditional Swedish massage to energy work to other complementary therapies (i.e.-homeopathy, herbs, aromatherapy, etc.)." **Pays on acceptance.** Publishes ms an average of 6 months after acceptance. Buys first North American serial rights and electronic rights or one-time rights. Editorial lead time 6 months. Submit seasonal material 6 months in advance. Accepts queries by mail, e-mail, fax, phone. Responds in 3 weeks to queries; 5 months to mss. Sample copy by mail. Writer's guidelines free.
Nonfiction: Essays, exposé, how-to (technique/modality), interview/profile, opinion, personal experience, technical, travel. No fiction. **Buys 60-75 mss/year.** Query with published clips. Length: 1,000-3,000 words. Pays writers with contributor copies or other premiums "when agreeable to both parties."
Reprints: Accepts previously published submissions "rarely."
Photos: State availability of photos with submission. Reviews contact sheets. Negotiates payment individually. Captions, model releases and identification of subjects required. Buys one-time rights.
Columns/Departments: Buys 20 mss/year.

Tips: "Know your topic. Offer suggestions for art to accompany your submission. *Massage & Bodywork* looks for interesting, tightly-focused stories concerning a particular modality or technique of massage, bodywork, somatic and esthetic therapies. The editorial staff welcomes the opportunity to review manuscripts which may be relevant to the field of massage, bodywork and esthetic practices, in addition to more general pieces pertaining to complementary and alternative medicine. This would include the widely varying modalities of massage and bodywork, (from Swedish massage to Polarity therapy), specific technique articles and ancillary therapies, including such topics as biomagnetics, aromatherapy and facial rejuvenation. Reference lists relating to technical articles should include the author, title, publisher and publication date of works cited. Word count: 1,500 to 4,000 words; longer articles negotiable.

N $ $ $ MEDICAL DEVICE APPROVAL LETTER, Washington Information Source Co., 6506 Old Stage Rd., Suite 100, Rockville MD 20852-4326. (301)770-5553. Fax: (301)468-0475. E-mail: wis@fdainfo.com. Website: www.fdainfo.com. **Contact:** Kenneth Reid, editor, publisher. Monthly newsletter covering regulation of pharmaceutical and medical devices. "We write to executives who have to keep up on changing FDA policies and regulations, and on what their competitors are doing at the agency." Estab. 1992. Pays on publication. Publishes ms an average of 1 month after acceptance. Byline given. Makes work-for-hire assignments. Editorial lead time 1 month. Submit seasonal material 1 month in advance. Accepts queries by e-mail, phone. Responds in 1 week to queries. Sample copy free. Writer's guidelines free.

Nonfiction: How-to, technical, regulatory. No lay interest pieces. **Buys 50-100 mss/year.** Query. Length: 600-1,500 words. **Pays $100/half day; $200 full day "to cover meetings and same rate for writing."** Sometimes pays expenses of writers on assignment.

Tips: "If you're covering a conference for non-competing publications, call me with a drug or device regulatory angle."

★ $ $ OPTICAL PRISM, Canada's Optical Business Magazine, Vezcom, Inc., 250 The Eastmall, Suite 1113, Toronto, Ontario M95 6L3 Canada. (905)475-9343. Fax: (905)477-2821. E-mail: prism@istar.ca. Website: www.opticalprism.com. **Contact:** Robert May, editor. **90% freelance written.** Magazine published 9 times/year covering the Canadian optical industry for "optometrists, opticians, ophthalmologists and optical suppliers and their sales staffs. Material covers clinical papers, practice management, contact lenses (clinical and practical), marketing, selling, motivation and merchandising." Estab. 1983. Circ. 7,800. **Pays on acceptance.** Publishes ms an average of 4 months after acceptance. Byline given. Not copyrighted. Buys one-time rights or second serial (reprint) rights. Editorial lead time 2 months. Submit seasonal material 3 months in advance. Accepts previously published submissions "with permission of original publisher in writing." Accepts queries by: mail, e-mail, fax. Responds in 2 weeks. Sample copy and writer's guidelines free.

• *Optical Prism* offers detailed writer's guidelines including a list of possible topics for future freelance articles.

Nonfiction: How-to, inspirational, interview/profile, new product (article), technical (article). "No U.S.-specific material. We try to concentrate on the Canadian market." **Buys 35-40 mss/year.** Query. Length: 500-10,000 words. **Pays $100-700 (25¢/word)(Canadian).**

Reprints: Accepts previously published submissions. Send tearsheet, photocopy or typed ms with rights for sale noted and information about when and where the article previously appeared. Pays 3¢/word.

Photos: Send photos with submission. Reviews transparencies and prints. Offers no additional payment for photos accepted with ms. Captions, model releases and indentification of subjects required. Buys one-time rights.

Tips: "Send query with reasonably detailed outline of the article to be written along with the 'slant' to be taken."

$ $ SUNWEAR, (formerly *Sun & Sport Eyewear*), Frames Data, 16269 Laguna Canyon Rd., Ste 100 Irvine CA 92618. (949)788-0150. Fax: (949)788-0130. E-mail: cwalker@framesdata.com. Website: www.framesdata.com. **Contact:** Christie Walker, editor. **20% freelance written.** Magazine published 3 times/year for the eye wear industry. "*Sunwear* brings readers current information on all the latest designs and innovations available in the field of fashion and sports sunwear." Estab. 1970. Circ. 30,000. Pays on publication. Publishes ms an average of 3 months after acceptance. Byline given. Buys first North American serial rights. Editorial lead time 3 months. Submit seasonal material 3 months in advance. Accepts simultaneous submissions. Responds in 2 weeks to queries; 1 month to mss. Sample copy for 8×10 SAE with 2 first-class stamps. Writer's guidelines free.

Nonfiction: How-to, new product. **Buys 10 mss/year.** Query with published clips. Length: 800-1,600 words. **Pays $300-500.** Sometimes pays expenses of writers on assignment.

Reprints: Accepts previously published submissions.

Photos: Send photos with submission. Offers no additional payment for photos accepted with ms. Captions and identification of subjects required. Buys one-time rights.

Tips: "Write for the doctor. How can doctors make more money selling sunwear?"

N $ $ $ VALIDATION TIMES, Washington Information Source Co., 6506 Old Stage Rd., Suite 100, Rockville MD 20852-4326. (301)770-5553. Fax: (301)468-0475. E-mail: wis@fdainfo.com. Website: www.fdainfo.com. **Contact:** Kenneth Reid, editor, publisher. Monthly newsletter covering regulation of pharmaceutical and medical devices. "We write to executives who have to keep up on changing FDA policies and regulations, and on what their competitors are doing at the agency." Estab. 1992. Pays on publication. Publishes ms an average of 1 month after acceptance. Byline given. Makes work-for-hire assignments. Editorial lead time 1 month. Submit seasonal material 1 month in advance. Accepts queries by e-mail, phone. Responds in 1 week to queries. Sample copy free. Writer's guidelines free.

Nonfiction: How-to, technical, regulatory. No lay interest pieces. **Buys 50-100 mss/year.** Query. Length: 600-1,500 words. **Pays $100/half day; $200 full day "to cover meetings and same rate for writing."** Sometimes pays expenses of writers on assignment.

Tips: "If you're covering a conference for non-competing publications, call me with a drug or device regulatory angle."

EDUCATION & COUNSELING

Professional educators, teachers, coaches and counselors—as well as other people involved in training and education—read the journals classified here. Many journals for educators are non-profit forums for professional advancement; writers contribute articles in return for a byline and contributor's copies. *Writer's Market* includes only educational journals that pay freelancers for articles. Education-related publications for students are included in the Consumer Career, College & Alumni; and Teen & Young Adult sections. Listings in the Childcare & Parental Guidance and Psychology & Self-Improvement sections of Consumer Magazines may also be of interest.

N $ $ ARTS & ACTIVITIES, Publishers' Development Corporation, Dept. WM, 591 Camino de la Reina, Suite 200, San Diego CA 92108-3104. (619)297-5352. Fax: (619)297-5353. Editor: Maryellen Bridge. **95% freelance written.** Eager to work with new/unpublished writers. Monthly (except July and August) art education magazine covering art education at levels from preschool through college for educators and therapists engaged in arts and crafts education and training. Estab. 1932. Circ. 24,000. Pays on publication. Publishes ms an average of 9-12 months after acceptance. Byline given. Buys first North American serial rights. Submit seasonal material 6 months in advance. Responds in 3 months. Sample copy for 9×12 SAE with 8 first-class stamps. Writer's guidelines for #10 SASE.

Nonfiction: Historical/nostalgic (arts, activities, history); how-to (classroom art experiences, artists' techniques); interview/profile (of artists); opinion (on arts activities curriculum, ideas on how to do things better, philosophy of art education); personal experience in the art classroom ("this ties in with the how-to, we like it to be *personal*, no recipe style"); articles on exceptional art programs. **Buys 80-100 mss/year.** Length: 200-2,000 words. **Pays $35-150.**

  • Editors here are seeking more materials for upper elementary and secondary levels on printmaking, ceramics, 3-dimensional design, weaving, fiber arts (stitchery, tie-dye, batik, etc.), crafts, painting and multicultural art.

Tips: "Frequently in unsolicited manuscripts, writers obviously have not studied the magazine to see what style of articles we publish. Send for a sample copy to familiarize yourself with our style and needs. The best way to find out if his/her writing style suits our needs is for the author to submit a manuscript on speculation. We prefer an anecdotal style of writing, so that readers will feel as though they are there in the art room as the lesson/project is taking place. Also, good quality photographs of student artwork are important. We are a *visual* art magazine!"

N $ THE ATA MAGAZINE, The Alberta Teachers' Association, 11010 142nd St., Edmonton, Alberta T5N 2R1 Canada. (780)447-9400. Fax: (780)455-6481. E-mail: postmaster@teachers.ab.ca. Website: www.teachers.ab.ca. Editor: Tim Johnston. **Contact:** Raymond Gariepy, associate editor. Quarterly magazine covering education. Estab. 1920. Circ. 39,500. Pays on publication. Publishes ms an average of 4 months after acceptance. Byline given. Offers kill fee of $75. Buys one-time rights. Editorial lead time 2 months. Submit seasonal material 2 months in advance. Accepts simultaneous submissions. Accepts queries by mail, e-mail, fax, phone. Responds in 2 months. Sample copy and writer's guidelines free.

Nonfiction: Education-related topics. Query with published clips. Length: 500-1,250 words. **Pays $75** (Canadian).

Photos: Send photos with submission. Reviews 4×6 prints. Negotiates payment individually. Captions required. Negotiates rights.

$ THE CHRISTIAN CLASSROOM, Great River Publishing Company, Inc., 2026 Exeter Rd., Suite 2, Germantown TN 38138. (901)624-5911. Fax: (901)624-5910. E-mail: tcc@grtriver.com. Website: www.grtriver.com. **Contact:** Sherry Campbell, editor. **25% freelance written.** "*The Christian Classroom* is the only national magazine devoted exclusively to the interests and issues of concern to teachers in Christian schools." Estab. 1997. Circ. 20,000. Pays on publication. Publishes ms an average of 6 months after acceptance. Byline given. Offers negotiable kill fee. Buys all rights. Editorial lead time 3 months. Submit seasonal material 3 months in advance. Accepts queries by mail, e-mail, fax, phone. Responds in 2 weeks to queries; 3 months to mss. Sample copy and writer's guidelines free.

Nonfiction: How-to, personal experience. "No articles that preach rather than give practical advice." **Buys 20 mss/ year.** Query. Length: 300-1,500 words. Pay is negotiable.

Photos: State availability of photos with submission. Reviews prints (up to 8×10). Offers no additional payment for photos accepted with ms. Model releases required. Buys one-time rights.

N INDICATES THAT the listing is new to this edition. New markets are often more receptive to freelance submissions.

Tips: "Submit articles of current interest to Christian school teachers."

$ THE CHRISTIAN SCHOOL ADMINISTRATOR, Great River Publishing Company, Inc., 2026 Exeter Rd., Suite 2, Germantown TN 38138. (901)624-5911. Fax: (901)624-5910. E-mail: csa@grtriver.com. Website: www.grtriver. com. **Contact:** Sherry Campbell, editor. **35% freelance written.** Bimonthly. *"The Christian School Administrator* provides Christian school administrators with news and information on such topics as legal issues, school financial management, parent and school relations, curriculum and educational materials, student recruitment, new technologies and school improvements. These administrators all face the same issues of budgeting, setting tuition rates, attracting new students, buying new equipment, fund raising and setting strong academic standards in a Christian environment." Estab. 1993. Circ. 13,000. Pays on publication. Publishes ms an average of 6 months after acceptance. Byline given. Offers negotiable kill fee. Buys all rights. Editorial lead time 3 months. Submit seasonal material 3 months in advance. Accepts queries by mail, e-mail, fax, phone. Responds in 2 weeks to queries; 3 months to mss. Sample copy and writer's guidelines free.
Nonfiction: How-to, personal experience. "No articles that preach rather than give advice or relate experiences." **Buys 20-30 mss/year.** Query. Length: 300-1,500 words. Pay is negotiable.
Photos: State availability of photos with submission. Reviews prints (up to 8×10). Offers no additional payment for photos accepted with ms. Model releases required. Buys one-time rights.
Tips: "Writers should be familiar with private Christian schools, their practices, problems and issues of interest and concern to them."

$ CLASS ACT, Class Act, Inc., P.O. Box 802, Henderson KY 42419. E-mail: classact@henderson.net. **Contact:** Susan Thurman, editor. **50% freelance written.** Educational newsletter published 9 times/year covering English/language arts education. "Our writers must know English as a classroom subject and should be familiar with writing for teens. If you can't make your manuscript interesting to teenagers, we're not interested." Estab. 1993. Circ. 300. **Pays on acceptance.** Publishes ms an average of 6 months after acceptance. Byline given. Offers 100% kill fee. Buys all rights. Editorial lead time 2 months. Submit seasonal material 3 months in advance. Accepts simultaneous submissions. Responds in 1 month. Sample copy for $3. Writer's guidelines for #10 SASE.
Nonfiction: How-to (games, puzzles, assignments relating to English education). "NO Masters theses; no esoteric articles; no poetry; no educational theory or jargon." **Buys 12 mss/year.** Send complete ms. Length: 100-2,000 words. **Pays $10-40.**
Columns/Departments: Writing assignments (innovative, thought-provoking for teens), 500-1,500 words; puzzles, games (English education oriented), 200 words; teacher tips (bulletin boards, time-saving devices), 100 words. "E-mailed manuscripts (not attachments) are encouraged. Articles on disk (MS Word or Works) also are encouraged." Send complete ms. **Pays $10-40.**
Fillers: Teacher tips. **Pays $10.**
Tips: "Please know the kind of language used by junior/senior high students. Don't speak above them. Also, it helps to know what these students *don't* know, in order to explain or emphasize the concepts. Clip art is sometimes used but is not paid extra for. We like material that's slightly humorous while still being educational. We are especially open to innovative writing assignments, educational puzzles and games, and instructions on basics. Again, be familiar with this age group. Remember we are geared for English teachers."

$ $ HISPANIC OUTLOOK IN HIGHER EDUCATION, 210 Rt 4 East, Ste 310., Paramus NJ 07652. (201)587-8800 ext 100. Fax: (201)587-9105. E-mail: sloutlook@aol.com. Website: www.Hispanicoutlook@aol.com. Editor: Adalyn Hixson. **Contact:** Sue Lopez-Isa, managing editor. **50% freelance written.** Biweekly magazine. "We're looking for higher education story articles, with a focus on Hispanics and the advancements made by and for Hispanics in higher education." Circ. 28,000. Pays on publication. Publishes ms an average of 2 months after acceptance. Byline given. Publication copyrighted. Editorial lead time 6 weeks. Submit seasonal material 3 months in advance. Accepts queries by mail, e-mail, fax, phone. Accepts simultaneous submissions. Sample copy free.
○─ Break with "issues articles such as new laws in higher education."
Nonfiction: Historical/nostalgic, opinion, personal experience, all regarding higher education only. **Buys 20-25 mss/ year.** Query with published clips. Length: 1,750-2,000 words. **Pays $400 minimum for assigned articles.** Pays expenses of writers on assignment (limit agreed upon in advance).
Photos: Send photos with submission. Reviews prints, black and white or color. Offers no additional payment for photos accepted with ms.
Tips: "Articles explore the Hispanic experience in higher education. Special theme issues address sports, law, health, corporations, heritage, women, and a wide range of similar issues; however, articles need not fall under those umbrellas. We are not looking for any more Affirmative Action articles at this time."

$ SCHOOL ARTS MAGAZINE, 50 Portland St., Worcester MA 01608-9959. Fax: (610)683-8229. Website: www.d avis-art.com. **Contact:** Eldon Katter, editor. **85% freelance written.** Monthly magazine (September-May), serving arts and craft education profession, K-12, higher education and museum education programs written by and for art teachers. Estab. 1901. Pays on publication. Publishes ms an average of 3 months "if timely; if less pressing, can be 1 year or more" after acceptance. Buys all rights. Accepts queries by: mail, phone. Responds in 3 months. Free sample copy and writer's guidelines.
○─ Break in with "professional quality photography to illustrate art lessons."

Nonfiction: Articles on art and craft activities in schools. Should include description and photos of activity in progress, as well as examples of finished artwork. Query or send complete ms and SASE. Length: 600-1,400 words. **Pays $30-150.**

■ The online version contains material not found in the print edition.

Tips: "We prefer articles on actual art projects or techniques done by students in actual classroom situations. Philosophical and theoretical aspects of art and art education are usually handled by our contributing editors. Our articles are reviewed and accepted on merit and each is tailored to meet our needs. Keep in mind that art teachers want practical tips, above all—more hands-on information than academic theory. Write your article with the accompanying photographs in hand." The most frequent mistakes made by writers are "bad visual material (photographs, drawings) submitted with articles, or a lack of complete descriptions of art processes; and no rationale behind programs or activities. Familiarity with the field of art education is essential. Review recent issues of *School Arts*."

$ TEACHER'S DISCOVERY, English, Foreign Language, Social Studies and Science editions, American Eagle, 2676 Paldan Dr., Auburn Hills MI 48326-1824. (248)340-7220, ext. 219. Fax: (248)276-1652. E-mail: Science@t eachersdiscovery.cnchost.com. **Contact:** Laurie Freeman. **10-20% freelance written.** Semiannual educational materials catalogues covering English, foreign language, social studies and science. Estab. 1969. Circ. 2,000,000. Pays on publication. Byline given. Buys first rights, electronic rights or all rights. Editorial lead time 2 months. Submit seasonal material 6 months in advance. Accepts queries by mail, e-mail, fax. Accepts simultaneous submissions. Responds in 1 month. Sample copy for $5.

Nonfiction: Nina Linebaugh, divisional manager/Social Studies. How-to articles with concrete examples, practical suggestions, first-person accounts of classroom experiences, quick teacher tips and ideas, seasonal and curriculum-related activities and projects, school humor, jokes, anecdotes, quips or quotes. **Buys 10 mss/year.** Query. Length: 100 words minimum. **Pays $25 minimum.**

Photos: State availability of photos with submission. Negotiates payment individually. Model releases, identification of subjects required. Buys one-time or all rights.

Nonfiction & Fiction: Laurie Freeman, divisional manager/Science & Math. Adventure, condensed novels, confession, ethnic, experimental, historical, humorous, mainstream, novel excerpts, religious, slice-of-life vignettes, suspense. No erotica. **Buys 2 mss/year.** Query. Length: 100 words minimum. **Pays $25 minimum.**

Poetry: Pat Naus, divisional manager/English. Avant-garde, free verse, haiku, light verse, traditional. No erotica. **Buys 5 mss/year.** Submit 5 poems/batch. Length: 1-13 lines. **Pays $25 minimum.**

Fillers: Pat Naus, divisional manager/English. Anecdotes, facts, gags to be illustrated by cartoonist, newsbreaks, short humor. **Buys 100 mss/year.** Length: 10-50 words. **Pays $25.**

Tips: "We like material that is slightly humorous while still being educational. All contributions must be original and not previously published. If you send your item electronically, remember to include your name, address and other information."

$ $ TEACHERS IN FOCUS, Focus on the Family, 8605 Explorer Dr., Colorado Springs CO 80920. (719)531-3372. Fax: (719)548-5860. Website: www.family.org/tif. Editor: Mark Hartwig. **Contact:** Heather Koerner, associate editor. **85% freelance written.** Magazine published 9 times/year covering education. "*Teachers in Focus* is designed to encourage and equip educators to live as Christians in every area of their lives." Estab. 1992. Circ. 28,000. **Pays on acceptance.** Byline given. Kill fee varies. Buys first rights. Editorial lead time 4 months. Submit seasonal material 4 months in advance. Accepts queries by mail, e-mail, fax, phone. Sample copy and writer's guidelines online at website.

Nonfiction: Book excerpts, how-to, humor, inspirational, interview/profile, religious, education issues. **Buys 20-25 mss/year.** Query. Length: 1,000-2,500 words. **Pays $100-500.** Sometimes pays expenses of writers on assignment.

Reprints: Accepts previously published submissions.

Photos: State availability of photos with submission.

Columns/Departments: Laughs From the Lounge (humorous teacher tales), 25-50 words; Guest Speaker (education or spiritual issues), 500 words; Teammates (profiles of inspirational staff), 500 words. **Buys 20 mss/year.** Query. **Pays $25-150.**

Fiction: Humorous, religious. **Buys 10 mss/year.** Query. Length: 1,000-2,000 words. **Pays $100-500.**

$ $ TEACHING THEATRE, Educational Theatre Association, 2343 Auburn Ave., Cincinnati OH 45219-2819. (513)421-3900. Fax: (513)421-7077. E-mail: jpalmarini@etassoc.org. Website: www.etassoc.org. **Contact:** James Palmarini, editor. **65% freelance written.** Membership benefit of the Educational Theatre Association. Quarterly magazine covering education theater K-12, primary emphasis on secondary level education. "*Teaching Theatre* emphasizes the teaching, theory, philosophy issues that are of concern to teachers at the elementary, secondary, and—as they relate to teaching K-12 theater—college levels. We publish work that explains specific approaches to teaching (directing, acting, curriculum development and management, etc.); advocates curriculum reform; or offers theories of theater education." Estab. 1989. Circ. 3,500. **Pays on acceptance.** Publishes ms an average of 1-3 months after acceptance. Byline given. Buys one-time rights. Editorial lead time 2 months. Submit seasonal material 3 months in advance. Accepts simultaneous and previously published submissions. Responds in 1 month to queries; 3 months to mss. Sample copy for $2. Writer's guidelines for #10 SASE.

Nonfiction: Book excerpts, essays, how-to, interview/profile, opinion, technical theater. *"Teaching Theatre*'s audience is well-educated and most have considerable experience in their field; *generalist* articles are discouraged; readers already *possess* basic skills." **Buys 20 mss/year.** Query. **Pays $100-300 for published articles.** "We generally pay cash and 5 copies of issue."

Reprints: Accepts previously published submissions.

Photos: State availability of photos with submission. Reviews contact sheets, 5×7 and 8×10 transparencies and prints. Offers no additional payment for photos accepted with ms.

Tips: Wants articles that address the needs of the busy but experienced high school theater educators. "Fundamental pieces, on the value of theater education are *not* of value to us—our readers already know that."

$ $ $ $ TEACHING TOLERANCE, The Southern Poverty Law Center, 400 Washington Ave., Montgomery AL 36104. (334)264-0286. Fax: (334)264-3121. Website: www.teachingtolerance.org. **Contact:** Elsie Williams, managing editor. **65% freelance written.** Semiannual magazine. *"Teaching Tolerance* is dedicated to helping K-12 teachers promote tolerance and understanding between widely diverse groups of students. Includes articles, teaching ideas, and reviews of other resources available to educators." Estab. 1991. Circ. 600,000. **Pays on acceptance.** Byline given. Buys all rights. Editorial lead time 6 months. Submit seasonal material 6 months in advance. Accepts queries by mail, fax. Sample copy and writer's guidelines free and on website.

Nonfiction: Features, essays, how-to (classroom techniques), personal classroom experiences, photo features. "No jargon, rhetoric or academic analysis. No theoretical discussions on the pros/cons of multicultural education." **Buys 6-8 mss/year.** Query with published clips. Length: 1,000-3,000 words. **Pays $500-3,000.** Pays expenses of writers on assignment.

Photos: State availability of photos with submission. Reviews contact sheets and transparencies. Captions and identification of subjects required. Buys one-time rights.

Columns/Departments: Essays (personal reflection, how-to, school program), 400-800 words; Idea Exchange (special projects, successful anti-bias activities), 250-500 words; Between the Lines, (using literature to teach tolerance), 1,200 words; Student Writings (short essays dealing with diversity, tolerance & justice), 300-500 words. **Buys 8-12 mss/year. Pays $50-1,000.** Query with published clips.

> The online magazine carries original content not found in the print edition and includes writer's guidelines. Contact: Tim Walker.

Tips: "We want lively, simple, concise writing. The writing style should be descriptive and reflective, showing the strength of programs dealing successfully with diversity by employing clear descriptions of real scenes and interactions, and by using quotes from teachers and students. We ask that prospective writers study previous issues of the magazine and writer's guidelines before sending a query with ideas. Most open to articles that have a strong classroom focus. We are interested in approaches to teaching tolerance and promoting understanding that really work—approaches we might not have heard of. We want to inform our readers; we also want to inspire and encourage them. We know what's happening nationally; we want to know what's happening in your neighborhood classroom."

$ TECH DIRECTIONS, Prakken Publications, Inc., P.O. Box 8623, Ann Arbor MI 48107-8623. (734)975-2800. Fax: (734)975-2787. E-mail: tom@techdirections.com. Website: www.techdirections.com. **Contact:** Tom Bowden, managing editor. **100% freelance written.** Eager to work with new/unpublished writers. Monthly magazine (except June and July) covering issues, trends and activities of interest to industrial, vocational, technical and technology educators at the elementary through post-secondary school levels. Estab. 1934. Circ. 43,000. Buys all rights. Pays on publication. Publishes ms an average of 18 months after acceptance. Byline given. No simultaneous submissions. Responds in 1 month. Sample copy $5. Writer's guidelines for #10 SASE or on website.

Nonfiction: Uses articles pertinent to the various teaching areas in industrial and technology education (woodwork, electronics, drafting, machine shop, graphic arts, computer training, etc.). Prefers authors who have direct connection with the field of industrial and/or technical education. "The outlook should be on innovation in educational programs, processes or projects that directly apply to the industrial/technical education area." Main focus: technical career and education. Buys general interest, how-to, opinion, personal experience, technical and think pieces, interviews and coverage of new products. **Buys 135 unsolicited mss/year.** Length: 2,000-3,000 words. **Pays $50-150.**

Photos: Send photos with accompanying query or ms. Reviews color prints. Payment for photos included in payment for ms. Will accept electronic art as well.

Columns/Departments: Direct from Washington (education news from Washington DC); Technology Today (new products under development); Technologies Past (profiles the inventors of last century); Mastering Computers, Technology Concepts (project orientation).

Tips: "We are most interested in articles written by industrial, vocational and technical educators about their class projects and their ideas about the field. We need more and more technology-related articles, especially written for the community college level. Will rough-read articles starting fall 2000."

$ VISION, Christian Educators Association, P.O. Box 41300, Pasadena CA 91114. (626)798-1124. Fax: (626)798-2346. E-mail: vision@ceai.org. Website: www.ceai.org. Editor: Forrest L. Turpen. Managing Editor: Denise Jones. **Contact:** Judy Turpen, contributing editor. **30% freelance written.** Newsletter published 9 times/year for Christian teachers in public education. *"Vision*'s articles inspire, inform and equip teachers and administrators in the educational arena. Readers look for organizational news and general interest education articles. Our audience is primarily public school educators. Other readers include teachers in private schools, university professors, school administrators, parents and school board members." Estab. 1953. Circ. 10,000. Pays on publication. Publishes ms an average of 6 months after acceptance. Byline given. Buys first North American serial or second serial (reprint) rights. Editorial lead time 6 months. Submit seasonal material 4 months in advance. Accepts simultaneous submissions. Accepts queries by mail, e-mail, fax, phone. Responds in 1 month to queries; 6 months to mss. Sample copy for 9×12 SAE and 4 first-class stamps. Writer's guidelines for #10 SASE and on website.

Nonfiction: How-to, inspirational, interview/profile, personal experience, religious. "Nothing preachy." **Buys 15-20 mss/year.** Query or send complete ms if 2,000 words or less. Length: 600-2,500 words. **Pays $30-40.**

Reprints: Accepts previously published submissions. **Pays $30.**

Photos: State availability of photos with submission. Offers no additional payment for photos accepted with ms. Buys one-time and reprint rights.

Columns/Departments: Query. **Pays $30-40.**

Fillers: Send with a SASE—must relate to public education.

Tips: "We are looking for material on living out one's faith in appropriate, legal ways in the public school setting."

ELECTRONICS & COMMUNICATION

These publications are edited for broadcast and telecommunications technicians and engineers, electrical engineers and electrical contractors. Included are journals for electronic equipment designers and operators who maintain electronic and telecommunication systems. Publications for appliance dealers can be found in Home Furnishings & Household Goods.

$ THE ACUTA JOURNAL OF TELECOMMUNICATIONS IN HIGHER EDUCATION, ACUTA, 152 W. Zandale Dr., Suite 200, Lexington KY 40503-2486. (606)278-3338. Fax: (606)278-3268. E-mail: pscott@acuta.org. Website: www.acuta.org. **Contact:** Patricia Scott, communications manager. **20% freelance written.** Quarterly professional association journal covering telecommunications in higher education. "Our audience includes, primarily, middle to upper management in the telecommunications department on college/university campuses. They are highly skilled, technology-oriented professionals who provide data, voice and video communications services for residential and academic purposes." Estab. 1997. Circ. 2,200. Pays on publication. Publishes ms an average of 6 months after acceptance. Byline given. Buys first rights. Editorial lead time 5-6 months. Accepts queries by mail, e-mail, fax, phone. Responds in 2-4 weeks to queries; 1-2 months to mss. Sample copy for 9×12 SASE and 6 first-class stamps; writer's guidelines free.

    O—¬ Break in with a campus study or case profile.

Nonfiction: How-to (telecom), technical (telecom), case study (college/university application of technology). "Each issue has a focus. Available with writer's guidelines. We are only interested in articles described in article types." **Buys 6-8 mss/year.** Query. Length: 1,200-4,000 words. **Pays 8-10¢/word.** Sometimes pays expenses of writers on assignment.

Photos: State availability of photos with submission. Reviews prints. Offers no additional payment for photos accepted with ms. Captions and model releases required.

Tips: "Our audience expects every article to be relevant to telecommunications on the college/university campus, whether it is related to technology, facilities, or management. Writers must read back issues to understand this focus and the level of technicality we expect."

N $ $ DIGITAL OUTPUT, The Business Guide for Electronic Publishers, The Doyle Group, 13000 Sawgrass Village Center, Suite 18, Ponte Vedra Beach FL 32082. (904)285-6020. Fax: (904)285-9944. E-mail: digout@mindspring.com. Website: www.digitalout.com. Associate Editor: Laura Lee Smith. **Contact:** Gregory Sharpless, editor-in-chief. **50% freelance written.** Monthly trade magazine covering electronic publishing and digital imaging, with articles ranging from digital capture and design to electronic prepress and digital printing. "*Digital Output* is a national business publication for electronic publishers and digital imagers, providing monthly articles which examine the latest technologies and digital methods and discuss how to profit from them. Our readers include service bureaus, prepress and reprographic houses, designers, printers, ad agencies, corporate communications and others." Estab. 1994. Circ. 30,000. Pays on publication. Publishes ms an average of 2 months after acceptance. Byline given. Offers 10-20% kill fee. Buys one-time rights including electronic rights for archival posting. Editorial lead time 3 months. Submit seasonal material 3 months in advance. Accepts queries by mail, e-mail. Responds in 2 weeks to queries; 1 month to mss. Sample copy for $4.50 or online at website. Writer's guidelines for #10 SASE.

Nonfiction: Book excerpts, how-to, interview/profile, technical. **Buys 36 mss/year.** Query with published clips. Length: 1,500-4,000 words. **Pays $250-600.**

Photos: State availability of photos and graphics with submission.

Columns/Departments: Pays $400.

Tips: "We're a business publication for professional digital imagers, so the writer should always keeps in mind that our readers want the business angle in every story—profits and economics, management tips and so on."

$ $ $ GLOBAL WIRELESS, The international newspaper for the wireless communications industry, Crain Communications, Inc., 777 E. Speer Blvd., Denver CO 80203. (303)733-2500. Fax: (303)733-9941. E-mail: swendelk@crain.com. Website: www.globalwirelessnews.com. **Contact:** Sandra Wendelken, editor. **80% freelance**

written. Magazine published 7 times/year covering international wireless telecommunications. Estab. 1998. Circ. 11,500. Pays on publication. Buys first and second serial (reprint) rights and makes work-for-hire assignments. Editorial lead time 3 months. Accepts queries by mail, e-mail, fax. Responds in 2 weeks. Sample copy for $7.

Nonfiction: Interview/profile, technical, news/news analysis. "No articles that are too general. You can't write for this publication unless you are very experienced in reporting on telecommunications and can write detailed, topical, analysis-oriented articles." **Buys 70-90 mss/year.** Query with published clips. Length: 200-1,400 words. **Pays 50-70¢/word.** Pays expenses of writers on assignment.

Photos: State availability of photos with submission. Reviews contact sheets and 4×6 prints. Negotiates payment individually. Captions and identification of subjects required. Buys one-time rights.

$ $ $ SOUND & VIDEO CONTRACTOR, Intertec Publishing, 9800 Metcalf Ave., Overland Park KS 66212-2286. (913)341-1300. Fax: (913)967-1905, publisher; or (818)780-6040, editor. E-mail: nat_hecht@intertec.com. Website: www.svconline.com. **Contact:** Nathaniel Hecht, editor. **60% freelance written.** Monthly magazine covering "professional audio, video, security, acoustical design, sales and marketing." Estab. 1983. Circ. 24,000. **Pays on acceptance.** Publishes ms an average of 3 months after acceptance. Byline given. Buys one-time or all rights. Editorial lead time 3 months. Accepts simultaneous submissions. Accepts queries by mail, e-mail, fax, phone. Reports ASAP on mss and queries. Sample copy and writer's guidelines free.

Nonfiction: Historical, how-to, photo feature, technical, professional audio/video applications, installations. No product reviews, opinion pieces, advertorial, interview/profile, exposé/gossip. **Buys 60 mss/year.** Query. Length: 1,000-2,500 words. **Pays $200-1,200 for assigned articles; $200-650 for unsolicited articles.**

Reprints: Accepts previously published submissions "if not previously or simultaneously published in our market segment."

Photos: Send photos with submission. Reviews transparencies and prints. Offers no additional payment for photos accepted with ms. Identification of subjects required.

Columns/Departments: Security Technology Review (technical install information); Sales & Marketing (techniques for installation industry); Video Happenings (Pro video/projection/storage technical info), all 1,500 words. **Buys 30 mss/year.** Query. **Pays $200-350.**

Tips: "We want materials and subject matter that would be of interest to audio/video/security/low-voltage product installers/contractors/designers professionals. If the piece allows our readers to save time, money and/or increases their revenues, then we have reached our goals. Highly technical is desirable."

ENERGY & UTILITIES

People who supply power to homes, businesses and industry read the publications in this section. This category includes journals covering the electric power, natural gas, petroleum, solar and alternative energy industries.

$ $ ELECTRICAL APPARATUS, The Magazine of Electromechanical & Electronic Application & Maintenance, Barks Publications, Inc., 400 N. Michigan Ave., Chicago IL 60611-4198. (312)321-9440. Fax: (312)321-1288. **Contact:** Elsie Dickson, editorial director. Senior Editor: Kevin N. Jones. Monthly magazine for persons working in electrical and electronic maintenance, chiefly in industrial plants, who install and service electrical motors, transformers, generators, controls and related equipment. Estab. 1967. Circ. 17,000. **Pays on acceptance.** Publishes ms an average of 3 months after acceptance. Byline given. Buys all rights unless other arrangements made. Accepts queries by mail, fax. Responds in 1 week to queries; 1 month to mss. Sample copy for $4.

Nonfiction: Technical. Length: 1,500-2,500. **Pays $250-500 for assigned articles.** Pays authorized expenses.

Tips: "All feature articles are assigned to staff and contributing editors and correspondents. Professionals interested in appointments as contributing editors and correspondents should submit résumé and article outlines, including illustration suggestions. Writers should be competent with a camera, which should be described in résumé. Technical expertise is absolutely necessary, preferably an E.E. degree, or practical experience. We are also book publishers and some of the material in *EA* is now in book form, bringing the authors royalties. Also publishes an annual directory, subtitled *ElectroMechanical Bench Reference*."

[N] $ $ ELECTRICAL WORLD MAGAZINE, McGraw-Hill, 20140 Scholar Dr., Suite 212, Hagerstown MD 21742. (301)745-5742. Fax: (301)745-8815. E-mail: editorew@aol.com. Website: www.electricalworld.com. **Contact:** Patricia Irwin, executive editor. **80% freelance written.** Bimonthly magazine covering electrical transmission and distribution. "Our audience consists mainly of electric utility engineers, substation and line personnel. Articles cover all angles of T&D work." Estab. 1875. Circ. 41,000. Pays on publication. Byline given. Buys all rights and makes work-for-hire assignments. Editorial lead time 3-4 months. Accepts queries by mail, e-mail, fax, phone. Responds in 3 weeks to queries; 1 month to mss. Sample copy online at website. Writer's guidelines by e-mail.

Nonfiction: Technical. "No articles that only mention one manufacturer or consultant and no long advertisements that look like articles. **Buys 60 mss/year.** Query. Length: 800-2,500 words. **Pays $300 minimum for assigned articles.** Sometimes pays expenses of writers on assignment.

Photos: State availability of photos with submission. Reviews contact sheets, negatives, transparencies and prints. Offers no additional payment for photos accepted with ms. Captions required. Buys one-time rights.

Columns/Departments: Automation (utility automation), 300-800 words; Power Puzzles (brain teasers), 300-800 words; Engineer's Notebook (technical explanation), 800 words. **Buys 20 mss/year.** Query. **Pays $50-300.**

Tips: "If you have experience in the T&D field and are willing to work hard on improving your writing, query me. Article angles most likely to succeed: info that is immediately useful to readers; how others solve their T&D problems; critical industry developments. No editorials."

$ $ HYDRO REVIEW, HCI Publications, 410 Archibald St., Kansas City MO 64111. (816)931-1311. Fax: (816)931-2015. E-mail: hci@aol.com. **Contact:** Marla Barnes, managing editor. **20% freelance written.** Magazine published 8 times/year covering hydroelectric power. "*Hydro Review* is the magazine for the North American hydroelectric industry. It covers all aspects of the industry, including dam safety. Our readers include a wide range of hydroelectric industry personnel, including utility executives, managers and operators, federal power producers, developers, regulators, consultants, engineers, designers, and other technicians, as well as providers of goods and services to the industry." Estab. 1982. Circ. 5,000. **Pays on acceptance.** Publishes ms an average of 2 months after acceptance. Byline sometimes given. Buys one-time, second serial (reprint) and electronic rights. Editorial lead time 6 months. Accepts queries by mail, e-mail, fax, phone. Sample copy for $25. Writer's guidelines free.

Nonfiction: General interest, historical/nostalgic, how-to, interview/profile, new product, opinion, technical. **Buys 10 mss/year.** Query. Length: 1,000-4,000 words. **Pays $150-600.**

Photos: Send photos with submission. Reviews 3×5 prints. Negotiates payment individually. Captions, model releases and identification of subjects required. Buys all rights.

Columns/Departments: Tech Briefs (technical news, reports), 300-500 words; R&D Forum (research findings), 300-500 words. **Buys 2 mss/year.** Query. **Pays $50-300.**

Tips: "In addition to writing, I hire freelancers to edit/rewrite articles from hydropower professionals."

$ $ PUBLIC POWER, Dept. WM, 2301 M St. NW, Washington DC 20037-1484. (202)467-2948. Fax: (202)467-2910. E-mail: jlabella@appanet.org. Website: www.appanet.org. **Contact:** Jeanne Wickline LaBella, chief editor. **60% freelance written.** Prefers to work with published/established writers. Bimonthly. Estab. 1942. **Pays on acceptance.** Publishes ms an average of 3 months after acceptance. Byline given. Accepts queries by mail, e-mail, fax. Responds in 6 months. Sample copy and writer's guidelines free.

Nonfiction: Features on municipal and other local publicly owned electric utilities. **Pays $400 and up.**

Photos: Reviews transparencies, slides and prints.

$ $ $ TEXAS CO-OP POWER, Texas Electric Cooperatives, Inc., Box 9589, Austin TX 78766. (512)454-0311, ext. 240. Fax: (512)467-9442. E-mail: ccook@texas-ec.org. Deputy Editor: Lisa Germany. **Contact:** Christopher Cook, editor. **60% freelance written.** Monthly magazine of the state's electric cooperatives. With more than 700,000 subscribers, it is the largest subscriber-based magazine in Texas and publishes general-interest articles designed to appeal to a predominantly rural, small-town audience." Estab. 1944. Circ. 725,000. **Pays on acceptance.** Publishes ms an average of 2 months after acceptance. Byline given. Offers 25% kill fee. Buys first rights. Editorial lead time 3 months. Submit seasonal material 3 months in advance. Accepts queries by mail, e-mail, fax, phone. Accepts simultaneous submissions. Responds in 3 weeks. Sample copy and writer's guidelines free.

Nonfiction: Essays, general interest, historical/nostalgic, humor, personal experience, photo feature. **Buys 30 mss/year.** Query with published clips or send complete ms. Length: 600-2,000 words. **Pays $250-750.** Pays expenses of writers on assignment.

Reprints: Accepts previously published submissions.

Photos: State availability of photos with submission. Reviews contact sheets. Negotiates payment individually. Captions, model releases and identification of subjects required. Buys one-time rights.

Tips: "We're looking for Texas-related, rural-based articles, often first-person, always lively and interesting."

N $ UTILITY AND TELEPHONE FLEETS, Practical Communications, Inc., 2615 Three Oaks Rd., P.O. Box 183, Cary IL 60013-0183. (847)639-2200. Fax: (847)639-9542. E-mail: curtis@pracom.com. Website: www.utfmag.com. **Contact:** Curt Marquardt, editor/publisher. **20% freelance written.** Magazine published 8 times/year for fleet managers and maintenance supervisors for electric gas and water utilities, telephone, interconnect and cable TV companies, public works departments and related contractors. "Case history/application features are also welcome." Estab. 1987. Circ. 18,000. Pays on publication. Publishes ms an average of 1 month after acceptance. Byline given. Buys all rights. Submit seasonal material 2 months in advance. Responds in 2 months. Free sample copy and writer's guidelines.

Nonfiction: How-to (ways for performing fleet maintenance/improving management skills/vehicle tutorials), technical, case history/application features. No advertorials in which specific product or company is promoted. **Buys 4-5 mss/year.** Query with published clips. Length: 1,000-2,800 words. **Pays 30¢/word.**

Photos: Send photos with submission. Reviews contact sheets, negatives, 3×5 transparencies and prints. Offers no additional payment for photos accepted with ms. Captions required. Buys one-time rights.

Tips: "Working with a utility or telephone company and gathering information about a construction, safety or fleet project is the best approach for a freelancer."

N **$ $ $UTILITY BUSINESS**, Intertec/PRIMEDIA, 9800 Metcalf, Overland Park KS 66212. Website: utilityb usiness.com. **Contact:** Dawn Hightower, managing editor. Editor: Martin Rosenberg. Monthly magazine covering electric, natural gas, telephone and water utilities for executives and managers. Estab. 1998. Circ. 50,000. Pays on publication. Publishes ms an average of 2 months after acceptance. Byline given. Buys all rights. Editorial lead time 3 months. Submit seasonal material 2 months in advance. Accepts queries by mail, e-mail, fax. Responds in 2 weeks to queries. Sample copy for 11×14 SAE.

Nonfiction: General interest, interview/profile, technical. **Buys 24 mss/year.** Query with published clips. Length: 1,500-2,500 words. **Pays 50¢/word.** Sometimes pays expenses of writers on assignment.

Photos: Send photos with submission. Negotiates payment individually. Buys one-time rights.

ENGINEERING & TECHNOLOGY

Engineers and professionals with various specialties read the publications in this section. Publications for electrical, electronics and telecommunications engineers are classified separately under Electronics & Communication. Magazines for computer professionals are in the Information Systems section.

N **$ $CABLING SYSTEMS**, Southam Inc., 1450 Don Mills Rd., Don Mills, Ontario M3B 2X7 Canada. (416)442-2124. Fax: (416)442-2214. E-mail: jstrom@corporate.southam.ca. Website: www.cablingsystems.com. **Contact:** Janine Strom, editor. **50% freelance written.** Magazine published 8 times/year covering structured cabling/telecommunications industry. *"Cabling Systems* is written for engineers, designers, contractors, and end users who design, specify, purchase, install, test and maintain structured cabling and telecommunications products and systems." Estab. 1998. Circ. 11,000. Pays on publication. Publishes ms an average of 1 month after acceptance. Byline given. Buys all rights. Editorial lead time 3 months. Submit seasonal material 1 month in advance. Accepts queries by mail, e-mail, phone. Accepts simultaneous submissions. Sample copy online at website. Writer's guidelines free.

Nonfiction: Technical (case studies, features). "No reprints or previously written articles. All articles are assigned by editor based on query or need of publication." **Buys 20 mss/year.** Query with published clips. Length: 1,500-2,500 words. **Pays 40-50¢/word.** Sometimes pays expenses of writers on assignment.

Photos: State availability of photos with submission. Reviews contact sheets and prints. Negotiates payment individually. Captions and identification of subjects required.

Columns/Departments: Focus on Engineering/Design, Focus on Installation, Focus on Maintenance/Testing, all 1,500 words. **Buys 7 mss/year.** Query with published clips. **Pays 40-50¢/word.**

Tips: "Visit our website to see back issues, and visit links on our website for background."

$ $ $CASS RECRUITMENT MEDIA, 9071 Mill Creek Rd., Suite 419, Levittown PA 19054. (215)269-8190. Fax: (847)733-3990. E-mail: paula.lipp@casscom.com. Website: www.casscom.com. **Contact:** Paula Lipp, editorial manager. **50% freelance written.** "Recruitment publications for college science students. Our readers are smart, savvy and hip. The writing must be, too." Circ. varies. **Pays on acceptance.** Publishes ms an average of 2 months after acceptance. Byline given. Offers $50 kill fee. Buys all rights. Editorial lead time 2 months. Submit seasonal material 6 months in advance. Accepts queries by mail, e-mail. Accepts simultaneous submissions. Responds in 2 weeks to queries; 3 months to mss. Sample copies and writer's guidelines free.

Nonfiction: Book excerpts, exposé, interview/profile, personal experience. Special issues: Minorities; Women. **Buys 40 mss/year.** Send complete ms. Length: 1,500-3,000 words. **Pays $200-800 for assigned articles; $50-300 for unsolicited articles.** Sometimes pays expenses of writers on assignment.

Photos: Send photos with submission. Reviews 3×5 prints. Offers no additional payment for photos accepted with ms. Identification of subjects required. Buys one-time rights.

Columns/Departments: Industry Focus (analysis of hiring market within particular industry), 1,500 words. **Buys 6 mss/year.** Query. **Pays $200-300.**

Tips: "Know the hiring market for entry-level professionals and be able to communicate to college students at their level."

N **$ $FLOW CONTROL, The Magazine of Fluid Handling Systems**, Witter Publishing Corp., 84 Park Ave., Flemington NJ 08822. (908)788-0343, ext. 141. Fax: (908)788-8416. E-mail: flowcontrol@witterpublishing.com. Website: www.flowcontrolnetwork.com. Managing Editor: Mary Beth Binder. **Contact:** Ron Piechota, editor. **90% freelance written.** Monthly magazine covering fluid handling systems. *"Flow Control* is the technology resource for the fluid handling industry's critical disciplines of control, containment and measurement. *Flow Control* provides solutions for system design, operational and maintenance challenges in all process and OEM applications." Estab. 1995. Circ. 40,000. Pays on publication. Publishes ms 1 month after acceptance. Byline given. Buys all rights. Accepts queries by mail, e-mail, fax, phone.

Nonfiction: How-to (design or maintenance), technical. No glorified product releases. **Buys 18 mss/year.** Query with published clips or send complete ms. Length: 1,00-2,500 words. **Pays $250-350.** Sometimes pays writers with contributor copies or other premiums.

Photos: State availability of or send photos with submission. Offers no additional payment for photos accepted with ms. Captions required and identification of subjects required.

Columns/Departments: Query with published clips or send complete ms. **Pays $250.**

Tips: "Anyone involved in flow control technology and/or applications may submit a manuscript for publication. Articles should be informative and analytical, containing sufficient technical data to support statements and material presented. Articles should not promote any individual product, service, or company. Case history features, describing the use of flow control technologies in specific applications, are welcomed."

$ $LIGHTING DESIGN & APPLICATION, Illuminating Engineering Society of North America, 120 Wall St., 17th Floor, New York NY 10005-4001. (212)248-5000. Fax: (212)248-5018. E-mail: ldanewman@aol.com. **Contact:** Mark A. Newman, editor. **40% freelance written.** Monthly magazine. "*LD&A* is geared to professionals in lighting design and the lighting field in architecture, retail, entertainment, etc. From designers to educators to sales reps, *LD&A* has a very unique, dedicated and well-educated audience." Estab. 1971. Circ. 10,000. **Pays on acceptance.** Publishes ms an average of 4 months after acceptance. Byline given. Buys first rights. Editorial lead time 4 months. Submit seasonal material 6 months in advance. Accepts simultaneous submissions. Accepts queries by mail, e-mail, fax, phone. Responds in 2 weeks. Sample copy free.

Nonfiction: Historical/nostalgic, how-to, opinion, personal experience, photo feature, technical. "Every year we have entertainment, outdoor, retail and arts and exhibits issues. No articles blatantly promoting a product, company or individual." Buys 6-10 mss/year. Query. Length: 1,500-2,200 words. **Pays $300-400 for assigned articles.** Pays writers with contributor copies or other premiums if writer is a member of IESNA or article promotes his/her own interest.

Photos: Send photos with submission. Reviews 4×5 transparencies. Offers no additional payment for photos accepted with ms. Captions required.

Columns/Departments: Essay by Invitation (industry trends), 1,200 words. Query. Does not pay.

Tips: "Most of our features detail the ins and outs of a specific lighting project. From Ricky Martin at the Grammys to the Getty Museum, *LD&A* gives its readers an in-depth look at how the designer(s) reached their goals."

$ $ $MINNESOTA TECHNOLOGY, Inside Technology and Manufacturing Business, Minnesota Technology, Inc., 111 Third Ave. S., Minneapolis MN 55401. (612)672-3412. Fax: (612)339-5214. E-mail: lball@mntech.org. Website: mntechnologymag.com. **Contact:** Linda Ball, editor. **75% freelance written.** "*Minnesota Technology* is read bimonthly by owners and top management of Minnesota's technology and manufacturing companies. The magazine covers technology trends and issues, global trade, management techniques and finance. We profile new and growing companies, new products and the innovators and entrepreneurs of Minnesota's technology sector." Estab. 1991. Circ. 20,000. **Pays on acceptance.** Publishes ms an average of 5 months after acceptance. Byline given. Offers 25% kill fee. Buys first North American serial rights. Editorial lead time 6 months. Submit seasonal material 1 year in advance. Accepts queries by mail, e-mail, fax. Responds in 1 month. Sample copy for 9×12 SAE and 5 first-class stamps. Writer's guidelines for #10 SASE.

Nonfiction: General interest, how-to, interview/profile. **Buys 60 mss/year.** Query with published clips. Length: 500-2,000 words. **Pays $175-800.** Pays expenses of writers on assignment.

Reprints: Accepts previously published submissions.

Columns/Departments: Viewpoint (Q&A format, provocative ideas from business and industry leaders), 700 words; Tech Watch (cutting edge, gee whiz technology), 250-500 words. **Buys 10 mss/year.** Query with published clips. **Pays $150-300.**

The online magazine carries original content not found in the print edition and includes writers guidelines. Contact: Linda Ball.

Tips: "Query with ideas for short profiles of fascinating Minnesota technology people and business written to interest even the most nontechnical person."

$ $MINORITY ENGINEER, An Equal Opportunity Career Publication for Professional and Graduating Minority Engineers, Equal Opportunity Publications, Inc., 1160 E. Jericho Turnpike, Suite 200, Huntington NY 11743. (516)421-9421. Fax: (516)421-0359. E-mail: info@aol.com. Website: www.eop.com. **Contact:** James Schneider, editor. **60% freelance written.** Prefers to work with published/established writers. Triannual magazine covering career guidance for minority engineering students and minority professional engineers. Estab. 1969. Circ. 15,000. Pays on publication. Publishes ms an average of 6 months after acceptance. Byline given. Buys first rights. Accepts queries by mail, e-mail, fax, phone. Accepts simultaneous submissions. Sample copy and writer's guidelines for 9×12 SAE with 5 first-class stamps.

Nonfiction: Book excerpts; articles (on job search techniques, role models); general interest (on specific minority engineering concerns); how-to (land a job, keep a job, etc.); interview/profile (minority engineer role models); new product (new career opportunities); opinion (problems of ethnic minorities); personal experience (student and career experiences); technical (on career fields offering opportunities for minority engineers). "We're interested in articles dealing with career guidance and job opportunities for minority engineers." No career-guidance strategies or role-model profiles. Query. Length: 1,000-2,000 words. Sometimes pays expenses of writers on assignment. **Pays 10¢/word.**

Reprints: Send typed ms with rights for sale noted and information about when and where the article previously appeared. Pays 100% of amount paid for an original article.

Photos: State availability of photos with submission. Reviews transparencies and prints. Captions required. Buys all rights. **Pays $15.**

Tips: "Articles should focus on career guidance, role model and industry prospects for minority engineers. Prefer articles related to careers, not politically or socially sensitive."

■ **$ $ PROGRESSIVE ENGINEER**, Buck Mountain Publishing Co., P.O. Box 20305, Roanoke VA 24018. (540)772-2225. Fax: (540)776-0871. E-mail: progress@rev.net. Website: www.progressiveengineer.com. **Contact:** Tom Gibson, editor. **75% freelance written.** Bimonthly online magazine. "*Progressive Engineer* is written for all disciplines of engineers in the Mid-Atlantic region (VA, NC, MD, WV, DE). We take a less technical slant than most engineering magazines and cover the engineers behind the technology as well as the technology itself. Promotes the profession of engineering by writing about engineers, projects and related activities." Estab. 1997. Pays on publication. Publishes ms an average of 4 months after acceptance. Byline given. Offers $25 kill fee. Buys first North American serial rights and second serial (reprint) rights. Editorial lead time 6 months. Accepts queries by mail, e-mail. Accepts simultaneous submissions. Responds in 3 weeks to queries; 1 month to mss. Writer's guidelines on request.

Nonfiction: Book excerpts, expose, general interest, historical/nostalgic, how-to, interview/profile, new product, technical, travel. **Buys 50 mss/year.** Query with published clips. Length: 750-2,000 words. **Pays $150-350.** Sometimes pays expenses of writers on assignment. The editor reports a need for more profiles of engineers.

Reprints: Accepts previously published submissions. Send photocopy or typed ms with rights for sale noted and information about when and where the article previously appeared. **Pays 50% of amount paid for original article.**

Photos: State availability of photos with submission. Reviews contact sheets, transparencies, prints. **Offers $25.** Captions, identification of subjects required. Buys one-time rights.

Columns/Departments: Profiles (individual engineers), 1,000 words; Business/Career Topics (affecting engineers), 1,000 words; Travel, Places to Visit (see technology in action), 1,000 words. Query with published clips. **Pays $150.**

Tips: "If you know of an engineer doing something interesting or unique in your area, we'd like to hear about it."

$ $ WOMAN ENGINEER, An Equal Opportunity Career Publication for Graduating Women and Experienced Professionals, Equal Opportunity Publications, Inc., 1160 E. Jericho Turnpike, Suite 200, Huntington NY 11743. (516)421-9478. Fax: (516)421-0359. E-mail: eopclaudia@aol.com. Website: www.eop.com. **Contact:** Claudia Wheeler, editor. **60% freelance written.** Works with a small number of new/unpublished writers each year. Triannual magazine covering career guidance for women engineering students and professional women engineers. Estab. 1968. Circ. 16,000. Pays on publication. Publishes ms up to 1 year after acceptance. Byline given. Buys First North American serial rights. Accepts queries by e-mail. Responds in 3 months. Free sample copy and writer's guidelines.

Nonfiction: "Interested in articles dealing with career guidance and job opportunities for women engineers. Looking for manuscripts showing how to land an engineering position and advance professionally. We want features on job-search techniques, engineering disciplines offering career opportunities to women; companies with career advancement opportunities for women; problems facing women engineers and how to cope with such problems; and role-model profiles of successful women engineers, especially in major U.S. corporations." Query. Length: 1,000-2,500 words. **Pays 10¢/word.**

Photos: Prefers color slides but will accept b&w. Captions and identification of subjects required. Buys all rights. **Pays $15.**

Tips: "We are looking for 800-1,000 word first-person 'As I See It, personal perspectives.' "

ENTERTAINMENT & THE ARTS

The business of the entertainment/amusement industry in arts, film, dance, theater, etc. is covered by these publications. Journals that focus on the people and equipment of various music specialties are listed in the Music section, while art and design business publications can be found in Art, Design & Collectibles. Entertainment publications for the general public can be found in the Consumer Entertainment section.

N $ AMUSEMENT BUSINESS, Billboard Publications, Inc., P.O. Box 24970, Nashville TN 37202. (615)321-4250. Fax: (615)327-1575. **Contact:** Linda Deckard, managing editor. **15% freelance written.** Works with a small number of new/unpublished writers each year. Weekly tabloid emphasizing hard news of the amusement park, sports arena, concert and fair industries for top management. Circ. 15,000. Pays on publication. Publishes ms an average of 3 weeks after acceptance. Byline sometimes given; "it depends on the quality of the individual piece." Buys all rights. Submit seasonal/holiday material 3 weeks in advance. Sample copy for 11×14 SAE with 5 first-class stamps.

● *Amusement Business* is placing an increased emphasis on international developments and looking for shorter news stories.

Nonfiction: How-to (case history of successful advertising campaigns and promotions); interviews (with leaders in the areas we cover highlighting appropriate problems and issues of today, i.e., insurance, alcohol control, etc.). Likes lots of financial support data: grosses, profits, operating budgets and per-cap spending. Also needs lots of quotes. No personality pieces or interviews with stage stars. **Buys 50-100 mss/year.** Query. Phone queries OK. Length: 400-700 words.

Photos: State availability of photos with query. Captions and model release required. Buys all rights.

Columns/Departments: Auditorium Arenas; Fairs; Parks & Attractions; Food Concessions; Merchandise; Marketing; Carnivals; Talent & Touring; Management Changes; Sports; Profile; Eye On Legislation; Commentary and International News.

Tips: "There will be more and more emphasis on financial reporting of areas covered. Submission must contain the whys and whos, etc., and be strong enough that others in the same field will learn from it and not find it naive. We will be increasing story count while decreasing story length."

N: $ $ BACK STAGE, The Performing Arts Weekly, BPI Communications, 1515 Broadway, 14th Floor, New York NY 10036. Fax: (212)536-5318. E-mail: seaker@backstage.com. Website: www.backstage.com. Managing Editor: David Sheward. **Contact:** Sherry Eaker, editor-in-chief. **X% freelance written.** Weekly newspaper covering performing arts with its main focus on stage. "*Backstage* focuses for opportunities on performing and creative markets and how to take advantage of those opportunities, including the skills and talents required." Estab. 1960. Circ. 33,000. Pays on publication. Byline given. Offers 50% kill fee. Buys all rights or makes work-for-hire assignments. Accepts queries by mail, e-mail, fax. Sample copy on website.

Nonfiction: How-to, interview/profile. Does not want to see general entartainment. Query. **Pays $500.**

Photos: State availability of photos with submission. Offers no additional payment for photos accepted with ms.

Columns/Departments: Query.

$ $ BOXOFFICE MAGAZINE, RLD Publishing Co., 155 S. El Molino Ave., Suite 100, Pasadena CA 91101. (626)396-0250. Fax: (626)396-0248. E-mail: boxoffice@earthlink.net. Website: www.boxoffice.com. **Contact:** Kim Williamson, editor-in-chief. **15% freelance written.** Monthly business magazine about the motion picture industry for members of the film industry: theater owners, film producers, directors, financiers and allied industries. Estab. 1920. Circ. 8,000. Pays on publication. Publishes ms an average of 4 months after acceptance. Byline given. Buys all rights, including electronic publishing. Submit seasonal material 4 months in advance. Accepts queries by mail, fax. Sample copy for $5.50.

Nonfiction: Investigative, interview, profile, new product, photo feature, technical. "We are a general news magazine about the motion picture industry and are looking for stories about trends, developments, problems or opportunities facing the industry. Almost any story will be considered, including corporate profiles, but we don't want gossip or celebrity coverage." Query with published clips. Length: 800-2,500 words. **Pays 10¢/word or set price.**

Photos: State availability of photos. Pays $10 maximum for 8×10 b&w prints. Captions required.

Tips: "Request a sample copy, indicating you read about *Boxoffice* in *Writer's Market*. Write a clear, comprehensive outline of the proposed story and enclose a résumé and clip samples."

$ CALLBOARD, Monthly Theatre Trade Magazine, Theatre Bay Area, 870 Market St., #375, San Francisco CA 94102-3002. (415)430-1140. Fax: (415)430-1145. E-mail: tba@theatrebayarea.org. Website: www.theatrebayarea.org. **Contact:** Belinda Taylor, editor. **50% freelance written.** Monthly magazine for local theater in the SF Bay area. "We publish news, views, essays and features on the Northern California theater industry. We also include listings, audition notices and job resources." Estab. 1976. Circ. 5,000. Pays on publication. Publishes ms an average of 4 months after acceptance. Byline given. Offers 50% kill fee. Buys first rights. Editorial lead time 6 weeks. Submit seasonal material 2 months in advance. Accepts simultaneous submissions. Accepts queries by mail, e-mail, phone. Responds in 1 month to queries. Sample copy for $6.

Nonfiction: Book excerpts, essays, opinion, personal experience, technical (theater topics only), features. No reviews. *No profiles of actors.* **Buys 12-15 mss/year.** Query with published clips. Length: 800-2,000 words. **Pays $100-200 for assigned articles.** Pays other for unsolicited articles. **Pays $35-75** for department articles. Sometimes pays expenses of writers on assignment (phone calls and some travel).

Reprints: Send tearsheet of article or typed ms with rights for sale noted and information about when and where the article previously appeared. **Pays 25% of amount paid for an original article.**

Photos: State availability of photos with submission. Reviews contact sheets or 5×7 prints. Offers no additional payment for photos accepted with ms. Identification of subjects required. Buys one-time rights.

N: $ CAMPUS ACTIVITIES, Cameo Publishing Group, P.O. Box 509, Prosperity SC 29127. (800)728-2950. Fax: (803)321-2049. E-mail: cameopub@aol.com. Website: www.cameopub.com or campusactivities.org. Editor: Laura Moore. Managing Editor: Robin Hellman. **Contact:** WC Kirby, publisher. **75% freelance written.** Trade magazine published 8 times/year covering entertainment on college campuses. *Campus Activities* goes to entertainment buyers on every campus in the US. Features stories on artists (national and regrional), speakers and the programs at individual schools. Estab. 1991. Circ. 5,200. Pays on publication. Publishes ms an average of 2 months after acceptance. Byline given. Offers 15% kill fee if accepted and not run. Buys first, second serial (reprint) and electronic rights. Editorial lead time 2 months. Submit seasonal material 2 months in advance. Accepts queries by mail, e-mail, fax. Accepts simultaneous submissions. Responds in 1 month to queries; 2 months to mss. Sample copy for $3.30. Writer's guidelines free.

Nonfiction: Interview/profile, photo feature. Accepts no unsolicited articles. **Buys 40 mss/year.** Query. Length: 1,400-3,000 words. **Pays $250.** Sometimes pays expenses of writers on assignment.

Photos: State availability of photos with submission. Reviews contact sheets, negatives, 3×5 transparencies and 8×10 prints. Negotiates payment individually. Identification of subjects required. Buys one-time rights.

Tips: "Writers who have ideas, proposals and special project requests should contact the publisher prior to any commitment to work on such a story. The publisher welcomes innovative and creative ideas for stories and works with writers on such proposals which have significant impact on our readers."

N $ THE COMIC BIBLE, PMS Productions, 222 W. 233rd St., Suite 4G, Bronx NY 10463. (718)548-7907. Fax: (718)548-2325. E-mail: comicbible@aol.com. Website: www.comicbible.com. **Contact:** Mary Ann Pierro, editor. **30% freelance written.** Bimonthly magazine covering comedy. Estab. 1997. Circ. 10,000. Pays on publication. Publishes ms an average of 4 months after acceptance. Byline given. Buys all rights. Editorial lead time 4 months. Accepts queries by mail, e-mail, fax. Sample copy for $4. Writer's guidelines free.
Nonfiction: Book excerpts, exposé, how-to, humor, inspirational, interview/profile, opinion, personal experience. Query. Length: 250-2,500 words. **Pays $100 maximum for assigned articles.** Sometimes pays expenses of writers on assignment.
Reprints: Accepts previously published submissions.
Photos: Send photos with submission. Reviews prints. Offers no additional payment for photos accepted with ms. Model releases required. Buys one-time rights.
Columns/Departments: California Scene/Roz Browne (California comedy scene), 1,000 words; Tips (how-to for comedians and writers), 1,500 words; Law & Laughter (legal tips/advice for entertainment industry), 1,500 words; Interesting Info (events and pertinent information regarding comedy), 1,500 words. **Buys 6 mss/year.** Query. **Pays up to $100.**
Fillers: Anna Beans, public relations director. Anecdotes, facts, gags to be illustrated by cartoonist, newsbreaks, short humor. Length: 2-1,000 words. Unpaid.
Tips: "Must be knowledgdable of comedy industry/scene."

$ $ $ EMMY MAGAZINE, Academy of Television Arts & Sciences, 5220 Lankershim Blvd., North Hollywood CA 91601-3109. (818)754-2800. Fax: (818)761-8524. E-mail: emmymag@emmys.org. Website: www.emmys.org. **Contact:** Gail Polevoi, editor. **90% freelance written.** Prefers to work with published established writers. Bimonthly magazine on television for TV professionals. Circ. 12,000. Pays on publication or within 6 months. Publishes ms an average of 4 months after acceptance. Byline given. Offers 25% kill fee. Buys first North American serial rights. Responds in 1 month. Sample copy for 9×12 SAE with 6 first-class stamps or on website. Writer's guidelines on website.
Nonfiction: Articles on contemporary issues, trends, and VIPs (especially those behind the scenes) in broadcast and cable TV; programming and new technology. "Looking for profiles of fascinating people who work 'below the line' in television. Also, always looking for new writers who understand technology and new media and can write about it in an engaging manner. We require TV industry expertise and clear, lively writing." Query by mail only with published clips. Length: 1,700 words. **Pay $900-1,000.** Pays some expenses of writers on assignment.
● Ranked as one of the best markets for freelance writers in *Writer's Yearbook* magazine's annual "Top 100 Markets," January 1999.
Columns/Departments: Most written by regular contributors, but newcomers can break into Labors of Love. Query by mail only with published clips. Length: 500-1,500 words, depending on department. **Pays $250-750.**
Tips: "Please review recent issues before querying us. Query in writing with published, television-related clips. No fanzine, academic or nostalgic approaches, please. Demonstrate experience in covering the business of television and your ability to write in a lively and compelling manner about programming trends and new technology. Identify fascinating people behind the scenes, not just in the executive suites but in all ranks of the industry."

$ $ RELEASE PRINT, The Magazine of Film Arts Foundation, Film Arts Foundation, 346 9th St., 2nd Floor, San Francisco CA 94103. (415)552-8760. Fax: (415)552-0882. E-mail: releaseprint@filmarts.com. Website: www.filmarts.org. **Contact:** Thomas J Powers, editor. **80% freelance written.** Monthly trade magazine covering US independent filmmaking. "We have a knowledgeable readership of film and videomakers. They are interested in the financing, production, exhibition and distribution of independent films and videos. They are interested in practical and technical issues and, to a lesser extent, aesthetic ones." Estab. 1977. Circ. 5,000. Pays on publication. Publishes ms an average of 3 months after acceptance. Byline given. All rights for commissioned works. For works submitted on spec, buys first rights and requests acknowledgement of release print in any subsequent publication. Editorial lead time 3 months. Responds in 3 weeks to queries; 2 months to mss. Writer's guidelines for 9×12 SASE with $1.47 postage.
O→ Break in with a proposal for an article or interview of an American experimental, documentary or very low budget feature film/video maker with ties to the San Francisco Bay area (or an upcoming screening in this area). Submit at least 3 months prior to publication date.
Nonfiction: Interview/profile, personal experience, technical, book reviews. No film criticism or reviews. **Buys 30-35 mss/year.** Query. Length: 300-2,000 words. **Pays 10¢/word.** Sometimes pays expenses of writers on assignment.
Photos: Send photos with submission. Reviews prints. Offers no additional payment for photos accepted with ms. Identification of subjects required. Buys one time rights.
Columns/Departments: Book Reviews (independent film & video), 800-1,000 words. **Buys 4 mss/year.** Query. **Pays 10¢/word.**

N $ SCREEN MAGAZINE, Screen Enterprises Inc., 16 W. Erie St., Chicago IL 60610. (312)664-5236. Fax: (312)664-8425. E-mail: screen@screenmag.com. **Contact:** Ruth L. Ratny. **10% freelance written.** Weekly magazine covering the audiovisual industry, exclusively Chicago area. "*Screen* is written for Chicago-area producers (and all involved) of commercials, AV, features, independent corporate and multimedia." Estab. 1979. Circ. 15,000. Pays on publication. Publishes ms an average of a few weeks after acceptance. Byline given. Offers 50% kill fee. Makes work-for-hire assignments. Accepts queries by mail, e-mail, fax. Responds in 3 weeks to queries. Sample copy online at website. Writer's guidelines for SAE and 1 first-class stamp.

Nonfiction: Interview/profile, new product, technical. "No general AV; specific to other markets; no-brainers and opinion." **Buys 50 mss/year.** Query with published clips. Length: 535-750 words. **Pays $100-150.** Sometimes pays expenses of writers on assignment.

Photos: Send photos with submission. Reviews prints. Offers no additional payment for photos accepted with ms. Captions required.

Tips: "Our readers want to know facts and figures. They want to know the news about a company or an individual. We provide exclusive news of this market, in as much depth as space allows without being boring, with lots of specific information and details. We are authoritative, and write knowledgably about the market we serve. We recognize the film/video-making process is a difficult one because it 1) is often technical, 2) has implications not immediately discerned and 3) calls for careful writing to maintain our authority."

FARM

The successful farm writer focuses on the business side of farming. For technical articles, editors feel writers should have a farm background or agricultural training, but there are opportunities for the general freelancer too. The following farm publications are divided into seven categories, each specializing in a different aspect of farming: equipment; crops & soil management; dairy farming; livestock; management; miscellaneous; and regional.

Agricultural Equipment

$ $IMPLEMENT & TRACTOR, Freiberg Publishing, 2302 W. First St., Cedar Falls IA 50613. (319)277-3599. Fax: (319)277-3783. E-mail: mshepherd@cfu.net. Website: www.ag-implements.com. **Contact:** Mary Shepherd, editor. **15% freelance written.** Bimonthly magazine covering farming equipment, light construction, commercial turf and lawn and garden equipment. "*Implement & Tractor* offers technical and business news for equipment dealers, manufacturers, consultants and others involved as suppliers to the industry. Writers must know US and global machinery and the industry trends." Estab. 1895. Circ. 10,000. **Pays on acceptance.** Publishes ms an average of 6 months after acceptance. Byline given. Buys all rights. Editorial lead time 4 months. Submit seasonal material 4 months in advance. Accepts queries by mail, e-mail, fax. No simultaneous submissions. Responds in 2 months to queries. Sample copy for $6.

Nonfiction: Interview/profile, new product, photo feature, technical. No lightweight technical articles, general farm machinery articles, "Isn't farm life great!" articles. Query with published clips. Length: 200-600 words. **Pays $100-250.** Sometimes pays expenses of writers on assignment.

Photos: State availability of photos with submission. Reviews contact sheets. Offers no additional payment for photos accepted with ms. Captions and identification of subjects required. Buys one-time rights.

Tips: "Know the equipment industry, have an engineer's outlook for analyzing machinery and a writer's skills to communicate that information. Technical background is helpful, as is mechanical aptitude."

Crops & Soil Management

N $ $AMERICAN FRUIT GROWER, Meister Publishing, 37733 Euclid Ave., Willoughby OH 44094. (440)942-2000. Fax: (440)942-0662. E-mail: afg_edit@meisternet.com. **Contact:** Laurie Sanders, managing editor. **30% freelance written.** Annual magazine covering commercial fruit growing. "How-to" articles are best. Estab. 1880. Circ. 50,000. Pays on publication. Publishes ms an average of 4 months after acceptance. Byline given. Buys first rights. Editorial lead time 2 months. Submit seasonal material 4 months in advance. Accepts queries by mail, e-mail, fax, phone. Responds in 2 weeks to queries; 2 months to mss. Sample copy free. Writer's guidelines free.

Nonfiction: How-to better grow fruit crops. **Buys 6-10 mss/year.** Query with published clips or send complete ms. Length: 800-1,200 words. **Pays $200-250.** Sometimes pays expenses of writers on assignment.

Photos: Send photos with submission. Reviews prints and slides. Negotiates payment individually. Buys one-time rights.

N $ $COTTON GROWER MAGAZINE, Meister Publishing Co., 65 Germantown Court, #220, Cordova TN 38018. (901)756-8822. Fax: (901)756-8879. Editor: Bill Sepencer. **Contact:** Al Fava, senior editor. **15% freelance written.** Monthly magazine covering cotton production, cotton markets and related subjects. Readers are mostly cotton producers who seek information on production practices, equipment and products related to cotton. Estab. 1901. Circ.

50,000. **Pays on acceptance**. Publishes ms an average of 2 months after acceptance. Byline given. Buys first rights. Editorial lead time 2 months. Submit seasonal material 2 months in advance. Accepts queries by mail, e-mail, fax, phone. Accepts simultaneous submissions. Sample copy free. Writer's guidelines not available.

Nonfiction: Interview/profile, new product, photo feature, technical. No fiction or humorous pieces. **Buys 5-10 mss/year.** Query with published clips. Length: 500-800 words. **Pays $200-400.** Pays expenses of writers on assignment.

Photos: State availability of photos with submission. Reviews transparencies. Offers no additional payment for photos accepted with ms. Captions and identification of subjects required. Buys all rights.

N $ $ THE FRUIT GROWERS NEWS, Great American Publishing, P.O. Box 128, Sparta MI 49345. (616)887-9008. Fax: (616)887-2666. E-mail: dean@iserv.net. Editor: Matt McCollum. **Contact:** Lee Dean, managing editor. **25% freelance written.** Monthly tabloid covering agriculture. "Our objective is to provide commercial fruit and vegetable growers of all sizes information to help them succeed." Estab. 1970. Circ. 28,000. Pays on publication. Publishes ms an average of 2 months after acceptance. Makes work-for-hire assignment. Editorial lead time 1 month. Submit seasonal material 1 month in advance. Accepts queries by mail, e-mail, fax, phone. Accepts simultaneous submissions. Responds in 2 weeks to queries; 1 month to mss. Sample copy free.

Nonfiction: Essays, general interest, how-to, interview/profile, new product, opinion, technical. No advertorials, other "puff pieces." **Buys 72 mss/year.** Query with published clips. Length: 800-1,100 words. **Pays $100-200.** Sometimes pays expenses of writers on assignment.

Photos: Send photos with submission. Reviews prints. Offers $10-20/photo. Captions required. Buys one-time rights.

$ GRAINEWS, Farm Business Communications (division of United Grain Growers), P.O. Box 6600, Winnipeg, Manitoba REC 3A7 Canada. (204)944-5587. Fax: (204)944-5416. E-mail: asirski@fbc.unitedgrain.ca or dbedard@fbc.unitedgrain.ca. **Contact:** Andy Sirski, editor-in-chief or David Bedard, managing editor. **80% freelance written.** Newspaper published 18 times/year covering agriculture/agribusiness. **Pays on acceptance.** Publishes ms an average of 1 month after acceptance. Byline given. Buys first rights. Editorial lead time 1 month. Submit seasonal material 1 month in advance. Accepts queries by mail, e-mail, fax, phone. Responds in 2 weeks to queries. Sample copy free.

Nonfiction: Indepth how-to articles on various aspects of farming, general interest, historical/nostalgic, humor, new product, opinion, personal experience, technical. "Every article should be written from the farmer's perspective." Query. **Pays $150 for assigned articles; $25 for unsolicited articles.** Sometimes pays expenses of writers on assignment.

Reprints: Accepts previously published submissions.

Photos: State availability of photos with submission. Offers no additional payment for photos accepted with ms. Captions and identification of subjects required. Buys one-time rights.

Poetry: Andy Sirski, editor. Traditional. **Pays $25.**

Tips: "We want writers who are farmers. We love 'how-to' articles on farm-related repairs, etc. Ask yourself how your story will help or entertain other farmers, and if it doesn't, don't send it."

N $ $ GRAPE GROWER MAGAZINE, Western Ag Publishing Co., 4969 E. Clinton Way #119, Fresno CA 93727. (559)252-7000. Fax: (559)252-7387. E-mail: westag@psnw.com. Website: **Contact:** Paul Baltimore, editor. Managing Editor: Melinda Warner. **20% freelance written.** Monthly magazine covering viticulture and winerys. Estab. 1968. Circ. 12,000. Pays on publication. Publishes ms an average of 4 months after acceptance. Byline sometimes given. Buys all rights, makes work-for-hire assignments. Editorial lead time 2 months. Submit seasonal material 3 months in advance. Accepts queries by mail, e-mail, fax, phone. Accepts simultaneous submissions. Responds in 2 weeks to queries; 1 month to mss. Sample copy free by e-mail.

Nonfiction: How-to, interview/profile, new product, personal experience. Query or send complete ms. Length: 450-1,600 words. **Pays $300-400.** Sometimes pays expenses of writers on assignment.

Photos: Send photos with submission. Reviews transparencies and prints. Buys all rights.

$ ONION WORLD, Columbia Publishing, P.O. Box 9036, Yakima WA 98909-0036. (509)248-2452. Fax: (509)248-4056. **Contact:** D. Brent Clement, editor. **50% freelance written.** Monthly magazine covering the world of onion production and marketing for onion growers and shippers. Estab. 1985. Circ. 5,500. Pays on publication. Publishes ms an average of 1 month after acceptance. Byline given. Not copyrighted. Buys first North American serial rights. Submit seasonal material 1 month in advance. Accepts simultaneous submissions. Responds in 1 month. Sample copy for 9 × 12 SAE with 5 first-class stamps.

● Columbia Publishing also produces *Fresh Cut*, *The Tomato Magazine*, *Potato Country* and *Carrot Country*.

Nonfiction: General interest, historical/nostalgic, interview/profile. **Buys 60 mss/year.** Query. Length: 1,200-1,500 words. **Pays 5¢/word for assigned articles.**

Reprints: Send photocopy of article and information about when and where the article previously appeared. Pays 50% of amount paid for an original article.

Photos: Send photos with submission. Offers no additional payment for photos accepted with ms unless it's a cover shot. Captions, identification of subjects required. Buys all rights.

Tips: "Writers should be familiar with growing and marketing onions. We use a lot of feature stories on growers, shippers and others in the onion trade—what they are doing, their problems, solutions, marketing plans, etc."

N $ $ RICE JOURNAL, SpecCom International, Inc., 3000 Highwoods Blvd., Raleigh NC 27604-1029. (919) 872-5040. Fax: (919)876-6531. E-mail: editor@ricejournal.com. Website: www.ricejournal.com. Editor: Mary Evans.

Contact: Mary Ann Rood, managing editor. **5% freelance written.** Monthly (January-June) magazine covering rice farming. "Articles must discuss rice production practices. Readers are rice farmers. Include on-farm interview with one or more farmers who use the featured agronomic practice. Must include photo of the farmer involved in a farming activity." Estab. 1897. Circ. 10,000. Pays on publication. Byline given. Buys first rights. Editorial lead time 2 months. Accepts queries by mail, e-mail, fax. Responds in 2 weeks to queries; 2 months to mss. Sample copy online at website. Writer's guidelines for #10 SASE.

Nonfiction: Book excerpts, how-to, personal experience, photo feature, technical, farmer production tips. January: land preparation; February water management; March: weed control; April: rice diseases and management; May: insect control, tracked vehicles; June: harvest, curing. No recipes, cooking. **Buys 2 mss/year.** Query. Length: 600-2,000 words. **Pays $50-400.**

Reprints: Accepts previously published submissions.

Photos: State availability of photos with submission. Offers no additional payment for photos accepted with ms. Captions and identification of subjects required. Buys one-time rights.

N **$ $ SEED TRADE NEWS,** Ball Publishing, 335 N. River St., Batavia IL 60510. (630)208-9080. Fax: (630)208-9350. E-mail: sbruhn@seedtradenews.com. Website: www.seedtradenews.com. **Contact:** Sherri Bruhn, editor. **15% freelance written.** Monthly magazine covering seed breeding. Estab. 1923. Circ. 6,809. Pays on publication. Publishes ms an average of 4 months after acceptance. Byline given. Offers 25% kill fee. Buys first North American serial rights. Editorial lead time 4 months. Submit seasonal material 4 months in advance. Accepts queries by mail, e-mail. Accepts simultaneous submissions.

Nonfiction: Interview/profile, technical. **Buys 10 mss/year.** Query with published clips. Length: 300-1,800 words. **Pays $125-800.** Sometimes pays expenses of writers on assignment.

Photos: Send photos with submission. Reviews slides. Negotiates payment individually. Captions and identification of subjects required. Buys one-time rights.

Columns/Departments: Industry Watch (industry, company, association news); Seed Strategies (business tips, market trends); Genetic Edge (agricultural biotechnology news, patents); Ground Work (agronomics, turf, vegetable, ornamentals), all 350 words. **Buys 10 mss/year.** Send complete ms. **Pays $100-400.**

N **$ $ THE VEGETABLE GROWERS NEWS,** Great American Publishing, P.O. Box 128, Sparta MI 49345. (616)887-9008. Fax: (616)887-2666. E-mail: dean@iserv.net. Editor: Matt McCollum. **Contact:** Lee Dean, managing editor. **25% freelance written.** Monthly tabloid covering agriculture. "Our objective is to provide commercial fruit and vegetable growers of all sizes information to help them succeed." Estab. 1970. Circ. 28,000. Pays on publication. Publishes ms an average of 2 months after acceptance. Makes work-for-hire assignment. Editorial lead time 1 month. Submit seasonal material 1 month in advance. Accepts queries by mail, e-mail, fax, phone. Accepts simultaneous submissions. Responds in 2 weeks to queries; 1 month to mss. Sample copy free.

Nonfiction: Essays, general interest, how-to, interview/profile, new product, opinion, technical. No advertorials, other "puff pieces." **Buys 72 mss/year.** Query with published clips. Length: 800-1,100 words. **Pays $100-200.** Sometimes pays expenses of writers on assignment.

Photos: Send photos with submission. Reviews prints. Offers $10-20/photo. Captions required. Buys one-time rights.

Dairy Farming

$ DAIRY GOAT JOURNAL, P.O. Box 10, 128 E. Lake St., Lake Mills WI 53551. (920)648-8285. Fax: (920)648-3770. **Contact:** Dave Thompson, editor. **45% freelance written.** Monthly. "We are looking for clear and accurate articles about dairy goat owners, their herds, cheesemaking, and other ways of marketing products. Some readers own two goats; others own 1,500 and are large commercial operations." Estab. 1917. Circ. 8,000, including copies to more than 70 foreign countries. Pays on publication. Please query first.

Nonfiction: Information on personalities and on public issues affecting dairy goats and their owners. How-to articles with plenty of practical information. Health and husbandry articles should be written with appropriate experience or academic credentials. **Buys 100 mss/year.** Query with published clips. Makes assignments. Length: 750-2,500 words. **Pays $50-150.** Pays expenses of writers on assignment.

Photos: Color or b&w. Vertical or horizontal for cover. Goats and/or people. Pays $100 maximum for 35mm slides for covers; $20 to $70 for inside use or for b&w. Accurate identification of all subjects required.

Tips: "We love good articles about dairy goats and will work with beginners, if you are cooperative."

$ $ HOARD'S DAIRYMAN, W.D. Hoard and Sons, Co., 28 Milwaukee Ave. W, Fort Atkinson WI 53538-0801. (920)563-5551. Fax: (920)563-7298. E-mail: hoards@hoards.com. Website: www.hoards.com. Editor: W.D. Knox. **Contact:** Steven A. Larson, managing editor. Tabloid published 20 times/year covering dairy industry. "We publish semi-technical information published for dairy-farm families and their advisors." Estab. 1885. Circ. 100,000. **Pays on acceptance.** Publishes ms an average of 2-4 months after acceptance. Byline given. Buys first rights. Editorial lead time 2 months. Submit seasonal material 3 months in advance. Accepts queries by mail, e-mail, fax. Responds in 2 weeks to queries; 1 month to mss. Sample copy for 12×15 SAE and $3. Writer's guidelines for #10 SASE.

Nonfiction: How-to, technical. **Buys 60 mss/year.** Query. Length: 800-1,500 words. **Pays $150-350.**

Photos: Send photos with submission. Reviews 2×2 transparencies. Offers no additional payment for photos accepted with ms.

Livestock

N **$** **$**ANGUS BEEF BULLETIN, Angus Productions, Inc., 3201 Frederick Ave., St. Joseph MO 64506. (816)383-5200. Fax: (816)233-6575. E-mail: shermel@angus.org. Website: www.angusebeefbulletin.com. **Contact:** Shauna Hermel, editor. **15% freelance written.** Trade tabloid published 4 times/year covering commercial cattle industry. "The *Bulletin* is mailed free to commercial cattlemen who have purchased an Angus bull, and had the registration transferred to them within the last 3 years." Estab. 1985. Circ. 63,000. Pays on publication. Publishes ms an average of 3 months after acceptance. Byline given. Buys first and electronic rights. Editorial lead time 3 months. Submit seasonal material 3 months in advance. Accepts queries by mail, e-mail. Accepts simultaneous submissions. Responds in 3 weeks to queries; 3 months to mss. Sample copy for $5. Writer's guidelines for #10 SASE.
Nonfiction: How-to (cattle production), interview/profile, technical (cattle production). **Buys 10 mss/year.** Query with published clips. Length: 800-2,500 words. **Pays $50-600.** Pays expenses of writers on assignment.
Photos: Send photos with submission. Reviews 5×7 transparencies and 5×7 glossy prints. Offers $25/photo. Identification of subjects required. Buys all rights.
Tips: "Read the publication *Angus Journal* and have a firm grasp of the commercial cattle industry and how the Angus breeds fit in that industry."

N **$** **$** **$**ANGUS JOURNAL, Angus Productions Inc., 3201 Frederick Ave., St. Joseph MO 64506-2997. (816)383-5200. Fax: (816)233-6575. E-mail: shermel@angusjournal.com. Website: www.angusjournal.com. **Contact:** Shauna Hermal, editor. **20% freelance written.** Trade magazine published monthly (except June) covering Angus cattle. "The *Angus Journal* is the official magazine of the American Angus Association. Its primary function as such is to report to the membership association activities and information pertinent to raising Angus cattle." Estab. 1919. Circ. 22,500. Pays on publication. Publishes ms an average of 3 months after acceptance. Byline given. Buys first and electronic rights. Editorial lead time 2 months. Submit seasonal material 3 months in advance. Accepts queries by mail, e-mail. Accepts simultaneous submissions. Responds in 3 weeks to queries; 2 months to mss. Sample copy for $5. Writer's guidelines for #10 SASE.
Nonfiction: How-to (cattle production), interview/profile, technical (related to cattle). **Buys 20-30 mss/year.** Query with published clips. Length: 800-3,500 words. **Pays $50-1,000.** Pays expenses of writers on assignment.
Photos: Send photos with submission. Reviews 5×7 glossy prints. Offers $25-400/photo. Identification of subjects required. Buys all rights.
Tips: "Read the magazine and have a firm grasp of the cattle industry."

N **$** **$**THE BRAHMAN JOURNAL, Sagebrush Publishing Co., Inc., P.O. Box 220, Eddy TX 76524-0220. Phone/fax: (817)859-5451. Editor: Joe Ed Brockett. **10% freelance written.** Monthly magazine covering Brahman cattle. Estab. 1971. Circ. 4,000. Pays on publication. Publishes ms an average of 2 months after acceptance. Byline given. Not copyrighted. Buys first North American serial, one-time and second serial (reprint) rights or makes work-for-hire assignments. Submit seasonal/holiday material 3 months in advance. Sample copy for 9×12 SAE with 5 first-class stamps.
Nonfiction: General interest, historical/nostalgic, interview/profile. Special issues: Herd Bull (July); Texas (October). **Buys 3-4 mss/year.** Query with published clips. Length: 1,200-3,000 words. **Pays $100-250.**
Reprints: Send typed ms with rights for sale noted. Pays 50% of amount paid for an original article.
Photos: Photos needed for article purchase. Send photos with submission. Reviews 4×5 prints. Offers no additional payment for photos accepted with ms. Captions required. Buys one-time rights.

$** **$THE CATTLEMAN, Texas and Southwestern Cattle Raisers Association, 1301 W. 7th, Ft. Worth TX 76102-2660. Fax: (817)332-5446. E-mail: sharla@thecattlemanmagazine.com. Website: www.thecattlemanmagazine.com. Editor: Lionel Chambers. Managing Editor: Susan Wagner. **Contact:** Sharla Ishmael, editorial director. **25% freelance written.** Monthly magazine covering the Texas/Oklahoma beef cattle industry. "We specialize in in-depth, management-type articles related to range and pasture, beef cattle production, animal health, nutrition and marketing. We want 'how-to' articles." Estab. 1914. Circ. 18,000. **Pays on acceptance.** Publishes ms an average of 2 months after acceptance. Byline given. Buys exclusive and one-time rights. Editorial lead time 2 months. Submit seasonal material 6 months in advance. Accepts queries by mail, e-mail, fax. Sample copy and writer's guidelines free.
    O— Break in with "clips from other cattle magazines and demonstrated knowledge of our audiences."
Nonfiction: How-to, humor, interview/profile, new product, personal experience, technical, ag research. Editorial calendar theme issues include: Horses (January); Range and Pasture (February); Livestock Marketing (July); Hereford and Wildlife (August); Feedlots (September); Bull Buyers (October); Mexican Marketing (December). Does not want to see anything not specifically related to beef production in the Southwest. **Buys 20 mss/year.** Query with published clips. Length: 1,500-2,000 words. **Pays $200-350 for assigned articles; $100-350 for unsolicited articles.** Sometimes pays expenses of writers on assignment.

Photos: State availability of photos with submission or send photos with submission. Reviews transparencies and prints. Offers no additional payment for photos accepted with ms. Identification of subjects required. Buys one-time rights.

Fiction: Humorous, slice-of-life vignettes, western. "No fiction unrelated to cattle/ranching in the Southwest." **Buys 5 mss/year.** Send complete ms. Length: 700-1,000 words. **Pays $100.**

Tips: "In our most recent readership survey, subscribers said they were most interested in the following topics in this order: range/pasture, property rights, animal health, water, new innovations and marketing. *The Cattleman* prefers to work on an assignment basis. However, prospective contributors are urged to write the editorial director of the magazine to inquire of interest on a proposed subject. Occasionally, the editor will return a manuscript to a potential contributor for cutting, polishing, checking, rewriting or condensing. Be able to demonstrate background/knowledge in this field. Include tearsheets from similar magazines."

N $ $ FARM INDUSTRY NEWS, Primedia Intertec Publishing, 7900 International Dr., #300, Minneapolis MN 55425. (612)851-4609. Fax: (612)851-4601. E-mail: fin@intertec.com. Website: www.homefarm.com. Managing Editor: Karen McMahon. **Contact:** Kurt Lawton, editor. **10% freelance written.** Trade journal published 13 times/year covering agriculture. "*Farm Industry News* is written for high-income row-crop and livestock farmers in the 12 Midwest states." Estab. 1967. Circ. 255,000. **Pays on acceptance.** Publishes ms an average of 2 months after acceptance. Byline given. Buys all rights. Editorial lead time 2 months. Submit seasonal material 2 months in advance. Accepts queries by mail, e-mail. Accepts simultaneous submissions. Responds in 1 month. Sample copy free.

Nonfiction: General interest, how-to, interview/profile, new product, technical. No opinion, humor, inspirational. **Buys 10 mss/year.** Query with published clips. Length: 1,200-2,400 words. **Pays $400-700.** Pays expenses of writers on assignment.

Photos: Send photos with submission. Reviews contact sheets, negatives, 4×6 4-color photos, slides. Offers $200-500/photo. Captions required, model releases and identification of subjects required. Buys one-time rights.

Tips: We prefer that writers have a background in agriculture. When sending a query, a writer should include samples of work published in other agricultural journals or those dealing with agriculture-related subjects."

$ $ FEED LOT MAGAZINE, Feed Lot Limited Partnership, P.O. Box 850, Dighton KS 67839. (316)397-2838. Editor: Robert A. Strong. **40% freelance written.** Bimonthly magazine. "The editorial information content fits a dual role: large feedlots and their related cow/calf, operations, and large 500+ cow/calf, stocker operations. The information covers all phases of production from breeding, genetics, animal health, nutrition, equipment design, research through finishing fat cattle. *Feed Lot* publishes a mix of new information and timely articles which directly effect the cattle industry." Estab. 1993. Circ. 12,000. Pays on publication. Publishes ms an average of 2 months after acceptance. Byline given. Offers 50% kill fee. Buys all rights. Editorial lead time 2 months. Submit seasonal material 6 months in advance. Responds in 1 month. Sample copy and writer's guidelines for $1.50.

Nonfiction: Interview/profile, new product (cattle-related). Send complete ms. Length: 100-400 words. **Pays 10¢/word.**

Reprints: Send tearsheet or typed ms with rights for sale noted and information about when and where the article previously appeared. Pays 50% of amount paid for an original article.

Photos: State availability of or send photos with submission. Reviews contact sheets. Negotiates payment individually. Captions, model releases required. Buys all rights.

Tips: "Know what you are writing about—have a good knowledge of the subject."

$ SHEEP! MAGAZINE, P.O. Box 10, 128 E. Lake St., Lake Mills WI 53551. (920)648-8285. Fax: (920)648-3770. **Contact:** Dave Thompson, editor. **35% freelance written.** Prefers to work with published/established writers. Monthly magazine. "We're looking for clear, concise, useful information for sheep raisers who have a few sheep to a 1,000 ewe flock." Estab. 1980. Circ. 15,000. Pays on publication. Byline given. Offers $30 kill fee. Buys all rights. Makes work-for-hire assignments. Submit seasonal material 3 months in advance. Please query first.

Nonfiction: Book excerpts; information (on personalities and/or political, legal or environmental issues affecting the sheep industry); how-to (on innovative lamb and wool marketing and promotion techniques, efficient record-keeping systems or specific aspects of health and husbandry). Health and husbandry articles should be written by someone with extensive experience or appropriate credentials (i.e., a veterinarian or animal scientist); profiles (on experienced sheep producers who detail the economics and management of their operation); features (on small businesses that promote wool products and stories about local and regional sheep producers' groups and their activities); new products (of value to sheep producers; should be written by someone who has used them); technical (on genetics, health and nutrition); first-person narratives. **Buys 80 mss/year.** Query with published clips or send complete ms. Length: 750-2,500 words. **Pays $45-150.** Pays expenses of writers on assignment.

Reprints: Send tearsheet or photocopy of article. Pays 40% of amount paid for an original article.

Photos: Color—vertical compositions of sheep and/or people—for cover. Use only b&w inside magazine. Black and white, 35mm photos or other visuals improve chances of a sale. Pays $100 maximum for 35mm color transparencies; **$20-50** for 5×7 b&w prints. Identification of subjects required. Buys all rights.

Tips: "Send us your best ideas and photos! We love good writing!"

Management

$ $ NEW HOLLAND NEWS, P.O. Box 1895, New Holland PA 17557-0903. Fax: (717)355-3600. Editor: Gary Martin. **50% freelance written.** Works with a small number of new/unpublished writers each year. Magazine published 8 times/year on agriculture; designed to entertain and inform farm families. Estab. 1960. **Pays on acceptance.** Publishes ms an average of 10 months after acceptance. Byline given. Offers negotiable kill fee. Buys first North American serial, one-time and second serial (reprint) rights. Submit seasonal material 6 months in advance. Accepts queries by mail. Responds in 2 months. Sample copy and writer's guidelines for 9 × 12 SAE with 2 first-class stamps.

Nonfiction: "We need strong photo support for articles of 1,200-1,700 words on farm management and farm human interest." Buys 40 mss/year. Query. **Pays $700-900.** Pays the expenses of writers on assignment.

Reprints: Accepts previously published submissions.

Photos: Send photos with query when possible. Reviews color transparencies. Pays $50-300, $500 for cover shot. Captions, model release and identification of subjects required. Buys one-time rights.

Tips: "We thrive on good article ideas from knowledgeable farm writers. The writer must have an emotional understanding of agriculture and the farm family and must demonstrate in the article an understanding of the unique economics that affect farming in North America. We want to know about the exceptional farm managers, those leading the way in agriculture. We want new efficiencies and technologies presented through the real-life experiences of farmers themselves. Use anecdotes freely. Successful writers keep in touch with the editor as they develop the article."

$ SMALL FARM TODAY, The How-to Magazine of Alternative and Traditional Crops, Livestock, and Direct Marketing, Missouri Farm Publishing, Inc., Ridge Top Ranch, 3903 W. Ridge Trail Rd., Clark MO 65243-9525. (573)687-3525. Fax: (573)687-3148. E-mail: smallfarm@socket.net. Website: www.smallfarmtoday.com. Editor: Ron Macher. **Contact:** Paul Berg, managing editor. Bimonthly magazine "for small farmers and small-acreage landowners interested in diversification, direct marketing, alternative crops, horses, draft animals, small livestock, exotic and minor breeds, home-based businesses, gardening, vegetable and small fruit crops." Estab. 1984 as *Missouri Farm Magazine*. Circ. 12,000. Pays 60 days after publication. Publishes ms an average of 6 months after acceptance. Byline given. Buys first serial and nonexclusive reprint rights (right to reprint article in an anthology). Submit seasonal/holiday material 4 months in advance. Accepts queries by mail (preferred), e-mail, fax. Responds in 3 months. Sample copy for $3. Writer's guidelines available.

O➤ Break in with a detailed "how-to" story with budget information on a specific crop or animal.

Nonfiction: Practical and how-to (small farming, gardening, alternative crops/livestock). Special issues: Wool & Fiber (February); Equipment (April). Query letters recommended. Length: 1,200-2,600 words. **Pays 3½¢/word.**

Reprints: Send photocopy or typed ms with rights for sale noted and information about when and where the article previously appeared. Pays 57% of amount paid for an original article.

Photos: Send photos with submission. Offers $6 for inside photos and $10 for cover photos. Captions required. Pays $4 for negatives or slides. Buys one-time rights and nonexclusive reprint rights (for anthologies).

Tips: "No poetery or humor—we don't publish these, but keep getting submissions. Your topic must apply to the small farm or acreage. It helps to provide more practical and helpful information without the fluff. We need 'how-to' articles (how to grow, raise, market, build, etc.), as well as articles about small farmers who are experiencing success through diversification, specialty/alternative crops and livestock, and direct marketing."

Regional

Ⓝ $ $ FLORIDA GROWER, The Oldest Spokesman For Florida Agriculture, Meister Publishing Co., 1555 Howell Branch Rd., Suite C-204, Winter Park FL 32789. (407)539-6552. E-mail: michael-allen@meisternet.com. Editor: Michael Allen. **10% freelance written.** Monthly magazine "edited for the Florida farmer with commercial production interest primarily in citrus, vegetables, and other ag endeavors. Our goal is to provide articles which update and inform on such areas as production, ag financing, farm labor relations, technology, safety, education and regulation." Estab. 1907. Circ. 14,500. Pays on publication. Byline given. Buys all rights. Editorial lead time 2 months. Submit seasonal material 3 months in advance. Accepts queries by mail, e-mail, fax, phone. Responds in 1 month. Sample copy for 9 × 12 SAE with 5 first class stamps. Writer's guidelines free.

Nonfiction: Interview/profile, photo feature, technical. Query with published clips. Length: 750-1,000 words. **Pays $150-250.**

Photos: Send photos with submission.

Ⓝ $ FLORIDAGRICULTURE, Florida Farm Bureau Federation, 5700 SW 34th St., Gainesville FL 32608. (352)374-1521. Fax: (352)374-1530. E-mail: ealbanesi@sfbcic.com. Website: www.fb.com/flfb. **Contact:** Ed Albanesi, editor. **Less than 5% freelance written.** Monthly tabloid covering Florida agriculture. Promotes agriculture to its 125,000 member families. Estab. 1943. Circ. 125,000. **Pays on acceptance.** Publishes ms an average of 3 months after acceptance. Byline sometimes given. Buys all rights. Editorial lead time 3 months. Submit seasonal material 3 months in advance. Accepts queries by mail, e-mail. Responds in 1 week to queries; 1 month to mss. Sample copy for $3.

Nonfiction: Sportsmen articles with a Florida connection. **Buys fewer than 2 mss/year.** Query. Length: 500-1,500 words. **Pays $50-100 for assigned articles.**

Photos: State availability of photos with submission. Negotiates payment individually. Captions and identification of subjects required. Buys up to 3 uses.

$ THE LAND, Minnesota's Favorite Ag Publication, Free Press Co., P.O. Box 3169, Mankato MN 56002-3169. (507)345-4523. E-mail: kschulz@the-land.com. Website: www.the-land.com. **Contact:** Kevin Schulz, editor. **40% freelance written.** Weekly tabloid "covering farming in Minnesota. Although we're not tightly focused on any one type of farming, our articles must be of interest to farmers. In other words, will your article topic have an impact on people who live and work in rural areas?" Estab. 1976. Circ. 40,000. **Pays on acceptance.** Publishes ms an average of 2 months after acceptance. Byline given. Buys first North American serial rights. Editorial lead time 2 months. Submit seasonal material 2 months in advance. Accepts queries by mail, e-mail. Responds in 3 weeks to queries; 2 months to mss. Prefer to work with Minnesota writers. Sample copy free. Writer's guidelines for #10 SASE.
Nonfiction: General interest (ag), how-to (crop, livestock production, marketing). **Buys 80 mss/year.** "Nothing that doesn't pertain to Minnesota agricultural or rural life." Query. Length: 750-1,200 words. **Pays $30-60 for assigned articles.**
Photos: Send photos with submission. Reviews contact sheets. Negotiates payment individually. Buys one-time rights.
Columns/Departments: Query. **Pays $10-50.**
Tips: "Be enthused about rural Minnesota life and agriculture and be willing to work with our editors. We try to stress relevance. When sending me a query, convince me the story belongs in a Minnesota farm publication."

$ $ MAINE ORGANIC FARMER & GARDENER, Maine Organic Farmers & Gardeners Association, RR 2, Box 594, Lincolnville ME 04849. (207)763-3043. E-mail: jenglish@midcoast.com. Website: www.mofga.org. **Contact:** Jean English, editor. **40% freelance written.** Prefers to work with published/established local writers. Quarterly magazine. "*MOF&G* promotes and encourages sustainable agriculture and environmentally sound living. Our primary focus is organic farming, gardening and forestry, but we also deal with local, national and international agriculture, food and environmental issues." Estab. 1976. Circ. 10,000. Pays on publication. Publishes ms an average of 8 months after acceptance. Byline and bio given. Buys first North American serial, one-time, first serial or second serial (reprint) rights. Submit seasonal material 1 year in advance. Accepts simultaneous submissions. Accepts queries by mail, e-mail. Responds in 2 months. Sample copy for $2 and SAE with 7 first-class stamps. Writer's guidelines free.
Nonfiction: Book reviews; how-to based on personal experience, research reports, interviews. Profiles of farmers, gardeners, plants. Information on renewable energy, recycling, nutrition, health, non-toxic pest control, organic farm management and marketing. "We use profiles of New England organic farmers and gardeners and news reports (500-1,000 words) dealing with US/international sustainable ag research and development, rural development, recycling projects, environmental and agricultural problems and solutions, organic farms with broad impact, cooperatives and community projects." **Buys 30 mss/year.** Query with published clips or send complete ms. Length: 1,000-3,000 words. **Pays $20-200.**
Reprints: Send typed ms with rights for sale noted and information about when and where the article previously appeared. Pays 50% of amount paid for an original article.
Photos: State availability of b&w photos with query; send 3×5 b&w photos with ms. Captions, model releases, identification of subjects required. Buys one-time rights.
Tips: "We are a nonprofit organization. Our publication's primary mission is to inform and educate, but we also want readers to enjoy the articles."

N $ $ TODAY'S FARMER, MFA Incorporated, 201 Ray Young Dr., Columbia MO 65201. (314)876-5252. Editor: Chuck Lay. **Contact:** Chuck Lay. **50% freelance written.** Company publication. Magazine published 10 times/year "owned and published by MFA Incorporated, an agricultural cooperative. We examine techniques and issues that help farmers and ranchers better meet the challenges of the present and future." Estab. 1908. Circ. 46,000. **Pays on acceptance.** Publishes ms an average of 2 months after acceptance. Byline given. Offers 100% kill fee. Publication not copyrighted. Buys first North American serial rights. Editorial lead time 2 months. Submit seasonal material at least 3 months in advance. Sample copy for $2. Writer's guidelines available by phone.
Nonfiction: How-to (ag technical), interview/profile, photo feature, technical. "No fiction, articles on MFA competitors, or subjects outside our trade territory (Missouri, Iowa, Arkansas)." **Buys 30 mss/year.** Query with published clips. Length: 1,000-2,000 words. **Pays $250-300 minimum (features).** Sometimes pays expenses of writers on assignment.
Photos: Send photos with submission. Reviews contact sheets. Negotiates payment individually. Identification of subjects required. Buys one-time rights.
Tips: "Freelancers can best approach us by knowing our audience (farmers/ranchers who are customers of MFA) and knowing their needs. We publish traditional agribusiness information that helps farmers do their jobs more effectively. Know the audience. We edit for length, AP style."

FINANCE

These magazines deal with banking, investment and financial management. Publications that use similar material but have a less technical slant are listed under the Consumer Business & Finance section.

$ $ BANK DIRECTOR, Board Member, Inc., 2 Maryland Farms, Suite 123, Brentwood TN 37027. (615)309-3200. Fax: (615)371-0899. E-mail: bankdirector@boardmember.com. Editor: Deborah Scally. **Contact:** Chantel DeDominicis, assistant editor. **75% freelance written.** *"Bank Director* is the only magazine written for directors of financial companies. Each quarterly issue focuses on the information directors need, from mergers and acquisitions to retail strategies, compensation and technology." Estab. 1990. Circ. 42,000. Pays on publication. Publishes ms an average of 2 months after acceptance. Byline given. Offers negotiable (20% average) kill fee. Buys all rights. Editorial lead time 3 months. Submit seasonal material 3 months in advance. Accepts queries by: mail, fax, phone. Responds in 3 weeks to queries; 2 months to mss. Sample copy free.

Nonfiction: Financial/banking. **Buys 16-20 mss/year.** Query with published clips. Length: 2,000-5,000 words. **Pays 30-75¢/word.** Sometimes pays expenses of writers on assignment.

Photos: State availability of photos with submission. Negotiates payment individually. Identification of subjects required. Buys one-time rights.

Columns/Departments: For You Review, 250-500 words; Boardroom Basics, 2,000-3,000 words; Perspective (opinion), 2,000-3,000 words. **Buys 10 mss/year.** Query with published clips. **Pays 30-50¢/word.**

Tips: "Call or write with a story idea relevant to our audience—bank directors."

N $ $ $ $ BANKING STRATEGIES, Bank Administration Institute (BAI), 1544 Bishop Hollow Run, Dunwoody GA 30338. Website: www._bai.org/bankingstrategies. **Contact:** Kenneth Cline, senior editor. **70% freelance written.** Covers banking and financial services. "Magazine covers banking from a strategic and managerial perspective for its senior financial executive audience. Each issue includes in-depth trend articles and interviews with influential executives." Offers variable kill fee. Buys all rights. Accepts queries by mail, e-mail. Responds almost immediately to queries.

Nonfiction: How-to (articles that help institutions be more effective and competitive in the marketplace), interview/profile (executive interviews). "No topic queries, we assign stories to freelancers. I'm looking for qualifications as opposed to topic queries. I need experienced writers/reporters." **Buys 30 mss/year.** E-queries preferred. **Pays $1.20/word for assigned articles.**

Tips: "Demonstrate ability and experience. I'm looking for freelancers who can write according to our standards, which are quite high."

N $ $ $ $ BLOOMBERG WEALTH MANAGER, Bloomberg L.P., P.O. Box 888, Princeton NJ 08542-0888. (609)279-3000. Fax: (609)279-7150. E-mail: wealthmanager@bloomberg.net. Website: www.wealth.bloomberg.com. Editor: Robert Casey. **Contact:** Mary Ann McGuigan, managing editor. **90% freelance written.** Magazine published 10 times/year for financial advisers. "Stories should provide insight and information for the financial adviser. Put yourself on the adviser's side of the table and cover the issues thoroughly from his/her perspective. The piece should delve beneath the surface. We need specific examples, professional caveats, advice from professionals." Estab. 1999. Circ. 45,000. **Pays on acceptance.** Publishes ms an average of 3 months after acceptance. Byline given. Offers 30% kill fee. Buys first North American serial rights. Editorial lead time 2 months. Submit seasonal material 2 months in advance. Accepts queries by mail, e-mail, fax, phone. Responds in 1 month.

Nonfiction: Book excerpts, interview/profile, technical. Do not submit anything that does not deal with financial planning issues or the financial markets. **Buys 30-40 mss/year.** Query with published clips. Length: 1,500-3,000 words. **Pays $1.50-$2/word for assigned articles.** Sometimes pays expenses of writers on assignment.

Columns/Departments: Expertly Speaking, Tax Strategies, Retirement, Executive Compensation (all finannnnncial planning), all 1,900 words. **Buys 10-15 mss/year.** Query with published clips. **Pays $1.50-$2/word.**

　■ The online version contains material not found in the print edition. Contact: Matt Stichnoth.

Tips: *"Wealth Manager* is a trade magazine. All pieces should be written from the perspective of a financial adviser who has wealthy clients."

N $ $ $ COLLECTIONS & CREDIT RISK, The Monthly Magazine for Collections and Credit Policy Professionals, Faulkner & Gray Inc., 300 S. Wacker Dr., Suite 1800, Chicago IL 60606. (312)913-1334. Fax: (312)913-1365. E-mail: jesse.snyder@faulknergray.com. Website: www.collectionsworld.com. Editor: David E. Whiteside. **Contact:** Jesse Snyder, deputy editor. **33% freelance written.** Monthly trade journal covering debt collections and credit risk management. *"Collections & Credit Risk* reports and analyzes events and trends affecting consumer and commercial credit practices and debt collections. The entire credit cycle is covered from setting credit policy and making loan decisions to debt recovery, collections, bankruptcy and debt sales." Estab. 1996. Circ. 22,000. **Pays on acceptance.** Publishes ms an average of 3 months after acceptance. Byline given. Kill fee determined case by case. Buys one-time or all rights. Editorial lead time 3 months. Accepts queries by mail, e-mail, fax. "Contact us first, then work on assignment." Sample copy free or online at website.

　O⊶ Break in with a "a query with clips of business trend stories using 8-10 sources and demonstrating strong analysis."

Nonfiction: Interview/profile, technical, business news and anaylsis. "No unsolicited submissions accepted—freelancers work on assignment only." **Buys 30-40 mss/year.** Query with published clips. Length: 1,800-3,000 words. **Pays $800-1,000.** Sometimes pays expenses of writers on assignment.

Photos: Send photos with submission. Negotiates payment individually. Identification of subjects required. Buys one-time rights.

　■ The online version contains material not found in the print version.

Tips: "This is a business news and analysis magazine focused on events and trends affecting the credit-risk management and collections industry. Our editorial approach is modeled after *Business Week, Forbes, Fortune, Wall Street Journal.* No fluff accepted."

$ $ $ CONTINGENCIES, American Academy of Actuaries, 1100 17th St. NW, 7th Floor, Washington DC 20036. (202)223-8196. Fax: (202)872-1948. E-mail: sullivan@actuary.org. **Contact:** Steven Sullivan, editor. **15% freelance written.** Bimonthly. "Though our membership is primarily actuaries, we are a magazine designed to be read by an outside audience. We look for nontechnical articles about what actuaries do and how it affects public policy." Estab. 1988. Circ. 23,296. Pays on publication. Publishes ms an average of 3 months after acceptance. Byline given. Buys first North American serial and second serial rights. Editorial lead time 2 months. Responds in 2 weeks to queries; 1 month to mss. Sample copy and writer's guidelines free.

Nonfiction: Humor, interview/profile, opinion, personal experience. "*Contingencies* is not an academic journal or newsletter. Features should be written for, and accessible to, the educated laymen, while technical pieces are directed principally to actuaries. Even those articles, however, should not be so burdened by equations and tables that they're prohibitively uninviting to the general reader." **Buys 6 mss/year.** Query with published clips. Length: 2,000 words. **Pays $800-1,000.** Pays writers with contributor copies or other premiums. Sometimes pays expenses of writers on assignment.

Tips: "I'm always looking for good ideas, and I'm willing to listen to any ideas relating to insurance, risk management, actuaries' involvement in public policy."

$ $ EQUITIES MAGAZINE CO., 160 Madison Ave., 3rd Floor, New York NY 10016. (212)213-1300. Fax: (212)213-5872. **Contact:** Robert J. Flaherty, editor. **50% freelance written.** "We are a seven-issues-a-year financial magazine covering the fastest-growing companies in the world. We study the management of companies and act as critics reviewing their performances. We aspire to be 'The Shareholder's Friend'. We want to be a bridge between quality public companies and sophisticated investors." Estab. 1951. Circ. 18,000. Pays on publication. Publishes ms an average of 2 months after acceptance. Byline given. Buys first and reprint rights. Accepts queries by mail. Sample copy for 9×12 SAE with 5 first-class stamps.

Nonfiction: New product, technical. **Buys 30 mss/year.** "We must know the writer first as we are careful about whom we publish. A letter of introduction with résumé and clips is the best way to introduce yourself. Financial writing requires specialized knowledge and a feel for people as well, which can be a tough combination to find." Query with published clips. Length: 300-1,500 words. **Pays $150-750 for assigned articles,** more for very difficult or investigative pieces. Carries guest columns by famous money managers who are not writing for cash payments, but to showcase their ideas and approach. Pays expenses of writers on assignment.

Photos: Send color photos with submission. Reviews contact sheets, negatives, transparencies and prints. Offers no additional payment for photos accepted with ms. Identification of subjects required.

Columns/Departments: Pays $25-75 for assigned items only.

Tips: "Give us an idea for a story on a specific publically-owned company, whose stock is traded on NASDAQ, or the NYSE or American Stock Exchange. Anyone who enjoys analyzing a business and telling the story of the people who started it, or run it today, is a potential *Equities* contributor. But to protect our readers and ourselves, we are careful about who writes for us. Business writing is an exciting area and our stories reflect that. If a writer relies on numbers and percentages to tell his story, rather than the individuals involved, the result will be numbingly dull."

$ $ $ THE FEDERAL CREDIT UNION, National Association of Federal Credit Unions, P.O. Box 3769, Washington DC 20007-0269. (703)522-4770. Fax: (703)524-1082. E-mail: tfcu@nafcunet.org. Website: www.nafcunet.org. Executive Editor: Patrick M. Keefe. **Contact:** Robin Johnston, publisher/managing editor. **25% freelance written.** "Looking for writers with financial, banking or credit union experience, but will work with inexperienced (unpublished) writers based on writing skill. Published bimonthly, *The Federal Credit Union* is the official publication of the National Association of Federal Credit Unions. The magazine has a unique focus among credit union publications, one which is well-suited to the large institutions that make up its primary reader base. Its editorial concentrates on Washington, D.C., and the rapidly changing regulatory and legislative environment affecting credit unions. More importantly, it covers how this environment will affect credit union strategy, operations, management, technology, and human resources." Estab. 1967. Circ. 11,136. Pays on publication. Publishes ms an average of 3 months after acceptance. Byline given. Buys first North American serial rights. Submit seasonal material 5 months in advance. Accepts simultaneous submissions. Accepts queries by mail, e-mail, fax (2 pages max). Responds in 2 months. Sample copy for 10×13 SAE with 5 first-class stamps. Writer's guidelines for #10 SASE.

O── Break in with "pithy, informative, thought-provoking items for our 'Briefs' section (for free or a small fee of $50-100."

Nonfiction: Query with published clips and SASE. Length: 1,200-2,000 words. Query. **Pays $400-800.**

Photos: Send photos with submission. Reviews 35mm transparencies and 5×7 prints. Offers no additional payment for photos accepted with ms. Model releases and identification of subjects required. Pays $250-$500. Buys all rights.

◼ The online magazine carries original content not found in the print edition. Contact: Robin Johnston.

Tips: "We would like more articles on how credit unions are using technology to serve their members and more articles on leading-edge technologies they can use in their operations. We have legislative and regulator experts on staff. If you can write on current trends in technology, human resources, or strategic planning, you stand a better chance of being published than if you wrote on other topics."

$ $ $ FINANCIAL PLANNING, Securities Data Publishing, 40 W. 57th St., 11th Fl., New York NY 10019. (212)765-5311. Fax: (212)765-8189. Website: www.financial-planning.com. Editor: Evan Simonoff. **Contact:** Thomas W. Johnson, executive editor. **30-40% freelance written.** Magazine published monthly covering stocks, bonds, mutual funds, retirement and estate planning insurance. Estab. 1971. Circ. 100,000. Pays on publication. Publishes ms an average of 3 months after acceptance. Byline given. Offers 15% kill fee. Buys all rights. Editorial lead time 3 months. Submit seasonal material 4 months in advance. Responds in 3 weeks to queries; 1 month to mss. Sample copy for $10. Writer's guidelines free on request.

Nonfiction: Book excerpts, interview/profile, new product, opinion, technical. No product endorsements. **Buys 25-30 mss/year.** Query with published clips. Length: 1,800-2,500 words. **Pays 50¢/word.** Sometimes pays expenses of writers on assignment (limit agreed upon in advance).

Photos: State availability of photos with submission. Reviews contact sheets, prints (any size). Offers no additional payment for photos accepted with ms. Identification of subjects required.

Tips: "Avoid articles that are too general—ours is a professional readership who require thoughtful, in-depth analysis of financial issues. A submission that includes charts, graphs and statistical data is much more likely to pique our interest than overviews of investing."

N $ $ INCOME FUND OUTLOOK; THE INSIDERS; MARKET LOGIC; MUTUAL FUND BUYER'S GUIDE; MUTUAL FUND FORECASTER, Time Inc., 2200 SW 10th St., Deerfield Beach FL 33442. (954)333-5204. Fax: (810)958-8413. E-mail: adam_martin@timeinc.com. **Contact:** Adam J. Martin, editor. **10-20% freelance written.** Biweekly finance newsletters covering stocks, mutual funds, stock market. "We're looking for 300- to 600-word stories on stocks and funds written for relatively sophisticated investors. We're also in need of stock market commentary." Circ. 80,000. Pays on publication. Publishes ms an average of 2 weeks after acceptance. Byline sometimes given. Pays negotiable kill fee. Buys all rights. Editorial lead time 3 weeks. Submit seasonal material 2 months in advance. Accepts queries by mail, e-mail, fax, phone. Sample copy free.

Nonfiction: Financial book excerpts, essays, opinion. **Buys 5-10 mss/year.** Query with published clips. Length: 300-600 words. **Pays $50-600.**

$ $ $ MORTGAGE BANKING, The Magazine of Real Estate Finance, Mortgage Bankers Association of America, 1919 Pennsylvania Ave., NW, Washington DC 20006. (202)557-2853. Fax: (202)721-0245. E-mail: janet_hewitt@mbaa.org. Website: www.mbaa.org. **Contact:** Janet Reilley Hewitt, editor in chief. Associate Editor: Lesley Hall. Monthly magazine covering real estate finance. "Timely examination of major news and trends in the business of mortgage lending for both commercial and residential real estate. Estab. 1939. Circ. 10,000. **Pays on acceptance.** Publishes ms an average of 2 months after acceptance. Byline given. Negotiates kill fee. Buys one-time rights or makes work-for-hire assignments. Editorial lead time 2 months. Submit seasonal material 3 months in advance. Accepts queries by mail, fax, phone. Accepts simultaneous submissions. Responds in 1 month to queries; 4 months to mss. Sample copy and writer's guidelines free.

Nonfiction: Book excerpts, essays, interview/profile, opinion. Commercial real estate special supplemental issue published each February. **Buys 30 mss/year.** Query. Length: 3,000-4,000 words. **Pays $1,000-3,000.** Sometimes pays expenses of writers on assignment.

Reprints: Accepts previously published submissions.

Photos: State availability of photos with submission. Reviews prints. Negotiates payment individually. Model releases and identification required. Buys one-time rights.

Columns and Departments: Book reviews (current, relevant material), 300 words; executive essay (industry executive's personal views on relevant topic), 750-1,000 words. **Buys 2 mss/year.** Query. Pay negotiated.

Tips: "Trends in technology, current and upcoming legislation that will affect the mortgage industry are good focus."

N $ $ $ $ ON WALL STREET, Thomson Financial, 40 W. 57th St., New York NY 10019. (212)765-5311. Fax: (212)765-8189. E-mail: evan.cooper@tfn.com. Executive Editor: Thomas Johnson. **Contact:** Evan Cooper, editor. **50% freelance written.** Monthly magazine for stockbrokers. "We help 90,000 stockbrokers build their business." Estab. 1991. Circ. 90,000. Pays on publication. Publishes ms an average of 1 month after acceptance. Byline given. Offers 50% kill fee. Buys first North American serial rights. Editorial lead time 2 months. Submit seasonal material 2 months in advance. Accepts queries by mail, e-mail. Accepts simultaneous submissions. Responds in 1 week to queries; 1 month to mss. Sample copy and writer's guidelines free.

Nonfiction: How-to, interview/profile. "Don't want investment-related articles about hot stocks, nor funds or hot alternative investments." **Buys 30 mss/year.** Query. Length: 1,000-3,000 words. **Pays $1/word.**

Photos: State availability of photos with submission. Reviews contact sheets. Negotiates payment individually. Identification of subjects required. Buys one-time rights.

Tips: "Writers should know what stockbrokers need to expand their business—industry-specific knowledge of cold-calling, selling investment ideas."

N $ $ SERVICING MANAGEMENT, The Magazine for Loan Servicing Professionals, LDJ Corp., P.O. Box 2330, Waterbury CT 06722-2330. (800)325-6745, ext. 241. Fax: (203)755-3480. E-mail: fabrini@sm-online.com. Website: www.sm-online.com. **Contact:** Julius Fabrini, editor. **15% freelance written.** Monthly magazine covering residential mortgage servicing. Estab. 1989. Circ. 22,000. **Pays on acceptance**. Publishes ms an average of 2 months after acceptance. Byline given. Accepts queries by mail, e-mail, fax, phone. Responds in 1 week to queries. Sample copy and writer's guidelines free.

Nonfiction: How-to, interview/profile, new product, technical. **Buys 10 mss/year.** Query. Length: 1,500-2,500 words. **Pays $200-550.** Will pay industry experts with contributor copies or other premiums rather than a cash payment.

Photos: State availability of photos with submission. Reviews contact sheets. Offers no additional payment for photos accepted with ms. Identification of subjects required. Buys all rights.

Columns/Departments: Buys 5 mss/year. Query. **Pays $200.**

FISHING

$ $ PACIFIC FISHING, Salmon Bay Communications, 1515 NW 51st St., Seattle WA 98107. (206)789-5333. Fax: (206)784-5545. E-mail: Brad@salmonbay.com. Website: www.pfmag.com. **Contact:** Brad Warren, editor. **75% freelance written.** Works with some new/unpublished writers. Monthly business magazine for commercial fishermen and others in the West Coast commercial fishing industry. "*Pacific Fishing* views the fisherman as a small businessman and covers all aspects of the industry, including harvesting, processing and marketing." Estab. 1979. Circ. 11,000. Pays on publication. Publishes ms an average of 2 months after acceptance. Byline given. Offers 10-15% kill fee on assigned articles deemed unsuitable. Buys one-time rights. Accepts queries by mail, e-mail, fax, phone. Responds in 3 weeks. Sample copy and writer's guidelines for 9×12 SAE with 10 first-class stamps.

Nonfiction: Interview/profile, technical (usually with a business hook or slant). "Articles must be concerned specifically with *commercial* fishing. We view fishermen as small businessmen and professionals who are innovative and success-oriented. To appeal to this reader, *Pacific Fishing* offers 4 basic features: technical, how-to articles that give fishermen hands-on tips that will make their operation more efficient and profitable; practical, well-researched business articles discussing the dollars and cents of fishing, processing and marketing; profiles of a fisherman, processor or company with emphasis on practical business and technical areas; and in-depth analysis of political, social, fisheries management and resource issues that have a direct bearing on West Coast commercial fishermen." Editors here are putting more focus on local and international seafood marketing, technical coverage of gear and vessels. **Buys 20 mss/ year.** Query noting whether photos are available, and enclosing samples of previous work and SASE. Length varies, one-paragraph news items to 3,000-word features. **For most assignments pays 10-15¢/word.** Sometimes pays the expenses of writers on assignment.

Reprints: Send photocopy of article and information about when and where the article previously appeared. Pays 100% of the amount paid for an original article.

Photos: "We need good, high-quality photography, especially color, of West Coast commercial fishing. We prefer 35mm color slides. Our rates are $200 for cover; $50-100 for inside color; $25-75 for b&w and $10 for table of contents."

FLORISTS, NURSERIES & LANDSCAPERS

Readers of these publications are involved in growing, selling or caring for plants, flowers and trees. Magazines geared to consumers interested in gardening are listed in the Consumer Home & Garden section.

$ GROWERTALKS, Ball Publishing, 335 N. River St., P.O. Box 9, Batavia IL 60510. (630)208-9080. Fax: (630)208-9350. E-mail: beytes@growertalks.com. Website: www.growertalks.com. **Contact:** Chris Beytes, editor. **50% freelance written.** Monthly magazine. "*GrowerTalks* serves the commercial greenhouse grower. Editorial emphasis is on floricultural crops: bedding plants, potted floral crops, foliage and fresh cut flowers. Our readers are growers, managers and owners. We're looking for writers who've had experience in the greenhouse industry." Estab. 1937. Circ. 9,500. Pays on publication. Publishes ms an average of 3 months after acceptance. Byline given. Buys first North American serial rights. Editorial lead time 4 months. Submit seasonal material 3 months in advance. Responds in 1 month. Sample copy and writer's guidelines free.

Nonfiction: How-to (time- or money-saving projects for professional flower/plant growers); interview/profile (ornamental horticulture growers); personal experience (of a grower); technical (about growing process in greenhouse setting). "No articles that promote only one product." **Buys 36 mss/year.** Query. Length: 1,200-1,600 words. **Pays $125 minimum for assigned articles; $75 minimum for unsolicited articles.** Sometimes pays in other premiums or contributor copies.

Photos: State availability of photos with submission. Reviews 2½×2½ slides and 3×5 prints. Negotiates payment individually. Captions, model releases and identification of subjects required. Buys one-time rights.

Tips: "Discuss magazine with ornamental horticulture growers to find out what topics that have or haven't appeared in the magazine interest them."

$ $ THE GROWING EDGE, New Moon Publishing Inc., 341 SW Second, Suite 201, P.O. Box 1027, Corvallis OR 97339-1027. (541)757-2511. Fax: (541)757-0028. E-mail: Doug@growingedge.com. Website: www.growingedge.com.

Contact: Dough Peckenpaugh, editor. **85% freelance written.** Bimonthly magazine signature covering indoor and outdoor high-tech gardening techniques and tips. Estab. 1980. Circ. 20,000. Pays on publication. Publishes ms an average of 3 months after acceptance. Byline given. Buys first serial and reprint rights. Submit seasonal material at least 6 months in advance. Accepts queries by mail, e-mail. Responds in 3 months. Sample copy for $7 or on website. Writer's guidelines for #10 SASE or on website..

Nonfiction: Book excerpts and reviews relating to high-tech gardening, general horticulture and agriculture, how-to, interview/profile, personal experience, must be technical. Query first. Length: 500-3,500 words. **Pays 20¢/published word. (10¢ first rights, 5¢ non-exclusive reprint rights, 5¢ non-exclusive electronic rights.)**

Reprints: Send tearsheet, photocopy or typed ms with rights for sale noted and information about when and where the article previously appeared. Payment negotiable.

Photos: Pays $175/color cover photos; $25-50/inside photo. Pays on publication. Credit line given. Buys first and reprint rights.

Tips: Looking for more hydroponics articles and information which will give the reader/gardener/farmer the "growing edge" in high-tech gardening and farming on topics such as high intensity grow lights, water conservation, drip irrigation, advanced organic fertilizers, new seed varieties and greenhouse cultivation.

$ $ LANDSCAPE TRADES, Landscape Ontario, 7856 Fifth Line S, RR4, Milton, Ontario L9T 2X8 Canada. (905)875-1805. Fax: (905)875-0183. E-mail: lo@hort-trades.com. Website: www.hort-trades.com. **Contact:** Linda Erskine, editor. Magazine published 9 times/year for the horticultural industry. "*Landscape Trades* is written for landscape contractors, grounds maintenance, growers and retail garden centers." Estab. 1979. Circ. 8,275. Pays on publication. Publishes ms an average of 2 months after acceptance. Byline given. Buys all rights. Editorial lead time 2 months. Submit seasonal material 3 months in advance. Accepts queries by mail, e-mail, fax, phone. Sample copy and writer's guidelines free.

Nonfiction: How-to, interview/profile, technical. "No consumer-based articles." **Buys 10 mss/year.** Query with published clips. Length: 1,000-2,500 words. **Pays 15-25¢/word for assigned articles; 15¢/word for unsolicited articles.** Sometimes pays expenses of writers on assignment.

Reprints: Accepts previously published submissions.

Photos: Send photos with submission. Reviews negatives, transparencies and prints. Negotiates payment individually. Captions and identification of subjects required. Buys all rights.

Columns/Departments: Grower's Six Pack, 700 words; CompuFacts (computer tech), 1,000 words. **Buys 5 mss/year.** Send complete ms. **Pays 15-25¢/word.**

Tips: "Submit query and article outline first."

$ $ ORNAMENTAL OUTLOOK, Your Connection To The South's Horticulture Industry, Meister Publishing Co., 1555 Howell Branch Rd., Suite C204, Winter Park FL 32789. (407)539-6552. Fax: (407)539-6544. E-mail: oo_edit@meisterpubl.com. **Contact:** Kris Sweet, managing editor. **50% freelance written.** Monthly magazine. "*Ornamental Outlook* is written for commercial growers of ornamental plants in the Southeast U.S. Our goal is to provide interesting and informative articles on such topics as production, legislation, safety, technology, pest control, water management and new varieties as they apply to Southeast growers." Estab. 1991. Circ. 12,500. Pays 30 days after publication. Publishes ms an average of 4 months after acceptance. Byline given. Buys all rights. Editorial lead time 2 months. Submit seasonal material 3 months in advance. Accepts queries by: mail, e-mail, fax, phone. Responds in 1-3 months. Sample copy for 9 × 12 SAE with 5 first-class stamps. Writer's guidelines free.

Nonfiction: Interview/profile, photo feature, technical. "No first-person articles. No word-for-word meeting transcripts or all-quote articles." Query with published clips. Length: 750-1,000 words. **Pays $250/article including photos.**

Photos: Send photos with submission. Reviews contact sheets, transparencies and prints. Captions and identification of subjects required. Buys one-time rights.

Tips: "I am most impressed by written queries that address specific subjects of interest to our audience, which is the *Southeast* grower of *commercial* horticulture. Our biggest demand is for features, about 1,000 words, that follow subjects listed on our editorial calendar (which is sent with guidelines). Please do not send articles of national or consumer interest."

$ $ TREE CARE INDUSTRY MAGAZINE, National Arborist Association, P.O. Box 1094, Amherst NH 03031-1094. (800)733-2622. (603)673-3311. E-mail: garvin@natlarb.com. Website: www.natlarb.com. **Contact:** Mark Garvin, editor. **50% freelance written.** Monthly magazine covering tree care and landscape maintenance. Estab. 1990. Circ. 28,500. Pays within 30 days of publication. Publishes ms an average of 3 months after acceptance. Byline given. Buys first North American serial rights. Editorial lead time 10 weeks. Submit seasonal material 3 months in advance. Accepts queries by mail, e-mail, fax, phone. Responds in 2 weeks to queries; 2 months to mss. Sample copy for 9 × 12 SAE with 6 first-class stamps. Writer's guidelines free.

Nonfiction: Book excerpts, general interest, historical/nostalgic, humor, interview/profile, new product, personal experience, technical. **Buys 40 mss/year.** Query with published clips Length: 900-3,500 words. Payment negotiable.

Photos: Send photos with submission. Reviews prints. Negotiates payment individually. Captions, identification of subjects required. Buys one-time and web rights.

Columns/Departments: Management Exchange (business management-related), 1,200-1,800 words; Industry Innovations (inventions), 1,200 words; From The Field (OP/ED from practitioners), 1,200 words. **Buys 40 mss/year.** Send complete ms. **Pays $100 and up.**

Tips: "Preference is given to writers with background and knowledge of the tree care industry; our focus is relatively narrow. Preference is also given to photojournalists willing to work on speculation."

GOVERNMENT & PUBLIC SERVICE

Listed here are journals for people who provide governmental services at the local, state or federal level or for those who work in franchised utilities. Journals for city managers, politicians, bureaucratic decision makers, civil servants, firefighters, police officers, public administrators, urban transit managers and utilities managers are listed in this section.

N **$** **AMERICAN FIRE JOURNAL**, Fire Publications, Inc., 9072 Artesia Blvd., Bellflower CA 90706. Fax: (562)867-6434. E-mail: afjm@accessl.net. Editor: Carol Carlsen Brooks. **Contact:** John Ackenman, publisher. **90% freelance written.** Monthly magazine covering fire service. "Written by firefighters for firefighters." Estab. 1940s. Circ. 6,000. Pays on publication. Publishes ms an average of 6 months after acceptance. Byline given. Buys first rights. Editorial lead time 3 months. Submit seasonal material 3 months in advance. Accepts queries by mail, e-mail, fax, phone. Responds in 2 weeks to queries; 2 months to mss. Sample copy for $3.50. Writer's guidelines free.
Nonfiction: Historical/nostalgic, how-to, new product, opinion, photo feature, technical. **Buys 50 mss/year.** Send complete ms. Any length. **Pays $150 maximum.** Pays writers with contributor copies or other premiums "if material is written on department time or auspices."
Reprints: Accepts previously published submissions.
Photos: Send photos with submission. Reviews contact sheets, negatives, transparencies and prints; any size. Offers $5-50/photo. Captions required. Buys one-time rights.
Columns/Departments: Hot Flashes (news/current events), 100-300 words; Innovations (new firefighting tricks and techniques), 300-1,000 words. **Buys 2-4 mss/year.** Send complete ms. **Pays $10 maximum.**
Fillers: Anecdotes, facts, newsbreaks. **Buys 2-4/year.** Length: 300-1,000 words. **Pays $25 maximum.**
Tips: "Content of articles is generally technical, tactical, educational or related to fire service legislation, current events or recent emergency incidents. We do not publish fiction or people profiles. We do, however, accept manuscripts for a monthly column of fire-service-related humor. Your punctuation, grammar and spelling are not our primary concerns. We have editors to correct these. We are more interested in your expertise, knowledge and experience in fire service subjects. However, it is important to spell names, places and organizations correctly, as our editors may not be familiar with them. Do not include opinions (unless you are submitting a Guest Editorial), unsubstantiated statements or untested tactics in your article. Accuracy is essential. Be sure of your facts, and always attribute information and identify sources."

$ **CHIEF OF POLICE MAGAZINE**, National Association of Chiefs of Police, 3801 Biscayne Blvd., Miami FL 33137. (305)573-0070. **Contact:** Jim Gordon, executive editor. Bimonthly trade journal for law enforcement commanders (command ranks). Circ. 13,500. **Pays on acceptance.** Publishes ms an average of 6 months after acceptance. Byline given. Buys first rights. Submit seasonal material 6 months in advance. Accepts simultaneous submissions. Accepts queries by mail, e-mail, fax. Responds in 2 weeks. Sample copy for $3 and 9 × 12 SAE with 5 first-class stamps. Writer's guidelines for #10 SASE.
O→ Break in with "a story concerning command officers or police family survivors."
Nonfiction: General interest, historical/nostalgic, how-to, humor, inspirational, interview/profile, new product, personal experience, photo feature, religious, technical. "We want stories about interesting police cases and stories on any law enforcement subject or program that is positive in nature. No exposé types. Nothing anti-police." **Buys 50 mss/year.** Send complete ms. Length: 600-2,500 words. **Pays $25-75 for assigned articles; $25-100 for unsolicited articles.** Payment includes publication on the organization's website at editor's discretion. Sometimes (when pre-requested) pays expenses of writers on assignment.
Reprints: Accepts previously published submissions.
Photos: Send photos with submission. Reviews 5 × 6 prints. Pays $5-10 for b&w; $10-25 for color. Captions required. Buys one-time rights.
Columns/Departments: New Police (police equipment shown and tests), 200-600 words. **Buys 6 mss/year.** Send complete ms. **Pays $5-25.**
Fillers: Anecdotes, short humor, law-oriented cartoons. **Buys 100/year.** Length: 100-1,600 words. **Pays $5-25.**
Tips: "Writers need only contact law enforcement officers right in their own areas and we would be delighted. We want to recognize good commanding officers from sergeant and above who are involved with the community. Pictures of the subject or the department are essential and can be snapshots. We are looking for interviews with police chiefs and sheriffs on command level with photos."

$** **$ **CORRECTIONS TECHNOLOGY & MANAGEMENT**, Hendon Publishing, Inc., 1000 Skokie Blvd, Suite 500, Wilmette IL 60091. (847)256-8555. Fax: (847)256-8574. E-mail: tim@hendonpub.com. Website: www.ctmmag.com. **Contact:** Tim Burke, editor-in-chief. **40% freelance written.** Trade magazine covering correctional facility management. "We focus on positive stories of corrections professionals doing their job. For stories . . . lots of quotes, dramatic photos. Make it real. Make it useful." Estab. 1997. Circ. 21,000. Pays 30 days after publication. Publishes ms an average of 3 months after acceptance. Byline given. Buys first North American serial rights. Editorial lead time 4 months. Submit seasonal material 6 months in advance. Reports 1 month on mss. Sample copy for 9×12 SAE and 6 first-class stamps.

Nonfiction: Facility design; technology; management; health care; food services, safety; training; interview/profile; photo features. "Nothing 'general market.' Must be corrections-specific." **Buys 30 mss/year.** Query with published clips. Length: 2,000-2,500 words.

Photos: Send photos with submission. Reviews transparencies and prints 8×10. Negotiates payment individually. Captions, model releases and identification of subjects required. Buys all rights.

Columns and Departments: Corrections Profile (spotlight on one facility), 2,000 words; Tactical Profile (products in corr. tactics), 1,000 words. **Buys 3 mss/year.** Query with published clips. **Pays 10-15¢/word.**

$ $ FIRE CHIEF, Intertec Publishing Corp., 35 E. Wacker Dr., Suite 700, Chicago IL 60601. (312)726-7277. Fax: (312)726-0241. E-mail: scott_baltic@intertec.com. Website: www.firechief.com. Editor: Scott Baltic. **90% freelance written.** Monthly. "*Fire Chief* is the management magazine of the fire service, addressing the administrative, personnel, training, prevention/education, professional development and operational issues faced by chiefs and other fire officers, whether in paid, volunteer or combination departments. We're potentially interested in any article that can help them do their jobs better, whether that's as incident commanders, financial managers, supervisors, leaders, trainers, planners, or ambassadors to municipal officials or the public." Estab. 1956. Circ. 50,000. Pays on publication. Publishes ms an average of 6 months after acceptance. Byline given. Kill fee negotiable. Buys first, one-time, second serial (reprint) or all rights. Editorial lead time 2 months. Submit seasonal material 4 months in advance. Accepts queries by mail, e-mail, fax. Responds in 1 month to queries; 2 months to mss. Sample copy and writer's guidelines free or on website.

Nonfiction: How-to, technical. "If your department hasmade some chagnes in its structure, budget, mission or organizational culture (or really did reinvent itself in a serious way), an account of that process, including the mistakes made and lessons learned, could be a winner. Similarly, if you've observed certain things that fire departments typicallys could do a lot of better and you think you have the solution, let us know." **Buys 50-60 mss/year.** Query with published clips. Length: 1,500-8,000 words. **Pays $50-400.** Sometimes pays expenses of writers on assignment.

Photos: State availability of photos with submissions. Reviews transparencies, prints. Negotiates payment individually. Captions, identification of subjects required. Buys one-time or reprint rights.

Columns/Departments: Training Perspectives, EMS Viewpoints, Sound Off, 1,000 to 1,800 words.

Tips: "Writers who are unfamiliar with the fire service are very unlikely to place anything with us. Many pieces that we reject are either too unfocused or too abstract. We want articles that help keep fire chiefs well informed and effective at their jobs."

$ $ FIREHOUSE MAGAZINE, Cygnus Business Media, 445 Broad Hollow Rd., Suite 21, Melville NY 11747. (631)845-2700. Fax: (631)845-7109. E-mail: peter@firehouse.com. Website: www.firehouse.com. Editor-in-Chief: Harvey Eisner. **Contact:** Peter Matthews, editorial assitant. **85% freelance written.** Works with a small number of new/unpublished writers each year. Monthly magazine. "*Firehouse* covers major fires nationwide, controversial issues and trends in the fire service, the latest firefighting equipment and methods of firefighting, historical fires, firefighting history and memorabilia. Fire-related books, fire safety education, hazardous materials incidents and the emergency medical services are also covered." Estab. 1976. Circ. 127,000. Pays on publication. Byline given. Exclusive submissions only. Accepts queries by mail, e-mail, fax, phone. Sample copy for 9×12 SAE with 7 first-class stamps. Writer's guidelines free or on website.

Nonfiction: Book excerpts (of recent books on fire, EMS and hazardous materials); historical/nostalgic (great fires in history, fire collectibles, the fire service of yesteryear); how-to (fight certain kinds of fires, buy and maintain equipment, run a fire department); technical (on almost any phase of firefighting, techniques, equipment, training, administration); trends (controversies in the fire service). No profiles of people or departments that are not unusual or innovative, reports of nonmajor fires, articles not slanted toward firefighters' interests. No poetry. **Buys 100 mss/year.** Query with or without published clips. Length: 500-3,000 words. **Pays $50-400 for assigned articles; $50-300 for unsolicited articles.**

Photos: Send photos with query or ms. Pays $15-45 for b&w prints; $20-200 for transparencies and color prints. Cannot accept negatives. Captions and identification of subjects required.

Columns/Departments: Training (effective methods); Book Reviews; Fire Safety (how departments teach fire safety to the public); Communicating (PR, dispatching); Arson (efforts to combat it). **Buys 50 mss/year.** Query or send complete ms. Length: 750-1,000 words. **Pays $100-300.**

Tips: "Have excellent fire service credentials and be able to offer our readers new information. Read the magazine to get a full understanding of the subject matter, the writing style and the readers before sending a query or manuscript. Send photos with manuscript or indicate sources for photos. Be sure to focus articles on firefighters."

$ FOREIGN SERVICE JOURNAL, 2101 E St. NW, Washington DC 20037-2990. (202)944-5511. Fax: (202)338-8244. E-mail: guldin@afsa.org. Website: www.afsa.org. **Contact:** Bob Guldin, editor. **75% freelance written.** Monthly magazine for Foreign Service personnel and others interested in foreign affairs and related subjects. Estab. 1924. Pays on publication. Publishes ms an average of 3 months after acceptance. Byline given. Buys first North American serial rights. Responds in 1 month. Sample copy for $3.50 and 10×12 SAE with 6 first-class stamps. Writer's guidelines for SASE.

Nonfiction: Uses articles on "diplomacy, professional concerns of the State Department and Foreign Service, diplomatic history and articles on Foreign Service experiences. Much of our material is contributed by those working in the profession. Informed outside contributions are welcomed, however." Query. **Buys 15-20 unsolicited mss/year.** Length: 1,000-4,000 words. Offers honoraria.

Fiction: Publishes short stories about foreign service life in the annual August fiction issue.

Tips: "We're more likely to want your article if it has something to do with diplomacy or U.S. foreign policy."

$ $ THE JOURNAL OF SAFE MANAGEMENT OF DISRUPTIVE AND ASSAULTIVE BEHAVIOR, Crisis Prevention Institute, Inc., 3315-K N. 124th St., Brookfield WI 53005. Fax: (262)783-5906. E-mail: info@crisispre vention.com. Website: www.crisisprevention.com. **Contact:** Diana B. Kohn, editor. **20% freelance written.** Quarterly journal covering safe management of disruptive and assaultive behavior. "Our audience is human service and business professionals concerned about workplace violence issues. *CPI* is the world leader in violence prevention training." Estab. 1980. Circ. 12,000. Pays on publication. Publishes ms an average of 6 months after acceptance. Byline given. Offers 50% kill fee. Buys one-time and second serial (reprint) rights. Editorial lead time 6 months. Submit seasonal material 3 months in advance. Responds in 1 month to queries. Sample copy and writer's guidelines free.

Nonfiction: Interview/profile, new product, opinion, personal experience, research. Inquire for editorial calendar. **Buys 5-10 mss/year.** Query. Length: 1,500-3,000 words. **Pays $50-300 for assigned articles; $50-100 for unsolicited mss.** "Each quarterly issue is specifically devoted to one topic. Inquire about topics by e-mail."

Reprints: Accepts previously published submissions.

Tips: "For more information on CPI, please refer to our website."

$ LAW AND ORDER, Hendon Co., 1000 Skokie Blvd., Wilmette IL 60091. (847)256-8555. Fax: (847)256-8574. E-mail: 71171.1344@compuserve.com. **Contact:** Bruce W. Cameron, editor. **90% freelance written.** Prefers to work with published/established writers. Monthly magazine covering the administration and operation of law enforcement agencies, directed to police chiefs and supervisors. Estab. 1952. Circ. 38,000. Pays on publication. Publishes ms an average of 6 months after acceptance. Byline given. Buys first North American serial rights. Submit seasonal material 3 months in advance. Responds in 1 month. Sample copy for 9×12 SAE. Free writer's guidelines.

Nonfiction: General police interest; how-to (do specific police assignments); new product (how applied in police operation); technical (specific police operation). Special issues: Communications (January); Buyers Guide (February); International (March); Community Relations (April); Administration (May); Science & Technology (June); Mobile Patrol (July); Uniforms & Equipment (August); Weapons (September); Investigations (November); Training (December). No articles dealing with courts (legal field) or convicted prisoners. No nostalgic, financial, travel or recreational material. **Buys 150 mss/year.** Length: 2,000-3,000 words. Query; no simultaneous queries. **Pays 15¢/word for professional writers; 10¢/word for others.**

Photos: Send photos with ms. Reviews transparencies and prints. Identification of subjects required. Buys all rights.

Tips: "*L&O* is a respected magazine that provides up-to-date information that police chiefs can use. Writers must know their subject as it applies to this field. Case histories are well received. We are upgrading editorial quality—stories *must* show some understanding of the law enforcement field. A frequent mistake is not getting photographs to accompany article."

N $ $ LAW ENFORCEMENT TECHNOLOGY, Cygnus Publishing, Inc. & Affiliates, P.O. Box 803, 1233 Janesville Ave., Fort Atkinson WI 53538-0803. (920)563-1726. Fax: (920)563-1702. E-mail: Ronnie.Paynter@cygnuspu bs.com. **Editor:** Ronnie Paynter. **50% freelance written.** Monthly magazine covering police management and technology. Estab. 1974. Circ. 35,000. Pays on publication. Publishes ms an average of 6 months after acceptance. Byline given. Offers 25% kill fee. Buys first North American serial rights. Editorial lead time 6 months. Submit seasonal material 6 months in advance. Responds in 1 month to queries; 2 months to mss. Sample copy for SAE with 6 first-class stamps. Writer's guidelines for #10 SASE.

Nonfiction: Book excerpts, how-to, humor, interview/profile, photo feature, police management and training. **Buys 15 mss/year.** Query. Length: 800-1,800 words. **Pays $75-400 for assigned articles.**

Reprints: Send typed ms with rights for sale noted and information about when and where the article previously appeared. Payment negotiable.

Photos: Send photos with submission. Reviews contact sheets, transparencies, 5×7 or 8×10 prints. Offers no additional payment for photos accepted with ms. Captions required. Buys one-time rights.

Fiction: Adventure, condensed novels, historical, humorous, mystery, novel excerpts, slice-of-life vignettes, suspense, (all must be police oriented). Buys 4 mss/year. Send complete ms. Length: 1,000-2,000 words. **Pays $150-400.**

Tips: "Writer should have background in police work or currently work for a police agency. Most of our articles are technical or supervisory in nature. Please query first after looking at a sample copy."

N $ $ NATIONAL FIRE & RESCUE, SpecComm International, Inc., 3000 Highwoods Blvd., Suite 300, Raleigh NC 27604. (919)872-5040. Fax: (919)876-6531. E-mail: editor@nfrmag.com. Website: www.nfrmag.com. **Contact:** Phil Powell, managing editor. **80% freelance written.** "*National Fire & Rescue* is a bimonthly magazine devoted to informing the nation's fire and rescue services, with special emphasis on fire departments serving communities of less than 25,000. It is the *Popular Science* for fire and rescue with easy-to-understand information on science, technology and training." Estab. 1980. Circ. 35,000. Pays on publication. Publishes ms an average of 5 months after acceptance.

Byline given. Offers 50% kill fee. Buys first North American serial rights. Editorial lead time 2 months. Submit seasonal material 3 months in advance. Accepts simultaneous submissions. Responds in 1 month. Sample copy for $6. Call for writer's guidelines.

Nonfiction: Book excerpts, how-to, humor, inspirational, interview/profile, new product, personal experience, photo feature. No pieces marketing specific products or services. **Buys 40 mss/year.** Query with published clips. Length: 600-2,000 words. **Pays $100-350 for assigned articles; $100-200 for unsolicited articles.** Pays expenses of writers on assignment.

Photos: State availability of photos with submission. Offers $35-150/photo. Identification of subjects required. Buys one-time rights.

Columns/Departments: Leadership (management); Training; Special Operations, all 800 words. **Buys 16 mss/year.** Send complete ms. **Pays $100-150.**

Tips: "Discuss your story ideas with the editor."

N **$ $ $ $ NFPA JOURNAL**, National Fire Protection Association, P.O. Box 9101, Quincy MA 02269-9101. Fax: (617)984-7090. E-mail: nfpajournal@nfpa.org. Website: www.nfpa.org. Executive Editor: Jenna Padula. Managing Editor: Denise Laitinen. **Contact:** Liz MacDonald, secretary. **40% freelance written.** Bimonthly magazine covering fire safety, fire science, fire engineering. "The *NFPA Journal*, the official journal of the NFPA, reaches all of the association's various fire safety professionals. Covering major topics in fire protection and suppression, the bimonthly *Journal* carries investigation reports; special NFPA statistical studies on large-loss and multiple-death fires, fire fighter deaths and injuries, and other annual reports; articles on fire protection advances and public education; and information of interest to NFPA members. Fire fighting techniques and fire department management are also covered." Estab. 1969. Circ. 66,000. **Pays on acceptance.** Publishes ms an average of 1 year after acceptance. Byline given. Buys all rights. Editorial lead time 6 months. Accepts queries by mail, e-mail, fax, phone. Responds in 2 weeks. Sample copy and writer's guidelines free (call or e-mail).

Nonfiction: Technical. No fiction or human interest. **Buys 10 mss/year.** Query. Length: 2,000-5,000 words. **Pays $800-3,000.**

Tips: "Query or call us. We appreciate and value quality writers who can provide well-written material on technical subjects related to fire safety and prevention."

$ $ 9-1-1 MAGAZINE, Official Publications, Inc., 18201 Weston Place, Tustin CA 92780-2251. (714)544-7776. Fax: (714)838-9233. E-mail: publisher@9-1-1magazine.com. Website: www.9-1-1magazine.com. **Contact:** Randall Larson, editor. **85% freelance written.** Bimonthly magazine for knowledgeable emergency communications profession-als and those associated with this respected profession. "*9-1-1 Magazine* is published to provide information valuable to all those interested in this exciting and rewarding profession." Estab. 1947. Circ. 13,000. Pays on publication. Publishes ms an average of 2 months after acceptance. Byline given. Offers 20% kill fee. Buys one-time and second serial (reprint) rights. Submit seasonal material well in advance. Accepts queries by mail, e-mail, fax. Accepts simultaneous submissions. Responds in 2 months to queries; 3 months to mss. Sample copy for 9×12 SAE with 5 first-class stamps. Writer's guidelines for #10 SASE.

The online version of this magazine contains material not found in the print version.

Nonfiction: Incident report, new product, photo feature, technical. **Buys 20-30 mss/year.** Query with SASE. "We prefer queries, but will look at manuscripts on speculation. Most positive responses to queries are considered on spec, but occasionally we will make assignments." Length: 1,000-2,500 words. **Pays $100-300 for unsolicited articles.**

Photos: Send photos with submission. Reviews color transparencies and prints. Offers $25-100/interior, $300/cover. Captions and identification of subjects required. Buys one-time rights.

Fillers: Cartoons. **Buys 10/year. Pays $25.**

Tips: "What we don't need are 'my first call' articles, or photography of a less-than-excellent quality. We seldom use poetry or fiction. *9-1-1 Magazine* is published for a knowledgeable, upscale professional. Our primary considerations in selecting material are: quality, appropriateness of material, brevity, knowledge of our readership, accuracy, accompanying photography, originality, wit and humor, a clear direction and vision, and proper use of the language."

$ $ $ PLANNING, American Planning Association, 122 S. Michigan Ave., Suite 1600, Chicago IL 60603. (312)431-9100. Fax: (312)431-9985. E-mail: slewis@planning.org. Website: www.planning.org. **Contact:** Sylvia Lewis, editor. **25% freelance written.** Monthly magazine emphasizing urban planning for adult, college-educated readers who are regional and urban planners in city, state or federal agencies or in private business or university faculty or students. Estab. 1972. Circ. 30,000. Pays on publication. Publishes ms an average of 2 months after acceptance. Buys all rights. Byline given. Accepts queries by mail, e-mail, fax. Responds in 2 months. Sample copy and writer's guidelines for 9×12 SAE with 5 first-class stamps.

Nonfiction: Exposé (on government or business, but topics related to planning, housing, land use, zoning); general interest (trend stories on cities, land use, government); how-to (successful government or citizen efforts in planning, innovations, concepts that have been applied); technical (detailed articles on the nitty-gritty of planning, zoning, transpor-tation but no footnotes or mathematical models). Also needs news stories up to 500 words. "It's best to query with a fairly detailed, one-page letter. We'll consider any article that's well written and relevant to our audience. Articles have a better chance if they are timely and related to planning and land use and if they appeal to a national audience. All articles should be written in magazine feature style." **Buys 2 features and 1 news story/issue.** Length: 500-2,000 words. **Pays $150-1,000.** "We pay freelance writers and photographers only, not planners."

Photos: "We prefer that authors supply their own photos, but we sometimes take our own or arrange for them in other ways." State availability of photos. Pays $100 minimum for 8×10 matte or glossy prints and $300 for 4-color cover photos. Captions required. Buys one-time rights.

\$ \$ POLICE AND SECURITY NEWS, DAYS Communications, Inc., 15 W. Thatcher Rd., Quakertown PA 18951-2503. (215)538-1240. Fax: (215)538-1208. E-mail: P&SN@netcarrier.com. **Contact:** James Devery, editor. **40% freelance written.** Bimonthly tabloid on public law enforcement and private security. "Our publication is designed to provide educational and entertaining information directed toward management level. Technical information written for the expert in a manner that the non-expert can understand." Estab. 1984. Circ. 21,000. Pays on publication. Publishes ms an average of 2 months after acceptance. Byline given. Buys first North American serial rights. Accepts simultaneous submissions. Accepts queries by: mail, e-mail, fax, phone. Sample copy and writer's guidelines for 9×12 SAE with $1.93 postage.
Nonfiction: Al Menear, articles editor. Exposé, historical/nostalgic, how-to, humor, interview/profile, opinion, personal experience, photo feature, technical. **Buys 12 mss/year.** Query. Length: 200-4,000 words. **Pays 10¢/word.** Sometimes pays in trade-out of services.
Reprints: Accepts previously published submissions. Send photocopy of article or short story or typed ms with rights for sale noted and information about when and where the article previously appeared.
Photos: State availability of photos with submission. Reviews 3×5 prints. Offers $10-50/photo. Buys one-time rights.
Fillers: Facts, newsbreaks, short humor. **Buys 6 mss/year.** Length: 200-2,000 words. **Pays 10¢/word.**

\$ POLICE TIMES, American Federation of Police & Concerned Citizens, Inc., 3801 Biscayne Blvd., Miami FL 33137. (305)573-0070. Fax: (305)573-9819. **Contact:** Jim Gordon, executive editor. **80% freelance written.** Eager to work with new/unpublished writers. Quarterly magazine covering "law enforcement (general topics) for men and women engaged in law enforcement and private security, and citizens who are law and order concerned." Circ. 55,000. **Pays on acceptance.** Publishes ms an average of 6 months after acceptance. Byline given. Buys second serial (reprint) rights. Submit seasonal material 4 months in advance. Accepts queries by mail, e-mail, fax. Accepts simultaneous submissions. Sample copy for $2.50 and 9×12 SAE with 3 first-class stamps. Writer's guidelines for #10 SASE.
Nonfiction: Book excerpts; essays (on police science); exposé (police corruption); general interest; historical/nostalgic; how-to; humor; interview/profile; new product; personal experience (with police); photo feature; technical—all police-related. "We produce a special edition on police killed in the line of duty. It is mailed May 15 so copy must arrive six months in advance. Photos required." No anti-police materials. **Buys 50 mss/year.** Send complete ms. Length: 200-4,000 words. **Pays $25-100.** Payment includes right to publish on organization's website.
Reprints: Accepts previously published submissions.
Photos: Send photos with submission. Reviews 5×6 prints. Offers $5-25/photo. Identification of subjects required. Buys all rights.
Columns/Departments: Legal Cases (lawsuits involving police actions); New Products (new items related to police services); Awards (police heroism acts). **Buys variable number of mss/year.** Send complete ms. Length: 200-1,000 words. **Pays $5-25.**
Fillers: Anecdotes, facts, newsbreaks, cartoons, short humor. **Buys 100 mss/year.** Length: 50-100 words. **Pays $5-10.** Fillers are usually humorous stories about police officer and citizen situations. Special stories on police cases, public corruptions, etc., are most open to freelancers.

N \$ \$ THE PUBLIC PURCHASER, The Journal of the Procurement Professional, Congressional Quarterly Inc., 1100 Connecticut Ave., Suite 1100, Washington DC 20036. (202)862-8802. Fax: (202)862-0032. E-mail: plemov@governing.com. Website: www.publicpurchaser.com. **Contact:** Penelope Lemor, editor. **50% freelance written.** Bimonthly magazine covering government purchasing of goods and services. "We Write for government employees involved in buying goods and services for federal, state and local governments, overseeing contracts and managing contracting." Estab. 1998. Circ. 25,000. Pays on publication. Publishes ms an average of 2 months after acceptance. Byline given. Offers 25% kill fee. Buys first rights. Editorial lead time 3 months. Submit seasonal material 3 months in advance. Accepts queries by mail, e-mail, fax. Responds in 2 months. Sample copy free. Writer's guidelines free.
Nonfiction: How-to deal with purchasing problems, interview/profile, personal experience, technical. No consumer-oriented stories. **Buys 5-6 mss/year.** Length: 1,500-2,500 words. **Pays $500-800.** Sometimes pays expenses of writers on assignment.
Photos: State availability of photos with submission. Offers no additional payment for photos accepted with ms. Identification of subjects required. Buys one-time rights.

\$ \$ TRANSACTION/SOCIETY, Bldg. 4051, Rutgers University, New Brunswick NJ 08903. (732)445-2280 ext. 83. Fax: (732)445-3138. E-mail: horowitz@transaction.pub. Website: www.transactionpub.com. **Contact:** Irving Louis Horowitz, editor. Publisher: Jonathan B. Imber. **10% freelance written.** Prefers to work with published/established writers. Bimonthly magazine for social scientists (policymakers with training in sociology, political issues and economics). Estab. 1962. Circ. 45,000. Pays on publication. Buys all rights. Byline given. Publishes ms an average of 6 months after acceptance. Responds in 3 months. Sample copy and writer's guidelines for 9×12 SAE with 5 first-class stamps.

Nonfiction: Andrew McIntosh, managing editor. "Articles of wide interest in areas of specific interest to the social science community. Must have an awareness of problems and issues in education, population and urbanization that are not widely reported. Articles on overpopulation, terrorism, international organizations. No general think pieces." Query. Payment for assigned articles only; *no payment for unsolicited articles.*

Photos: Douglas Harper, photo editor. Pays $200 for photographic essays done on assignment or upon publication.

Tips: "Submit an article on a thoroughly unique subject, written with good literary quality. Present new ideas and research findings in a readable and useful manner. A frequent mistake is writing to satisfy a journal, rather than the intrinsic requirements of the story itself. Avoid posturing and editorializing."

GROCERIES & FOOD PRODUCTS

In this section are publications for grocers, food wholesalers, processors, warehouse owners, caterers, institutional managers and suppliers of grocery store equipment. See the section on Confectionery & Snack Foods for bakery and candy industry magazines.

$ $ CANADIAN GROCER, Maclean-Hunter Ltd., Maclean Hunter Building, 777 Bay St., Toronto, Ontario M5W 1A7 Canada. (416)596-5772. Fax: (416)593-3162. E-mail: gcondon@mhpublishing.com. Website: www.mhbizlink.com/grocer. Managing Editor: Denise Foote. **Contact:**Julia Drake, editor. **20% freelance written.** Prefers to work with published/established writers. Monthly magazine about supermarketing and food retailing for Canadian chain and independent food store managers, owners, buyers, executives, food brokers, food processors and manufacturers. Estab. 1886. Circ. 19,500. **Pays on acceptance.** Publishes an average of 2 months after acceptance. Byline given. Buys first Canadian rights. Submit seasonal material 2 months in advance. Responds in 2 months. Sample copy for $6.

Nonfiction: Interview (Canadian trendsetters in marketing, finance or food distribution); technical (store operations, equipment and finance); news features on supermarkets. "Freelancers should be well versed on the supermarket industry. We don't want unsolicited material. Writers with business and/or finance expertise are preferred. Know the retail food industry and be able to write concisely and accurately on subjects relevant to our readers: food store managers, senior corporate executives, etc. A good example of an article would be 'How a dairy case realignment increased profits while reducing prices, inventory and stock-outs.' " Query with published clips. No phone queries please. **Pays 35¢/word.** Pays expenses of writers on assignment.

Reprints: Send typed ms with rights for sale noted and information about when and where the article previously appeared. Pays 50% of amount paid for an original article.

Photos: State availability of photos. Pays $10-25 for prints or slides. Captions preferred. Buys one-time rights.

Tips: "Suitable writers will be familiar with sales per square foot, merchandising mixes and efficient consumer response."

$ $ $ DISTRIBUTION CHANNELS, AWMA's Magazine for Candy, Tobacco, Grocery and General Merchandise Marketers, American Wholesale Marketers Association, 1128 16th St. NW, Washington DC 20036. (202)463-2124. Fax: (202)467-0559. E-mail: jillk@awmanet.org. Website: www.awmanet.org. **Contact:** Jill Kosko, editor-in-chief. **75% freelance written.** Magazine published 10 times/year. "We cover trends in candy, tobacco, groceries, beverages, snacks and other product categories found in convenience stores, grocery stores and drugstores, plus distribution topics. Contributors should have prior experience writing about the food, retail and/or distribution industries. Editorial includes a mix of columns, departments and features (2-6 pages). We also cover AWMA programs." Estab. 1948. Circ. 10,000. **Pays on acceptance.** Publishes ms an average of 2 months after acceptance. Byline given. Editorial lead time 4 months. Accepts queries by: mail, e-mail, fax.

Nonfiction: How-to, technical, industry trends; also profiles of distribution firms. No comics, jokes, poems or other fillers. **Buys 80 mss/year.** Query with published clips. Feature length: 1,200-3,600 words. **Pays $200-1,200, generally.** Sometimes pays industry members who author articles. Pays expenses of writers on assignment.

Photos: Authors must provide artwork (with captions) with articles.

Tips: "We're looking for reliable, accurate freelancers with whom we can establish a long-term working relationship. We need writers who understand this industry. We accept very few articles on speculation. Most are assigned. To consider a new writer for an assignment, we must first receive his or her résumé, at least two writing samples and references. We only work with full-time freelancers."

$ $ $ $ FOOD PRODUCT DESIGN MAGAZINE, Weeks Publishing, 3400 Dundee Rd., Suite 100, Northbrook IL 60062. (947)559-0385. Fax: (847)559-0389. E-mail: weeksfpd@aol.com. **Contact:** Lynn Kuntz, editor. **50% freelance written.** Monthly trade magazine covering food processing industry. "The magazine written for food technologists by food technologists. No foodservice/restaurant, consumer or recipe development." Estab. 1991. Circ. 30,000. Pays on publication. Publishes ms an average of 2 months after acceptance. Byline given. Offers 50% kill fee. Buys one-time rights, all rights or makes work-for-hire assignments. Editorial lead time 4 months. No queries all feature assignments. Sample copy for 9×12 SASE and 5 first-class stamps.

Nonfiction: Technical. **Buys 30 mss/year.** Query with published clips. Length: 1,500-7,000 words. **Pays $100-1,500.** Sometimes pays expenses of writers on assignments.

Reprints: Accepts previously published submissions depending on where it was published.

Photos: State availability of photos with submission. Reviews transparencies and prints. Offers no additional payment for photos accepted with ms. Captions required. Buys rights depending on photo.

Columns and Departments: Pays $100-150.

Tips: "If you haven't worked in the food industry in Research & Development, or QA/QC, don't bother to call us. If you can't communicate technical information in a way that is clear, easy-to-understand and well organized, don't bother to call us. While perfect grammar is not expected, good grammar and organization is."

⟨N⟩ $ $ FOODSERVICE DIRECTOR, Bill Communications, 355 Park Ave. S., New York NY 10010. (212)592-6533. Fax: (212)592-6539. **Contact:** Walter J. Schruntek, editor. Executive Editor, James Pond. Feature Editor: Karen Weisberg. News Editor: Amanda Chater. **20% freelance written.** Monthly tabloid on non-commercial foodservice operations for operators of kitchens and dining halls in schools, colleges, hospitals/health care, office and plant cafeterias, military, airline/transportation, correctional institutions. Estab. 1988. Circ. 45,000. Pays on publication. Byline sometimes given. Offers 25% kill fee. Buys all rights. Submit seasonal material 3 months in advance. Accepts simultaneous submissions. Free sample copy.

Nonfiction: How-to, interview/profile. **Buys 60-70 mss/year.** Query with published clips. Length: 700-900 words. **Pays $250-500.** Sometimes pays the expenses of writers on assignment.

Photos: Send photos with submission. Reviews transparencies. Offers no additional payment for photos accepted with ms. Identification of subjects required. Buys all rights.

Columns/Departments: Equipment (case studies of kitchen/serving equipment in use), 700-900 words; Food (specific category studies per publication calendar), 750-900 words. **Buys 20-30 mss/year.** Query. **Pays $250-500.**

$ $ FRESH CUT MAGAZINE, The Magazine for Value-added Produce, Columbia Publishing, P.O. Box 9036, Yakima WA 98909-0036. (509)248-2452. Fax: (509)248-4056. E-mail: ken@freshcut.com. **Contact:** Ken Hodge, editor. **40% freelance written.** Monthly magazine covering minimally processed fresh fruits and vegetables, packaged salads, etc. "We want informative articles about processing produce. We also want stories about how these products are sold at retail, in restaurants, etc." Estab. 1993. Circ. 9,500. Pays on publication. Publishes ms an average of 2 months after acceptance. Byline given. Buys all rights. Editorial lead time 2 months. Submit seasonal material 3 months in advance. Accepts queries by mail, e-mail, fax, phone. Responds in 1 month to queries; 2 months to mss. Sample copy for 9 × 12 SASE. Writer's guidelines for #10 SASE.

Nonfiction: Historical/nostalgic, new product, opinion, technical. **Buys 2-4 mss/year.** Query with published clips. Special issues: Retail (May 99); Foodservice (February 99); Packaging Technology (December). **Pays $5/column inch for assigned articles; $75-125 for unsolicited articles.**

Reprints: Send tearsheet of article with rights for sale noted and information about when and where the article previously appeared. Pays 50% of aount paid for an original article.

Photos: Send photos with submission. Reviews transparencies. Offers no additional payment for photos accepted with ms. Identification of subjects required. Buys one-time rights.

Columns/Departments: Packaging; Food Safety; Processing/engineering. **Buys 20 mss/year.** Query. **Pays $125-200.**

Fillers: Facts. Length: 300 words maximum. **Pays $25-50.**

$ $ HEALTH PRODUCTS BUSINESS, CYGNUS Business Media Inc., 445 Broad Hollow Rd., Suite 21, Melville NY 11747. (631)845-2700. Fax: (631)845-2723. Website: www.healthproductsbusiness.com. **Contact:** Susan Alberto, editor. **70% freelance written.** Monthly trade magazine covering health foods. "The business magazine for natural products retailers." Estab. 1953. Circ. 16,000. Pays on publication. Publishes ms an average of 3 months after acceptance. Byline given. Buys first North American serial rights. Editorial lead time 4 months. Submit seasonal material 3 months in advance. Accepts queries by mail, fax. Sample copy for $3. Writer's guidelines free.

Nonfiction: Store profile. Query. **Pays $200-250.**

Photos: State availability of photos with submissions.

Tips: "We are always looking for well-written store profiles with a lot of detailed information, but new writers should always query first to receive writer's guidelines and other directions. We prefer writers with industry experience/interest."

$ $ PRODUCE MERCHANDISING, Vance Publishing Corp., 10901 W. 84th Terrace, Lenexa KS 66214. (913)438-8700. Fax: (913)438-0691. E-mail: jkresin@producemerchandising.com. Website: www.producemerchandising.com. Editor: Elaine Symanski. **Contact:** Janice M. Kresin, managing editor. **33% freelance written.** Monthly. "The magazine's editorial purpose is to provide information about promotions, merchandising and operations in the form of ideas and examples. *Produce Merchandising* is the only monthly journal on the market that is dedicated solely to produce merchandising information for retailers." Circ. 12,000. **Pays on acceptance.** Publishes ms an average of 3 months after acceptance. Byline given. Buys all rights. Editorial lead time 2-3 months. Accepts queries by: mail. Responds in 2 weeks to queries. Sample copy free. Writer's guidelines for #10 SASE.

Nonfiction: How-to, interview/profile, new product, photo feature, technical (contact the managing editor for a specific assignment). **Buys 48 mss/year.** Query with published clips. Length: 1,000-1,500 words. **Pays $200-600.** Pays expenses of writers on assignment.

Photos: State availability of photos with submission or send photos with submission. Reviews color slides and 3×5 or larger prints. Offers no additional payment for photos accepted with ms. Captions, model releases and identification of subjects required. Buys all rights.

Columns/Departments: Contact managing editor for a specific assignment. **Buys 30 mss/year.** Query with published clips. **Pays $200-450.**

Tips: "Send in clips and contact the managing editor with specific story ideas. Story topics are typically outlined up to a year in advance."

$ $ PRODUCE NEWS, 2185 Lemoine Ave., Fort Lee NJ 07024-6003. Fax: (201)592-0809. E-mail: prod2185@aol.com. **Contact:** John Groh, managing editor. Editor: Gordon Hochberg. **10% freelance written.** Works with a small number of new/unpublished writers each year. Weekly magazine for commercial growers and shippers, receivers and distributors of fresh fruits and vegetables, including chain store produce buyers and merchandisers. Estab. 1897. Pays on publication. Publishes ms an average of 2 weeks after acceptance. Deadline is 2 weeks before Thursday press day. Accepts queries by mail, e-mail, fax. Responds in 1 month. Sample copy and writer's guidelines for 10×13 SAE with 4 first-class stamps.

Nonfiction: News stories (about the produce industry). Buys profiles, spot news, coverage of successful business operations and articles on merchandising techniques. Query. **Pays $1/column inch minimum.** Sometimes pays expenses of writers on assignment.

Photos: Black and white glossies or color prints. Pays $8-10/photo.

Tips: "Stories should be trade-oriented, not consumer-oriented. As our circulation grows in the next year, we are interested in stories and news articles from all fresh-fruit-growing areas of the country."

N $ $ THE SERVER FOODSERVICE NEWS, Group Publications, Ltd., 157 S. 26th St., Pittsburgh PA 15203. (412)381-5029. Fax: (412)381-5205. E-mail: editorial@theservernews.com. Website: www.theservernews.com. **Contact:** Lori Monahan, editor. **10-15% freelance written.** Monthly tabloid covering food service, restaurant industry, C-stores, supermarket chains. "*The Server Foodservice News* is edited for the food service industry. It is edited for restaurant personnel, liquor licenses, chain operation, personnel, etc. *The Server* provides pertinent data about new products, trends and other vital information. *The Server Foodservice News* is a national publication with a regional focus and a local flair. Michigan, Ohio, West Virginia, Maryland, Delaware, New Jersey, New York, and Pennsylvania are states that are covered with editorial features, current events and the people who make them happen in the foodservice industry." Estab. 1979. Circ. 25,000. Pays on publication. Byline given. Buys all rights. Accepts queries by mail, e-mail, fax. Sample copy for $3.95. Writer's guidelines free.

Nonfiction: General interest, historical/nostalgic, interview/profile, new product. No restaurant reviews. Query. Length: 400-800 words. **Pays 10-15¢/word.**

Photos: Send photos with submission. Reviews contact sheets. Offers $5/photo. Captions, model releases and identification of subjects required. Buys all rights.

■ The online version contains materials not found in the print edition. Contact: Lori Monahan.

N TODAY'S GROCER, F.G. Publications, Inc., P.O. Box 430760, South Miami FL 33243-0760. (305)441-1138. Fax: (305)661-6720. **Contact:** Dennis Kane, editor. **3% freelance written.** "*Today's Grocer* is a monthly trade newspaper, serving members of the food industry in Alabama, Florida, Georgia, Louisiana, Mississippi, North Carolina and South Carolina. Our publication is edited for chain and independent food store owners and operators as well as members of allied industries." Estab. 1956. Circ. 19,500. **Pays on acceptance.** Byline given. Buys all rights. Submit seasonal material 3 months in advance. Responds in 2 months. Sample copy for 10×14 SAE with 10 first-class stamps.

Nonfiction: Book excerpts, exposé, general interest, humor, features on supermarkets and their owners, new product, new equipment, photo feature, video. **Buys variable number of mss/year.** Query with or without published clips or send complete ms. **Pay varies.**

Photos: State availability of photos with submission. Terms for payment on photos "included in terms of payment for assignment."

Tips: "We prefer feature articles on new stores (grand openings, etc.), store owners, operators; food manufacturers, brokers, wholesalers, distributors, etc. We also publish a section in Spanish and also welcome the above types of materials in Spanish (Cuban)."

N WHOLE FOODS, Informing and Educating Natural Product Retailers, WFC, Inc., 3000 Hadley Rd., South Plainfield NJ 07080-1117. Fax: (908)769-1171. E-mail: user886276@aol.com. Website: www.wfcinc.com. **Contact:** Alan Richman, editor. Assistant Editor: Caroline Krastek. Monthly magazine covering the natural products industry. "Virtually all stories should in some way enable retailers of natural products (i.e., health foods, vitamins, herbs, etc.) to do their work more easily or more effectively." Estab. 1978. Circ. 14,000. Pays on publication. Publishes ms an average of 9 months after acceptance. Byline given. Buys all rights. Editorial lead time 3 months. Submit seasonal material 6-12 months in advance. Responds in 3 weeks to queries; 2 months to mss. Sample copy for $10.

Nonfiction: Book excerpts, essays, how-to, interview/profile. All must relate to natural products industry. **Buys 2-5 mss/year.** Query with published clips. Length: 1,000-3,000 words. **Pay varies.** "Some stories are published and payment is in the form of an author's box."

Photos: State availability of photos with submission. Offers no additional payment for photos accepted with ms. Captions, model releases and identification of subjects required. Photo credits are available when requested. Buys all rights.

HARDWARE

Journals for general and specialized hardware wholesalers and retailers are listed in this section. Journals specializing in hardware for a certain trade, such as plumbing or automotive supplies, are classified with other publications for that trade.

N **$ $ $ FASTENING**, McGuire Fasteners, Inc., 293 Hopewell Dr., Powell OH 43065-9350. (614)848-3232. Fax: (614)848-5045. E-mail: mmcguire@mail.fastening.com. Website: www.fastening.com. **Contact:** Mike McGuire, editor/publisher. **50% freelance written.** "Quarterly magazine seeking to advance fastener design and application engineering. Readership is made up of OEM design/application engineers and PAS." Estab. 1995. Circ. 28,000. Pays 30 days after publication. Publishes ms an average of 1 month after acceptance. Byline given. Buys all rights. Editorial lead time 2 months. Submit seasonal material 2 months in advance. Accepts simultaneous submissions. Sample copy and writer's guidelines free.
Nonfiction: How-to (fastening), new product. "No company profiles that are ads." **Buys 10-12 mss/year.** Query with published clips. Length: 500-2,000 words. **Pays $200-800.** Pays expenses of writers on assignment.
Photos: Send photos with submission. Reviews negatives. Offers no additional payment for photos accepted with ms. Captions, model releases and identification of subjects required. Buys all rights.
Columns/Departments: Case Study (history of applications), 800-1,000 words; Company Profile, 1,800-2,000 words with photos. **Buys 8-10 mss/year.** Query with published clips. **Pays $200-800.**
Fillers: Anecdotes. **Buys 2-3/year.** Length: 200-600 words. **Pays $50-100.**
Tips: *Fastening* seeks technical articles in regards to fasteners and applications.

HOME FURNISHINGS & HOUSEHOLD GOODS

Readers rely on these publications to learn more about new products and trends in the home furnishings and appliance trade. Magazines for consumers interested in home furnishings are listed in the Consumer Home & Garden section.

$ HOME LIGHTING & ACCESSORIES, P.O. Box 2147, Clifton NJ 07015. (973)779-1600. Fax: (973)779-3242. Website: www.homelighting.com. **Contact:** Linda Longo, editor. **25% freelance written.** Prefers to work with published/established writers. Monthly magazine for lighting showrooms/department stores. Estab. 1923. Circ. 10,000. Pays on publication. Publishes ms an average of 6 months after acceptance. Buys first rights. Submit seasonal material 6 months in advance. Accepts queries by: mail, e-mail. Responds in 2 months. Sample copy for 9×12 SAE with 4 first-class stamps.
Nonfiction: Interview (with lighting retailers); personal experience (as a businessperson involved with lighting); profile (of a successful lighting retailer/lamp buyer); technical (concerning lighting or lighting design). Special issues: Outdoor (March); tribute to Tiffanies (August). **Buys less than 10 mss/year.** Query.
Reprints: Send tearsheet of article and information about when and where the article previously appeared.
Photos: State availability of photos with query. Offers no additional payment for 5×7 or 8×10 b&w glossy prints. Captions required.
Tips: "Have a unique perspective on retailing lamps and lighting fixtures. We often use freelancers located in a part of the country where we'd like to profile a specific business or person. Anyone who has published an article dealing with any aspect of home furnishings will have high priority."

HOSPITALS, NURSING & NURSING HOMES

In this section are journals for medical and nonmedical nursing home personnel, clinical and hospital staffs and medical laboratory technicians and managers. Journals publishing technical material on medical research and information for physicians in private practice are listed in the Medical category.

N **AMERICAN JOURNAL OF NURSING**, 345 Hudson St., 16th Floor, New York NY 10014. (212)886-1200. Fax: (212)886-1206. E-mail: ajn@lww.com. Website: www.nursingcenter.com. Editorial Director: Fran Rosen. **Contact:** Thomas Schwarz, clinical director. Eager to work with new/unpublished nurse-authors. Monthly magazine covering nursing and health care. Estab. 1900. Circ. 325,000. Pays on publication. Publishes ms an average of 8 months after acceptance. Byline given. Responds in 2 weeks to queries, 10 weeks to mss. Sample copy and writer's guidelines free.

Nonfiction: Practical, hands-on clinical articles of interest to hospital staff nurses; professional issues; personal experience. Now accepting poetry, short stories and personal essays. Nurse-authors only accepted for publication.

Photos: Reviews b&w and color transparencies and prints. Model release and identification of subjects required. Now accepting paintings, drawings, photos of sculpture and other artwork. Buys variable rights.

Tips: "Everything we publish is written by nurses and edited inhouse. *American Journal of Nursing* is particularly interested in articles dealing with current health issues and implications for nursing care. Send an outline with query letter."

N **$** **JOURNAL OF CHRISTIAN NURSING, Nurses Christian Fellowship**, a division of InterVarsity Christian Fellowship, 430 E. Plaza Dr., Westmont IL 60559. (630)734-4030. Fax: (630)734-4200. E-mail: jcn@ivpress.com. Website: www.ncf-jcn.org. Editor: Judith Allen Shelly. **Contact:** Melodee Yohe, managing editor. **30% freelance written.** Quarterly professional journal/magazine covering spiritual care, ethics, crosscultural issues, etc. "Our target audience is Christian nurses in the U.S., and we are nondenominational in character. We are prolife in position. We strive to help Christian nurses view nursing practice through the eyes of faith. Articles must be relevant to Christian nursing and consistent with our statement of faith." Estab. 1984. Circ. 10,000. Pays on publication. Publishes ms 1-2 years after acceptance. Byline given unless subject matter requires pseudonym. Offers 50% kill fee. Not copyrighted. Buys first rights; second serial (reprint) rights, rarely; all rights, only multiple-authored case studies. Editorial lead time up to 2 years. Submit seasonal material 1 year in advance. Accepts queries by mail, e-mail, fax. Responds in 1 month to queries; 2 months to mss. Sample copy for $5 and SAE with 4 first-class stamps. Writers guidelines for #10 SASE.

Nonfiction: How-to, humor, inspirational, interview/profile, opinion, personal experience, photo feature, religious. All must be appropriate for Christian nurses. Poetry not accepted. No purely academic articles, subjects not appropriate for Christian nurses, devotionals, Bible study. **Buys 20-30 mss/year.** Send complete ms. Length: 6-12 pages (typed, double spaced). **Pays $25-80** and up to 8 complimentary copies.

Reprints: Occasionally accepts previously published submissions. Send tearsheet or photocopy of article and information about when and where the article previously appeared.

Photos: State availability of photos or send photos with submission. Offers no additional payment for photos accepted with ms. Model releases and identification of subjects required. No rights purchased; all photos returned.

Columns/Departments: Book Reviews (Resources). No payment for Book Reviews.

Tips: "Unless an author is a nurse, it will be unlikely that he/she will have an article accepted—unless they write a very interesting story about a nurse who is involved in creative ministry with a strong faith dimension."

$ $ $ LONG TERM CARE, The Ontario Nursing Home Assoc., 345 Renfrew Dr., Suite 102-202, Markham, Ontario L3R 9S9 Canada. (905)470-8995. Fax: (905)470-9595. E-mail: heather_runtz@sympatico.ca. Assistant Editor: Tracey Ann Schofield. **Contact:** Heather Lang-Runtz, editor. Quarterly magazine covering "practical articles of interest to staff working in a long term care setting (nursing home, retirement home); professional issues; information must be applicable to a Canadian setting; focus should be on staff and for resident well-being." Estab. 1990. Circ. 4,600. Pays on publication. Publishes ms an average of 4 months after acceptance. Byline given. Buys one-time rights. Editorial lead time 3 months. Submit seasonal material 5 months in advance. Responds in 3 months. Sample copy and writer's guidelines free.

Nonfiction: General interest, how-to (practical, of use to long term care practitioners), inspirational, interview/profile. No product-oriented articles. Query with published clips. Length: 800-1,500 words. **Pays up to $1,000.**

Reprints: Send photocopy of article or short story and information about when and where the article previously appeared. Pays 50% of amount paid for an original article.

Photos: Send photos with submission. Reviews contact sheets, 5×5 prints. Offers no additional payment for photos accepted with ms. Captions, model releases required. Buys one-time rights.

Columns/Departments: Resident Health (nursing, rehabilitation, food services); Resident Life (activities, volunteers, spiritual and pastoral care); Environment (housekeeping, laundry, maintenance, safety, landscape and architecture, staff health and well being); all 800 words. Query with published clips. **Pays up to $1,000.**

Tips: "Articles must be positive, upbeat, and contain helpful information that staff and managers working in the long term care field can use. Focus should be on staff and resident well being. Articles that highlight new ways of doing things are particularly useful. Please call the editor to discuss ideas. Must be applicable to Canadian settings."

$ $ $ NURSING SPECTRUM, Florida Edition, Nursing Spectrum, 1001 W. Cypress Creek Rd., Ste. 300, Ft. Lauderdale FL 33309. (954)776-1455. Fax: (954)776-1456. E-mail: pclass@nursingspectrum.com. Website: www.nursingspectrum.com. **Contact:** Phyllis Class, RN, editor. **80% freelance written.** Biweekly magazine covering registered nursing. "We support and recognize registered nurses. All articles must have at least one RN in byline. We prefer articles that feature nurses in our region, but articles of interest to all nurses are welcome, too. We look for substantive, yet readable articles. Our bottom line—timely, relevant, and compelling articles that support nurses and help them excel in their clinical and professional careers." Estab. 1991. Circ. 53,928. **Pays on acceptance.** Byline given. Buys all rights. Editorial lead time 3 months. Submit seasonal material 4 months in advance. Accepts queries by mail, e-mail, fax, phone. Responds in 1 month to queries; 4 months to mss. Sample copy free. Writer's guidelines free.

➤ "Having an original idea is paramount and the first step in writing an article. We are looking for success stories, nurses to be proud of, and progress that is helping patients. If you and your colleagues have dealt with and learned from a thorny issue, tell us how. What is new in your field? Consider your audience: all RNs, well-educated, and of various specialties. Will they relate, be inspired, learn something? The best articles are both interesting and informative."

Nonfiction: General interest, how-to (career management), humor, interview/profile, personal experience, photo feature. Special issues: Critical Care, nursing management. "No articles that do not have at least one RN on the byline." **Buys 125+ mss/year.** Length: 700-1,200 words. **Pays $50-800 maximum for assigned articles.** Sometimes pays expenses of writers on assignment (limit agreed upon in advance).

Photos: Negotiates payment individually. Captions required, model releases and identification of subjects required. Buys one-time all rights.

Columns/Departments: Management Perspectives (nurse managers); Advanced Practice (advanced practice nurses); Humor Infusion (cartoon, amusing anecdotes); Career Fitness (career tips, types of careers). **Buys 75 mss/year.** Query with published clips. **Pays $50-120.**

Tips: "Write in 'magazine' style—as if talking to another RN. Use to-the-point, active language. Narrow your focus. Topics such as 'The Future of Nursing' or 'Dealing With Change' are too broad and non-specific. Use informative but catchy titles and subheads (we can help with this). If quoting others be sure quotes are meaningful and add substance to the piece. To add validity, you may use statistics and up-to-date references. Try to paint a complete picture, using pros and cons. Be both positive and realistic."

$ $ $ NURSING SPECTRUM, Greater Philadelphia/Tri-State edition, Nursing Spectrum, 2002 Renaissance Blvd., Suite 250, King of Prussia PA 19406. (610)292-8000. Fax: (610)292-0179. E-mail: rhess@nursingspectrum. com. Website: www.nursingspectrum.com. **Contact:** Cheryl Barrett, RN, editor. **80% freelance written.** Biweekly magazine covering registered nursing. "We support and recognize registered nurses. All articles must have at least one RN in byline. We prefer articles that feature nurses in our region, but articles of interest to all nurses are welcome, too. We look for substantive, yet readable articles. Our bottom line—timely, relevant, and compelling articles that support nurses and help them excel in their clinical and professional careers." Estab. 1992. Circ. 59,553.

• See *Nursing Spectrum, Florida Edition.*

$ $ $ NURSING SPECTRUM, New England edition, Nursing Spectrum, 1050 Waltham St., Suite 510, Waltham MA 02421. (781)863-2300. Fax: (781)863-6277. E-mail: jborgatti@nursingspectrum.com. Website: www.nursi ngspectrum.com. **Contact:** Joan Borgatti, RN, editor. **80% freelance written.** Biweekly magazine covering registered nursing. "We support and recognize registered nurses. All articles must have at least one RN in byline. We prefer articles that feature nurses in our region, but articles of interest to all nurses are welcome, too. We look for substantive, yet readable articles. Our bottom line—timely, relevant, and compelling articles that support nurses and help them excel in their clinical and professional careers." Estab. 1997. Circ. 114,555. Accepts queries by mail, e-mail, fax, phone.

• See *Nursing Spectrum, Florida Edition.*

▣ The online version carries original content not bound in the print edition. Contact: Cynthia Saver, RN, editor.

$ $ $ NURSING SPECTRUM, Washington, DC/Baltimore edition, Nursing Spectrum, 803 W. Broad St., Ste. 500, Falls Church VA 22046. (703)237-6515. Fax: (703)237-6299. E-mail: lesposito@nursingspectrum.com. Website: www.nursingspectrum.com. **Contact:** Cindy Saver, RN, editor. **80% freelance written.** Trade journal published biweekly covering registered nursing. "We support and recognize registered nurses. All articles must have at least one RN in byline. We prefer articles that feature nurses in our region, but articles of interest to all nurses are welcome, too. We look for substantive, yet readable articles. Our bottom line—timely, relevant, and compelling articles that support nurses and help them excel in their clinical and professional careers." Estab. 1990. Circ. 55,000.

• See *Nursing Spectrum, Florida Edition.*

Ⓝ $ $ NURSING2000, Springhouse Corporation, 1111 Bethlehem Pike, P.O. Box 908, Springhouse PA 19477-0908. (215)646-8700. Fax: (215)653-0826. E-mail: nursing@springnet.com. Website: www.springnet.com. **Contact:** Pat Wolf, editorial dept. administrator. Vice President Journals and Continuing Education: Patricia Nornhold. Managing Editor: Jane Benner. **100% freelance written by nurses.** Monthly magazine "written by nurses for nurses; we look for practical advice for the direct caregiver that reflects the author's experience. Estab. 1971. Circ. over 300,000. Pays on publication. Publishes ms an average of 18 months after acceptance. Byline given. Offers 50% kill fee. Buys all rights. Submit seasonal material 8 months in advance. "Any form acceptable, but focus must be nursing." Responds in 2 weeks to queries; 3 months to mss. Sample copy for $4. Call 800-346-7844, ext. 300 for free writers' guidelines. Guidelines also available on our website.

Nonfiction: Book excerpts, exposé, how-to (specifically as applies to nursing field), inspirational, new product, opinion, personal experience, photo feature. No articles from patients' point of view, poetry, etc. **Buys 100 mss/year.** Query. Length: 100 words minimum. **Pays $50-400 for feature articles.**

Reprints: Send photocopy of article and information about when and where the article previously appeared. Pays 50% of amount paid for an original article.

Photos: State availability of photos with submission. Offers no additional payment for photos accepted with ms. Model releases required. Buys all rights.

Tips: "Basically, *Nursing2000* is a how-to journal, full of hands-on, practical articles. We look for the voice of experience from authors and for articles that help our readers deal with problems they face. We're always interested in taking a look at manuscripts that fall into the following categories: clinical articles, drug articles, charting/documentation, emotional problems, legal problems, ethical dilemmas, difficult ot challenging cases."

HOTELS, MOTELS, CLUBS, RESORTS & RESTAURANTS

These publications offer trade tips and advice to hotel, club, resort and restaurant managers, owners and operators. Journals for manufacturers and distributors of bar and beverage supplies are listed in the Beverages & Bottling section.

$ $ BARTENDER MAGAZINE, Foley Publishing, P.O. Box 158, Liberty Corner NJ 07938. (908)766-6006. Fax: (908)766-6607. E-mail: barmag@aol.com. Website: www.bartender.com. Editor: Jaclyn M. Wilson. **Contact:** Jackie Foley, publisher. Quarterly magazine emphasizing liquor and bartending for bartenders, tavern owners and owners of restaurants with full-service liquor licenses. **100% freelance written.** Prefers to work with published/established writers; eager to work with new/unpublished writers. Circ. 147,000. Pays on publication. Publishes ms an average of 3 months after acceptance. Buys first serial, first North American serial, one-time, second serial (reprint), all or simultaneous US rights. Byline given. Submit seasonal material 3 months in advance. Accepts simultaneous submissions. Responds in 2 months. Sample copies for 9×12 SAE with 4 first-class stamps.
Nonfiction: General interest, historical, how-to, humor, interview (with famous bartenders or ex-bartenders), new products, nostalgia, personal experience, unique bars, opinion, new techniques, new drinking trends, photo feature, profile, travel, bar sports or bar magic tricks. Special issue: 1999 Calendar and Daily Cocktail Recipe Guide. Send complete ms and SASE. Length: 100-1,000 words.
Reprints: Send tearsheet of article and information about when and where the article previously appeared. Pays 25% of amount paid for an original article.
Photos: Send photos with ms. Pays $7.50-50 for 8×10 b&w glossy prints; $10-75 for 8×10 color glossy prints. Caption preferred and model release required.
Columns/Departments: Bar of the Month; Bartender of the Month; Drink of the Month; Creative Cocktails; Bar Sports; Quiz; Bar Art; Wine Cellar; Tips from the Top (from prominent figures in the liquor industry); One For The Road (travel); Collectors (bar or liquor-related items); Photo Essays. Query by mail only with SASE. Length: 200-1,000 words. **Pays $50-200.**
Fillers: Clippings, jokes, gags, anecdotes, short humor, newsbreaks, anything relating to bartending and the liquor industry. Length: 25-100 words. **Pays $5-25.**
Tips: "To break in, absolutely make sure that your work will be of interest to all bartenders across the country. Your style of writing should reflect the audience you are addressing. The most frequent mistake made by writers in completing an article for us is using the wrong subject."

$ $ CHEF, The Food Magazine for Professionals, Talcott Communications Corp., 20 N. Wacker Dr., Suite 1865, Chicago IL 60606. (312)849-2220. Fax: (312)849-2174. E-mail: chefmag@aol.com. Website: www.chefmagazine.com. **Contact:** Brent T. Frei, editor-in-chief. Managing Editor: Kate Harrigan. **40% freelance written.** Monthly magazine covering chefs in all food-service segments. "*Chef* is the one magazine that communicates food production to a commercial, professional audience in a meaningful way." Circ. 50,000. **Pays on acceptance.** Byline given. Offers 10% kill fee. Buys first North American serial rights and second serial (reprint) rights. Editorial lead time 2 months. Submit seasonal material 4 months in advance. Accepts queries by: mail, e-mail, fax. Responds in 3 weeks to queries; 2 months to mss. Sample copy free. Writer's guidelines free.
Nonfiction: Book excerpts, essays, expose, general interest, historical/nostalgic, how-to (create a dish or perform a technique), humor, inspirational, interview/profile, new product, opinion, personal experience, photo feature, technical, travel. **Buys 24-36 mss/year.** Query. Length: 750-1,500 words. **Pays $250-500.** Sometimes pays expenses of writers on assignment.
Reprints: Accepts previously published submissions.
Photos: State availability of photos with submission. Reviews transparencies. Negotiates payment individually. Captions, identification of subjects required. Buys one-time rights.
Columns/Departments: Taste (modern versions of classic dishes), 1,000-1,200 words; Dish (professional chef profiles), 1,000-1,200 words; Savor (themed recipes), 1,000-1,500 words; Spin (menu trends), 750-1,250 words. **Buys 12-18 mss/year.** Query. **Pays $250-400.**
Tips: "Know food and apply it to the business of chefs. Always query first, *after* you've read our magazine. Tell us how your idea can be used by our readers to enhance their businesses in some way."

$ $ CHRISTIAN CAMP & CONFERENCE JOURNAL, Christian Camping International U.S.A., P.O. Box 62189, Colorado Springs CO 80962-2189. (719)260-9400. Fax: (719)260-6398. E-mail: dridings@cciusa.org. Website: www.cciusa.org. **Contact:** Dean Ridings, editor. **75% freelance written.** Prefers to work with published/established writers. Bimonthly magazine emphasizing the broad scope of organized camping with emphasis on Christian camping.

"All who work in youth camps and adult conferences read our magazine for inspiration and to get practical help in ways to serve in their operations." Estab. 1963. Circ. 7,500. Pays on publication. Publishes ms an average of 4 months after acceptance. Byline given. Rights negotiable. Submit seasonal material queries 6 months in advance. Query by mail, e-mail. Responds in 1 month. Sample copy for $2.25 plus 9×12 SASE. Writer's guidelines for #10 SASE.

Nonfiction: General interest (trends in organized camping in general, Christian camping in particular); how-to (anything involved with organized camping from motivating staff, to programming, to record keeping, to camper follow-up); inspirational (interested in profiles and practical applications of Scriptural principles to everyday situations in camping); interview (with movers and shakers in Christian camping; submit a list of basic questions first); and opinion (letter to the editor). **Buys 20-30 mss/year.** Query required. Length: 500-3,000 words. **Pays 12¢/word.**

Reprints: Send photocopy of article and information about when and where the article previously appeared. Pays 50% of amount paid for an original article.

Photos: Send photos with ms. Pays $25-250 for 5×7 b&w contact sheet or print; price negotiable for 35mm color transparencies. Rights negotiable.

Tips: "The most frequent mistake made by writers is that they send articles unrelated to our readers. Ask for our publication guidelines first. Profiles/interviews are the best bet for freelancers."

N **CLUB MANAGEMENT, The Resource for Successful Club Operations**, Finan Publishing Company, 107 W. Pacific Ave., St. Louis MO 63119-2323. (314)961-6644. Fax: (314)961-4809. E-mail: teri@finan.com. Website: www.club-mgmt.com. **Contact:** Teri Finan, managing editor. Bimonthly magazine covering club management, private club market, hospitality industry. Estab. 1925. Circ. 16,702. **Pays on acceptance.** Publishes ms an average of 2 months after acceptance. Buys first North American serial rights, electronic rights. Accepts queries by mail, e-mail, fax.

Nonfiction: Buys 100 mss/year. Query with published clips. Length: 1,500-2,500 words.

Photos: State availability of photos with submission.

Columns/Departments: Sports (private club sports: golf, tennis, yachting, fitness, etc.)

Tips: "We don't accept blind submissions. Please submit a résumé and clips of writer's work."

$ $ **FLORIDA HOTEL & MOTEL JOURNAL, The Official Publication of the Florida Hotel & Motel Association**, Accommodations, Inc., P.O. Box 1529, Tallahassee FL 32302-1529. (850)224-2888. Fax: (850)222-FHMA. Editor: Mrs. Jayleen Woods. **Contact:** Janet Litherland, associate editor. **10% freelance written.** Prefers to work with published/established writers. Magazine published 10 times/year for managers in every licensed hotel, motel and resort in Florida. Estab. 1978. Circ. 8,000. Pays on publication. Publishes ms an average of 2 months after acceptance. Byline given. Offers $50 kill fee. Buys all rights and makes work-for-hire assignments. Submit seasonal material 2 months in advance. Responds in 6 weeks. Sample copy and writer's guidelines for 9×12 SAE with 4 first-class stamps.

Nonfiction: General interest (business, finance, taxes); historical/nostalgic (old Florida hotel reminiscences); how-to (improve management, housekeeping procedures, guest services, security and coping with common hotel problems); humor (hotel-related anecdotes); inspirational (succeeding where others have failed); interview/profile (of unusual hotel personalities); new product (industry-related and non-brand preferential); photo feature (queries only); technical (emerging patterns of hotel accounting, telephone systems, etc.); travel (transportation and tourism trends only—no scenics or site visits); property renovations and maintenance techniques. "We would like to run more humorous anecdotes on hotel happenings than we're presently receiving." **Buys 10-12 mss/year.** Query by mail only with proposed topic and clips of published work. Length: 750-2,500 words. **Pays $75-250** "depending on type of article and amount of research."

Reprints: Send tearsheet of article and information about when and where the article previously appeared. **Pays flat fee of $55.**

Photos: Send photos with ms. Captions, model release and identification of subjects required.

Tips: "We prefer feature stories on properties or personalities holding current membership in the Florida Hotel and Motel Association. We're open to articles showing how hotel management copes with energy systems, repairs, renovations, new guest needs and expectations. The writer may have a better chance of breaking in at our publication with short articles and fillers because the better a writer is at the art of condensation, the better his/her feature articles are likely to be."

N **FOOD & SERVICE NEWS**, (formerly Food & Service), Texas Restaurant Association, P.O. Box 1429, Austin TX 78767-1429. (512)457-4100 (in Texas, 1-800-395-2872). Fax: (512)472-2777. E-mail: fsninfo@tramail.org. Website: www.txrestaurant.org. **Contact:** Michael Lyttel, editor. **40% freelance written.** Magazine published 12 times/year providing business solutions to Texas restaurant owners and operators. Estab. 1941. Circ. 6,000. Pays on publication. Responds in 1 month. Byline given. Buys first rights. Pay varies. Sample copy and editorial calendar for 11×14 SAE with 6 first-class stamps. Writer's guidelines free.

Nonfiction: Features must provide business solutions to problems in the restaurant and food service industries. Topics vary but always have business slant; usually particular to Texas. No restaurant critiques, human interest stories or seasonal copy. Quote members of the Texas Restaurant Association; substantiate with facts and examples. Query in writing. Length: 1,500-2,500 words, features; shorter articles sometimes used; product releases, 300-word maximum. **Pay varies.**

Reprints: Send tearsheet or photocopy of article and information about when and where the article previously appeared. Pays 50% of amount paid for an original article.

Photos: State availability of photos, but photos usually assigned.

$ $HOSPITALITY TECHNOLOGY, Edgell Communications, 10 W. Hanover Ave., Suite 107, Randolph NJ 07869. (973)895-3300. Fax: (973)895-9363. E-mail: erubinstein@edgellmail.com. Website: www.htmagazine.com. **Contact:** Ed Rubinstein, senior editor. **85% freelance written.** Bimonthly magazine covering technology in foodservice and lodging. "We are a bimonthly magazine covering the computer technology used in foodservice and lodging. Our readers are the end-users, who have varying degrees of technical knowledge." Estab. 1996. Circ. 12,500. **Pays on acceptance.** Publishes ms an average of 1 month after acceptance. Byline given. Offers 100% kill fee. Makes work-for-hire assignments. Editorial lead time 2 months. Submit seasonal material 3 months in advance. Accepts queries by mail, e-mail, fax, phone. Responds in 2 weeks. Sample copy and writer's guidelines free.

Nonfiction: How-to, interview/profile, new product, technical. "Our Buyer's Guide includes editorial material on market overviews. Published in November of each year." No unsolicited mss. **Buys 30 mss/year.** Query with published clips. Length: 1,000-1,200 words. **Pays $600.** Sometimes pays expenses of writers on assignment.

Photos: State availability of or send photos with submission. Reviews contact sheets, negatives, 5×7 transparencies and 5×7 prints. Offers no additional payment for photos accepted with ms or offers $100-200/photo, or negotiates payment individually. Captions required, model releases and identification of subjects required. Buys one-time rights **or** all rights.

N $ $RESORT MANAGEMENT & OPERATIONS, The Resort Resource, Finan Publishing Company, 107 W. Pacific Ave., St. Louis MO 63119-2323. (314)961-6644. Fax: (314)961-4809. E-mail: teri@finan.com. Website: www.resort-mgmt.com. **Contact:** Teri Finan, managing editor. Bimonthly magazine covering resort management and operations, hospitality industry. Estab. 1998. Circ. 15,116. **Pays on acceptance.** Buys first North American serial rights and electronic rights. Accepts queries by mail, e-mail, fax.

Nonfiction: "Do not send blind submissions. We assign pieces based on queries and clips *only*." **Buys 100 mss/year.** Query with published clips. Length: 1,500-2,500 words. **Pays $151-750/article.**

Tips: "Plese submit résumé and clips of writer's work."

$ $VACATION INDUSTRY REVIEW, Interval International, P.O. Box 431920, South Miami FL 33243-1920 or 6262 Sunset Dr., Miami FL 33143. (305)666-1861, ext. 7022. Fax: (305)668-3408. E-mail: gleposky@interval-intl.com. Website: www.resortdeveloper.com. **Contact:** George Leposky, editor. **30% freelance written.** Prefers to work with published/established writers. Bimonthly magazine covering leisure lodgings (timeshare resorts, fractionals, and other types of vacation-ownership properties). "The readership of *VIR* consists of people who develop, finance, market, sell, and manage timeshare resorts and mixed-use projects such as hotels, resorts, and second-home communities with a vacation-ownership component; and suppliers of products and services to the vacation-ownership industry." Estab. 1982. Circ. 15,000. Pays on publication. Publishes ms an average of 6 months after acceptance. Byline given. Buys all rights and makes work-for-hire assignments. Submit seasonal material at least 6 months in advance. Query by mail, e-mail, fax, phone. Responds in 1 month. Writer's guidelines for #10 SASE. Sample copy for 9×12 SAE and 3 first-class stamps or on website.

   O— Break in by writing a letter to tell us about yourself, and enclosing two or three (non-returnable) samples of published work that show you can meet our specialized needs.

Nonfiction: Essays, how-to, interview/profile, new product, opinion, personal experience, technical, travel. No consumer travel, hotel, or non-vacation real-estate material. **Buys 6-8 mss/year.** Query with published clips. Length: 1,000-1,500 words. **Pays 30¢/word.** Pays expenses of writers on assignment, if previously arranged.

Photos: Send photos with submission. Reviews 35mm transparencies, 5×7 or larger prints. Generally offers no additional payment for photos accepted with ms. Captions and identification of subjects required. Buys one-time rights.

Tips: "We *do not* want consumer-oriented destination travel articles. We want articles about the business aspects of the vacation-ownership industry: entrepreneurship, project financing, design and construction, sales and marketing, operations, management—anything that will help our readers plan, build, sell and run a quality vacation-ownership property that satisfies the owners/guests and earns a profit for the developer and marketer. We're also interested in owner associations at vacation-ownership resorts (not residential condos). Requires electronic submissions. Query for details."

INDUSTRIAL OPERATIONS

Industrial plant managers, executives, distributors and buyers read these journals. Some industrial management journals are also listed under the names of specific industries. Publications for industrial supervisors are listed in Management & Supervision.

ALWAYS CHECK the most recent copy of a magazine for the address and editor's name before you send in a query or manuscript.

N **$ $ CANADIAN PLASTICS**, Southam Publishing Magazine Group, 1450 Don Mills Rd, Don Mills Ontario M1E 1E8, Canada. (416)442-2290. Fax: (416)442-2213. E-mail: mlegault@corporate.southam.com. **Contact:** Michael LeGault, editor. Associate Editor: Cindy Macdonald. **20% freelance written.** Monthly trade magazine, tabloid covering plastics. "*Canadian Plastics Magazine* reports on and interprets development in plastics markets and technologies for plastics processors and end-users based in Canada." Estab. 1942. Circ. 11,000. Pays on publication. Publishes ms an average of 3 months after acceptance. Byline sometimes given. Offers 25% kill fee. Editorial lead time 2 months. Submit seasonal material 4 months in advance. Responds in 2 weeks to queries; 1 month to mss. Sample copy free.
Nonfiction: Technical, industry news (Canada only). **Buys 6 mss/year.** Query with published clips. Length: 400-1600 words. **Pays $120-350.** Sometimes pays expenses of writers on assignment.
Reprints: Accepts previously published submissions.
Photos: State availability of photos with submission.
Columns and Departments: Pays $100-300.
Tips: "Give the editor a call."

N **INDUSTRIAL FABRIC PRODUCTS REVIEW**, Industrial Fabrics Association International, 1801 County Rd. B W, Roseville MN 55113-4052. (651)222-2508. Fax: (651)225-6966. E-mail: gdnordstrom@ifai.com. Website: www.ifai.com. **Contact:** Galynn Nordstrom, editorial director. **50% staff- and industry-written.** Monthly magazine covering industrial textiles and products made from them for company owners, salespeople and researchers in a variety of industrial textile areas. Estab. 1915. Circ. 11,000. Pays on publication. Publishes ms an average of 2 months after acceptance. Byline given. Buys all rights. Accepts queries by mail, e-mail, fax, phone. Responds in 1 month.
Nonfiction: Technical, marketing and other topics related to any aspect of industrial fabric industry from fiber to finished fabric product. Special issues: new products, new fabrics and equipment. No historical or apparel-oriented articles. **Buys 8-10 mss/year.** Query with phone number. Length: 1,200-3,000 words.
Tips: "We encourage freelancers to learn our industry and make regular, solicited contributions to the magazine. We do not buy photography."

$ $ $ PHOTONICS SPECTRA, Laurin Publishing Co., Inc., 2 South St., Pittsfield MA 01201. (413)499-0514. Fax: (413)442-3180. E-mail: editorial@laurin.com. Website: www.Photonics.com. **Contact:** Aaron J. Hand, managing editor. **10% freelance written.** Monthly magazine covering photonics: optics, lasers, fiber optics and imaging. "*Photonics Spectra* covers the application of photonic technologies to solving real-world problems. Its audience includes developers, manufacturers and users of these technologies and its mission is to provide a dialogue among those groups to enable the proliferation of light-based technologies." Estab. 1960. Circ. 98,000. Pays on publication. Publishes ms an average of 1 month after acceptance. Byline given. Buys all rights. Editorial lead time 2 months. Accepts queries by: mail, e-mail, fax. Responds in 1 week to queries; 1 month to mss. Sample copy for $2.
Nonfiction: Opinion, technical. No technical journal-type articles with footnotes and lots of technical jargon and acronyms. Query with published clips. Length: 200-2,000 words. **Pays 50¢/word.** Sometimes pays expenses of writers on assignment.
Photos: Send photos with submission. Offers no additional payment for photos accepted with ms. Captions required. Buys negotiable rights.
Columns/Departments: Columns that detail trends in photonics technology and business/marketing, 700-1,000 words; news, 300-400 words; Accent on Applications (case studies of how specific companies used photonics to solve a problem), 400 words. **Buys 12-30 mss/year.** Query with published clips. **Pays 50¢/word.**
Fillers: Newsbreaks, short humor. Must be related to photonics technology, preferably "newsy." **Buys 12-30/year.** Length: 200 words. **Pays 50¢/word.**
Tips: "Reading the magazine is the key! Every *Photonics Spectra* article must answer four questions: 1. What problem does this technology solve? 2. How is it better than previous solutions? 3. What are some other potential commercial applications? 4. Where does the technology go from here? Articles must be written in *English,* not in engineering-ese. We also prefer regular over occasional contributors."

$ $ WAREHOUSING MANAGEMENT, Cahners Business Information, 275 Washington St., Newton MA 02458. (617)558-4569. E-mail: mlearolimpi@cabners.com. Website: www.warehousemag.com. **Contact:** John Johnson, chief editor. **40% freelance written.** Controlled-circulation business/trade magazine published 10 times/year covering warehousing, distribution centers, inventory. "*Warehousing Management* is a 10 times-a-year glossy national magazine read by managers of warehouses and distribution centers. We focus on lively, well-written articles telling our readers how they can achieve maximum facility productivity and efficiency. Heavy management components. We cover technology, too." Estab. 1994. Circ. 50,000. Pays on acceptance (allow 4 to 6 weeks for invoice processing). Publishes ms an average of 1 month after acceptance. Byline given. Editorial lead time 3 months. Accepts queries by: mail, e-mail, fax. Sample copy and writer's guidelines free.
Nonfiction: How-to, new product, technical. Special issues: State-of-the-Industry Report, Peak Performer, Salary and Wage survey, Warehouse of the Year. Doesn't want to see anything that doesn't deal with our topic—warehousing. Articles must be on-point, how-to pieces for managers. No general-interest profiles or interviews. **Buys 25 mss/year.** Query with published clips. **Pays $300-650.**
Photos: State availability of photos with submission. Reviews negatives, transparencies or prints. Offers no additional payment for photos accepted with ms. Captions and identification of subjects required. Buys all rights.
   ■ The online magazine carries original content not found in the print edition and includes writer's guidelines.

Tips: "Learn a little about warehousing, distributors and write well. We typically don't accept specific article queries, but welcome introductory letters from journalists to whom we can assign articles. But authors are welcome to request an editorial calendar and develop article queries from it."

$ $WEIGHING & MEASUREMENT, Key Markets Publishing Co., P.O. Box 270, Roscoe IL 61073-0270. (815)636-7739. Fax: (815)636-7741. E-mail: dwam34@inwave.com. Website: www.weighingandmeasurement.com. **Contact:** David M. Mathieu, editor. Bimonthly magazine for users of industrial scales. Estab. 1914. Circ. 12,000. **Pays on acceptance.** Buys all rights. Offers 20% kill fee. Byline given. Accepts queries by: mail, e-mail, fax, phone. Responds in 2 weeks. Sample copy for $2.
Nonfiction: Interview (with presidents of companies); personal opinion (guest editorials on government involvement in business, etc.); profile (about users of weighing and measurement equipment); product reviews; technical. **Buys 15 mss/year.** Query on technical articles; submit complete ms for general interest material. Length: 1,000-2,500 words. **Pays $175-300.**

INFORMATION SYSTEMS

These publications give computer professionals more data about their field. Consumer computer publications are listed under Personal Computers.

N $ $ $ $BOARDWATCH MAGAZINE, Penton Media, Inc., 13949 W. Colfax Avd., Suite 250, Golden CO 80401. Fax: (303)235-9502. E-mail: terickson@boardwatch.com. Website: www.boardwatch.com. Editor: Bill McCarthy. **Contact:** Todd Erickson, managing editor. **70% freelance written.** Monthly magazine covering Internet/information technology/networking. Estab. 1987. Circ. 29,000. **Pays on acceptance.** Publishes ms an average of 2 months after acceptance. Byline given. Offers $300 kill fee. Buys first North American serial rights, second serial (reprint) rights, electronic rights, and first worldwide rights. Editorial lead time 2 months. Submit seasonal material 2 months in advance. Accepts queries by e-mail. Accepts simultaneous submissions. Sample copy online at website. Writer's guidelines free.
Nonfiction: Exposé, interview/profile, new product, opinion, personal experience, technical. "No general interest internet—this is a trade publication for technical readers." **Buys 12 mss/year.** Query. Length: 800-3,000 words. **Pays $800-3,000.**
Photos: State availability of photos with submission. Negotiates payment individually. Identification of subjects required. Buys one-time rights.
Columns/Departments: "Columns on all issues of internet access providers and telecommunications are welcome." **Buys 180 mss/year.** Query. **Pays $100-500.**
Tips: "Submissions by e-mail are best; technical knowledge and experience in providing access or telecommunications very helpful."

N $ $ $CARD TECHNOLOGY, Tracking the future of card systems and applications, Faulkner & Gray, 3005 Wacker Dr., 18th Floor, Chicago IL 60606. Fax: (312)913-1340. E-mail: don.davis@faulknergray.com. Website: www.cardtech.faulknergray.com. Managing Editor: Dan Balaban. **Contact:** Don Davis, editor. **20% freelance written.** Monthly magazine covering smart cards. "*Card Technology* covers all uses of smart cards worldwide, as well as other advanced plastic card technologies. Aimed at senior management, not technical staff. Our readership is global, as is our focus." Estab. 1996. Circ. 25,000. **Pays on acceptance.** Byline given. Offers negotiable kill fee. Buys all rights. Editorial lead time 1 month. Submit seasonal material 2 months in advance. Accepts queries by mail, e-mail. Responds in 1 week to queries; 1 month to mss. Sample copy free.
Nonfiction: Interview/profile, opinion. **Buys 15 mss/year.** Query with published clips. Length: 2,000-4,000 words. **Pays $500-1,500.** Sometimes pays expenses of writers on assignment.
Photos: State availability of photos with submission. Reviews contact sheets, negatives, transparencies, prints. Negotiates payment individually. Identification of subjects required. Rights negotiable.
Tips: "We are especially interested in finding freelancers outside of North America who have experience writing about technology issues for business publications."

N $ $ $ $CLEC MAGAZINE, Penton Media, Inc., 13949 W. Colfax Ave., Suite 250, Golden CO 80401. Fax: (303)235-9502. E-mail: terickson@boardwatch.com. Website: www.clecmag.com. Editor: Bill McCarthy. **Contact:** Todd Erickson, managing editor. **70% freelance written.** Monthly magazine covering Internet/information technology/networking. Estab. 1987. Circ. 29,000. **Pays on acceptance.** Publishes ms an average of 2 months after acceptance. Byline given. Offers $300 kill fee. Buys first North American serial rights, second serial (reprint) rights, electronic rights, and first worldwide rights. Editorial lead time 2 months. Submit seasonal material 2 months in advance. Accepts queries by e-mail. Accepts simultaneous submissions. Sample copy online at website. Writer's guidelines free.
Nonfiction: Exposé, interview/profile, new product, opinion, personal experience, technical. "No general interest internet—this is a trade publication for technical readers." **Buys 12 mss/year.** Query. Length: 800-3,000 words. **Pays $800-3,000.**
Photos: State availability of photos with submission. Negotiates payment individually. Identification of subjects required. Buys one-time rights.

Columns/Departments: "Columns on all issues of internet access providers and telecommunications are welcome." **Buys 180 mss/year.** Query. **Pays $100-500.**

Tips: "Submissions by e-mail are best; technical knowledge and experience in providing access or telecommunications very helpful."

N $ $ $ $ COMPUTER CURRENTS, Real World Solutions for Business Computing, Computer Currents Publications, 1250 Ninth St., Berkeley CA 94710. Fax: (510)527-4106. E-mail: editorial@currents.net. Website: www.computercurrents.com. **Contact:** Robert Luhn, editor. Managing Editor: Keri Troutman. **90% freelance written.** Monthly magazine covering business computing. "*Computer Currents* is the 411/911 magazine. It's a source of help and information for business users of all stripes. *Computer Currents* doesn't torture-test 200 modems or devote space to industry chitchat. Instead, it focuses on real-world solutions for PC and Mac business users, showing them how to buy, what to buy, where to buy, and how to use computer products. *Computer Currents* is fundamentally proconsumerist, and we'll go undercover to ferret out sloppy service and scams." Estab. 1983. Circ. 550,000. Pays on publication. Byline given. Offers 20% kill fee. Buys first North American serial rights, electronic rights and second serial (reprint) rights. Editorial lead time 2 months. Submit seasonal material 3 months in advance. Accepts queries by mail, e-mail, fax. Accepts simultaneous submissions. Responds in 1 month to queries; 1 month to mss. Sample copy for $5 or online at website. Writer's guidelines for #10 SASE, online at website or by e-mail.

    O-→ Freelance opportunities are available in three areas: short reviews for our *Previews & Reviews* section, buyers' buides, and feature-length cover stories.

Nonfiction: Exposé, how-to. Also publishes annual gift guide (November). "No opinion, essays, fiction, 'why I hate my PC' pieces." **Buys 50 mss/year.** Length: 250-5,000 words. **Pays $50-2,500.**

Reprints: Accepts previously published submissions.

Photos: State availability of photos with submission. Reviews transparencies. Negotiates payment individually. Captions, model releases, identification of subjects required.

Columns/Departments: Previews & Reviews (hardware, services), 400 words. **Buys 50 mss/year. Pays $500-700.**

Tips: "Have technical and writing experience. Know your topic and have a point of view. Our readers run small businesses, manage midsized firms, and serve as department heads in large corporations. Although our style is informal and lively, every story has to deliver assistance, opinion, and resource information to the reader. Eighty percent of our readers use PCs and Windows 95/98, while the rest use the Mac."

N $ $ COMPUTER GRAPHICS WORLD, PennWell, 98 Spit Brook Rd., Nashua NH 03062-2801. (603)891-9160. Fax: (603)891-0539. E-mail: phill@pennwell.com. Website: www.cgw.com. **Contact:** Phil Lo Piccolo, editor. **25% freelance written.** Monthly magazine. "*Computer Graphics World* specializes in covering computer-aided 3D modeling, animation, and visualization and their uses in engineering, science, and entertainment applications." Estab. 1978. Circ. 70,000. **Pays on acceptance.** Publishes ms an average of 4 months after acceptance. Byline given. Offers 20% kill fee. Buys all rights. Editorial lead time 4 months. Submit seasonal material 3 months in advance. Sample copy free.

Nonfiction: General interest, how-to (how-to create quality models and animations), interview/profile, new product, opinion, technical, user application stories. "We do not want to run articles that are geared to computer programmers. Our focus as a magazine is on users involved in specific applications." **Buys 36 mss/year.** Query with published clips. Length: 1,200-3,000 words. **Pays $500 minimum.** Sometimes pays expenses of writers on assignment.

Columns/Departments: Technology stories (describes innovation and its implication for computer graphics users), 750-1,000 words; Reviews (offers hands-on review of important new products), 750 words; and Application Stories (highlights unique use of the technology by a single user), 800 words. **Buys 36-40 mss/year.** Query with published clips. **Pays $300-500.**

Tips: "Freelance writers will be most successful if they have some familiarity with computers and know how to write from a user's perspective. They do not need to be computer experts, but they do have to understand how to explain the impact of the technology and the applications in which a user is involved. Our technology stories, feature section, and our application story section are quite open to freelancers. The trick to winning acceptance for your story is to have a well-developed idea that highlights a fascinating new trend or development in computer graphics technology or profiles a unique and fascinating use of the technology by a single user or a specific class of users."

$ $ COMPUTING CHANNELS, CompTIA, 450 E. 22nd St., Ste. 230, Lombard IL 60148-6158. (630)268-1818. Fax: (630)268-1384. E-mail: info@comptia.org. Website: www.comptia.org. **Contact:** Kate Nemchausky, editor. **20-30% freelance written.** Monthly magazine format covering the computing industry. "We are dedicated to providing the most accurate and interesting information possible. Our audience consists of computer resellers, manufacturers and distributors." Circ. 7,800. Pays on publication. Publishes ms an average of 2 months after acceptance. Byline given. Offers 50% or $300 kill fee. Editorial lead time 2-3 months. Submit seasonal material 2 months in advance. Accepts queries by mail, e-mail, fax, phone. Accepts simultaneous submissions. Sample copy free. Writer's guidelines free.

Nonfiction: Query.

Photos: Send photos with submission. Reviews 8½×11 transparencies and 5×7 prints, largest. Offers no additional payment for photos accepted with ms. Buys one-time rights.

Tips: "Send us submissions, or simply call and request an editorial calendar, then send submissions. Show that you can write about the computing industry, get the facts you need, and provide sources."

$ $ $ DESKTOP ENGINEERING, Complete Computer Resource for Engineers, Helmers Publishing, 174 Concord St., Peterborough NH 03458. (603)924-9631. Fax: (603)924-4004. E-mail: de-editors@helmers.com. Website: www.deskeng.com. **Contact:** Anthony J. Lockwood, editor. Managing Editor: Vinoy Laughner. **90% freelance written.** Monthly magazine covering microcomputer hardware/software for engineers. Estab. 1995. Circ. 60,000. Pays on publication. Publishes ms an average of 4 months after acceptance. Byline given. Buys all rights. Editorial lead time 3 months. Accepts queries by: mail, e-mail, fax, phone. Responds in 6 weeks to queries; 6 months to mss. Sample copy and writer's guidelines free; editorial calendar on website.

Nonfiction: How-to, new product, technical, reviews. "No fluff." **Buys 120 mss/year.** Query. Length: 750-3,000 words. **Pays 60¢/word for assigned articles.** Negotiates fee for unsolicited articles. Sometimes pays expenses of writers on assignment.

Photos: Send photos with submission. Negotiates payment and rights purchased individually. Captions required.

Columns/Departments: Product Briefs (new products), 50-100 words; Reviews (software, hardware, books), 500-1,500 words. **Buys 30 mss/year.** Query. Pay varies.

    ■ The online magazine carries original content not found in the print edition. Contact: Vinoy Laughner.

Tips: "Call the editor or e-mail him for submission tips."

$ $ $ GAME DEVELOPER, CMP Media Inc., 600 Harrison St., San Francisco CA 94107. (415)905-2200. Fax: (415)905-2228. E-mail: editors@gdmag.com. Website: www.gdmag.com and www.gamasutra.com. Managing Editor: Kimberley Van Hoose. Departments Editor: Jennifer Olsen. **Contact:** Alex Dunne, editorial director **95% freelance written.** Monthly magazine covering computer game development. Estab. 1994. Circ. 30,000. Pays on publication. Publishes ms an average of 3 months after acceptance. Byline given. Buys first North American serial, first, all, and electronic rights. Editorial lead time 3 months. Submit seasonal material 4 months in advance. Accepts queries by e-mail. Sample copy and writer's guidelines free.

Nonfiction: How-to, personal experience, technical. **Buys 50 mss/year.** Query. Length: 3,000-5,000 words. **Pays $150 page.**

Photos: State availability of photos with submission.

    ■ The online magazine carries original content not found in the print edition and includes writer's guidelines. Contact: Alex Dunne, online editor.

Tips: "We're looking for writers who are game developers with published game titles."

N $ $ $ $ GOVERNMENT COMPUTER NEWS, 8601 Georgia Ave., Suite 300, Silver Spring MD 20910. (301)650-2100. Fax: (301)650-2111. E-mail: editor@gen.com. Website: www.gcn.com. **Contact:** Wilson Dizard, state/local; Julie Britt, news or Susan Menke, chief tech editor. Published biweekly for government information technology managers. **Pays on acceptance.** Byline given. Kill fee varies. Buys all rights. Responds in 1 month. Sample copy free. Writer's guidelines for #10 SASE.

Nonfiction: **Buys 30 mss/year.** Query. Length: 700-1,200 words. **Pays $800-2,000.** Pays expenses of writers on assignment.

Columns/Departments: Length: 400-600 words. **Buys 75 mss/year.** Query. **Pays $250-400.** No freelance columns accepted.

Fillers: **Buys 10 mss/year.** Length: 300-500 words. **Pays $250-450.**

Tips: Needs "technical case histories of applications of computers to governmental missions and trends in information technology."

$ $ $ INFORM, The Magazine of Information and Image Management, Association for Information and Image Management, 1100 Wayne Ave., Silver Spring MD 20910. (301)587-8202. Fax: (301)587-5129. E-mail: hduhon@aiim.org. Website: www.aiim.org/inform. **30% freelance written.** Prefers to work with writers with business/high tech experience. Monthly trade magazine on document and information management. "Specifically we feature coverage of the business issues surrounding implementation and use of document and information management technologies." Estab. 1943. Circ. 30,000. Pays on submission. Publishes ms an average of 3 months after acceptance. Byline given. Offers $50 kill fee. Buys first North American serial and second serial (reprint) rights. Accepts simultaneous submissions. Query by mail, e-mail, fax, phone. Sample copy and writer's guidelines free or on website.

Nonfiction: Interview/profile, photo feature, technical. **Buys 10-20 mss/year.** Query. Length: 1,500 words. **Pays 70¢/word.** Sometimes pays expenses of writers on assignment.

Reprints: Send tearsheet, photocopy of article or typed ms with rights for sale noted.

Photos: State availability of photos with submission. Reviews negatives, 4×5 transparencies and prints. Offers no additional payment for photos accepted with ms. Captions, identification of subjects required. Buys all rights.

Columns/Departments: Trends (developments across industry segments); Technology (innovations of specific technology); Management (costs, strategies of managing information); Point/Counterpoint. Query. Length: 500-1,500 words. **Pays $250.**

Fillers: Facts, newsbreaks. Length: 150-500 words. **Pays $50-250.**

Tips: "We would encourage freelancers who have access to our editorial calendar to contact us regarding article ideas, inquiries, etc. Our feature section is the area where the need for quality freelance coverage of our industry is most desirable. The most likely candidate for acceptance is someone who has a proven background in business writing, and/or someone with demonstrated knowledge of high-tech industries as they relate to information management."

$ $ $ $ INFORMATION WEEK, 600 Community Dr., Manhasset NY 11030. (516)562-5000. Fax: (516)562-5036. E-mail: speterso@cmp.com. Website: www.informationweek.com. Editor-in-Chief: Bob Evans. **Contact:** Frances Witkowski, editorial assistant. **20% freelance written.** Weekly magazine for information systems managers. Estab. 1985. Circ. 400,000. **Pays on acceptance.** Publishes ms an average of 1 month after acceptance. Byline given. Offers 25% kill fee. Buys first and non-exclusive serial rights. Accepts simultaneous submissions, if noted. Responds in 1 month. Sample copy free. Writer's guidelines for #10 SASE.

Nonfiction: Book excerpts, how-to, interview/profile, new product, technical, news analysis, company profiles. **Buys 30 mss/year.** Query with published clips. Length: 1,500-4,000 words. **Pays $1.10/word minimum.** Pays expenses of writers on assignment.

Reprints: Considers previously published submissions.

Tips: Needs "feature articles on technology trends—all with a business angle. We look at implementations by users, new products, management issues, intranets, the Internet, web, networks, PCs, objects, workstations, sewers, etc. Our competitors are tabloids—we're better written, more selective, and more analytical."

$ $ $ INTELLIGENT ENTERPRISE, Enterprise Solutions for Business Intelligence, CMP Media Inc., 411 Borel Ave., Suite 100, San Mateo CA 94402. Fax: (650)655-4350. E-mail: iemagazine@cmp.com. Website: www.intelligententerprise.com. **Contact:** Justin Kestelyn, editor in chief. **98% freelance written.** Magazine published 18 times/year covering e-business and business intelligence. "*Intelligent Enterprise* is a new magazine covering the strategies, trends and products for managing enterprise information solutions in a cohesive, coherent infrastructure—what we call the information supply chain. Most of our readers work within or are consultants serving the needs of corporate information systems organizations. Our readers are educated, technically astute, and experienced; they use their knowledge to guide them through a dynamic, market-driven industry. They are exploring business intelligence, data warehousing, knowledge management, multitier client/server, the Internet/intranet, and object technology. Estab. 1998. Circ. 100,000. Pays on publication. Publishes ms an average of 3 months after acceptance. Byline given. Buys all rights. Accepts queries by mail, e-mail, phone. Submit seasonal material 4 months in advance. Sample copy and writer's guidelines online at website.

 ■ The online version of *Intelligent Enterprise* contains material not found in the print edition.

Nonfiction: Technical. **Buys 60 mss/year.** Query. Length: 350-3,000 words. **Pays $0-1,000.** Sometimes pays expenses of writers on assignment.

Tips: "To write for *Intelligent Enterprise*, you must have a minimum of three years field experience. You must also have a working knowledge of theories and techniques beyond your own personal experience (unless you've done absolutely everything there is to do). Be familiar with the magazine in terms of style, content, and editorial focus. *Intelligent Enterprise* readers make the best *Intelligent Enterprise* writers and have enthusiasm for the job."

N $ $ ITrecruitermag.com, Employment opportunities and career news for information technology professionals, Quantum Communications Group, Inc., 1493 Chain Bridge Rd., #100, McLean VA 22101. (703)714-9462. Fax: (708)714-9482. E-mail: articles@itrecruitermag.com. Website: www.itrecruitermag.com. Editor: Loretta W. Prencipe. Senior Editor: Rima Assaker. **Contact:** (by e-mail) articles@itrecruitermag.com. **50% freelance written.** Bimonthly magazine covering information technology recruitment. "*ITrecruitermag.com* is the multimedia source for IT career news and opportunities. Every article must help the IT professional gain an insight into IT work force, career advancement or industry trends." Pays on publication. Publishes ms an average of 2 months after acceptance. Byline given. Kill fee negotiated. Negotiates rights purchased. Editorial lead time 3 months. Submit seasonal material 4 months in advance. Accepts queries by mail, e-mail, fax. Accepts simultaneous submissions. Sample copy and writer's guidelines free.

Nonfiction: Book excerpts, how-to, interview/profile, opinion, technical. "Our sections include: Community Focus; Tech Training; Career Advancement; Money Matters; Management 101; Industry Trends; and News Briefs. No "rehashing of the fact that there is an IT labor shortage. Our readers know that." **Buys approximately 60 mss/year.** Query with published clips. Length: 700-2,100 words. **Pays 30¢/word.** Sometimes pays expenses of writers on assignment.

Reprints: Accepts previously published submissions.

Photos: Send photos with submission. Offers no additional payment for photos accepted with ms. Captions and identification of subjects required.

Columns/Departments: Recruiters' Corner (how-to and advice for technical recruiters and hiring managers). **Buys 6 mss/year.** Query. **Pays 30¢/word.**

Tips: All articles should include quotes from IT professionals—our readers' colleagues. Writing should be clear, crisp, simple, informal and direct. Use active verbs. Each article should answer at least two of the following questions. Does this piece: assist the IT professional in managing his career?; assist the IT professional in managing his staff?; convey cutting-edge IT workforce issues?

$ $ $ JAVA PRO, Fawcette Technical Publications, 209 Hamilton Ave., Palo Alto CA 94301. (650)833-7100. Fax: (650)853-0230. E-mail: java-pro@fawcette.com. Website: www.java-pro.com. Managing Editor: Janaya Reitz. Assistant Editor: Charles Ferrara. **Contact:** Kay Keppler, executive editor. **100% freelance written.** Monthly magazine covering Java computer programming. "*Java Pro* speaks directly to the technical concerns of Java developers. Most of our readers write programs for use by others, and many develop applications for sale. We provide practical, hands-on technical information for Java Programmers to use in their work. Your articles should show readers how to do something they couldn't do before, overcome some problem, or do something better, faster, or more effectively. This holds true whether you're writing feature articles, columns, or product reviews. However, each section goes at the charter somewhat differently, and the format varies accordingly." Estab. 1997. Circ. 35,000. **Pays on acceptance**. Byline given. Offers 33% kill fee. Buys all rights. Editorial lead time 3 months. Accepts queries by mail, e-mail, fax, phone. Writer's guidelines free or on website.

Nonfiction: Book excerpts, how-to, opinion. Does not want to see news. **Buys 100 mss/year.** Query. Length: 1,200-5,000 words. **Pays $850-1,200.** Sometimes pays expenses of writers on assignment.

Photos: State availability of photos with submission.

Columns/Departments: Buys 60 mss/year. Query. **Pays $850-1,050.**

■ The online magazine carries original content not found in the print edition and includes writer's guidelines. **Contact:** Sean Gallagher, online editor.

N $ $ $ JAVA® REPORT, Independent Source for Java Development, 101 Communications LLC, 1250 Broadway, New York NY 10010. (212)268-7766. Fax: (212)268-0516. **Contact:** Dwight Deugo (deugo@scs.carkton.ca), editor-in-chief. Managing Editor: Anna M. Kanson (akanson@sigs.com). **100% freelance written.** Monthly magazine covering technical writing for Java development. Article must satisfy the need of the Java community. Estab. 1996. Circ. 35,000. Pays on publication. Byline given. Offers 50% kill fee. Buys all rights. Editorial lead time 3 months. Submit seasonal material 4 months in advance. Accepts simultaneous submissions. Responds in 6 weeks to queries; 6 months to mss. Sample copy and writer's guidelines free.

Nonfiction: How-to, interview/profile, new product, technical, case study. Query. Length: 2,500-5,000 words. **Pays $250-1,000.**

Photos: Send photos with submission. Reviews transparencies. Offers no additional payment for photos accepted with ms. Identification of subjects required. Buys one-time rights.

Columns/Departments: Pooh Review; Product Review; interviews, case study, all 2,500 words. **Buys 16-20 mss/year.** Query. **Pays $50-750.**

Fillers: Facts, newsbreaks. **Buys 12 mss/year.** Length: 350-500 words. **Pays $50.**

Tips: "Send abstracts to editor; articles are published on need basis."

N $ JOURNAL OF INFORMATION ETHICS, McFarland & Co., Inc., Publishers, Box 611, Jefferson NC 28640. (336)246-4460. Fax: (336)246-5018. Website: www.mcfarlandpub.com. **Contact:** Robert Hauptman, LRTS, editor, 720 Fourth Ave. S., St. Cloud State University, St. Cloud MN 56301. (320)255-4822. Fax: (320)255-4778. **90% freelance written.** Semiannual scholarly journal. "Addresses ethical issues in all of the information sciences with a deliberately interdisciplinary approach. Topics range from electronic mail monitoring to library acquisition of controversial material. The journal's aim is to present thoughtful considerations of ethical dilemmas that arise in a rapidly evolving system of information exchange and dissemination." Estab. 1992. Circ. 500. Pays on publication. Publishes ms an average of 9 months after acceptance. Byline given. Buys all rights. Submit seasonal material 8 months in advance. Accepts queries by mail, fax, phone. Sample copy for $21. Writer's guidelines free.

Nonfiction: Essays, opinion, book reviews. **Buys 10 mss/year.** Send complete ms. Length: 500-3,500 words. **Pays $25-50 (depending on length).**

Tips: "Familiarize yourself with the many areas subsumed under the rubric of information ethics, e.g., privacy, scholarly communication, errors, peer review, confidentiality, e-mail, etc. Present a well-rounded discussion of any fresh, current or evolving ethical topic within the information sciences, or involving real-world information collection/exchange."

$ $ NEWS/400, Duke Communications International, 221 E. 29th St., Loveland CO 80538. (970)663-4700. Fax: (970)663-3285. E-mail: editors@news400.com. Website: www.news400.com. Acquisitions Editor: Lori Piotrowski. **40% freelance written.** Magazine published 14 times/year. "Programming, networking, IS management, technology for users of IBM AS/400 platform." Estab. 1982. Circ. 30,000 (international). Pays on publication. Publishes ms an average of 3 months after acceptance. Byline given. Offers 50% kill fee. Buys first, second serial (reprint) and all rights. Editorial lead time 4 months. Submit seasonal material 4 months in advance. Accepts queries by: mail, e-mail, fax, phone. Responds in 3 weeks to queries; 5 weeks to mss. Writer's guidelines available online.

Nonfiction: Book excerpts, opinion, technical. **Buys 70 mss/year.** Query. Length: 1,500-2,500 words. **Pays 17-50¢/word.** Pays in copies upon request of author. Sometimes pays expenses of writers on assignment.

Reprints: Accepts previously published submissions, if published in a noncompeting market. Send photocopy of story. Payment negotiable.

Photos: State availability of photos with submission. Offers no additional payment for photos accepted with ms.

Columns/Departments: Dialog Box (computer industry opinion), 1,500 words; Load'n'go (complete utility). **Buys 24 mss/year.** Query. **Pays $250-1,000.**

■ The online magazine carries original content not found in the print edition and includes writer's guidelines.

Tips: "Be familiar with IBM AS/400 computer platform."

N ■ $ $ $ PLANET IT, The Community for IT Professionals, CMP Media, 600 Community Dr., Manhasset NY 11030. E-mail: pkrass@cmp.com. Website: www.PlanetIT.com. Managing Editor: Joy Blake. **Contact:** Peter Krass, editor. **25% freelance written.** Website covering information technology. "Our audience consists of information technology professionals in business, government, education and healthcare." Estab. 1998. Circ. 140,000. **Pays on acceptance**. Byline given. Offers 25% kill fee. Buys first or electronic rights. Editorial lead time 1 month. Accepts queries by e-mail. Responds in 2 weeks to queries; 1 month to mss. Sample copy online at website.

Nonfiction: How-to, new product, opinion, technical. No poetry, fiction, essays. Query with published clips. Length: 1,500 words. **Pays 75¢-$1.** Pays expenses of writers on assignment.

N **SYS ADMIN**, CMP Media, Inc., 1601 W. 23rd St., Suite 200, Lawrence KS 66046. (785)838-7555. Fax: (785)841-2047. E-mail: REndsley@MFI.com. Website: www.sysadminmag.com. Editor: Ralph Barker. **Contact:** Rikki Endsley, associate managing editor. **90% freelance written.** Monthly magazine. "*Sys Admin* is written for UNIX systems administrators. Articles are practical and technical. Our authors are practicing UNIX systems administrators." Estab. 1992. Circ. 60,000. Pays on publication. Publishes ms an average of 6 months after acceptance. Byline given. Kill fee $150. Buys all rights. Editorial lead time 4 months. Accepts queries by mail, e-mail, fax, phone. Query for electronic submissions. Responds in 1 month to queries. Sample copy and writer's guidelines free or on website.
Nonfiction: Technical. **Buys 40-60 mss/year.** Query. Length: 1,000 words minimum. **Pay varies.**

N **WINDOWS DEVELOPER'S JOURNAL**, CMP Media, Suite 200, 1601 W. 23rd St., Lawrence KS 66046. (785)838-7552. Fax: (785)841-2047. E-mail: wdletter@cmp.com. Website: www.wdj.com. Editor: Ron Burk. **Contact:** Pam Van Schmus, managing editor. **90% freelance written.** Monthly magazine. "*WDJ* is written for advanced Windows programmers. Articles are practical, advanced, code-intensive, and not product-specific. We expect our authors to be working Windows programmers." Estab. 1990. Circ. 23,000. **Pays on acceptance.** Publishes ms an average of 6 months after acceptance. Byline given. Kill fee $150. Buys all rights. Editorial lead time 3 months. Query for electronic submissions. Responds in 2 weeks to queries. Sample copy and writer's guidelines free.
Nonfiction: Technical. **Buys 70-80 mss/year.** Query. Length: varies. Pay varies.

INSURANCE

N **$ $ ADVISOR TODAY**, NAIFA Service Corp., 1922 F St. NW, Washington DC 20006. (202)331-6054. Fax: (202)835-9608. E-mail: jkosnett@naifa.org. Website: www.advisortoday.com. **Contact:** Jeffrey R. Kosnett, editor. Deputy Editor: Amy S. Friedman. **25% freelance written.** Monthly magazine covering life insurance and financial planning. "Writers must demonstrate an understanding at what insurance agents and financial advisors do to earn business and serve their clients." Estab. 1906. Circ. 110,000. Pays on acceptance or publication (by mutual agreement with editor). Publishes ms an average of 3 months after acceptance. Makes-work-for-hire assignments. Editorial lead time 3 months. Submit seasonal material 6 months in advance. Accepts queries by mail, e-mail, fax, phone. Sample copy free.
　　○→ Break in with queries for "pieces about sales techniques and product disclosure issues."
Nonfiction: Insurance. **Buys 8 mss/year.** Query. Length: 1,500-6,000 words. **Pays $800-2,000.**
Tips: Prior to January 2000, *Advisor Today* was published under the title *LAN* (Life Association News).

$ $ $ BUSINESS & HEALTH, Keys to Workforce Productivity, Medical Economics Publishing Co., 5 Paragon Dr., Montvale NJ 07645-1742. (201)358-7276. Fax: (201)772-2676. E-mail: rickservice@medec.com. Website: www.businessandhealth.com. Editor: Richard Service. **90% freelance written.** Monthly magazine. "*B&H* carries articles about how employers can cut their health care costs and improve the quality of care they provide to workers. We also write about health care policy at the federal, state and local levels." Estab. 1983. Circ. 52,000. **Pays on acceptance.** Publishes ms an average of 2 months after acceptance. Byline given. Offers 20% kill fee. Buys all rights. Editorial lead time 2 months. Submit seasonal material 4 months in advance. Accepts queries by: mail, fax. Responds in 3 months. Sample copy for 9 × 12 SAE with 6 first-class stamps. Writer's guidelines for #10 SASE.
Nonfiction: How-to (cut health care benefits costs, provide better care); case studies (of successful employer-led efforts); trend piece on broad issues such as 24-hour coverage or benefits for retirees. **Buys approx. 50 mss/year.** Query with published clips and SASE. Length: 2,000-3,500 words. **Pays $1,000-1,700 for features.** Pays expenses of writers on assignment.
Columns/Departments: Primarily staff-written but will consider queries.
Tips: "Please be familiar with *B&H* and follow writer's guidelines. Articles should combine a business angle with a human interest approach and address both cost-containment and quality of care. Include cost-benefit analysis data and material for charts or graphs whenever possible."

$ FLORIDA UNDERWRITER, National Underwriter Co., 9887 Fourth St., N., Suite 230, St. Petersburg FL 33702-2488. (727)576-1101. Fax: (727)577-4002. Editorial Director: Ian Mackenzie. **Contact:** James E. Seymour, editor. **20% freelance written.** Monthly magazine. "*Florida Underwriter* covers insurance for Florida insurance professionals: producers, executives, risk managers, employee benefit administrators. We want material about any insurance line, Life & Health or Property & Casualty, but *must* have a Florida tag—Florida authors preferred." Estab. 1984. Circ. 10,000. Pays on publication. Publishes ms an average of 3 months after acceptance. Byline given. Buys all rights. Submit seasonal material 3 months in advance. Accepts queries by mail, fax. Accepts simultaneous submissions. Responds in 1 month. Free sample copy and writer's guidelines.
Nonfiction: Essay, exposé, historical/nostalgic, how-to, interview/profile, new product, opinion, technical. "We don't want articles that aren't about insurance for insurance people or those that lack Florida angle. No puff pieces. Note:

Most non-inhouse pieces are contributed gratis by industry experts." **Buys 6 mss/year.** Query with or without published clips, or send complete ms. Length: 500-1,500 words. **Pays $50-150 for assigned articles; $25-100 for unsolicited articles.** "Industry experts contribute in return for exposure." Sometimes pays expenses of writers on assignment.

Reprints: Send tearsheet or photocopy of article or typed ms with rights for sale noted and information about when and where the article previously appeared. Pays 40% of amount paid for an original article.

Photos: State availability of photos with submission. Send photos with submission. Reviews 5×7 prints. Offers no additional payment for photos accepted with ms. Identification of subjects required.

$ $GEICO DIRECT, K.L. Publications, 2001 Killebrew Dr., Suite 105, Bloomington MN 55425-1879. **Contact:** Jan Brenny, editor. **60% freelance written.** Semiannual magazine published for the Government Employees Insurance Company (GEICO) policyholders. Estab. 1988. Circ. 3,000,000. **Pays on acceptance.** Byline given. Buys first North American serial rights. Responds in 2 months. Writer's guidelines for #10 SASE.

○┰ Break in by submitting clips that prove ability to research and provide attention to detail on technical/specialized topics. For lifestyle and travel show an ability to make people want to go to destinations in short entries. Typically, the editors pick themes for travel (i.e. zoos, national parks) and provide up to 10 selected destinations.

Nonfiction: Americana, home and auto safety, car care, financial, lifestyle, travel. Query with published clips. Length: 1,000-2,200 words. **Pays $300-650.**

Photos: Reviews 35mm transparencies. Payment varies.

Columns/Departments: Moneywise, 50+, Your Car. Query with published clips. Length: 500-600 words. **Pays $175-350.**

Tips: "We prefer work from published/established writers, especially those with specialized knowledge of the insurance industry, safety issues and automotive topics."

JEWELRY

$ $AJM: THE AUTHORITY ON JEWELRY MANUFACTURING, (formerly American Jewelry Manufacturing), Manufacturing Jewelers and Suppliers of America, One State St., 6th Floor, Providence RI 02908. (401)274-3840. Fax: (401)274-0265. E-mail: ajm@ajm-magazine.com. Website: www.ajm-magazine.com. **Contact:** Rich Youmans, editor/associate publisher. **75% freelance written.** "*AJM* is a monthly magazine providing technical, marketing and business information for finished jewelry manufacturers and supporting industries." Estab. 1956. **Pays on acceptance.** Publishes ms an average of 6 months after acceptance. Byline given. Buys all rights for limited period of 18 months. Editorial lead time 1 year. Submit seasonal material 6 months in advance. Accepts queries by mail, e-mail, fax. Responds in 2 months. Sample copy and writer's guidelines free.

Nonfiction: How-to, new product, technical. All articles should focus on jewelry manufacturing techniques, especially how-to and technical articles. "No generic articles for a wide variety of industries, articles for hobbyists, or articles written for a consumer audience or for retailers. Our focus is professional jewelry manufacturers and designers, and articles for *AJM* should be carefully targeted for this audience." **Buys 40 mss/year.** Query. Length: 2,500-3,000 words. **Pays $300-500 for assigned articles.** Sometimes pays expenses of writers on assignment.

Reprints: Occasionally accepts previously published submissions. Query.

Photos: State availability of photos with submission. Negotiates payment individually. Captions required. Buys one-time rights.

Tips: "Because our editorial content is highly focused and specific, we assign most article topics rather than relying on outside queries. We are, as a result, always seeking new writers comfortable with business and technical topics who will work with us long term and whom we can develop into 'experts' in jewelry manufacturing. We invite writers to send an introductory letter and clips highlighting business and technical writing skills if they would like to be considered for a specific assignment."

$THE DIAMOND REGISTRY BULLETIN, 580 Fifth Ave., #806, New York NY 10036. (212)575-0444. Fax: (212)575-0722. E-mail: diamond58@aol.com. Website: www.diamondregistry.com. **Contact:** Joseph Schlussel, editor-in-chief. **50% freelance written.** Monthly newsletter. Estab. 1969. Pays on publication. Buys all rights. Submit seasonal material 1 month in advance. Accepts simultaneous submissions. Accepts queries by mail, e-mail, fax. Responds in 3 weeks. Sample copy for $5.

Nonfiction: Prevention advice (on crimes against jewelers); how-to (ways to increase sales in diamonds, improve security, etc.); interview (of interest to diamond dealers or jewelers). Submit complete ms. Length: 50-500 words. **Pays $75-150.**

Reprints: Accepts previously published submissions.

▣ The online magazine carries original content not found in the print edition.

Tips: "We seek ideas to increase sales of diamonds."

$ $THE ENGRAVERS JOURNAL, 26 Summit St., P.O. Box 318, Brighton MI 48116. (810)229-5725. Fax: (810)229-8320. E-mail: editor@engraversjournal.com. Website: www.engraversjournal.com. Co-Publisher: Michael J. Davis. Administrative Editor: Rosemary Farrell. **Contact:** Jessica Haessler, managing editor. **15% freelance written.** "We are eager to work with published/established writers as well as new/unpublished writers." Monthly magazine covering the recognition and identification industry (engraving, marking devices, awards, jewelry, and signage.) "We provide practical information for the education and advancement of our readers, mainly retail business owners." Estab. 1975. **Pays on acceptance.** Publishes ms an average of 1 year after acceptance. Byline given "only if writer is recognized authority." Buys one-time rights and makes work-for-hire assignments. Accepts queries by: mail, e-mail, fax. Responds in 2 weeks. Writer's guidelines free. Sample copy to "those who send writing samples with inquiry."

O→ To break in, submit well written, fairly in-depth general business articles. Topics and article style should focus on the small retail business owner, and should be helpful and informative.

Nonfiction: General interest (industry-related); how-to (small business subjects, increase sales, develop new markets, use new sales techniques, etc.); technical. No general overviews of the industry. Length: 1,000-5,000 words. **Pays $100-500 for articles.**

Reprints: Accepts previously published submissions. Send photocopy of article or typed ms with rights for sale noted and information about when and where the article previously appeared. Pays 50-100% of amount paid for original article.

Photos: Send photos with query. Pays variable rate. Captions, model release, identification of subjects required.

Tips: "Articles should always be down to earth, practical and thoroughly cover the subject with authority. We do not want the 'textbook' writing approach, vagueness, or theory—our readers look to us for sound practical information. We use an educational slant, publishing both trade-oriented articles and general business topics of interest to a small retail-oriented readership."

$ $ FASHION ACCESSORIES, S.C.M. Publications, Inc., P.O. Box 859, Mahwah NJ 07430-0859. (201)684-9222. Fax: (201)684-9228. Publisher: Samuel Mendelson. Monthly newspaper covering costume or fashion jewelry. Published for executives in the manufacturing, wholesaling and retail volume buying of fashion jewelry and accessories. Estab. 1951. Circ. 9,500. **Pays on acceptance.** Byline given. Not copyrighted. Buys first rights. Submit seasonal material 3 months in advance. Sample copy for $2 and 9×12 SAE with 4 first-class stamps.

Nonfiction: Essays, general interest, historical/nostalgic, interview/profile, new product. **Buys 20 mss/year.** Query with published clips. Length: 1,000-2,000 words. **Pays $100-300.**

Photos: Send photos with submission. Reviews 4×5 prints. Offers no additional payment for photos accepted with ms. Identification of subjects required. Buys one-time rights.

Columns/Departments: Fashion Report (interviews and reports of fashion news), 1,000-2,000 words.

Tips: "We are interested in anything that will be of interest to costume jewelry buyers."

[N] $ $ LUSTRE, The Jeweler's Magazine on Design & Style, Cygnus Publishing Company, 445 Broad Hollow Rd., Melville NY 11747. (516)845-2700. Fax: (516)845-7109. Managing Editor: Matthew Kramer. **Contact:** Lorraine DePasque. Bimonthly trade magazine covering fine jewelry and related accessories. "*LUSTRE* is dedicated to helping the retail jeweler stock, merchandise, sell and profit from upscale, high-quality brand name and designer jewelry. Many stories are how-to. We also offer sophisticated graphics to showcase new products." Estab. 1997. Circ. 12,500. Pays on publication. Publishes ms an average of 4 months after acceptance. Byline given. Offers 50% kill fee. Buys all rights. Editorial lead time 4 months. Submit seasonal material four months in advance. Responds in 4 weeks to queries; 2 months to mss. Sample copy free.

Nonfiction: How-to, new product. **Buys 18 mss/year.** Query with published clips. Length: 1,000-2,500 words. **Pays $500.** Sometimes pays expenses of writers on assignment.

Photos: State availability of photos with submission. Offers no additional payment for photos accepted with ms. Captions and identification of subjects required. Buys one time rights plus usage for one year after publication date (but not exclusive usage).

Columns and Departments: Celebrity Link (tie in designer jewelry with celebrity), 500 words; Details (news about designer jewelry), 200-500 words. **Buys 8 mss/year.** Query. **Pays $200-500.**

Fillers: Facts, newsbreaks. **Buys 4 mss/year.** Length: 200-300 words. **Pays $200.**

Tips: "Step 1: Request an issue sent to them; call (212) 921-1091; ask for assistant. Step 2: Write a letter to Lorraine with clips. Step 3: Lorraine will call back."

JOURNALISM & WRITING

Journalism and writing magazines cover both the business and creative sides of writing. Writing publications offer inspiration and support for professional and beginning writers. Although there are many valuable writing publications that do not pay, we list those that pay for articles.

$ AUTHORSHIP, National Writers Association, 3140 S. Peoria, #295, Aurora CO 80014. (303)841-0246. E-mail: sandywrter@aol.com. Editor: Sandy Whelchel. Quarterly magazine covering writing articles only. "Association magazine targeted to beginning and professional writers. Covers how-to, humor, marketing issues." Estab. 1950s. Circ. 4,000. **Pays on acceptance.** Byline given. Buys first North American serial or second serial (reprint) rights. Editorial lead time 3 months. Submit seasonal material 6 months in advance. Accepts simultaneous submissions. Disk and e-mail submissions given preference. Responds in 2 months to queries. Sample copy for #10 SASE.

Nonfiction: Writing only. Poetry (January/February). **Buys 25 mss/year.** Query or send complete ms. Length: 900 words. **Pays $10** or discount on memberships and copies.

Photos: State availability of photos with submission. Reviews 5×7 prints. Offers no additional payment for photos accepted with ms. Model releases and identification of subjects required. Buys one-time rights.

Reprints: Accepts previously published submissions.

Tips: "Members of National Writers Association are given preference."

$ BOOK DEALERS WORLD, North American Bookdealers Exchange, P.O. Box 606, Cottage Grove OR 97424. Phone/fax: (541)942-7455. Editorial Director: Al Galasso. **50% freelance written.** Quarterly magazine covering writing, self-publishing and marketing books by mail. Circ. 20,000. Pays on publication. Publishes ms an average of 3 months after acceptance. Byline given. Buys first serial and second serial (reprint) rights. Accepts simultaneous submissions. Responds in 1 month. Sample copy for $3.

Nonfiction: Book excerpts (writing, mail order, direct mail, publishing); how-to (home business by mail, advertising); interview/profile (of successful self-publishers). Positive articles on self-publishing, new writing angles, marketing, etc. **Buys 10 mss/year.** Send complete ms. Length: 1,000-1,500 words. **Pays $25-50.**

Reprints: Send typed ms with rights for sale noted and information about when and where the article previously appeared. Pays 80% of amount paid for an original article.

Columns/Departments: Print Perspective (about new magazines and newsletters); Self-Publisher Profile (on successful self-publishers and their marketing strategy). **Buys 20 mss/year.** Send complete ms. Length: 250-1,000 words. **Pays $5-20.**

Fillers: Fillers concerning writing, publishing or books. **Buys 6/year.** Length: 100-250 words. **Pays $3-10.**

Tips: "Query first. Get a sample copy of the magazine."

$ BYLINE, P.O. Box 130596, Edmond OK 73013-0001. (405)348-5591. E-mail: bylinemp@flash.net. Website: www. bylinemag.com. **Contact:** Marcia Preston, editor/publisher. **80% freelance written.** Eager to work with new/unpublished writers. Magazine published 11 times/year for writers and poets. Estab. 1981. **Pays on acceptance.** Publishes ms an average of 3 months after acceptance. Byline given. Buys first North American serial rights. Editorial lead time 3 months. Submit seasonal material 6 months in advance. Accepts simultaneous submissions. Accepts queries by mail, e-mail. Responds in 2 months or less. Sample copy for $4 postpaid. Writer's guidelines for #10 SASE or on website.

O-n "First sale is probably the easiest way to break in."

Nonfiction: Essays, how-to, humor, inspirational, personal experience, interview, *all* connected with writing and selling. No profiles of writers. "We're always searching for appropriate, well-written features on topics we haven't covered for a couple of years." **Buys approximately 75 mss/year.** Prefers queries; will read complete mss. Send SASE. Length: 1,500-1,800 words for features. **Pays $75.**

Columns/Departments: End Piece (humorous, philosophical or motivational personal essay related to writing), 700-750 words, **pays $35;** First Sale (account of a writer's first sale), 200-300 words, **pays $20;** Only When I Laugh (writing-related humor), 50-600 words; pays $15-25; Great American Bookstores (unique, independent bookstores), 500-600 words. Send complete ms. **Pays $30-40.**

Fiction: Open to genre, mainstream and literary. No science fiction, erotica or extreme violence. **Buys 11 mss/year.** Send complete ms: 2,000-4,000 words preferred. **Pays $100.**

Poetry: Sandra Soli, poetry editor. Free verse, haiku, light verse, traditional. "All poetry should connect in some way with the theme of writing or writers." **Buys 100 poems/year.** Submit 3 poems max. Preferred length: under 30 lines. **Pays $10** plus free issue.

Tips: "We're open to freelance submissions in all categories. We're always looking for clear, concise feature articles on topics that will help writers write better, market smarter, and be more successful. Strangely, we get many more short stories than we do features, but we buy more features. If you can write a friendly, clear and helpful feature on some aspect of writing better or selling more work, we'd love to hear from you."

$ CANADIAN WRITER'S JOURNAL, P.O. Box 5180, New Liskeard, Ontario P0J 1P0 Canada. (705)647-5424. Fax: (705)647-8366. E-mail: cwj@ntl.sympatico.ca. Website: www.nt.net/~cwj/index.htm. **Contact:** Carole Manseau, managing editor. Accepts well-written articles by inexperienced writers. Bimonthly magazine for writers. Estab. 1982. Circ. 350. **75% freelance written.** Pays on publication. Publishes ms an average of 9 months after acceptance. Byline given. Accepts queries by mail, e-mail, fax, phone. Responds in 2 months. Sample copy for $4 and $1 postage. Writer's guidelines for #10 SAE and IRC or on website.

• *Canadian Writer's Journal* has a new owner and a new address.

Nonfiction: How-to articles for writers. Looking for articles on hot to break into niche markets. **Buys 50-55 mss/year.** Query optional. Length: 500-2,000 words. **Pays $5/published magazine page (approx. 450 words).**

Reprints: Send typed ms with rights for sale noted and information about when and where the article previously appeared.

Fiction: Requirements currently being met by annual contest. SASE for rules, or see guidelines on website.

Poetry: Short poems or extracts used as part of articles on the writing of poetry.

Tips: "We prefer short, tightly written, informative how-to articles. U.S. writers note that U.S. postage cannot be used to mail from Canada. Obtain Canadian stamps, use IRCs or send small amounts in cash."

$ $ FREELANCE WRITER'S REPORT, CNW Publishing, Inc., Main St., P.O. Box A, North Stratford NH 03590-0167. (603)922-8338. Fax: (603)922-8339. E-mail: danakcnw@ncia.net. Website: www.writers-editors.com. **Contact:** Dana K. Cassell, editor. **25% freelance written.** Monthly. "*FWR* covers the marketing and business/office management aspects of running a freelance writing business. Articles must be of value to the established freelancer; nothing basic." Estab. 1982. Pays on publication. Publishes ms an average of 6 months after acceptance. Byline given. Buys one-time rights. Editorial lead time 2 months. Submit seasonal material 2 months in advance. Accepts simultaneous submissions. Accepts queries by mail, e-mail. Responds in 1 week to queries; 1 month to mss. Sample copy for 6×9 SAE with 2 first-class stamps (for back copy); $4 for current copy. Guidelines on website.
Nonfiction: Book excerpts, how-to (market, increase income or profits). No articles about the basics of freelancing. **Buys 50 mss/year.** Send complete ms. Length: 500 words. **Pays 10¢/word.**
Reprints: Accepts previously published submissions.
        ▣ The online magazine carries original content not found in the print edition and includes writer's guidelines.
Tips: "Write in a terse, newsletter style."

N $ GOTTA WRITE NETWORK LITMAG, Maren Publications, 515 E. Thacker, Hoffman Estates IL 60194. E-mail: netera@aol.com. Website: http://members.aol.com/gwnlitmag/. **Contact:** Denise Fleischer, editor. **80% freelance written.** Semiannual literary magazine covering writer's techniques, markets. "Any article should be presented as if openly speaking to the reader. It should inform from the first paragraph to the last." Estab. 1988. Circ. 300. Pays after publication. Publishes ms an average of 6 months after acceptance. Byline given. Buys first North American serial rights and first electronic rights or makes work-for-hire assignments. Editorial lead time 6 months. Accepts queries by mail, e-mail. Responds in 3 months. Sample copy for $6. Writer's guidelines for #10 SASE.
Nonfiction: Articles (on writing), how-to (on writing techniques), interview/profile (for Behind the Scenes section), new product (books, software, computers), photo feature (on poets/writers/editors big and small press). "Don't want to see 'My First Sale,' 'When I Can't Write,' 'Dealing With Rejection,' 'Writer's Block,' a speech from a writers convention, an article published 10 times by other editors." **Buys 25 mss/year.** Query with published clips or send complete ms. Accepts e-mail queries and submissions but no attached mail. Length: 3-5 pages. **Pays $5** and contributor's copy.
Photos: State availability of photos with submission. Offers $10 (more for cover art). Captions, model releases and identification of subjects required. Buys one-time rights.
Fiction: Adventure, ethnic, experimental, fantasy, historical, horror, humorous, mainstream, mystery, romance, science fiction, slice-of-life vignettes, suspense, western. No dark fantasy. **Buys 15 and up mss/year.** Query with published clips. Send complete ms. Page length: 5-10. **Pays $10 maximum.**
Poetry: Avant-garde, free verse, haiku, beat—experimental. No poetry no one can understand or that has no meaning. Open to editor's news releases.
Tips: Send hard-hitting poetry and short stories that grab the reader's attention beginning with the first paragraph. Open to life's challenges, science-fiction, fantasy, romance, Twilight Zone and paranormal manuscripts. Bring the experience or scene to life through expressive sensory details.

N ▣ $ GREETING CARD WRITER MAGAZINE, Summerland, Ltd., P.O. Box 43523, Cincinnati OH 45243-0523. E-mail: editor@greetingcardwriter.com. Website: www.greetingcardwriter.com. **Contact:** Terri See, editor/publisher. **90% freelance written.** Online monthly magazine covering how to write and sell greeting cards and related products. "Our readers are serious freelance writers and artists—people who make their living in this and related kinds of work. The magazine is an online viewable subscription-based publication." Estab. 1999. **Pays on acceptance.** Byline given. Offers 100% kill fee. Buys all rights, electronic rights, archival rights. Editorial lead time 2 months. Submit seasonal material 3 months in advance. Accepts queries by mail, e-mail. Accepts simultaneous submissions. Reports in 1 month. Writer's guidelines on website.
Nonfiction: How-to (write and sell greeting cards). **Buys 50 mss/year.** Query. Length: 200-750 words. **Pays $30.**
Reprints: Accepts previously published submissions.
Photos: Contact: Aaron Butler, art director via e-mail at design@greetingcardwriter.com. State availability of photos with submission. Reviews GIF or JPEG format. Negotiates payment individually.
Fillers: Anecdotes, facts. **Buys 10/year.** Length: 20-50 words. **Pay varies.**
Tips: "We prefer articles from experienced greeting card industry professionals."

N ★ ▣ $ INKLINGS, Inkspot's Newsletter for Writers, Inkspot, 67 Mowat Ave., Ste. 239, Toronto, Ontario M6K3E3 Canada. E-mail: editor@inkspot.com. Website: www.inkspot.com. **Contact:** submissions@inkspot.com. Editor: Debbie Ridpath Ohi. Associate Editor: Moira Allen. **75% freelance written.** Biweekly electronic newsletter for writers of all levels of experience. Estab. 1995. Circ. 45,000. Pays on publication. Publishes ms an average of 3 months after acceptance. Byline given. Buys exclusive worldwide first-time rights plus non-exclusive right to archive the article online. Submissions and queries accepted only by e-mail.Responds in 2 weeks to queries; 1 month to mss. For free subscription, send e-mail to subscribe@inkspot.com or see website for back issues. For writer's guidelines send e-mail to guidelines@inkspot.com or on website.
Nonfiction: How-to (focus on writing, selling and promoting), interview/profile. Also accepts material for website and other Inkspot publications. Guidelines on website. **Buys 50-60 mss/year.** Query by e-mail. Length: 500-1,000 words. **Pays 6¢/word.**
Tips: "Focus should be heavily 'how to' with examples. Query with article idea/slant, publishing credits (if any), sample of writing style."

N ◻ **$ INSCRIPTIONS**, Mylitta Publishing, 432 S. B St., Lake Worth FL 33460. E-mail: Editor@inscriptionsma gazine.com. Website: www.inscriptionsmagazine.com. **Contact:** Pamela Wilfinger, editor. **100% freelance written.** E-zine covering writing, editing, publishing. "*Inscriptions* is the weekly e-zine for professional writers. Our focus is to help working writers and editors find work, paying markets and contests offering cash prizes." Estab. 1998. Pays on publication. Publishes ms an average of 2 months after acceptance. Byline given. Buys one-time rights and electronic rights. Editorial lead time 2-3 months. Submit seasonal material 3 months in advance. Accepts queries by e-mail. Responds in 2 weeks to queries. Sample copy free. Writer's guidelines online at website or by e-mail.

Nonfiction: Book excerpts, how-to, humor, interview/profile. **Buys 150 mss/year.** Query. Length: 500-1,500 words. **Pays $5-40.** "Authors can opt for advertising in lieu of payments."

Fillers: Buys 50/year. Length: 25-300 words. No pay.

Tips: "Articles must focus on writing or publishing-related issues (including interviews, how to's, troubleshooting, etc.). Inscriptions does not publish fiction, poetry or other nonfiction articles, unless the submissions have won our sponsored monthly contest. Interviews should be conducted with working writers, authors, writing teachers, editors, agents or publishers. All interviews must be approved in advance. Inscriptions accepts reprints of writing-related articles. The publication where the article originally appeared will be credited. However, you must hold the copyright to the article, in order to submit it to us."

N **$ MAINE IN PRINT, Maine Writers and Publishers Alliance**, 12 Pleasant St., Brunswick ME 04011. (207)729-6333. Fax: (207)725-1014. Editor: John Cole. Monthly newsletter for writers, editors, teachers, librarians, etc., focusing on Maine literature and the craft of writing. Estab. 1975. Circ. 5,000. Pays on publication. Publishes ms an average of 2 months after acceptance. Byline given. Buys one-time rights. Editorial lead time 1 month. Accepts simultaneous submissions. Responds in 2 weeks to queries; 1 month to mss. Sample copy and writer's guidelines free.

Nonfiction: Essays, how-to (writing), interview/profile, technical writing. No creative writing, fiction or poetry. **Buys 20 mss/year.** Query with published clips. Length: 400-1,500 words. **Pays $25-75 for assigned articles.**

Reprints: Send tearsheet of article or short story and information about when and where the article previously appeared. Pays $25 for reprints.

Photos: State availability of photos with submission. Offers no additional payment for photos accepted with ms.

Columns/Departments: Front-page articles (writing related), 500-1,500 words. Buys 20 mss/year. Query. Pays $25 minimum.

Tips: "Become a member of Maine Writers & Publishers Alliance. Become familiar with Maine literary scene."

◤◢ **$ NEW WRITER'S MAGAZINE**, Sarasota Bay Publishing, P.O. Box 5976, Sarasota FL 34277-5976. (941)953-7903. E-mail: newriters@aol.com. Website: www.newriters.com. **Contact:** George J. Haborak, editor. **95% freelance written.** Bimonthly magazine. "*New Writer's Magazine* believes that *all* writers are *new* writers in that each of us can learn from one another. So, we reach pro and non-pro alike." Estab. 1986. Circ. 5,000. Pays on publication. Byline given. Buys first rights. Accepts queries by mail. Responds in 3 weeks to queries; 1 month to mss. *Writer's Market* recommends allowing 2 months for reply. Sample copy for $3. Writer's guidelines for #10 SASE.

Nonfiction: General interest, how-to (for new writers), humor, interview/profile, opinion, personal experience (with pro writer). **Buys 50 mss/year.** Send complete ms. Length: 700-1,000 words. **Pays $10-50.**

Photos: Send photos with submission. Reviews 5×7 prints. Offers no additional payment for photos accepted with ms. Captions required.

Fiction: Experimental, historical, humorous, mainstream, slice-of-life vignettes. "Again, we do *not* want anything that does not have a tie-in with the writing life or writers in general." **Buys 2-6 mss/year.** "We offer a special fiction contest held each year with cash prizes." Send complete ms. Length: 700-800 words. **Pays $20-40.**

Poetry: Free verse, light verse, traditional. Does not want anything *not* for writers. **Buys 10-20 poems/year.** Submit maximum 3 poems. Length: 8-20 lines. **Pays $5 maximum.**

Fillers: Anecdotes, facts, newsbreaks, short humor. **Buys 5-15 mss/year.** Length: 20-100 words. **Pays $5 maximum.** Cartoons, writing lifestyle slant. **Buys 20-30/year. Pays $10 maximum.**

Tips: "Any article *with photos* has a good chance, especially an *up close and personal* interview with an established professional writer offering advice, etc. Short profile pieces on new authors also receive attention."

$ OHIO WRITER, Poets League of Greater Cleveland, P.O. Box 91801, Cleveland OH 44101. **Contact:** Ron Antonucci, editor. **75% freelance written.** Bimonthly magazine covering writing and Ohio writers. Estab. 1987. Pays on publication. Publishes ms an average of 4 months after acceptance. Byline given. Buys one-time rights and second serial (reprint) rights. Editorial lead time 4 months. Submit seasonal material 4 months in advance. Accepts queries by mail. Responds in 6 weeks. Sample copy for $2.50. Writer's guidelines for SASE.

Nonfiction: Essays, how-to, humor, inspirational, interview/profile, opinion, personal experience—"all must relate to the writing life or Ohio writers, or Ohio publishing scene." **Buys 24 mss/year.** Send complete ms and SASE. Length: 2,000-2,500 words. **Pays $25 minimum, up to $50 for lead article;** other payment under arrangement with writer.

Reprints: Send typed ms with rights for sale noted and information about when and where the article previously appeared. Pays 50% of amount paid for an original article.

Columns/Departments: Subjectively Yours (opinions, controversial stance on writing life), 1,500 words; Reviews (Ohio writers, publishers or publishing), 400-600 words; Focus On (Ohio publishing scene, how to write/publish certain kind of writing, e.g., travel), 1,500 words. **Buys 6 mss/year.** Send complete ms. **Pays $25-50; $5/book review.**

Tips: "We look for articles about writers and writing, with a special emphasis on activities in our state. However, we publish articles by writers throughout the country that offer something helpful about the writing life. Profiles and interviews of writers who live in Ohio are always needed. *Ohio Writer* is read by both beginning and experienced writers and hopes to create a sense of community among writers of different genres, abilities and backgrounds. We want to hear a personal voice, one that engages the reader. We're looking for intelligent, literate prose that isn't stuffy."

[N] $ $ ONLINE PUBLISHERS DIGEST, Digest Publications, 29 Fostertown Rd., Medford NJ 08055. (606)953-4900. Fax: (609)953-4905. Website: www.limodigest.com. **Contact:** Don Truax, editor. Trade journal covering internet publishing. Pays on publication. Publishes ms an average of 2 months after acceptance. Byline given. Makes work-for-hire assignments. Editorial lead time 1 year. Submit seasonal material 2 months in advance. Accepts queries by mail, e-mail, fax. Accepts simultaneous submissions. Responds in 2 weeks to queries.
Nonfiction: Historical/nostalgic, how-to (start company marketing), humor, inspirational, interview/profile, new product, personal experience, photo feature, technical. **Buys 1-2 mss/year.** Length: 700-1,900 words. **Pays 7-22¢/word.** Sometimes pays writers with advertising trade-outs.
Reprints: Accepts previously published submissions.
Photos: Send photos with submission. Reviews negatives. Negotiates payment individually. Captions, model releases, identification of subjects required. Buys all rights.
Columns/Departments: Pays 7-22¢.
Fillers: Facts, gags to be illustrated by cartoonist, newsbreaks. **Buys 24/year.** Length: 25-100 words. **Pays 7-22¢.**

[N] $ $ POETS & WRITERS, 72 Spring St., 3rd Floor, New York NY 10012. Fax: (212)226-3963. E-mail: editor@pw.org. Website: www.pw.org. **Contact:** Therese Eiben, editor. **100% freelance written.** Bimonthly professional trade journal for poets and fiction writers. No poetry or fiction. Estab. 1973. Circ. 70,000. **Pays on acceptance** of finished draft. Publishes ms an average of 4 months after acceptance. Byline given. Offers 20% kill fee. Buys first North American serial and first rights or makes work-for-hire assignments. Submit seasonal material at least 4 months in advance. Responds in 6 weeks to mss. Sample copy for $4.95 to Circulation Dept. Writer's guidelines for #10 SASE.
Nonfiction: Personal essays about literature, how-to (craft of poetry or fiction writing), profiles with poets or fiction writers (no Q&A), regional reports of literary activity, reports on small presses, service pieces about publishing trends. **Buys 35 mss/year.** Query by mail only with published clips or send complete ms. "We do *not* accept submissions by fax or e-mail." Length: 500-3,600 words (depending on topic).
Photos: State availability of photos with submission. Reviews b&w prints. Offers no additional payment for photos accepted with ms.
Columns/Departments: Literary and publishing news, 500-600 words; profiles of emerging and established poets and fiction writers, 2,400-3,600 words; regional reports (literary activity in US), 1,800-3,600 words. Query by mail only with published clips, or send complete ms. **Pays $100-300.**

[N] $ THE QUILL MAGAZINE QUARTERLY, The e-zine for beginning writers, Austin Aerospace Ltd. 2900 Warden Ave., P.O. Box 92207, Toronto, Ontario M1W 3Y9 Canada. (416)410-0277. Fax: (416)293-6148. E-mail: austin@thequill.com. Website: www.thequill.com. Editor: Charlotte Austin. **Contact:** Sue Elliott, assistant editor. **100% freelance written.** Quarterly online magazine. "*The Quill*'s readers are sophisticated and well-educated. The magazine is read by beginning and experienced writers alike. Use a concise, journalistic style. Feature articles should answer the particular concerns of beginning writers. Query first." Estab. 1988. Circ. 2,700. **Pays on acceptance.** Publishes ms an average of 2 months after acceptance. Byline given. Buys first, exclusive, one-time electronic rights and archive rights. Editorial lead time 3 months. Accepts queries by e-mail. Responds in 1 week to queries; 2 weeks to mss. Sample copy free on website. Writer's guidelines free on website.
Nonfiction: Charlotte Austin, editor. How-to, interview/profile, technical. "No personal experience; humor; opinion; essays; how I sold my first novel. **Buys 30-40 mss/year.** Query. Length: 800-1,200 words. **Pays $50-60.**
Columns/Departments: Sue Elliot, assistant editor. The Craft of Writing (technical; word usage) 500-1,200 words, Book Review Section (reviews) 350-450 words. **Pays $5/review. Buys 36 mss/year.** Query. **Pays $25-30.**
Fiction: Charlotte Austin, editor. Mainstream. "No experimental fiction, science fiction or mystery." **Buys 20 mss/year.** Send complete ms. Length: 800-1,200 words. **Pays $25-30.**
Tips: "*The Quill* has developed a particular writing style. You *must* study the magazine before submitting any material. Always query first and know our publication before querying wildly. Know your market and your audience."

$ SCAVENGER'S NEWSLETTER, 833 Main, Osage City KS 66523-1241. (913)528-3538. E-mail: foxscav1@jc.net. Website: www.jlgiftsshop.com/scav/index.html. **Contact:** Janet Fox, editor. **15% freelance written.** Eager to work with new/unpublished writers. Monthly newsletter covering markets for science fiction/fantasy/horror/mystery materials especially with regard to the small press. Estab. 1984. Circ. 850. **Pays on acceptance.** Publishes ms an average of 8 months after acceptance. Byline given. Not copyrighted. Buys one-time rights. Accepts simultaneous submissions. Accepts queries by: mail, e-mail, phone. Responds in 1 month if SASE included. Sample copy for $2.50. Writer's guidelines for #10 SASE. Now accepting e-mail submissions for everything except art.
Nonfiction: Essays, general interest, how-to (write, sell, publish science fiction/fantasy/horror/mystery), humor, interview/profile (writers, artists in the field), opinion. **Buys 12-15 mss/year.** Send complete ms. Length: 1,000 words maximum. **Pays $5.**

Reprints: Send information about when and where the article previously appeared. Pays 100% of amount paid for an original article.

Fiction: "Seeking a few (4-6) outstanding pieces of flash fiction to 1,200 words in the genre of SF/fantasy/horror/mystery. Looking for work that uses poetry techniques to make a short piece seem like a complete story." **Pays $5.**

Poetry: Avant-garde, free verse, haiku, traditional. All related to science fiction/fantasy/horror/mystery genres. **Buys 24 poems/year.** Submit maximum 3 poems. Length: 10 lines maximum. **Pays $3.**

Tips: "Because this is a small publication, it has occasional overstocks. We're especially looking for articles."

N ⊡ $ WORKING WRITERS NEWSLETTER, BSK Communications & Associates, P.O. Box 543, Oradell NJ 07649. E-mail: freelancewriting@abac.com. Website: www.freelancewriting.com. **Contact:** Brian Konradt, editor. **100% freelance written.** Online trade journal published weekly covering freelance writing. "*Working Writers* is a weekly e-mail newsletter that covers the creative and business sides of freelance writing." Estab. 1999. **Pays on acceptance.** Publishes ms an average of 2 months after acceptance. Byline given. Offers 10%. Buys first North American serial rights and electronic right. Editorial lead time 2 months. Submit seasonal material 2 months in advance. Accepts queries by e-mail. Responds in 2 weeks. Sample copy free. Writer's guidelines free.

Nonfiction: How-to, interview/profile. No very basic, beginner-type articles on freelance writing. **Buys 72-80 mss/year.** Query with published clips. Length: 100-700 words. **Pays 5¢/word. Sometimes pays expenses of writers on assignment.**

Tips: "Since articles are bulleted, short paragraphs or important information, writers should focus on providing essential, how-to information, rather than concentrating on proper writing style. Focus on short, solution-savvy, info-dense sentences. Always use specifics, solutions, step-by-steps, and experiences in your article."

$ WRITE, Canada's Writing Magazine, (formerly The Lazy Writer), The Lazy Writer, Inc., Box 977, Station F, 50 Charles St. E., Toronto, Ontario M4Y 3N9 Canada. (416)538-7170. E-mail: lzwriter@interlog.com. **Contact:** Chris Garbutt, editor. **80-100% freelance written.** Quarterly magazine covering writing. Estab. 1996. Circ. 2,500. Pays on publication. Publishes ms 4 months after acceptance. Byline given. Offers 50% kill fee. Buys first North American serial rights and second serial (reprint) rights. Editorial lead time 6 months. Submit seasonal material 8 months in advance. Accepts queries by mail, e-mail, phone. Accepts simultaneous submissions. Responds in 2 months to queries, 3 months to mss. Sample copy for $5.30 (Canadian). Writer's guidelines via e-mail only.

Nonfiction: Book excerpts, essays, exposé, general interest, how-to, humor, inspirational, interview/profile, opinion, personal experience, photo feature, travel. **Buys 20 mss/year.** Query. Length: 300-3,000 words. **Pays $25-200.** Rarely pays expenses of writers on assignment.

Photos: State availability of photos with submission. Offers $0-25/photo; negotiates payment individually. Buys one-time rights.

Columns/Departments: Person (interview), 500-1,500 words; Place (interview/profile), 500-1,500 words; Thing (interview/profile), 500-1,500 words; Text (review), 500-750 words; Word (essay), 500-1,500 words; Stuff, 500-1,000 words; Reviews, 300 words; Opinion, 750 words; Focus (practical), 500-1,000 words; Obituary, 200-800 words. **Buys 8 mss/year.** Query with published clips or send complete ms. **Pays $25-50.**

Fiction: Alexandra Leggat, portfolio editor. Adventure, confession, erotica, ethnic, experimental, fantasy, historical, horror, humorous, mainstream, mystery, novel excerpts, science fiction, slice-of-life vignettes, suspense. **Buys 4 mss/year.** Send complete ms. Length: 500-5,000 words. **Pays $25-200.**

Poetry: Alexandra Leggat, portfolio editor. Avant-garde, free verse, haiku. No limericks and the like. **Buys 15 poems/year.** Length: open. **Pays $25-50.**

★ ⊡ $ WRITER ON LINE, Newsletter of the Writer's Software Companion, Novation Learning Systems, 190 Mt. Vernon Ave., Rochester NY 14620. Fax: (716)340-0193. E-mail: email@novalearn.com. Website: www.novalearn.com/wol. **Contact:** Terry Boothman, editor. **60% freelance written.** Online "ezine" covering art and craft of writing. "Articles address the profession of writing—all kinds, including fiction, technical writing, business writing, public relations. Audience is *writers.*" Estab. 1998. Circ. 35,000. Pays on publication. Publishes ms an average of 1-2 months after acceptance. Byline given. Buys one-time, reprint, and archival rights. Editorial lead time 2 months. Submit seasonal material 2-3 months in advance. Accepts queries by mail, e-mail. Accepts simultaneous submissions. Responds in 2 months. Sample copy continuously online. Writer's guidelines by e-mail autoresponder at writers@novalearn.com.

Nonfiction: Essays, how-to (write fiction, essay, etc.), technical writing, marketing your writing. No fiction, personal memoirs, poetry. **Buys approximately 50 mss/year.** Query. Length: 800-2,000 words. **Pays $50 maximum for assigned articles; $20 for reprinted articles.**

Reprints: Accepts previously published submissions. **Pays $20 for reprints.**

Columns/Departments: Any genre of fiction: "Mystery Writer" "Romance Writer" "SF etc." Encourage material on "new writer's markets." **Buys 10-20 mss/year.** Query. **Pays $50 maximum.**

Tips: "We are always looking for concrete advice on how to break into new writers' markets—from credible sources. Also fresh, illustrated, well-written advice on the craft of writing and marketing of one's writing."

$ $ THE WRITER, 120 Boylston St., Boston MA 02116-4615. E-mail: writer@user1.channel1.com. Website: www.channel1.com/thewriter/. Editor-in-Chief/Publisher: Sylvia K. Burack. **20% freelance written.** Prefers to buy work of published/established writers. Monthly. Estab. 1887. **Pays on acceptance.** Publishes ms an average of 8 months after acceptance. Buys first serial rights. Accepts queries by: mail, e-mail. "No phone queries!" Sample copy for $4.

Nonfiction: Practical articles for writers on how to write for publication, and how and where to market manuscripts in various fields. Considers all submissions promptly. No assignments. Length: 2,000 words maximum.

Reprints: Occasionally buys previously published submissions from the *New York Times* and *Washington Post* book review sections. Send tearsheet or photocopy of article and information about when and where the article previously appeared.

Tips: "We are looking for articles with plenty of practical, specific advice, tips, techniques that aspiring and beginning writers can apply to their own work. New types of publications and our continually updated market listings in all fields will determine changes of focus and fact."

$ $ WRITER'S DIGEST, 1507 Dana Ave., Cincinnati OH 45207. (513)531-2222. Fax: (513)531-2902. E-mail: writersdig@fwpubs.com. Website: www.writersdigest.com. **Contact:** Dawn Simonds Ramirez, senior editor or Melanie Rigney, editor. **70% freelance written.** Monthly magazine about writing and publishing. "Our readers write fiction, poetry, nonfiction, plays and scripts. They're interested in improving writing skills and the ability to sell their work and find new outlets for their talents." Estab. 1920. Circ. 215,000. **Pays on acceptance.** Publishes ms an average of 6 months after acceptance. Buys first North American serial rights for one-time editorial use, possible electronic posting, microfilm/microfiche use and magazine promotional use. Pays 25% reprint fee and 10% for electronic use in fee-charging mediums. Pays 20% kill fee. Byline given. Submit seasonal material 8 months in advance. Accepts queries by mail, e-mail. Responds in month. Sample copy for $4. Writer's guidelines, editorial calendar available on website.

> Oー "We want articles about issues that concern writers today (electronic publishing and rights, for example) and are likely to reflect today's market conditions."

Nonfiction: "Our mainstay is the how-to article—that is, how to get more out of your writing. For instance, how to write compelling leads and conclusions, how to improve your character descriptions, how to become more efficient and productive. We like plenty of examples, anecdotes and details in our articles—so other writers can actually see what's been done successfully by the author of a particular piece. We like our articles to speak directly to the reader through the use of the first-person voice. We are seldom interested in author interviews and 'evergreen' topics are not accepted unless they are timely and address industry trends. For example, we'd only accept an article on query letters if it addressed concerns about the changing marketplace. We're looking for timely articles dealing with publishing as a dynamic, changing business. Don't send articles today that would have fit in *WD* five years ago. No articles titled 'So You Want to Be a Writer,' and no first-person pieces without something readers can learn from in the sharing of the story." **Buys 60 mss/year.** Queries are preferred. We only accept electronic final manuscripts. Length: 500-2,000 words. **Pays 25-40¢/word.** Sometimes pays expenses of writers on assignment. Must have fax to receive galleys.

Tips: "Two-thirds of assignments are based on staff-generated ideas. Only about 25 unsolicited queries for features are assigned per year."

$ WRITER'S FORUM, Writer's Digest School, 1507 Dana Ave., Cincinnati OH 45207. (513)531-2690, ext. 345. Fax: (513)531-0798. E-mail: wds@fwpubs.com. Website: www.writersdigestschool.com. **Contact:** Joe Squance, editor. **100% freelance written.** Tri-annual newsletter covering writing techniques, marketing and inspiration for students enrolled in fiction and nonfiction writing courses offered by Writer's Digest School. Estab. 1970. Circ. 10,000. **Pays on acceptance.** Publishes ms an average of 6 months after acceptance. Byline given. Buys first serial or second serial (reprint) rights. Accepts simultaneous submissions. Responds in 2 months. Sample copy free.

Nonfiction: How-to (write or market short stories, or articles, novels and nonfiction books); articles that will motivate beginning writers. **Buys 12 mss/year.** Prefers complete mss to queries. "If you prefer to query, please do so by mail or e-mail, not phone." Length: 500-1,000 words. **Pays $25.**

Reprints: Accepts previously published submissions.

[N] $ WRITERS INFORMATION NETWORK, The Professional Association for Christian Writers, P.O. Box 11337, Bainbridge Island WA 98110. (206)842-9103. Fax: (206)842-0536. E-mail: writersinfonetwork@juno.com. Website: www.bluejaypub.com/win. Editor: Elaine Wright Colvin. **33⅓% freelance written.** Bimonthly magazine covering religious publishing industry. Estab. 1983. Circ. 1,000. **Pays on acceptance.** Publishes ms 1-4 months after acceptance. Byline given. Buys first North American serial rights. Editorial lead time 2 months. Submit seasonal material 2 months in advance. Accepts queries by mail, e-mail. Responds in 1 month. Sample copy $5 for 9×12 SAE with 4 first-class stamps. Writer's guidelines for #10 SASE.

> Oー Break in by "getting involved in the Christian publishing (CBA) industry; interview CBA published authors, CBA editors or CBA bookstore managers."

Nonfiction: How-to (writing), humor, inspirational, personal experience. Send complete ms. Length: 50-800 words. **Pays $5-50.** Sometimes pays other than cash. Sometimes pays expenses of writers on assignment.

Columns/Departments: Industry News, Market News, Changes in the Industry, Watch on the World, Poetry News, Speakers Microphone, Conference Schedule, Look Over My Shoulder, new books reviewed or announced, Bulletin Board, Computer Corner. Send complete ms.

[N] $ WRITERS' JOURNAL, The Complete Writer's Magazine, Val-Tech Media, P.O. Box 394, Perham MN 56573-0394. (218)346-7921. Fax: (218)346-7924. E-mail: writersjournal@wadena.net. Website: www.writersjournal.com. Managing Editor: John Ogroske. **Contact:** Leon Ogroske, editor. **90% freelance written.** Bimonthly trade magazine covering writing. "*Writers' Journal* is read by thousands of aspiring writers whose love of writing has taken them to the next step: writing for money. We are an instructional manual giving writers the tools and information necessary to get their work published. We also print works by authors who have won our writing contests." Estab. 1980. Circ. 26,000. Pays on publication. Publishes ms an average of 10 months after acceptance. Byline given. Buys one-time rights. Editorial lead time 8 months. Submit seasonal material 8 months in advance. Accepts simultaneous submissions. Responds in 6 weeks to queries; 3 months to mss. Sample copy for $5. Writer's guidelines for #10 SASE.

Nonfiction: Book excerpts, essays, exposé, general interest (to writers), how-to (write, get published, interview, research), humor, inspirational, interview/profile, new product, opinion, personal experience, photo feature, technical. No erotica. Looking for articles on fiction writing (plot development, story composition and character development) and writing "how-to." **Buys 45 mss/year.** Send complete ms. Length: 800-2,500 words. **Pays $12-40.** Pays in contributor copies or other premiums if author agrees.

Photos: State availability of photos with submission. Reviews contact sheets, prints. Negotiates payment individually. Model releases required. Buys one-time rights.

Columns/Departments: Book and Software Reviews, 200 words; For Beginners Only (helpful advice to beginners), 800-2,500 words. **Buys 30 mss/year.** Send complete ms. **Pays $12-40.**

Fiction: "We only publish winners of our fiction writing contests—16 contests/year."

Poetry: Esther Leiper-Jefferson, poetry editor. No erotica. **Buys 25 poems/year.** Submit maximum 4 poems. Length: 25 lines. **Pays $5.**

Fillers: Anecdotes, facts, gags to be illustrated by cartoonist, short humor. **Buys 20/year.** Length: 200 words. **Pays up to $10.**

Tips: "Appearance must be professional with no grammatical or spelling errors submitted on white paper, double spaced with easy-to-read font."

WRITERS' POTPOURRI, Mea Productions, 55 Binks Hill Rd., Plymouth NH 03264. Fax: (603)536-4851. E-mail: me.allen@juno.com. Website: http://homepage.fcgnetworks.net/jetent/mea. **Contact:** Mary Emma Allen, editor. **25% freelance written.** Newsletter for writers covering writing and publishing. "This is a self-help, how-to publication for and by writers on writing and publishing in print and on the Internet." Estab. 1996. Circ. 100. **Pays on acceptance.** Publishes ms 6 months after acceptance. Byline given. Editorial lead time 6 months. Submit seasonal material 6 months in advance. "No queries; prefer complete manuscript." Accept simultaneous submissions. Responds in 2 months to mss. Sample copy for $1 and #10 SASE. Writer's guidelines for #10 SASE, online at website, by e-mail.

Nonfiction: How-to, personal experience. **Buys 6-8 mss/year.** Send complete ms with short bio. Length: 250-500 words. **Pays $5-10** plus 2 copies.

Reprints: Accepts previously published submissions.

Columns/Departments: Book Nook (reviews of writing books), 250 words. **Buys 4 mss/year. Pays $5.**

Fillers: Newsbreaks "about writers' own books, classes, workshops, accomplishments." Length: 25-100 words. "No pay because they are announcements of the writer's work."

Tips: "The articles need to be within the word limitation and you'll have more success with the 250 word articles. I seldom use long articles. The articles must be how-to tips and information for writers on writing, selling manuscripts, self-publishing, teaching workshops, giving author visits, promotion, book signings,etc."

$ $ $ WRITTEN BY, The Magazine of the Writers Guild of America, west, 7000 W. Third St., Los Angeles CA 90048. (323)782-4522. Fax: (323)782-4802. E-mail: writtenby@wga.org. **Contact:** Richard Stayton, editor. **40% freelance written.** "*Written By* is the premier monthly magazine written by and for America's screen and TV writers. We focus on the craft of screenwriting and cover all aspects of the entertainment industry from the perspective of the writer. We are read by all screenwriters and most entertainment executives." Estab. 1987. Circ. 17,000. **Pays on acceptance.** Publishes ms an average of 2 months after acceptance. Byline given. Offers 10% kill fee. Buys first North American serial and electronic rights. Editorial lead time 3-4 months. Submit seasonal material 4 months in advance. Accepts queries by mail, e-mail, fax. Responds in 2 months. Sample copy for $5. Writer's guidelines for SASE.

Break in with "an exclusive profile or Q&A with a major TV or screenwriter."

Nonfiction: Essays, humor, interview/profile, opinion. No "how to break into Hollywood," "how to write scripts"-type beginner pieces. **Buys 5-8 mss/year.** Query with published clips. Length: 500-2,500 words. **Pays $500-1,500.** Sometimes pays expenses of writers on assignment.

Reprints: Accepts previously published submissions.

Photos: State availability of photos with assignment. Reviews transparencies and prints. Offers no additional payment. Captions, model releases, identification of subjects required. Buys one-time rights.

Columns/Departments: Pays $250 maximum.

The online version of this publication contains material not found in the print edition. Contact: Scott Roeben.

Tips: "We are looking for more theoretical essays on screewriting past and/or present. Also the writer must *always* keep in mind that our audience is made up primarily of working writers who are inside the business, therefore all articles need to have an 'insider' feel and not be written for those who are still trying to break in to Hollywood. We prefer submissions on diskette or e-mail."

LAW

While all of these publications deal with topics of interest to attorneys, each has a particular slant. Be sure that your subject is geared to a specific market—lawyers in a single region, law students, paralegals, etc. Publications for law enforcement personnel are listed under Government & Public Service.

$ $ $ $ ABA JOURNAL, The Lawyer's Magazine, American Bar Association, 750 N. Lake Shore Dr., Chicago IL 60611. (312)988-6018. E-mail: abajournal@abanet.org. Website: www.abanet.org/journal/home.html. Editor: Gary Hengstler. **Contact:** Debra Cassens, managing editor. **10% freelance written.** Monthly magazine covering law. "The *ABA Journal* is an independent, thoughtful and inquiring observer of the law and the legal profession. The magazine is edited for members of the American Bar Association." Circ. 377,000. **Pays on acceptance.** Byline given. Pays kill fee. Buys all rights and makes work-for-hire assignments. Accepts queries by mail, e-mail. Sample copy and writer's guidelines free.

Nonfiction: Legal news and features. "We don't want anything that does not have a legal theme. No poetry or fiction." **Buys 10 mss/year (most are assigned).** Query with published clips. Length: 750-3,500 words. **Pays $350-2,000.**

Columns/Departments: Law Beat (reports on legal news and trends) 750-1,500 words; Solo Network (advice for solo practitioners) 1,000 words; In the Office (life on the job for lawyers) 750-1,500 words; In re Technology (technology for lawyers) 750-1,500 words. **Buys 50 mss/year (most are assigned).** Query with published clips. **Pays $350-700.**

$ $ $ BENCH & BAR OF MINNESOTA, Minnesota State Bar Association, 600 Nicollet Ave., Suite 380, Minneapolis MN 55402-1641. (612)333-1183. Fax: (612)333-4927. **Contact:** Judson Haverkamp, editor. **10% freelance written.** Magazine published 11 times/year. "Audience is mostly Minnesota lawyers. *Bench & Bar* seeks reportage, analysis, and commentary on trends and issues in the law and the legal profession, especially in Minnesota. Preference to items of practical/human interest to professionals in law." Estab. 1931. Circ. 16,000. **Pays on acceptance.** Publishes ms an average of 3 months after acceptance. Byline given. Buys first North American serial rights and makes work-for-hire assignments. Responds in 1 month. Sample copy for 9×12 SAE with 4 first-class stamps. Writer's guidelines free.

Nonfiction: General interest, historical/nostalgic, how-to (how to handle particular types of legal, ethical problems in office management, representation, etc.), humor, interview/profile, technical/legal. "We do not want one-sided opinion pieces or advertorial." **Buys 2-3 mss/year.** Query with published clips or send complete ms. Length: 1,500-3,000 words. **Pays $300-800.** Sometimes pays expenses of writers on assignment.

Photos: State availability of photos with submission. Reviews 5×7 or larger prints. Offers $25-100/photo upon publication. Model releases and identification of subjects required. Buys one-time rights.

Tips: "Articles should open with an interesting, 'catchy' lead, followed by a 'thesis paragraph' that tersely states the gist of the article. The exposition of the topic should then follow with a summary as the conclusion. Don't overwrite. If it only takes 8 pages to cover your subject, don't write a 12-page article."

$ $ $ $ CALIFORNIA LAWYER, Daily Journal Corporation, 1145 Market St., 8th Floor, San Francisco CA 94103. (415)252-0500. Fax: (415)252-2482. E-mail: tema_goodwin@dailyjournal.com. Managing Editor: Tema Goodwin. **Contact:** Peter Allen, editor. **85% freelance written.** Monthly magazine of law-related articles and general-interest subjects of appeal to lawyers and judges. "Our primary mission is to cover the news of the world as it affects the law and lawyers, helping our readers better comprehend the issues of the day and to cover changes and trends in the legal profession. Our readers are all 140,000 California lawyers, plus judges, legislators and corporate executives. Although we focus on California and the West, we have subscribers in every state. *California Lawyer* is a general interest magazine for people interested in law. Our writers are journalists." Estab. 1981. Circ. 140,000. **Pays on acceptance.** Publishes ms an average of 3 months after acceptance. Byline given. Pays 25% kill fee. Buys North American serial rights, electronic rights. Editorial leadtime 3 months. Accepts queries by mail, fax. Sample copy and writer's guidelines with SASE.

○▸ Break in by "showing us clips—we usually start people out on short news stories."

Nonfiction: Essays, interview/profile, general interest, news and feature articles on law-related topics. "We are interested in concise, well-written and well-researched articles on issues of current concern, as well as well-told feature narratives with a legal focus. We would like to see a description or outline of your proposed idea, including a list of possible sources." **Buys 36 mss/year.** Query with published clips or send ms. Length: 500-5,000 words. **Pays $250-2,000.** Pays expenses of writers on assignment.

Photos: Louise Kollenbaum, art director. State availability of photos with query letter or ms. Reviews prints. Identification of subjects and releases required.

Columns/Departments: California Esq. (current legal trends), 300 words. **Buys 30 mss/year.** Query with published clips if available. Length: 750-1,500 words. **Pays $50-250.**

COLORADO JOURNAL, A Daily Journal Corp. Publication, Daily Journal Corp., 717 17th St., Suite 2710, Denver CO 80202. (303)292-2575. Fax: (303)292-5821. E-mail: Brenda_McGann@dailyjournal.com. Website: www.dailyjournal.com. Editor: Katrina Dewey. **Contact:** Brenda McGann, executive editor. **20-30% freelance written.**

Weekly tabloid covering legal issues. Estab. 1996. Circ. 2,000. Pays on publication. Byline given. Buys all rights. Editorial lead time 1 month. Submit seasonal material 1 month in advance. Accepts queries by mail, e-mail, fax, phone. Responds in 1 month. Sample copy and writer's guidelines free.

Nonfiction: Exposé, general interest, how-to, interview/profile, photo feature, technical. Query. Length: 1,200-2,000 words. Sometimes pays expenses of writers on assignment.

Photos: State availability of photos with submission. Reviews contact sheets. Negotiates payment individually. Identification of subjects required. Buys all rights.

Columns/Departments: Ethel Bennet, legal editor. Query.

$ $ JOURNAL OF COURT REPORTING, National Court Reporters Association, 8224 Old Courthouse Rd., Vienna VA 22182. (703)556-6272. Fax: (703)556-6291. E-mail: pwacht@ncrahq.org. Editor: Peter Wacht. **20% freelance written.** Monthly (bimonthly July/August and November/December) magazine. "The *Journal of Court Reporting* has two complementary purposes: to communicate the activities, goals and mission of its publisher, the National Court Reporters Association; and, simultaneously, to seek out and publish diverse information and views on matters significantly related to the information/court reporting profession." Estab. 1905. Circ. 34,000. **Pays on acceptance.** Publishes ms an average of 3 months after acceptance. Byline given. Buys one-time rights and makes work-for-hire assignments. Editorial lead time 3 months. Accepts simultaneous submissions. Sample copy for $5. Writer's guidelines free.

Nonfiction: Essays, historical/nostalgic, how-to, interview/profile, new product, technical. **Buys 10 mss/year.** Query. Length: 1,200 words. **Pays $55-1,000.** Sometimes pays expenses of writers on assignment.

Reprints: Accepts previously published submissions.

Photos: State availability of photos with submission. Offers no additional payment for photos accepted with ms. Captions, model releases and identification of subjects required. Buys one-time rights.

$ $ $ LAW OFFICE COMPUTING, James Publishing, 3505 Cadillac Ave., Suite H, Costa Mesa CA 92626. (714)755-5468. Fax: (714)751-5508. E-mail: editorloc@jamespublishing.com. Website: www.lawofficecomputing.com. **Contact:** Jay Seidel, editor. **90% freelance written.** Bimonthly magazine covering legal technology industry. "*Law Office Computing* is a magazine written for attorneys and other legal professionals. It covers the legal technology field and features software reviews, profiles of prominent figures in the industry and 'how to' type articles." Estab. 1991. Circ. 8,000. Pays on publication. Publishes ms an average of 2 months after acceptance. Byline given. Buys first North American serial rights. Editorial lead time 2-4 months. Submit seasonal material 4 months in advance. Accepts queries by mail, e-mail, fax. Sample copy and writer's guidelines free.

Nonfiction: How-to, humor, interview/profile, new product, technical. Looking for Macintosh and Linux articles. **Buys 30 mss/year.** Query. Length: 2,000-4,000 words. **Pays $500-1,000.** Sometimes pays expenses of writers on assignment.

Photos: State availability of photos with submission.

Columns/Departments: Tech profile (profile firm using technology), 1,200 words; My Solution, 1,500 words; Software reviews: Short reviews (a single product), 400-500 words; Software Shootouts (two or three products going head-to-head), 1,000-1,500 words; Round-Ups/Buyer's Guides (8 to 15 products), 300-500 words per product. Each type of software review article has its own specific guidelines. Request the appropriate guidelines from your editor. **Buys 6 mss/year.** Query. **Pays $300-500.**

Tips: "If you are a practicing attorney, legal MIS or computer consultant, try the first-person My Solution column or a short review. If a professional freelance writer, technology profiles or a news story regarding legal technology are best; since most of our other copy is written by legal technology professionals."

$ $ LEGAL ASSISTANT TODAY, James Publishing, Inc., 3505 Cadillac Ave., Suite H, Costa Mesa CA 92626. (714)755-5468. Fax: (714)755-5508. E-mail: editorlat@jamespublishing.com. Website: www.legalassistanttoday.com. **Contact:** Rod Hughes, editor in chief. Bimonthly magazine "geared toward all legal assistants/paralegals throughout the United States and Canada, regardless of specialty (litigation, corporate, bankruptcy, environmental law, etc.). How-to articles to help paralegals perform their jobs more effectively are most in demand, as is career and salary information, and timely news and trends pieces." Estab. 1983. Circ. 13,000. **Pays on acceptance.** Byline given. Buys First North American Serial Rights on an exclusive basis, non-exclusive electronic/Internet right and non-exclusive rights to use the article, author's name, image and biographical data in advertising and promotion. Editorial lead time 10 weeks. Submit seasonal material at least 3 months in advance. Accepts simultaneous submissions. Accepts queries by mail, e-mail, fax. Responds in 1 month to queries; 2 months to mss. Sample copy and writer's guidelines free.

Nonfiction: News: brief, hard news topics regarding paralegals. Profiles: unique and interesting paralegals in unique and particular work-related situations. Features: present information to help paralegals advance their careers. **Payments for all submissions are determined on a case by case basis** and are at the discretion of the editor. All payment decisions are final.

Photos: Send photos with submission.

Tips: "Fax a detailed outline of a 3,000 to 4,500-word feature about something useful to working legal assistants. Writers *must* understand our audience. There is some opportunity for investigative journalism as well as the usual features, profiles and news. How-to articles are especially desired. If you are a great writer who can interview effectively, and really dig into the topic to grab readers' attention, we need you!"

N LOS ANGELES DAILY JOURNAL, Daily Journal Corporation, 915 E. First St., Los Angeles CA 90012. (213)229-5300. Fax: (213)625-0945. Website: www.dailyjournal.com. Editor: Katrina Dewey. **Contact:** Bob Emmers, managing editor. **5% freelance written.** Daily newspaper covering legal affairs. "Must be of interest to lawyers and others interested in legal and governmental affairs." Estab. 1877. Circ. 17,500. Pays on publication. Byline given. Kill fee varies. Buys first rights, electronic rights and makes work-for-hire assignments. Lead time varies. Accepts queries by mail, e-mail, fax, phone. Accepts simultaneous submissions.

Nonfiction: Book excerpts, essays, exposé, humor, interview/profile, opinion. **Number of mss bought/year varies.** Query with published clips. Length: 500-5,000 words. **Pay varies (individually negotiated).** Sometimes pays expenses of writers on assignment.

Photos: State availability of photos with submission. Negotiates payment individually. Captions and identification of subjects required. Buys all rights.

$ $ THE PENNSYLVANIA LAWYER, Pennsylvania Bar Association, P.O. Box 186, 100 South St., Harrisburg PA 17108-0186. Executive Editor: Marcy Carey Mallory. Editor: Geoff Yuda. **Contact:** Donald C. Sarvey, editorial director. **25% freelance written.** Prefers to work with published/established writers. Bimonthly magazine published as a service to the legal profession and the members of the Pennsylvania Bar Association. Estab. 1979. Circ. 30,000. **Pays on acceptance.** Publishes ms an average of 6 months after acceptance. Byline given. Generally buys first rights or one-time rights. Submit seasonal material 6 months in advance. Responds in 2 months. Sample copy for $2. Writer's guidelines for #10 SASE.

Nonfiction: Law-practice management, how-to, interview/profile, technology. All features *must* relate in some way to Pennsylvania lawyers or the practice of law in Pennsylvania. **Buys 8-10 mss/year.** Query. Length: 600-1,500 words. **Pays $50 for book reviews; $75-400 for assigned articles, $150 for unsolicited articles.** Sometimes pays expenses of writers on assignment.

Photos: State availability of photos with submission. Reviews contact sheets. Negotiates payment individually. Identification of subjects required. Buys one-time rights.

N $ $ $ STUDENT LAWYER, The magazine of the Law Student Division, American Bar Association, 750 N. Lake Shore Dr., Chicago IL 60611. (312)988-6048. Fax: (312)988-6081. E-mail: abastulawyer@abanet.org. Website: www.abanet.org/lsd. **Contact:** Ira Pilchen, editor. **85% freelance written.** Works with a small number of new writers each year. Monthly magazine (September-May). "*Student Lawyer* is not a legal journal. It is a legal-affairs features magazine that competes for a share of law students' limited spare time, so the articles we publish must be informative, lively, well-researched good reads." Estab. 1972. Circ. 35,000. **Pays on acceptance.** Buys first rights. Byline given. Editorial lead time 5 months. Submit seasonal material 6 months in advance. Publishes ms an average of 3 months after acceptance. Accepts queries by mail, e-mail, phone. Sample copy for $8. Writer's guidelines free on website.

Nonfiction: Features cover legal education and careers and social/legal subjects. Also profiles (prominent persons in law-related fields); opinion (on matters of current legal interest); essays (on legal affairs); interviews. Query with published clips. **Buys 25 mss/year.** Length: 2,500-4,000 words. **Pays $500-1,200 for features.** Covers some writer's expenses. *No fiction, please!*

Columns/Departments: Esq. (profiles out-of-the-ordinary lawyers), 1,200 words; Coping (dealing with law school), 1,200 words; Online (Internet and the law), 1,200 words; Legal-ease (language and legal writing), 1,200 words; Jobs (marketing to legal employers), 1,200 words; Opinion (opinion on legal issue), 800 words. **Buys 45 mss/year.** Query with published clips. **Pays $200-500.**

Tips: "*Student Lawyer* actively seeks good new reporters and writers eager to prove themselves. Legal training definitely not essential; writing talent is. The writer should not think we are a law review; we are a features magazine with the law (in the broadest sense) as the common denominator. Find issues of national scope and interest to write about; be aware of subjects the magazine—and other media—have already covered and propose something new. Write clearly and well. Expect to work with editor to polish manuscripts to perfection. We do not make assignments to writers with whose work we are not familiar. If you're interested in writing for us, send a detailed, thought-out query with three previously published clips. We are always willing to look at material on spec. Sorry, we don't return manuscripts."

LEATHER GOODS

N $ $ SHOWCASE INTERNATIONAL, The source for luggage, business cases and accessories, Luggage & Leather Goods Manufacturers of America, 350 Fifth Ave., Suite 2624, New York NY 10118. (212)695-2340. Fax: (212)643-8021. E-mail: showcase@llgma.org. Website: www.llgma.org. Editor: Michele M. Pittenger. **Contact:** John Misiano, senior editor. **5-10% freelance written.** Bimonthly magazine covering luggage, leather goods, accessories, trends and new products. "*Showcse* contains articles for retailers, dealers, manufacturers and suppliers, about luggage, business cases, personal leathergoods, handbags and accessories. Special articles report on trends in fashion promotions, selling and marketing techniques, industry statistics and other educational and promotional improvements and advancement. Estab. 1975. Circ. 14,500. **Pays on acceptance.** Publishes ms an average of 2 months after acceptance. Byline given. Offers $50 kill fee. Editorial lead time 2-3 months. Submit seasonal material 2 months in advance. Writer's guidelines free.

Nonfiction: Interview/profile, technical, travel. "No manufacturer profiles." **Buys 3 mss/year.** Query with published clips. Length: 1,200-1,600 words. **Pays $200-500.**

LUMBER

$ $ SOUTHERN LUMBERMAN, Greysmith Publishing, Inc., P.O. Box 681629, Franklin TN 37068-1629. (615)791-1961. Fax: (615)591-1035. E-mail: ngregg@southernlumberman.com. **Contact:** Nanci P. Gregg, editor. **20% freelance written.** Works with a small number of new/unpublished writers each year. Monthly trade journal for the sawmill industry. Estab. 1881. Circ. 15,000. Pays on publication. Publishes ms an average of 3 months after acceptance. Byline given. Buys first North American rights. Submit seasonal material 6 months in advance. Responds in 1 month to queries; 2 months to mss. Sample copy for $3 and 9×12 SAE with 5 first-class stamps. Writer's guidelines for #10 SASE.

Nonfiction: How-to (sawmill better), interview/profile, equipment analysis, technical. Sawmill features. **Buys 10-15 mss/year.** Query with or without published clips, or send complete ms. Length: 500-2,000 words. **Pays $150-350 for assigned articles; $100-250 for unsolicited articles.** Sometimes pays expenses of writers on assignment.

Reprints: Send tearsheet or photocopy of article and information about when and where the article previously appeared. Pays 25-50% of amount paid for an original article.

Photos: Send photos with submission. Reviews transparencies, 4×5 color prints. Offers $10-25/photo. Captions and identification of subjects required. Always looking for news feature types of photos featuring forest products, industry materials or people.

Tips: "Like most, we appreciate a clearly-worded query listing merits of suggested story—what it will tell our readers they need/want to know. We want quotes, we want opinions to make others discuss the article. Best hint? Find an interesting sawmill operation owner and start asking questions—I bet a story idea develops. We need color photos too. Find a sawmill operator and ask questions—what's he doing bigger, better, different. We're interested in new facilities, better marketing, improved production."

MACHINERY & METAL

$ ANVIL MAGAZINE, Voice of the Farrier & Blacksmith, P.O. Box 1810, 2770 Sourdough Flat, Georgetown CA 95634. (530)333-2142. Fax: (530)333-2906. E-mail: anvil@anvilmag.com. Website: www.anvilmag.com. **Contact:** Rob Edwards, publisher; Andy Juell, editor. **40% freelance written.** Monthly magazine featuring "how-to articles on hoof care and horseshoeing and blacksmithing, tips on running your own farrier or blacksmith business and general articles on those subjects." Estab. 1978. Circ. 4,000. Pays on publication. Publishes ms an average of 1 year after acceptance. Byline sometimes given. Buys first North American serial rights. Editorial lead time 3 months. Submit seasonal material 6 months in advance. Accepts simultaneous submissions. Accepts queries by mail, e-mail, fax. Sample copy for $6. Writer's guidelines free.

Nonfiction: General interest, how-to, humor, new product, photo feature, technical, book reviews of farrier/blacksmithing publications. Material has to be specific to the subjects of horseshoeing, hoof care, farrier interests, blacksmithing interests. **Buys 8-10 mss/year.** Send complete ms. Length: 1,200-1,600 words. **Pays $25-200.** Sometimes pays expenses of writers on assignment.

Reprints: Accepts previously published submissions.

Photos: Send photos with submission. Reviews transparencies and prints. Offers $25 additional payment for photos accepted with ms. Negotiates payment individually if photos only, such as for a how-to article. Identification of subjects required. Buys one-time rights.

Poetry: Traditional on blacksmithing and farriery subjects only. No cowboy poetry. **Buys 5-6 poems/year.** Submit maximum 1-2 poems. Length: 20-40 lines. **Pays $25.**

Tips: "Write clearly and concisely. Our readers are professionals. Stay away from generic topics or general horsemanship. Our most popular features are "how to's" and interviews. For interviews, don't be bashful—ask the tough questions."

[N] $ $ $ CUTTING TOOL ENGINEERING, CTE Publications, 400 Skokie Blvd., Suite 395, Northbrook IL 60062-7903. Fax: (847)559-4444. Website: www.ctemag.com. **Contact:** Don Nelson, editor. **50% freelance written.** Monthly magazine covering industrial metal cutting tools and metal cutting operations. "*Cutting Tool Engineering* serves owners, managers and engineers who work in manufacturing, specifically manufacturing that involves cutting or grinding metal or other materials. Writing should be geared toward improving manufacturing processes." Circ. 35,000. Pays 1 week before publication. Publishes ms an average of 2 months after acceptance. Byline given. Offers 50% kill fee. Buys all rights. Editorial lead time 2 months. Accepts queries by mail, fax. Accepts simultaneous submissions. Responds in 1 week to queries; 2 months to mss. Sample copy and writer's guidelines free.

Nonfiction: How-to, interview/profile, opinion, personal experience, technical. "No fiction, articles that don't relate to manufacturing." **Buys 30 mss/year.** Length: 1,500-3,000 words. **Pays $450-1,000.** Pays expenses of writers on assignment.

Photos: State availability of photos with submission. Reviews transparencies, prints. Negotiates payment individually. Captions required. Buys all rights.

Columns/Departments: Talking Points (interview with industry subject), 600 words; Cutting Remarks (opinion piece), 900 words; Manager's Desk (shop owner), 700 words; Back To Basics (tool review), 500 words. **Buys 28 mss/year.** Query with published clips. **Pays $150-300.**

Tips: "For queries, write two clear paragraphs about how the proposed article will play out. Include sources that would be in the article."

N $ NORTHWEST METALWORKER, The Magazine for Machinists & Related Tradesmen, Keithtoon Publishing, P.O. Box 903, Everett WA 98206-0903. (425)258-8960. Fax: (425)258-4703. E-mail: mtalworker@aol.com. Editor: Keith Ellis. **65% freelance written.** Monthly tabloid covering metalworking. "We are particularly interested in how-to in machining, welding, sheet metal fabrication or composite fabrication. As a regional pub, we like to do profiles of successful shops in Oregon, Idaho, California, Alaska, Montana or Washington. We'll take a look at humorous articles with a metalworking slant. Estab. 1989. Circ. 10,000. Pays on publication. Publishes ms an average of 1 month after acceptance. Byline given. Offers 50% kill fee. Buys first North American serial rights. Accepts queries by mail, e-mail, fax, phone. Responds in 2 months to queries; 1 month to mss. Sample copy for 10 × 13 SAE and 3 first-class stamps.
Nonfiction: Historical/nostalgic, how-to, humor, interview/profile. "No fiction. No 'machinists from space' or 'welders in love.' " **Buys 24 mss/year.** Query. Length: 500-1,500 words. **Pays $100-150.** Sometimes pays expenses of writers on assignment.
Reprints: Accepts previously published submissions.
Photos: State availability of photos with submissions. Offers $10. Captions, model releases, identification of subjects required. Buys one-time rights.
Fillers: Anecdotes, facts, short humor. **Buys 12/year.** Length: 10-250 words. **Pays $10-25.**
Tips: "Know about some aspect of metalworking. We print how-to articles for the tyro and pro."

$ $ ORNAMENTAL AND MISCELLANEOUS METAL FABRICATOR, National Ornamental And Miscellaneous Metals Association, 532 Forest Pkwy., Suite A, Forest Park GA 30297. Fax: (404)363-2857. E-mail: nomma2@aol .com. **Contact:** Todd Daniel, editor. **20% freelance written.** Bimonthly trade magazine "to inform, educate and inspire members of the ornamental and miscellaneous metalworking industry." Estab. 1959. Circ. 10,000. Pays when article is actually received. Byline given. Buys one-time rights. Editorial lead time 2 months. Submit seasonal material 2 months in advance. Accepts queries by mail, e-mail, fax. Responds in 1 month to queries. Sample copy for 9 × 12 SAE and 6 first-class stamps. Writer's guidelines for $1.
Nonfiction: Book excerpts, essays, exposé, general interest, historical/nostalgic, how-to, humor, inspirational, interview/profile, new product, opinion, personal experience, photo feature, technical. **Buys 5-7 mss/year.** Query. Length: 1,200-2,000 words. **Pays $250-275 for assigned articles; $50 minimum for unsolicited articles.** Pays expenses of writers on assignment.
Reprints: Send photocopy of article, typed ms with rights for sale noted and information about when and where the article previously appeared. Pays 100% of amount paid for an original article.
Photos: State availability of photos with submission. Reviews contact sheets, negatives, transparencies, prints. May offer additional payment for photos accepted with ms. Model releases required.
Tips: "Make article relevant to our industry. Don't write in passive voice."

$ $ WIRE ROPE NEWS & SLING TECHNOLOGY, VS Enterprises, P.O. Box 871, Clark NJ 07066. (908)486-3221. Fax: (732)396-4215. E-mail: vsent@aol.com. Website: www.wireropenews.com. **Contact:** Edward J. Bluvias, publisher. Editor: Barbara McGrath. Managing Editor: Conrad Miller. **100% freelance written.** Bimonthly magazine "published for manufacturers and distributors of wire rope, chain, cordage, related hardware, and sling fabricators. Content includes technical articles, news and reports describing the manufacturing and use of wire rope and related products in marine, construction, mining, aircraft and offshore drilling operations." Estab. 1979. Circ. 3,400. **Pays on acceptance.** Publishes ms an average of 6 months after acceptance. Byline sometimes given. Buys all rights. Editorial lead time 2 months. Submit seasonal material 2 months in advance. Accepts simultaneous submissions. Accepts queries by mail, fax.
Nonfiction: General interest, historical/nostalgic, interview/profile, photo feature, technical. **Buys 30 mss/year.** Send complete ms. Length: 2,500-5,000 words. **Pays $300-500.**
Reprints: Accepts previously published submissions.
Photos: Send photos with submission. Reviews contact sheets, 5 × 7 prints. Offers no additional payment for photos accepted with ms. Identification of subjects required. Buys all rights.

MAINTENANCE & SAFETY

N $ $ AMERICAN WINDOW CLEANER MAGAZINE, Voice of the Professional Window Cleaner, 27 Oak Creek Rd., El Sobrante CA 94803. (510)222-7080. Fax: (510)223-7080. E-mail: awcmag@aol.com. Website: www.awcmag.com. **Contact:** Richard Fabry, editor. **20% freelance written.** Bimonthly trade magazine covering window cleaning. "Articles to help window cleaners become more profitable, safe, professional and feel good about what they do." Estab. 1986. Circ. 9,000. **Pays on acceptance.** Publishes ms an average of 4 months after acceptance. Byline given. Offers 33% kill fee. Buys first rights. Editorial lead time 2 months. Submit seasonal material 3 months in advance. Responds in 2 weeks to queries; 1 month to mss. Sample copy and writer's guidelines free.

Nonfiction: How-to, humor, inspirational, interview/profile, personal experience, photo feature, technical, add-on businesses. Special issues: Covering a window cleaner, convention in February 2001 in Washington, DC. "Do not want PR-driven pieces. Want to educate not push a particular product." **Buys 20 mss/year.** Query. Length: 500-5,000 words. **Pays $50-250.** Sometimes pays expenses of writers on assignment.

Reprints: Accepts previously published submissions.

Photos: State availability of photos with submission. Reviews contact sheets, transparencies and 4×6 prints. Offers $10 per photo. Captions required. Buys one time rights.

Columns/Department: Window Cleaning Tips (tricks of the trade), 1,000-2,000 words; Humor-anecdotes-feel good-abouts (window cleaning industry); Computer High-tech (tips on new technology), all 1,000 words. **Buys 12 mss/year.** Query. **Pays $50-100.**

Tips: "*American Window Cleaner Magazine* covers an unusual niche that gets peoples' curiosity. What could possibly be covered in the international magazine for window cleaners? We are open to a wide varietyof articles as long as they are in some way connected to our industry. This would include: window cleaning unusual buildings, landmarks; working for well-known people/celebrities; window cleaning in resorts/casinos/unusual cities; humor or satire about our industry or the public's perception of it. If you have a good idea for a story, there is a good chance we will be interested in you writing it. At some point, we make phone contact and chat to see if our interests are compatible."

N **$ $ $ CANADIAN OCCUPATIONAL SAFETY**, Clifford/Elliot Ltd., 3228 S. Service Rd., Suite 209, Burlington, Ontario L7N 3H8 Canada. (905)634-2100. Fax: (905)634-2238. E-mail: mgault@cos-mag.com. Website: www.cos-mag.com. **Contact:** Michelle Gault, editor. **40% freelance written.** Bimonthly magazine. "We want informative articles dealing with issues that relate to occupational health and safety." Estab. 1989. Circ. 13,000. Pays on publication. Publishes ms an average of 3 months after acceptance. Byline given. Buys one-time rights. Editorial lead time 4 months. Submit seasonal material 4 months in advance. Responds in 3 weeks to queries; 1 month to mss. Sample copy and writer's guidelines free.

Nonfiction: How-to, interview/profile. **Buys 30 mss/year.** Query with published clips. Length: 750-3,500 words. **Pay varies.** Sometimes pays expenses of writers on assignment.

Photos: State availability of photos with submission. Reviews transparencies. Negotiates payment individually. Captions required. Buys one-time rights.

N **$ CLEANING BUSINESS**, P.O. Box 1273, Seattle WA 98111. (206)622-4241. Fax: (206)622-6876. E-mail: wgriffin@cleaningconsultants.com. Website: www.cleaningconsultants.com. Publisher: William R. Griffin. Associate Editor: Jim Saunders. **80% freelance written.** Quarterly magazine. "We cater to those who are self-employed in any facet of the cleaning and maintenance industry and seek to be top professionals in their field. *Cleaning Business* is published for self-employed cleaning professionals, specifically carpet, upholstery and drapery cleaners; janitorial and maid services; window washers; odor, water and fire damage restoration contractors. Our readership is small but select. We seek concise, factual articles, realistic but definitely upbeat." Circ. 6,000. Pays 1 month after publication. Publishes ms an average of 3 months after acceptance. Byline given. Buys first serial, second serial (reprint) and all rights or makes work-for-hire assignments. Submit seasonal material 6 months in advance. Responds in 3 months. Sample copy for $3 and 8×10 SAE with 3 first-class stamps. Writer's guidelines for #10 SASE.

Nonfiction: Exposé (safety/health business practices); how-to (on cleaning, maintenance, small business management); humor (clean jokes, cartoons); interview/profile; new product (must be unusual to rate full article—mostly obtained from manufacturers); opinion; personal experience; technical. Special issues: "What's New?" (February). No "wordy articles written off the top of the head, obviously without research, and needing more editing time than was spent on writing." **Buys 40 mss/year.** Query with or without published clips. Length: 500-3,000 words. **Pays $5-80.** ("Pay depends on amount of work, research and polishing put into article much more than on length.") Pays expenses of writers on assignment with prior approval only.

Photos: State availability of photos or send photos with ms. **Pays $5-25** for "smallish" b&w prints. Captions, model release and identification of subjects required. Buys one-time rights and reprint rights. "Magazine size is 8½×11—photos need to be proportionate. Also seeks full-color photos of relevant subjects for cover."

Columns/Departments: "Ten regular columnists now sell four columns per year to us. We are interested in adding Safety & Health and Fire Restoration columns (related to cleaning and maintenance industry). We are also open to other suggestions—send query." **Buys 36 columns/year;** department information obtained at no cost. Query with or without published clips. Length: 500-1,500 words. **Pays $15-85.**

Fillers: Jokes, gags, anecdotes, short humor, newsbreaks, cartoons. **Buys 40/year.** Length: 3-200 words. **Pays $1-20.**

Tips: "We are constantly seeking quality freelancers from all parts of the country. A freelancer can best break in to our publication with fairly technical articles on how to do specific cleaning/maintenance jobs; interviews with top professionals covering this and how they manage their business; and personal experience. Our readers demand concise, accurate information. Don't ramble. Write only about what you know and/or have researched. Editors don't have time to rewrite your rough draft. Organize and polish before submitting."

MANAGEMENT & SUPERVISION

This category includes trade journals for middle management business and industrial managers, including supervisors and office managers. Journals for business executives and owners are classified under Business Management. Those for industrial plant managers are listed in Industrial Operations.

$ $ HR MAGAZINE, On Human Resource Management, Society for Human Resource Management, 1800 Duke St., Alexandria VA 22314-3497. (703)548-3440. Fax: (703)548-9140. E-mail: hrmag@shrm.org. Website: www.shrm.org. Editor: Leon Rubis. **Contact:** Stacy VanDerWall, editorial assistant. **70% freelance written.** Monthly magazine covering human resource management professions with special focus on business news that affects the workplace including compensation and benefits, recruiting, training and development, management trends, court decisions, legislative actions and government regulations. Estab. 1948. Circ. 130,000. **Pays on acceptance.** Publishes ms an average of 2 months after acceptance. Byline given. Buys first or all rights. Editorial lead time 4 months. Responds in 1 month to queries, 2 months to mss. Sample copy free. Writer's guidelines for #10 SASE or free on website.
Nonfiction: Expert advice and analysis, news features, technical. **Buys 50 mss/year.** Query. Length: 1,800-2,500 words. Pays expenses of writers on assignment.
Photos: State availability of photos with submission. Model releases and identification of subjects required. Buys one-time rights.
Tips: "Readers are members of the Society for Human Resource Management (SHRM), mostly HR managers with private employers."

[N] $ $ HR NEWS, Society for Human Resource Management, 1800 Duke St., Alexandria VA 22314. (703)548-3440. Fax: (703)548-9140. E-mail: hrnews@shrm.org. Website: www.shrm.org. Editor: Leon Rubis. Monthly tabloid covering human resource professions "with special focus on business news that affects the workplace including court decisions, legislative actions and government regulations." Estab. 1982. Circ. 130,000. Pays on publication. Publishes ms an average of 1 month after acceptance. Byline given. Buys first or one-time rights or makes work-for-hire assignments. Editorial lead time 2 months. Responds in 1 month to queries. Sample copy and writer's guidelines free.
Nonfiction: News features, business trends. **Buys 8-12 mss/year.** Query with published clips. Length: 300-1,000 words. Pays expenses of writers on assignment.
Photos: State availability of photos with submission. Reviews contact sheets, any prints. Negotiates payment individually. Captions and identification of subjects required. Buys one-time rights.
Tips: "Experienced business/news writers should send some clips and story ideas for our file of potential writers in various regions and for various subjects. Local/state business news or government actions affecting HR management of potentially national interest is an area open to freelancers."

$ $ $ HUMAN RESOURCE EXECUTIVE, LRP Publications Magazine Group, 747 Dresher Rd., P.O. Box 980, Dept. 500, Dresher PA 19044. (215)784-0910. Fax: (215)784-0275. E-mail: dshadovitz@lrp.com. Website: www.workindex.com. **Contact:** David Shadovitz, editor. **30% freelance written.** "Monthly magazine serving the information needs of chief human resource professionals/executives in companies, government agencies and nonprofit institutions with 500 or more employees." Estab. 1987. Circ. 45,000. **Pays on acceptance.** Publishes ms an average of 2 months after acceptance. Byline given. Offers 50% kill fee on assigned stories. Buys first and all rights including reprint rights. Accepts queries by: mail, e-mail, fax. Responds in 1 month. Sample copy for 10×13 SAE with 2 first-class stamps. Writer's guidelines for #10 SAE with 1 first-class stamp.
Nonfiction: Book excerpts, interview/profile. **Buys 16 mss/year.** Query with published clips. Length: 1,700-2,000 words. **Pays $200-900.** Sometimes pays expenses of writers on assignment.
Photos: State availability of photos with submission. Reviews contact sheets. Offers no additional payment for photos accepted with ms. Identification of subjects required. Buys first and repeat rights.

[N] $ $ INCENTIVE, Managing & Marketing Through Motivation, Bill Communications, 355 Park Ave. S., New York NY 10010. (212)592-6453. Fax: (212)592-6459. Editor: Vincent Alonzo. **Contact:** Joan Steinauer, executive editor. **10-15% freelance written.** Monthly magazine covering sales promotion and employee motivation: managing and marketing through motivation. Estab. 1905. Circ. 40,000. Pays on publication. Publishes ms an average of 3 months after acceptance. Byline always given. Buys all rights. Editorial lead time 3 months. Submit seasonal material 3 months in advance. Accepts queries by mail, fax. Accepts simultaneous submissions. Responds in 1 month to queries; 2 months to mss. Sample copy for #10 SASE. Writer's guidelines free.
  ● *Incentive* won the *Folio* Award of Excellence in 1994, 1995, 1996, as well as a certificate of merit from the Jesse H. Neal Award.
Nonfiction: How-to (types of sales promotion, buying product categories, using destinations), interview/profile (sales promotion executives), new products, travel (incentive-oriented). **Buys 4-5 mss/year.** Query. Length: 500-3,000 words. **Pays $100-500.** Pays the expenses of writers on assignment.
Photos: State availability of photos with submission. Reviews transparencies. Negotiates payment individually. Identification of subjects required. Buys all rights.

Ⓝ $ MANAGE, 2210 Arbor Blvd., Dayton OH 45439. (937)294-0421. Fax: (937)294-2374. E-mail: doug@n-ma1.org. Website: www.nma1.org. **Contact:** Douglas E. Shaw, editor-in-chief. **60% freelance written.** Works with a small number of new/unpublished writers each year. Quarterly magazine for first-line and middle management and scientific/technical managers. Estab. 1925. Circ. 40,000. **Pays on acceptance.** Publishes ms an average of 6 months after acceptance. Buys North American magazine rights with reprint privileges; book rights remain with the author. Responds in 3 months. Sample copy and writer's guidelines for 9×12 SAE with 3 first-class stamps.
Nonfiction: "All material published by *Manage* is in some way management-oriented. Most articles concern one or more of the following categories: communications, executive abilities, human relations, job status, leadership, motivation and productivity and professionalism. Articles should be specific and tell the manager how to apply the information to his job immediately. Be sure to include pertinent examples, and back up statements with facts. *Manage* does not want essays or academic reports, but interesting, well-written and practical articles for and about management." **Buys 6 mss/issue.** Phone queries OK. Submit complete ms. Length: 600-1,000 words. **Pays 5¢/word.**
Reprints: Accepts previously published submissions. Send photocopy of article or short story. Pays 100% of amount paid for an original article.
Tips: "Keep current on management subjects; submit timely work. Include word count on first page of manuscript."

Ⓝ $ $ SECURITY WATCH: Protecting People, Property & Assets, Bureau of Business Practice, 7201 McKinney Circle, Frederick MD 21704-8356. Fax: (860)437-0796. E-mail: richard.dann@aspenpubl.com. Website: www.bbpnews.com. **Contact:** Dick Dann, editor. **50% freelance written.** Bimonthly publication focusing on such issues as loss prevention, new court rulings and pending laws that affect security, control of risk of workplace violence, fraud, shoplifting and burglarizing." Circ. 3,000. Pays when article assigned to future issue. Buys all rights. Sample copy and writer's guidelines free.
Nonfiction: Interview (with security professionals only). "Articles should be tight and specific. They should deal with new security techniques or new twists on old ones." **Buys 2-5 mss/issue.** Query by phone. Length: 500-800 words. **Pays 20¢/word.**
Tips: "*Security Watch* targets managers responsible for security primarily in the fields of manufacturing, retail, and office organizations, but also in hospitals, colleges, military installations, and museums."

$ SUPERVISION, 320 Valley, Burlington IA 52601-5513. Fax: (319)752-3421. Publisher: Michael S. Darnall. **Contact:** Teresa Levinson, editor. **95% freelance written.** Monthly magazine for first-line foremen, supervisors and office managers. "*Supervision*'s objective is to provide informative articles which develop the attitudes, skills, personal and professional qualities of supervisory staff, enabling them to use more of their potential to maximize productivity, minimize costs, and achieve company and personal goals." Estab. 1939. Circ. 2,620. Pays on publication. Publishes ms an average of 6 months after acceptance. Buys all rights. Accepts queries by: mail, fax, phone. Responds in 1 month. Sample copy and writer's guidelines for 9×12 SAE with 4 first-class stamps; mention *Writer's Market* in request.
Nonfiction: How-to (cope with supervisory problems, discipline, absenteeism, safety, productivity, goal setting, etc.); personal experience (unusual success story of foreman or supervisor). No sexist material written from only a male viewpoint. Include biography and/or byline with ms submissions. Author photos requested. **Buys 12 mss/issue.** Query. Length: 1,500-1,800 words. **Pays 4¢/word.**
Tips: "Following AP stylebook would be helpful." Uses no advertising. Send correspondence to Editor.

MARINE & MARITIME INDUSTRIES

$ $ MARINE BUSINESS JOURNAL, The Voice of the Marine Industries Nationwide, 330 N. Andrews Ave., Ft. Lauderdale FL 33301. (954)522-5515. Fax: (954)522-2265. E-mail: sboating@icanect.com. Executive Editor: David Strickland. **Contact:** Liz Haworth. **25% freelance written.** Bimonthly magazine that covers the recreational boating industry. "*The Marine Business Journal* is aimed at boating dealers, distributors and manufacturers, naval architects, yacht brokers, marina owners and builders, marine electronics dealers, distributors and manufacturers, and anyone involved in the US marine industry. Articles cover news, new product technology and public affairs affecting the industry." Estab. 1986. Circ. 26,000. Pays on publication. Publishes ms an average of 1 month after acceptance. Byline given. Buys first North American serial, one-time or second serial (reprint rights). Accepts queries by mail. Responds in 2 weeks to queries. Sample copy for $2.50 and 9×12 SAE with 7 first-class stamps. Writer's guidelines for #10 SASE.
Nonfiction: Buys 20 mss/year. Query with published clips. Length: 500-2,000 words. **Pays $100-200 for assigned articles.** Sometimes pays expenses of writers on assignment.
Photos: State availability of photos with submission. Reviews 35mm or larger transparencies, 5×7 prints. Offers $25-50/photo. Captions, model releases, identification of subjects required. Buys one-time rights.
Tips: "Query with clips. It's a highly specialized field, written for professionals by professionals, almost all on assignment or by staff."

Ⓝ $ $ PROFESSIONAL MARINER, Journal of the Maritime Industry, Navigator Publishing, 18 Danforth St., Portland ME 04101. (207)772-2466. Fax: (207)772-2879. E-mail: editors@professionalmariner.com. **Contact:** Evan

True, editor. **50% freelance written.** Bimonthly magazine covering professional seamanship and maritime industry news. Estab. 1993. Circ. 29,000. Pays on publication. Byline given. Buys all rights. Editorial lead time 3 months. Accepts simultaneous submissions.

Nonfiction: For professional mariners on vessels and ashore. Seeks submissions on industry news, regulations, towing, piloting, technology, engineering, business, maritime casualties and feature stories about the maritime industry. Does accept "sea stories" and personal professional experiences as correspondence pieces. **Buys 15 mss/year.** Query. Length varies: short clips to long profiles/features. **Pays 15¢/word.** Sometimes pays expenses of writers on assignment.

Reprints: Accepts previously published submissions.

Photos: Send photos and photo captions with submission. Reviews slides and prints. Negotiates payment individually. Identification of subjects required. Buys one-time rights.

MEDICAL

Through these journals physicians, therapists and mental health professionals learn how other professionals help their patients and manage their medical practices. Publications for nurses, laboratory technicians and other medical personnel are listed in the Hospitals, Nursing and Nursing Home section. Publications for drug store managers and drug wholesalers and retailers, as well as hospital equipment suppliers, are listed with Drugs, Health Care and Medical Products. Publications for consumers that report trends in the medical field are found in the Consumer Health and Fitness categories.

$ $ $ AMA ALLIANCE TODAY, American Medical Association Alliance, Inc., 515 N. State St., Chicago IL 60610. (312)464-4470. Fax: (312)464-5020. E-mail: amaa@ama-assn.org. Editor: Catherine Potts, MSJ. **10% freelance written.** Work with both established and new writers. Quarterly magazine for physicians' spouses. Estab. 1965. Circ. 60,000. **Pays on acceptance.** Publishes ms an average of 6 months after acceptance. Buys first rights. Accepts simultaneous submissions. Accepts queries by mail, e-mail, fax. Sample copy for 9×12 SAE with 2 first-class stamps.

Nonfiction: All articles must be related to the experiences of physicians' spouses. Current health issues; financial topics, physicians' family circumstances, business management and volunteer leadership how-to's. Query with clear outline of article—what points will be made, what conclusions drawn, what sources will be used. Length: 1,000 words. **Pays $300-800.**

Photos: State availability of photos with query. Uses all color visuals.

Tips: "The writing will be more mass appeal. Yet, the magazine will still focus on public health issues and report on the events of state and county alliances which are made up of physician's spouses."

[N] AMERICAN MEDICAL NEWS, American Medical Association, 515 N. State St., Chicago IL 60610. (312)464-4429. **Contact:** Kathryn Trombatore. "*American Medical News* is the nation's most widely circulated newspaper focusing on socioeconomic issues in medicine." Circ. 375,000. Pays on publication. Buys first rights. Responds in 1 month. Writer's guidelines for #10 SASE.

Nonfiction: Health, business. Needs "market driven features reporting developments that affect the structure of the health care industry." **Buys 20-25 mss/year.** Query with SASE. Length: 1,500-2,000 words. **Pay varies.**

[N] $ $ CONTINUING CARE, Stevens Publishing, 5151 Beltline Rd., Dallas TX 75240. (972)687-6748. Fax: (972)687-6770. E-mail: ksteinhauser@stevenspublishing.com. Website: www.ccareonline.com. **Contact:** Kyle Steinhauser, editor. **10% freelance written.** Monthly trade journal covering care management. "*Continuing Care* provides practical information for managed care professionals in case management and discharge planning of high-risk, high-cost patient cases in home health care, rehabilitation and long-term care settings. *Continuing Care* encourages practical articles on case management, focusing on quality outcome of patient care at a cost-effective price to the health care payer. The magazine also informs readers on professional and business news, insurance and reimbursement issues and legal and legislative news." Estab. 1971. Circ. 22,000. Pays on publication. Byline given. Offers no kill fee. Buys all rights. Editorial lead time 4 months. Submit seasonal material 4 months in advance. Accepts queries by mail, e-mail, fax, phone. Accepts simultaneous submissions. Responds in 6 weeks to queries; 1 month to mss. Sample copy and writer's guidelines free.

Nonfiction: Essays, exposé, general interest, new product, opinion, technical. **Buys 4 mss/year.** Query with published clips. Length: 2,500-5,000 words. **Pays $0-500.** Somtetimes pays in contributor copies.

Photos: Send photos with submission. Offers $0-500/photo. Captions and identification of subjects required.

Columns/Departments: Managed Care, 3,000 words. **Buys 3 mss/year.** Query with published clips. **Pays $0-50.**

[N] $ $ EMS MAGAZINE, Journal of Emergency Care, Rescue and Transportation, Summer Communications, 7626 Densmore Ave., Van Nuys CA 91311. Fax: (818)786-9246. E-mail: emseditor@aol.com. Website: www.ems magazine.com. **Contact:** Nancy Perry, editor. **50% freelance written.** Monthly magazine covering prehospital emergency medicine. Articles are designed to service the educational needs of EMTs and paramedics. They cover clinical care, current news items and psychosocial issues. Estab. 1972. Circ. 47,000. Pays on publication. Publishes ms an average of 8 months after acceptance. Byline given. Buys first North American rights and electronic rights. Editorial lead time 6 months. Submit seasonal material 6 months in advance. Accepts queries by mail, e-mail, fax. Responds in 1 week to queries; 1 month to mss. Sample copy free. Writer's guidelines free.

Nonfiction: Book excerpts, essays, interview/profile, opinion, personal experience, technical and clinical mss. **Buys 50 mss/year.** Query with published clips. Length: 1,000-4,000 words. **Pays $300-400. Sometimes pays writers in trade advertisement.**

Photos: State availability of photos with submission. Reviews contact sheets and 5×7 transparencies. Negotiates payment individually. Captions required. Buys one-time rights.

Columns/Departments: Guest Editorial, 1,000 words. **Buys 50 mss/year.** Query with published clips. **Pays $75-125.**

⭐ **$ $ JEMS, The Journal of Emergency Medical Services**, Jems Communications, 1947 Camino Vida Roble, Suite 200, Carlsbad CA 92008-2789. (760)431-9797. Fax: (760)930-9567. Website: www.jems.com. **Contact:** A.J. Heightman, editor. **95% freelance written.** Monthly magazine directed to personnel who serve the pre-hospital emergency medicine industry: paramedics, EMTs, emergency physicians and nurses, administrators, EMS consultants, etc. Estab. 1980. Circ. 45,000. Pays on publication. Publishes ms an average of 6 months after acceptance. Byline given. Buys all North American serial rights. Submit seasonal material 6 months in advance. Accepts queries by mail, e-mail, fax. Responds in 6 weeks to queries. Sample copy and writer's guidelines free.

Nonfiction: Essays, exposé, general interest, how-to, continuing education, humor, interview/profile, new product, opinion, personal experience, photo feature, technical. **Buys 50 mss/year.** Query. Length: 1,500-2,500 words. **Pays $200-400.**

Photos: State availability of photos with submission. Reviews 4×6 prints. Offers $25 minimum per photo. Model releases and identification of subjects required. Buys one-time rights.

Columns/Departments: "Columns and departments are staff-written with the exception of commentary on EMS issues and practices." Length: 850 words maximum. Query with or without published clips. **Pays $50-250.**

Tips: "Please submit a one-page query letter before you send a manuscript. Your query should answer these questions: 1) What specifically are you going to tell *JEMS* readers? 2) Why do *JEMS* readers need to know this? 3) How will you make your case (i.e., literature review, original research, interviews, personal experience, observation)? Your query should explain your qualifications, as well as include previous writing samples."

$ $ $ $ MANAGED CARE, 275 Phillips Blvd., Trenton NJ 08618-1426. (609)882-5700. Fax: (609)882-3213. E-mail: editors@managedcaremag.com. Website: www.managedcaremag.com. **Contact:** John Marcille, editor. **40% freelance written.** Monthly magazine. "We emphasize practical, usable information that helps the physician or HMO administrator cope with the options, challenges and hazards in the rapidly changing health care industry. Our regular readers understand that 'health care reform' isn't a piece of legislation; it's an evolutionary process that's already well under way. But we hope to help our readers also keep the faith that led them to medicine in the first place." Estab. 1992. Circ. 60,000. **Pays on acceptance.** Publishes ms an average of 1 month after acceptance. Byline given. Offers 20% kill fee. Buys all rights. Editorial lead time 3 months. Submit seasonal material 4 months in advance. Accepts queries by mail, e-mail, fax, phone. Responds in 3 weeks to queries; 2 months to mss. Sample copy free.

Nonfiction: Book excerpts, general interest, how-to (deal with requisites of managed care, such as contracts with health plans, affiliation arrangements, relationships with staffers, computer needs, etc.), technical. Also considered occasionally are personal experience, opinion, interview/profile and humor pieces, *but these must have a strong managed care angle and draw upon the insights of* (if they are not written by) *a knowledgeable MD or other managed care professional.* Don't waste those stamps on "A Humorous View of My Recent Gall Bladder Operation." **Buys 40 mss/year.** Query with clips. Length: 1,000-3,000 words. **Pays 50 to 60¢/word.** Pays expenses of writers on assignment.

Photos: State availability of photos with submissions. Reviews contact sheets, negatives, transparencies, prints. Negotiates payment individually. Buys first-time rights.

Columns/Departments: Michael Dalzell, senior editor. News/Commentary (usually staff-written, but factual anecdotes involving managed care's effect on providers are welcome. 100-300 words. **Pays $100.** Employer Update (focuses on practical advice for purchasers of healthcare) 800-1,000 words; State Initiatives (looks at state-level trends in managed care with national implications). **Pays $300-600.**

🖳 The online magazine carries original content not found in the print edition. Contact: John Marcille.

Tips: "We're looking for reliable freelancers who can write for our audience with our approach, so 'breaking in' may yield assignments. Do this by writing impeccably and with flair, and try to reflect the interests and perspective of the practicing physician or the active managed care executive. (Cardinal rule: The reader is busy, with many things vying for his/her reading time. Be sprightly, but don't waste our readers' time.) Review back issues on our website."

$ $ $ $ MEDICAL ECONOMICS, 5 Paragon Dr., Montvale NJ 07645. (201)358-7367. Fax: (201)722-2688. E-mail: helen.mckenna@medec.com. Website: www.medec.com. **Contact:** Helen A. McKenna, outside copy editor. **2% freelance written.** Biweekly magazine. "*Medical Economics* is a national business magazine read by M.D.s and D.O.s in office-based practice. Our purpose is to be informative and useful to practicing physicians in the professional and financial management of their practices. We look for contributions from writers who know—or will make the effort to learn—the non-clinical concerns of today's physician. These writers must be able to address those concerns in feature articles that are clearly written and that convey authoritative information and advice. Our articles focus very narrowly on a subject, and explore it in depth." Circ. 192,000. **Pays on acceptance.** Byline given. Offers 25% kill fee. Buys first world publication rights. Accepts queries by mail, e-mail, fax. Responds in 1 month to queries. Sample copy free.

Nonfiction: Articles about private physicians in innovative, pioneering and/or controversial situations affecting medical care delivery, patient relations or malpractice prevention/litigation; personal finance topics. "We do not want overviews or pieces that only skim the surface of a general topic. We address physician readers in a conversational, yet no-nonsense tone, quoting recognized experts on office management, personal finance, patient relations and medical-legal issues." **Buys 40-50 mss/year.** Query with published clips. Length: 1,500-3,000 words. **Pays $1,200-2,500 for assigned articles.** Pays expenses of writers on assignment; expenses over $100 must be approved in advance—receipts required.

● Ranked as one of the best markets for freelance writers in *Writer's Yearbook* magazine's annual "Top 100 Markets," January 2000.

Tips: "We look for articles about physicians who run high-quality, innovative practices suited to the age of managed care. We also look for how-to service articles—on practice-management and personal-finance topics—which must contain anecdotal examples to support the advice. Read the magazine carefully noting its style and content. Then send detailed proposals or outlines on subjects that would interest our mainly primary-care physician readers."

$ $ MODERN PHYSICIAN, Essential Business News for the Executive Physician, Crain Communications, 740 N. Rush St., Chicago IL 60611-2590. (312)649-5324. Fax: (312)649-5393. Website: www.modernphysician.com. **Contact:** Karen Petitte, editor. **40% freelance written.** Monthly magazine covering business and management news for doctors. "*Modern Physician* offers timely topical news features with lots of business information—revenues, earnings, financial data." Estab. 1997. Circ. 31,000. **Pays on acceptance.** Publishes ms an average of 2 months after acceptance. Byline given. Buys all rights. Editorial lead time 2 months. Accepts queries by mail, e-mail, fax, phone. Responds in 6 weeks to queries. Sample copy free. Writer's guidelines sent after query.

O─┐ Break in with a regional story involving business or physicians.

Nonfiction: Length: 1,000-2,000 words. **Pays 40-50¢/word.**

[N] $ $ OHIO MEDICINE, Ohio State Medical Association, 3401 Mill Run Dr., Hilliard OH 43026. (614)527-6762. Fax: (614)527-6763. E-mail: ohiomed@osma.org. Website: www.osma.org. **Contact:** Karen Edwards, editor. **75% freelance written.** Monthly tabloid covering medical news. "*Ohio Medicine* is written specifically for Ohio physicians and features the latest legislative, legal, and reimbursement news in addition to practical information on running a practice more efficiently." Estab. 1905. Circ. 15,000. **Pays on acceptance.** Byline given. Buys first North American serial rights. Editorial lead time 2 months. Submit seasonal material 4 months in advance. Accepts queries by mail, e-mail, fax. Accepts simultaneous submissions. Responds in 1 month to queries. Sample copy free.

Nonfiction: General interest, how-to, humor, interview/profile. No clinical or scientific. **Buys 72-80 mss/year.** Query with published clips. Length: 300-1,500 words. **Pays $100-500.** Pays expenses of writers on assignment.

Photos: State availability of photos with submission. Reviews 5×7 prints. Negotiates payment individually. Identification of subjects required. Buys one-time rights.

Columns/Departments: Your Practice Guide (hands-on practice management information) 500-800. **Buys 48-50 mss/year.** Query with published clips. **Pays up to $300.**

Tips: "Ask your physician for his or her concerns about practicing medicine in today's managed-care climate. Those are the topics we cover. Learn what doctors and your area are doing to address these issues. We need news especially from Cleveland, Akron, Dayton, Youngstown. I'd love to see more marketplace stories—what specific practices are doing to compete and even thrive in managed care. Also, ideas for our 'Portrait' column which features physicians who volunteer their time in other pursuits or with unique outside interests. Also, I see far too many stories that are interesting from a patient's perspective, not from a physician's. If it interests you as a patient, chances are, it won't interest us."

$ $ PHYSICIAN, Focus on the Family, 8605 Explorer Dr., Colorado Springs CO 80920. (719)531-3400. Fax: (719)531-3499. E-mail: physician@macmail.fotf.org Website: www.family.org. **Contact:** Susan Stevens, editor. Managing Editor: Charles Johnson. **20% freelance written.** Bimonthly. "The goal of our magazine is to encourage physicians in their faith, family and medical practice. Writers should understand the medical lifestyle." Estab. 1989. Circ. 83,000. **Pays on acceptance.** Publishes ms an average of 6 months after acceptance. Byline given. Buys first North American serial rights. Editorial lead time 1 year. Accepts queries by mail, e-mail, fax, phone. Responds in 2 months. Sample copy free with SASE.

Nonfiction: General interest, interview/profile, personal experience, religious, technical. "No patient's opinions of their doctor." **Buys 20-30 mss/year.** Query. Length: 900-2,400 words. **Pays $100-500.** Sometimes pays expenses of writers on assignment.

Reprints: Accepts previously published submissions.

Photos: State availability of photos with submission. Reviews transparencies. Negotiates payment individually. Buys one-time rights.

Tips: "Most writers are M.D.'s."

[N] $ $ $ PHYSICIANS' TRAVEL & MEETING GUIDE, Quadrant HealthCom, Inc., 26 Main St., Chatham NJ 07928. Fax: (973)701-8895. **Contact:** Bea Riemschneider, editor-in-chief. Managing Editor: Susann Tepperberg. **60% freelance written.** Monthly magazine covering travel for physicians and their families. *Physicians' Travel &*

Meeting Guide supplies continuing medical education events listings and extensive travel coverage of international and national destinations. Circ. 142,833. **Pays on acceptance.** Byline given. Buys first North American serial rights. Submit seasonal material 4-6 months in advance. Responds in 3 months.

Nonfiction: Photo feature, travel. **Buys 25-35 mss/year.** Query with published clips. Length: 450-3,000 words. **Pays $150-1,000 for assigned articles.**

Photos: State availability of photos with submission. Send photos with submission. Reviews 35mm or 4×5 transparencies. Captions and identification of subjects required. Buys one-time rights.

$ $ PODIATRY MANAGEMENT, Kane Communications, Inc., P.O. Box 750129, Forest Hills NY 11375. (718)897-9700. Fax: (718)896-5747. E-mail: bblock@prodigy.net. Website: www.podiatryMGT.com. **Contact:** Barry Block, editor. Publisher: Scott C. Borowsky. Magazine published 9 times/year for practicing podiatrists. "Aims to help the doctor of podiatric medicine to build a bigger, more successful practice, to conserve and invest his money, to keep him posted on the economic, legal and sociological changes that affect him." Estab. 1982. Circ. 13,000. Pays on publication. Byline given. Buys first North American serial and second serial (reprint) rights. Submit seasonal material 4 months in advance. Accepts queries by mail, e-mail. Accepts simultaneous submissions. Responds in 2 weeks. Sample copy for $3 and 9×12 SAE. Writer's guidelines for #10 SASE.

Nonfiction: General interest (taxes, investments, estate planning, recreation, hobbies); how-to (establish and collect fees, practice management, organize office routines, supervise office assistants, handle patient relations); interview/ profile about interesting or well-known podiatrists; and personal experience. "These subjects are the mainstay of the magazine, but offbeat articles and humor are always welcome." Send tax and financial articles to Martin Kruth, 5 Wagon Hill Lane, Avon CT 06001 or e-mail mgoldberg@avonct. **Buys 25 mss/year.** Query. Length: 1,000-2,500 words. **Pays $150-600.**

Reprints: Send photocopy of article. Pays 33% of amount paid for an original article.

Photos: State availability of photos. Pays $15 for b&w contact sheet. Buys one-time rights.

Tips: "We are looking for articles on minorities in podiatry."

⚑ $ $ STRATEGIC HEALTH CARE MARKETING, Health Care Communications, 11 Heritage Lane, P.O. Box 594, Rye NY 10580. (914)967-6741. Fax: (914)967-3054. E-mail: healthcomm@aol.com. Website: www.strategich ealthcare.com. **Contact:** Michele von Dambrowski, editor. **90% freelance written.** Works with published/established writers only. Monthly newsletter covering health care marketing and management in a wide range of settings including hospitals and medical group practices, home health services and managed care organizations. Emphasis is on strategies and techniques employed within the health care field and relevant applications from other service industries. Estab. 1984. Pays on publication. Publishes ms an average of 2 months after acceptance. Byline given. Offers 25% kill fee. Buys first North American serial rights. Accepts queries by mail, e-mail. Responds in 1 month. Sample copy for 9×12 SAE with 3 first-class stamps. Guidelines sent with sample copy only.

● *Strategic Health Care Marketing* is specifically seeking writers with expertise/contacts in managed care, patient satisfaction and demand management.

Nonfiction: How-to, interview/profile, new product, technical. "Preferred format for feature articles is the case history approach to solving marketing problems. Crisp, almost telegraphic style." **Buys 50 mss/year.** Query with published clips. *No unsolicited mss.* Length: 700-3,000 words. **Pays $100-500 plus.** Sometimes pays expenses of writers on assignment with prior authorization.

Photos: State availability of photos with submissions. (Photos, unless necessary for subject explanation, are rarely used.) Reviews contact sheets. Offers $10-30/photo. Captions and model releases required. Buys one-time rights.

▣ The online magazine contains content not found in the print edition. Contact: Mark Gothberg.

Tips: "Writers with prior experience on business beat for newspaper or newsletter will do well. We require a sophisticated, indepth knowledge of health care and business. This is not a consumer publication—the writer with knowledge of both health care and marketing will excel. Absolutely no unsolicited manuscripts; any received will be returned or discarded unread."

$ $ $ UNIQUE OPPORTUNITIES, The Physician's Resource, U O Inc., Suite 1236, 455 S. Fourth Ave., Louisville KY 40202. Fax: (502)587-0848. E-mail: bett@uoworks.com. Website: www.u0works.com. **Contact:** Bett Coffman, associate editor. Editor: Mollie Vento Hudson. **45% freelance written.** Bimonthly magazine covering physician relocation and career development. "Published for physicians interested in a new career opportunity. It offers physicians useful information and first-hand experiences to guide them in making informed decisions concerning their first or next career opportunity. It provides regular features and columns about specific aspects of the search process." Estab. 1991. Circ. 80,000 physicians. **Pays on acceptance.** Publishes ms an average of 2 months after acceptance. Byline given. Offers 15-33% kill fee. Buys first North American serial and electronic rights. Editorial lead time 3 months. Submit seasonal material 6 months in advance. Responds in 2 months to queries. Sample copy for 9×12 SAE with 6 first-class stamps. Writer's guidelines for #10 SASE.

Nonfiction: Practice options and information of interest to physicians in career transition. **Buys 14 mss/year.** Query with published clips. Length: 1,500-3,500 words. **Pays $750-2,000.** Sometimes pays expenses of writers on assignment.

Photos: State availability of photos with submission. Negotiates payment individually. Model releases and identification of subjects required. Buys one-time and electronic rights.

Columns/Departments: Remarks (opinion from physicians and industry experts on physician career issues), 500-1,000 words; Technology (technical articles relating to medicine or medical practice and business) 1,000-1,500 words. Payment negotiated individually. Query with published clips.

▣ The online version of this publication contains material not found in the print edition.

Tips: "Submit queries via letter or e-mail with ideas for articles that directly pertain to physician career issues, such as specific or unusual practice opportunities, relocation or practice establishment subjects, etc. Feature articles are most open to freelancers. Physician sources are most important, with tips and advice from both the physicians and business experts. Physicians like to know what other physicians think and do and appreciate suggestions from other business people."

MINING AND MINERALS

N̄ $ $ CANADIAN MINING JOURNAL, Southam Magazine Group Limited, 1450 Don Mills Rd., Don Mills Ontario, M3B 2X7 Canada. (416)510-6742. Fax: (416)442-2175. E-mail: jwerniuk@southam.ca. **Contact:** Jane Werniuk, editor. **5% freelance written.** Bimonthly magazine covering mining and mineral exploration by Canadian companies. "*Canadian Mining Journal* provides articles and information of practical use to those who work in the technical, administrative and supervisory aspects of exploration, mining and processin in the Canadian mineral exploration and mining industry." Estab. 1879. Circ. 10,000. Pays on publication. Publishes ms an average of 3 months after acceptance. Byline given. Buys one-time rights, electronic rights, and makes work-for-hire-assignments. Submit seasonal material 3 months in advance. Accepts queries by mail, e-mail, fax, phone. Reports in 1 week on queries; 1 months on mss.

Nonfiction: Opinion, technical, operation descriptions. **Buys 6 mss/year.** Query with published clips. Length: 500-1,400 words. **Pays $100-600.** Pays expenses of writers on assignment.

Photos: State availability of photos with submission. Reviews 4×6 prints. Negotiates payment individually. Captions, identification of subjects required. Buys one-time rights.

Columns/Departments: Guest editorial (opinion on controversial subject related to mining industry), 600 words. **Buys 3 mss/year.** Query with published clips. **Pays $150.**

Tips: "I need articles about mine sites that it would be expensive/difficult for me to reach. I also need to know that writer is competent to understand and describe the technology in an interesting way."

MUSIC

Publications for musicians and for the recording industry are listed in this section. Other professional performing arts publications are classified under Entertainment & the Arts. Magazines featuring music industry news for the general public are listed in the Consumer Entertainment and Music sections. (Markets for songwriters can be found in *Songwriter's Market*, Writer's Digest Books.)

N̄ $ CLASSICAL SINGER MAGAZINE, (formerly *The New York Opera Newsletter*), P.O. Box 278, Maplewood NJ 07040. (973)348-9549. Fax: (973)378-2372. E-mail: freeman6@classicalsinger.com. Website: www.classicalsinger.c om. **Contact:** Freeman Günter, managing editor. Monthly trade magazine covering classical singers. Estab. 1988. Circ. 5,000. Pays on publication. Publishes ms an average of 3 months after acceptance. Byline given. Offers 35% kill fee. Not copyrighted. Buys one-time rights or second serial (reprint) rights. Editorial lead time 3 months. Submit seasonal material 3 months in advance. Accepts queries by mail, e-mail, fax. Responds in 4 weeks to queries. Sample copy and writer's guidelines free.

○┳ Break in with a well-written review of a performance—written in a helpful tone with attention paid to all singers.

Nonfiction: Book excerpts, expose (carefully done), how-to, humor, interview/profile, new product, personal experience, photo feature, religious, technical, travel. Editorial calendar available on request. "Looking for material about unions, novel ways to make money as a singer and getting applause. No advertorial, agenda-tainted, complaints." Query with published clips. Length: 1,000-2,500 words. **Pays 5¢/word.** Sometimes pays expenses of writers on assignment.

Reprints: Accepts previously published submissions.

Photos: Send photos with submission. Negotiates payment individually. Captions required. Buys one time rights.

▣ The online magazine carries original content not found in the print edition.

Tips: "*Classical Singer Magazine*, is a 36+ page monthly magazine for singers and about singers. Our purpose is to increase respect for the profession and to connect the classical singer to opportunities, information, and support. Non-singers are welcome to submit queries but will need singers as their source."

N̄ $ CLAVIER MAGAZINE, The Instrumentalist Publishing Co., 200 Northfield Rd., Northfield IL 60093. Fax: (847)446-6263. **Contact:** Judy Nelson, editor. **1% freelance written.** "Published 10 times/year featuring practical information on teaching subjects that are of value to studio piano teachers and interviews with major artists." Estab.

1937. Circ. 16,000. Pays on publication. Publishes ms an average of 18 months after acceptance. Byline given. Buys all rights. Submit seasonal material 6 months in advance. Responds in 6 weeks. Sample copy and writer's guidelines free.

Nonfiction: "Articles should be of interest and direct practical value to concert pianists, harpsichordists and organists who are teachers of piano, organ, harpsichord and electronic keyboards. Topics may include pedagogy, technique, performance, ensemble playing and accompanying." Length: 10-12 double-spaced pages. Pays "a small honorarium."

Reprints: "Occasionally we will reprint a chapter in a book."

Photos: Send photos with submission. Reviews negatives, 2¼ × 2¼ transparencies and 3 × 5 prints. Offers no additional payment for photos accepted with ms. Identification of subjects required. Buys all rights.

$ CONTEMPORARY SONGWRITER MAGAZINE, (formerly *Songwriter Magazine*), P.O. Box 25879, Colorado Springs CO 80936-5879. (719)232-4489. E-mail: contemporarysong@yahoo.com. Website: www.contemporary.big step.com or www.angelfire.com/co2/contempo. **Contact:** Roberta Redford, editor. **100% freelance written.** Monthly trade magazine covering songwriting. "The purpose of *Songwriter Magazine* is to educate readers on the business and craft of songwriting. I'm looking for writers who can share their expertise on all aspects of songwriting from the first seeds of an idea, through the publishing and recording of the song. Most of our readers are at the beginning on intermediate stages of their careers and look to us for answers to all their questions. We're here to serve." Estab. 1998. Circ. 5,000. **Pays on acceptance.** Publishes ms an average of 3 months after acceptance. Byline given. Offers 20% kill fee. Buys first North American serial rights. Editorial lead time 4 months. Submit seasonal material 8 months in advance. Accepts queries by mail, e-mail. No simultaneous submissions. Responds in 3 weeks to queries; 1 month to mss. Sample copy for $3.00; writer's guidelines for #10 SASE or on website.

　　O—¬ Break in with personal experiences for Open Mike, interviews with successful songwriters, product or book reviews.

Nonfiction: Essays, how-to (contacts, record demo, etc . . .), humor, interview/profile (songwriters), new product (relating to songwriting/recording), opinion, personal experience. Interested in seeing articles about what to do after your song is written (i.e., how to get it to people who will publish and record it). **Buys 80 mss/year.** Query with published clips. Length: 50-2,500 words. **Pays 5¢/word for all articles.** Sometimes pays expenses for writers on assignment.

Photos: State availability of photos with submission. Reviews contact sheets. Negotiates payment individually. Identification of subjects required. Buys one time rights.

Columns and Departments: Book Report (books for songwriters), New Product Review (as relate to songwriting), all 250 words; Open Mike (personal experience as a songwriter), 500-1,500 words. **Buys 36 mss/year.** Query for reviews or send complete ms for Open Mike. **Pays 5¢/word.**

Fillers: Anecdotes, facts. **Buys 60/year.** Length: 50-250 words. **Pays $5-25.**

Tips: "Writers should have some experience in the music business. Our readers come to us for answers to all kinds of questions. Anticipate these and answer them clearly and concisely. We're always open to fresh ideas and new slants on old ideas. Good writing always has a place here."

$ $ MIX MAGAZINE, Intertec Publishing, 6400 Hollis St., Suite 12, Emeryville CA 94608. Fax: (510)693-5143. E-mail: 74673.3872@compuserve.com. Website: www.mixmag.com. Editor: George Petersen. **Contact:** Blair Jackson, executive editor. **50% freelance written.** Monthly magazine covering pro audio. "*Mix* is a trade publication geared toward professionals in the music/sound production recording and post-production industries. We include stories about music production, sound for picture, live sound, etc. We prefer in-depth technical pieces that are applications-oriented." Estab. 1977. Circ. 50,000. Pays on publication. Publishes ms an average of 3 months after acceptance. Byline given. Offers 50% kill fee. Buys first North American serial rights. Editorial lead time 10 weeks. Submit seasonal material 3 months in advance. Responds in 2 weeks to queries; 1 month to mss. Sample copy for $6. Writer's guidelines free on request.

Nonfiction: How-to, interview/profile, new product, technical, project/studio spotlights. Special issues: Sound for picture supplement (April, September), Design issue. **Buys 60 mss/year.** Query. Length 500-2,000 words. **Pays $300-600 for assigned articles; $300-400 for unsolicited articles.**

Photos: State availability of photos with submissions. Reviews 4 × 5 transparencies, prints. Negotiates payment individually. Captions, identification of subjects required. Buys one-time rights.

Tips: "Send Blair Jackson a letter outlining the article, including a description of the topic, information sources, what qualifies writers for the story, and mention of available graphics. A writing sample is also helpful."

N: MUSIC CONNECTION, The West Coast Music Trade Magazine, Music Connection, Inc., 4731 Laurel Canyon Blvd., North Hollywood CA 91607. (818)755-0101. Fax: (818)755-0102. E-mail: muscon@earthlink.net. Website: www.musicconnection.com. **Contact:** Jeremy M. Helfgot, associate editor. Senior Editor: Steven P. Wheeler. **50% freelance written.** "Biweekly magazine geared toward working musicians and/or other industry professionals, including producers/engineers/studio staff, managers, agents, publicists, music publishers, record company staff, concert promoters/bookers, etc." Estab. 1977. Circ. 70,000. Pays on publication. Publishes ms an average of 2 months after acceptance. Byline given. Kill fee varies. Buys all rights. Editorial lead time 2 months. Submit seasonal material 2 months in advance. Sample copy for $5. Writer's guidelines free.

Nonfiction: How-to (music industry related), interview/profile, new product, technical. Query with published clips. Length: 1,000-5,000 words. Pay varies. Sometimes pays expenses of writers on assignment.

Photos: State availability of photos with submission or send photos with submission. Reviews transparencies and prints. Negotiates payment individually. Identification of subjects required. Buys one-time rights.

Tips: "Articles must be informative music/music industry-related pieces, geared toward a trade-reading audience comprised mainly of musicians."

$ SONGWRITER'S MONTHLY, The Stories Behind Today's Songs, 332 Eastwood Ave., Feasterville PA 19053. Phone/fax: (215)953-0952. E-mail: a1foster@aol.com. www.lafay.com/sm. **Contact:** Allen Foster, editor. **30% freelance written.** Monthly magazine covering songwriting. Estab. 1992. Circ. 2,500. **Pays on acceptance.** Publishes ms an average of 6 months after aceptance. Byline given. Offers 100% kill fee. Buys first rights or one-time rights. Editorial lead time 3 months. Submit seasonal material 6 months in advance. Query by mail, e-mail, fax. Responds in 2 weeks to queries, 1 month to mss. Sample copy free. Writer's guidelines free.

    O⇥ Break in with "a great how-to article."

Nonfiction: How-to (write better songs, get a deal, etc.), technical. No interviews or reviews. **Buys 36 mss/year.** Query. Length: 300-800 words. **Pays $15.**

Reprints: Send information about when and where the article previously appeared. **Pays $15.**

Photos: State availability of photos with submission. Reviews prints. Offers no additional payment for photos accepted with ms. Identification of subjects required.

Fillers: Anecdotes, facts, newsbreaks, short humor. **Buys 60/year.** Length: 25-300 words. **Pays $0-5.**

Tips: "Currently *Songwriter's Monthly* is interested in 500-800 'How-To' articles which deal with some aspect of songwriting or the music business. Be friendly. Be knowledgeable. Keep the focus of the article tight. I will take a fresh idea that is poorly written over a brilliantly written piece that rehashes old territory every time. There is a lot of false information floating around, it's easy to see if you don't know your topic, so please write from honest experience or research. Again, I will publish raw writing from a songwriter before I publish pristine writing from someone with no 'hands on' experience."

OFFICE ENVIRONMENT & EQUIPMENT

N $ $ OFFICE DEALER, Updating the Office Products Industry, P.O. Box 1028, Mt. Airy NC 27030. Fax: (336)783-0045. E-mail: lbouchey@advi.net. Website: www.os-od.com. **Contact:** Lisa M. Bouchey, editor. **80% freelance written.** Bimonthly magazine covering the office products, industry. "*Office dealer* is an industry publication serving subscribers involved in the reselling of office supplies, furniture and equipment." Estab. 1987. Circ. 17,000. Pays on publication. Byline given. Buys first North American serial rigihts. Editorial lead time 4 months. Submit seasonal material 6 months in advance. Accepts queries by mail, e-mail, fax. Accepts simultaneous submissions. Responds in 1 month to queries; 2 months to mss. Sample and writer's guidelines are free.

Nonfiction: Book excerpts, interview/profile, new product, technical. "We do not publish a great deal of computer-related information—although that will continue to change as the digital age evolves." **Buys 30 mss/year.** Length: 1,500-2,200 words. **Pays $400-650.** Sometimes pays expenses of writers on assignment.

Photos: State availability of photos with submission. Reviews contact sheets, prints. Negotiates payment individually. Captions, model releases, identification of subjects required. Buys one-time rights.

Columns/Departments: Selling Power (sales tips/techniques), 800-1,000 words. **Buys 6 mss/year.** Query. **Pays $150-300.**

Tips: "Feature articles for the year are outlined in an editorial calendar published each fall. Although changes can occur, we make every effort to adhere to the published calendar. Feature articles are written by our staff or by freelance writers. We do not accept corporate 'byline' articles. We seek publishable stories written to an agreed-upon length, with text for agreed-upon components—such as sidebars. Stories should be as generic as possible, free of jargon, vague statements, unconfirmed facts and figures, and corporate superlatives. Each query should include the primary focus of the proposed article, the main points of discussion, and a list of any sources to be described or interviewed in the story. Samples of a writer's past work and clips concerning the proposed story are helpful."

$ $ OFFICE SOLUTIONS, The Magazine for Office Professionals, Quality Publishing, P.O. Box 1028, Mt. Airy NC 27030. Fax: (336)783-0045. E-mail: lbouchey@advi.net. Website: www.os.od.com. **Contact:** Lisa M. Bouchey, editor. **80% freelance written.** Monthly magazine covering the office environment. "*Office Solutions* subscribers are responsible for the management of their office environments." Estab. 1984. Circ. 107,000. Pays on publication. Publishes ms 2 months after acceptance. Byline given. Buys first North American serial rights. Editorial lead time 2-3 months. Submit seasonal material 4 months in advance. Accepts queries by mail, e-mail, fax. Accepts simultaneous submissions. Responds in 3 weeks to queries; 2 months to mss. Sample copy and writer's guidelines free.

Nonfiction: Book excerpts, interview/profile, new product, technical. "Our audience is responsible for general management of an office environment, so articles should be broad in scope and not too technical in nature." **Buys 75 mss/year.** Query. Length: 1,500-2,200 words. **Pays $400-650.** Sometimes pays expenses of writers on assignment.

Photos: State availability of photos with submission. Reviews contact sheets, prints. Negotiates payment individually. Captions, model releases, identification of subjects required. Buys one-time rights.

Columns/Departments: Cyberspeak (computer terminology), 800-1,000 words; Do It Yourself ('how to run' the office better), 1,000-1,200 words; Wireless World (wireless technology development), 1,000-1,200 words. **Buys 20 mss/ year.** Query. **Pays $150-400.**

Fillers: Facts, short humor. **Buys 10-15/year. Length: 500-800 words. Pays $150-250.**

Tips: "Feature articles for the year are outlined in an editorial calendar published each fall. Although changes can occur, we make every effort to adhere to the published calendar. Feature articles are written by our staff or by freelance writers. We seek publishable stories written to an agreed-upon length, with text for agreed-upon components—such as sidebars. Stories should be as generic as possible, free of jargon, vague statements, unconfirmed facts and figures, and corporate superlatives. Each query should include the primary focus of the proposed article, the main points of discussion, and a list of any sources to be described or interviewed in the story. Queries should be a single page or less and include a SASE for reply. Samples of a writer's past work and clips concerning the proposed story are helpful."

N $ OFFICEPRO™, (formerly *The Secretary*®), Stratton Publishing & Marketing, Inc., 5501 Backlick Rd., Suite 240, Springfield VA 22151. Fax: (703)914-6777. E-mail: officepromag@strattonpub.com. Website: www.iaap-hg.org. Publisher: Debra J. Stratton. **Contact:** Angela Hickman Brady, managing editor. **90% freelance written unpaid.** Magazine published 9 times/year covering the administrative support profession. Estab. 1946. Circ. 40,000. Publishes ms an average of 6-18 months after acceptance. Byline given. Buys first rights. Editorial lead time 3 months. Submit seasonal material 5 months in advance. Accepts simultaneous submissions. For electronic (IBM) PC-compatible, Word Perfect or ASCII on disk. Responds in 2-3 months. Sample copy $3 through (816)891-6600 ext. 235. Writer's guidelines free.

Nonfiction: Book excerpts, general interest, how-to (buy and use office equipment, advance career, etc.), interview/ profile, new product, personal experience. Query. Length: 2,000 words. **Pays $50 minimum.** Pays expenses of writers on assignment.

Reprints: Send typed ms with rights for sale noted (on disk, preferred) and information about when and where the article previously appeared.

Photos: Send photos with submission. Reviews transparencies and prints. Negotiable payment for photos accepted with ms. Identification of subjects required. Buys one-time rights.

Columns/Departments: Product News (new office products, non promotional), 500 words maximum; On The Run (general interest—career, woman's, workplace issues), 500 words maximum; Virtual Office, 800 words; Office Entrepreneur, 800 words; Electronic Office Suite, 800 words. Send complete ms.

Tips: "We're in search of articles addressing travel; meeting and event-planning; office recycling programs; computer hardware and software; workplace issues; international business topics. Must be appropriate to office professionals."

PAPER

N $ $ THE PAPER STOCK REPORT, News and Trends of the Paper Recycling Markets, McEntee Media Corp., 13727 Holland Rd., Cleveland OH 44142. (216)362-7979. E-mail: psr@recycle.cc. Website: www.recycle. cc. **Contact:** Ken McEntee, editor. Biweekly newsletter covering "market trends, news in the paper recycling industry. Audience is interested in new innovative markets, applications for recovered scrap paper as well as new laws and regulations impacting recycling." Estab. 1990. Circ. 2,000. Pays on publication. Publishes ms an average of 1 month after acceptance. Byline given. Buys first or all rights. Editorial lead time 2 months. Submit seasonal material 2 months in advance. Accepts simultaneous submissions. Responds in 1 month to queries. Sample copy for #10 SAE with 55¢ postage.

Nonfiction: Book excerpts, essays, exposé, general interest, historical/nostalgic, interview/profile, new product, opinion, technical, all related to paper recycling. **Buys 0-13 mss/year.** Send complete ms. Length: 250-1,000 words. **Pays $50-250 for assigned articles; $25-250 for unsolicited articles.** Pays expenses of writers on assignment.

Reprints: Accepts previously published submissions.

Photos: State availability of photos with submissions. Reviews contact sheets. Negotiates payment individually. Identification of subjects required.

Tips: "Article must be valuable to readers in terms of presenting new market opportunities or cost-saving measures."

N $ $ RECYCLED PAPER NEWS, Independent Coverage of Environmental Issues in the Paper Industry, McEntee Media Corporation, 13727 Holland Rd., Brook Park OH 44142. (216)362-7979. Fax: (216)362-6553. E-mail: rpn@recycle.cc. Website: www.recycle.cc. **Contact:** Ken McEntee, editor. **10% freelance written.** Monthly newsletter. "We are interested in any news impacting the paper recycling industry as well as other environmental issues in the paper industry, i.e., water/air pollution, chlorine-free paper, forest conservation, etc., with special emphasis on new laws and regulations." Estab. 1990. Pays on publication. Publishes ms an average of 2 months after acceptance. Buys first or all rights. Editorial lead time 1 month. Submit seasonal material 1 month in advance. Accepts simultaneous submissions. Responds in 2 months. Sample copy for 9×12 SAE and 55¢ postage. Writer's guidelines for #10 SASE.

Nonfiction: Book excerpts, essays, interview/profile, new product, opinion, personal experience, technical, new business, legislation, regulation, business expansion. **Buys 0-5 mss/year.** Query with published clips. Length: 100-5,000 words. **Pays $10-500.** Pays writers with contributor copies or other premiums by prior agreement.

Reprints: Accepts previously published submissions.

Columns/Departments: Query with published clips. **Pays $10-500.**

Tips: "We appreciate leads on local news regarding recycling or composting, i.e., new facilities or businesses, new laws and regulations, unique programs, situations that impact supply and demand for recyclables, etc. International developments are also of interest."

PETS

Listed here are publications for professionals in the pet industry—pet product wholesalers, manufacturers, suppliers, and retailers, and owners of pet specialty stores, grooming businesses, aquarium retailers and those interested in the pet fish industry. Publications for pet owners are listed in the Consumer Animal section.

[N] $ $ GROOM & BOARD H.H. Backer Associates Inc., 200 S. Michigan Ave., Suite 840, Chicago IL 60604-2404. (312)663-4040. Fax: (312)663-5676. E-mail: groomboard@aol.com. Editor: Karen Long MacLeod. **90% freelance written.** Magazine published 9 times/year. "*Groom & Board* is the only national trade publication for pet-care professionals, including pet groomers, boarding kennel operators and service-oriented veterinarians. Features emphasize professional development, including progressive business management, animal handling procedures, emerging business opportunities and profiles of successful pet-care operations. Estab. 1980. Circ. 14,186. **Pays on acceptance.** Publishes ms an average of 3 months after acceptance. Byline given. Buys first North American serial, one-time, or exclusive to industry. Sample copy available.

Nonfiction: How-to (groom specific breeds of pets, run business, etc.), interview/profile (successful grooming and/or kennel operations), technical. No consumer-oriented articles or stories about a single animal (animal heroes, grief, etc.). **Buys 40 mss/year.** Query by phone after 3 pm CST. Length: 1,000-2,000 words. **Pays $100-400 for assigned articles; $70-125 for unsolicited articles.** Sometimes pays expenses of writers on assignment.

Photos: Reviews slides, transparencies, 5×7 color glossy prints. Captions, identification of subjects required. Buys one-time rights.

[N] $ $ PET AGE, H.H. Backer Associates, Inc., 200 S. Michigan Ave., Suite 840, Chicago IL 60604-2383-2404. (312)663-4040. Fax: (312)663-5676. E-mail: petage@aol.com. Editor: Karen Long MacLeod. **90% freelance written.** Prefers to work with published/established writers. Monthly magazine for pet/pet supplies retailers, covering the complete pet industry. Estab. 1971. Circ. 23,022. **Pays on acceptance.** Publishes ms an average of 6 months after acceptance. Byline given. Buys first North American serial, one-time, or exclusive industry rights. Submit seasonal material 6 months in advance. Sample copy available.

Nonfiction: Profile (of a successful, well-run pet retail operation), how-to, business management, technical—all trade-related. Query by phone after 3 pm CST. Query with the name and location of a pet operation you wish to profile and why it would make a good feature. No general retailing articles or consumer-oriented pet articles. **Buys 120 mss/year.** Length: 1,000-2,500 words. **Pays $200-500 for assigned articles.** Sometimes pays the expenses of writers on assignment.

Photos: Reviews slides, transparencies, 5×7 color glossy prints. Captions, identification of subjects required. Buys one-time rights.

Tips: "This is a business publication for busy people, and must be very informative in easy-to-read, concise style. Articles about animal care or business practices should have the pet-retail angle or cover issues specific to this industry."

PLUMBING, HEATING, AIR CONDITIONING & REFRIGERATION

$ $ HEATING, PLUMBING, AIR CONDITIONING, 1370 Don Mills Rd., Suite 300, Don Mills, Ontario M3B 3N7 Canada. (416)759-2500. Fax: (416)759-6979. E-mail: lizmills@home.com. Publisher: Bruce Meacock. **Contact:** Liz Mills, vice president. **20% freelance written.** Monthly magazine for mechanical contractors; plumbers; warm air and hydronic heating, refrigeration, ventilation, air conditioning and insulation contractors; wholesalers; architects; consulting and mechanical engineers who are in key management or specifying positions in the plumbing, heating, air conditioning and refrigeration industries in Canada. Estab. 1923. Circ. 16,500. Pays on publication. Publishes ms an average of 3 months after acceptance. Accepts queries by mail, e-mail, fax, phone. Responds in 2 months. For a prompt reply, "enclose a sheet on which is typed a statement either approving or rejecting the suggested article which can either be checked off, or a quick answer written in and signed and returned." Sample copy free.

   O— Break in with technical, "how-to," Canadian-specific applications/stories.

Nonfiction: News, technical, business management and "how-to" articles that will inform, educate, motivate and help readers to be more efficient and profitable who design, manufacture, install, sell, service, maintain or supply all mechanical components and systems in residential, commercial, institutional and industrial installations across Canada. Length: 1,000-1,500 words. **Pays 25¢/word.** Sometimes pays expenses of writers on assignment.

Reprints: Send tearsheet or photocopy of article or typed ms with rights for sale noted and information about when and where article appeared.

Photos: Photos purchased with ms. Prefers 4×5 or 5×7 glossies.

Tips: "Topics must relate directly to the day-to-day activities of *HPAC* readers in Canada. Must be detailed, with specific examples, quotes from specific people or authorities—show depth. We specifically want material from other parts of Canada besides southern Ontario. Not really interested in material from US unless specifically related to Canadian readers' concerns. We primarily want articles that show *HPAC* readers how they can increase their sales and business step-by-step based on specific examples of what others have done."

N **$ $ WESTERN HVACR NEWS**, Trade, News International, 4444 Riverside Dr., #202, Burbank CA 91505-4048. Fax: (818)848-1306. E-mail: News@hvacrnews.com. Website: www.hvacrnews.com. **Contact:** Gary McCarty. Monthly tabloid covering heating, ventilation, air conditioning and refrigeration. "We are a trade publication writing about news and trends for those in the trade." Estab. 1981. Circ. 31,000. Pays on publication. Byline sometimes given. Buys first North American serial rights. Editorial lead time 2 months. Submit seasonal material 2 months in advance. Accepts queries by mail, e-mail. Responds in 1 month to queries. Sample copy online at website. Writer's guidelines by e-mail.
Nonfiction: General interest, how-to, interview/profile, photo feature, technical. **Buys 25 mss/year.** Query with published clips. Length: 250-1,000 words. **Pays 25¢/word.** Sometimes pays expenses of writers on assignment.
Reprints: Accepts previously published submissions.
Photos: Send photos with submission. Offers $10 minimum. Negotiates payment individually. Identification of subjects required. Buys one-time rights.
Columns/Departments: Technical onlly. **Buys 24 mss/year. Pays 20¢/word.**
Tips: "Writers must be knowledgeable about the HVACR industry."

PRINTING

$ $ PRINT & GRAPHICS; PRINTING JOURNAL; SOUTHERN GRAPHICS; PRINTING VIEWS, 1818 Pot Spring Rd., #102, Timonium MD 21093. (410)628-7826. Fax: (410)628-7829. E-mail: spencecom1@aol.com. Website: www.spencercygnus.com. Publisher: Kaj Spencer. **Contact:** David Lindsay, editor. **50% freelance written.** Eager to work with new/unpublished writers. Monthly tabloid of the commercial printing industry for owners and executives of graphic arts firms. Circ. 20,000. Pays on publication. Publishes ms an average of 2 months after acceptance. Byline given. Buys one-time rights. Accepts simultaneous submissions. Accepts queries by mail, fax, e-mail, phone. Responds in 2 months. Sample copy for $2.
Nonfiction: Book excerpts, historical/nostalgic, how-to, interview/profile, new product, opinion, personal experience, photo feature, technical. "All articles should relate to graphic arts management or production." **Buys 200 mss/year.** Query with published clips. Length: 750-1,500 words. **Pays $250-350.**
Reprints: Send photocopy of article and information about when and where the article previously appeared. Pays $150 flat fee. Publishes trade book excerpts.
Photos: State availability of photos. Captions, identification of subjects required.

$ $ SCREEN PRINTING, 407 Gilbert Ave., Cincinnati OH 45202-2285. (513)421-2050. Fax: (513)421-5144. E-mail: tfrecska@stpubs.com. Website: www.screenweb.com. Editor: Tom Frecska. **30% freelance written.** Works with a small number of new/unpublished writers each year. Monthly magazine for the screen printing industry, including screen printers (commercial, industrial and captive shops), suppliers and manufacturers, ad agencies and allied professions. Estab. 1953. Circ. 17,000. Pays on publication. Publishes ms an average of 3 months after acceptance. Byline given. Buys all rights. Accepts queries by mail, e-mail, fax. Reporting time varies. Sample copy available. Writer's guidelines for SAE.
Nonfiction: "Because the screen printing industry is a specialized but diverse trade, we do not publish general interest articles with no pertinence to our readers. Subject matter is open, but should fall into one of four categories—technology, management, profile, or news. Features in all categories must identify the relevance of the subject matter to our readership. Technology articles must be informative, thorough, and objective—no promotional or 'advertorial' pieces accepted. Management articles may cover broader business or industry specific issues, but they must address the screen printer's unique needs. Profiles may cover serigraphers, outstanding shops, unique jobs and projects, or industry personalities; they should be in-depth features, not PR puff pieces, that clearly show the human interest or business relevance of the subject. News pieces should be timely (reprints from non-industry publications will be considered) and must cover an event or topic of industry concern." **Buys 10-15 mss/year.** Query. Unsolicited mss not returned. Length: 2,000-3,000 words. **Pays $300** minimum for major features.
Photos: Cover photos negotiable; b&w or color. Published material becomes the property of the magazine.
　■ The online magazine carries information from the print edition, as well as original content not found in the print edition. Contact: John Tymoski.
Tips: "Be an expert in the screen-printing industry with supreme or special knowledge of a particular screen-printing process, or have special knowledge of a field or issue of particular interest to screen-printers. If the author has a working knowledge of screen printing, assignments are more readily available. General management articles are rarely used."

N **$ $ SERIF, THE MAGAZINE OF TYPE & TYPOGRAPHY**, Quixote Digital Typography, PMV 377 2038 N. Clark St., Chicago IL 60614. (312)953-3679. Fax: (312)803-0698. E-mail: serif@quixote.com. Website: www.quixote

.com/serif. **Contact:** D.A. Hosek, editor. **80-100% freelance written.** Quarterly magazine "covering the full spectrum of type and typography from classical to radical." Estab. 1994. Circ. 2,000. Pays on publication. Byline given. Buys first North American serial rights and the option to reprint in book form. Editorial lead time 6 months. Accepts previously published submissions. Sample copy for 9×12 SASE and 6 first-class stamps. Writer's guidelines for #10 SASE.

Nonfiction: Book excerpts, essays, exposé, historical/nostalgic, how-to, humor, interview/profile, new product, opinion, personal experience, photo feature, technical. **Buys 12 mss/year.** Send complete ms. Length: 500-5,000 words. **Pays 10¢/word.**

Photos: Send photos with submission. Reviews negatives and transparencies. Offers no additional payment for photos accepted with ms. Captions required. Buys one-time rights.

Tips: "Do not send generic articles."

PROFESSIONAL PHOTOGRAPHY

Journals for professional photographers are listed in this section. Magazines for the general public interested in photography techniques are in the Consumer Photography section. (For listings of markets for freelance photography use *Photographer's Market*, Writer's Digest Books.)

N $ THE PHOTO REVIEW, 301 Hill Ave., Langhorne PA 19047-2819. (215)757-8921. Fax: (215)757-6421. E-mail: info@photoreview.org. **Contact:** Stephen Perloff, editor. **50% freelance written.** Quarterly magazine on photography with reviews, interviews and articles on art photography. Estab. 1976. Circ. 2,500. Pays on publication. Publishes ms an average of 3 months after acceptance. Byline given. Buys one-time rights. Accepts simultaneous submissions. Responds in 1 month to queries; 2 months to mss. Sample copy for 9×12 SAE with 6 first-class stamps. Writer's guidelines for #10 SASE.

Nonfiction: Essays, historical/nostalgic, interview/profile, opinion. No how-to articles. **Buys 10-15 mss/year.** Query. **Pays $25-200.**

Reprints: Send tearsheet, photocopy or typed ms with rights for sale noted and information about when and where the article previously appeared. Payment varies.

Photos: Send photos with submission. Reviews 8×10 prints. Offers no additional payment for photos accepted with ms. Captions and identification of subjects required. Buys one-time rights.

$ $ PHOTOGRAPHIC PROCESSING, Cygnus Publishing, 445 Broad Hollow Rd., Melville NY 11747. (516)845-2700. Fax: (516)845-2797. E-mail: bill.schiffner@cygnuspub.com. Website: www.labsonline.com. **Contact:** Bill Schiffner, editor. **30% freelance written.** Monthly magazine covering photographic (commercial/minilab) and electronic processing markets. Estab. 1965. Circ. 23,000. Pays on publication. Publishes ms an average of 4 months after acceptance. Byline given. Offers $75 kill fee. Editorial lead time 3 months. Submit seasonal material 3 months in advance. Accepts simultaneous submissions. Sample copy and writer's guidelines free.

Nonfiction: How-to, interview/profile, new product, photo processing/digital imaging features. **Buys 30-40 mss/year.** Query with published clips. Length: 1,500-2,200 words. **Pays $275-350 for assigned articles; $250-300 for unsolicited articles.**

Photos: Send photos with submission. Reviews 4×5 transparencies, 4×6 prints. Offers no additional payment for photos accepted with ms. Captions required. Buys one-time rights. Looking for digitally manipulated covers.

Columns/Departments: Surviving in 2000 (business articles offering tips to labs on how make their businesses run better), 1,500-1,800 words; Business Side (getting more productivity out of your lab). **Buys 10 mss/year.** Query with published clips. **Pays $150-250.**

N $ $ TODAY'S PHOTOGRAPHER INTERNATIONAL, American Image Press Inc., P.O. Box 777, Lewisville NC 27023. (336)945-9867. Fax: (336)945-3711. Website: www.aipress.com. **Contact:** Vonda H. Blackburn, editor. **100% freelance written.** Bimonthly; "The make money with your camera magazine." Estab. 1984. Circ. 93,000. Pays on publication. Publishes ms an average of 4 months after acceptance. Byline given. Buys simultaneous rights. Editorial lead time 4 months. Submit seasonal material 8 months in advance. Accepts simultaneous submissions. Responds in 1 month to queries; 2 months to mss. Sample copy for $3. Writer's guidelines free.

Nonfiction: How freelance photographers make money. How-to (make money with your camera). Nothing outside making money with a camera. Query. Length: 800-2,000 words. **Pays $50-200.**

Reprints: Accepts previously published submissions.

Photos: State availability of photos with submission. Reviews contact sheets, transparencies and prints. Offers no additional payment for photos accepted with ms. Captions, model releases and identification of subjects required. Buys one-time rights.

Columns/Departments: Query with published clips.

REAL ESTATE

$ $ AREA DEVELOPMENT MAGAZINE, Sites and Facility Planning, Halcyon Business Publications, Inc., 400 Post Ave., Westbury NY 11590. (516)338-0900. Fax: (516)338-0100. E-mail: Gerriarea@aol.com or geni@area-development.com. Website: www.area-development.com. Managing Editor: Pam Karr. **Contact:** Geraldine Gambale, editor. **80% freelance written.** Prefers to work with published/established writers. Monthly magazine covering corporate facility planning and site selection for industrial chief executives worldwide. Estab. 1965. Circ. 45,000. Pays on publication. Publishes ms an average of 2 months after acceptance. Byline given. Buys all rights. Accepts queries by mail, e-mail, fax, phone. Responds in 3 months. Free sample copy. Writer's guidelines for #10 SASE.
Nonfiction: How-to (experiences in site selection and all other aspects of corporate facility planning); historical (if it deals with corporate facility planning); interview (corporate executives and industrial developers); and related areas of site selection and facility planning such as taxes, labor, government, energy, architecture and finance. **Buys 75 mss/year.** Query. Length: 1,500-2,000 words. **Pays 30¢/word.** Sometimes pays expenses of writers on assignment.
Photos: State availability of photos with query. Reviews transparencies. Captions, identification preferred. Negotiates payment individually.

$ $ $ $ COMMERCIAL INVESTMENT REAL ESTATE, Commercial Investment Real Estate Institute, 430 N. Michigan Ave., Suite 800, Chicago IL 60611-4092. (312)321-4460. Fax: (312)321-4530. E-mail: magazine@ccim.com. Website: www.ccim.com/magazine. **Contact:** Barbara Stevenson, editor. **10% freelance written.** Bimonthly magazine. *"CIRE* offers practical articles on current trends and business development ideas for commercial investment real estate practitioners." Estab. 1982. Circ. 12,500. **Pays on acceptance.** Publishes ms an average of 4 months after acceptance. Byline given. Buys all rights. Editorial lead time 4 months. Submit seasonal material 4 months in advance. Accepts queries by mail, e-mail, fax. Responds in 2 weeks to queries; 1 month to mss. Sample copy for 9 × 12 SAE with 5 first-class stamps or on website. Writer's guidelines for #10 SASE or on website.
   O─ Break in by sending résumé and clips, "including feature-length commercial real estate-related clips if available. We keep writers' materials on file for assigning articles."
Nonfiction: How-to, business strategies, technical. **Buys 6-8 mss/year.** Query with published clips. Length: 2,000-3,500 words. **Pays $1,000-2,000.**
Photos: Send photos with submission. Reviews prints. Offers no additional payment for photos accepted with ms. Buys all rights.
Tips: "Always query first with a detailed outline and published clips. Authors should have a background in writing on real estate or business subjects."

$ $ THE COOPERATOR, The Co-op and Condo Monthly, Yale Robbins, LLC, 31 E. 28th St., 12th Floor, New York NY 10016. (212)683-5700. Fax: (212)696-1268. E-mail: judy@cooperator.com. Website: www.cooperator.com. **Contact:** Judith C. Grover, managing editor. **20% freelance written.** Monthly tabloid covering real estate. *"The Cooperator* covers condominium and cooperative issues in New York and beyond. It is read by unit owners and shareholders, board members and managing agents. We have just become a national publication and are interested in receiving articles from states outside of New York." Estab. 1980. Circ 60,000. Pays on publication. Publishes ms an average of 3 months after acceptance. Byline given. Buys all rights and makes work-for-hire assignments. Submit seasonal material 3 months in advance. Accepts queries by mail, e-mail, fax. Responds in 2 weeks to queries. Sample copy free. Writer's guidelines not available.
Nonfiction: Interview/profile, new product, personal experience; all related to co-op and condo ownership. No submissions without queries. **Buys 20 mss/year.** Query with published clips. Length: 1,000-2,000 words. **Pays $150-250.** Sometimes pays expenses of writers on assignment.
Photos: State availability of photos with submission. Reviews contact sheets, negatives, transparencies and prints. Negotiates payment individually. Captions and identification of subjects required. Rights purchased vary.
Columns/Departments: Management profile (profile of prominent management company); Building finance (investment and financing issues); Buying and selling (market issues, etc.), all 1,500 words. Buys 20 mss/year. Query with published clips. Pays $150-250.
Tips: "You must have experience doing journalistic reporting, especially real estate, business, legal or financial. Must have published clips to send in with résumé and query."

[N] $ $ FLORIDA REALTOR MAGAZINE, Florida Association of Realtors, 7025 Augusta National Dr., Orlando FL 32822-5017. (407)438-1400. Fax: (407)438-1411. E-mail: FLRealtor@Fl.realtorUSA.com. Website: www.Floridarealtormagazine.com. Assistant Editor: Jamie Floer. **Contact:** Tracey Lawton, editor. **30% freelance written.** Trade journal published 11 times/year covering Florida real estate. "As the official publication of the Florida Association of Realtors, we provide helpful articles for our 65,000 members. We try to stay up on the trends and issues that affect business in Florida's real estate market." Estab. 1925. Circ. 65,000. Pays on publication. Publishes ms an average of 1 month after acceptance. Byline given. Editorial lead time 2½ months. Accepts queries by mail, e-mail, fax, phone. Accepts simultaneous submissions. Sample copy free online at website.
Nonfiction: Book excerpts, how-to, inspirational, interview/profile, new product (all with a real estate angle—Florida-specific is good). "No fiction, poetry." **Buys varying number of mss/year.** Query with published clips. Length: 800-1,500 words. **Pays $200-400.** Sometimes pays expenses of writers on assignment.

Reprints: Accepts previously published submissions.

Photos: State availability of photos with submission. Negotiates payment individually. Captions, model releases, identification of subjects required. Buys one-time rights.

Columns/Departments: "Rarely used." Occasionally publishes: Promotional Strategies, 900 words; Technology & You, 1,000 words; Realtor Advantage, 1,500 words. Buys varying number of mss/year. Pay varies.

Fillers: Short humor. Buys varying number.

Tips: "Build a solid reputation for specializing in real estate-specific writing in state/national publications."

$ $ JOURNAL OF PROPERTY MANAGEMENT, Institute of Real Estate Management, P.O. Box 109025, Chicago IL 60610-9025. (312)329-6058. Fax: (312)661-7958. E-mail: mevans@irem.org. Website: www.irem.org. **Contact:** Mariwyn Evans, executive editor. **30% freelance written.** Bimonthly magazine covering real estate management. "The *Journal* has a feature/information slant designed to educate readers in the application of new techniques and to keep them abreast of current industry trends." Circ. 23,000. **Pays on acceptance.** Publishes ms an average of 3 months after acceptance. Byline given. Buys all rights. Accepts queries by mail, e-mail, fax. Responds in 6 weeks to queries; 1 month to mss. Sample copy and writer's guidelines free.

Nonfiction: How-to, interview, technical (building systems/computers), demographic shifts in business employment and buying patterns, marketing. "No non-real estate subjects, personality or company, humor." **Buys 8-12 mss/year.** Query with published clips. Length: 1,200-1,500 words. Sometimes pays the expenses of writers on assignment.

Reprints: Send photocopy of article or short story. Pays 35% of amount paid for an original article.

Photos: State availability of photos with submission. Reviews contact sheets. May offer additional payment for photos accepted with ms. Model releases, identification of subjects required. Buys one-time rights.

Columns/Departments: Insurance Insights, Tax Issues, Investment and Finance Insights, Legal Issues. **Buys 6-8 mss/year.** Query. Length: 500-750 words.

N $ $ MULTIFAMILY EXECUTIVE, MGI Publications, 301 Oxford Valley Rd., Suite 804, Yardley PA 19067. (215)321-5112. Fax: (215)321-5122. E-mail: ibromberg@mgipublications.com. Website: www.multifamilyexecutive.com. Editor: Edward J. McNeill, Jr., **Contact:** Jodi A. Bromberg, group editorial editor. **35% freelance written.** Magazine published 12 times/year. "We target senior level executives in the multifamily housing industry—builders, developers, owners and managers." Circ. 25,000. Pays on publication. Publishes ms an average of 2 months after acceptance. Byline given. Buys first North American serial rights. Editorial lead time 3 months after acceptance. Submit seasonal material 4 months in advance. Accepts queries by mail, e-mail, fax, phone. Responds in 2 months to queries. Sample copy for 9×12 SAE with 8 first-class stamps. Writer's guidelines free.

Nonfiction: Book excerpts, how-to, interview/profile, new product, opinion. **Buys 15-20 mss/year.** Query with published clips. Length: 750-1,500 words. **Pays $100-1,000 for assigned articles; $100-500 for unsolicited articles.** Sometimes pays expenses of writers on assignment.

Photos: State availability of photos with submission. Reviews transparencies. Negotiates payment individually. Model releases, identification of subjects required. Buys all rights.

Columns/Departments: Financial, Legal, Senior Housing, Affordable Housing (all written to an advanced level of multifamily executives); all 750-850 words. Buys 8 mss/year. Query with published clips. Pays $100-400.

$ $ $ NATIONAL RELOCATION & REAL ESTATE, RIS Publishing Inc., 50 Water St., Norwalk CT 06854. (203)855-1234. Fax: (203)852-7208. E-mail: frank:rismedia.com. Website: rismedia.com. Editor: Frank Sziros. **30-50% freelance written.** Monthly magazine covering residential real estate and corporate relocation. "Our readers are professionals within the relocation and real estate industries; therefore, we require our writers to have sufficient knowledge of the workings of these industries in order to ensure depth and accuracy in reporting." Estab. 1980. Circ. 33,000. Pays on publication. Byline sometimes given. Offers 20-50% kill fee. Buys all rights. Editorial lead time 4 months. Responds in 2 weeks to queries. Sample copy free.

Nonfiction: Exposé, how-to (use the Internet to sell real estate, etc.), interview/profile, new product, opinion, technical. Query with published clips. Length: 250-1,500 words. Pays unsolicited article writers with contributor copies upon use. Sometimes pays expenses of writers on assignment.

Photos: Send photos with submission. Reviews transparencies. Offers no additional payment for photos accepted with ms. Captions required.

Columns/Departments: Query with published clips.

　　■ The online magazine carries original content not found in the print edition. Contact: Carol King. "Website features daily news service, written submissions and other information on publication."

Tips: "All queries must be done in writing. Phone queries are unacceptable. Any clips or materials sent should indicate knowledge of the real estate and relocation industries. In general, we are open to all knowledgeable contributors."

N $ $ $ OFFICE BUILDINGS MAGAZINE, Yale Robbins, Inc., 31 E. 28th St., New York NY 10016. (212)683-5700. E-mail: peg@yizine.com. Website: www.yizine.com. **Contact:** Peg Rivard, managing editor. **15% freelance written.** "Annual magazine covering market statistics, trends and thinking of area professionals on the current and future state of the real estate market." Estab. 1987. Circ. 10,500. Pays half on acceptance and half on publication. Byline sometimes given. Offers 25% kill fee. Buys all rights. Editorial lead time 2 months. Accepts queries by mail, e-mail, fax. Sample copy and writer's guidelines free.

Nonfiction: Survey of specific markets. **Buys 15-20 mss/year.** Query with published clips. Length: 1,200-2,000 words. **Pays $500-1,200.** Sometimes pays expenses of writers on assignment.

N $ $ $ REAL ESTATE FORUM, Real Estate Media, Inc., 111 Eighth Ave., Suite 1511, New York NY 1001-5201. Fax: (212)929-7124. E-mail: jsal@REMediaInc.com. Website: www.reforum.com. **Contact:** John Salustri, editor. **40% freelance written.** Magazine published 13 times a year with special international issue is October covering commercial real estate. "*Real Estate Forum* is a publication that speaks to senior level executives involved in the finance, investment, development, sales and leasing of commercial real estate on a global basis. We deal almost exclusively with office, multifamily, retail, industrial and hotel project, and all articles must be carefully targeted to this audience." Circ. 35,000. Pays on publication. Publishes ms an average of 4 months after acceptance. Byline sometimes given. Buys all rights. Editorial lead time 4 months. Accepts queries by mail. Responds in 1 month to queries. Sample copy free.
Nonfiction: Technical. Query with published clips. Length: 1,000-3,000 words. **Pays $400-1,500.**
Photos: Send photos with submission. Reviews 4×5 transparencies, 4×5 prints. Offers no additional payment for photos accepted with ms. Identification of subjects required. Buys one-time rights.

N $ $ RETIREMENT COMMUNITY BUSINESS, Great River Publishing Company, Inc., 2026 Exeter Rd., Suite 2, Germantown TN 38138. (901)624-5911. Fax: (901)624-5910. E-mail: rcb@grtriver.com. Website: www.grtriver. com. **Contact:** Sherry Campbell, editor. **25% freelance written.** Quarterly magazine covering management of retirement and assisted living communities. Estab. 1992. Circ. 13,000. Pays on publication. Publishes ms an average of 6 months after acceptance. Byline given. Offers negotiable kill fee. Buys all rights. Editorial lead time 3 months. Submit seasonal material 3 months in advance. Accepts queries by mail, e-mail, fax, phone. Responds in 2 weeks to queries; 3 months to mss. Sample copy and writer's guidelines free.
Nonfiction: How-to (management and operational issues of seniors housing), personal experience. Only articles specific to industry. **Buys 20-30 mss/year.** Query with published clips. Length: 300-1,500 words. Pay is negotiated.
Photos: State availability of photos with submission. Offers no additional payment for photos accepted with ms. Model releases required. Buys one-time rights.
Tips: "Writers should have basic knowledge of the industry sufficient to understand some management issues. Writer should understand what a retirement or assisted living community is and isn't."

N $ $ $ SETTLEMENT SERVICES TODAY, (formerly *Title Technology*), Condell & Co., P.O. Box 7768, Hilton Head Island SC 29938. (843)686-6636. Fax: (843)686-6515. E-mail: s2t@condell.com. Website: www.condell.c om. **Contact:** Mike Thompson, editor. **50% freelance written.** Monthly magazine covering the title and settlement services industry. "We consider the magazine to be a training tool for managers and owners of title insurance agencies." Estab. 1993. Circ. 5,000. Pays on publication. Publishes ms an average of 2 months after acceptance. Byline given. Buys one-time rights. Editorial lead time 4 months. Accepts queries by mail, e-mail, fax, phone. Accepts simultaneous submissions. Responds in 2 weeks to queries; 2 months to mss. Sample copy and writer's guidelines free.
　　O— Break in with "an article about a core process improvement within a settlement services office—a factual article with quantitative analysis of the improvement, including graphs and charts."
Nonfiction: How-to, interview/profile, new product, personal experience, technical. No thinly veiled commercials for a specific product or service—or worse, a blatant commercial for a product or service. **Buys 24 mss/year.** Query with published clips. Length: 1,000-4,000 words. **Pays $250-800 for assigned articles; $175-750 for unsolicited articles.**
Photos: Send photos with submission. Reviews prints smaller than 8×10. Offers no additional payment for photos accepted with ms. Captions, model releases and identification of subjects required.
Columns/Departments: Image Technology (use of imaging systems in title ops), 750-1,250 words; Electronic Commerce (news, tips, guidelines, breakthroughs in e-commerce), 1,000 words; Hardware (news, reviews, how-to, trends in small office automation), 1,000 words. **Buys 24 mss/year.** Query with published clips. **Pays $150-400.**
Tips: "Avoid trying to cover too much ground. An article that focuses on a single point or principle, elaborates on that point, and uses several examples and illustrations of the point, makes excellent reading. Use pictures, charts, and graphics whenever possible and as many as you like. *Settlement Services Today* can handle graphic files containing .tif or .eps file extensions."

N $ $ U.S. SITES MAGAZINE, XpansionLab, Inc., 2700 Second Ave., Suite 3, Birmingham AL 35233-2704. (404)881-6420. Fax: (404)881-6313. E-mail: editor@acn.net. Website: www.globalcommunitynetwork.net and www.acn .net. **Contact:** Robert Pittman, Ph.D., executive editor. **25% freelance written.** Monthly magazine covering all phases of business expansion planning and execution. Includes community research, site selection, commercial and industrial real estate, economic development issues, growth by acquisitions, foreign trade, etc. Estab. 1996. Circ. 50,000 controlled circulation. Pays on acceptance of final ms. Byline given. Buys first North American serial rights and electronic rights.

Editorial lead time 2½ months. Submit seasonal material 3 months in advance. Accepts queries by mail, e-mail, fax, phone. Accepts simultaneous submissions. Responds in 2 weeks to queries; 1 month to mss. Sample copy for 8×10 SAE and 4 first-class stamps.

Nonfiction: Interview/profile, technical, tax and finance. **Buys 20-30 mss/year.** Query with published clips. Length: 1,000-3,000 words. **Pays $300 minimum** (much more for well developed content). Pays expenses of writers on assignment.

Photos: Send photos with submission. Reviews contact sheets, negatives, transparencies and any prints. Offers no additional payment for photos accepted with ms. Captions, model releases and identification of subjects required. Buys all rights.

Columns/Departments: "An Interview with . . ." (one-on-one interviews with corporate execs re: business expansion experiences, planning, etc.); "Government Watch" (snippets re: federal, state and local government activities that affect a community's business-friendly reputation); "Obscure No More" (in-depth profile of business-friendly communities that most people have never heard of before).

RESOURCES & WASTE REDUCTION

[N] $ $ COMPOSTING NEWS, The Latest News in Composting and Scrap Wood Management, McEntee Media Corporation, 13727 Holland Rd., Brook Park OH 44142. (216)362-7979. Fax: (216)362-6553. E-mail: cn@recycle.cc. **Contact:** Ken McEntee, editor. **5% freelance written.** Monthly newsletter. "We are interested in any news impacting the composting industry including new laws, regulations, new facilities/programs, end-uses, research, etc." Estab. 1992. Circ. 1,000. Pays on publication. Publishes ms an average of 1 month after acceptance. Buys first or all rights. Editorial lead time 1 month. Submit seasonal material 1 month in advance. Accepts simultaneous and previously published submissions. Accepts queries by mail, e-mail, fax, phone. Responds in 2 months. Sample copy for 9×12 SAE and 55¢ postage. Writer's guidelines for #10 SASE.

Nonfiction: Book excerpts, essays, interview/profile, new product, opinion, personal experience, technical, new business, legislation, regulation, business expansion. **Buys 0-5 mss/year.** Query with published clips. Length: 100-5,000 words. **Pays $10-500.** Pays writers with contributor copies or other premiums by prior agreement.

Columns/Departments: Query with published clips. **Pays $10-500.**

■ The online version of this publication contains material not found in the print edition. Contact: Ken McEntee.

Tips: "We appreciate leads on local news regarding composting, i.e., new facilities or business, new laws and regulations, unique programs, situations that impact supply and demand for composting. International developments are also of interest."

$ $ EROSION CONTROL, The Journal for Erosion and Sediment Control Professionals, Forester Communications, Inc., 5638 Hollister Ave., Suite 301, Santa Barbara CA 93117. (805)681-1300. Fax: (805)681-1311. E-mail: erosion@ix.netcom.com. Website: www.erosioncontrol.net. **Contact:** John Trotti, editor. **60% freelance written.** Magazine published 9 times/year covering all aspects of erosion prevention and sediment control. "*Erosion Control* is a practical, hands-on, 'how-to' professional journal. Our readers are civil engineers, landscape architects, builders, developers, public works officials, road and highway construction officials and engineers, soils specialists, farmers, landscape contractors and others involved with any activity that disturbs significant areas of surface vegetation." Estab. 1994. Circ. 20,000. Pays on publication. Publishes ms an average of 3 months after acceptance. Byline given. Buys all rights. Editorial lead time 4 months. Submit seasonal material 4 months in advance. Accepts queries by mail, e-mail. Responds in 3 weeks. Accepts simultaneous submissions. Sample copy and writer's guidelines free.

Nonfiction: Photo feature, technical. **Buys 15 mss/year.** Query with published clips. Length: 3,000-4,000 words. **Pays $350-650.** Sometimes pays expenses of writers on assignment.

Photos: Send photos with submission. Reviews transparencies, prints. Offers no additional payment for photos accepted with ms. Captions, model releases, identification of subjects required. Buys all rights.

■ The online version of *Erosion Control* contains material not found in the print edition. Contact: John Trotti.

Tips: "Writers should have a good grasp of technology involved, good writing and communication skills, unbounded curiosity and no hidden agenda. Think like your audience. Put yourself in an erosion control professional's boots. What makes this subject important enough that you would take time out from your busy schedule to stop and read the article? Where's the hook? How best to bait it, cast it, troll it and sink it? When you've satisfied yourself on those scores, you're ready to write. Engage your reader. Leave no doubt in anyone's mind who your audience is and why what you have to say is important. Rivet your full attention on your readers and drag them into the middle of your subject; address them directly and personally. For instance, instead of saying, 'Sediment can be kept out of the watercourse in a number of ways,' you might say, 'If you want to keep sediment out of the streambed, here are some things you can do.' "

$ $ MSW MANAGEMENT, The Journal for Municipal Solid Waste Professionals, Forester Communications, Inc., 5638 Hollister Ave., Suite 301, Santa Barbara CA 93117. (805)681-1300. Fax: (805)681-1311. E-mail: erosion@ix.netcom.com. Website: www.mswmanagement.net. Editor: John Trotti. **70% freelance written.** Bimonthly magazine. "*MSW Management* is written for *public sector* solid waste professionals—the people working for the local counties, cities, towns, boroughs and provinces. They run the landfills, recycling programs, composting, incineration. They are responsible for all aspects of garbage collection and disposal; buying and maintaining the associated equipment;

and designing, engineering and building the waste processing facilities, transfer stations and landfills." Estab. 1991. Circ. 25,000. Pays on publication. Byline given. Buys all rights. Editorial lead time 4 months. Submit seasonal material 4 months in advance. Accepts queries by mail, e-mail. Accepts simultaneous submissions. Responds in 6 weeks to queries; 2 months to mss. Sample copy and writer's guidelines free.

Nonfiction: Photo feature, technical. "No rudimentary, basic articles written for the average person on the street. Our readers are experienced professionals with years of practical, in-the-field experience. Any material submitted that we judge as too fundamental will be rejected." **Buys 15 mss/year.** Query. Length: 3,000-4,000 words. **Pays $350-650.** Sometimes pays expenses of writers on assignment.

Photos: Send photos with submission. Reviews transparencies, prints. Offers no additional payment for photos accepted with ms. Captions, model releases, identification of subjects required. Buys all rights.

■ The online version of *MSW Management* includes material not found in the print edition. Contact: John Trotti.

Tips: "We're a small company, easy to reach. We're open to any and all ideas as to possible editorial topics. We endeavor to provide the reader with usable material, and present it in full color with graphic embellishment whenever possible. Dry, highly technical material is edited to make it more palatable and concise. Most of our feature articles come from freelancers. Interviews and quotes should be from public sector solid waste managers and engineers—*not* PR people, *not* manufacturers. Strive to write material that is 'over the heads' of our readers. If anything, attempt to make them 'reach.' Anything submitted that is too basic, elementary, fundamental, rudimentary, etc. cannot be accepted for publication."

$ $ WASTE AGE MAGAZINE, The Business Magazine For Waste Industry Professionals, (formerly *World Wastes Magazine*), Intertec Publishing, 6151 Powers Ferry Rd. NW, Atlanta GA 30339-2941. (770)618-0112. Fax: (770)618-0349. E-mail: bill_wolpin@intertec.com. Editorial Director: Bill Wolpin. **Contact:** Patti Tom, managing editor. **90% freelance written.** Monthly magazine. "*Waste Age* reaches individuals and firms engaged in the removal, collection, processing, transportation, and disposal of solid/hazardous liquid wastes. This includes: private refuse contractors; landfill operators; municipal, county and other government officials; recyclers and handlers of secondary materials; major generators of waste, such as plants and chain stores; engineers, architects and consultants; manufactures and distributors of equipment; universities, libraries and associations; and legal, insurance and financial firms allied to the field. Readers include: owners, presidents, vice-presidents, directors, superintendents, engineers, managers, supervisors, consultants, purchasing agents and commissioners." Estab. 1958. Circ. 43,000. Pays on publication. Publishes ms an average of 4 months after acceptance. Byline given. Buys all rights. Editorial lead time 2 months. Responds in 1 week to queries; 1 month to mss. Sample copy and writer's guidelines free.

Nonfiction: How-to (practical information on improving solid waste management, i.e., how to rehabilitate a transfer station, how to improve recyclable collection, how to manage a landfill, etc.), interview/profile (of prominent persons in the solid waste industry). "No feel-good 'green' articles about recycling. Remember our readers are not the citizens but the governments and private contractors. No 'why you should recycle' articles." **Buys over 50 mss/year.** Query. Length: 700-2,500 words. **Pays $75 flat rate to $175/printed page.** Will pay for expenses of writers on assignment.

Photos: Send photos with submission. Reviews contact sheets, negatives, transparencies, prints. Negotiates payment individually. Identification of subjects required.

Tips: "Read the magazine and understand our audience. Write useful articles with sidebars that the readers can apply to their jobs. Use the Associated Press style book. Freelancers can send in queries or manuscripts or can fax a letter of interest (including qualifications/resume) in possible assignments. Writers must be deadline-oriented."

N $ $ WATER WELL JOURNAL, National Ground Water Association, 601 Dempsey Rd., Westerville OH 43081. Fax: (614)898-7786. E-mail: jross@ngwa.org. Website: www.ngwa.org. **Contact:** Jill Ross, editor. **25% freelance written.** Monthly magazine covering the ground water industry; well drilling. "Known worldwide as 'the voice of the ground water industry,' this premier journal reports the latest news and events needed by the successful 21stcentury contractor. Each month the *Water Well Journal* covers the topics of drilling, rigs and heavy equipment, pumping systems, water quality, business management, water supply, on-site waste water treatment, and diversification opportunities, including geoexchange installations, environmental remediation, irrigation, dewatering and foundation installation. It also offers updates on regulatory issues that impact the ground water industry." Estab. 1948. Circ. 30,000. Pays on publication. Publishes ms an average of 3 months after acceptance. Byline given. Buys all rights. Editorial lead time 2 months. Submit seasonal material 3 months in advance. Accepts queries by mail, fax. Responds in 2 weeks to queries; 1 month to mss. Sample copy for 9×12 SAE and 2 first-class stamps. Writer's guidelines free.

Nonfiction: Essays (sometimes), historical/nostalgic (sometimes), how-to (new technologies), business management, personal experience, photo feature, technical. No company profiles; extended product releases. **Buys up to 20 mss/ year.** Query with published clips. Length: 1,000-4,000 words. **Pays $100-600.**

Photos: State availability of photos with submission. Offers $50-250/photo. Captions and identification of subjects required.

Tips: "Knowledge of ground water industry helpful. We prefer action photos."

SELLING & MERCHANDISING

Sales personnel and merchandisers interested in how to sell and market products successfully consult these journals. Publications in nearly every category of Trade also buy sales-related materials if they are slanted to the product or industry with which they deal.

N̲ $ $ THE AMERICAN SALESMAN, 320 Valley, Burlington IA 52601-5513. Fax: (319)752-3421. Publisher: Michael S. Darnall. **Contact:** Teresa Levinson, editor. Monthly magazine for distribution through company sales representatives. Estab. 1955. Circ. 1,500. Publishes ms an average of 4 months after acceptance. Sample copy and writer's guidelines for 6×9 SAE with 3 first-class stamps; mention *Writer's Market* in request. Accepts queries by mail, fax.
Nonfiction: Sales seminars, customer service and follow-up, closing sales, sales presentations, handling objections, competition, telephone usage and correspondence, managing territory, new innovative sales concepts. No sexist material. Written from a salesperson's viewpoint. Public relations articles or case histories reviewed. Length: 900-1,200 words. Uses no advertising. Follow AP Stylebook. Include biography and/or byline with ms submissions. Author photos used. Send correspondence to Editor.

N̲ $ $ CARD TRADE, Krause Publications, 700 E. State St., Iola WI 54990. (715)445-2214. Fax: (715)445-4087. E-mail: cardtrade@krause.com. Website: www.krause.com. Editor: Scott Kelnhofer. **20% freelance written.** Monthly magazine covering the sports collectible industry. "We're looking for experts in small business retailing and collectible-related sales." Estab. 1994. Circ. 9,000. Pays on publication. Buys perpetual non-exclusive rights. Accepts queries by mail, e-mail, fax, phone. Editorial lead time 1 month.
Nonfiction: How-to (retail advice), new product. **Buys 6-10 mss/year.** Query. Length: 1,000-2,500 words. **Pays $125-300.**
Reprints: Send photocopy of article and information about when and where the article previously appeared. Pays 50% of amount paid for an original article.
Columns/Departments: Buys 30 mss/year. Query. **Pays $125-200.**

N̲ $ $ $ CONSUMER GOODS TECHNOLOGY, Edgell Communications, 4 Middlebury Blvd., Randolph NJ 07867. (973)252-0100. Fax: (973)252-9020. Website: www.consumergoods.com. **Contact:** Angie Pantages, managing editor. **65% freelance written.** Monthly tabloid covering improving business performance using technology. Estab. 1987. Circ. 25,000. Pays on publication. Publishes ms an average of 2 months after acceptance. Byline given. Buys first North American serial rights and electronic rights, second serial (reprint) rights or all rights. Editorial lead time 3 months. Accepts queries by e-mail. Sample copy online at website. Writer's guidelines by e-mail.
Nonfiction: Essays, exposé, how-to, humor, interview/profile. "We create several supplements annually, often using freelance." **Buys 80 mss/year.** Query with or without published clips. Length: 700-1,900 words. **Pays $600-1,200.** Pays expenses of writers on assignment agreed upon in advance.
Photos: State availability of or send photos with submission. Negotiates payment individually. Model release, identification of subjects required. Buys all rights.
Columns/Departments: News/Trends (analysis of news/trends), 150-300 words. **Buys 4 mss/year.** Query with published clips. **Pays $100-300.**
Tips: "We're always on the lookout for new talent. We look in particular for writers with an in-depth understanding of the business issues faced by retailers and/or their suppliers. We also look for familiarity with business technology as a key to addressing those business issues successfully. 'Bits and bytes' tech writing is not wanted; our focus is on improving business performance, as enabled by technology. Most of our readers are not MIS executives (although about a third are from IS departments); copy must address their business focus. Case histories and 'technical round-up' articles are common assignments."

$ $ CONVENIENCE STORE DECISIONS, Donohue-Meehan Publishing, Two Greenwood Square, Suite 410, Bensalem PA 19020. (215)245-4555. Fax: (215)245-4060. E-mail: jgordon@penton.com. **Contact:** Jay Gordon, editor. **40% freelance written.** Monthly magazine. "*CSD* is read by executives of convenience store companies and seeks to be the 'idea store' by reporting on all facets of these specialized retail businesses, such as the marketing and merchandising of gasoline, food and merchandise." Estab. 1990. Circ. 42,000. Pays on publication. Byline given. Makes work-for-hire assignments. Editorial lead time 2 months. Submit seasonal material 4 months in advance. Accepts queries by mail, e-mail, fax. Sample copy free.
○⊶ Break in with a "demonstrated knowledge of finance and business, with special emphasis on retail. Keen powers of observation and attention to detail are also prized."
Nonfiction: How-to, interview/profile, new product, technical. **Buys 24 mss/year.** Query with published clips. Length: 500-2,500 words. **Pays $600.** Pays expenses of writers on assignment.
Photos: State availability of photos with submission. Negotiates payment individually.
Columns/Departments: Query. **Pays $350-500.**
Tips: "Writers with strong retail/business writing experience should write or call Jay Gordon, editor. We will work to find an acceptable 'trial' assignment (for pay) to assess the writer's abilities. Do not send boiler plate features on finance and human resource topics that are customized for our market by adding the words convenience store. Don't waste our time!"

N̲ $ $ DATA CAPTURE RESELLER, The Channels Source For Auto ID Solutions, Edgell Communications, Inc., 10 W. Hanover Ave., Suite 107, Randolph NJ 07869. (973)895-3300. Fax: (973)895-7711. E-mail: kcarson@edgellmail.com. Website: www.datacapturereseller.com. Editor: Michael Kachmar. **Contact:** Kathleen Carson, managing editor. **60% freelance written.** Bimonthly journal covering auto ID for the channel. "*Data Capture Reseller* is the channels source for Auto ID solutions. Covers warehousing, healthcase, supply chain, RFID, etc." Estab. 1996. Circ.

12,500. **Pays on acceptance**. Publishes ms an average of 2 months after acceptance. Byline given. Buys first North American serial rights. Editorial lead time 3 months. Accepts queries by mail, e-mail, fax. Accepts simultaneous submissions. Responds in 2 weeks to queries; 2 months to mss. Sample copy free.

Nonfiction: Interview/profile, opinion, technical, case histories/application stories. See our website for upcoming theme issues. **Buys 24 mss/year.** Query with published clips. Length: 600-1,700 words. **Pays $200-600 for assigned articles.** Sometimes pays in publicity for vendor articles.

Photos: Send photos with submission. Offers no additional payment for photos accepted with ms. Model releases and identification of subjects required.

Tips: "Understand the Auto ID channel for the resale market."

N $ EVENTS BUSINESS NEWS, S.E.N. Inc., 523 Route 38, Suite 207, Cherry Hill NJ 08002. (609)488-5255. Fax: (609)488-8324. **Contact:** Norman Zelnick, assistant to the editor. **20% freelance written.** Bimonthly glossy magazine covering special events across North America, including festivals, fairs, auto shows, home shows, trade shows, etc. Covers 15 categories of shows/events. Byline given. Buys first rights. Accepts queries by mail. Submit seasonal material 3 months in advance. Sample copy and writers guidelines free.

Nonfiction: How-to, interview/profile, event review, new product. Special issues: annual special event directory, covering over 38,000 events. No submissions unrelated to selling at events. Query. Length: 400-750 words. **Pays $2.50/ column inch.**

Reprints: Send photocopy of article and information about when and where the article previously appeared.

Photos: Send photos with submission. Reviews contact sheets. Offers $20/photo. Captions required. Buys one-time rights.

Columns/Departments: Five columns monthly (dealing with background of event, vendors or unique facets of industry in North America). Query with published clips. Length: 400-700 words. **Pays $3 column inch.**

N $ $ GIFTWARE NEWS, Talcott Corp., 20 N. Walker Dr., Suite 1865, Chicago IL 60606. (312)849-2220. Fax: (312)849-2174. **Contact:** John Saxtan, editor. **55% freelance written.** Monthly magazine covering gifts, collectibles, and tabletops for giftware retailers. Estab. 1976. Circ. 45,000. Pays on publication. Publishes ms an average of 2 months after acceptance. Byline given. Buys all rights. Submit seasonal/holiday material 4 months in advance. Responds in 2 months to mss. Sample copy for $5.

Nonfiction: How-to (sell, display), new product. Buys 50 mss/year. Send complete ms. Length: 1,500-2,500 words. **Pays $200-350 for assigned articles; $150-250 for unsolicited articles.**

Photos: Send photos with submission. Reviews 4×5 transparencies and 5×7 prints. Offers no additional payment for photos accepted with ms. Identification of subjects required.

Columns/Departments: Stationery, giftbaskets, collectibles, holiday merchandise, tabletop, wedding market and display—all for the gift retailer. **Buys 36 mss/year.** Send complete ms. Length: 1,500-2,500 words. **Pays $100-250.**

Tips: "We are not looking so much for general journalists but rather experts in particular fields who can also write."

N $ $ NEW AGE RETAILER, Continuity Publishing, 1300 N. State St., #105, Bellingham WA 98225. (800)463-9243. Fax: (360)676-0932. E-mail: molly@newageretailer.com. Website: www.newage.retailer.com. **Contact:** Molly Trimble, editor. **90% freelance written.** Bimonthly trade magazine for retailers of New Age books, music and merchandise. "The goal of the articles in *New Age Retailer* is usefulness—we strive to give store owners and managers practical, in-depth information they can begin using immediately. We have three categories of articles: retail business methods that give solid information about the various aspects of running an independent store; inventory articles that discuss a particular New Age subject or trend and include lists of books, music, and products suitable for store inventory; and education articles that help storeowners and managers gain knowledge and stay current in New Age subjects." Estab. 1987. Circ. 6,000. Pays on publication. Publishes ms an average of 4 months after acceptance. Byline given. Offers 10% kill fee. Buys first North American serial rights, second serial (reprint) rights, simultaneous rights and electronic rights. Editorial lead time 4 months. Submit seasonal material 4 months in advance. Accepts queries by mail, e-mail, fax, phone. Accepts simultaneous submissions. Responds in 1 month to queries; 2 months to mss. Sample copy for $5. Writer's guidelines for SAE and 1 first-class stamp.

Nonfiction: Book excerpts, how-to, interview profile, new product, opinion, personal experience, religious, technical, business principles. No self-promotion for writer's company or product. Writer must understand independent retailing and New Age subjects. **Buys 50 mss/year.** Query with published clips. Length: 1,500-5,000 words. **Pays $150-300 for assigned articles; $75-250 for unsolicited articles.** Sometimes pays writers with advertisement space in magazine. Sometimes pays expenses of writers on assignment.

Reprints: Accepts previously published submissions.

Photos: State availability of photos or send photos with submission. Reviews 2×3 prints (minimum size). Negotiates payment individually. Captions required. Buys one-time rights.

Columns/Departments: Mara Applebaum, associate editor. The Inspired Enterprise (New Age business tips for independent retailers), 2,500 words. **Buys 5-7 mss/year.** Query with published clips. **Pays $200-300.**

Tips: "E-mail Molly Trimble (molly@newageretailer.com), or phone her at (800)463-9243, ext. 3014. Describe your expertise in the New Age market and independent retailing. Have an idea for an article ready to pitch. Promise only what you can deliver."

N $ $ NICHE, The Magazine For Progressive Retailers, The Rosen Group, 3000 Chestnut Ave., Suite 304, Baltimore MD 21211. (410)889-3093. Fax: (410)243-7089. E-mail: hoped@rosengrp.com. **Contact:** Hope Daniels, editor. **75% freelance written.** Quarterly business-to-business magazine for the progressive craft gallery retailer. Each issue includes retail gallery profiles, store design trends, management techniques and merchandising strategies for small business owners. Estab. 1988. Circ. 20,000. Pays on publication. Publishes ms an average of 6 months after acceptance. Byline given. Buys first North American serial rights. Editorial lead time 4 months. Submit seasonal material 9 months in advance. Accepts queries by mail, e-mail, fax. Responds in 6 weeks to queries; 1 month to mss. Sample copy for $3.
Nonfiction: Interview/profile, photo feature, and articles targeted to independent retailers and small business owners. *Niche* is looking for in-depth articles on store security, innovative merchandising/display or marketing and promotion. Stories of interest to independent retailers, such as gallery owners, may be submitted. **Buys 20-28 mss/year.** Query with published clips. Length: 500-1,500 words. **Pays $300-700.** Sometimes pays expenses of writers on assignment.
Photos: Send photos with submission. Reviews 4×5 transparencies or slides. Negotiates payment individually. Identification of subjects required.
Columns/Departments: Retail Details (general retail information); Artist Profiles (biographies of American Craft Artists); Resources (book/video/seminar reviews pertaining to retailers). Query with published clips. **Pays $25-300.**

$ $ $ OPERATIONS & FULFILLMENT, Target Communications Corp., 11 Riverbend Dr. S., Stamford CT 06907-2524. (203)358-9900, ext. 166. Fax: (203)854-2956. E-mail: ramaswami@opsandfulfillment.com. Associate Editor: Barbara Arnn. **Contact:** Rama Ramaswami, editor. **50% freelance written.** Bimonthly magazine covering catalog/direct mail operations. *"Operations & Fulfillment (O&F)* is a bimonthly publication that offers practical solutions for catalog and direct response operations management. The magazine covers such critical areas as material handling, bar coding, facility planning, transportation, call centers, warehouse management, information systems, online fulfillment and human resources." Estab. 1993. Circ. 13,000. **Pays 50% on acceptance;** 50% on publication. Publishes ms an average of 2 months after acceptance. Buys first North American serial rights. Editorial lead time 2 months. Responds in 1 week to queries; 1 month to mss. Sample copy and writer's guidelines free.
Nonfiction: Book excerpts, how-to, interview/profile, new product, technical. **Buys 4-6 mss/year.** Query with published clips. Length: 2,750-3,000 words. **Pays $1,000-1,800.**
Photos: Send photos with submission. Captions and identification of subjects required. "In addition to the main article, you must include at least one sidebar of about 400 words that contains a detailed example or case study of how a catalog company implements or benefits from the process you're writing about; a checklist or set of practical guidelines (e.g., "Twelve Ways to Ship Smarter") that describe how to implement what you suggest in the article; supporting materials such as flow charts, graphs, diagrams, illustrations and photographs (these must be clearly labeled and footnoted); and an author biography of no more than 75 words."
Tips: "Writers need some knowledge of the mail order or catalog industry. They should be able to deal clearly with highly technical material; provide attention to detail and painstaking research."

N $ $ OUTFITTER MAGAZINE, The Monthly Trade Journal of Outdoor Gear, Virgo Publishing Inc., 3300 N. Central Ave., Suite 2500, Phoenix AZ 85012. (480)990-1101. Fax: (480)990-0819. E-mail: outfit@upico.com. Website: www.outfittermag.com. Editor: Martin Vilaboy. **Contact:** Tony Jones, managing editor. **5-10% freelance written.** Monthly magazine covering business and products of outdoor recreation. *"Outfitter* is a monthly trade journal dedicated to enhancing the business of retailers and manufacturers of outdoor apparel, footwear, equipment and accessories. Knowledge of outdoor activities, products, fabric and/or retailing is helpful." Estab. 1994. Circ. 20,000. Pays on publication. Publishes ms an average of 2 months after acceptance. Byline given. We publish on assignment. Buys first, one-time or all rights. Editorial lead time 2 months. Submit seasonal material 2 months in advance. Accepts queries by mail, e-mail, fax. Sample copy online at website. Writer's guidelines for 10×13 SAE and 5 first-class stamps.
Nonfiction: Interview/profile, new product, technical. Editorial calendar available on website. "No prewritten stories for publication. Submit story ideas and clips. Do not send articles aimed at consumers." **Buys 12-15 mss/year.** Query with published clips. Length: 500-1,500 words. **Pays $150-250.** Sometimes pays writers with advertising bio notes or trade for advertising.
Photos: State availability of photos with submission. Negotiates payment individually. Buys one-time rights or all rights.
Tips: "Have knowledge and experience in the outdoor industry, either in retailing or manufacturing of product. Submit story ideas based on our editorial calendar and enclose sample clips (no more than 3) if available."

$ $ PARTY & PAPER RETAILER, 107 Mill Plain Rd., Suite 204, Danbury CT 06811-6100. (203)730-4090. Fax: (203)730-4094. E-mail: editor@partypaper.com. Website: www.partypaper.com. **Contact:** Trisha McMahon Drain, editor-in-chief. **90% freelance written.** Monthly magazine for "every aspect of how to do business better for owners of party and fine stationery shops. Tips and how-tos on display, marketing, success stories, merchandising, operating costs, e-commerce, retail technology, etc." Estab. 1986. Circ. 20,000. Pays on publication. Offers 15% kill fee. Buys first North American serial rights. Editorial lead time 6 months. Submit seasonal material 6 months in advance. Accepts queries by mail, e-mail, fax. Responds in 2 months. Sample copy for $6.
○→ Especially interested in news items on party retail industry for our Press Pages. Also, new column on Internet retailing ("Cyberlink") which covers all www-related topics.

Nonfiction: Book excerpts, how-to (retailing related), new product. No articles written in first person. **Buys 100 mss/ year.** Query with published clips. Length: 800-1,800 words. **Pay "depends on topic, word count expertise, deadline."** Pays telephone expenses of writers on assignment.

Reprints: Send tearsheet or photocopy of article and information about when and where the article previously appeared.

Photos: State availability of photos with submission. Reviews transparencies. Negotiates payment individually. Captions, identification of subjects required. Buys one-time rights.

Columns/Departments: Shop Talk (successful party/stationery store profile), 1,800 words; Storekeeping (selling, employees, market, running store), 800 words; Cash Flow (anything finance related), 800 words; On Display (display ideas and how-to). **Buys 30 mss/year.** Query with published clips. Pay varies.

◼ The online magazine carries original content not found in the print edition.

N $ $ $ RETAIL SYSTEMS RESELLER, The news source for channel management, Edgell Communications, Inc., 10 W. Hanover Ave., Suite 107, Randolph NJ 07869-4214. (973)895-3300. Fax: (973)895-7711. E-mail: edgell@edgellmail.com. Website: www.retailsystemsreseller.com. Editor: Michael Kachmar. **Contact:** Kathleen Carson, managing editor. **60% freelance written.** Trade journal published 9 times/year covering retail technology and products for the channel. "The news source for retail channel management." Estab. 1992. Circ. 17,000. **Pays on acceptance.** Publishes ms an average of 2 months after acceptance. Byline given. Editorial lead time 3 months. Accepts queries by mail, e-mail, fax. Accepts simultaneous submissions. Responds in 2 weeks to queries; 2 months to mss. Sample copy free online at website.

Nonfiction: Interview/profile, opinion, technical, technology/channel issues. **Buys 36 mss/year.** Query with published clips. Length: 1,000-1,700 words. **Pays $200-800 for assigned articles.** Sometimes pays in publicity for vendor-contributed articles. Sometimes pays expenses of writers on assignment.

Photos: Send photos with submission. Offers no additional payment for photos accepted with ms. Model releases and identification of subjects required.

Tips: "Understand the retail resale channel and target to appropriate issues—service, technology, products as applied, etc."

N $ $ SHOWCASE INTERNATIONAL, The source for luggage, business cases and accessories, Luggage & Leather Goods Manufacturers of America, 350 Fifth Ave, Suite 2624, New York NY 10118. (212)695-2340. Fax: (212)643-8021. E-mail: showcase@llgma.org. Website: www.llgma.org. Editor: Michele M. Pittenger. **Contact:** John Misiano, senior editor. **5-10% freelance written.** Bimonthly magazine covering luggage, leather goods, accessories, trends and new products. "*SHOWCASE* contains articles for retailers, dealers, manufacturers and suppliers, about luggage, business cases, personal leather goods, handbags and accessories. Special articles report on trends in fashion promotions, selling and marketing techniques, industry statistics and other educational and promotional improvements and advancement." Estab. 1975. Circ. 14,500. **Pays on acceptance.** Publishes ms 2 months after acceptance. Byline given. Offers $50 kill fee. Editorial lead time 2-3 months. Submit seasonal material 2 months in advance. Accepts queries by mail, e-mail. Responds in 2 weeks to queries; 1 month to mss. Sample copy and writer's guidelines free.

Nonfiction: Interview/profile, technical, travel, "No manufacturer profiles." **Buys 3 mss/year.** Query with published clips. Length: 1,200-1,600 words. **Pays $200-500.**

N $ $ SPECIALTY COFFEE RETAILER, The Coffee Business Monthly, Adams Business Media, 2101 S. Arlington Heights Rd., Suite 150, Arlington Heights IL 60005. (847)427-2003. Fax: (847)427-2041. E-mail: sgillerlain@ mail.aip.com. Website: www.specialty-coffee.com. Managing Editor: Jenifer Everley. **Contact:** Sue Gillerlain, editor-in-chief. **60% freelance written.** Monthly magazine covering coffee—retail and roasting, tea. "*Specialty Coffee Retailer* is the business monthly for the specialty coffee industry. The magazine provides practical business information for the profitable operation of a coffeehouse, cart/kiosk/drive-through or tea house. Featured topics include business management and finance, marketing and promotion, site selection, store design, equipment selection and maintenance, drink preparation, tea trends, new products and more." Estab. 1994. Circ. 7,500. Pays on publication. Publishes ms an average of 2 months after acceptance. Byline given. Buys first North American serial and electronic rights. Editorial lead time 2 months. Submit seasonal material 5 months in advance. Accepts queries by mail, e-mail, fax. Accepts simultaneous submissions. Sample copy by e-mail.

Nonfiction: How-to (select a roaster, blend coffees, purchase tea, market chai). No opinion, essays, book reviews, humor, personal experience. **Buys 36 mss/year.** Query with published clips. Length: 1,800-2,500 words. **Pays $300-425.** Sometimes pays expenses of writers on assignment.

Photos: Send photos with submission. Reviews transparencies and 3×5 prints. Offers no additional payment for photos accepted with ms.

Tips: "Be willing to contact industry experts for inclusion in stories."

$ $ STORE EQUIPMENT & DESIGN, Macfadden Business Communications Group, 417 S. Dearborn St., 6th Floor, Chicago IL 60605. (312)935-2300. Fax: (312)935-2315. E-mail: storeequip@aol.com. Website: www.storequip.c om. Editor: David Litwak. **Contact:** Monica Buckley, managing editor. **45% freelance written.** Monthly magazine covering design and equipping of supermarkets and other retail formats. "The editorial objective of *Store Equipment & Design* (SE&D) is to be the idea source for retail design professionals. SE&D approaches store planning issues both from a 'business' and a 'design' perspective. The primary criteria for evaluating the success of a particular new store or remodeling project is how well the business strategy of a retailer is embodied in the physical look and organization of the store." Estab. 1991. Circ. 23,000. **Pays on acceptance**. Publishes ms an average of 1-3 months after acceptance. Byline given. Offers $100 kill fee. Buys first and second serial (reprint) rights. Editorial lead time 3 months. Submit seasonal material 6 months in advance. Accepts queries by mail, e-mail, fax, phone. Responds in 3 weeks. Sample copy for #10 SASE.

Nonfiction: Interview/profile, new product, technical. **Buys 36 mss/year.** Query with published clips. Length: 500-700 words. **Pays $300-600.** Sometimes pays expenses of writers on assignment.

Photos: State availability of photos with submission. Captions and identification of subjects required. Buys one-time rights.

Tips: "Stories must reach two audiences at the same time. Senior management need a general overview of every story, an executive summary per se of the general trend we're writing about in a story. What are the ideas which emerge from the merchandising core? Hands-on people need specific information, technical information, details, details, details, on what has worked and what hasn't."

SPORT TRADE

Retailers and wholesalers of sports equipment and operators of recreation programs read these journals. Magazines about general and specific sports are classified in the Consumer Sports section.

N $ $ AQUATICS INTERNATIONAL, Leisure Publications Inc., 4160 Wilshire Blvd., Los Angeles CA 90010. Website: www.aquaticsintl.com. **Contact:** Mark Edelstein, editor. Trade magazine published 9 times/year covering public swimming pools and waterparks. Estab. 1989. Circ. 30,000. Pays on publication. Publishes ms an average of 3 months after acceptance. Byline given. Buys international rights in perpetuity and makes work-for-hire assignments. Editorial lead time 3 months. Responds in 1 month to queries. Sample copy for $10.50.

Nonfiction: How-to, interview/profile, technical. **Buys 6 mss/year.** Query with published clips. Length: 1,500-2,500 words. **Pays $425 for assigned articles.**

Columns and Departments: Pays $250.

Tips: "Query letter with samples."

N $ $ ARROWTRADE MAGAZINE, A Magazine For Retailers, Distributors & Manufacturers of Bowhunting Equipment, Arrow Trade Publishing Corporation, 2295 E. Newman Rd., Lake City MI 49651. Fax: (231)328-3006. E-mail: atrade@freeway.net. **Contact:** Tim Dehn, editor. **20% freelance written.** Bimonthly magazine covering the archery industry. "Our readers are interested in articles that help them operate their business better. They are primarily owners or managers of sporting goods stores and archery pro shops." Estab. 1996. Circ. 10,000. **Pays on acceptance.** Publishes ms an average of 2 months after acceptance. Byline given. Buys first North American serial rights. Editorial lead time 2 months. Accepts queries by mail, e-mail, fax. Responds in 3 weeks to queries; 1 month to mss. Sample copy for 9×12 SAE and 10 first-class stamps. Writer's guidelines for #10 SASE.

　　O— *ArrowTrade Magazine* needs queries from veterans interested in writing for our industry audience. Our readers are primarily retailers of bowhunting equipment.

Nonfiction: Interview/profile, new product. "Generic business articles won't work for our highly specialized audience." **Buys 12 mss/year.** Query with published clips. Length: 1,800-2,800 words. **Pays $350-550.**

Photos: Send photos with submission. Reviews contact sheets, negatives, 35mm transparencies and 4×6 prints. Offers no additional payment for photos accepted with ms. Captions required.

Columns/Departments: Dealer Workbench (repair and tuning of bows), 1,600 words; Bow Report (tests and evaluations of current models), 2,400 words. **Buys 6 mss/year.** Query with published clips. **Pays $300-475.**

Tips: "Our readers are hungry for articles that help them decide what to stock and how to do a better job selling or servicing it. Articles needed typically fall into one of these categories: business profiles on outstanding retailers, manufacturers or distributors; equipment articles that cover categories of gear, citing trends in the market and detailing why products have been designed a certain way and what type of use they're best suited for; basic business articles that help dealers do a better job of promoting their business, managing their inventory, training their staff, etc. Good interviewing skills are a must, as especially in the equipment articles we like to see a minimum of six sources."

$ $ $ CASINO EXECUTIVE MAGAZINE, G.E.M. Communications, 1771 E. Flamingo Rd., Suite 207A, Las Vegas NV 89119. (702)735-0446. Fax: (702)735-0344. **Contact:** Rex Buntain, editor. Managing Editor: David McKee. Monthly magazine covering the US gaming industry. "*Casino Executive* is a business magazine covering the gaming industry in the U.S. Contributors should be knowledgeable about the workings of the gaming industry, its companies and personalities." Estab. 1995. Circ. 20,000. Pays on publication. Publishes ms an average of 3 months after acceptance. Byline given. Buys first rights. Editorial lead time 2 months. Submit seasonal material 4 months in advance. Responds in 1 month. Sample copy and writer's guidelines free.

Nonfiction: General interest, how-to, interview/profile, new product, technical (relating to gaming industry). **Buys 20-30 mss/year.** Query by mail only with published clips. Length: 800-2,500 words. **Pays $100-1,000.**

Photos: State availability of photos with submission. Reviews transparencies. Negotiates payment individually. Buys negotiable rights.

Columns/Departments: Gaming Law; Marketing (casino marketing); Compensation (industry salaries); Corporate Cultures (company environment); Food & Beverage (management of); Managing the Casino Hotel (management of); Retail & Entertainment (management-casino), all 800 words. **Buys 60-70 mss/year.** Query by mail only. **Pays $200.**

Tips: "Writers should be familiar with casino executive magazine and the gaming industry. We are a business magazine, and queries and submissions should reflect that. Most of the content is assigned so writers should query the editor with ideas, rather than submitting material."

N$ CROSSFIRE, Paintball Digest, Digest Publications, 29 Fostertown Rd., Medford NJ 08055. (609)953-4900. Fax: (609)953-4905. **Contact:** Melissa Sowers, publisher/editor-in-chief. **100% freelance written.** Monthly magazine covering paintball sport. "*Crossfire* will cover all aspects of the paintball industry from tactics to safety." Pays on publication. Byline given. Makes work-for-hire assignments. Editorial lead time 1 year. Submit seasonal material 2 months in advance. Accepts queries by mail, e-mail, fax. Accepts simultaneous submissions. Responds in 2 weeks to queries. Sample copy free.

Nonfiction: How-to, humor, interview/profile, new product, personal experience, photo feature, technical, travel, tournament coverage, industry news. **Buys 1-3 mss/year.** Send complete ms. Length: 700-1,900 words. **Pays 7-22¢.** Will pay authors in advertising trade outs.

Reprints: Accepts previously published submissions.

Photos: Send photos with submission. Reviews negatives. Negotiates payment individually. Captions, model release, identification of subjects required. Buys all rights.

Fillers: Facts, gags to be illustrated by cartoonist, newsbreaks. **Buys 24/year.** Length: 25-100 words. **Pays 7-22¢.**

$$ FITNESS MANAGEMENT, Issues and Solutions in Fitness Services, Leisure Publications, Inc., 215 S. Highway 101, Suite 110, P.O. Box 1198, Solana Beach CA 92075-0910. (858)481-4155. Fax: (858)481-4228. E-mail: fmedit@fitnessworld.com. Website: www.fitnessworld.com. Co-Publisher: Edward H. Pitts. **Contact:** Ronale Tucker, editor. **50% freelance written.** Monthly magazine. "Readers are owners, managers and program directors of physical fitness facilities. *FM* helps them run their enterprises safely, efficiently and profitably. Ethical and professional positions in health, nutrition, sports medicine, management, etc., are consistent with those of established national bodies." Estab. 1985. Circ. 26,000. Pays on publication. Publishes ms an average of 5 months after acceptance. Byline given. Pays 50% kill fee. Buys all rights (all articles published in *FM* are also published and archived on its website). Submit seasonal material 6 months in advance. Accepts queries by mail, e-mail, fax. Responds in 3 months. Sample copy for $5. Writer's guidelines for #10 SASE.

Nonfiction: Book excerpts (prepublication); how-to (manage fitness center and program); new product (no pay); photo feature (facilities/programs); technical; other (news of fitness research and major happenings in fitness industry). No exercise instructions or general ideas without examples of fitness businesses that have used them successfully. **Buys 50 mss/year.** Query. Length: 750-2,000 words. **Pays $60-300 for assigned articles.** Pays expenses of writers on assignment.

Photos: Send photos with submission. Reviews contact sheets, 2×2 and 4×5 transparencies; prefers glossy prints, 5×7 to 8×10. Captions, model releases required.

The online magazine carries original content not found in the print edition. Contact: Ronale Tucker. Includes sample articles.

Tips: "We seek writers who are expert in a business or science field related to the fitness-service industry or who are experienced in the industry. Be current with the state of the art/science in business and fitness and communicate it in human terms (avoid intimidating academic language; tell the story of how this was learned and/or cite examples or quotes of people who have applied the knowledge successfully)."

N $$ GOLF COURSE NEWS, The Newspaper for the Golf Course Industry, United Publications Inc., P.O. Box 997, 102 Lafayette St., Yarmouth ME 04096. (207)846-0600. Fax: (207)846-0657. E-mail: pblais@golfcoursen ews.com. Website: www.golfcoursenews.com. Managing Editor: Peter Blais. **Contact:** Mark Leslie, editor. **15% freelance written.** Monthly tabloid "written with the golf course superintendent in mind. Our readers are superintendents, course architects and builders, owners and general managers." Estab. 1989. Circ. 25,000. **Pays on acceptance.** Publishes ms an average of 2 months after acceptance. Byline given. Buys first North American serial rights. Editorial lead time 1 month. Submit seasonal material 2 months in advance. Accepts queries by mail, e-mail, fax, phone. Responds in 2 weeks to queries; 2 months to mss. Free sample copy and writer's guidelines.

Nonfiction: Book excerpts, general interest, interview/profile, new product, opinion, photo feature. "No how-to articles." **Buys 24 mss/year.** Query with published clips. Length: 500-1,000 words. **Pays $200.** Sometimes pays expenses of writers on assignment.

Photos: Send photos with submission. Reviews negatives, transparencies, prints. Offers no additional payment for photos accepted with ms. Identification of subjects required. Buys one-time rights.

Columns/Departments: On the Green (innovative ideas on the golf course), 500-800 words; Shop Talk (in the maintenance facility). Buys 4 mss/year. Query with published clips. Pays $200-500.

Tips: "Keep your eye out for news affecting the golf industry. Then contact us with your story ideas. We are a national paper and accept both national and regional interest articles. We are interested in receiving features on development of golf projects. We also have an international edition covering the golf industry in the Asia-Pacific retion—aptly called *Golf Course News International* published six times per year."

[N] $ $ HOCKEY BUSINESS NEWS, Transcontinental Sports Publications, 777 Bay St., #2700, Toronto, Ontario M5G 2N1 Canada. (416)340-8000, ext. 253. Fax: (416)340-2786. E-mail: karlw@transcontinental.ca. **Contact:** Wayne Karl, editor. **70% freelance written.** Trade journal published 8 times/year covering the hockey industry. Estab. 1994. Circ. 6,000. Pays on publication. Publishes ms an average of 1 month after acceptance. Byline given. Kill fee negotiated. Buys first North American serial, electronic or all rights. Editorial lead time 2 months. Accepts queries by mail, e-mail, fax, phone. Accepts simultaneous submissions. Responds in 2 weeks to queries; 1 month to mss. Writer's guidelines by e-mail.

Nonfiction: Exposé, general interest, how-to, interview/profile, new product, opinion, technical. Query with published clips. Length: 300-2,000 words. **Pays 35¢/word "or terms discussed."** Sometimes pays expenses of writers on assignment.

Photos: State availability of photos with submission or send photos with submission. Reviews transparencies and prints. Negotiates payment individually. Identification of subjects required. Buys all rights.

Columns/Departments: Buys 8 mss/year. Query with published clips. **Pays 35¢/word "or terms discussed."**

[N] IDEA HEALTH & FITNESS SOURCE, (formerly *Idea Today*), IDEA Inc., Dept. WM, 6190 Cornerstone Court E., Suite 204, San Diego CA 92121. (619)535-8979. Fax: (619)535-8234. E-mail: zamoram@ideafit.com. **Contact:** Michelle Zamora, editorial assistant. Executive Editor: Diane Lofshult. **70% freelance written.** Magazine published 10 times/year "for fitness professionals—aerobics instructors, one-to-one trainers and studio and health club owners—covering topics such as aerobics, nutrition, injury prevention, entrepreneurship in fitness, fitness-oriented research and exercise programs." Estab. 1984. Circ. 23,000. **Pays on acceptance.** Publishes ms an average of 4 months after acceptance. Byline given. Buys all rights. Accepts simultaneous submissions. Responds in 2 months to queries. Sample copy for $4.

Nonfiction: How-to, technical. No general information on fitness; our readers are pros who need detailed information. **Buys 15 mss/year.** Query. Length: 1,000-3,000 words. Pay varies.

Photos: State availability of photos with submission. Offers no additional payment for photos with ms. Model releases required. Buys all rights.

Columns/Departments: Research (detailed, specific info; must be written by expert), 750-1,500 words; Industry News (short reports on research, programs and conferences), 150-300 words; Fitness Handout (exercise and nutrition info for participants), 750 words. **Buys 80 mss/year.** Query. Length: 150-1,500 words. Pay varies.

Tips: "We don't accept fitness information for the consumer audience on topics such as why exercise is good for you. Writers who have specific knowledge of, or experience working in, the fitness industry have an edge."

$ $ NSGA RETAIL FOCUS, National Sporting Goods Association, 1699 Wall St., Suite 700, Mt. Prospect IL 60056-5780. (847)439-4000. Fax: (847)439-0111. E-mail: nsga1699@aol.com. Website: www.nsga.org. **Contact:** Larry N. Weindruch, editor/publisher. **25% freelance written.** Works with a small number of new/unpublished writers each year. "*NSGA Retail Focus* serves as a monthly trade journal for presidents, CEOs and owners of more than 22,000 retail sporting goods firms." Estab. 1948. Circ. 5,000. Pays on publication. Publishes ms an average of 1 month after acceptance. Byline given. Offers 50% kill fee. Buys first rights and second serial (reprint) rights. Submit seasonal material 6 months in advance. Accepts queries by mail, e-mail. Sample copy for 9×12 SAE with 5 first-class stamps.

Nonfiction: Interview/profile, photo feature. "No articles written without sporting goods retail businesspeople in mind as the audience. In other words, no generic articles sent to several industries." **Buys 12 mss/year.** Query with published clips. **Pays $75-500.** Sometimes pays the expenses of writers on assignment.

Photos: State availability of photos with submission. Reviews contact sheets, negatives, transparencies and 5×7 prints. Payment negotiable. Buys one-time rights.

Columns/Departments: Personnel Management (succinct tips on hiring, motivating, firing, etc.); Sales Management (in-depth tips to improve sales force performance); Retail Management (detailed explanation of merchandising/inventory control); Advertising (case histories of successful ad campaigns/ad critiques); Legal Advisor; Computers; Store Design; Visual Merchandising; all 1,500 words. **Buys 12 mss/year.** Query. Length: 1,000-1,500 words. **Pays $75-300.**

$ $ PADDLE DEALER, The Trade Magazine for Paddlesports, Paddlesport Publishing, Inc., P.O. Box 5450, Steamboat Springs CO 80477-5450. (970)879-1450. Fax: (970)870-1404. E-mail: editor@aca-paddler.org. Website: www.paddlermagazine.com. Editor: Eugene Buchanan. **Contact:** Tom Bie, managing editor. **70% freelance written.** Quarterly magazine covering the canoeing, kayaking and rafting industry. Estab. 1993. Circ. 7,500. Pays on publication. Publishes ms an average of 1-6 months after acceptance. Byline given. Buys first North American serial and one time electronic rights. Editorial lead time 2 months. Submit seasonal material 6 months in advance. Accepts queries by mail, e-mail, fax. Accepts simultaneous submissions (queries only). Responds in 3 months. Sample copy for 8½×11 SAE and $1.78. Writer's guidelines free for #10 SASE.

Nonfiction: Book excerpts, general interest, how-to, interview/profile, new product, technical, business advice. **Buys 8 mss/year.** Query or send complete ms. Length: 2,300 words. **Pays 20-25¢/word.** Sometimes pays expenses of writers on assignment.

Reprints: Accepts previously published submissions.

Photos: State availability of photos with submission. Reviews transparencies and 5×7 prints. Buys one-time rights.

Columns/Departments: Profiles, how-to, great ideas, computer corner. **Buys 12 mss/year.** Query or send complete ms. **Pays 10-20¢/word.**

N ⭐ **$ $ REFEREE**, Referee Enterprises, Inc., P.O. Box 161, Franksville WI 53126. Fax: (262)632-5460. E-mail: jarehart@referee.com. Website: www.referee.com. Editor: Bill Topp. **Contact:** Jim Arehart, associate editor. **75% freelance written.** Monthly trade magazine covering sports officiating. "*Referee* is a magazine for and read by sports officials of all kinds with a focus on baseball, basketball, football, softball and soccer officiating. Estab. 1976. Circ. 40,000. **Pays on acceptance.** Publishes ms an average of 6 months after acceptance. Byline given. Kill fee negotiable. Buys all rights. Editorial lead time 6 months. Accepts queries by mail, e-mail, fax. Responds in 2 weeks to queries; 1 month to mss. Sample copy for #10 SASE; writer's guidelines free.

Nonfiction: Book excerpts, essays, historical/nostalgic, how-to (sports officiating related), humor, interview/profile, opinion, photo feature, technical (as it relates to sports officiating). "We don't want to see articles with themes not relating to sport officiating. General sports articles, although of interest to us, will not be published." **Buys 40 mss/year.** Query with published clips. Length: 500-2,500 words. **Pays $100-400.** Sometimes pays expenses of writers on assignment.

Reprints: Accepts previously published submissions.

Photos: State availability of photos with submission. Reviews contact sheets, negatives, transparencies and prints. Offers $35-40 per photo. Identification of subjects required. Purchase of rights negotiable.

Tips: "Query first and be persistent. We may not like your idea but that doesn't mean we won't like your next one. Professionalism pays off."

N **$ $ SKI AREA MANAGEMENT**, Beardsley Publications, P.O. Box 644, 45 Main St. N, Woodbury CT 06798. (203)263-0888. Fax: (203)266-0452. E-mail: sam@saminfo.com. Website: www.saminfo.com. Editor: Jennifer Rowan. **Contact:** Jonathan Gourlay, managing editor. **85% freelance written.** Bimonthly magazine covering everything involving the management and development of ski resorts. "We are the publication of record for the North American ski industry. We report on new ideas, developments, marketing and regulations with regard to ski and snowboard resorts. Everyone from the CEO to the lift operator of winter resorts reads our magazine to stay informed about the people and procedures that make ski areas successful." Estab. 1962. Circ. 4,500. Pays on publication. Byline given. Offers kill fee. Buys all rights. Editorial lead time 2 months. Submit seasonal material 3 months in advance. Accepts queries by mail, e-mail. Responds in 2 weeks to queries; 1 month to mss. Sample copy for 9×12 SAE with $3 postage or on website. Writer's guidelines for #10 SASE.

Nonfiction: Historic/nostalgic, how-to, interview/profile, new product, opinion, personal experience, technical. "We don't want anything that *does not* specifically pertain to resort operations, management or financing." **Buys 25-40 mss/year.** Query. Length: 500-2,500 words. **Pays $50-400.**

Reprints: Accepts previously published submissions.

Photos: Send photos with submission. Reviews transparencies and prints. Offers no additional payment for photos accepted with ms. Identification of subjects required. Buys one-time rights OR all rights.

　■ The online magazine carries original content not found in the print edition. Contact: Olivia Rowan.

Tips: "Know what you are writing about. We are read by people dedicated to skiing and snowboarding and to making the resort experience the best possible for their customers."

N **$ $ WHITETAIL BUSINESS**, Krause Publications, Inc., 700 E. State St., Iola WI 54990. (715)445-2214, ext. 425. Fax: (715)445-4087. Website: www.whitetailbusiness.com. **Contact:** Pat Durkin, editor. Associate Editors: Jennifer Pillath and Dan Schmidt. Annual magazine. "*Whitetail Business* targets the hunting industry's driving force, the white-tailed deerhunting market. Archery, modern firearm and muzzleloader retail dealers make their largest profit from whitetail hunters, and *Whitetail Business* devotes itself to this largest profit category." Estab. 1997. Circ. 11,000. **Pays on acceptance.** Byline given. Offers $50 kill fee. Buys first North American serial rights. Editorial lead time up to 1 year. Submit seasonal material up to 1 year in advance. Accepts queries by mail, fax. Sample copy and writer's guidelines free.

Nonfiction: Retail management, personal experience, technical. Also topics relating to trade shows and the outdoor industry. No humor. Query with or without published clips. Length: 400-1,500 words. **Pays $200-350.**

Photos: State availability of photos with submission. Reviews transparencies. Offers $25-300/photo. Identification of subjects required. Buys one-time rights.

Columns/Departments: Archery, Firearms/Muzzleloaders, Marketing (all dealing with white-tailed deer hunting); all 400 words. Query with published clips. **Pays $250 maximum.**

Fillers: Anecdotes. Length: 100 words maximum. **Pays $25 maximum.**

Tips: "Keep it short."

STONE, QUARRY & MINING

N **$ $ COLORED STONE**, Lapidary Journal/Primedia Inc., 60 Chestnut Ave., Suite 201, Devon PA 19333-1312. (610)964-6300. Fax: (610)293-0977. E-mail: CSeditorial@primediasi.com. **Contact:** Morgan Beard, editor-in-chief. **50% freelance written.** Bimonthly magazine covering the colored gemstone industry. "*Colored Stone* covers all aspects of the colored gemstone (i.e., no diamonds) trade. Our readers are manufacturing jewelers and jewelry designers, gemstone dealers, miners, retail jewelers and gemologists." Estab. 1987. Circ. 11,000. **Pays on acceptance.** Publishes ms an average of 2 months after acceptance. Byline given. Buys one-time rights or all rights. Editorial lead time 2 months. Submit seasonal material 3-4 months in advance. Accepts queries by mail, e-mail, fax. Accepts simultaneous submissions. Responds in 1 month to queries; 2 months to mss. Sample copy and writer's guidelines free.

Nonfiction: Exposé, interview/profile, technical. "No articles intended for the general public." **Buys 35-45 mss/year.** Query with published clips. Length: 400-2,200 words. **Pays $200-600.**

Photos: State availability of photos with permission. Reviews any size transparencies, 4×6 prints and up. Offers $15-50/photo. Captions, model release, identification of subjects required. Buys one-time rights.

Tips: "Demonstrating a background in the industry or willingness to learn is helpful. So is attention to detail, i.e., if you've read that we're a trade magazine, don't send us a consumer-oriented 'puff' piece."

[N] $ $ $ MINING VOICE, National Mining Association, 1130 17th St., NW, Washington DC 20036-4677. (202)463-2625. Fax: (202)857-0135. E-mail: jchircop@nma.org. Website: www.nma.org. **Contact:** Jeanne Chircop, editor. **60% freelance written.** Bimonthly. "*Mining Voice* magazine is intended to serve as the 'voice' of America's hardrock and coal mining industries, informing and educating readers about business issues impacting mining companies. Stories should be written to appeal to those both inside and outside the industry." Estab. 1995. Circ. 10,000. **Pays on acceptance.** Publishes ms an average of 3 months after acceptance. Byline given. Offers $50 kill fee. Buys all rights. Editorial lead time 3 months. Submit seasonal material 3 months in advance. Responds in 1-2 months. Sample copy and writer's guidelines free.

Nonfiction: General interest, interview/profile, business interest. No promotional articles, satire, anti-mining, religious, technical. **Buys 50 mss/year.** Query with published clips. Length: 250-3,000 words. **Pays $50-1,200.** Sometimes pays expenses of writers on assignment.

Photos: State availability of photos with submission. Reviews prints. Negotiates payment individually. Identification of subjects required. Buys one-time rights.

Columns/Departments: Mineral Focus (the use of minerals in everyday life), 750 words; Personalities (mining industry employees with interesting outside accomplishments), 750 words; Briefings (soft news items pertaining to mining), 250-350 words. **Buys 25 mss/year.** Query with published clips. **Pays $50-300.**

Tips: "Writers should familiarize themselves with business, political and social trends affecting American business in general and mining in particular. Each issue is theme-based, so obtain a copy of our editorial calendar (available on our website) and guidelines before querying."

[N] $ $ PIT & QUARRY, Advanstar Communications, 7500 Old Oak Blvd., Cleveland OH 44130. (440)891-2607. Fax: (440)891-2675. E-mail: pitquar@en.com. Website: www.pitandquarry.com. **Contact:** Mark S. Kuhar, editor. Managing Editor: Darren Constantino. **20-30% freelance written.** Monthly magazine covering nonmetallic minerals, mining and crushed stone. Audience has "knowledge of construction-related markets, mining, minerals processing, etc." Estab. 1918. Circ. 25,000. **Pays on acceptance.** Publishes ms an average of 6 months after acceptance. Byline given. Buys first North American serial rights. Editorial lead time 6 months. Accepts queries by mail, e-mail, fax, phone. Accepts simultaneous submissions. Responds in 1 month to queries; 4 months to mss. Sample copy for 9×12 SAE and 4 first-class stamps. Writer's guidelines free.

Nonfiction: How-to, interview/profile, new product, technical. No humor or inspirational articles. **Buys 12-15 mss/year.** Query. Length: 1,200-2,500 words. **Pays $250-700 for assigned articles; $250-500 for unsolicited articles.** Pays writers with contributor copies or other premiums for simple news items, etc. Sometimes pays expenses of writers on assignment.

Photos: State availability of photos with submission or send photos with submission. Offers no additional payment for photos accepted with ms. Model releases and identification of subjects required. Buys one-time rights.

Columns/Departments: Environmental, economics. Length: 700 words. Buys 5-10 mss/year. Query. Pays $250-300.

    ■ The online magazine carries original content not found in the print edition.

Tips: "Be familiar with quarry operations (crushed stone or sand and gravel), not coal or metallic minerals mining. Know construction markets. We need more West Coast-focused stories."

TRANSPORTATION

These publications are for professional movers and people involved in transportation of goods. For magazines focusing on trucking see also Auto & Truck.

[N] $ BUS CONVERSIONS, The First and Foremost Bus Converters Magazine, MAK Publishing, 3431 Cherry Ave., Long Beach CA 90807. (562)492-9394. Fax: (562)492-1345. E-mail: editor@busconversions.com. Website: www.busconversions.com. **Contact:** Teresa Hagen, senior editor. Monthly magazine covering the bus conversion industry. **95% freelance written.** Estab. 1992. Circ. 20,000. Pays on publication. Buys first North American serial rights. Guidelines sent on request. Encourages first-time writers. Accepts queries by mail, e-mail.

Nonfiction: How-to articles on the electrical, plumbing, mechanical, decorative and structural aspects of bus conversions (buses that are converted into RVs). Each month, *Bus Conversions* publishes a minimum of two coach reviews, usually anecdotal stories told by those who have completed their own bus conversion. Publishes some travel/destination stories (all of which are related to bus/RV travel). Looking for articles on engine swaps, exterior painting and furniture. Accepts unsolicited mss. **Pays $25-50.**

Photos: Include color photos (glossy) or slides with submission. Photos/slides not returned unless an SASE is included.
Columns/Departments: Industry Update; Products of Interest; Electrical Shorts; Building a Balanced Energy System; Ask the Experts; One For the Road; Road Fix.
Tips: "Most of our writers are our readers. Knowledge of bus conversions and the associate lifestyle is a prerequisite."

[N] $ $ $ $ COMMERCIAL CARRIER JOURNAL, for Professional Fleet Managers, Cahners Business Information, 201 King of Prussia Rd., Radnor PA 19089. (610)964-4626. Fax: (610)964-4273. E-mail: prichards@cahner s.com. Managing Editor: Parry Desmond. **Contact:** Paul Richards, editor. **20% freelance written.** Monthly journal covering trucking. "We cover issues of importance to fleet managers from safety to information solutions." Estab. 1911. Circ. 65,000. Publishes ms an average of 1 month after acceptance. Byline sometimes given. Buys second serial (reprint) rights and electronic rights or all rights. Editorial lead time 1 year. Submit seasonal material 2 months in advance. Accepts queries by mail, e-mail, fax, phone.
Nonfiction: New product, technical, business issues. Special issues: "Maintenance for the New Millenium, custom supplements, custom applications." No fiction. **Buys 12 mss/year.** Query with published clips. Length: 500-4,000 words. **Pays $1,000-6,000.** Sometimes pays expenses of writers on assignment.
Photos: Send photos with submission. Reviews contact sheets, negatives and transparencies. Negotiates payment individually. Captions, model releases and identification of subjects required. Buys one-time rights.
Columns/Departments: Buys 12 mss/year. Query with published clips. **Pays $1,000-5,000.**

[N] $ $ ITS WORLD, Technology and applications for intelligent transportation systems, Scranton Gillette Communications, 380 E. Northwest Highway, Suite 200, Des Plaines IL 60016. (847)391-1000. Fax: (847)390-0408. E-mail: itsnews@itsworld.com. Website: www.itsworld.com. **Contact:** Tim Gregorski, managing editor. **50% freelance written.** Bimonthly tabloid covering intelligent transporation systems (the application of communications and computer technologies to surface transportation). "We focus on ITS based global projects, and the logistics of these projects." Estab. 1996. Circ. 25,000. Pays on publication. Publishes ms an average of 2 months after acceptance. Byline given. Buys all rights. Editorial lead time 2 months. Submit seasonal material 2 months in advance. Accepts queries by mail, e-mail, fax, phone. Accepts simultaneous submissions. Responds in 6 weeks to queries; 1 month to mss. Sample copy and writer's guidelines free.
Photos: Send photos with submission. Reviews negatives, 2×7 transparencies and prints. Offers no additional payment for photos accepted with ms. Captions and identification of subjects required.
Columns/Departments: World Watch (trends, activities and market opportunities in intelligent transportation systems in a country or region outside the U.S.); Washington Watch (ITS issues/Washington D.C. perspective); editorials (ITS issues/opinions), all 1,500 words. **Pays $500-1,000.** Query.
Tips: "Expertise in surface transportation and/or the application of advanced technologies (telecommunications, computers, etc.) to surface transportation is a must. Writers who demonstrate this through published works and other background information will be given highest consideration."

[N] LIMOUSINE DIGEST, Digest Publications, 29 Fostertown Rd., Medford NJ 08055. (609)953-4900. Fax: (609)953-4905. E-mail: info@limodigest.com. Website: www.limodigest.com. **Contact:** Melissa Sowers, editor-in-chief. **33% freelance written.** Monthly magazine covering ground transportation. "*Limousine Digest* is 'the voice of the limousine industry.' We cover all aspects of ground transportation from vehicles to operators, safety issues and political involvement." Estab. 1990. Circ. 22,000. Pays on publication. Publishes ms 1-2 months an average of 1-2 months after acceptance. Byline given. Makes work-for-hire assignments. Editorial lead time 1 year. Submit seasonal material 2 months in advance. Accepts queries by mail, e-mail, fax. Accepts simultaneous submissions. Sample copy free.
Nonfiction: Historical/nostalgic, how-to (start a company, market your product), humor, inspirational, interview/profile, new product, personal experience, photo feature, technical, travel, industry news, business. **Buys 1-3 mss/year.** Send complete ms. Length: 700-1,900 words. **Pays 7-22¢/word.** Will pay authors in advertising trade-outs.
Reprints: Accepts previously published submissions.
Photos: Send photos with submission. Reviews negatives. Negotiates payment individually. Captions, model release, identification of subjects required. Buys all rights.
Columns/Departments: New Model Showcase (new limousines, sedans, buses), 1,000 words; Player Profile (industry members profiled), 700 words; Hall of Fame (unique vehicles featured), 500-7,000 words; Association News (association issues), 400 words. **Buys 5 mss/year.** Query. **Pays 7-22¢.**
Fillers: Facts, gags to be illustrated by cartoonist, newsbreaks. **Buys 24/year.** Length: 25-100 words. **Pays 7-22¢.**

TRAVEL

Travel professionals read these publications to keep up with trends, tours and changes in transportation. Magazines about vacations and travel for the general public are listed in the Consumer Travel section.

[N] $ $ $ CRUISE INDUSTRY NEWS, Cruise Industry News, 441 Lexington Ave., New York NY 10017. (212)986-1025. Fax: (212)986-1033. Website: www.cruiseindustrynews.com. **Contact:** Oivind Mathisen, editor. **20%**

freelance written. Quarterly magazine covering cruise shipping. "We write about the *business* of cruise shipping for the industry. That is, cruise lines, shipyards, financial analysts, etc." Estab. 1991. Circ. 10,000. **Pays on acceptance** or on publication. Publishes ms an average of 4 months after acceptance. Byline given. Offers 25% kill fee. Buys first rights. Editorial lead time 3 months. Accepts queries by mail. Reporting time varies. Sample copy for $10. Writer's guidelines for #10 SASE.

Nonfiction: Interview/profile, new product, photo feature, technical, business. No travel stories. **Buys more than 20 mss/year.** Query with published clips. Length: 500-1,500 words. **Pays $500-1,000** for assigned articles. Sometimes pays expenses of writers on assignment.

Photos: State availability of photos with submission. Offers $25-50/photo. Buys one-time rights.

[N] $ $ $ DESTINATIONS, The Magazine of North American Motorcoach Tours & Travel, American Bus Association, 1100 New York Ave. NW, Suite 1050, Washington DC 20005. (202)842-1645. E-mail: vchao@buses.org. Website: www.buses.org. **Contact:** Veronica Chao, editor-in-chief. **70% freelance written.** Monthly magazine. "*Destinations* covers the cities, regions, attractions, and themed tours appropriate for bus groups. Its audience is the people who plan and run motorcoach tours." Estab. 1979. Circ. 6,000. **Pays on acceptance.** Publishes ms an average of 2 months after acceptance. Byline given. Buys one-time rights. Accepts queries by mail, e-mail. Editorial lead time 15 weeks. Submit seasonal material 6 months in advance. Sample copy for $5.75. Writers' guidelines for #10 SASE.

○┐ Break in by demonstrating an understanding of our content and submitting creative ideas.

Nonfiction: Interview/profile, photo feature, travel. No personal accounts of bus travel or travel outside the US and Canada. **Buys 48-75 mss/year.** Query with published clips. Length: 700-2,500 words. **Pays $60/ms page.** Sometimes pays expenses of writers on assignment.

Photos: State availability of photos with submission. Offers $25-200/photo. Identification of subjects required. Buys one-time rights.

$ $ $ RV BUSINESS, Affinity Group, Inc., 2575 Vista del Mar Dr., Ventura CA 93001. (800)765-1912. Fax: (805)667-4484. E-mail: rvb@tl.com. **Contact:** John Sullaway, editor. **50% freelance written.** Monthly magazine. "*RV Business* caters to a specific audience of people who manufacture, sell, market, insure, finance, service and supply, components for recreational vehicles." Estab. 1972. Circ. 21,000. **Pays on acceptance.** Publishes ms an average of 2 months after acceptance. Byline given. Offers kill fee. Buys first North American serial rights. Editorial lead time 3 months. Accepts queries by mail, e-mail. Sample copy free.

Nonfiction: New product, photo feature, industry news and features. "No general articles without specific application to our market." **Buys 300 mss/year.** Query with published clips. Length: 125-2,200 words. **Pays $35-1,500.** Sometimes pays expenses of writers on assignment.

Photos: Send photos with submission. Reviews 35mm transparencies. Offers $25-400/photo. Captions, identification of subjects required. Buys one-time rights.

Columns/Departments: Top of the News (RV industry news), 75-400 words; Business Profiles, 400-500 words; Features (indepth industry features), 800-2,000 words. **Buys 300 mss/year.** Query. **Pays $35-1,500.**

Tips: "Query. Send one or several ideas and a few lines letting us know how you plan to treat it/them. We are always looking for good authors knowledgeable in the RV industry or related industries. We need more articles that are brief, factual, hard hitting and business oriented. Review other publications in the field, including enthusiast magazines."

$ $ SPECIALTY TRAVEL INDEX, Alpine Hansen, 305 San Anselmo Ave., #313, San Anselmo CA 94960. (415)455-1643. Fax: (415)459-4974. E-mail: info@specialtytravel.com. Website: www.specialtytravel.com. Editor: C. Steen Hansen. **Contact:** Susan Kostrzewa, managing editor. **90% freelance written.** Semiannual magazine covering adventure and special interest travel. Estab. 1980. Circ. 45,000. Pays on receipt and acceptance of all materials. Byline given. Buys one-time rights. Editorial lead time 3 months. Submit seasonal material 3 months in advance. Accepts queries by mail, e-mail. Writer's guidelines on request.

Nonfiction: How-to, personal experience, photo feature, travel. **Buys 15 mss/year.** Query. Length: 1,250 words. **Pays $200 minimum.**

Reprints: Send tearsheet of article. Pays 100% of amount paid for an original article.

Photos: State availability of photos with submission. Reviews 35mm transparencies, 5×7 prints. Negotiates payment individually. Captions, identification of subjects required.

Tips: "Write about group travel and be both creative and factual. The articles should relate to both the travel agent booking the tour and the client who is traveling."

$ STAR SERVICE, Reed Travel Group, 500 Plaza Dr., Secaucus NJ 07090. (201)902-2000. Fax: (201)319-1797. E-mail: sgordon@cahners.com. Website: www.checkstarfirst.com. **Contact:** Steven R. Gordon, editor-in-chief. "Eager to work with new/unpublished writers as well as those working from a home base abroad, planning trips that would allow time for hotel reporting, or living in major ports for cruise ships." Worldwide guide to accommodations and cruise ships founded in 1960 (as *Sloane Travel Agency Reports*) and sold to travel agencies on subscription basis. Pays 15 days after publication. No byline. Buys all rights. Accepts queries by mail, e-mail, fax, phone. Responds in 3 months. Writer's guidelines and list of available assignments for #10 SASE.

○┐ Break in by "being willing to inspect hotels in remote parts of the world."

Nonfiction: Objective, critical evaluations of hotels and cruise ships suitable for international travelers, based on personal inspections. Freelance correspondents ordinarily are assigned to update an entire state or country. "Assignment involves on-site inspections of all hotels and cruise ships we review; revising and updating published reports; and reviewing new properties. Qualities needed are thoroughness, precision, perseverance and keen judgment. Solid research skills and powers of observation are crucial. Travel and travel writing experience are highly desirable. Reviews must be colorful, clear, and documented with hotel's brochure, rate sheet, etc. We accept no advertising or payment for listings, so reviews should dispense praise and criticism where deserved." Now accepting queries for destination assignments with deadlines in March 2001. Query should include details on writer's experience in travel and writing, clips, specific forthcoming travel plans, and how much time would be available for hotel or ship inspections. **Buys 2,000 reports/year. Pays $25/report used.** Sponsored trips are acceptable.

Tips: "We may require sample hotel or cruise reports on facilities near freelancer's hometown before giving the first assignment. No byline because of sensitive nature of reviews."

$ $ VACATION INDUSTRY REVIEW, Interval International, P.O. Box 431920, South Miami FL 33243-1920 or 6262 Sunset Dr., Miami FL 33143. (305)666-1861, ext. 7022. Fax: (305)668-3408. E-mail: gleposky@interval-intl.com. Website: www.resortdeveloper.com. **Contact:** George Leposky, editor. **30% freelance written.** Prefers to work with published/established writers. Bimonthly magazine covering leisure lodgings (timeshare resorts, fractionals, and other types of vacation-ownership properties). "The readership of *VIR* consists of people who develop, finance, market, sell, and manage timeshare resorts and mixed-use projects such as hotels, resorts, and second-home communities with a vacation-ownership component; and suppliers of products and services to the vacation-ownership industry." Estab. 1982. Circ. 15,000. Pays on publication. Publishes ms an average of 6 months after acceptance. Byline given. Buys all rights and makes work-for-hire assignments. Submit seasonal material at least 6 months in advance. Query by mail, e-mail, fax, phone. Responds in 1 month. Writer's guidelines for #10 SASE. Sample copy for 9×12 SAE and 3 first-class stamps or on website.

○┐ Break in by writing a letter to tell us about yourself, and enclosing two or three (non-returnable) samples of published work that show you can meet our specialized needs.

Nonfiction: Essays, how-to, interview/profile, new product, opinion, personal experience, technical, travel. No consumer travel, hotel, or non-vacation real-estate material. **Buys 6-8 mss/year.** Query with published clips. Length: 1,000-1,500 words. **Pays 30¢/word.** Pays expenses of writers on assignment, if previously arranged.

Photos: Send photos with submission. Reviews 35mm transparencies, 5×7 or larger prints. Generally offers no additional payment for photos accepted with ms. Captions and identification of subjects required. Buys one-time rights.

Tips: "We *do not* want consumer-oriented destination travel articles. We want articles about the business aspects of the vacation-ownership industry: entrepreneurship, project financing, design and construction, sales and marketing, operations, management—anything that will help our readers plan, build, sell and run a quality vacation-ownership property that satisfies the owners/guests and earns a profit for the developer and marketer. We're also interested in owner associations at vacation-ownership resorts (not residential condos). Requires electronic submissions. Query for details."

VETERINARY

[N] $ $ VETERINARY ECONOMICS, Business solutions for practicing veterinarians, Veterinary Medicine Publishing Group, 15333 W. 95th St., Lenexa KS 66219. (913)492-4300. Fax: (913)492-4157. E-mail: ve@vetmedpub.com. Website: www.vetmedpub.com. Managing Editor: Elizabeth Brown. **Contact:** Marnette Falley, editor. **20% freelance written.** Monthly magazine covering veterinary medicine. "We address the business concerns and management needs of practicing veterinarians." Estab. 1960. Circ. 52,000. Pays on publication. Publishes ms an average of 3 months after acceptance. Byline given. Buys first rights. Editorial lead time 3 months. Submit seasonal material 3 months in advance. Accepts queries by mail, e-mail, fax. Accepts simultaneous submissions. Responds in 3 months. Sample copy and writer's guidelines free.

Nonfiction: How-to, interview/profile, new product, personal experience. **Buys 35 mss/year.** Query or send complete ms. Length: 1,000-2,000 words. **Pays $50-400.**

Photos: Send photos with submission. Reviews transparencies and prints. Offers no additional payment for photos accepted with ms. Captions and identification of subjects required. Buys one-time rights.

Columns/Departments: Practice Tips (easy, unique business tips), 200-300 words. Send complete ms. **Pays $35.**

Tips: "Among the topics we cover: veterinary hospital design, client relations, contractual and legal matters, investments, day-to-day management, marketing, personal finances, practice finances, personnel, collections, and taxes. We also cover news and issues within the veterinary profession; for example, articles might cover the effectiveness of Yellow Pages advertising, the growing number of women veterinarians, restrictive-covenant cases, and so on. Freelance writers are encouraged to submit proposals or outlines for articles on these topics. Most articles involve interviews with a nationwide sampling of veterinarians; we will provide the names and phone numbers if necessary. We accept only a small number of unsolicited manuscripts each year; however, we do assign many articles to freelance writers. All material submitted by first-time contributors is read on speculation, and the review process usually takes 12 to 16 weeks. Our style is concise yet conversational, and all manuscripts go through a fairly rigorous editing process. We encourage writers to provide specific examples to illustrate points made throughout their articles."

Scriptwriting

Everyone has a story to tell, something to say. In telling that story as a play, movie, TV show or educational video you have selected that form over other possibilities. Scriptwriting makes some particular demands, but one thing remains the same for authors of novels, nonfiction books and scripts: you'll learn to write by rewriting. Draft after draft your skills improve until, hopefully, someone likes your work enough to hire you.

Whether you are writing a video to train doctors in a new surgical technique, alternative theater for an Off-Broadway company or you want to see your name on the credits of the next Harrison Ford movie, you must perfect both writing and marketing skills. A successful scriptwriter is a talented artist and a savvy business person. But marketing must always be secondary to writing. A mediocre pitch for a great script will still get you farther than a brilliant pitch for a mediocre script. The art and craft of scriptwriting lies in successfully executing inspiration.

Writing a script is a private act. Polishing it may involve more people as you ask friends and fellow writers to take a look at it. Marketing takes your script public in an effort to find the person willing to give the most of what you want, whether it's money, exposure or control, in return for your work.

There are accepted ground rules to presenting and marketing scripts. Following those guidelines will maximize your chances of getting your work before an audience.

Presenting your script professionally earns a serious consideration of its content. Certain scripts have a definite format and structure. An educational video written in a one-column format, a feature film much longer than 120 pages or an hour-long TV show that peaks during the first 20 minutes indicates an amateur writer. There are several sources for correct formats, including *Formatting & Submitting Your Manuscript*, by Jack and Glenda Neff and Don Prues (Writer's Digest Books) and *The Complete Guide to Standard Script Formats*, by Cole and Haig.

Submission guidelines are similar to those for other types of writing. The initial contact is a one-page query letter, with a brief synopsis and a few lines as to your credits or experience relevant to the subject of your script. Never send a complete manuscript until it is requested. Almost every script sent to a producer, studio, or agent must be accompanied by a release form. Ask the producer or agent for this form when invited to submit the complete script. Always include a self-addressed stamped envelope if you want your work returned; a self-addressed stamped postcard will do for acknowledgement or reply if you do not need your script returned.

Most writers break in with spec scripts, written "for free," which serve as calling cards to show what they can do. These scripts plant the seeds of your professional reputation by making the rounds of influential people looking to hire writers, from advertising executives to movie moguls. Good writing is more important than a specific plot. Make sure you are sending out your best work; a first draft is not a finished product. Have several spec scripts completed, as a producer will often decide that a story is not right for him, or a similar work is already in production, but will want to know what else you have. Be ready for that invitation.

Writing a script is a matter of learning how to refine your writing so that the work reads as a journey, not a technical manual. The best scripts have concise, visceral scenes that demand to be presented in a specific order and accomplish definite goals.

Educational videos have a message that must be expressed economically and directly, engaging the audience in an entertaining way while maintaining interest in the topic. Theatrical plays are driven by character and dialogue that expose a thematic core and engender enthusiasm or involvement in the conflict. Cinematic screenplays, while more visually-oriented, are a series of discontinuous scenes stacked to illuminate the characters, the obstacles confronting them and the resolution they reach.

A script is a difficult medium—written words that sound natural when spoken, characters that are original yet resonate with the audience, believable conflicts and obstacles in tune with the end result. One theater added to their listing the following tip: "Don't write plays. Write novels, short stories, anything but plays. But if you *must* write plays. . . ." If you are compelled to present your story visually, be aware of the intense competition. Hone it, refine it, keep working on it until it can be no better, then look for the best home you can find. That's success.

BUSINESS & EDUCATIONAL WRITING

"It's no longer the plankton of the filmmaking food chain," says Kirby Timmons, creative director of the video production company CRM Films. Scripts for corporate training, business management and education videos have become as sophisticated as those designed for TV and film, and they carry the additional requirement of conveying specific content. With an audience that is increasingly media literate, anything that looks and feels like a "training film" will be dead in the water. The trick is to produce a script that engages, compels *and* informs about the topic, whether it's customer relations, listening skills or effective employee management, while staying on a tight budget.

This can create its own challenges, but is an excellent way to increase your skills and exercise your craft. Good scriptwriters are in demand in this field. There is a strong emphasis on producing a polished complete script before filming begins, and a writer's involvement doesn't end until the film is "in the can."

A remarkably diverse industry, educational and corporate video is a $18-25 billion business, compared to theatrical films and TV, estimated at $5 billion. And there is the added advantage that opportunities are widespread, from large local corporations to small video production houses in your area. Larger companies often have inhouse video production companies, but others rely on freelance writers. Your best bet would be to find work with companies that specialize in making educational and corporate video while at the same time making yourself known to the creative directors of in-house video staffs in large corporations. Advertising agencies are also a good source of work, as they often are asked by their clients for help in creating films and use freelance writers and producers.

Business and educational video is a market-driven industry, with material created either in response to a general need or a specific demand. The production company usually identifies a subject and finds the writer. As such, there is a perception that a spec script will not work in this media. While it is true that, as in TV and theatrical films, a writer's spec script is rarely produced, it is a good résumé of qualifications and sample of skills. It can get you other work even though it isn't produced. Your spec script should demonstrate a knowledge of this industry's specific format. For the most part video scripts are written in two-columns, video on the left, audio on the right. A variety of references cover the basics of video script format. Computer software is available to format the action and dialogue.

Aside from the original script, another opportunity for the writer is the user's guide that often accompanies a video. If you are hired to create the auxiliary material you'll receive a copy of the finished video and write a concurrent text for the teacher or implementor to use.

Networking is very important. There is no substitute for calling companies and finding out what is in your area. Contact local training and development companies and find out who they serve and what they need. It pays to join professional organizations such as the Association of Visual Communicators and the Association for Training and Development, which offer seminars and conventions. Making the rounds at a business convention of video producers with your business card could earn you a few calls and invitations to submit writing samples.

Budgets are tighter for educational or corporate videos than for theatrical films. You'll want to work closely with the producer to make sure your ideas can be realized within the budget. Your fee will vary with each job, but generally a script written for a production house in a subject area with broad marketability will pay $5,000-7,000. A custom-produced video for a specific company will usually pay less. The pay does not increase exponentially with your experience; large increases come if you choose to direct and produce as well as write.

With the expansion of cable TV-based home shopping opportunities, direct response TV (informercials) is an area with increasing need for writers to create the scripts that sell the products. Production companies are located across the country, and more are popping up as the business grows. Pay can range from $5,000-18,000, depending on the type, length and success of the program.

The future of business and educational video lies in interactive media or multimedia. Interactive media combines computer and video technology to create a product that doesn't have to progress along a linear path. Videos that offer the viewer the opportunity to direct the course of events hold exciting possibilities for corporate training and educational applications. Writers will be in high demand as stories offer dozens of choices in storylines. Interactive video will literally eat up pages of script as quickly as a good writer produces them. A training session may last only 20 minutes, but the potential untapped story lines could add up to hours worth of script that must be written, realized and made available. From training salespeople to doctors, or teaching traffic rules to issues in urbanization, corporate and educational video is about to undergo a tremendous revolution.

Information on business and educational script markets listed in the previous edition of *Writer's Market* but not included in this edition can be found in the General Index.

◻ ABS ENTERPRISES, P.O. Box 5127, Evanston IL 60204-5127. Phone/fax: (847)982-1414. E-mail: absenterprises @mindspring.com. **Contact:** Alan Soell, president. "We produce material for all levels of corporate, medical, cable and educational institutions for the purposes of training and development, marketing and meeting presentations. We also are developing programming for the broadcast areas." **75% freelance written.** "We work with a core of three to five freelance writers from development to final drafts." All scripts are unagented submissions. Buys all rights. Accepts previously produced material. Responds in 2 weeks to queries.
Needs: Videotape, multimedia, realia, Internet audio, tapes and cassettes, television shows/series. Currently interested in "sports instructional series that could be produced for the consumer market on tennis, gymnastics, bowling, golf, aerobics, health and fitness, cross-country skiing and cycling. Also motivational and self-improvement type videos and film ideas to be produced. These could cover all ages '6-60' and from professional to blue collar jobs. These two areas should be 30 minutes and be timeless in approach for long shelf life. Sports audience, age 25-45; home improvement, 25-65. Cable TV needs include the two groups of programming detailed here. We are also looking for documentary work on current issues, nuclear power, solar power, urban development, senior citizens—but with a new approach." Query or submit synopsis/outline and résumé. Pays by contractual agreement.
Tips: "I am looking for innovative approaches to old problems that just don't go away. The approach should be simple and direct so there is immediate audience identification with the presentation. I also like to see a sense of humor used. Trends in the media field include interactive video with disk—for training purposes."

A/V CONCEPTS CORP., 30 Montauk Blvd., Oakdale NY 11769-1399. (631)567-7227. Fax: (631)567-8745. E-mail: editor@edconpublishing.com. Website: www.edconpublishing.com. **Contact:** Deborah Densen, editor. Estab. 1971. Produces supplementary materials for elementary-high school students, either on grade level or in remedial situations. **100% freelance written.** "All scripts/titles by assignment only. Do not send manuscripts." Employs video, book and personal computer media. Buys all rights. Responds in 1 month to outline, 6 weeks on final scripts. Writing samples returned with 9×12 SAE with 5 first-class stamps. **Pays $300 and up.**
Needs: Main concentration in language arts, mathematics and reading. "Manuscripts must be written using our lists of vocabulary words and meet our readability formula requirements. Specific guidelines are devised for each level. Student activities required. Length of manuscript and subjects will vary according to grade level for which material is prepared. Basically, we want material that will motivate people to read."
Tips: "Writers must be highly creative and disciplined. We are interested in high interest/low readability materials. Send writing samples, published or unpublished."

CRM FILMS, 1801 Avenue of the Stars, #715, Los Angeles CA 90067-5802. Fax: (310)789-5392. E-mail: kirby@crmfil ms.com. Website: www.crmfilms.com. **Contact:** Kirby Timmons, creative director. Estab. 1960. Material for business

and organizational training departments. **Buys 2-4 scripts/year. Works with 6-8 writers/year**. Buys all rights and interactive training rights. No previously produced material. Responds in 1 month. Catalog for 10×13 SAE with 4 first-class stamps. Query with résumé and script sample of writer's work in informational or training media. **Makes outright purchase of $4,000-7,000, or in accordance with WGA standard**. "We accept WGA standard one-page informational/interactive agreement which stipulates *no* minimum but qualifies writer for pension and health coverage."
Needs: Videotapes, multimedia kits. "CRM is looking for short (10- 20-minute) scripts on management topics such as communication, decision making, team building and customer service. No 'talking heads,' prefer drama-based, 'how to' approach as opposed to awareness style, but will on occasion produce either."
Tips: "Know the *specific* training need which your idea or script fulfills! Recent successes relate real-life events as basis for organizational or team learning—The Challenger incident to illustrate how groupthink can negatively impact team decisions, for example. Other titles document the challenges of retaining skilled employees in an active job market and compliance with ADA and other laws in hiring and evaluation."

N EDUCATIONAL VIDEO NETWORK, 1401 19th St., Huntsville TX 77340. (409)295-5767. Fax: (409)294-0233. E-mail: evn@edvidnet.com. Website: www.edvidnet.com. President: Debbie Henke. **Contact**: Anne Russell, executive editor. Estab. 1953. Produces material for junior high, senior high, college and university audiences. Works with **10 third-party scripts/year**. Buys all rights or pays royalty on gross retail and wholesale. Accepts previously produced material. Responds in 2 months. Free catalog and writer's guidelines.
Needs: Video for educational purposes. Query. Royalty varies.
Tips: "Educational video productions fall into two basic divisions. First are the curriculum-oriented programs that teachers in the various academic disciplines can use to illustrate or otherwise enhance textbook material in their subjects. Such programs should either be introductory overviews or concentrate on specific segments of lesson plans. Curriculum-oriented recent titles: *Monuments of Paris*; *The Internet: Cruising the Information Superhighway*; *Acids, Bases, and Salts*. Guidance & Development recent titles: *Teenage Alcohol Abuse, Teenage Conflict Resolution, 1st Aid & CPR, How to Get the Job You Want*. The second type of educational program deals with guidance and personal development areas. These programs need to reflect enough edutainment values to keep visually-sophisticated teens engaged while providing the real and valuable information that could help students with school and life. Recent titles: *Efficient Time Management*, *Making the Grade*, *Developing Your Self Esteem*, and *Dealing with Anger*. EVN is always looking for writers/producers who can write and illustrate for educational purposes."

HAYES SCHOOL PUBLISHING CO., INC., 321 Pennwood Ave., Wilkinsburg PA 15221-3398. (412)371-2373. Fax: (412)371-6408. E-mail: chayes@hayspub.com. Website: www.hayespub.com. Contact: Clair N. Hayes III, president. Estab. 1940. Produces material for school teachers and principals, elementary through high school. Also produces charts, workbooks, teacher's handbooks, posters, bulletin board material and reproducible blackline masters (grades K-12). **25% freelance written**. Prefers to work with published/established writers. **Buys 5-10 scripts/year from unpublished/unproduced writers. 100% of scripts produced are unagented submissions**. Buys all rights. Responds in 3 months. Catalog for SAE with 3 first-class stamps. Writer's guidelines for #10 SAE with 2 first-class stamps.
Needs: Educational material only. Particularly interested in foreign language material and educational material for elementary school level. Query. **Pays $25 minimum.**

JIST PUBLISHING, (formerly Jist Works, Inc.), 8902 Otis Ave., Indianapolis IN 46216. (317)613-4200. Fax: (317)613-4309. E-mail: jistworks@aol.com. Website: www.jistworks.com. **Contact**: Kelli Lawrence, video production manager. Estab. 1981. Produces career counseling, motivational materials (youth to adult) that encourage good planning and decision making for a successful future. **Buys 6-8 scripts/year. Works with 4-5 writers/year**. Buys all rights. Accepts previously produced material. Responds in 3 months. Catalog free. Query with synopsis. **Makes outright purchase of $500 minimum**.
Needs: Videotapes, multimedia kits. 15-30 minute video VHS tapes on job search materials and related markets.
Tips: "We need writers for long formats, such as scripts and instructor's guides, as well as short formats for catalogs, press releases, etc. We pay a royalty on finished video productions. We repackage, market, duplicate and take care of all other expenses when we acquire existing programs. Average sell price is $139. Producer gets a percentage of this and is not charged for any costs. Contact us, in writing, for details."

PALARDO PRODUCTIONS, 1807 Taft Ave., Suite 4, Hollywood CA 90028. Phone/fax: (323)469-8991. E-mail: palardo@Netscape.net. Website: www.palardo.com. **Contact**: Paul Ardolino, director. Estab. 1971. Produces material for youth ages 13-35. **Buys 3-4 scripts/year**. Buys all rights. Responds in 2 weeks to queries; 1 month on scripts.
Needs: Multimedia kits, tapes and cassettes, videotapes. "We are seeking comedy feature scripts involving technology and coming of age; techno-shortform projects." Submit synopsis/outline and résumé. Pays in accordance with WGA standards.
Tips: "Do not send a complete script—only synopsis of four pages or less *first*."

PHOTO COMMUNICATION SERVICES, INC., 6055 Robert Dr., Traverse City MI 49684. (231)943-5050. (231)943-5050. E-mail: writers@photocomm.net. Website: www.photocomm.net. President: (Ms.) M'Lynn Hartwell. Produces commercial, industrial, sales, training material, websites etc. **95% freelance written. No scripts from unpublished/unproduced writers. 100% of scripts produced are unagented submissions**. Buys all rights and first serial rights. Responds in 1 month.

Needs: Multimedia kits, tapes and cassettes, video presentations. Query with samples or submit completed script and résumé. Pays by agreement.

Tips: "I need to see the full range of each individual. One good piece does not demonstrate that this writer may meet the requirements of the project. Often time is of the essence and we do not have the privilege of time to correspond with a potential writer."

SPENCER PRODUCTIONS, INC., 736 West End Ave., New York NY 10025. Phone/fax: (212)222-8108. General Manager: Bruce Spencer. Creative Director: Alan Abel. Produces material for high school students, college students and adults. Occasionally uses freelance writers with considerable talent. Responds in 1 month. Payment negotiable.

Needs: Prerecorded tapes and cassettes. Satirical material only. Query.

Tips: "For a comprehensive view of our humor requirements, we suggest viewing our feature film production, *Is There Sex After Death* (Rated R), starring Buck Henry. It is available at video stores. Or read 'Don't Get Mad . . . Get Even' and 'How To Thrive On Rejection' by Alan Abel (published by W.W. Norton), both available from Barnes & Noble or Amazon." Also Books-on-Tape. "Send brief synopsis (one page) and outline (2-4 pages)."

TALCO PRODUCTIONS, 279 E. 44th St., New York NY 10017-4354. (212)697-4015. Fax: (212)697-4827. President: Alan Lawrence. Vice President: Marty Holberton. Estab. 1968. Produces variety of material for TV, radio, business, trade associations, nonprofit organizations, public relations (chiefly political and current events), etc. Audiences range from young children to senior citizens. **20-40% freelance written. Buys scripts from published/produced writers only.** Buys all rights. No previously published material. Responds in 3 weeks to queries.

● Talco reports that it is doing more public relations-oriented work: print, videotape and radio.

Needs: Films, radio tapes and cassettes, videotape, CDs. "We maintain a file of writers and call on those with experience in the same general category as the project in production. *We do not accept unsolicited manuscripts.* We prefer to receive a writer's résumé listing credits. If his/her background merits, we will be in touch when a project seems right." Makes outright purchase/project and in accordance with WGA standards (when appropriate). Sometimes pays expenses of writers on assignment.

Tips: "Concentration is now in TV productions. Production budgets will be tighter."

ULTITECH, INC., Foot of Broad St., Stratford CT 06497. (203)375-7300. Fax/BBS: (203)375-6699. E-mail: comcowic@meds.com. Website: www.meds.com. **Contact:** William J. Comcowich, president. Estab. 1993. Designs, develops and produces online services and interactive communications programs including video, multimedia, expert systems, software tools, computer-based training and audience response meetings. Specializes in medicine, science and technology. Prefers to work with published/established writers with video, multimedia and medical experience. **90% freelance written. Buys writing for approximately 15-20 programs/year.** Electronic submissions onto BBS or via ftp or e-mail attachment. Buys all rights. Responds in 1 month.

Needs: Currently producing about 10 interactive health and medical programs. Submit résumé and complete script. Makes outright purchase. Pays expenses of writers on assignment.

Tips: "Interactive media for learning and entertainment is a growing outlet for writers—acquiring skills for interactive design and development will pay back in assignments."

VISUAL HORIZONS, 180 Metro Park, Rochester NY 14623. (716)424-5300. Fax: (716)424-5313. E-mail: slides1@aol.com. Website: www.visualhorizons.com. **Contact:** Stanley Feingold, president. Produces material for general audiences. **Buys 5 programs/year.** Responds in 5 months. Free catalog.

Needs: Business, medical and general subjects. Produces silent and sound filmstrips, multimedia kits, slide sets, videotapes. Query with samples. Payment negotiable.

Tips: "We offer materials to help our audience make powerful presentations, train staff or customers, sell products or services and inspire audiences."

PLAYWRITING

TV and movies are visual media where the words are often less important than the images. Writing plays uses different muscles, different techniques. Plays are built on character and dialogue—words put together to explore and examine characters.

The written word is respected in the theater by producer, cast, director and even audience, to a degree unparalleled in other formats. While any work involving so many people to reach its final form is in essence a collaboration, it is presided over by the playwright and changes can be made only with her approval, a power many screenwriters can only envy. If a play is worth producing, it will be produced "as is."

Counterbalancing the greater freedom of expression are the physical limitations inherent in live performance: a single stage, smaller cast, limited sets and lighting and, most importantly, a strict, smaller budget. These conditions affect not only what but also how you write.

Start writing your play by reading. Your local library has play anthologies. Check the listings in this section for play publishers such as Baker's Plays and Samuel French. Reading gives you a feel for how characters are built, layer by layer, word by word, how each interaction presents another facet of a character. Exposition must mean something to the character, and the story must be worth telling for a play to be successful.

There are plenty of books, seminars and workshops to help you with the writing of your play. The development of character, setting, dialogue and plot are skills that will improve with each draft. The specific play format is demonstrated in *Formatting & Submitting Your Manuscript*, by Jack and Glenda Neff and Don Prues (Writer's Digest Books) and *The Complete Book of Standard Script Formats*, by Cole and Haig.

Once your play is finished you begin marketing it, which can take as long (or longer) than writing it. Before you begin you must have your script bound (three brads and a cover are fine) and copyrighted at the Copyright Office of the Library of Congress or registered with the Writers Guild of America. Write either agency and ask for information and an application.

Your first goal will be to get at least a reading of your play. You might be lucky and get a small production. Community theaters or smaller regional houses are good places to start. Volunteer at a local theater. As prop mistress or spotlight operator you will get a sense of how a theater operates, the various elements of presenting a play and what can and cannot be done, physically as well as dramatically. Personal contacts are important. Get to know the literary manager or artistic director of local theaters, which is the best way to get your script considered for production. Find out about any playwrights' groups in your area through local theaters or the drama departments of nearby colleges and universities. Use your creativity to connect with people that might be able to push your work higher.

Contests can be a good way to get noticed. Many playwriting contests offer as a prize at least a staged reading and often a full production. Once you've had a reading or workshop production, set your sights on a small production. Use this as a learning experience. Seeing your play on stage can help you view it more objectively and give you the chance to correct any flaws or inconsistencies. Incorporate any comments and ideas from the actors, director or even audience that you feel are on the mark into revisions of your script.

Use a small production also as a marketing tool. Keep track of all the press reviews, any interviews with you, members of the cast or production and put together a "press kit" for your play that can make the rounds with the script.

After you've been produced you have several directions to take your play. You can aim for a larger commercial production; you can try to get it published; you can seek artistic grants. After you have successfully pursued at least one of those avenues you can look for an agent. Choosing one direction does not rule out pursuing others at the same time. *The Dramatists Sourcebook*, published annually by Theatre Communications Group (355 Lexington Ave., New York NY 10017) lists opportunities in all these areas. The Dramatists Guild (234 W. 45th St., New York NY 10036) has three helpful publications: a bimonthly newsletter with articles, news and up-to-date information and opportunities; a quarterly journal; and an annual directory, a resource book for playwrights listing theaters, agents, workshops, grants, contests, etc.

Good reviews in a smaller production can get you noticed by larger theaters paying higher royalties and doing more ambitious productions. To submit your play to larger theaters you'll put together a submission package. This will include a one-page query letter to the literary manager or dramaturg briefly describing the play. Mention any reviews and give the number of cast members and sets. You will also send a two to three-page synopsis, a ten-page sample of the most interesting section of your play, your résumé and the press kit you've assembled. Do not send your complete manuscript until it is requested.

You can also explore publishing your play. *Writer's Market* lists many play publishers. When your script is published your play will make money while someone else does the marketing. You'll be listed in a catalog that is sent out to hundreds or thousands of potential performance spaces—high schools, experimental companies, regional and community theaters—for possible production. You'll receive royalty checks for both performance fees and book sales. In contacting publishers you'll want to send your query letter with the synopsis and reviews.

There are several sources for grants. Some are federal or state, but don't overlook sources closer to home. The category "Arts Councils and Foundations" in Contests and Awards in this book lists a number of sources. On the national level contact the NEA Theater Program Fellowship for Playwrights (1100 Pennsylvania Ave. NW, Washington DC 20506). State arts commissions are another possible source, and also offer opportunities for involvement in programs where you can meet fellow playwrights. Some cities have arts and cultural commissions that offer grants for local artists. PEN publishes a comprehensive annual book, *Grants and Awards Available to American Writers* that also includes a section for Canadian writers. The latest edition is available from the PEN American Center (568 Broadway, New York NY 10012).

Once you have been produced on a commercial level, your play has been published or you have won an important grant, you can start pursuing an agent. This is not always easy. Fewer agents represent playwrights alone—there's more money in movies and TV. No agent will represent an unknown playwright. Having an agent does *not* mean you can sit back and enjoy the ride. You will still need to get out and network, establishing ties with theaters, directors, literary managers, other writers, producers, state art agencies and publishers, trying to get your work noticed. You will have some help, though. A good agent will have personal contacts that can place your work for consideration at a higher level than your efforts alone might.

There is always the possibility of moving from plays to TV and movies. There is a certain cachet in Hollywood surrounding successful playwrights. The writing style will be different—more visually oriented, less dependent on your words. The money is better, but you will have less command over the work once you've sold that copyright. It seems to be easier for a playwright to cross over to movies than for a screenwriter to cross over to plays.

Writing can make you feel isolated, even when your characters are so real to you they seem to be in the room as you write. Sometimes the experience and companionship of other playwrights is what you need to get you over a particular hurdle in your play. Membership and service organizations such as The Dramatists Guild, The International Women's Writing Guild and local groups such as the Playwright's Center in Minneapolis and the Northwest Playwright's Guild in Seattle can help you feel still a part of this world as you are off creating your own.

Information on playwriting markets listed in the previous edition of *Writer's Market* but not included in this edition can be found in the General Index.

A.S.K. THEATER PROJECTS, 11845 W. Olympic Blvd., Suite 1250W, Los Angeles CA 90064. (310)478-3200. Fax: (310)478-5300. E-mail: info@askplay.org. Website: www.askplay.org. **Contact**: Mead Hunter, director of literary programs. Estab. 1989. **Produces 16 rehearsed public readings and 2 workshop productions/year.** "We utilize three theater facilities in the Los Angeles area with professional directors and casts. Our rehearsed readings and workshop productions are offered year-round. Our audience is the general public *and* theater professionals." Query with synopsis and sample pages. Obtains no rights. Responds in 4 months. **Pays $150 for staged readings; $1,000 for workshop productions**. Workshops are selected from plays previously presented in the reading series.
   ● A.S.K. publishes a biannual magazine, *Parabasis*, which focuses on news and issues surrounding the art, business and craft of contemporary playwriting. Playwrights are asked to query about proposed articles.
Needs: "We need full-length original plays that have not yet had full productions, and which would benefit from a rehearsed reading as a means of further developing the play."
Tips: "We are a nonprofit organization dedicated to new plays and playwrights. We do not produce plays for commercial runs, nor do we request any future commitment from the playwright should their play find a production through our reading or workshop programs."

ABOUT FACE THEATRE, 3212 North Broadway, Chicago IL 60657. (773)549-7943. Fax: (773)935-4483. E-mail: faceline1@aol.com. Website: www.aboutface.base.org. Co-Artistic Directors: Kyle Hall and Eric Rosen. **Contact:** Carl Hippensteel, literary manager. Estab. 1995. **Produces 4 plays/year.** "We are a self producing 99-seat professional theater." Query with synopsis or submit first 10 pages of script. Responds in 3 months.

Needs: One acts, full lengths, musicals and performance art. "Queer scripts only (especially interested in lesbian plays). We have a flexible thrust stage and limited shop facilities."

Tips: "We're looking for material that challenges self conceptions, moral expectations, and ideas about gender and sexuality in historical or contemporary contexts. We need scripts that are imaginative and of literary caliber with strong dramatic action, theatrically and dynamic unpredictable characters that break traditional ideas about dramatic form, structure and presentation. No unsolicited scripts. Will consider second productions. Adaptations accepted. Agent submissions are encouraged."

ACTORS & PLAYWRIGHTS' INITIATIVE, P.O. Box 50051, Kalamazoo MI 49005-0051. (616)343-8090. Fax: (616)343-8450. E-mail: api@telecity.org. **Contact:** Robert C. Walker, producing artistic director. Estab. 1989. **Produces 9 full lengths plus 'Late Night' 1 acts/year**. Produces professional, regional material for an academic audience age 25-45. Write for submission information.

Needs: Character driven, social/political provocative and adaptations—primarily non-musical. "Our theater is a small, 60-seat black box thrust stage; absolute minimum tech—sets, props, etc." Limit cast to 10.

Tips: "Study the greats—from Sophocles to Mamet."

ACTORS THEATRE OF LOUISVILLE, 316 W. Main St., Louisville KY 40202-4218. (502)584-1265. Estab. 1964. **Produces approximately 30 new plays of varying lengths/year**. Professional productions are performed for subscription audience from diverse backgrounds. Agented submissions only for full-length plays; open submissions to National Ten-Minute Play Contest (plays 10 pages or less). Buys variable rights. Responds in 9 months to submissions, mostly in the fall. Offers variable royalty.

Needs: "We are interested in full-length, one-act and ten-minute plays and in plays of ideas, language, humor, experiment and passion."

N ALABAMA SHAKESPEARE FESTIVAL, 1 Festival Dr., Montgomery AL 36117-4605. Fax: (334)271-5348. Website: www.asf.net. Artistic Director: Kent Thompson. **Contact:** Gwen Orel, literary manager. **Produces 14 plays/year**. Inhouse productions, general audience, children audience. Responds in 1 year. **Pays royalty**. Unsolicited scripts accepted for the Southern Writers' Project only.

Needs: "Through the Southern Writers' Project, ASF develops works by Southern writers, works that deal with the South and/or African-American themes, and works that deal with Southern and/or African-American history."

ALLEYWAY THEATRE, 1 Curtain Up Alley, Buffalo NY 14202-1911. (716)852-2600. Fax: (716)852-2266. E-mail: alleywayth@aol.com. Website: www.alleyway.com. Dramaturg: Kevin Stevens. Estab. 1980, competition 1990. **Produces 4 full-length, 10-15 short plays/year**. Submit complete script; include tape for musicals. Buys first production, credit rights. Responds in 6 months. **Pays 7% royalty** plus travel and accommodations for opening.

● Alleyway Theatre also sponsors the Maxim Mazumdar New Play Competition. See the Contest & Awards section for more information.

Needs: "Theatrical" work as opposed to mainstream TV.

Tips: Sees a trend toward social issue-oriented works. Also interested in "non-traditional" children's pieces. "Plays on social issues should put action of play ahead of political message. Not interested in adapted screen plays. Theatricality and setting are central."

N AMERICAN RENEGADE THEATRE CO., 11136 Magnolia Blvd., North Hollywood CA 91601. (818)763-1834. Fax: (818)509-3703. **Contact**: Barry Thompson, dramaturg; David A. Cox, artistic director. Estab. 1991. **Produces 6-8 plays/year**. Plays will be performed in an Equity 99 seat plan for adult audiences; 99 seat theater and 45 seat theater in the heart of thriving Noho Arts District. Query and synopsis (with SASE) or submit complete ms. **Pays 6% royalty.**

Needs: "Predominantly naturalistic, contemporary full length, but also one-acts and more experimental material on smaller stage. Mostly American authors and subject matter." No one-person plays.

N APPLE TREE THEATRE, 595 Elm Pl., Suite 210, Highland Park IL 60035. (847)432-8223. Fax: (847)432-5214. Website: www.appletreetheatre.com. Artistic Directors: Eileen Boevers and Gary Griffin. **Contact:** Nikki Sansone, administrative assistant. Estab. 1983. **Produces 5 plays/year**. "Professional productions intended for an adult audience mix of subscriber base and single-ticket holders. Our subscriber base is extremely theater-savvy and intellectual. We produce a mixture of musicals, dramas, classical, contemporary and comedies. Length: 90 minutes-2½ hours. Small space, unit set required. No fly space, 3¼ thrust stage. Maximum actors: 15." Submit query and synopsis, along with tapes for musicals. Rights obtained vary. **Pays variable royalty**. Return SASE submissions only if requested.

Tips: "No farces or large-scale musicals. Theater needs small shows with one-unit sets due to financial concerns. Also note the desire for non-linear pieces that break new ground. Please do not submit unsolicited manuscripts—send letter and description; if we want more, we will request it."

ARENA PLAYERS REPERTORY COMPANY, 296 Route 109, East Farmingdale NY 11735. (631)293-0674. Producer/Director: Frederic Defeis. **Contact:** Audrey Perry, literary manager. Estab. 1954. **Produces 19 plays/year** (at least 1 new play). Professional production on either Arena Players' Main Stage or Second Stage Theatres. Intended for a conventional, middle-class audience. Query with synopsis or submit complete ms. Responds in 1 year. **Pays flat fee of $400-600**.

Needs: Main Stage season consists of Neil Simon-type comedies. Christie-esque mysteries and contemporary dramas. Prefers single set plays with a minimal cast (2 to 8 people). Only full-length plays will be considered.
Tips: No one-acts and musicals.

ARENA STAGE, 1101 Sixth St. NW, Washington DC 20024. (202)554-9066. Fax: (202)488-4056. E-mail: cmadison@ arenastage.org. Artistic Director: Molly Smith. **Contact:** Cathy Madison, literary manager. Estab. 1950. **Produces 8 plays/year**. This is a professional theater. The Kreeger Theater seats 514. The Fichandler Stage seats 827. The Old Vat Room seats 110. Query with synopsis and bio of author. Responds in 1 year.
Needs: Full length comedy, drama, satire, musicals, plays by writers of color. We are beginning to consider one-person shows. We prefer cast sizes under 10, unless the play is a musical.
Tips: "Best for writer if he/she is agent-represented."

N ARIZONA THEATRE COMPANY, P.O. Box 1631, Tucson AZ 85702. (520)884-8210. Fax: (520)628-9129. **Contact:** Samantha K. Wyer, associate artistic director. Estab. 1966. **Produces 6 plays/year**. Arizona Theatre Company is the State Theatre of Arizona and plans the season with the population of the state in mind. Agented submissions only, though Arizona writers may submit unsolicited scripts. Responds in 6 months to submissions. Pay negotiated.
Needs: Full length plays of a variety of genres and topics and full length musicals.
Tips: No one-acts. "Please include in the cover letter a bit about your current situation and goals. It helps in responding to plays."

N ARKANSAS REPERTORY THEATRE, P.O. Box 110, Little Rock AR 72203-0110. (501)378-0445. Fax: (501)378-0012. E-mail: therep@alltel.net. Website: www.therep.org. Producing Director: Robert Hupp. **Contact:** Brady Moody, literary manager. Estab. 1976. **Produces 8-10 plays/year**. "Professional productions for adult audiences. No kids' shows please. We produce plays for a general adult audience. We do everything from intense dramas to farce. Only full-length plays. We look for shows with less than 10 characters, but we have done epics as well. Keeps 5% rights for 5 years." Submit query and synopsis only. Responds in 6 months. **Payment varies** on the script, number of performances, if it was commissioned, which stage it's produced on.
Tips: "No one-acts or children's shows. Smaller casts are preferred."

ART STATION THEATRE, P.O. Box 1998, 5834 Manor Dr., Stone Mountain GA 30086. (770)469-1105. Fax: (705)469-0355. E-mail: info@artstation.org. Website: www.artstation.org. **Contact:** David Thomas, artistic director. Estab. 1986. **Produces 5 plays/year**. "ART Station Theatre is a professional theater located in a contemporary arts center in Stone Mountain, which is part of Metro Atlanta. Audience consists of middle-aged to senior, suburban patrons." Query with synopsis or submit complete ms. Responds in 6 months. **Pays 5-7% royalty**.
Needs: Full length comedy, drama and musicals, preferably relating to the human condition in the contemporary South." Cast size no greater than 6.

ARTISTS REPERTORY THEATRE, 1516 S.W. Alder St., Portland OR 97205. (503)241-9807. Fax: (503)241-8268. E-mail: allen@artistsrep.org. Website: www.artistsrep.com. **Contact:** Allen Nause, artistic director. Estab. 1982. **Produces 6 plays/year**. Plays performed in professional theater with a subscriber-based audience. Responds in 6 months. **Pays royalty**. Send synopsis, sample and résumé. No unsolicited mss accepted.
Needs: "Full-length, hard-hitting, emotional, intimate, actor-oriented shows with small casts (rarely exceeds 10-13, usually 2-7). Language and subject matter are not a problem."
Tips: "No one-acts or children's scripts."

ASOLO THEATRE COMPANY, 5555 N. Tamiami Trail, Sarasota FL 34234. (941)351-9010. Fax: (941)351-5796. E-mail: bruce_rodgers@asolo.org. Website: www.asolo.org. **Contact:** Bruce E. Rodgers, associate artistic director. Estab. 1960. **Produces 7-8 plays/year**. A LORT theater with 2 intimate performing spaces. No unsolicited scripts. Send a letter with 1-page synopsis, 1 page of dialogue and SAE. Responds in 8 months. **Negotiates rights and payment**.
Needs: Play must be *full length*. "We operate with a resident company in rotating repertory. We have a special interest in adaptations of great literary works."

BAILIWICK REPERTORY, Bailiwick Arts Center, 1229 W. Belmont Ave., Chicago IL 60657-3205. (773)883-1090. Fax: (773)525-3245. E-mail: bailiwickr@aol.com. Website: www.bailiwick.org. **Contact:** David Zak, artistic director. Estab. 1982. **Produces 5 mainstage plays** (classic and newly commissioned) each year; **5 new full-length** in New Directions series; **50 1-acts** in annual Directors Festival; pride performance series (gay and lesbian plays, poetry), includes one acts, poetry, workshops, and staged adaptations of prose. Submit year-round. One acts should be submitted *before* April 1. (One-act play fest runs July-August). Responds in 9 months for full-length only. **Pays 6% royalty**.
Needs: "We need daring scripts that break the mold. Large cast or musicals are OK. Creative staging solutions are a must."
Tips: "Know the rules, then break them creatively and *boldly*! Please send SASE for manuscript submission guidelines before you submit or get manuscript guidelines at our website."

BAKER'S PLAYS PUBLISHING CO., P.O. Box 699222, Boston MA 02269-9222. (617)745-0805. Fax: (617)745-9891. E-mail: info@bakersplays.com. Website: www.bakersplays.com. **Contact:** Ray Pape, associate editor. Estab.

1845. **80% freelance written**. Plays performed by amateur groups, high schools, children's theater, churches and community theater groups. **75% of scripts unagented submissions. Publishes 20-30 straight plays and musicals. Works with 2-3 unpublished/unproduced writers annually**. Submit complete script with news clippings, résumé. Submit complete cassette of music with musical submissions. Responds in 4 months. **Pay varies; negotiated royalty split of production fees; 10% book royalty**.

Needs: "We are finding strong support in our new division—plays from young authors featuring contemporary pieces for high school production."

Tips: "We are particularly interested in adaptation of lesser-known folk tales from around the world. Also of interest are plays which feature a multicultural cast and theme. Collections of one-act plays for children and young adults tend to do very well. Also, high school students: Write for guidelines for our High School Playwriting Contest."

MARY BALDWIN COLLEGE THEATRE, Mary Baldwin College, Staunton VA 24401. Website: www.mbc.edu. **Contact:** Virginia R. Francisco, professor of theater. Estab. 1842. **Produces 5 plays/year. 75% of scripts are unagented submissions. Works with 0-1 unpublished/unproduced writer annually**. An undergraduate women's college theater with an audience of students, faculty, staff and local community (adult, conservative). Query with synopsis. Buys performance rights only. Responds in 1 year. **Pays $10-50/performance**.

Needs: Full-length and short comedies, tragedies, musical plays, particularly for young women actresses, dealing with women's issues both contemporary and historical. Experimental/studio theater not suitable for heavy sets. Cast should emphasize women. No heavy sex; minimal explicit language.

Tips: "A perfect play for us has several roles for young women, few male roles, minimal production demands, a concentration on issues relevant to contemporary society, and elegant writing and structure."

BILINGUAL FOUNDATION OF THE ARTS, 421 North Ave., #19, Los Angeles CA 90031. (323)225-4044. Fax: (323)225-1250. E-mail: bfa2001@earthlink.net. Artistic Director: Margarita Galban. **Contact:** Augustin Coppola, dramaturg/literary manager. Estab. 1973. **Produces 3-5 plays plus 9-10 staged readings/year**. "Productions are presented at home theater in Los Angeles, California. Our audiences are largely Hispanic and all productions are performed in English and Spanish. The Bilingual Foundation of the Arts produces plays in order to promote the rich heritage of Hispanic history and culture. Though our plays must be Hispanic in theme, we reach out to the entire community." Submit complete script. Responds in 6 months. Rights negotiable. **Pays royalty**.

Needs: "Plays must be Hispanic in theme. Comedy, drama, light musical, children's theater, etc., are accepted for consideration. More plays in Spanish are needed. Theater is 99-seater, no flies."

N CALIFORNIA THEATER CENTER, P.O. Box 2007, Sunnyvale CA 94087. (408)245-2978. Fax: (408)245-0235. E-mail: ctc@ctcinc.org. Website: www.ctcing.org. **Contact:** Will Huddleston, literary manager/resident director. Estab. 1976. **Produces 15 plays/year**. "Plays are for young audiences in both our home theater and for tour." Query with synopsis. Responds in 6 months. **Negotiates set fee**.

Needs: All plays must be suitable for young audiences, must be around 1 hour in length. Cast sizes vary. Many shows require touring sets.

Tips: "Almost all new plays we do are for young audiences, one-acts with fairly broad appeal, not over an hour in length, with mixed casts of two to eight adult, professional actors. We read plays for all ages, though plays for kindergarten through fourth grade have the best chance of being chosen. Plays with memorable music are especially looked for, as well as plays based upon literary works or historical material young people know from school. Serious plays written in the style of psychological realism must be especially well written. Satires and parodies are difficult for our audiences unless they are based upon material familiar to children. Anything "cute" should be avoided. In the summer we seek large cast plays that can be performed entirely by children in our Summer Conservatory programs. We particularly look for plays that can do well in difficult venues, such as high school gymnasiums, multi-purpose rooms, etc."

CELEBRATION THEATRE, 7985 Santa Monica Blvd., Suite 109-1, West Hollywood CA 90046. (323)957-1884. E-mail: tjacobson@LACMA.ORG. Artistic Director: Richard Israel. **Contact:** Tom Jacobson, literary manager. Estab. 1983. **Produces 6 plays/year**. "We are a 64-seat professional community-based theater which celebrates gay and lesbian culture and provides a forum for professional and emerging writers, directors, designers and performers." Query with synopsis. Responds in 6 months. **Pays variable royalty**.

Needs: Gay and lesbian stage plays including full-lengths, one-acts, musicals, solo shows, performance pieces and experimental works. Celebration Theater has a thrust stage 16 feet wide and 20 feet deep with a 12-foot ceiling.

Tips: "Although Celebration accepts unsolicited ms, we prefer a letter of inquiry with a brief description of the play and SASE. Plays are accepted year-round. We do consider second productions, but prefer premiering work by Southern California lesbian and gay writers."

N CENTER STAGE, 700 N. Calvert St., Baltimore MD 21202-3686. (410)685-3200. **Contact:** Charlotte Standt. resident dramaturg. Estab. 1963. **Produces 6-8 plays/year**. "LORT 'B' and LORT 'C' theaters; audience is both subscription and single-ticket. Wide-ranging audience profile." Query with synopsis, 10 sample pages and résumé, or submit through agent. Responds in 3 months. **Rights and payment negotiated**.

Needs: Produces dramas, comedies, musical theater works. No one-act plays. "Casts over 12 would give us pause. Be inventive, theatrical, not precious; we like plays with vigorous language and stage image. Domestic naturalism is

discouraged; strong political or social interests are encouraged. Plays about bourgeois adultery, life in the suburbs, Amelia Earhart, Alzheimer's, midlife crises, 'wacky southerners', fear of intimacy, Hemingway, Bible stories, backstage life, are unacceptable, as are spoofs and mysteries."
Tips: "We are interested in reading adaptations and translations as well as original work. Strong interest in plays about the African-American experience."

☒ CENTER THEATER, 1346 W. Devon Ave., Chicago IL 60660. (773)508-0200. Fax: (773)508-9584. E-mail: cntrth@aol.com. **Contact:** Dale Calandna, creative director. Estab. 1984. **Produces 4 plays/year.** "We run professional productions in our Chicago 'off-Loop' theaters for a diverse audience.." *Agented submissions only.* Responds in 3 months.
• This theater holds professional seminars in playwriting and screenwriting.

CHARLOTTE REPERTORY THEATRE, 129 W. Trade St., Charlotte NC 28202. (704)333-8587. Fax: (704)333-0224. E-mail: info@charlotterep.org. Website: www.charlotterep.org. Literary Manager: Claudia Carter Covington. Literary Associate: Carol Bellamy. Estab. 1976. "We are a not-for-profit regional theater." Submit complete script with SASE. Responds in 3 months. Writers receive free plane fare and housing for festival, stipend.
Needs: Need full-length scripts not previously produced professionally. No limitations in cast, props, staging, etc. No musicals, children's theater.

CHILDREN'S STORY SCRIPTS, Baymax Productions, 2219 W. Olive Ave., PMB 130, Burbank CA 91506-2648. (818)563-6105. Fax: (818)563-2968. E-mail: baymax@earthlink.net. **Contact:** Deedra Bébout, editor. Estab. 1990. "Our audience consists of children, grades K-8 (5-13-year-olds)." Send complete script with SASE. Licenses all rights to story; author retains copyright. Responds in 1 month. **Pays graduated royalty based on sales**.
Needs: "We add new titles as we find appropriate stories. We look for stories which are fun for kids to read, involve a number of readers throughout, and dovetail with school subjects. This is a must! Not life lessons . . . school subjects."
Tips: "The scripts are not like theatrical scripts. They combine dialogue and prose narration, à la Readers Theatre. If a writer shows promise, we'll work with him. Our most important goal is to benefit children. We want stories that bring alive subjects studied in classrooms. Facts must be worked unobtrusively into the story—the story has to be fun for the kids to read. Send #10 SASE for guidelines with samples. We do not respond to submissions without SASE."

CHILDSPLAY, INC., P.O. Box 517, Tempe AZ 85280. (480)350-8101. Fax: (480)350-8584. Website: www.tempe.gov/childsplay. **Contact:** David P. Saar, artistic director. Estab. 1978. **Produces 5-6 plays/year.** "Professional: Touring and in-house productions for youth and family audiences." Submit synopsis, character descriptions and 7- 10-page dialogue sample. Responds in 6 months. "On commissioned work we hold a small percentage of royalties for 3-5 years." **Pays royalty of $20-35/performance (touring) or pays $3,000-8,000 commission**.
Needs: Seeking *theatrical* plays on a wide range of contemporary topics. Touring shows: 5-6 actors; van-size. Inhouse: 6-10 actors; no technical limitations. "Innovative, theatrical and *small* is a constant need."
Tips: No traditionally-handled fairy tales. "Theater for young people is growing up and is able to speak to youth and adults. The material *must* respect the artistry of the theater and the intelligence of our audience. Our most important goal is to benefit children. If you wish your materials returned send SASE."

CIRCUIT PLAYHOUSE/PLAYHOUSE ON THE SQUARE, 51 S. Cooper, Memphis TN 38104. (901)725-0776. **Contact:** Jackie Nichols, artistic director. **Produces 16 plays/year.** Professional plays performed for the Memphis/Mid-South area. Member of the Theatre Communications Group. **100% of scripts unagented submissions. Works with 1 unpublished/unproduced writer/year**. Contest held each fall. Submit complete script. Buys percentage of royalty rights for 2 years. Responds in 6 months. **Pays $500**.
Needs: All types; limited to single or unit sets. Cast of 20 or fewer.
Tips: "Each play is read by three readers through the extended length of time a script is kept. Preference is given to scripts for the southeastern region of the U.S."

CITY THEATRE COMPANY, 57 S. 13th St., Pittsburgh PA 15203. E-mail: caquiline@citytheatre-pgh.org. Website: www.citytheatre-pgh.org. **Contact:** Carlyn Ann Aquiline, resident dramaturg/literary manager. **Produces 8 full productions/year**. "City Theatre is a LORT D company, whose mission is to provide an artistic home for the development and production of contemporary plays of substance and ideas that engage and challenge diverse audiences. We seek plays that engage the intellect as well as the emotions, and that challenge pre-conceptions about both life and theatre. We are particularly interested in new stories and new types of stories (sitcoms and kitchen sink drama rarely appear on our stage), innovation in form and in staging techniques and/or a new or different take on an old story. Our facilities include a 270-seat Mainstage theatre with flexible stage and seating configurations, state-of-the-art lighting and sound systems and the 99-seat Hamburg Studio Theatre." Query with synopsis or submit through agent and include synopsis and character breakdown, 15-20 page dialogue sample and development/production history. Obtains no rights. **Pays commission and/or royalty**. Responds in 9 months. No unsolicited or e-mail submissions. No phone calls.
Needs: Normal cast limit 8. "We are not presently considering one-acts or children's plays."

I.E. CLARK PUBLICATIONS, P.O. Box 246, Schulenburg TX 78956-0246. Website: www.ieclark.com. **Contact:** Donna Cozzaglio, general manager. Estab. 1956. **Publishes 10-15 plays/year** for educational theater, children's theater, religious theater, regional professional theater and community theater. **Publishes unagented submissions**. Submit complete script, 1 at a time with SASE. Responds in 6 months. Buys all available rights; "We serve as an agency as well as a publisher." **Pays standard book and performance royalty**, amount and percentages dependent upon type and marketability of play. Catalog for $3. Writer's guidelines for #10 SASE.

Needs: "We are interested in plays of all types—short or long. Audiotapes of music or videotapes of a performance are requested with submissions of musicals. We require that a play has been produced (directed by someone other than the author); photos, videos, and reviews of the production are helpful. No limitations in cast, props, staging, etc. Plays with only one or two characters are difficult to sell. We insist on literary quality. We like plays that give new interpretations and understanding of human nature. Correct spelling, punctuation and grammar (befitting the characters, of course) impress our editors."

- "One of our specialties is "Young Adult Awareness Drama"—plays for ages 13 to 25 dealing with sex, drugs, popularity, juvenile, crime, and other problems of young adults. We also need plays for children's theatre, especially dramatizations of children's classic literature."

Tips: Publishes plays only. "Entertainment value and a sense of moral responsibility seem to be returning as essential qualities of a good play script. The era of glorifying the negative elements of society seems to be fading rapidly. Literary quality, entertainment value and good craftsmanship rank in that order as the characteristics of a good script in our opinion. 'Literary quality' means that the play must—in beautiful, distinctive, and un-trite language—say something; preferably something new and important concerning man's relations with his fellow man or God; and these 'lessons in living' must be presented in an intelligent, believable and creative manner. Plays for children's theater are tending more toward realism and childhood problems, but fantasy and dramatization of fairy tales are also needed."

N CLEVELAND PUBLIC THEATRE, 6415 Detroit Ave., Cleveland OH 44102. (216)631-2727. Fax: (216)631-2575. E-mail: cpt@en.com. Website: www.en.com/cpt. **Contact:** Literary Manager. Estab. 1982. **Produces 6-8 full productions/year**. Also sponsors Festival of New Plays. 150-seat "Main Stage" and 700-seat Gordon Square Theatre. "Our audience believes that art touches your heart and your nerve endings." Query with synopsis and dialogue sample for full season. Rights negotiable. **Pays $15-100/performance**.

Needs: Poetic, experimental, avant-garde, political, multicultural works that need a stage (not a camera); interdisciplinary cutting-edge work (dance/performance art/music/visual); works that stretch the imagination and conventional boundaries. CPT presents performed work that addresses the issues and challenges of modern life. Particular focus is given to alternative, experimental, poetic, political works, with particular attention to those created by women, people of color, gays/lesbians.

Tips: "No conventional comedies, musicals, adaptations, children's plays—if you think Samuel French would love it, we probably won't. No TV sitcoms or soaps masquerading as theater. Theater is *not* TV or films. Learn the impact of what live bodies do to an audience in the same room. We are particularly interested in artists from our region who can grow with us on a longterm basis."

COLONY STUDIO THEATRE, 1944 Riverside Dr., Los Angeles CA 90039. Website: www.colonytheatre.org. **Contact**: Wayne Liebman, literary consultant. **Produces 6 plays/year**, 3 mainstage productions, 3 second stage productions/year. Professional 99-seat theater with thrust stage. Casts from resident company of professional actors. No unsolicited scripts. Send SASE for submission guidelines. Responds only if interested. Negotiated rights. **Pays royalty for each performance**.

Needs: Full length (90-120 minutes) with a cast of 4-12. No musicals or experimental works.

Tips: "A polished script is the mark of a skilled writer. Submissions should be in professional (centered) format."

CONTEMPORARY DRAMA SERVICE, Meriwether Publishing Ltd., P.O. Box 7710, Colorado Springs CO 80933. Fax: (719)594-9916. E-mail: merpcds@aol.com. Website: www.contemporarydrama.com. Editor-in-Chief: Arthur Zapel. **Contact**: Theodore Zapel, associate editor. Estab. 1969. **Publishes 50-60 plays/year**. "We publish for the secondary school market and colleges. We also publish for mainline liturgical churches—drama activities for church holidays, youth activities and fundraising entertainments. These may be plays, musicals or drama-related books." Query with synopsis or submit complete script. Obtains either amateur or all rights. Responds in 6 weeks. **Pays 10% royalty or negotiates purchase**.

- Contemporary Drama Service is now looking for play or musical adaptations of classic children's stories, for example: *The Secret Garden, Huckleberry Finn, Heidi*.

Needs: "Most of the plays we publish are one acts, 15-45 minutes in length. We also publish full-length two-act musicals or three-act plays 90 minutes in length. We prefer comedies. Musical plays must have name appeal either by prestige author or prestige title adaptation. Musical shows should have large casts for 20 to 25 performers. Comedy sketches, monologues and plays are welcomed. We prefer simple staging appropriate to middle school, high school, college or church performance. We like playwrights who see the world positively and with a sense of humor. Offbeat themes and treatments are accepted if the playwright can sustain a light touch and not take himself or herself too seriously. In documentary or religious plays we look for good research and authenticity. We are publishing many scenebooks for actors (which can be anthologies of great works excerpts), scenebooks on special themes and speech and theatrical arts textbooks. We are especially interested in authority-books on a variety of theater-related subjects."

Tips: Contemporary Drama Service is looking for creative books on: comedy, staging amateur theatricals and Christian youth activities.

A **A CONTEMPORARY THEATRE**, 700 Union St., Seattle WA 98101. (206)292-7660. Fax: (206)292-7670. Website: www.acttheatre.org. **Contact:** Gordon Edelstein, artistic director. Estab. 1965. **Produces 6-7 mainstage plays/ year**. "Our plays are performed in our 2 mainstages and third smaller space for our local Seattle audience. Sometimes our world premieres move onto other cities to play at regional theatres across the country." *Agented submissions only* or through theatre professionals recommendation. Query and synopsis only for Northwest playwrights. Responds in 6 months. **Pays 5-10% royalty**.

Needs: "We produce full length plays of varying sizes and shapes: anywhere from a one person play in our smaller house to a much larger ensemble. We tend to produce contemporary work, as the title of our theatre suggests; stories with current concerns. We are open to casting concerns—we often try to produce a 'big play' (over 10 characters) in every season, though we do have budgetary restrictions, and cannot produce more than one a season."

Tips: "At times it feels that 'telling the story' becomes less of a concern and gets subsumed by how it's told. At ACT, we look for the compelling story, and want to be compelled and brought in. Often we find this gets lost in stylistic grandiosity."

CREEDE REPERTORY THEATRE, P.O. Box 269, Creede CO 81130-0269. (719)658-2541. **Contact:** Richard Baxter, director. Estab. 1966. **Produces 6 plays/year**. Plays performed for a summer audience. Query with synopsis. Responds in 1 year. **Royalties negotiated** with each author—paid on a per performance basis.

Needs: One-act children's scripts. Special consideration given to plays focusing on the cultures and history of the American West and Southwest.

Tips: "We seek new adaptations of classical or older works as well as original scripts."

N **CROSSROADS THEATRE COMPANY**, 7 Livingston Ave., New Brunswick NJ 08904. (908)249-5581. Artistic Director: Ricardo Khan. Estab. 1978. **Produces 5 full productions**, plus an end-of-the-year festival of play readings intended for all audiences. Submit query, synopsis and ten-page dialogue sample. Responds in 9 months. **Pays royalty**.

Needs: Full-length plays, one-acts, translations, adaptations, musicals, cabaret/revues. Especially interested in African-American, African and West Indian issue-oriented, experimental plays. No limitations.

Tips: "Please be patient in awaiting a response."

MICHAEL D. CUPP, P.O. Box 256, Dept. SWV, Hazelhurst WI 54531-0256. (715)356-7173, ext. 958. Fax: (715)356-1851. E-mail: nlplays@newnorth.net. **Contact:** Claude A. Giroux, artistic director. Estab. 1976. **Produces 6 plays/year**. Professional Summer Theatre & Professional Dinner Theatre. Audience mostly senior-family oriented. Query with synopsis, cast breakdown and set requirements. Responds in 6 months. **Pays royalty**, per performance or makes outright purchase.

Needs: Comedies (2 hours), children's theatre (1 hour). Prefers cost efficient productions.

Tips: No sexy, racy or lewd productions, no dramas. "Remember you are writing for the audience. Be commercial."

DALLAS CHILDREN'S THEATER, 2215 Cedar Springs, Dallas TX 75201. Website: www.dct.org. Executive Director: Robyn Flatt. Estab. 1984. **Produces 11 plays/year**. Professional theater for family and student audiences. Query with synopsis. No materials will be returned without a SASE included. Responds in 8 months. Rights negotiable. **Pays negotiable royalty**.

Needs: Substantive material appropriate for youth and family audiences. Most consideration given to full-length, non-musical works, especially classic & contemporary adaptions of literature. Also interested in social, topical issue-oriented material. Very interested in scripts which enlighten diverse cultural experiences, particularly Hispanic and African-American experiences. Prefer scripts with no more than 15 cast members; 6-12 is ideal.

Tips: No adult experience material. "We are a family theater." Not interested in material intended for performance by children or in a classroom. Productions are performed by professional adults. Children are cast in child-appropriate roles. We receive far too much light musical material that plays down to children and totally lacks any substance. "Be patient. We receive an enormous amount of submissions. Most of the material we have historically produced has had previous production. We are not against perusing non-produced material, but it has rarely gone into our season unless we have been involved in its development."

DINER THEATRE, 2015 S. 60th St., Omaha NE 68106. (402)553-4715. E-mail: dmarr10523@aol.com. **Contact:** Doug Marr, artistic director. Estab. 1983. **Produces 5 plays/year**. Professional productions, general audience. Query with synopsis. Responds in 2 months to submissions. **Pays $15-30/performance**.

Needs: Comedies, dramas, musicals—original unproduced works. Full length, all styles/topics. Small casts, simple sets.

N **A** **DORSET THEATRE FESTIVAL**, Box 510, Dorset VT 05251-0510. (802)867-2223. Fax: (802)867-0144. E-mail: theatre@sover.net. Website: www.theatredirectories.com. **Contact:** Jill Charles, artistic director. Estab. 1976. **Produces 5 plays/year**, 1 a new work. "Our plays will be performed in our Equity summer stock theatre and are intended for a sophisticated community." *Agented submissions only*. **Rights and compensation negotiated**. Responds in 6 months.

Needs: "Looking for full-length contemporary American comedy or drama. Limited to a cast of six."
Tips: "Language and subject matter appropriate to general audience."

DRAMATIC PUBLISHING, 311 Washington St., Woodstock IL 60098. (815)338-7170. Fax: (815)338-8981. E-mail: plays@dramaticpublishing.com. Website: www.dramaticpublishing.com. Editor: Linda Habjan. Publishes paperback acting editions of original plays, musicals, adaptations and translations. **Publishes 50-70 titles/year.** Receives 250-500 queries and 600 mss/year. **Pays 10% royalty on scripts; performance royalty varies.** Publishes play 18 months after acceptance of ms. Responds in 1 month to queries, 6 months to mss. Catalog and ms guidelines free.
   ● Dramatic Publishing is seeking more material for the high school market and community theater.
Needs: Interested in playscripts appropriate for children, middle and high schools, colleges, community, stock and professional theaters. Send full ms.
Tips: "We publish all kinds of plays for the professional stock and amateur market: full lengths, one acts, children's plays, musicals, adaptations."

DRAMATICS MAGAZINE, 2343 Auburn Ave., Cincinnati OH 45219. (513)421-3900. Fax: (513)421-7077. E-mail: dcorathers@etassoc.org. Website: www.etassoc.org. **Contact:** Don Corathers, editor. Estab. 1929. **Publishes 5 plays/year.** For high school theater students and teachers. Submit complete ms. Responds in 3 months. Buys first North American serial rights only. Accepts previously published plays. Send tearsheet, photocopy or typed ms with rights for sale noted and information about when and where the work previously appeared. **For reprints, pays 50% of the amount paid for an original piece. Purchases only one-time publication rights for $100-400.**
Needs: "We are seeking one-acts to full-lengths that can be produced in an educational theater setting. No musicals."
Tips: "No melodrama, farce, children's theater, or cheap knock-offs of TV sitcoms or movies. Fewer writers are taking the time to learn the conventions of theater—what makes a piece work on stage, as opposed to film and television—and their scripts show it. We're always looking for good interviews with working theatre professionals."

ELDRIDGE PUBLISHING CO., P.O. Box 1595, Venice FL 34284. (941)496-4679. Fax: (941)493-9680. E-mail: info@histage.com. Website: www.histage.com. Editor: Susan Shore. Acquisitions Editor: Chris Augermann. Estab. 1906. **Publishes 100-110 new plays/year** for junior high, senior high, church and community audience. Query with synopsis (acceptable) or submit complete ms (preferred). Please send cassette tapes with any musicals. Buys all rights. Responds in 2 months. **Pays 50% royalties and 10% copy sales in general market. Makes outright purchase of $200-600 in religious market.** Writer's guidelines and catalog for #10 SASE or on website.
Needs: "We are most interested in full-length plays and musicals for our school and community theater market. Nothing lower than junior high level, please. We always love comedies but also look for serious, high caliber plays reflective of today's sophisticated students. We also need one-acts and plays for children's theater. In addition, in our religious market we're always searching for holiday or any time plays."
Tips: "Submissions are welcomed at any time. Authors are paid royalties twice a year. They receive complimentary copies of their published plays, the annual catalog and 50% discount if buying additional copies."

THE EMPTY SPACE THEATRE, 3509 Fremont Ave. N, Seattle WA 98103. (206)547-7633. Fax: (206)547-7635. E-mail: emptyspace@speakeasy.org. Website: www.emptyspace.org. Artistic Director: Eddie Levi Lee. **Contact:** Adam Greenfield, literary manager. Estab. 1970. **Produces 5 plays/year** between October and July. Professional productions. *Agented submissions only.* Responds in 2 months. Typically, we ask for something close to 5% of the author's royalties for 5 years. **Pays 6-10% royalty or $2,500-10,000 playwright commission.**
Needs: Full-length plays, full-length musicals, solo pieces, translations, adaptations. "The Empty Space strives to make theatre an event—bold, provocative, celebratory—brings audience and artists to a common ground through an uncommon experience." Prefer small casts.
Tips: The Empty Space produces work that specifically supports our artistic vision—generally rough and bold plays that seek to engage audiences on a visceral level. We therefore often find ourselves turning down scripts that are quite good only because they do not meet this need.

ENCORE PERFORMANCE PUBLISHING, P.O. Box 692, Orem UT 84059-0692. (801)225-0605. Fax: (801)765-0489. E-mail: encoreplay@aol.com. Website: www.encoreplay.com. **Contact:** Michael C. Perry, editor. Estab. 1979. **Publishes 40 plays/year.** "Our audience consists of all ages with emphasis on the family; educational institutions from elementary through college/university, community theaters and professional theaters." No unsolicited mss. Query with synopsis, production history and SASE. Responds in 1 month to queries; 3 months to scripts. **Pays 50% performance royalty; 10% book royalty.** Submit from May-August.
Needs: "We are looking for plays with strong message about or for families, plays with young actors among cast, any length, all genres. We prefer scripts with at least close or equal male/female roles, could lean to more female roles." Plays must have had at least 2 fully staged productions. Unproduced plays can be read with letter of recommendation accompanying the query.
Tips: "No performance art pieces or plays with overtly sexual themes or language. Looking for adaptations of Twain and other American authors."

ENSEMBLE THEATRE OF CINCINNATI, 1127 Vine St., Cincinnati OH 45248. (513)421-3555. Fax: (513)421-8002. E-mail: etcin@aol.com. Website: cincyetc.com. **Contact:** D. Lynn Meyers, producing artistic director. Estab. 1987. **Produces 9 plays/year**. Professional-year round theater. Query and sysnopsis, submit complete ms or submit through agent. Responds in 6 months. **Pays 5-10% royalty.**
Needs: Dedicated to good writing, any style for a contemporary, small cast. Small technical needs, big ideas.

N: EUREKA THEATRE COMPANY, 555 Howard St., Suite 201A, San Francisco CA 94105. (415)243-9899. Fax: (415)243-0789. Estab. 1972. **Produces 3-5 full productions/year.** Plays performed in professional-AEA, year-round for socially involved adult audiences.
Needs: Intelligent, provocative plays for adult general audiences. Plays with fewer production complexities preferred. Smaller casts (less than 8) preferred.
Tips: "We are looking for works that explore important human, social and political issues and that somehow reflect the diversity of experience of the San Francisco Bay area."

FIRST STAGE, P.O. Box 38280, Los Angeles CA 90038. (323)850-6271. Fax: (323)850-6295. E-mail: firststge@aol.com. **Contact:** Dennis Safren, literary manager. Estab. 1983. First Stage is a non-profit organization dedicated to bringing together writers, actors and directors in the development of new material for stage and screen. **Produces 50 plays/year**. Submit complete ms. Responds in 6 months.
Needs: Original non-produced plays in any genre. Correct play format. No longer than two hours.
Tips: No TV sitcoms. "We are a development organization."

N: A FLORIDA STAGE, 262 S. Ocean Blvd., Manalapan FL 33462. (561)585-3404. Fax: (561)588-4708. **Contact:** Des Gallant, literary manager. Estab. 1985. **Produces 5 plays/year**. Professional equity productions; 250 seat thrust; looking for edgy work that deals with issues and ideas; stylistically innovative. *Agented submissions only.* Responds in 1 year. Buys production rights only. **Pays royalty.** Include SASE for return of script.
Needs: "We need drama and comedy; issue-oriented plays, innovative in their use of language, structure and style." No more than 8 actors.
Tips: No kitchen sink; Neil Simon type comedy; TV sitcom type material. "We see a propensity for writing scripts that forget the art of the theater and that are overly influenced by TV and film. Theater's most important asset is language. It is truly refreshing to come across writers who understand that Eric Overmyer is a great example.

FLORIDA STUDIO THEATRE, 1241 N. Palm Ave., Sarasota FL 34236. (941)366-9017. Fax: (941)955-4137. E-mail: james@fst2000.org. **Contact**: James Ashford, casting and literary coordinator. **Produces 7 established and 6 new plays/year**. FST is a professional, not-for-profit theater. Plays are produced in 173-seat mainstage and 109-seat cabaret theater for subscription audiences. FST operates under a small professional theater contract of Actor's Equity. Query with synopsis. Responds in 2 months to queries; 6 months to mss. **Pays $200 for workshop production** of new script.
Needs: Contemporary plays, musicals, musical revues. Prefer casts of no more than 8 and single sets on mainstage, 3-4 in cabaret.
Tips: "We are looking for material for our Cabaret Theatre—musical revues, one-two character musicals. All should be in two acts and run no longer than 90 minutes, including a 10 to 15-minute intermission."

THE FOOTHILL THEATRE COMPANY, P.O. Box 1812, Nevada City CA 95959. (530)265-9320. Fax: (530)265-9325. E-mail: ftc@foothilltheatre.org. Website: www.foothilltheatre.org. **Contact:** Gary Wright, associate artist. Estab. 1977. **Produces 6-9 plays/year**. "We are a professional theater company operating under an Actors' Equity Association contract for part of the year, and performing in the historic 246-seat Nevada Theatre (built in 1865) and at an outdoor amphitheatre on the north shore of Lake Tahoe. We also produce a new play development program called New Voices of the Wild West that endeavors to tell the stories of the non-urban Western United States. The audience is a mix of locals and tourists." Query with synopsis or submit complete script. Responds in 6 months or less. Buys negotiable rights. **Pay varies.**
Needs: "We are most interested in plays which speak to the region and its history, as well as to its current concerns. No melodramas. Theatrical, above all." No limitations.
Tips: "At present, we're especially interested in unproduced plays that speak to the rural and semi-rural American West for possible inclusion in our new play reading and development program, New Voices of the Wild West. History plays are okay, as long as they don't sound like you wrote them with an encyclopedia open in your lap. The best way to get our attention is to write something we haven't seen before, and write it well."

FOUNTAIN THEATRE, 5060 Fountain Ave., Los Angeles CA 90029. (323)663-2235. Fax: (323)663-1629. E-mail: ftheatre@aol.com. Website: fountaintheatre.com. Artistic Directors: Deborah Lawlor, Stephen Sachs. **Contact:** Simon Levy, dramaturg. Estab. 1990. Produces both a theater and dance season. Produced at Fountain Theatre (99-seat equity plan). Query through agent or recommendation of theater professional. Query with synopsis to: Simon Levy, producing director/dramaturg. Rights acquired vary. Responds in 6 months. **Pays royalty.**
Needs: Original plays, adaptations of American literature, "material that incorporates dance or language into text with unique use and vision."

N **THE FREELANCE PRESS**, P.O. Box 548, Dover MA 02030-2207. (508)785-8250. Fax: (508)785-8291. **Contact**: Narcissa Campion, managing director. Estab. 1984. **Publishes 4 plays/year** for children/young adults. Submit complete ms with SASE. Responds in 4 months. **Pays 70% of performance royalties to authors. Pays 10% script and score royalty.**
Needs: "We publish original musical theater to be performed by young people, dealing with issues of importance to them. Also adapt 'classics' into musicals for 8- to 16-year-old age groups to perform." Large cast; flexible.

SAMUEL FRENCH, INC., 45 W. 25th St., New York NY 10010. (212)206-8990. Fax: (212)206-1429. E-mail: samuelfrench@earthlink.net. Website: www.samuelfrench.com. **Contact:** Lawrence Harbison, senior editor. Estab. 1830. Publishes paperback acting editions of plays. **Publishes 30-40 titles/year. Receives 1,500 submissions/year, mostly from unagented playwrights. 10% of publications are from first-time authors; 20% from unagented writers.** Publishes play an average of 6 months after acceptance. Accepts simultaneous submissions. Allow *minimum* of 4 months for reply. Catalog for $3.50. **Pays 10% royalty on retail price.**
Needs: Comedies, mysteries, children's plays, high school plays.
Tips: "Broadway and Off-Broadway hit plays, light comedies and mysteries have the best chance of selling to our firm. Our market is comprised of theater producers—both professional and amateur—actors and students. Read as many plays as possible of recent vintage to keep apprised of today's market; write plays with good female roles; and be 100% professional in approaching publishers and producers. No plays with all-male casts, radio plays or verse plays."

WILL GEER THEATRICUM BOTANICUM, P.O. Box 1222, Topanga CA 90290. (310)455-2322. Fax: (310)455-3724. **Contact:** Ellen Geer, artistic director. Estab. 1973. **Produces 3 classical and 1 new play** if selected/year. Professional productions for summer theater. Send synopsis, sample dialogue and tape if musical. Responds in 6 months. **Pays 6% royalty or $150 per show.**
Needs: Socially relevant plays, musicals; all full-length. Cast size of 4-10 people. "We are a large outdoor theatre—small intimate works could be difficult."

GENERIC PLAYS, P.O. Box 81, Bristol TN 37621-0081. **Contact:** Cody Miller, publisher. Estab. 1999. **Publishes 20 plays/year.** Audience is professional, college and community groups. Submit complete ms. Include score and tape/CD for musicals. Enclose SASE for return of materials or #10 SASE for notification. Responds in 6 months. **Pays 75% royalty plus 25% script/book royalty.**
Needs: 'We are very interested in plays/musicals by minorities or dealing with minority issues (women, gay/lesbian, persons of color)."
Tips: "No one-acts which are not part of a series or would constitute a full evening."

N **GEORGE STREET PLAYHOUSE**, 9 Livingston Ave., New Brunswick NJ 08901. (908)846-2895. Website: www.swirftweare.com/georgestreet. Producing Artistic Director: Gregory Hurst. **Contact:** Tricia Roche, literary manager. **Produces 7 plays/year.** Professional regional theater (LORT C). *No unsolicited scripts.* Agent or professional recommendation only. Responds to scripts in 10 months. "We also accept synopsis, dialogue sample and demo tape."
Needs: Full-length dramas, comedies and musicals with a fresh perspective on society. Prefers cast size under 9. Also presents 40-minute social issue-plays appropriate for touring to school-age children; cast size limited to 4-5 actors.
Tips: "We produce up to four new plays and one new musical each season. It is our firm belief that theater reaches the mind via the heart and the funny bone. Our work tells a compelling, personal, human story that entertains, challenges and stretches the imagination."

N **GEVA THEATRE**, 75 Woodbury Blvd., Rochester NY 14607. (716)232-1366. **Contact:** Marge Betley, literary manager. **Produces 7-10 plays/year.** Professional and regional theater, modified thrust, 552 seats. Subscription and single-ticket sales; no children's shows. Query with synopsis. Responds in 2 months.
Needs: Full-length plays, translations and adaptations.

THE GOODMAN THEATRE, 200 S. Columbus Ave., Chicago IL 60603. (312)443-3811. Fax: (312)443-7472. E-mail: staff@goodman-theatre.org. Website: www.goodman~theatre.org. **Contact:** Robert Falls, artistic director. Director of New Play Development: Susan V. Booth. Estab. 1925. **Produces 9 plays/year.** "The Goodman is a professional, not-for-profit theater producing both a mainstage and studio series for its subscription-based audience. The Goodman does not accept unsolicited scripts from playwrights or agents, nor will it respond to synopses of plays submitted by playwrights, unless accompanied by a stamped, self-addressed postcard. The Goodman may request plays to be submitted for production consideration after receiving a letter of inquiry or telephone call from recognized literary agents or producing organizations." Buys variable rights. Responds in 6 months. **Pays variable royalty.**
Needs: Full-length plays, translations, musicals; special interest in social or political themes.

A **GRETNA THEATRE**, P.O. Box 578, Mt. Gretna PA 17064. (717)964-3322. Fax: (717)964-2189. **Contact:** Pat Julian, producing director. Estab. 1977. "Plays are performed at a professional equity theater during summer." **Pays negotiable royalty, (6-12%).**
Needs: "We produce full-length plays for a summer audience—subject, language and content are important." Prefer "Package" or vehicles which have "Star" role.
Tips: "No one-acts." Comedy is popular.

HEUER PUBLISHING CO., 210 2nd St., Suite 301, Cedar Rapids IA 52406-0248. (319)364-6311. Fax: (319)364-1771. E-mail: editor@hitplays.com. Website: www.hitplays.com. Owner/Editor: C. Emmett McMullen. **Contact:** Geri Albrecht, associate editor. Estab. 1928. Publishes plays, musicals and theatre texts for junior and senior high schools and community theatres. Query with synopsis or submit complete script. Responds in 2 months. Purchases amateur rights only. **Pays royalty or makes outright purchase**.
Needs: "One-, two- and three-act plays and musicals suitable for middle, junior and senior high school productions. Preferably comedy or mystery/comedy with a large number of characters and minimal set requirements. Please avoid controversial or offensive subject matter. "

N HORIZON THEATRE COMPANY, P.O. Box 5376, Atlanta GA 31107. (404)523-1477. E-mail: horizonco@min dspring.com. Website: www.mindspring.com/~horizonco/. **Contact:** Jennifer Hebblethwaite, literary manager. Artistic Director: Lisa Adler. Estab. 1983. **Produces 4 plays/year**. Professional productions. Query with synopsis and résumé. Responds in 2 years. Buys rights to produce in Atlanta area. **Pays 6-8% royalty or $50-75/performance**.
Needs: "We produce contemporary plays with realistic base, but which utilize heightened visual or language elements. Interested in comedy, satire, plays that are entertaining and topical, but also thought provoking. Also particular interest in plays by women or with Southern themes." No more than 10 in cast.
Tips: "No plays about being in theater or film; no plays without hope; no plays that include playwrights as leading characters; no all-male casts; no plays with all older (50 plus) characters. Southern theme plays considered for New South for the New Century new play festival."

INDIANA REPERTORY THEATRE, 140 W. Washington St., Indianapolis IN 46204-3465. (317)635-5277. Fax: (317)236-0767. Artistic Director: Janet Allen. **Contact:** Literary Manager. Estab. 1972. **Produces 9 plays/year**. Plays are produced and performed at the Indiana Repertory Theatre, the state's only professional, nonprofit resident theatre. Audiences range from child to adult, depending on show. Query with synopsis. "We prefer a letter, résumé or short bio, production history, one page synopsis, and 10-page dialogue sample with SASE." Responds in 2 months to synopsis; 6 months on ms. **Rights and payment negotiated individually**.
Needs: Full-length plays; adaptations of well-known literary works; plays about Indiana and the Midwest; African-American plays; Native American plays; contemporary comedies; plays with compelling characters, situations, language and theatrical appeal. Prefer casts of 8 or fewer.
Tips: No musicals or plays that would do as well in film and on TV.

N INTERNATIONAL READERS' THEATRE, 73 Furby St., Winnipeg, Manitoba R3C 2A2 Canada. (204)775-2923. Fax: (204)775-2947. Website: www.blizzard.mb.ca/catalog/IRT.html. **Contact:** David Fuller, production coordinator. Estab. 1996. **Publishes 20-30 plays/year**. IRT is the publish-on-demand script service of Blizzard Publishing. Audience is primarily students (all ages) and theater groups. Query and synopsis. Responds in 6 months. "We obtain a license to publish the manuscript and handle amateur performance rights on the playwright's behalf." **Pays royalty**.
Needs: "We are open to submissions of all genres and styles. We prefer script lenghts of 2 hours or less. Scripts must be post-production drafts (even if only an amateur production). No unproduced plays."
Tips: Submission guidelines available on website.

JEWEL BOX THEATRE, 3700 N. Walker, Oklahoma City OK 73118-7099. (405)521-1786. Fax: (405)525-6562. **Contact:** Charles Tweed, production director. Estab. 1956. **Produces 6 plays/year**. Amateur productions. For 3,000 season subscribers and general public. Submit complete script. Responds in 4 months. **Pays $500 contest prize**.
Needs: Send SASE for entry form during September-October. We produce dramas and comedies. Only full-length plays can be accepted. Our theater is in-the-round, so we adapt plays accordingly." Deadline: mid-January.

N JEWISH REPERTORY THEATRE, 1395 Lexington Ave., New York NY 10128. (212)415-5550. Fax: (212)415-5575. E-mail: jrep@echonyc.com. Website: www.jrt.org. **Contact:** Ran Avni, artistic director. Estab. 1974. **Produces 4 plays, 15 readings/year**. New York City professional off-Broadway production. Submit complete script. Does not return scripts. Responds in 1 month. First production/option to move to Broadway or off-Broadway. **Pays royalty**.
Needs: Full-length only. Straight plays, musicals. Must have some connection to Jewish life, characters, history. Maximum 7 characters. Limited technical facilities.
Tips: No biblical plays.

N KUMU KAHUA, 46 Merchant St., Honolulu HI 96813. (808)536-4222. Fax: (808)536-4226. **Contact:** Harry Wong, artistic director. Estab. 1971. **Produces 5 productions, 3-4 public readings/year**. "Plays performed at new Kumu Kahua Theatre, flexible 120-seat theater, for community audiences." Submit complete script. Responds in 4 months. **Pays royalty of $50/performance**; usually 12 performances of each production.
Needs: "Plays must have some interest for local Hawai'i audiences, preferably by being set in Hawai'i or dealing with some aspect of the Hawaiian experience. Prefer small cast, with simple staging demands."
Tips: "We need time to evaluate scripts (our response time is four months)."

LARK THEATRE COMPANY/PLAYWRIGHTS WEEK, 939 Eighth Ave., New York NY 10019. (212)246-2676. Fax: (212)246-2609. E-mail: larkco@aol.com. Website: www.larktheatre.com. **Contact:** Todd Rosen, managing director. Producing Director: John C. Eisner. Estab. 1994. **Produces 5 plays/year, 8 during Playwrights Week**. "Our mission is to 'ready new plays for production.' Hence, we are a play development organization. We offer readings and developmental workshops, sometimes in limited runs off-Broadway." Submit complete manuscript. Responds in 8 months. No rights purchased at outset for Playwrights Week. Usually an off-Broadway option at next level of developmental production. **Pays 5½-7½% royalty (off-Broadway) or per performance (workshops)**. Sometimes pays travel per diem for Playwrights Week.

Needs: "We focus on the language of live theatre. Although we have no specific restrictions, we like to see creative use of language and theatrical innovation. Our taste is for simple staging and resonant, truthful language."

Tips: No television scripts or screenplays. "It is time to hear new voices for the theater. The focus should be on storytelling, not bells and whistles. We seek long-term developmental relationships with playwrights. Sometimes we choose a play because we are interested in the writer's voice as much as the work in question."

LILLENAS PUBLISHING CO., P.O. Box 419527, Kansas City MO 64141-6527. (816)931-1900. Fax: (816)753-4071. E-mail: drama@lillenas.com. Website: www.lillenas.com/drama. **Contact**: Kim Messer, product manager. Estab. 1926. "We publish on two levels: (1) Program Builders—seasonal and topical collections of recitations, sketches, dialogues and short plays; (2) Drama Resources which assume more than one format: (a) full-length scripts, (b) one-acts, shorter plays and sketches all by one author, (c) collection of short plays and sketches by various authors. All program and play resources are produced with local church and Christian school in mind. Therefore there are taboos." Queries are encouraged, but synopses and complete scripts are read. "First rights are purchased for Program Builder scripts. For Drama Resources, we purchase all print rights." Responds in 3 months. Writer's guidelines for #10 SASE.

• This publisher is more interested in one-act and full-length scripts—both religious and secular. Monologues are of lesser interest than previously. There is more interest in Readers' Theatre.

Needs: 98% of Program Builder materials are freelance written. Scripts selected for these publications are outright purchases; verse is minimum of 25¢/line, prose (play scripts) are minimum of $5/double-spaced page. "Lillenas Drama Resources is a line of play scripts that are, for the most part, written by professionals with experience in production as well as writing. However, while we do read unsolicited scripts, more than half of what we publish is written by experienced authors whom we have already published." **Drama Resources are paid on a 10% royalty, whether full-length scripts, one-acts, or sketches.** No advance.

Tips: "All plays need to be presented in standard play script format. We welcome a summary statement of each play. Purpose statements are always desirable. Approximate playing time, cast and prop lists, etc. are important to include. We are interested in fully scripted traditional plays, reader's theater scripts, choral speaking pieces. Contemporary settings generally have it over Biblical settings. Christmas and Easter scripts must have a bit of a twist. Secular approaches to these seasons (Santas, Easter bunnies, and so on), are not considered. We sell our product in 10,000 Christian bookstores and by catalog. We are probably in the forefront as a publisher of religious drama resources." Request a copy of our newsletter and/or catalog.

A LONG WHARF THEATRE, 222 Sargent Dr., New Haven CT 06511. (203)787-4284. Fax: (203)776-2287. Website: www.longwharf.org. **Contact:** Stephen Lanfer, literary associate. Estab. 1965. **Produces 8 plays/year**. Professional regional theatre. Query with synopsis, sample dialogue (first 10 pages) and SASE. *Agented submissions only.* Responds in 1 month to queries.

Needs: *Types of material:* full-length plays, translations, adaptations. *Special interest:* dramatic plays and comedies about human relationships, social concerns, ethical and moral dilemmas.

MAGIC THEATRE, INC., Bldg. D, Fort Mason, San Francisco CA 94123. (415)441-8001. Fax: (415)771-5505. E-mail: magicthtre@aol.com. Artistic Director: Larry Eilenberg. **Contact:** Laura Owen, literary manager. Estab. 1967. **Produces 6 plays/year** plus numerous co-productions. Regional theater. Query with synopsis and dialogue sample (10 pages). Responds in 6 months. **Pays royalty or per performance fee.**

Needs: "Plays that are innovative in theme and/or craft, cutting-edge political concerns, intelligent comedy. Full-length only, strong commitment to multicultural work."

Tips: "Not interested in classics, conventional approaches and cannot produce large-cast plays. Send query to Laura Owen, literary manager."

MANHATTAN THEATRE CLUB, 311 W. 43rd St., 8th Floor, New York NY 10036. Website: www.mtc-nyc.org. **Contact:** Christian Parker, literary manager. Director of Artistic Development: Robyn Goodman. **Produces 8 plays/ year**. Two-theater performing arts complex classified as off-Broadway, using professional actors. No unsolicited scripts. No queries. Responds in 6 months.

Needs: "We present a wide range of new work, from this country and abroad, to a subscription audience. We want plays about contemporary concerns and people.All genres are welcome. Multiple set shows are discouraged. Average cast is eight. MTC also maintains an extensive play development program."

N A McCARTER THEATRE, 91 University Place, Princeton NJ 08540. Website: www.mccarter.org. **Contact:** Charles McNulty, literary manager. **Produces 5 plays/year; 1 second stage play/year**. Produces professional productions for a 1,077-seat theater. Query with synopsis; *agented submissions only.* Responds in 1 month; agent submissions 3 months. **Pays negotiable royalty.**

Needs: Full length plays, musicals, translations.

MERIWETHER PUBLISHING LTD. (Contemporary Drama Service), Dept. WM, 885 Elkton Dr., Colorado Springs CO 80907-3557. Fax: (719)594-9916. E-mail: Merpcds@aol.com. Website: meriwetherPublishing.com. President: Mark Zapel. Editor: Arthur L. Zapel. **Contact:** Ted Zapel, associate eidtor. Estab. 1969. "We publish how-to materials in book and video formats. We are interested in materials for middle school, high-school and college level students only. Our Contemporary Drama Service division **publishes 60-70 plays/year." 80% written by unpublished writers. Buys 40-60 scripts/year from unpublished/unproduced writers. 90% of scripts are unagented submissions**. Responds in 1 month to queries; 2 months on full-length mss. Query with synopsis/outline, résumé of credits, sample of style and SASE. Catalog available for $2 postage. **Offers 10% royalty or makes outright purchase**.
Needs: Musicals for a large cast of performers. 1 act or 2 act comedy plays with large casts. Book mss on theatrical arts subjects, especially books of short scenes for amateur and professional actors. "We are now looking for scenebooks with special themes: 'scenes for young women,' 'comedy scenes for two actors', etc. These need not be original, provided the compiler can get letters of permission from the original copyright owner. We are interested in all textbook candidates for theater arts subjects. Christian children's activity book mss also accepted. We will consider elementary level religious materials and plays, but no elementary level children's secular plays. Query.
Tips: "We publish a wide variety of speech contest materials for high-school students. We are publishing more full length play scripts and musicals based on classic literature or popular TV shows, provided the writer includes letter of clearance from the copyright owner. Our educational books are sold to teachers and students at college and high-school levels. Our religious books are sold to youth activity directors, pastors and choir directors. Our trade books are directed at the public with a sense of humor. Another group of buyers is the professional theater, radio and TV category. We will be especially interested in full length (two- or three-act) plays with name recognition, either the playwright or the adaptation source."

METROSTAGE, 1201 N. Royal St., Alexandria VA 22314. (703)548-9044. Fax: (703)548-9089. **Contact:** Carolyn Griffin, producing artistic director. Estab. 1984. **Produces 4-5 plays/year**. Professional productions for 150 seat theatre, general audience. Query with synopsis and 10 page dialogue sample play production history. Responds in 3 months. **Payment negotiable, sometimes royalty percentage, sometimes per performance**.
Needs: Contemporary themes, small cast (up to 6 actors), unit set.

MILL MOUNTAIN THEATRE, Market Square, Center in Square, Roanoke VA 24011-1437. (703)342-5730. Fax: (540)342-5745. E-mail: mmtmail@intrlink.com. Website: www.intrlink.com/MMT. Executive Director: Jere Lee Hodgin. **Contact:** Literary Manager. **Produces 8 established plays, 10 new one-acts and 2 new full-length plays/year**. "Some of the professional productions will be on the main stage and some in our alternative Theater B." Send letter with SASE. Responds in 8 months. **Payment negotiable**. Send SASE for play contest guidelines; cast limit 15 for play and 24 for musicals. Do not include loose stamps or money.
Needs: "We are interested in plays with racially mixed casts, but not to the exclusion of others. We are constantly seeking one-act plays for 'Centerpieces', our lunch time program of script-in-hand productions. Playing time should be between 25-35 minutes. Cast limit 6."
Tips: "Subject matter and character variations are open, but gratuitous language and acts are not acceptable unless they are artistically supported. A play based on large amounts of topical reference or humor has a very short life. Be sure you have written a play and not a film script."

THE NATIONAL PLAYWRIGHTS CONFERENCE/NEW DRAMA FOR MEDIA PROJECT AT THE EUGENE O'NEILL THEATER CENTER, 234 W. 44th St., Suite 901, New York NY 10036-3909. (212)382-2790. Fax: (212)921-5538. E-mail: acthuman@aol.com. Artistic Director: James Houghton. **Contact:** Mary F. McCabe, managing director. Estab. 1965. **Develops staged readings of 9-12 stage plays, 2-3 screenplays or teleplays/year**. "We accept unsolicited scripts with no prejudice toward either represented or unrepresented writers. Our theater is located in Waterford, Connecticut, and we operate under an Equity LORT contract. We have three theaters: Barn—250 seats, Amphitheater—300 seats, Edith Oliver Theater—150 seats. Submission guidelines for #10 SASE in the fall. Complete bound, professionally unproduced, original plays are eligible (no adaptations). Decision by late April. **Pays stipend plus room, board and transportation**. We accept script submissions September 15-November 15 of each year. Conference takes place during July each summer."
● Scripts are selected on the basis of talent, not commercial potential.
Needs: "We use modular sets for all plays, minimal lighting, minimal props and no costumes. We do script-in-hand readings with professional actors and directors. Our focus is on new play/playwright development."

NEBRASKA THEATRE CARAVAN, 6915 Cass St., Omaha NE 68132. (402)553-4890. Fax: (402)553-6288. **Contact:** Marya Lucca-Thyberg, director. Estab. 1976. **Produces 4-5 plays/year**. "Nebraska Theatre Caravan is a touring

---

FOR LISTINGS OF OVER 500 literary and script agents, consult the *Guide to Literary Agents*.

company which produces professional productions in schools, arts centers, and small and large theaters for elementary, middle, high school and family audiences." Query with synopsis. Responds in 3 weeks. **Pays $20-50 per performance**. Negotiates production rights "unless the work is commissioned by us."

Needs: "All genres are acceptable bearing in mind the student audiences. We are truly an ensemble and like to see that in our choice of shows; curriculum ties are very important for elementary and high school shows; musicals are good. No more than eight in cast. Preferred lengths: 60 minute for elementary school shows; 75 minutes for middle/high school shows. No sexually explicit material."

Tips: "We tour eight months of the year to a variety of locations. Flexibility is important as we work in both beautiful performing arts facilities and school multipurpose rooms."

N **THE NEW AMERICAN THEATER CENTER**, 118 N. Main St., Rockford IL 61101. (815)963-9454. Fax: (815)963-7215. **Contact:** Richard Raether, associate artistic director: Produces a spectrum of American and international work in 10-month season. The New American Theater Center is a professional equity theater company performing on two stages, a thrust stage with 282-seat house and a 100-seat second stage.

Needs: New works for "New Voices in the Heartland," an annual play festival of staged readings. The works may have been workshopped, but not previously produced. Submit synopsis with SASE, full scripts only when requested.

Tips: "We look for new work that addresses contemporary issues; we do not look for work of any one genre or production style."

N **NEW JERSEY REPERTORY COMPANY**, Lumia Theatre, 179 Broadway, Long Branch NJ 07740. (732)229-3166. Fax: (732)229-3167. **Contact:** Gabor Barabas, executive producer. Estab. 1997. **Produces 6 plays/year**. Professional productions year round. Submit complete ms. Responds in 1 year. Rights negotiable. **Makes outright purchase**.

Needs: Prefers small cast unit or simple set.

NEW PLAYS INCORPORATED, P.O. Box 5074, Charlottesville VA 22905. (804)979-2777. Fax: (804)984-2230. E-mail: patwhitton@aol.com. Website: www.newplaysforchildren.com. **Contact:** Patricia Whitton, artistic director. Estab. 1964. **Publishes 3-6 plays/year**. Publishes for children's or youth theaters. Submit complete ms or for adaptations, query first. Responds in 2 months or longer. Buys all semi-professional and amateur rights in U.S. and Canada. **Pays 50% royalty**.

Needs: "I have eclectic taste—plays must have quality and originality in whatever genres, topics, styles or lengths the playwright chooses."

Tips: "No adaptations of stuff that has already been adapted a million times, e.g., *Tom Sawyer, A Christmas Carol*, or plays that sound like they've been written by the guidance counselor. There will be more interest in youth theater productions with moderate to large casts (15+). Plays must have been produced, directed by someone other than the author or author's spouse. People keep sending us material suitable for adults. This is not our market!"

N **NEW REPERTORY THEATRE**, P.O. Box 610418, Newton Highlands MA 02161-0418. (617)332-7058. Fax: (617)527-5217. E-mail: newrepth@aol.com. Website: www.Newrep.org. **Contact:** Rick Lombardo, producing artistic director. Estab. 1984. **Produces 5 plays/year**. Professional theater, general audience. Query with synopsis. Production, subsidiary. **Pays 5-10% royalty**.

Needs: Idea laden, all styles, full-length only. Small cast, unit set.

Tips: No sit-coms like comedies. Incorporating and exploring styles other than naturalism.

NEW STAGE THEATRE, 1100 Carlisle, Jackson MS 39202. (601)948-0143. Fax: (601)948-3538. **Contact:** John Maxwell, artistic director. Estab. 1965. **Produces 9 plays/year**. "Professional productions, 8 mainstage, 1 in our 'second space.' We play to an audience comprised of Jackson, the state of Mississippi and the Southeast." Query with synopsis. Responds in 6 weeks. Exclusive premiere contract upon acceptance of play for mainstage production. **Pays royalty of 5-8% or $25-60/performance**.

Needs: Southern themes, contemporary issues, small casts (5-8), single set plays.

• The New Stage no longer accepts children's theater.

NEW TUNERS THEATRE, 1225 W. Belmont Ave., Chicago IL 60657. (773)929-7367, ext. 22. E-mail: tbtuners@aol.com. Website: http://adamczyk.com/newtuners. **Contact:** John Sparks, artistic director. **Produces monthly readings of new works, 4 skeletal productions**, and the "Stages Festival of New Works" each year in July. Mostly developed in our New Tuners workshop. "Some scripts produced are unagented submissions. Plays performed in 3 small off-Loop theaters seating 148 for a general theater audience, urban/suburban mix. Submit synopsis, cover letter and cassette selections of the score, if available. Responds in 3 months. Next step is script and score (reports in 6 months).

Needs: "We're interested in all forms of musical theater including more innovative styles. Our production capabilities are limited by the lack of space, but we're very creative and authors should submit anyway. The smaller the cast, the better. We are especially interested in scripts using a younger (35 and under) ensemble of actors. We mostly look for authors who are interested in developing their script through workshops, readings and production. No casts over 12. No one-man shows or 'single author' pieces."

Tips: "We would like to see the musical theater articulating something about the world around us, as well as diverting an audience's attention from that world." Script Consultancy—A new program designed to assist authors and composers in developing new musicals through private feedback sessions with professional dramaturgs and musical directors. For further info contact (773)929-7367, ext. 17.

N: NORTH SHORE MUSIC THEATRE, 62 Dunham Rd., Beverly MA 01915. (978)232-7203. Fax: (978)921-0793. **Contact:** John La Rock. Estab. 1955. **Produces 7 musicals, 1 Shakespeare/year.** Arena theater, Beverly MA, 23,000 subscribers. Submit complete ms. Responds in 4 months. **Pay and rights negotiable.**
Needs: Musicals only (adult and children's).
Tips: No straight plays, opera.

N: NORTHLIGHT THEATRE, 9501 Skokie Blvd., Skokie IL 60077. (847)679-9501. Fax: (847)679-1879. **Contact:** Russell Vandenbroucke, artistic director. Estab. 1975. **Produces 5 plays/year.** "We are a professional, Equity theater, LORT D. We have a subscription base of over 6,000, and have a significant number of single ticket buyers." Query with synopsis and SASE. Responds in 3 months. Buys production rights plus royalty on future mountings. **Pays royalty.**
Needs: "Full-length plays, translations, adaptations, musicals. Interested in plays of 'ideas', plays that are passionate and/or hilarious, stylistic exploration, intelligence and complexity. Generally looking for cast size of eight or less, but there are always exceptions made for the right play."
Tips: "Please, do not try to do what television and film do better! Also, no domestic realism."

ODYSSEY THEATRE ENSEMBLE, 2055 S. Sepulveda Blvd., Los Angeles CA 90025. (310)477-2055. Fax: (310)444-0455. **Contact:** Sally Essex-Lopresti, director of literary programs. Estab. 1965. **Produces 9 plays/year.** Plays performed in a 3-theater facility. "All three theaters are Equity 99-seat theater plan. We have a subscription audience of 4,000 for a nine-play main season, and they are offered a discount on our rentals and co-productions. Remaining seats are sold to the general public." Query with résumé, synopsis, cast breakdown and 8-10 pages of sample dialogue and cassette if a musical. Scripts must be securely bound. Responds in 1 month to queries; 6 months on scripts. Buys negotiable rights. **Pays 5-7% royalty.** Does *not* return scripts without SASE.
Needs: "Full-length plays only with either an innovative form and/or provocative subject matter. We desire highly theatrical pieces that explore possibilities of the live theater experience. We are seeking full-length musicals and some plays with smaller casts (2-4). We are not reading one-act plays or light situation comedies."

N: OMAHA THEATER COMPANY FOR YOUNG PEOPLE, 2001 Farnam St., Omaha NE 68102. (402)345-4852. **Contact:** James Larson, artistic director. **Produces 6 plays/year.** "Our target audience is children, preschool-high school and their parents." Query with synopsis and SASE. Responds in 9 months. **Pays negotiable royalty.**
Needs: "Plays must be geared to children and parents (PG rating). Titles recognized by the general public have a stronger chance of being produced." Cast limit: 25 (8-10 adults). No adult scripts.
Tips: "Unproduced plays may be accepted only after a letter of inquiry (familiar titles only!)."

THE OPEN EYE THEATER, P.O. Box 959, Margaretville NY 12455. Phone/fax: (914)586-1660. E-mail: openeye@c atskill.net. Website: www.theopeneye.com. **Contact:** Amie Brockway, producing artistic director. The Open Eye is a not-for-profit professional theater company working in New York City since 1972, in the rural villages of Delaware County, NY since 1991, and on tour. The theater specializes in the development of new plays for multi-generational audiences (children ages 8 and up, and adults of all ages). Ensemble plays with music and dance, culturally diverse and historical material, myth, folklore, and stories with universal themes are of interest. Program includes readings, developmental workshops, and fully staged productions.
Tips: Send one-page letter with one-paragraph plot synopsis, cast breakdown and setting, résumé and SAE. "We will provide the stamp and contact you *if we want to see the script*."

N: OREGON SHAKESPEARE FESTIVAL, P.O. Box 158, Ashland OR 97520. (541)482-2111. Fax: (541)482-0446. Website: www.orshakes.org. Director of Literary Development and Dramaturgy: Doug Langworthy. Estab. 1935. **Produces 11 plays/year.** The Angus Bowmer Theater has a thrust stage and seats 600. The Black Swan is an experimental space and seats 140. The Elizabethan Outdoor Theatre seats 1,200 (stages almost exclusively Shakespearean productions there, mid-June-September). Professional recommendation only. Negotiates individually for rights with the playwright's agent. Response in 6 months. **Pays royalty.** "Most plays run within our ten-month season for 6-10 months, so royalties are paid accordingly."
Needs: "A broad range of classic and contemporary scripts. One or two fairly new scripts/season. Also a play readings series which focuses on new work. Plays must fit into our ten-month rotating repertory season. Black Swan shows usually limited to seven actors." No one-acts. Small musicals OK. Submissions from women and minority writers are strongly encouraged.
Tips: "We're always looking for a good comedy which has scope. We tend to prefer plays with a literary quality. We want plays to explore the human condition with language, metaphor and theatricality. We encourage translations of foreign plays as well as adaptations of non-dramatic material."

N: JOSEPH PAPP PUBLIC THEATER, 425 Lafayette St., New York NY 10003. (212) 539-8500. Website: www.pu blictheater.org. Producer: George C. Wolfe. **Contact:** Mervin P. Antonio, literary manager. Estab. 1964. **Produces 5 plays/year**. Professional productions. No unsolicited scripts. Query with synopsis and 10-page sample. Responds in 1 month to queries; 6 months to scripts.
Needs: All genres, no one-acts.

A: THE PASADENA PLAYHOUSE, 39 S. El Molino Ave., Pasadena CA 91101. (626)792-8672. Fax: (626)792-7343. Artistic Director: Sheldon Epps. **Contact:** David A. Tucker II, literary manager. Estab. 1917. **Produces 6 plays/ year**. Professional equity productions in a 676 seat historic theatre. *Agented submissions only*. Responds in 9 months.
Needs: Musicals, full-length dramas, comedies. No larger than 8 cast members unless it is a musical. No one act plays.
Tips: There are a number of organizations that do readings or workshops of new material. It would be helpful for a writer to have gone through a reading prior to submitting the work. Direct all submissions to our literary manager.

N: PEGASUS THEATRE, 3916 Main St., Dallas TX 75226-1228. (214)821-6005. Fax: (214)826-1671. E-mail: comedy@pegasustheatre.org. Website: www.pegasustheatre.com. **Contact:** Steve Erwin, new plays manager. Estab. 1985. **Produces 4 full productions, 4-6 readings/year**. Produces plays under an Umbrella Agreement with AEA. "Our productions are presented for the general public to attend." Query with synopsis; include 10 sample pages. Responds in 6 months. **Pays 5-8% royalty**.
Needs: New and original comedies with a satiric slant. Limit cast size to under 10, single set.
Tips: "No murder-mysteries, please. We'd rather not look at one-acts that don't have companion pieces or at plays that read and play like extended-length sitcoms. Neatness and proper formatting always make a better impression—even with the best of scripts."

PIONEER DRAMA SERVICE, INC., P.O. Box 4267, Englewood CO 80155-4267. (303)779-4035. Fax: (303)779-4315. E-mail: playwrights@pioneerdrama.com. Website: www.pioneerdrama.com. Publisher: Steven Fendrich. **Contact:** Beth Somers, submissions editor. Estab. 1963. **Publishes 30 new plays/year**. Plays are performed by schools, colleges, community theaters, recreation programs, churches and professional children's theaters for audiences of all ages. Query preferred; unsolicited scripts with proof of production accepted. Retains all rights. Responds in 2 weeks to queries, in 6 months to scripts. Guidelines for SASE. **Pays royalty**. All submissions automatically entered in Shubert Fendrich Memorial Playwriting Contest.
Needs: "Musicals, comedies, mysteries, dramas, melodramas and children's theater. Two-acts up to 90 minutes; children's theater, 1 hour. Prefers many female roles, simple sets. "Plays need to be appropriate for amateur groups." Prefers secular plays.
Tips: Interested in adaptations of classics of public domain works appropriate for children and teens. Also plays that deal with social issues for teens and preteens. "Check out the website to see what we carry and if your material would be appropriate. Make sure to include query letter, proof of productions and an SASE."

PLAYERS PRESS, INC., P.O. Box 1132, Studio City CA 91614-0132. **Contact:** Robert W. Gordon, editorial vice president. "We deal in all entertainment areas and handle publishable works for film and television as well as theater. Performing arts books, plays and musicals. All plays must be in stage format for publication." Also produces scripts for video and material for cable television. **20-30 scripts/year unagented submissions; 5-15 books also unagented. Works with 1-10 unpublished/unproduced writers annually**. Query. "Include #10 SASE, reviews and proof of production. All play submissions must have been produced and should include a flier and/or program with dates of performance." Buys negotiable rights. "We prefer all area rights." Responds in 1 month to queries; 1 year to mss. **Pays variable royalty according to area; approximately 10-75% of gross receipts. Also makes outright purchase of $100-25,000 or $5-5,000/performance**.
Needs: "We prefer comedies, musicals and children's theater, but are open to all genres. We will rework the script after acceptance. We are interested in the quality, not the format. Performing Arts Books that deal with theater how-to are of strong interest."
Tips: "Send only material requested. Do not telephone."

PLAYS, The Drama Magazine for Young People, 120 Boylston St., Boston MA 02116-4615. (617)423-3157. Fax: (617)423-2168. E-mail: writer@user1.channel1.com. Website: www.channel1.com/plays. **Contact:** Elizabeth Preston, managing editor. Estab. 1941. **Publishes 70 one-act plays** and dramatic program material in seven issues (Oct.-May) each school year to be performed by junior and senior high, middle grades, lower grades. "Scripts should follow the general style of *Plays*. Stage directions should not be typed in capital letters or underlined. No incorrect grammar or dialect." Desired lengths are: junior and senior high—15-18 double-spaced pages (20-30 minutes playing time); middle grades—10-12 pages (15-20 minutes playing time); lower grades—6-10 pages (8-15 minutes playing time). Buys all rights. Submit complete ms (except for dramatized classics, works in the public domain, for which we would liked to be queried first). Responds in 2 weeks. Sample copy $4. Send SASE for guidelines. **Pays on acceptance from $75**.
Needs: "Can use comedies and dramas, plays for holidays and other special occasions, such as Book Week; historical plays." Set and props should be kept as simple as possible. No monologues or plays with only a few characters.
Tips: "No material on drugs, sex, alcohol, very dysfunctional families. Plays are wholesome, positive."

PLAYS-IN-PROGRESS, 615 4th St., Eureka CA 95501. (707)443-3724. Artistic Director: Susan Bigelow-Marsh. Estab. 1988. **Produces 5 plays/year.** Non-profit, with adult audiences. Submit complete manuscript. Responds in 6 months. **Pays maximum of 10% royalty.**
Needs: Innovative, socially relevant, full-length drama and comedies. Simple scenes; cast limit 8.
Tips: Do not want to see musicals, children plays. "Bound scripts only. All must contain SASE."

THE PLAYWRIGHTS' CENTER'S PLAYLABS, 2301 Franklin Ave. E., Minneapolis MN 55406. (612)332-7481. Fax: (612)332-6037. E-mail: pwcenter@mtn.org. Website: www.pwcenter.org. Playwrights' Services Director: Megan Monaghan. Estab. 1971. "Playlabs is a 2-week developmental workshop for new plays. The program is held in Minneapolis and is open by script competition. It is an intensive two-week workshop focusing on the development of a script and the playwright. Four to six new plays are given rehearsed public readings at the site of the workshop." Announcements of playwrights by May 1. Playwrights receive honoraria, travel expenses, room and board.
Needs: "We are interested in playwrights with talent, ambitions for a sustained career in theater and scripts which could benefit from an intensive developmental process involving professional dramaturgs, directors and actors." US citizens or permanent residents, only. Participants must attend all of conference. No previously produced materials. Send SASE after Oct. 15 for application. Submission deadline: December 1. Call for information on competitions.
Tips: "We do not buy scripts or produce them. We are a service organization that provides programs for developmental work on scripts for members."

PLAYWRIGHTS HORIZONS, 416 W. 42nd St., New York NY 10036. (212)564-1235. Fax: (212)594-0296. Website: www.playwrightshorizons.org. **Contact:** Sonya Sobieski, literary manager (plays); send musicals Attn: Musical Theatre Program. Artistic Director: Tim Sanford. Estab. 1971. **Produces 6 plays/year** plus a reading series. Plays performed off-Broadway for a literate, urban, subscription audience. Send complete ms with author bio; include tape with musicals. Responds in 6 months. Negotiates for future rights. **Pays outright sum, then percentage after a certain run**.
Needs: "We are looking for new, full-length plays and musicals by American authors."
Tips: "No adaptations, children's theater, biographical or historical plays. We look for plays with a strong sense of language and a clear dramatic action that truly use the resources of the theater."

PLAYWRIGHTS THEATRE OF NEW JERSEY, 33 Green Village Rd., Madison NJ 07940. (973)514-1787. Fax: (973)514-2060. E-mail: playNJ@aol.com. Website: www.PTNJ.org. Producing Artistic Director: John Pietrowski. Artistic Director: Joseph Megel. Contact: Peter Hays, literary manager. Estab. 1986. **Produces 3 productions, 6 staged readings and 10 round-table readings/year.** "We operate under a Small Professional Theatre Contract (SPT) a development theatre contract with Actors Equity Association. Readings are held under a staged reading code." Submit synopsis, first 10 pages, short bio and production history and a SASE. Responds in 1 year. "For productions we ask the playwright to sign an agreement that gives us exclusive rights to the play for the production period and for 30 days following. After the 30 days we give the rights back with no strings attached, except for commercial productions. We ask that our developmental work be acknowledged in any other professional productions." **Pays $750 for productions**.
● Scripts are accepted September 1 through April 30 only. Write for guidelines before submitting.
Needs: Any style or length; full length, one acts, musicals.
Tips: "We are looking for American plays in the early stages of development—plays of substance, passion, and light (comedies and dramas) that raise challenging questions about ourselves and our communities. We prefer plays *that can work only on the stage* in the most theatrical way possible—plays that are not necessarily 'straight-on' realistic, but rather ones that use imagery, metaphor, poetry and musicality in new and interesting ways. Plays go through a three-step development process: a roundtable (inhouse reading), a public concert reading and then a workshop production."

N A PLOWSHARES THEATRE CO., 2870 E. Grand Blvd., Suite 600, Detroit MI 48202-3146. (313)872-0279. Fax: (313)872-0067. **Contact:** Gary Anderson, producing artistic director. Estab. 1989. **Produces 5 plays/year.** Professional productions intended for African-American audience and those who appreciate African-American culture. Query with synopsis. *Agented submissions only.* Responds in 8 months.

N POLARIS NORTH, % Martella, 1265 Broadway #803, New York NY 10001. (212)684-1985. **Contact:** Diane Martella, treasurer. Estab. 1974. **Workshops 15-20 plays/year.** "We have a studio workshop with professional actors and directors and mixed general-theater and professional audiences." Submit complete ms. Responds in 2 months. No payment. "Workshops are to assist writers—no charge to audience. **No payment.**"
Needs: "We workshop one-acts only. (Less than 30 minutes, not previously produced or workshopped. No musicals; no monologues, no situational skits; good writing and characters more important than genre or topic)."
Tips: No sexually oriented plays, no stage nudity. "The mission of our One Acts in Performance Project is to encourage and develop new playwrights by giving them an opportunity to see their work done (and be involved in the creative process) and to get audience feedback on their work."

PORTLAND STAGE COMPANY, P.O. Box 1458, Portland ME 04104. (207)774-1043. Fax: (207)774-0576. E-mail: portstage@aol.com. Artistic Director: Anita Stewart. **Contact:** Lisa DiFranza, literary manager. Estab. 1973. **Produces 7 plays/year.** Professional productions at the Portland Performing Arts Center. Send first 10 pages with synopsis. Responds in 3 months. Buys 3 or 4 week run in Maine. Pays standard LORT D royalty.

Needs: 1999-2000 season: *Blithe Spirit*; *Nixon's Nixon*; *Christmas Carol*; *Collected Stories*; *Waiting For Godot*; *Travels with my Aunt*; *Blues for an Alabama Sky*. Also Developmental Staged Readings: Little Festival of the Unexpected.
Tips: "Work developed in Little Festival generally will be more strongly considered for future production."

PRIMARY STAGES COMPANY, INC., 584 Ninth Ave., New York NY 10036. (212)333-7471. Fax: (212)333-2025. Website: www.NYTheatre.com/primary.htm. **Contact:** Tricia McDermott, literary manager. Estab. 1983. **Produces 4 plays, several readings and workshops/year.** All plays are produced professionally off-Broadway at Primary Stages Theatre, 99 seat proscenium stage; Phil Bosakowski Theatre, 65 seat proscenium stage. *Agented submissions* or synopsis and description of dramatic structure, 10 page dialogue sample, résumé and query with SASE for response; include cassette or CD for musicals. No unsolicited scripts. Responds in 2 months to query. Guidelines for SASE. **Pays flat fee**.
Needs: Full-length plays, small cast (6 or less) musicals. New York City or American Premiers only, written by American playwrights. Small cast (2-8), unit set or simple changes, no fly or wing space.
Tips: Best submission time: September-June. Chances: over 2,000 scripts read, 4-5 produced. Women and minorities encouraged to submit. Submission policy on website.

PRISM INTERNATIONAL, Buch E462-1866 Main Mall, University of British Columbia, Vancouver, British Columbia V6T 1Z1 Canada. (604)822-2514. Fax: (604)822-0231. E-mail: prism@interchange.ubc.ca; for drama contest: respriz e@interchange.ubc.ca. Website: www.arts.ubc.ca/prism. **Contact:** Steven Galloway, drama prize coordinator; Jennica Harper, editor; Kiera Miller, editor. UBC's Creative Writing Residency Prize in Stageplay. New biannual prize for drama, worth $25,000 and a one-month residency at UBC. Details online, or by written request.
Needs: No restrictions on genre, style or topic. Full length plays only, for this contest.
Tips: No screenplay-type material, situation comedy type writing, or stock characters. Tendency toward shorter pieces, for new play development, experimental structuring (structure that serves the material, specifically). "Do not have manuscripts bound. Read some back issues of the magazine to get an idea about what kind of material is usually published by *Prism*."

THE PURPLE ROSE THEATRE CO., P.O. Box 220, Chelsea MI 48118. (313)475-5817. Fax: (313)475-0802. E-mail: purplerose@earthlink.net. Website: www.purplerosetheatre.org. **Contact:** Anthony Caselli, literary manager. Estab. 1990. **Produces 4 plays/year.** PRTC is a regional theater with an S.P.T. Equity contract which produces plays intended for Midwest/Middle American audience. Query with synopsis, character breakdown, and 10-page dialogue sample. Expect replies in 9 months. **Pays 5-10% royalty**.
Needs: Modern, topical full length, 75-120 minutes. Prefer scripts that use comedy to deal with serious subjects. 8 cast maximum. No fly space, unit set preferable but not required. Intimate 119 seat ¾ thrust house.

RESOURCE PUBLICATIONS, INC., 160 E. Virginia St., #290, San Jose CA 95112-5876. (408)286-8505. Fax: (408)287-8748. Website: www.rpinet.com. **Contact:** Nicholas Wagner, editorial director. Estab. 1973. Audience is middle-school, high-school and adult settings. Query with synopsis. Responds in 6 weeks. **Pays 8% royalty**.
Needs: "We publish resources for teachers, counselors, group leaders, and other leaders in education and ministry. Short teaching parables, plays and skits that can be discussion starters, and curriculum resources for character development, are some areas we need work in."
Tips: "We are interested in material that can help teens grow into responsible adults."

[N] DUDLEY RIGGS THEATRES, 1586 Burton, St. Paul MN 55108. (651)647-6748. Artistic Director: Dudley Riggs. Estab. 1961. **Produces 7-8 plays/year.** "Comedy only! Revue and small musicals too. We have a wide range of audiences from teenage to seniors. We do some nonprofessional productions, but most are with a paid company and on a professional stage. Query and synopsis on longer works. Send full scripts for revue or musicals. Responds in 6 months. Obtains performance rights for our area and limited rights for touring. **Each project negotiated separately; commissioned work on a percentage of ticket sales are common**.
Needs: "We need revues of current events (social and political satire) and capsule musicals (3-7 actors). We have minimal staging—stage is 300 sq. ft. total—and a resident company of seven artists."
Tips: "No dramas, pageants, long-winded shows or large cast productions. There are too many dark plays, too few new musicals, and there's too much 'political correctness.' We only do comedy. It needs to be current or timeless and should be based on truth. There are no taboo subjects but they must have tasteful treatment."

SALTWORKS THEATRE COMPANY, 2553 Brandt School Rd., Wexford PA 15090-7931. (724)934-2820. Fax: (724)934-2815. Website: www.saltworks.org. **Contact:** Scott Kirk, artistic director. Estab. 1981. **Produces 8-10 plays/ year.** Educational tour: 200+ performance in PA, OH, WV, MD, NJ; mainstage: local amateur productions. Query with synopsis. Responds in 2 months. Obtains regional performance rights for educational grants. **Pays $25/performance**.
Needs: Social issues addressing violence prevention, sexual responsibility, peer pressures, drug and alcohol abuse (grades 1-12). Limited to 5 member cast, 2 men/3 women.

N SEATTLE CHILDREN'S THEATRE, 13003 20th Ave. NE, Seattle WA 98109. (206)443-0807. **Contact:** Deborah L. Frockt, literary manager/dramaturg. Estab. 1975. **Produces 6 plays/year**. Professional (adult actors) performing for young audiences, families and school groups. Resident company—not touring. Agented submissions only or professional recommendation with SASE. Responds in 8 months. **Pay varies**.
Needs: Full-length plays for young and family audiences.

SEATTLE REPERTORY THEATRE, 155 Mercer St., Seattle WA 98109. Website: www.seattlerep.org. Artistic Director: Sharon Ott. **Contact:** Christine Sumption, artistic associate. Estab. 1963. **Produces 9 plays/year**: 5 in the 800 seat Bagley Wright Theatre, 4 in the 300-seat Leo K Theatre. Agent submissions, or send query, résumé, synopsis, and 10 pages. No unsolicited mss or phone calls. Responds in 6 months. Buys percentage of future royalties. **Pays royalty**.
Needs: "The Seattle Repertory Theatre produces eclectic programming. We welcome a wide variety of writing."

N SECOND STAGE THEATRE, P.O. Box 1807, Ansonia Station, New York NY 10023. (212)787-8302. Fax: (212)877-9886. **Contact:** Christopher Burney, associate artistic director. Estab. 1979. **Produces 4 plays/year**. Professional off-Broadway productions. Adult and teen audiences. Query with synopsis and ten-page writing sample or agented submission. Responds in 6 months. **Pay varies**.
Needs: "We need socio-political plays, comedies, musicals, dramas—full lengths for full production, one-acts for workshops (comedies only)."
Tips: "No biographical or historical dramas. Writers are realizing that audiences can be entertained while being moved. Patience is a virtue but persistence is appreciated."

SOUTH COAST REPERTORY, P.O. Box 2197, Costa Mesa CA 92628-1197. (714)708-5500. Fax: (714)545-0391. Website: www.scr.org. Dramaturg: Jerry Patch. Literary Manager: John Glore. Estab. 1964. **Produces 6 plays/year on mainstage, 5 on second stage**. Professional nonprofit theater; a member of LORT and TCG. "We operate in our own facility which houses a 507-seat mainstage theater and a 161-seat second stage theater. We have a combined subscription audience of 21,000." Query with synopsis and 10 sample pages of dialogue. Scripts considered if submitted by agent. Acquires negotiable rights. Responds in 4 months. **Pays negotiable royalty**.
Needs: "We produce full lengths. We prefer plays that address contemporary concerns and are dramaturgically innovative. A play whose cast is larger than 15-20 will need to be extremely compelling, and its cast size must be justifiable."
Tips: "We don't look for a writer to write for us—he or she should write for him or herself. We look for honesty and a fresh voice. We're not likely to be interested in writers who are mindful of *any* trends. Originality and craftsmanship are the most important qualities we look for."

SOUTHERN APPALACHIAN REPERTORY THEATRE (SART), Mars Hill College, P.O. Box 1720, Mars Hill NC 28754. (828)689-1384. E-mail: sart@mhc.edu. Artistic Director: James W. Thomas. Managing Director: Milli Way. Estab. 1975. **Produces 6 plays/year**. "Since 1975 the Southern Appalachian Repertory Theatre has produced 43 world premieres in the 166-seat Owen Theatre on the Mars Hill College campus. The theater's goals are quality, adventurous programming and integrity, both in artistic form and in the treatment of various aspects of the human condition. SART is a professional summer theater company whose audiences range from students to senior citizens." It also conducts an annual Southern Appalachian Playwrights' Conference in which 5 playwrights are invited for informal readings of their new scripts. Deadline for submission is December 15 and conference is held the first weekend in April. If script is selected for production during the summer season, pays honorarium. Enclose SASE for return of script.
Needs: Since 1975, one of SART's goals has been to produce at least one original play each summer season. To date, 43 original scripts have been produced. Plays by southern Appalachian playwrights or about southern Appalachia are preferred, but by no means exclusively. Complete new scripts welcomed.

STAGE ONE: The Louisville Children's Theatre, 501 W. Main St., Louisville KY 40202-3300. (502)589-5946. Fax: (502)588-5910. E-mail: stageone@kca.org. Website: www.stageone.org. Contact: Moses Goldberg, producing director. Estab. 1946. **Produces 6-7 plays/year**. 20% freelance written; 15-20% unagented submissions (excluding work of playwright-in-residence). Plays performed by an Equity company for young audiences ages 4-18; usually does different plays for different age groups within that range. Submit complete script. Responds in 4 months. **Pays negotiable royalty or $25-75/performance**.
Needs: "Good plays for young audiences of all types: adventure, fantasy, realism, serious problem plays about growing up or family entertainment. Cast: ideally, twelve or less. Honest, visual potentiality, worthwhile story and characters are necessary. An awareness of children and their schooling is a plus. No campy material or anything condescending to children. Musicals if they are fairly limited in orchestration."

STAGES REPERTORY THEATRE, 3201 Allen Parkway, Houston TX 77091. (713)527-0220. Fax: (713)527-8669. Website: www.stagestheatre.com. **Contact:** Rob Bundy, artistic director. Estab. 1975. **Produces 12-14 plays/year** (6-7 main stage, 6-7 children's theatre). Query with synopsis. Responds in 8 months. **Pays 3-10% royalty**. Enclose SASE.
Needs: Full-length, theatrical, non-realistic work. Cast 6-8 maximum. "Unit set with multiple locations is preferable." No "kitchen sink" dramas. Plays also accepted October 1-December 31 for submission into the Southwest Festival of New Plays, held every June. Categories include Women's Playwrights' Division, Texas Playwrights' Division, Children's Theatre Playwrights' Division and Latino Playwrights' Division. More information on this can be found on website.

N STATE THEATER COMPANY, (formerly Live Oak Theatre), 719 Congress Ave., Austin TX 78701. (512)472-5143. Fax: (512)472-7199. E-mail: admin@statetheatercompany.com. **Contact:** John Walch, artistic associate. Estab. 1982. **Produces 6 professional plays/season**. "Strong commitment to and a history of producing new work." Responds in late summer. Send SASE for guidelines. Pays royalty.
Needs: Full length, translations, adaptations.
Tips: Also sponsors annual new play awards. Submit first 15 pages of plays, brief synopsis, and resume.

STEPPENWOLF THEATRE COMPANY, 758 W. North Ave., Chicago IL 60610. (312)335-1888. Fax: (312)335-0808. Artistic Director: Martha Lavey. **Contact:** Michele Volansky, dramaturg/literary manager. Estab. 1976. **Produces 9 plays/year**. 500 + 300 seat subscriber audience. Many plays produced by Steppenwolf have gone to Broadway. "We currently have 20,000 savvy subscribers." Query with synopsis, 10 pages sample dialogue. Agented submissions only or letter of recommendation from theater professional. Responds in 6 months. Buys commercial, film and television in addition to production rights. **Pays 6-8% royalty**.
Needs: "Actor-driven works are crucial to us, plays that explore the human condition in our time. We max at around ten characters."
Tips: No musicals or romantic/light comedies. Plays get produced at STC based on ensemble member interest.

SYRACUSE STAGE, 820 E. Genesee, Syracuse NY 13210-1508. (315)443-4008. Fax: (315)443-9846. E-mail: geisler @syr.edu. Website: www.syracusestage.org. **Contact:** Garrett Eisler, literary manager. Estab. 1974. **Produces 6-7 plays/year**. Professional LORT productions. Rights defined in contracts. Submit full script.
Needs: Full-length plays.
Tips: "Do not send computer disks or submit via e-mail. Let the script speak for itself."

N TADA!, 120 W. 28th St., New York NY 10001. (212)627-1732. Fax: (212)243-6736. E-mail: tada@ziplink.net. Website: www.tadatheater.com. Artistic Director: Janine Nina Trevens. Estab. 1984. **Produces 2-4 plays/year**. "TADA! produces original musicals and plays performed by children at our 95-seat theater. Productions are for family audiences." Submit complete script and tape, if musical. Responds in 6 months. **Pays 5% royalty or commission fee (varies)**.
 ● TADA! also sponsors a one-act play competition for their Spring Staged Reading Series. Works must be original, unproduced and unpublished one-acts. Plays may be geared toward teen audiences. Call for deadlines.
Needs: "Generally pieces run from 45-70 minutes. Must be enjoyed by children and adults and performed by a cast of children ages 8-17."
Tips: "No redone fairy tales or pieces where children are expected to play adults. Be careful not to condescend when writing for children's theater."
Tips: "No material written by non-Latino writers."

THE TEN-MINUTE MUSICALS PROJECT, P.O. Box 461194, West Hollywood CA 90046. (323)651-4899. Producer: Michael Koppy. Estab. 1987. **Produces 1-10 plays/year**. "Plays performed in Equity regional theaters in the US and Canada." Submit complete script, lead sheets and cassette. Deadline August 31; notification by December 15. Buys performance rights. Submission guidelines for #10 SASE. **Pays $250 royalty advance upon selection, against equal share of performance royalties when produced**.
Needs: Looking for complete short stage musicals playing between 7-14 minutes. Limit cast to 10 (5 women, 5 men).

TENNESSEE STAGE COMPANY AND ACTOR'S CO-OP, P.O. Box 1186, Knoxville TN 37901. (423)546-4280. Fax: (423)546-9677. **Contact:** Tom Parkhill, artistic director. Estab. 1989 Tennessee Stage Company; 1997 Actor's Co-op. **TSC produces 5 plays/year; Co-op produces 8 plays/year**. "Neither company owns a theater building. Each uses a variety of venues in the Knoxville area depending on the needs of the play, the budget, availability, etc. They are professional productions (non-Equity) for a general audience in the Knoxville area." Submit complete ms. Responds in 3 months. **Pays small royalty**.
Needs: The Tennessee Stage Company runs toward comedy, and prefers a play with a subtle approach and feel if there is a message intended. The Actor's Co-op is a broader based company producing mainstream work, off-beat material and experimental work. Any material will be considered. "We try to procure a venue that is suitable for a play we want to do but generally our productions run toward more simple staging. While heavily technical plays will be considered a more simple piece will have a stronger chance of getting an opportunity here."

ANTHONY TERRY JR., 7010 E. Broadway, Tucson AZ 85710. (520)886-9428. Fax: (520)722-6232. E-mail: Nancyla viola@gci-net.com. **Contact:** Nancy LaViola, general manager. Estab. 1976. **Produces 5 plays/year**. Professional productions. Audience is from 5 to 75 years old. Family fun entertainment. Query with synopsis. Responds in 1 month. **Usually makes outright purchase at producer's discretion**.
Needs: Musical melodramas—always fun, funny, slapstick comedy, westerns, 50s, spy spoofs. Total length is 2 hours, includes a 18 minute olio (song and dance theme after the show). Melodrama style—hero and villain and heroine. Cast: 3 women, 5-6 men.
Tips: "We like to use lots of music. We also use a lot of audience participation. Remember a conflict must be in the script. Something the hero has that the villian wants. We like to use fun sets, i.e., volcanoes, elevators, dancing camels, waves, helicopter rides, space ships, etc."

THE THEATER AT MONMOUTH, P.O. Box 385, Monmouth ME 04259. (207)933-9999. E-mail: tamoffice@theatr emonmouth.org. Website: www.theatreatmonmouth.org. **Contact:** David Greenham, managing director: Estab. 1970. **Produces 5-6 titles/year**. "Productions are professional. Children's productions are non-equity, mainstage productions are non-equity." Query with synopsis and character list. Responds in 2 months. **Pays negotiable royalties.**
Needs: "Children's theater (non-musical), productions based on classic fairy tales and children's stories for 4-7 actors, simple set. Also new, full-length, large cast adaptations of classic literature for adult and family audiences.
Tips: "Clear and concise synopsis and character list will get faster response."

THE THEATER OF NECESSITY, 11702 Webercrest, Houston TX 77048. (713)733-6042. Estab. 1981. **Produces 8 plays/year**. Plays are produced in a small professional theater. Submit complete script. Buys performance rights. Responds in 2 years. **Pays standard royalties** (average $500/run) based on size of house for small productions or individual contracts for large productions. "We usually keep script on file unless we are certain we will never use it." Send SASE with script and #10 SASE for response.
Needs: "Any play in a recognizable genre must be superlative in form and intensity. Experimental plays are given an easier read. We move to larger venue if the play warrants the expense."

THEATRE RHINOCEROS, 2926 16th St., San Francisco CA 94103. Website: www.therhino.org. **Contact:** Doug Holsclaw, acting artistic director. Estab. 1977. **Produces 5 plays/year**. Gay and lesbian audience, professional non-equity productions. Query with synopsis. Responds in 6 months. **Pays negotiable royalty**.
Needs: Gay and lesbian works. Cast size no larger than 10.

THEATRE THREE, P.O. Box 512, 412 Main St., Port Jefferson NY 11777-0512. (631)928-9202. Fax: (631)928-9120. Artistic Director: Jeffery Sanzel. Estab. 1969. "We produce an Annual Festival of One-Act Plays on our Second Stage." Deadline for submission, September 30. "We ask for exclusive rights up to and through the festival." Responds in 6 months. SASE for festival guidelines. **Pays $70 for the run of the festival**.
Needs: One-act plays. Maximum length: 40 minutes. "Any style, topic, etc. We require simple, suggested sets and a maximum cast of six. No adaptations, musicals or children's works."
Tips: "Too many plays are monologue-dominant. Please—reveal your characters through action and dialogue."

THEATRE THREE, 2800 Routh St., Dallas TX 75201. (214)871-2933. Fax: (214)871-3139. Contact: Natalie Gaupp, dramaturg. Estab. 1961. **Produces 7 plays/year**. Professional regional theatre, in-the-round. Audience is college age-senior citizens. Query with synopsis. No unsolicited scripts. Responds in 6 months. **Contractual agreements vary**.
Needs: Musicals, dramas, comedies, bills of related one-acts. Modest production requirement; casts no larger than 10.
Tips: No parodies or political commentary/comedy.

THEATRE WEST, 3333 Cahuenga W., Los Angeles CA 90068-1365. (323)851-4839. Fax: (323)851-5286. E-mail: theatrewest@earthlink.net. Website: www.theatrewest.org. **Contact:** Chris DiGiovanni or Doug Haverty. Estab. 1962. "99-seat waiver productions in our theater. Audiences are primarily young urban professionals." Full-length plays only, no one-acts. Submit script, résumé and letter requesting membership. Responds in 4 months. Contracts a percentage of writer's share to other media if produced on MainStage by Theatre West. **Pays royalty** based on gross box office, "equal to all other participants."
Needs: Uses minimalistic scenery.
Tips: "TW is a dues-paying membership company. Only members can submit plays for production. So you must seek membership prior to action for a production. The writers workshop is a weekly developmental workshop, so members should live in southern California."

THEATRE WEST VIRGINIA, P.O. Box 1205, Beckley WV 25802-1205. (304)256-6800. Fax: (304)256-6807. E-mail: twv@cwv.net. Website: http://wvweb.com/www/TWV. **Contact:** Marina Dolinger, artistic director. Estab. 1955. **Produces 6 plays/year**. Professional educational touring theatre—K-6 and 7-12 grade levels. Outdoor drama, musicals. Query with synopsis. Responds in 3 months. **Pays 3-6% royalty**.
Needs: Appropriate material for K through 12. Cast limited to 6 actors/van and truck tour.
Tips: Material needs to be educational, yet entertaining.

N **THEATREWORKS/USA**, 151 W. 26th St., 7th Floor, New York NY 10001. (212)647-1100. Fax: (212)924-5377. **Contact:** Barbara Pasternack, associate artistic director. Estab. 1965. **Produces 3-6 new productions/year**. Professional Equity productions for young audiences. Audition at Equitalle Towers, weekend series. Query with synopsis. Responds in 6 months. Obtains performing rights. **Pays 6% royalty**.
Needs: "One-hour musicals or plays with music written for K-3rd or 3rd-7th grade age groups. Subjects: historical, biography, classic literature, fairy tales with specific point of view, contemporary literature. Limited to 5-6 actors and a portable set. Do not rely on lighting or special effects."
Tips: "No campy, 'fractured' fairy tales, shows specifically written to teach or preach, shows relying heavily on narrators or 'kiddy theater' filled with pratfalls, bad jokes and audience participation. Write smart. Kids see a lot these days, and they are sophisticated. Don't write down to them. They deserve a good, well-told story. Seeing one of our shows will provide the best description."

THEATRICAL OUTFIT, P.O. Box 1555, Atlanta GA 30301. **Contact:** Kate Warner, artistic associate. Estab. 1978. **Produces 4-5 plays/year**. Year round productions. Query with 1 page synopsis, first 10 pages, letter of reference or 1 page résumé and a SAS postcard. Responds in 2 months. **Pays 5-8% royalty**.
Needs: Adaptations of classic works, new plays. Plays that focus on southern literature. Minimal sets.

TROUPE AMERICA INC., 528 Hennepin Ave., Suite 206, Minneapolis MN 55403. (612)333-3302. Fax: (612)333-4337. Contact: Curt Wollan, president/executive director. Estab. 1987. **Produces 10-12 plays/year**. Professional production in Minneapolis or on the road. Intended for general and family audiences as well as community arts series and University Arts Series audiences. Query with synopsis. Responds in 1 year. Buys the right to perform and license the production for 10 years. **Pays 2½-5% royalty**.
Needs: Family holiday musicals—2 hours with intermission and small cast musicals. Biographic musicals—2 hours with intermission. Musical adaptations of famous works—2 hours with intermission. Smaller contained musicals get attention and single set scripts do as well.
Tips: No heavy dramas, political plays (unless satirical) and any play dealing with sex, drugs or violence. The size of the cast is important. The smaller the size, the more likely it will get produced. Economics is a priority.

N TRUSTUS THEATRE, P.O. BOX 11721, Columbia SC 29211-1721. (803)254-9732. Fax: (803)771-9153. **Contact:** Jon Tuttle, literary manager. Estab. 1984. **Produces 13-20 plays/year**. Trustus Mainstage Theatre—T.C.G. Professional Company. Query and synopsis. Responds in 3 months. All rights revert to author after production. **Pays standard royalty**.
Needs: Experimental, hard-hitting, off-the-wall one-act comedies or "dramadies"suitable for open-minded Late-Night series audiences; no topic taboo; no musicals or plays for young audiences. Small cast modest production demands.

N UBU REPERTORY THEATER PUBLICATIONS, 95 Wall St., 21st Floor, New York NY 10005. (212)509-1455. Fax: (212)509-1635. E-mail: uburep@spacelab.net. Website: www.uburep.org. **Contact:** Françoise Kourilsky, artistic director. Estab. 1982. **Produces 4-5 plays/year; publishes 1-2 books/year**. Plays are performed off-Broadway at La Mama E.T.C., New York and Florence Gould Tinker Auditorium. Publishes books by Francophone, contemporary playwrights from Africa, Caribbean, etc. Query with synopsis or submit complete ms. Responds in 3 months. Buys performance, publication and translation rights. **Pays 10% royalty or $50 minimum performance.**
Needs: Contemporary French-language plays. No translations. Prefers small cost.
Tips: "No plays originally written in any language other than French! English translations of French-language plays may be submitted, provided translation rights have been obtained."

UNICORN THEATRE, 3828 Main St., Kansas City MO 64111. (816)531-7529, ext. 18. Fax: (816)531-0421. Website: www.unicorntheatre.org. Producing Artistic Director: Cynthia Levin. **Contact:** Herman Wilson, literary assistant. **Produces 6-8 plays/year**. "We are a professional Equity Theatre. Typically, we produce plays dealing with contemporary issues." Send full script with cover letter, bio, synopsis, character breakdown and SASE. Responds in 8 months.
Needs: Prefers contemporary (post-1950) scripts. No musicals, one-acts, or historical plays. Query (to Herman Wilson) with script, brief synopsis, bio, character breakdown, SASE if script is to be returned, SASP if acknowledgement of receipt is desired. A royalty/prize of $1,000 will be awarded the playwright of any play selected through this process, The National Playwright Award. This script receives production as part of the Unicorn's regular season.

N URBAN STAGES, 17 E. 47th St., New York NY 10017. (212)421-1380. Fax: (212)421-1387. E-mail: UrbanStage @aol.com. Website: www.mint.net/urbanstages.com. **Contact:** T.L. Reilly, producing director. Artistic Director: Frances Hill. Literary Manager: David Sheppard. Estab. 1986. **Produces 2-4 plays/year**. Professional productions off or off off-Broadway—throughout the year. General audience. Submit complete script, one play only. Responds in 4 months. If produced, option for 6 months. **Pays royalty**.
Needs: Both one-act and full-length; generally 1 set or styled playing dual. Good imaginative, creative writing. Cast limited to 3-7.
Tips: "We tend to reject 'living-room' plays. We look for imaginative settings. Be creative and interesting with intellectual content. All submissions should be bound. Send SASE. We are looking for plays with ethnic backgrounds."

WALNUT STREET THEATRE, Ninth and Walnut Streets, Philadelphia PA 19107. (215)574-3550. Fax: (215)574-3598. Producing Artistic Director: Bernard Havard. **Contact:** Beverly Elliott, literary manager. Estab. 1809. **Produces 5 mainstage and 5 studio plays/year**. "Our plays are performed in our own space. WST has 3 theaters—a proscenium (mainstage), 1,052 seats; 2 studios, 79-99 seats. We have a subscription audience, largest in the nation." Query with synopsis, 10-20 pages of dialogue, character breakdown and bio. Writer's must be members of the Dramatists' Guild. Responds in 5 months. Rights negotiated per project. **Pays negotiable royalty or makes outright purchase.**
Needs: "Full-length dramas and comedies, musicals, translations, adaptations and revues. The studio plays must have a cast of no more than four, simple sets."
Tips: "Bear in mind that on the mainstage we look for plays with mass appeal, Broadway-style. The studio spaces are our off-Broadway. No children's plays. Our mainstage audience goes for work that is entertaining and light. Our studio season is where we look for plays that have bite and are more provocative." Include SASE for return of materials.

WATERLOO COMMUNITY PLAYHOUSE, P.O. Box 433, Waterloo IA 50704-0433. (319)235-0367. Fax: (319)235-7489. E-mail: wcpbhct@cedarnet.org. **Contact:** Charles Stilwill, managing artistic director. Estab. 1917. Plays performed by Waterloo Community Playhouse with a volunteer cast. **Produces 11 plays** (7 adult, 4 children's); 1-2 musicals and 9-10 nonmusicals/year; 1-3 originals. **Most unagented submissions**. Works with 1-3 unpublished/unproduced writers annually. "We are one of few theaters with a commitment to new scripts. We do at least one and have done as many as four a year. We have 4,300 season members. We do a wide variety of plays. Our public isn't going to accept nudity, too much sex, too much strong language. We don't have enough Black actors to do all-Black shows. Theater has done plays with as few as 2 characters, and as many as 98. On the main stage, **we usually pay between $400 and $500**. We also produce children's theater. Submit complete script. Please, no loose pages. Reports negatively within 1 year, but acceptance sometimes takes longer if we like it but cannot immediately find the right slot for it. For scripts to be returned, must send proper size SASE."
Needs: "For our Children's Theater and our Adult Annual Holiday (Christmas) show, we are looking for good adaptations of name stories. Most recently: *Miracle on 34th Street, Best Christmas Pageant Ever* and *It's A Wonderful Life*."

WEST COAST ENSEMBLE, P.O. Box 38728, Los Angeles CA 90038. (323)876-9337. Fax: (323)876-8916. Website: http://wcensemble.org. **Contact:** Les Hanson, artistic director. Estab. 1982. **Produces 6 plays/year**. Plays performed at a Hollywood theater. Submit complete script. Responds in 9 months. Obtains exclusive rights in southern California to present the play for the period specified. All ownership and rights remain with the playwright. **Pays $25-45/performance**.
Needs: Prefers a cast of 6-12.
Tips: "Submit the script in acceptable dramatic script format."

SCREENWRITING

Practically everyone you meet in Los Angeles, from your airport cabbie on, is writing a script. It might be a feature film, movie of the week, TV series or documentary, but the sheer amount of competition can seem overwhelming. Some will never make a sale, while others make a decent living on sales and options without ever having any of their work produced. But there are those writers who make a living doing what they love and see their names roll by on the credits. How do they get there? How do *you* get there?

First, work on your writing. You'll improve with each script, so there is no way of getting around the need to write and write some more. It's a good idea to read as many scripts as you can get your hands on. Check your local bookstores and libraries. Script City (8033 Sunset Blvd., Suite 1500, Hollywood CA 90046, (800)676-2522) carries thousands of movie and TV scripts, classics to current releases, as well as books, audio/video seminars and software in their $2 catalog. Book City (6631 Hollywood Blvd., Hollywood CA 90028, (800)4-CINEMA) has film and TV scripts in all genres and a large selection of movie books in their $2.50 catalog.

There are lots of books that will give you the "rules" of format and structure for writing for TV or film. Samuel French (7623 Sunset Blvd., Hollywood CA 90046 (213)876-0570) carries a number of how-to books and reference materials on these subjects. The correct format marks your script as a professional submission. Most successful scriptwriters will tell you to learn the correct structure, internalize those rules—and then throw them away and write intuitively.

Writing for TV

To break into TV you must have spec scripts—work written for free that serves as a calling card and gets you in the door. A spec script showcases your writing abilities and gets your name in front of influential people. Whether a network has invited you in to pitch some ideas, or a movie producer has contacted you to write a first draft for a feature film, the quality of writing in your spec script got their attention and that may get you the job.

It's a good idea to have several spec scripts, perhaps one each for three of the top five shows in the format you prefer to work in, whether it's sitcom (half-hour comedies), episodic (one hour series) or movie of the week (two hour dramatic movies). Perhaps you want to showcase the breadth of your writing ability; your portfolio could include a few prime time sitcoms (i.e., *Friends, Everybody Loves Raymond, Will & Grace, Drew Carey*), and one or two episodics in a particular genre (i.e., *The Sopranos, Law and Order, NYPD Blue* or *Dawson's Creek, Felicity, Buffy the Vampire Slayer*). These are all "hot" shows for writers and can demonstrate your abilities to create believable dialogue for characters already familiar to your intended readers. For TV and cable movies you should have completed original scripts (not sequels to existing movies) and you might also have a few for episodic TV shows.

In choosing the shows you write spec scripts for you must remember one thing: don't write a script for a show you want to work on. If you want to write for *Will & Grace*, for example, you'll send a *Dharma & Greg* script and vice versa. It may seem contradictory, but it is standard practice. It reduces the chances of lawsuits, and writers and producers can feel very proprietary about their show and their stories. They may not be objective enough to fairly evaluate your writing. In submitting another similar type of show you'll avoid those problems while demonstrating comparable skills.

In writing your TV script you must get *inside* the show and understand the characters' internal motivations. You must immerse yourself in how the characters speak, think and interact. Don't introduce new characters in a spec script for an existing show—write believable dialogue for the characters as they are portrayed. Be sure to choose a show that you like—you'll be better able to demonstrate your writing ability through characters you respond to.

You must also understand the external factors. How the show is filmed bears on how you write. Most sitcoms are shot on videotape with three cameras, on a sound stage with a studio audience. Episodics are often shot on film with one camera and include on-location shots. *Dharma and Greg* has a flat, evenly-lit look and takes place in a limited number of locations. *NYPD Blue* has a gritty realism with varying lighting and a variety of settings.

Another important external influence in writing for TV is the timing of commercials in conjunction with the act structure. There are lots of sources detailing the suggested content and length of acts, but generally a sitcom has a teaser (short opening scene), two acts and a tag (short closing scene), and an episodic has a teaser, four acts and a tag. Each act closes with a turning point. Watching TV analytically and keeping a log of events will reveal some elements of basic structure. *Successful Scriptwriting*, by Wolff & Cox (Writer's Digest Books), offers detailed discussions of various types of shows.

Writing for the movies

With feature films you may feel at once more liberated and more bound by structure. An original movie script contains characters you have created, with storylines you design, allowing you more freedom than you have in TV. However, your writing must still convey believable dialogue and realistic characters, with a plausible plot and high-quality writing carried through the roughly 120 pages. The characters must have a problem that involves the audience. When you go to a movie you don't want to spend time watching the *second* worst night of a character's life. You're looking for the big issue that crystallizes a character, that portrays a journey with important consequences.

At the same time you are creating, you should also be constructing. Be aware of the basic three act structure for feature films. Scenes can be of varying lengths, but are usually no longer than three to three and a half pages. Some writers list scenes that must occur, then flesh them out from beginning to end, writing with the structure of events in mind. The beginning and climactic scenes are the easiest; it's how they get there from here that's difficult.

Many novice screenwriters tend to write too many visual cues and camera directions into their scripts. Your goal should be to write something readable, like a "compressed novella." Write succinct resonant scenes and leave the camera technique to the director and producer. In action/adventure movies, however, there needs to be a balance since the script demands more visual direction.

It seems to be easier for TV writers to cross over to movies. Cable movies bridge the two, and are generally less derivative and more willing to take chances with a higher quality show designed to attract an audience not interested in network offerings. Cable is also less susceptible to advertiser pullout, which means it can tackle more controversial topics.

Feature films and TV are very different and writers occupy different positions. TV is a medium for writers and producers; directors work for them. Many TV writers are also producers. In feature films the writers and producers work for the director and often have little or no say about what happens to the work once the script has been sold. For TV the writer pitches the idea; for feature films generally the producer pitches the idea and then finds a writer.

Marketing your scripts

If you intend to make writing your profession you must act professionally. Accepted submission practices should become second nature.

- The initial pitch is made through a query letter, which is no longer than one page with a one paragraph synopsis and brief summary of your credits if they are relevant to the subject of your script.
- Never send a complete manuscript until it is requested.
- Almost every script sent to a producer, studio or agent must be accompanied by a release form. Ask for that company's form when you receive an invitation to submit the whole script. Mark your envelope "release form enclosed" to prevent it being returned unread.
- Always include a self-addressed stamped envelope (SASE) if you want your work returned; a disposable copy may be accompanied by a self-addressed stamped postcard for reply.
- Allow four to six weeks from receipt of your manuscript before writing a follow-up letter.

When your script is requested, be sure it's written in the appropriate format. Unusual binding, fancy covers or illustrations mark an amateur. Three brass brads with a plain or black cover indicate a pro.

There are a limited number of ideas in the world, so it's inevitable that similar ideas occur to more than one person. Hollywood is a buyer's market and a release form states that pretty clearly. An idea is not copyrightable, so be careful about sharing premises. The written expression of that idea, however, can be protected and it's a good idea to do so. The Writers Guild of America can register scripts for television and theatrical motion pictures, series formats, storylines and step outlines. You need not be a member of the WGA to use this service. Copyrighting your work with the Copyright Office of the Library of Congress also protects your work from infringement. Contact either agency for more information and an application form.

If you are a writer, you should write—all the time. When you're not writing, read. There are numerous books on the art, craft and business of screenwriting. See the Publications of Interest at the end of *Writer's Market* for a few or check the catalogs of companies previously mentioned. The different industry trade papers such as *Daily Variety* and *Hollywood Reporter* can keep you in touch with the day to day news and upcoming events. Specialty newsletters such as *Hollywood Scriptwriter* (P.O. Box 10277, Burbank CA 91510, (818)845-5525, http://www.hollywoodscript writer.com) offer tips from successful scriptwriters and agents. The *Hollywood Creative Directory* is an extensive list of production companies, studios and networks that also lists companies and talent with studio deals.

Computer services have various bulletin boards and chat hours for scriptwriters that provide contact with other writers and a chance to share information and encouragement.

It may take years of work before you come up with a script someone is willing to take a chance on. Those years need to be spent learning your craft and understanding the business. Polishing scripts, writing new material, keeping current with the industry and networking constantly will keep you busy. When you do get that call you'll be confident in your abilities and know that your hard work is beginning to pay off.

Information on screenwriting markets listed in the previous edition of *Writer's Market* but not included in this edition can be found in the the General Index.

ALLIED ARTISTS, INC., 859 N. Hollywood Way, Suite 377, Burbank CA 91505. (818)594-4089. **Contact:** John Nichols, vice president, development. Estab. 1990. Produces material for broadcast and cable television, home video and film. **Buys 3-5 scripts/year. Works with 10-20 writers/year**. Buys first rights or all rights. Accepts previously produced material. Responds in 2 months to queries; 3 months to scripts. Submit synopsis/outline. **Pays in accordance with WGA standards** (amount and method negotiable). Written queries only—*no phone pitches.*
Needs: Films, videotapes. Social issue TV special (30-60 minutes); special interest home video topics; instruction and entertainment; positive values feature screenplays.
Tips: "We are looking for positive, up-lifting dramatic stories involving real people situations. Future trend is for more reality-based programming, as well as interactive television programs for viewer participation."

ANGEL FILMS, 967 Highway 40, New Franklin MO 65274-9778. Phone/fax: (573)698-3900. E-mail: angelfilm@aol.com. **Contact:** Matthew Eastman, vice president production. Estab. 1980. Produces material for feature films, television. **Buys 10 scripts/year. Works with 20 writers/year**. Buys all rights. Accepts previously published material (if rights available). Responds in 1 month to queries; 2 months to scripts. Query with synopsis. **Makes outright purchase.** "Our company is a low-budget producer, which means people get paid fairly, but don't get rich."
Needs: Films (35mm), videotapes. "We are looking for projects that can be used to produce feature film and television feature film and series work. These would be in the areas of action adventure, comedy, horror, thriller, science fiction, animation for children." Also looking for direct to video materials.
Tips: "Don't copy others. Try to be original. Don't overwork your idea. As far as trends are concerned, don't pay attention to what is 'in.' By the time it gets to us it will most likely be on the way 'out.' And if you can't let your own grandmother read it, don't send it. Slow down on western submissions. They are not selling. If you wish material returned, enclose proper postage with all submissions. Send SASE for response to queries and return of scripts."

ANGEL'S TOUCH PRODUCTIONS, 4872 Toponga Canyon Blvd., Suite 344, Woodland Hills CA 91364. **Contact:** Phil Nemy, director of development. Estab. 1986. Professional screenplays and teleplays. Send synopsis. Rights negotiated between production company and author. Responds in 8 months. **Payment negotiated.**
Needs: All types, all genres, only full-length teleplays and screenplays—no one-acts.
Tips: "We only seek feature film screenplays, television screenplays, and episodic teleplays. *No phone calls!*"

[N] BAUMGARTEN-PROPHET ENTERTAINMENT, 1640 S. Sepulveda Blvd., Suite 218, Los Angeles CA 90025. (310)996-1885. Fax: (310)996-1892. **Contact:** Adam Merims, producer or John Kapral, creative executive. E-mail: bpeproduction@aol.com. Estab. 1994. Audience is motion picture and television viewers. **Buys 35 scripts/year. Works with 100 writers/year**. Buys motion picture and television rights. Accepts previously published material. Does not return submissions. Responds in 1 month. Query with synopsis. **Pays in accordance with WGA standards** where applicable or through Internal Development Fund.
Needs: Produces 35mm films and videotapes. "We have feature projects in development at Disney, Sony, Sony Family, Fox, Warner Brothers and Bel Air. We have TV projects with Showtime, HBO, TNT and Sony Television. We are always looking for good material."
Tips: Interested in original motion picture, television and cable material. Movies and dramatic series.

BIG EVENT PICTURES, (formerly StoneRoad Production, Inc.), 11288 Ventura Blvd., #909, Studio City CA 91604. E-mail: bigevent1@hotmail.com. **Contact:** Michael Cargile, president. Produces feature films for theaters, cable TV and home video. PG, R, and G-rated films. Responds in 1 month to queries if interested; 2 months requested on submissions. Query with SASE and synopsis.
Needs: Films. All genres. Looking for good material from writers who have taken the time to learn the unique and difficult craft of scriptwriting.
Tips: "Interesting query letters intrigue us—and tell us something about the writer. Query letter should include a short 'log line' or 'pitch' encapsulating 'what this story is about' and should be no more than 1 page in length. We look for unique stories with strong characters and would like to see more action and science fiction submissions. We make movies that we would want to see. Producers are known for encouraging new (e.g. unproduced) screenwriters and giving real consideration to their scripts."

[A] BIG STAR MOTION PICTURES LTD., 13025 Yonge St., #201, Richmond Hill, Ontario L4E 1Z5 Canada. (416)720-9825. Fax: (905)773-3153. E-mail: bigstar@pathcom.com. **Contact:** Frank A. Deluca. Estab. 1991. **Buys 5 scripts/year. Works with 5-10 writers/year**. Responds in 3 months to queries; 3 months to scripts. Submit synopsis first. Scripts should be submitted by agent or lawyer.
Needs: Films (35mm). "We are very active in all medias, but are primarily looking for television projects, cable, network, etc. Family Films are of special interest."

CLC PRODUCTIONS, 1223 Wilshire Blvd., Suite 404, Santa Monica CA 90403. (310)454-0664. Fax: (310)459-2889. E-mail: cathylee@cathylee.com. Website: www.cathylee.com. **Contact:** Alison Doyle, CLC Productions. Est. 1994. T.V. and film. "We are interested in suspense, comedy. action/adventure with a strong female role age 35-45." **Buys 4-5 scripts/year. Works with 5-10 writers/year.** Buys all rights. Responds in 1 month to submissions. Has own financing. Open to co-productions with established companies or producers.

▣ COBBLESTONE FILMS, 1484 Reeves St., Suite 203, Los Angeles CA 90035. E-mail: cstonefilms@aol.com. **Contact:** Jacqui Adler, producer. Estab. 1997. TV and film. Options material 3-12 months. Accepts previously published material. Reponds in 1 month. Query with synopsis. **Pays in accordance with WGA standards**.
Needs: Films 35mm. Looking for completed screenplays only for the following genres: family entertainment, drama, horror, suspense-thrillers.

CODIKOW FILMS, 8899 Beverly Blvd., #719, Los Angeles CA 90048. (310)246-9388. Fax: (310)246-9877. E-mail: codikowflm@aol.com. Website: www.codikowfilms.com. **Contact:** Stacy Codikow, producer. Estab. 1990. **Buys 6 scripts/year. Works with 12 writers/year.** Buys all rights. Responds in 2 months to submissions. Query or résumé. **Pays in accordance with WGA standards.** Submit a synopsis no longer than 1 page via fax, e-mail or letter.
Needs: Films (35mm). Commercial and independent screenplays; good writing—all subjects.
Tips: "Screenwriters should submit ideas for finished screenplays in the form of a one-page synopsis that clearly captures the essence of the story. We are open to developing ideas with writers; however, we prefer completed screenplays."

CPC ENTERTAINMENT, 840 N. Larrabee St., #2322, Los Angeles CA 90069. (310)652-8194. Fax: (310)652-4998. E-mail: chane@compuserve.com. Producer/Director: Peggy Chene. Vice President, Creative Affairs: Sylvie de la Riviere. Development Associate: Louis Farber. Feature and TV. **Buys 15 scripts/year. Works with 24 writers/year.** Buys all rights. Recent production: "In the Eyes of a Stranger," CBS-TV thriller starring Richard Dean Anderson, CBS-TV. Responds in 2 months to written queries; 3 months to submissions. Query with 1 sentence premise, 3 sentence synopsis and résumé. Prefers queries by e-mail. **Makes outright purchase in accordance with WGA minimum.**
 ● CPC Entertainment is looking for scripts of wider budget range, from low independent to high studio.
Needs: Needs feature and TV movie screenplays: small independent, or any budget for thrillers, true stories, action/adventure, character driven stories of any genre.

EAST EL LAY FILMS, 12041 Hoffman St., Studio City CA 91604. (818)769-4565. (818)769-1917. **Contact:** Daniel Kuhn, president. Co-President: Susan Coppola (director). Estab. 1992. Low-budget feature films for television markets. Buys first rights and options for at least 1 year with refusal rights. Query with synopsis and résumé. Pays royalty, makes outright purchase or option fee. Produces and directs own features and documentaries.
Needs: Film loops (35mm), videotapes.

ENTERTAINMENT PRODUCTIONS, INC., 2118 Wilshire Blvd., #744, Santa Monica CA 90403. (310)456-3143. Fax: (310)456-8950. Producer: Edward Coe. **Contact:** M.E. Lee, story editor. Estab. 1971. Produces films for theatrical and television (worldwide) distribution. Material acceptable only if Writer Submission Release, made in any form, is included. Responds in 1 month only if SASE is enclosed.
Needs: Screenplay originals. Query with synopsis and SASE. Price negotiated on a project-by-project basis. Will consider participation, co-production..
Tips: "State what genre the script is and why it has great potential."

▣ JOSEPH FEURY ENTERTAINMENT, 230 West 41st St., Suite 1400, New York NY 10036. (212)221-9090. Fax: (212)221-0606. **Contact:** Joseph Feury, executive producer. Estab. 1982. Buys all rights. Accepts previously produced material. Query with synopsis. Pays negotiated option.
Needs: Films.

FILMSAAVY ENTERTAINMENT, 16931 Dearborn St., Northridge CA 91343. E-mail: filmsaavy@aol.com. Website: www.FilmSaavy.Saavedra.com. **Contact:** Michael Eastin, story editor. Estab. 1995. **Buys 2-5 scripts/year. Works with 5 writers/year.** Buys all rights. Accepts previously published material. Responds in 2 months to queries, 3 months to submissions. Query with synopsis. **Pays in accordance with WGA standards**.
Needs: Produces films (35mm). Feature length motion-picture screenplays based on original ideas. Any genre accepted, but prefer comedies, dramas and historical biographies.
Tips: "Teen slasher films and stories are out. Literary stories with strong characters, fresh ideas and life-affirming themes are what gets our attention."

▣ FOUNTAIN PRODUCTIONS, 500 S. Buena Vista, Burbank CA 91521-0180. **Contact:** Peter M. Green, president. Estab. 1999. Audience is kids, teens, family. **Buys 10 scripts/year. Works with 20 writers/year.** Buys first rights or all rights. Responds in 1 month. Submit completed script. **Pays in accordance with WGA standards.**
Needs: Produces 35mm films.

JACK FREEDMAN PRODUCTIONS, 14225 Ventura Blvd., #200, Sherman Oaks CA 91423. (818)789-9306. **Contact:** Patricia Herskovic, president. Estab. 1988. Commercial films. **Buys 0-10 scripts/year. Works with 10-15 writers/year.** Buys all rights. Accepts previously published material. Responds in 1 week to queries, 1 month to submissions. Query with synopsis, résumé, writing samples, production history. Payment varies.
Needs: Films (35mm).

N **GALLANT ENTERTAINMENT**, 16161 Ventura Blvd., #664, Encino CA 91436. **Contact:** Leslie Parness, vice president. **Works with 10 writers/year.** Buys all rights. Accepts previously published material. Responds to queries immediately. Query with synopsis.
Tips: "We are interested in character-driven scripts. No children stories and no scripts with a lot of violence."

BETH GROSSBARD PRODUCTIONS, 5168 Otis Ave., Tarzana CA 91356. Fax: (818)705-7366 or (310)841-5934. Producer: Beth Grossbard. **Contact:** K. Jacobs, development associate. Estab. 1994. **Buys 6 scripts/year. Works with 20 writers/year.** First rights and true life story rights. Responds in 3 months or less to queries and treatments; 4 months to submissions. Query with synopsis or treatment/outline. **Pays in accordance with WGA standards.**
Needs: Films (35mm).
Tips: "Develops material for television, cable and feature film markets. Areas of interest include: true stories, family dramas, social issues, young adult themed and children's stories, historical/biographical accounts. Will also consider outline/treatments for unpublished manuscripts, small press books, or concept pages for film development."

HBO FILMS, 2049 Century Park E., Suite 3600, Los Angeles CA 90067. Fax: (310)201-9552. Website: www.hbo.com. **Contact:** Bettina Moss, story editor. Contact by fax or mail only. Responds in 1 month. Query with synopsis one page or shorter. **Payment varies.**
Needs: Features for TV. Looks at all genres except family films or films with children as main protagonists. Focus on socially relevant material.
Tips: "Make sure industry standards are adhered to. Not interested in looking at work that is unprofessionally presented. Only submit synopsis if you have a true story or a fiction completed script or book. Not interested in partially completed projects."

HINTERLAND ENTERTAINMENT, 13547 Ventura Blvd. #294, Sherman Oaks CA 91423. E-mail: hinterent@aol.com. **Contact:** Karen Lee Arbeeny, producer/director. Estab. 1996. All audiences. Buys film, TV, novelization rights. Accepts previously published material. Responds in 2 months. Query. **Payment varies.**
Needs: Character-driven, large budget action or thriller, romantic comedy, female-driven, historical drama/epic. Screenplays for theatrical or MOW accepted; TV scripts for 1 hour drama or sitcom accepted.

INTERNATIONAL HOME ENTERTAINMENT, 1440 Veteran Ave., Suite 650, Los Angeles CA 90024. (323)663-6940. **Contact:** Jed Leland, Jr., assistant to the president. Estab. 1976. Buys first rights. Responds in 2 months. Query. **Pays in accordance with WGA standards.**
● Looking for material that is international in scope.
Tips: "Our response time is faster on average now (3-6 weeks), but no replies without a SASE. *No unsolicited scripts.*We do not respond to unsolicited phone calls."

MARTY KATZ PRODUCTIONS, 1250 6th St., Suite 205, Santa Monica CA 90401. (310)260-8501. Fax: (310)260-8502. **Contact:** Frederick Levy, vice president, development. Estab. 1992. Produces material for all audiences. Buys first, all and film rights. Accepts previously produced material. Responds in 1 month. "One page query letter by fax or mail. We will respond if interested in reading."
Needs: Films (35mm).

N **THE KAUFMAN COMPANY**, 808 Wilshire Blvd, 3rd Floor, Santa Monica CA 90401. Website: www.thekaufmancompany.com. **Contact:** Gregg Tilson, director of development or Lynn DiPaola, story editor. Estab. 1990. Intended for all audiences. **Buys 5-10 scripts/year. Works with 10 writers/year.** Buys all rights. Responds in 3 weeks to queries, 3 months to submissions. Query with synopsis. **Pays in accordance with WGA standards.**
Needs: We option screenplays and manuscripts for television, cable and film. "Must be a truly engaging story—no personal slice-of-life melodramas."

LICHT/MUELLER FILM CORP.. E-mail: LichtMueller@hotmail.com. Website: http://recoil.simplenet.com/lm/. **Contact:** Winston Stromberg, creative assistant. Estab. 1983. Produces material for all audiences. Accepts previously produced material. Responds in 1 month to queries; 3 months to submissions. Query with synopsis.
Needs: Films (35mm). "Scripts for feature films."
Tips: "We tend to focus on comedy, but are open to most other genres. As per our new policy, submissions may only be made via our website e-mail. We are looking for treatments and screenplays for feature films."

LOCKWOOD FILMS (LONDON) INC., 12569 Boston Dr., RR #41, London, Ontario N6H 5L2 Canada. Phone/fax: (519)657-3994. E-mail: mark.mccurdy@odyssey.on.ca. President: Nancy Johnson. Estab. 1974. Audience is entertainment and general broadcast for kids 9-12 and family viewing. **Works with 5-6 writers/year.** Submit query with synopsis, résumé or sample scripts. "Submissions will not be considered unless a proposal submission agreement is signed. We will send one upon receiving submissions." **Pays negotiated fee.**
Needs: Family entertainment: series, seasonal specials, mini-series, and movies of the week. Also feature films, documentaries.

Tips: "Potential contributors should have a fax machine and should be prepared to sign a 'proposal submission agreement.' We are in development with national broadcaster on live-action family drama series. Looking for international co-production opportunities."

N A LUMIERE, 8079 Selma Ave., Los Angeles CA 90046. (323)650-6773. Fax: (323)650-7339. E-mail: steve@lumiere-films.com. **Contact:** Steve Shedd, executive assistant. Estab. 1984. Produces material for the general audience. **Buys 5 scripts/year. Works with 10 writers/year.** Accepts previously produced material. Responds in 2 months. Query through known agent or attorney. **Pay negotiated on case by case bases.**
Needs: Films (35mm). "Screenplays which will attract major directing and acting talent, regardless of genre or perceived commerciality."

MEDIACOM DEVELOPMENT CORP., P.O. Box 6331, Burbank CA 91510-6331. (818)594-4089. **Contact:** Felix Girard, director/program development. Estab. 1978. **80% freelance written. Buys 8-12 scripts/year from unpublished/unproduced writers. 50% of scripts produced are unagented submissions.** Buys all rights or first rights. Query with samples. Responds in 1 month. Written query only. Please do not call.
Needs: Produces films, multimedia kits, tapes and cassettes, slides and videotape with programmed instructional print materials, broadcast and cable television programs. Publishes software ("programmed instruction training courses"). Negotiates payment depending on project. Looking for new ideas for CD-ROM titles.
Tips: "Send short samples of work. Especially interested in flexibility to meet clients' demands, creativity in treatment of precise subject matter. We are looking for good, fresh projects (both special and series) for cable and pay television markets. A trend in the audiovisual field that freelance writers should be aware of is the move toward more interactive video disc/computer CRT delivery of training materials for corporate markets."

N MEGA FILMS, INC., P.O. Box 6732, Beverly Hills CA 90212. (818)985-6342. **Contact:** Betsy Chory, vice president. Audience is women, ages 18-49. Buys all rights. Responds in 1 month to queries, 2 months to submissions. Query with synopsis, followed by a signed submission release. **Pays in accordance with WGA standards.**
Needs: Films (35mm). "Our primary focus is Movies for Television. We also look for feature, low-budget, independent film material."

N MICHAEL MELTZER PRODUCTIONS, 8530 Holloway Dr., #327, Los Angeles CA 90069. (310)289-0702. E-mail: melmax@aol.com. **Contact:** Michael Meltzer, producer. Responds in 1 month to queries; 2 months to submissions. Query with synopsis.
Needs: Produces 35mm films.

N MENDILLO/FORM PRODUCTIONS, 4262 Wilshire Blvd., Los Angeles CA 91604. (323)965-1884. **Contact:** Tag Mendillo, CEO. Estab. 1995. Film/TV. **Buys 1-2 scripts/year. Works with 20 writers/year.** Buys first rights or all rights. Accepts previously published material. Responds in 1 month. Catalog for #10 SASE. Query with synopsis or submit completed script. **Pays 1½-2% minimum; 3-5% maximum royalty or makes outright purchase $25,000.**
Needs: Produces 35mm films. Motion picture scripts, treatments or books that are cinematic and well written.

N MINDSTORM LLC, 1434 Sixth St., Suite 1, Santa Monica CA 91401. **Contact:** Karina Duffy, president. Estab. 1998. Audience is mid 20s-30s. **Buys 6 scripts/year. Works with 8 writers/year.** Buys all rights. Responds in 1 month. Query with synopsis with résumé, writing samples, production history. **Pays in accordance with WGA standards.**
Needs: Videotapes.
Tips: "Create a script that is unique, has good character development and a solid point to it." Looking for talented young up and coming directors with shorts. Looking for female driven scripts/mostly drama or romantic comedy.

N MONAREX HOLLYWOOD CORPORATION, 9421½ W. Pico Blvd., Los Angeles CA 90035. **Contact:** Chris D. Nebe, president. Estab. 1978. All audiences. **Buys 3-4 scripts/year. Works with 5-10 writers/year.** Buys all rights. Responds in 1 month. Query with synopsis. **Makes outright purchase in accordance with WGA standards or as negotiated.**
Needs: Produces 35mm film, videotapes. Needs dramatic material with strong visuals, action, horror, dance, romantic comedies, anything commercially viable. We are only interested in completed screenplays.

N NHO ENTERTAINMENT, 550 Euclid St., Santa Monica CA 90402. E-mail: nho_ent@hotmail.com. Website: www.nhoentertainment.com. **Contact:** Mark Costa, partner. Estab. 1999. All audiences. **Buys 5-10 scripts/year. Works with 10-15 writers/year.** Buys all rights. Accepts previously pubished material. Responds in 1 month. Catalog for #10 SASE. Prefers query with synopsis with résumé, optional writing samples, production history. **Pays in accordance with WGA standards.**
Needs: Films, videotapes, multimedia kits, tapes and cassettes. "We are currently accepting all forms of submissions and encourage all writers with material to send query letters."

ORBIT PICTURES, 714 N. LaBrea Ave., Hollywood CA 90038. (213)525-2626. E-mail: orbit@orbitEG.com. **Contact:** Kevin Moreton, vice president, production. Estab. 1987. Feature film; theatrical audience. **Buys 5 scripts/year. Works with 15 writers/year.** Buys all rights. Accepts previously published material. Responds in 1 month. Query with synopsis. **Buys option and writing fees against a purchase price.**
Needs: Films (35mm).
Tips: "Looking for well-written, distinctive stories in script form, or suitable for adaptation to script form, to serve as the basis for our feature film projects: drama, comedy, sci-fi, thrillers and horror."

■ **TOM PARKER MOTION PICTURES**, 3941 S. Bristol, #285, Santa Ana CA 92704. (714)549-9210. Fax: (714)549-9219. President: Tom Parker. **Contact:** Jennifer Phelps, script/development. Produces and distributes feature-length motion pictures worldwide for theatrical, home video, pay and free TV. Also produces short subject special interest films (30, 45, 60 minutes). **Works with 5-10 scripts/year.** Responds in 6 months. "Follow the instructions herein and do not phone for info or to inquire about your script."
Needs: "Complete script *only* for low budget (under $1 million) "R" or "PG" rated action/thriller, action/adventure, comedy, adult romance (R), sex comedy (R), family action/adventure to be filmed in 35mm film for the theatrical and home video market. (Do not send TV movie scripts, series, teleplays, stage plays). *Very limited dialogue.* Scripts should be action-oriented and fully described. Screen stories or scripts OK, but no camera angles please. No heavy drama, documentaries, social commentaries, dope stories, weird or horror. Violence or sex OK, but must be well motivated with strong story line." Submit synopsis and description of characters with finished scripts. Makes outright purchase: $5,000-25,000. Will consider participation, co-production.
Tips: "Absolutely will not return scripts or report on rejected scripts unless accompanied by SASE."

[N] [□] [A] PHASE I PRODUCTIONS, 429 Santa Monica Blvd., Suite #610, Santa Monica CA 90401. Executive Vice President: Kristine Schwarz. **Contact:** Dr. Ransom, director of development. Estab. 1995. Film and TV audiences. **Buys 12 scripts/year.** Buys all rights. Responds in 2 weeks to queries; 2 months to submissions. Submissions must not be unsolicited. Must come through agent or attorney or will be returned. **Pays in accordance with WGA standards.**
Needs: Films. Feature film and television and cable movies.

POP/ART FILM FACTORY, 513 Wilshire Blvd., #215, Santa Monica CA 90401. E-mail: dzpff@earthlink.net. Website: www.home.earthlink.net/~dzpff. **Contact:** Daniel Zirilli, director. Estab. 1990. Produces material for "all audiences/ features films." Query with synopsis. **Pays on per project basis.**
Needs: Film (35mm), documentaries, multimedia kits. "Looking for interesting productions of all kinds. We're producing 3 feature films/year, and 15-20 music-oriented projects. Also exercise and other special interest videos."
Tips: "Be original. Do not play it safe. If you don't receive a response from anyone you have ever sent your ideas to, or you continually get rejected, don't give up if you believe in yourself. Good luck and keep writing!" Will look at "reels" ¾ or VHS.

■ **PROMARK ENTERTAINMENT GROUP**, 3599 Cahuenga Blvd. W., Los Angeles CA 90026. (213)878-0404. Fax: (213)878-0486. E-mail: gwishnick@promarkgroup.com. **Contact:** Gil-Adrienne Wishnick, vice president creative affairs. Promark is a foreign sales company, producing theatrical films for the foreign market. **Buys 8-10 scripts/year. Works with 8-10 writers/year.** Buys all rights. Responds in 1 month to queries, 2 months to submissions. Query with synopsis. **Makes outright purchase.**
● Promark is concentrating on action-thrillers in the vein of *The Net* or *Marathon Man*. They are not looking for science fiction as much this year and are concentrating on suspense/action stories.
Needs: Film (35mm). "We are looking for screenplays in the action thriller genre. Our aim is to produce lower budget (3 million and under) films that have a solid, novel premise—a smart but smaller scale independent film. Our films are male-oriented, urban in setting. We try to find projects with a fresh premise, a clever hook and strong characters. We will also consider a family film, but not a drama or a comedy. Again, these family films need to have an element of action or suspense. We are not interested in comedies, dramas or horror films, ever. Among the recent films we've produced are: "Contaminated Man," a medical thriller, starring William Hurt and Peter Weller; "Pilgrim" with Ray Liotta, which follows an amnesiac's search for himself and a fortune he has stolen; "After Alice," a quirky tale of homicide and betrayal starring Kiefer Sutherland."

■ **RANDWELL PRODUCTIONS, INC.**, 1608 Pacific Ave., Suite 205, Venice CA 90291. **Contact:** Tom Kageff, vice president. Estab. 1997. TV and features audience. **Buys 3-4 scripts/year. Works with 2-3 writers/year.** Buys all rights. Responds in 2 weeks to queries; 3 months to submissions. Query with synopsis. **Pays in accordance with WGA standards.**
Needs: Films (35mm). No sci-fi, no westerns. Good character pieces with a strong plot and/or strong concepts.
Tips: "Please keep synopsis to no more than one page. We hardly if ever request a copy of unsolicited material so don't be surprised if we pass."

■ **REEL LIFE WOMEN**, 10158 Hollow Glen Circle, Bel Air CA 90077. (310)271-4722. E-mail: reellifewomen@co mpuserve.com. Co-President: Joanne Parrent. Estab. 1996. Mass audiences. **Buys 3-4 scripts/year.** Accepts previously produced material. Responds in 2 months. Query with synopsis, résumé and SASE for response to query. **Pays in accordance with WGA standards.**

Needs: Films. Looking for full-length scripts for feature films or television movies only. (No series or episode TV scripts.) Must be professionally formatted (courier 12pt.) and under 130 pages. All genres considered particularly drama, comedy, action, suspense.

Tips: "Must be professional screenwriters. We are not interested in writers who don't know their craft well. That said, we are looking for interesting, unique stories, which have good roles for actresses. We are not interested in women in stereotypical roles, as the male hero's sidekick, as passive helpmates, etc."

[N] TIM REID PRODUCTIONS, One New Millennium Dr., Petersburg VA 23805. (804)957-4200. E-mail: jarenef@ nmstudios.com. **Contact:** Jarene Fleming, development executive. Estab. 1996. **Produces 2 films/year.** MOW's for network TV. Query with synopsis. Buys film rights in perpetuity. Responds in 3 weeks to submissions. **Makes outright purchase of $40,000-75,000.**
Needs: Multicultural TV movies with positive black images.
Tips: Does not want to see stereotypical urban dysfunctional premises. "Our deal is with Procter & Gamble for a guarantee of 2 films/year with multicultural, conservative family values."

THE SHELDON/POST COMPANY, 1437 Rising Glen Rd., Los Angeles CA 90069. Producers: David Sheldon, Ira Post. Estab. 1989. Produces feature films as well as movies and series for television. Options and acquires all rights. Responds in 2 months. Query with 1-2 page synopsis, 2-3 sample pages and SASE. "Do not send scripts or books until requested. If the synopsis is of interest, you will be sent a release form to return with your manuscript. No phone inquiries." **Pays in accordance with WGA standards.**
Needs: "We look for all types of material, including comedy, family stories, suspense dramas, horror, sci-fi, thrillers, action-adventure." True stories should include news articles or other documentation.
Tips: "A synopsis should tell the entire story with the entire plot—including a beginning, a middle and an end. The producers have been in business with 20th Century Fox, Orion/MGM, Columbia Pictures and currently have contracts with Montel Williams, Columbia Tri-Star and Paramount Pictures. Most recent productions: "Grizzly Adams and the Legend of Dark Mountain" and "Secrets of a Small Town.""

SKYLARK FILMS, 1123 Pacific St., Santa Monica CA 90405. Phone/fax: (310)396-5753. E-mail: skylarkden@aol.c om. **Contact:** Brad Pollack, producer. Estab. 1990. **Buys 6 scripts/year.** *No unsolicited screenplays will be accepted.* Buys first or all rights. Accepts previously produced material. Responds in 1 month to queries; 2 months to submissions. Query with synopsis. Option or other structures depending on circumstances. **Pays in accordance with WGA standards.**
Needs: Films (TV, cable, feature).
 • Skylark Films is now seeking action, suspense and thrillers.
Tips: "True stories of romance or tragedy/redemption stories and contemporary issues for TV mows and cable. High concept, high stakes, action or romantic comedy for feature film."

SPECTACOR FILMS, 9000 Sunset Blvd., #1550, West Hollywood CA 90069. Fax: (310)247-0412. E-mail: spectacorfi lms@hotmail.com. **Contact:** David Newlon. Estab. 1988. HBO audiences. **Buys 3-4 scripts/year. Works with 10-12 writers/year.** Buys all rights. Responds in 1 month to queries; 3 months to submissions. Query with synopsis. **Pays small option money applicable to $40-50,000 purchase price.**
Needs: Films. Low budget action scripts. Should be 105 pages or less. Cop/action stories, buddy action stories. Unique hook or idea. Hero should be male in his 30's.
Tips: "Have an action script with something truly unique. Use proper script format with few attachments."

SPIRIT DANCE ENTERTAINMENT, 1023 North Orange Dr., Los Angeles CA 90038-2317. (323)512-7988. E-mail: meridian39301@earthlink.net. Contact: Robert Wheaton, story editor. Estab. 1997. Intelligent and hip persons between the ages of 15-50. **Buys 1-5 scripts/year. Works with 1-5 writers/year.** Buys all rights including motion picture and TV rights. Responds in 2 months. Query. **Pays in accordance with WGA standards.**
Needs: Films (35mm). "Feature length (approximately 90-120 pages) scripts that are well-crafted with a strong emotional core and well-developed characters. We are particularly interested in female driven stories and material that explores different cultures. Will consider material of almost any genre as long as it is presented with some level of sophistication. Think Oscar-caliber material for a general audience. As we also have a music division, we welcome music driven material with strong characters.
Tips: "Material should demonstrate not only a writer's passion for screenwriting, but also the writer's passion for the material. Don't be afraid to submit difficult material, but the writing must be exceptional. Of course all material must be submitted through a WGA signatory agent, entertainment attorney or a bona fide production company. As our needs change, the submitter should always contact the company first before sending anything longer than a logline or brief synopsis. Also look to the films that Forest Whitaker has been involved either as an actor or director as a guide."

[N] [A] STUDIO MERRYWOOD, 1199 Whitney Ave., Apt. G7, Hamden CT 06517-2804. Phone/fax: (203)777-6957. E-mail: merrywood@compuserve.com. Website: http://ourworld.compuserve.com/homepages/Merrywood. **Contact:** Raul daSilva, creative director. Estab. 1984. Produces feature films, documentaries. "We are not seeking any externally written screenplays for features but will engage produced screenwriters as consultants if they have been further recognized in the industry through leadership or international competitive festival prizes."

● STUDIO Merrywood is currently engaged in creating a database for Bardsworld.com, a registered, future website that can be seen in early development form at the above, second website listing.

Needs: "Proprietary material only. We seek writers, specifically with backgrounds in English education who can develop exercises in grammar, word and literary games and puzzles, to be published in Bardsworld.com. All rights will be purchased as a buyout with no royalties paid. For detail, see the website. As above, we are also seeking feature screenwriters who have taught screenwriting or have accomplished a profile in the industry. We seek script reviewers and editors for contracted fees."

Tips: "This is not a market for novice writers. We are a small, creative shop and cannot train neophyte, unpublished or unproduced writers who would best try larger markets and media facilities. We cannot return or even acknowledge any unsolicited material and will discard such material. Those qualified please contact us first by e-mail with your qualifications and your offerings."

N TOO NUTS PRODUCTIONS, L.P., 1511 Sawtelle Blvd., Suite 288, Los Angeles CA 90025. (310)967-4532. E-mail: toonutsproductions@yahoo.com. Website: www.anonymouse.net. **Contact:** Ralph Scott, president/co-executive producer. Estab. 1994. Audience is children. **Buys 4-10 scripts/year. Works with 4-6 writers/year.** Buys both first and all rights; project dependent. Responds in 3 months to queries; 6 months to submissions. Query with synopsis. Submit résumé, writing samples, production history, character, thumbnails if available. **Pays negotiable royalty or makes outright purchase.**
Needs: Videotapes, multimedia kits, CD-ROMs, CDs and cassettes. 1. 30 minute television edutainment with a twist. Our motto: "Creatively entertaining . . . while covertly educating." 2. Storylines for our current television and multimedia state, including "Toad Pizza," "The Salivating-Salamander," "The Contest-Ants," "The Suburban Cowbows," "The De-Stinktive Skunk," "Anonymous," etc. Serves in development: "Anonymouse," etc.
Tips: "Suggestion: Use the words 'Too Nuts' at least twice in your query. If you don't know how to giggle all the way to the bank, don't contact us. If you've already exorcised your inner child, don't contact us either!"

N IRA TRATTNER PRODUCTIONS, 6605 Iris Dr., Los Angeles CA 90068. **Contact:** Ira Trattner, president. Estab. 1985. **Buys 3-5 scripts/year. Works with 10 writers/year.** Buys motion picture rights. Accepts previously published material. Responds to queries in 1 month; to submissions in 3 months. Submit completed script with résumé and production history. **Payment negotiable.**
Needs: Produces 35mm films. "We need well written, unique screenplays with character development, story dialogue.
Tips: "I am only looking for screenplays that will attract A-List talent and directors for both studio and independent feature films."

VM BUTTERFLY—von Garnier-McCorkindale Entertainment. Fax: (323)954-8222. Producer: Laura McCorkindale. Director: Katja von Garnier. Estab. 1991. **Options 20 scripts/year.** Option includes purchase price which incorporates all rights. **Purchase price negotiable.** "Fax one page detailed synopsis of completed screenplay to the attention of Ilysoa Bozza. Also include genre type and 1-2 sentence logline at the top of synopsis and your phone number—all on the same one page. We will respond within 1 month if we want to see your screenplay."
Needs: Feature film screenplays. Our films range from medium budget intelligent, artistic independent films to big budget, commercial studio films. All genres accepted (favorites: dramas, sophisticated romantic comedies, drama-comedies, magical, metaphysical/spiritual).
Projects: In development: "Jump" at Tri Star, "Griffin and Sabine" at Interscope, "Rhinopsody" at Constantin, "Bandits" remake at Warner Brothers. Released: "Bandits" (released in U.S. 5/99) and "Makin Up!"
Tips: "Take time writing your synopsis and be detailed! Synopsis should be as well written as your screenplay and not more than one page. Although we are looking for all types of screenplays, we are especially drawn to commercial, innovative, magical and inspirational stories that enlighten, instill humanity and entertain. We do not accept unsolicited phone calls, so please correspond only via fax."

THE WOOFENILL WORKS, INC., 516 E. 81st St., Suite #3, New York NY 10028-2530. (212)734-2578. Fax: (212)734-3186. E-mail: woofenill@earthlink.net. Website: home.earthlink.net/~woofenill/. **Contact:** Kathy Winthrop, creative executive. Estab. 1990. Theatrical audience. **Buys 4-7 scripts/year. Works with 10 writers/year.** Buys all rights. No previously published material. Responds in 2 months to queries; 4 months to submissions. Query with synopsis. **Acquires option, then payment on production.**
Needs: Films (35mm).
Tips: "First review the company's website and in particular, the section General Business Parameters."

ZACHARY ENTERTAINMENT, 273 S. Swall Dr., Beverly Hills CA 90211-2612. Fax: (310)289-9788. E-mail: zacharyent@aol.com. **Contact:** David O. Miller, development associate. Estab. 1981. Audience is film goers of all ages, television viewers. **Buys 5-10 scripts/year. Works with 30 writers/year.** Rights purchased vary. Produced *The Tie That Binds*, feature film for Hollywood Pictures, a division of Walt Disney Studios and *Carriers*, CBS-TV movie. Responds in 2 weeks to queries; 3 months to submissions. Query with synopsis. **Payment varies.**
Needs: Films for theatrical, cable and network television release.
Tips: "Submit logline (one line description) and a short synopsis of storyline. Short biographical profile, focus on professional background. SASE required for all mailed inquiries. If submissions are sent via e-mail, subject must include specific information or else run the risk of being deleted as junk mail. All genres accepted but ideas must be commercially viable, high concept, original and marketable."

Syndicates

Newspaper syndicates distribute columns, cartoons and other written material to newspapers around the country—and sometimes around the world. Competition for syndication slots is stiff. The number and readership of newspapers are dropping. With paper costs high, there are fewer pages and less money to spend in filling them. Coveted spots in general interest, humor and political commentary are held by big-name columnists such as Ellen Goodman, Bob Herbert and Cal Thomas. And multitudes of aspiring writers wait in the wings, hoping one of these heavy hitters will move on to something else and leave the spotlight open.

Although this may seem discouraging, there are in fact many areas in which less-known writers are syndicated. Syndicates are not looking for general interest or essay columns. What they are looking for are fresh voices that will attract readers. As consumer interests and lifestyles change, new doors are being opened for innovative writers capable of covering emerging trends.

Most syndicates distribute a variety of columns, cartoons and features. Although the larger ones are usually only interested in running ongoing material, smaller ones often accept short features and one-shots in addition to continuous columns. Specialized syndicates—those that deal with a single area such as business—often sell to magazines, trade journals and other business publications as well as to newspapers.

THE WINNING COMBINATION

In presenting yourself and your work, note that most syndicated columnists start out writing for local newspapers. Many begin as staff writers, develop a following in a particular area, and are then picked up by a syndicate. Before approaching a syndicate, write for a paper in your area. Develop a good collection of clips that you feel is representative of your best writing.

New ideas are paramount to syndication. Sure, you'll want to study the popular columnists to see how their pieces are structured (most are short—from 500-750 words—and really pack a punch), but don't make the mistake of imitating a well-known columnist. Syndicates are looking for original material that is timely, saleable and original. Do not submit a column to a syndicate on a subject it already covers. The more unique the topic, the greater your chances. Most importantly, be sure to choose a topic that interests you and one you know well.

APPROACHING MARKETS

Request a copy of a syndicate's writer's guidelines. It will give you information on current needs, submission standards and response times. Most syndicates prefer a query letter and about six sample columns or writing samples and a SASE. You may also want to include a client list and business card if available. If you have a particular area of expertise pertinent to your submission, mention this in your letter and back it up by sending related material. For highly specialized or technical matter, provide credentials to show you are qualified to handle the topic.

In essence, syndicates act as agents or brokers for the material they handle. Writing material is usually sold as a package. The syndicate will promote and market the work to newspapers (and sometimes to magazines) and keep careful records of sales. Writers receive 40-60 percent of gross receipts. Some syndicates may also pay a small salary or flat fee for one-shot items.

Syndicates usually acquire all rights to accepted material, although a few are now offering writers and artists the option of retaining ownership. In selling all rights, writers give up ownership and future use of their creations. Consequently, sale of all rights is not the best deal for writers, and has been the reason many choose to work with syndicates that buy less restrictive rights. Before signing a contract with a syndicate, you may want to go over the terms with an attorney or with an agent who has a background in law. The best contracts will usually offer the writer a percentage of gross receipts (as opposed to net receipts) and will not bind the writer for longer than five years.

THE SELF-SYNDICATION OPTION

Many writers choose to self-syndicate. This route allows you to retain all rights, and gives you the freedom of a business owner. But as a self-syndicated writer, you must also act as your own manager, marketing team and sales force. You must develop mailing lists, and a pricing, billing and collections structure.

Payment is usually negotiated on a case-by-case basis. Small newspapers may offer only $10-20 per column, but larger papers may pay much more (for more information on pay rates, see How Much Should I Charge? on page 61). The number of papers you deal with is only limited by your marketing budget and your tenacity.

If you self-syndicate, be aware that some newspapers are not copyrighted, so you should copyright your own material. It's less expensive to copyright columns as a collection than individually. For more information on copyright procedures, see Copyrighting Your Writing in the Business of Writing section.

FOR MORE INFORMATION . . .

A complete listing of syndicates with contact names and the features they represent can be found in the *Editor & Publisher Syndicate Directory* (11 W. 19th St., New York NY 10011). The weekly magazine, *Editor & Publisher*, also has news articles about syndicates and can provide you with information about changes and events in the industry.

Information on syndicates listed in the previous edition of *Writer's Market* but not included in this edition can be found in the General Index.

N **ARKIN MAGAZINE SYNDICATE, INC.**, 300 Bayview Dr., Suite A-8, Sunny Isles Beach FL 33160-4747. **Contact:** Mitzi Roberg, editorial director. Estab. 1958. **20% freelance written by writers on contract; 80% freelance written on a one-time basis.** "We regularly purchase articles from several freelancers for syndication in trade and professional magazines." Accepts previously published submissions, if all rights haven't been sold. Responds in 3 weeks. Buys all North American magazine and newspaper rights. **Pays on acceptance.**
Needs: Magazine articles (nonfiction, 750-2,200 words), directly relating to business problems common to several different types of businesses and photos (purchased with written material). "We are in dire need of the 'how-to' business article." No article series or columns. Submit complete ms; SASE required. **Pays 3-10¢/word**; $5-10 for photos; "actually, line drawings are preferred instead of photos."
Tips: "Study a representative group of trade magazines to learn style, needs and other facets of the field."

ARTISTMARKET.COM , 35336 Spring Hill, Farmington Hills MI 48331-2044. (248)661-8585. Fax: (248)788-1022. E-mail: editor@artistmarket.com. Website: www.artistmarket.com. **Contact:** David Kahn, editor. Estab. 1996. Syndicates to magazines, newspapers and internet. Send samples. See guidelines on website.
Needs: Fillers, short humor features, cartoon panels, political cartoons, comic strips, puzzles. **Pays 50% author's percentage.** Currently syndicates cartoonists, comic strips, puzzles, fillers, etc. Publishes "www.artistmarket.com" website directed to newspaper, magazine editors and website publishers. Submit written features in 250 words or less via e-mail, postal mail or disk (PC format).

AUTO DIGEST, P.O. Box 459, Prineville OR 97754-0459. Phone: (541)923-4688. Fax: (815)346-9002. E-mail: adigest@iname.com. **Contact:** Bill Schaffer, co-owner. Estab. 1992. **17% written by writers on contract. Buys 100 features/year. Works with 3-4 writers/year.** Syndicates to newspapers and internet. Responds in 2 months. Buys first North American serial rights. Pays when paid by publication. Query only.
Needs: Uses newspaper columns and news items. **All writers equally split fee after expenses.** Currently syndicates: *New Car Reviews*, by Bill and Barbara Schaffer (800-1,000 words plus photo); *Auto Update* and *Car Quiz*, by Bill and Barbara Schaffer (400-500 words); *Auto Forum*, by Chip Keen (400-500 words); *Collector Cars*, by J.C. Chaney Jr. (800-1,000 words plus photo).

BLACK PRESS SERVICE, INC., 166 Madison Ave., New York NY 10016. (212)686-6850. Fax: (212)686-7308. **Contact:** Roy Thompson, editor. Estab. 1966. **10% written on contract; 10% freelance written on a one-time basis. Buys hundreds of features/year. Works with hundreds of writers/year.** Syndicates to magazines, newspapers and radio. Responds in 2 months. Buys all rights. Submit complete ms.
Needs: Magazine and newspaper columns; news items; magazine and newspaper features; radio broadcast material. Purchases single (one shot) features and articles series (current events oriented). **Pays variable flat rate.** Currently syndicates Bimonthly Report, by staff (roundup of minority-oriented news).

CLEAR CREEK FEATURES, P.O. Box 35, Rough & Ready CA 95975. **Contact:** Mike Drummond, editor. Estab. 1988. **50% written on contract; no one-shots. Works with 10 writers/year.** Syndicates to magazines and newspapers. Responds in 1 month. Buys first North American serial, all and second serial (reprint) rights. Submit clips of published work.
Needs: Fiction, magazine and newspaper columns, magazine features, maximum length 700 words. **Pays 50% author's percentage.** Currently syndicates *Coping in the Country* (humor); *The Voice of Experience*, by various authors (humor/commentary), *This Old Klutz*, by various authors (humor), *Another Senior Moment!* by various authors.
Tips: "Identify a niche and dig in! But before submitting a proposal do your homework—ask yourself, 'Why is this column's premise fresh and unique?' Book-length copies of the popular. 'Coping in the County' column are available for $5 postpaid."

CONTINENTAL FEATURES/CONTINENTAL NEWS SERVICE, 501 W. Broadway, P.M.B. #265, Plaza A, San Diego CA 92101-3802. (858)492-8696. E-mail: newstime@hotbot.com. Website: www.mediafinder.com/secure/cnstore.cfm?tp-con. **Contact:** Gary P. Salamone, editor-in-chief. Estab. 1981. **100% writers on contract.** "Writers who offer the kind and quality of writing we seek stand an equal chance regardless of experience." Syndicates to print media. Responds in 1 month with SASE. Writer's guidelines for #10 SASE.
Needs: Magazine and newspaper features. "Feature material should fit the equivalent of one-quarter to one-half standard newspaper page, and Continental News considers an ultra-liberal or ultra-conservative slant inappropriate." Query with SASE. **Pays 70% author's percentage.** Currently syndicates *News and Comment*, by Charles Hampton Savage (general news commentary/analysis); *Portfolio*, (cartoon/caricature art); *Sports and Families*, by former American League Pitcher David Frost; *Travelers' Checks*, by Ann Hattes; and *OnVideo*, by Harley Lond; over 50 features in all.
• This syndicate is considering fewer proposals for one-time projects. Virtually all of their new feature creators are signed to work on a continuing basis.
Tips: "*CF/CNS* is working to develop a feature package of greater interest and value to an English-speaking international audience. That is, those writers who can accompany their economic-social-political analyses (of foreign countries) with photo(s) of the key public figure(s) involved are particularly in demand. Official photos (8×10 down to 3×5) of key government leaders available from the information ministry/press office/embassy will be acceptable. *CF/CNS* emphasizes analytical/explanatory articles, but muckraking articles (where official-photo requests are inopportune) are also encouraged."

COPLEY NEWS SERVICE, P.O. Box 120190, San Diego CA 92112. (619)293-1818. Fax: (619)293-2322. **Contact:** Glenda Winders, editorial director. Most stories produced by news bureaus or picked up from Copley newspapers; **15% freelance written on a one-time basis. Offers 200 features/week.** Sells to newspapers and online services. Responds in 6 months. Buys first rights.
Needs: Comic strips, travel stories, columns on technology, new ideas. Query with clips of published work. **Pays $100/ story or negotiated monthly salary.** Only responds to queries accompanied by SASE.
Tips: "Writer needs to have a sense of competition for space in newspapers and offer features of broad, timely appeal. Competition is keen, but we are always on the lookout for good writers and fresh ideas."

CRICKET COMMUNICATIONS, INC., P.O. Box 527, Ardmore PA 19003-0527. (610)789-2480 or (610)924-9158. Fax: (610)924-9159. E-mail: crcktinc@aol.com. Editor: J.D. Krickett. **Contact:** E.A. Stern, senior editor. Estab. 1975. **10% written on contract; 10% freelance written on a one-time basis. Works with 2-3 previously unpublished writers/year.** Syndicates to trade magazines and newspapers. Responds in 1 month. Buys all rights.
Needs: Magazine and newspaper columns and features, news items—all tax and financial-oriented (700-1,500 words); also newspaper columns, features and news items directed to small business. Query with clips of published work. Pays $50-500. Currently syndicates *Hobby/Business*, by Mark E. Battersby (tax and financial); *Farm Taxes*, by various authors; and *Small Business Taxes*, by Mark E. Battersby.

N **DANY NEWS SERVICE**, 22 Lesley Dr., Syosset NY 11791. (516)921-4611. **Contact:** David Nydick, president and editor. **5% written on a one-time basis. Buys 10-20 features/year. Works with 5-10 writers/year.** Syndicates to newspapers. Responds in 2 weeks. Buys all rights. **Pays on acceptance.** Submit complete ms.
Needs: Newspaper features. **Pays flat fee, $100-500 and up.** Currently syndicates *You, Your Child and School*; *You, Your Child and Entertainment*; *You, Your Child and Sports*.

DEMKO'S AGEVENTURE SYNDICATED NEWS SERVICE, 21946 Pine Trace, Boca Raton FL 33428-3057 (561)482-6271. E-mail: demko@demko.com. Estab. 1983. **25% written by writers on contracts; 25% freelance**

written on a one-time basis. **Buys 52 features/year. Works with 27 writers/year.** Syndicates to magazines, radio, newspapers and internet-zines. Responds within 1 month. **Pays on acceptance.** Sends writer's guidelines via e-mail only. Query via e-mail.

Needs: Uses news items. Purchases single (one shot) features and article series (250-500 words). Currently syndicates *Senior Living* (500-750 words) lifestyle feature columns—staff writer; *Sonic Boomers* (150-200 words and photo) personal profiles (age 40-50); *Aging America* (50-75 words) mature market news items.

Tips: "Stick with what you know in order to avoid superficial content. Query via e-mail with 2-3 work samples. Be assertive and upfront—specify your product and costs/prices in advance."

EDITORIAL CONSULTANT SERVICE, P.O. Box 524, West Hempstead NY 11552-1206. Fax: (516)481-5487. E-mail: Alongo42033.com. **Contact:** Arthur A. Ingoglia, editorial director. Estab. 1964. **40% written on contract; 25% freelance written on a one-time basis. "We work with 75 writers in the U.S. and Canada." Adds about 10 new columnists/year.** Syndicates material to an average of 60 newspapers, magazines, automotive trade and consumer publications, and radio stations with circulation of 50,000-575,000. Responds in 1-2 months. Buys all rights. Writer's guidelines for #10 SASE.

Needs: Magazine and newspaper columns and features, news items, radio broadcast material. Prefers carefully documented material with automotive slant. Also considers automotive trade features. Will consider article series. No horoscope, child care, lovelorn or pet care. Query. **Author's percentage varies; usually averages 50%.** Additional payment for 8×10 b&w and color photos accepted with ms. Submit 2-3 columns. Currently syndicates *Let's Talk About Your Car*, by R. Hite.

Tips: "Emphasis is placed on articles and columns with an automotive slant. We prefer consumer-oriented features, how to save money on your car, what every woman should know about her car, how to get more miles per gallon, etc."

⒩ HISPANIC LINK NEWS SERVICE, 1420 N St. NW, Washington DC 20005. (202)234-0280. Fax: (202)234-4090. E-mail: zapoteco@aol.com. **Contact:** Charles A. Ericksen, publisher. Editor: Patricia Guadalupe. Estab. 1980. **50% freelance written on contract; 50% freelance written on a one-time basis. Buys 156 columns and features/year. Works with 50 writers/year; 5 previously unpublished writers.** Syndicates to 60 newspapers and magazines with circulations ranging from 5,000 to 300,000. Responds in up to 1 month. Buys second serial (reprint) or negotiable rights. For reprints, send photocopy of article. **Pays $25 for guest columns.** Writer's guidelines free.

Needs: Newspaper columns and features. "We prefer 650-700 word op/ed, analysis or new features geared to a general national audience, but focus on issue or subject of particular interest to Hispanics. Some longer pieces accepted occasionally." Query or submit complete ms. **Pays $25-100.** Currently syndicates *Hispanic Link*, by various authors (opinion and/or feature columns). Syndicated through Los Angeles Times Syndicate.

Tips: "We would especially like to get topical material and vignettes relating to Hispanic presence and progress in the US and Puerto Rico. Provide insights on Hispanic experience geared to a general audience. Of the columns we accept, 85 to 90% are authored by Hispanics; the Link presents Hispanic viewpoints and showcases Hispanic writing talent through its subscribing newspapers and magazines. Copy can be submitted in English or Spanish. We syndicate in both languages."

⒩ INTERNATIONAL PUZZLE FEATURES, 4507 Panther Pl., Charlotte NC 28269. **Contact:** Pat Battaglia, owner. Estab. 1990. **0% written on contract; 5-10% freelance written on a one-time basis. Buys 10 features/year. Works with 0 writers/year. Works with all new previously unpublished writers.** Syndicates to newspapers. Responds in 1 month. Writer's guidelines for #10 SASE. Submit complete ms.

Needs: Concisely written, entertaining word puzzles. **Pays $5 flat rate/puzzle.** Currently syndicates *If You're So Smart . . .*, by Pat Battaglia (word puzzles).

Tips: "We are not interested in crossword, word search, cryptogram, mathematical or trivia puzzles."

INTERPRESS OF LONDON AND NEW YORK, 90 Riverside Drive, New York NY 10026 (212)873-0772. **Contact:** Jeffrey Blyth, editor-in-chief. Estab. 1971. **10% freelance written on a one-time basis. Buys 10-12 features/year.** Syndicates to newspapers and radio. Responds in 1 week. Buys all rights. Writer's guidelines for #10 SASE. Query only.

Needs: Magazine features, newspaper features and off-beat feature stories. Purchases one shot features. **Pays 60% author's percentage.** Additional payment for photos. Currently syndicates *Destination America*, by various writers (travel) series; *Book World*, by Myrna Grier (book news/reviews); *Dateline NY*, by various writers (show biz news/features); *Music World* (news about new CDs and recordings). Also columns on media and medical news.

LEW LITTLE ENTERPRISES, INC., P.O. Box 47, Bisbee AZ 85603. (520)432-8003. Fax: (520)432-8004. **Contact:** Lewis A. Little, editor. Estab. 1986. **100% written on contract. Buys 2 features/year. Works with 10-20 writers/year. Works with 10-12 previously unpublished writers/year.** Syndicates to newspapers. Responds in 2 months. Buys all rights. Writer's guidelines for #10 SASE. "For cartoon features, I prefer that writers, after receiving my guidelines, submit an outline and about 12 finished and rough samples. For text features, submit six sample columns."

Needs: Newspaper columns and features. "I am open to all fresh ideas for text and comic features." No one-shot features. **Pays 50% author's percentage.** Currently syndicates *The Fusco Brothers*, by J.C. Duffy (comic strip); *Warped*, by Mike Cavna (comic strip).

Tips: "Unless a writer comes up with a truly fresh approach in a text or comic feature, his or her chances of landing a syndicate contract are virtually nonexistent."

MEGALO MEDIA, P.O. Box 1503, New York NY 10021. **Contact:** J. Baxter Newgate, president. Estab. 1972. **50% written on contract; 50% freelance written on a one-time basis. Works with 5 previously unpublished writers/ year.** Syndicates to newspapers, magazines. Query with SASE. Responds in 1 month. Buys all rights. Writer's guidelines for #10 SASE.
Needs: Crossword puzzles. Buys one-shot features. Submit complete ms. **Pays flat rate of $150 for Sunday puzzle.** Currently syndicates *National Challenge*, by J. Baxter Newgate (crossword puzzle); *Crossword Puzzle*, by J. Baxter Newgate.

MIDWEST FEATURES INC., P.O. Box 259907, Madison WI 53725-9907. E-mail: mfi@chorus.net. **Contact:** Mary Bergin. Estab. 1991. **80% written on contract; 20% freelance written on a one-time basis. Buys 1-2 features/year. Works with 6-8 writers/year.** Syndicates to Wisconsin newspapers. Responds in 2 months. Buys second serial (reprint) rights. Query with clips of published work.
Needs: Newspaper columns. Material *must* have a Wisconsin emphasis and already appear in a Wisconsin publication. Length: 500-1,000 words. Series in past have been book excerpts ("Nathan's Christmas") and seasonal material (spring gardening, Milwaukee Brewer spring training). **Pays 50% author's percentage when reprints of previously published work are sold.** Currently syndicates: *Midwest Gardening*, by Jan Riggenbach (gardening); *Beyond Hooks & Bullets*, by Pat Durkin (outdoor sports); *Images*, by Barbara Quirk (aging and older adults); *Consumer Watch*, by Bob Richards (consumer complaints).
Tips: "We do not consider 'generic' copy—what you write must have a specific Wisconsin emphasis."

MOTOR NEWS MEDIA CORPORATION, 7177 Hickman Rd., Suite 11-D, Urbandale IA 50322. (515)270-6782. Fax: (515)270-8752. E-mail: mnmedia@uswest.net. Website: www.motornewsmedia.com. Estab. 1995. **90% written by writers on contract; 10% freelance written on a one-time basis. Buys 132-150 features/year. Works with 10-12 writers/year. Works with 2-4 new previously unpublished writers/year.** Syndicates to newspapers and Internet. Responds in 6 weeks. Buys first North American serial or second serial (reprint) rights. Pays within 45 days of publication. Query only.
Needs: Newspaper features. "Maximum 650 words—automotive content only." Purchases single (one shot) features and automotive article series. **Pays minimum guarantee of $125.** Currently syndicates *Roadworthy*, by Ken Chester, Jr.; *Credit & Coverage*, by Tom Brownell; *Hard Bargains*, by Neal White; *Dateline: Detroit!*, by Kailoni Yates; *Street Talk*, by Mike Fornatero; *Neal's Garage*, by Neal White; *High & Mighty*, by Robin Bailey; *Ask Mr. Fix-It*, by Andy Mikonis; and others.

N **THE NATIONAL FINANCIAL NEWS SERVICES**, 331 W. Boot Rd., West Chester PA 19380. (610)344-7380. E-mail: brucenfns@aol.com. Website: www.nfns.com. **Contact:** Bruce Myers. Estab. 1985. **2% written by writers under contract. Buys 52 features/year. Works with 1 new previously unpublished writer/year.** Syndicates to newspapers. Does not return mss. Buys all rights. **Pays on acceptance.** Query only.
Needs: **Pays flat fee.** Currently syndicates *Mortgages This Week*, by Al Bowman.

NATIONAL NEWS BUREAU, P.O. Box 43039, Philadelphia PA 19129-0628. (215)849-9016. **Contact:** Harry Jay Katz, editor. **20% written by writers on contract; 35-40 freelance written on a one-time basis. Buys 100 features/ year. Works with 200 writers/year. Works with 50% new previously unpublished writers/year.** Syndicates to magazines and newspaper. Responds in 2 weeks. Buys all rights. Pays on publication. Writer's guidelines for 9 × 12 SAE with 3 first-class stamps.
Needs: Magazine features; newspaper columns and features. "We do many reviews and celebrity interviews. Only original, assigned material." One-shot features and article series; film reviews, etc. Query with clips. **Pays $5-200 flat rate or 50% author's percentage. Offers $5-200 additional payment for photos accompanying ms.**

N **NEWS USA**, 7777 Leesburg Pike, #307, Falls Church VA 22305. (703)734-6308. Website: www.newsusa.com. **Contact:** Katherine Egan, managing editor. Estab. 1988. **90% written by writers on contract; 1% freelance written on a one-time basis. Buys 200 features/year. Works with 20 writers/year.** Syndicates to radio, newspapers, internet. Responds in 2 months. Buys all rights. **Pays on acceptance.** Writer's guidelines for #10 SASE. Query only.
Needs: Newspaper features. "I only buy articles I commission from freelancers." **Pays flat rate $100.**

N **OASIS NEWSFEATURES**, P.O. Box 2144, Middletown OH 45044. (800)582-4391. E-mail: KWilliams@OASIS Newsfeatures.com. Website: www.OASISNewsfeatures.com. **Contact:** Kevin Williams. Estab. 1991. **95% written by writers on contract; 5% freelance written on a one-time basis. Buys very few features/year. Works with 3-5 writers/year. Works with 2-3 new previously unpublished writers/year.** Syndicates to newspapers. Responds in 2 months. Buys first North American serial rights. Pays on publication. Writer's guidelines for #10 SASE. Query with published clips.
Needs: Newspaper columns, comics. Purchases single (one shot) features and article series. Very rarely purchases "one-shots," but will if it is very compelling and unique. **Authors are paid monthly, 40% first year under contract, 45% second year, 50% and up third year and beyond.** Currently syndicates *The Amish Cook*, *The Handwriting Dr.*, *Family Daze*.

Tips: "This field is extremely competitive. Please, no slice-of-life Erma Bombeck type stuff. Come up with something specific and unique and please don't call me."

N **◼** **POWERPROSE.COM**, 16 E. Main St., Southborough MA 01772. (508)303-2481. E-mail: al@powerprose.c om. Website: www.PowerProse.com. **Contact:** A. Marsocci, vice president operations. Estab. 1998. **95% written by writers on contract. Buys 400-500 features/year. Works with 50-70 writers/year.** Syndicates to magazines, newspapers, websites. Responds in 3 weeks. Buys first North American serial rights, second serial (reprint) rights. Writer's guidelines on website. Query/samples via e-mail.
Needs: News items, magazine features, newspaper features. Purchases single (one shot) features, article series. General Features 600-800 words. "Our features span the gamut of what newspapers/magazines/websites offer—parenting, careers, fitness/health, auto, holidays, etc." **One-time payment for assigned or recycled works. Revenue split (50/50) for some reprint rights.** *The Driving Passion* (Auto), by Al Marcsocci; *Auto Mates* (Auto), by Al Marsocci and Holly Reich; *Motoring Decisively* (Auto), by Mike Covello.
Tips: Be persistent, send your best samples, don't be afraid to try something different.

PRESS ASSOCIATES, INC., 815 W. 15th St., Washington DC 20005. (202)638-0444. Fax: (202)638-0955. E-mail: palnews@bellatlantic.net. Website: www.pressassociates.com. **Contact:** Mark Gruenberg, president/editor. Estab. 1957. **5% written by writers on contract. Buys 100 features/year. Works with 2 writers/year.** Syndicates to union newspapers and publications. Responds in 2 months. Buys first North American serial rights. Pays on publication. Writer's guidelines available free. Query only.
Needs: News items. Buys one-shot features. **Pays 25¢/published word; maximum of $25.** Additional payment for photos accepted with ms.
Tips: "We do not syndicate outside of our subscribing readers."

N **SCRAMBL-GRAM INC.**, 41 Park Dr., Port Clinton OH 43452. (419)734-2600. Website: www.puzzlebuffs.com. **Contact:** S. Bowers, managing editor. Estab. 1978. **100% freelance written on a one-time basis. Buys 300 features/ year. Works with 20-30 writers/year. Works with 3-5 new previously unpublished writers/year.** Syndicates to magazines, newspapers, websites. Responds in 1 month. Buys all rights. **Pays on acceptance.** Guidelines for SASE.
Needs: "We accept only crossword puzzles. Submit one or two examples of your work and if interested, we will send you information and materials to produce puzzles for us." Rates are based on the size of the crosswords. **Pays $25-60.**
Tips: "Our crosswords appear weekly in *STAR Magazine, National Enquirer, Country Weekly* and numerous other magazines and newspapers. Crosswords should be edited to remove obscure and archaic words. Foreign words should be kept to a minimum. The puzzle should be fun and challenging but achievable."

N **THE SPORTS NETWORK**, 95 James Way, Southampton PA 18966. (215)942-7890. Fax: (215)942-7647. E-mail: kkipphut@sportsnetwork.com. Website: www.sportsnetwork.com. **Contact:** Kristine Kipphut, syndication editor. Estab. 1980. **30% written on contract; 10-15% freelance written on one-time basis; balance by in-house personnel. Buys 200-250 features/year. Works with 50-60 writers/year and 10-15 new previously unpublished writers/year.** Syndicates to magazines, newspapers, radio and has the additional benefit of being an international sports wire service with established awareness globally furnishing exposure world-wide for its writers/clients. Responds immediately. Buys all rights. Free writer's guidelines. Query with clips of published and/or sample works and SASE.
Needs: Fillers, magazine and newspaper columns and features, news items, radio and broadcast material, single features (timely sports pieces, from 700-1,000 words). Seeking ongoing coverage pieces of teams (professional) leagues (professional), conferences (college) and sports, 1-2 times weekly. **Payments variable.** Currently syndicates *The Sandlot Shrink*, by Dennis LePore; *Infosport*, by Julie Lanzillo; *The Women's Basketball Journal, Bball Stats*, by Robert Chaikin.
Tips: "The competition for sports is fast and furious, so right time and place, with a pinch of luck, are ingredients that complement talent. Making inroads to one syndicate for even one feature is an amazing door opener. Focus on the needs of that syndicate or wire service (as is the case with TSN) and use that as a springboard to establish a proven track record with quality work that suits specific needs. Don't give up and don't abandon the day job. This takes commitment, desire, knowledge of the topic and willingness to work at it while being able to handle rejection. No one who reads submissions really 'knows' and the history of great rejections would fill volumes, from *Gone With The Wind* to Snoopy and Garfield. We are different in that we are looking for specific items and not a magical cartoon (although sports cartoons will work), feature or story. Give us your best in sports and make certain that it is in tune with what is happening right now or is able to stand the test of time, be an evergreen and everlasting if it is a special feature."

TV DATA, 333 Glen St., Glens Falls NY 12801. (518)792-9914. Fax: (800)660-7185. E-mail: mskotnicki@tvdata.com. Website: www.tvdata.com. **Contact:** Monique Skotnicki, features managing editor. **70% written by full-time or contract writers; 30% freelance written on a one-time basis. Buys 100 features/year. Works with 20 writers/year.** Syndicates to newspapers and Internet. Does not return submissions. Responds in 1 month. Buys all rights. Pays on publication. Query with published clips.
Needs: Uses newspaper columns, features and fillers.
Tips: "Submissions should be television-related features about trends, stars, sports, movies, the Internet, etc. They should be approximately 1,000 words and written according to AP style."

Greeting Cards & Gift Ideas

How many greeting cards did you buy last year? Americans bought nearly six billion cards last year. That's according to figures published by The Greeting Card Association, a national trade organization representing the multi-billion dollar greeting card industry.

In fact, nearly 50 percent of all first class mail now consists of greeting cards. And, of course, card manufacturers rely on writers to supply them with enough skillfully crafted sentiments to meet the demand. The perfect greeting card verse is one that will appeal to a large audience, yet will make each buyer feel that the card was written exclusively for him or her.

Two greeting card companies dominate this industry; together, Hallmark and American Greetings supply 85 percent of all cards sold. The other 15 percent are published by nearly 2,000 companies who have found success mainly by not competing head to head with the big two but by choosing instead to pursue niche markets—regional and special-interest markets that the big two either cannot or do not supply.

A PROFESSIONAL APPROACH TO MARKETS

As markets become more focused, it's important to keep current on specific company needs. Familiarize yourself with the differences among lines of cards by visiting card racks. Ask retailers which lines are selling best. You may also find it helpful to read trade magazines such as *Gifts and Decorative Accessories* and *Party and Paper Retailer* (www.partypaper.com). These publications will keep you apprised of changes and events within the field, including seminars and trade shows.

Once you find a card line that appeals to you, write to the company and request its market list, catalog or submission guidelines (usually available for a SASE or a small fee). This information will help you determine whether or not your ideas are appropriate for that market.

Submission procedures vary among greeting card publishers, depending on the size and nature of the company. Keep in mind that many companies (especially the large ones) will not review your writing samples until you've signed and returned their disclosure contract or submission agreement, assuring them that your material is original and has not been submitted elsewhere.

Some editors prefer to see individual card ideas on 3×5 cards, while others prefer to receive a number of complete ideas on $8\frac{1}{2} \times 11$ bond paper. Be sure to put your best pieces at the top of the stack. Most editors do not want to see artwork unless it is professional, but they do appreciate conceptual suggestions for design elements. If your verse depends on an illustration to make its point or if you have an idea for a unique card shape or foldout, include a dummy card with your writing samples.

The usual submission includes from 5 to 15 card ideas and an accompanying cover letter, plus mechanical dummy cards, if necessary. Some editors also like to receive a résumé, client list and business card. Some do not. Be sure to check the listings and the company's writer's guidelines for such specifications before submitting material.

Payment for greeting card verse varies, but most firms pay per card or per idea; a handful pay small royalties. Some companies prefer to test a card first and will pay a small fee for a test card idea. In some instances, a company may even purchase an idea and never use it.

Greeting card companies will also buy ideas for gift products and may use card material for a number of subsequent items. Licensing—the sale of rights to a particular character for a variety of products from mugs to T-shirts—is a growing part of the industry. Because of this, however, note that most card companies buy all rights. We now include in this section markets for licensed product lines such as mugs, bumper stickers, buttons, posters and the like.

Information of interest to writers wishing to know more about working with the greeting card industry is available from the Greeting Card Association (1200 G Street NW, Suite 760, Washington, DC 20005).

MANAGING YOUR SUBMISSIONS

Because you will be sending out many samples, you may want to label each sample. Establish a master card for each verse idea and record where and when each was sent and whether it was rejected or purchased. Keep all cards sent to one company in a batch and give each batch a number. Write this number on the back of your return SASE to help you match up your verses as they are returned.

Information on greeting card companies listed in the previous edition of _Writer's Market_ but not included in this edition can be found in the General Index.

N AMBERLEY GREETING CARD CO., 11510 Goldcoast Dr., Cincinnati OH 45249-1695. (513)489-2775. Fax: (513)489-2857. Website: www.amberleygreeting.com. **Contact:** Editor. Estab. 1966. **90% freelance written. Bought 200 freelance ideas last year.** Responds in 1 month. Material copyrighted. Buys all rights. **Pays on acceptance.** Writer's guidelines for #10 SASE. Market list regularly revised.
  ● This company is now accepting alternative humor.
Needs: "Original, easy to understand, belly-laugh or outrageous humor. We sell to the 'masses, not the classes,' so keep it simple and to the point. Humor accepted in all captions, including general birthday, family birthday, get well, anniversary, thank you, friendship, etc. No non-humorous material needed or considered this year." **Pays $150/card idea.** Submit maximum 10 ideas/batch.
Tips: "Send SASE for our writer's guidelines before submitting. Amberley publishes humorous specialty lines in addition to a complete conventional line that is accented with humor. Since humor is our specialty, we are highly selective. Be sure your SASE has correct U.S. postage. Otherwise it will not be returned."

AMERICAN GREETINGS, Dept. WM, One American Rd., Cleveland OH 44144-2398. (216)252-7300. **Contact:** Leia Madden, creative recruitment department. No unsolicited material. "We are currently reviewing only humorous writing for our Humorous/Alternative card lines." Send letter of inquiry describing education or experience along with a #10 SASE for guidelines. Responds within 1 month. Buys all rights. **Pays on acceptance.**
Tips: "We're open to humorous verse, funny copy twists, and off-the-wall humor styles."

BLUE MOUNTAIN ARTS, INC., Dept. WM, P.O. Box 1007, Boulder CO 80306-1007. Fax: (303)447-0939. E-mail: bma@rmi.net.
  ● See the listing for SPS Studios in this section.

BRILLIANT ENTERPRISES, 117 W. Valerio St., Santa Barbara CA 93101-2927. **Contact:** Ashleigh Brilliant, preside nt. Estab. 1967. Buys all rights. Submit words and art in black on 3½×3½ horizontal, thin white paper in batches of no more than 15. Responds "usually in 2 weeks." Catalog and sample set for $2.
Needs: Postcards. Messages should be "of a highly original nature, emphasizing subtlety, simplicity, insight, wit, profundity, beauty and felicity of expression. Accompanying art should be in the nature of oblique commentary or decoration rather than direct illustration. Messages should be of universal appeal, capable of being appreciated by all types of people and of being easily translated into other languages. Because our line of cards is highly unconventional, it is essential that freelancers study it before submitting. No topical references or subjects limited to American culture or puns." Limit of 17 words/card. **Pays $50 for "complete ready-to-print word and picture design."**

CARDMAKERS, P.O. Box 236, 66 High Bridge Rd., Lyme NH 03768. (603)795-4422. Website: www.cardmakers.com. **Contact:** Peter D. Diebold, owner. Estab. 1978. Receives many submissions/year. Submit seasonal/holiday material 10 months in advance. Responds in 3 months. Buys all greeting cards rights. **Pays on acceptance.** Writer's guidelines/ market list for SASE.
Needs: Holiday (mostly) & everyday, humorous. "We like upbeat humor, skip sick or raunchy. Our customers use our cards to greet their customers so a positive approach/result is desirable." Prefers unrhymed verse.
Tips: "We are primarily a direct marketer of business to business greetings targeted to specific interest groups—i.e. Stockbrokers, Boaters, etc. . . . We also publish everyday cards for those same specific interests. We work with many free-lancers on design and have recently decided to solicit ideas from writers. Please don't call or e-mail. Send us a simple bio, samples if possible and SASE and we'll get in touch."

The Idea Dig

"Where do you get your ideas?" It's the question most frequently asked of greeting card writers (second only to "what do you really do for a living?"). Most people have never met someone who does this kind of writing, so they find it quite mysterious. They know those "sayings" get on the cards somehow, but don't associate them with the actions of real people. To their question, my usual reply is, "they come to me in dreams," or "elves deliver them under my door at night on teeny slips of paper," just to preserve folks' fantasies. Everyone needs something to believe in, right? Okay—the truth. The writing can be work. It often takes effort. Sometimes we have to go on a full-scale excavation for new ideas. When you are in need of inspiration, try mining some of the following resources. Maybe you'll hit pay dirt!

Look at catalogs & magazines: Devour catalogs like *Wireless*, and *Signals*, magazines like *Details*, *Martha Stewart Living*, *Good Housekeeping*, *GQ*, *Ladies' Home Journal*, *Esquire*, *Guideposts*, *Victoria*, *Reader's Digest*, *Highlights for Children*, *Self*, *People*, *Seventeen* . . . They're full of great ads and are good indicators of styles and trends.

Listen in on conversations: A candid comment on an airplane, elevator, bus, or even in the laundromat or grocery checkout line might make a sendable greeting card.

Listen to radio advertising: Tune in to language and slang.

Watch TV: The hit shows are hits because people relate to them; pick out themes; listen for punchlines you can put a new spin on.

Loiter in book stores: Read! Scan new-release titles and read the bestsellers list with an eye out for prevailing themes and topics.

Surf the Net: Check out all the greeting card websites you can turn up. Read the e-cards, look for new approaches you might want to try.

Browse gift and card shops: For general inspiration, visit the stores. Products change seasonally and might inspire holiday verse writing.

Read old letters: If you've ever had a pen-pal or ongoing written correspondence, you may have a treasure of good material stashed away. What could be more inspiring than old love letters?

Relocate: A change of scenery can be enormously inspiring. Try a coffee shop or cafe, a park or museum. New surroundings, new ideas!

Note: An advertising slogan is a terrible thing to waste, but mind your wording. If you find an idea to rewrite, make it a true rewrite. The plagiarism police are lurking about, cleverly disguised as editors.
    —*Terri See*

Terri See is the editor and publisher of Greeting Card Writer *magazine, www.greetingcardwriter.com, and former editor for Gibson Greetings. She teaches greeting card writing at writers' conferences and is production editor for* Writer's Market *and www.WritersMarket.com.*

COLORS BY DESIGN, 7723 Densmore Ave., Van Nuys CA 91436. (818)376-1226. Website: http://cbdcards.c om. **Contact:** Angie Novak, marketing director. Estab. 1985. **20% of material freelance written. Receives 500 submissions/year; bought 200 ideas/samples last year.** Does not return submissions not accompanied by SASE. Buys all rights. Pays on publication. Writer's guidelines/market list free. Please send SASE attention writers guidelines.
Needs: Announcements, informal, juvenile, conventional, invitations, soft line.
Tips: Submit on 3×5 cards, including your name and address on each. We are interested in soft, heartfelt sentiments of no longer than 3 lines. No humor.

DCI STUDIOS, 8010 State Line Rd., Leawood KS 66208. Website: www.emergemag.com. Managing Editor: Florestine Parnel. **Contact:** Scott Oppenheimer, freelance coordinator. Estab. 1992. Submit seasonal/holiday material 6 months in advance. Responds in 3 months. Buys greeting card rights. **Pays on acceptance.** Writers guidelines/market list for free. Market list issued one time only.
Needs: Inspirational, humorous, soft line. Prefers unrhymed verse. Submit 25-50 ideas/batch.
Tips: "We are looking for fresh, new, innovative humor. We divide our humor needs into general jokes and woman's humor. The only thing we remind writers of is that our market is mostly women between 19 and 55. So we need to create a product that will appeal to them."

DESIGNER GREETINGS, 250 Arlington Ave., Staten Island NY 10303. (718)981-7700. Estab. 1978. **Contact:** Fern Gimbelman, art director. **50% freelance written. Receives 200-300 submissions/year.** Submit seasonal/holiday submissions 6 months in advance. Responds in 2 months. Buys greeting card rights. **Pays on acceptance.** Guidelines free.
Needs: Humorous, inspirational, informal, juvenile, studio, conventional, sensitivity, and soft line. Accepts rhymed or unrhymed verse. Query with SASE.

DUCK AND COVER PRODUCTIONS, P.O. Box 21640, Oakland CA 94620. **Contact:** Jim Buser, editor. Estab. 1990. **50% freelance written. Receives 1,000 submissions/year. Bought 120 ideas/samples last year.** Responds in 3 weeks. Buys all rights on novelty products. Pays on publication. Guidelines for #10 SASE.
Other Product Lines: Novelty buttons and magnets **only.** "We do *not* make greeting cards." **Pays $35/idea.**
Tips: "Duck and Cover is a smorgasbord of existential angst, psychotic babble, dry wit and outrageous zingers. Our buttons and magnets appeal to anyone with an offbeat, irreverent sense of humor. We sell to novelty stores, head shops, record stores, bookstores, sex shops, comic stores, etc. There are no taboos for our writers; we encourage them to be as weird and/or rude as they like as long as they are funny. We feel buttons and magnets are commercial cousins to graffiti. Let your inner child thumb his nose at society. Cerebral material that makes use of contemporary pop vocabulary is a plus. We do *not* want to see old clichés or slogans already in the market."

EPHEMERA, INC., P.O. Box 490, Phoenix OR 97535. E-mail: ed@ephemera-inc.com. Website: www.ephemera-inc.com. **Contact:** Editor. Estab. 1979. **90% freelance written. Receives 2,500 submissions/year; bought 350 slogans for novelty buttons, stickers, magnets and keychains last year.** Responds in 3 months. Buys all rights. **Pays on acceptance.** Writer's guidelines for self addressed stamped envelope. Complete full color catalog available for $4.
Needs: Provocative, irreverent and outrageously funny slogans. "We want original, concise, high impact gems of wit that would sell in trendy card and gift shops, bookstores, record shops, political and gay shops, fashion boutiques, head shops, adult stores, amusement parks, etc! We've been in business for over 20 years and we have a reputation as *the* publisher of the wackiest slogans." **Pays $40/slogan.**
Tips: "We're looking for satirical slogans about current events, pop culture, political causes, the president, women's issues, job attitudes, coffee, booze, pot, drugs, sexual come-ons and put-downs, aging, slacker angst, gays and lesbians. But please don't limit yourself to these topics! Make us laugh out loud!"

KATE HARPER DESIGNS, P.O. Box 2112, Berkeley CA 94702. E-mail: kateharp@aol.com. Website: http://hometow n.aol.com/kateharp/myhomepage/index.html. **Contact:** Editor. Estab. 1993. 100% freelance written. Submit seasonal/ holiday material 1 year in advance. Responds in 3 months. **Pays flat fee for usage**, not exclusive, plus author's name credit. **Pays on acceptance.** Writer's guidelines/market list for SASE.
  ☛ Break in with samples on 3×5 index cards. Put name, address, fax, phone on back. Code reference number (on back or front). Don't use quotation marks. Don't use all caps. Writing by hand is OK. Request guidelines before submitting. See website for updated guidelines. Currently a strong need for submissions by children.
Needs: Humorous, informal, inspirational, sensitivity, everyday cards. Unrhymed verse only. Submit 10 ideas/batch. We are looking for birthday, valentine and love, thanks, humor.
Tips: "Quotes needed about work, family, love, kids, career, technology and marriage with a twist of humor. Something a working mom would laugh at and/or tips on how to have it all and still live to tell about it. Be adventurous and say what you really think in first person. What is ironic about this world we live in? What is the message you want to put out in the world? Don't be afraid to take risks and push beyond greeting card stereotypes. Nothing cute or sweet. Avoid quotes about women and weight, PMS, chocolate, diet, sex. Write as if you were talking to your best friend at the kitchen table. Be personal, and speak in an 'I' voice, like you've been there. We seek out new and unknown writers with a zing. Avoid traditional ideas of card quotes. Serious quotes also considered. Quotes must be 20 words or less. For front of card only. Do not send quotes for inside of card."

INSPIRATIONS UNLIMITED, P.O. Box 9097, Cedar Pines Park CA 92322. (800)337-6758. Estab. 1984. Bought 50 ideas/samples last year. Submit seasonal/holiday material 6 months in advance. Responds in 2 weeks. Pays on publication.
Needs: Informal, conventional, inspirational, sensitivity. Prefers unrhymed verse. Submit 10 ideas/batch.
Tips: "Send heart to heart messages—something that tugs at the heart."

J-MAR, P.O. Box 23149, Waco TX 76702. (254)751-0100. Fax: (254)751-0054. E-mail: Carla_Croce@tandycrafts. com. **Contact:** Carla Croce, assistant product marketing manager. Estab. 1984. **25% freelance written. Receives 200 submissions/year; bought 25 ideas/samples last year.** Submit seasonal/holiday material 10 months in advance. All submissions filed. Responds in 2 months. Buys all rights. **Pays on acceptance**.
Needs: Inspirational, soft line, friendship, birthdays, motivational, family, get well, sympathy, encouragement, humor, juvenile, seasonal, christenings, pastor/church thank you. Accepts either rhymed or unrhymed verse ideas. Submit each piece on a separate page, and include name, address, phone number, date and sample title on each page. Include an SASE. Our most focused attention will be on proposals for new topics/themes and/or product lines.
Other Product Lines: Bookmarks, gift books, greeting books, posters.
Tips: "J-Mar's target audience is the Christian market. J-Mar appreciates submissions focused on core inspirational Christian values, verses and themes. Keep a very positive, inspirational tone. Submissions can include biblical references or verses, poems and/or text."

N KOEHLER COMPANIES, INC., 4600 W. 77th St., Suite 301, Edina MN 55435-4909. (800)682-6965. Fax: (612)893-1934. E-mail: klrcompany@aol.com. President: Bob Koehler. **Contact:** Maria Rogers, operations manager. Estab. 1988. **65% of material freelance written. Receives 100 submissions/year; bought 28 ideas/samples last year.** Submit seasonal/holiday material 10 months in advance. Responds in 1 month. **Pays on acceptance.**
Needs: Juvenile, inspirational, sensitivity, humorous, cat, dog, golf, fishing, Celtic.
  ○ᴙ "Witty, concise, upbeat messages with a twist, unexpected turns or solid messages that are easy to understand and reach a large segment of our population are best suited for our plaques. Best selling themes are: humor, inspirational, cat, dog, golf, fishing, family, juvenile, sentiment of the heart."
Other Product Lines: Plaques pays $300; posters pays $300.
Tips: "We are gift and home decor industry manufacturers. Our finished products are plaques, clocks and mirrors. Our market is gift and home decor-based mail order catalogs. We begin projects with a saleable verse (humorous, family, Celtic, cat, dog, golf, fishing, inspirational) and work with artists to develop art that complements the verse without overpowering it. Because we sell only to mail order catalogs, both verse and art must be easy to see and understand when shrunk to a 1½″ square photo in a catalog."

OATMEAL STUDIOS, P.O. Box 138W3, Rochester VT 05767. (802)767-3171. **Contact:** Helene Lehrer, creative director. Estab. 1979. **85% freelance written. Buys 200-300 greeting card lines/year.** Responds within 6 weeks. **Pays on acceptance.** Current market list for #10 SASE.
Needs: Birthday, friendship, anniversary, get well cards, etc. Also Christmas, Hanukkah, Mother's Day, Father's Day, Easter, Valentine's Day, etc. Will review concepts. Humorous material (clever and *very* funny) year-round. "Humor, conversational in tone and format, sells best for us." Prefers unrhymed contemporary humor. Current pay schedule available with guidelines.
Other Product Lines: Notepads, stick-on notes.
Tips: "The greeting card market has become more competitive with a greater need for creative and original ideas. We are looking for writers who can communicate situations, thoughts, and relationships in a funny way and apply them to a birthday, get well, etc., greeting and we are willing to work with them in targeting our style. We will be looking for material that says something funny about life in a new way."

P.S. GREETINGS, 5060 N. Kimberly Ave., Chicago IL 60630. (773)725-9308. Fax: (773)725-8655. Website: www. psg-fpp.com. **Contact:** Jennifer Dodson, art director. **100% of material freelance written. Bought 200-300 ideas/ samples last year.** Submit seasonal/holiday material 6 months in advance. Responds in 1 month. Material not copyrighted. **Pays on acceptance.** Writer's guidelines/market list for #10 SASE or check them out on the website.
Needs: Juvenile, studio, conventional, inspirational, sensitivity, humorous, invitations, soft line. Accepts rhymed or unrhymed verse ideas. Submit 10 ideas/batch. **Pays one-time flat fee.**

THE PAPER MAGIC GROUP, INC., 401 Adams Ave., Scranton PA 18510. (800) 278-4085. Fax: (717)348-8389. **Contact:** Peggy Bernosky, product manager. Estab. 1907. **50% freelance written. Receives 500 submissions/year.** Submit seasonal/holiday material 6 months in advance. **Pays on acceptance**. No market list.
Nonfiction: Christmas boxed cards only. Submit Christmas sentiments only. No relative titles, no juvenile. Submit 6-12 ideas/batch.

PLUM GRAPHICS INC., P.O. Box 136, Prince Station, New York NY 10012. (212)337-0999. Fax: (212)633-9910. Website: http://plumgraphi@aol.com. President: Yvette Cohen. **Contact:** Michelle Reynoso, operations manager. Estab. 1983. **100% freelance written. Receives 500-1,000 submissions/year. Bought 30-40 samples last year.** Does not return samples unless accompanied by SASE. Responds in 4 months. Buys greeting card and stationery rights. Pays on publication. Guidelines sheet for SASE, "sent out about twice a year in conjunction with the development of new cards."
Needs: Fun copy to appeal to a wide range of ages. "We don't want general submissions. We want them to relate to our next line." Prefers unrhymed verse. Greeting cards pay $40-50.

Tips: "Humor is always appreciated. We want short, to-the-point lines."

N **PORTAL PUBLICATIONS**, 201 Alameda Del Prado, Novato CA 94941. (415)924-5652. Website: www.portal pub.com. **Contact:** Editorial Department. Estab. 1954. **25% freelance written. Receives 200 submissions/year; bought 50 freelance ideas/samples last year.** Responds in 3 months. Pays on publication. "Send an example of your work for us to keep on file. If we have a need for writers for our greeting cards or other products, we will contact you."
Needs: Conventional, humorous, informal, soft line, studio. Also copy for humorous and inspirational posters. Prefers unrhymed verse. Submit 12 ideas/batch.
Other Product Lines: Calendars, posters.
Tips: "Upscale, cute, soft, humorous cards for bookstores and college bookstores."

RENAISSANCE GREETING CARDS, P.O. Box 845, Springvale ME 04083. (207)324-4153. Fax: (207)324-9564. **Contact:** Janice Keefe, verse editor. Estab. 1977. **25% of material freelance written. Receives 75-100 submissions/year; bought 100 ideas/samples last year.** Submit seasonal/holiday material 16 months in advance. Responds in 2 months. Buys greeting card rights. Pays on publication. Writer's guidelines/market list for #10 SASE.
Needs: Informal, juvenile, inspirational, sensitive, humorous. Prefers unrhymed verse ideas. Submit no more than 25 ideas/batch.
Tips: "Verses that are sincere and complimentary in a conversational tone tend to do best. For humor, we avoid 'put down' type of jokes and try to stay positive. Target audience is women over 18 and Baby Boomers."

ROCKSHOTS, INC., 632 Broadway, 8th Floor, New York NY 10012. (212)420-1400. Fax: (212)353-8756. **Contact:** Bob Vesce, editor. Estab. 1979. **Buys 75 greeting card verse (or gag) lines/year.** Responds in 2 months. Buys rights for greeting-card use. Writer's guidelines for SASE.
Needs: Humorous ("should be off-the-wall, as outrageous as possible, preferably for sophisticated buyer"); soft line; combination of sexy and humorous come-on type greeting ("sentimental is not our style"); and insult cards ("looking for cute insults"). No sentimental or conventional material. "Card gag can adopt a sentimental style, then take an ironic twist and end on an off-beat note." Submit no more than 10 card ideas/samples per batch. Send to Attention: Submissions.
Pays $50/gag line. Prefers gag lines on 8×11 paper with name, address, and phone and social security numbers in right corner, or individually on 3×5 cards.
Tips: "Think of a concept that would normally be too outrageous to use, give it a cute and clever wording to make it drop-dead funny, and you will have commercialized a non-commercial message. It's always good to mix sex and humor. Our emphasis is definitely on the erotic. The trend is toward 'light' sexy humor, even cute sexy humor. 'Cute' has always sold cards, and it's a good word to think of even with the most sophisticated, crazy ideas. 80% of our audience is female. Remember that your gag line will be illustrated by a photographer, so try to think visually. If no visual is needed, the gag line *can* stand alone, but we generally prefer some visual representation. It is a very good idea to preview our cards at your local store if this is possible to give you a feeling of our style."

SPS STUDIOS, INC., publishers of BLUE MOUNTAIN ARTS PRODUCTS, Dept. WM, P.O. Box 1007, Boulder CO 80306-1007. Fax: (303)447-0939. E-mail: bma@rmi.net. **Contact:** Editorial Department. Estab. 1971. **Buys 100 items/year.** Responds in 3 months. Pays on publication. Writer's guidelines for #10 SASE.
Needs: "We are interested in reviewing poetry and writings that would be appropriate for greeting cards, which means that they should reflect a message, feeling, or sentiment that one person would want to share with another. We'd like to receive sensitive, original submissions about love relationships, family members, friendships, philosophies, and any other aspect of life. Poems and writings for specific holidays (Christmas, Valentine's Day, etc.) and special occasions, such as graduation, birthdays, anniversary, and get well are also considered." Submit seasonal material at least 4 months in advance. Enclose SASE with submission. **Buys worldwide, exclusive rights, $200/poem; anthology rights $25.**
Other Product Lines: Calendars, gift books, prints, mugs.
Tips: "Familiarize yourself with our products before submitting material, although we caution you not to study them too hard. We do *not* need more poems that sound like something we've already published. We're looking for poetry that expresses real emotions and feelings, so we suggest that you have someone specific in mind (a friend, relative, etc.) as you write. The majority of the poetry we publish *does not rhyme*. We do not wish to receive books, unless you are interested in having portions excerpted for greeting cards; nor do we wish to receive artwork or photography. We prefer that submissions be typewritten, one poem per page, with name and address on every page. Only a small portion of the freelance material we receive is selected each year, and the review process can also be lengthy, but please be assured that every manuscript is given serious consideration."

WEST GRAPHICS, 1117 California Dr., Burlingame CA 94010. (800)648-9378. Website: www.west-graphics.com. **Contact:** Production Department. Estab. 1980. **80% freelance written. Receives 20,000 submissions/year; bought 100 freelance ideas/samples last year.** Responds in 6 weeks. Buys greeting card rights. Pays 30 days after publication. Writer's guidelines/market list for #10 SASE.
Needs: "We are looking for outrageous adult humor that is on the cutting edge." Prefers unrhymed verse. Submit 20-30 ideas/batch. **Pays $60-100.**
Tips: "West Graphics is an alternative greeting card company which offers a diversity of humor from 'off the wall' to 'tastefully tasteless'. Our goal is to publish cards that challenge the limits of taste and keep people laughing. The majority of our audience is women in their 30s and 40s, ideas should be targeted to birthday sentiment."

Contests & Awards

The contests and awards listed in this section are arranged by subject. Nonfiction writers can turn immediately to nonfiction awards listed alphabetically by the name of the contest or award. The same is true for fiction writers, poets, playwrights and screenwriters, journalists, children's writers and translators. You'll also find general book awards, miscellaneous awards, arts council and foundation fellowships, and multiple category contests.

New contests and awards are announced in various writer's publications nearly every day. However, many lose their funding or fold—and sponsoring magazines go out of business just as often. We have contacted the organizations whose contests and awards are listed here with the understanding that they are valid through 2000-2001. If you are using this section in 2002 or later, keep in mind that much of the contest information listed here will not be current. Requirements such as entry fees change, as do deadlines, addresses and contact names.

To make sure you have all the information you need about a particular contest, always send a self-addressed, stamped, business-sized envelope (#10 SASE) to the contact person in the listing before entering a contest. The listings in this section are brief, and many contests have lengthy, specific rules and requirements that we could not include in our limited space. Often a specific entry form must accompany your submission. A response with rules and guidelines will not only provide specific instructions, it will also confirm that the award is still being offered.

When you receive a set of guidelines, you will see that some contests are not for some writers. The writer's age, previous publication, geographic location and the length of the work are common matters of eligibility. Read the requirements carefully to ensure you don't enter a contest for which you are not qualified. You should also be aware that every year, more and more contests, especially those sponsored by "little" literary magazines, are charging entry fees.

Contest and award competition is very strong. While a literary magazine may publish ten short stories in an issue, only one will win the prize in a contest. Give yourself the best chance of winning by sending only your best work. There is always a percentage of manuscripts cast off immediately as unpolished, amateurish or wholly unsuitable for the competition.

To avoid first-round rejection, make certain that you and your work qualify in every way for the award. Some contests are more specific than others. There are many contests and awards for a "best poem," but some award only the best lyric poem, sonnet or haiku.

Winning a contest or award can launch a successful writing career. Take a professional approach by doing a little extra research. Find out who the previous winner of the award was by investing in a sample copy of the magazine in which the prize-winning article, poem or short story appeared. Attend the staged reading of an award-winning play. Your extra effort will be to your advantage in competing with writers who simply submit blindly.

If a contest or award requires nomination by your publisher, ask your publisher to nominate you. Many welcome the opportunity to promote a work (beyond their own, conventional means). Just be sure the publisher has plenty of time before the deadline to nominate your work.

Further information on funding for writers is available at most large public libraries. See the *Annual Register of Grant Support* (National Register Publishing Co., a division of Reed-Elsevier, *Foundations and Grants to Individuals* (Foundation Center, 79 Fifth Ave., New York NY 10003) and *Grants and Awards Available to American Writers* (PEN American Center, 568 Broadway, New York NY 10012). For more listings of contests and awards for fiction writers, see *Novel & Short Story Writer's Market* (Writer's Digest Books). *Poet's Market* (Writer's Digest Books) lists contests and awards available to poets. *Children's Writer's & Illustrator's Market* (Writer's

Digest Books) has a section of contests and awards, as well. Two more good sources for literary contests are *Poets & Writers* (72 Spring St., New York NY 10012), and the *Associated Writing Programs Newsletter* (Old Dominion University, Norfolk VA 23529). Journalists should look into the annual Journalism Awards Issue of *Editor & Publisher* magazine (11 W. 19th St., New York NY 10011), published in the last week of December. Playwrights should be aware of the newsletter put out by The Dramatists Guild, (234 W. 44th St., New York NY 10036).

Information on contests and awards listed in the previous edition of *Writer's Market* but not included in this edition can be found in the General Index.

General

THE ANISFIELD-WOLF BOOK AWARDS, The Cleveland Foundation, 1422 Euclid Ave., Suite 1400, Cleveland OH 44115. (216)861-3810. Fax: (216)861-1729. E-mail: asktcf@clevefda.org. Website: www.clevelandfoundation.org. **Contact:** Marcia Bryant. "The Anisfield-Wolf Book Award annually honors books which contribute to our understanding or racism or our appreciation of the diversity of human culture published during the year of the award." Deadline: January 31. Guidelines for SASE. Prize: $20,000. Judged by five-member panel chaired by Dr. Henry Louis Gates of Harvard University and including Joyce Carol Oates, Rita Dove and Stephen Jay Gould. Any work addressing issues of racial bias or human diversity may qualify.

ARTS & LIFE PRIZE FOR HUMOR, International Literary Society, 18463 Blueberry Lane, Apt. C101, Monroe WA 98272-1379. (206)930-6588. Fax: (360)794-5104. E-mail: nccsteve@Juno.com. Contest Director: Steve Whalen. Offered annually for unpublished humorous anecdotes or jokes to gather material for a cultural magazine. Deadline: March 31. Guidelines for SASE. Charges $5 fee per entry; maximum 5 entries. Prize: 1st-$1,000, 2nd-$150, Honorable Mentions.

ARTS & LIFE PRIZE FOR RELIGION, International Literary Society, 18463 Blueberry Lane, Apt. C101, Monroe WA 98272-1379. (206)890-4422. Fax: (425)487-2633. E-mail: swhalen@mcwe.com. Contest Director: Steve Whalen. Offered annually for unpublished 1,500 word stories of a spiritual testimony or journey (nonfiction preferred, fiction accepted) to gather material for a cultural magazine. Deadline: November 30. Guidelines for SASE. Charges $18 fee. Prize: 1st-$1,000, 2nd-$150, Honorable Mentions.

ARTSLINK COLLABORATIVE PROJECTS AWARD, CEC International Partners, 12 W. 31st St., New York NY 10001. (212)643-1985. Fax: (212)643-1996. E-mail: artslink@cecip.org. Website: www.cecip.org. **Contact:** Susan Wyatt. Offered annually to enable artists of all media to work in eastern Europe with colleagues there on collaborative projects. Check on website for deadline and other information. Prize: up to $10,000.

BANTA AWARD, Wisconsin Library Association, % Literary Awards Comm., 5250 E. Terrace Dr., Suite A-1, Madison WI 53718-8345. (608)245-3640. Website: www.bratshb.uwc.edu/nwla/. **Contact:** Chair, Literary Award Committee. Offered annually for books published during the year preceding the award. The Literary Awards Committee reviews all works by Wisconsin authors that are not edited, revised editions, textbooks or written in foreign languages. Review copies or notification of books, along with verification of the author's ties to Wisconsin, may be submitted to the Committee, by the publisher or author. Deadline: March of calendar year following publication. Prize: $500, a plaque given by the Banta Corporation Foundation, and presentation at the Annual Conference of the Wisconsin Library Association between late October and early November. Only open to writers born, raised or currently living in Wisconsin.

FRIENDS OF THE DALLAS PUBLIC LIBRARY AWARD, The Texas Institute of Letters, Southwest Texas State University, San Marcos TX 78666. (512)245-2428. Fax: (512)245-7462. E-mail: mb13@swt.edu. Website: www.English. swt.edu/css/TIL/rules.htm. **Contact:** Mark Busby.. Offered annually for submissions published January 1-December 31 of previous year to recognize the writer of the book making the most important contribution to knowledge. Deadline: January 3. Guidelines for SASE. Prize: $1,000. Writer must have been born in Texas, have lived in the state at least 2 consecutive years at some time, or the subject matter of the book should be associated with the state.

STANLEY MARCUS AWARD FOR BEST BOOK DESIGN, Texas Institute of Letters, Southwest Texas State University, San Marcos TX 78666. (512)245-2428. Fax: (512)245-7462. E-mail: mb13@swt.edu. Website: www.English. swt.edu/css/TIL/rules.htm. **Contact:** Mark Busby. Offered annually for work published January 1-December 31. Deadline: First working day of new year. Guidelines for SASE. Prize: $750. Open to Texas residents or those who have lived in Texas for two consecutive years.

MATURE WOMAN GRANTS, The National League of American Pen Women, 1300 17th St. N.W., Washington DC 20036. (202)785-1997. Fax: (202)452-6868. E-mail: nlapw1@juno.com. Website: members.aol.com/penwomen/

pen.htm. **Contact:** Mary Jane Hillery, national scholarship chair, 66 Willow Rd., Sudbury MA 01776-2663. Offered every 2 years to further the 35+ age woman and her creative purposes in art, music and letters. Deadline: October 1, odd-numbered years. Award announced by March 1, even-numbered years. Send letter stating age, background and purpose for the monetary award. Send SASE for information. Charges $8 fee with entry. Prize: $1,000 each in art, letters and music.

MINNESOTA VOICES PROJECT COMPETITION, New Rivers Press, 420 N. Fifth St., #1180, Minneapolis MN 55401. (612)339-7114. Fax: (612)339-9047. E-mail: eric@newriverspress.org. Website: www.newriverspress.org. **Contact:** Eric Braun, editor. Offered annually for new and emerging writers of poetry, prose, essays, and memoirs (as well as other forms of creative prose) from Minnesota to be published in book form for the first time. Deadline: April 1. Guidelines for SASE. Prize: $500 plus publication.

MISSISSIPPI REVIEW PRIZE, Mississippi Review, U.S.M. Box 5144, Hattiesburg MS 39406. (601)266-4321. Fax: (601)266-5757. E-mail: rief@netdoor.com. Website: sushi.st.usm.edu/mrw. **Contact:** Ric Fortenberry, contest director. Offered annually for unpublished literary, short fiction and poetry. Guidelines available online or with SASE. Charges $15/story entry fee.

NEW WRITING AWARD, New Writing, Box 1812, Amherst NY 14226-7812. E-mail: info@newwriting.com. Website: www.newwriting.com. **Contact:** Sam Meade. Offered annually for unpublished work "to award the best of *new* writing. We accept short stories, poems, plays, novels, essays, films and emerging forms. All entries are considered for the award based on originality." Charges $10 + 10¢ per page reading fee for first entry; $5 + 10¢ per page per additional entry—no limit. Guidelines and form for SASE or available on website. Prize: Monetary award (up to $3,000 in cash and prizes) and possible publication. "We are looking for new, interesting or experimental work."

PEN CENTER WEST LITERARY AWARDS, PEN Center West, 672 S. Lafayette Park Place, #41, Los Angeles CA 90057. (213)365-8500. Fax: (213)365-9616. E-mail: pen@pen-usa-west.org. Website: www.pen-usa-west.org. Deadl ine: Jan. 31, 2001. **Contact:** Christina L. Apeles, awards coordinator. Estab. 1952. Offered for work published and produced in previous calendar year. Deadline: 4 copies must be received by January 31. Open to writers living west of the Mississippi River. Award categories: drama, screenplay, teleplay, journalism. Prize: $1,000 and awards.

TORONTO MUNICIPAL CHAPTER IODE BOOK AWARD, Toronto Municipal Chapter IODE, 40 St. Clair Ave. E., Toronto, Ontario M4T 1M9 Canada. (416)925-5078. Fax: (416)925-5127. Education Officer: Kathleen Bull. **Contact:** IODE Education Committee. Offered annually for previously published childrens' book published by a Canadian publisher. Deadline: early November. Prize: $1,000. Author and illustrator must be a Canadian citizen and reside in or around Toronto.

TOWSON UNIVERSITY PRIZE FOR LITERATURE, College of Liberal Arts, Towson University, Towson MD 21252. (410)830-2128. **Contact:** Dean, College of Liberal Arts. Estab. 1979. Book or book-length ms that has been accepted for publication, written by a Maryland author of no more than 40 years of age. Deadline: June 15. Guideline for SASE. Prize: $1,500.

FRED WHITEHEAD AWARD, Texas Institute of Letters, Southwest Texas State University, San Marcos TX 78666. (512)245-2428. Fax: (512)245-7462. E-mail: mb13@swt.edu. Website: www.English.swt.edu/css/TIL/rules.htm. **Contact:** Mark Busby. Offered annually for the best design for a trade book. Deadline: January 3. Guidelines for SASE. Prize: $750. Open to Texas residents or those who have lived in Texas for 2 consecutive years.

WORLD FANTASY AWARDS ASSOCIATION, P.O. Box 43, Mukilted WA 98275-0043. Website: www.worldfant asy.org. **Contact:** Peter Dennis Pautz. Estab. 1975. Offered annually for previously published work recommended by previous convention attendees in several categories, including life achievement, novel, novella, short story, anthology, collection, artist, special award-pro and special award non-pro. Deadline: July 1. Works are recommended by attendees of current and previous two years' conventions, and a panel of judges.

Nonfiction

AMWA MEDICAL BOOK AWARDS COMPETITION, American Medical Writers Association, 40 W. Gude Dr., Rockville MD 20850-1192. (301)493-0003. E-mail: amwa@amwa.org. Website: www.amwa.org. **Contact:** Book Awards Committee. Offered annually to honor the best medical book published in the previous year in 3 categories: Books for Physicians, Books for Allied Health Professionals, and Trade Books. Deadline March 1. Charges $20 fee.

MRS. SIMON BARUCH UNIVERSITY AWARD, United Daughters of the Confederacy® 328 N. Boulevard, Richmond VA 23220-4057. (804)355-1636. Fax: (804)353-1396. E-mail: hqudc@aol.com. **Contact:** Mrs. Sarah O. Dunaway, chairman. Offered biannially in even-numbered years for unpublished work for the purpose of encouraging research in Southern history, the United Daughters of the Confederacy® offers as a grant-aid of publication the Mrs. Simon Baruch

University Award. Deadline: May 1. Authors and publishers interested in the Baruch Award contest should ask for a copy of these rules. All inquiries should be addressed to the Chairman of the Mrs. Simon Baruch University Award Committee at the above address. Award: $2,000 and $500 author's award. Invitation to participate in the contest is extended (1) to anyone who has received a Master's, Doctoral, or other advanced degree within the past fifteen years, from a university in the United States; and (2) to any graduate student whose thesis or dissertation has been accepted by such an institution. Manuscripts must be accompanied by a statement from the registrar giving dates of attendance, and by full biographical data together with passport photograph of the authors.

BIRKS FAMILY FOUNDATION AWARD FOR BIOGRAPHY, Canadian Author's Association, Box 419, 320 S. Shores Rd., Campbellford, Ontario K0L 1L0 Canada. (705)653-0323. Fax: (705)653-0593. E-mail: canauth@redd en.on.ca. Website: www.canauthors.org. **Contact:** Alec McEachern. Offered annually for a previously published biography about a Canadian. Deadline: December 15. Guidelines for SASE. Charges $20 entry fee (Canadian). Prize: $2,500 and a silver medal.

BOWLING WRITING COMPETITION, American Bowling Congress Publications, 5301 S. 76th St., Greendale WI 53129-1127. Fax: (414)421-3013. E-mail: mmille@bowlinginc.com. Website: www.bowl.com. Editor: Bill Vint. **Contact:** Mark Miller, assistant editor. Estab. 1935. Feature, editorial and news all relating to the sport of bowling. Deadline: December 15. Prize: 1st Place in each division-$300. In addition, News and Editorial-$225, $200, $175, $150, $75 and $50; Feature-$225, $200, $175, $150, $125, $100, $75, $50 and $50; with five honorable mention certificates awarded in each category.

BRITISH COUNCIL PRIZE, North American Conference on British Studies, Dept. of History, University of Texas, Austin TX 78712-1163. (512)475-7204. Fax: (512)475-7222. E-mail: levack@mailiutexas.edu. **Contact:** Brian P. Levack, executive secretary. Offered annually for best books in any field of British Studies after publication by a North American in previous year. Previously published submissions. Deadline: April 1. Guidelines for SASE. Prize: $1,000. Open to American or Canadian writers.

THE BROSS PRIZE, Lake Forest College, 555 N. Sheridan, Lake Forest IL 60045. (847)735-5175. Fax: (847)735-6192. E-mail: rmiller@lfc.edu. **Contact:** Professor Ron Miller. Offered every 10 years for unpublished work "to award the best book or treatise on the relation between any discipline or topic of investigation and the Christian religion." Deadline: September 1, 2000. Guidelines for SASE. Prize: Award varies depending on interest earned. Manuscripts awarded prizes become property of the college. Open to any writer.

JOHN BULLEN PRIZE, Canadian Historical Association, 395 Wellington, Ottawa, Ontario K1A 0N3 Canada. (613)233-7885. Fax: (613)567-3110. E-mail: cha-shc@archives.ca. Website: www.yorku.ca/research/cha/cha-shc.html. **Contact:** Joanne Mineault. Offered annually for an outstanding historical dissertation for a doctoral degree at a Canadian university. Deadline: November 30. Guidelines for SASE. Prize: $500. Open only to Canadian citizens or landed immigrants.

CANADIAN AUTHORS ASSOCIATION LELA COMMON AWARD FOR CANADIAN HISTORY, Box 419, 320 S. Shores Rd., Campbellford, Ontario K0L 1L0 Canada. (705)653-0323. Fax: (705)653-0593. E-mail: canauth@redden.on.ca. **Contact:** Alec McEachern. Offered annually for a work of historical nonfiction on a Canadian topic by a Canadian. Deadline: December 15. Guidelines for SASE. Charges $20 entry fee (Canadian). Prize: $2,500 and a silver medal. Open to Canadian authors only.

CANADIAN LIBRARY ASSOCIATION STUDENT ARTICLE CONTEST, Canadian Library Association, 200 Elgin St., Suite 602, Ottawa, Ontario K2P 1L5 Canada. (613)232-9625, ext. 318. Fax: (613)563-9895. Website: www.cla.ca. **Contact:** Brenda Shields. Offered annually to "unpublished articles discussing, analyzing or evaluating timely issues in librarianship or information science." Deadline: March 15. Guidelines for SASE. Prizes: 1st-$150, publication in *Feliciter*, trip to CLA's annual conference; Runners-Up: $75 choice of CLA publications. "Open to all students registered in or recently graduated from a Canadian library school, a library techniques program or faculty of education library program." Submissions may be in English or French.

MORTON N. COHEN AWARD, Modern Language Association of America, 10 Astor Place, New York NY 10003-6981. (212)614-6324. Fax: (212)533-0680. E-mail: awards@mla.org. Website: www.mla.org. **Contact:** Robert Blondeau. Estab. 1989. Awarded in odd-numbered years for a previously published distinguished edition of letters. At least 1 volume of the edition must have been published during the previous 2 years. Deadline: May 1. Guidelines for SASE. Prize: $1,000 and certificate.

CARR P. COLLINS AWARD, The Texas Institute of Letters, Southwest Texas State University, San Marcos TX 78666. (512)245-2428. Fax: (512)245-7462. E-mail: mb13@swt.edu. Website: www.English.swt.ecu/css/TIL/rules.htm. **Contact:** Mark Busby. Offered annually for work published January 1-December 31 of the previous year to recognize the best nonfiction book by a writer who was born in Texas or who has lived in the state for at least 2 consecutive years at one point or a writer whose work has some notable connection with Texas. Deadline: January 3. Guidelines for SASE. Prize: $5,000.

COLORADO PRIZE, Colorado Review/Center for Literary Publishing, Department of English, Colorado State University, Ft. Collins CO 80523. (970)491-5449. E-mail: creview@vines.colostate.edu. Website: www.colostate.edu/Depts/English/english_ns4.htm. General Editor: David Milofsky. Offered annually to an unpublished collection. Deadline: January 8, 2001. Guidelines for SASE. Charges $25 fee. Prize: $2,000 and publication of book.

CREATIVE NON-FICTION CONTEST, *Event*, P.O. Box 2503, New Westminster, British Columbia V3L 5B2 Canada. (604)527-5293. Fax: (604)527-5095. E-mail: event@douglas.bc.ca. Offered annually for unpublished creative nonfiction. Deadline: April 15. Guidelines for SASE. Charges $20 entry fee. Prize: $500 plus payment for publication. Acquires First North American serial rights. Open to any writer, except Douglas College employees.

N: THE CREATIVE NON-FICTION CONTEST, *sub-TERRAIN* Magazine & Anvil Press Publishers, #204-A 175 E. Broadway, Vancouver, British Columbia V5T 1W2 Canada. (604)876-8710. Fax: (604)879-2667. E-mail: subter@portal.ca. **Contact:** Brian Kaufman. Offered annually for creative nonfiction, not limited to any specific topic or subject. Length: 2,000-4,000 words. Deadline: August 1st. Submissions to be accompanied by a SASE and a typed 8½×11 paper, double spaced (no disks or e-mail submissions, please). Charges $15/story. $250 cash prize plus publication in the fall issue of *sub-TERRAIN* magazine. All entrants receive a one-year subscription to *sub-TERRAIN*.

N: DEXTER PRIZE, Society for the History of Technology, 216B Ames Hall, John Hopkins University, Baltimore MD 21218. (410)516-8349. Fax: (410)516-7502. **Contact:** Society Secretary. Estab. 1968. For work published in the previous 3 years: for 1998—1995 to 97. "Award given to the best book in the history of technology." Deadline: April 15. Guidelines for SASE. Prize: $2,000 and a plaque from the Dexter Chemical Company.

ANNIE DILLARD AWARD IN NONFICTION, The Bellingham Review, M.S. 9053, Western Washington University, Bellingham WA 98225. Website: www.wwu.edu/~bhreview/. **Contact:** (Mr.) Robin Hemley. Offered for annually unpublished essay on any subject and in any style. Submissions from January 2-March 1. Charges $10 entry fee for first essay, $5 thereafter. Guidelines for SASE. Prize: 1st-$1,000; 2nd-$250; 3rd-$100, plus publication and copies.

N: GORDON W. DILLON/RICHARD C. PETERSON MEMORIAL ESSAY PRIZE, American Orchid Society, Inc., 6000 S. Olive Ave., West Palm Beach FL 33405-9974. (561)585-8666. Fax: (561)585-0654. E-mail: TheAOS@CompuServe.com. Website: www.orchidweb.org. **Contact:** Jane Mengel. Estab. 1985. "An annual contest open to all writers. The theme is announced each May in the *Orchids* magazine. All themes deal with aspect of orchids, such as repotting, growing, hybridizing, etc. Unpublished submissions only." Themes in past years have included Orchid Culture, Orchids in Nature and Orchids in Use. Deadline: November 30. Guidelines for SASE. Prize: Cash award and certificate. Winning entry usually published in the May issue of *Orchids* magazine. One-time rights.

EDUCATOR'S AWARD, The Delta Kappa Gamma Society International, P.O. Box 1589, Austin TX 78767-1589. (512)478-5748. Fax: (512)478-3961. E-mail: tfechek@deltakappagamma.org. **Contact:** Dr. Theresa Fechek, executive coordinator. Offered annually for quality research and nonfiction published January-December of previous year. This award recognizes educational research and writings of women authors whose book may influence the direction of thought and action necessary to meet the needs to today's complex society. Deadline: February 1. Guidelines for SASE. Prize: $1,500. The book must be written by one woman or by two women who are citizens of any country in which The Delta Kappa Gamma Society International is organized: Canada, Costa Rica, El Salvador, Finland, Germany, Great Britain, Guatemala, Iceland, Mexico, The Netherlands, Norway, Puerto Rico, Sweden, United States. Must request guidelines and directions.

EVERETT E. EDWARDS AWARD, Agricultural History Center for Agricultural History, Iowa State University, 618 Ross Hall, Ames IA 50011-1202. (515)294-1596. Fax: (515)294-6390. E-mail: rdhurt@iastate.edu. Website: www.iastate.edu/~history_info/aghistory.htm. **Contact:** R. Douglas Hurt, Dept. of History, Iowa State University, Ames, Iowa 50011. Offered annually for best ms on any aspect of agricultural and rural history, broadly interpreted, submitted by a graduate student. Deadline: December 31. Guidelines for SASE. Prize: Monetary award to the author and publication in the journal. Open to submission by any graduate student.

WILFRED EGGLESTON AWARD FOR NONFICTION, Writers Guild of Alberta, 11759 Groat Rd., Edmonton Alberta T5M 3K6 Canada. (708)422-8174 or (800)665-5354. Fax: (708)422-2663. E-mail: wga@oanet.com. **Contact:** Renate Donnovan or Miki Andrejevic, executive directors. Offered annually for a nonfiction book published in current year. Open to Alberta authors. Prize: $500 and leatherbound copy of book. Guidelines for SASE.

THE CHARLES C. ELDREDGE PRIZE OF THE NATIONAL MUSEUM OF AMERICAN ART, National Museum of American Art, Smithsonian Institution, Washington DC 20560. (202)357-1886. Fax: (202)786-2583. E-mail: plynagh@nmaa.si.edu. Website: www.nmaa.si.edu. **Contact:** Pat Lynagh. Offered annually for previously published outstanding scholarship in the field of American art in the previous 2 years. It seeks to recognize originality and thoroughness of research, excellence of writing, clarity of method, and significance for professional or public audiences. Deadline: December 1. Guidelines for SASE. Prize: $2,000. "Nominations cannot be accepted from the author or publisher of any nominated book."

DAVID W. AND BEATRICE C. EVANS BIOGRAPHY & HANDCART AWARDS, Mountain West Center for Regional Studies, Utah State University, 0735 Old Main Hill, Logan UT 84322-0735. (435)797-3632. Fax: (435)797-3899. E-mail: mwc@cc.usu.edu. Website: www.usu.edu/~pioneers/mwc.html. **Contact:** Jane Reilly, associate director, Mountain West Center. Estab. 1983. Offered to encourage the writing of biography about people who have played a role in Mormon Country. (Not the religion, the country: Intermountain West with parts of Southwestern Canada and Northwestern Mexico.) Deadline: December 1. Guidelines for SASE. Two prizes: $10,000 and $1,000. Publishers or author may nominate book. Criteria for consideration: Work must be a biography or autobiography on "Mormon Country"; must be submitted for consideration for publication year's award; new editions or reprints are not eligible; mss are not accepted. Submit 4 copies.

WALLACE K. FERGUSON PRIZE, Canadian Historical Association, 395 Wellington, Ottawa, Ontario K1A 0N3 Canada. (613)233-7885. Fax: (615)567-3110. E-mail: cha-shc@archives.ca Website: www.yorku.ca/research/cha/cha-shc.html. **Contact:** Joanne Mineault. Offered to a Canadian who has published the outstanding scholarly book in a field of history other than Canadian history. Deadline: December 1. Guidelines for SASE. Prize: $1,000. Open to Canadian citizens and landed immigrants only.

DIXON RYAN FOX MANUSCRIPT PRIZE, New York State Historical Association, P.O. Box 800, Cooperstown NY 13326. (607)547-1481. Fax: (607)547-1405. Website: www.nysha.org. **Contact:** Wendell Tripp, director of publications. Offered annually for the best unpublished book-length manuscript dealing with some aspect of the history of New York State. Deadline: January 20. Guidelines for SASE. Prize: $3,000 and assistance in finding a publisher. Open to any writer.

GEORGE FREEDLEY MEMORIAL AWARD, Theatre Library Association, Benjamin Rosenthal Library, Queens College, C.U.N.Y., 65-30 Kissena Blvd., Flushing NY 11367. (718)997-3672. Fax: (718)997-3672. E-mail: rlwqc@cuny vm.cuny.edu. Website: www.brown.edu/Facilities/University_Library/beyond/TLA/TLA.html. **Contact:** Richard Wall, Book Awards Committee Chair. Estab. 1968. Offered for a book published in the US within the previous calendar year on a subject related to live theatrical performance (including cabaret, circus, pantomime, puppetry, vaudeville, etc.). Eligible books may include biography, history, theory, criticism, reference or related fields. Prize: $250 and certificate to the winner; $100 and certificate for Honorable Mention. Submissions and deadline: Nominated books are requested from publishers; one copy should be received by each of three award jurors as well as the Chairperson by February 15 of the year following eligibility.

LIONEL GELBER PRIZE, Lionel Gelber Foundation, 112 Braemore Gardens, Toronto Ontario M6G 2C8 Canada. (416)652-1947 or (416)656-3722. Fax: (416)658-5205. E-mail: meisner@interlog.com. **Contact:** Susan Meisner, prize manager. Offered annually for the year's most outstanding work of nonfiction in the field of international relations. Books must be published in English or English translation September 1, 1999-August 31, 2000. Deadline: May 31. Guidelines for SASE. However, the publisher must submit the title on behalf of the author. Prize: $50,000 (Canadian funds).

ALBERT J. HARRIS AWARD, International Reading Association, Division of Research and Policy, 800 Barksdale Rd., P.O. Box 8139, Newark DE 19714-8139. (302)731-1600 ext. 226. Fax: (302)731-1057. Offered annually to recognize outstanding published works on the topics of reading disabilities and the prevention, assessment or instruction of learners experiencing difficulty learning to read. Deadline: September 15. Guidelines for SASE. Prize: monetary award and recognition at the International Reading Association's annual convention. Open to all writers.

HIGHSMITH LIBRARY LITERATURE AWARD, (formerly G.K. Hall Award for Library Literature), American Library Association, 50 E. Huron St., Chicago IL 60611. (312)280-3247. Fax: (312)280-3257. E-mail: awards@ala.org. Offered annually to previously published books that make an outstanding contribution to library literature. Deadline: December 1. Guidelines for SASE or by e-mail. Prize: $500 and framed citation.

THE KIRIYAMA PACIFIC RIM BOOK PRIZE, Kiriyama Pacific Rim Institute and University of San Francisco Center for the Pacific Rim, 2130 Fulton St., San Francisco CA 94117-1080. (415)422-5984. Fax: (415)422-5933. E-mail: cuevas@usfca.edu. Website: www.pacificrimvoices.org. **Contact:** Jeannine Cuevas, project coordinator. Offered for work published October 1-September 30 of the award year to promote books that will contribute to better understanding and increased cooperation throughout all areas of the Pacific Rim. Guidelines and entry form for SASE. Deadline: July 1. Prize: $30,000 to be divided equally between the author of one fiction and of one nonfiction book. Books must be submitted for entry by the publisher. Proper entry forms must be submitted. Contact the administrators of the prize for complete rules and entry forms.

KATHERINE SINGER KOVACS PRIZE, Modern Language Association of America, 10 Astor Place, New York NY 10003-6981. (212)614-6324. Fax: (212)533-0680. E-mail: awards@mla.org. Website: www.mla.org. **Contact:** Robert Blondeau. Estab. 1990. Offered annually for a book published during the previous year in English in the field of Latin American and Spanish Literatures and cultures. Books should be broadly interpretive works that enhance understanding of the interrelations among literarture, the other arts, and society. Authors need not be members of the MLA. Deadline: May 1. Guidelines for SASE. Prize: $1,000 and certificate.

N WALTER D. LOVE PRIZE, North American Conference on British Studies, Dept. of History, University of Texas, Austin TX 78712. (512)475-7204. Fax: (512)475-7222. E-mail: levack@mail.utexas.edu. **Contact:** Brian P. Levack, executive secretary. Offered annually for best article in any field of British Studies. Previously published submissions. Deadline: April 1. Guidelines for SASE. Prize: $150. Open to American or Canadian writers.

JAMES RUSSELL LOWELL PRIZE, Modern Language Association of America, 10 Astor Place, New York NY 10003-6981. (212)614-6324. Fax: (212)533-0680. E-mail: awards@mla.org. Website: www.mla.org. **Contact:** Robert Blondeau. Offered annually for literary or linguistic study, or critical edition or biography published in previous year. Open to MLA members only. Deadline: March 1. Guidelines for #10 SASE. Prize: $1,000 and certificate.

SIR JOHN A. MACDONALD PRIZE, Canadian Historical Association, 395 Wellington, Ottawa, Ontario K1A 0N3 Canada. (613)233-7885. Fax: (613)567-3110. E-mail: cha-shc@archives.ca. Website: www.yorku.ca/research/cha/cha-shc.html. **Contact:** Joanne Mineault. Offered annually to award a previously published nonfiction work of Canadian history "judged to have made the most significant contribution to an understanding of the Canadian past." Deadline: December 1. Guidelines for SASE. Prize: $1,000. Open to Canadian citizens only.

MACLEAN HUNTER ENDOWMENT LITERARY NON-FICTION PRIZE, PRISM international, Buch E462, 1866 Main Mall, Vancouver, British Columbia V6T 1Z1 Canada. (604)822-2514. Fax: (604)822-3616. E-mail: prism@in terchange.ubc.ca. Website: www.arts.ubc.ca/prism. **Contact:** Laisha Rosnau. Offered annually for published and unpublished writers to promote and reward excellence in literary nonfiction writing. Deadline: September 30. Guidelines for SASE. Charges $20 fee. Prize: $1,500 for the winning entry plus $20/page for the publication of the winner in *PRISM*'s winter issue. PRISM buys North American serial rights upon publication; "we also buy limited web rights for pieces selected for website." Open to anyone except students and faculty of the Creative Writing Program at UBC.

HOWARD R. MARRARO PRIZE and SCAGLIONE PRIZE FOR ITALIAN LITERARY STUDIES, Modern Language Association of America, 10 Astor Place, New York NY 10003-6981. (212)614-6324. Fax: (212)533-0680. E-mail: awards@mla.org. Website: www.mla.org. **Contact:** Robert Blondeau. Joint prize offered in even-numbered years for books or essays on any phase of Italian literature or comparative literature involving Italian, published in previous 2 years. Open to MLA members only. Deadline: May 1, 2000. Guidelines for SASE. Prize: $1,000 and certificate.

THE MAYFLOWER SOCIETY CUP COMPETITION, North Carolina Literary and Historical Association, 4610 Mail Service Center, Raleigh NC 27699-4610. (919)733-9375. **Contact:** Jerry C. Cashion, awards coordinator. Offered annually for volume of published nonfiction by a North Carolina resident. Deadline: July 15.

McLEMORE PRIZE, Mississippi Historical Society, P.O. Box 571, Jackson MS 39205-0571. (601)359-6850. Fax: (601)359-6975. Website: www.mdah.state.ms.us. **Contact:** Katie Blount. Estab. 1902. Offered for a scholarly book on a topic in Mississippi history/biography published in the year of competition. Deadline: November 1.

N MELCHER BOOK AWARD, Unitarian Universalist Association, 25 Beacon St., Boston MA 02108-2800. (617)742-2100. Fax: (617)742-7025. Website: www.uua.org. **Contact:** Sascha Galkin, publication assistant. Estab. 1964. Previously published book on religious liberalism. Deadline: January 31.

MID-LIST PRESS FIRST SERIES AWARD FOR CREATIVE NONFICTION, Mid-List Press, 4324 12th Ave. S., Minneapolis MN 55407-3218. Fax: (612)823-8387. E-mail: guide@midlist.org. Website: www.midlist.org. **Contact:** Lane Stiles, senior editor. Open to any writer who has never published a book of creative nonfiction. Submit either a collection of essays or a single book-length work; minimum length 50,000 words. Charges $20 fee. Submit entire ms beginning after March 31; must be postmarked by July 1. Accepts simultaneous submissions. Guidelines and entry form for SASE or from website. Awards include publication and an advance against royalties.

KENNETH W. MILDENBERGER PRIZE, Modern Language Association of America, 10 Astor Place, New York NY 10003-6981. (212)614-6324. Fax: (212)533-0680. E-mail: awards@mla.org. Website: www.mla.org. **Contact:** Robert Blondeau. Offered annually for a research publication (articles in odd-numbered years and books in even-numbered years) from the previous biennium in the field of teaching foreign languages and literatures. In 2000 the award will be given to a book published in 1998 or 1999. Deadline: May 1. Guidelines for SASE. Prize: $500 for articles and $1,000 for books, and a year's membership in the MLA. Author need not be a member.

MLA PRIZE FOR A DISTINGUISHED BIBLIOGRAPHY, 10 Astor Place, New York NY 10003-6981. (212)614-6324. Fax: (212)533-0680. E-mail: awards@mla.org. Website: www.mla.org. **Contact:** Robert Blondeau. Offered even-numbered years for enumerative and descriptive bibliographies published in monographic, book or electronic format in the previous biennium. Deadline: May 1, 2000. Guidelines for SASE. Prize: $1,000. Open to any writer or publisher.

MLA PRIZE FOR A DISTINGUISHED SCHOLARLY EDITION, Modern Language Association of America, 10 Astor Place, New York NY 10003-6981. (212)614-6324. Fax: (212)533-0680. E-mail: awards@mla.org. Website: www.mla.org. **Contact:** Robert Blondeau. Offered in odd-numbered years. Work published between 1999 and 2000 qualifies for the 2001 competition. To qualify for the award, an edition should be based on an examination of all available relevant textual sources; the source texts and the edited text's deviations from them should by fully described; the edition should employ editorial principles appropriate to the materials edited, and those principles should be clearly articulated in the volume; the text should be accompanied by appropriate textual and other historical contextual information; the edition should exhibit the highest standards of accuracy in the presentation of its text and apparatus; and the text and apparatus should be presented as accessibly and elegantly as possible. Deadline: May 1. Guidelines for SASE. Prize: $1,000 and certificate. Editor need not be a member of the MLA.

MLA PRIZE FOR A FIRST BOOK, Modern Language Association, 10 Astor Place, New York NY 10003-6981. (212)614-6324. Fax: (212)533-0680. E-mail: awards@mla.org. Website: www.mla.org. **Contact:** Robert Blondeau. Offered annually for the first book-length scholarly publication by a current member of the association. To qualify, a book must be a literary or linguistic study, a critical edition of an important work, or a critical biography. Studies dealing with literary theory, media, cultural history and interdisciplinary topics are eligible; books that are primarily translations will not be considered. Deadline: April 1. Guidelines for SASE. Prize: $1,000 and certificate.

MLA PRIZE FOR INDEPENDENT SCHOLARS, Modern Language Association of America, 10 Astor Place, New York NY 10003-6981. (212)614-6324. Fax: (212)533-0680. E-mail: awards@mla.org. Website: www.mla.org. **Contact:** Robert Blondeau. Offered annually for a book in the field of English or another modern language or literature published in previous year. Authors who are enrolled in a program leading to an academic degree or who hold tenured or tenure-track positions in higher education are not eligible. Authors do not need to be members of MLA to compete for this prize. Deadline: May 1. Guidelines and application form for SASE. Prize: $1,000 and a year's membership in the MLA.

NATIONAL WRITERS ASSOCIATION NONFICTION CONTEST, The National Writers Association, 3140 S. Peoria, #295, Aurora CO 80014. (303)841-0246. Fax: (303)751-8593. E-mail: sandywrter@aol.com. **Contact:** Sandy Whelchel, director. Annual contest "to encourage writers in this creative form and to recognize those who excel in nonfiction writing." Charges $18 fee. Deadline: December 31. Prizes: $200, $100, $50. Guidelines for #10 SASE.

THE FREDERIC W. NESS BOOK AWARD, Association of American Colleges and Universities, 1818 R St. NW, Washington DC 20009. (202)387-3760. Fax: (202)265-9532. E-mail: info@aacu.nw.dc.us. Website: www.aacu-edu.org. **Contact:** Karyn Hadfield. Offered annually for work previously published July 1-June 30 of the year in which it is being considered. "Each year the Frederic W. Ness Book Award Committee of the Association of American Colleges and Universities recognizes books which contribute to the understanding and improvement of liberal education." Deadline: August 15. Guidelines for SASE and on website. "Writers may nominate their own work; however, we send letters of invitation to publishers to nominate qualified books." Prize: $2,000 and presentation at the association's annual meeting. Transportation and one night hotel for meeting are also provided.

OUTSTANDING DISSERTATION OF THE YEAR AWARD, International Reading Association, 800 Barksdale Rd., P.O. Box 8139, Newark DE 19714-8139. (302)731-1600, ext. 226. Fax: (302)731-1057. E-mail: gkeating@reading.org. **Contact:** Gail Keating. Offered annually to recognize dissertations in the field of reading and literacy. Deadline: October 1. Guidelines for SASE. Prize: $1,000.

FRANK LAWRENCE AND HARRIET CHAPPELL OWSLEY AWARD, Southern Historical Association, Department of History, University of Georgia, Athens GA 30602-1602. (706)542-8848. Fax: (706)542-2455. Website: www.uga.edu/~sha. Managing Editor: John B. Boles. **Contact:** Secretary-Treasurer. Estab. 1934. Offered in odd-numbered years for recognition of a distinguished book in Southern history published in even-numbered years. Publishers usually submit the books. Deadline: March 1.

N PEN/ARCHITECTURAL DIGEST AWARD, 568 Broadway, New York NY 10012. Fax: (212)334-2181. E-mail: jm@pen.org. Website: www.pen.org. **Contact:** John Morrone, literary awards manager. Offered annually for an outstanding book, published in the US in 2000, of criticism or commentary on one or more of the visual arts, which may include architecture, interior design, landscape studies, painting, photography and sculpture. Deadline: December 15; earlier submissions strongly recommended. Prize: $10,000. Send 3 copies of each eligible book. Eligible books must have been published in the current calendar year. Open to US writers.

PEN/JERARD FUND, PEN American Center, 568 Broadway, New York NY 10012. (212)334-1660. Fax: (212)334-2181. E-mail: jm@pen.org. **Contact:** John Morrone. Estab. 1986. Biennial grant offered in odd-numbered years of $4,000 for American woman writer of nonfiction for a booklength work in progress. Guidelines for #10 SASE. Next award: 2001. Deadline: January 2.

PEN/MARTHA ALBRAND AWARD FOR FIRST NONFICTION, PEN American Center, 568 Broadway, New York NY 10012. (212)334-1660. Fax: (212)334-2181. E-mail: jm@pen.org. **Contact:** John Morrone, coordinator. Offered annually for a first published book of general nonfiction distinguished by qualities of literary and stylistic excellence. Eligible books must have been published in the calendar year under consideration. Authors must be American citizens or permanent residents. Although there are no restrictions on the subject matter of titles submitted, non-literary books will not be considered. Books should be of adult nonfiction for the general or academic reader. Deadline: December 15. Publishers, agents and authors themselves must submit *3* copies of each eligible title. Prize: $1,000.

PEN/MARTHA ALBRAND AWARD FOR THE ART OF THE MEMOIR, Pen American Center, 568 Broadway, New York NY 10012. (212)334-1660. Fax: (212)334-2181. E-mail: jm@pen.org. **Contact:** John Morrone. Offered annually to an American author for his/her memoir published in the current calendar year, distinguished by qualities of literary and stylistic excellence. Deadline: December 15. Send three copies of each eligible book. Prize: $1,000. Open to American writers.

N: PEN/SPIELVOGEL-DIAMONSTEIN AWARD, PEN American Center, 568 Broadway, New York NY 10012. (212)334-1660. Fax: (212)334-2181. E-mail: jm@pen.org. **Contact:** John Morrone. Offered for the best previously unpublished collection of essays on any subject by an American writer. "The $5,000 prize is awarded to preserve the dignity and esteem that the essay form imparts to literature." Authors must be American citizens or permanent residents. The essays included in books submitted may have been previously published in magazines, journals or anthologies, but must not have collectively appeared before in book form. Books will be judged on literary character and distinction of the writing. Publishers, agents, or the authors must submit four copies of each eligible title. Deadline: December 15.

JAMES A. RAWLEY PRIZE, Organization of American Historians. (812)855-9852. Fax: (812)855-0696. E-mail: kara@oah.org. Website: www.oah.org. **Contact:** Award and Prize Committee Coordinator. Offered annually for a book dealing with the history of race relations in the US. Deadline: October 1. Prize: $750 and certificate. Before submitting a nomination, a listing of current committee members and details about individual prizes must be obtained by sending SASE to: Award and Prize Committee Coordinator, Organization of American Historians, 112 N. Bryan Ave., Bloomington IN 47408-4199.

N: PHILLIP D. REED MEMORIAL AWARD FOR OUTSTANDING WRITING ON THE SOUTHERN ENVIRONMENT, Southern Environmental Law Center, 201 W. Main St., Charlottesville VA 22902. (804)977-4090. Fax: (804)977-1483. E-mail: cmccue@selcva.org. Website: www.southernenvironment.org. **Contact:** Cathryn McCue, award director. Offered annually for pieces published in the previous calendar year "to encourage and promote writing about natural resources in the South." Deadline: March. Guidelines for SASE. Prize: $1,000 in each category. Two categories: Journalistic non-fiction (newspaper and magazine articles) and Literary non-fiction (essays and books). Minimum length: 3,000 words.

N: EVELYN RICHARDSON MEMORIAL LITERARY AWARD, Writers' Federation of Nova Scotia, 1113 Martindale Rd., Halifax, Nova Scotia B3H 4P7 Canada. (902)423-8116. Fax: (902)422-0881. E-mail: talk@writers.ns.ca. **Contact:** Jane Buss, executive director. Contest is offered annually for best nonfiction book by Nova Scotian published during the previous calendar year. Deadline: December 10. Send four copies with letter. Prize: cash award and prize ceremony. Open to writers who were born and have spent a considerable portion of their lives, or have lived for the past two years in Nova Scotia.

ELLIOTT RUDWICK PRIZE, Organization of American Historians. (812)855-9852. Fax: (812)855-0696. E-mail: kara@oah.org. Website: www.oah.org **Contact:** Award and Prize Committee Coordinator. Offered every two years in even-numbered years for a book on the experience of racial and ethnic minorities in the United States. Books on interactions between two or more minority groups, or comparing the experience of two or more minority groups are especially welcome. Deadline: September 1. Prize: $2,000 and certificate. Final prize will be given in 2001. No book that has won the James A. Rawley Prize will be eligible for the Elliott Rudwick Prize. Before submitting a nomination, a listing of current committee members and details about individual prizes must be obtained by sending SASE to: Award and Prize Committee Coordinator, Organization of American Historians, 112 N. Bryan Ave., Bloomington IN 47408-4199.

THE CORNELIUS RYAN AWARD, The Overseas Press Club of America, 40 W. 45th St., New York NY 10036. (212)626-9220. Fax: (212)626-9210. **Contact:** Sonya Fry, executive director. Offered annually for excellence in a nonfiction book on foreign affairs. Deadline: January 31. Guidelines for SASE. Generally publishers nominate the work, but writers may also submit in their own name. Charges $100 fee. Prize: certificate and $1,000. The work must be published and on the subject of foreign affairs.

THEODORE SALOUTOS AWARD, Agricultural History Society, Iowa State University, 618 Ross Hall, Ames IA 50011-1202. (515)294-1596. Fax: (515)294-6390. E-mail: rdhurt@iastate.edu. Website: www.iastate.edu/~history_info/aghistry.htm. **Contact:** R. Douglas Hurt, Center for Agricultural History, Iowa State University, Ames, Iowa, 50011-1202. Offered annually for best book on US agricultural history broadly interpreted. Deadline: December 31. Prize: $500. Open nominations.

THE BARBARA SAVAGE "MILES FROM NOWHERE" MEMORIAL AWARD, The Mountaineers Books, 1001 SW Klickitat Way, Suite 201, Seattle WA 98134. (206)223-6303. Fax: (206)223-6306. E-mail: mbooks@mountaineers.org. Website: www.mountaineers.org. **Contact:** Margaret Foster or Mary Metz. Offered in even-numbered years for previously unpublished book-length nonfiction personal adventure narrative. Narrative must be based on an outdoor adventure involving hiking, mountain climbing, bicycling, paddle sports, skiing, snowshoeing, nature, conservation, ecology, or adventure travel not dependent upon motorized transport. Subjects *not* acceptable include hunting, fishing, or motorized or competitive sports. Deadline: May 1, 2000. Check for 2001 deadline. Guidelines for #10 SASE. Prize: $3,000 cash award, a $12,000 guaranteed advance against royalties and publication by The Mountaineers.

ALDO AND JEANNE SCAGLIONE PRIZE FOR STUDIES IN GERMANIC LANGUAGES, Modern Language Association of America, 10 Astor Place, New York NY 10003-6981. (212)614-6324. Fax: (212)533-0680. E-mail: awards@mla.org. Website: www.mla.org. **Contact:** Robert Blondeau. Offered in even-numbered years for outstanding scholarly work appearing in print in the previous two years and written by a member of the MLA, on the linguistics or literatures of the Germanic languages. Deadline: May 1, 2000. Guidelines for SASE. Prize: $1,000 and certificate. Works of literary history, literary criticism, and literary theory are eligible; books that are primarily translations are not.

ALDO AND JEANNE SCAGLIONE PRIZE FOR STUDIES IN SLAVIC LANGUAGES AND LITERATURES, Modern Language Association, 10 Astor Place, New York NY 10003-6981. (212)614-6324. Fax: (212)533-0680. E-mail: awards@mla.org. Website: www.mla.org. **Contact:** Robert Blondeau. Offered each odd-numbered year for books published in the previous 2 years. Books published in 1999 or 2000 are eligible for the 2001 award. Membership in the MLA is not required. Works of literary history, literary criticism, philology and literary theory are eligible; books that are primarily translations are not. Deadline: May 1. Guidelines for SASE. Prize: $1,000 and certificate.

ALDO AND JEANNE SCAGLIONE PRIZE IN COMPARATIVE LITERARY STUDIES, Modern Language Association of America, 10 Astor Place, New York NY 10003-6981. (212)614-6324. Fax: (212)533-0680. E-mail: awards@mla.org. Website: www.mla.org. **Contact:** Robert Blondeau. Offered annually for outstanding scholarly work published in the preceding year in the field of comparative literary studies involving at least 2 literatures. Deadline: May 1. Prize: $1,000 and certificate. Writer must be a member of the MLA. Works of scholarship, literary history, literary criticism and literary theory are eligible; books that are primarily translations are not.

ALDO AND JEANNE SCAGLIONE PRIZE IN FRENCH AND FRANCOPHONE STUDIES, 10 Astor Place, New York NY 10003-6981. (212)614-6324. Fax: (212)533-0680. E-mail: awards@mla.org. Website: www.mla.org. **Contact:** Robert Blondeau. Offered annually for work published in the preceding year that is an outstanding scholarly work in the field of French or francophone linguistic or literary studies. Deadline: May 1. Prize: $1,000 and certificate. Writer must be a member of the MLA. Works of scholarship, literary history, literary criticism and literary theory are eligible; books that are primarily translations are not.

SCIENCE-WRITING AWARD IN PHYSICS AND ASTRONOMY, American Institute of Physics, 1 Physics Ellipse, College Park MD 20740-3843. (301)209-3090. Fax: (301)209-0846. E-mail: pubinfo@aip.org. Website: www.aip.org. **Contact:** Karin Heineman. Previously published articles, booklets or books "that improve public understanding of physics and astronomy." Deadline: March 1 for professional writers, for physicists, astronomers, members of AIP, and affiliated societies, for articles or books intended for children, preschool-15 years old, for broadcast media involving radio or television.

SERGEANT KIRKLAND'S PRIZE IN AMERICAN HISTORY, Sergeant Kirkland's Museum and Historical Society, Inc., 8 Yakama Trail, Spotsylvania VA 22553-2422. (540)582-6296. Fax: (540)582-8312. **Contact:** Pia S. Seagrave, Ph.D., editor-in-chief. Offered annually for the best research work focusing on American history. Text must have been in publication during the 12 months prior to the June 1 deadline. Studies should be in scholarly form and based, in part, on primary sources, with the usual documentation and bibliography. Please submit three copies of the complete work. Must be at least 65,000 words. Prize: $500 and engraved plaque.

MINA P. SHAUGHNESSY PRIZE, Modern Language Association of America, 10 Astor Place, New York NY 10003-6981. (212)614-6324. Fax: (212)533-0680. E-mail: awards@mla.org. Website: www.mla.org. **Contact:** Robert Blondeau. Offered annually for research publication (book) in the field of teaching English language, literature, rhetoric and composition published during preceding year. Deadline: May 1. Guidelines for SASE. Prize: $1,000 and a year's membership in the MLA.

FRANCIS B. SIMKINS AWARD, Southern Historical Association, Department of History, University of Georgia, Athens GA 30602-1602. (706)542-8848. Fax: (706)542-2455. Managing Editor: John B. Boles. **Contact:** Secretary-Treasurer. Estab. 1934. Offered in odd-numbered years for recognition of the best first book by an author in the field of Southern history over a 2-year period. Deadline: March 1.

CHARLES S. SYDNOR AWARD, Southern Historical Association, Department of History, University of Georgia, Athens GA 30602. (706)542-8848. Fax: (706)542-2455. Website: www.uga.edu/~sha. **Contact:** Southern Historical Association. Offered in even-numbered years for recognition of a distinguished book in Southern history published in odd-numbered years. Publishers usually submit books. Deadline: March 1.

THE THEATRE LIBRARY ASSOCIATION AWARD, Theatre Library Association, Benjamin Rosenthal Library, Queens College, C.U.N.Y., 65-30 Kissena Blvd., Flushing NY 11367. (718)997-3672. Fax: (718)997-3672. E-mail: rlwqc@cunyvm.cuny.edu. Website: www.brown.edu/Facilities/University_Library/beyond/TLA/TLA.html. **Contact:** Richard Wall, book awards committee chair. Estab. 1973. Offered for a book published in the US within the previous calendar year on a subject related to recorded or broadcast performance (including motion pictures, television and radio). Eligible books may include biography, history, theory, criticism, reference or related fields. Prize: $250 and certificate to the winner; $100 and certificate for Honorable Mention. Submissions and deadline: Nominated books are requested from publishers; one copy should be received by each of three award jurors as well as the Chairperson by February 15 of the year following eligibility.

THIRTEENTH PRIZE FOR BIBLIOGRAPHY, International League of Antiquarian Booksellers, Hauptstrasse 19A, D-53604, Bad Honnef, Germany. **Contact:** Konrad Meuschel, director. Offered every four years for work published or unpublished January 1, 1997-December 12, 2000 for the best work published or unpublished, of learned bibliography or of research into the history of the books or of typography, and books of general interest on the subject. Deadline: December 31. Guidelines for SASE. Prize: $10,000. Open to any writer.

TRAVEL WRITING CONTEST, Val-Tech Media, Inc., P.O. Box 394, Perham MN 56573. (218)346-7921. Fax: (218)346-7924. E-mail: writersjournal@wadena.net. Website: www.writersjournal.com **Contact:** Leon Ogroske. Offered annually "for previously unpublished works." Deadline: November 30. Guidelines for SASE. Charges $5 fee. Prizes: 1st-$50, 2nd-$25, 3rd-$15 plus honorable mentions. Publication of prize winners and selected honorable mentions in *Writer's Journal* magazine. Buys one-time rights. Open to any writer.

HARRY S. TRUMAN BOOK AWARD, Harry S. Truman Library Institute for National & International Affairs, 500 West U.S. Hwy. 24, Independence MO 64050-1798. (816)833-0425. Fax: (816)833-2715. E-mail: library@truman.nara.g ov. Website: www.trumanlibrary.org. **Contact:** Book Award Administrator. Offered in even-numbered years for a book published January 1-December 31, dealing "primarily and substantially with some aspect of the history of the United States between April 12, 1945 and January 20, 1953, or with the public career of Harry S. Truman. Deadline January 20, 2002. Guidelines for SASE. Prize: $1,000.

FREDERICK JACKSON TURNER AWARD, Organization of American Historians. (812)855-9852. Fax: (812)855-0696. E-mail: kara@oah.org. Website: www.oah.org. **Contact:** Award and Prize Committee Coordinator. Offered annually for an author's first book on some significant phase of American history and also to the press that submits and publishes it. The entry must comply with the following rules: 1) the work must be the first book-length study of history published by the author; 2) if the author has a Ph.D., he/she must have received it no earlier than seven years prior to submission of the manuscript for publication; 3) the work must be published in the calendar year before the award is given; 4) the work must deal with some significant phase of American history. Deadline: September 1. Prize: $1,000, certificate and medal. Before submitting a nomination, a listing of current committee members and details about individual prizes must be obtained by sending SASE to: Award and Prize Committee Coordinator, Organization of American Historians, 112 N. Bryan Ave., Bloomington IN 47408-4199.

THE VIACOM CANADA WRITERS' TRUST NONFICTION PRIZE, The Writers' Trust of Canada, 40 Wellington St. E, Suite 300, Toronto, Ontario M5E 1C7 Canada. (416)504-8222. Fax: (416)504-9090. E-mail: writers.trust@sym patico.ca. Offered annually for a work of nonfiction published in the previous year. Deadline: late April and early September, depending on work's date of publication. Applications for SASE. Prize: $10,000 (Canadian), and up to 4 runner-up prizes of $1,000 (Canadian).

WEATHERFORD AWARD, Berea College Appalachian Center and Hutchins Library, C.P.O. 2166, Berea KY 40404. (606)985-3140. Fax: (606)985-3903. **Contact:** Gordon B. McKinney, director, Appalachian Center. Offered annually for outstanding writing published between January 1-December 31 which best illustrates the problems, personalities and unique qualities of the Appalachian South. Deadline: December 31. Guidelines for SASE. Prize: $500. Entries must have been first published during the year for which the award is made and may be nominated by its publisher, a member of the award committee or any reader.

WESTERN HISTORY ASSOCIATION AWARDS, Western History Association, Mesa Vista 1080, University of New Mexico, Albuquerque NM 87131-1181. (505)277-5234. Fax: (505)277-5275. E-mail: wha@unm.edu. Website: www.unm.edu/~wha. Director: Paul Hutton. Seventeen awards in various aspects of the American West. Guidelines for SASE.

JON WHYTE ESSAY COMPETITION, Writers Guild of Alberta, 11759 Groat Rd., Edmonton, Alberta T5M 3K6 Canada. (780)422-8174. Fax: (780)422-2663. E-mail: wga@oanet.com. Website: www.writersguild.ab.ca. **Contact:** Miki Andrejevic, executive director. Offered annually for unpublished work. Essay competition on announced theme; length 2,800 words. Winner announced in the spring of each year. Deadline: February 28. Guidelines for SASE. Charges $10 fee Canadian. Prize: $1,000, $500 for 2 runners up, plus publication in 2 newspapers and radio readings. Open to Alberta residents.

N **L. KEMPER AND LEILA WILLIAMS PRIZE**, The Historic New Orleans Collection and Louisiana Historical Association, 533 Royal St., New Orleans LA 70130-2179. Fax: (504)598-7108. Website: www.hnoc.org. Director: John H. Lawrence. **Contact:** Chair, Williams Prize Committee. Offered annually for the best published work on Louisiana history. Deadline: January 15. Prize: $1,500 and a plaque.

Fiction

EDWARD ABBEY SHORT FICTION AWARD, The Bear Deluxe Magazine, P.O. Box 10342, Portland OR 97296. (503)242-1047. Fax: (503)243-2645. E-mail: bear@teleport.com. Website: www.ovlo.com. **Contact:** Thomas L. Webb. Offered annually for unpublished short fiction to recognize new environmental writing in the spirit of Edward Abbey. New forms, styles and humor welcome. Deadline: postmark first Tuesday after Labor Day. Guidelines for SASE. Charges $5 fee. Prize: $500 and publication; publication to Honorable Mention winners. Acquires first North American serial rights. Open to any writer.

AIM MAGAZINE SHORT STORY CONTEST, P.O. Box 1174, Maywood IL 60153-8174. (773)874-6184. Fax: (206)543-2746. Website: www.AIMMagazine.org. **Contact:** Ruth Apilado, associate editor. Estab. 1974. Offered for unpublished short stories (4,000 words maximum) "promoting brotherhood among people and cultures." Deadline: August 15.

THE AMETHYST REVIEW ANNUAL WRITING CONTEST, The Amethyst Review/Marcasite Press, 23 Riverside Ave., Truro, Nova Scotia B2N 4G2 Canada. (902)895-1345. E-mail: amethyst@col.auracom.com (for information only). Website: www.col.auracom.com/~amethyst. **Contact:** Penny Ferguson, editor. Offered annually for unpublished (and not simultaneously submitted) fiction to encourage excellence in writing and to reward the writer. Deadline: January 31. Guidelines for SASE (include IRCs for SASEs from outside of Canada). Charges $12 Canadian, $14 U.S., $24 international fee. Prize: $100 for each category and publication. Acquires first North American serial rights for published works. After publication, rights revert to author. Open to any writer.

ANNUAL SHORT STORY CONTEST, sub-TERRAIN Magazine, P.O. Box 1575, Bentall Centre, Vancouver, British Columbia V6C 2P7 Canada. (604)876-8710. Fax: (604)879-2667. E-mail: subter@portal.ca. **Contact:** Brian Kaufman. Offered annually to foster new and upcoming writers. Deadline May 15. Guidelines for SASE. Charges $15 fee for first story, $5 for additional entries. Prize: $500 (Canadian), publication in summer issue and 3-issue subscription to sub-TERRAIN.

ANVIL PRESS INTERNATIONAL 3-DAY NOVEL WRITING CONTEST, Anvil Press, 204-A 175 E. Broadway, Vancouver, British Columbia V5T 1W2 Canada. (604)876-8710. Fax: (604)879-2667. E-mail: subter@portal.ca. Website: anvilpress.com. **Contact:** Brian Kaufman. Estab. 1988. Offered annually for the best novel written in three days (Labor Day weekend). Entrants return finished novels to Anvil Press for judging. Registration deadline: Friday before Labor Day weekend. Send SASE (IRC if from the US) for details. Charges $25 fee.

ARIADNE PRIZE, Ariadne Press, 4817 Tallahassee Ave., Rockville MD 20853. Phone/Fax: (301)949-2514. **Contact:** Carol Hoover. Offered annually dependent on financing to encourage and promote the publication of novels by emerging writers. Deadline: January 15-March 31. Guidelines for SASE. Charges $50 fee (includes brief critique). Prize: $500 plus publication by Ariadne Press. No rights are acquired by contest entry. Open to "non-established" writers.

AUTHORS IN THE PARK SHORT STORY CONTEST, Authors in the Park, P.O. Box 85, Winter Park FL 32790-0085. (407)658-4520. Fax: (407)275-8688. E-mail: foley@magicnet.net. Estab. 1985. **Contact:** David or Jennifer Foley. Offered annually to help expose fiction writers to literary journals. Deadline: April 30. Guidelines for SASE or by e-mail. Charges $12 fee. Prize: 1st-$1,000, 2nd-$500, 3rd-$250. Open to any writer.

BONOMO MEMORIAL LITERATURE PRIZE, (formerly Arcudi Fiction Award), Italian Americana, URI/CCE, 80 Washington St., Providence RI 02903. (401)277-5306. Fax: (401)277-5100. **Contact:** Carol Bonomo Albright. Offered annually for the best fiction, essay, or memoir that is published annually by an Italian American. Guidelines for SASE. Prize: $250. Acquires first North American serial rights. Open to Italian Americans only.

BOSTON REVIEW SHORT STORY CONTEST, *Boston Review*, E-53-407 MIT, Cambridge MA 02139. (617)494-0708. Website: http:bostonreview.mit.edu. **Contact:** Rob Mitchell, advertising and promotions manager. Stories should not exceed four thousand words and must be previously unpublished. Deadline: September 1. Charges $15 fee, payable to *Boston Review*, check or money order. Prize: $1,000 and publication in the December/January issue of *Boston Review*.

BOULEVARD SHORT FICTION CONTEST FOR EMERGING WRITERS, Boulevard Magazine, 4579 Laclede Ave., #332, St. Louis MO 63108-2103. (314)361-2986. **Contact:** Richard Burgin. Offered annually for unpublished short fiction to award a writer who has not yet published a book of fiction, poetry or creation nonfiction with a nationally distributed press. Deadline: December 15. Guidelines for SASE. Charges $15 fee. Prize: $1,200 and publication in one of the next year's issues. "We hold first North American rights on anything not previously published." Open to any writer with no previous publication by a nationally known press.

THE WILLIAM YOUNG BOYD MILITARY NOVEL AWARD, American Library Association Awards Program, 50 E. Huron St., Chicago IL 60611. (800)545-2433, ext. 3247. E-mail: awards@ala.com. Website: www.ala.org/work/awards/index.html. Offered annually for a previously published work that honors the best fiction set in a period when the United States was at war. It recognizes the service of American veterans and military personnel and encourages the writing and publishing of outstanding war-related fiction. Deadline: December 1. Prize: $5,000.

BRAZOS BOOKSTORE SHORT STORY AWARD, The Texas Institute of Letters, Southwest Texas State University, San Marcos TX 78666. (512)245-2428. Fax: (512)245-7462. E-mail: mb13@swt.edu. Website: www.English.swt.ecu/css/TIL/rules.htm. **Contact:** Mark Busby. Offered annually for work previously published January 1-December 31 of previous year to recognize the best short story. The story submitted must have appeared in print for the first time to be eligible. Deadline: January 3. Guidelines for SASE. Prize: $750. Writers must have been born in Texas, must have lived in Texas for at least two consecutive years or the subject matter of the work must be associated with Texas.

GEORGES BUGNET AWARD FOR FICTION (NOVEL), Writers Guild of Alberta, 11759 Groat Rd., Edmonton Alberta T5M 3K6 Canada. (708)422-8179 or (800)665-5354. Fax: (708)422-2663. E-mail: wga@oanet.com. **Contact:** Renate Donnovan or Miki Andrejevic, executive directors. Offered annually for work previously published January 1-December 31 of the past year. Deadline: December 31. Guidelines for SASE. Prize: $500 and leatherbound copy of book. Open to Alberta authors.

CANADIAN AUTHORS ASSOCIATION AWARD FOR FICTION, Box 419, 320 South Shores Rd., Campbellford, Ontario K0L 1L0 Canada. (705)653-0323. Fax: (705)653-0593. E-mail: canauth@redden.on.ca. **Contact:** Alec McEachern. Offered annually for a full-length novel by a Canadian. Deadline: December 15. Guidelines for IRC. Charges $20 fee (Canadian). Prize: $2,500 and a silver medal. Open to Canadian citizens only.

CANADIAN AUTHORS ASSOCIATION JUBILEE AWARD FOR SHORT STORIES, P.O. Box 419, 320 S. Shores Rd., Campbellford, Ontario K0L 1L0 Canada. (705)653-0323. Fax: (705)653-0593. E-mail: canauth@redden.on.ca. **Contact:** Alec McEachern. Offered annually for a collection of short stories by a Canadian author. Deadline: December 15. Guidelines for SASE. Charges $20 fee (Canadian). Prize: $2,500 and a medal. Open to Canadian citizens only.

COOP FICTION FELLOWSHIP, Arts Co-Operative, 725 Ashland, Houston TX 77007. E-mail: cottonwood@geocities.com. Website: www.geocities.com/~cottonwood. Director: Charli Buono de Valdez. Deadline: May 31. Charges $10 fee. Prize: $500-1,000 cash award and publication to support serious, aspiring writers of fiction from anywhere. For most recent information, please visit website or write for guidelines with SASE. Submit fiction portfolios up to 50 pages in length with cover sheet, bio and publications list. (For an additional ten dollars and SASE, feedback provided.) Competition received only 30 submissions in 1998!

DARK OAK MYSTERY CONTEST, Oak Tree Press, 915 W. Foothill Blvd., Suite 411, Claremont CA 91711-3356. (909)625-8400. Fax: (909)624-3930. E-mail: oaktreepub@aol.com. Website: http://oaktreebooks.com. **Contact:** Billie Johnson. Offered annually for an unpublished mystery ms (up to 85,000 words) of any sort from police procedurals to amateur sleuth novels. Deadline: June 30. Guidelines for SASE. Charges $35 fee. Prize: 1st-publishing contract from Oak Tree Press; 2nd-ms analysis; 3rd-selection of Oak Tree books. Acquires first North American, audio and film rights to winning entry. Open to authors not published in the past 3 years.

THE E.F.S. RELIGIOUS FICTION WRITING COMPETITION, E.F.S. Enterprises, Inc. 2844 Eighth Ave., Suite 6E, New York NY 10039. (212)283-8899. Website: www.efs-enterprises.com. **Contact:** Zeretha Jenkins, competition director. Offered annually for unpublished work to help writers of religious fiction in 2 categories (short fiction and book-length fiction) by giving them the opportunity to publish work online. Submissions must be unpublished. Applications and guidelines are required and are available upon request with SASE. Submissions accepted with applications from May 1-June 30. Deadline: June 30. Charges $15 fee. Does not return mss. Prize: 1st—$100 and online publishing contract; 2nd—$50. Writers retain all rights. Open to any writer. Authors do not have to be previously published.

ARTHUR ELLIS AWARDS, Crime Writers of Canada, 3007 Kingston Rd., Box 113, Scarborough, Ontario M1M 1P1 Canada. (416)461-9876. Fax: (416)461-4489. E-mail: ap113@freenet.toronto.on.ca. Website: www.crimewriterscanada.com. **Contact:** Secretary/Treasurer. Offered annually for crime literature published during the year of the award. Categories: Best Crime Novel, True Crime Novel, Crime Short Story, Crime Genre Criticism/Reference/Anthology, Play, Juvenile Crime Fiction. Deadline: January 31. Prize: a symbolic hanged person, cash prizes from year to year in certain categories. Open to Canadian writers or writer regardless of nationality, resident in Canada or Canadian writers resident abroad.

N THE WILLIAM FAULKNER CREATIVE WRITING COMPETITION, The Pirate's Alley Faulkner Society, 632 Pirate's Alley, New Orleans LA 70116-3254. (504)586-1609. E-mail: faulkhouse@aolcom. Website: www.wordsand music.com. Contest Director: Joseph J. DeSalvo, Jr. **Contact:** Rosemary James, editor. Offered annually for unpublished mss to encourage publisher interest in a promising writer's novel, novella, short story, personal essay, poem, or Louisiana high school student's short story. Deadline: April 15. Guidelines for SASE. Charges entry fee: novel-$35; novella-$30; short story $25; personal essay-$25; individual poem-$25; high school short story $10. Prize: novel-$7,500; novella-$2,500; short story-$1,500; personal essay-$1,000; individual poem-$750; high school-$750 for student and $250 for sponsoring teacher; and expenses for trip to New Orleans for Faulkner Celebration. Excerpts published in Society's Literary Quarterly, *The Double Dealer Redux*. The Society retains the right to publish excerpts of longer fiction; short stories in toto. Open to all US residents.

FICTION OPEN, Glimmer Train Press, 710 SW Madison St., #504, Portland OR 97205. (503)221-0836. Fax: (503)221-0837. Website: www.glimmertrain.com. **Contact:** Linda Burmeister Davies. Offered annually for unpublished stories as "a platform for all themes, all lengths, all writers." Deadline: June 30. Guidelines for SASE. Charges $15 fee per story. Prize: 1st-$2,000, publication in *Glimmer Train Stories* and 20 copies of that issue, 2nd-$1,000, possible publication in *Glimmer Train Stories*, 3rd-$600, possible publication in *Glimmer Train Stories*. Open to any writer.

ROBERT L. FISH MEMORIAL AWARD, Mystery Writers of America, Inc., 17 E. 47th St., 6th Floor, New York NY 10017. (212)888-8171. Fax: (212)888-8107. E-mail: mwa_org@earthlink.net. Website: www.mysterywriters.org. **Contact:** Mary Beth Becker, administrative director. Offered annually for the best first mystery or suspense short story published during the previous year. Deadline: December 1.

H.E. FRANCIS SHORT STORY AWARD, University of Alabama in Huntsville & Ruth Hindman Foundation, 301 Sparkman Dr. N.W., Huntsville AL 35805. E-mail: MaryH71997@aol.com. Website: www.uah.edu. **Contact:** Mary Hindman, editor. Offered annually for unpublished work. Deadline: December 31. Guidelines for SASE. Charges $15 reading fee. Prize: $1,000. Acquires first time publication rights.

GLIMMER TRAIN'S FALL SHORT-STORY AWARD FOR NEW WRITERS, Glimmer Train Press, Inc., 710 SW Madison St., Suite 504, Portland OR 97205-2900. (503)221-0836. Fax: (503)221-0837. Website: www.glimmertrain. com. **Contact:** Linda Burmeister Davies. Offered for any writer whose fiction hasn't appeared in a nationally-distributed publication with a circulation over 5,000. "Send original, unpublished short (1,200-8,000 words) story with $12 reader fee for each story entered. Guidelines available for SASE. Must be postmarked between August 1 and September 30. Title page to include name, address, phone, and Short Story Award for New Writers must be written on outside of envelope. No need for SASE as materials will not be returned. Notification on January 2. Winner receives $1,200, publication in *Glimmer Train Stories* and 20 copies of that issue. First/second runners-up receive $500/$300, respectively, and consideration for publication. All applicants receive a copy of *Writers Ask*, the newsletter for literary writers.

GLIMMER TRAIN'S SPRING SHORT-STORY AWARD FOR NEW WRITERS, Glimmer Train Press, Inc., 710 SW Madison St., Suite 504, Portland OR 97205-2900. (503)221-0836. Fax: (503)221-0837. Website: www.glimmert rain.com. **Contact:** Linda Burmeister Davies. Offered for any writer whose fiction hasn't appeared in a nationally-distributed publication with a circulation over 5,000. "Send original, unpublished short (1,200-8,000 words) story with $12 reader fee for each story entered. Guidelines available for SASE. Must be postmarked between February 1 and March 31. Title page to include name, address, phone, and Short Story Award for New Writers must be written on outside of envelope. No need for SASE as materials will not be returned. Notification on July 1. Winner receives $1,200, publication in *Glimmer Train Stories* and 20 copies of that issue. First/second runners-up receive $500/$300, respectively, and consideration for publication. All applicants receive a copy of *Writers Ask*, the newsletter for literary writers.

DRUE HEINZ LITERATURE PRIZE, University of Pittsburgh Press, 3347 Forbes Ave., Pittsburgh PA 15261. Website: www.pitt.edu/~press. **Contact:** Melanie Shrawder, assistant to the director. Estab. 1936. Collection of short fiction. Offered annually to writers who have published a book-length collection of fiction or a minimum of 3 short stories or novellas in commercial magazines or literary journals of national distribution. Does not return mss. Submit: May-June. Guidelines for SASE (essential). Prize: $10,000.

N ERNEST HEMINGWAY FOUNDATION PEN AWARD FOR FIRST FICTION, PEN New England, P.O. Box 725, North Cambridge MA 02140. (617)499-9550. Fax: (617)353-7134. E-mail: hemingway@pen-ne.org. Website: www.pen-ne.org. **Contact:** Mary Louise Sullivan. Offered for first-published novel or short story collection by an American author. Guidelines and entry form for SASE. Deadline: December 15.

LORIAN HEMINGWAY SHORT STORY COMPETITION, Hemingway Days Festival, P.O. Box 993, Key West FL 33041-0993. (305)294-0320. Fax: (305)292-3653. E-mail: calico2419@aol.com. Fax and e-mail for guideline requests only. **Contact:** Lorian Hemingway and Carol Shaughnessy, coordinators. Estab. 1981. Offered annually for unpublished short stories up to 3,000 words. Deadline: June 15. Charges $100 fee for each story postmarked by June 1, $15 for each story postmarked by June 15; no stories accepted after June 15. Guidelines for SASE. Prize: 1st-$1,000; 2nd and 3rd-$500 runner-up awards; honorable mentions will also be awarded.

N L. RON HUBBARD'S WRITERS OF THE FUTURE CONTEST, P.O. Box 1630WM, Los Angeles CA 90078. (323)466-3310. Fax: (323)466-6474. Website: www.writersofthefuture.com. **Contact:** Nathalie CordeBard, contest administrator. Offered annually for unpublished science fiction, fantasy and horror. Guidelines for #10 SASE. Prize: $2,250 quarterly prizes; $4,000 annual Grand Prize, with 5-day workshop and publication in major anthology. Authors retain all rights.

INTERNATIONAL IMITATION HEMINGWAY COMPETITION, PEN Center West, 672 S. La Fayette Park Place, Suite 41, Los Angeles CA 90057. (213)365-8500. Fax: (213)365-9616. E-mail: pen@pen-usa-west.org. Website: www.pen-usa-west.org. **Contact:** Christina L. Apeles, awards coordinator. Offered annually for unpublished one-page (500 words) parody of Hemingway. Must mention Harry's Bar and must be funny. Uncertain if will run in 2001. Write or call PEN for deadline or access. Winner receives round trip transportation for two to Florence, Italy and dinner at Harry's Bar & American Grill in Florence.

JAPANOPHILE ANNUAL SHORT STORY CONTEST, *Japanophile*, P.O. Box 7977, 415 N. Main St., Ann Arbor MI 48107-7977. (734)930-1553. Fax: (734)930-9968. E-mail: jpnhand@japanophile.com. Website: www.japanophile.com. **Contact:** Susan Lapp, director. Associate Editor: Ashby Kinch. Offered annually for unpublished work to encourage good fiction-writing that contributes to understanding of Japan and Japanese culture. Deadline: December 31. Guidelines for SASE. Charges $5 fee. Prize: $100, certificate, and usually publication.

JESSE H. JONES AWARD, The Texas Institute of Letters, Southwest Texas State University, San Marcos TX 78666. (512)245-2428. Fax: (512)245-7462. E-mail: mb13@swt.edu. Website: www.English.swt.ecu/css/TIL/rules.htm. **Contact:** Mark Busby. Offered annually for work previously published January 1-December 31 of year before award is given to recognize the writer of the best book of fiction entered in the competition. Deadline: January 3. Guidelines for SASE. Prize: $6,000. Writers must have been born in Texas, or have lived in the state for at least two consecutive years at some time, or the subject matter of the work should be associated with the state.

JAMES JONES FIRST NOVEL FELLOWSHIP, Wilkes University, English Department, Kirby Hall, Wilkes-Barre PA 18766. (570)408-4530. Fax: (570)408-7829. E-mail: english@wilkes1.wilkes.edu. **Contact:** Darin Fields, humanities chairman. Offered annually for unpublished novels, novellas and closely-linked short stories (all works-in-progress). "The award is intended to honor the spirit of unblinking honesty, determination and insight into modern culture exemplified by the late James Jones." Deadline: March 1. Guidelines for SASE. Charges $15 fee. Prize: $5,000. The competition is open to all American writers who have not previously published novels.

N HENRY KREISEL AWARD FOR BEST FIRST BOOK, Writers Guild of Alberta, Awards Program, Percy Page Centre, 11759 Groat Rd., Edmonton, Alberta T5M 3K6 Canada. (708)422-8174 or (800)665-5354. E-mail: guild@oanet.com. **Contact:** Renate Donnovan or Miki Andrejevic. Eligible books will have been published anywhere in the world between January 1 and December 31. The authors will have been residents of Alberta for at least 12 months of the 18 months prior to December 31. Unpublished mss, except in the drama category, are not eligible. Anthologies are not eligible. Full-length radio plays which have been published in anthologies are eligible. Five copies of each book must be mailed to the WGA office no later than December 31. Works may be submitted by authors, publishers or any interested parties. Winning authors will receive leather-bound copies of their books and $500.

N LAURIE, Smoky Mountain Romance Writers, P.O. Box 70268, Knoxville TN 37918. (865)922-7700. E-mail: questionrs@aol.com. Website: www.smrw.org. **Contact:** Deborah Ledgerwood. Offered annually to honor excellence in unpublished romance fiction. Deadline: March 1. Guidelines and entry forms for SASE or on website. Charges $25 fee. Prize: finalist have their entry read by an acquiring editor or agent. 1st Place wins a Laurie Pendant and finalist and winners receive certificates. Participants must furnish a valid Romance Writers of America membership number to enter.

N URSULA K. LEGUIN PRIZE FOR IMAGINATIVE FICTION, Rosebud, P.O. Box 459, Cambridge WI 53523. Website: www.rsbd.net. **Contact:** J. Rod Clark, editor. Annual contest for unpublished stories. Deadline: December 31. Guidelines for SASE. Charges $10/story fee. Prize: $1,000 plus publication in *Rosebud*. Acquires first rights. Open to any writer.

N LONG FICTION CONTEST, White Eagle Coffee Store Press, P.O. Box 383, Fox River Grove IL 60021. (847)639-9200. E-mail: wecspress@aol.com. Website: http://members.aol.com/wecspress. **Contact:** Frank E. Smith, publisher. Offered annually since 1993 for unpublished work to recognize and promote long short stories of 8,000-14,000 words (about 30-50 pages). Deadline: December 15. Guidelines for SASE. Charges $15 fee, $5 for second story in same envelope. A.E. Coppard Prize: $500 and publication plus 25 copies of chapbook. Open to any writer, no restrictions on materials. Sample of previous winner: $5.95, including postage.

THE MALAHAT REVIEW NOVELLA PRIZE, The Malahat Review, Box 1700 STN CSC, Victoria, British Columbia V8W 2Y2 Canada. (250)721-8524. E-mail: malahat@uvic.ca. Website: web.uvic.ca/malahat. **Contact:** Marlene

Cookshaw, editor. Offered every 2 years (even years) to promote unpublished novellas. Deadline: March 1. Guidelines for SASE. Charges $25 fee (includes a one-year subscription to *Malahat*, published quarterly). Prize: $400, plus payment for publication ($30/page). Obtains first world rights. After publication rights revert to the author. Open to any writer.

MARY MCCARTHY PRIZE IN SHORT FICTION, Sarabande Books, P.O. Box 4456, Louisville KY 40204. (502)458-4028. Fax: (502)458-4065. E-mail: sarabandeb@aol.com. Website: www.SarabandeBooks.org. **Contact:** Sarah Gorham, editor-in-chief. Offered annually to publish an outstanding collection of stories or novellas. Submissions accepted January 1-February 15. Guidelines for SASE. Charges $20 fee. Prize: $2,000 and publication, standard royalty contract. All finalists considered for publication.

MID-LIST PRESS FIRST SERIES AWARD FOR SHORT FICTION, Mid-List Press, 4324 12th Ave. S., Minneapolis MN 55407-3218. (612)822-3733. Fax: (612)823-8387. E-mail: guide@midlist.org. Website: www.midlist.org. **Contact:** Lane Stiles, senior editor. Open to any writer who has never published a book-length collection of short fiction (short stories, novellas); minimum 50,000 words. Submit entire ms beginning *after* March 31; must be postmarked by July 1. Accepts simultaneous submissions. Charges $20 fee. Enclose SAS postcard for acknowledgment of receipt of ms. Guidelines and entry form for SASE or from website. Awards include publication and an advance against royalties.

MID-LIST PRESS FIRST SERIES AWARD FOR THE NOVEL, Mid-List Press, 4324-12th Ave. S., Minneapolis MN 55407-3218. Fax: (612)823-8387. E-mail: guide@midlist.org. Website: www.midlist.org. **Contact:** Lane Stiles, senior editor. Offered annually for unpublished novels to locate and publish quality manuscripts by first-time writers, particularly those mid-list titles that major publishers may be rejecting. Deadline: February 1. Guidelines for SASE or from website. Charges $20 fee. Prize: $1,000 advance against royalties, plus publication. Open to any writer who has never published a novel.

MILKWEED NATIONAL FICTION PRIZE, Milkweed Editions, 1011 Washington Ave. S., Suite 300, Minneapolis MN 55415. (612)332-3192. Fax: (612)332-6248. **Contact:** Elisabeth Fitz, first reader. Estab. 1986. Annual award for unpublished works. "Milkweed is looking for a novel, novella, or a collection of short stories. Manuscripts should be of high literary quality and must be double-spaced and between 150-400 pages in length." Guidelines for SASE. "SAS mailer large enough to hold your manuscript must accompany submission for manuscript to be returned. If no SAS mailer is sent along, manuscript will be recycled." Prize: Publication by Milkweed Editions and a cash advance of $5,000 against any royalties or other payment agreed upon in the contractual arrangement negotiated at the time of acceptance. Winner will be chosen from the mss Milkweed accepts for publication each year. All mss submitted to Milkweed will automatically be considered for the prize. Submission directly to the contest is no longer necessary. "Must be written in English. Writers should have previously published a book of fiction or three short stories (or novellas) in magazines/journals with national distribution. Catalog available on request for $1.50.

C. WRIGHT MILLS AWARD, The Society for the Study of Social Problems, 906 McClung Tower, University of Tennessee, Knoxville TN 37996-0490. (865)974-3620. Fax: (865)974-7013. E-mail: mkoontz3@eutk.edu. Website: www.it.utk.edu/sssp. **Contact:** Michele Koontz, admistrative officer. Offered annually for fiction published January 1-December 31 to recognize fiction that critically addresses an issue of contemporary public importance. Deadline: January 15, 2000. Prize: $500 stipend.

Ⓝ MOSAIC ANNUAL FICTION CONTEST, *Mosaic*, Tenth Street Press, 300 W. 10th St., Morris MN 56267. Phone/fax: (320)589-0120. **Contact:** Heather Timmerman. Offered annually for previously published or unpublished work to reward outstanding fiction and support publication of the magazine. Each entrant receives a copy of the issue in which the winning story appears. Deadline: November 10. Guidelines for SASE. Charges $10/story fee. Prize: $300 plus publication in *Mosaic*. Acquires one-time rights. All entries considered for publication. Maximum length 5,000 words.

Ⓝ MOSAIC QUARTERLY FICTION CONTEST, *Mosaic*, Tenth Street Press, 300 W. 10th St., Morris MN 56267. Phone/fax: (320)589-0120. **Contact:** Heather Timmerman. Offered quarterly for previously published or unpublished work to reward outstanding fiction and support publication of the magazine. Each entrant receives a copy of the issue in which the winning story appears. Deadline: March 15, June 15, September 15, December 15. Guidelines for SASE. Charges $5/story fee. Prize: $100 plus publication in *Mosaic*. Acquires one-time rights. All entries considered for publication. Maximum length 5,000 words.

Ⓝ MOSAIC VERY SHORT FICTION CONTEST, *Mosaic*, Tenth Street Press, 300 W. 10th St., Morris MN 56267. Phone/fax: (320)589-0120. **Contact:** Heather Timmerman. Offered twice annually for previously published or unpublished work to reward outstanding fiction and support publication of the magazine. Each entrant receives a copy of the issue in which the winning story appears. Deadline: February 1, August 1. Guidelines for SASE. Charges $5/story fee. Prize: $100 plus publication in *Mosaic*. Acquires one-time rights. All entries considered for publication. Maximum length 2,000 words.

MYSTERY NOVEL AWARD, Salvo Press, P.O. Box 9095, Bend OR 97708. E-mail: sschmidt@bendnet.com. Website: www.salvopress.com. **Contact:** Scott Schmidt. Offered annually for the best unpublished mystery, suspense, thriller or espionage novel. Deadline: July 15. Guidelines for SASE or on website. Charges $25 fee. Prize: publication under a standard royalty contract by Salvo Press. Open to any writer.

NATIONAL WRITERS ASSOCIATION NOVEL WRITING CONTEST, The National Writers Association, 3140 S. Peoria, #295, Aurora CO 80014. (303)841-0246. Fax:(303)751-8593. E-mail: sandywrter@aol.com. **Contact:** Sandy Whelchel, director. Annual contest "to help develop creative skills, to recognize and reward outstanding ability and to increase the opportunity for the marketing and subsequent publication of novel manuscripts." Deadline: April 1. Guidelines for SASE. Charges $35 fee. Prizes: 1st-$500; 2nd-$300; 3rd-$200.

N **NATIONAL WRITERS ASSOCIATION SHORT STORY CONTEST**, The National Writers Association, 3140 S. Peoria, #295, Aurora CO 80014. (303)841-0246. Fax:(303)751-8593. E-mail: sandywrter@aol.com. **Contact:** Sandy Whelchel, director. Annual contest "to encourage writers in this creative form and to recognize those who excel in fiction writing." Deadline: July 1. Guidelines for SASE. Charges $15 fee. Prizes: $200, $100, $50, copy of *Writer's Market*.

N **NEW CENTURY WRITER AWARDS (FICTION)**, 32 Alfred St., Suite B, New Haven CT 06512-3927. (203)469-8824. Fax: (203)468-0333. E-mail: newcenturywriter@yahoo.com. Website: www.newcenturywriter.org. **Contact:** Jason J. Marchi, executive director. Offered annually to discover emerging writers of short stories and novels. No poetry of children's picture books. Deadline: January 31. Guidelines/entry forms for #10 SAE. Charges $30 entry fee. Prize: 1st—$3,000; 2nd—$1,000; 3rd—$500; 4th-10th—$100; free story development or scriptwriting software to selected finalists. All entrants receive 1-year subscription to *The Anvil*, educational newsletter for writers. Open to all writers, both non-produced and those with limited production history. Call if you doubt your eligibility.
  • Also provides an annual Fellowship for a short fiction writer to attend the Zoetrope Short Story Writers' Workshop at Francis Ford Coppola's Blancaneaux Lodge in Belize, Central America. Fellowship is separate and is *not* awarded to any of the Top 10 cash winners. Also provides other fellowships and tuition assistance to select writers' workshops and programs.
Tips: "We seek to encourage writers with cash awards and to connect writers to our numerous alliance companies in the film production and publishing industries. We also produce a popular reading series in New York City of works selected from annual finalists. Please call for application package—all submission details are included."

N **NEW MUSE AWARD**, Broken Jaw Press, Box 596 Station A, Fredericton, New Brunswick E3B 5A6 Canada. E-mail: jblades@nbnet.nb.ca. Website: www.brokenjaw.com. **Contact:** Joe Blades. Offered annually for unpublished fiction mss of 120 pages maximum to encourage development of book-length mss by Canadian writers without a first fiction book published. Deadline: February 28. Guidelines for SASE (with Canadian postage). Charges $20 fee (all entrants receive copy of winning book upon publication). Prize: book publication on trade terms.

NORTHWOODS JOURNAL'S ANNUAL NATIONAL SHORT FICTION CONTEST, Conservatory of American Letters, P.O. Box 298, Thomaston ME 04861. (207)354-0998. Fax: (207)354-8953. E-mail: cal@americanletters.org. Website: www.americanletters.org. **Contact:** Dr. Ken Sieben. Offered annually to find the best short fiction of the year. Deadline: November 15. Guidelines for SASE. Charges $7 fee/2,500 words or any part. Prize: 1st-$100 plus publication and further payment, 2nd-$50 and possible publication, 3rd-$25 and possible publication. Open to all writers.

THE FLANNERY O'CONNOR AWARD FOR SHORT FICTION, The University of Georgia Press, 330 Research Dr., Athens GA 30602-4901. (706)369-6135. Fax: (706)369-6131. E-mail: mnunnell@ugapress.uga.edu. Website: www.uga.edu/ugapress. **Contact:** Margaret Nunnelley, competition coordinator. Estab. 1981. Submission period: April-May 31. Charges $15 fee. Does not return mss. Manuscripts must be 200-275 pages long. Authors do not have to be previously published. Guidelines for SASE. Prize: $1,000 and publication under standard book contract.

HOWARD O'HAGAN AWARD FOR SHORT FICTION, Writers Guild of Alberta, 11759 Groat Rd., Edmonton Alberta T5M 3K6 Canada. (708)422-8174 or (800)665-5354. Fax: (708)422-2663. E-mail: wga@oanet.com. **Contact:** Renate Donnovan or Miki Andrejevic, executive directors. Short fiction book published in current year. Open to Alberta authors. Guidelines for SASE. Prize: $500 and leatherbound copy of book.

CHRIS O'MALLEY PRIZE IN FICTION, *The Madison Review*, Dept. of English, 600 N. Park St., Madison WI 53706. (608)263-0566, (608)263-3374. **Contact:** Josh Swedlow or Jessica Agneessens; fiction editors. Offered annually for previously unpublished work. Awarded to the best piece of fiction. Deadline: September 30. Charges $3 fee. Prize: $500, plus publication in the spring issue of *The Madison Review*. All contest entries are considered as submissions to *The Madison Review*, the literary journal sponsoring the contest. No simultaneous submissions to other publications.

WILLIAM PEDEN PRIZE IN FICTION, The Missouri Review, 1507 Hillcrest Hall, Columbia MO 65211. (573)882-4474. Fax: (573)884-4671. Website: www.missourireview.org. **Contact:** Greg Michalson, managing editor. Offered annually "for the best story published in the past volume year of the magazine. All stories published in *MR* are automatically considered." Prize: $1,000 cash prize; the winner is honored at a reading/reception in November.

PEN/FAULKNER AWARDS FOR FICTION, PEN/Faulkner Foundation, 201 E. Capitol St., Washington DC 20003. (202)675-0345. Fax: (202)608-1719. E-mail: delaney@folger.edu. Website: www.penfaulkner.org. **Contact:** Janice F. Delaney, executive director:. Offered annually for best book-length work of fiction by American citizen published in a calendar year. Deadline: October 31. Prize: $15,000 (one winner), 5,000 (4 nominees).

THE PEREGRINE PRIZE (fiction), *Peregrine,* the Literary Journal of Amherst Writers & Artists, P.O. Box 1076, Amherst MA 01004-1076. Phone/fax: (413)253-7764. E-mail: awapress@javanet.com. Website: www.javanet.com/~awapress. **Contact:** Nancy Rose. Offered annually for unpublished fiction. Deadline: April 1. Guidelines for SASE. Charges $10 fee. Prize: $500 plus publication in *Peregrine*. Open to any writer.
 • Entrants who reside in Western Massachusetts are also eligible for The Peregrine Prize: "Best of the Nest" Prize.

EDGAR ALLAN POE AWARD, Mystery Writers of America, Inc., 17 E. 47th St., New York NY 10017. (212)888-8171. Fax: (212)888-8107. E-mail: mwa_org@earthlink.net. Website: www.mysterywriters.org. **Contact:** Mary Beth Becker, administrative director. Entries must be produced/published in the year they are submitted. Deadline: December 1. Guidelines for SASE. Must request guidelines and entry forms. Entries for the book categories are usually submitted by the publisher but may be submitted by the author or his agent.

MARY RUFFIN POOLE AWARD FOR FIRST WORK OF FICTION, North Carolina Literary and Historical Association, 4610 Mail Service Center, Raleigh NC 27699-4610. (919)733-9375. **Contact:** Jerry C. Cashion, awards coordinator. Offered annually for first work of published book-length fiction by a North Carolina resident. Prize: $1,000 stipend. Deadline: July 15.

⚏ PRISM INTERNATIONAL FICTION CONTEST, *Prism International*, University of British Columbia, Buch E462, 1866 Main Mall, Vancouver, British Columbia V6T 1Z1 Canada. (604)822-2514. Fax: (604)822-3616. E-mail: prism@interchange.ubc.ca. Website: www.arts.ubc.ca/prism. Offered annually for previously unpublished fiction. Deadline: December 31. Maximum length: 25 pages. Story's title should appear on every page. Author's name and address must appear *only* on a separate cover page. Entry fee: $22 for one story, plus $5 for each additional story. Entrants from outside Canada pay in US funds. Entry fee includes one-year subscription. Works of translations are eligible. For complete guidelines, send SASE with Canadian postage or SAE with 1 IRC. Prize: 1st-$2,000; 5 honorable mentions of $200 each, plus publication payment.

QUARTERLY WEST NOVELLA COMPETITION, *Quarterly West*, University of Utah, 200 S. Central Campus Dr., Room 317, Salt Lake City UT 84112. (801)581-3938. Website: www.chronicle.utah.edu/qw. **Contact:** Margot Schilpp, editor. Estab. 1976. Offered biennially for 2 unpublished novellas of 50-125 pages. Charges $20 fee. Deadline: December 31 of even-numbered years. Guidelines for SASE. Prize: 2 writers receive $500 and publication in *Quarterly West*.

THOMAS H. RADDALL ATLANTIC FICTION PRIZE, Writers' Federation of Nova Scotia, 1113 Martindale Rd., Halifax, Nova Scotia B3H 4P7 Canada. (902)423-8116. Fax: (902)422-0881. E-mail: talk@writers.ns.ca. Website: www.writers.ns.ca. **Contact:** Jane Buss. Offered annually to fiction published during the year preceding the competition. The Prize "honors the best fiction writing by an Atlantic born (Nova Scotia, New Brunswick, Newfoundland, Prince Edward Island) or resident (1 year) writer." Deadline: December 10. Forward four copies of published book of fiction to the Writers' Federation of Nova Scotia. Prize: $5,000 (Canadian funds) and medal.

SIR WALTER RALEIGH AWARD, North Carolina Literary and Historical Association, 4610 Mail Service Center, Raleigh NC 27699-4610. (919)733-9375. **Contact:** Jerry C. Cashion, awards coordinator. Offered annually for published volume of fiction by a North Carolina resident. Deadline: July 15.

⚏ RAMBUNCTIOUS REVIEW, Rambunctious Review, 1221 W. Pratt Blvd., Chicago IL 60626. Annual themed contest for unpublished stories. Deadline: December 3. Guidelines for SASE. Charges $3/story fee or free entry with paid subscription. Prize: 1st-$100, 2nd-$75, 3rd-$50. Acquires first rights. Open to any writer.

HAROLD U. RIBALOW AWARD, Hadassah WZOA, 50 W. 58th St., New York NY 10019. (212)688-0227. Fax: (212)446-9521. **Contact:** Dorothy Silfen. Editor: Alan Tigay. English-language books of fiction on a Jewish theme published January 1-December 31 in a calendar year are eligible for the next year's award. Deadline: April. Prize: $1,000. Books should be submitted by the publisher.

⚏ GWEN PHARIS RINGWOOD AWARD FOR DRAMA, Writers Guild of Alberta, Awards Program, Percy Page Centre, 11759 Groat Rd., Edmonton, Alberta T5M 3K6 Canada. (708)422-8174 or (800)665-5354. E-mail: guild@oanet.com. **Contact:** Renate Donnovan or Miki Andrejevic. Registered plays having had a minimum of 3 consecutive public performances during premiere engagements may be entered. Eligible books will have been published anywhere in the world between January 1 and December 31. The authors will have been residents in Alberta for at least 1 year of 18 months prior to December 31. Eligible plays must be submitted with copies of contracts of performances. Unpublished mss, except in the drama category, are not eligible. Except in the drama category, anthologies are not eligible.

Full-length radio plays which have been published in anthologies are eligible. Five copies of each book or registered play must be mailed to the WGA office no later than December 31. Works may be submitted by authors, publishers or any interested parties. Winning playwrights will win a leather-bound copy of their entry and $500.

RIVER CITY WRITING AWARDS IN FICTION, The University of Memphis/Hohenberg Foundation, Dept. of English, Memphis TN 38152. (901)678-4591. Fax: (901)678-2226. Website: www.people.memphis.edu/~rivercity. Director: Dr. Thomas Russell. Offered annually for unpublished short stories of 7,500 words maximum. Deadline: January 20. Guidelines for SASE or visit our website. Charges $10, which is put toward a one year subscription for *River City*. Prize: 1st-$2,000; 2nd-$500; 3rd-$300. Open to any writer.

THE SANDSTONE PRIZE IN SHORT FICTION, Ohio State University Press and the MFA Program in Creative Writing at The Ohio State University, 1070 Carmack Rd., Columbus OH 43210-1002. (614)292-1462. Fax: (614)292-2065. E-mail: ohiostatepress@osu.edu. Website: ohiostatepress.org. **Contact:** Jeanette Rivard. Offered annually to published and unpublished writers. Accepts submissions in January only. Charges $20 fee. Prize: $1,500, publication under a standard book contract, an invitation to Ohio State University to give a public reading and direct a creative writing workshop. Submissions may include short stories, novellas or a combination of both. Manuscripts must be 150-300 typed pages; novellas must not exceed 125 pages. No employee or student of Ohio State University is eligible.

SEVENTEEN MAGAZINE FICTION CONTEST, 850 Third Ave., New York NY 10022. E-mail: www.seventeen.com. Estab. 1948. . Previously unpublished short stories from writers 13-21 years old. Deadline: April 30. Check the November issue or website. Prize: 1st-$1,000 and publication in the magazine; 2nd-$500; 3rd-$250; 5 honorable mentions-$50.

MICHAEL SHAARA AWARD FOR EXCELLENCE IN CIVIL WAR FICTION, US Civil War Center, LSU, Raphael Semmes Dr., Baton Rouge LA 70803. (225)388-3151. Fax: (225)388-4876. E-mail: lwood@lsu.edu. Website: www.lsu.edu. **Contact:** Leah Jewett, director. Offered annually for fiction published January 1-December 31 "to encourage examination of the Civil War from unique perspectives or by taking an unusual approach." Deadline: December 31. Guidelines for SASE. Prize: $1,000. "All Civil War fiction, including collections of short stories, is eligible. Nominations should be made by publishers, but authors and critics can nominate as well."

JOHN SIMMONS SHORT FICTION AWARD and IOWA SHORT FICTION AWARDS, Iowa Short Fiction Award, Iowa Writers' Workshop, 102 Dey House, Iowa City IA 52242-1000. Offered annually for a collection of short stories. Anyone who has not published a book of prose fiction is eligible to apply. Prize: publication by the University of Iowa Press. Guidelines for SASE. Submissions: August 1-September 30 only.

KAY SNOW WRITING AWARDS, Willamette Writers, 9045 SW Barbur Blvd., Suite 5a, Portland OR 97219. (503)452-1592. Fax: (503)452-0372. E-mail: wilwrite@teleport.com. Website: www.teleport.com/~wilwrite/. **Contact:** Liam Callen. Annual contest to "offer encouragement and recognition to writers with unpublished submissions." Deadline: May 14. Guidelines for SASE. Charges $15 fee; no fee for student writers. Prize: 1st-$300, 2nd-$150, 3rd-$50, excerpts published in Willamette Writers newsletter, and winners acknowledged at banquet during writing conference. Acquires right to publish excerpts from winning pieces one time in their newsletter.

N SOUL OF THE WRITER AWARD, Grammar Bytes, 3044 Shepherd of Hills PMB519, Branson MO 65616. E-mail: contest@grammarbytes.com. Website: www.grammarbytes.com. **Contact:** Shane Jeffries. Offered twice a year to unpublished submissions. "Soul of the Writer Award was created to aid writers in their journey toward ultimate literary goals—whatever they may be. We look at fiction of any genre, any style." Deadline for entry postmarked by December 31, 2000 and by June 30, 2001. Guidelines for SASE. Charges $15. Limit of 15,000 words. Prize: 1st-$250; 2nd-$100; 3rd-$25 plus honorable mention certificate. Previous winners will select semi-finalists, then a committee of 3 prominent writers will make final decision. Writers retain all rights. Open to any writer.

SOUTH CAROLINA FICTION PROJECT, South Carolina Arts Commission, 1800 Gervais St., Columbia SC 29201. (803)734-8696. Fax: (803)734-8526. Website: www.state.sc.us/arts. **Contact:** Sara June Goldstein, contest director. Offered annually for unpublished short stories of 2,500 words or less. Deadline: January 15. Guidelines for SASE. Prize: $500. *The Post and Courier* newspaper (Charleston SC) purchases first publication rights. Open to any writer who is a legal resident of South Carolina and 18 years of age or older. 12 stories are selected for monthly publication.

N THE SOUTHERN REVIEW/LOUISIANA STATE UNIVERSITY SHORT FICTION AWARD, Louisiana State University, 43 Allen Hall, Baton Rouge LA 70803. (225)388-5108. Fax: (225)388-5098. E-mail: davesm@unixl.sn cc.lsu.edu. **Contact:** Dave Smith, selection committee chairman. First collection of short stories by an American published in the US during previous year. Deadline: January 31. Publisher or author may enter by mailing 2 copies of the collection.

N THE STAND MAGAZINE SHORT STORY COMPETITION, *Stand Magazine*, Haltwhistle House, Reorge St., Newcastle on Tyne, NE4 7JL United Kingdom. (0191)-2733280. E-mail: dlatane@vcu.edu. **Contact:** Editors of *Stand Magazine*. "This competition is an open international contest for unpublished writing in the English language intended to foster a wider interest in the short story as a literary form and to promote and encourage excellent writing in it." Deadline: TBA. Check website or send SASE. "Please note that intending entrants enquiring from outside the UK should send IRCs, not stamps from their own countries. In lieu of an entry fee we ask for a minimum donation of £4 or $8 US per story entered." Editorial inquiries and requests for entry form should be made with SASE to: Prof. David Latane, English Dept., VCU, Richmond, VA 23284-2005.

N **SUDDEN FICTION CONTEST**, *Berkeley Fiction Review*, % Eshleman Library, 201 Heller Lounge, University of California, Berkeley CA 94720-4500. (510)642-2892. E-mail: bfreview@excite.com. Website: www.OCF.berkeley. edu/~bfr. **Contact:** Fiction Editor. Offered annually for unpublished short stories under 1,000 words to showcase the relatively new genre of sudden fiction. Deadline: November 10. Charges $6 fee/first entry, $4/subsequent entries. Prize: 1st-$200 and publication, 2nd and 3rd-publication.

TAMARACK AWARD, *Minnesota Monthly*, 10 S. Fifth St., #1000, Minneapolis MN 55402. (612)371-5842. Fax: (612)371-5801. E-mail: nnelson@mnmo.com. Website: www.minnesotamonthly.com. **Contact:** Nichol Nelson, editorial assistant. Offered annually for unpublished fiction. Deadline: May. Guidelines for SASE. Prize: $800 and publication. Buys one-time publication rights. Open to residents of MN, ND, SD, IA, WI and MI.

STEVEN TURNER AWARD, The Texas Institute of Letters, Southwest Texas State University, San Marcos TX 78666. (512)245-2428. Fax: (512)245-7462. E-mail: mb13@swt.edu. Website: www.English.swt.ecu/css/TIL/rules.htm. **Contact:** Mark Busby. Offered annually for work published January 1-December 31 for the best first book of fiction. Deadline: January 3. Guidelines for SASE. Prize: $1,000. Writers must have been born in Texas, or have lived in the state for at least two consecutive years at some time, or the subject matter of the work should be associated with the state.

VERY SHORT FICTION AWARD, Glimmer Train Press, Inc. 710 SW Madison St., Suite 504, Portland OR 97205-2900. (503)221-0836. Fax: (503)221-0837. **Contact:** Linda Burmeister Davies. Website: www.glimmertrain.com. Offered twice yearly to encourage the art of the very short story. "Send your unpublished very short story with $10 reading fee/story. Word count: 2,000 max. Must be postmarked April 1-July 31 (summer contest) or November 1-January 31 (winter contest). Cover letter optional. First page of story to include name, address, phone, word count. 'VSF' must be written on the outside of the envelope. Winners will be called by November 1 (for summer contest) or May 1 (for winter contest). For a list of winners, include SASE with your story." Prizes: 1st-$1,200, publication in *Glimmer Train Stories* (circulation 13,000), and 20 copies of that issue. Runners-up-$500, $300, respectively and consideration for publication.

PAUL A. WITTY SHORT STORY AWARD, Executive Office, International Reading Association, P.O. Box 8139, Newark DE 19714-8139. (302)731-1600, ext. 293. Fax: (302)731-1057. E-mail: jbutler@reading.org. Website: www.reading.org. **Contact:** Janet Butler, public information coordinator. Offered to reward author of an original short story published in a children's periodical which serves as a literary standard that encourages young readers to read periodicals. Write for deadlines and guidelines. Prize: $1,000.

THOMAS WOLFE FICTION PRIZE, North Carolina Writers' Network, 3501 Hwy. 54 W., Studio C, Chapel Hill NC 27516. (919)967-9540. Fax: (919)929-0535. E-mail: mail@ncwriters@org. Website: www.ncwriters.org. **Contact:** Frances O. Dowell, program coordinator. Offered annually for unpublished work "to recognize a notable work of fiction—either short story or novel excerpt—while honoring one of North Carolina's best writers—Thomas Wolfe." Deadline: August 31. Guidelines for SASE. Charges $7 fee. Prize: $1,000 and potential publication. Past judges have included Anne Tyler, Barbara Kingsolver, C. Michael Curtis and Randall Kenan.

TOBIAS WOLFF AWARD IN FICTION, The Bellingham Review, M.S.9053, Western Washington University, Bellingham WA 98225. E-mail: bhreview@cc.wwu.edu. Website: www.wwu.edu/~bhreview/. **Contact:** (Mr.) Robin Hemley. Offered annually for unpublished short stories or novel excerpts. Submissions from January 2-March 1. Guidelines for SASE. Charges $10 fee/first entry; $5 for subsequent entries. Prize: 1st-$1,000; 2nd-$250; 3rd-$100, plus publication and copies.

WRITERS' JOURNAL ANNUAL SHORT STORY CONTEST, Val-Tech Media, Inc., P.O. Box 394, Perham MN 56573. (218)346-7921. Fax: (218)346-7924. E-mail: writersjournal@wadena.net. Website: www.writersjournal.com. **Contact:** Leon Ogroske. Offered annually for previously unpublished short stories. Deadline: May 31. Send SASE for guidelines. Prizes: 1st-$250, 2nd-$100, 3rd-$50 plus honorable mentions. Publication of prize winners and selected honorable mentions in *Writers' Journal* magazine. Buys one-time rights. Open to any writer. Charges $5 reading fee.

WRITERS' JOURNAL FICTION CONTEST, Val-Tech Media, P.O. Box 394, Perham MN 56573. (218)346-7921. Fax: (218)346-7924. E-mail: writersjournal@wadena.net. Website: www.writersjournal.com. **Contact:** Leon Ogroske. Offered annually for previously unpublished fiction. Deadline: December 31. Send SASE for guidelines. Prizes: 1st-$50, 2nd-$25, 3rd-$15 plus honorable mentions. Publication of prize winners and selected honorable mentions in *Writers' Journal* magazine. Buys one-time rights. Open to any writer. Charges $5 reading fee.

WRITERS' JOURNAL HORROR/GHOST CONTEST, Val-Tech Media, Dept. HG-20, P.O. Box 394, Perham MN 56573. (218)346-7921. Fax: (218)346-7924. E-mail: writersjournal@wadena.net. Website: www.writersjournal.com. **Contact:** Leon Ogroske. Offered annually for previously unpublished works. Deadline: March 30. Guidelines for SASE. Prizes: 1st-$50, 2nd-$25, 3rd-$15 plus honorable mentions. Publication of prize winners and selected honorable mentions in *Writers' Journal* magazine. Buys one-time rights. Open to any writer. Charges $5 fee.

WRITERS' JOURNAL ROMANCE CONTEST, Val-Tech Media, Dept. HG-20, P.O. Box 394, Perham MN 56573. (218)346-7921. Fax: (218)346-7924. E-mail: writersjournal@wadena.net. Website: www.writersjournal.com. **Contact:** Leon Ogroske. Offered annually for previously unpublished works. Deadline: July 31. SASE for guidelines. Prizes: 1st-$50, 2nd-$25, 3rd-$15 plus honorable mentions. Publication of prize winners and selected honorable mentions in *Writers' Journal* magazine. Buys one-time rights. Open to any writer. Charges $5 fee.

N ZOETROPE SHORT STORY CONTEST, Zoetrope: All-Story, 1350 Avenue of the Americas, 24th Floor, New York NY 10019. (212)708-0400. Fax: (212)708-0475. Website: www.zoetrope-stories.com. **Contact:** Adrienne Brodeur, editor. Annual contest for unpublished short stories. Deadline: October 1. Guidelines for SASE. Charges $10 fee. Prize: 1st-$1,000, 2nd-$500, 3rd-$250. Acquires first serial rights and two-year option on movie rights. Open to any writer.

Poetry

THE MILTON ACORN PRIZE FOR POETRY, Poetry Forever, P.O. Box 68018, Hamilton, Ontario L8M 3M7 Canada. (905)312-1779. Fax: (905)312-8285. Offered annually for unpublished poems up to 30 lines. Charges $3 fee. Deadline: May 15. Prize: 3 prizes of up to $100 and broadsheet publication.

THE ACORN-RUKEYSER CHAPBOOK CONTEST, Mekler & Deahl, Publishers, 237 Prospect St., S., Hamilton, Ontario L8M 2Z6 Canada. (905)312-1779. Fax: (905)312-8285. E-mail: meklerdeahl@globalserve.net. Website: www.meklerdeahl.com. Offered annually for published or unpublished poetry manuscript up to 30 pages. Deadline: September 30. Charges $10 fee (US). Prize: 1st—$100 and 50 copies of the chapbook; runner-up—$100.

AKRON POETRY PRIZE, University of Akron Press, 374B Bierce Library, Akron OH 44325-1703. (330)972-5342. Fax: (330)972-5132. E-mail: press@uakron.edu. Website: www.uakron.edu/uapress. **Contact:** Elton Glaser, poetry editor. Annual book contest for unpublished poetry. "The Akron Poetry Prize brings to the public writers with original and compelling voices. Books must exhibit three essential qualities: mastery of language, maturity of feeling, and complexity of thought." Deadline: Entries must be postmarked between May 15-June 30. Guidelines available online or for SASE. Charges $25. Winning poet receives $1,000 and publication of book. The final selection will be made by a nationally prominent poet. The University of Akron Press has the right to publish the winning manuscript, inherent with winning the Poetry Prize. Open to all poets writing in English.

ANAMNESIS POETRY CHAPBOOK AWARD COMPETITION, Anamnesis Press, P.O. Box 51115, Palo Alto CA 94303. (415)255-8366. Fax: (510)481-7123. E-mail: anamnesis@compuserve.com. Website: http://ourworld.compuserve.com/homepages/anamnesis. **Contact:** Keith Allen Daniels. Offered annually to preserve and promote outstanding imaginative poetry. Deadline: March 15. Guidelines for SASE. Charges $15 fee. Prize: $1,000, certificate, 20 copies of winning chapbook. Acquires one-time right to publish chapbook in a limited edition of 200-300 copies. Open to all writers. Recommends that poets purchase a sample chapbook for $6 (postpaid) before submitting their work.

ANHINGA PRIZE FOR POETRY, Anhinga Press, P.O. Box 10595, Tallahassee FL 32302. (850)521-9920. Fax: (850)442-6363. E-mail: info@anhinga.org. Website: www.anhinga.org. **Contact:** Rick Campbell. Offered annually for a book-length collection of poetry by an author who has not published more than one book of poetry. Submit January 1-March 15. Guidelines for SASE or on website. Charges $20 fee. Prize: $2,000 and publication. Open to any writer writing in English.

ANNUAL POETRY CONTEST, National Federation of State Poetry Societies, 1220 W. Koradine Dr., South Jordan UT 84095. **Contact:** Patricia A. Kimber. Estab. 1959. Previously unpublished poetry. "Fifty categories. Flier lists them all." Deadline: March 15. Guidelines for SASE. Charges fees. See guidelines for fees and prizes; must have guidelines to enter. See guidelines for procedure. All awards are announced in June. Top awards only (not honorable mentions) published the following June.

ARTS & LIFE PRIZE FOR POETRY, International Literary Society, 18463 Blueberry Lane, Apt. C101, Monroe WA 98272-1379. (206)930-6588. Fax: (360)794-5704. E-mail: nhccsteve@juno.com. Contest Director: Steve Whalen. Offered annually for unpublished 1,500 word stories of a restaurant, party, wine-tasting or any event involving food to gather material for a cultural magazine. Deadline: July 31. Guidelines for SASE. Charges $5 fee/poem; maximum 5 entries. Prize: 1st—$750, 2nd—$150, Honorable Mentions.

THE HERB BARRETT AWARD, for Short Poetry in the Haiku Tradition, Mekler & Deahl, Publishers, 237 Prospect St., S., Hamilton, Ontario L8M 2Z6 Canada. (905)312-1779. Fax: (905)312-8285. E-mail: meklerdeahl@global serve.net. Website: www.meklerdeahl.com. Offered annually for short poems in the haiku tradition. Deadline: November 30. Charges $10 fee (US); maximum 10 entries. Prize: 1st—$200, 2nd—$100, 3rd—$50 (US); all entrants receive a copy of the published anthology, entrants with poetry in the anthology receive 2 copies. Writers retain all rights. Open to any writer.

BLUESTEM POETRY AWARD, Division of English, Emporia State University, 1200 Commercial, Box 4019, Emporia KS 66801. (316)341-5216. Fax: (316)341-5547. E-mail: bluestem@emporia.edu. Website: www.emporia.edu/ bluestem/index.htm. **Contact:** Philip Heldrich, award director. Offered annually "to recognize outstanding poetry." Deadline: March 1. Guidelines for SASE. Charges $15 fee. Prize: $1,000 and a published book. Full length, single author collections, at least 48 pages long.

THE FREDERICK BOCK PRIZE, *Poetry*, 60 W. Walton St., Chicago IL 60610. (312)255-3703. Website: poetry@poe trymagazine.org. **Contact:** Joseph Parisi, editor. Offered annually for poems published in *Poetry* during the preceding twelve months (October through September). Guidelines for SASE. Prize: $300. *Poetry* buys all rights to the poems published in the magazine. Copyrights are returned to the authors on request. Any writer may submit poems to *Poetry*. Only poems published in *Poetry* during the preceding year are considered for the annual prizes.

BOSTON REVIEW POETRY CONTEST, *Boston Review*, E-53-407 MIT, Cambridge MA 02139. (617)494-0708. Submit up to 5 unpublished poems, no more than 10 pages total. Deadline: June 1. Charges $15 fee, payable to *Boston Review*, check or money order. Prize: $1,000 and publication in the October/November 2000 issue of *Boston Review*.

⋈ BARBARA BRADLEY AWARD, New England Poetry Club, 11 Puritan Rd., Arlington MA 02174-7710. **Contact:** Virginia Thayer. Offered annually for a lyric poem under 21 lines, written by a woman. Deadline: June 30. Guidelines for SASE. Charges $5 entry fee for nonmembers. Prize: $200.

BRIGHT HILL PRESS ANNUAL CHAPBOOK COMPETITION, Bright Hill Press, P.O. Box 193, Treadwell NY 13846. E-mail: wordthur@catskill.net. **Contact:** Bertha Rogers. Poetry in odd-numbered years, fiction even years, 16-24 pages, including bio, contents, acknowledgment and title. Deadline: May 31. Guidelines for SASE. Charges $9 fee. Prize: $100 and publication.

BRITTINGHAM PRIZE IN POETRY/FELIX POLLAK PRIZE IN POETRY, University of Wisconsin Press, 2537 Daniels St., Madison WI 53718-6772. **Contact:** Ronald Wallace, contest director. Estab. 1985. Unpublished book-length mss of original poetry. Submissions must be *received* by the press *during* the month of September, accompanied by a SASE for contest results. Prizes: $1,000 and publication of the 2 winning mss. Guidelines for SASE. Does *not* return mss. Charges $20 fee, payable to University of Wisconsin Press. One entry fee covers both prizes.

⋈ CADENCE ANNUAL POETRY CONTEST, *Cadence*, Tenth Street Press, 300 W. 10th St., Morris MN 56267. Phone/fax: (320)589-0120. **Contact:** Heather Timmerman. Offered annually for previously published or unpublished work to reward outstanding poetry and support publication of the magazine. Each entrant receives a copy of the issue in which the winning poem appears. Deadline: November 1. Guidelines for SASE. Charges $10/3 poems fee. Prize: $300 and publication in *Cadence*. Acquires one-time rights. All entries considered for publication.

⋈ CADENCE CHAPBOOK CONTEST, *Cadence*, Tenth Street Press, 300 W. 10th St., Morris MN 56267. Phone/ fax: (320)589-0120. **Contact:** Heather Timmerman. Offered twice annually for previously published or unpublished work to reward the most outstanding poetry and support publication of the magazine. Each entrant receives a copy of the winning chapbook. Deadline: February 1, August 1. Guidelines for SASE. Charges $12/20-24 poems. Prize: $200 and 50 copies. Acquires one-time rights. All entries considered for publication.

⋈ CADENCE QUARTERLY POETRY CONTEST, *Cadence*, Tenth Street Press, 300 W. 10th St., Morris MN 56267. Phone/fax: (320)589-0120. **Contact:** Heather Timmerman. Offered quarterly for previously published or unpublished work to reward the most outstanding poetry and support publication of the magazine. Each entrant receives a copy of the issue in which the winning poem appears. Deadline: March 15, June 15, September 15, December 15. Guidelines for SASE. Charges $5/3 poems. Prize: $100 and publication in *Cadence*. Acquires one-time rights. All entries considered for publication.

☙ CANADIAN AUTHORS ASSOCIATION AWARD FOR POETRY, Box 419, 320 S. Shores Rd., Campbellford, Ontario K0L 1L0 Canada. (705)653-0323. Fax: (705)653-0593. E-mail: canauth@redden.on.ca. **Contact:** Alec McEachern. Offered annually for a volume poetry by a Canadian. Deadline: December 15. Guidelines for SASE. Charges $20 fee (Canadian). Prize: $2,500 and a silver medal. Canadian citizens only.

CLEVELAND STATE UNIVERSITY POETRY CENTER PRIZE, Cleveland State University Poetry Center, 1983 E. 24 St., Cleveland OH 44115-2440. (216)687-3986. Fax: (216)687-6943. E-mail: poetrycenter@csuohio.edu. Website: www.ims.csuohio.edu/poetry/poetrycenter.html. **Contact:** Rita Grabowski, poetry center coordinator. Estab. 1962. Offered annually to identify, reward and publish the best unpublished book-length poetry ms submitted. Deadline: Submissions accepted November-January only. Charges $20 fee. Prize: $1,000 and publication. "Submission implies willingness to sign standard royalty contract for publication if manuscript wins." One or more of the other finalist mss may also be published for standard royalty (no prize). Guidelines for SASE. Does not return mss.

CONTEMPORARY POETRY SERIES, University of Georgia Press, 330 Research Dr., Suite B100, Athens GA 30602-4901. (706)369-6135. Fax: (706)369-6131. E-mail: mnunnell@ugapress.uga.edu. **Contact:** Margaret Nunnelley. Offered 2 times/year. Two awards: for poets who have not had a full-length book of poems published (deadline in September), and poets with at least one full-length publication (deadline in January). Guidelines for SASE. Charges $15 fee.

CRAB ORCHARD AWARD SERIES IN POETRY, Crab Orchard Review and Southern Illinois University Press, Department of English, Carbondale IL 62901-4503. (618)453-6833. Website: www.siu.edu/~crborchd. **Contact:** Jon C. Tribble, series editor. Offered annually for collections of unpublished poetry. Visit our website for current deadlines. Charges $20 fee. Prize: 1st-$3,000 and publication; 2nd-$1,000 and publication. Open to US citizens and permanent residents.

EMILY DICKINSON AWARD IN POETRY, Universities West Press, P.O. Box 22310, Flagstaff AZ 86002-2310. (520)213-9877. E-mail: swamisam@aol.com. Website: popularpicks.com. **Contact:** Jane Armstrong. Offered annually for unpublished poem in any form or style, and on any subject. Deadline: August 31. Guidelines for SASE. Charges $10 fee. Prize: $1,000 and publication in an anthology of poems published by Universities West Press. All finalists and winners will be published. Winner grants UWP one-time rights to publish the award-winning poem in its anthology. "A submission should include 1-3 poems, total entry not to exceed 6 pages, short biographical statement, reading fee of $10, and a SASE or e-mail address for results. Award is open to all writers. (Current students and employees of Northern Arizona University may not enter.)

N **"DISCOVERY"/THE NATION, The Joan Leiman Jacobson Poetry Prizes**, The Unterberg Poetry Center of the 92nd Street YM-YWHA, 1395 Lexington Ave., New York NY 10128. Website: www.92ndsty.org. **Contact:** Jennifer Cayer, assistant to the director. Estab. 1973. Open to poets who have not published a book of poems (chapbooks, self-published books included). Deadline: January. Charges $5 fee. Must have guidelines; send SASE or call (212)415-5759.

MILTON DORFMAN POETRY PRIZE, Rome Art & Community Center, 308 W. Bloomfield St., Rome NY 13440. (315)336-1040. Fax: (315)336-1090. **Contact:** Deborah O'Shea, director. Estab. 1990. "The purpose of the Milton Dorfman Poetry Prize is to offer poets an outlet for their craft. All submissions must be previously unpublished." Entries accepted: July 1-November 1. Guidelines for SASE. Charges $5 fee per poem. Make checks payable to: Rome Art & Community Center. Prize: 1st-$500; 2nd-$200; 3rd-$100. Open to any writer. Include name, address and phone number.

N **ECKERD COLLEGE REVIEW POETRY CONTEST**, Eckerd College Review, 4200 54th Ave. S, St. Petersburg FL 33711. E-mail: siren@eckerd.edu. Offered annually for previously unpublished poems. Deadline: December 1. Guidelines for SASE or by e-mail. Charges $7/3 poems fee, $3 for each additional poem. Include SASE. Prize: 1st-$300, 2nd and 3rd-$50. All winning poems published in spring issue. Acquires first North American serial rights. Open to any writer. No simultaneous submissions.

EDITORS' PRIZE, Spoon River Poetry Review, Campus Box 4241, English Dept., Illinois State University, Normal IL 61790-4241. (309)438-7906. Website: www.litline.org/spoon. **Contact:** Lucia Cordell Getsi, editor. Offered annually to unpublished poetry "to identify and reward excellence." Deadline: April 15. Guidelines for SASE or on website. Charges $18/3 poem fee (entitles entrant to a year's subscription valued at $15). Prizes: 1st-$1,000, two $100 runner-up prizes; publication of first place, runners-up, and selected honorable mentions. Open to all writers.

T.S. ELIOT PRIZE FOR POETRY, Truman State University Press, New Odyssey Series, 100 E. Normal St., Kirksville MO 63501-4221. (660)785-7199. Fax: (660)785-4480. E-mail: tsup@truman.edu. Website: www2.truman.edu/tsup. **Contact:** Nancy Reschly. Offered annually for unpublished English-language poetry. Deadline: October 31. Charges $25 fee. Guidelines for SASE. Prize: $2,000 and publication.

ROBERT G. ENGLISH/POETRY IN PRINT, P.O. Box 30981, Albuquerque NM 87190-0981. Phone/fax: (505)888-3937. Website: www.poets.com/RobertEnglish.html. **Contact:** Robert G. English. Offered annually "to help a poetry writer accomplish their own personal endeavors. Hopefully the prize amount of the Poetry in Print award will grow to a higher significance." Deadline: August 1. Charges $5/poem. Prize: $500. "The contest is open to any writer of any age. Hopefully to prepare writers other than just journalists with a stronger desire to always tell the truth."

FIVE POINTS JAMES DICKEY PRIZE FOR POETRY, Five Points, Georgia State University, University Plaza, Atlanta GA 30303-3083. (404)651-0071. Fax: (404)651-3167. E-mail: msexton@gsu.edu. Website: www.webdelsol. com/Five-Points. **Contact:** Megan Sexton. Offered annually for unpublished poetry. Deadline: November 30. Guidelines for SASE. Charges $10 fee (includes 1 year subscription). Prize: $1,000 plus publication.

THE 49th PARALLEL POETRY AWARD, The Bellingham Review, M.S. 9053, Western Washington University, Bellingham WA 98225. Website: www.wwu.edu/~bhreview. **Contact:** (Mr.) Robin Hemley. Estab. 1977. Offered annually for unpublished poetry. Submit October 1-December 31. Guidelines for SASE. Charges $5 fee/poem; checks payable to The Western Foundation/Bellingham Review. Prize: 1st-$1,000, 2nd-$250, 3rd-$100, plus publication and copies.

FOUR WAY BOOKS POETRY PRIZES, Four Way Books, P.O. Box 535, Village Station, New York NY 10014. Phone/fax: (781)837-4887. Website: www.gypsyfish.com/fourway/. **Contact:** K. Clarke, contest coordinator. Submissions accepted through March 31. Prize: cash honorarium and book publication. Four Way runs different prizes annually. Guidelines for SASE.

GLIMMER TRAIN'S APRIL POETRY OPEN, Glimmer Train Press, 710 SW Madison St., #504, Portland OR 97205. (503)221-0836. Fax: (503)221-0837. Website: www.glimmertrain.com. **Contact:** Linda Burmeister Davies. Submissions must be unpublished and may be entered in other contests. There are no subject, form, or length restrictions. "Name, address and phone number need to appear on all submitted poems." Entry fee(s): $10 for up to 3 poems (sent together). Deadline: April 30. Winners contacted by September 1. Prize: 1st-$500, publication in *Glimmer Train Stories* and 20 copies of that issue; 2nd-$250; 3rd-$100.

GLIMMER TRAIN'S OCTOBER POETRY OPEN, Glimmer Train Press, 710 SW Madison St., #504, Portland OR 97205. (503)221-0836. Fax: (503)221-0837. Website: www.glimmertrain.com. **Contact:** Linda Burmeister Davies. Submissions must be unpublished and may be entered in other contests. There are no subject, form, or length restrictions. "Name, address and phone number need to appear on all submitted poems." Entry fee(s): $10 for up to 3 poems (sent together). Deadline: October 31. Winners contacted by March 1. Prize: 1st-$500, publication in *Glimmer Train Stories* and 20 copies of that issue; 2nd-$250; 3rd-$100.

GROLIER POETRY PRIZE, Grolier Poetry Book Shop, Inc. & Ellen LaForge Memorial Poetry Foundation, Inc., 6 Plympton St., Cambridge MA 02138. (617)547-4648. Fax: (617)547-4230. E-mail: grolierpoetrybookshop@compuserve .com. Website: www.grolier-poetry.com. **Contact:** Ms. Louisa Solano. Estab. 1973. Offered annually for previously unpublished work to encourage and recognize developing writers. Open to all poets who have not published with either a vanity, small press, trade, or chapbook of poetry. Opens January 15; deadline: May 1. Guidelines must be followed; send SASE. Charges $6 fee. Prize: honorarium of $200 for two poets. Also poems of each winner and four runners-up will be published in the Grolier Poetry Prize Annual.

CECIL HEMLEY MEMORIAL AWARD, Poetry Society of America, 15 Gramercy Park S., New York NY 10003. (212)254-9628. Fax: (212)673-2352. E-mail: rebecca@poetrysociety.org. Website: www.poetrysociety.org. **Contact:** Rebecca Wolff, programs associate. Unpublished lyric poem on a philosophical theme. Guidelines for SASE. Deadline: December 21. Open to members only. Prize: $500.

THE BESS HOKIN PRIZE, *Poetry*, 60 W. Walton St., Chicago IL 60610. (312)255-3703. E-mail: poetry@poetrymaga zine.org. **Contact:** Joseph Parisi, editor, *Poetry*. Offered annually for poems published in *Poetry* during the preceding year (October-September). Guidelines for SASE. Prize: $500. *Poetry* buys all rights to the poems published in the magazine. Copyrights are returned to the authors on request. Any writer may submit poems to *Poetry*. Only poems published in *Poetry* during the preceding year are considered for the annual prizes.

FIRMAN HOUGHTON AWARD, New England Poetry Club, 11 Puritan Rd., Arlington MA 02476-7710. **Contact:** Virginia Thayer. Offered annually for a lyric poem worthy of the former NEPC President. Deadline: June 30. Send SASE for guidelines. For nonmembers: entry fee $5 for each poem or 3 poems for $10. Prize: $250.

IOWA POETRY PRIZES, University of Iowa Press, 119 W. Park Rd., Iowa City IA 52242. (319)335-2000. Fax: (319)335-2055. E-mail: sharon-rebouche@uiowa.edu. Website: www.uiowa.edu/~uipress. **Contact:** Sharon Rebouche. Offered annually to encourage mature poets and their work. Submit mss in May; put name on title page only. Send SASE. Charges $15 fee. Open to writers of English (US citizens or not) who have published at least one previous book.

RANDALL JARRELL POETRY PRIZE, North Carolina Writers' Network, 3501 Highway 54 West, Studio C, Chapel Hill NC 27516. E-mail: mail@ncwriters.org. Website: www.ncwriters.org. **Contact:** Frances O. Dowell, program coordinator. Offered annually for unpublished work "to honor Randall Jarrell and his life at UNC-Greensboro by recognizing the best poetry submitted." Deadline: November 1. Guidelines for SASE. Charges $7 fee. Prize: $1,000 and publication in *Parnassus: Poetry in Review*.

THE CHESTER H. JONES FOUNDATION NATIONAL POETRY COMPETITION, P.O. Box 498, Chardon OH 44024-9996. E-mail: WFerris412@aol.com. Website: http://chjonespoetrycomp.org. Estab. 1982. **Contact:** Mary J. Ferris, manager. Offered annually to encourage unpublished poets. Winning poems plus others, called "commendations," are published in a chapbook available from the foundation. Deadline: March 31. Charges $2 fee/each poem. Maximum 10 entries, no more than 32 lines each; must be unpublished. Prize: 1st-$1,000; 2nd-$750; 3rd-$500; 4th-$250; 5th-$100; several honorable mentions-$50. All commendations printed in the winners book receive $10. Winners receive the book free. "We require the right to publish the poems first."

THE JUNIPER PRIZE, University of Massachusetts, Amherst MA 01003. (413)545-2217. Fax: (413)545-1226. Website: www.umass.edu/umpress. **Contact:** Stephanie Attia, assistant editor. Estab. 1964. Offered for poetry mss by previously published authors. Deadline: September 30. Charges $10 fee.

KALLIOPE'S ANNUAL SUE SANIEL ELKIND POETRY CONTEST, *Kalliope, a journal of women's art*, 3939 Roosevelt Blvd., Jacksonville FL 32205. (904)381-3511. Website: www.fccj.org.kalliope. **Contact:** Mary Sue Koeppel. Offered annually for unpublished work. "Poetry may be in any style and on any subject. Maximum poem length is 50 lines. Only unpublished poems and poems not submitted elsewhere are eligible." Deadline: November 1. Guidelines for SASE. Charges $4/poem or $10/3 poems fee. No limit on number of poems entered by any one poet. Prize: $1,000, publication of poem in *Kalliope*. The winning poem is published as are the finalists' poems. Copyright then returns to the authors.

BARBARA MANDIGO KELLY PEACE POETRY AWARDS, Nuclear Age Peace Foundation, PMB 121, 1187 Coast Village Rd., Suite 1, Santa Barbara CA 93108-2794. Fax: (805)568-0466. E-mail: wagingpeace@napf.org. Website: www.wagingpeace.org. **Contact:** Chris Pizzinat. Offered annually for unpublished poems "to encourage poets to explore and illuminate some aspect of peace and the human spirit." Deadline: Postmarked by July 1. Guidelines for SASE or available on website. Charges $5/poem, $10/2-3 poem fee. No fee for youth entries. Prize: Adult-$500, youth (13-18)-$250, youth (12 and under)-$250. The Nuclear Age Peace Foundation reserves the right to publish and distribute the award-winning poems. Open to any writer.

THE GEORGE KENT PRIZE, *Poetry*, 60 W. Walton St., Chicago IL 60610. (312)255-3703. E-mail: poetry@poetrym agazine.org. **Contact:** Joseph Parisi, editor, *Poetry*. Offered annually for poems by an Illinois author published in *Poetry* during the preceding year (October-September). Guidelines for SASE. Prize: $500. *Poetry* buys all rights to the poems published in the magazine. Copyrights are returned to the authors on request. Any writer may submit poems to *Poetry*. Only poems published in *Poetry* during the preceding year are considered for the annual prizes. Open only to any resident of Illinois.

(HELEN AND LAURA KROUT MEMORIAL) OHIOANA POETRY AWARD, Ohioana Library Association, 65 S. Front St., Suite 1105, Columbus OH 43215. (614)466-3831. Fax: (614)728-6974. E-mail: ohioana@winslo.state.oh.us. Website: www.oplin.lib.oh.us/OHIOANA/. **Contact:** Linda R. Hengst. Offered annually "to an individual whose body of published work has made, and continues to make, a significant contribution to the poetry and through whose work, interest in poetry has been developed." Deadline: December 31. Guidelines for SASE. Prize: $1,000. Recipient must have been born in Ohio or lived in Ohio at least 5 years.

LAST POEMS POETRY CONTEST, sub-TERRAIN Magazine, P.O. Box 1575, Bentall Centre, Vancouver, British Columbia V6C 2P7 Canada. (604)876-8710. Fax: (604)879-2667. E-mail: subter@portal.ca. Website: www.anvilpress.c om. Offered annually for unpublished poetry that encapsulates the North American experience at the close of the 20th Century. Deadline: January 31. Guidelines for SASE. Charges $15 fee, four poem limit. Prize: $250, publication in spring issue and 3-issue subscription to sub-TERRAIN.

THE JAMES LAUGHLIN AWARD, The Academy of American Poets, 584 Broadway, Suite 1208, New York NY 10012-3250. (212)274-0343. Fax: (212)274-9427. E-mail: academy@poets.org. Website: www.poets.org. **Contact:** Awards Administrator. Offered annually for a ms of original poetry, in English, by a poet who has already published one book of poems in a standard edition (40 pages or more in length and 500 or more copies). Only mss that have come under contract with a US publisher between May 1 of the preceding year and April 30 of the year of the deadline are eligible. Deadline: April 30. Guideline for SASE. Prize: $5,000 and the Academy will purchase at least 6,000 hardcover copies for distribution.

THE LEDGE ANNUAL POETRY CHAPBOOK CONTEST, *The Ledge Magazine*, 78-44 80th St., Glendale NY 11385. **Contact:** Timothy Monaghan. Offered annually to publish an outstanding collection of poems. Deadline: October 31. Guidelines for SASE. Charges $12 fee. Prize: $1,000 and publication of chapbook. All entrants receive a copy of winning chapbook. Winner receives 50 copies. Open to any writer.

THE LEDGE POETRY AWARDS, *The Ledge Magazine*, 78-44 80th St., Glendale NY 11385. **Contact:** Timothy Monaghan. Offered annually for unpublished poetry of exceptional quality and significance. Deadline: April 30. Guidelines for SASE. Charges $10/3 poems; $3/additional poem. Prize: $1,000 and publication in *The Ledge Magazine*; 2nd Prize: $250 and publication in *The Ledge Magazine*; 3rd Prize: $100 and publication in *The Ledge Magazine*. All poems considered for publication in the magazine. Open to any writer.

THE LEVINSON PRIZE, *Poetry*, 60 W. Walton St., Chicago IL 60610. (312)255-3703. E-mail: poetry@poetrymagazi ne.org. **Contact:** Joseph Parisi, editor, *Poetry*. Offered annually for poems published in *Poetry* during the preceding year (October-September). Guidelines for SASE. Prize: $500. *Poetry* buys all rights to the poems published in the magazine. Copyrights are returned to the authors on request. Any writer may submit poems to *Poetry*. Only poems published in *Poetry* during the preceding year are considered for the annual prizes.

THE RUTH LILLY POETRY PRIZE, The Modern Poetry Association, 60 W. Walton St., Chicago IL 60610-3305. E-mail: poetry@poetrymagazine.org. **Contact:** Joseph Parisi. Estab. 1986. Offered annually to poet whose accomplishments in the field of poetry warrant extraordinary recognition. No applicants or nominations are accepted. Deadline varies. Prize: $75,000.

LOCAL 7's ANNUAL NATIONAL POETRY COMPETITION, Santa Cruz/Monterey Local 7, National Writers Union, P.O. Box 2409, Aptos CA 95001-2409. Website: www.mbay.net/~nwu/contest7.htm. **Contact:** Contest Coordinator. Offered annually for previously unpublished poetry to encourage the writing of poetry and to showcase unpublished work of high quality. Proceeds support the work of Local 7 of the National Writers Union. Deadline varies. Guidelines for SASE or on website. Charges $4/poem fee. Prize: 1st-$500; 2nd-$300; 3rd-$200.

LOUISIANA LITERATURE PRIZE FOR POETRY, *Louisiana Literature*, SLU—Box 792, Southeastern Louisiana University, Hammond LA 70402. (504)549-5022. Fax: (504)549-5021. E-mail: lalit@selu.edu. Website: www.selu.edu/orgs/lalit/. **Contact:** Jack Bedell, contest director. Estab. 1984. Offered annually for unpublished poetry. Deadline: February 16. Guidelines for SASE. Prize: $400. All entries considered for publication.

⚫ PAT LOWTHER MEMORIAL AWARD, The League of Canadian Poets, 54 Wolseley St., Suite 204, Toronto, Ontario, N5T 1A5 Canada. (416)504-1657. Fax: (416)504-0096. E-mail: league@ican.net. Website: www.poets.ca. **Contact:** Sandie Drzewiecki, program manager. Offered annually for a book of poetry by a Canadian woman. Deadline: November 1. Guidelines for SASE. Charges $15 fee (Canadian). Prize: $1,000. Open to female Canadian citizens and landed immigrants only.

LYRIC POETRY AWARD, Poetry Society of America, 15 Gramercy Park, New York NY 10003. (212)254-9628. Fax: (212)673-2352. E-mail: rebecca@poetrysociety.org. Website: www.poetrysociety.org. **Contact:** Rebecca Wolff, programs associate. Offered annually for unpublished work to promote excellence in the lyric poetry field. Deadline: December 21. Guidelines for SASE. Prize: $500. Line limit 50. Open only to Poetry Society members.

NAOMI LONG MADGETT POETRY AWARD, Lotus Press, Inc., P.O. Box 21607, Detroit MI 48221. (313)861-1280. Fax: (313)861-4740. E-mail: nlmadgett@aol.com. **Contact:** Constance Withers. Offered annually to recognize an outstanding unpublished poetry ms by an African-American. Entries accepted from April 1-June 1. Guidelines for SASE or by e-mail. Charges $15 fee. Prize: $500 and publication by Lotus Press. Open to any African-American poet.

THE MALAHAT REVIEW LONG POEM PRIZE, The Malahat Review, Box 1700 STNCSC, Victoria, British Columbia V8W 2Y2 Canada. (250)721-8524. E-mail: malahat@uvic.ca (queries only). Website: web.uvic.ca/malahat. **Contact:** Marlene Cookshaw. Offered every two years to unpublished long poems. Deadline: March 1. Guidelines for SASE. Charges $25 fee (includes a one-year subscription to the *Malahat*, published quarterly.) Prize: $400, plus payment from publication ($30/page). Preliminary reading by editorial board; final judging by the editor and 2 recognized poets. Obtains first world rights. After publication rights revert to the author. Open to any writer.

THE LENORE MARSHALL POETRY PRIZE, *The Nation* and The Academy of American Poets, 584 Broadway, Suite 1208, New York NY 10012. (212)274-0343. E-mail: academy@poets.org. Website: www.poets.org. **Contact:** Awards Administrator. Offered for book of poems published in US during previous year and nominated by the publisher. Deadline: June 1. Guidelines for SASE. Prize: $10,000.

LUCILLE MEDWICK MEMORIAL AWARD, Poetry Society of America, 15 Gramercy Park S., New York NY 10003. (212)254-9628. Fax: (212)673-2352. E-mail: rebecca@poetrysociety.org. Website: www.poetrysociety.org. **Contact:** Rebecca Wolff, programs associate. Original poem in any form on a humanitarian theme. Guidelines for SASE. Guidelines subject to change. Prize: $500. Deadline: December 21. Open to Poetry Society members only.

MID-LIST PRESS FIRST SERIES AWARD FOR POETRY, Mid-List Press, 4324 12th Ave. S., Minneapolis MN 55407-3218. Fax: (612)823-8387. E-mail: guide@midlist.org. Website: www.midlist.org. **Contact:** Lane Stiles, senior editor. Estab. 1990. Offered annually for unpublished book of poetry to encourage new poets. Deadline: February 1. Guidelines for SASE or from website. Charges $20 fee. Prize: publication and an advance against royalties. Contest is open to any writer who has never published a book of poetry. ("We do not consider a chapbook to be a book of poetry.")

[N] MISSISSIPPI VALLEY NON-PROFIT POETRY CONTEST, P.O. Box 3188, Rock Island IL 61204-3188. (309)259-1057. President: Max Molleston. Estab. 1972. Unpublished poetry: adult general, student division, Mississippi Valley, senior citizen, religious, rhyming, jazz, humorous, haiku, history and ethnic. Deadline: April 1. Charges $5 fee, $3 for students. Up to 5 poems may be submitted with a limit of 50 lines/poem.

MORSE POETRY PRIZE, Northeastern University English Deptment, 406 Holmes Hall, Boston MA 02115. (617)437-2512. Website: www.casdn.neu.edu/~english/morse.htm. **Contact:** Guy Rotella. Offered annually for previously published poetry, book-length mss of first or second books. Deadline: September 15. Charges $15 fee. Prize: $1,000 and publication by Northeastern University Press.

KATHRYN A. MORTON PRIZE IN POETRY, Sarabande Books, P.O. Box 4456, Louisville KY 40204. (502)458-4028. Fax: (502)458-4065. E-mail: sarabandeb@aol.com. Website: www.SarabandeBooks.org. **Contact:** Sarah Gorham, editor-in-chief. Offered annually to publish an outstanding collection of poetry. Submissions accepted January 1-February 15. Guidelines for SASE. Charges $20 fee. Prize: $2,000 and publication under standard royalty contract. All finalists considered for publication.

SHEILA MOTTON AWARD, New England Poetry Club, 11 Puritan Rd., Arlington MA 02476-7710. For a poetry book published in the last two years. Send 2 copies of the book and $10 entry fee. Prize: $500.

MUDFISH POETRY PRIZE, Mudfish/Box Turtle Press, 184 Franklin St., New York NY 10013. (212)219-9278. Editor: Jill Hoffman. Offered annually for unpublished poems. Deadline: April 30. Guidelines for SASE. Charges $15/3 poems; $2/additional poem. Prize: $1,000 and publication. All entries considered for publication.

NATIONAL LOOKING GLASS POETRY CHAPBOOK COMPETITION, Pudding House Publications, 60 N. Main St., Johnstown OH 43031. (740)967-6060. E-mail: pudding@johnstown.net. Website: www.puddinghouse.com. **Contact:** Jennifer Bosveld. Offered twice/year for "a collection of poems that represents our editorial slant: popular culture, social justice, psychological, etc. Poems might be themed or not." Deadlines: June 30, September 30. Guidelines for SASE or on website. Charges $10 fee. Prize: $100, publication of chapbook, 20 free books, 10 more to the reviewer of the poet's choice. Past winners include Rebecca Baggett, Willie Abraham Howard Jr., Michael Day, Bill Noble, William Keener, Mark Taksa, Ron Moran and many others.

NATIONAL POETRY BOOK AWARD, Salmon Run Press, P.O. Box 672130, Chugiak AK 99567-2130. Phone/fax: (907)688-4268. E-mail: salmonrp@aol.com. **Contact:** John Smelcer. Offered annually to previously published or unpublished poetry. "Each year we invite poets nationwide to send their 68-96 page poetry ms. After the deadline, our judge/staff selects one ms to be published in a run of no fewer than 500 copies." Deadline: December 31. Guidelines for SASE. Charges $10 fee. Prize: $1,000, publication of ms (minimum 500 copies), advertising in national literary magazines (*Poets & Writer*, etc.), arrangements for national reviews with approximately 50-100 promotional copies sent. Acquires one-time rights. Open to any writer.

NATIONAL WRITERS ASSOCIATION POETRY CONTEST, The National Writers Association, 3140 S. Peoria, #295, Aurora CO 80014. (303)841-0246. Fax:(303)751-8593. E-mail: sandywrter@aol.com. **Contact:** Sandy Whelchel, director. Annual contest "to encourage the writing of poetry, an important form of individual expression but with a limited commercial market." Charges $10 fee. Prizes: $100, $50, $25. Guidelines for SASE.

HOWARD NEMEROV SONNET AWARD, *The Formalist: A Journal of Metrical Poetry*, 320 Hunter Dr., Evansville IN 47711. **Contact:** Mona Baer. Offered annually for an unpublished sonnet to encourage poetic craftsmanship and to honor the memory of the late Howard Nemerov, third US Poet Laureate. Deadline: June 15. Guidelines for SASE. Charges $3/sonnet fee. Final judge for year 2000: W.D. Snodgrass. Prize: $1,000 cash and publication in *The Formalist*; 11 other finalists also published. Acquires first North American serial rights for those sonnets chosen for publication. Upon publication all rights revert to the author. Open to the international community of writers.

THE JOHN FREDERICK NIMS MEMORIAL PRIZE, *Poetry*, 60 W. Walton St., Chicago IL 60610. (312)255-3703. E-mail: poetry@poetrymagazine.org. Website: www.poetrymagazine.org. **Contact:** Joseph Parisi, editor, *Poetry*. Offered annually for poems published in *Poetry* during the preceding year (October-September). Guidelines for SASE. Prize: $500. Judged by the editors of *Poetry*. *Poetry* buys all rights to the poems published in the magazine. Copyrights are returned to the authors on request. Any writer may submit poems to *Poetry*. Only poems published in *Poetry* during the preceding year are considered for the annual prizes.

NLAPW INTERNATIONAL POETRY CONTEST, The National League of American Pen Women (Palomar Branch), 11929 Caminito Corriente, San Diego CA 92128. **Contact:** Helen J. Sherry. Offered annually for unpublished work. All proceeds from this contest provide an annual scholarship for a student entering college in the fields of art, letters or music. Categories: haiku—any style, rhymed verse—30 line limit, free verse—30 line limit. Deadline: first Friday in March. Guidelines for SASE. Charges $5/poem or $5/2 haiku. Prize: $50, $25, $10 and honorable mentions in each category. Open to any writer.

THE FRANK O'HARA AWARD CHAPBOOK COMPETITION, Thorngate Road, Campus Box 4240, English Dept., Illinois State University, Normal IL 61790-4240. (309)438-7705. Fax: (309)438-5414. E-mail: jmelled@ilstu.edu. Website: www.litline.org/html/thorngate.html. **Contact:** Jim Elledge, director. Offered annually for published or unpublished poetry "to recognize excellence in poetry by gays, lesbians and bisexuals. Entrants may be beginners, emerging poets or those with a national reputation. Poems may be formal, free verse, post-modern, prose poems, etc." Deadline: February 1. Guidelines for SASE. Charges $15/ms fee. Prize: $500 and publication of the winning ms; author also receives 25 copies of the chapbook.

THE OHIO STATE UNIVERSITY PRESS/THE JOURNAL AWARD IN POETRY, The Ohio State University Press and *The Journal*, 1070 Carmack, Columbus OH 43210. (614)292-6930. Fax: (614)292-2065. E-mail: ohiostatepress @osu.edu. **Contact:** Priscilla Vitelli, poetry editor. Offered annually for unpublished work, minimum of 48 pages of original poetry. Entries accepted September 1-30. Charges $20 fee. Prize: $1,000 and publication.

ORION PRIZE FOR POETRY, Poetry Forever, P.O. Box 68018, Hamilton, Ontario L8M 3M7 Canada. (905)312-1779. Fax: (905)312-8285. Offered for unpublished poetry to fund the publication of a full-size collection by Ottawa poet Marty Flomen (1942-1997). Deadline: June 15. Guidelines for SASE. Charges $3/poem fee. Prize: $100 minimum. Open to any writer.

NATALIE ORNISH POETRY AWARD IN MEMORY OF WAYNE GARD, The Texas Institute of Letters, Southwest Texas State University, San Marcos TX 78666. (512)245-2428. Fax: (512)245-7462. E-mail: mb13@swt.edu. Website: www.English.swt.edu/css/TIL/rules.htm. **Contact:** Mark Busby. Offered annually for the best book of poems published January 1-December 31 of previous year. Deadline: January 3. Guidelines for SASE. Prize: $1,000. Poet must have been born in Texas, have lived in the state at some time for at least two consecutive years, or subject matter is associated with the state.

PAUMANOK POETRY AWARD, Visiting Writers Program, SUNY Farmingdale, Knapp Hall Farmingdale NY 11735. Fax: (516)420-2051. E-mail: brownml@farmingdale.edu. Website: www.farmingdale.edu/CampusPages/ArtsSci ences/EnglishHumanities/paward.html. **Contact:** Margery L. Brown, director, Visiting Writers Program. Offered annually for published or unpublished poems. Send cover letter, 1-paragraph bio, 1-5 poems (name and address on each poem). Include SASE for notification of winners. (Send photocopies only; mss will not be returned.) Deadline: September 15. Charges $12 fee, payable to SUNY Farmingdale VWP. Prize: 1st-$1,000 plus expenses for a reading in 2000-2001 series; 2 runners-up—$500 plus expenses for a reading in series.

THE PEREGRINE PRIZE (Poetry), *Peregrine*, the literary journal of Amherst Writers & Artists, P.O. Box 1076, Amherst MA 01004-1076. E-mail: awapress@javanet.com. Website: www.javanet.com/~awapress. **Contact:** Nancy Rose. Offered annually for unpublished poetry. Deadline: April 1. Guidelines for SASE. Charges $10 fee. Prize: $500, plus publication in *Peregrine*. Open to any writer. "We seek writing that is honest, unpretentious and memorable."
   ● Entrants who reside in Western Massachusetts are also eligible for The Peregrine Prize: "Best of the Nest" Prize.

THE RICHARD PHILLIPS POETRY PRIZE, The Phillips Publishing Co., 2721 N.E. Stephens St., Suite F, Roseburg OR 97470. **Contact:** Richard Phillips, Jr. Offered annually to give a modest financial reward to emerging poets who have not yet established themselves sufficiently to generate appropriate compensation for their work. Deadline: Postmarked by January 31. Guidelines for SASE. Charges $15 fee. Prize: $1,000 and publication. Open to all poets. "There are no anthologies to buy. No strings attached. Simply put, the poet who enters the best manuscript will win the prize of $1,000 and will receive a check in that amount within 60 days of the deadline." Recent winners: Kathryn Presley (Somerville TX) 1997; Jana Klenburg (New York, NY) 1998; Paul Davidson (Los Angeles CA) 1999.

POET LORE NARRATIVE POETRY CONTEST, *Poet Lore*, The Writer's Center, 4508 Walsh St., Bethesda MD 20815. (301)654-8664. Fax: (301)654-8667. E-mail: postmaster@writer.org. Website: www.writer.org. **Contact:** Geraldine Connolly. Estab. 1889. Offered annually for unpublished narrative poems of 100 lines or more. Deadline: November 30. Prize: $350 and publication in *Poet Lore*. "*Poet Lore* has first publication rights for poems submitted. All rights revert to the author after publication in *Poet Lore*." Open to any writer.

THE POETRY CENTER BOOK AWARD, The Poetry Center, San Francisco State University, 1600 Holloway Ave., San Francisco CA 94132-9901. (415)338-2227. Fax: (415)338-0966. E-mail: newlit@sfsu.edu. Website: www.sfsu.edu/ ~newlit/welcome.htm. Director: Steve Dickison. Estab. 1980. Offered annually for books of poetry and chapbooks, published in year of the prize. "Prize given for an extraordinary book of American poetry." Deadline December 31. Charges $10/book fee. Prize: $500 and an invitation to read in the Poetry Center Reading Series. Please include a cover letter noting author name, book title(s), name of person issuing check, and check number. Will not consider anthologies or translations.

N: POETRY SOCIETY OF VIRGINIA CONTESTS, Poetry Society of Virginia, 11027 Becontree Lake Dr., Apt. 303, Reston VA 20190-4130. (703)904-9671. E-mail: lorifraind@netscape.net. **Contact:** Lori C. Fraind, contest director. Annual contest for unpublished stories in several categories. Deadline: January 19. Guidelines for SASE. Charges $2/ poem for nonmembers, free for members, free for student categories. Cash prizes: $25-100 in each category. Some categories are open to any writer; others are open only to members or students.

▼: POET'S CORNER AWARD, Broken Jaw Press, Box 596 Stn. A, Fredericton, New Brunswick E3B 5A6 Canada. Phone/fax: (506)454-5127. E-mail: jblades@nbnet.nb.ca. Website: www.brokenjaw.com. Offered annually to recognize the best book-length ms by a Canadian poet. Deadline: December 31. Guidelines for SASE. Charges $20 fee (Canadian). Prize: Publication of poetry ms.

FELIX POLLAK PRIZE IN POETRY/BRITTINGHAM PRIZE IN POETRY, University of Wisconsin Press, 2537 Daniels St., Madison WI 53718-6772. **Contact:** Ronald Wallace, contest director. Estab. 1994. Offered annually for unpublished book-length ms of original poetry. Submissions must be received during September (postmark is irrelevant) and must be accompanied by SASE for contest results. Prize: $1,000 and publication to the 2 best submissions. Guidelines for SASE. Does not return mss. Charges $20 fee, payable to University of Wisconsin Press. One fee covers both competitions. Notification in February.

EZRA POUND POETRY AWARD, *Paintbrush: Journal of Poetry and Translation*, Division of Language and Literature, Truman State University, Kirksville MO 63501. (660)785-4185. Fax: (660)785-7486. E-mail: pbrush@truman .edu. Website: www.paintbrush.org. **Contact:** Ben Bennani. Offered annually. Prize: $2,000 and publication of 32 pages of ms. Open to any writer.

QUARTERLY REVIEW OF LITERATURE POETRY SERIES, 26 Haslet Ave., Princeton NJ 08540. (609)921-6976. Website: www.princeton.edu/~qrl. "QRL Poetry Series is a book publishing series chosen from an open competition." Publishes 4-6 titles/year. Prize: $1,000, publication and 100 copies to each winner for a book of miscellaneous poems, a single long poem, a poetic play or a book of translations. Charges $20 fee, includes subscription. Guidelines for SASE.

RAINMAKER AWARDS IN POETRY, ZONE 3, Austin Peay State University, P.O. Box 4565, Clarksville TN 37044. (931)221-7031. Fax: (931)221-7393. E-mail: wallacess@apsu01.apsu.edu. **Contact:** Susan Wallace, editor. Offered annually for unpublished poetry. Deadline: January 1. Guidelines for SASE. Charges $8 fee. Prize: 1st-$500, 2nd-$300, 3rd-$100. Previous judges include Carolyn Forché, Marge Piercy, Howard Nemerov and William Stafford. Open to any poet.

[N:] RAMBUNCTIOUS REVIEW, Rambunctious Review, 1221 W. Pratt Blvd., Chicago IL 60626. Annual themed contest for unpublished poems. Deadline: December 3. Guidelines for SASE. Charges $2/poem fee, or free entry with $12 subscription. Prizes: 1st-$100, 2nd-$75, 3rd-$50. Acquires first rights. Open to any writer.

RED ROCK POETRY AWARD, *Red Rock Review*/Community College of Southern Nevada, English Dept., 3200 E. Cheyenne Ave., North Las Vegas NV 89030. (702)651-4094. E-mail: rich_logsdon@ccsn.nevada.edu. Website: www. ccsn.nevada.edu/academics/departments/English/contest.htm. **Contact:** Rich Logsdon. Offered annually for unpublished poetry. Deadline: October 31. Guidelines for SASE. Charges $6/3 poems. Prize: $500. Open to any writer.

ROANOKE-CHOWAN AWARD FOR POETRY, North Carolina Literary and Historical Association, 4610 Mail Service Center, Raleigh NC 27699-4610. (919)733-9375. Fax: (919)733-8807. **Contact:** Jerry C. Cashion, awards coordinator. Offered annually for published volume of poetry by a NC resident. Deadline: July 15.

NICHOLAS ROERICH POETRY PRIZE, Story Line Press, Three Oaks Farm, P.O. Box 1240, Ashland OR 97520-0055. (541)512-8792. Fax: (541)512-8793. E-mail: mail@storylinepress.com. Website: www.storylinepress.com. **Contact:** Roerich Prize Coordinator. Estab. 1988. Offered annually for full-length book of poetry. Any writer who has not previously published a full-length collection of poetry (48 pages or more) in English is eligible to apply. Deadline: May 1-October 31. Guidelines for SASE or on website. Charges $20 fee. Prize: winner—$1,000, publication, and reading at the Nicholas Roerich Museum in New York; runner-up—scholarship to Wesleyan Writers Workshop.

ANNA DAVIDSON ROSENBERG AWARD FOR POEMS ON THE JEWISH EXPERIENCE, Judah L. Magnes Museum, 2911 Russell St., Berkeley CA 94705. **Contact:** Paula Friedman. Offered annually for unpublished work to encourage poetry of/on/from the Jewish experience. Deadline for requesting mandatory entry forms is July 15; deadline for receipt of poems is August 31. Guidelines and entry form for SASE; forms sent out after April 15. Submissions must include entry form. Charges $2 fee/up to 3 poems. Prize: 1st-$100; 2nd-$50; 3rd-$25; $25-New/ Emerging Poet Prize; $25-Youth Award; also, silver (Senior) Award and honorable mentions. All winners and honorable mentions receive certificate, and winning poems are read in an Awards Reading at the Museum.

THE SANDBURG-LIVESAY ANTHOLOGY CONTEST, Mekler & Deahl, Publishers, 237 Prospect St., S, Hamilton, Ontario L8M 2Z6 Canada. (905)312-1779. Fax: (905)312-8285. E-mail: meklerdeahl@globalserve.net. Website: www.meklerdeahl.com. Offered annually for published or unpublished poetry (up to 70 lines). Deadline: October 31. Charges $12 fee (US); maximum 10 entries. Prize: 1st—$250 (US) and anthology publication, 2nd—$150 (US) and anthology publication, 3rd—$100 (US) and anthology publication; all entrants receive a copy of the published anthology, entrants with poetry in the anthology receive 2 copies. Writers retain all rights. Open to any writer.

THE HELEN SCHAIBLE INTERNATIONAL SHAKESPEAREAN/PETRARCHAN SONNET CONTEST, sponsored by The Poets Club of Chicago, 3715 Chimney Hill Dr., Valparaiso IN 46383. **Contact:** Bernhard Hillala, chairperson. Offered annually for original and unpublished traditional sonnets. Estab. 1954. Deadline: September 1. Guidelines for SASE after March 1. Prizes: 1st-$50, 2nd-$35, 3rd-$15; 2 honorable mentions.

→ Easy-to-customize search settings make it a snap to search through thousands of markets in seconds. You'll get a quick list of target markets perfect for your manuscript or query letter.

→ Bookmarks allow you to return to your target markets easily, every time you visit www.WritersMarket.com. There's no need to search time and time again.

→ A click of the mouse hyperlinks you to a listing's Web site where you can see full submission guidelines, get a list of contacts, or just check out the market.

→ Enter your personal profile at "My Writers Market," and the latest market updates will be tailored to match your profile. If there's a new market out there that fits your interests, you'll know about it the second you sign on.

→ You'll also find hundreds more listings – markets that just couldn't fit in the book – giving you even more publishing opportunities.

→ You'll get the latest information right at your fingertips, from updates to existing markets to brand-new places to publish your work.

→ **AND SO MUCH MORE!**

VISIT www.WritersMarket.com AND SUBSCRIBE TODAY!

SLIPSTREAM ANNUAL POETRY CHAPBOOK COMPETITION, *Slipstream*, Box 2071, Niagara Falls NY 14301. (716)282-2616 after 5P.M. EST. E-mail: editors@slipstreampress.org. Website: www.slipstreampress.org. **Contact:** Dan Sicoli, director. Offered annually to help promote a poet whose work is often overlooked or ignored. Deadline: December 1. Guidelines for SASE. Charges $10 fee. Prize: $1,000 and 50 copies of published chapbook. Open to any writer.

N: PEREGRINE SMITH POETRY CONTEST, Gibbs Smith, Publisher, P.O. Box 667, Layton UT 84041. (801)544-2958. **Contact:** Gail Yngve, poetry editor. Offered annually to recognize and publish a previously unpublished work. Deadline: April 30. Submissions accepted only during the month of April. Guidelines for SASE. Charges $15 fee. Prize: $500 and publication.

THE SOW'S EAR CHAPBOOK PRIZE, *The Sow's Ear Poetry Review*, 19535 Pleasant View Dr., Abingdon VA 24211-6827. (540)628-2651. E-mail: richman@preferred.com. **Contact:** Larry K. Richman, contest director. Estab. 1988. 24-26 pages of poetry. Submit March-April. Guidelines for SASE or by e-mail. Charges $10 fee. Prize: 1st-$1,000, 25 copies and distribution to subscribers; 2nd-$200; 3rd-$100.

THE SOW'S EAR POETRY PRIZE, The Sow's Ear Poetry Review, 19535 Pleasant View Dr., Abingdon VA 24211-6827. (540)628-2651. E-mail: richman@preferred.com. **Contact:** Larry K. Richman, contest director. Estab. 1988. Previously unpublished poetry. Submit September-October. Guidelines for SASE or by e-mail. Charges $2 fee/poem. Prizes: $1,000, $250, $100 and publication, plus option of publication for 20-25 finalists. All submissions considered for publication.

ANN STANFORD POETRY PRIZE, The Southern California Anthology, % Master of Professional Writing Program, WPH 404, U.S.C., Los Angeles CA 90089-4034. (213)740-3252. Website: www.usc.edu/dept/LAS/mpw. **Contact:** James Ragan, contest director. Estab. 1988. Offered annually for previously unpublished poetry to honor excellence in poetry in memory of poet and teacher Ann Stanford. Submit cover sheet with name, address and titles of the 5 poems entered. Deadline: April 15. Guidelines for SASE. Charges $10 fee. Prize: 1st-$1,000; 2nd-$200; 3rd-$100. Winning poems are published in *The Southern California Anthology* and all entrants receive a free issue.

THE AGNES LYNCH STARRETT POETRY PRIZE, University of Pittsburgh Press, 3347 Forbes Ave., Pittsburgh PA 15261. Website: www.pitt.edu/~press. Series Editor: Ed Ochester. **Contact:** Melanie Shrauder. Estab. 1980. Offered annually for first book of poetry for poets who have not had a full-length book published. Charges $20 fee. Deadline: March and April only. Mandatory guidelines for SASE. Prize: $5,000.

◄► STEPHAN G. STEPHANSSON AWARD FOR POETRY, Writers Guild of Alberta, 11759 Groat Rd., Edmonton Alberta T5M 3K6 Canada. (708)422-8174 or (800)665-5354. Fax: (708)422-2663 or (800)665-5354. E-mail: wga@oanet.com. **Contact:** Renate Donnovan or Miki Andrejevic, executive directors. Poetry book published in current year. Must be an Alberta poet. Prize: a leatherbound copy of your book and $500. Send 5 copies of the submission by December 31.

TIDEPOOL PRIZE FOR POETRY, Poetry Forever, P.O. Box 68018, Hamilton, Ontario L8M 3M7 Canada. (905)312-1779. Fax: (905)312-8285. Offered for unpublished poetry to fund the publication of a full-size collection by Hamilton poet Herb Barrett (1912-1995). Deadline: July 15. Guidelines for SASE. Charges $3/poem fee. Prize: $100 minimum. Open to any writer.

THE EUNICE TIETJENS MEMORIAL PRIZE, *Poetry*, 60 W. Walton St., Chicago IL 60610. (312)255-3703. E-mail: poetry@poetrymagazine.org. Editor, *Poetry*: Joseph Parisi. Offered annually for poems published in *Poetry* during the preceding year (October-September). Guidelines for SASE. Prize: $200. *Poetry* buys all rights to the poems published in the magazine. Copyrights are returned to the authors on request. Any writer may submit poems to *Poetry*. Only poems published in *Poetry* during the preceding year are considered for the annual prizes.

UNION LEAGUE CIVIC AND ARTS POETRY PRIZE, *Poetry*, 60 W. Walton St., Chicago IL 60610. (312)255-3703. E-mail: poetry@poetrymagazine.org. Editor, *Poetry*, Joseph Parisi. Offered annually for poems published in *Poetry* during the preceding year (October-September). Guidelines for SASE. Prize: $1,000. *Poetry* buys all rights to the poems published in the magazine. Copyrights are returned to the authors on request. Any writer may submit poems to *Poetry*. Only poems published in *Poetry* during the preceding year are considered for the annual prizes.

DANIEL VAROUJAN AWARD, New England Poetry Club, 11 Puritan Rd., Arlington MA 02476-7710. **Contact:** Virginia Thayer. Offered annually for "an unpublished poem worthy of Daniel Varoujan, a poet killed by the Turks at the onset of the first genocide of this century which decimated three-fourths of the Armenian population." Send poems in duplicate. Charges $5 per poem or 3 poems for $10. Deadline: June 30. Send SASE for guidelines. Prize: $500. Open to any writer.

THE WASHINGTON PRIZE, The Word Works, Inc., P.O. Box 42164, Washington DC 20015. E-mail: wordworks@shirenet.com. Website: www.writer.org/wordwork/wordwrk1.htm. **Contact:** Miles David Moore. Offered annually "for the best full-length poetry manuscript (48-64 pp.) submitted to the Word Works each year. The Washington Prize contest is the only forum in which we consider unsolicited manuscripts." Submissions accepted in the month of February. Deadline: March 1 (postmark). Guidelines for SASE. Charges $20 fee. Prizes: $1,500 and book publication; all entrants receive a copy of the winning book. Acquires first and subsequent English-language publication rights. Open to any American writer.

WHITE PINE PRESS POETRY PRIZE, White Pine Press, P.O. Box 236, Buffalo NY 14201. E-mail: wpine@whitepine.org. Website: www.whitepine.org. **Contact:** Elaine LaMattina, managing editor. Offered annually for previously published or unpublished poets. Deadline: December 15. Guidelines for SASE. Manuscript: up to 96 pages of original work; translations are not eligible. Poems may have appeared in magazines of limited edition chapbooks. Charges $20 fee. Prize: $1,000 and publication. "We hold rights until the book is out of print; then rights revert to the author. With previously published work, the author is responsible for obtaining permission for publication by White Pine Press." Open to any US citizen.

THE WALT WHITMAN AWARD, The Academy of American Poets, 584 Broadway, Suite 1208, New York NY 10012-3250. (212)274-0343. Fax: (212)274-9427. E-mail: academy@poets.org. Website: www.poets.org. **Contact:** Awards Administrator. Offered annually to publish and support a poet's first book. Entries accepted from September 15-November 15. Guidelines for SASE. Charges $20 fee. Prize: $5,000, a residency for one month at the Vermont Studio Center, publication by Louisiana State University Press. Submissions must be in English by a single poet. Translations are not eligible. Contestants must be living citizens of the US and have neither published nor committed to publish a volume of poetry 40 pages or more in length in an edition of 500 or more copies.

WICK POETRY CHAPBOOK SERIES "OPEN" COMPETITION, Wick Poetry Program, Dept. of English, Kent State University, P.O. Box 5190, Kent OH 44242-0001. (330)672-2067. Fax: (330)672-3152. Website: www.kent.edu:80/english/wick/WickPoetry.htm. **Contact:** Maggie Anderson, director. Publication of a chapbook of poems by a poet currently living in Ohio. Deadline: October 31. Guidelines for SASE. Prize: Publication of the chapbook by the Kent State University Press.

WICK POETRY CHAPBOOK SERIES "STUDENT" COMPETITION, Wick Poetry Program, Dept. of English, Kent State University, P.O. Box 5190, Kent OH 44242-0001. (330)672-2067. Fax: (330)672-3152. Website: www.kent.edu:80/english/wick/WickPoetry.htm. **Contact:** Maggie Anderson, director. Offered annually for publication of a chapbook of poems by a poet currently enrolled in an Ohio college or university. Deadline: October 31. Guidelines for SASE. Prize: Publication of the chapbook by the Kent State University Press.

STAN AND TOM WICK POETRY PRIZE, Wick Poetry Program, Dept. of English, Kent State University, P.O. Box 5190, Kent OH 44242-0001. (330)672-2067. Fax: (330)672-3152. Website: www.kent.edu:80/english/wick/WickPoetry.htm. **Contact:** Maggie Anderson, director. First Book Prize open to anyone writing in English who has not previously published a full-length book of poems (a volume of 48 pages or more published in an edition of 500 or more copies). Deadline: May 1. Guidelines for SASE. Charges $15 fee. Prize: $2,000 and publication by the Kent State University Press.

THE RICHARD WILBUR AWARD, The University of Evansville Press, University of Evansville, Evansville IN 47722. (812)479-2963. **Contact:** The Editors. Offered annually for an unpublished poetry collection. Deadline: December 1. Guidelines for SASE. Charges $20 fee. Prize: $1,000 and publication by the University of Evansville Press.

WILLIAM CARLOS WILLIAMS AWARD, Poetry Society of America, 15 Gramercy Park S, New York NY 10003. (212)254-9628. Fax: (212)673-2352. Website: www.poetrysociety.org. **Contact:** Rebecca Wolff, programs associate. Offered annually for a book of poetry published by a small press, non-profit or university press. Deadline: December 21. Guidelines for SASE. Charges $10 fee. Prize: $500-1,000. Winning books are distributed to PSA members upon request and while supplies last.

ROBERT H. WINNER MEMORIAL AWARD, Poetry Society of America, 15 Gramercy Park S., New York NY 10003. (212)254-9628. Fax: (212)254-2352. Website: www.poetrysociety.org. **Contact:** Rebecca Wolff, programs associate. "Recognizing and rewarding the work of someone in midlife. Open to poets over 40, still unpublished or with one book." Guidelines for SASE; guidelines subject to change. Charges $5 fee for nonmembers; free to members. Deadline: December 21. Prize: $2,500.

THE J. HOWARD AND BARBARA M.J. WOOD PRIZE, *Poetry*, 60 W. Walton St., Chicago IL 60610. (312)255-3703. E-mail: poetry@poetrymagazine.org. **Contact:** Joseph Parisi, editor, *Poetry*. Offered annually for poems published in *Poetry* during the preceding year (October-September). Guidelines for SASE. Prize: $3,000. *Poetry* buys all rights to the poems published in the magazine. Copyrights are returned to the authors on request. Any writer may submit poems to *Poetry*. Only poems published in *Poetry* during the preceding year are considered for the annual prizes.

THE WRITER MAGAZINE/EMILY DICKINSON AWARD, Poetry Society of America, 15 Gramercy Park S., New York NY 10003. (212)254-9628. Fax: (212)673-2352. Website: www.poetrysociety.org. **Contact:** Rebecca Wolff, programs associate. Offered annually for a poem inspired by Emily Dickinson, though not necessarily in her style. Guidelines for SASE; guidelines subject to change. Deadline: December 21. Open to Poetry Society members only. Prize: $250.

YALE SERIES OF YOUNGER POETS, Yale University Press, P.O. Box 209040, New Haven CT 06520-9040. Website: www.yale.edu/yup/. **Contact:** Nick Raposo. Offered annually for first book of poetry by poet under the age of 40. Submit during February. Guidelines for SASE. Charges $15 fee. Winning manuscript is published by Yale University Press under royalty contact. The author receives royalties.

Playwriting & Scriptwriting

N **ALBERTA PLAYWRITING COMPETITION**, Alberta Playwrights' Network, 1134 Eighth Ave. SW, 2nd Floor, Calgary, Alberta T2P 1J5 Canada. (403)269-8564. Fax: (403)265-6773. E-mail: apn@nucleus.com. Website: www.nucleus.com/~apc. Offered annually for unproduced plays with full-length and Discovery categories. Discovery is open only to previously unproduced playwrights. Deadline: January 15. Charges $35 fee (Canadian). Prize: in each category: $3,500 written critique, workshop of winning play, reading of winning plays at a Showcase Conference. Open only to residents of Alberta.

N **THE ANNUAL BLANK THEATRE COMPANY YOUNG PLAYWRIGHTS FESTIVAL**, The Blank Theatre Company, 1301 Lucile Ave., Los Angeles CA 90026-1519. (323)662-7734. Fax: (323)661-3903. E-mail: steele@theblank.com. Website: www.theblank.com. **Contact:** Christopher Steele. Offered annually for unpublished work to encourage young writers to write for the theatre by presenting their work as well as through our mentoring programs. Deadline: April 1. Prize: Workshop of the winning plays by professional theatre artists. Open to all writers 19 or younger on the submission date.

ANNUAL INTERNATIONAL ONE PAGE PLAY COMPETITION, Lamia Ink! Inc., P.O. Box 202, Prince Street Station, New York NY 10012. **Contact:** Cortland Jessup, founder/artistic director. Offered annually for previously published or unpublished one page plays. Deadline: March 15. Guidelines for SASE. Charges $2/play or $5/3 plays. Prize: $200 and staged reading and publication of 12 finalists. Acquires "the rights to publish in our magazine and to be read or performed at the prize awarding festival." Playwright retains copyright.

N **ANNUAL ONE-ACT PLAY COMPETITION**, TADA!, 120 W. 28th St., New York NY 10001. (212)627-1732. Fax: (212)243-6736. E-mail: tada@tadatheater.com. Website: www.tadatheater.com. **Contact:** John Foster, literary manager. Offered annually for unpublished work to encourage playwrights, composers and lyricists to develop new plays for young audiences. Deadline: varies each year, usually in late winter. Call for guidelines. Prize: staged readings and honorarium for winners. Must address teen subjects and issues. Predominantly teen cast.

N **AURICLE AWARD**, Plays on Tape, P.O. Box 5789, Bend OR 97708. (541)923-6246. Fax: (541)923-9679. E-mail: theatre@playsontape.com. Website: www.playsontape.com. **Contact:** Silvia Gonzalez S. Annual contest to make available on tape and CD stage plays and to discover stage plays that have the components for audio production. Open to previously published and unpublished plays. Deadline: December 31. Guidelines for SASE or on website. Charges $3 fee. Prize: $100 award, then if the winning entry is audio published, an additional $500 plus royalty agreement. "We're looking for stage-play writers and radio-play writers. The concentration is on the adaptability of the stage play to audio. All writers encouraged regardless of résumé. We would like more minority submissions." Submit in any form: recycled paper, floppy disk, e-mail.

AUSTIN HEART OF FILM FESTIVAL FEATURE LENGTH SCREENPLAY COMPETITION, 1604 Nueces, Austin TX 78701. (512)478-4795. Fax: (512)478-6205. E-mail: austinfilm@aol.com. Website: www.austinfilmfestival.com. **Contact:** BJ Burrow, competition director. Offered annually for unpublished screenplays. The Austin Film Festival is looking for quality screenplays which will be read by industry professionals. The contest hopes to give unknown writers exposure to producers and other industry executives. Three competitions: (Adult/Mature Category, Children/Family Category, Comedy Category) and Best Feature Film Award. Deadline: screenplay: May 15th; film: August 1. Guidelines for SASE or call 1-800-310-3378. Charges $40 entry fee. Prize: Feature Length, Adult Prize: $4,000; Family Prize: $4,000; Comedy Prize: $1,000. The writer must hold the rights when submitted; it must be original work. The screenplay must be between 90 and 120 pages. It must be in standard screenplay format (industry standard).

N **BABYLON PLAYERS "WORLD PREMIERE" WRITING CONTEST**, Babylon Players, 386 High Point Dr., Edwardsville IL 62025. E-mail: babylon@inlink.com. **Contact:** Chas Melichar. Offered annually for unpublished work in 2 categories: One Act Plays and Full-Length Plays. Deadline: April 30. Guidelines for SASE. Charges $10/1-5 submissions, $20/6-10 submissions fee. Prize: full-length plays: $100 and production by Babylon Players; for one-acts, $50 and production. One full-length and one one-act play will be selected each year. Additional plays, or "runners-up" plays may be chosen for production, but only one prize for each category will be given. All rights remain with the author. Open to any writer. Material must be original, unproduced, and unpublished. Plays must utilize a simple set and common props. One-acts may range from 15 to 60 minutes. Full-length plays should be over approximately 1:45 with intermission. No period costumes or special effects. No more than six characters. Content/language should be acceptable to a general audience. Include SASE if return of materials is desired. Include SASE if you wish a list of winners. E-mail any queries.

BAKER'S PLAYS HIGH SCHOOL PLAYWRITING CONTEST, Baker's Plays, P.O. Box 699222, Quincy MA 02289-9222. (617)745-0805. Fax: (617)745-9891. E-mail: info@bakersplays.com. Website: www.bakersplays.com. **Contact:** Ray Pape, associate editor. Offered annually for unpublished work about the "high school experience," but can be about any subject, so long as the play can be reasonably produced on the high school stage. Plays may be of any length. Plays must be accompanied by the signature of a sponsoring high school drama or English teacher, and it is recommended that the play receive a production or a public reading prior to the submission. Multiple submissions and co-authored scripts are welcome. Teachers may not submit a student's work. The manuscript must be firmly bound, typed and come with SASE that includes enough postage to cover the return of the ms. Plays that do not come with an SASE will not be returned. Do not send originals; copies only. Deadline: postmarked by January 31, 2001. Guidelines for SASE. Prize: $500 and publication; $250, $100.

THE BEVERLY HILLS THEATRE GUILD-JULIE HARRIS PLAYWRIGHT AWARD COMPETITION, 2815 N. Beachwood Drive, Los Angeles CA 90068. (323)465-2703. **Contact:** Dick Dotterer. Estab. 1978. "Annual contest to discover new dramatists and to encourage established and aspiring playwrights to develop quality plays for the theatre." Original full-length plays, unpublished, unproduced and not currently under option. Plays must be written in English, no translations from foreign languages, adaptations from other media, or musicals are eligible. Also offers additional competition for plays written for children's theatre. Application and guidelines required, send SASE. Submissions accepted with applications from August 1-November 1. Prizes: 1st-$5,000, 2nd-$2,500, 3rd-$1,500; **The Marilyn Hall Awards**: for children: Category I (grades 6-8) $750; Category II: (grades 3-5) $250. Open to any writer who is a US citizen or legal resident. Co-authorships permissable.

THE BEVERLY HILLS THEATRE GUILD—PLAY COMPETITION FOR CHILDREN'S THEATRE: THE MARILYN HALL AWARDS, 2815 N. Beachwood Dr., Los Angeles CA 90068-1923. **Contact:** Dick Dotterer. Offered annually for unpublished, theatrical works suitable for the grades in 2 designated categories. Category I: plays for grades 6-8 (middle school), approximately 60 minutes or less; Category II: plays for grades 3-5 (upper elementary), approximately 30 minutes or less. Authors may enter up to 2 scripts, one in each category. Plays must be written in Standard English. They may be original, adaptations, or translations. Musicals are not eligible. Authors must be US citizens or legal residents. Co-authorship permissable. Deadline: entries must be postmarked January 15-February 28. Prizes: Category I-$750; Category II-$250. Send #10 SASE for guidelines and entry forms before submitting.

WALDO M. & GRACE C. BONDERMAN IUPUI/IRT NATIONAL YOUTH THEATRE PLAYWRITING COMPETITION AND DEVELOPMENT WORKSHOP, IUPUI Communication Studies Dept., 425 University Blvd., CA 309, Communication Studies, Indianapolis IN 46202. (317)274-2095. Fax: (317)278-1025. E-mail: dwebb@iupui.edu. Website: www.iupui.edu/~comstudy/playsym/symwork.html. **Contact:** Dorothy Webb. Offered every 2 years for unpublished plays to encourage writers to create artistic scripts for young audiences. "It provides a forum through which each playwright receives constructive criticism and the support of a development team consisting of a professional director and dramaturg. Plays will be cast from professional and experienced area actors." Deadline: postmarked by September 8, received by September 15. Guidelines for SASE or on website. Awards will be presented to 10 finalists. In addition to the development work, 4 cash awards of $1,000 each will be presented to the 4 playwrights whose plays are selected for development. "Plays should be intended for young audiences 1st grade through high school (no play is expected to appeal to all ages simultaneously). Playwrights must suggest the appropriate age category on official entry form."

CALIFORNIA YOUNG PLAYWRIGHTS CONTEST, Playwrights Project, 450 B St., Suite 1020, San Diego CA 92101-8093. (619)239-8222. Fax: (619)239-8225. E-mail: youth@playwright.com. Website: www.playwrightsproject.com. Contact: Laurel Withers. Offered annually for previously unpublished plays by young writers to stimulate young people to create dramatic works, and to nurture promising young writers (under age 19). Deadline: April 1. Guidelines for SASE. Prize: professional production of 3-5 winning plays at the Old Globe Theatre in San Diego, plus royalty. All entrants receive detailed evaluation letter. Scripts must be a minimum of 10 standard typewritten pages; send 2 copies. Writers must be California residents under age 19 as of the deadline date.

CANADIAN AUTHORS ASSOCIATION AWARD FOR DRAMA, Box 419, 320 S. Shores Dr., Campbellford, Ontario K0L 1L0 Canada. (705)653-0323. Fax: (705)653-0593. E-mail: canauth@redden.on.ca. **Contact:** Alec McEachern. Offered annually for a full-length play first published or performed that year. Deadline: December 15. Guidelines for SASE. Charges $20 fee (Canadian). Prize: $2,500 and a silver medal. Canadian citizens only.

CEC JACKIE WHITE MEMORIAL NATIONAL CHILDREN'S PLAYWRITING CONTEST, Columbia Entertainment Company, 309 Parkade Blvd., Columbia MO 65202. (573)874-5628. **Contact:** Betsy Phillips. Estab. 1988. Offered annually for "top notch unpublished scripts for theater school use, to challenge and expand the talents of our students, ages 10-15. Should be a full length play with speaking roles for 20-30 characters of all ages with at least 10 roles developed in some detail." Deadline: June 1. Prize: 1st-$250. "Production is usual, but the company reserves the right to grant the 1st place prize money without production. When produced, travel money is available for playwright." Guidelines for SASE. Entrants receive written evaluation of work. Charges $10 fee.

N: JANE CHAMBERS PLAYWRITING AWARD, Women and Theatre Program of Association for Theatre in Higher Education (WTP/ATHE), % Mary Donahoe, Department of Theatre Arts, Wright State University, Dayton OH 45435-0001. **Contact:** Mary Donahoe, director. Estab. 1983. Offered annually to recognize a woman playwright who has written a play with a feminist perspective, a majority of roles for women, and which experiments with the dramatic form. Deadline: February 15. Notification: May 31. Guidelines for #10 SASE. Prize: $1,000. Student award: $250. Synopses of both winners sent to all TCG-affiliated theatres. "Writer must be female. A recommendation from a theatre professional is helpful, but not required."

CHARLOTTE FESTIVAL/NEW PLAYS IN AMERICA, Charlotte Repertory Theatre, 129 W. Trade St., Charlotte NC 28202-2143. **Contact:** Carol Bellamy, literary associate. Four plays selected for each festival. Must be full scripts—no one acts or musicals. Must not have had any previous professional production. Accepted all year. Prize: staged reading of script, transportation to festival, small honorarium for expenses. Scripts *must be bound* and include SASE if need to be returned. No cassettes, international reply coupons or videos accepted.

CHILDREN'S THEATRE PLAYWRIGHT DIVISION, Stages Repertory Theatre, 3201 Allen Pkwy., Suite 101, Houston TX 77019. (713)527-0240. Fax: (713)527-8669. **Contact:** Rob Bundy, artistic director. Offered annually for original scripts or scripts designed on existing fairy tales or books designed specifically for family audiences. Deadline: October 1-December 31. Guidelines for SASE or on website. Prize: reading by professional actors and prizes awarded. Winners notified in May.

N: CLAUDER COMPETITION, in Playwriting Excellence, P.O. Box 383259, Cambridge MA 02238. (781)322-3187. **Contact:** Betsy Carpenter, director. Offered every 2 years for unproduced plays to encourage *New England* playwrights. Deadline: September 1, 2000. Guidelines for SASE. Prize: $3,000 and full production during the Mainstage Season at Portland Stage. Two finalists receive $500 and professional staged reading. Rights negotiated with author or author's agent.

N: CLEVELAND PUBLIC THEATRE NEW PLAYS FESTIVAL, Cleveland Public Theatre, 6415 Detroit Ave., Cleveland OH 44102-3011. (216)631-2727. Fax: (216)631-2575. E-mail: cpt@en.com. Website: www.clevelandartists.net/cpt. **Contact:** Literary Manager. Estab. 1983. Annual festival of staged readings of 10-15 alternative, experimental, poetic, political work, and plays by women, people of color, gays/lesbians. Deadline: September 1. Guidelines for SASE. Charges $10 fee. "We accept both full-length and one-acts, but emphasize shorter works, simple set, 10 actor cast maximum. Generally, half of the works in the New Plays Festival are by Ohio playwrights."

CUNNINGHAM PRIZE FOR PLAYWRITING, The Theatre School, DePaul University, 2135 N. Kenmore, Chicago IL 60614. (773)325-7938. Fax: (773)325-7920. E-mail: lgoetsch@wppost.depaul.edu. Website: theatreschool.depaul.edu. **Contact:** Lara Goetsch. Offered annually for published or unpublished work "to recognize and encourage the writing of dramatic works which affirm the centrality of religion, broadly defined, and the human quest for meaning, truth and community." Deadline: December 1. Guidelines for SASE. Prize: $5,000. Open to Chicago residents, defined as within 100 miles of the Loop.

WALT DISNEY STUDIOS FELLOWSHIP PROGRAM, Walt Disney Studios, 500 S. Buena Vista St., Burbank CA 91521. (818)560-6894. **Contact:** Troy Nethercott. Offering up to 8 positions for writers to work full-time developing their craft at Disney in feature film and television writing. Deadline: May 1-21, 2000. "Writing samples are required, as well as a résumé, completed application form and notarized standard letter agreement (available from the Program Administrator.)" A $33,000 salary for 1 year period beginning January 2001. Fellows outside of LA area will be provided with airfare and 1 month's accommodations. Members of the WGA should apply through the Guild's Employment Access Department at (323)782-4648. Information and application form available on the Internet at members.tripod.com/disfel.

N: DRAMARAMA PLAYWRIGHTING COMPETITION, Playwright's Center of San Francisco, P.O. Box 460466, San Francisco CA 94146-0466. (415)626-4603. Fax: (415)863-0901. **Contact:** Dr. S.B. Kominars. Annual contest for previously unpublished and unproduced plays. Two categories: Short Plays (under one hour) and Full-Length Plays (over one hour). Deadline: March 15, 2001. Guidelines for SASE. Charges $25 fee. Prize: $500 for winning play in each category. Open to any writer, but "staged readings" will not be considered.

DRURY UNIVERSITY ONE-ACT PLAY CONTEST, Drury University, 900 N. Benton Ave., Springfield MO 65802-3344. (417)873-7430. Fax: (417)873-7432. E-mail: sasher@lib.drury.edu. Website: www.drury.edu. **Contact:** Sandy Asher. Estab. 1986. Offered in even-numbered years for unpublished and professionally unproduced plays. One play per playwright. Deadline: December 1. Guidelines for SASE.

DUBUQUE FINE ARTS PLAYERS ANNUAL ONE-ACT PLAYWRITING CONTEST, 330 Clarke Dr., Dubuque IA 52001. (319)588-0646. E-mail: snakelady@mwci.net. **Contact:** Jennie G. Stabenow, contest coordinator.

Annual competition since 1977 for previously unpublished, unproduced plays. Adaptations must be of playwright's own work or of a work in the public domain. No children's plays or musicals. No scripts over 35 pages or 40 minutes performance time. Two copies of ms required. Script Readers' review sheets available. "Concentrate on character, relationships, and a good story." Deadline: January 31. Guidelines for #10 SASE. Charges $10 fee for each play submitted. Prizes: $600, $300, $200, plus possible full production of play. Buys rights to first full-stage production and subsequent local video rights. Reports by June 30.

EMERGING PLAYWRIGHT'S AWARD, Urban Stages, 17 E. 47th St., New York NY 10017. (212)421-1380. Fax: (212)421-1387. E-mail: urbanstages@aol.com. Website: www.mint.net/urbanstages. **Contact:** Brigitte Viellieu-Davis, programs director. Submissions required to be unpublished and unproduced in New York City. Send script, letter of introduction, production history, author's name résumé and SASE. Submissions accepted year-round. Plays selected in August and January for award consideration. Estab. 1983. Prize: $500 and New York showcase production. One play submission per person.

N EMPIRE SCREENPLAY CONTEST, Empire Productions, 12358 Ventura Blvd., #602, Studio City CA 91604-2508. (661)420-9919. Fax: (661)920-9916. E-mail: empiresc@aol.com. Website: www.geocities.com/hollywood/movie/7728. **Contact:** Michael J. Farrand. Annual contest to identify and develop motion picture projects for the Hollywood producers and to advance screenwriter careers worldwide through guidance, competitive selection, and publicity/promotion/marketing. Deadline: June 15, July 15, August 1. All contact and communication must be via e-mail and the website. Charges $40-50 fee. Prize: $2,000. Open to any writer. Scripts/projects must be narrative, feature length and available for option/purchase/development/production.

SHUBERT FENDRICH MEMORIAL PLAYWRITING CONTEST, Pioneer Drama Service, Inc., P.O. Box 4267, Englewood CO 80155. (303)779-4035. Fax: (303)779-4315. E-mail: playwrights@pioneerdrama.com. Website: www.pioneerdrama.com. **Contact:** Beth Somers, assistant editor. Offered annually for unpublished but previously produced submissions to encourage the development of quality theatrical material for educational and community theater. Deadline: March 1. Guidelines for SASE. Prize: $1,000 royalty advance, publication. Rights acquired only if published. People already published by Pioneer Drama are not eligible.

FESTIVAL OF FIRSTS, City of Carmel-by-the-Sea-Community and Cultural Dept., P.O. Box 1950, Carmel CA 93921-1950. (831)624-3996. Fax: (831)624-0147. **Contact:** Brian Donoghue, award director. Offered annually for unpublished plays to recognize and foster the art of playwriting. Deadline: June 15 through August 31. Guidelines for SASE. Charges $15/script. Prize: up to $1,000.

FESTIVAL OF NEW WORKS, Plays-In-Progress, 615 Fourth St., Eureka CA 95501. (707)443-3724. **Contact:** Susan Bigelow-Marsh. Offered fall and spring for unpublished/unproduced submissions to give playwrights an opportunity to hear their work and receive audience feedback. "We also produce a full season of new unproduced plays—submission deadline is June 1." Deadlines: August 1 and March 1. Guidelines for SASE. Prize: staged reading.

FULL-LENGTH PLAY COMPETITION, West Coast Ensemble, P.O. Box 38728, Los Angeles CA 90038. (323)876-9337. Fax: (323)876-8916. **Contact:** Les Hanson. Offered annually "to nurture, support and encourage" unpublished playwrights. Deadline: December 31. Guidelines for SASE. Prize: $500 and presentation of play. Permission to present the play is granted if work is selected as finalist.

JOHN GASSNER MEMORIAL PLAYWRITING COMPETITION, New England Theatre Conference, Inc., Northeastern University, 360 Huntington Ave., Boston MA 02115. E-mail: netc@world.std.com. Website: www.netheatreconference.org. **Contact:** Clinton Campbell, managing director. Offered annually to unpublished full-length plays and scripts. Deadline: April 15. Guidelines for SASE. Charges $10 fee. Prizes: 1st-$1,000; 2nd-$500. Open to New England residents NETC members. Playwrights living outside New England may participate by joining NETC.

GREAT PLATTE RIVER PLAYWRIGHTS FESTIVAL, University of Nebraska at Kearney, Theatre Department, 905 W. 25th St., Kearney NE 68849. (308)865-8406. Fax: (308)865-8806. E-mail: garrisonj@unk.edu. **Contact:** Jack Garrison. Estab. 1988. "Purpose of award is to develop original dramas and encourage playwrights to work in regional settings. There are five catagories: 1) Adult; 2) Youth (Adolescent); 3) Children's; 4) Musical Theater; 5) Native American. Entries may be drama or comedy." Deadline: April 1. Prize: 1st-$500; 2nd-$300; 3rd-$200; plus free lodging and a travel stipend. "The Festival reserves the rights to development and premiere production of the winning plays without payment of royalties." Contest open to entry by any writer "provided that the writer submits playscripts to be performed on stage—works in progress also acceptable. Works involving the Great Plains will be most favored. More than one entry may be submitted." SASE required for return of scripts. Selection announcement by July 31 only to writers who provide prepaid postcard or SASE.

PAUL GREEN PLAYWRIGHTS PRIZE, North Carolina Writers' Network, 3501 Hwy. 54 W., Studio C, Chapel Hill NC 27516. (919)967-9540. Fax: (919)929-0535. E-mail: mail@ncwriters.org. Website: www.ncwriters.org. **Con-**

tact: Frances O. Dowell, program coordinator. Offered annually for unpublished submissions to honor a playwright, held in recognition of Paul Green, North Carolina's dramatist laureate and Pulitzer Prize-winning playwright. Deadline: September 30. Guidelines for SASE. Charges $10 ($7.50 for NCWN members). Prize: $500. Open to any writer.

AURAND HARRIS MEMORIAL PLAYWRITING AWARD, The New England Theatre Conference, Inc., Northeastern University, 360 Huntington Ave., Boston MA 02115. (617)424-9275. Fax: (617)424-1057. E-mail: netc@world.st d.com. Website: www.netheatreconference.org. Offered annually for an unpublished full-length play for young audiences. Deadline: May 1. Guidelines for SASE. Charges $20 fee. "No phone calls, please." Prize: 1st-$1,000, 2nd-$500. Open only to New England residents and members of the New England Theatre Conference.

HENRICO THEATRE COMPANY ONE-ACT PLAYWRITING COMPETITION, Henrico Recreation & Parks, P.O. Box 27032, Richmond VA 23273. (804)501-5138. Fax: (804)501-5284. E-mail: per22@co.henrico.va.us. Website: www.co.henrico.va.us/rec. **Contact:** Amy A. Perdue. Offered annually for previously unpublished or unproduced plays or musicals to produce new dramatic works in 1-act form. Deadline: July 1. Guidelines for SASE. Prize: winner $300; runner-up $200; winning entries may be produced; videotape sent to author. "Scripts with small casts and simpler sets given preference. Controversial themes and excessive language should be avoided."

HISPANIC PLAYWRIGHTS' DIVISION: SOUTHWEST FESTIVAL OF NEW PLAYS, Stages Repertory Theatre, 3201 Allen Pkwy., Suite 101, Houston TX 77019. (713)527-0240. Fax: (713)527-8669. **Contact:** Rob Bundy, artistic director. Offered annually to provide an outlet for playwrights of Hispanic/Latino heritage. Deadline: October 1-December 31. Guidelines for SASE or on website. Prize: 1st-reading by professional actors; 2 runners-up-selected scenes read. Winners notified in May.

HISPANIC PLAYWRIGHTS' PROJECT, South Coast Repertory Theatre, P.O. Box 2197, Costa Mesa CA 92628-2197. (714)708-5500, ext. 5405. Fax: (714)545-0391. **Contact:** Juliette Carrillo. Offered annually for unpublished plays to develop work by Latino writers across the US. Deadline: January 15. Guidelines for SASE or call for a brochure and leave address. Prize: a workshop or reading of the play. Open to unproduced plays by Latino writers only.

INTERNATIONAL ONE-PAGE PLAY COMPETITION, *Lamia Ink!* Inc., P.O. Box 202, Prince St. Station, New York NY 10012. **Contact:** Cortland Jessup, founder. Offered annually to encourage and promote performance writers and to challenge all interested writers. Interested in all forms of theater and performance writing in one page format. Deadline: March 15. No phone calls. Guidelines for SASE. Charges $2/one-page play, $5/3 plays per author per competition. Prize: 1st-$200. Public reading given for top 12 in NYC. Publication in *Lamia Ink!*. If play has been previously published, playwright must have retained copyright.

JEROME FELLOWSHIP, The Playwrights' Center, 2301 Franklin Ave., E., Minneapolis MN 55406-1099. (612)332-7481. Fax: (612)332-6037. E-mail: pwcenter@mtn.org. Website: www.pwcenter.org. **Contact:** Megan Monaghan, director of playwright services. Offered annually to provide emerging American playwrights with funds and services to aid them in the development of their craft. Deadline: September 15. Guidelines for SASE. Prize: $7,200 Fellowship which includes access to Playwrights' Center services, including readings and workshops with professional directors, dramaturgs and actors. Applications are screened for eligibility by the Center's Playwright Services Director and then evaluated by a diverse panel of national theater artists. Applicants must be citizens or permanent residents of the US, and applicants may not have had more than two works fully produced by professional theaters at the time of application. Jerome Fellows spend a full year in residency in the Twin Cities.

JEWEL BOX THEATRE PLAYWRIGHTING COMPETITION, Jewel Box Theatre, 3700 N. Walker, Oklahoma City OK 73118-7099. (405)521-1786. **Contact:** Charles Tweed, production director. Estab. 1982. Offered annually for full-length plays. Deadline: January 15. Send SASE in October for guidelines. Prize: $500.

THE KENNEDY CENTER FUND FOR NEW AMERICAN PLAYS, J.F. Kennedy Center for the Performing Arts, Washington DC 20566. (202)416-8024. Fax: (202)416-8205. E-mail: rsfoster@kennedy-center.org. Website: kennedy-center.org/newwork/fnap. **Contact:** Rebecca Foster, manager, theater programming. Estab. 1988. Previously unproduced work. "Program objectives: to encourage playwrights to write, and nonprofit professional theaters to produce new American plays; to ease the financial burdens of nonprofit professional theater organizations producing new plays; to provide a playwright with a better production of the play than the producing theater would normally be able to accomplish." Deadline: May 5 (date changes from year to year). "Nonprofit professional theater organizations can mail in name and address to be placed on the mailing list or check website." Prize: grants to theaters based on scripts submitted by producing theaters and $10,000 for playwrights. A few encouragement grants of $2,500 may be given to promising playwrights chosen from the submitted proposals. Submissions and funding proposals only through the producing theater.

Ⓝ KEY WEST THEATRE FESTIVAL, Theatre Key West, P.O. Box 992, Key West FL 33041. (305)292-3725 or (800)741-6945. Fax: (305)293-0845. E-mail: theatrekw@attglobal.net. **Contact:** Joan McGillis, artistic director. Offered annually for unproduced submissions to develop new plays from either new or established playwrights. Deadline: March 31. Guidelines for SASE or by e-mail. Award: round trip airfare to Key West, lodging in Key West for a minimum of 1 week and small stipend. Open to any writer when submitted by agent or by professional recommendation.

MARC A. KLEIN PLAYWRITING AWARD FOR STUDENTS, Department of Theater Arts, Case Western Reserve University, 10900 Euclid Ave., Cleveland OH 44106-7077. (216)368-4868. Fax: (216)368-5184. E-mail: ksg3@po.cwru.edu. Website: www.cwru.edu/artsci/thtr/website/Home.htm. Chair, Reading Committee: John Orlock. Estab. 1975. Unpublished, professionally unproduced full-length play, or evening of related short plays by student in American college or university. Prize: $1,000, which includes $500 to cover residency expenses; production. Deadline: May 15.

KUMU KAHUA/UHM THEATRE DEPARTMENT PLAYWRITING CONTEST, Kumu Kahua Theatre Inc./University of Hawaii at Manoa, Department of Theatre and Dance, 46 Merchant St., Honolulu HI 96813. (808)536-4222. Fax: (808)536-4226. **Contact:** Harry Wong III. Offered annually for unpublished work to honor full-length and short plays. Deadline: January 1. Guidelines available every September. Prize: $500 (Hawaii Prize); $400 (Pacific Rim); $200 (Resident). First 2 categories open to residents and nonresidents. For Hawaii Prize, plays must be set in Hawaii or deal with some aspect of the Hawaiian experience. For Pacific Rim prize, plays must deal with Hawaii or the Pacific Islands, Pacific Rim or Pacific/Asian/American experience—short plays only considered in 3rd category!

LOVE CREEK ANNUAL SHORT PLAY FESTIVAL, Love Creek Productions, % Granville, 162 Nesbit St., Weehawken NJ 07087-6817. E-mail: creekread@aol.com. **Contact:** Cynthia Granville-Callahan, festival manager. Estab. 1985. Annual festival for unpublished plays, unproduced in New York in the previous year, under 40 minutes, at least 2 characters, larger casts preferred. "We established the Festival as a playwriting competition in which scripts are judged on their merits in performance." Deadline: ongoing. Guidelines for SASE. All entries must specify "festival" on envelope and must include letter giving permission to produce script, if chosen and stating whether equity showcase is acceptable. Cash prize awarded to winner. "We are giving strong preference to scripts featuring females in major roles in casts which are predominantly female."

LOVE CREEK MINI FESTIVALS, Love Creek Productions, % Granville, 162 Nesbit St., Weehawken NJ 07087-6817. E-mail: creekread@aol.com. **Contact:** Cynthia Granville-Callahan, festival literary manager. "The Mini Festivals are an outgrowth of our annual Short Play Festival in which we produce scripts concerning a particular issue or theme which our artistic staff selects according to current needs, interests and concerns of our members, audiences and playwrights submitting to our Short Play Festival throughout the year." Considers scripts unpublished, unproduced in New York City in past year, under 40 minutes, at least 2 characters, larger casts preferred. Guidelines for SASE. Submissions must list name of festival on envelope and must include letter giving permission to produce script, if chosen, and stating whether equity showcase is acceptable. Finalists receive a mini-showcase production in New York City. Winner receives a cash prize. Write for upcoming themes, deadlines ongoing. Fear of God: Religion in the 90s, Gay and Lesbian Festival will be presented again in 2000 along with others TBA. "We are giving strong preference to scripts featuring females in major roles in casts which are predominantly female."

MAXIM MAZUMDAR NEW PLAY COMPETITION, Alleyway Theatre, One Curtain Up Alley, Buffalo NY 14202-1911. (716)852-2600. Fax: (716)852-2266. E-mail: alleywayth@aol.com. Website: www.alleyway.com. **Contact:** Joyce Stilson, artistic director. Estab. 1990. Annual competition. Full Length: not less than 90 minutes, no more than 10 performers. One-Act: less than 40 minutes, no more than 6 performers. Children's plays. Musicals must be accompanied by audio tape. Deadline: July 1. Finalists announced January 1. "Playwrights may submit work directly. There is no entry form. Annual playwright's fee $5; may submit one in each category, but pay only one fee. Please specify if submission is to be included in competition." Prize: full length—$400, travel plus lodging, production and royalties; one-act—$100, production plus royalties. "Alleyway Theatre must receive first production credit in subsequent printings and productions."

McKNIGHT ADVANCEMENT GRANT, The Playwrights' Center, 2301 Franklin Ave. E., Minneapolis MN 55406-1099. (612)332-7481. Fax: (612)332-6037. E-mail: pwcenter@mtn.org. Website: www.pwcenter.org. **Contact:** Megan Monaghan, director of playwright services. Offered annually for either published or unpublished playwrights to recognize playwrights whose work demonstrates exceptional artistic merit and potential whose primary residence is in the state of Minnesota. The grants are intended to significantly advance recipients' art and careers, and can be used to support a wide variety of expenses. Applications available December 1. Deadline: February 1. Guidelines for SASE. Prize: $8,500 which can be used to support a wide variety of expenses, including writing time, artistic costs of residency at a theater or arts organization, travel and study, production or presentation. Additional funds of up to $1,500 are available for workshops and readings. The Playwrights' Center evaluates each application and forwards finalists to a panel of three judges from the national theater community. Applicant must have been a citizen or permanent resident of the US and a legal resident of the state of Minnesota for 6 months prior to the application deadline. (Residency must be maintained during fellowship year.) Applicant must have had a minimum of one work fully produced by a professional theater at the time of application.

McLAREN MEMORIAL COMEDY PLAYWRITING COMPETITION, Midland Community Theatre, 2000 W. Wadley, Midland TX 79705. (915)682-2544. Fax: (915)682-6136. Website: www.mct-cole.org. Estab. 1990. Offered annually for unpublished work. "Entry must be a comedy, one- or two-act. Number of characters or subject is not limited. Make us laugh." Deadline: January 31. Charges $5 fee. Guidelines for SASE. Prize: 4 finalists selected for Reader's Theatre presentation; winner receives cash prize.

MILL MOUNTAIN THEATRE NEW PLAY COMPETITION, Mill Mountain Theatre, Center in the Square, 1 Market Square, 2nd Floor, Roanoke VA 24011-1437. (540)342-5749. Fax: (540)342-5749. E-mail: mmtmail@millmount ain.org. Website: www.millmountain.org. **Contact:** New Play Competition Coordinator. Estab. 1985. Offered annually for previously unpublished and unproduced plays, both full length and 1 acts for up to 10 cast members. Plays must be agent submitted—or have the recommendation of a director, literary manager or dramaturg. Deadline: postmark January 1. Guidelines for SASE.

MOVING ARTS PREMIERE ONE-ACT COMPETITION, Moving Arts, 514 S. Spring St., Los Angeles CA 90013-2304. (213)622-8906. Fax: (213)622-8946. E-mail: rrasmussen@movingarts.org. Website: www.movingarts.org. Award Director: Rebecca Rasmussen. Offered annually for unpublished one-act plays and "is designed to foster the continued development of one-act plays." Deadline: February 28 (postmark). Guidelines for SASE. Charges $8 fee/ script. Prizes: 1st-$200 plus a full production with a 4-8 week run. 2nd and 3rd-program mention and possible production. All playwrights are eligible except Moving Arts company members.

MUSICAL STAIRS, West Coast Ensemble, P.O. Box 38728, Los Angeles CA 90038. (323)876-9337. Fax: (323)876-8916. **Contact:** Les Hanson. Offered annually for unpublished writers "to nurture, support and encourage musical creators." Deadline: June 30. Prize: $500 and presentation of musical. Permission to present the musical is granted if work is selected as finalist.

NANTUCKET SHORT PLAY COMPETITION AND FESTIVAL, Nantucket Theatrical Productions, Box 2177, Nantucket MA 02584. (508)228-5002. **Contact:** Jim Patrick. Offered annually for unpublished plays to "seek the highest quality of playwriting distilled into a short play format." Deadline: Ongoing. Charges $8 fee. Prize: $200 plus staged readings. Selected plays also receive staged readings. "We would like to see a wider range of works featuring kids, adolescents or multicultural casts." Plays must be less than 40 pages.

NATIONAL CHILDREN'S THEATRE FESTIVAL, Actors' Playhouse at the Miracle Theatre, 280 Miracle Mile, Coral Gables FL 33134. (305)444-9293. Fax: (305)444-4181. Website: www.actorsplayhouse.org. **Contact:** Earl Maulding. Offered annually for unpublished musicals for young audiences. Target age is between 5-12. Script length should be 45-60 minutes. Maximum of 8 actors to play any number of roles. Settings which lend themselves to simplified scenery. Bilingual (English/Spanish) scripts are welcomed. Deadline: August 1, 2000. Call for guidelines. Charges $10 fee. Prizes: 1st-full production, $1,000; runner-up-reading and $100. Open to any writer.

NATIONAL HISPANIC PLAYWRITING AWARD, Arizona Theatre Co. in affiliation with Centro Cultural Mexicano, P.O. Box 1631, Tucson AZ 85702. (520)884-8210. Fax: (520)628-9129. E-mail: ERomero@aztheatreco.org. Website: www.aztheatreco.org. **Contact:** Elaine Romero, contest director. Offered annually for unproduced, unpublished plays. "The plays may be in English, bilingual or in Spanish (with English translation). The award recognizes exceptional full-length plays by Hispanic playwrights on any subject." Deadline: October 31. Guidelines for SASE. Prize: $1,000 and possible inclusion in ATC's Genesis New Play Reading Series. Open to Hispanic playwrights currently residing in the US, its territories, and/or Mexico.

NATIONAL ONE-ACT PLAYWRITING COMPETITION, Little Theatre of Alexandria, 600 Wolfe St., Alexandria VA 22314. (703)683-5778. Fax: (703)683-1378. E-mail: ltlthtre@erols. **Contact:** Bonnie Jourdan, chairman. Estab. 1978. Offered annually to encourage original writing for theatre. Submissions must be original, unpublished, unproduced one-act stage plays. Deadline: Submit scripts for year 2001 contest from January 1, 2001 to June 30, 2001. Charges $5/ play fee; 2 play limit. Prizes: 1st-$350, 2nd-$250, 3rd-$150. "We usually produce top two or three winners." Guidelines for SASE.

NATIONAL PLAYWRIGHTS' AWARD, Unicorn Theatre, 3828 Main St., Kansas City MO 64111. (816)531-7529, ext. 18. Fax: (816)531-0421. Website: www.unicorntheatre.org. **Contact:** Herman Wilson, literary assistant. Offered annually for previously unproduced work. "We produce contemporary original scripts, preferring scripts that deal with social concerns. However, we accept (and have produced) comedies." Guidelines for SASE. Prize: $1,000 in royalty/ prize fee and mainstage production at the Unicorn as part of its regular season.

NATIONAL TEN-MINUTE PLAY CONTEST, Actors Theatre of Louisville, 316 W. Main St., Louisville KY 40202-4218. (502)584-1265. Fax: (502)561-3300. Website: www.actorstheatre.org. Contact: Michael Bigelow Dixon, literary manager. Estab. 1964. Offered annually for previously professionally unproduced ten-minute plays (10 pages or less). "Entries must *not* have had an Equity or Equity-waiver production." One submission per playwright. Scripts are not returned. Postmark deadline: December 1. Prize: $1,000. Please write or call for submission guidelines.

N: NEW CENTURY WRITER AWARDS (SCREENWRITING), 32 Alfred St., Suite B, New Haven CT 06512-3927. (203)469-8824. Fax: (203)468-0333. E-mail: newcenturywriter@yahoo.com. Website: www.newcenturywriter.o

rg. **Contact:** Jason J. Marchi, executive director. Offered annually for previously unproduced work or work with a limited production history to discover emerging writers of screenplays, stage plays, TV scripts, TV movie scripts and musicals. All genres. Deadline: January 31. Winners announced June/July. Guidelines/entry form for #10 SAE. Charges $30 entry fee. Prize: 1st—$5,000; 2nd—$2,000; 3rd—$1,000; 4th-10th—$250; free story development or scriptwriting software to selected finalists. All entrants receive 1-year subscription to *The Anvil*, educational newsletter for writers. Open to all writers, both non-produced and those with limited production history. Call if in doubt about your eligibility. **Tips:** "We seek to encourage writers with cash awards and to connect writers to our numerous alliance companies in the film production and publishing industries. We also produce a popular reading series in New York City of works selected from annual finalists. Please call for application package—all submission details are included."

THE NEW HARMONY PROJECT CONFERENCE/LABORATORY, The New Harmony Project, 613 N. East St., Indianapolis IN 46202. (317)464-1101. Fax: (317)635-4201. E-mail: newharmony@iquest.net. **Contact:** Anna D. Shapiro, artistic director. Offered annually for previously published or unpublished scripts. "The purpose is to identify new theater, TV, film and musical scripts that emphasize the dignity of the human spirit and celebrate the worth of the human experience." Deadline: Mid-November. "Writers participate in an intensive exploration of their work through rehearsals and various readings for two and one-half weeks in May. Of scripts submitted, four to six are selected."

N: NEW PROFESSIONAL THEATRE WRITERS FESTIVAL, New Professional Theatre, P.O. Box 799, New York NY 10108. (212)398-2666. Fax: (212)398-2924. **Contact:** Sheila Kay Davis. Offered annually for unpublished full-length plays for the theatre. Deadline: June 1. Submit entry with SASE if you want work returned. No entry fee. Prize: $2,000 grant, 1st and 2nd draft reading, 2 week residency, dramaturgical support, possible production. "We are seeking to encourage and promote African-American playwrights."

NEW VOICE SERIES, Remembrance Through the Performing Arts, P.O. Box 162446, Austin TX 78716. **Contact:** Marla Macdonald, director of new play development. Offered annually "to find talented central Texas playwrights who are in the early stages of script development. We develop these scripts on the page through a Work In Progress production." Deadline: ongoing. Playwrights need to send script, bio and a script size SASE. Prize: free development of their play with our company plus free representation of their plays to theaters nationally for world premieres. Open to central Texas playwrights only.

N: NEW WORKS FOR THE STAGE, COE College Theatre Arts Department, 1220 First Ave. NE, Cedar Rapids IA 52402. (319)399-8689. Fax: (319)399-8557. E-mail: swolvert@coe.edu. **Contact:** Susan Wolverton. Offered every 2 years (odd years) "to encourage new work, to provide an interdisciplinary forum for the discussion of issues found in new work, to offer playwright contact with theater professionals who can provide response to new work." Deadline: June 1. Prize: $325 plus travel, room and board for residency at the college. Full-length, original unpublished and unproduced scripts only. No musicals, adaptations, translations or collaborations. Submit one-page synopsis, résumé and SASE if the script is to be returned.

NEW YORK CITY HIGH SCHOOL PLAYWRITING CONTEST, Young Playwrights Inc., 321 W. 44th St., Suite 906, New York NY 10036. (212)307-1140. Fax: (212)307-1454. E-mail: writeaplay@aol.com. Website: http://youngplaywrights.org. Offered annually for plays by NYC public high school students only. Deadline: April 15. Guidelines for SASE. Prize: 3 cash prizes, staged readings, certificates, books and records. Must be New York City public high school student.

DON AND GEE NICHOLL FELLOWSHIPS IN SCREENWRITING, Academy of Motion Picture Arts & Sciences, 8949 Wilshire Blvd., Beverly Hills CA 90211-1972. (310)247-3059. E-mail: nicholl@oscars.org. Website: www.oscars.org/nicholl. **Contact:** Greg Beal, program coordinator. Estab. 1985. Offered annually for unproduced screenplays to identify talented new screenwriters. Deadline: May 1. Charges $30 fee. Guidelines for SASE, available January 1-April 30. Prize: $25,000 fellowships (up to 5/year). Recipients announced late October. Open to writers who have not earned more than $5,000 writing for films or TV.

OGLEBAY INSTITUTE TOWNGATE THEATRE PLAYWRITING CONTEST, Oglebay Institute, Stifel Fine Arts Center, 1330 National Rd., Wheeling WV 26003. (304)242-7700. Fax: (304)242-7747. **Contact:** Kate H. Crosbie, director of performing arts. Estab. 1976. Offered annually for unpublished works. Deadline: December 31. Guidelines for SASE. No entry fee. Prize: $300, limited-run production of play. "All full-length *non-musical* plays that have never been professionally produced or published are eligible." Winner announced May 31. Open to any writer.

MILDRED & ALBERT PANOWSKI PLAYWRITING AWARD, Forest A. Roberts Theatre, Northern Michigan University, Marquette MI 49855-5364. (906)227-2559. Fax: (906)227-2567. Website: www.nmu.edu/theatre. **Contact:** (Ms.) J. Love, award coordinator. Estab. 1978. Offered annually for unpublished, unproduced, full-length plays. Scripts must be *received* on or before the Friday before Thanksgiving. Guidelines and application for SASE. Prize: $2,000.

PERISHABLE THEATRE'S WOMEN'S PLAYWRITING FESTIVAL, P.O. Box 23132, Providence RI 02903. (401)331-2695. Fax: (401)331-7811. E-mail: perishable@as220.org. Website: www.perishable.org. **Contact:** Vanessa Gilbert, festival director. Offered annually for unpublished, one-act plays up to 45 minutes in length when fully produced to encourage women playwrights. Deadline: December 15. Guidelines for SASE. Charges $5 fee. Prize: 3 winners $500 each. Judged by reading committee, the Festival Director and the artistic director of the theater. Open to women playwrights exclusively.

ROBERT J. PICKERING AWARD FOR PLAYWRIGHTING EXCELLENCE, Coldwater Community Theater, % 89 Division, Coldwater MI 49036. (517)279-7963. Fax: (517)279-8095. **Contact:** J. Richard Colbeck, committee chairperson. Estab. 1982. Previously unproduced monetarily. "To encourage playwrights to submit their work, to present a previously unproduced play in full production." Deadline: end of year. Guidelines for SASE. Submit script with SASE. Prize: 1st-$300, 2nd-$100, 3rd-$50. "We reserve right to produce winning script."

PILGRIM PROJECT GRANTS, 156 Fifth, #400, New York NY 10010. (212)627-2288. Fax: (212)627-2184. **Contact:** Davida Goldman. Grants for a reading, workshop production or full production of plays that deal with questions of moral significance. Deadline: ongoing. Guidelines for SASE. Grants: $1,000-7,000.

PLAYHOUSE ON THE SQUARE NEW PLAY COMPETITION, Playhouse on the Square, 51 S. Cooper, Memphis TN 38104. **Contact:** Jackie Nichols. Submissions required to be unproduced. Deadline: April 1. Guidelines for SASE. Prize: $500 and production.

PLAYWRIGHT DISCOVERY PROGRAM, VSA Arts Connection, 1300 Connecticut Ave. NW, Suite 700, Washington DC 20036. (800)933-8721. Fax: (202)737-0725. E-mail: playwright@vsarts.org. Website: www.vsarts.org. **Contact:** Elena Widder, program manager. Invites individuals with disabilities to submit a one-act play that documents the experience of living with a disability. One play in each age category—age 21 and under; age 22 and up—will be selected for production at the John F. Kennedy Center for the Performing Arts. Prize: monetary award and a trip to Washington D.C. to view the production or staged reading. Deadline: late April. Guidelines for SASE.

PLAYWRIGHTS' CENTER McKNIGHT FELLOWSHIP, The Playwrights' Center, 2301 Franklin Ave. E, Minneapolis MN 55406. (612)332-7481. Fax: (612)332-6037. E-mail: pwcenter@mtn.org. Website: www.pwcenter.org. **Contact:** Megan Monaghan, playwrights' services director. Estab. 1982. Recognition of playwrights whose work has made a significant impact on the contemporary theater. Deadline: February 1. Open to professionally nominated playwrights only. Must have had a minimum of two different fully staged productions by professional theaters. Must spend 1 month at Playwrights' Center. Open to US citizens or permanent residents only. Prize: $10,000 fellowship award; up to $2,000 additional funds available for development expenses during residency, and up to $1,500 available for travel and housing for out-of-town Fellows.

GWEN PHARIS RINGWOOD AWARD FOR DRAMA, Writers Guild of Alberta, 11759 Groat Rd., Edmonton, Alberta T5M 3K6 Canada. (780)422-8174. Fax: (780)422-2663. E-mail: wga@oanet.com. Website: www.writerguild.ab.ca. **Contact:** Miki Andrejevic. Drama book published in current year or script of play produced three times in current year in a community theater. Must be an Alberta playwright. Eligible plays must be registered with the WGA-APN Drama Award Production Registry.

ROCHESTER PLAYWRIGHT FESTIVAL, Midwest Theatre Network, 5031 Tongen Ave. NW, Rochester MN 55901. (507)281-1472. E-mail: sweens@uswest.net. **Contact:** Joan Sween, executive director. Offered every two years for unpublished submissions to support emerging playwrights. No categories, but entries are considered for production by various types of theaters: community theater, dinner theater, issues theater, satiric/new format theater, children's theater, musical theater. Entry form required. Guidelines and entry form for SASE. No fee for first entry. Subsequent entries by same author, $10 fee. Prize: full production, travel stipend, accomodations, plus $300 cash prize. Open to any writer.

THE LOIS AND RICHARD ROSENTHAL NEW PLAY PRIZE, Cincinnati Playhouse in the Park, Box 6537, Cincinnati OH 45206-0537. (513)345-2242. Website: www.cincyplay.com. **Contact:** Associate Artistic Director. For playwrights and musical playwrights. Annual award. "The Lois and Richard Rosenthal New Play Prize was established in 1987 to encourage the development of new plays that are original, theatrical, strong in character and dialogue, and make a significant contribution to the literature of American theatre. Residents of Cincinnati, the Rosenthals are committed to supporting arts organizations and social agencies that are innovative and that foster social change."
Needs: Plays must be full-length in any style: comedy, drama, musical, etc. Translations, adaptations, individual one-acts and any play previously submitted for the Rosenthal Prize are not eligible. Collaborations are welcome, in which case prize benefits are shared. Plays must be unpublished prior to submission and may not have received a full-scale, professional production. Plays that have had a workshop, reading or non-professional production are still eligible. Playwrights with past production experience are especially encouraged to submit new work. Submit a two-page maximum abstract of the play including title, character breakdown, story synopsis and playwright information (bio or resume). Also include up to 5 pages of sample dialogue. If submitting a musical, please include a tape of selections from the score. All abstracts and dialogue samples will be read. From these, selected manuscripts will be solicited. Do not send a ms with or instead of the abstract. Unsolicited mss will not be read. Submitted materials, including tapes,will be returned only if a SAE with adequate postage is provided. The Rosenthal Prize is open for submission from July 1-

December 31. Only one submission per playwright/year. Prize: A full production at Cincinnati Playhouse in the Park as part of the annual season and regional and national promotion; and $10,000 award plus travel and residency expenses for the Cincinnati rehearsal period.

N SANTA FE SCREENPLAY COMPETITION, Santa Fe Screenwriting Conference, P.O. Box 28423, Santa Fe NM 87592-8423. (505)424-1501. E-mail: writeit@SFeSC.com. Website: www.sfesc.com. Annual contest. Prizes: 1st-$1,500, 2nd-$750, 3rd-$450, 4th-$300, 5th-$150, 6th-20th-$65 each. Top five winners receive tuition to the Santa Fe Screenwriting Conference.

THE SCREENWRITER'S PROJECT, Cyclone Entertainment Group/Cyclone Productions, P.O. Box 148849, Chicago IL 60614-8849. (773)665-7600. Fax: (773)665-7660. E-mail: cycprod@aol.com or cyclone@cyclone-ent.com. Website: www.cyclone-entertainment.com. **Contact:** Lee Alan, director. Offered annually to give both experienced and first-time writers the opportunity to begin a career as a screenwriter. Deadline: August 1. Guidelines for SASE. Charges $40 fee for July 1st deadline; $45 for August 1 deadline; $50 fee for September 1 deadline. Prizes: three $5,000 grants.

SIENA COLLEGE INTERNATIONAL PLAYWRIGHTS COMPETITION, Siena College Theatre Program, 515 Loudon Rd., Loudonville NY 12211-1462. (518)783-2381. Fax: (518)783-4293. E-mail: maciag@siena.edu. Website: www.siena.edu. **Contact:** Gary Maciag, director of theatre. Offered every 2 years for unpublished plays "to allow students to explore production collaboration with the playwright. In addition, it provides the playwright an important development opportunity. Plays should be previously unproduced, unpublished, full-length, non-musicals and free of copyright and royalty restrictions. Plays should require unit set or minimal changes and be suitable for a college-age cast of 3-10. There is a required 6-week residency." Deadline: February 1 to June 30 in even-numbered years. Guidelines for SASE. Guidelines are available after November 1 in odd-numbered years. Prize: $2,000 honorarium; up to $1,000 to cover expenses for required residency; full production of winning script. Winning playwright must agree that the Siena production will be the world premiere of the play.

DOROTHY SILVER PLAYWRITING COMPETITION, Halle Theatre of the Jewish Community Center, 3505 Mayfield Rd., Cleveland Heights OH 44118. (216)382-4000, ext. 274. Fax: (216)382-5401. **Contact:** Lisa Kollins, managing director of Halle Theatre. Estab. 1948. All entries must be original works, not previously produced, suitable for a full-length presentation; directly concerned with the Jewish experience. Deadline: April 15. Prize: Cash award plus staged reading.

SOUTHEASTERN THEATRE CONFERENCE NEW PLAY PROJECT, P.O. Box 9868, Greensboro NC 27429. (910)272-3645. Fax: (910)272-8810. Website: www.setc.org. **Contact:** Elizabeth Spicer. Offered annually for the discovery, development and publicizing of worthy new unproduced plays and playwrights. Eligibility limited to members of 10 state SETC Region: AL, FL, GA, KY, MS, NC, SC, TN, VA or WV. Submit March 1-June 1. Bound full-length or related one acts under single cover (one submission only). Send SASE with scripts for return. Guidelines available upon request. Prize: $1,000, staged reading at SETC Convention, expenses paid trip to convention and preferred consideration for National Playwrights Conference.

SOUTHERN APPALACHIAN PLAYWRIGHTS' CONFERENCE, Southern Appalachian Repertory Theatre, P.O. Box 1720, Mars Hill NC 28754. (828)689-1384. Fax: (828)689-1211. **Contact:** Milli Way, managing director. Offered annually for unpublished, unproduced plays to promote the development of new plays. Deadline: December 15. Guidelines for SASE. Prize: 5 playwrights are invited for informal readings in April, room and board provided. All plays are considered for later production with honorarium provided for the playwright.

SOUTHERN PLAYWRIGHTS COMPETITION, Jacksonville State University, 700 Pelham Rd. N., Jacksonville AL 36265-9982. (256)782-5411. Fax: (256)782-5441. E-mail: swhitton@jsucc.jsu.edu. Website: www.jsu.edu/depart/english/southpla.htm. **Contact:** Steven J. Whitton. Estab. 1988. Offered annually to identify and encourage the best of Southern Playwrighting. Deadline: February 15. Guidelines for SASE. Prize: $1,000 and a production of the play. Playwrights must be native to or resident of AL, AR, FL, GA, KY, LA, MO, NC, SC, TN, TX, VA or WV.

N SPRING STAGED READING PLAY CONTEST, TADA!, 120 W. 28th St., New York NY 10001. (212)627-1732. Fax: (212)243-6736. E-mail: tada@ziplink.net. Website: www.tadatheater.com. **Contact:** John Foster, contest coordinator. Offered annually for unpublished work to introduce the playwriting process to family audiences in a staged reading series featuring the winning entries. One-act plays should address teenage issues and subject matter, cast to be mostly children 8-17. Deadline: varies yearly; usually late winter, early spring. Send cover letter, 2 copies of the script and play with SASE for return, no application form necessary. Prize: $200 and a staged reading held in TADA!'s theater with TADA! cast and others hired by TADA! Open to any writer. Plays must be appropriate for family audiences.

N STANLEY DRAMA AWARD, Dept. of Theatre, Wagner College, Staten Island NY 10301. Fax: (718)390-3323. Contact: Elizabeth Terry, director. Offered for original full-length stage plays, musicals or one-act play sequences that have not been professionally produced or received trade book publication. Deadline: October 1. Guidelines for SASE. Award: $2,000.

TEXAS PLAYWRIGHT'S DIVISION, Stages Repertory Theatre, 3201 Allen Pkwy., Suite 101, Houston TX 77019. (713)527-0240. Fax: (713)527-8669. **Contact:** Rob Bundy, artistic director. Offered annually to provide an outlet for unpublished Texas playwrights. Entries received from October 1-December 31. Guidelines for SASE or on website. Prize: A reading by professional actors and prizes awarded. Writer must be a current or previous resident of Texas, or the play must be set in Texas or have a Texas theme.

⚠️ 🍁 THEATRE BC'S ANNUAL CANADIAN NATIONAL PLAYWRITING COMPETITION, Theatre BC, P.O. Box 2031, Nanaimo, British Columbia V9R 6X6 Canada. (250)714-0203. Fax: (250)714-0213. E-mail: pwc@th eatrebc.org. Website: www.theatrebc.org. **Contact:** Robb Mowbray, executive director. Offered annually to unpublished plays "to promote the development and production of previously unproduced new plays (no musicals) at all levels of theater. Categories: Full-Length (2 acts or longer); One Act (less than 60 minutes) and an open Special Merit (juror's discretion). Deadline: last Monday in July. Guidelines for SASE or on website. Charges $35/entry and optional $25 for written critique. Prize: Full-Length-$1,500; One Act-$1,000; Special Merit-$750. Winners are also invited to new play festival: 18 hours with a professional dramaturg, registrant actors and a public readings in Kamloops (every spring). Production and publishing rights remain with the playwright. Open to Canadian residents. All submissions are made under pseudonyms. E-mail inquiries welcome.

⚠️ TRUSTUS PLAYWRIGHTS' FESTIVAL, Trustus Theatre, Box 11721, Columbia SC 29211-1721. (803)254-9732. Fax: (803)771-9153. E-mail: trustus88@aol.com. Website: www.trustus.org. **Contact:** Jon Tuttle, literary manager. Offered annually for professionally unproduced full-length plays; cast limit of 8; prefer challenging, innovative dramas and comedies; no musicals, plays for young audiences or "hillbilly" southern shows. Deadline: March 1; no submissions before January 1. Send two copies of synopsis, résumé and completed application; send SASE for application and guidelines. Prize: public staged-reading and $250, followed after a one-year development period by full production, $500, plus travel/accommodations to attend opening.

UNICORN THEATRE NATIONAL PLAYWRIGHTS' AWARD, Unicorn Theatre, 3828 Main St., Kansas City MO 64111. (816)531-7529, ext. 18. Fax: (816)531-0421. Website: www.unicorntheatre.org. **Contact:** Herman Wilson, literary assistant. Offered annually to encourage and assist the development of an unpublished and unproduced play. Deadline: April 30. Guidelines for SASE. Prize: $1,000 and production. Acquires 2% subsidiary rights of future productions for a 5 year period.

UNIVERSITY OF ALABAMA NEW PLAYWRIGHTS PROGRAM, P.O. Box 870239, Tuscaloosa AL 35487-0239. (205)348-9032. Fax: (205)348-9048. E-mail: pcastagn@woodsquad.as.ua.edu. Website: www.as.ua.edu/theatre/npp.htm (includes guidelines). Director/Dramaturg: Dr. Paul C. Castagno. Estab. 1982. Full-length plays for mainstage; experimental plays for B stage. Workshops and small musicals can be proposed. Queries responded to quickly. Competitive stipend. Development process includes readings, visitations, and possible complete productions with faculty director and dramaturg. Guidelines for SASE. Up to 6 months assessment time. Submit August-March, by October for Janus Fest in January.

🍁 THE HERMAN VOADEN NATIONAL PLAYWRITING COMPETITION, Drama Department, Queen's University, Kingston, Ontario K7L 3N6 Canada. (613)533-2104. Fax: (613)533-6268. Website: www.queensu.ca/drama. **Contact:** Carol Anne Hanna. Offered every 2 years for unpublished plays to discover and develop new Canadian plays. See website for deadlines, guidelines. Charges $30 fee. Prize: $3,000, $2,000 and $1,000. Prize: 1st and 2nd prize winners are offered a one-week workshop and public reading by professional director and cast. Open to Canadian citizens or landed immigrants.

WE DON'T NEED NO STINKIN' DRAMAS, Mixed Blood Theatre Company, 1501 S 4th St., Minneapolis, MN 55454. (612)338-0937. E-mail: czar@mixedblood.com. **Contact:** Dave Kunz. Offered for full-length, contemporary comedies; particularly comedies about race, sports or containing political edge (or similarly themed musical comedies). Must remain unproduced as of October 1, 2000. No one-acts. Scripts must be a minimum of 65 pages long. Guidelines for SASE. Deadline: February 1. Prize: $2,000 if Mixed Blood chooses to produce the winning script, $1,000 if Mixed Blood declines production. Open to American citizens.

WEST COAST ENSEMBLE FULL-PLAY COMPETITION, West Coast Ensemble, P.O. Box 38728, Los Angeles CA 90038. (323)876-9337. Fax: (323)876-8916. **Contact:** Les Hanson, artistic director. Estab. 1982. Offered annually for unpublished plays in Southern California. No musicals or children's plays for full-play competition. No restrictions on subject matter. Deadline: December 31.

JACKIE WHITE MEMORIAL NATIONAL CHILDREN'S PLAYWRITING CONTEST, Columbia Entertainment Co., 309 Parkade, Columbia MO 65202. (573)874-5628. Contest Director: Betsy Phillips. Offered annually for unpublished plays. "Searching for good scripts suitable for audiences of all ages to be performed by the 25-40 students, grade 6-9, in our theater school." Deadline: June 1. Guidelines for SASE. Charges $10 fee. Prize: $250; full production, plus travel expenses to come see production is probable but company reserves the right to grant prize money without production."

WICHITA STATE UNIVERSITY PLAYWRITING CONTEST, University Theatre, Wichita State University, Wichita KS 67260-0153. (316)978-3368. Fax: (316)978-3951. E-mail: lclark@twsuvm.uc.twsu.edu. **Contact:** Bela Kiralyfalvi. Contest Director: Professor Leroy Clark, chair, school of performing arts. Estab. 1974. Unpublished, unproduced full-length or 2-3 short plays of at least 90 minutes playing time. No musicals or children's plays. Deadline: February 15. Guidelines for SASE. Prize: production of winning play (ACTF) and expenses paid trip for playwright to see final rehearsals and/or performances. Contestants must be graduate or undergraduate students in a US college or university. Information available on the Internet at www.mrc.twsu.edu/fineart/performing/theatre.html.

WOMEN'S PLAYWRIGHT'S DIVISION, Stages Repertory Theatre, 3201 Allen Pkwy., Suite 101, Houston TX 77019. (713)527-0240. Fax: (713)527-8669. Contact: Rob Bundy, artistic director. Offered annually to provide an outlet for unpublished women playwrights. Deadline: October 1. Guidelines for SASE or on website. Prize: A reading by professional actors and prizes awarded. Winners notified in May.

WORKING STAGES, A Festival of New Plays, Colorado Shakespeare Festival, University of Colorado, Boulder, Department of Theater & Dance, Campus Box 261, Boulder CO 80309-0261. Fax: (303)492-7722. E-mail: kevin.brown @colorado.edu. Website: www.tesser.com/csf/stages. **Contact:** Kevin Brown, dramaturg. Annual workshop for authors of unpublished plays allowing playwrights to work and rework scripts in collaboration with professional directors and Colorado Shakespeare Festival actors and dramaturgs for a one or two week intensive workshop that culminates in a staged reading of the play in process. Write or e-mail for guidelines and deadlines. Playwrights must live in CO, NM, AZ, UT, TX or CA.

YEAR END SERIES (YES) NEW PLAY FESTIVAL, Northern Kentucky Univ. Dept. of Theatre, Nunn Dr., Highland Heights KY 41099-1007. (606)572-6362. Fax: (606)572-6057. E-mail: forman@nku.edu. **Contact:** Sandra Forman, award director. Offered every 2 years (even years) for unpublished full-length plays and musicals. Deadline: October 31. Guidelines for SASE. Prize: $400 and an expense-paid visit to Northern Kentucky University to see the play produced. Open to all writers.

YOUNG PLAYWRIGHTS FESTIVAL, Young Playwrights Inc., Suite 906, 321 W. 44th St., New York NY 10036. (212)307-1140. Fax: (212)307-1454. E-mail: writeaplay@aol.com. Website: http://youngplaywrights.org. **Contact:** Sheri M. Goldhirsch, artistic director. Offered annually for stage plays (no musicals, screenplays or adaptations). "Writers aged 18 or younger are invited to send scripts for consideration in the annual Young Playwrights Festival. Winning plays will be performed in professional Off Broadway production." Deadline: December 1. Contest/award rules for SASE. Entrants must be 18 or younger as of the annual deadline.

N: ANNA ZORNIO MEMORIAL CHILDREN'S THEATRE PLAYWRIGHTING AWARD, University of New Hampshire, Dept. of Theatre and Dance, PCAC 30 College Rd., Durham NH 03824-3538. (603)862-2919. Fax: (603)862-0298. E-mail: jbrinker@hopper.unh.edu. **Contact:** Julie Brinker. Offered annually for unpublished well-written plays or musicals appropriate for young audiences with a maximum length of 60 minutes. Deadline: September 1. Guidelines and entry forms for SASE. Prize: up to $1,000 to winning playwright(s) and public production by the UNH Theatre for Youth Program. May submit more than one play, but not more than three. Open to all playwrights in US and Canada. All ages are invited to participate.

Journalism

N: AAAS SCIENCE JOURNALISM AWARDS, American Association for the Advancement of Science, 1333 H St. NW, Washington DC 20005. (202)326-6440. Fax: (202)789-0455. E-mail: tayers@aaas.org. Website: www.aaas.org. **Contact:** Tiffany Ayers. Offered annually for previously published work July 1-June 30 to reward excellence in reporting on science and its applications in daily newspapers with circulation over 100,000; newspapers with circulation under 100,000; general circulation magazines; radio; television and online." Deadline: August 1. Award: $2,500, plaque, trip to AAAS Annual Meeting. Sponsored by the Whitaker Foundation.

AMY WRITING AWARDS, The Amy Foundation, P.O. Box 16091, Lansing MI 48901. (517)323-6233. Fax: (517)323-7293. E-mail: amyfoundtn@aol.com. Website: www.amyfound.org. **Contact:** James Russell, president. Estab. 1985. Offered annually for nonfiction articles containing scripture published in the previous calendar year in the secular media. Deadline: January 31. Prize: $10,000, $5,000, $4,000, $3,000, $2,000 and 10 prizes of $1,000.

ARTS & LIFE PRIZE FOR CULINARY JOURNALISM, International Literary Society, 18463 Blueberry Lane, Apt. C101, Monroe WA 98272-1379. (206)930-6588. Fax: (425)487-2633. E-mail: nhccsteve@juno.com. **Contact:** Steve Whalen, contest director. Offered annually for unpublished 1,500 word stories of a restaurant, party, wine-tasting or any event involving food to gather material for a cultural magazine. Deadline: September 30. Guidelines for SASE. Charges $18 fee. Prize: 1st-$1,000, 2nd-$150, honorable mentions.

ARTS & LIFE PRIZE FOR JOURNALISM (ARTS), International Literary Society, 18463 Blueberry Lane, Apt. C101, Monroe WA 98272-1379. (206)930-6588. Fax: (425)487-2633. E-mail: nhccsteve@juno.com. **Contact:** Steve Whalen, contest director. Offered annually for unpublished 1,500 word stories of a play, concert, museum event any event involving the arts. Deadline: May 31. Guidelines for SASE. Charges $18 fee. Prize: 1st-$1,000, 2nd-$150, honorable mentions.

◪ ATLANTIC JOURNALISM AWARDS, School of Journalism, University of King's College, 6350 Coburg Rd., Halifax, Nova Scotia B3H 2A1 Canada. (902)422-1271, ext. 150. Fax: (902)425-8183. E-mail: pherod@is.dal.ca. Website: http://aja.ukings.ns.ca. **Contact:** Stephen Kimber or Pamela Herod. Offered annually to recognize excellence and achievement by journalists in Atlantic Canada. Deadline: January 15. Guidelines and entry forms available via mail request, or website (download entry form). Entries are usually nominated by editors, news directors, etc. Freelancers are eligible to enter. Prize: a plaque presented at an awards dinner. "We request permission from winning entrants to publish their work on our website. It is not published without their consent." The competition is open to any journalist living in Atlantic Canada whose entry was originally published or broadcast during the previous year in Atlantic Canada.

THE ERIC AND AMY BURGER AWARD, Overseas Press Club of America, 320 East 42 St., New York NY 10017. (212)626-9220. Fax: (212)626-9210. Executive Director: Sonya Fry. Offered annually for previously published best reporting in the broadcast medium dealing with human rights. Deadline: January 31. Charges $100 fee. Prize: certificate and $1,000. Work must be published by US-based publications or broadcast.

CONGRESSIONAL FELLOWSHIP PROGRAM, American Political Science Association, 1527 New Hampshire Ave., Washington DC 20036-1206. (202)483-2512. Fax: (202)483-2657. E-mail: cfp@apsanet.org. Website: www.apsanet.org/CFP. **Contact:** Jeffrey Biggs. Offered annually for professional journalists who have 2-10 years of full-time professional experience in newspaper, magazine, radio or television reporting at time of application to learn more about the legislative process through direct participation. Visit our website for deadlines. Awards $35,000 and travel allowance for 3 weeks' orientation and legislation aide assignments December through August. Open to journalists and scholars.

ROBIN GOLDSTEIN AWARD FOR WASHINGTON REGIONAL REPORTING, National Press Club, National Press Bldg., Washington DC 20045. (202)662-8744. Website: npc.press.org. **Contact:** Joann Booze. Offered annually for a Washington newspaper correspondent who best exemplifies the standards set by the late Robin Goldstein. Deadline: April 20. Prize: $1,000.

Ⓝ THE GREAT AMERICAN TENNIS WRITING AWARDS, *Tennis Week*, 341 Madison Ave., New York NY 10017. (212)808-4750. Fax: (212)983-6302. E-mail: tennisweek@tennisweek.com. **Contact:** Heather Holland or Kim Kodl, managing editors. Estab. 1974. Category 1: unpublished ms by an aspiring journalist with no previous national byline. Category 2: unpublished ms by a non-tennis journalist. Category 3: unpublished ms by a tennis journalist. Categories 4-6: published tennis-related articles and book award. Deadline: December 15.

O. HENRY AWARD, The Texas Institute of Letters, Southwest Texas State University, San Marcos TX 78666. (512)245-2428. Fax: (512)245-7462. E-mail: mb13@swt.edu. Website: www.English.swt.edu/css/TIL/rules.htm. **Contact:** Mark Busby, secretary. Offered annually for previously published work between January 1-December 31 of previous year to recognize the best-written work of journalism appearing in a magazine or weekly newspaper. Deadline: January 3. Guidelines for SASE. Prize: $1,000. Judged by a panel chosen by the TIL Council. Writer must have been born in Texas, have lived in Texas for at least two consecutive years at some time, or the subject matter of the work should be associated with Texas.

INVESTIGATIVE JOURNALISM GRANT, The Fund For Investigative Journalism, 5540 32nd St. N.W., Washington DC 20015-1621. (202)362-0260. E-mail: fundfij@aol.com. Website: www.fij.org. **Contact:** Peg Lotito. Offered three times/year for original investigative newspaper and magazine stories, radio and TV documentaries, books and media criticism. Deadline: February 1, June 1 and October 1. Guidelines on website or by e-mail. Prize: Grants of $500-10,000.
  • The Fund also offers an annual $25,000 FIJ Book Prize for the best book chosen by the board during the year.

DONALD E. KEYHOE JOURNALISM AWARD, Fund for UFO Research, P.O. Box 277, Mt. Rainier MD 20712. Phone/fax: (703)684-6032. E-mail: fufor@fufor.org. Website: www.fufor.org. **Contact:** Don Berliner, chairman. Estab. 1979. Offered annually for the best article or story published or broadcast in a newspaper, magazine, TV or radio news outlet during the previous calendar year. Separate awards for print and broadcast media; also makes unscheduled cash awards for published works on UFO phenomena research or public education.

◪ HERB LAMPERT STUDENT WRITING AWARD, Canadian Science Writers' Association, P.O. Box 75, Station A, Toronto, Ontario M5W 1A2 Canada. (416)408-4566. E-mail: cswa@interlog.com. Contest/Award Director: Andy F. Visser-deVries. Offered annually to any student science writer who has an article published in a student or other newspaper or magazine or aired on a radio or TV station in Canada. Deadline: February 15. Guidelines for SASE. Prize: $750 for print and broadcast winners. Open to any Canadian resident or citizen.

LIVINGSTON AWARDS FOR YOUNG JOURNALISTS, Mollie Parnis Livingston Foundation, Wallace House, 620 Oxford, Ann Arbor MI 48104. (734)998-7575. Fax: (734)998-7979. E-mail: LivingstonAwards@umich.edu. Website: www.livawards.org. **Contact:** Charles Eisendrath. Offered annually for journalism published between January 1-December 31 the previous year to recognize and further develop the abilities of young journalists includes print, online and broadcast. Visit our website for current guidelines. Prize: 3-$10,000: 1 each for local reporting, national reporting and international reporting. Previous judges include Mike Wallace, Ellen Goodman and Tom Brokaw. Open to journalists who are 34 years or younger as of December 31 of previous year and whose work appears in US controlled print or broadcast media.

MENCKEN AWARDS, Free Press Association, P.O. Box 63, Port Hadlock WA 98339. Fax: (360)384-3704. FPA Executive Director: R.W. Bradford. Estab. 1981. Honoring defense of human rights and individual liberties, or exposés of governmental abuses of power. Categories: News Story or Investigative Report, Feature Story or Essay/Review, Editorial or Op-Ed Column, Editorial Cartoon and Book. Entries *must* have been published or broadcast during previous calendar year. Deadline: June 1 (for work from previous year). Guidelines and form for SASE. Charges modest fee. Late deadline: June 15 with extra fee.

FRANK LUTHER MOTT-KAPPA TAU ALPHA RESEARCH AWARD IN JOURNALISM, University of Missouri, School of Journalism, Columbia MO 65211. (573)882-7685. E-mail: ktahq@showme.missouri.edu. **Contact:** Dr. Keith Sanders, executive director, Kappa Tau Alpha. Offered annually for best researched book in mass communication. Submit 6 copies; no forms required. Deadline: December 6. Prize: $1,000.

NATIONAL PRESS CLUB CONSUMER JOURNALISM AWARDS, National Press Club, National Press Bldg., Washington DC 20045. (202)662-8744. E-mail: jbooze@npcpress.org. Website: http://npc.press.org. **Contact:** Joann Booze. Offered annually to recognize excellence in reporting on consumer topics in the following categories: newspapers, periodicals, television and radio. Deadline: April 20. Prize: $500 for each category.

NATIONAL PRESS CLUB WASHINGTON CORRESPONDENCE AWARDS, National Press Club, National Press Bldg., Washington DC 20045. (202)662-8744. E-mail: jbooze@npcpress.org. Website: http://npc.press.org. **Contact:** Joann Booze. Offered annually to honor the work of reporters who cover Washington for the benefit of the hometown audience. Deadline: April 20. Prize: $1,000 award.

NEWSLETTER JOURNALISM AWARD, National Press Club, National Press Bldg., Washington DC 20045. (202)662-8744. E-mail: jbooze@npcpress.org. Website: http://npc.press.org. **Contact:** Joann Booze. Offered annually to acknowledge excellence in newsletter journalism in 2 categories: Best analytical or interpretive reporting piece or best exclusive story. Deadline: April 20. Prize: $2,000 for each category.

ALICIA PATTERSON JOURNALISM FELLOWSHIP, Alicia Patterson Foundation, 1730 Pennsylvania Ave. NW, Suite 850, Washington DC 20006. (202)393-5995. Fax: (301)951-8512. E-mail: apfengel@charm.net. Website: www.alic iapatterson.org. **Contact:** Margaret Engel. Offered annually for previously published submissions to give 8-10 print journalists or photojournalists a year of in-depth research and reporting. Applicants must have 5 years of professional print journalism experience and be US citizens. Fellows write 4 magazine-length pieces for the *Alicia Patterson Reporter*, a quarterly magazine, during their fellowship year. Fellows must take a year's leave from their jobs, but may do other freelance articles during the year. Deadline: October 1. Write, call, fax or check website for applications. Prize: $35,000 stipend for calendar year.

PRINT MEDIA AWARD, International Reading Association, P.O. Box 8139, Newark DE 19714-8139. (302)731-1600, ext. 293. Fax: (302)731-1057. E-mail: jbutler@reading.org. Website: www.reading.org. **Contact:** Janet Butler. Offered annually for journalism published January 1-December 31 to recognize outstanding reporting in newspapers, magazines and wire services. Deadline: January 15. Prize: Awards certificate, announced at annual convention. Open to professional journalists.

THE PULLIAM JOURNALISM FELLOWSHIPS, Central Newspapers, Inc., P.O. Box 145, Indianapolis IN 46206-0145. (317)633-9121. Fax: (317)630-9549. E-mail: rpulliam@starnews.com. Website: www.starnews.com/pjf. **Contact:** Russell B. Pulliam. Offered annually as an intensive 10-week summer "finishing school" for recent college graduates with firm commitments to, and solid training in, newspaper journalism. Deadline: March 1. "Call or e-mail us, and we'll send an application packet." Award: $5,500 for 10-week session. Applicants must receive their bachelor's degree during the August-June period preceding the June fellowship.

THE MADELINE DANE ROSS AWARD, Overseas Press Club of America, 320 East 42 St., New York NY 10017. (212)626-9220. Fax: (212)626-9210. Executive Director: Sonya Fry. Offered annually for previously published best foreign correspondent in any medium showing a concern for the human condition. Deadline: January 31. Charges $100 fee. Prize: certificate and $1,000. Work must be published by US-based publications or broadcast.

N: WILLIAM B. RUGGLES JOURNALISM SCHOLARSHIP, National Institute for Labor Relations Research, 5211 Port Royal Rd., Suite 510, Springfield VA 22151. (703)321-9820. **Contact:** Mary Kate Grover. Estab. 1974. "To honor the late William B. Ruggles, editor emeritas of the Dallas Morning News, who coined the phrase 'Right to Work.' " Deadline: January 1-March 31. Prize: $2,000 scholarship. "We do reserve the right to reprint the material/ excerpt from the essay in publicizing the award. Applicant must be a graduate or undergraduate student majoring in journalism in institutions of higher learning throughout the US."

SCIENCE IN SOCIETY JOURNALISM AWARDS, Canadian Science Writers' Association, P.O. Box 75, Station A, Toronto, Ontario M5W 1A2 Canada. (416)408-4566. Fax: (416)408-1044. E-mail: cswa@interlog.com. Website: www.interlog.con/~cswa. **Contact:** Andy F. Visser-deVries. Offered annually for work published/aired January 1-December 31 of previous year to recognize outstanding contributions to science journalism in all media. Three newspaper, 3 magazine, 2 TV, 2 radio, 1 special publication, student sciences writing award (Herb Lampert Student Writing Award). Deadline: January 31. Guidelines for SASE. Each prize: $1,000 and a plaque. Material becomes property of CSWA. Does not return mss. Open to Canadian citizens or residents of Canada.

SOVEREIGN AWARD OUTSTANDING NEWSPAPER STORY, OUTSTANDING FEATURE STORY, The Jockey Club of Canada, P.O. Box 156, Rexdale, Ontario M9W 5L2 Canada. (416)675-7756. Fax: (416)675-6378. E-mail: tjcc@ftn.net. **Contact**: Bridget Bimm, executive director. Estab. 1973. Offered annually to recognize outstanding achievement in the area of Canadian thoroughbred racing journalism published November 1-October 31 of the previous year. Newspaper Story: Appeared in a newspaper by a racing columnist on Canadian Racing subject matter. Outstanding Feature Story: Appeared in a magazine book or newspaper, written as feature story on Canadian Racing subject matter. Deadline: October 31. There is no nominating process other than the writer submitting no more than 1 entry per category. Special Criteria: Must be of Canadian racing content. A copy of the newspaper article or magazine story must be provided along with a 3¼" disk containing the story in an ASCII style format.

THE TEN BEST "CENSORED" STORIES OF 2001, Project Censored—Sonoma State University, Rohnert Park CA 94928. (707)664-2500. Fax: (707)664-2108. E-mail: censored@sonoma.edu. Website: www.sonoma.edu/projectcens ored/. **Contact:** Peter Phillips, director. Estab. 1976. Current published, nonfiction stories of national social significance that have been overlooked or under-reported by the news media. Deadline: October 1.

• Peter Phillips and Project Censored choose 25 stories that have been underreported to make up *Censored: The News That Didn't Make the News and Why*, published by Seven Stories Press.

THE LAWRENCE WADE JOURNALISM FELLOWSHIP, The Heritage Foundation, 214 Massachusetts Ave., NE, Washington DC 20002. (202)546-4400. **Contact:** Selection Committee. Offered annually to award a journalism student who best exemplifies the high ideals and standards of the late Lawrence Wade. Guidelines for SASE. Prize: $1,000 and 1 ten-week salaried internship at the Heritage Foundation. Applicants must be enrolled full-time in an accredited college or university.

STANLEY WALKER JOURNALISM AWARD, The Texas Institute of Letters, Southwest Texas State University, San Marcos TX 78666. (512)245-2428. Fax: (512)245-7462. E-mail: mb13@swt.edu. Website: www.English.swt.edu/ css/TIL/rules.htm. **Contact:** Mark Busby. Offered annually for work published January 1-December 31 of previous year to recognize the best writing appearing in a daily newspaper. Deadline: January 3. Guidelines for SASE. Prize: $1,000. Writer must have been born in Texas, or must have lived in the state for two consecutive years at some time, or the subject matter of the article must be associated with the state.

EDWARD WEINTAL PRIZE FOR DIPLOMATIC REPORTING, Georgetown University Inst. for the Study of Diplomacy, 1316 36th St. NW, Washington DC 20007. (202)965-5735 ext. 3010. Fax: (202)965-5811. E-mail: dolgas@gunet.georgetown.edu. Website: data.georgetown.edu/sfs/programs/isd. Contest/Award Director: Charles Dolgas. Offered annually to honor previously published journalists whose work reflects initiative, hard digging and bold thinking in the coverage of American diplomacy and foreign policy. Deadline: mid-January. Writer should place name on award mailing list to receive notice of nominations being sought. Prize: $5,000. "Nominations are made by the editor on the basis of a specific story or series or on the basis of a journalist's overall news coverage."

Writing for Children & Young Adults

AMERICAN ASSOCIATION OF UNIVERSITY WOMEN AWARD, NORTH CAROLINA DIVISION, North Carolina Literary and Historical Association, 4610 Mail Service Center, Raleigh NC 27699-4610. (919)733-9375. **Contact:** Jerry C. Cashion, awards coordinator. Offered annually for published volume of juvenile literature by a North Carolina resident. Deadline: July 15.

R. ROSS ANNETT AWARD FOR CHILDREN'S LITERATURE, Writers Guild of Alberta, 11759 Groat Rd., Edmonton, Alberta T5M 3K6 Canada. (708)422-8174 or (800)665-5354. Fax: (708)422-2663. E-mail: wga@oanet.com. **Contact:** Renate Donnovan or Miki Andrejevic, executive directors. Offered annually for children's book published in current year. Open to Albertan authors. Prize: a leather-bound copy of your book and $500. Send five copies of the submission by December 31.

THE GEOFFREY BILSON AWARD FOR HISTORICAL FICTION FOR YOUNG PEOPLE, The Canadian Children's Book Centre, 35 Spadina Rd., Toronto, Ontario M5R 2S9 Canada. (416)975-0010. Fax: (416)975-1839. E-mail: ccbc@sympatico.ca. Website: www3.sympatico.ca/ccbc. **Contact:** (Ms.) Hadley Dyer. Offered annually for a previously published "outstanding work of historical fiction for young people by a Canadian author." Prize: $1,000 and a certificate. Open to Canadian citizens and residents of Canada for at least two years.

IRMA S. AND JAMES H. BLACK AWARD, Bank Street College of Education, 610 W. 112th St., New York NY 10025. (212)875-4450. Fax: (212)875-4558. E-mail: lindag@bnkst.edu. Website: www.bankstreet.edu/html/library/isb.html. **Contact:** Linda Greengrass, director. Estab. 1972. Offered annually for a book for young children, for excellence of both text and illustrations. Entries must have been published during the previous calendar year. Deadline for entries: January 1 after book is published.

BOOK PUBLISHERS OF TEXAS AWARD FOR CHILDREN'S OR YOUNG PEOPLE'S BOOK, The Texas Institute of Letters, Southwest Texas State University, San Marcos TX 78666. (512)245-2428. Fax: (512)245-7462. E-mail: mb13@swt.edu. Website: www.English.swt.edu/css/TIL/rules.htm. **Contact:** Mark Busby. Offered annually for work published January 1-December 31 of previous year to recognize the best book for children or young people. Deadline: January 3. Guidelines for SASE. Prize: $250. Writer must have been born in Texas or have lived in the state for at least two consecutive years at one time, or the subject matter is associated with the state.

BOSTON GLOBE-HORN BOOK AWARD, *The Boston Globe*, 135 Morrissey Blvd, P.O. Box 2378, Boston MA 02107. Also: The Horn Book Magazine, 56 Roland St., Suite 200, Boston MA 02129. Offered annually for previously published work in children's literature. Awards for original fiction or poetry, picture book, and nonfiction. Publisher submits entry. Deadline: May 15. Prize: $500 in each category.

MARGUERITE DE ANGELI PRIZE, Bantam Doubleday Dell Books for Young Readers, Random House, Inc., 1540 Broadway, New York NY 10036. (212)782-9000. Fax: (212)782-9452. Website: www.randomhouse.com/kids. **Contact:** Diana Capriotti, editor. Estab. 1992. Offered annually for unpublished fiction manuscript suitable for readers 7-10 years of age, set in North America, either contemporary or historical. Deadline: April 1-June 30. Guidelines for SASE. Prize: $1,500 in cash, publication and $3,500 advance against royalties; world rights acquired.

DELACORTE PRESS PRIZE FOR A FIRST YOUNG ADULT NOVEL, Delacorte Press, 1540 Broadway, New York NY 10036. (212)354-6500. Fax: (212)782-9452. Website: www.randomhouse.com/kids. Executive Editor: Wendy Lamb. Estab. 1983. Previously unpublished young adult fiction. Submissions: October 1-December 31. Guidelines for SASE. Prize: $1,500 cash, publication and $6,000 advance against royalties. World rights acquired.

FRIENDS OF AMERICAN WRITERS YOUNG PEOPLE'S LITERATURE AWARDS, 400 E. Randolph St., Apt. 2123, Chicago IL 60601. (312)664-5628. **Contact:** Jane Larson, chairman. Estab. 1960. "Annual awards for children's books that were published in the past year. Entry must be first, second or third children's book published by the author. The author must be a resident or native of AR, IL, IN, IA, KS, MI, MN, MO, NE, ND, OH, SD or WI or story can be *set* in one of these states. No poetry." Prize: up to $400 each to 2 writers; certificates to publishers. Guidelines for SASE. Deadline: December 31.

GOLDEN KITE AWARDS, Society of Children's Book Writers and Illustrators (SCBWI), 8271 Beverly Blvd., Los Angeles CA 90048. (310)859-9887. E-mail: scbwi@juno.com. Website: www.scbwi.org. **Contact:** Mercedes Coats, coordinator. Estab. 1973. Offered annually for published children's fiction, nonfiction and picture illustration books by a SCBWI members only published in the calendar year. Deadline: December 15.

GUIDEPOSTS YOUNG WRITERS CONTEST, *Guideposts*, 16 E. 34th St., New York NY 10016. (212)251-8100. **Contact:** James McDermont. Offered annually for unpublished high school juniors and seniors. "We accept submissions after announcement is placed in the October issue each year." Deadline: Monday after Thanksgiving. Guidelines in October issue. Prizes: 1st-$10,000, 2nd-$8,000, $250 gift certificate for college supplies. "If the manuscript is placed, we require all rights to the story in that version." Open only to high school juniors or seniors.

HIGHLIGHTS FOR CHILDREN FICTION CONTEST, *Highlights for Children*, 803 Church St., Honesdale PA 18431-1824. Website: www.highlightsforchildren.com. **Contact:** Fiction Contest Editor. Manuscript Coordinator: Beth Troop. Estab. 1946. Stories for children ages 2-12; category varies each year. Guidelines for SASE. Stories should be limited to 900 words for older readers, 500 words for younger readers. No crime or violence, please. Prize: $1,000 to 3 winners. Specify that ms is a contest entry. All entries must be postmarked January 1-February 28.

INTERNATIONAL READING ASSOCIATION CHILDREN'S BOOK AWARDS, International Reading Association, P.O. Box 8139, Newark DE 19714-8139. (302)731-1600, ext. 293. Fax: (302)731-1057. E-mail: jbutler@reading.org. Website: www.reading.org. **Contact:** Janet Butler. Offered annually for an author's first or second published book in three categories: younger readers (ages 4-10); older readers (ages 10-17); to recognize newly published authors who show unusual promise in the children's book field. Guidelines and deadlines for SASE. Prize: $500 and a medal for each of 3 categories.

ANNE SPENCER LINDBERGH PRIZE IN CHILDREN'S LITERATURE, The Charles A. & Anne Morrow Lindbergh Foundation, 708 S. Third St., Suite 110, Anoka MN 55303. (612)576-1596. Fax: (612)576-1664. E-mail: lindbergh@lsd.net. Website: www.lindberghfoundation.org. **Contact:** Executive Director. Offered every two years in even years for children's fantasy novel published in that or the preceding year. Deadline: November 1. Entries must include four copies of the book and an application fee of $25, payable to the Lindbergh Foundation, for each title submitted. Open to any writer.

JUDY LOPEZ MEMORIAL AWARD, Women's National Book Association/Los Angeles, 1225 Selby Ave., Los Angeles CA 90024. (310)474-9917. **Contact:** Margaret Flanders. Offered annually to writers published during the previous calendar year for the award given each June to identify and publicize outstanding books for children each year. Deadline: third Monday in February. Guidelines for SASE. Prize: solid bronze medal by a noted sculptor; expense-paid trip to Los Angeles for award ceremony in June; $200 honorarium. Writers must have been published first in the US; writer must be a citizen or resident of the US and work must be appropriate for children ages 9 to 12.

VICKY METCALF BODY OF WORK AWARD, Canadian Authors Association, Box 419, 320 S. Shores Rd., Campbellford, Ontario K0L 1L0 Canada. (705)653-0323. Fax: (705)653-0593. E-mail: canauth@redden.on.ca. **Contact:** Alec McEachern. Offered annually for a Canadian author who has published a minimum of four books inspirational to young people. Deadline: December 31. Guidelines for IRCs. Prize: $10,000. Open to Canadian only.

VICKY METCALF SHORT STORY AWARD, Canadian Authors Association, Box 419, 320 S. Shores Rd., Campbellford, Ontario K0L 1L1 Canada. (705)653-0323. Fax: (705)653-0593. E-mail: canauth@redden.on.ca. **Contact:** Alec McEachern. Offered annually for a Canadian author of a short story for children. Deadline: December 31. Guidelines for IRCs. Prize: $3,000. Open to Canadian authors only.

MILKWEED PRIZE FOR CHILDREN'S LITERATURE, Milkweed Editions, 1011 Washington Ave. S, Suite 300, Minneapolis MN 55415. (612)332-3192. E-mail: books@milkweed.org. Website: www.milkweed.org. **Contact:** Elisabeth Fitz, first reader. Annual prize for unpublished works. Estab. 1993. "Milkweed is looking for a novel or biography intended for readers aged 8-13. Manuscripts should be of high literary quality and must be double-spaced, 90-200 pages in length. The Milkweed Prize for Children's Literature will be awarded to the best manuscript for children ages 8-13 that Milkweed accepts for publication during each calendar year by a writer not previously published by Milkweed Editions." Prize: $5,000 advance on any royalties agreed upon at the time of acceptance. Must send SASE for guidelines, both for regular children's submission policies and for the announcement of the restructured contest. Catalog for $1.50 postage.

MR. CHRISTIE'S BOOK AWARD, Christie Brown & Copy, 2150 Lakeshore Blvd. W., Toronto, Ontario M8V 1A3 Canada. (416)503-6050. Fax: (416)503-6034. E-mail: myustin@nabisco.ca. **Contact:** Marlene Yuston. Offered annually to honor excellence in "the writing and illustration of Canadian children's literature." Deadline: January 31. Guidelines for SASE. Prize: $7,500 awarded to six age categories. Open to Canadian citizens and landed immigrants.

THE NATIONAL CHAPTER OF CANADA IODE VIOLET DOWNEY BOOK AWARD, National Chapter of Canada IODE, 40 Orchard View Blvd., Suite 254, Toronto, Ontario M4R 1B9 Canada. (416)487-4416. Fax: (416)487-4417. Website: www.iodecanada.ca. **Contact:** Mrs. Marty Dalton, contest/award director. Offered annually for children's books of at least 500 words. Entries must have appeared in print January 1-December 31. Deadline: December 31. Guidelines for SASE. Prize: $3,000 (Canadian funds). Open only to Canadian citizens.

SCOTT O'DELL AWARD FOR HISTORICAL FICTION, 1700 E. 56th St., #3906, Chicago IL 60637. (773)752-7880. **Contact:** Zena Sutherland, director. Estab. 1981. Historical fiction book for children set in the Americas. Entries must have been published during previous year. Deadline: December 31.

PEN/NORMA KLEIN AWARD, PEN American Center, 568 Broadway, New York NY 10012. (212)334-1660. Fax: (212)334-2181. E-mail: jm@pen.org. **Contact:** John Morrone. Offered in odd-numbered years to recognize an emerging voice of literary merit among American writers of children's fiction. *Candidates may not nominate themselves.* Next award is 2001. Deadline: December 15. Guidelines for SASE. Award: $3,000.

TEDDY AWARD FOR BEST CHILDREN'S BOOK, Austin Writers' League, 1501 W. Fifth St., Suite E-2, Austin TX 78703. (512)499-8914. Fax: (512)499-0441. E-mail: awl@writersleague.org. Website: www.writersleague.org. **Contact:** Gus Gonzalez III, executive assistant. Offered annually for work published January 1-December 31 to honor an outstanding book for children published by a member of the Austin Writers' League. Deadline: March 1. Guidelines for SASE. Charges $10 fee. Prize: $1,000 and trophy. Austin Writers' League dues may accompany entry fee.

(ALICE WOOD MEMORIAL) OHIOANA AWARD FOR CHILDREN'S LITERATURE, Ohioana Library Association, 65 Front St., Suite 1105, Columbus OH 43215. (614)466-3831. Fax: (614)728-6974. E-mail: ohioana@wins lo.state.oh.us. Website: www.oplin.lib.oh.us/OHIOANA/. **Contact:** Linda R. Hengst. Offered to an author whose body of work has made, and continues to make, a significant contribution to literature for children or young adults and through their work as a writer, teacher, administrator or through community service, interest in children's literature has been encouraged and children have become involved with reading. Prize: $1,000. Deadline: December 31. Nomination forms for SASE. Recipient must have been born in Ohio or lived in Ohio at least 5 years.

WORK-IN-PROGRESS GRANT, Society of Children's Book Writers and Illustrators (SCBWI) and Judy Blume, 8271 Beverly Blvd., Los Angeles CA 90048. E-mail: scbwi@juno.com. Website: www.scbwi.org. Two grants—one designated specifically for a contemporary novel for young people—to assist SCBWI members in the completion of a specific project. Deadline: March 1. Guidelines for SASE. Open to SCBWI members only.

WRITING FOR CHILDREN COMPETITION, The Writers' Union of Canada, 24 Ryerson Ave., Toronto, Ontario M5T 2P3. (416)703-8982, ext. 223. Fax: (416)703-0826. E-mail: twuc@the-wire.com. Website: www.swifty. com/twuc. **Contact:** Cindy Newton. Offered annually "to discover developing Canadian writers of unpublished children's/young adult fiction or nonfiction." Deadline: April 23. Charges $15 entry fee. Prize: $1,500. The winner and 11 finalists' pieces will be submitted to a Canadian publisher of children's books. Open to Canadian citizens or landed immigrants who have not been published in book format and who do not currently have a contract with a publisher.

Translation

AMERICAN TRANSLATORS ASSOCIATION HONORS AND AWARDS, American Translators Association, 225 Reinekers Lane, Suite 590, Alexandria VA 22314. (703)683-6100. Fax: (703)683-6122. E-mail: ata@atanet.org. Website: www.atanet.org. **Contact:** Walter Bacak, executive director. Student award offered annually; other awards offered every 2 years. Categories: best student translation; best literary translation in German; and best literary translation in any language but German. Guidelines for SASE. Prize varies—usually $500-1,000 and a trip to annual conference.

ASF TRANSLATION PRIZE, The American-Scandinavian Foundation, 15 E. 65 St., New York NY 10021. (212)879-9779. Fax: (212)249-3444. E-mail: agyongy@amscan.org. Website: www.amscan.org. **Contact:** Adrienne Gyongy. Offered annually to a translation of Scandinavian literature into English of a Nordic author born within last 200 years. Deadline: June 1. Guidelines for SASE. Prizes: $2,000, publication of an excerpt in an issue of *Scandinavian Review* and a commemorative bronze medallion; the Inger Sjöberg Prize of $500. "The Prize is for an outstanding English translation of poetry, fiction, drama or literary prose originally written in Danish, Finnish, Icelandic, Norwegian or Swedish that has not been previously published in the English language."

THE BORDIGHERA BILINGUAL ITALIAN-AMERICAN POETRY PRIZE, Sonia Raiziss-Giop Foundation, P.O. Box 15, Andover NJ 07821-0015. E-mail: daniela@garden.net. Website: www.luc.edu/depts/modern_lang/italian/ bordighera. **Contact:** Daniela Gioseffi. Offered annually for an unpublished collection of poetry "to find the best manuscripts of poetry in English, by an American of Italian descent to be translated into quality Italian and published bilingually." Deadline: May 31. Guidelines for SASE. Prize: $2,000 and bilingual book publication to be divided between poet and translator. Open to mss of poetry in English by an American of Italian descent.

FELLOWSHIPS FOR TRANSLATORS, National Endowment for the Arts Literature Program, 1100 Pennsylvania Ave. NW, Washington DC 20506. (202)682-5428. Website: arts.endow.gov. **Contact:** Heritage and Preservation Division. Offered to published translators of exceptional talent.

SOEURETTE DIEHL FRASER TRANSLATION AWARD, The Texas Institute of Letters, Southwest Texas State University, San Marcos TX 78666. (512)245-2428. Fax: (512)245-7462. E-mail: mb13@swt.edu. Website: www.English. swt.edu/css/TIL/rules.htm. **Contact:** Mark Busby. Offered annually for work published January 1-December 31 of previous year to recognize the best translation of a literary book into English. Deadline: January 3. Guidelines for SASE. Prize: $1,000. Translator must have been born in Texas or have lived in the state for at least two consecutive years at some time.

GERMAN PRIZE FOR LITERARY TRANSLATION, American Translators Association, 225 Reinekers Lane, Suite 590, Alexandria VA 22314. (703)683-6100. Fax: (703)683-6122. E-mail: ata@atanet.org. Website: www.atanet.org. **Contact:** Walter Bacak, executive director. Offered in odd-numbered years for previously published book translated from German to English. In even-numbered years, the Lewis Galentière Prize is awarded for translations other than German to English. Deadline April 15. Prize: $1,000, a certificate of recognition, and up to $500 toward expenses for attending the ATA Annual Conference.

THE HAROLD MORTON LANDON TRANSLATION AWARD, The Academy of American Poets, 584 Broadway, Suite 1208, New York NY 10012-3250. (212)274-0343. Fax: (212)274-9427. E-mail: academy@poets.org. Website: www.poets.org. **Contact:** Awards Administrator. Offered annually to recognize a published translation of poetry from any language into English. Deadline: December 31. Guidelines for SASE. Prize: $1,000. Open to living US citizens. Anthologies by a number of translators are ineligible.

PEN/BOOK-OF-THE-MONTH CLUB TRANSLATION PRIZE, PEN American Center, 568 Broadway, New York NY 10012. (212)334-1660. Fax: (212)334-2181. E-mail: jm@pen.org. **Contact:** John Morrone. Prize: $3,000 for a literary book-length translation into English published in the calendar year. (No technical, scientific or reference books.) Deadline: December 15. Publishers, agents or translators may submit 3 copies of each eligible title.

THE RAIZISS/DE PALCHI TRANSLATION FELLOWSHIP, The Academy of American Poets, 584 Broadway, Suite 1208, New York NY 10012-3250. (212)274-0343. Fax: (212)274-9427. E-mail: academy@poets.org. Website: www.poets.org. **Contact:** Michael Tyrell. Offered every two years to recognize outstanding unpublished translations of modern Italian poetry into English. Accepts entries from September 1-November 1, 2000. Guidelines for SASE. Prize: $20,000 and a one-month residency at the American Academy in Rome. Applicants must verify permission to translate the poems or that the poems are in the public domain. Open to any US citizen.

LOIS ROTH AWARD FOR A TRANSLATION OF A LITERARY WORK, Modern Language Association, 10 Astor Place, New York NY 10003-6981. (212)614-6324. Fax: (212)533-0680. E-mail: awards@mla.org. Website: www.mla.org. Offered every 2 years (odd years) for an outstanding translation into English of a book-length literary work published the previous year. Deadline: April 1, 2000. Guidelines for SASE. Prize: $1,000. Open to members of the MLA.

ALDO AND JEANNE SCAGLIONE PRIZE FOR TRANSLATION OF A LITERARY WORK, Modern Language Association of America, 10 Astor Place, New York NY 10003-6981. (212)614-6324. Fax: (212)533-0680. E-mail: awards@mla.org. Website: www.mla.org. **Contact:** Robert Blondeau. Offered in even-numbered years for the translation of a book-length literary work appearing in print during the previous year. Deadline: May 1, 2000. Guidelines for SASE. Prize: $1,000 and a certificate. Translators need not be members of the MLA.

ALDO AND JEANNE SCAGLIONE PRIZE FOR TRANSLATION OF A SCHOLARLY STUDY OF LITERATURE, Modern Language Association, 10 Astor Place, New York NY 10003-6981. (212)614-6324. Fax: (212)533-0680. Offered in odd-numbered years "for an outstanding translation into English of a book-length work of literary history, literary criticism, philology or literary theory published during the previous biennium." Deadline: May 1. Guidelines for SASE. Prize: $1,000 and a certificate. Open to any translator.

STUDENT TRANSLATION PRIZE, American Translators Association, % Courtney Searls-Ridge, 225 Reinekers Lane, Suite 590, Alexandria VA 22314 (703)683-6100. Fax: (703)683-6122. E-mail: ata@atanet.org. Website: www.atanet.org. Support is granted for a promising project to an unpublished student enrolled in a translation program at a US college or university. Deadline: April 1. Must be sponsored by a faculty member. Prize: $500 and up to $500 toward expenses for attending the ATA Annual Conference.

Multiple Writing Areas

AMELIA STUDENT AWARD, *Amelia Magazine*, 329 E St., Bakersfield CA 93304. (805)323-4064. Fax: (805)323-5326. E-mail: amelia@lightspeed.net. **Contact:** Frederick A. Raborg, Jr., editor. Offered annually for previously unpublished poems, essays and short stories by high school students and undergraduates, one entry per student; each high school entry should be signed by parent, guardian *or* teacher to verify originality. Deadline: May 15. No entry fee; however, if guidelines and sample are required, please send SASE with $3 handling charge.

ANNUAL GIVE BACK TO SOCIETY WRITING COMPETITION, E.F.S. Enterprises, Inc., 2844 Eighth Ave., Suite 6E, New York NY 10039. (212)283-8899. Website: www.efs-enterprises.com. **Contact:** Zeretha Jenkins, competition awards coordinator. Offered annually to help young writers while stressing the significance of arts, particularly creative writing, in the schools. Offered in 2 categories (fiction, essays) to give writers the opportunity to publish work online. The competition stresses one's responsibility to society by emphasizing the need for young adults to help others by "giving back to society" in some meaningful way, or ways. Fiction submitted must be original, unpublished and copyrighted. Applications and guidelines are required and are available upon request with SASE. Letters of recommendation required. Submissions accepted with applications from February 1-March 31. Deadline: March 31. No entry fee. Does not return mss. Prize: 1st—$100 and online publishing contract. Writers retain all rights. Open to high school seniors.

ARIZONA AUTHORS' ASSOCIATION ANNUAL NATIONAL LITERARY CONTEST, Arizona Authors' Association, P.O. Box 87857, Phoenix AZ 85080-7857. (623)780-0053. Fax: (623)780-0468. E-mail: VijayaSchartz@az.rmci.net. Website: home.rmci.net/vijayaschartz/azauthors.htm. **Contact:** Vijaya Schartz. Offered annually for previously unpublished poetry, short stories, essays and movies. Deadline: July 1. Charges $10 fee for poetry; $15 for short stories and essays and $30 for novels. Winners announced at an Award Banquet in Phoenix in November, and short pieces published in Arizona Literary Magazine.

N THE ART OF MUSIC ANNUAL WRITING CONTEST, Piano Press, P.O. Box 85, Del Mar CA 92014-0085. (858)481-5650. Fax: (858)755-1104. E-mail: pianopress@aol.com. Website: http://pianopress.iuma.com. **Contact:**

Elizabeth C. Axford, M.A. Offered annually for unpublished work. Categories are: Essay Contest (ages 4-12, 13-17, and 18 and over), Short Story Contest (ages 4-12, 13-17, and 18 and over) and Poetry Contest (ages 4-12, 13-17, and 18 and over); nine total winners. All writings must be on music-related topics. The purpose of the contest is to promote the art of music through writing. Deadline: June 30. Charges $20/entry fee. Prize: medal, certificate, publication in the annual anthology/chapbook and free copy of the book. Acquires one-time rights. All entries must be accompanied by an entry form indicating category and age; parent signature is required of all writers under age 18. All writings must be in music-related topics. Poems may be of any length and in any style; essays and short stories should not exceed five double-spaced typewritten pages. All entries shall be previously unpublished and the original work of the author. SASE (#10 or e-mail) for entry form and writer's guidelines.

ARTS AND LETTERS COMPETITION, Government of Newfoundland and Labrador Culture and Heritage Division, Box 1854, St. John's, Newfoundland A1C 5P9 Canada. (709)729-5253. Fax: (709)729-5952. **Contact:** Regina Best, coordinator. Offered annually "to encourage creative talent of the residents of Newfoundland and Labrador. Senior Divison (19 years and older): poetry, fiction, nonfiction and dramatic scripts. Also in Senior Division: The Percy Janes 1st Novel Award for unpublished ms for unpublished novelists, minimum 30,000 words. Junior (E.J. Pratt) Division (12-18 years old): prose and poetry. All work submitted must be unpublished. Deadline: February of each year (exact date to be announced each year). Guidelines for SASE or call the Arts and Letters Competition office at (709)729-5253 (must have application form accompanying entry). Prizes: *Senior Division:* 1st-$600, 2nd-$300, 3rd-$150 for each category; *Percy Janes Prize:* $1,000; *Junior Division:* 1st-$300, 2nd-$200, 3rd-$100 for each category. Rights remain with the author, but the first place winner is usually published in an annual booklet. Open to residents of province of Newfoundland and Labrador. Blind judging.

AWP AWARD SERIES, Associated Writing Programs, Tallwood House, Mail Stop 1E3, George Mason University, Fairfax VA 22030. (703)993-4301. Fax: (703)993-4302. E-mail: awp@gmu.edu. Website: http://awpwriter.org. **Contact:** David Sherwin. Offered annually to foster new literary talent. Categories: poetry, short fiction, creative nonfiction, novel. Deadline: must be postmarked January 1-February 28. Guidelines for SASE. Charges $20-nonmembers, $10 for members. Prize: cash honorarium (novel-$10,000; other categories-$2,000) and publication by a participating press. Open to all writers.

BAKELESS LITERARY PUBLICATION PRIZES, Bread Loaf Writers' Conference/Middlebury College, Middlebury College, Middleburg VT 05753. (802)443-2018. Fax: (802)443-2087. E-mail: bakeless@middlebury.edu. Website: www.middlebury.edu/~blwc. **Contact:** Ian Pounds, contest director. Offered annually for unpublished authors of poetry, fiction and creative nonfiction. Submissions accepted January 1-March 1. Guidelines for SASE. Charges $10 fee. Prize: Publication of book length ms by University Press of New England and a Fellowship to attend the Bread Loaf Writers' Conference. Open to all writing in English who have not yet published a book in their entry's genre.

EMILY CLARK BALCH AWARD, *Virginia Quarterly Review*, 1 West Range, Charlottesville VA 22903. (804)924-3124. Fax:(804)924-1397. Website: www.virginia.edu/vqr. **Contact:** Staige D. Blackford, editor. Best short story/poetry accepted and published by the *Virginia Quarterly Review* during a calendar year. No deadline.

BYLINE MAGAZINE AWARDS, P.O. Box 130596, Edmond OK 73013-0001. Phone/fax: (405)348-5591. E-mail: bylinemp@flash.net. Website: www.bylinemag.com. **Contact:** Marcia Preston, award director. Contest includes several monthly contests, open to anyone, in various categories that include fiction, nonfiction, poetry and children's literature, an annual poetry chapbook award which is open to any poet and an annual ByLine Short Fiction and Poetry Award open only to our subscribers. Deadlines: chapbook—March 1; ByLine Short Fiction and Poetry Award—November 1; monthly contests have various deadlines. Guidelines for SASE. Charges $3-5 monthly contests and $12 chapbook. Prizes: monthly contests—cash and listing in magazine; chapbook award—publication of chapbook, 50 copies and $200; ByLine Short Fiction and Poetry Award—$250 in each category, plus publication in the magazine. For chapbook award and Subscriber Awards, publication constitutes part of the prize, and winners grant first NA rights to ByLine. Monthly contests and poetry chapbook competition are open to any writer.

CANADIAN AUTHORS ASSOCIATION AWARDS PROGRAM, P.O. Box 419, Campbellford, Ontario K0L 1L0 Canada. (705)653-0323. Fax: (705)653-0593. **Contact:** Alec McEachern. Offered annually for short stories, fiction, poetry, history, biography books inspirational to young people, short stories for children and to promising writers under age 30. Deadlines vary. Guidelines for SASE. Prizes range from air travel for two to $10,000. Entrants must be Canadians by birth, naturalized Canadians or landed immigrants.

CANADIAN HISTORICAL ASSOCIATION AWARDS, Canadian Historical Association, 395 Wellington, Ottawa, Ontario K1A 0N3 Canada. (613)233-7885. Fax: (613)567-3110. E-mail: cha-shc@archives.ca. Website: www.yorku.ca/research/cha/cha-shc.html. Offered annually. Categories: regional history, Canadian history, history (not Canadian), women's history (published articles, English or French), doctoral dissertations. Deadlines vary. Guidelines for SASE. Prizes: certificates of merit-$1,000. Open to Canadian writers.

THE CHELSEA AWARDS FOR POETRY AND SHORT FICTION, % Richard Foerster, Editor, P.O. Box 1040, York Beach ME 03910. Estab. 1958. Offered annually for previously unpublished submissions. "Two prizes awarded for the best work of short fiction and for the best group of 4-6 poems selected by the editors in anonymous competitions."

Deadline: June 15 for fiction; December 15 for poetry. Guidelines for SASE. Charges $10 fee (includes free subscription to *Chelsea*). Checks made payable to Chelsea Associates, Inc. Prize: $1,000, winning entries published in *Chelsea*. Include SASE for notification of competition results. Does not return mss. *Note:* General submissions and other business should be addressed to the Editor at *Chelsea*, P.O. Box 773, Cooper Station, New York NY 10276.

CHICANO/LATINO LITERARY CONTEST, Department of Spanish and Portuguese, University of California-Irvine, Irvine CA 92717. (949)824-5443. Fax: (949)824-2803. E-mail: fchee@nci.edu. Website: www.hnet.uci.edu/spanishandportugese./contest.html. **Contact:** Fabio Chee. Estab. 1974. Offered annually "to promote the dissemination of unpublished Chicano/Latino literature in Spanish or English, and to encourage its development. The call for entries will be genre specific, rotating through four categories: short story (2000), poetry (2001), drama (2002) and novel (2003)." Deadline: June 2. Prize: 1st-$1,000 and publication, transportation to receive the award; 2nd-$500; 3rd-$250. Guidelines for #10 SASE. The contest is open to all citizens or permanent residents of the US.

CNW/FLORIDA STATE WRITING COMPETITION, Florida Freelance Writers Association, P.O. Box A, North Stratford NH 03590-0167. (603)922-8338. Fax: (603)922-8339. E-mail: contest@writers-editors.com. Website: www.writers-editors.com. **Contact:** Dana Cassell, executive director. Deadline: March 15. Subject areas include: adult articles, adult short stories, writing for children, novels, poetry; categories within these areas vary from year to year. Guidelines for #10 SASE. Entry fees vary from year to year; in 2000 were $3-20. Prizes: cash, certificates. Open to any writer.

COLORADO BOOK AWARDS, Colorado Center for the Book, 2123 Downing, Denver CO 80205. (303)839-8320. Fax: (303)839-8319. E-mail: 103332.1376@compuserve.com. Website: www.aclin.org/~ccftb. **Contact:** Christiane H. Citron, director. Offered annually for work published by December of previous year or current calendar year. The purpose is to champion all Colorado authors and in particular to honor the award winners and a reputation for Colorado as a state whose people promote and support reading, writing and literacy through books. The categories are children, young adult, fiction, nonfiction & poetry, guidebooks, romance. Guidelines for SASE. Charges $40 fee. Prize: $500 cash prize in each category and an annual dinner event where winners are honored. Open to authors who reside or have resided in Colorado.

Ⓝ COMMONWEALTH CLUB OF CALIFORNIA BOOK AWARDS, 595 Market St., San Francisco CA 94105. (415)597-6700. Fax: (415)597-6729. E-mail: jimcwc@pacbell.net. Website: www.commonwealthclub.org. **Contact:** Jim Coplan, director. Estab. 1931. Offered annually for previously published submissions appearing in print January 1-December 31 of the previous year. "Purpose of award is the encouragement and production of literature in California. Categories include: fiction, nonfiction, poetry, first work of fiction, juvenile ages up to 10, juvenile 11-16, notable contribution to publishing and Californiana." Deadline: January 31. Guidelines for SASE. Can be nominated by publisher as well. Prize: Medals and cash prizes to be awarded at publicized event. Open to California residents (or residents at time of publication).

VIOLET CROWN BOOK AWARDS, Austin Writers' League, 1501 W. Fifth St., Suite E-2, Austin TX 78703. (512)499-8914. Fax: (512)499-0441. E-mail: awl@writersleague.org. Website: www.writersleague.org. **Contact:** Gus Gonzales III, director. Offered annually for work published July 1-June 30 to honor three outstanding books published in fiction, nonfiction and literary categories by Austin Writers' League members. Deadline: June 30. Guidelines for SASE. Charges $10 fee. Prize: 3 $1,000 cash prizes and trophies. Entrants must be Austin Writers' League members. Membership dues may accompany entry fee.

DOG WRITERS ASSOCIATION OF AMERICA ANNUAL WRITING CONTEST, Dog Writers Association of America, 173 Union Rd., Coatesville PA 19320-1326. (610)384-2436. Fax: (610)384-2471. E-mail: dwaa@dwaa.org. Website: dwaa.org. **Contact:** Janine Adams, contest chair, or Pat Santi, secretary. Offered annually for submissions published between September 1999-September 2000 in the following categories: Newspaper Articles, Books, Poems, Mystery, Club Newsletters, Videos and Children's Books. Deadline: September 1. Guidelines for SASE. Charges $10-12 fee. Prize: plaques and cash awards.

THE E.F.S. ANNUAL WRITING COMPETITION, E.F.S. Enterprises, Inc., 2844 Eighth Ave., Suite 6E, New York NY 10039. (212)283-8899. Website: www.efs-enterprises.com. **Contact:** Zeretha Jenkins, competition director. Offered annually for unpublished work in 5 categories (fiction, nonfiction, poetry, plays, screenplays). Provides writers the opportunity to publish online. Submissions must be unpublished, unproduced and currently not under option. Applications and guidelines are required and are available upon request with SASE. Submissions accepted with applications from March 1-April 30. Charges $20 fee. Does not return mss. Prize: 1st-$100 and online publishing contract; 2nd-$50. Writers retain all rights. Open to any writer. Authors do not have to be previously published.

EMERGING LESBIAN WRITERS FUND AWARD, ASTRAEA National Lesbian Action Foundation, 116 E. 16th St., 7th Floor, New York NY 10003. (212)529-8021. Fax: (212)982-3321. E-mail: info@astraea.org. Website: www.astraea.org. **Contact:** Christine Lipat, program officer. Offered annually to encourage and support the work of new lesbian writers of fiction and poetry. Deadline: International Women's Day, March 8. Guidelines for SASE. Charges $5 fee. Prize: $10,000 grants. Entrants must be a lesbian writer of either fiction or poetry, a US resident, work includes some lesbian content, at least one piece of writing (in any genre) has been published in a newspaper, magazine, journal or anthology, and not more than one book. (Published work may be in any discipline; self-published books are not included in the one book maximum.)

EXPLORATIONS PRIZES FOR LITERATURE, UAS Explorations, University of Alaska Southeast, 11120 Glacier Highway, Juneau AK 99801. (907)465-6418 (message only). Fax: (907)465-6406. E-mail: jfamp@uas.alaska.edu. **Contact:** Art Petersen, editor. Offered annually to provide a venue for poets and writers of prose fiction across Alaska, the US, Canada, England and Europe. Deadline: May 15. Guidelines for SASE. Charges $6/1-2 poems, $3/6 maximum; $6/story. Prize: 1st-$1,000, 2nd-$500, 3rd-$100. Open to any writer.

N: THE GREAT AMERICAN BOOK CONTEST, Book Deals, Inc., 20 N. Wacker Dr., Suite 1928, Chicago IL 60606. (312)372-0227. Fax: (312)372-0249. E-mail: BookDeals@aol.com. **Contact:** Caroline Francis Carney. Annual contest for unpublished work. Purpose of contest is to discover distinctive American authors of exceptional literary talent whose work equals or surpasses the finest of America's past and future. Three prizes: Grand Prize for Fiction; Grand Prize for Nonfiction; Honorable Mention for New Talent (writers under 30). Deadline: December 31. Guidelines for SASE. Charges $30 entry fee. Two Grand Prizes (one for fiction/one for nonfiction): $1,500, a meeting with a book editor and a meeting with a film development scout. One Honorable Mention (author 30 years and younger): $750. Open to any writer, but only book-length works of narrative adult fiction and nonfiction with American settings which have never been published, have not been accepted for publication and are not under contract before April 1, 2001 are eligible.

THE GREENSBORO REVIEW LITERARY AWARD IN FICTION AND POETRY, *The Greensboro Review*, English Department, 134 McIver Bldg., P.O. Box 26170, University of North Carolina-Greensboro, Greensboro NC 27402-6170. (336)334-5459. E-mail: jlclark@uncg.edu. Website: www.uncg.edu/eng/mfa. **Contact:** Jim Clark, editor. Offered annually for fiction and poetry recognizing the best work published in the spring issue of *The Greensboro Review*. Deadline: September 15. Sample copy for $5.

HACKNEY LITERARY AWARDS, *Writing Today*, Box 549003/Birmingham-Southern College, Birmingham AL 35254. (205)226-4921. E-mail: D.C.Wilson@bsc.edu. Website: www.bsc.edu/. **Contact:** D.C. Wilson. Estab. 1969. Offered annually for unpublished novel, short story (maximum 5,000 words) and poetry (50 line limit). Deadline: September 30 (novels), December 31 (short stories and poetry). Guidelines on website or for SASE. Charges $25 entry fee for novels, $10 for short story and poetry. Prize: $5,000 for each category.

ROBERT F. KENNEDY BOOK AWARDS, 1367 Connecticut Ave., NW, Suite 200, Washington DC 20036. (202)463-7575. Fax: (202)463-6606. E-mail: info@rfkmemorial.org. Website: www.rfkmemorial.org. **Contact:** Book Award Director. Offered annually for work published the previous year "which most faithfully and forcefully reflects Robert Kennedy's purposes—his concern for the poor and the powerless, his struggle for honest and even-handed justice, his conviction that a decent society must assure all young people a fair chance, and his faith that a free democracy can act to remedy disparities of power and opportunity." Deadline: January 31. Charges $25 fee. Prize: Grand Prize winner-$2,500 and a bust of Robert F. Kennedy.

■ HENRY KREISEL AWARD FOR BEST FIRST BOOK, Writers Guild of Alberta, 11759 Groat Rd., Edmonton Alberta T5M 3K6 Canada. (780)422-8174. Fax: (780)422-2663. E-mail: wga@oanet.com. Executive Director: Miki Andrejevic. Offered annually for a first book in any genre published in current year. Open to Alberta authors.

LARRY LEVIS EDITORS' PRIZE IN POETRY/THE MISSOURI REVIEW EDITOR'S PRIZE IN FICTION & ESSAY, The Missouri Review, 1507 Hillcrest Hall, Columbia MO 65211. (573)882-4474. Fax: (573)884-4671. Website: www.missourireview.org. **Contact:** Greg Michalson. Offered annually for unpublished work in 3 categories: fiction, essay and poetry. Deadline: October 15. Guidelines for SASE after June. Charges $15 fee (includes a 1 year subscription). Prize: fiction and poetry winner-$1,500 and publication in the spring issue; essay winner-$1,000 and publication. (3 finalists in each category receive a minimum of $100.)

MAMMOTH PRESS AWARDS, 7 S. Juniata St., Dubois PA 15801. E-mail: mammothbooks@hotmail.com. Website: http://cac.psu.edu/~dwm7/mammoth.htm. **Contact:** Antonio Vallone. Offered annually for unpublished works. Prose mss may be a collection of essays or a single long work of creative nonfiction, a collection of stories or novellas or a novel. Poetry mss may be a collection of poems or a single long poem. Translations are acceptable. "Manuscripts as a whole must not have been previously published. Some or all of each manuscript may have appeared in periodicals, chapbooks, anthologies or other venues. These must be identified. Authors are responsible for securing permissions." Deadline: prose March 1-August 31; poetry September 1-February 28. Guidelines for SASE or by e-mail. Charges $20 fee. Prize: $750 advance against royalties, standard royalty contract and publication.

N: ■ MANITOBA WRITING AND PUBLISHING AWARDS, % Manitoba Writers Guild, 206-100 Arthur St., Winnipeg, Manitoba R3B 1H3 Canada. (204)942-6134. Fax: (204)942-5754. E-mail: mbwriter@escape.ca. Website: www.m bwriter.mb.ca. **Contact:** Robyn Maharaj. Offered annually: the McNally Robinson Book of Year Award (adult); the McNally Robinson Book for Young People Awards (8 and under and 9 and older); the John Hirsch Award for Most Promising Manitoba Writer; The Mary Scorer Award for Best Book by a Manitoba Publisher; The Carol Shields Award; The Eileen

Sykes McTavish Award for Best First Book; two Book Publishers Awards, and the biennial Les Prix Des Caisse Populaires. Deadline for books is December 1st. Books published December 1-31 will be accepted until mid-January. Prize: $250-3,000. Guidelines and submission forms available upon request. Open to Manitoba writers only.

MASTERS LITERARY AWARDS, Center Press, P.O. Box 17897, Encino CA 91416. E-mail: usa11@usa.net. Website: http://members.xoom.com/CenterPress. **Contact:** Scott A. Sonders, managing editor. Offered annually and quarterly for work published within 2 years (preferred) and unpublished work (accepted). Fiction: 15 page, maximum; Poetry: 5 pages or 150 lines, maximum; Nonfiction: 10 page, maximum. Deadlines: March 15, June 15th, August 15th, December 15. Guidelines for SASE. Charges $15 reading/administration fee. Prizes: 4 quarterly honorable mentions from which is selected one yearly Grand Prize of $1,000. "A selection of winning entries will appear in our national literary publication." Winners also appear on the Internet. Center Press retains one time publishing rights to selected winners.

[N] MIDLAND AUTHORS AWARD, Society of Midland Authors, P.O. Box 10419, Chicago IL 60610-0419. E-mail: writercc@aol.com. Website: www.midlandauthors.org. **Contact:** Carol Carlson. Offered annually for published fiction, nonfiction, poetry, biography, children's fiction and children's nonfiction. Authors must reside in the states of IL, IN, IA, KS, MI, MN, MS, NE, ND, SD, WI or OH. Guidelines and submission at website. Deadline: March 1.

THE NEBRASKA REVIEW AWARDS IN FICTION AND POETRY, *The Nebraska Review*, FAB 212, University of Nebraska-Omaha, Omaha NE 68182-0324. (402)554-3159. E-mail: nereview@fa-cpacs.unomaha.edu. **Contact:** Susan Aizenberg (poetry), James Reed (fiction). Estab. 1973. Offered annually for previously unpublished fiction and a poem or group of poems. Deadline: November 30. Charges $10 fee (includes a subscription to *The Nebraska Review*). Prize: $500 for each category.

NEUSTADT INTERNATIONAL PRIZE FOR LITERATURE, "World Literature Today," University of Oklahoma, 110 Monnet Hall, Norman OK 73019-4033. (405)325-4531. Fax: (405)325-7495. Website: ou.edu/worldlit/. **Contact:** Prof. Robert Con Davis-Undiano, executive director. Offered every 2 years for outstanding achievement in fiction, poetry or drama. Nominations are made only by jurors for each prize. Prize: $40,000, a Silver Eagle Feather, an Award Certificate, and a special issue of *World Literature Today* is devoted to the writer and his/her work.

NEW MILLENNIUM WRITINGS AWARD, New Millennium Writings Journal, P.O. Box 2463, Knoxville TN 37901. (423)428-0389. Website: www.mach2.com/books or www.magamall.com. **Contact:** Don Williams, director. Offered twice annually for unpublished fiction, poetry, essays or nonfiction prose, to encourage new fiction writers, poets and essayists and bring them to attention of publishing industry. Deadline: January 31, June 15. Guidelines for SASE. Charges $15 fee. Entrants receive an issue of *NMW* in which winners appear. Prize: Fiction-$1,000; Poetry-$1,000; Essay or nonfiction prose-$1,000 and publication of winners and runners-up in *NMW* and at www.mach2.com, 25 honorable mentions listed.

NEW WRITERS AWARDS, Great Lakes Colleges Association New Writers Awards, English Dept., Denison University, Granville OH 43023. (740)587-5740. Fax: (740)587-5680. E-mail: krumholz@denison.edu. Website: www.glca.org. **Contact:** Prof. Linda Krumholz, award director. Offered annually to the best first book of poetry and the best first book of fiction among those submitted by publishers. Deadline: February 28. Guidelines for SASE. Prizes: Winning authors tour the GLCA colleges, where they will participate in whatever activities they and the college deem appropriate. An honorarium of at least $300 will be guaranteed the author by each of the colleges they visit. Open to any first book of poetry or fiction submitted by a publisher.

[N] NEW YORK UNIVERSITY PRESS PRIZES IN FICTION AND POETRY, New York University Press, 70 Washington Sq. S., New York NY 10012. (212)998-2575. Fax: (212)995-3833. E-mail: nyupress.info@nyu.edu. Website: www.nyupress.nyu.edu. Offered annually for unpublished writers "to support innovative, experimental and important fiction and poetry by authors whose work either has not yet appeared in book form or who remain unrecognized relative to the quality and ambition of their writing." Guidelines for SASE. Prizes: Publication of the work by New York University Press plus a $1,000 honorarium for both the fiction and poetry winners. Open to any writer.

NIMROD, The University of Tulsa, 600 S. College, Tulsa OK 74104-3189. (918)631-3080. Fax: (918)631-3033. E-mail: nimrod@utulsa.edu. Website: www.utulsa.edu/nimrod.html. **Contact:** Francine Ringold, editor. Offered annually for unpublished fiction and poetry for Katherine Anne Porter Prize for Fiction and Pablo Neruda Prize for Poetry. Theme issue in the spring. *Nimrod*/Hardman Awards issue in the fall. For contest or theme issue guidelines send SASE. Deadline: April 20. Charges $20 fee, includes 2 issues. Prize: 1st-$2,000 in each genre, 2nd-$1,000. Open to any writer.

OHIOANA BOOK AWARDS, Ohioana Library Association, 65 S. Front St., Room 1105, Columbus OH 43215. (614)466-3831. Fax: (614)728-6974. E-mail: ohioana@winslo.state.oh.us. Website: www.oplin.lib.oh.us/OHIOANA. **Contact:** Linda Hengst, director. Offered annually to bring national attention to Ohio authors and their books. Categories: fiction, nonfiction, juvenile, poetry, and books about Ohio or an Ohioan. Deadline: December 31. Guidelines for SASE. Writers must have been born in Ohio or lived in Ohio for at least 5 years.

KENNETH PATCHEN COMPETITION, Pig Iron Press, P.O. Box 237, Youngstown OH 44501. (330)747-6932. Fax: (330)747-0599. **Contact:** Jim Villani. Offered biannually for unpublished poetry or fiction (except for individual works published in magazines/journals). Alternates between poetry and fiction. Deadline: December 31. Guidelines for SASE. Charges $10 fee. Prize: trade paperback publication in an edition of 1,000 copies, 20 copies to author, and $500.

PEN CENTER USA WEST ANNUAL LITERARY AWARDS, PEN Center USA West, 672 S. Lafayette Park Place, #41, Los Angeles CA 90057. (213)365-8500. Fax: (213)365-9616. E-mail: pen@pen-usa-west.org. Website: www.pen-usa-west.org. **Contact:** Christina L. Apeles, awards coordinator. Offered annually for fiction, nonfiction, poetry, children's literature, translation published January 1-December 31 of the current year. Deadline: December 31. Charges $20 fee. Send SASE for guidelines or access. Prize: $1,000. Open to authors west of the Mississippi River.

N PEN WRITING AWARDS FOR PRISONERS, PEN American Center, 568 Broadway, New York NY 10012. (212)334-1660. Fax: (212)334-2181. E-mail: pen@echonyc.com. Website: www.pen.org. **Contact:** Jackson Taylor, coordinator. Offered annually to the authors of the best poetry, plays, short fiction and nonfiction received from prison writers in the US. Guidelines for SASE. Deadline: September 1. Prizes: 1st-$200; 2nd-$100; 3rd-$50 (in each category).

POSTCARD STORY COMPETITION, The Writers' Union of Canada, 24 Ryerson Ave., Toronto, Ontario M5T 2P3 Canada. (416)703-8982. Fax: (416)703-0826. E-mail: twuc@the-wire.com. Website: www.swifty.com/twuc. **Contact:** Cindy Newton. Offered annually for original and unpublished fiction, nonfiction, prose, verse, dialogue, etc. with a maximum 250 words in length. Deadline: February 14. Guidelines for SASE. Charges $5/entry fee. Prize: $500. Open to Canadian citizens or landed immigrants only.

THE PRESIDIO LA BAHIA AWARD, Sons of the Republic of Texas, 1717 Eighth St., Bay City TX 77414. Phone/ fax: (409)245-6644. E-mail: srttexas@srttexas.org. Website: www.srttexas.org. Offered annually "to promote suitable preservation of relics, appropriate dissemination of data, and research into our Texas heritage, with particular attention to the Spanish Colonial period." Deadline: June 1-September 30. Guidelines for SASE. Prize: $2,000 total; 1st-minimum of $1,200, 2nd and 3rd prizes at the discretion of the judges.

N QUINCY WRITER'S GUILD ANNUAL CREATIVE WRITING CONTEST, Quincy Writer's Guild, P.O. Box 433, Quincy IL 62306-0433. **Contact:** Contest Coordinator. Categories include serious poetry, light poetry, nonfiction, fiction. Deadline: January 1. Charges $2/poem; $4/fiction or nonfiction. "No identification should appear on manuscripts, but send a separate 3×5 card attached to each entry with name, address, phone number, word count, and title of work." Offered for previously unpublished work: serious or light poetry (2 page/poem maximum), fiction (3,000 words maximum), nonfiction (2,000 words maximum). Deadline: January 1-April 1. Guidelines for SASE or by e-mail at chillerbr@adams.net. Cash prizes.

QWF LITERARY AWARDS, (formerly QSPELL), Quebec Writers' Federation, 1200 Atwater Ave., Montreal, Quebec H3Z 1X4 Canada. (514)933-0878. Fax: (514)934-2485. E-mail: qspell@total.net. Website: www.qwf.org. **Contact:** Diana McNeill. Offered annually for work published October 1-September 30 to honor excellence in English-language writing in Quebec. Categories—fiction, nonfiction, poetry and First Book and translation. Deadline: May 31 and August 15 for finished proofs. Guidelines for SASE. Charges $10/title. Prize: $2,000 in each category; $1,000-First Book. Author must have resided in Quebec for 3 of the past 5 years.

SUMMERFIELD G. ROBERTS AWARD, Sons of the Republic of Texas, 1717 Eighth St., Bay City TX 77414. Phone/fax: (409)245-6644. E-mail: srttexas@srttexas.org. Website: www.srttexas.org. Offered annually for submissions published during the previous calendar year "to encourage literary effort and research about historical events and personalities during the days of the Republic of Texas, 1836-1846, and to stimulate interest in the period." Deadline: January 15. Guidelines for SASE. Prize: $2,500.

BRUCE P. ROSSLEY LITERARY AWARD, 96 Inc., P.O. Box 15558, Boston MA 02215. (617) 267-0543. Fax: (617)262-3568. E-mail: to96inc@ici.net. **Contact:** Vera Gold. Offered in even years to give greater recognition to a writer of merit. In addition to writing, accomplishments in the fields of teaching and community service are considered. Deadline: September 30. Nominations accepted August 1-September 30. Guidelines for SASE. Charges $10 fee. Prize: $1,000. Any writer may be nominated, but the focus is merit and those writers who have been under-recognized.

SHORT GRAIN WRITING CONTEST, Grain Magazine, P.O. Box 1154, Regina Saskatchewan S4P 3B4 Canada. (306)244-2828. Fax: (306)244-0255. E-mail: grain.mag@sk.sympatico.ca. Website: www.skwriter.com. Contest Director: Elizabeth Philips. **Contact:** Jennifer Still. Offered annually for unpublished dramatic monologues, postcard stories (narrative fiction) and prose (lyric) poetry and nonfiction creative prose. Maximum length for short entries: 500 words; Long Grain of Truth (nonfiction), 5,000 words or less. Deadline: January 31. Guidelines for SAE and IRC or Canadian stamps. Charges $22 fee for 2 entries, plus $5 for additional entries; US and international entries: $22, plus $4 postage in US funds (non-Canadian). Prizes: all categories 1st-$500, 2nd-$250, 3rd-$125. All entrants receive a one year subscription to *Grain*. *Grain* purchases first Canadian serial rights only; copyright remains with the author. Open to any writer. No fax or e-mail submissions.

◆ SHORT PROSE COMPETITION FOR DEVELOPING WRITERS, The Writers' Union of Canada, 24 Ryerson Ave., Toronto, Ontario M5T 2P3 Canada. (416)703-8982, ext. 223. Fax: (416)703-0826. E-mail: twuc@the-wire.com. Website: www.swifty.com/twuc. **Contact:** Cindy Newton, competition administrator. Offered annually "to discover developing Canadian writers of unpublished prose fiction and nonfiction." Deadline: November 3. Guidelines for SASE. Length: 2,500 words max. Charges $25/entry fee. Prize: $2,500 and publication in *Books in Canada* (a Canadian literary journal). Open to Canadian citizens or landed immigrants who have not been published in book format and who do not currently have a contract with a publisher.

ℕ SONORA REVIEW ANNUAL LITERARY AWARDS, *Sonora Review*, English Department, University of Arizona, Tucson AZ 85721. E-mail: sonora@u.Arizona.edu. **Contact:** poetry, fiction or nonfiction editor. $250 Fiction Award given each Spring to the best previously unpublished short story. Deadline: December 1. Charges $10 or $12 one-year subscription fee. $250 Poetry Award given each Fall to the best previously unpublished poem. Four poems/5 page maximum submission. Deadline: December 1. Charges $10 or $12 one-year subscription fee. $150 nonfiction award given each fall to the best previously unpublished essay. Deadline: December 1. Charges $10 reading fee or $12 one-year subscription. For all awards, all entrants receive a copy of the issue in which the winning entry appears. No formal application form is required; regular submission guidelines apply. SASE required for return of ms. Guidelines for #10 SASE. For samples, send $6.

SOUTHWEST REVIEW AWARDS, Southern Methodist University, 307 Fondren Library West, P.O. Box 750374, Dallas TX 75275-0374. (214)768-1036. Fax: (214)768-1408. E-mail: swr@mail.smu.edu. **Contact:** Elizabeth Mills. "The $1,000 John H. McGinnis Memorial Award is given each year for fiction and nonfiction that has been published in the *Southwest Review* in the previous year. Stories or articles are not submitted directly for the award, but simply for publication in the magazine. The Elizabeth Matchett Stover Award, an annual prize of $200, is awarded to the author of the best poem or group of poems published in the magazine during the preceding year."

WALLACE STEGNER FELLOWSHIPS, Creative Writing Program, Stanford University, Dept. of English, Stanford CA 94305-2087. (650)723-2637. Fax: (650)723-3679. E-mail: gay.pierce@leland.stanford.edu. Website: www.stanford.edu/dept/english/cw/. **Contact:** Gay Pierce, program administrator. Offered annually for a two-year residency at Stanford for emerging writers to attend the Stegner workshop and writer under guidance of the creative writing faculty. Deadline: December 1. Guidelines available. Charges $40 fee. Prize: living stipend (currently $15,000/year) and required workshop tuition of $6,000/year.

THE DONNA J. STONE NATIONAL LITERARY AWARDS, American Mothers, Inc. and the Matthew J. Pascal Foundation, 301 Park Ave., New York NY 10022. Phone/fax: (212)755-2539. E-mail: infor@americanmothers.org. Website: www.pascalfoundation.org/donnajstone/html. **Contact:** Yavonne Bagwell, literature chair, American Mothers, Inc. Offered annually for unpublished work in three categories: poetry (any style, 100 lines or less), short story (2,500 words or less) and essay or article (2,500 words or less). Family themes suggested. Deadline: February 15. Guidelines for SASE. Charges $20 entry fee. Prizes: 1st-$400, 2nd-$100, honorable mentions in each category, plus publication in Donna J. Stone Literature Awards Booklet. Entrants must be a mother, and a member of American Mothers, Inc.

◆ SUB-TERRAIN MAGAZINE AWARDS, *Sub-Terrain Magazine*, 175 E. Broadway, #204A, Vancouver, British Columbia V5T 1W2 Canada. (604)876-8710. Fax: (604)879-2667. E-mail: subter@portal.ca. Website: www.anvilpress.com. **Contact:** Brian Kaufman, managing editor. Offered annually for nonfiction, poems, short stories and photography. Contests include the Sub-Terrain Creative Nonfiction Writing Contest, The Not Quite the Cover of the Rolling Stone Award, Last Poems Poetry Contest and Annual Short Story Contest. Deadlines vary. Charges $15 fee including a subscription to magazine. Prize: Cash and publication. The magazine acquires one-time rights only; after publication rights revert to the author.

WESTERN HERITAGE AWARDS, National Cowboy Hall of Fame & Western Heritage Center, 1700 NE 63rd, Oklahoma City OK 73111. (405)478-2250, ext. 221. Fax: (405)478-4714. E-mail: editor@cowboyhalloffame.org. Website: www.cowboyhalloffame.org. **Contact:** M.J. VanDeventer, publications director. Offered annually for excellence in representation of great stories of the American West published January 1-December 31. Competition includes seven literary categories: Nonfiction; Western Novel; Juvenile Book; Art Book; Short Story; Poetry Book; and Magazine Article. Deadline: November 30.

ℕ ◆ WESTERN MAGAZINE AWARDS, Western Magazine Awards Foundation, Main Post Office, Box 2131, Vancouver, British Columbia V6B 3T8 Canada. (604)669-3717. Fax: (604)669-9920. **Contact:** Bryan Pike. Offered annually for magazine work published January 1-December 31 of previous calendar year. Entry categories include business, culture, science, technology and medicine, entertainment, fiction, political issues, and much more. Write or phone for rules and entry forms. Deadline: February 1. Entry fee: $27 for work in magazines with circulation under 20,000; $35 for work in magazines with circulation over 20,000. Prize: $500. Applicant must be Canadian citizen, landed immigrant, or fulltime resident of Canada. The work must have been published in a magazine whose main editorial office is in Western Canada, the Northwest Territories and Yukon.

N **⚑** **WINNERS' CIRCLE INTERNATIONAL WRITING CONTEST**, Canadian Authors Association, Metropolitan Toronto Branch, 33 Springbank Ave., Scarborough, Ontario M1N 1G2 Canada. Phone/fax: (416)698-8687. E-mail: caamtb@inforamp.net. Website: www3.sympatico.ca/gerry.penrose/tacob7. **Contact:** Bill Belfontaine. Offered annually to encourage new short stories and personal essays which help authors to get published. Charges $20, $10 from each entry can be used to discount cost of $115 plus GST for new memberships in the Canadian Authors Association. Prizes: Grand Prize-$1,000, 1st-$250, 2nd-$100, 3rd $50 and 5 honorary mention winners in short stories and same for essays. Winners of cash prizes and honorary mentions published in Winners' Circle Anthology. Deadline: July 1-November 30. First publishing rights required but copyright owned by writer. SAE plus 90 cents postage for "How to Write a Short Story" or "How to Write a Good Essay" booklet. Registration and rules only, send SASE.

WOMEN'S EMPOWERMENT AWARDS WRITING COMPETITION, E.F.S. Enterprises, Inc., 2844 Eighth Ave., Suite 6E, New York NY 10039. (212)283-8899. Website: www.efs-enterprises.com. **Contact:** Zeretha Jenkins, competition director. Offered annually for unpublished work by female writers in 3 categories (fiction, essays, playwriting) and designed to give female writers the opportunity to publish work online. Submissions must be unpublished, unproduced and not currently under option. Applications and guidelines are required and are available upon request with SASE. Submissions accepted with applications from September 1-October 31. Deadline: October 31. Charges $15 fee. Does not return mss. Prize: 1st-$100 and online publishing contract; 2nd-$50. Writers retain all rights. Open to any female writers. Authors do not have to be previously published.

N **WRITERS AT WORK FELLOWSHIP COMPETITION**, Writers at Work, P.O. Box 540370, North Salt Lake City UT 84054-0370. (801)292-9285. E-mail: w-at-w@hotmail.com. Website: www.ihi-env.com/watw.html. **Contact:** Maureen Clark. Offered annually for unpublished short stories, novel excerpts and poetry. Deadline: March 15. Guidelines for SASE. Charges $15 fee. Short stories or novel excerpts 20 double-spaced pages maximum; one story per entry. Poetry submissions limited to 6 poems, 10 pages maximum. No names on manuscript, please. Prize: $1,500, publication and partial conference tuition; $500, partial conference tuition.

Arts Councils & Foundations

ARIZONA COMMISSION OF THE ARTS FELLOWSHIP IN CREATIVE WRITING, Arizona Commission on the Arts, 417 W. Roosevelt, Phoenix AZ 85018. (602)255-5882. Fax: (602)256-0282. E-mail: general@ArizonaArts.org. Website: az.arts.asu.edu/artscomm. **Contact:** Jill Bernstein, literature director. Offered annually for previously published or unpublished fiction or poetry written within the last three years. Deadline: mid-September 2001 (fiction); September 14, 2000 (poetry). Prize: $5,000-7,500. Write, call or e-mail guideline request. Open to Arizona writers 18 years or older.

ARTIST ASSISTANCE FELLOWSHIP, Minnesota State Arts Board, Park Square Court, 400 Sibley St., Suite 200, St. Paul MN 55101-1928. (651)215-1600 or (800)866-2787. Fax: (651)215-1602. E-mail: msab@state.mn.us. Website: www.arts.state.mn.us. **Contact:** Artist Assistance Program Associate, (651)215-1607. Annual fellowships of $8,000 to be used for time, materials, living expenses. Literary categories include prose, poetry, playwriting and screenwriting. Open to Minnesota residents. Deadline: early Fall—call for deadline dates.

N **ARTIST FELLOWSHIP**, Connecticut Commission on the Arts, 755 Main St., Hartford CT 06103. (860)566-4770. Fax: (860)566-6462. Website: www.cs/net/ctstateu.edu/cca/. **Contact:** Linda Dente, senior program manager. Offered every 2 years for previously published or unpublished work to assist in the development and encouragement of Connecticut writers of substantial talent. Deadline: September 18, 2000. Guidelines for SASE. Prize: $2,500 or $5,000. Must be residents of CT for one or more years. Cannot be a student.

ARTIST FELLOWSHIP AWARDS, Wisconsin Arts Board, 101 E. Wilson St. 1st Floor, Madison WI 53702. (608)266-0190. Fax: (608)267-0380. E-mail: artsboard@arts.state.wi.us. Website: www.arts.state.wi.us. **Contact:** Mark Fraire, director. Offered every 2 years, rewrding outstanding, professionally active Wisconsin artists by supporting their continued development, enabling them to create new work, complete work in progress, or pursue activities which contribute to their artistic growth. Deadline: September 15th. If the deadline falls on a weekend, the deadline is extended to the following Monday. Contact the Arts Board for an application and guidelines. Prize: $8,000 fellowship awarded to eight Wisconsin writers. The Arts Board requires permission to use the work sample, or a portion thereof, for publicity or educational purposes. Contest open to professionally active artists who have resided in Wisconsin 1 year prior to application. Artists who are full-time students pursuing a degree in the fine arts at the time of application are not eligible.

ARTISTS FELLOWSHIP, Japan Foundation, 39th Floor, 152 W. 57th St., New York NY 10019. (212)489-0299. Fax: (212)489-0409. E-mail: yuika_goto@jfny.org. Website: www.jfny.org/. **Contact:** Yuika Goto. Offered annually. Deadline: December 1. "Contact us in September by mail or fax. Keep in mind that this is an international competition. Due to the breadth of the application pool only four artists are selected for awards in the US. Applicants need not submit a writing sample, but if one is submitted it must be brief. Three letters of recommendation must be submitted from peers. One letter will double as a letter of affiliation, which must be submitted by a *Japan-based* (not necessarily an ethnic Japanese) peer artist. The applicant must present a concise and cogent project objective and must be a professional writer/artist with accessible qualifications, i.e., a list of major works or publications."

ARTISTS' FELLOWSHIPS, New York Foundation for the Arts, 155 Avenue of the Americas, New York NY 10013-1507. (212)366-6900 ext. 217. Fax: (212)366-1778. Website: www.nyfa.org. **Contact:** Artists' Fellowships. "Artists' Fellowships are cash grants of $7,000 awarded in 16 disciplines on a biannual rotation. Nonfiction Literature and Poetry will be the literature disciplines under review in 2000-2001. Fiction and Playwriting will be reviewed in 2001-2002. Awards are based upon the recommendations of peer panels and are not project support. The fellowship may be used by each recipient as she/he sees fit. Call for application in July. Deadlines in October. Results announced in April. The New York Foundation for the Arts supports artists at all stages of their careers and from diverse backgrounds." All applicants must be 18 years of age and a New York resident for two years prior to the time of application.

ARTS RECOGNITION AND TALENT SEARCH, National Foundation for Advancement in the Arts, 800 Brickell Ave., Suite 500, Miami FL 33131. (305)377-1140 or (800)970-ARTS. Fax: (305)377-1149. E-mail: nfaapr@aol.com. Website: www.ARTSawards.org. **Contact:** Sonja Romany, communications coordinator or Elizabeth Estefan. Estab. 1981. For achievements in dance, music (classical, jazz and vocal), photography, theater, film & videos, visual arts and writing. Students fill in and return the application, available at every public and private high school around the nation, for cash awards of up to $3,000 each and scholarship opportunities worth more than $3 million. Deadline: early—June 1, regular—October 1. Charges $25 registration fee for June; $35 for October.

GEORGE BENNETT FELLOWSHIP, Phillips Exeter Academy, 20 Main St., Exeter NH 03833-2460. Website: www.exeter.edu. **Contact:** Charles Pratt, coordinator, selection committee. Estab. 1968. Annual award of $6,000 stipend, room and board for Fellow and family "to provide time and freedom from material considerations to a person seriously contemplating or pursuing a career as a writer. Applicants should have a manuscript in progress which they intend to complete during the fellowship period." Guidelines for SASE or on website. The committee favors writers who have not yet published a book with a major publisher. Deadline: December 1. Charges $5 fee. Residence at the Academy during the Fellowship period required.

BUSH ARTIST FELLOWS PROGRAM, The Bush Foundation, E-900 First National Bank Bldg., 332 Minnesota St., St. Paul MN 55101. (651)227-5222. **Contact:** Kathi Polley. Estab. 1976. Award for Minnesota, North Dakota, South Dakota, and western Wisconsin residents 25 years or older (students are not eligible) "to buy 12-18 months of time for the applicant to further his/her own work." Up to 15 fellowships/year, $40,000 each. Deadline: October. All application categories rotate on a two year cycle. Literature (fiction, creative nonfiction, poetry) and scriptworks (playwriting, screenwriting) will be offered next for the 2001 fellowships. Publishing, performance and/or option requirements for eligibility. Applications available August 2000.

ChLA RESEARCH FELLOWSHIPS & SCHOLARSHIPS, Children's Literature Association, P.O. Box 138, Battle Creek MI 49016-0138. (616)965-8180. Fax: (616)965-3568. E-mail: chla@mlc.lib.mi.us. Website: ebbs.english.vt.edu/chla. **Contact:** ChLA Scholarship Chair. Offered annually. "The fellowships are available for proposals dealing with criticism or original scholarship with the expectation that the undertaking will lead to publication and make a significant contribution to the field of children's literature in the area of scholarship or criticism." Deadline: February 1. Guidelines for SASE. Prize: $250-1,000. Funds are not intended for work leading to the completion of a professional degree.

DOCTORAL DISSERTATION FELLOWSHIPS IN JEWISH STUDIES, National Foundation for Jewish Culture, 330 7th Ave., 21st Floor, New York NY 10001. (212)629-0500, ext. 205. Fax: (212)629-0508. E-mail: kbistrong@jewishculture.org. Website: www.jewishculture.org. **Contact:** Kim Bistrong, grants administrator. Offered annually to students. Deadline varies, usually early January. Guidelines for SASE. Prize: $7,000-$10,000 grant. Open to students who have completed their course work and need funding for research in order to write their dissertation thesis or a Ph.D. in a Jewish field of study.

N FELLOWSHIP, William Morris Society in the US, P.O. Box 53263, Washington DC 20009. E-mail: biblio@aol.com. Website: www.ccny.cuny.edu/wmorris/morris.html. **Contact:** Mark Samuels Lasner. Offered annually "to promote study of the life and work of William Morris (1834-96), British poet, designer and socialist. Award may be for research or a creative project." Deadline: December 1. Curriculum vitae, 1-page proposal and two letters of recommendation required for application. Prize: up to $1,000, multiple, partial awards possible. Applicants must be US citizens or permanent residents.

FELLOWSHIP PROGRAM, New Jersey State Council on the Arts, 225 W. State St., P.O. Box 306, Trenton NJ 08625. (609)292-6130. Fax: (609)989-1440. Website: www.njartscouncil.org. **Contact:** Beth A. Vogel, program officer. Offered every other year. Writers may apply in either poetry, playwriting or prose. Fellowship awards are intended to provide support for the artist during the year to enable him or her to continue producing new work. Deadline: July 15. Send for guidelines and application. Awards: $5,000-12,000. Must be NJ residents; may *not* be undergraduate or graduate matriculating students.

N̄ FELLOWSHIP-LITERATURE, Alabama State Council on the Arts, 201 Monroe St., Montgomery AL 36130. (334)242-4076, ext. 224. Fax: (334)240-3269. **Contact:** Randy Shoults. Literature Fellowship offered every year, for previously published or unpublished work to set aside time to create and to improve skills. Two-year Alabama residency requirement. Deadline: March 1, 2000. Guidelines available. Prize: $10,000 or $5,000.

FELLOWSHIPS, DC Commission on the Arts & Humanities, 410 Eighth St. NW, Washington DC 20004. (202)724-5613. E-mail: dccah@erols.com. Website: www.capaccess.org/dccah. **Contact:** Sandra Maddox. Offered annually to reward excellence in an artistic endeavor. Deadline: early June, 2000. "Visit the website for updated deadline information and guidelines." Prize: $2,500. Writers must be residents of the District of Columbia for at least one year prior to application date.

FELLOWSHIPS FOR CREATIVE WRITERS, National Endowment for the Arts Literature Program, 1100 Pennsylvania Ave. NW, Washington DC 20506. (202)682-5428. Website: arts.endow.gov. **Contact:** Amy Stolls. Offered to published creative writers of exceptional talent. Deadline: Fiction/Creative Nonfiction, March 2001; poetry, call or write for guidelines in January 2002.

FELLOWSHIPS (LITERATURE), RI State Council on the Arts, 95 Cedar St., Suite 103, Providence RI 02903. (401)222-3883. Fax: (401)521-1351. E-mail: randy@risca.state.ri.us. Website: www.modcult.brown.edu/RISCA/. **Contact:** Randall Rosenbaum. Offered every two years for previously published or unpublished works of poetry, fiction, playwriting/screenwriting. Deadline: April 1, 1999. Guidelines for SASE. Prize: $5,000 fellowship; $1,000 runner-up. Open to Rhode Island residents only.

FELLOWSHIPS TO ASSIST RESEARCH AND ARTISTIC CREATION, John Simon Guggenheim Memorial Foundation, 90 Park Ave., New York NY 10016. (212)687-4470. Fax: (212)697-3248. E-mail: fellowships@gf.org. Website: www.gf.org. **Contact:** Patricia O'Sullivan. Offered annually to assist scholars and artists to engage in research in any field of knowledge and creation in any of the arts, under the freest possible conditions and irrespective of race, color, or creed. Application form is required. Deadline: October 1.

FLORIDA INDIVIDUAL ARTIST FELLOWSHIPS, Florida Department of State, Division of Cultural Affairs, The Capitol, Tallahassee FL 32399-0250. (850)487-2980. Fax: (850)922-5259. E-mail: vohlsson@mail.dos.state.fl.us. Website: www.dos.state.fl.us. **Contact:** Valerie Ohlsson, arts administrator. Prize: $5,000 each for fiction, poetry and children's literature. Open to Florida writers only. Deadline: February.

GAP (GRANTS FOR ARTIST PROJECTS); FELLOWSHIP, Artist Trust, 1402 Third Ave, Suite 404, Seattle WA 98101-2118. (206)467-8734. Fax: (206)467-9633. E-mail: info@artisttrust.org. **Contact:** Heather Dwyer, program director. "The GAP is awarded to 70 artists, including writers, per year. The award is meant to help finance a specific project, which can be in very early stages or near completion. Literature fellowships are offered every other year, and approximately six literature fellowships are awarded. The award is made on the basis of work of the past five years. It is 'no-strings-attached' funding." Guidelines for SASE. Prize: GAP: up to $1,200. Fellowship: $5,500. Fulltime students not eligible. Open to Washington state residents only.

HAWAI'I AWARD FOR LITERATURE, State Foundation on Culture and the Arts, 44 Merchant St., Honolulu HI 96813. (808)586-0306. Fax: (808)586-0308. E-mail: sfca@sfca.state.hi.us. Website: www.state.hi.us/sfca. **Contact:** Hawai'i Literary Arts Council (Box 11213, Honolulu HI 96828-0213). "The annual award honors the lifetime achievement of a writer whose work is important to Hawai'i and/or Hawai'i's people." Deadline: November. Nominations are a public process; inquiries should be directed to the Hawai'i Literary Arts Council at address listed. Prize: a governor's reception and cash award. "Cumulative work is considered. Self nominations are allowed, but not usual. Fiction, poetry, drama, certain types of nonfiction, screenwriting and song lyrics are considered. The award is not intended to recognize conventional academic writing and reportage, nor is it intended to recognize more commercial types of writing, e.g., advertising copy, tourist guides, and how-to manuals."

THE HODDER FELLOWSHIP, The Council of the Humanities, 122 E. Pyne, Princeton University, Princeton NJ 08544. (609)258-4713. Fax: (609)258-2783. E-mail: humcounc@princeton.edu. Website: www.princeton.edu/~humcounc/. **Contact:** Cass Garner. The Hodder Fellowship is awarded to a humanist in the early stages of a career for the pursuit of independent work at Princeton in the humanities. The recipient has usually written one book and is working on a second. Preference is given to applicants outside of academia. "The Fellowship is designed specifically to identify and nurture extraordinary potential rather than to honor distinguished achievement." Candidates for the Ph.D. are not eligible. Prize: approximately $45,600 stipend. Submit résumé, sample of work (up to 10 pages), proposal and SASE. Deadline: November 1.

INDIVIDUAL ARTIST FELLOWSHIP, Oregon Arts Commission, 775 Summer St. NE, Salem OR 97310. (503)986-0086. Fax: (503)986-0260. E-mail: michael.b.faison@state.or.us. Website: http://art.econ.state.or.us. **Contact:** Michael Faison, assistant director. Offered in even years to reward achievement in the field of literature. Deadline: September 1. Guidelines for SASE. Prize: $3,000. Writers must be Oregon residents, 18 years and older; degree candidate students not eligible.

INDIVIDUAL ARTISTS FELLOWSHIPS, Nebraska Arts Council, 3838 Davenport St., Omaha NE 68131-2329. (402)595-2122. Fax: (402)595-2334. Website: www.nebraskaartscouncil.org. **Contact:** Suzanne Wise. Estab. 1991. Offered every three years (literature alternates with other disciplines) to recognize exemplary achievements by originating artists in their fields of endeavor and supports the contributions made by Nebraska artists to the quality of life in this state. Deadline: November 15, 2002. "Generally, distinguished achievement awards are $5,000 and merit awards are $1,000-2,000. Funds available are announced in September prior to the deadline." Must be a resident of Nebraska for at least 2 years prior to submission date; 18 years of age; not enrolled in an undergraduate, graduate or certificate-granting program in English, creative writing, literature, or related field.

JOSEPH HENRY JACKSON AWARD, The San Francisco Foundation, Administered by Intersection for the Arts, 446 Valencia St., San Francisco CA 94103. (415)626-2787. Fax: (415)626-1636. E-mail: info@theintersection.org. **Contact:** Kevin B. Chen, program director. Estab. 1965. Offered annually for unpublished, work-in-progress fiction (novel or short story), nonfiction or poetry by author age 20-35, with 3-year consecutive residency in northern California or Nevada prior to submission. Deadline: November 15-January 31. Guidelines for SASE.

:N: ✂ JURIED PROGRAMS FOR ART PROFESSIONALS (all disciplines), New Brunswick Arts Board, P.O. Box 6000, Fredericton, New Brunswick E3B 5H1 Canada. (506)453-4307. Fax: (506)453-6043. **Contact:** Program Officer, New Brunswick Arts Board. Grants and awards programs: Excellence Awards, Creation, Documentation, Artist-in-Residence, NB Arts-by-Invitation and Arts Scholarships. Available to New Brunswick residents only. (Must have resided in New Brunswick 2 of past 4 years).

KENTUCKY ARTS COUNCILS FELLOWSHIPS IN WRITING, Kentucky Arts Council, Old Capitol Annex, 300 W. Broadway, Frankfort KY 40601. (502)564-3757 or toll free (888)833-2787. Fax: (502)564-2839. E-mail: lori.meadows@mail.state.ky.us. Website: www.kyarts.org. **Contact:** Lori Meadows. Offered in even-numbered years for development/artist's work. Deadline: September 15, 2000. Guidelines for SASE (3 months before deadline). Award: $5,000. Must be Kentucky resident.

WALTER RUMSEY MARVIN GRANT, Ohioana Library Association, 65 S. Front St., Suite 1105, Columbus OH 43215. (614)466-3831. Fax: (614)728-6974. E-mail: ohioana@winslo.state.oh.us. Website: www.oplin.lib.oh.us/ohioana. **Contact:** Linda Hengst, director. Offered annually. Deadline: January 31. Entries submitted may consist of up to 6 pieces of prose. No submission may total more than 60 pages or less than 10. No entries will be returned. Applicant must have been born in Ohio or have lived in Ohio for 5 years or more, must be 30 years of age or younger, and not have published a book.

MONEY FOR WOMEN, Barbara Deming Memorial Fund, Inc., P.O. Box 630125, The Bronx NY 10463. Contact: Susan Pliner. "Small grants to individual feminists in art, fiction, nonfiction and poetry, whose work addresses women's concerns and/or speaks for peace and justice from a feminist perspective." Deadlines: December 31 and June 30. Guidelines for SASE. Prize: grants up to $1,000: "The Fund does *not* give educational assistance, monies for personal study or loans, monies for dissertation, research projects, or self publication, grants for group projects, business ventures, or emergency funds for hardships." Open to citizens of the US or Canada.
  ● The fund also offers two awards, the "Gertrude Stein Award" for outstanding works by a lesbian and the "Fannie Lou Hamer Award" for work which combats racism and celebrates women of color. No special application necessary for these 2 awards. Recipients will be chosen from all the proposals.

LARRY NEAL WRITERS' COMPETITION, DC Commission on the Arts and Humanities, 410 Eighth St., NW 5th Floor, Washington DC 20004. (202)724-1475. Fax: (202)727-4135. E-mail: lionellt@hotmail.com. Website: www.capaccess.org/dccah. **Contact:** Lionell C. Thomas, grants and legislative officer. Offered annually for unpublished poetry, fiction, essay and dramatic writing. Call or visit website for current deadlines. Prize: cash awards. Open to Washington DC residents only.

NEW HAMPSHIRE INDIVIDUAL ARTISTS' FELLOWSHIPS, New Hampshire State Council on the Arts, 40 N. Main St., Concord NH 03301-4974. (603)271-2789. Fax: (603)271-3584. Website: www.state.nh.us/nharts. **Contact:** Audrey V. Sylvester. Estab. 1982. Offered to recognize artistic excellence and professional commitment. Literature eligible in 2000. Open only to New Hampshire residents 18 and older. No full-time students.

PEW FELLOWSHIPS IN THE ARTS, The University of the Arts, 230 S. Broad St., Suite 1003, Philadelphia PA 19102. (215)875-2285. Fax: (215)875-2276. Website: www.pewarts.org. **Contact:** Melissa Franklin, director. Offered annually to provide financial support directly to artists so that they may have the opportunity to dedicate themselves wholly to the development of their artwork for up to two years. Areas of interest have included fiction, creative nonfiction, poetry, playwriting and screenwriting. Deadline: December. Call for guidelines or view from the website. Prize: $50,000 fellowship. Open only to Pennsylvania residents 25 or older of Bucks, Chester, Delaware, Montgomery or Philadelphia counties for two years or longer. Current students are not eligible.

JAMES D. PHELAN LITERARY AWARD, The San Francisco Foundation, administered by Intersection for the Arts, 446 Valencia St., San Francisco CA 94103. (415)626-2787. Fax: (415)626-1636. E-mail: info@theintersection.org. **Contact:** Kevin B. Chen, program director. Estab. 1965. Offered annually for unpublished, work-in-progress fiction, nonfiction, short story, poetry or drama by California-born author age 20-35. Deadline: November 15-January 31. Guidelines for SASE.

REQUEST FOR PROPOSAL, Rhode Island State Council on the Arts, Suite 103, 95 Cedar St., Providence RI 02903. (401)277-3880. Fax: (401)521-1351. E-mail: randy@risca.state.ri.us. Website: www.risca.state.ri.us. **Contact:** Randall Rosenbaum, executive director. "Request for Proposal grants enable an artist to create new work and/or complete works-in-progress by providing direct financial assistance. By encouraging significant development in the work of an individual artist, these grants recognize the central contribution artists make to the creative environment of Rhode Island." Deadline: October 1 and April 1. Guidelines for 9×12 SASE. Prize: non-matching grants of $1,500-4,000. Open only to Rhode Island residents, age 18 or older; students not eligible.

SEATTLE ARTISTS PROGRAM, Seattle Arts Commission, 312 First Ave. N., 2nd Floor, Seattle WA 98109. (206)684-7171. Fax: (206)684-7172. Project Manager: Irene Gomez. Offered every 2 years. Next literary deadline will be in 2000. The Seattle Artists Program commissions new works by emerging, mid-career or established individual artists based in Seattle. Literary and performing arts disciplines are funded in alternating years. Award amounts are $7,500 and $2,000. Decided through open, competitive peer-panel review process and subject to approval by the full Commission. Applicants must be residents of or maintain studio space in the city of Seattle, Washington. Guidelines available in May with an application deadline on July 4.

STUDENT RESEARCH GRANT, the Society for the Scientific Study of Sexuality, Box 208, Mount Vernon IA 52314. (319)895-8407. Fax: (319)895-6203. E-mail: thesociety@worldnet.att.net. Website: www.ssc.wisc.edu/ssss. **Contact:** Howard J. Ruppel, executive director. Offered twice a year for unpublished works. "The student research grant award is granted twice yearly to help support graduate student research on a variety of sexually related topics." Deadline: February 1 and September 1. Guidelines and entry forms for SASE. Prize: $750. Open to students pursuing graduate study.

N **☑** **TRILLIUM BOOK AWARD/PRIX TRILLIUM**, Ontario Ministry of Citizenship, Culture and Recreation, 400 University Ave., 5th Floor, Toronto, Ontario M7A 2R9 Canada. (416)314-7745. Fax: (416)314-7460. Website: www.gov.on.ca/MCZCR. **Contact:** Edward Yanofsky, cultural industries officer. Offered annually for work previously published January 1-December 31. This is the Ontario government's annual literary award. There are 2 categories—an English language category and a French language category. Deadline: mid-December. Publishers submit books on behalf of authors. Prize: the winning author in each category receives $12,000; the winning publisher is each category receives $2,500. Authors must be an Ontario resident three of the last five years.

UCROSS FOUNDATION RESIDENCY, 30 Big Red Lane, Clearmont WY 82835. (307)737-2291. Fax: (307)737-2322. E-mail: ucross@wyoming.com. **Contact:** Sharon Dynak, executive director. Eight concurrent positions open for artists-in-residence in various disciplines (includes writers, visual artists, music, humanities) extending from 2 weeks-2 months. No charge for room, board or studio space. Deadline: March 1 for August-December program; October 1 for February-June program.

VERMONT ARTS COUNCIL, 136 State St., Drawer 33, Montpelier VT 05633-6001. (802)828-3291. Fax: (802)828-3363. E-mail: info@arts.vca.state.vt.us. Website: www.state.vt.us/vermont-arts. **Contact:** Michele Bailey. Offered quarterly for previously published or unpublished works. Opportunity Grants are for specific projects of writers (poetry, playwriters, fiction, nonfiction) as well as not-for-profit presses. Also available are Artist Development funds to provide technical assistance for VT Writers. Write or call for entry information. Prize: $250-5,000. Open to VT residents only.

WRITERS FELLOWSHIPS, NC Arts Council, Dept. of Cultural Resources, Raleigh NC 27601-2807. (919)733-2111, ext. 22. E-mail: dmcgill@ncacmail.dcr.state.nc.us. Website: www.ncarts.org. Literature Director: Deborah McGill. Offered every two years. "To serve writers of fiction, poetry, literary nonfiction and literary translation in North Carolina and to recognize the contribution they make to this state's creative environment." Deadline: November 1, 2000. Write for guidelines. We offer eleven $8,000 grants every two years. Writer must have been a resident of NC for at least a year and may not be enrolled in any degree-granting program at the time of application.

Are You Ready to Write Better and Get Paid For What You Write?

At **Writer's Digest School,** we want you to have both a "flair for words" *and* the marketing know-how it takes to give your writing the best shot at publication. That's why you'll work with a professional, published writer who has already mastered the rules of the game firsthand. A savvy mentor who can show you, through detailed critiques of the writing assignments you send in, how to effectively target your work and get it into the hands of the right editor.

Whether you write articles or short stories, nonfiction or novels, **Writer's Digest School** has a course that's right for you. Each provides a wealth of expertise and one goal: helping you break into the writing market.

So if you're serious about getting published, you owe it to yourself to check out **Writer's Digest School**. To find out more about us, simply fill out and return the card below. There's absolutely no obligation!

Course descriptions on the back ➡

Send Me Free Information!

I want to write better and sell more with the help of the professionals at **Writer's Digest School**. Send me free information about the course I've checked below:

☐ Novel Writing Workshop   ☐ Writing & Selling Short Stories

☐ Writing & Selling Nonfiction Articles   ☐ Writing Your Life Stories

☐ Writer's Digest Criticism Service   ☐ The Elements of Effective Writing

☐ Getting Started in Writing   ☐ Marketing Your Nonfiction Book

                                         ☐ Screenwriting Workshop

Name _____

Address _____

City _____ State _____ ZIP _____

Phone: (Day) (_____)_____ (Eve.) (_____)_____

Email Address _____

To get your package even sooner, call 1-800-759-0963
Outside the U.S. call 1-513-531-2690 ext. 342

IWMXX1X1

Novel Writing Workshop: Iron out your plot, create your main characters, develop a dramatic background, and complete the opening scenes and summary of your novel's complete story. Plus, you'll pinpoint potential publishers for your type of book.

NEW! **Getting Started in Writing:** From short fiction and novels to articles and nonfiction books, we'll help you discover where your natural writing talents lie.

Writing & Selling Short Stories: Learn how to create believable characters, write vivid, true-to-life dialogue, fill your scenes with conflict, and keep your readers on the edge of their seats.

Writing & Selling Nonfiction Articles: Master the components for effective article writing and selling. You'll learn how to choose attention-grabbing topics, conduct stirring interviews, write compelling query letters, and slant a single article for a variety of publications.

Writing Your Life Stories: Learn how to weave the important events of your personal or family's history into a heartfelt story. You'll plan a writing strategy, complete a dateline of events, and discover how to combine factual events with narrative flow.

Writer's Digest Criticism Service: Have an experienced, published writer review your manuscripts before you submit them for pay. Whether you write books, articles, short stories or poetry, you'll get professional, objective feedback on what's working well, what needs strengthening, and which markets you should pursue.

The Elements of Effective Writing: Discover how to conquer the pesky grammar and usage problems that hold so many writers back. You'll refresh your basic English composition skills through step-by-step lessons and writing exercises designed to help keep your manuscripts out of the rejection pile.

Marketing Your Nonfiction Book: You'll work with your mentor to create a book proposal that you can send directly to a publisher, develop and refine your book idea, write a chapter-by-chapter outline of your subject, line up your sources and information, write sample chapters, and complete your query letter.

Screenwriting Workshop: Learn to write for the silver screen! Work step by step with a professional screenwriter to craft your script, find out how to research the right agent or producer for your work, and get indispensable information about the Hollywood submission process.

More Great Books to Help You Sell Your Work!

Latest Edition! **2001 Novel & Short Story Writer's Market**
edited by Barbara Kuroff
Discover buyers hungry for your work! You'll find the names, addresses, pay rates and editorial needs of thousands of fiction publishers. Plus, loads of helpful articles and informative interviews with professionals who know what it takes to get published!
#10682/$24.99/688 p/pb *Available December 2000*

Totally Updated! **2001 Guide to Literary Agents**
edited by Donya Dickerson
Enhance your chances of publishing success by teaming up with an agent! You'll find more than 500 listings of literary and script agents, plus valuable information about how to choose the right agent to represent your work.
#10684/$21.99/368 p/pb *Available December 2000*

The Insider's Guide to Getting an Agent
by Lori Perkins
In today's fast-paced publishing industry, getting an agent is crucial—but where do you begin to find one that's right for you? Lori Perkins takes the mystery out of finding an agent by providing an industry overview, explaining the role and responsibilities of an agent, then guiding you through researching and contacting an agent.
#10630/$16.99/240 p/pb

Formatting & Submitting Your Manuscript
This easy-to-use guide offers dozens of charts, lists, models and sidebars to show you exactly what it takes to successfully submit your work. You'll find information on creating effective query letters, proposals, outlines, synopses and follow-up correspondence.
#10618/$18.99/208 p/pb

The Writer's Market Companion
by Joe Feiertag and Mary Carmen Cupito
This "how-to" guide provides solutions and guidelines for all your professional writing needs. An easy-to-reference format features crucial information, including lists, forms, sample letters and pricing guides you can use to get published.
#10653/$19.99/272 p/pb

The Writer's Online Marketplace
by Debbie Ridpath Ohi
Learn how to sell your fiction, reviews, nonfiction, poetry and just about any other type of writing on the Web. This guide has over 250 paying online markets, plus advice on the unique marketing and writing techniques needed to succeed in the online writing world. Discover what online markets are hot, how to write online queries — with examples of successful queries, copyright basics for the electronic market, what to look for in contracts and more.
#10697/$17.99/288 p/pb *Available October 2000*

Guerrilla Marketing for Writers
100 No-Cost, Low Cost Weapons to Help you Sell Your Work
by Jay Conrad Levinson, Rick Frishman and Michael Larsen
Packed with proven insights and techniques, this practical manual arms you with the tools needed to sell your book. You'll learn effective marketing techniques, including networking, using the media to generate free publicity, using the internet, getting the most from conferences and festivals, and more.
#10667/$14.99/224 p/pb *Available October 2000*

Order these helpful references today from your local bookstore, or use the handy order card on the reverse side.

Resources

Publications

In addition to newsletters and publications from local and national organizations, there are trade publications, books, and directories which offer valuable information about writing and about marketing your manuscripts and understanding the business side of publishing. Some also list employment agencies that specialize in placing publishing professionals, and some announce actual freelance opportunities.

TRADE MAGAZINES

ADVERTISING AGE, Crain Communications Inc., 740 N. Rush St., Chicago IL 60611. (312)649-5200. *Weekly magazine covering advertising in magazines, trade journals and business.*

AMERICAN JOURNALISM REVIEW, 2116 Journalism Bldg. University of Maryland, College Park MD 20742-7111. (301)405-8803. *10 issues/year magazine for journalists and communications professionals.*

DAILY VARIETY, Daily Variety Ltd./Cahners Publishing Co., 5700 Wilshire Blvd., Suite 120, Los Angeles CA 90036. (323)857-6600. *Trade publication on the entertainment industry, with helpful information for screenwriters.*

EDITOR & PUBLISHER, The Editor & Publisher Co., 11 W. 19th St., New York NY 10011. (212)675-4380. *Weekly magazine covering the newspaper publishing industry.*

FOLIO:, Cowles Business Media, 11 Riverbend Dr. South, P.O. Box 4272, Stamford CT 06907-0272. (203)358-9900. *Monthly magazine covering the magazine publishing industry.*

GIFTS & DECORATIVE ACCESSORIES, Cahners Publishing Co., 345 Hudson St., 4th Floor, New York NY 10014. (212)519-7200. *Monthly magazine covering greeting cards among other subjects, with an annual buyer's directory in September.*

HORN BOOK MAGAZINE, 56 Roland St., Suite 200, Boston MA 02129. (617)628-0225. *Bimonthly magazine covering children's literature.*

PARTY & PAPER RETAILER, 4 Ward Corp., 70 New Canaan Ave., Norwalk CT 06850. (203)730-4090. *Monthly magazine covering the greeting card and gift industry.*

POETS & WRITERS INC., 72 Spring St., New York NY 10012. (212)226-3586. *Bimonthly magazine, primarily for literary writers and poets.*

PUBLISHERS WEEKLY, Bowker Magazine Group, Cahners Publishing Co., 245 W. 17th St., New York NY 10011. (212)645-0067. *Weekly magazine covering the book publishing industry.*

SCIENCE FICTION CHRONICLE, P.O. Box 022730, Brooklyn NY 11202-0056. (718)643-9011. Website: http://www.sfsite.com/sfc. *Monthly magazine for science fiction, fantasy and horror writers.*

TRAVELWRITER MARKETLETTER, The Waldorf-Astoria, 301 Park Ave., Suite 1880, New York NY 10022. *Monthly newsletter for travel writers with market listings as well as trip information.*

THE WRITER, 120 Boylston St., Boston MA 02116. (617)423-3157. *Monthly writers' magazine.*

WRITER'S DIGEST, 1507 Dana Ave., Cincinnati OH 45207. (800)888-6880. *Monthly writers' magazine.*

BOOKS AND DIRECTORIES

AV MARKET PLACE, R.R. Bowker, A Reed Reference Publishing Co., 121 Chanlon Rd., New Providence NJ 07974. (908)464-6800.

BACON'S NEWSPAPER & MAGAZINE DIRECTORIES, Bacon's Information Inc., 332 S. Michigan Ave., Chicago IL 60604. (312)922-2400.

THE COMPLETE BOOK OF SCRIPTWRITING, by J. Michael Straczynski, Writer's Digest Books, 1507 Dana Ave., Cincinnati OH 45207. (800)289-0963.

THE COMPLETE GUIDE TO LITERARY CONTESTS, compiled by Literary Fountain, Prometheus Books, 59 John Glenn Dr., Amherst NY 14228-2197. (716)691-0133.

THE COMPLETE GUIDE TO SELF PUBLISHING, by Marilyn and Tom Ross, Writer's Digest Books, 1507 Dana Ave., Cincinnati OH 45207. (800)289-0963.

DRAMATISTS SOURCEBOOK, edited by Kathy Sova, Theatre Communications Group, Inc., 355 Lexington Ave., New York NY 10017. (212)697-5230.

EDITORS ON EDITING: What Writers Need to Know About What Editors Do, edited by Gerald Gross, Grove/Atlantic Press, 841 Broadway, New York NY 10003.

FORMATTING & SUBMITTING YOUR MANUSCRIPT, by Jack and Glenda Neff, Don Prues and the editors of *Writer's Market*, Writer's Digest Books, 1507 Dana Ave., Cincinnati OH 45207. (800)289-0963.

GRANTS AND AWARDS AVAILABLE TO AMERICAN WRITERS, PEN American Center, 568 Broadway, New York NY 10012. (212)334-1660.

GUIDE TO LITERARY AGENTS, edited by Donya Dickerson, Writer's Digest Books, 1507 Dana Ave., Cincinnati OH 45207. (800)289-0963.

HOW TO WRITE IRRESISTIBLE QUERY LETTERS, by Lisa Collier Cool, Writer's Digest Books, 1507 Dana Ave., Cincinnati OH 45207. (800)289-0963.

INTERNATIONAL DIRECTORY OF LITTLE MAGAZINES & SMALL PRESSES, edited by Len Fulton, Dustbooks, P.O. Box 100, Paradise CA 95967. (530)877-6110.

JUMP START YOUR BOOK SALES: A MONEY-MAKING GUIDE FOR AUTHORS, INDEPENDENT PUBLISHERS AND SMALL PRESSES, by Marilyn & Tom Ross, Writer's Digest Books, 1507 Dana Ave., Cincinnati OH 45207. (800)289-0963.

LITERARY MARKET PLACE and INTERNATIONAL LITERARY MARKET PLACE, R.R. Bowker, A Reed Reference Publishing Co., 121 Chanlon Rd., New Providence NJ 07974. (908)464-6800.

MAGAZINE WRITING THAT SELLS, by Don McKinney, Writer's Digest Books, 1507 Dana Ave., Cincinnati OH 45207. (800)289-0963.

MY BIG SOURCEBOOK, 66 Canal Center Plaza, Suite 200, Alexandria VA 22314-5507. (703)683-0683.

NATIONAL WRITERS UNION GUIDE TO FREELANCE RATES & STANDARD PRACTICE, by Alexander Kopelman, distributed by Writer's Digest Books, 1507 Dana Ave., Cincinnati OH 45207. (800)289-0963.

ONLINE MARKETS FOR WRITERS: Where and How to Sell Your Writing on the Internet, by Anthony Tedesco with Paul Tedesco (Spring 2000), Owl Books/Henry Holt, 61 E. Eighth St., Suite 272, New York NY 10003. (212)353-0455. E-mail: anthony@marketsforwriters.com.

STANDARD DIRECTORY OF ADVERTISING AGENCIES, National Register Publishing, A Reed Reference Publishing Co., 121 Chanlon Rd., New Providence NJ 07974. (908)464-6800.

SUCCESSFUL SCRIPTWRITING, by Jurgen Wolff and Kerry Cox, Writer's Digest Books, 1507 Dana Ave., Cincinnati OH 45207. (800)289-0963.

THE WRITER'S GUIDE TO BOOK EDITORS, PUBLISHERS & LITERARY AGENTS, by Jeff Herman, Prima Publishing, Box 1260, 3875 Atherton Rd., Rocklin CA 95677. (916)632-4400.

WRITER'S ONLINE MARKETPLACE, by Debbie Ridpath Ohi, Writer's Digest Books, 1507 Dana Ave., Cincinnati OH 45207. (800)289-0963.

WRITER'S MARKET COMPANION, by Joe Fiertag and Mary Carmen Cupito, Writer's Digest Books, 1507 Dana Ave., Cincinnati OH 45207. (800)289-0963.

Websites

The Internet provides a wealth of information for writers. The number of websites devoted to writing and publishing is vast and will continue to expand as the year progresses. Below is a short—and thus incomplete—list of websites that offer information and hypertext links to other pertinent sites relating to writing and publishing. Because the Internet is such an amorphous, evolving, mutable entity with website addresses launching, crashing and changing daily, some of these addresses may be obsolete by the time this book goes to print. But this list does give you a few starting points for your online journey. If, in the course of your electronic ventures, you find additional websites of interest, please let us know by e-mailing us at writersmarket@fwpubs.com.

Link sites

Books A to Z: www.booksatoz.com

Information on publications, services and leads to other useful websites, including areas for book research, production services, self-publishing, bookstores, organizations, and publishers.

Books and Writing Online: www.interzone.com/Books/books.html

A collection of sources directing you to other sites on the Web, this is a good place to jump to other areas with information pertaining to writing, literature and publishing.

Bookwire: www.bookwire.com

A gateway to finding information about publishers, booksellers, libraries, authors, reviews and awards. Also offers information about frequently asked publishing questions and answers, a calendar of events, a mailing list, and other helpful resources.

Pilot-search: www.pilot-search.com

This search engine features more than 11,000 literary links. Writing advice is given, and information is posted on workshops, fellowships and literary job openings.

Publishers' Catalogues Home Page: www.lights.com/publisher

A mammoth link collection of publishers around the world arranged geographically. This site is one of the most comprehensive directories of publishers on the Internet.

Zuzu's Petals Literary Resource: www.zuzu.com

Contains 7,000 organized links to helpful resources for writers, researchers and others. Zuzu's Petals also publishes an electronic quarterly.

Miscellaneous

Delphi Forum: www.delphi.com

This site hosts forums on many topics including writing and publishing. Just type "writing" in the search bar, and you'll find 30 pages where you can talk about your craft.

Freelance Online: www.freelanceonline.com

A directory of and resource center for freelancers in the field of communications. Jobs, message boards, a searchable directory of over 700 freelancers, frequently asked questions, resources, and networking for freelance professionals. The FAQ for freelancers has lots of useful information catalogued and linked especially for freelancing beginners.

Novel Advice: www.noveladvice.com

A cyber-journal devoted to the craft of writing. This site offers advice, online courses on the craft of writing (for a fee), and an extensive list of research resources.

Internet Entertainment Network: HollywoodNetwork.com

This site covers everything in Hollywood whether it's dealmaking, music, screenwriting, or profiles of agents and Hollywood executives.

ShawGuides: www.shawguides.com

A cyber-journal devoted to the craft of writing. This site offers advice, online courses on the craft of writing (for a fee), and an extensive list of research resources.
Searchable database of writers' conferences.

United States Postal Service: http://new.usps.com

Domestic and International postage rate calculator, stamp ordering, zip code look-up, express mail tracking, etc.

Multiple services

Authorlink: www.authorlink.com

An information and news service for editors, literary agents and writers. Showcasing and matching quality manuscripts to publishers' needs, this site also contains interviews with editors and agents, publishing industry news, links and writer's guidelines.

Book Zone: www.bookzone.com

A catalog source for books, audio books, and more, with links to other publishing opportunities, diversions and distractions such as news, classifieds, contests, magazines and trade groups.

BookWeb: www.ambook.org

This ABA site offers books news, markets, discussions groups, events, resources and other book-related information.

Children's Writing Resource Center: www.write4kids.com

Presented by Children's Book Insider, The Newsletter for Children's Writers. *Offers information on numerous aspects of publishing and children's literature, such as an InfoCenter, a Research Center, results of various surveys, and secrets on getting published.*

Creative Freelancers: www.freelancers.com

A meeting spot for freelancers and employers. Writers post their résumés for free, and employers post job listings in writing, editing, proofreading, etc.

Editor & Publisher: www.mediainfo.com

The Internet source for Editor & Publisher, *this site provides up-to-date industry news, with other opportunities such as a research area and bookstore, a calendar of events and classifieds.*

Inkspot: www.inkspot.com

An elaborate site that provides information about workshops, how-to information, copyright, quotations, writing tips, resources, contests, market information, publishers, booksellers, associations, mailing lists, newsletters, conferences and more.

International Online Writers Association (IOWA): www.project-iowa.org/

This site includes resources, events calendar and research aids.

Online Markets for Writers: www.marketsforwriters.com

Site rooted in groundbreaking book, Online Markets for Writers: Where And How To Sell Your Writing On The Internet *(Owl Books/Henry Holt & Co., Spring 2000), offering online market information, interviews, extensive resources and advice from expert contributors including the National Writers Union (NWU) and the American Society of Journalists and Authors (ASJA).*

RoseDog.com: www.rosedog.com

This site is for readers, writers, agents and publishers. Post excerpts from your unpublished work at no cost, to be reviewed by agents and publishers.

Small Publisher Association of North America (SPAN): www.SPANnet.org

This site includes membership information, publishing events and calendar, links, book sales and other services.

The Write Page: www.writepage.com

Online newsletter for readers and writers of genre fiction, featuring information on authors, books about writing, new releases, organizations, conferences, websites, research, public service efforts writers can partake in, and writer's rights.

Writer's Toolbox: www.writerstoolbox.com

Feataures resources for fiction writers, journalists, technical writers and screenwriters.

Research

AcqWeb: www.library.vanderbilt.edu/law/acqs/acqs.html

Although geared toward librarians and researchers, AcqWeb provides reference information useful to writers, such as library catalogs, bibliographic services, Books in Print, and other web reference resources.

The Currency Site Historical Tables, Current Rates an Forecasts for World Currencies: www.oanda.com

Find current names for the world's curencies and exchange rates.

The Electronic Newsstand: www.enews.com

One of the largest directories of magazines on the Web. The Electronic Newsstand not only provides links to their magazines, but also tracks the content of many major magazines on a continually updated basis. It also allows users to customize their own newsstands to view only the magazines of their choice.

FindLaw: www.findlaw.com

Contains information on landmark legal decisions, and includes legal publishers and state and local bar association information.

InfoNation: www.un.org/Pubs/CyberSchoolBus/infonation/e_infonation.htm

A two-step database that allows you to view and compare the most up-to-date statistical data for the Member States of the United Nations.

Information Please Almanac: www.infopls.com

General reference.

International Trademark Association: www.inta.org

Check the correct spelling of nearly 4,000 trademarks and service marks, and get the correct generic term.

Library of Congress: http://lcweb.loc.gov/homepage/lchp.html

Provides access to Library of Congress catalogues and other research vehicles, including full access to bills under consideration in the U.S. House of Representatives and Senate.

Media Resource Service: www.mediaresource.org

This service provided by the Scientific Research Society helps writers find reputable sources of scientific information at no charge.

Mediafinder: www.oxbridge.com

Contains basic facts about 100,000 publications.

Newswise: www.newswise.com
A comprehensive database of news releases from top institutions engaged in scientific, medical, liberal arts and business research.

The Polling Report: www.pollingreport.com
Includes recent public opinion poll results from leading U.S. polling firms on politics, business, social issues, news events, sports and entertainment.

ProfNet: www.profnet.com
Contains names of 6,000 news and information officers at colleges and universities, corporations, think tanks, national labs, medical centers, nonprofits and PR agencies courtesy of this PR Newswire service.

Publishing Law Center: www.publaw.com
Links and articles about intellectual property and other legal issues.

SharpWriter.com: www.sharpwriter.com
Dictionaries, encyclopedic references, grammar tips.

World Factbook: www.odci.gov/cia/publications/factbook/index.html
Includes facts on every country in the world, on subjects from population to exports.

World Wide Web Acronym and Abbreviation Server: www.ucc.ie/acronyms/acro.html
Research to find the names behind the acronyms or the acronyms for the names.

Writer's Digest: www.writersdigest.com
This site includes information about writing books and magazine pieces from Writer's Digest. It also has a huge, searchable database of writer's guidelines from thousands of publishers.

Retail

Amazon.com: www.amazon.com
Calling itself "A bookstore too big for the physical world," Amazon.com has more than 3 million books available on their website at discounted prices, plus a personal notification service of new releases, reader reviews, bestseller and suggested book information.

Barnes and Noble Online: www.barnesandnoble.com
The world's largest bookstore chain's website contains 600,000 in-stock titles at discount prices as well as personalized recommendations, online events with authors and book forum access for members.

Master Freelancer: www.masterfreelancer.com
Products and services for freelance writers.

Organizations

Whether you write nonfiction or science fiction, self-help or short stories, there are national organizations representing your field as a whole or representing their members in court. Hundreds more smaller, local groups are providing assistance from paragraph to paragraph. There is an organization—probably several—to suit your needs.

ACADEMY OF AMERICAN POETS, 584 Broadway, Suite 1208, New York NY 10012-3250. (212)274-0343. Fax: (212)274-9427. Website: www.poets.org. Contact: Michael Smith.

AMERICAN BOOK PRODUCERS ASSOCIATION, 160 Fifth Ave., Suite 625, New York NY 10010-7000. (212)645-2368.

AMERICAN MEDICAL WRITERS ASSOCIATION, 40 W. Gude Dr., Rockville MD 20850-1199. (301)294-5303.

AMERICAN SOCIETY OF JOURNALISTS AND AUTHORS (ASJA), 1501 Broadway, Suite 302, New York NY 10036. (212)997-0947. Fax: (212)768-7414. E-mail: asja@compuserve.com. Website: www.asja.org. Executive Director: Brett Harvey.

AMERICAN TRANSLATORS ASSOCIATION, 225 Reinekers Lane, Suite 590, Alexandria VA 22314-0214. (703)683-6100. Website: www.atanet.org.

ASIAN AMERICAN WRITERS' WORKSHOP, 37 St. Mark's Place, Suite B, New York NY 10003. (212)228-6718. Fax: (212)228-7718. Website: www.aaww.org.

ASSOCIATED WRITING PROGRAMS, Tallwood House MS1E3, George Mason University, Fairfax VA 22030.

ASSOCIATION OF AUTHORS' REPRESENTATIVES, P.O. Box 237201 Ansonia Station, New York NY 10003. Website: www.aar-online.org.

ASSOCIATION OF DESK-TOP PUBLISHERS, 3401-A800 Adams Ave., San Diego CA 92116-2490. (619)563-9714.

THE AUTHORS GUILD, 330 W. 42nd St., 29th Floor, New York NY 10036. (212)563-5904.

THE AUTHORS LEAGUE OF AMERICA, INC., 330 W. 42nd St., New York NY 10036. (212)564-8350.

CANADIAN AUTHORS ASSOCIATION, P.O. Box 419, Campbellford, Ontario, K0L 1L0, Canada. (705)653-0323. Fax: (705)653-0593. E-mail: canauth@redden.on.ca. Website: www.Canauthors.org. Contact: Alec McEachern.

THE DRAMATISTS GUILD, 1501 Broadway, Suite 701, New York NY 10036-5601. (212)398-9366. Fax: (212)944-0420. Website: www.dramaguild.com.

EDITORIAL FREELANCERS ASSOCIATION, 71 W. 23rd St., Suite 1910, New York NY 10010. (212)929-5400. Fax: (212)929-5439. Website: www.THE-EFA.org.

EDUCATION WRITERS ASSOCIATION, 1331 H. St. NW, Suite 307, Washington DC 20005. (202)637-9700. Fax: (202)637-9707. E-mail: ewa@ewa.org. Website: www.ewa.org.

FREELANCE EDITORIAL ASSOCIATION, P.O. Box 380835, Cambridge MA 02238-0835. E-mail: freelanc@tiac .net. Website: www.tiac.net/users/freelanc.

INTERNATIONAL ASSOCIATION OF BUSINESS COMMUNICATORS, One Hallidie Plaza, Suite 600, San Francisco CA 94102. (415)544-4700 or (800)776-4222. Website: www.iabc.com.

INTERNATIONAL ASSOCIATION OF CRIME WRITERS INC., North American Branch, P.O. Box 8674, New York NY 10116-8674. (212)243-8966. Fax: (815)361-1477.

INTERNATIONAL TELEVISION ASSOCIATION, Raybourn Group International, 9202 N. Meridian St., Suite 200, Indianapolis IN 46260-1810. (800)362-2546. Fax: (317)571-5603. E-mail: jhiler@itva.org. Website: www.itva.org.

INTERNATIONAL WOMEN'S WRITING GUILD, Box 810, Gracie Station, New York NY 10028-0082. (212)737-7536. Website: www.iwwg.com. Executive Director: Hannelore Hahn.

MYSTERY WRITERS OF AMERICA, INC., 17 E. 47th St., 6th Floor, New York NY 10017. Website: www.mystery writers.net. President: Donald E. Westlake. Executive Director: Priscilla Ridgeway.

NATIONAL ASSOCIATION OF SCIENCE WRITERS, Box 294, Greenlawn NY 11740. (631)757-5664.

NATIONAL WRITERS ASSOCIATION, 3140 S. Peoria #295, Aurora CO 80014.

NATIONAL WRITERS UNION, 113 University Plaza, 6th Floor, New York NY 10003. (212) 254-0279. Fax: (212) 254-0673. E-mail: nwu@nwu.org. Website: www.nwu.org. Contact: Karen Ford.

NEW DRAMATISTS, 424 W. 44th St., New York NY 10036. (212)757-6960.

NOVELISTS, INC., P.O. Box 1166, Mission KS 66222. Website: www.ninc.com

PEN AMERICAN CENTER, 568 Broadway, New York NY 10012. (212)334-1660.

POETRY SOCIETY OF AMERICA, 15 Gramercy Park, New York NY 10003. (212)254-9628. Website: www.poetry society.org

POETS & WRITERS, 72 Spring St., New York NY 10012. (212)226-3586. Fax: (212)226-3963. Website: www.pw.org.

PUBLIC RELATIONS SOCIETY OF AMERICA, 33 Irving Plaza, New York NY 10003. (212)995-2230.

ROMANCE WRITERS OF AMERICA, 3707 FM 1960 W., Suite 55, Houston TX 77068. (281)440-6885. Fax: (281)440-7510. Website: www.rwanational.com. Executive Director: Allison Kelley.

SCIENCE FICTION AND FANTASY WRITERS OF AMERICA, INC., 532 La Guardia Place, #632, New York NY 10012-1428. Website: www.sfwa.org/org/sfwa_info.htm. President: Michael Capobianco

SOCIETY OF AMERICAN BUSINESS EDITORS & WRITERS, University of Missouri, School of Journalism, 76 Gannett Hall, Columbia MO 65211. (573)882-7862. Fax: (573)884-1372. Website: www.sabew.org. Contact: Carolyn Guniss, executive director.

SOCIETY OF AMERICAN TRAVEL WRITERS, 4101 Lake Boone Trail, Suite 201, Raleigh NC 27607. (919)787-5181.

SOCIETY OF CHILDREN'S BOOK WRITERS AND ILLUSTRATORS, 8271 Beverly Blvd., Los Angeles CA 90048. (323)782-1010. Fax: (323)782-1892. Website: www.scbwi.org. President: Stephen Mooser. Executive Director: Lin Oliver.

SOCIETY OF PROFESSIONAL JOURNALISTS, 16 S. Jackson, Greencastle IN 46135-1514. (765)653-3333. Website: www.spj.org.

VOLUNTEER LAWYERS FOR THE ARTS, One E. 53rd St., 6th Floor, New York NY 10022. (212)319-2787. Fax: (212)752-6575.

WESTERN WRITERS OF AMERICA, % Ms. Rita Cleary, WWA Membership, 20 Cove Woods Rd., Oyster Bay NY 11771.

WOMEN WRITING THE WEST, P.O. Box 2199, Evergreen CO 80437. (303)674-5450.

WRITERS GUILD OF ALBERTA, 11759 Groat Rd., Edmonton, Alberta, T5M 3K6, Canada. (780)422-8174.

WRITERS GUILD OF AMERICA, East Chapter: 555 W. 57th St., New York NY 10019, (212)767-7800; West Chapter: 7000 Third St., Los Angeles CA 90048, (310)550-1000. Website: www.wga.org.

Glossary

Key to symbols and abbreviations appears on the front and back inside covers.

Advance. A sum of money a publisher pays a writer prior to the publication of a book. It is usually paid in installments, such as one-half on signing the contract; one-half on delivery of a complete and satisfactory manuscript. The advance is paid against the royalty money that will be earned by the book.

Advertorial. Advertising presented in such a way as to resemble editorial material. Information may be the same as that contained in an editorial feature, but it is paid for or supplied by an advertiser and the word "advertisement" appears at the top of the page.

Agent. A liason between a writer and editor or publisher. An agent shops a manuscript around, receiving a commission when the manuscript is accepted. Agents usually take a 10-15% fee from the advance and royalties, 10-20% if a co-agent is involved, such as in the sale of dramatic rights.

All rights. See Rights and the Writer in the Minding the Details article.

Anthology. A collection of selected writings by various authors or a gathering of works by one author.

Assignment. Editor asks a writer to produce a specific article for an agreed-upon fee.

Auction. Publishers sometimes bid for the acquisition of a book manuscript that has excellent sales prospects. The bids are for the amount of the author's advance, advertising and promotional expenses, royalty percentage, etc. Auctions are conducted by agents.

Avant-garde. Writing that is innovative in form, style or subject, often considered difficult and challenging.

B&W. Abbreviation for black and white photographs.

Backlist. A publisher's list of its books that were not published during the current season, but that are still in print.

Belles lettres. A term used to describe fine or literary writing—writing more to entertain than to inform or instruct.

Bimonthly. Every two months. See also *semimonthly*.

Bio. A sentence or brief paragraph about the writer. It can appear at the bottom of the first or last page of a writer's article or short story or on a contributor's page.

Biweekly. Every two weeks.

Boilerplate. A standardized contract. When an editor says "our standard contract," he means the boilerplate with no changes. Writers should be aware that most authors and/or agents make many changes on the boilerplate.

Book packager. Draws all elements of a book together, from the initial concept to writing and marketing strategies, then sells the book package to a book publisher. Also known as book producer or book developer.

Business size envelope. Also known as a #10 envelope, it is the standard size used in sending business correspondence.

Byline. Name of the author appearing with the published piece.

Category fiction. A term used to include all various labels attached to types of fiction. See also *genre*.

CD-ROM. Compact Disc-Read Only Memory. A computer information storage medium capable of holding enormous amounts of data. Information on a CD-ROM cannot be deleted. A computer user must have a CD-ROM drive to access a CD-ROM.

Chapbook. A small booklet, usually paperback, of poetry, ballads or tales.

Circulation. The number of subscribers to a magazine.

Clean copy. A manuscript free of errors, cross-outs, wrinkles or smudges.

Clips. Samples, usually from newspapers or magazines, of your *published* work.

Coffee table book. An oversize book, heavily illustrated.

Column inch. The amount of space contained in one inch of a typeset column.

Commercial novels. Novels designed to appeal to a broad audience. These are often broken down into categories such as western, mystery and romance. See also *genre*.

Commissioned work. See *assignment*.

Concept. A statement that summarizes a screenplay or teleplay—before the outline or treatment is written.

Confessional. Genre of fiction essay in which the author or first-person narrator confesses something shocking or embarassing.

Contact sheet. A sheet of photographic paper on which negatives are transferred so you can see the entire roll of shots placed together on one sheet of paper without making separate, individual prints.

Contributor's copies. Copies of the issues of magazines sent to the author in which the author's work appears.

Cooperative publishing. See *co-publishing*.

Co-publishing. Arrangement where author and publisher share publication costs and profits of a book. Also known as *cooperative publishing*. See also *subsidy publisher*.

Copyediting. Editing a manuscript for grammar, punctuation and printing style, not subject content.

Copyright. A means to protect an author's work. See Copyright in the Minding the Details section.

Cover letter. A brief letter, accompanying a complete manuscript, especially useful if responding to an editor's request for a manuscript. A cover letter may also accompany a book proposal. A cover letter is *not* a query letter; see Targeting Your Ideas in the Getting Published section.

Creative nonfiction. Nofictional writing that uses an innovative approach to the subject and creative language.

CV. Curriculum vita. A brief listing of qualifications and career accomplishments.

Derivative works. A work that has been translated, adapted, abridged, condensed, annotated or otherwise produced by altering a previously created work. Before producing a derivative work, it is necessary to secure the written permission of the copyright owner of the original piece.

Desktop publishing. A publishing system designed for a personal computer. The system is capable of typesetting, some illustration, layout, design and printing—so that the final piece can be distributed and/or sold.

Docudrama. A fictional film rendition of recent newsmaking events and people.

Eclectic. Publication features a variety of different writing styles of genres.

Electronic submission. A submission made by modem or on computer disk.

El-hi. Elementary to high school.

E-mail. Electronic mail. Mail generated on a computer and delivered over a computer network to a specific individual or group of individuals. To send or receive e-mail, a user must have an account with an online service, which provides an e-mail address and electronic mailbox.

Erotica. Fiction or art that is sexually oriented.

Experimental. See *avant-garde*.

Fair use. A provision of the copyright law that says short passages from copyrighted material may be used without infringing on the owner's rights.

Feature. An article giving the reader information of human interest rather than news. Also used by magazines to indicate a lead article or distinctive department.

Filler. A short item used by an editor to "fill" out a newspaper column or magazine page. It could be a timeless news item, a joke, an anecdote, some light verse or short humor, puzzle, etc.

First North American serial rights. See Rights and the Writer in the Minding the Details article.

First-person point of view. In nonfiction, the author reports from his or her own perspective; in fiction, the narrator tells the story from his or her point of view. This viewpoint makes frequent use of "I," or occasionally, "we."

Formula story. Familiar theme treated in a predictable plot structure—such as boy meets girl, boy loses girl, boy gets girl.

Frontlist. A publisher's list of its books that are new to the current season.

Galleys. The first typeset version of a manuscript that has not yet been divided into pages.

Genre. Refers either to a general classification of writing, such as the novel or the poem, or to the categories within those classifications, such as the problem novel or the sonnet. Genre fiction describes commercial novels, such as mysteries, romances and science fiction. Also called category fiction.

Ghostwriter. A writer who puts into literary form an article, speech, story or book based on another person's ideas or knowledge.

Gift book. A book designed as a gift item. Often small in size with few illustrations and placed close to a bookstore's checkout as an "impulse" buy, gift books tend to be written to a specific niche, such as golfers, mothers, etc.

Glossy. A black and white photograph with a shiny surface as opposed to one with a non-shiny matte finish.

Gothic novel. A fiction category or genre in which the central character is usually a beautiful young girl, the setting an old mansion or castle, and there is a handsome hero and a real menace, either natural or supernatural.

Graphic novel. An adaptation of a novel in graphic form, long comic strip or heavily illustrated story, of 40 pages or more, produced in paperback form.

Hard copy. The printed copy of a computer's output.

Hardware. All the mechanically-integrated components of a computer that are not software. Circuit boards, transistors and the machines that are the actual computer are the hardware.

High-lo. Material written for newer readers, generally adults, with a *high* interest level and *low* reading ability.

Home page. The first page of a World Wide Web document.

Honorarium. Token payment—small amount of money, or a byline and copies of the publication.

How-to. Books and magazine articles offering a combination of information and advice in describing how something can be accomplished. Subjects range widely from hobbies to psychology.

Hypertext. Words or groups of words in an electronic document that are linked to other text, such as a definition or a related document. Hypertext can also be linked to illustrations.

Illustrations. May be photographs, old engravings, artwork. Usually paid for separately from the manuscript. See also *package sale*.

Imprint. Name applied to a publisher's specific line or lines of books (e.g., Avon Eos is an imprint of HarperCollins).

Interactive. A type of computer interface that takes user input, such as answers to computer-generated questions, and then acts upon that input.

Interactive fiction. Works of fiction in book or computer software format in which the reader determines the path the story will take. The reader chooses from several alternatives at the end of a "chapter," and thus determines the structure of the story. Interactive fiction features multiple plots and endings.

Internet. A worldwide network of computers that offers access to a wide variety of electronic resources.

Invasion of privacy. Writing about persons (even though truthfully) without their consent.

Kill fee. Fee for a complete article that was assigned but which was subsequently cancelled.

Lead time. The time between the acquisition of a manuscript by an editor and its actual publication.

Libel. A false accusation or any published statement or presentation that tends to expose another to public contempt, ridicule, etc. Defenses are truth; fair comment on a matter of public interest; and privileged communication—such as a report of legal proceedings or client's communication to a lawyer.

List royalty. A royalty payment based on a percentage of a book's retail (or "list") price. Compare *net royalty*.

Literary fiction. The general category of serious, non-formulaic, intelligent fiction.

Little magazine. Publications of limited circulation, usually on literary or political subject matter.

LORT. An acronym for League of Resident Theatres. Letters from A to D follow LORT and designate the size of the theater.

Magalog. Mail order catalog with how-to articles pertaining to the items for sale.

Mainstream fiction. Fiction that transcends popular novel categories such as mystery, romance and science fiction. Using conventional methods, this kind of fiction tells stories about people and their conflicts with greater depth of characterization, background, etc., than the more narrowly focused genre novels.

Mass market. Nonspecialized books of wide appeal directed toward a large audience. Smaller and more cheaply produced than trade paperbacks, they are found in many non-bookstore outlets, such as drug stores or supermarkets.

Memoir. A narrative recounting a writer's (or fictional narrator's) personal or family history.

Microcomputer. A small computer system capable of performing various specific tasks with data it receives. Personal computers are microcomputers.

Midlist. Those titles on a publisher's list that are not expected to be big sellers, but are expected to have limited sales. Midlist books are mainstream, not literary, scholarly or genre, and are usually written by new or unknown writers.

Model release. A paper signed by the subject of a photograph (or the subject's guardian, if a juvenile) giving the photographer permission to use the photograph, editorially or for advertising purposes or for some specific purpose as stated.

Modem. A device used to transmit data from one computer to another via telephone lines.

Monograph. A detailed and documented scholarly study concerning a single subject.

Multimedia. Computers and software capable of integrating text, sound, photographic-quality images, animation and video.

Multiple submissions. Sending more than one poem, gag or greeting card idea at the same time. This term is often used synonymously with simultaneous submission.

Narrative nonfiction. A narrative presentation of actual events.

Narrative poem. Poetry that tells a story. One of the three main genres of poetry (the others being dramatic poetry and lyric poetry).

Net royalty. A royalty payment based on the amount of money a book publisher receives on the sale of a book after booksellers' discounts, special sales discounts and returns. Compare list royalty.

Network. A group of computers electronically linked to share information and resources.

New Age. A "fringe" topic that has become increasingly mainstream. Formerly New Age included UFOs and occult phenomena. The term has evolved to include more general topics such as psychology, religion and health, but emphasizing the mystical, spiritual or alternative aspects.

Newsbreak. A brief, late-breaking news story added to the front page of a newspaper at press time or a magazine news item of importance to readers.

Nostalgia. A genre of reminiscence, recalling sentimental events or products of the past.

Novella. A short novel, or a long short story; 7,000 to 15,000 words approximately. Also known as a novelette.

Novelization. A novel created from the script of a popular movie, usually called a movie "tie-in" and published in paperback.

On spec. An editor expresses an interest in a proposed article idea and agrees to consider the finished piece for publication "on speculation." The editor is under no obligation to buy the finished manuscript.

One-shot feature. As applies to syndicates, single feature article for syndicate to sell; as contrasted with article series or regular columns syndicated.

One-time rights. See Rights and the Writer in the Minding the Details article.

Online Service. Computer networks accessed via modem. These services provide users with various resources, such as electronic mail, news, weather, special interest groups and shopping. Examples of such providers include America Online and CompuServe.

Outline. A summary of a book's contents in 5 to 15 double-spaced pages; often in the form of chapter headings with a descriptive sentence or two under each one to show the scope of the book. A screenplay's or teleplay's outline is a scene-by-scene narrative description of the story (10-15 pages for a ½-hour teleplay; 15-25 pages for a 1-hour teleplay; 25-40 pages for a 90-minute teleplay; 40-60 pages for a 2-hour feature film or teleplay).

Over-the-transom. Describes the submission of unsolicited material by a freelance writer.

Package sale. The editor buys manuscript and photos as a "package" and pays for them with one check.

Page rate. Some magazines pay for material at a fixed rate per published page, rather than per word.

Parallel submission. A strategy of developing several articles from one unit of research for submission to similar magazines. This strategy differs from simultaneous or multiple submission, where the same article is marketed to several magazines at the same time.

Parody. The conscious imitation of a work, usually with the intent to ridicule or make fun of the work.

Payment on acceptance. The editor sends you a check for your article, story or poem as soon as he decides to publish it.

Payment on publication. The editor doesn't send you a check for your material until it is published.

Pen name. The use of a name other than your legal name on articles, stories or books when you wish to remain anonymous. Simply notify your post office and bank that you are using the name so that you'll receive mail and/or checks in that name. Also called a pseudonym.

Photo feature. Feature in which the emphasis is on the photographs rather than on accompanying written material.

Plagiarism. Passing off as one's own the expression of ideas and words of another writer.

Potboiler. Refers to writing projects a freelance writer does to "keep the pot boiling" while working on major articles— quick projects to bring in money with little time or effort. These may be fillers such as anecdotes or how-to tips, but could be short articles or stories.

Proofreading. Close reading and correction of a manuscript's typographical errors.

Proposal. A summary of a proposed book submitted to a publisher, particularly used for nonfiction manuscripts. A proposal often contains an individualized cover letter, one-page overview of the book, marketing information, competitive books, author information, chapter-by-chapter outline, 2-3 sample chapters and attachments (if relevant) such as magazine articles about the topic and articles you have written (particularly on the proposed topic).

Proscenium. The area of the stage in front of the curtain.

Prospectus. A preliminary written description of a book or article, usually one page in length.

Pseudonym. See *pen name*.

Public domain. Material that was either never copyrighted or whose copyright term has expired.

Query. A letter to an editor intended to raise interest in an article you propose to write.

Release. A statement that your idea is original, has never been sold to anyone else and that you are selling the negotiated rights to the idea upon payment.

Remainders. Copies of a book that are slow to sell and can be purchased from the publisher at a reduced price. Depending on the author's book contract, a reduced royalty or no royalty is paid on remainder books.

Reporting time. The time it takes for an editor to report to the author on his/her query or manuscript.

Reprint rights. See Rights and the Writer in the Minding the Details article.

Round-up article. Comments from, or interviews with, a number of celebrities or experts on a single theme.

Royalties, standard hardcover book. 10% of the retail price on the first 5,000 copies sold; 12½% on the next 5,000; 15% thereafter.

Royalties, standard mass paperback book. 4 to 8% of the retail price on the first 150,000 copies sold.

Royalties, standard trade paperback book. No less than 6% of list price on the first 20,000 copies; 7½% thereafter.

Scanning. A process through which letter-quality printed text or artwork is read by a computer scanner and converted into workable data.

Screenplay. Script for a film intended to be shown in theaters.

Self-publishing. In this arrangement, the author keeps all income derived from the book, but he pays for its manufacturing, production and marketing.

Semimonthly. Twice per month.

Semiweekly. Twice per week.

Serial. Published periodically, such as a newspaper or magazine.

Serial fiction. Fiction published in a magazine in installments, often broken off at a suspenseful spot.

Series fiction. A sequence of novels featuring the same characters.

Short-short. A complete short story of 1,500 words maximum, and around 250 words minimum.

Sidebar. A feature presented as a companion to a straight news report (or main magazine article) giving sidelights on human-interest aspects or sometimes elucidating just one aspect of the story.

Similar submission. See *parallel submission*.

Simultaneous submissions. Sending the same article, story or poem to several publishers at the same time. Some publishers refuse to consider such submissions.

Slant. The approach or style of a story or article that will appeal to readers of a specific magazine. For example, a magazine may always use stories with an upbeat ending.

Slice-of-life vignette. A short fiction piece intended to realistically depict an interesting moment of everyday living.

Slides. Usually called transparencies by editors looking for color photographs.

Slush pile. The stack of unsolicited or misdirected manuscripts received by an editor or book publisher.

Software. The computer programs that control computer hardware, usually run from a disk drive of some sort. Computers need software in order to run. These can be word processors, games, spreadsheets, etc.

Speculation. The editor agrees to look at the author's manuscript with no assurance that it will be bought.

Style. The way in which something is written—for example, short, punchy sentences or flowing narrative.

Subsidiary rights. All those rights, other than book publishing rights included in a book contract—such as paperback, book club, movie rights, etc.

Subsidy publisher. A book publisher who charges the author for the cost to typeset and print his book, the jacket, etc. as opposed to a royalty publisher who pays the author.

Synopsis. A brief summary of a story, novel or play. As part of a book proposal, it is a comprehensive summary condensed in a page or page and a half, single-spaced. See also *outline*.

Tabloid Newspaper format publication on about half the size of the regular newspaper page, such as *The Star* .

Tagline. A caption for a photo or a comment added to a filler.

Tearsheet. Page from a magazine or newspaper containing your printed story, article, poem or ad.

Teleplay. A play written for or performed on television.

TOC. Table of Contents.

Trade. Either a hardcover or paperback book; subject matter frequently concerns a special interest. Books are directed toward the layperson rather than the professional.

Transparencies. Positive color slides; not color prints.

Treatment. Synopsis of a television or film script (40-60 pages for a 2-hour feature film or teleplay).

Unsolicited manuscript. A story, article, poem or book that an editor did not specifically ask to see.

Vanity publisher. See *subsidy publisher*.

Word processor. A computer program that allows for easy, flexible manipulation and output of printed copy.

World Wide Web (WWW). An Internet resource that utilizes hypertext to access information. It also supports formatted text, illustrations and sounds, depending on the user's computer capabilities.

Work-for-hire. See Copyright in the Minding the Details article.

YA. Young adult books.

Book Publishers Subject Index

This index will help you find publishers that consider books on specific subjects—the subjects you choose to write about. Remember that a publisher may be listed here only under a general subject category such as Art and Architecture, while the company publishes *only* art history or how-to books. Be sure to consult each company's detailed individual listing, its book catalog and several of its books before you send your query or proposal. The page number of the detailed listing is provided for your convenience.

FICTION

Adventure: Alligator 134; Atheneum Bks for Yng Rdrs 144; Avon 147; Bantam Dell Pub Grp 149; Bantam Bks For Yng Rdrs 150; Berkley Pub Grp 154; Bethany 155; Blue Sky Pr 158; Books In Motion 159; Borealis 347; Boyds Mills 160; Bristol Fashion 162; Broadcast Interview 163; Caitlin 349; Cedar Fort 169; Citron 350; Cloud Peak 176; Dial Bks for Yng Rdrs 187; Doubleday 188; Electric Works 195; Floricanto 201; Ft Ross 203; Front St 205; Geringer, Laura 206; HAWK 216; HarperCollins Children's 214; Holiday House 222; Holt Bks for Yng Rdrs 222; Houghton Mifflin Adult 224; Houghton Mifflin Bks for Children 223; Journey 233; Le Gesse 239; Little, Brown Children's 243; McElderry, Margaret 250; Mesorah 253; Milkweeds for Yng Rdrs 254; Minstrel 255; Multnomah 258; Nelson, Tommy 260; Neshui 261; New Victoria 263; Onjinjinkta 268; Owen, Richard 271; Picasso 357; Piñata 279; Pontalba 281; Presidio 283; Pride & Imprints 284; Ragweed 358; Random House Trade 290; Review & Herald 292; Rising Tide 292; Scrivenery Press 301; Settel 382; Simon & Pierre 360; Snowapple 361; Soho 306; Trans-Atlantic 320; Turnstone 362; Turtle Books 321; Vandamere 330; Whispering Coyote 338; Willow Creek 340; Winslow 341; Wysteria Publishing 378; Whitman, Albert 338

Comic books: Amber 137; Edutainment Media 194; Neshui 261; Picasso 357; Doubleday 188; Houghton Mifflin Adult 224; Le Gesse 239; Neshui 261; Pontalba 281; Random House Trade 290; Soft Skull 306; Willowgate 340

Erotica: Alligator 134; Amber 137; Autonomedia 145; Blue Moon 157; Broadcast Interview 163; Carroll & Graf 167; Circlet 175; Citron 350; Doubleday 188; Éditions Logiques 352; Edutainment Media 194; Floricanto 201; Gay Sunshine & Leyland 205; Genesis 205; Neshui 261; New American Library 261; New Victoria 263; Pedlar 357; Picasso 357; Pontalba 281; Pride & Imprints 284; Rising Tide 292; Settel 382; Vandamere 330; Willowgate 340

Ethnic: Alligator 134; Arabesque 142; Arcade 142; Arte Publico 143; Atheneum Bks for Yng Rdrs 144; Avalon 146; Ballantine 149; Borealis 347; Bottom Dog 160; Boyds Mills 160; Branden 161; Citron 350; Confluence 179; Coteau 351; Doubleday 188; Dufour 190; Electric Works 195; Floricanto 201; Gay Sunshine & Leyland 205; Genesis 205; Guernica 353; HarperPerennial 215; Holiday House 222; Houghton Mifflin Adult 224; Houghton Mifflin Bks for Children 223; Le Gesse 239; Lee & Low 240; Little, Brown Children's 243; Mage 248; Neshui 261; New American Library 261; Northland 265; Picasso 357; Piñata 279; Pontalba 281; Pride & Imprints 284; Red Hen 290; Snowapple 361; Soho 306; Spinsters Ink 309; Stone Bridge 311; Third World 317; Turnstone 362; Turtle Books 321; UCLA Amer Indian Stud Ctr 322; Univ of Illinois 325; Univ of Texas 328; Willowgate 340; Winslow 341; YMAA 344

Experimental: Atheneum Bks for Yng Rdrs 144; Autonomedia 145; Beach Holme 346; Books Collective 347; Broadcast Interview 163; Citron 350; Coach House Books 350; Éditions Logiques 352; Electric Works 195; Gay Sunshine & Leyland 205; Goose Lane 352; Grove/Atlantic 211; House of Anansi 354; Jesperson 355; Le Gesse 239; Lintel 372; Livingston 244; Neshui 261; Pedlar 357; Pontalba 281; Pride & Imprints 284; Random House Trade 290; Red Hen 290; Ronsdale 359; Scrivenery Press 301; Snowapple 361; Soft Skull 306; Stone Bridge 311; Trans-Atlantic 320; Turnstone 362; Univ of Illinois 325; Willowgate 340; York 365

Fantasy: Ace 130; Allisone 135; Atheneum Bks for Yng Rdrs 144; Avon 147; Avon EOS 147; Baen 148; Bantam Dell Pub Grp 149; Bantam Bks For Yng Rdrs 150; Blue Sky Pr 158; Books Collective 347; Books In Motion 159; Bookworld/Blue Star 159; Brucedale 349; Circlet 175; Citron 350; Cloud Peak 176; Crossway 183; DAW 185; Del Rey 186; Dial Bks for Yng Rdrs 187; Edge SF&F 351; Éditions Logiques 352; Electric Works 195; Ft Ross 203; Front St 205; Geringer, Laura 206; Greenwillow 209; gynergy 353; HAWK 216; HarperCollins Children's 214; Holt Bks for Yng Rdrs 222; Houghton Mifflin Adult 224; Le Gesse 239; Little, Brown Children's 243; Milkweeds for Yng Rdrs 254; Minstrel 255; Neshui 261; New American Library 261; New Victoria 263; Onjinjinkta 268; Orchard 269; Overlook 270; Picasso 357; Pontalba 281; Pride & Imprints 284; Random House Trade 290; ROC 293; Settel 382; Simon & Schuster Bks for Yng Rdrs 304; Snowapple 361; St Martin's 297; Stone Bridge 311; Tor Books 318; Turtle Books 321; Warner Aspect 334; Warner Bks 334; Whispering Coyote 338; Whitman, Albert 338; Willowgate 340; Winslow 341; Wizards of the Coast 341; Write Way 343

Feminist: Alligator 134; Autonomedia 145; Bantam Dell Pub Grp 149; Books Collective 347; Brucedale 349; Calyx 368;

Circlet 175; Citron 350; Cleis 176; Coteau 351; Dunne, Thomas 190; Ediciones Nuevo Espacio 192; Firebrand 200; Four Walls Eight Windows 204; Front St 205; Goose Lane 352; Guernica 353; HarperPerennial 215; Houghton Mifflin Adult 224; House of Anansi 354; Jesperson 355; Kensington 235; Le Gesse 239; Little, Brown Children's 243; Mage 248; Naiad 259; Neshui 261; New Victoria 263; Pedlar 357; Picasso 357; Pontalba 281; Pride & Imprints 284; Red Hen 290; Snowapple 361; Soho 306; Spinsters Ink 309; Stone Bridge 311; Third World 317; Turnstone 362; Willowgate 340; Zebra 344

Gay/lesbian: Alligator 134; Alyson 136; Autonomedia 145; Bantam Dell Pub Grp 149; Books Collective 347; Calyx 368; Circlet 175; Citron 350; Cleis 176; Doubleday 188; Firebrand 200; Gay Sunshine & Leyland 205; Guernica 353; gynergy 353; Houghton Mifflin Adult 224; House of Anansi 354; Kensington 235; Le Gesse 239; Little, Brown Children's 243; Naiad 259; Neshui 261; New Victoria 263; Pedlar 357; Picasso 357; Pontalba 281; Pride & Imprints 284; Red Hen 290; Rising Tide 292; Spinsters Ink 309; Stone Bridge 311; Stonewall 312; Willowgate 340

Gothic: Atheneum Bks for Yng Rdrs 144; Citron 350; Edutainment Media 194; Electric Works 195; Le Gesse 239; Neshui 261; Picasso 357; Pontalba 281; Pride & Imprints 284; Willowgate 340; Wizards of the Coast 341

Hi-lo: Le Gesse 239; Neshui 261; Willowgate 340

Historical: Academy Chicago 130; Alexander 134; Arcade 142; Atheneum Bks for Yng Rdrs 144; Avalon 146; Ballantine 149; Bantam Dell Pub Grp 149; Barbour 150; Beach Holme 346; Beil, Frederic 153; Berkley Pub Grp 154; Bethany 155; Blue Sky Pr 158; Blue/Gray 158; Books In Motion 159; Bookwrights 379; Borealis 347; Boyds Mills 160; Branden 161; Bridge Works 162; Broadcast Interview 163; Brucedale 349; Caitlin 349; Carolrhoda 167; Cedar Fort 169; Chandler 170; Chariot/Victor 170; Christian Pub 173; Citron 350; Cloud Peak 176; Consortium 179; Cross Cultural 182; Crossway 183; Dial Bks for Yng Rdrs 187; Doubleday 188; Dry Bones 190; Dufour 190; Ediciones Nuevo Espacio 192; Edutainment Media 194; Electric Works 195; Forge 202; Front St 205; Gay Sunshine & Leyland 205; Geringer, Laura 206; Goose Lane 352; Greenwillow 209; HAWK 216; HarperCollins Children's 214; Hendrick-Long 219; Holiday House 222; Holt Bks for Yng Rdrs 222; Houghton Mifflin Adult 224; Houghton Mifflin Bks for Children 223; Jesperson 355; Kindred Prod 355; Le Gesse 239; Little, Brown Children's 243; Love Spell 246; MacAdam/Cage 248; Mage 248; McElderry, Margaret 250; Mesorah 253; Milkweeds for Yng Rdrs 254; Multnomah 258; Narwhal 259; Nautical & Aviation 260; Neshui 261; New American Library 261; New England 261; New Victoria 263; Pelican 275; Philomel 278; Picasso 357; Pineapple 279; Pleasant Co 280; Pontalba 281; Presidio 283; Pride & Imprints 284; Putnam's Bks for Yng Rdrs 286; Ragweed 358; Random House Trade 290; Red Hen 290; Review & Herald 292; Rising Tide 292; Saxon House Canada 359; Scrivenery Press 301; Settel 382; Simon & Schuster Bks for Yng Rdrs 304; Snowapple 361; Soft Skull 306; Soho 306; St Martin's 297; Third World 317; Tyndale 322; Toby Pr 362; Tor Books 318; Turtle Books 321; Whitman, Albert 338; Willowgate 340; Winslow 341; Wysteria Publishing 378

Horror: Alligator 134; Atheneum Bks for Yng Rdrs 144; Bantam Dell Pub Grp 149; Books Collective 347; Books In Motion 159; Citron 350; Cloud Peak 176; Design Image 186; Doubleday 188; Electric Works 195; Forge 202; Ft Ross 203; Front St 205; Gryphon Pub 211; HAWK 216; Le Gesse 239; Leisure 241; Midknight Club 253; Neshui 261; New American Library 261; Onjinjinkta 268; Picasso 357; Pontalba 281; Random House Trade 290; Rising Tide 292; ROC 293; St Martin's 297; Tor Books 318; Vista 333; Warner Bks 334; Willowgate 340; Write Way 343; Wysteria Publishing 378

Humor: Amber 137; American Atheist 137; Arcade 142; Archway 142; Atheneum Bks for Yng Rdrs 144; Bantam Bks For Yng Rdrs 150; Barbour 150; Blue Sky Pr 158; Books In Motion 159; Boyds Mills 160; Broadcast Interview 163; Brucedale 349; Caitlin 349; Cartwheel 168; Catbird 168; Cedar Fort 169; Christian Pub 173; Citron 350; Cloud Peak 176; Consortium 179; Dial Bks for Yng Rdrs 187; Doubleday 188; Dry Bones 190; Electric Works 195; Front St 205; Geringer, Laura 206; Greenwillow 209; HAWK 216; HarperCollins Children's 214; HarperEntertainment 215; Holiday House 222; Holt Bks for Yng Rdrs 222; Houghton Mifflin Adult 224; Houghton Mifflin Bks for Children 223; Jesperson 355; Le Gesse 239; Menus & Music 372; Little, Brown Children's 243; Milkweeds for Yng Rdrs 254; Multnomah 258; Neshui 261; New Victoria 263; Onjinjinkta 268; Pedlar 357; Picasso 357; Pontalba 281; Pride & Imprints 284; Review & Herald 292; Settel 382; Simon & Schuster Bks for Yng Rdrs 304; Turnstone 362; Willowgate 340; Winslow 341; Whitman, Albert 338; Wysteria Publishing 378

Juvenile: Absey 130; Alef 134; Ambassador 136; Annick Press Ltd. 346; Archway 142; Atheneum Bks for Yng Rdrs 144; Baker Bks 148; Bantam Bks For Yng Rdrs 150; Barron's Educ 151; Blue Sky Pr 158; Borealis 347; Boyds Mills 160; Brucedale 349; Candlewick 166; CandyCane 166; Carolrhoda 167; Cartwheel 168; Cedar Fort 169; Chronicle Bks for Children 174; Cloud Peak 176; Concordia 178; Coteau 351; Cricket Books 182; Crossway 183; Design Pr 380; Dial Bks for Yng Rdrs 187; Doral 188; Down East 189; Dutton Children's 191; Eakin Pr/Sunbelt Media 191; Eerdmans Bks for Yng Rdrs 194; Electric Works 195; Farrar Straus & Giroux 199; Farrar, Straus & Giroux Bks for Yng Rdrs 199; Fiesta City 370; Focus Pub 202; Forward Movement 203; Front St 205; Geringer, Laura 206; Godine, David 207; Great Quotations 209; Greenwillow 209; Grolier 210; Grosset & Dunlap 210; Gulf 212; HAWK 216; Harcourt Children's 214; HarperCollins Children's 214; HarperEntertainment 215; Hendrick-Long 219; Heritage House 353; Highsmith 220; Holiday House 222; Holt Bks for Yng Rdrs 222; Houghton Mifflin Bks for Children 223; Ideals Children's Bks 227; Illumination 370; Journey 233; Kar-Ben 235; Kindred Prod 355; Knopf & Crown Bks For Yng Rdrs 236; Le Gesse 239; Lee & Low 240; Lerner 241; Levine, Arthur 241; Little, Brown Children's 243; Manatee 249; McClanahan Book Co 381; McElderry, Margaret 250; Meadowbrook 251; Mesorah 253; Milkweed 254; Milkweeds for Yng Rdrs 254; Minstrel 255; Morehouse 256; Morrow, William 257; Narwhal 259; Nelson, Tommy 260; Neshui 261; North-South 266; Owen, Richard 271; Pauline Bks & Media 274; Peachtree Children's 275; Peachtree 275; Pelican 275; Perfection Learning 276; Philomel 278; Picasso 357; Piñata 279; Pleasant Co 280; Pride & Imprints 284; Puffin 286; Putnam's Bks for Yng Rdrs 286; Ragweed 358; Raincoast 358; Random House Bks for Yng Rdrs 289; Review & Herald 292; Ronsdale 359; Salina 297; Scholastic Canada 360; Scholastic Inc 300; Scholastic Pr 300; Seedling 302; Settel 382; Simon & Schuster Bks for Yng Rdrs 304; Skinner 305; Soundprints 307; Speech Bin 308; Third World 317; Tidewater

318; Tingley Books, Megan 318; Torah Aura 318; Tradewind 362; Tyndale 322; Vanwell 364; Viking Children's Bks 332; Walker & Co 334; What's Inside 337; Whispering Coyote 338; Whitman, Albert 338; Winslow 341

Literary: Absey 130; Algonquin 134; Alligator 134; Ambassador 136; Anvil 346; Arcade 142; Arte Publico 143; Autonomedia 145; Baker Bks 148; Ballantine 149; Bancroft 149; Bantam Dell Pub Grp 149; Beach Holme 346; Beil, Frederic 153; Berkley Pub Grp 154; Birch Brook 155; BK MK 156; Books Collective 347; Borealis 347; Bottom Dog 160; Bridge Works 162; Broadcast Interview 163; Broadway 163; Broken Jaw 348; Brucedale 349; Calyx 368; Carroll & Graf 167; Catbird 168; Cedar Fort 169; Citron 350; Cleis 176; Coach House Books 350; Coffee House 177; Confluence 179; Cormorant 351; Coteau 351; Delta 186; Dial Press 187; Doubleday 188; Dufour 190; Ecco Pr 192; Ediciones Nuevo Espacio 192; Éditions Logiques 352; Electric Works 195; Eriksson, Paul 196; Farrar, Straus & Giroux Bks for Yng Rdrs 199; Farrar, Straus & Giroux Paperbacks 199; Floricanto 201; Florida Academic 201; Four Walls Eight Windows 204; Front St 205; Genesis 205; Geringer, Laura 206; Godine, David 207; Goose Lane 352; Graywolf 208; Greenwillow 209; Grove/Atlantic 211; Guernica 353; HarperCollins Children's 214; HarperPerennial 215; HAWK 216; Heinemann 218; Houghton Mifflin Adult 224; Houghton Mifflin Bks for Children 223; House of Anansi 354; Jesperson 355; Knopf, Alfred 236; Knopf & Crown Bks For Yng Rdrs 236; Latin Amer Lit Review 239; Le Gesse 239; Little, Brown 243; Livingston 244; Longstreet 245; MacAdam/Cage 248; MacMurray & Beck 248; Mage 248; Marlowe 249; Milkweed 254; Neshui 261; New American Library 261; New Rivers 263; New York Univ 263; Northeastern Univ 265; Norton, WW 266; Ocean View 374; Overlook 270; Owl Bks 271; Passeggiata 273; Peachtree 275; Pedlar 357; Pelican 275; Permanent Pr/Second Chance 277; Picador 278; Picasso 357; Pineapple 279; Pontalba 281; Pride & Imprints 284; Puckerbrush 375; Ragweed 358; Raincoast 358; Red Hen 290; Rising Tide 292; Ronsdale 359; Ruminator 294; Sarabande 299; Saxon House Canada 359; Scribner 301; Scrivenery Press 301; Simon & Pierre 360; Smith, Gibbs 306; Snowapple 361; Soft Skull 306; Soho 306; Somerville 382; St Martin's 297; Southern Methodist Univ 308; Still Waters 311; Stone Bridge 311; Stonewall 312; Stormline 376; Story Line 312; Summit Pub Grp 313; Talese, Nan 315; Third World 317; Tidewater 318; Toby Pr 362; Trans-Atlantic 320; Turnstone 362; Univ of Georgia 325; Viking 332; Westminster John Knox 337; Willowgate 340; Wysteria Publishing 378; Zoland 344

Mainstream/contemporary: Absey 130; Academy Chicago 130; Alexander 134; Alligator 134; Arcade 142; Arte Publico 143; Atheneum Bks for Yng Rdrs 144; Autonomedia 145; Baker Bks 148; Ballantine 149; Bantam Dell Pub Grp 149; Bantam Bks For Yng Rdrs 150; Barbour 150; Berkley Pub Grp 154; Bethany 155; Blue Sky Pr 158; Blue Sky Pr 158; Books Collective 347; Books In Motion 159; Bookwrights 379; Bottom Dog 160; Broadcast Interview 163; Brucedale 349; Caitlin 349; Cedar Fort 169; Chariot/Victor 170; Christian Pub 173; Chronicle Bks for Children 174; Citron 350; Confluence 179; Cormorant 351; Coteau 351; Doubleday 188; Dry Bones 190; Dunne, Thomas 190; Dutton Plume 191; Eakin Pr/Sunbelt Media 191; Ecopress 369; Éditions Logiques 352; Electric Works 195; Evans & Co 197; Forge 202; Ft Ross 203; Genesis 205; Guernica 353; HAWK 216; Houghton Mifflin Adult 224; Jesperson 355; Le Gesse 239; Le Gesse 239; Little, Brown 243; Longstreet 245; MacAdam/Cage 248; Mage 248; McElderry, Margaret 250; Mesorah 253; Milkweeds for Yng Rdrs 254; Morrow, William 257; Narwhal 259; Neshui 261; Neshui 261; New American Library 261; Norton, WW 266; Onjinjinkta 268; Pantheon 272; Parabola Books 375; Peachtree 275; Permanent Pr/Second Chance 277; Picasso 357; Picasso 357; Pineapple 279; Pleasant Co 280; Pontalba 281; Rainbow (FL) 289; Random House Trade 290; Regan Bks 290; Review & Herald 292; Rising Tide 292; Scrivenery Press 301; Seven Stories 303; Simon & Pierre 360; Snowapple 361; Soft Skull 306; Soho 306; St Martin's 297; Third World 317; Toby Pr 362; Turnstone 362; Turtle Books 321; Univ of Illinois 325; Univ of Iowa 326; Univ Pr of Mississippi 329; Viking 332; Villard 332; Warner Bks 334; Westminster John Knox 337; Willowgate 340; Winslow 341

Military/war: Academy Chicago 130; Alligator 134; Broadcast Interview 163; Citron 350; Cloud Peak 176; Edutainment Media 194; Electric Works 195; Jesperson 355; Le Gesse 239; Narwhal 259; Naval Inst 260; Neshui 261; Onjinjinkta 268; Picasso 357; Pontalba 281; Presidio 283; Willowgate 340

Multicultural: Alligator 134; Bantam Bks For Yng Rdrs 150; Books Collective 347; Chronicle Bks for Children 174; Cloud Peak 176; Ediciones Nuevo Espacio 192; Electric Works 195; Highsmith 220; Holt Bks for Yng Rdrs 222; Kensington 235; Latin Amer Lit Review 239; Piñata 279; Ragweed 358; Red Hen 290; Trans-Atlantic 320; Vista 333

Multimedia: Cloud Peak 176; Coach House Books 350; Electric Works 195; Menus & Music 372; Neshui 261; Picasso 357; Pontalba 281; Serendipity 302; Willowgate 340

Mystery: Academy Chicago 130; Alexander 134; Alligator 134; Arcade 142; Atheneum Bks for Yng Rdrs 144; Avalon 146; Avon 147; Baker Bks 148; Ballantine 149; Bancroft 149; Bantam Dell Pub Grp 149; Berkley Pub Grp 154; Black Dog & Leventhal 156; Books In Motion 159; Boyds Mills 160; Brewers 162; Bridge Works 162; Brucedale 349; Carroll & Graf 167; Cartwheel 168; Christian Pub 173; Citron 350; Cloud Peak 176; Crossway 183; Cumberland 183; Dial Bks for Yng Rdrs 187; Doubleday 188; Dry Bones 190; Dunne, Thomas 190; Ediciones Nuevo Espacio 192; Electric Works 195; Forge 202; Ft Ross 203; Gay Sunshine & Leyland 205; Genesis 205; Greenwillow 209; Gryphon Pub 211; gynergy 353; HAWK 216; Holt Bks for Yng Rdrs 222; Houghton Mifflin Adult 224; Houghton Mifflin Bks for Children 223; Intercontinental 229; Island 232; Kensington 235; Le Gesse 239; Little, Brown Children's 243; McElderry, Margaret 250; Mesorah 253; Minstrel 255; Multnomah 258; Mysterious Pr 258; Naiad 259; Nelson, Tommy 260; Neshui 261; New American Library 261; New Victoria 263; Norton, WW 266; Onjinjinkta 268; Owen, Richard 271; Permanent Pr/Second Chance 277; Picasso 357; Platinum 280; Pocket Bks 281; Pontalba 281; Presidio 283; Pride & Imprints 284; Rainbow (FL) 289; Random House Bks for Yng Rdrs 289; Random House Trade 290; Rising Tide 292; Salvo 298; Scholastic Inc 300; Scribner 301; Scrivenery Press 301; Settel 382; Silver Dagger Mysteries 304; Simon & Pierre 360; Simon & Schuster Bks for Yng Rdrs 304; Snowapple 361; Soho 306; Spinsters Ink 309; St Martin's 297; Stone Bridge 311; Stonewall 312; Sudbury 313; Thorndike Press 317; Trans-Atlantic 320; Turnstone 362; Vandamere 330; Viking 332; Vista 333; Walker & Co 334; Warner Bks 334; Westminster John Knox 337; Whitman, Albert 338; Willowgate 340; Winslow 341; Write Way 343; Wysteria Publishing 378

Occult: Allisone 135; Citron 350; Electric Works 195; Floricanto 201; Holmes Pub Grp 222; Le Gesse 239; Llewellyn 244; Midknight Club 253; Neshui 261; New American Library 261; Pontalba 281; Pride & Imprints 284; Rising Tide 292; Willowgate 340; Write Way 343

Picture books: Ambassador 136; Baker Bks 148; Bantam Bks For Yng Rdrs 150; Blue Sky Pr 158; Boyds Mills 160; Carolrhoda 167; Cartwheel 168; Charlesbridge Publishing 171; Chronicle Bks for Children 174; Concordia 178; Consortium 179; Design Pr 380; Doubleday 188; Dutton Children's 191; Eerdmans Bks for Yng Rdrs 194; Farrar Straus & Giroux 199; Farrar, Straus & Giroux Bks for Yng Rdrs 199; Focus Pub 202; Front St 205; Geringer, Laura 206; Greenwillow 209; Grolier 210; Grosset & Dunlap 210; Gulf 212; HAWK 216; Harcourt Children's 214; HarperCollins Children's 214; Holiday House 222; Holt Bks for Yng Rdrs 222; Houghton Mifflin Bks for Children 223; Ideals Children's Bks 227; Illumination 370; Knopf & Crown Bks For Yng Rdrs 236; Le Gesse 239; Lee & Low 240; Levine, Arthur 241; Little, Brown Children's 243; Manatee 249; McClanahan Book Co 381; McElderry, Margaret 250; Morehouse 256; Nelson, Tommy 260; Northland 265; North-South 266; Orchard 269; Overmountain 270; Owen, Richard 271; Peachtree Children's 275; Pedlar 357; Philomel 278; Piñata 279; Puffin 286; Putnam's Bks for Yng Rdrs 286; Ragweed 358; Raincoast 358; Random House Bks for Yng Rdrs 289; Scholastic Inc 300; Scholastic Pr 300; Settel 382; Simon & Schuster Bks for Yng Rdrs 304; Snowapple 361; Third World 317; Tingley Books, Megan 318; Torah Aura 318; Tricycle 320; Vernon Pr 382; What's Inside 337; Whispering Coyote 338; Whitman, Albert 338; Willow Creek 340; Winslow 341

Plays: Anchorage 140; Anvil 346; Books Collective 347; Broadcast Interview 163; Brucedale 349; Coach House Books 350; Coteau 351; Discovery 187; Dry Bones 190; Ediciones Nuevo Espacio 192; Electric Works 195; Fiesta City 370; Hill & Wang 221; Le Gesse 239; Meriwether 252; Neshui 261; Owen, Richard 271; Players 280; Playwrights Canada 357; Pride & Imprints 284; Simon & Pierre 360; Smith & Kraus 306; Third World 317; Trans-Atlantic 320; UCLA Amer Indian Stud Ctr 322

Poetry (including chapbooks): Absey 130; Acropolis 130; Alligator 134; Allisone 135; Anhinga 367; Anvil 346; Arte Publico 143; Autonomedia 145; Bancroft 149; Beach Holme 346; Beacon Pr 152; Birch Brook 155; BOA 159; Books Collective 347; Bottom Dog 176; Broken Jaw 348; Brooks Books 163; Brucedale 349; Caitlin 349; Calyx 368; Candlewick 166; Cartwheel 168; China Bks 172; Cleveland State Univ Poetry Center 176; Cloud Peak 176; Coach House Books 350; Coffee House 177; Confluence 179; Copper Canyon 179; Dante Univ of America Pr 184; Dee, Ivan 186; Dry Bones 190; Ediciones Nuevo Espacio 192; Editions Du Noroit 352; Electric Works 195; Focus Pub 202; Front St 205; Godine, David 207; Graywolf 208; Great Quotations 209; Grove/Atlantic 211; Guernica 353; HarperPerennial 215; Hippocrene 221; Hohm 221; Jesperson 355; Knopf, Alfred 236; Latin Amer Lit Review 239; Le Gesse 239; Lintel 372; Little, Brown Children's 243; Livingston 244; Louisiana State Univ 246; March St 249; McElderry, Margaret 250; Meadowbrook 251; Menus & Music 372; Michigan State Univ 253; Milkweed 254; Morrow, William 257; Neshui 261; New Rivers 263; New York Univ 263; Norton, WW 266; Oberlin College 374; Ohio State Univ 267; Passeggiata 273; Pedlar 357; Pennywhistle 276; Piñata 279; Pride & Imprints 284; Puckerbrush 375; Ragweed 358; Ronsdale 359; Salina 297; Sarabande 299; Saxon House Canada 359; Smith, Gibbs 306; Still Waters 311; Stone Bridge 311; Stormline 376; Story Line 312; Third World 317; Tia Chucha 377; Truman State Univ 321; Turnstone 362; UCLA Amer Indian Stud Ctr 322; Univ of Akron 323; Univ of Arkansas 324; Univ of California 325; Univ of Iowa 326; Univ of North Texas 327; Univ of South Carolina 328; Vehicule 364; Vernon Pr 382; Vista 333; Wesleyan Univ 336; Whispering Coyote 338; Winslow 341; Wisdom 341; Wysteria Publishing 378; Yale Univ 343

Poetry in translation: BK MK 156; BOA 159; Dante Univ of America Pr 184; Ediciones Nuevo Espacio 192; Electric Works 195; Guernica 353; Hohm 221; Latin Amer Lit Review 239; Le Gesse 239; Menus & Music 372; Neshui 261; Red Hen 290; Univ of California 325; Weatherhill 336

Regional: Alexander 134; Beach Holme 346; Blair 157; Books Collective 347; Borealis 347; Cedar Fort 169; Down East 189; Down the Shore 189; Eakin Pr/Sunbelt Media 191; Electric Works 195; Florida Academic 201; Genesis 205; Hendrick-Long 219; Jesperson 355; Le Gesse 239; Neshui 261; New England 261; Northland 265; Onjinjinkta 268; Philomel 278; Picasso 357; Pineapple 279; Pontalba 281; Scrivenery Press 301; Simon & Pierre 360; Sunstone 313; TCU Press 315; Turtle Books 321; Univ of Maine 326; Univ of Tennessee 328; Univ Pr of Colorado 329; Univ Pr of New England 330; Willowgate 340; Woodholme 342; Wysteria Publishing 378

Religious: Alef 134; Allisone 135; Ambassador 136; Baker Bks 148; Barbour 150; Bethany 155; Books In Motion 159; Bookworld/Blue Star 159; Branden 161; Broadcast Interview 163; CandyCane 166; Cedar Fort 169; Chariot/Victor 170; Christian Pub 173; Concordia 178; Cross Cultural 182; Crossway 183; Doubleday 188; Doubleday Religious 188; Dry Bones 190; Eerdmans Bks for Yng Rdrs 194; Electric Works 195; Focus Pub 202; Forward Movement 203; Holt Bks for Yng Rdrs 222; Journey 233; Kar-Ben 235; Kindred Prod 355; Kregel 237; Le Gesse 239; Mesorah 253; Midknight Club 253; Multnomah 258; Nelson, Thomas 260; Nelson, Tommy 260; Neshui 261; Onjinjinkta 268; Parabola Books 375; Picasso 357; Resource Pub 291; Revell, Fleming 291; Review & Herald 292; Southern Methodist Univ 308; St Mary's 297; Summit Pub Grp 313; Torah Aura 318; Tyndale 322; UCLA Amer Indian Stud Ctr 322; Unity 323; Westminster John Knox 337

Romance: Alligator 134; Amber 137; Arabesque 142; Archway 142; Avalon 146; Avon 147; Ballantine 149; Bantam Dell Pub Grp 149; Barbour 150; Berkley Pub Grp 154; Bethany 155; Borealis 347; Brucedale 349; Cedar Fort 169; Citron 350; Cross Cultural 182; Ediciones Nuevo Espacio 192; Electric Works 195; Floricanto 201; Ft Ross 203; Front St 205; Genesis 205; Island 232; Kensington 235; Le Gesse 239; Leisure 241; Love Spell 246; Multnomah 258; Neshui 261; New American Library 261; New Victoria 263; Picasso 357; Pocket Bks 281; Pontalba 281; Rising Tide 292; Scholastic Inc 300; Settel 382; Silhouette 304; Steeple Hill 310; Thorndike Press 317; Warner Bks 334; Willowgate 340; Wysteria Publishing 378; Zebra 344

Science fiction: Ace 130; Alexander 134; Alligator 134; Atheneum Bks for Yng Rdrs 144; Autonomedia 145; Avon

147; Avon EOS 147; Baen 148; Bantam Dell Pub Grp 149; Berkley Pub Grp 154; Books Collective 347; Books In Motion 159; Carroll & Graf 167; Circlet 175; Citron 350; Cloud Peak 176; Cross Cultural 182; DAW 185; Del Rey 186; Edge SF&F 351; Éditions Logiques 352; Electric Works 195; Ft Ross 203; Four Walls Eight Windows 204; Front St 205; Gay Sunshine & Leyland 205; Gryphon Pub 211; gynergy 353; HAWK 216; Le Gesse 239; Little, Brown Children's 243; McElderry, Margaret 250; Midknight Club 253; Minstrel 255; Neshui 261; New American Library 261; New Victoria 263; Ocean View 374; Onjinjinkta 268; Orchard 269; Owen, Richard 271; Picasso 357; Pocket Bks 281; Pontalba 281; Pride & Imprints 284; Rising Tide 292; ROC 293; Simon & Schuster Bks for Yng Rdrs 304; St Martin's 297; Stone Bridge 311; Tor Books 318; Trans-Atlantic 320; Warner Aspect 334; Warner Bks 334; Wesleyan Univ 336; Willowgate 340; Winslow 341; Wizards of the Coast 341; Write Way 343

Short story collections: Allisone 135; Anvil 346; Arcade 142; Autonomedia 145; BK MK 156; Books Collective 347; Borealis 347; Bridge Works 162; Brucedale 349; Caitlin 349; Calyx 368; Chronicle 174; Circlet 175; Citron 350; Coffee House 177; Confluence 179; Cormorant 351; Coteau 351; Delta 186; Doubleday 188; Dufour 190; Ecco Pr 192; Ediciones Nuevo Espacio 192; Electric Works 195; Floricanto 201; Gay Sunshine & Leyland 205; Godine, David 207; Goose Lane 352; Gryphon Pub 211; Houghton Mifflin Adult 224; House of Anansi 354; Jesperson 355; Latin Amer Lit Review 239; Le Gesse 239; Livingston 244; Mage 248; Naiad 259; Neshui 261; New Rivers 263; Ohio State Univ 267; Owen, Richard 271; Pedlar 357; Puckerbrush 375; Red Hen 290; Resource Pub 291; Ronsdale 359; Sarabande 299; Scrivenery Press 301; Snowapple 361; Soft Skull 306; Somerville 382; Southern Methodist Univ 308; Stone Bridge 311; Third World 317; Toby Pr 362; Turnstone 362; Univ of Illinois 325; Univ of Missouri 326; Vista 333; Willow Creek 340; Willowgate 340; Wizards of the Coast 341; Woodholme 342; Wysteria Publishing 378; Zoland 344

Spiritual (New Age, etc.): Acropolis 130; Allisone 135; Ambassador 136; Barbour 150; Bookworld/Blue Star 159; Cedar Fort 169; Christian Pub 173; Electric Works 195; Focus Pub 202; Hampton Rds 213; Le Gesse 239; Llewellyn 244; Neshui 261; Onjinjinkta 268; Oughten House 374; Parabola Books 375; Picasso 357; Pontalba 281; Starburst 310; Westminster John Knox 337; Wilshire 340

Sports: Ambassador 136; Amber 137; Cedar Fort 169; Electric Works 195; Le Gesse 239; Mopam Publishing 373; Picasso 357; Pontalba 281; Turtle Books 321; Willowgate 340; Winslow 341

Suspense: Alligator 134; Arcade 142; Atheneum Bks for Yng Rdrs 144; Avon 147; Ballantine 149; Bantam Dell Pub Grp 149; Bantam Bks For Yng Rdrs 150; Berkley Pub Grp 154; Black Dog & Leventhal 156; Books In Motion 159; Boyds Mills 160; Carroll & Graf 167; Cedar Fort 169; Citron 350; Cloud Peak 176; DAW 185; Doubleday 188; Dunne, Thomas 190; Ediciones Nuevo Espacio 192; Electric Works 195; Forge 202; Ft Ross 203; Gryphon Pub 211; HAWK 216; Holt Bks for Yng Rdrs 222; Houghton Mifflin Adult 224; Houghton Mifflin Bks for Children 223; Intercontinental 229; Island 232; Kensington 235; Le Gesse 239; Leisure 241; Little, Brown Children's 243; Minstrel 255; Multnomah 258; Mysterious Pr 258; Neshui 261; New American Library 261; Onjinjinkta 268; Orchard 269; Picasso 357; Platinum 280; Pocket Bks 281; Pontalba 281; Presidio 283; Pride & Imprints 284; Random House Trade 290; Rising Tide 292; Salvo 298; Scribner 301; Scrivenery Press 301; Settel 382; Soho 306; St Martin's 297; Tor Books 318; Trans-Atlantic 320; Vandamere 330; Viking 332; Warner Bks 334; Winslow 341; Wysteria Publishing 378

Translation: Books Collective 347; Broadcast Interview 163; Catbird 168; Cormorant 351; Dante Univ of America Pr 184; Ediciones Nuevo Espacio 192; Electric Works 195; Gay Sunshine & Leyland 205; Grove/Atlantic 211; Guernica 353; Latin Amer Lit Review 239; Le Gesse 239; Overlook 270; Passeggiata 273; Pedlar 357; Scrivenery Press 301; Univ of California 325; Univ of Texas 328

Western: Alexander 134; Atheneum Bks for Yng Rdrs 144; Avalon 146; Avon 147; Berkley Pub Grp 154; Books In Motion 159; Boyds Mills 160; Broadcast Interview 163; Cedar Fort 169; Citron 350; Cloud Peak 176; Crossway 183; Electric Works 195; Jameson 232; Kensington 235; Le Gesse 239; Leisure 241; Multnomah 258; Neshui 261; New American Library 261; New Victoria 263; Pocket Bks 281; St Martin's 297; Thorndike Press 317; Tor Books 318; Turtle Books 321

Young adult: Absey 130; Alef 134; Ambassador 136; Annick Press Ltd. 346; Archway 142; Atheneum Bks for Yng Rdrs 144; Baker Bks 148; Bantam Bks For Yng Rdrs 150; Barron's Educ 151; Beach Holme 346; Berkley Pub Grp 154; Bethany 155; Borealis 347; Boyds Mills 160; Brucedale 349; Caitlin 349; Candlewick 166; Cedar Fort 169; Chronicle Bks for Children 174; Concordia 178; Coteau 351; Design Pr 380; Dial Bks for Yng Rdrs 187; Dutton Children's 191; Ediciones Nuevo Espacio 192; Eerdmans Bks for Yng Rdrs 194; Electric Works 195; Farrar Straus & Giroux 199; Farrar, Straus & Giroux Bks for Yng Rdrs 199; Focus Pub 202; Front St 205; Genesis 205; Geringer, Laura 206; HAWK 216; Harcourt Children's 214; HarperCollins Children's 214; Hendrick-Long 219; Holiday House 222; Holt Bks for Yng Rdrs 222; Houghton Mifflin Bks for Children 223; Journey 233; Knopf & Crown Bks For Yng Rdrs 236; Le Gesse 239; Listen & Live 243; Little, Brown Children's 243; McElderry, Margaret 250; Narwhal 259; Neshui 261; New England 261; Orchard 269; Peachtree Children's 275; Peachtree 275; Perfection Learning 276; Philomel 278; Picasso 357; Piñata 279; Pride & Imprints 284; Puffin 286; Putnam's Bks for Yng Rdrs 286; Ragweed 358; Random House Bks for Yng Rdrs 289; Scholastic Inc 300; Scholastic Canada 360; Simon & Schuster Bks for Yng Rdrs 304; Speech Bin 308; St Mary's 297; Third World 317; Tingley Books, Megan 318; Torah Aura 318; Trans-Atlantic 320; Tyndale 322; Viking Children's Bks 332; What's Inside 337; Winslow 341

NONFICTION

Agriculture/horticulture: American Pr 139; Ball 149; Boyds Mills 160; Bright Mountain 368; Broadcast Interview 163; Burford 164; Camino 166; Chelsea Green 171; China Bks 172; Cornell Univ 180; Doubleday 188; Dover 189; Electric Works 195; Hancock House 213; Haworth 217; Houghton Mifflin Bks for Children 223; Interstate 231; ISER 355; Le Gesse

239; Lebhar-Freidman 240; Libraries Unltd 241; Ohio Univ 267; Purdue Univ 286; Purich 358; Ronin Pub 293; Stipes 311; Universal 323; Univ of Alaska 324; Univ of Idaho 325; Univ of North Texas 327; Walsworth 334; Weidner & Sons 336; Whitman, Albert 338; Windward 341; Woodbridge 378

Alternative lifestyles: Beach Holme 346; Hunter House 226; Ronin Pub 293; Sterling 311

Americana: Adams Media 131; Addicus 132; Alaska Northwest 133; Ancestry 140; Arcadia 142; Arkansas 143; Atheneum Bks for Yng Rdrs 144; Avanyu 146; Bantam Dell Pub Grp 149; Bay 151; Bellwether-Cross 153; Berkshire 154; Black Dog & Leventhal 156; Blair 157; Blue/Gray 158; Bluewood 158; Boston Mills 348; Bowling Green 160; Branden 161; Brassey's Sports 161; Brevet 161; Broadcast Interview 163; Camino 166; Capstone 167; Caxton 169; Chandler 170; Clear Light 175; Cloud Peak 176; Confluence 179; Cornell Maritime 180; Country Music Found 180; Creative Pub 182; Cumberland 183; Doubleday 188; Dover 189; Down East 189; Down the Shore 189; Dutton Children's 191; Eagle's View 191; Eakin Pr/ Sunbelt Media 191; Eastern Nat'l 192; Electric Works 195; Eriksson, Paul 196; Facts on File 198; Filter 200; Fromm Int'l 204; Glenbridge 206; Godine, David 207; HarperPerennial 215; Heyday 220; HiddenSpring 220; Holiday House 222; Houghton Mifflin Bks for Children 223; Ideals Children's Bks 227; Krause 237; Lake Claremont 238; Le Gesse 239; Lebhar-Freidman 240; Lehigh Univ 241; Lion Bks 243; Longstreet 245; Lyons Pr 247; March Tenth 381; MBI 250; McDonald & Woodward 250; Menus & Music 372; Michigan State Univ 253; Middle Atlantic 373; Mustang Pub 258; Neshui 261; Northeastern Univ 265; Ohio Univ 267; Onjinjinkta 268; Overmountain 270; Pacific Bks 271; Parnassus 273; Pelican 275; Picasso 357; Picton 279; Pleasant Co 280; Pontalba 281; Pruett 285; Purdue Univ 286; Quill Driver/Word Dancer 287; Reynolds, Morgan 292; Sachem 382; Santa Monica 298; Sarpedon 299; Saxon House Canada 359; Scholastic Canada 360; Scrivenery Press 301; Sgt Kirklands 303; Settel 382; Shoreline 360; Soma 307; Southern Illinois Univ Pr 308; TCU Press 315; Towle House 319; Truman State Univ 321; TwoDot 322; Universal 323; Univ of Alaska 324; Univ of Arizona 324; Univ of Arkansas 324; Univ of Georgia 325; Univ of Idaho 325; Univ of Illinois 325; Univ of North Carolina 327; Univ of North Texas 327; Univ of Oklahoma 327; Univ of Pennsylvania 328; Univ of Tennessee 328; Univ Pr of Kansas 329; Univ Pr of Kentucky 329; Univ Pr of Mississippi 329; Univ Pr of New England 330; Upney 363; Utah State Univ Pr 330; Vandamere 330; Vanderbilt Univ 331; Vanderwyk & Burnham 377; Vernon Pr 382; Viking Studio 332; Voyageur 333; Washington State Univ 335; Westcliffe 337; Westernlore 337; Yale Univ 343

Animals: ABDO 129; Adams Media 131; Alpine 367; Atheneum Bks for Yng Rdrs 144; Autonomedia 145; Ballantine 149; Barron's Educ 151; Benefactory 153; Bick 155; Black Dog & Leventhal 156; Blackbirch 156; Boyds Mills 160; Burford 164; Capstone 167; Cartwheel 168; Chandler 170; Children's Pr 172; Chronicle Bks for Children 174; Dimi 187; Doral 188; Doubleday 188; Dover 189; Dutton Children's 191; Electric Works 195; Epicenter 196; Eriksson, Paul 196; Gollehon 207; Half Halt 212; Hancock House 213; HarperPerennial 215; Heritage House 353; Houghton Mifflin Bks for Children 223; IDG Lifestyle 227; Journey 233; Kesend, Michael 235; Krieger 237; Le Gesse 239; Lebhar-Freidman 240; Lifetime Bks 242; Lift Every Voice 371; Little, Brown Children's 243; Lone Pine 355; Lyons Pr 247; McDonald & Woodward 250; Millbrook 254; Mountain Pr 257; New American Library 261; Northland 265; Northword 266; Ohio Univ 267; Orchard 269; Ottenheimer 381; Picasso 357; Pineapple 279; Putnam's Sons 286; Rainbow (FL) 289; Raindbow (California) 288; Raincoast 358; Random House Bks for Yng Rdrs 289; Review & Herald 292; Seedling 302; Simon & Schuster Bks for Yng Rdrs 304; Soundprints 307; Sterling 311; Storey 312; Three Hawks 377; Totline 319; Trafalgar 319; Trans-Atlantic 320; Turtle Books 321; Universal 323; Univ of Alaska 324; Weidner & Sons 336; Weigl 365; Westcliffe 337; Whitecap 365; Whitman, Albert 338; Willow Creek 340; Windward 341; Wysteria Publishing 378

Anthropology/archaeology: Abique 129; American Pr 139; Autonomedia 145; Avanyu 146; Baker Bks 148; Baylor Univ 152; Baywood 152; Beacon Pr 152; Bergin & Garvey 154; Blackbirch 156; Bluewood 158; Broadview 348; Burnham 165; Children's Pr 172; Clear Light 175; Common Courage 178; Cornell Univ 180; Cross Cultural 182; Doubleday 188; Dover 189; Eagle's View 191; Electric Works 195; Encounter 196; Evans & Co 197; Fernwood 352; Filter 200; Floricanto 201; Gollehon 207; Greenwood 209; Greenwood Pub Grp 210; Gruyter, Aldine de 211; HAWK 216; Heritage House 353; HiddenSpring 220; Horsdal & Schubart 354; Houghton Mifflin Bks for Children 223; House of Anansi 354; Inner Traditions Int'l 228; ISER 355; Island Press 232; Johnson 233; Kent State Univ 235; Kroshka 237; Le Gesse 239; Lebhar-Freidman 240; Libraries Unltd 241; Lone Pine 355; Louisiana State Univ 246; Mage 248; Mayfield 250; McDonald & Woodward 250; Millbrook 254; Minnesota Hist Soc 254; Missouri Historical Society Press 373; Narwhal 259; Natural Heritage/Natural History 356; New York Univ 263; Northland 265; Ohio Univ 267; Parnassus 273; Pennsylvania Hist and Museum Comm 276; Pontalba 281; Quest Bks 287; Red Hen 290; Review & Herald 292; Rose 293; Routledge 294; Rutgers Univ 295; Schenkman 300; Sgt Kirklands 303; Stanford Univ 310; Texas A&M Univ 316; Third World 317; Truman State Univ 321; Universal 323; Univ of Alabama 323; Univ of Alaska 324; Univ of Arizona 324; Univ of Georgia 325; Univ of Idaho 325; Univ of Iowa 326; Univ of Nevada 326; Univ of New Mexico 326; Univ of North Carolina 327; Univ of Pennsylvania 328; Univ of Tennessee 328; Univ of Texas 328; Univ Pr of Kansas 329; Vanderbilt Univ 331; Wadsworth 333; Washington State Univ 335; Weatherhill 336; Westernlore 337; Whitman, Albert 338; Yale Univ 343

Art/architecture: Abrams 130; Alaska Northwest 133; Allworth 135; American Pr 139; Atheneum Bks for Yng Rdrs 144; Avanyu 146; Balcony 148; Barron's Educ 151; Beil, Frederic 153; Black Dog & Leventhal 156; Blackbirch 156; Bluewood 158; Boston Mills 348; Bowling Green 160; Branden 161; Brewers 162; Bucknell Univ 164; Bullfinch 164; Calyx 368; Camino 166; Chelsea Green 171; Children's Pr 172; China Bks 172; Chronicle 174; Chronicle Bks for Children 174; Clear Light 175; Coach House Books 350; Collectors Pr 177; Cornell Univ 180; C&T 166; Davis 185; Design Pr 380; Doubleday 188; Dover 189; Down the Shore 189; Electric Works 195; Epicenter 196; Eriksson, Paul 196; Fairleigh Dickinson 198; Family Album 370; Ft Ross 203; Four Walls Eight Windows 204; Fromm Int'l 204; Godine, David 207; Goose Lane 352; Guernica 353; HiddenSpring 220; Holmes & Meier 222; Home Planners 223; Horsdal & Schubart 354; Houghton Mifflin Bks for Children 223; Hudson Hills 225; Int'l Scholars 230; Kent State Univ 235; Kesend, Michael 235; Le Gesse 239; Lebhar-Freidman 240;

Lehigh Univ 241; Lerner 241; Libraries Unltd 241; Lift Every Voice 371; Little, Brown Children's 243; Louisiana State Univ 246; Loyola 247; Mage 248; March Tenth 381; Mayfield 250; McFarland & Co 251; Menus & Music 372; Meriwether 252; Minnesota Hist Soc 254; Missouri Historical Society Press 373; Monacelli 255; Morrow, William 257; Mount Ida 373; Natural Heritage/Natural History 356; New York Univ 263; North Light 264; Northland 265; Norton, WW 266; Ohio Univ 267; Orange Frazer 269; Overlook 270; Owen, Richard 271; Owl Bks 271; Parnassus 273; PBC Int'l 274; Pelican 275; Pennsylvania Hist and Museum Comm 276; Phaidon Press 278; Picasso 357; Pogo 375; Pontalba 281; Potter, Clarkson 282; Prairie Oak 283; Professional Pub 284; ProStar 285; Pruett 285; Quest Bks 287; Raincoast 358; Random House Trade 290; Running Pr 295; Sasquatch 299; Shoreline 360; Smith, Gibbs 306; Soft Skull 306; Sound View 376; Sourcebooks 307; Sterling 311; Stoddart 361; Stone Bridge 311; Summit Pub Grp 313; Sunstone 313; Talese, Nan 315; Teaching & Learning 315; Texas A&M Univ 316; Totline 319; Trans-Atlantic 320; Tricycle 320; Truman State Univ 321; Universal 323; Univ of Alaska 324; Univ of Alberta 363; Univ of Calgary 363; Univ of California 325; Univ of Georgia 325; Univ of Missouri 326; Univ of New Mexico 326; Univ of North Carolina 327; Univ of Pennsylvania 328; Univ of South Carolina 328; Univ of Tennessee 328; Univ of Texas 328; Univ Pr of Mississippi 329; Univ Pr of New England 330; Upney 363; Vernon Pr 382; Viking Studio 332; Visions Comm 332; Walch, J. Weston 334; Washington State Univ 335; Watson-Guptill 335; Weatherhill 336; Wesleyan Univ 336; Western NY 378; Whitman, Albert 338; Whitson 338; Williamson 339; Wonderland Pr 382; Wysteria Publishing 378; Yale Univ 343; Zoland 344

Astrology/psychic/New Age: Acropolis 130; Allisone 135; America West 137; American Fed of Astrologers 138; AngeLines 141; Bantam Dell Pub Grp 149; Bookworld/Blue Star 159; Broadway 163; Cassandra 368; Crossing Pr 183; Emerald Wave 369; Granite Publishing, LLC 208; Hampton Rds 213; Hay House 217; Holmes Pub Grp 222; In Print 371; Inner Traditions Int'l 228; Kramer, H.J. 236; Llewellyn 244; Marlowe 249; Ottenheimer 381; Prometheus 284; Quest Bks 287; Random House Trade 290; Skyfoot Technical 360; Sterling 311; Viking Studio 332; Weiser, Samuel 336; Whitford 378

Audiocassettes: Bantam Dell Pub Grp 149; Course Crafters 380; Walch, J. Weston 334

Autobiography: Consortium 179; Little, Brown 243; Norton, WW 266; Pantheon 272; Permanent Pr/Second Chance 277; Potter, Clarkson 282; Soho 306; Sudbury 313; Turnstone 362; Vehicule 364; Zondervan 344

Automotive: Bentley 154; Bonus 159; Fisher 200; Owen, Richard 271

Bibliographies: Family Album 370; Gryphon Pub 211; Locust Hill 244; Scarecrow 299; Whitson 338

Biography: 2M Comm 382; ABDO 129; Academy Chicago 130; Adams Media 131; Addax 132; Alexander 134; Algonquin 134; Ambassador 136; Amber 137; American Atheist 137; Arcade 142; Atheneum Bks for Yng Rdrs 144; Avanyu 146; Avisson 146; Avon 147; Baker Bks 148; Balcony 148; Bancroft 149; Bantam Dell Pub Grp 149; Barbour 150; Barricade 151; Beil, Frederic 153; Berkley Pub Grp 154; Bethany 155; Between the Lines 347; Black Dog & Leventhal 156; Blackbirch 156; Bliss 368; Blue/Gray 158; Bluewood 158; Bonus 159; Books Collective 347; Borealis 347; Bottom Dog 160; Bowling Green 160; Branden 161; Brassey's 161; Brassey's Sports 161; Brewers 162; Bridge Works 162; Bright Mountain 368; Broadcast Interview 163; Broadview 348; Broadway 163; Brucedale 349; Bryant & Dillon 164; Cadence 165; Caitlin 349; Camino 166; Carolrhoda 167; Carroll & Graf 167; Cedar Fort 169; Chandler 170; Chariot/Victor 170; Chelsea Green 171; Chicago Review 172; China Bks 172; Christian Pub 173; Chronicle Bks for Children 174; Clear Light 175; Cloud Peak 176; Collectors Pr 177; Common Courage 178; Companion 178; Cornell Univ 180; Country Music Found 180; Creative Pub 182; Cross Cultural 182; Dante Univ of America Pr 184; David, Jonathan 185; Dee, Ivan 186; Delta 186; Dial Press 187; Doubleday 188; Doubleday Religious 188; Doubleday/Image 189; Dover 189; Dufour 190; Dunne, Thomas 190; Dutton Plume 191; Eakin Pr/Sunbelt Media 191; Eastern Nat'l 192; ECW 351; Ecco Pr 192; Éditions Logiques 352; Edutainment Media 194; Electric Works 195; Encounter 196; Enslow 196; Epicenter 196; Equilibrium 369; Eriksson, Paul 196; Family Album 370; Farrar, Straus & Giroux Paperbacks 199; Fernwood 352; Floricanto 201; Ft Ross 203; Fromm Int'l 204; Genesis 205; Godine, David 207; Goose Lane 352; Grove/Atlantic 211; Guernica 353; HAWK 216; Hancock House 213; HarperBusiness 214; HarperEntertainment 215; HarperPerennial 215; HarperSanFrancisco 215; Hastings 216; Hendrick-Long 219; Heritage House 353; HiddenSpring 220; Holiday House 222; Holmes & Meier 222; Horsdal & Schubart 354; Houghton Mifflin Adult 224; Houghton Mifflin Bks for Children 223; House of Anansi 354; IBEX 226; Information Today 228; Int'l Scholars 230; ISER 355; Island Press 232; Jacobs, Lee 232; Jameson 232; Journey 233; Kamehameha 234; Kensington 235; Kent State Univ 235; Kesend, Michael 235; Kindred Prod 355; Knopf & Crown Bks For Yng Rdrs 236; Kregel 237; Kroshka 237; Le Gesse 239; Lebhar-Freidman 240; Lehigh Univ 241; Lerner 241; Lifetime Bks 242; Limelight 242; Lion Bks 243; Little, Brown 243; Lone Eagle 245; Longstreet 245; Louisiana State Univ 246; Loyola 247; Madison Bks 248; Mage 248; March Tenth 381; Marketscope 249; McDonald & Woodward 250; McElderry, Margaret 250; McGregor 251; Merriam Press 252; Mesorah 253; Middle Atlantic 373; Minnesota Hist Soc 254; Minstrel 255; Missouri Historical Society Press 373; Mitchell Lane 255; Momentum 255; Mopam Publishing 373; Morrow, William 257; Mountain N'Air 257; Narwhal 259; Naval Inst 260; Neshui 261; New American Library 261; New England 261; New Horizon 262; New Victoria 263; North Point 264; Northeastern Univ 265; Northfield 265; Northland 265; Norton, WW 266; NTC/Contemporary 266; Ohio Univ 267; Oliver 268; Orange Frazer 269; Oregon State Univ 269; Osprey 270; Overlook 270; Overmountain 270; Owl Bks 271; Ozark 374; Pacific Pr 271; Pantheon 272; Papier-Mache 272; Parlay Int'l 273; Pauline Bks & Media 274; Peachtree 275; Pelican 275; Pennsylvania Hist and Museum Comm 276; Perfection Learning 276; Permanent Pr/Second Chance 277; Picador 278; Picasso 357; Pineapple 279; Pocket Bks 281; Pontalba 281; Potter, Clarkson 282; Press at the Maryland Hist Soc 283; Pride & Imprints 284; Prometheus 284; Pruett 285; Publicom 381; Puffin 286; Purdue Univ 286; Putnam's Sons 286; Quest Bks 287; Quill Driver/Word Dancer 287; Ragweed 358; Ragweed 358; Rainbow (FL) 289; Random House Trade 290; Red Hen 290; Regan Bks 290; Regnery Pub 291; Republic of Texas 291; Revell, Fleming 291; Review & Herald 292; Reynolds, Morgan 292; Rising Star 376; Rockbridge 293; Ronin Pub 293; Ronsdale 359; Rutledge Hill 295; Safari 295; Sandlapper 298; Sarpedon 299; Schenkman 300; Scribner 301; Scrivenery Press 301; Sgt Kirklands 303; Settel 382; Seven Stories 303; Sheed & Ward 303; Shoreline 360; Skinner 305; Soft Skull 306; Soho

306; Southern Illinois Univ Pr 308; St Martin's 297; Stoddart 361; Summit Pub Grp 313; Talese, Nan 315; Taylor 315; Texas State Hist Assoc 316; Thunder's Mouth 318; Titan 361; Toby Pr 362; Towle House 319; Trans-Atlantic 320; Troitsa 321; Truman State Univ 321; Univ of Alabama 323; Univ of Alaska 324; Univ of Idaho 325; Univ of Illinois 325; Univ of Nevada 326; Univ of New Mexico 326; Univ of North Carolina 327; Univ of North Texas 327; Univ of South Carolina 328; Univ of Texas 328; Univ Pr of Kansas 329; Univ Pr of Kentucky 329; Univ Pr of Mississippi 329; Univ Pr of New England 330; Upney 363; Utah State Univ Pr 330; Vandamere 330; Vanderbilt Univ 331; Vanwell 364; Vehicule 364; Viking 332; Walker & Co 334; Warner Bks 334; Washington State Univ 335; Watts, Franklin 335; Weatherhill 336; Wesleyan Univ 336; Westernlore 337; Westminster John Knox 337; Wiley 339; Wonderland Pr 382; Woodholme 342; Wysteria Publishing 378; Yale Univ 343; Zoland 344; Zondervan 344

Booklets: American Catholic 367; Bureau for At-Risk Youth 164; Speech Bin 308

Business/economics: Accent 367; Adams Media 131; Adams-Blake 131; Adams-Hall 367; Addicus 132; AHA 132; Allworth 135; Amacom 136; America West 137; American Bar 137; American Coll of Physician Exec 138; American Pr 139; Anchor Pub 140; Atheneum Bks for Yng Rdrs 144; ATL 145; Auburn 145; Autonomedia 145; Avery 146; Avon 147; Ballantine 149; Bancroft 149; Bantam Dell Pub Grp 149; Barricade 151; Barron's Educ 151; Bellwether-Cross 153; Berkley Pub Grp 154; Betterway 155; Bloomberg 157; Bluewood 158; BNA 158; Bonus 159; Bookhome 159; Brevet 161; Broadcast Interview 163; Broadway 163; Bryant & Dillon 164; Business McGraw-Hill 165; Butterworth-Heinemann 165; Career Pr 167; Carroll & Graf 167; Carswell Thomson 350; Cato Inst 169; Cerier, Alison Brown 380; Chandler 170; China Bks 172; Consortium 179; Cross Cultural 182; Crown Business 183; Currency 184; Cypress 184; Dearborn 185; Doubleday 188; Eakin Pr/Sunbelt Media 191; Edutainment Media 194; Electric Works 195; EMC/Paradigm 195; Encounter 196; Equilibrium 369; Eriksson, Paul 196; Executive Excellence 197; Fairleigh Dickinson 198; Fell, Frederick 199; Fisher 200; Ft Ross 203; Forum 203; Forum Pub 203; Free Pr 204; Glenbridge 206; Glenlake 207; Gollehon 207; Government Inst 208; Graduate Grp 208; Great Quotations 209; Greenwood Pub Grp 210; Gulf 212; HAWK 216; HarperBusiness 214; HarperPerennial 215; Harvard Bus School 215; Hastings 216; Haworth 217; Health Comm 217; HiddenSpring 220; Holmes & Meier 222; IDG Business 227; ILR 227; Impact Publications 228; In Print 371; Information Today 228; Intercultural 229; Int'l Found Of Employee Benefit Plans 230; Int'l Wealth 231; Island Press 232; Jameson 232; Jewish Lights 233; Jist Works 233; Kogan Page 236; Krause 237; Kroshka 237; Kumarian 238; Le Gesse 239; Lebhar-Freidman 240; Libraries Unltd 241; Lifetime Bks 242; Lift Every Voice 371; Lighthouse Point 372; Listen & Live 243; LRP 247; March Tenth 381; Maximum 249; McFarland & Co 251; McGraw-Hill Ryerson 356; McGregor 251; Mesorah 253; Michigan State Univ 253; New World 263; New York Univ 263; Next Decade 373; Nichols 264; Nolo.com 264; Northfield 265; Norton, WW 266; NTC/Contemporary 266; Oasis 267; Ohio State Univ 267; Oliver 268; Oryx 269; Pacific View 272; Pacific View 375; Parlay Int'l 273; PBC Int'l 274; Pelican 275; Peterson's 277; Pilgrim 279; Pontalba 281; Possibility 281; Practice Mgmt 282; Praeger 282; Precept 283; Pride & Imprints 284; Productive 358; ProStar 285; Purdue Univ 286; Putnam's Sons 286; Quorum 288; Rainbow (FL) 289; Raincoast 358; Random House Trade 290; Regnery Pub 291; Reynolds, Morgan 292; Ronin Pub 293; Routledge 294; Russian Info 376; Self-Counsel (US) 302; Settel 382; Sourcebooks 307; South End 308; St. Martin's Scholarly & Reference 297; Starburst 310; Stipes 311; Stoddart 361; Stone Bridge 311; Storey 312; Stylus 313; Success Pub 313; Sudbury 313; Summit Pub Grp 313; Ten Speed 316; Texas A&M Univ 316; Thompson Educ 361; Tower 319; Transnational 320; United Church Pr 322; Universal 323; Univ of Calgary 363; Univ of Pennsylvania 328; Verso 331; VGM 331; Visions Comm 332; Vista 333; Walch, J. Weston 334; Walsworth 334; Warner Bks 334; Weidner & Sons 336; Wilshire 340; Wonderland Pr 382; Woodhead 365; Yale Univ 343; Ten Speed 316

Child guidance/parenting: Accent 367; Adams Media 131; Alba 133; Avery 146; Baker Bks 148; Ballantine 149; Bantam Dell Pub Grp 149; Barbour 150; Barron's Educ 151; Bay 151; Beacon Pr 152; Bergin & Garvey 154; Bethany 155; Black Dog & Leventhal 156; Bookhome 159; Broadway 163; Bureau for At-Risk Youth 164; Cambridge Educ 166; Camino 166; Capstone 167; Cedar Fort 169; Cerier, Alison Brown 380; Chandler 170; Chariot/Victor 170; Chicago Review 172; Child Welfare 172; Christian Pub 173; City & Co. 175; Conari 178; Concordia 178; Consortium 179; Consumer Pr 179; Doubleday 188; Doubleday Religious 188; Elder Bks 194; Electric Works 195; Encounter 196; Equilibrium 369; Fairview 198; Farrar, Straus & Giroux Paperbacks 199; Fell, Frederick 199; Fisher 200; Free Spirit 204; Gifted Educ 206; Great Quotations 209; Greenwood Pub Grp 210; Guilford 211; gynergy 353; HAWK 216; HarperPerennial 215; Harvard Common 215; Haworth 217; Hazelden 217; Health Comm 217; Heinemann 218; Hendricks, F.P. 353; Hensley 219; HiddenSpring 220; Humanics Pub 225; IDG Lifestyle 227; Illumination 370; Iron Gate 232; Kensington 235; Kroshka 237; Lawrence, Merloyd 239; Le Gesse 239; Lebhar-Freidman 240; Lifetime Bks 242; Lift Every Voice 371; Love and Logic 246; Lowell 246; Magni Grp 249; Manatee 249; Mayfield 250; McBooks 250; Meadowbrook 251; Mesorah 253; Moody 256; Multnomah 258; New American Library 261; New Hope 262; New Horizon 262; Newmarket Pr 381; Next Decade 373; Northfield 265; Norton, WW 266; Oughten House 374; Parlay Int'l 273; Pauline Bks & Media 274; Perigee 277; Phi Delta Kappa 278; Picasso 357; Prufrock 286; Publicom 381; Putnam's Sons 286; Rainbow (FL) 289; Resource Pub 291; Revell, Fleming 291; Review & Herald 292; Seal 301; Settel 382; Shaw, Harold 303; Soma 307; Sourcebooks 307; Starburst 310; Stoddart 361; Studio 4 Prod 376; Success Pub 313; Taylor 315; Ten Speed 316; Totline 319; 2M Comm 382; Tyndale 322; Universal 323; Viking 332; Vista 333; Weidner & Sons 336; Wiley 339; Williamson 339; Workman 342

Coffeetable book: Addax 132; Ambassador 136; American & World Geographic 379; American Quilters 139; A&B 128; Arcadia 142; Balcony 148; Bay 151; Beeman Jorbensen 153; Bentley 154; Black Dog & Leventhal 156; Boston Mills 348; Brassey's 161; Brassey's Sports 161; Bullfinch 164; China Bks 172; Chronicle 174; Clear Light 175; Collectors Pr 177; Countrysport 181; Cross Cultural 182; David, Jonathan 185; Design Pr 380; Dover 189; Down the Shore 189; Éditions Logiques 352; Epicenter 196; Godine, David 207; Ideals Pub 227; Jacobs, Lee 232; Judaica 234; Lark 238; Le Gesse 239; Lebhar-Freidman 240; Longstreet 245; Lynx Images 356; MacAdam/Cage 248; Mage 248; March Tenth 381; MBI 256; McDonald & Woodward 250; Menus & Music 372; Mesorah 253; Minnesota Hist Soc 254; Missouri Historical Society Press 373; Monacelli 255; Multnomah 258; Northland 265; Northword 266; Orange Frazer 269; Ottenheimer 381; Pelican 275;

Picasso 357; Pontalba 281; ProStar 285; Ragweed 358; Raincoast 358; Regan Bks 290; Revell, Fleming 291; Soma 307; Stoddart 361; Summit Pub Grp 313; Texas State Hist Assoc 316; Trans-Atlantic 320; Vernon Pr 382; Voyageur 333; Walsworth 334; Watson-Guptill 335; Weatherhill 336; Westcliffe 337; Westminster John Knox 337; Whitecap 365; Willow Creek 340; Wonderland Pr 382; Woodholme 342

Communications: Battelle 151; Baywood 152; Bonus 159; Butterworth-Heinemann 165; Eckert, J.K. 380; EMC/Paradigm 195; Focal 201; GATF Pr 205; Government Inst 208; Mayfield 250; Oak Knoll 267; Tiare 318; Univ of Alabama 323; Wadsworth 333

Community/public affairs: And Books 140; Lucent 247; Norton, WW 266; Overlook 270; PPI 282; Univ of Alabama 323; Univ of Nevada 326; Watts, Franklin 335

Computers/electronic: Adams-Blake 131; Alexander 134; Amacom 136; American Bar 137; And Books 140; A-R 142; Baywood 152; Bellwether-Cross 153; Branden 161; Broadcast Interview 163; Butterworth-Heinemann 165; Charles River Media 170; Cypress 184; Doubleday 188; Eckert, J.K. 380; Éditions Logiques 352; Electric Works 195; EMC/Paradigm 195; GATF Pr 205; Gifted Educ 206; Gleason Grp 380; Glenlake 207; Government Inst 208; Information Today 228; Jist Works 233; Kroshka 237; Le Gesse 239; Lebhar-Friedman 240; Liguori 242; Loompanics 245; Maximum 249; Neal-Schuman 260; New York Univ 263; No Starch 264; North Light 264; Norton, WW 266; Oasis 267; One on One 268; Osborne Media Group 269; Productive 358; PROMPT 285; Que 287; Sams 298; Self-Counsel (US) 302; Serendipity 302; Skyfoot Technical 360; Stoddart 361; Sybex 314; Teachers College 315; Tiare 318; Universal 323; Walch, J. Weston 334; Weidner & Sons 336; Whitman, Albert 338; Wilshire 340; Wordware 342

Consumer affairs: And Books 140; Bloomberg 157; Broadway 163; Int'l Found Of Employee Benefit Plans 230; Norton, WW 266; Oryx 269

Contemporary culture: Andrews McMeel 141; Ballantine 149; Bancroft 149; Brewers 162; Broadway 163; Carroll & Graf 167; Davis 185; Dial Press 187; DTP 190; Facts on File 198; Forum 203; Graywolf 208; HarperEntertainment 215; Kensington 235; Little, Brown 243; Madison Bks 248; McFarland & Co 251; NTC/Contemporary 266; Pelican 275; Picador 278; Random House Bks for Yng Rdrs 289; Rising Star 376; Schocken 300; Seal 301; Talese, Nan 315; Thunder's Mouth 318; Vanderwyk & Burnham 377; Viking Studio 332

Cooking/foods/nutrition: A&B 128; Accent 367; Adams Media 131; Alaska Northwest 133; Arcade 142; Avery 146; Ballantine 149; Barbour 150; Barnegat 150; Barron's Educ 151; Bay 151; Bellwether-Cross 153; Berkley Pub Grp 154; Berkshire 154; Black Dog & Leventhal 156; Bonus 159; Boston Mills 348; Brewers 162; Bright Mountain 368; Bristol Pub 163; Broadcast Interview 163; Broadway 163; Burford 164; Caitlin 349; Cambridge Educ 166; Camino 166; Capstone 167; Cassandra 368; Cerier, Alison Brown 380; Chelsea Green 171; Chelsea Green 171; Chicago Review 172; China Bks 172; Chronicle 174; Clear Light 175; Creation House 182; Cross Cultural 182; Crossing Pr 183; Cumberland 183; David, Jonathan 185; Design Pr 380; Doubleday 188; Doubleday Religious 188; Doubleday/Image 189; Dover 189; Eakin Pr/Sunbelt Media 191; Ecco Pr 192; Éditions Logiques 352; Electric Works 195; Elephant 195; Eriksson, Paul 196; Evans & Co 197; Fiesta City 370; Filter 200; Fisher 200; Floricanto 201; Glenbridge 206; Godine, David 207; Golden West 207; Gulf 212; Harbor 213; HarperPerennial 215; Harvard Common 215; Hastings 216; Haworth 217; Hay House 217; Healthwise 218; Heritage House 353; HiddenSpring 220; Hippocrene 221; Hoffman Pr 370; Howell Pr 224; IBEX 226; IDG Lifestyle 227; Inner Traditions Int'l 228; Interlink 229; Interweave 231; Krause 237; Kroshka 237; Lambrecht 355; Lark 238; Le Gesse 239; Lebhar-Friedman 240; Legacy 240; Lifetime Bks 242; Lift Every Voice 371; Little, Brown 243; Llewellyn 244; Longstreet 245; Lowell 246; Lyons Pr 247; Mage 248; Magni Grp 249; McBooks 250; Meadowbrook 251; Menus & Music 372; Mesorah 253; Middle Atlantic 253; Middle Atlantic 373; Minnesota Hist Soc 254; Momentum 255; Morrow, William 257; Mountain N'Air 257; New American Library 261; New World 263; Newmarket Pr 381; Next Decade 373; North Point 264; Northland 265; Norton, WW 266; NTC/Contemporary 266; Orange Frazer 269; Ottenheimer 381; Overmountain 270; Overmountain 270; Owl Bks 271; Pacific Pr 271; Parlay Int'l 273; Parnassus 273; Pelican 275; Picasso 357; Pocket Bks 281; Pontalba 281; Potter, Clarkson 282; Pride & Imprints 284; Pruett 285; Putnam's Sons 286; Ragged Mountain 288; Ragweed 358; Raindbow (California) 288; Raincoast 358; Random House Trade 290; Red Hen 290; Regan Bks 290; Republic of Texas 291; Review & Herald 292; Richboro 292; Ronin Pub 293; Running Pr 295; Rutledge Hill 295; Sandlapper 298; Sasquatch 299; Settel 382; Soma 307; St Martin's 297; Starburst 310; Stoddart 361; Storey 312; Ten Speed 316; Three Forks 317; Tidewater 318; Totline 319; Towle House 319; Trans-Atlantic 320; TwoDot 322; 2M Comm 382; Universal 323; Univ of North Carolina 327; Univ of South Carolina 328; Viking 332; Voyageur 333; Wadsworth 333; Warner Bks 334; Washington State Univ 335; Weatherhill 336; Whitecap 365; Whitman, Albert 338; Williamson 339; Willow Creek 340; Woodbridge 378; Workman 342; Wysteria Publishing 378; Wysteria Publishing 378

Counseling/career guidance: Amacom 136; Ballantine 149; Cambridge Educ 166; Executive Excellence 197; Facts on File 198; Ferguson 200; Graduate Grp 208; Jist Works 233; NASW 259; Owen, Richard 271; Peterson's 277; PPI 282; Professional Pub 284; Rosen Pub Grp 294; Starburst 310; Teachers College 315; Trilobyte 362; VGM 331; Zondervan 344

Crafts: Barron's Educ 151; Charlesbridge Pub 171; C&T 166; Davis 185; Down East 189; Eagle's View 191; Filter 200; Howell Pr 224; Interweave 231; Johnston Assoc 371; Lark 238; Naturegraph 259; North Light 264; Quilt Digest 287; Running Pr 295; Rutledge Hill 295; Stackpole 309; Standard 309; Sterling 311; Storey 312; Sunstone 313; Teaching & Learning 315; Viking Studio 332

Creative nonfiction: Academy Chicago 130; Allisone 135; Ambassador 136; American Quilters 139; Ballantine 149; Bellwether-Cross 153; BK MK 156; Bookhome 159; Books Collective 347; Boston Mills 348; Chicago Review 172;

Common Courage 178; David, Jonathan 185; DioGenes 187; Duquesne Univ 190; Electric Works 195; Encounter 196; Guernica 353; gynergy 353; HiddenSpring 220; Jesperson 355; Le Gesse 239; Lebhar-Freidman 240; Legacy 240; Lift Every Voice 371; Mesorah 253; Neshui 261; New Horizon 262; New Rivers 263; Onjinjinkta 268; Pathfinder 274; Pedlar 357; Picasso 357; Pontalba 281; Raindbow (California) 288; Ruminator 294; Scrivenery Press 301; Towle House 319; Trans-Atlantic 320; Universal 323; Univ of Calgary 363; Vanderwyk & Burnham 377; Vista 333

Educational: Abingdon 129; Absey 130; Accent 367; Alba 133; Albury 133; Allyn & Bacon 135; Althouse 346; Amacom 136; American Catholic 367; American Counseling 138; American Nurses 139; American Pr 139; Anchorage 140; ASA 143; Assoc for Supervision 144; ATL 145; Bandanna 367; Bantam Dell Pub Grp 149; Barron's Educ 151; Bay 151; Baywood 152; Beacon Pr 152; Bergin & Garvey 154; Between the Lines 347; Blackbirch 156; Blue Heron 157; Bonus 159; BPS 348; Broadcast Interview 163; Bryant & Dillon 164; Bureau for At-Risk Youth 164; Cambridge Educ 166; Can Educators 349; Cato Inst 169; Charlesbridge Pub 171; Charlesbridge Pub Trd 171; Chicago Review 172; Children's Pr 172; China Bks 172; Christian Ed 173; Church Growth 174; Cloud Peak 176; Cornell Univ 180; Corwin 180; Course Crafters 380; Dante Univ of America Pr 184; Davis 185; Doubleday 188; Eastern 369; ECS 192; Education Center 193; Educator's Int'l Pr 193; Edupress 193; Elder Bks 194; Electric Works 195; EMC/Paradigm 195; Encounter 196; ETC Pub 197; Evan Moor 197; Facts on File 198; Farrar, Straus & Giroux Paperbacks 199; Fell, Frederick 199; Fernwood 352; Free Spirit 204; Gessler 206; Gifted Educ 206; Graduate Grp 208; Greenhaven 209; Greenwood Pub Grp 210; Group Pub 210; Guilford 211; HAWK 216; HarperPerennial 215; Hay House 217; Heinemann 218; Hendricks, F.P. 353; Highsmith 220; Hi-Time 221; Human Kinetics 225; Humanics Pub 225; Hunter House 226; IDG Business 227; IDG Education 227; Incentive 228; Information Today 228; Intercultural 229; Int'l Scholars 230; Interstate 231; Jesperson 355; Kamehameha 234; Kent State Univ 235; Kroshka 237; Langenscheidt 238; Le Gesse 239; Learning Pub 240; Lebhar-Freidman 240; Libraries Unltd 241; Lifetime Bks 242; Lift Every Voice 371; Love and Logic 246; Lowell 246; LRP 247; Lucent 247; Manatee 249; Mayfield 250; Meriwether 252; Mesorah 253; Modern Language Assoc 255; Morehouse 256; Neal-Schuman 260; New Hope 262; New York Univ 263; Nichols 264; Oasis 267; Ohio State Univ 267; Orange Frazer 269; Oryx 269; Oughten House 374; Pencil Point 276; Perfection Learning 276; Peterson's 277; Phi Delta Kappa 278; Picasso 357; Pontalba 281; Prakken 375; Pride & Imprints 284; Prometheus 284; Prufrock 286; Publicom 381; Rainbow (FL) 289; Raindbow (California) 288; Reference Svce 290; Reidmore 359; Resource Pub 291; Review & Herald 292; Rising Star 376; Routledge 294; Rutgers Univ 295; Sagamore 296; Schocken 300; Scholastic Prof Pub 301; Scribner 301; Shoreline 360; Soma 307; South End 308; Speech Bin 308; Spence 308; St Anthony Messenger 296; Standard 309; Starburst 310; Stenhouse 310; Stylus 313; Teachers College 315; Teaching & Learning 315; Texas Western 317; Third World 317; Thompson Educ 361; Totline 319; Trilobyte 362; Turtle Books 321; Universal 323; Univ of Alaska 324; Univ of Ottawa 363; Vandamere 330; Vanderbilt Univ 331; Vanderwyk & Burnham 377; Wadsworth 333; Walch, J. Weston 334; Wall & Emerson 364; Weidner & Sons 336; Weigl 365; Westminster John Knox 337; Wonderland Pr 382; Wysteria Publishing 378; Yale Univ 343

Entertainment/games: Amber 137; Arden 143; Bonus 159; Brighton 162; Bristol Pub 163; Chess 171; Dover 189; Drew, Lisa 189; Facts on File 198; Gambling Times 370; HarperEntertainment 215; McFarland & Co 251; Meriwether 252; Minstrel 255; Piccadilly 279; Popular Culture 281; Speech Bin 308; Standard 309; Sterling 311; Univ of Nevada 326

Ethnic: Alban Inst 133; Alef 134; Arcadia 142; Arkansas 143; Arte Publico 143; Avanyu 146; Avisson 146; Balcony 148; Barricade 151; Beacon Pr 152; Behrman 153; Bethany 155; Blue Poppy 158; Bowling Green 160; Boyds Mills 160; Bryant & Dillon 164; Bucknell Univ 164; Calyx 368; Camino 166; Carolrhoda 167; Chicago Review 172; Children's Pr 172; China Bks 172; Clarity 368; Clear Light 175; Cleis 176; Common Courage 178; Companion 178; Confluence 179; Consortium 179; Cornell Univ 180; Cross Cultural 182; David, Jonathan 185; Delta 186; Doubleday 188; Eagle's View 191; Eakin Pr/Sunbelt Media 191; Eastern 369; Electric Works 195; Encounter 196; Epicenter 196; Fairleigh Dickinson 198; Fell, Frederick 199; Fernwood 352; Filter 200; Floricanto 201; Guernica 353; Hancock House 213; HarperPerennial 215; HarperSanFrancisco 215; Heyday 220; HiddenSpring 220; Hippocrene 221; Holmes & Meier 222; Holy Cross 223; Houghton Mifflin Bks for Children 223; Inner Traditions Int'l 228; Interlink 229; Int'l Scholars 230; ISER 355; Knopf & Crown Bks For Yng Rdrs 236; Lake Claremont 238; Le Gesse 239; Lebhar-Freidman 240; Lee & Low 240; Lerner 241; Libraries Unltd 241; Lifetime Bks 242; Lift Every Voice 371; Lion Bks 243; Little, Brown Children's 243; Locust Hill 244; Louisiana State Univ 246; Mage 248; March Tenth 381; McDonald & Woodward 250; McFarland & Co 251; McGregor 251; Mesorah 253; Michigan State Univ 253; Millbrook 254; Minnesota Hist Soc 254; Mitchell Lane 255; Natural Heritage/Natural History 356; Naturegraph 259; Neshui 261; New American Library 261; New World 263; New York Univ 263; Northeastern Univ 265; Northland 265; Ohio Univ 267; Oliver 268; Overmountain 270; Pacific View 272; Pacific View 375; Passeggiata 273; Pelican 275; Picasso 357; Piñata 279; Pontalba 281; Pruett 285; Purich 358; Raincoast 358; Red Hen 290; Reference Svce 290; Reidmore 359; Rosen Pub Grp 294; Routledge 294; Rutgers Univ 295; Salina 297; Schenkman 300; Schocken 300; Scribner 301; Seal 301; Sgt Kirklands 303; Shoreline 360; Simon & Schuster Bks for Yng Rdrs 304; South End 308; Stanford Univ 310; Sterling 311; Stoddart 361; Stone Bridge 311; Summit Pub Grp 313; Temple Univ 316; Texas A&M Univ 316; Texas A&M Univ 316; Third World 317; Totline 319; Tuttle 321; 2M Comm 382; Universal 323; Univ of Alaska 324; Univ of Arizona 324; Univ of Idaho 325; Univ of Manitoba 363; Univ of Nevada 326; Univ of New Mexico 326; Univ of North Texas 327; Univ of Oklahoma 327; Univ of Tennessee 328; Univ of Texas 328; Univ Pr of Kentucky 329; Univ Pr of Mississippi 329; Walsworth 334; Washington State Univ 335; Wesleyan Univ 336; Westminster John Knox 337; Whitman, Albert 338; Williamson 339; YMAA 344

Fashion/beauty: Amber 137; Owen, Richard 271; Quite Specific Media Grp 288; Storey 312

Feminism: Calyx 368; Cleis 176; Firebrand 200; gynergy 353; New Victoria 263; Spinsters Ink 309; Vehicule 364;

Film/cinema/stage: Allworth 135; Betterway 155; Bryant & Dillon 164; Companion 178; Dee, Ivan 186; Fairleigh Dickinson 198; Focal 201; Guernica 353; HarperEntertainment 215; Heinemann 218; Lifetime Bks 242; Limelight 242; Lone

Eagle 245; Mayfield 250; McFarland & Co 251; Meriwether 252; Overlook 270; Piccadilly 279; Players 280; Precept 283; Quite Specific Media Grp 288; Rutgers Univ 295; Santa Monica 298; Scarecrow 299; Simon & Pierre 360; Smith & Kraus 306; Teachers College 315; Titan 361; Univ of Texas 328; Wesleyan Univ 336

Gardening: Accent 367; Adams Media 131; Algonquin 134; Avery 146; Balcony 148; Ball 149; Barnegat 150; Black Dog & Leventhal 156; Boston Mills 348; Bullfinch 164; Burford 164; Camino 166; Chelsea Green 171; Chicago Review 172; China Bks 172; Chronicle 174; City & Co. 175; Cornell Univ 180; Countryman 180; Creative Homeowner 182; Doubleday 188; Electric Works 195; Fisher 200; Godine, David 207; Gollehon 207; Herbal Studies 370; HiddenSpring 220; Home Planners 223; Houghton Mifflin Bks for Children 223; Howell Pr 224; IDG Lifestyle 227; Interweave 231; Journey 233; Kesend, Michael 235; Lark 238; Le Gesse 239; Lebhar-Freidman 240; Legacy 240; Lone Pine 355; Longstreet 245; Lyons Pr 247; Menus & Music 372; Naturegraph 259; North Point 264; Ohio Univ 267; Ottenheimer 381; Owen, Richard 271; Owl Bks 271; Parnassus 273; Pineapple 279; Prairie Oak 283; Rainbow (FL) 289; Raindbow (California) 288; Red Eye 376; Richboro 292; Ronin Pub 293; Sasquatch 299; Sierra Club 304; Stackpole 309; Starburst 310; Steller Press Ltd. 361; Sterling 311; Stoddart 361; Storey 312; Summit Pub Grp 313; Taylor 315; Ten Speed 316; Totline 319; Tricycle 320; Universal 323; Univ of North Carolina 327; Vernon Pr 382; Weatherhill 336; Weidner & Sons 336; Westcliffe 337; Whitecap 365; Whitman, Albert 338; Willow Creek 340; Windward 341; Wonderland Pr 382; Woodbridge 378; Workman 342

Gay/lesbian: Alligator 134; Alyson 136; American Counseling 138; Autonomedia 145; Bantam Dell Pub Grp 149; Barricade 151; Beacon Pr 152; Berkley Pub Grp 154; Between the Lines 347; Broadview 348; Broadway 163; Cleis 176; Common Courage 178; Companion 178; Educator's Int'l Pr 193; Fernwood 352; Firebrand 200; Gay Sunshine & Leyland 205; Guernica 353; Guilford 211; gynergy 353; HarperPerennial 215; Haworth 217; Hazelden 217; Heinemann 218; Hidden-Spring 220; House of Anansi 354; Le Gesse 239; Lift Every Voice 371; Little, Brown Children's 243; Neal-Schuman 260; Neshui 261; New Victoria 263; New York Univ 263; Pedlar 357; Picasso 357; Pilgrim 279; Pontalba 281; Pride & Imprints 284; Red Hen 290; Routledge 294; Rutgers Univ 295; Scribner 301; Seal 301; Skinner 305; Soft Skull 306; South End 308; Stonewall 312; Trans-Atlantic 320; 2M Comm 382; United Church Pr 322; Universal 323; Wesleyan Univ 336; Westminster John Knox 337; Wonderland Pr 382

General nonfiction: American Atheist 137; Arcade 142; Ballantine 149; Beacon Pr 152; Beil, Frederic 153; Berkley Pub Grp 154; Broadway 163; Catbird 168; Countryman 180; Dutton Plume 191; ECW 351; Evans & Co 197; Harcourt Trade 214; Johnson 233; Johnston Assoc 371; Kent State Univ 235; Knopf, Alfred 236; Leisure 241; Morrow, William 257; Mustang Pub 258; Newmarket Pr 381; Nolo.com 264; Ohio State Univ 267; Pacific Bks 271; Pantheon 272; Peachtree 275; Pocket Bks 281; Prairie Oak 283; Quill Driver/Word Dancer 287; Republic of Texas 291; Seven Stories 303; Shaw, Harold 303; Sierra Club 304; Starburst 310; Taylor 315; Tiare 318; Villard 332

Gift books: Abingdon 129; Adams Media 131; American & World Geographic 379; Andrews McMeel 141; Baker Bks 148; Barbour 150; Bay 151; Bethany 155; Black Dog & Leventhal 156; Blue Sky 368; Boston Mills 348; Broadcast Interview 163; Bullfinch 164; Chandler 170; Christian Pub 173; Chronicle 174; City & Co. 175; Collectors Pr 177; Creation House 182; Cumberland 183; David, Jonathan 185; Design Pr 380; Doubleday 188; Doubleday Religious 188; Doubleday/Image 189; Down the Shore 189; Elder Bks 194; Epicenter 196; Equilibrium 369; Front St 205; gynergy 353; Hazelden 217; Health Comm 217; HiddenSpring 220; Honor 223; IDG Lifestyle 227; Kregel 237; Le Gesse 239; Lebhar-Freidman 240; Lifetime Bks 242; Lynx Images 356; MacAdam/Cage 248; Mage 248; March Tenth 381; MBI 250; Menus & Music 372; Mesorah 253; Moody 256; Multnomah 258; New World 263; Northland 265; Ohio Univ 267; Orange Frazer 269; Papier-Mache 272; Peachtree 275; Pedlar 357; Peter Pauper 277; Picasso 357; Pontalba 281; Raincoast 358; Regan Bks 290; Review & Herald 292; Santa Monica 298; Sheed & Ward 303; Soma 307; Sourcebooks 307; Starburst 310; Stoddart 361; Talese, Nan 315; Towle House 319; Vernon Pr 382; Watson-Guptill 335; Weatherhill 336; Westcliffe 337; Westminster John Knox 337; Wildcat Canyon 339; Workman 342

Government/politics: Abique 129; Adams Media 131; Alexander 134; Allegro 134; America West 137; American Atheist 137; American Pr 139; Arcade 142; Atheneum Bks for Yng Rdrs 144; Auburn 145; Austin & Winfield 145; Auto-nomedia 145; Avon 147; Bancroft 149; Bantam Dell Pub Grp 149; Barricade 151; Bellwether-Cross 153; Between the Lines 347; Bliss 368; Blue/Gray 158; Bluewood 158; Borealis 347; Branden 161; Brassey's 161; Broadway 163; Bryant & Dillon 164; Bucknell Univ 164; Burnham 165; Camino 166; Can Educators 349; Cassandra 368; Catholic Univ 168; Cato Inst 169; China Bks 172; Cleis 176; Common Courage 178; Consortium 179; CQ 181; Cross Cultural 182; Cumberland 183; Dee, Ivan 186; Discovery 187; Doubleday 188; Drew, Lisa 189; Dunne, Thomas 190; Dutton Plume 191; Electric Works 195; Encounter 196; Eriksson, Paul 196; Fairleigh Dickinson 198; Fernwood 352; Florida Academic 201; Forum 203; Four Walls Eight Windows 204; Glenbridge 206; Graduate Grp 208; Greenwood Pub Grp 210; Grove/Atlantic 211; Guernica 353; Guilford 211; HiddenSpring 220; Hill & Wang 221; Holmes & Meier 222; Horsdal & Schubart 354; House of Anansi 354; ILR 227; Interlink 229; Int'l City/County Mgmt. 229; Int'l Scholars 230; ISER 355; Jameson 232; Kroshka 237; Kumarian 238; Le Gesse 239; Lebhar-Freidman 240; Lion Bks 243; Loompanics 245; Louisiana State Univ 246; Marlowe 249; Michigan State Univ 253; Millbrook 254; Momentum 255; Naval Inst 260; Neshui 261; New England Pub Assoc 381; New Horizon 262; New York Univ 263; Northern Illinois Univ 265; Norton, WW 266; Ohio State Univ 267; Oliver 268; Oryx 269; Pantheon 272; Paragon 273; Pelican 275; Pennsylvania Hist and Museum Comm 276; Picasso 357; Pilgrim 279; Pontalba 281; PPI 282; Praeger 282; Prometheus 284; Purdue Univ 286; Purich 358; Ragweed 358; Reidmore 359; Reynolds, Morgan 292; Routledge 294; Rutgers Univ 295; Sachem 382; Sarpedon 299; Schenkman 300; Schocken 300; Sgt Kirklands 303; Sierra Club 304; Soft Skull 306; South End 308; Spence 308; St. Martin's Scholarly & Reference 297; Stanford Univ 310; Stoddart 361; Stone Bridge 311; Summit Pub Grp 313; Teachers College 315; Temple Univ 316; Texas A&M Univ 316; Third World 317; Thompson Educ 361; Thunder's Mouth 318; Towle House 319; Trans-Atlantic 320; Transnational 320; Truman State Univ 321; UCLA Amer Indian Stud Ctr 322; United Church Pr 322; Universal 323; Univ of Alabama 323; Univ of Alabama 323;

Univ of Alaska 324; Univ of Alberta 363; Univ of Arkansas 324; Univ of Georgia 325; Univ of Illinois 325; Univ of Missouri 326; Univ of North Carolina 327; Univ of North Texas 327; Univ of Oklahoma 327; Univ of Ottawa 363; Univ Pr of Kansas 329; Univ Pr of Mississippi 329; Utah State Univ Pr 330; Vanderbilt Univ 331; Vehicule 364; Verso 331; Walch, J. Weston 334; Washington State Univ 335; Watts, Franklin 335; Weigl 365; Westminster John Knox 337

Health/medicine: ABI 129; Abique 129; Adams Media 131; Adams-Blake 131; Addicus 132; AHA 132; Alban Inst 133; Allegro 134; Allyn & Bacon 135; Alyson 136; America West 137; American Coll of Physician Exec 138; American Counseling 138; American Nurses 139; American Pr 139; ASCP 144; ATL 145; Atheneum Bks for Yng Rdrs 144; Auburn 145; Avery 146; Avon 147; Ballantine 149; Bancroft 149; Bantam Dell Pub Grp 149; Barricade 151; Barron's Educ 151; Bay 151; Baywood 152; Berkley Pub Grp 154; Between the Lines 347; Bick 155; Black Dog & Leventhal 156; Blackbirch 156; Blue Poppy 158; Bluewood 158; Bonus 159; Branden 161; Brewers 162; Broadway 163; Butterworth-Heinemann 165; Butterworths Canada 349; Cambridge Educ 166; Capstone 167; Cassandra 368; Cato Inst 169; Cerier, Alison Brown 380; CHA 350; Chelsea Green 171; Chicago Review 172; Children's Pr 172; China Bks 172; Common Courage 178; Consortium 179; Consumer Pr 179; Cornell Univ 180; Creation House 182; Crossing Pr 183; Current Clinical Strategies 184; Delta 186; Doubleday 188; Dover 189; Dry Bones 190; Educator's Int'l Pr 193; Elder Bks 194; Electric Works 195; Emerald Wave 369; Emis 195; Empire 196; Encounter 196; Equilibrium 369; Eriksson, Paul 196; Evans & Co 197; Facts on File 198; Fairview 198; Fell, Frederick 199; Fernwood 352; Fisher 200; Floricanto 201; Forge 202; Free Spirit 204; Fromm Int'l 204; Gollehon 207; Government Inst 208; Graduate Grp 208; Guilford 211; HAWK 216; Hampton Rds 213; Harbor 213; Harvard Common 215; Hastings 216; Hatherleigh 216; Haworth 217; Hay House 217; Hazelden 217; Health Comm 217; Health Info 218; Healthwise 218; Hendricks, F.P. 353; Herbal Studies 370; HiddenSpring 220; Hohm 221; Holmes Pub Grp 222; Human Kinetics 225; Hunter House 226; IDG Lifestyle 227; In Print 371; Inner Traditions Int'l 228; Int'l Found Of Employee Benefit Plans 230; Int'l Medical 230; Iron Gate 232; Jewish Lights 233; Kali 371; Kensington 235; Kesend, Michael 235; Kramer, H.J. 236; Kroshka 237; Kumarian 238; Lawrence, Merloyd 239; Le Gesse 239; Lebhar-Freidman 240; Libraries Unltd 241; Lifetime Bks 242; Lippincott Williams & Wilkins 243; Llewellyn 244; Love and Logic 246; Lowell 246; Lyons Pr 247; Magni Grp 249; Marcus 356; Marketscope 249; Marlowe 249; Mayfield 250; McFarland & Co 251; Millbrook 254; NASW 259; New American Library 261; New Harbinger 262; New Horizon 262; New York Univ 263; Newmarket Pr 381; Next Decade 373; Norton, WW 266; NTC/Contemporary 266; Oliver 268; Oryx 269; Ottenheimer 381; Owl Bks 271; Pacific Pr 271; Pacific View 272; Pacific View 375; Parlay Int'l 273; Pathfinder 274; Peachtree 275; Perigee 277; Pilgrim 279; Possibility 281; Practice Mgmt 282; Precept 283; Productive 358; Prometheus 284; Purdue Univ 286; Putnam's Sons 286; QED 375; Quest Bks 287; Quest Bks Trade 290; Random House 290; Regnery Pub 291; Review & Herald 292; Rising Star 376; Ronin Pub 293; Rosen Pub Grp 294; Running Pr 295; Rutgers Univ 295; Sagamore 296; Santa Monica 296; Schocken 300; Scribner 301; Seal 301; Settel 382; Shoreline 360; Skidmore-Roth 305; Slack 305; Soma 307; South End 308; Southern Methodist Univ 308; Speech Bin 308; Starburst 310; Sterling 311; Storey 312; Summit Pub Grp 313; Taylor 315; Temple Univ 316; Ten Speed 316; Texas Western 317; Third World 317; Three Hawks 377; Trans-Atlantic 320; Tricycle 320; Trilobyte 362; Tuttle 321; 2M Comm 382; United Church Pr 322; Unity 323; Universal 323; Univ of Alaska 324; Univ of Calgary 363; Univ of North Carolina 327; Univ Pr of Mississippi 329; Vandamere 330; Vanderbilt Univ 331; VGM 331; Viking 332; Visions Comm 332; Vista 333; Vista 377; Vitesse 377; Volcano 333; Wadsworth 333; Walker & Co 334; Wall & Emerson 364; Warner Bks 334; Weidner & Sons 336; Weiser, Samuel 336; Whitman, Albert 338; Wiley 339; Woodbine 342; Woodbridge 378; Woodland 342; Workman 342; Wysteria Publishing 378; Yale Univ 343; YMAA 344

Hi-lo: Cambridge Educ 166; Rising Tide 292

History: A&B 128; ABDO 129; Abique 129; Absey 130; Academy Chicago 130; Adams Media 131; Alexander 134; Algonquin 134; Ambassador 136; American Atheist 137; American Pr 139; Ancestry 140; Appalachian Mountain 141; A-R 142; Arcade 142; Arcadia 142; Arkansas 143; Aronson 143; Atheneum Bks for Yng Rdrs 144; Autonomedia 145; Avanyu 146; Aviation Publishers (PA) 146; Avisson 146; Avon 147; Aztex 147; Balcony 148; Bandanna 367; Bantam Dell Pub Grp 149; Barricade 151; Bay 151; Baylor Univ 152; Beil, Frederic 153; Berkley Pub Grp 154; Berkshire 154; Between the Lines 347; Black Dog & Leventhal 156; Blackbirch 156; Blair 157; Bliss 368; Blue/Gray 158; Bluewood 158; Borealis 347; Boston Mills 348; Bowling Green 160; Boyds Mills 160; Branden 161; Brassey's 161; Brassey's Sports 161; Brevet 161; Brewers 162; Bridge Works 162; Bright Mountain 368; Bristol Fashion 162; Broadcast Interview 163; Broadview 348; Broadway 163; Broken Jaw 348; Brucedale 349; Bryant & Dillon 164; Bucknell Univ 164; Caitlin 349; Camino 166; Can Educators 349; Capstone 167; Carroll & Graf 167; Cartwheel 168; Catholic Univ 168; Caxton 169; Centerstream 170; CHA 350; Chandler 170; Chariot/Victor 170; Chicago Review 172; Children's Pr 172; China Bks 172; Christian Pub 173; Clear Light 175; Cloud Peak 176; Common Courage 178; Companion 178; Confluence 179; Consortium 179; Cornell Maritime 180; Cornell Univ 180; Country Music Found 180; Creative Pub 182; Cross Cultural 182; Cumberland 183; Dante Univ of America Pr 184; Darlington 184; Davis 185; Dee, Ivan 186; Discovery 187; Doubleday 188; Doubleday Religious 188; Dover 189; Down East 189; Down the Shore 189; Drew, Lisa 189; Dry Bones 190; Dufour 190; Dunne, Thomas 190; Dutton Children's 191; Eagle's View 191; Eakin Pr/Sunbelt Media 191; Eastern Nat'l 192; Edutainment Media 194; Eerdmans, William 194; Electric Works 195; Elephant 195; Encounter 196; Epicenter 196; Eriksson, Paul 196; ETC Pub 197; Facts on File 198; Fairleigh Dickinson 198; Family Album 370; Fernwood 352; Filter 200; Floricanto 201; Florida Academic 201; Forum 203; Four Walls Eight Windows 204; Fromm Int'l 204; Genesis 205; Glenbridge 206; Golden West 207; Goose Lane 352; Greenhaven 209; Greenwood Pub Grp 210; Grove/Atlantic 211; Guernica 353; HAWK 216; Hancock House 213; HarperPerennial 215; Hellgate 219; Hendrick-Long 219; Heritage 220; Heritage House 353; Heyday 220; HiddenSpring 220; Hill & Wang 221; Hippocrene 221; Holiday House 222; Holmes & Meier 222; Horsdal & Schubart 354; Houghton Mifflin Bks for Children 223; House of Anansi 354; Howell Pr 224; ILR 227; Inner Traditions Int'l 228; Interlink 229; Int'l Scholars 230; ISER 355; Jacobs, Lee 232; Jameson 232; Jesperson 355; Jewish Lights 233; Johnson 233; Journey 233; Judaica 234; Kamehameha 234; Kent State Univ 235; Kesend, Michael 235; Knopf & Crown Bks For Yng Rdrs 236; Krieger 237; Kroshka 237; Lake Claremont 238; Le Gesse

239; Lehbar-Freidman 240; Lehigh Univ 241; Lerner 241; Libraries Unltd 241; Lifetime Bks 242; Lift Every Voice 371; Limelight 242; Lion Bks 243; Little, Brown 243; Little, Brown Children's 243; Livingston 244; Longstreet 245; Louisiana State Univ 246; Loyola 247; Lucent 247; Lynx Images 356; Madison Bks 248; Mage 248; March Tenth 381; Marlowe 249; MBI 250; McDonald & Woodward 250; McElderry, Margaret 250; McFarland & Co 251; McGregor 251; Mesorah 253; Michigan State Univ 253; Middle Atlantic 253; Middle Atlantic 373; Millbrook 254; Minnesota Hist Soc 254; Missouri Historical Society Press 373; Momentum 255; Morningside 257; Morrow, William 257; Mount Ida 373; Mountain Pr 257; Narwhal 259; Natural Heritage/Natural History 356; Nautical & Aviation 260; Naval Inst 260; Neshui 261; New England 261; New England Pub Assoc 381; New Victoria 263; New York Univ 263; North Point 264; Northeastern Univ 265; Northern Illinois Univ 265; Northland 265; Norton, WW 266; Ohio State Univ 267; Ohio Univ 267; Oliver 268; Orange Frazer 269; Orchard 269; Oregon State Univ 269; Osprey 270; Overlook 270; Overmountain 270; Owen, Richard 271; Owl Bks 271; Pacific View 272; Pantheon 272; Parnassus 273; Passeggiata 273; Peachtree Children's 275; Peachtree 275; Pelican 275; Pennsylvania Hist and Museum Comm 276; Permanent Pr/Second Chance 277; Picasso 357; Picton 279; Pineapple 279; Pocket Bks 281; Pogo 375; Pontalba 281; Praeger 282; Prairie Oak 283; Presidio 283; Press at the Maryland Hist Soc 283; Pride & Imprints 284; Prometheus 284; ProStar 285; Pruett 285; Puffin 286; Purdue Univ 286; Purich 358; Quite Specific Media Grp 288; Ragweed 358; Raincoast 358; Random House Bks for Yng Rdrs 289; Random House Trade 290; Regnery Pub 291; Reidmore 359; Republic of Texas 291; Review & Herald 292; Reynolds, Morgan 292; Rockbridge 293; Ronsdale 359; Routledge 294; Rutgers Univ 295; Sachem 382; Sandlapper 298; Sarpedon 299; Sasquatch 299; Saxon House Canada 359; Schenkman 300; Schocken 300; Scholastic Canada 360; Scribner 301; Scrivenery Press 301; Sgt Kirklands 303; Settel 382; Shoreline 360; Simon & Schuster Bks for Yng Rdrs 304; Skinner 305; Soma 307; South End 308; Southern Illinois Univ Pr 308; Southern Methodist Univ 308; St Anthony Messenger 296; St. Augustine's 296; St Bede's 296; St. Martin's Scholarly & Reference 297; Stackpole 309; Stackpole 309; Stanford Univ 310; Steller Press Ltd. 361; Stoddart 361; Summit Pub Grp 313; Sunstone 313; Talese, Nan 315; Tamarack 377; Taylor 315; Teachers College 315; Temple Univ 316; Texas A&M Univ 316; Texas State Hist Assoc 316; Texas Western 317; Third World 317; Tidewater 318; Towle House 319; Trans-Atlantic 320; Trinity 320; Troitsa 321; Truman State Univ 321; Turtle Books 321; TwoDot 322; UCLA Amer Indian Stud Ctr 322; Universal 323; Univ of Akron 323; Univ of Alabama 323; Univ of Alaska 324; Univ of Alberta 363; Univ of Arkansas 324; Univ of California 325; Univ of Georgia 325; Univ of Idaho 325; Univ of Illinois 325; Univ of Iowa 326; Univ of Maine 326; Univ of Manitoba 363; Univ of Missouri 326; Univ of Nevada 326; Univ of New Mexico 326; Univ of North Carolina 327; Univ of North Texas 327; Univ of Oklahoma 327; Univ of Ottawa 363; Univ of Pennsylvania 328; Univ of South Carolina 328; Univ of Tennessee 328; Univ of Texas 328; Univ Pr of Kansas 329; Univ Pr of Kentucky 329; Univ Pr of Mississippi 329; Upney 363; Utah State Univ Pr 330; Vandamere 330; Vanderbilt Univ 331; Vanwell 364; Vehicule 364; Vernon Pr 382; Verso 331; Viking 332; Voyageur 333; Walch, J. Weston 334; Walker & Co 334; Walsworth 334; Warner Bks 334; Washington State Univ 335; Watts, Franklin 335; Weatherhill 336; Weigl 365; Wesleyan Univ 336; Western NY 378; Westernlore 337; Westminster John Knox 337; White Mane 338; Whitecap 365; Whitman, Albert 338; Wiener, Markus 339; Wiley 339; Winslow 341; Wonderland Pr 382; Yale Univ 343; Zondervan 344

Hobby: Adams Media 131; Alexander 134; American Quilters 139; Ancestry 140; Arkansas 143; Aviation Publishers (PA) 146; Bale 148; Barron's Educ 151; Bay 151; Berkshire 154; Betterway 155; Black Dog & Leventhal 156; Bonus 159; Boyds Mills 160; Brewers 162; Broadcast Interview 163; Burford 164; Chicago Review 172; Children's Pr 172; Creative Homeowner 182; C&T 166; Cypress 184; Doubleday 188; Dover 189; Eagle's View 191; Edutainment Media 194; Electric Works 195; Eriksson, Paul 196; Fell, Frederick 199; Fox Chapel 204; Gollehon 207; Gryphon Pub 211; HAWK 216; House of Collectibles 224; Interweave 231; Iron Gate 232; Jacobs, Lee 232; Kalmbach 234; Kesend, Michael 235; Krause 237; Lark 238; Le Gesse 239; Lehbar-Freidman 240; Legacy 240; Lifetime Bks 242; Little, Brown Children's 243; Lyons Pr 247; March Tenth 381; Marketscope 249; MBI 250; Menus & Music 372; Millbrook 254; Mustang Pub 258; Next Decade 373; No Starch 264; North Light 264; Northland 265; Norton, WW 266; Oak Knoll 267; Osprey 270; Parnassus 273; Pathfinder 274; Picasso 357; Picton 279; Popular Woodworking 281; Possibility 281; Productive 358; Quilt Digest 285; Rainbow (FL) 289; Scholastic Canada 360; Scrivenery Press 301; Settel 382; Skyfoot Technical 360; Soma 307; Stackpole 309; Sterling 311; Success Pub 313; Summit Pub Grp 313; Totline 319; Universal 323; Vernon Pr 382; Viking Studio 332; Voyageur 333; Weidner & Sons 336; Whitman, Albert 338; Willow Creek 340

House and home: Betterway 155; Blue Sky 368; Bonus 159; Brighton 162; Consumer Pr 179; Creative Homeowner 182; Home Planners 223; Pantheon 272; Sourcebooks 307; Sterling 311; Storey 312; Taylor 315; Warner Bks 334

How-to: aatec 366; ABDO 129; Absey 130; Accent 367; Adams Media 131; Adams-Blake 131; Addicus 132; Alexander 134; Allisone 135; Allworth 135; Alpine 367; Amacom 136; Amber 137; American Bar 137; American Correctional 138; American Quilters 139; Amherst Media 140; Ancestry 140; Anchor Pub 140; Andrews McMeel 141; Appalachian Mountain 141; Arkansas 143; ASA 143; Assoc for Supervision 144; Aviation Publishers (PA) 146; Avon 147; Aztex 147; Ball 149; Ballantine 149; Bancroft 149; Bantam Dell Pub Grp 149; Barnegat 150; Barricade 151; Bay 151; Bentley 154; Berkley Pub Grp 154; Bethany 155; Betterway 155; Black Dog & Leventhal 156; Bloomberg 157; Blue Sky 368; Bookhome 159; Bookwrights 379; Brighton 162; Bristol Fashion 162; Bristol Pub 163; Broadcast Interview 163; Bryant & Dillon 164; Burford 164; Business McGraw-Hill 165; Butterworth-Heinemann 165; Cambridge Educ 166; Camino 166; Career Pr 167; Cassandra 368; CCC 169; Cedar Fort 169; Cerier, Alison Brown 380; CHA 350; Chandler 170; Chelsea Green 171; Chicago Review 172; China Bks 172; Chosen Bks 173; Christian Pub 173; Church Growth 174; Circlet 175; Cloud Peak 176; Coaches 177; Concordia 178; Consortium 179; Consumer Pr 179; Cornell Maritime 180; Countryman 180; Countrysport 181; Craftsman 181; Creative Homeowner 182; C&T 166; Cumberland 183; Cypress 184; David, Jonathan 185; Dearborn 185; Doral 188; Doubleday 188; Doubleday/Image 189; Dover 189; Eagle's View 191; Ecopress 369; Éditions Logiques 352; Edupress 193; Edutainment Media 194; Elder Bks 194; Electric Works 195; Empire 196; Equilibrium 369; Eriksson, Paul 196; Fell, Frederick 199; Fiesta City 370; Florida Academic 201; Focal 201; Footprint Press 370; Fox Chapel 204; Gambling Times 370; GATF Pr 205; Gay

Sunshine & Leyland 205; Gollehon 207; Graduate Grp 208; Group Pub 210; Gulf 212; HAWK 216; Half Halt 212; Hamilton, Alexander 212; Hampton Rds 213; Hancock House 213; Hanser Gardner 213; HarperPerennial 215; HarperSanFrancisco 215; Hastings 216; Hazelden 217; Health Info 218; Heinemann 218; Herbal Studies 370; Heritage 220; Heritage House 353; HiddenSpring 220; Home Planners 223; House of Collectibles 224; Human Kinetics 225; IDG Business 227; IDG Education 227; IDG Lifestyle 227; Ideals Pub 227; In Print 371; Information Today 228; Int'l Wealth 231; Interweave 231; Iron Gate 232; Jacobs, Lee 232; Jelmar 371; Jist Works 233; Kalmbach 234; Kesend, Michael 235; Kogan Page 236; Krause 237; Lark 238; Laureate 371; Le Gesse 239; Lebhar-Freidman 240; Lifetime Bks 242; Limelight 242; Lion Bks 243; Llewellyn 244; Lone Eagle 245; Loompanics 245; March Tenth 381; Marketscope 249; Maximum 249; MBI 250; McDonald & Woodward 250; McGavick Field 372; McGraw-Hill Ryerson 356; McGregor 251; Meadowbrook 251; Meriwether 252; Midknight Club 253; Morrow, William 257; Mountain N'Air 257; Mountain Pr 257; Mountaineers Bks 258; Mustang Pub 258; Narwhal 259; Naturegraph 259; New American Library 261; New Hope 262; Next Decade 373; No Starch 264; Nolo.com 264; North Light 264; NTC/Contemporary 266; Oak Knoll 267; Oasis 267; One on One 268; Open Road 268; Pacesetter 375; Pacific Pr 271; Paladin 272; Phi Delta Kappa 278; Picasso 357; Piccadilly 279; Pineapple 279; Popular Woodworking 281; Possibility 281; Potter, Clarkson 282; PPI 282; PROMPT 285; Pride & Imprints 284; Productive 358; ProStar 285; Prufrock 286; Quill Driver/Word Dancer 287; Quilt Digest 287; Quite Specific Media Grp 288; Ragged Mountain 288; Rainbow (FL) 289; Red Eye 376; Resource Pub 291; Revell, Fleming 291; Richboro 292; Rocky Mountain 359; Running Pr 295; Safari 295; Santa Monica 298; Scrivenery Press 301; Self-Counsel (US) 302; Settel 382; Sierra Club 304; Skyfoot Technical 360; Soma 307; Sourcebooks 307; Speech Bin 308; Spotted Dog 309; Starburst 310; Sterling 311; Stoddart 361; Stoeger 311; Stone Bridge 311; Stoneydale 312; Success Pub 313; Summit Pub Grp 313; Sunstone 313; Taylor 315; Tech Books for the Layperson 377; Ten Speed 316; The Magni Group, Inc. 249; Tiare 318; Titan 361; Tricycle 320; Trilobyte 362; Turtle Pr 321; 2M Comm 382; Universal 323; Visions Comm 332; Watson-Guptill 335; Weatherhill 336; Weiser, Samuel 336; Westminster John Knox 337; Whitehorse 378; Whitford 378; Wilderness 339; Wiley 339; Williamson 379; Willow Creek 340; Wilshire 340; Wonderland Pr 382; Workman 342; Writer's Digest 343; Wysteria Publishing 378; YMAA 344

Humanities: Dante Univ of America Pr 184; Free Pr 204; Greenwood 209; Greenwood Pub Grp 210; Gruyter, Aldine de 211; Learning Pub 240; Roxbury 294; St. Martin's Scholarly & Reference 297; Stanford Univ 310; Univ of Arkansas 324; Whitson 338; Zondervan 344

Humor: Accent 367; Adams Media 131; Albury 133; Anchor Pub 140; Andrews McMeel 141; Atheneum Bks for Yng Rdrs 144; Ballantine 149; Bancroft 149; Bantam Dell Pub Grp 149; Barbour 150; Bay 151; Black Dog & Leventhal 156; Blue Sky 368; Bonus 159; Broadcast Interview 163; Brucedale 349; Catbird 168; CCC 169; Christian Pub 173; Cloud Peak 176; Common Courage 178; Cumberland 183; David, Jonathan 185; Doubleday 188; Doubleday/Image 189; Dover 189; DTP 190; Éditions Logiques 352; Electric Works 195; Empire 196; Epicenter 196; Eriksson, Paul 196; Fiesta City 370; Genesis 205; Gollehon 207; Great Quotations 209; HarperEntertainment 215; HarperPerennial 215; Houghton Mifflin Bks for Children 223; Jacobs, Lee 232; Jesperson 355; Kensington 235; Le Gesse 239; Lebhar-Freidman 240; Limelight 242; Longstreet 245; Marketscope 249; McGavick Field 372; Meadowbrook 251; Meriwether 252; Multnomah 258; Mustang Pub 258; NTC/Contemporary 266; Onjinjinkta 268; Orange Frazer 269; Owen, Richard 271; Paladin 272; Peachtree 275; Pedlar 357; Picasso 357; Piccadilly 279; Pocket Bks 281; Pontalba 281; Potter, Clarkson 282; Price Stern Sloan 283; Pride & Imprints 284; Ragged Mountain 288; Ragweed 358; Random House Trade 290; Republic of Texas 291; Review & Herald 292; Rutledge Hill 295; Sandlapper 298; Settel 382; Shoreline 360; Smith, Gibbs 306; Soma 307; Sound & Vision 361; Spectacle Lane 376; Sterling 311; Stoddart 361; Summit Pub Grp 313; Titan 361; 2M Comm 382; Warner Bks 334; Weatherhill 336; Westminster John Knox 337; Willow Creek 340; Wonderland Pr 382; Workman 342

Illustrated book: A&B 128; Abrams 130; Adams Media 131; Alpine 367; Ambassador 136; American & World Geographic 379; ASCP 144; Avanyu 146; Baker Bks 148; Balcony 148; Ballantine 149; Bandanna 367; Bantam Dell Pub Grp 149; Barbour 150; Bay 151; Beeman Jorbensen 153; Beil, Frederic 153; Betterway 155; Black Dog & Leventhal 156; Blackbirch 156; Bliss 368; Bluewood 158; Boston Mills 348; Branden 161; Broadway 163; Broken Jaw 348; Brucedale 349; Bullfinch 164; Burford 164; Caxton 169; Chandler 170; Chronicle Bks for Children 174; City & Co. 175; Collectors Pr 177; Common Courage 178; Consortium 179; Country Music Found 180; Countrysport 181; Creative Homeowner 182; C&T 166; Cumberland 183; Cypress 184; Darlington 184; David, Jonathan 185; Davis 185; Design Pr 380; Dial Bks for Yng Rdrs 187; Doubleday 188; Doubleday/Image 189; Dover 189; Down the Shore 189; Eakin Pr/Sunbelt Media 191; Éditions Logiques 352; Edutainment Media 194; Electric Works 195; Falcon 199; Ft Ross 203; Fromm Int'l 204; Front St 205; Godine, David 207; Goose Lane 352; Great Quotations 209; Grolier 210; gynergy 353; Hampton Rds 213; HarperPerennial 215; Health Info 218; Heritage House 353; Holt Bks for Yng Rdrs 222; Houghton Mifflin Bks for Children 223; Howell Pr 224; Humanics Pub 225; IDG Business 227; IDG Lifestyle 227; Ideals Pub 227; Ideals Pub 227; Jacobs, Lee 232; Jewish Lights 233; Judaica 234; Kalmbach 234; Kesend, Michael 235; Kramer, H.J. 236; Krause 237; Lark 238; Le Gesse 239; Lebhar-Freidman 240; Lee & Low 240; Limelight 242; Longstreet 245; Mage 248; Manatee 249; March Tenth 381; MBI 250; McDonald & Woodward 250; Merriam Press 252; Minnesota Hist Soc 254; Multnomah 258; New England 261; Northland 265; Northword 266; Orange Frazer 269; Orchard 269; Osprey 270; Ottenheimer 381; Pedlar 357; Pelican 275; Pennsylvania Hist and Museum Comm 276; Philomel 278; Picador 278; Picasso 357; Pogo 375; Pontalba 281; Popular Woodworking 281; Press at the Maryland Hist Soc 283; Pride & Imprints 284; ProStar 285; Puffin 286; Quest Bks 287; Ragweed 358; Raincoast 358; Random House Trade 290; Regan Bks 290; Sandlapper 298; Santa Monica 298; Saxon House Canada 359; Settel 382; Shoreline 360; Smith, Gibbs 306; Soma 307; Soundprints 307; Sourcebooks 307; Speech Bin 308; Standard 309; Stoddart 361; Tamarack 377; Texas State Hist Assoc 316; Third World 317; Tidewater 318; Titan 361; Totline 319; Trans-Atlantic 320; Truman State Univ 321; Turtle Books 321; Univ of New Mexico 326; Univ of South Carolina 328; Vernon Pr 382; Verso 331; Watson-Guptill 335; Weatherhill 336; Westcliffe 337; Whitman, Albert 338; Willow Creek 340; Windward 341; Wonderland Pr 382; Wysteria Publishing 378; Yale Univ 343

Juvenile books: A&B 128; ABDO 129; Abingdon 129; Absey 130; Addax 132; Alaska Northwest 133; Alef 134; Allegro 134; Ambassador 136; Amber 137; Annick Press Ltd. 346; Archway 142; Arte Publico 143; ATL 145; Atheneum Bks for Yng Rdrs 144; Baker Bks 148; Baker Bks 148; Barbour 150; Barron's Educ 151; Behrman 153; Beil, Frederic 153; Benefactory 153; Black Dog & Leventhal 156; Blackbirch 156; Borealis 347; Boyds Mills 160; Branden 161; Bristol Fashion 162; Brucedale 349; Camino 166; Candlewick 166; Capstone 167; Carolrhoda 167; Cartwheel 168; Chariot/Victor 170; Charlesbridge Pub 171; Charlesbridge Pub Trd 171; Chicago Review 172; Child Welfare 172; Children's Pr 172; China Bks 172; Christian Ed 173; Chronicle Bks for Children 174; Cloud Peak 176; Concordia 178; David, Jonathan 185; Design Pr 380; Dial Bks for Yng Rdrs 187; Doral 188; Dover 189; Down East 189; Down the Shore 189; Dutton Children's 191; Eakin Pr/Sunbelt Media 191; Eastern Nat'l 192; Éditions Logiques 352; Education Center 193; Edupress 193; Eerdmans Bks for Yng Rdrs 194; Eerdmans, William 194; Electric Works 195; Enslow 196; Evan Moor 197; Facts on File 198; Farrar Straus & Giroux 199; Fiesta City 370; Focus Pub 202; Free Spirit 204; Front St 205; Genesis 205; Godine, David 207; Gollehon 207; Greenhaven 209; Grolier 210; Grosset & Dunlap 210; Group Pub 210; HAWK 216; Harcourt Children's 214; HarperEntertainment 215; Hendrick-Long 219; Highsmith 220; Holt Bks for Yng Rdrs 222; Houghton Mifflin Adult 224; Houghton Mifflin Bks for Children 223; Humanics Pub 225; Ideals Children's Bks 227; Ideals Pub 227; Illumination 370; Incentive 228; Jewish Lights 233; Journey 233; Judaica 234; Kamehameha 235; Kar-Ben 235; Knopf & Crown Bks For Yng Rdrs 236; Kramer, H.J. 236; Lark 238; Le Gesse 239; Lee & Low 240; Legacy 240; Lerner 241; Lifetime Bks 242; Lift Every Voice 371; Liguori 242; Little, Brown Children's 243; Little Simon 244; Lucent 247; Mage 248; Manatee 249; McClanahan Book Co 381; McElderry, Margaret 250; Meadowbrook 251; Mesorah 253; Middle Atlantic 253; Millbrook 254; Minstrel 255; Mitchell Lane 255; Moody 256; Mountaineers Bks 258; Multnomah 258; Narwhal 259; Nelson, Tommy 260; New Hope 262; New Horizon 262; Northwood 266; Oliver 268; Onjinjinkta 268; Orchard 269; Orchard 269; Ottenheimer 381; Overmountain 270; Owen, Richard 271; Pacific Pr 271; Pacific View 272; Pacific View 375; Pauline Bks & Media 274; Peachtree Children's 275; Peachtree 275; Pelican 275; Perfection Learning 276; Philomel 278; Picasso 357; Piñata 279; Players 280; Pleasant Co 280; PPI 282; Press at the Maryland Hist Soc 283; Price Stern Sloan 283; Pride & Imprints 284; Prometheus 284; Prufrock 286; Puffin 286; Ragweed 358; Rainbow (FL) 289; Raincoast 358; Random House Bks for Yng Rdrs 289; Red Hen 290; Review & Herald 292; Ronsdale 359; Rosen Pub Grp 294; Running Pr 295; Salina 297; Sandlapper 298; Scholastic Canada 360; Scholastic Inc 300; Scholastic Pr 300; Scholastic Prof Pub 301; Seedling 302; Settel 382; Sierra Club 304; Simon & Schuster Bks for Yng Rdrs 304; Skinner 305; Smith, Gibbs 306; Soundprints 307; Speech Bin 308; St Anthony Messenger 296; Standard 309; Sterling 311; Success Pub 313; Summit Pub Grp 313; Teaching & Learning 315; Third World 317; Tidewater 318; Tingley Books, Megan 318; Torah Aura 318; Totline 319; Tricycle 320; Turtle Books 321; Twenty-First Century 322; Tyndale 322; Vanwell 364; Vernon Pr 382; Viking Children's Bks 332; Visions Comm 332; Volcano 333; Walker & Co 334; Watts, Franklin 335; Weigl 365; Westminster John Knox 337; White Mane 338; Whitecap 365; Whitman, Albert 338; Wiley 339; Williamson 339; Winslow 341; Zondervan 344

Labor: Amacom 136; Battelle 151; Baywood 152; Baywood 152; BNA 158; Brevet 161; Hamilton, Alexander 212; ILR 227; Intercultural 229; Michigan State Univ 253; Temple Univ 316

Language and literature: Absey 130; Adams Media 131; Alef 134; Alligator 134; Allyn & Bacon 135; Anchorage 140; Arte Publico 143; Avisson 146; Bandanna 367; Bantam Dell Pub Grp 149; Barron's Educ 151; Beil, Frederic 153; Birch Brook 155; Black Dog & Leventhal 156; Books Collective 347; Borealis 347; Bottom Dog 160; Bowling Green 160; Brewers 162; Bridge Works 162; Broadview 348; Broken Jaw 348; Brucedale 349; Bryant & Dillon 164; Bucknell Univ 164; Calyx 368; Catholic Univ 168; China Bks 172; Coach House Books 350; Confluence 179; Cornell Univ 180; Coteau 351; Course Crafters 380; Dante Univ of America Pr 184; Dee, Ivan 186; Doubleday 188; Dover 189; Duquesne Univ 190; Eastern 369; Ecco Pr 192; Ediciones Nuevo Espacio 192; Education Center 193; Educator's Int'l Pr 193; Educators Pub Svces 193; Electric Works 195; Encounter 196; Facts on File 198; Family Album 370; Farrar, Straus & Giroux Paperbacks 199; Fernwood 352; Floricanto 201; Four Walls Eight Windows 204; Fromm Int'l 204; Gessler 206; Gifted Educ 206; Goose Lane 352; Graywolf 208; Greenwood Pub Grp 210; Gryphon Pub 211; Guernica 353; HAWK 216; HarperPerennial 215; Heinemann 218; Hendricks, F.P. 353; Highsmith 220; Hippocrene 221; Houghton Mifflin Adult 224; Houghton Mifflin Bks for Children 223; House of Anansi 354; IBEX 226; Int'l Scholars 230; Kent State Univ 235; Langenscheidt 238; Latin Amer Lit Review 239; Le Gesse 239; Lebhar-Friedman 240; Lehigh Univ 241; Libraries Unltd 241; Lift Every Voice 371; Livingston 244; Locust Hill 244; Longstreet 245; Louisiana State Univ 246; MacMurray & Beck 248; Mage 248; March Tenth 381; Mayfield 250; Michigan State Univ 253; Milkweed 254; Missouri Historical Society Press 373; Modern Language Assoc 255; Neal-Schuman 260; Neshui 261; New American Library 261; New York Univ 263; Norton, WW 266; Ohio State Univ 267; Ohio Univ 267; Oregon State Univ 269; Oryx 269; Owl Bks 271; Passeggiata 273; Pedlar 357; Pencil Point 276; Perfection Learning 276; Picador 278; Picasso 357; Pontalba 281; Potter, Clarkson 282; Pride & Imprints 284; Prometheus 284; Puckerbrush 375; Purdue Univ 286; Red Hen 290; Reynolds, Morgan 292; Rising Star 376; Ronsdale 359; Roxbury 294; Ruminator 294; Russian Info 376; Rutgers Univ 295; Scribner 301; Scrivenery Press 301; Serendipity 302; Sierra Club 304; Simon & Pierre 360; St. Martin's Scholarly & Reference 297; Stanford Univ 310; Stoddart 361; Stone Bridge 311; Stormline 376; Story Line 312; TCU Press 315; Teaching & Learning 315; Texas Western 317; Third World 317; Torah Aura 318; Totline 319; Truman State Univ 321; Turtle Books 321; UCLA Amer Indian Stud Ctr 322; Universal 323; Univ of Alabama 323; Univ of Alaska 324; Univ of Arkansas 324; Univ of California 325; Univ of Georgia 325; Univ of Idaho 325; Univ of Illinois 325; Univ of Iowa 326; Univ of Nevada 326; Univ of North Carolina 327; Univ of North Texas 327; Univ of Oklahoma 327; Univ of Ottawa 363; Univ of Pennsylvania 328; Univ of South Carolina 328; Univ of Tennessee 328; Univ of Texas 328; Univ Pr of Kentucky 329; Univ Pr of Mississippi 329; Utah State Univ Pr 330; Vanderbilt Univ 331; Vehicule 364; Vernon Pr 382; Viking 332; Wadsworth 333; Walch, J. Weston 334; Weatherhill 336; Weidner & Sons 336; Wesleyan Univ 336; Whitman, Albert 338; Writer's Digest 343; Yale Univ 343; York 365; Zoland 344

Law: Allworth 135; American Bar 137; American Correctional 138; Beacon Pr 152; BNA 158; Butterworth-Heinemann

165; Butterworths Canada 349; Carswell Thomson 350; Catbird 168; Drew, Lisa 189; Government Inst 208; Graduate Grp 208; Hamilton, Alexander 212; Hein, William 218; Lawyers & Judges 239; LRP 247; Michigan State Univ 253; Nolo.com 264; Northeastern Univ 265; Norton, WW 266; Ohio State Univ 267; Phi Delta Kappa 278; Pilgrim 279; Purich 358; Quorum 288; Self-Counsel (US) 302; Spence 308; Temple Univ 316; Tower 319; Transnational 320; United Church Pr 322

Literary criticism: Broken Jaw 348; Bucknell Univ 164; Fairleigh Dickinson 198; Godine, David 207; Greenhaven 209; Greenwood 209; Guernica 353; Holmes & Meier 222; House of Anansi 354; Kent State Univ 235; Michigan State Univ 253; Northern Illinois Univ 265; Ohio State Univ 267; Passeggiata 273; Picador 278; Purdue Univ 286; Quite Specific Media Grp 288; Routledge 294; Simon & Pierre 360; Stanford Univ 310; TCU Press 315; Third World 317; Univ of Alabama 323; Univ of Arkansas 324; Univ of Missouri 326; Univ of Pennsylvania 328; Univ of Tennessee 328; Univ of Texas 328; Univ Pr of Mississippi 329; York 365; Doubleday 188

Marine subjects: Cornell Maritime 180; Howell Pr 224; Narwhal 259; Naval Inst 260

Memoirs: Between the Lines 347; Black Dog & Leventhal 156; Books Collective 347; Brucedale 349; Chelsea Green 171; Chicago Review 172; Cormorant 351; Cross Cultural 182; David, Jonathan 185; Delta 186; Doubleday Religious 188; Ediciones Nuevo Espacio 192; Edutainment Media 194; Electric Works 195; Encounter 196; Equilibrium 369; Filter 200; Ft Ross 203; Hazelden 217; HiddenSpring 220; Jacobs, Lee 232; Le Gesse 239; Lebhar-Freidman 240; Lift Every Voice 371; MacMurray & Beck 248; Mesorah 253; Middle Atlantic 373; Momentum 255; Narwhal 259; Neshui 261; Northeastern Univ 265; Orange Frazer 269; Pontalba 281; ProStar 285; St Mary's 297; Westminster John Knox 337; Wysteria Publishing 378

Military/war: Allegro 134; Ambassador 136; Bantam Dell Pub Grp 149; Black Dog & Leventhal 156; Bluewood 158; Brucedale 349; Capstone 167; Cloud Peak 176; Combined Pub 177; Common Courage 178; Cornell Univ 180; Cumberland 183; Darlington 184; Eakin Pr/Sunbelt Media 191; Eastern Nat'l 192; Elephant 195; Encounter 196; Flying 201; HarperPerennial 215; Le Gesse 239; Merriam Press 252; Morningside 257; Neshui 261; Ohio Univ 267; Picasso 357; Pontalba 281; Sarpedon 299; Soft Skull 306; Towle House 319; Universal 323; Univ of North Carolina 327; Walsworth 334

Money/finance: Accent 367; Adams Media 131; Adams-Blake 131; Adams-Hall 367; Amacom 136; American Bar 137; American Nurses 139; AngeLines 141; ATL 145; Avery 146; Bale 148; Bancroft 149; Barbour 150; Betterway 155; Bloomberg 157; Bonus 159; Broadcast Interview 163; Broadway 163; Bryant & Dillon 164; Business McGraw-Hill 165; Cambridge Educ 166; Career Pr 167; Cato Inst 169; Chandler 170; Chelsea Green 171; Consumer Pr 179; Crown Business 183; Cypress 184; Dearborn 185; Doubleday 188; Doubleday Religious 188; Elder Bks 194; Electric Works 195; Encounter 196; Equilibrium 369; Fell, Frederick 199; Forum Pub 203; Glenlake 207; Gollehon 207; Graduate Grp 208; Gulf 212; HAWK 216; HarperPerennial 215; Haworth 217; Hay House 217; Hensley 219; HiddenSpring 220; Houghton Mifflin Adult 224; IDG Business 227; Int'l Scholars 230; Int'l Wealth 231; Jacobs, Lee 232; Kroshka 237; Le Gesse 239; Lebhar-Freidman 240; Lifetime Bks 242; Lowell 246; March Tenth 381; Marketscope 249; McGraw-Hill Ryerson 356; McGregor 251; Moody 256; New American Library 261; New World 263; New York Univ 263; Newmarket Pr 381; Next Decade 373; Nolo.com 264; Northfield 265; NTC/Contemporary 266; Oasis 267; Pacesetter 375; Parlay Int'l 273; Picasso 357; Pride & Imprints 284; Productive 358; Quill Driver/Word Dancer 287; Rainbow (FL) 289; Reynolds, Morgan 292; Self-Counsel (US) 302; Settel 382; Sourcebooks 307; Starburst 310; Stoddart 361; Success Pub 313; Summit Pub Grp 313; Ten Speed 316; The Magni Group, Inc. 249; Universal 323; ULI 330; Wonderland Pr 382; Woodhead 365

Multicultural: Amber 137; Black Dog & Leventhal 156; Bluewood 158; Books Collective 347; Broadway 163; Can Educators 349; Capstone 167; Charlesbridge Pub 171; Chicago Review 172; Chronicle Bks for Children 174; Cloud Peak 176; Common Courage 178; Cross Cultural 182; David, Jonathan 185; Ediciones Nuevo Espacio 192; Electric Works 195; Encounter 196; Facts on File 198; Gessler 206; Guernica 353; HiddenSpring 220; Highsmith 220; Intercultural 229; ISER 355; Judson 234; Le Gesse 239; Lee & Low 240; Lift Every Voice 371; Missouri Historical Society Press 373; Mitchell Lane 255; New Hope 262; Next Decade 373; Ohio State Univ 267; Oryx 269; Pacific View 272; Pacific View 375; Parabola Books 375; Paragon 273; Passeggiata 273; Pelican 275; Picasso 357; Piñata 279; Pontalba 281; Rosen Pub Grp 294; Rutgers Univ 295; Turtle Books 321; Universal 323; Univ of North Carolina 327; Univ of Pennsylvania 328; Volcano 333

Multimedia: ATL 145; Baker Bks 148; Black Dog & Leventhal 156; Books Collective 347; BPS 348; Broadcast Interview 163; Butterworths Canada 349; Charles River Media 170; Coach House Books 350; Electric Works 195; EMC/Paradigm 195; Government Inst 208; Group Pub 210; HarperEntertainment 215; Hazelden 217; Human Kinetics 225; Int'l Medical 230; Iron Gate 232; Jist Works 233; Lebhar-Freidman 240; Liguori 242; Listen & Live 243; Lynx Images 356; Paladin 272; Parlay Int'l 273; Picasso 357; Pontalba 281; Precept 283; Professional Pub 284; Review & Herald 292; Serendipity 302; Univ of North Carolina 327; Wadsworth 333; Walch, J. Weston 334; YMAA 344

Music/dance: Abingdon 129; American Catholic 367; American Pr 139; And Books 140; A-R 142; Atheneum Bks for Yng Rdrs 144; Betterway 155; Birch Brook 155; Black Dog & Leventhal 156; Bliss 368; Branden 161; Bucknell Univ 164; Cadence 165; Cartwheel 168; Centerstream 170; Chicago Review 172; Children's Pr 172; China Bks 172; City & Co. 175; Consortium 179; Country Music Found 180; Delta 186; Doubleday 188; Dover 189; Eagle's View 191; ECW 351; Electric Works 195; Empire 196; Facts on File 198; Fairleigh Dickinson 198; Glenbridge 206; Greenwood Pub Grp 210; Guernica 353; HarperPerennial 215; HiddenSpring 220; Houghton Mifflin Adult 224; Houghton Mifflin Bks for Children 223; Inner Traditions Int'l 228; Interlink 229; Le Gesse 239; Libraries Unltd 241; Lift Every Voice 371; Limelight 242; Louisiana State Univ 246; Mage 248; March Tenth 381; Mayfield 250; McFarland & Co 251; Menus & Music 372; Meriwether 252; New York Univ 263; Northeastern Univ 265; Norton, WW 266; Onjinjinkta 268; Owen, Richard 271; Pelican 275; Pencil Point 276; Pontalba 281; Popular Culture 281; Quest Bks 287; Ragweed 358; Random House Trade 290; Resource Pub 291; Santa Monica 298; Saxon House Canada 359; Scarecrow 299; Schenkman 300; Simon & Pierre 360; Soft Skull 306; Sound & Vision 361; Stipes 311; Tiare 318; Totline 319; Universal 323; Univ of Illinois 325; Univ of Iowa 326; Univ of North Carolina 327;

Univ Pr of Mississippi 329; Univ Pr of New England 330; Vanderbilt Univ 331; Vernon Pr 382; Viking 332; Wadsworth 333; Walker & Co 334; Watson-Guptill 335; Weatherhill 336; Weiser, Samuel 336; Wesleyan Univ 336; Whitman, Albert 338; Writer's Digest 343; Yale Univ 343

Nature/environment: Abique 129; Abrams 130; Adams Media 131; Adirondack Mountain 132; Alaska Northwest 133; Algonquin 134; American Water Works 140; Appalachian Mountain 141; Arcade 142; ATL 145; Atheneum Bks for Yng Rdrs 144; Autonomedia 145; aatec 366; Backcountry 147; Ballantine 149; Bantam Dell Pub Grp 149; Barricade 151; Bay 151; Baywood 152; Beachway 152; Beacon Pr 152; Bellwether-Cross 153; Benefactory 153; Berkshire 154; Black Dog & Leventhal 156; Blackbirch 156; Blair 157; Bliss 368; BNA 158; Boston Mills 348; Bottom Dog 160; Boyds Mills 160; Broken Jaw 348; Brucedale 349; Burford 164; Capstone 167; Carolrhoda 167; Cartwheel 168; Charlesbridge Pub 171; Charlesbridge Pub Trd 171; Chelsea Green 171; Chicago Review 172; Children's Pr 172; China Bks 172; Chronicle 174; Chronicle Bks for Children 174; City & Co. 175; Clear Light 175; Common Courage 178; Confluence 179; Consortium 179; Cornell Maritime 180; Countryman 180; Cross Cultural 182; Dimi 187; Doubleday 188; Dover 189; Down East 189; Down the Shore 189; Dutton Children's 191; Eakin Pr/Sunbelt Media 191; Eastern Nat'l 192; Ecopress 369; Electric Works 195; Emerald Wave 369; Encounter 196; Epicenter 196; Eriksson, Paul 196; Facts on File 198; Falcon 199; Fernwood 352; Filter 200; Foghorn 202; Four Walls Eight Windows 204; Godine, David 207; Goose Lane 352; Government Inst 208; Great Quotations 209; Grosset & Dunlap 210; Gulf 212; HAWK 216; Hancock House 213; HarperPerennial 215; Hay House 217; Heritage House 353; Heyday 220; HiddenSpring 220; Horsdal & Schubart 354; Houghton Mifflin Adult 224; Houghton Mifflin Bks for Children 223; Ideals Children's Bks 227; In Print 371; Inner Traditions Int'l 228; Island Press 232; Jewish Lights 233; Johnson 233; Kali 371; Kesend, Michael 235; Knopf & Crown Bks For Yng Rdrs 236; Kroshka 237; Kumarian 238; Lark 238; Lawrence, Merloyd 239; Le Gesse 239; Lebhar-Freidman 240; Lerner 241; Little, Brown 243; Little, Brown Children's 243; Llewellyn 244; Lone Pine 355; Longstreet 245; Lynx Images 356; Lyons Pr 247; Marketscope 249; McDonald & Woodward 250; Milkweed 254; Millbrook 254; Mountain N'Air 257; Mountain Pr 257; Mountaineers Bks 258; Natural Heritage/Natural History 356; Naturegraph 259; New England Cartographics 373; New England 261; New Horizon 262; New World 263; New York Univ 263; North Point 264; Northland 265; Northword 266; Norton, WW 266; Oasis 267; Ohio Univ 267; Oliver 268; Onjinjinkta 268; Orange Frazer 269; Orchard 269; Oregon State Univ 269; Overmountain 270; Owen, Richard 271; Owl Bks 271; Pacific Pr 271; Paragon 273; Parnassus 273; Pilgrim 279; Pineapple 279; Plexus 280; Potter, Clarkson 282; ProStar 285; Pruett 285; Putnam's Sons 286; Quest Bks 287; Ragged Mountain 288; Ragweed 358; Rainbow (FL) 289; Raindbow (California) 288; Raincoast 358; Random House Bks for Yng Rdrs 289; Review & Herald 292; Rocky Mountain 359; Ronsdale 359; Rutgers Univ 295; Sagamore 296; Sasquatch 299; Scholastic Canada 360; Scribner 301; Scrivenery Press 301; Seal 301; Sierra Club 304; Simon & Schuster Bks for Yng Rdrs 304; Smith, Gibbs 306; Soma 307; Soundprints 307; South End 308; Spotted Dog 309; Stackpole 309; Stanford Univ 310; Starburst 310; Steller Press Ltd. 361; Sterling 311; Stipes 311; Stoddart 361; Storey 312; Summit Pub Grp 313; Ten Speed 316; Texas A&M Univ 316; Texas Western 317; Three Hawks 377; Totline 319; Trans-Atlantic 320; Tricycle 320; Turnstone 362; Turtle Books 321; United Church Pr 322; Universal 323; Univ of Alaska 324; Univ of Alberta 363; Univ of Arizona 324; Univ of Arkansas 324; Univ of California 325; Univ of Georgia 325; Univ of Idaho 325; Univ of Iowa 326; Univ of Nevada 326; Univ of North Carolina 327; Univ of North Texas 327; Univ of Oklahoma 327; Univ of Ottawa 363; Univ of Texas 328; Univ Pr of Colorado 329; Univ Pr of Kansas 329; Univ Pr of New England 330; Vanderbilt Univ 331; Venture 331; VGM 331; Voyageur 333; Wadsworth 333; Walker & Co 334; Washington State Univ 335; Watts, Franklin 335; Weatherhill 336; Weidner & Sons 336; Weigl 365; Westcliffe 337; Whitecap 365; Whitman, Albert 338; Wilderness 339; Williamson 339; Willow Creek 340; Windward 341; Zoland 344

Philosophy: Abique 129; Acropolis 130; Alba 133; Allegro 134; Allisone 135; American Atheist 137; AngeLines 141; Aronson 143; Austin & Winfield 145; Autonomedia 145; Bantam Dell Pub Grp 149; Beacon Pr 152; Behrman 153; Bellwether-Cross 153; Bookworld/Blue Star 159; Bridge Works 162; Broadview 348; Bucknell Univ 164; Can Educators 349; Cassandra 368; Catholic Univ 168; Clear Light 175; Cornell Univ 180; Cross Cultural 182; Design Pr 380; DioGenes 187; Doubleday 188; Doubleday/Image 189; Dover 189; Dry Bones 190; Duquesne Univ 190; Educator's Int'l Pr 193; Eerdmans, William 194; Electric Works 195; Emerald Wave 369; Encounter 196; Facts on File 198; Fairleigh Dickinson 198; Fernwood 352; Gifted Educ 206; Glenbridge 206; Greenwood Pub Grp 210; Guernica 353; Guilford 211; HAWK 216; HarperPerennial 215; Haven 216; Hay House 217; HiddenSpring 220; Hohm 221; Holmes Pub Grp 222; Houghton Mifflin Adult 224; House of Anansi 354; Humanics Pub 225; Inner Traditions Int'l 228; Inst of Psych Res 354; Int'l Scholars 230; Jewish Lights 233; Judaica 234; Kroshka 237; Larson/PBPF 239; Le Gesse 239; Lebhar-Freidman 240; Libraries Unltd 241; Lifetime Bks 242; Louisiana State Univ 246; Mayfield 250; Mesorah 253; Midknight Club 253; Neshui 261; New York Univ 263; Nicolas-Hays 374; Northern Illinois Univ 265; Ohio Univ 267; Omega 374; Oughten House 374; Parabola Books 375; Paragon 273; Paulist Pr 274; Picador 278; Pontalba 281; Pride & Imprints 284; Prometheus 284; Purdue Univ 286; Quest Bks 287; Rainbow (FL) 289; Review & Herald 292; Rising Star 376; Routledge 294; Saxon House Canada 359; Schenkman 300; Schocken 300; Scribner 301; Scrivenery Press 301; Settel 382; Soft Skull 306; Somerville 382; South End 308; Spence 308; St. Augustine's 296; St Bede's 296; St. Martin's Scholarly & Reference 297; Stone Bridge 311; Stonewall 312; Swedenborg 314; Talese, Nan 315; Teachers College 315; Texas A&M Univ 316; Third World 317; Trans-Atlantic 320; Truman State Univ 321; Turtle Pr 321; Unity 323; Universal 323; Univ of Alberta 363; Univ of Calgary 363; Univ of Illinois 325; Univ of North Carolina 327; Univ of Ottawa 363; Univ Pr of Kansas 329; Vanderbilt Univ 331; Verso 331; Viking 332; Viking Studio 332; Wadsworth 333; Wall & Emerson 364; Weiser, Samuel 336; Wesleyan Univ 336; Westminster John Knox 337; Wisdom 341; Wonderland Pr 382; Yale Univ 343; YMAA 344

Photography: Allworth 135; Amherst Media 140; Atheneum Bks for Yng Rdrs 144; Avanyu 146; Black Dog & Leventhal 156; Bottom Dog 160; Branden 161; Brucedale 349; Bullfinch 164; Butterworth-Heinemann 165; Caitlin 349; Charlesbridge Publishing 171; Charlesbridge Pub 171; Chronicle 174; Clear Light 175; Companion 178; Doubleday 188; Dover 189; Dutton Children's 191; Edutainment Media 194; Electric Works 195; Epicenter 196; Focal 201; Godine, David

207; Houghton Mifflin Adult 224; Hudson Hills 225; Jacobs, Lee 232; Le Gesse 239; Lebhar-Freidman 240; Longstreet 245; Louisiana State Univ 246; MBI 250; Menus & Music 372; Minnesota Hist Soc 254; Monacelli 255; Natural Heritage/Natural History 356; New York Univ 263; Northland 265; Norton, WW 266; Orange Frazer 269; Overmountain 270; Phaidon Press 278; Pontalba 281; Potter, Clarkson 282; Ragweed 358; Raincoast 358; Random House Trade 290; Stackpole 309; Stonewall 312; Stormline 376; Temple Univ 316; Trans-Atlantic 320; Tricycle 320; Universal 323; Univ of Iowa 326; Univ of North Carolina 327; Univ Pr of Mississippi 329; Vernon Pr 382; Viking Studio 332; Vintage Images 332; Warner Bks 334; Watson-Guptill 335; Weatherhill 336; Westcliffe 337; Western NY 378; Whitman, Albert 338; Willow Creek 340; Writer's Digest 343; Zoland 344

Psychology: Adams Media 131; Addicus 132; Alba 133; Allyn & Bacon 135; American Counseling 138; American Nurses 139; American Pr 139; And Books 140; AngeLines 141; Aronson 143; Atheneum Bks for Yng Rdrs 144; Avisson 146; Avon 147; Baker Bks 148; Ballantine 149; Bantam Dell Pub Grp 149; Barricade 151; Baywood 152; Berkley Pub Grp 154; Bethany 155; Bick 155; BPS 348; Bridge Works 162; Broadcast Interview 163; Broadway 163; Bucknell Univ 164; Burnham 165; Cassandra 368; Conari 178; Consortium 179; Cornell Univ 180; Cross Cultural 182; Cypress 184; DioGenes 187; Doubleday 188; Doubleday/Image 189; Duquesne Univ 190; Dutton Plume 191; Educator's Int'l Pr 193; Eerdmans, William 194; Elder Bks 194; Electric Works 195; EMC/Paradigm 195; Emerald Wave 369; Emis 195; Encounter 196; Eriksson, Paul 196; Evans & Co 197; Facts on File 198; Fairleigh Dickinson 198; Fairview 198; Floricanto 201; Free Spirit 204; Fromm Int'l 204; Gifted Educ 206; Glenbridge 206; Gollehon 207; Greenwood 209; Greenwood Pub Grp 210; Guernica 353; Guilford 211; HarperPerennial 215; HarperSanFrancisco 215; Hastings 216; Hatherleigh 216; Haven 216; Haworth 217; Hay House 217; Hazelden 217; Health Comm 217; Health Info 218; Healthwise 218; HiddenSpring 220; Hohm 221; Houghton Mifflin Adult 224; Human Kinetics 225; Hunter House 226; Inner Traditions Int'l 228; Inst of Psych Res 354; Int'l Scholars 230; Jacobs, Lee 232; Kroshka 237; Larson/PBPF 239; Lawrence, Merloyd 239; Le Gesse 239; Learning Pub 240; Lebhar-Freidman 240; Libraries Unltd 241; Lifetime Bks 242; Llewellyn 244; Love and Logic 246; Lowell 246; Mayfield 250; Neshui 261; New American Library 261; New Harbinger 262; New Horizon 262; New World 263; New York Univ 263; Newmarket Pr 381; Nicolas-Hays 374; Norton, WW 266; NTC/Contemporary 266; Ottenheimer 381; Oughten House 374; Parabola Books 375; Pathfinder 274; Pontalba 281; Praeger 282; Pride & Imprints 284; Prometheus 284; Quest Bks 287; Rainbow (FL) 289; Ronin Pub 293; Routledge 294; Schenkman 300; Scribner 301; Settel 382; Sourcebooks 307; Stanford Univ 310; Starburst 310; Stoddart 361; Swedenborg 314; Third World 317; 2M Comm 382; Unity 323; Universal 323; Vanderwyk & Burnham 377; Visions Comm 332; Wadsworth 333; Warner Bks 334; Weidner & Sons 336; Weiser, Samuel 336; Westminster John Knox 337; Wildcat Canyon 339; Wiley 339; Williamson 339; Williamson 339; Wilshire 340; Wisdom 341; Wonderland Pr 382; Woodbridge 378; Yale Univ 343

Real estate: Dearborn 185; Government Inst 208; NTC/Contemporary 266; Starburst 310; ULI 330

Recreation: Abrams 130; Accent 367; Adirondack Mountain 132; American & World Geographic 379; Appalachian Mountain 141; Atheneum Bks for Yng Rdrs 144; Aviation Publishers (PA) 146; Backcountry 147; Beachway 152; Berkshire 154; Betterway 155; Black Dog & Leventhal 156; Bliss 368; Boston Mills 348; Burford 164; Capstone 167; Career Pr 167; Cartwheel 168; Chandler 170; Chicago Review 172; Chronicle 174; City & Co. 175; Countryman 180; Cumberland 183; Doubleday 188; Down East 189; Ecopress 369; Electric Works 195; Enslow 196; Epicenter 196; Eriksson, Paul 196; Facts on File 198; Falcon 199; Foghorn 202; Footprint Press 370; Globe Pequot 207; Golden West 207; HAWK 216; HarperPerennial 215; Heritage House 353; Heyday 220; Horsdal & Schubart 354; Houghton Mifflin Adult 224; Houghton Mifflin Bks for Children 223; House of Collectibles 224; Human Kinetics 225; IDG Lifestyle 227; ISER 355; Jacobs, Lee 232; Johnson 233; Krause 237; Kroshka 237; Le Gesse 239; Lebhar-Freidman 240; Legacy 240; Lion Bks 243; Little, Brown Children's 243; Lone Pine 355; Lowell 246; March Tenth 381; Marketscope 249; McFarland & Co 251; Menus & Music 372; Meriwether 252; Middle Atlantic 253; Middle Atlantic 373; Mountain N'Air 257; Mountaineers Bks 258; Mustang Pub 258; Natural Heritage/Natural History 356; New England Cartographics 373; Next Decade 373; Orange Frazer 269; Owen, Richard 271; Parnassus 273; Peachtree 275; Picasso 357; Pontalba 281; Pruett 285; Ragged Mountain 288; Ragweed 358; Rainbow (FL) 289; Raindbow (California) 288; Raincoast 358; Rocky Mountain 359; Running Pr 295; Sagamore 296; Sasquatch 299; Scholastic Canada 360; Settel 382; Stackpole 309; Starburst 310; Sterling 311; Stipes 311; Summit Pub Grp 313; Ten Speed 316; Universal 323; Univ of Idaho 325; Venture 331; Vernon Pr 382; Whitecap 365; Whitman, Albert 338; Wilderness 339; Willow Creek 340; Windward 341

Reference: ABI 129; Abingdon 129; Abique 129; Adams Media 131; Adirondack Mountain 132; AHA 132; Alba 133; Alexander 134; Allworth 135; Allyn & Bacon 135; Alpine 367; Amacom 136; American Atheist 137; American Bar 137; American Correctional 138; American Counseling 138; American Nurses 139; American Quilters 139; Ancestry 140; Andrew/Noyes 141; Appalachian Mountain 141; Arkansas 143; Arte Publico 143; ASCP 144; ASM 144; ATL 145; Austin & Winfield 145; Avanyu 146; Avery 146; Avisson 146; Baker Bks 148; Ball 149; Ballantine 149; Barbour 150; Barricade 151; Beeman Jorbensen 153; Behrman 153; Beil, Frederic 153; Berkley Pub Grp 154; Bethany 155; Betterway 155; Between the Lines 347; Black Dog & Leventhal 156; Blackbirch 156; Bliss 368; Bloomberg 157; BNA 158; Borealis 347; Bowling Green 160; BPS 348; Branden 161; Brassey's 161; Brassey's Sports 161; Bristol Fashion 162; Broadcast Interview 163; Broadview 348; Broadway 163; Brucedale 349; Business McGraw-Hill 165; Butterworth-Heinemann 165; Butterworths Canada 349; Cadence 165; Career Pr 167; Carroll & Graf 167; Carswell Thomson 350; Cerier, Alison Brown 380; Chandler 170; Charles River Media 170; Charlton 350; Chelsea Green 171; Christian Pub 173; City & Co. 175; Coaches 177; Collectors Pr 177; Common Courage 178; Consortium 179; Cornell Univ 180; Coteau 351; Country Music Found 180; Countryman 180; CQ 181; Cross Cultural 182; Cumberland 183; Dante Univ of America Pr 184; Darlington 184; David, Jonathan 185; Dearborn 185; Discovery 187; Doral 188; Doubleday Religious 188; Doubleday/Image 189; Dry Bones 190; Eckert, J.K. 380; Ediciones Nuevo Espacio 192; Éditions Logiques 352; Eerdmans, William 194; Electric Works 195; Emis 195; Empire 196; Encounter 196; Enslow 196; Evans & Co 197; Facts on File 198; Fairleigh Dickinson 198; Fairview 198; Fell, Frederick 199; Ferguson 200; Fernwood

352; Fire Engineering 200; Floricanto 201; Florida Academic 201; Focal 201; Fromm Int'l 204; Gambling Times 370; GATF Pr 205; Gifted Educ 206; Government Inst 208; Graduate Grp 208; Greenwood 209; Greenwood Pub Grp 210; Grolier 210; Gryphon Pub 211; Gulf 212; Hancock House 213; HarperPerennial 215; HarperSanFrancisco 215; Hastings 216; Hatherleigh 216; Haworth 217; Health Info 218; Hein, William 218; Heinemann 218; Hendrickson 219; Herbal Studies 370; Heritage 220; Highsmith 220; Hippocrene 221; Holmes & Meier 222; Home Planners 223; House of Collectibles 224; Human Kinetics 225; Hunter Pub 226; IBEX 226; IDG Business 227; IDG Education 227; IDG Lifestyle 227; Impact Publications 228; Information Today 228; Intercultural 229; Int'l City/County Mgmt. 229; Int'l Found Of Employee Benefit Plans 230; Int'l Medical 230; Int'l Scholars 230; Iron Gate 232; ISER 355; Island Press 232; Jacobs, Lee 232; Jewish Lights 233; Jist Works 233; Judaica 234; Kamehameha 234; Kogan Page 236; Krause 237; Kregel 237; Krieger 237; Langenscheidt 238; Lawyers & Judges 239; Learning Pub 240; Lebhar-Freidman 240; Lehigh Univ 241; Libraries Unltd 241; Lifetime Bks 242; Lifetime Bks 242; Lift Every Voice 371; Lighthouse Point 372; Lippincott Williams & Wilkins 243; Locust Hill 244; Lone Eagle 245; Longstreet 245; Loompanics 245; Lowell 246; LRP 247; Madison Bks 248; March Tenth 381; McFarland & Co 251; McGraw-Hill Ryerson 356; Meadowbrook 251; Medical Physics 252; Meriwether 252; Merriam Press 252; Mesorah 253; Middle Atlantic 373; Minnesota Hist Soc 254; Missouri Historical Society Press 373; Narwhal 259; Nautical & Aviation 260; Neal-Schuman 260; Nelson, Thomas 260; New American Library 261; New England Pub Assoc 381; Next Decade 373; Nichols 264; No Starch 264; Nolo.com 264; Norton, WW 266; NTC/Contemporary 266; Oasis 267; Ohio Univ 267; Orange Frazer 269; Oryx 269; Ottenheimer 381; Our Sunday Visitor 270; Pacific Bks 271; Pacific View 272; Parlay Int'l 273; Pencil Point 276; Pennsylvania Hist and Museum Comm 276; Phi Delta Kappa 278; Picton 279; Pineapple 279; Plexus 280; Pocket Bks 281; Popular Culture 281; PROMPT 285; Practice Mgmt 282; Prakken 375; Precept 283; Pride & Imprints 284; Productive 358; Professional Pub 284; Prometheus 284; ProStar 285; Purich 358; Quill Driver/Word Dancer 287; Quite Specific Media Grp 288; Red Eye 376; Reference Svce 290; Regan Bks 290; Resource Pub 291; Review & Herald 292; Rising Star 376; Ronin Pub 293; Rose 293; Rosen Pub Grp 294; Routledge 294; Russian Info 376; Rutgers Univ 295; Sachem 382; Sagamore 296; Sandlapper 298; Santa Monica 298; Scarecrow 299; Self-Counsel (US) 302; Serendipity 302; Sgt Kirklands 303; Sheed & Ward 303; Shoreline 360; Simon & Pierre 360; Skidmore-Roth 305; Skyfoot Technical 360; Sound View 376; Sourcebooks 307; Southern Illinois Univ Pr 308; Speech Bin 308; St. Martin's Scholarly & Reference 297; St Martin's 297; Standard 309; Sterling 311; Stoeger 311; Stone Bridge 311; Tech Books for the Layperson 377; Ten Speed 316; Texas State Hist Assoc 316; Third World 317; Tidewater 318; Tower 319; Trans-Atlantic 320; Transnational 320; Trilobyte 362; UCLA Amer Indian Stud Ctr 322; Unity 323; Universal 323; Univ of Alaska 324; Univ of Idaho 325; Univ of Illinois 325; Univ of North Texas 327; Univ of Ottawa 363; Univ of South Carolina 328; Univ Pr of Kentucky 329; Upney 363; Utah State Univ Pr 330; Walker & Co 334; Wall & Emerson 364; Warner Bks 334; Watson-Guptill 335; Weatherhill 336; Weidner & Sons 336; Westcliffe 337; Westminster John Knox 337; Whitehorse 378; Whitford 378; Wiley 339; Wisdom 341; Wonderland Pr 382; Woodbine 342; Wordware 342; Wysteria Publishing 378; Yale Univ 343; York 365; Zondervan 344

Regional: Adams Media 131; Addicus 132; Adirondack Mountain 132; Alexander 134; Algonquin 134; Ambassador 136; American & World Geographic 379; Appalachian Mountain 141; Arcadia 142; Arkansas 143; Arte Publico 143; Avanyu 146; Avisson 146; Balcony 148; Bancroft 149; Barnegat 150; Baylor Univ 152; Berkshire 154; Black Dog & Leventhal 156; Blair 157; Bliss 368; Blue Sky 368; Bonus 159; Bookwrights 379; Borealis 347; Boston Mills 348; Bottom Dog 160; Bowling Green 160; Boyds Mills 160; Bright Mountain 368; Broken Jaw 348; Caitlin 349; Camino 166; Caxton 169; Chandler 170; Chelsea Green 171; Chicago Review 172; Chronicle 174; City & Co. 175; Clear Light 175; Confluence 179; Cornell Maritime 180; Cornell Univ 180; Coteau 351; Country Music Found 180; Countryman 180; Creative Pub 182; Cumberland 183; Design Pr 380; Doubleday 188; Down East 189; Down the Shore 189; Dry Bones 190; Eakin Pr/Sunbelt Media 191; Eerdmans, William 194; Electric Works 195; Epicenter 196; Family Album 370; Filter 200; Fisher 200; Footprint Press 370; Globe Pequot 207; Golden West 207; Goose Lane 352; Guernica 353; Gulf 212; Hancock House 213; HarperPerennial 215; Hendrick-Long 219; Heritage 220; Heritage House 353; Heyday 220; HiddenSpring 220; Horsdal & Schubart 354; Houghton Mifflin Adult 224; Houghton Mifflin Bks for Children 223; Howell Pr 224; Hunter Pub 226; ISER 355; Jameson 232; Johnson 233; Johnston Assoc 371; Kamehameha 234; Kent State Univ 235; Lahontan 371; Lake Claremont 238; Le Gesse 239; Lebhar-Freidman 240; Livingston 244; Lone Pine 355; Longstreet 245; Louisiana State Univ 246; Loyola 247; MacAdam/Cage 248; Marketscope 249; McBooks 250; McGraw-Hill Ryerson 356; McGregor 251; Michigan State Univ 253; Middle Atlantic 253; Middle Atlantic 373; Minnesota Hist Soc 254; Missouri Historical Society Press 373; Moon 256; Mount Ida 373; Mountain Pr 257; Mountaineers Bks 258; Natural Heritage/Natural History 356; New England Cartographics 373; New England 261; New York Univ 263; Northeastern Univ 265; Northern Illinois Univ 265; Northland 265; Ohio State Univ 267; Ohio Univ 267; Onjinjinkta 268; Orange Frazer 269; Oregon State Univ 269; Overlook 270; Overmountain 270; Owl Bks 271; Pacific Bks 271; Pacific View 272; Pacific View 373; Parnassus 273; Passeggiata 273; Peachtree Children's 275; Pelican 275; Pennsylvania Hist and Museum Comm 276; Pineapple 279; Plexus 280; Pontalba 281; Prairie Oak 283; Pruett 285; Purdue Univ 286; Quill Driver/ Word Dancer 287; Ragweed 358; Raincoast 358; Republic of Texas 291; Rising Star 376; Rockbridge 293; Rocky Mountain 359; Ronsdale 359; Rutgers Univ 295; Rutledge Hill 295; Sandlapper 298; Sasquatch 299; Sgt Kirklands 303; Shoreline 360; Simon & Pierre 360; Smith, Gibbs 306; Southern Illinois Univ Pr 308; Southern Methodist Univ 308; St Mary's 297; Steller Press Ltd. 361; Stormline 376; Summit Pub Grp 313; Sunstone 313; Syracuse Univ 314; Tamarack 377; TCU Press 315; Temple Univ 316; Texas A&M Univ 316; Texas Western 317; Third World 317; Tidewater 318; Towle House 319; Turtle Books 321; TwoDot 322; Universal 323; Univ of Akron 323; Univ of Alaska 324; Univ of Alberta 363; Univ of Arizona 324; Univ of Arkansas 324; Univ of Georgia 325; Univ of Idaho 325; Univ of Maine 326; Univ of Manitoba 363; Univ of Missouri 326; Univ of Nevada 326; Univ of North Carolina 327; Univ of North Texas 327; Univ of Oklahoma 327; Univ of Ottawa 363; Univ of South Carolina 328; Univ of Tennessee 328; Univ of Texas 328; Univ Pr of Colorado 329; Univ Pr of Kansas 329; Univ Pr of Kentucky 329; Univ Pr of Mississippi 329; Univ Pr of New England 330; Utah State Univ Pr 330; Vandamere 330; Vanderbilt Univ 331; Vanwell 364; Vehicule 364; Vernon Pr 382; Voyageur 333; Washington State Univ 335; Westcliffe 337; Westernlore 337; Whitecap 365; Woodholme 342; Wysteria Publishing 378; Zoland 344

Religion: Abingdon 129; ACTA 131; Accent 367; Acropolis 130; Alba 133; Alban Inst 133; Albury 133; Alef 134; Alexander 134; Allegro 134; Allisone 135; Ambassador 136; American Atheist 137; American Catholic 367; American Counseling 138; And Books 140; Aronson 143; Atheneum Bks for Yng Rdrs 144; Autonomedia 145; Baker Bks 148; Ballantine 149; Bantam Dell Pub Grp 149; Barbour 150; Bay 151; Baylor Univ 152; Beacon Pr 152; Behrman 153; Bethany 155; Bookworld/Blue Star 159; Bookwrights 379; Boyds Mills 160; Broadcast Interview 163; Broadview 348; Bucknell Univ 164; Can Educators 349; Cassandra 368; Catholic Univ 168; Cedar Fort 169; Chalice 170; Chariot/Victor 170; China Bks 172; Chosen Bks 173; Christian Ed 173; Christian Pub 173; Church Growth 174; College Pr 177; Concordia 178; Cornell Univ 180; Creation House 182; Cross Cultural 182; Crossway 183; David, Jonathan 185; Doubleday 188; Doubleday Religious 188; Doubleday/Image 189; Dover 189; Dry Bones 190; Duquesne Univ 190; Eerdmans Bks for Yng Rdrs 194; Eerdmans, William 194; Electric Works 195; Encounter 196; ETC Pub 197; Facts on File 198; Focus Pub 202; Forum 203; Forward Movement 203; Great Quotations 209; Greenwood Pub Grp 210; Group Pub 210; Guernica 353; HarperPerennial 215; HarperSanFrancisco 215; Haven 216; Hendrickson 219; Hensley 219; HiddenSpring 220; Hi-Time 221; Hohm 221; Holmes Pub Grp 222; Holy Cross 223; Honor 223; Houghton Mifflin Adult 224; Inner Traditions Int'l 228; Int'l Scholars 230; InterVarsity 231; Jewish Lights 233; Journey 233; Judaica 234; Judson 234; Kar-Ben 235; Kindred Prod 355; Kramer, H.J. 236; Kregel 237; Kroshka 237; Larson/PBPF 239; Le Gesse 239; Lebhar-Freidman 240; Legacy 240; Libraries Unltd 241; Lifetime Bks 242; Lift Every Voice 371; Liguori 242; Loyola 247; Mayfield 250; Meriwether 252; Mesorah 253; Midknight Club 253; Moody 256; More, Thomas 256; Morehouse 256; Morrow, William 257; Multnomah 258; Nelson, Thomas 260; Nelson, Tommy 260; Neshui 261; New Hope 262; New World 263; New York Univ 263; Nicolas-Hays 374; North Point 264; Norton, WW 266; Omega 374; Onjinjinkta 268; Ottenheimer 381; Our Sunday Visitor 270; Pacific Pr 271; Parabola Books 375; Paraclete 272; Paragon 273; Pauline Bks & Media 274; Paulist Pr 274; Pelican 275; Picasso 357; Pilgrim 279; Pontalba 281; Prometheus 284; Putnam's Sons 286; Quest Bks 287; Raindbow (California) 288; Random House Trade 290; Resource Pub 291; Revell, Fleming 291; Review & Herald 292; Rising Star 376; Rose 293; Rosen Pub Grp 294; Rutgers Univ 295; Saxon House Canada 359; Schocken 300; Scribner 301; Shaw, Harold 303; Sheed & Ward 303; Shoreline 360; Skinner 305; Soma 307; Spence 308; St Anthony Messenger 296; St. Augustine's 296; St Bede's 296; St. Martin's Scholarly & Reference 297; Standard 309; Starburst 310; Starburst 310; Summit Pub Grp 313; Swedenborg 314; Third World 317; Torah Aura 318; Towle House 319; Trinity 320; Troitsa 321; Truman State Univ 321; Tuttle 321; Tyndale 322; United Church Pr 322; Unity 323; Univ of Alabama 323; Univ of North Carolina 327; Univ of Ottawa 363; Univ of South Carolina 328; Univ of Tennessee 328; Vanderbilt Univ 331; Vernon Pr 382; Visions Comm 332; Wadsworth 333; Weiser, Samuel 336; Westminster John Knox 337; White Stone Circle 338; Whitman, Albert 338; Wilshire 340; Wisdom 341; Yale Univ 343; Zondervan 344

Scholarly: Abique 129; Baylor Univ 152; Baywood 152; Beacon Pr 152; BNA 158; Bucknell Univ 164; Burnham 165; Butterworth-Heinemann 165; Catholic Univ 168; Cato Inst 169; Cornell Univ 180; Dante Univ of America Pr 184; Duquesne Univ 190; Eastern 369; Fairleigh Dickinson 198; Focal 201; Greenwood 209; Greenwood Pub Grp 210; Gruyter, Aldine de 211; Harvard Bus School 215; Haworth 217; Holy Cross 223; Int'l Scholars 230; Johnson 233; Kent State Univ 235; Knopf, Alfred 236; Kumarian 238; Lehigh Univ 241; McFarland & Co 251; Michigan State Univ 253; Minnesota Hist Soc 254; Modern Language Assoc 255; Morehouse 256; Northeastern Univ 265; Ohio State Univ 267; Oregon State Univ 269; Pacific Bks 271; Passeggiata 273; Phi Delta Kappa 278; Pilgrim 279; Praeger 282; Purdue Univ 286; Routledge 294; Scarecrow 299; Schenkman 300; St. Martin's Scholarly & Reference 297; St Martin's 297; Stanford Univ 310; Stylus 313; TCU Press 315; Texas State Hist Assoc 316; Texas Western 317; Trinity 320; United Church Pr 322; Univ of Akron 323; Univ of Alabama 323; Univ of Alaska 324; Univ of Alberta 363; Univ of Arizona 324; Univ of Calgary 363; Univ of California 325; Univ of Illinois 325; Univ of Maine 326; Univ of Manitoba 363; Univ of Missouri 326; Univ of New Mexico 326; Univ of Ottawa 363; Univ of Pennsylvania 328; Univ of Tennessee 328; Univ of Texas 328; Univ Pr of Colorado 329; Univ Pr of Kansas 329; Univ Pr of Kentucky 329; Univ Pr of Mississippi 329; Utah State Univ Pr 330; Vanderbilt Univ 331; Venture 331; Wesleyan Univ 336; Westernlore 337; Whitson 338; Yale Univ 343; York 365

Science/technology: Abique 129; Abrams 130; Adams Media 131; Alban Inst 133; Allegro 134; Amacom 136; American Chemical 138; American Pr 139; American Water Works 140; Andrew/Noyes 141; ASCP 144; ATL 145; Atheneum Bks for Yng Rdrs 144; Bantam Dell Pub Grp 149; Battelle 151; Blackbirch 156; Bluewood 158; Brewers 162; Bucknell Univ 164; Butterworth-Heinemann 165; Cambridge Educ 166; Capstone 167; Carolrhoda 167; Cartwheel 168; Chandler 170; Charlesbridge Pub 171; Charlesbridge Pub Trd 171; Children's Pr 172; Chronicle Bks for Children 174; Common Courage 178; Consortium 179; Cornell Univ 180; Crown Business 183; Dimi 187; Doubleday 188; Dover 189; Dutton Children's 191; Dutton Plume 191; Ecopress 369; Edupress 193; Electric Works 195; Encounter 196; Enslow 196; Evans & Co 197; Facts on File 198; Focal 201; Four Walls Eight Windows 204; GATF Pr 205; Gifted Educ 206; Government Inst 208; Grosset & Dunlap 210; HarperPerennial 215; Haven 216; Health Info 218; Helix 219; Hendricks, F.P. 353; HiddenSpring 220; Holiday House 222; Houghton Mifflin Adult 224; Houghton Mifflin Bks for Children 223; House of Anansi 354; Ideals Children's Bks 227; Inst of Psych Res 354; Int'l Scholars 230; Island Press 232; Johnson 233; Kalmbach 234; Knopf & Crown Bks For Yng Rdrs 236; Krieger 237; Kroshka 237; Kumarian 238; Le Gesse 239; Lebhar-Freidman 240; Lehigh Univ 241; Lerner 241; Libraries Unltd 241; Little, Brown 243; Little, Brown Children's 243; Lyons Pr 247; McDonald & Woodward 250; Millbrook 254; Mountain Pr 257; Naturegraph 259; Naval Inst 260; Neshui 261; Norton, WW 266; Ohio Univ 267; Oliver 268; Oregon State Univ 269; Owen, Richard 271; Paladin 272; Pencil Point 276; Plexus 280; Pontalba 281; PROMPT 285; Practice Mgmt 282; Precept 283; Professional Pub 284; Purdue Univ 286; Putnam's Sons 286; Quest Bks 287; Rainbow (FL) 289; Random House Bks for Yng Rdrs 289; Rose 293; Rosen Pub Grp 294; Running Pr 295; Scholastic Canada 360; Scribner 301; Scrivenery Press 301; Skyfoot Technical 360; Somerville 382; South End 308; Stanford Univ 310; Sterling 311; Stipes 311; Stoddard 361; Summit Pub Grp 313; Teaching & Learning 315; Ten Speed 316; Texas Western 317; Three Hawks 377; Totline 319; Trans-Atlantic 320; Tricycle 320; Trilobyte 362; Universal 323; Univ of Akron 323; Univ of Alaska 324; Univ of Arizona 324; Univ of Maine 326; Univ of Texas 328; Visions Comm 332; Wadsworth 333; Walch, J. Weston 334; Walker & Co 334; Wall & Emerson 364; Watts, Franklin 335; Watts, Franklin 335; Weidner & Sons 336; Weigl 365; Whitman, Albert 338; Wiley 339;

Williamson 339; Windward 341; Woodhead 365; Wysteria Publishing 378; Yale Univ 343

Self-help: Accent 367; Adams Media 131; Addicus 132; Albury 133; Alexander 134; Alligator 134; Allisone 135; Amacom 136; Ambassador 136; Amber 137; AngeLines 141; Arkansas 143; Atheneum Bks for Yng Rdrs 144; Avery 146; Avisson 146; Avon 147; Baker Bks 148; Baker Bks 148; Ballantine 149; Bancroft 149; Bantam Dell Pub Grp 149; Barricade 151; Berkley Pub Grp 154; Bethany 155; Betterway 155; Black Dog & Leventhal 156; Blue Poppy 158; Blue Sky 368; Bonus 159; Bookhome 159; Bookwrights 379; Broadcast Interview 163; Bryant & Dillon 164; Business McGraw-Hill 165; Career Pr 167; Carroll & Graf 167; Cassandra 368; CCC 169; Cedar Fort 169; Cerier, Alison Brown 380; Chandler 170; Chelsea Green 171; China Bks 172; Chosen Bks 173; Christian Pub 173; Conari 178; Consortium 179; Consumer Pr 179; Cypress 184; David, Jonathan 185; Doubleday 188; Doubleday Religious 188; Doubleday/Image 189; DTP 190; Dutton Plume 191; Éditions Logiques 352; Edutainment Media 194; Elder Bks 194; Electric Works 195; Equilibrium 369; Eriksson, Paul 196; Executive Excellence 197; Fairview 198; Fell, Frederick 199; Fisher 200; Florida Academic 201; Free Spirit 204; Gollehon 207; Graduate Grp 208; Great Quotations 209; Guilford 211; Gulf 212; HAWK 216; Hampton Rds 213; Harbor 213; HarperPerennial 215; HarperSanFrancisco 215; Hastings 216; Hatherleigh 216; Hay House 217; Hazelden 217; Health Comm 217; Health Info 218; Hendricks, F.P. 353; Herbal Studies 370; HiddenSpring 220; Hohm 221; Holmes Pub Grp 222; Houghton Mifflin Adult 224; Human Kinetics 225; Humanics Pub 225; Hunter House 226; IDG Business 227; IDG Education 227; IDG Lifestyle 227; Ideals Pub 227; Impact Publications 228; Int'l Wealth 231; Jewish Lights 233; Jist Works 233; Kensington 235; Kesend, Michael 235; Kogan Page 236; Kramer, H.J. 236; Krause 237; Le Gesse 239; Lebhar-Freidman 240; Lifetime Bks 242; Liguori 242; Llewellyn 244; Loompanics 245; Love and Logic 246; March Tenth 381; Marketscope 249; Marlowe 249; McDonald & Woodward 250; McGavick Field 372; McGregor 251; Mesorah 253; Midknight Club 253; More, Thomas 256; Mustang Pub 258; Nelson, Thomas 260; Neshui 261; New American Library 261; New Harbinger 262; New Horizon 262; New World 263; Newmarket Pr 381; Next Decade 373; Nicolas-Hays 374; Nolo.com 264; Norton, WW 266; NTC/Contemporary 266; Ohio Univ 267; One on One 268; Onjinjinkta 268; Ottenheimer 381; Oughten House 374; Pacesetter 375; Pacific Pr 271; Parlay Int'l 273; Pathfinder 274; Pauline Bks & Media 274; Paulist Pr 274; Peachtree 275; Pelican 275; Picasso 357; Pontalba 281; Possibility 281; Potter, Clarkson 282; PPI 282; Pride & Imprints 284; Productive 358; Publicom 381; Putnam's Sons 286; Quest Bks 287; Rainbow (FL) 289; Random House Trade 290; Regan Bks 290; Resource Pub 291; Revell, Fleming 291; Review & Herald 292; Rising Star 376; Ronin Pub 293; Rosen Pub Grp 294; Running Pr 295; Schenkman 300; Seal 301; Self-Counsel (US) 302; Settel 382; Shaw, Harold 303; Skinner 305; Sourcebooks 307; St Martin's 297; Starburst 310; Stoddart 361; Studio 4 Prod 376; Success Pub 313; Summit Pub Grp 313; Swedenborg 314; Tech Books for the Layperson 377; Ten Speed Pr 316; The Magni Group, Inc. 249; Third World 317; Tricycle 320; Trilobyte 362; Turtle Pr 321; Tuttle 321; Tyndale 322; Unity 323; Universal 323; Vanderwyk & Burnham 377; Visions Comm 332; Volcano 333; Walker & Co 334; Warner Bks 334; Weatherhill 336; Weiser, Samuel 336; Westminster John Knox 337; Whitford 378; Wildcat Canyon 339; Wiley 339; Williamson 339; Wilshire 340; Wisdom 341; Wonderland Pr 382; Woodbridge 378; Zondervan 344

Sex: Black Dog & Leventhal 156; Blue Moon 157; Broadway 163; Companion 178; Encounter 196; Guernica 353; Le Gesse 239; Lift Every Voice 371; Neshui 261; Pedlar 357; Picasso 357; Pontalba 281; The Magni Group, Inc. 249; Trans-Atlantic 320; Universal 323

Social sciences: Burnham 165; Cambridge Educ 166; Eerdmans, William 194; ETC Pub 197; Free Pr 204; Greenwood 209; Greenwood Pub Grp 210; Lawrence, Merloyd 239; Northern Illinois Univ 265; Oryx 269; Pilgrim 279; Purdue Univ 286; Routledge 294; Roxbury 294; Stanford Univ 310; Teachers College 315; Texas Western 317; United Church Pr 322; Univ of California 325; Univ of Missouri 326; Walch, J. Weston 334; Whitson 338

Sociology: Abique 129; Allyn & Bacon 135; American Counseling 138; American Pr 139; Atheneum Bks for Yng Rdrs 144; Austin & Winfield 145; Avanyu 146; Bantam Dell Pub Grp 149; Barricade 151; Baywood 152; Bethany 155; Between the Lines 347; Black Dog & Leventhal 156; Branden 161; Bridge Works 162; Broadview 348; Bucknell Univ 164; Burnham 165; Can Educators 349; Cato Inst 169; Cedar Fort 169; Child Welfare 172; China Bks 172; Cleis 176; Consortium 179; Cornell Univ 180; Cross Cultural 182; DioGenes 187; Doubleday 188; Eerdmans, William 194; Electric Works 195; Encounter 196; Enslow 196; Eriksson, Paul 196; Evans & Co 197; Fairleigh Dickinson 198; Fairview 198; Fernwood 352; Free Spirit 204; Glenbridge 206; Greenwood 209; Greenwood Pub Grp 210; Gruyter, Aldine de 211; Guilford 211; HarperPerennial 215; Haven 216; Haworth 217; Hay House 217; HiddenSpring 220; Hill & Wang 221; Houghton Mifflin Adult 224; House of Anansi 354; ILR 227; Int'l Scholars 230; ISER 355; Kroshka 237; Kumarian 238; Le Gesse 239; Learning Pub 240; Lebhar-Freidman 240; Libraries Unltd 241; Louisiana State Univ 246; Love and Logic 246; Mage 248; Mayfield 250; McFarland & Co 251; NASW 259; New York Univ 263; Ohio State Univ 267; Ohio Univ 267; Owl Bks 271; Paragon 273; Pathfinder 274; Praeger 282; Purdue Univ 286; Rainbow (FL) 289; Random House Trade 290; Rising Star 376; Roxbury 294; Rutgers Univ 295; Schenkman 300; Settel 382; South End 308; Spence 308; St. Martin's Scholarly & Reference 297; Stanford Univ 310; Stoddart 361; Stonewall 312; Summit Pub Grp 313; Teachers College 315; Temple Univ 316; Third World 317; Thompson Educ 361; Trans-Atlantic 320; Truman State Univ 321; Universal 323; Univ of Alberta 363; Univ of Arkansas 324; Univ of Illinois 325; Univ of Ottawa 363; Univ Pr of Kansas 329; Vehicule 364; Venture 331; Verso 331; Wadsworth 333; Wesleyan Univ 336; Westminster John Knox 337; Yale Univ 343

Software: Adams-Blake 131; American Bar 137; American Water Works 140; A-R 142; ATL 145; Branden 161; Cypress 184; Doubleday 188; Eckert, J.K. 380; Educator's Int'l Pr 193; Electric Works 195; Family Album 370; Jist Works 233; Kroshka 237; Le Gesse 239; Lebhar-Freidman 240; Neal-Schuman 260; No Starch 264; One on One 268; Osborne Media Group 269; Productive 358; Richboro 292; SAS 299; Serendipity 302; Sybex 314; Universal 323; Wadsworth 333; Walch, J. Weston 334

Spiritual: Acropolis 130; Alba 133; Allisone 135; Alyson 136; Ambassador 136; AngeLines 141; Ballantine 149; Bantam Dell Pub Grp 149; Bethany 155; Bookworld/Blue Star 159; Cedar Fort 169; Chalice 170; Chosen Bks 173; Christian Pub 173;

Common Courage 178; Conari 178; Creation House 182; Cross Cultural 182; Crossing Pr 183; Crossway 183; David, Jonathan 185; Doubleday Religious 188; Doubleday/Image 189; Down the Shore 189; Electric Works 195; Encounter 196; Equilibrium 369; Focus Pub 202; Hampton Rds 213; HarperPerennial 215; HarperSanFrancisco 215; Hay House 217; Hazelden 217; Hendrickson 219; Hensley 219; HiddenSpring 220; Hohm 221; Honor 223; Humanics Pub 225; IDG Business 227; IDG Lifestyle 227; Ideals Pub 227; Jewish Lights 233; Judson 234; Kensington 235; Kramer, H.J. 236; Kregel 237; Le Gesse 239; Lebhar-Freidman 240; Legacy 240; Lift Every Voice 371; Liguori 242; Loyola 247; March Tenth 381; Mesorah 253; Midknight Club 253; More, Thomas 256; Morehouse 256; Nelson, Thomas 260; Onjinjinkta 268; Oughten House 374; Ozark 374; Parabola Books 375; Paraclete 272; Paragon 273; Pauline Bks & Media 274; Perigee 277; Pontalba 281; Putnam's Sons 286; Quest Bks 287; Raindbow (California) 288; Rising Star 376; Ronin Pub 293; Sheed & Ward 303; St Mary's 297; Taylor 315; Universal 323; Westminster John Knox 337; White Stone Circle 338

Sports: ABDO 129; Adams Media 131; Addax 132; Adirondack Mountain 132; Alaska Northwest 133; Algonquin 134; Ambassador 136; Amber 137; American Pr 139; Arcadia 142; Archway 142; Atheneum Bks for Yng Rdrs 144; Avisson 146; Avon 147; Backcountry 147; Ballantine 149; Bancroft 149; Bantam Dell Pub Grp 149; Barron's Educ 151; Beachway 152; Bentley 154; Birch Brook 155; Black Dog & Leventhal 156; Blackbirch 156; Bluewood 158; Bonus 159; Bowling Green 160; Boyds Mills 160; Brassey's 161; Brassey's Sports 161; Broadway 163; Burford 164; Capstone 167; Carolrhoda 167; Cartwheel 168; Cerier, Alison Brown 380; Chandler 170; Children's Pr 172; City & Co. 175; Cloud Peak 176; Coaches 177; Countrysport 181; Cumberland 183; David, Jonathan 185; Doubleday 188; Dover 189; Down East 189; Eakin Pr/Sunbelt Media 191; ECW 351; Ecco Pr 192; Ecopress 369; Electric Works 195; Emerald Wave 369; Eriksson, Paul 196; Facts on File 198; Fernwood 352; Foghorn 202; Footprint Press 370; Great Quotations 209; Greenwood Pub Grp 210; Half Halt 212; HarperEntertainment 215; HarperPerennial 215; Hendricks, F.P. 353; Heritage House 353; Houghton Mifflin Adult 224; Houghton Mifflin Bks for Children 223; Howell Pr 224; Human Kinetics 225; Ideals Children's Bks 227; Illumination 370; Journey 233; Kesend, Michael 235; Krause 237; Kroshka 237; Le Gesse 239; Lerner 241; Lifetime Bks 242; Lift Every Voice 371; Lion Bks 243; Little, Brown 243; Little, Brown Children's 243; Longstreet 245; Lowell 246; Lyons Pr 247; MBI 250; McBooks 250; McFarland & Co 251; McGregor 251; Middle Atlantic 253; Middle Atlantic 373; Millbrook 254; Missouri Historical Society Press 373; Momentum 255; Mountaineers Bks 258; Mustang Pub 258; New American Library 261; New York Univ 263; North Point 264; Norton, WW 266; NTC/Contemporary 266; Omega 374; Orange Frazer 269; Owen, Richard 271; Owl Bks 271; Parnassus 273; Pelican 275; Picasso 357; Pontalba 281; Prairie Oak 283; Pruett 285; Putnam's Sons 286; Ragged Mountain 288; Rainbow (FL) 289; Raincoast 358; Random House Bks for Yng Rdrs 289; Random House Trade 290; Safari 295; Santa Monica 298; Sasquatch 299; Scholastic Canada 360; Southern Illinois Univ Pr 308; Spectacle Lane 376; St Martin's 297; Stackpole 309; Sterling 311; Stoddart 361; Stoeger 311; Stoneydale 312; Summit Pub Grp 313; Taylor 315; Towle House 319; Trans-Atlantic 320; Troitsa 321; Turtle Pr 321; Universal 323; Univ of Illinois 325; Univ of Iowa 326; Vitesse 377; Walker & Co 334; Walsworth 334; Warner Bks 334; Whitman, Albert 338; Willow Creek 340; Wilshire 340; Windward 341; Workman 342; Wysteria Publishing 378

Technical: ABI 129; Adams-Blake 131; AHA 132; Allegro 134; Allyn & Bacon 135; American Bar 137; American Chemical 138; American Coll of Physician Exec 138; American Correctional 138; American Nurses 139; American Pr 139; American Quilters 139; American Soc of Civil Eng 139; Andrew/Noyes 141; ASA 143; ASM 144; ATL 145; Austin & Winfield 145; Aviation Publishers (PA) 146; aatec 366; Ball 149; Baywood 152; Baywood 152; Bentley 154; Black Dog & Leventhal 156; Bloomberg 157; Blue Poppy 158; Bookwrights 379; Branden 161; Brevet 161; Broadcast Interview 163; Business McGraw-Hill 165; Butterworth-Heinemann 165; Charles River Media 170; Chelsea Green 171; Consortium 179; Cornell Maritime 180; Craftsman 181; Current Clinical Strategies 184; Cypress 184; Darlington 184; Eckert, J.K. 380; Éditions Logiques 352; Electric Works 195; Empire 196; Fire Engineering 200; Focal 201; Ft Ross 203; GATF Pr 205; Government Inst 208; Guilford 211; Gulf 212; Hancock House 213; Hanser Gardner 213; Hatherleigh 216; Haven 216; Human Kinetics 225; IDG Business 227; Information Today 228; Int'l Found Of Employee Benefit Plans 230; Interweave 231; Jacobs, Lee 232; Jelmar 371; Krieger 237; Kroshka 237; Kumarian 238; Laureate 371; Le Gesse 239; Lebhar-Freidman 240; Lone Eagle 245; Maximum 249; McFarland & Co 251; Medical Physics 252; Merriam Press 252; Metal Powder Ind 253; Neal-Schuman 260; Nichols 264; No Starch 264; One on One 268; Osborne Media Group 269; Pacific Bks 271; Parlay Int'l 273; Pencil Point 276; Pennsylvania Hist and Museum Comm 276; Possibility 281; PROMPT 285; Practice Mgmt 282; Precept 283; Productive 358; Professional Pub 284; ProStar 285; Purich 358; SAS 299; Sams 298; Skyfoot Technical 360; Sourcebooks 307; Stipes 311; Sybex 314; Tech Books for the Layperson 377; Texas Western 317; Tiare 318; Transnational 320; Universal 323; Univ of Alaska 324; Univ of Idaho 325; ULI 330; Visions Comm 332; Vitesse 377; Weidner & Sons 336; Woodhead 365; Wordware 342; Wysteria Publishing 378

Textbook: ABI 129; Abingdon 129; AHA 132; Alba 133; Alef 134; Allyn & Bacon 135; Amacom 136; American Coll of Physician Exec 138; American Correctional 138; American Counseling 138; American Nurses 139; American Pr 139; Anchorage 140; Andrew/Noyes 141; ASCP 144; ASM 144; ATL 145; Austin & Winfield 145; Avisson 146; Baker Bks 148; Ball 149; Bandanna 367; Barron's Educ 151; Behrman 153; Bellwether-Cross 153; Between the Lines 347; Bliss 368; Blue Poppy 158; Bookwrights 379; Bowling Green 160; BPS 348; Branden 161; Brassey's 161; Broadcast Interview 163; Broadview 348; Burnham 165; Butterworth-Heinemann 165; Can Educators 349; CHA 350; Chalice 170; Charlesbridge Pub 171; Charlesbridge Pub Trd 171; China Bks 172; Christian Pub 173; College Pr 177; Common Courage 178; Consortium 179; Cornell Univ 180; Corwin 180; Course Crafters 380; Cross Cultural 182; Crossway 183; Current Clinical Strategies 184; Cypress 184; Dearborn 185; Dover 189; Eckert, J.K. 380; Éditions Logiques 352; Educator's Int'l Pr 193; Educators Pub Svces 193; Eerdmans, William 194; EMC/Paradigm 195; Empire 196; ETC Pub 197; Evan Moor 197; Fernwood 352; Fire Engineering 200; Focal 201; Free Pr 204; GATF Pr 205; Gessler 206; Gifted Educ 206; Gleason Grp 380; Greenwood Pub Grp 210; Group Pub 210; Gruyter, Aldine de 211; Guilford 211; Hanser Gardner 213; Haven 216; Haworth 217; Hendricks, F.P. 353; Human Kinetics 225; IBEX 226; Inst of Psych Res 354; Intercultural 229; Int'l City/County Mgmt. 229; Int'l Found Of Employee

Benefit Plans 230; Int'l Medical 230; Int'l Scholars 230; Interstate 231; Island Press 232; Jacobs, Lee 232; Jist Works 233; Kamehameha 234; Kogan Page 236; Krieger 237; Kumarian 238; Le Gesse 239; Learning Pub 240; Lebhar-Freidman 240; Libraries Unltd 241; Lippincott Williams & Wilkins 243; Loyola 247; Mayfield 250; Medical Physics 252; Meriwether 252; Mesorah 253; Metal Powder Ind 253; Missouri Historical Society Press 373; NASW 259; Neal-Schuman 260; Neshui 261; New Harbinger 262; Oasis 267; Orange Frazer 269; Pacific Bks 271; Pacific View 272; Paragon 273; Paulist Pr 274; Pencil Point 276; Perfection Learning 276; Picton 279; Plexus 280; Practice Mgmt 282; Precept 283; Press at the Maryland Hist Soc 283; Professional Pub 284; Prufrock 286; Publicom 381; Purich 358; Quite Specific Media Grp 288; Reidmore 359; Review & Herald 292; Rosen Pub Grp 294; Routledge 294; Roxbury 294; SAS 299; Sagamore 296; Salina 297; Sandlapper 298; Schenkman 300; Skidmore-Roth 305; Slack 305; Smith, Gibbs 306; Sourcebooks 307; Southern Illinois Univ Pr 308; Speech Bin 308; St. Augustine's 296; St Bede's 296; St Martin's 297; Stanford Univ 310; Stipes 311; Tech Books for the Layperson 377; Third World 317; Thompson Educ 361; Torah Aura 318; Transnational 320; Trilobyte 362; Trinity 320; Truman State Univ 321; Universal 323; Univ of Alaska 324; Univ of Alberta 363; Univ of Idaho 325; Univ of Ottawa 363; Utah State Univ Pr 330; Vanderbilt Univ 331; Venture 331; VGM 331; Visions Comm 332; Wadsworth 333; Wall & Emerson 364; Watson-Guptill 335; Weidner & Sons 336; Weigl 365; Westminster John Knox 337; Wiener, Markus 339; Wisdom 341; Wordware 342; Wysteria Publishing 378; Yale Univ 343; York 365; Zondervan 344

Translation: Abique 129; Alyson 136; Aronson 143; Arte Publico 143; Aztex 147; Bandanna 367; Barron's Educ 151; Broadcast Interview 163; Calyx 368; China Bks 172; Confluence 179; Cornell Univ 180; Cross Cultural 182; Dante Univ of America Pr 184; Doubleday 188; Dover 189; Dry Bones 190; Dry Bones 190; Dufour 190; Ecco Pr 192; Ediciones Nuevo Espacio 192; Eerdmans, William 194; Electric Works 195; ETC Pub 197; Fernwood 352; Free Pr 204; Goose Lane 352; Guernica 353; HarperPerennial 215; Harvard Common 215; Hohm 221; Holmes & Meier 222; Inst of Psych Res 354; Intercultural 229; ISER 355; Johnson 233; Kamehameha 234; Latin Amer Lit Review 239; Le Gesse 239; Mage 248; MBI 250; Mesorah 253; Mountaineers Bks 258; Northern Illinois Univ 265; Ohio Univ 267; Pacific Bks 271; Parlay Int'l 273; Passeggiata 273; Paulist Pr 274; Potter, Clarkson 282; Puckerbrush 375; Quite Specific Media Grp 288; Rutgers Univ 295; Scrivenery Press 301; St Bede's 296; Stone Bridge 311; Trinity 320; Universal 323; Univ of Alabama 323; Univ of Alaska 324; Univ of California 325; Univ of North Carolina 327; Univ of Ottawa 363; Univ of Texas 328; Vanderbilt Univ 331; Vernon Pr 382; Zoland 344

Transportation: ASA 143; Aviation Publishers (PA) 146; Aztex 147; Bentley 154; Boston Mills 348; Bristol Fashion 162; Howell Pr 224; Howell Pr 224; Iconografix 226; Kalmbach 234; Lerner 241; MBI 250; Norton, WW 266; Possibility 281

Travel: Academy Chicago 130; Accent 367; Adirondack Mountain 132; Alaska Northwest 133; Alexander 134; American & World Geographic 379; Appalachian Mountain 141; Arcade 142; Atheneum Bks for Yng Rdrs 144; Autonomedia 145; Ballantine 149; Barnegat 150; Barron's Educ 151; Bay 151; Beachway 152; Berkshire 154; Black Dog & Leventhal 156; Blackbirch 156; Blair 157; Boyds Mills 160; Burford 164; Camino 166; China Bks 172; City & Co. 175; Compass 178; Countryman 180; Cross Cultural 182; Cumberland 183; Doubleday 188; Dover 189; Electric Works 195; Epicenter 196; Eriksson, Paul 196; Falcon 199; Fodor's 202; Globe Pequot 207; Golden West 207; Grove/Atlantic 211; HarperPerennial 215; Harvard Common 215; Hastings 216; Hellgate 219; Heyday 219; HiddenSpring 220; Hippocrene 221; Houghton Mifflin Adult 224; Houghton Mifflin Bks for Children 223; Howell Pr 224; Hunter Pub 226; IDG Lifestyle 227; Ideals Pub 227; Impact Publications 228; Interlink 229; Johnson 233; Johnston Assoc 371; Kesend, Michael 235; Lake Claremont 238; Langenscheidt 238; Le Gesse 239; Lebhar-Freidman 240; Lonely Planet 245; Lynx Images 356; Lyons Pr 247; McDonald & Woodward 250; Menus & Music 372; Middle Atlantic 373; Momentum 255; Moon 256; Mountain N'Air 257; Mountaineers Bks 258; Mustang Pub 258; Neshui 261; New York Univ 263; North Point 264; Norton, WW 266; Open Road 268; Orange Frazer 269; Owl Bks 271; Pacific View 272; Parnassus 273; Pelican 275; Pennsylvania Hist and Museum Comm 276; Pogo 375; Pontalba 281; ProStar 285; Pruett 285; Putnam's Sons 286; Quest Bks 287; Raincoast 358; Red Hen 290; Rockbridge 293; Rocky Mountain 359; Russian Info 376; Rutledge Hill 295; Sasquatch 299; Seal 301; Settel 382; Shoreline 360; Sierra Club 304; Soho 306; Soma 307; Spotted Dog 309; Steller Press Ltd. 361; Stone Bridge 311; Studio 4 Prod 376; Travelers' Tales 320; Turnstone 362; Universal 323; Univ of Calgary 363; Upney 363; Vernon Pr 382; Westcliffe 337; Western NY 378; Whitecap 365; Whitehorse 378; Whitman, Albert 338; Workman 342; Wysteria Publishing 378; Zoland 344

True crime: Addicus 132; Ballantine 149; Bantam Dell Pub Grp 149; Berkley Pub Grp 154; Carroll & Graf 167; Kensington 235; McGregor 251; St Martin's 297; Stoddart 361

Women's issues/studies: Adams Media 131; Adams Media 131; Alban Inst 133; American Counseling 138; American Nurses 139; Arden 143; Arkansas 143; Arte Publico 143; Autonomedia 145; Avisson 146; Avon 147; Baker Bks 148; Ballantine 149; Bancroft 149; Bantam Dell Pub Grp 149; Barbour 150; Barricade 151; Baylor Univ 152; Baywood 152; Beacon Pr 152; Bellwether-Cross 153; Berkley Pub Grp 154; Bethany 155; Between the Lines 347; Blackbirch 156; Blair 157; Blue/Gray 158; Bluewood 158; Bonus 159; Bookwrights 379; Bottom Dog 160; Bowling Green 160; Brassey's 161; Broadcast Interview 163; Broadview 348; Broadway 163; Broken Jaw 348; Bryant & Dillon 164; Burford 164; Calyx 368; Cerier, Alison Brown 380; Chandler 170; China Bks 172; Cleis 176; Cloud Peak 176; Conari 179; Consortium 179; Consumer Pr 179; Cornell Univ 180; Cross Cultural 182; Doubleday 188; Doubleday/Image 189; Drew, Lisa 189; Ediciones Nuevo Espacio 192; Educator's Int'l Pr 193; Elder Bks 194; Electric Works 195; Encounter 196; Epicenter 196; Facts on File 198; Fairleigh Dickinson 198; Fairleigh Dickinson 198; Fernwood 352; Floricanto 201; Focus Pub 202; Forge 202; Goose Lane 352; Great Quotations 209; Greenwood Pub Grp 210; Guernica 353; Guilford 211; gynergy 353; HarperPerennial 215; HarperSanFrancisco 215; Haworth 217; Hay House 217; Health Comm 217; Heinemann 218; Hellgate 219; Hensley 219; HiddenSpring 220; Hill & Wang 221; Hippocrene 221; Holmes & Meier 222; Houghton Mifflin Adult 224; House of Anansi 354; Howell Pr 224; Hunter House 226; Inner Traditions Int'l 228; Int'l Scholars 230; ISER 355; Jesperson 355; Jesperson 355; Jewish

Lights 233; Kumarian 238; Latin Amer Lit Review 239; Le Gesse 239; Learning Pub 240; Lebhar-Freidman 240; Libraries Unltd 241; Lift Every Voice 371; Llewellyn 244; Locust Hill 244; Longstreet 245; Louisiana State Univ 246; Lowell 246; March Tenth 381; Mayfield 250; MBI 250; McFarland & Co 251; McGavick Field 372; McGraw-Hill Ryerson 356; Michigan State Univ 253; Minnesota Hist Soc 254; Missouri Historical Society Press 373; Momentum 255; Moody 256; More, Thomas 256; Morehouse 256; Narwhal 259; Natural Heritage/Natural History 356; Nautical & Aviation 260; Naval Inst 260; Neshui 261; New American Library 261; New Hope 262; New Horizon 262; New Victoria 263; New World 263; New York Univ 263; Nicolas-Hays 374; Northeastern Univ 265; NTC/Contemporary 266; Ohio State Univ 267; Ohio Univ 267; Oliver 268; Onjinjinkta 268; Orange Frazer 269; Osprey 270; Oughten House 374; Overmountain 270; Owen, Richard 271; Paladin 272; Papier-Mache 272; Paragon 273; Parlay Int'l 273; Pedlar 357; Picasso 357; Pontalba 281; Praeger 282; Presidio 283; Puffin 286; Putnam's Sons 286; Quest Bks 287; Rainbow (FL) 289; Red Hen 290; Reference Svce 290; Reference Svce 290; Republic of Texas 291; Review & Herald 292; Reynolds, Morgan 292; Rockbridge 293; Routledge 294; Rutgers Univ 295; Rutledge Hill 295; Sachem 382; Scarecrow 299; Schenkman 300; Schocken 300; Seal 301; Sgt Kirklands 303; Shoreline 360; Skinner 305; Sourcebooks 307; South End 308; Southern Illinois Univ Pr 308; Spence 308; Spinsters Ink 309; St. Martin's Scholarly & Reference 297; Stackpole 309; Stoddart 361; Stone Bridge 311; Summit Pub Grp 313; Teachers College 315; Temple Univ 316; Texas A&M Univ 316; Texas A&M Univ 316; Third World 317; Thompson Educ 361; Transnational 320; 2M Comm 382; Universal 323; Univ of Alaska 324; Univ of Arizona 324; Univ of Calgary 363; Univ of Idaho 325; Univ of Manitoba 363; Univ of North Carolina 327; Univ of North Texas 327; Univ of Oklahoma 327; Univ of Ottawa 363; Univ of Pennsylvania 328; Univ of South Carolina 328; Univ of Tennessee 328; Univ of Texas 328; Univ Pr of Kansas 329; Univ Pr of Kansas 329; Univ Pr of Kentucky 329; Univ Pr of Kentucky 329; Vandamere 330; Vanderbilt Univ 331; Vanwell 364; Vernon Pr 382; Verso 331; Viking 332; Visions Comm 332; Vista 333; Volcano 333; Westminster John Knox 337; White Mane 338; Wildcat Canyon 339; Wiley 339; Wiley 339; Yale Univ 343; Yale Univ 343; Zoland 344

World affairs: Beacon Pr 152; Brassey's 161; Clarity 368; Dee, Ivan 186; Family Album 370; Forum 203; Intercultural 229; Int'l Scholars 230; Kumarian 238; Lucent 247; McFarland & Co 251; New England 261; Stoddart 361; Univ of Arizona 324; Univ of Calgary 363; Univ of South Carolina 328; Wiener, Markus 339

Young adult: Archway 142; Atheneum Bks for Yng Rdrs 144; Avisson 146; Barron's Educ 151; Blackbirch 156; Blue Heron 157; Boyds Mills 160; Cambridge Educ 166; Candlewick 166; Christian Ed 173; Dial Bks for Yng Rdrs 187; Eerdmans Bks for Yng Rdrs 194; Enslow 196; Facts on File 198; Greenhaven 209; Group Pub 210; Hendrick-Long 219; Highsmith 220; Holt Bks for Yng Rdrs 222; Journey 233; Little, Brown Children's 243; Lucent 247; McElderry, Margaret 250; Mitchell Lane 255; New England 261; Oliver 268; Perfection Learning 276; Philomel 278; PPI 282; Price Stern Sloan 283; Reynolds, Morgan 292; Rosen Pub Grp 294; Scholastic Inc 300; Speech Bin 308; Twenty-First Century 322; Tyndale 322; Zondervan 344;

General Index

This index lists every market appearing in the book; use it to find specific companies you wish to approach. Markets that appeared in the 2000 edition of *Writer's Market*, but are not included in this edition are identified by a two-letter code explaining why the market was omitted: **(ED)**— Editorial Decision, **(NS)**—Not Accepting Submissions, **(NR)**—No or Late Response to Listing Request, **(OB)**—Out of Business, **(RR)**—Removed by Market's Request, **(UC)**—Unable to Contact, **(RP)**—Business Restructured or Purchased, **(NP)**—No Longer Pays in Copies Only, **(SR)** Subsidy/Royalty Publisher, **(UF)**—Uncertain Future, **(Web)**—a listing that appears on our website at www.WritersDigest.com

A

A.G.S. Incorporated (RR)
A Muse (NR)
A.S.K. Theater Projects 944
AAA Carolinas Go Magazine 647
AAA Going Places 778
AAA Midwest Traveler 778
AAA Today 780
AAAS Science Journalism Awards 1030
A&B Publishers Group 128
A&U, America's AIDS Magazine 447
aatec publications 366
ABA Journal 902
Abaco Life 660
Abbeville Publishing Group 129
Abbey Short Fiction Award, Edward 999
Abbott, Langer & Assoc. (NS)
ABC-CLIO (NS)
ABC-CLIO America: History and Life Award (NR)
ABDO Publishing Company 129
Aberdeen Group, The (RP)
Aberdeen's Concrete Construction (see Concrete Construction 843)
ABI Professional Publications 129
Abilities (NR)
Abingdon Press 129
Abique 129
Aboard Magazine 540
Aboriginal Science Fiction 706
About Face Theatre 944
Above & Beyond (NR)
Abrams, Inc., Harry N. 130
ABS Enterprises 940
Absey & Co. 130
Absolute Magnitude 706
Acada Books (NR)
Academy Chicago Publishers 130
Accent Books 367
Accent on Living 451
Access Internet Magazine 603
Accounting Today 828
Ace Science Fiction and Fantasy 130
ACM (NP)
Acme Press (Web)
Acorn Prize for Poetry, Milton 1008
Acorn-Rukeyser Chapbook Contest, The 1008

Acropolis Books, Inc. 130
Across the Board 413, 829
ACTA Publications 131
Action (Canada) Magazine 493
Active Living (NR)
Active Parenting Publishers (Web)
ActiveTimes Magazine 696
Actors & Playwrights' Initiative 945
Actors Theatre of Louisville 945
Acuta Journal of Telecommunications in Higher Education 852
Ad Astra 703
Adams Media Corporation 131
Adams Prize, Herbert Baxter (NR)
Adams-Blake Publishing 131
Adams-Hall Publishing 367
Addax Publishing Group, Inc. 132
Addicus Books, Inc. 132
Additions & Decks (NR)
Adirondack Life 644
Adirondack Mountain Club, Inc. 132
Adobe Magazine (NR)
Adventure Book Publishers (NR)
Adventure Cyclist 719
Adventure Journal (NR)
Advisor Today 892
Advocate, The 474
Aegis Publishing Group (Web)
African Access Magazine 460
African American Magazine 479
African American Pulpit, The 835
African American Review 558
Afrimax (NR)
Afterimage 447
Agni 559
AG-Pilot International Magazine 821
Agventures (NR)
AHA 132
Ahsahta Press (NR)
Aim Magazine 461
Aim Magazine Short Story Contest 999
Air and Space/Smithsonian 409
Air Cargo World (NR)
Air Force Times 584
Airbrush Action Magazine 814
Airline, Ship & Catering Onboard Services (NR)
Airwaves, Connections 541
AJM: The Authority on Jewelry Manufacturing 893

AKC Gazette (Web)
Akron Poetry Prize 1008
Aktrin Furniture Research (Web)
Alabama Game & Fish 740
Alabama Heritage 617
Alabama Living (Web)
Alabama Shakespeare Festival 945
Alaska 618
Alaska Business Monthly 417
Alaska Northwest Books 133
Alaska Parenting (OB)
Alaska Quarterly Review 559
Alba House 133
Alban Institute, The 133
Albemarle 658
Alberta Playwriting Competition 1019
Alberta Sweetgrass 461
AlbertaViews 661
Albury Publishing 133
Alef Design Group 134
Aletheia Publications (NR)
Alexander Books 134
Alexander/Enright and Assoc. (Web)
Algonquin Books of Chapel Hill 134
Alive! 696
All About You 770
Allegro Press 134
Allen Literary Agency, Linda 94
Allen Publishing (RR)
Allergy and Asthma Health 452
Alleyway Theatre 945
Alliance Theatre (NR)
Allied Artists, Inc. 969
Alligator Press, Inc. 134
Allison & Busby (Web)
Allisone Press 135
All-Stater Sports 730
Allworth Press 135
Allyn & Bacon 135
Almanac for Farmers & City Folk, The 529
Alpine Publications 367
Alternative Energy Retailer (Web)
Alternative Family Magazine 475
Althouse Press, The 346
Alyson Publications, Inc. 136
AMA Alliance Today 910
Amacom Books 136
Amazing Stories 707
Ambassador Books, Inc. 136

Ambassador Magazine 461
Amber Books Publishing 137
Amber Lane Press Limited (Web)
Amberley Greeting Card Co. 983
AMC Outdoors 593
Amelia Magazine 559
Amelia Student Award 1037
America 666
America West Airlines Magazine 541
America West Publishers 137
American & World Geographic Publishing 379
American Angler 740
American Archaeology 703
American Art Journal, The 394
American Association of University Women Award, North Carolina Division 1033
American Astronautical Society (Web)
American Atheist Press 137
American Baby Magazine 430
American Bar Association 137
American Brewer (NR)
American Careers 422
American Catholic Press 367
American Cheerleader 757
American Chemical Society 138
American Classics (RR)
American College of Physician Executives 138
American Correctional Assoc. 138
American Counseling Assoc. 138
American Country 588
American Demographics (NR)
American Drycleaner/Coin-Op/Clean Car/American Laundry News 829
American Eagle Publications (Web)
American Federation of Astrologers 138
American Fiction Awards (NR)
American Fire Journal 872
American Fitness 493
American Forests 593
American Fruit Grower 860
American Gardener, The 530
American Girl (Web)
American Greetings 983
American Heritage 504
American History 504
American Hockey Inc. 739
American Homestyle & Gardening Magazine 530
American Hunter 741
American Indian Art Magazine (OB)
American Ink Maker (NR)
American Institute of Certified Public Accountants (NR)
American International Syndicate (NR)
American Iron Magazine 405
American Jewelry Manufacturing (see AJM: The Authority on Jewelry Manufacturing 893)
American Journal of Nursing 880
American Legion Magazine, The 480
American Matchcover Collectors Club, The 507
American Medical News 910
American Moving Picture Co. (NR)
American Music Theater Festival (NR)
American Nurses Publishing 139

American Press 139
American Psychiatric Press, The (NS)
American Quilter's Society 139
American Regional History Publishing Awards (NR)
American Renaissance Theatre of Dramatic Arts (NR)
American Renegade Theatre Co. 945
American Salesman, The 926
American Salon (NR)
American Scholar, The 480
American Skating World 763
American Snowmobiler 763
American Society of Civil Engineers Press 139
American Songwriter 588
American Spectator 609
American Stage Festival (NR)
American Style 395
American Survival Guide 584
American Translators Association Honors and Awards 1036
American Turf Monthly 739
American Venture (NR)
American Visions 462
American Water Works Assoc. 140
American Way 541
American Window Cleaner Magazine 906
American Woman 796
American Woman Motorscene (see American Woman Road & Travel 405)
American Woman Road & Travel 405
America's Civil War 504
America's Cutter (OB)
America's Network (NR)
Amethyst Review Annual Writing Contest, The 999
Amherst Media, Inc. 140
Amicus Journal, The 596
Amigadget Publishing Co. (Web)
Ampersand Communications (Web)
Amster Literary Enterprises, Betsy 95
Amusement Business 857
AMWA Medical Book Awards Competition 990
Amwell Press, The (Web)
Amy Writing Awards 1030
Analog Science Fiction & Fact (NR)
Anamnesis Poetry Chapbook Award Competition 1008
Ancestry Incorporated 140
Anchor Publishing Maryland 140
Anchorage Press, Inc. 140
And Books 140
Andrew, Inc., William (see William Andrew/Noyes Publishing 141)
Andrew/Noyes Publishing, William 141
Andrews McMeel 141
Angel Films 969
Angeleno 620
AngeLines™ Productions (see AngeLines™ Publishing 141)
AngeLines Publishing 141
Angels on Earth 666
Angel's Touch Productions 969
Anglofile (NR)
Angus Beef Bulletin 863
Angus Journal 863
Anhinga Press 367
Anhinga Prize for Poetry 1008

Animals 386
Anisfield-Wolf Book Awards 989
Ann Arbor Observer 637
Annals of Saint Anne De Beaupre, The 667
Annett Award for Children's Literature, R. Ross 1033
Annick Press Ltd. 346
Annual Blank Theatre Company Young Playwrights Festival 1019
Annual Give Back to Society Writing Competition 1037
Annual International One Page Play Competition 1019
Annual National Playwriting Contest (NR)
Annual One-Act Play Competition 1019
Annual Poetry Contest 1008
Annual Short Story Contest 999
AnotheRealm 707
Anthem Essay Contest (NR)
Antietam Review (NR)
Antietam Review Literary Award (NR)
Antigonish Review, The 560
Antioch Review 560
Antique Review 508
Antique Trader Weekly, The (NR)
Antiqueweek 814
Anvil Magazine 905
Anvil Press 346
Anvil Press International 3-Day Novel Writing Contest 999
APDG Publishing (NR)
Appalachian Mountain Club Books 141
Appalachian Trailway News 596
Appaloosa Journal 386
Apparel Industry Magazine (NR)
Apple Tree Theatre 945
Appliance Service News (NR)
Aqua (OB)
Aquatics International 930
A-R Editions, Inc. 142
Arabesque 142
Arc 560
Arcade Publishing 142
Arcadia Publishing 142
Archaeology (Web)
Architecture Magazine (NR)
Archway Paperbacks 142
Arcudi Fiction Award (see Bonomo Memorial Literature Prize 999)
Arden Press Inc. 143
Area Development Magazine 921
Arena Players Repertory Company 945
Arena Stage 946
Ariadne Press (Web)
Ariadne Prize 999
Arizona Authors' Association Annual National Literary Contest 1037
Arizona Commission of the Arts Fellowship in Creative Writing 1044
Arizona Foothills Magazine 618
Arizona Highways 618
Arizona, The State of Golf 733
Arizona Theatre Company 946
Arkansas Repertory Theatre 946
Arkansas Research 143
Arkansas Sportsman 741
Arkansas Trucking Report (OB)

Arkin Magazine Syndicate, Inc. 977
Armenian International Magazine (NR)
Army Magazine 585
Army Times 585
Aronson, Inc., Jason 143
Arriving Magazine (OB)
ArrowTrade Magazine 930
Art & Antiques 395
Art Direction (NR)
Art Direction Book Co. (Web)
Art Materials Retailer (Web)
Art of Music Annual Writing Contest, The 1037
Art Revue Magazine 395
Art Spirit! 396
Art Station Theatre 946
Art Times (Web)
Arte Publico Press 143
Artemis Creations Publishing (Web)
Artemis Magazine 707
Arthritis Today 452
Artilleryman, The 505
Artist Assistance Fellowship 1044
Artist Fellowship 1044
Artist Fellowship Awards 1044
Artistmarket.com 977
Artists Fellowship 1044
Artists' Fellowships 1045
Artist's Magazine, The 396
Artists Repertory Theatre 946
Artnews 396
Arts & Activities 848
Arts and Letters Competition 1038
Arts & Life Prize for Culinary Journalism 1030
Arts & Life Prize for Humor 989
Arts & Life Prize for Journalism 1031
Arts & Life Prize for Poetry 1008
Arts & Life Prize for Religion 989
Arts Management (Web)
Arts Recognition and Talent Search 1045
ArtsLink Collaborative Projects Award 989
Art-Talk 396
Aruba Nights 780
ASA, Aviation Supplies & Academics 143
ASCP Press 144
ASF Translation Prize 1036
AS/400 Systems Management (NR)
Asian American Theater Co. (Web)
Asian Humanities Press (Web)
Asian Pages 462
Asimov's Science Fiction 708
ASM International 144
Asolo Theatre Company 946
ASPCA Animal Watch 386
Aspen Magazine 625
Asphalt Angels Magazine 405
Asphalt Contractor (NR)
Associate Reformed Presbyterian, The (Web)

Association for Supervision and Curriculum Development 144
Asthma Magazine 452
Astragal Press (Web)
Astro Communications Services (NS)
Astrology Your Daily Horoscope (NR)
Astronomy 704
ASU Travel Guide 781
ATA Magazine, The 848
Atheneum Books For Young Readers 144
At-Home Mother 430
ATI (Web)
ATL Press, Inc. 145
Atlanta 629
Atlanta Homes and Lifestyles 530
Atlanta Parent/Atlanta Baby 433
Atlanta Tribune: The Magazine 629
Atlantic Books Today 661
Atlantic Business Magazine (NR)
Atlantic Canadian Poetry Prize (UC)
Atlantic City Magazine 642
Atlantic Journalism Awards 1031
Atlantic Monthly, The 480
Atlantic Salmon Journal, The 596
Atlantic Writing Competition (UC)
Atlas Shrugged Essay Competition (NR)
Attaché Magazine 542
Auburn House 145
Audio (OB)
Audubon 597
Augsburg Books (NS)
Auricle Award 1019
Aurora Productions (NR)
Austin & Winfield Publishers 145
Austin Heart of Film Festival Feature Length Screenplay Competition 1019
Austin Home & Living (NR)
Australian Way, The (NR)
Authors in the Park Short Story Contest 999
Authorship 894
Auto & Flat Glass Journal 816
Auto Book Press (NR)
Auto Digest 977
Auto Racing Digest 760
Auto Rental News 816
Auto Restorer 406
Autograph Collector 508
Automated Builder (Web)
Automobile Quarterly 406
Autonomedia 145
AutoWeek 406
A/V Concepts Corp. 940
Avalanche Entertainment (Web)
Avalon Books 146
Avanyu Publishing Inc. 146
Avenue 645
Avery 146
Aviation Buyer's Directory (NR)
Aviation History (NR)

Aviation International News 821
Aviation Publishers 146
Aviation Publishing (NS)
Avisson Press, Inc. 146
Avon Books 147
Avon EOS 147
Avon Flare Books (OB)
Avon Twilight (OB)
AWP Award Series 1038
Aztex Corp. 147
Azure Design, Architecture and Art 397

B

B Street Theatre, The (NR)
Baby Talk 433
Babybug 545
Babylon Players "World Premiere" Writing Contest 1019
Back Home In Kentucky 634
Back Stage 858
Backcountry Guides 147
Backcountry Publications (see Backcountry Guides 147)
BackHome 531
Backpacker 738
Backroads 406
Backstretch, The 740
Badham Company (Web)
Baen Publishing Enterprises 148
Bailiwick Repertory 946
Bait Fisherman 741
Bakeless Literary Publication Prizes 1038
Baker Book House Company 148
Baker Books 148
Baker's Plays High School Playwriting Contest 1020
Baker's Plays Publishing Co. 946
Balch Award, Emily Clark 1038
Balcony Press 148
Baldwin College Theatre, Mary 947
Bale Books 148
Balian's Outdoor & Nature Photography 607
Ball Publishing 149
Ballantine Books 149
Balloon Life 410
Balloons and Parties Magazine (Web)
Baltimore Alternative 635
Baltimore Magazine 636
Bancroft Press 149
Bandanna Books 367
B&B Publishing (RR)
Bangtale Press (NR)
Bank Director 867
Bank Marketing Magazine (NR)
Banking Strategies 867
Banta Award 989
Bantam Dell Publishing Group 149
Bantam Doubleday Dell Books for Young Readers 150
Barbour Publishing, Inc. 150
Bark, The 387

Barker Playwriting Prize, Roy (UC)
Barnegat Light Press 150
Barnstorm Films (Web)
Barrett Award, The Herb 1009
Barrett Books Inc., Loretta 95
Barricade Books Inc. 151
Barron's Educational Series, Inc. 151
Bartender Magazine 883
Barter Theatre (NR)
Baruch University Award, Mrs. Simon 990
Basch Feature Syndicate, Buddy (Web)
Baseball America 719
Bass & Walleye Boats 721
Bassmaster Magazine 742
Batsford Brassey (see Brassey's 161)
Battelle Press 151
Battery Man, The (NR)
Baumgarten-Prophet Entertainment 969
Bay Area Baby (NR)
Bay Area Parent Magazine (NR)
Bay Books 151
Bay Windows 475
Baylor University Press 152
Baywood Publishing Co., Inc. 152
BBW 797
BC Business 417
BC Outdoors 742
Bcala Literary Awards (NR)
Beach Holme Publishers Ltd. 346
Beachway Press 152
Beacon Entertainment Syndicate of Tennessee (NR)
Beacon Hill Press of Kansas City (NR)
Beacon Press 152
Bear Deluxe Magazine, The 597
Beauty Store Business 822
Beaver, The 661
Beaver Pond Publishing (Web)
Bebi Das (NR)
Beckett Baseball Card Monthly (NR)
Beckett Baseball Card Monthly 508
Beckett Football Card Monthly (NR)
Beckett Hockey Collector 509
Beckett Pokemon Collector 509
Beckett Racing Monthly (NR)
Beckett Sports Collectibles and Autographs (NR)
Bedtimes 829
Bee Culture (NR)
Beeman Jorbensen, Inc. 153
Beer Prize, George Louis (NR)
Beer, Wine & Spirits Beverage Retailer (Web)
Behrman House Inc. 153
Beil, Publisher, Inc., Frederic C. 153
Bellwether-Cross Publishing 153
Bench & Bar of Minnesota 902
Bend of the River Magazine 648
Benefactory, Inc., The 153
Bennett Fellowship, George 1045
Bent, Literary Agent, Graybill & English, L.L.C., Jenny 95
Bentley Publishers 154
Berg Publishers (Web)
Bergin & Garvey 154
Berkley Publishing Group, Thep 154
Berkshire House Publishers, Inc. 154
Berman Boals and Flynn Inc. 114
Bernstein & Associates, Inc., Pam 96

Best Ideas for Christmas (NR)
Bethany House Publishers 155
Better Health 495
Better Homes and Gardens 531
Better Nutrition 496
Betterway Books 155
Between the Lines 347
Beverage Journal, The 825
Beverly Hills Theatre Guild—Julie Harris Playwright Award Competition, The 1020
Beverly Hills Theatre Guild—Play Competition for Children's Theatre: The Marilyn Hall Awards, The 1020
Bible Advocate 667
Bible Advocate Online 667
Bibliophilos 481
Bick Publishing House 155
Bicycling 720
Big Apple Parent/Queens Parent 433
Big Event Pictures 969
Big Star Motion Pictures Ltd. 969
Big World 781
Bike Magazine 720
Bilingual Foundation of the Arts 947
Billiards Digest (NR)
Billington Prize, Ray Allen (NR)
Bilson Award for Historical Fiction for Young People, The Geoffrey 1034
Bingham Prize, The Worth (NR)
Biomed Books (Web)
Birch Brook Press 155
Birch Lane Press (OB)
Bird Watcher's Digest 598
Birds & Blooms (NR)
Birdsall Prize In European Military & Strategic History (NR)
Birks Family Foundation Award for Biography 991
Birmingham Weekly 617
BK MK Press 156
Black & White 617
Black Award, Irma S. and James H. 1034
Black Belt 755
Black Collegian, The 422
Black Dog & Leventhal Publishers Inc. 156
Black Elegance (Web)
Black Heron Press (NR)
Black Press Service, Inc. 978
Black Romance Group, The 699
Black Secrets (RP)
Black Warrior Review 560
Blackbirch Press, Inc. 156
Blade Magazine 509
Blair, Publisher, John F. 157
Blate Assoc., Sam (Web)
Bleecker Street Associates 96
Bliss Publishing Co. 368
Blizzard Publishing (NR)
Bloodsongs (NR)
Bloomberg Press 157
Bloomberg Wealth Manager 867
Bloomsbury Review 826
Blue Heron Publishing 157
Blue Moon Books, Inc. 157
Blue Mountain Arts, Inc. 983
Blue Poppy Press 158
Blue Ridge Business Journal 418
Blue Ridge Country 614

Blue Sky Marketing, Inc. 368
Blue Sky Press, The 158
Bluegrass Unlimited 588
Blue/Gray Books 158
Bluestem Poetry Award 1009
Bluewood Books 158
BNA Books 158
B'nai B'rith International Jewish Monthly, The 462
BOA Editions, Ltd. 159
Boardwatch Magazine 887
Boarshead Theater (NR)
Boat and Motor Dealer (NR)
Boating Industry (Web)
Boating Life 722
Bobbin 842
Boca Raton Magazine 627
Bock Prize, The Frederick 1009
Bogin Memorial Award, George (NR)
Boise Magazine 631
Bomb Magazine (NR)
Bon Appetit 469
Bonaire Nights 781
Bonderman IUPUI/IRT National Youth Theatre Playwriting Competition and Development Workshop, Waldo M. & Grace C. 1020
Bone Memorial Playwriting Award, Robert (NR)
Bonomo Memorial Literature Prize 999
Bonus Books, Inc. 159
Book® 448
Book Dealers World 895
Book Publishers of Texas Award for Children's or Young People's Book 1034
Bookcraft (RP)
Bookedup.com (UC)
Bookhaven Press (Web)
Bookhome Publishing 159
BookPage 448
Books Collective, The 347
Books In Motion 159
Bookworld, Inc./Blue Star Productions 159
Bookwrights Press 379
Borderlines (NR)
Bordighera Bilingual Italian-American Poetry Prize, The 1036
Borealis Press, Ltd. 347
Boston Globe Magazine 636
Boston Globe-Horn Book Award 1034
Boston Magazine 636
Boston Mills Press, The 348
Boston Review 448
Boston Review Poetry Contest 1009
Boston Review Short Story Contest 999
Bosustow Media Group (NR)
Bottom Dog Press, Inc. 160
Boulder County Business Report 418
Boulevard (books) 160
Boulevard (magazine) 561
Boulevard Books (United Kingdom) (Web)
Boulevard Short Fiction Contest for Emerging Writers 999
Bow & Arrow Hunting 717
Bowhunter 718
Bowhunting World 718

Bowling Green State University Popular Press 160
Bowling Writing Competition 991
Boxoffice Magazine 858
Boyd Military Novel Award, The William Young 1000
Boyds Mills Press 160
Boys' Life 545
Boys Quest 545
Boz Productions (NR)
BPS Books 348
Bracket Racing USA (see Drag Racing USA 761)
Bradley Award, Barbara 1009
Bradley's Fantasy Magazine, Marion Zimmer (UF)
Brahman Journal, The 863
Brand Packaging 812
Branden Publishing Co., Inc. 161
Brassey's, Inc. 161
Brassey's Sports 161
Brazos Bookstore Short Story Award 1000
Brazzil 661
Bread for God's Children (Web)
Breasted Prize, James Henry (NR)
Brevet Press, Inc. 161
Brew Your Own 510
Brewers Publications 162
Brewing Techniques (NR)
Brewpub 825
Bridal Guide 797
Bride Again 798
Bridge Bulletin, The 474
Bridge Works Publishing Co. 162
Brigade Leader (Web)
Bright Hill Press Annual Chapbook Competition 1009
Bright Mountain Books, Inc. 368
Bright Ring Publishing, Inc. (NR)
Brighton Publications, Inc. 162
Brilliant Enterprises 983
Bristol Fashion Publications 162
Bristol Publishing Enterprises 163
Bristol Riverside Theatre (NR)
British Car Magazine (RR)
British Council Prize 991
Brittingham Prize in Poetry/Felix Pollak Prize in Poetry 1009
BRNTWD Magazine 621
Broadcast Interview Source, Inc. 163
Broadman & Holman Publishers (RR)
Broadview Press Ltd. 348
Broadway Books 163
Broken Jaw Press 348
Brookline Books (NS)
Brooklyn Bridge Magazine 645
Brooks Books 163
Bross Prize, The 991
Brown Limited, Curtis 96
Brucedale Press, The 349
Brushware (NR)
Brutarian (NR)
Bryant & Dillon Publishers, Inc. 164
Buchanan's Info Marketing Report, Jerry (OB)
Bucknell Seminar for Younger Poets (NR)
Bucknell University Press 164
Buffalo Spree Magazine 645
Bugle 742
Bugnet Award for Fiction (Novel)

Georges 1000
Bull Publishing Co. (Web)
Bullen Prize, John 991
Bulletin (see Fibre Focus 515)
Bullfinch Press 164
Bump & Grind 712
Buon Giorno (RR)
Bureau for At-Risk Youth, The 164
Burford Books 164
Burger Award, The Eric and Amy 1031
Burnham Publishers 165
Bus Conversions 934
Bus World (Web)
Bush Artist Fellows Program 1045
Business & Health 892
Business & Legal Reports (NS)
Business Asset, Business Sense, Smart Business, Your Business 413
Business Fleet 816
Business Journal of Central NY 418
Business Life Magazine 418
Business McGraw-Hill 165
Business New Haven 419
Business NH Magazine 419
Business North Carolina (RR)
Business 2.0 Magazine 413
Business Week 414
Butte Publications (Web)
Butterworth-Heinemann 165
Butterworths Canada 349
Buttime Stories 712
Bykofsky Associates, Inc., Sheree 97
Byline 895
ByLine Magazine Awards 1038

C

C 397
C&T Publishing 166
Cable Poetry Competition (NR)
Cabling Systems 855
Cadence Annual Poetry Contest 1009
Cadence Chapbook Contest 1009
Cadence Jazz Books 165
Cadence Quarterly Poetry Contest 1009
Cadmus Editions (NR)
Cafe Eighties (NR)
Caitlin Press, Inc. 349
California Computer News (NR)
California Game & Fish 743
California Journal 609
California Lawyer 902
California Theater Center 947
California Wild 598
California Writers' Club Conference and Contest (NR)
California Young Playwrights Contest 1020
Callboard 858
Calliope 546
Caltrux 817
Calyx Books 368
Cam Magazine (Web)
Cambridge Educational 166
Camelot Books (OB)
Cameron Agency, The Marshall 114
Camino Books, Inc. 166
Campbell's Texas Football, Dave (NR)
Camperways, Camp-Orama, Carolina

RV Traveler, Southern RV, Texas RV 782
Camping Canada's RV Lifestyles 782
Camping Today 782
Campus Activities 858
Campus Life 771
Canadian Authors Association Award for Drama 1020
Canadian Authors Association Award for Fiction 1000
Canadian Authors Association Award for Poetry 1009
Canadian Authors Association Awards Program 1038
Canadian Authors Association Jubilee Award for Short Stories 1000
Canadian Authors Association Lela Common Award for Canadian History 991
Canadian Biker Magazine 407
Canadian Chapbook Manuscript Contest (NR)
Canadian Consulting Engineer (Web)
Canadian Dimension 448
Canadian Educators' Press 349
Canadian Forest Service—Sault Ste. Marie Journalism Award (NR)
Canadian Geographic 662
Canadian Grocer 877
Canadian Guernsey Journal (NR)
Canadian Historical Association Awards 1038
Canadian Home Workshop, The Do-It-Yourself Magazine 531
Canadian Library Association (Web)
Canadian Library Association Student Article Contest 991
Canadian Mining Journal 914
Canadian Occupational Safety 907
Canadian Pharmaceutical Journal 846
Canadian Plains Research Center (Web)
Canadian Plastics 886
Canadian Rodeo News 758
Canadian Sportfishing Magazine 743
Canadian Writer's Journal 895
Canadian Youth Poetry Contest (NR)
Candlewick Press 166
CandyCane Press 166
Cannabis Culture (NR)
Canoe & Kayak Magazine 722
Canvas House Films (Web)
Capall Bann Publishing (Web)
Cape Cod Life (NR)
Capilano Review, The 561
Capper's 481
Capstone Press 167
Car and Driver 407
Caravan International (NR)
Card Technology 887
Card Trade 926
Cardmakers 983
Cardoza Publishing (NS)
Career Focus 422
Career Press, Inc., The 167
Careers & the disABLED 453
Carefree Enterprise Magazine 619
Caribbean Travel and Life 783
Carlink News 817
Carol Publishing (RP)
Carolina Alumni Review (RR)
Carolina Country (RR)
Carolina Novel Award (NR)

Carolrhoda Books, Inc. 167
Carousel Press (NR)
Carroll & Graf Publishers Inc. 167
Carstens Publications (Web)
Carswell Thomson Professional Publishing 350
Cartoon World (NR)
Cartwheel Books 168
Carver Short Story Contest (NR)
Cascades East 651
Casino Executive Magazine 930
Cass Recruitment Media 855
Cassandra Press 368
Cat Fancy 387
Catbird Press 168
Cathedral Art Metal Co. (NR)
Catholic Digest 668
Catholic Faith & Family 434
Catholic Forester 668
Catholic Near East Magazine 668
Catholic Parent (NR)
Catholic University of America Press 168
Cato Institute 169
Cats Magazine 388
Catsumer Report (OB)
Cattleman, The 863
Cave Books (Web)
Caxton Press 169
Caxton Printers, Ltd., The (see Caxton Press 169)
CBA Marketplace 830
CC Motorcycle Magazine (see CC Motorcycle Newsmagazine 407)
CC Motorcycle Newsmagazine 407
CCC Publications 169
CE Connection Communique 836
CEC Jackie White Memorial National Children's Playwriting Contest 1020
Cedar Fort, Inc. 169
Celebrate Life 669
Celebration Theatre 947
Celestial Arts (NR)
Centennial Publications (Web)
Center for African-American Studies (NR)
Center Stage 947
Center Theater 948
Centerstream Publications 170
Central PA 652
Century 708
Ceramics Monthly 510
Cerier Book Development, Inc., Alison Brown 380
Cessna Owner Magazine 410
CHA Press 350
Chalice Press 170
Challenging Destiny 708
Chamber Music 589
Chambers Playwriting Award, Jane 1021
Chance Magazine 730
Chandler House Press 170
Chapin Media Awards, Harry (NR)
Chariot Books (NR)
Chariot/Victor Publishing 170
Chariton Review, The 561
Charles Press (NR)
Charles River Media 170
Charlesbridge Publishing (School) 171
Charlesbridge Publishing (Trade) 171

Charleston Magazine 654
Charleston Regional Business Journal 419
Charlotte Festival/New Plays in America 1021
Charlotte Magazine 647
Charlotte Repertory Theatre 948
Charlton Press 350
Chatelaine 798
Chatham Press (NR)
Cheaters Club 712
Chef 883
Chelsea 561
Chelsea Awards for Poetry and Short Fiction, The 1038
Chelsea Green Publishing Co. 171
Chemical Publishing Co. (Web)
Chemtec Publishing (NR)
Chesapeake Bay Magazine 722
Chesapeake Life Magazine 636
Chess Enterprises 171
Chess Life (Web)
Chicago District Golfer 733
Chicago History (NR)
Chicago Life 631
Chicago Magazine 632
Chicago Parent 434
Chicago Reader 632
Chicago Review Press 172
Chicago Social 632
Chicago Theatre Co. (NR)
Chicago Tribune 783
Chicano/Latino Literary Contest 1039
Chickadee Magazine 546
Chief of Police Magazine 872
Child 434
Child Life 546
Child Welfare League of America 172
Children's Digest 546
Children's Ministry (NR)
Children's Playmate 546
Children's Press 172
Children's Story Scripts 948
Children's Theatre Playwright Division 1021
Childsplay, Inc. 948
Chile Pepper 469
China Books & Periodicals, Inc. 172
ChLa Research Fellowships & Scholarships 1045
Chosen Books Publishing Co. 173
Christian Camp & Conference Journal 883
Christian Century, The 669
Christian Classroom, The 848
Christian College Focus 423
Christian College Handbook (see Christian College Focus 423)
Christian Communicator, The 836
Christian Courier 669
Christian Ed. Publishers 173
Christian Education Counselor 670
Christian Education Leadership 836
Christian Home & School 670
Christian Literature Crusade (NS)
Christian Ministry, The (RR)
Christian Parenting Today 434
Christian Publications, Inc./Horizon Books. 173
Christian Reader 670
Christian Response, The (Web)

Christian School Administrator 849
Christian Science Monitor, The 482
Christian Social Action 671
Christianity Online Mag 671
Christianity Today 671
Chronicle Books 174
Chronicle Books for Children 174
Chronicle of the Horse, The 388
Chronogram 615
Chrysalis Reader 671
Church & State (Web)
Church Educator 836
Church Growth Institute 174
Church Worship (NR)
Cicada 562
Cicerone Press (Web)
Cigar Aficionado 581
Cigar Lifestyles (UC)
Cincinnati Magazine 649
Cincinnati Woman Magazine 798
Cineaste 455
Cine/Design Films (NR)
Cinefantastique Magazine (NR)
Circle K Magazine 423
Circle of Confusion Ltd. 114
Circlet Press Inc. 175
Circuit Playhouse/Playhouse on the Square 948
Citadel Press (RP)
Citron Press PLC 350
Citrus & Vegetable Magazine (NR)
City & Company 175
City AZ 619
City Limits 645
City of Toronto Book Awards (NR)
City Theatre Company 948
Civil War Times Illustrated 505
Civilization 482
Clarity Press Inc. 368
Clark Publications, I.E. 948
Class Act 849
Classic Toy Trains 510
Classic Trucks 408
Classical Singer Magazine 914
Clauder Competition 1021
Clavier Magazine 914
CLC Productions 969
Cleaning Business 907
Clear Creek Features 978
Clear Light Publishers 175
CLEC Magazine 887
Cleis Press 176
Cleveland Magazine (NR)
Cleveland Public Theatre 949
Cleveland Public Theatre New Plays Festival 1021
Cleveland State University Poetry Center 176
Cleveland State University Poetry Center Prize 1009
Cliffs Notes (NR)
Cloud Peak 176
Club Management 884
Clubhouse Magazine 547
Clubmex 783
CMYK Magazine (NR)
CNW/Florida State Writing Competition 1039
Coach House Books 350
Coaches Choice 177
Coast Business (Web)
Coast Magazine 639
Coast to Coast Magazine 783

Coast to Coast Theater Co. (NR)
Coastal Living (NR)
Cobblestone (NR)
Cobblestone Films 970
Codikow Films 970
Coe College Playwriting Festival (NR)
Coffee House Press 177
Cohen Award for Excellence In Theatre Criticism (NR)
Cohen Award, Morton N. 991
Cohen, Inc. Literary Agency, Ruth 97
Collectibles Canada 511
Collections & Credit Risk 867
Collector Books (NR)
Collector Editions 511
Collector's Mart 511
Collectors News & The Antique Reporter 511
Collectors Press, Inc. 177
College Board, The (NR)
College Bound 423
College Bound.NET 424
College Press Publishing Co. 177
College Preview 424
College Store (Web)
Collin Publishing, Peter (NR)
Collins Award, Carr P. 991
Colony Theatre Studio 949
Colorado Book Awards 1039
Colorado Homes & Lifestyles (NR)
Colorado Journal 902
Colorado Prize 992
Colored Stone 933
Colorlines 463
Colors By Design 985
Columbia 672
Columbiad (NR)
Columbus Book Discovery Award (NR)
Columbus Monthly 649
Columbus Screenplay Discovery Awards, The (NR)
Combined Publishing, Inc. 177
Come & Eat! 469
Comedy Writers Association Newsletter (OB)
Comic Bible, The 859
Comics Scene 444
Commercial Carrier Journal 935
Commercial Investment Real Estate 921
Common Courage Press 178
Commonweal 609
Commonwealth Club of California Book Awards 1039
Commune-A-Key Publishing (OB)
Communication Briefings (NR)
Communications News (NR)
Communications Systems Design (NR)
Community College Week 425
Community Press Service (NR)
Companion Press 178

Compass American Guides Inc. 178
Competition for Writers of B.C. History (NR)
Complete Woman 799
Composting News 924
Compressed Air (OB)
Computer Buyer's Guide & Handbook (Web)
Computer Currents 603, 888
Computer Dealer News (NR)
Computer Graphics World 888
ComputerCredible Magazine 603
Computing Channels 888
Computoredge 605
Comstock Cards (NR)
Conari Press 178
Concordia Publishing House 178
Concrete Construction 843
Concrete Homes (NR)
Concrete Producer, The 843
Condé Nast Bride's 799
Condé Nast Traveler 784
Confectioner, APC (NR)
Confluence Press, Inc. 179
Confrontation 562
Confrontations: A Literary Journal (Web)
Congress Monthly 463
Congressional Fellowship Program 1031
Connecticut Family (NR)
Connecticut Magazine 626
Conqueror, The 771
Conrad Concepts (NR)
Conscience 672
Consortium Publishing 179
Constable Publishers (NR)
Construction Bulletin (NR)
Construction Dimensions (NR)
Construction Equipment Guide 843
Consultant Press, The (Web)
Consumer Goods Manufacturer 830
Consumer Goods Technology 830, 926
Consumer Press 179
Contemporary Drama Service 949
Contemporary Poetry Series 1010
Contemporary Songwriter Magazine 915
Contemporary Stone & Tile Design (Web)
Contemporary Theatre, A 950
Continental (NR)
Continental Features/Continental News Service 978
Contingencies 868
Contingency Planning & Management 831
Continuing Care 910
Continuum International Publishing Group (Web)
Contract Professional (NR)
Contracting Profits 831
Convenience Store Decisions 926

Convention South 831
Conversely 664
Cooking & Entertaining (NR)
Cooking Light 472
Co-op Fiction Fellowship 1000
Co-op Poetry Fellowship (NR)
Cooperator, The 921
Copley News Service 978
Copper Canyon Press 179
Corel Magazine (NR)
Cormorant Books Inc. 351
Cornell Maritime Press, Inc. 180
Cornell University Press 180
Cornerstone 672
Cornfield Literary Agency, Robert 97
Correctional Foodservice (Web)
Corrections Technology & Management 872
Corwin Press, Inc. 180
Cosmetics 823
Cosmopolitan (NR)
Coteau Books 351
Coterie, The (NS)
Cottage Life 532
Cottage Magazine, The 662
Cotton Grower Magazine 860
Cottonwood Press (Web)
Council on Social Work Education (Web)
Counselor 547
Counterpoint (NS)
Country Connection, The 700
Country Folk 701
Country Home 532
Country Journal 532
Country Living 532
Country Living's Healthy Living 496
Country Music Foundation Press 180
Country Sampler (NR)
Country Woman 799
Countryman Press, The 180
Countrysport Press 181
County (NR)
Couples 664
Course Crafters, Inc. 380
Covenant Companion, The (Web)
Cowboy Magazine 582
CPC Entertainment 970
CQ Press 181
CQ VHF (RP)
Crab Orchard Award Series in Poetry 1010
Craft Patterns (NR)
Crafts Magazine 512
Crafts 'n' Things (NS)
Craftsman Book Company 181
Crain's Detroit Business (Web)
CrankMail 720
Craven Award, Avery O. (NR)
Crayola Kids Magazine (NR)
Creation House 182
Creative Bound Inc. (NR)
Creative Homeowner 182
Creative Non-Fiction Contest, The

(*Event*) 992
Creative Non-Fiction Contest
(*subTERRAIN Magazine* & Anvil
Press) 992
Creative Publishing Co. 182
Creativity Fellowship (NR)
Creator Magazine 837
Creede Repertory Theatre 950
Crescent Moon Publishing (Web)
Cricket 547
Cricket Books 182
Cricket Communications, Inc. 978
Christie's Book Award, Mr. 1035
Critical Ceramics 512
Critique Magazine 814
CRM Films 940
Crochet World 512
Cross & Quill 837
Cross Cultural Publications, Inc. 182
Crossfire 931
Crossing Press, The 183
Crossquarter Breeze (NR)
Crossroads Theatre Company 950
Crossway Books 183
Crossword.org (NR)
Crown Book Awards, Violet 1039
Crown Business 183
Cruise Industry News 935
Cruise Travel Magazine (NR)
Cruising In Style (RR)
Crusader Magazine 548
Crystal Ball, The 708
Culinary Trends (NR)
Cumberland House Publishing 183
Cummings & Hathaway (NR)
Cunningham Prize for Playwriting
1021
Cupp, Michael D. 950
Curaçao Nights 784
Curio (OB)
Curiocity (OB)
Currency 184
Current Clinical Strategies Publish-
ing 184
Current Health 1 (NR)
Currents 723
Curti Award In American Social and
Intellectual History (NR)
Curtis Associates, Inc., Richard 98
Curve Magazine 476
Custom Builder (RR)
Cutting Tool Engineering 905
CWW Annual Awards Competition
(NR)
Cycle California! 721
Cypress Publishing Group 184

D

DAC News (Web)
Dairy Goat Journal 862
Dakota Outdoors 656
Dallas Children's Theater 950
Dallas Family Magazine 435
Dallas/Fort Worth Special Occasions
(NR)
Dance International 455
Dance Spirit 455
Dance Spirits In Motion 456
Dance Teacher Now (NR)
Dancing USA (NR)
Dante University Of America Press,
Inc. 184
DANY News Service 978

Darhansoff & Verrill Literary Agents
98
Dark Oak Mystery Contest 1000
Dark Skin Art 512
Darlington Productions, Inc. 184
Data Capture Reseller 926
Davenport, Publishers, May (Web)
Daves Agency, Joan 98
David Publishers, Inc., Jonathan 185
Davis Publications, Inc. 185
DAW Books, Inc. 185
Dawn Publications (Web)
Daybreak Books (NR)
Dayspa 823
Dayton Playhouse Futurefest (NR)
DBMS (NR)
DBS Productions (Web)
DCI Studios 985
de Angeli Prize, Marguerite 1034
Dead Letter (RR)
Dealer and Applicator (NR)
Dealmaker, The (Web)
Dearborn 185
Deca Dimensions 812
Decision 673
Decorating Ideas (NR)
Decorative Artist's Workbook 513
Dee, Inc., Ivan R. 186
Deep Outside SFFH 709
Deer & Deer Hunting 743
Del Rey Books 186
Del Rey Prize, The Premio (NR)
Delacorte Press 186
Delacorte Press Prize for a First
Young Adult Novel 1034
Delicious! 496
Delta 186
Demko's AgeVenture Syndicated
News Service 978
Denali Press, The (Web)
Denison & Co., T.S. (RR)
Denny Poetry Award (OB)
Denver Center Theatre Co. (NR)
Dermascope Magazine 823
Descant (NR)
Design Concepts (RR)
Design Design. (NR)
Design Image Group Inc., The 186
Design Press 380
Design Times 532
Designer Greetings 985
Desktop Engineering 889
Destinations 936
Detective Cases (NR)
Detective Dragnet (NR)
Detective Files (NR)
Detroit Repertory Theatre (NR)
Dexter Prize 992
DH Literary, Inc. 98
DHS Literary, Inc. 99
Di Castagnola Award, Alice Fay (NR)
Diabetes Interview (NR)
Diabetes Self-Management 453
Dial Books For Young Readers 187
Dial Press 187
Dialogue 453
Diamond Registry Bulletin, The 893
Dickinson Award in Poetry, Emily
1010
Digital Output 852
Dijkstra Literary Agency, Sandra 99
Dillard Award in Nonfiction, Annie
992

Dillon/Richard C. Peterson Memorial
Essay Prize, Gordon W. 992
Dimefast Limited, USA/UK (UC)
Dimensions (NR)
Dimi Press 187
Diner Theatre 950
DioGenes Publishing 187
Direct AIM 425
Disaster News Network 609
Discipleship Journal 673
Discoveries 548
Discovering and Exploring New Jer-
sey's Fishing Streams and the
Delaware River 743
Discovery Enterprises, Ltd. 187
Discovery Trails 548
"Discovery"/The Nation 1010
Diskotech, Inc. 369
Disney Studios Fellowship Program,
Walt 1021
Distribution Channels 877
Diver 767
Diver, The 767
Diversion 482
Diversity: Career Opportunities & In-
sights 425
Divorce Magazine 665
Dobbins Productions, Steve (NS)
Doctoral Dissertation Fellowships in
Jewish Studies 1045
Dog Fancy 388
Dog Sports Magazine (Web)
Dog World 389
Dog Writers Association of America
Annual Writing Contest 1039
DogGone 389
Do-It-Yourself Legal Publishers
(Web)
Doll World 513
Dollars and Sense (Web)
Dollhouse Miniatures 513
Dollmaking 514
Dolls 514
Dolphin Log (NR)
Donadio and Olson, Inc. 100
Donner Prize, The (NR)
Door, The (NR)
Doral Publishing, Inc. 188
Dorchester Publishing Co., Inc. 188
Dorfman Poetry Prize, Milton 1010
Dornstein Memorial Creative Writing
Contest for Young Adult Writers
(NR)
Dorset Theatre Festival 950
Doubleday 188
Doubleday Religious Publishing 188
Doubleday/Image 189
DoubleTake 562
Douroux & Co. 115
Dover Publications, Inc. 189
Dovetail 673
Dow Jones Investment Advisers (NR)
Dowling Press (Web)
Down East Books 189
Down the Shore Publishing 189
Down There Press (RR)
Drag Racing USA 761
Drainie-Taylor Biography Prize (NR)
Drake Magazine 743
DramaRama Playwrighting Competi-
tion 1021
Dramatic Publishing 951
Dramatics Magazine 456, 951

Dreams & Visions 562
Dreams of Decadence 563
Dressage Today (NS)
Drew Books, Lisa 189
Drummer (NR)
Drury University One-Act Play Contest 1021
Dry Bones Press 190
DTP 190
Dubuque Fine Arts Players Annual One-Act Playwriting Contest 1021
Duck and Cover Productions 985
Dufour Editions 190
Dummies Trade Press (RP)
Dunne Books, Thomas 190
Duquesne University Press 190
Dutton Children's Books 191
Dutton Plume 191
DWAA Annual Writing Competition (NR)
Dystel Literary Management, Jane 100

E

E.F.S. Annual Writing Competition, The 1039
E.F.S. Religious Fiction Writing Competition 1000
E The Environmental Magazine 598
Eagle's View Publishing 191
Eakin Press/Sunbelt Media, Inc. 191
Early American Homes 533
Early Childhood News (NR)
East Bay Monthly, The 621
East El Lay Films 970
East End Lights 456
Eastern National 192
Eastern Press 369
Eastland Press (Web)
Ecco Press, The 192
Eckerd College Review Poetry Contest 1010
Eckert & Co., Inc., J.K. 380
Economic Facts 445
Ecopress 369
Ecrits des Forges 351
ECS Learning Systems, Inc. 192
ECW Press 351
Edge Science Fiction and Fantasy Publishing 351
Ediciones Nuevo Espacio 192
Editions du Noroît 352
Éditions Logiques/Logical Publishing 352
Editorial Consultant Service 979
Editors' Book Award (NR)
Editors' Prize 1010
Educated Traveler, The 784
Education Center, Inc., The 193
Education in Focus 483
Educational Systems Assoc. (NR)
Educational Technology Publications (RP)
Educational Video Network 941
Educator's Award 992
Educator's International Press 193
Educators Publishing Service 193
Edupress 193
Edutainment Media 194
Edwards Award, Everett E. 992
Eerdmans Books for Young Readers 194

Eerdmans Publishing Co., 194
Eggleston Award for Nonfiction, Wilfred 992
1812 563
Einstein Award, The Alfred (UC)
El Restaurante Mexicano (NR)
Elder Books 194
Eldredge Prize of the National Museum of American Art, The Charles C. 992
Eldridge Publishing Co. 951
Electric Perspectives (NR)
Electric Works Publishing 195
Electrical Apparatus 853
Electrical World Magazine 853
Electron, The 704
Electronic Distribution Today (RR)
Electronic Servicing & Technology (NR)
Electronics Now (see Poptronis 521)
Element Books (NR)
Elephant Books 195
Eliot Prize for Poetry, T.S. 1010
Elks Magazine, The 399
Ellis Awards, Arthur 1000
Ellis Memorial Award (NR)
Ellis Publishing, Aidan (Web)
EMC/Paradigm Publishing Inc. 195
Emerald Wave 369
Emerge 463
Emergency (NR)
Emerging Lesbian Writers Fund Award 1039
Emerging Playwright's Award 1022
Emis, Inc. 195
Emmy Magazine 859
Emphasis on Faith & Living (NS)
Empire Publishing Service 196
Empire Screenplay Contest 1022
Empire State Report 610
Empty Space Theatre, The 951
Empyreal Press (NR)
EMS Magazine 910
Encore Performance Pubishing 951
Encounter 771
Encounter Books 196
Endless Knot Productions 369
Endless Vacation 785
English/Poetry in Print, Robert G. 1010
Engravers Journal, The 893
Ensemble Studio Theatre, The (NR)
Ensemble Theatre of Cincinnati 952
Enslow Publishers Inc. 196
Entertainment Productions, Inc. 970
Entertainment Today 457
Entrepreneur Magazine 414
Entrepreneur's Business Start-Ups 414
Environment (Web)
Ephemera, Inc. 985
Epicenter Press, Inc. 196
Equal Opportunity 426
Equilibrium Press, Inc. 369
Equine Journal 389
Equinox 483
Equipment Journal 843
Equities Magazine Co. 868
Eriksson, Publisher, Paul S. 196
Erosion Control 924
ESI International (OB)
Esquire 582
Essence 800

Estylo Magazine 464
ETC Publications 197
Eureka Theatre Company 952
Europe 610
Evangel 674
Evangelical Baptist, The 674
Evangelical Missions Quarterly 674
Evangelizing Today's Child 675
Evan-Moor Educational Publishers 197
Evans and Co., Inc., M. 197
Evans Biography & Handcart Award, David W. and Beatrice C. 993
Event 563
Events Business News 927
EXPO 831
Excalibur Publications (Web)
Excelsior Cee Publishing (Web)
Exchange (NR)
Executive Excellence Publishing 197
Executive Update 832
Exotic Magazine 713
Explorations Prizes for Literature 1040
Explore! (RR)
Extra Mile, The (NR)
Eyenet Magazine (NR)

F

Fabricating Equipment News Magazine (NR)
Fabrics & Architecture (NR)
Faces (NR)
Facts On File, Inc. 198
Fairbank Prize In East Asian History (NR)
Fairleigh Dickinson University Press 198
Fairview Press 198
Faith Publishing Company (OB)
Faith Today 675
Falcon Publishing, Inc. 199
Family Album, The 370
Family Circle Magazine 800
Family Digest (California) 435
Family Digest, The (Indiana) 435
Family Life 436
Family Motor Coaching 785
Family Times (see MetroKids 439)
Family Tree Magazine 514
FamilyFun 436
Fanfare (RP)
Fangoria 457
Farm & Country (NR)
Farm & Ranch Living 701
Farm Industry News 864
Farm Journal (RR)
Farm Times 701
Farmweek (Web)
Farrar, Straus & Giroux Books for Young Readers 199
Farrar, Straus & Giroux, Inc. 199
Farrar, Straus & Giroux Paperbacks 199
Fashion Accessories 894
Fast and Healthy Magazine (see Come & Eat! 469)
Fastening 880
Fate 402
Faulkner Creative Writing Competition, The William 1001
Fawcett Juniper (OB)
FDA Consumer (NR)

GENERAL INDEX

Federal Credit Union, The 868
Feed Lot Magazine 864
Feis Award for Nonacademically-Affiliated Historians (NR)
Fell Publishers, Inc., Frederick 199
Fellow Script (NR)
Fellowship 1045
Fellowship Program 1045
Fellowship-Literature 1046
Fellowships 1046
Fellowships (Literature) 1046
Fellowships for Creative Writers 1046
Fellowships for Translators 1036
Fellowships to Assist Research and Artistic Creation 1046
Feminist Press at the City University of New York, The (NR)
Fencers Quarterly Magazine 758
Fendrich Memorial Playwriting Contest, Shubert 1022
Ferguson Prize, Wallace K. 993
Ferguson Publishing Company 200
Fernhurst (Web)
Fernwood Publishing Ltd. 352
Festival of Emerging American Theatre, The (NR)
Festival of Firsts 1022
Festival of New Works 1022
Feury Entertainment, Joseph 970
Fiddlehead, The (NR)
Fiberarts 514
Fibre Focus 515
Fiction Open 1001
Field & Stream 744
FIELD Magazine 563
Field Trial Magazine 390
Fiesta City Publishers, ASCAP 370
Fifty-Five Plus 696
Filipinas 464
Film Comment (RR)
Film House Inc., The (RP)
FilmSaavy Entertainment 970
Filter Press 200
Financial Freedom Report Quarterly (OB)
Financial Planning 869
Financial Sentinel 445
Fine Gardening 533
Fine Homebuilding 533
Fine Tool Journal 515
Fine Woodworking 516
Finescale Modeler 516
Fire Chief 873
Fire Engineering Books & Videos 200
Firebrand Books 200
Firehouse Magazine 873
Fire-Rescue Magazine (NR)
Fireweed (NR)
First Hand (NR)
First Opportunity 426
First Stage 952
First Things 449
First Word Bulletin (UF)
Fish Memorial Award, Robert L. 1001
Fisher Books 200
Fisherman, The 744
Fit 497
Fitness Magazine 497
Fitness Management 931
Fitnesslink 497

Fitzwarren Publishing (NR)
Five Points James Dickey Prize for Poetry 1010
Five Stones, The 675
Fjord Press (RR)
Fleet Executive 817
Flesh and Blood 709
Flicks Books (Web)
Florida Academic Press 201
Florida Game & Fish 744
Florida Grower 865
Florida Hotel & Motel Journal 884
Florida Individual Artist Fellowships (Florida) 1046
Florida Leader (for college students) (Web)
Florida Leader (for high school students) (Web)
Florida Living Magazine 628
Florida Realtor Magazine 921
Florida Sportsman 744
Florida Stage 952
Florida Studio Theatre 952
Florida Underwriter 892
Florida Wildlife 745
Floricanto Press 201
FloridAgriculture 865
Florist, The (Web)
Flow Control 855
Flower and Garden Magazine 534
Fly Fishing in Salt Waters 745
Fly Fishing Quarterly 746
Flyer 411
Flyfishing & Tying Journal 746
Flying Books 201
FMCT's Biennial Playwrights Competition (Mid-West) (NR)
Focal Press 201
Focus Publishing, Inc. 202
Focuskansas City 640
Fodor's Travel Publications, Inc. 202
Foghorn Outdoors 202
Fons and Porter's Sew Many Quilts (Web)
Food & Service News 884
Food & Wine (NR)
Food People (NR)
Food Product Design Magazine 877
Foodservice and Hospitality (NR)
Foodservice Director 878
Foothill Theatre Company, The 952
Footprint Press 370
Foreign Language Book and Foreign Language Article Prizes (NR)
Foreign Service Journal 873
Forest Landowner (Web)
ForeWord Magazine 826
Forge 202
Forkosch Prize, Morris D. (NR)
Fort Ross Inc. Russian-American Publishing Projects 203
Fortress Press (NS)
49th Parallel Poetry Award, The 1011
Forum (California) 203
Forum Publishing Company (New York) 203
Forward in Christ (Web)
Forward Movement Publications 203
Foster Publishing, Walter (NR)
Foul Play (OB)
Fountain Productions 970
Fountain Theatre 952
Fountainhead Essay Contest (NR)

Four Walls Eight Windows 204
Four Way Books Poetry Prizes 1011
Foursquare World Advance (Web)
Fourth Estate Award (NR)
Fox Chapel Publishing 204
Fox Magazine 713
Fox Manuscript Prize, Dixon Ryan 993
FRAMESdata.com 846
France Today 449
Francis Short Story Award, H.E. 1001
Franciscan University Press (Web)
Frank 563
Fraser Translation Award, Soeurette Diehl 1036
Fredericks Literary Agency, Inc., Jeanne 100
Free Press, The 204
Free Spirit Magazine 402
Free Spirit Publishing Inc. 204
Freed Co., The Barry 115
Freedley Memorial Award, George 993
Freedman Productions, Jack 970
Freelance (NR)
Freelance Press, The 953
Freelance Writer's Report 896
Freeman, The (see Ideas on Liberty 610)
French, Inc., Samuel 115, 953
Fresh Cut Magazine 878
Friend, The 548
Friendly Exchange 483
Friends of American Writers Young People's Literature Awards 1034
Friends of the Dallas Public Library Award 989
Friends United Press (Web)
Fromm International Publishing Corp. 204
Front Row Experience (Web)
Front Street 205
Front Street Productions (NR)
Frontier Magazine 785
Fruit Growers News, The 861
Full-Length Play Competition 1022
Fulton Opera House (NR)
Funny Times (Web)
Funworld (NR)
Fur-Fish-Game 746
FUSE Magazine 397
Futures Magazine 564

G
Gaited Horse, The (NR)
Gallant Entertainment 971
Gallery Magazine 713
Gambling Times, Inc. 370
Game & Fish Publications 746
Game Developer 889
Gamepro (RR)
Games Magazine 474
GAP (Grants for Artist Projects) Fellowship 1046
Garden Design 534
Gardening & Outdoor Living Ideas (NR)
Gassner Memorial Playwriting Competition, John 1022
Gateway Heritage 505
GATF Press 205
Gay Sunshine Press and Leyland Publications 205

Geer Theatricum Botanicum, Will 953
GEICO Direct 893
Gelber Prize, Lionel 993
Gem Guides Book Co. (Web)
Genealogical Computing 516
General Publishing Group (OB)
Generic Plays 953
Genesis 714
Genesis Press, Inc. 205
Genre 476
Gent 714
George Street Playhouse 953
Georgetown Review Fiction and Poetry Contest (NR)
Georgia Magazine 630
Georgia Sportsman 747
Georgia State University Review Writing Contest (NR)
Geringer Books, Laura 206
German Life 464
German Prize for Literary Translation 1036
Gershoy Award, Leo (NR)
Gessler Publishing Co., Inc. 206
Gettysburg Review, The 564
Geva Theatre 953
Giant Crosswords 474
Gibson Greetings (RP)
Gift & Collectibles Retailer (OB)
Gifted Education Press 206
Gifted Psychology Press (Web)
Giftware News 927
Girlfriends Magazine 476
Girl's Life 549
GIS World (UC)
Glamour (NR)
Glass Digest 817
Glass Magazine (NR)
Glassco Translation Prize, John (NR)
Gleason Group, Inc. 380
Glenbridge Publishing Ltd. 206
Glenlake Publishing Company 207
Glimmer Train Stories 564
Glimmer Train's April Poetry Open 1011
Glimmer Train's Fall Short-Story Award for New Writers 1001
Glimmer Train's October Poetry Open 1011
Glimmer Train's Spring Short-Story Award for New Writers 1001
Glines, The (Web)
Global Technology Business 832
Global Wireless 852
Globe Pequot Press, Inc., The 207
Gnosis (OB)
Go Boating Magazine 723
Go Magazine (Web)
Godine, Publisher, Inc., David R. 207
Golden Kite Awards 1034
Golden West Publishers 207
Goldstein Award for Washington Regional Reporting, Robin 1031

Golf & Travel (NR)
Golf Canada 734
Golf Course News 931
Golf Digest Woman 734
Golf Illustrated (NR)
Golf News Magazine 734
Golf Tips 735
Golf Traveler 735
Golfer, The 735
Gollehon Press, Inc. 207
Good Book Publishing Co. (Web)
Good Dog! 390
Good Housekeeping 801
Good Old Days 505
Goodman Theatre, The 953
Goose Lane Editions 352
Gotta Write Network LitMag 896
Gottschalk Prize, Louis (NR)
Government Computer News 889
Government Finance Review (NP)
Government Institutes/Abs. 208
Grace 801
Grade A Entertainment (NR)
Graduate Group, The 208
Grain Journal (NR)
Grain Literary Magazine 564
Grainews 861
Granite Publishing, LLC 208
Granta 565
Grape Grower Magazine 861
Gray, Stephen (ED)
Graywolf Press 208
Great American Book Contest 1040
Great American Crafts 516
Great American Tennis Writing Awards, The 1031
Great Expectations 437
Great Plains Game & Fish 747
Great Plains Play Contest (NR)
Great Platte River Playwrights Festival 1022
Great Quotations Publishing 209
Green Grass Blue Sky Co. (NR)
Green Playwrights Prize, Paul 1022
Greenburger Associates, Inc., Sanford J. 101
Greene Bark Press (Web)
Greenhaven Press, Inc. 209
Greensboro Review Literary Award in Fiction and Poetry, The 1040
Greenwillow Books 209
Greenwood 209
Greenwood Publishing Group 210
Greeting Card Writer Magazine 896
Gretna Theatre 953
Greyhound Review, The 390
Grit 484
Grocery Distribution Magazine (NR)
Grolier Poetry Prize 1011
Grolier Publishing 210
Groom & Board 918
Grossbard Productions, Beth 971
Grosset & Dunlap Publishers 210
Group Magazine 675, 837

Group Publishing, Inc. 210
Grove/Atlantic, Inc. 211
GrowerTalks 870
Growing Edge, The 870
Growing Parent 437
Gruyter, Aldine de 211
Gryphon House (Web)
Gryphon Publications 211
GSE Today 822
Guernica Editions 353
GuestLife 615
Guide® 549
Guide, The 477
Guideposts for Kids 549
Guideposts for Teens 772
Guideposts Magazine 676
Guideposts Young Writers Contest 1034
Guilford Publications, Inc. 211
Guitar Magazine 589
Guitar One 589
Gulf Coast & Texas Boating 723
Gulf Coast Condo Owner (NR)
Gulf Coast Golfer 735
Gulf Coast Poetry & Short Fiction Prizes (NR)
Gulf Publishing Company 212
Gulfshore Life 628
Gun Digest 737
Guns Magazine 737
Guys (OB)
gynergy books 353

H

Hachai Publishing (Web)
Hackney Literary Awards 1040
Hadassah Magazine 465
Half Halt Press, Inc. 212
Hall Award for Library Literature, G.K. (see Highsmith Library Literature Award 993)
Halsey North, Reece 101
Hamilton Institute, Alexander 212
Hampton Roads Publishing Company, Inc. 213
Hancock House Publishers 213
Handprint Entertainment (NR)
Hand/The Theatrex, Kai (NR)
Hanser Gardner Publications 213
Happy 565
Harbor Press 213
Harcourt Inc., Children's 214
Harcourt Inc., Trade 214
Hard Hat News 844
Hardboiled 591
HardPressed Publishing (UC)
Haring Prize, Clarence (NR)
Harlan Davidson (RR)
Harlequin Enterprises (NR)
Harper Designs, Kate 985
HarperBusiness 214
HarperCollins Children's Books 214
HarperCollins Publishers (Web)
HarperEntertainment 215

HarperLibros (RR)
HarperPerennial 215
Harper's Bazaar 801
Harper's Magazine 484
HarperSanFrancisco 215
Harris Award, Albert J. 993
Harris Memorial Playwriting Award, Aurand 1023
Hartford Stage Co. (NR)
Harvard Business School Press 215
Harvard Common Press, The 215
Hastings House 216
Hatherleigh Press 216
Haven Publications 216
Hawai'i Award for Literature 1046
HAWK Publishing Group 216
Haworth Press, Inc., The 217
Hay House, Inc. 217
Hayes School Publishing Co. 941
Hazelden Publishing 217
HBO films 971
Headquarters Detective (NR)
Headwaters Literary Competition (UC)
Headway (OB)
Healing Retreats & Spas 786
Health 497
Health Communications, Inc. 217
Health for Women (OB)
Health Information Press (HIP) 218
Health Press (Web)
Health Products Business 878
HealthPlan (NR)
Healthwise Publications 218
Healthy Kids 437
Hearing Health 453
Heart & Soul 498
Heartland Boating 724
Heartland USA 582
Heating, Plumbing, Air Conditioning 918
Heavy Equipment News 844
Hedgerow Theatre (NR)
Heekin Group Foundation Writing Fellowships Program (NR)
Hein & Co., Inc., William S. 218
Heinemann 218
Heinz Literature Prize, Drue 1001
Helix Books 219
Hellgate Press 219
Helter Skelter Publishing (Web)
Hemingway Foundation Pen Award for First Fiction, Ernest 1001
Hemingway Short Story Competition, Lorian 1001
Hemingway Western Studies Series (Web)
Hemispheres 542
Hemley Memorial Award, Cecil 1011
Hendrick-Long Publishing Co. 219
Hendricks Manuscript Award (NR)
Hendrickson Publishers Inc. 219
Hendriks Publishing, F.P. 353
Henrico Theatre Company One-Act Playwriting Competition 1023
Henry Award, O. 1031
Henshaw Group, Richard 101
Hensley Publishing 219
Hensley, Virgil (see Hensley Publishing 219)
Herb Companion, The 534
Herb Quarterly 534
Herbal Studies Library 370

Heritage Books, Inc. 220
Heritage Florida Jewish News 465
Heritage House Publishing Co. 353
Hero Magazine 477
Heuer Publishing Co. 954
Heyday Books 220
Hi Willow Research & Publishing (Web)
HiddenSpring 220
High Country News 599
High Plains Literary Review 565
High Plains Press (Web)
High School Playwriting Contest (NR)
High Technology Careers (NR)
High Times 449
Highlander, The (NR)
Highlights for Children 550
Highlights for Children Fiction Contest 1034
Highroads Magazine 786
Highsmith Library Literature Award 993
Highsmith Press 220
Highways 786
Hill and Wang 221
Hilton Head Monthly 655
Hinterland Entertainment 971
Hippocrene Books Inc. 221
Hippopotamus Press (Web)
Hispanic Link News Service 979
Hispanic Outlook in Higher Education 849
Hispanic Playwrights' Division 1023
Hispanic Playwrights' Project 1023
Historic Traveler (OB)
Hitchcock's Mystery Magazine, Alfred 592
Hi-Time Pflaum 221
Hi-Time Publishing (see Hi-Time Pflaum 221)
Hoard's Dairyman 862
Hockey Business News 932
Hodder Fellowship, The 1046
Hodges Agency, Carolyn 115
Hoffman Press, The 370
Hohm Press 221
Hokin Prize, The Bess 1011
Holiday House, Inc. 222
Hollis Publishing Co. (Web)
Holmes & Meier Publishers, Inc. 222
Holmes Publishing Group 222
Holt & Company Books for Young Readers, Henry 222
Holt & Company, Inc., Henry 223
Holvoe Books (OB)
Holy Cross Orthodox Press 223
Home Business Magazine 445
Home Care Magazine 846
Home Cooking 472
Home Digest 535
Home Education Magazine 437
Home Energy (NR)
Home Furnishings Executive (NR)
Home Lighting & Accessories 880
Home Planners, LLC 223
Home Remodeling (NR)
Home Shop Machinist, The 517
Home Times 676
Homes & Cottages 535
Homeschooling Today 438
Honolulu 631
Honor Books 223

Hood Award for Diplomatic Correspondence, Edwin M. (NR)
Hope Magazine 484
Hopscotch 550
Horizon Air Magazine 543
Horizon Theatre Company 954
Horn Book Magazine, The 826
Horsdal & Schubart Publishers 354
Horse, The 391
Horse & Country Canada 390
Horse & Rider 390
Horse Illustrated 391
Horses All 391
Horticulture 535
Hospitality Technology 885
Hot Boat 724
Hot Toys (see Beckett Pokemon Collector 509)
Hot Water 767
Hotelier (NR)
HotRead.com 565
Houghton Award, Firman 1011
Houghton Mifflin Books for Children 223
Houghton Mifflin Company 224
Hour Detroit 637
House of Anansi Press 354
House of Collectibles 224
Houston Press 656
Howell Book House (NR)
Howell Press, Inc. 224
Howells House (Web)
HOW 815
HR Briefing (NR)
HR Magazine 908
HR News 908
Hubbard's Writers of the Future Contest, L. Ron 1002
Hudson Agency 116
Hudson Hills Press, Inc. 225
Hudson River Classics Annual Contest (NR)
Human Kinetics Publishers, Inc. 225
Human Resource Executive 908
Humanics Publishing Group 225
Humpty Dumpty's Magazine 551
Hungry Mind Press (see Ruminator Books 294)
Hunt Publishing, John (NR)
Hunter House 226
Hunter Publishing, Inc. 226
Hustler 714
Hustler Busty Beauties 715
Hyde Park Media (NR)
Hydro Review 854

I

I Love Cats 392
I Love My Job! 426
IBEX Publishers 226
ICC Publishing (NR)
Icon Editions (Web)
Iconografix, Inc. 226
ICS Publications (Web)
ID Magazine (UC)
ID Systems (NR)
Idaho Writer-In-Residence (NR)
Idea Health & Fitness Source 932
Idea Today (see Idea Health & Fitness 932)
Ideals Children's Books 227
Ideals Magazine 485
Ideals Publications Inc. 227

Ideas on Liberty 610
IDG Books Worldwide, Business Group 227
IDG Books Worldwide, Education Group 227
IDG Books Worldwide, Lifestyle Group 227
Idyll Arbor (Web)
IFM Film Assoc. (NR)
Illinois Entertainer 632
Illinois Game & Fish 747
Illumination Arts 370
ILR Press 227
Image Books (see Doubleday/Image 189)
Immersed Magazine 767
Impact Publications 228
Impact Publishers (Web)
Implement & Tractor 860
Implosion (NR)
In Business Windsor 419
In Print Publishing 371
In Step 477
In Tents (NR)
In the Family 477
In the Flesh (RR)
In Touch/Indulge for Men 715
Incentive 908
Incentive Publications, Inc. 228
Income Fund Outlook 869
Independent Business (RR)
Independent Energy (NR)
Independent Publisher 826
Indian Artist (OB)
Indian Life 465
Indiana Game & Fish 747
Indiana Historical Society (NR)
Indiana Repertory Theatre 954
Indiana Review 566
Indiana University Press (NR)
Indianapolis Monthly 633
Indianapolis Woman Magazine 801
Indigenous Fiction 566
Individual Artist Fellowship (Oregon) 1046
Individual Artist Fellowship (Tennessee) (NR)
Individual Artists Fellowships (Nebraska) 1047
Individual Artists Grants (NR)
Individual Investor 415
Individual Project Fellowship (NR)
Indoor Comfort News (Web)
Industrial Fabric Products Review 886
IndustryWeek 415
Info Net Publishing (Web)
Inform 889
Information Management Journal (NR)
Information Today, Inc. 228
Information Week 890
Ingram's 419
Inklings (United States) (NR)
Inklings (Canada) 896
Inland Empire Business Journal (RR)
Inner Traditions International 228
Innisfree Press (Web)
In-Plant Graphics (Web)
Inscriptions 897
Inside Automotives (NR)
Inside Journal 676
Inside Kung-Fu 755

Inside Technology Training (NR)
Inside Texas Running 761
Insight 772
Inspirations Unlimited 986
Institute of Psychological Research, Inc./Institut de Recherches Psychologiques, Inc. 354
Instructor Magazine (NR)
Insurance Journal (NR)
Intelligent Enterprise 890
Interact Theatre Company (Web)
Interactive Technologies, Inc. (NR)
Intercontinental Publishing 229
Intercultural Press, Inc. 229
Interior Business Magazine 815
Interline Adventures 787
Interlink Publishing Group, Inc. 229
International, The 582
International Artistic Writing Awards (NR)
International Bluegrass (Web)
International City/County Management Association 229
International Creative Management 102
International Fiber Journal (NR)
International Foundation of Employee Benefit Plans 230
International Gymnist (NS)
International Home Entertainment 971
International Imitation Hemingway Competition 1002
International Living (NR)
International Marine 230
International Medical Publishing 230
International Narrative Contest (NR)
International News Group (NR)
International One-Page Play Competition 1023
International Performance Theatre (NR)
International Photo News (Web)
International Publishers Co. (Web)
International Puzzle Features 979
International Railway Traveler 787
International Readers' Theatre 954
International Reading Association Children's Book Awards 1034
International Scholars Publications 230
International Wealth Success 231
International Wildlife 599
International Wristwatch Magazine 517
Interpress of London and New York 979
Interstate Publishers, Inc. 231
Intertext (Web)
InterVarsity Press 231
Interweave Press 231
Interzone 872
Intimacy/Black Romance (see Black Romance Group 699)
Intimacy/Bronze Thrills (see Black Romance Group 699)
Investigative Journalism Grant 1031
Iowa Game & Fish 747
Iowa Poetry Prizes 1011
Iowa Review, The 566
Iron Gate Publishing 232
ISER Books 355
Island 232

Island Press 232
Islands 787
Islesboro Island News (Web)
It Takes Two (NR)
Italian America 466
Italica Press (Web)
ITrecruitermag.com 890
ITS World 935
Ivy League Press (Web)

J

Jack and Jill 551
Jackson Award, Joseph Henry 1047
Jacksonville 628
Jacobs Productions, Lee 232
Jain Publishing Co. (Web)
James Peter Associates, Inc. 102
Jameson Books Inc. 232
Japanophile Annual Short Story Contest 1002
Japanophile Press 567
Jarrell Poetry Prize, Randall 1011
Java Pro 890
Java™ Report 891
JCA Literary Agency, Inc. 102
Jefferson University Press, Thomas (see Truman State University Press 321)
Jelmar Publishing Co., Inc. 371
JEMS 911
Jerome Fellowship 1023
Jesperson Publishing, Ltd. 355
Jewel Box Theatre 954
Jewel Box Theatre Playwrighting Competition 1023
Jewish Action 466
Jewish Book Awards (NR)
Jewish Ensemble Theatre (NR)
Jewish Lights Publishing 233
Jewish Publication Society (NS)
Jewish Repertory Theatre 954
Jist Publishing 233, 941
Jist Works, Inc. (see Jist Publishing 233, 941)
Jive (RP)
J-Mar 986
Johnson Books 233
Johnson County Business Times (NR)
Johnston Associates, International 371
Joiners' Quarterly 844
Jones Award, Jesse H. 1002
Jones First Novel Fellowship, James 1002
Jones Foundation National Poetry Competition, The Chester H. 1011
Jones, M.D. Award, Anson (NR)
Jossey-Bass/Pfeiffer (NR)
Journal, The 567
Journal of Accountancy (NR)
Journal of Adventist Education 838
Journal of Asian Martial Arts 756
Journal of Christian Nursing 881
Journal of Court Reporting 903
Journal of Information Ethics 891
Journal of Property Management 922
Journal of Safe Management of Disruptive and Assaultive Behavior, The 874
Journey 427
Journey Books 233

Joy of Collecting 517
Joyful Woman (Web)
Judaica Press 234
Judson Press 234
Jump 772
Junior Baseball 719
Juniper Prize, The 1012
Juried Programs for Art Professionals 1047

K

Kafenio 788
Kaleidoscope 454
Kali Press 371
Kalliope 567
Kalliope's Annual Sue Saniel Elkind Poetry Contest 1012
Kalmbach Publishing Co. 234
Kamehameha Schools Press 234
Kanin Playwriting Awards Program (NR)
Kansas! 633
Kansas Alumni 427
Kansas City Magazine 640
Karate/Kung Fu Illustrated 756
Kar-Ben Copies, Inc. 235
Kashrus Magazine 472
Katz Productions, Marty 971
Kaufman Company, The 971
Kelly Memorial Prize in Women's History (NR)
Kelly Peace Poetry Awards, Barbara Mandigo 1012
Kenkeldey Award, The Otto (NR)
Kennedy Book Awards, Robert F. 1040
Kennedy Center Fund for New American Plays, The 1023
Kensington Publishing Corp. 235
Kent Prize, The George 1012
Kent State University Press 235
Kentucky Arts Councils Fellowships in Writing 1047
Kentucky Game & Fish 747
Kentucky Living 634
Kentucky Monthly 634
Kenyon Review, The 568
Kesend Publishing, Ltd., Michael 235
Ketz Agency, Louise B. (NR)
Key Club 715
Key West Theatre Festival 1023
Keyhoe Journalism Award, Donald E. 1031
Keynoter 773
Kids' Ministry Ideas 838
Kidz Chat (NR)
Kindred Productions 355
King Features Syndicate (NR)
Kingsley Publishers, Jessica (Web)
Kinseeker Publications (Web)
Kiplinger's Personal Finance 445
Kiriyama Pacific Rim Book Prize, The 993
Kit-Cat Review, The 568
Kitchens & Baths (NR)
Kitchenware News (NR)
Kitplanes 518
Kiwanis 399
Klein Playwriting Award for Students, Marc A. 1024
Klein Publications, B. (Web)
Klinger, Inc., Harvey 103
Kluwer Academic Publishing (NR)

Knight Agency, The 103
Knitting Digest (NR)
Knives Illustrated 518
K'n'k Productions (Web)
Knopf and Crown Books For Young Readers 236
Knopf, Inc., Alfred A. 236
Know Atlanta Magazine 630
Knowledge, Ideas & Trends (NS)
Kodansha America (OB)
Koehler Companies, Inc. 986
Kogan Page U.S. 236
Kouts, Literary Agent, Barbara S. 103
Kovacs Prize, Katherine Singer 993
Kozik Award for Environmental Reporting (NR)
KPBS On Air Magazine (Web)
KQED Books (see Bay Books 151 and Soma Books 307)
Kramer, Inc., H.J. 236
Krater Quarterly 568
Krause Publications 237
Kregel Publications 237
Kreisel Award for Best First Book, Henry 1002, 1040
Krieger Publishing Co. 237
Kroshka Books 237
Krout Memorial Ohioana Poetry Award, Helen and Laura 1012
Kumarian Press, Inc. 238
Kumu Kahua 954
Kumu Kahua/UHM Theatre Department Playwriting Contest 1024
Kurian Reference Books (NR)
Kwihi 543

L

L.A. Architect 397
L.A. Designers' Theatre-Commissions (NR)
L.A. Parent (NR)
L.A. Weekly 621
Ladies' Home Journal 802
Ladybug 552
Lahontan Images 371
Lake Claremont Press 238
Lake Country Journal Magazine 638
Lake Superior Magazine 639
Lake View Press (NS)
Lakeland Boating (Web)
Lambda Book Report 478
Lambrecht Publications 355
Lampert Memorial Award, Gerald (NR)
Lampert Student Writing Award, Herb 1031
Lamppost Press Inc. (NR)
Land, The 866
Landmark Specialty Books (UC)
Landon Translation Award, The Harold Morton 1036
Landscape Trades 871
Lane Publishers, Inc., Mitchell 255
Lane Report, The 420
Lang Publishing, Peter (SR)
Langenscheidt Publishing Group 238
Lansing City Limits (RR)
Lapidary Journal (NR)
Lapis (PR)
Larchmont Literary Agency 116
Lark 238
Lark Theatre Company/Playwrights Week 954

Larsen/Elizabeth Pomada Literary Agents, Michael 103
Larson Publications/PBPF 239
Las Vegas Family Magazine 438
Laser Focus World Magazine (Web)
Last Poems Poetry Contest 1012
Latest Jokes (OB)
Latin American Literary Review Press 239
Laughlin Award, The James 1012
Laureate Press 371
Laurel Books (RP)
Lauren Productions, Andrew (NR)
Laurie 1002
Law and Order 874
Law Enforcement Technology 874
Law Office Computing 903
Lawrence Books, Merloyd 239
Lawyers & Judges Publishing 239
Lazy Writer, The (see Write 899)
Le Gesse Stevens Publishing 239
Leacock Memorial Award for Humour, Stephen (NR)
Leader Guide Magazine 485
Leadership 838
Leadership Publishers (Web)
League of Canadian Poets Awards (NR)
Learning Publications, Inc. 240
Leather Crafters & Saddlers Journal, The 518
Lebhar-Friedman Books 240
Ledge Annual Poetry Chapbook Contest, The 1012
Ledge Poetry Awards, The 1012
Lee & Low Books 240
Lee Co., J & L (Web)
Legacy Press 240
Legal Assistant Today 903
Legal Intelligencer, The (Web)
Legions of Light 568
LeGuin Prize for Imaginative Fiction, Ursula K. 1002
Lehigh University Press 241
Leiden Calligraphy, Laura (NR)
Leisure Books 241
Leisure World 788
Leo Films (Web)
Leopold Prize, Richard W. (NR)
Lerner Publishing Group 241
Lerner-Scott Prize (NR)
Let's Live Magazine 498
Letter Arts Review 815
Levant & Wales, Literary Agency, Inc. 104
Levine Books, Arthur 241
Levine Literary Agency, Ellen 104
Levinson Prize, The 1012
Levis Editors' Prize in Poetry/The Missouri Review Editor's Prize in Fiction & Essay, Larry 1040
Libido 569
Libraries Unlimited, Inc. 241
Licht/Mueller Film Corp. 971
Life Extension Magazine 498
Lifeglow 677
Lifelines Section/Military Times 585
Lifetime Books, Inc. 242
Lift Every Voice 371
Light and Life Magazine (Web)
Lighthouse Point Press 372
Lighting Design & Application 856
Liguori Publications 242

Liguorian 677
Lillenas Publishing Co. 955
Lilly Poetry Prize, The Ruth 1013
Limelight Editions 242
Limousine Digest 935
Lindbergh Prize in Children's Literature, Anne Spencer 1035
Lines in the Sand Short Fiction Contest (NR)
Link & Visitor, The 802
Link Magazine (NR)
Linn's Stamp News 519
Lintel 372
Lion, The 400
Lion Books 243
Lion Publishing (NS)
Lippincott Williams & Wilkins 243
Listen & Live Audio, Inc. 243
Listen Magazine 773
Literal Latte Fiction Award (NR)
Literal Latte Poetry Award (NR)
Literary Competition (NR)
Literary Magazine Review 569
Little, Brown and Co., Children's Books 243
Little, Brown and Co., Inc. 243
Little Enterprises, Inc., Lew 979
Little Simon 244
Littleton-Griswold Prize (NR)
Live Oak Theatre (see State Theater Co. 963)
LIVE 773
Live Wire 677
Living 485
Living Church, The 677
Living Light News 678
Living Magazines, The (NS)
Living Safety 446
Livingston Awards for Young Journalists 1032
Livingston Press 244
Llamas Magazine (NR)
Llewellyn Publications 244
Local 7's Annual National Poetry Competition 1013
Lockwood Films (London) Inc. 971
Locust Hill Press 244
Loeb Awards, The Gerald (NR)
Log Home Design Ideas (Web)
Log Home Living 536
Log Homes Illustrated 536
Lone Eagle Publishing Co. 245
Lone Pine Publishing 355
Lonely Planet Publications 245
Long Fiction Contest 1002
Long Term Care 881
Long Wharf Theatre 955
Longstreet Press, Inc. 245
Lookout, The 678
Loompanics Unlimited 245
Lopez Memorial Award, Judy 1035
Lorimer & Co., James (NR)
Los Angeles Daily Journal 903
Los Angeles Magazine 621

Los Angeles Times Book Review 827
Los Angeles Times Magazine 622
Lost Treasure, Inc. 519
Lothrop, Lee & Shepard Books (OB)
Louisana Literature Prize for Poetry 1013
Louis/Emily F. Bourne Student Poetry Award, Louise (NR)
Louisiana Game & Fish 747
Louisiana Literary Award (NR)
Louisiana State University Press 246
Louisville Magazine 635
Love and Logic Press, Inc., The 246
Love Creek Annual Short Play Festival 1024
Love Creek Mini Festivals 1024
Love Prize, Walter D. 994
Love Spell 246
Loving More Magazine 665
Low-Budget Feature Project, The (NR)
Lowell House 246
Lowell Prize, James Russell 994
Lowenstein Associates, Inc. 105
Lowther Memorial Award, Pat 1013
Loyola Press 247
LRP Publications, Inc. 247
Lubricants World (NR)
Lucent Books 247
Lumiere 972
Lustre 894
Lutheran, The 678
Lutheran Digest, The 679
Lutheran Journal, The 679
Lutheran Partners 679
Lutheran Witness, The 680
Lynx Images, Inc. 356
Lyons Press, The 247
Lyric Poetry Award 1013

M

MacAdam/Cage Publishing Inc. 248
Macaddict 606
MacDonald Prize, Sir John A. 994
Maclean Hunter Endowment Literary Nonfiction Prize 994
Macmillan Brands (RP)
Macmillan Computer Publishing USA 248
Macmillan Consumer Reference (RP)
Macmillan General Reference (RP)
Macmillan Travel (RP)
MacMurray & Beck 248
MacWEEK 606
Mad Magazine 540
Mad Rhythms 458
Made to Measure 842
Mademoiselle 802
Madgett Poetry Award, Naomi Long 1013
Madison (NS)
Madison Books 248
Magazine Antiques, The 398
Magazine of Fantasy & Science Fic-

tion, The 709
Mage Publishers Inc. 248
Magic Theatre, Inc. 955
Magical Blend Magazine (NR)
Magni Group, Inc., The 249
Magnus Press (NR)
Mailbox Teacher, The (OB)
Main Street Books (OB)
Main Theatre Co. (NR)
Maine In Print 897
Maine Magazine 635
Maine Organic Farmer & Gardener 866
Maine Sportsman, The 747
Malahat Review, The 569
Malahat Review Long Poem Prize, The 1013
Malahat Review Novella Prize, The 1002
Mama's Little Helper Newsletter (NR)
Mamm Magazine 499
Mammoth Press Awards 1040
Manage 909
Managed Care 911
Management Review (NR)
Manatee Publishing 249
Manhattan Arts International Magazine 815
Manhattan Theatre Club 955
Manitoba Writing and Publishing Awards 1040
Mann Agency, Carol 105
Manoa 569
Manus & Associates Literary Agency 105
March Street Press 249
March Tenth, Inc. 381
Marcus Award for Best Book Design, Stanley 989
Marcus Books 356
Marine Business Journal 909
Marine Corps Times 586
Mariner Books (NR)
Maritimes Arts Projects Productions (see Broken Jaw Press 348)
Marketscope Books 249
Markson Literary Agency, Elaine 106
Marlboro Prize in Poetry, The (UC)
Marlin 747
Marlor Press (Web)
Marlowe & Company 249
Marlton Publishers (Web)
Marraro Prize, Howard R. (AHA) (NR)
Marraro Prize, Howard R. and Scaglione Prize for Italian Literary Studies 994
Marsh Entertainment (NR)
Marshall Poetry Prize, Lenore 1013
Martial Arts Training 757
Marvin Grant, Walter Rumsey 1047
Masquerade Books (OB)
Mass High Tech 420

Massachusetts Review, The 570
Massage & Bodywork 846
Massage Magazine 499
Masters Literary Awards 1041
Masters Press (RP)
Masthead (NS)
Mature Living 697
Mature Outlook 697
Mature Woman Grants 989
Mature Years 697
Maupin House Publishing (Web)
Maximum Press 249
May Trends (NR)
Mayfield Publishing Company 250
Mayflower Society Cup Competition, The 994
Mazumdar New Play Competition, Maxim 1024
MBI Publishing 250
MC Magazine 844
McBooks Press 250
McBride Literary Agency, Margret 106
McCall's 803
McCarter Theatre 955
McCarthy Prize in Short Fiction, Mary 1003
McClanahan Book Company Inc. 381
McClelland & Stewart (NR)
McDonald & Woodward Publishing Co. 250
McElderry Books, Margaret K. 250
McFarland & Company, Inc., Publishers 251
McGavick Field Publishing 372
McGraw-Hill Companies, The (NR)
McGraw-Hill Ryerson Limited 356
McGregor Publishing 251
McKnight Advancement Grant 1024
McLaren Memorial Comedy Playwriting Competition 1024
McLemore Prize 994
Meadowbrook Press 251
Media Inc. 812
Mediacom Development Corp. 972
Medical Device Approval Letter 847
Medical Economics 911
Medical Physics Publishing 252
Medwick Memorial Award, Lucille 1013
Meetings in the West 832
Mega Films, Inc. 972
Mega Media Press (NR)
Megalo Media 980
Mekler & Deahl, Publishers (NR)
Melcher Book Award 994
Meltzer Productions, Michael 972
Memory Makers 519
Memphis 656
Mencken Awards 1032
Mendillo/Form Productions 972
Mennonite Brethren Herald 680
Men's Fitness (NR)
Men's Health 499
Men's Journal 583
Menus and Music 372
Mercat Press (NR)
Mercator's World 519
Mercury House (RR)
Meriwether Publishing Ltd. 252, 956
Merlyn's Pen 570
Merriam Press 252
Merrimack Repertory Theatre (NR)

Mesorah Publications, Ltd. 253
Message Company, The (Web)
MESSAGE Magazine 680
Messenger of the Sacred Heart 681
Metal Powder Industries Fed. 253
Metamorphous Press (Web)
Metcalf Body of Work Award, Vicky 1035
Metcalf Short Story Award, Vicky 1035
Metro 622
Metro Journal (see Oklahoma Business Monthly 420)
Metro Parent Magazine 438
Metro Santa Cruz 622
Metro Sports Magazine (NR)
Metrojournal (OB)
MetroKids Magazine 439
Metropolis 398
MetroSource 478
MetroStage 956
Meyerbooks, Publisher (Web)
MH-18 774
MHQ (NR)
Michener Prize in Writing, James A. (NR)
Michigan Contractor & Builder 845
Michigan Links 736
Michigan Living 788
Michigan Out-of-Doors 748
Michigan Quarterly Review 570
Michigan Sportsman 748
Michigan State University Press 253
Microstation Manager (NR)
Mid West Outdoors 748
Midatlantic Antiques Magazine (NR)
Mid-Atlantic Game & Fish 748
Middle Atlantic Press 253, 373
Midknight Club, The 253
Midland Authors Award 1041
Mid-List Press (Web)
Mid-List Press First Series Award for Creative Nonfiction 994
Mid-List Press First Series Award for Poetry 1013
Mid-List Press First Series Award for Short Fiction 1003
Mid-List Press First Series Award for the Novel 1003
Midmarch Arts Press (NS)
Midstream (NR)
Midwest Express Magazine 543
Midwest Features Inc. 980
Midwest Home and Garden 536
Midwest Motorist, The (see AAA Midwest Traveler 778)
Mildenberger Prize, Kenneth W. 994
Military History (NR)
Military Space (NR)
Military.com 586
Milkweed Editions 254
Milkweed National Fiction Prize 1003
Milkweed Prize for Children's Literature 1035
Milkweeds for Young Readers 254
Mill Mountain Theatre 956
Mill Mountain Theatre New Play Competition 1025
Millbrook Press Inc., The 254
Millennium Science Fiction & Fantasy 709
Miller Prize In Poetry, Vassar (UC)

miller's pond 570
Mills Award, C. Wright 1003
Milton Center Post-Graduate Fellowship, The (NR)
Milwaukee Filmworks (OB)
Milwaukee Magazine 659
Mindstorm LLC 972
Miniature Donkey Talk 392
Miniature Quilts 520
Mining Voice 934
Mini-Storage Messenger (NR)
Minnesota Christian Chronicle 681
Minnesota Golfer 736
Minnesota Historical Society Press 254
Minnesota Hockey Journal 739
Minnesota Monthly 639
Minnesota Sportsman 748
Minnesota Technology 856
Minnesota Voices Project Competition 990
Minority Advancement Profile (NR)
Minority Business Entrepreneur 832
Minority Engineer 856
Minstrel Books 255
Miraculous Medal, The 681
Mirimar Enterprises (NR)
Mississippi Game & Fish 748
Mississippi Magazine 640
Mississippi Review Prize 990
Mississippi Valley Non-Profit Poetry Contest 1013
Missouri Game & Fish 748
Missouri Historical Society Press 373
Missouri Review, The 571
Mix 398
Mix Magazine 915
Mixxzine (NR)
MLA Prize for a Distinguished Bibliography 994
MLA Prize for a Distinguished Scholarly Edition 994
MLA Prize for a First Book 995
MLA Prize for Independent Scholars 995
MNC Films (NR)
Mobile Bay Monthly 617
Model Railroader 520
Model Retailer (Web)
Modern Bride 803
Modern Drummer 589
Modern Language Association of America 255
Modern Machine Shop (Web)
Modern Maturity 698
Modern Physician 912
Mom Guess What Newspaper 478
Moment 466
Momentum 839
Momentum Books, Ltd. 255
Monacelli Press 255
Monarch Publications (Web)
Monarex Hollywood Corporation 972
Money for Women 1047
Money Saving Ideas 446
Monitoring Times 520
Montador Award, The Gordon (NR)
Montage Magazine 643
Montana Catholic, The (Web)
Montana Magazine 641
Monteiro Rose Agency 116
Moody Magazine 682
Moody Press 256

Moon Publications, Inc. 256
Moore Studio, Marlene (NR)
Mopam Publishing 373
More Magazine 803
More Publishing, Thomas 256
Morehouse Publishing Co. 256
Morley Journalism Competition, Felix (NR)
Morningside House, Inc. 257
Morris Agency, Inc., William 106
Morrison, Inc., Henry 107
Morrow Junior Books (OB)
Morrow, William, 257
Morse Poetry Prize 1013
Mortgage Banking 869
Morton Prize in Poetry, Kathryn A. 1014
Mosaic Annual Fiction Contest 1003
Mosaic Press Miniature Books (Web)
Mosaic Quarterly Fiction Contest 1003
Mosaic Very Short Fiction Contest 1003
Mother Earth News 702
Mother Jones 449
Motor News Media Corporation 980
Motorcycle Tour & Cruiser 408
Motorhome 788
Mott-Kappa Tau Alpha Research Award in Journalism, Frank Luther 1032
Motton Award, Sheila 1014
Mount Ida Press 373
Mountain Drive (NR)
Mountain Living 536
Mountain N'Air Books 257
Mountain Pilot Magazine 411
Mountain Press Publishing Co. 257
Mountain Sports & Living (OB)
Mountaineers Books, The 258
Mountainfreak 599
Movie Reps Int'l (NR)
Moving Arts Premiere One-Act Competition 1025
Moxie Magazine 804
MR Magazine (NR)
MRTW Annual Radio Script Contest (NR)
Ms. Magazine 804
MSW Management 924
Mudfish Poetry Prize 1014
Muir Publications, John (see Avalon Publishing Group 146)
Multifamily Executive 922
Multnomah Publishers, Inc. 258
Mumford Prize, Erika (NR)
Murderous Intent 592
Muscle & Fitness 500
Muscle Mag International 500
Muse 552
Mushing 392
Music Connection 915
Music for the Love of It 590
Music, Inc. (NR)
Musical Stairs 1025
Musky Hunter Magazine 748
Mustang & Fords Magazine (NR)
Mustang Publishing Co. 258
Muzzle Blasts 737
My Daily Visitor 682
My Friend 552
Mysterious Press, The 258
Mystery Novel Award 1004

Mystery Review, The 592
Mystic Seaport Museum (Web)

N

Na'amat Woman 467
Naggar Literary Agency, Jean V. 107
Naiad Press, Inc., The 259
Nailpro 823
Nails 824
Nantucket Short Play Competition and Festival 1025
Narwhal Press, Inc. 259
NASW Press 259
Nation, The 610
National Awards for Education Reporting (NR)
National Bus Trader (NR)
National Chapter of Canada IODE Violet Downey Book Award 1035
National Children's Theatre Festival 1025
National Children's Theatre Festival Contest (NR)
National Examiner 458
National Financial News Services, The 980
National Fire & Rescue 874
National Geographic Magazine 486
National Geographic Traveler 789
National Hispanic Playwriting Award 1025
National Jesuit Book Award (UC)
National Jewish Book Award—Autobiography/Memoir (NR)
National Jewish Book Award—Children's Literature (NR)
National Jewish Book Award—Children's Picture Book (NR)
National Jewish Book Award—Contemporary Jewish Life (NR)
National Jewish Book Award—Holocaust (NR)
National Jewish Book Award—Israel (NR)
National Jewish Book Award—Jewish Christian Relations (NR)
National Jewish Book Award—Jewish History (NR)
National Jewish Book Award—Jewish Thought (NR)
National Jewish Book Award—Scholarship (NR)
National Jewish Book Award—Visual Arts (NR)
National Looking Glass Poetry Chapbook Competition 1014
National Neighborhood News 537
National News Bureau 980
National One-Act Playwriting Competition 1025
National Parks 600
National Play Award (NR)
National Playwrights' Award 1025
National Playwrights Conference/ New Drama for Media Project at the Eugene O'Neill Theater Center, The 956
National Poetry Book Award 1014
National Poetry Contest (NR)
National Poetry Series, The (NR)
National Press Club Consumer Journalism Awards 1032
National Press Club Online Journal-

ism Awards (NR)
National Press Club Washington Correspondence Awards 1032
National Relocation & Real Estate 922
National Review (NR)
National Ten-Minute Play Contest 1025
National Theatre Artist Residency Program (NR)
National Voter, The 611
National Wildlife 600
National Writers Association Nonfiction Contest 995
National Writers Association Novel Writing Contest 1004
National Writers Association Poetry Contest 1014
National Writers Association Short Story Contest 1004
National Writers Literary Agency 107
Native Peoples Magazine 467
Natural Health 500
Natural Heritage/Natural History 356
Natural History 601
Naturally 789
Nature Canada 601
Nature Friend 553
Nature Photographer 607
Naturegraph Publishers, Inc. 259
Nautical & Aviation Publishing Co., The 260
Naval History 586
Naval Institute Press 260
Navy Times 587
Neal Writers' Competition, Larry 1047
Neal-Schuman Publishers, Inc. 260
Nebraska Review Awards in Fiction and Poetry, The 1041
Nebraska Theatre Caravan 956
Neighborhood Works, The (OB)
Nelson Publishers, Thomas 260
Nelson, Tommy 260
Nelson-Hall Publishers (see Burnham Publishers 165)
Nemerov Sonnet Award, Howard 1014
Neshui Publishing 261
Ness Book Award, The Frederic W. 995
Network Journal, The 415
Neustadt International Prize for Literature 1041
Nevada Lawyer (NP)
Nevada Magazine 642
New Age 402
New Age Retailer 927
New American Comedy Showcase (NR)
New American Library 261
New American Theater Center 957
New Century Writer Awards (Fiction) 1004
New Century Writer Awards (Screenwriting) 1025
New Choices 501
New England Booming (OB)
New England Cartographics, Inc. 373
New England Game & Fish 749
New England Mechanic (NR)
New England Poetry Club Contests (UC)

New England Press, Inc., The 261
New England Printer & Publisher (NR)
New England Publishing Associates, Inc. 108, 381
New England Review 571
New Era, The 774
New Hampshire Individual Artists' Fellowships 1047
New Hampshire Magazine 642
New Harbinger Publications 262
New Harmony Project Conference/ Laboratory, The 1026
New Haven Advocate (Web)
New Holland News 865
New Hope Publishers 262
New Horizon Press 262
New Humor Magazine (UC)
New Jersey Lake Survey Fishing Maps Guide 749
New Jersey Monthly 643
New Jersey Outdoors 643
New Jersey Repertory Company 957
New Jersey Reporter 611
New Letters 571
New Mexico Magazine 644
New Millenniam Writings Award 1041
New Moon 553
New Moon Network (Web)
New Muse Award 1004
New Mystery (NR)
New Physician, The (NR)
New Plays Incorporated 957
New Playwrights' Program (Web)
New Professional Theatre Writers Festival 1026
New Repertory Theatre 957
New Rivers Press 263
New Stage Theatre 957
New Steel Magazine (NR)
New Theatre (Web)
New Times Los Angeles 623
New Tuners Theatre 957
New Victoria Publishers 263
New Voice Series 1026
New Works for a New World (NR)
New Works for the Stage 1026
New World Library 263
New World Outlook (RR)
New Writers Awards 1041
New Writer's Magazine 897
New Writing Award 990
New York City High School Playwriting Contest 1026
New York Daily News (NS)
New York Family (NR)
New York Game & Fish 749
New York Magazine 646
New York Nightlife 646
New York Opera Newsletter, The (see Classical Singer Magazine 914)
New York Runner 762
New York State Theatre Institute (NR)
New York Theatre Workshop (NR)
New York Times, The (NR)
New York University Press 263
New York University Press Prizes in Fiction and Poetry 1041
New Yorker, The (NR)
Newcastle Publishing Co. (NR)
NeWest Publishers Ltd. (NR)

Newfoundland Herald, The 458
Newjoy Press (Web)
Newmarket Press 381
News USA 980
News/400 891
Newsage Press (NR)
Newsday 646
Newsletter Journalisim Award 1032
NewStar Press (UF)
Newsweek 486
Next Decade, Inc. 373
NFPA Journal 875
NHO Entertainment 972
NICHE 928
Nichol Chapbook Award (NR)
Nicholl Fellowships in Screenwriting, Don and Gee 1026
Nichols Publishing 264
Nicolas-Hays 374
Nightshade Press (NS)
Nimrod 1041
Nims Memorial Prize, The John Frederick 1014
9-1-1 Magazine 875
Njema Magazine 467
NLAPW International Poetry Contest 1014
No Starch Press 264
Nodin Press (Web)
Nolo Press (see Nolo.Com 264)
Nolo.com 264
Noonday Press (see Farrar Straus & Giroux Paperbacks 199)
Norbry Publishing (NR)
North American Fisherman (NR)
North American Review, The 572
North American Whitetail 749
North & South (RR)
North Carolina Game & Fish 749
North Carolina Literary Review (NR)
North Dakota REC/RTC Magazine 648
North Georgia Journal 630
North Light Books 264
North Point Press 264
North Shore (NR)
North Shore Music Theatre 958
North Texas Golfer 736
Northeast Export 832
Northeast Magazine 626
Northeast Outdoors 790
Northeastern University Press 265
Northern Aquaculture (NR)
Northern Breezes, Sailing Magazine 725
Northern Centinel, The (NR)
Northern Illinois University Press 265
Northern Ohio Live 649
Northfield Publishing 265
Northland Publishing Co., Inc. 265
Northlight Theatre 958
North-South Books 266
Northwest Family Magazine 439
Northwest Metalworker 906
Northwest Motor 818
Northwest Travel 790
Northwoods Journal's Annual National Short Fiction Contest 1004
NorthWord Press, Inc. 266
Norton Co., Inc., W.W. 266
Nostalgia 572
Notorious (NR)

Notre Dame Magazine 427
Nottingham University Press (NR)
Nova Press (Web)
Now and Then 615
NSGA Retail Focus 932
NTC/Contemporary Publishing Group 266
Nugget 715
Nurseweek (NR)
Nursing Spectrum, Florida 881
Nursing Spectrum, Greater Chicago (NR)
Nursing Spectrum, Greater Philadelphia/Tristate 882
Nursing Spectrum, New York/New Jersey Metro (NR)
Nursing2000 882

O

Oak Knoll Press 267
O&A Marketing News 818
Oasis Newsfeatures 980
Oasis Press 267
Oatmeal Studios 986
Oberlin College Press 374
Oblates 682
Observer Magazine, The (NR)
Ocean View Books 374
O'Connor Award for Short Fiction, The Flannery 1004
O'Dell Award for Historical Fiction, Scott 1035
Odyssey Theatre Ensemble 958
Off Duty Magazine (NR)
Office Buildings Magazine 922
Office Dealer 916
Office Solutions 916
OfficePRO® 917
Off-Off-Broadway Original Short Play Festival (NR)
Offshore 725
Oglebay Institute Towngate Theatre Playwriting Contest 1026
O'Hagan Award for Short Fiction, Howard 1004
O'Hara Award Chapbook Competition, The Frank 1014
Ohio Farmer (NR)
Ohio Game & Fish 749
Ohio Magazine 649
Ohio Medicine 912
Ohio State University Press 267
Ohio State University Press/The Journal Award in Poetry, The 1015
Ohio University Press 267
Ohio Writer 897
Ohioana Book Awards 1041
Oklahoma Business Monthly 420
Oklahoma Game & Fish 749
Oklahoma Today 650
Old Cars Weekly 818
Old House Interiors (NR)
Oldcastle Theatre Co. (NR)
Oliver Press, Inc., The 268
Olson & Co., C. (NR)
Olympian Magazine (OB)
Omaha Theater Company for Young People 958
O'Malley Prize in Fiction, Chris 1004
Omega Publications 374
On Mission 682
On Spec Magazine 572, 710
On the Downlow (NR)

On the Line 554
On the Scene Magazine (NR)
On Wall Street 869
Once Upon A Time Films (NR)
One On One Computer Training 268
One World (NR)
One-Act Playwriting Competition (NR)
104 Zone, The (NR)
OneWorld Publications (Web)
Onion World 861
Onjinjinkta Publishing 268
Online Publishers Digest 898
Ontario Out Of Doors 749
Open Door Entertainment (NR)
Open Eye Theater, The 958
Open Road Publishing 268
Open Spaces 486
Operations & Fulfillment 928
Opportunities For Actors & Models (OB)
Optical Prism 847
Optical Technology 21st Century (see FRAMESdata.com 846)
Optimist, The (Web)
Options 715
Opus Magnum Discovery Award (NR)
Orange Coast Magazine 623
Orange County Woman 623
Orange Frazer Press, Inc. 269
Orbis Books (NS)
Orbit Pictures 973
Orchard Books 269
Orchises Press (Web)
Oregon Coast 651
Oregon Outside 651
Oregon Quarterly 428
Oregon Shakespeare Festival 958
Oregon State University Press 269
Oregon Stater 428
Organic Gardening (NR)
Origin of Books, The (NR)
Orion Prize for Poetry 1015
Orlando Weekly (RR)
Ormonde Wedding Style, Grace 804
Ornamental and Miscellaneous Metal Fabricator 906
Ornamental Outlook 871
Ornish Poetry Award in Memory of Wayne Gard, Natalie 1015
Oryx Press 269
Osborne Media Group 269
Osprey Publishing Limited 270
Other Side, The 683
Ottenheimer Publishers, Inc. 381
Oughten House Foundation, Inc. 374
Our Family 683
Our State 647
Our Sunday Visitor (magazine) 684
Our Sunday Visitor, Inc. (books) 270
Out West (PR)
Outdoor America 601
Outdoor Canada Magazine 662

Outdoor Life 750
Outfitter Magazine 928
Outlaw Biker 408
Outside 738
Outside (literary sci-fi) (see Deep Outside SFFH 709)
Outsmart 479
Outstanding Dissertation of the Year Award 995
Over the Back Fence 650
Overdrive 818
Overlook Press, The 270
Overmountain Press, The 270
Owen Publishers Inc., Richard C. 271
Owl Books 271
Owl Magazine 554
Owsley Award, Frank Lawrence and Harriet Chappell 995
Oxford American, The 486
Oxford University Press (NR)
Oxygen! 501
Ozark Mountain Publishing, Inc. 374

P

P. I. Magazine 451
P.O.V. (OB)
P.S. Greetings 986
Pacesetter Publications 375
Pacific Bakers News 842
Pacific Books, Publishers 271
Pacific Business News (NR)
Pacific Educational Press (NR)
Pacific Fishing 870
Pacific Press Publishing Assoc. 271
Pacific View Press 272, 375
Pacific Yachting 725
Packer/Shipper (OB)
Pack-O-Fun 521
Paddle Dealer 932
Paddler Magazine 768
Pagemill Press (RP)
Paine Prize, Robert Troup (NR)
Paint Dealer, The (NR)
Paint Horse Journal (Web)
Paladin Press 272
Palardo Productions 941
Palm Springs Life 624
Palo Alto Weekly (Web)
Panda Talent 117
PanGaia 403, 684
Panowski Playwriting Award, Mildred & Albert 1026
Pantheon Books 272
Paper Magazine 450
Paper Magic Group, Inc., The 986
Paper Stock Report, The 917
Papercity (Web)
Papier-Mache Press 272
Papp Public Theater, Joseph 959
Parabola 403
Parabola Books 375
Paraclete Press 272
Parade 487
Paragon House Publishers 273

Parameters: US Army War College Quarterly 587
Paramount Cards (NR)
Parenting Bay Area Teens (NR)
Parenting Magazine 439
Parents' Press 440
Parent.Teen 440
Paris Review, The (NR)
Parker Motion Pictures, Tom 973
Parkway Publishers (Web)
Parlay International 273
Parnassus 572
Parnassus Imprints 273
Parrot Press (NR)
Partners In Publishing (Web)
Parts & People 818
Party & Paper Retailer 928
Pasadena Playhouse, The 959
Passeggiata Press 273
Passport Press (Web)
Pastoral Life 839
Patchen Competition, Kenneth 1042
Pathfinder Publishing of California 274
Pathfinders 790
Pathway National Playwriting Contest (NR)
Patterson Journalism Fellowship, Alicia 1032
Patterson's California Beverage Journal 825
Paula Company, C.M. (NR)
Pauline Books & Media 274
Paulist Press 274
Paumanok Poetry Award 1015
Pavilion Books (Web)
PBC International Inc. 274
Peace Playwriting Contest (NR)
Peachtree Children's Books 275
Peachtree Publishers, Ltd. 275
Peden Prize in Fiction, William 1004
Pediatrics for Parents 440
Pedlar Press 357
Pegasus Theatre 959
Pelican Publishing Company 275
Pelzer Memorial Award, Louis (NR)
PEN Center USA West Annual Literary Awards 1042
PEN Center West Literary Awards 990
PEN Writing Awards for Prisoners 1042
PEN/Architectural Digest Award 995
PEN/Book-of-the-Month Club Translation Prize 1037
Pencil Point Press, Inc. 276
PEN/Faulkner Awards for Fiction 1005
Penguin Books Canada Ltd. 357
Penguin Putnam Inc. 276
PEN/Jerard Fund 995
PEN/Martha Albrand Award for First Nonfiction 995
PEN/Martha Albrand Award for the

Art of the Memoir 996
PEN/Norma Klein Award 1035
Penn Stater, The 428
Pennsylvania 652
Pennsylvania Angler & Boater 750
Pennsylvania Game & Fish 751
Pennsylvania Heritage 653
Pennsylvania Historical and Museum Commission 276
Pennsylvania Lawyer, The 904
Pennywhistle Press 276
PEN/Spielvogel-Diamonstein Award 996
Pentecostal Evangel 684
Pentecostal Messenger, The 684
Penthouse 716
People's Light & Theatre Co. (NR)
Perdido 415
Peregrine Prize, The (fiction) 1005
Peregrine Prize, The (poetry) 1015
Perfection Learning Corp. 276
Performing Arts Magazine 458
Perigee Books 277
Periodical Writers Association of Canada Annual Nonfiction Writing Contest, The (NR)
Perishable Theatre's Women's Playwriting Festival 1026
Permanent Buildings & Foundations 845
Permanent Press/Second Chance Press, The 277
Persimmon Hill 506
Perspective (Web)
Perspectives (NR)
Perspectives Press (Web)
Pest Control Magazine (NR)
Pet Age 918
Pet Product News (NR)
Peter Pauper Press, Inc. 277
Peterkin Award, The Julia (NR)
Peters, A.K. (RR)
Petersen's Bowhunting 718
Petersen's Hunting 751
Peterson's 277
Pets Magazine 393
Pew Fellowships in the Arts 1047
PFI World Report (RR)
Phaidon Press 278
Phase 1 Productions 973
Phelan Literary Award, James D. 1048
Phi Delta Kappa Educational Foundation 278
Philadelphia Enterpriser (NR)
Philadelphia Magazine 653
Phillips Poetry Prize, The Richard 1015
Philomel Books 278
Phoenix 619
Phoenix Theatre, The (NR)
Photo Communication Services 941
Photo Life 608
Photo Review, The 920
Photo Techniques 608
Photographic Processing 920
Photonics Spectra 886
Physician 912
Physician and Sports Medicine, The (Web)
Physicians' Travel & Meeting Guide 912
Picador USA 278

Picasso Publications, Inc. 357
Piccadilly Books Ltd. 279
Pickering Award for Playwrighting Excellence, Robert J. 1027
Picton Press 279
Picture Entertainment Corp. (NR)
PieceWork Magazine 521
Pier One Theatre (NR)
Pig Iron Series (NR)
Pilgrim Press, The 279
Pilgrim Project Grants 1027
Pilot Books (UC)
Pime World (NR)
Piñata Books 279
Pinder Lane & Garon-Brooke Associates, Ltd. 108
Pineapple Press, Inc. 279
Pinter Publishers Ltd. (see Continuum International Publishing Group (Web))
Pioneer Drama Service, Inc. 959
Pipers Magazine 411
Pippin Press (Web)
Pit & Quarry 934
PitchWeekly (RR)
Pittsburgh Business Times (NR)
Pittsburgh Magazine 653
Pizza Today (NR)
Plain Truth, The 685
Plan Sponsor (NR)
Plane and Pilot 412
Planet IT 891
Planners Press (Web)
Planning 875
Planning/Communications (Web)
Platinum Press Inc. 280
Play the Odds (OB)
Playboy College Fiction Contest (NR)
Players Press, Inc. 280, 959
Playgirl (NR)
Playhouse on the Square New Play Competition 1027
Playlabs (NR)
Plays 959
Plays for the 21st Century (NR)
Plays-In-Progress 960
Playwright Discovery Program 1027
Playwrights' Arena (NR)
Playwrights Canada Press 357
Playwrights' Center McKnight Fellowship 1027
Playwrights' Center's Playlabs 960
Playwrights Horizons 960
Playwrights Theatre of New Jersey 960
Pleasant Company Publications 280
Pleiades 572
Plexus Publishing, Inc. 280
Ploughshares 573
Plowshares Theatre Co. 960
Plum Graphics Inc. 986
Plus 698
PML 819
Pocket Books 281
Pockets 554
Podiatry Management 913
Poe Award, Edgar Allan 1005
Poet Lore Narrative Poetry Contest 1015
Poetry Center Book Award, The 1015
Poetry Center Summer Residency Program (NR)

Poetry Society of Virginia Contests 1015
Poets & Writers 898
Poet's Corner Award 1015
Pogo Press, Incorporated 375
Point of View (NR)
Polaris North 960
Polestar Books Publishers (NR)
Police and Security News 876
Police Times 876
Policy Review 611
Pollak Prize in Poetry/Brittingham Prize in Poetry, Felix 1016
Polo Players' Edition 758
Pontalba Press 281
Pontoon & Deck Boat 726
Pool & Spa News (Web)
Poole Award for First Work of Fiction, Mary Ruffin 1005
Pop Culture Collecting 521
Pop/Art Film Factory 973
Poptronis 521
Popular Communications 522
Popular Culture Ink 281
Popular Electronics (NR)
Popular Home Automation (NR)
Popular Mechanics 522
Popular Science 704
Popular Woodworking (magazine) 522
Popular Woodworking Books 281
Portable Restroom Operator 833
Portal Publications 987
Porthole Cruise Magazine 791
Porthole Press (NR)
Portland Stage Company 960
Possibility Press 281
Post-Apollo Press, The (NR)
Postcard Story Competition 1042
Pot Shard Press (NR)
Potentials Development (NR)
Potter, Clarkson 282
Pottersfield Portfolio 573
Pound Poetry Award, Ezra 1016
Powder 764
Power and Light (NR)
Power & Motoryacht 726
Power Boating Canada 726
Power for Living 685
PowerProse.com 981
PPI Publishing 282
Practice Management Information Corp. (PMIC) 282
Practice Strategies (NR)
Praeger Publishers 282
Prairie Journal, The 573
Prairie Messenger (Web)
Prairie Oak Press 283
Prakken Publications, Inc. 375
Precept Press 283
Preferred Artists Talent Agency 117
Presbyterian Record 685
Presbyterians Today 686
PresenceSense Magazine 487
Preservation Magazine 506
Preserving Christian Homes 686
Presidio La Bahia Award, The 1042
Presidio Press 283
Press (OB)
Press Associates, Inc. 981
Press at the Maryland Historical Society, The 283
Press Gang Publishers (NR)

Prevention (NR)
Prevention Update 441
Pride & Imprints 284
Price Stern Sloan, Inc. 283
Priest, The 839
Priest Literary Agency, Aaron M. 108
Prima Publishing (NR)
Primary Stages Company, Inc. 961
Prime Health & Fitness (NR)
Prime Time Sports & Fitness 759
Prime Times 698
Princess Grace Awards Playwright
    Fellowship (NR)
Print & Graphics, Printing Journal
    919
Print Media Award 1032
Prism International Annual Short Fic-
    tion Contest (NR)
Prism International Fiction Contest
    1005
Prism International 574, 961
Prism Magazine 686
Private Pilot 412
Prix Alvine-Belisle (NR)
Pro/Am Music Resources (Web)
Proceedings 587
Processing Magazine (NR)
Produce Merchandising 878
Produce News 879
Productive Publications 358
Professional Collector 833
Professional Mariner 909
Professional Pilot 822
Professional Publications, Inc. 284
Professional Selling (OB)
Professional Tool & Equipment News
    (NR)
Profile (NR)
Profit (Canada) 420
Progressive, The 611
Progressive Engineer 857
Progressive Rentals 833
Promark Entertainment Group 973
Prometheus Books 284
Promising Playwright Award (UC)
Promo Magazine (Web)
PROMPT Publications 285
Properties (Web)
Prorodeo Sports News (Web)
ProStar Publications Inc. 285
Provincetown Arts 637
Pruett Publishing 285
Prufrock Press 286
Psychology Today (NR)
Public Citizen News 612
Public Power 854
Public Purchaser, The 876
Publicom, Inc. 381
Puckerbrush Press 375
Puffin Books 286
Pulitzer Prizes (NR)
Pulliam Journalism Fellowships 1032
Pulp & Paper Canada (Web)
Pulp Eternity Online 710
Pulse 839
Puppetoon Studios, The (Web)
Puppy House Publishing (NR)
Purdue Alumnus, The 428
Purdue University Press 286
Purich Publishing Ltd. 358
Purple Rose Theatre Co., The 961
Purpose 686
Putnam's Sons Books for Young

Readers, G.P. 286
Putnam's Sons, G.P. 286
PWC 828

Q
QED Press 375
Qspell Literary Awards (see QWF
    Literary Awards 1042)
QSR (NR)
Qualified Remodeler 828
Quality Digest (NR)
Quality Management (NR)
Quarter Horse Journal, The 393
Quarter Racing Journal, The 740
Quarterly Review of Literature
    Poetry Series 1016
Quarterly West 574
Quarterly West Novella Competition
    1005
Que 287
Queen of All Hearts 687
Queen's Mystery Magazine, Ellery
    593
Queen's Quarterly 574
Quest Books 287
Quick Frozen Foods International
    (NR)
Quick Printing (RR)
Quiet Hour, The 687
Quill & Quire (NR)
Quill Driver Books/Word Dancer
    Press 287
Quill Magazine Quarterly, The 898
Quilt Digest Press, The 287
Quilt World (NR)
Quilter's Newsletter Magazine (NR)
Quilting Today Magazine 523
Quincy Writer's Guild Annual Cre-
    ative Writing Contest 1042
Quintet Publishing Limited (NR)
Quite Specific Media Group Ltd. 288
Quorum Books 288
QWF Literary Awards 1042

R
Race Point Press (RP)
Racing Milestones (NR)
Racquetball Magazine 759
Raddall Atlantic Fiction Prize,
    Thomas H. 1005
Radiance 807
Radio World International (NR)
Radio World Newspaper (NR)
Ragged Mountain Press 288
Ragweed Press 358
Railmodel Journal 523
Rain Crow 574
Rainbow Books (California) 288
Rainbow Books, Inc. (Florida) 289
Raincoast Book Distribution Ltd. 358
Rainmaker Awards in Poetry 1016
Raiziss/de Palchi Translation Fellow-
    ship, The 1037
Raleigh Award, Sir Walter 1005
Rambunctious Review (fiction) 1005
Rambunctious Review (poetry) 1016
Random House Books for Young
    Readers 289
Random House Children's Publishing
    (see Random House Books for
    Young Readers 289)
Random House, Inc. 289
Random House of Canada (NR)

Random House Trade Publishing
    Group 290
Random Lengths 487
Randwell Productions, Inc. 973
Rap Sheet (NR)
Raritan 575
Rawley Prize, James A. 996
Rawson Assoc. (NR)
Rev. 839
React (OB)
Reader's Digest 488
Reader's Digest (Canada) 488
Readers Review 489
Readers Showcase, The 459
Real Estate Forum 923
Real People 489
Real You 807
Reason, Free Minds and Free Markets
    (see Reason 612)
Reason 612
Recreation News 404
Recycled Paper News 917
Red Deer Press (NS)
Red Eye Press, Inc. 376
Red Hen Press 290
Red Hots Entertainment (Web)
Red Rock Poetry Award 1016
Redbook Magazine 808
Reed Memorial Award for Outstand-
    ing Writing on the Southern Envi-
    ronment, Phillip D. 996
Reel Life Women 973
Rees Literary Agency, Helen 109
Reeves Journal (NR)
Referee 933
Reference Press International (Web)
Reference Publications (NS)
Reference Service Press 290
Reform Judaism 687
Regan Books 290
Regnery Publishing, Inc. 291
Reid Productions, Tim 974
Reidmore Books Inc. 359
Relay Magazine (NR)
Release Magazine 590
Release Print 859
Relix Magazine 590
REMEDY Magazine 501
Remodeling (Web)
Remote Control Productions (NR)
Renaissance Books 291
Renaissance Greeting Cards 987
Renaissance Magazine 523
Reno Air Approach (OB)
Rental Management 833
Report on Business Magazine (Web)
Reporter, The 688
Reptile & Amphibian Hobbyist 393
Republic of Texas Press 291
Request for Proposal 1048
Research and Writing Grants for Indi-
    viduals (NR)
Resort Management & Operations
    885
Resource Publications, Inc. 291, 961
Response, Multi-Channel Direct Ad-
    vertising (NR)
Restaurant Greeting Cards (NR)
Resurrection Press, Ltd. (Web)
Retail Info Systems News 834
Retail Systems Reseller 929
Retired Officer Magazine, The 587
Retirement Community Business 923

Retriever Journal, The (NR)
Reunions Magazine 489
Revell Publishing, Fleming H. 291
Review and Herald Publishing Association 292
Review for Religious 688
Reynolds Publishing, Morgan 292
Rhode Island Monthly 654
Rhyme Time Creative Writing Competition (NR)
Rider 408
Ribalow Award, Harold U. 1005
Rice Journal 861
Richardson Memorial Literary Award, Evelyn 996
Richboro Press 292
Richulco, Inc. (see Avalanche Entertainment (Web))
Riehle Foundation, The (OB)
Riggs Theatres, Dudley 961
Right On! (Web)
Rilke Poetry Competiton (NR)
Rinaldi Literary Agency, Angela 109
Rinehart Fund, Mary Roberts (NR)
Ringwood Award for Drama, Gwen Pharis 1027
Ripon College Magazine (Web)
Rising Star Press 376
Rising Tide Press 292
Ristorante 473
River City Writing Awards in Fiction 1006
River Hills Traveler 641
River Oak Poetry Contest (NR)
River Styx 575
Road & Track 409
Road King Magazine 819
Roads to Adventure 791
Roanoke-Chowan Award for Poetry 1016
Roanoker, The 658
Robb Report 490
Roberts Award, Summerfield G. 1042
ROC Books 293
Rochester Playwright Festival 1027
Rock & Gem 524
Rockbridge Publishing Co. 293
Rockshots, Inc. 987
Rocky Mountain Books 359
Rocky Mountain Game & Fish 751
Rocky Mountain Rider Magazine 394
Rocky Mountain Sports Magazine 731
Rodale (NR)
Roerich Poetry Prize, Nicholas 1016
Rogers Communications Writers' Trust Fiction Prize, The (NR)
RoMANtic, The 665
Romantic Homes 537
Rom/Con (NR)
Ronin Publishing, Inc. 293
Ronsdale Press 359
Room of One's Own 575
Rose Publishing 293
Rosebud 575
Rosemont Productions (NR)
Rosen Publishing Group, The 294
Rosenberg Award for Poems on the Jewish Experience, Anna Davidson 1016
Rosenthal New Play Prize, The Lois and Richard 1027
Rosicrucian Digest 613

Ross Award, The Madeline Dane 1032
Ross Literary Agency, The Gail 109
Rossley Literary Award, Bruce P. 1042
Rotarian, The 400
Roth Award for a Translation of a Literary Work, Lois 1037
Routledge, Inc. 294
Rowland Agency, The Damaris 109
Rowland Prize for Fiction, The Pleasant T. (NR)
Rowman & Littlefield Publishing Group 294
Rowse Award for Press Criticism, Arthur (NR)
Roxbury Publishing Co. 294
Rudi Publishing (OB)
Rudwick Prize, Elliott 996
Rug Hooking Magazine 524
Rugby Magazine 760
Ruggles Journalism Scholarship, William B. 1032
Ruminator Books 294
Runner's World 762
Running Press Book Publishers 295
Rural Heritage 702
Ruralite 703
Russell, James (Web)
Russian Information Services 376
Russian Life 467
Rutgers Magazine (NR)
Rutgers University Press 295
Rutledge Hill Press 295
RV Business 936
RV Trade Digest 819
Ryan Award, The Cornelius 996

S

Sachem Publishing Associates 382
Sacramento Business Journal (Web)
Sacramento Magazine 624
Sacramento News & Review 624
SAE International (NR)
Safari Magazine 751
Safari Press Inc. 295
Safety & Health (NR)
Sagamore Publishing 296
Sail 726
Sailing Magazine 727
Sailing World 727
St. Anthony Messenger 688
St. Anthony Messenger Press 296
St. Augustine's Press 296
St. Bede's Publications 296
St. James Awards, The Ian (UF)
St. Jerome's Press (UC)
St. Joseph's Messenger & Advocate of the Blind 688
St. Louis Construction News & Review 845
St. Maarten Nights 792
St. Martin's Press 297
St. Martin's Press Scholarly & Reference Division 297
St. Mary's Press 297
Salina Bookshelf 297
Saloutos Award, Theodore 996
Salt Hill Journal Poetry Prize (NR)
Salt Lake City (RR)
Salt Water Sportsman Magazine 751
Saltworks Theatre Company 961
Salvo Press 298

Sams 298
San Diego Family Magazine 441
San Diego Home/Garden Lifestyles 537
San Diego Magazine 624
San Francisco 624
San Francisco Peninsula Parent (NR)
San Jose 625
San Jose Repertory Theatre (NR)
Sand Sports Magazine 761
Sandburg-Livesay Anthology Contest, The 1016
Sanders & Associates, Victoria 110
Sandlapper 655
Sandpaper, The (Web)
Sandlapper Publishing Co., Inc. 298
Sandstone Prize in Short Fiction 1006
Santa Fe Screenplay Competition 1028
Santa Monica Press LLC 298
Sarabande Books, Inc. 299
Sarett National Playwriting Competition (NR)
Sarpedon Publishers 299
SAS Institute Inc. 299
Sasquatch Books 299
Saturday Evening Post, The 490
Saturday Night (NS)
Savage "Miles From Nowhere" Memorial Award, The Barbara 996
Saxon House Canada 359
Say Amen Magazine 689
Scaglione Prize for Studies in Germanic Languages, Aldo and Jeanne 997
Scaglione Prize for Studies in Slavic Languages and Literatures, Aldo and Jeanne 997
Scaglione Prize for Translation of a Literary Work, Aldo and Jeanne 1037
Scaglione Prize for Translation of a Scholarly Study of Literature, Aldo and Jeanne 1037
Scaglione Prize in Comparative Literary Studies, Aldo and Jeanne 997
Scaglione Prize in French and Francophone Studies, Aldo and Jeanne 997
Scale Auto Enthusiast 524
Scandinavian Review 468
Scarecrow Press, Inc. 299
Scavenger's Newsletter 898
Schaible International Shakespearean/Petrarchan Sonnet Contest, The Helen 1016
Schenkman Books, Inc. 300
Schirmer Books (RP)
Schocken Books 300
Scholastic (NR)
Scholastic Canada Ltd. 360
Scholastic Inc. 300
Scholastic Press 300
Scholastic Professional Publishing 301
School Arts Magazine 849
School Bus Fleet (Web)
School Mates (Web)
Schurman Co., Marcel (NR)
Science in Society Journalism Awards 1033
Science of Mind Magazine 614
Science Spectra (NR)

Science Writing Award in Physics and Astronomy by Scientists (NR)
Sciences, The 704
Science-Writing Award in Physics and Astronomy 997
Scientific American 705
Sci-Fi Entertainment 459
Sci-Fi TV (OB)
Score 736
Scott Publishing, D & F (RR)
Scottsdale Life 620
Scouting 400
SCP Journal and SCP Newsletter (Web)
Scrambl-Gram Inc. 981
Screen Magazine 859
Screen Printing 919
Screenwriter's Project, The 1028
Scribner 301
Scrivenery Press 301
Scroll (OB)
Sea Kayaker 727
Sea Magazine 768
Seal Press 301
Seastone (RR)
Seattle Artists Program 1048
Seattle Children's Theatre 962
Seattle Homes and Lifestyles 538
Seattle Magazine 659
Seattle Repertory Theatre 962
Seattle Weekly 659
Seaworthy Publications (Web)
Second Nature Ltd. (NR)
Second Stage Theatre 962
Secret Place, The 689
Secretary, The (see OfficePRO™ 917)
Security Dealer 834
Security Watch: Protecting People, Property & Assets 909
Seed Trade News 862
Seedling Publications, Inc. 302
Seek 689
Self-Counsel Press (Canada) (NR)
Self-Counsel Press (United States) 302
Self 808
Senior Living Newspapers 699
Senior Magazine (see Plus 698)
Senior Voice of Florida 628
Senior Wire (NR)
Sensors (NR)
Serendipity Systems 302
Sergeant Kirkland's Press 303
Sergeant Kirkland's Prize in American History 997
Serif, The Magazine of Type & Typography 919
Server Foodservice News, The 879
Servicing Management 869
Sesame Street Parents 441
Settel Associates Inc. 382
Settlement Services Today 923

Seven Stories Press 303
7ball Magazine 590
Seventeen 775
Seventeen Magazine Fiction Contest 1006
Severn House Publishers (Web)
Shaara Award for Excellence in Civil War Fiction, Michael 1006
Shaman's Drum 404
Shape Magazine 502
Sharing the Victory 690
SharpMan.com 583
Shaughnessy Prize, Mina P. 997
Shaw Festival Theatre (NR)
Shaw, Harold 303
Sheed & Ward Book Publishing 303
Sheep! Magazine 864
Sheldon/Post Company, The 974
Shelley Memorial Award (ED)
Shenandoah 576
Sherman Associates, Inc., Wendy 110
Shofar Magazine (OB)
Shopping Center World (RR)
Shoreline 360
Short Grain Writing Contest 1042
Short Prose Competition for Developing Writers 1043
Short Stuff 576
Shotgun News (NR)
Shotgun Sports Magazine 752
Showcase International 904, 929
Showtime Publishers (NR)
Shuttle Spindle & Dyepot 524
Sidran Press, The (Web)
Siena College International Playwrights Competition 1028
Sierra 601
Sierra Club Books 304
Sign Builder Illustrated 813
Signcraft 813
Signs of the Times (religious) 690
Signs of the Times (advertising) 813
Silent News 454
Silent Sports 731
Silhouette Books 304
Silver Dagger Mysteries 304
Silver Filmworks (NR)
Silver Lion (NR)
Silver Moon Press (NR)
Silver Playwriting Competition, Dorothy 1028
Silver Web, The 710
Simkins Award, Francis B. 997
Simmons Short Fiction Award and Iowa Short Fiction Awards 1006
Simon & Pierre Publishing Co. 360
Simon & Schuster 304
Simon & Schuster Books for Young Readers 304
Simon Tse Productions (NR)
Sing Heavenly Muse! (OB)
Singles Lifestyle & Entertainment Magazine 665
Sisters Today 691

Skating 764
Ski Area Management 933
Ski Magazine 764
Skidmore-Roth Publishing, Inc. 305
Skiing 764
Skin Inc. Magazine 824
Skinner House Books 305
Skolnick Literary Agency, Irene 110
Sky (NR)
Sky & Telescope 705
Sky Publishing Corp. (Web)
Skydiving 760
Skyfoot Technical 360
Skylark Films 974
Skyline Partners (Web)
Slack Inc. 305
Slam (NR)
Slipstream Annual Poetry Chapbook Competition 1017
Small Business News (Web)
Small Farm Today 865
Small Press Review (NP)
Smart Computing 606
Smiley Prize (NR)
Smith, The (NS)
Smith and Kraus Publishers, Inc. 306
Smith Poetry Contest, Peregrine 1017
Smith, Publisher, Gibbs 306
Smith Style, B. 797
Smithee Films, Alan (Web)
Smithsonian Magazine 490
Smoke Magazine 584
Snafu Designs (NR)
Snips Magazine (Web)
Snow Goer 765
Snow Week 765
Snow Writing Awards, Kay 1006
Snowapple Press 361
SnoWest Magazine 765
Snowy Egret 602
Soap Opera Update 459
Soccer Digest 766
Soccer Jr. 766
Soccer Now 766
Social Justice Review 691
Social Science Education Consortium (Web)
Soft Skull Press Inc. 306
Soho Press, Inc. 306
Solimar (OB)
Soma Books 307
Some Like It Hot: An Erotic Romance Contest (UC)
Somerville House Books Limited 382
Songwriter Magazine (see Contemporary Songwriter Magazine 915)
Songwriter's Monthly 916
Sonora Review Annual Literary Awards 1043
Soul of the Writer Award 1006
Sound & Video Contractor 853
Sound and Vision Publishing Limited 361
Sound View Press 376

Markets that appeared in the 2000 edition of *Writer's Market*, but are not included in this edition, are listed in this General Index with the following codes explaining why these markets were omitted: (ED)— Editorial Decision, (NS)—Not Accepting Submissions, (NR)—No (or late) Response to Listing Request, (OB)—Out of Business, (RR)—Removed by Market's Request, (UC)—Unable to Contact, (RP)—Business Restructured or Purchased, (NP)—No Longer Pays or Pays in Copies Only, (SR)—Subsidy/Royalty Publisher, (UF)—Uncertain Future, (Web)—a listing that appears on our website at www.WritersMarket.com

Soundprints 307
Sourcebooks, Inc. 307
South Carolina Fiction Project 1006
South Carolina Game & Fish 752
South Carolina Playwrights' Festival
   (see Trustus Playwrights' Festival
   1029)
South Carolina Wildlife 752
South Coast Repertory 962
South End Press 308
South Florida Parenting 442
South Fork Productions (Web)
Southeastern Theatre Conference
   New Play Project 1028
Southern Accents 538
Southern Appalachian Playwrights'
   Conference 1028
Southern Appalachian Repertory
   Theatre (SART) 962
Southern Boating Magazine 728
Southern Illinois University Press
   308
Southern Lumberman 905
Southern Methodist University Press
   308
Southern Playwrights Competition
   1028
Southern Review, The 576
Southern Review/Louisiana State
   University Short Fiction Award,
   The 1006
Southern Traveler, The 792
Southfarm Press (Web)
Southwest Airlines Spirit 543
Southwest Review Awards 1043
Sovereign Award Outstanding News-
   paper Story, Outstanding Feature
   Story 1033
Sow's Ear Chapbook Prize, The 1017
Sow's Ear Poetry Prize, The 1017
SPS Studios, Inc. 987
Space and Time 711
Spare Time Magazine 446
Specialty Coffee Retailer 929
Specialty Travel Index 936
Spectacle Lane Press Inc. 376
Spectacor Films 974
Spectra (RP)
Speech Bin, Inc., The 308
Speedway Illustrated 761
Spence Publishing Company 308
Spencer Productions, Inc. 942
Spider 555
Spike 732
Spin 591
Spinsters Ink 309
Spirit (religious) 691
Spirit (teen religious) 775
Spirit Dance Entertainment 974
Spirit of Aloha 544
Spirit That Moves Us, The (Web)
Spiritual Life 691
Sport 732
Sport Diver 768
Sport Fishing 752
Sport Literate 576
Sport Truck & SUV Accessory Busi-
   ness 820
Sporting Life, The 732
Sports Afield (NR)
Sports Collectors Digest 525
Sports Etc 732
Sports Illustrated 733

Sports Illustrated for Kids 555
Sports Network, The 981
Sports Spectrum 691
Spotlight Magazine 646
Spotted Dog Press, Inc. 309
Spring Staged Reading Play Contest
   1028
Springfield! Magazine 641
Springs (NR)
SPSM&H 577
Spy Gaze Pictures Inc. (NR)
Squire Syndication Service (NR)
STUDIO Merrywood 974
Stackpole Books 309
Stage Directions (NR)
Stage One 962
Stagebill 450
Stages Repertory Theatre 962
Stained Glass 827
Sta-Kris (Web)
Stamp Collector 525
Stand Magazine 577
Stand Magazine Short Story Compe-
   tition, The 1006
Standard 692
Standard Publishing 309
Stanford Poetry Prize, Ann 1017
Stanford University Press 310
Stanley Drama Award 1028
Stanton & Associates Literary
   Agency 117
Star Date 705
Star Service 936
Starburst Publishers 310
Starlog Magazine 711
Starrett Poetry Prize, The Agnes
   Lynch 1017
Starship Earth (NR)
Startling Detective (NR)
State Journal, The 834
State Theater Company 963
Steamboat Magazine 625
Steel Balls Press (NR)
Steeple Hill 310
Stegner Fellowships, Wallace 1043
Steller Press Ltd. 361
Stemmer House Publishers (Web)
Stenhouse Publishers 310
Stephansson Award for Poetry, Ste-
   phan G. 1017
Steppenwolf Theatre Company 963
Steppin' Out Magazine (NR)
Stereo Review (see Stereo Review's
   Sound & Vision 459)
Stereo Review's Sound & Vision 459
Sterling Publishing 311
Sticky Buns 716
Still Waters Poetry Press 311
Still Waters Press Poetry Chapbook
   Competitions (NR)
Stipes Publishing Co. 311
Stock Car Racing Magazine (NR)
Stoddart Kids (RR)
Stoddart Publishing Co., Ltd. 361
Stoeger Publishing Company 311
Stone Award for Student Journalism,
   I.F. (NR)
Stone Bridge Press 311
Stone National Literary Awards, The
   Donna J. 1043
Stone Soup 555
Stone World (Web)
StoneRoad Production (see Big Event

Pictures 969)
Stonewall Inn 312
Stoneydale Press 312
Store Equipment & Design 929
Storey Publishing 312
Stormline Press 376
Story Friends 556
Story Line Press 312
Straight (see Encounter 771)
Strain, The 577
Strand Magazine, The 578
Strategic Health Care Marketing 913
Strategic Sales Management (OB)
Stratum Entertainment (NR)
Straus Agency, Inc., Robin 110
Student Lawyer 904
Student Leader (for college students)
   (Web)
Student Research Grant 1048
Student Translation Prize 1037
Studio 4 Productions 376
Style at Home 538
Stylus Publishing, LLC 313
Sub-Terrain Magazine Awards 1043
Succeed 429
Success 416
Success Publishing 313
Successful Student 442
Succulent (NR)
Sudbury Press 313
Sudden Fiction Contest 1007
Sugar Hill Press, The (NR)
Summers Press (Web)
Summit Publishing Group, The 313
Sun, The 491
Sun & Sport Eyeware (see Sunwear
   847)
Sunday Advocate Magazine (Web)
Sunrise Publications (NR)
Sunset Magazine 616
Sunshine Artist (Web)
Sunshine: The Magazine of South
   Florida (NR)
Sunstone Press 313
Sunwear 847
Supervision 909
Surfer (NR)
Swank 716
Swan-Raven & Co. (Web)
Swedenborg Foundation 314
Swim Magazine 769
Swimming Technique 769
Swimming World 769
Sybex, Inc. 314
Sydnor Award, Charles S. 997
Sydra Technique Corp. 117
Symbol (NR)
Symphony 591
Syracuse New Times 646
Syracuse Stage 963
Syracuse University Press 314
Sys Admin 892
Systems Co. (Web)
Systemsware Corp., The (Web)

T

TADA! 963
T'ai Chi 757
Take Pride! Community 468
Take That Ltd. (NR)
Talbot Prize Fund for African Anthro-
   pology, Amaury (NR)
Talco Productions 942

Talent Source 117
Talese, Nan A. 315
Talking Rings Entertainment (Web)
Tallahassee Magazine 629
Tamarack Award 1007
Tamarack Books, Inc. 377
Tambra Publishing (Web)
Tampa Bay Business Journal 421
Tampa Review (NR)
Tar Assoc., Ed (NR)
Tarcher, Jeremy P. (NR)
Tattoo Revue 525
Taylor Manuscript Competition, Sydney (NR)
Taylor Playwriting Award, Marvin (NR)
Taylor Publishing Company 315
TCU Press 315
Teachers College Press 315
Teacher's Discovery 850
Teachers in Focus 850
Teachers Interaction 840
Teaching & Learning Company 315
Teaching K-8 (NR)
Teaching Theatre 850
Teaching Tolerance 851
Team NYI Magazine 840
Teatro Vision (Web)
Tech Directions 851
Technical Analysis of Stocks & Commodities 416
Technical Books for the Layperson, Inc. 377
Techniques (NR)
Technology & Learning (NR)
Teddy Award for Best Children's Book 1035
Teddy Bear Review 526
Teen Life (NS)
Tel-Air Interests (NR)
Tele Revista 459
Telescene Film Group (NR)
Temple University Press 316
Ten Best "Censored" Stories of 2001, The 1033
Ten Speed Press 316
Ten-Minute Musicals Project 963
Tennessee Sportsman 753
Tennessee Stage Company and Actor's Co-op 963
Tennessee Writers Alliance Literary Competition (NR)
Tennis Week 766
Terry Jr., Anthony 963
Texas A&M University Press 316
Texas Architect (NR)
Texas Co-op Power 854
Texas Gardener 538
Texas Highways 657
Texas Parks & Wildlife 657
Texas Playwright's Division 1029
Texas Sportsman 753
Texas State Historical Association 316
Texas Technology 421
Texas Western Press 317
Textile Rental 835
Theater at Monmouth, The 964
Theater By the Blind (Web)
Theater of Necessity, The 964
Theater of The First Amendment (Web)
Theatre & Co. (NR)

Theatre BC's Annual Canadian National Playwriting Competition 1029
Theatre Conspiracy Annual New Play Contest (NR)
Theatre de la Jeune Lune (Web)
Theatre Library Association Award, The 998
Theatre Residency Program for Playwrights (NR)
Theatre Rhinoceros 964
Theatre Three (New York) 964
Theatre Three (Texas) 964
Theatre West 964
Theatre West Virginia 964
TheatreForum 460
TheatreVirginia (NR)
Theatreworks/USA 964
Theatrical Outfit 965
Thema 578
Theodore Ward Prize for Playwriting (NR)
These Days 692
Third World Press 317
Thirteenth Prize for Bibliography 998
33 Metalproducing (NR)
This Magazine 662
This People Magazine (NR)
Thomas Travel Journalism Competition, Lowell (NR)
Thompson Educational Publishing Inc. 361
Thorndike Press 317
Thoroughbred Times (NR)
Threads 526
Three Forks Books 317
Three Hawks Publishing LC 377
Three Ring Circus Films (NR)
Threepenny Review, The 578
Thunder's Mouth Press 318
Tide Magazine 753
Tidepool Prize for Poetry 1017
Tidewater Parent 442
Tidewater Publishers 318
Tia Chucha Press 377
Tiare Publications 318
Tickled by Thunder 578
Tide-Mark Press (RR)
Tietjens Memorial Prize, The Eunice 1017
Timber Homes Illustrated 539
Time (NR)
Time Out New York 647
Timeline 506
Times Books (NR)
Times Business (see Crown Business 183)
Times of the Islands 792
Tin House 579
Tingley Books, Megan 318
Tippen Davidson (NR)
Titan Books Ltd. 361
Title Technology (see Settlement Services Today 923)
Toastmaster, The 401
Toby Press Ltd., The 362
Today's Bride (Web)
Today's Catholic Teacher 840
Today's Christian Preacher (Web)
Today's Christian Senior (NR)
Today's Christian Teen 776
Today's Christian Woman 808
Today's Collector 526

Today's Farmer 866
Today's Grocer 879
Today's Homeowner 539
Today's Photographer International 608, 920
Today's Trucking 820
Todd Publications (Web)
Together 692
Together Time 556
Toledo Area Parent News 443
Tomorrow's Christian Graduate 429
Too Nuts Productions, L.P. 975
Tor Books 318
Torah Aura Productions 318
Toronto Book Award (NR)
Toronto Life 663
Toronto Municipal Chapter IODE Book Award 990
Totem Books (RP)
Totline Publications 319
Touch 556
Toward Freedom 612
Tower Publishing 319
Towing & Recovery Phootnotes 820
TowleHouse Publishing Co. 319
Town & Country 491
Towson University Prize for Literature 990
Toy Cars & Vehicles 527
Toy Farmer 527
Toy Shop 527
Toy Trucker & Contractor 527
ToyFare 528
Traces of Indiana and Midwestern History 507
Traders Magazine (Web)
Tradewind Books 362
Tradition (Web)
Traditional Quilter 528
Traditional Quiltworks 528
Trafalgar Square Publishing 319
Trail Runner 762
Trailer Boats Magazine 728
Trailer Life 793
Training Magazine (Web)
Transaction/Society 876
Trans-Atlantic Publications, Inc. 320
Transitions Abroad 793
Transnational Publishers, Inc. 320
Transworld Stance 765
Trapper & Predator Caller 753
Trattner Productions, Ira 975
Travel America 794
Travel Impulse 794
Travel + Leisure 794
Travel Smart (Web)
Travel World International 795
Travel Writing Contest 998
Travelers' Tales 320, 795
Travelin' Magazine (UC)
Traverse 638
Treasure Chest 528
Treasure Learning Systems (NS)
Tree Care Industry Magazine 871
Treks & Journeys 795
Trentham Books (Web)
Triathlete Magazine 762
Tricycle Press 320
Tricycle: The Buddhist Review 692
Trillium Book Award/Prix Trillium 1048
Trilobyte Press & Multimedia 362
Trilobyte Press (see Trilobyte Press &

Multimedia 362)
Trilogy Books (NS)
Trinity Press International 320
trips 795
Triquarterly 579
Troika 491
Troitsa Books 321
Troupe America Inc. 965
Trucker, The (Web)
Truckin' (NR)
Trucking Times & Sport Utility 820
True Confessions 699
True Experience (OB)
True Life Stories (OB)
True Police Cases (NR)
True Romance 700
True Story 700
True West 507
Truman Book Award, Harry S. 998
Truman State University Press 321
Trustus Playwrights' Festival 1029
Trustus Theatre 965
TSL 733
TSR (see Wizards of The Coast 341)
Tucson Lifestyle 620
Tuesday's Child (UC)
Tufts Discovery Award for Poetry, Kate (NR)
Tufts Poetry Award at the Claremont Graduate School, Kingsley (NR)
Turkey & Turkey Hunting 753
Turkey Call 753
Turner Award, Frederick Jackson 998
Turner Award, Steven 1007
Turnstone Press 362
Turtle Books 321
Turtle Magazine for Preschool Kids 557
Turtle Press 321
Tuttle Publishing, Charles E. (see Tuttle Publishing 321)
Tuttle Publishing 321
TV Data 981
TV Guide Celebrity Dish 473
TWA Ambassador 544
Twain Award for Short Fiction (NR)
Twenty-First Century Books 322
29th Street Press (OB)
Twins 443
Twist 776
TwoDot 322
2M Communications Ltd. 382
Tyndale House Publishers, Inc. 322

U

U.S. Art 399
U.S. Catholic 693
U.S. Distribution Journal (NR)
U.S. Kids 557
U.S. Sites Magazine 923
UBU Repertory Theater Publications 965
UCLA American Indian Studies Center 322
Ucross Foundation Residency 1048
UDM 835
UFO Universe (RR)
Ukrainian Weekly, The (NR)
Ultimate Audio (Web)
UltiTech, Inc. 942
Ulysses Press (RR)
Underground Shopper, The 446
Ungroom'd (NR)

Unicorn Theatre National Playwrights' Award 1029
Unicorn Theatre 965
Unifilms (NR)
Union League Civic and Arts Poetry Prize 1017
Unique Greetings (NR)
Unique Opportunities 913
United Church Observer, The 693
United Church Press 322
United Church Publishing House, The (NR)
United Tribes 112
Unity Books 323
Univelt (Web)
Universal Publishers 323
University Affairs (RR)
University of Akron Press 323
University of Alabama 323
University of Alabama New Playwrights Program (NR)
University of Alabama New Playwrights Program 1029
University of Alaska Press 324
University of Alberta Press, The 363
University of Arizona Press 324
University of Arkansas Press 324
University of Calgary Press 363
University of California Press 325
University of Chicago Press (NS)
University of Georgia Press 325
University of Idaho Press 325
University of Illinois Press 325
University of Iowa Press 326
University of Maine Press 326
University of Manitoba Press 363
University of Missouri Press 326
University of Nevada Press 326
University of New Mexico Press 326
University of North Carolina Press, The 327
University of North Texas Press 327
University of Oklahoma Press 327
University of Ottawa 363
University of Pennsylvania Press 328
University of Scranton Press (Web)
University of South Carolina 328
University of Tennessee Press 328
University of Texas Press 328
University of Western Ontario, The (see Althouse Press 346)
University Press of Colorado 329
University Press of Kansas 329
University Press of Kentucky 329
University Press of Mississippi 329
University Press of New England 330
Up Here 663
Upney Editions 363
Upper Room, The 693
Upscale Magazine 468
Uptown Health and Spirit (OB)
Urban Land Institute, The 330
Urban Stages 965
Urbanite, The 711
US Black Engineer/Hispanic Engineer (Web)
US Glass, Metal & Glazing 827
US Weekly 460
USA Cycling Magazine 721
USA Gymnastics (Web)
Utah Business 421
Utah State University Press 330
Utility and Telephone Fleets 854

Utility Business 855
Utne Reader 450

V

Vacation Industry Review 885, 937
Validation Times 847
Valiant Press (Web)
Valley Parent Magazine (NR)
Valleykids Parent News (NR)
Van Der Plas Publications (Web)
Vandamere Press 330
Vanderbilt University Press 331
Vanderwyk & Burnham 377
Vanwell Publishing Limited 364
Variations 717
Varoujan Award, Daniel 1017
Vegetable Growers News, The 862
Vegetarian Times (NR)
Véhicule Press 364
VeloNews 721
Ventura County Reporter (Web)
Venture Publishing, Inc. 331
Vermont Arts Council 1048
Vermont Business Magazine (NR)
Vermont Life Magazine 657
Vermont Playwright's Award (NR)
Vernon Press, Inc. 382
Verso (United Kingdom) (NR)
Verso (United States) 331
Very Short Fiction Award 1007
Veterinary Economics 937
Vette Magazine (NR)
VFW Magazine 401
VGM Career Horizons 331
Videomaker (NR)
Via (NR)
Viacom Canada Writers' Trust Nonfiction Prize, The 998
Vibe 591
Vibrant Life 502
Victor Books (see Chariot/Victor Publishing 170)
Victorian Homes 539
Viener Prize, Saul (NR)
Vietnam (NR)
Viking 332
Viking Children's Books 332
Viking Studio 332
Village Profile 616
Villard Books 332
Vim & Vigor 502
Vineyard & Winery Management 825
Vintage Anchor Publishing (NR)
Vintage Images 332
Viper Magazine 409
Virginia Dynamics (NR)
Virginia Game & Fish 754
Virginia Golfer 737
Virginia Quarterly Review 579
Virginia Stage Co. (NR)
Vision 841, 851
Visions Communications 332
Vista Magazine 468
Vista Publishing, Inc. 333
Visual Horizons 942
Vital Ministry (see Rev. 839)
Vitality Magazine (NR)
Vitesse Press 377
VM Butterfly 975
Voaden National Playwriting Competition, The Herman 1029
Vogue Knitting (NR)
Vogue 809

Volcano Press, Inc. 333
Vows: The Bridal & Wedding Business Journal (NR)
Voyageur 796
Voyageur Press 333

W

Wade Journalism Fellowship, The Lawrence 1033
Wadsworth Publishing Company 333
Wake Boarding Magazine (Web)
Walch, Publisher, J. Weston 334
Walker and Co. 334
Walker Journalism Award, Stanley 1033
Walking Magazine, The 502
Wall & Emerson, Inc. 364
Wallace Award, The Bronwen (NR)
Walls, Windows & Floors (NR)
Walnut Street Theatre 965
Walsworth Publishing Co. 334
War Cry, The 694
Ward's Auto World (NP)
Warehousing Management 886
Warmwater Fly Fishing 754
Warner Aspect 334
Warner Books 334
Warner Press (NR)
Warren Poetry Prize Competition, The Robert Penn (NR)
Wascana Review (NR)
Washington Blade, The (NR)
Washington City Paper 626
Washington Flyer Magazine (NR)
Washington Monthly 613
Washington Post, The 627
Washington Prize, The 1017
Washington State University Press 335
Washingtonian, The 627
Washington-Oregon Game & Fish 754
Waste Age Magazine 925
Water Skier, The 770
Water Well Journal 925
Waterloo Community Playhouse 966
Waterway Guide 728
Watson-Guptill Publications 335
Watts, Franklin 335
Wave-Length Paddling Magazine 729
Waxman Agency, Inc., Scott 113
Wayfinder Press (Web)
WEDDINGBells (Web)
We Don't Need No Stinkin' Dramas 1029
Weatherford Award 998
Weatherhill, Inc. 336
Weatherwise 706
Weekend Woodcrafts (NR)
Weidner & Sons Publishing 336
Weighing & Measurement 887
Weight Watchers Magazine 503
Weigl Educational Publishers 365
Weintal Prize for Diplomatic Reporting, Edward 1033

Weiser, Inc., Samuel 336
Weiss Associates, Daniel (NR)
Welcome Home Magazine (RR)
Wescott Cove Publishing Co. (Web)
Wesleyan Advocate, The 694
Wesleyan University Press 336
Wesleyan Woman, The 694
West Coast Ensemble 966
West Coast Ensemble Full-Play Competition 1029
West Graphics 987
West Group (NR)
West Virginia Game & Fish 754
WestArt 399
Westbeth Theatre Center (RR)
Westchester Family (NR)
Westcliffe Publishers 337
Western Canada Highway News 821
Western Heritage Awards 1043
Western History Association Awards 998
Western Horse, The 394
Western Horseman, The (RR)
Western Humanities Review 579
Western HVACR News 919
Western Magazine Awards 1043
Western New York Family 443
Western New York Wares Inc. 377
Western Outdoors 754
Western People 663
Western Psychological Services (Web)
Western RV News 796
Western Sportsman (NR)
Western States Book Awards (NR)
Westernlore Press 337
Westminster John Knox Press 337
Westsylvania 654
Westview Press (RR)
WestWind Press 337
Westworld Magazine 664
Whap! (OB)
What Magazine 776
What Makes People Successful 429
What's Inside Press 337
Where & When 654
Where Chicago (Web)
Where Dallas 657
Whetstone 580
Which? Ltd. (NR)
Whispering Coyote Press 338
Whispers from Heaven 695
White Cliffs Media (NR)
White Mane Books 338
White Memorial National Children's Playwriting Contest, Jackie 1029
White Pine Press Poetry Prize 1018
White Review, The James 479
White Stone Circle Press 338
Whitecap Books Ltd. 365
Whitehead Award, Fred 990
Whitehorse Press 378
Whitetail Business 933

Whitford Press 378
Whitman and Co., Albert 338
Whitman Award, The Walt 1018
Whitman Citation of Merit for Poets, Walt (NR)
Whitson Publishing Co., Inc. 338
Whittlesey Agency, Peregrine 118
Who Cares Magazine (NR)
Whole Earth 602
Whole Foods 879
Whole Life Times 404
Whyte Essay Competition, Jon 998
Wichita State University Playwriting Contest 1030
Wick Poetry Chapbook Series "Open" Competition 1018
Wick Poetry Chapbook Series "Student" Competition 1018
Wick Poetry Prize, Stan and Tom 1018
Wicked Fetishes 717
Wicked Mystic Magazine (NR)
Wiener Publishers Inc., Markus 339
Wiese Productions, Michael (Web)
Wiesel Ethics Essay Contest, The Elie (NR)
Wilbur Award, The Richard 1018
Wild Flower Press (see Granite Publishing 208)
Wild Outdoor World (NR)
Wild West (NR)
Wildcat Canyon Press 339
Wilder Publishing Center (Web)
Wilderness Press 339
Wildlife Art (NR)
Wiley & Sons, Inc., John 339
Williams Award, William Carlos 1018
Williams Prize, L. Kemper and Leila 999
Williams/New Orleans Literary Festival One-Act Contest, Tennessee (NR)
Williamson Publishing Co. 339
Willow Creek Press 340
Willow Springs 580
Willowgate Press 340
Willows Theatre Co. (NR)
Wilma Theater, The (NR)
Wilmington Magazine (NR)
Wilshire Book Co. 340
Wind Magazine Contests (NR)
Window Fashions (NR)
Windows Developers Journal 892
Windows Magazine (RP)
Windrush Press Ltd. (Web)
Windsor Books (Web)
Windward Publishing, Inc. 341
Windy City Sports Magazine (NR)
Wine Business Monthly (NR)
Wine Spectator (NR)
Wine X Magazine 473
Wingtips (see Airwaves, Connections 541)

Markets that appeared in the 2000 edition of *Writer's Market*, but are not included in this edition, are listed in this General Index with the following codes explaining why these markets were omitted: (ED)—Editorial Decision, (NS)—Not Accepting Submissions, (NR)—No (or late) Response to Listing Request, (OB)—Out of Business, (RR)—Removed by Market's Request, (UC)—Unable to Contact, (RP)—Business Restructured or Purchased, (NP)—No Longer Pays or Pays in Copies Only, (SR)—Subsidy/Royalty Publisher, (UF)—Uncertain Future, (Web)—a listing that appears on our website at www.WritersMarket.com

Winner Memorial Award, Robert H. 1018
Winners' Circle International Writing Contest 1044
Winslow Press 341
Wire Rope News & Sling Technology 906
Wired Magazine 607
Wisconsin Agriculturist (NR)
Wisconsin Outdoor Journal 659, 755
Wisconsin Sportsman 755
Wisconsin Trails 660
Wisdom Publications 341
WIT (Women In Touch) (OB)
With 776
Witty Short Story Award, Paul A. 1007
Wizard: The Comics Magazine 444
Wizards of the Coast 341
Wolfe Fiction Prize, Thomas 1007
Wolff Award in Fiction, Tobias 1007
Woman Engineer 857
Woman Pilot 412
Woman's Day (NR)
Woman's Life 809
Woman's Own 809
Woman's Touch 695
Woman's World 809
Women in Business 810
Women Police (NP)
Women with Wheels (Web)
Women's Empowerment Awards Writing Competition 1044
Women's Playwright's Division 1030
Women's Playwriting Festival (NR)
Women's Project and Productions, The (Web)
Women's Sports + Fitness Magazine (NR)
Wonder Time 558
Wonderful Ideas (NR)
Wonderland Entertainment Group (NR)
Wonderland Press, The 382
Wood Memorial Ohioana Award for Children's Literature, Alice 1035
Wood Prize, The J. Howard and Barbara M.J. 1018
Woodberry Productions (Web)
Woodbine House 342
Woodbridge Press 378
Woodenboat Magazine 729
Woodhead Publishing Ltd. 365
Woodholme House Publishers 342
Woodland Publishing Inc. 342
Woodshop News 528
Woodwork 529
Woofenill Works, Inc., The 975

Worcester Foothills Theatre Co. (NR)
Worcester Magazine 637
Words For Sale 416, 540
Wordware Publishing, Inc. 342
Working Mother Magazine 444
Working Stages 1030
Working Woman 810
Working Writers Newsletter 899
Work-In-Progress Grant 1036
Workman Publishing Co. 342
World, The (NR)
World & I, The 492
World Christian 695
World Fantasy Awards Assoc. 990
World Film Services (NR)
World Leisure (Web)
World News Syndicate (Web)
World Policy Journal (Web)
World Pulse 695
World Trade 835
World War II (NR)
World Wastes Magazine (see Waste Age Magazine 925)
Worship Leader Magazine 841
WPI Journal 429
Wrestling World 770
Wright Concept, The 118
Write 899
Writer, The 899
Write Way Publishing 343
Writer Magazine/Emily Dickinson Award, The 1018
Writer OnLine 899
Writers & Artists Agency 118
Writers at Work Fellowship Competition 1044
Writer's Block Magazine 580
Writers Community Residency Awards, The (NR)
Writer's Digest 900
Writer's Digest Books 343
Writer's Digest National Self-Published Book Awards (NR)
Writer's Digest Writing Competition (NR)
Writers Fellowships 1048
Writer's Forum 900
Writer's Guidelines & News (OB)
Writers House 113
Writers Information Network 900
Writers' International Forum (RR)
Writers' Journal 900
Writers' Journal Annual Short Story Contest 1007
Writers' Journal Fiction Contest 1007
Writers' Journal Horror/Ghost Contest 1008
Writers' Journal Romance Contest

1008
Writers' Potpourri 901
Writer's Publishing, The (NR)
Writer's Yearbook (NR)
Writing for Children Competition 1036
Written By 901
Wuerz Publishing, Ltd. (NR)
Wyoming Rural Electric News (Web)
Wysteria Publishing 378

X

XXL Magazine (NR)

Y

Yachting 729
Yale Repertory Theatre (NR)
Yale Review, The 581
Yale Series of Younger Poets 1019
Yale University Press 343
Yankee 616
Year End Series (YES) New Play Festival 1030
Yellow Silk (NR)
Yes! 450
Yesterday's Magazette (RR)
YM 777
YMAA Publication Center 344
Yoga Journal 503
York Press Ltd. 365
Young & Alive 777
Young Connecticut Playwrights Festival (NR)
Young Playwrights Festival 1030
Young Prizes In Poetry, Phyllis Smart (NR)
Young Salvationist 777
Your Baby (OB)
Your Church 841
Your Health & Fitness 503
Your Money 417
Youth Update 778

Z

Zachary Entertainment 975
Zebra Books 344
Zeckendorf Assoc. Inc., Susan 114
Zed Books (Web)
Zoetrope 581
Zoetrope Short Story Contest 1008
Zoland Books, Inc. 344
Zondervan Publishing House 344
Zoom! Magazine 544
Zornio Memorial Children's Theatre Playwriting Award, Anna 1030
ZYZZYVA 581